ROTHMANS FOOTBALL YEARBOOK 1976-77

COMPILED BY
LESLIE VERNON AND JACK ROLLIN

QUEEN ANNE PRESS
LONDON

Edited by **Peter Dunk**

Front Cover: Action from the 1975 Charity Shield match at Wembley between
West Ham United and Derby County.
Photo courtesy of Colorsport.
All other photos courtesy of Syndication International.

Published by Queen Anne Press Limited
12 Vandy Street, London EC2A 2EN

Typeset in Times Roman by
Waterlow London

Printed and bound in England by
Hazell Watson & Viney Limited
Aylesbury, Bucks

CONTENTS

THE FOOTBALL LEAGUE: THE CLUBS

THE FOOTBALL LEAGUE: STATISTICS

THE FA CUP

THE FOOTBALL LEAGUE CUP

SCOTTISH FOOTBALL

IRISH AND WELSH FOOTBALL

MISCELLANEOUS

BRITISH INTERNATIONAL FOOTBALL

INFORMATION SECTION

FOREWORD BY ROTHMANS OF PALL MALL

Rothmans Football Yearbook is now seven years old, and football in Britain has certainly seen some drastic changes since our first edition was published at the beginning of the 1970-71 season.

Following Scotland's qualification for the World Cup Final Tournament in Germany, Wales became Britain's only representative in this year's European Championship quarter finals and England's reputation as a first class soccer power has been severely dented.

Three Second Division clubs have reached the FA Cup Final within the last four seasons and have produced two winners, while no First Division club reached the Football League Cup Semi-Final in season 1974-75 and non-league clubs such as Wimbledon, Leatherhead, Wycombe Wanderers, and Hendon held their own in FA Cup clashes against First Division opposition.

All the facts and figures showing the ever-changing face of football are presented in this year's Yearbook and there is no doubt that with the World Cup qualifying matches under way, the coming season will be vital to Britain's international teams.

All the post-war Football League tables are included in the Yearbook this season, and it is fascinating to follow the progress of individual clubs throughout the years. The consistency of Liverpool stands out like a beacon, and we can only hope that this season they can lift English morale with a successful run in the European Cup.

The publication of the new Rothmans Football Yearbook coincides with the exciting time when all players, officials and supporters are full of high hopes for their favourites in the competitions to come. We hope you enjoy this year's publication and that this season brings the much needed success to our British club and international sides who will be representing us in the months ahead.

EDITORIAL BOARD

Brian James (*Chairman*)**, Bobby Charlton, C.B.E., David Coleman, Ted Croker, Jimmy Hill, Jack Rollin, Leslie Vernon.**

ADVISORY PANEL

Denis Follows, C.B.E.

Denis Compton, C.B.E.: *Arsenal & England*

Phil Issacs: *Sportsman Club*

Walter Winterbottom, O.B.E.: *Director, Sports Council*

John Morgan: *Daily Express*

John Bromley: *London Weekend Television*

Cliff Lloyd: *Secretary, Professional Footballers' Association*

Bernard Audley: *AGB Research*

Tony Williams: *Rothmans of Pall Mall*

Tom Finney, O.B.E.: *Preston North End & England*

Tony Pullein: *Founder, England Football Supporters Association*

Joe Mercer, O.B.E.: *Director, Coventry City*

Sam Leitch: *BBC Television*

Jarvis Astaire: *Anglo-America Sporting Club*

Neville Holtham: *Sports Editor The Sunday People*

Brian Moore: *London Weekend Television*

R. E. Hadingham, O.B.E., M.C.: *Slazengers Ltd.*

Geoffrey Irvine: *The Bagenal Harvey Organisation Ltd.*

J. N. H. Rice.

7

INTRODUCTION

As the compilers of *Rothmans Football Yearbook 1976-77* – the seventh edition – we have found our usual problem to be one of deciding the balance between new material and the retention of established sections. Among the innovations are a Who's Who of leading Football League managers, a South American section, and a list of the top goalscorers in English football since the war. The South American section includes some interesting tables at both national and club level which we consider are of special significance in view of the next World Cup being held in Argentina in 1978. Naturally the features which have become synonymous with the essentials of Rothmans are included again. These include the line-ups of every match played in the Football League and Scottish League and the associated cup competitions in our usual easy-to-read style. Full coverage is also given to the European Championship and other international fixtures and the draw for the 1978 World Cup qualifying competition. The popular day-by-day diary section is also again prominent, as are the graphical record of eight great goals of the season. Football League attendances since the last war are also listed with the new features of the current edition.

Of course, it is not possible to compile such a wealth of information without the invaluable assistance we receive from various organisations, club secretaries, and officials. We are especially grateful to Mrs Sandra Whiteside of the Football League, Mr John Carvosso and Mr Mike McNamara of the Football Association, and Mr Tom Maule of the Scottish League, all of whom were extremely helpful.

We trust that this seventh edition will again maintain the standards of previous issues of the Rothmans Football Yearbook.

LESLIE VERNON
JACK ROLLIN

ACKNOWLEDGEMENTS

The compilers wish to thank the many individuals and organisations whose ready co-operation has produced material for this volume, and in particular:

Lionel Francis
Malcom Brodie
Tony Pullein
The Football Association
The Scottish Football Association
The Welsh Football Association
The Football League
The Scottish Football League
The Secretaries of all Football League Clubs

Glyn Evans (The English Schools FA)
A. E. Evans (UAU)
A. Elliott
Maurice Golesworthy
Martin Tyler
John Pyke
Ken Goldman
Paul Buckle
Morley Farror

ROTHMANS FOOTBALL AWARDS 1976

The following six people are to receive special awards from Rothmans for having made a worthwhile contribution to the wide spectrum of the game in season 1975-76.

EMLYN HUGHES. The greatest single argument against reducing the number of competitive fixtures in a season must surely be the achievement of Liverpool, who wrestled with League, League Cup, FA Cup and UEFA Cup commitments and won honours in the first and last mentioned. Captaining them with his own individual brand of enthusiastic example in the heart of the defence was Hughes, now the most capped of Liverpool players with 40 appearances for England. No longer a current international he is still as firm a favourite at Anfield as ever, with more than 500 matches to his credit and further proof that Liverpool is the capital of English football *c*. 1976.

GEOFFREY GREEN. Retiring this year as football correspondent of *The Times*, he will leave behind him a wealth of readable matter covering the game; no journalist could ask more from a lifetime in the game; few, however, achieve it. Radio listeners, too, have been able to share his love of the round ball game so happily obvious from lyrical, flowing phrases released by a pleasant voice which never palled. Covering football matches and events around the world is not in itself a passport to knowing the game, but his understanding of it will live along with the memories both written and verbal, so elegantly reported.

DON MASSON. Entering First Division football for the first time at the age of 28 in December 1974, he gave the impression that a decade. had been wasted for this gifted Scottish midfield player. Queen's Park Rangers paid something in the region of £100,000 for him from Notts County, his second senior English club after he had been introduced into League football by Middlesbrough. A midfield player with apparent time to find his openings and distribute with precision and style, he is now in his 30th year and carries newly won honours at international level for the country of his birth. He is yet another example of talent finding its own reward no matter at what level it is exposed.

ALEX STEPNEY. Manchester United injected a breath of fresh air into the game last season with their swashbuckling approach to attacking football. It was not wholly successful in the end, but it won them many new friends. At the back of the defence their carefree system needed some safe goalkeeping which was entrusted again to a young veteran in his 30s and in his 13th year as a professional, with previous terms as an amateur in a career gracing Tooting & Mitcham, Millwall, and briefly Chelsea, too. He also had his moments of crisis, being dropped for a spell in 1975-76, but he came back as strongly and resolute as ever, as one might expect from his character.

TERRY PAINE. At the end of last season he made his 800th League appearance certainly a record and a feat unlikely to be achieved again. During the term he broke Jimmy Dickinson's long-standing record of matches for Portsmouth, which seemed unassailable at one time. He was able to couple this event with helping Hereford United gain promotion having spent the greater part of his career with Southampton and for England, too, as a winger. Now operating more in midfield, the advancing years have been borne lightly by this sprightly performer in his mid-30s. Football in modern terminology might be a young man's game but fortunately the expertise of the experienced remains with us.

MIKE CHANNON. When Southampton descended into the Second Division at the end of 1973-74 season there were many who thought that it might be the beginning of the end of this man's career as an England international. Though the Saints won the FA Cup last season in commendable fashion, they stayed in Division Two, but far from losing his status, Channon established himself in England's colours, scoring vital goals in what was a difficult transitional season for the national side. A direct, confident dribbler with acceleration and finish, he has provided much of the optimism which has quietly existed about England's future prospects.

9

EDITORIAL

Brian James

Is it not time for Britons to sink their pride in their football and admit that we need help from outside? And isn't that, in fact, exactly what Arsenal and Spurs have already done?

Tottenham manager Terry Neill made no bones about his reasons for making a bold attempt to sign Barcelona's Dutch forward Johann Cruyff: 'I need a player of great individual skill, both to improve my team and to add an extra element to our matches for our public. Such a man is not available anywhere in the English League.'

Arsenal chairman Denis Hill-Wood said of his club's attempt to sign the Yugoslav coach Miljanic: 'I suppose we could find an Englishman now to help us win matches. To be a great team you need something else, something extra. I was hoping that, by signing the man who rebuilt Real Madrid, I could import new ideas to Arsenal. I have to admit I could not see anyone available in England who might have done as much.'

By these statements Britain, for a century the main exporters of football playing and teaching talent, seems to have been placed among the importing nations. We may, instinctively, dislike the trend – I feel we should be foolish to condemn it. Most coaches admit our football is flying full-pelt up a cul-de-sac, and most also admit they lack the power to change its direction. A new coach or two, a few fresh players from abroad, brought up to different disciplines could provide the catalyst for change.

The point was made, more specifically, by the events of two European cup finals within a week of each other at the end of our season. First, West Ham lost to Anderlecht in the final of the Cup-winners' Cup. They played well, but weeks of the wearing, tearing grind of the English League had made them ill-prepared for the tests when the Belgians turned on the individual skills. Then, a week later, Bayern took the European champions Cup against St Etienne – and both winners and losers of this Hampden Park match looked a class above their English rivals.

It was in a Glasgow hotel later that night that a group of English managers sat discussing what they'd seen. 'I have to face the fact,' said one, 'that none of my blokes could have done some of the things we saw tonight . . . forwards taking on opponents in two's and three's . . . defenders coming forward and looking as clever on the ball as our best forwards.'

'That's right,' said another. 'We've lost it . . . and I don't think we're easily going to get it back. I'll tell you now I'd buy a couple of Continental players this summer if I got the chance. Not because they've got skills we haven't, but because they are prepared to *use* those skills, even in the tightest matches. Get a couple like that in your side, and I think this confidence would rub off on the rest.'

The Common Market makes it likely that British clubs will get their chance to import in the near future – some clubs are already girding themselves for test cases against the League's existing ban on foreign footballers. The League might argue that the ban is there to protect the jobs of British players: that is a short-term view. What is the point of having job-security in an industry in decline? The interest of our players would be better served by any move to improve the quality, appeal and presentation of our ailing national game.

The demand in Europe and even further afield for British coaches and British players is no contradiction. We still have great virtues in our football . . . high morale, endurance, fitness, discipline. These all have a high price in the Common Market, where, often, *too* much emphasis is placed on the sophisticated skills. We need, in effect, to balance the trading figures, bartering our guts for their guile.

It is not as though we have *never* copied from abroad. Formations like 4-2-4 were Brazilian inventions: the use of the 'sweeper' in defence something picked up – a shade too readily – from the Italians. Visiting coaches and managers, like a group of carrion crows, are there at every football match of a standard where something new may be seen.

Formation and tactics, though, are easy to copy. You can come back with a new free-kick trick or a corner caper scribbled on the back of an envelope. This other matter, the mental attitude of players who seem unafraid to apply their skills, cannot be carried back through customs on paper or in a package. We need the men themselves, so that, as the man said, 'something may rub off.'

Spurs didn't get Cruyff. Arsenal failed to tempt Miljanic. That doesn't mean failure – just a couple of false starts on a trail that seems certain to be blazed, then broadened. The only shame in the notion of Britain having to learn about football from abroad is that we have taken so long to recognise the need.

DIARY 1975-76

June

The FA announces a new disciplinary code . . . Leeds are banned from European competitions . . . the managerial merry-go-round starts again.

10 A strong statement from the Football Association establishes a disciplinary code for the 1975–76 season. The *Daily Telegraph* writes: 'The Football Association yesterday brought a heavy disciplinary foot down on those players and clubs who have been flouting the appeals system. Next season, any player accumulating 20 penalty points will be banned – and there will be no delaying tactics by clubs to free players for vital matches. Under the new system, agreed yesterday by representatives of the FA, Football League, Professional Footballers' Association, and the Managers' and Secretaries' Association, players on 20 points will be called before an FA commission. They will be entitled to enter a plea in mitigation but, unless the player's previous record persuades the commission to waive a ban, the only point in question will be the length of suspension. Depending on the nature of the player's offences, he may be banned for one, two, or three matches. Any player sent off next season will not be able to contest the referee's decision but, instead of the present three-match ban, he will miss only one match – and also collect 12 penalty points. Clubs will have to bear their share of responsibility for the conduct of their players. A club will be called before an FA commission, should their players accumulate 100 penalty points.'

12 Gordon Lee (Blackburn) is the new manager of Newcastle. Joe Harvey becomes general manager.

13 Mike Summerbee, the Manchester City winger, joins Burnley . . . The UEFA Disciplinary Commission places a four-year ban on Leeds United for the misbehaviour of their supporters at the European Cup final in May. Leeds will be excluded from Europe on two occasions during the four-year period . . . Dave Watson moves to Manchester C. from Sunderland in a deal involving £175,000 cash plus Jeff Clarke . . . Willie Morgan is back with Burnley from Manchester U.

20 New managers are appointed at several clubs – Jim Smith takes the place of Gordon Lee at Blackburn, and his job at Colchester goes to Bobby Roberts. John McNamee is the new boss at Workington.

27 Leicester sign Steve Kember from Chelsea for £80,000.

July

Charlie George goes to Derby . . . Jock Stein seriously injured in a car crash . . . ex-Doncaster manager Maurice Setters is awarded damages for unfair dismissal . . . there will be no more replays in the European Cup final – penalties will decide the result if extra time doesn't . . . the government working party on crowd control announces its findings.

1 Cardiff are taken over by a group of businessmen . . . A snag occurs in the reported transfer of Charlie George from Arsenal to Tottenham. After the medical has been satisfactorily completed, Derby County express an interest in the player. Terry Neill says, 'I am very disappointed, but I don't think anything can be gained by going mad. It could still work out.'

2 Derby sign Charlie George for £90,000 . . . Stockport County are in danger of going out of business. The club is heavily in debt and must find £25,000 to ward off closure . . . Giorgio Chinaglia, the Lazio striker says that he is finished with Italian football and will continue his career in the USA.

4 John Hollins, the former Chelsea captain, signs for QPR in an £80,000 deal . . . Mick Dennehy goes to Walsall from Nottingham F. and Barney Daniels (Manchester C.)

agrees to join Chester.

5　Jock Stein, the Celtic manager, is involved in a car accident. His condition is described as 'serious' . . . Johnny Giles is the player/manager of WBA.

7　Bill Glazier, the veteran Coventry 'keeper, signs for Brentford (£12,500).

10　Bob McNab, the Arsenal defender, goes to Wolves on a free transfer . . . Frank Lord leaves Crystal Palace, and Terry Venables is their new chief coach.

11　Maurice Setters is awarded £1340 compensation for unfair dismissal against Doncaster Rovers. After the court case Setters says, 'What has happened today will make the business of being a football manager or coach more comfortable. We should have the same protection enjoyed by people in other jobs.'

14　Bohemians Dublin are making precautionary arrangements in connection with the Rangers European Cup-Winners' Cup tie. They say that ᴜnless they receive a 'good conduct guarantee' from the Scottish club regarding their supporters, Bohemians will only allocate the compulsory 200 tickets to Rangers.

15　Mike Channon hands in a written transfer request at Southampton . . . Liverpool sign the young Wrexham full-back, Joey Jones, for £110,000. John Neal, manager of the Welsh club, says that he was not consulted about the deal, and it is not in the best interests of his club . . . Peter Latchford, who has been on loan to Celtic from West Bromwich, signs permanently for the Scottish club for £25,000 . . . Terry Brisley and Barry Fairbrother move to Millwall from Orient in exchange for winger Doug Allder – no cash is involved in the deal.

17　'There will be no European Cup final replays in future', reports the *Daily Express*. 'A meeting of UEFA decided that if scores are level after 30 minutes extra time, the title will be decided by penalty kicks.　The same rule will apply to the Cup-Winners' Cup' . . . Leicester sign Brian Alderson of Coventry for £150,000.

22　John Phillips, the Chelsea goalkeeper, is badly injured in training, and will miss the first half of the forthcoming season . . . Southend will print their own programme in the future, and the cost to fans will be only 5p each . . . Stoke report a loss of £450,000 for the 1974–75 season.

24　Ipswich Town declares war on the hooligans who smear the name of British football abroad.　In a four-point statement, the club set out their plan to ensure good behaviour from their supporters when they go with the team on UEFA Cup missions.　1.　No-one under 18 will be allowed on any official trip abroad unless accompanied by an adult.　2.　Inflammatory flags, banners and the drinking of alcohol will be banned.　3.　Fans making their own travel arrangements will only be sold tickets if they sign a form holding themselves responsible for any damage they do.　4.　European travel cards, issued to supporters, will be withdrawn if they get into trouble.

25　Arsenal will fine players booked for dissent.　Manager Bertie Mee explains his decision, and says that the club will follow the lead set by Chelsea and Manchester C.

29　Graham Cross is suspended at Leicester.　The veteran defender is playing county cricket and hasn't reported for training . . . Alan Ball Sr is dismissed by Southport. Ball is working in Sweden and has failed to return to Lancashire to take up his duties with the club.

30　Minister of Sport, Denis Howell, announces the findings of the working party on crowd behaviour with particular emphasis on control and safety of First Division grounds.　These clubs are to arrange meetings with local police, magistrates, and court clerks so as to work out a uniform policy in the treatment of soccer hooligans. Clubs playing in Europe were told to follow the lead of Ipswich, and introduce strict control on their ticket allocations and travel arrangements.　Sales of alcohol should be banned on foreign trips.　The working party agrees that the use of detention centres could act as a deterrent.　'We feel that depriving youngsters of football or their leisure might be more effective than fining them.'　Safety at the grounds is of paramount importance, and the findings of the Wheatley report will be implemented.　This means that football grounds will be licensed by the local authority.　The government – possibly through some kind of a levy – might

help to cover the expenditure involved in converting football grounds to comply with the stiff safety regulations . . . Leeds United are beaten 4–1 by St Etienne in a pre-season friendly – their second heavy defeat in four days.

31   Alan Foggon is suspended for two weeks at Middlesbrough for being absent from training . . . Graham Cross is back at Leicester, but he is not in the team for the opening game of the Anglo-Scottish Tournament. Alan Birchenall is given an opportunity to establish himself in the defence . . . Jimmy Melia is the new manager of Southport.

August

Derby win the Charity Shield . . . Bill Nicholson joins West Ham as a 'consultant' . . . Gerry Francis will captain England for the rest of the season . . . Bobby Charlton resigns at Preston . . . hooliganism is in the headlines again.

2   The season opens on a very hot afternoon with the Anglo-Scottish Cup and friendly matches . . . Arsenal lose a friendly at Dundee, where Eddie Kelly captains the side in place of the transfer-listed Alan Ball . . . The best crowd of the day is in Glasgow where Celtic beat Derby 1–0 in a friendly in front of 44,000 . . . Jock Stein is out of hospital where he has been recovering from serious injuries sustained in a car accident.

3   Jim Holton is sent off in a friendly in Denmark. Manchester U. win 3–0 there, and their travelling fans behave impeccably . . . Ipswich finish third in a pre-season tournament, after beating Spartak Trnava 2–1 . . . Everton winger John Connolly breaks his left leg in a game at Deventer, Holland, and will be out of football until Christmas.

5   Jimmy Meadows resigns as Stockport manager – Eddie Hopkinson takes over on a temporary basis . . . John Holsgrove leaves Sheffield W. and joins Stockport on a free transfer.

7   Goalkeeper Bryan King goes to Coventry from Millwall for the bargain price of £57,000. Only a year ago Millwall were asking £150,000 for King. Bertie Mee says, 'The transfer fee involved in Bryan King's move is one of the most significant things to happen. It seems to me to represent the moment when football finally moved out of cloud cuckoo land'. . . Ipswich win 6–0 in Norway in a friendly, but West Ham only scrape home 2–1 against Bergen . . . Lou Macari is sent off in Denmark – the second Manchester U. player to be dismissed in warm-up friendlies.

9   Derby win the Charity Shield. Despite the tropical weather, 59,000 turn up at Wembley, where the Champions beat West Ham 2–0 with goals by Hector and McFarland. Charlie George makes a promising debut for Derby. For the first time in England, numbered placards are used to signal substitutions . . . Player-manager Johnny Giles is injured in a friendly and will not be fit to open the season with West Bromwich.

10   Arsenal starlets come under attack from the club's chief scout Gordon Clark. He says, 'Some of our youngsters need a kick up the backside. Nobody is more anxious for them to make the grade than I am, but they will have to pull their fingers out. . . . In the meantime Arsenal are beaten 2–0 in Split by the Yugoslav champions, Hajduk . . . Gerry Queen is transfer-listed by Orient.

13   Malcolm Allison receives an offer from Stockport, but decides to stay with Crystal Palace . . . John Lacy (Fulham) misses the start of the season due to cartilage trouble . . . Carlisle refuse a reported six-figure offer from Tottenham for their centre-back Bill Green.

15   Bill Nicholson joins West Ham in a general executive capacity. He will help with the youth sides and also do some scouting.

16   The season opens with the usual surprises on the field, and crowd trouble off it. Over 70 fans are arrested at Wolverhampton where Manchester U. are the visitors, and at Leicester who are at home to Birmingham . . . Brian Clough, the Forest manager, runs on to the pitch to stop an invasion, and orders the Plymouth supporters back to the stands . . . At Peterborough a female 'streaker' livens up the

proceedings . . . But attendances are down – especially in the lower divisions . . . An excellent day for London and Manchester but a sad .t for the Liverpool clubs. The four First Division London clubs collect seven points, with Q.P.R. (home to Liverpool) and West Ham (away to Stoke) recording convincing victories. Manchester U. mark their return to the top flight with a 2–0 win at Wolves. Newcastle win 3–0 at Ipswich, and Coventry beat Everton 4–1 at Goodison with David Cross getting the season's first hat-trick. Holders Derby draw 1–1 at Sheffield United. Both Sunderland and Southampton in the second division open their promotion bids with easy wins at the expense of Chelsea and West Bromwich respectively.

18 Geoff Hurst, 33, signs for WBA for £20,000.

19 Arsenal's Sammy Nelson is ordered off at Sheffield United, but Arsenal win 3–1. Nelson is automatically suspended for one match and collects 12 penalty points according to the new disciplinary system . . . Manchester U. win 2–0 away at Birmingham and are the only team with maximum points in Division One after two matches. Stepney is taken to hospital during the match with a dislocated jaw – reportedly sustained while shouting at a team-mate! . . . 26 United supporters are arrested.

20 Mike England, back in football as a player, cannot prevent his new club Cardiff going down 2–1 to Bristol R. in the first leg of their League Cup tie . . . Arsenal pay £30,000 to Crewe for goalkeeper Brian Parker . . . Gerry Francis is named as the new England captain. Alan Ball, the previous skipper, is not included in the squad for the friendly against Switzerland . . . Martin Buchan is back in the Scotland squad for the European Championship tie v Denmark.

21 Bill Nicholson advocates a new points system in the league, in an address given to the Press at the Rothmans lunch. He proposes a system with 10 points for a win, five for a draw, and a point for each goal scored . . . Bobby Charlton resigns as manager of Preston following a transfer dispute with the directors. He says: 'It is a sad day for me. But I refuse to have players at the club that I don't want. It was a matter of principle. The directors decided that a deal with Newcastle must go through. But I do not think it was a realistic deal. If they want to have somebody to carry out their decisions, they can get anyone to do that!' The proposed deal is the transfer of defender John Bird, to Newcastle, for £40,000 plus either Micky Burns or ex-North Ender Alex Bruce . . . Doug Livermore (Norwich) joins Cardiff for a £20,000 fee.

23 Stan Bowles scores a hat-trick for QPR in their 5–1 defeat of Derby at the Baseball Ground. Ted MacDougall also gets three goals for Norwich, who defeat Aston Villa 5–3.

25 Nobby Stiles refuses the offer to take over as manager of Preston North End and leaves the club. 'My decision had nothing to do with my close friendship with Bobby Charlton', he says, 'It is a matter of principle.'

26 Liverpool win 3–0 at Leeds with goals from Ray Kennedy and Ian Callaghan (2). During the match Leeds substitute Norman Hunter clashes with boss Jimmy Armfield, and walks away from the bench in apparent disgust. However, Armfield says, 'Norman and I are of entirely different temperaments, but now the incident is closed. A substitute would have made no difference' . . . Peter Bonetti agrees to help out Chelsea in their present goalkeeping shortage. He signs a monthly contract until John Phillips is back in action, but the veteran ex-Chelsea player is still available on a free transfer.

27 At Derby, the Champions beat Newcastle 3–2 in a controversial game, which sees the dismissal of Micky Burns following a disputed goal. Manager Gordon Lee says, 'What went on out there was a disgrace to the First Division, and a disgrace to football' . . . Joe Kinnear signs for Brighton for a £5000 fee . . . Harry Catterick is the new manager of Preston. His first transfer deal is the one which has caused Charlton's resignation. John Bird to Newcastle for £50,000 plus Alec Burns.

28 Nottingham F. buy Tony Curran from Doncaster. Peacock and Miller plus a £50,000 cheque go to the Yorkshire club . . . Terry Hibbit moves to Birmingham

from Newcastle for £100,000.

29 Nobby Stiles returns to Preston as chief coach.

30 Hooliganism makes the headlines again. Hundreds of Chelsea fans invade the pitch at Luton in an attempt to get the match abandoned because their team is losing 3-0. Some of them also attack Keith Barber, the Luton goalkeeper. But referee Eric Reed suspends play, and after the riot is quelled, completes the match. The Chelsea fans also vandalize the town after the game and their train back to London is wrecked ... Other trouble spots are Stoke, where there were 50 arrests– the visitors being Manchester U., Glasgow where there are 60 arrests following the first ever Rangers v Celtic Premier Division game and Crewe, where the railway is closed after a fire in a football special ... Tony Waddington criticises Don Revie for not selecting Alan Hudson for the England squad. 'He has knocked the stuffing out of Alan's game. I think it is unfair that Don should recall players like Hudson and Ball and then drop them as he has'.

31 Don Revie replies to Tony Waddington's criticisms by saying 'I want men who are proud to pull on the England shirt. I don't want any players with me in the World Cup who go running for the plane home if they are left out of one match. We want less talking off the pitch and more on it. I won't have managers using me as an excuse for their own mediocre start to the season. Stoke pay Hudson's wages and it is Tony Waddington's job, not mine, to motivate his players' ... There is strong reaction to the chaos and hooliganism of last Saturday. Chelsea chairman, Brian Mears, calls an emergency Board meeting to discuss measures to deal with the situation. Referee Eric Reed says, 'Bring back the birch or the cat. That would stop the hooligans.' And an MP proposes that grounds should be closed as a punishment for crowd disturbances ... Barry Powell (Wolves) goes to Coventry for £75,000 ... Roy Chapman is the new manager of Stockport County.

September

British Rail soccer specials are cancelled for the remainder of the season ... Wally Barnes dies aged 55 ... Bremner and others involved in Copenhagen nightclub rumpus—they are banned for life by Scotland ... outline proposals are announced for granting freedom of contract to players ... Gianna Rivera 'buys' AC Milan ... big bonuses for England players if they do well in the European Championship.

1 'Identity cards for football fans and the ending of British Rail specials become imminent as the soccer authorities, politicians and magistrates act in an attempt to halt hooliganism.' writes the *Daily Mail*. 'The Football Association urged a two-point plan for transporting fans to and from away matches. 1. Trains would be chartered by either official supporters' clubs or the football clubs themselves, and the organisers would be responsible for the behaviour of the fans. 2. The trips would be available only to registered supporters carrying an identity card and a ticket for the match.'

2 George Miller takes over as manager of Falkirk.

3 England beat Switzerland 2-1 in Basle, but play below form ... Scotland win in Denmark to keep their faint hopes alive in the European Championship, but N. Ireland lose at home to Sweden ... UEFA makes it clear that there will be no European finals of any kind staged at Wembley, Hampden Park, or any British ground until they erect 8ft fences all round the ground ... British Railways cancel all football specials for the rest of the season, and there won't be any 'cheap day returns' on Saturdays until 3 p.m. Clubs may charter their own trains but they will be responsible for any damage. Alan Hardaker says, 'This regulation came about three or four years too late. And I don't like the expression 'soccer hooligans' – they are merely hooligans, no-one wants them in football.'

4 Wally Barnes, the ex-Wales and Arsenal full-back, dies at the age of 55 after a short illness ... Wembley officials say that the erection of fences will not create a problem, and England could stage the finals of the current European Championship.

6   There are no arrests and no hooliganism is reported – perhaps a result of the disappearance of B.R. 'football specials' . . . Ted MacDougall of Norwich scores a hat-trick against Everton . . . Crystal Palace win at Cardiff 1-0 and are the only team to have won all their league matches this season. . . . Billy Bremner, Willie Young, Arthur Graham, Joe Harper and Pat McCluskey face a Scottish FA disciplinary enquiry following alleged incidents in a Copenhagen nightclub. Bremner says, 'I have heard about these rumours. They are nonsense. There was no row in the club, no fight, and no trouble about the bill. Anyway, what we do in our spare time is nothing to do with anyone else.'

8   The five Scottish players who were allegedly involved in the 'Copenhagen incidents' are banned for life by the Scottish FA. Billy Bremner and the others will never play again for Scotland on any level. Bremner says, 'I am staggerd. I don't know if I shall be allowed to appeal.' In addition, Ronnie McKenzie of Falkirk who has been with the squad says that he does not want to be considered again for selection as trainer to the Scottish team . . . A new scheme is proposed following discussions between the Football League and the Professional Footballers' Association. This scheme, which might start next season, includes the introduction of compensation payments, which will replace transfer fees when a player moves to a new club at the end of his contract. The compensation has computer-like dimensions, being based on the basic salary offered by the new club, multiplied by a factor determined by the player's age and the Division he has been playing in. The multiplying factor has yet to be decided by the Secretaries of the League and PFA, Alan Hardaker and Cliff Lloyd respectively. Contracts end on June 30 and clubs must notify players by March 1 whether they intend to re-engage them, and on what terms. If the terms are less favourable than those which the player has been receiving he can move to a new club without compensation being paid. The League will publish a list of players offered terms by their clubs, and as soon as they do so, players can start negotiations with interested clubs. Restrictions on signing-on fees will be abolished and any such fees will be paid in weekly instalments over the entire period of the contract. There will be no transfer deadline under the new system. Another far-reaching step is the proposed abolition of the apprentice system for 16-year-olds. In future all players between 16 and 18 may sign only as part-time contract players. Clubs will have to train such players in an outside job or make adequate provision for their further education. There will be no maximum wage for them, and the minimum wage for all full-time contract players will be £30 a week, instead of a scale varying with age and Division. But the entire system is to be the subject of further discussions with all interested parties.

9   Arthur Horsfield joins Watford from Charlton . . . Paul Crossley (Tranmere) and John James (Chester) change clubs . . . Jimmy Adamson, the Burnley manager, says that the new 'freedom of contract' system would kill football if introduced in its proposed form.

10 Poland beat World Cup silver medallists Holland 4-1 in the European Championship . . . Chelsea lose at Crewe through a disputed penalty and Lincoln defeat Stoke in the League Cup. . . . Leeds United reprimand Billy Bremner and warn him about his future conduct as a consequence of his being banned by Scotland.

11 Leeds are warned by the FA that if their disciplinary record does not improve, they will be fined. The Yorkshire club, in the company of eight others including Birmingham and Southampton, appear in front of a special committee . . . England manager Don Revie advocates the birching of 'soccer hooligans' in a broadcast. 'We have tried everything, we might as well try this drastic deterrent' . . . Norwich manager John Bond attacks Manchester City's over-defensive methods in the League Cup tie against his team at Norwich, and says that football has no future if teams persist in boring the public . . . It is announced that there will be a train and bus strike in West London on Saturday as a defensive measure against the invading Manchester U. fans on their way to Q.P.R.

13 Another high-scoring day in the First Division underlines the bright opening to

16

the season. Manchester U. lose their unbeaten record at QPR, but West Ham cling to theirs with a last minute equalizer at Leicester having been 3-0 down at half-time . . . Peter Noble scores all four goals for Burnley in their 4-4 draw with Norwich. Jim Holton of Manchester U. breaks a leg in a reserve match.

15 In the first European match of the season, Duisberg beat Paralimni of Cyprus 7-1.

16 Tottenham pay £100,000 for Willie Young the Aberdeen centre-back, recently banned by Scotland.

17 A mixed start for English clubs in Europe. At Goodison, A.C. Milan draw 0-0 with Everton in the UEFA Cup. Four Italians are booked, and Everton's Mike Bernard is sent off. A.C. Milan's club President Buticchi has been ousted and a group of businessmen have bought up his shares for over £1 million. Ex-player Gianna Rivera will run the club with the help of the veteran coach Nereo Rocco

18 Freddie Goodwin is sacked by Birmingham. He has been with the club for five years, and brought it up from the Second Division in his second season, but they have collected only two points in their first seven matches this year. Goodwin says: 'I've no regrets about my years at St. Andrews. I've always given 100% and had faith in my methods. But a bad start to the season meant that the board and myself have been increasingly on trial'. Willie Bell takes over as caretaker manager until a new man is appointed.

19 Sheffield United sign Chris Calvert, the York City full-back for £30,000 . . . Frank Worthington – dropped by Leicester for last Wednesday's League Cup tie – asks for a transfer, but manager Bloomfield says that he won't be allowed to leave the club.

20 Managerless Birmingham beat Burnley 4-0. Burnley's Doug Collins is taken off with a serious leg injury and Leighton James is carried off . . . Alan Gowling gets a hat-trick in Newcastle's 5-1 win over Wolves . . . Tony Currie of Sheffield U. is substituted at West Ham for the first time in his career.

21 Ian Brennan, the young Burnley full-back, sustains a broken leg in a car accident . . . Eddie McCreadie fines the Chelsea players booked for dissent – Hutchinson and Garner – £25 each.

22 It is announced following an FA Council meeting that England players will get £5000 each if they win the European Championship. There will be a £2000 bonus payment for reaching the quarter-finals, and £1000 each for victories in the semi-final and the Final. Don Revie says, 'Let me make it quite clear that when I ask players to pull on the England shirt I expect them to do it first of all for the pride of playing for their country. But football is a short career and the players' rewards should be proportionate to the amount of money the national association collects as the result of their efforts' . . . The same FA Council meeting agrees to raise Cup final ticket prices – the gate receipts in 1976 will be £420,000.

23 Marcus Lipton MP attacks the bonus plan for the England team. 'Apart from any other consideration, this business of bribing players to play better or rougher than they otherwise would, is going to kill this sport' he says. 'This is sheer prostitution of the game of football. How the devil can we expect ordinary people to have £6 maximum increase when these vast sums are being offered to soccer players?' . . . In the evening fixtures, QPR beat Leicester 1-0 and move to second place – still undefeated . . . But Crystal Palace's run ends at home when they are beaten by Brighton . . . Sheffield U. register their first win of the season and Birmingham collect two more points – four in as many days under caretaker manager Willie Bell . . . Aston Villa pay £100,000 for Blackpool's 23-year-old goalkeeper John Burridge.

24 Brighton manager, Peter Taylor, suspends four players following a 'disgraceful display' in a recent reserve match . . . Mick Jones, the Leeds striker, whose career ended due to a knee injury, will get £20,000 golden handshake as part of an insurance settlement . . . Bobby Charlton takes a job with a travel agency. He has turned down several offers inside the game, and says, 'I'm not leaving the game with ill-will. It has been good to me. I don't think I did a bad job as a manager'.

. . . Hungary beat Austria 2-1 in the European Championship — Wales need only one point to reach the quarter-finals.

25 Welsh referee Ron Jones is killed in a car accident. The 37-year-old official, who was due to referee his first European match in four days' time, was on his way home from the Hereford v Swindon game . . . Norwich manager John Bond signs Forest centre-back David Jones for £40,000 . . . Jimmy Melia resigns at Southport. They had a gate of 871 for a league match on Wednesday . . . Don Revie takes on Ken Burton as a full-time assistant. Burton was in charge of the UEFA Youth Cup-winning side last season, and will be mainly concerned with the development of young talent . . . Tommy Baldwin is released by Chelsea on a free transfer.

27 Andy Gray, Dundee United's 19-year-old striker is Villa's second big signing of the week — £110,000 . . . Italy draw 0-0 with Finland in Rome, and the 50,000 crowd demonstrate against their own players . . . Leicester still haven't won a league game this season . . . Tottenham boss Terry Neill apologises to the fans for his team's poor display against Arsenal. 'It made me feel ashamed. I can't apologise enough to the spectators. It was the kind of stuff that will kill football.'

29 Seven players are booked and one sent off in the Mansfield v Ayr U. Anglo-Scottish Cup tie . . . The FA announce an enquiry concerning the pitch invasion during the recent Luton v Chelsea match.

October

Sheffield United sack manager Ken Furphy . . . Dynamo Kiev win the European Supercup . . . Rodney Marsh is transfer listed . . . Terry Paine establishes a new League appearances record . . . . England lose in Czechoslavakia in the European Championship.

1 Gerry Summers is sacked at Oxford after seven years as manager. He says, 'I kept a Third Division side in Division Two. Last season when we sold two of my best players — Curran and Roberts — I wanted to resign, but they wouldn't let me go' . . . Steve Burtenshaw is also dismissed at Sheffield Wednesday.

2 Bobby Svarc signs for Blackburn Rovers from Colchester for £25,000 — a record for Colchester.

4 West Ham and QPR lose their unbeaten records. The former lose at home to Everton and the latter are beaten at Leeds. Leicester draw for the seventh time in 11 league matches . . . Bury are still undefeated . . . Three players are sent off including Len Badger of bottom-of-the-table Sheffield U. . . . Dave Cunningham (Southend) is the first player to collect 20 disciplinary points — he'll start a three match suspension on Monday . . . Phil Walker, a 20-year-old amateur who only signed for Millwall five days ago scores the winning goal on his debut for the London club . . . Goalkeeper Pat Jennings establishes a new appearance record for Tottenham. The 2-2 draw against Newcastle is his 419th league game for the club.

6 Sheffield United dismiss manager Ken Furphy after 11 league matches this season which have yielded only three points. Now the town of Sheffield has two league teams without a manager . . . The FA Charity Shield match will be sponsored by Pontins Holiday Camp firm for the next three years . . . Oleg Blochin scores twice for Dynamo Kiev in their 2-0 Supercup victory over Bayern Munich. The Soviet champions win the trophy on a 3-0 aggregate.

7 Chelsea will issue identity cards to their terrace supporters in an effort to stop hooliganism.

8 Notts Co. provide a major shock by beating Leeds 1-0 at Elland Road in the League Cup. The scorer is Ian Scanlon.

13 Rodney Marsh is put on the transfer list by Manchester City for 'not giving 100% to the club'. Marsh denies the allegation and says that he does not wish to leave . . . Stuart Pearson of Manchester U. and John Gidman, the Aston Villa defender, are included in the England squad for the Czechoslovakia match, but neither

Hudson nor Bowles is included ... Following a trial period, Willie Bell is appointed manager of Birmingham. Chairman Keith Coombs says, 'We didn't realize that we had such a jewel in our midst!'

15   A night of European Championship football—Holland take revenge on Poland by winning 3-0 in Amsterdam, Yugoslavia strengthen their position on top of Group 3 and Austria beat Luxembourg 6-2 ... Len Ashurst is the new manager of struggling Sheffield Wednesday ... Jimmy Sirrel leaves Notts Co. and takes over Ken Furphy's old job at Sheffield U. Sirrel had no contract with County, but the 53-year-old Scot gave a month's notice to the club. 'I can do both jobs for a few weeks', he says, 'there is plenty of time' ... Gillingham want compensation for Ashurst, who has a contract which still has 19 months unfulfilled ... Manager Alan Ashman resigns at Carlisle.

16   An Aston Villa bid for Rodney Marsh is turned down by Manchester City.

18   Bury, the last unbeaten club in the Football League, lose 4-0 at Peterborough ... Manchester U. are back on top of Division One following their 3-1 win over Arsenal ... Frank Casper of Burnley scores his 100th league goal in his first game for 19 months ... Crowd riots stop two games in Scotland, at Motherwell and Celtic Park. Motherwell beat Rangers 2-1, but the Celtic v Hibernian game with the visitors leading 2-0 is abandoned due to thick fog with five minutes left to play.

20   David McCreery, Manchester United's 18-year-old striker is included in the Irish squad against Norway ... Terry Naylor is suspended for two matches ... Syd Owen leaves Leeds, because the club has refused to give him a written contract. 'I was happy at Leeds,' says the coach, 'but I am looking for security' ... The England squads—38 players—travelling to Czechoslovakia, are insured for around 10 million pounds.

23   Archie Gemmill is recalled into the Scotland squad following his excellent displays for Derby.

24   Brian Little, the Aston Villa striker, is out of football with cartilage trouble ... Eric Sykes, comedian and scriptwriter, accepts an invitation to join the Oldham Board of Directors.

25   Referee Peter Reeves takes the players off the pitch and the West Ham v Manchester U. match is suspended for 18 minutes. There is a pitch invasion caused partly by an overspill from the terraces, partly by fighting. ... West Ham win 2-1 and the two teams plus QPR are locked on top of the table with 19 points each ... Terry Paine, 36, the Hereford player-coach establishes a new league appearance record— 765! The previous holder of the record was Jimmy Dickinson of Portsmouth.

26   Several players are doubtful for the England trip to Czechoslovakia and Don Revie calls in Frank Lampard to join the senior squad ... Withdrawals from the Scottish squad include Hay, Harvey, Buchan, and Sandy Jardine.

27   Don Revie selects an attacking formation against Czechoslovakia ... Gerry Summers, the ex-Oxford manager, is appointed as the new boss of Gillingham ... The Sports Council is considering a gambling levy and using the money to develop football grounds as community sports centres.

28   The England U-23 side draws in Trnava—substitute Peter Taylor equalizes an earlier Czech goal ... Scotland beat Denmark 4-1 in the same competition with Andy Gray of Aston Villa getting a hat-trick.

29   The Czechoslovakia v England match is suspended because of fog after 16 minutes This is only the second time that an England match has been postponed in 103 years of international football ... In the other matches, both Scotland and N. Ireland win convincingly ... Don Givens scores four times in the Republic of Ireland's 4-0 win over Turkey. Givens now has eight goals in the European Championship and he leads the chart of goal-getters. Givens equals a 41-year-old record set by Paddy Moore ... Adrian Alston joins Cardiff from Luton for £30,000.

30   Czechoslovakia beat England 2-1 in Bratislava – their first victory against England since 1934. Channon puts England ahead, but Nehoda equalizes seconds before half-time. Gallis gets the winner early in the second period. Gillard and two Czech

players are booked. Following an incident on the field the Czech substitute goal-keeper Vencel remonstrates with the referee from the substitute's bench and is shown the red disc and told to go into the dressing-room. McFarland is injured and substituted by Watson. This is the first England defeat since Don Revie took over as manager.

31 Don Howe is the new coach of Leeds. The ex-West Bromwich manager has been helping the Turkish side, Galatasaray during the last few months on the under-standing that if a job in England was offered to him, he was free to take it.

November
Derby and Rangers go out of Europe . . . George Best is released by Manchester United and plans a comeback . . . the World Cup draw is made . . . England are out of Europe.

1 Two ex-England internationals, Francis Lee and Norman Hunter, are sent off at Derby. After the players are dismissed by referee Derek Nippard for fighting, they resume the battle as they are leaving the field, and have to be separated by team-mates. Derby win 3-2 by a late Roger Davies goal . . . The Manchester City bus taking the players to Sheffield is involved in an accident and goalkeeper Corrigan is injured . . . West Ham beat Birmingham 5-1 at St Andrews, but Manchester U. are back on top with a narrow 1-0 win over Norwich. Docherty attacks Norwich: 'They play parasitic football', he says, 'living-off other peoples' mistakes' . . . Givens scores for Q.P.R. in their 1-1 draw at Coventry – his sixth goal in eight days . . . After the Millwall v Colchester match, linesman Gerald Colyer is attacked by a group of youths when getting into his car. He receives treatment for concussion and bruises.

4 Crystal Palace winger Peter Taylor is sent off at Swindon. He admits that referee Jack Taylor was right, but the Swindon management protest against the dismissal of Moss who was involved in the incident. Palace win 2-1 and are now four points clear at the top of Division 3 . . . Liverpool beat Real Sociedad 6-0 at Anfield with teenagers Brian Kettle and Dave Fairclough in the side.

5 A depressing night for Britain in Europe. Real beat Derby 5-1 with an extra-time goal in the European Cup, and Rangers go out of the same competition with a 2-1 defeat against St Etienne . . . Ipswich lose 4-0 at Bruges . . . However, the Cup-Winners' Cup is dominated by British clubs as all three reach the quarter-finals. West Ham (3-1 v Ararat), Celtic (3-1 v Boavista) and Wrexham (1-1 v Stal Rzeszow) are through . . . Both W. German clubs make the last eight in the Champions' Cup, but in the UEFA Cup no less than 13 countries are represented in the last 16! Only the USSR, Italy, and Poland have two clubs left and only W. Germany and Holland have teams still remaining in all three tournaments.

7 Lee and Hunter will be charged by the F.A. with 'bringing the game into disrepute' . . . George Best is suspended from playing in any country under the jurisdiction of FIFA . . . Stan Bowles, Q.P.R.'s controversial star, is included in the England squad for the forthcoming Portugal match.

8 Phil Dwyer of Cardiff is given mouth-to-mouth resuscitation at Gillingham by trainer Ron Durham and is taken to hospital suffering from concussion. 'Phil would have died if I didn't help him', said Durham . . . Comedian Eric Morecambe resigns from the Luton Board . . . Three ex-Chelsea players – Weller, Kember, and Garland score for Leicester in their 3-2 win over Burnley – their first league win of the season! . . . George Best is released by Manchester United and is free to sign for any club in any country as the FIFA ban on him is lifted automatically.

10 George Best signs for Stockport Co. for a month and plays against Stoke in an exhibition match. 8000 people see Best score, and the Fourth Division club get a 1-1 draw . . . Mike England of Cardiff City is recalled into the Wales squad.

11 Norman Hunter is suspended for three matches as he has accumulated 20 penalty points . . . Goalkeeper Dai Davies is out of the Welsh squad with a broken thumb . . . Ron Davies former Welsh International striker signs for Millwall on temporary transfer.

12 Colin Bell is seriously injured and is out of the England squad for the match against Portugal . . . Gordon Hill of Millwall joins Manchester United for £70,000. 'He is the last piece of the jigsaw in my team-building,' says manager Tommy Docherty . . . Portugal draw 1-1 with the Czechs, but England still lead the European Championship group with better goal difference.

15 John Richards scores after 16 seconds' play for Wolves at Burnley, and the Midlanders record a 5-1 away win . . . Two ex-Arsenal players score vital goals in the race for the Championship. Charlie George gets Derby's winner against West Ham, and Ray Kennedy scores in the last minute at Newcastle giving a 2-1 win to Liverpool. Derby are on top for the first time this season with Liverpool and Manchester United one point behind. The London challengers – QPR and West Ham – are in fourth and fifth place . . . Peter Bonetti plays his 500th game for Chelsea in their 2-0 win over Notts County . . . Billy Hughes of Sunderland is taken off with a broken leg at Charlton, but substitute Mel Holden scores twice in their 2-1 away win . . . Bell, Bowles, and McFarland are definitely out of the England squad with injuries and several other players are doubtful for the vital game against Portugal . . . Brentford Chairman, Dan Tana, makes a 'citizen's arrest' during the home game against Watford. 'Some louts used bad language near the directors' box,' said Tana, 'I was embarrassed for my wife and children. So, I nabbed the worst offender and handed him over to a policeman.'

16 Alan Ball withdraws his transfer request at Arsenal . . . West Ham defender Kevin Lock is called into the England squad . . . The Welsh FA offer a special bonus payment to the players if they qualify for the last eight of the European Championship.

17 UEFA fine the F.A. of Ireland £900 because of bad crowd behaviour during the Eire v Turkey match in Dublin . . . Chairman Len Hawkins and director Richard Banks resign from the Board at Luton . . . The Argentinian Government promises to provide financial backing for the 1978 World Cup.

18 The England U-23 team qualify for the quarter-finals of the European Championship by beating Portugal 2-0 at Crystal Palace.

19 England draw 1-1 at Lisbon, and are now on the brink of elimination from the European Championship . . . Don Revie suggests England need more time to prepare for these matches . . . Wales go into the quarter-finals by beating Austria 1-0 at Wrexham. 33-year-old Arfon Griffiths gets the winning goal. . . . Both Yugoslavia and W. Germany win 1-0 against N. Ireland and Bulgaria respectively, and are certain qualifiers . . . The Rodney Marsh transfer to Anderlecht is off, because the player feels that the language difficulties would create too many problems . . . Jimmy Johnstone, the ex-Celtic and Scotland winger, signs for Sheffield United.

20 Unseeded England are drawn with Italy, Luxembourg, and Finland in the 1978 World Cup. Wales and Scotland are in the same group as each other together with Czechoslovakia . . . N. Ireland have the difficult task of competing with Holland, Belgium and Iceland. Don Revie says: 'We are very fortunate to be in a section like this. Italy will be the test. They have a lot of great players. But we're given a chance and it's entirely up to us to get busy and qualify. ' . . Tony Currie comes back from Lisbon in a wheelchair suffering from appendicitis and will have to undergo an operation . . . Alan Hardaker attacks Revie, 'It would not have made a scrap of difference to England's performance if League matches had been postponed. We smacked of excuses before we even left for Portugal. At present it is all money, money, money! Wales got exactly the same co-operation as England and they have done well.' Revie answers: 'This is one of the biggest shocks of my life. It is hard to believe that a person in a responsible position should say such things. The players have never discussed money – they have run themselves into the ground. If you get a chance to prepare and you don't qualify, then you have no excuses. But you must get the chance to prepare properly!'

22 Ten League clubs fail to defeat non-League clubs in the First Round of the FA Cup. Six League clubs are beaten and four can only draw. Among the surprises are Coventry Sporting's win over Tranmere, and Hendon's defeat of Reading . . . Sammy McIlroy is carried off with a jaw injury at Highbury, where Manchester United lose 3-1 . . . In the first division only four points separate the top eight clubs . . . Italy beat Holland 1-0, but the Dutch national side are in the last eight of the European Championship as group winners on goal average over Poland.

23 Czechoslovakia win 3-0 in Limassol and as a result England are out of the European Championship.

24 In answer to Alan Hardaker's criticisms, the England players led by Gerry Francis volunteer to donate their match fees against Italy to charity . . . The PFA annual meeting backs Derek Dougan's proposals concerning the 'freedom of contract' issue . . . George Best, once again on the comeback trail, scores twice in the Peter Osgood Testimonial match at Chelsea.

25 Millwall draw with Yeovil in an FA Cup replay, and Millwall manager Gordon Jago reportedly launches an attack on his players: 'They were disgraceful, not an ounce of character. If I could stop their appearance money, I would.'

26 Dover become the fourteenth non-League club to reach Round Two of the FA Cup. They beat Colchester 4-1 in extra time in their replay . . . The Irish club Home Farm complains that Aston Villa have illegally approached their 17-year-old player Martin Murray.

27 Bryan Hamilton joins Everton from Ipswich for £40,000 . . . A revised form of freedom of contract system is accepted by the Joint Committee and will be recommended to the clubs and the players . . . Alan Hardaker assures Don Revie that the England squad will have sufficient time to prepare for the World Cup qualifying matches . . . Wales will also be given assistance to have all their players available for the European Championship quarter-finals.

28 Derby pay £300,000 for Leighton James of Burnley. Dave Mackay says: 'I would have taken us to win the championship again. But now we must be even a better bet. James will give our attack extra width' . . . George Best scores twice against Swansea, in his first League game for Stockport.

29 Bill Garner of Chelsea is sent off at Bristol Rovers – his second dismissal this season . . . Sunderland and Crystal Palace are drawing clear of their challengers in Division Two and Three respectively.

December

'Freedom of contract' draws nearer . . . Francis Lee's knuckles are rapped . . . Derek Dougan makes a comeback . . . attendances on the increase.

2 The transfer market becomes more active, as Middlesbrough pay £75,000 for Phil Boersma of Liverpool, and Jimmy McIlvraith signs for Bury . . . Bill Garner of Chelsea is suspended for four games.

3 Luton are facing a grave financial crisis, and they call a special meeting of the shareholders.

4 Andy Grey of Aston Villa is included in the Scotland senior squad for the international against Rumania . . . Chelsea are reported to be considering a bid for George Best – on a special match fee basis linked to attendances.

5 Luton Town are in serious financial difficulties. A First Division club less than nine months ago, they will go out of business if they cannot get additional finance within a few days. Their bankers have refused to extend their credit, and the directors have to pay the wages bill this week from their own pockets . . . Bobby Gould rejoins Wolves for £30,000 from West Ham . . . Only Leeds win of the top eight teams and now only one point separates the first six clubs in Division One . . . Three players are sent off in four minutes at the Brentford v Rochdale match . . . Southport win their first League match of the season.

7   Luton's Peter Anderson signs for Antwerp in an £80,000 deal. The money will help Luton's financial problems. Their chief executive Davies Mortimer says: 'Now we can get on with other measures needed to set the club to rights.'

9   Francis Lee of Derby is banned for four games and fined £200 for 'bringing the game into disrepute'. Leeds defender Norman Hunter who had been involved with Lee in the incident is cleared of the same charge . . . Derek Dougan is back in football as player/manager of Kettering . . . Alan Ashman is the new manager of Workington.

10 Liverpool reach the quarter-finals of the UEFA Cup by beating Slask Wroclaw 3-0 (agg. 5-1) with a hat-trick scored by reserve striker, 21-year-old Jimmy Case. Surprise of the round – Levski Spartak's victory over Ajax Amsterdam . . . West Ham lose 1-0 at home to Fiorentina, and the Italians collect the re-incarnated Anglo-Italian Cup . . . Derek Dougan says that a 'football levy board' must be set up by the Government to save clubs from going out of business . . . Wales are to consider an offer to stage their European Championship quarter-final at Wembley. Secretary Trevor Morris says: 'Money is not everything. A move from Cardiff or Wrexham would be a betrayal' . . . It is announced that England will play in a four-nations tournament in America in May. Italy, Brazil, and the U.S.A. are the other likely participants.

11 An informal meeting of club chairmen endorses the 'freedom of contract' proposals. But Arsenal chairman, Dennis Hill-Wood warns: 'When Jimmy Hill got rid of the maximum wage, 5000 professional footballers became 2500. If freedom of contract goes through now, the 2500 could become 1000 within a year.' At the same meeting, the FA and Football League agree on a new system to give the international squad more time for preparation – details of the plan will be released later . . . Peter Marinello goes to Motherwell for a £35,000 fee . . . Martin Murray, the Home Farm player, who has been watched by several League clubs, signs for Everton.

13 Scarborough are the only non-league club to reach the third round of the F.A. Cup, but four other non-league clubs are involved in re-plays. In the League, four teams share first place and only 3 points separate the top eight . . . Two ex-internationals, Peter Storey and Johnny Giles are sent off, and as he is leaving the pitch, Storey is attacked by an irate Stoke fan at the Victoria Ground.

14 Important decisions are approved at the Football League meeting. The peace formula between the clubs and Don Revie will enable the England squad to spend nine days together before a midweek international, providing the players will be released to play for their clubs on the intervening Saturday. From next season, referees will use the yellow and red cards system in domestic football. . . . Alun Evans (Aston Villa) signs for Walsall for £3000.

15 The Football League refuses to allow Rodney Marsh to be registered with an American Club and play for Crystal Palace on loan. Marsh says: 'It is costing me a fortune. I certainly feel the Football League are depriving me of my livelihood' . . . West Ham are told to build a wall, to rule out pitch invasion, at a cost of around £40,000.

16 Local referee Alan Turvey abandons the Tooting v Leatherhead F.A. Cup re-play in the 57th minute due to ground conditions . . . The FA turns down the request of three clubs to switch their Third Round ties to January 1 in order to avoid clashes with other games in their area. One of the clubs concerned is Chelsea and their chairman Brian Mears says that he'll fight the ban. Orient boss Brian Winston says: 'They are trying to kill us. We would have 15,000 on New Year's Day, but with West Ham and Tottenham playing at home, we'll be lucky to get 3000 against Cardiff City.'

17 Scotland draw with Rumania 1-1 in their last European Championship match. Rioch scores from a free-kick, but Crisas equalises. Doyle of Ayr U. and Andy Grey, the young Aston Villa striker, collect their first full caps.

18 The FA yield to pressure and allow two cup ties to be played on New Year's Day

... A fund in the region of £500,000 will be available for the clubs to improve safety conditions at the grounds. The money will be provided by the Pools Promoters Association.

20 Liverpool are back on top after beating QPR 2-0 with a John Toshack goal and a Phil Neal penalty . . . Allan Clarke scores his 100th goal for Leeds – the only goal in the match v Aston Villa . . . Crystal Palace lose their unbeaten away record at Millwall . . . Billy Jennings scores a hat-trick for West Ham against Stoke's England international goalkeeper Peter Shilton.

22 It is announced that the Cup Final will be played late in May next season to give the England squad more time together. Other plans include permission for teams to cancel their League matches if two or more of their players are involved in a midweek international and the playing of a round of the League Cup before the start of the Championship . . . Alec Stock says that referees are spoiling football by booking players for innocuous offences.

23 Aston Villa pay £175,000 for Dennis Mortimer of Coventry. Jimmy Hill says: 'Our supporters might be disappointed but this sale ensures Coventry's future for the next five years' . . . Bobby Collins resigns at Huddersfield.

26 Despite the B.R. shut-down, 630,367 people watch Boxing Day football and seven clubs have the highest attendances of the season. Liverpool are back on top after their 1-1 draw at Stoke. Leeds win at Maine Road – a first home defeat for Manchester City and the first defeat of any kind for 18 matches . . . City's Peter Barnes goes off with a hairline fracture of the shoulder . . . Leighton James scores his first goal for Derby, but the Champions are beaten 2-1 at Leicester . . . Warwick Rimmer of Crewe is sent off a few days after his club was warned by the FA concerning their players' behaviour.

27 The increase in attendances continues – 777,627 spectators attend League matches . . . Keith Robson is sent off as West Ham are defeated by Ipswich. Liverpool are still on top, but Leeds collect maximum points in the holiday games and are only one point behind with a game in hand . . . Ron Moore of Tranmere scores four goals in a match for the second time this season . . . Jimmy Greaves makes his debut for Brentwood in the Essex Senior League.

29 Derby's David Nish has an exploratory operation on his knee but is assured that there are no permanent problems . . . John Deacon, the chairman of Portsmouth, refuses to resign at the club's annual meeting, despite strong pressure from the directors . . . Don Revie calls the peace formula with the League a 'great breakthrough' and says 'there are no excuses now if we do badly in the World Cup qualifying matches.'

January

FA Cup-holders go out at first hurdle . . . Jimmy Adamson resigns at Burnley . . . the 'kissing and cuddling' scandal . . . Bowles transfer-listed again . . . Newcastle and Manchester City for League Cup final.

1 Oleg Blochin of Russia is the European 'Footballer of the Year'. Beckenbauer, Cruyff, Vogts, and Maier are placed in the first five . . . Colin Todd is ninth.

2 Allen Brown is appointed manager of Southport, who are at the bottom of the fourth division.

3 Both last year's finalists, West Ham and Fulham, are beaten in the third round of the FA Cup – the first time this has happened for 43 years . . . Tooting draw 2-2 at Swindon having been 2-0 down until the last six minutes . . . Manchester United beat Oxford with the help of two penalties scored by Gerry Daly – Oxford were leading 1-0 at half-time.

6 Tooting beat Swindon 2-1 and progress into Round 4. An early Tooting goal in this FA Cup replay is cancelled out by an own goal headed 'home' by defender Bobby Green, but five minutes from time, Alan Ives, a 27-years-old sales rep. gets

the winner . . . Jimmy Adamson leaves Burnley after 29 years' association with the club. Following last Saturday's Cup defeat at Blackpool it was reported that there were scuffles in the dressing room between players and staff. Adamson was locked out and now he has decided to resign.

7 Peterborough beat Nottingham Forest in a Cup replay and will meet Manchester United in the next round . . . Stan Bowles misses a penalty for QPR at Newcastle, and Tommy Craig scores one, so Newcastle go through to the next round . . . Don Revie asks 28 players to keep themselves free for England's international programme at the end of May and early June . . . Joe Brown, Jimmy Adamson's former assistant at Burnley, takes over the managerial job at the club.

8 Roy Greenwood of Hull signs for Sunderland for £120,000.

10 Bobby Charlton makes another 'comeback' – he is to play a few matches for Irish club Waterford . . . Manchester United are back on top of Division One after their 2-1 victory over QPR . . . Alan Gowling scores his third hat-trick of the season in Newcastle's 5-0 defeat of Everton . . . Portsmouth gain their first home win of the season by beating Carlisle 1-0 . . . Not a single player is sent off in the League.

11 In a *Sunday People* exclusive, Alan Ball attacks Don Revie's training methods and says that yes-men are selected for England instead of players of ability and imagination. 'Some of the players picked are donkeys. Give them a lump of sugar and they run all day and play bingo all night.'

12 Don Revie answers Ball: 'I am disappointed to hear a player for whom I have a great deal of admiration criticizing his fellow professionals. Alan Ball should concentrate on helping Arsenal. I often wish certain players would stop talking about how good they are and what they are going to do in a match . . . and actually get out on the pitch and do it' . . . Eddie Kelly is put on the transfer list at Arsenal . . . Scunthorpe manager Dicky Rooks is sacked . . . The Rodney Marsh saga is over – he signs for Tampa Bay Rowdies of Florida. In future the ex-Manchester City forward will spend six months in the USA and six in Britain, where he'll be available to play for non-League clubs.

13 Six players refuse to turn out for Ramsgate in a Kent Cup tie as a demonstration of solidarity with sacked manager, Alf Bentley . . . The FA are considering a £2 million deal for the 190 acre Ambassador College in Hertfordshire. They would convert the college into a National Football Training Centre . . . The FA's Match and Ground Committee are recommending to the executive that 'kissing and cuddling and making gestures to the crowd when a goal is scored should be stopped and that players who continue to act this way should be charged with bringing the game into disrepute.' Committee member Dan Tana explains: 'We feel the biggest problem is the players running behind the goal and throwing their fists into the air after scoring This could incite trouble among the fans' . . . Hickton scores the only goal of the match at Middlesbrough where Manchester City are beaten in the first leg of the League Cup semi-final . . .

14 In the European Championship draw Wales are drawn against highly-rated Yugoslavia. England U-23 will face Hungary, Liverpool play Dynamo Dresden – a repeat of their 1973 meeting, and West Ham are drawn against Den Haag, a middle of-the-table Dutch team.

15 Peterborough spend £25,000 on buying Ernie Moss of Chesterfield – a record for the club . . . Ron Ashman is back as manager of Scunthorpe . . . Dennis Tueart of Manchester City is suspended for two matches following his FA Cup 'punch-up' with Hartlepool player, George Potter.

17 Willie Bell, the Birmingham manager, withdraws skipper Kenny Burns at half-time against QPR. Burns was booked earlier, and then was involved in an off-the-ball incident with Hollins. Bell says: 'I cannot tolerate that sort of thing. I want my men to play the game as it should be played'.

19 Stan Bowles is on the transfer list at QPR at his own request. His wife and children have moved back to Manchester and the player wishes to join them. This is the

third time that Bowles has been on the list.

21 There will be an all-Northern League Cup Final at Wembley. Newcastle beat Tottenham 3-1 with the help of hotly disputed early goal by Alan Gowling and further scores by Keeley and Nulty. Manchester City easily dispose of Middlesbrough's challenge with a 4-0 win at Maine Road ... Sir Alf Ramsey joins Birmingham City as a club director. He will advise the Board, but will have no executive function – Willie Bell continues to have full control of all the playing affairs of the club ... Ken Furphy the ex-Sheffield United manager is appointed coach to New York Cosmos, the club in the USA for which Pele plays.

24 Third Division Crystal Palace defeat First Division Leeds 1-0 at Leeds thus creating the sensation of Round 4. David Swindlehurst scores in the first half. Non-Leaguers Tooting lose at Bradford.

25 There are bitter complaints from Tooting concerning the behaviour of Bradford – the club and its alleged supporters – yesterday. It is claimed that hidden microphones were put in one side of the ground to increase the volume of vocal support for the home team. After the match the Bradford hooligans attacked the Tooting fans with bricks and stones causing several injuries.

26 Kettering are the first English club to carry advertising on their jerseys during a match. Manager Derek Dougan has arranged a contract with a local tyre company. Football League Secretary Alan Hardaker does not approve of this development. He says: 'Those who go to soccer want to see a game of football, not to be reminded every time they look at a player that they must go home and tell the wife to change her soap powder.'

28 Charlton win 3-0 at Portsmouth in an FA Cup replay and reach the Fifth Round for the first time in 14 years ... Ladbrokes are said to be prepared to sponsor the Home International Championship for three years... FIFA will organize a World Cup for Under-20-year-old players in Tunisia in 1977, and thereafter every two years.

29 Ian St John, the Portsmouth manager, makes a verbal attack on his players following the defeat by Charlton: 'We had over 30,000 people at the ground – the best attendance for years. But my players must have thought that the game would be on the following day. Even my youth team would have beaten us today' ... Hereford announce an early kick-off v Crystal Palace to accommodate television transmission ... But the Football League intervene to prevent the game from being televised, because the BBC and the Football League have an agreement not to publicise in advance the venue of a televised match ... Mike Pejic of Stoke and Willie Donachie of Manchester City are sent off in an eventful Cup tie at Stoke. Jimmy Greenhoff's late goal puts Stoke into Round 5 ... Colin Viljoen is out of football for the rest of the season with an Achilles tendon injury.

30 George Best is no longer wanted by Cork Celtic. He has played three times for the Irish club, and although he has drawn the crowds his football has lacked enthusiasm.

February

Ian Hutchinson retires from football ... Palace storm on in the FA Cup – but slip in the League ... Derek Dougan's Kettering Town get into trouble over advertising ... More shocks in the FA Cup ... Pat Jennings is PFA Footballer of the Year.

2 Bowles is back in the QPR team. He plays a leading part in the Londoners' 4-0 win over Red Star Belgrade in Mick Leach's testimonial ... Sunderland reach the Fifth Round of the Cup by beating Hull 1-0.

3 Tony Morley signs for Burnley from Preston for £100,000 – a club record ... Bob Latchford will have a cartilage operation ... Two players – Taylor and Derek Jeffries – are sent off as Crystal Palace are beaten 4-1 at Rotherham.

4 The 'no-kissing-and-cuddling' recommendation is rejected by the FA as 'not practicable'.

6   Liverpool are back on top of the table following their 2-0 win over Leeds – once
    again Toshack and Keegan get the goals . . . Change in Division 2 also – Bolton
    take over from Sunderland, who lose 2-0 at Fulham . . . Hereford and Lincoln are
    leading the lower divisions . . . Jenny Baseley creates football history. A mother
    of two, she is the first woman to referee a football match between men. She officiates
    in Thornton Heath, Surrey.

9   The shattered glass of the team coach's window injures Southend goalkeeper
    Malcolm Webster. Reserve 'keeper Sean Rafter plays in the 1-1 draw at Port Vale.

10 Ian Hutchinson, the Chelsea striker retires from football. One of the unluckiest
    men in the game, Hutchinson has sustained two broken legs during his career,
    two cartilage operations, a broken arm, and a broken toe. He retires on medical
    advice. Chelsea manager Eddie McCreadie says: 'I watched him struggle for four
    years of terrible injuries where no-one else would have survived. The club will
    look after "Hutch" financially' . . . Don Revie selects an extremely powerful
    looking U-23 squad against Hungary. Gerry Francis, Kevin Beattie and over-age
    players, Alan Hudson and Jimmy Greenhoff are included.

11 The Norwich v Bradford City tie is postponed because a 'flu epidemic hits the
    Fourth Division club . . . Peter Taylor of Crystal Palace and Peter Osgood of
    Southampton are suspended for two matches each for reaching 20 disciplinary
    points.

12 The FA pay £500 compensation to a London Transport worker, who was attacked
    by Scottish fans travelling to Wembley in 1973 . . . Ron Greenwood, chairman of
    the Managers and Secretaries Association, warns that 'freedom of contract' would
    lead to increased admission charges. The managers believe that a simpler form of
    the current proposals would help the players to keep their jobs and would also
    help the financial structure of the clubs. Derek Dougan, PFA chairman reacts:
    'I am a little disappointed. They are against members of another Trade Union
    trying to better conditions. All we are trying to do is to give players the same rights
    as managers.'

13 John Manning, 34-year-old Crewe trainer-coach, who hasn't played a league match
    for 18 months, returns against Southport and scores a hat-trick! . . . Alan Buckley
    goes one better – he gets four in Walsall's 5-1 win over Rotherham . .   Johan
    Cruyff has a disagreement with Barcelona manager Hennes Weisweiler, and seems
    likely to leave the Spanish club next summer.

14 Crystal Palace defeat Chelsea in the fifth round of the FA Cup. Palace are 2-0
    up at half time, but Wilkins and Wicks equalise for Chelsea. A Peter Taylor
    free-kick puts Palace into the last 8 for the second time in their history . . . Sub.
    John Richards scores a hat-trick for Wolves v Charlton and a solitary Bruce
    Rioch goal is enough for Derby to defeat Southend . . . There are scenes of violence
    off the pitch at Chelsea – several arrests, hospital cases, and a mounted police
    patrol is needed to quell the riot . . . QPR take advantage of the inactivity of their
    rivals, and by winning 3-0 at Tottenham reduce the gap at the top to one point . . .
    Jimmy Greaves, now with Brentwood, is sent off for making a remark to a linesman.

16 Crystal Palace player Nick Chatterton will be 'sponsored' by a local firm. They
    will pay his wages, and use him for promoting the company's products. All the
    other Crystal Palace players are up 'for sale' for similar schemes . . . Terry Neill
    says that Tottenham are negotiating to sign Johan Cruyff. He is trying to raise the
    necessary finance from commercial enterprises.

18 Derby close the gap on the leaders with a 2-0 win over Arsenal. Recent signing
    Leighton James scores twice . . . Manchester U. draw with Liverpool at Old Trafford
    in front of 59,709 people . . . Another crowd of over 50,000 see the Newcastle v.
    Bolton FA Cup replay end in a 0-0 draw . . . In the first of European Championship
    U-23 quarter-finals, Holland beat Scotland 2-0.

19 The Police Superintendents' Association suggest that football matches should be
    given certificates like films. An X-certificate match – where crowd trouble is likely –
    would be banned for fans under 16 unless they are accompanied by an adult.

The idea doesn't please the clubs. Brian Mears of Chelsea said: 'Who would decide which matches should be selected?' . . . A sizeable crowd demonstrates in Barcelona on behalf of Johan Cruyff. They want the player to stay, and the manager, Hennes Weisweiler, to leave.

21 Referee P. Richardson of Lincolnshire sends off three Oxford United players – Shuker, Tait and Houseman at Blackpool . . . Liverpool take a two point lead as Manchester United lose at Villa in front of the day's biggest crowd – 50,094 . . . Graham Tutt of Charlton is carried off at Sunderland after five minutes' play, and the home team score four times against sub. goalkeeper, striker Derek Hales . . . Glen Hoddle, a 17-year-old, scores Tottenham's winning goal at Stoke in his first full appearance for the league side.

23 The twice-postponed Norwich v Bradford City FA Cup tie provides a shock result. The Fourth Division club wins 2-1 through an 87th minute goal by 21-year-old Billy McGinley. This is only the third time that a team from Division 4 has reached the last 8 of the FA Cup . . . The twice replayed Newcastle v Bolton tie is won by Newcastle, 2-1. . . . Kettering Town are told to remove advertising slogans from their jerseys. Manager Derek Dougan is said to be considering a test case in court against the FA to decide how far football sponsorship is allowed to go . . . Colin Bell loses his battle against injury and will not play for Manchester City in the League Cup Final.

24 Bristol City go on top of Division Two, following their 1-0 win over Oldham and Hereford lengthen their lead in Division Three . . . Brighton beat Palace 2-0 at home in front of 33,000 people. Palace have collected six points only in their last 12 league games and have slipped into fifth place.

25 The championship race becomes even more tense as QPR win at Leicester and Manchester United draw with Derby at Old Trafford. Now only one point separates the top four! . . . It is announced that Geoff Hurst will manage Southern League Telford next season . . . Newcastle are hit by a 'flu epidemic a few days before the League Cup Final. A request for postponement is considered, but manager Gordon Lee says that the game must be played on Saturday.

27 'Freedom of Contract' for the player is a step nearer as the 92 club chairmen agree on principle to accept the proposals . . . Derek Dougan says that the Kettering team will continue to carry advertising on their jerseys in defiance of the warning letter from the FA, but at the end compromises with just the letter 'T' instead of 'Tyres'.

28 Manchester City win 2-1 in an excellent League Cup Final with goals by wingers Barnes and Tueart. Gowling scores the Newcastle goal . . . Manchester United slam West Ham 4-0 . . . Derby, Liverpool and QPR draw . . . Leeds are back in the reckoning after a 1-0 win at Coventry . . . W. Germany beat Malta 8-0 in the last of the European Championship qualifying matches and now they will meet Spain in the quarter-finals.

29 Pat Jennings is the PFA 'Footballer of the Year'. He is selected from a short list of six which also included Kevin Keegan, Lou Macari, Archie Gemmill, Don Masson, and Duncan McKenzie. Peter Barnes, the Manchester City winger and son of ex-player Ken Barnes is the 'Young Player of the Year'. George Eastham is presented with the meritorious award for past services to football.

March

Controversy over Ladbroke's offer to sponsor the Home International Championship . . . Peter Storey says he'll never play for Arsenal again . . . England flop in the European U-23 Championship . . . Bertie Mee announces his retirement . . . Crystal Palace start sliding.

3 Penalties play vital parts in the British clubs' games in European football. Mansveld scores two penalties in Den Haag's 4-2 defeat of West Ham in the European Cup Winners' Cup. Ray Clemence saves a penalty at Dresden in Liverpool's 0-0 draw in the UEFA Cup. Bobby Lennox misses a penalty at Glasgow in Celtic's 1-1 draw

with the East German team Zwickau. Wrexham lose at Anderlecht 1-0. The top tie of the evening ends in a 2-2 draw between Moenchengladbach and Real Madrid . . . Newcastle sign Roger Jones and Graham Oates from Blackburn in a £100,000 package deal.

4   Both Terry Venables and Jim Cannon, respectively Crystal Palace's coach and player, are found guilty of bringing the game into disrepute by the FA . . . Brentford sign Andy McCulloch from Oxford for £25,000.

5   Don Rogers re-joins Swindon from QPR in a £30,000 transfer deal . . . The FA turns down Ladbroke's offer to sponsor the Home International Championship. But Trevor Morris, Welsh FA Secretary, says: 'They cannot decide without consulting the other three Associations. We would benefit by £18,000 per year from the sponsorship, and as far as we are concerned, the deal is on'.

6   Crystal Palace reach the semi-finals – the fourth Third Division side since the war to do so, and the first since 1959. Alan Whittle scores the only goal of the match at Sunderland . . . Bradford City lose 1-0 against Southampton . . . Derby beat injury-hit Newcastle 4-2, Manchester United are held to draw by Wolves . . . In the League, a surprise Liverpool home defeat enables QPR to go two points clear at the top of the first division.

7   Malcolm Allison is reported to be in line for the USA team manager job during the coming summer. He would coach and select the team for the four-cornered tournament which also involves England. He says: 'I would only go if I could take Terry Venables with me. In a month coaching the best players in America, I could teach them more than they have learned in the history of the game there'. . . Don Revie adds four players to the U-23 squad for the match against Hungary in Budapest – Dodd, Mills, Wilkins and new boy Paul Jones of Bolton. But only Dodd, who takes the place of the injured Beattie, is included in the team which will start the game.

8   Peter Storey is suspended for 14 days by Arsenal. The ex-England player has allegedly not reported for training for 10 days . . . The FA Cup semi-final draw ensures that a team outside the First Division will appear in the Final for the third time in four years.

9   QPR buy Peter Eastoe, the 22-year-old Swindon striker for £80,000 . . . Crystal Palace drop yet another home point – they haven't won a League match at Selhurst Park since November . . . In a pulsating Cup re-play, Manchester United beat Wolves 3-2 with an extra-time Sammy McIlroy goal. Tommy Docherty: 'This is the first time that the Cup Final will be played at Hillsbrough – for what else can you call our semi-final match against Derby? The other semi-final is a bit of a joke really'.

10   England U-23 flop in Hungary in the first leg of their European Championship tie. The 3-0 defeat is described in the Press as "hopeless", Jeff Powell writes in the *Daily Mail:* 'The real message from this match is that the 1978 World Cup Finals could be moved from Argentina to the Moon for all it will matter to most of these England players'. . . On the last day before the transfer deadline, Sunderland sign Ray Train for £80,000 from Carlisle. Brighton pay £30,000 for Brian Horton of Port Vale and Dennis Nelson goes to Reading from Crewe for £10,000. Newport collect a club record £15,000 from Swindon for Steve Aizlewood.

11   Coach Ian McFarlane leaves Manchester City, the League Cup winners, and signs as chief coach for Sunderland . . . Bobby Moore is dropped by Fulham – he is said to be contemplating a contract with a club in the USA.

13   All four championship aspirants win in Division 1 . . . Manchester United build up a 3-0 lead against Leeds at Old Trafford in front of yet another near 60,000 crowd, but two late goals by the visitors make the score more respectable . . . Dennis Tueart misses two penalties against Burnley, and is involved in an incident with Jim Thompson, who is sent off. The match ends in a goalless draw . . . Crystal Palace are the only team with promotion hopes to win in Division 3. . . .

16   Peter Storey says that he'll never play for Arsenal again. The ex-international defender is 'fed-up' with reserve team football and feels unwanted at Highbury . . .

Crystal Palace win their first home League match since late November.

17 Both English teams – West Ham and Liverpool – progress into the semi-finals of the UEFA competitions. West Ham score three times in the first half, but a second half Den Haag goal opens up the game again. Finally West Ham win with the help of the 'away goals' ruling – 5-5 . . . Jimmy Case and Kevin Keegan score in Liverpool's 2-1 win over Dynamo Dresden. Wrexham and Celtic lose against Anderlecht and Zwickau respectively . . . a surprise result in the European Cup is St Etienne 3 Dynamo Kiev 0. The other Eastern European side Hajduk Split also eliminated by PSV Eindhoven by the same score . . . Real Madrid are in the semi-final with an 'away goal' win over Moenchengladbach . . . Bulgaria provide the strangest score of the night—Levski 5 Barcelona 4. Barcelona win on an 8-5 aggregate and join Bruges, Hamburg and Liverpool in the UEFA-Cup draw . . . In front of a miserly 8,874 people, a patched-up Football League side beat the Scottish League 1-0 . . . Manchester United drop a point at Norwich, but in the Second Division Bristol City strengthen their position at the top with a surprising 1-0 win at West Bromwich.

18 Don Revie names his England squads, for the matches against Wales and Hungary U-23 but his plans are soon altered, because the Derby v Stoke match is rearranged for the same week. Five players drop out of the senior squad, and four others, including Bolton and Bristol City footballers drop out of the U-23 squad. Revie says: 'I don't blame Derby manager Dave Mackay. I know how difficult it is for him. But this is yet another chance lost of getting our best team together. No one should be surprised if England don't succeed in internationals' . . . Dave Watson will miss the rest of the season with a back injury.

19 Ray Kennedy, Dave Clement and Phil Parkes of QPR are called into the full England squad . . . Kevin Lock and John Middleton are the new members of the U-23 Squad.

20 Aston Villa's Chris Nicholl scores all four goals in the Leicester v Aston Villa (2-2) match. Brian Kidd gets a hat-trick in Arsenal's 6-1 win over West Ham United . . . Alan Buckley also gets a hat-trick, taking his season's total to 29 in the League.

22 Gary Jones of Everton is put on the transfer list . . . Peter Taylor of Crystal Palace is selected for the England squad to play Wales, and four Manchester United players are selected for U-23 match against Hungary at Old Trafford . . . Bertie Mee, manager of Arsenal, announces that he will retire at the end of the season.

23 England are out of the U-23 European Championship. Although a late rally gives them a 3-1 win over Hungary, they go out on a 4-3 aggregate in front of a 33,410 crowd at Old Trafford – a record for a U-23 fixture in England . . . Bolton lose again at home to Blackburn and are slipping in the Second Division race.

24 A depleted England side beat Wales 2-1 in the Centenary match at Wrexham. Including the substitutes, eight players are capped for the first time. Ray Kennedy and Peter Taylor score their first goals for England. He is the first Third Division player to be selected for England since Johnny Byrne – also of Crystal Palace – 15 years ago . . . Alan Mullery, the 34-year-old Fulham captain says he will retire at the end of the season. He also says that he would like to go into football management . . . Charlie George suffers a dislocated shoulder injury as Derby drop a home point against Stoke. In the same match Stoke's Alan Hudson cracks a bone in his foot and is out for the rest of the season . . . Scotland beat Holland 2-0 to make the aggregate 2-2 in the U-23 international but lose the penalty contest 4-3 and are out of the European Championship . . .

25 Dave Clement of QPR is suspended for two matches by the FA . . . In an emotional Press Conference, Bertie Mee reveals his reason for leaving club management. 'The pressures on an Arsenal manager are sometimes intolerable' he says, 'and I was not quite as motivated in the last two years as I should have been'. He added that his dearest wish is to stay with Arsenal in some capacity.

27 The top clubs in Division One all win. Asa Hartford of Manchester City is sent off at QPR and David Webb gets the only goal of the match . . . Liverpool sub. Fairclough scores twice in their 2-0 win over Burnley . . . Manchester U. beat

Middlesbrough after a goalless first half and Derby defeat Birmingham . . . Sheffield United are definitely relegated following their 5-0 thrashing at Spurs . . . Allan Clarke scores his 200th league goal – against Arsenal in Leeds' 3-0 home win . . . Mark Wallington, Leicester's U-23 international goalkeeper fractures his ankle.

30 A brilliant John Toshack goal gives Liverpool a surprising 1-0 win at Barcelona in the UEFA Cup. Toshack says: 'When my career is over and I look back on all the goals I scored, this one will probably stand out' . . . More than 38,000 people see Peter Taylor of Crystal Palace miss a penalty in the vital Third Division promotion match against Millwall which ended in a 0-0 draw. Palace wanted to play a day earlier because of their forthcoming Cup semi-final, but Millwall's manager Gordon Jago refused their request . . . Alan King moves to Everton from Luton for £35,000.

31 Graham Paddon gives West Ham the lead against Frankfurt, in the Cup Winners Cup, but the Londoners lose the match 2-1 – a result greeted with satisfaction by manager John Lyall . . . Elsewhere in Europe, Real Madrid draw with Bayern Munich 1-1 and St Etienne beat PSV 1-0 in the European Cup. After the match at Madrid, a spectator attacks the referee, and knocks down Bayern's Gerd Muller, who goes to rescue the official . . . Glasgow Rangers are in the Scottish Cup Final. Two goals down at half-time to Motherwell, they fight back and goals by Miller and Johnstone (2) put them through.

April

Southampton and Manchester U. are this year's Cup Finalists . . . Barcelona's manager resigns after their UEFA Cup defeat by Liverpool . . . Bobby Moore goes to the USA . . . Miljan Miljanic might come to Arsenal . . . Sunderland are promoted.

3 Crystal Palace fail to make football history by reaching the FA Cup Final as a Third Division club. In a lacklustre game, they lose to Southampton 2-0. Southampton's second half goals are scored by Gilchrist and Peach (pen), and their appearance in the Final will be their first since 1902. Their opponents, Manchester United, will be making their fifth post-war Wembley FA Cup Final appearance. They beat Derby 2-0. Gordon Hill scores both goals . . . In the League, both Liverpool and QPR win through late goals. Sub. David Fairclough helps out Liverpool once again, and Stan Bowles gets the QPR winner at Newcastle 20 seconds from the end . . . Barcelona manager Hennes Weisweiler resigns following the midweek defeat against Liverpool in the UEFA-Cup.

5 Ted MacDougall opts out of Scotland's Home International fixtures. He says that he needs a rest, and would rather go on a tour with Norwich . . . Bobby Moore goes to the USA to play for San Antonio.

6 Liverpool are level on points with QPR on top of the table. Kevin Keegan scores the winning goal for them against Leicester . . . Three Southampton players, Osgood, McCalliog and Steel are disciplined by the club for 'celebrating' the semi-final victory too long and not obeying the curfew. Without them Southampton beat Portsmouth 1-0 in a league match. David Peach is booked and may be banned from playing at Wembley.

7 Scotland beat Switzerland 1-0 in a friendly with an early goal by Willy Pettigrew . . . In the Third Division promotion battle Crystal Palace and Brighton both lose, Cardiff win and Millwall gain a point against Bury in a goalless draw.

8 QPR manager Dave Sexton fines winger Dave Thomas for his involvement in the incident which cost Asa Hartford a two-match ban. Sexton says: 'This question of clubs being responsible for players' conduct is difficult. It is better if the discipline comes from within the player himself' . . . Several First Division clubs pledge to release players for Wales's European Championship match on April 24 – the last Saturday of the league season!

9 A record crowd for soccer of 58,128 see Pele's team the New York Cosmos play Seattle Sounders in the new Seattle Stadium – an important step for the game in the USA. 29-year-old Jim Shoulder, an ex-Sunderland player, takes over the

Australian national team . . . Colin Barrett of Manchester City signs for Notts Forest.

10   A useful Saturday for QPR – they are the only winning side in the top five. Middlesbrough go ahead at Loftus Road but a penalty awarded for a foul on Dave Clement gives Gerry Francis the opportunity to level the score. Givens, Francis and Bowles score further goals to give QPR a 4-2 victory. Derby lose at Manchester City 4-3 and City's Mick Doyle is sent off early in the match for allegedly punching Leighton James, Ipswich beat Manchester United comfortably, and Liverpool drop a point at Aston Villa . . . In Division Two, only Sunderland win of the promotion contenders, and in Division Three Crystal Palace lose at home to Cardiff . . . A goal by Geoff Aslett wins the FA Vase at Wembley for Billericay the Essex Senior League Champions . . . Stan Bowles is offered a six-years contract by QPR worth £100,000.

12   According to a *Daily Express* exclusive, Miljan Miljanic, the current Yugoslav manager of Real Madrid is negotiating with Arsenal with a view to becoming their manager.

13   There are more set-backs for teams hoping for promotion. Bolton in the Second Division lose at home to York, and Third Division Crystal Palace drop a point against Halifax at Selhurst Park.

14   Two English clubs reach European Finals! West Ham break the deadlock against Eintracht Frankfurt at Upton Park with a Trevor Brooking goal in the 49th minute, and run out 4-3 aggregate winners. 'Our best display in the club's history. Everything I hoped for when I took the job came true tonight' says manager John Lyall . . . Liverpool draw with Barcelona 1-1, but the solitary Toshack goal from the first leg takes them into their second UEFA-Cup Final . . . Gerd Muller scores twice for Bayern's 2-0 win over Real in the European Cup, and St. Etienne drew 0-0 at Eindhoven to become the first French club to reach the European Cup Final since Rheims in 1959 . . . In England, Second Division WBA and Third Division Cardiff strengthen their promotion bids with conclusive victories over Fulham and Hereford respectively. 35,549 people see Cardiff's match at Ninian Park – their best league attendance for 15 years . . . Don Revie names a squad of 30 players for the next seven internationals which are scheduled before the end of the season. Eight uncapped players are included, and five more who gained their first caps in the recent game against Wales. Revie says: 'I wanted to include both skills and workrate. It is a matter of grafting one to the other. Skill is no good alone. I have picked the players for these qualities. I know they will play their guts out for England' . . . Dave Smith, manager, leaves Mansfield – at the end of the club's best run of results for years.

16   Terry Shanahan joins Millwall on a free transfer from Chesterfield, and Hereford pay £8,000 to Luton for Peter Spiring . . . Millwall gain an important 3-1 win over Brighton . . . In other Good Friday fixtures, Southampton lose at Plymouth – a severe blow to their promotion hopes, and two Bristol clubs draw in front of a 26,000 crowd . . . Lincoln score two more goals and become the first club to score more than 100 league goals in a season for nine years.

17   The second day of the Easter programme solves quite a few problems. Hereford are definitely promoted to Division Two – in their fourth season as a Football League club! . . . Derby are out of the First Division championship race after their home draw against Leicester, QPR lose at Norwich, and as Liverpool beat Stoke 5-3, they go to the top of Division One . . . Birmingham beat Tottenham, and both Wolves and Burnley seem certain to be relegated . . . Southampton are out of the Second Division promotion race . . . Ron Moore of Tranmere scores a hat-trick and joins Buckley of Walsall as top league scorer on 32 . . . Youngsters who earn headlines include Tony McAndrew (Middlesbrough) with a hat-trick against Sheffield United, Keith Bertshin (Ipswich), with a goal at Highbury with his first touch of the ball as sub., and David McNiven by scoring a goal for Leeds against Manchester City . . . Bayern Munich want their European Cup Final to be moved

from Glasgow, because of the Scotland v England fixture which might affect the attendance.

19 Sunderland are promoted to Division One! They beat Bolton 2-1 in front of a 52,000 crowd . . . Burnley are relegated to Division Two after losing to Manchester United . . . Liverpool are favourites to win the league – they beat Manchester City 3-0, with the help of two goals by David Fairclough, who has now scored seven league goals! . . . QPR defeat Arsenal 2-1 with a Gerry Francis penalty in the 87th minute.

20 Millwall win again, and finish their league programme on 56 points. Now promotion from Division Three depends on the remaining results of Cardiff and Crystal Palace . . . A Glasgow garage owner, Jack Gillespie pays nearly £300,000 for shares in Glasgow Rangers . . . Portsmouth sack coach Pat Wright as an economy measure.

21 Manchester United are out of the championship race after a home defeat by Stoke . . . Bristol City are back in the First Division after 65 years' absence . . . Francis Lee of Derby announces his retirement at the end of the season . . . Terry Yorath, who was sent off against Leicester on Tuesday, will still captain Wales against Yugoslavia in Zagreb . . . Reading are certain to be promoted from Division Four after their draw at Cambridge.

24 QPR beat Leeds 2-0, with goals by Thomas and Bowles, on the last Saturday of the league season. But the championship decider will be played on May 4 at Wolverhampton, where Wolves must win to have a hope of avoiding relegation, and Liverpool need a low scoring draw or a win to finish on top of the First Division . . . Lincoln are sure to set an all-time points record in Division Four. They have 73 points with one game to play . . . Francis Lee finishes his playing career with two late goals in Derby's 6-2 win at Ipswich . . . Trevor Anderson scores a hat-trick of penalties for Swindon v Walsall, a feat last achieved by Ken Barnes for Manchester City in 1957 v Everton . . . Rangers clinch the Scottish Premier Division title . . . Kevin Keegan is elected 'Footballer of the Year' . . . In the European Championship, Wales lose 2-0 in Yugoslavia . . . Czechoslovakia beat Russia by the same score . . Spain and W. Germany draw 1-1 in Madrid . . . Sunderland are Second Division champions, WBA are promoted with them and Bristol City and Oxford U. are relegated to Division Three.

25 Stan Bowles is involved in yet another controversy with manager Dave Sexton. As QPR leave for a short tour of Israel, Bowles refuses to board the plane and stays at home. It is reported that the German club SV Hamburg is making a bid for Bowles.

27 Arsenal place Brian Kidd, Eddie Kelly and young Brian Hornsby on the transfer list . . . Cyril Knowles of Tottenham, 31, retires because of knee trouble.

28 Two early Bruges goals surprise Liverpool at Anfield, but during a five minute second-half spell, Kennedy, Case and Keegan (pen), put the home side ahead in the first leg of the UEFA-Cup Final. A highly entertaining match ends in a 3-2 win for Liverpool . . . Millwall are back in Division Two after just one season in the Third . . . Crystal Palace fail to beat Chesterfield at home and now cannot overhaul their South London neighbours . . . Dixie McNeil gets another hat-trick for Hereford, and is the joint highest league scorer with 34, for the second year in succession.

29 Palace give Alan Whittle a free transfer, and put Peter Taylor on the transfer list. Several clubs are interested in the England international at £250,000 . . . Kevin Keegan, when presented with the 'Footballer of the Year' award at the annual dinner says: 'I know I am not the most popular footballer in the country. I have done things wrong in my time. But I have learnt from my mistakes'.

30 Sheffield W. escape relegation to Division Four by beating Southend. Aldershot go down.

Southampton win the Cup . . . Liverpool win the League Championship and the UEFA Cup . . . Scotland are British Champions . . . Malcolm Allison leaves Crystal Palace . . . England do well in the American Bicentennial Tournament.

1   It is Cup Final day in Britain. In England Southampton gain a shock victory over clear favourites Manchester United. Bobby Stokes scores the only goal of the match in the 83rd minute. Manager Lawrie McMenemy says: 'We've won the Cup because we deserved to. Everybody called us homely and hospitable. What they forgot to say is that we are also professional, ruthless, determined and have a lot of ability'. United manager Tommy Docherty says: 'We lost because they scored so late in the match. I'd much have preferred to get an early goal and we would then have got right into it'. It is the first time that Southampton have won the FA cup. In Scotland Rangers complete a League, League Cup, FA Cup hat-trick by beating Hearts 3-1. The first goal is scored after 41 seconds play by Derek Johnstone.

3   29,508 people attend Mick Channon's testimonial at Southampton – a record crowd at The Dell still celebrating the Cup victory . . . Colin Bell undergoes a cartilage operation.

4   On a night of high drama, Liverpool clinch the League Championship, establishing a new record of nine title wins . . . Kindon puts Wolves ahead in the vital match at Wolverhampton, but Keegan equalizes in the 76th minutes, Toshack and Kennedy make it 3-1 . . . Wolves are relegated and Birmingham escape relegation . . . Cardiff win at Bury and ensure their promotion to Division Two.

5   Anderlecht beat West Ham 4-2 in the European Cup Winners Cup Final in the Heysel Stadium, Brussels. Pat Holland puts West Ham ahead but Rensenbrink equalizes before half time. Van Der Elst and Robson add further goals, but Rensenbrink scores from a penalty and Van Der Elst adds another goal. This is the first victory for a Belgian club in European competition . . . Allan Brown is the new manager of Blackpool, taking over from Harry Potts the ex-Burnley boss.

6   Two managers lose their jobs – Walter Joyce leaves Rochdale and Roy Chapman is sacked at Stockport. But contrary to speculation Malcolm Allison states that he'll stay with Crystal Palace . . . Real Madrid is banned for a year by the UEFA. A spectator attacked the referee and a Bayern player at the end of the first half at the Bernabeau Stadium . . . Scotland open the Home Championship with a convincing 3-1 win over under-strength Wales.

8   England field an untried team at Cardiff. After early Welsh pressure, the game becomes more evenly balanced, and a Peter Taylor goal gives England a 1-0 win. At Hampden, Scotland beat N. Ireland 3-0, Don Masson of QPR scores one of the goals in his second game for his country.

9   Jimmy Rimmer, the Arsenal goalkeeper, is in the England squad. He takes the place of Phil Parkes, who has asked to be omitted for personal reasons . . . David Smith is the new manager of relegated Southend. Former manager Arthur Rowley will work as a scout.

10   Jimmy Adamson joins Sparta Rotterdam as manager . . . Real Madrid appeal against the European ban.

11   England beat N. Ireland 4-0 at Wembley . . . Pop singer Elton John is elected as chairman of Watford. John says: 'I'm really serious about this. I hope people will not treat this as a gimmick. I've supported this club since I was seven years old'.

12   Bayern Munich win the European Cup for the third year running, equalling Ajax's record. Roth scores the only goal of the match in the second-half following a free-kick . . . The Football League propose to introduce a 'goal-bonus' system next season, but it must be ratified by the clubs at their annual meeting . . . Doug Collins, freed by Burnley, signs for Plymouth.

13   Bill McGarry is sacked at Wolves after seven and a half years as manager . . . Rod Thomas is dropped by Wales for the first time in eight years . . . Bertie Mee is leaving Highbury for good. Contrary to expectations, he is not offered an adminis-

trative post by Arsenal.

14 Leighton James scores for Wales to beat N. Ireland 1-0 at Swansea . . . Bob Paisley is the 'Manager of the Year'. Paisley says: 'My old headmaster Bill Shankly must take much of the credit. After working with him for 14 years I could not fail to learn a tremendous amount' . . . Peter Shilton pulls out of the England party, and asks not to be considered for selection in the future . . . Terry Yorath, captain of Wales, is put on the transfer list by Leeds . . . Pat Jennings now has 61 caps for N. Ireland – an all-time record!

15 Scotland win the Home Championship outright for the first time since 1967 by beating England 2-1 at Hampden Park. Channon opens the scoring, but Don Masson equalizes with a header. In the second-half a Kenny Dalglish shot beats Clemence – a rare bad mistake by the goalkeeper. Don Revie says: 'It was a good match and I think Scotland just deserved to win. Our second-half performance pleased me. We can build on it'.

17 The FA Council proposes that the two-years qualification for foreign players should be scrapped. But the Football League could still veto the signing of players from abroad.

19 Liverpool repeat their 1973 double by winning the UEFA Cup after clinching the championship. They go a goal behind at Bruges when Lambert scores from a penalty, but Keegan equalizes following a free kick. The 1-1 draw gives Liverpool a 4-3 winning aggregate . . . Cardiff win the Welsh Cup and will play in European football next season . . . Malcolm Allison leaves Crystal Palace. He says: 'I had desperately wanted the club to win something this season and we failed however narrowly. I have also become increasingly disillusioned at the way English football is heading. This is not an excuse. It is just that I am sad and frustrated by some of the trends in the game'.

21 Carlisle sign Bill Rafferty from Plymouth for £30,000 . . . George Best and Rodney Marsh fail to turn up in time for 'Team America' and are dropped from the squad against Italy.

22 In an incident packed match at Ninian Park Cardiff, Wales draw 1-1 with Yugoslavia. The visitors take the lead from a penalty and then Ian Evans equalizes. In the second half referee R. Gloeckner of E. Germany disallows a Welsh goal and when objects are thrown on the pitch, suspends the game for five minutes. Invading fans are taken away by the police. When play resumes, yet another Welsh goal is disallowed and a Terry Yorath penalty is saved by goalkeeper Maric. Four players are booked. Now Yugoslavia are in the semi-finals of the European Championship, where they are joined by W. Germany 2-0 (3-1 aggregate) winners over Spain, Czechoslovakia who drew 2-2 in Russia (4-2 aggregate), and Holland who did the double against Belgium by winning the second leg 2-1.

23 England lose to a last minute goal against Brazil in Los Angeles. In the opening game of the American Bicentennial Tournament, Roberto gets the winner following a corner, but the England team's performance is praised. Don Revie says: 'I've had some disappointments in football but this is the most disappointing result in 14 years. It was a great performance and I was proud of every one of my players. The pleasing thing to me is that I've really got something to build on.'

24 Malcolm Macdonald reportedly wants to leave Newcastle . . . Carlisle pay £50,000 for St Johnstone's Scottish U-23 defender Ian McDonald.

25 Ian Hamilton, the Aston Villa striker is to play in USA. He is joining Minnesota Kicks for a £30,000 transfer fee . . Jimmy Adamson is back in England. The ex-Burnley coach leaves Sparta Rotterdam because he says he cannot settle in Holland.

26 Two Don Givens goals give a surprise 2-0 win to the Republic of Ireland in Poland. The QPR forward is now the all-time top-scorer for the Irish National team.

27 Arsenal draw-up a short list for their managerial vacancy . . . Vernon Stokes, chairman of League's Disciplinary Committee says that the 'no appeals' system has worked well . . . On a tour match, Manchester United draw 2-2 with 'Chicago Sting' in the USA . . . Elton John, new chairman of Watford brings Tom Walley

back to the club from Orient . . . Elton's uncle, ex-Fulham player Roy Dwight takes over Dartford as manager . . . Rimmer, Wilkins and Gordon Hill are the new caps in a much-changed England team against Italy. Hill's international debut means that an extra £10,000 transfer fee is due to Millwall from Manchester United.

28 In New York's Yankee Stadium, where the pitch is designed for baseball, England beat Italy 3-2. Graziani scores twice in the first-half, but a quick goal by Channon immediately after the interval and a Thompson header make the score 2-2. Following an excellent pass by Brooking, Channon scores the winner. Unsavoury incidents spoil the last half-an-hour of the match and three Italian players are booked for fouls. Towers is cautioned for dissent. Rimmer is replaced by Corrigan at half-time, and Mick Mills comes in for Phil Neal . . . Don Revie says: 'I chose this team because I wanted to give players a game and because we play Italy twice in the World Cup during the next 18 months. It could have gone wrong but it didn't, and for that I have to thank the character of my players. ' . . Gil scores twice for Brazil against Team America in the other game of this Bicentennial Tournament.

30 Wales lose 1-0 against Hungary in the UEFA Youth Tournament.

31 England complete the USA tour with a comfortable 3-1 over Team America. Kevin Keegan scores twice in the first half, and a fine individual effort by skipper Gerry Francis makes the score 3-0. Stewart Scullion gets the consolation goal for the home side, which includes Pele, Bobby Moore, the Italian international Chinaglia and Mike England . . . Brazil take the Cup by beating Italy 4-1. Uruguayan referee Baretto sends off Causio and Bettega from Italy and Lula of Brazil.

June

Stan Bowles signs a 6-year contract with QPR . . . Some interesting decisions in the League AGM . . . Jimmy Hill is appointed as soccer supremo in Saudi Arabia.

1 Tony Waiters, manager of Plymouth, raises £4,000 for the club by a sponsored marathon run. Waiters, a former international goalkeeper, completes the course in just over 35 minutes . . . Wales beat Italy 1-0 in the UEFA Tournament, but fail to reach the semi-finals . . . The FA state that they do not regard the match against 'Team America' as a full international, and no caps will be given to the players involved. 'It was a training match' says an FA official.

3 Stan Bowles signs a six-year contract for QPR . . . Martin Chivers is wanted by the Swiss club Servette.

4 The Football League's AGM decide that from next season, goal difference will decide League positions instead of goal average. But the 'goal bonus' idea is thrown out . . . The four bottom clubs are re-elected to the Fourth Division. Workington have the narrowest escape, collecting 21 votes as opposed to Yeovil's 18. Chairman Lord Westwood announces that in the future only two clubs – one from the Southern and one from the Northern Premier League – will attempt to obtain FL status . . . The 65p minimum entrance charge remains unaltered . . . Don Revie calls up Paul Madeley into the England squad for the Finland match . . . Hosts, Hungary and the USSR reach the Final of the UEFA Youth Tournament.

7 Jimmy Hill signs a long-term contract with Saudi Arabia. He will act as a 'football supremo' appointing coaches and organising the game generally. Hill will stay in London, but there will be jobs for several English coaches, referees and administrators.

8 Tony Currie signs for Leeds. Jimmy Armfield says about his £240,000 purchase: 'Tony is a crowd puller. He is one of the game's personalities. We've needed a midfield player of his calibre since Johnny Giles left ' . . . West Ham buys Bill Green from Carlisle for £75,000 . . . Fulham lodges a complaint with the Football League regarding the fixtures for season '76/77. They object to having home games on the same dates as QPR while neighbours Chelsea will have West London to themselves.

EIGHT
GREAT
GOALS
OF 1975-76

**Diagrams illustrating eight memorable
goals from the past season**

Eight Great Goals of 1975-76

Once again eight goals have been selected to represent the memorable moments of the season and the teams which have been successful within its context. The year 1975-76 provided more intensive competition than most; the League Championship bobbed about like a cork on the waves until reaching the haven of Anfield; the European dream was pursued with ultimate success by Liverpool and almost matched by West Ham; Wales unexpectedly made their competitive mark; the League Cup final produced one of Wembley's most flamboyant goals while the FA Cup offered a Third Division semi-finalist and a Second Division winner. This selection of eight goals reflects, in essence, this type of season.

The tiny Welshman Arfon Griffiths was hardly cast in the mould of international star, but at an age when many professionals are pondering on their post-playing futures, Griffiths discovered an ability to play and score at such a level. His goal against Austria at Wrexham ensured the principality a place, as Great Britain's only representatives, in the European Championship quarter-finals; his intuition led him to reach a through pass before the Austrian defenders and his finish was emphatic.

Lincoln City provided a milestone of their own in becoming the first club for nine years to score more than a hundred League goals. John Ward and Percy Freeman provided much of the firepower and Freeman's goal against Cambridge United was characteristic of his work. On this occasion his simple task was to finish off some play of authentic class from the former Welsh international Dick Krzwycki.

In any context, Dennis Tueart's overhead-kick against Newcastle United would have been totally memorable but against a Wembley backcloth it was unforgettable. The build-up had been well-rehearsed – Donachie's cross directed back across goal by the tall Tommy Booth – but this time Tueart and Booth were slightly out of tune until Tueart won the League Cup with an athletic piece of improvisation.

Crystal Palace proved the quality of their play, despite their inexplicable inability to clinch promotion, by eliminating Leeds Utd., Chelsea and Sunderland from the FA Cup. Peter Taylor figured prominently in all three victories and his direct running paved the way for the only goal at Roker Park. His pedigree was matched by Alan Whittle who, back to goal, killed the ball and swivelled to score in classic vein.

It looked for all the world that Keith Robson had ruined a moment of class from Trevor Brooking when West Ham were battling to make something out of their European Cup-Winners' Cup semi-final second leg against Eintracht Frankfurt. Brooking sent Robson clear only to see him miss the ball completely; amazingly the forward recovered possession, realised that his route was now blocked and responded by scoring with a sensational 25-yard shot.

In Scotland, Rangers monopolised the three competitions, sealing their invincibility by taking the Scottish Cup. They showed their authority from the kick-off, taking the lead after just 40 seconds with an exhilarating header from Derek Johnstone, one of the most versatile players in the country who enjoyed a spectacular season as a striker.

Undoubtedly the most unexpected goal of the season came from Southampton and Bobby Stokes to beat Manchester United at Wembley. But it also illustrated the class in the Second Division side. Channon laid the ball off to McCalliog, who swept it forward first time; Stokes' finish may have owed more to an in-built goal sense than a moment of deliberation but it beat Alex Stepney who appeared to have every eventuality covered.

Voted Footballer of the Year, Kevin Keegan again established an understanding with John Toshack which mystified First Division and European defences alike. Not surprisingly it was a Toshack flick and Keegan's uncanny appearance on the end of it which brought the goal that won Liverpool the League Championship. That it came a mere 14 minutes from the end of the League season and at the same time expelled Wolves into Second Division exile typified the remarkable competition of 1975-76.

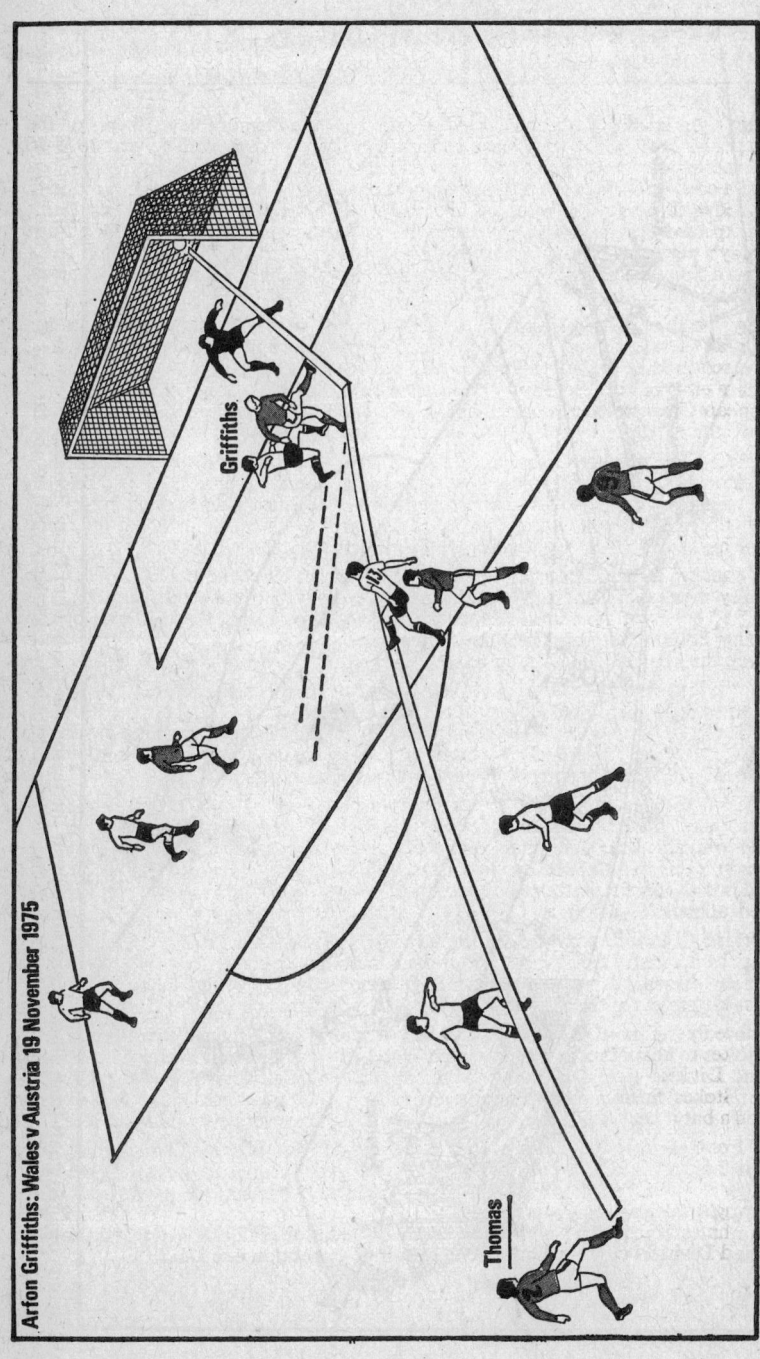

Arfon Griffiths: Wales v Austria 19 November 1975

Griffiths

Thomas

The moment of triumph for Wales came when full-back Rod Thomas pushed a precise pass into the Austrian penalty area. Arfon Griffiths timed his run to perfection to reach the ball in front of his marker and his first-time shot flashed inside the near post.

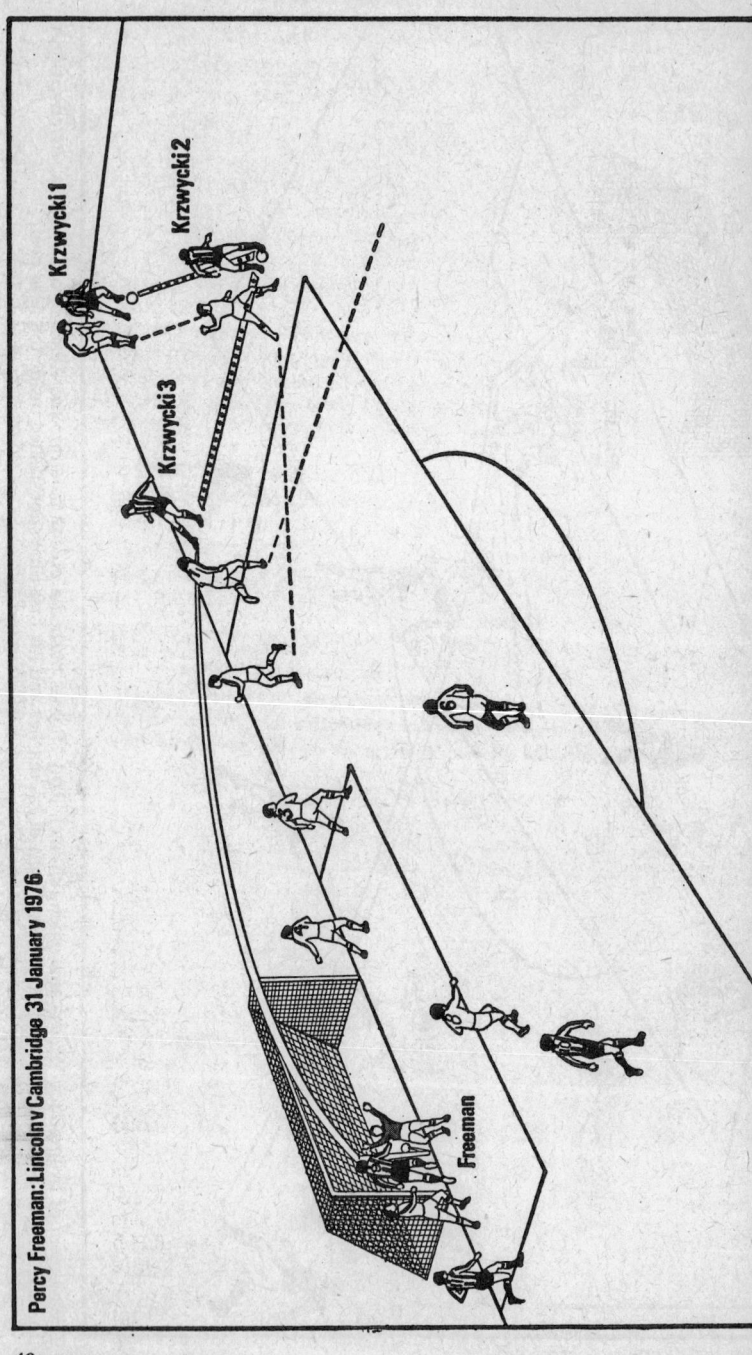

Percy Freeman: Lincoln v Cambridge 31 January 1976.

Krzwycki 1

Krzwycki 2

Krzwycki 3

Freeman

Lincoln conjured goals from all positions throughout the season but the head of Percy Freeman provided a focal point for the attack. Against Cambridge the big forward benefited from a twisting dribble by Dick Krzwycki; at the far post Freeman had only to guide home the cross.

Dennis Tueart : Man. City v Newcastle 28 February 1976

Booth

Tueart

A move that was well rehearsed except for the flamboyant finish. Willie Donachie's long cross was knocked across goal by Tommy Booth but slightly behind Dennis Tueart. Improvising, Tueart fashioned a spectacular overhead kick that totally beat Mahoney and provided a Wembley setting with a perfect winner.

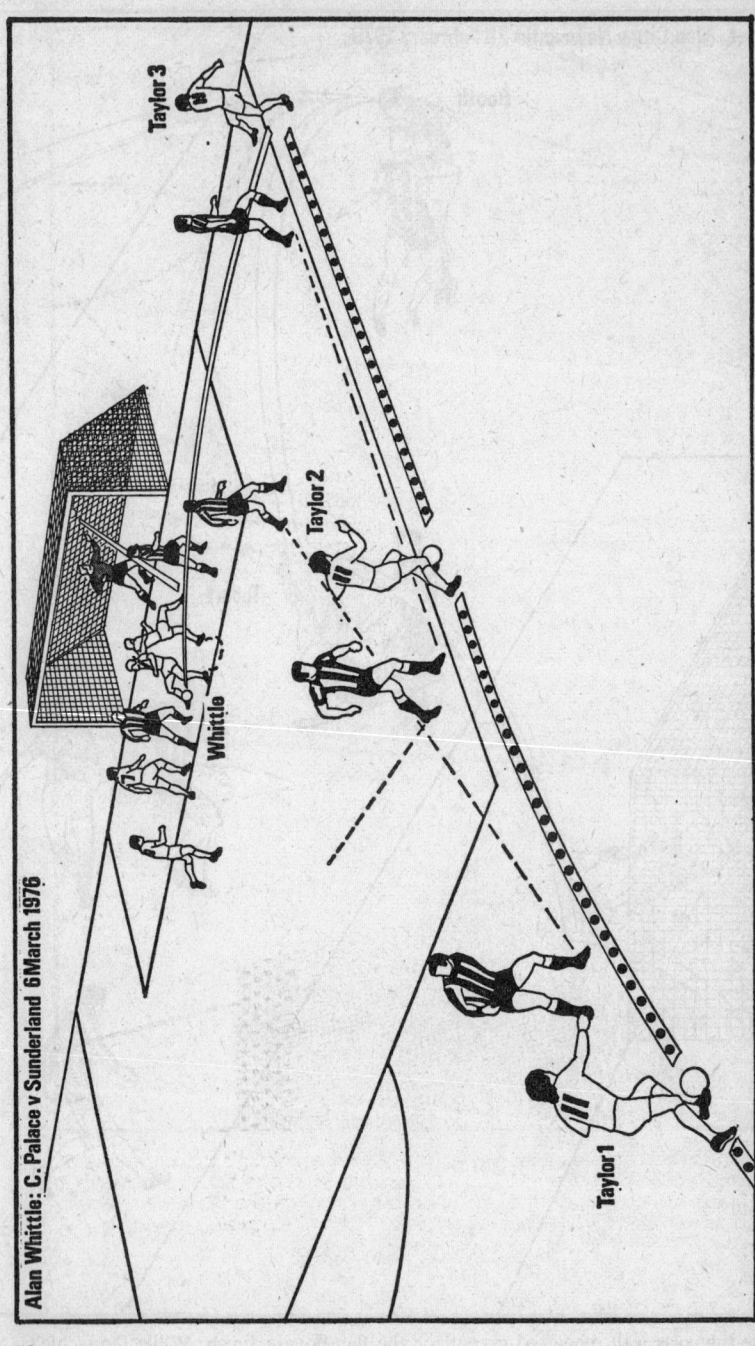

Alan Whittle: C. Palace v Sunderland 6 March 1976

Taylor 3

Taylor 2

Whittle

Taylor 1

Sunderland's defence became vulnerable the moment Peter Taylor received the ball from his goalkeeper. His pace exposed Bolton and the covering Moncur, and when he crossed from the by-line Whittle controlled the ball with his first touch and slammed it high into the net with his second.

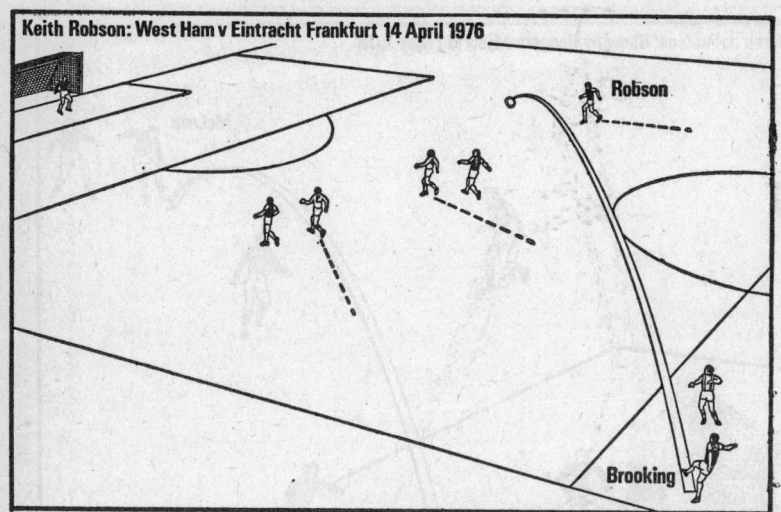

Robson

Brooking

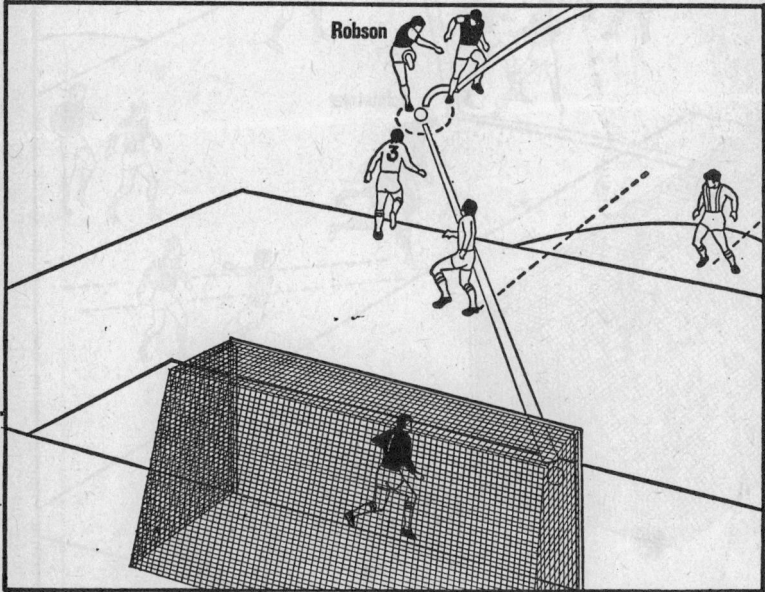

Robson

The upper section of the diagram shows how Trevor Brooking's perceptive pass gave Keith Robson a clear run to goal. The chance seemed to have evaporated when Robson mis-controlled, but in a remarkable recovery the West Ham forward turned to collect the ball and then scored with a shot of staggering power.

43

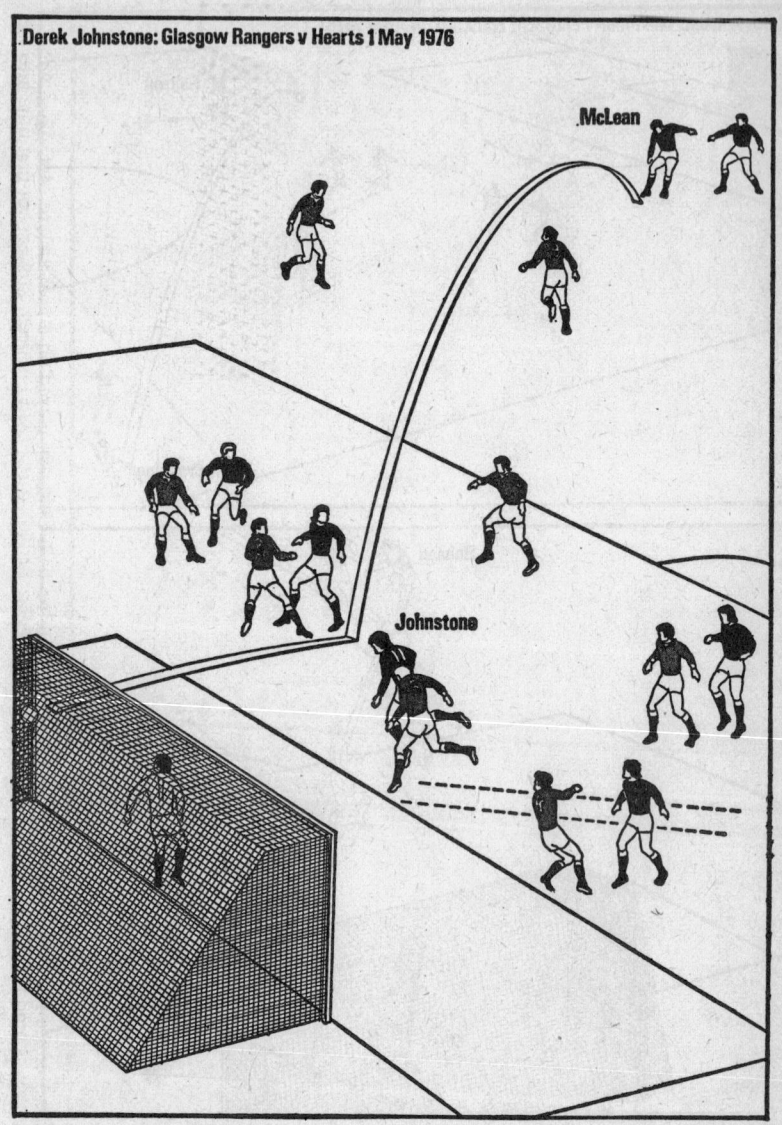

Derek Johnstone: Glasgow Rangers v Hearts 1 May 1976

McLean

Johnstone

Bidding for the treble, Rangers made a perfect start to their Scottish Cup Final against Hearts. McLean's free-kick caught the defenders cold and Derek Johnstone stole a yard on his marker; he reached the curling cross and directed his header to perfection before the goalkeeper could raise an arm to stop it.

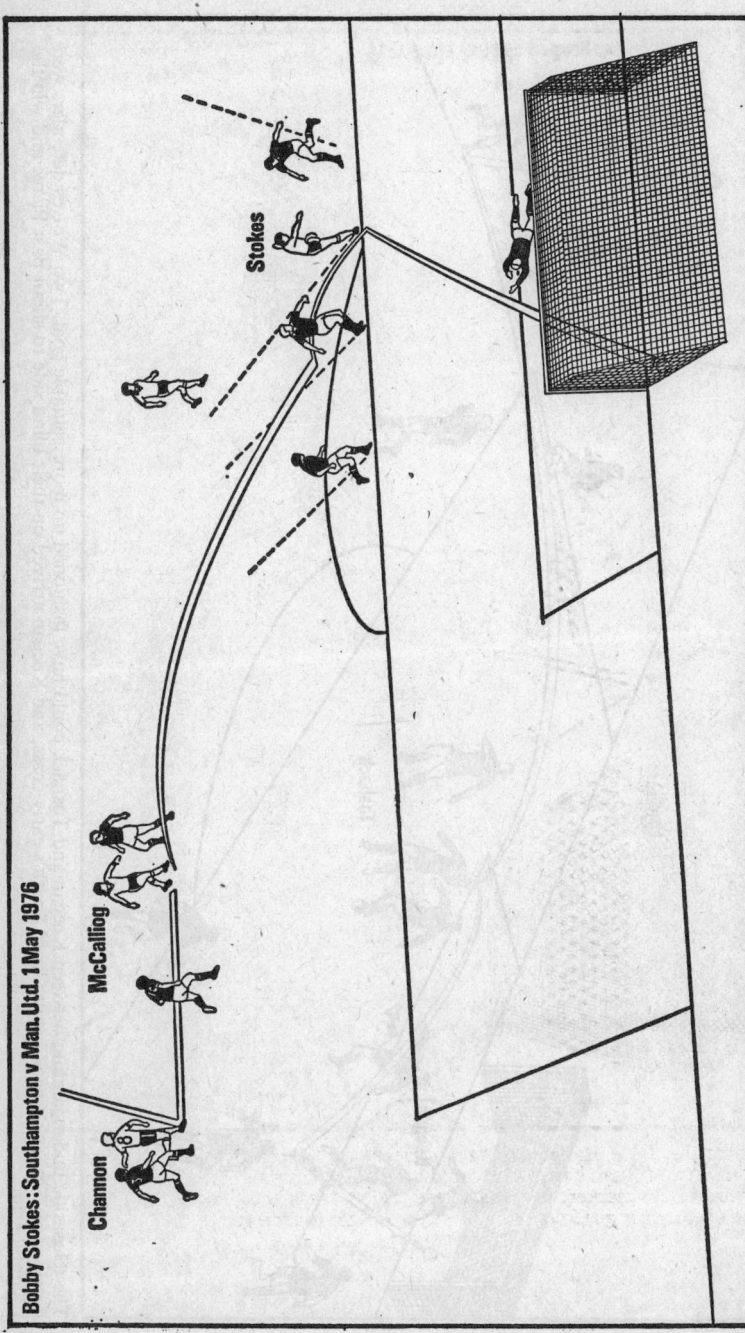

Bobby Stokes: Southampton v Man. Utd. 1 May 1976

Channon

McCalliog

Stokes

The sensational moment of the FA Cup Final was a tribute to first-time football. Channon played off a goal-kick to McCalliog, who struck an immediate pass behind the Manchester United defence. Reaching the ball after it had bounced, Stokes shot first time into the only space Stepney could not cover.

45

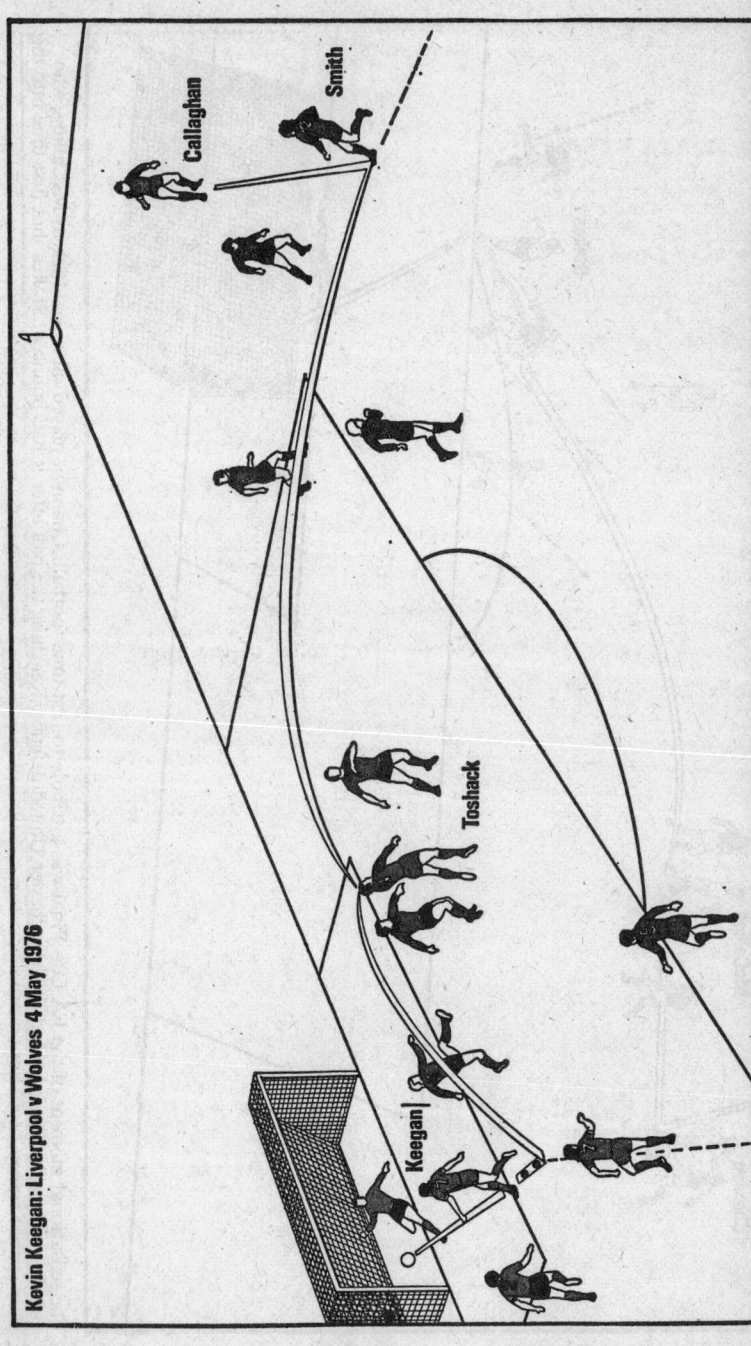

Kevin Keegan: Liverpool v Wolves 4 May 1976

Callaghan

Smith

Toshack

Keegan

The telepathic understanding between Keegan and Toshack could have fashioned no more valuable goal. Two Wolves defenders were deceived by Toshack's back-header from Smith's early cross, and Keegan arrived on their blind side to shoot past Pierce and win the Championship.

FOOTBALL AWARDS 1975-76

The Footballer of the Year

The PFA Player of the Year

The Manager of the Year

The European Footballer of the Year

FOOTBALLER OF THE YEAR

The Football Writers Association was founded in 1947, and it was proposed that the members should elect the Footballer of the Year at the end of each season. The first recipient of the Award, a statuette of a footballer on a square plinth, was one of the all-time greats, Stanley Matthews. The Award, presented at a dinner held in London during Cup Final week, is given 'to the the Player, who by precept and example on and off the field, shall have been considered to have done most for football during that season'. To this day, this Award has remained the most prestigious for any player, and the dinner in his honour is an important occasion for English football.

This season, Kevin Keegan became only the second Liverpool player to receive the accolade, following in the footsteps of Ian Callaghan, who was elected in 1973-74. It had been a great season for Keegan, who not only established himself as a regular and valuable England international player, but also figured prominently in Liverpool's 'Double' of League Championship and UEFA Cup triumphs.

Award Winners

1947-48 Stanley Matthews (Blackpool), 1948-49 Johnny Carey (Manchester U.), 1949-50 Joe Mercer (Arsenal), 1950-51 Harry Johnston (Blackpool), 1951-52 Billy Wright (Wolverhampton), 1952-53 Nat Lofthouse (Bolton), 1953-54 Tom Finney (Preston), 1954-55 Don Revie (Manchester C.), 1955-56 Bert Trautmann (Manchester C.), 1956-57 Tom Finney (Preston), 1957-58 Danny Blanchflower (Tottenham), 1958-59 Syd Owen (Luton), 1959-60 Bill Slater (Wolverhampton), 1960-61 Danny Blanchflower (Tottenham), 1961-62 Jimmy Adamson (Burnley), 1962-63 Stanley Matthews (Stoke), 1963-64 Bobby Moore (West Ham), 1964-65 Bobby Collins (Leeds), 1965-66 Bobby Charlton (Manchester U.), 1966-67 Jackie Charlton (Leeds), 1967-68 George Best (Manchester U.), 1968-69 Dave Mackay (Derby) shared with Tony Book (Manchester C.), 1969-70 Billy Bremner (Leeds), 1970-71 Frank McLintock (Arsenal), 1971-72 Gordon Banks (Stoke), 1972-73 Pat Jennings (Tottenham), 1973-74 Ian Callaghan (Liverpool), 1974-75 Alan Mullery (Fulham).

THE P.F.A. AWARDS 1975

Once again, the members of the Professional Footballers' Association were asked to vote for several individual awards and to select four teams representing the divisions of the Football League.

Player of the Year—Pat Jennings (Tottenham H.)
Previous Winners—1974—Colin Todd (Derby Co.)
          1973—Norman Hunter (Leeds U.)
Young Player of the Year—Peter Barnes (Manchester C.)
Previous Winners—1974—Mervyn Day (West Ham U.)
          1973—Kevin Beattie (Ipswich T.)
PFA Merit Award—George Eastham
Previous Winners—1974—Dennis Law
          1973—Bobby Charlton

DIVISION 1: Pat Jennings (Tottenham H.); Paul Madeley (Leeds U.), Kevin Beattie (Ipswich T.), Don Masson (Q.P.R.), Roy McFarland (Derby Co.), Colin Todd (Derby Co.), Kevin Keegan (Liverpool), Alan Hudson (Stoke C.), Duncan McKenzie (Leeds U.), John Toshack (Liverpool), Dennis Tueart (Manchester C.).

DIVISION 2: Jim Montgomery (Sunderland); Gary Locke (Chelsea), John Gorman (Carlisle U.), Tony Towers (Sunderland), Paul Jones (Bolton W.), Geoff Merrick (Bristol C.), Bobby Kerr (Sunderland), Mike Channon (Southampton), Paul Cheesley (Bristol C.), Johnny Giles (W.B.A.), Peter Thompson (Bolton W.).

DIVISION 3: Eric Steele (Peterborough U.); Ray Evans (Millwall), Clive Charles (Cardiff C.), Dennis Burnett (Brighton & H.A.), Ian Evans (C. Palace), Derek Jeffries (C. Palace), Peter O'Sullivan (Brighton & H.A.), David Gregory (Peterborough U.), Dixie McNeil (Hereford U.), Alan Buckley (Walsall), Peter Taylor (C. Palace).

DIVISION 4: Peter Grotier (Lincoln C.); Ian Branfoot (Lincoln C.), Ken Sanderock (Torquay U.), Geoff Hutt (Huddersfield T.), Sam Ellis (Lincoln C.), Terry Cooper (Lincoln C.), Ian Miller (Doncaster R.), John Ward (Lincoln C.), Ron Moore (Tranmere R.), Mike Kitchen (Doncaster R.), Tony Whelan (Rochdale).

Bob Paisley is Manager of the Year

Bob Paisley of Liverpool – England's First Division League Champions and UEFA Cup winners – was named Football Manager of the Year by the Bell's Scotch Whisky Football Managers Awards panel of 25 leading British soccer journalists.

Paisley, one of soccer's longest-serving one-club men (he signed for the Merseyside club in 1939) received a cheque for £1000 at the Bell's Scotch Whisky Football Managers Awards luncheon at the Albany Hotel in Glasgow. The presentation was made by Mr R C Miquel, chairman and managing director of Arthur Bell & Sons.

Paisley, from Hetten-le-Hole in County Durham, joined Liverpool from Bishop Auckland where he had won an FA Amateur Cup medal, the first of eight winners medals he has won as a player, coach, trainer and finally manager – the latest being his fifth Football League Championship medal. On that occasion Paisley paid tribute to his 'Headmaster', Bill Shankly, the former Liverpool manager, and a former Manager of the Year. Naming a list of star internationals who had played under Shankly's leadership, Paisley said: 'Bill set such a high standard – and I'd like to think that he tutored me too.'

DIVISIONAL MANAGERS OF THE SEASON 1975-76

Tommy Docherty (Manchester United) in Division One, Lawrie McMenemy (Southampton) in Division Two, John Sillett (Hereford United) in Division Three, Graham Taylor (Lincoln City) in Division Four. Each received an inscribed salver and a cheque for £250. A special award went to Bob Stokoe of Sunderland, the Second Division champions, who received a cheque for £250.

DIVISIONAL MANAGERS OF THE MONTH 1975-76

AUGUST: MANAGER OF THE MONTH: Tommy Docherty (Manchester U.); Division Two: Alec Stock (Fulham); Division Three: David Smith (Mansfield T.); Division Four: Peter Madden (Darlington). SEPTEMBER: MANAGER OF THE MONTH: Dave Sexton (Queen's Park Rangers); Division Two: Jimmy Sirrel (Notts Co.); Division Three: Bobby Smith (Bury); Division Four: Graham Taylor (Lincoln C.). OCTOBER: MANAGER OF THE MONTH: Dave Mackay (Derby Co.); Division Two: Don Megson (Bristol R.); Division Three: Noel Cantwell (Peterborough U.); Division Four: Stan Anderson (Doncaster Rovers). NOVEMBER: MANAGER OF THE MONTH: Tony Book (Manchester C.); Division Two: Eddie McCreadie (Chelsea); Division Three: John Sillet (Hereford U.); Division Four: Graham Taylor (Lincoln C.). DECEMBER: MANAGER OF THE MONTH: Bob Paisley (Liverpool); Division Two: Lawrie McMenemy (Southampton); Division Three: Jimmy Andrews (Cardiff C.); Division Four: Graham Taylor (Lincoln C.). JANUARY: MANAGER OF THE MONTH: Gordon Lee (Newcastle U.); Division Two: Ian Greaves (Bolton W.); Division Three: Malcolm Allison (Crystal Palace); Division Four: Bobby Kennedy (Bradford C.). FEBRUARY: MANAGER OF THE MONTH: Tony Book (Manchester C.); Division Two: Lawrie McMenemy (Southampton); Division Three: Alan Durban (Shrewsbury T.); Division Four: Bobby Kennedy (Bradford C.). MARCH: MANAGER OF THE MONTH: Tommy Docherty (Manchester U.); Division Two: Alan Dicks (Bristol C.) Division Three: Gordon Jago (Millwall); Division Four: Bill Dodgin (Northampton T.). APRIL: MANAGER OF THE MONTH: Bob Paisley (Liverpool); Division Two: Bob Stokoe (Sunderland); Division Three: Jimmy Andrews (Cardiff C.); Division Four: Graham Taylor (Lincoln C.).

European Footballer of the Year 1975

Oleg Blokhin, the Dynamo Kiev and Soviet Union international left-winger, became in 1975 only the second of his countrymen to win the European Footballer of the Year award. Lev Yashin, the Moscow Dynamo goalkeeper, had been the previous Russian holder of the title in 1963. Blokhin won by a massive 80 points margin.

For the 23-year-old, helping Kiev to win the Cup-Winners' Cup, the so-called Super Cup, and being included with his club colleagues *en bloc* in the national side, it was a memorable ending to an eventful and successful year.

Blokhin figures chiefly on the left side in attack but is equally happy striking from the centre or right and undoubtedly his clever, close control and expert finish have lifted him into world class rating in a comparatively short time.

He was 18 when he won a place in the Kiev side and played for Russia in the 1972 Olympics. In the past three seasons he has been top scorer in the First Division and for the last two has won the Footballer of the Year award in his own country.

Johan Cruyff, the winner of the European Footballer title for the last two seasons, finished third, while Franz Beckenbauer, second in 1974 and the winner in 1972, was again runner-up.

British players were again only seen in the minor placings. Colin Todd, the Derby County and England extra cover defender, was highest, finishing ninth with 10 points. Peter Lorimer of Leeds United and Scotland was joint 11th with nine points, Don Givens and Pat Jennings from respective sides of the Irish border were level 27th and last with one point.

Points awarded

122 Oleg Blokhin (Dynamo Kiev)

42 Franz Beckenbauer (Bayern Munich)

27 Johan Cruyff (Barcelona)

25 Berti Vogts (Borussia Moenchengladbach)

20 Sepp Maier (Bayern Munich)

18 Ruud Geels (Ajax)

17 Jupp Heynckes (Borussia Moenchengladbach)

14 Paul Breitner (Real Madrid)

12 Colin Todd (Derby County)

11 Dudu Georgescu (Dinamo Bucharest)

9 Jose Pirri (Real Madrid), Peter Lorimer (Leeds United), Branko Oblak (Schalke 04)

6 Dino Zoff (Juventus), Ralf Edstrom (PSV Eindhoven), Gunter Netzer (Real Madrid)

4 Josip Katalinski (Nice), Gerd Müller (Bayern Munich), Grzegorz Lato (Stal Mielec), Ivo Viktor (Dukla Prague), Christo Bonev (Lokomotiv Plovdiv)

3 Jan Pivarnik (Slovan Bratislava)

2 Jurgen Croy (Sachsenring Zwickau), Jean-Marc Guillou (Nice), Burjak (Dynamo Kiev), Johan Neeskens (Barcelona).

1 Don Givens (Queen's Park Rangers), Pat Jennings (Tottenham Hotspur), Allan Simonsen (Borussia Moenchengladbach), Dragan Dzajic (Bastia), Giacinto Facchetti (Inter-Milan), Jose Alves (Boavista)

Previous winners

1956	Stanley Matthews	1962	Josef Masopust	1968	George Best
1957	Alfredo Di Stefano	1963	Lev Yashin	1969	Gianni Rivera
1958	Raymond Kopa	1964	Denis Law	1970	Gerd Müller
1959	Alfredo Di Stefano	1965	Eusebio	1971	Johan Cruyff
1960	Luis Suarez	1966	Bobby Charlton	1972	Franz Beckenbauer
1961	Omar Sivori	1967	Florian Albert	1973	Johan Cruyff
				1974	Johan Cruyff

THE FOOTBALL LEAGUE CLUBS

Featuring a review of the 1975-76 League season, and full details of each of the 92 clubs in the Football League.

Officials, statistics, ground information, full 1975-76 League record, career details of the players.

THE FOOTBALL LEAGUE OFFICIALS

President
Lord Westwood (*Newcastle United*)

Vice-Presidents
R. W. Lord (*Burnley*),
R. Wragg (*Sheffield United*)

Management Committee
J. F. Wiseman (*Birmingham City*),
Sir Matt Busby (*Manchester United*),
L. T. Shipman M.B.E. (*Leicester City*),
J. B. Mears (*Chelsea*)
Dr. C. S. Grossmark

Life Members
F. A. Would (*Grimsby Town*)
E. M. Gliksten (*Charlton Athletic*),
S. Bolton (*Leeds United*)
D. F. Wiseman O.B.E.

Secretary
A. Hardaker O.B.E., Lytham St Annes, Lancashire

Review of the Season

The events of the final evening of the 1975-1976 season brought a dramatic end to a League competition sometimes obscured by a lack of really top-class technique. On that night the denouement of an intriguing plot of promotion and relegation was finally completed, including the ultimate 'who wunnit?' the Championship itself.

By then the issue, for so long as unfathomable as a tangled ball of string, had resolved itself into a straightforward premise: Liverpool needed to win, or to achieve a low-scoring draw in their final match against Wolverhampton at Molineux, to claim their ninth League title, at the expense of Queen's Park Rangers. Even then there were greater connotations, for Wolves themselves were in desperate need of a victory to preserve their First Division status – but only if, on that same evening, Birmingham failed to take a point at Bramall Lane against the already-doomed Sheffield United.

With a perfect sense of theatre, Wolves struck the first blow as the games unfolded simultaneously, with Kindon shooting a 14th minute lead. Minutes later, in Sheffield, Woodward sent Birmingham behind; if the half-time scores had remained unaltered, Rangers would have been champions, while Birmingham were relegated. But Liverpool, with a characteristic show of strength, responded with a devastating three-goal burst in the game's last 14 minutes to lift the crown and send Wolves through the trapdoor.

The champions and the runners-up had shaken off their closest pursuers with a burst of spring-time invincibility. Liverpool, criticised for their functional approach to away matches, dropped just one point from their final nine games. Rangers, the popular favourites, forfeited their first title by letting only three points out of their last 30 evade their grasp. Manchester United, who had returned to the top flight, seemed to be precariously successful on a prayer and the wing power of Coppell and Hill, but their exuberant industry contributed greatly to a season in which there was a small but definite switch of emphasis towards attack.

But Tommy Docherty's youngsters could not match this final flourish. Nor could Derby County who lost, at a vital time, the goal scoring panache of Charlie George, who at last revealed a mature consistency in his new surrounds. Nor could Leeds United, at times unable to conceal the odd crack of vulnerability in an ageing squad.

Yorkshire's discomfort was increased by the demise of Sheffield United, who neither under Ken Furphy nor his successor Jimmy Sirrel could produce football of sufficient quality to gain points or fill the impressive new stand that ended Bramall Lane's dual existence as a football and cricket ground. Burnley failed for once to conjure enough pedigree youngsters from their astute resources, and they, along with Wolves, failed to survive.

The dramas of the final evening were not confined to Division One. Indeed the Third Division produced arguably the most fascinating of all the dog-fights. On that evening defeat for Crystal Palace at Chester cost them a return to higher things while Cardiff won at Bury to earn the last promotion place. Palace's failure remained one of the season's imponderables. Retaining all the trappings of a big-time organisation, much of their football was styled, by Malcolm Allison and Terry Venables, along similarly ambitious lines. Towards the season's half-way mark they towered above their rivals by seven clear points; and even as that lead was eroded they sustained some remarkable performances to become only the fifth Third Division side to reach the F.A. Cup semi-final. But an inability to win at home finally had a malignant effect on the players' confidence.

Pressures on Palace grew greater in the face of a remarkable rise across South London by Millwall – unbeaten in their last fifteen games – where Gordon Jago manufactured a revival on a double brace of signings; the coloured forwards Lee and Walker early in the campaign, and then the on-loan Seasman and McGrath at the time for a final impetus. Cardiff similarly timed their run to perfection to pip stayers like Palace and Peter Taylor's Brighton, but the divisional championship went to Hereford who completed a remarkable rise from the Southern League to the Second Division in four years. In the course of their triumph Terry Paine, at 37 still a force in midfield, overtook Jimmy Dickinson's record of 764 League appearances.

The Second Division race itself was barely less exciting. Sunderland after many a stutter finally returned to Division One after disappointing failure each season since their momentous FA Cup win. Bristol City, spurred by prolific goalscoring in the

early weeks from Cheesley and later from Ritchie, accompanied them after 65 years in the lower echelons. And the First Division will have a rare player-manager next season following the success of Johnny Giles in his first season in that role at West Bromwich Albion. His experienced side showed more resilience in the final analysis than Bolton, who for so long seemed certain to go up, Southampton, who took 38 out of 42 home points but found travelling unprofitable, and Luton, who projected a cheerful front even in the real face of bankruptcy.

Luton, who in November were given just one month to live, faced the most severe financial difficulties. But their problems were by no means untypical. Portsmouth, relegated along with York and Oxford, faced debts of over £300,000, and the general lack of profitability among the League clubs again provoked discussions of a restructuring of competition and a turn towards part-time football.

But the Fourth Division clubs, the most financially oppressed, did more than most to portray the commercial quality of the product: Lincoln City became the first side for nine years to score 100 League goals, and in doing so they shattered the points record for the Division, an achievement which reflects considerable credit on their young manager Graham Taylor. Northampton almost matched Lincoln and they too were promoted along with Reading and Tranmere Rovers. And the Division was even graced by a George Best comeback. This time it was with Stockport, in carefully selected home matches. But sadly, like the others, it remained abortive.

In fact the clubs did cope with the increase in admission charges – the minimum up to 65p – which hovered gloomily on the horizon at the start of the year. Goalscoring was up, if only marginally in all four divisions, though the philanthropy of the Daily Express, with their offer of £10,000 to any scorer of 30 *League* goals in the First or Second Divisions, remained untested; this despite a lone, brave challenge by Derek Hales of Charlton who reached 28 with two games to go, then dried up.

Discipline took on a smoother style in the wake of legislation which made provision for automatic suspensions when an offender reached 20 penalty points and for most sending-off transgressions. And even though it was a season in which the talents of Rodney Marsh were sacked by Manchester City and allowed to be exported to the United States, and even though Liverpool, still the most machine-like of the very best sides, became the ultimate winners, there was, at least, lip-service paid to the needs of the paying customer.

The present-day chestnut of football – 'do you want us to entertain or win?' – began to lose some of its polarisation, even if performances at national level continued to question the value of such intense domestic competition.

Introduction to Club Section

Having reached in last year's edition what we considered to be an improved form for the club section, enabling a particular line-up to be found quickly by reference to the number of the match itself appearing on 'page 2' and 'page 3', the formula is again much on the same lines.

We must again emphasise that the arrangement we have for denoting substitutes who have actually taken part in League matches is not entirely satisfactory. Regular readers will know that the example of a player's appearances being 14+1 means he made 14 full appearances and one as a substitute. Players not making full appearances but turning out as substitute and actually getting on the field of play are listed: 0+1.

It would be much better if we could take the view of every country outside the British Isles and include appearances as substitutes in with the full appearances. It would be easier for us to do this, as we have stated previously, but because there remains considerable disinterest in many places in this country over the value of the substitute in records, we intend to retain this method of discrimination.

Happily, thanks to some notable goalscoring achievements by players who have come on the field with the No. 12 shirt on their backs, the role has suddenly been given a new form of respectability – so perhaps there is hope even yet!

All appearances and goals represent League matches only in the cumulative figures on 'page 4'. As before, we are including the League position of each club throughout the season as on the Saturdays shown on 'page 2'.

Players not making full or substitute appearances have been given the notation (−) after their names. Full international players are listed with the country of their honour in brackets underneath their name.

All players retained at the end of the 1975–76 season are included under the respective club. They include those whose registration is still retained by the club even though they may not have played for some while. An asterisk denotes players given a free transfer at the end of the 1975–76 season. Line-ups have been checked with clubs and the Football League and Scottish League. In Scotland, where two substitutes are permitted, suitable notation has been given.

Once again transfer fees may differ from the figures published originally in the Press, but we have tried as always to keep to those supplied by the clubs themselves.

We are grateful again for the patience and assistance of Club secretaries who were kind enough to supply the relative data. We would particularly like to thank once more those clubs who allowed us to reproduce their badges.

On the question frequently asked of us concerning players ages, we have complied with those clubs who were not disposed towards this end, quite understandably in our view, and have decided for uniformity's sake not to include any of them.

Our final 'copy date' for compiling information was, with a few exceptions, June 1. Thus some additional details concerning transfers, changes of colours, etc., will not have been recorded.

President: S. C. Salter.

Chairman: R. J. Driver

Vice-Chairman: F. G. Wiltshire, F.S.V.A.

Directors: S. R. Hooker, Dr. W. Brown, M.B., B.S., L. C. Eustace, M. E. J. Hall.

Team Manager: Tom McAnearney.

Secretary/Commercial Manager: M. A. Cosway

Year Formed: 1926. *Turned Professional:* 1927.

Limited Company: 1927.

Honours: *Football League:* best season: 8th Division 3, 1973–74. *F.A. Cup,* best season: 5th Rd. 1932–33. *Football League Cup:* best season: Never past 2nd Rd.

Record Victory: 8-1 v Gateshead, Division 4, 1958–59.

Record Defeat: 0-9 v Bristol C., Division 3(S), Dec. 28th, 1946.

Most League Points: 56, Division 4, 1972–73.

Most League Goals: 83, Division 4, 1963–64.

Highest League Scorer in Season: Jack Howarth, 25, Division 3, 1973–74.

Most League Goals in Total Aggregate: Jack Howarth, 168, 1965–76.

Most Capped Player: None.

Most League Appearances: Len Walker, 450, 1964–76.

Record Transfer Fee Received: £30,000 and 2 players from Leicester City for Joe Jopling, Sept. 1970.

Record Transfer Fee Paid: Not disclosed by Club.

Managers Since the War: Bill McCracken, Gordon Clark, Harry Evans, Dave Smith, Tom McAnearney, Jimmy Melia, Cliff Huxford.

Address of Supporters Club: 127 High Street, Aldershot.

Recreation ground: High St., Aldershot, GU11 1TW. Telephone Aldershot 20211. *Record attendance:* 19,138 v Carlisle U., F.A. Cup 4th Rd. Replay, January 1970. *Record receipts:* £8,355.50 v Manchester U., 2nd Rd. Lg. Cup, September 9, 1970. *Ground capacity:* 20,000 (18,000 under cover). *Pitch measurements:* 117 yds × 76 yds.

How to get there: Aldershot railway station is on the main line from London's Waterloo; the ground is five minutes walk from the station. Many buses run from the town centre on match days.

Match tickets: Can be booked in advance by telephoning ground. Available 2 weeks prior to match.

Car parking: Car parks within ¼ mile of the ground.

Entertainments/catering facilities: Members' club. Social club scheduled to open during 1976–77.

Club shop: Run by Supporters' Club; sells all types of souvenirs.

Handbooks/programmes: Programmes only available on sale.

Extra information: Harry Brooks scored five goals for Aldershot in each of two successive F.A. Cup ties in the 1945–46 season.

Club Colours: Red Shirts, blue collars and cuffs, blue shorts red socks with blue trim.
Change Colours: All Yellow
Club Captain:
Trainer/Coach: John Anderson.
Club Nickname: 'Shots'.

ALDERSHOT 1975-76 LEAGUE RECORD

Match No.	Date	Venue	Opponents	Result	H/T Score	League Pos'n	Goalscorers	Attendance
1	Aug 16	A	Wrexham	L 1-3	1-1	—	Morrissey	3315
2	23	H	Halifax T.	L 1-2	1-1	23	Howarth	3221
3	30	A	Bury	D 1-1	1-0	23	Howarth	4372
4	Sept 6	H	Mansfield T.	W 2-1	1-0	18	Brodie 2	3289
5	13	A	Peterborough U.	D 1-1	0-0	15	Howarth	6201
6	20	H	Preston N.E.	D 1-1	1-0	17	Morrissey	3883
7	24	H	Millwall	D 1-1	0-0	—	Bell	4935
8	27	A	Grimsby T.	L 0-1	0-0	19		5139
9	Oct 4	H	Southend U.	W 2-1	0-1	15	Howarth, Crosby	3579
10	11	A	Chester	L 0-1	0-1	19		3375
11	18	H	Colchester U.	D 2-2	2-1	20	Howarth, Bell	3586
12	22	H	Cardiff C.	W 2-1	1-1	—	Morrissey, Bell	3687
13	25	A	Rotherham U.	D 2-2	0-0	16	Richardson, Bell	4428
14	Nov 1	H	Gillingham	W 3-0	1-0	10	Warnock, Morrissey, Howarth	4290
15	3	A	Port Vale	W 1-0	0-0	—	Walton	3917
16	8	A	Chesterfield	L 2-5	0-2	10	Bell 2	4374
17	15	H	Sheffield W.	D 1-1	0-0	11	Morrissey	5181
18	29	H	Walsall	W 3-2	2-0	8	Morrissey, Walton, Howitt	4010
19	Dec 6	A	Shrewsbury T.	L 3-5	1-3	11	Bell 2, Howarth	3061
20	20	H	Hereford U.	L 0-2	0-0	15		4113
21	27	H	Crystal Palace	W 1-0	1-0	15	Morrissey	13,997
22	30	A	Brighton & H.A.	L 1-4	1-3	—	Howarth	18,818
23	Jan 10	H	Bury	D 1-1	0-0	17	Howarth	4202
24	17	A	Preston N.E.	L 0-1	0-1	17		6196
25	31	A	Cardiff C.	L 0-1	0-1	17		8934
26	Feb 7	H	Port Vale	W 2-0	1-0	17	Howarth, Bell	3446
27	10	A	Swindon T.	L 3-6	0-5	—	Walton 2, Morrissey	7323
28	14	H	Chesterfield	W 3-1	2-1	17	Howarth, Brodie, Bell	3362
29	21	A	Sheffield W.	L 1-3	1-2	18	Walton	8286
30	25	A	Millwall	L 1-4	0-0	—	Richardson	5904
31	28	H	Rotherham U.	W 3-0	1-0	17	Warnock, Derrett (og), Bell	3538
32	Mar 6	A	Gillingham	D 1-1	0-0	17	Warnock	5028
33	8	A	Southend U.	W 2-0	0-0	—	Crosby, Bell	3874
34	13	H	Chester	D 1-1	1-0	15	Howarth	3831
35	16	A	Colchester U.	L 0-2	0-1	—		3040
36	20	A	Walsall	L 1-4	1-1	17	Morrissey	5206
37	24	H	Peterborough U.	W 1-0	0-0	—	Morrissey	3001
38	27	H	Shrewsbury T.	D 1-1	1-1	15	Morrissey	3883
39	31	A	Hereford U.	L 1-2	0-2	—	Warnock	7497
40	Apr 3	H	Wrexham	L 2-3	1-1	18	Bell 2	3506
41	7	H	Grimsby T.	L 0-3	0-1	—		3069
42	10	A	Mansfield T.	L 0-1	0-0	19		7179
43	14	H	Swindon T.	L 0-1	0-1	—		4226
44	17	H	Brighton & H.A.	D 1-1	0-0	20	Warnock	11,666
45	20	A	Crystal Palace	D 0-0	0-0	—		25,549
46	24	A	Halifax T.	W 3-1	1-1	20	Howarth 2, Rhodes (og)	1608

Goalscorers

League (59): Howarth 14, Bell 14, Morrissey 11, Warnock 5, Walton 5, Brodie 3, Crosby 2, Richardson 2, Howitt 1, own goals 2.

League Cup (2): Warnock 2.

F.A. Cup (7): Howarth 3, Morrissey 2 (1 a pen), Richardson, Warnock.

League Cup	First Round	Portsmouth (h)	1-1
	Second Leg	(a)	1-2
F.A. Cup	First Round	Wealdstone (h)	4-3
	Second Round	Bishops Stortford (h)	2-0
	Third Round	Lincoln C. (h)	1-2

Johnson	Walden	Wallace, J.	Wallace, R.	Walker	Jopling	Bell	Morrissey	Howarth	Brodie	Walton	Sainty	Warnock	Crosby	Richardson	Howitt	Lally	Earls	Godfrey	Marlowe	Goldthorpe	Brown	Match No.
1	2	3	4	5	6	7	8	9	10	11												1
1	2	3		5	6	10	8	9				7	4	11*	12							2
1	2	3	12		6	10	8	9				7	11*	4	5							3
1	2	3	12		6		8*	9	10			7	11	4	5							4
1	2	3	12		6		8	9	10			7	11*	4	5							5
1	2	3	12		6		8	9	10			7*	11	4	5							6
1	2	3	4		6	10	8	9*				7	11	5	12							7
1	2	3	4	5	6	10	8	9		12		7*	11									8
1	2	3		5	6	10	8	9		11		7	4									9
1	2		10		6*	7	8	9		11	12	4	5	3								10
1		3			6	10	8	9		11		7	4	5	2							11
1	2	3			6	10*	8	9		11		7	4	5	12							12
1	2				6	10	8	9		11		7	4	5	3							13
1	2	3			6	10	8	9		11		7	4	5								14
1	2	3			6		8	9	10			7	4	5	11							15
1	2	3			6*	12	8	9		11		7	4	5	10							16
1	2	12	3		6	10	8	9		11			4	5*	7							17
1	2	3			6	10	8	9		7*	11		4		12		5					18
1	2	12	4	3	6	11	8	9				7		10	5*							19
1	2	7	3		6*	10	8	9				4	5	11	12							20
	2	11	3		6	10	8	9		7*		4	5	12					1			21
	2	7*	3		6	10	8	9	11			4	5	12					1			22
	12	7	3			8	9	11				4	6*	2	5		1	10				23
1		3	4		6	10	8		11	7			2			5		9				24
1		3	7		6	10	8	9		11		4		2			5					25
1		4	3			10	8	9		7	11	6	2				5					26
1		3	4		6	10	8	9	11*	7		12	2				5					27
1		3	4		6	10	8	9	11*	7		12	2				5					28
1		3	4*		11	8	9		7	10		5	2	12						6		29
1		3				10	8	9	12	11		6	2	4*						5	7	30
1		3	4			10	8	9	7	11		6	2							5		31
1		3	4			10	8	9	7	11		6	2							5		32
1		3	4			10	8	9	7*	11	12	6	2							5		33
1		3	4			10	8	9	11	7		6	2							5		34
1		3	4			10	8	9	11	7		6	2							5*	12	35
1		3	12	4		10	8	9	7			6	2							5	11*	36
1		3	7	4		10	8	9	11			6	2							5		37
1		3	7	4*		10	8	9	11	12		6	2							5		38
1		3	7	4*	12		8	9	11	10		6	2							5		39
1		3	4	5		10	8	9	11	7*12		6	2									40
1		3	4*	5		10	8	9	11	7	12	6	2									41
1		3	4	2	12	10*	8	9	11	7							5			6		42
1		3	4			10	8	9	11*	7	12		2				5			6		43
1		3	4			10*	8	9	11	7			2				5			6	12	44
1		3	4		12		8	9	11	10			2					6*		5	7	45
1		4	3		6		8	9	11	7			10	2						5		46
43	21	31	22	35	24	37	46	45	25	18	1	28	32	31	27	3	13	3	2	16	3	
	+3s	+1s	+4s	+3s	+1s			+2s				+2s	+7s		+5s		+2s			+2s		

Player and position	Ht.	Wt.	Birthplace	Clubs	League Appearances	Goals
Goalkeepers						
*Tony Godfrey	5 7	12 0	Pangbourne	Southampton	140	—
				Aldershot	172	—
				Rochdale	71	—
				Aldershot	68	—
Gerry Gurr	6 1	12 8	Brighton	Southampton	42	—
				Aldershot	55	—
Glen Johnson	6 0	12 0	Barrow	Arsenal	—	—
				Doncaster R.	95	—
				Walsall (on loan)	3	—
Defenders				Aldershot	116	—
Jim Wallace	5 11	12 0	Bridge of Allen	Dunfermline	73	3
				Aldershot	31+3	—
David Howitt	5 11	12 5	Birmingham	Birmingham C.	2	—
				Bury	11+9	4
				Workington	30+5	1
				Aldershot	27+5	1
Joe Jopling	6 0	11 8	South Shields	Aldershot	35	2
				Leicester C.	2+1	—
				Torquay U. (on loan)	6	—
				Aldershot	54+6	—
*Len Walker	5 11	12 4	Darlington	Newcastle U.	1	—
				Aldershot	440+10	23
John Richardson	6 0	11 0	Ashington	Millwall	1	—
				Brentford	83+2	7
				Fulham	61+9	6
				Aldershot	119+1	6
Michael Earls	6 0	11 10	Limerick	Southampton	8	—
				Aldershot	13+2	—
Alan Wooler	5 10	11 0	Poole	Reading	38	—
				West Ham U.	3+1	—
Midfield				Aldershot	—	—
Malcolm Crosby	5 10	10 10	South Shields	Aldershot	60+14	4
Bob Wallace	5 8	10 12	Huddersfield	Huddersfield	4	—
				Halifax	190+11	16
				Chester	41	9
				Aldershot	64+3	1
John Sainty	5 10	13 4	Poplar	Tottenham H.	—	—
(Now Norwich C. youth coach)				Reading	63+8	20
				Bournemouth	111+7	21
				Mansfield T. (on loan)	3	—
Forwards				Aldershot	26+3	—
Murray Brodie	11	11 2	Glasgow	Leicester C.	3	2
				Aldershot	221+6	35
Terry Bell		10 10	Sherwood	Hartlepool	113+6	34
				Reading	82+5	20
				Aldershot	70+10	29
Jack Howarth	6 0	13 6	Crook	Chelsea	—	—
				Swindon T.	2	—
				Aldershot	258+1	113
				Rochdale	40	12
				Aldershot	146	55
Pat Morrissey	5 7	10 5	Eire	Coventry C.	6+4	—
				Torquay U.	19+2	—
				Crewe Alex.	95+1	28
				Chester	9	1
				Watford	101+6	27
				Aldershot	68	18
Ronnie Walton	5 10	11 6	Plymouth	Northampton T.	1	—
				Carlisle U.	1	—
				Crewe Alex.	2	—
				Aldershot	190+5	41
				Cambridge U.	62	9
				Aldershot	80+4	14
Neil Warnock	5 9½	10 10	Sheffield	Chesterfield	19+3	2
				Rotherham U.	46+8	5
				Hartlepool	58+2	5
				Scunthorpe U.	63+9	7
				Aldershot	29+2	5

Chairman: D. J. C. Hill-Wood, M.C., M.A.

Directors: Sir G. Bracewell Smith, Bart., M.B.E., B.A., Sir Robert Bellinger, C.B.E., D.Sc., S. C. McIntyre, M.B.E., F.C.I.S., The Rev. N. F. Bone, T.D., P. D. Hill-Wood, A. Wood.

General Manager: W. R. Wall.

Manager: *Secretary:* K. J. Friar.

Coach: Bobby Campbell

Year Formed: 1886. *Turned Pro.* 1891. *Ltd. Co.* 1893.

Former Names: 1886–91, Royal Arsenal; 1891–1914, Woolwich Arsenal.

Former ,Grounds: 1886–87, Plumstead Common; 1887–88, Sportsman Ground; 1888–90, Manor Ground; 1890–93, Invicta Ground; 1893–1913, Manor Ground; 1913– Highbury.

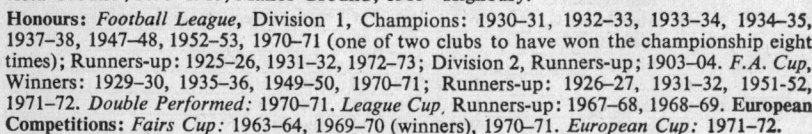

Honours: *Football League,* Division 1, Champions: 1930–31, 1932–33, 1933–34, 1934–35, 1937–38, 1947–48, 1952–53, 1970–71 (one of two clubs to have won the championship eight times); Runners-up: 1925–26, 1931–32, 1972–73; Division 2, Runners-up: 1903–04. *F.A. Cup,* Winners: 1929–30, 1935–36, 1949–50, 1970–71; Runners-up: 1926–27, 1931–32, 1951-52, 1971–72. *Double Performed:* 1970–71. *League Cup,* Runners-up: 1967–68, 1968–69. **European Competitions:** *Fairs Cup:* 1963–64, 1969–70 (winners), 1970–71. *European Cup:* 1971–72.

Record Victory: 12-0 v Loughborough T., Division 2, Mar. 12th, 1900.

Record Defeat: 0-8 v Loughborough T., Division 2, Dec. 12th, 1896.

Most League Points: 66, Division 1, 1930–31.

Most League Goals: 127, Division 1, 1930–31.

Highest League Scorer in Season: Ted Drake, 42, 1934–35.

Most League Goals in Total Aggregate: Cliff Bastin, 150, 1930–47.

Most Capped Player: Terry Neill, 44 (59), Northern Ireland.

Most League Appearances: George Armstrong, 463, 1960–76.

Record Transfer Fee Received: £180,000 from Liverpool for Ray Kennedy, July 1974.

Record Transfer Fee Paid: £220,000 to Everton for Alan Ball, Dec. 1971.

Managers Since the War: George Allison, Tom Whittaker, Jack Crayston, George Swindin, Billy Wright, Bertie Mee.

Address of Club Shop or Boutique: Gunners Shop, Arsenal Stadium, Highbury, N.5.

Arsenal Stadium, Highbury, London N.5. Telephone 01-226-0304. *Ground capacity:* 60,000. *Record attendance:* 73,295 v Sunderland, Div 1, March 9, 1935. *Record receipts:* £51,477 v Anderlecht, Fairs Cup Final, April 28, 1970. *Telegraphs:* 'Gunneretic London N.5.' *Pitch measurements:* 110 yds × 71 yds.

How to get there: Arsenal Underground Station (Piccadilly Line) is within one minute of the ground. Finsbury Park (Piccadilly and Victoria) and Drayton Park (Northern) are also within walking distance. Buses 4a, 19, 106, 141a, 236.

Match tickets: Postal application one calendar month prior to the match. Prices and availability of tickets can be checked with the club on their Ansafone Service (01)-359-0131.

Car parking: Parking is allowed in the adjacent streets under the control of the Police.

Entertainments/catering facilities: West Stand restaurant is open Mon.–Fri. for the general public and on match days for ticket holders in the West Stand Upper tier. East Stand restaurant is open on match days only for ticket holders in the East Stand Upper tier. Reservations for both restaurants can be made by telephoning (01)-226-4968. There are also extensive refreshment bars around the ground.

Club shop: Shop in Avenell Road, Highbury, is open Mon.–Fri. 9.30 am. - 5 pm. On Saturday first team matches it is open from 1.00 pm. - 5.30 pm. Other shops in the ground are open on match days.

Handbooks/programmes: Handbooks and programmes can be obtained from the club shop. Programmes available on subscription.

Extra information: In 1970–71 Arsenal became the fourth club to achieve the Football League and F.A. Cup double.

Club Colours: Red shirts with white sleeves, white shorts, red and white stockings.

Change Colours: Yellow shirts with blue shorts, yellow stockings.

Club Captain: Alan Ball.

Club Nickname: 'Gunners'.

ARSENAL 1975-76 LEAGUE RECORD

Match No.	Date	Venue	Opponents	Result	H/T Score	League Pos'n	Goalscorers	Attendance
1	Aug 16	A	Burnley	D 0-0	0-0	—		18,603
2	19	A	Sheffield U.	W 3-1	1-1	—	Brady, Rice, Kidd	23,344
3	23	H	Stoke C.	L 0-1	0-1	7		28,025
4	26	H	Norwich C.	W 2-1	1-1	—	Ball (pen), Kelly	22,613
5	30	A	Wolverhampton W.	D 0-0	0-0	7		18,144
6	Sept 6	H	Leicester C.	D 1-1	1-0	7	Stapleton	22,005
7	13	A	Aston Villa	L 0-2	0-0	11		34,474
8	20	H	Everton	D 2-2	0-2	11	Kidd, Stapleton	24,864
9	27	A	Tottenham H.	D 0-0	0-0	15		37,092
10	Oct 4	H	Manchester C.	L 2-3	0-2	15	Ball, Cropley	24,928
11	11	H	Coventry C.	W 5-0	4-0	13	Cropley 2, Ball, Kidd 2	19,234
12	18	A	Manchester U.	L 1-3	1-1	16	Kelly	52,958
13	25	H	Middlesbrough	W 2-1	1-0	13	Stapleton, Cropley	23,591
14	Nov 1	A	Newcastle U.	L 0-2	0-1	14		32,824
15	8	H	Derby Co.	L 0-1	0-1	17		32,012
16	15	A	Birmingham C.	L 1-3	0-0	18	Ball	21,652
17	22	H	Manchester U.	W 3-1	2-0	15	Ball, Greenhoff (og), Armstrong	40,102
18	29	A	West Ham U.	L 0-1	0-1	18		31,012
19	Dec 2	A	Liverpool	D 2-2	1-1	—	Ball (pen), Kidd	27,447
20	6	H	Leeds U.	L 1-2	0-0	18	Brady	36,003
21	13	A	Stoke C.	L 1-2	0-0	18	Armstrong	18,628
22	20	H	Burnley	W 1-0	0-0	18	Radford	16,459
23	26	A	Ipswich T.	L 0-2	0-1	18		28,457
24	27	H	Q.P.R.	W 2-0	0-0	17	Ball, Kidd	39,021
25	Jan 10	H	Aston Villa	D 0-0	0-0	18		24,501
26	17	A	Leicester C.	L 1-2	0-0	18	Ross	21,331
27	31	H	Sheffield U	W 1-0	0-0	18	Brady	14,477
28	Feb 7	A	Norwich C.	L 1-3	1-2	18	Kidd	23,038
29	18	A	Derby Co.	L 0-2	0-0	—		24,875
30	21	H	Birmingham C.	W 1-0	1-0	18	Brady	20,907
31	24	H	Liverpool	W 1-0	0-0	—	Radford	36,127
32	28	A	Middlesbrough	W 1-0	0-0	16	Radford	20,000
33	Mar 13	H	Coventry C.	D 1-1	1-0	17	Powling	13,938
34	16	H	Newcastle U.	D 0-0	0-0	—		18,424
35	20	H	West Ham U.	W 6-1	4-1	13	Ball 2 (1 a pen), Armstrong, Kidd 3	34,011
36	27	A	Leeds U.	L 0-3	0-2	14		26,657
37	Apr 3	H	Tottenham H.	L 0-2	0-2	15		42,134
38	10	A	Everton	D 0-0	0-0	17		20,774
39	13	H	Wolverhampton W.	W 2-1	1-1	—	Brady, Mancini	19,518
40	17	H	Ipswich T.	L 1-2	1-0	15	Stapleton	26,973
41	19	A	Q.P.R.	L 1-2	0-0	—	Kidd	30,362
42	24	A	Manchester C.	L 1-3	1-1	17	Armstrong	31,003

Goalscorers

League (47): Kidd 11, Ball 9 (3 pens), Brady 5, Stapleton 4, Cropley 4, Armstrong 4, Radford 3, Kelly 2
Rice 1, Ross 1, Powling 1, Mancini 1, own goal 1.
League Cup (2): Cropley, Stapleton.

League Cup	Second Round	Everton (a)	2-2
		(h)	0-1
F.A. Cup	Third Round	Wolverhampton W. (a) 0-3	

Rimmer	Rice	Nelson	Kelly	Mancini	O'Leary	Armstrong	Cropley	Hornsby	Kidd	Brady	Storey	Ball	Radford	Stapleton	Rostron	Simpson	Powling	Matthews	Barnett	Ross	Match No.
1	2	3	4	5	6	7	8	9	10	11											1
1	2	3	4	5	6	7	8	9	10	11											2
1	2	3	4	5	6	7	8	9	10	11											3
1	2			4	5	6	7	8	10	11	3	9									4
1	2	3	4	5	6		8		10	11		7	9								5
1	2	3	4	5	6		8		10	11		7	9								6
1	2	3	4	5	6		8		10	11		7	9								7
1	2	3	4	5	6		8		10	11		7	9								8
1	2	3	4	5	6		8		10	12		7	9	11*							9
1	2	3	4*		6		8		10	11		7	9	12	5						10
1	2	3			6		8*		10	11		7	9	12	5	4					11
1	2	3	4	5			8		10	11		7	9				6				12
1	2	3	4*		6		8		10	11		7	9		5	12					13
1	2	3	4		6				10	11		7	9		5	8					14
1	2		4	5			8		10	11	3	7	9				6				15
1	2		4	5			8*		10	11	3	7	9			12	6				16
1	2		4	5			8		10	11	3	7	9				6				17
1	2	3		5			8		10	11	4	7	9				6				18
1	2		4	5			8		10	11	3	7	9				6				19
1	2	3			5	7			10	11	4	8		9			6				20
	2	3*			5	7			10	11	4	8		9		12	6		1		21
1	2		4		5	7			10	11*		8		9	12	3	6				22
1	2		4		5	7			10	11	3	8		9			6				23
1	2	3			5	7			10	11	4	8		9			6				24
1	2	3		5	6	7			10	11		8		9		4					25
1	2	3		5	6	7			10	11		8		9						4	26
1	2	3*			5	7			10	11		8		9		12	6			4	27
1	2				5	7			10	11	3	8		9			6			4	28
1	2	3			5	7			10	11		8		9			6			4	29
1	2	3			5	7			10	11*		8		9		12	6			4	30
1	2	3			5	7			10	11		8		9			6			4	31
1	2	3			5	7			10	11		8		9			6			4	32
1	2	3			5	7			10	11		8		9			6			4	33
1	2	3			5	7			10	11		8		9			6			4	34
1	2*	3			5	7			10	11		8		9		12	6			4	35
1	2	3			5	7			10	11		8		9			6			4	36
1	2	3			5	7			10	11		8		9			6			4	37
1	2	3			5	7			10	11		8		9			6			4	38
1	2	3			5	7			10	11		8		9			6			4	39
1	2	3			5				10	11		8		9	7		6			4	40
1	2	3			5	7			10	11		8		9*	12		6			4	41
1	2	3			5	7			10	11		8		9			6			4	42
41	42	36	17	26	27	28	20	4	37	41	11	39	15	23	2	7	28	—	1	17	
					+1s							+1s		+2s	+3s	+2s	+1s	+1s			

ARSENAL—PLAYERS

Player and position	Ht.	Wt.	Birthplace	Clubs	League Appearances	Goals
Goalkeepers						
Geoff Barnett	6 0	11 12	Northwich	Everton	10	—
				Arsenal	39	—
				(contract cancelled Feb. 1976)		
Jimmy Rimmer (England)	5 11	11 12	Southport	Manchester U.	34	—
				Swansea C. (on loan)	17	—
				Arsenal	82	—
Brian Parker	5 10	11 0	Chorley	Crewe Alex.	26	—
				Liverpool (on loan)	—	—
				Arsenal	—	—
Defenders						
Terry Mancini (Eire)	6 0	12 0	London	Watford	66	—
				Orient	167	16
				Q.P.R.	94	3
				Arsenal	52	1
Sammy Nelson (N. Ireland)	5 10	11 0	Belfast	Arsenal	105+8	2
Pat Rice (N. Ireland)	5 8	11 7	Belfast	Arsenal	246+3	5
Peter Simpson	5 10½	11 9	Gorleston	Arsenal	328+13	10
David MacKinnon	5 10	11 7	Scotland	Arsenal	—	—
				(contract cancelled March 1976)		
David O'Leary	5 11	11 3	London	Arsenal	27	—
Midfield						
Alan Ball (England)	5 6	10 5	Farnworth	Blackpool	116	41
				Everton	208	66
				Arsenal	163	44
Alex Cropley (Scotland)	5 8	10 4	Aldershot	Hibernian	110+4	24
				Arsenal	27	5
Graham Rix	5 9	11 0	Doncaster	Arsenal	—	—
John Matthews	5 11	11 13	London	Arsenal	20+1	—
Eddie Kelly	5 7	12 0	Glasgow	Arsenal	168+7	13
Peter Storey (England)	5 9	11 7	Farnham	Arsenal	380	9
David Price	5 11	12 2	Caterham	Arsenal	3+3	—
				Peterborough U. (on loan)	6	1
Richie Powling	5 7	11 6	Barking	Arsenal	35+4	1
Liam Brady (Eire)	5 7	10 7	Dublin	Arsenal	80+7	9
Forwards						
George Armstrong	5 6	11 2	Hebburn	Arsenal	453+10	51
Brian Hornsby	5 8	10 7	Cambridge	Arsenal	23+3	5
Brian Kidd (England)	6 0	12 12	Manchester	Manchester U.	195+8	52
				Arsenal	77	30
Frank Stapleton	5 11	12 7	Dublin	Arsenal	24+2	4
Wilf Rostron	5 6	11 2	Sunderland	Arsenal	8+3	2
John Radford (England)	5 11	12 12	Pontefract	Arsenal	374+3	111
Trevor Ross	5 8	10 12	Co. Durham	Arsenal	18+1	1
*Gary Goodchild	5 10	11 2	Chelmsford	Arsenal	—	—
Warwick Bean	5 10	11 2	Epsom	Arsenal	—	—

Chairman: Sir William Dugdale.   *Vice-Chairman:* J. H. Kartz.

Vice Chairman: R. F. Bendall.

Directors: A. C. Smith, W. E. Houghton, H. G. Cressman,
H. D. Ellis, J. H. Kartz.

Manager: Ron Saunders   *Secretary:* Alan Bennett.

Commercial Manager: Eric Woodward.   *Year Formed:* 1874.

Turned Professional: 1885.   *Limited Company:* 1896.

Previous Grounds: 1874–76, Aston Park; 1876–97, Perry Barr;
1897–, Villa Park.

Honours: *League*, Division 1, Champions: 1893–94, 1895–96,
1896–97, 1898–1899, 1899–1900, 1909–10; Runners-up: 1888–89,
1902–03, 1907–08, 1910–11, 1912–13, 1913–14, 1930–31, 1932–33.
Division 2, Champions: 1937–38, 1959–60; Runners-up 1974-75.
Division 3, Champions: 1971–72. *F.A. Cup*, Winners: 1887, 1895,
1897, 1905, 1913, 1920, 1957 (seven wins stands as the record);
Runners-up: 1892–94. *Football League Cup*, Winners: 1961, 1975; Runners-up: 1963, 1971.
European Competitions: UEFA Cup 1975–76.

Record Victory: 13-0 v Wednesbury Old Athletic, F.A. Cup 1st Rd., 1886.

Record Defeat: 1-8 v Blackburn R., F.A. Cup 3rd Rd., 1888–89.

Most League Points: 70, Division 3, 1971–72.

Most League Goals: 128, Division 1, 1930–31.

Highest League Scorer in Season: 49, 'Pongo' Waring, Division 1, 1930–31.

Most League Goals in Total Aggregate: 213, Harry Hampton, 1904–20 and Billy Walker,
1919–34.

Most League Appearances: 560, Charlie Aitken 1961–76.

Most Capped Player: Peter McParland, 33 (34), Ireland.

Record Transfer Fee Received: £200,000 from Derby Co. for Bruce Rioch, March 1974.

Record Transfer Fee Paid: £175,000 to Coventry C. for Dennis Mortimer, Dec. 1975.

Managers Since the War: Alex Massie, George Martin, Eric Houghton, Joe Mercer, Dick
Taylor, Tommy Cummings, Tommy Docherty, Vic Crowe.

Address of Supporters Club: c/o Villa ground.

Address of Club Shop or Boutique: c/o Villa ground.

Villa Park, Trinity Rd., Birmingham B6 6HE. Telephone 021-327 6604. 24 hour answering
service 021-238 1722. *Telegraphic Address:* 'Villa, Birmingham 6'. *Ground capacity:* 58,182.
Record attendance: 76,588 v Derby County, F.A. Cup, 6th Rd., March 2, 1946. *Record
receipts:* £88,000, F.A. Cup semi-final, Ipswich T. v West Ham U., April 5, 1975. *Club
record:* £46,518 F.L. Div. 1 v Birmingham C. September 27, 1975. *Pitch measurements:*
115 yds × 75 yds.

How to get there: Bus 5 from Corporation Street to Witton Square. Special buses from Priory Ringway and
Hall of Memory (city centre). Birmingham New Street railway station is near the centre. The ground is
½ mile from link to the motorway.

Match tickets: Postal applications one month in advance, personal applications two weeks in advance.

Car parking: Serpentine Car Park in Aston Hall Road. Side-street parking also available.

Entertainments/catering facilities: Lions Club (members only) adjacent to the ground. Many refreshment
points around the ground.

Club Shop: Adjacent to the ground; sells all types of souvenirs.

Handbooks/programmes: Programmes available on seasonal subscription.

Extra information: Aston Villa are one of only four clubs to achieve the Football League and F.A. Cup
double; they did so in 1896–97.

Club Colours: Claret shirts with light blue sleeves, white shorts, blue stockings.   *Change Colours:* White
shirts with claret and light blue collar and cuffs, blue shorts, white stockings.   *Club Nickname:* 'The Villans'

ASTON VILLA 1975-76 LEAGUE RECORD

Match No.	Date	Venue	Opponents	Result	H/T Score	League Pos'n	Goalscorers	Attendance
1	Aug16	H	Leeds U.	L 1-2	1-1	—	Phillips	46,026
2	19	A	Q.P.R.	D 1-1	0-0	—	Leonard	21,986
3	23	A	Norwich C.	L 3-5	1-4	18	Graydon 2 (1 a pen), Aitken	21,797
4	27	H	Manchester C.	W 1-0	0-0	12	Leonard	35,212
5	30	H	Coventry C.	W 1-0	0-0	12	Graydon	41,026
6	Sept 6	A	Newcastle U.	L 0-3	0-2	17		34,668
7	13	H	Arsenal	W 2-0	0-0	14	Phillips, Leonard	34,474
8	20	A	Liverpool	L 0-3	0-0	16		42,779
9	23	A	Wolverhampton W.	D 0-0	0-0	—		33,344
10	27	H	Birmingham C.	W 2-1	0-1	13	Hamilton, Little	53,782
11	Oct 4	A	Middlesbrough	D 0-0	0-0	8		24,102
12	11	H	Tottenham H.	D 1-1	0-0	12	Gray	40,048
13	18	A	Everton	L 1-2	0-2	15	Nicholl	30,376
14	25	H	Burnley	D 1-1	0-0	15	Noble (og)	34,242
15	Nov 1	A	Ipswich T.	L 0-3	0-1	12		24,691
16	8	H	Sheffield U.	W 5-1	1-0	13	Gray, Hamilton 2, Deehan, Graydon (pen)	30,053
17	15	A	Manchester U.	L 0-2	0-1	15		51,682
18	22	H	Everton	W 3-1	1-0	14	Gray 2, McNaught (og)	33,949
19	29	H	Leicester C.	D 1-1	0-1	13	Graydon	36,388
20	Dec 6	A	Stoke C.	D 1-1	1-1	14	Graydon	28,492
21	13	H	Norwich C.	W 3-2	2-1	12	Graydon, Deehan 2	30,478
22	20	A	Leeds U.	L 0-1	0-1	12		29,118
23	26	H	West Ham U.	W 4-1	2-1	12	Deehan 2, Hamilton, Gray	51,300
24	27	A	Derby Co.	L 0-2	0-0	13		37,230
25	Jan 10	A	Arsenal	D 0-0	0-0	13		24,501
26	17	H	Newcastle U.	D 1-1	1-1	13	Mahoney (og)	36,387
27	31	H	Q.P.R.	L 0-2	0-0	16		32,223
28	Feb 7	A	Manchester C.	L 1-2	1-0	17	Gray	32,331
29	14	A	Sheffield U.	L 1-2	1-1	17	Graydon	21,152
30	21	H	Manchester U.	W 2-1	1-1	17	McDonald, Gray	50,094
31	24	H	Wolverhampton W.	D 1-1	0-0	—	Graydon	47,693
32	28	A	Burnley	D 2-2	2-1	17	Graydon, Gray	17,123
33	Mar 6	H	Ipswich T.	D 0-0	0-0	14		32,477
34	13	A	Tottenham H.	L 2-5	1-3	18	Graydon, Gray	23,169
35	20	A	Leicester C.	D 2-2	1-1	18	Nicholl 2	24,663
36	27	H	Stoke C.	D 0-0	0-0	18		32,359
37	Apr 3	A	Birmingham C.	L 2-3	1-1	18	Gray, Graydon (pen)	46,251
38	10	H	Liverpool	D 0-0	0-0	18		44,250
39	13	A	Coventry C.	D 1-1	0-1	—	Nicholl	27,586
40	17	A	West Ham U.	D 2-2	2-2	18	Deehan, Hunt	21,642
41	19	H	Derby Co.	W 1-0	0-0	—	McDonald	39,241
42	24	H	Middlesbrough	W 2-1	1-1	16	Deehan, Carrodus	33,241

Goalscorers

League (51): Graydon 12 (3 pens), Gray 10, Deehan 7, Nicholl 4, Hamilton 4, Leonard 3, Phillips 2, McDonald 2, Aitken 1, Little 1, Hunt 1, Carrodus 1, own goals 3.
League Cup (3): Leonard, Nicholl, Gray.
F.A. Cup (2): Gray, Graydon.

League Cup	Second Round	Oldham Ath. (h)	2-0
	Third Round	Manchester U. (h)	1-2
F.A. Cup	Third Round	Southampton (a)	1-1
		(h)	1-2 (a.e.t.)

Cumbes	Gidman	Aitken	Ross	Nicholl	Phillips	Graydon	Little	Leonard	Hamilton	Carrodus	Robson	Morgan	McDonald	Findlay	Pimblett	Hunt	Burridge	Gray	Deehan	Mortimer	Overton	Cowans	Masefield	Match No.
1	2	3	4	5	6	7	8	9	10	11														1
1	2	3	4	5	6	7	8	9	10	11														2
1	2	3	4	5	6	7	8	9	10	11														3
1	2*	3	4	5	6	7	8	9	10	11	12													4
1		3	4	5	6	7	8	9	10	11	2													5
1		3	4	5	6	7	8	9*	10	11	2	12												6
1	2	3	4	5	6	7		9	10			8	11											7
	2	3	4	5	6	7	8			11		9		1	10*	12								8
	2	3	4	5	6	7	8		10	11	9			1										9
	2	3	4	5	6	7	8		10	11	9			1										10
	2	3	6	5	7		8		10	11	4						1	9						11
	2	3	4	5	6	7	8		10	11							1	9						12
	2	3	4	5	6	7	8*		10	11	12						1	9						13
	2	3	4	5	6	7			10	11	8						1	9						14
	2	3	4	5	6*	7				11	8	12					1	9	10					15
	2	3	4	5		7				11	8				6		1	9	10					16
	2	3	4	5	12	7				11	8				6*		1	9	10					17
	2		4	5	6	7			10	11	3						1	9	8					18
	2		4	5	6	7			10	11	3						1	9	8					19
	2		4	5	10	7				11	3	9			6		1		8					20
	2		4	5	6	7			10	11	3						1	9	8					21
		3	4	5	8	7			10*	11	2			12	6		1	9						22
	2		4	5		7			10	11	3						1	9	8	6				23
	2		4	5		7			10	11	3						1	9	8	6				24
	2	3	4	5	6				10	11	8						1	9		7				25
	2	3	4	5	12					11	7	8					1	9	10	6*				26
	2	3	4	5*	6	7			10	11	8						1	9	12					27
	2		4	5		7			10	11	3					8*	1	9		6	12			28
	2		4	5	6	7			12	11	3		10			8	1	9*						29
	2		4	5	6	7	8			11	3		10				1	9						30
	2		4	5	6	7	8			11	3		10*				1	9			12			31
	2		4		6	7	8			11	3		10				1	9	5					32
	2		4	5	6	7	8*			11	3		12				1	9	10					33
	2		4	5	6*	7	8		12	11	3						1	9	10					34
	2		4	5		7	8		10	11	3						1	9		6				35
	2		4	5		7	8		10	11	3						1	9		6				36
	2		4	5		7	8		10	11	3						1	9		6				37
	2		5	4		7				11	3		10			8	1	9		6				38
	2		5	4		7				11	3		10			8	1	9*		6	12			39
	2		5	4						11	3		10	1		8		9	7	6				40
	2		5	4		7				11	3					8	1	9	10	6				41
	2		4	5		7				11	3					8	1	9	10	6				42
7	39	21	38	40	33	38	20	7	29	39	34	2	10	5	7	3	30	30	14	14	2	—	—	
					+2s			+2s	+2s	+1s	+3s						+1s		+1s	+1s	+1s	+1s		

Player and position	Ht.	Wt.	Birthplace	Clubs	League Appearances	Goals
Goalkeepers						
John Burridge	5 10	11 0	Custon	Workington	27	—
				Blackpool	134	—
				Aston V.	30	—
Jim Cumbes	6 2	13 0	Manchester	Tranmere R.	136	—
				W.B.A.	64	—
				Aston V.	157	—
				(contract cancelled April 1976)		
John Findlay	6 1	14 1	Blairgowrie	Aston V.	7	—
Defenders						
*Charlie Aitken	5 10	11 0	Edinburgh	Aston V.	558+2	13
John Gidman	5 10	11 0	Liverpool	Liverpool	—	—
				Aston V.	95+1	1
Chris Nicholl	6 2	12 7	Macclesfield	Halifax T.	42	3
(N. Ireland)				Luton T.	97	6
				Aston V.	175	9
John Robson	5 7½	9 2	Consett	Derby Co.	171+1	3
				Aston V.	106+2	1
Ian Ross	5 9½	11 9	Glasgow	Liverpool	42+5	2
				Aston V.	175	3
Keith Masefield	5 7	11 9	Birmingham	Aston V.	0+2	—
Ron Armstrong	5 8	11 10	Birmingham	Aston V.	—	—
				(contract cancelled Dec. 1975)		
David Evans	5 10	11 13	West Bromwich	Aston V.	—	—
David Hughes	5 9	10 11	Birmingham	Aston V.	—	—
Charles Young	5 11	11 2	Nicosia	Aston V.	—	—
Leighton Phillips	5 8	10 9	Briton Ferry	Cardiff C.	169+9	10
(Wales)				Aston V.	56+4	4
Midfield						
Bob McDonald	5 9	10 8	Aberdeen	Aston V.	33+6	3
Dennis Mortimer	5 10	11 5	Liverpool	Coventry C.	179+14	10
				Aston V.	14	—
Frank Carrodus	5 8	10 10	Manchester	Manchester C.	33+9	1
				Aston V.	75	4
Pat McMahon	5 11	10 10	Glasgow	Celtic	2+1	2
				Aston V.	121+7	25
				(contract cancelled March 1976)		
*Frank Pimblett	5 9	12 0	Liverpool	Aston V.	9	—
				Newport Co. (on loan)	7	—
Keith Williams	5 8	11 3	Burtwood	Aston V.	—	—
Forwards						
Ray Graydon	5 9	11 0	Bristol	Bristol R.	132+2	33
				Aston V.	171+4	61
Ian Hamilton	5 10	10 6	Streatham	Chelsea	3+3	2
				Southend	35+2	11
				Aston V.	189+17	39
*John Overton	5 10	10 12	Rotherham	Aston V.	2+1	—
				Halifax T. (on loan)	14	2
Keith Leonard	5 11	13 7	Birmingham	Aston V.	36+2	11
				Port Vale (on loan)	12+1	1
Brian Little	5 8	11 2	Durham	Aston V.	107+5	33
(England)						
Andy Gray	5 10	11 2	Glasgow	Dundee U.	61+1	36
(Scotland)				Aston V.	30	10
Steve Hunt	5 7	10 11	Birmingham	Aston V.	4+2	1
John Deehan	5 10	11 2	Solihull	Aston V.	14+1	7
Gordon Cowans	5 9	11 4	County Durham	Aston V.	0+1	—

BARNSLEY

Chairman: E. S. Dennis.

Directors: A. Raynor, J.P., R. F. Potter, G. Pallister, G. Buckle, N. W. B. Moody, J.P.

General Manager/Secretary: Johnny Steele.

Team Manager: Jim Iley.

Year Formed: 1887. *Turned Professional:* 1888.

Limited Company: 1899.

Previous Name: Barnsley St. Peter's.

Honours: *Football League,* best season: 3rd, Division 2, 1914–15, 1921–22. Division 3(N) Champions: 1933–34, 1938–39, 1954–55. Runners-up: 1953–54. Division 4, Runners-up: 1967–68. Division 3(N). *F.A. Cup,* Winners: 1912; Runners-up: 1910. *Football League Cup,* best season: 3rd Rd., 1962–63.

Record Victory: 9-0 v Loughborough T. Div. 2, Jan. 28th, 1899 and v Accrington Stanley at Accrington, Division 3(N), Feb. 3rd, 1934.

Record Defeat: 0-9 v Notts. Co., Division 2, Nov. 19th, 1927.

Most League Points: 67, Division 3(N), 1938–39.

Most League Goals: 118, Division 3(N), 1933–34.

Highest League Scorer in Season: Cecil McCormack, 33, Division 2, 1950–51.

Most League Goals in Total Aggregate: Ernest Hine, 123, 1921–26, 1934–38.

Most Capped Player: Eddie McMorran, 9 (15), Ireland.

Most League Appearances: Eric Winstanley, 409, 1961–73.

Record Transfer Fee Received: £40,000 from Newcastle U. for Stewart Barrowclough, Aug. 1970.

Record Transfer Fee Paid: £20,000 to Cardiff C. (joint fee) for Frank Sharp and Leslie Lea, Aug. 1970.

Managers Since the War: Angus Seed, Tim Ward, Johnny Steele, John McSeveney.

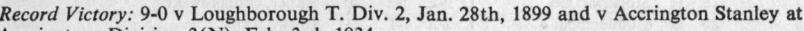

Oakwell Ground, Grove St., Barnsley. Telephone Barnsley 84113. *Ground capacity:* 38,500 (15,000 under cover). *Record attendance:* 40,255 v Stoke C. February 15, 1936 F.A. Cup 5th Round. *Record receipts:* £9,620 v Manchester U., February 1964. *Pitch measurements:* 111 yds × 75 yds.

How to get there: Fairly frequent train service from Sheffield and Leeds to Exchange Station Barnsley. No special buses, just the normal services, and no buses from town centre because the ground is so close.

Match tickets: Stand seats bookable two weeks in advance.

Car parking: Official club park adjacent to the ground holds 600 cars; parking fee 5p. The Yorkshire Traction Company Park, also adjacent, holds another 800 at the same fee. There is a free public park in Queens Road, two minutes from the ground. The M1 runs approximately two miles from the ground.

Entertainments/catering facilities: Football club social club is adjacent to the ground. Seven tea bars sited around the ground sell hot drinks and pies; six of them sell alcoholic drinks.

Club shop: Inside the ground; sells all types of souvenirs.

Handbooks/programmes: Programmes available on subscription.

Extra information: For post-match entertainment, there is the Ba-Ba night club in Queens Road.

Club Colours: Red shirts, white shorts, white stockings.

Change Colours: All white or yellow and blue.

Club Captain:

Club Nickname: 'The Tykes'.

BARNSLEY 1975–76 LEAGUE RECORD

Match No.	Date	Venue	Opponents	Result	H/T Score	League Pos'n	Goalscorers	Attendance
1	Aug 16	H	Watford	W 1-0	0-0	—	Butler	3690
2	23	A	Southport	D 0-0	0-0	5		1316
3	30	H	Northampton T.	W 3-1	1-1	2	Butler 2, Peachey	3525
4	Sept 6	A	Brentford	L 0-1	0-0	5		5600
5	12	H	Crewe Alex.	D 1-1	0-0	6	Butler	4243
6	19	A	Tranmere R.	L 0-1	0-1	10		2638
7	24	H	Doncaster R.	L 0-1	0-1	—		6557
8	27	H	Workington	D 0-0	0-0	16		2843
9	Oct 4	A	AFC Bournemouth	D 1-1	1-0	15	Chambers	4408
10	11	A	Newport Co.	L 0-1	0-0	17		3043
11	18	H	Reading	W 4-2	2-1	15	Butler, Peachey, Price 2	2814
12	21	H	Exeter C.	D 0-0	0-0	—		3619
13	25	A	Hartlepool	L 0-1	0-1	17		2324
14	Nov 1	H	Swansea C.	D 0-0	0-0	15		2709
15	5	A	Torquay U.	L 0-2	0-2	—		1457
16	8	A	Darlington	L 0-2	0-1	20		2066
17	15	H	Stockport Co.	D 2-2	2-2	20	Butler, Otulakowski	2534
18	29	H	Huddersfield T.	L 2-3	1-1	21	Brown, Price	5007
19	Dec 6	A	Bradford C.	L 1-2	1-2	21	Otulakowski	3285
20	20	A	Cambridge U.	D 1-1	0-1	21	Harris	2180
21	26	H	Rochdale	W 2-1	1-1	21	Brown, Millar	3362
22	27	A	Lincoln C.	L 1-2	0-1	21	Butler	12,074
23	Jan 3	H	Scunthorpe U.	W 1-0	0-0	21	Doyle (pen)	2823
24	10	A	Northampton T.	L 0-5	0-3	21		6132
25	17	H	Tranmere R.	W 1-0	0-0	20	James (og)	2689
26	23	A	Crewe Alex.	D 1-1	1-0	—	Price	2291
27	31	A	Exeter C.	L 0-2	0-1	20		2449
28	Feb 7	H	Torquay U.	D 0-0	0-0	21		2229
29	14	A	Darlington	W 1-0	1-0	20	Price	2440
30	20	A	Stockport Co.	D 1-1	0-0	20	Gorry	2707
31	24	A	Doncaster R.	D 2-2	1-1	—	Felton, Butler	8250
32	28	H	Hartlepool	W 3-1	2-0	19	Price, Doyle (pen), Gorry	2648
33	Mar 5	A	Swansea C.	L 1-3	0-1	19	Butler	2510
34	9	H	AFC Bournemouth	W 2-0	1-0	—	Brown, Felton	2550
35	13	H	Newport Co.	W 3-1	0-1	15	Peachey 2, Doyle (pen)	2587
36	17	A	Reading	D 0-0	0-0	—		6579
37	20	A	Huddersfield T.	W 2-1	2-0	14	Burke, Brown	10,049
38	27	H	Bradford C.	D 1-1	1-1	14	Peachey	5206
39	30	H	Cambridge U.	W 4-0	1-0	—	Peachey, Price, Brown, Seddon (og)	3066
40	Apr 3	A	Watford	L 0-1	0-1	13		4203
41	7	A	Workington	W 7-1	4-1	—	Peachey 3, Price 2 (1 a pen), Saunders, Doyle (pen)	1057
42	10	H	Brentford	D 1-1	1-0	12	Doyle (pen)	3753
43	17	A	Rochdale	D 0-0	0-0	12		1386
44	19	H	Lincoln C.	L 0-1	0-1	—		8573
45	20	A	Scunthorpe U.	L 0-1	0-0	—		4770
46	24	H	Southport	W 2-0	1-0	12	Peachey, Doyle	2995

Goalscorers

League (52): Peachey 10, Butler 9, Price 9 (1 a pen), Doyle 6 (5 pens), Brown 5, Felton 2, Gorry 2, Otulakowski 2, Burke 1, Chambers 1, Harris 1. Millar 1, Saunders 1, own goals 2.
League Cup (2): Butler, Price.
F.A. Cup (1): Butler.

League Cup	First Round	Huddersfield T. (a)	1-2
	Second Leg	(h)	1-1
F.A. Cup	First Round	Marine (a)	1-3

Springett	Yates	Chambers	Doyle	Burke	Murphy	Millar	Butler, M.	Price	Walker	Brown	Peachey	Pickering	Riley	Lea	Harris	Deere	Butler, I.	Otulakowski	Gorry	Saunders	Felton	Match No.
1	2	3	4	5	6	7	8	9*	10	11	12											1
1		3	4	5	2	7*	8	9	10	11	12	6										2
1		3	4	5	2	11	9	10	8	7*	12	6										3
1		3	4	5	2	9	10	11*	7	8	12	6										4
1	2	3	4	5	10*	7	8			11	9	6	12									5
1		3	4	5	2	7	8			11	9	6		10								6
1		3	4	5	2	7	8	10*	12	9		6		11								7
1		3	4	5	2	11	9		8	7*		6		12	10							8
1	2	3	4	5			8	7	9	10		6		11								9
1	2	3	4	5	11	10	7	8	*		12	6		9*								10
1	2	3	4		6	7	8			10	9	5				11						11
1	2	3	4	5		7	8			10	9	6				11						12
1	2	3	4		6	7	8			11*	9			12	5	10						13
1	2	3	4	5	10*		11			8				12	9	6	7					14
1	2	3	4	5			8	7		10	12			9		6	11*					15
1	2	3	4	5	11	7						6		8	10			9				16
1	2	3	4	5	11	7					9	6		10	8							17
1			4	5	2	11	7		8	10		6						9	3			18
1		3	4	5	6	11	9*	12	8			7						10	2			19
1		3	4				12	8	10	11		6		9				7*	2	5		20
1		3	4				12	8	10*	11		6		9				7	2	5		21
1			4		2		10	8		11		6		9				7	3	5		22
1		3	4				11	10	9		7	6						8	2	5		23
1		3	4				11*	7	9	10		6		12				8	2	5		24
1	2	3	4				11	8*	10			6		9	12			7		5		25
1	2	3	4				10	9	8	11		6						7		5		26
1	2	3	4				7	10	9	11*		6		12				8		5		27
1	2	3	4				11*	7	9	10		6		12				8		5		28
1			4	5	2			11	9	10		6						8	3		7	29
1			4	5	2			8	9	11		6						10	3		7	30
1			4	5	2			8	9	11		6						10	3		7	31
1			4	5	2			8	9*	11		6		12				10	3		7	32
1			4	5	2			8	9	12	11	6						10	3		7*	33
1			4	5	2			8	9	11		6						10	3		7	34
1			4	5	2			8		11	9	6						10	3		7	35
1		3	4	5	2			8		11	9	6						10			7	36
1		3	4	5	2			8		11	9	6						10			7	37
1		3	4	5	2			8		11	9	6						10			7	38
1			4		2			8		11	9	6						10	3	5	7	39
1			4		2			8		11	9	6		12				10	3	5	7*	40
1			4		2			8		11*	9	6	7	12				10	3	5		41
1			4		2		12		8*		9	6	7	11				10	3	5		42
1			4		2		11		8*	7	9	6		12				10	3	5		43
1			4		2			7		11	9	6		8				10	3	5		44
1			4		2			7		11	9	6		8				10	3	5		45
1			4		2			8		11	9	6		7				10	3	5		46
46	15	29	46	26	36	27	31	31	11	38	19	41	3	7	9	4	5	31	22	17	12	
			+1s	+2s				+2s	+2s	+5s		+1s	+2s	+9s								

BARNSLEY—PLAYERS

Player and position	Ht.	Wt.	Birthplace	Clubs	League Appearances	Goals
Goalkeepers						
Peter Springett	5 10	11 6	Fulham	Q.P.R.	139	—
				Sheffield W.	180	—
				Barnsley	46	—
Defenders						
Philip Chambers	5 7	11 0	Barnsley	Barnsley	176+1	6
Martin Gorry	5 11	10 2	Derby	Barnsley	22	2
Barrie Murphy	5 11	11 6	Crookham	Barnsley	420+5	2
Peter Burke	6 0	11 10	Rotherham	Barnsley	28	1
David Yates	5 9	10 0	Barnsley	Barnsley	99	2
Michael Pickering	6 0	11 4	Huddersfield	Barnsley	55	—
John Saunders	6 1	12 6	Worksop	Mansfield T.	90	2
				Huddersfield T.	123	1
				Barnsley	17	1
Midfield						
Kenny Brown	5 8	8 7	Barnsley	Barnsley	197+10	19
Graham Collingwood	5 10	10 7	Barnsley	Barnsley	12+2	—
Robert Doyle	5 11	10 7	Dunbarton	Barnsley	148+1	16
Alistair Millar	5 9	10 7	Glasgow	Barnsley	178+12	7
Leslie Lea	5 8	10 2	Manchester	Blackpool	158+1	13
				Cardiff C.	75+1	7
				Barnsley	198+7	33
				(contract cancelled April 1976)		
Brian Mahoney	5 11	12 11	Huddersfield	Huddersfield T.	18+2	2
				Barnsley	82+8	15
Forwards						
Peter Price	5 8	10 10	Wrexham	Liverpool	—	—
				Peterborough U.	114+5	61
				Northampton T. (on loan)	—	—
				Portsmouth	13+1	2
				Peterborough U. (on loan)	2	—
				Barnsley	53+1	21
Glyn Riley				Barnsley	1+1	1
Antoni Otulakowski				Barnsley	32	2
John Peachey	6 0	12 1	Cambridge	York C.	6+2	3
				Barnsley	43+6	15
				Darlington (on loan)	5+1	3
Philip Sanderson				Barnsley	2	1
Larry McGettigan	5 9	10 5	London	Watford	40+20	3
				Barnsley	—	—
				(contract cancelled Aug. 75)		
*Paul Walker	5 9½	11 3	Bradford	Wolverhampton W.	16+11	—
				Watford (on loan)	2+1	—
				Swindon T. (on loan)	2+3	—
				Peterborough U.	75+3	3
				Barnsley	11+2	—
Glyn Riley	5 10	11 11	Barnsley	Barnsley	3+1	—
Leslie Harris	5 9	10 5	Sheffield	Barnsley	9+9	1

BIRMINGHAM CITY

Chairman: C. K. Coombs.

Directors: Sir Alf Ramsey, L. J. Morris, H. Dare, J. F. Wiseman, Ald. N. Bosworth, B.A., D. M. Coombs.

Manager: Willie Bell. *Limited Company:* 1888.

Secretary: Alan Instone. *Coach:* Syd Owen.

Year Formed: 1875. *Turned Professional:* 1885.

Previous Grounds: Waste ground near Arthur St., 1875; Muntz St., Small Heath, 1877; St. Andrew's, 1906.

Previous Name: 1875–88, Small Heath Alliance; 1888, dropped 'Alliance'; became Birmingham, 1905; became Birmingham City, 1945.

Honours: Football League, best season: 6th, Division 1, 1955–56. Division 2, Champions: 1892–93, 1920–21, 1947–48, 1954–55; Runners-up: 1893–94, 1900–01, 1902–03, 1971–72. *F.A. Cup,* Runners-up: 1931, 1956. *Football League Cup,* Winners: 1963. **European Competitions:** *European Fairs Cup:* 1955–58, 1958–60 (Finalists), 1960–61 (Finalists), 1961–62.

Record Victory: 12-0 v Walsall Town Swifts, Division 2, Dec. 17th, 1892 and v Doncaster R., Division 2, Apr. 11th, 1903.

Record Defeat: 1-9 v Sheffield W., Division 1, Dec. 13th, 1930.

Most League Points: 59, Division 2, 1947–48.

Most League Goals: 103, Division 2, 1893–94 (only 28 games).

Highest League Scorer in Season: Joe Bradford, 29, Division 1, 1927–28.

Most Capped Player: Harry Hibbs, 25, England.

Most League Appearances: Gil Merrick, 486, 1946–60.

Most League Goals in Total Aggregate: Joe Bradford, 249, 1920–35.

Record Transfer Fee Received: £350,000 from Everton for Bob Latchford, Feb. 1974 (including Archie Styles and Howard Kendall in part exchange).

Record Transfer Fee Paid: £180,000 to Everton for Howard Kendall, Feb. 1974.

Managers Since the War: Ted Goodier, Harry Storer, Bob Brocklebank, Arthur Turner, Pat Beasley, Gil Merrick, Joe Mallett, Stan Cullis, Fred Goodwin.

Address of Supporters Club: St. Andrew's Club, St. Andrew's, Birmingham 9.

Address of Club Shop or Boutique: The Beautique, 26 Cattell Road, Birmingham 9.

St. Andrews, Birmingham B9 4NH. Telephone 021-772 0101/2689. *Telegraphic Address:* 'Heathen Birmingham'. *Ground capacity:* 52,500 (9,579 seats). *Record Attendance:* 66,844 v Everton, F.A. Cup, 5th Round, February 11, 1939. *Record Receipts:* £29,739 v Middlesbrough, F.A. Cup 6th Round, March 8, 1975. *Pitch measurements:* 115 yds × 75 yds.

How to get there: Buses 53, 54 from Carr's Lane, City Centre. Specials from Albert Street and Hall of Memory, Broad Street. Nearest railway station, Birmingham New Street. By road; via M1, M45, and A45 to Small Heath area of Birmingham and via Cattell Road (sixth turning on the right past Small Heath Park) to the ground; via M6 (exit 6, Gravelly Hill) and A38M (Aston Expressway) leave Expressway at first exit, left into Dartmouth Street, and then via Lawley Street and Watery Lane onto the Coventry Road. Turn left and then take left fork into Cattell Road.

Match tickets: Bookable three weeks in advance.

Car parking: Public car park in Coventry Road.

Entertainments/catering facilities: Catering points inside the ground.

Club shop: Sells all types of souvenirs.

Handbooks/programmes: Programmes on sale on match days in and outside the ground; subscription rates available on request.

Extra information: In their away League programme in 1947–48, Birmingham let in only 11 goals; this is the best away performance in Division 2 since World War II.

Club Colours: Royal blue shirts, with broad white vertical stripe, white collars and cuffs, blue shorts, white stockings.

Change colours: Red shirts, white shorts, red and white stockings. *Club Trainer/Coach:* George Dalton.

Club Nickname: 'Blues'. *Club Captain:* Howard Kendall. *Chief Scout:* Don Dorman.

BIRMINGHAM CITY 1975-76 LEAGUE RECORD

Match No.	Date	Venue	Opponents	Result	H/T Score	League Pos'n	Goalscorers	Attendance
1	Aug 16	A	Leicester C.	D 3-3	1-1	—	Hatton, Kendall 2 (1 a pen)	25,547
2	19	H	Manchester U.	L 0-2	0-0	—		33,177
3	23	H	Everton	L 0-1	0-1	19		26,794
4	26	A	Middlesbrough	L 0-2	0-0	—		22,423
5	30	A	Ipswich T.	L 2-4	0-4	21	Hatton 2	22,649
6	Sept 6	H	Q.P.R.	D 1-1	1-0	21	Kendall	27,305
7	13	A	Woverhampton W.	L 0-2	0-0	21		25,142
8	20	H	Burnley	W 4-0	0-0	21	Campbell, Withe, Kendall, Francis	25,830
9	23	H	Newcastle U.	W 3-2	3-1	—	Withe 2, Francis (pen)	31,166
10	27	A	Aston Villa	L 1-2	1-0	18	Francis	53,782
11	Oct 4	H	Sheffield U.	W 2-0	1-0	17	Hatton, Francis	26,121
12	11	A	Liverpool	L 1-3	0-1	19	Hatton	36,532
13	18	H	Leeds U.	D 2-2	2-2	19	Francis, Gallagher	33,775
14	25	A	Norwich C.	L 0-1	0-1	19		20,178
15	Nov 1	H	West Ham U.	L 1-5	1-2	20	Francis	28,474
16	8	A	Manchester C.	L 0-2	0-2	21		28,329
17	15	H	Arsenal	W 3-1	0-0	21	Francis (pen), Withe, Hatton	21,652
18	22	A	Leeds U.	L 0-3	0-1	21		26,640
19	29	A	Coventry C.	L 2-3	1-3	21	Burns, Kendall (pen)	21,687
20	Dec 6	H	Derby Co.	W 2-1	0-1	19	Burns, Page	30,620
21	13	A	Everton	L 2-5	1-2	21	Kendall, Withe	20,188
22	20	A	Leicester C.	W 2-1	1-0	19	Francis (pen) Withe	21,890
23	26	A	Tottenham H.	W 3-1	2-0	19	Francis 2, Withe	21,657
24	27	H	Stoke C.	D 1-1	1-1	19	Hatton	37,166
25	Jan 10	H	Wolverhampton W.	L 0-1	0-0	19		28,552
26	17	A	Q.P.R.	L 1-2	0-2	19	Francis	16,759
27	31	A	Manchester U.	L 1-3	0-2	20	Withe	50,274
28	Feb 7	H	Middlesbrough	W 2-1	0-0	19	Kendall, Hatton	18,599
29	14	H	Manchester C.	W 2-1	1-1	19	Gallagher, Kendall	22,445
30	21	A	Arsenal	L 0-1	0-1	19		20,907
31	28	H	Norwich C.	D 1-1	1-0	19	Francis (pen.)	22,359
32	Mar 6	A	West Ham U.	W 2-1	1-0	19	Withe, Emmanuel	19,868
33	13	H	Liverpool	L 0-1	0-0	19		31,797
34	20	H	Coventry C.	D 1-1	0-1	19	Francis (pen.)	22,956
35	27	A	Derby Co.	L 2-4	0-1	19	Francis, Needham	28,161
36	Apr 3	H	Aston Villa	W 3-2	1-1	19	Hibbitt, Burns, Francis	46,251
37	7	A	Newcastle U.	L 0-4	0-2	—		18,547
38	10	A	Burnley	L 0-1	0-0	20		13,668
39	13	H	Ipswich T.	W 3-0	1-0	19	Francis (pen.), Hibbitt, Burns	20,497
40	17	H	Tottenham H.	W 3-1	0-0	19	Gallagher, Francis, Burns	30,616
41	19	A	Stoke C.	L 0-1	0-1	—		19,918
42	May 4	A	Sheffield U.	D 1-1	0-1	—	Hibbitt	28,782

Goalscorers

League (57): Francis 17 (6 pens), Withe 9, Hatton 8, Kendall 8 (2 pens), Burns 5, Gallagher 3, Hibbitt 3, Campbell 1, Page 1, Emmanuel 1, Needham 1.
League Cup (4): Gallagher, Hatton, Morton, Want.
F.A. Cup (1): Francis.

League Cup	Second Round	Orient (h)	4-0
	Third Round	Wolverhampton W. (h)	0-2
F.A. Cup	Third Round	Portsmouth (a)	1-1
		(h)	0-1

Latchford	Osborne	Bryant	Kendall	Gallagher	Roberts	Calderwood	Phillips	Hendrie	Hatton	Taylor	Want	Hynd	Burns	Francis	Pendrey	Martin	Hope	Withe	Hibbitt	Campbell	Page	Styles	Emmanuel	Smith	Needham	Match No.
1	2	3	4	5	6	7	8	9	10	11																1
1	2	3	4	5		8*	9	7	10	11	6	12														2
1		3	4	5	12		9	7*	10		2		6	8	11											3
1		3	4	5	12		9*	7	10	8	2		6		11											4
1		3	4	5					10				6	8	11	2	7	9								5
1		3	4	5					10				6	8		2	7	9	11							6
1		3	4	5	6				10					8		2	7	9	11							7
1		3	4	5					10				6	8		2		9	11	7						8
1		3	4	5					10				6	8	12	2*		9	11	7						9
1	2		4	5					10		3		6	8	12			9*	11	7						10
1		3	4	5					10				6	8		2		9	11	7						11
1		3		5					10	11	12		6	8*	4	2		9		7						12
1			4	5					10		12		6	8	3	2		9*	11	7						13
1			4	5	6				10	11			8		3	2		9		7						14
1			4	5*	6				10		12		9	8	3	2			11	7						15
1			4	5					10				6	8	3	2		9	11	7						16
1	2	3	4	5					10	11			6	8		7		9								17
1	2	3	4	5		8		11	10				6			7		9								18
1	8		4	5		7			10		3		6			2		9	11							19
1	2		4	5					10		3		6	8				9	11		7					20
1	2	12	4	5					10		3		6	8				9	11*		7					21
1	2		4	5					10		3		6	8	7			9	11							22
1	2	7	4	5					10		3		6	8				9	11							23
1	2	7	4	5					10		3		6	8				9	11							24
1				5		4			10		3		6	8		2		9				7	11			25
1				5		12			10		3		6*	8		2		9				7	11			26
1			4	5		10			12				6	8		2		9	11*		7	3				27
1		3	4	5					10	11			6	8		2		9			7					28
1			4	5	11				10				6	8		2		9			7	3				29
1			4	5	11*		9						6	8		2		10			7	3	12			30
1			4	5	11		10						6	8				9		2	3	7				31
1			4	5	12								6	8		2		9	11*	10	3	7				32
			4*	5		7			12		3		8	6	2			9	11	10			1			33
			4	5					10				8	6	2				11		7	3	1	9		34
1			4	5					9		3		8	6	2				11		7*	10		12		35
1			4	5*		2			12		6		9	8					11			3	7	10		36
1		4*		6					9		5		10		12			8	11	2	3	7				37
1	10			5		2							6	8				9	11	4	3	7				38
1				5		2					6		9	8				10	11	4	3	7				39
1				5		2			12		6		9	8				10	11*	4	3	7				40
1	11			5		2					6		9	8				10		4	3	7				41
1			4	5		12					6		9	8				10	11*	2	3	7				42
40	10	19	36	41	5	15	4	5	33	7	20	—	36	35	14	22	3	32	27	9	19	16	10	2	2	
	+1s			+2s	+3s								+4s	+2s	+1s	+1s		+3s				+1s	+1s			

BIRMINGHAM CITY—PLAYERS

Player and position	Ht.	Wt.	Birthplace	Clubs	League Appearances	Goals
Goalkeeper						
Mike Kelly	6 0	12 7	Wimbledon	Q.P.R.	54	—
				Birmingham C.	62	—
				(contract cancelled March 1976)		
Dave Latchford	6 2	12 9	Birmingham	Birmingham C.	175	—
				Wolverhampton W. (on loan)	—	—
*Gary Sprake (Wales)	6 0	13 3	Swansea	Leeds U.	381	—
				Birmingham C.	16	—
Steve Smith	6 0	12 5	Lynde	Birmingham C.	2	—
Defenders						
*David Dyer	6 0	10 13	Dorking	Birmingham C.	—	—
*Bob Atkins	6 2	11 7	Tipton	Birmingham C.	—	—
Ray Martin	5 8	11 8	Wolverhampton	Birmingham C.	331+8	1
				(contract cancelled April 1976)		
*Ian Osborne	5 8	10 6	Leicester	Birmingham C.	10	—
John Roberts (Wales)	6 0	12 0	Swansea	Swansea C.	36+1	16
				Northampton T.	62	11
				Arsenal	56+3	4
				Birmingham C.	61+5	1
Archie Styles	5 9	11 0	Liverpool	Everton	22+1	—
				Birmingham C.	42+2	2
Ricky Sbragia	6 0	11 0	Levroxtown	Birmingham C.	1	—
Steve Bryant	5 8	10 4	Islington	Birmingham C.	34+2	1
Joe Gallagher	6 2	11 3	Liverpool	Birmingham C.	100+5	6
Gary Pendrey	5 9	11 0	Birmingham	Birmingham C.	217+13	3
Tony Want	5 7	11 1	London	Tottenham H.	46+4	—
				Birmingham C.	51+3	1
Malcolm Page (Wales)	5 9	10 11	Knicklas, Rads	Birmingham C.	231+10	9
Midfield						
Roy Morton	5 6	11 0	Birmingham	Manchester U.	—	—
				Birmingham C.	3	—
Ken Burns (Scotland)	5 10½	11 0	Glasgow	Birmingham C.	127+7	26
Bobby Hope (Scotland)	5 7½	11 3	Glasgow	W.B.A.	324+4	33
				Birmingham C.	33+1	5
				(contract cancelled April 1976)		
Jimmy Calderwood	5 9	11 0	Glasgow	Birmingham C.	52+5	3
Howard Kendall	5 8½	10 9	Durham	Preston N.E.	104	13
				Everton	227+3	21
				Birmingham C.	90	13
Terry Hibbitt	5 6	9 10	Bradford	Leeds U.	32+13	9
				Newcastle U.	138	7
				Birmingham C.	27	3
Forwards						
Trevor Francis	5 9	11 7	Plymouth	Birmingham C.	186+1	69
Bob Hatton	5 11	12 0	Hull	Wolverhampton W.	10	7
				Bolton W.	23	2
				Northampton T.	29+4	8
				Carlisle U.	93	38
				Birmingham C.	170+5	58
Gary Emmanuel	5 8	10 8	Swansea	Birmingham C.	19+1	2
Paul Hendrie	5 6	9 8	Glasgow	Birmingham C.	19+4	1
				(contract cancelled April 1976)		
*Andy Needham	5 11	11 6	Oldham	Birmingham C.	2+1	1
Danny Conway	5 9	10 0	Dublin	Birmingham C.	—	—
Ian Smith	6 1	12 6	Edinburgh	Queen's Park	15+4	7
				Birmingham C.	0+2	—
Peter Withe	6 3	12 0	Liverpool	Southport	3	—
				Barrow	1	—
				Arcadia Shepherds	not known	—
				Wolverhampton W.	12+5	3
				Birmingham C.	32	9

BLACKBURN ROVERS DIV. 2

Chairman: W. H. Bancroft.

Directors: C. R. Davies, A. L. Fryars, E. Pickering, D. T. Keighley, D. Brown, W. I. Hubert.

Secretary: J. W. Howarth.

Manager: Jim Smith.   *Year Formed:* 1875.

Limited Company: 1897.   *Turned Professional:* 1880.

Previous Grounds: 1875, Brookhouse Ground; 1876, Alexandra Meadows; 1881 Leamington Road; 1890, Ewood Park.

Previous Name: Blackburn Grammar School O.B.

Honours: *Football League,* Division 1, Champions: 1911–12, 1913–14. Division 2, Champions: 1938–39; Runners-up: 1957–58. Division 3, Champions 1974–75. *F.A. Cup,* Winners: 1884, 1885, 1886, 1890, 1891, 1928; Runners-up: 1882, 1960.   *Football League Cup,* Semi-Finalists: 1961–62.

Record Victory: 11-0 v Rossendale U., F.A. Cup, 1884–85.

Record Defeat: 0-8 v Arsenal, Division 1, Feb. 25th, 1933.

Most League Points: 60, Division 3, 1974–75.

Most League Goals: 114, Division 2, 1954–55.

Highest League Scorer in Season: Ted Harper, 43, Division 1, 1925–26.

Most Capped Player: Bob Crompton, 41, England.

Most League Appearances: Ronnie Clayton, 580, 1950–69 (and 57 F.A. Cup games).

Most League Goals in Total Aggregate: Tommy Briggs, 140, 1952–58.

Record Transfer Fee Received: £95,000 from Tottenham H. for Mike England. Aug. 1966.

Record Transfer Fee Paid: £60,000 to Bury for James Kerr, May 1970.

Managers Since the War: Eddie Hapgood, Will Scott, Jack Bruton, Jackie Bestall, John Carey, Dally Duncan, Jack Marshall, Eddie Quigley, John Carey, Ken Furphy, Gordon Lee.

Ewood Park, Blackburn BB2 4JF. Telephone Blackburn 55432/55433.   *Telegraphic Address:* 'Rovers, Blackburn'.   *Ground capacity:* 47,500.   *Record attendance:* 61,783 v Bolton W. F.A. Cup 6th Rd., March 2, 1929.   *Record receipts:* £13,280 v Manchester C., F.A. Cup 5th Rd., February 24, 1969.   *Pitch measurements:* 116 yds 2 ft × 72 yds 2ft.

How to get there: Blackburn is the nearest railway station and Corporation buses run from there to the ground.

Match tickets: Seats can be booked 14 days in advance.

Car parking: Ample street parking around the ground.

Entertainments/catering facilities: Licensed refreshment bars in all parts of the ground.

Club shop: Open on match days selling all types of souvenirs.

Handbook/programmes: No handbook. Programmes available on subscription from the club shop.

Extra information: In 1881–82, Blackburn Rovers were unbeaten for 35 successive matches.

Club Colours: Blue and white halved shirts, white shorts, blue stockings with two white rings.

Change Colours: Red shirts, black shorts, red stockings with white ring.

Club Nickname: 'Blue and Whites'.

BLACKBURN ROVERS 1975–76 LEAGUE RECORD

Match No.	Date	Venue	Opponents	Result	H/T Score	League Pos'n	Goalscorers	Attendance
1	Aug 16	A	Orient	D 1-1	0-1	—	Beamish	6054
2	23	H	Oldham Ath.	W 4-1	0-1	6	Beamish, Martin, Metcalfe (pen) Parkes	12,688
3	30	A	Carlisele U.	W 1-0	0-0	5	Hickman	8683
4	Sept 6	H	Bristol C.	L 1-2	0-0	9	Parkes	10,281
5	13	A	Southampton	L 1-2	0-2	12	Hird (pen)	13,279
6	20	H	Sunderland	L 0-1	0-1	14		15,773
7	24	H	Blackpool	L 0-2	0-1	—		11,048
8	27	A	Luton T.	D 1-1	0-0	16	Kenyon	8458
9	Oct 4	H	Fulham	L 0-1	0-1	18		10,190
10	11	H	W.B.A.	D 0-0	0-0	18		9973
11	18	A	Oxford U.	D 0-0	0-0	18		5388
12	21	A	Plymouth Arg.	D 2-2	1-0	—	Beamish, Hutt	14,371
13	25	H	Chelsea	D 1-1	0-1	18	Metcalfe	12,128
14	Nov 1	A	Bristol R.	D 1-1	1-1	18	Svarc	10,534
15	4	H	Hull C.	W 1-0	1-0	—	Oates	8816
16	8	H	Bolton W.	D 1-1	1-1	14	Oates	24,480
17	15	A	Portsmouth	W 1-0	0-0	13	Beamish	7323
18	22	H	Oxford U.	D 0-0	0-0	13		9279
19	29	H	Charlton Ath.	W 2-0	1-0	11	Metcalfe (pen), Svarc	8776
20	Dec 6	A	Notts Co.	L 0-3	0-3	15		10,252
21	13	A	Oldham Ath.	L 1-2	1-2	16	Beamish	10,193
22	20	H	Orient	D 1-1	0-0	15	Metcalfe	7136
23	26	A	York C.	L 1-2	0-1	15	Svarc	6597
24	27	H	Nottingham F.	L 1-4	0-2	19	Parkes	10,724
25	Jan 17	A	Bristol C.	L 0-1	0-1	19		12,168
26	28	H	Southampton	D 1-1	0-1	—	Svarc	8786
27	31	H	Plymouth Arg.	W 3-1	2-1	18	Svarc 2, Hird	8525
28	Feb 6	A	Hull C.	W 1-0	1-0	19	Oates	6205
29	21	H	Portsmouth	L 0-3	0-1	19		8067
30	24	A	Blackpool	D 1-1	1-1	—	Parkes	8772
31	28	A	Chelsea	L 1-3	1-1	19	Oates	14,855
32	Mar 6	H	Bristol R.	L 1-2	1-0	19	Hawkins	6765
33	13	A	W.B.A.	D 2-2	2-1	19	Fazackerley, Parkes	16,969
34	20	A	Charlton Ath.	L 1-2	0-0	19	Beamish	9704
35	23	H	Bolton W.	W 1-0	1-0	—	Waddington	24,780
36	27	H	Notts Co.	W 2-1	0-0	19	Hird 2 (pens)	8472
37	Apr 3	H	Luton T.	W 3-0	1-0	18	Parkes, Waddington, Beamish	7895
38	10	A	Sunderland	L 0-3	0-1	19		33,523
39	16	H	Carlisle U.	W 1-0	1-0	18	Hird (pen)	11,215
40	17	H	York C.	W 4-0	1-0	17	Hird, Parkes, Metcalfe, Waddington	8952
41	20	A	Nottingham F.	L 0-1	0-0	—		13,006
42	24	A	Fulham	D 1-1	1-0	15	Taylor	5914

Goalscorers

League (45): Beamish 7, Parkes 7, Hird 6 (4 pens), Svarc 6, Metcalfe 5 (2 pens), Oates 4, Waddington 3, Fazackerley 1, Hawkins 1, Kenyon 1, Hickman 1, Hutt 1, Martin 1, Taylor 1.

League Cup	First Round	Preston N.E. (a)	0-2
	Second Leg	(h)	0-0
F.A. Cup	Third Round	Luton T. (a)	0-2

Jones	Heaton	Burgin	Hird	Hawkins	Fazackerley	Beamish	Oates	Hickman	Waddington	Martin	Hoy	Metcalfe	Parkes	Wood	Hutt	Wilkinson	Kenyon	Svarc	Hindson	Bradshaw	Mullen	Wagstaffe	Bailey	Taylor	Downes	Match No.
1	2	3	4	5	6	7	8	9	10*	11	12															1
1	2	3		5	6	7	11	8		9			4	10												2
1	2	7		5	6		8	9		11			4	10	3											3
1	2	3		5	6	7	8	9		11	12		4*	10												4
1	2	3*	4	5	6	7	8	11		9			10	12												5
1	2			5	6	7	8		9	11			4	10	3											6
1				5	6	7	8			11	9*		4	10	3	2	12									7
1			4	5	8	7	12			9		6	11		3	2	10*									8
1				5*	6	7	8			11			4	10	3	2	12	9								9
1					6	7*	11	12			5		4	10	3	2		8	9							10
1					6	7	9				5		4	10	3	2		8	11							11
1					6	7	8				5		4	11	3	2		10	9							12
1					6	7	8				5		4	11	3	2		10	9							13
1					6	7*	10				5	12	4	11	3	2		8	9							14
1					6	7	8				5	12	4	11	3	2		10	9*							15
1					6	7	8				5	11	4	10	3	2			9							16
1		12			6	7	10				5		4	11	3	2*		8	9							17
1	2				6	7	10				5	12	4	11	3			8	9*							18
1	2				6	7	10				5		4	11	3			8	9							19
1	2				6	7	10				5	12	4	11	3			8*	9							20
	2		8	4	6	7	9				5	11		10	3					1						21
1	2				6	7	9				5	11	4	10	3			8								22
1	2		9	5*	6	7	8				12		4	11	3			10								23
1	2				6	7*	8				5	11	4	10	3	12		9								24
1		12	5	6			8						4	10	3	2		9				7*	11			25
1		7	5	6			9						4	10	3	2		8				11				26
1		7	5	6			8						4	10	3	2		9				11				27
1		7	5	6			9						4	10	3	2		8				11				28
1		11	5	6	7*	8							4	10	3	2	12	9								29
1		7	5	6	8	9							4	10	3	2						11				30
1		11	5	6	9	8		7*					4	10	3		2	12				3				31
		9	5	6	8								4	10	3	2	7			1		11				32
			5	6	9		12						4	10	3	2				1	11*		7	8		33
		7	5	6	9		2						4*	10	3					1		12	8	11		34
		7	5	2	9		6						4	10	3					1			8	11		35
		7	5	2	9		6						4	10	3	12				1			8	11*		36
		11	5	6	9		2						4	10	3					1			7	8		37
		7	5	6	9		2						4	10	3					1		12	11	8*		38
		10	5	6	9		2						4	11	3					1		8		7		39
		11	5	6	9		2						4*	10	3			12		1		8		7		40
		8	5	6	9*		2							10	3			12		1		11	4	7		41
		8	5	2	9		6						4	10	3					1		11		7		42
30	13	5	20	29	42	37	31	5	25	8	7	38	41	28	10	19	3	19	10	12	1	9	4	10	6	
		+1s	+1s				+2s	+1s	+2s	+5s		+1s			+2s	+6s						+2s				

77

Player and position	Ht.	Wt.	Birthplace	Clubs	League Appearances	Goals
Goalkeepers						
Paul Bradshaw	6 2	12 0	Altrincham	Blackburn R.	30	—
John Butcher	6 2	12 3	Newcastle	Blackburn R.	—	—
Defenders						
Andy Burgin	5 8½	9 8	Sheffield	Sheffield W.	1	—
				Rotherham U.	9	—
				Halifax T.	243	9
				Blackburn R.	45	1
Derek Fazackerley	5 11	11 6	Preston	Blackburn R.	209+1	8
Michael Heaton	5 6	10 10	Sheffield	Sheffield U.	31+2	—
				Blackburn R.	169+2	1
Neil Wilkinson	5 7	10 0	Blackburn	Blackburn R.	26+2	—
Mick Wood	5 11	10 13	Bury	Blackburn R.	112+3	—
Graham Hawkins	6 0	11 10	Darlaston	Wolverhampton W.	28+6	—
				Preston N.E.	241+4	3
				Blackburn R.	71+1	2
John Waddington	5 11	11 7	Darwen	Liverpool	—	—
				Blackburn R.	76+1	8
John Bailey	5 8	10 9	Liverpool	Blackburn R.	4+2	—
Midfield						
*Mick Higgins	5 8	10 2	Haslingden	Blackburn R.	—	—
Stuart Metcalfe	5 7	9 0	Blackburn	Blackburn R.	259+8	16
Tony Parkes	5 10	11 0	Sheffield	Blackburn R.	200+2	27
Gordon Taylor	5 6	11 2	Ashton under Lyme	Bolton W.	254+5	41
				Birmingham C.	156+10	9
				Blackburn R.	10	1
Forwards						
*Bobby Hoy	5 7½	10 0	Halifax	Huddersfield T.	140+4	20
				Blackburn R.	13+6	—
*John Kenyon	5 8½	11 1	Blackburn	Blackburn R.	32+14	7
Kevin Hird	5 6	9 0	Colne	Blackburn R.	27+2	6
*Jimmy Mullen	5 8½	10 10	Oxford	Reading	8	1
				Charlton Ath.	7	—
				Rotherham U.	173+3	24
				Blackburn R.	6+4	—
Ken Beamish	6 0	12 6	Bebbington	Tranmere R.	175+1	49
				Brighton	86+10	27
				Blackburn R.	80	19
Bobby Svarc	5 7	11 2	Leicester	Leicester C.	13	2
				Lincoln C.	40+5	16
				Barrow (on loan)	15	3
				Boston U. (Non-league)	—	—
				Colchester U.	116	59
				Blackburn R.	19	6
David Wagstaffe	5 8	10 8	Manchester	Manchester C.	144	8
				Wolverhampton W.	324	24
				Blackburn R.	9	—

President: A. E. Parkinson. *Chairman:* W. Cantwell.

Vice Chairman: W. B. Gregson.

Directors: T. Brennard, S. Davies, G. S. Parr, W. Helmn.

Manager: Allan Brown *Secretary:* D. McBain.

Year Formed: 1887. *Limited Company:* 1896.

Turned Professional: 1887.

Previous Grounds: 1887, Raikes Hall Gardens; 1897, Athletic Grounds; 1899, Raikes Hall Gardens; 1899, Bloomfield Road.

Previous Name: 'South Shore' combined with Blackpool in 1899, twelve years after the latter had been formed on the breaking up of the old 'Blackpool St. Johns' club.

Honours: *Football League,* Division 1, Runners-up: 1955–56. Division 2, Champions: 1929–30; Runners-up: 1936–37, 1969–70. *F.A. Cup,* Winners: 1953; Runners-up: 1948, 1951. *Football League Cup,* best season: semi-final, 1962. *Anglo-Italian Cup,* Winners 1971; Runners-up: 1972.

Record Victory: 8-4 v Charlton Ath., Division 1, Sept. 27th, 1952.

Record Defeat: 1-10 v Huddersfield, Division 1, Dec. 13th, 1930.

Most League Points: 58, Division 2, 1929–30 and 1967–68.

Most League Goals: 98, Division 2, 1929–30.

Highest League Scorer in Season: Jimmy Hampson, 45, Division 2, 1929–30.

Most League Goals in Total Aggregate: Jimmy Hampson, 247, 1927–38.

Most Capped Player: Jimmy Armfield, 43, England.

Most League Appearances: Jimmy Armfield, 568, 1952–71.

Record Transfer Fee Received: £166,000 from Newcastle U. for Mick Burns, July 1974

Record Transfer Fee Paid: £60,000 to Newcastle U. for Alan Suddick, Dec. 1966.

Managers Since the War: Joe Smith, Ron Suart, Stan Mortensen, Les Shannon, Jimmy Meadows, Bob Stokoe. Harry Potts.

Address of Supporters Club: Blackpool F.C., Supporters Club, Bloomfield Road, Blackpool, Lancs. (*Shop:* Same address as ground.)

Bloomfield Rd. Ground, Blackpool FY1 6JJ. Telephone Blackpool 46118. *Telegraphic address:* 'Football Blackpool'. *Ground capacity:* 38,000. *Record attendance:* 39,118 v Manchester U., Division 1, April 1952. *Record receipts:* £15,118 v Burnley, F.A. Cup 3rd Rd., January 1, 1976. *Pitch measurements:* 111 yds × 73 yds.

How to get there: Coliseum bus station, Lytham Road, 10 minutes' walk. Railway: South station (a few minutes' walk from ground) and North station.

Match tickets: Bookable four weeks in advance of the match.

Car parking: Car park for 1,000 cars. Street parking available.

Entertainments/catering facilities: Refreshment and licensed bars. Entertainment after the game at the Supporters' Club by prior arrangement.

Club shop: In Bloomfield Road sells all types of souvenirs.

Handooks/programmes: Programmes available from the development shop.

Extra information: When England lost 6-3 to Hungary in November 1953, there were four Blackpool players – Stanley Matthews, Stan Mortensen, Harry Johnston, and Ernie Taylor – in the team.

Club Colours: Tangerine shirts with white collars and cuffs, white shorts, white stockings.

Change Colours: White shirts, tangerine shorts and tangerine stockings.

Club Captain: Dave Hatton.

First Team Trainer: Len Graham.

Club Nickname: 'The Seasiders'.

BLACKPOOL 1975–76 LEAGUE RECORD

Match No.	Date	Venue	Opponents	Result	H/T Score	League Pos'n	Goalscorers	Attendance
1	Aug 16	A	Fulham	D 0-0	0-0	—		8863
2	19	A	Hull C.	L 0-1	0-1	—		5304
3	23	H	Orient	W 1-0	0-0	7	Tong	6626
4	30	A	Sunderland	L 0-2	0-1	16		24,000
5	Sept 6	H	Oldham Ath.	D 1-1	1-0	16	Walsh	8862
6	13	A	Charlton Ath.	D 1-1	1-1	13	Walsh	9190
7	20	H	Southampton	W 4-3	4-1	10	Walsh 3, (1 a pen), Moore	9564
8	24	A	Blackburn R.	W 2-0	1-0	—	Walsh, Moore	11,048
9	27	A	Bristol C.	L 0-2	0-2	9		10,240
10	Oct 4	H	Luton T.	W 3-2	1-1	8	Hart, Suddaby, Walsh	7854
11	11	H	Portsmouth	D 0-0	0-0	8		8351
12	18	A	Chelsea	L 0-2	0-0	9		16,924
13	25	H	Bristol R.	L 1-4	0-1	13	Suddick	9019
14	Nov 1	A	Bolton W.	L 0-1	0-0	17		17,274
15	4	H	Nottingham F.	D 1-1	0-1	—	Ainscow	5851
16	8	H	W.B.A.	L 0-1	0-0	18		8271
17	15	A	Oxford U.	W 3-1	1-1	17	Walsh, Suddaby, Ainscow	4316
18	22	H	Chelsea	L 0-2	0-1	18		8595
19	29	H	Notts Co.	W 1-0	1-0	18	Walsh	6103
20	Dec 6	A	Plymouth Arg.	W 2-1	1-0	18	Walsh 2	12,422
21	12	A	Orient	W 1-0	0-0	13	Tong	4337
22	20	H	Fulham	D 1-1	1-0	12	Weston	6379
23	26	A	Carlisle U.	L 0-1	0-0	13		11,532
24	27	H	York C.	D 0-0	0-0	14		7939
25	Jan 10	A	Charlton Ath.	W 2-1	2-1	11	Walsh 2 (1 a pen)	5748
26	17	A	Oldham Ath.	L 0-1	0-1	13		11,734
27	31	H	Hull C.	D 2-2	1-2	11	Alcock, Ronson	4966
28	Feb 7	A	Nottingham F.	L 0-3	0-0	13		8582
29	21	H	Oxford U.	W 2-0	1-0	13	Walsh, Smith	4423
30	24	H	Blackburn R.	D 1-1	1-1	—	Hart	8772
31	28	A	Bristol R.	D 1-1	0-1	15	Smith	6686
32	Mar 6	H	Bolton W.	D 1-1	1-0	14	Smith	18,548
33	13	A	Portsmouth	L 0-2	0-0	16		8394
34	20	A	Notts Co.	W 2-1	0-0	15	Smith 2	10,427
35	27	H	Plymouth Arg.	D 0-0	0-0	15		5497
36	31	A	W.B.A.	D 0-0	0-0	—		20,729
37	Apr 3	H	Bristol C.	W 2-1	1-1	10	Moore, Walsh	8273
38	10	A	Southampton	L 1-3	0-2	13	Suddaby	21,758
39	17	H	Carlisle U.	W 2-1	0-1	10	Walsh, Hart	8382
40	19	A	York C.	D 1-1	0-0	—	Ronson	3800
41	20	H	Sunderland	W 1-0	1-0	—	Walsh	16,768
42	24	A	Luton T.	L 0-3	0-2	10		8757

Goalscorers

League (40): Walsh 17 (2 pens), Smith 5, Hart 3, Moore 3, Suddaby 3, Ainscow 2, Ronson 2, Tong 2, Alcock 1, Suddick 1, Weston 1.

F.A. Cup (2): Bentley, Alcock.

League Cup	Second Round	Peterborough U. (a)	0-2
F.A. Cup	Third Round	Burnley (h)	1-0
	Fourth Round	Southampton (a)	1-3

Burridge	Curtis	Harrison	Suddaby	Tong	Alcock	Walsh	Suddick	Ronson	Moore	Ainscow	Hart	Bentley	Dyson	Hatton	Wood	Evanson	Betts	Weston	McEwan	Smith	Match No.
1	2	3	4	5	6	7	8	9	10	11											1
1	2	3	5	8	6	9	4		10	7	11										2
1	2	3	5	7	6	10	4	9	8	11											3
1	2	3	5	7*	6	9	4		12	11	8	10									4
1	2	3	5	11*	6	7	4	12		8		10	9								5
1	2		6	7		12	8		10	11	4	3	9*	5							6
1	2		5			7	8	9	10	11	4	3		6							7
	2		5		9	8	7	11	10		4	3		6	1						8
	2*	12	5		9	8	7	11	10		4	3		6	1						9
	2	11	5		9	8	7		10		4	3		6	1						10
	2	12	5	7*	9	8			10	11	4	3		6	1						11
	2	3			6	7	8	11	9		4	10		5	1						12
	2	3	5		12	9	8		7		4	10		6	1	11*					13
	2	3	5		9	8		7	11	6		10		4	1						14
	2	3	5		9	7	10	11	8	6				4	1						15
		3	5		2	9	7	10	11	8	6			4	1						16
	2	5	6		9	10	8*	11	7	4		3			1		12				17
	3	5	7	12	9	6	8*	10	11	4		2			1						18
	3*	5	7	4	9	8		10	6			2			1		11	12			19
		5	7	4	9		10*	6	3			2			1	12	11	8			20
		5	7	6	9			3				2			1	8	11	10	4		21
			7	4	9		11*	6	3			2			1	10	12	8	5		22
	12	5	7	6	9		4		3			2			1	8	11	10*			23
	3	5	7*	4	9		8		6	10		2			1	11		12			24
	3	5		6	7		9	10				2			1	11		8	4		25
	8		6	9		2	5*	7	3						1	11	12	10	4		26
	3		6	9	12	8		5	2						1	7*		11	4	10	27
	4	11		6	9		7	8		5	3				1		2	10			28
	3	6		9		7	8	4	5	10		2			1		11				29
	3	5		9		7	11	8	4	6		2			1		10				30
	3	5		9		7	6	10			2				1	8		4	11		31
	3	5		9		8	4	11	2						1	7		6	10		32
	3	5		4	9	8		11			2				1	12	9*	6	10		33
	3	5		6	9		7		11		2				1	8		4	10		34
	3	5		6	9	8		7		10	2				1	11		4			35
		5		6	9	8	11	10		3	2				1	7		4			36
		5		6	9	8		10	11		3	2			1	7		4			37
	12	5		6	9	8		11	10		3	2			1	7*		4			38
	3	5		9	8		11		6	10	2				1	7		4			39
	6	5		9	8	11		10	4	3	2				1	7					40
	3	5		9	8	4		7	6	10	2				1	11					41
	3	5		9	8	4		11	6	10	2				1	7*	12				42
7	15	30	38	15	23	41	27	17	20	35	33	36	2	34	35	17	4	10	15	8	

Substitute appearances: Suddaby +4s; Tong +2s, Alcock +1s; Walsh +2s, Suddick +1s; Hatton +2s, Wood +3s, Evanson +1s, Betts +2s.

BLACKPOOL—PLAYERS

Player and position	Ht.	Wt.	Birthplace	Clubs	League Appearances	Goals
Goalkeepers						
George Wood	5 11	11 0	Douglas	East Stirling	22	—
				Blackpool	75	—
Colin King	6 1	13 0	Edinburgh	Blackpool	—	—
Defenders						
Terry Alcock	6 0	11 8	Hanley	Port Vale	112	—
				Blackpool	188+6	21
				Bury (on loan)	6	1
Dave Hatton	5 10	11 10	Farnworth	Bolton W.	231	7
				Blackpool	250+1	6
Peter Suddaby	5 11	12 2	Stockport	Blackpool	192+1	6
Glyn James (Wales)	5 11½	12 5	Llangollen	Blackpool (contract cancelled Jan 1976)	394+6	22
John Curtis	5 9	11 4	Poulton	Blackpool	76+6	—
Steve Harrison	5 7	11 1½	Blackpool	Blackpool	84+6	—
Midfield						
Bill Bentley	5 11	13 0	Longton	Stoke C.	44+4	1
				Blackpool	250+7	7
Kevin Moore	5 9	10 9	Blackpool	Blackpool	25+3	3
*John Evanson	5 9½	10 12	Newcastle under Lyme	Oxford U.	145+13	10
				Blackpool	63+4	—
Paul Hart	6 0	12 0	Manchester	Stockport Co.	88	5
				Blackpool	73	8
Alan Suddick	5 11	11 0	Chester le Street	Newcastle U.	144	41
				Blackpool	293+5	62
Alan Ainscow	5 6½	9 3½	Bolton	Blackpool	126+14	22
Forwards						
Keith Dyson	5 10	11 12	Durham	Newcastle U.	74+2	21
				Blackpool (contract cancelled March 1976)	91+3	30
David Tong	5 8	10 1	Blackpool	Blackpool	39+3	4
Michael Betts	5 10	12 10	Barnsley	Blackpool (contract cancelled Feb. 1976)	4+3	—
Michael Walsh (Eire)	5 9	11 5	Chorley	Blackpool	92+8	32
Willie Ronson	5 6	9 9	Fleetwood	Blackpool	19+2	2
Jimmy Weston	5 9	10 7	Skelmersdale	Blackpool	10+1	1
Stanley McEwan	5 11	12 2	Cambusrethan	Blackpool	15+3	—
Brian Wilson	5 9	10 5	Newcastle	Blackpool	—	—
Paul Gardner	5 9	11 8	Southport	Blackpool	—	—
Laurence Milligan	5 7	12 0	Liverpool	Blackpool	—	—

BOLTON WANDERERS   DIV. 2

President: H. D. Warburton.
Chairman: G. Warburton.
Vice-Chairman: J. W. Woods
Directors: J. Battersby, H. T. Tyldesley, J. W. Woods,
B. Cowsill, W. G. Isherwood.
Manager: Ian Greaves.
Asst. Manager: George Mulhall.
Secretary: E. Rothwell.   *Year Formed:* 1874.
Turned Professional: 1880.   *Limited Company:* 1895.
Previous Grounds: Park Recreation Ground and Cockle's
Field before moving to Pike's Lane Ground 1881; Burnden
Park 1895.
Previous Name: 1874–77, Christ Church F.C.; 1877, became Bolton Wanderers.
Honours: Football League: best season: 3rd, Div. 1, 1891–92, 1920–21, 1924–25. Division 2,
Champions: 1908–09; Runners-up: 1899–1900, 1904–05. 1910–11, 1934–35. Division 3 Champions 1972-73. *F.A. Cup,* Winners: 1923, 1926, 1929, 1958; Runners-up: 1894, 1904, 1953.
Football League Cup, best season: 4th Rd. (replay) 1971–72.
Record Victory: 13-0 v Sheffield U., F.A. Cup, 2nd Rd., Feb. 1st, 1890.
Record Defeat: 0-7 v Manchester C., Division 1, Mar. 21st, 1936.
Most League Points: 61, Division 3, 1972–73.
Most League Goals: 96, Division 2, 1934–35.
Highest League Scorer in Season: Joe Smith, 38, Division 1, 1920–21.
Most Capped Player: Nat Lofthouse, 33, England.
Most League Appearances: Eddie Hopkinson, 519, 1956–70.
Most League Goals in Total Aggregate: Nat Lofthouse, 255, 1946–61.
Record Transfer Fee Received: £85,000 from Newcastle U. for Wyn Davies, Oct. 1966.
Record Transfer Fee Paid: £60,000 to Wolverhampton W. for Terry Wharton, Oct. 1967.
Managers Since the War: Walter Rowley, Bill Ridding, Nat Lofthouse, Jimmy McIlroy,
Jimmy Meadows, Nat Lofthouse, Jimmy Armfield.
Address of Supporters Club: Supporters Club, Burnden Park, Manchester Road, Bolton.
Address of Club Shop or Boutique: 'The Happy Shop', Burnden Park, Bolton.

Burnden Park, Bolton, BL3 2QR. Telephone Bolton 21101.   *Ground capacity:* 60,136.   *Record
attendance:* 69,912 v Manchester C., F.A. Cup, February 18, 1933.   *Record receipts:* £42,000
Leeds U. v Manchester U., F.A. Cup Semi-Final Replay, March, 1970.   *Pitch measurements:*
113 yds × 76 yds.

How to get there: Local buses 8, 524, 523, 542, 543. The nearest station is Trinity St. in the town centre.
Match tickets: Bookable two weeks in advance.
Car parking: Private car parking only on Burnden forecourt. Large park only 200 yards from the ground.
Limited street parking in the vicinity. Multi-storey parks in the town centre.
Entertainments/catering facilities: Prerecorded programmes of news, interviews, and record requests.
Burnden Sporting Club open before matches and cabarets there on Friday and Saturday evenings. Refreshment bars in each section of the ground and in the Sporting Club.
Club shop: Open match days only. Postal applications and price lists available on request.
Handbooks/programmes: Programmes available on subscription from club shop.
Extra information: History of club written by Dr Percy Young.

Club Colours: White shirts, dark blue shorts, white stockings.
Change Colours: Red shirts, white trimmings, blue shorts.
Club Captain: John Ritson.
Club Coach: Jim Conway.
First Team Trainer: Bert Sproston.
Club Nickname: 'Trotters'.

BOLTON WANDERERS 1975–76 LEAGUE RECORD

Match No.	Date	Venue	Opponents	Result	H/T Score	League Pos'n	Goalscorers	Attendance
1	Aug 16	A	Bristol C.	L 0-1	0-0	—		10,510
2	20	A	Oxford U.	L 0-2	0-2	—		5277
3	23	H	Fulham	D 2-2	1-2	19	Jones (G.), Byrom	8786
4	30	A	York C.	W 2-1	0-1	15	Jones (P.), Jones (G.)	5640
5	Sept 6	H	Southampton	W 3-0	1-0	10	Curran, Jones (G.), Byrom	9188
6	13	A	Luton T.	W 2-0	1-0	7	Futcher (P.), (og), Curran	11,217
7	20	H	Orient	D 1-1	0-0	6	Greaves	10,218
8	23	A	Bristol R.	D 2-2	1-1	—	Jones (P.), Greaves	7992
9	27	A	Nottingham F.	W 2-1	1-0	6	Whatmore, Jones (P.) (pen)	10,775
10	Oct 4	H	Charlton Ath.	W 5-0	2-0	4	Ritson 2, Whatmore 2, Byrom	9895
11	11	A	Plymouth Arg.	W 3-2	0-1	4	Whatmore 2, Reid	14,595
12	18	H	Notts Co.	W 2-1	0-0	3	Allardyce, Whatmore	16,080
13	25	A	Hull C.	D 2-2	1-2	3	Byrom, Jones (G.)	7369
14	Nov 1	H	Blackpool	W 1-0	0-0	3	Ritson	17,274
15	4	H	Portsmouth	W 4-1	1-1	—	Jones (P.), Jones (G.) 2, Whatmore	18,538
16	8	A	Blackburn R.	D 1-1	1-1	2	Jones (G.)	24,480
17	15	H	Carlisle U.	D 0-0	0-0	2		14,556
18	22	A	Notts. Co.	D 1-1	1-1	2	Jones (G.)	12,064
19	29	H	W.B.A.	L 1-2	1-1	3	Greaves	18,710
20	Dec 6	A	Chelsea	W 1-0	1-0	2	Greaves	20,896
21	13	A	Fulham	W 2-1	1-1	2	Whatmore, Jones (G.)	8720
22	20	H	Bristol C.	W 1-0	0-0	2	Whatmore	18,503
23	26	A	Oldham Ath.	L 1-2	0-0	2	Whatmore	24,537
24	27	H	Sunderland	W 2-1	0-1	2	Allardyce, Byrom	42,680
25	Jan 17	A	Southampton	D 0-0	0-0	3		20,363
26	27	H	Luton T.	W 3-0	3-0	—	Jones (G.), Byrom, Allardyce	21,358
27	Feb 7	A	Portsmouth	W 1-0	1-0	1	Went (og)	8958
28	21	A	Carlisle U.	L 2-3	1-1	2	Reid, Allardyce	12,809
29	28	H	Hull C.	W 1-0	1-0	1	Thompson	21,789
30	Mar 2	H	Oxford U.	L 0-1	0-0	—		22,340
31	6	A	Blackpool	D 1-1	0-1	2	Jones, (G.)	18,548
32	13	H	Plymouth Arg.	D 0-0	0-0	2		21,147
33	20	A	W.B.A.	L 0-2	0-1	3		25,319
34	22	H	Blackburn R.	L 0-1	0-1	—		24,780
35	27	H	Chelsea	W 2-1	0-0	3	Hay (og), Wilkins (G.), (og)	20,817
36	Apr 3	H	Nottingham F.	D 0-0	0-0	4		21,464
37	10	A	Orient	D 0-0	0-0	3		6294
38	13	H	York C.	L 1-2	0-0	—	Nicholson	19,048
39	17	H	Oldham Ath.	W 4-0	2-0	4	Greaves 2, Jones (P.) 2 (2 pens)	22,455
40	19	A	Sunderland	L 1-2	0-2	—	Allardyce	51,983
41	24	A	Charlton Ath.	W 4-0	1-0	—	Whatmore, Greaves, Byrom 2	14,415
42	28	H	Bristol R.	W 3-1	3-0	—	Nicholson, Byrom 2	12,815

Goalscorers

League (64): Jones, G. 11, Whatmore 11, Byrom 10, Greaves 7, Jones, P. 6 (3 pens), Allardyce 5, Ritson 3, Curran 2, Nicholson 2, Reid 2, Thompson 1, Own Goals 4.

League Cup (1): Byrom.

F.A. Cup (7): Whatmore 2, Jones, G. 2, Reid, Allardyce, Jones P.

League Cup	Second Round	Coventry C. (h)	1-3
F.A. Cup	Third Round	Brentford (a)	0-0
		(h)	2-0
	Fourth Round	Huddersfield T. (a)	1-0
	Fifth Round	Newcastle U. (h)	3-3
		(a)	0-0 (a.e.t.)
			1-2 (at Leeds)

Siddall	Ritson	Dunne	Reid	Jones, P.	Walsh	Byrom	Greaves	Curran	Jones, G.	Thompson	Nicholson	Allardyce	Waldron	Whatmore	Taylor	Smith	Morgan	Match No.
1	2	3	4	5	6	7	8	9	10	11								1
1	2	3	10	5	6	7	4	9*	8	11	12							2
1	2	3	4	5		7	10	9	8	11		6						3
1	2	3	10	5		7	4	9	8	11		6						4
1	2	3	4	5		7	8	9	10	11		6						5
1	2		10	5		7	4	8	9	11	3	6						6
1	2	3	10	5		7	4	9*	8	11		6	12					7
1	2	3	10	5		7	4		9	11		6		8				8
1		3	10	5		7	4		8	11	2	6		9				9
1	2	3	10	5		7*	4		8	11		6	12	9				10
1		3	10	5	12	7	4		8*	11	2	6		9				11
1	2	3	10	5			4		8	11		6	7	9				12
1	2	3	8	5		7	4		9	11		6		10				13
1	2	3	8	5		7	4		9	11		6		10				14
1	2	3	10	5		7	4		9	11		6		8				15
1	2	3	8	5		7	4		9	11		6		10				16
1	2	3	10	5		7*	4	12	9	11		6		8				17
1	2	3	10	5		7			9	11	4	6		8				18
1	2	3	10	5			4	9*		11		6	7	8		12		19
1	2	3	10	5		7			9	11		6	4	8				20
1	2	3	10	5		7			9	11*		6	4	8		12		21
1	2	3	10	5	12	7			9	11*		6	4	8				22
1	2	3	10	5	12		4		9	11		6	7*	8				23
1	2	3	10	5		7	4		9	11		6		8				24
1	2	3	10	5		7	4		9	11		6		8				25
1	2	3	10	5		7*	4		9	11	12	6		8				26
1	2	3	10	5		7	4		9	11		6		8				27
1	2	3	10			7	4		9	11	5	6		8				28
1	2	3	10	5	12	7*	4		9	11		6		8				29
1		3	10	5			4		9	11	2	6		8*		12	7	30
1	2*	3	10	5	12		4		9	11		6		8			7	31
1		3	10	5	2	7	4		9	11		6		8*		12		32
1		3	10	5			4		9	11	2	6		8			7	33
1		3	10	5			4		9	11	2	6		8*		12	7	34
1		3	10	5			4		9	11	2	6		8			7	35
1		3	10	5			4		9	11*	2	6		8		12	7	36
1	2	3*	10				4		9	11	12	6		8			7	37
1	2		10	5			4		9	11	3	6		8			7	38
1	2		10	5	12		4		9*	11	3	6		8			7	39
1	2		10	5	12		4		9*	11	3	6		8			7	40
1	2		10	5			4		9	11	3	6		8			7	41
1	2		10	5			4		9	11	3	6		8			7	42
42	32	35	42	41	6	29	42	8	36	38	15	40	6	35	—	5	10	
						+3s	+4s	+1s	+1s		+3s		+2s	+3s		+1s	+1s	

85

Player and position	Ht.	Wt.	Birthplace	Clubs	League Appearances	Goals
Goalkeepers						
Barry Siddall	6 0	13 2	Ellesmere Port	Bolton W.	130	—
*Ian Holbrook	5 10	13 0	Warrington	Bolton W.	—	—
Defenders						
Tony Dunne (Eire)	5 6½	9 11	Dublin	Manchester U.	415	2
				Bolton W.	79+2	—
John Ritson	5 8½	10 5	Liverpool	Bolton W.	287+3	8
Paul Jones	5 11	10 10	Warrington	Bolton W.	208+1	19
Andrew Clements	5 11	11 2	Swinton	Bolton W.	—	—
Michael Walsh	5 11	11 7	Manchester	Bolton W.	10+4	—
Sam Allardyce	6 1½	13 4	Dudley	Bolton W.	64+1	8
Garry Johnston	5 11	10 11	Tottington	Bolton W.	—	—
Midfield						
Peter Nicholson	5 11½	11 8½	Cleator Moor	Blackpool	3+3	—
				Bolton W.	160+10	11
Peter Reid	5 8	11 3	Huyton	Bolton W.	66+3	2
Alan Waldron	5 7½	9 8	Bury	Bolton W.	110+12	5
Roy Greaves	5 11	11 12	Farnworth	Bolton W.	344+6	52
Geoffrey Gay	5 10	10 9	Romford	Bolton W.	—	—
Michael Beckett	5 9	11 3	Swinton	Bolton W.	—	—
Willie Morgan (Scotland)	5 8	11 2	Glasgow	Burnley	183	19
				Manchester U.	236+2	23
				Burnley	12+1	—
				Bolton W.	10+1	—
Forwards						
John Byrom	5 9	11 12	Blackburn	Blackburn R.	106+2	45
				Bolton W.	296+8	113
Garry Jones	5 9	10 2	Manchester	Bolton W.	175+3	38
				Sheffield U. (on loan)	3	1
Peter Thompson (England)	5 9	11 10	Carlisle	Preston N.E.	122	20
				Liverpool	317+5	42
				Bolton W.	103	2
Neil Whatmore	5 9	11 3	Ellesmere Port	Bolton W.	81+7	25
Hugh Curran (Scotland)	5 9	11 8	Glasgow	Third Lanark	9	4
				Millwall	57	27
				Norwich C.	112	46
				Wolverhampton W.	77+5	40
				Oxford U.	69+1	26
				Bolton W.	40+4	13
Brian Smith	5 7	11 5	Bolton	Bolton W.	11+2	1
Steven Taylor	5 9	11 2	Royston	Bolton W.	3+5	—
				Port Vale (on loan)	4	2

AFC BOURNEMOUTH DIV. 4

President: W. J. Peek.

Chairman: H. G. Walker, LL.B.

Directors: C. M. Pardy, E. M. A. Lane, E. G. Keep, P. Hayward, W. J. L. MacKeen, L. Smart, H. G. Berwick, S. F. Holtum, G. P. Pound, F. Ward.

Secretary: W. H. Stace.

Player-Manager: John Benson.

Commercial Manager: D. Dowsett.

Year Formed: 1899.   *Turned Professional:* 1912.

Limited Company: 1914.

Previous Names: Boscombe St. Johns, 1880–89; Boscombe F.C., 1899–1923.

Previous Grounds: 1899–1910, Castlemain Road, Pokesdown, Dean Court 1910.

Honours: *Football League,* best season in Division 3, 3rd 1961–62, 1971–72. Division 3(S), Runners-up: 1947–48. Promotion from Division 4: 1970–71. (2nd). *F.A. Cup,* best season: 6th Rd., 1956–57. *Football League Cup,* best season: 4th Rd., 1962, 1964.

Record Victory: 11-0 v Margate, F.A. Cup 1st Rd., Nov. 20th, 1971.

Record Defeat: 1-8 v Bradford C., Division 3, Jan. 24th, 1970.

Most League Points: 62, Division 3, 1971–72.

Most League Goals: 88, Division 3(S), 1956–57.

Highest League Scorer in Season: Ted MacDougall 42, 1970–71.

Most League Goals in Total Aggregate: Ron Eyre. 202, 1924–33.

Most Capped Player: Tommy Godwin, 4 (13), Eire.

Most League Appearances: Ray Bumstead, 412, 1958–70.

Record Transfer Fee Received: £195,000 from Manchester U. for Ted MacDougall, Sept. 1972.

Record Transfer Fee Paid: £70,000 to Cardiff C. for Brian Clark, Oct. 1972.

Managers Since the War: Harry Kinghorn, Harry Lowe, Jack Bruton, Freddie Cox, Don Welsh, Bill McGarry, Reg Flewin, Freddie Cox, John Bond, Trevor Hartley.

Address of Supporters Club Shop: The Cherry Bees Shop, Dean Court, Bournemouth, Hants.

Dean Court Ground, Bournemouth. Telephone Bournemouth 35381.   *Telegraphic address:* 'Football Bourn'th'.   *Ground capacity:* 22,000.   *Record attendance:* 28,799 v Manchester U., F.A. Cup 6th Rd., March 2, 1957.   *Record Receipts:* £7,326 v Brighton, Division 3, April 1, 1972.   *Pitch measurements:* 115 yds × 75 yds.

How to get there: Nearest station Bournemouth on the main line from London (Waterloo). Corporation bus 25.

Car parking: Adequate parking for 1500 cars.

Entertainments/catering facilities: Refreshment points around the ground.

Club shop: Sells all types of souvenirs.

Handbooks/programmes: No handbook. Programmes available on subscription.

Extra information: The club did not compete in the F.A. Cup in 1923–24, their first League season, because their election came too late for them to be exempt from the preliminary rounds.

Club Colours: Red shirts with white trim, white shorts, black stockings with red and white tops.
Change Colours: All white with red trim on shirts.
Club Captain: Keith Miller.   *Club Coach:* Fred Davies.   *Club Nickname:* 'Cherries'.   *Trainer:* John Kirk.

AFC BOURNEMOUTH 1975–76 LEAGUE RECORD

Match No.	Date	Venue	Opponents	Result	H/T Score	League Pos'n	Goalscorers	Attendance
1	Aug 16	A	Hartlepool	D 1-1	0-0	—	Goddard	2225
2	23	H	Darlington	L 1-2	1-1	17	Goddard	4298
3	30	A	Bradford C.	W 1-0	0-0	11	Goddard	2210
4	Sept 6	H	Doncaster R.	L 0-1	0-0	18		3511
5	12	A	Stockport Co.	D 0-0	0-0	18		3605
6	20	H	Newport Co.	W 2-0	0-0	12	Morgan, Reeves	3993
7	24	H	Brentford	W 3-0	2-0	—	Hague, Reeves, Goddard	4113
8	27	A	Reading	L 1-2	0-0	12	Reeves	7226
9	Oct 4	H	Barnsley	D 1-1	0-1	12	Nightingale (pen)	4408
10	10	A	Southport	W 2-0	0-0	8	Nightingale (pen), Goddard	1044
11	18	H	Transmere R.	W 4-2	3-1	8	Nightingale (pen), Goddard 2, Hague	5226
12	22	H	Rochdale	W 2-1	0-1	—	Cunningham, Morgan	4395
13	25	A	Lincoln C.	L 0-1	0-0	8		7431
14	Nov 1	H	Cambridge U.	W 3-0	1-0	6	Ashworth, Nightingale, Reeves	4863
15	5	A	Crewe Alex.	L 0-1	0-0	—		2000
16	8	A	Watford	D 1-1	0-0	8	Goddard	4714
17	15	H	Scunthorpe U.	W 1-0	0-0	8	Reeves	4333
18	29	H	Northampton T.	D 0-0	0-0	8		5890
19	Dec 6	A	Workington	W 3-1	1-0	5	Hague, Goddard, Rickard	1219
20	20	H	Huddersfield T.	W 1-0	1-0	5	Goddard	4012
21	27	H	Swansea C.	W 2-0	0-0	5	Buttle, Ashworth	6714
22	30	A	Torquay U.	L 1-2	0-1	—	Howard	3265
23	Jan 2	A	Exeter C.	L 0-1	0-1	5		3031
24	10	H	Bradford C.	W 2-1	1-0	5	Buttle, Reeves	4559
25	17	A	Newport Co.	L 1-3	0-1	5	Payne	1496
26	24	H	Stockport Co.	W 2-0	1-0	5	Steele, Howard	3927
27	Feb 7	H	Crewe Alex.	W 1-0	0-0	5	Morgan	3933
28	10	A	Rochdale	D 2-2	1-1	—	Reeves, Hague	1393
29	14	H	Watford	W 4-1	2-0	5	Goddard, Buttle, Steele (pen), Reeves	4897
30	21	A	Scunthorpe U.	L 0-2	0-1	5		2068
31	23	A	Brentford	W 2-1	0-1	—	Goddard, Reeves	4590
32	Mar 6	A	Cambridge U.	W 1-0	1-0	5	Rickard	2055
33	9	A	Barnsley	L 0-2	0-1	—		2550
34	13	H	Southport	D 3-3	0-2	8	Reeves, Goddard, Miller	4433
35	15	A	Tranmere R.	L 0-2	0-1	—		3660
36	20	A	Northampton T.	L 0-6	0-6	8		6780
37	27	H	Workington	W 1-0	1-0	8	Buttle	3564
38	30	A	Huddersfield T.	D 0-0	0-0	—		5834
39	Apr 3	H	Hartlepool	W 4-2	1-0	7	Morgan 2, Reeves, Grapes	3102
40	7	H	Reading	L 0-1	0-0	—		5372
41	10	A	Doncaster R.	D 1-1	1-0	8	Reeves	4097
42	16	H	Exeter C.	W 1-0	1-0	6	Cunningham	4651
43	17	H	Torquay U.	D 0-0	0-0	6		4180
44	20	A	Swansea C.	D 1-1	0-0	—	Reeves	2354
45	24	A	Darlington	L 0-2	0-1	6		2249
46	26	H	Lincoln C.	D 1-1	1-1	—	Reeves	4284

Goalscorers

League (57): Reeves 14, Goddard 13, Morgan 5, Buttle 4, Hague 4, Nightingale 4 (3 pens), Ashworth 2, Cunningham 2, Howard 2, Rickard 2, Steele 2 (1 a pen), Grapes 1, Miller 1, Payne 1.
League Cup (1): Rickard.
F.A. Cup (4): Ashworth 3, Goddard.

League Cup	First Round	Plymouth Arg. (a)	0-2
	Second Leg	(h)	1-2
F.A. Cup	First Round	Sutton (a)	1-1
		(h)	1-0
	Second Round	Hereford U. (h)	2-2
		(a)	0-2

Baker	Russo	Benson	Payne	Morgan	Hague	Cunningham	Howard	Goddard	Rickard	Nightingale	Miller	Buttle	Redknapp	Reeves	Ashworth	Impey	Best	Steele	Butler	Grapes	Chalk	Match No.
1	2	3	4	5	6	7	8	9	10	11												1
1		3	2	5	6	12	4*	9	10	7	8	11										2
1		3	2	5	6			9	10	8	4	11	7									3
1			2	5	6		4	9	8*	10	3	11	7	12								4
1			2	5	6		4	9	12	10	3	11	7*	8								5
1				5	6	2	4	9			7	3	11	8	10							6
1			2	5	6		4	9			7	3	11	8	10							7
1			2	5	6		4	9			7	3	11	8	10							8
1			2	5	6	12	4	9			7	3*	11	8	10							9
1			2	5	6		4	9			7	3	11	8	10							10
1			2	5	6	12	4*	9			7	3	11	8	10							11
1			2	5	6	12	4	9*			7	3	11	8	10							12
1	9		2	5	6	12	4*				7	3	11	8	10							13
1			2	5	6	9	4				7	3	11*12	8	10							14
1			2	5	6		4	9			7	3	11	8	10							15
1			2	5			4	9			7	3	11	8	10	6						16
			2	6	5		4	9			7	3	11	8	10		1					17
1			2		6		4	9			7	3	11	8	10	5						18
1			2	5	6		4	9	12		7	3	11	8	10*							19
1			2	5	6		4	9			7	3	11	8	10							20
1			2	5	6		4	9			7	3	11*12	8	10							21
1				5	6		4	9			7	3	11	8	10	2						22
1	2*			5	6		4	9			7	3	11	12	8	10						23
1			2	5	6		4				8	3	11	7	10	9						24
			2	5*	6	7	4					3	11	12	9	10		8				25
			2	5	6	7	4					3	11	9	10		1	8				26
1				5	6	2	4				7	3	11	9	10			8				27
1			2	5	6	7*	4		10	12		3	11	9				8				28
1			2	5	6	7	4		10			3	11	9				8				29
1			2	7	5	6	4*	9		12		3	11		10			8				30
1	2*			5	6	7			10		4	3	11	9	12			8				31
1			2	5	6	7	8		10		4	3	11	9								32
1			2		6	7	4		10		8	3	11	9	5							33
1			2	4	6			9	8*	12		11	10		5				3	7		34
1			4	5	6		2		10		7	8		9					3	11		35
1			2	5	6		4	9	10		11		8						3	7		36
1				5	6	10		9			4	3	11	8					2	7		37
1	10			5	6		4				8	3	11	9					2	7		38
1				5	6	2	4		10			11	8	9					3	7		39
1				5	6	2	4*				8		11	9	10	12			3	7		40
				5	6	8	4				7	3	11	9	10				2		1	41
1				5	6	7	4				8	3	11	9	10				2			42
1				5	6		4	8			7	3	11*	9	10	12			2			43
1				5*	6	7	4		11	12	8	3		9	10				2			44
1					6	7	4		10	12	8*	3		9	11	5			2			45
1					6	7	4		11		8	3		9	10	5			2			46
43	1	6	32	40	46	22	42	35	8	35	43	40	5	41	30	7	2	7	13	7	1	
							+5s			+6s	+1s		+4s	+1s	+1s	+2s						

AFC BOURNEMOUTH—PLAYERS

Player and position	Ht.	Wt.	Birthplace	Clubs	League Appearances	Goals
Goalkeepers						
Kieron Baker	6 0	12 4	Ryde	Fulham	—	—
				Mansfield T. (on loan)	—	—
				Brentford (on loan)	6	—
				Bournemouth	135	—
Stephen Chalk	6 1	12 3	Southampton	Bournemouth	1	—
Defenders						
John Benson	5 10	11 10	Arbroath	Manchester C.	44	—
				Torquay U.	233+8	7
				Bournemouth	85+8	
				Exeter C. (on loan)	4	—
				Norwich C.	29+2	—
				Bournemouth	16	
*Les Parodi	5 10	10 10	Lambeth	Bournemouth	45+4	2
John Impey	6 0	12 7	Exeter	Cardiff C.	13+8	—
				Bournemouth	7+2	
*Neil Hague	6 0¼	12 7	Rotherham	Rotherham U.	134+11	23
				Plymouth Arg.	98	15
				Bournemouth	89	7
Clive Payne	5 9	11 4	Burgh	Norwich C.	122+3	—
				Bournemouth	101	3
Stuart Morgan	5 11	12 7	Glamorgan	West Ham U.	—	—
				Torquay U. (on loan)	14	—
				Reading	42+4	1
				Colchester U.	79+2	10
				Bournemouth	52	5
Ian Cunningham	5 11	10 11	Glasgow	Bournemouth	23+5	2
*Martin Bridge	6 1	11 10	Hartley Wintney	Bournemouth	—	—
Geoff. Butler	5 7	11 0		Middlesbrough	54+1	1
				Chelsea	8+1	—
				Sunderland	0+2	—
				Norwich C.	151+2	1
				Bournemouth	13	—
Midfield						
Steve Buttle	5 7	10 5	Norwich	Ipswich T.	—	—
				Bournemouth	112+3	11
Keith Miller	5 9½	10 10	Lewisham	West Ham U.	1+2	—
				Bournemouth	226+1	17
Mark Nightingale	5 10	10 7	Salisbury	Bournemouth	44+5	4
*Trevor Howard	5 7	10 10	Kings Lynn	Norwich C.	81+43	13
				Bournemouth	86	11
Hughen Riley	5 8	10 6	Accrington	Rochdale	81+12	12
				Crewe A.	116+5	9
				Bury	47+4	4
				Bournemouth	—	—
Forwards						
John Rudge	6 0	12 4	Carlisle	Huddersfield T.	5	—
				Carlisle U.	45+5	16
				Torquay U.	93+2	36
				Bristol R.	50+20	17
				Bournemouth	7	—
*Derek Rickard	5 8	10 10	Plymouth	Plymouth Arg.	101+9	41
				Bournemouth	22+10	6
*Howard Goddard	5 8½	10 6	Over Wallop	Bournemouth	62+2	18
*Phillip Ashworth	6 0	12 0	Burnley	Blackburn R.	—	—
				Bournemouth	30+1	2
Kevin Reeves	5 10	12 0	Burley	Bournemouth	41+2	14
Tom Patterson	5 10	11 0	Newcastle	Leicester C.	—	—
				Middlesbrough	1	—
				Bournemouth	—	—
Stephen Gritt	5 10	10 8	Bournemouth	Bournemouth	—	—

BRADFORD CITY DIV. 4

President: Lord Feather.
Chairman: R. Martin.
Vice-Chairman: J. Dunne.
Directors: K. D. Morrison, J. C. Tordoff, D. W. Wilkinson,
W. T. Davidson. J. H. Garside, R. Stead, W. Roper.
Team Manager: Bobby Kennedy.
General Manager/Secretary: C. S. Thompson.
Year Formed: 1903.
Turned Professional: 1903.
Limited Company: 1908.
Relegated to Division 4: 1971–72.
Honours: *Football League,* highest League position, 5th Division
1, 1910–11. Division, 2 Champions: 1907–08. Division 3(N),
Champions: 1928–29. *F.A. Cup,* Winners: 1911 (first holders of
the present trophy). *Football League Cup* best season: 5th Rd.,
1965.

Record Victory: 11-1 v Rotherham U., Division 3(N), Aug. 25th, 1928.

Record Defeat: 1-9 v Colchester U., Division 4, Dec. 30th, 1961.

Most League Points: 63, Division 3(N), 1928–29.

Most League Goals: 128, Division 3(N), 1928–29.

Highest League Scorer in Season: David Layne, 34, Division 4, 1961–62.

Most League Goals in Total Aggregate: Frank O'Rourke, 88, 1906–13.

Most Capped Player: Harry Hampton, 9, Ireland.

Most League Appearances: John Hall, 430, 1962–74.

Record Transfer Fee Received: £20,000 from Bristol Rovers for Bruce Bannister, Nov. 1971.

Record Transfer Fee Paid: £12,500 to Aston Villa for Trevor Hockey, June 1974.

Managers Since the War: Jack Barker, John Milburn, David Steele, Ivor Powell, Peter
Jackson, Bob Brocklebank, Bill Harris, Willie Watson, Grenville Hair, Jimmy Wheeler,
Bryan Edwards.

Address of Supporters Club: Bradford City Supporters' Club, Corwall Terrace, Bradford.

Valley Parade Ground, Bradford BD8 7DY. Telephone Bradford 26565. *Ground capacity:*
23,469. *Record attendance:* 39,146 v Burnley, F.A. Cup 4th Rd., March 11, 1911. *Record
receipts:* £6,893 v Tottenham H., F.A. Cup 3rd Rd., January 3, 1970. *Pitch measurements:*
110 yds × 70 yds.

How to get there: Ground situated approximately ¾ mile from city centre along Manningham Lane. Cor-
poration buses 23–26 from Cheapside plus specials. West Yorkshire buses from Chester St. bus station.
The nearest railway station is Bradford Exchange. By road, the ground is approximately ¼ mile from Ring
Road towards Bradford.
Car parking: Club car park off Valley Parade holds 100 cars. Street parking in most side-streets. No parking
in Valley Parade or South Parade.
Entertainments/catering facilities: Members' club adjacent to ground; this admits adult members of visiting
supporters' clubs on production of member's card. Hot drinks, pies, crisps, etc available at snack bars in
the ground.
Club shop: Adjacent to ground entrance; sells all types of souvenirs.
Handbooks/programmes: Programmes will be sent on receipt of remittance and S.A.E. c/o City Shop,
Valley Parade.
Extra information: A Bradford firm designed the present F.A. Cup, the third actual trophy, in 1910. The
first club to win it was Bradford City in 1911.

Club Colours: All white with claret and amber stripes, trim.
Change Colours: Amber shirts, claret shorts.
Club Captain: Rod Johnson,
First Team Trainer:
Club Nickname: 'The Paraders'.

BRADFORD CITY 1975–76 LEAGUE RECORD

Match No.	Date	Venue	Opponents	Result	H/T Score	League Posn'	Goalscorers	Attendance
1	Aug 16	H	Brentford	D 1-1	1-1	—	McGinley	2385
2	23	A	Cambridge U.	D 0-0	0-0	9		3027
3	30	H	AFC Bournemouth	L 0-1	0-0	20		2210
4	Sept 5	A	Northampton T.	L 2-4	1-2	—	Cooke, Ingram	3675
5	13	H	Tranmere R.	W 3-0	1-0	16	Ingram, Mathias (og), Cooper	2046
6	20	A	Rochdale	D 0-0	0-0	17		2004
7	24	H	Huddersfield T.	D 2-2	1-0	—	Watson, Johnson	4476
8	27	H	Watford	W 1-0	0-0	14	Cooke	2308
9	Oct 3	A	Southport	W 2-1	1-1	10	Cooke, Watson	1150
10	11	A	Reading	L 1-2	1-2	13	Cooke	5885
11	18	H	Stockport Co.	L 1-2	1-0	16	McGinley (pen)	2527
12	22	H	Doncaster R.	L 3-4	0-3	—	Cooke 2, Hall	3687
13	25	A	Swansea C.	L 1-3	1-0	20	Hutchins	3380
14	Nov 1	H	Darlington	W 2-0	1-0	16	Hutchins, Cooke	1916
15	4	A	Exeter C.	D 0-0	0-0	—		2723
16	8	A	Newport Co.	L 1-3	0-3	18	Ingram (pen)	2747
17	15	H	Hartlepool	L 1-2	0-0	19	Ingram	2009
18	29	A	Torquay U.	L 0-1	0-0	20		1868
19	Dec 6	H	Barnsley	W 2-1	2-1	17	McGinley, Cooke	3285
20	20	A	Lincoln C.	L 2-4	1-2	19	Cooke 2	6780
21	26	H	Scunthorpe U.	D 0-0	0-0	20		3465
22	27	H	Crew Alex.	W 3-1	1-0	19	McGinley (pen), Bevan (og), Ingram	3415
23	Jan 10	A	AFC Bournemouth	L 1-2	0-1	20	McGinley	4559
24	14	H	Workington	W 1-0	1-0	—	Cooke	2567
25	17	H	Rochdale	W 3-0	0-0	18	Hutchins, Cooke, Ingram	3059
26	30	A	Doncaster R.	D 1-1	0-0	19	Cooke	4484
27	Feb 7	H	Exeter C.	D 0-0	0-0	19		3049
28	21	A	Hartlepool	D 2-2	0-0	19	Ingram (pen), Hall	1865
29	28	H	Swansea C.	D 0-0	0-0	20		6672
30	Mar 10	H	Southport	D 1-1	1-1	—	Cooke	2706
31	13	H	Reading	D 1-1	0-0	20	Cooke	2916
32	15	A	Stockport Co.	L 1-2	0-0	—	Watson	2326
33	20	H	Torquay U.	W 3-1	2-1	20	Cooke 2, Ingram	2498
34	22	A	Darlington	D 2-2	0-1	—	Ingram, Johnson	1368
35	27	A	Barnsley	D 1-1	1-1	19	Hutchins	5206
36	31	H	Lincoln C.	L 1-5	0-0	—	Grotier (o.g.)	4019
37	Apr 3	A	Brentford	D 2-2	2-1	19	Ingram, Cooke	3450
38	6	A	Watford	L 0-3	0-2	—		3745
39	10	H	Northampton T.	L 1-2	1-1	20	Cooke	3175
40	16	A	Workington	W 3-0	0-0	19	Johnson, McGinley, Hutchins	1224
41	17	A	Scunthorpe U.	L 0-2	0-1	19		3254
42	19	H	Crewe Alex.	W 4-1	1-1	—	Hutchins, Cooke, McGinley, Cooper	2102
43	24	H	Cambridge U.	L 1-2	1-1	20	Johnson	2320
44	26	A	Tranmere R.	D 3-3	2-2	—	Cooke 2, McGinley	5867
45	29	A	Huddersfield T.	D 0-0	0-0	—		4779
46	May 3	H	Newport Co.	W 3-0	1-0	—	McFadzean 2, Watson	1676

Goalscorers

League (63): Cooke 22, Ingram 10 (2 pens), McGinley 8 (2 pens), Hutchins 6, Johnson 4, Watson 4, Cooper 2, Hall 2, McFadzean 2, Own Goals 3.
League Cup (2): Cooper, Johnson.
F.A. Cup (11): Hutchins 5, Ingram 2, Cooke 2, Middleton, McGinley.

League Cup	First Round	York C. (h)	2-0
	Second Leg	(a)	0-3
F.A. Cup	First Round	Chesterfield (h)	1-0
	Second Round	Rotherham U. (a)	3-0
	Third Round	Shrewsbury T. (a)	2-1
	Fourth Round	Tooting & Mitcham (h)	3-1
	Fifth Round	Norwich C. (a)	2-1
	Sixth Round	Southampton (h)	0-1

Downsborough	Podd	Cooper	Hockey	Middleton	Fretwell	Rayner	Johnson	Ingram	McGinley	Hall	Nicholls	Watson	Hutchins	Cooke	Ratcliffe	Punton	McFadzean	Jones	Match No.
	2	3	4	5	6	7*	8	9	10	11	12								1
1	2	3		5	6	7*		9	11	10	12	4	8						2
1	2	3	4	5	6		8	9	11	7			10						3
1	2	3	4	5	6		8	9	7	10			11						4
1	2	3	4	5	6		10	9	7	8*	12		11						5
1	2	3	4	5	6		7	10	9		12	8	11*						6
1	2	3	4	5	6		8	9	7			10	11*	12					7
1	2	3	4	5		12	8	9*	7	6		10	11						8
1	2	3	4	5			10	9	7	6		8	11						9
1	2	3	4	5	12		8	9*	7	6		11	10						10
1	2	3	4	5	12		8		7	6		10*	9	11					11
1	2	3	4	5	12		10		7*	6		8	11	9					12
1	2	3	4	5	6		7			8		10	11	9					13
1	2	3	4		6		8	9				7	11	10	5				14
1	2	3	4		6		10	7				8	11	9	5				15
1	2	3	4		6		10	7				8	11	9	5				16
1	2	3	4	5	6		8*	9	12			7	11	10					17
1	2	3		5	6		7	10	8			4	11	9					18
1	2	3	4*	5	6		8			7	10	12	11	9					19
	2	3		5	6		4	8	7	10			11	9		1			20
	2	3		5	6		4	8	7	10			11	9		1			21
	2	3		5	6		4	10	8	7			11	9		1			22
1	2	3		ɔ	6		4	10	8	7			11	9					23
1	2	3	4	5*	6		8	7	10			12	11	9					24
1	2	3			6		4	10	7			8	11	9	5				25
1	2	3	8	5	6		4		7	10			11	9					26
1	2	3		5	6		4	8	7	10			11	9					27
1	2	3		5	6		4	10	7	8			11	9					28
1	2	3		5	6		4	8	7	10			11	9					29
1	2	3	12	5	6		4	8	7*	10			11	9					30
1	2	3		5	6		4	10	7	8			11	9					31
1	2	3		5	6		4	8	7	10		12	11*	9					32
1	2	3		5	6		4	8		10		7	11	9					33
1	2	3		5	6		4	8	12	10		7	11	9*					34
1	2	3		5	6		4	8		10		7	11	9					35
1	2	3		5	6		4	8		10		7	11	9					36
1	2	3*		5	6		4	8		10		7	11	9	12				37
	2	3		5	6		4	8		10		7	11	9		1			38
	2	3		5	6		4	8	7			10	11	9		1			39
1	2	3		5	6	8	4		10			7	11	9					40
1	2	3		5	6	8*	4		10	12		7	11	9					41
1	2	3		5	6		4	8		10		7	11	9					42
1	2	3		5	6*		4	7	10	8			11	9		12			43
1	2	3		5	6*		4	8	10	7			11	9	12				44
1	2			5	6		4	8	10*	12		7	11		3		9		45
		3			6	12	4	8	10			7	11*		5	1	9	2	46
40	45	45	19	42	39	5	44	34	35	36	—	28	38	41	6	6	2	1	
				+1s		+3s	+2s		+2s	+1s	+4s	+4s		+1s	+2s		+1s		

Player and position	Ht.	Wt.	Birthplace	Clubs	League Appearances	Goals
Goalkeepers						
Peter Downsborough	5 10½	13 2	Halifax	Halifax T.	148	—
				Swindon T.	274	—
				Brighton (on loan)	3	—
				Bradford C.	109	—
Bill Punton				Bradford C.	6	—
Defenders						
Ian Cooper	5 10	11 12	Bradford	Bradford C.	437+1	4
Cec Podd	5 9	10 0	St. Kitts, W. Indies	Bradford C.	193+3	—
Graham Jones				Bradford C.	1	—
John Middleton	5 10	11 7	Rawmarsh	Bradford C.	85+2	2
Midfield						
David Fretwell	5 9	10 9	Normanton	Bradford C.	166+5	2
Trevor Hockey (Wales)	5 6½	10 4	Keighley	Bradford C.	53	5
				Nottingham F.	75	6
				Newcastle U.	52	3
				Birmingham C.	195	8
				Sheffield U.	68	4
				Norwich C.	13	—
				Aston V.	24	1
				Bradford C.	43+1	1
				(contract cancelled March 1976)		
Garry Watson	5 8	10 6	Bradford	Bradford C.	48+9	8
Rodney Johnson	5 7½	11 4	Leeds	Leeds U.	18+3	4
				Doncaster R.	106+1	23
				Rotherham U.	108+2	8
				Bradford C.	106	9
David Hall	5 11	12 0	Sheffield	Sheffield W.	—	—
				Bradford C.	36+1	2
David Ratcliffe	5 11	11 7		Bradford C.	6+6	—
Warren Rayner	6 0	11 0		Bradford C.	12+2	—
Forwards						
Joseph Cooke	5 11	12 0	Dominica	Bradford C.	100+10	30
Don Hutchins	5 7	10 2	Leicester	Leicester C.	4	—
				Plymouth Arg.	94+2	23
				Blackburn R.	37+3	6
				Bradford C.	81	11
Gerry Ingram	5 10	12 8	Hull	Blackpool	33+1	18
				Preston N.E.	107+3	40
				Bradford C.	156+1	51
Billy McGinley	5 5	9 10	Dumfries	Leeds U.	0+1	—
				Huddersfield T.	11+4	1
				Bradford C.	35+2	8
Clive McFadzean	5 10	11 5	Kilmarnock	Bradford C.	2+1	2
David Nichols				Bradford C.	0+4	—

BRENTFORD DIV. 4

President: F. A. Davis.
Chairman: Dan Tana.
Directors: L. F. Davey, P. L. Davey, P. H. Pond-Jones,
B. J. Poyton, C. W. Wheatley, R. J. J. Blindell.
Team Manager: John Docherty.
General Manager/Secretary: D. R. Piggott.
Year Formed: 1889.
Turned Professional: 1899. *Limited Company:* 1901.
Previous Grounds: Clifden Road 1889-91; Benns Fields,
Little Ealing 1891-95; Shotters Field 1895-98; Cross
Road, S. Ealing 1898-1900; Boston Park 1900-04; Griffin
Park 1904.
Honours: *Football League,* Highest Position in Division 1,
5th, 1935–36. Division 2, Champions: 1934–35. Divi-
sion 3(S), Champions: 1932–33; Runners-up: 1929–30,
1957–58. Division 4, Champions: 1962–63. *F.A. Cup,*
best season: 6th Rd., 1938, 1946, 1949. *Football League
Cup,* best season: 3rd Rd., 1961, 1969.

Brentford FC

© Brentford Football and Sports
Club Limited, 1975

Record Victory: 9-0 v Wrexham, Division 3, Oct. 15th,
1963.
Record Defeat: 0-7 v Swansea T., Division 3(S), Nov. 8th, 1924; 0-7 v Walsall, Division 3(S)
Jan. 19th, 1957.
Most League Points: 62, Division 3(S), 1932–33; 62, Division 4, 1962–63.
Most League Goals: 98, Division 4, 1962–63.
Highest League Scorer in Season: Jack Holliday, 36, Division 3(S), 1932–33.
Most League Goals in Total Aggregate: Jim Towers, 153, 1954–61.
Most Capped Player: Idris Hopkins, 12, Wales.
Most League Appearances: Ken Coote, 514, 1949–64.
Record Transfer Fee Received: £40,000 from Manchester U. for Stewart Houston, Dec. 1973.
Record Transfer Fee Paid: £25,000 to Oxford U. for Andy McCulloch, March 1976.
Managers Since the War: Harry Curtis, Jackie Gibbons, Jimmy Bain, Tom Lawton, Bill
Dodgin (Snr.), Malcolm McDonald, Tommy Cavanagh, Billy Gray, Jimmy Sirrel, Frank
Blunstone, Mike Everitt.
Address of Supporters Club: Same as Football Club.
Address of the Club Shop or Boutique: c/o the Club.

Griffin Park, Braemar Rd., Brentford, Middlesex TW8 0NT. Telephone 01-560-2021. *Ground
capacity:* 37,000 (30,500 under cover). *Record attendance:* 39,626 v Preston N.E., F.A. Cup
6th Rd., March 5, 1938. *Record receipts:* £8,032 v Bolton W., F.A. Cup 3rd Rd., January
3, 1976. *Pitch measurements:* 114 yds × 75 yds.
How to get there: South Ealing (Underground, Piccadilly line). Southern Region trains from Waterloo to
Brentford Central. Buses 91, 65, 116, 117, E1, E2, 267. The ground is within a mile of the M4 and A4 roads.
Match tickets: All admission by cash through turnstiles for league games. Cup-tie seats may be booked in
advance.
Car parking: Mainly confined to streets around the ground. A small park at Ealing Road entrance and a
larger one at the junction of Brook Road and Clifden Road; charges 25–30p. Access to the latter may be
gained only by the gate in Clifden Road approaching from the Boston Manor Road end.
Entertainments/catering facilities: Catering kiosks in the ground. A members' social club, the Bees Club
in Braemar Road, provides entertainment throughout the year.
Club-shop: The Supporters' Club sells all souvenir items. Applications for price lists, etc should be sent to
the Sales Secretary, Brentford Football Supporters & Social Club, c/o Brentford F.C., accompanied by
S.A.E.
Handbooks/programmes: Programmes not available on subscription.
Extra information: One of only six clubs to win all their home games in a season; Brentford accomplished
this feat in 1929–30.
Club Colours: Red and white striped shirts, black shorts.
Change Colours: All green, with black trimmings.
First Team Trainer: A. E. Lyons.
Club Nickname: 'Bees'.

BRENTFORD 1975-76 LEAGUE RECORD

Match No.	Date	Venue	Opponents	Result	H/T Score	League Pos'n	Goalscorers	Attendance
1	Aug 16	A	Bradford C.	D 1-1	1-1	—	Johnson	2385
2	23	H	Hartlepool	D 1-1	1-0	10	Cross	4950
3	30	A	Torquay U.	W 3-2	1-1	8	Cross, Allen, Graham	3011
4	Sept 6	H	Barnsley	W 1-0	0-0	4	Cross	5600
5	15	A	Doncaster R.	D 1-1	0-0	—	Johnson	6353
6	20	H	Stockport Co.	W 2-1	1-1	3	Simmons, Riddick	6280
7	24	A	AFC Bournemouth	L 0-3	0-2	—		4113
8	27	A	Huddersfield T.	L 1 2	0-0	11	Sweetzer	4160
9	Oct 4	H	Newport Co.	L 1-3	1-2	14	Graham	5680
10	11	A	Lincoln C.	L 1-3	0-2	15	Graham	6312
11	18	H	Southport	W 1-0	1-0	14	Johnson	4510
12	21	A	Northampton T.	L 1-3	0-2	—	Scales	6225
13	25	A	Cambridge U.	L 1-2	1-1	18	French	2596
14	Nov 1	H	Scunthorpe U.	W 5-2	2-0	14	French, Johnson, Cross 2, Graham	4220
15	3	H	Workington	W 4-0	2-0	—	French, Sweetzer, Johnson (pen), Cross	5380
16	7	A	Tranmere R.	L 1-5	1-2	15	Cross	4327
17	15	H	Watford	W 1-0	0-0	14	Scales	6930
18	29	A	Crewe Alex.	L 0-1	0-1	15		2248
19	Dec 6	H	Rochdale	W 3-0	1-0	14	Johnson (pen), Cross, Riddick	4850
20	20	H	Darlington	W 3-0	1-0	11	Sweetzer 2, Cross	4170
21	26	A	Exeter C.	D 0-0	0-0	13		4912
22	27	H	Reading	D 2-2	1-0	11	Johnson, Scales	6934
23	Jan 10	H	Torquay U.	D 1-1	1-1	11	Johnson	5680
24	16	A	Stockport Co.	L 0-2	0-1	15		2267
25	24	H	Doncaster R.	L 0-1	0-1	17		4900
26	31	H	Northampton T.	W 2-1	1-0	14	Johnson (pen), Cross	4110
27	Feb 7	A	Workington	D 1-1	1-0	14	French	1231
28	14	H	Tranmere R.	L 0-1	0-1	16		4720
29	21	A	Watford	L 2-3	2-1	18	Bristow o.g., Sweetzer	6223
30	23	H	AFC Bournemouth	L 1-2	1-0	—	Graham	4590
31	28	H	Cambridge U.	D 0-0	0-0	17		4080
32	Mar 6	A	Scunthorpe U.	L 1-2	0-1	18	Sharp	3225
33	8	A	Newport Co.	L 0-1	0-1	—		1150
34	13	H	Lincoln C.	W 1-0	1-0	18	Cross	5380
35	16	A	Southport	L 0-2	0-0	—		1506
36	20	H	Crewe Alex.	D 0-0	0-0	18		3840
37	27	A	Rochdale	W 2-1	1-0	18	McCulloch, French	1088
38	29	A	Darlington	L 0-2	0-1	—		1758
39	Apr 3	H	Bradford C.	D 2-2	1-2	18	McCulloch, Cross	3450
40	5	H	Huddersfield T.	D 0-0	0-0	—		4410
41	10	A	Barnsley	D 1-1	0-1	18	Cross	3753
42	16	H	Swansea C.	W 1-0	0-0	17	Johnson	4360
43	17	H	Exeter C.	W 5-1	2-0	15	Bence, French 2, McCulloch, Cross	3980
44	19	A	Reading	L 0-1	0-0	—		12,772
45	24	A	Hartlepool	L 0-1	0-1	17		1272
46	26	A	Swansea C.	D 2-2	1-0	—	French, Johnson	1311

Goalscorers

League (56): Cross 14, Johnson 11 (3 pens), French 8, Graham 5, Sweetzer 5, McCulloch 3, Scales 3, Riddick 2, Allen 1, Bence 1, Sharp 1, Simmons 1, Own Goal 1.
League Cup (4): Cross 2, Johnson 1 (pen), Lawrence.
F.A. Cup (4): Sweetzer 2, Johnson 2 (1 a pen).

League Cup:	First Round	Brighton & H.A. (h)	2-1	
	Second Leg	(a)	1-1	
	Second Round	Manchester U. (a)	1-2	
F.A. Cup	First Round	Northampton T. (h)	2-0	
	Second Round	Wimbledon (a)	2-0	
	Third Round	Bolton W. (h)	0-0	
		(a)	0-2	

Glazier	Nelmes	Allen	Scales	Lawrence	Smith	Bence	Graham	Simmons	French	Johnson	Cross	Riddick	Priddy	Sweetzer	Poole	Horn	Sharp	Salman	McCulloch	Match No.
1	2	3	4	5	6	7	8	9	10	11										1
1	2	3	4	5	6	7	8	9		11	10*	12								2
1	2	3	8	5	6	4	7	9		11	10									3
1	2	3	8	5	6	4	7	9*	12	11	10									4
1	2	3	8	5	6	4	7	9	10	11										5
1	2	3	8	5	6	4	7	9	10	11*		12								6
1	2	3	8*	5	6	4	7	10	9	11		12								7
	2	3	8		6	4	7	9*		11	10	5	1	12						8
1	2	3	8	5	6	4	7	9*	12	11	10									9
1		3	8	5	6	4	7			11	9	2*		10	12					10
		3	8	5	6	2	7	9*		11	10	4	1	12						11
	2*	3	8	5		4	7	12		11	9	6	1	10						12
		3	8	5	6	2	7		4	11	9		1	10						13
		3	8	5	4	2	7			11	6	9	1	10						14
		3	8	5	6	2	7		4	11	9		1	10						15
		3	8	5*	6	2	7		4	11	9			10	12	1				16
		3	8		6	2	7		4	11	9	5*		10		1	12			17
	2	3	6	5	8	4	7			11	9			10		1				18
	2	3	5	6	8	7				11	9	4	1	10						19
	2	3	8	5	6	4	7			11	9		1	10						20
	2	3	8	5	6	4	7			11	9		1	10						21
	4	3	8	5	6	2	7			11	9		1	10						22
	2	3	8	5	6	4*	7			11	9			10		1	12			23
	2	3	8	5*	6	4	7			11	9			10		1	12			24
		3	8		4	2	7		11	6*	9	5	1	10	12					25
		3	8		6	2	7		11	4	9	5	1	10						26
		3	8		6*	2	7		11	4	9	5	1	10	12					27
		3	8		6	2	7		11	4	9	5	1	10						28
12		3	8			2	7		11	4	9	5*	1	10		6				29
		3	8	5		2	7		11	4	9*		1	10	12	6				30
		3	8	5	6*	2	7		11	4	9		1	10	12					31
		3	8	5	6	2	7		11	4			1	10	9*	12				32
		3	8	5	6	2	7		11	4			1	10					9	33
		3	8		6	2	7		4	11	5*		1	10	12				9	34
		3	5		6	2	7		4	11*	8		1	10	12				9	35
8		3			6	2	7		4	11*	5		1	10	12				9	36
	2	3	8	5	4		7			11	10	6	1						9	37
	2*	3	8	5	4				11	10	7	6	1		12				9	38
	2	3	8	5	6*		7		12	11	10	4	1						9	39
	2	3	8	5		4	7		10	11	6*		1		12				9	40
	2	3	8	5	6	4	7*		10	11			1		12				9	41
	2	3	8	5		4	7		10	11	6		1						9	42
	2	3	8		6	4	7			11	10	5	1						9	43
	2	3	8		6	4	7		10	11	5*		1		12				9	44
	2	6	8	5		4	7*			11			1	10	12			3	9	45
	2		8		6	4	7		10	11	9	5	1					3		46
9	28	45	43	35	37	46	38	10	27	46	37	23	34	25	2	3	2	3	13	
	+1s								+4s			+3s	+2s	+5s			+10s	+3s		

BRENTFORD—PLAYERS

Player and position	Ht.	Wt.	Birthplace	Clubs	League Appearances	Goals
Goalkeepers						
Bill Glazier	6 0	13 3	Nottingham	C. Palace	106	—
				Coventry C.	346	—
				Brentford	9	—
Paul Priddy	6 0	11 8	Isleworth	Brentford	84	—
Defenders						
*Alan Nelmes	6 0	11 0	Hackney	Brentford	311+5	2
*Keith Lawrence	6 1	13 6	Farnborough, Kent	Chelsea	—	—
				W.B.A. (on loan)	—	—
				Brentford	78	1
Nigel Smith	5 10	11 3	Banstead	Brentford	39	—
Denis Salman	5 9	11 0	Famagusta	Brentford	3+3	—
Tom Sharp	5 11	11 0	Newmains	Everton	—	—
				Brentford	2+10	1
Mike Allen	5 11	10 8	S. Shields	Middlesbrough	32+3	1
				Brentford	157+8	10
Midfield						
Paul Bence	5 9	11 0	Littlehampton	Brighton	0+1	—
				Reading	12+1	2
				Brentford	228+5	6
Terry Scales	5 10	11 5	Stratford	West Ham U.	—	—
				Brentford	200	5
Jackie Graham	5 7	10 12	Glasgow	Morton	6	1
				Dundee U.	21+2	10
				Guildford C. (not known)		
				Brentford	229+1	30
Forwards						
Gordon Riddick	6 0	12 6	Watford	Luton T.	101+1	16
				Gillingham	114	24
				Charlton Ath.	26+3	5
				Orient	13+8	3
				Northampton T.	28	3
				Brentford	91+4	5
Roger Cross	6 0	13 7	London	West Ham U.	5+2	1
				Orient (on loan)	4+2	2
				Brentford	62	20
				Fulham	39+1	8
				Brentford	120+4	43
*Richard Poole	6 1	12 9	Hefton	Brentford	12+9	1
Mickey French	5 11	12 2	Eastbourne	Q.P.R.	—	—
				Brentford	41+5	12
Terry Johnson	5 9	10 13	Newcastle	Newcastle U.	—	—
				Darlington (on loan)	4	1
				Southend U.	155+2	34
				Brentford	74	19
Andy McCulloch	6 2	13 6	Northampton	Q.P.R.	30+12	10
				Cardiff C.	58	24
				Oxford U.	41	9
				Brentford	13	3
Gordon Sweetzer	6 0	11 8	Toronto	Brentford	25+2	5

BRIGHTON & HOVE ALBION   DIV. 3

Chairman: M. K. Bamber.

Vice-chairman: H. Bloom.

Directors: N. J. Hyams, W. Smith, D. Sizen, K. Wickenden, T. Appleby.

Manager: Peter Taylor.

Asst. Manager: Brian Daykin.

Secretary: Kenneth Calver.   *Year Formed:* 1900.

Turned Professional: 1900.   *Limited Company:* 1901.

Previous Name: Brighton & Hove Rangers.

Previous Grounds: 1900, Withdean; 1901, County Ground; 1902, Goldstone Ground.

Honours: Football League: best season: 12th, Div. 2, 1958–59. Division 3(S), Champions: 1957–58; Runners-up: 1953–54, 1955–56, Division 3: 1971–72. Division 4, Champions: 1964–65. *F.A. Cup,* best season: 5th Rd., 1929–30, 1932–33, 1945–46, 1959–60, old 3rd Rd., 1913–14, 1923–24. *Football League Cup,* best season: 4th Rd., 1966–67.

Record Victory: 10-1 v Wisbech, F.A. Cup, 1st Rd., Nov. 13th, 1965.

Record Defeat: 0-9 v Middlesbrough, Division 2, Aug. 23rd, 1958.

Most League Points: 65, Division 3(S), 1955–56, and Division 3, 1971–72.

Most League Goals: 112, Division 3(S), 1955–56.

Highest League Scorer in Season: Hugh Vallance, 30, Division 3(S), 1929–30.

Most League Goals in Total Aggregate: Tommy Cook, 113, 1922–29.

Most Capped Player: Jack Jenkins, 8, Wales.

Most League Appearances: 'Tug' Wilson, 509, 1922–36.

Record Transfer Fee Received: £26,000 from Blackburn R. for Ken Beamish, May 1974.

Record Transfer Fee Paid: £40,000 to Norwich C. for Ian Mellor, April. 1974.

Managers Since the War: Tommy Cook, Don Welsh, Billy Lane, George Curtis, Archie Macaulay, Freddie Goodwin, Pat Saward, Brian Clough.

Address of Supporters Club: Albion Shop, Goldstone Ground, Hove.

Goldstone Ground, Old Shoreham Rd., Hove, Sussex, BN3 7DE. Telephone Brighton 739535. *Ground capacity:* 36,000.   *Record attendance:* 36,747 v Fulham, Division 2, December 27, 1958.   *Record receipts:* £23,000 v Crystal Palace, Div. 3, February 24, 1976.   *Pitch measurements:* 112 yds × 75 yds.

How to get there: Buses 5, B5, 9, 26, 40, 55, 19 from Old Steyne and 11 via Brighton station and Old Shoreham Rd. Hove station is five minutes walk from the ground.

Match tickets: Postal bookings for tickets two weeks in advance.

Car parking: Car parking facilities are available a few minutes away at the Greyhound Stadium, Neville Road, and in Hove Station Goods Yard, Sackville Road. There is limited street parking adjacent to the stadium.

Entertainments/catering facilities: Bars and tea stands around the ground.

Club shop: At the ground; sells all types of souvenirs.

Handbooks/programmes: Programmes available by post from the club shop.

Extra information: In 1933–34 Oliver Brown was Brighton's leading scorer with 12 goals; yet he played in only 8 matches!

Club Colours: Blue and white striped shirts, blue shorts, white socks with 2 blue hoops.

Change Colours: Green shirts, white shorts, green stockings.

Physiotherapist: Glen Wilson.

First Team Coach: Ken Gutteridge.

Club Nickname: 'The Albion' or 'The Dolphins'.

BRIGHTON & HOVE ALBION 1975–76 LEAGUE RECORD

Match No.	Date	Venue	Opponents	Result	H/T Score	League Pos'n	Goalscorers	Attendance
1	Aug 16	H	Rotherham U.	W 3-0	3-0	—	Binney, Machin, Martin	10,138
2	23	A	Sheffield W.	D 3-3	1-2	5	Martin 2, Turner	10,326
3	30	H	Cardiff C.	L 0-1	0-0	10		11,353
4	Sept 6	A	Port Vale	D 1-1	1-0	10	Binney	3289
5	10	H	Walsall	L 1-2	1-1	—	Binney	8592
6	13	H	Chester	W 6-0	2-0	7	Binney 2, O'Sullivan, Mellor, Fell 2	7924
7	20	A	Colchester U.	L 0-2	0-0	11		3176
8	23	A	Crystal Palace	W 1-0	1-0	—	Butlin	25,606
9	27	H	Chesterfield	W 3-0	2-0	6	O'Sullivan, Butlin, Binney	8784
10	Oct 4	A	Shrewsbury T.	W 2-1	2-0	3	Binney, O'Sullivan	4198
11	11	H	Preston N.E.	W 1-0	1-0	3	Rollings	14,375
12	18	A	Grimsby T.	L 1-2	0-0	4	Martin	4938
13	25	H	Wrexham	W 3-2	1-1	5	Towner, Martin, Fell	12,059
14	Nov 1	A	Peterborough U.	L 0-1	0-1	5		8630
15	4	H	Bury	W 2-1	2-1	—	Binney 2	14,603
16	8	H	Southend U.	W 2-0	1-0	3	O'Sullivan, Fell	13,500
17	15	A	Halifax T.	W 3-1	1-1	2	Martin, Binney, Fell	2201
18	29	A	Swindon T.	L 2-3	1-0	3	Binney, Melior	6792
19	Dec 6	H	Hereford U.	W 4-2	2-1	2	Binney, Mellor, Martin 2	17,811
20	20	A	Walsall	L 0-2	0-0	4		5435
21	27	A	Gillingham	L 0-1	0-1	6		9294
22	30	H	Aldershot	W 4-1	3-1	—	O'Sullivan 2, Mellor, Binney	18,818
23	Jan 10	A	Cardiff C.	W 1-0	0-0	3	Mellor	17,728
24	17	H	Colchester U.	W 6-0	3-0	2	Mellor, Rollings, Binney 2, Fell 2	16,302
25	24	A	Chester	L 0-3	0-0	4		5099
26	31	H	Mansfield T.	W 1-0	0-0	3	Machin	11,918
27	Feb 3	H	Millwall	W 1-0	0-0	—	Binney	15,332
28	7	A	Bury	D 1-1	0-0	3	Mellor	6217
29	17	A	Southend U.	L 0-4	0-1	—		4784
30	21	H	Halifax T.	W 1-0	0-0	3	Binney	13,685
31	24	H	Crystal Palace	W 2-0	1-0	—	Morgan 2	33,300
32	28	A	Wrexham	L 0-3	0-1	2		4662
33	Mar 1	A	Mansfield T.	L 0-1	0-0	—		8321
34	6	H	Peterborough U.	W 5-0	2-0	2	Binney 2, Mellor, Rollings, Morgan	16,398
35	10	A	Shrewsbury T.	D 2-2	0-2	—	Morgan, Binney	21,423
36	13	A	Preston N.E.	L 0-1	0-0	2		6720
37	17	H	Grimsby T.	W 4-2	1-2	—	Morgan, Wilson (pen), Binney (pen), O'Sullivan	17,384
38	20	H	Swindon T.	W 2-0	0-0	2	Morgan 2	18,208
39	27	A	Hereford U.	D 1-1	1-0	2	Ward	12,160
40	Apr 3	A	Rotherham U.	D 1-1	1-0	2	Ward	4309
41	7	A	Chesterfield	L 1-2	0-1	—	Kinnear (pen)	4500
42	10	H	Port Vale	W 3-0	1-0	3	Binney, Mellor, Ward	19,171
43	16	A	Millwall	L 1-3	0-2	—	Binney	23,008
44	17	A	Aldershot	D 1-1	0-0	4	Ward	11,666
45	19	H	Gillingham	D 1-1	0-1	—	Ward	19,142
46	24	H	Sheffield W.	D 1-1	0-1	4	Ward	11,859

Goalscorers

League (78): Binney 23 (1 a pen), Mellor 9, Martin 8, O'Sullivan 7, Fell 7, Morgan 7, Ward 6, Rollings 3, Machin 2, Butlin 2, Wilson 1 (pen), Kinnear 1 (pen).
League Cup (2): Binney (pen), own goal 1.
F.A. Cup (5): Binney 3, Martin, Fell.

League Cup	First Round	Brentford (a)	1-2
	Second Leg	(h)	1-1
F.A. Cup	First Round	Watford (a)	3-0
	Second Round	Gillingham (a)	1-0
	Third Round	Southend U.	1-2

Grummitt	Tiler	Wilson	Beal	Piper	Winstanley	Towner	Machin	Binney	Martin	O'Sullivan	Kinnear	Fell	Burnett	Walker	Mellor	Butlin	Rollings	Morgan	Horton	Ward	Match No.
1	2	3	4	5	6	7	8	9	10	11											1
1	2	3	4	5	6	7	8	9	10	11											2
1		3	4	5	6	7	8	9		11	2	10									3
1		3	4		6	7	8	9		11	2	10	5								4
1	2	3			6	7	8	9	10	11	12	5		4*							5
1	2	3		5		7	4	9		11		10	6		8						6
1	2	3		5	11		4	9*	12	8		7	6		10						7
1	2	3	11				4*	9	12	8		7	6		10		5				8
1	2	3					4	8		11		10	6		7	9	5				9
1	2	3					4	8		11		7	5		10	9	6				10
1	2	3					4	8*	12	11		10	5		7	9	6				11
1	2	3				7	4		10	11		8	6		9		5				12
1	2	3	12			7	4	9		8		10	6		11*		5				13
1	2	3	10			7	4	9		11		8	6				5				14
1	2	3	11				4	9	10	8		7	6				5				15
1	2	3	11				4	9	10	8		7	6				5				16
1	2	3	11				4	8	9	10		7	6				5				17
1	2	3					4	9	10	8		7	6		11		5				18
1	2	3					4	9	10	8		7	6		11		5				19
1		3					4	9	10	8	2	7	6		11		5				20
1		3					4	9		8	2	7	6		11		5	10			21
1		3					4	9		8	2	7	6		11		5	10			22
1	2	3					4	9		8		7	6		11		5	10			23
1	2	3					4	9		8		7	6		11		5	10			24
1	2	3			12		4	9		8		7	6		11*		5	10			25
1	2	3					4	9	12	8		7	6		11		5	10*			26
1	2	3			12		4*	9	10	8		7	6		11		5				27
1	2	3	10	9		7	4			8			6		11		5				28
1	2	3	10	11		7	4			8			6		9		5				29
1	2	3				7	4	9		10			6		11		5	8			30
1	2	3				7	4	9		8			6		11		5	10			31
1	2	3				7	4	9		8			6		11		5	10			32
1	2	3*			12	7	4	9		8			6		11		5	10			33
1	2	3				7	4	9		8			6		11		5	10			34
1	2	3				7	4	9		8		12	6		11		5*	10			35
1		3		5		7		9		8	2		6		11			10	4		36
1		3		5		7	4*	9		8	2		6		12			10	11		37
1		3		5		7		9		8	2		6		11			10	4		38
1		3		11		7				8	2		6				5	10	4	9	39
1		3		6		7				8	2				11		5	10	4	9	40
1		3		6		7				8	2				11	9	5		4	10	41
1		3		6		7		9		8	2				11		5		4	10	42
1		3		6		7		9		8	2	12			11*		5		4	10	43
1		3		6		7*		9		8	2	12			11		5		4	10	44
1		3		6		7		9		8	2*	12			11		5		4	10	45
1		3		6		7		9*		8	2	12			11		5		4	10	46
46	30	46	8	19	8	28	36	38	13	46	15	25	36	1	33	5	36	18	11	8	
			+1s	+2s	+1s	+1s		+4s				+1s	+4s		+1s						

BRIGHTON—PLAYERS

Player and position	Ht.	Wt.	Birthplace	Clubs	League Appearances	Goals
Goalkeepers						
Peter Grummitt	5 10	11 1	Bourne	Nottingham F.	313	—
				Sheffield W.	121	—
				Brighton	105	—
*Derek Forster	5 9	11 2	Newcastle	Sunderland	18	—
				Charlton Ath.	9	—
				Brighton	3	—
Defenders						
Dennis Burnett	5 11	11 12	Bermondsey	West Ham U.	48+2	—
				Millwall	259	3
				Hull C.	46	2
				Millwall (on loan)	6	2
				Brighton	36	—
Ken Tiler	5 11	10 12½	Sheffield	Chesterfield	138+1	1
				Brighton	58	—
Andy Rollings	6 0	11 8	N. Weston	Norwich C.	4	—
				Brighton	61	3
Phil Beal	5 10	11 9	Godstone	Tottenham H.	330+3	1
				Brighton	8+1	—
Graham Winstanley	5 11	11 3	Croxdale	Newcastle U.	5+2	—
				Carlisle U.	165+1	8
				Brighton	37+1	2
Alan Lewis	5 9	10 6	Oxford	Derby Co.	2	—
				Peterborough U. (on loan)	10	—
				Brighton	3	—
Steve Piper	5 10	11 10	Brighton	Brighton	99+2	2
Ian Goodwin	6 0	12 11	Irlam	Coventry C.	4	—
				Brighton	52+4	—
Harry Wilson	5 9½	10 12	Hetton-le-Hole	Burnley	12	—
				Brighton	113	4
Joe Kinnear (Eire)	5 8	11 6	Dublin	Tottenham H.	189+7	2
				Brighton	15+1	1
Midfield						
Brian Horton	5 10	11 4	Hednesford	Port Vale	232+4	33
				Brighton	11	—
Ernie Machin	5 8½	11 0	Bolton	Coventry C.	255+2	32
				Plymouth Arg.	57	6
				Brighton	64	2
*Thomas Mason	5 3	10 4	Buxton	Derby Co.	—	—
				Brighton	23+2	2
Peter O'Sullivan (Wales)	5 6	10 0	Colwyn Bay	Manchester U.	—	—
				Brighton	254	28
Forwards						
Fred Binney	5 10	11 7	Plymouth	Torquay U.	5+4	1
				Exeter C.	17	11
				Torquay U.	19+3	9
				Exeter C.	161	79
				Brighton	62+2	32
*Ricky Marlowe	6 0	11 4	Edinburgh	Derby Co.	—	—
				Shrewsbury T.	31	4
				Brighton	24+1	5
				Aldershot (on loan)	2	—
Tony Towner	5 7	9 11	Brighton	Brighton	103+4	16
Ian Mellor	6 1	10 12	Manchester	Manchester C.	36+4	7
				Norwich C.	28+1	2
				Brighton	59+3	15
Gerrie Fell	5 9	11 9	Newark	Brighton	45+4	12
Sammy Morgan (N. Ireland)	6 1	11 0	Gorleston	Port Vale	109+4	24
				Aston V.	35+5	9
				Brighton	18	7
Peter Ward	5 10	11 3	Derbyshire	Brighton	8	6

BRISTOL CITY   DIV. 1

Chairman: Robert Hobbs.
Vice-Chairman: N. B. Jones.
Directors: S. F. Kew, W. G. Garland, A. R. Hobbs,
O. F. L. Brown, G. C. Griffiths.
Manager: Alan Dicks. *Commercial Manager/Secretary:*
A. E. Rance
Coach: Ken Wimshurst. *Year Formed:* 1894.
Turned Professional: 1897. *Limited Company:* 1897.
Previous Grounds: 1894, St. John's Lane; 1904, Ashton Gate.
Previous Name: 1894–97, Bristol South End.
Honours: *Football League,* Division 1, Runners-up: 1906–07.
Division 2, Champions: 1905–06. Runners-up: 1975-76. Division
3(S), Champions: 1922–23, 1926–27, 1954–55; Runners-up:
1937–38. Division 3, Runners-up: 1964–65. *F.A. Cup,* Runners-
up: 1909. *Football League Cup,* Semi-final: 1970-71.

Record Victory: 11-0 v Chichester, F.A. Cup, 1st Rd., Nov. 5th, 1960.

Record Defeat: 0-9 v Coventry C., Division 3(S), Apr. 28th, 1934.

Most League Points: 70, Division 3(S), 1954–55.

Most League Goals: 104, Division 3(S), 1926–27.

Highest League Scorer in Season: Don Clark, 36, Division 3(S), 1946–47.

Most Capped Player: Billy Wedlock, 26, England.

Most League Appearances: John Atyeo, 597, 1951–1966 (+ 48 cup ties).

Most League Goals in Total Aggregate: John Atyeo, 315, 1951–66.

Record Transfer Fee Received: £110,000 from Chelsea for Chris Garland, Sept. 1971.

Record Transfer Fee Paid: £62,000 to W.B.A for Bobby Gould, Dec. 1972.

Managers Since the War: Bob Hewison, Bob Wright, Pat Beasley, Peter Doherty, Fred Ford.

Address of Supporters Club: Supporters Club, Bristol City F.C., Ashton Gate, Bristol BS3 2EJ.

Address of Club Shop or Boutique: Robbie Robin Shop, Ashton Gate, Bristol BS3 2EJ.

Ashton Gate, Bristol BS3 2EJ. Telephone Bristol 664093 and 665428. *Telegraphic address:*
'City Bristol'. *Ground capacity:* 37,000. *Record attendance:* 43,335 v Preston N.E., F.A. Cup
5th Rd., February 16th, 1935. *Record receipts:* £28,000 v Leeds U., F.A. Cup 5th Rd., February 16, 1974. *Pitch measurements:* 115 yds × 75 yds.

How to get there: Buses 6, 7, 9, 19, 22. Parson St. railway station is within walking distance. By special
arrangement Ashton Gate station is open to visiting supporters' trains.

Match tickets: Tickets can be booked any length of time before the match; they will be issued 14 days prior
to kick-off. Postal application must include remittance and S.A.E. Seats can also be reserved by personal
application or by telephone; tickets booked by telephone must be collected 30 minutes before the start of
the game.

Car parking: Season-ticket holders park at the ground. Coaches can park in the ground for 25p. Ample
street parking around the ground.

Entertainments/catering facilities: Social club in the main stands. Tea bars in the ground. Alcoholic bev-
erages only obtainable by members of a bona-fide Supporters' Club. There is a wide variety of pre-
match entertainment, and some matches are sponsored, so throw-away gifts to the crowd, and
programme prizes, are a regular feature.

Club shop: Run by the Supporters' Club; sells all types of souvenirs.

Handbooks/programmes: Supporters' Club produce a handbook. Programmes not available on subscription but postal applications are accepted.

Extra information: Indoor bowling area in the main stand. Large room available for functions caters for
200 people.

Club Colours: Red shirts, white shorts, red stockings.

Change Colours: All white.

Club Captain: Geoff Merrick.

Club Nickname: 'Robins'.

BRISTOL CITY 1975–76 LEAGUE RECORD

Match No.	Date	Venue	Opponents	Result	H/T Score	League Pos'n	Goalscorers	Attendance
1	Aug 16	H	Bolton W.	W 1-0	0-0	—	Sweeney (pen)	10,510
2	19	H	Sunderland	W 3-0	2-0	—	Brolly, Mann 2	12,199
3	23	A	Hull C.	L 1-3	0-2	3	Ritchie	5076
4	26	A	Southampton	L 1-3	0-2	—	Gow	16,833
5	30	H	Bristol R.	D 1-1	1-1	6	Cheesley	17,918
6	Sept 6	A	Blackburn R.	W 2-1	0-0	5	Sweeney (pen), Mann	10,281
7	12	H	Oxford U.	W 4-1	1-0	4	Cheesley 2, Ritchie 2	10,374
8	20	A	Chelsea	D 1-1	1-1	4	Cheesley	17,661
9	27	H	Blackpool	W 2-0	2-0	4	Cheesley, Gow (pen)	10,240
10	Oct 4	A	Notts Co.	D 1-1	0-0	5	Mann	10,802
11	7	A	Oldham Ath.	W 4-2	1-1	—	Mann, Gillies, Cheesley, Whitehead	9572
12	11	H	Charlton Ath.	W 4-0	2-0	2	Whitehead, Gow (pen), Cheesley 2	12,701
13	18	A	York C.	W 4-1	3-1	1	Cheesley 3 (1 a pen), Ritchie	4661
14	25	H	W.B.A.	L 0-2	0-0	2		19,132
15	Nov 1	A	Luton T.	D 0-0	0-0	2		11,466
16	7	H	Orient	D 0-0	0-0	3		14,553
17	15	A	Nottingham F.	L 0-1	0-1	3		11,583
18	22	H	York C.	W 4-1	2-1	3	Ritchie 3, Merrick	11,228
19	29	A	Fulham	W 2-1	2-0	2	Ritchie 2	11,400
20	Dec 6	H	Carlisle U.	D 0-0	0-0	3		12,466
21	13	H	Hull C.	W 3-0	1-0	3	Ritchie, Mann, Cheesley	10,796
22	20	A	Bolton W.	L 0-1	0-0	3		18,503
23	26	H	Plymouth Arg.	D 2-2	1-1	3	Merrick, Collier	21,471
24	27	A	Portsmouth	W 1-0	1-0	3	Ritchie	14,315
25	Jan 10	A	Oxford U.	D 1-1	1-0	3	Cheesley	7335
26	17	H	Blackburn R.	W 1-0	1-0	2	Mann	12,168
27	24	A	Plymouth Arg.	D 0-0	0-0	2		17,887
28	Feb 7	A	Southampton	D 1-1	1-0	2	Ritchie	23,316
29	14	A	Orient	W 1-0	0-0	2	Ritchie	5785
30	21	H	Nottingham F.	L 0-2	0-2	3		15,302
31	24	H	Oldham Ath.	W 1-0	1-0	—	Cheesley	14,361
32	Mar 6	H	Luton T.	W 3-0	0-0	1	Ritchie 2, Cheesley	15,870
33	13	A	Charlton Ath.	D 2-2	0-0	1	Gow, Sweeney	12,683
34	17	A	W.B.A.	W 1-0	1-0	—	Sweeney	26,640
35	20	H	Fulham	D 0-0	0-0	1		19,935
36	23	A	Sunderland	D 1-1	0-0	—	Sweeney	38,395
37	27	A	Carlisle U.	W 1-0	1-0	1	Gow (pen)	7563
38	Apr 3	A	Blackpool	L 1-2	1-1	1	Ritchie	8273
39	10	H	Chelsea	D 2-2	1-1	2	Ritchie 2	24,710
40	16	A	Bristol R.	D 0-0	0-0	2		26,430
41	20	H	Portsmouth	W 1-0	1-0	—	Whitehead	27,300
42	24	H	Notts Co.	L 1-2	0-1	2	Whitehead	24,614

Goalscorers

League (59): Ritchie 18, Cheesley 15 (1 a pen), Mann 7, Gow 5 (3 pens), Sweeney 5 (2 pens), Whitehead , Merrick 2, Brolly 1, Collier 1, Gillies 1.

League Cup (1): Cheesley.

F.A. Cup (1): Brolly.

League Cup	Second Round	West Ham U. (a)	0-0
		(h)	1-3
F.A. Cup	Third Round	Coventry C. (a)	1-2

Cashley	Sweeney	Drysdale	Gow	Collier	Merrick	Tainton	Ritchie	Cheesley	Mann	Brolly	Emanuel	Gillies	Harding	Whitehead	Fear	McNeil	Match No.
1	2	3	4	5	6	7	8	9	10	11							1
1	2		4	5	6	7	8	10	9	11	3						2
1	2		4	5	6	7	8	10	9	11	3						3
1	2		4	5	6	7	8	10	9	11*	3	12					4
1	2	3	4	5	6	7	8	10	9	11							5
1	2	3	4	5	6	7	8	10	9	11							6
1	2*	3	4		6	7	8	10		11	12	9	5				7
1		3	4	5	6	7	8	9	10	11		2					8
1		3	4	5	6	7	8	10*	9	11		2		12			9
1		3	4	5	6	7	8	9	10	11		2					10
1		3	4	5	6	7	8	10	9	11*		2		12			11
1		3	4	5	6	7	8	9	10			2		11			12
1		3	4	5	6	7	8	10	9			2		11			13
1	12	3	4	5	6	7	8	9	10			2*		11			14
1		3	4	5	6	7	8	9	10			2		11			15
1		3	4	5	6	7	8	10	9			2		11*	12		16
1	12	3	4	5	6	7	8	10	9			2		11*			17
1	2	3	4	5	6	7	8	10*	9					11	12		18
1	2	3*	4		6	7	8	10	9				5	11	12		19
1	2	3	4	5	6	7	8	10	9					11			20
1	2	3	4	5	6	7	8	10	9					11			21
1	2	3	4	5	6	7	8	10*	9	12				11			22
1	2	3	4	5	6	7	8	10*	9	12				11			23
1	2	3	4	5	6	7	8	9	10					11			24
1	2	3	4	5	6	7	8	10	9					11			25
1	2	3	4	5	6	7	8	9						11	10		26
1	2	3	4	5	6	7	8	9						11	10		27
1	2	3	4	5	6	7	8	10	9					11			28
1	2	3	4	5	6	7	8	10*	9	12				11			29
1	2	3	4	5	6	7	8	10	9	12				11*			30
1	2	3	4	5	6	7	8	10	9					11			31
1	9	3	4	5	6	7	8	10				2		11			32
1	2	3	4	5	6	7	8	10*	9					11	12		33
1	2	3	4	5	6	7	8	10	12			9		11*			34
1	10	2	4	5	6	7	8	9				3		11			35
1	10	3	4	5	6	7	8	9*	12			2		11			36
1	10	3	4	5	6	7	8	12				2		11	9*		37
1	10	3	4	5	6	7	8	9*	12			2		11			38
1	7	3	4	5	6		8	9	10	12		2		11*			39
1	2	3	4	5	6	7	8	10				9		11			40
1	2	3	4	5	6	7	8	10	9					11			41
1	10	3	4	5	6	7	8	9	12			2*		11			42
42	32	39	42	40	42	42	42	38	30	14	3	22	2	19	13	—	
		+2s								+6s	+1s	+1s	+3s	+3s	+2s	+2s	

Player and position	Ht.	Wt.	Birthplace	Clubs	League Appearances	Goals
Goalkeepers						
Len Bond	5 9	12 0	Ilminster	Bristol C.	28	—
				Exeter C. (on loan)	30	—
				Cardiff C. (on loan)	—	—
				Torquay U. (on loan)	3	—
				Scunthorpe U. (on loan)	8	—
				Colchester U. (on loan)	3	—
Ray Cashley	5 10	11 0	Bristol	Bristol C.	183	1
John Shaw	6 1	13 7	Stirling	Leeds U.	—	—
				Bristol C.	—	—
Defenders						
Brian Drysdale	5 7	11 0	Wingate	Lincoln C.	14	—
				Hartlepool	169+1	2
				Bristol C.	269+2	3
Geoff Merrick	5 9	11 0	Bristol	Bristol C.	226+5	8
Garry Collier	6 1	12 0	Bristol	Bristol C.	115	2
David Rodgers	6 1½	13 2	Bristol	Bristol C.	78+2	3
Gerry Sweeney	5 10	10 10	Glasgow	Celtic	—	—
				Morton	137+2	16
				Bristol C.	188+7	19
Charlie Williamson	5 9	9 5	Glasgow	Bristol C.	—	—
Steve Harding	6 2	12 13	Bristol	Bristol C.	2	—
				Southend U. (on loan)	2	—
Brian McNeil	5 9	10 12	Newcastle	Bristol C.	0+2	—
Colin Lee	6 1	11 9	Plymouth	Bristol C.	—	—
				Hereford U. (on loan)	7+2	—
Don Gillies	5 10	11 5	Glencoe	Morton	45+2	23
				Bristol C.	89+12	18
Midfield						
*John Emanuel (Wales)	5 11	13 7	Ferndale	Bristol C.	124+4	10
				Swindon T. (on loan)	6	—
				Gillingham (on loan)	4	—
Trevor Tainton	5 8	11 7	Bristol	Bristol C.	255+23	15
Mike Brolly	5 9	10 4	Galston	Chelsea	7+1	1
				Bristol C.	27+3	2
James Mann	5 6	11 1	Poole	Leeds U.	2	—
				Bristol C.	59+7	13
John Bain	5 7	9 3	Glasgow	Bristol C.	—	—
Gerry Gow	5 8	10 8	Glasgow	Bristol C.	224+3	34
Kevin Mabbutt	5 7	10 2	Bristol	Bristol C.	—	—
Forwards						
Tom Ritchie	5 11	12 8	Scotland	Bristol C.	137+8	32
Paul Cheesley	5 11	11 4	Bristol	Norwich C.	10+3	1
				Bristol C.	58+3	19
Keith Fear	5 7	10 8	Bristol	Bristol C.	109+16	27
Kevin Griffin	5 9	12 0	Plymouth	Bristol C.	5+3	—
				Mansfield T. (on loan)	4	2
				Cambridge U. (on loan)	7+1	1
				(contract cancelled April 1976)		
Shaun Penny	5 8	10 13	Bristol	Bristol C.	—	—
Clive Whitehead	5 9	10 7	Birmingham	Bristol C.	38+10	6
Michael Simmons	5 6	9 9	Bristol	Bristol C.	—	—

BRISTOL ROVERS   DIV. 2

President: Duke of Beaufort.   *Chairman:* D. Mearns Milne.

Directors: H. E. L. Brown, J. P. Hare, C. A. L. Stevens, P. W. Hort, A. I. Seager, E. W. H. Godfrey, G. A. W. Holmes, I. S. P. Stevens.

Team Manager: Don Megson.

Secretary: Peter Terry.

Year Formed: 1883.   *Turned Professional:* 1897.

Limited Company: 1896.

Previous Names: 1883, Black Arabs; 1884, Eastville Rovers; 1897, Bristol Eastville Rovers; 1898, Bristol Rovers.

Previous Grounds: Purdown, Ashley Hill and Ridgeway Ground

Honours: Football League, highest League position: 6th Division 2, 1955–56, 1958–59. Division 3(S), Champions: 1952–53.   Division 3 Runners-up 1973–74   *F.A. Cup,* best season: 6th Rd. 1950–51 and 1957–58

Football League Cup, best season: 5th Rd., 1970–71, 1971–72.

Record Victory: 7-0 v Swansea Town, Division 2, Oct. 2, 1954; v Brighton Division 3(S), Nov. 29, 1952 and v Shrewsbury Town, Division 3, Mar. 21, 1964.

Record Defeat: 0-12 v Luton T., Division 3(S), Apr. 13th, 1936.

Most League Points: 64, Division 3(S), 1952–53.

Most League Goals: 92, Division 3(S), 1952–53.

Highest League Scorer in Season: Geoff Bradford, 33, Division 3(S), 1952–53.

Most League Goals in Total Aggregate: Geoff Bradford, 245, 1949–64.

Most Capped Player: Matt O'Mahoney, 6, Eire, 1, Ireland.

Most League Appearances: Harry Bamford, 487, 1946–58.

Record Transfer Fee Received: £55,000 from Portsmouth for Phil Roberts, May 1973.

Record Transfer Fee Paid: £38,000 to Sheffield U. for Alan Warboys, March 1973.

Managers Since the War: Brough Fletcher, Bert Tann, Fred Ford, Bill Dodgin (Snr).

Address of Supporters Club: 468 Stapleton Road, Bristol.

Address of Club Shop or Boutique: The Rovers Shop, 414 Stapleton Road, Bristol 5.

Bristol Stadium, Eastville, Bristol BS5 6NN. Telephone Bristol 558620.   *Ground capacity:* 39,333 (21,000 covered).   *Record attendance:* 38,472 v Preston N.E., F.A. Cup 4th Rd., January 30, 1960.   *Record receipts:* £16,116 v Stoke F.L. Cup 5th Rd., November 23, 1971. *Pitch measurements:* 112 yds × 76 yds.

How to get there: Buses 44, 45, 11 from Temple Meads Station to Stapleton Rd., five minutes from ground. By car, leave M4 or M5 at M32 junction; M32 runs direct to the ground.

Match tickets: Stand tickets available two weeks prior to the match.

Car parking: Large car parks at Stapleton Rd. and Muller Rd. entrances.

Entertainments/catering facilities: Bars open to the public in both stands. Tea bars on the terraces.

Club shop: In Stapleton Rd.; sells all types of souvenirs.

Handbooks/programmes: Handbooks and programmes available from club shop; programmes can be ordered on subscription.

Extra information: Bristol Rovers went 27 games without defeat in 1952–53, a Third Division (South) record, and 27 games in Division 3 from the start of the season 1973-74 (a Div. 3 record).

Club Colours: Blue and white quartered shirts, white shorts, blue stockings with a white band at top.

Change Colours: White shirts, black shorts and red stockings.

Club Nickname: 'The Pirates'.

BRISTOL ROVERS 1975–76 LEAGUE RECORD

Match No.	Date	Venue	Opponents	Result	H/T Score	League Pos'n	Goalscorers	Attendance
1	Aug 16	A	Oldham Ath.	L 0-2	0-1	—		6993
2	23	H	York C.	W 2-1	0-0	15	Bannister, McMordie (og)	8142
3	30	A	Bristol C.	D 1-1	1-1	14	Bannister	17,918
4	Sept 6	H	Charlton Ath.	D 0-0	0-0	13		7718
5	13	H	Fulham	W 2-0	0-0	10	Warboys 2	11,516
6	20	H	Carlisle U.	L 0-1	0-0	13		8223
7	23	H	Bolton W.	D 2-2	1-1	—	Bannister, Prince	7992
8	26	A	Orient	D 0-0	0-0	11		4978
9	Oct 4	H	Nottingham F.	W 4-2	1-0	9	Prince 2, Powell, Bannister	7689
10	11	A	Hull C.	D 0-0	0-0	9		5642
11	18	H	Sunderland	W 1-0	1-0	7	Bannister	13,577
12	21	A	Portsmouth	W 2-1	0-0	—	Staniforth, Bannister	9078
13	25	A	Blackpool	W 4-1	1-0	4	Smith, Fearnley 2, Bannister (pen)	9019
14	Nov 1	H	Blackburn R.	D 1-1	1-1	5	Staniforth	10,534
15	4	H	W.B.A.	D 1-1	1-1	—	Fearnley	13,105
16	8	A	Notts Co.	D 1-1	1-1	5	Staniforth	10,930
17	15	H	Plymouth Arg.	D 0-0	0-0	4		14,121
18	22	A	Sunderland	D 1-1	1-0	4	Williams	31,356
19	29	H	Chelsea	L 1-2	0-0	4	Williams	16,277
20	Dec 6	A	Oxford U.	L 1-2	0-1	7	Bannister	6532
21	13	A	York C.	D 0-0	0-0	7		3112
22	20	H	Oldham Ath.	W 1-0	0-0	5	Bannister	7389
23	26	A	Southampton	L 0-3	0-1	10		19,556
24	27	H	Luton T.	L 0-1	0-0	10		11,044
25	Jan 10	H	Fulham	W 1-0	0-0	9	Bannister	7863
26	17	A	Charlton Ath.	L 0-3	0-2	9		8598
27	31	H	Portsmouth	W 2-0	2-0	9	Britten, Bannister	6133
28	Feb 7	A	W.B.A.	L 0-3	0-1	10		17,201
29	14	H	Notts Co.	D 0-0	0-0	9		7754
30	21	A	Plymouth Arg.	L 0-3	0-1	10		11,183
31	28	H	Blackpool	D 1-1	1-0	12	Taylor	6686
32	Mar 6	A	Blackburn R.	W 2-1	0-1	10	Staniforth, Bannister	6765
33	13	H	Hull C.	L 0-1	0-0	12		6236
34	20	A	Chelsea	D 0-0	0-0	13		16,132
35	27	H	Oxford U.	L 0-1	0-0	14		5952
36	Apr 3	H	Orient	D 1-1	1-1	16	Bannister (pen)	5182
37	10	A	Carlisle U.	L 2-4	1-1	17	Smith, Staniforth	5928
38	16	H	Bristol C.	D 0-0	0-0	16		26,430
39	17	H	Southampton	W 2-0	2-0	14	Prince 2 (1 a pen)	11,834
40	19	A	Luton T.	L 1-3	1-0	—	Britten	7646
41	24	A	Nottingham F.	L 0-3	0-0	18		12,127
42	27	A	Bolton W.	L 1-3	0-3	—	Warboys	12,815

Goalscorers

League (38): Bannister 13 (2 pens), Prince 5 (1 a pen), Staniforth 5, Fearnley 3, Warboys 3, Britten 2, Smith 2, Williams 2, Powell 1, Taylor 1, own goal 1.

League Cup (5): Warboys, Bannister, Stephens, Fearnley, Staniforth.

F.A. Cup (1): Warboys.

League Cup	First Round	Cardiff C. (a)	2-1
	Second Leg	(h)	1-1
	Second Round	Southampton (a)	1-0
	Third Round	Newcastle U. (h)	1-1
		(a)	0-2
F.A. Cup	Third Round	Chelsea (a)	1-1
		(h)	0-1

Eadie	Smith	Williams	Aitken	Taylor	Prince	Stephens	Stanton	Warboys	Bannister	Evans	Pulis	Fearnley	Day	Bater	Dobson	Britten	Powell	Parsons	Staniforth	Jacobs	Lewis	*Match No.*
1	2	3	4	5	6	7	8	9	10	11												1
1	2	3	4	5	6	8	7	9	10	11												2
1	2	3	4	5	6	7*		9	10	11	8	12										3
1	2	3	4	5	6	7		9	10*	11	8	12										4
1	2	3	6	5	8	7*		9	10	11		12	4									5
1	2	3	6	5	8	7		9	10	11*		12	4									6
1*	2	3		5	8	7		9	10	11		12	4	6								7
1	2	3	6	5	8	7		9	10				4		11							8
1	8	3	2*	5	6	7		9	10				4			11	12					9
1	8	2		5	6	7			10				4			11*	12	3	9			10
1	8	2		5	6	7*		9	10				4			11		3	12			11
1	6	2		5	8				10			7	4		11			3	9			12
1	8	2		5	6				10			7	4		11			3	9			13
1	8	2		5	6				10			7	4		11*	12		3	9			14
1	6	2		5	8			9*	10			7	4			12		3	11			15
1	8	3		5	6	12	7		10			11	4*					2	9			16
1	8	2		5	6	7		9	10			11	4					3				17
1	7	2		5	6		8	9	10			11	4					3				18
1	6	2		5	8	12	7	9*	10			11	4					3				19
1	8	2		5	6		7*	9	10				4	12				3	11			20
1	7	8		5	6			9	10			11	4	2				3				21
1	7	3		5	8			9	10			11	4	2				6				22
1	6	5			11		7		10			8	4	2				3	9			23
1	6	8				7		9	10	11			5	4				3		2		24
1		3	5			7	8		12			9*	4	2	11			6	10			25
1		8	6	5		7		9*	10				4	2	11		12	3				26
1	8	3	4	5	6	7		9	10					2		11						27
1	8	3	4	5	6	7		9	10					2		11*			12			28
1	7	3		5	6			9					4	2	11		8		10			29
1	8			5	6*	7		9	10				4	3	11				12	2		30
1	8	3		5		7		9	10	11	6		4	2								31
1	7	6		5				9	10	11			4					3	8	2		32
1	8	6		5		7		12	10	11			4					3	9	2*		33
1	8*	6		5		7		9	10	12			4					3	11	2		34
1	8	6		5		7			10				4*			11	12	3	9	2		35
1	4	6		5		7*		12	10	9						11		3	8	2		36
1	8	6		5		12		9		11*				4		7		3	10	2		37
1	8	2		5	6	7		9	10				4	3		11						38
1	9	3		5	7	12				10			4	6*		11		2	8			39
1	8*	2		5		12				11	6	10	4			7		3	9			40
1		8	4	5	6	7		9					12			11*		3	10	2		41
	7	4	11*	5	6	12		9	10					2				3	8		1	42
41	39	41	14	39	31	25	8	30	36	15	4	13	32	16	8	12	1	27	20	9	1	
						+ 6s		+ 2s	+ 1s	+ 1s		+ 5s	+ 1s	+ 1s		+ 2s	+ 4s		+ 3s			

BRISTOL ROVERS—PLAYERS

Player and position	Ht.	Wt.	Birthplace	Clubs	League Appearances	Goals
Goalkeepers						
Jim Eadie	6 2	14 1	Kirkintilloch	Cardiff C.	43	—
				Chester (on loan)	6	—
				Bristol R.	142	—
*Paul Lewis	6 1	11 7	Rhondda	Bristol R.	1	—
Glyn Jones	5 11	11 8	Newport	Bristol R.	—	—
Defenders						
Lindsay Parsons	5 9	11 8	Bristol	Bristol R.	328+6	—
*Tom Stanton	5 9	11 9	Edinburgh	Arsenal	—	—
				Mansfield T.	37	1
				Bristol R.	160+11	7
Peter Aitken	6 0	10 11	Penarth	Bristol R.	89+1	—
Stuart Taylor	6 4	14 0	Bristol	Bristol R.	404	24
*Trevor Jacobs	5 9	11 10	Bristol	Bristol C.	130+1	2
				Plymouth Arg. (on loan)	4	—
				Bristol R.	82	3
Phil Bater	5 9	11 0	Cardiff	Bristol R.	46+1	—
Graham Day	6 0	10 6	Bristol	Bristol R.	41+1	—
David Williams	5 9	11 6	Cardiff	Bristol R.	41	2
Tony Pulis	5 10	10 8	Newport	Bristol R.	4	—
Midfield						
Frankie Prince	5 9	11 7	Cardiff	Bristol R.	257+2	20
Wilf Smith	5 10	11 3	Germany	Sheffield W.	206	4
				Coventry C.	132+3	1
				Brighton (on loan)	5	—
				Millwall (on loan)	5	—
				Bristol R.	49	2
Gordon Fearnley	5 10	11 12	Bradford	Sheffield W.	—	—
				Bristol R.	73+26	16
Lawrence Paul	5 9	10 9	Rhondda	Bristol R.	—	—
Martyn Britten	5 7	10 5	Bristol	Bristol R.	15+2	2
Forwards						
Bruce Bannister	5 11	11 3	Yorkshire	Bradford C.	199+9	61
				Bristol R.	184+3	76
Ken Stephens	5 7½	10 12	Bristol	W.B.A.	21+1	2
				Walsall	5+2	—
				Bristol R.	170+9	12
Dave Staniforth	6 0	11 5	Chesterfield	Sheffield U.	22+4	3
				Bristol R.	43+13	9
Colin Dobson	5 8	10 12	Eston	Sheffield W.	177	49
				Huddersfield T.	149+5	50
				Brighton (on loan)	2+2	—
				Bristol R.	62	4
Alan Warboys	6 0	14 5	Goldthorpe	Doncaster R.	39+2	11
				Sheffield W.	66+5	13
				Cardiff C.	57+4	27
				Sheffield U.	7	—
				Bristol R.	115+3	42
Wayne Powell	5 11	11 0	Newport	Bristol R.	1+4	1
Andrew Evans	5 10	10 6	Swansea	Bristol R.	15+1	—
Ray Guscott	5 9	11 2	Newport	Bristol R.	—	—

BURNLEY

Chairman: R. W. Lord.

Directors: Dr. R. D. Iven, M.R.C.S.(Eng.), L.R.C.P. (Lond.), M.R.C.G.P., R. Hargreaves, F.R.V.A., J. Harrison.

Team Manager: Joe Brown.

Secretary: A. Maddox,

Commercial Manager: J. Butterfield.

Year Formed: 1882. *Turned Professional:* 1883.

Limited Company: 1897.

Previous Name: 1881–82, Burnley Rovers.

Previous Grounds: 1881, Calder Vale; 1882, Turf Moor.

Honours: *Football League,* Division 1, Champions: 1920–21, 1959–60; Runners-up: 1919–20, 1961–62. Division 2, Champions: 1897–98, 1972–73; Runners-up: 1912–13, 1946–47. *F.A. Cup,* Winners: 1913–14; Runners-up: 1946–47, 1961–62. *Football League Cup,* best season: Semi-Final, 1960–61, 1968–69.

European Competitions: *European Cup,* 1960-61; *European Fairs Cup,* 1966-67.

Record Victory: 9-0 v Darwen, Division 1, Jan. 9th, 1892, v C. Palace, F.A. Cup, 2nd Rd. Replay 1908–09 and v New Brighton, F.A. Cup, 4th Rd., Jan. 26th, 1957.

Record Defeat: 0-10 v Aston Villa, Division 1, Aug. 29th, 1925 and v Sheffield U., Division 1, Jan. 19th, 1929.

Record 30 consecutive Division 1 games without defeat 1920–21

Most League Points: 62, Division 2, 1972–73.

Most League Goals: 102, Division 1, 1960–61.

Highest League Scorer in Season: George Beel, 35, Division 1, 1927–28.

Most League Goals in Total Aggregate: George Beel, 178, 1923–32.

Most Capped Player: Jimmy McIlroy, 52 (55) Ireland.

Most League Appearances: Jerry Dawson, 530, 1906–29.

Record Transfer Fee Received: £300,000 from Everton for Martin Dobson, August 1974; and from Derby Co. for Leighton James, Nov. 1975.

Record Transfer Fee Paid: £100,000 to Preston N.E. for Tony Morley, Feb. 1976.

Managers Since the War: Cliff Britton, Frank Hill, Alan Brown, Billy Dougall, Harry Potts, Jimmy Adamson.

Address of Club Shop or Boutique: The Claret and Blue Shop, Brunshaw Road, Burnley, Lancs.

Turf Moor, Burnley BB10 4BX. *Telephones: Office:* Burnley (0282) 27777/38021 *Ticket Office and Shop:* Burnley 27777 ext. 46. *Ground capacity:* 38,000. *Record attendance:* 54,775 v Huddersfield T., F.A. Cup 3rd Rd., February 23, 1924. *Record receipts:* £21,619 v Wrexham, F.A. Cup 6th Rd., March 9 1974. *Pitch measurements:* 115 yds × 73 yds.

How to get there: Central bus station and the Central railway station are both within 5 minutes walk of the ground, which is near the town centre.

Match tickets: Bob Lord Stand reserved seats £2.00; Cricket Field Stand (behind goals) £1.50. Pre-match bookings for seats one month prior to game.

Car parking: parks in Church St. and Fulledge Recreation Ground are both chargeable. Each holds about 500 cars, and both are about 5 minutes' walk from stadium.

Entertainments/catering facilities: 'Centre Spot' Social Club underneath Bob Lord Stand—open every night except Monday. Seating for 300. Members and bona-fide guests only on match days. Snack, licensed, hamburger, and chippy bars are sited around the ground and under the stands.

Club shop: Attached to the Development Office in Brunshaw Rd., Burnley. Telephone: Burnley 27777 ext. 46.

Handbooks/programmes: No handbooks. There is a subscription list for League programmes on a seasonal basis; enquiries c/o Club shop.

Club Colours: Claret shirts with sky blue 'V' white shorts and stockings.

Change Colours: White shirts, claret shorts, blue stockings.

Club Captain: Keith Newton.

First Team Trainer: Brian Miller.

Club Nickname: 'Clarets'.

BURNLEY 1975–76 LEAGUE RECORD

Match No.	Date	Venue	Opponents	Result	H/T Score	League Pos'n	Goalscorers	Attendance
1	Aug 16	H	Arsenal	D 0-0	0-0	—		18,603
2	19	H	Everton	D 1-1	0-0	—	Hankin	23,041
3	23	A	West Ham U.	L 2-3	1-0	15	James, Noble	27,075
4	26	A	Ipswich T.	D 0-0	0-0	—		23,548
5	30	H	Middlesbrough	W 4-1	2-1	10	Noble 3, Hankin	17,016
6	Sept 6	A	Derby Co.	L 0-3	0-2	14		24,086
7	13	H	Norwich C.	D 4-4	3-1	16	Noble 4 (2 pens)	15,496
8	20	A	Birmingham C.	L 0-4	0-0	17		25,830
9	23	A	Sheffield U.	L 1-2	1-1	—	Noble	21,477
10	27	H	Leeds U.	L 0-1	0-1	19		23,190
11	Oct 4	A	Coventry C.	W 2-1	0-0	18	Hankin, James	15,432
12	11	A	Manchester C.	D 0-0	0-0	17		35,003
13	18	H	Q.P.R.	W 1-0	0-0	17	Casper	20,409
14	25	A	Aston Villa	D 1-1	0-0	17	Noble	34,242
15	Nov 1	H	Stoke C.	L 0-1	0-0	18		18,269
16	8	A	Leicester C.	L 2-3	1-2	18	Noble (pen), James	18,344
17	15	H	Wolverhampton W.	L 1-5	0-3	20	Hankin	14,559
18	22	A	Q.P.R.	L 0-1	0-0	20		17,390
19	29	A	Tottenham H.	L 1-2	1-0	20	Hankin	21,222
20	Dec 6	H	Liverpool	D 0-0	0-0	21		18,426
21	13	H	West Ham U.	W 2-0	2-0	19	Hankin, Kennerley	14,907
22	20	A	Arsenal	L 0-1	0-0	20		16,459
23	26	H	Newcastle U.	L 0-1	0-0	20		22,458
24	27	A	Manchester U.	L 1-2	1-0	20	Hankin	59,726
25	Jan 10	A	Norwich C.	L 1-3	0-2	21	Newton	18,059
26	17	H	Derby Co.	L 1-2	0-1	21	Fletcher	21,082
27	31	A	Everton	W 3-2	1-0	21	Noble, Flynn, Scott	21,389
28	Feb 7	H	Ipswich T.	L 0-1	0-0	21		17,307
29	14	A	Middlesbrough	D 1-1	1-1	21	Hankin	18,000
30	17	H	Leicester C.	W 1-0	0-0	21	Newton	13,516
31	21	A	Wolverhampton W.	L 2-3	0-1	21	Fletcher, Hankin	19,390
32	24	H	Sheffield U.	W 3-1	1-1	—	Hankin, Scott, Flynn	14,387
33	28	H	Aston Villa	D 2-2	1-2	20	Flynn 2	17,123
34	Mar 6	A	Stoke C.	L 1-4	1-3	20	Hankin	16,065
35	13	H	Manchester C.	D 0-0	0-0	21		24,278
36	20	H	Tottenham H.	L 1-2	0-0	21	Waldron	15,465
37	27	A	Liverpool	L 0-2	0-1	21		36,708
38	Apr 3	A	Leeds U.	L 1-2	1-1	21	Hankin	25,384
39	10	H	Birmingham C.	W 1-0	0-0	21	Hankin	13,668
40	17	A	Newcastle U.	W 1-0	1-0	21	Noble	23,984
41	19	H	Manchester U.	L 0-1	0-0	—		27,411
42	24	H	Coventry C.	L 1-3	1-0	21	Parker	11,636

Goalscorers

League (43): Hankin 13, Noble 13 (3 pens), Flynn 4, James 3, Newton 2, Fletcher 2, Scott 2, Casper 1, Kennerley 1, Waldron 1, Parker 1.
League Cup (8): Noble 4 (1 a pen), Flynn 2, Morgan (1 a pen), Hankin.

League Cup	Second Round	Hereford U. (a)	4-1
	Third Round	Liverpool (a)	1-1
		(h)	1-0
	Fourth Round	Leicester C. (h)	2-0
	Fifth Round	Middlesbrough (h)	0-2
F.A. Cup	Third Round	Blackpool (a)	0-1

Stevenson	Docherty	Newton	Noble	Waldron	Thomson	Morgan	Hankin	Summerbee	Collins	James	Flynn	Brennan	Ingham	Casper	Fletcher	Bradshaw	Peyton	Kennerley	Loggie	Scott	Morris	Rodaway	Morley	Pashley	Jakub	Parker	Match No.
1	2	3	4*	5	6	7	8	9	10	11	12																1
1	2	3	4	5	6		8	9	10*	11	7	12															2
1	2	3	4	5	6	12	8	9	10*	11	7																3
1	2	3	4	5	6		8	9	10	11	7																4
1	2	3	4	5	6	7	8	9	10	11																	5
1	2	3	7	5	6	4	8	9	10	11																	6
1		3	4	5	6		8	9	10	11	7	2															7
1	2	7	5	6			8	9	10*	11	4	3	12														8
1	2	3	4	5	6		8	9		11	7		10														9
1	2	3		5	6	4	8	9		11	7		10														10
1	2	3	10	5	6	4	8*	9		11	7		12														11
1	2	3	4	5	6	7	8	9		11	10																12
1		3	4	5	6	7		9		11	10			2	8												13
1	2	3	8	5	6		7			11	4			10	9												14
1	2	3	4	5	6		7			11	10			8	9												15
1	2	3	9*	5	6	10	8	7		11	4		12														16
1	2*	3		5	6	7	8	9	10	11	4		12														17
1	2	3		5	6	7		9	8	10	4				11												18
1	2	3		5	6	7		9	8	10*	4				11	12											19
	2	3		5	6			9	7	10	4				11		1	8									20
	2	3		5	6			9	7	10	4				11		1	8									21
	2	3		5	6			9	7	10	4				11		1	8									22
	2	3	12	5*	6			9	7	10	4				11		1	8									23
	2	3		5	6		8	9	7		4*		10	12	11		1										24
1	2	3		5	6		8				4				11		7			9	10						25
		3	11	5	6		8				4		10		7		1	9		2							26
		3	8	5	6					11	4				9		1			2		7	10				27
		3	11	5	6	9	8				4		10				1			2		7					28
		3	8*	5	6			9	7		12		10				1			2		4	11				29
		3		5	6		8			11			10		9		1			2		4	7				30
		3		5	6		8			11	12		10*		9		1			2		4	7				31
1		3		5	6		8			11			10		9					2		7	4				32
1		3		5	6		8			11			10		9					2		7	4				33
		3		5	6		8			11	12		10		9		1			2		7	4*				34
		3		5			8	9			4		10		11		1			2		6	7				35
		3		5			8	9			4		10		11		1			2		6	7				36
		3	4	5			8	9					10		11		1			2		6	7				37
		3*	10	5			8	9			12		4		11		1			2		7	6				38
			10	5			8	9			4				11		1			2		7	6	3			39
		3		5			8	9			4		10		11		1			2		7	6				40
		3	4	5			8	9*			12		10		11		1			2		7	6				41
		3		5		7		9			4						1			2		6	10		8	11	42
22	22	41	25	36	40	12	34	39	14	17	37	2	14	4	17	8	20	6	1	17	8	15	8	1	1	1	

+1s (Noble)   +1s (Thomson)   +2s (Flynn) +1s (Brennan) +6s (Ingham) +2s (Casper)   +1s (Fletcher)   +1s (Rodaway)

BURNLEY—PLAYERS

Player and position	Ht.	Wt.	Birthplace	Clubs	League Appearances	Goals
Goalkeepers						
*Michael Finn	5 7¼	11 5½	Liverpool	Burnley	4	—
Alan Stevenson	6 1	12 2½	Staveley	Chesterfield	104	—
				Burnley	160	—
Gerry Peyton	6 2	13 11	Birmingham	Burnley	20	—
Defenders						
Terry Pashley	5 8	10 12	Chesterfield	Burnley	1	—
Keith Newton	5 11	11 2	Manchester	Blackburn	307	9
(England)				Everton	49+1	1
				Burnley	161	4
Ian Brennan	5 10	11 4½	Easington	Burnley	37+1	1
*Richard Dixey	6 0	12 1	Wigston	Burnley	3	—
				Stockport Co. (on loan)	14	1
Jim Thomson	5 11½	12 0	Glasgow	Chelsea	33+6	1
				Burnley	172+3	2
Colin Waldron	6 0	11 6	Bristol	Bury	20	—
				Chelsea	9	—
				Burnley	308	16
				(contract cancelled April 1976)		
Derek Scott	5 8	11 12	Gateshead	Burnley	19	2
William Rodaway	5 9	12 12	Liverpool	Burnley	54+1	1
Midfield						
Wilf Wrigley	5 9½	11 8	Clitheroe	Burnley	6	1
Peter Noble	5 9	10 6	Newcastle	Newcastle U	22+3	7
				Swindon T.	212+4	62
				Burnley	107+2	25
Brian Flynn	5 2	8 8	Port Talbot	Burnley	62+5	4
(Wales)						
David Loggie	6 0	11 8	Newbiggin	Burnley	1	—
William Ingham	5 5½	9 10	Stakeford	Burnley	81+25	7
Joe Jakub	5 6	9 3	Falkirk	Burnley	1	—
Forwards						
Paul Bradshaw	5 6½	10 4	Sheffield	Burnley	8+2	—
*Frank Casper	5 9½	10 7	Barnsley	Rotherham U.	99	26
				Burnley	231+7	74
Paul Fletcher	5 9½	12 10	Bolton W.	Bolton W.	33+3	5
				Burnley	180	51
Colin Morris	5 6	10 1	Blyth	Burnley	9+1	—
Ray Hankin	5 10	10 10	Wallsend	Burnley	104+2	35
Derek Parker	5 9	9 11	Wallsend	Burnley	5+1	2
Mike Summerbee	5 10½	11 4	Preston	Swindon T.	218	39
(England)				Manchester C.	355+2	46
				Burnley	39	—
Tony Morley	5 7	10 0	Ormskirk	Preston N.E.	78+6	15
				Burnley	8+1	—
Glynn Chamberlain	5 8	10 7	Chesterfield	Burnley	—	—

BURY

Chairman: W. H. Allen.

Vice-Chairman: R. A. Clarke B.Sc.Tech., F.I.O.B.

Directors: G. Black, Canon J. R. Smith.

Team Manager: Bobby Smith.

Secretary: Gordon Hurst.

Year Formed: 1885. *Turned Professional:* 1885.

Limited Company: 1897.

Honours: *Football League,* Highest League Position: 4th, Division 1, 1925–26. Division 2, Champions: 1894–95; Runners-up: 1923–24. Division 3, Champions: 1960–61; Runners-up: 1967–68. *F.A. Cup,* Winners, 1900, 1903. *Football League Cup,* best season, semi-finalists: 1963.

Record Victory: 12-1 v Stockton, F.A. Cup, 1st Rd. Replay, 1896–97.

Record Defeat: 0-10 v Blackburn R., F.A. Cup, 1887–88.

Most League Points: 68, Division 3, 1960–61.

Most League Goals: 108, Division 3, 1960–61.

Highest League Scorer in Season: Norman Bullock, 31, Division 1, 1925–26.

Most League Goals in Total Aggregate: Norman Bullock, 124, 1920–35.

Most Capped Player: Bill Gorman, 11 (14), Eire and (4), Ireland.

Most League Appearances: 506, Norman Bullock, 1920–35.

Record Transfer Fee Received: £68,000 from Liverpool for Alec Lindsay, Mar. 1969.

Record Transfer Fee Paid: £25,000 to Motherwell for Jim McIlwraith, Dec. 1975.

Managers Since the War: Norman Bullock, John McNeil, Dave Russell, Bob Stokoe, Bert Head, Les Shannon, Jack Marshall, Les Hart, Colin McDonald, Tom McAnearney, Allan Brown.

Address of Club Shop or Boutique: Bury F.C., Souvenir Shop, Gigg Lane.

Gigg Lane, Bury BL9 9HR. Telephone 061-764 4881/2. *Ground capacity:* 35,000. *Record attendance:* 35,000 v Bolton, F.A. Cup 3rd Rd., January 9, 1960. *Record receipts:* £7,423 v Leeds U., League Cup 3rd Rd., Oct. 9 1974. *Pitch measurements:* 112 yds × 72 yds.

How to get there: Buses 1, 2, 29, 35, 37, 38, 48, 52 from Kay Gardens to within walking distance. The nearest railway station is Bury. Buses run from the station to the ground.

Match tickets: 500 seats in the Reserved Chair section of the main stand may be booked two weeks before the match.

Car parking: Season-ticket holders only may use the car park on match days. But there is ample parking space in the side-streets around the ground.

Entertainments/catering facilities: Social club open during normal licensing hours.

Club shop: At the ground; sells all types of souvenirs.

Handbooks/programmes: Programmes available from club shop.

Extra information: The social club has large dance hall, lounge, and cocktail bars. These facilities may be hired for private functions; tel. 061-764-6771.

Club Colours: White shirts, royal blue shorts, royal blue stockings with white band.

Change Colours: Yellow shirts, yellow shorts, yellow stockings.

Club Captain: John Hulme.

First Team Trainer: Les Hart.

Club Nickname: 'Shakers'.

BURY 1975–76 LEAGUE RECORD

Match No.	Date	Venue	Opponents	Result	H/T Score	League Pos'n	Goalscorers	Attendance
1	Aug 16	H	Gillingham	W 2-0	0-0	—	Hulme, Rowland (pen)	3932
2	23	A	Cardiff C.	D 1-1	0-1	4	Riley	6664
3	30	H	Aldershot	D 1-1	0-1	3	Spence	4372
4	Sept 6	A	Rotherham U.	D 3-3	2-2	7	Spence 2, Rowland	4070
5	13	H	Chesterfield	W 3-1	0-1	4	Spence, Rowland, Hamstead	4368
6	20	A	Walsall	W 1-0	0-0	2	Hulme	4845
7	23	H	Mansfield T.	W 2-1	1-0	—	Rowland, Phillips	5896
8	27	H	Millwall	W 2-0	1-0	2	McIlwraith, Phillips	5682
9	Oct 4	A	Colchester U.	D 0-0	0-0	2		3035
10	11	H	Southend U.	W 1-0	0-0	2	Williams	6268
11	18	A	Peterborough U.	L 0-4	0-2	3		7271
12	21	H	Swindon T.	W 5-0	4-0	—	Rowland 2 (1 a pen), Phillips, Hulme, Williams	5737
13	25	H	Halifax T.	D 0-0	0-0	2		7516
14	Nov 1	A	Grimsby T.	D 0-0	0-0	2		5189
15	4	A	Brighton & H.A.	L 1-2	1-2	—	Smith	14,603
16	8	H	Wrexham	L 0-1	0-0	4		6063
17	15	A	Preston N.E.	D 0-0	0-0	3		11,017
18	29	A	Hereford U.	L 0-2	0-1	5		6867
19	Dec 6	H	Crystal Palace	L 0-1	0-0	6		10,035
20	20	A	Shrewsbury T.	W 3-1	0-1	5	Rowland, Williams, Buchan	3735
21	26	H	Sheffield W.	D 0-0	0-0	4		9657
22	27	A	Port Vale	L 1-2	1-1	7	Riley	5376
23	Jan 10	A	Aldershot	D 1-1	0-0	7	Hulme	4202
24	17	H	Walsall	D 1-1	1-0	7	Rowland	8068
25	31	A	Swindon T.	L 1-2	1-1	12	Rowland	5408
26	Feb 7	H	Brighton & H.A.	D 1-1	0-0	15	Williams	6217
27	11	A	Chesterfield	L 2-3	1-1	—	Rowland 2	3024
28	14	A	Wrexham	L 1-2	0-1	16	Rowland	3109
29	21	H	Preston N.E.	W 2-0	1-0	14	Rowland 2	7049
30	23	A	Mansfield T.	D 1-1	0-1	—	Spence	6610
31	28	A	Halifax T.	W 2-0	2-0	11	Woolfall, Rowland	3606
32	Mar 6	H	Grimsby T.	D 1-1	0-1	11	McIlwraith	4821
33	13	A	Southend U.	L 0-2	0-0	13		3844
34	16	H	Peterborough U.	W 2-1	1-0	—	Hoolickin, Rowland	4493
35	20	H	Hereford U.	L 2-3	0-1	14	Williams, Buchan	6384
36	27	A	Crystal Palace	L 0-1	0-0	14		21,328
37	30	H	Shrewsbury T.	W 2-1	0-1	—	Spence, Irvine (og)	4626
38	Apr 3	A	Gillingham	L 0-2	0-2	13		4732
39	7	A	Millwall	D 0-0	0-0	—		10,001
40	10	H	Rotherham U.	W 4-0	1-0	14	Spence 2, Buchan, MIlwraith	5141
41	12	H	Colchester U.	D 0-0	0-0	—		4505
42	16	A	Chester	D 0-0	0-0	—		5045
43	17	A	Sheffield W.	L 0-1	0-0	13		10,585
44	19	H	Port Vale	L 1-2	1-1	—	Spence	4609
45	27	H	Chester	W 1-0	0-0	—	Woolfall	3748
46	May 4	H	Cardiff C.	L 0-1	0-1	—		7135

Goalscorers

League (51): Rowland 16 (2 pens), Spence 9, Williams 5, Hulme 4, Phillips 3, McIlwraith 3, Buchan 3, Riley 2, Woolfall 2, Hamstead 1, Smith 1, Hoolickin 1, own goal 1.
League Cup (5): Nicholson 2, Rowland 2, Spence.
F.A. Cup (10): Rowland 3, Riley, Hamstead, Kennedy, Buchan, McIlwraith, Hulme, own goal 1.

League Cup	First Round	Rochdale (h)	2-0
	Second Leg	(a)	2-0
	Second Round	Middlesbrough (h)	1-2
F.A. Cup	First Round	Doncaster R. (h)	4-2
	Second Round	Spennymoor (h)	3-0
	Third Round	Middlesbrough (a)	0-0
		(h)	3-2
	Fourth Round	Leicester C. (a)	0-1

Forrest	Keenan	Kennedy	Nicholson	Hulme	Bailey	Buchan	Williams	Rowland	Phillips	Hamstead	Riley	Hoolickin	Spence	Rudd	Woolfall	McIlwraith	Smith	Farrell	Brown	Thomson	Match No.
1	2	3	4	5	6	7	8	9	10	11*	12										1
1		3	4	5	6		11*	8	10		7	2	9	12							2
1		3	4	5	6	7*12	8	11	10			2	9								3
1		3	4	5	6		8	10	7	11*		2	9	12							4
1		3	4	5	6		7	10	8	11		2	9								5
1		3	4	5	6		7	8	10	11*12		2	9								6
1		3	4	5	6		7	10	8	11		2			12	9*					7
1		3	4	5	6		7	10	11	8		2			12	9*					8
1		3	4	5	6		11	9	7	10		2	8								9
1		3	4	5	6	7*11	8	9		10		2			12						10
1		3	4	5	6		11	8	7	10		2	9*12								11
1		3	4	5	6		7	9	10	8	11	2									12
1		3	4	5	6	12	11	9	8	10		2				7*					13
1		3	4	5	6		9	11	8	10		2				7					14
1		3	4	5	6	12	9	8	10*	11		2				7					15
1		3	4	5	6	12	9	8	10*	11		2				7					16
1		3	4	5	6		10	9	7	11		2				8					17
1		3	4	5	6		9	10	8	11	7	2									18
1		3	4*	5	6		11	10	8	12		2	9			7					19
1		3	12	5	6	7*	4	8		10		2	9		11						20
1		3		5	6	7	11	9	4			2	10		8						21
1		3	4	5	6	7	10	9			8	2	11								22
1	12	3		5	6*		11	9	4			2	10	8	7						23
1		3		5	6	12	11	9	4*			2	10	8	7						24
1		3		5	6			8		10	12	2	9	4	11*	7					25
1		3	5*	6			11	9		10	4	2	8		7	12					26
1		3		6	12		11	10		8*	4	2	7	9					5		27
1	4	3	12	5*	6			10	9	11			8	7				2			28
1		3	4	5	6	12	11	9	7			2	10	8*							29
1		3	4	5	6		11	9	8		12	2	10	7*							30
1		3	4	5	6		11	9	8			2	10*		7	12					31
1		3	4	5	6		11	9	8			2	10*		7	12					32
1		3	4	5	6	12	11	9	10			2			7*	8					33
1		3	4	5	6	7	11	9	8			2	10								34
1		3	4*	5	6	7	11	9	8			2	10			12					35
1		3	4	5	6	7	11	9	8			2	10								36
1		3	4*	5	6	7	11	9	8		12	2	10								37
1		3		5	6	7	11	9	8		4*	2	10			12					38
1		3		5	6	7	11	9	8			2	10	4							39
1		3*		5	6	7	11	9	8			2	10	12	4						40
1		3		5	6	7	11	9*	8			2	10	12	4						41
1		3	4	5	6		11	9	8				10		7				2		42
1	12	3		5	6		11	9	8				10		7*	4			2		43
1		3		5	6	7	11	9	8				10			4			2		44
1		3		5			11	9	8		12		10*		7		4		2	6	45
1		3		5			11	9	8		12	2		4*	7	10				6	46
46	2	46	30	45	44	16	45	46	41	5	20	41	29	7	10	19	5	1	5	3	
	+2s		+2s			+7s	+1s		+1s	+3s	+4s				+2s	+6s	+4s	+1s			

117

BURY—PLAYERS

Player and position	Ht.	Wt.	Birthplace	Clubs	League Appearances	Goals
Goalkeepers						
Colin Darcy	6 3	13 9	Wirral	Everton	—	—
				Bury	4	—
John Forrest	5 9	11 6	Bury	Bury	241	—
Defenders						
Tony Bailey	5 10	11 2	Burton	Derby Co.	1	—
				Oldham Ath.	26	1
				Bury	65+1	1
Steve Hoolickin	5 11	11 2	Manchester	Oldham Ath.	8	—
				Bury	130	4
John Thomson	5 11	12 3	Newcastle	Newcastle U.	—	—
				Bury	19+5	—
John Hulme	6 0½	12 1	Mobberley	Bolton W.	186+2	7
				Notts Co. (on loan)	8	—
				Reading	86+1	—
				Bury	86	5
Keith Kennedy	5 7	10 8	Sunderland	Newcastle U.	1	—
				Bury	168	2
Gerry Keenan	5 9	11 2	Liverpool	Bury	3+2	—
Malcolm Brown	6 2	12 6	Salford	Bury	5	—
Midfield						
*Billy Rudd	5 6	10 3	Manchester	Manchester U.	—	—
				Birmingham C.	24	3
				York C.	193	30
				Grimsby T.	59+1	9
				Rochdale	108	8
				Bury	155+12	17
*George Buchan	5 7	10 11	Aberdeen	Manchester U.	0+3	—
				Bury	57+8	6
				Motherwell (on loan)	—	—
*Jimmy Nicholson	5 9	11 8	Belfast	Manchester U.	58	5
(N. Ireland)				Huddersfield T.	280+1	26
				Bury	79+4	—
Peter Farrell	5 7	9 12	Liverpool	Bury	1+1	—
Ron Phillips	5 6½	10 3	Worsley	Bolton W.	135+9	17
				Chesterfield (on loan)	5	—
				Bury	41+1	3
Forwards						
George Hamstead	5 6½	10 13	Rotherham	Rotherham U.	—	—
				York C.	32+3	1
				Barnsley	147+2	23
				Bury	165+7	28
Derek Spence	6 0	11 0	Belfast	Oldham Ath.	5+1	—
(N. Ireland)				Bury	131	42
Brian Williams	5 7	10 13	Manchester	Bury	116+11	16
Andy Rowland	5 9	11 6	Derby	Derby Co.	—	—
				Bury	76+5	26
Alan Woolfall	5 6	9 12	Liverpool	Bury	10+8	2
Jimmy McIlwraith				Motherwell	21+7	2
				Bury	19+4	3
Brian Stanton	5 7	10 7	Liverpool	Bury	—	—

CAMBRIDGE UNITED   DIV. 4

Chairman: D. A. Ruston.

Vice-Chairman: S. Tanner.

Directors: S. J. Starr, A. Douglas, B. Moore, R. H. Smart, A. E. Harris.

Manager: Ron Atkinson.   *Secretary:* J. C. Benson.

Asst. Manager: Paddy Sowden.

Year Formed: 1919.   *Turned Professional:* 1946.

Limited Company: 1948.

Previous Name: Abbey United until 1949.

Honours: Football League, highest position: 21st, Division 3, 1973–74. *F.A. Cup,* best season: 2nd Rd., 1953–54, 1970–71, 1971–72. *Football League Cup* never beyond 1st Rd.

Record Victory: 6-0 v Darlington, Sept. 18, 1971.

Record Defeat: 0-6 v Aldershot, Division 3, April 13 1974, and v Darlington, Division 4, September 28 1974.

Most League Points: 57, Division 4, 1972–73.

Most League Goals: 67, 1972–73.

Highest League Scorer in a Season: Brian Greenhalgh, 19, 1971–72.

Most League Goals in Total Aggregate: Brian Greenhalgh, 47, 1971–74.

Most Capped Player: None.

Most League Appearances: Terry Eades, 240, 1970–76.

Record Transfer Fee Received: £35,000 from AFC Bournemouth for Brian Greenhalgh Feb 8, 1974.

Record Transfer Fee Paid: £22,000 to Oxford United for Nigel Cassidy, March 1974; and to Walsall for Bobby Shinton, March 1974.

Managers Since the War: Bill Whittaker, Gerald Williams, Bert Johnson, Roy Kirk, Alan Moore, Bill Leivers.

Address of Supporters Club: 530, Newmarket Rd., Cambridge.

Abbey Stadium, Newmarket Rd., Cambridge. Telephone Teversham (02205) 2170. *Ground capacity:* 12,000. *Record attendance:* 14,000 v Chelsea, Friendly, May 1, 1970. *Record receipts:* £3392 v Mansfield T., April 23, 1973. *Pitch measurements:* 115 yds × 75 yds.

How to get there: Nearest railway station; Cambridge. Buses 180 and 181 run from the station to the town centre; then buses 182 and 183 to the ground, which is situated on the east side of the city.

Match tickets: Reserved seats bookable 14 days in advance. Postal applications must be accompanied by remittance and S.A.E.

Car parking: Limited parking at main entrance; off-street parking allowed, and at Coldhams Common.

Entertainments/catering facilities: Entertainments each evening organised by Supporters' Club. Three canteens open in the ground on match days.

Club shop: Two shops, one at the main entrance, the other inside the ground.

Handbooks/programmes: Handbooks not available.

Extra information: Cambridge are the second youngest professional club in the Football League; they turned professional in 1946.

Club Colours: Amber shirts with black collar and cuffs, black shorts, amber stockings.

Change Colours: White.

CAMBRIDGE UNITED 1975–76 LEAGUE RECORD

Match No.	Date	Venue	Opponents	Result	H/T Score	League Pos'n	Goalscorers	Attendance
1	Aug 16	A	Doncaster R.	W 2-0	0-0	—	Horsfall, Biley	2990
2	23	H	Bradford C.	D 0-0	0-0	4		3027
3	30	A	Swansea C.	L 0-1	0-0	9		2082
4	Sept 6	H	Stockport Co.	L 0-1	0-1	16		2677
5	13	A	Exeter C.	W 2-1	1-0	13	Hodge (og), Lill	2471
6	20	H	Huddersfield T.	D 0-0	0-0	10		3150
7	23	H	Watford	W 4-1	2-1	—	Cassidy 2, Spriggs, Shinton	3234
8	27	A	Newport Co.	L 0-2	0-0	13		2244
9	Oct 4	H	Darlington	W 1-0	1-0	8	Griffin	2695
10	11	H	Crewe Alex.	D 1-1	1-1	9	Horsfall	2835
11	18	A	Workington	L 0-1	0-1	10		1122
12	21	A	Lincoln C.	L 2-4	1-3	—	Tully, Howell	3330
13	25	H	Brentford	W 2-1	1-1	12	Horsfall 2	2596
14	Nov 1	A	AFC Bournemouth	L 0-3	0-1	13		4863
15	4	H	Scunthorpe U.	W 1-0	0-0	—	Watson (pen)	1526
16	8	H	Northampton T.	L 0-1	0-0	14		5560
17	14	A	Rochdale	D 1-1	0-1	14	Lyon	1562
18	29	A	Southport	W 4-2	2-1	13	Horsfall 2, Simmons, Lyon	1001
19	Dec 6	H	Tranmere R.	D 3-3	1-1	13	Simmons, Horsfall 2	2588
20	13	A	Darlington	D 1-1	0-0	13	Simmons	1184
21	20	H	Barnsley	D 1-1	1-0	13	Batson	2180
22	26	A	Reading	L 0-1	0-1	14		7783
23	27	H	Torquay U.	W 2-1	2-0	12	Simmons, Horsfall	2921
24	Jan 1	A	Stockport Co.	W 1-0	1-0	9	Eades	2789
25	10	H	Swansea C.	W 3-1	3-1	7	Horsfall 2, Shinton	2534
26	17	A	Huddersfield T.	L 0-2	0-0	8		5195
27	24	H	Exeter C.	L 0-1	0-0	12		2188
28	31	A	Lincoln C.	L 0-3	0-0	12		7440
29	Feb 7	H	Scunthorpe U.	D 2-2	0-0	13	Lyon, Biley	1777
30	14	A	Northampton T.	L 2-4	1-1	15	Simmons, Spriggs	5969
31	18	A	Hartlepool	D 2-2	1-2	—	Lyon, Seddon	1400
32	21	H	Rochdale	D 0-0	0-0	12		2048
33	24	A	Watford	L 0-1	0-1	—		4888
34	28	A	Brentford	D 0-0	0-0	12		4080
35	Mar 6	H	AFC Bournemouth	L 0-1	0-1	15		2055
36	13	A	Crewe Alex.	W 2-1	2-0	14	Shinton, Horsfall	2009
37	15	H	Workington	W 4-1	2-1	—	Seddon, Lyon, Watson, Spriggs	1415
38	20	H	Southport	D 2-2	0-1	12	O'Donnell, Biley	1789
39	26	A	Tranmere R.	L 2-3	0-3	13	Lyon, Horsfall	4005
40	30	A	Barnsley	L 0-4	0-1	—		3006
41	Apr 3	H	Doncaster R.	D 3-3	2-1	14	Horsfall, Smith, Shinton	1633
42	6	H	Newport Co.	L 0-1	0-0	—		1361
43	16	H	Hartlepool	W 4-0	3-0	16	Lyon 2, Shinton, Smith	2136
44	19	A	Torquay U.	D 0-0	0-0	—		3090
45	21	H	Reading	D 2-2	1-2	—	Spriggs, Fallon	3245
46	24	A	Bradford C.	W 2-1	1-1	13	Horsfall, Lyon	2320

Goalscorers

League (58): Horsfall 15, Lyon 9, Shinton 5, Simmons 5, Spriggs 4, Biley 3, Cassidy 2, Seddon 2, Smith 2, Watson 2 (1 a pen), Batson 1, Eades 1, Fallon 1, Griffin 1, Howell 1, Lill 1, O'Donnell 1, Tully 1, Own Goal 1. *League Cup* (1): Biley.

League Cup	First Round	Charlton Ath. (h)	1-1
	Second Leg	(a)	0-3
F.A. Cup	First Round	Leatherhead (a)	0-2

Team line-up / appearance grid (shirt numbers by player and match). An asterisk (*) denotes a substitute appearance.

Smith, G.	Howell	Batson	Lyon	Eades	Smith, P.	Watson	Shinton	Horsfall	Cassidy	Spriggs	Biley	Fallon	Tully	Lill	Griffin	Walker	Seary	Gilder	Simmons	O'Donnell	Cleary	Seddon	Tuddenham	Baldry	Match No.
1	2	3*	4	5	6	7	8	9	10	11	12														1
1	2	6	5	3	4	7	8	9*	10	11	12														2
1	2	3	4		7	6	9	10*	12	8		5		11											3
1	2	6	4	5	7	8	11	9*	10					3	12										4
1	2		4	5	6	7	11			9	8			3	10										5
1	2	6	4		7		11			9	8	5		3	10										6
1	2	7	3	4	6		11			9	8	5			10										7
1	2	7	6	3	4*		10	12	9	8		5		11											8
1	2	7	4		6		11			9	8	5		3	10										9
1	2	8	4		6		11	9			5	7		3	10										10
1	2	7	4		6		11			9	8	5	12	3	10*										11
1	2	6	4		7*		9	10	12	8		5	11	3											12
1	2	6		5		7	10	9		8		4	11	3											13
1	2	6		5		7	10	9	4	8		12	11*	3											14
	2		4	5		7	11	9*	8	10		6			1	3	12								15
	2	6		5		7	11	10		8		4			1	3		9							16
	2	6	4	5			11	10		8		7			1	3		9							17
1	2	6	4	5	7		11	9		8					3	10									18
1	2	6	4	5	7		11*	10		8		12			3	9									19
1	2	6	4	5	12		10*	8		7		11			3	9									20
1	2	7	4	5			11			8		10*	6		3	9	12								21
1		2	4	5			11	7		8					3	9	6	10							22
1		2	4	5			11	7		8					3	9	6	10							23
1	12	2	4	5			11	7		8					3	9	6*	10							24
1	2	6	4	5		7	11	9		8					3			10							25
1	2	6	4	5		7*	11	10		8					3	9		12							26
	12	2	4	5		7*	11	10		6					1	3	9	8							27
	2	6	4	5	7		11	10		8		3				1		9*	12						28
	2	6	4	5		7	11	10		8*	12	3				1		9							29
1	2		4	5			11	10		8	7	3			12			9	6*						30
		4	5				10	7		8	11	3			1		9	2	6						31
		4	5				10	7		8	11	3			1		9	2	6						32
12		2	4	5			10	9		8	11	3			1	7*			6						33
	2		4	5		11	10	9		8		3			1		7		6						34
	2		4	5		11	10	7		8	12	3			1		9*		6						35
		3	4	5		11	10	9		7	8				1		2		6						36
	4	9	5			11	10	7		8		3			1		2		6						37
	4	9	5			11*	10	7		8	12	3			1		2		6						38
	4	9	5			11	10	7		8		3			1		2		6						39
	4	9				11	10	7		8	12	3			1		2*		6	5					40
	2	5	9		6		10	7		8	11	4			1		3								41
	2	5	9		6		10	7		8	11	4			1		3								42
1		4	9		6		7	10		8		5										11	2	3	43
1		4	9		6		7	10		8		5										11	2	3	44
1		4			6	9	7	10		8		5							12			11	2*	3	45
1	2		10		4	7	9	11		8		6										5		3	46
28	29	41	41	33	20	22	45	39	9	45	7	33	5	12	7	18	16	—	16	13	5	14	4	4	
+3s					+1s		+1s	+2s		+5s	+3s	+1s		+1s		+1s	+1s	+1s			+3s				

CAMBRIDGE UNITED—PLAYERS

Player and position	Ht.	Wt.	Birthplace	Clubs	League Appearances	Goals
Goalkeepers						
Graham Smith	5 11	12 0	Liverpool	Notts Co.	10	—
				Colchester U.	94	—
				W.B.A.	10	—
				Cambridge U.	85	—
Phil Walker	6 1	12 8	Sheffield	Sheffield U.	—	—
				Cambridge U.	19	—
Defenders						
Brendan Batson	5 10	11 7	Trinidad	Arsenal	6+4	—
				Cambridge U.	91+1	6
David Lyon	6 3½	14 7	Northwich	Bury	65+6	—
				Huddersfield T.	24+1	—
				Mansfield T. (on loan)	2	—
				Cambridge U.	83	11
*John O'Donnell	5 10	11 10	Leeds	Leeds U.	—	—
				Cambridge U.	79	8
				Colchester U. (on loan)	1	—
Terry Eades	6 1	12 1	Banbridge, N.I.	Cambridge U.	240	5
Steve Fallon	6 1	11 2	Whittlesey	Cambridge U.	39+5	1
*Graham Howell	5 8	10 13	Manchester	Manchester C.	—	—
				Bradford C.	45	—
				Brighton	40+4	—
				Cambridge U.	68+3	3
*Ray Seary	5 9	10 7	Wallingford	Q.P.R.	0+1	—
				Cambridge U.	55+2	—
Tony Tuddenham	5 10	11 9	Reepham	Cambridge U.	4	—
William Baldry	6 0	11 10	Luton	Cambridge U.	4	—
Midfield						
*Paul Smith	5 5	10 0	Doncaster	Huddersfield T.	1	—
				Cambridge U.	35+3	3
Stephen Spriggs	5 2	9 0	Doncaster	Huddersfield T.	2+2	—
				Cambridge U.	45	4
Graham Watson	5 9	10 7	Doncaster	Doncaster R.	152+4	34
				Cambridge U.	151+2	12
*David Lill	6 0	12 12	Aldbrough	Hull C.	16+2	2
				Rotherham U.	33+7	5
				Cambridge U.	156+6	22
*George Cleary	5 7	10 3	Bedford	Cambridge U.	5+3	—
Forwards						
*Nigel Cassidy	5 10	12 6	Sudbury	Norwich C.	2+1	—
				Scunthorpe U.	88	35
				Oxford U.	111+3	33
				Cambridge U.	52+2	13
Bobby Shinton	5 11	11 0	West Bromwich	Walsall	78+1	20
				Cambridge U.	99	25
Thomas Horsfall	5 9	11 11	Hamilton	Southend U.	11+5	1
				Bury (on loan)	0+1	—
				Scunthorpe U. (on loan)	5	2
				Cambridge U.	57+3	22
*Carl Gilder	5 11	11 0	Newport	Cambridge U.	0+2	—
Alan Biley	5 8	10 9	Leighton Buzzard	Luton T.	—	—
				Cambridge U.	7+5	3
Dave Simmons	5 11	12 13	Gosport	Arsenal	—	—
				Bournemouth	7	3
				Aston Villa	13+4	7
				Walsall (on loan)	5	2
				Colchester U.	52+5	11
				Cambridge U.	19+5	3
				Brentford	47+5	17
				Cambridge U.	16+1	5
Keith Bowker	5 9	10 7	W. Bromwich	Birmingham C.	19+2	5
				Exeter C.	110	38
				Cambridge U.	—	—

122

CARDIFF CITY   DIV. 2

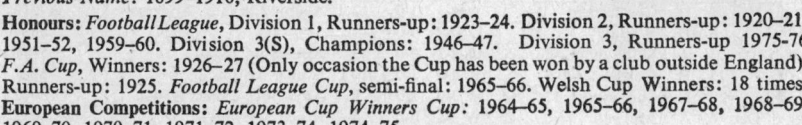

Chairman: Stefan Terlezki, M.H.C.I.

Vice-Chairman: J. A. Clemo, Dip.P.E.

Directors: C. Griffiths, R. Grogan, W. J. Jarvis, E. Jones, J. Latner, J. P. Leonard.

Team Manager: Jimmy Andrews.

Asst. Manager: Ken Whitfield.

Secretary: L. G. Hayward.

Year Formed: 1899.   *Turned Professional:* 1910.

Limited Company: 1910.

Previous Grounds: Riverside, Sophia Gardens, Old Park and Fir Gardens. Moved to Ninian Park, 1910.

Previous Name: 1899–1910, Riverside.

Honours: *Football League,* Division 1, Runners-up: 1923–24. Division 2, Runners-up: 1920–21, 1951–52, 1959–60. Division 3(S), Champions: 1946–47.   Division 3, Runners-up 1975–76 *F.A. Cup,* Winners: 1926–27 (Only occasion the Cup has been won by a club outside England). Runners-up: 1925. *Football League Cup,* semi-final: 1965–66. Welsh Cup Winners: 18 times. **European Competitions:** *European Cup Winners Cup:* 1964–65, 1965–66, 1967–68, 1968–69, 1969–70, 1970–71, 1971–72, 1973–74, 1974–75.

Record Victory: 9-2 v Thames, Division 3(S), Feb. 6th, 1932.

Record Defeat: 2-11 v Sheffield U., Division 1, Jan. 1st, 1926.

Most League Points: 66, Division 3(S), 1946–47.

Most League Goals: 93, Division 3(S), 1946–47.

Highest League Scorer in Season: Stan Richards, 31, Division 3(S), 1946–47.

Most Capped Player: Alf Sherwood, 39 (41), Wales.

Most League Appearances: Tom Farquharson, 445, 1922–35.

Most League Goals in Total Aggregate: Len Davies, 127, 1921–29.

Record Transfer Fee Received: £110,000 for John Toshack from Liverpool, Nov. 1970.

Record Transfer Fee Paid: £60,500 to Leicester City for John Farrington, Nov. 1973.

Managers Since the War: Bill McCandless, Cyril Spiers, Trevor Morris, Bill Jones, George Swindin, Jimmy Scoular, Frank O'Farrell.

Address of Supporters Club: Bluebirds Club, Bluebirds Office, Ninian Park, Cardiff CF1 8SX.

Address of Club Shop or Boutique: Bluebirds Shop, Ninian Park, Cardiff CF1 8SX.

Ninian Park, Cardiff CF1 8SX. Telephone Cardiff 28501/33230. *Telegraphic address:* 'Soccer Cardiff'.   *Ground capacity:* 46,000.   *Record attendance:* 61,566, Wales v England, October 14, 1961.   *Club record:* 57,800 v Arsenal, Division 1, April 22, 1953.   *Record receipts:* £22,000 v Leeds U. F.A. Cup 5th Rd., February 26, 1972.   *Pitch measurements:* 112 yds × 76 yds.

How to get there: Corporation bus 2 runs past the ground; special buses run to Ninian Park from the bus station, returning after the match. Nearest railway station, Cardiff Central.

Match tickets: Bookable 14 days in advance by postal application. Details from Ticket Office (tel: Cardiff 397997).

Entertainments/catering facilities: Visiting supporters welcome at the Bluebirds Club on production of their supporters' club card or a rail or bus ticket. Refreshment points around the ground.

Club shop: Open on match days; souvenirs available during the week from the Pools Office.

Handbooks/programmes: No handbook. Back numbers of programmes available from Programme Dept., Ninian Park.

Extra information: In 1928–29 Cardiff conceded the least number of goals in the First Division – but were relegated!

Club Colours: Blue shirts with single yellow and white stripe, blue shorts and stockings with yellow and white trim.

Change Colours: All yellow.

Club Captain: Gil Reece.

Club Nickname: 'Bluebirds'.

CARDIFF CITY 1975–76 LEAGUE RECORD

Match No.	Date	Venue	Opponents	Result	H/T Score	League Pos'n	Goalscorers	Attendance
1	Aug 16	A	Grimsby T.	L 0-2	0-1	—		6283
2	23	H	Bury	D 1-1	1-0	19	Villars	6664
3	30	A	Brighton & H.A.	W 1-0	0-0	15	Villars	11,353
4	Sept 6	H	Crystal Palace	L 0-1	0-0	19		10,479
5	13	A	Mansfield T.	W 4-1	1-0	12	Giles, Dwyer, Reece 2 (1 a pen)	6682
6	20	H	Halifax T.	D 0-0	0-0	13		8035
7	22	A	Port Vale	L 1-2	0-1	—	Attley	5143
8	27	A	Preston N.E.	L 1-3	0-2	17	Evans	8103
9	Oct 4	H	Wrexham	W 3-0	1-0	14	Dwyer 2, Evans	7653
10	11	A	Rotherham U.	L 0-1	0-1	17		4272
11	18	H	Sheffield W.	W 2-0	0-0	15	Evans, Quinn (og)	7930
12	22	A	Aldershot	L 1-2	1-1	—	Anderson	3687
13	25	A	Chester	D 1-1	1-1	17	Evans	5348
14	Nov 1	H	Chesterfield	W 4-3	3-0	12	Alston 2, Evans, Anderson	7512
15	4	H	Walsall	D 0-0	0-0	—		8884
16	8	A	Gillingham	D 2-2	0-0	13	Anderson, Evans	5762
17	15	H	Colchester U.	W 2-0	1-0	10	Evans, Alston	6781
18	29	H	Shrewsbury T.	W 3-0	1-0	7	Anderson, Evans, Alston	8002
19	Dec 6	A	Millwall	W 3-1	0-0	5	Reece 2, Evans	6092
20	22	H	Southend U.	W 3-1	1-0	—	Evans 2, Alston	9342
21	26	A	Swindon T.	L 0-3	0-2	7		10,003
22	27	H	Peterborough U.	W 5-2	1-1	3	Anderson, Dwyer 2, Evans 2	16,094
23	Jan 10	H	Brighton & H.A.	L 0-1	0-0	6		17,728
24	17	A	Halifax T.	D 1-1	0-0	6	England	2399
25	20	H	Mansfield T.	W 1-0	0-0	—	Evans	10,161
26	31	H	Aldershot	W 1-0	1-0	6	Alston	8934
27	Feb 4	A	Hereford U.	L 1-4	0-3	—	Buchanan	12,962
28	7	A	Walsall	W 3-2	0-2	5	Alston 2, Dwyer	7109
29	14	H	Gillingham	W 4-1	1-1	5	Livermore, Buchanan, Evans, Alston	11,025
30	21	A	Colchester U.	L 2-3	1-0	6	Dwyer, Anderson	3248
31	25	H	Port Vale	D 1-1	0-1	—	Livermore	9129
32	28	H	Chester	W 2-0	0-0	5	Alston, Buchanan	10,000
33	Mar 6	A	Chesterfield	D 1-1	1-0	5	Alston	4095
34	8	A	Wrexham	D 1-1	0-0	—	Evans	5674
35	13	H	Rotherham U.	D 1-1	1-1	4	Alston	11,072
36	17	A	Sheffield W.	W 3-1	0-0	—	Evans, Charles, Clark	8867
37	20	A	Shrewsbury T.	L 1-3	0-0	5	Evans	7573
38	27	H	Millwall	D 0-0	0-0	6		12,511
39	29	A	Southend U.	W 2-0	2-0	—	Dwyer, Evans	4596
40	Apr 3	A	Grimsby T.	W 2-1	0-1	5	Evans, Buchanan	9645
41	7	H	Preston N.E.	W 1-0	0-0	—	Evans	12,447
42	10	A	Crystal Palace	W 1-0	0-0	—	Alston	25,603
43	14	H	Hereford U.	W 2-0	0-0	—	Livermore, Campbell	35,549
44	17	H	Swindon T.	D 0-0	0-0	2		23,428
45	19	A	Peterborough U.	D 0-0	0-0	—		6846
46	May 4	A	Bury	W 1-0	1-0	—	Alston	7135

Goalscorers

League (69): Evans 21, Alston 14, Dwyer 8, Anderson 6, Reece 4 (1 a pen.), Buchanan 4, Livermore 3, Villars 2, Clark 1, Giles 1, Attley 1, England 1, Charles 1, Campbell 1, own goal 1.
League Cup (2): Reece (1 pen), Clark.
F.A. Cup (9): Alston 4, Evans 3, Reece 2.

League Cup	First Round	Bristol R. (h)	1-2
	Second Leg	(a)	1-1
F.A. Cup	First Round	Exeter C. (h)	6-2
	Second Round	Wycombe W. (h)	1-0
	Third Round	Orient (a)	1-0
	Fourth Round	Southend U. (a)	1-2

Healey	Attley	Charles	Buchanan	Larmour	Dwyer	Villars	Clark	Reece	Pethard	Durrell	England	Livermore	Evans	Showers	Morgan	Giles	Anderson	Alston	Irwin	Sayer	Campbell	Match No.
1	2	3	4	5	6	7	8	9	10	11												1
1	4	3	6	2	8		10	9		11*	5	7	12									2
1	2	3	6	4	7		10				5	8	11	9								3
1	2	3	6	4	7		8	12			5*10	11		9								4
1	2	3	6	4			10	9			7	11			5	8						5
1	2	3	6	4			10	9			5	7	11			8						6
1	2	3	6	4	7		8	9			5	10	11									7
1	2*	3	6	4	7		10	9			5	8	11			12						8
1	2	3	8	6	4			9			5	7	10				11					9
1	2	3	8	6	4			9			5	7	10				11					10
1	2	3	8	6	4		12	9*			5	7	10				11					11
1	2	3	7*	6	4		8		12		5	10	9				11					12
1	2	3	7*	6	4		8	9			5	10	11			12						13
1	2	3	6	4	7						5	8	9				11	10				14
12		3	6	4	7*			2			5	8	9				11	10	1			15
		3	6	4*	12			2			5	7	10			8	11	9	1			16
		3	12	6	2			7			5	4	10			8*	11	9	1			17
		3	4	6	2			7			5	8	10				11	9	1			18
		3	4	6	2			7			5	8	10				11	9	1			19
		3	7*	6	2			4			5	8	9			12	11	10	1			20
		3		6	2			4			5	8	9			7	11	10	1			21
		3	7	6	2			4			5	8	9				11	10	1			22
		3	8	6	2			4			5	7	10				11	9	1			23
		3	4	6	2	7					5	8	9				11	10	1			24
		3	7	6	2			4			5	8	9				11	10	1			25
		3	7	6	2			4			5	8	9				11	10	1			26
		3	7	6		4			2		5	8	9				11	10	1			27
1		3	8	6	2			4			7	9			5		11	10				28
1		3	8	6	2			4			7	9			5			10	11			29
1		3*		6	2			4			7	9			5	8	11	10	12			30
1		3	7*	6	2			4				8	9		5	12	11	10				31
1		3	4		2				12		5	8	9		6	11*10			7			32
1		3	4		2		11				5	8	9		6			10			7	33
1		3	7	6	2		11				5	8	9					10			4	34
1		3	4		2		11				5	8	9		6			10			7	35
1		3	7		2		11				5	8	9		6			10			4	36
1		3	7		2		11		12		5	8	9		6*			10			4	37
1		3			4		11	2			5	8	9			7*		10		12	6	38
1		3	7		6		11	2			5	8	9					10			4	39
1				7	6		2		3		5	8	9				11	10			4	40
1				7*	6		2		3		5	8	9				11	10		12	4	41
1					6		2		3		5	8	9				11	10		7	4	42
1					6		2	12	3		5	8	9					10		7*	4	43
1					6	12	2	11	3		5	7	9					10		8*	4	44
1					6		2		3		5	8	9			7	11	10			4	45
1					6		2		3		5	8	9			7	11	10			4	46
33	14	39	27	39	45	10	19	18	17	2	40	45	44	2	10	8	28	33	13	6	14	
+1s		+1s			+2s	+3s	+3s						+1s			+3s	+1s		+3s			

125

CARDIFF CITY—PLAYERS

Player and position	Ht.	Wt.	Birthplace	Clubs	League Appearances	Goals
Goalkeepers						
Billy Irwin	6 2	13 8½	Newtonards	Bangor	—	—
				Cardiff C.	147	—
Ron Healey	5 11	11 3	Manchester	Manchester C.	30	—
				Coventry C. (on loan)	3	—
				Preston N.E. (on loan)	6	—
				Cardiff C.	49	—
Defenders						
*Mike England (Wales)	6 2	13 2	Greenfields	Blackburn R.	166	21
				Tottenham H.	299	14
				Cardiff C.	40	1
Phil Dwyer	5 11	11 4	Cardiff	Cardiff C.	155	13
Albert Larmour	5 10½	11 12	Belfast	Cardiff C.	76+2	—
Freddie Pethard	5 7	9 8	Glasgow	Cardiff C.	88+3	—
Clive Charles	5 9	10 4	London	West Ham U.	12+2	—
				Cardiff C.	61+1	3
Richie Morgan	5 11	12 6	Cardiff	Cardiff C.	66	—
Brian Attley	5 8	10 4	Cardiff	Cardiff C.	25+2	1
Keith Pontin	6 1	11 7	Pontyclun	Cardiff C.	—	—
Midfield						
John Buchanan	5 9	10 7	Dingwall	Northampton T.	104+10	25
				Cardiff C.	56+1	7
Doug Livermore	5 8½	10 5	Liverpool	Liverpool	13+2	—
				Norwich C.	113+1	4
				Bournemouth (on loan)	10	—
				Cardiff C.	45	3
*Martin Morgan	5 9	10 5	Neath	Cardiff C.	—	—
*Gil Reece (Wales)	5 6¾	9 9	Cardiff	Newport Co.	32	9
				Sheffield U.	197+13	59
				Cardiff C.	94+6	23
David Giles	5 5	10 4	Cardiff	Cardiff C.	11+4	1
Alan Campbell	5 8	10 7	Arbroath	Charlton Ath	196+2	28
				Birmingham C.	39+1	6
				Cardiff C.	14	1
Forwards						
Peter Sayer	5 6	10 2	Cardiff	Cardiff C.	14+8	1
Derek Showers (Wales)	5 11	11 4	Merthyr Tydfil	Cardiff C.	61+6	6
Tony Villars (Wales)	5 6½	9 10½	Cwmbran	Cardiff C.	66+7	4
Willie Anderson	5 9	11 0	Liverpool	Manchester U.	7	—
				Aston Villa	229+2	36
				Cardiff C.	107+3	12
*Brian Clark	5 11	12 0	Bristol	Bristol C.	195	81
				Huddersfield T.	28+1	11
				Cardiff C.	178+7	78
				Bournemouth	28+2	12
				Millwall	66+5	16
				Cardiff C.	19+2	1
Tony Evans	5 8	11 7	Liverpool	Blackpool	4+2	—
				Cardiff C.	44+1	21
Adrian Alston (Australia)	6 0	11 7	Preston	Luton T.	26+3	8
				Cardiff C.	33	14

CARLISLE UNITED DIV. 2

Chairman: E. G. Sheffield.

Directors: H. Sherrard, J. C. Monkhouse, J. W. Cullen, H. A. Jenkins, T. L. Sibson, J. Johnston, J. A. Bendall, Dr. T. Gardner, M.B., ChB.

Team Manager: Dick Young.

Secretary: J. D. Dent.

Year Formed: 1904. *Limited Company:* 1921.

Previous Grounds: 1903–5, Milholme Bank; 1906–9, Devonshire Park; 1910– Brunton Park.

Honours: *Football League, highest position:* 22nd Division 1, 1974–75. Promoted from Division 2 (3rd) 1973–74. Division 3, Champions: 1964–65. Division 4, runners-up: 1963–64. *F.A. Cup,* 6th Rd., 1974–75.

Football League Cup, Semi-Finalists: 1969–70.

Record Victory: 8-0 v Hartlepools U., Division 3(N), Sept. 1st, 1928 and v Scunthorpe U. Division 3(N), Dec. 25th, 1952.

Record Defeat: 1-11 v Hull C., Division 3(N), Jan. 14th, 1939.

Most League Points: 62, Division 3(N), 1950–51.

Most League Goals: 113, Division 4, 1963–64.

Highest League Scorer in Season: Jimmy McConnell, 42, Division 3(N), 1928–29.

Most Capped Player: Eric Welsh, 4, Ireland.

Most League Appearances: Alan Ross, 420, 1963-76.

Most League Goals in Total Aggregate: Jimmy McConnell, 126, 1928–32.

Record Transfer Fee Received: £100,000 from Q.P.R. for Stan Bowles, Sept. 1972.

Record Transfer Fee Paid: £52,000 to Coventry C. for Bobby Parker, June 1974.

Managers Since the War: W. Clark, Ivor Broadis, Bill Shankly, Fred Emery, Ivor Broadis, Andy Beattie, Ivor Powell, Alan Ashman, Tim Ward, Bob Stokoe, Ian MacFarlane, Alan Ashman.

Brunton Park, Carlisle, CA1 1LL. Telephone Carlisle 26237. *Record attendance:* 27,500 v Birmingham C., F.A. Cup 3rd Rd., January 5, 1957, and v. Middlesbrough, F.A. Cup, 5th Rd., February 7, 1970. *Record Receipts:* £12,303 v Sunderland, Division 2, February 24, 1976. *Ground capacity* 28,000. *Pitch measurements:* 117 yds × 78 yds.

How to get there: City centre one mile away. Ribble buses from the Town Hall. Nearest railway station Carlisle. By road—exit 43 from the M6, ground ¾ mile away; this avoids the town centre.

Match tickets: Bookable 1–2 weeks in advance by post or personal application.

Car parking: Car park holding 1500 vehicles adjacent to the ground. Limited street parking available.

Entertainments/catering facilities: Supporters Club with extensive bar facilities. Refreshment points around the ground.

Club shop: Caravan in car park open on match days.

Handbooks/programmes: No handbook. Programmes available on subscription.

Extra information: In 1949, Carlisle's player-manager Ivor Broadis transferred himself to Sunderland for £18,000.

Club Colours: Blue shirts with broad white vertical stripe and red piping, white shorts, red stockings.

Change Colours: Yellow shirts, blue shorts, yellow stockings.

Club Captain: Bill Green.

Club Trainer/Coach: Hugh Neil.

Club Nickname: 'Cumbrians'

CARLISLE UNITED 1975–76 LEAGUE RECORD

Match No.	Date	Venue	Opponents	Result	H/T Score	League Pos'n	Goalscorers	Attendance
1	Aug 16	H	Oxford U.	D 1-1	1-1	—	Laidlaw (pen)	8505
2	20	A	Fulham	L 0-3	0-1	—		7443
3	23	A	Chelsea	L 1-3	0-1	20	Barry	19,165
4	30	H	Blackburn R.	L 0-1	0-0	22		8683
5	Sept 6	A	Notts Co.	L 0-1	0-1	22		8005
6	13	H	Portsmouth	W 2-1	1-1	22	Prudham, Clarke	7316
7	20	A	Bristol R.	W 1-0	0-0	18	Barry	8223
8	23	A	Sunderland	L 2-3	0-2	—	Barry, Laidlaw (pen)	28,185
9	27	H	W.B.A.	D 1-1	0-0	19	Laidlaw	6625
10	Oct 4	A	Plymouth Arg.	L 1-2	0-1	20	Clarke	12,875
11	11	H	Luton T.	D 1-1	1-1	21	Clarke	6621
12	18	A	Orient	L 0-1	0-1	22		4600
13	25	H	Charlton Ath.	D 1-1	0-1	20	O'Neill	7008
14	Nov 1	A	Nottingham F.	L 0-4	0-2	20		11,894
15	4	H	Oldham Ath.	W 2-1	2-0	—	McCartney, Clarke	6389
16	8	H	York C.	W 1-0	1-0	19	Laidlaw	7021
17	15	A	Bolton W.	D 0-0	0-0	19		14,556
18	22	H	Orient	L 1-2	0-0	19	Laidlaw (pen)	6502
19	29	H	Southampton	W 1-0	0-0	19	Clarke	6977
20	Dec 6	A	Bristol C.	D 0-0	0-0	19		12,466
21	12	H	Chelsea	W 2-1	1-1	18	McCartney 2	8065
22	20	A	Oxford U.	D 0-0	0-0	18		4241
23	26	H	Blackpool	W 1-0	0-0	16	Train	11,532
24	27	H	Hull C.	W 3-2	3-0	15	Green, Clarke, O'Neill	7056
25	Jan 10	A	Portsmouth	L 0-1	0-0	16		11,430
26	17	H	Notts Co.	L 1-2	0-1	17	Martin	7600
27	31	H	Fulham	D 2-2	2-1	17	Barry, Owen	6247
28	Feb 7	A	Oldham Ath.	D 2-2	1-1	18	Clarke 2	8870
29	14	A	York C.	W 2-1	0-0	11	Barry, McVitie	3850
30	21	H	Bolton W.	W 3-2	1-1	11	Ritson (og), Lathan, Spearritt	12,809
31	24	H	Sunderland	D 2-2	1-2	—	Train, Barry	20,001
32	27	A	Charlton Ath.	L 2-4	2-2	16	Owen, Martin	10,370
33	Mar 6	A	Nottingham F.	D 1-1	0-1	15	Martin	7153
34	13	A	Luton T.	L 0-3	0-1	17		8856
35	20	A	Southampton	D 1-1	0-0	18	Lathan	18,304
36	27	H	Bristol C.	L 0-1	0-1	18		7563
37	Apr 3	A	W.B.A.	L 0-3	0-2	19		17,136
38	10	H	Bristol R.	W 4-2	1-1	18	Barry, Owen, Martin, Lathan	5928
39	16	A	Blackburn R.	L 0-1	0-1	19		11,215
40	17	A	Blackpool	L 1-2	1-0	19	Laidlaw	8382
41	20	H	Hull C.	D 0-0	0-0	—		8185
42	24	H	Plymouth Arg.	W 2-0	1-0	19	Clarke, McVitie	7038

Goalscorers

League (45): Clarke 9, Barry 7, Laidlaw 6 (3 pens), Martin 4, Lathan 3, McCartney 3, Owen 3, McVitie 2, O'Neill 2, Train 2, Green 1, Prudham 1, Spearritt 1, own goal 1.

League Cup (2): Laidlaw, own goal 1.

F.A. Cup (1): Own goal 1

League Cup	Second Round	Gillingham (h)	2-0
	Third Round	Everton (a)	0-2
F.A. Cup	Third Round	W.B.A. (a)	1-3

Burleigh	Carr	Gorman	O'Neill	Green	Parker	Martin	Train	Owen	Laidlaw	Clarke	Barry	Spearritt	Prudham	McCartney	Hindson	Ross	McVitie	Lathan	Bonnyman	Match No.
1	2	3	4	5	6	7	8	9	10	11										1
1	2	3	4	5	6	11	8	7	10	9										2
1	2	3	4	5	6	7	8	9	10	11*	12									3
1	2	11	4	5	6*	7		12	10		8	3	9							4
1	2	3	4	5	6	7		9	11		8		10*	12						5
1	6	3	12	5		7			10	11	4	2	9	8*						6
1	6	3	4	5		7			10	11	8	2	9							7
1	6	3	10	5		7			11	9	4	2	8*	12						8
1	6	3	4	5		7*			10	11	8	2	9	12						9
1		3	4	5	6	7		12	11	10	8*	2	9							10
1	6	3	4	5		7			10	11	8	2	9							11
1	6	3	4	5	2			12	10	11	8	9*	7							12
1	6	3	4	5	2	7		8	10	9	11									13
1	6	3	10	5	2	7		4		11	9		8							14
	2	3	10	5	6	8		4	11	9	12	7*				1				15
	2	3*	10	5	6	7		4	12	11	9	8				1				16
	2	3	10*	5	6	7		4	11	9	12	8				1				17
	2	3	10	5	6	7		4	11	9		8				1				18
	2	3*		5	6	7		4	12	11	9	8	10			1				19
	2	3		5	6	8	4	12	9*	10	11					1	7			20
	2	3		5	6	11	8	9	4	10						1	7			21
	2	3		5	6	11	4	9	8	12	10*					1	7			22
	2	3	12	5	6	11	8	9*	4	10						1	7			23
	2	3	4	5	6	8	11	9	10							1	7			24
	2	3	4	5	6	11	8	12	9	10*						1	7			25
	2	3	4*	5	6	11	8	10	9	12						1	7			26
	2	3		5	6	11	8	10	12	9	4*					1	7			27
	6	3		5	11	8		10	9	4	2					1	7			28
	6	3		5	11	8	12	10*	9	4	2					1	7			29
		3		5	11	8	6	10	9	4	2					1	7			30
	12	3		5	11	8	6	10	9*	4	2					1	7			31
	5	3			11	8	6	10	9	4	2					1	7			32
		3	12	5	11	8	6	10		4	2					1	7*	9		33
		3	8		11		6	10	9	4	2*					1	12	7	5	34
	2	3	4	5	11		6	10	9							1	7	8		35
	2	3	4*	5	11		6	10	9							1	12	7	8	36
	2	3		5	10		6	9	4							1	7	11	8	37
	2	3	6	5	10		12	9*	4							1	7	11	8	38
	2	3	8	5	11		9	12	4							1	7	10*	6	39
	2	3	8	5	11		9	10	4							1	7*	12	6	40
		3	8	5	11		9	10	4		2					1	7		6	41
	2	3	8	5	11		10	9	4							1	7		6	42
14	36	42	28	40	22	39	24	20	30	36	28	16	9	13	1	28	17	10	9	
+1s		+3s						+7s	+4s	+3s	+1s	+1s	+1s	+2s		+2s	+1s			

Player and position	Ht.	Wt.	Birthplace	Clubs	League Appearances	Goals
Goalkeepers						
Alan Ross	5 10¾	10 7½	Glasgow	Luton T.	—	—
				Carlisle U.	419+1	—
Martin Burleigh	5 10	13 1	Durham	Newcastle U.	11	—
				Darlington	30	—
				Carlisle U.	14	—
Defenders						
John Gorman	5 8	11 10	Winchburon	Celtic	—	—
				Carlisle U.	215+1	4
Peter Carr	5 9	10 0	Bishop Middleham	Darlington	131+4	1
				Carlisle U.	135+1	1
Bob Parker	5 9	10 12	Coventry	Coventry C.	78+3	—
				Carlisle U.	64	1
*Eddie Spearritt	5 8	11 9	Lowestoft	Ipswich T.	62+10	13
				Brighton	202+7	22
				Carlisle U.	29+2	1
Philip Bonnyman	5 11	12 1	Glasgow	Rangers	—	—
				Hamilton A.	65+6	7
				Carlisle U.	9	—
Ian MacDonald	6 1	12 4	Rinteln, W. Germany	St Johnstone	107+1	2
				Carlisle U.	—	—
Midfield						
Les O'Neill	5 7	10 10	Hartford Colliery	Newcastle U.	1	—
				Darlington	178+1	35
				Bradford C.	95+2	17
				Carlisle U.	130+4	18
Mike McCartney	5 7	10 12	Edinburgh	W.B.A.	—	—
				Carlisle U.	15+5	3
Mike Barry	5 7	10 10	Hull	Huddersfield T.	21+5	—
				Carlisle U.	45+8	7
John Latham	5 7	11 0	Sunderland	Sunderland	43+11	14
				Mansfield T.	72+2	14
				Carlisle U.	10+1	3
Dennis Martin	5 11	10 12	Edinburgh	W.B.A.	14+2	1
				Carlisle U.	234+3	44
Forwards						
Bobby Owen	5 10	10 7	Farnworth	Bury	81+2	38
				Manchester C.	18+4	3
				Swansea C. (on loan)	5+1	1
				Carlisle U.	182+18	51
Joe Laidlaw	5 8	10 12	Wallsend	Middlesbrough	104+7	20
				Carlisle U.	146+5	44
Frank Clarke	5 11½	11 0	Wolverhampton	Shrewsbury T.	189	77
				Q.P.R.	67	17
				Ipswich T.	63+4	14
				Carlisle U.	102+2	29
Eddie Prudham	5 8½	10 6	Gateshead	Sheffield W.	14+5	2
				Carlisle U.	14+2	2
George McVitie	5 9¾	11 1	Carlisle	Carlisle U.	124+4	21
				W.B.A.	42	5
				Oldham Ath.	108+5	19
				Carlisle U.	17+2	2
Bill Rafferty	5 10	10 7	Glasgow	Coventry C.	27	3
				Blackpool	35+1	9
				Plymouth Arg.	89+1	35
				Carlisle U.	—	—

CHARLTON ATHLETIC DIV. 2

Chairman: E. M. Gliksten.

Directors: W. J. Jenner, A. T. G. Pocock O.B.E., C. W. Wheeler, D. Follows, C.B.E., F. W. Boswell.

General Manager/Secretary: Rodney Stone.

Manager: Andy Nelson *Ass. Secretary:* Mrs J. P. Doble.

Year Formed: 1905. *Turned Professional:* 1920.

Limited Company: 1919.

Previous Grounds: 1906, Siemen's Meadow; 1907, Woolwich Common; 1909, Pound Park; 1913, Horn Lane; 1920, The Valley; 1922, Catford; 1922, The Valley.

Honours: *Football League,* Division 1, Runners-up: 1936–37. Division 2, Runners-up: 1935–36. Division 3(S), Champions: 1928–29, 1934–35. Promoted from Division 3 (3rd) 1974–75. *F.A. Cup,* Winners: 1947; Runners-up: 1946. *Football League Cup,* best season: 4th Rd., 1962–63, 1964–65.

Record Victory: 8-1 v Middlesbrough. Division 1, Sept. 12th, 1953.

Record Defeat: 1-11 v Aston Villa, Division 2, Nov. 14th, 1959.

Most League Points: 61, Div 3(S) 1934-5.

Most League Goals: 107, Div. 2, 1957-8.

Highest League Scorer in Season: Ralph Allen, 32, Division 3(S), 1934–35.

Most Capped Player: John Hewie, 19, Scotland.

Most League Appearances: Sam Bartram, 583, 1934–56.

Most Goals in Total Aggregate: Stuart Leary, 153, 1953–62.

Record Transfer Fee Received: £80,000 from Leicester C. for Len Glover, Nov. 1967.

Record Transfer Fee Paid: £25,000 to Orient for Paul Went, June 1967 and £25,000 to Tottenham H. for Dennis Bond, Oct. 29th, 1970.

Managers Since the War: James Seed, Jimmy Trotter, Frank Hill, Bob Stokoe, Eddie Firmani, Theo Foley.

Address of Supporters Club: Same address as Club.

Address of Club Shop or Boutique: 'The Valley Shop', The Valley, Floyd Road, London SE7 8AW.

The Valley, Floyd Rd., Charlton, London SE7 8AW. Telephone 01-858-3711/2. *Ground capacity:* 66,000 (largest capacity in Football League). *Record attendance:* 75,031 v Aston Villa, F.A. Cup 5th Rd., February 12, 1938. *Record receipts:* £21,185 v Q.P.R., League Cup 3rd Rd., October 14, 1975. *Pitch measurements:* 114 yds × 78 yds.

How to get there: Buses 53, 54, 75, 177, 180. Nearest railway station, Charlton, is on the line from London from Charing Cross and Waterloo East. The ground is 3 minutes walk from the station.

Match tickets: Advance bookings for seats restricted to all Cup matches and selected League games.

Car parking: In ground for season-ticket holders only. Ample off-street parking available.

Entertainments/catering facilities: The Valley Club, Harvey Gardens, and Beer and Snack Bars in the ground.

Club shop: The Valley Shop in ground is open on match days.

Handbooks/programmes: Both available in shops, and programmes on subscription.

Extra information: Charlton are the only club to go from the third to the first division in successive seasons (1934-36) and then finish runners-up.

Club Colours: Red shirts, white shorts.

Change Colours: Yellow and black.

Club Captain: David Young.

Club Coach: Peter Shearing.

First Team Trainer/Physiotherapist: Charlie Hall.

Club Nickname: 'Haddicks', 'Robins', or 'Valiants'.

CHARLTON ATHLETIC 1975–76 LEAGUE RECORD

Match No.	Date	Venue	Opponents	Result	H/T Score	League Pos'n	Goalscorers	Attendance
1	Aug 16	H	Notts Co.	L 1-2	1-1	—	Bowman (pen)	9612
2	23	A	Plymouth Arg.	L 0-1	0-1	22		14,201
3	29	H	Oxford U.	W 2-1	2-1	—	Flanagan, Hunt	8748
4	Sept 6	A	Bristol R.	D 0-0	0-0	19		7718
5	13	H	Blackpool	D 1-1	1-1	15	Hales	9190
6	20	A	W.B.A.	D 1-1	0-1	15	Warman	10,563
7	24	A	Nottingham F.	W 2-1	1-0	—	Warman, Harrison	10,588
8	26	H	Hull C.	W 1-0	1-0	8	Hales	10,305
9	Oct 4	A	Bolton W.	L 0-5	0-2	12		9895
10	11	A	Bristol C.	L 0-4	0-2	13		12,701
11	18	H	Oldham Ath.	W 3-1	2-0	13	Flanagan, Hales 2	8582
12	21	A	York C.	W 3-1	1-1	—	Hunt, Hales 2	4345
13	25	A	Carlisle U.	D 1-1	1-0	9	Hales	7008
14	31	H	Southampton	W 4-1	1-0	9	Hales 2, Fisher (og), Warman	16,036
15	Nov 8	A	Fulham	D 1-1	0-1	8	Giles	15,466
16	15	H	Sunderland	L 1-2	0-1	11	Hales	22,307
17	22	A	Oldham Ath	L 0-2	0-1	15		8059
18	29	A	Blackburn R.	L 0-2	0-1	17		8776
19	Dec 3	H	Luton T.	L 1-5	1-1	18	Flanagan	8703
20	12	H	Plymouth Arg	W 2-0	2-0	17	Flanagan, Darke (og)	7095
21	20	A	Notts Co.	L 0-2	0-1	18		10,017
22	26	H	Portsmouth	L 1-3	0-2	19	Flanagan	10,736
23	27	A	Chelsea	W 3-2	2-0	17	Warman, Hales 2	25,367
24	Jan 10	A	Blackpool	L 1-2	1-2	18	Warman	5748
25	17	H	Bristol R.	W 3-0	2-0	16	Hope, Hales 2	8598
26	31	H	York C.	W 3-2	1-0	15	Warman, Giles, Hunt	6916
27	Feb 17	H	Fulham	W 3-2	1-0	—	Hales 3	11,536
28	21	A	Sunderland	L 1-4	1-1	16	Bowman	30,173
29	24	H	Nottingham F.	D 2-2	1-0	—	Hales 2	10,655
30	27	H	Carlisle U.	W 4-2	2-2	14	Owen (og), Hales, Hope, Powell	10,370
31	Mar 2	A	Orient	W 1-0	0-0	—	Hales	9754
32	12	H	Bristol C.	D 2-2	0-0	13	Berry, Young, T.	12,683
33	20	H	Blackburn R.	W 2-1	0-0	11	Peacock, Powell	9704
34	23	H	Orient	D 1-1	1-1	—	Harrison	10,625
35	27	A	Luton T.	D 1-1	0-1	9	Hales	9947
36	Apr 3	A	Hull C.	D 2-2	1-0	9	Hales, Giles	4148
37	9	H	W.B.A.	W 2-1	1-0	9	Hales, Flanagan	14,252
38	12	A	Southampton	L 2-3	0-2	—	Hales 2	23,686
39	16	A	Oxford U.	L 0-1	0-0	9		7930
40	17	A	Portsmouth	D 2-2	0-0	9	Hales 2	7992
41	19	H	Chelsea	D 1-1	0-0	—	Curtis	23,263
42	24	H	Bolton W.	L 0-4	0-1	9		14,415

Goalscorers

League (61): Hales 28, Flanagan 6, Warman 6, Giles 3, Hunt 3, Bowman 2 (1 a pen), Harrison 2, Hope 2, Powell 2, Berry 1, Curtis 1, Peacock 1, Young, T. 1, Own Goals 3.

League Cup (12): Hales, 3 Bowman 2 (1 a pen), Peacock 2, Flanagan 2, Hope, Giles, Powell.

F.A. Cup (6): Peacock, Warman, Curtis (pen), Powell, Flanagan, Hope.

League Cup	First Round	Cambridge U. (a)	1-1
	Second Leg	(h)	3-0
	Second Round	Oxford U. (h)	3-3
		(a)	1-1
		(a)	3-2 (a.e.t.)
	Third Round	Q.P.R. (a)	1-1
		(h)	0-3
F.A. Cup	Third Round	Sheffield W. (h)	2-1
	Fourth Round	Portsmouth (h)	1-1
		(a)	3-0
	Fifth Round	Wolverhampton W. (a)	0-3

Tutt	Penfold	Warman	Bowman	Giles	Young	Powell	Flanagan	Hunt	Horsfield	Peacock	Cripps	Hales	Hope	Harrison	Curtis	Goldthorpe	Young, T	Wood	Berry	Campbell	Match No.
1	2	3	4	5	6	7	8	9*	10	11	12										1
1	2	3	4	5	6	7	10	9		11		8									2
1	2	3	4	5	6		11	10		7		8	9								3
1	2	3	4	5	6		11	9		7		8	10								4
1	2	3	4	5	6	12	11	10		7		8	9*								5
1	2	3	4	5	6	7	10	9		11		8									6
1	2	3	4	5	6		9	10		11		8		7							7
1	2	3	4	5	6		9	10		11		8		7							8
1	2	3	4	5	6	7	9	10		11		8									9
1	2	3	4	5	6	7	9	10				8						11			10
1	2	3	4	5	6	7	9	10		11		8									11
1	2	3	4	5	6	7	9	10		11		8									12
1	2	3	4	5	6	7	9	10		11		8									13
1	2	3	4	5	6	7	9	10		11*		8			12						14
1	2	3	4	5	6*	7	9	10		11		8			12						15
1	2	3	4	5	6	7	9	10		11		8									16
1	2		4	5	6	7	9			11			8*	3	10		12				17
1	2	3	4	5	6	7	9	10		11		8									18
1	2	3	4	5	6	7	9	10		11		8									19
1		3	4	5		7	9	10		11		8			2	6					20
1		3	4	5		7	9	10		11		8			2	6					21
1		3	4	5		7	9	10		11		8			2	6					22
1		3	4	5	6	7	9	10		11		8			2						23
1	2		4	5	6	7	9	10		11		8			3						24
1	2	3		5		7	10	4		11		8	9		6						25
1	2	3		5		7	11	4		10		8	9		6						26
1	2	3		5		7		4		10		8	9		6		11				27
1	2	3	12	5		7		4		10		8*	9		6		11				28
	2	3		5		7		4		10		8	9		6		11	1			29
			4	5	3	7	10					8	9		6		11	1	2		30
				5	3	7	11	10				8	9		6		4	1	2		31
				5	3	7	11	10				8	9		6		4	1	2		32
			10*	5	3	7	11					8	9		6		4	1	2	12	33
				5	3	7	9	12		11		8		10*	6		4	1	2		34
			12	5	3	7	9	10		11		8			6*		4	1	2		35
				5	3	7	9	10		11		8			6		4	1	2		36
				5	3	7	9	10		11		8			6		4	1	2		37
				5	3	7	9	10		11		8			6		4	1	2		38
				5	3	7	9	10		11		8			6		4	1	2		39
			12	5		7	9	10				8		11	6*		4	1	3	2	40
				5	2	7	9	10		11		8			6		4	1	3		41
	2			5		7	9	10		11		8			6		4*	1	3	12	42
28	24	29	26	42	32	37	38	36	1	39	—	40	12	5	24	4	16	14	14	1	
			+3s		+1s		+1s			+1s					+2s		+1s	+2s			

133

CHARLTON ATHLETIC—PLAYERS

Player and position	Ht.	Wt.	Birthplace	Clubs	League Appearances	Goals
Goalkeepers						
Graham Tutt	6 4	13 3	London	Charlton Ath.	65	—
				Workington (on loan)	4	—
Jeff Wood	5 11	11 8		Charlton Ath.	14	—
Defenders						
Harry Cripps	5 10	13 8	Plaistow	West Ham U.	—	—
				Millwall	387+10	38
				Charlton Ath.	17+3	4
Jimmy Giles	6 0	12 0	Kidlington	Swindon T.	12+1	—
				Aldershot	81+1	3
				Exeter C.	183	6
				Charlton Ath.	42	3
Bob Curtis	5 9½	11 0	Derby	Charlton Ath.	294+12	29
Mark Penfold	5 7	10 1	London	Charlton Ath.	45+2	—
				Manchester U. (on loan)	—	—
Phil Warman	5 6	10 4	London	Charlton Ath.	174+3	12
*Ray Tumbridge	5 10	11 10	London	Charlton Ath.	43+3	—
				Northampton T. (on loan)	11	—
David Young	5 9¾	10 9	Newcastle	Newcastle U.	41+2	2
				Sunderland	24+6	1
				Charlton Ath.	76	—
Leslie Berry	6 0	11 4	Plumstead	Charlton Ath.	14+1	1
David Campbell				Charlton Ath.	1+2	—
*Bob Goldthorpe	6 0¾	12 4	Osterley	C. Palace	1	—
				Charlton Ath.	70+9	6
				Aldershot (on loan)	16	—
Midfield						
Tony Young	5 10	10 13	Urmston	Manchester U.	69+14	1
				Charlton Ath.	16	1
Richard Bowman	5 6	10 1	London	Charlton Ath.	82+3	6
John Harrison	5 10	11 2	London	Charlton Ath.	5	2
Keith Peacock	5 6½	10 7	Barnhurst	Charlton Ath.	408+16	80
Peter Hunt	5 7	10 0	London	Southend U.	31+8	1
				Charlton Ath.	105+17	6
Forwards						
Michael Flanagan	5 9	11 8	Ilford	Tottenham H.	—	—
				Charlton Ath.	142+13	33
Derek Hales	5 10	11 2	Lower Halston	Luton T.	5+2	1
				Charlton Ath.	110+3	57
Colin Powell	5 10	11 10	Hendon	Charlton Ath.	135+6	16
George Hope	5 10	11 1	Haltwhistle	Newcastle U.	6	1
				Charlton Ath.	12	2

CHELSEA   DIV. 2

President: The Right Hon. Earl Cadogan, M.C., D.L.

Chairman: J. B. Mears.

Directors: Viscount Chelsea, L. J. Mears, G. M. Thomson, R. Attenborough, C.B.E.

General Manager: Ron Suart.

Team Manager: Eddie McCreadie

Secretary: Christine Matthews.

Year Formed: 1905.   *Turned Pro.* 1905.

Limited Company: 1905.

Honours: *Football League,* Division 1, Champions: 1954–55. Division 2, Runners-up: 1906–07, 1911–12, 1929–30, 1962–63.   *F.A. Cup,* Winners: 1970; Runners-up: 1914–15, 1966–67. *Football League Cup,* Winners: 1964–65. Runners-up: 1971–72, Semi-finalists 1972–73

European Competitions: *European Fairs Cup:* 1958–60, 1965–66, 1968–69. *European Cup-Winners' Cup:* 1970–71 (winners), 1971–72.

Record Victory: 13-0 v Jeunesse Hautcharage, European Cup Winners' Cup, 1st Rd., Sept. 29th, 1971.

Record Defeat: 1-8 v Wolverhampton W., Division 1, Sept. 26th, 1953.

Most League Points: 57, Division 2, 1906–07.

Most League Goals: 98, Division 1, 1960–61.

Highest League Scorer in Season: Jimmy Greaves, 41, 1960–61.

Most Goals in Total Aggregate: Bobby Tambling, 164, 1958–70.

Most Capped Player: Eddie McCreadie, 23, Scotland.

Most League Appearances: Peter Bonetti, 522, 1960–76.

Record Transfer Fee Received: £240,000 from Southampton for Peter Osgood, March 1974.

Record Transfer Fee Paid: £225,000 to Celtic for David Hay, July 1974.

Managers Since the War: Billy Birrell, Ted Drake, Tommy Docherty, Dave Sexton.

Address of Supporters Club: Same as Football Club.

Address of Club Shop or Boutique: Stamford Bridge, S.W.6.

Stamford Bridge, London S.W.6. Telephone 01-385-5545/6. *Telegraphic address:* 'Chelstam, London S.W.6.'   *Ground capacity:* 60,000 (31,500 covered).   *Record attendance:* 82,905 v Arsenal, Division 1, October 12, 1935.   *Record receipts:* £110,000, F.A. Cup semi-final, Southampton v Crystal Palace, April 3, 1976.   *Pitch measurements:* 114 yds × 71 yds.

How to get there: Nearest station is Fulham Broadway on the Underground (District Line). London Transport regular buses to Fulham Broadway, Kings Road, Fulham Road, or Stamford Bridge.

Match tickets: Advance tickets available by postal or personal application. No telephone bookings.

Car parking: Street parking only.

Entertainments/catering facilities: Licensed bars at all points of the ground.

Club shop: Run by the Football Club; sells all types of souvenirs.

Handbooks/programmes: Programmes available on subscription. The club also produces an annual magazine.

Extra information: Stamford Bridge, which remained largely unaltered from its construction until the late sixties, is being rebuilt into a luxurious super-stadium.

Club Colours: All royal blue with white strip on shorts. White stockings.

Change Colours: Red shirts, white shorts, green stockings.

Team Captain: 'Butch' Wilkins

First Team Trainer: Norman Medhurst.

Club Nickname: 'Blues'.

CHELSEA 1975–76 LEAGUE RECORD

Match No.	Date	Venue	Opponents	Result	H/T Score	League Pos'n	Goalscorers	Attendance
1	Aug 16	A	Sunderland	L 1-2	1-1	—	Garner	28,689
2	20	A	W.B.A.	D 0-0	0-0	—		18,014
3	23	H	Carlisle U.	W 3-1	1-0	8	Maybank 2, Bason	19,165
4	27	H	Oxford U.	W 3-1	2-1	—	Wilkins, R 2, Swain	22,841
5	30	A	Luton T.	L 0-3	0-1	7		19,024
6	Sept 6	H	Nottingham F.	D 0-0	0-0	8		21,023
7	13	A	Oldham Ath.	L 1-2	1-1	11	Wilkins, R	10,406
8	20	H	Bristol C.	D 1-1	1-1	9	Garner	17,661
9	23	A	Portsmouth	D 1-1	1-1	—	Garner	16,144
10	27	A	Fulham	L 0-2	0-0	14		22,921
11	Oct 4	H	York C.	D 0-0	0-0	11		15,323
12	11	A	Southampton	L 1-4	0-1	12	Wilkins, R.	21,227
13	18	H	Blackpool	W 2-0	0-0	12	Wilkins, R (pen), Langley	16,924
14	25	A	Blackburn R.	D 1-1	1-0	12	Hutchinson	12,128
15	Nov 1	H	Plymouth Arg.	D 2-2	1-0	14	Britton, Wilkins, R	20,096
16	8	A	Hull C.	W 2-1	1-1	12	Britton, Hutchinson	9,097
17	15	H	Notts Co.	W 2-0	0-0	10	Garner, Wilkins, R (pen)	18,229
18	22	A	Blackpool	W 2-0	1-0	9	Droy, Maybank	8595
19	29	A	Bristol R.	W 2-1	0-0	8	Maybank, Hutchinson	16,277
20	Dec 6	H	Bolton W.	L 0-1	0-1	10		20,896
21	13	A	Carlisle U.	L 1-2	1-1	12	Wilkins R.	8065
22	22	H	Sunderland	W 1-0	0-0	11	Britton	22,802
23	26	A	Orient	L 1-3	0-1	11	Maybank	15,509
24	27	H	Charlton Ath.	L 2-3	0-2	13	Swain, Britton	25,367
25	Jan 10	A	Oldham Ath.	L 0-3	0-1	15		16 464
26	17	A	Nottingham F.	W 3-1	1-1	12	Garner, Wilkins, R, Hutchinson	14,172
27	31	H	W.B.A.	L 1-2	1-1	14	Britton	15,896
28	Feb 7	A	Oxford U.	D 1-1	0-0	12	Garner	11,162
29	18	H	Hull C.	D 0-0	0-0	—		10,254
30	21	A	Notts Co.	L 2-3	2-1	15	Stanley, Finnieston	14,528
31	25	H	Portsmouth	W 2-0	2-0	—	Cooke, Locke	12,709
32	28	H	Blackburn R.	W 3-1	1-1	11	Wilkins, R., 2, Finnieston	14,855
33	Mar 6	A	Plymouth Arg.	W 3-0	1-0	9	Stanley, Britton, Swain	20,638
34	13	H	Southampton	D 1-1	0-0	9	Finnieston	29,011
35	20	H	Bristol R.	D 0-0	0-0	9		16,132
36	27	A	Bolton W.	L 1-2	0-0	11	Britton	20,817
37	Apr 6	H	Fulham	D 0-0	0-0	—		23,605
38	10	A	Bristol C.	D 2-2	1-1	11	Swain, Stanley	24,710
39	16	H	Luton T.	D 2-2	1-1	11	Finnieston, Hay	19,878
40	17	H	Orient	L 0-2	0-1	11		17,679
41	19	A	Charlton Ath.	D 1-1	0-0	—	Berry (og)	23,263
42	24	A	York C.	D 2-2	0-1	11	Britton (pen), Finnieston	4914

Goalscorers

League (53): Wilkins, R. 11 (2 pens), Britton 8 (1 a pen), Garner 6, Finnieston 5, Maybank 5, Hutchinson 4, Swain 4, Stanley 3, Bason 1, Cooke 1, Droy 1, Hay 1, Langley 1, Locke 1, Own Goal 1.

F.A. Cup (6): Garner 2, Swain, Hutchinson, Wilkins R., Wicks.

League Cup	Second Round	Crewe Alex. (a)	0-1
F.A. Cup	Third Round	Bristol R. (h)	1-1
		(a)	1-0
	Fourth Round	York C. (a)	2-0
	Fifth Round	Crystal Palace (h)	2-3

Sherwood	Wilkins G.	Sparrow	Stanley	Droy	Dempsey	Britton	Wilkins R.	Maybank	Garner	Cooke	Swain	Bason	Harris	Hay	Langley	Hutchinson	Wilks	Locke	Bonetti	Finnieston	Lewington	Phillips	Match No.
1	2	3	4	5	6	7	8	9	10	11													1
1	2	3	4	5	6	7	8	9	10*	11	12												2
1	2	3		6	5	7*	8	9		11	10	4	12										3
1	2	3		5	6		8	9		11	10	4	7										4
1	2*	3		5	6	7	8	9		11	10	4	12										5
1		3	7	5	4		8	9		11	10		6	2									6
1			4	5	6	7	8			11	10		2	3	9								7
1			4	6	5	7	8			11		9	2	3	10								8
1			4	5	6	7	8			11		9	2	3	10								9
1			4	5	6	7	8					9*	2	3	11	10	12						10
1		3	6	5	11	8						7	2	4	9	10							11
1			6	5		7	8			11		9*	3	4	12	10		2					12
			6	5		7	8	9*		11			3	4	12	10		2	1				13
			6	5		7	8	9		11			3	4	12	10		2*	1				14
			4	6	5	7	8	9		11			3			10		2	1				15
			4	5	6	7	8	9		11			3			10		2	1				16
			4	5	6	7	8	9		11			3			10		2	1				17
			4	6	5	7	8	9		11*			3		12	10		2	1				18
			4	5	6	7	8	9		11			3			10		2	1				19
			4	6	5	7	8	9		11			3			10		2	1				20
				5	6	7	8	9		11			3	4		10		2	1				21
			4	5	6	7	8	9		11			3		12	10*		2	1				22
	12		4	5	6	7	8	9		11			3			10*		2	1				23
			4	5	6*	7	8	9	10	11			3		12			2	1				24
				5		7	8	9		11	12		3	4		10	6*	2	1				25
						7	8	9		11	4		3	6		10	5	2	1				26
						7	8	9		11	4		3	6		10	5	2	1				27
		3				7	8	9		11	4			6		10	5	2	1				28
						7	8			11	4		3	6		10	5	2	1	9			29
			4*			7	8		11	10			3	6			5	2	1	9	12		30
			4			7	8		11	10			3	6			5	2	1	9			31
			4			7	8*		11	10			3	6		12	5	2	1	9			32
			4			7	8			10			3	6			5	2	1	9	11		33
			4			7	8		12	10			3	6			5	2*	1	9	11		34
	3		4			7	8		12	10*			2	6			5		1	9	11		35
	2		4			7	8	9	10				3	6			5		1		11		36
	3		4			7	8	9	10				2	6			5		1		11		37
	3		4			7	8		10				2	6			5		1	9	11		38
	3		4			7	8		12	10			2	6			5		1*	9	11		39
	3		4			7	8		12	10			2	6			5			9	11*	1	40
	3		4			7	8		11	10			2	6			5			9		1	41
	3*		4			7	8		11	10	12		2	6			5			9		1	42
12	13	8	29	25	24	40	42	22	21	16	24	8	38	27	4	18	18	23	27	12	8	3	
	+1s								+4s	+1s	+1s	+1s	+2s	+1s	+6s	+1s			+1s				

Player and position	Ht.	Wt.	Birthplace	Clubs	League Appearances	Goals
Goalkeepers						
Peter Bonetti (England)	5 10	11 8	Putney	Chelsea	522	—
John Phillips (Wales)	6 0	10 8	Shrewsbury	Shrewsbury T.	51	—
				Aston Villa	15	—
				Chelsea	96	—
Steve Sherwood	6 3	14 0	Selby	Chelsea	16	—
				Brighton (on loan)	—	—
				Millwall (on loan)	1	—
				Brentford (on loan)	62	—
Les Briley	5 6	9 11	Southwark	Chelsea		.
				(contract cancelled March 1976)		
Defenders						
Ron Harris	5 7½	11 10	Hackney	Chelsea	518+2	10
Gary Locke	5 10½	10 8	London	Chelsea	112+1	2
Micky Droy	6 4	12 2	Highbury	Chelsea	98+2	4
*Marvin Hinton	5 10½	12 7	Croydon	Charlton Ath.	130	2
				Chelsea	257+8	3
Graham Wilkins	5 6	9 4	Hayes	Chelsea	19	—
John Dempsey (Eire)	6 0	11 1	London	Fulham	150	4
				Chelsea	161+4	4
John Sparrow	5 10	12 0	London	Chelsea	28+1	1
Steve Wicks	6 2	13 0	Reading	Chelsea	19+1	—
Midfield						
Charlie Cooke (Scotland)	5 8	12 6	St. Monance	Aberdeen	125	27
				Dundee	44	11
				Chelsea	204+8	15
				C. Palace	42+2	—
				Chelsea	71+2	7
David Hay (Scotland)	5 11	11 7	Paisley	Celtic	111+1	8
				Chelsea	61+1	1
Ray Wilkins (England)	5 7	10 0	Hillingdon	Chelsea	66+3	13
Steve Perkins	5 11	11 0	London	Chelsea	—	—
Ray Lewington	5 6	10 5	London	Chelsea	8+1	—
Brian Bason	5 9	11 1	Epsom	Chelsea	12+1	1
Garry Stanley	5 9	10 10	Burton-on-Trent	Chelsea	29	3
Forwards						
*Tommy Baldwin	5 8½	11 7	Gateshead	Arsenal	17	6
				Chelsea	181+3	74
				Millwall (on loan)	6	1
				Manchester U. (on loan)	2	—
Ian Britton	5 5	9 2	Dundee	Chelsea	82+4	11
Steve Finnieston	5 11	11 2	Edinburgh	Chelsea	21	7
				Cardiff C. (on loan)	9	2
John Sissons	5 7	10 8	Hayes	West Ham U.	212+2	37
				Sheffield W.	114+1	14
				Norwich C.	52+1	2
				Chelsea	10+1	—
				(contract cancelled March 1976)		
*Ian Hutchinson	6 0½	12 13	Derby	Chelsea	112+7	44
Bill Garner	6 0	12 0	Leicester	Notts Co.	2	—
				Bedford	Non-League	
				Southend U.	101+1	41
				Chelsea	78+8	26
Ken Swain	5 11	11 7	Liverpool	Chelsea	28+4	5
				W.B.A. (on loan)	—	—
Ted Maybank	5 10	10 12	London	Chelsea	25	6
Tommy Langley	5 11	11 7	London	Chelsea	9+9	2
Clive Walker	5 8	11 4	Oxford	Chelsea	—	—

President: T. Sarl-Williams, Esq.   *Chairman:* R. Rowlands.

Directors: A. E. Cheshire, C. Thompson, L. Lloyd, R. H. Clark, E. J. Owen.

Manager: Ken Roberts.   *Secretary:* S. Gandy.

Year Formed: 1884.   *Turned Professional:* 1902.

Limited Company: 1909.

Previous Grounds: Faulkner Street; Old Showground; 1904, Whipcord Lane; 1906, Sealand Road.

Honours: *Football League,* highest position: 17th, Division 3, 1975–76. Division 3(N), Runners-up: 1935–36. *F.A. Cup,* best season: 4th Rd., 1932–33, 1936–37, 1938–39, 1946–47, 1947–48, 1969–70. *Football League Cup:* best season, semi-final, 1974–75.

Record Victory: 12-0 v York C., Division 3(N), Feb. 1st, 1936.

Record Defeat: 2-11 v Oldham Ath., Division 3(N), Jan. 19th 1952.

Most League Points: 56, Division 3(N), 1946–47; Division 4, 1964–65.

Most League Goals: 119, Division 4, 1964–65.

Highest League Scorer in Season: Dick Yates, 36, Division 3(N), 1946–47.

Most League Goals in Total Aggregate: Gary Talbot, 83, 1963–67, 1968–70.

Most Capped Player: Bill Lewis, 9 (30), Wales.

Most League Appearances: Ray Gill, 408, 1951–62.

Record Transfer Fee Received: £100,000 from Luton T. for Paul Futcher, June 1974.

Record Transfer Fee Paid: £20,000 to Manchester C. for Barney Daniels, June 1975.

Managers Since the War: Frank Brown, Louis Page, John Harris, Stan Pearson, Bill Lambton, Peter Hauser.

Address of Supporters Club: 7 Bridge Street Row, Chester.

Address of Club Shop or Boutique: Club Shop, 7 Bridge Street Row, Chester.

The Stadium, Sealand Rd, Chester CH1 4LW. Telephone Chester 21048.   *Ground capacity:* 20,000.   *Record attendance:* 20,500 v Chelsea, F.A. Cup 3rd Rd., Replay, January 16 1952. *Record receipts:* £15,854 v Aston Villa, F.L. Cup semi-final first leg, January 15 1975. *Pitch measurements:* 114 yds × 76 yds.

How to get there: Nearest railway station, Chester. Corporation bus to Town Hall Square, where special buses run from the Odeon Cinema to the ground.

Match tickets: No advance booking.

Car parking: Extensive parking at ground.

Entertainments/catering facilities: Catering facilities on ground.

Club shop: In town centre; stocks all types of souvenirs.

Handbooks/programmes: Programmes not available on subscription.

Extra information: Additional programme shop inside the ground.

Club Colours: Royal blue shirts with white stripes, royal blue shorts.

Change Colour: Yellow shirts white shorts.

First Team Trainer: Vincent Pritchard.

Coach: Reg Mathewson.

Youth Team Manager: Cliff Sear.

Club Nickname: 'The Seals'.

CHESTER 1975-76 LEAGUE RECORD

Match No.	Date	Venue	Opponents	Result	H/T Score	League Pos'n	Goalscorers	Attendance
1	Aug 16	A	Crystal Palace	L 0-2	0-1	—		13,009
2	23	H	Southend U.	D 1-1	1-0	20	Daniels	4781
3	30	H	Mansfield T.	D 1-1	0-0	20	Redfern	6164
4	Sept 6	A	Grimsby T.	L 1-2	0-1	22	Owen	4092
5	13	A	Brighton & H.A.	L 0-6	0-2	23		7924
6	20	H	Peterborough U.	D 1-1	1-0	24	Crossley	4063
7	24	H	Colchester U.	W 1-0	1-0	—	Owen	3954
8	27	A	Halifax T.	L 2-5	1-3	23	Owen, Whitehead	2240
9	Oct 4	H	Hereford U.	L 0-1	0-0	24		4144
10	11	H	Aldershot	W 1-0	1-0	22	Storton	3375
11	18	A	Walsall	L 0-1	0-0	24		4146
12	21	H	Sheffield W.	W 1-0	0-0	—	Owen	6248
13	25	H	Cardiff C.	D 1-1	1-1	23	Pugh	5348
14	Nov 1	A	Shrewsbury T.	L 0-2	0-0	23		4567
15	4	A	Rotherham U.	W 1-0	1-0	—	Lennard	4282
16	8	H	Millwall	W 3-1	2-1	20	Redfern, Lennard, Owen	4811
17	15	A	Port Vale	W 1-0	1-0	16	Lennard	3908
18	29	A	Chesterfield	D 1-1	0-1	17	Storton	4338
19	Dec 6	H	Gillingham	D 2-2	1-0	15	Owen, Edwards	4451
20	20	H	Swindon T.	W 2-1	0-0	13	Delgado, Storton	3674
21	26	A	Wrexham	D 1-1	1-1	14	Lennard	10,486
22	27	H	Preston N.E.	W 3-0	1-0	9	Pugh, McMahon (og), Owen	8137
23	Jan 10	H	Mansfield T.	D 1-1	1-1	13	Delgado	4623
24	17	A	Peterborough U.	L 0-3	0-1	16		8674
25	24	H	Brighton & H.A.	W 3-0	0-0	13	Pugh, Redfern, Owen	5099
26	31	A	Sheffield W.	L 0-3	0-2	15		7558
27	Feb 7	H	Rotherham U.	W 3-1	1-0	14	Redfern (pen), Lennard, Loska	4573
28	14	A	Millwall	L 0-1	0-0	15		4965
29	21	H	Port Vale	W 1-0	0-0	13	Redfern (pen)	5707
30	24	A	Colchester U.	L 0-1	0-0	—		3534
31	28	A	Cardiff C.	L 0-2	0-0	16		10,000
32	Mar 6	H	Shrewsbury T.	W 1-0	1-0	14	Owen	5916
33	10	A	Hereford U.	L 0-5	0-3	—		7103
34	13	A	Aldershot	D 1-1	0-1	14	Edwards	3831
35	16	H	Walsall	D 1-1	0-1	—	Edwards	4059
36	20	H	Chesterfield	W 2-1	1-0	13	Redfern (pen), Owen	4018
37	27	A	Gillingham	L 0-2	0-1	13		4983
38	30	A	Swindon T.	L 1-2	1-2	—	Owen	5117
39	Apr 7	H	Halifax T.	W 2-1	0-1	—	Storton, Redfern	3369
40	10	A	Grimsby T.	L 0-2	0-2	17		4644
41	16	H	Bury	D 0-0	0-0	—		5045
42	17	H	Wrexham	L 1-3	0-1	17	Draper	6553
43	19	A	Preston N.E.	D 0-0	0-0	—		6719
44	23	A	Southend U.	L 0-2	0-1	18		3553
45	27	A	Bury	L 0-1	0-0	—		3748
46	4	H	Crystal Palace	W 2-1	1-1	—	Crossley 2	6702

Goalscorers

League (43): Owen 11, Redfern 7 (3 pens), Lennard 5, Storton 4, Crossley 3, Pugh 3, Edwards 3, Delgado 2, Daniels 1, Whitehead 1, Loska 1, Draper 1, Own goal 1.

F.A. Cup (3): Moore, Redfern, Edwards.

League Cup	First Round	W.rexham (a)	0-3
	Second Leg	(h)	0-0
F.A. Cup	First Round	Darlington (a)	0-0
		(h)	2-0
	Second Round	Shrewsbury T. (a)	1-3

Millington	Edwards	Loska	Matthewson	Dunleavy	Seddon	Whitehead	Pugh	Draper	James	Lennard	Moore	Storton	Mason	Daniels	Redfern	Owen	Craven	Crossley	Watling	Delgado	Dearden	Nickeas	Match No.
1	2	3	4	5	6	7	8	9	10	11													1
1	2	3*		5	8	7		9		11	12	4	6		10								2
1		3		5	6		8			11	9	4	2		7	10							3
1		3		5	6		8			11*	9	4	2	12	7	10							4
		3		5	6		12			10	8	4	2		7*	9	1	11					5
	2	3		5			8			12		4	6	10	7	9		11*	1				6
	2	3		5			8			11		4	6	9	7	10			1				7
	2	3		5	12	7	8			11		4	6		10	9*			1				8
	2	3		5	12	7		10		11*	9	4	6		8				1				9
	2	3		5			8	9		11		4	6	10	7				1				10
1	2	3		5*	12		8	9		11		4	6	10	7								11
1	2*	3		5	12		8	9		10		4	6		7			11					12
1		3		5	2	12	10	8		11		4	6		7*	9							13
1	2	3					6	9		11	8	4			7	10				5			14
1	2	3					8	6		10	9	4			7			11		5			15
1	2	3					6	9		11	8	4			7	10				5			16
1	2	3					6	8		11	9	4			7	10				5			17
1	2	3					8			10	9	4	6	11	7*			12		5			18
1	2	3					6	8		11	9*	4			7	10		12		5			19
1	2	3					6	8		10		4			7	9		11		5			20
1	2	3					8	6		10		4			7	9		11		5			21
1	2	3					6	8		10		4			7	9		11		5			22
1	2	3					8	6		10		4			7	9		11		5			23
1	2	3					8	6		10		4			7	9		11		5			24
1	2	3					8	6		10		4			7	9		11		5			25
1	2	3					8	6		10		4	12		7	9		11*		5			26
1		3	12				8	6*		10		4	2		7	9		11		5			27
1	12	3					8	6		10		4	2		7	9		11*		5			28
1	2	3		5			8	6				4	10		7	9		11					29
1	2	3	4				8	6		10					7	9		11		5			30
1		3		5			8	6		10*	12		2		7	9		11		4			31
1		3		5			8	6		11	10	4	2		7*	9		12					32
1		3*		5			8	6		11	9	10	2		7			12		4			33
1	2						8	6		10		4	3		7	9		11		5			34
1	2						8	6		12	10*	4	3		7	9		11		5			35
1	2	3		5			8	6		10		4			7	9		11					36
1	2	3		5			8	6		10		4			7*	9		11		12			37
1	2	3		5			8	12				4	6		7	9		11		10*			38
1	2	3		5		7	8	6				4	10*			9		11		12			39
1	2*	3		5			8	6		11		4			7	9		12		10			40
1		3	12				8*	6		10	11	2			9	7				5	4		41
1		3		5	12	7*		6		10		2				9		11		8	4		42
1	2					7	8	6		10		4	3			9		11		5			43
1	2				12	7	8	6		10			3			9		11*		5	4		44
1		3	2				8*			10	11	4	6		7	9		12		5			45
1		3	2				8			10		4	6		7	9		11		5			46
40	36	37	7	23	5	7	42	37	1	39	17	40	29	8	37	40	1	22	5	28	2	3	
	+1s		+2s	+3s	+3s	+2s				+2s	+3s		+1s	+1s				+6s	+2s				

Player and position	Ht.	Wt.	Birthplace	Clubs	League Appearances	Goals
Goalkeepers						
Gren Millington	5 10	11 6	Queensferry	Chester	1	—
				Brighton	—	—
				Chester	109	—
Michael Craven	5 11	10 6	Chester	Chester	1	—
Defenders						
Chris Dunleavy	5 10	11 6	Liverpool	Everton	—	—
				Southport	145+2	9
				Chester	66+2	—
Nigel Edwards	5 11	11 10	Wrexham	Chester	224+8	13
				Rotherham U. (on loan)	—	—
Bob Delgado	6 0	11 7	Cardiff	Luton T.	—	—
				Carlisle U.	25+10	3
				Workington (on loan)	7	—
				Rotherham U.	69+1	5
				Chester	28+2	2
Tony Loska	5 8	11 0	Stoke	Shrewsbury T.	12	—
				Port Vale	74+6	5
				Chester	100+6	5
*Reg Matthewson	5 11	11 12	Sheffield	Sheffield U.	146+3	3
				Fulham	156+2	1
				Chester	86+1	1
Stuart Mason	5 8½	10 9	Whitchurch	Wrexham	28	—
				Liverpool	—	—
				Doncaster R.	1	—
				Wrexham	145+13	3
				Chester	106+3	4
*Gary Potter	5 11	10 12	Chester	Chester	11	—
Trevor Storton	6 1	12 4	Keighley	Tranmere R.	112+6	8
				Liverpool	5	—
				Chester	85	6
Paul Raynor	5 11	11 0	Chester	Chester	—	—
Midfield						
*Dave Lennard	5 9	11 0	Manchester	Bolton W.	114+5	3
				Halifax T.	97	16
				Blackpool	42+3	9
				Cambridge U.	39+1	6
				Chester	73+2	11
Terry Owen	5 7	11 1	Liverpool	Everton	2	—
				Bradford C.	41+11	6
				Chester	131+10	36
Graham Pugh	5 7	11 2	Hoole	Sheffield W.	137+4	8
Huddersfield T. 80(1) Chester 59+2(3)						
Mark Nickeas	5 9	10 11	Southport	Plymouth Arg.	—	—
				Chester	3	—
Derek Draper	5 8	10 8	Swansea	Swansea	61	10
Derby Co. 8(1) Bradford P.A. 60+3(9) Chester 316+3(55)						
Forwards						
*Barney Daniels	5 8	11 0	Salford	Manchester U.	—	—
Manchester C. 9+4(2) Chester 8+1(1)						
Jim Redfern	5 7	10 2	Kirby	Bolton W.	19+5	2
				Chester	93+4	13
*Ian Seddon	5 8½	10 0	Prestbury	Bolton W.	51+13	4
Chester 62+11(7) Stockport Co. (on loan) 4 Chesterfield (on loan) 2 Cambridge C. (on loan) 14(2)						
*Norman Whitehead	5 9	10 9	Liverpool	Southport	7+1	—
Rochdale 154+2(11) Rotherham U. 29+4(2) Chester 66+8(5)						
*Gary Moore	6 2	12 0	South Hetton	Sunderland	11	2
				Grimsby T.	52	15
				Southend U.	157+6	46
				Colchester U. (on loan)	11	7
				Chester	29+14	4
Paul Crossley	5 7	11 5	Rochdale	Rochdale	17	2
				Preston N.E.	3	—
				Southport	10	2
				Tranmere R.	186+17	37
				Chester	22+6	3

CHESTERFIELD

President: His Grace the Duke of Devonshire, M.C., D.L., J.P.

Vice-President: G. Kenning, D.F.C., T.D., M.A.

Chairman: D. B. Newton.

Vice-Chairman: P. C. J. T. Kirkman, O.B.E.

Directors: F. Tuckley, A. Bates, E. Brocklehurst, E. I. Gaunt, J. Leedham.

Team Manager: Joe Shaw.

General Manager/Secretary: A. G. Sutherland.

Year Formed: 1866. *Turned Professional:* 1891.

Limited Company: 1871.

Previous Name: Chesterfield Town, 1904.

Honours: *Football League,* highest position in Division 2: 4th, 1946–47. Division 3(N). Champions: 1930–31, 1935–36; Runners-up: 1933–34. Division 4, Champions: 1969–70, *F.A. Cup,* best season: 5th Rd., 1932–33, 1937–38, 1949–50. *Football League Cup,* best season, 4th Rd., 1964–65.

Record Victory: 10-0 v Glossop North End, Division 2, Jan. 17th, 1903.

Record Defeat: 1-9 v Port Vale, Division 2, Sept. 24th, 1932.

Most League Points: 64, Division 4, 1969–70.

Most League Goals: 102, Division 3(N), 1930–31.

Highest League Scorer in Season: Jimmy Cookson, 44, Division 3(N), 1925–26.

Most League Goals in Total Aggregate: Herbert Munday, 112, 1899–1909.

Most Capped Player: Walter McMillen, 4 (7), Ireland.

Most League Appearances: Dave Blakey, 613, 1948–67.

Record Transfer Fee Received: £60,000 for Jim Brown from Sheffield U., March 1974.

Record Transfer Fee Paid: £15,000 to Sheffield U. for Frank Barlow, July 1972.

Managers Since the War: Bob Brocklebank, Bob Marshall, Ted Davison, Duggie Livingstone, Tony McShane, Jimmy McGuigan.

Address of Club Shop: The Club Shop, Chesterfield F.C.

Recreation Ground, Chesterfield. Telephone Chesterfield 32318. *Ground capacity:* 28,500 (12,000 covered). *Record attendance:* 30,968 v Newcastle U., Division 2, April 7, 1939. *Record receipts:* £4,600 v Aston Villa F.L. Div. 3 August 15, 1970. *Pitch measurements:* 114 yds × 72 yds.

How to get there: Chesterfield railway station is one mile from the ground, via Corporation St., Holywell St., to Saltergate.

Match tickets: Seats in the Centre and Wing Stands may be booked in advance.

Car parking: Street parking permitted around the ground. Also car parks in Saltergate within ½ mile of the ground.

Entertainments/catering facilities: A social club is sited on the ground at the Saltergate entrance. Entertainment provided at the Aquaries Club, Whittington Moor.

Club shop: At the ground; stocks all types of souvenirs.

Handbooks/programmes: Programmes available on subscription.

Extra information: Arnold Birch, Chesterfield's goalkeeper, scored five goals in 1923–24, all from penalties.

Club Colours: Blue shirts, white shorts, royal blue stockings, white tops.

Change Colours: All amber.

Club Trainer/Coach: Harold Roberts.

Club Nickname: 'Blues' or 'Spireites'.

CHESTERFIELD 1975–76 LEAGUE RECORD

Match No.	Date	Venue	Opponents	Result	H/T Score	League Pos'n	Goalscorers	Attendance
1	Aug 16	A	Swindon T.	W 1-0	0-0	—	Burrows (og)	7675
2	23	H	Crystal Palace	L 1-2	0-1	11	Darling	5386
3	30	A	Wrexham	L 0-1	0-1	18		3519
4	Sept 6	H	Peterborough U.	D 1-1	1-0	16	Moss	2570
5	13	A	Bury	L 1-3	1-0	22	Fern	4368
6	20	H	Hereford U.	L 2-3	0-0	22	Darling (pen), Burton	3000
7	24	H	Sheffield W.	W 1-0	1-0	—	Darling	12,959
8	27	A	Brighton & H.A.	L 0-3	0-2	22		8784
9	Oct 4	A	Preston N.E.	W 3-0	0-0	19	Darling, Kowalski, Moss	4000
10	11	H	Shrewsbury T.	W 2-1	0-1	14	Moss, Shanahan	4060
11	18	A	Port Vale	D 1-1	0-0	16	Winstanley	3892
12	21	A	Gillingham	D 2-2	0-1	—	Hunter, Winstanley	5573
13	25	H	Millwall	D 2-2	0-1	15	McEwan, Shanahan	3500
14	Nov 1	A	Cardiff C.	L 3-4	0-3	30	O'Neill, McElvaney, Shanahan	7512
15	5	H	Colchester U.	W 6-1	3-1	—	Darling 2, Shanahan 3, Moss	2906
16	8	H	Aldershot	W 5-2	2-0	9	Hunter, Shanahan 2, Moss, McEwan	4374
17	15	A	Walsall	L 0-1	0-0	14		4175
18	29	H	Chester	D 1-1	1-0	14	Shanahan (pen)	4338
19	Dec 6	A	Rotherham U.	L 0-2	0-1	17		6474
20	20	H	Halifax T.	L 1-2	0-0	19	Shanahan (pen)	3703
21	26	A	Mansfield T.	W 1-0	1-0	19	Shanahan (pen)	8607
22	27	H	Southend U.	L 1-2	0-2	19	Fern	4670
23	Jan 3	A	Grimsby T.	L 0-3	0-2	20		4024
24	10	H	Wrexham	D 1-1	0-0	20	Shanahan	3732
25	17	A	Hereford U.	L 2-4	0-3	20	Bailey, Shanahan (pen.)	5999
26	24	H	Port Vale	L 0-1	0-0	20		4052
27	31	H	Gillingham	L 0-1	0-1	22		21,000
28	Feb 7	A	Colchester U.	W 3-2	2-0	18	Cammack, Fern, Darling	2245
29	11	H	Bury	W 3-2	1-1	—	Darling 2, Cammack	3024
30	14	H	Aldershot	L 1-3	1-2	18	Shanahan (pen)	3362
31	21	H	Walsall	W 2-1	0-0	17	Darling, Shanahan	4595
32	28	A	Millwall	L 0-2	0-2	18		6476
33	Mar 6	H	Cardiff C.	D 1-1	0-1	19	Fern	4095
34	9	A	Preston N.E.	L 1-3	0-2	—	Cammack	4621
35	13	A	Shrewsbury T.	W 2-0	1-0	19	Fern, Bentley	4967
36	20	A	Chester	L 1-2	0-1	20	Darling (pen)	4018
37	24	H	Sheffield W.	W 3-1	2-1	—	Darling 2 (1 a pen), Fern	10,653
38	27	H	Rotherham U.	W 1-0	1-0	18	Cammack	5595
39	30	A	Halifax T.	L 0-1	0-1	—		1975
40	Apr 3	H	Swindon T.	W 4-0	2-0	17	O'Neill, Fern 2, Darling	3646
41	7	A	Brighton & H.A.	W 2-1	1-0	—	Darling (2 pens)	4500
42	10	A	Peterborough U.	W 1-0	0-0	15	Cammack	5830
43	16	H	Grimsby T.	W 4-3	1-2	—	Fern 2, Darling (pen), Welch	5483
44	17	H	Mansfield T.	L 1-2	1-0	15	Darling	10,616
45	19	A	Southend U.	D 1-1	1-1	—	Fern	3917
46	28	A	Crystal Palace	D 0-0	0-0	—		27,961

Goalscorers

League (69): Darling 18 (6 pens), Shanahan 15 (5 pens), Fern 11, Cammack 5, Moss 5, Hunter 2, Winstanley 2, McEwan 2, O'Neill 2, Kowalski 1, Burton 1, McElvaney 1, Bailey 1, Bentley 1, Welch 1, own goals 1.
League Cup (5): Darling, Kowalski, Fern, Hunter, own goal 1.

League Cup	First Round	Lincoln C. (a)	2-4
	Second Leg	(h)	3-2
F.A. Cup	First Round	Bradford C. (a)	0-1

Tingay	Holmes	Burton	McEwan	Hunter	Barlow	Bellamy	Moss	Darling	Bentley	Fern	Kowalski	Shanahan	O'Neill	Winstanley	McElvaney	Wann	Roberts	Badger	Seddon	Bailey	Welch	McIntosh	Cammack	Hardwick	Cross	Charlton	Match No.
1	2	3	4	5	6	7	8	9	10	11																	1
1	2	3	4	5	6	7	8	9	10	11																	2
1	2	3	4	5	6		8	9	10	11			7														3
1	2	3	4	5	6		8	9	10*	11			7	12													4
1	2	3	4	5	6	10	7	9		11			8														5
1	2	3	4	5	6	10	7	8*	11	12			9														6
1		3	8	4	6	7		9	10	11	2	5															7
1		3	4	10	6	8	7	9		11	2	5															8
1		3	4		6	7	8	9	10	11	2	5															9
1		3	12	4	6		8	9	10*	7	11	2	5														10
1		3	4		6	7	8	9		11	2	5	10														11
1		3	10	4	6		8	9		11	2	5	7														12
1		3	10	4	6		8	12	9*	11	2	5	7														13
1		3	10	4	6		8	9		11	2	5	7														14
1	2		7	4	6		8	9	10	11	3	5															15
1	2	8	4		6		7		10	11	3	5			9												16
1	2	8		4	6		7	9		11	3	5			10												17
1	2				6		8	7	10		4	9	3	5	11												18
1	12	2	5	6			8	7	11	10*	4	9	3														19
1		3	4	5	6		8	10	7	9	2				11												20
1	2			5	6		8	9	10	7	4	11	3														21
1	2			5	6		8	9	10	7	4	11	3														22
1	12	3	2*	5			7	8	11	10	4	9	6														23
1		3		5			8	7		11	4	9	6					2	10								24
1	2	3		5				10	7		4	11	6								8	9*	12				25
1	2	3		5				10	11		4	9	6								7	8					26
1		3		5			12	11	10		4	9	6					2			7		8*				27
1		3		5			12	11	10		4	9	6					2*			7		8				28
1		6		5				11	10	7	4	9	3					2					8				29
1		3		5				7	10	11	4	9	6					2					8				30
1		3	4	5				7	10	11		9	6					2					8				31
1		3	4	5					10	11		9	6					2			7		8				32
1		3*	4	5				7	10	11		9	6					2			12		8				33
1		6		5				11	10*	7	12	9	3					2			4		8				34
			4	5				9	10	11			3					2			7		8	1	6		35
		3	4	5				9	10	11*								2			7		8	1	6	12	36
		3		5				9	10	11								2			7		8	1	6	4	37
		3		5				9	10	11								2			7		8	1	6	4	38
		3		5				9	10	11								2			7		8	1	6	4	39
			4	5			12	9	10	11			3					2					8	1	6	7*	40
		7		5				9	10	11			3					2	4				8	1	6		41
		7		5				9	10	11			3					2	4				8	1	6		42
		7		5				9	10	11			3					2	4				8	1	6		43
		7		5				9	10	11			3					2	4				8	1	6		44
		7		5				9	10	11			3					2					8	1	6	4	45
		7		5			8	9	10	11			3					2						1	6	4	46
34	11	28	35	45	22	7	21	36	28	36	29	29	41	12	4	3	1	15	2	1	13	3	20	12	12	6	
+1s	+1s	+1s						+2s	+1s	+2s	+2s										+2s				+1s		

CHESTERFIELD—PLAYERS

Player and position	Ht.	Wt.	Birthplace	Clubs	League Appearances	Goals
Goalkeepers						
Phillip Tingay	5 11	11 12	Chesterfield	Chesterfield	117	—
				Barnsley (on loan)	8	—
Steve Hardwick	5 10	11 6	Mansfield	Chesterfield	17	—
Defenders						
Ken Burton	5 7½	11 8	Sheffield	Sheffield W.	54+2	2
				Peterborough U. (on loan)	3+1	—
				Chesterfield	108+1	2
Len Badger	5 8	10 8	Sheffield	Sheffield U.	457+1	7
				Chesterfield	15	—
Albert Holmes	5 9	12 0	Sheffield	Chesterfield	468+3	9
				(contract cancelled March 1976)		
Eric Winstanley	6 1	12 8	Barnsley	Barnsley	409	36
				Chesterfield	97+1	7
Sean O'Neill	5 9	12 2	Belfast	Leeds U.	—	—
				Chesterfield	77+2	3
Leslie Hunter	6 2	11 10	Middlesbrough	Chesterfield	45	2
Midfield						
Frank Barlow	5 10	11 9½	Mexborough	Sheffield U.	116+5	2
				Chesterfield	140+1	3
Bill McEwan	5 10	11 2	Cleland	Hibernian	59+2	2
				Blackpool	4	—
				Brighton	27	3
				Chesterfield	57+1	3
David Bentley	5 8½	10 0	Worksop	Rotherham U.	243+7	13
				Mansfield T. (on loan)	1+3	1
				Chesterfield	29+2	1
Arthur Bellamy	5 8½	9 10½	Blackhill	Burnley	205+12	30
				Chesterfield	133	12
				(contract cancelled April 1976)		
Ronald Welch	5 6½	10 7	Chesterfield	Burnley	1	—
				Brighton	35+1	4
				Chesterfield	16+5	1
David McElvaney	5 8	11 2	Chesterfield	Chesterfield	4	1
Forwards						
Malcolm Darling	5 7½	10 0	Arbroath	Blackburn R.	114+13	31
				Norwich C.	16	5
				Rochdale	82+4	16
				Bolton W.	6+2	—
				Chesterfield	80+2	26
Rod Fern	5 11	11 0	Burton on Trent	Leicester C.	132+17	27
				Luton T.	34+5	5
				Chesterfield	36	11
Andrew Kowalski	5 10	11 0	Mansfield	Chesterfield	99+6	12
Peter Roberts	5 7	10 12	Chesterfield	Chesterfield	2	—
Steve Cammack	5 11	11 1	Sheffield	Sheffield U.	21+15	5
				Chesterfield	20	5
David Bailey	6 1	11 9	Worksop	Chesterfield	1	1

COLCHESTER UNITED DIV. 4

President: A. Buck, M.P.

Chairman: J. W. Rippingale.

Vice-Chairman: G. H. Parker.

Directors: T. C. M. Dodwell, S. G. Firth, N. F. Fitch.

Manager: Bobby Roberts. *Secretary:* Mrs. E. Scott.

Year Formed: 1937. *Turned Professional:* 1937.

Limited Company: 1937.

Honours: *Football League,* Highest position in Division 3(S) 3rd, 1956–57. Division 4, Runners-Up; 1961–62. *F.A. Cup,* best season: 1970–71, 6th Rd. (Record for a Fourth Division club, shared with Oxford United.) *Football League Cup,* best season: 5th Rd., 1974–75.

Record Victory: 9-1 v Bradford C., Division 4, Dec. 30th, 1961.

Record Defeat: 0-7 v Leyton Orient, Division 3(S), Jan. 5th, 1952; 0-7 v Reading, Division 3(S), Sept. 18th, 1957.

Most League Points: 60, Division 4, 1973–74.

Most League Goals: 104, Division 4, 1961–62.

Most League Goals in a Season: Bobby Hunt, 37, Division 4, 1961–62.

Most League Goals in Total Aggregate: Martyn King, 131, 1959–65.

Most Capped Player: None.

Most League Appearances: Feter Wright, 421, 1952–64.

Record Transfer Fee Received: £19,000 from Blackburn R. for Bobby Svarc, October, 1975.

Record Transfer Fee Paid: £12,000 to Bournemouth for Paul Aimson, August, 1973.

Managers Since the War: Ted Fenton, Jimmy Allen, Jack Butler, Benny Fenton, Neil Franklin, Dick Graham, Jim Smith.

Layer Rd. Ground, Colchester. Telephone 74042. *Telegraphic address:* 'United Colchester'. *Ground capacity:* 16,150. *Record attendance:* 19,072 v Reading F.A. Cup 1st Rd., November 27, 1948. *Record receipts:* £10,500 v Leeds U., F.A. Cup 5th Rd., February 13, 1971. *Pitch measurements:* 110 yds × 73 yds.

How to get there: Buses from Butt Road in Colchester, which is about 2 miles from the railway station. Also buses from town centre and bus station.

Match tickets: Stand seats can be booked two weeks in advance (Ticket Office tel: Colchester 72202 or 74042.)

Car parking: Parking facilities in Butt Road and Layer Road, approximately 150 yards past the ground on the south side of Colchester. Free parking in Army Barracks (150 yards).

Entertainments/catering facilities: Refreshment points on the ground.

Club shop: Sells all types of souvenirs; mailing list on request.

Handbooks/programmes: Back numbers of programmes can be ordered from the club shop.

Extra information: In 1947–48, Colchester, then a non-League side, reached the 5th round of the F.A. Cup.

Club Colours: Blue and white vertical stripes, blue shorts, white stockings.

Change Colours: Red shirts, black shorts, red stockings.

Club Trainer/Coach: Ray Hartford.

Club Nickname: 'The U's.

COLCHESTER UNITED 1975–76 LEAGUE RECORD

Match No.	Date	Venue	Opponents	Result	H/T Score	League Pos'n	Goalscorers	Attendance
1	Aug 16	A	Preston N. E.	L 1-2	1-0	—	Svarc	6324
2	23	H	Mansfield T.	L 0-2	0-2	24		3333
3	30	A	Crystal Palace	L 2-3	2-2	24	Svarc, Bunkell	13,713
4	Sept 6	H	Halifax T.	L 0-1	0-0	24		2819
5	13	A	Hereford U.	D 0-0	0-0	24		5577
6	20	H	Brighton & H.A.	W 2-0	0-0	21	Froggatt, Svarc	3176
7	24	A	Chester	L 0-1	0-1	—		3954
8	27	A	Swindon T.	W 1-0	0-0	21	Packer	5750
9	Oct 4	H	Bury	D 0-0	0-0	21		3035
10	11	H	Walsall	W 2-0	1-0	18	Froggatt, Dominey	2980
11	18	A	Aldershot	D 2-2	1-2	19	Foley 2	3586
12	21	H	Rotherham U.	D 0-0	0-0	—		3468
13	25	H	Port Vale	W 1-0	1-0	14	Foley	3053
14	Nov 1	A	Millwall	D 1-1	0-1	14	Smith	7492
15	5	A	Chesterfield	L 1-6	1-3	—	Smith	2906
16	8	H	Shrewsbury T.	D 1-1	0-1	18	Smith	3088
17	15	A	Cardiff C.	L 0-2	0-1	20		6781
18	29	A	Gillingham	W 1-0	0-0	18	Foley	5402
19	Dec 6	H	Sheffield W.	W 2-1	0-0	14	Smith, Cook	3534
20	13	A	Wrexham	D 1-1	0-1	12	Froggatt	2143
21	20	H	Wrexham	L 0-2	0-2	18		2608
22	26	A	Southend U.	L 0-2	0-1	19		6267
23	27	H	Grimsby T.	W 1-0	0-0	18	Foley	3136
24	Jan 10	H	Crystal Palace	L 0-3	0-2	19		6240
25	14	A	Peterborough U.	L 1-3	0-1	—	Packer	7453
26	17	A	Brighton & H.A.	L 0-6	0-3	19		16,302
27	24	H	Hereford U.	L 1-4	1-3	19	Telford	2626
28	31	A	Rotherham U.	L 0-2	0-1	21		3943
29	Feb 7	H	Chesterfield	L 2-3	0-2	23	Bunkell (pen), Leslie	2245
30	14	A	Shrewsbury T.	L 0-1	0-0	23		4485
31	21	H	Cardiff C.	W 3-2	0-1	22	Garwood 2, Froggatt	3248
32	24	H	Chester	W 1-0	0-0	—	Gough	3534
33	28	A	Port Vale	L 2-3	1-1	19	Dyer 2	3803
34	Mar 13	A	Walsall	D 1-1	0-1	24	Leslie	5371
35	16	H	Aldershot	W 2-0	1-0	—	Gough, Leslie	3040
36	20	H	Gillingham	D 2-2	0-0	21	Bunkell (pen), Leslie	3981
37	23	H	Millwall	L 0-1	0-1	—		4573
38	27	A	Sheffield W.	L 0-1	0-0	23		6905
39	Apr 3	H	Preston N.E.	D 1-1	1-1	24	Leslie	2657
40	6	H	Swindon T.	L 1-2	1-2	—	Leslie	2694
41	12	A	Bury	D 0-0	0-0	—		4505
42	16	H	Peterborough U.	D 1-1	1-0	—	Bunkell	3687
43	17	H	Southend U.	W 2-1	0-1	23	Gough, Froggatt	4260
44	19	A	Grimsby T.	W 1-0	1-0	—	Gough	4862
45	24	A	Mansfield T.	D 0-0	0-0	22		7407
46	26	A	Halifax T.	D 1-1	1-0	—	Gough	856

Goalscorers

League (41): Leslie 6, Froggatt 5, Foley 5, Gough 5, Smith 4, Bunkell 4 (2 pens), Svarc 3, Packer 2, Garwood 2, Dyer 2, Dominey 1, Cook 1. Telford 1.
League Cup (3): Svarc 2, Smith.
F.A. Cup (4): Leslie, Dominey, Smith, Packer (pen).

League Cup	First Round	Crystal Palace (a)	0-3
	Second Leg	(h)	3-1
F.A. Cup	First Round	Dover (h)	3-3
		(a)	1-4

Walker	O'Donnell	Cook	Bunkell	Packer	Harrison	Thomas	Svarc	Froggatt	Smith	Dyer	Dominey	Williams	Anderson	Leslie	Foley	Bright	Allinson	Gough	Bond	Telford	Garwood	Match No.
1	2	3	4	5	6	7	8	9	10	11*	12											1
1		7	4	6	2		8	9	10	12	5*	3	11									2
1		7	4	10	5	2	8	9	11*	6		3	12									3
1		7	4	5*	2		8	9		12	6	3	11	10								4
1		7*	5	2			8	9	4	6	3	11	10	12								5
1		7	6	10			8	9	2	5	3	11		4*	12							6
1		7	6	10*			8	9	2	5	3	11		4	12							7
1		7	12	6			8	9	2	5		11*	4	10								8
1		7	4	6				9	11	2	5	3		8	10							9
1		7	4	6				9	11	2	5	3		8	10							10
1		7	4	6				9	11	2	5	3		8	10							11
1		7	4	6				9	11	2	5	3	12	8	10*							12
1		7	4	6				9	11	2	5	3*	12	8	10							13
1		7	4	6				9	11	2	5	3	12	8	10*							14
1		7	4	6				9	11	2	5	3		10	8							15
1		7	4	6				9*	11	2	5	3	12	10	8							16
1		7	4	6				12	10	2	5	3	11*	9	8							17
1		7	4	6				9	11	2	5	3		8	10							18
1		7	4	6*	12			9	11	2	5	3		8	10							19
1		7	4	6	12			9	11*	2	5	3		8	10							20
1		7	4	6				9	11	2	5	3		8	10							21
1		7		6					11	2*	5	3	9	8	10	4	12					22
1		7	4	6					11		5	3		10	8	9	2					23
1		7	4	6				9	11	2*	5	3	12	10				8				24
1		7	4	6				11	12	2*	5	3	9	10				8				25
1		7		6				11		2	5	3	9	4	10			8				26
		7*	4	6					11	12	5	3		10		2		8	1	9		27
			4	6	5			9	10	11	12	3		7	2			8*	1			28
1		7	4	5*				9	11	6		3		10	2			8	12			29
		3	4	6				9	11	7	5	2						8	1		10	30
1		3	4	5				9	11		6	2		7				8			10	31
1		3	4	6				9	11		5	2	12	10				8*			7	32
1		3	4	6				9	11		5	2	12	10				8			7*	33
1		3	4	5				9	11		6	2		10				8			7	34
1		3	4	6				9	11		5	2		10				8			7	35
1		3	4	6				9	11		5	2		10				8			7	36
1		3	4	6				9	11		5	2		10				8			7	37
1		3	4	6				9	11		5	2	12	10				8*			7	38
1		7*	4	6				9	11	2	5	3	12	10				8				39
1			4	6				9	11	2	5	3		10				8			7	40
1			4	6				9	11	2	5	3	12	10				8*			7	41
1			4	6					11	2	5	3	12	10	9*			8			7	42
1		10*	4	6				9	11	2	5	3	12		7			8				43
1			4	6				9	11	2	5	3		10				8			7	44
1			4	6				9	11	2	5	3		10				8			7	45
1			4	6				9	11	2	5	3		10				8			7	46
43	1	39	40	44	5	7	8	41	39	34	32	36	13	36	26	18	3	22	3	1	15	
		+1s		+2s	+1s				+2s	+2s	+6s		+3s	+3s	+3s	+2s	+2s			+1s		

COLCHESTER UNITED—PLAYERS

Player and position	Ht.	Wt.	Birthplace	Clubs	League Appearances	Goals
Goalkeepers						
Mike Walker	6 1	13 2	Colwyn Bay	Shrewsbury T.	7	—
				York C.	60	—
				Watford	137	—
				Charlton Ath. (on loan)	1	—
				Colchester U.	135	—
Defenders						
Michael Cook	5 7	10 11	Enfield	Colchester U.	261+4	9
John Williams	5 10	11 10	Tottenham	Watford	371+4	2
				Colchester U.	36	—
Mike Packer	5 10	11 0	London	Watford	57+11	2
				Crewe Alex. (on loan)	12	—
				Colchester U.	106+1	4
Barry Dominey	6 0	12 0	Edmonton	Colchester U.	55+13	3
Lindsay Smith	5 11	11 1	London	Colchester U.	140+27	10
Stewart Bright	5 8	10 10	Colchester	Colchester U.	18+2	—
Paul Dyer	5 9	12 0	Leicester	Notts Co.	1+6	—
				Colchester U.	34+2	2
*Derek Harrison	6 0	11 8	Leicester	Leicester C.	—	—
				Torquay U.	124+3	—
				Colchester U.	5+2	—
Midfield						
Ray Bunkell	5 9	11 3	Tottenham	Tottenham H.	—	—
				Swindon T.	52+4	3
				Colchester U.	68+8	5
Steve Leslie	5 10	11 0	Brentwood	Colchester U.	158+12	30
Philip Thomas	5 10	10 8	Sherbourne	Bournemouth	—	—
				Colchester U.	103+5	8
				(contract cancelled April 1976)		
*Terry Anderson	5 9	11 4	Woking	Arsenal	25	7
				Norwich C.	118+18	16
				Colchester U. (on loan)	4	—
				Scunthorpe U.	10	—
				Bournemouth	—	—
				Colchester U.	13+3	—
Steve Dowman	5 11	12 4	Manor Park	Colchester U.	—	—
Forwards						
Stephen Foley	6 0	11 4	Clacton	Colchester U.	127+5	28
John Froggatt	5 11	12 3	Sutton-in-Ashfield	Notts Co.	2	—
				Colchester U.	87	21
Bobby Gough	5 7	11 0	Birmingham	Walsall	1	—
				Port Vale	189+21	33
				Stockport Co. (on loan)	6	—
				Southport	61	6
				Colchester U.	22	5
Colin Garwood	5 9	10 13	Heacham	Peterborough U.	58+8	31
				Oldham Ath.	83+9	36
				Huddersfield T.	22+6	8
				Colchester U.	15	2
Ian Allinson	5 10	11 0	Hitchin	Colchester U.	3+3	—

COVENTRY CITY

DIV. 1

Patron: The Right Rev. Dr. Cuthbert K. N. Bardsley, C.B.E., M.A., D.D. (Lord Bishop of Coventry).
President: D. H. Robins.
Chairman: Sir Jack Scamp, D.L., J.P. *Vice-Chairman:* J. R. Mead, J.P. *Managing Director:* J. W. T. Hill.
Directors: M. F. French, F.C.A., J. W. Jamieson, J. Mercer, O.B.E., P. D. H. Robins, T. Sergeant, F.R.C.S.
Team Manager: Gordon Milne.
Asst. Managers: Bob Dennison and Ron Wylie.
General Secretary: Eddie Plumley.
Commercial Manager: George Curtis.
Year Formed: 1883. *Turned Professional:* 1908.
Limited Company: 1907. *Former Names:* 1883–98 Singers F.C.; 1898 Coventry City F.C.
Honours: *Football League,* highest League position: 6th, Division 1, 1969–70. Division 2, Champions: 1966–67. Division 3, Champions: 1963–64. Division 3(S), Champions: 1935–36; Runners-up: 1933–34. Division 4, Runners-up: 1958–9. *F.A. Cup,* best season: 6th Rd., 1962–63, 1966–67, 1972–73; old 4th Rd., 1909–10. *Football League Cup,* best season: 5th Rd., 1964–65, 1970–71, 1973–74. **European Competition:** *European Fairs Cup:* 1970–71.
Record Victory: 9-0 v Bristol C., Division 3(S), Apr. 28th, 1934.
Record Defeat: 2-10 v Norwich C., Division 3(S), Mar. 15th, 1930.
Most League Points: 60, Division 4, 1958–59; and Division 3, 1963–64.
Most League Goals: 108, Division 3(S), 1931–32.
Highest League Scorer in Season: Clarrie Bourton, 49, Division 3(S), 1931–32.
Most Goals in Total Aggregate: 171, Clarrie Bourton, 1931–37.
Most Capped Player: Dave Clements, 21 (44), N. Ireland.
Most League Appearances: George Curtis, 486, 1956–70.
Record Transfer Fee Received: £200,000 from Arsenal for Jeff Blockley, Oct. 1972.
Record Transfer Fee Paid: £210,000 to Liverpool for Larry Lloyd, August 1974.
Managers Since the War: Dick Bayliss, Billy Frith, Harry Storer, Jack Fairbrother, Jesse Carver, Harry Warren, Billy Frith, Jimmy Hill, Noel Cantwell, Bob Dennison.
Address of Supporters Club: Thackhall Street, Coventry.
Address of Club Shop: 'Sky Blue Shop', Highfield Road, Coventry.

Highfield Rd., Coventry. Telephone Coventry 57171. *Telegraphic address:* 'City Football Coventry'. *Ground capacity:* 48,000 (16,000 covered). *Record attendance:* 51,457 v Wolverhampton W., Division 2, April 29, 1967. *Record receipts:* £29,674 v Newcastle U., F.A. Cup 4th Rd., Jan. 24, 1976. *Pitch measurements:* 110 yds × 75 yds.
How to get there: Buses from Coventry railway station to town centre (Pool Meadow bus station). Then buses 1, 4, 7, 8, 8A to ground. Also taxi service from station.
Match tickets: Stand seat tickets can be booked 28 days in advance of any home League fixture. Postal applications accepted if sent with correct remittance to the Ticket Office Manager, Coventry City F.C. Highfield Rd. Stadium, Coventry.
Car parking: Street parking permitted all around the ground. Special coach/car park situated at Gosford Green (200 yards from stadium) on Walsgrave Road. (A46.)
Entertainments/catering facilities: Pre-match entertainment at all League and Cup games by Radio Sky Blue; live entertainment from groups and bands at special matches. The Sky Blue Buttery is open for hot and cold snacks before matches for main stand patrons. There are 16 licensed refreshment rooms and lounges, and 11 unlicensed refreshment rooms and lounges around the ground; all are open before the game, at half-time, and after the match. The Grandstand restaurant, recommended by Egon Ronay, is open for lunch Mon. to Fri. and is available in the evening for private dinner parties. On match days it is used as the Vice-Presidents' Club. An executive suite, with accommodation for 60 and full buffet facilities, can also be hired on match days, during the afternoon. Applications should be made to Giovanni, Maitre d'hotel, Grandstand Restaurant, c/o Coventry City F.C.
Club shop: Sited in the main stand; sells all types of souvenirs. There is a smaller shop at the Thackhall St. side of the stadium attached to the Pools Office.
Handbooks/programmes: Programmes available through a postal service.
Extra information: Coventry City Supporters' Club under the Sky Blue stand, Thackhall St. welcome visiting supporters on production of the membership card of their own club. They can attend the evening entertainment if they give 48-hours' notice by post to the secretary, Jim Wrigley, Coventry City S.C., Thackhall St., Coventry.
Club Colours: Sky blue shirts and shorts with navy and white trim, sky blue stockings.
Change Colours: Red shirts and shorts with navy and white trim, red stockings.
Club Captain: John Craven. *Club Nickname:* 'Sky Blues'.

COVENTRY CITY 1975–76 LEAGUE RECORD

Match No.	Date	Venue	Opponents	Result	H/T Score	League Pos'n	Goalscorers	Atten- dance
1	Aug 16	A	Everton	W 4-1	2-1	—	Cross 3, Green	33,200
2	19	H	Derby Co.	D 1-1	0-0	—	Coop	24,161
3	23	H	Manchester C.	W 2-0	1-0	4	Green 2	21,097
4	27	A	Manchester U.	D 1-1	0-1	—	Green	52,169
5	30	A	Aston Villa	L 0-1	0-0	6		41,026
6	Sept 6	H	Ipswich T.	D 0-0	0-0	6		17,622
7	13	A	Sheffield U.	W 1-0	1-0	4	Ferguson	20,153
8	20	H	Stoke C.	L 0-3	0-1	9		18,965
9	23	H	Middlesbrough	L 0-1	0-1	—		15,124
10	27	A	Leicester C.	W 3-0	1-0	7	Craven, Cross 2	20,411
11	Oct 4	H	Burnley	L 1-2	0-0	11	Cross	15,432
12	11	A	Arsenal	L 0-5	0-4	14		19,234
13	18	H	Liverpool	D 0-0	0-0	13		20,695
14	25	A	Leeds U.	L 0-2	0-0	16		25,956
15	Nov 1	H	Q.P.R.	D 1-1	0-0	16	Cross	17,845
16	8	A	West Ham U.	D 1-1	0-0	16	Powell	29,501
17	15	H	Norwich C.	W 1-0	1-0	12	Mortimer	14,897
18	22	A	Liverpool	D 1-1	0-1	13	Powell	36,929
19	29	H	Birmingham C.	W 3-2	3-1	10	Powell, Cross, Murphy	21,687
20	Dec 6	A	Newcastle U.	L 0-4	0-2	15		26,372
21	13	A	Manchester C.	L 2-4	0-1	16	Cross Ferguson	27,256
22	19	H	Everton	L 1-2	0-0	17	Coop (pen)	14,394
23	26	A	Wolverhampton W.	W 1-0	1-0	15	Craven	21,224
24	27	H	Tottenham H.	D 2-2	1-1	14	Cross, Hutchison	21,094
25	Jan 10	H	Sheffield U.	W 1-0	0-0	14	Green	13,796
26	17	A	Ipswich T.	D 1-1	1-1	14	Murphy	23,516
27	31	A	Derby Co.	L 0-2	0-0	17		24,253
28	Feb 7	H	Manchester U.	D 1-1	1-0	16	Cartwright	33,821
29	14	H	West Ham U.	W 2-0	1-0	14	Powell, Coop	16,173
30	21	A	Norwich C.	W 3-0	1-0	10	Ferguson, Craven, Cross	20,798
31	24	A	Middlesbrough	L 0-2	0-0	—		19,000
32	28	H	Leeds U.	L 0-1	0-0	13		25,563
33	Mar 6	A	Q.P.R.	L 1-4	0-1	16	Powell	19,731
34	13	H	Arsenal	D 1-1	0-1	15	Green	13,938
35	20	A	Birmingham C.	D 1-1	1-0	16	Powell	22,956
36	27	H	Newcastle U.	D 1-1	1-1	17	Murphy	14,144
37	Apr 3	H	Leicester C.	L 0-2	0-1	17		18,135
38	10	A	Stoke C.	W 1-0	0-0	15	Powell	16,059
39	13	H	Aston Villa	D 1-1	1-0	—	Coop (pen)	27,586
40	40	H	Wolverhampton	W 3-1	1-1	12	Green 3	18,678
41	19	A	Tottenham H.	L 1-4	0-2	—	Murphy	21,107
42	24	A	Burnley	W 3-1	0-1	14	Cross 3	11,636

Goalscorers

League (47): Cross 14, Green 9, Powell 7, Coop 4 (2 pens), Murphy 4, Ferguson 3, Craven 3, Mortimer 1 Hutchison 1, Cartwright 1.
League Cup: (3): Cross, Green, Ferguson.
F.A. Cup (3): Cross, Murphy, own goal 1.

League Cup	Second Round	Bolton W. (a)	3-1
	Third Round	Mansfield T. (a)	0-2
F.A. Cup	Third Round	Bristol C. (h)	2-1
	Fourth Round	Newcastle U. (h)	1-1
		(a)	0-5

King	Oakey	Brogan	Craven	Holmes	Dugdale	Coop	Mortimer	Green	Cross	Hutchison	Ferguson	Lloyd	Powell	Murphy	Hindley	Blyth	Cartwright	Cattlin	Roberts	Match No.
1	2	3	4	5	6	7	8	9	10	11										1
1	2	3	4	6	5	7	8	10	9	11										2
1	2	3	4	6		7	8	10	9	11		5								3
1	2	3	4	6		7	8	10	9	11	12	5*								4
1	2	3	4	6	5	7	8	10	9	11										5
1	2	3	4	6	5	7	8	10	9	11										6
1		3	4	6	5	2	7		9	11	10		8							7
1		3	4	6	5	2	7	10	9	11	12		8*							8
1	2	3	4	6	5	7	8	10	9	11										9
1	2	3	4	6	5	7	8	10*	9	11		12								10
1	2	3	4	6	5	8	7		9	11	10									11
1		3	4	6		2	8	10	9	11		5	7							12
1		3		6	4	2	7	10	9	11		5	8							13
1		3		6	4	2	7	10	9	11		5	8							14
1		3		6	4	2	8	10	9	11		5	7							15
1		3		6	4	2	8		9	11		5	7	10						16
1		3		6	4	2	8		9	11		5	7	10						17
1		3		6	4	2	8		9	11		5	7	10						18
1		3		6	4	2	8		9	11		5	7	10						19
1		3		6	4*	2	8	10	9	11	12		7		5					20
1*		3	12	6	4	2	8		9	11		5	7	10						21
		3		6		2	4		9	11	10	5	7	8		1				22
1		3	4	6	5	2		12	9	11			8	10*			7			23
1		3	4	6	5	2		10	9	11			7				8			24
		3	4	6	5	2		10	9	11		12	8			1	7*			25
	12	3	4	6	5	2		8	9	11		7*	10			1				26
		3		6	5	2		8	9	11		4	10			1	7			27
		3*	4	6	5	2		8	9	11		7	10			1	12			28
	2		4		5	6			9	11			8	10		1	7	3		29
	2		4	12	5	6			9	11	10		8			1	7*	3		30
	2		4	7	5	6			9	11*	10		8	12		1		3		31
	2		4		5	6		12	9	11	8*	7	10			1		3		32
	2		4*		5	6		10		11	9	8	7			1	12	3		33
	2		4		5	6*		10		11	12	8	7			1	9	3		34
	2				5	6		10	9	11		7	8			1	4	3		35
	2				5	6		8		11	4	10	9			1	7	3		36
	2				5	6		10	12	11	9*	7	8			1	4	3		37
	2		4	6	5			8		11	9	7				1	10	3		38
	2		4		5	6		8	9	11		10				1	7	3		39
	2		4*		5	6		10	9	11			8	12		1	7	3		40
			4		5	6		8	9	11		10		12		1		3*	7	41
			4		5	6		10	9	11		7	8			1		3	2	42
23	22	28	27	34	34	42	22	29	37	42	11	11	32	19	1	19	13	14	2	
+1s		+1s	+1s					+2s	+1s				+4s	+2s		+3s	+2s			

153

COVENTRY CITY—PLAYERS

Player and position	Ht.	Wt.	Birthplace	Clubs	League Appearances	Goals
Goalkeepers						
Bryan King	6 2	11 6	Bishop's Stortford	Millwall	302	—
				Coventry C.	23	—
James Blyth	5 11	12 0	Perth	Preston N.E.	1	—
				Coventry C.	19	—
				Hereford U. (on loan)	7	—
Defenders						
*Chris Cattlin	5 11	12 5½	Milnrow	Huddersfield T.	59+2	1
				Coventry C.	213+4	—
Michael Coop	5 11	10 9½	Leamington	Coventry C.	245+11	9
				York C. (on loan)	4	—
*Peter Hindley	5 11	12 0	Worksop	Nottingham F.	366	10
				Coventry C.	33	—
James Holmes (Eire)	5 9	11 7	Dublin	Coventry C.	97+5	7
Larry Lloyd (England)	6 2	12 4	Bristol	Bristol R.	43	1
				Liverpool	150	4
				Coventry C.	45	5
Graham Oakey	5 6	9 5	Worcester	Coventry C.	53+1	—
Alan Dugdale	5 9	11 9	Kirkby	Coventry C.	113+3	—
Jim Brogan	5 10	11 8	Scotland	Celtic	208+3	6
				Coventry C.	28	—
Brian Roberts	5 10	11 5	Manchester	Coventry C.	2	—
Midfield						
Barry Powell	5 6	10 0	Kenilworth	Wolverhampton W.	58+6	7
				Coventry C.	32+2	7
Tom Hutchison (Scotland)	5 11½	11 2	Cardenden	Alloa Ath.	68	4
				Blackpool	164+2	10
				Coventry C.	155	10
John Craven	5 11	13 12	St. Annes	Blackpool	154+9	24
				C. Palace	56+7	14
				Coventry C.	82+2	8
Leslie Cartwright (Wales)	5 7½	10 10	Aberdare	Coventry C.	39+10	2
Forwards						
David Cross	5 11	12 0	Bury	Rochdale	50+9	21
				Norwich C.	83+1	21
				Coventry C.	88+1	29
Tom O'Brien	5 4	10 2	Cork	Coventry C.	—	—
Michael Ferguson	6 1	12 3	Newcastle	Coventry C.	23+4	5
James Wilson	5 7	10 4	Falkirk	Coventry C.	—	—
Alan Green	5 5½	10 6	Worcester	Coventry C.	68+11	20
Donal Murphy	5 9	10 8	Dublin	Coventry C.	19+3	4
Donato Nardiello	5 10	10 11	Cardiganshire	Coventry C.	—	—

CREWE ALEXANDRA

DIV. 4

President: D. Plastow.

Chairman: N. Rowlinson.

Directors: J. McHugh, K. Potts, D. Irving, E. Tagg, C. Humphrey.

Manager: Harry Gregg.

Secretary: Chris Jones.

Year Formed: 1877.

Turned Professional: 1893.

Limited Company: 1892.

Honours: *Football League:* Best season Division 2, 10th, 1892–93. *F.A. Cup,* best season: semi-finalists: 1888. *Football League Cup,* 1974–75. 1975-76 3rd Rd.

Record Victory: 8-0 v Rotherham U., Division 3(N), Oct. 1st, 1932.

Record Defeat: 2-13 v Tottenham H., F.A. Cup, 4th Rd. Replay, Feb. 3rd, 1960.

Most League Points: 59, Division 4, 1962–63.

Most League Goals: 95, Division 3(N), 1931–32.

Highest League Scorer in Season: Terry Harkin, 34, Division 4, 1964–65.

Most League Goals in Total Aggregate: Bert Swindells, 126, 1928–37.

Most Capped Player: Bill Lewis, 12 (30), Wales.

Most League Appearances: Peter Leigh, 430, 1963–72.

Record Transfer Fee Received: £30,000 from Arsenal for Brian Parker, August, 1975.

Record Transfer Fee Paid: £5,000 for Gordon Wallace to Liverpool, Oct. 1967.

Managers Since the War: George Lillycrop, Frank Hill, Arthur Turner, Harry Catterick, Ralph Ward, Maurice Lindley, Harry Ware, Jimmy McGuigan, Ernie Tagg, Dennis Viollet, Jimmy Melia, Ernie Tagg.

Address of Supporters Club: Registered Office, Crewe Alexandra, Supporters' Association, 131 Edleston Road, Crewe, Cheshire.

Address of Club Shop or Boutique: Gresty Road, Crewe.

Football Ground, Gresty Rd., Crewe. Telephone Crewe 3014. *Telegraphic address:* 'Alex Football Crewe'. *Ground capacity:* 17,000. *Record attendance:* 20,000 v Tottenham H. F.A. Cup 4th Rd., January 30, 1960. *Record receipts:* £3,377 v Coventry C., F.A. Cup 4th Rd., February 12, 1966. *Pitch measurements:* 113 yds × 75 yds.

How to get there: Local bus services from outlying districts. The ground is situated just five minutes' walk from Crewe railway station.

Match tickets: Advance booking for important cup ties only.

Car parking: Parking at the ground for 120 cars.

Entertainments/catering facilities: The Alexandra Club adjoining the ground is owned by the club. Refreshment points inside the ground.

Club shop: Situated at the ground; sells all types of souvenirs.

Handbooks/programmes: Handbooks on sale at matches.

Extra information: In 1956–57 the club set an unenviable League record of playing 30 successive games without a win.

Club Colours: Red shirts, black shorts, red stockings.

Change Colours: Sky blue shirts and stockings, white shorts.

Club Nickname: 'The Railwaymen'.

CREWE ALEXANDRA 1975–76 LEAGUE RECORD

Match No.	Date	Venue	Opponent	Result	H/T Score	League Pos'n	Goalscorers	Attendance
1	Aug 16	A	Stockport Co.	D 0-0	0-0	—		3443
2	23	H	Reading	D 3-3	2-1	11	Bowles, Evans, Nicholls	2057
3	30	A	Doncaster R.	L 1-3	0-1	19	Purdie	2467
4	Sept 6	H	Torquay U.	W 6-0	4-0	13	Davies, Lee (og), Nelson, Humphreys, Evans, Purdie	1751
5	12	A	Barnsley	D 1-1	0-0	12	Davies	4243
6	20	H	Darlington	W 2-0	1-0	7	Nelson 2	2501
7	24	H	Rochdale	D 0-0	0-0	—		3500
8	27	A	Exeter	D 2-2	2-0	9	Davies, Purdie	2116
9	Oct 4	H	Hartlepool	D 0-0	0-0	7		2326
10	11	A	Cambridge U.	D 1-1	1-1	9	Nelson	2835
11	18	H	Scunthorpe U.	W 1-0	1-0	9	Humphreys	1939
12	22	A	Workington	W 3-0	2-0	—	Davies, Humphreys, Nelson (pen)	1333
13	25	A	Watford	L 1-2	1-0	7	Nicholls	4252
14	Nov 1	H	Lincoln C.	L 2-3	1-1	11	Melledew, Bowles	2707
15	5	H	AFC Bournemouth	W 1-0	0-0	—	Davies	2000
16	7	A	Southport	D 2-2	0-1	9	Davies, Nelson	1445
17	15	H	Tranmere R.	W 1-0	1-0	9	Humphreys (pen)	2832
18	29	H	Brentford	W 1-0	1-0	6	Nelson	2248
19	Dec 6	A	Northampton T.	L 1-2	0-1	8	Bowles	5705
20	20	H	Swansea C.	W 2-1	1-1	6	Humphreys, Davies	2088
21	26	A	Newport Co.	D 2-2	0-1	6	Nelson, Humphreys	3788
22	27	H	Bradford C.	L 1-3	0-1	7	Bevan	3415
23	Jan 3	A	Swansea C.	L 0-4	0-0	11		2513
24	10	H	Doncaster R.	L 1-2	0-0	11	Humphreys (pen)	2501
25	17	A	Darlington	D 0-0	0-0	12		1497
26	23	H	Barnsley	D 1-1	0-1	11	Purdie	2291
27	27	A	Huddersfield T.	L 0-1	0-1	—		4459
28	31	H	Workington	D 0-0	0-0	9		1752
29	Feb 7	A	AFC Bournemouth	L 0-1	0-0	12		3933
30	13	H	Southport	W 4-0	1-0	10	Nelson, Manning 3	1966
31	20	A	Tranmere R.	L 1-2	1-0	11	Nelson	4306
32	Mar 3	H	Watford	D 2-2	1-1	—	Nelson 2	2068
33	6	A	Lincoln C.	L 0-2	0-2	14		7211
34	10	A	Hartlepool	W 3-1	3-0	—	Bowles, Bevan, Purdie	1506
35	13	H	Cambridge U.	L 1-2	0-2	13	Manning	2009
36	16	A	Scunthorpe U.	L 0-1	0-1	—		3126
37	20	A	Brentford	D 0-0	0-0	15		3840
38	22	A	Rochdale	W 1-0	0-0	—	Bevan	1128
39	27	H	Northampton T.	L 0-1	0-0	12		2865
40	Apr 3	H	Stockport Co.	W 3-1	1-0	12	Davies, Manning, Evans	2530
41	7	H	Exeter C.	D 0-0	0-0	—		2034
42	10	A	Torquay U.	L 1-2	0-1	14	Davies	2293
43	14	H	Huddersfield T.	L 0-2	0-0	—		2750
44	17	H	Newport Co.	W 4-0	3-0	13	Purdie 2, Bowles, Nicholls	1971
45	19	A	Bradford C.	L 1-4	1-1	—	Nicholls	2102
46	24	A	Reading	L 1-3	0-1	16	Purdie	12,229

Goalscorers

League (58): Nelson 12 (1 a pen), Davies 9, Purdie 8, Humphreys 7 (2 pens), Bowles 5, Manning 5, Nicholls 4, Bevan 3, Evans 3, Melledew 1, Own Goal 1.
League Cup (4): Nicholls 2, Nelson, Humphreys (1 a pen).
F.A. Cup (1): Bevan.

League Cup	First Round	Transmere R. (h)	2-1
	Second Leg	(a)	1-2
	Second Round	Chelsea (h)	1-0
	Third Round	Tottenham H. (h)	0-2
F.A. Cup	First Round	Rotherham U. (a)	1-2

Crudgington	Lowry	Evans	Davies	Bowles	Lugg	Humphreys	Reed	Nicholls	Rimmer	Bevan	Nelson	Melledew	Purdie	Kelley	McGuire	Tully	Cheetham	Manning	Mayman	Hughes	Match No.
1	2	3	4	5	6	7	8*	9	10	11	12										1
1	2	3	7	4	5	11		10	6	8	9										2
1	2	3	7	5	4	11	10*			6	9	8	12								3
1	2	3	8	5	4	11	6			7	9		10								4
1	2	3	7	5	4	11	6			8		10*	12	9							5
1	2	3	8	5	4	11	6*			9		7	12	10							6
1		3	7	5	4	11	12			8	10	6*	9	2							7
1		3	7	5	4	11	12			8	10*	6	9	2							8
1	2	3	7	5	4	11	12			6	9	8	10*								9
1	2	3	7	5	4	11	12	6*		8	10	9									10
1	2	3	8	5	4	11	10			6	9	7									11
1	2	3	7	5	4	11	6			8	10	9									12
1	2	3	7	5	4	11	6			8	10	9									13
1		3	9	5	4	8	6			7	11	10		2							14
1	2*	3	7	5	4	11	12	6		8	10	9									15
1		3	7	5	4	11	8	6		10	9			2							16
1			8	5	4	11	10	6		7	9	3		2							17
1	2	7*		5	4	11				6	8	10	9	12	3						18
1	2*	3	7	5	4	11				6	8	10	9	12							19
1	2	3	8*	5	4	11	12	6		7	10	9									20
1	2	3	7*	5	4	11	12	6		8	10	9									21
1	2	3		5	4	11	12	6		7	10		9		8*						22
1	2	3	7	5	6	11		4*		8	12		9	10							23
1	2	3	7	5	4	11	8*			6	12		9	10							24
1	2	3	7	5	4	11				6	9	10	8								25
1	2	3	7	5	4	11*				8	10		6	9		12					26
1	2	3	7	5	4	12	6*			8	10		9			11					27
1	2	3	8	5	4	10	12	6		7	9*					11					28
1	2	3	7	5	4	11	10*	6		8	12					9					29
1	2	3	7	5	4			6		10						11	8	9			30
1	2	3	7*	5	4	12		6		8	10					11		9			31
1	2	3		5	4	10		6		9						11	7	8			32
1	2	3	8	5	4			6		12	9					11*	7	10			33
1	2	7*		5	4	11	10	6		3			9			12	8				34
1	2			5	4	11	10	6*			12		7			3	8	9			35
1	2			5	4	7	12	8	6				9*	3		11	10				36
1	2	3		5			7	10*	4	6	8		12			11	9				37
1	2	3		5			8	10*	4	6	7		12			11	9				38
1	2	3	7			11	5			6	8		9			12	4		10*		39
1	2	3	7	4			5	6		8						11	9	10			40
1	2	3	7	4		12	5	6		9*						11	8	10			41
1	2	3	7	5	4	11	10	6		9*						12	8				42
1	2	3	7	6	4	11	5	8*				9	12			10					43
1	2	3	7*	5		11		4	6				9			8			10	12	44
1	2	3		5	4	7	10*						9			11	8		6	12	45
1	2	3	7	5	4	11*	10			12	9					8			6		46
46	41	41	39	43	42	40	3	29	27	37	29	20	20	7	1	14	16	7	4	—	
			+3s	+3s	+7s			+1s	+4s	+6s	+4s					+4s			+2s		

CREWE ALEXANDRA—PLAYERS

Player and position	Ht.	Wt.	Birthplace	Clubs	League Appearances	Goals
Goalkeepers						
Geoff Crudgington	6 0	12 6	Wolver-hampton	Aston V.	4	—
				Bradford C. (on loan)	1	—
				Crewe A.	172	—
				Preston N.E. (on loan)	—	—
Defenders						
Paul Bevan	5 11	10 9	Shrewsbury	Shrewsbury T.	67+5	1
				Swansea C.	77+2	5
				Crewe A.	37+1	3
Micky Evans	6 0	12 6	West Bromwich	Walsall	229+3	7
				Swansea C.	77+2	5
				Crewe A.	41	3
Tommy Lowry	5 9	10 3	Liverpool	Liverpool	1	—
				Crewe A.	388+1	2
Warwick Rimmer	5 8¼	10 13	Birkenhead	Bolton W.	462+6	17
				Crewe A.	37	—
Alan Kelley	5 7	10 8	Liverpool	Southport	17+6	2
				Crewe A.	105+2	—
				(contract cancelled April 1976)		
Phillip Nicholls	5 11	11 6	Bilston	Wolverhampton W.	—	—
				Crewe A.	137+8	1
Midfield						
Ray Lugg	5 9	10 10	Jarrow	Middlesbrough	34+3	3
				Watford	51+8	3
				Plymouth Arg.	22+2	1
				Crewe A.	116+1	3
*Steve Melledew	5 8	12 0	Rochdale	Rochdale	88+8	23
				Everton	—	—
				Aldershot	90+2	27
				Bury	14+6	2
				Crewe A.	49+7	2
Kevin Tully	5 9	11 4	Manchester	Blackpool	10+1	—
				Cambridge U.	40+4	8
				Crewe A.	14+4	—
Paul Mayman	5 8	10 0	Crewe	Crewe A.	4	—
Hughie Cheetham	5 10	10 5	Manchester	Crewe A.	16	—
Paul Bowles				Crewe A.	51+1	5
David Davies	6 0	13 5	Rhondda Valley	Swansea C.	0+1	—
				Crewe A.	39	9
Forwards						
Gerry Humphreys	5 8	11 4	Llandudno	Everton	12	2
				C. Palace	4+7	—
				Crewe A.	164+9	27
*Tommy Maguire				Crewe A.	23+4	1
*Bernard Purdie	5 9	11 0	Wrexham	Wrexham	7+3	3
				Chester	54+9	14
				Crewe A.	76+8	24
*Hugh Reed	5 4	10 1	Alexandria	W.B.A.	5+4	2
				Plymouth Arg.	44+12	9
				Brentford (on loan)	3+1	—
				Crewe A.	38+9	9
John Manning	5 11	12 9	Liverpool	Tranmere R.	130	70
				Shrewsbury T.	39	18
				Norwich C.	60	21
				Bolton W.	27+2	7
				Walsall	13+1	6
				Tranmere R. (on loan)	5	1
				Crewe A.	37+1	6
				Barnsley	41+4	7
				Crewe A.	7	5
Stephen Hughes	5 11	11 0	Warrington	Crewe A.	0+2	—

CRYSTAL PALACE DIV. 3

Chairman: R. E. Bloye.

Directors: K. B. Sinclair, E. J. Swann, B. Bishop, R. S. Briggs, R. R. Varey.

Manager: Malcolm Allison.

Secretary: Alan Leather.

Commercial Manager: Tony Shaw.

Year Formed: 1905.   *Limited Company:* 1905.

Turned Professional: 1905.

Previous Grounds: 1905, Crystal Palace; 1915, Herne Hill; 1919, The Nest; 1924, Selhurst Park.

Honours: *Football League,* best season in Division 1: 18th 1970–71. Division 2, Runners-up: 1968–69. Division 3, Runners-up: 1963–64.   Division 3(S), Champions: 1920–21; Runners-up: Division 3(S), 1928–29, 1930–31, 1938–39. Division 4, Runners-up: 1960–61.   *F.A. Cup,* best season: semi-final 1975–76.   *Football League Cup:* 5th Rd., 1968–69, 1970–71.

Record Victory: 9-0 v Barrow, Division 4, Oct. 10th, 1959.

Record Defeat: 4-11 v Manchester C., F.A. Cup, 5th Rd., Feb. 20th, 1926.

Most League Points: 64, Division 4, 1960–61.

Most League Goals: 110, Division 4, 1960–61.

Highest League Scorer in Season: Peter Simpson, 46, Division 3(S), 1930–31.

Most Goals in Total Aggregate: Peter Simpson, 154, 1930–36.

Most Capped Player: Ian Evans, 6, Wales.

Most League Appearances: Terry Long, 432, 1956–69.

Record Transfer Fee Received: £150,000 from Chelsea for Steve Kember, Sept. 1971.

Record Transfer Fee Paid: £150,000 to Swindon T. for Don Rogers, Oct. 1972.

Managers Since the War: George Irwin, Jack Butler, Ronnie Rooke, Fred Dawes, Charlie Slade, Laurie Scott, Cyril Spiers, George Smith, Arthur Rowe, Dick Graham, Bert Head.

Address of Social Section: Social Hall, Selhurst Park, S.E.25, 6PU.

Address of Club Shop or Boutique: Social Hall and in New Stand; Programme Shop in Old Stand.

Selhurst Park, London, SE25 6PU. Telephone 01-653-2223/4.   *Ground capacity:* 51,000 (21,000 covered).   *Record attendance:* 49,498 v Chelsea, Division 1, December 27, 1969. *Record receipts:* £22,000 v Chelsea, F.A. Cup 3rd Rd., January 2 1971. *Pitch measurements:* 110 yds × 75 yds.

How to get there: Ground served by three stations—Selhurst (5 minutes walk), Norwood Junction (7 minutes) and Thornton Heath (10 minutes). Buses 68, 75, 154, 157, 12 (to Norwood Junction).

Match tickets: Seats bookable in advance in Old Stand; postal applications accepted one month in advance and personal application two weeks in advance. Postal applications must be accompanied by S.A.E. and the correct remittance. Cheques must be made payable to Crystal Palace F.C. and name and address must be written on the back. Separate application must be made for each match.

Car parking: Large car park at the ground.

Entertainments/catering facilities: A social hall and catering facilities within the ground.

Club shops: Two shops sell all types of souvenirs.

Handbooks/programmes: Programmes available on subscription.

Extra information: Vic Rouse, the Crystal Palace goalkeeper, was the first Fourth Division player to be capped when he played for Wales v Ireland in 1959.

Club Colours: Royal blue and red vertical striped shirts, royal blue shorts, royal blue stockings with red and white bands.

Change Colours: All white.

First Team Coach: Terry Venables.   *Club Captain:* Peter Taylor.   *Club Nickname:* 'The Eagles'.

CRYSTAL PALACE 1975–76 LEAGUE RECORD

Match No.	Date	Venue	Opponents	Result	H/T Score	League Pos'n	Goalscorers	Attendance
1	Aug 16	H	Chester	W 2-0	1-0	—	Chatterton, Kemp	13,009
2	23	A	Chesterfield	W 2-1	1-0	1	Kemp, Holder	5386
3	30	H	Colchester U.	W 3-2	2-2	1	Evans 3	13,713
4	Sept 6	A	Cardiff C.	W 1-0	0-0	1	Kemp	10,479
5	13	H	Rotherham U.	W 2-0	1-0	1	Evans, Kemp	16,421
6	16	A	Walsall	D 1-1	0-0	—	Evans	5496
7	20	A	Shrewsbury T.	W 4-2	3-0	1	Swindlehurst, Kemp, Taylor, Durban (og)	7480
8	23	H	Brighton & H.A.	L 0-1	0-1	—		25,606
9	27	H	Sheffield W.	D 1-1	0-1	1	Kemp	14,840
10	Oct 4	A	Port Vale	D 0-0	0-0	1		6121
11	11	H	Grimsby T.	W 3-0	1-0	1	Evans, Kemp, Swindlehurst	15,552
12	18	A	Preston N.E.	D 0-0	0-0	1		10,971
13	21	H	Hereford U.	D 2-2	1-0	—	Swindlehurst, Taylor (pen)	20,232
14	25	H	Southend U.	D 1-1	1-0	1	Taylor	18,438
15	Nov 1	A	Halifax T.	W 3-1	2-0	1	Cannon, Swindlehurst, Taylor	3282
16	4	A	Swindon T.	W 2-0	0-0	—	Swindlehurst 2	10,599
17	8	H	Peterborough U.	D 1-1	1-0	1	Chatterton	19,000
18	15	A	Wrexham	W 3-1	1-0	1	Swindlehurst 2, Kemp	5878
19	29	H	Mansfield T.	W 4-1	3-0	1	Swindlehurst 2, Hinshelwood, M., Evans	15,701
20	Dec 6	A	Bury	W 1-0	0-0	1	Kemp	10,035
21	20	A	Millwall	L 1-2	0-1	1	Swindlehurst	9841
22	27	A	Aldershot	L 0-1	0-1	1		13,997
23	30	H	Gillingham	L 0-1	0-0	—		20,919
24	Jan 6	H	Walsall	L 0-1	0-1	—		16,181
25	10	A	Colchester U.	W 3-0	2-0	1	Taylor (pen), Swindlehurst, Whittle	6240
26	17	H	Shrewsbury T.	D 1-1	0-0	1	Johnson (J.)	16,531
27	31	A	Hereford U.	D 1-1	0-0	1	Swindlehurst	12,970
28	Feb 3	A	Rotherham U.	L 1-4	0-0	—	Swindlehurst	7633
29	7	H	Swindon T.	D 3-3	2-1	2	Taylor (pen), Chatterton 2	15,844
30	18	A	Peterborough U.	L 0-2	0-1	—		13,308
31	21	H	Wrexham	D 1-1	1-1	5	Chatterton	16,944
32	24	A	Brighton & H.A.	L 0-2	0-1	—		33,300
33	27	A	Southend U.	W 2-1	1-1	3	Wall, Taylor (pen)	13,500
34	Mar 9	H	Port Vale	D 2-2	2-1	—	Chatterton, Swindlehurst	23,014
35	13	A	Grimsby T.	W 2-1	1-1	3	Taylor 2	8412
36	16	H	Preston N.E.	W 2-0	0-0	—	Taylor, Swindlehurst	22,213
37	20	A	Mansfield T.	D 1-1	0-1	3	Taylor	12,990
38	27	H	Bury	W 1-0	0-0	3	Chatterton	21,328
39	30	H	Millwall	D 0-0	0-0	—		34,893
40	Apr 7	A	Sheffield W.	L 0-1	0-0	—		11,909
41	10	H	Cardiff C.	L 0-1	0-0	5		25,603
42	13	H	Halifax T.	D 1-1	1-1	—	Martin	19,175
43	17	A	Gillingham	W 2-1	2-0	5	Cannon, Ley (og)	12,880
44	20	H	Aldershot	D 0-0	0-0	—		25,549
45	28	H	Chesterfield	D 0-0	0-0	—		27,961
46	May 4	A	Chester	L 1-2	1-1	—	Taylor (pen)	6702

Goalscorers

League (61): Swindlehurst 16, Taylor 12 (5 pens), Kemp 9, Chatterton 7, Evans 7, Cannon 2, Holder 1, Johnson (J.) 1, Hinshelwood (M.) 1, Whittle 1, Wall 1, Martin 1, own goals 2.
League Cup (5): Kemp 2, Swindlehurst, Chatterton, Johnson.
F.A. Cup (11): Taylor 4 (1 a pen), Kemp 2, Swindlehurst 2, Evans, Chatterton, Whittle.

League Cup	First Round	Colchester U. (h)	3-0
	Second Leg	(a)	1-3
	Second Round	Doncaster R. (a)	1-2
F.A. Cup	First Round	Walton (h)	1-0
	Second Round	Millwall (a)	1-1
		(h)	2-1
	Third Round	Scarborough (a)	2-1
	Fourth Round	Leeds U. (a)	1-0
	Fifth Round	Chelsea (a)	3-2
	Sixth Round	Sunderland (a)	1-0
	Semi-Final	Southampton	0-2 (at Stamford Bridge)

Burns	Wall	Johnson, J.	Holder	Jeffries	Hinshelwood, M.	Hill	Chatterton	Kemp	Swindlehurst	Taylor	Evans	Cannon	Hammond	Hinshelwood, P.	Jump	Whittle	Johnson, P.	Sansom	Martin	Match No.
1	2	3	4	5	6	7	8	9	10	11										1
1	2	3	11	5	4	7	8	9	10		6									2
1	2		8	5	4		7	9	10	11	6	3								3
	2		4	5	8		7	10	9	11	6	3	1							4
	2		8	5	4		7	9	10	11	6	3	1							5
	2		8	5	4		7	9	10	11	6	3	1							6
	2		8	5	4		7	10	9	11	6	3	1							7
	2	12	8	5	4		7*	9	10	11	6	3	1							8
	2	8	7	5	4*			10	9	11	6	3	1	12						9
	2	10	7	5	4			9		11	6	3	1	8						10
	2	8	7	5	4			9	10*	11	6		1	12	3					11
		8	7	5	4			9	10	11	6	3	1		2					12
		4	8	5			12	9	10	11	6	3*	1		2	7				13
	2	8	4	5				9	10	11*	6	3	1	12		7				14
	2		8		4		7	9	10	11	6	5	1		3					15
	2	4	8	5			7	9	10	11	6	3	1							16
	2		8	4	5		7	9	10		6	3	1			11				17
	2		8	4	5		7	9	10	11	6	3	1							18
	2	4		5	8*		7	9	10	11	6	3	1		12					19
	2		8		4		7	9	10	11	6	3	1		5					20
	2		8	5	4		7	9	10	11	6	3	1							21
	2	4	12	5	8		7	9*	10	11	6	3	1							22
	2	12	4	5	8		7		10*	11	6	3	1		9					23
	2		8				7	9	10	11	6	3	1		5	4				24
	2	4	8				7		10	11	6	3	1		5	9				25
	2	4	8				7		10	11	6	3	1		5	9				26
	2		4		8		7		10	11	6	3	1		5	9				27
	2		4		8		7		10	11	6	3	1		5	9				28
	2		4		8		7		10	11	6	3	1		5	9				29
	2	11	4		8		7	9	10		6	3	1		5					30
	2	11	4*		8		7	9	10		6	3	1		5	12				31
	2	11	4		8		7		10	9	6	3	1		5					32
	2		5	4	8		7		10	11	6	3	1		9					33
	2		4	5	8*		7	12	10	11	6	3	1		9					34
			8	6	4		7		10	11	5	3	1		9		2			35
	2		8		4*		7		10	11	6	3	1		5	9	12			36
	2		8		4		7		10	11	6	3	1		5*	12		9		37
	2*	12	4	5			7		10	11	6	3	1			9		8		38
			8	4	5		7		10	11	6	3	1		2	9				39
	2		8	4	5		7		10		6	3	1			9		11		40
	2		8	4	5		7		10	11	6	3	1			9				41
	2	7					12		10*	11	6	3	1		5	9		4	8	42
	2	7							10	11	6	3	1		5	9		4	8	43
	2		8				12		10*	11	6	3	1		5	9		4	7	44
	2	7					9			11	6	3	1		5	10		4	8	45
	2	7					9			11	6	3	1		5	10		4	8	46
3	42	26	30	35	28	4	36	27	43	41	45	40	43	2	25	20	2	6	8	
		+3s	+1s				+1s	+3s						+3s		+2s	+1s		+1s	

CRYSTAL PALACE—PLAYERS

Player and position	Ht.	Wt.	Birthplace	Clubs	League Appearances	Goals
Goalkeepers						
Paul Hammond	6 0	12 7	Nottingham	C. Palace	92	—
Tony Burns	6 0	12 11	Tonbridge	Arsenal	31	—
				Brighton	39	—
				Charlton Ath.	10	—
				C. Palace	41	—
Defenders						
Stewart Jump	5 9	10 2	Crumpsall	Stoke C.	36+8	1
				C. Palace	67+1	2
Peter Wall	5 11	12 4	Shrewsbury	Shrewsbury T.	18	—
				Wrexham	15+7	—
				Liverpool	31	—
				Orient (on loan)	10	—
				C. Palace	146+6	3
Ken Sansom				C. Palace	7	—
Ian Evans	6 2	11 2	Egham	Q.P.R.	39	2
(Wales)				C. Palace	83	10
Jimmy Cannon	5 11	12 0	Glasgow	C. Palace	90+3	7
Derek Jefferies	5 10½	11 3	Manchester	Manchester C.	64+9	—
				C. Palace	108	1
*John Love	5 9	11 0	Harrow	C. Palace	1	—
Midfield						
Philip Holder	5 3	10 6	Kilburn	Tottenham H.	9+4	1
				C. Palace	40+1	1
*Jeffrey Johnson	5 7	10 0	Cardiff	Manchester C.	4+2	—
				Swansea C. (on loan)	37+2	4
				C. Palace	82+5	4
Terry Venables	5 9	11 6	Dagenham	Chelsea	203	26
(England)				Tottenham	114+1	5
				Q.P.R.	176+1	19
				C. Palace	14	—
				(contract cancelled April 1976)		
*Alan Whittle	5 7	10 4	Liverpool	Everton	72+2	21
				C. Palace	103+5	19
Martin Hinshelwood	5 10½	12 2	Reading	C. Palace	61+2	3
Nick Chatterton	5 9	11 4	Norwood	C. Palace	64+5	13
Mark Lindsay	5 7	10 7	Lambeth	Millwall	—	—
				C. Palace	27+3	—
				(contract cancelled April 1976)		
Forwards						
Peter Taylor	5 9	11 7	Southend	Southend U.	57+18	12
(England)				C. Palace	116	32
Mick Hill	6 0	11 10	Hereford	Sheffield U.	35+2	9
(Wales)				Ipswich T.	47+1	14
				Colchester U. (on loan)	—	—
				C. Palace	43+2	6
				(contract cancelled Feb. 1976)		
David Swindlehurst	6 1	11 8	Edgware	C. Palace	82+8	30
Paul Hinshelwood	5 11	11 8	Bristol	C. Palace	16+4	4
Ken Ayres	5 8	11 6	Oxford	Manchester U.	—	—
				C. Palace	3+3	—
				Charlton Ath. (on loan)	—	—
				(contract cancelled April 1976)		
Peter Johnson	5 8	10 10	Islington	Orient	1+2	—
				C. Palace	5+2	—
David Kemp				C. Palace	28+3	9
Neil Martin	6 0	11 3	Alloa	Alloa	not known	
(Scotland)				Queen of South	61	33
				Hibernian	65	53
				Sunderland	85	38
				Coventry C.	106	40
				Nottingham F.	116+3	28
				Brighton	13+4	8
				C. Palace	8+1	1

DARLINGTON

Chairman: George A. Tait.

Directors: F. T. Walker, W. Nicholson, D. Mason, M. C. Robson, J. Hunter.

Manager: Peter Madden.

Secretary: Andrew W. Rowell.

Year Formed: 1883. *Turned Professional:* 1908.

Limited Company: 1891.

Honours: *Football League,* highest position: 15th, Division 2, 1925–26. Division 3(N), Champions: 1924–25; Runners-up: 1921–22. Division 4, Runners-up: 1965–66. *F.A. Cup,* best season: 3rd Rd., 1910–11; 5th Rd., 1957–58. *Football League Cup,* best season: 5th Rd., 1967–68.

Record Victory: 9-2 v Lincoln C., Division 3 (N), Jan. 7, 1928.

Record Defeat: 0-10 v Doncaster R., Division 4, Jan. 25th, 1964.

Most League Points: 59, Division 4, 1965–66.

Most League Goals: 108, Division 3(N), 1929–30.

Highest League Scorer in Season: David Brown, 39, Division 3(N), 1924–25.

Most League Goals in Total Aggregate: David Brown, 74, 1923–26.

Most Capped Player: None.

Most League Appearances: Ron Greener, 442, 1955–68.

Record Transfer Fee Received: £15,555 from Lincoln C. for Alan Harding, March 1973.

Record Transfer Fee Paid: £7,000 to Lincoln C. for Frank McMahon, Mar. 1973.

Managers Since the War: Bill Forrest, George Irwin, Bob Gurney, Dick Duckworth, Eddie Carr, Lol Morgan, Jimmy Greenhalgh, Ray Yeoman, Len Richley, Frank Brennan, Allan Jones, Ralph Brand, Dick Conner, Billy Horner.

Address of Supporters Club: Same as Football Club.

Feethams Ground, Darlington. Telephone Darlington 65097/67712. *Ground capacity:* 20,000. *Record attendance:* 21,023 v Bolton W., League Cup 3rd Rd., November 14, 1960. *Record receipts:* £4,195 v Arsenal, F.A. Cup 3rd Rd., January 9, 1965. *Pitch measurements:* 110 yds × 74 yds.

How to get there: Darlington railway station, five minutes walk.

Match tickets: Postal and telephone bookings accepted in advance of the match.

Car parking: Ample parking in surrounding side-streets.

Entertainments/catering facilities: Four nearby cafés. Three snack bars in the ground.

Club shop: Shop inside the ground sells all types of souvenirs.

Handbooks/programmes: No handbook. Programmes available on subscription.

Extra information: The club will make every effort to cater for the disabled, the blind, or any person who has some difficulty seeking entrance because of illness.

Club Colours: White shirts with red trim, black shorts, black stockings.

First Team Trainer/Coach: Bill Atkins.

Club Nickname: 'The Quakers'.

DARLINGTON 1975–76 LEAGUE RECORD

Match No.	Date	Venue	Opponents	Result	H/T Score	League Pos'n	Goalscorers	Attendance
1	Aug 16	H	Scunthorpe U.	W 2-0	1-0	—	Sinclair, Holbrook	1920
2	23	A	AFC Bournemouth	W 2-1	1-1	2	Crosson, Lowery	4298
3	30	H	Watford	W 1-0	1-0	1	Young	2998
4	Sept 5	A	Tranmere R.	L 0-2	0-0	3		2403
5	13	H	Northampton T.	L 0-1	0-1	9		3788
6	20	A	Crewe Alex.	L 0-2	0-1	16		2501
7	22	A	Stockport Co.	D 0-0	0-0	—		3054
8	27	H	Lincoln C.	D 0-0	0-0	15		2580
9	Oct 4	A	Cambridge U.	L 0-1	0-1	17		2695
10	11	H	Exeter C.	D 0-0	0-0	14		2314
11	18	A	Torquay U.	W 4-2	1-1	12	Sinclair 4	2413
12	21	A	Swansea C.	L 0-2	0-1	—		2200
13	25	H	Doncaster R.	D 2-2	2-1	15	Uzelac (og), Craig	3725
14	Nov 1	A	Bradford C.	L 0-2	0-1	19		1916
15	3	H	Hartlepool	L 1-2	0-1	—	Webb	4275
16	8	H	Barnsley	W 2-0	1-0	16	Sinclair (pen), Lowery	2066
17	15	A	Huddersfield T.	L 0-1	0-0	16		4133
18	29	H	Reading	L 0-1	0-1	18		1761
19	Dec 6	A	Newport Co.	L 1-4	1-1	19	Sinclair	1878
20	13	H	Cambridge U.	D 1-1	0-0	19	Peachey	1184
21	20	A	Brentford	L 0-3	0-1	20		4170
22	26	H	Workington	W 1-0	1-0	18	Young	2128
23	27	A	Rochdale	L 0-1	0-0	20		1659
24	Jan 3	H	Southport	W 2-0	0-0	17	Peachey 2	1368
25	10	A	Watford	L 0-2	0-1	19		3865
26	17	H	Crewe Alex.	D 0-0	0-0	21		1497
27	24	A	Northampton T.	L 2-3	0-3	21	Holbrook, Webb	5136
28	Feb 7	A	Hartlepool	W 3-2	0-2	20	Nattress, Coulson, Sinclair	3655
29	14	A	Barnsley	L 0-1	0-1	21		2440
30	21	H	Huddersfield T.	L 0-3	0-3	21		2052
31	23	H	Stockport Co.	L 0-1	0-0	—		1302
32	27	A	Doncaster R.	L 2-3	1-2	21	Webb, Sinclair	5587
33	Mar 13	A	Exeter C.	D 1-1	0-1	22	Young	3196
34	15	H	Torquay U.	W 1-0	0-0	—	Ferguson	1313
35	20	A	Reading	L 1-4	0-2	22	Sinclair	5350
36	22	H	Bradford C.	D 2-2	1-0	—	Sinclair 2	1368
37	27	H	Newport Co.	W 4-0	1-0	21	Sinclair 2, Rowles, Nattress	1312
38	29	H	Brentford	W 2-0	1-0	—	Crosson, Sinclair	1758
39	Apr 3	A	Scunthorpe U.	L 1-2	0-2	22	Sinclair	2492
40	7	A	Lincoln C.	L 1-2	0-2	—	Sinclair	10,658
41	10	H	Tranmere R.	W 2-0	1-0	22	Sinclair 2 (1 a pen)	2023
42	16	A	Southport	L 0-2	0-0	22		2149
43	17	A	Workington	D 0-0	0-0	22		1178
44	20	H	Rochdale	W 4-0	2-0	—	Webb, Craig 2, Sinclair	1957
45	24	H	AFC Bournemouth	W 2-0	1-0	21	Sinclair (pen), Ferguson	2249
46	28	H	Swansea C.	D 1-1	0-0	—	Webb	4295

Goalscorers

League (48): Sinclair 21 (3 pens), Webb 5, Craig 3, Peachey 3, Young 3, Crosson 2, Ferguson 2, Holbrook 2, Lowery 2, Nattress 2, Coulson 1, Rowles 1, own goal 1.
League Cup (4): Webb 2, Holbrook, Sinclair.

League Cup	First Round	Sheffield W. (h)	0-2
	Second Leg	(a)	2-0
	Second Round	Luton T. (h)	2-1
	Third Round	West Ham U. (a)	0-3
F.A. Cup	First Round	Chester (h)	0-0
		(a)	0-2

164

Ogley	Nattress	Cochrane	Cattrell	Noble	Smith	Holbrook	Sinclair	Webb	Crosson	Young	Rowles	Lees	Lowery	Blant	Craig	Cowan	Peachey	Coulson	Ferguson	Match No.
1	2	3	4	5	6	7	8*	9	10	11	12									1
1	2	5	4		3	7		9*	8	11	10	6	12							2
1	2	3	4	5		7		9	8	11	10		6							3
1	2	3	4	5		7	8	9	10*	11	12		6							4
1	2	3		5		7	8	9	10	11	12		6			4*				5
1	2	3	4		6*	7	12	9	10	11	8		5							6
1	2	3	4	5	7*		8	9	10	11	12		6							7
1	2	3	4	5		7	8	9*	10	11	12		6							8
1	2	3	4*	5		7		9	10	11	8	12	6							9
1	2	3	4	5			8	9	10	11*	7	12	6							10
1	2	3		5		10		9	8	11	7				6	4				11
1	2	3*		5			8	9	4	11	7		12		6	10				12
1	2		4				8	9	10	11	7		3		5	6				13
1	2			5			8	9	4*	11	7		3	12	6	10				14
1	2			5			8	9	6	11	7		3	10	4					15
1	2			5			8	9		11	7		3	10	6	4				16
1	2			5		7	8			11	9		3	10	4	6				17
1	2	3		5		7		9		12	4*	10	11	8	6					18
1	2*	3	4	5		7		9		11			10	8	6	12				19
1	2	3	4		6		8	12	7				10*	11	5				9	20
1	2	3	4			7	8	12	11*				10	5	6				9	21
1	2	3	4			7	8			11	12		10*	6	5				9	22
1	6	3	4	5	7*		8		2	11	12		10						9	23
1	2	3	4	5		7	10			11			12	6*	8				9	24
1	4	3	6			7	8	9	2	11			10		5					25
1	7	3	4				8	9	2	11			10		5	6				26
1	6	3	7*			12	10	11	2		9				5	4		8		27
1	2	3	6			7		9			8		10		5	4		11		28
1	2	3	6			10	12	9	11				8		5	4*	7			29
1	2	3	6				8	9			11			5	10	4		7		30
1	2	3					8	9	10				7	6	5	4		11		31
1	2	3	12				8	9		10		4	7*	6	5			11		32
1	2	3	6			7	8	9		11	10	4*			5			12		33
1	2	3	6			7*	8			10	4	12			5		11		9	34
1	2*	3	6			7	8		10	11	4				5		12		9	35
1	2	3	6				8	12		4	10				5	7*	11		9	36
1	2	3	4	6			10		8	11	7				5				9	37
1	2	3	7*	6		12	8		10	11	4				5				9	38
1	2	3	7	6			8		10	11*	4				5		12		9	39
1	2	3	6				8	9	7		4				5	10		11		40
1	2	3	6				8	9	7		4				5	10		11		41
1	2	3	6	12		8			7		4				5	11		10*	9	42
1	9	3	6			7	8			11	4				5	10	2			43
1	2	3		5			8	11	10		4			6	7				9	44
1	2	3	6				8	9	7		4				5	11		10		45
1	2	3		5			8	11	10		4			6	7				9	46
46	46	41	20	35	6	22	43	27	31	34	29	12	14	33	31	10	5	11	10	
	+				+	+	+	+	+	+	+				+	+		+		
	1s				3s	1s	4s	1s	7s	1s	6s				1s	2s		1s		

165

Player and position	Ht.	Wt.	Birthplace	Clubs	League Appearances	Goals
Goalkeepers						
Alan Ogley	5 10	11 8	Barnsley	Barnsley	9	—
				Manchester C.	51	—
				Stockport Co.	240	—
				Darlington	46	—
Defenders						
*Colin Blant	6 1½	13 4	Rawtenstall	Burnley	46+6	7
				Portsmouth	64	1
				Rochdale	51	—
				Darlington	89	—
*Billy Horner	5 8	11 0	Cassop	Middlesbrough	182+3	11
				Darlington	111+7	5
Clive Nattress	6 0	12 4½	Durham	Blackpool	—	—
				Darlington	138+4	4
Gordon Jones	5 8	11 0	Darlington	Middlesbrough	457+5	4
				Darlington	80+5	5
				(contract cancelled April 1976)		
Alex Smith	5 9	11 8	Middlesbrough	Middlesbrough	123+2	—
				Bangor C.	Non-league	
				Darlington	43	—
				(contract cancelled Oct. 1975)		
Bobby Noble	5 11	12 0	Newcastle	Newcastle U.	—	—
				Bury	6	—
				Barrow	91+1	8
				Colchester U.	25+2	—
				Southport	61+2	6
				Darlington	35	—
Derek Craig	6 0	11 9	Durham	Newcastle U.	13+2	—
				Darlington	31	3
Jimmy Cochrane	5 9	11 0	Glasgow	Middlesbrough	3	—
				Darlington	54	—
Midfield						
Norman Lees	5 9	11 0	Newcastle	Hull C.	4+1	—
				Hartlepool (on loan)	—	—
				Darlington	108+10	5
Steve Holbrook	5 5½	10 12	Richmond, Yorks	Hull C.	2+1	—
				Darlington	89+8	9
*Don Burluraux	5 10	11 0	Skelton	Middlesbrough	4+1	—
				York C. (on loan)	3	1
				Darlington	105+7	13
David Crosson	5 9	11 11	Durham	Newcastle U.	6	—
				Darlington	31	2
*Eddie Rowles	5 9	11 2	Gosport	Bournemouth	58+8	12
				York C.	61+6	14
				Torquay U.	54+5	13
				Darlington	29+7	1
*John Cowan (N. Ireland)	5 9	9 8	Belfast	Newcastle U.	6+1	—
				Darlington	10	—
Forwards						
*Patrick Lowery	5 8	12 3	Newcastle	Sunderland	12+2	3
				Darlington	14+6	2
Gordon Cattrell	5 6½	9 2½	Sunderland	Leeds U.	—	—
				Darlington	96+6	5
Colin Sinclair	5 10	11 2	Edinburgh	Raith R.	45+4	14
				Darlington	194+2	57
Stan Webb	6 0	12 0	Middlesbrough	Middlesbrough	20+7	6
				Carlisle U.	16+10	5
				Brentford	37+2	8
				Darlington	69+5	21
Eric Young	5 6½	10 3	Stockton on Tees	Manchester U.	—	—
				Peterborough U. (on loan)	24+1	2
				Walsall (on loan)	8	—
				Stockport Co. (on loan)	16	—
				Darlington	76+2	7

DERBY COUNTY   DIV. 1

President: Sir Robertson King, K.B.E.

Chairman: Sam Longson.

Vice-Chairman: S. C. Bradley.

Directors: F. W. Innes, R. J. Moore, G. Hardy.

Manager: Dave Mackay.   *Asst-Manager:* Des Anderson.

Secretary: A. S. Webb.

Year Formed: 1884.   *Turned Professional:* 1884.

Badge
copyright
reserved

Limited Company: 1896.

Former Grounds: 1884–95, Racecourse Ground; 1895, Baseball Ground.

Honours: *Football League:* Division 1, Champions: 1971–72; 1974–75; runners-up: 1895–96, 1929–30, 1935–36. Division 2, Champions: 1911–12, 1914–15, 1968–69; runners-up: 1925–26. Division 3(N), Champions: 1956–57; runners-up: 1955–56. *F. A. Cup,* Winners: 1945–46; runners-up: 1897–98, 1898–99, 1902–03. *Football League Cup.* best season: semi-final, 1967–68. *Charity Shield winners:* 1975.

European Competitions: European Cup 1972–73 (semi-finalists), 1975–76; UEFA Cup 1974–75.

Record Victory: 9-0 v Wolverhampton W., Division 1, Jan. 10th, 1891 and v Sheffield W., Division 1, Jan. 21st, 1899.

Record Defeat: 2-11 v Everton, 1st Rd., F.A. Cup, 1889–90.

Most League Points: 63, Division 2, 1968–69 and 63, Division 3(N), 1955–56, 1956–57.

Most League Goals: 111, Division 3(N), 1956–57.

Highest League Scorer in Season: Jack Bowers, 37, Division 1, 1930–31 and Ray Straw, 37, Division 3(N), 1956–57.

Most Goals in Total Aggregate: Steve Bloomer, 291, 1892–1906 and 1910–14.

Most League Appearances: Jack Parry, 478, 1949–66.

Most Capped Player: Alan Durban, 27, Wales.

Record Transfer Fee Received: £90,000 from Aston Villa for John Robson, Dec. 1972.

Record Transfer Fee Paid: £300,000 to Burnley for Leighton James, Nov. 1975.

Managers Since the War: Stuart McMillan, Jack Barker, Harry Storer, Tim Ward, Brian Clough.

Address of Supporters Club: Baseball Ground, Derby.

Address of Club Shop or Boutique: The Ramtique, 55 Osmaston Road, Derby DE1 2JH.

Baseball Ground, Shaftesbury Crescent, Derby DE3 8NB. Telephone Derby 40105. *Telegraphic address:* 'Football Derby'.   *Ground capacity:* 38,500 (30,000 covered, 15,250 seats.) *Record attendance:* 41,826 v Tottenham H., Division 1, September 20, 1969.   *Record receipts:* £65,000 v Juventus. European Cup semi-final April 25, 1973. *Pitch measurements:* 110 yds × 71 yds.

How to get there: Buses from town centre 60, 88 and 89.   Nearest railway station Derby.

Match tickets: Available 14 days prior to game (£1.50, £1.20, £1.00).

Car parking: Eight car parks within half a mile of the ground run by the club in connection with the local corporation. Street parking half a mile from the ground.

Entertainments/catering facilities: Sportsman Club (members only). Licensed and refreshment bars in all parts of the ground.

Club shop: The Ramtique in Osmaston Road open every week day. Shop on the ground open on match days.

Handbooks/programmes: Yearbook published annually. "The Ram", the club newspaper and official programme, available on subscription c/o The Programme Editor, Derby County F.C. or from local newsagents.

Club Colours: White shirts, blue shorts, white stockings.

Change Colours: Blue and white striped shirts, white shorts, blue stockings.

Club Captain: Roy McFarland.

Club Nickname: 'The Rams'.

Match No.	Date	Venue	Opponents	Result	H/T Score	League Pos'n	Goalscorers	Attendance
1	Aug 16	A	Sheffield U.	D 1-1	0-0	—	George	31,316
2	19	A	Coventry C.	D 1-1	0-0	—	McFarland	24,161
3	23	H	Q.P.R.	L 1-5	0-3	17	McFarland	27,590
4	27	H	Newcastle U.	W 3-2	0-1	19	Craig T. (og), Hector, Lee	27,858
5	30	A	Everton	L 0-2	0-0	19		32,483
6	Sept 6	H	Burnley	W 3-0	2-0	12	Lee 2, Gemmill	24,086
7	13	A	Tottenham H.	W 3-2	1-2	8	George, Hector, Lee	28,455
8	20	H	Manchester C.	W 1-0	1-0	7	Lee	23,250
9	24	H	Manchester U.	W 2-1	1-0	—	George 2	33,187
10	27	A	Stoke C.	L 0-1	0-1	6		25,097
11	Oct 4	H	Ipswich T.	W 1 0	0-0	5	Lee	26,056
12	11	A	Norwich C.	D 0-0	0-0	5		23,022
13	18	H	Wolverhampton W.	W 3-2	3-0	4	Hector 2, Lee	25,861
14	25	A	Liverpool	D 1-1	0-1	4	Lee	46,324
15	Nov 1	H	Leeds U.	W 3-2	2-1	4	Gemmill, George (pen), Davies	33,107
16	8	A	Arsenal	W 1-0	1-0	2	George	32,012
17	15	H	West Ham U.	W 2-1	1-1	1	Rioch, George	31,172
18	22	A	Wolverhampton W.	D 0-0	0-0	1		26,690
19	29	H	Middlesbrough	W 3-2	1-2	1	Lee, Newton, Gemmill	27,745
20	Dec 6	A	Birmingham C.	L 1-2	1-0	2	George	30,620
21	13	A	Q.P.R.	D 1-1	0-0	4	Rioch	25,465
22	20	H	Sheffield U.	W 3-2	2-1	3	Nish, George, Garner (og)	26,455
23	26	A	Leicester C.	L 1-2	0-2	5	James	26,870
24	27	H	Aston Villa	W 2-0	0-0	4	Powell, Gemmill (pen)	37,230
25	Jan 10	H	Tottenham H.	L 2-3	2-3	4	Powell, Davies	28,085
26	17	A	Burnley	W 2-1	1-0	4	James, George	21,082
27	31	H	Coventry C.	W 2-0	0-0	3	George 2 (1 a pen)	24,253
28	Feb 7	A	Newcastle U.	L 3-4	0-1	4	Powell, George, Rioch	44,488
29	18	H	Arsenal	W 2-0	0-0	—	James 2	24,875
30	21	A	West Ham U.	W 2-1	0-1	4	George, Rioch	26,941
31	25	A	Manchester U.	D 1-1	0-1	—	Rioch	59,632
32	28	H	Liverpool	D 1-1	0-0	4	George (pen)	32,800
33	Mar 2	A	Leeds U.	D 1-1	1-1	—	Gemmill	40,608
34	13	H	Norwich C.	W 3-1	0-1	4	Gemmill, Rioch, James	27,005
35	20	H	Middlesbrough	W 2-0	1-0	4	George, Hector	24,000
36	24	H	Stoke C.	D 1-1	1-1	—	Rioch (pen)	30,156
37	27	H	Birmingham C.	W 4-2	1-0	3	James, Rioch, Davies, Nish	28,161
38	Apr 10	A	Manchester C.	L 3-4	1-3	4	Rioch 2, Todd	42,061
39	17	H	Leicester C.	D 2-2	1-0	5	Lee 2	29,085
40	19	A	Aston Villa	L 0-1	0-0	—		39,241
41	21	H	Everton	L 1-3	0-2	—	Rioch	22,488
42	24	A	Ipswich T.	W 6-2	3-2	4	Hector 2, Rioch 2 (1 a pen) Lee 2	26,702

Goalscorers

League (75): George 16 (3 pens), Rioch 13 (2 pens), Lee 13, Hector 7, James 6, Gemmill 6 (1 a pen), Powell 3, Davies 3, McFarland 2, Nish 2, Newton 1, Todd 1, own goals 2.
League Cup (2): Rioch, George.
F.A. Cup (8): George 3, Rioch 3, Davies, Newton.

League Cup	Second Round	Huddersfield T. (h	2-1
	Third Round	Middlesbrough (a)	0-1
F.A. Cup	Third Round	Everton (h)	2-1
	Fourth Round	Liverpool (h)	1-0
	Fifth Round	Southend U. (h)	1-0
	Sixth Round	Newcastle U. (h)	4-2
	Semi-Final	Manchester U	0-2 (at Hillsboro)

Boulton	Thomas	Nish	Rioch	McFarland	Todd	Newton	Gemmill	Lee	Bourne	George	Hinton	Hector	Webster	Moseley	Davies	Powell	James	Daniel	Macken	King	Match No.
1	2	3	4	5	6	7	8*	9	10	11	12										1
1	2	3	4	5	6	7	8	9	10	11											2
1	2	3	4	5	6	7	8	9*		11	12	10									3
1	2	3	4	5	6	7	8	9		11		10									4
1	5	3	4		6	7	8	9*		11	12	10	2								5
1	5	3	4		6	7	8	9		11		10	2								6
	2	3	4	5	6	7	8	9		11		10		1							7
1	2	3	4	5	6	7	8	9		11		10									8
1	2	3	4	5	6	7	8	9*		11		10			12						9
1	2	3	4	5	6	7	8		9	11		10									10
1	2	3	4	5	6		8	9		11		10				7					11
1	2	3	4	5	6		8	9*		11		10			12	7					12
1	2	3	4	5	6	7	8	9		11*		10			12						13
1	2	3	4	5	6	7*	8	9		11		10			12						14
1	5	3	4*		6	7	8	9		11		10	2		12						15
1	2	3	4	5	6	7	8	9		11		10									16
1	2	3	4	5	6	7	8	9		11		10									17
1	5	3	4		6	7	8	9		11		10	2								18
1	2	3	4	5	6	7	8	9		11		10									19
1	2	3	4	5	6	7*	8	9		11		10			12						20
1	2	3	4	5	6	7	8	9	10	11											21
1	2	3	4	5	6	7	8			12		10*			9	11					22
1	2		4*	5	6	7	8			12		10			9	11		3			23
1	2	6	3				8					10			9	7	11	5	4		24
1	2		4	5	6	3	8			12		10			9	7*	11				25
	2	3	4	5	6		8	9				10		1		7	11				26
	2		4	5	6	3	8	9*				10		1	12	7	11				27
	2	3	4	5	6		8	9*				10		1	12	7	11				28
	2	3	4	5	6		8					10		1	9	7	11				29
	2	3	4	5	6		8					10		1	9	7	11				30
	2	3	4	5	6		8					10		1	9	7	11				31
	2	3	4	5	6		8					10		1	9	7*	11				32
	2	3	4	5	6		8					10		1	9	7	11*				33
		3	4	5	6		8					10	2	1	9	7	11				34
	2	3	4	5	6		8					10		1	9	7	11				35
	2	3	4	5	6		8					10*		1	9	7	11				36
	2	3	4	5*	6	12	8					10		1	9	7	11				37
	2*	3	4	5	6	12	8					10		1	9	7	11				38
	2	3	4*	5	6	12	8					10		1	9	7	11				39
	2		4	5	6	3	8			12		9		1		7	11		10*		40
	2*		4	5	6	3	8			12		10		1	9	7	11				41
			4	5*	6	3	8			12		10	2	1	9	7				11	42

| 24 | 40 | 35 | 38 | 37 | 42 | 30 | 42 | 28 | 4 | 35 | — | 29 | 6 | 18 | 8 | 20 | 21 | 2 | 2 | 1 | |
| | | | | | | +3s | | | | +3s | +3s | | | | +13s | +1s | | | | | |

DERBY COUNTY—PLAYERS

Player and position	Ht.	Wt.	Birthplace	Clubs	League Appearances	Goals
Goalkeepers						
Colin Boulton	5 10½	12 6	Cheltenham	Derby Co.	234	—
Graham Moseley	6 0	11 8	Manchester	Blackburn R.	—	—
				Derby Co.	20	—
				Aston V. (on loan)	3	—
Defenders						
Peter Daniel	5 10	11 2	Stanley	Derby Co.	145+2	3
David Nish	5 11	11 3	Burton on	Leicester C.	228	25
(England)			Trent	Derby Co.	147	6
Ron Webster	5 8½	11 0	Belper	Derby Co.	432+1	7
Roy McFarland	5 11½	11 2	Liverpool	Tranmere R.	35	—
(England)				Derby Co.	310	33
Rod Thomas	6 0	12 10	Glyncorrwg	Swindon T.	296	5
(Wales)				Derby Co.	66	—
Colin Todd	5 9	11 5	Chester le	Sunderland	170+3	3
(England)			Street	Derby Co.	216	4
Midfield						
Henry Newton	5 8	11 4	Nottingham	Nottingham F.	282	17
				Everton	75	5
				Derby Co.	86+4	5
Bruce Rioch	5 11	12 5	Aldershot	Luton T.	147+1	47
(Scotland)				Aston V.	149+6	34
				Derby Co.	93	30
Steve Powell	5 8	11 0	Derby	Derby Co.	85+5	8
Archie Gemmill	5 5	11 2	Paisley	St. Mirren	65+2	9
(Scotland)				Preston N.E.	93+9	13
				Derby Co.	226	16
Jeff King	5 9	11 0	Fauld House	Albion R.	40+2	7
				Derby Co.	1	—
				Notts Co. (on loan)	3	—
				Portsmouth (on loan)	4	—
Tony Macken	5 18	12 6	Waterford	Derby Co.	2	—
				Portsmouth (on loan)	10	1
Forwards						
Charlie George	5 11	11 9	London	Arsenal	113+20	31
				Derby Co.	35	16
Jeff Bourne	5 9	11 5	Linton	Derby Co.	32+10	9
Eric Carruthers	5 5	10 2		Hearts	45+5	9
				Derby Co.	—	—
Roger Davies	6 2	12 0	Wolver-	Worcester C.	Non-league	
			hampton	Preston N.E. (on loan)	2	—
				Derby Co.	98+16	31
Kevin Hector	5 8	10 9	Leeds	Bradford P.A.	176	113
(England)				Derby Co.	387+3	140
*Alan Hinton	5 11	11 12	Wednesbury	Wolverhampton W.	75	29
(England)				Nottingham F.	108+4	24
				Derby Co.	240+13	63
*Francis Lee	5 7½	12 2	Bolton	Bolton W.	189	92
(England)				Manchester C.	248+1	112
				Derby Co.	62	25
*Chris Egan	5 9	11 0	Ireland	Cork Celtic	League of Ireland	
				Derby Co.	—	—
Leighton James	5 9	10 3	Llwchwr, Glam.	Burnley	180+1	44
(Wales)				Derby Co.	21+1	6

DONCASTER ROVERS DIV. 4

President: J. S. Garnham. *Vice-President:* J. C. Morris.
Chairman: B. Rayner.
Directors: H. Bates, K. Jackson, B. Bailey, A. Phillips, T. R.
Jones.
Team Manager: Stan Anderson.
General Manager/Secretary: G. Thompson.
Promotions Manager: Harry Barton. (tel: 59679, mornings only).
Year Formed: 1879. *Turned Professional:* 1885.
Limited Company: 1905 and 1920.
Previous Grounds: 1880–1916, Intake Ground; 1920–22, Benet-
thorpe Ground; 1922, Low Pasture, Belle Vue.
Honours: *Football League,* highest position: Division 2, 7th,
1901–02. Division 3(N), Champions: 1934–35 1946–47, 1949–50;
Runners-up: 1937–38, 1938–39. Division 4, Champions: 1965–
66, 1968–69. *F.A. Cup,* best season: 5th Rd., 1951–52, 1953–54, 1954–55, 1955–56. *Football
League Cup,* best season: 5th Rd., 1975–76.

Record Victory: 10-0 v Darlington, Division 4, Jan. 25th, 1964.

Record Defeat: 0-12 v Small Heath, Division 2, Apr. 11th, 1903.

Most League Points: 72, Division 3(N), 1946–7 (record any Division).

Most League Goals: 123, Division 3(N), 1946–47.

Highest League Scorer in Season: Clarrie Jordan, 42, Division 3(N), 1946–47.

Most League Goals in Total Aggregate: Tom Keetley, 180, 1923–29.

Most Capped Player: Len Graham, 14, Ireland.

Most League Appearances: Fred Emery, 406, 1925–36.

Record Transfer Fee Received: £70,000 from Preston N.E. for Mike Elwiss, Feb. 1974.

Record Transfer Fee Paid: £10,000 to Stoke C. for John Flowers, Aug. 1966.

Managers Since the War: Bill Marsden, Jackie Bestall, Peter Doherty, Jack Hodgson, Syd
Bycroft, Jack Crayston, Jack Bestall, Norman Curtis, Danny Malloy, Oscar Hold, Bill
Leivers, Keith Kettleborough, George Raynor, Lawrie McMenemy, Maurice Setters.

Address of Supporters Club: Secretary, K. J. Avis, 64 Harrowden Road, Doncaster.

Address of Club Shop or Boutique: On ground.

Belle Vue Ground, Doncaster. Telephone Doncaster 55281. *Telegraphic address:* 'Rovers
Doncaster'. *Ground capacity:* 30,000. *Record attendance:* 37,149 v Hull C., Division 3(N),
October 2, 1948. *Record receipts:* £8936 v Liverpool, F.A. Cup 3rd Rd., Jan. 8, 1974.
Pitch measurements: 118 yds × 79 yds.

How to get there: Buses from town centre (Duke St.)—Race Course, Hyde Park, and Cantley Estate
services. Doncaster railway station is near the town centre.

Match tickets: No advance booking except for Cup ties.

Car parking: Very large car and coach park adjoining the ground. Entrance direct from Great North Road.

Entertainments/catering facilities: Refreshment bars in Main Stand and around the ground, including
licensed bars. Social club adjoining ground.

Club shop: In Main Stand, stocks all types of souvenirs.

Handbooks/programmes: Annual handbook on sale at 20p post free or at shop or Supporters Club office
Programmes on sale at shop but not on subscription.

Extra information: Development Association office on ground. Supporters' Club office on ground—
minimum subscription 15p (Cihldren and OAPs 10p). Handbook free to members. Phone 59679.

Club Colours: Red shirts with white stripe on sleeves, red shorts and red stockings.

Change Colours: Red shirts with white facings, white shorts with red stripe, white stockings.

First Team Trainer: John Quigley.

Club Nickname: 'Rovers'.

DONCASTER ROVERS 1975-76 LEAGUE RECORD

Match No.	Date	Venue	Opponents	Result	H/T Score	League Pos'n	Goalscorers	Attendance
1	Aug 16	H	Cambridge U.	L 0-2	0-0	—		2990
2	22	A	Tranmere R.	D 2-2	1-0	19	Curran 2	2013
3	30	H	Crewe Alex.	W 3-1	1-0	12	Chappell, O'Callaghan, Alseinoye	2467
4	Sept 6	A	AFC Bournemouth	W 1-0	0-0	10	Kitchen	3511
5	15	H	Brentford	D 1-1	0-0	—	Uzelac	6353
6	20	A	Watford	L 1-2	0-0	14	Murray	4228
7	24	A	Barnsley	W 1-0	1-0	—	O'Callaghan	6557
8	27	H	Southport	W 5-2	2-2	7	Kitchen 3 (1 a pen), O'Callaghan 2	5219
9	Oct 3	A	Northampton T.	L 1-2	0-0	9	Chappell	6155
10	10	A	Stockport Co.	W 2-1	0-1	7	Kitchen, O'Callaghan	3159
11	18	H	Swansea C.	W 2-1	0-0	7	O'Callaghan, Kitchen	6640
12	22	A	Bradford C.	W 4-2	3-0	—	O'Callaghan 3, Chappell	3687
13	25	A	Darlington	D 2-2	1-2	5	Chappell, Murray	3725
14	Nov 1	H	Reading	D 1-1	0-1	5	Uzelac	7293
15	4	H	Huddersfield T.	W 4-1	1-0	—	O'Callaghan, Ternent, Miller, Kitchen	10,650
16	8	A	Hartlepool	L 1-2	0-1	6	Murray	3567
17	15	H	Newport Co.	W 5-1	1-0	5	Miller 3, O'Callaghan 2	7793
18	28	A	Exeter C.	L 0-1	0-1	7		2848
19	Dec 6	A	Torquay U.	L 0-1	0-0	9		7667
20	13	H	Tranmere R.	W 3-0	1-0	5	Murray, Kitchen, O'Callaghan	5684
21	20	A	Workington	L 1-3	0-2	7	Kitchen	1642
22	26	H	Lincoln C.	L 2-4	1-2	8	Kitchen, Miller	14,353
23	27	A	Scunthorpe U.	L 1-2	1-1	9	Kitchen	5801
24	Jan 10	A	Crewe Alex.	W 2-1	0-0	8	O'Callaghan, Kitchen	2501
25	17	H	Watford	L 1-2	1-0	11	Kitchen	5845
26	20	H	Rochdale	L 1-2	0-2	—	Kitchen	3586
27	24	A	Brentford	W 1-0	1-0	8	O'Callaghan	4900
28	30	H	Bradford C.	D 1-1	0-0	8	Miller	4484
29	Feb 7	A	Huddersfield T.	W 2-1	1-1	8	Murray, O'Callaghan	6305
30	14	H	Hartlepool	W 3-0	2-0	7	Kitchen 2, O'Callaghan	5035
31	21	A	Newport Co.	W 3-2	2-1	8	O'Callaghan 2, Kitchen	1543
32	24	H	Barnsley	D 2-2	1-1	—	O'Callaghan, Miller	8250
33	28	H	Darlington	W 3-2	2-1	8	Kitchen 2 (1 a pen), O'Callaghan	5587
34	Mar 6	A	Reading	W 1-0	0-0	7	Chappell	6441
35	9	H	Northampton T.	L 0-4	0-1	—		8737
36	13	A	Stockport Co.	W 3-1	1-0	7	Balderstone, Chappell, Kitchen	4231
37	16	A	Swansea C.	L 1-2	0-1	—	Miller	3128
38	20	H	Exeter C.	D 0-0	0-0	7		4149
39	27	A	Torquay U.	D 2-2	1-2	7	Kitchen, Murray	1975
40	30	A	Workington	W 1-0	1-0	—	Miller	4081
41	Apr 3	A	Cambridge U.	D 3-3	1-2	6	Kitchen, Robinson, Wignall, D.	1633
42	6	A	Southport	D 1-1	1-1	—	O'Callaghan	1599
43	10	H	AFC Bournemouth	D 1-1	0-1	6	Taylor	4097
44	16	A	Rochdale	L 0-1	0-0	7		1462
45	17	A	Lincoln C.	L 0-5	0-3	7		14,096
46	19	H	Scunthorpe U.	L 0-1	0-1	—		4097

Goalscorers

League (75): Kitchen 22 (2 pens), O'Callaghan 22, Miller 9, Chappell 6, Murray 6, Curran 2, Uzelac 2, Alseinoye 1, Balderstone 1, Robinson 1, Taylor 1, Ternent 1, Wignall, D. 1.
League Cup (13): O'Callaghan 6, Kitchen 2, Chappell, Reed, Balderstone, Ternent, Murray.
F.A. Cup (2): Uzelac 2.

League Cup	First Round	Grimsby T. (h)	3-1
	Second Leg	(a)	0-0
	Second Round	C. Palace (h)	2-1
	Third Round	Torquay U. (a)	1-1
		(h)	3-0
	Fourth Round	Hull C. (h)	2-1
	Fifth Round	Tottenham H. (a)	2-7
F.A. Cup	First Round	Bury (a)	2-4

172

Peacock	Ternent	Wignall, S.	Chappell	Uzelac	Brookes	Curran	Alseinoye	O'Callaghan	Kitchen	Higgins	Murray	Reed	Miller	Robinson	Balderstone	Brown	Creamer	Taylor	Binch	Wignall, D.	Jones	McConville	Match No.
1	2	3	4	5	6	7	8*	9	10	11	12												1
1	3		4	5	6	7	8*	9	10	11	12	2											2
1	3		4	5	6		8	9	10	11*		2	7	12									3
1			4	5	6		8	9	10			2	7	3	11								4
1			4	5	6		8*	9	10		12	2	7	3	11								5
1	3		4	5	6		8*	9	10		12	2	7		11								6
1			4	5	6		8	9	10		7	2		3	11								7
1			4	5*	6		8	9	10		12	2	7	3	11								8
1			4	5	6		8*	9	10		12	2	7	3	11								9
1			4	5	6			9	10		8	2	7	3	11								10
1			4	5	6			9	10		8	2	7	3	11								11
1			4	5	6			9	10		8	2	7		11								12
1	8		4	5	6			9	10		11	2	7	3									13
1	12		4	5	6*			9	8		10	2	7	3	11								14
1	4			5	6			9	10		8	2	7	3	11								15
1	4	12		5	6*			9	10		8	2	7	3	11								16
1	4	12		5	6			9	10		8	2*	7	3	11								17
	12		4	5	6			9	10		8	2	7	3	11*	1							18
	4	10	5					9				8	7	3	11	1	2	6					19
	4		5	12				9	10			8	7	3	11*	1	2	6					20
	4		5	12				9	10			8*	7	6	11	1	2	3					21
1	8	4	11	5				9	10			7		3	12		2	6*					22
	8	5	4					9	10			2	7	3	11	1		6					23
	8		4	5	6			9	10			7			11	1	2	3					24
	8		4	5*	3			9	10			7	12		11	1	2	6					25
1					3			9	10		8	2	7	4	11		5	6					26
1		6	4		3			9	10*	12	8	2	7		11		5						27
1	12	6	4		3			9	10		8	2*	7		11		5						28
1		6	4		3			9	10		8	2	7		11		5						29
1		6			3		4*	9	10		8	2	7	12	11		5						30
1		6	4		3		11	9	10		8	2	7				5						31
1		6	4		3		12	9	10			2	7		11*		5						32
1		6	4		3			9	10		8	2	7		11		5						33
1		6	4		3			9	10		8	2	7		11		5						34
1		6	4		3			9*	10		8	2	7		11		5	12					35
1		6	4		3			9	10		8	2	7		11		5						36
1		6	8		3			9	10		12	2	7		11*		5	4					37
1		6	4		3*			9	8		10		7	12	11		2	5					38
1			4		3			9	10		8		7		11		2	5	6				39
			4		3			9	10		8		7		11	1	2	6	5				40
			4		3			9	10		8*		7	12	11	1	2	6	5				41
			4		3			9	10*		12		7	8		1	2	5		6	11		42
			4		3			9	10				7	8	11	1	2	6	5				43
					3			9	10			2	7	8	11	1	5	6	4				44
		5			3				10			8	7			1	2*	6	9	4	12	11	45
1	12	5			3				10			2	7	4	11			6*	9	8			46
33	13	21	33	25	41	2	13	42	43	4	30	30	43	26	38	13	26	18	2	8	1	1	
+3s	+2s	+1s	+2s		+1s			+1s	+8s					+5s	+1s			+1s		+1s			

173

DONCASTER ROVERS—PLAYERS

Player and position	Ht.	Wt.	Birthplace	Clubs	League Appearances	Goals
Goalkeepers						
*Graham Brown	6 1½	12 7	Bromley	Millwall	—	—
				Mansfield	142	—
				Doncaster R.	53	—
Dennis Peacock	6 3	12 10	Lincoln	Nottingham F.	22	—
				Walsall (on loan)	10	—
				Doncaster R.	33	—
Defenders						
*David Carver	6 1	11 10	Rotherham	Rotherham U.	83	—
				Cardiff C.	210+1	1
				Swansea C. (on loan)	3	—
				Hereford U.	14	—
				Doncaster R.	29+1	—
Peter Creamer	5 11	11 4	Hartlepool	Middlesbrough	9	—
				York C. (on loan)	4	—
				Doncaster R.	26	—
Brian Taylor	5 11	11 9	Hodthorpe	Middlesbrough	11+4	1
				Doncaster R.	18	1
Ray Ternent	5 9	11 0	Gateshead	Burnley	13+1	—
				Southend U.	82	1
				Doncaster R.	76+5	3
Steve Uzelac	6 0	11 7	Doncaster	Doncaster R.	161+2	8
				Mansfield T. (on loan)	2	—
				Liverpool	—	—
Steve Wignall	5 9	10 4	Liverpool	Doncaster R.	116+3	1
Stephen Reed	5 9	10 9	Doncaster	Doncaster R.	81	1
Fred Robinson	5 10	11 4	Rotherham	Doncaster R.	26+5	1
Stanley Brookes	5 11	11 0	Doncaster	Doncaster R.	188+4	5
Midfield						
Alan Murray	5 8	10 8	Newcastle	Middlesbrough	6+4	1
				York (on loan)	4	—
				Brentford	42+3	7
				Doncaster R.	97+12	18
Chris Balderstone	5 11	12 10	Huddersfield	Huddersfield T.	117	23
				Carlisle U.	377+7	67
				Doncaster R.	38+1	1
*Peter Woods	5 9	10 8	Sale	Manchester U.	—	—
				Luton T.	—	—
				Southend U.	25	—
				Doncaster R.	41+8	1
David Wignall	5 10	11 0	Liverpool	Doncaster R.	8	1
*Leslie Chappell	5 8	10 5	Nottingham	Rotherham U.	106+2	37
				Blackburn R.	7	—
				Reading	193+8	78
				Doncaster R.	57+1	10
Michael Kitchen	5 8½	10 5	Mexborough	Doncaster R.	178+7	66
Forwards						
*Peter Higgins	5 9	10 10	Cardiff	Bristol R.	36+1	5
				Doncaster R.	63+5	10
				Torquay U. (on loan)	3+1	1
Bren O'Callaghan	6 2	13 9	Bradford	Doncaster R.	108+3	43
Ian Miller	5 9	12 1	Perth	Bury	9+6	—
				Nottingham F.	—	—
				Doncaster R.	43	9
*Martin Alesinoye	5 10	11 7	Middlesbrough	Doncaster R.	13+1	1
David Binch	5 9	10 12	Doncaster	Doncaster R.	2+1	—
Mark Jones	6 1	11 12	Doncaster	Doncaster R.	1+1	—
Ian McConville	5 9	11 0	Doncaster	Doncaster R.	1	—

Chairman: A. W. Waterworth.

Vice-Chairman: John Moores, C.B.E.

Directors: N. W. Coffey, T. H. W. Scott, J. C. Sharp, G. A. Watts, K. M. Tamlin.

Manager: Billy Bingham.

Secretary: Jim Greenwood.

Year Formed: 1878. *Limited Company:* 1892.

Turned Professional: 1885.

Former Grounds: 1878, Stanley Park; 1882, Priory Road; 1884, Anfield Road; 1892, Goodison Park.

Honours: Football League, Division 1, Champions: 1890–91, 1914–15, 1927–28, 1931–32, 1938–39, 1962–63, 1969–70; Runners-up: 1889–90, 1894–95, 1901–02, 1904–05, 1908–09, 1911–12. Division 2, Champions: 1930–31; Runners-up: 1953–54. *F.A. Cup,* Winners: 1906, 1933, 1966; Runners-up: 1893, 1897, 1907, 1968. *Football League Cup,* best season: 1960–61, 5th Rd.

European Competitions: *European Cup:* 1963–64, 1970–71; *European Cup Winners Cup:* 1966–67. *European Fairs Cup:* 1962–63, 1964–65, 1965–66. *UEFA Cup:* 1975–76.

Record Victory: 11-2 v Derby Co., F.A. Cup, 1st Rd., 1889–90.

Record Defeat: 4-10 v Tottenham H., Division 1, Oct. 11th, 1958.

Most League Points: 66, Division 1, 1969–70.

Most League Goals: 121, Division 2, 1930–31.

Highest League Scorer in Season: Dixie Dean, 60, 1927–28.

Most Goals in Total Aggregate: Dixie Dean, 349, 1925–37.

Most League Appearances: Ted Sagar, 465, 1929–53.

Most Capped Player: Alan Ball, 39 (72), England.

Record Transfer Fee Received: £220,000 from Arsenal for Alan Ball, Dec. 1971.

Record Transfer Fee Paid: £350,000 to Birmingham C. for Bob Latchford, Feb. 1974.

Managers Since the War: Theo Kelly, Cliff Britton, Ian Buchan, John Carey, Harry Catterick.

Address of Supporters Club: 38 City Rd., Liverpool 4.

Goodison Park, Liverpool L4 4EL. Telephone 051-525-5263/4. *Ground capacity:* 58,000. (25,000 seats.) *Record attendance:* 78,299 v Liverpool, Division 1, September 18, 1948. *Record receipts:* £56,462 Arsenal v Stoke, F.A. Cup semi-final replay, April 1972. *Pitch measurements:* 112 yds × 78 yds.

How to get there: Corporation buses 19 and 44 from Pierhead, 68 from Old Swan 3, 22, 25, 500 from South End of the City and 30, 92, 92a, 92b, 93 from City centre. Nearest railway station, Liverpool Lime Street.

Match tickets: Reserved stand seats are available for all home fixtures (except the match v Liverpool) at any time during the season, either by post or by personal application to the Box Office at the Bullens Rd. side of the ground (tel: 051-525-0080). The Box Office is open each weekday from 9 a.m. to 5 p.m. Postal applications should be addressed to the Box Office manager and contain the correct remittance and S.A.E.

Car parking: Extensive parking facilities on site at the corner of Priory Rd. and Utting Ave.

Entertainments/catering facilities: Royal Blue Social Club offers cabaret entertainment each Saturday and Sunday; visiting parties by arrangement. Royal Blue Restaurant open to the public for lunch on Mondays to Fridays but restricted to members on match days.

Club shop: All souvenirs available from The Toffee Shops in Goodison Rd. and Bullens Rd.; send S.A.E. for mail order list.

Handbooks/programmes: Match-day magazine available on seasonal subscription.

Club Colours: Blue shirts with white collars, white shorts and stockings.

Change Colours: Amber shirts, royal blue shorts.

Club Coach: Steve Burtonshaw.

Team Captain: Roger Kenyon.

First Team Trainer: Stewart Imlach.

Club Nickname: 'Toffeemen' or 'Blues'.

EVERTON 1975–76 LEAGUE RECORD

Match No.	Date	Venue	Opponents	Result	H/T Score	League Pos'n	Goalscorers	Attendance
1	Aug16	H	Coventry C.	L 1-4	1-2	—	Kenyon	33,200
2	19	A	Burnley	D 1-1	0-0	—	Smallman	23,041
3	23	A	Birmingham C.	W 1-0	1-0	14	Smallman	26,794
4	26	H	Sheffield U.	W 3-0	2-0	—	Smallman (pen), Lyons, Latchford	25,848
5	30	H	Derby Co.	W 2-0	0-0	4	Lyons, Latchford	32,483
6	Sept 6	A	Norwich C.	L 2-4	0-2	10	Latchford, Pearson	20,407
7	13	H	Newcastle U.	W 3-0	2-0	5	Latchford, Lyons, Clements	28,938
8	20	A	Arsenal	D 2-2	2-0	5	Jones G, Buckley	24,864
9	27	H	Liverpool	D 0-0	0-0	9		55,570
10	Oct 4	A	West Ham U.	W 1-0	0-0	7	Jones G	31,005
11	11	A	Q.P.R.	L 0-5	0-2	9		23,855
12	18	H	Aston Villa	W 2-1	2-0	8	Jones G 2 (1 a pen)	30,376
13	25	A	Wolverhampton W.	W 2-1	1-0	7	Dobson, Jones G	20,063
14	Nov 1	H	Leicester C.	D 1-1	1-0	6	Smallman (pen)	24,930
15	8	A	Stoke C.	L 2-3	0-1	10	Telfer, Pearson	24,657
16	15	H	Manchester C.	D 1-1	0-1	10	Telfer	32,077
17	22	A	Aston Villa	L 1-3	0-1	10	Telfer	33,949
18	29	A	Leeds U.	L 2-5	1-3	11	Clements (pen), Latchford	30,879
19	Dec 6	H	Ipswich T.	D 3-3	2-1	10	Dobson 2, Latchford	24,601
20	10	A	Tottenham H.	D 2-2	0-1	—	Telfer, Latchford	18,638
21	13	H	Birmingham C.	W 5-2	2-1	9	Latchford, Jones G, Dobson, Hamilton, Telfer	20,188
22	19	A	Coventry C.	W 2-1	0-0	9	Jones G pen, Latchford	14,394
23	23	H	Manchester U.	D 1-1	1-1	—	Latchford	41,732
24	27	A	Middlesbrough	D 1-1	1-0	9	Latchford	30,000
25	Jan 10	A	Newcastle U.	L 0-5	0-2	11		32,076
26	17	H	Norwich C.	D 1-1	0-0	11	Dobson	23,164
27	31	H	Burnley	L 2-3	0-1	11	Hamilton 2	21,389
28	Feb 7	A	Sheffield U.	D 0-0	0-0	12		20,113
29	21	A	Manchester C.	L 0-3	0-2	15		33,148
30	24	H	Tottenham H.	W 1-0	0-0	—	Lyons	18,126
31	28	H	Wolverhampton W.	W 3-0	3-0	8	Telfer 2, Hamilton	21,827
32	Mar 6	A	Leicester C.	L 0-1	0-1	10		18,490
33	13	H	Q.P.R.	L 0-2	0-1	12		25,186
34	20	H	Leeds U.	L 1-3	0-0	14	Lyons	28,566
35	27	A	Ipswich T.	L 0-1	-01	16		22,368
36	Apr 3	A	Liverpool	L 0-1	0-0	16		54,632
37	7	H	Stoke C.	W 2-1	1-0	—	Hamilton, Bernard (pen)	16,974
38	10	H	Arsenal	D 0-0	0-0	13		20,774
39	17	A	Manchester U.	L 1-2	1-0	16	Telfer	61,879
40	19	H	Middlesbrough	W 3-1	2-1	—	Pearson, Latchford, Connolly	18,204
41	21	A	Derby Co.	W 3-1	2-0	—	King 2, Pearson	22,488
42	24	H	West Ham U.	W 2-0	2-0	11	Bernard (pen), Pearson	26,101

Goalscorers

League (60): Latchford 12, Telfer 8, Jones G 7 (2 pens), Lyons 5, Pearson 5, Dobson 5, Hamilton 5, Smallman 4 (2 pens), Clements 2 (1 a pen), Bernard 2 (2 pens), King 2, Kenyon 1, Buckley 1, Connolly 1.
League Cup (7): Smallman, Lyons, Kenyon, Latchford, Dobson, Irving, Jones.
F.A. Cup (1): Jones.

League Cup	Second Round	Arsenal (h)	2-2	
		(a)	1-0	
	Third Round	Carlisle U. (h)	2-0	
	Fourth Round	Notts Co. (h)	2-2	
		(a)	0-2	
F.A. Cup	Third Round	Derby Co. (a)	1-2	

Lawson	Bernard	Seargeant	Clements	Kenyon	Hurst	Lyons	Dobson	Latchford	Smallman	Pearson	Marshall	Darracott	Buckley	Telfer	Jones, G.	Davies	McLaughlan	McNaught	Jones, D.	Irving	Brand	Hamilton	Goodlass	Connolly	Robinson	King	Match No.
1	2	3	4	5	6	7	8	9	10	11																	1
1	2	3	4	5		6	8	9	10	11	7																2
1		3		5	12	6	8	9	10	4	11*	2	7														3
1	2	3		5		6	8	9	10	4	11*		7	12													4
1	2	3		5		6	8	9	10	4	11*		7	12													5
1	2	3		5		6	8	9	10	4			7			11											6
1	2	3	12	5		6	8	9	10	4*			7			11											7
1	2	3	12	5		6	8	9	10	4*			7			11											8
		3	12	5		6	8	9	10	4			7			11	1	2*									9
	2	3		5		6	8	9		4*			7	10		11	1		12								10
	2	3	10	5		6	8	9		4			7			11		1									11
	2	3	10	5			8	9	12	4			7*			11		1	6								12
	2	3		5*		6	8	9	10	4			7			11		1	12								13
		3				6	8	9	10	4			7			11*	1	2	5	12							14
		3	4	5			8	11	9			2	7*	12	1			6	10								15
1		3				6	8		10	4		2	7	12		11		5	9*								16
1		3	4			6	8	9		12		2*	7	10		11		5									17
		3	4	5		6	8	9		12		2	7*			11		1	10								18
1	4	3		5		6	8	9		12		2		10		11						7*					19
	4	3*		5		6	8	9				2	12			11		1				7					20
	2			5		6	8	9				3	7	10		11		1				4					21
	2			5	12	6	8	9				3	7	10*		11		1				4					22
	2			5	6	4	8	9	10			3						1				7		11			23
	2			5	6	4	8	9	10			3*				11		1	12			7					24
	2			5	6	4	8	9	10			3				11*		1				7	12				25
1	2			5		4	8	9	10*			3	6			11			12			7					26
1		3		5		6	8	9				4	10			11		5				7			2		27
1		3				6	8	9				2	4	10				5				7		11			28
1	2			5*	6	4	8					3			9	11			12			7		10			29
1	2					4	8					3	6		9	11		5				7		10			30
1	2					4	8					3	6		9	11		5				7		10			31
1	2					4	8						6		9	10		5	3			7		11			32
1	2					4	8						6		9	11*		5	3			7	12	10*			33
1	2	12				4	8						6		9	11*		5	3			7		10			34
1	2					4	8			11			6		9			5	3			7		10			35
	2	12				6	8	9				4	10		5*			1	3			7		11			36
	2			6		4	8	9							5	11		1	3			7		10			37
	2	12				4	8	9		6					5	11		1	3			7*		10			38
				6		4	8	9				2	7*		5	11		1	3			12		10			39
				5	12	4	8	9		11		2						1	3			7*		10		6	40
	12			5*		4	8	9		11		2						1	3			7		10		6	41
1	2					4	8	9		11		7			5				3					10		6	42
22	29	17	11	28	6	42	42	31	14	26	4	20	30	20	24	19	2	18	11	3	1	22	2	14	1	3	
+ 1s	+ 1s	+ 3s	+ 2s	+ 3s		+ 1s	+ 3s					+ 1s	+ 4s	+ 1s				+ 1s	+ 2s	+ 2s		+ 1s	+ 1s	+ 1s			

177

Player and position	Ht.	Wt.	Birthplace	Clubs	League Appearances	Goals
Goalkeepers						
Dai Davies (Wales)	6 0½	13 4½	Ammanford	Swansea C.	9	—
				Everton	57	—
				Swansea C. (on loan)	6	—
Dave Lawson	6 0¾	11 0	Newcastle	Bradford P.A.	13	—
				Huddersfield T.	51	—
				Everton	108	—
Andrew Brand	6 1	11 1	Edinburgh	Everton	1	—
Defenders						
John McLaughlan	5 5	9 10	Stirling	Falkirk	104+4	10
				Everton	59+2	1
				(contract cancelled April 1976)		
Roger Kenyon	6 0	11 8	Blackpool	Everton	229+14	5
Steve Seargeant	5 8	11 0	Liverpool	Everton	73+2	1
Mike Bernard	5 9	10 10	Shrewsbury	Stoke C.	124+12	6
				Everton	125+7	7
Terry Darracott	5 9	11 6	Liverpool	Everton	92+6	—
Neil Robinson	5 7	9 11	Liverpool	Everton	1	—
David Jones	5 10	12 7	Liverpool	Everton	11+2	—
Michael Lyons	6 0	12 2	Liverpool	Everton	115+17	28
Midfield						
Mike Buckley	5 5	9 6	Manchester	Everton	109+3	8
Dave Clements (N. Ireland)	5 10	11 9	Millbrook	Wolverhampton W.	—	—
				Coventry C.	227+2	26
				Sheffield W.	78	—
				Everton	81+4	6
				(contract cancelled Feb. 1976)		
Martin Dobson (England)	5 11¾	11 8	Blackburn	Bolton W.	—	—
				Burnley	220+3	42
				Everton	72	10
Ronald Goodlass	5 7	10 12	Liverpool	Everton	2+1	—
Kenneth McNaught	5 11	11 1	Kirkcaldy	Everton	22+2	—
Bryan Hamilton (N. Ireland)	5 8	10 4	Belfast	Ipswich T.	142+11	43
				Everton	22+1	5
Andy King	5 9	10 13	Luton	Luton T.	30+3	9
				Everton	3	—
Jim Pearson	5 10	11 2	Falkirk	St. Johnstone	96+9	39
				Everton	43+15	8
Forwards						
John Connolly (Scotland)	5 9	10 7	Glasgow	St. Johnstone	96	41
				Everton	105+3	15
Garry Jones	5 9	11 7	Liverpool	Everton	76+6	13
*John Smith	5 6	9 6	Liverpool	Everton	2	—
Bob Latchford	6 0	12 0	Birmingham	Birmingham C.	158+2	68
				Everton	80	36
*Cliff Marshall	5 10	11 2	Liverpool	Everton	6+1	—
David Smallman (Wales)	5 8	10 4	Connah's Quay	Wrexham	100+1	38
				Everton	18+1	5
George Telfer	5 10	11 5	Liverpool	Everton	46+8	13

President: F. E. J. Dart.

Chairman: L. G. Vallance.

Vice-Chairman: C. Hill.

Directors: J. R. Cowley, W. O. Rice, M.A., A.I.B., F.R.G.S.

Manager: John Newman.

Secretary: P. R. Wakeham.

Commercial Manager: Ray Ellis.

Year Formed: 1904. *Turned Professional:* 1908.

Limited Company: 1908.

Honours: *Football League,* highest position in Division 3: 17th, 1964–65. Division 3(S), Runners-up: 1932–33. *F.A. Cup,* best season: 6th Rd. Replay, 1931. *Football League Cup,* best year: Never beyond 3rd Rd. Division 3(S) Cup Winners: 1944.

Record Victory: 8-1 v Coventry C., Division 3(S), Dec. 4th, 1926 and v Aldershot, Division 3(S), May 4th, 1935.

Record Defeat: 0-9 v Notts Co., Division 3(S), Oct. 16th, 1948, 0-9 v Northampton, Division 3(S) Apr. 12, 1958.

Most League Points: 58, Division 3(S), 1932–33; Division 4, 1963–64.

Most League Goals: 88, Division 3(S), 1932–33.

Highest League Scorer in Season: Fred Whitlow, 34, Division 3(S), 1932–33.

Most Goals in Total Aggregate: Alan Banks, 105, 1963–66, 1967–73.

Most Capped Player: Dermot Curtis, 1 (17), Eire.

Most League Appearances: Arnold Mitchell, 495, 1952–66.

Record Transfer Fee Received: £42,000 from Brighton & H.A. for Fred Binney, May 1974.

Record Transfer Fee Paid: £10,000 to Brighton & H.A. for Lammie Robertson and John Templeman (£10,000 each) May 1974.

Managers Since the War: George Roughton, Norman Kirkman, Norman Dodgin, Bill Thompson, Frank Broome, Glen Wilson, Cyril Spiers, Jack Edwards, Ellis Stuttard, Jock Basford, Frank Broome.

Address of Supporters Club: Same as Football Club.

Address of Club Shop or Boutique: The 'Near Post', 2 Blackbury Rd. Exeter.

St. James Park, Exeter. Telephone Exeter 54073. *Ground capacity:* 18,500. *Record attendance:* 20,984 v Sunderland. F.A. Cup 6th Rd. replay, March 4, 1931. *Record receipts:* £5,872 v Manchester U., F.A. Cup 3rd Rd., January 4, 1969. *Pitch measurements:* 114 yds × 73 yds.

How to get there: City buses A, D, J, K, S from city centre to The Fountain (one-minute walk to the ground). Routes G and J pass both railway stations—Exeter St David's and Exeter Central.

Match tickets: Tickets may be booked in advance usually two weeks before home matches.

Car parking: No car park at the ground. Limited street parking permitted.

Entertainments/catering facilities: Members social club. Subscription £1.00; joint membership £1.50. The club is situated at the ground.

Club shop: Sells all types of souvenirs.

Handbooks/programmes: Handbooks available at 20p; programmes can be ordered on subscription.

Extra information: Membership of the Supporters Association at 25p per year.

Club Colours: Red and white striped shirts, black shorts, red and white stockings. *Change Colours:* Blue and white striped shirts, blue shorts, blue and white stockings. *Club Captain:* Lammie Robertson *Club Nickname:* 'The Grecians'.

EXETER CITY 1975–76 LEAGUE RECORD

Match No.	Date	Venue	Opponents	Result	H/T Score	League Pos'n	Goalscorers	Attendance
1	Aug 16	H	Southport	W 2-0	2-0	—	Beer, Hodge	2844
2	23	A	Scunthorpe U.	W 1-0	1-0	1	Bowker	1660
3	29	H	Tranmere R.	L 0-2	0-0	—		3861
4	Sept 6	A	Workington	L 0-1	0-1	14		1004
5	13	H	Cambridge U.	L 1-2	0-1	17	Beer	2471
6	20	A	Lincoln C.	L 1-4	0-1	20	Robertson	5088
7	24	A	Torquay U.	L 0-1	0-1	—		3705
8	27	H	Crewe Alex.	D 2-2	0-2	21	Saxton, Bowker	2116
9	Oct 4	A	Rochdale	W 1-0	1-0	19	Bowker	1234
10	11	A	Darlington	D 0-0	0-0	18		2314
11	13	A	Hartlepool	L 1-2	0-2	—	Bowker	1323
12	18	H	Hartlepool	W 3-1	2-1	18	Beer, Jennings, Potter (og)	2406
13	21	H	Barnsley	D 0-0	0-0	—		3619
14	25	A	Newport Co.	D 3-3	0-2	16	Beer, 2 Bowker	2871
15	31	H	Stockport Co.	W 2-0	0-0	12	Beer, Hodge	2856
16	Nov 4	H	Bradford C.	D 0-0	0-0	—		2723
17	8	A	Reading	L 3-4	1-0	12	Beer 2, Hodge	6341
18	14	H	Swansea	W 3-0	2-0	13	Wingate, Harris (og), Bowker	2967
19	28	H	Doncaster R.	W 1-0	1-0	11	Bowker	2848
20	Dec 6	A	Huddersfield T.	W 1-0	0-0	10	Morrin	4981
21	13	H	Northampton T.	D 0-0	0-0	10		3394
22	20	A	Northampton T.	L 1-3	1-0	10	Beer	5212
23	26	H	Brentford	D 0-0	0-0	10		4912
24	27	A	Watford	L 0-2	0-2	13		5055
25	Jan 2	H	AFC Bournemouth	W 1-0	1-0	10	Templeman	3031
26	9	A	Tranmere R.	D 1-1	0-1	9	Beer	4661
27	17	H	Lincoln C.	D 0-0	0-0	9		3858
28	24	A	Cambridge U.	W 1-0	0-0	7	Jordan	2188
29	31	H	Barnsley	W 2-0	1-0	7	Hatch, Bowker	2449
30	Feb 7	A	Bradford C.	D 0-0	0-0	6		3049
31	13	H	Reading	W 4-1	4-1	6	Robertson, Jordan, Beer, Templeman	3641
32	20	A	Swansea C.	W 3-0	1-0	7	Beer 2, Bowker	4252
33	25	H	Torquay U.	D 0-0	0-0	—		8112
34	28	H	Newport Co.	W 3-0	1-0	5	Templeman, Bowker, Jennings	3447
35	Mar 5	A	Stockport Co.	L 1-2	1-1	8	Bowker	2440
36	9	H	Rochdale	W 1-0	0-0	—	Morrin	3102
37	13	H	Darlington	D 1-1	1-0	6	Beer	3196
38	20	A	Doncaster R.	D 0-0	0-0	6		4149
39	27	H	Huddersfield T.	W 4-1	3-0	6	Beer 2, Robertson, Bowker	3925
40	Apr 2	A	Southport	L 0-1	0-1	8		1514
41	7	A	Crewe Alex.	D 0-0	0-0	—		2034
42	10	H	Workington	W 1-0	0-0	7	Beer	2603
43	16	A	AFC Bournemouth	L 0-1	0-1	8		4651
44	17	A	Brentford	L 1-5	0-2	8	Jordan	3980
45	19	H	Watford	L 1-3	1-1	—	Bowker	2480
46	23	H	Scunthorpe U.	W 5-4	2-2	7	Beer 3, Robertson, Wingate	1863

Goalscorers

League (56): Beer 20, Bowker 13, Robertson 4, Hodge 3, Jordan 3, Templeman 3, Jennings 2, Morrin 2, Wingate 2, Hatch 1, Saxton 1, own goals 2.
League Cup (5): Bowker 2, Beer 2, Hatch.
F.A. Cup (2): Beer, Robertson.

League Cup	First Round	Newport Co. (a)		1-1
	Second Leg	(h)		2-0
	Second Round	Torquay U. (a)		1-1
		(h)		1-2
F.A. Cup	First Round	Cardiff C. (a)		2-6

180

Wilson	Templeman	Hooker	Joy	Wingate	Hatch	Hodge	Beer	Robertson	Bowker	Jennings	Morrin	Jordan	Moxham	Key	Saxton	Munks	Hore	Clapham	Rutter	Match No.
1	2	3	4	5	6	7	8	9	10	11										1
1	2	3	4	5	6	8	11	9	10	7										2
1	2	3	4	5	6		11	9	8	7	10									3
1	2	3	4	5	6		11	10	9	7*	8	12								4
1	2	3		5	6	7*	10	9	8	11	4		12							5
1	2	3		5	6	7	10	9	8	11	4									6
	2	3		5	6	7	10	9	8		4		11	1						7
	2	3			6	7	10	9	8		4		11	1	5					8
	2	3		7	6		10	9	8	11	4			1	5					9
	2	3		7	6		10	9	8	11	4			1	5					10
	2	3	4	7	6		10	9	8	11				1	5					11
	2	3	4		6	7	10	9	8	11				1	5					12
	2	3		7	6	4	10	9	8	11				1	5					13
	2	3	4		6	7	10	9	8	11				1	5					14
1	2	3		7	6	4	10	9	8	11					5					15
1	2	3		7	6	4	10	9	8	11					5					16
1	2	3	4		6	7	10	9	8	11					5					17
	2*	3		7	6	4	10	9	8	11				1	5			12		18
	2	3		7	6		10*	9	8	11	4	12		1	5					19
	2			7	6		10	9	8	11	4			1	5	3				20
	2			7	6		10	9	8	11	4			1	5	3				21
12	2*		4		6	7	10	9	8	11				1	5	3				22
	2			7	6	4	10	9	8	11				1	5	3				23
	2	4	3	7			10	9	8	11				1	5	6				24
	2	3		7			10	9	8	11	4			1	5	6				25
	2	3		7			9	10	8	11	4			1	5	6				26
	2	3		7		12	10	9	8*	11	4			1	5	6				27
	2	3		8	7		10	9		4	11			1	5	6				28
	2	3		7	6		10	9	8	4	11			1	5					29
	2	3		7	6		10	9	8	4	11			1	5					30
	2	3		7	6	4	10	9	8	11				1	5					31
	2	3		7	6		10	9	8	4	11			1	5					32
	2	3		7	6		10	9	8	4	11			1	5					33
	2	3		7	6		10	9	8	11	4			1	5					34
	2	3		7	6		10	9	8	11	4			1	5					35
	2			7	6		10	9	8	11	4			1	5		3			36
	2			7	6		10	9	8	11	4			1	5		3			37
	2			7	6		10	9	8	11	4			1	5		3			38
	2	12		7	6		10	9	8	11	4			1	5		3*			39
	2			7	6		10	9	8	11	4			1	5		3			40
	2			7	6		10	9	8	11	4			1	5		3			41
	2	12		7	6		10	9	8	11	4*			1	5		3			42
	2	3		7	6	11	10	9	8					1	5		4			43
	2	3		7*	6	8	10	9		11				1	5		4	12		44
	2	3	12		6	7	10	9	8*	11				1	5		4			45
	2			7	6	12	10	9	8	11	4*			1	5		3			46
9	42	26	15	44	43	23	46	44	42	34	28	10	4	37	39	9	11	—	—	
+1s	+2s		+1s	+2s							+1s	+2s					+1s	+1s		

Player and position	Ht.	Wt.	Birthplace	Clubs	League Appearances	Goals
Goalkeepers						
Richard Key	6 0	12 4	Coventry	Coventry C.	—	—
				Exeter C.	37	—
*Bob Wilson	6 0	11 9	Birmingham	Aston Villa	9	—
				Cardiff C.	114	—
				Bristol C.	1	—
				Exeter C.	205	—
Defenders						
Peter Hatch	5 10½	10 8	Reading	Oxford U.	15+4	2
				Exeter C.	108	2
Bob Saxton	5 10	11 4	Doncaster	Derby Co.	94+2	1
				Plymouth Arg.	224+7	7
				Exeter C.	39	1
Brian Joy	5 8	11 0	Birmingham	Blackburn R.	—	—
				Torquay U.	26+1	—
				Tranmere R.	21	1
				Doncaster R.	28+6	1
				Exeter C.	89+1	2
				(contract cancelled March 1976)		
*David Munks	5 10	11 10	Sheffield	Sheffield U.	108+4	1
				Portsmouth	132+5	2
				Swindon T.	21	—
				Exeter C.	20	—
Michael Balson	5 11	11 10	Bridport	Exeter C.	274+2	9
Allan Hooker	5 7	11 4	Exmouth	Exeter C.	33+4	—
John Templeman	5 11	11 7	Yapton	Brighton	229+7	16
				Exeter C.	81+1	5
Midfield						
Keith Clapham	5 10	11 3	Fareham	Bournemouth	—	—
				Exeter C.	72+10	—
Tony Morrin	5 8	11 3	Swinton	Stockport Co.	27+5	2
				Barrow	97+3	6
				Exeter C.	165+2	15
*Hedley Steele	5 9	11 0	Exeter	Exeter C.	6+1	1
Bob Hodge	5 9	11 1	Exeter	Exeter C.	50+7	7
*Graham Moxham	5 8	11 3	Exeter	Exeter C.	4+2	—
Graham Weeks	5 9	10 9	Exeter	Exeter C.	—	—
Mike Green	5 8	11 1	London	Exeter C.	—	—
Forwards						
Nicky Jennings	5 6	9 1	Wellington	Plymouth Arg.	98	10
				Portsmouth	198+8	43
				Aldershot (on loan)	4	1
				Exeter C.	53	6
*John Rutter	5 7	10 7	Warrington	Wolverhampton W.	—	—
				Bournemouth	2+2	—
				Exeter C.	31+1	1
Lammie Robertson	5 9	10 4	Paisley	Burnley	—	—
				Bury	3+2	—
				Halifax T.	142+8	20
				Brighton	42+4	9
				Exeter C.	86	14
*John Wingate	6 1½	12 4	Budleigh Salterton	Plymouth Arg.	1	—
				Exeter C.	185+14	32
				Bournemouth	30+3	3
				Exeter C.	44+1	2
Alan Beer	5 7	10 7	Swansea	Swansea C.	9+5	3
				Exeter C.	73	29
Mike Jordan	5 9	11 1	Exeter	Exeter C.	10+1	3

FULHAM

DIV. 2

Chairman: T. Trinder.

Directors: R. A. Dean, C. B. Dean, E. M. Miller, J.P., E. Libby, B.A. D. E. Budden

Manager: Alec Stock.

Secretary: G. I. S. Hortop.   *Year Formed:* 1880.

Turned Professional: 1898.   *Limited Company:* 1903.

Previous Name: 1880–98, Fulham St. Andrew's.

Previous Grounds: Lillie Road, Fulham Cross; Barn Elms, Barnes; Ranelagh House; Stansfield's Field, Fulham Road; Half-moon Cricket Ground, Putney; 1896, Craven Cottage.

Honours: *Football League,* highest position in Division 1: 10th, 1959–60. Division 2, Champions: 1948–49; Runners-up: 1958–59. Division 3(S), Champions: 1931–32. Division 3, Runners-up 1970–71.   *F.A. Cup,* best season: Runners-up 1974-5.

Football League Cup, best season: 5th Rd., 1967–68, 1970–71.

Record Victory: 10-1 v Ipswich T., Division 1, Dec. 26th, 1963.

Record Defeat: 0-9 v Wolverhampton W., Division 1, Sept. 16th, 1959.

Most League Points: 60, Division 2, 1958–59, and Division 3, 1970–71.

Most League Goals: 111, Division 3(S), 1931–32.

Highest League Scorer in Season: Frank Newton, 41, Division 3(S), 1931–32.

Most Goals in Total Aggregate: Johnny Haynes, 159, 1952–70.

Most Capped Player: Johnny Haynes, 56, England.

Most League Appearances: Johnny Haynes, 598, 1952–70.

Record Transfer Fee Received: £155,000 from Portsmouth for Paul Went, Dec. 1973.

Record Transfer Fee Paid: £80,000 to Charlton Ath. for Paul Went, July 1972.

Managers Since the War: Jack Peart, Frank Osborne, Doug Livingstone, Bedford Jezzard, Vic Buckingham, Bobby Robson, Johnny Haynes, Bill Dodgin (Jnr.).

Address of Supporters Club: Fulham Travel Club, Craven Cottage, Stevenage Road, S.W.6.

Craven Cottage, Stevenage Rd., Fulham, London S.W.6. Telephone 01-736 5621/7035/0511. Pools Office: 736 4634.   *Telegraphic address:* 'Fulhamish, London S.W.6.'   *Ground capacity:* 42,000.   *Record attendance:* 49,335 v Millwall, Division 2, October 8 1938.   *Record receipts:* £18,756 v West Ham U., Football League Cup 3rd Rd., October 8 1974.   *Pitch measurements:* 110 yds × 75 yds.

How to get there: Underground stations, Putney Bridge (District Line) and Hammersmith (District, Metropolitan, Piccadilly). Then by bus—30, 74, 85, 93, 220.

Match tickets: The Box Office is now computerised, and seats are bookable at any time during the season.

Car parking: Plentiful parking in streets around the ground.

Entertainments/catering facilities: Social amenities available. Snack bars and licensed bars around the ground.   The Riverside Suite is available for conferences, weddings, parties, etc.

Club shop: Sells all types of souvenirs.

Handbooks/programmes: Both handbooks and programmes available.

Extra information: Fulham Travel Club runs trips to away matches. The Box Office computer is also geared to obtain tickets for the theatre and other London entertainments.

Club Colours: White shirts, black shorts with two white stripes, white stockings.

Change Colours: Red and black stripes, black shorts, black stockings.

Club Captain:

First Team Trainer/Coach: Bill Taylor.

Club Nickname: 'Cottagers'.

FULHAM 1975–76 LEAGUE RECORD

Match No.	Date	Venue	Opponents	Result	H/T Score	League Pos'n	Goalscorers	Attendance
1	Aug 16	H	Blackpool	D 0-0	0-0	—		8863
2	20	H	Carlisle U.	W 3-0	1-0	2	Conway, Barrett, Slough	7443
3	23	A	Bolton W.	D 2-2	2-1	1	Busby, Mitchell	8786
4	26	A	Sunderland	L 0-2	0-2	—		25,450
5	30	H	W.B.A.	W 4-0	2-0	3	Mitchell, Howe 2, Busby	9910
6	Sept 6	A	Oxford U.	W 3-1	2-0	2	Clarke C. (og), Conway, Busby	7318
7	13	H	Bristol R.	L 0-2	0-0	5		11,516
8	20	A	Hull C.	W 2-1	0-1	3	Busby, Lloyd	8471
9	27	H	Chelsea	W 2-0	0-0	3	Howe, Conway	22,921
10	Oct 4	A	Blackburn R.	W 1-0	1-0	3	Howe	10,190
11	11	H	Nottingham F.	D 0-0	0-0	3		10,149
12	18	A	Luton T.	L 0-1	0-1	4		14,086
13	25	H	Orient	D 1-1	0-1	6	Howe	10,464
14	Nov 1	H	Portsmouth	W 1-0	0-0	4	Slough	11,441
15	8	H	Charlton Ath.	D 1-1	1-0	6	Lloyd	15,466
16	15	A	York C.	L 0-1	0-1	7		3414
17	22	H	Luton T.	W 2-0	1-0	6	Conway 2	9626
18	29	H	Bristol C.	L 1-2	0-2	7	Mullery (pen)	11,400
19	Dec 6	A	Oldham Ath.	D 2-2	0-1	6	Howe, Conway	8746
20	13	H	Bolton W.	L 1-2	1-1	8	Slough	8720
21	20	A	Blackpool	D 1-1	0-1	9	Mullery	6379
22	26	H	Notts Co.	W 3-2	1-0	8	Mitchell 2, Slough	11,887
23	27	A	Plymouth Arg.	L 0-4	0-4	9		24,054
24	Jan 10	A	Bristol R.	L 0-1	0-0	10		7863
25	17	H	Oxford U.	D 1-1	1-0	10	Mitchell	6783
26	31	A	Carlisle U.	D 2-2	1-2	10	Mitchell 2	6247
27	Feb 7	H	Sunderland	W 2-0	1-0	9	Busby 2	12,839
28	17	A	Charlton Ath.	L 2-3	0-1	—	Mullery 2	11,536
29	21	H	York C.	W 2-0	1-0	9	Lloyd, Slough	6686
30	24	A	Southampton	L 1-2	1-1	—	Lacy	23,575
31	28	A	Orient	L 0-2	0-1	10		7558
32	Mar 6	H	Portsmouth	L 0-1	0-0	13		6928
33	9	H	Southampton	W 1-0	1-0	—	Mitchell	8731
34	13	A	Nottm. F.	L 0-1	0-0	11		11,445
35	20	A	Bristol C.	D 0-0	0-0	12		19,935
36	27	H	Oldham Ath.	W 1-0	1-0	10	Conway	5856
37	Apr 6	A	Chelsea	D 0-0	0-0	—		23,605
38	10	H	Hull C.	D 1-1	0-1	10	Mitchell	5624
39	14	A	W.B.A.	L 1-3	0-2	—	Scrivens (pen)	18,234
40	17	A	Notts. Co.	L 0-4	0-2	12		8819
41	19	H	Plymouth Arg.	D 0-0	0-0	—		6913
42	24	H	Blackburn R.	D 1-1	0-1	12	Howe	5914

Goalscorers

League (45): Mitchell 9, Conway 7, Howe 7, Busby 6, Slough 5, Mullery 4 (1 a pen), Lloyd 3, Berrett 1, Lacy 1, Scrivens 1 (pen), Own Goal 1.

League Cup (2): Conway, Mullery (pen).

F.A. Cup (2): Conway, Busby.

League Cup	Second Round	W.B.A. (a)	1-1
		(h)	1-0
	Third Round	Peterborough U. (h)	0-1
F.A. Cup	Third Round	Huddersfield T. (h)	2-3

Mellor	Cutbush	Strong	Mullery	Howe	Moore	Conway	Mitchell	Busby	Lloyd	Barrett	Dowie	Slough	James	Kerslake	Lacy	Fraser	Camp	Bullivant	Scrivens	Margerrison	Match No.
1	2	3	4	5	6	7	8*	9	10	11	12										1
1	2	3	4	5	6	7		9		11	8	10									2
1	2	3	4	5	6	7	11	9			8	10									3
1	2	3	4	5	6	8	12	9	7	11		10*									4
1	2	3	4	5	6	8	7	9		11		10									5
1	2	3	4	5	6	7	11	9			8	10									6
1	2	3	4	5	6	7	8	9		11		10									7
1	2	3	4	5	6	7	11	9	8			10									8
1	2	3	4	5	6	8		9	7	11		10									9
1	2	3	4	5	6	8		9	7	11		10									10
1	2	3	4	5	6	8	7	9		11		10									11
1			4	5	6	8	7*	9	10	11	12	3	2								12
1			4	11	6	7		9	10			8	2	3	5						13
1		3	4		6	7		9		11	8	10	2		5						14
1			4		6	7		9	10	11	8	3	2		5						15
1		3	4	10	6	7		9	8	11			2		5						16
1		3	4	5	6	7		9		11	8	10	2								17
1		3	4	5	6	8		9		11	7	10	2								18
1		3	4	5	6	7		9		11	8*	10	2		12						19
1		3*	4	2	6	8		9		11	7	10			5	12					20
1	2	3	4		6	8				11	7	10*	12		5		9				21
1	2	3	4		6	8	7	9		11		10			5						22
1	2	3	4	12	6*	7	8	9		11		10			5						23
1	2	3	4		6	7	8	9		11		10			5						24
1	2	3	4	12	6	8	7	9		11*		10			5						25
1	2		4	5	6	7	8	9	10	11			3								26
1		3	4		6	8		9	7	11		10	2		5						27
1		3	4		6	8		9	7	11		10	2		5						28
1		3	4		6	8		9	7	11*		10	2		5	12					29
1		3	4		6	8		9	7	11		10	2		5						30
1		3	4		6	8*		9	7	11		10	2		5	12					31
1	2	8	4		6	7		9	10	11*	12	3			5						32
1	2	3	4		6	8	7	9		11		10			5						33
1	2	3	4		6	8		9*	7	11	12	10			5						34
1	2	3	4		6	7	8	9		11		10			5						35
1	2	3			6	8	10	9	7	11		4			5						36
1		3	4		6	8	7	9	10	11			2		5						37
1		3			6	7	8	9	10	11			2		5	4*	12				38
1		3*	12		6	8	7	9	4			10	2		5				11		39
1	2				6	7	8	9	4	11		10	3		5						40
1					6	8*	7	9	4	11	12	10	2		5	3	9				41
1		3			6	9*			4		10	8	2		5	7		11	12		42
42	23	36	36	28	33	39	26	37	25	32	14	40	14	1	26	4	3	1	2	—	
			+1s	+2s		+1s				+1s	+4s	+1s			+1s		+1s	+2s	+1s	+1s	

185

FULHAM—PLAYERS

Player and position	Ht.	Wt.	Birthplace	Clubs	League Appearances	Goals
Goalkeepers						
Peter Mellor	6 1	14 0	Manchester	Manchester C.	—	—
				Burnley	69	—
				Chesterfield (on loan)	4	—
				Fulham	176	—
Defenders						
*John Fraser	5 9	10 0	London	Fulham	54+1	1
John Lacy	6 1	12 4	Liverpool	Fulham	100+3	3
John Cutbush	5 10	10 10	Malta	Tottenham H.	—	—
				Fulham	115+2	3
Bobby Moore	6 0	12 13	London	West Ham U.	544+1	24
(England)				Fulham	84	1
Ernie Howe	6 1	12 12	London	C. Palace	—	—
				Fulham	35+2	8
Leslie Strong	5 9	10 7	London	C. Palace	—	—
				Fulham	110+3	2
Tyrone James	6 4½	10 8	London	Fulham	14+1	—
Michael Kerslake	5 10	11 1	London	Fulham	1	—
Midfield						
Alan Slough	5 10	12 5	Luton	Luton T.	265+10	28
				Fulham	112	9
John Dowie	6 0	11 7	Scotland	Fulham	29+5	2
Barry Lloyd	5 7	10 5	Hillingdon	Chelsea	8+2	—
				Fulham	249+9	28
*Alan Mullery	5 9	12 4	Notting Hill	Fulham	199	13
(England)				Tottenham H.	312	25
				Fulham	164+1	24
John Margerrison	5 10	12 2	Bushey	Tottenham H.	—	—
				Fulham	0+1	—
Forwards						
Les Barrett	5 8	10 3	London	Fulham	401+3	71
Viv Busby	5 11½	11 6	High Wycombe	Luton T.	64+13	16
				Newcaslte U. (on loan)	4	2
				Fulham	109+4	29
Jimmy Conway	5 7	10 9	Dublin	Fulham	299+4	66
(Eire)						
John Mitchell	5 11	11 7	London	Fulham	81+11	27
Steven Scrivens	5 8	8 12	London	Fulham	3+1	1
Terry Bullivant	5 9	8 9	London	Fulham	1+3	—
Steve Camp	5 11	11 4	Manchester	Fulham	3+1	—

GILLINGHAM

Chairman: Dr. C. S. Grossmark.

Directors: S. H. Martin, C. A. L. Cox, J. W. Leech, B. B. Moore.

Manager: Gerry Summers. *Club Secretary:* M. A. Bramley.

Assistant Manager: Alan Hodgkinson.

Financial Secretary: R. F. Swan.

Year Formed: 1893. *Turned Professional:* 1894.

Limited Company: 1893.

Previous Name: New Brompton, 1893–1913.

Honours: *Football League,* highest position in Division 3: 6th, 1965–66. Division 4, Champions: 1963–64. Runners-up 1973–74. *F.A. Cup,* best season: 5th Rd., 1969–70. *Football League Cup,* best season: 4th Rd., 1964.

Record Victory: 10-1 v Gorleston, F.A. Cup, 1st Rd., Nov. 16th, 1957.

Record Defeat: 2-9 v Nottingham F., Division 3(S), Nov. 18th, 1950.

Most League Points: 62, Division 4, 1973–74.

Most League Goals: 90, Division 4, 1973–74.

Highest League Scorer in Season: Ernie Morgan, 31, Division 3(S), 1954–55. Brian Yeo, 31, Division 4, 1973–74.

Most League Goals in Total Aggregate: Brian Yeo, 135, 1963–75.

Most Capped Player: Frank Fox, 1, England; Damien Richardson, 1(2), Eire.

Most League Appearances: John Simpson, 571, 1957–72.

Record Transfer Fee Received: £50,000 from Southampton for David Peach, Jan. 1974.

Record Transfer Fee Paid: £18,000 to Q.P.R. for Danny Westwood, Dec. 1975.

Managers Since the War: Archie Clark, Harry Barratt, Freddie Cox, Basil Hayward, Andy Nelson, Len Ashurst.

Address of Supporters Club: Gillingham F.C. Supporters' Association, Gordon Road, Gillingham.

Priestfield Stadium, Gillingham. Telephone Medway 51854. *Telegraphic address:* 'Football, Gillingham, Kent'. *Ground capacity:* 22,000. *Record attendance:* 23,002 v Q.P.R., F.A. Cup 3rd Rd., January 10, 1948. *Record receipts:* £7035 v Crystal Palace, Division 3, December 28, 1974. *Pitch measurements:* 114 yds × 75 yds.

How to get there: Gillingham railway station (six or seven minutes' walk). Bus services are 10 minutes from ground.

Match tickets: Can be reserved by postal application enclosing correct remittance and S.A.E.

Car parking: Park for 500 cars adjoining the ground, entrance in Toronto Rd.

Entertainments/catering facilities: A club house, and several bars around the ground.

Club shop: Sells all types of souvenirs.

Handbooks/programmes: Programmes available on subscription. Handbooks also available.

Extra information: Enquiries about supporters association to Gillingham F.C. Supporters Association Gordon Rd., Gillingham.

Club Colours: Blue shirts, white shorts, blue stockings, white and blue trim.

Change Colours: Yellow shirts with blue collar and cuffs, blue shorts, yellow socks.

Club Captain: Dick Tydeman.

Club Nickname: 'The Gills'.

GILLINGHAM 1975–76 LEAGUE RECORD

Match No.	Date	Venue	Opponents	Result	H/T Score	League Pos'n	Goalscorers	Attendance
1	Aug 16	A	Bury	L 0-2	0-0	—		3932
2	23	H	Grimsby T.	W 3-0	2-0	8	Weatherly 2, Richardson (pen)	4407
3	30	A	Swindon T.	D 2-2	1-1	12	Galvin, Feely	6786
4	Sept 6	H	Preston N.E.	W 1-0	1-0	6	Feely	5786
5	13	A	Wrexham	L 0-2	0-0	13		2654
6	20	H	Mansfield T.	W 3-1	1-0	10	Feely, Jacks, Hilton	5742
7	23	H	Rotherham U.	D 0-0	0-0	—		5498
8	27	A	Hereford U.	D 1-1	0-0	9	Shipperley	5512
9	Oct 4	A	Halifax T.	D 1-1	0-0	10	Gauden	5934
10	11	H	Port Vale	W 2-1	1-0	5	Feely, Shipperley	5041
11	18	A	Shrewsbury T.	L 0-1	0-1	8		3242
12	21	H	Chesterfield	D 2-2	1-0	—	Hill, Feely	5573
13	25	H	Walsall	L 2-3	1-1	10	Richardson, Feely	5942
14	Nov 1	A	Aldershot	L 0-3	0-1	15		4290
15	5	A	Sheffield W.	L 0-1	0-0	—		8235
16	8	H	Cardiff C.	D 2-2	0-0	17	Richardson (pen), Jacks	5762
17	15	A	Millwall	D 2-2	1-1	18	Jacks, Richardson	6838
18	29	H	Colchester U.	L 0-1	0-0	19		5402
19	Dec 6	A	Chester	D 2-2	0-1	20	Westwood, Davies	4451
20	20	H	Peterborough U.	D 2-2	2-1	20	Richardson, Durrell	4086
21	27	H	Brighton & H.A.	W 1-0	1-0	20	Richardson	9294
22	30	A	Crystal Palace	W 1-0	0-0	—	Westwood	20,919
23	Jan 10	H	Swindon T.	W 3-2	1-0	14	Durrell, Westwood, Richardson	6459
24	17	A	Mansfield T.	D 1-1	0-1	13	Westwood	5939
25	24	H	Wrexham	D 1-1	0-0	14	Shipperley	5849
26	31	A	Chesterfield	W 1-0	1-0	11	Westwood	2100
27	Feb 7	H	Sheffield W.	D 0-0	0-0	11		8090
28	14	A	Cardiff C.	L 1-4	1-1	12	Morgan (og)	11,025
29	21	H	Millwall	W 3-1	2-0	11	Wiltshire, Shipperley, Westwood	9111
30	24	A	Rotherham U.	L 0-2	0-0	—		4404
31	27	A	Walsall	L 0-4	0-1	14		5493
32	Mar 1	A	Southend U.	D 2-2	1-2	—	Westwood 2	4722
33	6	H	Aldershot	D 1-1	0-0	13	Durrell	5028
34	9	A	Halifax T.	D 1-1	1-0	—	Knight	1886
35	13	A	Port Vale	D 1-1	1-0	12	Durrell	3516
36	16	H	Shrewsbury T.	W 2-1	0-0	—	Knight, Weatherley	5139
37	20	A	Colchester U.	D 2-2	0-0	12	Richardson (pen), Durrell	3981
38	27	H	Chester	W 2-0	1-0	11	Knight, Weatherley	4983
39	31	A	Peterborough U.	D 1-1	1-1	—	Weatherley	4594
40	Apr 3	H	Bury	W 2-0	2-0	11	Galvin, Durrell	4732
41	6	H	Hereford U.	L 3-4	2-1	—	Durrell 2, Ritchie (og)	7914
42	10	A	Preston N.E.	L 0-4	0-1	12		6349
43	13	H	Southend U.	L 1-2	1-0	—	Shipperley	5776
44	17	H	Crystal Palace	L 1-2	0-2	14	Richardson (pen)	12,880
45	19	A	Brighton & H.A.	D 1-1	1-0	—	Westwood	19,142
46	24	A	Grimsby T.	L 1-2	0-0	13	Shipperley	4415

Goalscorers

League (58): Richardson 9 (4 pens), Westwood 9, Durrell 8, Feely 6, Shipperley 6, Weatherley 5, Jacks 3, Knight 3, Galvin 2, Hilton 1, Gauden 1, Hill 1, Davies 1, Wiltshire 1, own goals 2.
League Cup (2): Richardson, own goal 1.
F.A. Cup (2): Richardson 2.

League Cup	First Round	Reading (a)	1-0
	Second Leg	(h)	1-1
	Second Round	Carlisle U. (a)	0-2
F.A. Cup	First Round	Weymouth (a)	2-0
	Second Round	Brighton & H.A. (h)	0-1

Hillyard	Wiltshire	Ley	Tydeman	Galvin	Hill	Jacks	Gauden	Richardson	Wilks	Feely	Weatherley	O'Donnell	Knight	Fogarty	Shipperley	Hilton	Durrell	Westwood	Davies	Emanuel	Hughes	Owers	Armstrong	Match No.
1	2	3	4	5	6	7	8	9	10	11*	12													1
1	2	3	6	4	5	7*	8	9	10	11	12													2
1	2	3	6*	4	5	7	8	9	10	11	12													3
1		3	6	4	5	7	8	9	10*	11			2	12										4
1	2	3	6	4	5	7	8	9	10*	11	12													5
1	2	3	6	4		7	8	9	12	11					5*	10								6
1	2	3	6	4		7	8	9	12	11					5	10*								7
1	2	3	6	4		7*	8	9		11	12				5	10								8
1	2	3	6	4*		7	8	9	10	11	12				5									9
1		3	6	4		7*	8	9	12	11			2		5	10								10
1	12	3	6	4			8	9		11		7	2		5	10*								11
1	12	3	6	4		7*	8	9		11			2		5	10								12
1	2	3		4		7	8	9		11			6		5	10								13
1	2	3	6	4		7*	8	9		11			10		5	12								14
1	4	3	6			7	8	9		10*			2	12	5		11							15
1	4	3	6			7	8	9		10*			2		5	12	11							16
1	4	3	6			7*	8	9			12		2		5		11	10						17
1		3	6			7	8	9	12				4		5		11*	10	2					18
1		3	4	6			8	9			11		7		5			10	2					19
1		3	7	4		8		9			12		2	6	5		11*	10						20
1		3	6	4		7		9					2	8	5		11	10						21
1		3	6	4		7		9					2	8	5		11	10						22
1		3	6	4		7		9					2	8	5		11	10						23
1		3	6	4		7		9					2	8	5		11	10						24
1		3	6	4		7*		9			12		2	8	5		11	10						25
1	12	3	6	4*		7		9					2	8	5		11	10						26
1		3	7		6			9					2	8	5		11	10		4				27
1		3	7		6			9					2	8	5		11	10		4				28
1	4	3	6					9					2	8	5		11	10		7				29
1	4	3	6					9					2	8	5	12	11	10		7*				30
1	4	3	6		5	7*			9				2	8		12	11	10						31
1	2	3	6	4				9					7	8	5	11		10						32
1	12	3	6	4*				9					2	8	5	7	11	10						33
1	4	3	6			7		9			12		2	8*	5		11	10						34
1	4	3	6	12		7*			9				2	8	5		11	10						35
1	2	3	6	4				9		11			7	8	5			10						36
1	2	3	6	4				9		11*			7	8	5	12		10						37
1	2*	3	6	4				9			10		7	8	5	12	11							38
1		3	6	4		7		9			10		2	8	5		11							39
1		3	6	4				9			7		2	8	5		11	10						40
1	2*	3	6	4				9			12		7	8	5		11	10						41
1		3	6	4	5	7		9					2	8		12	11*	10						42
1		3*	6	4				9			7			8*	5	2	11	10		12				43
1		3	4		6			9			12		7	8*	5	2	11	10						44
		3	6		4			9					7	8	5	2	11	10				1		45
			6		4			9					7	8	5	2	11	10*	12			1	3	46
44	23	45	45	28	16	30	18	44	7	14	11	1	39	24	39	15	26	28	2	4	—	2	1	

| | | + 4s | | + 1s | | | | | | + 4s | + 7s | + 1s | + 3s | + 3s | | + 6s | + 1s | | | + 1s | + 1s | | | |

GILLINGHAM—PLAYERS

Player and position	Ht.	Wt.	Birthplace	Clubs	League Appearances	Goals
Goalkeepers						
Ron Hillyard	5 10½	11 0	Rotherham	York C.	61	—
				Hartlepool (on loan)	23	—
				Bury (on loan)	—	—
				Brighton (on loan)	—	—
				Gillingham	90	—
*Phil Owers	5 11	10 9	Shildon	Darlington	45	—
				Gillingham	2	—
Mervyn Cawston	6 1	11 6	Norwich	Norwich C.	4	—
				Southend U. (on loan)	10	—
				Leicester C. (on loan)	—	—
				Newport Co. (on loan)	4	—
				Gillingham	—	—
Defenders						
David Galvin	6 1	11 11	Denaby Main	Wolverhampton W.	5	—
				Gillingham	202+6	14
Kenny Hill	6 0	11 3	Canterbury	Gillingham	119+5	7
				Lincoln C. (on loan)	1	—
*George Ley	5 9	11 12	Exeter	Exeter C.	91	7
				Portsmouth	183+1	10
				Brighton	47	—
				Gillingham	87	2
				(contract cancelled April 1976)		
*David Wiltshire	5 11	12 0	Folkestone	Gillingham	55+8	2
Graham Knight	5 11	11 9½	Gillingham	Gillingham	155+15	8
Dave Shipperley	6 2½	13 8	Hillingdon	Charlton Ath.	92+8	8
				Plymouth Arg. (on loan)	1	—
				Gillingham	76	9
Gary Armstrong	5 8	10 7	London	Gillingham	1	—
*John Davis	5 11	12 2	Hackney	Gillingham	2+1	1
Midfield						
Dick Tydeman	5 11	11 0	Gillingham	Gillingham	277+2	12
Mark Weatherly	5 11	11 8	Ramsgate	Gillingham	13+10	6
Bill Fogarty	5 9	10 10	London	Gillingham	24+3	—
Alan Muskett	5 6	10 4	London	Gillingham	—	—
Billy Hughes	5 10	10 8	Folkestone	Gillingham	0+1	—
Forwards						
Joe Durrell	5 7	10 1	London	West Ham U.	5+1	—
				Bristol C.	5+3	2
				Cardiff C. (on loan)	2	—
				Gillingham	26+1	8
Pat Hilton	5 8	11 0	Aylesham	Brighton	18+2	1
				Blackburn R.	16	2
				Gillingham	15+6	1
*Alan Wilks	5 10½	10 6	Slough	Q.P.R.	45+5	14
				Gillingham	138+13	29
Brian Yeo	5 10	12 6	Worthing	Portsmouth	—	—
				Gillingham	345+11	135
				(contract cancelled Jan. 1976)		
*George Jacks	5 7	10 13	Stepney	Q.P.R.	1	—
				Millwall	143+7	5
				Gillingham	158	20
Damien Richardson	5 11½	12 0	Dublin	Gillingham	160	59
Allan Gauden	5 8	10 3	Langley Park	Sunderland	40+3	6
				Darlington	125+3	39
				Grimsby T.	54+1	12
				Hartlepool	63	15
				Gillingham	41	3
				(contract cancelled March 1976)		
Danny Westwood	5 10	11 5	Dagenham	Q.P.R.	0+1	1
				Gillingham	28	9

GRIMSBY TOWN DIV. 3

Chairman: H. C. Hamilton.

Vice-Chairman: J. R. Atkinson.

Directors: F. A. Would, J. Evans, M.B.E., R. Middleton, T. Wilkinson, T. L. Lindley.

Manager: Tommy Casey, *Secretary:* Mrs. D. Edwards.

Year Formed: 1878. *Turned Professional:* 1890.

Limited Company: 1890. *Previous Name:* Grimsby Pelham.

Previous Grounds: Clee Park; Abbey Park.

Honours: *Football League,* highest position: Division 1, 5th, 1934–35. Division 2, Champions: 1900–01, 1933–34; Runners-up: 1928–29. Division 3(N), Champions: 1925–26, 1955–56; Runners-up: 1951–52. Division 3, Runners-up: 1961–62. Division 4, Champions: 1971–72. *F.A. Cup,* best season: Semi-finalists, 1936, 1939. *Football League Cup,* best season: 5th Rd. Replay, 1966.

Record Victory: 9-2 v Darwen, Division 2, Apr. 15th, 1899.

Record Defeat: 1-9 v Arsenal, Division 1, Jan. 28th, 1931.

Most League Points: 68, Division 3(N), 1955–56.

Most League Goals: 103, Division 2, 1933–34.

Most Capped Player: Pat Glover, 7, Wales.

Highest League Scorer in Season: Pat Glover, 42, Division 2, 1933–34.

Most League Goals in Total Aggregate: Pat Glover, 182, 1930–39.

Most League Appearances: Keith Jobling, 448, 1953–69.

Record Transfer Fee Received: £20,000 from Burnley for Doug Collins, Sept. 1968.

Record Transfer Fee Paid: £20,000 Rotherham U. for Ron Wigg, January 1975.

Managers Since the War: Charlie Spencer, Bill Shankly, Billy Walsh, Allenby Chilton, Tim Ward, Tom Johnston, Jimmy McGuigan, Don McEvoy, Bill Harvey, Bobby Kennedy, Laurie McNenemy, Ron Ashman.

Address of Club Shop: Junior Club Souvenir Shop, Blundell Park, Cleethorpes.

Blundell Park, Cleethorpes, Lincolnshire. Telephone Cleethorpes 61420 and 61803. *Telegraphic address:* 'Football Grimsby'. *Ground capacity:* 28,000. *Record attendance:* 31,657 v Wolverhampton W., F.A. Cup, February 20, 1937. *Record Receipts:* £7005 v Norwich C., League Cup 4th Rd., October 26, 1971. *Pitch measurements:* 111 yds × 74 yds.

How to get there: Buses 3, 3A, 3F, 9 run to the ground; also football specials from the town centre. Nearest railway stations are Cleethorpes and Grimsby Town.

Match tickets: Seating can be booked one month in advance.

Car parking: Parking permitted in all side streets around the ground.

Entertainments/catering facilities: A licensed bar and several snack bars.

Club shop: There are 3 club shops, run by the Grimsby Town Junior Club, selling all types of souvenirs.

Handbooks/programmes: Programmes on sale at matches.

Extra information: Grimsby have played in all six divisions of the Football League—First, Second, Third, Third South, Third North and Fourth.

Club Colours: Black and white striped shirts, black shorts, red stockings.

Change Colours: All white.

Club Captain: David Booth.

Coach:

Club Nickname: 'The Mariners'.

GRIMSBY TOWN 1975-76 LEAGUE RECORD

Match No.	Date	Venue	Opponents	Result	Score	H/T Score	League Pos'n	Goalscorers	Attendance
1	Aug 16	H	Cardiff C.	W 2-0		1-0	—	Lewis Hubbard	6283
2	23	A	Gillingham	L 0-3		0-2	16		4407
3	30	H	Shrewsbury T.	W 3-2		2-0	9	Lewis 2, Barton	4709
4	Sept 6	A	Chester	W 2-1		1-0	5	Lewis ,Boylen	4092
5	13	H	Millwall	W 2-1		0-1	2	Czuczman, Wigg	6466
6	20	A	Sheffield W.	L 0-4		0-2	6		11,345
7	23	H	Halifax T.	D 2-2		2-0	16	Hubbard, Lewis	6130
8	27	H	Aldershot	W 1-0		0-0	5	Partridge	5139
9	Oct 4	A	Walsall	L 0-2		0-1	8		4113
10	11	A	Crystal Palace	L 0-3		0-1	10		15,552
11	18	H	Brighton & H.A.	W 2-1		0-0	7	Wigg, Lewis	4938
12	25	A	Swindon T.	L 0-3		0-1	13		5873
13	Nov 1	H	Bury	D 0-0		0-0	11		5189
14	4	A	Peterborough U.	L 2-4		1-2	—	Partridge 2	7646
15	8	A	Hereford U.	L 2-3		0-1	19	Wigg, Barton	6391
16	11	H	Wrexham	W 3-2		1-1	—	Boylen, Young, Lewis	4850
17	15	H	Mansfield T.	W 4-1		3-1	9	Partridge 2, Wigg, Lewis	4659
18	29	H	Preston N.E.	D 0-0		0-0	9		4519
19	Dec 5	A	Southend U.	L 2-5		0-2	12	Partridge, Lewis	3925
20	20	A	Port Vale	L 3-4		2-0	17	Lewis, Ridley (og), Wigg	2789
21	26	H	Rotherham U.	W 4-1		3-1	13	Partridge, Boylen, Lewis, Oldridge	6919
22	27	A	Colchester U.	L 0-1		0-0	17		3136
23	Jan 3	H	Chesterfield	W 3-0		2-0	10	Boylen (pen), Walton, Marley	4024
24	10	A	Shrewsbury T.	L 0-1		0-0	15		3344
25	17	H	Sheffield W.	D 1-1		0-0	15	Wigg	7167
26	24	A	Millwall	D 1-1		0-0	15	Waters	5486
27	31	A	Wrexham	L 0-1		0-0	16		2808
28	Feb 7	H	Peterborough U.	D 1-1		0-1	16	Partridge	5482
29	14	H	Hereford U.	W 1-0		1-0	14	Lewis	5944
30	21	A	Mansfield T.	L 0-1		0-1	16		6094
31	24	A	Halifax T.	L 1-2		1-1	—	Czuczman (pen)	2229
32	28	H	Swindon T.	W 1-0		1-0	13	Partridge	5218
33	Mar 6	A	Bury	D 1-1		1-0	15	Barton	4821
34	9	H	Walsall	L 1-2		1-0	—	Partridge	5300
35	13	H	Crystal Palace	L 1-2		1-1	17	Hubbard	8412
36	17	A	Brighton & H.A.	L 2-4		2-1	—	Marley, Hubbard	17,384
37	20	A	Preston N.E.	D 0-0		0-0	18		6586
38	27	H	Southend U.	D 2-2		2-2	19	Waters, Booth	4158
39	30	H	Port Vale	D 1-1		1-0	—	Lewis	4322
40	Apr 3	A	Cardiff C.	L 1-2		1-0	19	Lewis	9645
41	7	A	Aldershot	W 3-0		1-0	—	Barton 2, Booth	3069
42	10	H	Chester	W 2-0		2-0	16	Hubbard, Cumming	4644
43	16	A	Chesterfield	L 3-4		2-1	—	Booth, Hubbard, Lewis	5483
44	17	A	Rotherham U.	L 0-3		0-2	18		4414
45	19	H	Colchester U.	L 0-1		0-1	—		4862
46	24	H	Gillingham	W 2-1		0-0	17	Cumming, Wigg	4415

Goalscorers

League (62): Lewis 15, Partridge 10, Wigg 7, Hubbard 6, Barton 5, Boylen 4 (1 a pen), Booth 3, Marley 2, Waters 2, Cumming 2, Czuczman 2 (1 a pen), Young 1, Oldridge 1, Walton 1, own goal 1.
League Cup (1): Wigg.
F.A. Cup (1): Booth.

League Cup	First Round	Doncaster R. (a)	1-3
	Second Leg	(h)	0-0
F.A. Cup	First Round	Gateshead (h)	1-3

Freeman	Booth	Govier	Cumming	Young	Gray	Partridge	Hubbard	Wigg	Boylen	Lewis	Brown	Baker	Czuczman	Barton	Wainman	Marley	Ford	Oldridge	Walton	Waters	Parkin	Match No.
1	2	3*	4	5	6	7	8	9	10	11	12											1
	3	12		5	4*		8	11	9	10	7	1	2	6								2
	3			5	6	8	4	9	10	11			2	7	1							3
	3			5	6	8	4	9	10	11			2	7	1							4
	3			5	6	8	4	9	10	11			2	7	1							5
	8	3		5	6		11		10	9			2	7	1	4						6
	8	3		5	6		9		10	7	11		4	1	2							7
	4	3		5	6	8	11		10	9			7	1	2							8
	8	3		5	6	10	4*	9		11			7	1	2	12						9
	7	3		5	6	8		9	10	11			2		1	4						10
	7	3		5	6		8	9	10*	11			2		1	4	12					11
	5	12	10		3	4*	9		11				6	7	1	2	8					12
	4	3*			6	10	12	9		11			5	7	1	2	8					13
	3				6	9		11	10	8			5	4	1	2	7					14
1	3			5	6	9		11	10	8			4		2	7						15
1	3			5	6	9	8	11	10	7			4		2							16
1	8			5	6	3	7	11	10	9			4		2							17
1	3	6		4		8	7	11	10	9			5		2							18
1	3	6		4		9	8	11	10	7			5		2							19
1	4	6	3	5		8	7	11	10	9			2									20
	3	6	4*	5		9	8	11	10	7			2	1			12					21
	3	6		5	7	8	11	10	9				2	1					4			22
	3	12		6	7	11	10	9		5			1	2	8		4*					23
	3	4		6	8	11	10	9		5			7	1	2							24
	3	12		6	7	11	10	9		5			4	1	2		8*					25
	3	11*		6	7	12	10	9		5			4	1	2					8		26
	3	6	11		9	10	7			5			4	1	2					8		27
	3			6	7	9	10	11		5			4	1	2					8		28
	3	12		6	8	9	10	11*		5			7	1	2					4		29
	3	12		6	8	7*	11	10	9	5			4	1	2							30
	3	11	4	6	9	12	10	7		5			8	1	2*							31
	3			6	8	11	10	9		5			7	1	2					4		32
	3			6	8	11	10	9		5			7	1	2					4		33
	3			6	7	11	10*	8	5	9			1	2	12					4		34
	3			6	7	9	11	10	8	5			1	2						4		35
10	3		4	6	11	9*	12	7		5			1	2						8		36
	3	8		6	7	9	12	10	11	5			1	2*						4		37
	3	12		6	7*	9	10	11		5			1	2	8					4		38
	3	11*	4	6	9	12	10			5			1	2	7					8		39
	3	12	5	6	11		9*						2	7	1	8				4	10	40
	3	11	5	6	9								4	1	2	7				8	10	41
	3	11	5	6	9								4	1	2	7				8	10	42
	3*	11	5	6	12	9			7				4	1	2					8	10	43
1	3	11*	5	6		12	9						4		2	7				8	10	44
1	3	11*	5	6	9	12	10						4		2	7				8		45
1	3	11	5*	6	9	12	7						2	4						8	10	46
10	41	10	25	30	40	33	31	30	33	44	1	1	34	32	35	36	11	2	2	19	6	
		+1s	+7s		+1s	+1s	+8s		+1s							+3s	+1s					

GRIMSBY TOWN—PLAYERS

Player and position	Ht.	Wt.	Birthplace	Clubs	League Appearances	Goals
Goalkeepers						
*Neil Freeman	6 2	13 9	Northampton	Arsenal	—	—
				Northampton (on loan)	—	—
				Grimsby T.	33	—
Harry Wainman	6 0	13 1	Hull	Grimsby T.	346	—
				Rochdale (on loan)	9	—
Defenders						
David Booth	5 10	11 7	Darton	Barnsley	162+3	8
				Grimsby T.	166	7
Steve Govier	6 0	12 0	Watford	Norwich C.	22	1
				Brighton	12	1
				Grimsby T.	22+1	—
*Alan Marley	5 8	11 1	Durham	Grimsby T.	39+1	2
Martin Young				Grimsby T.	50+1	2
Michael Czuczman	6 2	12 0	Carlisle	Preston N.E.	—	—
				Grimsby T.	108+6	6
Midfield						
Frank Barton	5 9½	11 11½	Barton on Humber	Scunthorpe U.	93	26
				Carlisle U.	161+4	22
				Blackpool	18	1
				Grimsby T.	123	15
Keith Brown	5 10	11 5	Grimsby	Nottingham F.	—	—
				Grimsby T.	32+7	5
				(contract cancelled Jan. 1976)		
Roy Coyle (N. Ireland)	5 9	11 4	Ireland	Glentoran	not known	
				Sheffield W.	38+2	2
				Grimsby T.	24	1
Stewart Gray	5 9	11 0	Doncaster	Doncaster R.	53+5	—
				Grimsby T.	232+1	2
David Boylen	5 3	9 3	Manchester	Grimsby T.	336+12	32
Jack Lewis	5 9	10 9	Long Eaton	Lincoln C.	47+15	9
				Grimsby T.	197+26	66
Robert Cumming				Grimsby T.	30+7	2
Joe Waters	5 5	10 5	Limerick	Leicester C.	11+2	1
				Grimsby T.	19	2
Tony Ford				Grimsby T.	11+3	—
*Ian Walton				Grimsby T.	2	1
Forwards						
Alan Woodward	5 9	11 6	Stamford Hill	Grimsby T.	55	12
Phil Hubbard	6 0	12 5	Lincoln	Lincoln C.	150+1	41
				Norwich C.	6+4	1
				Grimsby T.	144+2	37
Ron Wigg	6 0	11 5	Dunmow	Orient	—	—
				Ipswich T.	36+2	8
				Watford	92+6	20
				Rotherham U.	65	22
				Grimsby T.	35+10	8
Malcolm Partridge	6 0½	12 3	Calow	Mansfield T.	66+3	20
				Leicester C.	24+11	4
				Charlton Ath. (on loan)	1+1	—
				Grimsby T.	44+1	10
Bob Oldridge				Barton-on-Humber Grimsby T.	2+1	1

HALIFAX TOWN

DIV. 4

Chairman: P Albon.

Directors: T. H. Scott, H. Taylor, J. Turner, J. Wilson, J. S. Crowther.

Manager: Alan Ball.   *Secretary:* D. Holland

Year Formed: 1911.   *Turned Professional:* 1911.

Limited Company: 1911.

Previous Grounds: Sandhall and Exley.

Honours: *Football League,* highest position in Division 3: 3rd 1970–71. Division 3(N), Runners-up: 1934–35. Division 4, Runners-up: 1968–69.   *F.A. Cup,* best season: 5th Rd., 1932–33, 1952–53.   *Football League Cup,* best season: 4th Rd., 1964.

Record Victory: 7-0 v Bishop Auckland, F.A. Cup 2nd Rd. Replay, Jan. 10th, 1967.

Record Defeat: 0-13 v Stockport Co., Division 3(N), Jan. 6th, 1934.

Most League Points: 57, Division 4, 1968–69.

Most League Goals: 83, Division 3(N), 1957–58.

Most Capped Player: Mick Meagan. Eire, 1.

Most League Appearances: John Pickering, 367, 1965–74.

Highest League Scorer in Season: Albert Valentine, 34 Division 3(N), 1934–35.

Most League Goals in Total Aggregate: Ernest Dixon, 129, 1922–30.

Record Transfer Fee Received: £40,000 from Liverpool for Alan Waddle, June, 1973.

Record Transfer Fee Paid: £13,500 to Blackpool for Fred Kemp, Dec. 1971.

Managers Since the War: Jack Breedon, W. Wootton, Jimmy Thomson, Gerald Henry, Bobby Browne, Willie Watson, Billy Burnicle, Harry Hooper, Willie Watson, Vic Metcalfe, Alan Ball, George Kirby, Ray Henderson, George Mulhall, John Quinn.

Address of Supporters Club: Same as Football Club.

Address of Club Shop or Boutique: Club Shop, 11 Horton Street, Halifax, Yorks.

Shay Ground, Halifax HX1 2YS. Telephone Halifax 53423.   *Ground capacity:* 25,000.   *Record attendance:* 36,885 v Tottenham H., F.A. Cup 5th Rd., February 14, 1953.   *Record receipts:* £4,898 v Tottenham H., F.A. Cup 5th Rd., February 14, 1953.   *Pitch measurements:* 110 yds × 70 yds.

How to get there: Near the town centre within a few minutes walking distance of the bus station and railway station.

Match tickets: Advance booking on application to the secretary.

Car parking: Car park is available; entrance in Shaw Hill.

Entertainments/catering facilities: Social club adjacent to the club office. Catering facilities at points inside the ground.

Club shop: Sells all types of souvenirs.

Handbooks/programmes: Handbooks and programmes available from Supporters Club, c/o Halifax Town A.F.C.

Extra information: In 1929, Halifax played a goalkeeper, Bob Suter, who was 47 years old!

Club Colours: Royal blue shirts with white collar and cuffs, white shorts, blue stockings with white tops.

Change Colours: Green and black striped shirts, black shorts, black stockings.

Team Captain: Tony Rhodes.

Coach: Syd Farrimond.

Club Nickname: 'Town'.

HALIFAX TOWN 1975–76 LEAGUE RECORD

Match No.	Date	Venue	Opponents	Result	H/T Score	League Pos'n	Goalscorers	Attendance
1	Aug 16	H	Millwall	L 1-2	0-2	—	Downes	2460
2	23	A	Aldershot	W 2-1	1-1	12	McHale, Gwyther	3221
3	30	H	Walsall	W 2-1	1-1	7	Ford, Gwyther	2076
4	Sept 6	A	Colchester U.	W 1-0	0-0	3	McHale (pen)	2819
5	13	H	Shrewsbury T.	D 0-0	0-0	6		2501
6	20	A	Cardiff C.	D 0-0	0-0	3		8035
7	23	A	Grimsby T.	D 2-2	0-2	—	Bell 2	6130
8	27	H	Chester	W 5-2	3-1	4	Bell, Rhodes 2, McHale, Phelan	2240
9	Oct 4	A	Gillingham	D 1-1	0-0	5	Bell	5934
10	11	A	Swindon T.	L 1-3	0-1	7	McHale	6214
11	18	H	Hereford U.	L 0-1	0-1	9		2667
12	20	A	Southend U.	L 1-4	1-2	—	McHale	3089
13	25	A	Bury	D 0-0	0-0	11		7516
14	Nov 1	H	Crystal Palace	L 1-3	0-2	16	McHale	3282
15	4	H	Preston N.E.	W 2-1	1-0	—	Bell, Rhodes	3366
16	8	A	Mansfield T.	D 1-1	0-0	11	McHale	5288
17	15	H	Brighton & H.A.	L 1-3	1-1	15	Ford	2201
18	29	A	Wrexham	D 1-1	0-0	15	McHale	3063
19	Dec 6	H	Peterborough U.	L 0-1	0-1	19		2289
20	20	A	Chesterfield	W 2-1	0-0	16	Bell, Gwyther	3703
21	26	H	Port Vale	L 1-3	1-1	18	Bell	2959
22	27	A	Rotherham U.	W 1-0	1-0	16	Gwyther	7614
23	Jan 10	A	Walsall	L 0-2	0-2	18		7167
24	17	H	Cardiff C.	D 1-1	0-0	18	Phelan	2399
25	24	A	Shrewsbury T.	L 0-2	0-2	18		3398
26	Feb 7	A	Preston N.E.	L 1-2	0-0	21	McHale	5480
27	14	H	Mansfield T.	L 1-2	0-0	22	Downes	2378
28	21	A	Brighton & H.A.	L 0-1	0-0	23		13,686
29	24	A	Grimsby T.	W 2-1	1-1	—	Downes, McHale (pen)	2229
30	28	H	Bury	L 0-2	0-2	23		3606
31	Mar 2	H	Sheffield W.	D 0-0	0-0	—		5876
32	9	H	Gillingham	D 1-1	0-1	—	Jones (G)	1886
33	13	H	Swindon T.	L 0-2	0-1	23		1864
34	17	A	Hereford U.	W 2-1	0-0	—	Jones (G.) 2	7395
35	20	H	Wrexham	L 0-1	0-0	24		2970
36	23	H	Southend U.	W 1-0	0-0	—	McHale	1450
37	27	A	Peterborough U.	L 0-1	0-1	22		4933
38	30	H	Chesterfield	W 1-0	1-0	—	Overton	1975
39	Apr 3	A	Millwall	L 0-1	0-0	20		7237
40	7	A	Chester	L 1-2	1-0	—	Overton	3369
41	13	A	Crystal Palace	D 1-1	1-1	—	McHale	19,175
42	17	A	Port Vale	D 1-1	1-0	22	Phelan	3169
43	19	H	Rotherham U.	L 0-1	0-1	—		2614
44	20	A	Sheffield W.	L 0-1	0-1	—		13,143
45	24	H	Aldershot	L 1-3	1-1	24	Harris	1608
46	26	H	Colchester U.	D 1-1	0-1	—	Smith (og)	856

Goalscorers

League (41): McHale 12 (2 pens), Bell 7, Gwyther 4, Downes 3, Phelan 3, Rhodes 3, Jones (G.) 3, Ford 2, Overton 2, Harris 1, Own Goal 1.
League Cup (7): Bell 2, Downes 2, Phelan, Albeson, Rhodes.
F.A. Cup (7): McHale 4 (3 pens), Rhodes, Downes, Gwyther.

League Cup	First Round	Hartlepool (h)	4-1
	Second Leg	(a)	1-2
	Second Round	Sheffield U. (h)	2-4
F.A. Cup	First Round	Altrincham (h)	3-1
	Second Round	Stafford (a)	3-1
	Third Round	Ipswich T. (a)	1-3

Gennoe	Smith, A.	Luckett	McHale	Rhodes	Phelan	Jones	Downes	Ford	Gwyther	Pugh	Harrold	Collins	Bell	Veitch	Harris	Blair	Smith, A.	McGill	Bullock	Jones, G.	Favell	Overton	Match No.
1	2	3*	4	5	6	7	8	9	10	11	12												1
1	2		4	5	6	7	11	9	10	8													2
1	2		4	5	6	7	11	9*	10	8		3	12										3
1	2		4	5	6	7		9	10	11		3	8										4
1	2		4	5	6	7	12	9	10	11*		3	8										5
1	2		4	5	6	7		9*	10	11		3	8	12									6
1	2		4	5	6	7				11		3	9	8	10								7
1	2		4	5	6	7			11			3	9	8	10								8
1	2		4	5	6	7			10	11		3	9	8									9
1	2		4	5	6	7			10	11		3	9	8									10
1			10	5	6	7				11	2	3	9	8	4								11
1			4	5	6	7			10	11*	12	3	9	2	8								12
1	2		8	5	6	7			10			3	9	4		11							13
1			4	5	6				10		2	3	9	8	7	11							14
1			4	5	6				10	12	2	3	9	8	7*	11							15
1			4*	5	6			12	10	7	2	3	9	8		11							16
1			4	5	6			12	7	10	2	3	9	8	11*								17
1			4	5	6		8	7	10	11		3	9	2									18
1	12		4	5	6		8	7	10	11		3	9	2*									19
1	2		4	5	6	7	8*		10	11		3	9	12									20
1	2		4	5	6	7			10	11		3	9	8									21
1	2		4	5	6	7			10	8		3	9		11								22
	8	12	4		6	7			10	5		3	9	2	11*	1							23
	2*		4	5	6	7	12		10	11		3	9	8		1							24
	2	3	4	5	6	7	12		10	11*			9	8		1							25
	2		4	5	6	7			10		12	3	9	8	11*	1							26
	2		4	5	6	7	11		10			3	9	8*	12	1							27
	2		4	5	6	7	11		10			3			12	1		8*	9				28
1	2		4	5*	6	7			10	11		3			12			8	9				29
1	2		4		6	7			12	11*		3			5			8	9	10			30
1	2		4		6	7				11		3			5			8	9	10			31
	2		4		6	7				5		3			11	1		8	9	10			32
	2*		4		6	7				5					12	1		8	9	10	3	11	33
			4	5	6	7						3				1		8	9	10	2	11	34
			4	5	6	7						3				1		8	9	10	2	11	35
			4	5	6	7						3				1		8	9	10	2	11	36
			4*	5	6	7					12	3				1		8	9	10	2	11	37
			8	5	6				4			3		7		1			9	10	2	11	38
			4	5	6				10	8		3		7		1			9		2	11	39
			8			7	12		6			3	11			1	4	9	10*		2	5	40
			8	5	6	7			4			3	10			1			9		2	11	41
			8	5	6	7			4			3	10			1			9		2	11	42
			8	5	6	7	9		4			3	10			1			9		2	11	43
			8	5	6*	7	12		4			3	10			1			9		2	11	44
	2		4*	5				9	8			3	10	12	7	1					11	6	45
1	2		8	5				9	4				10		7	11					3	6	46
26	27	2	46	40	43	36	12	10	24	36	5	42	30	20	10	12	20	11	16	10	14	14	

```
 +  +            +  +        +  +      +  +  +  +
1s 1s           6s 2s       3s 2s     1s 2s 4s 1s
```

HALIFAX TOWN—PLAYERS

Player and position	Ht.	Wt.	Birthplace	Clubs	League Appearances	Goals
Goalkeepers						
*Alex Smith	5 9	11 0	Lancaster	Accrington S.	33	—
				Bolton W.	19	—
				Halifax T.	341	—
Terrence Gennoe	6 2	12 5	Shrewsbury	Bury	3	—
				Blackburn R. (on loan)	—	—
				Leeds U. (on loan)	—	—
				Halifax T.	26	—
Defenders						
*Syd Farrimond	5 9¼	11 4	Hindley	Bolton W.	363+1	1
				Shrewsbury T.	—	—
				Tranmere R.	132+2	—
				Halifax T.	—	—
John Collins	5 8	10 10	Rhymney	Tottenham H.	—	—
				Portsmouth	71+3	—
				Halifax T.	82	1
Tony Rhodes	5 11	11 6	Dover	Derby Co.	5	—
				Halifax T.	233	9
Albert Phelan	6 0	11 13	Sheffield	Chesterfield	384+4	14
				Halifax T.	79	4
John Quinn	5 6	10 10	St. Helens	Sheffield W.	164+8	19
				Rotherham U.	114	7
				Halifax T.	88+4	1
				(contract cancelled April 1976)		
*Alex Smith	5 11	11 9	Dewsbury	Bradford C.	59+2	2
				Huddersfield T.	29	—
				Southend U.	130+1	1
				Colchester U.	51	1
				Halifax T.	46+1	1
Bobby Flavell	5 7	9 10	Berwick	Burnley	—	—
Midfield				Halifax T.	14	—
*David Ford	5 7	10 7	Sheffield	Sheffield W.	118+5	31
				Newcastle U.	24+2	3
				Sheffield U.	21+6	2
				Halifax T.	83+2	6
*Kenny Blair	5 9	11 0	Lancs.	Derby Co.	—	—
				Halifax T.	42+1	4
				Stockport Co. (on loan)	7	—
*David Pugh	5 10½	11 7	Markham	Newport	73+4	9
				Chesterfield	212+1	12
				Halifax T.	91+5	3
Jimmy McGill	5 8	11 12	Glasgow	Arsenal	6+4	—
				Huddersfield T.	161+3	8
				Hull C.	141+6	3
				Halifax T.	11	—
*Tommy Veitch	5 10	11 3	Scotland	Hearts	37+10	—
				Tranmere R.	76+3	5
Forwards				Halifax T.	20+2	—
*Steve Downes	5 10	11 7	Leeds	Rotherham U.	54+8	18
				Sheffield W.	26+4	4
				Chesterfield	37+4	11
				Halifax T.	38+12	12
				Blackburn R. (on loan)	6	—
Alan Jones	5 5	9 11½	Grimethorpe	Huddersfield T.	30+2	—
				Halifax T.	104	6
Ray McHale	5 7	11 6	Sheffield	Chesterfield	123+1	27
				Halifax T.	82	19
*Mark Harrold	5 11	11 0	Halifax	Halifax T.	8+5	1
Micky Bullock	5 10¼	12 0	Stoke	Birmingham C.	27	10
				Oxford U.	58+1	15
				Orient	267+10	64
				Halifax T.	16	—
George Jones	5 11	12 0	Radcliffe	Bury	65	14
				Blackburn R.	36+2	14
				Bury	249+7	100
				Oldham Ath.	63+8	19
				Halifax T.	10	3
Derek Bell	5 8	11 5	Wyberton	Derby Co.	—	—
				Halifax T.	30+1	7
				Sheffield W. (on loan)	5	1
Geoff Harris	5 10	11 1	Manchester	Oldham Ath.	—	—
				Halifax T.	10+4	1

198

HARTLEPOOL   DIV. 4

President: S. Spaldin.

Chairman: E. Ord.

Vice-Chairman: B. H. Crosby.

Directors: E. B. Young, N. S. Armstrong, J. O. Curry.

Manager: Ken Hale.   *Secretary:* W. P. Hillan.
Year Formed: 1908.   *Turned Professional:* 1908.

Limited Company: 1908.

Previous Name: Hartlepools United until 1968.

Honours: *Football League,* highest position in Division 3:
22nd, 1968–69. Division 3(N), Runners-up: 1956–57.
F.A. Cup, best season: 4th Rd. 1954–55. *F.L. Cup,* best season: 4th Rd. 1974–75.
Record Victory: 10-1 v Barrow, Division 4, Apr. 4th, 1959.
Record Defeat: 1-10 v Wrexham, Division 4, Mar. 3rd, 1962.
Most League Points: 69, Division 4, 1967–68.
Most League Goals: 90, Division 3(N), 1956–57.
Highest League Scorer in Season: William Robinson, 28, Division 3(N), 1927–28.
Most League Goals in Total Aggregate: Ken Johnson, 98, 1949–64.
Most Capped Player: Ambrose Fogarty, 1 (11), Eire.
Most League Appearances: Wattie Moore, 448, 1948–64.
Record Transfer Fee Received: £10,000 from Reading for Terry Bell, Mar. 1970.
Record Transfer Fee Paid: £10,000 to Sunderland for Ambrose Fogarty, Nov. 1963.
Managers Since the War: Fred Westgarth, Ray Middleton, Bill Robinson, Allenby Chilton. Bob Gurney, Alvan Williams, Geoff Twentyman, Brian Clough, Angus McLean, John Simpson, Len Ashurst.

Club Shop: On ground.

The Victoria Ground. Telephone Hartlepool 72584. 18 Scarborough Street, Hartlepool. Telephone 3492 (Office).   *Ground capacity:* 16,500.   *Record attendance:* 17,426 v Manchester U., F.A. Cup 3rd Rd., January 5, 1957.   *Record receipts:* £5000 v Aston Villa, Football League Cup 4th Rd., November 13 1974.   *Pitch measurements:* 113 yds × 77 yds.

How to get there: Hartlepool railway station is only a few hundred yards from the ground. Local bus services run scheduled services to Hartlepool.
Match tickets: No pre-booking of tickets.
Car parking: Ample side-street parking.
Entertainments/catering facilities: Two refreshment kiosks inside the ground.
Club shop: Open on match days; stocks all types of souvenirs.
Handbooks/programmes: No handbooks. Programmes available on subscription.
Extra information: Just three years after finishing second in Division III(N) in 1956–57 the club conceded a Fourth Division record 109 goals.

Club Colours: Blue shirts, white shorts, blue stockings.
Change Colours: Yellow shirts and shorts with green trim, yellow stockings.
Club Nickname: 'The Pool'.

HARTLEPOOL 1975–76 LEAGUE RECORD

Match No.	Date	Venue	Opponents	Result	H/T Score	League Pos'n	Goalscorers	Attendance
1	Aug 16	H	AFC Bournemouth	D 1-1	0-0	—	Smith, D.	2225
2	23	A	Brentford	D 1-1	0-1	12	Goad	4950
3	30	H	Lincoln C.	D 2-2	2-0	13	Smith, D. 2	1895
4	Sept 6	A	Watford	L 1-2	0-2	17	Skillen	3998
5	13	H	Scunthorpe U.	L 1-2	0-1	20	Johnson	1970
6	19	A	Southport	W 4-2	2-1	18	Johnson, McMahon, Moore, Smith, D.	1012
7	22	H	Reading	L 2-4	1-1	—	Rowlands, Smith, R.	2261
8	27	H	Tranmere R.	L 1-2	1-2	19	Rowlands	1544
9	Oct 4	A	Crewe Alex.	D 0-0	0-0	20		2326
10	11	H	Torquay U.	L 0-1	0-1	22		1695
11	13	H	Exeter C.	W 2-1	2-0	—	Moore, Smith, D.	1323
12	18	A	Exeter C.	L 1-3	1-2	19	Goad	2406
13	22	H	Stockport Co.	W 3-0	1-0	—	Moore, Smith, D., McMahon	1683
14	25	H	Barnsley	W 1-0	1-0	13	Smith, D.	2324
15	Nov 1	A	Huddersfield T.	L 0-2	0-0	17		4183
16	3	A	Darlington	W 2-1	1-0	—	McMahon, Scaife	4275
17	8	H	Doncaster R.	W 2-1	1-0	12	Rowlands, McMahon	3567
18	15	A	Bradford C.	W 2-1	0-0	12	Johnson, Honour	2009
19	29	H	Newport Co.	W 4-1	2-0	10	Moore, Screen (og), Johnson, McMahon	2780
20	Dec 6	A	Swansea C.	L 1-3	0-0	12	McMahon	2253
21	20	A	Rochdale	D 1-1	0-1	12	Scaife	1168
22	26	H	Northampton T.	W 3-0	1-0	11	McMahon, Smith, D. 2	5077
23	27	A	Workington	W 2-1	1-0	8	McMahon, Moore	2553
24	Jan 10	A	Lincoln C.	L 0-3	0-0	12		7581
25	17	H	Southport	D 0-0	0-0	13		2950
26	30	A	Stockport Co.	L 0-2	0-1	15		1565
27	Feb 7	H	Darlington	L 2-3	2-0	16	Rowlands, Smith. D.	3655
28	14	A	Doncaster R.	L 0-3	0-2	18		5035
29	18	H	Cambridge U.	D 2-2	2-1	—	Goad, Moore	1400
30	21	H	Bradford C.	D 2-2	0-0	16	Smith, D. 2	1865
31	25	A	Reading	L 0-1	0-0	—		6288
32	28	A	Barnsley	L 1-3	0-2	18	Scaife	2648
33	Mar 2	A	Scunthorpe U.	L 1-5	0-2	—	Smith, D.	2966
34	6	H	Huddersfield T.	D 1-1	0-0	16	Rowlands	2044
35	10	H	Crewe Alex.	L 1-3	0-3	—	Moore	1506
36	13	A	Torquay U.	D 1-1	0-1	19	Moore	2676
37	20	A	Newport Co.	W 1-0	0-0	17	Moore	1230
38	27	H	Swansea C.	W 1-0	1-0	17	Rowlands	1708
39	31	H	Rochdale	W 3-0	1-0	—	Spelman, Moore 2	1525
40	Apr 3	A	AFC Bournemouth	L 2-4	0-1	16	Endean, Johnson	3102
41	6	A	Tranmere R.	W 2-1	1-0	—	Endean, Griffiths (og)	3450
42	10	H	Watford	W 2-1	1-1	13	Endean, Moore	1993
43	16	A	Cambridge U.	L 0-4	0-3	13		2136
44	17	A	Northampton T.	L 2-5	1-4	16	Moore, Johnson (pen)	7555
45	20	H	Workington	L 0-2	0-1	—		1731
46	24	H	Brentford	W 1-0	1-0	14	Scaife	1272

Goalscorers

League (62): Moore 13, Smith, D. 13, McMahon 8, Johnson 6 (1 a pen), Rowlands 6, Scaife 4, Endean 3, Goad 3, Honour 1, Skillen 1, Smith, R. 1, Spelman 1, own goals 2.
League Cup (3): Johnson, McMahon, Skillen.
F.A. Cup (10): Moore 3, Scaife 2, Smith, D., McMahon, Potter, Johnson (pen), Rowlands.

League Cup	First Round	Halifax T. (a)	1-4
	Second Leg	(h)	2-1
F.A. Cup	First Round	Stockport Co. (h)	3-0
	Second Round	Marine (a)	1-1
		(h)	6-3
	Third Round	Manchester C. (a)	0-6

200

Hope	Smith, R.	Crowther	Dawes	Goad	Potter	Smith, D.	Honour	Moore	McMahon	Johnson	Skillen	Richardson	Embleton	Watling	Spelman	Scaife	Rowlands	Bielby	Maggiore	Charlton	Elliott	Wann	Jacques	Luckett	Rylands	Endean	Match No.
1	2	3	4*	5	6	7	8	9	10	11	12																1
	6	4		2	5	7	10	12	9	11	8	1	3*														2
	2	3		5	6	7	4	10	9	11	8	1															3
	2				6	5	7*	9	10	11	8	1				3	4	12									4
	2				5	6	7*	10	9	11	8	1				3	4	12									5
	3			2		8		9	10	11		1		6	7	4	5										6
	3			2		8		9	10	11		1		6	7	4	5										7
1	3			6	2	8		9	10	11	12				7	4*	5										8
1	2				6	10	8	9		11		3			7	4	5										9
1	2				6	7	8	9*	12	11		3			10	4	5										10
1	2			3	4	8	7	9	10	6					11	5											11
1	2			3	5	8	4	9	10	11					7	6											12
1	2			3	4	8	7	9	10	6					11	5											13
1	2			3	4	8	7	9	10	6					11	5											14
1	2			3	4	8	7*	9	10	6					11	12	5										15
1	2			3	5	8	7	10	9	4					11	6											16
1	2			3	5	8	7	9	10	11					4	6											17
1	2			3	6	8	7*	9	10	4					11	5	12										18
1	2			3	5*	7		9	10	8					11	6	4	12									19
1	2			3	5	7		9	10	8					11	6	4										20
1	2			3	4	8		9	10	6*					7	11	5	12									21
1	2			3	4	8	7	9	10	6					11	5											22
1	2			3	4	8	6	9	10*	7					11	5	12										23
1	2			3		8				10					11	5	6	4	7	9							24
1	2			3		8				10					11	6	4	5	7		9						25
1	2					8	7	9	10	6					11	5	3						4				26
1	2			5		8	7	9	10*	4					11	6	3		12								27
	3			5				9	10	4		1			7	11	6	12	2	8*							28
	2			3	4	8		9	10	6		1			7*	11	5	12									29
	2			3	4	8	7	9				1			10	11	5				6						30
	2			3	4	8	7	9				1			10	11	5				6						31
	2			3	4	8	7	9				1			10*	11	5		12		6						32
1				3	4	8		9		6					7	11		2	10				5				33
	2			3	4	8		9	10	6		1			7	11	5										34
	2			3	4	8*		9	10	6		1			7	11	5	12									35
	2				6			9		4		1			7	11	10		12					3*	5	8	36
	2			4				9		6		1			7	11	10							3	5	8	37
	2				6			9		4		1			7	11	10							3	5	8	38
	2			4				9		6		1			7	11	10							3	5	8	39
	2			5				10	9	4		1			7	11								3	6	8	40
	2			4				9	10			1			7	11	6							3	5	8	41
	2			5				9	10			1			7	11*	12		4					3	6	8	42
	2			4				9	10			1*			7	12	11		6					3	5	8	43
1				4				9	10			2			7	11	6							3	5	8	44
				4				9		6		2			10	11	12					7		3	5*	8	45
	2			4			9*					1			7	10	11		12			6		3	5	8	46
23	34	3	1	37	43	35	20	43	29	38	4	21	5	2	34	37	33	8	10	2	4	2	5	11	11	11	

Totals annotations: Potter +1s, Smith, D. +1s, Moore +2s; Spelman +2s, Scaife +2s, Rowlands +8s, Bielby +4s, Maggiore +1s.

Player and position	Ht.	Wt.	Birthplace	Clubs	League Appearances	Goals
Goalkeepers						
*John Hope	6 0	11 7	Shildon	Darlington	14	—
Newcastle U. 1(—)				Sheffield U. 63(—) Preston N.E. (on loan) —(—) Hartlepool 23(—)		
Graham Richardson				Hartlepool	21	—
Defenders						
Kenneth Ellis	5 9	10 10	Newcastle	Hartlepool	32+2	4
Alan Goad	5 10	10 10	Hailsham	Exeter C.	—	—
				Hartlepool	330+1	9
George Potter	5 8	10 8	Arbroath	Luton T.	3+4	—
				Torquay U.	32+6	—
				Hartlepool	211+1	4
Paul Luckett	5 8	10 3		Coventry C.	—	—
				Halifax T.	26+1	—
				Hartlepool	11	—
*Joe Jacques	5 11	11 10	Consett	Preston N.E.		
Lincoln C. 22(—)				Darlington 150+3(5) Southend U. 75+2(—) Gillingham 73(1)		
Hartlepool 5(—)						
Tony Maggiore				Hartlepool	10+4	—
John Rowlands	5 10	10 9	Riddings	Mansfield T.	11+1	3
Torquay U. 18(4)				Exeter C. (on loan) 1(—) Stockport Co. 45+1(13) Barrow 52+2(6)		
Workington 50+1(11)				Crewe A. 31+4(1) Hartlepool (contract cancelled April 1976) 33+2(6)		
*Robert Smith	5 6	10 2	Hull	Hull C.	—	—
Grimsby T. 10+1(—)				Hartlepool 141+11(4)		
Midfield						
Don Heath	5 8	12 0	Stockton	Middlesbrough	—	—
Norwich C. 80+3(15)				Swindon T. 82+6(2) Oldham A. 43+2(2) Peterborough U. 43+1(4)		
Hartlepool 36+1(2)						
Michael Spelman	5 9	10 9	Newcastle	Wolverhampton W.	—	—
Watford —(—)				Hartlepool 106+6(4) Darlington (on loan) 4(—)		
Kevin Johnson	5 5	9 12	Doncaster	Sheffield W.	0+1	—
Southend U. 13+4(1)				Gillingham (on loan) 1(—) Workington 15(1) Hartlepool 56+1(9)		
Forwards						
*Kevin McMahon	6 0	12 2	Tantosie	Newcastle U.	—	—
York C. 85+8(31)				Bolton W. (on loan) 4+2(1) Barnsley 4+1(—) Hartlepool 104+3(28)		
*David Smith	5 9	10 9	Sheffield	Huddersfield T.	27+7	7
Stockport Co. (on loan) 7+1(—)				Halifax T. (on loan) 12+1(4) Cambridge U. 15+2(3)		
Hartlepool 42(13)						
Robert Scaife	6 0	12 4	Northallerton	Middlesbrough	—	—
Halifax T. (on loan) 5+1(1)				Hartlepool 37+2(4)		
Paul Bielby	5 9	12 4	Darlington	Manchester U.	2+2	—
				Hartlepool	8+6	—
Keith Skillen	5 9	11 12	Cockermouth	Workington	56+8	9
				Hartlepool	4+2	1
Malcolm Moore	5 10	12 0	Sunderland	Sunderland	11+2	3
Crewe Alex. (on loan) 8(—)				Tranmere R. 83+9(21) Hartlepool 127+2(34)		
Barry Endean	5 10	11 0	Chester le Street	Watford	72+5	28
Charlton Ath. 27(1)				Blackburn R. 65+14(18) Huddersfield T. 8+4(1) Workington (on loan) 8(2)		
Hartlepool 11(3)						
Kevin Elliott				Hartlepool	4	—

HEREFORD UNITED   DIV. 2

Chairman: F. L. Miles.

Directors: H. Nield, J. Jackson, D. Vaughan, P. Hill,
M. Roberts, P. Edmunds.

Manager: John Sillett.

Secretary: Bill Stevens.

Assistant-Secretary: Jim Finney.

Year Formed: 1924. *Turned Professional:* 1924.

Limited Company: 1939.

Ground: Edgar Street Athletic Ground.

Honours: Best season *Football League:* Division 3 Champions,
1975-76. *F.A. Cup* best season 4th Rd. 1971-72. *F.L. Cup*
Best season 3 Rd. 1974-5. Division 4, Runners-up, 1972–73.
Welsh Cup finalists: 1967–68 1975-76.

Record Victory: 11-0 v Thynnes (F.A. Cup), Sept. 1947.

Record Defeat: 0-5 v Wrexham, Dec. 1973, 1-6 v Tranmere R., Jan. 1975.

Most League Points: 58, Division 4, 1972–73.

Most League Goals: 56, Division 4 1972–73.

Highest League Scorer in Season: Dixie McNeil, 35, 1975-76.

Most League Appearances: Billy Tucker, 117, 1972-75.

Most League Goals in Total Aggregate: Dixie McNeil, 66, 1974–76.

Most Capped Player: Brian Evans, 1(7) Wales.

Record Transfer Fee Received: £20,000 for Dudley Tyler from West Ham U., May 1972.

Record Transfer Fee Paid: £20,000 to Plymouth Arg. for Jim Hinch, Oct. 1973; to Lincoln C.
or Dixie McNeil, August 1974.

Managers Since the War: George Tranter, Alex Massie, Joe Wade, Ray Daniel, Bob Dennison,
John Charles, Colin Addison.

Address of Supporters' Club: Edgar Street, Hereford.

Address of Club Shop: Edgar Street, Hereford.

Edgar Street, Hereford. Telephone Hereford (0432) 4037. *Telegraphic Address:*
Ground Capacity: 17,500. *Record Attendance:* 18,114 v Sheffield W., January 1958. *Record
receipts:* £12,666 Bristol C., F.A. Cup 4th Rd., Jan. 26 1974. *Pitch measurements:* 111 yds ×
80 yds.

How to get there: Ground very close to town centre, within five minutes walking distance from Hereford
railway station and the bus station.

Match tickets: Tickets can be booked in advance.

Car parking: Parking is available around the ground for approximately 1,000 vehicles.

Entertainments/catering facilities: Canteens on the ground. A social club is in the process of construction.

Club shop: All types of souvenirs sold.

Handbooks/programmes: Programmes available on application to the club shop.

Extra information: As a non-League Club, Hereford reached the first round proper of the F.A. Cup for 21
consecutive seasons.

Club Colours: White shirts, black shorts, black and white stockings. *Change Colours:* Yellow, blue,
yellow. *Club Trainer:* Peter Isaac. *Club Nickname:* 'United'.

HEREFORD UNITED 1975–76 LEAGUE RECORD

Match No.	Date	Venue	Opponents	Result	H/T Score	League Pos'n	Goalscorers	Attendance
1	Aug 16	H	Port Vale	D 0-0	0-0	—		6219
2	23	A	Rotherham U.	D 1-1	1-1	13	Carter	3825
3	30	H	Sheffield W.	W 3-1	1-0	4	Tucker, McNeil 2 (1 a pen)	7017
4	Sept 6	A	Millwall	L 0-1	0-0	11		6066
5	13	H	Colchester U.	D 0-0	0-0	11		5577
6	20	A	Chesterfield	W 3-2	0-0	8	McNeil, Silkman, Redrobe	3000
7	24	H	Swindon T.	W 1-0	1-0	—	Emery	6423
8	27	H	Gillingham	D 1-1	0-0	7	Davey	5512
9	Oct 4	A	Chester	W 1-0	0-0	4	Davey	4144
10	11	H	Wrexham	W 2-0	1-0	4	Layton, Davey	6228
11	18	A	Halifax T.	W 1-0	1-0	2	Tyler	2667
12	21	A	Crystal Palace	D 2-2	0-1	—	Layton, Tyler	20,232
13	25	A	Peterborough U.	L 2-4	1-1	3	Lindsay (pen), Davey	8471
14	Nov 1	A	Preston N.E.	W 4-3	2-1	3	Davey, Tucker, McNeil, Lindsay	9682
15	8	H	Grimsby T.	W 3-2	1-0	2	McNeil 2, Davey	6391
16	19	H	Bury	W 2-0	1-0	2	Davey, McNeil (pen)	6867
17	Dec 6	A	Brighton & H.A.	L 2-4	1-2	4	Tyler, Carter	17,811
18	20	A	Aldershot	W 2-0	0-0	2	McNeil, Walker	4113
19	26	H	Walsall	L 1-3	1-1	3	Davey	10,891
20	27	A	Shrewsbury T.	L 1-2	0-2	4	Walker	9488
21	Jan 10	A	Sheffield W.	W 2-1	1-1	4	Davey, McNeil	8155
22	17	H	Chesterfield	W 4-2	3-0	5	Hunter (o.g.), Layton, McNeil 2	5999
23	24	A	Colchester U.	W 4-1	3-1	3	McNeil 2, Dominey (o.g.), Davey	2626
24	26	A	Southend U.	W 3-1	2-0	—	McNeil 2, Layton	3722
25	31	H	Crystal Palace	D 1-1	0-0	2	McNeil	12,970
26	Feb 4	H	Cardiff C.	W 4-1	3-0	—	McNeil 2, Emery, Layton	12,962
27	7	A	Mansfield T.	D 2-2	0-0	1	McNeil 2	5997
28	11	H	Mansfield T.	W 1-0	1-0	—	Ritchie	8302
29	14	A	Grimsby T.	L 0-1	0-1	1		5944
30	21	H	Southend U.	W 2-1	1-1	1	McNeil, Galley	7264
31	24	A	Swindon T.	W 1-0	1-0	—	Davey	10,691
32	27	A	Peterborough U.	W 3-0	2-0	1	McNeil, Carter, Davey	14,106
33	Mar 10	H	Chester	W 5-0	3-0	—	McNeil 4 (1 a pen.), Davey	7103
34	13	H	Wrexham	L 1-2	1-2	1	McNeil	7621
35	17	H	Halifax T.	L 1-2	0-0	—	Galley	7395
36	20	A	Bury	W 3-2	1-0	1	Davey, Carter, McNeil	6384
37	27	H	Brighton & H.A.	D 1-1	0-1	1	McNeil	12,160
38	31	H	Aldershot	W 2-1	2-0	—	Richardson (o.g.), Paine	7497
39	Apr 3	A	Port Vale	D 1-1	0-0	1	Davey	4424
40	6	A	Gillingham	W 4-3	1-2	—	Davey 2, McNeil, Layton	7914
41	10	H	Millwall	D 0-0	0-0	1		10,176
42	14	A	Cardiff C.	L 0-2	0-0	—		35,549
43	17	A	Walsall	D 0-0	0-0	1		9225
44	19	H	Shrewsbury T.	W 3-1	0-0	—	Carter, Davey, McNeil	12,314
45	24	H	Rotherham U.	W 3-2	3-0	1	McNeil, Tyler 2	8950
46	28	H	Preston N.E.	W 3-1	0-1	—	McNeil 3	7592

Goalscorers
League (86): McNeil 34 (3 pens), Davey 18, Layton 6, Carter 5, Tyler 5, Lindsay 2 (1 a pen), Tucker 2, Emery 2, Walker 2, Galley 2, Ritchie 1, Paine 1, Silkman 1, Redrobe 1, Own Goals 3.
League Cup (5): Lindsay 2, Carter 2, Ritchie.
F.A. Cup (7): Layton 2, McNeil 2, Carter, Tucker, Tyler.

League Cup	First Round	Port Vale (a)	2-4	
	Second Leg	(h)	2-0	
	Second Round	Burnley (h)	1-4	
F.A. Cup	First Round	Torquay U. (h)	2-0	
	Second Round	A.F.C. Bournemouth (a)	2-2	
		(h)	2-0	
	Third Round	York C. (a)	1-2	

204

Hughes	Emery	Ritchie	Layton	Galley	Lindsay	Paine	Walker	Davey	McNeil	Tyler	Charlton	Tucker	Carter	Silkman	Redrobe	Rudge	Byrne	Rylands	Spring	McCafferty	Sheedy	Match No.
1	2	3	4	5	6	7	8	9	10	11												1
	2	3	6		4	12	8	9	10*		1	5	7	11								2
	2	3	4	8	6			9	10		1	5	7	11								3
	2	3	4		6	12	7	9	10		1	5	8	11*								4
	2	3	4		6	8	12		10		1	5		11	9*	7						5
	2	3	4		6	7			10	8	1	5		11	9							6
	2	3	4		6	7		12	10*	8	1	5		11	9							7
	2	3	4		6	7		12	10	8	1	5		11*	9							8
	2	3	5	4	6	7			10	8	1			11	9							9
	2	3	5*	4	6	7		12	10	8	1			11	9							10
	2	3	5	4	6	7			10	8	1	12		11	9*							11
	2*	3	5	4	6	7			10	8	1	12		11	9							12
		3	5	4	6	7		10	12	8	1			11	9*				2			13
	2	3	4		6	7		9	10	8	1	5		11								14
	2	3	4		6	7		9	10	8	1	5		11								15
	2	3	4		6	7		9	10	8	1	5		11								16
	2	3*	4		6	8		9	10	11	1	5	7		12							17
	2	3*	4		6	7	11	9	10	8	1	5			12							18
	2	3*	4		6	7	11	9	10	8	1	5	12									19
	2	3	4		6	7*	11	9		8	1	5			10		12					20
1	2	3	4		6	7		9	10	8			11						5			21
1	2	3	4		6	7		9	10	8			11						5			22
1	2	3	5	4	6	7*		9	10	8			11	12								23
1	2	3	4	5	6	7*		9	10	8			11	12								24
1	2	3	4	5	6	7		9	10	8*			11	12								25
1	2	3	4	5	6	7*		9	10				11		8				12			26
1	2	3	4	5	6		8*	9	10				7	11				12				27
1	2	3	4	5	6	7		9	10				11	12					8*			28
1	2	3	4	5	6	7		9	10				11						8			29
1	2	3	4	5	6	7		9	10				11	12					8*			30
	2	3	4	5	6	7		9	10*	8	1		11	12								31
	2	3	4	5	6	7		9	10*		1		11	12					8			32
	2	3	4	5	6	7		9	10	8*	1		11	12								33
	2	3*	4	5	6	7		9	10	8	1		11	12								34
	2	3	4	5	6	7*		9	10	8	1		11						12			35
	2	3	4	5	6	7		9	10	8	1		11									36
	2	3	4	5	6	7		9	10	8	1		11									37
	2	3	4	5	6	7		9	10	8*	1		11						12			38
	2	3	4	5	6	7*		9	10	8	1		11	12								39
	2	3	4	5	6			9	10	8	1		11		7							40
	2	3	4	5	6	12		9	10	8	1		11		7*							41
	2	3	4	5	6	7*		9	10	8	1		11						12			42
	2	3	4*	5	6	7	12	9	10		1		11		8							43
	2	3		5	6	7*		9	10	8	1	4		11	12							44
	2	3	4		6	7*		9	10	8	1	5		11	12							45
	2	3	4		6	12		9	10		1	5		11					7*		8	46
11	45	46	38	35	46	40	7	42	40	34	35	17	33	12	15	1	1	2	5	—	1	
					+4s	+2s	+3s	+1s			+2s		+10s	+5s	+1s	+1s			+1s	+3s		

Player and position	Ht.	Wt.	Birthplace	Clubs	League Appearances	Goals
Goalkeepers						
Tommy Hughes	6 1	12 4	Dalmuir	Chelsea	11	—
				Aston V.	16	—
				Brighton (on loan)	3	—
				Hereford U.	93	—
Kevin Charlton	5 9	11 8	Atherstone	Wolverhampton W.	—	—
				Bournemouth	21	—
				Hereford U.	35	—
Defenders						
Tony Byrne	5 7	10 2	Rathdowney	Millwall	1	—
(Eire)				Southampton	80+12	3
				Hereford U.	46+1	—
John Layton	6 0	13 2	Hereford	Hereford U.	57	7
Billy Tucker	5 11	11 10	Kidderminster	Hereford U.	130+2	12
Steve Ritchie	5 11	13 3	Glasgow	Bristol C.	1	—
				Morton	54	2
				Hereford U.	46	1
*David Rylands	6 0	11 7	Liverpool	Liverpool	—	—
				Hereford U.	22	—
				Newport Co. (on loan)	3	1
				Hartlepool (on loan)	11	—
Stephen Emery	5 11	11 10	Hereford	Hereford U.	96	2
John Galley	6 1	12 7	Clowne	Wolverhampton W.	5	2
				Rotherham U.	111	48
				Bristol C.	175	82
				Nottingham F.	31+6	6
				Peterborough U. (on loan)	7	1
				Hereford U.	57	8
Midfield						
Terry Paine	5 8	10 5	Winchester	Southampton	709+4	160
(England)				Hereford U.	83+4	5
Dudley Tyler	5 10	11 9	Salisbury	West Ham U.	29	1
				Hereford U.	93+3	10
Shane Walker	5 9	11 4	Pontypool	Arsenal	—	—
				Hereford U.	10+2	2
Forwards						
Jimmy Lindsay	5 7½	10 2	Hamilton	West Ham U.	35+3	2
				Watford	64+1	12
				Colchester U.	45	6
				Hereford U.	46	2
Dixie McNeil	5 10	11 12	Melton Mowbray	Leicester C.	—	—
				Exeter C.	31	11
				Corby T.	(Non-League)	
				Northampton T.	84+1	33
				Lincoln C.	96+1	53
				Hereford U.	84+1	66
*Eric Redrobe	6 1	12 6	Wigan	Bolton W.	4	1
				Southport	186+6	55
				Hereford U.	75+11	17
Roy Carter	6 0	10 8	Torpoint	Hereford U.	34	5
Steve Davey	5 7	10 3	Plymouth	Plymouth Arg.	214+12	48
				Hereford U.	42+3	18
*Bary Silkman	5 9	10 3	London	Hereford U.	18+19	2
Brian Preece				Hereford U.	2	—
*Jim McCafferty	5 7	10 0	Motherwell	Bristol C.	—	—
				Hereford U.	0+3	—
Kevin Sheedy	5 7	9 2	Hereford	Hereford U.	1	—
Peter Spring	5 8	11 0	Glastonbury	Bristol C.	57+5	16
				Liverpool	—	—
				Luton T.	12+3	2
				Hereford U.	5+1	—

HUDDERSFIELD TOWN

Chairman: K. S. Longbottom.
Directors: S. Kinder, O.B.E., E. Simpson, G. Hill.
M. Bland, J. Christie, W. F. Brook.
General Manager: T. D. Johnston.
Secretary: G. S. Binns.
Year Formed: 1908.
Turned Professional: 1908. *Limited Company:* 1908.
Honours: *Football League,* Division 1, Champions:
1923–24, 1924–25, 1925–26; Runners-up: 1926–27,
1927–28, 1933–34. Division 2, Champions: 1969–70;
Runners-up; 1919–20, 1952–53. *F.A. Cup,* Winners:
1922; Runners-up: 1920, 1928, 1930, 1938. *Football
League Cup,* best season: Semi-finalists, 1967–68.
Record Victory: 10-1 v Blackpool, Division 1. Dec. 13th,
1930.

Record Defeat: 0-8 v Middlesbrough, Division 1, Sept. 30, 1950.

Most League Points: 64, Division 2, 1919–20.

Most League Goals: 97, Division 2, 1919–20.

Highest Scorer in Season: Sam Taylor. 35, Division 2, 1919–20; George Brown, 35, Division 1
1925–26.

Most Capped Player: Jimmy Nicholson, 31 (41) N. Ireland.

Most League Appearances: Billy Smith, 520, 1914–34.

Most League Goals in Total Aggregate: George Brown, 142, 1921–29.

Record Transfer Fee Received: £100,000 from Leeds U. for Trevor Cherry, June 1972.

Record Transfer Fee Paid: £65,000 to Manchester U. for Alan Gowling, June 1972.

Managers Since the War: David Steele, George Stephenson, Andy Beattie, Bill Shankly,
Eddie Boot, Tom Johnston, Ian Greaves, Bobby Collins.

Address of Supporters Club: Supporters Club Office 286 Leeds Road, Huddersfield, Yorkshire.

Address of Club Shop or Boutique: The Terriers Souvenir Shop, 286 Leeds Road, Huddersfield.

Leeds Rd., Huddersfield HD1 6PE. Telephone Huddersfield 20335/6. *Ground capacity:* 48,000.
Record attendance: 67,037 v Arsenal, F.A. Cup 6th Rd., February 27, 1932. *Record receipts:*
£17,577.73p v Bolton W., F.A. Cup 4th Rd., Jan. 24, 1976. *Pitch measurements:* 115 yds ×
75 yds.

How to get there: The ground is one mile from the town centre via Corporation buses 40, 41, 42. On match
days special buses run from the centre. By road, the ground can be reached along Leeds Road either from
the town centre or from Leeds.
Match tickets: Admission to all parts is by payment at the turnstiles except for special matches. (tel:
Huddersfield 36100).
Car parking: Ample parking accommodation on all four sides of the ground; in the region of 6,000 cars can
be parked within 200 yards of the turnstiles.
Entertainments/catering facilities: No social club, but there are 11 unlicensed snack bars around the ground.
Club shop: Close to the ground; sells all types of souvenirs (tel: Huddersfield 31028). Open match days.
Handbooks/programmes: Programmes available on subscription from the club shop.
Extra information: In 1952–53 the club fielded an unchanged defensive line-up throughout the season.

Club Colours: Blue shirts with twin white stripes down sleeves, white shorts and stockings.
Change Colours: All yellow.
Club Captain: Rod Belfitt.
Coach: John Haselden.
Physiotherapist: Bryan Edwards.
Club Nickname: 'The Terriers'.

HUDDERSFIELD TOWN 1975–76 LEAGUE RECORD

Match No.	Date	Venue	Opponents	Result	H/T Score	League Pos'n	Goalscorers	Attendance
1	Aug 16	H	Northampton T.	D 1-1	1-0	—	Gray	3595
2	23	A	Watford	W 2-0	1-0	6	O'Neil (pen), Gray	4500
3	30	H	Rochdale	D 0-0	0-0	5		4185
4	Sept 6	A	Scunthorpe U.	W 1-0	1-0	1	Campbell	1992
5	13	H	Lincoln C.	L 0-1	0-1	5		5209
6	20	A	Cambridge U.	D 0-0	0-0	6		3150
7	24	A	Bradford C.	D 2-2	0-1	—	Gray 2	4476
8	27	H	Brentford	W 2-1	0-0	5	Gray, Garwood	4160
9	Oct 4	A	Workington	W 2-0	0-0	5	Maitland, Garwood	1158
10	11	A	Swansea C.	D 1-1	1-1	6	Garwood	3230
11	18	H	Newport Co.	W 2-1	1-0	4	Garwood, Gray	5477
12	21	H	Torquay U.	L 2-3	1-2	—	Belfitt, Garwood	5777
13	25	A	Reading	L 0-2	0-0	9		6679
14	Nov 1	H	Hartlepool	W 2-0	0-0	7	Garwood (pen), Smith	4183
15	4	A	Doncaster R.	L 1-4	0-1	—	Gray	10,650
16	8	A	Stockport Co.	W 1-0	1-0	7	Gray	2789
17	15	H	Darlington	W 1-0	0-0	6	Smith	4133
18	29	A	Barnsley	W 3-2	1-1	5	Lawson 2, Smith	5007
19	Dec 6	H	Exeter C.	L 0-1	0-0	6		4981
20	20	A	AFC Bournemouth	L 0-1	0-1	8		4012
21	26	H	Tranmere R.	W 1-0	0-0	7	Belfitt	6672
22	27	A	Southport	W 2-1	0-0	6	Belfitt, Smith	2546
23	Jan 17	H	Cambridge U.	W 2-0	0-0	6	Smith, Hart	5195
24	27	H	Crewe Alex.	W 1-0	1-0	—	Newton	4459
25	Feb 7	H	Doncaster R.	L 1-2	1-1	7	Gray	6305
26	14	H	Stockport Co.	D 2-2	1-1	8	Newton 2	5307
27	17	A	Torquay U.	W 3-1	1-0	—	Gray 2, Baines	2019
28	21	A	Darlington	W 3-0	3-0	6	Firth, Gray, Sweeney	2052
29	28	H	Reading	W 3-0	2-0	7	Newton, Gray 2	6546
30	Mar 1	A	Rochdale	D 0-0	0-0	—		3791
31	6	A	Hartlepool	D 1-1	0-0	6	Gray	2044
32	9	H	Workington	W 2-0	2-0	—	Hughes (og), Lawson	5010
33	13	H	Swansea C.	W 2-0	0-0	5	Butler, Firth	6393
34	17	A	Newport Co.	W 2-1	1-0	—	Jones, R. (og), Sidebottom	1374
35	20	H	Barnsley	L 1-2	0-2	5	Goldthorpe	10,049
36	23	A	Lincoln C.	D 0-0	0-0	5		11,290
37	27	A	Exeter C.	L 1-4	0-3	5	Sidebottom	3925
38	30	H	AFC Bournemouth	D 0-0	0-0	—		5834
39	Apr 3	A	Northampton T.	D 1-1	0-1	5	Belfitt	7218
40	5	A	Brentford	D 0-0	0-0	—		4410
41	10	H	Scunthorpe U.	D 1-1	0-0	5	Dolan	6502
42	14	A	Crewe Alex.	W 2-0	0-0	—	Belfitt, Newton	2750
43	17	A	Tranmere R.	L 0-3	0-1	5		8308
44	19	H	Southport	L 1-2	1-1	—	Belfitt	6324
45	24	H	Watford	W 1-0	0-0	5	Goldthorpe	3787
46	29	H	Bradford C.	D 0-0	0-0	—		4779

Goalscorers

League (56): Gray 15, Belfitt 6, Garwood 6 (1 a pen), Newton 5, Smith 5, Lawson 3, Firth 2, Goldthorpe 2, Sidebottom 2, Baines 1, Butler 1, Campbell 1, Dolan 1, Hart 1, Maitland 1, O'Neil 1 (pen), Sweeney 1, Own Goals 2.
League Cup (4): Gray 2, Dolan, Campbell.
F.A. Cup (6): Belfitt 2, Gray 2, Baines, Lawson.

League Cup	First Round	Barnsley (h)	2-1
	Second Leg	(a)	1-1
	Second Round	Derby Co. (a)	1-2
F.A. Cup	First Round	Walsall (a)	1-0
	Second Round	Port Vale (h)	2-1
	Third Round	Fulham (a)	3-2
	Fourth Round	Bolton W. (h)	0-1

Taylor	Hutt	Garner	Smith	Baines	Saunders	Gray	O'Neil	Belfitt	Campbell	Lawson	Dolan	Newton	Sweeney	Garwood	Endean	Maitland	Fowler	Simpkin	Poole	Coulson	Goldthorpe	McGifford	Hart	Firth	Sidebottom	Butler	Match No.
1	2	3	4	5	6	7	8	9	10	11																	1
1	2	3	4	5	6	7	8	9	10		11																2
1	2	3	4	5	6	7	8	9	10		11																3
1	2	3	4	5	6	7	8	9	10		11																4
1	2	3	4	5	6	7	8	9	10*		11	12															5
1		3	4	5	6	7	8	10*	9	11		2				12											6
1		3	4	5	6	7	8		10	11		2	9														7
1		3	4*	5	6	7	8		10	11		2	9	12													8
1		3		5	6			8		11	4	2	10	7	9												9
1		3		5	6			8	9		4	2	10	11	7												10
1		3		5	6	7	8	10*			4	2	9	12		11											11
1		3		5	6	7	8	10			4	2	9	12			4*										12
1		3		5		7	8	10			4	2	9	12		11*		6									13
	3	4		5		7	8	10		12	11	2	9*					6	1								14
	3	4			6	7	8	10		12	11	2		9*				5	1								15
1	3	4	5			7	8					2	9					6	10	11							16
1	3	4	5			7	8					2	10	9				6	11								17
1	3	4	5			7	9	11	8			2	10					6									18
1	3	4	5			7	10	11	8			2	9*	12				6									19
1	2	4	5			7	9	11	8			3	10					6									20
1	3	4	5			10	7	9	11	8		2						6									21
1	3	4	5			7	8	9	11	10		2						6									22
1		4	5			7	8	9	11*	10		2						6					3	12			23
1	3	4	5			7	8	9		10	11	2						6									24
1	3	4	5			7*	8	9		10	11	2				12		6									25
1	3	4	5			7	8	9	11	10		2						6									26
1	3	4	5			7	8	9		10	11	2						6									27
1	3	4	5			7	8			10	11	2						6						9			28
1	3	4	5			7	8			11	10	2						6		2*	12			9			29
1	3	4	5			7	8			11	9	2						6					2	10			30
1	3	4		5		7*	8			11	12	2						6					2	10	9		31
1	3*	4		5				8		10	11					12					9		2	7	6		32
1		4		5				8		11		2									9		3	10	6	7	33
1		4		5				8		11		9	3										2	7	6	10	34
1		4		5				8		11		9*	3								12		2	10	6	7	35
1		4		5				8		11		2				7					9		3		6	10	36
1		4		5				8		12	11	2				7					9*		3		6	10	37
1		4		5				8	9	11		2						6					3	7		10	38
1		4		5				8	9	11		2				12		6					3	7*		10	39
1		4		5				8	9	11	10	2						6					3	7			40
1		4		5					9	11*	8	12	2					6					3			10	41
1		4		5					9	11	8	10	2					6					3	7			42
1		4		5					9	8	10*	2				12	11	6					3	7			43
1		4		5				8	9	11	10*	2						6					3	7	6	12	44
		4		5					9					8			11	1	12	2			3	7	6*	10	45
		4		5		6				10		2		7		8		1			9		3	11			46
42	20	16	41	41	17	29	38	28	11	22	29	16	36	12	2	9	6	25	4	2	6	3	17	16	9	9	
									+3s	+1s	+2s		+2s	+6s	+2s						+2s		+2s			+1s	

Player and position	Ht.	Wt.	Birthplace	Clubs	League Appearances	Goals
Goalkeepers						
Terry Poole	5 10½	10 10	Chesterfield	Huddersfield T.	183	—
Richard Taylor				Huddersfield T.	68	—
Defenders						
*Geoff Hutt	5 8	12 0	Hazelwood	Huddersfield T.	245	4
				Blackburn R. (on loan)	10	1
Stephen Baines	6 0	12 12	Newark	Nottingham F.	2	—
				Huddersfield T.	41	1
*Grahame McGifford	5 7	10 7	Wallington	Huddersfield T.	41+1	—
Peter Hart	5 10	11 12	Hexborough	Huddersfield T.	31+2	1
Martin Fowler	5 10	11 8	York	Huddersfield T.	21+5	1
Alan Sweeney	5 5	9 5	Glasgow	Huddersfield T.	37	2
Chris Simpkin	5 11½	12 13	Hull	Hull C.	284+1	19
				Blackpool	31+3	1
				Scunthorpe U.	61	2
				Huddersfield T.	25	—
Arnie Sidebottom	6 1	12 1	Barnsley	Manchester U.	16	—
				Huddersfield T.	9	2
Paul Cooper	5 9	10 6	Birmingham	Huddersfield T.	—	—
Peter Oliver	5 9	10 8	Dunfermline	Hearts	76+2	—
				York C.	41	—
				Huddersfield T.	—	—
Midfield						
*Brian O'Neil	5 8	11 7½	Bedlington	Burnley	231+4	22
				Southampton	148+1	16
				Huddersfield T.	60+1	3
Alan Ogden	5 10	11 11	Thrybergh	Sheffield U.	6+6	—
				York C.	7	—
				Huddersfield T.	—	—
				(contract cancelled Dec 1975)		
Terry Gray	5 8	9 2	Bradford	Chelsea	—	—
				Huddersfield T.	62+12	19
Franny Firth	5 10	11 0	Dewsbury	Huddersfield T.	18+1	2
Terry Dolan	6 1	11 3	Bradford	Bradford C.	—	—
				Bradford P. A.	46+2	—
				Huddersfield T.	157+5	14
Steve Smith	5 9	10 3	Huddersfield	Huddersfield T.	286+9	26
				Bolton W. (on loan)	3	—
Forwards						
Mick Butler	5 9	10 0	Barnsley	Barnsley	118+2	58
				Huddersfield T.	9+1	1
*Rod Belfitt	5 11	11 11	Doncaster	Leeds U.	58+19	17
				Ipswich T.	40	13
				Everton	14+2	2
				Sunderland	36+3	4
				Fulham (on loan)	6	1
				Huddersfield T.	34	8
Mick Fairclough	5 9	10 6	Drogheda	Huddersfield T.	25+10	2
				(contract cancelled Oct 1975)		
*Jimmy Lawson	5 8	10 10	Middlesbrough	Middlesbrough	20+6	3
				Huddersfield T.	236+10	42
Bob Newton	5 11	12 6	Chesterfield	Huddersfield T.	22+3	5
Lloyd Maitland	5 7	11 2	Birmingham	Huddersfield T.	21+6	2
Bobby Campbell	5 11	12 7	Ireland	Aston V.	7+3	1
				Halifax T. (on loan)	14+1	—
				Huddersfield T.	11	1
Wayne Goldthorpe	6 10	12 6	Staincross	Huddersfield T.	6+2	2
Peter Howey	5 4	9 8	Kinsley	Huddersfield T.	—	—

HULL CITY DIV. 2

Chairman: G. H. Christopher Needler, B.A., A.C.A.

Directors: John Needler, S. T. Kershaw, O.B.E., J.P., G. Needler, F.R.I.C.S., J.P., R. E. Chapman, B.Sc., T. G. C. Thomas, M.A., A.C.A., M. J. Kay, Dip.Arch., J.P.

Team Manager: John Kaye.

Assistant Manager: Andy Davidson.

Secretary: M. T. Stone.

Year Formed: 1904. *Turned Professional:* 1905.

Limited Company: 1905.

Previous Grounds: 1904, Boulevard Ground (Hull R.F.C.); 1905, Anlaby Road (Hull C.C.); 1946, Boothferry Park.

Honours: Football League, highest position in Div. 2: 3rd, 1909–10. Division 3(N), Champions: 1932–33, 1948–49. Division 3, Champions: 1965–66; Runners-up: 1958–59. *F.A. Cup,* best season: Semi-finalists, 1930. *Football League Cup,* best season: 4th Rd. 1973–74, 1975–76.

Record Victory: 11-1 v Carlisle U., Division 3(N), Jan. 14th, 1939.

Record Defeat: 0-8 v Wolverhampton W., Division 2, Nov. 4th, 1911.

Most League Points: 69, Division 3, 1965–66.

Most League Goals: 109, Division 3, 1965–66.

Highest League Scorer in Season: Bill McNaughton, 39, Division 3(N), 1932–33.

Most Capped Player: Terry Neill, 15 (59), N. Ireland.

Most League Goals in Total Aggregate: Chris Chilton 195, 1960–71.

Most League Appearances: Andy Davidson, 511, 1947–67.

Record Transfer Fee Received: £200,000 from Manchester U. for Stuart Pearson, May 1974.

Record Transfer Fee Paid: £75,000 to Millwall for Alf Wood, November 1974.

Managers Since the War: Ernest Blackburn, Major Frank Buckley, Raich Carter, Bob Jackson, Bob Brocklebank, Cliff Britton, Terry Neill.

Club Shop: Club Shop, Boothferry Park, Hull.

Boothferry Park, Hull HU4 6EU. Telephone 0482 52195/6/7. *Telegraphic address:* 'Tigers Hull'. *Ground capacity:* 42,000. *Record attendance:* 55,019 v Manchester U., F.A. Cup 6th Rd., February 26, 1949. *Record receipts:* £22,229 v Stoke City F.A. Cup 6th Rd., March 6, 1971. *Pitch measurements:* 112 yds × 75 yds.

How to get there: Buses 55, 57, 43, 48 from coach station, Ferensway, Hull. Nearest railway stations, Hull and Boothferry Park Halt. Special trains on match days from Hull Paragon to Boothferry Park Halt; admittance to ground through turnstiles on station. Ground situated on A63 to the west of the city.

Match tickets: Tickets for League games may be booked two weeks in advance of the match.

Car parking: Official car park at ground for season passholders only. Public car park, Kempton Road park three minutes walk away; coach park in Pickering Road five minutes from ground.

Entertainments/catering facilities: Catering facilities at points around the ground.

Club shop: In the South Stand, open on League match days, and at ticket office on weekdays.

Handbooks/programmes: Programmes available on subscription.

Extra information: The club's 31 wins in 1965–66 was a Third Division record.

Club Colours: Black and amber stripes, white shorts, white stockings.

Change Colours: White shirts, black shorts.

Club Captain: Dave Roberts.

Club Nickname: 'Tigers'.

HULL CITY 1975–76 LEAGUE RECORD

Match No.	Date	Venue	Opponents	Result	H/T Score	League Pos'n	Goalscorers	Attendance
1	Aug 16	A	Luton T.	L 0-2	0-2	—		10,389
2	19	H	Blackpool	W 1-0	1-0	—	Galvin	5304
3	23	H	Bristol C.	W 3-1	2-0	2	Greenwood 2, Fletcher	5076
4	30	A	Oldham Ath.	L 0-1	0-0	9		6365
5	Sept 6	A	Orient	W 1-0	1-0	7	Wood	5194
6	13	A	Nottingham F.	W 2-1	0-1	6	Galvin, Greenwood	12,191
7	20	H	Fulham	L 1-2	1-0	7	Grimes	8471
8	23	H	Notts Co.	L 0-2	0-1	—		8068
9	26	A	Charlton Ath.	L 0-1	0-1	13		10,305
10	Oct 4	H	Southampton	D 0-0	0-0	10		6342
11	11	H	Bristol R.	D 0-0	0-0	10		5642
12	18	A	Portsmouth	D 1-1	0-0	11	Grimes	8155
13	25	H	Bolton W.	D 2-2	2-1	11	Lord, Wagstaff	7369
14	Nov 1	A	Oxford U.	W 3-2	1-0	10	Galvin, Wagstaff, Grimes	4701
15	4	A	Blackburn R.	L 0-1	0-1	—		8816
16	8	H	Chelsea	L 1-2	1-1	17	Grimes	9097
17	15	A	W.B.A.	L 0-2	0-1	18		13,780
18	22	H	Portsmouth	W 1-0	0-0	16	Galvin	4549
19	29	H	Plymouth Arg.	W 4-0	2-0	13	Greenwood 2, Wood, Grimes	5098
20	Dec 6	A	York C.	W 2-1	1-0	12	Fletcher, Greenwood	6657
21	13	A	Bristol C.	L 0-3	0-1	14		10,796
22	20	H	Luton T.	L 1-2	0-1	16	Wood	5449
23	26	A	Sunderland	L 1-3	1-2	17	Hawley	32,210
24	27	H	Carlisle U.	L 2-3	0-3	18	Wood (pen), Hawley	7056
25	Jan 10	H	Nottingham F.	W 1-0	0-0	17	Wood	6465
26	17	A	Orient	L 0-1	0-1	18		3876
27	31	A	Blackpool	D 2-2	2-1	19	Fletcher, Wood	4966
28	Feb 6	H	Blackburn R.	L 0-1	0-1	19		6205
29	18	A	Chelsea	D 0-0	0-0	—		10,254
30	21	H	W.B.A.	W 2-1	1-1	17	Fletcher, Lyall	6137
31	24	A	Notts Co.	W 2-1	1-0	—	Hawley, Sunley	15,293
32	28	A	Bolton W.	L 0-1	0-1	18		21,789
33	Mar 6	H	Oxford U.	W 2-0	0-0	18	Clarke, C (og), Daniel	4820
34	13	A	Bristol R.	W 1-0	0-0	14	Sunley	6236
35	20	A	Plymouth Arg.	D 1-1	1-1	14	McIntosh	10,631
36	27	H	York C.	D 1-1	0-0	13	Daniel (pen)	6306
37	Apr 3	H	Charlton Ath.	D 2-2	0-1	14	Hemmerman, Sunley	4148
38	10	A	Fulham	D 1-1	1-0	14	Hemmerman	5624
39	16	A	Oldham Ath.	W 3-0	1-0	12	Hemmerman, Lyall, Sunley	5546
40	17	H	Sunderland	L 1-4	1-3	13	Croft	21,296
41	20	A	Carlisle U.	D 0-0	0-0	—		8185
42	24	A	Southampton	L 0-1	0-1	14		18,272

Goalscorers

League (45): Greenwood 6, Wood 6 (1 a pen), Grimes 5, Fletcher 4, Galvin 4, Sunley 4, Hawley 3, Hemmerman 3, Daniel 2 (1 a pen), Lyall 2, Wagstaff 2, Croft 1, Lord 1, McIntosh 1, Own Goal 1.

League Cup (7): Greenwood 3, Wood 2, Lord, Hawley.

F.A. Cup (5): Wood 2, Grimes, Hawley, Own Goal 1.

League Cup	Second Round	Preston N. E. (h)	4-2
	Third Round	Sheffield U. (h)	2-0
	Fourth Round	Doncaster R. (a)	1-2
F.A. Cup	Third Round	Plymouth Arg. (h)	1-1
		(a)	4-1
	Fourth Round	Sunderland (a)	0-1

Wealands	Banks	Devries	Croft	Roberts	Galvin	Grimes	Lord	Wood	Wagstaff	Greenwood	Fletcher	McGill	Hawley	Daniel	Stewart	Haigh	Gibson	Lyall	Staniforth	Sunley	Hemmerman	McIntosh	Dobson	Match No.
1	2	3	4	5	6	7	8	9	10	11														1
1	2	3	5	6	7	4	8	9	10	11														2
1	2	3	5*	6	4	8	7	9		11	10	12												3
1	2	3	5	4	6	7	8	9		11	10													4
1	2*	3	5	6	4	7	8	9		11	10	12												5
1	2	3	5	6	4	7	8	9		11	10*	12												6
1	2	3	5	6	4	7	8*	9		11	10	12												7
1	2	3	5	6	4	7*		9		11	10	8	12											8
1	2	3	5	6	4			9		11		8	10	7										9
1	2	3	5	6	4			9	12	11		7	10	8*										10
1	2	3	5	6	12			9	10	11		7	8		4*									11
1	2	3	5	6	4	9	7			10	11	8												12
1	2	3	5	6	4	9	7			10	11	8												13
1	2	3	5	6	4	8	7*	12		10	11		9											14
1	2	3	5	6*	4	7		12		10	11	8	9											15
1	2	3	5		4	8				10	11			9		6	7							16
1		3	5		4	7		9		11		8	10	2		6								17
1		3			4	8		5		10	11		9	2		6	7							18
1		3	5	6	4	8		10		11	9	12		2		7*								19
1		3	5	6	4	8		10		11*	9	12		2		7								20
1	2		5	6	4	8		9		11	10	12		3		7*								21
1		3*	5		4			10		11	9	8		2		6	12	7						22
1			5	6			7	9		11		8	4	2		3		10						23
1			5	6			7	10		11		2	4			3		8	9					24
1		3	5	6	4	7		10			12	9		2				8		11*				25
1		3	5	6	4			9			12	10		2				8	7	11*				26
1		3	5	6	4			10			9*			2	11			7		8	12			27
1		3	5	6	4			9			10	12		2				8*		11	7			28
1		3	5	6	4	7		9			10			2				8		11				29
1		3	5	6	4	7		9			10			2				8		11				30
1		3	5	6	4	7		9			10			2				8		11				31
1		3	5	6	4	7		10			9*	8		2						11	12			32
1		3	5	6	4	7		9*			12	10		2				8		11				33
1		3	5	6	4	7		9						2				8		10	11			34
1		3	5	6	4	7		9*						2				8		10	12	11		35
1		3	5	6	4	7		9			10			2				8			12	11*		36
1		3	5	6	4	7					12	10*		2				8		11	9			37
1		3	5		4	7					12			2				8		10*	9	11	6	38
1		3		6	4*					11	12			2				8		9	10	7	5	39
1		3		6	4					11	12			2				8		9	10	7*	5	40
1		3	4	6			5			11	10			2				8		9	7			41
1		3	5	6						11	10			2	4			8		9	7			42
42	18	38	41	34	37	37	10	28	9	24	20	10	17	27	3	7	6	20	4	15	6	6	3	
			+1s					+2s	+1s	+7s	+4s	+5s						+1s		+4s				

HULL CITY—PLAYERS

Player and position	Ht.	Wt.	Birthplace	Clubs	League Appearances	Goals
Goalkeepers						
Jeff Wealands	6 0½	12 0	Darlington	Wolverhampton W.	—	—
				Northampton (on loan)	—	—
				Darlington	28	—
				Hull C.	147	—
Edwin Blackburn	5 9	10 5	Houghton Le Spring	Hull C.	2	—
Defenders						
Roger DeVries	5 8½	11 5	Hull	Hull C.	177+4	—
Steve Deere	6 0	11 6	Burnham	Norwich C.	—	—
				Scunthorpe U.	232+6	21
				Hull C.	65+1	2
				Barnsley (on loan)	4	—
				Stockport Co. (on loan)	6	—
Peter Daniel	5 8	10 10	Hull	Hull C.	46	2
David Roberts (Wales)	5 11	11 5	Southampton	Fulham	21+1	—
				Oxford U.	160+1	8
				Hull C.	47	—
Paul Haigh	5 10	11 6	Scarborough	Hull C.	8	—
Ian Dobson	5 10	11 1	Hull C.	Hull C.	3	—
Midfield						
Chris Galvin	5 10	12 3	Huddersfield	Leeds U.	7+1	—
				Hull C.	84+3	6
Stuart Blampey	5 8½	11 4½	Hull	Hull C.	61+11	1
George Lyall	5 8	11 2	Wick	Raith R.	27	21
				Preston N.E.	92+15	16
				Nottingham F.	108+8	24
				Hull C.	20	2
Malcolm Lord	5 7½	11 10	Driffield	Hull C.	215+24	17
Stuart Croft	5 11	11 5	Ashington	Hull C.	60+3	2
Dave Gibson	5 7	9 0	Seaham	Hull C.	6+1	—
Vincent Grimes	5 8	11 5	Scunthorpe	Hull C.	70+2	8
Jim McIntosh	5 8	11 2	Forfar	Montrose	15	—
				Nottingham F.	45+8	2
				Chesterfield (on loan)	3	—
				Hull C.	6	1
Forwards						
Jeff Hemmerman	5 11	11 0	Hull	Hull C.	19+9	4
				Scunthorpe U. (on loan)	4+1	1
Gordon Staniforth	5 6	9 12	Hull	Hull C.	6+1	1
*Ken Wagstaff	5 9½	12 10	Longworth	Mansfield T.	181	96
				Hull C.	374+4	174
*John Hawley	5 11	11 2	Beverley	Hull C.	67+7	13
Alf Wood	5 11½	12 2	Macclesfield	Manchester C.	24+1	—
				Shrewsbury T.	257+1	64
				Millwall	99+1	38
				Hull C.	50+2	11
David Sunley	5 9	11 0	Shelton	Sheffield W.	122+12	21
				Nottingham F. (on loan)	1	—
				Hull C.	15	4
Dave Stewart	5 8	9 3	Belfast	Hull C.	3	—

IPSWICH TOWN

President: Lady Blanche Cobbold.

Chairman: P. M. Cobbold.

Directors: W. Kerr, H. R. Smith, J. M. Sangster, K. H. Brightwell, J. C. Cobbold.

Manager: Bobby Robson.

Secretary: D. C. Rose.

P. R. O.: Mel Henderson.

Year Formed: 1887. *Turned Professional:* 1936.

Limited Company: 1936.

Honours: *Football League:* Division 1, Champions: 1961–62. Division 2, Champions: 1960–61, 1967–68. Division 3(S), Champions: 1953–54, 1956–57. *F.A. Cup*, best season: Semi-final, 1974–75.

Football League Cup, best season: 5th Rd., 1966, 1974.

European Competitions: *European Cup*, 1962–63. UEFA Cup, 1973–74, 1974–75, 1975–76.

Record Victory: 10-0 v Floriana, Malta, European Cup, 1st Rd., 1962–63.

Record Defeat: 1-10 v Fulham, Division 1, Dec. 26th, 1963.

Most League Points: 64, Division 3(S), 1953–54, 1955–56.

Most League Goals: 106, Division 3(S), 1955–56.

Highest League Scorer in Season: Ted Phillips, 41, Division 3(S), 1956–57.

Most Goals in Total Aggregate: Ray Crawford, 203, 1958–63, 1966–69.

Most Capped Player: Allan Hunter, 30(36), N. Ireland.

Most League Appearances: Tom Parker, 428, 1946–57.

Record Transfer Fee Received: £90,000 from W.B.A. for Danny Hegan, May 1969.

Record Transfer Fee Paid: £70,000 to Blackburn R. for Allan Hunter, Sept. 1971.

Managers Since the War: A. Scott Duncan, Alf Ramsey, Jackie Milburn, Bill McGarry.

Address of Supporters Club: Same as Football Club.

Address of Club Shop or Boutique: Same as Football Club.

Portman Rd., Ipswich, Suffolk IP1 2DA. Telephone: Ipswich 51306 and 57107. *Ground capacity:* 38,000. *Record attendance:* 38,010 v Leeds U., F.A. Cup 6th Rd., March 8 1975. *Record receipts:* £23,500 v Leeds U., FA Cup 6th Rd., March 8 1975. *Pitch measurements:* 112 yds × 72 yds.

How to get there: The ground is central and only two minutes walk from Ipswich railway station; the town centre is five minutes away. Local buses run past the ground.

Match tickets: All seats sold as season tickets.

Car parking: Large parks in Portman Road, Portman's Walk, and off Princes Street at Greyfriars Park.

Entertainments/catering facilities: 'Centre Spot' bar in Portman Road. Bars ground the ground.

Club shops: Four on the ground stock all types of souvenirs.

Handbooks/programmes: Programmes available on subscription and an Annual is published.

Extra information: When Ipswich won the First Division title in 1962, five of the side – Bailey, Carberry Phillips, Elsworthy, and Leadbetter – had been regulars in the Third Division side of the middle fifties.

Club Colours: Blue shirts, white shorts, and blue stockings.

Change Colours: Yellow shirts, blue shorts, yellow stockings.

Club Captain: Mick Mills.

First Team Trainer: Cyril Lea.

Club Nickname: 'Town' or 'Blues'.

IPSWICH TOWN 1975–76 LEAGUE RECORD

Match No.	Date	Venue	Opponents	Result	H/T Score	League Pos'n	Goalscorers	Attendance
1	Aug16	H	Newcastle U.	L 0-3	0-2	—		27,579
2	20	A	Tottenham H.	D 1-1	0-0	—	Viljoen	28,311
3	23	A	Leeds U.	L 0-1	0-0	22		30,912
4	26	H	Burnley	D 0-0	0-0	—		23,548
5	30	H	Birmingham C.	W 4-2	4-0	17	Johnson, Whymark 2 (1 a pen), Hamilton	22,649
6	Sept 6	A	Coventry C.	D 0-0	0-0	15		17,622
7	13	H	Liverpool	W 2-0	1-0	12	Johnson, Austin	28,132
8	20	A	Manchester U.	L 0-1	0-1	15		50,513
9	23	H	Norwich C.	W 2-0	0-0	—	Beattie, Hamilton	34,825
10	27	H	Middlesbrough	L 0-3	0-1	16		22,334
11	Oct 4	A	Derby Co.	L 0-1	0-0	16		26,056
12	11	H	Stoke C.	W 1-0	1-0	15	Hamilton	21,975
13	18	H	Leicester C.	D 1-1	1-1	14	Whymark	23,373
14	25	A	Manchester C.	D 1-1	1-1	14	Hamilton	30,644
15	Nov 1	H	Aston Villa	W 3-0	1-0	12	Peddelty, Whymark, Hamilton	24,691
16	8	A	Wolverhampton W.	L 0-1	0-0	12		16,191
17	15	H	Q.P.R.	D 1-1	1-0	11	Peddelty	25,540
18	22	A	Leicester C.	D 0-0	0-0	12		20,115
19	29	H	Sheffield U.	D 1-1	0-1	12	Whymark	20,796
20	Dec 6	A	Everton	D 3-3	1-2	12	Lambert, Johnson, Clements (og)	24,601
21	13	H	Leeds U.	W 2-1	0-0	11	Lambert, Peddelty	26,858
22	20	A	Newcastle U.	D 1-1	1-0	11	Talbot	25,098
23	26	H	Arsenal	W 2-0	1-0	11	Woods, Hunter	28,457
24	27	A	West Ham U.	W 2-1	0-0	11	Lambert, Peddelty	32,741
25	Jan 10	A	Liverpool	D 3-3	1-2	9	Whymark 2, Gates	40,547
26	17	H	Coventry C.	D 1-1	1-1	10	Osborne	23,516
27	31	H	Tottenham H.	L 1-2	0-1	10	Johnson	24,072
28	Feb 7	A	Burnley	W 1-0	0-0	8	Beattie (pen)	17,307
29	17	H	Wolverhampton W.	W 3-0	2-0	8	Beattie 2, Whymark	19,293
30	21	A	Q.P.R.	L 1-3	0-0	8	Lambert	22,593
31	Mar 6	A	Aston Villa	D 0-0	0-0	8		32,477
32	13	H	Stoke C.	D 1-1	0-0	9	Osborne	22,812
33	20	A	Sheffield U.	W 2-1	2-1	7	Johnson, Mills	15,220
34	27	A	Everton	W 1-0	1-0	7	Whymark (pen)	22,368
35	31	A	Norwich C.	L 0-1	0-1	—		31,024
36	Apr 3	A	Middlesbrough	L 0-2	0-1	10		15,000
37	7	H	Manchester C.	W 2-1	1-0	—	Lambert, Whymark	21,290
38	10	H	Manchester U.	W 3-0	1-0	6	Lambert, Whymark, Johnson	34,889
39	13	A	Birmingham C.	L 0-3	0-1	—		20,497
40	17	A	Arsenal	W 2-1	0-1	6	Bertschin, Sharkey	26,973
41	19	H	West Ham	W 4-0	2-0	—	Bertschin, Talbot, Whymark, Peddelty	28,217
42	24	H	Derby Co.	L 2-6	2-3	6	Lambert, Whymark	26,702

Goalscorers

League (54): Whymark 13 (2 pens), Lambert 7, Johnson 6, Hamilton 5, Peddelty 5, Beattie 4 (1 a pen), Talbot 2, Osborne 2, Bertschin 2, Viljoen 1, Hunter 1, Austin 1, Woods 1, Gates 1, Mills 1, Sharkey 1, own goal 1.
League Cup (2): Johnson, Hunter.
F.A. Cup (3): Lambert 3.

League Cup	Second Round	Leeds U. (a)	2-3
F.A. Cup	Third Round	Halifax T. (h)	3-1
	Fourth Round	Wolverhampton W. (h)	0-0
		(a)	0-1

Sivell	Burley	Mills	Talbot	Wark	Beattie	Hamilton	Viljoen	Johnson	Whymark	Lambert	Osborne	Cooper	Hunter	Austin	Woods	Peddelty	Gates	Turner	Sharkey	Roberts	Tibbott	Bertschin	Match No.
1	2	3	4	5	6	7	8	9	10*	11	12												1
	2	3	4		6	7	8			11	10	1	5	9									2
	2	3	4		6	7	8	9	10*	11	12	1	5										3
	2	3	4		6	7		9	10	11*	8	1	5	12									4
	2	3	4		6	7		9	10	11*	8	1	5	12									5
	2	3	4		6	7		9	10*	11	8	1	5		12								6
	2	3				7	8	9*	10		4	1	5	12	11	6							7
	2	3			6	7*	8	9	10	12	4	1	5	11									8
	2	3			6*	7	8	9	10		4	1	5	12	11								9
	2	3			6	7	8	9*	10		4	1	5	11	12								10
	2	3				7		9	10		4*	1	5	11	6	8	12						11
	2	3			6	7	8	9	10		4	1	5	12	11*								12
	2	3			6	7	8	9	10		4	1	5	11									13
	2	8	3*			7			10		4	1	5	9	11	6	12						14
	2	3				7		12	10		4	1	5	9*	11	6	8						15
	2	8	3			7		9	10*		4	1	5	12	11	6							16
	2	8	3			7		9	10		4	1	5		11	6							17
	2	8	3			7		9	10		4	1	5		11	6							18
	2	8	3*					9	10	11	4	1	5	12	7	6							19
	2	8	4*	3				9	10	11		1	5		7	6	12						20
	2	8	4	3				9	10	11		1	5		7	6							21
	2	8	4	3				9	10	11		1	5		7	6							22
	2	8*	4	3				9	10	11	12	1	5		7	6							23
	2	8	4	3					10	11		1	5	9	7	6							24
	2	8	4*	3				9	10		7	1	5	12	6	11							25
	2	8	4		6			9	10	11*	7	1	5	12						3			26
	2	3	4*		6			9	10	11	8	1	5		7		12						27
	2	4	6	3				9		11	8	1	5	10	7								28
	2	8	3						10	11	4	1	5	9	7*	6	12						29
	2	4	6	3*				12	10	11	8	1		9	7	5							30
1*	2	3						9	10	11	8		5	12	7	6			4				31
	2	3						9	10	11	8	1	5	12	7*	6			4				32
	2	8	3*					9	10	11	7	1	5	12		6			4				33
	2	3	8					9*	10	11	7	1	5	12		6			4				34
	2	3	8					9	10	11	7*	1	5	12		6			4				35
	2	11	8			7			10*			1	5	9	6		12		4		3		36
	2	8	3					9	10	11		1	5			6	7		4				37
	2	3						9	10	11	8	1	5	12		6	7*		4				38
	2	3						9	10	11	8*	1	5	12		6	7		4				39
	2	3						9	10	11	8	1	5			6	7*		4		12		40
	2	3				7			10	11	8	1	5			6			4			9	41
	2	3	8					12	10	11	7*	1	5			6			4			9	42
2	42	42	19	3	29	18	9	32	40	30	33	40	40	8	24	27	7	—	12	1	2	2	
								+3s		+1s	+3s			+9s	+7s		+6s	+1s	+1s		+1s		

217

IPSWICH TOWN—PLAYERS

Player and position	Ht.	Wt.	Birthplace	Clubs	League Appearances	Goals
Goalkeepers						
Paul Cooper	5 9	10 10	Brierley Hill	Birmingham C.	17	—
				Ipswich T.	43	—
Laurie Sivell	5 8	11 0	Lowestoft	Ipswich T.	103	—
David McKeller	6 1	12 3	Irvine	Ipswich T.	—	—
				Colchester U. (on loan)	—	—
				Peterborough U. (on loan)	—	—
				(contract cancelled April 1976)		
Glenn Ellis	5 10	12 10	Dagenham	Ipswich T.	—	—
Defenders						
George Burley	5 8	10 5	Cumnock	Ipswich T.	93	—
Colin Harper	5 8	10 7	Ipswich	Ipswich T.	143+4	5
Allan Hunter	5 11	12 7	Sion Mills	Oldham Ath.	83	1
(N. Ireland)				Blackburn R.	84	2
				Ipswich T.	186	6
Mick Mills	5 6	10 8	Godalming	Ipswich T.	352+4	10
(England)						
*Ian Collard	5 7	11 7	South Hetton	W.B.A.	63+5	7
				Ipswich T.	82+9	5
				Portsmouth (on loan)	1	—
Leslie Tibbott	5 10	10 6	Oswestry	Ipswich T.	2	—
John Peddelty	5 10	10 12	Bishop Auckland	Ipswich T.	40	5
Dale Roberts	5 8	10 5	Ashington	Ipswich T.	2	—
Kevin Beattie	5 10	12 2	Carlisle	Ipswich T.	145+1	17
(England)						
John Wark	5 8	10 4	Glasgow	Ipswich T.	6	—
Russell Osman	5 9	10 10	Repton	Ipswich T.	—	—
Glen Westley	5 11	11 8	Ipswich	Ipswich T.	—	—
Midfield						
Colin Viljoen	5 8	10 10	Johannesburg	Ipswich T	293+2	46
(England)						
Brian Talbot	5 8	11 9	Ipswich	Ipswich T.	74	13
Roger Osborne	5 9	10 11	Otley	Ipswich T.	46+11	5
Eric Gates	5 5	10 4	Ferryhill	Ipswich T.	7+18	1
Pat Sharkey	5 8	10 7	Omagh	Portadown	N.I.	
(N. Ireland)				Ipswich T.	12+1	1
John Stirk	5 6	9 11	Consett	Ipswich T.	—	—
Clive Woods	5 9	9 10	Norwich	Ipswich T.	93+48	9
Steve Gardner	5 8	11 3	Barnsley	Ipswich T.	—	—
Alec Jamieson	5 7	10 10	Clydebank	Ipswich T.	—	—
Forwards						
Michael Lambert	5 8	10 12	Cambridge	Ipswich T.	172+15	36
Trevor Whymark	5 9	10 5	Norfolk	Ipswich T.	186+5	50
David Johnson	5 10	11 0	Liverpool	Everton	47+3	11
(England)				Ipswich T.	134+3	35
Terence Austin	6 1	11 10	Isleworth	C. Palace	—	—
				Ipswich T.	10+9	1
Robin Turner	5 9	10 8	Carlisle	Ipswich T.	0+1	—
Tommy Parkin	5 7	9 6	Gateshead	Ipswich T.	—	—
				Grimsby T. (on loan)	6	—
Keith Bertschin	6 1	11 8	Enfield	Ipswich T.	2+1	2
David Geddis	5 11	11 2	Carlisle	Ipswich T.	—	—

LEEDS UNITED   DIV. 1

President: The Right Hon. The Earl of Harewood, LL.D.

Chairman: M. Cussins.
Directors: S. Bolton, S. G. Simon, R. R. Roberts, P. A. Woodward.

Manager: Jimmy Armfield. *Secretary:* K. Archer.

Year Formed: 1919, as Leeds United after disbandment (by F.A. Order) of Leeds City 1904.

Turned Professional: 1920. *Limited Company:* 1920.

Honours: *Football League,* Division 1, Champions: 1968–69, 1973–74; Runners-up: 1964–65, 1965–66, 1969–70, 1970–71, 1971–72. Division 2, Champions: 1923–24, 1963–64; Runners-up: 1927–28, 1931–32, 1955–56. *F.A. Cup,* Winners: 1971–72. Runners-up: 1964–65, 1969–70, 1972–73. *Football League Cup,* Winners: 1967–68.

European Competitions: *European Cup:* 1969–70, Finalists 1974–75. *European Cup-Winners' Cup:* Finalists 1972–73. *European Fairs Cup:* 1965–66, 1966–67, 1967–68 (winners), 1968–69; 1970–71 (winners), Finalists 1966–67. *UEFA Cup:* 1971–72.

Record Victory: 10-0 v Lyn Oslo, European Cup, 1st Rd., 1st Leg, Sept. 17th, 1969.

Record Defeat: 1-8 v Stoke C., Division 1, Aug. 27th, 1934.

Most League Points: 67, Division 1, 1968–69 (First Division Record).

Most League Goals: 98, Division 2, 1927–28.

Highest League Scorer in Season: John Charles, 42, Division 2, 1953–54.

Most League Goals in Total Aggregate: John Charles, 154, 1948–57 and 1962.

Most Capped Player: Billy Bremner, 54, Scotland.

Most League Appearances: Jack Charlton, 629, 1953–73.

Record Transfer Fee Received: £100,000 from Birmingham C. for Gary Sprake, Sept. 1973.

Record Transfer Fee Paid: £250,000 to Nottingham F. for Duncan McKenzie, August 1974.

Managers Since the War: Billy Hampson, Willis Edwards, Major Frank Buckley, Raich Carter, Bill Lambton, Jack Taylor, Don Revie O.B.E., Brian Clough.

Address of Supporters Club: Leeds United Supporters Club, Fullerton Park, Elland Road, Leeds 11.

Address of Club Shop: Leeds United Club Shop, Elland Road, Leeds 11.

Elland Rd., Leeds LS11 0ES. Telephone Leeds 716037/8/9. *Telegraphic Address:* 'Football Leeds'. *Ground Capacity:* 50,000. *Record attendance:* 57,892 v Sunderland, F.A. Cup 5th Rd., Replay, March 15, 1967. *Record receipts:* £90,000 v Barcelona, European Cup semi-final first leg, April 9 1975. *Pitch measurements:* 117 × 76 yds.

How to get there: Nearest railway station, Leeds. The city centre is within walking distance from the station and then by Corporation buses to the ground.

Match tickets: Season 1975–76, 8,000 tickets were available for advance sale; this number may be revised for season 1976–77. The number will depend on demand for season tickets.

Car parking: Within one minute of the ground there is a large park owned by the Leeds Greyhound Association; this holds about 1,000 cars. Street parking in the immediate vicinity. Large park on the Beeston Ring Road owned and operated by the club.

Entertainments/catering facilities: Supporters' social club adjacent to the ground. Snack bars around the ground.

Club shop: This operates at the ground next to the Pools Office and stocks all types of souvenirs.

Handbooks/programmes: Both handbooks and programmes are available from the club shop; programmes are available on subscription.

Extra information: In 1968–69, Leeds collected 67 First Division points and were beaten only twice; both these feats are First Division records. The club have a Robotphone Answering System – the Leeds United Information Service: Leeds 702621. New Football League record established in 1973–74 with a 29-game run of matches without defeat from the beginning of the season.

Club Colours: All white.
Change Colours: All yellow.
Club Captain: Billy Bremner.
Coach: Don Howe.

LEEDS UNITED 1975-76 LEAGUE RECORD

Match No.	Date	Venue	Opponents	Result	H/T Score	League Pos'n	Goalscorers	Attendance
1	Aug 16	A	Aston Villa	W 2-1	1-1	—	Lorimer 2 (1 a pen)	46,026
2	20	A	Norwich C.	D 1-1	0-0	—	Cherry	25,301
3	23	H	Ipswich T.	W 1-0	0-0	5	Lorimer	30,912
4	26	H	Liverpool	L 0-3	0-1	—		36,186
5	30	A	Sheffield U.	W 2-0	1-0	5	McKenzie, Clarke	29,966
6	Sept 6	H	Wolverhampton W.	W 3-0	2-0	3	McQueen, Clarke, McKenzie	24,460
7	13	A	Stoke C.	L 2-3	0-2	6	Lorimer 2 (1 a pen)	23,139
8	20	H	Tottenham H.	D 1-1	1-0	6	Lorimer	27,372
9	27	A	Burnley	W 1-0	1-0	4	Cherry	23,190
10	Oct 4	H	Q.P.R.	W 2-1	0-0	4	Clarke, Lorimer	30.943
11	11	H	Manchester C.	L 1-2	0-1	6	Clarke	40,264
12	18	A	Birmingham	D 2-2	2-2	7	Cherry, Hunter	33,775
13	25	H	Coventry C.	W 2-0	0-0	6	Yorath, Clarke	25,946
14	Nov 1	A	Derby Co.	L 2-3	1-2	7	Cherry, McKenzie	33,107
15	8	H	Newcastle U.	W 3-0	2-0	6	McKenze 2, Yorath	39,304
16	15	A	Middlesbrough	D 0-0	0-0	6		33,000
17	22	H	Birmingham C.	W 3-0	1-0	6	Bremner, McKenzie 2	26,640
18	29	H	Everton	W 5-2	3-1	5	Lorimer 2 (1 a pen), Clarke 2, Gray, E.	30,879
19	Dec 6	A	Arsenal	W 2-1	0-0	3	McKenzie 2	36,003
20	13	A	Ipswich T.	L 1-2	0-0	6	McKenzie	26,858
21	20	H	Aston Villa	W 1-0	1-0	5	Clarke	29,118
22	26	A	Manchester C.	W 1-0	0-0	4	Madeley	48,077
23	27	H	Leicester C.	W 4-0	1-0	3	Clarke, McKenzie 2, Lorimer	45,139
24	Jan 17	A	Stoke C.	W 2-0	2-0	2	McKenzie, Bremner	36,906
25	17	A	Wolverhampton W.	D 1-1	1-0	2	McAlle (og)	34,925
26	31	H	Norwich C.	L 0-3	0-1	4		27,254
27	Feb 7	A	Liverpool	L 0-2	0-1	5		54,525
28	21	H	Middlesbrough	L 0-2	0-1	5		32,994
29	23	A	West Ham U.	D 1-1	0-0	—	McKenzie	28,025
30	28	A	Coventry C.	W 1-0	0-0	5	Gray, F.	25,563
31	Mar 2	H	Derby Co.	D 1-1	1-1	—	Gray, F. (pen)	40,608
32	9	H	West Ham U.	D 1-1	0-0	—	Jordan	28,453
33	13	H	Manchester U.	L 2-3	0-2	5	Cherry, Bremner	59,42℃
34	20	A	Everton	W 3-1	0-0	5	Bremner, Jordan, Harris	28,566
35	27	H	Arsenal	W 3-0	2-0	5	Clarke 2, Bremner	26,657
36	31	H	Newcastle U.	W 3-2	2-1	—	Oates (og), Cherry, Harris	32,685
37	Apr 3	H	Burnley	W 2-1	1-1	5	McKenzie, Hampton	25,384
38	10	A	Tottenham H.	D 0-0	0-0	5		40,359
39	14	H	Sheffield U.	L 0-1	0-0	—		22,799
40	17	H	Manchester C.	W 2-1	0-1	4	McNiven, Harris	33,514
41	20	A	Leicester C.	L 1-2	0-0	—	McKenzie	24,240
42	24	A	Q.P.R.	L 0-2	0-0	5		31,002

Goalscorers

League (65): McKenzie 16, Clarke 11, Lorimer 10 (3 pens), Cherry 6, Bremner 5, Harris 3, Yorath 2, Gray, F. 2 (1 a pen), Jordan 2, McQueen 1, |Hunter 1, Gray, E. 1, Madeley 1, Hampton 1, McNiven 1, own goals 2.
League Cup (3): McKenzie, Lorimer, Clarke.
F.A. Cup (1): Clarke.

League Cup	Second Round	Ipswich T. (h)	3-2
	Third Round	Notts Co. (h)	0-1
F.A. Cup	Third Round	Notts Co. (a)	1-0
	Fourth Round	C. Palace (h)	0-1

Harvey	Reaney	Gray, F.	Bremner	McQueen	Cherry	Lorimer	Clarke	McKenzie	Yorath	Madeley	Hunter	Gray, E.	Harris	Stewart	Jordan	Stevenson	Parkinson	Bates	Hampton	McNiven	Match No.
1	2	3	4	5	6	7	8	9	10	11											1
1	2	3	4	5	6	7	8	9	10	11											2
1	2	3		5	6	7	8	9	10		4	11									3
1	2	3	4	5	6	7	8	9	10	11											4
1		3	4	5	2	7	8	9	10	11	6										5
1		3	4	5	2	7	8	9	10	11	6										6
1		3	4	5	2	7	8	9*	10	11	6	12									7
1		3	4	5	2	7*	8	9	10	11	6	12									8
1	2	3	9		6	7	8		10	5	4	11									9
1	12	3	4	5*	2	7	8	9	10	11	6										10
	2	3	4			7	8	9*	10	5	6	11	12	1							11
1	2	3	4			7	8	9	10	5	6	11									12
1	2	3	4	11		7	8	9	10	5	6										13
1	2	3	4	5		7	8	9	10	11	6										14
1	2	3	4	5*	8	7		9	10	6		11	12								15
1	2	3	4		6	7	8	9	10	5		11									16
1	2	3	4		6	7	8	9	10	5		11									17
1	2	3	4		6	7	8	9	10*	5		11			12						18
1	2	3	4		6	7	8	9	10	5		11									19
1	2	3	4		6	7	8	9	10	5		11									20
1	2	3	4		6	7	8	9	10	5		11									21
1	2	3	4		6	7	8	9	10	5		11									22
1	2*	3	4		10	7	8	9		5	6	11	12								23
1	2	3*	4		11	7	8	9	10	5	6	12									24
1	2	3	4		11	7	8	9	10	5	6										25
1	2	3			4	7*	8	9	10	5	6	11				12					26
1	2*	3			4	8	7		10	5	6	11			9	12					27
1	2	3			4*	8	7		10	5	6	11			9		12				28
1	2	3				8	7		10	5	6	11			9			4			29
1	2	3				8	12	7	10	5	6	11*			9			4			30
1	2	3		11		8	7		10	5	6				9			4			31
1	2*	3		11		8	7		10	5	6	12			9			4			32
1		3	4	2	10	8	7			5	6	11			9						33
1		3	4	2	8				10	5	6	11	7		9						34
1	2	3	4		10		8	12		5	6	11	7		9*						35
1	2	3	4		10		8			5	6	11	7		9						36
	2	3	4		10		8	11*		5	6		7	1	9				12		37
1		3	4	2	8				10		6	11	7		9		5				38
1		3	4	2	12		8	9	10		6	11	7*				5				39
1		3	4	2	10		8				6	11*	7		9		5*			12	40
1		3	4	2	10		8			5	6	11*	7		9					12	41
1	2	3*	4				8	12	10	5	6	11	7		9						42
40	31	42	34	10	40	27	35	38	35	39	31	27	9	2	15	—	3	4	—	—	
+1s					+2s	+1s	+1s					+2s	+5s		+2s	+1s	+1s		+1s	+2s	

LEEDS UNITED—PLAYERS

Player and position	Ht.	Wt.	Birthplace	Clubs	League Appearances	Goals
Goalkeepers						
David Harvey (Scotland)	5 11	11 10	Leeds	Leeds U.	177	—
David Stewart	6 1	12 10	Glasgow	Ayr U.	157	—
				Leeds U.	19	—
Glan Letheren	6 1	12 4	Briton Ferry	Leeds U.	1	—
Defenders						
Paul Madeley (England)	6 0	12 13	Leeds	Leeds U.	380+10	23
Paul Reaney (England)	5 10	11 3	Fulham	Leeds U.	502+6	5
Peter Hampton	5 6¼	9 5½	Bishop Auckland	Leeds U.	2+3	1
Gordon McQueen (Scotland)	6 2	13 0	Scotland	St. Mirren	57	5
				Leeds U.	85	3
Norman Hunter (England)	5 11½	12 8	Eighton Banks	Leeds U.	534	18
Byron Stevenson	5 10	10 0	Llanelli	Leeds U.	1+1	—
Frankie Gray (Scotland)	5 7¼	9 13¼	Glasgow	Leeds U.	66+4	5
Midfield						
Trevor Cherry (England)	5 8½	11 2	Huddersfield	Huddersfield T.	184+2	10
				Leeds U.	139+5	10
Billy Bremner (Scotland)	5 5½	9 13	Stirling	Leeds U.	581+1	92
Terry Yorath (Wales)	5 10	10 12	Cardiff	Leeds U.	109+23	10
Mick Bates	5 7	10 7	Doncaster	Leeds U.	106+21	4
Tony Currie (England)	5 11	12 5	Edgware	Watford	17+1	9
				Sheffield U.	313	55
				Leeds U.	—	—
Forwards						
Allan Clarke (England)	6 0	11 1	Willenhall	Walsall	72	41
				Fulham	85+1	45
				Leicester C.	36	12
				Leeds U.	242+2	103
Eddie Gray (Scotland)	5 10	11 5	Glasgow	Leeds U.	233+7	35
Carl Harris (Wales)	5 9	10 8	Neath	Leeds U.	10+7	4
Mick Jones (England)	5 10	11 9	Worksop	Sheffield U.	149	63
				Leeds U. (contract cancelled Oct 1975)	215+4	76
Gary Liddell	5 9	9 11½	Bannockburn	Leeds U.	2+1	—
Peter Lorimer (Scotland)	5 10	11 2	Dundee	Leeds U.	278+14	142
Duncan McKenzie	5 8	11 3	Luton	Nottingham F.	105+6	41
				Mansfield T. (on loan)	6	7
				Leeds U.	64+2	27
Joe Jordan (Scotland)	5 11¾	11 12	Carluke	Morton	7+3	1
				Leeds U.	87+31	22
David McNiven	5 6	11 4	Stonehouse	Leeds U.	0+2	1
Keith Parkinson	5 11	11 2	Preston	Leeds U.	3+1	—
David Thomas	5 8	11 0	Swansea	Leeds U.	0+1	—

Directors: W. S. G. Needham, T. W. Shipman, D. E. Sharp, A. E. Pallett, L. T. Shipman, T. E. Bloor, T. S. Bloor.

Turned Professional and Limited Company: 1894.

Manager: Jimmy Bloomfield.   *Secretary:* J. R. Smith.

Year Formed: 1884.

Previous Grounds: 1884, Victoria Park; 1887, Belgrave Road; 1888, Victoria Park; 1891, Filbert Street.

Previous Name: 1884–1919, Leicester Fosse.

Honours: Football League, Division 1, Runners-up: 1928–29. Division 2, Champions: 1924–25, 1936–37, 1953–54, 1956–57; 1970–71. Runners-up: 1907–08. *F.A. Cup,* Runners-up: 1949, 1961, 1963, 1969. *Football League Cup,* Winners: 1964; Runners-up: 1965.

European Competitions: *European Cup Winners Cup:* 1961–62.

Record Victory: 10-0 v Portsmouth, Division 1, Oct. 20th, 1928.

Record Defeat: 0-12 (as Leicester Fosse) v Nottingham F., Division 1, Apr. 21st, 1909.

Most League Points: 61, Division 2, 1956–57.

Most League Goals: 109, Division 2, 1956–57.

Highest League Scorer in Season: Arthur Rowley, 44, Division 2, 1956–57.

Most Capped Player: Gordon Banks, 37 (73), England.

Most League Appearances: Adam Black, 530, 1919–35.

Most Goals in Total Aggregate: Arthur Chandler, 262, 1923–35.

Record Transfer Fee Received: £325,000 from Stoke C. for Peter Shilton, November 1974.

Record Transfer Fee Paid: £150,000 to Fulham for Allan Clarke, June 1968.

Managers Since the War: Johnny Duncan, Norman Bullock, David Halliday, Matt Gillies, Frank O'Farrell.

Address of Club Shop: City Stadium, Filbert Street.

City Stadium, Filbert St., Leicester. Telephone Leicester 57111/2 (Match information Leicester 539199). *Record attendance:* 47,298 v Tottenham, F.A. Cup 5th Rd., February 18, 1928. *Record receipts:* £23,000 v Arsenal, F.A. Cup 5th Rd., second replay, Feb. 24, 1975. *Pitch measurements:* 112 yds × 75 yds.

How to get there: Corporation buses from Humberstone Gate and Waterloo St. (opposite railway station) in city centre. Nearest station Leicester. Midland Red run bus services to the town centre from outlying districts.

Match tickets: Seats can be booked from two matches in advance.

Car parking: Parking adjacent to the ground is for season-ticket holders only. There is nearby street parking and also a public car park about five minutes walk from the ground.

Entertainments/catering facilities: A private season-ticket members bar in the main stand, and catering bars in all sections of the ground.

Club shop: Situated under the main stand; sells all types of souvenirs.

Handbooks/programmes: Both handbooks and programmes are available from the club shop.

Extra information: A league inquiry after Leicester's record defeat discovered that the players had been celebrating a team-mate's wedding!

Club Colours: Blue shirts with white collar and cuffs, white shorts, white stockings.

Change Colours: Red shirts, white shorts, navy stockings.

Club Captain: Jon Sammels.

Physiotherapist: George Preston.

Club Nickname: 'Filberts' and 'Foxes'.

LEICESTER CITY 1975–76 LEAGUE RECORD

Match No.	Date	Venue	Opponents	Result	H/T Score	League Pos'n	Goalscorers	Attendance
1	Aug 16	H	Birmingham C.	D 3-3	1-1	—	Sammels (pen), Alderson, Roberts (og)	25,547
2	20	A	Manchester C.	D 1-1	0-0	—	Lee	28,557
3	23	A	Newcastle U.	L 0-3	0-2	16		37,471
4	27	H	Stoke C.	D 1-1	0-1	—	Garland	22,878
5	30	H	Liverpool	D 1-1	0-0	18	Weller	25,007
6	Sept 6	A	Arsenal	D 1-1	0-1	16	Sammels	22,005
7	13	H	West Ham U.	D 3-3	3-0	17	Worthington, Sammels 2	21,413
8	20	A	Norwich C.	L 0-2	0-1	18		22,799
9	23	A	Q.P.R.	L 0-1	0-0	—		19,292
10	27	H	Coventry C.	L 0-3	0-1	20		20,411
11	Oct 4	A	Manchester U.	D 0-0	0-0	20		47,878
12	11	H	Middlsbrough	D 0-0	0-0	21		19,095
13	18	A	Ipswich T.	D 1-1	1-1	20	Lee	23,373
14	25	H	Tottenham H.	L 2-3	1-1	20	Weller 2	22,088
15	Nov 1	A	Everton	D 1-1	0-1	19	Lee	24,930
16	8	H	Burnley	W 3-2	2-1	19	Weller, Kember, Garland	18,344
17	15	A	Sheffield U.	W 2-1	1-0	17	Alderson, Rofe	20,165
18	22	H	Ipswich T.	D 0-0	0-0	17		20,115
19	29	A	Aston Villa	D 1-1	1-0	17	Worthington	36,388
20	Dec 6	H	Wolverhampton W.	W 2-0	0-0	17	Weller, Worthington	20,012
21	13	H	Newcastle U.	W 1-0	0-0	14	Weller	18,130
22	20	A	Birmingham C.	L 1-2	0-1	15	Lee	21,890
23	26	H	Derby Co.	W 2-1	2-0	14	Lee, Worthington	26,870
24	27	A	Leeds U.	L 0-4	0-1	15		45,139
25	Jan 10	A	West Ham U.	D 1-1	0-0	16	Lee	24,615
26	17	H	Arsenal	W 2-1	0-0	15	Alderson, Lee	21,331
27	31	H	Manchester C.	W 1-0	0-0	13	Lee	21,723
28	Feb 7	A	Stoke C.	W 2-1	1-1	13	Worthington, Lee	21,001
29	17	A	Burnley	L 0-1	0-1	—		13,516
30	21	H	Sheffield U.	D 1-1	1-0	11	Blockley	18,698
31	25	H	Q.P.R.	L 0-1	0-1	—		24,340
32	28	A	Tottenham H.	D 1-1	0-1	11	Kember	21,427
33	Mar 6	H	Everton	W 1-0	1-0	11	Worthington	18,490
34	13	A	Middlesbrough	W 1-0	1-0	8	Boam (og)	18,000
35	20	A	Aston Villa	D 2-2	1-1	10	Nicholl (2 og's)	24,663
36	27	A	Wolverhampton W.	D 2-2	1-2	9	Sammels (pen), Worthington	18,113
37	Apr 3	A	Coventry C.	W 2-0	1-0	8	Weller, Lee	18,135
38	6	A	Liverpool	L 0-1	0-0	—		35,290
39	10	H	Norwich C.	D 0-0	0-0	9		19,856
40	17	A	Derby Co.	D 2-2	0-1	9	Alderson, Garland	29,085
41	20	H	Leeds U.	W 2-1	0-0	—	Worthington 2	24,240
42	24	H	Manchester U.	W 2-1	1-0	7	Lee, Garland	31,053

Goalscorers

League (48): Lee 11, Worthington 9, Weller 7, Sammels 5 (2 pens), Alderson 4, Garland 4, Kember 2, Rofe 1, Blockley 1, own goals 4.
League Cup (4): Sammels 2 (1 a pen), Garland, Weller.
F.A. Cup (5): Garland 3, Lee 2.

League Cup	Second Round	Portsmouth (a)	1-1
		(h)	1-0 (a.e.t.)
	Third Round	Lincoln C. (h)	2-1
	Fourth Round	Burnley (a)	0-2
F.A. Cup	Third Round	Sheffield U. (h)	3-0
	Fourth Round	Bury (h)	1-0
	Fifth Round	Manchester U. (h)	1-2

224

Wallington	Whitworth	Rofe	Sammels	Blockley	Birchenall	Kember	Alderson	Lee	Garland	Tomlin	Earle	Sims	Cross	Weller	Worthington	Woollett	Glover	Match No.
1	2	3	4	5	6	7	8	9	10	11*	12							1
1	2	3	10		6	4	7	9		11	8	5*	12					2
1	2	3	10		6	4	7	9			8*	5		12	11			3
1	2	3	10		6	4	8	11				5		7	9			4
1	2	3	10		6	4	12	8*	11			5		7	9			5
1	2	3	10		6	4	8	12	11			5*		7	9			6
1	2	3	10			4	8	11				5		7	9	6		7
1	2	3	8			4	12	10*	11			5		7	9	6		8
1	2	3	8			4	10	11				5		7	9	6		9
1	2	3	8		6	4	11	10				5		7	9			10
1	2	3	10			4	8	11				5		7	9	6		11
1	2	3	10			4	8*	12	11			5		7	9	6		12
1	2	3	8	5		4	10	11						7	9	6		13
1	2	3	10	5		4*	8	11	12					7	9	6		14
1	2	3	8	5		4	10	11	9					7		6		15
1	2	3	8	5		4	10*	9	11					7	12	6		16
1	2	3	8	5		4	10	12	9*					7	11	6		17
1	2	3	8	5		4	10	9						7	11	6		18
1	2	3	10	5		4	8	11						7	9	6		19
1	2	3	8*	5		4	10	12	11					7	9	6		20
1	2	3	5	12		4	10	8	9*					7	11	6		21
1	2	3		5		4	10	11			8			7	9	6		22
1	2	3		5		4	10	8	9					7	11	6		23
1	2	3	4	5			8	10	9					7	11	6		24
1	2	3	12	5		4	8	10	9*					7	11	6		25
1	2	3		5		4	10	8	9					7	11	6		26
1	2	3		5		4	8	10	9					7	11	6		27
1	2	3	8	5		4	10		11					7	9	6		28
1	2	3	10	5		4	8	11						7	9	6		29
1	2	3		5		4	10	8	11					7	9	7		30
1	2	3	12	5		4	10	8	11*					7	9	6		31
1	2	3	11	5		4	10	8						7	9	6		32
1	2	3	8	5		4	10*	9	12					7	11	6		33
1	2	3	10	5		4	8	9						7	11	6		34
1	2	3	8	5		4	10	9						7	11	6		35
1	2	3	8	5		4	10	9	12					7*	11	6		36
1	2	3	8	5		4	10	9						7	11	6		37
1	2	3	11	5		4	10	8						7	9	6		38
1	2	3	11	5		4	10*	8	12					7	9	6		39
1	2	3		5		4	8	9	10					7	11	6		40
1	2	3		5		4	10	8	11					7	9	6		41
1	2	3		5		4	10	8	11					7	9	6		42
42	42	42	31	31	7	41	37	34	28	2	3	10	1	38	38	35	—	
	+2s		+1s			+2s	4	+2			+1s	+1s		1	1	+2		

LEICESTER CITY—PLAYERS

Player and position	Ht.	Wt.	Birthplace	Clubs	League Appearances	Goals
Goalkeepers						
Mark Wallington	6 0	12 0	Sleaford	Walsall	11	—
				Leicester C.	78	—
Carly Jayes	6 0	12 6	Leicester	Leicester C.	5	—
Defenders						
Jeff Blockley	6 0½	12 6	Leicester	Coventry C.	144+2	6
(England)				Arsenal	52	1
				Leicester C.	47	1
Steve Whitworth	5 9	11 1	Coalville	Leicester C.	247	—
(England)						
Alan Woollett	5 11	11 3	Leicester	Leicester C.	170+15	—
Dennis Rofe	5 7	10 11	Fulham	Orient	170+1	6
				Leicester C.	150	2
Malcolm Munro	6 0	12 0	Leicester	Leicester C.	69+1	1
Stephen Yates	6 0	13 0	Leicester	Leicester C.	11+4	—
Steve Trice	5 11	11 12	London	Leicester C.	—	—
Tom Williams	5 10	10 4	Leicester	Leicester C.	—	—
Steve Sims	6 0	13 6	Lincoln	Leicester C.	10	—
Midfield						
*Graham Cross	6 0	13 0	Leicester	Leicester C.	496+3	29
				Chesterfield (on loan)	12	—
Jon Sammels	5 9½	11 5	Ipswich	Arsenal	212+3	39
				Leicester C.	183+3	17
Keith Weller	5 10	12 1	Islington	Tottenham H.	19+2	1
(England)				Millwall	121	38
				Chelsea	34+4	14
				Leicester C.	191+1	30
Steve Kember	5 8	10 8	Croydon	C. Palace	216+2	34
				Chelsea	125+5	13
				Leicester C.	41	2
Alan Birchenall	6 0	12 8	East Ham	Sheffield U.	106+1	31
				Chelsea	74+1	20
				C. Palace	41	11
				Leicester C.	145+1	12
				Notts Co. (on loan)	5	—
Andy Gould	5 9	10 7	Leicester	Leicester C.	—	—
Adie Green	6 0	10 9	Leicester	Leicester C.	—	—
Richard Wilcox	5 7	9 6	Leicester	Leicester C.	—	—
Forwards						
Brian Alderson	5 7	10 7	Dundee	Coventry C.	116+11	29
				Leicester C.	37+2	4
Steve Earle	5 9	10 13	Feltham	Fulham	286+6	96
				Leicester C.	56+2	7
Chris Garland	5 11	10 12	Bristol	Bristol C.	141	32
				Chelsea	89+3	22
				Leicester C.	38+2	12
Len Glover	5 9	12 0	London	Charlton Ath.	177	20
				Leicester C.	246+7	38
Robert Lee	6 1	12 5	Leicester	Leicester C.	51+6	17
				Doncaster R. (on loan)	14	4
David Tomlin	5 10	11 9	Nuneaton	Leicester C.	20+7	2
Frank Worthington	5 10½	11 10	Halifax	Huddersfield T.	166+5	42
(England)				Leicester C.	161+1	57
Alan Hoult	5 8	10 8	Burbage	Leicester C.	—	—

LINCOLN CITY   DIV. 3

Chairman: H. W. Dove.
Vice-Chairman: R. Brearley.
Directors: G. Blades, A. C. Davey, D. W. Houlston,
H. C. Sills.
Manager: Graham Taylor.
Secretary: R. Chester.
Year Formed: 1883.   *Turned Professional:* 1892.
Limited Company: 1892.
Previous Grounds: 1883, John O'Gaunt's; 1894, Sincil
Bank.
Honours: *Football League,* highest position in Division 2:
5th, 1901–02. Division 3(N), Champions: 1931–32,
1947–48, 1951–52; Runners-up: 1927–28, 1930–31, 1936–
37. Division 4 Champions 1975/6.   *F.A. Cup,* best
season: 1st Rd. of Second Series (5th Rd. equivalent),
1886–87, 2nd Rd. (5th Rd. equivalent), 1889–90, 1901–02. *Football League Cup,* best season:
4th Rd., 1967–68.

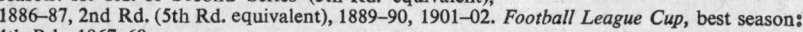

Record Victory: 11-1 v Crewe Alex., Division 3(N), Sept. 29th,1951.

Record Defeat: 3-11 v Manchester C., Division 2, Mar. 23rd, 1895.

Most League Points: 74, Division 4, 1975-76.

Most League Goals: 121, Division 3(N), 1951–52.

Highest League Scorer in Season: Allan Hall, 42, Division 3(N), 1931–32.

Most League Goals in Aggregate: Andy Graver, 144, 1950–55 and 1958–61.

Most Capped Players: David Pugh, 3 (7), Wales; Con Moulson, 3 (6) Eire; George Moulson,
3, Eire.

Most League Appearances: Tony Emery, 402, 1946–59.

Record Transfer Fee Received: £29,500 from Leicester C. for Andy Graver, Dec. 1954.

Record Transfer Fee Paid: £16,666 to West Ham U. for Peter Grotier, September 1974.

Managers Since the War: Bill Anderson, Bob Chapman, Ron Gray, Bert Loxley, David Herd.

Address of Club Shop or Boutique: Red Imps Shop on Ground.

Sincil Bank, Lincoln. Telephone Lincoln 21912 and 21298.   *Ground capacity:* 25,300.
Record attendance: 23,196 v Derby Co., League Cup 4th Rd., Nov. 15, 1967.   *Record
receipts:* £8,567 v Stoke C., League Cup 2nd Rd., Sept. 10 1975.   *Pitch Measurements:*
110 yds × 75 yds.

How to get there: There is a regular bus service from Lincoln Central Station to the ground, although there
are no special buses. Nearest stations are Lincoln Central and Lincoln St Marks.
Car parking: Limited to 150 cars at the ground.
Entertainments/catering facilities: Social club at the ground with light catering before and after the match.
Club shop: Sited on the ground; sells all types of souvenirs.
Handbooks/programmes: Programmes available at each game or by subscription.
Extra information: Frank Keetley scored six times in 21 minutes for Lincoln against Halifax Town, January
16, 1932. Most points, most wins and fewest defeats in a season in division 4.

Club Colours: Red and white striped shirts, black shorts, red and white stockings.
Change Colours: Yellow shirts, blue shorts, yellow stockings.
Club Trainer/Coach: George Kerr.
Physiotherapist: Bert Loxley.
Club Nickname: The 'Red Imps'.

LINCOLN CITY 1975–76 LEAGUE RECORD

Match No.	Date	Venue	Opponents	Result	H/T Score	League Pos'n	Goalscorers	Attendance
1	Aug 16	A	Newport Co.	L 1-3	1-3	—	Freeman	2797
2	23	H	Torquay U.	W 4-2	2-2	13	Ward, Fleming, Branfoot, Freeman	4128
3	30	A	Hartlepool	D 2-2	0-2	14	Smith, Fleming	1895
4	Sept 6	H	Reading	W 3-1	0-1	9	Ellis, Harding, Graham	4327
5	13	A	Huddersfield T.	W 1-0	1-0	4	Fleming	5209
6	20	H	Exeter C.	W 4-1	1-0	2	Freeman, Ward 2, Cooper	5008
7	24	A	Southport	W 2-1	0-1	—	Ward, Freeman	871
8	27	A	Darlington	D 0-0	0-0	2		2580
9	Oct 4	H	Swansea C.	W 4-0	3-0	2	Freeman, Smith, Ward 2	5323
10	11	H	Brentford	W 3-1	2-0	2	Ward 2, Ellis (pen)	6312
11	18	A	Northampton T.	L 0-1	0-1	1		6566
12	21	A	Cambridge U.	W 4-2	3-1	—	Graham, Freeman 2, Ward	3330
13	25	H	AFC Bournemouth	W 1-0	0-0	2	Ellis (pen)	7431
14	Nov 1	A	Crewe Alex.	W 3-2	1-1	1	Graham 3	2707
15	4	H	Tranmere R.	D 2-2	0-1	—	Graham, Ward	11,026
16	8	H	Rochdale	W 2-0	1-0	2	Krzywicki, Graham	7063
17	15	A	Workington	W 3-0	2-0	2	Freeman, Graham, Fleming	1237
18	28	H	Scunthorpe U.	W 3-0	3-0	1	Freeman 2, Graham	8494
19	Dec 6	A	Watford	W 3-1	1-0	1	Harding, Graham 2	4178
20	20	H	Bradford C.	W 4-2	1-2	2	Harding 2, Ward, Ellis	6780
21	26	A	Doncaster R.	W 4-2	2-1	1	Freeman 2, Ward 2	14,353
22	27	H	Barnsley	W 2-1	1-0	1	Ellis (pen), Cooper	12,074
23	Jan 10	H	Hartlepool	W 3-0	0-0	1	Smith, Ellis (pen), Ward	7581
24	17	A	Exeter C.	D 0-0	0-0	1		3858
25	31	H	Cambridge U.	W 3-0	0-0	1	Ward, Freeman, Fleming	7440
26	Feb 6	A	Tranmere R.	L 0-2	0-0	1		4869
27	14	A	Rochdale	D 0-0	0-0	2		2051
28	21	H	Workington	W 4-1	2-1	2	Kirby (og), Neale, Ward, Freeman	7069
29	25	H	Southport	W 6-0	2-0	—	Neale 2, Ellis, Bowery, Woodcock, Ward	8080
30	Mar 6	H	Crewe Alex.	W 2-0	2-0	2	Ward, Smith	7211
31	9	A	Swansea C.	D 2-2	1-2	—	Branfoot, Ward	4000
32	13	A	Brentford	L 0-1	0-1	2		5380
33	17	H	Northampton T.	W 3-1	2-0	—	Fleming, Krzywicki, Smith	13,880
34	20	A	Scunthorpe U.	W 2-0	2-0	2	Ellis, Ward	10,329
35	23	H	Huddersfield T.	D 0-0	0-0	—		11,290
36	26	H	Watford	W 5-1	3-1	1	Freeman 2, Fleming, Branfoot, Smith	8798
37	31	A	Bradford C.	W 5-1	0-0	—	Harding, Ellis (pen), Freeman 2, Neale	4019
38	Apr 3	H	Newport Co.	W 4-1	2-0	1	Ward 2, Harding, Fleming	8178
39	7	A	Darlington	W 2-1	2-0	—	Booth, Smith	10,658
40	10	A	Reading	D 1-1	1-1	1	Ward	15,683
41	12	A	Stockport Co.	W 3-0	2-0	—	Krzywicki, Harding, Smith	3703
42	16	H	Stockport Co.	W 2-0	0-0	1	Freeman, Ellis (pen)	10,906
43	17	H	Doncaster R.	W 5-0	3-0	1	Branfoot, Freeman 2, Harding, Ellis (pen)	14,096
44	19	A	Barnsley	W 1-0	1-0	—	Freeman	8573
45	24	A	Torquay U.	D 2-2	0-1	1	Ellis, Freeman	4151
46	26	A	AFC Bournemouth	D 1-1	1-1		Ward	4284

Goalscorers

League (111): Ward 24, Freeman 23, Ellis 12 (7 pens), Graham 11, Fleming 8, Harding 8, Smith 8, Branfoot 4, Neale 4, Krzywicki 3, Cooper 2, Booth 1, Bowery 1, Woodcock 1, Own Goal 1.
League Cup (9): Ward 4, Graham, Ellis (pen), Harding, Booth, Smith.
F.A. Cup (7): Freeman 2, Ellis 2 (2 pens), Branfoot, Ward, Fleming.

League Cup	First Found	Chesterfield (h)	4-2
	Second Leg	(a)	2-3
	Second Round	Stoke C. (h)	2-1
	Third Round	Leicester C. (a)	1-2
F.A. Cup	First Round	Boston U. (a)	1-0
	Second Round	Mansfield T. (a)	2-1
	Third Round	Aldershot (a)	2-1
	Fourth Round	W.B.A. (a)	2-3

Grotier	Branfoot	Leigh	Fleming	Cooper	Wiggett	Krzywicki	Freeman	Graham	Smith	Harding	Ward	Ellis	Neale	Booth	Sellars	Bowery	Woodcock	Match No.
1	2	3	4*	5	6	7	8	9	10	11	12							1
1	2	3	4	6		7	12	9*	10	11	8	5						2
1	6	3	7				12	9*	10	11	8	5	2	4				3
1	2	3	7*	6			9	12	10	11	8	5		4				4
1	2	3	7	6			9		10	11	8	5		4				5
1	2	3	7	6			9	12	10	11*	8	5		4				6
1	2	3	7	6			9	12	10	11*	8	5		4				7
1	2	3	7	6			9*	12	10	11	8	5		4				8
1	2	3	7	6			9	12	10	11*	8	5		4				9
1	2	3	7	6			12	10*	9	11	8	5		4				10
1	2	3	7	6		11	10	12	8	9*		5		4				11
1	2	3	7	6			10		9	11	8	5		4				12
1	2	3	7	6			12	10	9*	11	8	5		4				13
1	2		7	6			9		10	11	8	5	3	4				14
1	2		7*	6		12	9		10	11	8	5	3	4				15
1	2	3	10	6		7	12	9		11	8*	5		4				16
1	2	3	7	6			10	9	8	11		5		4				17
1	2	3		6		7	8	9	10	11	12	5*		4				18
1	5	3*	7	6			8	9	10	11	12		2	4				19
1	2		7	6			8*	9	10	11	12	5	3	4				20
1	2	3	7	6			9		10	11	8	5		4				21
1	2	3	7	6		11	9		10		8	5		4				22
1	2	3	7	6		11	9		10		8	5		4				23
1	2	3	7	6		11	9		10		8	5		4				24
1	2	3	7	6		11	9		10		8	5		4				25
1	2	3	7	6		11	9		10		8	5		4				26
1	2	3		6		7	9		10	11	8	5		4				27
1	2	3	6*			7	9		10	11	8	5		4	12			28
1	2	3	12	6					10		8	5	4	7*		9	11	29
1	2	3		6					10	11	8	5	4	7		9		30
1	2	3		6		9			10	11	8	5	7*	4	12			31
1	2*	3		6					10	11	8	5	4	7	12	9		32
1	2		7	6		9*			10	11	8	5	3	4	12			33
1	2		7	6		9*			10	11	8	5	3	4	12			34
1	2		7	6		9*12			10	11	8	5	3	4				35
1	2		7	6		12	9		10	11	8*	5	3	4				36
1	2		7	6		12	9*		10	11	8	5	3	4				37
1	2		7	6		9			11	10	8	5	3	4				38
1	2		7	6		9			10	11	8	5	3	4				39
1	2		7	6		9			10	11	8	5	3	4				40
1	2		7	6		9			10	11	8	5	3	4				41
1	2		7	6	12	4	9		10	11	8	5	3*					42
1	2		7	6		9			10	11	8	5	3	4				43
1	2		7	6		12	9		10	11	8*	5	3	4				44
1	2		7	3	6	12	9		10	11	8	5		4				45
1	2		7*	6	3	12	9		10	11	8	5		4*				46
46	46	29	39	45	3	21	30	13	45	36	41	44	22	42	—	2	2	
			+		+	+	+	+		+			+	+	+			
			1s		1s	7s	5s	6s		4s			1s	2s	2s			

229

LINCOLN CITY PLAYERS

Player and position	Ht.	Wt.	Birthplace	Clubs	League Appearances	Goals
Goalkeepers						
Peter Grotier	5 11	12 2	Stratford	West Ham U.	50	—
				Cardiff C. (on loan)	2	—
				Lincoln C.	92	—
Defenders						
Dennis Booth	5 7½	10 5	Stenley Common	Charlton Ath.	66+10	5
				Blackpool	12	—
				Southend U.	77+1	1
				Lincoln C.	104	6
Ian Branfoot	5 10	12 2	Gateshead	Sheffield W.	33+3	—
				Doncaster R.	156	5
				Lincoln C.	133	11
Dennis Leigh	5 8½	10 11	Doncaster	Doncaster R.	33+2	1
				Rotherham U.	154+5	10
				Lincoln C.	120+1	—
Sam Ellis	6 0	13 5	Ashton under Lyme	Sheffield W.	155+2	1
				Mansfield T.	64	7
				Lincoln C.	134	26
Kevin Scott				Lincoln C.	1	—
David Wiggett	6 0	11 12	Sheffield	Lincoln C.	4+2	—
Phil Neale	5 8	10 6	Scunthorpe	Lincoln C.	28+4	4
Midfield						
John Fleming	5 8	10 2	Nottingham	Oxford U.	67+8	2
				Lincoln C.	39+1	8
Peter Sellers			Market Rasen	Lincoln C.	0+1	—
Jackie Gallacher			Wisbech	Lincoln C.	—	—
Terry Cooper	5 9	11 0	Cwmbran	Newport Co.	64+4	1
				Notts Co.	3+6	—
				Lincoln C.	167	7
Forwards						
Alan Harding	5 9	11 0	Sunderland	Darlington	125+4	38
				Lincoln C.	109+4	26
Peter Graham	5 10	10 4	Barnsley	Barnsley	16+3	—
				Halifax (on loan)	6	—
				Darlington	118+1	43
				Lincoln C.	77+11	25
Percey Freeman	6 0½	13 10	Newark	W.B.A.	2	—
				Lincoln C.	76+4	30
				Reading	53+7	13
				Lincoln C.	41+7	26
Dick Krzywicki (Wales)	5 10	11 0	Flints	W.B.A.	51+6	9
				Huddersfield T.	39+8	7
				Scunthorpe U. (on loan)	2	—
				Northampton T. (on loan)	8	3
				Lincoln C.	55+13	11
Dave Smith	5 7	10 7	Thornaby	Middlesbrough	1	—
				Lincoln C.	302+8	46
John Ward	5 8	10 10	Lincoln	Lincoln C.	143+16	68
				Workington (on loan)	9+2	3

LIVERPOOL DIV. 1

Chairman: J. W. Smith, J.P.

Directors: C. J. Hill, E. A. F. Sawyer, S. C. Reakes J.P., H. Cartwright, J. T. Cross, W. D. Corkish, F.C.A.

Team Manager: Bob Paisley. *Secretary:* P. B. Robinson.

Year Formed: 1892. *Turned Professional:* 1892.

Limited Company: 1892.

Honours: *Football League,* Division 1, Champions: 1900–01, 1905–06, 1921–22, 1922–23, 1946–47, 1963–64 1965–66, 1972–73, 1975-76 (Liverpool now have a record number of nine League Championship wins.) Runners-up: 1898–99, 1909–10, 1968–69, 1973-74. 1974-75 Division 2, Champions: 1893–94, 1895–96, 1904–05, 1961–62. *F.A. Cup,* Winners: 1965, 1973-74. Runners-up: 1914, 1950, 1971. *Football League Cup,* best season: 5th Rd., 1972–73, 1973–74.

European Competitions: *European Cup:* 1964–65, 1966–67, 1973-74. *European Cup Winners' Cup:* 1965–66 (Finalists) 1971–72, 1974–75. *European Fairs Cup:* 1967–68, 1968–69, 1969–70, 1970–71. *UEFA Cup,* 1972–73 (winners), 1975–76 (winners).

Record Victory: 11-0 v Strömsgodset, European Cup-Winners' Cup, Sept. 17th, 1974.

Record Defeat: 1-9 v Birmingham C., Division 2, Dec. 11th, 1954.

Most League Points: 62, Division 2, 1961–62.

Most League Goals: 106, Division 2, 1895–96.

Highest League Scorer in Season: Roger Hunt, 41, Division 2, 1961–62.

Most League Goals in Total Aggregate: Roger Hunt, 245, 1959–69.

Most Capped Player: Emlyn Hughes, 40, England.

Most League Appearances: Ian Callaghan, 581, 1960–76.

Record Transfer Fee Received: £240,000 from Coventry C. for Larry Lloyd, August 1974.

Record Transfer Fee Paid: £180,000 to Arsenal for Ray Kennedy, July 1974.

Managers Since the War: George Kay, Don Welsh, Phil Taylor, Bill Shankly.

Address of Supporters Club: 1 Lower Breck Rd.

Address of Club Shop or Boutique: Same as ground.

Anfield Road, Liverpool 4. Telephone 051–263–2361. *Telegraphic address:* 'Goalkeeper Liverpool'. *Ground capacity:* 56,318. *Record attendance:* 61,905 v Wolverhampton W., F.A. Cup 4th Rd., February 2, 1952. *Record receipts:* £79,000 v F.C. Bruges U.E.F.A. Cup Final 1st leg 28 April, 1972. *Pitch measurements:* 110 yds × 75 yds.

How to get there: Buses 17d from Pier Head and 26, 27 from Castle Street. Nearest stations, Bankhall and Kirkdale.

Match tickets: Postal applications 19 days before the match.

Car parking: Limited street parking around the ground. Large privately owned car park in Priory Road within five minutes walk of the ground.

Entertainments/catering facilities: Licensed refreshment bars in all parts of the ground.

Club shop: Main shop run by the Development Association open Monday–Saturday. Small kiosks in the ground open on match days only.

Handbooks/programmes: No handbook. Programmes available on subscription from the secretary.

Extra information: Liverpool's defensive record of only 24 goals conceded in 1968–69 is the best in First Division history.

Club Colours: All red with white facings.
Change Colours: White shirts with red collars and cuffs, black shorts, white stockings.
Captain: Emlyn Hughes.
First Team Trainer: Ron Moran.
Club Nickname: 'Reds' or 'Pool'

LIVERPOOL 1975–76 LEAGUE RECORD

Match No.	Date	Venue	Opponents	Result	H/T Score	League Pos'n	Goalscorers	Attendance
1	Aug 16	A	Q.P.R.	L 0-2	0-1	—		27,113
2	19	H	West Ham U.	D 2-2	1-1	—	Callaghan, Toshack	40,564
3	23	H	Tottenham H.	W 3-2	0-2	13	Keegan (pen), Case, Heighway	42,729
4	26	A	Leeds U.	W 3-0	1-0	—	Keenedy, Callaghan 2	36,186
5	30	A	Leicester C.	D 1-1	0-0	8	Keegan	25,007
6	Sept 6	H	Sheffield U.	W 1-0	0-0	5	Kennedy	37,340
7	13	A	Ipswich T.	L 0-2	0-1	7		28,132
8	20	H	Aston Villa	W 3-0	0-0	4	Toshack, Case, Keegan	42,779
9	27	A	Everton	D 0-0	0-0	8		55,570
10	Oct 4	H	Wolverhampton W.	W 2-0	0-0	6	Hall, Case	36,391
11	11	H	Birmingham C.	W 3-1	1-0	4	Toshack 3	36,532
12	18	A	Coventry C.	D 0-0	0-0	5		20,695
13	25	H	Derby Co.	D 1-1	1-0	5	Toshack	46,324
14	Nov 1	A	Middlesbrough	W 1-0	0-0	5	McDermott	30,952
15	8	H	Manchester U.	W 3-1	1-0	4	Heighway, Toshack, Keegan	49,136
16	15	A	Newcastle U.	W 2-1	1-1	2	Hall, Kennedy	39,686
17	22	H	Coventry C.	D 1-1	1-0	3	Toshack	36,929
18	29	H	Norwich C.	L 1-3	0-0	6	Hughes	34,780
19	Dec 2	H	Arsenal	D 2-2	1-1	—	Neal 2 (2 pens)	27,447
20	6	A	Burnley	D 0-0	0-0	5		18,426
21	13	A	Tottenham H.	W 4-0	1-0	2	Keegan, Case, Neal, Heighway	29,891
22	20	H	Q.P.R.	W 2-0	1-0	1	Toshack, Neal (pen)	39,182
23	26	A	Stoke C.	D 1-1	1-0	1	Toshack	32,092
24	27	H	Manchester C.	W 1-0	0-0	1	Cormack	53,386
25	Jan 10	H	Ipswich T.	D 3-3	2-1	3	Keegan 2, Case	40,547
26	17	A	Sheffield U.	D 0-0	0-0	3		31,255
27	31	A	West Ham U.	W 4-0	0-0	2	Toshack 3, Keegan	26,741
28	Feb 7	H	Leeds U.	W 2-0	1-0	1	Keegan, Toshack	54,525
29	18	A	Manchester U.	D 0-0	0-0	—		59,709
30	21	H	Newcastle U.	W 2-0	1-0	1	Keegan, Case	43,404
31	24	A	Arsenal	L 0-1	0-0	—		36,127
32	28	A	Derby Co.	D 1-1	0-0	1	Kennedy	32,800
33	Mar 6	A	Middlesbrough	L 0-2	0-2	2		41,391
34	13	A	Birmingham C.	W 1-0	0-0	2	Neal (pen)	31,397
35	20	A	Norwich C.	W 1-0	0-0	3	Fairclough	29,013
36	27	H	Burnley	W 2-0	1-0	4	Fairclough 2	36,708
37	Apr 3	H	Everton	W 1-0	0-0	2	Fairclough	54,632
38	6	H	Leicester C.	W 1-0	0-0	2	Keegan	35,290
39	10	A	Aston Villa	D 0-0	0-0	2		44,250
40	17	H	Stoke C.	W 5-3	2-1	1	Neal (pen), Toshack, Kennedy, Hughes, Fairclough	44,069
41	19	A	Manchester C.	W 3-0	0-0	—	Heighway, Fairclough 2	50,439
42	May 4	A	Wolverhampton W.	W 3-1	0-1	—	Keegan, Toshack, Kennedy	48,900

Goalscorers

League (66): Toshack 16, Keegan 12 (1 a pen), Fairclough 7, Case 6, Kennedy 6, Neal 6 (5 pens), Heighway 4, Callaghan 3, Hall 2, Hughes 2, McDermott 1, Cormack 1.
League Cup (2): Lindsay, Case.
F.A. Cup (2): Keegan, Toshack.

League Cup	Second Round	York C. (a)	1-0
	Third Round	Burnley (h)	1-1
		(a)	0-1
F.A. Cup	Third Round	West Ham U. (a)	2-0
	Fourth Round	Derby Co. (a)	0-1

Clemence	Neal	Jones	Thompson	Cormack	Hughes	Keegan	McDermott	Heighway	Toshack	Callaghan	Case	Boersma	Hall	Kennedy	Lindsay	Smith	Fairclough	Kettle	Match No.
1	2	3	4	5	6	7	8	9	10	11									1
1	2	3	4	5	6	7	8	9	10	11									2
1	2	3	4	5	6	7	8	9	10		11								3
1	2	3	4	5	6	7	8			11		9*	12	10					4
1	2	3*	4	5	6	7	8	9		11			12	10					5
1	2		4	5	6	7	8	9		11				10	3				6
1	2	3		5	6	7	8	9		11				10		4			7
1	2		4	5	6	7		9	10	11			8		3				8
1	2		4	5	6	7		9	10	11			8		3				9
1	2		4	5	6	7			10	11	9		8		3				10
1	2		4	12	6	7		9	10	11	5*		8		3				11
1	2		4	5	6	7		9	10	11			8		3				12
1	2	3	4	5	6*	7		9	10	11	12		8						13
1	2	3	4			7	12		10	11	8*		6	5				9	14
1	2	3	4		6	7		9	10	11			8	5					15
1	2	3	4		6	7		9	10	11			8	5					16
1	2	3	4		6			9	10	11	7		8	5					17
1	3		4		6	7		9	10	11			8	5		2			18
1	2		4		6	7		9	10	11			8	5			3		19
1	2	3	4		6	7		9	10	11	8			5					20
1	3		4	5*	6	7		9	10	11	8					2	12		21
1	3		4	5	6	7		9	10	11	8					2			22
1	3		4	5*	6	7		9	10	11	8		12			2			23
1	3		4	5	6	7		9	10	11	8					2			24
1	3		4		6	7		9	10	11	8			5		2			25
1	3		4		6	7		9	10	11	8*			5		2	12		26
1	3		4		6	7		9	10	11	8			5		2			27
1	3		4		6	7	12	9	10*	11	8			5		2			28
1	3		4		6	7		9	10	11	8			5		2			29
1	3		4		6	7		9	10	11	8			5		2*	12		30
1	3	2	4		6	7		9	10	11	8			5					31
1	3		4		6	7		9		11	8			5		2	10		32
1	3		4		6	7		9		11	8			5		2	10		33
1	3		4		6	7		9	10	11	8			5		2			34
1	3		4		6	7		9		11	8			5		2	10		35
1	3		4		6	7		9*	10	11	8			5		2	12		36
1	3		4		6	7		9	10*	11	8			5		2	12		37
1	3		4		6	7		9	10	11	8*			5		2	12		38
1	3		4		6	7		9	10*	11	8			5		2	12		39
1	3		4		6	7		9	10	11	8*			5		2	12		40
1	3		4		6	7		9	10	11				5		2	8		41
1	3		4		6	7		9	10	11	8*			5		2	12		42
42	42	13	41	16	41	41	7	39	35	40	27	1	12	29	6	24	5	1	
			+		+						+	+	+			+			
			1s		2s						2s	1s	1s			9s			

LIVERPOOL—PLAYERS

Player and position	Ht.	Wt.	Birthplace	Clubs	League Appearances	Goals
Goalkeepers						
Ray Clemence (England)	5 11½	12 0	Skegness	Scunthorpe U.	48	—
				Liverpool	264	—
Peter McDonnell	6 1	12 1	Bury	Bury	1	—
				Liverpool	—	—
Defenders						
Joe Jones (Wales)	5 10	11 1	Llandudno	Wrexham	98	2
				Liverpool	13	—
Brian Kettle	5 9	10 7	Prescot	Liverpool	1	—
Alec Lindsay (England)	5 8	10 10	Bury	Bury	126	14
				Liverpool	167+2	12
Phil Neal (England)	5 11	10 12	Irchester	Northampton T.	184+4	29
				Liverpool	65	6
Tommy Smith (England)	5 10½	11 7	Liverpool	Liverpool	429	35
Phil Thompson (England)	6 0	10 7	Liverpool	Liverpool	120+3	2
Emlyn Hughes (England)	5 10½	11 13	Barrow	Blackpool	27+1	—
				Liverpool	377	34
Jeff Ainsworth	5 9	11 0	Liverpool	Liverpool	—	—
Colin Irwin	6 0	11 0	Liverpool	Liverpool	—	—
Ray Jones	5 10	11 7	Liverpool	Liverpool	—	—
Clifford Woof	5 10	11 7	Liverpool	Liverpool	—	—
Max Thompson	6 1	12 10	Liverpool	Liverpool	1	—
Midfield						
Ian Callaghan (England)	5 7	11 1	Liverpool	Liverpool	579+2	48
John McLaughlin	5 8	10 3	Liverpool	Liverpool	38+2	2
				Portsmouth (on loan)	5	—
				(Contract cancelled April 1976)		
Brian Hall	5 7	10 6	Glasgow	Liverpool	140+14	15
Peter Cormack (Scotland)	5 8	10 12	Edinburgh	Hibernian	182	75
				Nottingham F.	74	15
				Liverpool	119+6	21
Terry McDermott	5	10 10	Kirby	Bury	83+7	8
				Newcastle U.	55+1	6
				Liverpool	21+3	3
Ray Kennedy (England)	5 11	13 4	Seaton Delavel	Arsenal	156+2	53
				Liverpool	52+3	11
Forwards						
Steve Heighway (Eire)	5 10½	11 7	Dublin	Liverpool	213+8	32
Kevin Keegan (England)	5 8	10 10	Armthorpe	Scunthorpe U.	120+4	18
				Liverpool	192	56
Kevin Kewley	5 8	10 7	Liverpool	Liverpool	—	—
John Toshack (Wales)	6 0	11 7	Cardiff	Cardiff C.	159+2	74
				Liverpool	145+2	64
Jimmy Case	5 9	11 7	Liverpool	Liverpool	28	6
*Derek McClatchey	5 8	10 7	Whiston	Liverpool	—	—
				Southport (on loan)	2+1	—
Thomas Tynan	5 8	10 7	Liverpool	Liverpool	—	—
				Swansea (on loan)	6	2
Alan Waddle	6 3	12 12	Newcastle	Halifax T.	33+6	4
				Liverpool	11+5	1
David Fairclough	5 8	11 0	Liverpool	Liverpool	5+9	7
Trevor Birch	5 11	11 7	Ormskirk	Liverpool	—	—
Sammy Lee	5 7	10 7	Liverpool	Liverpool	—	—
William McClure	5 9	11 0	Liverpool	Liverpool	—	—

LUTON TOWN

DIV. 2

President: T. Hodgson.

Chairman: D. Mortimer.

Directors: H. Richardson, R. J. Smith, E. S. Pearson, R. L. Banks, J. R. Yates.

Secretary: D. G. Lygo, A.C.M.A.

Team Manager: Harry Haslam.

Year Formed: 1885. *Turned Professional:* 1890.

Limited Company: 1897.

Previous Grounds: 1885, Excelsior, Dallow Lane; 1897, Dunstable Road; 1905, Kenilworth Road.

Honours: Football League, highest position in Division 1: 8th, 1957–58. Division 2, Runners-up: 1954–55, 1973–74. Division 3, Runners-up: 1969–70. Division 4, Champions: 1967–68. Division 3(S), Champions: 1936–37; Runners-up: 1935–36. *F.A. Cup,* best season: Runners-up: 1959. *Football League Cup,* best season: 4th Rd., 1963.

© L.T.F.C. 1972

Record Victory: 12-0 v Bristol R., Division 3(S), Apr. 13th, 1936.

Record Defeat: 1-9 v Swindon T., Division 3(S), Aug. 28th, 1920.

Most League Points: 66, Division 4, 1967–68 (equalled Division 4 record).

Most League Goals: 103, Division 3(S), 1936–37.

Highest League Scorer in Season: Joe Payne, 55, Division 3(S), 1936–37.

Most Goals in Total Aggregate: 243, Gordon Turner, 1949–64.

Most Capped Player: George Cummins, 19, Eire.

Most League Appearances: Bob Morton, 494, 1948–64.

Record Transfer Fee Received: £180,000 from Newcastle U. for Malcolm Macdonald, May 1971.

Record Transfer Fee Paid: £100,000 to Burnley for Alan West, Oct. 1973, and to Chester for Paul Futcher, May 1974.

Managers Since the War: George Martin, Dally Duncan, Syd Owen, Sam Bartram, Bill Harvey, Allan Brown, Alec Stock.

Address of Supporters Club: Bobbers Club, Beech Hill Path, Luton.

70–72 Kenilworth Rd. Luton. Telephone Luton 411622. *Telegraphic Address:* 'Football, Luton'. *Ground capacity:* 25,000 (17,000 covered). *Record attendance:* 30,069 v Blackpool F.A. Cup 6th Rd. Replay, March 4, 1959. *Record receipts:* £16,100 v Chelsea Div. 1, Jan. 11 1975. *Pitch measurements:* 112 yds × 72 yds.

How to get there: Nearest railway station, Luton (six minutes walk). There is also a frequent bus service to and from the town centre to the ground, but the ground is central.

Match tickets: Seats can be booked one month before the game.

Car parking: Ample parking facilities adjacent to the ground entrance in Maple Road.

Entertainments/catering facilities: Licensed bars and refreshment bars on ground.

Club shop: Sells all types of souvenirs.

Handbooks/programmes: Handbooks and programmes can be obtained from club shop.

Extra information: Joe Payne scored 10 goals against Bristol Rovers in April 1936, a record individua score in a Football League match.

Club Colours: Orange shirt with one navy and one white vertical stripe on left side. Navy blue shorts. Orange stockings.
Change Colours: White shirts, navy shorts, white stockings.
Club Captain: Alan West.
First Team Trainer: Reg Game.
Club Nickname: 'Hatters'.

LUTON TOWN 1975–76 LEAGUE RECORD

Match No.	Date	Venue	Opponents	Result	H/T Score	League Pos'n	Goalscorers	Atten-dance
1	Aug 16	H	Hull C.	W 2-0	2-0	—	Futcher, R., King	10,389
2	23	A	W.B.A.	L 0-1	0-0	18		13,875
3	30	H	Chelsea	W 3-0	1-0	8	Anderson, Buckley (pen) Futcher, R.	19,024
4	Sept 6	A	Portsmouth	W 2-0	1-0	6	Alston, King	9835
5	13	H	Bolton W.	L 0-2	0-1	9		11,217
6	20	A	Notts Co.	L 0-1	0-0	11		11,173
7	24	H	Plymouth Arg.	D 1-1	1-0	—	Husband	9226
8	27	H	Blackburn R.	D 1-1	0-0	10	Husband	8458
9	Oct 4	A	Blackpool	L 2-3	1-1	13	Anderson, Spiring	7854
10	11	A	Carlisle U.	D 1-1	1-1	11	Seasman	6621
11	18	H	Fulham	W 1-0	1-0	10	Chambers	14,086
12	21	A	Nottingham F.	D 0-0	0-0	—		12,290
13	25	A	Sunderland	L 0-2	0-0	10		28,338
14	Nov 1	H	Bristol C.	D 0-0	0-0	12		11,466
15	4	H	York C.	W 4-0	1-0	—	Husband, West, King, Anderson	7982
16	8	A	Southampton	L 1-3	0-2	11	John Ryan	13,885
17	15	H	Oldham Ath.	L 2-3	1-2	15	Husband, Chambers	8237
18	22	A	Fulham	L 0-2	0-1	17		9626
19	29	H	Orient	W 1-0	1-0	15	Husband	7897
20	Dec 3	A	Charlton Ath.	W 5-1	1-1	13	Anderson 2, Husband 2, Chambers	8703
21	13	H	W.B.A.	W 2-1	1-0	10	King, Aston	10,203
22	20	A	Hull City	W 2-1	1-0	10	Husband, King	5449
23	26	H	Oxford U.	W 3-2	2-0	9	Futcher, R. 2, King	13,111
24	27	A	Bristol R.	W 1-0	0-0	6	King	11,044
25	Jan 17	H	Portsmouth	W 3-1	2-0	8	Faulkner, King, Futcher, R.	10,464
26	27	A	Bolton W.	L 0-3	0-3	—		21,358
27	31	H	Nottingham F.	D 1-1	0-0	7	Futcher, R.	8503
28	Feb 7	A	York C.	W 3-2	2-1	7	Chambers, Futcher, R., Fuccillo	3132
29	21	A	Oldham Ath.	D 1-1	0-1	7	Husband	8808
30	24	A	Plymouth Arg.	L 0-3	0-1	—		13,927
31	28	H	Sunderland	W 2-0	0-0	7	Moncur (og), Futcher R.	15,338
32	Mar 2	H	Southampton	W 1-0	0-0	—	Husband	13,737
33	6	A	Bristol C.	L 0-3	0-0	7		15,870
34	13	H	Carlisle U.	W 3-0	1-0	6	Husband 2, King	8856
35	20	A	Orient	L 0-3	0-2	7		5544
36	27	H	Charlton Ath.	D 1-1	1-0	5	John Ryan	9947
37	Apr 3	A	Blackburn R.	L 0-3	0-1	6		7895
38	10	H	Notts Co.	D 1-1	1-0	8	West	8277
39	16	A	Chelsea	D 2-2	1-1	8	Husband, Chambers	19,878
40	17	A	Oxford U.	W 3-1	1-1	7	Buckley, Fuccillo, Husband	7633
41	19	H	Bristol R.	W 3-1	0-1	—	Price, Chambers, Hill	7646
42	24	H	Blackpool	W 3-0	2-0	7	Futcher, R. 2, Fuccillo	8757

Goalscorers

League (61): Husband 14, Futcher, R. 10, King 9, Chambers 6, Anderson 5, Fuccillo 3, Buckley 2 (1 a pen), John Ryan 2, West 2, Alston 1, Aston 1, Faulkner 1, Hill 1, Price 1, Seasman 1, Spiring 1, Own Goal 1.

League Cup (1): Futcher, R.

F.A. Cup (2): Futcher, R., Chambers.

League Cup	Second Round	Darlington (a)	1-2
F.A. Cup	Third Round	Blackburn R.	2-0
	Fourth Round	Norwich C. (a)	0-2

Barber	Ryan, John	Buckley	Faulkner	Litt	Anderson	King	West	Alston	Futcher, R.	Aston	Futcher, P.	Chambers	Spiring	Ryan, Jim	Husband	Seasman	Thomson	Pollock	Price	Fuccillo	Hill	Jones	Match No.
1	2	3	4	5	6	7	8	9	10	11													1
1	2	3	5		4	7	10	8	9	11	6												2
1	2	3	5		4	7	10*	8	9	11	6	12											3
1	2	3	5		4	7	11		9		6	8	10										4
1	2	3	6		4	7	9	10	11	5		8											5
1	2	3	5		4	7	9	10	11*		6	8	12										6
1	2	3	5		4	7	9				6	10		8	11								7
1	2	3	5		4	10	9				6			7	8	11							8
1	2	3	5		4	10	8				6	12	9	7	11*								9
1	2		5		4	12	9				6	10	8*	7	11		3						10
1	2		5		4	12	9				6	10	8	7	11*		3						11
1	2		5		4	11	9				6	10	8	7			3						12
1	2		5		4	12	10	11*			6	8		7		9	3						13
1	2		5		4	7	10	11			6	9		8*	12		3						14
1	2		5		9	8	10	11			6	4			7		3						15
1	2		5		9	8	10	11			6	4		12	7*		3						16
1	2		5			7	10	9*	11		6	4		12	8		3						17
1	2		5			7	10		11		6	4		8	9		3						18
1	2	3	5		8*	10		11			6	4		12	7		9						19
1	2	3	5	8		7	10	11			6	4			9								20
1	2	3	5			7	10	9	11		6	4*		12	8								21
1	2	3	5			7	8	10	11		6	4			9								22
1	2	3	5			8	10		9	11	6	4			7								23
1	2	3	5			8	10		9	11	6	4			7								24
1	2	3	5			8	10		9	11	6	4			7								25
1	2	3	5			8	10		9	11	6	4		7									26
1	2	3	5			8	10		9	11	6	4			7								27
1	2	3				8	10		9		6	4			11				5	7			28
1	2	3	5			8	10		12		6	4			7			9*		11			29
1	2	3	5*			8	10		11		6	4			7			12		9			30
1	2	3	5			8	10		9		6	4			7					11			31
1	2	3	5			8	10		9		6	4			7					11			32
1	2	3	5			8	10		9	12	6	4			7					11*			33
1	2	3				7	10		9	11	6				8					4			34
1	2	3	5*			7	10		9	11	6				8			12		4			35
1	2	3				7	10		9	11	6				8				5	4			36
1	2	3					10		9	11	6	12	8*		7			4	5				37
1	2	3					10		9	11	6	7			8				5	4			38
1	2	3					10		9	11	6	4			7				5	8			39
1	2	3					10		9	11*	6	7			8			12	5	4			40
1	11	3	5*				10		9		6	4			7				2	8	12		41
1		3					10		9		6	4			8				2	7	11	5	42
42	41	33	35	1	17	30	36	8	31	28	41	30	7	12	28	6	9	3	8	14	1	1	
					+2s	+1s				+2s		+3s	+1s	+3s	+2s		+3s			+1s			

LUTON TOWN—PLAYERS

Player and position	Ht.	Wt.	Birthplace	Clubs	League Appearances	Goals
Goalkeepers						
Keith Barber	5 11	10 12	London	Luton T.	127	—
Graham Horn	6 1	12 5	London	Arsenal	—	—
				Porstmouth (on loan)	22	—
				Luton T.	58	—
				Brentford (on loan)	3	—
				(contract cancelled April 1976)		
Defenders						
Paul Price	5 11	11 12	St Albans	Luton T.	8+1	1
John Ryan	5 10	12 6	London	Fulham	41+4	1
				Luton T.	271+3	10
Bobby Thomson (England)	5 11¾	12 2	Smethwick	Wolverhampton W.	277	3
				Birmingham C.	62+1	—
				Walsall (on loan)	9	1
				Luton T.	110	1
				(contract cancelled April 1976)		
John Faulkner	6 0	12 3	Orpington	Leeds U.	2	—
				Luton T.	138	4
Steve Litt	6 1	13 0	Carlisle	Blackpool	—	—
				Luton T.	15	—
				Arsenal (on loan)	—	—
				(contract cancelled April 1976)		
*Alex Malcolm	5 10	11 3	Hamilton	Luton T.	—	—
Paul Futcher	5 10	10 6	Chester	Chester	20	—
				Luton T.	60	—
Stephen Buckley	5 11	12 4	Brinsley	Luton T.	57	2
Graham Jones	6 0	12 7	Worsley	Luton T.	1	—
Wayne Morgan	5 7	10 0	Pirton	Luton T.	—	—
Peter Mead	5 6	10 1	Luton T.	Luton T.	—	—
Midfield						
Peter Anderson	5 10	11 3	Hendon	Luton T.	178+3	34
				(transferred to Royal Antwerp Dec. 1975)		
Maitland Pollock	5 8	11 0	Dumfries	Walsall	1+1	—
				Luton T.	3+3	—
Brian Chambers	5 10	10 12	Newcastle	Sunderland	53+10	5
				Arsenal	1	—
				Luton T.	36+3	6
Pasqualle Fuccillo	5 11	11 4	Bedford	Luton T.	14+1	3
Ricky Hill	5 9	11 10	London	Luton T.	1+1	1
Tim Smith	5 7	11 3	Gloucester	Luton T.	—	—
Alan West	5 8½	10 7½	Hyds	Burnley	41+4	3
				Luton T.	111+1	4
Forwards						
Gordon Hindson	5 9	11 4	Durham	Newcastle U.	7	1
				Luton T.	62+6	3
				Carlisle U. (on loan)	1+2	—
				Blackburn R. (on loan)	10	—
				(contract cancelled April 1976)		
Jimmy Husband	5 8	11 0	Newcastle	Everton	158+7	44
				Luton T.	82+2	25
Jim Ryan	5 9	10 11	Stirling	Manchester U.	21+3	4
				Luton T.	163+12	21
Ron Futcher	5 10	10 3	Chester	Chester	4	—
				Luton T.	47+1	17
John Aston	5 9½	11 6	Manchester	Manchester U.	139+17	25
				Luton T.	135+2	21
Ian Donnelly	5 8	11 12	Hitchin	Luton T.	—	—
Sandor Simon	5 8	11 0	Rawtenshall	Luton T.	—	—

MANCHESTER CITY

Chairman: P. J. Swales.

Vice-Chairman: S. H. Cussons.

Directors: S. Rose, A. E. Alexander, J. J. H. Humphreys, R. Harris, J. B. Muir, I. L. G. Niven.

Secretary: J. B. Halford

Manager: Tony Book.

Chief Coach: Bill Taylor

Year Formed: 1887 as Ardwick F.C.; 1895 as Manchester City.

Limited Company: 1894.

Turned Professional: 1887 as Ardwick F.C.

Previous Names: 1887–94, Ardwick F.C. (Formed through the amalgamation of West Gorton and Gorton Athletic, the latter having been formed in 1880.)

Previous Grounds: 1880–81, Clowes Street; 1881–82, Kirkmanshulme Cricket Ground; 1882–84, Queens Road; 1884–87, Pink Bank Lane; 1887–94, Hyde Road; (1894–1923, as City); 1923. Maine Rd.

Honours: *Football League,* Division 1, Champions: 1936–37, 1967–68; Runners-up: 1903–04, 1920–21. Division 2, Champions: 1898–99, 1902–03, 1909–10, 1927–28, 1946–47, 1965–66; Runners-up: 1895–96, 1950–51. *F.A. Cup,* Winners: 1904, 1934, 1956, 1969; Runners-up: 1926, 1933, 1955. *Football League Cup,* Winners: 1970, 1976. Finalists: 1973–74. **European Competitions:** *European Cup:* 1968–69. *European Cup-Winners' Cup:* 1969–70 (Winners): 1970–71. *UEFA Cup:* 1972–73.

Record Victory: 11-3 v Lincoln C., Division 2, Mar. 23rd, 1895.

Record Defeat: 1-9 v Everton, Division 1, Sept. 3rd, 1906.

Most League Points: 62, Division 2, 1946–47.

Most League Goals: 108, Division 2, 1926–27.

Highest League Scorer in Season: Tommy Johnson, 38, Division 1, 1928–29.

Most League Goals in Total Aggregate: Tommy Johnson, 158, 1919–30.

Most Capped Player: Colin Bell, 46, England.

Most League Appearances: Alan Oakes, 565 1959-76.

Record Transfer Fee Received: £125,000 from Torino, Italy, for Denis Law, June, 1961.

Record Transfer Fee Paid: £275,000 to Sunderland for Dennis Tueart, March 1974.

Managers Since the War: Wilf Wild, Sam Cowan, Jock Thomson, Les McDowall, George Poyser, Joe Mercer, Malcolm Allison, John Hart, Ron Saunders.

Address of Club Shop or Boutique: The City Souvenir Shops, Maine Road, Moss Side.

Maine Road, Moss Side, Manchester M14 7WN. Telephone 061-226-1191/2. *Telegraphic address:* 'Football, Manchester 14'. *Capacity crowd:* 52,500. *Record attendance:* 84,569 v Stoke C., F.A. Cup 6th Rd., March 3, 1934 (British record for any game outside London or Glasgow). *Record receipts:* £70,000 Leeds U. v Wolverhampton W., F.A. Cup Semi-Final, April 7, 1973. *Pitch measurements:* 117 yds × 79 yds.

How to get there: Corporation specials from Aytoun Street, Piccadilly, in centre of city. Nearest railway station, Manchester Piccadilly.
Match tickets: Advance booking 14 days prior to the match.
Car parking: Kippax Street car park holds approximately 400 cars. Also street parking.
Entertainments/catering facilities: Social club can be used by visiting supporters (contact Mr Roy Clarke). Licensed refreshment points around the ground.
Club shop: Open all week at the ground.
Handbook/programmes: Handbook available. Programmes can be obtained on a mailing list.
Extra information: Manchester City scored more goals in 1937–38 than any other First Division side – but were relegated!

Club Colours: Sky blue shirts with white collars and cuffs, sky blue shorts, sky blue stockings.
Change Colours: white shirts with red/black stripe across chest, white shorts, black socks.
Club Captain: Mike Doyle.
Club Nickname: 'Citizens'.

MANCHESTER CITY 1975–76 LEAGUE RECORD

Match No.	Date	Venue	Opponents	Result	H/T Score	League Pos'n	Goalscorers	Attendance
1	Aug 16	H	Norwich C.	W 3-0	0-0	—	Bell, Tueart 2	29,103
2	20	H	Leicester C.	D 1-1	0-0	—	Birchenall (og)	28,557
3	23	A	Coventry C.	L 0-2	0-1	8		21,097
4	27	A	Aston Villa	L 0-1	0-0	—		35,212
5	30	H	Newcastle U.	W 4-0	1-0	9	Tueart 2 (2 pens), Royle 2	31,875
6	Sept 6	A	West Ham U.	L 0-1	0-0	13		29,752
7	13	H	Middlesbrough	W 4-0	3-0	9	Royle, Marsh 2, Tueart	30,353
8	20	A	Derby Co.	L 0-1	0-1	14		23,250
9	24	H	Stock C.	W 1-0	0-0	—	Marsh	28,915
10	27	H	Manchester U.	D 2-2	2-2	11	Nicholl (og), Royle	46,931
11	Oct 4	A	Arsenal	W 3-2	2-0	9	Hartford, Royle, Marsh	24,928
12	11	H	Burnley	D 0-0	0-0	8		35,003
13	18	A	Tottenham H.	D 2-2	1-2	9	Watson, Bell	30,502
14	25	H	Ipswich T.	D 1-1	1-1	9	Bell	30,644
15	Nov 1	A	Sheffield U.	D 2-2	2-1	9	Booth, Barnes	24,670
16	8	H	Birmingham C.	W 2-0	2-0	8	Bell 2	28,329
17	15	A	Everton	D 1-1	1-0	8	Booth	32,077
18	22	H	Tottenham H.	W 2-1	0-0	8	Tueart, Oakes	31,456
19	29	A	Wolverhampton W.	W 4-0	2-0	7	Hartford 2, Barnes, Tueart	20,867
20	Dec 6	A	Q.P.R.	D 0-0	0-0	7		36,066
21	13	H	Coventry C.	W 4-2	1-0	5	Oakes, Barnes, Booth, Tueart	27,256
22	20	A	Norwich C.	D 2-2	2-0	7	Tueart, Royle	19,692
23	26	H	Leeds U.	L 0-1	0-0	7		48,077
24	27	A	Liverpool	L 0-1	0-0	7		53,386
25	Jan 10	A	Middlesbrough	L 0-1	0-1	8		23,000
26	17	H	West Ham U.	W 3-0	2-0	6	Royle 2 (1 a pen), Oakes	32,147
27	31	A	Leicester C.	L 0-1	0-0	7		21,723
28	Feb 7	H	Aston Villa	W 2-1	0-1	7	Booth, Hartford	32,331
29	14	A	Birmingham C.	L 1-2	1-1	7	Hartford	22,445
30	21	H	Everton	W 3-0	2-0	6	Hartford, Tueart (pen), Royle	33,148
31	Mar 6	H	Sheffield U.	W 4-0	0-0	7	Hartford 2, Tueart, Royle	33,510
32	13	A	Burnley	D 0-0	0-0	6		24,278
33	20	H	Wolverhampton W.	W 3-2	0-1	6	Keegan, Tueart (pen) Doyle	32,761
34	27	A	Q.P.R.	L 0-1	0-0	6		29,883
35	Apr 2	A	Stoke C.	D 0-0	0-0	7		18,798
36	7	A	Ipswich T.	L 1-2	0-1	—	Keegan	21,290
37	10	H	Derby Co.	W 4-3	3-1	7	Tueart 2, Royle, Power	42,061
38	14	A	Newcastle U.	L 1-2	1-1	—	Royle	21,095
39	17	A	Leeds U.	L 1-2	1-0	7	Bell	33,514
40	19	H	Liverpool	L 0-3	0-0	—		50,439
41	24	H	Arsenal	W 3-1	1-1	8	Booth 2, Hartford	31,003
42	May 4	A	Manchester U.	L 0-2	0-0	—		59,528

Goalscorers

League (64): Tueart 14 (4 pens), Royle 12 (1 a pen), Hartford 9, Bell 6, Booth 6, Marsh 4, Barnes 3, Oakes 3, Keegan 2, Watson 1, Power 1, Doyle 1, Own Goals 2.
League Cup (25): Tueart 8 (3 pens), Royle 6, Hartford 2, Barnes 2, Oakes 2, Watson, Doyle, Bell, Keegan, Own Goal 1.
F.A. Cup (6): Tueart 2 (1 a pen), Booth 2, Hartford, Oakes.

League Cup	Second Round	Norwich C. (a)	1-1
		(h)	2-2 (a.e.t.)
			6-1 (at Stamford Bridge
	Third Round	Nottingham F. (h)	2-1
	Fourth Round	Manchester U. (h)	4-0
	Fifth Round	Mansfield T. (h)	4-2
	Semi-Final	Middlesbrough (a)	0-1
		(h)	4-0
	Final	Newcastle U.	2-1
F.A. Cup	Third Round	Hartlepool (jh)	6-0
	Fourth Round	Stoke C. (a)	0-1

Corrigan	Hammond	Donachie	Doyle	Watson	Oakes	Hartford	Bell	Marsh	Royle	Tueart	Telford	Clements	Power	Leman	Barnes	Booth	MacRae	Keegan	Barrett	Owen	Docherty	Match No.
1	2	3	4	5	6	7	8	9	10	11												1
1	2	3	4	5	6	7	8	9	10	11												2
1	2	3	4	5	6	7	8	9	10*	11	12											3
1		3	4	5	6	7	8	9		11		2	10									4
1		3	4	5	6	7	8	9	10	11		2										5
1		3	4	5	6	7	8		10	11		2		9								6
1		3	4	5	6	7	8	10	9	11		2										7
1		3	4	5	6	7	8	10	9	11		2										8
1		3	4	5	6	7	8	10	9	11		2										9
1		3	4	5	6	7	8	10	9*	11		2	12									10
1		3	4	5	6	7	8	10	9	11*		2	12									11
1		3	4	5	6	7	8	9	10*			2	12		11							12
1		3	4	9	6	10	8			11		2	7		5							13
1		3	4	9	6	7	8			11		2	10		5							14
		3	4	5	6	10	8			11		2	7		9		1					15
1		3	4	5	6	7	8	10	9			2	11									16
1		3	4	5	6	7		10		11*		2	12		8	9						17
1		3	4	5	6	10			9	11		2			8	7						18
1		3	4	5	6	10			9	11		2			8	7						19
1		3	4	5	6	10			9	11		2			7	8						20
1	2	3	4	5	6	10			9	11			12		7	8*						21
1		3	4	5	6	10			9	11		2			7	8						22
1		3	4	5	6	10			9	11		2	12		7*	8						23
1		3	4	5	6*	10			9	11		2	7			8		12				24
1		3	4	5	6	10			9				7			8		11	2			25
1		3	4		6	10			9			5	7		11	8		2				26
1		3	4	5	6*	10			9	11			7		12	8		2				27
1		3	4	5	6	10			9	11		2*			8	12		7				28
1		3	4	5	6	10			9			2			11	8		7				29
1		3	4	5	6	10			9	11					7	8		2				30
1		3	4	5	6	10			9	11					7	8		2				31
1		3	4	5	6	10			9	11					7	8		2				32
1		3	4			10			9	11		5			7	8		2	6			33
1		3	4		6	10			9*	11		12			7	5		2		8		34
1	2	3	4		6				9	11		10			7	5		8				35
1	2	3	4		6				9	11		6			7	5		8				36
1	12	3	4		6		2		9	11		10			7*	5		8				37
1	2	3							9	11		4	10		7	5		8	6			38
1	2		4	3	10	8			9	11					7	5		6				39
1	2		4	3*	10	8			9	11		12			7	5		6				40
1		3	4		10	8			9	12		6*			7	5		2		11		41
1		4*		12	10				9	11		2	8		7	5		6			3	42
41	7	40	41	31	38	39	20	12	37	37	—	26	14	1	27	25	1	17	3	4	1	

+1s (Corrigan) +1s (Watson) +1s +1s +1s +5s +2s +1s +1s +1s

MANCHESTER CITY—PLAYERS

Player and position	Ht.	Wt.	Birthplace	Clubs	League Appearances	Goals
Goalkeepers						
Joe Corrigan (England)	6 4½	15 11½	Manchester	Manchester C.	207	—
Keith MacRae	6 0	11 9	Glasgow	Motherwell	111	—
				Manchester C.	53	—
Defenders						
Tommy Booth	6 1	11 12½	Manchester	Manchester C.	252+1	21
Willie Donachie (Scotland)	5 9	11 3	Glasgow	Manchester C.	209+4	2
Mike Doyle (England)	6 0	11 9	Manchester	Manchester C.	395+7	31
Glyn Pardoe	5 9½	10 12	Winsford	Manchester C.	302+2	17
*Geoff Hammond	5 10	11 4	Sudbury	Ipswich T.	53+3	2
				Manchester C.	33+1	2
Dave Watson (England)	5 11½	11 7	Nottingham	Notts. Co.	22+1	1
				Rotherham	121	19
				Sunderland	177	27
				Manchester C.	31	1
Kenny Clements	6 1	12 6	Manchester	Manchester C.	26+1	—
Mike Docherty	5 6	9 8	Preston	Burnley	149+4	—
				Manchester C.	1	—
Midfield						
Alan Oakes	6 0	12 10	Winsford	Manchester C.	562+3	26
Asa Hartford (Scotland)	5 7	10 6	Clydebank	W.B.A.	206+8	18
				Manchester C.	68+1	11
Michael Lester	5 10	11 5	Manchester	Oldham Ath.	26+1	1
				Manchester C.	1	—
				Stockport Co. (on loan)	8+1	1
Colin Bell (England)	5 11½	11 6½	Hesleden	Bury	82	25
				Manchester C.	367	115
Gerard Keegan	5 7	10 2	Manchester	Manchester C.	20+3	2
Peter Barnes	5 10	11 4	Manchester	Manchester C.	30+1	4
Tony Henry	5 11	11 12	Newcastle	Manchester C.	—	—
Forwards						
Dennis Leman	5 5	10 2	Newcastle	Manchester C.	10+7	1
*George McBeth	5 6½	9 11	Belfast	Manchester C.	—	—
Rodney Marsh (England)	6 0	12 0	London	Fulham	63	22
				Q.P.R.	211	106
				Manchester C.	116+2	36
				(transferred to Tampa Bay Jan. 1976)		
Joe Royle (England)	6 1	13 8	Liverpool	Everton	229+2	102
				Manchester C.	53	13
Dennis Tueart (England)	5 8	11 0	Newcastle	Sunderland	173+9	46
				Manchester C.	84+1	29
Gary Owen	5 9	9 9	St Helens	Manchester C.	4	—
Paul Power	5 11	10 13	Manchester	Manchester C.	14+5	1

MANCHESTER UNITED   DIV. 1

Chairman: L. C. Edwards.
Directors: J. A. Gibson, W. A. Young, D. D. Haroun, J.P.,
C. M. Edwards., Sir Matt Busby, C.B.E.
Manager: Tommy Docherty.   *Secretary:* R. L. Olive.
Ass. Manager: Frank Blunstone.
Year Formed: 1878 as Newton Heath; 1902, Manchester United.
Turned Professional: 1885.   *Limited Company:* 1907.
Previous Name: Newton Heath, 1880–1902.
Previous Grounds: 1880–93, North Road, Monsall Road;
1893, Bank Street; 1910, Old Trafford; 1946, Maine Rd.;
1947, Old Trafford.
Honours: Football League, Division 1, Champions: 1907–08,
1910–11, 1951–52, 1955–56, 1956–57, 1964–65, 1966–67;
Runners-up: 1946–47, 1947–48, 1948–49, 1950–51, 1958–59,
1963–64, 1967–68. Division 2, Champions: 1935–36; 1974–75; Runners-up; 1896–97, 1905–06,
1924–25, 1937–38.   *F.A. Cup,* Winners: 1909, 1948, 1963; Runners-up: 1957, 1958, 1976.
Football League Cup, best season: Semi-Finalists; 1969–70, 1970–71, 1974–75. **European
Competitions:** *European Cup,* Semi-finalists: 1956–57, 1957–58, 1965–66, 1968–69; Winners:
1967–68.   *European Cup Winners' Cup:* 1963–64.   *European Fairs Cup,* Semi-finalists:
1964–65.
Record Victory: 10-0 v Anderlecht, European Cup, preliminary Rd., 1956–57.
Record Defeat: 0-7 v Aston Villa, Division 1, Dec. 27th, 1930.
Most League Points: 64, Division 1, 1956–57.
Most League Goals: 103, Division 1, 1956–57 and 1958–59.
Highest League Scorer in Season: Dennis Viollet, 32, 1959–60.
Most Goals in Total Aggregate: Bobby Charlton, 198, 1956–73.
Most Capped Player: Bobby Charlton, 106, England.
Most League Appearances: Bobby Charlton, 606, 1956–1973.
Record Transfer Fee Received: £170,000 from West Ham U. for Ted MacDougall, Feb. 1973.
Record Transfer Fee Paid: £200,000 for Ian Moore to Nottingham F., March 1972; £200,000
to Celtic for Lou Macari, Jan. 1973. £200,000 for Stuart Pearson to Hull C. May 1974.
Managers Since the War Matt Busby, Wilf McGuinness, Sir Matt Busby, Frank O'Farrell.
Address of Club Shop or Boutique: Red Devils Souvenir Shop, Old Trafford.

Old Trafford, Manchester M16 0RA. Telephone 061-872-1661/2. *Telegraphic address:*
'Stadium Manchester'.   *Ground capacity:* 60,500.   *Record attendance:* 76,962 Wolves v
Grimsby T., F.A. Cup Semi-final, March 25, 1939.   *Club record:* 70,504 v Aston Villa,
Division 1, December 27, 1920.   *Record receipts:* £104,000, F.A. Cup semi-final, Leicester C.
v Liverpool, March 30, 1974.   *Club record:* £63,430 v Estudiantes, World Club Champion-
ship. *Pitch measurements:* 116 yds × 76 yds.

How to get there: Special buses from Aytoun Street, Cannon Street, and various points in Manchester and
Salford. Frequent train service from Manchester Oxford Road station direct to the Football Ground
station, returning after the match. Schedule services from Oxford Road and Knott Mill, Manchester, or
from Altrincham, Timperley, and intermediate stations, run to Warwick Road station, only a few minutes
walk from the ground.
Match tickets: Seats can be booked from two calendar months before the match. Any not sold by
Monday before a Saturday match can be reserved by personal application. For up-to-date ticket information, tel.: 061-872 7771.
Car parking: Large car parks within easy reach of the ground at Chester Road municipal park (500 cars),
Lancashire County Cricket Ground, Talbot Road and Great Stone Road (1,200), White City Stadium,
Chester Road (900), British Car Auctions, Talbot Road (100), and the former Deaf and Dumb School,
entrance Talbot Road/Boyer Street (300). Alternatively, cars can be parked in Manchester, Altrincham, or
at outside intermediate stations and the rest of the journey made by the above train services.
Entertainments/catering facilities: Licensed bars around the ground. Restaurant (not match days).
Club shop: The souvenir shop alongside the ticket office is open throughout the week. Price lists sent on
receipt of S.A.E.
Programmes: Available on subscription and application with remittance can be sent to the ground for
individual matches. The supporters' club publishes an annual handbook.
Extra information: The Manchester United Development Association has monthly draws for special
prizes and a weekly draw. New agents are always welcome; tel.: 061-872 4676/5208 for full details. There is a
travel club for away matches.
Club Colours: Red shirts with red and white trim, white shorts, black stockings with red tops and white
band.   *Change Colours:* White shirts with 3 black stripes, black shorts with red and white stripes, white
stockings with red and black top. *Trainer:* Tommy Cavanagh *Club Nickname:* 'Red Devils'.

MANCHESTER UNITED 1975-76 LEAGUE RECORD

Match No.	Date	Venue	Opponents	Result	H/T Score	League Pos'n	Goalscorers	Attendance
1	Aug16	A	Wolverhampton W.	W 2-0	0-0	—	Macari 2	31,973
2	19	A	Birmingham C.	W 2-0	0-0	—	McIlroy 2	33,177
3	23	H	Sheffield U.	W 5-1	3-0	1	Pearson 2, Badger (og), Daly, McIlroy	55,949
4	27	H	Coventry C.	D 1-1	1-0	—	Pearson	52,169
5	30	A	Stoke C.	W 1-0	1-0	1	Dodd (og)	33,337
6	Sept 6	H	Tottenham H.	W 3-2	2-1	1	Pratt (og), Daly 2 (1 a pen)	51,641
7	13	A	Q.P.R.	L 0-1	0-1	1		29,237
8	20	H	Ipswich T.	W 1-0	1-0	1	Houston	50,513
9	24	A	Derby Co.	L 1-2	0-1	—	Daly	33,187
10	27	A	Manchester C.	D 2-2	2-2	3	McCreery, Macari	46,931
11	Oct 4	H	Leicester C.	D 0-0	0-0	1		47,878
12	11	A	Leeds U.	W 2-1	1-0	2	McIlroy 2	40,264
13	18	H	Arsenal	W 3-1	1-1	1	Coppell 2, Pearson	52,958
14	25	A	West Ham U.	L 1-2	0-1	2	Macari	38,528
15	Nov 1	H	Norwich C.	W 1-0	0-0	1	Pearson	50,587
16	8	A	Liverpool	L 1-3	0-1	5	Coppell	49,136
17	15	H	Aston Villa	W 2-0	1-0	3	Coppell, McIlroy	51,682
18	22	A	Arsenal	L 1-3	0-2	5	Pearson	40,102
19	29	H	Newcastle U.	W 1-0	0-0	4	Daly	52,624
20	Dec 6	A	Middlesbrough	D 0-0	0-0	4		33,000
21	13	A	Sheffield U.	W 4-1	2-0	3	Pearson 2, Hill, Macari	32,003
22	20	H	Wolverhampton W.	W 1-0	0-0	2	Hill	44,269
23	23	A	Everton	D 1-1	1-1	—	Macari	41,732
24	27	H	Burnley	W 2-1	0-1	2	McIlroy, Macari	59,726
25	Jan 10	A	Q.P.R.	W 2-1	1-1	1	Hill, McIlroy	58,312
26	17	A	Tottenham H.	D 1-1	1-0	1	Hill	49,387
27	31	H	Birmingham C.	W 3-1	2-0	1	Forsyth, Macari, McIlroy	50,274
28	Feb 7	A	Coventry C.	D 1-1	0-1	2	Macari	33,821
29	18	H	Liverpool	D 0-0	0-0	—		59,709
30	21	A	Aston Villa	L 1-2	1-1	3	Macari	50,094
31	25	H	Derby Co	D 1-1	1-0	—	Pearson	59,632
32	28	H	West Ham U.	W 4-0	0-0	3	Forsyth, Macari, McCreery, Pearson	57,240
33	Mar13	H	Leeds U.	W 3-2	2-0	3	Houston, Pearson, Daly	59,429
34	17	A	Norwich C.	D 1-1	1-0	—	Hill	30,000
35	20	A	Newcastle U.	W 4-3	2-3	2	Pearson 2, Bird (og), Howard (og)	41,427
36	27	H	Middlesbrough	W 3-0	0-0	2	Daly (pen), McCreery, Hill	58,527
37	Apr 10	A	Ipswich T.	L 0-3	0-1	3		34,889
38	17	H	Everton	W 2-1	0-1	3	Kenyon (og), McCreery	61,879
39	19	A	Burnley	W 1-0	0-0	—	Macari	27,411
40	21	H	Stoke C.	L 0-1	0-0	—		53,879
41	24	A	Leicester C.	L 1-2	0-1	3	Coyne	31,053
42	May 4	H	Manchester C.	W 2-0	0-0	—	Hill, McIlroy	59,528

Goalscorers

League (68): Pearson 13, Macari 12, McIlroy 10, Daly 7 (2 pens), Hill 7, McCreery 4, Coppell 4, Houston 2, Forsyth 2, Coyne 1, own goals 6.
League Cup (4): Macari 2, McIlroy, Coppell.
F.A. Cup (13): Daly 4 (2 pens), Hill 3, McIlroy 2, Forsyth, Macari, Pearson, Greenhoff.

League Cup	Second Round	Brentford (h)	2-1
	Third Round	Aston Villa (a)	2-1
	Fourth Round	Manchester C. (a)	0-4
F.A. Cup	Third Round	Oxford U. (h)	2-1
	Fourth Round	Peterborough U. (h)	3-1
	Fifth Round	Leicester C. (a)	2-1
	Sixth Round	Wolverhampton W.	
		(h)	1-1
		(a)	3-2 (a.e.t.)
	Semi-Final	Derby Co.	2-0 (at Hillsborough)
	Final	Southampton	0-1

Stepney	Forsyth	Houston	Jackson	Greenhoff	Buchan	Coppell	McIlroy	Pearson	Macari	Daly	Nicholl	McCreery	Young	Albiston	Grimshaw	Roche	Hill	Kelly	Coyne	Match No.
1	2	3	4	5	6	7	8	9*	10	11	12									1
1	2	3	4	5*	6	7	8		10	11	12	9								2
1	2*	3	4	5	6	7	8	9	10	11	12									3
1	2	3	4	5	6	7	8	9	10	11										4
1	2	3	4	5	6	7	8	9	10	11										5
1		3	4	5	6	7	8	9	10	11	2									6
1		3	4*		6	7	8	9	10	11	2	12		5						7
1		3		5	6	7	8	9	10	11	2	4								8
1		3		5	6	7	8	9	10	11	2	4								9
1		3		5	6	7	8	9	10	11	2	4								10
1		3	4*	5	6	7	8	9	10	11	2	12								11
1		3*	4	5	6	7	8	9	10	11	2	12								12
1		3	4	5	6	7	8	9	10	11	2									13
1		3	4	5	6	7	8	9	10	11*	2	12								14
		3	4	5	6	7	8	9	10	11	2					1				15
		3	4*	5	6	7	8	9	10	11	2	12				1				16
		3		5	6	7	8*	9	10	4	2	12				1	11			17
		3		5	6	7	8*	9	10	4	2	12				1	11			18
1		3		5	6	7	8	9*	10	4	2	12					11			19
1	2*	3		5	6	7	8	9	10	4		12					11			20
1	2	3		5	6	7	8*	9	10	4		12					11			21
1	2	3		5*	6	7	8	9	10	4							11	12		22
1	2	3		5	6	7	8	9	10	4							11			23
1	2	3		5	6	7	8	9*	10	4		12					11			24
1	2	3		5	6	7	8	9	10	4							11			25
1	2	3		5	6	7	8*	9	10	4		12					11			26
1	2	3		5	6	7	8	9*	10	4		12					11			27
1	2	3		5	6	7	8	9*	10	4		12					11			28
1	2	3		5	6	7	8*	9	10	4		12					11			29
1	2	3		5	6	7	8	9*	10	4							11	12		30
1	2	3		5	6	7	8	9	10	4		12					11*			31
1	2	3		5	6	7	8*	9	10	4		12					11			32
1	2	3		5	6	7	8	9		4	10						11			33
1	2	3		5	6	7	8	9		4	10						11			34
1	2	3		5	6	7	8	9		4	10						11			35
1	2	3		5	6	7	8	9		4	10						11			36
1	2	3		5	6	7	8	9		4	10						11			37
1	2	3		5	6	7*	8	9	10	4	12						11			38
1	2	3	12	5	6		8	9*	10	4		7					11			39
1	2	3	7*	5	6		8		10	4	12	9					11			40
1	2	3*	7	5	6			10		4	8	12					11		9	4
1	2	3	10		6	7	8	9*		4	12			5			11			42
38	28	42	16	40	42	39	41	39	36	41	15	12	—	2	—	4	26	—	1	
	+1s										+5s	+16s	+1s	+1s	+1s		+1s	+1s		

Player and position	Ht.	Wt.	Birthplace	Clubs	League Appearances	Goals
Goalkeepers						
Alex Stepney (England)	6 0	13 3	Mitcham	Millwall	137	—
				Chelsea	1	—
				Manchester U.	370	2
Paddy Roche (Eire)	6 1	11 5	Dublin	Shelbourne	not known	
				Manchester U.	6	—
*David Ryan	6 0	12 4		Manchester U.	—	—
				Port Vale (on loan)	1	—
				Southport (on loan)	14	—
Defenders						
*Clive Griffiths	5 10	12 0	Pontypridd	Manchester U.	7	—
				Plymouth Arg. (on loan)	10+1	—
				Tranmere R. (on loan)	28	—
Alex Forsyth (Scotland)	5 9	11 1	Swinton, Scotland	Partick T.	52	5
				Manchester U.	93+1	4
Jim Holton (Scotland)	6 1	13 5	Lesmanagow	W.B.A.	—	—
				Shrewsbury T.	67	4
				Manchester U.	63	5
Martin Buchan (Scotland)	5 10	11 11	Aberdeen	Aberdeen	129+2	10
				Manchester U.	180	1
*Alan Kirkup	5 10	11 13	Reading	Manchester U.	—	—
Stewart Houston (Scotland)	5 11	11 8	Argyle	Chelsea	6+3	—
				Brentford	77	9
				Manchester U.	102	10
Arthur Albiston	5 7	11 0	Scotland	Manchester U.	4+1	—
David Bradley	5 11	12 7	Manchester	Manchester U.	—	—
*Isaac McKeown	5 8	11 4	Belfast	Manchester U.	—	—
James Nicholl (N. Ireland)	5 8	11 1	Canada	Manchester U.	15+6	—
Brian Greenhoff (England)	5 10	11 11	Barnsley	Manchester U.	115+2	7
Tony Grimshaw	5 5	10 5	Manchester	Manchester U.	0+1	—
Midfield						
Tommy Jackson (N. Ireland)	5 7	11 0	Belfast	Everton	30+1	—
				Nottingham F.	73+8	6
				Manchester U.	16+1	—
James Kelly	5 7	10 0	Carlisle	Manchester U.	0+1	—
Ray Storey	5 7	10 7	Sheffield	Manchester U.	—	—
Gerry Daly (Eire)	5 9	10 0	Dublin	Bohemians	not known	
				Manchester U.	91+3	19
Lou Macari (Scotland)	5 5½	10 9	Edinburgh	Celtic	51+5	27
				Manchester U.	122+3	33
Forwards						
Ron Davies (Wales)	6 0	12 6	Holywell	Chester	94	45
		Luton T. 32(21)	Norwich C. 113(58)	Southampton 239+1(134)	Portsmouth 59(18)	
		Manchester U. 0+8(—)	Millwall (on loan) 3(—)	(contract cancelled April 1976)		
Sammy McIlroy (N. Ireland)	5 9½	10 9	Belfast	Manchester U.	128+20	27
Stephen Coppell	5 6	10 0	Liverpool	Tranmere R.	35+3	10
				Manchester U.	48+1	5
Stuart Pearson (England)	5 9	12 7	Hull	Hull C.	126+3	44
				Manchester U.	69+1	30
Ray Botham	5 7	10 0	Manchester	Manchester U.	—	—
Peter Loughnane	5 9	10 4	Shrewsbury	Manchester U.	—	—
John Lowey	5 10	11 4	Manchester	Manchester U.	—	—
David Morris	5 5	9 10	Wales	Manchester U.	—	—
David McCreery (N. Ireland)	5 6	9 7	Belfast	Manchester U.	12+8	4
Gordon Hill (England)	5 7	10 12	Sunbury	Millwall	79+7	20
				Manchester U.	26	7
*Ged Coyne	6 0	12 0	Manchester	Manchester C.	—	—
				Manchester U.	1+1	1

MANSFIELD TOWN   DIV. 3

Chairman: A. F. Patrick.

Directors: J. A. Brown, B. Chambers, J. B. Almond,
J. W. Pratt.

Manager: *Secretary:* J. D. Eaton.

Year Formed: 1905.

Turned Professional: 1905.   *Limited Company:* 1905.

Honours: *Football League*, highest position in Division
3: 3rd, 1964–65. Division 3(N), Runners-up: 1950–51.
Div. 4 Champions 1974-75. *F.A. Cup*, best season: 6th
Rd., 1968–69.   *Football League Cup*, best season: 5th Rd.,
1975–76.

Record Victory: 9-2 v Rotherham U., Division 3(N)
Dec. 27th, 1932 and v Hounslow T., F.A. Cup, 1st Rd.
Replay, Nov. 5th, 1962.

Record Defeat: 1-8 v Walsall, Division 3(N), Jan. 19th, 1933.

Most League Points: 68, Division 4, 1974–75.

Most League Goals: 108, Division 4, 1962–63.

Highest League Scorer in Season: Ted Harston, 55, Division 3(N), 1936–37.

Most League Goals in Total Aggregate: Harry Johnson, 104, 1931–36.

Most League Appearances: Don Bradley, 417, 1949–62.

Most Capped Player: None.

Record Transfer Fee Received: £50,000 from Leicester C. for Malcolm Partridge, Sept. 1970
and £50,000 from Middlesbrough for Stuart Boam, June 1971.

Record Transfer Fee Paid: £10,000 to W.B.A. for Bill Williams, Jan. 1966.

Managers Since the War: Roy Goodall, Freddie Steele, Stan Mercer, Charlie Mitten, Sam
Weaver, Raich Carter, Tommy Cummings, Tommy Eggleston, Jock Basford, Danny Williams,
David Smith.

Address of Supporters Club: Jackpot Office, c/o the ground.

Field Mill Ground, Quarry Lane, Mansfield. Telephone Mansfield 23567. *Telegraphic
address:* 'Football, Mansfield'. *Ground capacity:* 23,500. *Record attendance:* 24,467 v
Nottingham F., F.A. Cup 3rd Rd., January 10, 1953.   *Record receipts:* £13,317 v Carlisle U.,
F.A. Cup 5th Rd., February 1, 1975. *Pitch measurements:* 115 yds × 72 yds.

How to get there: Buses from town centre to within 300 yards of the ground. Nearest railway station
Alfreton and Mansfield Parkway.

Match tickets: Advance booking 5 days prior to match.

Car parking: Room for 500 cars at the ground and another 3,000 within 500 yards.

Entertainments/catering facilities: No Club room. Licensed tea bars in the ground.

Club shop: Adjacent to the ground; sells all types of souvenirs.

Handbooks/programmes: Both on sale at the club shop.

Extra information: Mansfield became famous giant-killers as a non-League side in 1929. They went to
Molineux in the FA Cup 3rd round and beat Wolves 1-0.

Club Colours: Amber shirts, blue shorts, amber stockings.
Change Colours: White shirts with blue and amber trimmings, blue shorts, white stockings.
Club Trainer/Coach: John Haselden.
Club Nickname: 'The Stags'.

MANSFIELD TOWN 1975–76 LEAGUE RECORD

Match No.	Date	Venue	Opponents	Result	H/T Score	League Pos'n	Goalscorers	Attendance
1	Aug 16	H	Shrewsbury T.	L 1-2	0-1	—	McDonald	6951
2	23	A	Colchester U.	W 2-0	2-0	9	Bird, Clarke	3333
3	30	H	Chester	D 1-1	0-0	11	McDonald (pen)	6164
4	Sept 6	A	Aldershot	L 1-2	0-1	15	Hodgson	3289
5	13	H	Cardiff C.	L 1-4	0-1	21	Eccles (pen)	6682
6	20	A	Gillingham	L 1-3	0-1	23	Eccles (pen)	5742
7	23	A	Bury	L 1-2	0-1	—	McDonald	5896
8	27	H	Walsall	W 4-1	2-0	20	Clarke 3, Hodgson	5450
9	Oct 4	A	Millwall	L 0-1	0-0	23		6792
10	11	H	Peterborough U.	D 1-1	0-1	23	Clarke	6983
11	17	A	Southend U.	D 2-2	2-1	22	Clarke, Bird	3248
12	25	H	Preston N.E.	L 0-1	0-0	24		6677
13	Nov 1	A	Wrexham	L 0-1	0-0	24		2701
14	8	H	Halifax T.	D 1-1	0-0	24	Bird	5288
15	15	A	Grimsby T.	L 1-4	1-3	24	Bird	4659
16	29	A	Crystal Palace	L 1-4	0-3	24	Hodgson	15,701
17	Dec 6	H	Swindon T.	W 3-1	1-0	24	Bird, Randall, Clarke	5487
18	20	A	Rotherham U.	L 1-2	0-0	24	Hodgson	6067
19	26	H	Chesterfield	L 0-1	0-1	24		8607
20	27	A	Sheffield W.	D 0-0	0-0	24		15,430
21	Jan 3	H	Port Vale	W 3-1	2-1	24	Clarke 2, Randall	5417
22	10	A	Chester	D 1-1	1-1	24	Randall	4623
23	17	H	Gillingham	D 1-1	1-0	24	Shipperley (o.g.)	5939
24	20	A	Cardiff C.	L 0-1	0-0	—		10,161
25	31	A	Brighton & H. A.	L 0-1	0-0	24		11,918
26	Feb 7	H	Hereford U.	D 2-2	0-0	24	Bird, Clarke	5997
27	11	A	Hereford U.	L 0-1	0-1	—		8302
28	14	A	Halifax T.	W 2 1	0 0	24	Clarke, Saxby	2378
29	21	H	Grimsby T.	W 1 0	1 0	24	Clarke	6094
30	23	H	Bury	D 1 1	1-0	—	Clarke	6610
31	28	A	Preston N E	W 2-0	0-0	24	Matthews, Clarke	6945
32	Mar 1	A	Brighton & H. A.	W 1-0	0-0	—	McDonald	8321
33	6	H	Wrexham	D 0-0	0-0	21		6473
34	8	H	Millwall	D 1-1	0-1	—	McCaffrey	7435
35	13	A	Peterborough U.	W 3-0	1-0	18	Clarke 2, McCafffrey	7497
36	15	H	Southend U.	W 3-1	1-0	—	Clarke 3	8043
37	20	H	Crystal Palace	D 1-1	1-0	16	Laverick	12,990
38	27	A	Swindon T.	W 2-0	2-0	16	Clarke, Laverick	6789
39	29	H	Rotherham U.	D 1-1	0-1	—	Foster, C.	9098
40	Apr 2	A	Shrewsbury T.	W 2-1	0-1	14	Hodgson, Clarke	4580
41	6	A	Walsall	W 1-0	0-0	—	Hodgson	6481
42	10	H	Aldershot	W 1-0	0-0	13	Mackenzie	7179
43	17	A	Chesterfield	W 2-1	0-1	12	Laverick, Eccles (pen.)	10,616
44	19	H	Sheffield W.	W 3-0	1-0	—	Pate, Hodgson, Clarke	13,410
45	20	A	Port Vale	D 2-2	1-0	—	Clarke 2	4239
46	24	H	Colchester U.	D 0-0	0-0	11		7407

Goalscorers

League (58): Clarke 24, Hodgson 7, Bird 6, McDonald 4 (1 a pen.), Laverick 3, Eccles 3 (3 pens.), Randall 3 McCaffrey 2, Foster, (C.) 1, Saxby 1, Mackenzie 1, Pate 1, Matthews 1, own goal 1.
League Cup (13): Bird 3, McDonald 3, Clarke 3, Laverick 2, Eccles, Lathan.
F.A. Cup (5): Eccles 2, Laverick, McDonald, own goal 1.

League Cup	First Round	Scunthorpe U. (h)		4-0
	Second Leg		(a)	2-0
	Second Round	Wrexham (a)		2-1
	Third Round	Coventry C. (h)		2-0
	Fourth Round	Wolverhampton W. (h)		1-0
	Fifth Round	Manchester C. (a)		2-4
F.A. Cup	First Round	Wrexham (h)		1-1
			(a)	1-1 (a.e.t.)
				2-1 (at Villa Park)
	Second Round	Lincoln C. (h)		1-2

248

Arnold	O'Brien	Foster, B.	McDonald	Mackenzie	Bird	McCaffrey	Matthews	Clarke	Lathan	Hodgson	Foster, C.	Eccles	Laverick	Pate	Wood	Evans	Madden	Randall	Saxby	Uzelac	Brown, R. E.	Match No.
1	2	3	4	5	6	7	8	9	10*	11	12											1
1	4	3	7	5*	2	11		9	10	6	12	8										2
1	4	3	7	5	2	11*		9	12	10	6	8										3
1	8	3	7	5	4*			9	12	10	6	11		2								4
1	8	3	9*	5	4	11		7	10	6	12			2								5
1	4	3	8	5				9	7	11	6	12	10*	2								6
1	4	3	8	5	2		11	7*	10	6	9	12										7
1		3	11	5*	4		8	9	10	6	7	12		2								8
1		3	11	5	4			9	10	6	8	7		2								9
1			11*		6	12	4	9	10	5	8	7	2	3								10
1		3	11		6	7		9		10	5	8	4	2								11
1		3	7		6	11	4	9		10	5	8*	12	2								12
		3	6	12	5	11*	7	9		10	4	8		2	1							13
		3	11	5	6	7		9		10	8			2	1	4						14
		3	4	11	6		8	9		10				2		1	5	7				15
		3	4		6	7		9		10	8			2		5		11			1	16
		3	4*	5	6	11	7	9		8	12	2				1		10				17
		3	4	5	2	11	8	9		10	6			2		1		7				18
		3	4	5*	2	11	7	9		10	6	12				1		8				19
1		3	6		4	11		9		7	10	5		2				8				20
1		3	4		6	11		9		7	10	5		2				8				21
1		3	4	5				9		7	10	6	11	2				8				22
1		3	4	5		11		9		7	10	6		2				8				23
1		3	4	5	6	11		9		7	10			2				8				24
1		3	4*	5	6	11	12	9		7	10			2				8				25
1				5	6	11	4	9		10	8			2			3	7				26
1		3	12	5	6*	11	4	9		10	8			2				7				27
1		3		5		11	4	9		10	8			2				7	6			28
1		3		5		11	4	9		10	8			2				7		6		29
1		3	12	5		11	4	9		10	8			2				7*		6		30
1		3	7	5		11	4*	9		10	6	8		2				12				31
1		3	7	5		11		9		10	6	8	4	2								32
1		3	7	5		11		9		10	6	8	4	2								33
1		3	7	5		11		9		10	6	8	4	2								34
1		3	7	5		11		9		10	6	8	4	2								35
1		3	7	5		11		9		10	6		4	2				8				36
1		3	7	5		11		9		10	6	8	4	2								37
1		3		5		11	4	9		10	6	8	7	2								38
1		3		5		11	7	9		10	6		4	2				8				39
1		3		5		11	7	9		10	6	8	4	2								40
1		3		5		11	7	9		10	6	8	4	2								41
1		3		5		11	7	9		10	6	8	4	2								42
1		3		5		11	7	9		10	6	8	4	2								43
1		3		5		11	7	9		10	6	8	4	2								44
1		3	12	5		11	7*	9		10	6	8	4	2								45
1		3	12	5		11	7	9		10	6	8	4	2*								46
39	7	44	32	36	26	35	28	45	10	46	34	29	22	40	2	6	3	18	1	2	1	
		+2s	+1s	+2s	+1s	+1s		+2s		+2s	+3s	+3s	+1s					+1s				

MANSFIELD TOWN—PLAYERS

Player and position	Ht.	Wt.	Birthplace	Clubs	League Appearances	Goals
Goalkeepers						
Rod Arnold	5 10	11 4	Wolver-hampton	Wolverhampton W.	—	—
				Mansfield T.	144	—
Paul Evans	5 9	10 7	Sheffield	Mansfield T.	6	—
Defenders						
Sandy Pate	5 10	10 10	Glasgow	Watford	14	
				Mansfield T.	389+1	1
Ian Mackenzie	6 0	10 10	Rotherham	Sheffield U.	43+2	1
				Southend (on loan)	5+1	—
				Mansfield T.	36+1	1
Kevin Bird	5 9	10 12	Doncaster	Doncaster R.	—	—
				Mansfield T.	124+2	23
Barry Foster	5 9	10 4	Worksop	Mansfield T.	123+5	—
Lawrence Madden				Mansfield T.	9+1	—
*Noel O'Brien	5 8	10 11	London	Arsenal	—	—
				Mansfield T.	7	—
Ian Wood	5 10	10 7	Kirkby in Ashfield	Mansfield T.	2	—
Colin Foster	5 9	11 0	Nottingham	Mansfield T.	107+6	5
Midfield						
Mike Laverick	5 8	10 0	Trimdon	Mansfield T.	73+16	13
Paul Matthews	5 9	10 3	Leicester	Leicester C.	56+5	5
				Southend U. (on loan)	1	—
				Mansfield T.	100+2	4
Ian McDonald	5 7	10 5	Barrow	Barrow	30+5	2
				Workington	42	4
				Liverpool	—	—
				Colchester U. (on loan)	5	2
				Mansfield T.	32+2	4
Gordon Hodgson	5 11	12 9	Newcastle	Newcastle U.	8+1	—
				Mansfield T.	90	17
Jim McCaffrey	5 7	9 11	Luton	Nottingham F.	2+6	1
				Mansfield T.	154+6	18
Forwards						
Ray Clarke	5 11	11 0	Hackney	Tottenham H.	0+1	—
				Swindon T.	11+3	2
				Mansfield T.	91	52
Terry Eccles	6 0½	13 0	Leeds	Blackburn R.	33+13	6
				Mansfield T.	105+3	40
Michael Saxby	6 0	10 0	Mansfield	Mansfield T.	1+1	1
Kevin Randall	5 10½	12 9	Ashton under Lyne	Bury	4	—
				Chesterfield	257	97
				Notts Co.	119+2	38
				Mansfield T.	18	3

MIDDLESBROUGH

DIV. 1

Chairman: C. Amer.

Vice-Chairman: Dr. U. N. Phillips.

Directors: G. T. Kitching, E. Varley, J. D. Hatfield, M. McCullagh, K. Amer, E. K. Varley.

Manager: Jack Charlton, O.B.E.

Asst. Manager: Harold Shepherdson, M.B.E.

Secretary: T. H. C. Green.

Year Formed: 1876.

Turned Professional: 1889; became amateur 1892, and professional again, 1899.

Limited Company: 1892.

Previous Grounds: 1877, Old Archery Ground, Linthorpe Rd; 1903, Ayresome Park.

Honours: Football League, highest position in Division 1: 3rd, 1913–14. Division 2, Champions: 1926–27, 1928–29, 1973–74; Runners-up: 1901–02. Division 3, Runners-up: 1966–67. *F.A. Cup,* best season: 6th Rd., 1935–36, 1946–47, 1969–70, 1974–75, old last eight, 1900–01, 1903–04. *Football League Cup,* Semi-final: 1975–76. *Amateur Cup,* Winners: 1895, 1898. Anglo-Scottish Cup Winners: 1975–76.

Record Victory: 9-0 v Brighton & H.A. Division 2, Aug. 23rd, 1958.

Record Defeat: 0-9 v Blackburn R., Division 2, Nov. 6th, 1954.

Most League Points: 65, Division 2, 1973–74.

Most League Goals: 122, Division 2, 1926–27.

Highest League Scorer in Season: George Camsell, 59, Division 2, 1926–27 (record for Division 2).

Most Capped Player: Wilf Mannion, 26, England.

Most League Appearances: Tim Williamson, 563, 1902–23.

Most League Goals in Total Aggregate: George Camsell, 326, 1925–39.

Record Transfer Fee Received: £57,500 from Chelsea for Geoff Butler, Sept. 1967.

Record Transfer Fee Paid: £72,000 to Liverpool for Phil Boersma, Dec. 1975.

Managers Since the War: David Jack, Walter Rowley, Bob Dennison, Raich Carter, Stan Anderson.

Address of Club Shop or Boutique: 64 Kensington Road, Middlesbrough, and Warwick Street.

Ayresome Park, Middlesbrough, Teesside. Telephone Middlesbrough 89659/85996. *Telegraphic address:* 'Football, Middlesbrough'. *Ground capacity:* 42,000. *Record attendance:* 53,596 v Newcastle U., Division 1, December, 1949. *Record receipts:* £29,491.25p v Manchester C., League Cup Semi-final, Jan. 21, 1976. *Pitch measurements:* 115 yds × 75 yds.

How to get there: Regular buses from the Exchange in Middlesbrough to the ground. Buses also from bus station next to Middlesbrough railway station.
Match tickets: By postal or personal application two weeks prior to the match.
Car parking: Off-street parking near the ground.
Entertainments/catering facilities: Social club (members only); refreshment bars around the ground.
Handbooks/programmes: Programmes available on subscription.
Extra information: When Middlesbrough bought Alf Common from Sunderland in 1905, they paid the first £1,000 transfer fee.

Club Colours: Red shirts with 2in. wide white band round chest, red shorts with white stripe down sides, red stockings with white tops.
Change Colours: Black and royal blue vertical striped shirts, black shorts and stockings.
Club Captain: Stuart Boam.
First Team Trainer: Jim Headridge.
Club Coaches: J. Coddington, J. Greenhalgh.
Club Nickname: 'The Boro'.

MIDDLESBROUGH 1975–76 LEAGUE RECORD

Match No.	Date	Venue	Opponents	Result	H/T Score	League Pos'n	Goalscorers	Attendance
1	Aug16	A	Tottenham H.	L 0-1	0-0	—		25,502
2	20	A	Newcastle U.	D 1-1	1-0	—	Gowling (og)	41,482
3	23	H	Wolverhampton W.	W 1-0	1-0	9	Hickton	22,595
4	26	H	Birmingham C.	W 2-0	0-0	—	Hickton, Mills	22,423
5	30	A	Burnley	L 1-4	1-2	13	Armstrong	17,016
6	Sept 6	H	Stoke C.	W 3-0	1-0	9	Hickton, Mills 2	21,975
7	13	A	Manchester C.	L 0-4	0-3	15		30,353
8	20	H	Q.P.R.	D 0-0	0-0	13		24,867
9	23	A	Coventry C.	W 1-0	1-0	—	Mills	15,124
10	27	A	Ipswich T.	W 3-0	1-0	5	Foggon, Armstrong, Hickton (pen)	22,334
11	Oct 4	H	Aston Villa	D 0-0	0-0	8		24,102
12	11	A	Leicester C.	D 0-0	0-0	7		19,095
13	18	H	West Ham U.	W 3-0	1-0	6	Souness, Armstrong, Foggon	25,851
14	25	A	Arsenal	L 1-2	0-1	8	Mills	23,591
15	Nov 1	H	Liverpool	L 0-1	0-0	10		30,952
16	8	A	Norwich C.	W 1-0	0-0	9	Souness	19,793
17	15	H	Leeds U.	D 0-0	0-0	9		33,000
18	22	A	West Ham U.	L 1-2	1-1	9	Mills	26,914
19	29	A	Derby Co.	L 2-3	2-1	9	Boam, Craggs	27,745
20	Dec 6	H	Manchester U.	D 0-0	0-0	9		33,000
21	13	A	Wolverhampton W.	W 2-1	2-1	10	Armstrong, Mills	13,548
22	20	H	Tottenham H.	W 1-0	1-0	10	Hickton (pen)	22,000
23	26	A	Sheffield U.	D 1-1	1-0	10	Foggon	28,538
24	27	H	Everton	D 1-1	0-1	10	Maddren	30,000
25	Jan 10	H	Manchester C.	W 1-0	1-0	7	Armstrong	23,000
26	17	‡A	Stoke C.	L 0-1	0-0	9		21,009
27	31	H	Newcastle U.	D 3-3	1-0	8	Mills, Keeley (og), Maddren	31 000
28	Feb 7	A	Birmingham C.	L 1-2	0-0	10	Mills	18,599
29	14	H	Burnley	D 1-1	1-1	9	Boam	18,000
30	21	A	Leeds U.	W 2-0	1-0	7	Hickton 2	32,994
31	24	H	Coventry C.	W 2-0	0-0	—	Boam, Souness	19,000
32	28	H	Arsenal	L 0-1	0-0	6		20 000
33	Mar 6	A	Liverpool	W 2-0	2-0	6	Cooper, Hickton	41,391
34	13	H	Leicester C.	L 0-1	0-1	7		18,000
35	20	H	Derby Co.	L 0-2	0-1	8		24,000
36	27	A	Manchester U.	L 0-3	0-0	10		58,527
37	Apr 3	H	Ipswich T.	W 2-0	1-0	9	Mills, Armstrong	15,000
38	6	H	Norwich C.	L 0-1	0-0	—		16,000
39	10	A	Q.P.R.	L 2-4	0-0	10	Boersma Brine	24,342
40	17	H	Sheffield U.	W 3-0	2-0	10	McAndrew 3	17,000
41	19	A	Everton	L 1-3	1-2	—	Woof	18,204
42	24	A	Aston Villa	L 1-2	1-1	13	Hickton	33,241

Goalscorers

League (46): Mills 10, Hickton 9 (2 pens), Armstrong 6, Foggon 3, Souness 3, Boam 3, McAndrew 3, Maddren 2, Craggs 1, Brine 1, Cooper 1, Boersma 1, Woof 1, own goals 2.
‡Played at Port Vale.
League Cup (9): Hickton 3 (1 a pen), Mills 2, Foggon, Boam, Armstrong, Maddren
F.A. Cup (2): Brine, Hickton (pen).

League Cup	Second Round	Bury (a)	2-1
	Third Round	Derby Co. (h)	1-0
	Fourth Round	Peterborough U. (h)	3-0
	Fifth Round	Burnley (a)	2-0
	Semi-Final	Manchester C. (h)	1-0
		(a)	0-4
F.A. Cup	Third Round	Bury (h)	0-0
		(a)	2-3

252

Platt	Craggs	Cooper	Souness	Boam	Maddren	Murdoch	Mills	Hickton	Willey	Armstrong	Brine	Taylor	Foggon	Spraggon	Boersma	Bailey	McAndrew	Woof	Smith	Cuff	Coleman	Ramage	Match No.
1	2	3	4	5	6	7	8	9	10	11													1
1	2	3	4	5	6	7	8	9		11	10												2
1	2	3	4		6	7	8	9*	12	11	10	5											3
1	2	3	4		6*	7	8	9	12	11	10	5											4
1	2	3	4		6	7	8	9*	12	11	10	5											5
1	2	3	4	5	6	7	8	9	10*	11	12												6
1	2	3	4	5	6	7	8	9	10*	11	12												7
1	2	3	4	5	6		8	9		11	7		10										8
1	2		4	5	6		8	9		11	7		10	3									9
1	2	3	4	5	6		8	9		11	7		10										10
1		3	4	5	6	12	8	9		11	7*		10	2									11
1	2	3	4	5	6		8	9		11	7		10										12
1	2	3	4	5	6	7	8	9		11	10												13
1	2	3	4	5	6		8	9		11	7		10										14
1	2	3	4	5	6	7	8	9		11			10*	12									15
1	2	10	4	5	6		8	9		11	7			3									16
1	2	10	4*	5	6	7	8	9		11	12			3									17
1	2	10		5	6	4	8	9*		11	7		12	3									18
1	2	3		5	6	4	8	10		11	7		9										19
1	2	3		5	6	7	8	10	9	11					4								20
1	2	3		5	6	7	8	10	9	11					4								21
1	2	10		5	6	7		9	8	11	12				4	3*							22
1	2	3		5	6	7	8	10		11	12		9*		4								23
1	2	3		5	6	7	8	10		11			9		4								24
1	2	10	12	5	6	7	8		9*	11					4	3							25
1	2	3	4	5	6		10	9		11	7		8										26
1		10	4	5	6	7		9		11			2		8	3							27
1	2	10	4	5	6	7*	8	12		11					9	3							28
1		10	4	5	6		8*	9	12	11			2		7	3							29
1	2	3	4	5	6		8	9		11					10*		7	12					30
1	2	3	4	5	10		8	9		11					7*		6	12					31
1	2	3	4	5	10		8	9		11					7*		6	12					32
1	2	3	4	5	10		8	9		11					7		6						33
1		7	4	5	6		10	9*	12	11			2		8	3							34
1		3	4	5	10		8	9		11	12		2*		7		6						35
1	2		4	5	10		8	3		11	12				7*		6	9					36
	2	3	4	5			8			11	7				6		9	10		1			37
1	2	3	4	5	10*		8			11	12				7		6		9				38
1		3	4	5	10		8	2		11	7				9		6						39
1	2	3	4	5	10	7	8*			11					6		9		12				40
1	2	3	4	5	6		8			11*	7				10		9		12				41
1	2	9	4	5	6		8			11	7						3				10*	12	42
41	36	40	34	39	41	21	38	35	9	42	18	3	11	9	19	6	12	3	3	1	1	—	
		+1s			+1s		+1s	+5s		+2s			+7s	+1s	+3s	+2s					+1s		

MIDDLESBROUGH—PLAYERS

Player and position	Ht.	Wt.	Birthplace	Clubs	League Appearances	Goals
Goalkeepers						
Pat Cuff	5 10	10 12	Middlesbrough	Middlesbrough	3	—
				Grimsby T. (on loan)	2	—
Jim Platt (N. Ireland)	6 1	12 10	Ballymoney	Middlesbrough	198	—
Defenders						
Terry Cooper (England)	5 7½	10 9	Castleford	Leeds U.	240+10	7
				Middlesbrough	49	1
John Craggs	5 8	12 0	Flinthill	Newcastle U.	50+2	1
				Middlesbrough	195	8
Bill Maddren	5 11	12 0	Billingham	Middlesbrough	250+2	19
Stuart Boam	6 0½	11 0	Kirkby	Mansfield T.	175	2
				Middlesbrough	201	10
*Frank Spraggon	5 9	12 2	Marley Hill	Middlesbrough	276+3	3
Ian Bailey	5 9	10 6	Middlesbrough	Middlesbrough	6	—
*John Symon	5 7	11 2	Middlesbrough	Middlesbrough	—	—
*Michael Taylor	5 10	10 1	Middlesbrough	Middlesbrough	3	—
Midfield						
Tony McAndrew	5 10	11 4	Lanark	Middlesbrough	14	3
Bobby Murdoch (Scotland)	5 10	12 8	Bothwell	Celtic	287+3	62
				Middlesbrough	93+2	6
Graham Souness (Scotland)	5 9½	11 6	Edinburgh	Tottenham H.	—	—
				Middlesbrough	127+2	17
Peter Brine	5 10	11 0	London	Middlesbrough	31+17	4
Dave Armstrong	5 8	10 0	Durham	Middlesbrough	150+2	17
Harry Charlton	5 7	9 4	Gateshead	Middlesbrough	8+2	—
				Hartlepool (on loan)	2+1	—
				Chesterfield (on loan)	6+1	—
Forwards						
John Hickton	6 0	12 0	Birmingham	Sheffield W.	52+1	21
				Middlesbrough	386+7	159
David Mills	5 8	10 0	Whitby	Middlesbrough	185+16	44
Malcolm Smith	5 8	11 0	Stockton	Middlesbrough	32+24	11
				Bury (on loan)	5	1
				Blackpool (on loan)	8	5
Alan Foggon	5 9	13 3	West Pelton	Newcastle U.	54+6	13
				Cardiff C.	14+3	1
				Middlesbrough	105+10	45
William Woof	5 10	11 9	Gateshead	Middlesbrough	3+4	1
				Brighton (on loan)	—	—
Alan Willey	5 11	11 2	Houghton le Spring	Middlesbrough	16+15	3
Graeme Hedley	5 7	8 6	Easington	Middlesbrough	—	—
Phil Boersma	5 10	11 7	Liverpool	Liverpool	73+10	18
				Wrexham (on loan)	3+2	—
				Middlesbrough	19	1
Edward Coleman	5 9	10 7	Middlesbrough	Middlesbrough	1	—
Alan Ramage	6 0	11 5	Guisborough	Middlesbrough	0+1	—

MILLWALL

Chairman: H. T. J. Burnidge, F.R.I.C.S.

Directors: N. Weedon, W. J. Nelan, L. Eppel, J. B. Rickard,

Manager: Gordon Jago.   *Secretary:* D. G. Borland.

Year Formed: 1885.   *Turned Professional:* 1890.

Limited Company: 1890.

Previous Grounds: 1885, Glengall Road, Millwall; 1886, Back of 'Lord Nelson'; 1890, East Ferry Road; 1901, North Greenwich; 1910, The Den.

Previous Names: 1885, Millwall Rovers; 1893, Millwall Athletic; 1920 Millwall.

Honours: *Football League*, Highest position in Division 2: 3rd, 1971–72. Division 3(S), Champions: 1927–28, 1937–38. Division 3, Runners-up: 1965–66. Division 4, Champions: 1961–62; Runners-up: 1964–65.   Longest unbeaten home run: Aug. 24, 1964 to Jan. 14, 1967.   *F.A. Cup*, best season: semi-finalists, 1900, 1903, 1937 (First Division 3 side to reach Semi-Final.)   *Football League Cup*, best season: 5th Rd., 1973–74.

Record Victory: 9-1 v Torquay U., Division 3(S), Aug. 29th, 1927; v Coventry C., Division 3(S), Nov. 19th, 1927.

Record Defeat: 1-9 v Aston Villa, F.A. Cup, 4th Rd., Jan. 28th, 1946.

Most League Points: 65, Division 3(S), 1927–28; Division 3, 1965–66.

Most League Goals: 127, Division 3(S), 1927–28.

Highest League Scorer in Season: Richard Parker, 37, Division 3(S), 1926–27.

Most Capped Player: Eamonn Dunphy, 26 (27), Eire.

Most League Appearances: Harry Cripps, 397, 1961–74.

Most League Goals in Total Aggregate: Derek Possee, 79, 1967–73.

Record Transfer Fee Received: £118,000 from Crystal Palace for Derek Possee, Jan. 1973.

Record Transfer Fee Paid: £45,000 to Shrewsbury T. for Alf Wood, May 1972.

Managers Since the War: Jack Cock, Charlie Hewitt, Ron Gray, Jimmy Seed, Reg. Smith, Ron Gray, Billy Gray, Benny Fenton.

Address of Supporters Club: Same as Ground.

Address of Club Shop or Boutique: Same.

The Den, Cold Blow Lane, London, SE14 5RH. Telephone 01-639 3143/4.   *Ground capacity:* 40,000.   *Record attendance:* 48,672 v Derby Co., F.A. Cup 5th Rd., February 20, 1937. *Record receipts:* £13,500 v Brighton & H.A., Division 3, April 16, 1976.   *Pitch measurements:* 112 yds × 74 yds.

How to get there: Buses from Central London and West End: 36, 36A, 36B, 53, 141, 163, 171, 177, 182 From City: 21. Nearest Underground stations, New Cross or New Cross Gate (Metropolitan Line). Also New Cross Gate British Rail station.

Match tickets: Bookable 10-14 days in advance from club office.

Car parking: N.C.P. car park near the ground. Also ample street parking.

Entertainments/catering facilities: Several licensed refreshment points around the ground.

Club shop: Two shops at the ground open on match days.

Handbooks/programmes: Programmes not available on subscription.

Extra information: Millwall went unbeaten for 59 successive League matches at the Den between 1964 and 1967.

Club Colours: Blue and white.

Change Colours: White shirts, white shorts, white stockings.

Club Captain: Barry Kitchener.

First Team Trainer/Physiotherapist: Jack Blackman.

Club Nickname: 'Lions'.

MILLWALL 1975–76 LEAGUE RECORD

Match No.	Date	Venue	Opponents	Result	H/T Score	League Pos'n	Goalscorers	Attendance
1	Aug 16	A	Halifax T.	W 2-1	2-0	—	Saul, Salvage	2460
2	23	H	Wrexham	W 2-1	1-0	3	Welsh, Hill	6784
3	30	A	Preston N.E.	L 1-2	0-1	8	Hill	7707
4	Sept 6	H	Hereford U.	W 1-0	0-0	4	Hill	6066
5	13	A	Grimsby T.	L 1-2	1-0	9	Summerill	6466
6	20	H	Southend U.	W 2-1	2-0	5	Hill 2	6418
7	24	A	Aldershot	D 1-1	0-0	—	Kitchener	4935
8	27	A	Bury	L 0-2	0-1	11		5682
9	Oct 4	H	Mansfield T.	W 1-0	0-0	7	Walker	6792
10	11	A	Sheffield W.	L 1-4	1-1	8	Salvage	10,144
11	18	H	Rotherham U.	W 3-1	1-1	6	Kitchener, Lee, Hill	6327
12	21	A	Walsall	D 1-1	0-0	—	Summerill	4884
13	25	A	Chesterfield	D 2-2	1-0	6	Hill, Lee	3500
14	Nov 1	A	Colchester U.	D 1-1	1-0	7	Hill	7492
15	4	H	Shrewsbury T.	D 0-0	0-0	—		7528
16	8	A	Chester	L 1-3	1-2	8	Lee	4811
17	15	H	Gillingham	D 2-2	1-1	8	Salvage (pen), Lee	6838
18	29	A	Port Vale	L 0-2	0-1	12		3580
19	Dec 6	A	Cardiff C.	L 1-3	0-0	13	Brisley	6092
20	20	H	Crystal Palace	W 2-1	1-0	12	Summerill, Walker	9841
21	26	A	Peterborough U.	D 1-1	1-1	12	Lee	10,653
22	27	H	Swindon T.	D 0-0	0-0	14		7022
23	Jan 3	A	Wrexham	D 1-1	1-0	11	May (og)	2779
24	10	H	Preston N.E.	W 2-0	1-0	9	Summerill, Saul	6057
25	16	A	Southend U.	D 0-0	0-0	10		7746
26	24	H	Grimsby T.	D 1-1	0-0	10	Kitchener	5486
27	31	H	Walsall	W 2-1	0-0	8	Brisley, Salvage	4747
28	Feb 3	A	Brighton & H.A.	L 0-1	0-0	—		15,332
29	7	A	Shrewsbury T.	L 0-1	0-0	9		4453
30	14	H	Chester	W 1-0	0-0	9	Kitchener	4965
31	21	A	Gillingham	L 1-3	0-2	10	McGrath	9111
32	25	H	Aldershot	W 4-1	0-0	—	Walker, Salvage, Seasman, Hazell	5904
33	28	H	Chesterfield	W 2-0	2-0	9	Evans, Salvage (pen)	6476
34	Mar 8	A	Mansfield T.	D 1-1	1-0	—	Summerill	7435
35	13	H	Sheffield W.	W 1-0	1-0	10	Kitchener	6769
36	16	A	Rotherham U.	W 2-1	0-1	—	McGrath, Summerill	4556
37	20	H	Port Vale	W 1-0	1-0	8	Summerill	7116
38	23	A	Colchester U.	W 1-0	1-0	—	Brisley	4573
39	27	A	Cardiff C.	D 0-0	0-0	5		12,511
40	30	A	Crystal Palace	D 0-0	0-0	—		34,893
41	Apr 3	H	Halifax T.	W 1-0	0-0	4	Moore	7237
42	7	H	Bury	D 0-0	0-0	—		10,001
43	10	A	Hereford U.	D 0-0	0-0	4		10,176
44	16	H	Brighton & H.A.	W 3-1	2-0	—	Lee, Seasman, Brisley	23,008
45	17	H	Peterborough U.	W 2-0	2-0	3	Walker, McGrath	11,377
46	20	A	Swindon T.	W 2-0	0-0	—	Seasman, Summerill	13,756

Goalscorers

League (54): Hill, 8 Summerill 8, Salvage 6 (2 pens), Lee 6, Kitchener 5, Walker, 4, Brisley 4, McGrath 3, Seasman 3, Saul 2, Welsh 1, Moore 1, Hazell 1, Evans 1, own goal 1.
League Cup (1): Summerill.
F.A. Cup (6): Kitchener, Salvage, Welsh, Hart, Summerill, Moore.

League Cup	First Round	Swindon T. (a)	1-2
	Second leg	(h)	0-1
F.A. Cup	First Round	Yeovil (a)	1-1
		(h)	2-2
			1-0 (at Aldershot)
	Second Round	Crystal Palace (h)	1-1
		(a)	1-2

Goddard	Evans	Moore	Jones	Kitchener	Hazell	Fairbrother	Brisley	Saul	Summerill	Salvage	Welsh	Hill	Dorney	Hart	Donaldson	Lee	Walker	Davies	McGrath	Seasman	Match No.
1	2	3	4	5	6	7	8	9	10	11											1
1	2	3		5	6		4	7	10	11		8	9								2
1	2	3	8	5	6		4		10	9	11*	7	12								3
1	2	3	8	5	6	7	4		10*	9	12	11									4
1	2	3	8	5	6		4		10	9		7	11								5
1	2	3	8	5	6		4		10	9	12	7*	11								6
1	2	3		5	6	7	4		12	9	10	11		8*							7
1	2	3		5	6	7	4		12	9	10*	11		8							8
1	2			5	6		4		9	12	11			8*	3	7	10				9
1	2	3	6	5			4*	8	10	11	12					9	7				10
1	2*	3		5	6		4	8	9	12		11				7	10				11
1		3		5	6		4	8	9	11		2				7	10				12
1	2	3		5	6		4	8	9	11						7	10				13
1	2	3		5	6		4	8	10*	11	12					9	7				14
1	2	3		5	6		4		9	11		8	12			7	10*				15
1	6	3		5	7		8*		12	10	11	4			2	9					16
1	2	8		5	6		4	10		11					3	7	9				17
1	2	3		5			8	10	11	12		4				7	6*	9			18
1	2	3		5			4	10	12	11	8*		6			7	9				19
1	2	3	4	5	6				12	9*11				10		7	8				20
1	2	3	4	5	6				9	11				8		7	10				21
1	2	3		5	6				9	11	12			8	4*	10	7				22
1	2	3		5	6		4		12	9		11		8*		7	10				23
1	2	3		5	6		4		12	9*11				8		7	10				24
1	2	3		5	6		4		9	11				8		7	10				25
1	2	3		5	6		4	8	9	11						7	10				26
1	2	3		5	6		4		12	9		11		8*		7	10				27
1	2	3		5	6		4		9	11				8		7	10				28
1	2	3		5*	6		4		9	11	12			8		7	10				29
1	2	3		5	6		4		12	9	11*			8		7	10				30
1	2	3		5	6		4			11						7	10		8	9	31
1	2	3		5	6		4		9	11							10		7	8	32
1	2	3		5	6		4		9	11							10		7	8	33
1		3		5	6		4		9			12			2	11*10			7	8	34
1		3		5	6		4		9*11						2	12	10		7	8	35
1		3		5	6		4		9	11*					2	12	10		7	8	36
1		3		5	6		4		9						2	11	10		7	8	37
1		3		5	6		4		9						2	11	10		7	8	38
1		3		5	6		4		9	12					2	11*10			7	8	39
1		3		5	6		4		9	12					2	11	10		7	8*	40
1		3		5	6		4		9						2	11	10		7	8	41
1		3		5	6		4		9	12					2	11	10		7*	8	42
1		3		5	6		4		9*12						2	11	10		7	8	43
1		3		5	6		4		9						2	11	10		7	8	44
1		3			6		4		9			5			2	11	10		7	8	45
1		3		5	6		4		9	7					2	11	10			8	46
46	32	34	15	45	45	4	43	18	38	27	5	15	6	13	17	34	35	3	15	16	

+7s +1s +8s +4s   +2s +3s   +2s

MILLWALL—PLAYERS

Player and position	Ht.	Wt.	Birthplace	Clubs	League Appearances	Goals
Goalkeepers						
Ray Goddard	5 10	11 9	Fulham	Orient	279	—
				Morton (on loan)	1	—
				Millwall	46	—
Defenders						
David Donaldson	5 10	11 2	London	Arsenal	—	—
				Millwall	72	1
Alan Dorney	5 11½	12 4	Bermondsey	Millwall	243+3	1
*Eddie Jones	5 6	10 8	Finchley	Tottenham H.	—	—
				Millwall	58+1	—
Ray Evans	5 10½	12 4	Edmonton	Tottenham H.	132+4	2
				Millwall	45	2
Barry Kitchener	6 1½	13 8	Dagenham	Millwall	378+2	20
Jon Moore	5 10	11 3	Cardiff	Bristol R.	—	—
				Millwall	56	3
Midfield						
Terry Brisley	5 7	10 2	Stepney	Orient	133+9	10
				Southend U. (on loan)	8	—
				Millwall	43	4
Tony Hazell	5 10	11 6	High Wycombe	Q.P.R.	361+7	4
				Millwall	66	3
Barry Salvage	5 11	11 10	Bristol	Fulham	7	—
				Millwall	1+1	—
				Q.P.R.	16+5	1
				Brentford	87	8
				Millwall	27+8	6
Frank Saul	5 10½	11 2	Canvey Island	Tottenham H.	112+4	37
				Southampton	46+7	2
				Q.P.R.	58+5	7
				Millwall	85+11	4
				(contract cancelled March 1976)		
Barrie Fairbrother	5 8	11 7	Hackney	Orient	171+18	41
				Millwall	4	—
Forwards						
Phil Summerill	5 10½	11 2	Birmingham	Birmingham C.	107+8	46
				Huddersfield T.	48+6	11
				Millwall	58+1	14
*Alan Hart	5 7	10 3	London	Charlton Ath.	3	2
				Millwall	13+3	—
Alan Welsh	5 8	11 0	Edinburgh	Millwall	3	—
				Torquay U.	139+9	45
				Plymouth Arg.	64+2	14
				Bournemouth	33+2	3
				Millwall	5+4	1
Terry Shanahan	5 10	11 0	Paddington	Tottenham H.	—	—
				Ipswich T.	3+1	—
				Blackburn R. (on loan)	6	—
				Halifax T.	88+8	23
				Chesterfield	56+4	28
				Millwall	—	—
John Seasman	5 9	10 7	Liverpool	Tranmere R.	15+2	—
				Luton T.	7+1	2
				Millwall	16	3
Trevor Lee	5 11	11 9	London	Millwall	34+2	6
Phillip Walker	5 9	11 9	London	Millwall	35	4

NEWCASTLE UNITED   DIV. 1

Chairman: Rt. Hon. Lord Westwood, J.P., F.C.I.S.
Vice-Chairman: R. J. Rutherford.
Directors: G. S. Seymour, F. Braithwaite, O.B.E., J. Rush,
H. H. Dickson, W. G. McKeag.
General Manager: Joe Harvey.
Team Manager: Gordon Lee.
Secretary: R. Cushing.
Assistant Secretary: A. J. Garvie.
Year Formed: 1882. *Turned Professional:* 1889.
Limited Company: 1890.
Previous Name: Newcastle East End until Newcastle U. in 1892.
Previous Grounds: Chillingham Road, Heaton, until 1892.

Honours: *Football League:* Division 1, Champions: 1904–05,
1906–07, 1908–09, 1926–27. Division 2, Champions: 1964–65;
Runners-up: 1897–98, 1947–48. *F.A. Cup,* Winners: 1910,
1924, 1932, 1951 1952, 1955; Runners-up: 1905, 1906, 1908, 1911, 1974. *Football League Cup:*
Runners-up, 1975–76. **European Competitions:** *European Fairs Cup:* 1968–69 (Winners),
1969–70, 1970–71. *Anglo-Italian Cup,* Winners 1973. *Texaco Cup* Winners, 1973–74, 1974–75.

Record Victory: 13–0 v Newport Co., Division 2, Oct. 5th 1946.
Record Defeat: 0–9 v Burton Wanderers, Division 2, April, 15, 1895
Most League Points: 57, Division 2, 1964–65.
Most League Goals: 98, Division 1, 1951–52.
Highest League Scorer in Season: Hughie Gallacher, 36, Division 1, 1926–27.
Most Capped Player: Alf McMichael, 40, Ireland.
Most League Appearances: Jim Lawrence, 432, 1904–22.
Most League Goals in Total Aggregate: Jackie Milburn, 178, 1946–57.
Record Transfer Fee Received: £175,000 from Liverpool for Terry McDermott Nov. 1974.
Record Transfer Fee Paid: £180,000 to Luton T. for Malcolm Macdonald, May 1971.
Managers Since the War: George Martin, Duggie Livingstone, Charlie Mitten, Norman
Smith, Joe Harvey.
Address of Club Shop or Boutique: Magpie Shop, St. James' Park, Newcastle-upon-Tyne
NE1 4ST.
Address of Supporters' Club: Newcastle United Supporters' Club, 2 St. James Street, New-
castle-upon-Tyne, NE1 4NF.

St, James' Park, Newcastle-upon-Tyne NE1 4ST Telephone Newcastle 28361/2. Information
service 611571. *Telegraphic address:* 'Football, Newcastle-upon-Tyne'. *Ground capacity:*
56,000 (35,000 covered). *Record attendance:* 68,386 v Chelsea, Division 1, September 3, 1930.
Record receipts: £42,415 v Ujpest Dozsa, European Fairs Cup Final, May 29, 1969. *Pitch
measurements:* 115 yds × 75 yds.
How to get there: The ground is central and within walking distance of the railway station and the town
centre.
Match tickets: Postal and personal applications accepted 10 days before the match.
Car parking: Car park on the north side of the ground. Street parking available.
Entertainments/catering facilities: Excellent facilities in the New Stand. Refreshments available in all parts
of the ground.
Club shop: Open Saturdays 9.30–3.00. Run by the Supporters' Club.
Handbooks/programmes: Handbook, 'Magpie', published by Supporters' Club. Programmes if available
can be ordered from the secretary up to three weeks after the match.
Extra information: United's 13–0 win over Newport County in 1946 was a Second Division record score.

Club Colours: Black and white striped shirts, black shorts, black and white stockings. *Change Colours:*
Yellow shirts, green shorts, yellow and green stockings. *First Team Trainer/Coach:* R. Dinns. *Club
Nickname:* 'Magpies'.

NEWCASTLE UNITED 1975-76 LEAGUE RECORD

Match No.	Date	Venue	Opponents	Result	H/T Score	League Pos'n	Goalscorers	Attendance
1	Aug 16	A	Ipswich T.	W 3-0	2-0	—	Macdonald 2, Craig, T. (pen)	27,579
2	20	H	Middlesbrough	D 1-1	0-1	—	Macdonald	41,481
3	23	H	Leicester C.	W 3-0	2-0	2	Macdonald 2, Burns	37,471
4	27	A	Derby Co.	L 2-3	1-0	—	Bruce, Macdonald	27,858
5	30	A	Manchester C.	L 0-4	0-1	11		31,875
6	Sept 6	H	Aston Villa	W 3-0	2-0	8	Macdonald 2, Craig, T.	34,668
7	13	A	Everton	L 0-3	0-2	10		28,938
8	20	H	Wolverhampton W.	W 5-1	1-1	8	Gowling 3, Tudor, Cassidy	29,834
9	23	A	Birmingham C.	L 2-3	1-3	—	Nulty, Craig T.	31,166
10	27	A	Q.P.R.	L 0-1	0-1	14		22,981
11	Oct 4	H	Tottenham H.	D 2-2	1-0	14	Tudor, Barrowclough	32,235
12	11	A	West Ham U.	L 1-2	0-1	16	Howard	30,400
13	18	H	Norwich C.	W 5-2	1-1	11	Macdonald 2, Gowling 2, Jones (og)	31,868
14	25	A	Stoke C.	D 1-1	0-0	12	Gowling	24,057
15	Nov 1	H	Arsenal	W 2-0	1-0	11	Gowling, Nattrass	32,824
16	8	A	Leeds U.	L 0-3	0-2	11		39,304
17	15	H	Liverpool	L 1-2	1-1	13	Nulty	39,686
18	22	A	Norwich C.	W 2-1	0-1	11	Nulty 2	19,700
19	29	A	Manchester U.	L 0-1	0-0	14		52,624
20	Dec 6	H	Coventry C.	W 4-0	2-0	11	Craig, D., Craig, T. 2 (1 a pen) Burns	26,372
21	13	A	Leicester C.	L 0-1	0-0	15		18,310
22	20	H	Ipswich T.	D 1-1	0-1	13	Nulty	25,098
23	26	A	Burnley	W 1-0	0-0	13	Craig T.	22,458
24	27	H	Sheffield U.	D 1-1	0-0	12	Macdonald	30,730
25	Jan 10	A	Everton	W 5-0	2-0	12	Nattrass, Gowling 3, Nulty	32,076
26	17	A	Aston Villa	D 1-1	1-1	12	Gowling	36,387
27	31	A	Middlesbrough	D 3-3	0-1	12	Gowling, Kennedy, Nattress	31,000
28	Feb 7	H	Derby Co.	W 4-3	1-0	9	Todd (og), Nulty, Craig, T. (pen) Macdonald	44,488
29	21	A	Liverpool	L 0-2	0-1	12		43,404
30	Mar 3	H	Stoke C.	L 0-1	0-1	—		37,459
31	13	H	West Ham U.	W 2-1	1-1	14	Macdonald, Craig, T. (pen)	32,842
32	16	A	Arsenal	D 0-0	0-0	—		18,424
33	20	H	Manchester U.	L 3-4	3-2	15	Burns, Macdonald, Gowling	41,427
34	27	A	Coventry C.	D 1-1	1-1	13	Bird	14,144
35	31	H	Leeds U.	L 2-3	1-2	—	Craig, T. (pen), Gowling	32,685
36	Apr 3	H	Q.P.R.	L 1-2	1-1	14	Gowling	30,134
37	7	H	Birmingham C.	W 4-0	2-0	—	Burns, Gowling, Macdonald 2	18,547
38	10	A	Wolverhampton W.	L 0-5	0-0	14		20,083
39	14	H	Manchester C.	W 2-1	1-1	—	Cassidy, Macdonald	21,095
40	17	H	Burnley	L 0-1	0-1	13		23,984
41	19	A	Sheffield U.	L 0-1	0-1	—		18,906
42	24	A	Tottenham H.	W 3-0	0-0	15	Burns, Macdonald 2	30,049

Goalscorers

League (71): Macdonald 19, Gowling 16, Craig, T. 9 (5 pens), Nulty 7, Burns 5, Nattrass 3, Tudor 2, Cassidy 2, Bruce 1, Barrowclough 1, Howard, 1 Craig, D. 1, Kennedy 1, Bird 1, Own Goals 2.
League Cup (17): Gowling 7, Cannell 2, Nulty 2, Craig, T. (1 a pen), Nattrass, Keeley, Burns, Macdonald, Own Goal 1.
F.A. Cup (13): Gowling 7, Macdonald 4, Burns 2, Craig, T. (1 a pen), Cassidy.

League Cup	Second Round	Southport (h)	6-0
	Third Round	Bristol R. (a)	1-1
		(h)	2-0
	Fourth Round	Q.P.R. (a)	3-1
	Fifth Round	Notts Co. (h)	1-0
	Semi-Final	Tottenham H. (a)	0-1
		(h)	3-1
	Final	Manchester C.	1-2
F.A. Cup	Third Round	Q.P.R. (a)	0-0
		(h)	2-1
	Fourth Round	Coventry C. (a)	1-1
		(h)	5-0
	Fifth Round	Bolton W. (a)	3-3
		(h)	0-0 (a.e.t.)
			2-1 (at Leeds)
	Sixth Round	Derby Co. (a)	2-4

Mahoney	Nattrass	Kennedy	Nulty	Howard	Hibbitt	Burns	Bruce	Macdonald	Gowling	Craig, T.	Barrowclough	Bird	Cassidy	Tudor	Keeley	Craig, D.	Blackhall	Hudson	Cannell	Jones	Oates	McCaffrey	McLean	Match No.
1	2	3	4	5	6	7	8	9	10	11														1
1	2	3	4	5	6	7	8*	9	10	11	12													2
1	2	3	4	5	6	7	8	9	10	11														3
1	2	3	4	5	6	7	8*	9	10	11	12													4
1	2	3	4	6			8	9	10	11	7	5												5
1	2	3	4	6		7		9	10	11		5	8											6
1	2	3	4	6			8		10	11	12	5	7	9*										7
1	2	3	4	6		7			10	11		5	8	9										8
1	2	3	4	6		7			10	11		5	8	9										9
1	2	3	11	6		7		9	10			4		8	5									10
1	2	3	4	6		7		9	10	11	12	5		8*										11
1	2	3	4	6			8	9	10	11	7	5												12
1	2	3	4	6		7		9	10	11		8				5								13
1	4	3	6	5		7*		9	10	11		8	12			2								14
1	2	3	4	6		7		9	10	11		8				5								15
1	4	3	6	5		7		9	10	11		8				2								16
1	4	3	6	5		7		9	10	11		8				2								17
1	2	3	4	6		7		9	10	11		8				5								18
1	2	3	4	6		7*		9	10	11		8		12		5								19
1	2	3	4	6		7		9	10	11		8				5								20
1	2	3	4	6		7		9	10	11		8				5								21
1	2	3	4	6		7		9	10	11		8				5								22
1	2	3	4	6		12		9	10	11			7	8*		5								23
1	2	3	4	6				9	10	11		8	7			5								24
1	2	3	4	6		7		9	10	11		5	8											25
1	2	3	4	6		7		9	10*	11	12	5	8											26
1	2	3	4	6			8	9	10	11			7	5										27
1	2	3	4	6		7		9	10	11				5	8									28
1	2	3		6		7		9	10	11	4		8	12	5*									29
1		3		6		7		9*		11	4		8	5			2	12	10					30
		3		6		7		9	10	11	4	5	8				2		1					31
		3		6		7		9	10	11	4	5	8				2		1					32
	2	3		6		7		9	10	11	4	5	8*							1	12			33
1	2	3		6*		7		9	10	11	4	5				12					8			34
1	2	3				7		9	10	11	4	5									8	6		35
1	2	3				7		9	10	11	4	5									8	6		36
1	2	3				7		9	10	11	4	5									8	6		37
1	2	3				7		9	10	12	4*	5				11					8	6		38
1	2	3				7		9	10	11	5*	4									8	6	12	39
1	2	3				7		9	10	11		4									8	6	5	40
	2	3				7		9	10	11		4	8							1	6*	5	12	41
	2	3				7		9	10	11		4								1	6	5	8	42
37	39	42	28	34	4	40	4	39	41	39	23	19	20	6	4	14	3	7	1	5	9	3	1	
							+1s		+1s	+5s	+1s		+1s	+1s			+2s				+1s	+1s	+1s	

Player and position	Ht.	Wt.	Birthplace	Clubs	League Appearances	Goals
Goalkeepers						
Iam McFaul (N. Ireland)	5 9½	12	Coleraine	Linfield	not known	—
				Newcastle U.	290	—
Mike Mahoney	5 11	11 10	Bristol	Bristol C.	4	—
				Torquay U.	157	—
				Newcastle U.	39	—
Roger Jones	5 11	12 4	Upton on Severn	Bournemouth	160	—
				Blackburn R.	242	—
				Newcastle U.	5	—
*Edward Edgar	5 11	12 4	Bristol	Newcastle U.	—	—
Kevin Carr	5 10	10 9	Ashington	Newcastle U.	—	—
Defenders						
John Bird	6 0	12 0	Doncaster	Doncaster R.	48+2	3
				Preston N.E.	166	9
				Newcastle U.	19+1	1
David Craig (N. Ireland)	5 9½	11 3	Belfast	Newcastle U.	338+4	8
Pat Howard	5 11	12 0	Dodworth	Barnsley	176+1	6
				Newcastle U.	182+1	7
Aiden McCaffery	5 11	11 2	Newcastle	Newcastle U.	5+2	—
Glen Keeley	5 10	12 0	Barking	Ipswich T.	4	—
				Newcastle U.	43+1	2
Alan Kennedy	5 9	10 7	Sunderland	Newcastle U.	87+3	4
Allan Barker	5 9	10 8	Newcastle	Newcastle U.	2	—
Peter Kelly	5 7	10 0	Lothian	Newcastle U.	1	—
Irving Nattrass	5 10	11 6	Fishburn	Newcastle U.	128+11	9
Danny Close	5 8	10 4	Newcastle	Newcastle U.	—	—
Mel Owens	5 6	9 4	Durham	Newcastle U.	—	—
Ray Blackhall	5 9	11 8	Ashington	Newcastle U.	4	—
Midfield						
Tom Craig (Scotland)	5 7½	11 7	Aberdeen	Aberdeen	43+2	8
				Sheffield W.	211+3	38
				Newcastle U.	58+1	11
Stewart Barrowclough	5 7	9 0	Barnsley	Barnsley	9	—
				Newcastle U.	130+15	16
Geoff Nulty	5 10	10 9	Prestcott	Burnley	123+7	20
				Newcastle U.	48	8
Jim Smith (Scotland)	5 11	11 8	Glasgow	Aberdeen	103+1	21
				Newcastle U.	124+5	13
Ray Hudson	5 11	11 3	Dunston	Newcastle U.	8+3	—
Tony Smith	5 11	11 6	Sunderland	Newcastle U.	—	—
Graham Oates	6 2	12 4	Bradford	Bradford C.	158+3	19
				Blackburn R.	76	10
				Newcastle U.	9+1	—
Forwards						
Micky Burns	5 7	10 8½	Blackpool	Blackpool	173+6	53
				Newcastle U.	61+2	10
Tom Cassidy (N. Ireland)	5 11½	13 1	Belfast	Coleraine	not known	—
				Newcastle U.	70+9	9
Alan Gowling	6 0	11 10	Stockport	Manchester U.	64+7	18
				Huddersfield T.	128	58
				Newcastle U.	41	16
Malcolm Macdonald (England)	5 8	11 3	London	Fulham	10+3	5
				Luton T.	88	49
				Newcastle U.	187	95
John Tudor	5 10	11 10	Ilkeston	Coventry C.	63+6	13
				Sheffield U.	64+7	30
				Newcastle U.	160+3	53
Paul Cannell	5 10	10 12	Newcastle	Newcastle U.	10	1
*Alan Barker	5 10	10 10	Durham	Newcastle U.	—	—
Ken Mitchell	5 11	11 8	Sunderland	Newcastle U.	—	—
Colin Chambers	5 7	10 11	Newcastle	Newcastle U.	—	—
Alan Guy	5 9	10 0	Jarrow	Newcastle U.	—	—
David McLean	5 7	9 12	Newcastle	Newcastle U.	1+1	—

NEWPORT COUNTY DIV. 4

Chairman: C. Rogers.

Directors: B. D. Mills, R. Warry, J. C. O'Dwyer, Frank Catson (Executive Director).

Manager: Jimmy Scoular.

Secretary: K. L. Saunders.

Commercial Manager: Alf Buckley.

Year Formed: 1912. *Turned Professional:* 1912.

Limited Company: 1912.

Honours: *Football League,* highest position in Division 3: 13th, 1959–60, 1960–61. Division 3(S), Champions: 1938–39. *F.A. Cup,* best season: 5th Rd. 1948–49. *Football League Cup:* never past 3rd Rd.

Record Victory: 10-0 v Merthyr Town, Division 3(S), Apr. 10th, 1930.

Record Defeat: 0-13 v Newcastle U., Division 2, Oct. 5th, 1946.

Most League Points: 56, Division 4, 1972–73.

Most League Goals: 85, Division 4, 1964–65.

Highest League Scorer in Season: Tudor Martin, 34, Division 3(S), 1929–30.

Most League Goals in Total Aggregate: Reg Parker, 99, 1948–54.

Most Capped Players: Fred Cook, 2 (9), Jack Nicholls, 2 (4), Alf Sherwood, 2 (41), Bill Thomas 2, Harold Williams 2 (all for Wales).

Most League Appearances: Ray Wilcox, 530, 1946–60.

Record Transfer Fee Received: £15,000 from Swindon T. for Steve Aizlewood, March, 1976.

Record Transfer Fee Paid: £10,000 to Bristol Rovers for Brian Godfrey, June 1973.

Managers Since the War: Billy McCandless, Tom Bromilow, Fred Stansfield, Bill Lucas, Bobby Evans, Bill Lucas, Trevor Morris, Les Graham, Bob Ferguson, Bill Lucas, Brian Harris, Dave Elliott.

Address of Supporters Club: Same as Football Club.

Somerton Park, Newport, Mon. Telephone 71543 and 71271. *Ground capacity:* 22,060 (seating 672). *Record attendance:* 24,268 v Cardiff C., Division 3(S), October 16, 1937. *Record receipts:* £4,069 v Cardiff C., Welsh Cup, February 20, 1973. *Pitch measurements:* 112 yds × 78 yds.

How to get there: Nearest railway station, Newport. By bus: the Chepstow Road bus to Beechwood and walk down over Somerton Hill; the Corporation Road bus to Cromwell Road and Somerton Park. All buses from bus centre in Dock Street.

Match tickets: Seats can be reserved from the club secretary.

Car parking: Car park at the back of the Social Club Stand in Cromwell Road. Otherwise street parking.

Entertainments/catering facilities: Licensed bar in Supporters' Club. Licensed bar in the Social Club at Cromwell Road; both membership only. Licensed bars on both sides of ground.

Club shop: Sells all types of souvenirs.

Handbooks/programmes: Back issues of programmes available from programme shop. Club history available from Vice-President's club, Somerton Park. Match programmes available on subscription.

Extra information: Newport hold the unenviable record of most defeats in the Third Division—31 in 1961–62.

Club Colours: Sky blue and white striped shirts, sky blue shorts, black stockings

Change Colours: Tangerine shirts, black shorts, tangerine stockings.

First Team Trainer: Ronnie Bird.

Club Nickname: 'The Ironsides'.

NEWPORT COUNTY 1975–76 LEAGUE RECORD

Match No.	Date	Venue	Opponents	Result	H/T Score	League Pos'n	Goalscorers	Attendance
1	Aug 16	H	Lincoln C.	W 3-1	3-1	—	Jones 2, Woods	2797
2	23	A	Workington	W 2-1	1-0	3	Woods, Jones	1425
3	30	H	Scunthorpe	D 0-0	0-0	3		2375
4	Sept 6	A	Rochdale	L 3-4	0-3	7	Woods 2, Jones	1119
5	13	H	Southport	W 2-0	1-0	1	Godfrey, White	2342
6	20	A	AFC Bournemouth	L 0-2	0-0	8		3993
7	23	A	Swansea C.	D 2-2	2-2	—	Aizlewood 2	4500
8	27	H	Cambridge U.	W 2-0	0-0	8	Parson 2	2244
9	Oct 4	A	Brentford	W 3-1	2-1	6	Jones, Bell, Hooper	5680
10	11	H	Barnsley	W 1-0	0-0	4	Woods	3043
11	18	A	Huddersfield T.	L 1-2	0-1	6	Parsons	5477
12	20	H	Reading	D 0-0	0-0	—		2955
13	25	H	Exeter C.	D 3-3	0-2	6	Parsons 2, Jones	2871
14	Nov 1	A	Torquay U.	D 1-1	1-0	9	Parsons	2163
15	3	A	Stockport Co.	W 1-0	0-0	—	Fogarty (og)	2208
16	8	H	Bradford C.	W 3-1	3-0	5	Hooper, Love, White	2747
17	15	A	Doncaster R.	L 1-5	0-1	7	Parsons	7793
18	29	A	Hartlepool	L 1-4	0-2	9	Godfrey	2780
19	Dec 6	H	Darlington	W 4-1	1-1	7	Craig (og), Jones, Parsons, White	1878
20	20	A	Watford	L 1-3	1-2	9	Parsons	3261
21	26	H	Crewe Alex	D 2-2	1-0	9	Woodruff, Parsons	3788
22	27	A	Northampton	L 0-3	0-2	10		8448
23	Jan 3	H	Tranmere R.	L 1-5	0-1	13	Parsons	2074
24	10	A	Scunthorpe U.	W 2-1	2-0	10	Woods 2	1739
25	17	H	AFC Bournemouth	W 3-1	1-0	7	Morgan o.g., Parsons, White	1496
26	24	A	Southport	L 0-3	0-0	9		1268
27	Feb 7	H	Stockport Co.	D 2-2	1-0	9	White, Aizlewood (pen)	1652
28	21	H	Doncaster R.	L 2-3	1-2	14	Parsons, Woods	1543
29	23	H	Swansea C.	L 1-2	0-2	—	Aizlewood (pen)	2040
30	28	A	Exeter C.	L 0-3	0-1	16		3447
31	Mar 2	A	Reading	L 0-1	0-1	—		6211
32	5	H	Torquay U.	L 0-2	0-1	17		1588
33	8	H	Brentford	W 1-0	1-0	—	Parsons	1150
34	13	A	Barnsley	L 1-3	1-0	17	Woods	2587
35	17	H	Huddersfield T.	L 1-2	0-1	—	Parsons	1374
36	20	H	Hartlepool	L 0-1	0-0	18		1230
37	27	A	Darlington	L 0-4	0-1	20		1312
38	31	H	Watford	L 0-2	0-2	—		1092
39	Apr 3	A	Lincoln C.	L 1-4	0-2	20	Morgan	8178
40	6	A	Cambridge U.	W 1-0	0-0	—	Love	1361
41	10	H	Rochdale	D 1-1	1-1	19	Jones	1331
42	14	A	Tranmere R.	L 1-3	0-2	—	Jones	2629
43	17	A	Crewe Alex.	L 0-4	0-3	21		1971
44	20	H	Northampton T.	D 1-1	0-0	—	Jones	1728
45	24	H	Workington	L 2-3	0-1	22	Woods, Jones	1226
46	May 3	A	Bradford C.	L 0-3	0-1	—		1676

Goalscorers

League (57): Parsons 15, Jones 11, Woods 10, White 5, Aizlewood 4 (2 pens), Godfrey 2, Hooper 2, Love 2, Bell 1, Morgan 1, Woodruff 1, own goals 3.
League Cup (1): Love.
F.A. Cup (2): Godfrey, Parsons.

League Cup	First Round	Exeter C. (h)		1-1
	Second Leg	(a)		0-2
F.A. Cup	First Round	Swindon T. (h)		2-2
		(a)		0-3

Macey	Screen	Bell	Love	Aizlewood, S.	Elliott	Hooper	Jones	Woodruff	Woods	White	Godfrey	Parsons	Hancock	Relish	Passey	Preece	Cawston	Powell	Hayes	Pimblett	Morgan	Aizlewood, M.	Dowler	Match No.
1	2	3	4	5	6	7	8	9	10	11														1
1	2	3	4	5	6	7	8	9	10	11														2
1	2	3	4*	5	6	7	8	9	10	11	12													3
1	2	3	8	5	6	7	12	9*	10	11	4													4
1	2	3	9	5	6	7	8		10	11	4													5
1	2	3	8	5	6	7	10		9	11	4													6
1	2	3	9	5	6	7	8		10	11	4													7
1	2	3	8	6	7	5			10	11	4	9												8
1	2	3	8	5	7	6			10	11	4	9												9
1	2	3	8	5	7	6			10	11	4	9												10
1	2	3	10	5	8	7			6	11	4	9												11
1	2	3	9	5*	7	6			10	11	4	8	12											12
1	2	3	8	5	6	7			10	11	4	9												13
1	2	3*	8	5	11	7	10	12	4	9	6													14
1	2		9	5	11	7	10	12	4*	8	6	3												15
1	2		8	5	4	7	10		11	9	6	3												16
1	2		8	5	4	7	10		11	9	6	3												17
1	2		8	5					9	11	4		6	3	7	10								18
1	2		8	5		7			10	11	4	9			3	6								19
1	2		8	5*		7			9	11	4	10	12		3	6								20
1		7*	5	8	6				10	11	4	9	12	3	2									21
1		7	5	8	6				10	11	4	9		3*	2	12								22
1		3	8	5*	7				10	11	4	9	2	6	12									23
		3	5			7		9	10	11	8	6	4				1	2						24
		3	4	5				9	10	11	8	6	7				1	2						25
		3*	8	5					10	11	4	9	6	7			1	2	12					26
		3	9	5	6				10	11	4	8	2		7		1							27
1	2	3	5						10	11	4	8	6		9	7								28
1	8	3	5						9	11	4	10	6		2	7								29
1	8	3	7	5					9	11	4		6		2									30
1	2	3	10	5					9	11	4	8	12		6	7*								31
1		3	10	5	6				9	11	4	8	12		2	7*								32
1		3	10	5					9	11	4	8	6		7		2							33
1		3	7	5					10	11	4	9	6				2			8				34
1		3	10	5					9	11		8	12		6*	7	2	4						35
1		3	7		11				10		12	8	5		9*		2	6		4				36
1		3	7						10	11		9	6		2			12		4	5	8*		37
1	2	3	10*						9	11	4	8	6		7					5	12			38
1	2	3	10						9		4	8	6		7					5	11			39
		3	12						10		9	4	8		2		6			7	5	11*	1	40
		3	7						9	11	4	8			2		6	12			5	10*	1	41
		3	7						9	11	4	8			2		6*	12		10	5		1	42
	2		8						10	11	4	9	7		6		3				5		1	43
			7				8		10	11	4	9			2		3			5	6		1	44
		3	7	5			8		10	11	4	9	2*		6	12							1	45
	2	3	10	5			8		12	11	4	9			6	7*							1	46
35	31	35	41	30	21	17	35	11	32	39	35	38	20	8	22	13	4	7	4	7	9	5	7	
			+1s			+1s	+1s			+3s	+1s				+6s	+5s				+1s		+1s	+1s	

265

NEWPORT COUNTY—PLAYERS

Player and position	Ht.	Wt.	Birthplace	Clubs	League Appearances	Goals
Goalkeepers						
*John Macey	5 9	11 6	Bristol	Bristol C.	—	—
				Grimsby T.	36+1	—
				Newport Co.	194	—
Don Payne	5 10	10 0	Swansea	Swansea C.	11	—
				Torquay U.	—	—
				Newport Co.	32	—
Mike Dowler	5 8	11 0	Caldicot	Hereford U.	—	—
				Newport Co.	7	—
Defenders						
Gary Bell	5 7	10 10	Stourbridge	Cardiff C.	219+2	10
				Hereford U. (on loan)	8	—
				Newport Co.	69	3
*Peter Passey	5 8	9 13	Birmingham	Birmingham C.	—	—
				Newport Co.	136	2
Graham Coldrick	5 11	12 0	Newport	Cardiff C.	91+5	2
				Newport Co.	156+1	10
				(contract cancelled Oct 1975)		
John Relish	5 9	11 0	Liverpool	Chester	10+1	1
				Bury (on loan)	—	—
				Newport Co.	26+4	—
Michael Powell	5 10	11 7	Newport	Newport Co.	7	—
Billy Screen	5 7	9 8	Swansea	Swansea C.	134+9	14
				Newport Co.	137+5	7
Peter Morgan	5 10	11 12	Cardiff	Cardiff Co.	16	—
				Hereford U. (on loan)	16	—
				Newport Co.	9+1	1
Midfield						
*Michael Hancock	5 10	11 0	Newport	Newport Co.	51+9	1
*Dave Elliott	5 8	12 3	Durham	Sunderland	30+1	—
				Newcastle U.	77+2	4
				Southend U.	163+4	10
				Newport Co.	21	—
Mark Aizlewood	6 0	11 7	Newport	Newport Co.	5+1	—
*Paul Preece	5 8	9 6	Penarth	Newport Co.	17+6	—
John Parsons	5 8	10 11	Cardiff	Cardiff C.	7+8	6
				Bournemouth	6+1	1
				Newport Co	48+2	19
Michael Hayes	5 11	12 0	Newport	Newport Co.	4+1	—
*Brian Godfrey (Wales)	5 8	11 7	Flint	Everton	1	—
				Scunthorpe	87	24
				Preston N.E.	126+1	52
				Aston Villa	139+4	22
				Bristol R.	79+2	16
				Newport Co.	117+1	14
Forwards						
Wynne Hooper	5 9	10 12	Neath	Newport Co.	163+13	21
Roderick Jones	5 9	11 6	Rhiwderin	Newport Co.	206+8	62
*Alistair Love	5 7	10 1	Edinburgh	W.B.A.	—	—
				Southend U.	6+5	—
				Newport Co.	41+1	2
Andy White	5 7	10 6	Newport	Newport Co.	209+24	25
*Bobby Woodruff	5 11	11 4	Highworth	Swindon T.	184	19
				Wolverhampton	63	18
				C. Palace	123+2	48
				Cardiff C.	141+9	22
				Newport Co.	52	7
Edward Woods	6 0	15 0	Ferndale	Bristol C.	1+1	—
				Scunthorpe U. (on loan)	4	2
				Newport Co.	73	31

Life Vice-President: W. R. Penn.

Chairman: N. J. Ronson.

Directors: C. R. Brett, N. J. Ronson, T. C. Hadland, R. P. Dilliegh, E. P. Northover, J. D. Adkins, G. Taylor, L Jaffa.

Secretary/General Manager: Dave Bowen.

Team Manager: Bill Dodgin.

Year Formed: 1897.   *Turned Professional:* 1901. *Limited Company:* 1901.

Honours: Football League, highest position in Division 1: 21st, 1965–66. Division 2, Runners-up: 1964–65. Division 3, Champions: 1962–63. Division 3(S), Runners-up: 1927–28, 1949–50. Division 4, Promoted: 1960–61 (3rd). Runners-up 1975-76 *F.A. Cup,* best season: 5th Rd., 1933–34, 1949–50, 1969–70. *Football League Cup,* best season: 5th Rd., 1964–65, 1966–67.

Record Victory: 10-0 v Walsall, Division 3(S), Nov. 5th, 1927.

Record Defeat: 0-10 v Bournemouth, Division 3(S), Sept. 2, 1939.

Most League Points: 62, Division 3(S), 1952–53; Division 3, 1962–63.

Most League Goals: 109, Division 3, 1962–63; Division 3(S), 1952–53.

Highest League Scorer in Season: Cliff Holton, 36, Division 3, 1961–62.

Most League Goals in Total Aggregate: Jack English, 135, 1947–60.

Most Capped Player: E. Lloyd Davies, 12 (16), Wales.

Most League Appearances: Tommy Fowler, 521, 1946–61 (39 F.A. Cup ties).

Record Transfer Fee Received: £65,000 from Liverpool for Phil Neal, November 1974.

Record Transfer Fee Paid: £20,000 to Coventry C. for George Hudson, Mar. 1966.

Managers Since the War: T. Smith, Bob Dennison, David Smith, Dave Bowen, Tony Marchi, Ron Flowers, Bill Baxter.

Address of Supporters Club: 195, Abington Avenue, Northampton.

County Ground, Abington Avenue, Northampton NNI 4PS. Telephone Northampton 31553. *Ground capacity:* 20,000 (Seating 1,959).   *Record attendance.* 24,523 v Fulham, Division 1, April 23, 1966.   *Record receipts:* £17,438 v Manchester U.   *Pitch measurements:* 120 yds × 75 yds.

How to get there: Nearest railway station, Northampton. Any bus to the town centre, then from Mercer's Row, buses 1, 21, 2 and 14, though only 2 goes right to the ground.

Match tickets: No pre-match booking.

Car parking: No car park, but ample space in nearby side-streets.

Entertainments/catering facilities: Refreshment in hotel and tea bars on ground.

Club shop: Run by the Supporters Club; sells all types of souvenirs.

Handbooks/programmes: Programmes available from the Supporters Club.

Extra information: Ground is shared with Northamptonshire County Cricket Club.

Club Colours: White shirts, claret trim, claret shorts and claret and white tops on stockings.

Change Colours: Blue shirts and stockings, white shorts.   *Club Nickname:* 'Cobblers'.

NORTHAMPTON TOWN 1975–76 LEAGUE RECORD

Match No.	Date	Venue	Opponents	Result	H/T Score	League Pos'n	Goalscorers	Attendance
1	Aug 16	A	Huddersfield T.	D 1-1	0-1	—	Tucker	3595
2	22	A	Stockport Co.	W 3-1	3-1	—	Hall 2, Farrington	3032
3	30	A	Barnsley	L 1-3	1-1	15	Hall	3525
4	Sept 5	H	Bradford C.	W 4-2	2-1	8	Christie, Gregory, Robertson, McGowan	3675
5	13	A	Darlington	W 1-0	1-0	3	Gregory	3788
6	19	A	Swansea C.	D 0-0	0-0	4		5428
7	23	H	Workington	W 2-1	0-0	—	Stratford, Best	4677
8	27	A	Torquay U.	W 1-0	0-0	3	Best	1919
9	Oct 3	H	Doncaster R.	W 2-1	0-0	3	Hall, Stratford	6155
10	10	A	Tranmere R.	L 0-2	0-1	5		4808
11	18	H	Lincoln C.	W 1-0	1-0	3	Stratford	6566
12	21	H	Brentford	W 3-1	2-0	—	Farrington, Best 2	6225
13	25	A	Scunthorpe U.	W 2-0	1-0	3	Stratford 2	1965
14	Nov 1	H	Watford	W 3-0	1-0	2	Hall, Felton, Phillips	6656
15	3	A	Rochdale	W 2-0	1-0	—	Robertson, Stratford	2995
16	8	A	Cambridge U.	W 1-0	0-0	1	Hall	5560
17	15	H	Southport	W 1-0	1-0	1	Farrington	6089
18	29	A	AFC Bournemouth	D 0-0	0-0	2		5890
19	Dec 6	H	Crewe Alex	W 2-1	1-0	2	Hall, McGowan	5705
20	13	A	Exeter C.	D 0-0	0-0	1		3394
21	20	H	Exeter C.	W 3-1	0-1	1	Hall 2, Phillips	5212
22	26	A	Hartlepool	L 0-3	0-1	2		5077
23	27	H	Newport Co	W 3-0	2-0	2	Phillips, Robertson, Hall	8448
24	Jan 3	A	Reading	L 0-1	0-1	2		10,139
25	10	H	Barnsley	W 5-0	3-0	2	Carlton, Robertson, Hall 2, Best	6132
26	16	A	Swansea C.	D 1-1	0-1	2	Mayes	3656
27	24	H	Darlington	W 3-2	3-0	1	Robertson, Hall 2	5135
28	31	A	Brentford	L 1-2	0-1	2	Hall	4110
29	Feb 7	H	Rochdale	D 1-1	0-0	2	Stratford	5393
30	14	H	Cambridge U.	W 4-2	1-1	1	Smith (og), Mayes 2, Robertson	5969
31	21	A	Southport	W 1-0	0-0	1	Farrington	1332
32	25	A	Workington	L 0-1	0-1	—		1135
33	27	H	Scunthorpe U.	W 2-1	1-1	1	Mayes, Martin (pen)	6804
34	Mar 6	A	Watford	W 1-0	1-0	1	Hall	7389
35	9	A	Doncaster R.	W 4-0	1-0	—	Stratford 2, McGowan 2	8737
36	12	H	Tranmere R.	D 1-1	0-1	1	Phillips	8047
37	17	A	Lincoln C.	L 1-3	0-2	—	Stratford	13,880
38	20	H	AFC Bournemouth	W 6-0	6-0	1	Hall 3, Best 2, Stratford	6780
39	27	A	Crewe Alex.	W 1-0	0-0	2	Best	2865
40	Apr 3	H	Huddersaeld T.	D 1-1	1-0	2	Phillips	7218
41	6	H	Torquay U.	D 2-2	2-1	—	Phillips, Gregory	6263
42	10	A	Bradford C.	W 2-1	1-1	2	Hall 2	3175
43	15	H	Reading	W 4-1	0-1	—	McGowan, Stratford 2, Martin	9548
44	17	H	Hartlepool	W 5-2	4-1	2	Starling (pen), Martin 3 (1 a pen), Robertson	7555
45	20	A	Newport Co.	D 1-1	0-0	—	Martin (pen)	1728
46	23	H	Stockport Co.	W 4-0	2-0	2	Stratford 3, Martin	7680

Goalscorers

League (87): Hall 21, Stratford 16, Best 8, Martin 7 (3 pens), Robertson 7, Phillips 6, McGowan 5, Farrington 4, Mayes 4, Gregory 3, Carlton 1, Christie 1, Felton 1, Starling 1 (pen), Tucker 1, own goal 1.
League Cup (1): Hall

League Cup	First Round	Watford (a)	0-2
	Second Leg	(h)	1-1
F.A. Cup	First Round	Brentford (a)	0-2

268

Parton	Tucker	Anderson	Carlton	Robertson	Gregory	Farrington	Best	Hall	Christie	Stratford	Mabee	McGowan	Starling	Davids	Phillips	Felton	Martin	Mayes	Match No.
1	2	3	4*	5	6	7	8	9	10	11	12								1
1	2	3	7	5	6	4	8	9	10	11									2
1	3	2	4	5	6*	7	8	9	10	11		12							3
3				5	6	7	2	9	8	11		10	1	4					4
3	12			5	6	7*	2	9	8	11		10	1	4					5
3				5	6	7	2	9	8	11		10	1	4					6
3	12			5	4	7	2	9	8*	11		10	1	6					7
6	4			5	3	7	8	9		11		10	1	2					8
3	8			5	6	7	2	9	12	11*		10	1	4					9
3	8			5	6	7	2	9		11		10	1	4					10
3	4*			5	6	7	2	9		11		10	1		8	12			11
3				5	2	7	8	9		11		10	1	4	6				12
3				5	2	7	4	9*		11		8	1	6	10	12			13
3	6			5	2		4	9		11		8	1		10	7			14
3	6			5	2		4	9		11		8	1		10	7			15
3	6			5	2		4	9		11		8	1		10	7			16
3	6			5	2	11*	4	9	12			8	1		10	7			17
3	6			5	2	7	4	9				8	1		10	11			18
3	6			5	2	7	4	9				8	1		10	11			19
3	6			5	2	7	4	9				8	1		10	11			20
3	6			5	2	7	4	9				8	1		10	11			21
3	6			5	2	11	4	7				10	1		8	9			22
3	6*			5	2	7	4	9	12			8	1		10	11			23
3	6			5	2	7	4	9				8	1		10	11			24
3	6			5	2	7	4	9					1		10	11	8		25
3	6			5		7*	4	9	12			11	1		10	2	8		26
3				5	6*	7	4	9	12			11	1		10	2	8		27
3	6			5	2	7*	4	9				12	1		10	11	8		28
3	6			5	2		4	9		11			1		10	7	8		29
3	6*			5	2	7	4			11		12	1		10	9	8		30
3*	6			5	2	7	4			11		12	1		10	9	8		31
3	6			5	2	7	4			12		11	1		10*	9	8		32
3	6*			5	2	7	4	9		11		10	1			12	8		33
3				5	2	7	4	9		11		10	1			6	8		34
3	12			5	2	7		9	6*	11		10	1		8	4			35
3	12			5	2	7		9	6	11*		10	1		8	4			36
3				5	2	7	4	9		11		10	1		8	6			37
3				5	2	7*	4	9	12	11		10	1		8	6			38
3	11			5	2		4	9	7			8	1		10	6			39
3	11			5	2		4	9	7			10	1		8	6			40
3	6		7*		2	12	4	9		11		8	1		10	5			41
3	6				2	7	4	9		11		8	1		10	5			42
3					2	6	4	9		11		10	1		8	7	5		43
3				5	2*	12	4	9		11		10	1		8	7	6		44
3				5	2		4	9		11		10	1		8	7	6		45
3				5	2		4	9		11		10	1		8	7	6		46
3	46	3	30	44	45	36	44	43	12	30	—	38	43	9	34	8	28	10	

+4s (Carlton)   +2s (Gregory)   +7s (Christie)   +1s +4s (Mabee / McGowan)   +2s +1s (Phillips / Felton)

NORTHAMPTON TOWN—PLAYERS

Player and position	Ht.	Wt.	Birthplace	Clubs	League Appearances	Goals
Goalkeepers						
Alan Starling	6 0	11 6	Dagenham	Luton T.	7	—
				Torquay U. (on loan)	6	—
				Northampton T.	212	1
Jeff Parton	5 11	12 7	Swansea	Burnley	3	—
				Northampton T.	3	—
Defenders						
*Gary Anderson	5 7	10 9	Bow	Tottenham H.	—	—
				Northampton T.	14	—
Stuart Robertson	5 11	12 12	Nottingham	Nottingham F.	—	—
				Doncaster R.	225+3	8
				Northampton T.	137	13
Billy Best	5 6	10 9	Scotland	Northampton T.	38+2	11
				Southend U.	223+1	106
				Northampton T.	128+1	24
*Alan Oman	5 9	11 0	Newcastle	Northampton T.	83+5	3
Kenneth Parker	6 0	12 10	Newcastle	Northampton T.	—	—
Barry Tucker	5 8	11 0	Swansea	Northampton T.	144+5	2
John Gregory	6 1	11 0	Scunthorpe	Northampton T.	132	4
Midfield						
David Carlton	5 10½	11 2	London	Fulham	5+4	—
				Northampton T.	93+5	6
Don Martin	5 10	10 7	Corby	Northampton T.	135	52
				Blackburn R.	218+6	58
				Northampton T.	28+1	7
Derrick Christie	5 8	10 10	Bletchley	Northampton T.	25+11	1
Steve Phillips	5 8	10 7	Edmonton	Birmingham C.	15+5	1
				Torquay U. (on loan)	6	—
				Northampton T.	34	6
Forwards						
*Graham Felton	5 7	10 8	Cambridge	Northampton T.	142+13	25
				Barnsley (on loan)	12	2
Peter Hawkins	5 4	9 13	Swansea	Northampton T.	49+9	9
*Gary Mabee	5 9	10 12	Oxford	Tottenham H.	—	—
				Northampton T.	29+4	13
*Eric Ross (N. Ireland)	5 9	10 8	Belfast	Newcastle U.	2	—
				Northampton T.	51+7	5
				Hartlepool (on loan)	2	—
Paul Stratford	5 9		Northampton	Northampton T.	127+1	46
Robin Wainwright	5 11	11 13	Luton	Luton T.	15+1	3
				Cambridge U. (on loan)	1	—
				Millwall	2+2	—
				Northampton T.	23+9	5
John Farrington	5 10	10 6	Lynemouth	Wolverhampton W.	31+3	2
				Leicester C.	114+3	19
				Cardiff C.	23	6
				Northampton T.	70+2	7
Jim Hall	6 0	12 4	Northampton	Northampton T.	54+2	7
				Peterborough U.	298+4	120
				Northampton T.	48	25
Andrew McGowan	5 8	10 8	Corby	Northampton T.	38+4	5

President: J. L. Hanly, J.P.   *Chairman:* Sir A. South, J.P.
Directors: G. F. B. Fish, W. M. Young, G. C. Watling, J. S. Murray, E. A. Burrell.
Asst. Manager: Ken Brown.
Manager: John Bond.   *Secretary:* A. E. Westwood, J.P.
Year Formed: 1905.   *Turned Professional:* 1905.
Limited Company: 1905.
Previous Grounds: 1905, Newmarket Road; 1908, The Nest, Rosary Road; 1935, Carrow Road.
Honours: *Football League,* best season 10th Div. 1, 1975–76. Division 2, Champions: 1971–72. Division 3(S), Champions: 1933–34. Division 3, Runners-up: 1959–60. *F.A. Cup,* best season: semi-finalists, 1959 (Division 3 side). *Football League Cup,* best season, Winners: 1962. Runners-up 1973, 1975.

NORWICH CITY FC

Record Victory: 10-2 v Coventry C., Division 3(S), Mar. 15th, 1930.
Record Defeat: 2-10 v Swindon T., Southern League, Sept. 5th, 1908.
Most League Points: 64, Division 3(S), 1950–51.
Most League Goals: 99, Div. 3(S), 1952–53.
Highest League Scorer in Season: Ralph Hunt, 31, Division 3(S), 1955–56.
Most Capped Player: Ted MacDougall, 7, Scotland
Most League Appearances: Ron Ashman, 590, 1947–64 (plus 72 Cup games).
Most League Goals in Total Aggregate: Johnny Gavin, 122, 1945–54; 1955–58.
Record Transfer Fee Received: £150,000 from Coventry C. for David Cross, Nov. 1973.
Record Transfer Fee Paid: £145,000 to West Ham U. for Ted MacDougall, Dec. 1973.
Managers Since the War: Cyril Spiers, Dugald Lockhead, Norman Low, Tom Parker, Archie Macauley, Willie Reid, George Swindin, Ron Ashman, Lol Morgan, Ron Saunders.
Address of Supporters Club: 50 King Street, Norwich.
Address of Club Shop or Boutique: 50 King Street, Norwich, also shop on ground.

Carrow Rd., Norwich NOR 22. Telephone Norwich 21514/5.   *Telegraphic address:* 'Football, Norwich'.   *Ground capacity:* 33,000.   *Record attendance:* 43,984 v Leicester C., F.A. Cup 6th Rd., March 30, 1963.   *Record receipts:* £20,853 v Manchester U., Football League Cup semi-final second leg, January 22, 1975.   *Pitch measurements:* 114 yds × 74 yds.

How to get there: Norwich railway station is eight minutes walk from the ground; British Rail run trains from outlying districts on match days. Coach firms also operate special services from surrounding parts Any scheduled bus to the station and then walk.
Match tickets: Personal applications only at the previous first-team match to the Advance Ticket Office on the ground.
Car parking: Several private car parks within walking distance of the ground. Multi-storey parks in Malt House Road and St Andrews Street. Street parking in Rouen Road, Carrow Hill, Kerrison Road, Cousins Road, and side streets off King Street. Coaches may park at Martineau Lane off the City Ring Road to the south of the city.
Entertainments/catering facilities: Supporters' Club in Rosary Road within walking distance of the ground. Numerous licensed bars in the ground.
Club shop: Sells all types of souvenirs.
Handbooks/programmes: Supporters Club produce a handbook. Programmes available on demand but not on subscription.
Extra information: In 1958–59 Norwich became one of only four clubs from the Third Division to reach the FA Cup semi-final.

Club Colours: Yellow shirts, green collars and cuffs, green shorts with yellow stripe, yellow stockings.
Change Colours: All white.
Club Captain: Duncan Forbes.
Club Nickname: 'Canaries'.

NORWICH CITY 1975–76 LEAGUE RECORD

Match No.	Date	Venue	Opponents	Result	H/T Score	League Pos'n	Goalscorers	Attendance
1	Aug 16	A	Manchester C.	L 0-3	0-0	—		29,103
2	20	H	Leeds U.	D 1-1	0-0	—	Madeley (og)	25,301
3	23	H	Aston Villa	W 5-3	4-1	12	MacDougall 3 (1 a pen), Forbes, Grapes	21,797
4	26	A	Arsenal	L 1-2	1-1	—	Peters	22,613
5	30	A	Tottenham H.	D 2-2	0-1	16	Boyer, MacDougall	23,145
6	Sept 6	H	Everton	W 4-2	2-0	11	MacDougall 3, Suggett	20,407
7	13	A	Burnley	D 4-4	1-3	13	MacDougall 2 (1 a pen) Peters, Boyer	15,496
8	20	H	Leicester C.	W 2-0	1-0	10	MacDougall 2 (1 a pen)	22,799
9	23	A	Ipswich T.	L 0-2	0-0	—		34,825
10	27	A	Sheffield U.	W 1-0	0-0	10	MacDougall	20,624
11	Oct 4	H	Stoke C.	L 0-1	0-0	12		22,318
12	11	H	Derby Co.	D 0-0	0-0	10		23,022
13	18	A	Newcastle U.	L 2-5	1-1	12	McGuire, MacDougall	31,868
14	25	H	Birmingham C.	W 1-0	1-0	11	Boyer	20,178
15	Nov 1	A	Manchester U.	L 0-1	0-0	13		50,587
16	8	H	Middlesbrough	L 0-1	0-0	15		19,793
17	15	A	Coventry C.	L 0-1	0-1	16		14,897
18	22	H	Newcastle U.	L 1-2	1-0	18	Sullivan	19,700
19	29	A	Liverpool	W 3-1	0-0	16	Suggett, Peters, MacDougall	34,780
20	Dec 6	H	West Ham U.	W 1-0	0-0	16	MacDougall	27,020
21	13	A	Aston Villa	L 2-3	1-2	17	Peters, MacDougall	30,478
22	20	H	Manchester C.	D 2-2	0-2	16	Boyer 2	19,692
23	26	A	Q.P.R.	L 0-2	0-1	17		21,774
24	27	H	Wolverhampton W.	D 1-1	0-1	18	Peters	25,115
25	Jan 10	H	Burnley	W 3-1	2-0	17	Peters, Forbes, Boyer	18,059
26	17	A	Everton	D 1-1	0-0	17	Boyer	23,164
27	31	H	Leeds U.	W 3-0	1-0	15	MacDougall 2, McGuire	27,254
28	Feb 7	H	Arsenal	W 3-1	2-1	14	Peters 2, MacDougall	23,038
29	21	H	Coventry C.	L 0-3	0-1	16		20,798
30	28	A	Birmingham C.	D 1-1	0-1	18	Peters	22,359
31	Mar 6	H	Tottenham H.	W 3-1	0-0	13	Suggett, MacDougall (pen), Boyer	21,220
32	13	A	Derby Co	L 1-3	1-0	16	Forbes	27,005
33	17	H	Manchester U.	D 1-1	0-1	—	Boyer	30,000
34	20	H	Liverpool	L 1-1	0-0	17		29,013
35	27	A	West Ham U.	W 1-0	1-0	15	MacDougall	20,628
36	31	H	Ipswich T.	W 1-0	1-0	—	Peters	31,024
37	Apr 3	H	Sheffield U.	L 1-3	1-3	12	Boyer	19,937
38	6	A	Middlesbrough	W 1-0	0-0	—	Steele	16,000
39	10	A	Leicester C.	D 0-0	0-0	11		19,856
40	17	H	Q.P.R.	W 3-2	1-1	11	MacDougall, Morris, Boyer	31,231
41	19	A	Wolverhampton W.	L 0-1	0-1	—		16,168
42	24	A	Stoke C.	W 2-0	0-0	10	MacDougall, Suggett	15,598

Goalscorers

League (58): MacDougall 23 (4 pens), Boyer 11, Peters 10, Suggett 4, Forbes 3, McGuire 2, Grapes 1, Sullivan 1, Steele 1, Morris 1, own goal 1.

League Cup (4): MacDougall 3, Peters

F.A. Cup (6): MacDougall 2 (2 pens), Peters 2, Jones, Suggett.

League Cup	Second Round	Manchester C. (h)	1-1
		(a)	2-2 (a.e.t.)
			1-6 (at Stamford Bridge)
F.A. Cup	Third Round	Rochdale (h)	1-1
		(a)	0-0 (a.e.t.)
		(h)	2-1
	Fourth Round	Luton T. (h)	2-0
	Fifth Round	Bradford C. (h)	1-2

Keelan	Machin	Sullivan	Morris	Forbes	Powell	Grapes	MacDougall	Peters	Suggett	McGuire	Boyer	Butler	Stringer	Steele	Miller	Jones	Wilson	Davids	Bond	Match No.
1	2	3	4	5	6	7	8	9	10	11										1
1	2	3	4	5	6	7	8	10	9	11										2
1	2	3	4	5	6	7	8	10	9	11										3
1	2	3	4	5	6	7	8	9	10		11									4
1	2	3	4	5	6	7	8	11	10	9										5
1	2	3	4	5	6	7	10	11	8	9										6
1	2		4	5	6		8	11	10*	7	9		3	12						7
1	2		4	5	6		8	11	10	7	9		3							8
1	2		4	5	6		8*	11	10	7	9		3	12						9
1	2		4	5	6		8	11	10	12	9		3	7*						10
1	2	3		5	6		8	11	10	4	9			12	7*					11
1	2			5	6	7	8	11		4	9		3	10						12
1	2			5	6	7	8	11	10*	4	9		12		3					13
1	10	3		5	6	7	8	11		4	9				2					14
1	10	3		5	6		8	11		4	9		2	7						15
1	4	3		5	6	7	8	11	10		9				2*	12				16
1		3	4	5	6		8	11	10		9			7	2					17
1		3	4	5	6*		8	11	10		9			7	2	12				18
1	7	3	4	5	6		8	11	10		9					2				19
1	7	3	4	5	6		8	11	10		9					2				20
1	7	3	4	5	6		8	11	10		9					2				21
1	7	3	4	5	6		8	11	10		9					2				22
1	7	3	4	5	6		8	11	10		9					2				23
1	7	3	4	5	6		8	11	10		9					2				24
1	7	3	4	5	6		8	11	10		9					2				25
1	7	3		5	6		8	11	10	4	9					2				26
1	7	3		5	6		8	11	10	4	9					2				27
1	7	3		5	6		8	11	10	4	9					2				28
1	7	3		5	6		8	11	10	4	9					2				29
1		3		5	6		8	11	10	4	9			7		2				30
1		3		5	6		8	11	10	4	9			7		2				31
1		3		5	6		8	11	10	4	9			7		2				32
1		3		5	6		8	11	10	4	9			7*12		2				33
1		3		5	6		8	11	10	4	9			7		2				34
1		3		5	6		8	11	10	4	9			7		2				35
1		3	2		6		8*	11	10	4	9			12	7			5		36
1		3	2		6		8	11	10	4	9			7				5		37
1			2		6		8	11	10	4	9		3	7	5					38
1		3		5	6		8	11	10	4	9		7*		2			12		39
1			4	5	6		8	11	10	7	9		3		2					40
1	2		3	5	6	12	8	11	10	4	9		7*							41
1		3		5	6		8	11	10	4	9			7		2				42
42	28	31	26	39	31	10	42	42	38	29	39	8	12	12	8	23	—	2	—	
			+1s						+1s		+1s	+2s	+3s	+1s		+1s		+1s		

Player and position	Ht.	Wt.	Birthplace	Clubs	League Appearances	Goals
Goalkeepers						
Kevin Keelan	5 11	12 10	Calcutta	Aston Villa	5	—
				Wrexham	68	—
				Norwich C.	459	—
Roger Hansbury	5 11	12 0	Barnsley	Norwich C.	4	—
Defenders						
David Jones (Wales)	6 1	12 8	Bristol	Bournemouth	128+6	5
				Nottingham F.	36	1
				Norwich C.	23	—
Mel Machin	5 10	12 0	Newcastle under Lyne	Port Vale	29+1	6
				Gillingham	154+1	11
				Bournemouth	110	7
				Norwich C.	67	3
Tony Powell	5 11	11 1	Thornley	Bournemouth	214+5	10
				Norwich C.	71	2
David Stringer	5 10	11 6	Gt. Yarmouth	Norwich C.	416+2	19
Colin Sullivan	5 7½	10 11	Saltash	Plymouth Arg.	225+5	7
				Norwich C.	66+1	2
Duncan Forbes	5 11½	11 7	Edinburgh	Colchester U.	270	2
				Norwich C.	266+5	9
*Christopher Watts	5 7	10 0	Watton	Norwich C.	—	—
*Paul Wilson	5 9	12 0	Norwich	Norwich C.	0+1	—
Neil Davids	6 0	11 3	Keighley	Leeds U.	—	—
				Norwich C.	2	—
				Northampton T. (on loan)	9	—
				Stockport Co. (on loan)	5	1
Kevin Bond	6 0	12 0	London	Norwich C.	0+1	—
Marl Alcock	5 9	10 8	Bolton	Norwich C.	—	—
David Burden	5 9	10 8	Chichester	Norwich C.	—	—
Jim Fleeting	6 1	11 5	Glasgow	Norwich C.	—	—
Midfield						
Peter Morris	5 8	11 3	Mansfield	Mansfield T.	285+1	50
				Ipswich T.	213+7	13
				Norwich C.	66	1
*Paul Kent	5 9	11 0	Rotherham	Norwich C.	1+2	—
Billy Steele	5 9	10 8	Kirkmuirhill	Norwich C.	27+8	1
				Bournemouth (on loan)	7	2
Mike McGuire	5 8	10 0	Blackpool	Coventry C.	60+12	1
				Norwich C.	45+1	4
Martin Peters (England)	6 0½	11 10½	Plaistow	West Ham U.	302	79
				Tottenham H.	189	46
				Norwich C.	52	12
Colin Suggett	5 9	10 12	Washington	Sunderland	83+3	24
				W.B.A.	123+5	20
				Norwich C.	131+1	16
Forwards						
Ted MacDougall (Scotland)	5 10	11 11	Inverness	Liverpool	—	—
				York C.	84	34
				Bournemouth	146	103
				Manchester U.	18	5
				West Ham U.	24	5
				Norwich C.	109	51
Steve Grapes	5 6	9 0	Norwich	Norwich C.	31+7	3
				Bournemouth (on loan)	7	1
John Miller	5 8	10 9	Ipswich	Ipswich T.	37+13	3
				Norwich C.	22+1	3
Phil Boyer (England)	5 8	10 4	Nottingham	Derby C.	—	—
				York C.	108+1	27
				Bournemouth	140+1	46
				Norwich C.	94	29
Ian Davies	5 8	10 8	Bristol	Norwich C.	0+1	—
Douglas Evans	5 10	11 0	Swansea	Norwich C.	—	—
Norman Brown	5 8	11 2	Falkirk	Norwich C.	—	—
Andy Proudlove	5 10	11 9	Buxton	Sheffield W.	10+5	—
				Norwich C.	—	—

NOTTINGHAM FOREST

DIV. 2

President: G. N. Watson, J.P.
Chairman: B. J. Appleby, Q.C.
Vice-Chairman: S. M. Dryden, J.P.
Committee: J. H. Wilmer, H. W. Alcock, F.C.A., H. Levy, G. E. Macpherson, J.P., G. T. Thorpe, F. Reacher, F. T. C. Pell, F.C.A.
Manager: Brian Clough. *Sec./Treasurer:* K. Smales.

Year Formed: 1865. *Turned Professional:* 1889.
This is a club (200 members) *not* a limited company.
Previous Grounds: 1865, Forest Racecourse; 1879, The Meadows; 1880, Trent Bridge Cricket Ground; 1882, Parkside, Lenton; 1885, Gregory, Lenton; 1890, Town Ground; 1898, City Ground.

Honours: Football League, Division 1, Runners-up: 1966–67. Division 2, Champions: 1906–07, 1921–22; Runners-up: 1956–57. Division 3(S), Champions: 1950–51. *F.A. Cup,* Winners: 1898, 1959.
Football League Cup, best season, 4th Rd.: 1960–61, 1969–70.
European Competitions: Fairs Cup: 1961–62, 1967–68.

Record Victory: 14-0 v Clapton, F.A. Cup, 1st Rd., 1890–91.

Record Defeat: 1-9 v Blackburn R., Division 2. Apr 10th, 1937.

Most League Points: 70, Div. 3(S), 1950–51.

Most League Goals: 110, Div. 3(S), 1950–51

Highest League Scorer in Season: Wally Ardron, 36, Division 3(S), 1950–51.

Most Capped Player: Liam O'Kane, 20, N. Ireland.

Most League Appearances: Bob McKinlay, 614, 1951–70.

Most Goals in Total Aggregate: Grenville Morris, 199, 1898–1913. (+18 F.A. Cup).

Record Transfer Fee Received: £240,000 from Leeds U. for Duncan McKenzie, August 1974,

Record Transfer Fee Paid: £122,000 to Luton T. for Barry Butlin, October 1974.

Managers Since the War: Billy Walker, Andy Beattie, John Carey, Matt Gillies, Dave Mackay, Allan Brown.

Address of Supporters Club: 'Forest House', 6 Pavilion Road, West Bridgford, Nottingham.

Address of Club Shop or Boutique: Pools Office, City Ground, Nottingham NG2 5FJ.

City Ground, Nottingham NG2 5FJ. Telephone Nottingham 868236-7-8. Information Desk: 861121. *Telegraphic Address:* 'Forestball, Nottingham'. *Ground capacity:* 49,000 (26,500 covered). *Record attendance:* 49,945 v Manchester U., Division 1, October 28, 1967. *Record receipts:* £19,550 Leeds U. v Man. Utd., F.A. Cup Semi-Final replay, March 31, 1965. *Pitch measurements:* 115 yds × 78 yds.

How to get there: From Nottingham station any bus marked 'Trent Bridge'. Corporation specials from Parliament Street.
Match tickets: Bookable 14 days in advance of the match.
Car parking: Room for 300 cars in the East Stand car park and street parking off the Loughborough and Radcliffe Roads.
Entertainments/catering facilities: Only match-day refreshment bars. Social club situated just outside the ground.
Club shop: Two shops on the ground sell all types of souvenirs.
Handbooks/programmes: Programmes available on subscription from Carrington Publications Ltd., 20 Carrington St., Nottingham.
Extra information: Forest hold the record for the highest away win in the F.A. Cup proper; they beat Clapton 14-0 in 1890-91. They were also the first club to adopt shinguards (1874), the Referee's whistle (1878), three half-backs (1885), the crossbar instead of tape (1891), and oval section goal-posts. Nottingham Forest claim to be the only club to have played against clubs from all four home countries in the F.A. Cup. They are the only club in the Football League which is not a limited company.

Club Colours: Red shirts, white shorts, red and white stockings.
Change Colours: All yellow.
Club Captain: Bob Chapman.
First Team Trainer: Jimmy Gordon. Second Team: John Sheridan
Club Nickname: 'Reds'.

NOTTINGHAM FOREST 1975-76 LEAGUE RECORD

Match No.	Date	Venue	Opponents	Result	H/T Score	League Pos'n	Goalscorers	Attendance
1	Aug 16	H	Plymouth Arg.	W 2-0	1-0	—	Horswill (og), O'Hare	13,083
2	23	A	Portsmouth	D 1-1	1-0	11	Bowyer	10,655
3	30	H	Notts Co.	L 0-1	0-0	12		19,757
4	Sept 6	A	Chelsea	D 0-0	0-0	12		21,023
5	13	H	Hull C.	L 1-2	1-0	14	Robertson	12,191
6	20	A	Oxford U.	W 1-0	0-0	12	Lyall	5068
7	24	H	Charlton Ath.	L 1-2	0-1	—	Robertson	10,588
8	27	H	Bolton W.	L 1-2	0-1	17	Lyall	10,775
9	Oct 4	A	Bristol R.	L 2-4	0-1	19	Robertson, Bowyer	7689
10	11	A	Fulham	D 0-0	0-0	20		10,149
11	18	H	Southampton	W 3-1	2-0	16	O'Neill, O'Hare, Cottam	12,677
12	21	H	Luton T.	D 0-0	0-0	—		12,290
13	25	A	Oldham Ath.	D 0-0	0-0	15		11,324
14	Nov 1	H	Carlisle U.	W 4-0	2-0	11	Butlin, O'Hare 2, Curran (pen)	11,894
15	4	A	Blackpool	D 1-1	1-0	—	O'Neill	5851
16	8	A	Sunderland	L 0-3	0-2	13		31,227
17	15	H	Bristol C.	W 1-0	1-0	12	Butlin	11,583
18	22	A	Southampton	W 3-0	0-0	10	Bowyer 2, Richardson	14,245
19	29	H	York C.	W 1-0	1-0	10	Butlin	13,108
20	Dec 6	A	Orient	D 1-1	0-1	9	Bowyer	5629
21	13	H	Portsmouth	L 0-1	0-0	11		11,343
22	20	A	Plymouth Arg.	L 0-1	0-0	13		10,545
23	26	H	W.B.A.	L 0-2	0-0	14		19,395
24	27	A	Blackburn R.	W 4-1	2-0	11	Bowery 2, Robertson, Bowyer	10,724
25	Jan 10	A	Hull C.	L 0-1	0-0	13		6465
26	17	H	Chelsea	L 1-3	1-1	15	Bowyer	14,172
27	31	A	Luton T.	D 1-1	0-0	16	Curran	8503
28	Feb 7	H	Blackpool	W 3-0	0-0	11	Curran, Butlin, Bowyer	8582
29	21	A	Bristol C.	W 2-0	1-0	12	Curran, O'Hare	15,302
30	24	A	Charlton Ath.	D 2-2	0-1	—	Bowyer, McCann	10,655
31	28	H	Oldham Ath.	W 4-3	2-1	9	Butlin, O'Neill 2, Curran (pen)	11,509
32	Mar 6	A	Carlisle U.	D 1-1	1-0	11	Barry (og)	7153
33	13	H	Fulham	W 1-0	0-0	8	O'Hare	11,445
34	17	H	Sunderland	W 2-1	2-1	—	Bowyer, O'Hare	16,995
35	20	A	York C.	L 2-3	0-1	8	O'Hare, Downing (og)	5571
36	27	H	Orient	W 1-0	1-0	8	Bowyer	11,127
37	Apr 3	A	Bolton W.	D 0-0	0-0	8		21,464
38	10	H	Oxford U.	W 4-0	0-0	6	Butlin, O'Neill, Curran (pen), Robertson	11,259
39	13	A	Notts Co.	D 0-0	0-0	—		28,766
40	17	A	W.B.A.	L 0-2	0-0	8		26,447
41	20	H	Blackburn R.	W 1-0	0-0	—	Butlin	13,006
42	24	H	Bristol R.	W 3-0	0-0	8	O'Hare, Bowyer 2	12,127

Goalscorers

League (55): Bowyer 13, O'Hare 9, Butlin 7, Curran 6 (3 pens), O'Neill 5, Robertson 5, Bowery 2, Lyall 2, Cottam 1, McCann 1, Richardson 1, Own Goals 3.

League Cup (9): Bowyer 3, Lyall 2 (2 pens), Richardson 2, McGovern, Chapman.

League Cup	First Round	Rotherham U. (a)	2-1
	Second Leg	(h)	5-1
	Second Round	Plymouth Arg. (h)	1-0
	Third Round	Manchester C. (a)	1-2
F.A. Cup	Third Round	Peterborough U. (h)	0-0
		(a)	0-1

Middleton	Anderson	Clark	Chapman	O'Kane	McGovern	Lyall	Richardson	O'Hare	Robertson	Bowyer	O'Neill	Gunn	Curran	Cottam	Sunley	Butlin	Wells	McIntosh	Bowery	McCann	Barrett	Match No.
1	2	3	4	5	6	7	8	9	10	11												1
1	2	3		4*	8	11	6	9	7	10	12											2
1	2		4	5	8		6	9	10	11		3	7									3
1	2		5	4	8		10	9	6	11		3	7									4
1	2	6	5	4	8			9	10	11		3	7									5
1	2		4	5	8	12	6	9	10	11*		3	7									6
1	2		4	5	8		10		6	11	9	3	7									7
1		3	6	4	10	8		9		11		2	7	5								8
1		3	5	4	12	8		9	10	11		2	7*	6								9
1	2	3	4		8	10	6		12	11			7*	5	9							10
1	2	3	4		6			9		11	8		7	5		10						11
1	2	3	4		6			9		11	8		7	5		10						12
1	2	3	4		6			9		11	8		7	5		10						13
1	2	3	4		6*		9		12	11	8		7	5		10						14
1	2	3	4		6			9	7	11	8			5		10						15
1	2	3	5		4		6	9	8	11			7			10						16
1	2	3	5		4		6	9	8	11			7			10						17
1	2	3	5		4		6	9	8	11			7			10						18
	2	3	5		4		6	9	8	11			7			10	1					19
	2	3	5		4			9	6	11	8		7			10	1					20
	2	3	5		4			9	6	11	8		7			10	1					21
	2	3	5		4		6	9	12	11	8		7*			10	1					22
		3	5	2	4		6	9		11	8		7			10	1					23
		3	5	2	4			9	6	11						10	1	7	8			24
	2*	3	5		4		6	9	8	11			7			10	1	12				25
	4	5	2		6			9		11	8	3	7			10	1					26
		3	5	2	4			9	11	6	8		7			10	1					27
		3	5	2	4			9	11	6	8		7			10	1					28
		3	5	2*	4			10	11	6	8		7			9	1	12				29
		3	5		4			9	11	6	8	2	7			10*	1	12				30
		3	5		4			9	11	6	8	2	7			10	1					31
1		3	5		4			9	11	6		2	7			10			8			32
	2	3			4			9	11	6	8		7			10	1			5		33
		3	5		4			9	11	6	8		7			10	1				2	34
		3	5		4			9	11	6	8		7			10*	1			12	2	35
		3	5		4			9	11	6	8		7*			10	1			12	2	36
		3	5		4			9	11	6	8		7			10	1				2	37
		3	5		4			9	11	6	8		7			10	1				2	38
		3	5		4			9	11	6	8		7			10	1				2	39
		3	5		4		12	9	11*	6	8		7			10	1				2	40
		3	5		4			9	11	6	8		7			10	1				2	41
		3	5		4			9	11	6	8		7			10	1				2	42
19	21	42	37	8	41	5	23	39	37	40	29	11	33	8	1	32	23	1	1	1	10	
				+2s	+1s	+1s	+2s		+1s							+1s	+4s					

NOTTINGHAM FOREST—PLAYERS

Player and position	Ht.	Wt.	Birthplace	Clubs	League Appearances	Goals
Goalkeepers						
John Middleton	6 2		Lincoln	Nottingham F.	47	—
Peter Wells	6 0		Nottingham	Nottingham F.	23	—
Defenders						
Paddy Greenwood	5 10½	12 0	Hull	Hull C.	137+12	1
				Barnsley	110+1	6
				Nottingham F.	15	—
				(contract cancelled March 1976)		
Liam O'Kane (N. Ireland)	5 10	12 1	Derry	Nottingham F.	186+3	—
Bob Chapman	5 11	12 0	Walsall	Nottingham F.	316+11	15
John Cottam	5 10	11 10	Nottingham	Nottingham F.	92+3	4
				Mansfield (on loan)	2	1
				Lincoln C. (on loan)	1	—
Viv Anderson	5 11	10 4	Nottingham	Nottingham F.	35+2	—
Bryn Gunn	5 9	10 5	Corley	Nottingham F.	3	—
Frank Clark	6 0	12 2	Durham	Newcastle U.	388+1	—
				Nottingham F.	42	—
Colin Barrett	5 11	11 7	Stockport	Manchester C.	50+3	—
				Nottingham F.	10	—
Midfield						
John McGovern	5 10	10 13	Montrose	Hartlepool	69+3	5
				Derby C.	186+4	16
				Leeds U.	4	—
				Nottingham F.	49	—
Jim McCann	5 8	11 8	Dundee	Nottingham F.	2+4	1
				Stockport Co. (on loan)	4+1	—
				Chesterfield (on loan)	—	—
John Robertson	5 8	10 9	Uddinston	Nottingham F.	100+11	9
Paul Richardson	5 10	10 11	Nottingham	Nottingham F.	198+22	17
Ian Bowyer	5 11	11 2½	Ellesmere Port	Manchester C.	42+8	13
				Orient	75+3	18
				Nottingham F.	98+2	25
Forwards						
John O'Hare (Scotland)	5 8½	11 7	Renton	Sunderland	51	14
				Derby C.	247+1	65
				Leeds U.	6	1
				Nottingham F.	49+1	11
Barry Butlin	5 11½	10 4	Roslington	Notts Co.	30+1	13
				Derby Co.	4	—
				Luton T.	56+1	24
				Nottingham F.	61+1	14
				Brighton (on loan)	5	2
Terry Curran	5 10	11 3	Kinsley	Doncaster R.	67+1	11
				Nottingham F.	33	6
Martin O'Neill (N. Ireland)	5 10	11 3	Kilrea	Nottingham F.	108+14	15
Tony Woodcock	5 10	11 0	Nottingham	Nottingham F.	7+4	—
				Lincoln C. (on loan)	2+2	1
Bert Bowery	6 1	13 10	St. Kitts	Nottingham F.	1	2
				Lincoln C. (on loan)	2+2	1

NOTTS COUNTY

Chairman: J. J. Dunnett, M.A., LL.D.(Cantab.), M.P.

Directors: W. A. Hopcroft, L. S. Levin, J.P., R. Sweet, J. W. Maitland.

Manager: Ron Fenton.   *Player/Coach:* Colin Addison.

Commercial Manager: Stuart J. Burgan.

Secretary: Dennis Marshall.

Year Formed: 1862 (the oldest club in the Football League).

Turned Professional: 1885. *Limited Company:* 1888.

Previous Grounds: 1862, The Park; 1863, The Meadows; 1881, Trent Bridge; 1910, Meadow Lane.

Honours: *Football League,* best season in Division 1: 3rd, 1890–91, 1900–01. Division 2, Champions: 1896–97, 1913–14, 1922–23; Runners-up: 1894–95. Division 3(S), Champions: 1930–31, 1949–50; Runners-up: 1936–37.   Division 4, Champions 1970–71; Runners-up: 1959–60.   *F.A. Cup,* Winners: 1893–94; Runners-up: 1890–91. *Football League Cup,* best season: 5th Rd., 1963–64, 1972–64, 1972–73, 1975–76.

Record Victory: 15–0 v Thornhill U., F.A. Cup 1st Rd., Oct. 24th, 1885.

Record Defeat: 1-9 v Blackburn R., Division 1, Nov. 16th, 1889; v Aston Villa, Division 1, Sept. 29th, 1888; v Portsmouth, Division 2, Apr. 9th, 1927.

Most League Points: 69, Division 4, 1970–71.

Most League Goals: 107, Division 4, 1959–60.

Highest League Scorer in Season: Tom Keetley, 39, Division 3(S), 1930–31.

Most League Goals in Total Aggregate: Tony Hateley, 109, 1960–63, 1970–72.

Most Capped Player: Bill Fallon, 7 (10), Eire.

Most League Appearances: Albert Iremonger, 564, 1904–26.

Record Transfer Fee Received: £100,000 from Q.P.R. for Don Masson, December 1974.

Record Transfer Fee Paid: £45,000 to Manchester United for Ray O'Brien, March, 1974.

Managers Since the War: Arthur Stollery, Eric Houghton, George Poyser, Tommy Lawton, Frank Hill Tim Coleman, Eddie Lowe, Jack Burkitt, Andy Beattie, Billy Gray, Jimmy Sirrel.

Address of Supporters Club: c/o Club.

Address of Club Shop or Boutique: Supporters Association Kop Shop, c/o the Ground.

County Ground, Meadow Lane, Nottingham NG2 3HJ.   *Telegraphic address:* 'Notts County F.C. Nottingham'. Telephone General Office: Nottingham 868494; Manager: Nottingham 868364. Information Service tel: 864152. *Ground capacity:* 40,000. *Record attendance:* 47,310 v York C., F.A. Cup 6th Rd., March 12, 1955. *Record receipts:* £23,215.62p v Leeds U., F.A. Cup 1st Rd., Jan. 3, 1976. *Pitch measurements:* 117 yds × 76 yds.

How to get there: Corporation Specials from Parliament Square. Nearest railway station Nottingham from there any bus marked 'Trent Bridge'.

Match tickets: Advance bookings can be accepted by post or by personal application 14 days before each home game. S.A.E. must be sent with remittance in postal applications.

Car parking: No street parking around the ground, but ample space in the City of Nottingham Corporation car park on the Cattle Market, Meadow Lane, just 400 yards from the main entrances. There is a small club car park at the rear of the Spion Kop on Iremonger Road.

Entertainments/catering facilities: No social club. Tea bars and refreshment points on all sides of the ground.

Club shop: Open only on match days; situated at the ground.

Handbooks/programmes: The club produces its own official newspaper—Magpie—which is available on the day prior to a first team home game. Back copies and subscription rates available from the club.

Extra information: When Notts County won the F.A. Cup in 1893–94, they became the first winners from the Second Division.

Club Colours: Black and white striped shirts, black shorts, blue and white stockings
Change Colours: Yellow shirts with broad green vertical stripe, green shorts with yellow stripe, yellow stockings.
Club Captain: Brian Stubbs.
First Team Trainer: Jack Wheeler.
Club Nickname: 'Magpies'.

NOTTS COUNTY 1975–76 LEAGUE RECORD

Match No.	Date	Venue	Opponents	Result	H/T Score	League Pos'n	Goalscorers	Attendance
1	Aug 16	A	Charlton Ath.	W 2-1	1-1	—	Bradd, Probert	9612
2	19	A	Orient	D 1-1	1-0	—	Probert	5223
3	23	H	Southampton	D 0-0	0-0	4		8495
4	30	A	Nottingham F.	W 1-0	0-0	4	Bradd	19,757
5	Sept 6	H	Carlisle U.	W 1-0	1-0	1	Probert	8005
6	13	A	York C.	W 2-1	1-0	1	Scanlon (pen), McVay	5586
7	20	H	Luton T.	W 1-0	0-0	1	Scanlon	11,173
8	23	A	Hull C.	W 2-0	1-0	—	Bradd 2	8068
9	27	A	Sunderland	L 0-4	0-1	2		27,565
10	Oct 4	H	Bristol C.	D 1-1	0-0	2	Needham	10,802
11	11	H	Oxford U.	L 0-1	0-1	5		11,742
12	18	A	Bolton W.	L 1-2	0-0	5	Bolton	16,080
13	25	H	Portsmouth	W 2-0	0-0	5	Scanlon (pen), Probert	9597
14	Nov 1	A	W.B.A.	D 0-0	0-0	6		12,595
15	4	H	Plymouth Arg.	W 1-0	0-0	—	Scanlon	9239
16	8	H	Bristol R.	D 1-1	1-1	4	Bradd	10,930
17	15	A	Chelsea	L 0-2	0-0	5		18,229
18	22	H	Bolton W.	D 1-1	1-1	5	Bradd	12,064
19	29	A	Blackpool	L 0-1	0-1	5		6103
20	Dec 6	H	Blackburn R.	W 3-0	3-0	4	Bolton, Bradd, Scanlon	10,252
21	13	A	Southampton	L 1-2	1-1	4	Vinter	12,571
22	20	H	Charlton Ath.	W 2-0	1-0	4	O'Brien, Sims	10,017
23	26	A	Fulham	L 2-3	0-1	5	Vinter, Scanlon	11,887
24	27	H	Oldham Ath.	W 5-1	1-1	5	Bradd, Scanlon 2, Sims	14,706
25	Jan 10	H	York C.	W 4-0	3-0	4	Sims 2, Bradd, Vinter	10,136
26	17	A	Carlisle U.	W 2-1	1-0	4	Bradd, 2 Vinter	7600
27	Feb 7	A	Plymouth Arg.	W 3-1	2-0	4	Probert, Scanlon, Vinter	11,576
28	14	A	Bristol R.	D 0-0	0-0	4		7754
29	21	H	Chelsea	W 3-2	1-2	4	Scanlon, Sims, Bradd	14,528
30	24	H	Hull C.	L 1-2	0-1	—	Bolton	15,293
31	28	A	Portsmouth	W 3-1	1-0	4	Bradd 2, Scanlon	9135
32	Mar 6	H	W.B.A.	L 0-2	0-0	4		20,032
33	13	A	Oxford U.	L 1-2	0-2	4	Sims	5516
34	20	H	Blackpool	L 1-2	0-0	6	Mann	10,427
35	27	A	Blackburn R.	L 1-2	0-0	6	Mann	8472
36	Apr 3	H	Sunderland	D 0-0	0-0	5		14,811
37	10	A	Luton T.	D 1-1	0-1	7	Sims	8277
38	13	H	Nottingham F.	D 0-0	0-0	—		28,766
39	17	H	Fulham	W 4-0	2-0	6	Bradd, O'Brien, Scanlon, Benjamin	8819
40	19	A	Oldham Ath.	D 2-2	1-0	—	Bradd, Mann	7341
41	24	A	Bristol C.	W 2-1	1-0	7	O'Brien, Benjamin	24,614
42	27	H	Orient	W 2-0	1-0	—	Needham, Sims	8515

Goalscorers

League (60): Bradd 16, Scanlon 12 (2 pens), Sims 8, Probert 5, Vinter 5, Bolton 3, Mann 3, O'Brien 3, Benjamin 2, Needham 2, McVay 1.

League Cup (7): Bradd 3, Stubbs 2, Scanlon 2 (1 a pen).

League Cup	Second Round	Sunderland (h)	2-1	
	Third Round	Leeds U. (a)	1-0	
	Fourth Round	Everton (a)	2-2	
		(h)	2-0	
	Fifth Round	Newcastle U. (a)	0-1	
F.A. Cup	Third Round	Leeds U. (h)	0-1	

McManus	Brindley	Richards P.	Bolton	Needham	Stubbs	Carter	McVay	Bradd	Probert	Scanlon	Randall	Mann	O'Brien	Vinter	Sims	King	Lane	Birchenall	Smith	Richards L. G.	Benjamin	Match No.
1	2*	3	4	5	6	7	8	9	10	11	12											1
1	2	4		5	6	7	10	9	8	11			3									2
1	2	4		5	6	7	10	9*	8	11	12		3									3
1	2	4		5	6	7	10	9	8	11			3									4
1	2	4		5	6	7	10	9	8	11			3									5
1	2	4		5	6	7*	10	9	8	11			3	12								6
1	2	4		5	6	7	10	9	8	11			3									7
1	2	4		5	6	7	10	9	8	11			3									8
1	2	4*		5	6	7	10	9	8	11			3	12								9
1	2	4		5	6	7*	10	9	8	11			3	12								10
1	2	3	4*	5	6	7	8	9		11		10	12									11
1	2	4		5	6			8	9	11	7	10	3									12
1	2	4		5	6		8	9	10	11	7*		3	12								13
1	12	2	4	5	6	7	9*	8		11		10	3									14
1	2	12		5	6*	7	8	9	4	11		10	3									15
1	2			5	6	7	8	9	4	11		10	3									16
1	12	2		5	6	7*	8	9	4	11		10	3									17
1	2	4		5	6*	7	12	9	8	11		10	3									18
1	2	4		5	6	7	9	8*		11		10	3	12								19
1	2	4		5	6		9	8		11		10	3	7								20
1	2	4		5	6	12	9	8		11		10	3	7*								21
1	2	4		5	6		9	8		11		10	3		7							22
1	2	7		5	6			9	4	11		10	3*	12	8							23
1	2	7		5	6	4		9		11		10	3		8							24
1	2			5	6	12	9	4				10	3	11	7*	8						25
1	2	12		5	6		9*	4		11		10	3	7		8						26
1	2			5	6		9	4		11		10*	3	12	8	7						27
1	2	4		5	6		9	8		11*		10	3	12	7							28
1	2			5	6	12	9*	4		11		10	3	7	8							29
1	2*	12		5	6	7	9	4		11		10	3	8								30
1	2	7		5	6		9	4		11		10	3	12	8*							31
1	2	4*		5	6		8	9		11		10	3	12	7							32
	2			5	6		9	4*		11		10	3	12	7		1	8				33
	2			5	6	4	12			11		10	3	9	7*		1	8				34
1	2			5	6	12	4*	9				10	3	11	7			8				35
1	2			5	6	11		9				10	3		7			8	4			36
1	2			5	6	11		9	12			10*	3		7			8	4			37
1	2			5	6	7*		9	11			10	3		8				4	12		38
1	2			5	6	8		9	11			10	3		7*				4	12		39
1	2			5	6	7		9	11			10	3		8*				4	12		40
1	2			5	6	8		9	11*			10	3		7				4	12		41
1	2			5	6	7		9*				10	3		8				4	12	11	42
40	12	32	24	42	40	21	25	41	30	37	2	31	40	8	19	3	2	5	7		1	
	+2s	+3s			+3s	+2s	+1s		+1s	+2s			+12s						+1s	+4s		

NOTTS COUNTY—PLAYERS

Player and position	Ht.	Wt.	Birthplace	Clubs	League Appearances	Goals
Goalkeepers						
Eric McManus	6 0	11 2	Linabidy, N.I.	Coventry C.	6	—
				Notts Co.	103	—
Frank Lane	6 1	12 10	Wallasey	Tranmere R.	76	—
				Liverpool	1	—
				Notts Co.	2	—
Defenders						
*John Brindley	5 8	11 11	Nottingham	Nottingham F.	8+8	1
				Notts Co.	221+2	—
David McVay	6 1	11 11	Workington	Notts Co.	64+3	2
David Needham	6 1	12 7	Leicester	Notts Co.	387+1	26
Pedro Richards	5 8	10 8	Nottingham	Notts Co.	39	—
Brian Stubbs	5 10	11 10	Keyworth	Notts Co.	276+1	18
Tristan Benjamin	6 0	11 1	St. Kitts	Notts Co.	3+4	2
Ray O'Brien	5 9	10 10	Sherbourne	Manchester U.	—	—
(Eire)				Notts Co.	83	4
Steven Towle	5 6	10 6	Nottingham	Notts Co.	—	—
Midfield						
Steve Carter	5 8	10 10	Gt. Yarmouth	Manchester C.	4+2	2
				Notts Co.	103+11	7
Arthur Mann	5 9	10 10	Burntisland	Hearts	32	—
				Manchester C.	32+3	—
				Blackpool (on loan)	3	—
				Notts Co.	137+4	10
Eric Probert	5 7½	10 9½	South Kirby	Burnley	63+5	11
				Notts Co.	104	11
Lloyd Richards	5 8	11 0	West Indies	Notts Co.	0+1	—
Dave Smith	5 5	10 6	Nottingham	Notts Co.	7	—
Forwards						
Ian Bolton	6 0	11 9	Leicester	Notts Co.	58+7	4
Les Bradd	6 0	12 12	Rotherham	Rotherham U.	3	—
				Notts Co.	317+14	101
Mick Vinter	5 9	11 0	Boston	Notts Co.	23+27	11
Ian Scanlon	5 8	10 11	Stirling	E. Stirling	25+2	15
				Notts Co.	71+5	26
John Sims	5 11	11 10	Belper	Derby Co.	2+1	—
				Luton T. (on loan)	3	1
				Oxford U. (on loan)	6+1	1
				Colchester U. (on loan)	2	—
				Notts Co.	19	8

OLDHAM ATHLETIC DIV. 2

Chairman: H. Wilde.
Vice-Chairman: R. Schofield.
Directors: J. Kershaw, F. D. Whitehead, I. H. Stott, G. T. Butterworth, G. A. Hudson, E. Sykes.

Manager: Jimmy Frizzell.

Secretary/General Manager: W. Griffiths.

Year Formed: 1894. *Turned Professional:* 1899.

Limited Company: 1906.

Previous Names: 1894, Pine Villa; 1899, Oldham Athletic.

Previous Ground: Sheepfoot Lane; 1905, Boundary Park.

Honours: *Football League*, Division 1, Runners-up: 1914–15. Division 2, Runners-up: 1909–10. Division 3(N), Champions: 1952–53. Division 3, Champions: 1973–74. Division 4, Runners-up: 1962–63. *F.A. Cup*, best season, semi-finalists: 1913. *Football League Cup*, best season: never past 2nd Rd.

Record Victory: 11-0 v Southport, Division 4, Dec. 26th, 1962.

Record Defeat: 4-13 v Tranmere R., Division 3(N), Dec. 26th, 1935.

Most League Points: 62, Division 3, 1973–74.

Most League Goals: 95, Division 4, 1962–63.

Highest League Scorer in Season: Tom Davis, 33, Division 3(N), 1936–37.

Most League Goals in Total Aggregate: Eric Gemmell, 110, 1947–54.

Most Capped Player: Albert Gray, 9 (23), Wales.

Most League Appearances: Ian Wood, 388, 1966–76.

Record Transfer Fee Received: £80,000 from W.B.A. for David Shaw, March 1973.

Record Transfer Fee Paid: £36,000 to Bury for David Holt, December 1974.

Managers Since the War: Bob Mellor, Billy Wootton, George Hardwick, Ted Goodier, Peter McKennan, Norman Dodgin, Jack Rowley, Les McDowall, Gordon Hurst, Jimmy McIlroy, Jack Rowley, Gordon Hurst.

Address of Supporters Club: Same as Football Club.

Address of Club Shop or Boutique: 'Latique', Boundary Park, Oldham.

Boundary Park, Oldham. Telephone 061-624 4972. *Ground capacity:* 30,000 (16,000 covered). *Record attendance:* 47,671 v Sheffield W., F.A. Cup 4th Rd., January 25, 1930. *Record receipts:* £15,952 v Bolton W., Division 2, December 26, 1975. *Pitch measurements:* 110 yds × 74 yds.

How to get there: Oldham Werneth is the nearest railway station; ordinary bus routes and specials link the station to the ground at Boundary Park.

Match tickets: Tickets can be booked in advance and collected before the day of the match; or, if required, they can be sent through the post.

Car parking: Parking for 1,000 cars at the Chadderton End and Ford Stand side of the ground.

Entertainments/catering facilities: A new social club has been built and it holds 350–400 people. It is open after matches and every evening except Mondays, when it is available for private parties. Catering stands around the ground sell hot drinks and pies.

Club shop: A new shop has been opened and sells all the usual souvenirs.

Handbooks/programmes: Programmes on sale at the ground or through the post for 10p plus postage and packing.

Extra information: Oldham's record victory in 1962 is the record for the Fourth Division.

Club Colours: Blue shirts, white shorts, white stockings.
Change Colours: Tangerine shirts, blue shorts, tangerine stockings.
Club Captain: Ian Wood.
Trainer/Physiotherapist: R. Jay. *Club Nickname:* 'The Latics'.

OLDHAM ATHLETIC 1975–76 LEAGUE RECORD

Match No.	Date	Venue	Opponents	Result	H/T Score	League Pos'n	Goalscorers	Attendance
1	Aug 16	H	Bristol R.	W 2-0	1-0	—	Aitken (og) Jones	6993
2	23	A	Blackburn R.	L 1-4	1-0	13	Blair	12,688
3	30	H	Hull C.	W 1-0	0-0	10	Whittle	6365
4	Sept 6	A	Blackpool	D 1-1	0-1	11	Whittle	8862
5	13	H	Chelsea	W 2-1	1-1	8	Wood, Jones	10,406
6	20	A	Portsmouth	D 1-1	1-1	8	Groves	8079
7	27	H	Plymouth Arg.	W 3-2	1-1	7	Jones, Horswill (og) Robins	8227
8	Oct 4	A	W.B.A.	D 1-1	1-1	7	Blair	9500
9	7	H	Bristol C.	L 2-4	1-1	—	Whittle (pen), Jones	9572
10	11	H	York C.	W 2-0	1-0	7	Chapman, Robins	8704
11	18	A	Charlton Ath.	L 1-3	0-2	8	Robins	8582
12	21	H	Southampton	W 3-2	3-0	—	Shaw 3	11,219
13	25	H	Nottingham F.	D 0-0	0-0	8		11,324
14	Nov 1	A	Orient	L 0-2	0-0	8		4576
15	4	A	Carlisle U.	L 1-2	0-2	—	Bell	6389
16	8	H	Oxford U.	D 1-1	1-1	9	Blair	8063
17	15	A	Luton T.	W 3-2	2-1	8	Chapman, McVitie, Shaw	8237
18	22	H	Charlton Ath.	W 2-0	1-0	7	Jones, Goldthorpe (og)	8059
19	29	A	Sunderland	L 0-2	0-1	9		28,220
20	Dec 6	H	Fulham	D 2-2	1-0	8	Shaw, Hicks	8746
21	13	H	Blackburn R.	W 2-1	2-1	6	Whittle, Shaw	10,193
22	20	A	Bristol R.	L 0-1	0-0	7		7389
23	26	H	Bolton W.	W 2-1	0-0	6	Shaw 2	24,537
24	27	A	Notts Co.	L 1-5	1-1	8	Young	14,706
25	Jan 10	A	Chelsea	W 3-0	1-0	7	Young 2, Shaw	16,464
26	17	H	Blackpool	W 1-0	1-0	6	Blair	11,734
27	31	A	Southampton	L 2-3	2-1	8	Young, Shaw	14,297
28	Feb 7	H	Carlisle U.	D 2-2	1-1	8	Whittle (pen), Groves	8870
29	14	A	Oxford U.	D 1-1	1-0	8	Wood	4786
30	21	H	Luton T.	D 1-1	1-0	8	Shaw	8808
31	24	A	Bristol C.	L 0-1	0-1	—		14,361
32	28	A	Nottingham F.	L 3-4	1-2	8	Shaw, Bell, Hicks	11,505
33	Mar 6	H	Orient	D 1-1	1-1	8	Whittle	6851
34	13	A	York C.	L 0-1	0-1	10		4132
35	20	H	Sunderland	D 1-1	1-1	10	Bell	13,704
36	27	A	Fulham	L 0-1	0-1	12		5856
37	Apr 3	A	Plymouth Arg.	L 1-2	0-1	15	Whittle	9782
38	10	H	Portsmouth	W 5-2	3-0	12	Hicks, Robins, Groves, Whittle Shaw	6672
39	16	A	Hull C.	L 0-3	0-1	14		5546
40	17	A	Bolton W.	L 0-4	0-2	18		22,455
41	19	H	Notts Co.	D 2-2	0-1	—	Robins, Groves	7341
42	24	H	W.B.A.	L 0-1	0-0	17		22,356

Goalscorers

League (57): Shaw 13, Whittle 8 (2 pens), Jones 5, Robins 5, Blair 4, Groves 4, Young 4, Bell 3, Hicks 3, Chapman 2, Wood 2, McVitie 1, Own Goals 3.

League Cup (6): Jones 3, Robins, Groves, Holt.

League Cup	First Round	Workington (h)	3-0
	Second Leg	(a)	3-1
	Second Round	Aston Villa (a)	0-2
F.A. Cup	Third Round	Sunderland (a	0-2

Ogden	Wood	Whittle	Bell	Holt	Blair	Chapman	Jones	Young	Groves	Edwards	Hicks	McVitie	Robins	Branagan	Shaw	Platt	Dungworth	Carroll	Match No.
1	2	3	4	5	6	7	8	9	10	11									1
1	2	3	7	6	4	10	8*		11		5	12	9						2
1		3	7	6	4	10	8*	12	11		5		9	2					3
1	12	3	4*	6	7	10	8		11		5		9	2					4
1	9	3	7	6	4*	10	8		11		5	12		2					5
1	9	3	4	6	7	10	8		11*		5	12		2					6
1		3	4	6	7	8	9		11		5	10		2					7
1	12	3	7	6	4	10	8		11*		5		9	2					8
1	4	3	7	6		10	9*	12	11		5		8	2					9
1	9	3	4	6		10	7		11		5		8	2					10
1	4	3	7	6		10			11		5		9	2	8				11
	2		4	6	3	10			11		5		7	9	8	1			12
	2		4	6	3	10		12	11*		5		7	9	8	1			13
	2	12	4	6	3*	10			11		5		7	9	8	1			14
	2	12	4	6	3	10			11		5		7	9*	8	1			15
	2	3	4	6	9	10*			11		5		7		8	1	12		16
	2	3	4	6	9	10			11		5		7		8	1			17
1	2	3	4	6	9	10	8		11		5		7						18
1	2*		4	6	3	10	8	12	11		5		7	9					19
1		3	4	6		10	7		11*		5	12	9	2	8				20
1		3	4	6		10	9		11		5		7	2	8				21
1	2	3	4*	6	12	10	9		11		5		7		8				22
	2	3	6	4		10	8		11		5		7	9		1			23
	2	3			4	10	8	9	11		6	5	7*			1	12		24
	2	3	4		7	10	9		11		5		6		8	1			25
	2	3	4		7	10	8		11		5		6		9	1			26
	2	3	4		7	10	9		11		5		6		8	1			27
	2	3	4	6	7	10	8		11		5				9	1			28
	2	3	4*	6	7		9		11		5	12	10		8	1			29
	2	3	4	6	7	10	8*		11		5	12	9			1			30
	2	3	4	6	7	10			11		5		9		8	1			31
	2	3	4	6	7*	12			11		5		10		8	1	9		32
	2	3	4	6		10			11		5				8	1	9	7	33
	2	3	4	6	8	10					5		7		9	1		11	34
	3	3	7	6					11		5	4	9		8	1		10	35
	2	3	8	6	12	10*			11		5	4	7		9	1			36
	2	3	8	6		10			11		5	4	7		9	1			37
	2	3	7	6		10			11		5	4	9		8	1			38
	2	3	4	6	12	10			11		5		7	9	8*	1			39
	2*	3	4	12	7	10			11		5		6	9	8	1			40
1		3	4*	6	2	10			11		5		9		7	8	12		41
1	2	3	4		7	10*			11		5		6	9	12	8			42
18	35	37	40	36	30	40	15	10	40	28	27	8	28	12	29	24	2	3	
+2s	+2s		+1s	+3s	+1s		+4s				+2s	+1s	+3s	+1s	+2s	+1s			

Player and position	Ht.	Wt.	Birthplace	Clubs	League Appearances	Goals
Goalkeepers						
John Platt	5 10	11 7	Oldham	Oldham Ath.	24	—
Chris Ogden	5 10½	12 5	Oldham	Oldham Ath.	101	—
Defenders						
Maurice Whittle	5 8	10 11	Wigan	Blackburn R.	5	—
				Oldham Ath.	282+5	36
Ian Wood	5 9	10 12	Radcliffe	Oldham Ath.	382+6	17
David Holt	5 10	11 0	Padiham	Bury	174+5	9
				Oldham Ath.	57+1	—
Keith Hicks	6 0	12 0	Oldham	Oldham Ath.	152+2	6
Paul Edwards	5 10	10 4	Crompton	Manchester U.	52+2	—
				Oldham Ath.	84+3	7
Jim Branagan	5 10	11 5	Barton	Oldham Ath.	15+3	—
Colin Johnson	5 11	10 10	Stretford	Oldham Ath.	—	—
Gary Hoolickin	5 11	10 11	Middleton	Oldham Ath.	—	—
Midfield						
Ronnie Blair	5 9	11 0	Coleraine	Oldham Ath.	74+2	1
(N. Ireland)				Preston N.E. (on loan)	—	—
				Rochdale	66+5	3
				Oldham Ath.	136+5	21
Graham Bell	5 9	10 6	Middleton	Oldham Ath.	72+3	3
John Hurst	5 10	12 7	Blackpool	Everton	336+13	29
				Oldham Ath.	—	—
John Dungworth	6 0	10 7	Rotherham	Huddersfield T.	18+5	1
				Barnsley (on loan)	2+1	1
				Oldham Ath.	2+2	—
Les Chapman	5 7	10 4	Oldham	Oldham Ath.	75+2	9
				Huddersfield T.	120+13	8
				Oldham Ath.	64+1	2
Forwards						
Alan Groves	5 10	10 12	Southport	Southport	10+4	2
				Chester	21	3
				Shrewsbury T.	76	11
				Bournemouth	31+5	4
				Oldham Ath.	93+2	11
*Andy Lochhead	6 0	12 6	Minngie	Burnley	224+1	102
				Leicester C.	40+4	12
				Aston V.	127+4	34
				Oldham Ath.	44+1	10
Ian Robins	5 9	10 8	Bury	Oldham Ath.	169+14	37
Alan Young	6 0	12 0	Kirkcaldy	Oldham Ath.	31+10	11
David Shaw	5 10	11 3	Huddersfield	Huddersfield T.	24+2	2
				Oldham Ath.	155	69
				W.B.A.	65+17	17
				Oldham Ath.	29	13
Joe Carroll	5 9	10 7	Radcliffe	Oldham Ath.	3+1	—
Carl Valentine	5 9	10 7	Manchester	Oldham Ath.	—	—
Stephen Edwards	5 9	10 2	Birkenhead	Oldham Ath.	—	—
David Irving	5 9	10 8	Maryport	Workington	57+8	16
				Everton	4+2	—
				Sheffield U. (on loan)	0+2	—
				Oldham Ath.	—	—

Chairman: Brian Winston.
Directors: F. F. Harris, H. S. Zussman, M. E. Page, M.A.
Manager: George Petchey.   *Secretary:* Peter Barnes.
Year Formed: 1881.   *Turned Professional:* 1901.
Limited Company: 1906.
Previous Names: 1881–46, Clapton Orient; 1946–66, Leyton Orient.
Previous Grounds: Millfields Road, Homerton, Millfields, and Lea Bridge Road.
Honours: *Football League,* best season in Division 1: 22nd, 1962–63. Division 2, Runners-up: 1961–62. Division 3, Champions: 1969–70. Division 3(S), Champions: 1955–56; Runners-up: 1954–55.   *F.A. Cup,* best season: 6th Rd., 1925–26, 1953–54, 1971–72.   *Football League Cup,* best season: 5th Rd., 1963.
Record Victory: 9-2 v Aldershot, Division 3(S), Feb. 10th, 1934 and v Chester, League Cup, 3rd Rd., Oct. 17th, 1962.
Record Defeat: 0-8 v Aston Villa, F.A. Cup, 4th Rd., Jan. 30th, 1929.
Most League Points: 66, Division 3(S), 1955–56.
Most League Goals: 106, Division 3(S), 1955–56.
Highest League Scorer in Season: Tom Johnston, 35, Division 2, 1957–58.
Most League Goals in Total Aggregate: Tom Johnston, 119, 1956–58, 59–61.
Most Capped Player: 'Taffy' Evans, 3 (4), Wales; Ernest Morley, 3 (4) Wales.
Most League Appearances: Peter Allen, 380, 1965-76.
Record Transfer Fee Received: £112,000 from Leicester C. for Dennis Rofe, Aug. 1972.
Record Transfer Fee Paid: £60,000 to C. Palace for Gerry Queen, Sept. 1972, and £60,000 to C. Palace for Derek Possee, July 1974.
Managers Since the War: Charles Hewitt, Neil McBain, Alec Stock, Les Gore, Alec Stock, John Carey, Benny Fenton, Dave Sexton, Dick Graham, Jimmy Bloomfield.
Address of Sportsman's Club: Same as Ground.
Address of Club Shop: 'The Orient Shop', Leyton Stadium, Brisbane Rd., London, E10 5NE.

Leyton Stadium, Brisbane Road, Leyton, London, E10 5NE.   Telephone 01-539 2223/4.   *Telegraphic address:* 'The Orient', Leyton E.10.   *Ground capacity:* 34,000 (3400 seats).   *Record attendance:* 34,345 v West Ham U., F.A. Cup 4th Rd., January 25, 1964.   *Record receipts:* £22,440 v Arsenal, F.A. Cup 6th Rd., March 18, 1972.   *Pitch measurements:* 110 yds × 80 yds.

How to get there: Buses 69, 58, 278, 241 pass the ground. From the centre of London, journey by underground (Central Line) to Leyton station; the ground is a few minutes walk.   Nearest BR station is Leyton Midland Road (10 minutes' walk).
Match tickets: Can be booked at least two weeks in advance.
Car parking: Street parking around the ground. A National Car Park five minutes from Brisbane Road (off Oliver Road).
Entertainments/catering facilities: Supporters' Section Club and snack bar points around the ground.
Club shop: Sells all types of souvenirs.
Handbooks/programmes: Programmes can be obtained on subscription, and back numbers can be ordered from the club shop.
Extra information: The club operates a Pools Section and Travel Service. All enquiries to Mr. B. Blower, commercial manager, club address (tel 01-539 6092).

Club Colours: Red shirts with white insert, white shorts, black stockings, with red and white tops.
Change Colours: Yellow shirts, blue shorts.
Club Captain: Peter Allen.
Trainer: Terry Long.
Club Nickname: 'The O's'.

ORIENT 1975–76 LEAGUE RECORD

Match No.	Date	Venue	Opponents	Result	H/T Score	League Pos'n	Goalscorers	Attendance
1	Aug 16	H	Blackburn R.	D 1-1	1-0	—	Waddington (og)	6054
2	19	H	Notts Co.	D 1-1	0-1	—	Bullock	5223
3	23	A	Blackpool	L 0-1	0-0	14		6626
4	29	H	Portsmouth	L 0-1	0-1	—		5056
5	Sept 6	A	Hull C.	L 0-1	0-1	21		5194
6	13	H	Plymouth Arg.	W 1-0	0-0	16	Grealish	5010
7	20	A	Bolton W.	D 1-1	0-0	16	Roeder	10,218
8	23	H	York C.	W 1-0	1-0	—	Bennett	4290
9	26	H	Bristol R.	D 0-0	0-0	12		4978
10	Oct 4	A	Oxford U.	L 1-2	0-0	15	Bennett	4569
11	11	A	Sunderland	L 1-3	0-1	15	Queen	28,327
12	18	H	Carlisle U.	W 1-0	1-0	14	Heppolette	4600
13	25	A	Fulham	D 1-1	1-0	17	Cunningham	10,464
14	Nov 1	H	Oldham Ath.	W 2-0	0-0	13	Roeder, Holt (og)	4576
15	7	A	Bristol C.	D 0-0	0-0	15		14,553
16	15	H	Southampton	W 2-1	0-1	14	Queen, Rodrigues (og)	6332
17	22	A	Carlisle U.	W 2-1	0-0	12	Mooney, Cunningham	6502
18	29	A	Luton T.	L 0-1	0-1	14		7897
19	Dec 6	H	Nottingham F.	D 1-1	1-0	14	Cunningham	5629
20	12	H	Blackpool	L 0-1	0-0	15		4337
21	20	A	Blackburn R.	D 1-1	0-0	14	Hoadley	7136
22	26	H	Chelsea	W 3-1	1-0	12	Possee, Bennett, Cunningham	15,509
23	27	A	W.B.A.	D 1-1	1-0	12	Possee	20,626
24	Jan 10	A	Plymouth Arg.	L 0-3	0-2	14		11,934
25	17	H	Hull C.	W 1-0	1-0	11	Cunningham	3876
26	Feb 14	H	Bristol C.	L 0-1	0-0	15		5785
27	21	A	Southampton	L 0-3	0-1	18		17,230
28	24	A	York C.	W 2-0	1-0	—	Scott (og), Queen	2857
29	28	H	Fulham	W 2-0	0-0	17	Cunningham, Queen	7558
30	Mar 2	H	Charlton Ath.	L 0-1	0-0	—		9754
31	6	A	Oldham Ath.	D 1-1	1-1	16	Walley	6851
32	13	H	Sunderland	L 0-2	0-2	18		7954
33	20	H	Luton T.	W 3-0	2-0	16	Bennett 2, Heppolette	5544
34	23	A	Charlton Ath.	D 1-1	1-1	—	Queen	10,625
35	27	A	Nottingham F.	L 0-1	0-1	16		11,127
36	Apr 3	A	Bristol R.	D 1-1	1-1	17	Mooney	5182
37	10	H	Bolton W.	D 0-0	0-0	15		6294
38	13	A	Portsmouth	L 1-2	0-2	17	Queen	5069
39	17	A	Chelsea	W 2-0	1-0	15	Possee, Cunningham	17,679
40	20	H	W.B.A.	D 0-0	0-0	—		10,857
41	24	H	Oxford U.	W 2-1	1-0	11	Cunningham, Mooney	5014
42	27	A	Notts. Co.	L 0-2	0-1	—		8515

Goalscorers

League (37): Cunningham 8, Queen 6, Bennett 5, Mooney 3, Possee 3, Heppolette 2, Roeder 2, Bullock 1, Grealish 1, Hoadley 1, Walley 1, Own Goals 4.

League Cup	Second Round	Birmingham C. (a)	0-4
F.A. Cup	Third Round	Cardiff C. (h)	0-1

Jackson	Fisher	Grealish	Allen	Hoadley	Walley	Cunningham	Bennett	Bullock	Heppolette	Allder	Roffey	Roeder	Queen	Mooney	Cotton	Possee	Beason	Payne	Gray	Everett	Hibbs	Match No.
1	2	3	4	5	6	7	8	9	10	11												1
1	2	4		5	6	7	8	9	10	11	3											2
1	2	4		5	6	7	8*	9	10	11	3	12										3
1	2	3		5	6	7	8	9	10	11			4									4
1	2	8		5	6	7	4	9	10	11*	3	12										5
1	2	8		5	6		4			11	3	7	9*	10	12							6
1	2	8		5	6		4	12		11*	3	7	9	10								7
1	2	8		5	6	11	4	12			3*	7	10	9								8
1	2	8*		5	6		4	9		11	3	7	10		12							9
1	2	8		5	6	12	4	9		11*	3	7	10									10
1	2	3		5	6	11	4	9	8			7	10									11
1	2	3		5	6	11	4	9*	8			7	10	12								12
1	2	3		5	6	11	4		10			7	9	8								13
1	2	3		5	6	11	4*		10			7	9	8	12							14
1	2	3		5	6	7	4			11			8	10	9							15
1	2	3		5	6	11	4		10			7	9	8								16
1	2	3		5	6	11	4		10			7	9	8								17
1	2	3		5	6	7	4			11	12		8	9	10*							18
1	2	3		5	6	7	4			11			8	10*	12	9						19
1	2	3		5	6	7	4*	9		11	12		8		10							20
1	2	3		5	6	7	4	9			12		8	10		11*						21
1	2	3		5	6	7	4	9					8	10		11						22
1	2	3		5	6	7	4	9		11			8	10								23
1	2				6	7	4	9		11			8	10				3	5			24
1				5	6	7	4	9	10	3			8			11		2				25
1	2*	4		5	6	7		9	10	12			8			11		3				26
1	2	8		5	6	7		9	10				4*	12		11		3				27
1	2	8		5	6	7	4		10				9			11		3				28
1		8*		5	6	7				11	4	2	9	10				3		12		29
1	12		4	5	6	7*				11	8	2	9	10				3				30
1		8	4	5	6					11	7	3	9	10				2				31
1		8*	4	5	6				10	11	3		9	7	12			2				32
1				5		7	4	3	9*	10	6	8	11	12				2				33
1	2		4	5	6		8			11	10*	12	9			7		3				34
1	2	8*	3		6	11		9	10				5	12		7		4				35
1	2	8		5	6	11	4		10				9			7		3				36
1	3	8		5	6		4			11			10	9		7		2				37
1	2	8		5	6		4		10	12			11	9*		7		3				38
1	2	8		5	6	7	12		10		4*		9			11		3				39
1	2	8		5	6	7			10		4		9			11		3				40
1	3	8		5	6	7			10		4	12	9			11*		2				41
1	3	8		5	6	7					4	12	9*			11		2			10	42
42	36	38	7	40	42	33	33	16	34	19	13	20	32	15	—	21	—	19	1	—	1	

Substitute appearances:

Jackson						Cunningham	Bennett	Bullock		Heppolette	Allder	Roffey	Queen	Mooney	Cotton	Possee		Payne
1s +						+ 1s	+ 1s	+ 2s		+ 4s	+ 1s	+ 5s	+ 4s	+ 3s	+ 1s	+ 1s		+ 1s

ORIENT—PLAYERS

Player and position	Ht.	Wt.	Birthplace	Clubs	League Appearances	Goals
Goalkeepers						
John Jackson	6 2	13 2	London	C. Palace	346	—
				Orient	100	—
John Smeulders	5 10	12 10	Hackney	Orient	—	—
Defenders						
Peter Bennett	5 10½	11 3	Hillingdon	West Ham U.	36+3	3
				Orient	140+2	6
Phil Hoadley	5 11	12 2	Battersea	C. Palace	62+11	1
				Orient	194	6
David Payne	5 9	10 13	Croydon	C. Palace	281+3	9
				Orient	55+2	—
Bill Roffey	5 11	12 6	Stepney	C. Palace	24	—
				Orient	39+2	1
Nigel Gray	6 3	12 8	Fulham	Orient	3	—
Bobby Fisher	5 8	10 1	Wembley	Orient	82+5	—
Midfield						
Peter Allen	5 9	10 13	Hove	Orient	376+4	27
Tom Walley (Wales)	5 10	11 6	Caernarvon	Arsenal	10+4	1
				Watford	202+1	17
				Orient	155+2	5
Ricky Heppolette	5 9	11 5	Bolton	Preston N.E.	149+5	13
				Orient	105	10
Doug Allder	5 10	10 7	Hammersmith	Millwall	191+11	10
				Orient	19+4	—
Tony Grealish (Eire)	5 7	11 7	Paddington	Orient	62+1	3
Gary Hibbs	5 8	11 4	Hammersmith	Orient	1	—
Glenn Roeder	6 1	12 2	Woodford	Orient	23+8	2
*Malcolm Beason	5 7	11 1	Dulwich	Orient	0+1	—
Forwards						
Gerry Queen	6 0	11 1	Glasgow	S. Mirren	63	10
				Kilmarnock	94	29
				C. Palace	101+7	24
				Orient	131+4	32
*Roy Cotton	6 0	12 3	Fulham	Brentford	1+1	—
				Orient	0+3	—
Laurie Cunningham	5 8	10 13	Archway	Orient	48+3	9
Dean Mooney	6 1	12 4	Paddington	Orient	16+6	3
Derek Possee	5 5	9 8	Southwark	Tottenham H.	19	4
				Millwall	222+1	79
				C. Palace	51+2	12
				Orient	55+2	10
Mike Everett	5 11	11 2	Mile End	C. Palace	—	—
				Orient	0+1	—

OXFORD UNITED DIV. 3

President: The Duke of Marlborough.

Chairman: A. E. R. Rosser.

Vice-Chairman: G. E. Coppock.

Directors: D. J. Meeson, A. T. Lees, W. H. Reeves, G. Pritchard.

Manager: Mike Brown.

Secretary: Brian Truscott.

Year Formed: 1896. *Turned Professional:* 1949.

Limited Company: 1949.

Previous Name: 1896, Headington United; 1960, Oxford United.

Honours: *Football League,* best season in Division 2: 8th, 1972–73. Division 3, Champions: 1967–68. Division 4, Promoted: 1964–65 (4th). *F.A. Cup,* best season: 6th Rd., 1963–64. (Record for 4th Division Club). *Football League Cup,* best season: 5th Rd., 1969–70.

Record Victory: 7-1 v Barrow, Division 4, Dec. 19th, 1964.

Record Defeat: 0-5 v Cardiff C., Division 2, Feb. 8th, 1969, and v Cardiff C., Division 2, Sept. 12, 1973.

Most League Points: 61, Division 4, 1964–65.

Most League Goals: 87, Division 4, 1964–65.

Highest League Scorer in Season: Colin Booth, 23, Division 4, 1964–65.

Most League Appearances: John Shuker, 450, 1962–76.

Most League Goals in Total Aggregate: Graham Atkinson, 73, 1962–73.

Most Capped Player: David Roberts, 6 (11), Wales.

Record Transfer Fee Received: £70,000 from Hull C. for David Roberts, February 1975.

Record Transfer Fee Paid: £75,000 to Cardiff C. for Andy McCulloch, July 1974.

Managers Since Election to Football League: Arthur Turner, Ron Saunders, Gerry Summers.

Address of the Supporters Club: Supporters Club Offices, Manor Ground Beech Road, Headington, Oxford.

Address of Club Shop: On ground on match days.

Manor Ground, Beech Road, Headington, Oxford. Telephone Oxford 61503. *Ground capacity:* 18,000. *Record attendance:* 22,730 v Preston N.E., F.A. Cup 6th Rd., February 29, 1964. *Record receipts:* £9,302 v Liverpool F.A. Cup 3rd Rd., January 15, 1972. *Pitch measurements:* 112 yds × 78 yds.

How to get there: Bus 580/1/2 from the city centre. Nearest railway station is Oxford General. From the station take Bus 1 to Queens Lane and then take Bus 581/2/3. By road, take Oxford ring road to the east of the city, following the signs for Headington. Leave the ring road at Green Road roundabout into London Road; the ground is on the right after going straight across at the traffic lights.

Match tickets: Subject to availability tickets may be booked 14 days prior to the match.

Car parking: Parking is available in certain streets around the ground.

Entertainments/catering facilities: Cinema, public houses, and cafés, all just minutes from the ground. Refreshments available inside the ground.

Club shop: Open Mon.–Fri. offering all types of souvenirs.

Handbook/programmes: Programmes available from the club shop.

Extra information: In five years from joining the Fourth Division, Oxford reached Division Two.

Club Colours: Blue and yellow striped shirts, blue shorts with yellow stripe, yellow stockings.

Change Colours: White shirts, white shorts, white stockings.

Club Captain: John Shuker.

First Team Trainer: Ken Fish.

Club Nickname: The U's.

OXFORD UNITED 1975–76 LEAGUE RECORD

Match No.	Date	Venue	Opponents	Result	H/T Score	League Pos'n	Goalscorers	Attendance
1	Aug 16	A	Carlisle U.	D 1-1	1-1	—	Tait	8505
2	20	H	Bolton W.	W 2-0	2-0	—	Clarke, D., Gibbins	5277
3	23	H	Sunderland	D 1-1	0-0	5	Clarke, D.	9069
4	27	A	Chelsea	L 1-3	1-2	—	McGrogan	22,841
5	29	A	Charlton Ath.	L 1-2	1-2	—	Tait	8748
6	Sept 6	H	Fulham	L 1-3	0-2	14	Clarke, D.	7318
7	12	A	Bristol C.	L 1-4	0-1	17	Tait	10,374
8	20	H	Nottingham F.	L 0-1	0-0	22		5068
9	27	A	York C.	L 0-2	0-0	22		3190
10	Oct 4	H	Orient	W 2-1	0-0	21	Clarke, D., Heron	4569
11	11	A	Notts Co.	W 1-0	1-0	16	Clarke, D.	11,742
12	18	H	Blackburn R.	D 0-0	0-0	17		5388
13	25	A	Plymouth Arg.	L 1-2	0-0	19	Tait	12,491
14	Nov 1	H	Hull C.	L 2-3	0-1	19	McGrogan, Foley	4701
15	8	A	Oldham Ath.	D 1-1	1-1	20	Tait	8063
16	12	H	W.B.A.	L 0-1	0-1	—		5685
17	15	H	Blackpool	L 1-3	1-1	20	Shuker (pen)	4316
18	22	A	Blackburn R.	D 0-0	0-0	20		9279
19	29	A	Portsmouth	W 2-0	2-0	20	Tait 2	8648
20	Dec 6	H	Bristol R.	W 2-1	1-0	20	Tait, McCulloch	6532
21	13	A	Sunderland	L 0-1	0-0	20		22,501
22	20	H	Carlisle U.	D 0-0	0-0	20		4241
23	26	A	Luton T.	L 2-3	0-2	20	Shuker, Jeffrey	13,111
24	27	H	Southampton	L 1-2	1-1	20	Tait	12,004
25	Jan 10	H	Bristol C.	D 1-1	0-1	20	Clarke, C.	7355
26	17	A	Fulham	D 1-1	0-1	20	Foley	6783
27	Feb 7	H	Chelsea	D 1-1	0-0	20	Tait	11,162
28	14	H	Oldham Ath.	D 1-1	0-1	20	Foley	4786
29	21	A	Blackpool	L 0-2	0-1	20		4423
30	25	A	W.B.A.	L 0-2	0-1	—		14,159
31	28	H	Plymouth Arg.	D 2-2	0-1	20	Tait 2	5778
32	Mar 2	A	Bolton W.	W 1-0	0-0	—	Briggs	22,340
33	6	A	Hull C.	L 0-2	0-0	20		4820
34	13	H	Notts. Co.	W 2-1	2-0	20	Clarke, C., Aylott	5516
35	20	H	Portsmouth	W 1-0	0-0	20	Foley	6928
36	27	A	Bristol R.	W 1-0	0-0	20	Gibbins	5952
37	Apr 3	H	York C.	W 1-0	0-0	20	Clarke, D.	4926
38	10	A	Nottingham F.	L 0-4	0-0	20		11,259
39	16	A	Charlton Ath.	W 1-0	0-0	20	Lowe	7930
40	17	H	Luton T.	L 1-3	1-1	20	Clarke, D.	7633
41	19	A	Southampton	L 1-2	1-1	—	Shuker (pen)	18,870
42	24	A	Orient	L 1-2	0-1	20	Jeffrey	5014

Goalscorers

League (39): Tait 12, Clarke, D. 7, Foley 4, Shuker 3 (2 pens), Clarke, C. 2, Gibbins 2, Jeffrey 2, McGrogan 2, Aylott 1, Briggs 1, Heron 1, Lowe 1, McCulloch 1.

League Cup (6): Jeffrey 2, Foley, Aylott, Heron, Lowe.

F.A. Cup (1): Clarke D.

League Cup	Second Round	Charlton Ath. (a)	3-3
		(h)	1-1
		(h)	2-3 (a.e.t.)
F.A. Cup	Third Round	Manchester U. (a)	1-2

Burton	Light	Shuker	Lowe	Clarke, C.	Jeffrey	Houseman	Tait	Clarke, D.	Gibbins	Heron	Aylott	McGrogan	Taylor	Milkins	Foley	Bodel	Duncan	Briggs	Hynd	McCulloch	Match No.
1	2	3	4	5	6	7	8	9	10	11											1
1		3	4	5	6	7	8	9	10	11	2										2
1		3	4	5	6	7	8*	9	10	11	2	12									3
1		3	4	5	6	11	8	9	10		2	7									4
	2	3	4	5	6	11	8	9	10			7		1							5
		3	4*	5	6	11	8	9	10		2	7		1	12						6
	2	3		5	6		12	9		11		7		1	10*	4	8				7
1		3	4	5	10*	8		9		11	7	12	2		6						8
1		3	4	5	6		12	9		11	7		2		10	8*					9
1		3		5	6	7		9		11	8		2		10		4				10
1		3		5	6	7	12	9		11*	8		2		10		4				11
1		3		5	6*	7	8	9		11	12		2		10		4				12
1		3		5	6*	7	8	9		11	12		2		10		4				13
1		3		5	6	7	8	9		11*	12		2		10		4				14
1		3	4	5	6	7	8	9		11			2		10						15
1		3	4	5	6	7	8		12	11	8*		2		10						16
1		3	4	5	6	7	10	9		11			2		8						17
1		3		5	6	7	10	9		11	12		2		8*	4					18
1		3	4	5	6	7*	8	9		11			2		12					10	19
1		3	4	5	6	7	8	9		11			2							10	20
1		3		5	6	7	8	9		11			2		4					10	21
1		3	4	5	6	7	8	9*		11			2		12					10	22
1		3	4	5	6	7	11			8			2		9					10	23
1		3	4	5	6*	7	11	9		8			2		12					10	24
1		3	4	5	11*	7		9		8			2		12			6		10	25
1		3	4	5		7	11	9			12		2*		8			6		10	26
1		3	4	5		7	11	9					2		8			6		10	27
1		3	4	5		7	11	9					2		8			6		10	28
1		3	4	5		7	11	9			12		2		8			6*		10	29
1			4	5		7		9	12	3			2		8		11*	6		10	30
1		3	4	5	6	7	10	9*	12				2		8		11				31
1		3	4	5		7	11	9	10				2		8			6			32
1			4	5		7		9	10	3			2		8		11	6			33
1		3	4	5		7		9	10	11			2		8			6			34
1		3	4	5		7	11	9	10				2		8			6			35
1		3	4	5		7	11	9	10				2		8			6			36
1		3	4	5	7		11	9	10		12		2		8*			6			37
1		3	4	5		7	11	9	10				2		8			6			38
1		3	4	5		7	11	9	10				2		8			6			39
1		3	4	5		7	11	9	10*		12		2		8			6			40
1		3	4	5		8	10	9		11	7*		2		12			6			41
1		3	4	5	11	7	10		9				2		8			6			42
39	3	40	35	41	29	37	34	39	16	7	28	6	35	3	27	3	5	18	5	12	
							+3s		+3s	+4s	+6s				+6s						

OXFORD UNITED—PLAYERS

Player and position	Ht.	Wt.	Birthplace	Clubs	League Appearances	Goals
Goalkeepers						
Roy Burton	5 10	12 2	Wantage	Oxford U.	152	—
John Milkins	6 0½	13 7½	Dagenham	Portsmouth	344	—
				Oxford U.	31	—
*Keith Baker	5 11	12 6	Oxford	Oxford U.	—	—
				Grimsby T. (on loan)	1	—
				Millwall (on loan)	—	—
Defenders						
John Shuker	5 9	11 5	Manchester	Oxford U.	444+6	45
Colin Clarke	6 1½	11 7	Glasgow	Arsenal	—	—
				Oxford U.	382+1	20
Andy Bodell	5 11	11 13	Clydebank	Oxford U.	3	—
Nick Lowe	5 10	12 10	Headington	Oxford U.	57	1
				Halifax T. (on loan)	9	—
*Jimmy Light	5 8	11 7	Oxford	Oxford U.	64	1
Les Taylor	5 9	10 9	North Shields	Oxford U.	40	—
Midfield						
*Steve Aylott	5 11	11 3½	Ilford	Orient	—	—
				West Ham	—	—
				Oxford U.	143+11	8
Max Briggs	5 8½	10 8	Barmerton	Norwich C.	127+8	—
				Oxford U.	57+3	1
Billy Jeffrey	5 10	11 0	Clydebank	Oxford U.	63	4
Colin Duncan	5 10	10 13	Plymouth	Oxford U.	28	—
Peter Houseman	5 8	11 7	Battersea	Chelsea	252+17	20
				Oxford U.	37	—
Forwards						
Derek Clarke	5 8½	10 7	Whillenhall	Walsall	6	2
				Wolverhampton W.	2+3	—
				Oxford U.	172+7	35
Brian Heron	5 8	10 12	Dumbarton	Rangers	—	—
				Motherwell	75	20
				Dumbarton	33+3	10
				Oxford U.	37+2	8
Peter Foley	5 11	10 7	Bicester	Oxford U.	29+6	4
*Roger Gibbins	5 10	11 3	Enfield	Tottenham H.	—	—
				Oxford U.	16+3	2
Hughie McGrogan	5 9	9 12	Dumbarton	Oxford U.	13+8	3
Mick Tait	5 11	11 8	North Shields	Oxford U.	38+3	12
Archie White	5 7	10 8	Dumbarton	Oxford U.	—	—

PETERBOROUGH UNITED   DIV. 3

Chairman: G. H. Woodcock.

Vice-Chairman: H. W. Wright.

Directors: S. E. Nicholas, W. O'Neill Wilde, C. Duddington.

Manager: Noel Cantwell.

Secretary: A. V. Blades.

Commercial Manager: P. F. Mowforth.

Year Formed: 1923.

Turned Professional: 1934.

Limited Company: 1934.

Previous Name: Peterborough and Fletton United until 1934.

Honours: *Football League,* best season in Division 3: 5th, 1961–62. Division 4, Champions: 1960–61, 1973–74.   *F.A. Cup,* best season: 6th Rd., 1965.   *Football League Cup,* best season, semi-finalists: 1966.

Record Victory: 8-1 v Oldham Ath., Division 4, Nov. 26th, 1969.

Record Defeat: 1-8 v Northampton T., F.A. Cup, 2nd Rd. (2nd Replay), 1946–47.

Most League Points: 66, Division 4, 1960–61.

Most League Goals: 134, Division 4, 1960–61.

Highest League Scorer in Season: Terry Bly, 52, Division 4, 1960–61.

Most League Goals in Total Aggregate: Jim Hall, 120, 1967–75

Most Capped Player: Ollie Conmy, 6, Eire.

Most League Appearances: Jim Hall, 302, 1967–75.

Record Transfer Fee Received: £30,000 from W.B.A. for John Wile, Dec. 1970.

Record Transfer Fee Paid: £25,000 to Chesterfield for Ernie Moss, Nov. 1975.

Managers Since Joining Football League: Jimmy Hagan, Jack Fairbrother, Gordon Clark, Norman Rigby, Jim Iley.

Address of Supporters Club: Same as Football Club.

London Road Ground, Peterborough PE2 8AL. Telephone Peterborough (0733) 63947. *Ground capacity:* 30,000. *Record attendance:* 30,096 v Swansea T., F.A. Cup 5th Rd., February 20, 1965. *Record receipts:* £17,215 v Leeds U., F.A. Cup 4th Rd., Jan 26 1974. *Pitch measurements:* 112 yds × 76 yds.

How to get there: Peterborough Station (20 minutes' walking distance). Bus terminal 400 yards.

Match tickets: Bookable 14 days in advance.

Car parking: Ample parking available at the ground.

Entertainments/catering facilities: Supporters' Club provides entertainments. Licensed refreshment kiosks in the ground.

Club shop: Sells all types of souvenirs (postal requests to Commercial Manager).

Handbooks/programmes: Handbooks available and programmes can be ordered on subscription.

Extra information: Since joining the Football League in 1960, Peterborough United have scored more goals than any other League club over the corresponding period.

Club Colours: Royal blue shirts and shorts, red stockings.

Change Colours: Yellow shirts, sky blue shorts, yellow stockings.

Club Captain: Chris Turner.

First Team Trainer/Coach: John Barnwell.

Club Nickname: 'The Posh'.

PETERBOROUGH UNITED 1975-76 LEAGUE RECORD

Match No.	Date	Venue	Opponents	Result	H/T Score	League Pos'n	Goalscorers	Attendance
1	Aug 16	H	Walsall	D 0-0	0-0	—		7174
2	23	A	Shrewsbury T.	L 1-3	0-1	21	Nixon	4473
3	30	H	Port Vale	D 0-0	0-0	21		6065
4	Sept 6	A	Chesterfield	D 1-1	0-1	20	Nixon	2570
5	13	H	Aldershot	D 1-1	0-0	18	Telford	6201
6	20	A	Chester	D 1-1	0-1	18	Robson	4063
7	24	H	Wrexham	W 2-0	1-0	—	Robson, Gregory	5888
8	27	H	Rotherham U.	L 1-3	1-0	14	Telford	6543
9	Oct 4	A	Sheffield W.	D 2-2	1-1	16	Jones, Gregory	11,412
10	11	A	Mansfield T.	D 1-1	1-0	15	Turner	6983
11	18	H	Bury	W 4-0	2-0	11	Robson 3, Turner	7271
12	21	A	Preston N.E.	L 1-2	0-1	—	Robson	9597
13	25	A	Hereford U.	W 4-2	1-1	9	Gregory, Turner 2, Nixon	8471
14	Nov 1	A	Brighton & H.A.	W 1-0	1-0	8	Gregory	8630
15	4	H	Grimsby T.	W 4-2	2-1	—	Gregory 3, Nixon	7646
16	8	A	Crystal Palace	D 1-1	0-1	6	Robson	19,000
17	15	H	Swindon T.	W 3-1	3-1	5	Eustace (pen), Robson 2	7287
18	29	A	Southend U.	W 3-2	1-1	4	Nixon, Robson, Eustace	7393
19	Dec 6	A	Halifax T.	W 1-0	1-0	3	Murray	2289
20	20	A	Gillingham	D 2-2	1-2	3	Robson, Eustace	4086
21	26	H	Millwall	D 1-1	1-1	2	Cozens	10,653
22	27	A	Cardiff C.	L 2-5	1-1	2	Hughes, Gregory	16,094
23	Jan 10	A	Port Vale	L 0-2	0-1	5		3892
24	14	A	Colchester U.	W 3-1	1-0	—	Gregory, Hughes, Turner	7453
25	17	H	Chester	W 3-0	1-0	3	Cozens, Delgado (og), Robson	8674
26	31	H	Preston N.E.	W 2-0	1-0	4	Moss 2	7728
27	Feb 7	A	Grimsby T.	D 1-1	1-0	4	Hughes	5482
28	18	H	Crystal Palace	W 2-0	1-0	—	Robson, Eustace (pen)	13,308
29	21	A	Swindon T.	W 3-0	2-0	4	Moss, Eustace, Gregory	7477
30	23	A	Wrexham	L 0-3	0-1	—		3640
31	27	H	Hereford U.	L 0-3	0-2	6		14,106
32	Mar 6	A	Brighton & H.A.	L 0-5	0-2	8		16,398
33	10	H	Sheffield W.	D 2-2	1-1	—	Oakes, Nixon	8209
34	13	H	Mansfield T.	L 0-3	0-1	9		7497
35	16	A	Bury	L 1-2	0-1	—	Gregory	4493
36	19	A	Southend U.	D 0-0	0-0	9		4561
37	24	A	Aldershot	L 0-1	0-0	—		3001
38	27	H	Halifax T.	W 1-0	1-0	9	Moss	4933
39	31	H	Gillingham	D 1-1	1-1	—	Cozens	4594
40	Apr 3	A	Walsall	D 2-2	1-2	9	Hughes, Gregory	6266
41	6	A	Rotherham U.	D 1-1	1-0	—	Moss	3872
42	10	H	Chesterfield	L 0-1	0-0	10		5830
43	16	A	Colchester U.	D 1-1	0-1	—	Leslie (og)	3687
44	17	A	Millwall	L 0-2	0-2	9		11,377
45	19	H	Cardiff C.	D 0-0	0-0	—		6846
46	24	H	Shrewsbury T.	W 3-2	3-1	10	Gregory 2, Moss	5023

Goalscorers

League (63): Gregory 14, Robson 13, Nixon 6, Moss 6, Turner 5, Eustace 5 (2 pens), Hughes 4, Cozens 3, Telford 2, Jones 1, Murray 1, Oakes 1, own goals 2.
League Cup (6): Gregory 2, Robson 2, Turner, Cozens.
F.A. Cup (10): Nixon 3, Cozens 2, Gregory, Turner, Hughes, Jones, M, own goal 1.

League Cup	First Round	Southend U. (a)	0-2
	Second Leg	(h)	3-0
	Second Round	Blackpool (h)	2-0
	Third Round	Fulham (a)	1-0
	Fourth Round	Middlesbrough (a)	0-3
F.A. Cup	First Round	Winsford (h)	4-1
	Second Round	Coventry Spts. (a)	4-0
	Third Round	Nottingham F. (a)	0-0
		(h)	1-0
	Fourth Round	Manchester U. (a)	1-3

Steele	Bradley	Lee	Fustace	Oakes	Murray	Nixon	Gregory	McCormick	Hughes	Robson	Carmichael	Turner	Cozens	Hodson	Merrick	Telford	Jones	Walker	Rogers	Moss	Heeley	Match No.
1	2	3	4*	5	6	7	8	9	10	11	12											1
1	2	3	4		6	7	9		11	10		5	8									2
1		3	4	5	2	7	8		10	11	6			9								3
1	12	3	4	5	2	7	8		10	11	6				9*							4
1		3	4	5	2	7	8		10	11	6				9*	12						5
1		3		5	2	7	8		4	11	6				9	10*	12					6
1		3			2	7	8		10	11*	6	12	4	9	5							7
1		3	12		2	7*	8		4	11	5			10	9	6						8
1	9	3	4		2	7	8		10	11	6						5					9
1		3	2	4		7	8		10	11*	6	9					5	12				10
1		3	4		2	7	8		10	11	6	9					5					11
1		3	4		2	7	8		10	11	6	9					5					12
1		3	2	4		7	8		10	11	6	9					5					13
1		3	4*		2	7	8		10	11	6	9					5	12				14
1		3	4		2	7	8		10	11	6	9					5					15
1		3*	4		2	7	8		10	11	6	9					5	12				16
1	2		4		3	7	8		10	11	6	5	9									17
1		3	4		2	7	8		10	11	6	5	9*				12					18
1		3	4		2	7	8*		10	11	6	5	9				12					19
1		3	4		2	7	8		10	11	6	5	9									20
1		3	4		2	7*	8		10	11	6	5	9				12					21
1		3	4		2	7	8		10	11	6	5	9									22
1	2		4*		3		8		10	11	6	5	9				7	12				23
1			4		2		8		10	11	6	5	9					3		7		24
1			4		2		8		10	11	6	5	9					3		7		25
1			4		2		8		10	11	6	5	7					3		9		26
1	3		4		2		8		10		6	5	7				11			9		27
1	3		4		2	12	8*		10	11	6	5	7							9		28
1			4		2	7	8		10	3	6	5					11			9		29
1	12		4	3	2		8		10	11	6	5	7*							9		30
1	12		4		2	7	8		10	11	6	5						3		9*		31
1	2		4		12	7	8		10	11	6	5*						3		9		32
1			4	5	2	7	8			11	6			10			3	12		9*		33
1			4	5		7	8*		10	11	6	2					3	12		9		34
1	3		4	10*	2	7	8		12		6	5					11			9		35
1		3	4		2	7	8		10	11	6	5	9*				12					36
1		3	4		2*	7	8		10	11	6	5					12			9		37
1		3	4			7*	8		10	11	6	2	5				12			9		38
1		3	4			7	8		10	11*	6	5	4	2			12			9		39
1		3	4				8		10	11*	6	5	7	2			12			9		40
1			4				8		10	12	6	5	7	2*			11	3		9		41
1			4				8		10*12		6	5	7	2			11	3		9		42
1	12		4			7	8		10		6*	5		2			11	3		9		43
1		3	4			7	8		10		6	5					11	2		9		44
1		3	2			7	8		10	11	6	5		4*				12		9		45
1		3	4			7	8		10*	11	6	5		2				9		12		46
46	9	30	42	9	36	33	46	1	42	39	45	31	21	11	5	3	22	13	1	21	—	
		+ 3s	+ 1s	+ 1s	+ 2s				+ 3s	+ 1s				+ 1s			+ 1s	+ 5s	+ 7s	+ 4s	+ 1s	

PETERBOROUGH UNITED—PLAYERS

Player and position	Ht.	Wt.	Birthplace	Clubs	League Appearances	Goals
Goalkeepers						
*Michael Drewery	6 0	12 0	Snettisham	Peterborough J.	209	—
Eric Steele	5 11	11 3	Newcastle	Newcastle U.	—	—
				Peterborough U.	112	—
Defenders						
*Michael Jones	5 11	10 11	Sunderland	Derby Co.	—	—
				Notts Co.	82+20	1
				Peterborough U.	82+6	4
Jeff Lee	5 8	9 13	Norristhorpe	Halifax T.	231+9	2
				Peterborough	106+1	8
Jack Carmichael	5 10	12 11½	Newcastle	Arsenal	—	—
				Peterborough U.	196+16	—
Chris Turner	6 1	12 9	St. Neots	Peterborough U.	223+7	27
*Keith Bradley	5 9	10 10	Ellesmere Port	Aston V.	116+7	2
				Peterborough U.	106+3	—
Stuart Hodson	6 0	12 6	Peterborough	Peterborough U.	22+9	—
Bert Murray	5 9	11 7	Shoreditch	Chelsea	156+3	39
				Birmingham C.	127+11	22
				Brighton	99+3	25
				Peterborough U.	123	10
Midfield						
Keith Oakes	5 10	12 2	Bedworth	Peterborough U.	21+8	1
Jim Walker	5 9	10 10	Northwich	Derby Co.	35+6	3
				Brighton	24+4	4
				Peterborough U.	13+7	—
*Peter Eustace	5 11½	11 11	Scotsbridge	Sheffield W.	189+3	20
				West Ham U.	41+2	6
				Rotherham U. (on loan)	6	1
				Sheffield W.	48+8	4
				Peterborough U.	42+1	5
Lyndon Hughes	5 11	11 5	Smethwick	W.B.A.	89+9	3
				Peterborough U.	42	4
Tommy Robson	5 8	10 0	Gateshead	Northampton T.	73+1	20
				Chelsea	6+1	—
				Newcastle U.	46+1	11
				Peterborough U.	310+11	84
Forwards						
Jon Nixon	5 6	10 0	Preston	Notts Co.	167+12	32
				Peterborough U.	71+3	11
John Cozens	6 0	12 0	London	Notts Co.	41+5	13
				Peterborough U.	95	33
David Gregory	5 10	11 6	Peterborough	Peterborough U.	90+9	23
Ernie Moss	6 1	12 11	Chesterfield	Chesterfield	271	94
				Peterborough U.	21	6
*Bill Telford	5 11	11 3	Ellesmere Port	Tranmere R.	—	—
				Manchester C.	0+1	—
				Peterborough U.	3+1	2
				Colchester (on loan)	1+1	1
				Crewe A. (on loan)	—	—
David McCormick				Peterborough U.	1	—
Andrew Rogers	5 7	9 4	Chatteris	Peterborough U.	1+4	—
Mark Heeley				Peterborough U.	0+1	—

PLYMOUTH ARGYLE DIV. 2

President: G. H. Gillin, Esq. *Chairman:* R. Daniel.
Vice-Chairman: P. W. Skinnard.
Directors: B. S. Williams, S. J. Williams, B. Ford, L.
C. Lovick.

Team Manager: Tony Waiters.

Secretary: Graham Little.

Year Formed: 1886. *Turned Professional:* 1903.

Limited Company: 1903.

Previous Name: 1886–1903, Argyle Athletic Club.

The Pilgrims

P·A·F·C

Honours: *Football League,* best season in Division 2:
4th, 1931–32, 1952–53. Division 3(S), Champions:
1929–30, 1951–52; Runners-up: 1921–22, 1922–23,
1923–24, 1924–25, 1925–26, 1926–27. (Record of six
consecutive years.) Division 3, Champions: 1958–59.
F.A. Cup, best season: 5th Rd., 1952–53. *Football
League Cup,* best season: semi-finalists, 1965, 1974.

Record Victory: 8-1 v Millwall, Division 2, Jan. 16th, 1932.

Record Defeat: 0-9 v Stoke C., Division 2, Dec. 17th, 1960.

Most League Points: 68, Division 3(S), 1929–30.

Most League Goals: 107, Division 3(S), 1925–26 and 1951–52.

Highest League Scorer in Season: Jack Cock, 32, Division 3(S), 1925–26.

Most League Goals in Total Aggregate: Sammy Black, 180, 1924–38.

Most Capped Player: Moses Russell, 20 (23) Wales.

Most League Appearances: Sammy Black, 470, 1924–38.

Record Transfer Fee Received: £70,000 from Norwich C. for Colin Sullivan, June 1974.

Record Transfer Fee Paid: £45,000 to Swansea C. for Barrie Jones, Sept. 1964.

Managers Since the War: Jack Tresadern, Jimmy Rae, Jack Rowley, Neil Dougall, Ellis
Stuttard, Andy Beattie, Malcolm Allison, Derek Ufton, Billy Bingham. Ellis Stuttard.

Address of Supporters Association: Same as Football Club.

Address of Club Shop or Boutique: The Pilgrim Shop, Home Park, Plymouth, Devon.

Home Park, Plymouth, Devon. Telephone Plymouth (0752) 52561/2/3. *Ground capacity:*
40 000 (30,000 covered). *Record attendance:* 43,596 v Aston Villa, Division 2, October 10,
1936. *Record receipts:* over £10,000 (official figure not disclosed by club) v Manchester C.,
League Cup semi-final, Jan. 23, 1974. *Pitch measurements:* 112 yds × 75 yds.

How to get there: Special City buses from the Plymouth bus station at Bretonside. Nearest railway station
Plymouth.
Match tickets: Grand Stand and Mayflower Stand tickets are available 2–3 weeks before each first-team
game.
Car parking: Car park adjoining the ground holds 2,000 cars.
Entertainments/catering facilities: Eight refreshment bars around the ground.
Club shop: Situated on the ground; sells all types of souvenirs.
Handbooks/programmes: Handbook published annually and sold by the Supporters Association. Pro-
grammes sent to all parts of the world.
Extra information: In 1920–21, Plymouth Argyle established a Third Division record by drawing 21
matches.
Club Colours: White shirts, green and black trimmings, white shorts, white socks.
Club Nickname: 'The Pilgrims'.

PLYMOUTH ARGYLE 1975–76 LEAGUE RECORD

Match No.	Date	Venue	Opponents	Result	H/T Score	League Pos'n	Goalscorers	Attendance
1	Aug 16	A	Nottingham F.	L 0-2	0-1			13,083
2	23	H	Charlton Ath.	W 1-0	1-0	17	Johnson	14,201
3	29	A	Southampton	L 0-1	0-1	—		18,000
4	Sept 6	H	Sunderland	W 1-0	0-0	15	Rafferty	18,304
5	13	A	Orient	L 0-1	0-0	18		5010
6	20	H	York C.	D 1-1	0-1	17	Rafferty	12,818
7	24	A	Luton T.	D 1-1	0-1	—	Johnson	9226
8	27	A	Oldham Ath.	L 2-3	1-1	18	Mariner, Horswill	8227
9	Oct 4	H	Carlisle U.	W 2-1	1-0	14	McAuley, Burrows	12,875
10	11	H	Bolton W.	L 2-3	1-0	14	Johnson 2 (1 a pen)	14,595
11	18	A	W.B.A.	L 0-1	0-1	19		11,149
12	21	H	Blackburn R.	D 2-2	0-1	—	Delve, Rafferty	14,371
13	25	H	Oxford U.	W 2-1	0-0	16	Mariner 2	12,491
14	Nov 1	A	Chelsea	D 2-2	0-1	16	Mariner 2	20,096
15	4	A	Notts Co.	L 0-1	0-0	—		9234
16	8	H	Portsmouth	W 3-1	0-0	16	Johnson, Rafferty 2	13,885
17	15	A	Bristol R.	D 0-0	0-0	16		14,121
18	22	H	W.B.A.	W 2-1	1-0	14	Wile (og), Mariner	17,380
19	29	A	Hull C.	L 0-4	0-2	16		5098
20	Dec 6	H	Blackpool	L 1-2	0-1	17	Mariner	12,422
21	12	A	Charlton Ath.	L 0-2	0-2	19		7095
22	20	H	Nottingham F.	W 1-0	0-0	17	Mariner	10,545
23	26	A	Bristol C.	D 2-2	1-1	18	Mariner 2	21,471
24	27	H	Fulham	W 4-0	4-0	16	Randell, Rafferty 2, Johnson	24,054
25	Jan 10	H	Orient	W 3-0	2-0	12	Randell, Rafferty, Mariner	11,934
26	17	A	Sunderland	L 1-2	1-0	14	Mariner	29,737
27	24	H	Bristol C.	D 0-0	0-0	11		17,887
28	31	A	Blackburn R.	L 1-3	1-2	13	Foster	8525
29	Feb 7	H	Notts. Co.	L 1-3	0-2	15	Rafferty	11,576
30	14	A	Portsmouth	L 0-2	0-1	17		9509
31	21	H	Bristol R.	W 3-0	1-0	14	Johnson, Rafferty, Mariner	11,183
32	24	H	Luton T.	W 3-0	1-0	—	Rafferty 2, Randell	13,927
33	28	A	Oxford U.	D 2-2	1-0	13	Mariner, McAuley	5778
34	Mar 6	H	Chelsea	L 0-3	0-1	17		20,638
35	13	A	Bolton W.	D 0-0	0-0	15		21,147
36	20	H	Hull C.	D 1-1	1-1	17	Johnson (pen)	10,631
37	27	A	Blackpool	D 0-0	0-0	17		5497
38	Apr 3	H	Oldham Ath.	W 2-1	1-0	13	Randell, Burrows	9782
39	10	A	York C.	L 1-3	0-1	16	Mariner	3646
40	16	H	Southampton	W 1-0	0-0	13	Darke	25,305
41	19	A	Fulham	D 0-0	0-0	—		6913
42	24	A	Carlisle U.	L 0-2	0-1	16		7038

Goalscorers

League (48): Mariner 15, Rafferty 12, Johnson 8 (2 pens), Randell 4, Burrows 2, McAuley 2, Darke 1, Delve 1, Foster 1, Horswill 1, Own Goal 1.

League Cup (4): Rafferty, Burrows, Mariner, Own Goal 1.

F.A. Cup (2): Rafferty, Green.

League Cup	First Round	A.F.C. Bournemouth (h) 2-0	
	Second Leg	(a) 2-1	
	Second Round	Nottingham F. (a)	0-1
F.A. Cup	Third Round	Hull C. (a)	1-1
		(h)	1-4

Aleksic	Hore	Burrows	Horswill	Green	Delve	Randell	Johnson	Rafferty	McAuley	Saxton	Mariner	Pearson	Foster	Vassallo	Darke	Rioch	Sutton	Furnell	Harrison	Hardcastle	Match No.
1	2	3	4	5	6	7*	8	9	11	12	10										1
1	2	3	7	5	6	4	10	9	11*	8	12										2
1	2	3	7	5	6	4		11	12	8	9*	10									3
1	2	3	7	5	6	4	8*10	11			9		12								4
1	2	3	7	5	4		8	10	11	6	9										5
1	2	3	4	5	6		8	10	11		9		7								6
1	2	3	4	5	6	7	8	10	11		9*		12								7
1	2	3	4	5	6*	7	8	10	11		9		12								8
1	2	3	4	5	6	7	8	10	11		9										9
1	2	3	4*	5	6	7	8	10	11		9		12								10
1	2	3	4	5	6	7	8	10	11		9										11
1	2	3	4	5	6	7	8	10	11		9										12
1		3	4	5	6*	7	8	10	11		9		12		2						13
1		3		5	6	7	8	10	11		9				2		4				14
1		3		6	4	7	8	10	11*		9		12		2		5				15
1		3		6	4		8	10			9	11	7		2		5				16
1		3	4	5	6	7	8*10				9	11			2	12					17
1		3	4	5	6	7	8	10	11		9				2						18
1		3	4	5	6	7	8	10	11		9				2*12						19
1		3	4	5	6	7*	8	10	11		9		12		2						20
1		3	4		6	7	8*10	11			9		12		2		5				21
1		3	4		6	7	8	10	11		9				2		5				22
1		3		5	6	7	8	10	11		9				2		4				23
1		3		5	6	7	8	10	11		9				2		4				24
1		3		5	6	7	8	10	11		9				2		4				25
1		3	12	5	6	7	8	10	11		9*				2		4				26
1		3	8	5	6	7*12	10	11			9				2		4				27
1		3	7	5	6		8		11		9		10		2		4				28
1		3	8	5	6*	7		12	11		9		10		2		4				29
		3	2	5	6	7		10	11		9		8				4	1			30
		3	2	5	6	7	8	10	11		9						4	1			31
		3	2	5	6	7	8	10*11			9		12				4	1			32
		3	6	5			8	10	11		9		7		2		4	1			33
		3	6	5			8	10	11		9*		7		2		4	1		12	34
		3	6	5		7	8	10*11			9	12			2		4	1			35
		3	6	5		7	8	10*11	9	12	2						4	1			36
		3		5	4	7	8	10	11*		9	12			2		6	1			37
		3		5	6	7	8	10	11		9				2		4	1			38
		3		5	6	7	8	10	11		9				2		4	1			39
		3	8	5	6	7		10	11		9				2		4	1			40
		3	8	5	6	7	12	10*11			9				2		4	1			41
		3	8	5	6	7		11	9		10						4	1	2		42
29	12	42	32	40	38	36	35	38	40	1	38	6	9	1	26	3	22	13	1		

+1s   +2s +1s   +2s   +4s 7s 2s   +2s   +1s

Player and position	Ht.	Wt.	Birthplace	Clubs	League Appearances	Goals
Goalkeepers						
Jim Furnell	6 2	14 6	Manchester	Burnley	2	—
				Liverpool	28	—
				Arsenal	141	—
				Rotherham	76	—
				Plymouth Arg.	183	—
Milijia Aleksic	6 0	13 11	Stafford	Plymouth Arg.	32	—
Defenders						
Geoff. Banton	5 11	11 7	Ashton-under-Lyne	Bolton W.	—	—
				Plymouth Arg.	—	—
Phil Burrows	5 8	10 6	Stockton	Manchester C.	—	—
				York C.	333+2	14
				Plymouth Arg.	81	2
Mike Green	6 1	12 4	Carlisle	Carlisle U.	2	—
				Gillingham	131+1	24
				Bristol R.	74+3	2
				Plymouth Arg.	86	6
*Peter Hardcastle	5 8	11 13	Leeds	Blackpool	29+7	—
				Plymouth Arg.	12+2	1
David Sutton	5 11	11 0	Tarleton	Plymouth Arg.	26	—
*John Hore	5 7½	11 2	St. Austell	Plymouth Arg.	393+4	17
				Exeter C. (on loan)	11	—
Christopher King	5 9	11 4	Plymouth	Plymouth Arg.	—	—
Peter Darke	5 10½	11 9	Exeter	Plymouth Arg.	79+6	2
Graeme Hurn	5 9	11 1	Ivybridge	Plymouth Arg.	—	—
Midfield						
John Delve	5 8	10 7	Hanworth	Q.P.R.	9+6	—
				Plymouth Arg.	80	6
Colin Randall	5 8½	11 0	Skewen	Coventry C.	—	—
				Plymouth Arg.	103+1	9
Chris Harrison	5 8	10 6	Launceston	Plymouth Arg.	1	—
George Foster	5 10	11 0	Plymouth	Plymouth Arg.	11+10	1
*Barrie Vassallo	5 8	10 7	Newport, Mon.	Arsenal	—	—
				Plymouth Arg.	6+7	2
Neil Rioch	5 10	12 0	Paddington	Luton T.	—	—
				Aston V.	17+6	1
				York C. (on loan)	0+1	—
				Northampton T. (on loan)	14	4
				Plymouth Arg.	3+2	—
				(contract cancelled April 1976)		
Michael Horswill	5 10½	11 0	Anfield Plain	Sunderland	68+1	3
				Manchester C.	11+3	—
				Plymouth Arg.	32+1	1
Doug Collins	5 8	9 9	Newton	Grimsby T.	95+6	11
				Burnley	173+15	18
				Plymouth Arg.	—	—
Forwards						
Brian Johnson	5 10	11 6	London	Plymouth Arg.	81+2	18
Hugh McAuley	5 7	9 7	Bootle	Liverpool	—	—
				Tranmere R. (on loan)	13	1
				Plymouth Arg.	72	7
Paul Mariner	5 11	11 2	Bolton	Plymouth Arg.	124+1	49
Alan Rogers	5 10	11 4	Plymouth	Plymouth Arg.	26+5	1
Ian Pearson	5 10	11 0	Leeds	Plymouth Arg.	6+6	—
Jim Hamilton	5 10	10 7	Uddingston	Sunderland	9+8	2
				Plymouth Arg.	—	—

PORTSMOUTH DIV. 3

Vice-Presidents: R. Vernon Stokes, A. L. Blake, M.C., LL.B.

Chairman: B. J. Deacon.

Vice-Chairman: P. D. Clark.

Directors: J. D. P. Collett, D. K. Deacon, J. R. Parkhouse

Manager: Ian St. John.

Assistant Manager: Billy Hunter.

Secretary: Jimmy Dickinson, M.B.E.

Year Formed: 1898.

Turned Professional: 1898.   *Limited Company:* 1898.

Honours: *Football League,* Division 1, Champions: 1948–49, 1949–50. Division 2, Runners-up: 1926–27. Division 3(S), Champions: 1923–24. Division 3, Champions: 1961–62.   *F.A. Cup,* Winners: 1939; Runners-up: 1929, 1934.   *Football League Cup,* best season: 5th Rd., 1961.

Record Victory: 9-1 v Notts Co., Division 2, Apr. 9th, 1927.

Record Defeat: 0-10 v Leicester C., Division 1, Oct. 20th, 1928.

Most League Points: 65, Division 3, 1961–62.

Most League Goals: 87, Division 3(S), 1923–24, Division 2, 1926–27 and Division 3, 1961–62.

Highest League Scorer in Season: Billy Haines, 40, Division 2, 1926–27.

Most League Appearances: 764, Jimmy Dickinson, 1946–65.

Most Capped Player: Jimmy Dickinson, 48, England.

Most League Goals in Total Aggregate: Peter Harris, 194, 1946–60.

Record Transfer Fee Received: £50,000 from Middlesbrough for George Smith, Jan. 1969.

Record Transfer Fee Paid: £155,000 to Fulham for Paul Went, Dec. 1973.

Managers Since the War: Jack Tinn, Bob Jackson, Eddie Lever, Freddie Cox, George Smith.

Address of Supporters Club: Frogmore Road, Portsmouth.

Address of Club Shop or Boutique: The Club Shop, Portsmouth F.C. Supporters Club, 42 Frogmore Road, Portsmouth.

Fratton Park, Frogmore Rd., Portsmouth PO4 8RA. Telephone Portsmouth 31204/5.   *Telegraphic address:* 'Pompey Portsm'th'.   *Ground capacity:* 46,000 (14,200 covered).   *Record attendance:* 51,385 v Derby Co., F.A. Cup 6th Rd., February 26, 1949.   *Record receipts:* £18,002 v Arsenal, F.A. Cup 4th Rd., January 23, 1971.   *Pitch measurements:* 116 yds × 73 yds.

How to get there: Fratton station on main line from London Waterloo is just four minutes walk from the ground. Buses 17 and 18 from Portsmouth Harbour station and Gosport Ferry Terminal to the ground. Buses also from Portsmouth station.

Match tickets: South Stand centre section (the best seats) bookable 10 days in advance.

Car parking: Only side-street parking.

Entertainments/catering facilities: The Pompey public house and reception rooms adjoin the ground and are owned by the club. The Supporters' Club is open to members of the visiting Supporters' Club before and after the match. There are also several bars around the ground.

Club shop: 42 Frogmore Road.

Handbooks/programmes: No handbook. The match-day magazine available on subscription.

Extra information: Portsmouth were the first club to come out of the Third Division to win the League Championship.

Club Colours: Blue shirts with white collars and cuffs, white shorts, red socks.

Change Colours: Red shirts with two white vertical stripes, red shorts, red socks with blue and white trim.

Club Captain: Paul Went.   *Club Coach:*   *First Team Trainer:* Gordon Neave.

Club Nickname: 'Pompey'.

PORTSMOUTH 1975–76 LEAGUE RECORD

Match No.	Date	Venue	Opponents	Result	H/T Score	League Pos'n	Goalscorers	Attendance
1	Aug 16	A	York C.	L 1-2	1-1	—	Piper	4602
2	23	H	Nottingham F.	D 1-1	0-1	21	Went	10,665
3	29	A	Orient	W 1-0	0-1	—	Fisher (og)	5056
4	Sept 6	H	Luton T.	L 0-2	0-1	20		9835
5	13	A	Carlisle U.	L 1-2	1-1	21	McGuinness	7316
6	20	H	Oldham Ath.	D 1-1	1-1	21	Piper	8079
7	23	H	Chelsea	D 1-1	1-1	—	Reynolds	16,144
8	27	A	Southampton	L 0-4	0-1	21		17,310
9	Oct 4	H	Sunderland	D 0-0	0-0	22		13,098
10	11	A	Blackpool	D 0-0	0-0	22		8351
11	18	H	Hull C.	D 1-1	0-0	20	Piper	8155
12	21	H	Bristol R.	L 1-2	0-0	—	Marinello	9078
13	25	A	Notts Co.	L 0-2	0-0	21		9597
14	Nov 1	H	Fulham	L 0-1	0-0	21		11,441
15	4	A	Bolton W.	L 1-4	1-1	—	Kamara	18,538
16	8	A	Plymouth Arg.	L 1-3	0-0	21	Piper	13,885
17	15	H	Blackburn R.	L 0-1	0-0	22		7323
18	22	A	Hull C.	L 0-1	0-0	22		4549
19	29	H	Oxford U.	L 0-2	0-2	22		8648
20	Dec 6	A	W.B.A.	L 1-3	0-1	22	Marinello	15,325
21	13	A	Nottingham F.	W 1-0	0-0	22	McGuinness	11,343
22	20	H	York C.	L 0-1	0-1	22		7093
23	26	A	Charlton Ath.	W 3-1	2-0	22	Piper, Graham, Roberts	10,736
24	27	H	Bristol C.	L 0-1	0-1	22		14,315
25	Jan 10	H	Carlisle U.	W 1-0	0-0	22	Eames	11,430
26	17	A	Luton T.	L 1-3	0-2	22	Piper	10,464
27	31	A	Bristol R.	L 0-2	0-2	22		6133
28	Feb 7	H	Bolton W.	L 0-1	0-1	22		8958
29	14	H	Plymouth Arg.	W 2-0	1-0	21	Busby, Macken	9509
30	21	A	Blackburn R.	W 3-0	1-0	21	Graham, Piper 2	8067
31	24	A	Chelsea	L 0-2	0-2	—		12,709
32	28	H	Notts Co.	L 1-3	0-1	21	Kamara	9135
33	Mar 6	A	Fulham	W 1-0	0-0	21	Piper	6928
34	13	H	Blackpool	W 2-0	0-0	21	Kamara (pen), Piper	8394
35	20	A	Oxford U.	L 0-1	0-0	21		6928
36	27	H	W.B.A.	L 0-1	0-0	21		10,617
37	Apr 6	H	Southampton	L 0-1	0-0	—		24,115
38	10	A	Oldham Ath.	L 2-5	0-3	22	Piper, Kamara (pen)	6672
39	13	H	Orient	W 2-1	2-0	—	Wilson, McGuinness	5069
40	17	H	Charlton Ath.	D 2-2	0-0	22	Mellows 2	7992
41	20	A	Bristol C.	L 0-1	0-1	—		27,300
42	24	A	Sunderland	L 0-2	0-2	22		40,515

Goalscorers

League (32): Piper 11, Kamara 4 (2 pens), McGuinness 3, Graham 2, Marinello 2, Mellows 2, Busby 1, Eames 1, Macken 1, Reynolds 1, Roberts 1, Went 1, Wilson 1, Own Goal 1.

League Cup (4): Graham, Marinello, Reynolds, Eames.

F.A. Cup (3): Eames, McGuinness, Piper.

League Cup	First Round		Aldershot (a)	1-1
	Second Leg		(h)	2-1
	Second Round		Leicester C. (h)	1-1
			(a)	0-1 (a.e.t.)
F.A. Cup	Third Round		Birmingham C. (h)	1-1
			(a)	1-0
	Fourth Round		Charlton Ath. (a)	1-1
			(h)	0-3

Lloyd	Roberts	Ellis	Piper	Went	Hand	Marinello	Kane	Graham	McGuinness	Mellows	Reynolds	Foster	Kamara	Collard	Eames	Cahill	Wilson	McLaughlin	Lawler	Stewart	Macken	Busby	Figgins	Viney	Denyer	King	Pullar	Mate No.
1	2	3	4	5	6	7	8*	9	10	11	12																	1
1	2	3	4	5	6	7	8	9	10*	11	12																	2
1	2	12	3	5	6	7	8	9		11*	4	10																3
1	2		3	5	6	11	8	9			4	10	7															4
1	2		3	5	6		8	9	10*	7	4				11	12												5
1	2		4	5	6			9	10	11	7					3	8											6
1	2		4	5	6	12		9	7*	11	8					3	10											7
1	2		4	5	6	12		9	7*	11	8					3	10											8
1	2		4	5	6	7		9*		11	8	12				3	10											9
1	2		4	5	6	7*		9		11	8	12				3	10											10
1	2		4	5	6	7		9	10	11						3	8											11
1	2		4	5	6	7		9		11	8					3	10											12
1	2			5	6			9		11		10			8	3	12	7*	4									13
1	2		6	5		7		9	11*		8	10				3		4	12									14
1	2			5	6	7		9		11	8	10				3		4										15
1	8	2		5	6	7		9	10*	11					12	3		4										16
1	2			5	6	7		9	10*	11	8	12				3		4										17
1			4	5		7		9	10*	3	8	12				6			2		11							18
1		4	8	5		7	3	12	9	10*						6			2		11							19
1		4	8	5		7		9		3	10					6			2		11							20
1		4	7	5				9	10	3	8*	12				6			2		11							21
1		4*	8	5	9	7		3	12	10						6			2		11							22
1		4	7	5				9		11	3	10	8			6			2									23
1		4	8	5	12	11*	3	10	9	7						6			2									24
1		4	8	5	9	7	3	10		11						6			2									25
1		4	8	5	9	7	3	10		11						6		12	2*									26
1		4	10	5	9	7	3	8		11						6			2									27
1		4	8	5		7		9		11						6	3		2		10							28
1		4*	8	5				9		11		12				6	3		2		10	7						29
1			8	5				9		11		10				6	3		2		4	7						30
1			8	5		7		9		11						6	3		2		4	10						31
1			8					9	7*	11	12	10			5	3			2		4	6						32
			8					9	10	11					5		3		2		4*	6	1	7	12			33
			8					9		4*	11	10				6	3		2				1	5	12	7		34
			10					9		12	8	11				5	3*		2				1	7	6	4		35
			8					9	7*	12	11	10				5	3		2				1		6	4		36
1		4	3		8			9		11	10					5			2						6	7		37
	4*		5					9	10	3	8	11				6			2				1	7	12			38
		2	8			7		9*		11	10		4		5		3						1		6	12		39
	4	2	8			7		9		11	10				5		3*						1	12	6			40
	3	2	8			7		9		11	10					6	5						1			4		41
	2	3	8	5		7		9		11	10					6*	12						1			4		42
33	33	8	39	29	17	15	5	39	26	39	19	8	21	1	9	32	18	5	26	—	10	6	9	6	5	4	—	
			+1s		+1s	+2s		+2s	+3s	+3s	+3s					+3s	+1s	+3s	+1s				+1s	+3s		+1s		

305

PORTSMOUTH—PLAYERS

Player and position	Ht.	Wt.	Birthplace	Clubs	League Appearances	Goals
Goalkeepers						
Grahame Lloyd	5 9	11 6	Liverpool	Liverpool	—	—
				Motherwell	9	—
				Portsmouth	33	—
Phil Figgins	5 11	11 4	Portsmouth	Portsmouth	11	—
Defenders						
Chris Lawler	6 0	12 10	Liverpool	Liverpool	406	41
(England)				Portsmouth	26	—
Eoin Hand	6 0	12 0	Dublin	Portsmouth	259+1	12
(Eire)				(contract cancelled March 1976)		
Malcolm Manley	6 0	11 2	Johnston	Leicester C.	108+11	5
				Portsmouth	11	—
				(contract cancelled April 1976)		
Peter Ellis	5 11	11 2	Portsmouth	Portsmouth	25+3	—
Billy Wilson	5 9	11 1	Seaton Delaval	Blackburn R.	246+1	—
				Portsmouth	124+3	3
Phil Roberts	5 10	11 0	Cardiff	Bristol R.	175+1	6
(Wales)				Portsmouth	105+1	1
Paul Went	6 0	12 10	Bromley by Bow	Orient	48+2	5
				Charlton Ath.	160+2	15
				Fulham	58	3
				Portsmouth	84	4
Paul Cahill	5 9	10 2	Liverpool	Coventry C.	—	—
				Portsmouth	39+1	—
Peter Denyer	5 11	11 9	Hazlemere	Portsmouth	5+3	—
Keith Viney	5 11	11 12	Portsmouth	Portsmouth	6+1	—
Midfield						
Norman Piper	5 6½	9 11	North Tawton	Plymouth Arg.	215	35
				Portsmouth	245	47
Mick Mellows	5 10	11 6		Reading	14+2	2
				Portsmouth	95+4	10
Billy Eames	5 8	11 0	Malta	Portsmouth	9+3	1
George Graham	5 11	12 3	Bargeddie	Aston V.	8	2
(Scotland)				Chelsea	72	35
				Arsenal	219+8	60
				Manchester U.	41+2	2
				Portsmouth	58	5
Forwards						
Peter Marinello	5 8	10 8¾	Edinburgh	Hibernian	42+3	5
				Arsenal	32+6	3
				Portsmouth	92+3	7
				(transferred to Motherwell Dec. 1975)		
Richard Reynolds	5 11	12 6	Looe	Plymouth Arg.	123+4	24
				Portsmouth	134+7	24
Bobby McGuinness	5 11	11 8	Motherwell	Motherwell	2+1	—
				Portsmouth	26+2	3
*Andy Stewart	5 5	10 5	Letchworth	Portsmouth	14+5	3
Allan Kane	5 8	11 0	Edinburgh	Hibernian	—	—
				Portsmouth	6+1	—
				(contract cancelled Jan. 1976)		
Chris Kamara	6 0	12 6	Middlesex	Portsmouth	21+3	4
Stephen Foster	6 0	12 8	Portsmouth	Portsmouth	8+3	—
David Pullar				Portsmouth	0+1	—

PORT VALE DIV. 3

Chairman: M. J. Singer.

Directors: J. Burgess, L. W. Cliff, A. McPherson. D. Ratcliffe J.P., D. Attwood.

Manager: Roy Sproson.   *Secretary:* Richard Dennison.

Year Formed: 1876.   *Turned Professional:* 1885.

Limited Company: 1911.

Previous Name: Burslem Port Vale; became Port Vale, 1913.

Previous Grounds: 1876, Limekin Lane, Longport; 1881, Westport; 1884, Moorland Road, Burslem; 1886, Athletic Ground, Cobridge; 1913, Recreation Ground, Hanley; 1950, Vale Park.

Honours: Football League, best season in Division 2: 5th, 1930–31. Division 3(N), Champions: 1929–30, 1953–54; Runners-up: 1952–53. Division 4, Champions: 1958–59; Promoted 1969–70 (4th). *F.A. Cup*, best season, semi-finalists: 1954, when in Division 3. *Football League Cup*, best season: never past 2nd Rd.

Record Victory: 9-1 v Chesterfield, Division 2, Sept. 24th, 1932.

Record Defeat: 0-10 v Sheffield U., Division 2, Dec. 10th, 1892 and v Notts Co., Division 2, Feb. 26th, 1895.

Most League Points: 69, Div. 3(N), 1953–54.

Most League Goals: 110, Division 4, 1958–59.

Highest League Scorer in Season: Wilf Kirkham, 38, Division 2, 1926–27.

Most League Goals in Total Aggregate: Wilf Kirkham, 154, 1923–29, 1931–33.

Most Capped Player: Sammy Morgan, 7 (17) N. Ireland.

Most League Appearances: Roy Sproson, 761, 1950–72.

Record Transfer Fee Received: £30,000 from Brighton for Brian Horton, March 1976.

Record Transfer Fee Paid: £15,000 to Leicester C. for Albert Cheeseborough, July 1963; £15,000 to Everton for Billy Bingham, Aug. 1963.

Managers Since the War: Billy Frith, Gordon Hodgson, Ivor Powell, Freddie Steele, Norman Low, Freddie Steele, Jackie Mudie, Sir Stanley Matthews, Gordon Lee.

Address of Supporters Club: Hamil Rd., Burslem, Stoke on Trent, ST6 1AW.

Vale Park, Burslem, Stoke-on-Trent. Telephone Stoke on Trent 87626.   *Telegraphic address:* 'Port Vale Burslem'.   *Ground Capacity:* 50,000.   *Record attendance:* 50,000 v Aston Villa, F.A. Cup 5th Rd., February 20, 1960.   *Record receipts:* £8,600 v West Ham U., F.A. Cup 3rd Rd., Jan. 13 1973.   *Pitch measurements:* 116 yds × 76 yds.

How to get there: Nearest railway station, Stoke-on-Trent; there are frequent bus services from the town centre to Burslem.

Match tickets: Not bookable in advance.

Car parking: Parking is available behind the Railway Stand on Hamil Road, and on the Lorne Street side of the ground.

Entertainments/catering facilities: Light refreshments served on the ground. Social club on the Hamil Road side of the ground provides entertainment on certain evenings; membership by subscription.

Club shop: Sells all types of souvenirs.

Handbooks/programmes: Programmes are available on application to the club office or to the club shop.

Extra information: Port Vale are one of only four clubs to reach the F.A. Cup semi-final while in the Third Division; they did so in the 1953–54 season.

Club Colours: White shirts, black shorts.

Change Colours: All yellow, with blue and white trim.

Trainer: Lol Hamlett.

Club Nickname: 'Valiants'.

PORT VALE 1975-76 LEAGUE RECORD

Match No.	Date	Venue	Opponents	Result	H/T Score	League Pos'n	Goalscorers	Attendance
1	Aug 16	A	Hereford U.	D 0-0	0-0	—		6219
2	23	H	Preston N.E.	D 1-1	0-1	14	Cullerton	4282
3	30	A	Peterborough U.	D 0-0	0-0	13		6065
4	Sept 6	H	Brighton & H.A.	D 1-1	0-1	13	Morris	3289
5	13	A	Southend U.	D 3-3	0-3	14	Dulson, Cullerton (pen), Tartt	4455
6	20	H	Swindon T.	W 3-0	1-0	7	Bailey 2, Cullerton	3720
7	22	A	Cardiff C.	W 2-1	1-0	—	Cullerton, Lees	5143
8	27	A	Wrexham	L 0-1	0-1	8		3853
9	Oct 4	H	Crystal Palace	D 0-0	0-0	9		6121
10	11	A	Gillingham	L 1-2	0-1	11	Chadwick	5041
11	18	H	Chesterfield	D 1-1	0-0	10	Cullerton	3892
12	21	A	Shrewsbury T.	L 0-1	0-0	—		4673
13	25	A	Colchester U.	L 0-1	0-1	—		3053
14	Nov 1	H	Rotherham U.	W 1-0	1-0	14	Ridley	3921
15	3	H	Aldershot	L 0-1	0-0	—		3917
16	8	A	Sheffield W.	W 3-0	1-0	12	Chadwick, Taylor 2	10,880
17	15	H	Chester	L 0-1	0-1	17		3908
18	29	H	Millwall	W 2-0	1-0	13	Horton 2	3580
19	Dec 6	A	Walsall	L 1-3	0-2	16	Horton	4526
20	20	H	Grimsby T.	W 4-3	0-2	14	Harris, Lees, Cullerton 2	2789
21	26	A	Halifax T.	W 3-1	1-1	10	Brownbill, Cullerton 2	2959
22	27	H	Bury	W 2-1	1-1	8	Cullerton, Bailey	5376
23	Jan 3	A	Mansfield T.	L 1-3	1-2	8	Cullerton	5417
24	10	H	Peterborough U.	W 2-0	1-0	8	Cullerton, Horton	3892
25	17	A	Swindon T.	L 1-2	0-0	11	Brownbill	5557
26	24	A	Chesterfield	W 1-0	0-0	7	Cullerton	4052
27	31	H	Shrewsbury T.	D 0-0	0-0	9		3835
28	Feb 7	A	Aldershot	L 0-2	0-1	10		3446
29	9	H	Southend U.	D 1-1	0-1	—	Harris	3494
30	16	H	Sheffield W.	W 1-0	0-0	—	Brownbill	5557
31	21	A	Chester	L 0-1	0-0	9		5707
32	25	H	Cardiff C.	D 1-1	1-0	—	Williams	9129
33	28	H	Colchester U.	W 3-2	1-1	10	Cullerton, Brownbill, Bailey	3803
34	Mar 6	A	Rotherham U.	W 2-1	2-0	9	Dulson, Williams	4280
35	9	A	Crystal Palace	D 2-2	1-2	—	Cullerton, Tartt	23,014
36	13	H	Gillingham	D 1-1	0-1	8	Williams	3516
37	20	A	Millwall	L 0-1	0-1	10		7116
38	27	H	Walsall	L 1-2	0-2	12	Bailey	4863
39	30	A	Grimsby T.	D 1-1	0-1	—	Cullerton	4322
40	Apr 3	H	Hereford U.	D 1-1	0-0	12	Griffiths	4424
41	5	H	Wrexham	W 3-1	2-0	—	Bailey 2, Tartt	3604
42	10	A	Brighton & H.A.	L 0-3	0-1	11		19,171
43	17	H	Halifax T.	D 1-1	0-1	11	Beech	3169
44	19	A	Bury	W 2-1	1-1	—	Cullerton, McLaren	4609
45	20	H	Mansfield T.	D 2-2	0-1	—	Bailey, Tartt	4239
46	24	A	Preston N.E.	L 0-3	0-1	12		5783

Goalscorers

League (55): Cullerton 17 (1 a pen), Bailey 8, Tartt 4, Brownbill 4, Horton 4, Williams 3, Dulson 2, Lees 2, Chadwick 2, Taylor 2, Harris 2, Morris 1, Ridley 1, Griffiths 1, Beech 1, McLaren 1.
League Cup (4): Cullerton 3 (1 a pen), Bailey.
F.A. Cup (7): Brownbill 5, Cullerton, Tartt.

League Cup	First Round	Hereford U. (h)		4-2
	Second Leg	(a)		0-2
F.A. Cup	First Round	Grantham (a)		2-2
		(h)		4-1
	Second Round	Huddersfield T. (a)		1-2

Connaughton	Tartt	Dulson	Ridley	Harris	Horton	Morris	Lees	Cullerton	Bailey	Brownbill	Chadwick	McLaren	Williams	Griffiths	Betts	Taylor	Brodie	Ryan	Beech	Robson	Match No.
1	2	3	4	5	6	7	8	9	10	11											1
1	2	3	4	5	6*	7	8	9	10	11	12										2
1	2	3	4	5			6	9	10	8	12	7	11*								3
1	2	3	4	5	11		6	9*			12	7	10	8							4
1	2	6	4	5	12		8	9	10*			7	11	3							5
1	2	3	5	4	6		8	9	10			7	11								6
1	2	3	4	5	6		8	9	10			7	11								7
1	2	3	5	6	4	12	7	9	8	10*			11								8
1	2	3	5	6	4	7	8	9*	10		12		11								9
1	2	3	4	5	6		8	10	9		12	7	11*								10
1	2*	3	4	5	6	12	10	9	11	8		7									11
1	8	7	4	5	6	2	9	10			12		11*	3							12
1	2	3	4	5	6		8*	11	10		12	7	9								13
1	2	3	4	5	6		8	9	11			7				10					14
1		3	4	5	6*	12	2	9	11			7	8			10					15
1	2	3	6	5	4		10	8				7	9		11						16
1	2	3	5	6	4		8	12	9			7*	11			10					17
1	2		5	6	4		7	9	8	10			11	3							18
1	2		4	5	6		8*	9	10	11		7	12	3							19
1	2*		5	6	4		8	9	10	11		7	12	3							20
1			4	5	6		7	10	11	9		2	8	3							21
1			5	6	4		8	9	10	11		2	7	3							22
1	7		5	6	4		9	8	11			2	10	3							23
1	8		5	6	4		7*	9	10	11	12			3			2				24
	8		5	6	4		7	9	10	11				3			2	1			25
1	8		5	6	4		9	10	11			7		3			2				26
1	8		5	6	4		9	10	11			7		3			2				27
1	8		4	5	6	12	9	10	11			7*		3			2				28
1	8		4	5	6	7	9	10			12		11	3			2*				29
1	2		4	5	6		8	9	10	11		7		3							30
1	2		4	5	6*		8	9	10	11	12	7		3							31
1	2	6*	4	12	5		9	10	11			7		3					8		32
1	2	6*	4	12	5		9	10	11			7		3					8		33
1	2	6	4	8	5		9	10	11			7		3							34
1	2	8*	4	6	5		9	10	11		12	7		3							35
1	2	8	4	5			9	10	11		12	7		3					6*		36
1	6	8	4	5			9	10	11		12	7*		3			2				37
1	7	8	4	5*	6		9	10	11		12			3			2				38
1	7		4	8	5		9	10	11*		12	6		3			2				39
1	6		4	7	5		9	10	11*		12	8		3			2				40
1	7		4	8	5		9	10	11			6		3			2				41
1	7	12	4	8	5		10	11	9			6		3			2*				42
1	8*	3	4	5			9	10	11			7					2		6	12	43
1	8	3	4	5			9	10	11			7					2		6		44
1	8	3	4	5			9	10	11			7					2		6		45
1	4	3	5	6			8	11				7	9				2		10		46
45	42	29	46	32	30	10	40	41	42	34	4	28	26	32	1	4	12	1	7	—	
	+1s		+1s	+5s	+1s			+1s	+2s	+10s	+3s	+3s							+1s		

PORT VALE—PLAYERS

Player and position	Ht.	Wt.	Birthplace	Clubs	League Appearances	Goals
Goalkeepers						
John Connaughton	5 11	10 12	Wigan	Manchester U.	3	—
				Halifax T. (on loan)	3	—
				Torquay U. (on loan)	22	—
				Sheffield U.	12	—
				Port Vale	89	—
Defenders						
John Brodie	5 10	11 9	Bedlington	Carlisle U.	8+1	—
				Bradford P.A.	43	—
				Port Vale	172+4	2
Garry Dulson	5 10	11 10	Nottingham	Nottingham F.	—	—
				Port Vale	61+1	2
Neil Griffiths	5 10	10 12	Stoke	Chester	89+1	4
				Port Vale	68	1
Dave Harris	6 2	12 4	Stoke	Port Vale	84	6
Keith Chadwick	6 0	11 4	Stoke	Port Vale	29+11	7
Terry Lees	5 8	11 0	Stoke	Stoke C.	17+7	—
				Crewe A. (on loan)	6	—
				Port Vale	40+1	2
John Ridley	6 1	11 12	Consett	Port Vale	68+6	2
Midfield						
Terry Bailey	5 5	11 7	Stafford	Port Vale	86+1	21
Colin Tartt	5 11	11 8	Liverpool	Port Vale	146+4	4
Kevin Kennerley	5 10	11 8	Chester	Burnley	6	1
				Port Vale	—	—
Forwards						
Tony Betts	5 10	11 7	Derby	Aston V.	1+3	—
				Southport (on loan)	8	1
				Port Vale	1	—
Derek Brownbill	5 9	10 10	Liverpool	Liverpool	1	—
				Port Vale	50+2	8
Tom McLaren	5 9	11 6	Livingstone	Port Vale	266+32	28
Ray Williams	5 10	10 11	Staffordshire	Port Vale	146+6	37
Ken Beech	5 8	10 0	Stoke	Port Vale	8	1
Mike Cullerton	5 9	12 0	Edinburgh	Port Vale	95+2	22
				Chester (on loan)	5+2	—
				Stafford R. (non-league)		
				Port Vale	41	17
*Geoff Morris	5 5	9 12	Birmingham	Walsall	171+5	35
				Shrewsbury T.	71+4	9
				Port Vale	10+5	1
Trevor Robson	5 9	11 6	Stoke-on-Trent	Port Vale	0+1	—

PRESTON NORTH END   DIV. 3

President: Tom Finney;   *Chairman:* Alan R. W. Jones.

Vice-Chairman: T. J. Hemmings.

Directors: R. B. Bolton, J. G. Brown, T. H. Gore, E. Griffith, M. Johnson, M. H. McCann, A. C. Pilkington.

Manager: Harry Catterick.

Secretary: Chris Hassell.

Year Formed: 1862.   *Turned Professional:* 1885.

Limited Company: 1893.

Honours: *Football League,* Division 1, Champions: 1888–89 (first champions), 1889–90; Runners-up: 1890–91, 1891–92, 1892–93, 1905–06, 1952–53, 1957–58. Division 2, Champions: 1903–04, 1912–13, 1950–51; Runners-up: 1914–15, 1933–34. Division 3, Champions 1970–71. *F.A. Cup,* Winners: 1889, 1938; Runners-up: 1888, 1922, 1937, 1954, 1964. *Football League Cup,* best season: 4th Rd., 1963, 1966, 1972.

Record Victory: 26-0 v Hyde, F.A. Cup 1st Series, 1st Rd., Oct. 15th, 1887.

Record Defeat: 0-7 v Blackpool, Division 1, May 1st, 1948.

Most League Points: 61, Division 3, 1970-71.

Most League Goals: 100, Division 2, 1927–28 and Division 1, 1957–58.

Highest League Scorer in Season: Ted Harper, 37, Division 2, 1932–33.

Most Capped Player: Tom Finney, 76, England.

Most League Appearances: Alan Kelly, 447, 1961–75.

Most League Goals in Total Aggregate: Tom Finney, 187, 1946–60.

Record Transfer Fee Received: £150,000 from Newcastle U. for Alex Bruce, Jan. 1974.

Record Transfer Fee Paid: £70,000 to Doncaster R., for Mike Elwiss, Feb. 1974.

Managers Since the War: W. Scott, Scot Symon, Frank Hill, Cliff Britton, Jimmy Milne, Bobby Seith, Alan Ball snr, Bobby Charlton C.B.E.

Address of Supporters Club: Deepdale Road, Preston.

Address of Club Shop or Boutique: Lilywhite Shop, Deepdale, Preston.

Deepdale, Preston PR1 6RU. Telephone Preston 795919. *Telegraphic address:* 'Football Preston'. *Ground capacity:* 38,000. *Record attendance:* 42,684 v Arsenal, Division 1, April 23, 1938. *Record receipts:* £20,022 v Manchester U., F.A. Cup 4th Rd., February 5, 1972. *Pitch measurements:* 112 yds × 78 yds.

How to get there: Special buses to Deepdale from outlying areas and town centre bus station. Nearest railway station: Preston.

Match tickets: Postal applications, including remittance and S.A.E., may be made 14 days before the match.

Car parking: Club car park on the Deepdale Road (West Stand) side of the ground, holds 1,000 vehicles. Only limited off-street parking.

Entertainments/catering facilities: Entertainments provided by the Supporters' Club. The ground is well-equipped for normal match-day refreshments.

Club shop: Open on match days. All postal enquiries to: The Commercial Manager, Preston North End Development Association, Deepdale Road, Preston (Tel: Preston 795465).

Handbooks/programmes: No handbook. Programmes available on subscription from the Commercial Manager.

Extra information: The first club to do the League and F.A. Cup double; Preston accomplished this feat in 1888–89.

Club Colours: White shirts, with blue collars and cuffs, white shorts with blue stripes, white stockings.

Change Colours: Yellow shirts, blue shorts, yellow stockings.

Chief Coach: Nobby Stiles, Second Team: Alan Kelly.

Team Captain: Alex Spark.

First Team Trainer: Harry Hubbick.

Club Nickname: 'The Lilywhites'.

PRESTON NORTH END LEAGUE RECORD 1975–76

Match No.	Date		Venue	Opponents	Result	H/T Score	League Pos'n	Goalscorers	Attendance
1	Aug 16	H		Colchester U.	W 2-1	0-1	—	Treacy 2	6324
2		23	A	Port Vale	D 1-1	1-0	6	Treacy	4282
3		30	H	Millwall	W 2-1	1-0	2	Elwiss, Treacy	7707
4	Sept 6	A		Gillingham	L 0-1	0-1	8		5786
5		13	H	Walsall	W 3-1	1-0	3	Elwiss, Bruce, Treacy	7015
6		20	A	Aldershot	D 1-1	0-1	4	Bruce	3883
7		22	A	Southend U.	W 2-0	1-0	—	Morley, Coleman	4583
8		27	H	Cardiff C.	W 3-1	2-0	3	Elwiss, Treacy, Morley (pen)	8103
9	Oct 4	A		Chesterfield	L 0-3	0-0	6		4000
10		11	A	Brighton & H.A.	L 0-1	0-1	6		14,375
11		18	H	Crystal Palace	D 0-0	0-0	5		10,971
12		21	H	Peterborough U.	W 2-1	1-0	—	Treacy, Bruce	9597
13		25	A	Mansfield T.	W 1-0	0-0	4	Elwiss	6677
14	Nov 1	H		Hereford U.	L 3-4	1-2	4	Baxter, Morley (pen), Treacy	9682
15		4	A	Halifax T.	L 1-2	0-1	—	Morley	3366
16		8	A	Swindon T.	W 3-1	3-0	5	Bruce, Elwiss, Taylor (og)	6332
17		15	H	Bury	D 0-0	0-0	6		11,017
18		29	A	Grimsby T.	D 0-0	0-0			4519
19	Dec 6	H		Wrexham	L 0-1	0-0	7		7438
20		20	A	Sheffield W.	D 2-2	0-0	6	Smith, Elwiss	8553
21		27	A	Chester	L 0-3	0-1	10		8137
22	Jan 10	A		Millwall	L 0-2	0-1	16		6057
23		13	H	Rotherham U.	W 3-2	2-1	—	Morley, Smith, Elwiss	6289
24		17	H	Aldershot	W 1-0	1-0	9	Earls (og)	6196
25		24	A	Walsall	L 1-3	0-3	12	Treacy	6721
26		31	A	Peterborough U.	L 0-2	0-1	13		7728
27	Feb 3	H		Shrewsbury T.	L 0-2	0-0	—		4995
28		7	H	Halifax T.	W 2-1	0-0	13	Elwiss, Doyle	5480
29		14	H	Swindon T.	W 4-2	3-2	10	Bruce, Treacy, Brown (pen) Smith	5868
30		21	A	Bury	L 0-2	0-1	12		7049
31		24	H	Southend U.	W 5-1	0-0	—	Smith 2, Treacy, Elwiss 2	5210
32		28	H	Mansfield T.	L 0-2	0-0	12		6945
33	Mar 9	H		Chesterfield	W 3-1	2-0	—	Elwiss, Bruce 2	4621
34		13	H	Brighton & H.A.	W 1-0	0-0	11	Bruce (pen)	6720
35		16	A	Crystal Palace	L 0-2	0-0	—		22,213
36		20	H	Grimsby T.	D 0-0	0-0	11		6586
37		27	A	Wrexham	W 2-1	1-1	10	Smith, Bruce	4906
38		30	H	Sheffield Wed.	W 4-2	1-0	—	Elwiss, McMahon, Bruce 2	6899
39	Apr 3	A		Colchester U.	D 1-1	1-1	10	Elwiss	2657
40		7	A	Cardiff C.	L 0-1	0-0	—		12,447
41		10	H	Gillingham	W 4-0	1-0	9	McMahon, Bruce 2 (1 a pen), Smith	6349
42		17	A	Shrewsbury T.	L 0-1	0-1	10		3547
43		19	H	Chester	D 0-0	0-0	—		6719
44		20	A	Rotherham U.	D 1-1	1-1	—	Coleman	4874
45		24	H	Port Vale	W 3-0	1-0	8	Elwiss, Bruce 2	5783
46		28	A	Hereford U.	L 1-3	1-0	—	Elwiss	7592

Goalscorers

League (62): Elwiss 15, Bruce 15 (2 pens), Treacy 11, Smith 7, Morley 5 (2 pens), Coleman 2, McMahon 2, Baxter 1, Doyle 1, Brown 1 (pen), own goals 2.

League Cup (4): Morley 2, Treacy 2.

F.A. Cup (4): Smith 2, Morley (pen), Elwiss.

League Cup	First Round	Blackburn R. (h)	2-0
	Second Leg	(a)	0-0
	Second Round	Hull C. (a)	2-4
F.A. Cup	First Round	Scunthorpe U. (h)	2-1
	Second Round	Scarborough (a)	2-3

312

Tunks	McMahon	Williams	Doyle	Bird	Spark	Lamb	Burns	Treacy	Elwiss	Morley	Baxter, M. J.	Sadler	Bruce	Coleman	Taylor	Brown	Thompson	Smith	Lawrenson	Clarke	Robinson	Cameron	Match No.
1	2	3	4	5	6	7	8	9	10	11													1
1	2	3		5	6	7	11	9	10	8	4												2
1	2	3	4		6	7	8	9	10	11	5												3
1	2	3	7*		5		8	9	10	11	6	4	12										4
1	2	3			6	4	8	9	10	11	5		7										5
1	2	3			6	4	8	9	10	11	5		7										6
1	2	3			6	4*	8	9	10	11	5		7	12									7
1	2	3			6		8	9	10	11	5	12	7	4*									8
1		3			6		8	9	10	11	5	2	7	12	4*								9
1		3			6	7	11	9	10*		5	2	8	4	12								10
1	2	3			6		8	11	9	10	5		7	4									11
1	2	3			6		8	9	10	11	5		7	4									12
1	2	3			6		8	9	10	11	5		7	4									13
1	2	3			6		8	9	10	11	5		7*	4	12								14
1	2	3			6		8	9	10	11	5		7	4									15
1	2	3			6		8	9	10	11		5	7	4									16
1	2	3			6		7	9	10	11		5	8	4									17
1	2	3			6		7	9	10	11		5	8	4									18
1		3			6		7	9*	10	11	5		8	12				4	2				19
1	2	3	8		6	7		10	11	4	5							9					20
	2	3	4	6		8		9	10		5					7		11		1			21
	2*	3		4		10		9	11		5	8	12			7		6		1			22
	2	3				8	9	10	11	5	12		6*			7		4		1			23
1	2	3		4		8	9	10	11	5			6			7							24
1	2	3			6		8	9	10		5	11	7	4									25
1	2	3			6		7		10	11	5		8	4				9					26
1		3			6		8*	12	10		5	11	7	4				9	2				27
1	2	3	4		6			9	10		5		8			11		7					28
1	2	3	4					9	10		5		8			11		7	6				29
1	2	3	4					9	10		5	11	8					7	6				30
1	2	3	4					9	10		5		7			8		11	6				31
1	2	3	4*					9	10		5	7	12			8		11	6				32
1	2	3	4						10		5	11	8			7		9	6				33
1	2	3	4						10		5	8	7			11		9	6				34
1	2	3	4						10		5	11	8			7		9	6				35
1	2	3	4					9			5	11	7			8		10	6				36
1	2	3	4	12				9			5	11	7			10		8	6*				37
1	2	3	4						10		5	11	8			7		9	6				38
1	2*	3	4	12				9			5	8	7			11		10	6				39
1			4		6				10	12	5	11	2			7		9	3		8*		40
1	2*	6	4	12					10		5	11	8			7		9	3				41
1	2		4	3				9			5	11	8			7		10	6				42
1	2	3	4						10		5	11	8			7*		9	6			12	43
1	2	3	4			7			10		5	11	8					9	6				44
1	2	3	4					9			5	11	7			10		8	6				45
1	2	3	4			8			10		5	11	7*					9	6			12	46
43	41	44	24	2	29	8	27	27	46	25	21	28	38	15	3	29	1	27	24	3	1	—	

+3s (Doyle)   +1s (Burns)   +1s +1s +2s +5s (Morley, Baxter, Sadler, Bruce)   +1s +1s (Smith, Lawrenson)   +1s +1s (Clarke, Robinson)

313

PRESTON NORTH END—PLAYERS

Player and position	Ht.	Wt.	Birthplace	Clubs	League Appearances	Goals
Goalkeepers						
Roy Tunks	6 0	12 0	Wuppertall	Rotherham J.	138	—
				York C. (on loan)	4	—
				Ipswich T. (on loan)	—	—
				Newcastle U. (on loan)	—	—
				Preston N.E.	70	—
*Tom Clarke	5 10	12 12	Ardrossan	Airdrieonians	6	—
				Carlisle U.	23	—
				Preston N.E.	3	—
Defenders						
David Sadler	6 0	12 3	Yalding	Manchester U.	265+5	22
(England)				Preston N.E.	84+1	2
John McMahon	5 9	11 2	Manchester	Preston N.E.	187	6
				Southend U. (on loan)	4	—
Michael Baxter	6 1	11 12	Birmingham	Preston N.E.	1+1	—
Daniel Cameron	5 7	11 7	Dundee	Sheffield W.	31	1
				Colchester U. (on loan)	5	—
				Preston N.E.	0+1	—
Mark Lawrenson	5 10	10 10	Preston	Preston N.E.	27	—
Stuart Baxter	6 0	11 12	Wolverhampton	Preston N.E.	55+7	2
				(transferred to Dundee U. Oct. 1975)		
Gary Williams	5 10	11 0	Liverpool	Preston N.E.	63+5	2
Midfield						
Alex Bruce	5 8	10 3	Dundee	Preston N.E.	55+7	22
				Newcastle J.	16+4	3
				Preston N.E.	38+2	15
Francis Burns	5 8	10 10	Coatbridge	Manchester U.	111+8	6
(Scotland)				Southampton	20+1	—
				Preston N.E.	114	8
Stephen Doyle	5 9	10 12	Neath	Preston N.E.	36+1	1
Richard Thomson	5 9	10 8	Edinburgh	Preston N.E.	7+2	—
Jimmy Brown	5 10	11 10	Birmingham	Aston V.	72+4	2
				Preston N.E.	29	1
*Alex Spark	5 10	11 2	Stenhousemuir	Preston N.E.	208+18	6
Alan Lamb	5 8	10 4	Falkirk	Preston N.E.	73+3	2
Michael Robinson	5 11	12 0	Leicester	Preston N.E.	1+1	—
*Roy Taylor	5 10	11 3	Preston	Preston N.E.	3	—
Forwards						
*Ray Treacy	5 9	10 2	Dublin	W.B.A.	2+1	1
(Eire)				Charlton Ath.	144+5	43
				Swindon T.	55	16
				Preston N.E.	54+4	11
				Oldham (on loan)	3	1
Gordon Coleman	5 8	10 7	Nottingham	Preston N.E.	32+12	4
Mike Elwiss	5 10½	11 3	Doncaster	Doncaster R.	106+1	30
				Preston N.E.	100+1	30
John Smith	5 9	10 3	Coatbridge	Preston N.E.	31+6	8

QUEEN'S PARK RANGERS DIV. 1

Chairman: J. A. Gregory.

Directors: R. A. Starnes, A. D. Farmer, F. S. Wade, B. P. Baker, B. A. Henson, J. C. Gregory.

Manager: Dave Sexton.   *Secretary:* R. J. Phillips.

Asst. Manager: Frank Sibley.

Year Formed: 1885.   *Turned Professional:* 1898.

Limited Company: 1899.

Previous Name: 1885–87, St. Jude's; 1887, became Queen's Park Rangers.

Previous Grounds: 1885, Welford's Fields; 1888, London Scottish Ground, Brondesbury: Home Farm: Kensal Rise Green: Gun Club, Wormwood Scrubs: Kilburn Cricket Ground; 1899, Kensal Rise Athletic Ground; 1901, Latimer Road, Notting Hill; 1904, Agricultural Society, Park Royal: 1907, Park Royal Ground; 1917, Loftus Road; 1931, White City; 1933, Loftus Road; 1962, White City; 1963, Loftus Road.

Honours: Football League, best season in Division 1: 2nd, 1975–76. Division 2, Runners-up: 1967–68, 1972–73. Division 3(S), Champions: 1947–48, Runners-up: 1946–47. Division 3, Champions: 1966–67. *F.A. Cup:* best season: 6th Rd. (or equivalent) 1910, 1914, 1923, 1948, 1970, 1974.   *Football League Cup,* Winners: 1966–67. Double: 1966–67, won Division 3 and Football League Cup.

Record Victory: 9-2 v Tranmere R., Division 3, December 3rd, 1960.

Record Defeat: 1-8 v Mansfield T., Division 3, Mar. 15th, 1965, and 1-8 v Manchester U. Division 1, Mar. 19, 1969.

Most League Points: 67, Division 3, 1966–67.

Most League Goals: 111, Division 3, 1961–62.

Highest League Scorer in Season: George Goddard, 37, Division 3(S), 1929–30.

Most League Goals in Total Aggregate: George Goddard, 172, 1926–34.

Most Capped Player: Don Givens, 32, Eire.

Most League Appearances: Tony Ingham, 519, 1950–63.

Record Transfer Fee Received: £200,000 from Manchester C. for Rodney Marsh, March 1972.

Record Transfer Fee Paid: £165,000 to Burnley for David Thomas, Oct. 1972.

Managers Since the War: Dave Mangnall, Jack Taylor, Alec Stock, Tommy Docherty, Les Allen, Gordon Jago.

Address of Supporters Club: c/o Football Club.

Address of Club Shop or Boutique: Supporters Club Shop, Queen's Park Rangers F.C., South Africa Road, London W.12.

South Africa Road, W12 7PA. Telephone 01-743-2618.   *Telegraphic address:* 'Queu Pear' *Ground capacity:* 30,000 (23,000 covered).   *Record attendance:* 35,353 v Leeds U., F.L., April 28, 1974.   *Record receipts:* £34,718 v Leeds U., Division 1, April 24, 1976. *Pitch measurements:* 112 yds × 72 yds.

How to get there: Buses 12 and 207. Nos. 11, 49, 72, 88, 105, 220 go near Shepherd's Bush (Metropolitan and Central Lines) and White City (Central Line—five to ten minutes walk). *Match tickets:* Seats bookable one month in advance of the match. *Car parking:* No club car park, but the White City park, adjacent to the ground, is recommended. Limited parking in side-streets. *Entertainments/catering facilities:* Various bars around the ground. *Club shop:* Programme shop in South Africa Road and kiosks inside the ground. *Handbooks/programmes:* Available from programme shop. *Extra information:* Queen's Park Rangers have had more home grounds than any other present Football League club; 12 in all, plus one game at Highbury in 1930.

Club Colours: Blue and white hooped shirts, white shorts, white stockings. *Change Colours:* Red and white halved shirts, black shorts, red socks. *Club Captain:* Gerry Francis. *First Team Trainer:* Frank Sibley. *Club Nickname* 'Rangers' or 'R's.

QUEEN'S PARK RANGERS 1975–76 LEAGUE RECORD

Match No.	Date	Venue	Opponents	Result	H/T Score	League Pos'n	Goalscorers	Attendance
1	Aug 16	H	Liverpool	W 2-0	1-0	—	Francis, Leach	27,113
2	19	H	Aston Villa	D 1-1	0-0	—	Francis	21,986
3	23	A	Derby Co.	W 5-1	3-0	3	Thomas, Bowles 3 (1 a pen), Clement	27,590
4	26	A	Wolverhampton W.	D 2-2	2-2	—	Givens 2	19,380
5	30	H	West Ham U.	D 1-1	1-0	3	Givens	28,408
6	Sept 6	A	Birmingham C.	D 1-1	0-1	4	Thomas	27,305
7	13	H	Manchester U.	W 1-0	1-0	3	Webb	29,237
8	20	A	Middlesbrough	D 0-0	0-0	3		24,867
9	23	H	Leicester C.	W 1-0	0-0	—	Leach	19,292
10	27	H	Newcastle U.	W 1-0	1-0	1	Leach	22,981
11	Oct 4	A	Leeds U.	L 1-2	0-0	2	Bowles (pen)	30,943
12	11	H	Everton	W 5-0	2-0	1	Givens, Masson, Francis 2, Thomas	23,022
13	18	A	Burnley	L 0-1	0-0	2		20,409
14	25	H	Sheffield U.	W 1-0	0-0	1	Givens	21,161
15	Nov 1	A	Coventry C.	D 1-1	0-0	3	Givens	17,845
16	8	H	Tottenham H.	D 0-0	0-0	3		28,454
17	15	A	Ipswich T.	D 1-1	0-1	4	Givens	25,540
18	22	H	Burnley	W 1-0	0-0	2	Bowles	17,390
19	29	H	Stoke C.	W 3-2	1-0	2	Masson, Clement, Webb	22,328
20	Dec 6	A	Manchester C.	D 0-0	0-0	1		36,066
21	13	H	Derby Co.	D 1-1	0-0	1	Nutt	25,465
22	20	A	Liverpool	L 0-2	0-1	4		39,182
23	26	H	Norwich C.	W 2-0	1-0	3	Masson, Bowles	21,774
24	27	A	Arsenal	L 0-2	0-0	5		39,021
25	Jan 10	A	Manchester U.	L 1-2	1-1	5	Givens	58,312
26	17	H	Birmingham C.	W 2-1	2-0	5	Masson 2	16,759
27	24	A	West Ham U.	L 0-1	0-1	5		26,677
28	31	A	Aston Villa	W 2-0	0-0	5	Hollins, Francis	32,223
29	Feb 7	H	Wolverhampton W.	W 4-2	2-1	3	Givens 2, Thomas, Francis (pen)	17,153
30	14	A	Tottenham H.	W 3-0	0-0	3	Givens, Francis 2	28,200
31	21	H	Ipswich T.	W 3-1	0-0	2	Wark (og), Webb, Thomas	22,593
32	25	A	Leicester C.	W 1-0	1-0	—	Thomas	24,340
33	28	A	Sheffield U.	D 0-0	0-0	2		21,949
34	Mar 6	H	Coventry C.	W 4-1	1-0	1	Thomas, Francis, Givens, Masson	19,731
35	13	A	Everton	W 2-0	1-0	1	Bowles, Leach	25,186
36	20	A	Stoke C.	W 1-0	1-0	1	Webb	22,848
37	27	H	Manchester C.	W 1-0	0-0	1	Webb	29,883
38	Apr 3	A	Newcastle U.	W 2-1	1-1	1	McLintock, Bowles	30,134
39	10	H	Middlesbrough	W 4-2	0-0	1	Francis 2 (1 a pen), Givens, Bowles	24,342
40	17	A	Norwich C.	L 2-3	1-1	2	Thomas, Powell (og)	31,231
41	19	H	Arsenal	W 2-1	0-0	—	McLintock, Francis (pen)	30,362
42	24	H	Leeds U	W 2-0	0-0	1	Thomas, Bowles	31,002

Goalscorers

League (67): Givens 13, Francis 12 (3 pens), Bowles 10 (2 pens), Thomas 9, Masson 6, Webb 5, Leach 4, Clement 2, McLintock 2, Nutt 1, Hollins 1, Own Goals 2.
League Cup (9): Masson 2, Bowles 2, Leach 2, Thomas 2, Webb.
F.A. Cup (1): Masson.

League Cup	Second Round	Shrewsbury T. (a)	4-1
	Third Round	Charlton Ath. (h)	1-1
		(a)	3-0
	Fourth Round	Newcastle U. (h)	1-3
F.A. Cup	Third Round	Newcastle U. (h)	0-0
		(a)	1-2

Parkes	Clement	Gillard	Hollins	McLintock	Webb	Thomas	Francis	Masson	Bowles	Givens	Leach	Beck	Abbott	Tagg	Nutt	Shanks	Match No.
1	2	3	4*	5	6	7	8	9	10	11	12						1
1	2	3		5*		7	8	9	10	11	4	12	6				2
1	2	3				7*	8	9	10	11	4	12	5	6			3
1	2	3				7	8	9	10	11	4		5	6			4
1	2	3	12			7	8*	9	10	11	4		5	6			5
1	2	8		3		7		9	10	11	4		5	6			6
1	2	3		5	6	7	8	9	10	11	4						7
1	2	3	12	5	6	7	8	9	10	11*	4						8
1	2	3		5	6	7	8	9	10	11	4						9
1	2	3		5	6	7	8	9	10	11	4						10
1	2	3	4	5	6	7	8	9	10	11							11
1	2	3		5	6	7	8	9	10	11	4						12
1	2	3	5		6	7	8	9	10	11	4						13
1	2	3		5	6	7	8	9	10	11	4						14
1	2	3		5	6	7	8	9	10	11	4						15
1	2	3		5	6	7	8	9	10	11	4						16
1	2	3	10	5	6	7	8	9		11	4						17
1	2	3		5	6	7	8	9	10	11	4						18
1	2	3	4	5	6	7		9	10	11*	8			12			19
1	2	3	4	5	6	7	8	9		11	10						20
1	2	3	4	5	6	7	8	9*		11	10			12			21
1	2	3	4	5	6	7	8	9	10	11							22
1	2	3		5	6	7	8	9	10	11	4						23
1	2	3	4	5	6	7	8	9	10	11							24
1	2	3	4	5	6		8	9	10*	11	7	12					25
1	2	3	4	5	6	7		9	10	11	8						26
1	2	3	4	5*	6	7		9		11	10	8		12			27
1	2	3	4	5	6	7	8	9		11	10						28
1	2	3	5		6	7	8	9	10	11	4						29
1	2	3	5		6	7	8	9	10	11	4						30
1	2	3	5	12	6	7	8	9	10	11	4*						31
1	2	3	4	5	6	7	8	9	10	11							32
1	2	3	4	5	6	7		9	10	11	8						33
1	2	3	4	5	6	7	8	9	10	11							34
1	2	3	4	5	6	7	8*	9	10	11	12						35
1	2	3	4	5	6	7		9	10	11	8						36
1		3	4	5*	6	7	8	9	10	11	12					2	37
1		3	4	5	6	7	8	9	10	11						2	38
1	2	3	4	5	6	7	8	9	10	11							39
1	2	3·	4	5	6	7	8	9	10	11							40
1	2	3	4	5	6	7	8	9	10	11							41
1	2	3	4	.5	6	7	8	9	10	11							42
42	40	41	28	34	38	41	36	42	37	41	28	3	5	4	—	2	
			+	+							+	+	+		+		
			2s	1s							3s	2s	1s		3s		

317

QUEEN'S PARK RANGERS—PLAYERS

Player and position	Ht.	Wt.	Birthplace	Clubs	League Appearances	Goals
Goalkeepers						
Phil Parkes (England)	6 2½	14 0	Sedgeley	Walsall	52	—
				Q.P.R.	249	—
Richard Teale	6 1	13 7	Millam	Q.P.R.	1	—
Derek Richardson	6 1	14 4	London	Chelsea	—	—
				Q.P.R.	—	—
Defenders						
David Clement (England)	5 10	11 5	London	Q.P.R.	313+2	19
Ian Gillard (England)	5 11	12 0	London	Q.P.R.	172+3	3
Frank McLintock (Scotland)	5 10	11 2	Glasgow	Leicseter C.	170	25
				Arsenal	312+2	26
				Q.P.R.	90+1	3
*Keith Pritchett	5 7	11 9	Glasgow	Wolverhampton W.	—	—
				Doncaster R.	6	—
				Q.P.R.	3	—
Don Shanks	5 9	10 8	London	Luton T.	89+1	2
				Q.P.R.	14	—
David Webb	5 10½	12 11	London	Orient	62	3
				Southampton	75	2
				Chelsea	230	21
				Q.P.R.	71	5
Stephen Jones	6 1	12 1	Eastbourne	Q.P.R.	—	—
Tony Tagg	6 1	11 0	Epsom	Q.P.R.	4	—
Ron Abbott	6 0	11 0	London	Q.P.R.	14+8	1
Tommy Cunningham	6 0	11 3	London	Chelsea	—	—
				Q.P.R.	—	—
Tony Martin	5 6	10 0	London	Q.P.R.	—	—
Midfield						
Martyn Busby	6 1	12 4	Slough	Q.P.R.	70+7	6
				Portsmouth (on loan)	6+1	—
Don Masson (Scotland)	5 8	10 12	Banchory	Middlesbrough	51+3	6
				Notts Co.	273	81
				Q.P.R.	63	7
Gerry Francis (England)	5 10	10 8	Hammersmith	Q.P.R.	235+5	46
John Hollins (England)	5 8	11 7	Guildford	Chelsea	436	47
				Q.P.R.	28+2	1
Forwards						
Dave Thomas (England)	5 8	9 13	Kirkby in Ashfield	Burnley	152+4	19
				Q.P.R.	151	28
John Beck	5 10	11 7	Edmonton	Q.P.R.	32+8	1
Mike Leach	6 0	12 0	London	Q.P.R.	269+16	60
Don Givens (Eire)	5 11	11 2	Dublin	Manchester U.	4+4	1
				Luton T.	80+3	19
				Q.P.R.	164	62
Stan Bowles (England)	5 10	11 4	Manchester	Manchester C.	15+2	2
				Bury	5	—
				Crewe A.	51	18
				Carlisle U.	33	12
				Q.P.R.	147	56
Peter Eastoe	5 10	11 3	Tamworth	Wolverhampton W.	4+2	—
				Swindon T.	91	43
				Q.P.R.	—	—
Steve Adams	5 4	9 0	Windsor	Q.P.R.	—	—
Phil Nutt	5 11	11 8	London	Q.P.R.	0+3	1

READING

President: A. E. Smith. *Chairman:* F. V. Waller.

Directors: W. T. D. Vincent, L. Davies, E. T. Harrison, O.B.E., J. Brooks.

Manager: Charlie Hurley.

Secretary/Manager: F. May.

Year Formed: 1871. *Turned Professional:* 1895.

Limited Company: 1895.

Previous Grounds: 1871, Reading Recreation; Reading Cricket Ground; 1882, Coley Park; 1889, Caversham Cricket Ground; 1896, Elm Park.

Honours: Football League, best season in Division 2: 14th, 1926–27. Division 3(S), Champions: 1925–26; Runners-up: 1931–32, 1934–35, 1948–49, 1951–52. *F.A. Cup,* best season: semi-finalists, 1927. *Football League Cup,* best season: 4th Rd., 1965, 1966.

Record Victory: 10-2 v C. Palace, Division 3(S), 1946–47.

Record Defeat: 0-18 v Preston N.E., F.A. Cup, 1st Rd., 1893–94.

Most League Points: 61, Division 3(S), 1951–52.

Most League Goals: 112, Division 3(S), 1951–52.

Highest League Scorer in Season: Ronnie Blackman, 39, Division 3(S), 1951–52.

Most League Goals in Total Aggregate: Ronnie Blackman, 156, 1947–54.

Most Capped Player: Pat McConnell, 8, Ireland.

Most League Appearances: Dick Spiers, 453, 1955–70 (and 41 F.A. Cup-ties).

Record Transfer Fee Received: £60,000 from Southampton for Tommy Jenkins, Dec. 1969.

Record Transfer Fee Paid: £20,000 to West Ham U. for Steve Death, Sept. 1970.

Managers Since the War: Joe Edelston, Ted Drake, Jack Smith, Harry Johnston, Roy Bentley, Jack Mansell.

Address of Supporters Club: Reading Football Supporters Club, Elm Park, Norfolk Road, Reading.

Elm Park, Norfolk Road, Reading. Telephone Reading 57878/9/0. *Ground capacity:* 27,200. *Record attendance:* 33,042 v Brentford, F.A. Cup 5th Rd., February 19, 1927. *Record receipts:* £17,509 v Arsenal, F.A. Cup 4th Rd., February 5, 1972. *Pitch measurements:* 112 yds × 77 yds.

How to get there: Corporation specials from St. Mary's Butts (town centre) and from Northumberland Avenue. Usual buses within a few minutes of the ground. Nearest railway station, Reading.

Match tickets: Stand tickets are bookable in advance for all first-team matches 14 days before the match.

Car parking: Space is available for approximately 300 cars adjoining the ground entrance in Norfolk Road and Tilehurst Road.

Entertainments/catering facilities: Catering is available in each of the five stands and also on the terraces.

Club shop: Shops in Norfolk Road and on the West Terrace are open on match days selling all types of souvenirs.

Handbooks/programmes: The Supporters' Club produce a handbook and these are available on application to the club. Unsold programmes are available after each match at the programme shop on the West Terrace.

Extra information: Reading first appeared in the F.A. Cup 1st Rd. in 1877; only Notts County of the present League clubs played so long ago.

Club Colours: Blue and white hoops, white shorts, white stockings, two blue rings.

Change Colours: Yellow and blue.

First Team Trainer: Jimmy Wallbanks.

Club Nickname: 'Biscuitmen'.

READING 1975–76 LEAGUE RECORD

Match No.	Date	Venue	Opponents	Result	H/T Score	League Pos'n	Goalscorers	Attendance
1	Aug 16	H	Rochdale	W 2-0	1-0	—	Youlden, Hetzke	4534
2	23	A	Crewe Alex.	D 3-3	1-2	8	Hiron 2, Friday	2057
3	30	H	Southport	W 1-0	1-0	4	Murray	4595
4	Sept 6	A	Lincoln C.	L 1-3	1-0	11	Friday	4327
5	13	H	Watford	W 3-0	0-0	2	Barker, Murray, Friday	5521
6	20	A	Workington	W 2-0	0-0	1	Murray (pen), Friday	1712
7	22	A	Hartlepool	W 4-2	1-1	—	Whithams 3, Smith R (og)	2261
8	27	H	AFC Bournemouth	W 2-1	0-0	1	Dunphy 2	7226
9	Oct 4	A	Scunthorpe	L 1-2	0-0	4	Friday	2177
10	11	H	Bradford C.	W 2-1	2-1	3	Murray, Hiron	5885
11	18	A	Barnsley	L 2-4	1-2	5	Friday, Henderson	2814
12	20	A	Newport Co.	D 0-0	0-0	—		2955
13	25	H	Huddersfield T.	W 2-0	0-0	4	Cumming, Stuckey	6679
14	Nov 1	A	Doncaster R.	D 1-1	1-0	4	Hiron	7293
15	5	H	Swansea C.	W 1-0	0-0	—	Murray	5499
16	8	H	Exeter C.	W 4-3	0-1	4	Friday, Murray 2 (1 a pen), Hiron	6341
17	15	A	Torquay U.	D 0-0	0-0	3		2220
18	29	A	Darlington	W 1-0	1-0	3	Peters	1761
19	Dec 6	A	Stockport Co.	W 5-0	1-0	3	Murray 3, Friday 2	6701
20	13	H	Scunthorpe U.	W 1-0	0-0	3	Murray	5575
21	19	A	Tranmere R.	L 0-2	0-1	3		3170
22	26	H	Cambridge U.	W 1-0	1-0	3	Hiron	7783
23	27	A	Brentford	D 2-2	0-1	3	Peters, Stuckley	6934
24	Jan 3	H	Northampton T.	W 1-0	1-0	3	Barker	10,139
25	10	A	Southport	W 2-1	0-1	3	Hiron, Henderson	1167
26	17	H	Workington	W 1-0	1-0	3	Friday	7183
27	24	A	Watford	L 1-2	0-0	3	Friday	5944
28	Feb 6	A	Swansea C.	L 1-5	0-1	3	Friday	2750
29	13	A	Exeter C.	L 1-4	1-4	3	Friday	3641
30	21	H	Torquay U.	D 0-0	0-0	4		6259
31	25	H	Hartlepool	W 1-0	0-0	—	Friday	6288
32	28	A	Huddersfield T.	L 0-3	0-2	4		6546
33	Mar 2	H	Newport Co.	W 1-0	1-0	—	Murray (pen)	6211
34	6	H	Doncaster R.	L 0-1	0-0	3		6441
35	13	A	Bradford C.	D 1-1	0-0	3	Nelson	2916
36	17	H	Barnsley	D 0-0	0-0	—		6579
37	20	H	Datlington	W 4-1	2-0	3	Friday 2, Hollis, Hiron	5350
38	26	A	Stockport Co.	D 1-1	1-1	4	Friday	2319
39	31	H	Tranmere R.	W 5-0	2-0	—	Murray 3 (2 pens), Friday 2	10,961
40	Apr 3	A	Rochdale	D 0-0	0-0	3		1063
41	7	A	AFC Bournemouth	W 1-0	0-0	—	Nelson	5372
42	10	H	Lincoln C.	D 1-1	1-1	3	Hiron	15,683
43	15	A	Northampton T.	L 1-4	1-0	3	Hiron	3548
44	19	H	Brentford	W 1-0	0-0	4	Hiron	12,772
45	21	A	Cambridge U.	D 2-2	2-1	—	Friday, Carnaby	3245
46	24	H	Crewe Alex.	W 3-1	1-0	3	Friday, Dunphy, Nelson	12,229

Goalscorers

League (70): Friday 21, Murray 15 (5 pens), Hiron 11, Dunphy 3, Nelson 3, Whitham 3, Barker 2, Henderson 2, Peters 2, Stuckey 2, Carnaby 1, Cumming 1, Hetzke 1, Hollis 1, Youlden 1, own goal 1.
League Cup (1): Friday.

League Cup	First Round	Gillingham (h)		0-1
	Second Leg	(a)		1-1
F.A. Cup	First Round	Hendon	(a)	0-1

Death	Peters	Alleyne	Cumming	Hetzke	Youlden	Carnaby	Dunphy	Hiron	Whitham	Friday	Murray	Henderson	Stuckey	Moreline	Barker	Lennarduzzi	Cooper	Turner	Hollis	Nelson	Match No.
1	2	3	4	5	6	7	8	9	10	11											1
1	2	3	4	5	6		11	8	7*	9	10	12									2
1	2		4	5	6			8		9	11	3	7	10							3
1	2		4	5	6		12	8		9	7	3	11*	10							4
1	2		4		6*		10	8	7	9	12	11	3	5							5
1	2		4				11	9*	8	10	12	7	3	5	6						6
1	2		4				10	7		9	8	11	3	5	6						7
1	2		4				10	12	7*	9	8	11	3	5	6						8
1	2		4				7	10	12	9	8*	11	3	5	6						9
1	2		4				11	10		9	8	7	3	5	6						10
1	2		4				11	10	9	8*	12	7	3	5	6						11
1			4		6		10	8	7	9	2	11	3	5							12
1			4		6		11	8	10	9	2*	7	3	5	12						13
1	2*		4		6		10	8	7	9		11	3	5	12						14
1			4		6		10*	8	12	9	7	11	3	5	2						15
1			4		6		11*	10	12	9	8	7	3	5	2						16
1			4		6		11	9	10	8	7		3	5	2						17
1	10		4		6		11			9	8	7	3	5	2						18
1			4		6		11	10		9	8	7	3	5	2						19
1			4		6		11	10		9	8	7	3	5	2						20
1	12		4		6		10	8		9	7	11*	3	5	2						21
1			4		6		10	8	9	7	2	11	3	5							22
1	12		4		6		11*	10	9	8	2	7	3	5							23
1	7				6		10	8	9	4	2	11	3	5							24
1			4		6		10	8	9	7	2	11	3	5							25
1			4		6	8	11	10	12	9	7*	2	3	5							26
1	12		4		6		11*	8	10	9	2	7	3	5							27
1	2				6	11*	10	8	12	9	7	4	3	5							28
1	12		4		6		10	8	9	7	2	11*	3	5							29
1	2		4		6		10	8*	12	9	7	11	3	5							30
1	2		11*	5	6		12	8	10	9		4	3				7				31
1	2			5	6		11	8	10*	9	12	4	3				7				32
	2			5	6		11	10	8	9	7	4	3					1			33
	2			5	6	7	11	8*		9	10	4	3					1	12		34
	2			5	6	7	10	11				4	3					1	8	9	35
	2			5	6		10	11		9	12	4*	3					1	7	8	36
	12		4		6		10	8		9	7	2	3*	5				1		11	37
					6		10	11	8	9	4	2	3	5				1		7	38
				5*	6		10	11	8	9	4	2	3					1	12	7	39
				5	6		10	11*	8	9	4	2	3					1	12	7	40
				5	6		10	11	8	9	4	2	3					1		7	41
				5	6		10	11	8	9	4	2	3					1		7	42
				5	6		10	11	8	9	4	2	3					1		7	43
	2			5	6		10	11	8	9	4*		3					1	12	7	44
	2		4	5	6		10	11*	3	9			3	12				1		7	45
	2		4		6		10	11	8	9		3	5					1		7	46
32	25	2	30	17	40	18	43	42	13	44	33	25	26	44	29	13	2	14	4	10	
+5s							+2s	+1s	+6s	+4s	+2s		+1s	+3s				+3s			

Player and position	Ht.	Wt.	Birthplace	Clubs	League Appearances	Goals
Goalkeepers						
Steve Death	5 7½	11 0	Elmswell	West Ham U.	1	—
				Reading	261	—
John Turner	5 11	12 0	Peterlee	Derby Co.	—	—
				Doncaster R. (on loan)	4	—
				Brighton (on loan)	—	—
				Peterborough U. (on loan)	—	—
				Huddersfield T. (on loan)	1	—
				Reading	14	—
Defenders						
Geoffrey Barker	6 0	12 0	Hull	Hull C.	29+1	2
				Southend U. (on loan)	25	—
				Darlington	151	6
				Reading	45+1	2
Dave Moreline	5 9	10 8	Stepney	Fulham	63+7	—
				Reading	75	—
Tommy Youlden	6 0¼	12 9	London	Arsenal	—	—
				Portsmouth	82+8	1
				Reading	144+1	3
*Andy Alleyne	5 4	10 7	Barbados	Reading	46+2	2
Stewart Henderson	5 6	10 11	Bridge of Allan	Chelsea	—	—
				Brighton	201	1
				Reading	112+2	6
Stephen Hetzke	6 2	11 10	Marlborough	Reading	55+4	2
Garry Peters				Reading	25+5	2
Bob Lenarduzzi	5 11	11 7	Vancouver	Reading	63+4	2
				(contract cancelled Apr 1976)		
Midfield						
Eamonn Dunphy	5 7½	8 13	Dublin	York C.	22	3
(Eire)				Millwall	267+7	24
				Charlton Ath.	39+3	3
				Reading	43+2	3
*Adrian Cooper				Reading	14	2
Brian Carnaby	5 9	11 0	Plymouth	Reading	118+8	9
Gordon Cumming	5 5	9 4	Johnstone near Glasgow	Arsenal	—	—
				Reading	220+16	46
Forwards						
John Murray	5 8½	11 0	Newcastle	Burnley	20+2	6
				Blackpool	6+2	1
				Bury	117+9	37
				Reading	75+6	27
Robin Friday	5 10	12 0	London	Reading	105	43
John Ashton				Reading	10+3	1
				(contract cancelled Feb 1976)		
Bruce Stuckey	5 8	11 6	Torquay U.	Exeter C.	37+1	6
				Sunderland	24+2	2
				Torquay U.	69+17	6
				Reading	75+3	6
				Torquay U. (on loan)	4	—
Ray Hiron	6 2	11 0	Gosport	Portsmouth	324+7	110
				Reading	42+1	11
*Jack Whitham	5 11½	12 0	Burnley	Sheffield W.	57+6	28
				Liverpool	15	7
				Cardiff C.	12+2	3
				Reading	13+6	3
Dennis Nelson	5 8	10 4	Edinburgh	Dunfermline	38+10	17
				Crewe A.	65+6	18
				Reading	10	3
Mick Hollis	5 10	11 5	Loughborough	Leicester	—	—
				Barrow	88+3	13
				Chester	34+3	8
				Stockport Co.	106+6	33
				Reading	4+3	1

ROCHDALE DIV. 4

Chairman: F. S. Ratcliffe.
Directors: J. S. Stoney, R. Brierley, E. Lord, K. J. Leary, H. Carter.
Manager: Bill Green.   *Secretary:* A. McLean.
Year Formed: 1907.   *Turned Professional:* 1907.
Limited Company: 1910.
Previous Name: Rochdale Town.

Honours: *Football League,* best season in Division 3: 9th, 1969–70. Division 3(N), Runners-up: 1923–24, 1926–27. *F.A. Cup,* best season: 4th Rd., 1970–71. *Football League Cup:* Runners-up, 1962 (record for 4th Division Club).
Record Victory: 8-1 v Chesterfield, Division 3(N), Dec. 18th, 1926.
Record Defeat: 0-8 v Wrexham, Division 3(N), Dec. 28th, 1929.
Most League Points: 62, Division 3(N), 1923–24.
Most League Goals: 105, Division 3(N), 1926–27.
Highest League Scorer in Season: Albert Whitehurst, 44, Division 3(N), 1926–27.
Most League Goals in Total Aggregate: Albert Whitehurst, 117, 1923–28.
Most Capped Player: None.
Most League Appearances: Graham Smith, 316 (+1), 1966–74.
Record Transfer Fee Received: £40,000 plus Malcolm Darling from Norwich C. for David Cross, Oct. 1971.
Record Transfer Fee Paid: £8,000 to Aldershot for Jack Howarth, Jan. 1972.
Managers Since the War: Ted Goodier, Jack Warner. Harry Catterick, Jack Marshall, Tony Collins, Bob Stokoe, Len Richley, Dick Conner, Walter Joyce.
Address of Club Shop: Rochdale A.F.C. Soccer Shop, Spotland, Sandy Lane, Rochdale.

Spotland, Willbutts Lane, Rochdale. Telephone 44648/9.   *Ground capacity:* 28,000.   *Record attendance:* 24,231 v Notts County, F.A. Cup 2nd Rd., December 10, 1949.   *Record receipts:* £3996.83p v Coventry C., F.A. Cup 3rd Rd., January 11, 1971.   *Pitch measurements:* 113 yds × 75 yds.

How to get there: Football specials run from The Esplanade in the town centre, which is five minutes' walk from Rochdale railway station. Specials also run from the same place for evening matches.
Match tickets: Seats can be reserved in advance.
Car parking: Car parking at the ground and in the adjacent side-streets.
Entertainments/catering facilities: A social club in the car park.
Club shop: Sells all types of souvenirs.
Handbooks/programmes: Programmes not available on subscription.
Extra information: In 1931–32 the club lost 17 Division Three (North) games in a row.

Club Colours: Royal blue shirts with white trimmings, white shorts with blue stripe, blue stockings.
Change Colours: Yellow shirts, blue shorts, yellow stockings.   *Club Nickname:* 'The Dale'.

ROCHDALE 1975–76 LEAGUE RECORD

Match No.	Date	Venue	Opponents	Result	H/T Score	League Pos'n	Goalscorers	Attendance
1	Aug 16	A	Reading	L 0-2	0-1	—		4534
2	23	H	Swansea C.	W 2-1	1-0	16	Mountford 2	1169
3	30	A	Huddersfield T.	D 0-0	0-0	17		4185
4	Sept 6	H	Newport Co.	W 4-3	3-0	12	Cooper 2, Mountford 2	1119
5	13	A	Torquay U.	L 0-1	0-1	15		1679
6	20	H	Bradford C.	D 0-0	0-0	15		2004
7	24	A	Crewe Alex.	D 0-0	0-0	—		3500
8	26	A	Stockport Co.	W 1-0	0-0	15	Mountford	3200
9	Oct 4	H	Exeter C.	L 0-1	0-1	13		1234
10	11	A	Scunthorpe U.	W 3-1	2-0	11	Mountford 2, Whelan	2508
11	18	H	Watford	W 2-1	0-0	10	Summerscales, Tobin	1528
12	22	A	AFC Bournemouth	L 1-2	1-0	—	Tobin	4396
13	25	A	Southport	W 1-0	0-0	10	Tobin	1447
14	Nov 1	H	Tranmere R.	W 4-1	3-0	8	Tobin, Whelan, Mountford 2	2047
15	3	H	Northampton T.	L 0-2	0-1	—		2995
16	8	A	Lincoln C.	L 0-2	0-1	11		7063
17	14	H	Cambridge U.	D 1-1	1-0	10	Mulvaney	1562
18	29	H	Workington	D 1-1	0-0	12	Tobin	1361
19	Dec 6	A	Brentford	L 0-3	0-1	15		4850
20	20	H	Hartlepool	D 1-1	1-0	15	Murty	1156
21	26	A	Barnsley	L 1-2	1-1	15	Mountford	3362
22	27	H	Darlington	W 1-0	0-0	15	Murty	1659
23	Jan 17	A	Bradford C.	L 0-3	0-0	19		3059
24	20	A	Doncaster R.	W 2-1	2-0	—	Hanvey, Fielding	3586
25	24	H	Torquay U.	D 2-2	2-1	15	Hanvey, Whelan	1443
26	Feb 7	A	Northampton T.	D 1-1	0-0	17	Whelan	5393
27	10	H	AFC Bournemouth	D 2-2	1-1	—	Whelan, Mountford	1393
28	14	H	Lincoln C.	D 0-0	0-0	14		2051
29	21	A	Cambridge U.	D 0-0	0-0	15		2048
30	28	H	Southport	W 2-0	0-0	11	Mountford, Summerscales	1261
31	Mar 1	H	Huddersfield T.	D 0-0	0-0	—		3791
32	6	A	Tranmere R.	W 1-0	1-0	11	Mullington	3354
33	9	A	Exeter C.	L 0-1	0-0	—		3102
34	12	H	Scunthorpe U.	D 1-1	1-1	12	Cooper	1430
35	16	A	Watford	L 0-3	0-0	—		3886
36	20	A	Workington	D 0-0	0-0	13		1009
37	22	H	Crewe Alex.	L 0-1	0-0	—		1128
38	27	H	Brentford	L 1-2	0-1	15	Boslem	1088
39	31	A	Hartlepool	L 0-3	0-1	—		1525
40	Apr 3	H	Reading	D 0-0	0-0	15		1063
41	5	H	Stockport Co.	L 2-3	1-1	—	Mountford, Whelan (pen)	1287
42	10	A	Newport Co.	D 1-1	1-1	15	Mullington	1331
43	16	H	Doncaster R.	W 1-0	0-0	14	Mountford	1462
44	17	H	Barnsley	D 0-0	0-0	14		1386
45	20	A	Darlington	L 0-4	0-2	—		1957
46	23	A	Swansea C.	D 1-1	0-1	15	Cooper	1604

Goalscorers

League (40): Mountford 14, Whelan 6 (1 pen), Tobin 5, Cooper 4, Hanvey 2, Mullington 2, Murty 2, Summerscales 2, Boslem 1, Fielding 1, Mulvaney 1.
F.A. Cup (9): Mountford 3, Ferguson, Whelan, Tobin, Mullington, own goal 2.

League Cup	First Round	Bury (a)	0-2	
	Second Leg	(h)	0-2	
F.A. Cup	First Round	Workington (a)	1-1	
		(h)	2-1	(a.e.t.)
	Second Round	Gateshead (a)	1-1	
		(h)	3-1	
	Third Round	Norwich C. (a)	1-1	
		(h)	0-0	(a.e.t.)
		(a)	1-2	

Poole	Hallows	Townsend	Mulvaney	Summerscales	Hanvey	Fielding	Mountford	Whelan	Sweeney	Lacey	Cooper	Ferguson	Tobin	Murty	Duffy	Hulmes	Mullington	Boslem	Oliver	Ainsworth	Brears	Match No.
1	2	3	4	5	6	7*	8	9	10	11	12											1
1	2	3		5	6		9	8	11	7	10	4										2
1	2	3	4	5	6		9	11	8		10	7										3
1	2	3	5	4	6		11	9	8		10	7										4
1	2		4	5	6	12	8	9	11*	3	10	7										5
1	2		4	5	6		9	8	11	3	10	7										6
1	2		4	5	6		8	10	11	3	9	7										7
1	2		4	5	6	12	8	10	11*	3	9	7										8
1	2		4	5	6	12	9	8	11	3*	10	7										9
1	2*			5	6		8	9	10	3	11	7	4	12								10
1	2			5	6	4	9	11		3	10	7	8									11
1		2		5	6	11	8	10		3	9	7	4									12
1	2			5	6	11	8	10		3	9	7	4									13
1	2			5	6	4	9	11		3	10	7	8									14
1	2			5	6	4*	8	10		3	9	7	11			12						15
1	2			5	6	11*	8	10	12	3	9	7	4									16
1	2			5	6		8	10	7*	3	9	11	4	12								17
1	2	4		5			8	10		3	9	7	6	11								18
1	2	12		5	6		8	9		3*	10	4	11	7								19
1	2		4	5	6			11		3	8	7	10	9								20
1	2			5	6		8	9		3	4	10*	7				12	11					21
1	2	3		5	6	7	9	4			8	10					11					22
1	2		4	5	6	10	8	9		3	7						11					23
1	2		4	5	6	10	8	9	12	3	7*						11					24
1	2*			5	6		8	9	10	3	7					12	11	4				25
1	2		4	5	6		8	9	10	3	7						11					26
1	2		4	5	6	10	8	9		3	7						11					27
1	2		4	5			8	9		3	10	7					11					28
	2		4	5	6		8	9	7	3	10*	12					11		1			29
1	2		4	5			8	9	7	3	10	6					11					30
1	2		4	5		7	8	9		3	10	11					6					31
1	2		4	5		7	8	9		3	10	11					6					32
1	2		4	5	6		8	9*		3	10	7				12	11					33
1	2		4	5	6		8	9		3	10	7					11					34
1	2		4	5	6		8	9		3	7						11	10*	12			35
1	2			5			8	9		3	10	7				11	6	4				36
1	2			5			8	9	12	3	7		10		6*		11	4				37
	2	3	4	5	6		8				7*	10					11	12	1		9	38
	2	3	4	5		7	8	9			10						11	6	1			39
1	2		4	5			8	9		3	7						11	6			10	40
1	2		4	5		10	8	9		3	7	6					11					41
1	2		4	5	6	7		9		3	10						11	7				42
1	2		4	5	6	12	8	9		3	7						11	10*				43
1	2		4	5	6	7*	9	10		3	11	8						12				44
1	2		4	5	6		8	9		3	7						11	10				45
1	2		4	5	6	7	8		12	3	10	9					11*					46
43	45	8	38	43	28	26	44	44	12	41	40	26	13	12	2	3	25	8	3	—	2	

+1s (Mulvaney) +4s (Hanvey) +5s (Whelan) +1s 1s (Lacey, Cooper) +23 (Ferguson) +2s (Hulmes) +1s (Mullington) +2s (Boslem)

Player and position	Ht.	Wt.	Birthplace	Clubs	League Appearances	Goals
Goalkeepers						
Mike Poole	6 0	12 7	Leeds	Coventry C.	—	—
				Rochdale	124	—
Brian Oliver	5 11	12 10	Liverpool	Burnley	—	—
				Peterborough U.	—	—
				Bury	—	—
				Rochdale	3	—
Defenders						
Keith Hanvey	6 1	13 0	Manchester	Manchester C.	—	—
				Swansea C.	11	1
				Rochdale	102	6
Tony Lacey	5 8	11 3	Leek	Stoke C.	2+2	—
				Port Vale	193+7	9
				Rochdale	41	—
Dick Mulvaney	6 0	12 7	Sunderland	Blackburn R.	135+6	4
				Oldham Ath.	88+4	2
				Rochdale	68	4
*George Townsend	5 11	12 0	Ashton	Rochdale	31+1	—
Bill Boslem	6 0	11 6	Middleton	Rochdale	8+1	1
Bill Summerscales	6 1	11 0	Stoke	Port Vale	126+3	4
				Rochdale	43	2
Midfield						
Mike Ferguson	5 10½	11 7	Burnley	Accrington S.	49	2
				Blackburn R.	220	30
				Aston Villa	38	2
				Q.P.R.	67+1	2
				Cambridge U.	39	4
				Rochdale	68+1	5
				(contract cancelled Mar 1976)		
Paul Hallows	5 7	10 9	Chester	Bolton W.	44+2	—
				Rochdale	91	1
Stan Horne	5 10	12 6	Clanfield	Aston Villa	6	—
				Manchester C.	48+2	—
				Fulham	73+6	—
				Chester	17+1	—
				Rochdale	48	5
				(contract cancelled Jan 1976)		
*Paul Brears	5 6	10 0	Oldham	Oldham Ath.	—	—
				Rochdale	26+1	—
Philip Mullington	5 10	11 10	Oldham	Oldham Ath.	—	—
				Rochdale	25	2
Forwards						
Bob Mountford	5 11	10 10	Stoke	Port Vale	64+13	9
				Scunthorpe U. (on loan)	1+2	—
				Crewe A. (on loan)	5	—
				Rochdale	60	24
*Andy Sweeney	5 6	10 7	Oldham	Oldham Ath.	37+5	2
				Bury (on loan)	2	—
				Rochdale	12+5	—
*Paul Fielding	5 8	10 0	Rochdale	Rochdale	65+7	5
Gary Cooper	5 11	11 4	Horwich	Rochdale	64+5	9
*Donald Tobin	5 7	10 7	Liverpool	Rochdale	46+2	5
Tony Whelan	6 1	11 8	Salford	Manchester U.	—	—
				Manchester C.	3+3	—
				Rochdale	90	16
*Gary Hulmes	5 8	10 7	Manchester	Rochdale	4+6	1
*Joe Murty	5 10	11 6	Glasgow	Rochdale	15+5	2
*David Ainsworth	5 6	11 8	Bolton	Rochdale	0+2	—

ROTHERHAM UNITED   DIV. 3

Chairman: E. Purshouse.

Directors: L. D. Purshouse, C. R. Wright, A. H. Steel.

Manager: Jimmy McGuigan   *Secretary:* J. E. Bennison.

Year Formed: 1884.   *Turned Professional:* 1905.

Limited Company: 1920.

Previous Names: 1884, Thornhill United; 1905, Rotherham County; 1925, amalgamated Rotherham Town under Rotherham United.

Previous Grounds: Red House Ground; 1907, Millmoor.

Honours: *Football League,* best season in Division 2: 3rd, 1954–55 (equal points with Champions and Runners-up). Division 3(N), Champions: 1950–51; Runners-up: 1946–47, 1947–48, 1948–49. *F.A. Cup,* best season: 5th Rd., 1953, 1968. *Football League Cup,* best season, Runners-up: 1961.

Record Victory: 8-0 v Oldham Ath., Division 3(N), May 26th, 1947.

Record Defeat: 1-11 v Bradford C., Division 3(N), Aug. 25th, 1928.

Most League Points: 71, Division 3(N), 1950–51.

Most League Goals: 114, Division 3(N), 1946–47.

Highest League Scorer in Season: Wally Ardron, 38, Division 3(N), 1946–47.

Most League Goals in Total Aggregate: Gladstone Guest, 130, 1946–56.

Most Capped Player: Harold Millership, 6, Wales.

Most League Appearances: Danny Williams, 459, 1946–62.

Record Transfer Fee Received: £100,000 from Sunderland for Dave Watson, Dec. 1970.

Record Transfer Fee Paid: £27,000 to Sheffield W. for John Quinn, Nov. 1967.

Managers Since the War: Reg Freeman, Andy Smailes, Tom Johnston, Danny Williams, Jack Mansell, Tommy Docherty, Jimmy McAnearney.

Address of Supporters Club: Red and White Shop, c/o Millmoor, Rotherham.

Millmoor Ground, Rotherham. Telephone Rotherham 2434. *Telegraphic address:* 'Holmes Millmoor, Rotherham'. *Ground capacity:* 24,000. *Record attendance:* 25,000 v Sheffield U., Division 2, December 13, 1952 and v Sheffield W., Division 2, January 26, 1952. *Record receipts:* £7,666 v Leeds U., F.A. Cup 3rd Rd., January 11, 1971. *Pitch measurements:* 115 yds × 76 yds.

How to get there: Corporation buses from town centre. Also regular service buses from Sheffield to town centre. Nearest railway station, Rotherham on the line from Sheffield.

Match tickets: Seats can be reserved one month before the match.

Car parking: There are parks in Kimberworth Road and Main St. (the municipal car park); both are within easy reach of the ground.

Entertainments/catering facilities: There are refreshment kiosks on all four sides of the ground and also behind the grandstand, and the 'Windmill' where meals may be obtained if booked in advance, and drinks are served during licensing hours.

Club shop: Sited on the forecourt of the ground; stocks all types of souvenirs.

Handbooks/programmes: No handbook, but programmes may be obtained from the club or the club shop.

Extra information: Rotherham full-back Irvine Rhodes scored twice on his debut for Rotherham against Hartlepools in March 1937.

Club Colours: Red shirts, white collar, white sleeves, white shorts, red stockings.

Change Colours: Blue shirts and shorts with yellow trim, yellow stockings.

Club Coach: Charlie Bell.

Club Nickname: 'The Merry Millers'.

ROTHERHAM UNITED 1975–76 LEAGUE RECORD

Match No.	Date	Venue	Opponents	Result	H/T Score	League Pos'n	Goalscorers	Attendance
1	Aug 16	A	Brighton & H.A.	L 0-3	0-3	—		10,138
2	23	H	Hereford U.	D 1-1	1-1	22	Breckin	3825
3	30	A	Southend U.	W 2-1	0-0	16	Finney, Leng	4219
4	Sept 6	H	Bury	D 3-3	2-2	14	Habbin, Finney 2	4070
5	13	A	Crystal Palace	L 0-2	0-1	19		16,421
6	20	H	Wrexham	W 2-1	1-0	15	Spencer, Wagstaff	3776
7	23	A	Gillingham	D 0-0	0-0	—		5498
8	27	A	Peterborough U.	W 3-1	0-1	12	Habbin 2, Phillips	6543
9	Oct 4	H	Swindon T.	L 0-2	0-2	13		4731
10	11	H	Cardiff C.	W 1 0	1 0	9	England (og)	4272
11	18	A	Millwall	L 1-3	1-1	14	Habbin	6327
12	21	A	Colchester U.	D 0-0	0-0	—		3468
13	25	H	Aldershot	D 2-2	0-0	12	Crawford (pen), Stancliffe	4428
14	Nov 1	A	Port Vale	L 0-1	0-1	18		3921
15	4	H	Chester	L 0-1	0-1	—		4282
16	8	H	Walsall	W 3-1	1-1	14	Phillips 2, Finney	4454
17	15	A	Shrewsbury T.	W 2-0	0-0	12	Phillips 2	3775
18	29	A	Sheffield W.	D 0-0	0-0	11		18,691
19	Dec 6	H	Chesterfield	W 2-0	1-0	9	Goodfellow, Rhodes	6474
20	20	H	Mansfield T.	W 2-1	0-0	7	Phillips, Spencer	6067
21	26	A	Grimsby T.	L 1-4	1-3	9	Finney	6919
22	27	H	Halifax T.	L 0-1	0-1	13		7614
23	Jan 10	A	Southend U.	W 2-0	0-0	12	Womble, Finney	4390
24	13	A	Preston N.E.	L 2-3	1-2	—	Womble, Finney	6289
25	17	A	Wrexham	L 0-3	0-2	14		2897
26	31	H	Colchester U.	W 2-0	1-0	14	Spencer, Leng	3943
27	Feb 3	H	Crystal Palace	W 4-1	0-0	—	Spencer, Rhodes, Finney 2	7633
28	7	A	Chester	L 1-3	0-1	12	Stancliffe	4573
29	13	A	Walsall	L 1-5	1-1	13	Habbin	4989
30	21	H	Shrewsbury T.	L 0-1	0-1	15		4947
31	24	H	Gillingham	W 2-0	0-0	—	Habbin, Gwyther	4404
32	28	A	Aldershot	L 0-3	0-1	15		3538
33	Mar 6	H	Port Vale	L 1-2	0-2	16	Rhodes	4280
34	9	A	Swindon T.	D 1-1	1-1	—	Goodfellow	9866
35	13	A	Cardiff C.	D 1-1	1-1	16	Gwyther	11,072
36	16	H	Millwall	L 1-2	1-0	—	Womble	4556
37	20	H	Sheffield W.	W 1-0	1-0	15	Habbin	13,500
38	27	A	Chesterfield	L 0-1	0-1	17		5595
39	29	A	Mansfield T.	D 1-1	1-0	—	Crawford	9098
40	Apr 3	H	Brighton & H.A.	D 1-1	0-1	15	Spencer	4309
41	6	H	Peterborough U.	D 1-1	0-1	—	Crawford (pen)	3872
42	10	A	Bury	L 0-4	0-1	18		5141
43	17	H	Grimsby T.	W 3-0	2-0	16	Finney, Crawford 2	4414
44	19	A	Halifax T.	W 1-0	1-0	—	Gwyther	2614
45	20	H	Preston N.E.	D 1-1	1-1	—	Crawford	4874
46	24	A	Hereford U.	L 2-3	0-3	16	Finney, Crawford	8950

Goalscorers

League (54): Finney 11, Crawford 7 (2 pens), Habbin 7, Phillips 6, Spencer 5, Rhodes 3, Womble 3, Gwyther 3, Leng 2, Stancliffe 2, Goodfellow 2, Breckin 1, Wagstaffe 1, own goal 1.

League Cup (2): Crawford (1 a pen), Goodfellow.

F.A. Cup (2): Crawford, Stancliffe.

League Cup	First Round	Nottingham F. (h)		1-2
	Second Leg	(a)		1-5
F.A. Cup	First Round	Crewe Alex. (h)		2-1
	Second Round	Bradford C. (h)		0-3

McDonagh	Leng	Breckin	Wagstaff	Stancliffe	Spencer	Finney	Phillips	Habbin	Goodfellow	Crawford	Haslam	Derrett	Delgado	Green	Eades	Rhodes	Womble	Watling	McAllister	Gwyther	Match No.
1	2	3	4	5	6	7	8	9	10	11											1
	3	2	4	5		7	8*	9	10	11	1	6	12								2
	7	3	4	5		8		9	10	11	1	6		2							3
1	7	3	4	5		8		9	10	11		6		2							4
1	7	3	4	5		8		9	10	11		6		2							5
1	7	3	4	5	6	8		9	10	11				2							6
1	7	3	4*	5	6	8	12	9	10	11				2							7
1	4	3		5	6	8	7	9	10	11				2							8
1	4	3		5	6		7	9	10	11		12		2	8*						9
1	4	3		5	6	8	7	9	10	11				2							10
1	4	3		5	6	8	7	9	10	11				2							11
1	7	3		5	6	8	4	9	10	11				2							12
1	4	3		5	6	8	7	9	10	11				2							13
1	7	3		5	6	8	4	9	10	11				2							14
1	7	3		5	6	8	4	9	10	11				2							15
1		3		5	6	7	8	9	10	11				2		4					16
1		3		5	6	7	8	9	10	11				2		4					17
1		3		5	6	7	8	9	10	11				2		4					18
1*		3		5	6	7	8	9	10	11				2		4	12				19
		3		5	6	7	8	9	10	11				2		4		1			20
		3		5	6	7	8	9	10	11				2		4		1			21
	7	3		5	6	9	8		10	11				2		4		1			22
		3		5	6	7	8		10	11				2		4	9	1			23
12		3		5	6	7	8*		10	11				2		4	9	1			24
		3		5	6	8	7		10	11				2		4	9		1		25
	7	3		5	6	8		9	10	11				2		4			1		26
	7	3		5	6	8		9	10	11				2		4			1		27
	7	3		5	6	8	12	9*	10	11				2		4			1		28
12		3		5	6	7	8	9	10	11				2*		4			1		29
		3	4	5		7		9	10	11		6		2					1	8	30
		3		5	6*	7	8		10	11	12			2		4			1	9	31
		3		5		7		9	10	11		6		2		4			1	8	32
12		3		5*		7	8		10	11		6		2		4			1	9	33
		3		5		7			10	11		6		2		4	8		1	9	34
		3			6			9	10	11		5		2		4	7		1	8	35
12		3		5		7			10	11		6		2		4	8*		1	9	36
		3		5	6	8	7		10	11				2		4			1	9	37
		3		5	6	12	8*	7	10	11				2		4			1	9	38
		3	4	5	6	8			10	11				2			7		1	9	39
		3	4	5	6	8			10	11				2			7		1	9	40
		3	4	5	6	8*	12	7	10	11				2					1	9	41
		3	4	5	6	8	7		10	11				2					1	9	42
		3	4	5		7	8		10	11		6		2					1	9	43
12		3		5	6	7*	8		10	11				2		4			1	9	44
	7	3		5	6	9	8		10	11				2		4			1		45
	9	3		5	6	7	8		10	11				2		4			1		46
17	21	46	18	42	34	37	26	40	46	46	2	16	—	38	1	28	6	5	22	15	
+5s					+1s	+3s					+2s	+1s						+1s			

ROTHERHAM UNITED—PLAYERS

Player and position	Ht.	Wt.	Birthplace	Clubs	League Appearances	Goals
Goalkeepers						
Jim McDonagh	5 11½	13 0	Rotherham	Rotherham U.	121	—
				Manchester U. (on loan)	—	—
Tom McAlister	6 0	11 1	Clydebank	Sheffield U.	63	—
				Rotherham U.	22	—
Graham Haslam	5 8	10 1	Doncaster	Rotherham U.	2	—
Defenders						
John Breckin	5 9½	11 9	Rotherham	Rotherham U.	145+3	5
				Darlington (on loan)	4	—
*Steve Derrett (Wales)	5 8	11 12	Cardiff	Cardiff C.	62+4	1
				Carlisle U.	13	—
				Aldershot (on loan)	4	—
				Rotherham U.	79+2	2
*Michael Leng	5 9½	10 11	Rotherham	Rotherham U.	94+7	2
Tommy Spencer	5 11	12 9	Glasgow	Celtic	—	—
				Southampton	3	—
				York C.	54+3	20
				Workington	167	10
				Lincoln C.	67+7	10
				Rotherham U.	80+1	6
*Trevor Swift	5 11	12 5	Rotherham	Rotherham U.	283+5	21
Raymond Mielczarek (Wales)	5 11½	11 8	Caernarvon	Wrexham	76	—
				Huddersfield T.	25+1	1
				Rotherham U.	114+1	7
				(contract cancelled Feb 1976).		
John Green	5 10	12 1	Rotherham	Rotherham U.	38	—
Paul Stancliffe	6 0	11 10	Sheffield	Rotherham U.	42	2
Midfield						
Eddie Ferguson	5 10	12 7	Dumbarton	Dumbarton	50+2	9
				Rotherham U.	64+3	5
				Grimsby T. (on loan)	1+1	—
Jimmy Goodfellow	5 8	10 7	Bishop Auckland	Port Vale	77+8	11
				Workington	199	15
				Rotherham U.	105	6
Alan Crawford	5 7½	9 10	Rotherham	Rotherham U.	120+4	17
				Mansfield (on loan)	1+1	—
Barrie Wagstaff	5 10¾	11 8	Brampton	Sheffield U.	160+10	5
				Reading	198+6	23
				Rotherham U.	29+1	1
Mark Rhodes	5 9	10 11	Sheffield	Rotherham U.	28	3
Kevin Eades	5 5	8 3	Rawmarsh	Rotherham U.	1	—
Forwards						
Carl Gilbert	6 0	12 8	Folkestone	Gillingham	28+2	11
				Bristol R.	38+7	15
				Rotherham U.	78+16	37
Richard Habbin	5 7	10 6	Cambridge	Reading	204+14	42
				Rotherham U.	61	17
Richard Finney	5 7	10 4	Rotherham	Rotherham U.	79	26
Trevor Phillips	5 6½	10 3	Rotherham	Rotherham U.	156+33	38
Trevor Womble	5 8	10 0	Durham	Rotherham U.	155+21	36
				Crewe Alex. (on loan)	4	1
				Halifax T. (on loan)	9+1	2
John Woodall	5 9	11 7	Goole	Rotherham U.	25+1	6
*David Stenson	5 8	10 5	Sheffield	Rotherham U.	—	—
David Gwyther	5 10	13 4	Birmingham	Swansea C.	213+4	59
				Halifax T.	104	26
				Rotherham U.	15	3

SCUNTHORPE UNITED   DIV. 4

President: Ald. Alec Moore.   *Chairman:* J. T. Empson.

Vice-Chairman: J. S. Wharton.

Directors: W. H. Archer, A. Harvey, C. Smith, T. Belton, G. E. Johnson, B. Collen.

Manager: Ron Ashman.

Secretary: Mrs. S. Louth.

Year Formed: 1904.   *Turned Professional:* 1912.

Limited Company: 1912.

Previous Name: Amalgamated with Lindsey United to become Scunthorpe United, 1910.

Honours: *Football League*, best season in Division 2: 4th, 1961–62. Division 3(N), Champions: 1957–58.   *F.A. Cup*, best season: 5th Rd., 1957–58 1969–70.   *Football League Cup*, best season: never past 3rd Rd.

Record Victory: 9-0 v Boston U., F.A. Cup, 1st Rd., Nov. 21st, 1953.

Record Defeat: 0-8 v Carlisle U., Division 3(N), 1952–53.

Most League Points: 66, Division 3(N), 1957–58.

Most League Goals: 88, Division 3(N), 1957–58.

Highest League Scorer in Season: Barrie Thomas, 31, Division 2, 1961–62.

Most League Goals in Total Aggregate: Barrie Thomas, 92, 1959–62, 1964–66.

Most Capped Player: None.

Most League Appearances: Jack Brownsword, 600, 1950–65.

Record Transfer Fee Received: £45,000 from W.B.A. for John Kaye, May 1963.

Record Transfer Fee Paid: £20,000 to Newcastle U. for Barrie Thomas, Nov. 1964.

Managers Since the War: Leslie Jones, Bill Corkhill, Ron Suart, Tony McShane, Bill Lambton (3 days, shortest ever term of office), Frank Soo, Dick Duckworth, Freddie Goodwin, Ron Ashman, Ron Bradley, Dickie Rooks.

Address of Supporters Club: Scunthorpe U. Supporters and Social Club at Ground.

Old Show Ground, Scunthorpe, South Humberside. Telephone Scunthorpe 2954.   *Ground capacity:* 27,000.   *Record attendance:* 23,935 v Portsmouth, F.A. Cup 4th Rd., January 30, 1954.   *Record receipts:* £7895 v Newcastle U., F.A. Cup 4th Rd., replay, Jan. 30 1974. *Pitch measurements:* 112 yds × 78 yds.

How to get there: Buses 211, 212, 213, 118 run near the ground. Nearest railway station is Scunthorpe. By road along A18 from Doncaster via Berkeley Circle, Doncaster Road Hill, and Henderson Avenue; A18 from Grimsby; A15 from Lincoln via Queensway Circle, Ashby Road, Station Roundabout, Church Lane, Exeter Road, and Doncaster Road; via A1 on A638 to Retford, A620 to Gainsborough, A159 to Scunthorpe.

Match tickets: Tickets are bookable up to the day before the match unless advertised otherwise in the local press. No telephone bookings accepted.

Car parking: Club car park adjoining the ground holds 40–50 cars. Ample street parking around the ground.

Entertainments/catering facilities: Catering sub-let to an outside firm; hot drinks and light refreshments served on first-team match days.

Club shop: Three club shops on the ground sell all types of souvenirs.

Handbooks/programmes: Programmes available on match days.

Extra information: The club have their own personality competition for the title, 'Miss Scunthorpe United' The club song 'Scunthorpe United', is available on record.

Club Colours: All red.

Change Colours: All yellow.

Club Nickname: 'The Irons'.

SCUNTHORPE UNITED 1975–76 LEAGUE RECORD

Match No.	Date	Venue	Opponents	Result	H/T Score	League Posn'	Goalscorers	Attendance
1	Aug 16	A	Darlington	L 0-2	0-1	—		1920
2	23	H	Exeter C.	L 0-1	0-1	23		1660
3	30	A	Newport Co.	D 0-0	0-0	21		2735
4	Sept 6	H	Huddersfield T.	L 0-1	0-1	24		1992
5	13	A	Hartlepool	W 2-1	1-0	20	Hemmerman, Collier	1970
6	20	H	Torquay U .	W 3-1	2-0	19	Collier, Woodward 2	1989
7	22	A	Tranmere R.	L 1-2	1-2	—	Money	2308
8	27	A	Swansea C.	L 0-2	0-2	20		3098
9	Oct 4	H	Reading	W 2-1	0-0	18	Keeley, Collier	2177
10	11	H	Rochdale	L 1-3	0-2	20	Green	2508
11	18	A	Crewe Alex.	L 0-1	0-1	21		1939
12	21	A	Watford	L 0-1	0-1	—		3581
13	25	H	Northampton T.	L 0-2	0-1	22		1965
14	Nov 1	A	Brentford	L 2-5	0-2	22	Charnley, Green	4220
15	4	H	Cambridge U.	L 0-1	0-0	—		1526
16	8	H	Workington	W 3-0	0-0	22	Keeley, Green 2	1503
17	15	A	AFC Bournemouth	L 0-1	0-0	22		4333
18	28	A	Lincoln C.	L 0-3	0-3	22		8494
19	Dec 6	H	Southport	L 1-2	0-1	22	Collier	1817
20	13	A	Reading	L 0-1	0-0	22		5575
21	20	H	Stockport Co.	D 0-0	0-0	22		1570
22	26	A	Bradford C.	D 0-0	0-0	22		3465
23	27	H	Doncaster R.	W 2-1	1-1	22	Davidson, Woodward	5801
24	Jan 3	A	Barnsley	L 0-1	0-0	22		2823
25	10	H	Newport Co.	L 1-2	0-2	22	Money	1739
26	17	A	Torquay U.	L 0-1	0-1	22		2776
27	Feb 7	A	Cambridge U.	D 2-2	0-0	22	Keeley, Davidson	1777
28	10	H	Watford	L 0-1	0-1	—		2200
29	14	A	Workington	W 3-2	2-2	22	Green 2, Davidson	1273
30	21	H	AFC Bournemouth	W 2-0	1-0	22	Money, Charnley	2068
31	24	A	Tranmere R.	D 2-2	1-1	—	Wiggington (pen), O'Connor	3049
32	27	A	Northampton T.	L 1-2	1-1	22	O'Connor	6804
33	Mar 2	H	Hartlepool	W 5-1	2-0	—	Collier 2, Green 2, Oates	2966
34	6	H	Brentford	W 2-1	1-0	21	Green, O'Connor	3225
35	12	A	Rochdale	D 1-1	1-1	21	Green	1430
36	16	H	Crewe Alex.	W 1-0	1-0	—	Green	3126
37	20	H	Lincoln C.	L 0-2	0-2	21		10,329
38	26	A	Southport	D 1-1	1-1	22	Collier	1805
39	29	A	Stockport Co.	D 0-0	0-0	—		2078
40	Apr 3	H	Darlington	W 2-1	2-0	21	Irvine, Davidson	2492
41	6	H	Swansea C.	D 1-1	0-1	—	Green	3015
42	10	A	Huddersfield T.	D 1-1	0-0	21	Davidson	6502
43	17	H	Bradford C.	W 2-0	1-0	20	Green, O'Connor	3254
44	19	A	Doncaster R.	W 1-0	1-0	—	Green	4097
45	20	H	Barnsley	W 1-0	0-0	—	O'Connor	4770
46	23	A	Exeter C.	L 4-5	2-2	18	Green, Woodward 2, Wiggington	1863

Goalscorers

League (50): Green 15, Collier 7, Davidson 5, O'Connor 5, Woodward 5, Keeley 3, Money 3, Charnley 2, Wigginton 2 (1 a pen), Hemmerman 1, Irvine 1, Oates 1.
F.A. Cup (1): Green.

League Cup	First Round	Mansfield T. (a)	0-4
	Second Leg	(h)	0-2
F.A. Cup	First Round	Preston N.E. (a)	1-2

Norris	Markham	Peacock	Irvine	Wigginton	Money	Charnley	Robinson	Keeley	Pilling	Davidson	Oates	Collier	Roberts	O'Connor	Hemmerman	Woodward	Welbourne	Green	O'Meara	Farrell	Bond	Ferguson	Dale	Match No.
1	2	3	4	5	6	7	8*	9	10	11	12													1
1	2	3	6	5	4	11		8		9		7		10										2
1	2	3		5	4	11		10	8	9	6	7												3
1	2	3		6	5	10		11	8	9	4*	7			12									4
1	2		4	6	5			9		3	8	7				10	11							5
1	2		4	6	5	12		11		3*	9	8				10	7							6
1	2*		6	5	4	9		8		3		7				10	11	12						7
1	2		12	6	3			8		4		7				10	11*	5	9					8
1	2	3	4	6	5			10	11	8	7							9						9
1	2	3	4	6	5			10	11*	8	7				12			9						10
	2		4	5	6			11		3		7				9	10	8	1					11
	2		6	5	3	12		8		9		7		11*		4		10	1					12
	2		6	5	3	12		8		7		9		11*		4		10	1					13
	2		6	4	3	9		8				7		11			5	10	1					14
	2		6		5	8		10		3		7		9*	12	4	11		1					15
	2	3		5	10			7		9		6		11		4*		8	1			12		16
	2	3		5	7			10	12	8		6		11		4*		9	1					17
	2	3	4	10	12			8		6		7		9*		5	11		1					18
	2	3		5	4	11		8		6		7				10		9			1			19
	2	3		5	6			8		4	12	7				9	11*				1	10		20
	2		5	4	3			8		6	12	7				9*	11				1	10		21
	2			5	4			8	3	9	6	7				10					1	11		22
			5	4	2			10	3	7	8	6				9	11				1			23
			5	4	2			10	3	7	8	6				9	11				1			24
			5	4	2			10	3	7	8	6		12		9*	11				1			25
	2	8		5	4			10		3	6	7		11*		12		9			1			26
	2	3	6	5	4	12		8		9		7		11				10*	1					27
	2	3	6	5	4	12		8		9		7		11*				10	1					28
	2	3	7	5	4			8		9		6		11				10	1					29
	2	3	6	5	4	12		8		9		7		11				10*	1					30
	2	3	6	5	4	12		8		9		7		11*				10	1					31
	2	3	6	5	4			8		9		7		11				10	1					32
	2	3		5	4			8		9	6*	7		11			12	10	1					33
	2	3		5	4			8		9	6	7		11				10	1					34
	2	3	4	5				8		9	7	6		11			12	10*	1					35
	2	3		5	6			8		9	4	7		11				10	1					36
	2*	3		5	4	12		8		9	7	6		11				10	1					37
	2	3		5	4			8		9	7	6		11				10	1					38
	2	3		5	6			8		9	4	7		11				10	1					39
	2	3	11	5	6			8		9	4	7						10	1					40
	2	3	11	5	6			8		9	4	7						10	1					41
	2	3	11*	5	6	12		8		9	4	7						10	1					42
		3		5	6	2		8		9	4	7		11				10	1					43
	2	3		5	6			8		9	4	7		11				10	1					44
	2	3		5	6			8*		9	4	7		11			12	10	1					45
	2	3		5	6	8					4	7		9				10	1				11	46
10	**42**	**31**	**22**	**42**	**45**	**18**	**1**	**42**	**11**	**45**	**22**	**45**	**4**	**18**	**4**	**16**	**9**	**39**	**28**	**—**	**8**	**3**	**1**	
				+1s	+9s			+1s	+1s		+3s			+3s	+1s	+3s	+1s		+2s					

SCUNTHORPE UNITED—PLAYERS

Player and position	Ht.	Wt.	Birthplace	Clubs	League Appearances	Goals
Goalkeepers						
*Michael Norris	6 0	10 9	Retford	Scunthorpe U.	25	—
Alan O'Meara	5 11	10 10	Grantham	Scunthorpe U.	28	—
Defenders						
Clive Wigginton	6 0	11 5	Sheffield	Grimsby T.	163+8	6
				Scunthorpe U.	42	2
Peter Markham	5 7	10 0	Scunthorpe	Scunthorpe U.	102+1	1
John Peacock	5 9	10 4	Leeds	Scunthorpe U.	48+2	—
Midfield						
*Donald Welbourne	5 10	11 0	Scunthorpe	Scunthorpe U.	253+4	5
Angus Davidson	5 7	11 0	Forfar	Grimsby T.	46+3	1
				Scunthorpe U.	269+11	41
Richard Money	5 11	10 12	Lowestoft	Scunthorpe U.	109+8	4
*Archie Irvine	5 5	10 4	Coatbridge	Airdrieonians	24	—
				Sheffield W.	25+3	1
				Doncaster R.	219+8	16
				Scunthorpe U.	22+1	1
Alan Robinson	5 9	9 10	Grantham	Coventry C.	—	—
				Sheffield W.	—	—
				Scunthorpe U.	1	—
Doug O'Connor	5 10	10 5	Barnsley	Barnsley	27+9	7
				Mansfield T.	11+6	2
				Scunthorpe U.	18+3	5
Robert Oates	5 11	10 10	Leeds	Scunthorpe U.	36+3	1
Forwards						
*Dudley Roberts	6 0½	12 2	Coventry	Coventry C.	11+1	6
				Mansfield T.	194+6	67
				Doncaster R. (on loan)	7	—
				Scunthorpe U.	56+3	17
Nolan Keeley	5 11	11 12	Barsham	Scunthorpe U.	117+4	16
Graham Collier	5 11	10 13	Nottingham	Nottingham F.	13+2	2
				Scunthorpe.	127+3	19
Stuart Pilling	5 11	10 12	Sheffield	Hull C.	—	—
				Scunthorpe U.	84+2	6
Derek Charnley	5 10	10 4	Doncaster	Scunthorpe U.	28+10	3
*John Woodward	6 0	11 0	Stoke	Stoke C.	10+1	1
				Aston Villa	22+5	7
				Walsall	116+10	23
				Port Vale	88+11	30
				Scunthorpe U.	16+3	5
Rick Green	6 0	10 9	Scunthorpe	Scunthorpe U.	39	15
Alan Dale	5 10	11 0	Thorne	Scunthorpe U.	1	—
Mick Farrell	5 8	9 13	Ilkley	Scunthorpe U.	0+2	—

SHEFFIELD UNITED

Chairman: J. C. Hassall.

Vice-Chairman: A. Jackson, J.P. F.R.C.I.S.

Directors: M. Board, F.C.A., J.P., F. Melling, D.Ip.Arch., F.R.I.B.A., G. Price, M.I.Min.E., F.G.S., K. Lee, F. J. P. O'Gorman, F.R.C.S., J. W. Sterland, O.B.E., J.P., A. Jackson, J.P., F.R.I.C.S., R. Wragg, M.Inst. B.M.

Manager: Jimmy Sirrell.

Coach: Cecil Coldwell. *Secretary:* Keith Walker.

Commercial Manager: Derek Dooley.

Year Formed: 1889. *Turned Professional:* 1889.

Limited Company: 1899.

Honours: *Football League.* Division 1, Champions: 1897–98; Runners-up: 1896–97, 1899–1900. Division 2, Champions: 1952–53; Runners-up: 1892–93, 1938–39, 1960–61, 1970–71. *F.A. Cup,* Winners: 1899, 1902, 1915, 1925; Runners-up: 1901, 1936. *Football League Cup,* best season: 5th Rd., 1961–62, 1966–67.

Record Victory: 11-2 v Cardiff C., Division 1, Jan. 1st, 1926.

Record Defeat: 0-13 v Bolton W., F.A. Cup, 2nd Rd., Feb. 1st, 1890.

Most League Points: 60, Division 2, 1952–53.

Most League Goals: 102, Division 1, 1925–26.

Highest League Scorer in Season: Jimmy Dunne, 41, Division 1, 1930–31.

Most League Goals in Total Aggregate: Harry Johnson, 205, 1919–30.

Most Capped Player: Billy Gillespie, 25, Ireland.

Most League Appearances: Joe Shaw, 629, 1948–66.

Record Transfer Fee Received: £165,000 from Stoke C. for Geoff Salmons, July 1974.

Record Transfer Fee Paid: £100,000 to Southend U. for Chris Guthrie, May 1975.

Managers Since the War: Ted Davison, Reg Freeman, Joe Mercer, John Harris, Arthur Rowly, John Harris, Ken Furphy.

Address of Supporters Club: Secretary, c/o S.U.F.C., Bramall Lane, Sheffield S2 4SU.

Address of Club Shop or Boutique: Lane Souvenir Shop, John Street, Sheffield S2 4SU.

Bramall Lane Ground, Sheffield, S2 4SU. Telephone Sheffield 25585/730630. *Telegraphic address:* 'United, Sheffield'. *Ground capacity:* 49,000 (15,300 seats). *Record attendance:* 68,287 v Leeds U., F.A. Cup 5th Rd., February 15, 1936. *Record receipts:* £32,000 v Manchester U., Division 1, Dec. 13, 1975. *Pitch masurements:* 117 yds × 75 yds

How to get there: Buses 34, 35, 38, 42, 45 from the central bus station. Sheffield railway station is within walking distance of the town centre.

Match tickets: Tickets bookable 14 days prior to the match.

Car parking: The ground is five minutes from car parks in the city centre. Ample parking in side-streets around Bramall Lane.

Entertainments/catering facilities: Numerous bars and buffets in the ground.

Club shop: Sells all types of souvenirs.

Handbook/programmes: Mail order service available through the club shop.

Extra information: Lane Social Club offers restaurant, lounge bars, bier keller, sauna baths, and keep-fit facilities.

Club Colours: Red, white and thin black striped shirts, black shorts, white stockings, two red bands on top.

Change Colours: White with green/black sash across front of shirt, green shorts, green stockings with white tops.

Club Captain: Tony Currie.

Club Trainer/Coach: Cecil Coldwell.

Club Nickname: 'Blades'.

SHEFFIELD UNITED 1975-76 LEAGUE RECORD

Match No.	Date	Venue	Opponents	Result	H/T Score	League Pos'n	Goalscorers	Attendance
1	Aug 16	H	Derby Co	D 1-1	0-0	—	Eddy (pen)	31,316
2	19	H	Arsenal	L 1-3	1-1	—	Eddy (pen)	23,344
3	23	A	Manchester U.	L 1-5	0-3	21	Guthrie	55,949
4	26	A	Everton	L 0-3	0-2	—		25,846
5	30	H	Leeds U.	L 0-2	0-1	22		33,337
6	Sept 6	A	Liverpool	L 0-1	0-0	22		37,340
7	13	H	Coventry C.	L 0-1	0-1	22		20,153
8	20	A	West Ham U.	L 0-2	0-0	22		28,924
9	23	H	Burnley	W 2-1	1-1	—	Guthrie, Field	21,477
10	27	H	Norwich C.	L 0-1	0-0	22		20,624
11	Oct 4	A	Birmingham C.	L 0-2	0-1	22		26,121
12	11	A	Wolverhampton W.	L 1-5	0-2	22	Flynn	16,162
13	18	H	Stoke C.	L 0-2	0-0	22		23,410
14	25	A	Q.P.R.	L 0-1	0-0	22		21,161
15	Nov 1	H	Manchester C.	D 2-2	1-2	22	Guthrie, Eddy (pen)	24,670
16	8	A	Aston Villa	L 1-5	0-1	22	Guthrie	30,053
17	15	H	Leicester C.	L 1-2	0-1	22	Woodward	20,165
18	22	A	Stoke C.	L 1-2	0-2	22	Woodward	21,959
19	29	A	Ipswich T.	D 1-1	1-0	22	Peddelty (og)	20,796
20	Dec 6	H	Tottenham H.	L 1-2	0-1	22	Bradford	23,909
21	13	H	Manchester U.	L 1-4	0-2	22	Dearden	32,003
22	20	A	Derby Co.	L 2-3	1-2	22	Woodward 2	26,455
23	26	H	Middlesbrough	D 1-1	0-1	22	Garner	28,538
24	27	A	Newcastle U.	D 1-1	0-0	22	Woodward	30,730
25	Jan 10	A	Coventry C.	L 0-1	0-0	22		13,796
26	17	H	Liverpool	D 0-0	0-0	22		31,255
27	31	A	Arsenal	L 0-1	0-0	22		14,477
28	Feb 7	H	Everton	D 0-0	0-0	22		20,113
29	14	H	Aston Villa	W 2-1	1-1	22	Woodward, Guthrie	21,152
30	21	A	Leicester C.	D 1-1	0-1	22	Woodward (pen)	18,698
31	24	H	Burnley	L 1-3	1-1	4	Guthrie	14,387
32	28	A	Q.P.R.	D 0-0	0-0	22		21,949
33	Mar 6	A	Manchester C.	L 0-4	0-0	22		33,510
34	13	H	Wolverhampton W.	L 1-4	1-3	22	Johnstone	17,661
35	20	H	Ipswich T.	L 1-2	1-2	22	Colquhoun	15,220
36	27	A	Tottenham H.	L 0-5	0-1	22		21,370
37	Apr 3	A	Norwich C.	W 3-1	3-1	22	Guthrie, Stainrod, Currie	19,937
38	10	H	West Ham U.	W 3-2	0-1	22	Woodward, Guthrie, Stainrod	18,797
39	14	A	Leeds U.	W 1-0	0-0	—	Woodward	22,799
40	17	A	Middlesbrough	L 0-3	0-2	22		17,000
41	19	H	Newcastle U.	W 1-0	1-0	—	Guthrie	18,906
42	May 4	H	Birmingham C.	D 1-1	1-0	—	Woodward	28,782

Goalscorers

League (33): Woodward 10 (1 a pen), Guthrie 9, Eddy 3 (3 pens), Stainrod 2, Field 1, Flynn 1, Bradford 1, Dearden 1, Garner 1, Johnstone 1, Colquhoun 1, Currie 1, Own Goal 1.
League Cup (4): Guthrie 3, Own Goal 1.

League Cup	Second Round	Halifax T. (a)	4-2
	Third Round	Hull C. (a)	0-2
F.A. Cup	Third Round	Leicester C. (a)	0-3

Brown	Badger	Bradford	Eddy	Franks	Flynn	Woodward	Speight	Guthrie	Garbett	Field	Cammack	Colquhoun	Currie	Goulding	Hemsley	Irving	Calvert	Dearden	McAllister	Garner	Johnstone	Ludlam	McGeady	Faulkner	Edwards	Stainrod	Kenworthy	Match No.
1	2	3	4	5	6	7	8	9	10	11																		1
1	2	3	4	5	6*	7	8	9	10	11	12																	2
1	2*	3	4		6	7	8	9	12	11		5	10															3
1		8	4			7	3	9	6	11		5	10		2													4
1	12	8	4			7	3	9	6	11		5	10		2*													5
1	2		4		6	7	11	9	8			5	10		3													6
1	2		4*		6	7	11	9	8			5	10		3		12											7
1		6	4	2		7	8	9		11		5	10*				12	3										8
1		3	4		6	7	11*	9	8	12		5	10		2													9
1	2	11	4		6	7	8	9				5	10		3													10
1	2		12		6	7	8	9		11		5*	10		3			4										11
1	2	8			6	7		9		11		5	10		3			4										12
1	2		4		6	9	7	12	8			5	10		3*		11											13
	2		4		6	7		9				5	10		3		8	11									1	14
	2		4		6	7	8	9	12			5	10		3		11*										1	15
	2		4		6	7	8	9	12			5	10		3		11*										1	16
1	2	8	4		6	7		9				5	10				11	3										17
1	2	10	4		6		11	9	12			5					8	7*		3								18
1	2	8	4		6		11	9	10*			5					12	7		3								19
1	2	8	4		6		11	9	12			5						7		3			10*					20
1	2	8	4		6		11		12			5					9*	7		3			10					21
		6	4			7	12	9		11		5	10*		2		1			3		8						22
		8	4				12	9		11		5	10		2*		1	7		3	6							23
1	7	4	2				12	9		11		5	10					8*		3	6							24
1		4	6	2		7		9				5	10							3		8	11					25
1		8	2				11	9				5	10					7		3	6		4					26
1		8	2				11	9				5	10					7		3	6		4					27
1		8	2	4			11	9	12			5	10*					7		3	6							28
1		8	2	4			11	9	10			5						7		3	6							29
1		10	2		6		11	9	8									7	4	3			5					30
1		8	2	4			11	9	10			5						7		3	6*		12					31
1			2	4	6		11	9				5*	10					7	8	3			12					32
1		8	2	4			11	9					10					7	6	3			5					33
1		4	2		6		11	9				5	10					7		3						8		34
1			4		6	7	12	9				5*	10	2						3	8		11					35
1		6	4			7		9				5	10	2			11			3						8		36
1	11	12	2	4		7		9				5	10							3*					6	8		37
1		8	2	4		7		9				5	10							3					6	11		38
1		8	2	5		7		9					10						4	3					6	11		39
1		8	2	5		7		9					10				12		4	3					6*	11		40
1		8	2*	12		7		9				5	10						4	3					6	11		41
1		8	2			7		9				5	10	2					4	3					6	11		42
37	17	31	23	32	18	41	17	37	9	11	6	36	33	6	9	—	14	7	5	25	6	12	11	4	2	7	6	
	+1s			+1s	+2s	+2s	+2s	+1s	+3s	+6s		+1s				+2s	+1s							+1s	+1s			

SHEFFIELD UNITED—PLAYERS

Player and position	Ht.	Wt.	Birthplace	Clubs	League Appearances	Goals
Goalkeepers						
Jim Brown (Scotland)	5 11	12 4	Coatbridge	Albion Rovers	79	—
				Chesterfield	47	—
				Sheffield U.	89	—
Steven Conroy	5 11	12 2	Chesterfield	Sheffield U.	—	—
Defenders						
Eddie Colquhoun (Scotland)	6 0	12 2	Prestonpans	Bury	81	2
				W.B.A.	46	1
				Sheffield U.	302+1	21
Terry Garbett	5 9	11 12	Malton	Middlesbrough	7	1
				Watford	196+4	47
				Blackburn R.	90	6
				Sheffield U.	26+5	—
				(contract cancelled Feb. 1976)		
Stephen Faulkner	6 3	13 5	Sheffield	Sheffield U.	9+1	—
John Flynn	6 0	11 4	Workington	Workington	35+3	—
				Sheffield U.	142+3	8
Stephen Goulding	5 8	10 9	Hexborough	Sheffield U.	28	—
Ted Hemsley	5 8	11 5	Stoke	Shrewsbury T.	234+1	21
				Sheffield U.	246	8
Paul Garner	5 6	9 10	Doncaster	Huddersfield T.	96	2
				Sheffield U.	25	1
Colin Franks	5 11	12 8	Wembley	Watford	99+14	8
				Sheffield U.	59+7	—
Midfield						
David Bradford	5 5	9 8	Manchester	Blackburn R.	58+6	3
				Sheffield U.	53+4	2
Michael Speight	5 9½	11 2½	Upton	Sheffield U.	80+9	3
Keith Eddy	5 11	11 10	Barrow	Barrow	127+1	5
				Watford	239+1	26
				Sheffield U.	113+1	16
				(contract cancelled Jan. 1976)		
Stephen Ludlam	5 6	9 11	Chesterfield	Sheffield U.	12	—
Cliff Calvert	5 7	10 6	Wombwell	York C.	62+5	—
				Sheffield U.	14	—
Tony Kenworthy	5 8	10 8	Leeds	Sheffield U.	6	—
Forwards						
Bill Dearden	5 10	10 13	Oldham	Oldham Ath.	29+3	2
				Crewe Alex.	45+3	7
				Chester	85	22
				Sheffield U.	170+5	61
				Chester (on loan)	2	—
Tony Field	5 7	11 0	Halifax	Halifax T.	21	3
				Barrow	36+2	16
				Southport	127+6	41
				Blackburn R.	104+2	46
				Sheffield U.	63+3	13
				(contract cancelled Feb. 1976)		
Alan Woodward	5 8½	11 8½	Sheffield	Sheffield U.	452+2	136
Chris Guthrie	6 1	13 5	Gramlington	Newcastle U.	3	—
				Southend U.	107+1	35
				Sheffield U.	37+2	9
Jimmy Johnstone	5 4	10 0	Viewpark	Celtic	298+10	81
				Sheffield U.	6	1
Keith Edwards	5 7	10 3	Stockton	Sheffield U.	2+1	—
John McGeady	5 6	10 0	Glasgow	Sheffield U.	11	—
Simon Stainrod	5 10	11 1	Sheffield	Sheffield U.	7	2

SHEFFIELD WEDNESDAY   DIV. 3

President: The Rt. Hon. The Lord Netherthorpe, LL.D.

Vice-president: Sir Andrew Stephen, M.B., Ch.B.

Chairman: H. E. McGee.

Vice-Chairman: M. Sheppard, J.P., F.C.A.

Directors: C. Turner, C. Woodward, S. Speight,
R. Whitehead, K. T. Addy.

Manager: Len Ashurst.

Secretary: Eric England.

Year Formed: 1867 (fifth oldest League Club).

Turned Professional: 1887.   *Limited Company:* 1899.

Previous Grounds: 1867, Highfield; 1869, Myrtle Road; 1877, Sheaf House; 1887, Olive
Grove; 1899, Owlerton (since 1912 known as Hillsborough). Some games were played at
Endcliffe in the 1880's. Until 1895 Bramall Lane was used for some games.

Honours: *Football League,* Division 1, Champions: 1902–03, 1903–04, 1928–29, 1929–30,
runners-up: 1960–61. Division 2, Champions: 1899–1900, 1925–26, 1951–52, 1955–56,
1958–59; Runners-up: 1949–50. *F.A. Cup,* Winners: 1896, 1907, 1935; Runners-up: 1890,
1966.   *Football League Cup,* best season: 4th Rd., 1967–68.

European Competitions: *Fairs Cup:* 1961–62.

Record Victory: 12-0 v Halliwell, F.A. Cup, 1st Rd., Jan. 17th, 1891.

Record Defeat: 0-10 v Aston Villa, Division 1, Oct. 5th, 1912.

Most League Points: 62, Division 2, 1958–59.

Most League Goals: 106, Division 2, 1958–59.

Highest League Scorer in Season: Derek Dooley, 46, Division 2, 1951–52.

Most Capped Player: Ron Springett, 33, England.

Most League Appearances: Andy Wilson, 502, 1900–20.

Most League Goals in Total Aggregate: Andy Wilson, 200, 1900–20.

Record Transfer Fee Received: £120,000 from Newcastle U. for Tommy Craig, January 1975.

Record Transfer Fee Paid: £100,000 to Aberdeen for Tommy Craig, May 1969.

Managers Since the War: Secretary/Manager Eric Taylor, Harry Catterick, Vic Buckingham,
Alan Brown, Jack Marshall, Danny Williams, Derek Dooley, Steve Burtenshaw.

Address of Supporters Club: Same as Football Club.

Address of Club Shop or Boutique: Owl Shop, Hillsborough, Sheffield S6 1SW.

Club Restaurant: Adjoining South stand.

Hillsborough, Sheffield, S6 1SW. Telephone Sheffield 343123. (Box Office: Sheffield 343122).
Telegraphic address: 'Wednesday, Sheffield 6'. *Ground capacity:* 55,000. *Record attendance:*
72,841 v Manchester C., F.A. Cup 5th Rd., February 17, 1934. *Record receipts:* £140,300,
Derby Co. v Manchester U., F.A. Cup Semi-final, April 3 1976. (Record for F.A. Cup-tie
other than the Final.) *Pitch measurements:* 115 yds × 75 yds.

How to get there: Buses 42, 53, 81, 2 from the city centre. Sheffield railway station is close to the centre.

Match tickets: Seats can be booked in advance in the South and North Stands. Postal applications to the
Box Office not more than 21 days before the match. Tickets are offered subject to being unsold when the
application is received. Remittance and S.A.E. must be enclosed.

Car parking: Street parking available. Also a park at the training ground in Middlewood Road.

Entertainments/catering facilities: Refreshment bars in all parts of the ground.

Club shop: Two shops in the ground sell all types of souvenirs.

Handbooks/programmes: Handbooks available from the secretary. Programmes available on subscription.

Extra information: When Sheffield Wednesday won the First Division title in 1929–30, they finished 10
points ahead of the runners-up.

Club Colours: Royal blue/white striped shirts, royal blue shorts, white stockings. *Change Colours:* Yellow
shirts with blue trim, blue shorts, yellow socks with blue band. *Club Captain:* Allan Thompson. *First
Team Coach:* Tony Toms. *Club Nickname:* 'Owls'.

SHEFFIELD WEDNESDAY 1975–76 LEAGUE RECORD

Match No.	Date	Venue	Opponents	Result	H/T Score	League Pos'n	Goalscorers	Attendance
1	Aug 16	A	Southend U.	L 1-2	1-0	—	Prendergast	6775
2	23	H	Brighton & H.A.	D 3-3	2-1	17	Prendergast, Joicey, Herbert	10,326
3	30	A	Hereford U.	L 1-3	0-1	22	Henson	7017
4	Sept 6	H	Wrexham	W 1-0	0-0	17	Herbert	7585
5	13	A	Swindon T.	L 1-2	1-0	20	Herbert	6993
6	20	H	Grimsby T.	W 4-0	2-0	16	Prendergast, Herbert, Potts, Gray (og)	11,345
7	24	A	Chesterfield	L 0-1	0-1	—		12,959
8	27	A	Crystal Palace	D 1-1	1-0	16	Potts	14,840
9	Oct 4	A	Peterborough U.	D 2-2	1-1	18	Prendergast, Lee (og)	11,412
10	11	H	Millwall	W 4-1	1-1	12	Potts 2, Henson 2	10,144
11	18	A	Cardiff C.	L 0-2	0-0	18		7930
12	21	A	Chester	L 0-1	0-0	—		6248
13	25	H	Shrewsbury T.	D 1-1	1-0	19	Joicey	12,045
14	Nov 5	H	Gillingham	W 1-0	0-0	—	Joicey	8235
15	8	H	Port Vale	L 0-3	0-1	22		10,880
16	15	A	Aldershot	D 1-1	0-0	21	Henson	5181
17	29	H	Rotherham U.	D 0-0	0-0	21		18,691
18	Dec 2	A	Walsall	D 2-2	1-0	—	Prendergast 2	4148
19	6	A	Colchester U.	L 1-2	0-0	21	Potts	3534
20	20	H	Preston N.E.	D 2-2	0-0	21	Potts, Herbert	8553
21	26	A	Bury	D 0-0	0-0	20		9657
22	27	H	Mansfield T.	D 0-0	0-0	22		15,430
23	Jan 10	H	Hereford U.	L 1-2	1-1	22	Shaw	8155
24	17	A	Grimsby T.	D 1-1	0-0	22	Wylde	7167
25	24	H	Swindon T.	L 0-2	0-1	22		8342
26	31	H	Chester	W 2-0	2-0	19	Nimmo, Prendergast	7558
27	Feb 7	A	Gillingham	D 0-0	0-0	19		8090
28	16	A	Port Vale	L 0-1	0-0	—		5557
29	21	H	Aldershot	W 3-1	2-1	20	Nimmo, Prendergast, Feely	8286
30	Mar 2	A	Halifax T.	D 0-0	0-0	—		5876
31	6	H	Walsall	W 2-1	0-0	18	Henson, Nimmo	9713
32	10	A	Peterborough U.	D 2-2	1-1	—	Nimmo, O'Donnell	8209
33	13	A	Millwall	L 0-1	0-1	21		6769
34	17	H	Cardiff C.	L 1-3	0-0	—	Quinn	8867
35	20	A	Rotherham U.	L 0-1	0-1	22		13,500
36	24	H	Chesterfield	L 1-3	1-2	—	Prendergast	10,653
37	27	H	Colchester U.	W 1-0	0-0	21	Henson	6905
38	30	A	Preston N.E.	L 2-4	0-1	—	Bell, Henson	6899
39	Apr 7	H	Crystal Palace	W 1-0	0-0	—	Prendergast	11,909
40	10	A	Wrexham	L 0-3	0-0	21		4190
41	13	A	Shrewsbury T.	D 0-0	0-0	—		2968
42	17	H	Bury	W 1-0	0-0	21	Nimmo	10,585
43	19	A	Mansfield T.	L 0-3	0-1	—		13,410
44	20	H	Halifax T.	W 1-0	1-0	—	Henson	13,143
45	24	A	Brighton & H.A.	D 1-1	1-0	21	Potts	11,859
46	29	H	Southend U.	W 2-1	2-0	—	Prendergast, Potts	25,802

Goalscorers

League (48): Prendergast 11, Potts 8, Henson 8, Nimmo 5, Herbert 5, Joicey 3, Shaw 1, Wylde 1, Feely 1, O'Donnell 1, Quinn 1, own goals 2.
League Cup (2): Prendergast, Potts.
F.A. Cup (6): Sunley 2, Proudlove, Knighton, Prendergast, Nimmo+.

League Cup	First Round	Darlington (a)	2-0
	Second Leg	(h)	0-2
F.A. Cup	First Round	Macclesfield (h)	3-1
	Second Round	Wigan (h)	2-0
	Third Round	Charlton Ath. (a)	1-2

Fox	Cameron	Quinn	Mullen	Thompson	Harvey	Potts	Henson	Joicey	Prendergast	Brown	Knighton	Ramsbottom	Dowd	McIver	Herbert	Shaw	Proudlove	Sunley	Cusack	O'Donnell	Wylde	Walden	Nimmo	Watling	Feely	Hull	Bell	Match No.
1	2	3	4	5	6	7	8	9	10	11*	12																	1
	2	3	4		8*	7	11	9	10				1	5	6	12												2
	2	3	6		8	7	11		10*		12		1	5	4	9												3
	2	3	4		8	7	6		10	11*	12		1	5	9													4
	2		6		8	7	11		10		12	3	1	5	4*	9												5
	2	3	4		8	7	11		10*				1	5	9	6	12											6
	2	3	4		8	7	10*	9					1	5	11	6	12											7
	2	3	4		8	7	11						1	5	9*	6	12	10										8
		3	4		8	7	11	12	10*				1	5	9	2	6											9
	2*		4		8	7	11		10		12		1	5	6	9	3											10
	2	3			8	7	11		10*		12		1	5	6	9	4											11
	2	3			6	11	12	9					1	4	10*	7	8	5										12
		3	2		8	7	11	9	10				1	4	6			5										13
		3	4	7		11	8*	9				1			12	2		10	5	6								14
		3	4	8		7		9				1			12	2	11	10*	5	6								15
	2		4*	7		10	11					1		12	3	8	9		5	6								16
		3	11	4	7			9	10		8*	1			12	2			5	6								17
		3	7	4		11		9	10		8	1				2			5	6								18
		3	4	8	7	11		9*	10			1			12	2			5	6								19
1		3	7	4		11								9	2	8*	10		5	6	12							20
1		3	7	4		11						12			2	9*	8		5	6	10							21
1		3	7	4		11						12		9	2	8*	10		5	6								22
1		3	7*	4		11		9	12						8				5	6	10	2						23
1		3	4	7			10*								8	11			5	6	9	2	12					24
		3	4	7			10								8	11			5	6	9	2*	12	1				25
1		3	4*	7		10	11								8	2			5	6	12	9						26
1		3	4	7		10	11								8	2			5	6		9						27
1		3	4			11	8	9						7*		2			5	6	12				10			28
1						11									8	3			5	6	7	2	9		10	4		29
1		3	4					9						7		2			5	6	8	11			10			30
1		3	4			11	8	9						7*		2			5	6	12				10			31
1		3	4			7	8	9								2			5	6	11				10			32
1		3	4			7	8*	9								2			5	6	11				10	12		33
1		3	4	7			8	12								2			5	6	9	11*			10			34
1		3	4	2		11		9						7					5	6	8*				10	12		35
1		3	4			7	12	9						8					5	6	2*	10			11			36
1		3			6	7	10	9						4*					5	8	12				2	11		37
1		3	4				8	9	10										5	6*	7				12	2	11	38
1		3	4			11	8	9											5	6	7				12	2	10*	39
1		3	4			11	8												5	6*	7		12		9	2	10	40
1			4		6	11		9							8	3			5	7		10			2			41
1		3	4			11	8	9							6	2			5	7	12		10*					42
1	3*		8	4		11			10					6	12	2			5	7	9							43
1			4		7	11		9								3			5	6	8		2		10			44
1			4		7	10	11									3			5	6	8		2		9			45
1			4			11	8		10							3			5	6	7		2		9			46
27	8	36	41	21	15	42	29	13	32	2	5	18	12	13	10	37	10	8	37	29	18	8	13	1	10	6	5	
							+2s	+1s	+2s	+1s	+5s		+1s	+1s	+5s		+5s				+3s		+6s		+2s	+2s		

SHEFFIELD WEDNESDAY—PLAYERS

Player and position	Ht.	Wt.	Birthplace	Clubs	League Appearances	Goals
Goalkeepers						
Barry Watling	5 9	11 12	Walthamstow	Orient	—	—
				Bristol C.	2	—
				Notts Co.	65+1	—
				Hartlepool	139	—
				Chester (on loan)	5	—
				Crewe A. (on loan)	—	—
				Rotherham U. (on loan)	5	—
				Sheffield W.	1	—
				(contract cancelled April 1976)		—
Neil Ramsbottom	6 0	12 0	Blackburn	Bury	174	—
				Blackpool	12	—
				Crewe A. (on loan)	3	—
				Coventry C.	51	—
				Sheffield W.	18	—
Peter Fox	5 11	11 8	Scunthorpe	Sheffield W.	48	—
Defenders						
Richard Walden	5 11	12 9	Hereford	Aldershot	401+4	16
				Sheffield W.	8	—
*Bernard Shaw	5 6½	10 12½	Sheffield	Sheffield U.	135+1	2
				Wolverhampton W.	113+3	2
				Sheffield W.	100+4	3
*Jim Quinn	5 9	11 0	Kilsyth	Celtic	21+1	—
				Sheffield W.	46	1
*Alan Thompson	5 10	11 9	Liverpool	Sheffield W.	150+6	3
Neil O'Donnell	5 10	10 8	Glasgow	Norwich C.	31+19	2
				Gillingham	18+6	—
				Sheffield W.	29	1
David Cusack	6 0	12 1	Rotherham	Sheffield W.	37	—
James Mullen	5 9½	9 6	Jarrow	Sheffield W.	106+6	3
Hugh Dowd (N. Ireland)	6 0	13 0	Lurgan	Sheffield W.	39+2	—
Midfield						
*Colin Harvey (England)	5 7½	11 0	Liverpool	Everton	317+4	18
				Sheffield W.	45	2
Ken Knighton	5 9	11 5	Barnsley	Wolverhampton W.	13+3	—
				Oldham Ath.	45	5
				Preston N.E.	62	3
				Blackburn R.	70	11
				Hull C.	79+1	9
				Sheffield W.	71+5	2
				(contract cancelled Jan. 76)		
*Fred McIver	5 7	11 0	Newcastle	Sunderland	1	—
				Sheffield W.	34+3	—
Gary Hull	5 9	11 2	Sheffield	Sheffield W.	6+2	—
Philip Henson	5 10	9 12	Manchester	Manchester C.	12+5	—
				Swansea C. (on loan)	1	—
				Sheffield W.	43+2	8
*David Herbert	5 10	11 0	Sheffield	Sheffield W.	12+6	5
Eric Potts	5 5	10 2	Liverpool	Sheffield W.	131+9	19
Forwards						
Peter Feely	6 0	12 0	London	Chelsea	4+1	2
				Bournemouth	8+1	2
				Fulham	—	—
				Gillingham	41	22
				Sheffield W.	10+2	1
*Brian Joicey	5 11½	12 2	Winlaton	Coventry C.	31+8	9
				Sheffield W.	144+1	48
Mike Prendergast	5 7	12 4	Denaby Main	Sheffield W.	155+7	49
Roger Wylde	5 11	11 0	Sheffield	Sheffield W.	27+9	2
				Burnley (on loan)	—	—
*Bobby Brown	5 7	11 4	Plymouth	Chelsea	—	—
				Sheffield W.	17+5	3
				Aldershot (on loan)	3+2	—
*Ronnie Ferguson	6 0	12 5	Accrington	Sheffield W.	15+1	1
				Scunthorpe U. (on loan)	3	—
				Darlington (on loan)	10+1	2
Ian Nimmo	5 9	11 3	Boston	Sheffield W.	13+6	5

SHREWSBURY TOWN DIV. 3

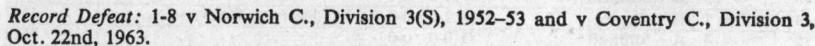

President: Sydney Yates. *Chairman:* H. S. Yates.

Directors: L. Tudor-Owen, A. C. Williams, F. C. G. Fry, K. R. Woodhouse.

Manager: Alan Durban. *Secretary:* M. J. Starkey.

Year Formed: 1886. *Turned Professional:* 1905 (approx.).
Limited Company: 1936.

Previous Ground: Old Shrewsbury Racecourse.

Honours: *Football League,* best season in Division 3: 3rd, 1959–60, 1967–68. Runners-up Division 4, 1974–75.
F.A. Cup, best season; 5th Rd., 1965 and 1966.
Football League Cup, best season, semi-finalists: 1961.

Record Victory: 7-0 v Swindon T., Division 3(S), 1954–55.

Record Defeat: 1-8 v Norwich C., Division 3(S), 1952–53 and v Coventry C., Division 3, Oct. 22nd, 1963.

Most League Points: 62, Division 4, 1974–75.

Most League Goals: 101, Division 4, 1958–59.

Highest League Scorer in Season: Arthur Rowley, 38, Division 4, 1958–59.

Most League Goals in Total Aggregate: Arthur Rowley, 152, 1958–65. (While with Shrewsbury T., Arthur Rowley completed his League scoring record of 434 goals.)

Most Capped Player: Jimmy McLaughlin, 5 (12) Ireland.

Most League Appearances: Joe Wallace, 329, 1954–63.

Record Transfer Fee Received: £90,000 from Manchester U. for Jim Holton, Jan. 1973.

Record Transfer Fee Paid: £30,000 to Chester for Graham Turner, Jan. 1973.

Managers Since the War: Sam Crooks, Walter Rowley, Harry Potts, John Spuhler, Arthur Rowley, Harry Gregg, Maurice Evans.

Address of Supporters Club and Shop: c/o Football Club.

Gay Meadow, Shrewsbury. Telephone Shrewsbury 56068. *Ground capacity:* 20,050. *Record attendance:* 18,917 v Walsall, Division 3, April 26, 1961. *Record receipts:* £4,962 v Arsenal, F.A. Cup January 27, 1968. *Pitch measurements:* 116 yds × 76 yds.

How to get there: Midland Red schedule bus services from main bus station in Barker Street to the ground. Special coach facilities are arranged by local companies from neighbouring districts. Shrewsbury railway station is 10 minutes walk from the ground.

Car parking: A park adjacent to the ground and a free public car park five minutes walk away.

Entertainments/catering facilities: Buffets are situated on each side of the ground.

Club shop: Sells all types of souvenirs.

Handbooks/programmes: No handbook. Programmes can be obtained through the post at 10p each plus S.A.E.

Extra information: In 1960–61 Shrewsbury met Swindon Town six times in League, F.A. Cup, and League Cup and did not lose once.

Club Colours: Blue with amber trim.
Change Colours: Amber with blue trim.
Club Nickname: 'Town'.

SHREWSBURY TOWN 1975–76 LEAGUE RECORD

Match No.	Date	Venue	Opponents	Result	H/T Score	League Pos'n	Goalscorers	Attendance
1	Aug 16	A	Mansfield T.	W 2-1	1-0	—	Bates, Haywood	6951
2	23	H	Peterborough U.	W 3-1	1-0	2	Bradley (og), Collier (pen) Durban	4473
3	30	A	Grimsby T.	L 2-3	0-2	6	Haywood 2	4709
4	Sept 6	H	Swindon T.	W 3-0	1-0	2	Collier 2 (2 pens), Haywood	4062
5	13	A	Halifax T.	D 0-0	0-0	3		2501
6	20	H	Crystal Palace	L 2-4	0-3	9	Collier (pen), Kearney	7480
7	22	A	Walsall	L 0-2	0-2	—		4866
8	27	A	Southend U.	W 3-1	1-0	10	Durban 2, Duffey	2922
9	Oct 4	A	Brighton & H.A.	L 1-2	0-2	11	Kearney	4198
10	11	A	Chesterfield	L 1-2	1-0	13	Kearney	4060
11	18	H	Gillingham	W 1-0	1-0	12	Durban	3242
12	21	H	Port Vale	W 1-0	0-0	—	Irvine	4673
13	25	A	Sheffield W.	D 1-1	0-1	7	Tarbuck	12,045
14	Nov 1	H	Chester	W 2-0	0-0	6	Kearney, Haywood	4567
15	4	A	Millwall	D 0-0	0-0	—		7528
16	8	A	Colchester	D 1-1	1-0	7	Bates	3088
17	15	H	Rotherham U.	L 0-2	0-0	7		3775
18	29	A	Cardiff C.	L 0-3	0-1	10		8002
19	Dec 6	A	Aldershot	W 5-3	3-1	8	Kearney, Durban 2, Atkens, Bates	3061
20	20	H	Bury	L 1-3	1-0	10	McGregor	3735
21	27	H	Hereford U.	W 2-1	2-0	11	Durban 2	9488
22	Jan 10	H	Grimsby T.	W 1-0	0-0	10	McGregor	3344
23	17	A	Crystal Palace	D 1-1	0-0	12	Durban	16,531
24	24	H	Halifax T.	W 2-0	2-0	8	Bates, Irvine	3398
25	31	H	Port Vale	D 0-0	0-0	10		3835
26	Feb 3	A	Preston N.E.	W 2-0	0-0	—	Irvine, Durban	4995
27	7	H	Millwall	W 1-0	0-0	6	Bates	4453
28	9	A	Wrexham	W 3-2	2-1	—	Irvine, Kearney, Atkins	5356
29	14	A	Colchester U.	W 1-0	0-0	3	Kearney	4486
30	21	A	Rotherham U.	W 1-0	1-0	2	Stancliffe (og)	4947
31	24	H	Walsall	D 1-1	1-0	—	Bates	9085
32	Mar 6	A	Chester	L 0-1	0-1	4		5916
33	10	A	Brighton & H.A.	D 2-2	2-0	—	Haywood, Burnett (og)	21,423
34	13	H	Chesterfield	L 0-2	0-1	7		4967
35	16	A	Gillingham	L 1-2	0-0	—	Irvine	5139
36	20	H	Cardiff C.	W 3-1	0-0	7	Atkins (pen), Irvine, McGregor	7573
37	27	A	Aldershot	D 1-1	1-1	7	Kearney	3883
38	30	A	Bury	L 1-2	1-0	—	Atkins	4626
39	Apr 2	H	Mansfield T.	L 1-2	1-0	8	Bates	4580
40	6	H	Southend U.	W 3-1	2-0	—	Turner, Kearney 2 (1 a pen)	2493
41	10	A	Swindon T.	L 0-3	0-1	8		5869
42	13	H	Sheffield W.	D 0-0	0-0	—		2968
43	17	H	Preston N.E.	W 1-0	1-0	8	King	3547
44	19	A	Hereford U.	L 1-3	0-0	—	Kearney	12,314
45	21	H	Wrexham	L 1-2	1-2	—	Kearney	3097
46	24	A	Peterborough U.	L 2-3	1-3	9	Griffin, Kearney	5023

Goal scorers

League (61): Kearney 13 (1 a pen), Durban 10, Bates 7, Haywood 6, Irvine 6, Atkins 4 (1 a pen), Collier 4 (4 pens), McGregor 3, Tarbuck 1, Duffey 1, Turner 1, King 1, Griffin 1, own goals 3.
League Cup (3): Tarbuck, Duffey (pen), Bates.
F.A. Cup (5): Bates 3, Durban, Kearney.

League Cup	First Round	Walsall (a)	0-0
	Second Leg	(h)	2-1
	Second Round	Q.P.R. (h)	1-4
F.A. Cup	First Round	Rossendale (a)	1-0
	Second Round	Chester (h)	3-1
	Third Round	Bradford C. (h)	1-2

Mulhearn	King	Gregory	Durban	Turner	Kearney	O'Loughlin	McGregor	Haywood	Bates	Tarbuck	Collier	Irvine	Duffey	Lawrence	Roberts, Ian	Atkins	Leonard	Griffin	Moore	Hayes	Dolby	Roberts, Lee	Match No.
1	2	3	4	5	6	7	8	9	10	11													1
1		3	4	6	5	12	11*	9	8	10	2	7											2
1	2	3	4	6	5		8*	9	11	10		7	12										3
1		3	4	5	6		8	9*	11	10	2	7	12										4
1		3	4	6	5	7	9*	10	11		2		12			8							5
1		3	4	6	5	11*	8	9	10		2	7	12										6
1		3	4	6	5	7	9	10			2					8*	11		12				7
1			4	6	5	12	9	10	11		2	7*			3	8							8
1	2		4	6	5		9	10	11			7			3	8*	12						9
1			4	6	5		9	10	11		2	7			3	8*	12						10
1			4	6	5		9	10	11		2	7			3	8							11
1			4	6	5	12	9	10	11*		2	7			3	8							12
1			4	6	5	12	9	10	11		2	7			3	8*							13
1			4	6	5		9	10	11		2	7			3	8							14
1			4	6	5		9	10	11		2	7			3	8							15
1	8		4	6	5		9	10	11		2	7			3								16
1			4	5	6	8	9	10	11		2*	7	12		3								17
1			4	5	6	8	9	10	11		2*	7			3		12						18
1	2		4	6	5	11	9	10	12			7			3	8*							19
1	2		4	6	5	11	9	10	12			7			3*	8							20
1	2	3	4	6	5	11*	9	10	12			7				8							21
1	2			6		11	9	10	12	4					3	8		5	7*				22
1	2		4	5		11	9*	10	12			7			3	8	6						23
1	2		4	6		9	11		10			7			8	3		5					24
1	2		4	6		9	11		10			7			8	3		5					25
1	2		4	6		9*	11		10	12		7			8	3		5					26
1	2		4	6		9	11*		10	12		7			8	3		5					27
1	2		4	6		9	11*	12	10			7			8	3		5					28
1	2			6		9	11		10	4		7			8	3		5					29
1	2	4*		6		9	11		10			7			8	3		5	12				30
1	2		4	6		9	11*	12	10			7			8	3		5					31
1	2		4	5		9	11		10	12		7			8	3*		6					32
1	2		4	6		11*	9		10			7			8	3		5					33
1	2		4	6		11	9		10	12		7			8	3*		5					34
1	2		4	6			9*	10	12			7	11		8	3		5					35
1	2		4	6		11	9		10			7			3	8		5					36
1	3		4	6		9		10	11		2	7				8		5					37
1	2	10	9		6	8						7	12		3*	11			5	4			38
1	2		4		6	8	12	11	9*	10		7			3			5					39
1	2	4*		8		9	11		10			7			3			5	12	6			40
1	2			9		8	12		10	11	3	7						5	4*	6			41
1	2			9	4	11*		10				7			8	3		5		6		12	42
1	2	12		9	7	11*		10			4				8	3		5		6			43
1	2		4	6		9	11		10			7			8*	3		5	12				44
1	2		4	8		9	11*				7		10		12	3		5		6			45
1	2		4	10		9			12			7			8	3		5		6		11*	46
46	31	10	41	43	40	9	28	28	43	19	16	41	4	3	23	29	17	25	3	6	—	1	
	+1s				+3s	+3s	+2s		+12s				+4s	+2s		+3s	+1s		+2s	+1s	+1s	+1s	

SHREWSBURY TOWN—PLAYERS

Player and position	Ht.	Wt.	Birthplace	Clubs	League Appearances	Goals
Goalkeepers						
Ken Mulhearn	6 0	13 11	Liverpool	Everton	—	—
				Stockport Co.	100	—
				Manchester C.	50	—
				Shrewsbury T.	237	—
Robert Wardle	5 11	11 2	Leeds	Bristol C.	—	—
				Shrewsbury T.	—	—
Defenders						
*Tony Gregory	5 11	11 12	Dawley	Shrewsbury T.	285+5	—
Colin Griffin	6 0	11 7	Dudley	Derby Co.	—	—
				Shrewsbury T.	25	1
John King	5 10	11 0	Glasgow	Shrewsbury T.	105+1	1
Graham Turner	5 10	11 13	Ellesmere Port	Wrexham	77	—
				Chester	215+3	5
				Shrewsbury T.	146+2	1
Ian Atkins	5 10	11 0	Birmingham	Shrewsbury T.	29+3	4
Stephen Hickenbottom	6 1	12 7	Walsall	Shrewsbury T.	—	—
*Ian Roberts	5 10	10 8	Glasgow	Shrewsbury T.	93+3	—
David Collier	5 7	11 3	Bangor, Wales	Shrewsbury T.	17	4
Carleton Leonard	5 9	10 3	Oswestry	Shrewsbury T.	17+1	—
Midfield						
*Peter Dolby	6 1	11 2	Derby	Shrewbury T.	304+22	17
				Crewe Alex. (on loan)	—	—
Alan Durban (Wales)	5 9	10 8	Port Talbot	Cardiff C.	52	9
				Derby Co.	336+10	91
				Shrewsbury T.	119+2	30
Michael Kearney	5 11	13 5	Glasgow	Shrewsbury T.	116+6	29
Steve Hayes	5 10	11 6	Smethwick	Shrewsbury T.	32+3	4
				Torquay U. (on loan)	1	—
Forwards						
Chic Bates	6 0	11 2	West Bromwich	Shrewsbury T.	89	24
Ray Haywood	6 0	11 0	Dudley	Shrewsbury T.	74+2	27
Sam Irvine	5 6	9 12	Glasgow	Shrewsbury T.	118+8	8
*Alan Tarbuck	5 6	10 0	Liverpool	Crewe Alex.	79+5	18
				Chester	69	22
				Preston N.E.	42+6	17
				Shrewsbury T.	107+17	17
*Nigel O'Loughlin	5 8½	10 10	Denbigh	Shrewsbury T.	23+10	7
Lee Roberts	6 0	11 2	Wolverhampton	Shrewsbury T.	4+5	—
*Alexander McGregor	5 10	10 8	Glasgow	Hibernian	—	—
				Shrewsbury T.	46+3	7
Leslie Lawrence	6 3	12 3	Rowley Regis	Shrewsbury T.	3+2	—
Chris Duffey	5 8	9 10	Kirby	Bolton W.	8	—
				Crewe A.	60+3	12
				Bury	17+4	8
				Shrewsbury T.	4+4	1
				Rochdale (on loan)	2	—
				(Contract cancelled Febuary 1976)		
Kevin Moore	5 7	9 8	Loughborough	Shrewsbury T.	3+3	—

SOUTHAMPTON DIV. 2

President: H. G. Blagrave. *Chairman:* G. Reader.

Directors: E. C. Chaplin, J. Corbett, Lt.-Col. Sir George Meyrick (Bart), M.C., T.D., B. G. W. Bowyer, J.P., F. G. L. Askham, F.C.A., A. A. Woodford.

Chief Executive: Ted Bates. *Manager:* Lawrie McMenemy.

Secretary: K. F. Honey.

Year Formed: 1885.

Turned Professional: 1894. *Limited Company:* 1897.

Previous Name: Southampton St. Mary's until 1885.

Previous Grounds: 1885, Antelope Ground; 1897, County Cricket Ground; 1898, The Dell.

S•F•C

Honours: Football League, best season in Division 1; 7th, 1968–69, 1970–71. Division 2, Runners-up: 1965–66 Division 3(S), Champions: 1921–22, Runners-up, 1920–21. Division 3, Champions: 1959–60. *F.A. Cup,* Winners 1975–76; Runners-up: 1900, 1902. *Football League Cup,* best season: 5th Rd., 1960–61, 1968–69.

European Competitions: *European Fairs Cup:* 1969–70. *UEFA Cup:* 1971–72.

Record Victory: 11-0 v Northampton, Southern League, Dec. 28th, 1901.

Record Defeat: 0-8 v Tottenham H., Division 2, Mar. 28th, 1936, and v Everton, Division 1 Nov. 20 1971.

Most League Points: 61, Division 3(S), 1921–22, and Division 3, 1959–60.

Most League Goals: 112, Div 3(S), 1957–58.

Highest League Scorer in Season: Derek Reeves, 39, Division 3, 1959–60.

Most Capped Player: Mike Channon, 35, England.

Most League Appearances: Terry Paine, 713, 1956–74.

Most League Goals in Total Aggregate: Terry Paine, 160, 1956–74.

Record Transfer Fee Received: £125,000 from Tottenham H. for Martin Chivers, Jan. 1968.

Record Transfer Fee Paid: £275,000 to Chelsea for Peter Osgood, March 1974.

Managers Since the War: Bill Dodgin (Snr.), Sid Cann, George Roughton, Ted Bates.

Address of Supporters Club: Same as Football Club.

The Dell, Milton Road, Southampton SO9 4XX. Telephone Southampton 23408. *Ground capacity:* 31,000. *Record attendance:* 31,044 v Manchester U., Division 1, October 8, 1969. *Record receipts:* £21,997 v W.B.A. F.A. Cup 4th Rd. Replay February 17, 1976. *Pitch measurements:* 110 yds × 72 yds.

How to get there: The ground is 10 minutes walk from Southampton Central station via Hill Lane. Buses 2 and 5 from the city centre pass the ground, which is only 10 minutes walk from the centre.

Match tickets: No seats available, all seats being sold to season-ticket holders. Room on the terraces for 24,000 standing, and admission is through the turnstiles on the day of the match.

Car parking: Only street parking in the vicinity of the ground. Municipal car parks in the city centre.

Entertainments/catering facilities: Licensed bars inside the ground.

Club shop: Situated in the private car park alongside the ground.

Handbooks/programmes: Handbooks not published annually. Programmes available on subscription.

Extra information: In 1921–22, Southampton lost only four league games and conceded only 21 goals, both Division Three (South) records.

Club Colours: Red and white striped shirts, black shorts, red and white stockings.

Change Colours: Gold shirts, blue shorts, gold stockings.

Club Captain: Peter Rodrigues. *Physiotherapist:* Don Taylor, M.C.S.P., S.R.P.

First Team Trainer: Jim Clunie *Club Nickname:* 'Saints'.

SOUTHAMPTON 1975-76 LEAGUE RECORD

Match No.	Date	Venue	Opponents	Result	H/T Score	League Pos'n	Goalscorers	Attendance
1	Aug 16	H	W.B.A.	W 3-0	2-0	—	Holmes, Channon 2	14,246
2	23	A	Notts Co.	D 0-0	0-0	9		8495
3	26	H	Bristol C.	W 3-1	2-0	—	Stokes 2, Peach	16,833
4	29	H	Plymouth Arg.	W 1-0	1-0	—	Channon	18,000
5	Sept 6	A	Bolton W.	L 0-3	0-1	3		9188
6	13	H	Blackburn R.	W 2-1	2-0	2	Stokes, Peach	13,279
7	20	A	Blackpool	L 3-4	1-4	5	Rodrigues, Steele, Holmes	9564
8	27	H	Portsmouth	W 4-0	1-0	5	Channon 3, Peach	17,310
9	Oct 4	A	Hull C.	D 0-0	0-0	6		6342
10	11	H	Chelsea	W 4-1	1-0	6	Channon 2 (1 a pen), Stokes, Holmes	21,227
11	18	A	Nottingham F.	L 1-3	0-2	6	Osgood	12,677
12	21	A	Oldham Ath.	L 2-3	0-3	—	Holmes 2	11,219
13	25	H	York C.	W 2-0	1-0	7	Channon (pen), McCalliog	13,501
14	31	A	Charlton Ath.	L 1-4	0-1	7	Osgood	16,036
15	Nov 8	H	Luton T.	W 3-1	2-0	7	McCalliog, Stokes, Channon	13,885
16	15	A	Orient	L 1-2	1-0	9	McCalliog	6332
17	22	H	Nottingham F.	L 0-3	0-0	11		14,245
18	29	A	Carlisle U.	L 0-1	0-0	12		6977
19	Dec 6	H	Sunderland	W 4-0	0-0	11	Osgood 2, Holmes, Blyth	17,598
20	13	H	Notts Co.	W 2-1	1-1	9	McCalliog (pen), Holmes	12,571
21	19	A	W.B.A.	W 2-0	1-0	6	Peach, Blyth	17,071
22	26	H	Bristol R.	W 3-0	1-0	4	Holmes, Stokes, Channon	19,556
23	27	A	Oxford U.	W 2-1	1-1	4	Stokes, Holmes	12,004
24	Jan 17	H	Bolton W.	D 0-0	0-0	7		20,363
25	28	A	Blackburn R.	D 1-1	1-1	—	Osgood	8786
26	31	H	Oldham Ath.	W 3-2	1-2	5	Osgood, Stokes, Channon	14,297
27	Feb 7	A	Bristol C.	D 1-1	0-1	6	Holmes	23,216
28	21	H	Orient	W 3-0	1-0	5	McCalliog 2 (1 a pen), Stokes	17,230
29	24	H	Fulham	W 2-1	1-1	—	Blyth, Channon	23575
30	28	A	York C.	L 1-2	1-1	5	Channon	3777
31	Mar 2	A	Luton T.	L 0-1	0-0	—		13,737
32	9	A	Fulham	L 0-1	0-1	—		8731
33	13	A	Chelsea	D 1-1	0-0	7	Channon	29,011
34	20	H	Carlisle U.	D 1-1	0-0	5	Peach	18,304
35	27	A	Sunderland	L 0-3	0-1	7		34,946
36	Apr 6	A	Portsmouth	W 1-0	0-0	—	Channon	24,115
37	10	H	Blackpool	W 3-1	2-0	5	Holmes, Channon, Peach (pen)	21,758
38	12	H	Charlton Ath.	W 3-2	2-0	—	Channon 2, McCalliog	23,686
39	16	A	Plymouth Arg.	L 0-1	0-0	5		25,305
40	17	A	Bristol R.	L 0-2	0-2	5		11,834
41	19	H	Oxford U.	W 2-1	1-1	—	Clarke, C. (og), Rodrigues	18,870
42	24	H	Hull C.	W 1-0	1-0	6	Stoke.	18,272

Goalscorers

League (66): Channon 19 (2 pens), Holmes 11, Stokes 10, McCalliog 7 (2 pens), Osgood 6, Peach 6 (1 a pen), Blyth 3, Rodrigues 2, Steele 1, Own Goal 1.

F.A. Cup (15): Channon 5 (1 a pen), McCalliog 3, Stokes 3, Gilchrist 2, Peach (1 a pen), Fisher.

League Cup	Second Round	Bristol R. (h)	0-1
F.A. Cup	Third Round	Aston Villa (h)	1-1
		(a)	2-1 (a.e.t.)
	Fourth Round	Blackpool (h)	3-1
	Fifth Round	W.B.A. (a)	1-1
		(h)	4-0
	Sixth Round	Bradford C. (a)	1-0
	Semi-Final	C. Palace	2-0 (at Stamford Bridge)
	Final	Manchester U.	1-0

Middleton	Rodrigues	Steele	Holmes	Bennett	Blyth	O'Brien	Channon	Stokes	Peach	McCalliog	Osgood	Fisher	Gilchrist	Waldron	Crabb	Andruszewski	Turner	Earles	Williams	Mills	Match No.
1	2	3	4	5	6	7	8	9	10	11											1
1	2	3	4	5	6	7	8	9	11	10											2
1	2	3	4	5	6	7	8	9	11	10											3
1	2	3	4	5	6	7*	8	9	11	10	12										4
1	2	3	4	5	6	7	8		11*	10	9	12									5
1	2	3	4	5	6	11	8	7	10		9										6
1	2	3	4	5	6	11*	8	7	10		9	12									7
1	2		4	5	6		8	11	3	10	9	7									8
1	2		4	5	6		8	11	3	10	9	7									9
1	2		4	5	6		8	11	3	10	9	7									10
1	2		4	5	6		8	11	3	10	9	7*	12								11
1	2	3*	4	5			8		11	10	9	7	6	12							12
1	2		4	5	6		8	9	10	11	12	7	3*								13
1	2		4	5	6		8	11	3	10	9	7									14
1	2*	3	4		6	12	8	7	10	11	9					5					15
1	2	3	4	5			8	7	10	11	9					6					16
1	2	3	4	5		12	8	7	10*	11	9					6					17
	2	5	4				8	12	3	10	9	7	11			6*	1				18
	2	6	4		5		8		3	10	9	7	11				1				19
	2	6	4		5		8		3	10	9	7	11				1				20
	2	6*	4		5		8	9	3	10		7	11	12			1				21
	2	6	4		5		8	9	3	10	12	7*	11				1				22
	2	6	4		5		8	9	3	10		7	11				1				23
	2	6	4		5		8	11	3	10	9	7					1				24
	2	6	4		5		8	11	3	10	9	7					1				25
	2	6	4		5		8	11	3	10	9	7					1				26
	2	6	4		5		8	11	3	10	9	7					1				27
	2	6	4		5		8	11	3	10	7	9					1				28
	2	6	4		5		8	11	3	10	12	7	9*				1				29
	2	6	4		5		8	11	3	10	7	9					1				30
	2	4	6		5		8	11	3	10	9	7					1				31
	2		6		5		8	11	3	10	9	7	4				1				32
	2	6			5		8	11	3	10	9	7	4				1				33
	2	6			5		8	11*	3	10	9	7	4				1		12		34
	2*	6	4		5		8	11	3	10	7	9					1		12		35
	2	4	6		5		8	11	3			7					1	9	10		36
	2*	6	4		5		8	11	3	10	9	7					1		12		37
		6	4		5		8	11	3	10	9	7				2	1				38
	2	6	4		5		8	11	3	10	9						1				39
	2	10			5		8	11	3		9	4*	7			6	1		12		40
	2	6	4		5		8	11	3		9	7*	10				1		12		41
	2	6	4		5		8	11		10	9	7					1			3	42
17	41	32	39	20	37	7	42	37	41	37	29	27	20	2	—	6	25	1	1	1	
						+2s		+1s			+4s	+2s	+1s			+2s			+5s		

SOUTHAMPTON—PLAYERS

Player and position	Ht.	Wt.	Birthplace	Clubs	League Appearances	Goals
Goalkeepers						
Ian Turner	6 0	12 5	Middlesbrough	Huddersfield T.	—	—
				Grimsby T.	26	—
				Walsall (on loan)	3	—
				Southampton	61	—
Steve Middleton	6 0	12 7	Portsmouth	Southampton	20	—
				Torquay U. (on loan)	10	—
Defenders						
Mel Blyth	6 1	11 11	Norwich	Scunthorpe U.	27	3
				C. Palace	213+3	9
				Southampton	71+1	4
Steve Mills	5 7	10 2	Portsmouth	Southampton	55+4	—
Peter Rodrigues (Wales)	5 9	11 1	Cardiff	Cardiff C.	85	2
				Leicester C.	138	6
				Sheffield W.	162	2
				Southampton	41	2
Paul Bennett	6 0	12 6	Southampton	Southampton	116	1
David Peach	5 9	11 6	Bedford	Gillingham	186+1	30
				Southampton	89+3	12
Jim Steele	6 0	12 2	Edinburgh	Dundee	73+3	4
				Southampton	147+1	2
Malcolm Waldron	5 9	10 12	Emsworth	Southampton	4+1	—
Manny Andruszewski	5 10	10 9	Eastleigh	Southampton	22	—
Michael Berry	5 8	10 8	Newbury	Southampton	2	—
Midfield						
Nicholas Holmes	5 11	11 7	Southampton	Southampton	60+5	13
Hugh Fisher	5 8½	10 3	Glasgow	Blackpool	51+3	1
				Southampton	284+5	7
Jim McCalliog (Scotland)	5 9	10 5	Glasgow	Chelsea	7	2
				Sheffield W.	150	19
				Wolverhampton W.	158+5	34
				Manchester U.	31	7
				Southampton	50+1	7
Paul Gilchrist	5 11	12 5	Dartford	Charlton Ath.	5+2	—
				Fulham (on loan)	—	—
				Doncaster R.	22	8
				Southampton	94+11	17
Forwards						
Mick Channon (England)	6 0½	11 6	Orcheston	Southampton	348+4	138
Peter Osgood (England)	6 1½	12 6	Windsor	Chelsea	267+3	103
				Southampton	79+4	20
Bobby Stokes	5 7	10 2	Portsmouth	Southampton	186+21	39
Stephen Crabbe	5 7	10 6	Weymouth	Southampton	8+3	—
Patrick Earles	5 7½	10 10	Titchfield	Southampton	1+6	—
Steve Williams	5 10	11 8	London	Southampton	1	—

SOUTHEND UNITED   DIV. 4

President: N. L. Mitchell. *Chairman:* W. W. Rubin.
Vice-chairman: F. H. Walton.
Directors: J. N. Woodcock, L. H. Lesser, F.C.A., D. A.
Smith, G. C. Janes.
Manager: David Smith. *Secretary:* K. Holmes.
Commercial Manager: Harold Rumsey.
Year Formed: 1906. *Turned Professional:* 1906.
Limited Company: 1919.
Previous Grounds: 1906, Roots Hall, Prittlewell; 1920,
Kursaal; 1934, Southend Stadium; 1955, Roots Hall
Football Ground.
Honours: *Football League,* best season in Division 3(S):
3rd. 1931–32, 1949–50. *F.A. Cup,* best season: old
3rd Rd., 1920–21, 5th Rd., 1925–26, 1951–52, 1975–76.
Football League Cup: best season: never past 3rd Rd.

Record Victory: 10-1 v Golders Green, F.A. Cup, 1st
Rd., Nov. 24th, 1934, 10-1 v Brentwood, F.A. Cup 2nd Rd., Dec. 7th, 1968.

Record Defeat: 1-11 v Northampton, Southern League, Dec. 30th, 1909.

Most League Points: 60, Division 4, 1971-72.

Most League Goals: 92, Division 3(S), 1950–51.

Highest League Scorer in Season: Jim Shankly, 31, 1928–29 and Sammy McCrory 1957–58,
both of Division 3(S).

Most League Goals in Total Aggregate: Roy Hollis, 122, 1953–60.

Most Capped Player: George Mackenzie, 9, Eire.

Most League Appearances: Sandy Anderson, 451, 1950–63.

Record Transfer Fee Received: £120,000 from C. Palace for Peter Taylor, Oct. 1973.

Record Transfer Fee Paid: £25,000 to C. Palace for Tony Taylor, August 1974.

Managers Since the War: Harry Warren, Eddie Perry, Frank Broome, Ted Fenton, Alvan
Williams, Ernie Shepherd, Geoff Hudson, Arthur Rowley.

Address of Supporters Club: 374 Victoria Ave., Southend-on-Sea, Essex.

Address of Club Shop or Boutique: 374 Victoria Avenue, Southend-on-Sea.

Roots Hall Football Ground, Victoria Avenue, Southend-on-Sea. Telephone Southend 40707.
Ground capacity: 35,000 (16,000 covered). *Record attendance:* 28,059 v Birmingham C., F.A.
Cup 4th Rd., January 26, 1957. *Record receipts:* £10,038 v Chelsea, F.L. Cup,
September 6, 1972. *Pitch measurements:* 110 yds × 74 yds.

How to get there: Regular buses from Southend Central station in the High Street; the station is on the
London line from Fenchurch Street. Southend Victoria, five minutes walk from the ground, is served by
trains from Liverpool Street, London.

Match tickets: Seats can be purchased 14 days before the match.

Car parking: Two car parks at the ground hold approximately 700 cars. Ample parking in side-streets.

Entertainments/catering facilities: Tea bars all around the ground. There is a social club for members and
bona fide visitors.

Club shop: Situated in Victoria Avenue opposite the ground; sells all types of souvenirs.

Handbooks/programmes: Both handbooks and programmes are available from the club shop; programmes
are available on subscription.

Extra information: In 1921–22 full-back Jimmy Evans topped Southend's scorers' list with 10 penalties.

Club Colours: Royal blue shirts, blue shorts, with white stripes, red stockings.
Change Colours: White shirts with blue trim, white shorts, white stockings.
Club Captain: Neil Townsend.
Club Trainer/Coach: Jack Burkett.
Club Nickname: 'The Shrimpers'.

SOUTHEND UNITED 1975-76 LEAGUE RECORD

Match No.	Date	Venue	Opponents	Result	H/T Score	League Pos'n	Goalscorers	Attendance
1	Aug 16	H	Sheffield W.	W 2-1	0-1	—	Parker, Moody	6775
2	23	A	Chester	D 1-1	0-1	7	Silvester	4781
3	30	H	Rotherham U.	L 1-2	0-0	14	Brace	4219
4	Sept 6	A	Walsall	W 3-2	2-1	9	Silvester 3	4380
5	13	H	Port Vale	D 3-3	3-0	10	Parker, Silvester 2	4455
6	20	A	Millwall	L 1-2	0-2	14	Little	6418
7	22	H	Preston N.E.	L 0-2	0-1	—		4583
8	27	H	Shrewsbury T.	L 1-3	0-1	18	Moody (pen)	2922
9	Oct 4	A	Aldershot	L 1-2	1-0	20	Silvester	3579
10	11	A	Bury	L 0-1	0-0	24		6268
11	17	H	Mansfield T.	D 2-2	1-2	24	Silvester, Foggo	3248
12	20	H	Halifax T.	W 4-1	2-1	—	Nicholl, Parker, Moody (pen), Little	3089
13	25	A	Crystal Palace	D 1-1	0-1	20	Foggo	18,438
14	31	H	Swindon T.	W 3-0	2-0	18	Nicholl, Parker, Brace	4256
15	Nov 8	A	Brighton & H.A.	L 0-2	0-1	21		13,500
16	29	A	Peterborough U.	L 2-3	1-1	22	Foggo, Brace	7393
17	Dec 5	H	Grimsby T.	W 5-2	2-0	22	Silvester 3, Foggo, Ford	3925
18	22	A	Cardiff C.	L 1-3	0-1	—	Little	9342
19	26	H	Colchester U.	W 2-0	1-0	22	Brace 2	6267
20	27	A	Chesterfield	W 2-1	2-0	21	Foggo, Silvester	4670
21	Jan 10	A	Rotherham U.	L 0-2	0-0	21		4390
22	16	H	Millwall	D 0-0	0-0	21		7746
23	26	A	Hereford U.	L 1-3	0-2	—	Moody (pen)	3722
24	Feb 6	H	Wrexham	W 2-1	1-0	22	Brace, Silvester	4162
25	9	A	Port Vale	D 1-1	1-0	—	Silvester	3494
26	17	H	Brighton & H.A.	W 4-0	1-0	—	Silvester 4	4784
27	21	A	Hereford U.	L 1-2	1-1	19	Silvester	7264
28	24	A	Preston N.E.	L 1-5	0-0	—	Parker	5210
29	27	H	Crystal Palace	L 1-2	1-1	20	Pountney	13,500
30	Mar 1	H	Gillingham	D 2-2	2-1	—	Little, Parker	4722
31	6	A	Swindon T.	D 0-0	0-0	20		5585
32	8	A	Aldershot	L 0-2	0-0	—		3874
33	13	H	Bury	W 2-0	0-0	20	Parker, Brace	3844
34	15	A	Mansfield T.	L 1-3	0-1	—	Brace	8043
35	19	H	Peterborough U.	D 0-0	0-0	19		4561
36	23	A	Halifax T.	L 0-1	0-0	—		1450
37	27	A	Grimsby T.	D 2-2	2-2	20	Keeffe, Goodwin	4158
38	29	H	Cardiff C.	L 0-2	0-2	—		4596
39	Apr 6	A	Shrewsbury T.	L 1-3	0-2	—	Parker	2493
40	9	H	Walsall	D 2-2	1-1	23	Parker, Nicholl	3723
41	13	A	Gillingham	W 2-1	0-1	—	Parker, Little	5776
42	17	A	Colchester U.	L 1-2	1-0	24	Moody (pen)	4260
43	19	H	Chesterfield	D 1-1	1-1	—	Moody (pen)	3917
44	23	H	Chester	W 2-0	1-0	—	Foggo, Moody (pen)	3553
45	27	A	Wrexham	D 2-2	0-1	—	Moody (pen), Little	1965
46	29	A	Sheffield W.	L 1-2	0-2	—	Moody	25,802

Goalscorers

League (65): Silvester 19, Parker 10, Moody 9 (7 pens), Brace 8, Little 6, Foggo 6, Nicholl 3, Ford 1, Pountney 1, Keefe 1, Goodwin 1.
League Cup (2): Silvester, Little.
F.A. Cup (10): Parker 5, Silvester 3, Moody (pen), Brace.

League Cup	First Round	Peterborough U (h)	2-0
	Second Leg	(a)	0-3
F.A. Cup	First Round	Swansea C. (h)	2-0
	Second Round	Dover (h)	4-1
	Third Round	Brighton & H.A. (h)	2-1
	Fourth Round	Cardiff C. (h)	2-1
	Fifth Round	Derby Co. (a)	0-1

Webster	Wothington	Taylor	Little	Dyer	Moody	Pountney	Brace	Parker	Nicholl	Silvester	Ford	Cunningham	Townsend	Coulson	Foggo	Rafter	Lamb	Hadley	Glover	Harding	Banks	Goodwin	Keefe	Match No.
1	2	3	4	5	6	7	8	9	10	11														1
1	2	`	7	5	6	10*	8	9	4	11	3	12												2
1	2	3	4		6	8	7	10	9	11			5											3
1	2	3	4		6		8	9	7	11		10	5											4
1	2	3	4		6	7	12	9	11	10		8*	5											5
1	2	3	4		6		12	9	11	10		8	5	7*										6
1	2	3	4		6		7	9	11	10		8	5											7
1	2	3	4	8	6		7	12	9*	11	10		5											8
1	2		4	8	6		7*	12	11	10	3	9	5											9
1	2		4		6		7	8	10	9	3		5		11									10
1	2		4		6		8	9	11	10*	3		5		7									11
	2		4		6		7	9	11		3		5		8	1		10				12		12
1	2		4	12	6	7		9	11	10*	3		5		8									13
1	2		4		6		8	9	11	10	3		5		7									14
1	2		4	12	6		8	9	11*	10	3		5		7									15
1	2		4		6		8	9	10	11	3		5		7									16
1	2		4		6	12	8	9*	11	10	3		5		7									17
1	2		4		6		8	9	11	10	3				7			5						18
1	2		4		6		8	9	11	10	3				7			5						19
1	2		4		6		8	9	11	10	3				7			5						20
	2		4	12	6		8	9	11	10	3	5*			7	1								21
	2		4		6	12	8	9	11	10*	3				7	1		5						22
1	2		4		6		8	9*	11	10	3				7			5	12					23
1	2		4		6		8	9	11	10	3				7			5						24
			4	2	6			9	11	10	3	8			7	1		5						25
1	2		4		6		8	9	11	10	3				7			5						26
1	2		4		6			9	11	10	3	7			8			5						27
1	2		4		6			9	11	10	3	8			7			5						28
1	2		4		6		8	9	11	10	3				7			5						29
1	2		4		6		8	9	11	10	3				7			5						30
1			4	2	6		8	9	11		3	10			7			5						31
1	2				6		8	9	11	10	3	4			7			5						32
1			4		6		11	9		10	3	7			8			5			2			33
1			4	2	6	12	8	9*	11	10	3				7			5						34
1			4	2	6		8	9*	7	10	3	11						5				12		35
1		11	4		6	12	8			10	3				7			5			2	9*		36
1		11	4		6		8	9			3							5			2	10	7	37
1		11	4		6		8	9			3				7			5			2		10	38
1			4	8	6	7	12	9	11*		3							5			2	10		39
1	2		4		6		8	9	11	10	3	7						5						40
1	2	11	4		6		8	9		10	3	7						5						41
1	2	7	4		6		8	9		10	3	11						5						42
	2	11	4		6		8	9	7		3						1	5		10				43
	2	11	4		6			9	7	10	3				8	1		5						44
	2	11	4	5	6			9	8	10	3				7	1								45
	2	11	4		6	12		9	7	10	3				8*	1		5						46
38	37	16	45	14	42	16	27	43	40	40	39	15	16	1	30	8	1	25	—	2	5	4	2	
			+3s		+5s	4s	1s					+1s							+1s		+1s	1s		

Player and position	Ht.	Wt.	Birthplace	Clubs	League Appearances	Goals
Goalkeepers						
*Malcolm Webster	5 10½	12 6	Rossington	Arsenal	3	—
				Fulham	95	—
				Southend	96	—
Sean Rafter	6 1	11 4	Rochford	Southend U.	8	—
Defenders						
Alan Moody	6 0	10 4	Middlesbrough	Middlesbrough	44+2	—
				Southend U.	162+1	18
Neil Townsend	6 0	12 0	Long Buckby	Northampton T.	65+2	1
				Southend U.	99	3
Andrew Ford	6 0	12 0	Minehead	Bournemouth	—	—
				Southend U.	89+2	3
*Tony Taylor	5 9	11 7	Glasgow	Morton	20+2	7
				C. Palace	192+3	8
				Southend U.	56	1
*David Worthington	5 10	11 0	Halifax	Halifax T.	37	8
				Barrow	60+1	7
				Grimsby T.	292+1	14
				Halifax T. (on loan)	5	—
				Southend U.	92+3	—
*Graham Byford	5 9	11 6	Chelmsford	Southend U.	—	—
Anthony Hadley	6 0	11 8	Southend	Southend U.	29	—
Steve Dyer	5 9	11 4	Chelmsford	Southend U.	59+7	—
Frank Banks	5 9	11 7	Hull	Southend U.	4	—
				Hull C.	284+4	6
				Southend U.	5	—
Midfield						
Alan Little	5 10	12 3	Co. Durham	Aston V.	2+1	—
				Southend U.	69	7
*William Coulson	5 9½	11 9	N. Shields	Newcastle U.	—	—
				Southend U.	51+2	4
				Aldershot (on loan)	3	—
				Huddersfield T. (on loan)	2	—
				Darlington (on loan)	11+2	1
David Cunningham	5 5	9 5	Kirkcaldy	Brechin City	44+5	6
				Southend U.	43+3	3
Terry Nicholl	5 9	10 8	Wilmslow	Crewe Alex.	46	7
				Sheffield U.	12+10	1
				Southend U.	40	3
Forwards						
*Peter Silvester	5 11	11 8	Wokingham	Reading	76+2	26
				Norwich C.	99+1	36
				Colchester U. (on loan)	4	—
				Southend U.	78+2	32
				Reading (on loan)	2	
Ron Pountney	5 6	9 4	Bilston	Walsall	1	—
				Port Vale	—	—
				Southend U.	20+5	1
*Stuart Brace	5 8	10 4	Taunton	Plymouth Arg.	9	—
				Watford	16	4
				Mansfield T.	55+1	25
				Peterborough U.	22+1	5
				Grimsby T.	205+18	2
				Southend U.	106+6	37
David Keefe	5 4	8 9	Dagenham	Southend U.	4+2	1
Stuart Parker	6 1	11 9	Preston	Blackpool	10+6	2
				Southend U.	43+1	10
*Ken Foggo	5 5	10 8	Perth	W.B.A.	128+2	29
				Norwich C.	182+4	54
				Portsmouth	47+13	3
				Brentford	—	
				Southend U.	30	6
Steve Goodwin	5 9	11 0	Oldham	Norwich C.	2+1	—
				Scunthorpe U. (on loan)	2	
				Southend U.	4+1	1

SOUTHPORT DIV. 4

President: H. K. Latham.

Chairman: J. Church.

Directors: G. Troy, G. Davies, E. J. Scott, C. Rimmer, J. F. Carr.

Life Members: J. Church, C. Rimmer.

Manager: *Secretary:* D. T. Raybould.

Year Formed: 1888.   *Turned Professional:* 1888

Limited Company: 1912.   *Present Company:* 1921.

Previous Names: 1894–95, Southport Wanderers; 1918, Southport Vulcan; 1919, Southport.

Previous Grounds: Sussex Road Sports Ground 1888-1889; Scarisbrick New Road 1889-1905

Honours: Football League, Best Season in Division 3: 8th, 1968–69. 1972–73, Runners up: 1966–67. *F.A. Cup,* best season: 6th Rd. *Cup,* best season: never past 2nd Rd.

Record Victory: 8-1 v Nelson, Division 3(N), Jan. 1st, 1931.

Record Defeat: 0-11 v Oldham Ath., Division 4, Dec. 26th, 1962.

Most League Points: 62, Division 4, 1972–73.

Most League Goals: 88, Division 3(N), 1930–31.

Highest League Scorer in Season: Archie Waterston, 31, Division 3(N), 1930–31.

Most League Goals in Total Aggregate: Alan Spence, 98, 1962–69.

Most Capped Player: Terry Harkin, 2 (4), Northern Ireland

Most League Appearances: Arthur Peat, 401, 1962–72.

Record Transfer Fee Received: £16,000 from Blackburn R. for Tony Field, Oct. 1971.

Record Transfer Fee Paid: £6,000 to Halifax T. for Malcolm Russell, Aug. 1968.

Managers Since the War: Gordon Hunt, Trevor Hitchen, Wally Fielding, Lem Newcomb, Willie Cunningham, Billy Bingham, Don McEvoy, Arthur Peat, Alex Parker, Jimmy Meadows, Alan Ball, Jimmy Melia, Alan Ball, Allan Brown.

Address of Supporters Club and Shop: c/o The Ground.

Haig Avenue, Southport PR8 6JZ. Telephone Secretary, Southport 33422; *Ground capacity:* 21,000 (11,000 covered). *Record attendance:* 20,010 v Newcastle U., F.A. Cup 4th Rd. Replay, January 26, 1932. *Record receipts:* £6,175 v Everton, F.A. Cup 3rd Rd., January 26, 1968. *Pitch measurements:* 113 yds × 77 yds.

How to get there: By road; from Liverpool via Formby by-pass, town centre, Palace cinema, Eastbank, Scarisbrick New Road, to Haig Avenue; from Liverpool via Maghull and Halsall, Scarisbrick New Road, to Haig Avenue; from East Lancashire via Ormskirk and then via Maghull and Halsall as above from Preston and the North via town centre and Scarisbrick New Road. The ground is signposted.

Match tickets: Reserved seats for special matches only.

Car parking: Certain side-streets are available.

Entertainments/catering facilities: Kiosks on the ground.

Club shop: Sells all types of souvenirs.

Handbooks/programmes: No handbooks. Programmes available on subscription.

Extra information: Jack Lindsay scored three goals in three minutes for Southport against Scunthorpe United in February 1952.

Club Colours: Old gold shirts with blue trim, royal blue shorts and blue stockings.

Change Colour: All blue.   *Club Captain:*

Club Nickname: 'The Sandgrounders'.

SOUTHPORT 1975–76 LEAGUE RECORD

Match No.	Date	Venue	Opponents	Result	H/T Score	League Pos'n	Goalscorers	Attendance
1	Aug 16	A	Exeter C.	L 0-2	0-2	—		2844
2	23	H	Barnsley	D 0-0	0-0	21		1316
3	30	A	Reading	L 0-1	0-1	22		4595
4	Sept 5	H	Swansea C.	D 1-1	0-1	23	Sibbald	1017
5	13	A	Newport Co.	L 0-2	0-1	24		2342
6	19	H	Hartlepool	L 2-4	1-2	23	Martin 2 (1 a pen)	1012
7	24	H	Lincoln C.	L 1-2	0-1	—	Jones	871
8	27	A	Doncaster R.	L 2-5	2-2	24	Gough 2	5219
9	Oct 3	H	Bradford C.	L 1-2	1-1	24	Gough	1150
10	10	H	AFC Bournemouth	L 0-2	0-0	24		1044
11	18	A	Brentford	L 0-1	0-1	24		4510
12	20	A	Tranmere R.	L 0-1	0-0	—		3896
13	25	H	Rochdale	L 0-1	0-0	24		1447
14	Nov 1	A	Workington	L 1-2	0-0	24	Wilson	1017
15	4	H	Watford	L 1-2	0-2	—	Gough	1046
16	7	H	Crewe Alex.	D 2-2	1-0	24	Gough 2	1445
17	15	A	Northampton T.	L 0-1	0-1	24		6089
18	29	H	Cambridge U.	L 2-4	1-2	24	Wilson, Martin (pen)	1001
19	Dec 6	A	Scunthorpe U.	W 2-1	1-0	24	Wilson, Dewsnip	1817
20	19	H	Torquay U.	L 1-3	0-2	24	O'Neil	1013
21	26	A	Stockport Co.	L 0-1	0-1	24		6321
22	27	H	Huddersfield T.	L 1-2	0-0	24	Galley	2546
23	Jan 3	A	Darlington	L 0-2	0-0	24		1368
24	10	H	Reading	L 1-2	1-0	24	Martin	1167
25	17	A	Hartlepool	D 0-0	0-0	24		2950
26	24	H	Newport Co.	W 3-0	0-0	24	Dewsnip, Galley 2	1268
27	31	H	Tranmere R.	D 0-0	0-0	24		2632
28	Feb 7	A	Watford	L 0-2	0-0	24		4334
29	13	A	Crewe Alex.	L 0-4	0-1	24		1966
30	21	H	Northampton T.	L 0-1	0-0	24		1332
31	25	A	Lincoln C.	L 0-6	0-2	—		8080
32	28	A	Rochdale	L 0-2	0-0	24		1261
33	Mar 5	H	Workington	W 2-1	0-0	24	Galley 2	1226
34	10	A	Bradford C.	D 1-1	1-1	—	Dewsnip	2706
35	13	A	AFC Bournemouth	D 3-3	2-0	24	Dewsnip, Galley, Taylor	4433
36	16	H	Brentford	W 2-0	0-0	—	Galley, Wilson	1506
37	20	A	Cambridge U.	D 2-2	1-0	23	Hughes 2 (1 a pen)	1789
38	26	H	Scunthorpe U.	D 1-1	1-1	23	O'Riley	1805
39	31	A	Torquay U.	L 1-2	0-0	—	Dewsnip	1974
40	Apr 2	H	Exeter C.	W 1-0	1-0	23	Galley	1514
41	6	H	Doncaster R.	D 1-1	1-1	—	O'Neil	1599
42	10	A	Swansea C.	L 0-2	0-1	23		2147
43	16	H	Darlington	W 2-0	0-0	23	Snookes, Johnston	2149
44	17	H	Stockport Co.	W 2-0	1-0	23	Dewsnip, Higham	2108
45	19	A	Huddersfield T.	W 2-1	1-1	—	Galley, Taylor	6324
46	24	A	Barnsley	L 0-2	0-1	23		2995

Goalscorers

League (41): Galley 9, Gough 6, Dewsnip 6, Martin 4 (2 pens), Wilson 4, Hughes 2 (1 a pen), Taylor 2, Higham 1, Johnston 1, Jones 1, O'Neil 2, O'Riley 1, Sibbald 1, Snookes 1.
League Cup (5): Gough 2, Snookes, O'Riley, Wilson.
F.A. Cup (1): O'Neil.

League Cup	First Round	Stockport Co. (h)	3-1	
	Second Leg	(a)	2-1	
	Second Round	Newcastle U. (a)	0-6	
F.A. Cup	First Round	Spennymoor (a)	1-4	

Thomas	O'Neil	Snookes	Hughes	James	Welbourne	Johnston	Gough	O'Riley	Dewsnip	Wilson	Sibbald	Wain	Jones	Martin	Taylor	Galley	O'Brien	Oliver	Farrell	Johnson	Higham	McClatchey	Ryan	Lafite	Match No.
1	2	3	4	5	6	7	8	9	10	11															1
1	6	3	4	5	12	7	8*	10		9	2	11													2
1	4	3	6	12	11	7*		10		9	2	8	5												3
1	6*	3	4	12		7	8	10		9	2		5	11											4
1	6	3	7	4		8*	12		10	9	2		5	11											5
1	6	3	10	4		8	12			9	2	11	5*	7											6
1	11	3	6	4		8		10*		2	12	5	7	9											7
1	4	3	6	10		8*				9	2	12	5	7	11										8
1	2		4	10	7	8	12	6		3		5	11	9*											9
1	6	3	4	5		7	8			9	2			11	10										10
1	4	3	6	5		7	8			9	2			11	10										11
1	6	3	4	5	10	7*	8	12		9	2			11											12
1	4	3	5			8	9	7	10	2				11	6										13
1	4	3	6	5		8	7			9	2			11	10										14
1	6	3	4			10	8	7		9	2			11	5										15
1	6	3	4			10	8	7		9	2			11	5										16
1	6	3	4			10	8	12		7	9	2		11*	5										17
1		3	4	6		10	8			7	9	2		11	5										18
1	4	3	6			10	8			7	9	2		11	5										19
1	6	3	4			10	8			7	9	2		11*	5		12								20
1	6	3	4			10	8			7	11	2		12	5	9*									21
1	4		5			10*	8			7	11	3		12	6	9	2								22
	6		4			8*				7	10	3		11	5	9	2	1	12						23
	4	3	6			8	10			7	9*	2		11	5	12		1							24
	4		8			3	10			7		2		11	6	9				1	5				25
	4		8			3	10			7		2		11	6	9				1	5				26
	4		8			3	10	12		7		2		11	6	9				1	5*				27
	4	3				2	10			8	7	11		12	6	9*	5			1					28
1	4					3	10			7	9	2		11	6		12				5*	8			29
	2		7				10			11	4	3		6	9	5		1				8			30
	4		8			3				7	10	2		11	6	9				1	5				31
	4	3	8			1				7	10	2		11*	6	9					5	12			32
12	3	4				8				7	10	2		11	6*	9					5		1		33
10	3	6				11				7	4	2			8	9					5		1		34
8	3	6				10	12			7	4	2		11	9*						5		1		35
10	3	6				11				7	4	2			8	9					5		1		36
2		6				10	12			7	4	3		8*	9						5		1	11	37
2		6				10				8	7	4	3		9						5		1	11	38
10	3	6				11				8	7	4	2		9						5		1		39
10	3	6				11				8	7	4	2		9						5		1		40
6	3	4				10				8	7	5	2		9							11	1		41
6	3	4				10	8*			7	5	5	2		9	12						11	1		42
10	3	6				11				7	4	2		9	8						5		1		43
8	3	6				10				7	4	2	11		9						5		1		44
10	3	6				11				7	4	2		8	9						5		1		45
10	3	6				11				7	4	2		8	9						5		1		46
23	44	35	40	11	16	39	21	11	35	43	44	3	7	27	33	24	4	2	—	6	20	2	14	2	
+1s				+2s	+1s		+7s	+1s			+2s			+3s	+1s	+2s				+2s			+1s		

357

SOUTHPORT—PLAYERS

Player and position	Ht.	Wt.	Birthplace	Clubs	League Appearances	Goals
Goalkeepers						
Kevin Thomas	6 0	12 13	Prescott	Blackpool	12	—
				Tranmere R.	18	—
				Oxford U.	5	—
				Southport	67	—
Defenders						
Bobby Sibbald	5 8	10 7	Newcastle	Leeds U.	1	—
				York C.	73+5	7
				Southport	214	12
*Joe James	6 0	12 0	Bootle	Liverpool	—	—
				Southport	11+2	—
*Duncan Welbourne	5 9	11 5	Scunthorpe	Grimsby T.	129	3
				Watford	404+7	22
				Southport	52+1	2
Alan Jones	5 11	12 4	Swansea	Swansea C.	59	6
				Hereford U.	52+1	2
				Southport	49	2
				(contract cancelled Oct. 1975)		
Eric Snookes	5 7	10 0	Birmingham	Preston N.E.	20	1
				Crewe A.	33+1	—
				Southport	35	1
John Higham	6 0	11 7	Liverpool	Liverpool	—	—
				Southport	20	1
Midfield						
Tom O'Neil	5 6½	10 4	St. Helens	Manchester U.	53	—
				Blackpool (on loan)	7	—
				Southport	109+6	4
*John Johnston	5 8	10 4	Belfast	Blackpool	19+5	2
				Halifax (on loan)	3+1	1
				Bradford C.	55+4	4
				Southport	82	6
Paul Taylor				Sheffield W.	5+1	—
				York C.	4	—
				Hereford U. (on loan)	0+1	—
				Colchester U. (on loan)	6+3	—
				Southport	65	14
*Les Wain	5 7	11 0	Crewe	Crewe A.	48+6	1
				Southport	3+2	—
Alan Wilson	5 9	11 5	Liverpool	Everton	2	—
				Southport	43	4
Forwards						
David Hughes	5 10	11 4	Blackburn	Preston N.E.	22+9	—
				Southport	40	1
				Bury	12	3
				Southport	87+4	3
*Johnny Martin	5 9	10 2	Ashington	Aston Villa	1	—
				Colchester U.	76+1	11
				Workington	206+1	32
				Southport	54+9	7
Paul O'Riley	5 9	11 11	Liverpool	Hull C.	19+11	2
				Scunthorpe U. (on loan)	11	4
				Barnsley	11+3	2
				Southport	18+9	4
George Dewsnip	5 7	8 11	Little Hulton	Preston N.E.	—	—
				Southport	41+3	6
Tony O'Brien				Southport	8+2	—
*Paul Meachin				Southport	3	—
Keith Galley				Southport	24+1	9
†Graham Lafite	5 10	11 5	Wolverhampton	Shrewsbury T.	27	1
				Swindon T.	5	—
				Luton T.	180+2	22
				Reading (on loan)	3	—
				Southport	2	—
Paul Farrell				Southport	0+2	—

†formerly known as French.

STOCKPORT COUNTY

DIV. 4

President: A. N. Kirk.

Joint Chairmen: P. Lukic, F. Pye.

Directors: W. C. Adams, G. Hopwood, A. Barlow, J. Lewis.

Manager:　　　*Secretary:* T. R. McCreery.

Asst. Manager: Eddie Hopkinson.

Year Formed: 1883.　*Turned Professional:* 1891.

Limited Company: 1908.

Previous Name: Heaton Norris Rovers, 1883–91.

Previous Grounds: 1884, Chorlton's Farm, Didsbury Road; 1885, Ash Inn; 1887, Belmont Street; 1890, Green Lane; 1902, Edgeley Park.

Honours: *Football League*, best season in Division 2: 10th, 1905–06. Division 3(N), Champions: 1921–22, 1936–37; Runners-up: 1928–29, 1929–30. Division 4, Champions: 1966–67.　*F.A. Cup,* best season: 5th Rd., 1935, 1950.　*Football League Cup,* best season: 4th Rd., 1972–73.

Record Victory: 13-0 v Halifax T., Division 3(N), Jan. 6th, 1934.

Record Defeat: 1-8 v Chesterfield, Division 2, Apr., 19th, 1902.

Most League Points: 64, Division 4, 1966–67.

Most League Goals: 115, Div. 3(N), 1933–34.

Highest League Scorer in Season: Alf Lythgoe, 46, Division 3(N), 1933–34.

Most League Goals in Total Aggregate: Jackie Connor, 132, 1951–56.

Most Capped Player: Harry Hardy, 1, England.

Most League Appearances: Bob Murray, 465, 1952–63.

Record Transfer Fee Received: £30,000 from Blackpool for Paul Hart, May 1973.

Record Transfer Fee Paid: £15,000 to Glentoran for Alex Young, Nov. 1968.

Managers Since the War: Bob Marshall, Andy Beattie, Dick Duckworth, Willie Moir, Reg Flewin, Trevor Porteous, Bert Trautmann, Eddie Quigley, Jimmy Meadows, Walter Galbraith, Matt Woods, Brian Doyle, Jimmy Meadows, Roy Chapman.

Address of Supporters Club: Same as Football Club.

Edgeley Park, Stockport, Cheshire. SK3 9DD. Telephone Stockport 8888/9.　*Ground capacity:* 24,904.　*Record attendance:* 27,833 v Liverpool, F.A. Cup 5th Rd., February 11, 1950.　*Record receipts:* £6,700 v Norwich C., F.L. Cup 4th Rd., November 1, 1972.　*Pitch measurements:* 110 yds × 75 yds.

How to get there: Edgeley Park is situated within a mile of Mersey Square, the town centre; a few minutes walk via Wellington Road South and Greek Street. The main line railway station lies just off Greek Street and is only five minutes from the ground. By road, there are RAC signs to ground on all the main routes around the town centre.

Match tickets: Seats can be reserved in the Main Stand by post or telephone two weeks before the match.

Car parking: Ample street parking around the ground.

Entertainments/catering facilities: Modern licensed club adjoining the ground.

Club shop: Adjacent to the ground; sells all types of souvenirs.

Handbooks/programmes: Programmes available for match only.

Extra information: In May 1921, Stockport County were forced to play a home match at Old Trafford because their ground was under suspension; the attendance for this match was 13!

Club Colours: White shirts, blue collars, white shorts, white stockings with blue ring at top.　*Change Colours:* Blue and black striped shirts, black shorts, black and blue stockings.　*Club Captain:* Alan McNeill.　*Club Nickname:* 'The Hatters'.

STOCKPORT COUNTY 1975–76 LEAGUE RECORD

Match No.	Date	Venue	Opponents	Result	H/T Score	League Pos'n	Goalscorers	Attendance
1	Aug 16	H	Crewe Alex.	D 0-0	0-0	—		3443
2	22	H	Northampton T.	L 1-3	1-3	20	Lawther	3032
3	30	H	Workington	W 4-1	3-1	10	Massey, Davies, Hollis, McNab	1678
4	Sept 6	A	Cambridge U.	W 1-0	1-0	6	Howell (og)	2677
5	12	H	AFC Bournemouth	D 0-0	0-0	8		3605
6	20	A	Brentford	L 1-2	1-1	13	Lester	6280
7	22	H	Darlington	D 0-0	0-0	—		3054
8	26	H	Rochdale	L 0-1	0-0	17		3200
9	Oct 4	A	Watford	D 1-1	0-1	16	Price	4143
10	10	A	Doncaster R.	L 1-2	1-0	16	Hollis	3159
11	18	A	Bradford C.	W 2-1	0-1	17	Bradley, Massey (pen)	2527
12	22	A	Hartlepool	L 0-3	0-1	—		1683
13	24	H	Torquay U.	W 1-0	0-0	14	Massey	2670
14	31	H	Exeter C.	L 0-2	0-0	18		2856
15	Nov 3	H	Newport Co.	L 0-1	0-0	—		2208
16	8	H	Huddersfield T.	L 0-1	0-1	21		2789
17	15	A	Barnsley	D 2-2	2-2	20	Hollis 2	2534
18	28	H	Swansea C.	W 3-2	1-0	17	Potter (og), Bradley, Best	9220
19	Dec 6	A	Reading	L 0-5	0-1	18		6701
20	12	H	Watford	D 2-2	1-1	17	Best, Lawther	5055
21	20	A	Scunthorpe U.	D 0-0	0-0	17		1570
22	26	H	Southport	W 1-0	1-0	17	Hollis	6321
23	27	A	Tranmere R.	L 0-5	0-0	18		4701
24	Jan 1	H	Cambridge U.	L 0-1	0-1	19		2789
25	9	A	Workington	W 2-1	0-1	18	Davies, Cross	1917
26	16	H	Brentford	W 2-0	1-0	17	Hollis, Sutcliffe	2267
27	24	A	AFC Bournemouth	L 0-2	0-1	18		3927
28	30	H	Hartlepool	W 2-0	1-0	18	Hughes, Davids	1565
29	Feb 7	A	Newport Co.	D 2-2	0-1	18	Davies, Hughes	1652
30	14	A	Huddersfield T.	D 2-2	1-1	17	Davies, Massey	5307
31	20	H	Barnsley	D 1-1	0-0	17	Massey (pen)	2707
32	23	A	Darlington	W 1-0	0-0	—	Fogarty (pen)	1302
33	28	A	Torquay U.	L 1-4	1-0	15	Bradley	2072
34	Mar 5	A	Exeter C.	W 2-1	1-1	13	Davies, Hollis	2440
35	13	A	Doncaster R.	L 1-3	0-1	16	McNeill	4231
36	15	H	Bradford C.	W 2-1	0-0	—	Cross, Dixey	2326
37	19	A	Swansea C.	L 0-5	0-3	16		2692
38	26	H	Reading	D 1-1	1-1	16	Hughes	2319
39	29	H	Scunthorpe U.	D 0-0	0-0	—		2078
40	Apr 3	A	Crewe Alex.	L 1-3	0-1	17	Davies (pen)	2530
41	5	A	Rochdale	W 3-2	1-1	—	Davies, Bradley, Hardman	1287
42	12	H	Lincoln C.	L 0-3	0-2	—		3703
43	16	A	Lincoln C.	L 0-2	0-0	18		10,906
44	17	A	Southport	L 0-2	0-1	18		2108
45	19	H	Tranmere R.	L 0-2	0-0	—		2973
46	23	A	Northampton T.	L 0-4	0-2	19		7680

Goalscorers

League (43): Davies 7 (1 a pen), Hollis 7, Massey 5 (2 pens), Bradley 4, Hughes 3, Best 2, Cross 2, Lawther 2, Davids 1, Dixey 1, Fogarty 1 (pen), Hardman 1, Lester 1, McNab 1, McNeill 1, Price 1, Sutcliffe 1, own goals 2.
League Cup (2): Lester, Massey (pen).

League Cup	First Round	Southport (a)	1-3
	Second Leg	(h)	1-2
F.A. Cup	First Round	Hartlepool (a)	0-3

Brown	Smith	Cross	Fogarty	Holsgrove	Lawther	McNeill	Coleman	Buckley	Hollis	Davies	Lester	Price	Massey	McNab	Bradley	Turner	Vernon	Hopkinson	McCann	Seddon	Taylor	Best	Coyne	Deere	Sutcliffe	Davids	Hughes	Dixey	Duddy	Blair	Hardman	
1	2	3	4	5	6	7	8*	9	10	11	12																					1
1	2	3	4	5	6	8			10	11			7	9																		2
1	2	7	6			8			10	11		4	12	9*	3	5																3
1	2	7	6			11			8	9*		4	12	10	3	5																4
1	2	7	6			11*			8	9		4	12	10	3	5																5
1	2	4	8*			11			12	9		3	7	10	6	5																6
1	2		6			10			11	9		4	7	8	3	5																7
1	2		6			8			11*	9	12	4	7	10	3	5																8
1	2		6			9*			12	11	10	4	7	8	3	5																9
1	2		6			12			11	10	9	4	7	8	3*	5																10
1	2	4	5						11	9		7	8	3	6	10																11
1	2		6		4				11	9*	12	7	8	3	5	10																12
	2		6	4					11			7	10	3*	5	8	12	1	9													13
	2		6	4	3							7	10	5	8	11		1	9													14
	3		6	4					11			8	12	7	5	2		1	9	10*												15
	2	3		4					10	11	12	7	9		5			1	8*	6												16
	8*		6	5	4	3			11			10	9		2			12	7		1											17
	6		4			11				3		9	10*		5	2		1		8		7	12									18
	2	10	6		4	7		3	8	11*		12	5					1						9								19
	2	10	6		4	7		3	8			12	5					1					11	9*								20
	2	10	6	8		7		3	12	11		4						1						9*	5							21
	2	10	6			7		3	8	9			5					1					11	4								22
	2	10	6			7		3	8	11		9	5					1						4								23
	2	11	6	5		7		3	8	9*		10						1					4	12								24
	2	11	6		4			3	8	9		10						1							5	7						25
	2	11	6		4			3*	8	9		12			10			1							5	7						26
	2	10	6		4	7		3	8	9					5			1							11							27
	2	10	6		4	3		9							8			1							7	5	11					28
	2	10	6		4	3		9*					12		8			1							7	5	11					29
	2	10	6		4	3		9					12		8*			1							7	5	11					30
	2	10	6		4	3		9				7			8			1								5	11					31
	2	10	6		4	3		9				7			8			1								5	11					32
	2	10	6		4	3		9				7*	12		8			1								5	11					33
	2	10	6		4	3		9				7	12		8			1								5	11*					34
	2	11	6		4	3*		9				7	10		8			1								5		12				35
	2	3	6		4			9				7	11*		12			1								5		10			8	36
	2	3	6		4			9				7	11*					1								5	8	10	12			37
	2	3	6		4			9				7						1								5	11	10		8		38
	2	3	6		4			9*				7						1								5	11	10		8	12	39
1	2		6		3			9				12						11								5	10*		4	8	7	40
1	2		6		4	3		9				10			8											5	11				7	41
1	2		6		4	3		9				10			8											5	12			11*	7	42
	2		6		4	3		9				10			8			1							7	5					11	43
	2	11	6		4	3		9				10						1							7	5				8		44
	2	10	6		4	3		9							8			1							7	5					11	45
	2	10	6		4	3		9							8			1							7	5					11	46
15	44	27	44	9	14	33	6	36	22	28	8	21	30	12	39	8	1	30	4	4	1	3	3	6	9	5	11	14	6	7	6	
			+1s	+1s	+1s	+3s	+2s	+1s	+5s	+5s			+1s		+2s			+1s				+1s			+2s		+1s				+2s	

R.F.76/77–19

Player and position	Ht.	Wt.	Birthplace	Clubs	League Appearances	Goals
Goalkeepers						
Paul Hopkinson	5 10	11 10	Royton	Stockport Co.	30	—
*John Brown	5 11	11 10	Bradford	Preston N.E.	67	—
				Stockport Co.	41	—
*John Taylor	5 11	11 6	Birmingham	Chester	70	—
				Rochdale (on loan)	3	—
				Stockport Co.	1	—
Defenders						
*James McNab	5 11	11 6	Denny	Sunderland	284+1	12
				Preston N.E.	222+2	6
				Stockport Co.	30	1
Graham Smith	5 10	11 0	Pudsey	Leeds U.	—	—
				Rochdale	316+1	2
				Stockport Co.	83	—
Derek Loadwick	5 7	10 8	Middlesbrough	Leeds U.	—	—
				Stockport Co.	—	—
Ian Buckley	5 8	11 0	Oldham	Oldham Ath.	—	—
				Stockport Co.	36+1	—
*Ian Lawther (N. Ireland)	5 10	11 9	Belfast	Sunderland	75	41
				Blackburn R.	59	21
Scunthorpe U. 60(21) Brentford 138+1(43) Halifax T 87+14(23) Stockport Co. 158+6(29)						
*Mark Turner	5 8	11 0	Stockport	Everton	—	—
				Stockport Co.	8	—
Midfield						
Alan McNeill	5 1	11 2	Belfast	Middlesbrough	3	—
				Huddersfield T.	1+1	—
				Oldham Ath.	154+16	19
				Stockport Co.	33+1	1
Ken Fogarty	5 10	11 1	Manchester	Stockport Co.	165+3	2
*Tony Coleman	5 8	12 0	Liverpool	Doncaster R.	58	11
Manchester C. 82+3(12) Sheffield W. 25+1(2) Blackpool 17 Southport 22+1(1) Stockport Co. 28+2(3)						
*Peter Olinyk	5 6	10 4	Bolton	Bolton W.	7+3	—
				Stockport Co.	4	—
Lee Bradley	5 11	11 5	Manchester	Stockport Co.	39+1	4
Mike Cross	5 6	10 4	Little Hulton	Bolton W.	—	—
				Stockport Co.	27	2
John Duddy	5 9	11 1	Oldham	Oldham Ath.	—	—
				Stockport Co.	6	—
Forwards						
*John Griffiths	5 7	10 6	Oldbury	Aston Villa	0+2	—
				Stockport Co.	167+16	31
*Wyn Davies	6 1	12 5	Caerarvon	Wrexham	55	22
Bolton W. 155(66) Newcastle U. 181(40) Manchester C. 45(8) Manchester U. 15+1(4) Blackpool 34+2(5) C. Palace (on loan) 3 Stockport Co. 28+2(7)						
*John Price	5 4	10 4	Co. Durham	Burnley	20	2
Stockport Co. 241+6(23) Blackburn R. 63+13(12) Stockport Co. 51+15(1)						
Stephen Massey	5 11	11 0	Stockport	Stockport Co.	36+7	7
*John Vernon	5 11	11 2	S. Africa	Stockport Co.	4+2	—
Peter Sutcliffe	5 6	9 0	Manchester	Manchester U.	—	—
				Stockport Co.	9+2	1
Peter Fletcher	6 0	11 6	Manchester	Manchester U.	2+5	—
				Hull C.	26+10	5
				Stockport Co.	—	—
*John Hughes	5 8	11 4	Bangor, N. Wales	Blackpool	5+3	—
				Southport (on loan)	7+1	1
				Altrincham	Non-League	—
				Stockport Co.	11+1	3
Colin Hardman	5 10	11 7	Workington	Workington	6+2	1
John Coyne	5 11	11 2	Liverpool	Tranmere R.	12+3	3
				U.S.A.		
				Wigan Ath.	Non-League	—
				Blackpool	—	—
				Stockport Co.	3+1	—

362

STOKE CITY DIV. 1

President: G. W. Taylor. *Chairman:* A. A. Henshall.

Directors: T. H. Degg, P. Axon, J. A. M. Humphreys, A. W. Clubb.

Manager: Tony Waddington. *Asst. Manager:* George Eastham.

Secretary: W. C. Williams. *Coach:* Alan A'Court.

Year Formed: 1863 (second oldest League Club).

Turned Professional: 1885. *Limited Company:* 1908.

Previous Grounds: 1875, Sweeting's Field; 1878, Victoria Ground (previously known as the Athletic Club Ground).

Honours: *Football League,* best season in Division 1: 4th, 1935–36, 1946–47. Division 2, Champions: 1932–33, 1962–63; Runners-up: 1921–22. Division 3(N), Champions: 1926–27. *F.A. Cup,* best season: semi-finalist; 1899, 1971, 1972. *Football League Cup,* best season: Winners: 1971–72.

European Competitions: *UEFA Cup:* 1972–73, 1974–75.

Record Victory: 10-3 v W.B.A., Division 1, Feb. 4th, 1937.

Record Defeat: 0-10 v Preston N.E., Division 1, Sept 14th, 1889.

Most League Points: 63, Division 3(N), 1926–27.

Most League Goals: 92, Division 3(N), 1926–27.

Highest League Scorer in Season: Freddie Steele, 33, Division 1, 1936–37.

Most League Appearances: Eric Skeels, 506, 1958–76.

Most Capped Player: Gordon Banks 36 (73), England.

Most League Goals in Total Aggregate: Freddie Steele, 142, 1934–49.

Record Transfer Fee Received: £125,000 from Everton, for Mike Bernard, May 1972.

Record Transfer Fee Paid: £325,000 to Leicester C. for Peter Shilton, November 1974.

Managers Since the War: Bob McGrory, Frank Taylor.

Address of Social Club: c/o Football Club.

Victoria Ground, Stoke-on-Trent. Telephone Stoke-on-Trent 44660. *Telegraphic address:* 'Football, Stoke-on-Trent'. *Ground capacity:* 50,500. *Record attendance:* 51,380 v Arsenal, Division 1, March 29, 1937. *Record receipts:* £20,580 v Manchester U., F.A. Cup, 6th Rd. replay, March 22, 1972. *Pitch measurements:* 116 yds × 75 yds.

How to get there: Stoke-on-Trent railway station, on the main line from London, is five minutes walk from the ground. No special buses from the town centre because the ground is central. By road, Stoke is well served by the M6 which passes just two miles from the city.

Match tickets: Bookable two weeks before the match.

Car parking: The official car park in Wheildon Road holds 2,000 cars. Street parking permitted.

Entertainments/catering facilities: Social club. Refreshments obtainable on the ground.

Club shop: Sells all types of souvenirs.

Handbooks/programmes: Programmes available on subscription.

Extra information: Neville Coleman scored seven goals for Stoke against Lincoln City in 1957, a record for a winger in English senior football.

Club Colours: Red and white striped shirts, white shorts and stockings. *Change Colours:* White shirts, black shorts, white stockings with white tops. *Club Captain:* Jimmy Greenhoff. *First Team Trainer:* Frank Mountford. *Club Nickname:* 'Potters'.

STOKE CITY 1975–76 LEAGUE RECORD

Match No.	Date	Venue	Opponents	Result	H/T Score	League Pos'n	Goalscorers	Attendance
1	Aug 16	H	West Ham U.	L 1-2	0-2	—	Moores	23,744
2	20	H	Wolverhampton W.	D 2-2	0-1	—	Bowers, Conroy (pen)	22,551
3	23	A	Arsenal	W 1-0	1-0	10	Hudson	28,025
4	27	A	Leicester C.	D 1-1	1-0	—	Hudson	22,878
5	30	H	Manchester U.	L 0-1	0-1	15		33,337
6	Sept 6	A	Middlesbrough	L 0-3	0-1	19		21,975
7	13	H	Leeds U.	W 3-2	2-0	18	Conroy, Pejic, Greenhoff	23,139
8	20	A	Coventry C.	W 3-0	1-0	12	Greenhoff, Moores 2	18,965
9	24	A	Manchester C.	L 0-1	0-0	—		28,915
10	27	H	Derby Co.	W 1-0	1-0	12	Greenhoff	25,097
11	Oct 4	A	Norwich C.	W 1-0	0-0	10	Haslegrave	22,318
12	11	H	Ipswich T.	L 0-1	0-1	11		21,975
13	18	A	Sheffield U.	W 2-0	0-0	10	Greenhoff 2	23,410
14	25	H	Newcastle U.	D 1-1	0-0	10	Greenhoff	24,057
15	Nov 1	A	West Ham U.	W 1-0	0-0	8	Moores	18,269
16	8	H	Everton	W 3-2	1-0	7	Salmons, Darracott (og), Robertson	24,657
17	15	A	Tottenham H.	D 1-1	0-0	7	Moores	25,698
18	22	H	Sheffield U.	W 2-1	2-0	7	Salmons 2 (1 a pen)	21,959
19	29	A	Q.P.R.	L 2-3	0-1	8	Moores, Bloor	22,328
20	Dec 6	H	Aston Villa	D 1-1	1-1	8	Greenhoff	28,492
21	13	H	Arsenal	W 2-1	0-0	8	Salmons, Greenhoff	18,628
22	20	A	West Ham U.	L 1-3	1-2	8	Bloor	21,135
23	26	H	Liverpool	D 1-1	0-1	8	Salmons	32,092
24	27	A	Birmingham C.	D 1-1	1-1	8	Moores	37,166
25	Jan 10	A	Leeds U.	L 0-2	0-2	10		36,906
26	17	‡H	Middlesbrough	W 1-0	0-0	7	Moores	21,009
27	31	A	Wolverhampton W.	L 1-2	0-1	9	Conroy	24,960
28	Feb 7	H	Leicester C.	L 1-2	1-1	11	Moores	21,001
29	21	H	Tottenham H.	L 1-2	1-2	13	Greenhoff	17,113
30	Mar 3	A	Newcastle U.	W 1-0	0-0	—	Burns (og)	37,459
31	6	H	Burnley	W 4-1	3-1	9	Smith 2, Greenhoff, Mahoney	16,069
32	13	A	Ipswich T.	D 1-1	0-0	10	Smith	22,812
33	20	H	Q.P.R.	L 0-1	0-1	11		22,848
34	24	A	Derby Co.	D 1-1	1-1	—	Bloor	30,156
35	27	A	Aston Villa	D 0-0	0-0	11		32,359
36	Apr 2	H	Manchester C.	D 0-0	0-0	11		18,798
37	7	A	Everton	L 1-2	0-1	—	Greenhoff (pen)	16,974
38	10	H	Coventry C.	L 0-1	0-0	12		16,059
39	17	A	Liverpool	L 3-5	1-2	14	Conroy, Moores, Bloor	44,069
40	19	H	Birmingham C.	W 1-0	1-0	—	Gallagher (og)	19,918
41	21	A	Manchester U.	W 1-0	0-0	—	Bloor	53,879
42	24	H	Norwich C.	L 0-2	0-0	12		15,598

Goalscorers

League (48): Greenhoff 11 (1 a pen), Moores 10, Salmons 5 (1 a pen), Bloor 5, Conroy 4 (1 a pen), Smith 3, Hudson 2, Bowers 1, Pejic 1, Haselgrave 1, Robertson 1, Mahoney 1, own goals 3.

League Cup (1): Greenhoff.

F.A. Cup (5): Mahoney, Moores, Salmons (1 a pen), Greenhoff, Smith.

League Cup	Second Round	Lincoln C. (a)	1-2
F.A. Cup	Third Round	Tottenham H. (a)	1-1
		(h)	2-1
	Fourth Round	Manchester C. (h)	1-0
	Fifth Round	Sunderland (h)	0-0
		(a)	1-2

‡Owing to storm damage, game played on Port Vale's ground.

Shilton	Dodd	Pejic	Mahoney	Smith	Bloor	Skeels	Moores	Conroy	Hudson	Salmons	Haslegrave	Marsh	Bowers	Greenhoff	Lewis	Goodwin	Robertson	Lumsden	Crooks	Sheldon	Match No.
1	2	3	4	5	6	7*	8	9	10	11	12										1
1	6	3	7*	5			12	9	10	11		2	4	8							2
1	6	3	4	5				9	10	11		2	7	8							3
1	6	3	4	5			12	9*	10	11		2	7	8							4
1	5	3	4		6		12	9	10	11*		2	7	8							5
1	5	3	4			6		9	10	11	7			8	2						6
1	5	3	4			6	9	11	10		7	2		8							7
1	5	3	4			6		9	10	11	7	2		8							8
1	6	3	4*	5				9	10	11	7	2		8		12					9
1	4	3		5	6			9	10	11	7	2		8							10
1	5	3	4			6		9	10	11	7	2		8							11
1	2	3	4	5	6			9	10	11*	7	12		8							12
1	5	3	4			6		9	10	11	7	2		8							13
1	5	3	4			6		9	10	11	7	2		8							14
1	5	3	4			6		9	10	11	7	2		8							15
1	6	3	4					9	10	11	7*	2		8	5	12					16
1	5	3	4					9	10	11	7*			8	6	12	2				17
1	5	3	4			6		9	10	11				8	2	7					18
1	5	3	4			6		9	10	11	12			8	2	7*					19
1	5	3	4			6		9	10	11				8	2	7					20
1	5	3	4			6		9	10	11		2		8		7					21
1	5	3	4			6		9*	10	11	12	2		8		7					22
1		3	4			6	9		10	11		2		8	5	7					23
1		3	4			6		9	10	11		2		8	5	7					24
1	5	3	4			6		9	10	11	7*			8	2	12					25
1	2	3*	4	5	6			9	10	11				8		7	12				26
1	5		4			6		9	10	11	12	2	3	8		7*					27
1	5	3	4			6		9	10	11	7*	2		8		12					28
1		3		5	6	4		9	10	12	11*			8		7	2				29
1	6	3	4	5		7		9	10	11		2		8							30
1	6	3	4	5		7		9	10	11		2		8							31
1	6	3	4	5				9	10	11	7	2		8							32
1	6	3	4	5					10	11*	7	2		8		9	12				33
1	7	3	4	5	6			10*		11		8		9			12	2			34
1	7	3	4	5	6					11*		8		9		10	12	2			35
1	7	3	4	5	6			9	10	11				8				2			36
1	6	3	4	5				9	10	11				8		7		2			37
1	12	3	4	5*	6			9		11	7			8				2	10		38
1	5	3	4			6	10	9		11		2		8		7					39
1	5	3	4			6		9		7	12	2		8					10*	11	40
1	4			5	6			9	10	11		3		8				2		7	41
1	4	3	5*			6		9	10	11	12			8				2		7	42
42	39	39	38	19	32	4	29	16	34	39	23	25	6	40	9	2	12	9	2	3	
	+1s				+3s			+1s	+5s	+1s	+1s				+2s	+6s	+1s				

365

STOKE CITY—PLAYERS

Player and position	Ht.	Wt.	Birthplace	Clubs	League Appearances	Goals
Goalkeepers						
Peter Shilton (England)	6 0	12 10	Leicester	Leicester C.	286	1
				Stoke C.	67	—
*John Farmer	6 1	13 0	Biddulph	Stoke C.	163	—
				Leicester C. (on loan)	2	—
Michael McDonald	6 2	13 8	Glasgow	Clydebank	108	—
				Stoke C.	5	—
				(transferred to Hibernian Jan. 1976)		
Alan Ryder	6 1	12 0	Stoke	Stoke C.	—	—
Defenders						
John Marsh	5 8	10 4	Stoke	Stoke C.	272+7	2
Mike Pejic (England)	5 6	10 5	Chesterton	Stoke C.	253	6
Kevin Lewis	5 9	10 10	Hull	Manchester U.	—	—
				Stoke C.	15	—
Paul Johnson	5 6	11 10	Stoke	Stoke C.	—	—
Kenneth Raper	5 7	10 8	Consett	Stoke C.	—	—
John Lumsden	5 6	9 2	Stoke	Stoke C.	9+1	—
Danny Bowers	5 7	9 13	Audley	Stoke C.	16+1	1
Steven Waddington	5 3	8 11	Crewe	Stoke C.	—	—
Alan Bloor	6 0	13 0	Stoke	Stoke C.	338+3	15
Dennis Smith	5 11½	12 0	Stoke	Stoke C.	246+1	22
Alan Dodd	5 10	10 12	Stoke	Stoke C.	112+1	—
Martin Brown	5 8	9 0	Stoke	Stoke C.	—	—
Stefan Feniuk	5 9	10 9+	Manchester	Stoke C.	—	—
Michael Smith	5 9	10 0	Stoke	Stoke C.	—	—
Steven Wilshaw	5 9	10 0	Stoke	Stoke C.	—	—
Midfield						
Alan Hudson (England)	5 10½	12 1	Chelsea	Chelsea	144+1	10
				Stoke C.	94	9
Geoff Salmons	5 10¾	11 10½	Mexborough	Sheffield U.	170+10	8
				Stoke C.	81+1	13
*Eric Skeels	5 8	10 9	Manchester	Stoke C.	494+12	7
John Mahoney (Wales)	5 7½	11 1	Cardiff	Crewe Alex.	16+2	5
				Stoke C.	248+12	25
*Steven Matthews	5 9	9 12	Stoke	Stoke C.	—	—
Kevin Sheldon	5 3	8 9	Leek	Stoke C.	3	—
Brian Bithell	5 7	10 9	Winsford	Stoke C.	—	—
Sean Haslegrave	5 9	9 2	Stoke	Stoke C.	106+7	5
Forwards						
*Deano Martin	5 7	10 9	Stoke	Stoke C.	—	—
Terry Conroy (Eire)	5 10½	11 0	Dublin	Stoke C.	187+19	43
Jimmy Greenhoff	5 10	11 2	Barnsley	Leeds U.	89+6	19
				Birmingham C.	31	14
				Stoke C.	260	74
Keith Brookes	5 6	9 0	Stoke	Stoke C.	—	—
Ian Challinor	5 8	10 3	Swinnerton	Stoke C.	—	—
John Ritchie	6 0	12 4	Kettering	Stoke C.	110	64
				Sheffield W.	88+1	35
				Stoke C.	151+9	71
Jimmy Robertson (Scotland)	5 8	9 7	Glasgow	Cowdenbeath	25	7
				St. Mirren	52	14
				Tottenham H.	153+4	26
				Arsenal	45+1	7
				Ipswich T.	87	10
				Stoke C.	85+15	12
David Goodwin	5 11	11 7	Alsager	Stoke C.	6+3	2
Ian Moores	6 2	13 8	Chesterton	Stoke C.	40+10	14
John Ruggiero	5 10	11 5	Stoke-on-Trent	Stoke C.	—	—
				Workington (on loan)	3	—
Garth Crooks	5 8	8 9	Stoke	Stoke C.	2	—
Raymond Draper	5 7	8 7	Stoke	Stoke C.	—	—
Martin Penny	5 7	9 0	Manchester	Stoke C.	—	—
David Perkin	5 8	8 9	Macclesfield	Stoke C.	—	—

SUNDERLAND

DIV. 1

President: S. S. Collings.

Vice-Presidents: J. Cooke, S. Ritson, F.R.C.S., J.P.

Chairman: K. I. Collings.

Vice-Chairman: J. M. Ditchburn.

Directors: E. M. Evans, R. Thompson, M. E. Bewick, A. D. S. Martin, F. Stewart.

Manager: Bob Stokoe.   *Secretary:* R. M. Linney.

Year Formed: 1879.   *Turned Professional:* 1886.

Limited Company: 1906.

Previous Grounds: 1879, Blue House Field, Hendon; 1881, Ashbrooke; 1883, site of Cooper Street; 1884, Abbs Field, Fulwell; 1886, Newcastle Road; 1898, Roker Park.

Previous Name: 1879–81, Sunderland and District Teachers' A.F.C.

Honours: Football League, Division 1, Champions: 1891–92, 1892–93, 1894–95, 1901–02, 1912–13, 1935–36; Runners-up: 1893–94, 1897–98, 1900-01, 1922–23, 1934–35. Division 2, Champions: 1975–76; Runners-up: 1963–64. *F.A. Cup,* Winners: 1937, 1973; Runners-up: 1913. *Football League Cup,* best season: semi-finalists: 1963. **European Competitions:** Cup-Winners' Cup 1973–74.

Record Victory: 11-1 v Fairfield, F.A. Cup, 1st Rd., 1894–95.

Record Defeat: 0-8 v West Ham U., Division 1, Oct. 1968.

Most League Points: 61, Division 2, 1963–64.

Most League Goals: 109, Division 1, 1935–36.

Highest League Scorer in Season: Dave Halliday, 43, Division 1, 1928–29.

Most League Appearances: Jim Montgomery, 531, 1962-1976.

Most Capped Player: Billy Bingham, 33 (56), N. Ireland, Martin Harvey, 33, N. Ireland.

Most League Goals in Total Aggregate: Charlie Buchan, 209, 1911–25.

Record Transfer Fee Received: £275,000 from Manchester C. for Dennis Tueart, March 1974.

Record Transfer Fee Paid: £145,000 to West Ham U. for Bryan Robson, July 1974.

Managers Since the War: Bill Murray, Alan Brown, George Hardwick, Ian McColl, Alan Brown.

Address of the Supporters Club: c/o Football Club

Roker Park Ground, Sunderland. Telephone Sunderland 72077 and 58638. *Telegraphic address:* 'Football, Sunderland'. *Ground capacity:* 53,500. *Record attendance:* 75,118 v Derby Co., F.A. Cup 6th Rd. Replay, March 8, 1933. *Record receipts:* £42,846.45p v Crystal Palace, F.A. Cup 6th Rd., March 6, 1976.

How to get there: From Sunderland railway station and Seaburn railway station take buses 23 and 24 to Redby Community Centre: the ground is five minutes walk away. Special buses from the town centre. By road via M1, A690 to Sunderland, and then route to Roker Park is signed.

Match tickets: Seats may be booked 10 days prior to the match.

Car parking: Limited parking close to the ground.

Entertainments/catering facilities: Hot and cold drinks, pies, sandwiches, etc. available in the ground.

Club shop: Open on match days; sells all types of souvenirs.

Handbooks/programmes: Programmes are obtainable on subscription; details from the Club Offices.

Extra information: Sunderland share the highest First Division away win, beating Newcastle United 9-1 in 1908; Newcastle went on to win the League that season!

Club Colours: Red and white striped shirts, black shorts, red stockings with white tops.

Change Colours: White shirts with single red and black stripe, white shorts with single red and black stripe, white socks with single red and black hoop.

Club Coach: Ian MacFarlane.

Club Nickname: 'Rokerites'.

SUNDERLAND 1975–76 LEAGUE RECORD

Match No.	Date	Venue	Opponents	Result	H/T Score	League Pos'n	Goalscorers	Attendance
1	Aug 16	H	Chelsea	W 2-1	1-1	—	Robson, Longhorn	28,689
2	19	A	Bristol C.	L 0-3	0-2	—		12,199
3	23	A	Oxford U.	D 1-1	0-1	10	Moncur	9069
4	26	H	Fulham	W 2-0	2-0	—	Holden, Gibb	25,450
5	30	H	Blackpool	W 2-0	1-0	2	Towers 2	24,000
6	Sept 6	A	Plymouth Arg.	L 0-1	0-0	4		18,304
7	13	H	W.B.A.	W 2-0	0-0	3	Halom, Hughes	25,159
8	20	A	Blackburn R.	W 1-0	1-0	2	Towers	15,773
9	23	H	Carlisle U.	W 3-2	2-0	—	Robson, Towers (pen), Hughes	28,185
10	27	H	Notts Co.	W 4-0	1-0	1	Robson 2, Kerr, Halom	27,565
11	Oct 4	A	Portsmouth	D 0-0	0-0	1		13,098
12	11	H	Orient	W 3-1	1-0	1	Towers (pen), Hughes, Robson	28,327
13	18	A	Bristol R.	L 0-1	0-1	2		13,577
14	25	H	Luton T.	W 2-0	0-0	1	Kerr, Robson	28,338
15	Nov 1	A	York C.	W 4-1	3-0	1	Hughes 2, Hunter (og), Towers (pen)	15,232
16	8	H	Nottingham F.	W 3-0	2-0	1	Robson, Halom 2	31,227
17	15	A	Charlton Ath.	W 2-1	1-0	1	Holden 2	22,307
18	22	H	Bristol R.	D 1-1	0-1	1	Kerr	31,356
19	29	H	Oldham Ath.	W 2-0	1-0	1	Robson 2	28,220
20	Dec 6	A	Southampton	L 0-4	0-0	1		17,598
21	13	H	Oxford U.	W 1-0	0-0	1	Porterfield	22,051
22	20	A	Chelsea	L 0-1	0-0	1		22,802
23	26	H	Hull C.	W 3-1	2-1	1	Holden, Finney, Henderson	32,210
24	27	A	Bolton W.	L 1-2	1-0	1	Dunne (og)	42,680
25	Jan 10	A	W.B.A.	D 0-0	0-0	1		25,399
26	17	H	Plymouth Arg.	W 2-1	0-1	1	Holden, Kerr	29,737
27	Feb 7	A	Fulham	L 0-2	0-1	3		12,839
28	21	H	Charlton Ath.	W 4-1	1-1	1	Holden, Moncur, Robson, Towers	30,173
29	24	A	Carlisle U.	D 2-2	2-1	—	Towers (pen), Holden	20,001
30	28	A	Luton T.	L 0-2	0-0	3		15,338
31	Mar 13	A	Orient	W 2-0	2-0	3	Kerr 2	7954
32	17	A	Nottingham F.	L 1-2	1-2	—	Holden	16,995
33	20	A	Oldham Ath.	D 1-1	1-1	2	Hughes	13,704
34	23	H	Bristol C.	D 1-1	0-0	—	Holden	38,395
35	27	H	Southampton	W 3-0	1-0	2	Greenwood, 2 Holden	34,946
36	30	H	York C.	W 1-0	1-0	—	Kerr	33,462
37	Apr 3	A	Notts Co.	D 0-0	0-0	2		14,811
38	10	H	Blackburn R.	W 3-0	1-0	1	Holden, Parkes (og), Robson	33,523
39	17	A	Hull C.	W 4-1	3-1	1	Robson, Rowell, Dobson (og), Holden	21,296
40	19	H	Bolton W.	W 2-1	2-0	—	Towers (pen), Robson	51,983
41	20	A	Blackpool	L 0-1	0-1	—		16,768
42	24	H	Portsmouth	W 2-0	2-0	1	Bolton, Hughes	40,515

Goalscorers

League (67): Robson 13, Holden 12, Towers 9 (5 pens), Hughes 7, Kerr 7, Halom 4, Greenwood 2, Moncur 2, Bolton 1, Finney 1, Gibb 1, Henderson 1, Longhorn 1, Porterfield 1, Rowell 1, Own Goals 4.

League Cup (1): Holden.

F.A. Cup (5): Holden 2, Robson 2, Finney.

League Cup	Second Round	Notts Co. (a)	1-2
F.A. Cup	Third Round	Oldham Ath. (h)	2-0
	Fourth Round	Hull C. (h)	1-0
	Fifth Round	Stoke C. (a)	0-0
		(h)	2-1
	Sixth Round	C. Palace (h	0-1

Swinburne	Ashhurst	Bolton	Longhorn	Clarke	Moncur	Kerr	Gibb	Halom	Robson	Porterfield	Holden	Montgomery	Malone	Towers	Hughes	Henderson	Rowell	Finney	Mitchell	Greenwood	Train	Match No.
1	2	3	4	5	6	7	8*	9	10	11	12											1
1	2	3	4	5	6	7	12	9	10	11*	8											2
		3		5	6	7	4	9	10	12	8*	1	2	11								3
		3		5	6	7	8	12	10	11	9*	1	2	4								4
		3		5	6	7*	4	12	9	10	8	1	2	11								5
		3		5	6	7	4	8	10	12	9*	1	2	11								6
		3	4	5	6	7		8	10	11	9*	1	2	12								7
		3		5	6	7		9	10	11		1	2	4	8							8
		3		5	6	7		9	10	11		1	2	4	8							9
		3		5	6	7		9	10	11		1	2	4	8							10
		3		5	6	7		9	10	11		1	2	4	8							11
	6	3		5		7			10	11	9	1	2	4	8							12
		3		5	6	7*		9	10	11	12	1	2	4	8							13
		3		5	6	7		9	10	11	12	1	2	4*	8							14
				5	6	7		9	10	11		1	2	4	8	3						15
				5	6	7		9	10	11		1	2	4	8	3						16
				5	6	7		9	10	11	12	1	2	4	8*	3						17
				5	6	7		9	10	11	8	1	2	4		3						18
				5	6	7		9	10	11	8	1	2	4		3						19
	12			5	6	7		9	10	11*	8	1	2	4		3						20
			10	5	6	7		9		11	8*	1	2	4		3				12		21
		3		5	6	7		9	10	11*	12	1	2	4		8						22
	6	3		5		7			10		9	1	2	4		11				8*	12	23
	6	3		5		7			10		9	1	2	4		11				8		24
		3		5	6	7			10		9	1	2	4		8*		12		11		25
		3	4	5	6	7*		9	10		8	1	2					12		11		26
		3	12	5	6		8*		10		9	1	2	4				7		11		27
	8*	3		5	6	7			10		9	1	2	4		11				12		28
	8	3		5	6	7			10		9	1	2	4		11						29
	8	3		5	6	7			10		9	1	2	4		11*				12		30
		3	12	5	6	7			10		9	1	2	4*						11	8	31
	5	3	4*		6	7			10		9	1	2					12		11	8	32
	5	3			6	7	12				9*	1	2	10	4					11	8	33
	5	3			6	7			10		9	1	2		8					11	4	34
	5	3			6	7			10		9	1	2	4						11	8	35
	5	3			6	7			10*		9	1	2	4				12		11	8	36
	5	3			6	7			10		9	1	2	4						11	8	37
	5	3			6	7			10		9	1	2	4						11	8	38
	5	3			6	7			10		9	1	2		8					11	4	39
	5	3			6	7			10		9	1	2	4				12		11*	8	40
1	5	3			6				10		9*	4	11	2	7					12	8	41
1	5	3			6	7			10		9		2		8	11					4	42
4	20	34	6	31	39	40	5	21	40	20	31	38	39	34	14	11	3	7	—	13	12	
+1s	+2s				+1s	+3s		+2s	+5s					+3s	+2s	+1s	+1s	+1s		+3s		

369

SUNDERLAND—PLAYERS

Player and position	Ht.	Wt.	Birthplace	Clubs	League Appearances	Goals
Goalkeepers						
Jim Montgomery	5 10½	11 9	Sunderland	Sunderland	531	—
Trevor Swinburne	6 0	12 12	East Rainton	Sunderland	8	—
Defenders						
Joe Bolton	5 11	11 12	Birtley	Sunderland	93+9	4
Dick Malone	6 0	12 2	Ayr	Ayr U.	163	5
				Sunderland	226+1	2
Jack Ashurst	6 0	11 0	Coatbridge	Sunderland	49+8	1
Bobby Moncur	5 9¾	10 9	Perth	Newcastle U.	293+3	3
(Scotland)				Sunderland	81	2
*Stan Ternent	5 8	11 6	Felling on Tyne	Burnley	5	—
				Carlisle U.	186+2	5
				Sunderland	—	—
Jeffrey Clarke	5 11	12 1	Pontefract	Manchester C.	13	—
				Sunderland	31	—
Midfield						
Dennis Longhorn	5 11	11 0	Bournemouth	Bournemouth	23+8	1
				Mansfield T.	93+3	5
				Sunderland	33+5	3
Tony Towers	5 8½	11 2½	Manchester	Manchester C.	117+5	10
(England)				Sunderland	83	15
Gary Rowell	5 8	10 9	Seaham	Sunderland	3+1	1
Ian Porterfield	5 11	11 6	Dunfermline	Raith R.	117	17
				Sunderland	218+13	17
Bobby Kerr	5 4½	9 3	Alexandria	Sunderland	288+8	51
Michael Henderson	5 9	10 8	Gosforth	Sunderland	11+2	1
Tommy Gibb	5 10¾	11 1	West Lothian	Partick T.	112	13
				Newcastle U.	190+9	12
				Sunderland	5+1	1
Ray Train	5 7	10 9	Nuneaton	Walsall	67+7	11
				Carlisle U.	154+1	8
				Sunderland	12	—
Forwards						
Tom Finney	5 11	11 8	Belfast	Luton T.	13+1	5
(N. Ireland)				Sunderland	8+7	1
Bill Hughes	5 9	10 2	Coatbridge	Sunderland	246+22	71
(Scotland)						
*Robert Mitchell	5 8	10 12	Hebburn	Sunderland	1+2	—
Bryan Robson	5 8	11 8	Sunderland	Newcastle U.	205+1	81
				West Ham U.	120	47
				Sunderland	82	32
Peter Stronach	5 6	12 0	Seaham	Sunderland	—	—
Vic Halom	5 10	10 10	Burton	Charlton Ath.	8+3	—
				Orient	53	12
				Fulham	66+6	22
				Luton T.	57+2	17
				Sunderland	110+3	35
*Alan Crompton	5 9	10 8	Manchester	Sunderland	—	—
Shaun Elliott	5 11	10 6	Haydin Bridge	Sunderland	—	—
*Thomas Mason	5 8	10 6	Washington	Sunderland	—	—
Mel Holden	6 1	10 4	Dundee	Preston N.E.	69+3	22
				Sunderland	31+5	12
Roy Greenwood	5 10	11 0	Leeds	Hull C.	118+8	24
				Sunderland	13+3	2

SWANSEA CITY

DIV. 4

President: P. E. Holden. *Chairman:* M. Struel.

Vice-Chairman: T. J. Phillips.

Directors: E. P. Walters, I. C. Pursey, P. L. W. Owen, R. J. Jones, W. C. Floyd.

Team Manager: Harry Griffiths. *Secretary:* G. J. Daniels.

Year Formed: About 1900. *Turned Professional:* 1911.

Limited Company: 1912.

Previous Name: Swansea Town until Feb. 1970

Honours: *Football League,* best season in Division 2: 5th, 1925–26. Division 3(S), Champions: 1924–25, 1948–49. Division 4, Promoted: 1969–70 (3rd). *F.A. Cup,* best season, semi-finalists: 1926, 1964. *Football League Cup,* best season: 4th Rd., 1965. **European Competitions:** *European Cup Winners Cup,* 1961–2, 1966–7. *Welsh Cup,* Winners 4 times.

Record Victory: 8-1 v Bristol R., Division 3(S), Apr. 15th. 1922 and v Bradford C., Division 2, Feb. 22nd, 1926.

Record Defeat: 1-8 v Fulham, Division 2, Jan. 22nd, 1938.

Most League Points: 62, Division 3(S), 1948–49.

Most League Goals: 90, Division 2, 1956–57.

Highest League Scorer in Season: Cyril Pearce, 35, Division 2, 1931–32.

Most League Goals in Total Aggregate: Ivor Allchurch, 166, 1949–58, 1965–68.

Most Capped Player: Ivor Allchurch, 42 (68), Wales.

Most League Appearances: Wilfred Milne, 585, 1919–37.

Record Transfer Fee Received: £45,000 from Plymouth Arg. for Barrie Jones, Sept. 1964.

Record Transfer Fee Paid: £26,000 to Nottingham F., for Ron Rees, Jan. 1972.

Managers Since the War: Bill McCandless, Ron Burgess, Trevor Morris, Glyn Davies, Bill Lucas, Roy Bentley, Harry Gregg.

Address of Supporters Club: Elysium Buildings, High Street, Swansea.

Vetch Field, Swansea. Telephone Swansea 42855. *Ground capacity:* 35,000. *Record attendance:* 32,796 v Arsenal, F.A. Cup 4th Rd., February 17, 1968. *Record receipts:* £9,377 v Arsenal, F.A. Cup, February 17, 1968. *Pitch measurements:* 110 yds × 70 yds.

How to get there: 10 minutes' walk from bus depot. South Wales Transport Co. Ltd. services from High Street General station to Lower Oxford Street.

Match tickets: Tickets can be reserved in advance.

Car parking: Car park 200 yards from the ground in The Kingsway. Side-street parking available.

Entertainments/catering facilities: Disc jockey programme prior to the match. Licensed bar and refreshment kiosk inside the ground.

Club shop: Situated in William Street; sells all types of souvenirs.

Handbooks/programmes: No handbook. Programmes can be obtained from the Secretary by sending remittance and S.A.E.

Club Colours: All white.

Change Colours: All red, with white collars.

Club Coach: R. Saunders.

Club Nickname: 'Swans'.

Youth Team Manager: J. Charles.

SWANSEA CITY 1975-76 LEAGUE RECORD

Match No.	Date	Venue	Opponents	Result	H/T Score	League Pos'n	Goalscorers	Attendance
1	Aug 16	H	Tranmere R.	D 1-1	1-0	—	Evans W.	2866
2	23	A	Rochdale	L 1-2	0-1	18	Leitch	1169
3	30	H	Cambridge U.	W 1-0	0-0	16	Bekker	2082
4	Sept 5	A	Southport	D 1-1	1-0	15	Curtis	1017
5	13	H	Workington	W 1-0	1-0	10	James	2126
6	19	A	Northampton T.	D 0-0	0-0	9		5428
7	23	H	Newport Co.	D 2-2	2-2	—	Thomas, Bruton (pen)	4500
8	27	H	Scunthorpe U.	W 2-0	2-0	6	Thomas, Bray	3098
9	Oct 4	A	Lincoln C.	L 0-4	0-3	11		5323
10	11	H	Huddersfield T.	D 1-1	1-1	12	Bray	3230
11	18	A	Doncaster R.	L 1-2	0-0	13	Tynan	6640
12	21	H	Darlington	W 2-0	1-0	—	Bray, Bruton	2200
13	25	H	Bradford C.	W 3-1	0-1	11	Tynan, Bray 2	3380
14	Nov 1	A	Barnsley	D 0-0	0-0	10		2709
15	5	A	Reading	L 0-1	0-0	—		5499
16	8	H	Torquay U.	W 3-0	2-0	10	James 2, Bray	3170
17	14	A	Exeter C.	L 0-3	0-2	11		2967
18	28	A	Stockport Co.	L 2-3	0-1	14	Curtis, Bruton	9220
19	Dec 6	H	Hartlepool	W 3-1	0-0	11	Bray (pen), Leitch 2	2253
20	20	A	Crewe Alex.	L 1-2	1-1	14	Bray (pen)	2088
21	26	H	Watford	W 4-2	2-2	12	Joslyn (og), Garner (og), Leitch, Curtis	4091
22	27	A	AFC Bournemouth	L 0-2	0-0	14		6714
23	Jan 3	H	Crewe Alex.	W 4-0	0-0	12	Leitch 2, Bray 2	2513
24	10	A	Cambridge U.	L 1-3	1-3	14	James	2534
25	16	H	Northampton T.	D 1-1	1-0	14	Bray	3656
26	24	A	Workington	D 1-1	0-1	13	Davies	1270
27	Feb 6	H	Reading	W 5-1	1-0	11	Bray, Conway, James, Curtis 2	2750
28	14	A	Torquay U.	W 2-0	1-0	9	Curtis 2	2670
29	20	H	Exeter C.	L 0-3	0-1	10		4252
30	23	A	Newport Co.	W 2-1	2-0	—	Bruton, Bray	2040
31	28	A	Bradford C.	D 0-0	0-0	9		6672
32	Mar 5	A	Barnsley	W 3-1	0-1	9	Bray, Thomas, James	2510
33	9	H	Lincoln C.	D 2-2	2-1	—	Thomas, Curtis	4000
34	13	A	Huddersfield T.	L 0-2	0-0	10		6393
35	16	H	Doncaster R.	W 2-1	1-0	—	Bray, Wignall (og)	3128
36	19	H	Stockport Co.	W 5-0	3-0	9	Bray, Bartley, Curtis, Harris, Williams	2692
37	27	A	Hartlepool	L 0-1	0-1	9		1708
38	Apr 2	A	Tranmere R.	L 0-3	0-1	11		3475
39	6	A	Scunthorpe U.	D 1-1	1-0	—	Lally	3015
40	10	H	Southport	W 2-0	1-0	11	Evans, W., James	2147
41	16	A	Brentford	L 0-1	0-0	11		4360
42	17	A	Watford	L 1-2	0-1	11	James	4536
43	20	H	AFC Bournemouth	D 1-1	0-0	—	Bray	2354
44	23	A	Rochdale	D 1-1	1-0	11	Bruton	1604
45	26	H	Brentford	D 2-2	0-1	—	Bray 2 (1 a pen)	1311
46	28	A	Darlington	D 1-1	0-0	—	Evans, W.	4295

Goalscorers

League (66): Bray 19 (3 pens), Curtis 9, James 8, Leitch 6, Bruton 5 (1 a pen), Thomas 4, Evans, W. 3, Tynan 2, Bartley 1, Bekker 1, Conway 1, Davies 1, Harris 1, Lally 1, Williams 1, own goals 3.
League Cup (4): Leitch 2, Bekker, Bruton (pen).

League Cup	First Round	Torquay U. (h)	1-2
	Second Round	(a)	3-5
F.A. Cup	First Round	Southend U. (a)	0-2

Potter	Evans, W.	Bartley	Smith	Harris	Bruton	Curtis	Lally	James	Thomas	Bray	Bekker	Davies	Leitch	Dalling	Griffiths	Tynan	Evans, P.	Abbott	Conway	Williams	Morris	Stevenson	Harvey	Match No.
1	2	3	4	5	6	7	8	9	10	11*	12													1
1	2	11	6	5	4	7*12		8		9		3	10											2
1	2	3	4	6	5	7		11		10	12	9	8*											3
1	2	3	4	7	5	8		11		6*10	12	9												4
1	2	11	4	6	5	7		8		12	10*	3	9											5
1	2	11	4	6	5	7		9	10	8		3												6
1	2	11*	4	6	5	8		9	7	10		3	12											7
1	2	11	4	6	5	7		9	8	10		3												8
1	2	11*	4	6	5	7		9	8	10	12	3												9
1	2	3	4	6	5	7		11*	8	10	12	9												10
1	2		4	6	5	7	3	10*11		9	12					8								11
1	2		4	6	5	8		7	11	10		3				9								12
1	2		4	6	5	7		10	11	9		3				8								13
1	2		4	6	5	8		7	11	10		3				9								14
1	2	12	4	6	5	8		7	11*10			3				9								15
1	2		4	6	5	8		7*11	10			3	12			9								16
1	2	11	4	6	5	8		9*	7	10	12	3												17
1	2		4	6	12	8	7	9		10		3	11*				5							18
1	2		4	6		7*	8	11		10		3	9				5		12					19
1	3		6	4	12	8	7	9		10*		2	11				5							20
1	2	11	4	6		8		7		10		3	9				5							21
1	2	11	4	6	12	7		8*		10		3	9				5							22
1	2		4	6		7		8		10		3	9				5		11					23
1	2		4	6	12	8	7			10		3	9				5*		11					24
1	2		4	6	5	7		8	10	12		3	9						11*					25
1	2	12	4	6	5	8		7		10		3	9*						11					26
1	2	11	4	6	5	8*		9	10			3	12						7					27
1	6	11	4	5	2	8		9		3	10								7					28
1	2	11	6	5		8		3	10	4*	9								12 7					29
1	2	3	4	6	5	11		9	8	10									7					30
1	2	3	4	6	5	11		9	8	10									7					31
1	2	3	4	6	5	8		9	7	10									11					32
1	2	3	4	6	5	8		9	7	10									11*12					33
1	2	3	4	6	5	8		10	11	9									7*12					34
1	2	3	4	6	5	8		9	7	10									11					35
1	2	11	6		5	8		9	4	10		7	3											36
1	2	3	4	6	5	8	10	9	7		12								11*					37
1	2*	3	4	6	5	8		9	7	10									11 12					38
1	2	11	4	6	5	8	7		3	10	9													39
1	2	3	4			8	10	9		12		7	11*	5	6									40
1	2	3	4	6	5	8		9	7	10									11					41
1	5	3	2	6		8	11	9	4	10									7*	12				42
1	2	3	4	6*9		8		7		12		5							11 10					43
1	8	3	4	9		7	2	10				5							11	6				44
1	2	3		6		8	4	10		5		9							7*11 12					45
1	2		4	6*		9	8	10	3	7									11 5	12				46
46	46	32	43	43	37	41	9	44	31	40	4	26	15	2	1	6	9	—	20	7	2	2	—	
		+2s		+4s			+1s			+3s	5s	4s	2s				+3s		+3s	2s		+1s		

Player and position	Ht.	Wt.	Birthplace	Clubs	League Appearances	Goals
Goalkeepers						
Steve Potter	6 1	12 2	Belper	Manchester C.	—	—
				Swansea C.	73	—
Defenders						
Paul Harris	5 10	11 4	Hackney	Orient	96	4
				Swansea C.	43	1
David Bruton	6 2	14 0	Gloucester	Bristol C.	16+1	—
				Swansea C.	124+5	16
Wyndham Evans	5 9	12 0	Llanelli	Swansea C.	189+5	16
*Glen Davies	5 9	10 4½	Swansea	Swansea C.	140+12	13
Danny Bartley	5 8	10 10	Paulton	Bristol C.	93+6	7
				Swansea C.	63+2	1
Steven Morris				Swansea C.	2+2	—
Phillip Evans				Swansea C.	9	—
Nigel Stevenson				Swansea C.	2	—
Midfield						
Pat Lally	5 10	10 9	Paddington	Millwall	1	—
				York C.	64+8	5
				Swansea C.	74+6	6
				Aldershot (on loan)	3	—
Barry Hole	5 11	11 4	Swansea	Cardiff C.	211	16
(Wales)				Blackburn R.	79	13
				Aston Villa	47	6
				Swansea C.	78	3
*Geoff Thomas	5 8	11 4	Swansea	Swansea C.	346+15	52
				Manchester U. (on loan)	—	—
Carl Slee	6 0	10 10	Swansea	Swansea C.	111+4	—
George Smith	5 7	10 8	Newcastle	Barrow	91+1	11
				Portsmouth	64	3
				Middlesbrough	74	—
				Birmingham	36+3	—
				Cardiff C.	43+2	1
				Swansea C.	43	—
Forwards						
Alan Curtis	5 11	12 3	Rhondda	Swansea C.	125+4	13
(Wales)						
Peter Abbot	6 1	12 8	Rotherham	Manchester U.	—	—
				Swindon T. (on loan)	—	—
				Swansea C.	34+7	3
				(contract cancelled March 1976)		
Geoff Bray	5 8	11 13	Chatham	Gillingham	—	—
				Oxford U.	22+11	6
				Swansea C.	40+3	19
Mickey Conway	5 7	10 3	Sheffield	Brighton	—	—
				Swansea C.	20	1
Robbie James	5 10	11 1	Swansea	Swansea C.	115+2	18
*Jan Bekker	5 6	10 6	Cardiff	Swansea C.	16+6	4
Nigel Dalling				Swansea C.	2+3	—
Andy Leitch	6 2	10 7	Bristol	Swansea C.	15+2	6
Steven Williams				Swansea C.	7+3	1
Jeff Griffiths				Swansea C.	1	—

SWINDON TOWN

DIV. 3

President: W. H. Castle. *Chairman:* C. J. Green.

Directors: C. Day, A. W. Done, C. Cowley, H. Cowley, T. J. R. Kearsley, R. Stephenson, M. W. Earle, W. H. Dore.

Team Manager: Danny Williams.

Admin. Manager/Secretary: R. Jefferies.

Finance Manager: R. A. Morse.

Year Formed: 1881. *Turned Professional:* 1894.

Limited Company: 1894. *Previous Ground:* 1881–96, The Croft. **Honours:** *Football League,* best season in Division 2: 5th, 1969–70. Division 3, Runners-up: 1962–63, 1968–69. *F.A. Cup,* best season, semi-finalists: 1910, 1912. *Football League Cup,* best season, Winners: 1968–69. Anglo-Italian Cup, Winners: 1970.

Record Victory: 10-1 v Farnham United Breweries, F.A. Cup, 1st Rd., Nov. 28th, 1925.

Record Defeat: 1-10 v Manchester C., F.A. Cup, 4th Rd. Replay, Jan. 25th, 1930.

Most League Points: 64, Division 3, 1968–69.

Most League Goals: 100, Division 3(S), 1926–27.

Highest League Scorer in Season: Harry Morris, 47 Division 3(S), 1926–27.

Most League Goals in Total Aggregate: Harry Morris, 216, 1926–33.

Most Capped Player: Rod Thomas, 29, Wales.

Most League Appearances: John Trollope, 658, 1960–76.

Record Transfer Fee Received: £150,000 from C. Palace for Don Rogers, Oct. 1972.

Record Transfer Fee Paid: £88,000 to Wolverhampton W. for Peter Eastoe, March 1974.

Managers Since the War: Louis Page, Maurice Lindley, Bert Head, Danny Williams, Fred Ford, Dave Mackay, Les Allen.

Address of Supporters Club: Swindon Town Supporters Club, County Ground, Swindon, Wilts.

Address of Club Shop: Souvenir and Sports Shop, Swindon Town F.C., County Ground, Swindon.

County Ground, Swindon, Wiltshire. Telephone Ground Swindon 22118. *Ground capacity:* 28,000 (6500 seats). *Record attendance:* 32,000 v Arsenal F.A. Cup 3rd Rd., January 15, 1972. *Record receipts:* £12,594 v Arsenal, F.A. Cup 3rd Rd., January 15, 1972. *Pitch measurements:* 114 yds × 72 yds.

How to get there: Both Swindon bus and railway stations are half a mile from the ground.

Match tickets: Available 3 weeks in advance.

Car parking: Corporation car park adjacent to the west end of the ground, off County Road.

Club shop: Postal enquiries welcome. All types of souvenirs are stocked.

Handbooks/programmes: Programmes available by postal application, or subscription.

Entertainments/catering facilities: The Supporters' Club. Rendezvous Club in the North Stand. Refreshment kiosks in all parts of the ground. No licensed bars.

Extra information: Harold Fleming of Swindon Town played 11 times for England before World War 1 when the club were still a non-League side. Separate terrace enclosure available for adults and accompanied children only.

Club Colours: Red shirts, white shorts, red and white stockings.

Change Colours: All blue.

Club Nickname: 'Robins'.

SWINDON TOWN 1975-76 LEAGUE RECORD

Match No.	Date	Venue	Opponents	Result	H/T Score	League Pos'n	Goalscorers	Attendance
1	Aug 16	H	Chesterfield	L 0-1	0-0	—		7675
2	23	A	Walsall	D 1-1	1-1	18	Eastoe	5146
3	30	H	Gillingham	D 2-2	1-1	17	Moss (pen), Eastoe	6786
4	Sept 6	A	Shrewsbury T.	L 0-3	0-1	23		4062
5	13	H	Sheffield W.	W 2-1	0-1	17	Anderson, Eastoe	6993
6	20	A	Port Vale	L 0-3	0-1	20		3720
7	24	A	Hereford U.	L 0-1	0-1	—		6423
8	27	H	Colchester U.	L 0-1	0-0	24		5750
9	Oct 4	A	Rotherham U.	W 2-0	2-0	22	Anderson, Moss (pen)	4731
10	11	H	Halifax T.	W 3-1	1-0	20	Anderson 2, Stroud	6214
11	18	A	Wrexham	L 0-2	0-0	21		2893
12	21	A	Bury	L 0-5	0-4	—		5737
13	25	H	Grimsby T.	W 3-0	1-0	22	Eastoe 2, Anderson	5873
14	31	A	Southend U.	L 0-3	0-2	22		4258
15	Nov 4	H	Crystal Palace	L 1-2	0-0	—	Moss	10,599
16	8	H	Preston N.E.	L 1-3	0-3	23	Trollope	6332
17	15	A	Peterborough U.	L 1-3	1-3	23	Eastoe	7287
18	29	H	Brighton & H.A.	W 3-2	0-1	23	Syrett, Dixon, Eastoe	6792
19	Dec 6	A	Mansfield T.	L 1-3	0-1	23	Eastoe	5487
20	20	A	Chester	L 1-2	0-0	23	Anderson	3674
21	26	H	Cardiff C.	W 4-0	2-0	23	Anderson, Eastoe, Burrows, Dixon	10,003
22	27	A	Millwall	D 0-0	0-0	23		7022
23	Jan 10	A	Gillingham	L 2-3	0-1	23	Anderson, Burrows	6459
24	17	H	Port Vale	W 2-1	0-0	23	McLaughlin, Syrett	5557
25	24	A	Sheffield W.	W 2-0	1-0	23	Dixon, Syrett	8342
26	31	H	Bury	W 2-1	1-1	20	Stroud, Rudd (og)	5408
27	Feb 7	A	Crystal Palace	D 3-3	1-2	20	Stroud, Syrett 2	15,844
28	10	H	Aldershot	W 6-3	5-0	23	Syrett, Dixon, Stroud, Anderson (2 pens), Moss	7323
29	14	A	Preston N.E.	L 2-4	2-3	19	Dixon, Butler	5868
30	21	H	Peterborough U.	L 0-3	0-2	21		7477
31	24	H	Hereford U.	L 0-1	0-1	—		10,691
32	28	A	Grimsby T.	L 0-1	0-1	22		5218
33	Mar	H	Southend U.	D 0-0	0-0	22		5585
34	9	H	Rotherham U.	D 1-1	1-1	—	Rogers	9866
35	13	A	Halifax T.	W 2-0	1-0	22	Syrett 2	1864
36	20	A	Brighton & H.A.	L 0-2	0-0	23		18,208
37	27	H	Mansfield T.	L 0-2	0-2	24		6789
38	30	H	Chester	W 2-1	2-1	—	Moss, Syrett	5117
39	Apr 3	A	Chesterfield	L 0-4	0-2	23		3646
40	6	A	Colchester U.	W 2-1	2-1	—	Anderson (pen), Syrett	2694
41	10	H	Shrewsbury T.	W 3-0	1-0	20	Syrett, Anderson, Stroud	5869
42	14	A	Aldershot	W 1-0	1-0	—	Dixon	4226
43	17	A	Cardiff C.	D 0-0	0-0	19		23,428
44	20	H	Millwall	L 0-2	0-0	—		13,756
45	24	H	Walsall	W 5-1	2-1	19	Anderson (3 pens), Moss, Syrett	7363
46	29	H	Wrexham	D 2-2	1-1	—	Syrett 2	9007

Goalscorers

League (62) Anderson 15 (6 pens), Syrett 14, Eastoe 9, Moss 6 (2 pens), Dixon 6, Stroud 5, Burrows 2, McLaughlin 1, Trollope 1, Butler 1, Rogers 1, own goal 1.
League Cup (7): Eastoe 2, Moss 2 (1 a pen), Trollope 2 (1 a pen), Stroud.
F.A. Cup (9): Moss 2 (1 a pen), Dixon 2, Syrett 2, Trollope, Eastoe, own goal 1.

League Cup	First Round	Millwall (h)	2-1
	Second Leg	(a)	1-0
	Second Round	Wolverhampton W. (h)	2-2
		(a)	2-3
F.A. Cup	First Round	Newport Co. (a)	2-2
		(h)	3-0
	Second Round	Hendon (a)	1-0
	Third Round	Tooting & Mitcham (h)	2-2
		(a)	1-2

Barron	McLaughlin	Trollope	Hubbard	Burrows	Prophett	Moss	Stroud	Eastoe	Jenkins	Anderson	Dixon	Butler	Syrett	Allan	Taylor	Gilligan	Emanuel	Farr	Chalklin	Rogers	Aizlewood	O'Brien	Match No.
1	2	3	4	5	6	7	8	9	10	11													1
1	7	3	4	5			8	9	12	11	2	6	10*										2
	8	3	4		6	7	5	9	12	11	2	10*		1									3
	4	3	7*	12	6	8	5	9		11	2	10		1									4
1	8	3		5	6*	7	4	9	12	11	2	10											5
	8	3	4	5	6	7		9		11	2	10*	12	1									6
	8	3	4*	5		7	6	9	12	11	2	10		1									7
	8	3	4*	5		7	6	9	12	11	2	10		1									8
	4	3		5		7	6	9	8	11	2	10		1									9
	4	3		5		7	6	9	10	11	2	8		1									10
	4	3		5		7	6	9	8	11	2	10		1									11
	8	3	7*	5	12	6	9	4		11	2	10		1									12
	8	3		5		7	4	9	10	11	2			1	6								13
1	8	3		5		7	10	9	4*	11	2				6	12							14
1	8	3		5		7		9		11	2	4*	10		6	12							15
1	8	3		5			10	9		11*	2				6	7	4	12					16
1	8	3		5		7	6	9		10	12		2			4*	11						17
1		3		5		7	6	9		11	10		8		2	4							18
1		3		5		7		9	10*	11	6		8		2	12	4						19
1	8	3		5			6	9		11	7	12	10		2	4*							20
1	6	3		5		7	4	9		11	8	10			2								21
1	7	3		5			4	9	12	11	8		10		2*	6							22
1	6	3		5		7	4			11	8		10		2				9				23
1	6	3		5		7	4			11	8		10		2				9				24
1	6	3		5		7	4		12	11	8		10		2				9*				25
1	9	3		5	6	7	4			11	8		10		2								26
1	9	3		5	6	7	4			11	8		10		2								27
1	10	3		5	6	7	4			11	8		9		2								28
1	10	3		5	6	7*	4			11	8	12	9		2								29
1	6	3		5			4	9	7	11	10		8		2								30
1	10	3		5	6		4	9		11	8		7		2								31
1	10	3		5	6	7	4*	9		11	8	2	12										32
1	10	3		5	6	7	4	9		11*	8	2	12										33
1	4	3		5	6	7	12			11	10	2*	9						8				34
1	2	3			6	7	4			10			9						11	5		8	35
1	2	3			6	7	4			10		12	9						11*	5		8	36
1	2	3			6	7	4			11		12	9						10*	5		8	37
1	2	3			6	7	4			11		8	9								5	10	38
1	2	3			6	7	4			11		8	9						12	5*		10	39
1	2	3		5	6	7				11		8	9							4		10	40
1	2	3		5	6	7	12			11		4	9*							8		10	41
1	2	3		5	6	7	12			11*		8	9							4		10	42
1	2	3		5	6	12	7			11		8	9							4*		10	43
1	2	3		5	6	7				11		8	9							4		10	44
1	2	3		5	6	7	4			11		8	9									10	45
1	2	3		5	6	7	4			11		8	9									10	46
36	44	46	8	37	26	37	39	26	10	46	41	16	28	10	19	2	6	—	3	9	5	12	
			+1s			+2s	+3s		+7s		+3s	+2s	+3s		+3s		+1s		+1s				

SWINDON TOWN—PLAYERS

Player and position	Ht.	Wt.	Birthplace	Clubs	League Appearances	Goals
Goalkeepers						
Jimmy Allan	5 11	11 7	Inverness	Swindon T.	71	—
Jim Barron	5 11½	11 7	Co. Durham	Wolverhampton W.	8	—
				Chelsea	1	—
				Oxford U.	152	—
				Nottingham F.	155	—
				Swindon T.	76	—
Defenders						
Will Dixon	5 8	10 6	London	Arsenal	—	—
				Reading	150+3	—
				Colchester U.	—	—
				Swindon T.	96+5	8
John McLaughlin	5 10	10 12	Edmonton	Colchester U.	66	2
				Swindon T.	99+2	5
John Trollope	5 10	11 13	Wroughton	Swindon T.	662+1	20
*Joe Butler	5 7½	11 0	Newcastle	Newcastle U.	3	—
				Swindon T.	355+5	17
Colin Prophett	5 11	12 2	Crewe	Sheffield W.	113+6	7
				Norwich C.	34+1	—
				Swindon T.	67+1	3
Geoff Chalklin	5 7	11 0	Swindon	Swindon T.	3	—
Keith Tanner	5 11	12 3	Swindon	Swindon T.	—	—
Mark Thompson	5 11	12 3	Swindon	Swindon T.	—	—
Steve Aizlewood	5 11	12 6	Newport	Newport Co.	191+6	17
				Swindon T.	5	—
Frank Burrows	6 1	12 8	Larkhall	Raith R.	75	1
				Scunthorpe	106	4
				Swindon T.	290+4	9
				Mansfield T. (on loan)	6	—
Midfield						
Trevor Anderson (N. Ireland)	5 8½	9 11	Belfast	Portadown	not known	
				Manchester U.	13+6	2
				Swindon T.	70+1	17
Kenneth Stroud	5 11	12 0	London	Swindon T.	78+8	6
Terry Hubbard	5 9	10 12	Sebastopol	Swindon T.	81+1	3
				(contract cancelled Feb. 1976)		
Trevor Brinkworth	5 11	12 0	Swindon	Swindon T.	—	—
Gerry O'Brien	5 6	9 9	Glasgow	Clydebank	not known	
				Southampton	66+12	2
				Bristol R. (on loan)	3	—
				Swindon T.	12	—
Forwards						
Dave Moss	5 9	11 7	Witney	Swindon T.	129+12	30
Tom Jenkins	5 9	10 8	London	Orient	1	—
				Reading	21	5
				Southampton	84	4
				Swindon T.	89+11	4
				(contract cancelled April 1976)		
Dave Syrett	5 11	11 13	Salisbury	Swindon T.	67+12	22
				Wolverhampton W. (on loan)—		
Don Rogers	5 10	12 10	Paulton	Swindon T.	400	147
				C. Palace	69+1	28
				Q.P.R.	13+5	5
				Swindon T.	9+1	1
Ian Farr	5 9	11 0	Swindon	Swindon T.	0+1	—
Clive Gardner	5 11	12 0	Wellington	Swindon T.	—	—
John Gilligan	5 10	12 0	Abingdon	Swindon T.	2+3	—

TORQUAY UNITED   DIV. 4

Chairman: A. J. Boyce.
Vice-Chairman: M. C. Spedding.

Directors: C. W. S. Williams, H. G. Lidstone, J. H. Perry, Lt.-Col. W. J. Elliott, M.B.E., F.C.I.S.

Manager: Malcolm Musgrove.   *Secretary:* D. J. Easton.

Player-Coach: Lew Chatterley.

Year Formed: 1898.   *Turned Professional:* 1921.

Limited Company: 1921.

Previous Name: 1910, Torquay Town; 1921, Torquay United.

Previous Grounds: 1898, Teignmouth Road; 1901, Torquay Recreation Ground; 1905, Cricket Field Road; 1907, Torquay Cricket Ground; 1910, Plainmoor.

Honours: *Football League,* best season in Division 3: 4th, 1967–68. Division 3(S), Runners-up: 1956–57. Division 4, Promoted: 1959–60, 1965–66.   *F.A. Cup,* best season: 4th Rd. 1949, 1955, 1971.   *Football League Cup,* never past 3rd Rd.

Record Victory: 9-0 v Swindon T., Division 3(S), March 8th, 1952.

Record Defeat: 2-10 v Fulham, Division 3(S), Sept. 7th, 1931 and v Luton T., Division 3(S), Sept. 2nd, 1933.

Most League Points: 60, Division 4, 1959–60.

Most League Goals: 89, Div. 3(S), 1956–57.

Highest League Scorer in Season: Sammy Collins, 40, Division 3(S), 1955–56.

Most League Goals in Total Aggregate: Sammy Collins, 204, 1948–58.

Most Capped Player: None.

Most League Appearances: Dennis Lewis, 443, 1947–59.

Record Transfer Fee Received: £35,000 from Newcastle U. for Mike Mahoney, March 1975.

Record Transfer Fee Paid: £15,000 to Leicester C. for David Tearse, Nov. 1971.

Managers Since the War: Jack Butler, John McNeil, Bob John, Alex Massie, Eric Webber, Frank O'Farrell, Allan Brown, Jack Edwards.

Address of Supporters Association: Plainmoor, Torquay, Devon.

Address of Club Shop: The Gull Shop, Torquay United Supporters Association, Plainmoor, Torquay, Devon.

Plainmoor Ground, Torquay, Devon, TQ1 3PS. Telephone Torquay (0803) 38666–7.   *Ground capacity:* 22,000.   *Record attendance:* 21,908 v Huddersfield T., F.A. Cup 4th Rd., January 29, 1955.   *Record receipts:* £10,326 v Tottenham H., F.L. Cup, 3rd Rd., October 6, 1971.   *Pitch measurements:* 112 yds × 74 yds.

How to get there: Train to Torquay railway station. Bus 30 runs every 12 minutes from the station to the ground.

Match tickets: Stand seats available a fortnight before the match. Postal applications accepted provided correct remittance and S.A.E. are enclosed.

Car parking: Some street parking. Coaches park at Lymington Road coach station.

Entertainments/catering facilities: 200 Club—a match day venue luxury club—membership £10 (48 hours notice required for membership). Supporters' Social Club—open all week—now completely up-dated with luxury furnishings—membership 75p (48 hours notice required).

Club shop: Sells all types of souvenirs.

Handbooks/programmes: For programmes contact the club shop.

Extra information: Running commentaries of home matches to local hospitals. Twelve free seats supplied to members of the local Rehabilitation Centre of the Royal National Institute for the Blind who can listen to the hospital commentary while experiencing the match atmosphere.

Club Colours: All white with blue/yellow stripe on side of shirts, blue and yellow ring on sock turnover.
Change Colours: Yellow shirts with blue trim, blue shorts with yellow stripe down side, yellow socks with blue turnover.
Club Captain: Clint Boulton.   *Club Nickname:* 'The Gulls'.   *Team Captain:* Lew Chatterley.

TORQUAY UNITED 1975–76 LEAGUE RECORD

Match No.	Date	Venue	Opponents	Result	H/T Score	League Pos'n	Goalscorers	Attendance
1	Aug 16	H	Workington	W 1-0	0-0	—	Sandercock (pen)	2552
2	23	A	Lincoln C.	L 2-4	2-2	15	Twitchin, Boulton	4128
3	30	H	Brentford	L 2-3	1-1	18	Lane, Kruse	3011
4	Sept 6	A	Crewe Alex.	L 0-6	0-4	22		1751
5	13	H	Rochdale	W 1-0	1-0	19	Summerscales (og)	1679
6	20	A	Scunthorpe U.	L 1-3	0-2	22	Provan	1989
7	24	H	Exeter C.	W 1-0	1-0	—	Brown	3705
8	27	H	Northampton T.	L 0-1	0-0	18		1919
9	Oct 3	A	Tranmere R.	L 1-7	1-3	21	Brown	2870
10	11	A	Hartlepool	W 1-0	1-0	19	Chatterley	1695
11	18	H	Darlington	L 2-4	1-1	20	Sandercock (pen), Kruse	2413
12	21	A	Huddersfield T.	W 3-2	2-1	—	Parker, Brown 2	5777
13	24	A	Stockport Co.	L 0-1	0-0	21		2670
14	Nov 1	H	Newport Co.	D 1-1	0-1	21	Lynch	2163
15	5	H	Barnsley	W 2-0	2-0	—	Sandercock (pen), Myers	1457
16	8	A	Swansea C.	L 0-3	0-2	19		3170
17	15	H	Reading	D 0-0	0-0	18		2220
18	29	H	Bradford C.	W 1-0	0 0	16	Boulton	1868
19	Dec 6	A	Doncaster R.	W 1-0	0 0	16	Sandercock	7667
20	19	A	Southport	W 3-1	2 0	16	Kennedy, Lynch, Brown	1013
21	27	A	Cambridge U.	L 1-2	0 2	16	Provan	2921
22	30	H	AFC Bournemouth	W 2-1	1-0	—	Provan 2	3265
23	Jan 3	H	Watford	W 1-0	1-0	14	Chatterley	2515
24	10	A	Brentford	D 1-1	1-1	13	Sandercock (pen)	5680
25	17	H	Scunthorpe U.	W 1-0	1-0	10	Brown	2776
26	24	A	Rochdale	D 2-2	1-2	10	Chatterley, Brown	1443
27	Feb 7	A	Barnsley	D 0-0	0-0	10		2229
28	14	H	Swansea C.	L 0-2	0-1	13		2670
29	17	H	Huddersfield T.	L 1-3	0-1	—	Brown	2019
30	21	A	Reading	D 0-0	0-0	13		6259
31	25	A	Exeter C.	D 0-0	0-0	—		8112
32	28	H	Stockport Co.	W 4-1	0-1	13	Kennedy, Brown, Rudge, Lane	2072
33	Mar 5	A	Newport Co.	W 2-0	1-0	10	Brown, Twitchin	1588
34	10	H	Tranmere R.	W 2-1	0-0	—	Lane, Kennedy	2597
35	13	H	Hartlepool	D 1-1	1-0	9	Higgins	2676
36	15	A	Darlington	L 0-1	0-0	—		1313
37	20	A	Bradford C.	L 1-3	1-2	11	Goslin	2498
38	27	H	Doncaster R.	D 2-2	2-1	11	Goslin, Morrall	1975
39	31	H	Southport	W 2-1	0-0	—	Sandercock (pen), Morrall	1974
40	Apr 3	A	Workington	W 3-1	2-0	10	Brown, Kennedy, Rudge	1003
41	6	A	Northampton T.	D 2-2	1-2	—	Chatterley, Kruse	6263
42	10	H	Crewe Alex.	W 2-1	1-0	9	Brown, Provan	2293
43	16	A	Watford	D 0-0	0-0	9		5137
44	17	A	AFC Bournemouth	D 0-0	0-0	10		4180
45	19	H	Cambridge U.	D 0-0	0-0	—		3090
46	24	H	Lincoln C.	D 2-2	1-0	9	Brown 2	4151

Goalscorers

League (55): Brown 14, Sandercock 6 (5 pens), Provan 5, Chatterley 4, Kennedy 4, Kruse 3, Lane 3, Boulton 2, Goslin 2, Lynch 2, Morrall 2, Rudge 2, Twitchin 2, Higgins 1, Myers 1, Parker 1, own goal 1.
League Cup (11): Lane 3, Brown 3, Boulton 2, Kennedy, Twitchin, Provan.

League Cup	First Round	Swansea C. (a)	2-1
	Second Leg	(h)	5-3
	Second Round	Exeter C. (h)	1-1
		(a)	2-1
	Third Round	Doncaster R. (h)	1-1
		(a)	0-3
F.A. Cup	First Round	Hereford U. (a)	0-2

Lee	Parker	Sandercock	Chatterie	Kruse	Stocks	Provan	Myers	Boulton	Brown	Kennedy	Twitchin	Lane	Morrall	Lynch	Hayes	Kellard	Bond	Hickman	Goslin	Kudge	Higgins	Crabtree	Dunne	Match No.
1	2	3	4*	5	6	7	8	9	10	11	12													1
1	2	3	4	5	6*	7	8	9	10	11	12													2
1	2	3		5		7*	6	4	10	11	8	9	12											3
1		3		5			6*	9	10	11	7	8	12	2	4									4
1		3		5		9	6	4	11	8	7	10*	12	2										5
1		3		5		11	6	4	10	9	7	12	8*	2										6
1		3	4	5		7	6	9	10	11	8			2										7
1	12	3	4	5		7	6*	9	10	11	8			2										8
1	12	3	4	5			6	10	11	8	9		2*	7										9
		3	4	5		7		6	10	11	12	9*		2		8	1							10
8*		3	4	5		7	12	6	10	11				2			1	9						11
	2	3	4	5		7*	12	6	10	11	8						1	9						12
1	2	3	4	5		7	6*	10	11	8	12							9						13
1	2	3	6	5		8		10	11	4	7*	12						9						14
1	2	3		5		12	6	10	11*	8	7	4						9						15
1	2	3		5		12	8	6	10	11	7	4*						9						16
1		3	4	5		12	8*	6	10	11	7			2				9						17
1	7*	3		5		10		4	12	11	6	9		2				8						18
1		3	4	5		7		6	10	11	8			2				9						19
1		3	4	5		7		6	10	11	8	12	9*	2										20
1		3	4	5		7		6*	10	11	8	12	9	2										21
1		3	4	5		7		6	10	11	8	9*	12	2										22
1		3	4	5		7*		6	10		8		12	2				9			11			23
1		3	4	5		7		6	10		8		12	2				9*		11				24
1		3	4	5		7		6	10		8		12	2				9*		11				25
1		3	4	5		7		6	10	12	8			2				9		11*				26
1		3	12	5		7*		6	10	11	4			2				9		8				27
1		3	4	5		7		6	10	11	7	12		2				9*		8				28
1		3		5		7		6	10	4	8	9	12	2						11*				29
1		8		5		7		6	10	4	3	9*	12	2						11				30
1		3		5		7*		6	10	11	4	9	12	2						8				31
1		3		5				6	10	11	4	9	7	2						8				32
1		3	4	5				6	10	11	8	9		2						7				33
1		3		5				6	10	4	8	9		2						7	11			34
1		3	12	5				6	10	8	4	9*		2						7	11			35
1		3	7	5				6	10	4	8	9		2					12	11*				36
1		3	7*	5				6	10	4	11			2					9	8	12			37
1		3		5				6	10	4	8	12	7*	2					9	11				38
1		3		5		12		6	10	4*	8		7	2					9	11				39
		3		5		7		6	10	4	8		11*	2					12	9		1		40
1		3		5				6	10	4	8		11*	2					12	7				41
1		3		5		9		6	11	4	8		10	2						7				42
1		3	11	5		9		6*	10	4	8		12	2						7				43
1		3	4	5		10*		6	9	8	12		11	2						7				44
1		3	4	5		9		6	10	8	12		11*	2						7				45
1		6		5		11*		9	10	4	8		12	2						7			3	46
42	10	44	29	46	2	29	13	44	45	38	43	15	15	39	1	2	3	14	4	23	3	1	1	
+2s		+2s				+4s	2s			1s	1s	3s	8s	12s	1s				+3s	+1s				

TORQUAY UNITED—PLAYERS

Player and position	Ht.	Wt.	Birthplace	Clubs	League Appearances	Goals
Goalkeepers						
Terry Lee	5 11	11 0	Stepney	Tottenham H.	1	—
				Cardiff C. (on loan)	—	—
				Gillingham (on loan)	—	—
				Torquay U.	42	—
Richard Crabtree	5 10	11 7	Exeter	Bristol R.	—	—
				Doncaster R. (on loan)	1	—
				Northampton T. (on loan)	—	—
				Torquay U.	1	—
Defenders						
Clinton Boulton	5 10	11 3	Stoke	Port Vale	244	11
				Torquay U.	177+1	27
Phil Sandercock	5 10	11 0	Hollymouth	Torquay U.	172+6	11
David Stocks	5 11	11 13	Dulwich	Charlton Ath.	26	—
				Gillingham	45	—
				Bournemouth	221	2
				Torquay U.	146	3
Ian Twitchin	5 6	10 0	Teignmouth	Torquay U.	183+22	6
*Graham Parker	5 7	10 5	Coventry	Aston Villa	16+1	1
				Rotherham U.	3	—
				Lincoln C.	4+1	—
				Exeter C.	180+2	12
				Torquay U.	41+2	3
Pat Kruse	5 11	12 4	Biggleswade	Leicester C.	2	—
				Mansfield T. (on loan)	6	1
				Torquay U.	56	3
Jimmy Dunne (Eire)	5 9	10 11	Dublin	Millwall	—	—
				Torquay U.	125	13
				Fulham	142+1	1
				Torquay U.	1	—
Barry Lynch	5 11	11 13	Northfield	Aston V.	2	—
				Oldham (on loan)	—	—
				Grimsby T.	10+5	—
				Scunthorpe U.	62+2	—
				Torquay U.	39+1	2
Midfield						
Lew Chatterley	6 0	11 7	Birmingham	Aston Villa	149+5	25
				Doncaster R. (on loan)	9	—
				Northampton T.	23	2
				Grimsby T.	72+1	15
				Southampton	7+2	—
				Torquay U.	42+2	6
*Richard Goslin	5 11	11 12	Bovey Tracey	Torquay U.	14+5	4
Forwards						
*Cliff Myers	5 10	10 10	London	Charlton Ath.	15+2	2
				Yeovil T.	(Southern League)	
				Torquay U.	80+6	12
David Kennedy	5 7	10 4	Birkenhead	Tranmere R.	16+1	—
				Chester	79+9	9
				Torquay U.	107+6	4
Andy Provan	5 5	10 0	Greenock	St. Mirren	8	—
				Barnsley	3	—
				York C.	159+1	49
				Chester	77+3	19
				Wrexham	49+2	10
				Southport	82+1	28
				Torquay U.	64+7	11
Steve Morrall	5 9	11 0	Torquay	Torquay U.	100+28	10
				Norwich C. (on loan)	—	—
Billy Brown	5 9	11 4	Falkirk	Burnley	0+1	—
				Carlisle U.	16+3	8
				Newport Co.	166+2	49
				Hereford U. (on loan)	9	6
				Brentford	16	9
				Torquay U.	55+1	17
Mike Hickman	5 10	11 3	Elstead	Brighton	12+2	—
				Grimsby T.	247+6	48
				Blackburn R.	23+3	8
				Torquay U.	14	—
Kevin Lane	5 9	10 8	Wolverhampton	Walsall	—	—
				Torquay U.	15+8	3
David Rudge	5 7	10 10	Wolverhampton	Aston V.	49+6	10
				Hereford U.	75+7	8
				Torquay U.	23	2

TOTTENHAM HOTSPUR
DIV. 1

Chairman: S. A. Wale.

Directors: C. F. Cox (*Vice-Chairman*), A. Richardson, H. G. S. Groves, G. A. Richardson.

Manager: Terry Neill. *Secretary:* G. W. Jones.

Asst. Manager: Wilf Dixon.

Year Formed: 1882. *Turned Professional:* 1895.

Limited Company: 1898.

Previous Grounds: 1882, Tottenham Marshes; 1885, Northumberland Park; 1898, White Hart Lane.

Previous Name: 1882–85, Hotspur Football Club.

Honours: *Football League,* Division 1. Champions: 1950–51, 1960–61; Runners-up: 1921–22, 1951–52, 1956–57 1962–63. Division 2, Champions: 1919–20, 1949–50; Runners-up: 1908–09, 1932–33. *F.A. Cup,* Winners: 1901 (as non-league club), 1921, 1961, 1962, 1967. *Football League Cup,* Winners: 1970–71, 1972–73.

European Competitions: *European Cup:* 1961–62 (semi-finalists). *European Cup Winners Cup:* 1962–63 (winners), 1963–64, 1967–68. *UEFA Cup:* 1971–72 (winners), 1972–73 (semi-finalists), 1973–74 (finalists).

Record Victory: 13-2 v Crewe Alex, F.A. Cup, 4th Rd. Replay, Feb. 3rd, 1960.

Record Defeat: 2-7 v Liverpool, Division 1, Oct. 31st, 1914; v Newcastle U., Division 1. Sept. 1st, 1951; v Blackburn R., Division 1, Sept. 7th, 1963. and v Burnley, Division 1, Apr. 22nd, 1964.

Most League Points: 70, Division 2, 1919–20.

Most League Goals: 115, Division 1, 1960–61.

Highest League Scorer in Season: Jimmy Greaves, 37, Division 1, 1962–63.
Most League Appearances: Pat Jennings 449, 1964-1976.

Most Capped Player: Pat Jennings, 59 (61), N. Ireland.

Most League Goals in Total Aggregate: Jimmy Greaves, 220, 1961–70.

Record Transfer Fee Received: £70,000 for Terry Venables from Q.P.R., June 1969.

Record Transfer Fee Paid: £200,000 to West Ham U. for Martin Peters, Mar. 1970.

Managers Since the War: Joe Hulme, Arthur Rowe, Jimmy Anderson, Bill Nicholson.

Address of Supporters Club: 744 High Road, N.17.

---

748 High Rd., Tottenham, N.17. Telephone 01-808 2046. *Ground capacity:* 52,000. *Record attendance:* 75,038 v Sunderland, F.A. Cup 6th Rd., March 5, 1938. *Record receipts:* £49,920 v Feyenoord, UEFA Cup Final 1st leg, May 21, 1974. *Pitch measurements:* 110 yds × 73 yds.

How to get there: Underground to Manor House (Piccadilly line) or Seven Sisters (Victoria line). From Manor House, buses 279, 259; from Seven Sisters 67, 149, 171, 243, 259, 123, 279. White Hart Lane station is three minutes walk from the ground and is served by trains from Liverpool St.

Match tickets: For League matches, seats can be booked not earlier than 21 days before the match. At the Park Lane and Paxton Road ends, there are seats available at the turnstiles.

Car parking: No street parking within a ¼ mile radius of the ground.

Entertainments/catering facilities: Hot food available at snack and chicken bars in the ground.

Club Shop: There is a shop on corner of Park Lane and High Road, and a kiosk on the ground which stocks over 400 items.

Handbooks/programmes: Programmes available on subscription to shop.

Extra information: Supporters' Club with a present membership of over 7,000 is open to new members; information from the Secretary, Mrs. M. Ellam. (Tel: 808-7430).

Club Colours: White shirts, blue shorts, white stockings.
Change Colours: All yellow with blue trims.
Club Captain: Steve Perryman.
First Team Trainer: Keith Burkinshaw.
Club Nickname: 'Spurs'.

TOTTENHAM HOTSPUR 1975–76 LEAGUE RECORD

Match No.	Date	Venue	Opponents	Result	H/T Score	League Pos'n	Goalscorers	Attendance
1	Aug16	H	Middlesbrough	W 1-0	0-0	—	Perryman	25,502
2	20	H	Ipswich T.	D 1-1	0-0	—	Duncan	28,311
3	23	A	Liverpool	L 2-3	2-0	11	Duncan, Jones	42,729
4	25	A	West Ham U.	L 0-1	0-1	—		35,914
5	30	H	Norwich C.	D 2-2	1-0	14	Pratt, Duncan	23,145
6	Sept 6	A	Manchester U.	L 2-3	1-2	18	Jones, Chivers	51,641
7	13	H	Derby Co.	L 2-3	2-1	20	Duncan, Chivers	28,455
8	20	A	Leeds U.	D 1-1	0-1	19	Pratt	27,372
9	27	H	Arsenal	D 0-0	0-0	17		37,092
10	Oct 4	A	Newcastle U.	D 2-2	0-1	19	Pratt, Duncan	32,235
11	11	A	Aston Villa	D 1-1	0-0	18	Pratt	40,048
12	18	H	Manchester C.	D 2-2	2-1	18	Jones 2	30,502
13	25	A	Leicester C.	W 3-2	1-1	18	Coates, Chivers, Perryman	22,088
14	Nov 1	H	Wolverhampton W.	W 2-1	1-0	15	Neighbour, Young	26,102
15	8	A	Q.P.R.	D 0-0	0-0	14		28,454
16	15	H	Stoke C.	D 1-1	0-0	14	Jones	25,698
17	22	A	Manchester C.	L 1-2	0-0	16	Osgood	31,456
18	29	H	Burnley	W 2-1	0-1	15	Duncan 2	21,222
19	Dec 6	A	Sheffield U.	W 2-1	1-0	13	Duncan 2	23,909
20	10	H	Everton	D 2 2	1-0	—	Pratt, Duncan	18,638
21	13	H	Liverpool	L 0-4	0-1	13		29,891
22	20	A	Middlesbrough	L 0-1	0-1	14		22,000
23	26	H	Birmingham C.	L 1-3	0-2	16	Chivers (pen)	21,651
24	27	A	Coventry C.	D 2-2	1-1	16	Duncan 2	21,094
25	Jan 10	A	Derby Co.	W 3-2	3-2	15	Neighbour, Perryman, McAllister	28,085
26	17	H	Manchester U.	D 1-1	0-1	16	Duncan	49,387
27	31	A	Ipswich T.	W 2-1	1-0	14	Coates, Osgood (pen)	24,072
28	Feb 7	H	West Ham U.	D 1-1	0-0	15	Duncan	32,832
29	14	H	Q.P.R.	L 0-3	0-0	16		28,200
30	21	A	Stoke C.	W 2-1	2-1	14	Duncan, Hoddle	17,113
31	24	A	Everton	L 0-1	0-0	—		18,126
32	28	H	Leicester C.	D 1-1	1-0	12	Chivers	21,427
33	Mar 6	A	Norwich C.	L 1-3	0-0	15	Chivers	21,220
34	13	H	Aston Villa	W 5-2	3-1	13	Nicholl (og), Perryman, Duncan, McAllister, Robinson	23,169
35	16	A	Wolverhampton W.	W 1-0	0-0	—	Pratt	21,544
36	20	A	Burnley	W 2-1	0-0	9	Duncan, Pratt	15,465
37	27	H	Sheffield U.	W 5-0	1-0	8	Young, Duncan, Perryman 2, Chivers	21,370
38	Apr 3	A	Arsenal	W 2-0	2-0	6	Pratt, Duncan	42,134
39	10	H	Leeds U.	D 0-0	0-0	8		40,359
40	17	A	Birmingham C.	L 1-3	0-0	8	Pratt	30,616
41	19	H	Coventry C.	W 4-1	2-0	—	Osgood, Neighbour, Pratt, Duncan	21,107
42	24	H	Newcastle U.	L 0-3	0-0	9		30,049

Goalscorers

League (63): Duncan 20, Pratt 10, Chivers 7 (1 a pen), Perryman 6, Jones 5, Neighbour 3, Osgood 3 (1a pen), Coates 2, McAllister 2, Young 2, Hoddle 1, Robinson 1, own goal 1.
League Cup (14): Duncan 4, Pratt 3, Chivers 2, Conn, Jones, Young, McAllister, own goal 1.
F.A. Cup (2): Duncan, Perryman.

League Cup	Second Round	Watford (a)	1-0	
	Third Round	Crewe Alex. (a)	2-0	
	Fourth Round	West Ham U. (h)	0-0	
		(a)	2-0	(a.e.t.)
	Fifth Round	Doncaster R. (h)	7-2	
	Semi-Final	Newcastle U. (h)	1-0	
		(a)	1-3	
F.A. Cup	Third Round	Stoke C. (h)	1-1	
		(a)	1-2	

Appearances grid (shirt number worn by each player in each match; `*` denotes substitute/captain marker as printed). Blank = did not appear.

Jennings	Kinnear	Naylor	Pratt	Osgood	McAllister	McNab	Perryman	Chivers	Jones	Neighbour	Duncan	Knowles	Conn	Smith	Hoddle	Young	Coates	Walford	McGrath	Stead	Robinson	Brotherston	Daines	Match
1	2	3	4	5	6	7	8	9	10	11														1
1		2*	4	5	6	7	8	9	10	11	12	3												2
1		2	4	5	6		8	9	10	11		3	7											3
1		2	4	5	6	12	8	9	10	11*		3	7											4
1		8	4	5	6	7			10	11	9	3*		2	12									5
1		3	4	5	6	7	8	12	10	9	11			2*										6
1		3	2	5	6	7	8	4	10	11	9													7
1		2	4	6		7	8		10	11	9	3				5								8
1		2	4	6		7	8	12	10	11	9*	3				5								9
1		2	4	6		7	8		10	11	9	3*				5	12							10
1		2	4	6	3		8	9	12	11	7*		10			5								11
1		4	6	2			8	9	10	11		3	7			5								12
1			2	6	3		8	9	10	11			7			5	4							13
1			2	6	3	12	8	9	10	11			7*			5	4							14
1		2	4	6	3		8	9*	10	11	12					5	7							15
1		2	4	6	3*		8		10	11	9					5	7	12						16
1		2	4	6	3		8		10	11	9*	12				5	7							17
1		2	4	6	12		8		10	11*	9	3				5	7							18
1		2	4	6	3	8			10	11	9					5	7							19
1		2	4	6	12		8		10	11	9	3				5	7*							20
1		2	4	6	3	7	8		10*	11	9					5	12							21
1		2	4	6	3		8	9		11	10					5	7							22
1		2	4	6	3	11	8	9	12		10					5	7*							23
1		2	4	6	3		8	9	12	11	10					5	7*							24
1		2	4	6	3		8	9		11	10					5	7							25
1		2	4	6	3		8	9		11	10					5	7							26
1			4	6	3		8		10	11	9					5	7		2					27
1		2	4	6	3		8	12	10	11*	9					5	7							28
1		2	4	6	3		8	12	10	11	9					5	7*							29
1			4	6	3		8	10	12	11	9*		7			5			2					30
1			4	6	3		8	10		11	9		7			5			2					31
1		2	4*	6			8	9		11	10	3	7			5	12							32
1		2*	4	6	3		8	10	12	11	9					5	7							33
1		2		6	3		8	9	10		4					5	7				12	11*		34
1		2	4	6	3		8	9	10	11						5	7							35
		2	4	6	3		8	9	10	11						5	7						1	36
		2	4	6	3		8	9	12	11	10					5	7*						1	37
1		2	4	6	3		8	9	7	11	10					5								38
1		2	4	6	3		8	9	7*	11	10					5	12							39
1		2	4	6	3		8	9	12	11*	10					5	7							40
1		2	4	6	3		8	9*	12	11	10					5	7							41
1		2	4	6			8	9*	12	11	10					5	7			3				42
40	**1**	**36**	**41**	**42**	**35**	**11**	**40**	**28**	**25**	**35**	**35**	**10**	**7**	**2**	**6**	**35**	**21**	**1**	**3**	**4**	**1**	**1**	**2**	
					+4s					+4s	+9s		+2s		+1s		+3s	+1s	+1s	+1s				

385

TOTTENHAM HOTSPUR—PLAYERS

Player and position	Ht.	Wt.	Birthplace	Clubs	League Appearances	Goals
Goalkeepers						
Pat Jennings	6 0	12 6	Newry	Watford	48	—
(N. Ireland)			Co. Down	Tottenham H.	449	—
Barry Daines	5 11½	11 8	Whitham	Tottenham H.	11	—
Mark Kendall	5 11	13 0	Blackwood	Tottenham H.	—	—
Defenders						
*Cyril Knowles	6 0	11 13	Fitzwilliam	Middlesbrough	37	—
(England)				Tottenham H.	400+1	14
Willie Young	6 3	12 10	Scotland	Aberdeen	132	10
				Tottenham H.	35	2
Michael Dillon	5 10½	11 8	Highgate	Tottenham H.	21+3	1
				Millwall (on loan)	4	—
				Swindon T. (on loan)	7+2	—
				(contract cancelled Oct. 1975)		
Don McAllister	5 10	11 2	Radcliffe	Bolton W.	155+1	2
				Tottenham H.	42+1	2
Terry Naylor	5 10	11 10	Islington	Tottenham H.	132+5	—
Keith Osgood	5 11	11 2	Ealing	Tottenham H.	52+1	3
*Ian Smith	5 10	10 12	Rotherham	Tottenham H.	2	—
Fred Barwick	5 9	11 0	Dagenham	Tottenham H.	—	—
Steve Cavanagh	5 9	10 13	Hackney	Tottenham H.	—	—
Mike Stead	5 9	11 8	West Ham	Tottenham H.	—	—
Roger Wade	5 8	10 7	Lambeth	Tottenham H.	—	—
Midfield						
Alfie Conn	5 10	11 5	Kirkaldy	Rangers	78+16	21
(Scotland)				Tottenham H.	23+2	6
Ralph Coates	5 7½	11 9½	Hetton-le-Hole	Burnley	213+2	26
(England)				Tottenham H.	144+10	10
Steve Perryman	5 8	10 10	Ealing	Tottenham H.	266	20
John Pratt	5 8¾	10 3	London	Tottenham H.	181+13	22
Noel Brotherston	5 10	10 6	Dundonald	Tottenham H.	1	—
Andrew Keeley	5 10	11 5	Basildon	Tottenham H.	—	—
Neil McNab	5 7	10 0	Greenock	Morton	11+3	—
				Tottenham H.	13+5	—
Terry Boyle	5 10	11 6	Ammerford	Tottenham H.	—	—
Glen Hoddle	6 0	11 6	Hayes	Tottenham H.	6+1	1
Steve Walford	6 1	11 7	Highgate	Tottenham H.	1+1	—
Forwards						
Martin Chivers	6 1½	12 12½	Southampton	Southampton	173+1	97
(England)				Tottenham H.	268+10	118
John Duncan	5 11	11 4	Lochee	Dundee	121+3	62
				Tottenham H.	63+2	32
Chris Jones	5 11	10 7	Jersey	Tottenham H.	41+9	6
Chris McGrath	5 9	10 11	Belfast	Tottenham H.	30+8	5
(N. Ireland)				Millwall (on loan)	15	3
Jimmy Neighbour	5 7	10 10	Chingford	Tottenham H.	97+15	8
Gerry Armstrong	5 11	13 2	Belfast	Tottenham H.	—	—
Martin Robinson	5 11	11 3	Ilford	Tottenham H.	1+1	1
Kevin Stead	5 10	11 0	West Ham	Tottenham H.	4	—
*Ian Cranstone	6 0	11 12	Rochford	Tottenham H.	—	—
				Charlton Ath. (on loan)	—	—

TRANMERE ROVERS

Chairman: W. A. Bothwell.

Vice-Chairman: H. B. Thomas.

Directors: H. B. Thomas, H. A. Bainbridge, F.C.A., G. A. Gould, J.P., F.C.A., R. Moffat, J.P., G. E. Williams, A. W. Brew.

Secretary & General Manager: D. W. Russell.

Team Manager: John King.

Year Formed: 1883. *Turned Professional:* 1912.

Limited Company: 1920.

Honours: *Football League,* best season in Division 2: 22nd, 1938–39. Division 3(N), Champions: 1937–38. *F.A. Cup,* best season: 5th Rd., 1967–68. *Football League Cup,* best season: 4th Rd., 1961.

Record Victory: 13-4 v Oldham Ath., Division 3(N), Dec. 26th, 1935.

Record Defeat: 1-9 v Tottenham H., F.A. Cup, 3rd Rd. Replay, Jan. 14th, 1953.

Most League Points: 60, Division 4, 1964–65.

Most League Goals: 111, Division 3(N), 1930–31.

Highest League Scorer in Season: Bunny Bell, 35, Division 3(N), 1933–34 (the same player scored 9 v Oldham Ath. Dec. 26th, 1935).

Most League Goals in Total Aggregate: Bunny Bell, 104, 1931–36.

Most Capped Player: Joe Brown, 3 (4), Ireland; Albert Gray, 3 (23), Wales.

Most League Appearances: Harold Bell, 595, 1946–64 (including League record of 401 consecutive appearances).

Record Transfer Fee Received: £34,000 from W.B.A. for Jim Cumbes, Aug. 1969.

Record Transfer Fee Paid: £9,000 to Northampton T. for George Hudson, Jan. 1967.

Managers Since the War: Ernie Blackburn, Noel Kelly, Peter Farrell, Walter Galbraith, Dave Russell, Jackie Wright, Ron Yeats.

Address of Supporters Club: Supporters Assn., Prenton Park, Prenton Road West, Birkenhead.

Prenton Park, Prenton Road West, Birkenhead. Telephone 051-608 3677/4194. *Ground capacity:* 25,000. *Record attendance:* 24,424 v Stoke C., F.A. Cup 4th Rd., February 5, 1972. *Record receipts:* £8,982 v Stoke City F.A. Cup 4th Rd., February 5, 1972. *Pitch measurements:* 112 yds × 74 yds.

How to get there: Special buses from railway stations, Hamilton Square and Rock Ferry. Mersey Railway Liverpool, to Hamilton Square, then buses 80 to 90 or 64.

Match tickets: Seats can be booked in advance.

Car parking: Large car park at the back of the stand.

Entertainments/catering facilities: Snack bars in ground. Social club with bar facilities.

Club shop: Run by Supporters' Association.

Handbooks/programmes: Programmes available on subscription.

Extra information: Tranmere's record victory equals the highest score in a League game; in the 13-4 win over Oldham, centre-forward Bunny Bell scored nine goals.

Club Colours: All white with blue facings, blue shorts and white stockings with blue tops.

Change Colours: Red shirts, red shorts, red stockings.

First Team Trainer/Coach:

Club Nickname: 'Rovers'.

TRANMERE ROVERS 1975–76 LEAGUE RECORD

Match No.	Date	Venue	Opponents	Result	H/T Score	League Pos'n	Goalscorers	Attendance
1	Aug 16	A	Swansea C.	D 1-1	0-1	—	Moore	2866
2	22	H	Doncaster R.	D 2-2	0-1	14	Brookes (og), Mathias	2013
3	29	A	Exeter C.	W 2-0	0-0	6	Moore, Allen	3861
4	Sept 5	H	Darlington	W 2-0	0-0	2	Moore, Tynan	2403
5	13	A	Bradford C.	L 0-3	0-1	11		2046
6	19	H	Barnsley	W 1-0	1-0	5	Tynan	2638
7	22	H	Scunthorpe U.	W 2-1	2-1	—	Peplow, Tynan	2308
8	27	A	Hartlepool	W 2-1	2-1	4	Peplow, Moore	1544
9	Oct 3	H	Torquay U.	W 7-1	3-1	2	James 2, Mitchell 2, Moore 2, Young	2870
10	10	H	Northampton T.	W 2-0	1-0	1	James, Moore	4808
11	18	A	AFC Bournemouth	L 2-4	1-3	2	James, Kenny (pen)	5226
12	20	H	Southport	W 1-0	0-0	—	James	3896
13	24	H	Workington	W 6-0	4-0	1	Moore, James, Young, Peplow 3	4045
14	Nov 1	A	Rochdale	L 1-4	0-3	3	James	2047
15	4	A	Lincoln C.	D 2-2	1-0	—	James, Peplow	11,206
16	7	H	Brentford	W 5-1	2-1	3	James, Moore 4	4327
17	15	A	Crewe Alex.	L 0-1	0-1	4		2832
18	28	H	Watford	W 3-0	2-0	4	Moore 2, Peplow	3473
19	Dec 6	A	Cambridge U.	D 3-3	1-1	4	Kenny, James, Peplow	2588
20	13	A	Doncaster R.	L 0-3	0-1	4		5684
21	19	H	Reading	W 2-0	1-0	4	Peplow, Mitchell	3170
22	26	A	Huddersfield T.	L 0-1	0-0	4		6672
23	27	H	Stockport Co.	W 5-0	0-0	4	Moore 4, Peplow	4701
24	Jan 3	A	Newport Co.	W 5-1	1-0	4	Moore 4, Palios	2074
25	9	H	Exeter C.	D 1-1	1-0	4	Moore (pen)	4661
26	17	A	Barnsley	L 0-1	0-0	4		2689
27	31	A	Southport	D 0-0	0-0	4		2632
28	Feb 6	H	Lincoln C.	W 2-0	0-0	4	Moore (pen), James	4869
29	14	A	Brentford	W 1-0	1-0	4	James	4720
30	20	H	Crewe Alex.	W 2-1	0-1	3	James, Mitchell	4306
31	24	A	Scunthorpe U.	D 2-2	1-1	—	Philpotts, Mathias	3049
32	28	A	Workington	W 1-0	0-0	3	Palios	1369
33	Mar 6	H	Rochdale	L 0-1	0-1	4		3354
34	10	A	Torquay U.	L 1-2	0-0	—	Moore	2597
35	12	A	Northampton T.	D 1-1	1-0	4	Mitchell	8047
36	15	H	AFC Bournemouth	W 2-0	1-0	—	Moore, James	3660
37	20	A	Watford	D 2-2	0-2	4	James, Moore (pen)	5449
38	26	H	Cambridge U.	W 3-2	3-0	3	Moore (pen), Palios, Philpotts	4005
39	31	A	Reading	L 0-5	0-2	—		10,961
40	Apr 2	H	Swansea C.	W 3-0	1-0	4	Tynan, Palios, Allen	3475
41	6	H	Hartlepool	L 1-2	0-1	—	Tynan	3450
42	10	A	Darlington	L 0-2	0-1	4		2023
43	14	H	Newport Co.	W 3-1	2-0	—	James, Moore, Peplow	3629
44	17	H	Huddersfield T.	W 3-0	2-0	3	Moore 3 (2 pens)	8308
45	19	A	Stockport Co.	W 2-0	0-0	—	Philpotts, Moore	2973
46	26	H	Bradford C.	D 3-3	2-2	—	Philpotts, Moore (pen), James	5867

Goalscorers

League (89): Moore 34 (7 pens), James 17, Peplow 11, Mitchell 5, Tynan 5, Palios 4, Philpotts 4, Allen 2, Kenny 2 (1 a pen), Mathias 2, Young 2, own goal 1.
League Cup (3): Moore 3.

League Cup	First Round	Crewe Alex. (a)	1-2
	Second Leg	(h)	2-1
F.A. Cup	First Round	Coventry Spts. (a)	0-2

Johnson	Mathias	Flood	Parry	Philpotts	Palios	Young	Tynan	Moore	Kenny	Peplow	Mitchell	Crossley	Allen	James	Griffiths	Match No.
1	2	3	4	5	6	7	8	9	10	11						1
1	2	3	4	5	6	11	10	9		7*	8	12				2
1	2	3	4	5	6	11*	10	9		7	8	12				3
1	2	3	4	5	6		10	9		7	8			11		4
1	2	3	4	5	6		10	9		7	8			11		5
1	2	3	4	5	6		10	9		7	8			11		6
1	2	3	4	5	6		10*	9		7	8	12		11		7
1	2	3	4	5			10	9	6	7	8	12		11*		8
1	2	3	4	5	6			9	10	7	8			11		9
1	2	3	4	5	12	6	10	9		7*	8			11		10
1	2	3	4	5	6	8*	10	12	9	7				11		11
1	2	3	4	5	6		10	9		7	8			11		12
1	2	3	4	5	6		10	9		7	8			11		13
1	2	3	4	5	6	9	10	12		7*	8			11		14
1	2	3	4	5	6		10	9		7	8			11		15
1	2	3	4	5	6		10	9		7	8			11		16
1	2	3	4	5	6	9	11	12		7*	8			10		17
1	2	3	4	5	6		10	9*	8	7	12			11		18
1	3		2	5	6			9	10	7	8			11	4	19
1	2		4	5	6	12		9	10	7	8			11*	3	20
1	3		2	5		6	10	9		7	8			11	4	21
1	2	3		5		6	10	9		7	8			11	4	22
1	2	3		5		6	10*	9	12	7	8			11	4	23
1	2	3		5		6	10	9		7	8			11	4	24
1	2	3		5		6	10*	9	12	7	8			11	4	25
1	2	3		5		6*	10	9	12	7	8			11	4	26
1	2	3		5		6	12	10	9	7*	8			11	4	27
1	2	3		5		6	10	9		7	8			11	4	28
1	2	3		5		6	10	9		7	8			11	4	29
1	2	3		5		6	10	9		7	8			11	4	30
1	2	3		5		6	10	9	12	7	8			11*	4	31
1	2	3		5		6	10	9		7	8			11	4	32
1	2	3		5		6*	10	9	12	7	8			11	4	33
1	2	3		5		6	10	9		7	8			11	4	34
1	2	3		5		6*	10	9	12	7	8			11	4	35
1	2	3		5		6	10	9		7	8			11	4	36
1	2	3		5*	12	6	10	9	8	7				11	4	37
1	2	3		5		6	10	9	8	7				11	4	38
1	2	3		5		6	10	9		7	8			11	4	39
1	2	3		5		6	10	9	12	7*	8			11	4	40
1	2	3		5		6	10	9*		7	8	12		11	4	41
1	2	3		5		6	10	9		7*	8	12		11	4	42
1	2	3		5		6		9		7	8		11	10	4	43
1	2	3		5		6		9		7	8		11	10	4	44
1	2	3		5		6		9		7	8		11	10	4	45
1	2	3		5	12	6		9		7	8		11	10*	4	46
46	46	43	21	46	20	25	42	46	8	46	42	—	9	38	28	

+2s (Palios) +2s (Young) +1s (Tynan) +10s (Kenny) +1s (Mitchell) +1s (Crossley) +5s (Allen)

TRANMERE ROVERS—PLAYERS

Player and position	Ht.	Wt.	Birthplace	Clubs	League Appearances	Goals
Goalkeepers						
Dickie Johnson	6 1	12 10	Liverpool	Tranmere R.	139	—
*David Johnson	6 5	14 7	Birkenhead	Tranmere R.	3	—
				Southport (on loan)	6	—
				Preston N.E. (on loan)	—	—
Gordon West			Darfield	Blackpool	31	—
(England)				Everton	335	—
				Tranmere R.	—	—
Defenders						
Ray Mathias	5 9	11 4	Liverpool	Tranmere R.	320+5	5
Eddie Flood	5 7	10 0	Liverpool	Liverpool	—	—
				Tranmere R.	120+1	3
Leslie Parry	5 11	11 0	Wallasey	Tranmere R.	34+3	—
Midfield						
Steve Peplow	5 8	10 4	Liverpool	Liverpool	2	—
				Swindon T.	37+3	11
				Nottingham F.	3	—
				Mansfield T. (on loan)	4	3
				Tranmere R.	78+3	16
David Philpotts	5 11½	11 7	Bramborough	Coventry C.	3	—
				Southport (on loan)	8	—
				Tranmere R.	85	4
Mark Palios	5 8	10 13	Birkenhead	Tranmere R.	90+5	13
Tommy Young	5 11	12 7	Glasgow	Falkirk	83+9	33
				Tranmere R.	149+2	23
Forwards						
Paul Crossley	5 7	11 5	Rochdale	Rochdale	17	2
				Preston N.E.	3	—
				Southport	10	2
				Tranmere R.	186+16	37
Russell Allen	5 10	11 7	Smethwick	Arsenal	—	—
				W.B.A.	—	—
				Cambridge U. (on loan)	—	—
				Tranmere R.	51+19	15
John James	6 0	11 0	Stoke	Port Vale	201+7	40
				Chester	97+1	40
				Tranmere R.	38	17
Bill Kenny	5 8	10 2	Liverpool	Everton	8+3	—
				Tranmere R.	20+11	2
Barrie Mitchell	6 0	11 6	Aberdeen	Dunfermline	136+3	32
				Aberdeen	14	1
				Tranmere R.	77+6	10
Bobby Tynan	5 10	11 0	Liverpool	Tranmere R.	105+2	16
Ronnie Moore	6 0	12 9	Liverpool	Tranmere R.	136	38

Chairman: K. E. Wheldon.

Directors: J. A. Harris, S. E. Boler, R. Homden.

Manager: Doug Fraser

Secretary and Commercial Manager: H. J. Westmancoat.

Year Formed: 1888.

Turned Professional: 1888.

Limited Company: 1921.

Previous Names: Walsall Swifts (Founded 1877) and Walsall Town (Founded 1879) amalgamated in 1888 and were known as Walsall Town Swifts until 1895.

Honours: *Football League,* best season in Division 2: 6th, 1898–99. Division 4, Champions: 1959–60. Division 3, Runners-up: 1960–61. *F.A. Cup,* best season: 5th Rd., 1939 and last 16, 1888–89. *Football League Cup,* best season: 4th Rd., 1966–67.

Record Victory: 10-0 v Darwen, Division 2, Mar. 4th, 1899.

Record Defeat: 0-12 v Small Heath, Dec. 17th, 1892 and v Darwen, Dec. 26th, 1896, both Division 2.

Most League Points: 65, Division 4, 1959–60.

Most League Goals: 102, Division 4, 1959–60.

Highest League Scorer in Season: Gilbert Alsop, 40, Division 3(N), 1933–34 and 1934–35.

Most League Goals in Total Aggregate: Tony Richards, 184, 1954–63, and Colin Taylor, 184 1958–72.

Most Capped Player: Alf Jones, 3, England.

Most League Appearances: Colin Taylor, 459, 1958–63, 1964–68, 1969–73.

Record Transfer Fee Received: £35,000 from Fulham for Allan Clarke, Mar. 1966.

Record Transfer Fee Paid: £17,000 to Birmingham C. for Trevor Smith, Oct. 1964.

Managers Since the War: Harry Hibbs, Tony McPhee, Brough Fletcher, Major Buckley, John Love, Billy Moore, Alf Wood, Ray Shaw, Ron Lewin, Dick Graham, Billy Moore, John Smith, Ronnie Allen.

Address of Supporters Club: 61 Bradford Street, Walsall, Staffs.

Fellows Park, Walsall. Telephone 0922 22791. *Telegraphic address:* 'Walsall F.C., Walsall'. *Ground capacity:* 24,100. *Record attendance:* 25,453 v Newcastle U., Division 2, August 29 1961. *Record receipts:* £12,775.35p v Newcastle U., F.A. Cup 4th Rd., January 25 1975. *Pitch measurements:* 113 yds × 73 yds.

How to get there: Corporation specials from Bradford Place. Buses 37 and 38 within walking distance of the ground. Nearest railway stations, Bescot (10 minutes' walk from ground) and Walsall.

Match tickets: Seats can be booked at any time by postal, personal, or telephone application to the secretary's office.

Car parking: Car park in Hillary Street for 200 cars. Side-street parking available.

Entertainments/catering facilities: Supporters' club adjacent to ground. Four tea bars and three licensed bars inside the ground.

Club shop: The Boutique, run by the Supporters' Club, is open on match days.

Handbooks/programmes: Annual handbook published by the supporters' club. Programmes available on subscription.

Extra information: In 1947, Walsall set a Division 3(S) record by winning 8-0 away at Northampton.

Club Colours: White shirts with red facings, red shorts, white stockings.
Change Colour: Blue shirts, black shorts, blue stockings.
Club Captain: Dave Robinson.
Club Nickname: 'Saddlers'.

WALSALL 1975–76 LEAGUE RECORD

Match No.	Date	Venue	Opponents	Result	H/T Score	League Pos'n	Goalscorers	Attendance
1	Aug 16	A	Peterborough U.	D 0-0	0-0	—		7174
2	23	H	Swindon T.	D 1-1	1-1	15	Buckley	5146
3	30	A	Halifax T.	L 1-2	1-1	19	Harrison	2076
4	Sept 6	H	Southend U.	L 2-3	1-2	21	Buckley (pen), Dennehy	4380
5	10	A	Brighton & H.A.	W 2-1	1-1	—	Wright, Andrews	8592
6	13	H	Preston N. E.	L 1-3	0-1	16	Buckley	7015
7	16	H	Crystal Palace	D 1-1	0-0	—	Wright	5496
8	20	H	Bury	L 0-1	0-0	19		4845
9	22	H	Shrewsbury T.	W 2-0	2-0	—	Taylor, Buckley (pen)	4866
10	27	A	Mansfield T.	L 1-4	0-2	15	Wright	5450
11	Oct 4	H	Grimsby T.	W 2-0	1-0	12	Buckley (pen), Spinner	4113
12	11	A	Colchester U.	L 0-2	0-1	16		2980
13	18	H	Chester	W 1-0	0-0	13	Buckley	4146
14	21	H	Millwall	D 1-1	0-0	—	Wright	4884
15	25	A	Gillingham	W 3-2	1-1	8	Wiltshire (og), Buckley, Andrews	5942
16	Nov 4	A	Cardiff C.	D 0-0	0-0	—		8884
17	8	A	Rotherham U.	L 1-3	1-1	15	Buckley	4454
18	15	H	Chesterfield	W 1-0	0-0	13	Wright	4175
19	29	A	Aldershot	L 2-3	0-2	16	Dennehy, Wright	4010
20	Dec 2	H	Sheffield W.	D 2-2	0-1	—	Buckley, Wright	4148
21	6	H	Port Vale	W 3-1	2-0	10	Andrews, Birch, Wright	4526
22	20	H	Brighton & H.A.	W 2-0	0-0	8	Buckley 2	5435
23	26	A	Hereford U.	W 3-1	1-1	5	Evans, Buckley 2	10,891
24	27	H	Wrexham	D 2-2	1-1	5	Dennehy, Buckley	9028
25	Jan 6	A	Crystal Palace	W 1-	1-0	—	Dennehy	16,181
26	10	H	Halifax T.	W 2-0	2-0	2	Robinson, Wright	7167
27	17	A	Bury	D 1-1	0-1	4	Andrews	8068
28	24	H	Preston N.E.	W 3-1	3-0	2	Evans, Buckley 2	6721
29	31	A	Millwall	L 1-2	0-0	5	Dennehy	4747
30	Feb 7	H	Cardiff C.	L 2-3	2-0	7	Buckley 2	7109
31	13	H	Rotherham U.	W 5-1	1-1	6	Buckley 4, Dennehy	4989
32	21	A	Chesterfield	L 1-2	0-0	7	Andrews	4595
33	24	A	Shrewsbury T.	D 1-1	0-1	—	Wright	9085
34	27	H	Gillingham	W 4-0	1-0	7	Buckley 3 (1 a pen), Andrews	5493
35	Mar 6	A	Sheffield W.	L 1-2	0-0	6	Hynd	9713
36	9	A	Grimsby T.	W 2-1	0-1	—	Dennehy, Taylor	5300
37	13	H	Colchester U.	D 1-1	1-0	6	Andrews	5371
38	16	A	Chester	D 1-1	1-0	—	Buckley	4059
39	20	H	Aldershot	W 4-1	1-1	4	Buckley 3, Andrews	5206
40	27	A	Port Vale	W 2-1	2-0	4	Atthey, Buckley	4863
41	Apr 3	H	Peterborough U.	D 2-2	2-1	6	Wright, Andrews	6266
42	6	H	Mansfield T.	L 0-1	0-0	—		6481
43	9	A	Southend U.	D 2-2	1-1	6	Buckley 2	3723
44	17	H	Hereford U.	D 0-0	0-0	7		9225
45	19	A	Wrexham	W 3-0	1-0	—	Dennehy, Wright, Buckley	5482
46	24	A	Swindon T.	L 1-5	1-2	7	Buckley (pen)	7363

Goalscorers

League (74): Buckley 34 (5 pens), Wright 12, Andrews 9, Dennehy 8, Taylor 2, Evans 2, Harrison 1, Spinner 1, Birch 1, Robinson 1, Hynd 1, Atthey 1, Own Goal 1.
League Cup (1): Buckley.

League Cup	First Round	Shrewsbury T. (h)	0-0
	Second Leg	(a)	1-2
F.A. Cup	First Round	Huddersfield T. (h)	0-1

Kearns	Fry	Harrison	Robinson	Atthey	Caswell	Dennehy	Andrews	Wright	Buckley	Taylor	Spinner	Saunders	Birch	Serella	Clarke	Hynd	Evans	Shelton	Match No.
1	2	3	4	5	6	7	8	9	10	11									1
1	2	3	5	4	6	7	8*	9	10	11	12								2
1	2	3	4		6	7	8	9	10	11*		5	12						3
1	2	3	4	6*		7	8	9	10		12	5	11						4
1	2	3	4		6	7	8	9	10	12		5	11*						5
1	2	3*	4		6	7	8	9	10			5	11	12					6
1	2	3*	4		6	7	9	12	10	8		11	5						7
1	2		4		6	7	8	12	10	9		11*	5		3				8
1	3		4	2		7	8	9	10	6			11	5					9
1	3		4	2		7	8	9	10	11			6	5					10
1	3		4	2*		7	8	9	10	11	12		6	5					11
1	3	6	4	2		7		9	10	11	8*		12	5					12
1	2	3	4	6*		7	12	8	10	11			9	5					13
1	2	3	4			7	8	9	10	6			11	5					14
1	2	3	4			7	8	9	10	6			11	5					15
1	2	3	4			7	8	9	10	6		12	11	5*					16
1	2	3	4			7		9	10	8	12	6	11	5*					17
1	2	3	4			7	8	9	10	11		5	6						18
1	2	3	4	12		7	8*	9	10	6			11	5					19
1	2	3	4	12		7	8*	9	10	6			11	5					20
1	2	3	4			7	8	9	10	6			11			5			21
1	2	3	4			7*	8	9	10	6	12					5	11		22
1	2	3	4			7	8	9	10	6						5	11		23
1	2	3	4			7*	8	9	10	6	12					5	11		24
1	2	3	4			7	8	9	10	6						5	11		25
1	2	3	4			7	8	9	10	6						5	11		26
1	2	3		12		7	8	9	10	6					4	5	11*		27
1	2	3	4			7	8	9	10	6						5	11		28
1	2	3	4			7	8	9	10	6						5	11		29
1	2	3	4			7	8*	9	10	6	12					5	11		30
1	2	3	4			7	8	9	10	6			11			5			31
1	2	3	4			7	8	9	10	6			11*			5	12		32
1	2	3	4			7	8	9	10	6						5	11		33
1	2	3	4			7	8	9	10	6						5	11		34
1		3	4			7	8	9	10	6				2		5	11		35
1		3	4	11		7	8		10	6				2		5	9		36
1		3	4	11*		7	8	12	10	6				2		5	9		37
1		3	4	6	11	7	8		10					2		5	9		38
1		3	4	6	11*	7		9	12	10				2		5	8		39
1		3	4	6		7	8	9	10					2		5	11		40
1	2	3	4	6		7	8	9	10							5	11		41
1	2	3	4	6		7		9	12	10			11*			5	8		42
1	2	3	4	6			8	9	10				5			7	11		43
1	2	3	4	6		7	8	9	10		12					5	11*		44
1	2	3	4	6		7	8*	9	10		12					5	11		45
1	2	3		6*		7	8	9	10	4						5	11	12	46
46	40	42	44	14	14	45	43	39	46	34	3	13	18	13	2	26	23	1	

```
            +          +   +          +   +   +   +   +   +          +   +
            3s         1s  5s         1s  4s  1s  6s  1s  1s         1s  1s
```

Player and position	Ht.	Wt.	Birthplace	Clubs	League Appearances	Goals
Goalkeepers						
Mick Kearns (Eire)	6 3	13 12	Banbury	Oxford U.	67	—
				Plymouth A. (on loan)	1	—
				Charlton Ath. (on loan)	4	—
				Walsall	137	—
Defenders						
Roger Hynd	6 0	13 1	Falkirk	Rangers	22+2	1
				C. Palace	30+1	—
				Birmingham C.	162+9	4
				Oxford U. (on loan)	5	—
				Walsall	26	1
Roger Fry	5 10	11 7	Southampton	Southampton	23	—
				Walsall	112	1
Colin Harrison	5 10	11 8	Pelsall	Walsall	355+15	32
*John Saunders	5 11	10 12	Newport	Newport C.	26+1	—
				Leeds U.	—	—
				Walsall	94+5	2
Dave Robinson	5 11½	12 0	Birmingham	Birmingham C.	110+2	2
				Walsall	133	3
David Serella	5 9	10 10	King's Lynn	Nottingham F.	65+3	—
				Walsall	16+1	—
Midfield						
Brian Caswell	5 10	10 7	Wednesbury	Walsall	50+8	1
Nicholas Atthey	5 8	11 8	Newcastle-upon-Tyne	Walsall	399+7	14
Alan Birch	5 5	10 2	West Bromwich	Walsall	60+10	4
Alun Evans	5 9	11 0	Kidderminster	Wolverhampton W.	20+1	4
				Liverpool	77+2	21
				Aston V.	53+9	11
				Walsall	23+1	2
Alan Buckley	5 5	9 11	Mansfield	Nottingham F.	16+2	1
				Walsall	138	76
Brian Taylor	5 10	11 7	Gateshead	Coventry C.	—	—
				Walsall	160+10	23
Forwards						
Bernie Wright	5 11	13 0	Liverpool	Walsall	15	2
				Everton	10+1	2
				Walsall	122+7	33
George Andrews	6 0	12 0	Dudley	Cardiff C.	43	21
				Southport	116+2	39
				Shrewsbury T.	123+1	50
				Walsall	128+2	30
Terry Spinner	5 9	10 4	Woking	Southampton	1+1	—
				Walsall	10+6	5
				(contract cancelled Jan. 1976)		
Kelvin Clarke				Walsall	2+2	—
Miah Dennehy (Eire)	5 9	10 13	Ireland	Nottingham F.	37+4	4
				Walsall	45	8
Gary Shelton				Walsall	1+1	—

WATFORD   DIV. 4

President: His Worship the Mayor.

Chairman: E. John.

Directors: J. Harrowell, E. John, H. M. Stratford, G. A. Smith, J. Reid, W. A. Wells.

Team Manager: Mike Keen.

General Manager/Secretary: R. E. Rollitt.

Year Formed: 1891.   *Turned Professional:* 1897.

Limited Company: 1909.

Previous Grounds: 1899, Cassio Road; 1919, Vicarage Road.

Honours: Football League, best season in Division 2: 18th, 1970–71. Division 3, Champions: 1968–69. Promoted from Division 4 1959–60. *F.A. Cup,* best season, semi-finalists: 1970. *Football League Cup,* best season: never past 3rd Rd.

Record Victory: 10-1 v Lowestoft Town, F.A. Cup, 1st Rd., Nov. 27th, 1926.

Record Defeat: 0-10 v Wolverhampton W., F.A. Cup, 1st Rd. Replay, Jan. 13th, 1912.

Most League Points: 64, Division 3, 1968–69.

Most League Goals: 92, Division 4, 1959–60.

Highest League Scorer in Season: Cliff Holton, 42, Division 4, 1959–60.

Most League Goals in Total Aggregate: Tom Barnett, 144, 1928–39.

Most Capped Player: Frank Hoddinott, 2, Wales; Pat Jennings, 2 (54), Ireland.

Most League Appearances: Duncan Welbourne, 411, 1963–74.

Record Transfer Fee Received: £110,000 from West Ham U. for Billy Jennings, September 1974.

Record Transfer Fee Paid: £40,000 to C. Palace for Ross Jenkins, June 1972.

Managers Since the War: Jack Bray, Eddie Hapgood, Haydn Green, Ron Gray, Len Goulden, Neil McBain, Ron Burgess, Bill McGarry, Ken Furphy, George Kirby.

Address of Supporters Club: Watford F.C. Supporters Club, Vicarage Road, Watford.

Address of Club Shop or Boutique: Same as Football Club.

Vicarage Road Ground, Watford. WD1 8ER. Telephone Watford 21759.   *Ground capacity:* 36,500.   *Record attendance:* 34,099 v Manchester U., F.A. Cup 4th Rd., February 3, 1969. *Record receipts:* £18,400 v Liverpool, F.A. Cup 6th Rd., February 21, 1970.   *Pitch measurements:* 113 yds × 73 yds.

How to get there: Bus 385 from Watford Junction. This and Watford High Street station are both within walking distance of the ground. Trains from London leave Euston station.

Match tickets: Stand seats bookable 10 days before each League match. The Police insist that visiting supporters who wish to stand must use the Vicarage Road terracing.

Car parking: Parking for season-ticket holders only at the ground, but there are several multi-storey car parks a few minutes away.

Entertainments/catering facilities: Tea kiosks and hot dog stands inside the ground.

Club shops: Four shops on the ground sell all types of souvenirs.

Handbooks/programmes: Handbook porduced annually, price 10p, and programmes are available on subscription.

Extra information: In 1968–69 Watford conceded only 34 goals, a record for the Third Division.

Club Colours: Gold shirts, black shorts, gold stockings.
Change Colours: All red.
Club Nickname: 'Hornets'.

WATFORD 1975–76 LEAGUE RECORD

Match No.	Date	Venue	Opponents	Result	H/T Score	League Pos'n	Goalscorers	Attendance
1	Aug 16	A	Barnsley	L 0-1	0-0	—		3690
2	23	H	Huddersfield T.	L 0-2	0-1	24		4500
3	30	A	Darlington	L 0-1	0-1	24		2988
4	Sept 6	H	Hartlepool	W 2-1	0-0	21	Mercer, Bond	3998
5	13	A	Reading	L 0-3	0-0	23		5521
6	20	H	Doncaster R.	W 2-1	0-0	21	Horsfield, Jenkins	4228
7	23	A	Cambridge U.	L 1-4	1-2	—	Jenkins	3234
8	27	A	Bradford C.	L 0-1	0-0	22		2308
9	Oct 4	H	Stockport Co.	D 1-1	1-0	22	Jenkins	4143
10	11	H	Workington	W 2-0	0-0	21	Scullion (pen), Bond	3872
11	18	A	Rochdale	L 1-2	0-0	22	Jenkins	1528
12	21	H	Scunthorpe U.	W 1-0	1-0	—	Horsfield	3581
13	25	H	Crewe Alex.	W 2-1	0-1	19	Lees, Horsfield	4252
14	Nov 1	A	Northampton T.	L 0-3	0-1	20		6656
15	4	A	Southport	W 2-1	2-0	—	Jenkins, Horsfield	1046
16	8	H	AFC Bournemouth	D 1-1	0-0	17	Jenkins	4714
17	15	A	Brentford	L 0-1	0-0	17		6930
18	28	A	Tranmere R.	L 0-3	0-2	19		3473
19	Dec 6	H	Lincoln C.	L 1-3	0-1	20	Jenkins	4178
20	12	A	Stockport Co.	D 2-2	1-1	20	Horsfield, Jenkins	5055
21	20	H	Newport Co.	W 3-1	2-1	18	Jenkins 2, Horsfield	3261
22	26	A	Swansea C.	L 2-4	2-2	19	Horsfield, How	4091
23	27	H	Exeter C.	W 2-0	2-0	17	Bond 2	5055
24	Jan 3	A	Torquay U.	L 0-1	0-1	18		2515
25	10	H	Darlington	W 2-0	1-0	17	Horsfield, Scullion	3865
26	17	A	Doncaster R.	W 2-1	0-1	16	Horsfield 2	5845
27	24	H	Reading	W 2-1	0-0	16	Jenkins, Horsfield	5944
28	Feb 7	H	Southport	W 2-0	0-0	15	Mercer 2	4334
29	10	A	Scunthorpe U.	W 1-0	1-0	—	Bond	2200
30	14	A	AFC Bournemouth	L 1-4	0-2	12	Bond (pen)	4897
31	21	H	Brentford	W 3-2	1-2	9	Horsfield, Jenkins, Downes	6223
32	24	H	Cambridge U.	W 1-0	1-0	—	Coffill	4888
33	Mar 3	A	Crewe Alex.	D 2-2	1-1	—	Bond 2 (pens)	2068
34	6	H	Northampton T.	L 0-1	0-1	12		7389
35	13	A	Workington	W 3-1	1-0	11	Mercer, Jenkins 2	1209
36	16	H	Rochdale	W 3-0	1-0	—	McCarthy, Jenkins 2	3886
37	20	H	Tranmere R.	D 2-2	2-0	10	Jenkins, Coffill	5449
38	26	A	Lincoln C.	L 1-5	1-3	10	Mercer	8798
39	31	A	Newport Co.	W 2-0	2-0	—	Jenkins, Downes	1092
40	Apr 3	H	Barnsley	W 1-0	1-0	9	Bond (pen)	4203
41	6	H	Bradford C.	W 3-0	2-0	—	Bond, Mercer, Jenkins	3745
42	10	A	Hartlepool	L 1-2	1-1	10	Mercer	1993
43	16	H	Torquay U.	D 0-0	0-0	10		5137
44	17	H	Swansea C.	W 2-1	1-0	9	Coffill, Blissett	4536
45	19	A	Exeter C.	W 3-1	1-1	—	Mercer 3	2480
46	24	A	Huddersfield T.	L 0-1	0-0	8		3787

Goalscorers

League (62): Jenkins 19, Horsfield 12, Bond 10 (4 pens), Mercer 10, Coffill 3, Downes 2, Scullion 2 (1 a pen), Blissett 1, How 1, Lees 1, McCarthy 1.

League Cup (3): Downes, Greenhalgh, Goodeve.

League Cup	First Round	Northampton T. (h)	2-0
	Second Leg	(a)	1-1
	Second Round	Tottenham H. (h)	0-1
F.A. Cup	First Round	Brighton & H.A. (h)	0-3

Rankin	How	Akers	Joslyn	Goodeve	Garner	Downes	Bond	Jenkins	Greenhalgh	Mayes	Mercer	Lees	Butler	Scullion	Horsfield	Walsh	Cofill	McCarthy	Bristow	Blissett	Gibbs	Match No.
1	2	3	4	5	6	7	8	9	10	11												1
1	2	3	4*	5	6	7	8	9	10	11	12											2
1	2	3	4	5	6	8	7	9	10*	11		12										3
1		3	4		6	8	7	9			11	5	2	10								4
1		3	4		6	11	8	12		10		5	2	7*	9							5
1		3	2		6	10	7	11				5		8	9	4						6
1		3	12	2	6	11*	4	10				5		8	9	7						7
1		3	2		6	11	7	10	8			5			9	4						8
1		3	2		6	4	11			12		5		8	9*	7	10					9
1	11		2		6	12	7	10				5		8	9	4	3*					10
1	6		2	3		11	7	10				5		8	9	4						11
1		3	2		6	11	8	10				5		7	9	4						12
1		3*	2		6	11	8	10		12		5		7	9	4						13
1		3	12	2	6	11	8*	10				5		7	9	4						14
1	2	3	8	4	6		10		9					7	5	11						15
1		3	2		6	4	10		9*	12		5		7	8	11						16
1		3	5	2	6	4	10		9	12				7	8	11*						17
1	2	3	4	8*	6		10		9	12					5		7	11				18
1	2	3	4		5		9		10					8	6		7	11				19
1	2	3	4		6		10				12	5		7	9*		11	8				20
1	2	3	4		6		9					5		7	10		11	8				21
1	2	3	4		6		12		10			5		7*	9		11	8				22
1	2		4	3	6	11	7	10							9		8		5			23
1	2	4*		3	6		10	11							7	9	12	8	5			24
1	2	3			6	4	10								7	9	11	8	5			25
1	2				6	4	11							8	9	3	7	10	5			26
1	2				6	4		10			12			8	9	3	7*	11	5			27
1	2				6	4		10			12			7	9	3	11	8*	5			28
1	2				6		7	10			12			11	9*	3	8	4	5			29
1	2				6		7	10			12			11*	9	3	8	4	5			30
1	2				6	11	7	10			12				9	3	8*	4	5			31
1	2				6	11	7	10							9	3	8	4	5			32
1	2				6	11	7	9							10	3	8	4	5			33
1	2				6	11	7	9			12				10	3	8	4	5*			34
1	2					11	7	10			12			9	6	3	8	4*	5			35
1	2				6	11	7	10			12				9*	3	8	4	5			36
1	2				6	11	7	10*			12				9	3	8	4	5			37
1	2				6	11	7	9				5			10	3	8	4				38
1	2				6	11	7	10						9	5	3	8*	4	12			39
1	2				6	11	7	9						10	5	3	8*	4	12			40
1	2				6	11*	7	10						9	5	3	8	4	12			41
1	2	12			6	11	7	9							10	3*	8	4	5			42
1	12				6	11	7	10						9	5	3	8*	4	2			43
	2				6	12	7	10*						9	5	3	8	4		11	1	44
	2	4			6	11	7	10							9	3	8	5			1	45
	2	7			6	11*		10						9	5	3	8	4	12		1	46
43	32	22	16	21	43	28	39	39	5	11	12	16	2	24	41	33	29	28	18	1	3	
+1s		+3s			+2s	+1s	+1s	+1s		+3s	+1s	+2s				+1s		+2s	+2s			

Player and position	Ht.	Wt.	Birthplace	Clubs	League Appearances	Goals
Goalkeepers						
Andy Rankin	6 0	12 0	Liverpool	Everton	85	—
				Watford	192	—
Peter Gibbs	5 11	12 0	London	Watford	3	—
Defenders						
*David Butler	5 8	11 5	Stockton	Workington T.	195+4	7
				Watford	168	2
Guy Bristow	5 9	11 1	London	Watford	18+4	—
Jimmy Walsh	5 9	11 0	London	Watford	45+1	—
Alan Garner	6 0	12 4	Lambeth	Millwall	2	—
				Luton T.	88	3
				Watford	56	2
*Ken Goodeve	5 10	10 10	Manchester	Manchester U.	—	—
				Luton	9+6	—
				Brighton	5+1	—
				Watford	67	4
*Walter Lees	5 10	11 4	Glasgow	Watford	219+6	10
Trevor How	5 10	12 2		Watford	43+1	1
*Vic Akers	5 9	11 2	London	Cambridge U.	122+7	5
				Tooting & M.	non-league	
				Watford	22	—
Midfield						
Dennis Bond	5 7	10 10	Waltham Forest	Watford	93	17
				Tottenham H.	20+3	1
				Charlton Ath.	70+5	3
				Watford	129+1	15
Roger Joslyn	5 10	11 2	Colchester	Colchester U.	91+5	4
				Aldershot	186	17
				Watford	43+3	2
Laurence Craker	5 9	11 0	Aylesbury	Chelsea	—	—
				Watford	51+6	3
Bobby Downes	5 10	11 5	Bloxwich	W.B.A.	—	—
				Peterborough U.	24+2	3
				Rochdale	164+10	10
				Watford	71+2	6
Kevin McCarthy	5 7	9 0	London	Watford	28	1
Forwards						
Ian Morgan	5 8½	11 0	London	Q.P.R.	161+11	26
				Watford	15+1	1
				(contract cancelled Aug. 1975)		
Alan Mayes	5 7	10 0	London	Q.P.R.	—	—
				Watford	29+7	2
				Northampton T. (on loan)	10	4
Ross Jenkins	6 2	12 2	Kensington	C. Palace	15	2
				Watford	114+8	36
Keith Mercer	5 10	11 7	Lewisham	Watford	23+16	11
Stewart Scullion	5 7½	10 6	Bo Ness	Watford	217+8	30
				Sheffield U.	53+4	7
				Watford	87	19
				(contract cancelled Feb. 1976)		
*Brian Greenhalgh	5 11	11 6	Birmingham	Preston N.E.	19	9
				Aston Villa	37+3	12
				Leicester C.	2+2	—
				Huddersfield T.	15	—
				Cambridge U.	116	47
				Bournemouth	23+1	7
				Torquay U. (on loan)	9	1
				Watford	17+1	1
Arthur Horsfield	5 11	11 4	Newcastle	Middlesbrough	107+4	51
				Newcastle	7+2	3
				Swindon	107+1	41
				Charlton Ath.	139	53
				Watford	41	12
Luther Blissett	5 11	12 0	Jamaica	Watford	1+2	1
Peter Coffill	5 9	10 3	Romford	Watford	29+1	3

WEST BROMWICH ALBION   DIV. 1

Chairman: F. A. Millichip.

Directors: T. H. Silk, J. Gordon, C. I. Edwards, J. W. Gaunt, J. S. Lucas.

Player-Manager: Johnny Giles.   *Secretary:* A. Everiss, J.P.

Commercial Manager: Gordon Dimbleby.

Statistician: Tony Matthews.

Year Formed: 1879.   *Turned Professional:* 1885.

Limited Company: 1891.

Previous Grounds: 1879, Coopers Hill; 1879, Dartmouth Park; 1881, Bunn's Field, Walsall Street; 1882, Four Acres (Dartmouth Cricket Club); 1885, Stoney Lane; 1900, The Hawthorns.   *Previous Name:* 1879–80, West Bromwich Strollers.

Honours: *Football League,* Division 1, Champions: 1919–20; Runners-up: 1924–25, 1953–54. Division 2, Champions: 1901–02, 1910–11; Runners-up; 1930–31, 1948–49.   *F.A. Cup,* Winners: 1888, 1892, 1931, 1954, 1968; Runners-up: 1886, 1887, 1895, 1912, 1935.   *Football League Cup,* Winners: 1965–66; Finalists: 1966–67, 1969–70.

European Competitions: *European Cup-Winners Cup;* 1968–69.   *European Fairs Cup:* 1966–67.

Record Victory: 12-0 v Darwen, Division 1, April 4th, 1892.

Record Defeat: 3-10 v Stoke C., Division 1, Feb. 4th, 1937.

Most League Points: 60, Division 1, 1919–20.

Most League Goals: 105, Division 2, 1929–30.

Highest League Scorer in Season: William 'Ginger' Richardson, 39, Division 1, 1935–36.

Most Capped Player: Stuart Williams, 33 (43), Wales.

Most League Appearances: Jesse Pennington, 455, 1903–22, (39 F.A. Cup appearances).

Most League Goals in Total Aggregate: Ronnie Allen, 208, 1950–61.

Record Transfer Fee Received: £225,000 from Manchester City for Asa Hartford Aug. '74.

Record Transfer Fee Paid: £138,000 to Rangers for Willie Johnston, Dec. 1972.

Managers Since the War: Jack Smith, Vic Buckingham, Gordon Clark, Archie Macaulay, Jimmy Hagan, Alan Ashman, Don Howe.

Address of Supporters Club: Throstle Club, Birmingham Road, West Bromwich, Staffs.

Address of Club Shop or Boutique: Albion Club Shop, same address as club.

The Hawthorns, West Bromwich B71 4LF. Telephone 021-553 0095. Box Office 021 553 5472. *Ground capacity:* 50,500.   *Record attendance:* 64,815 v Arsenal, F.A. Cup 6th Rd., March 6, 1937.   *Record receipts:* £32,024 v Southampton, F.A. Cup 5th Rd., Feb. 14 1976.   *Pitch measurements:* 115 yds × 75 yds.

How to get there: Buses 72, 74, 75, and 79 from outside Birmingham New Street station run directly to the ground. A special bus service from the centre of West Bromwich to the ground runs every three minutes on match days.

Match tickets: Advance bookings for Centre and Wing Stands accepted six weeks in advance by post including remittance and S.A.E. Telephone bookings are accepted but not before two days prior to the match; tickets reserved by telephone must be collected at least 30 minutes before kick-off. A limited number of unreserved seats in the Paddock are available at Door E1 on the day of the match.

Car parking: Street parking permitted in certain areas, all within 10 minutes walk of the ground.

Entertainments/catering facilities: Post-match entertainment in the Supporters' Club adjoining the ground; Excellent facilities at The Hawthorns Throstle Club alongside the ground includes a full-course lunch. several restaurants within walking distance of the ground. Snack bars in the ground.

Club shop: Situated in the Pools Office in Halfords Lane, and open from 9–5 Mon.–Sat. Stocks over 200 different articles. Excellent mailing service. Price list available on request.

Handbooks/programmes: No handbook. Programmes available on subscription.

Extra information: There are six Throstle Clubs in the surrounding areas, and the club runs a Junior Throstle Club for the under-15s.

Club Colour: Navy blue and white striped shirts, white shorts and white stockings.

Change Colours: Yellow and green striped shirts, blue shorts, yellow stockings.

Club Captain: John Wile.

Coaches: Albert McPherson and Brian Whitehouse.

Club Nicknames: 'Baggies', 'Throstles', 'Albion'.

WEST BROMWICH 1975–76 LEAGUE RECORD

Match No.	Date		Venue Opponents	Result	H/T Score	League Pos'n	Goalscorers	Attendance
1	Aug 16	A	Southampton	L 0-3	0-2	—		14,246
2	20	H	Chelsea	D 0-0	0-0	—		18,014
3	23	H	Luton T.	W 1-0	0-0	12	Trewick	13,875
4	30	A	Fulham	L 0-4	0-2	17		9,910
5	Sept 6	H	York C.	D 2-2	2-0	17	Brown, T., Hurst	11,028
6	13	A	Sunderland	L 0-2	0-0	20		25,159
7	20	H	Charlton Ath.	D 1-1	1-0	19	Hurst	10,563
8	27	A	Carlisle U.	D 1-1	0-0	20	Brown, A.	6625
9	Oct 4	H	Oldham Ath.	D 1-1	1-1	17	Johnston	9500
10	11	A	Blackburn R.	D 0-0	0-0	17		9973
11	18	H	Plymouth Arg.	W 1-0	1-0	15	Brown, A.	11,149
12	25	A	Bristol C.	W 2-0	0-0	14	Brown, A., Brown, T.	19,132
13	Nov 1	H	Notts Co.	D 0-0	0-0	15		12,595
14	4	A	Bristol R.	D 1-1	1-1	—	Edwards	13,105
15	8	A	Blackpool	W 1-0	0-0	10	Johnston	8271
16	12	A	Oxford U.	W 1-0	1-0	—	Mayo	5685
17	15	H	Hull C.	W 2-0	1-0	6	Martin, Brown, T.	13,780
18	22	A	Plymouth Arg.	L 1-2	0-1	8	Giles	17,380
19	29	A	Bolton W.	W 2-1	1 1	6	Mayo, Robson	18,710
20	Dec 6	H	Portsmouth	W 3-1	1-0	5	Brown, A. 2, Brown, T.	15,225
21	13	A	Luton T.	L 1-2	0-1	6	Martin	10,203
22	19	H	Southampton	L 0-2	0-1	8		17,071
23	26	A	Nottingham F.	W 2-0	0-0	7	Giles, Johnston	19,395
24	27	H	Orient	D 1-1	0-1	7	Mayo	20,626
25	Jan 10	A	Sunderland	D 0-0	0-0	6		25,399
26	17	A	York C.	W 1-0	1-0	5	Brown, A.	5628
27	31	A	Chelsea	W 2-1	1-1	6	Martin, Brown, T.	15,896
28	Feb 7	H	Bristol R.	W 3-0	1-0	5	Cantello, Mayo, Brown, A.	17,201
29	21	A	Hull C.	L 1-2	1-1	6	Johnston	6137
30	25	H	Oxford U.	W 2-0	1-0	—	Brown, T., Robertson	14,159
31	Mar 6	A	Notts Co.	W 2-0	0-0	5	Mayo, Johnston	20,032
32	13	H	Blackburn R.	D 2-2	1-2	5	Mayo, Wile	16,969
33	17	H	Bristol C.	L 0-1	0-1	—		26,640
34	20	H	Bolton W.	W 2-0	1-0	4	Mayo, Wile	25,319
35	27	A	Portsmouth	W 1-0	0-0	4	Cantello	10,617
36	31	H	Blackpool	D 0-0	0-0	—		20,729
37	Apr 3	H	Carlisle U.	W 3-0	2-0	3	Brown, A., Martin, Mayo	17,136
38	9	A	Charlton Ath.	L 1-2	0-1	4	Brown, T. (pen)	14,252
39	14	H	Fulham	W 3-1	2-0	—	Brown, A. 2, Cantello	18,234
40	17	H	Nottingham F.	W 2-0	0-0	3	Martin, Johnston	26,447
41	20	A	Orient	D 0-0	0-0	—		10,857
42	24	A	Oldham Ath.	W 1-0	0-0	3	Brown, T.	22,356

Goalscorers

League (50): Brown, A. 10, Brown, T. 8 (1 a pen), Mayo 8, Johnston 6, Martin 5, Cantello 3, Giles 2, Hurst 2, Wile 2, Edwards 1, Robertson 1, Robson 1, Trewick 1.
League Cup (1): Johnston.
F.A. Cup (7): Brown, T. 4 (1 a pen.), Brown A., Martin, Robson.

League Cup	Second Round	Fulham (h)	1-1
		(a)	0-1
F.A. Cup	Third Round	Carlisle U. (h)	3-1
	Fourth Round	Lincoln C. (h)	3-2
	Fifth Round	Southampton (h)	1-1
		a)	0-4

Osborne	Nisbet	Wilson	Cantello	Wile	Robertson	Trewick	Brown, A.	Mayo	Merrick	Johnston	Brown, T.	Hurst	Giles	Robson	Thompson	Rushbury	Glover	Martin	Mulligan	Edwards	Match No.
1	2	3	4	5	6	7	8	9*	10	11	12										1
1	2	3	4	5	6	7				11	8	9	10								2
1	2	3		5	6	7				11	8	9	10	4							3
1	2	3	4	5	6	7				11	8*	9	10	12							4
1	2		4	5	6	7				11	8	9	10	3							5
1	2		4	5	6	7				11*	8	9	10	12	3						6
1		3	4	5				12		11	8*	9	10	2	6	7					7
1		3	4	5	6			8		11	12	9*	10	2		7					8
1		3	4	5	6			8		11	12	9*		2		7	10				9
1		3	4	5	6			8		11		9	10					7	2		10
1		3	4	5	6			8		11		9	10					7	2		11
1		3	4	5	6			9		11	8		10					7	2		12
1		3	4	5	6			9		11	8		10					7*	2	12	13
1		3	4	5	6			9		11	8		10*					7	2	12	14
1		3	4*	5	6	12		9		11	8		10					7	2		15
1		3		5	6	4		9			8		10					7	2	11	16
1		3		5	6	4		9			8		10					7	2	11	17
1		3		5	6	4*	9	10		11	8							7	2	12	18
1		3		5	6		8	9		11	7		10	4					2		19
1		3		5			9	8		11	7		10	6				4	2		20
1		3		5			8	9		11	4		10	6				7	2		21
1			4		6	10	9			11	8			5	3			7	2		22
1		3		5	6		9	8		11	7		10	4					2		23
1		3		5	6		9	8		11	7		10	4					2		24
1			4	5	6		9	3		11	7		10					8	2		25
1			4	5	6		9	3		11	7		10					8	2		26
1				5	6		9	3		11	7		10	4				8	2		27
1			4	5	6		9	3		11	7		10					8	2		28
1			8*	5	6		12	3		11	4		10	9				7	2		29
1		3		5			8	9		11	4		10	6				7	2		30
1			8	5	6			3		11	9		10	4				7	2		31
1			8	5	6			3		11	9		10	4				7	2		32
1			8	5	6		12	9*		11	4		10	3				7	2		33
1			8	5	6		12	9		11	4		10*	3				7	2		34
1			8	5	6			9		11	4		10	3				7	2		35
1			8	5	6		12	9		11	4		10	3*				7	2		36
1		3		5	6		8	9		11	4		10					7	2		37
1		3		5	6		8	9		11	4		10					7	2		38
1		3		5	6		8	9		11	4		10					7	2		39
1		3		5	6		8	9		11	4		10					7	2		40
1		3		5	6		8	9		11	4		10					7	2		41
1		3		5	6		8	9		11	4		10					7	2		42
42	6	19	34	37	42	10	26	28	1	39	37	10	38	14	5	2	3	34	33	2	
						+1s	+5s				+3s		+2s						+3s		

WEST BROMWICH ALBION—PLAYERS

Player and position	Ht.	Wt.	Birthplace	Clubs	League Appearances	Goals
Goalkeepers						
John Osborne	6 1	11 6	Balborough	Chesterfield	110	—
				W.B.A.	216	—
				Walsall (on loan)	3	—
Bob Ward	6 1	12 0	W. Bromwich	W.B.A.	7	—
Tony Godden	6 1	12 2	Gillingham	Gillingham	—	—
				W.B.A.	—	—
Defenders						
Ray Wilson	5 3	9 9	Grangemouth	W.B.A.	231+2	3
Paddy Mulligan	5 9	11 0	Dublin	Chelsea	55+3	2
(Eire)				C. Palace	57	2
				W.B.A.	33	—
Gordon Nisbet	5 10	11 4	Wallsend on Tyne	W.B.A.	136	—
Alistair Robertson	5 9	10 3	Philipstown	W.B.A.	182+2	3
John Wile	6 1	11 12	Sherburn	Sunderland	—	—
				Peterborough	116+2	7
				W.B.A.	220	12
Trevor Thompson	5 9	10 12	N. Shields	W.B.A.	20	—
David Rushbury	5 10	11 4	Wolverhampton	W.B.A.	28	—
Tony Cooper	5 9	11 0	Crewe	W.B.A.	—	—
Derek Statham	5 5	11 0	Wolverhampton	W.B.A.	—	—
Brian Clarke	6 0	12 0	Dawley	W.B.A.	—	—
Martyn Davies	5 11	12 2	Swansea	W.B.A.	—	—
Midfield						
Johnny Giles	5 7	10 0	Dublin	Manchester U.	98	10
(Eire)				Leeds U.	378+3	86
				W.B.A.	38	2
Len Cantello	5 9½	10 8½	Manchester	W.B.A.	221+4	9
Bryan Robson	5 9	11 1	Chester-le-Street	W.B.A.	17+2	3
John Trewick	5 9	10 10	Bedlington	W.B.A.	12+2	1
Wayne Hughes	6 0	12 5	Port Talbot	W.B.A.	—	—
Colin Gregson	5 6	10 10	Newcastle-on-Tyne	W.B.A.	—	—
Mick Martin	5 9	10 11	Belfast	Manchester U.	33+7	2
(Eire)				W.B.A.	34	5
Forwards						
Alistair Brown	6 0	11 0	Musselburgh	Leicester C.	93+8	31
				W.B.A.	80+10	19
Tony Brown	5 6½	11 6	Oldham	W.B.A.	443+6	179
(England)						
Alan Glover	5 9	11 2	Staines	Q.P.R.	5+1	—
				W.B.A.	83+8	8
				Southend U. (on loan)	0+1	—
Joe Mayo	6 1	12 3	Tipton	Walsall	2+5	1
				W.B.A.	58+4	16
Willie Johnston	5 7	11 0	Glasgow	Rangers	210+2	90
(Scotland)				W.B.A.	134	14
Ian Edwards	6 1	12 5	Wrexham	W.B.A.	9+2	3
Steve Lynex	5 5	10 3	West Bromwich	W.B.A.	—	—
Kevin Summerfield	5 11	10 7	Walsall	W.B.A.	—	—
Mark Trenter	6 0	12 0	Bridgend	W.B.A.	—	—

Manager: John Giles; there is no assistant manager; *Extra director on board:* Mr S. Lucas; *Assistant secretary:* Mr Ray Fairfax; *Promoted to Division One 1975-76; FA Youth Cup winners 1975-76; Ground capacity now is 45,500 (Seats 12,000); Record gate receipts:* £32,024 (v Southampton, FA Cup 5th Rd. Feb. 14 1976); *Pitch measurements:* 115½ yards × 75½ yards; there are ONLY Five Throstle clubs now in the vicinity of the ground.

WEST HAM UNITED
DIV. 1

Chairman: R. H. Pratt.

Directors: L. C. Cearns, W. F. Cearns, R. G. Brandon, B. R. Cearns, F.C.I.S.

General Manager: Ron Greenwood. *Secretary:* Eddie Chapman.

Team Manager: John Lyall.

P.R.O.: Jack Helliar. *Year Formed:* 1900.

Turned Professional: 1900. *Limited Company:* 1900.

Previous Grounds: Memorial Recreation Ground, Canning Town; 1904. Boleyn Ground.

Honours: Football League, best season in Division 1: 6th, 1926–27, 1958–59, 1972–73. Division 2, Champions: 1957–58; runners-up: 1922–23. *F.A. Cup,* Winners: 1964, 1975; runners-up: 1922–23. *Football League Cup,* runners-up: 1966. **European Competitions:** *European Cup-Winners' Cup:* 1964–65 (Winners), 1965–66, 1975–76 (finalist)

Record Victory: 8-0 v Rotherham U., Division 2, 1957–58 and Sunderland, Division 1, Oct. 19th, 1968.

Record Defeat: 2-8 v Blackburn R., Division 1, Dec. 26th, 1963.

Most League Points: 57, Division 2, 1957–58.

Most League Goals: 101, Division 2, 1957–58.

Highest League Scorer in Season: Vic Watson, 41, Division 1, 1929–30.

Most Capped Player: Bobby Moore, 108, England.

Most League Appearances: Bobby Moore, 545, 1958–1974.

Most League Goals in Total Aggregate: Vic Watson, 306, 1920–35.

Record Transfer Fee Received: £200,000 from Tottenham H. (including Jimmy Greaves in part exchange) for Martin Peters, Mar. 1970.

Record Transfer Fee Paid: £170,000 to Manchester U. for Ted MacDougall, Feb. 1973.

Managers Since the War: Charlie Paynter, Ted Fenton.

Address of Supporters Club: Castle St., Upton Park, E.13.

Address of Club Shop or Boutique: Hammers Shop, Boleyn Ground, Green Street, Upton Park, London E.13.

Boleyn Ground, Green Street, Upton Park, London E.13. Telephone 01-472 0704. *Ground capacity:* 41,000. *Record attendance:* 42,322 v Tottenham H., Division 1, October 17, 1970. *Record receipts:* £33,000 v Ararat Erevan, European Cup-Winners' Cup 2nd Rd., Nov. 5 1975. *Pitch measurements:* 110 yds × 70 yds.

How to get there: Nearest station Upton Park (Underground, District Line)—five minutes' walk. Buses from Barking Road, Romford Road and Green Street.

Match tickets: Advance booking, by personal application only, 12 days prior to League matches.

Car parking: Ample side-street parking available.

Entertainments/catering facilities: Refreshment points around the ground.

Club shop: Situated on the ground; sells all types of souvenirs.

Handbooks/programmes: No handbook. Programmes available by post from either Sales Service c/o West Ham United F.C. or from Helliar & Sons, 237, Barking Road, London E13 8EQ.

Extra information: Vic Watson's 306 League goals for West Ham is the fourth highest total scored with one club in the history of the competition.

Club Colours: Claret shirts, blue sleeves, white shorts and white stockings.
Change Colours: Sky blue shirts with two claret bands, sky blue shorts and stockings.
Club Captain: Billy Bonds.
First Team Trainer: David Jenkins.
Club Nickname: 'Hammers'.

WEST HAM UNITED 1975–76 LEAGUE RECORD

Match No.	Date	Venue	Opponents	Result	H/T Score	League Pos'n	Goalscorers	Attendance
1	Aug 16	A	Stoke C.	W 2-1	2-0	—	Gould, Taylor, A.	23,744
2	19	A	Liverpool	D 2-2	1-1	—	Taylor, A. 2	40,564
3	23	H	Burnley	W 3-2	0-1	6	Taylor, A. 2, Paddon	27,075
4	25	H	Tottenham H.	W 1-0	1-0	—	Robson	35,914
5	30	A	Q.P.R.	D 1-1	0-1	2	Jennings	28,408
6	Sept 6	H	Manchester C.	W 1-0	0-0	2	Lampard	29,752
7	13	A	Leicester C.	D 3-3	0-3	2	Bonds, Lampard, Holland	21,413
8	20	H	Sheffield U.	W 2-0	0-0	2	Taylor, T., Best	28,924
9	27	A	Wolverhampton W.	W 1-0	0-0	2	Paddon	18,455
10	Oct 4	H	Everton	L 0-1	0-0	3		31,005
11	11	H	Newcastle U.	W 2-1	1-0	3	Curbishley, Taylor, A.	30,400
12	18	A	Middlesbrough	L 0-3	0-1	3		25,851
13	25	H	Manchester U.	W 2-1	1-0	3	Taylor, A., Gould	38,528
14	Nov 1	A	Birmingham C.	W 5-1	2-1	2	Brooking, Pendrey (og), Lampard, Taylor, A. 2	28,474
15	8	H	Coventry C.	D 1-1	0-0	1	Robson	29,501
16	15	A	Derby Co.	L 1-2	1-1	5	Brooking	31,172
17	22	H	Middlesbrough	W 2-1	1-1	4	Jennings, Holland	26,914
18	29	H	Arsenal	W 1-0	1-0	3	Taylor, A.	31,012
19	Dec 6	A	Norwich C.	L 0-1	0-0	6		27,020
20	13	A	Burnley	L 0-2	0-2	7		14,907
21	20	H	Stoke C.	W 3-1	2-1	6	Jennings 3	21,135
22	26	A	Aston Villa	L 1-4	1-2	6	Jennings	51,300
23	27	H	Ipswich T.	L 1-2	0-0	6	Taylor, T. (pen)	32,741
24	Jan 10	H	Leicester C.	D 1-1	0-0	6	Taylor, A	24,615
25	17	A	Manchester C.	L 0-3	0-2	6		32,147
26	24	H	Q.P.R.	W 1-0	1-0	6	Taylor, A	26,677
27	31	H	Liverpool	L 0-4	0-0	6		26,741
28	Feb 7	A	Tottenham H.	D 1-1	0-0	6	Brooking	32,832
29	14	A	Coventry C.	L 0-2	0-1	6		16,173
30	21	H	Derby Co.	L 1-2	0-0	9	Brooking	24,941
31	23	H	Leeds U.	D 1-1	0-0	—	Taylor, A	28,025
32	28	A	Manchester U	L 0-4	0-0	9		57,240
33	Mar 6	H	Birmingham C.	L 1-2	0-1	12	Martin (og)	19,868
34	9	A	Leeds U.	D 1-1	0-0	—	Jennings	26,453
35	13	A	Newcastle U.	L 1-2	1-1	11	Jennings	32,842
36	20	A	Arsenal	L 1-6	1-4	12	Jennings	34,011
37	27	H	Norwich C.	L 0-1	0-1	12		20,628
38	Apr 3	H	Wolverhampton W.	D 0-0	0-0	13		16,769
39	10	A	Sheffield U.	L 2-3	1-0	16	Jennings 2	18,797
40	17	H	Aston Villa	D 2-2	1-2	17	Robson, Brooking	21,642
41	19	A	Ipswich T.	L 0-4	0-2	—		28,217
42	24	A	Everton	L 0-2	0-2	18		26,101

Goalscorers

League (48): Taylor, A. 13, Jennings 11, Brooking 5, Robson 3, Lampard 3, Gould 2, Paddon 2, Holland 2, Taylor, T. 2 (1 a pen), Bonds 1, Best 1, Curbishley 1, own goals 2.
League Cup (6): Brooking, Best, Taylor, A., Paddon, Bonds (1 a pen), Robson.

League Cup	Second Round	Bristol C. (h)	0-0
		(a)	3-1
	Third Round	Darlington (h)	3-0
	Fourth Round	Tottenham H. (a)	0-0
		(h)	0-2 (a.e.t.)
F.A. Cup	Third Round	Liverpool (h)	0-2

Day	McDowell	Lampard	Holland	Taylor, T.	Lock	Taylor, A.	Paddon	Gould	Brooking	Robson	Jennings	Ayris	Bonds	Best	Coleman	Curbishley	Orhan	McGiven	Wooler	Pike	Ferguson	Match No.
1	2	3	4	5	6	7	8	9	10	11												1
1	2	3	4	5	6	7	8	9*	10	11	12											2
1	2	3	4	5	6	7	8		10	11	9*	12										3
1	2	3	4	5	6	7	8		10	11	9											4
1	2	3	4	5	6	7	8		10	11	9											5
1	2	3	4	5	6	7*	8		10	11	9	12										6
1	2	3	7	5	6		8		10	11	9		4									7
1	2	3	11	5	6	9*	8		10		7		4	12								8
1	2	3	11	5	6	7	8		10				4	9								9
1	2	3	11	5	6	12	8		10		7		4	9*								10
1	6	3	7	5		9	8						4	11	2	10						11
1	2	3*	11	5		7	8		10				4	9	6	12						12
1	6	3	4	5		7	8	9	10	11					2							13
1	2	3	9	5		7	8		10	11			4		6							14
1	6		7	5	3	9	8	12	10	11			4*		2							15
1	2	3	9	5	4	7	8*		10	11	12				6							16
1	2		4	5	3	7	8		10	11	9				6							17
1	2	3	9	5	6	7	8		11	10			4									18
1	4	3	11	5	6	7	8		10	9					2							19
1		3	11	5	6	7	8		10	9	12				2	4*						20
1	4	3	9	5	6	7	8		11	10					2							21
1	4	3	9	5	6	7	8		11	10					2							22
1		3	4	5	6	7	8		10	11	9				2*	12						23
1	2	3	4	5	6	7			10		9		8		11							24
1	2	3	4	5	6	7*	8		10		9		12		11							25
1	2	3	4	5		7	8		9	10					6	11						26
1	2	3	4	5		7	8		10	12	9*				6	11						27
1		3	4	5		7	8		10	11	9				2			6				28
1	2	3	4	5		7	8		10	11	9							6				29
1	7	3	4	5			8		10	11	12				2	9*		6				30
1	2	3	4*	5		7	8		10	11	12				9	6						31
1	2			5	3	7*	8		10	11	12		4		9	6						32
1		3		5		7	8			11			4		2	9	10*	6	12			33
1		3		5		6	8			11	9	7*	4	2	10			12				34
1	12	3*		5		6	8			11	9	7	4		2	10						35
1		3		5		6	7		10	11	9	4	2*	8		12						36
1	10	3		5	6	7			11	9		4	2	8								37
1	4	3	7	5	6*	8			10	11	9	12	2									38
1	6	3	7	5		8			10	11*	9	12	4		2							39
	6	3	7	5	4*	8			10	11	9	12			2						1	40
1	6		5			8			10	11	7	2			4	9*	3		12			41
1	6	3	7	5		12	8		10	11*	9		4		2							42
41	36	37	35	42	26	33	39	4	34	33	26	3	17	5	26	12	5	6	1	—	1	
	+1s					+2s		+1s	+1s	4s	6s	1s	2s		+2s		+1s	+3s				

Player and position	Ht.	Wt.	Birthplace	Clubs	League Appearances	Goals
Goalkeepers						
Mervyn Day	6 3	13 0	Chelmsford	West Ham U.	116	—
Bobby Ferguson (Scotland)	5 10½	11 11	Ardrossan	Kilmarnock	73	—
				West Ham U.	208	—
				Sheffield W. (on loan)	5	—
				Leicester C. (on loan)	—	—
Defenders						
Keith Coleman	5 9	11 0	Washington	Sunderland	49	2
				West Ham U.	84+4	—
Frank Lampard (England)	5 10	12 1	West Ham	West Ham U.	287	11
John McDowell	5 9	11 9½	East Ham	West Ham U.	205+2	5
Kevin Lock	6 0	11 6	London	West Ham U.	91+9	1
Tommy Taylor	6 1	13 0	Hornchurch	Orient	112+2	6
				West Ham U.	230	6
Bill Green	6 3	12 8	Newcastle	Hartlepool	128+3	9
				Carlisle U.	119	4
				West Ham U.	—	—
Midfield						
Alan Curbishley	5 9	11 0	Forest Gate	West Ham U.	13+3	1
Billy Bonds	6 0½	12 10	Woolwich	Charlton Ath.	95	1
				West Ham U.	327+1	32
Mike McGiven	5 10½	11 4	Newcastle	Sunderland	107+6	9
				West Ham U.	27+1	—
Trevor Brooking (England)	6 0½	12 10	Barking	West Ham U.	278+7	52
Pat Holland	5 8	11 1	Limehouse	West Ham U.	118+10	10
				Bournemouth (on loan)	10	—
Graham Paddon	5 7	10 8	Manchester	Coventry C.	3+1	1
				Norwich C.	162	19
				West Ham U.	103	10
Geoff Pike	5 9	11 2	Clapton	West Ham U.	0+3	—
Forwards						
Clyde Best (Bermuda)	6 1	12 0	Bermuda	West Ham U.	178+8	47
				(contract cancelled Feb. 1976)		
Ronnie Boyce	5 9	11 4	West Ham	West Ham U.	275+7	21
Ade Coker	5 9	10 7	Lagos	West Ham U.	9+1	3
				Lincoln C. (on loan)	6	1
				(contract cancelled April 1967)		
Billy Jennings	5 9	11 4	Hackney	Watford	81+12	33
				West Ham U.	58+4	24
John Ayris	5 7	9 0	Poplar	West Ham U.	40+14	1
Yilmaz Orhan	5 7	11 0	Nicosia	West Ham U.	5	—
Keith Robson	5 9½	9 12	Hetton-le-Hole	Newcastle U.	14	3
				West Ham U.	58+1	13
Alan Taylor	5 7	11 0	Lancaster	Rochdale	55	7
				West Ham U.	44+5	15

WOLVERHAMPTON WANDERERS DIV. 2

Chairman: J. R. Ireland.

Directors: W. C. Sproson, G. S. Clark, H. J. Marshall, G. P. Devine.

Manager: *Secretary:* P. A. Shaw.

Year Formed: 1877. *Turned Professional:* 1888.

Limited Company: 1923.

Previous Grounds: 1877, Goldthorn Hill; 1884, Dudley Road; 1889, Molineux.

Previous Name: 1880, St. Luke's, Blakenhall combined with The Wanderers to become Wolverhampton Wanderers.

Honours: Football League, Division 1, Champions: 1953–54, 1957–58, 1958–59; Rs-up: 1937–38, 1938–39, 1949–50, 1954–55, 1959–60. Division 2, Champions: 1931–32; Runners-up; 1966–67. Division 3(N), Champions: 1923–24. *F.A. Cup,* Winners: 1893, 1908, 1949, 1960; Runners-up: 1889, 1896, 1921, 1939. *Football League Cup,* Winners, 1973–74, semi-finalists 1972–73.

European Competitions: European Cup: 1958–59, 1959–60. *European Cup-Winners Cup:* 1960–61. *UEFA Cup:* 1971–72 (finalists), 1973–74, 1974–75.

Record Victory: 14-0 v Crosswell's Brewery, F.A. Cup, 2nd Rd., 1886–87.

Record Defeat: 1-10 v Newton Heath, Division 1, Oct. 15th, 1892.

Most League Points: 64, Division 1, 1957–58.

Most League Goals: 115, Division 2, 1931–32.

Highest League Score in Season: Dennis Westcott, 37, Division 1, 1946–47.

Most Capped Player: Billy Wright, 105, England (70 consecutive).

Most League Appearances: Billy Wright, 491, 1946–59.

Most League Goals in Total Aggregate: Bill Hartill, 164, 1928–35.

Record Transfer Fee Received; £100,000 from Liverpool for Alun Evans, Sept. 1968.

Record Transfer Fee Paid: £100,000 to Burnley for Steve Kindon, Aug. 1972.

Managers Since the War: Ted Vizard, Stan Cullis, Andy Beattie, Ron Allen, Bill McGarry.

Address of Club Shop or Boutique: 'The Lair', Wolverhampton W. F.C., Molineux Grounds, Wolverhampton, Staffordshire.

Molineux Grounds, Wolverhampton WV1 4QR. Telephone Wolverhampton 24053/4. *Telegraphic address:* 'Wanderers, Wolverhampton'. *Ground capacity:* 53,000. *Record attendance:* 61,315 v Liverpool, F.A. Cup 5th Rd., February 11, 1939. *Record receipts:* £44,891 v Manchester U., F.A. Cup 6th Rd. replay, March 9 1976. *Pitch measurements:* 115 yds × 72 yds.

How to get there: The ground is within easy walking distance of both Wolverhampton High Level railway station and the town centre. For this reason the local bus company does not operate special services on match days.

Match tickets: Seats are bookable by post one month before the match.

Car parking: Parking is available around 'The West Park', in various side streets, and at the Molineux Hotel (15p per match).

Entertainments/catering facilities: Entertainment at the Wolves Social Club a few yards from the ground. Bars are provided all around the ground.

Club shop: The club shop is situated on the official car park at the ground.

Handbooks/programmes: No handbook. Programmes available on subscription.

Extra information: Wolves scored over 100 First Division goals in four successive seasons (1957–58 to 1960–61).

Club Colours: Old gold shirts, black collar and cuffs, black shorts, old gold stockings. *Change Colours:* White shirt, light blue shorts, white stockings. *Club Captain:* Mike Bailey. *First Team Trainer/Coach:* Sammy Chung. *Club Nickname:* 'Wolves'.

WOLVERHAMPTON WANDERERS 1975–76 LEAGUE RECORD

Match No.	Date	Venue	Opponents	Result	H/T Score	League Pos'n	Goalscorers	Attendance
1	Aug 16	H	Manchester U.	L 0-2	0-0	—		31,973
2	20	A	Stoke C.	D 2-2	1-0	—	Carr, Richards	22,551
3	23	A	Middlesbrough	L 0-1	0-1	20		22,595
4	26	H	Q.P.R.	D 2-2	2-2	—	Richards, Hibbit (pen)	19,380
5	30	H	Arsenal	D 0-0	0-0	20		18,144
6	Sept 6	A	Leeds U.	L 0-3	0-2	20		24,460
7	13	H	Birmingham C.	W 2-0	0-0	19	Carr 2	25,142
8	20	A	Newcastle U.	L 1-5	1-1	20	Daley	29,834
9	23	H	Aston Villa	D 0-0	0-0	—		33,344
10	27	H	West Ham U.	L 0-1	0-0	21		18,455
11	Oct 4	A	Liverpool	L 0-2	0-0	21		36,391
12	11	H	Sheffield U.	W 5-1	2-0	20	Richards 2, Hibbitt 2, Carr	16,162
13	18	A	Derby Co.	L 2-3	0-3	21	Kindon, Richards	25,861
14	25	H	Everton	L 1-2	0-1	21	Hibbitt	20,063
15	Nov 1	A	Tottenham H.	L 1-2	0-1	21	Daley	26,102
16	8	H	Ipswich T.	W 1-0	0-0	20	Daley	16,191
17	15	A	Burnley	W 5-1	3-0	19	Richards 2, Daley 2, Hibbitt	14,559
18	22	H	Derby Co.	D 0-0	0-0	19		26,690
19	29	H	Manchester C.	L 0-4	0-2	19		20,887
20	Dec 6	A	Leicester C.	L 0-2	0-0	20		20,012
21	13	H	Middlesbrough	L 1-2	1-2	20	Hibbitt (pen)	13,548
22	20	A	Manchester U.	L 0-1	0-0	21		44,269
23	26	H	Coventry C.	L 0-1	0-1	21		21,224
24	27	A	Norwich C.	D 1-1	1-0	21	Bell	25,115
25	Jan 10	A	Birmingham C.	W 1-0	0-0	20	Carr (pen)	28,552
26	17	H	Leeds U.	D 1-1	0-1	20	Gould	34,925
27	31	H	Stoke C.	W 2-1	1-0	19	Carr (pen), Bell	24,960
28	Feb 7	A	Q.P.R.	L 2-4	1-2	20	Gould 2	17,153
29	17	A	Ipswich T.	L 0-3	0-2	—		19,293
30	21	H	Burnley	W 3-2	1-0	20	Richards 2, Bell	19,390
31	24	A	Aston Villa	D 1-1	0-0	—	Richards	47,693
32	28	A	Everton	L 0-3	0-3	21		21,827
33	Mar 13	A	Sheffield U.	W 4-1	3-1	20	Richards, Palmer, Kindon 2	17,661
34	16	H	Tottenham H.	L 0-1	0-0	—		21,544
35	20	A	Manchester C.	L 2-3	1-0	20	Daley, Kindon	32,761
36	27	H	Leicester C.	D 2-2	2-1	20	Richards, Hibbitt	18,113
37	Apr 3	A	West Ham U.	D 0-0	0-0	20		16,769
38	10	H	Newcastle U.	W 5-0	0-0	19	Richards 3, Hibbitt, Carr	20,083
39	13	A	Arsenal	L 1-2	1-1	—	Richards	19,518
40	17	A	Coventry C.	L 1-3	1-1	20	Bell	18,678
41	19	H	Norwich C.	W 1-0	1-0	—	Richards	16,168
42	May 4	H	Liverpool	L 1-3	1-0	—	Kindon	48,900

Goalscorers

League (51): Richards 17, Hibbitt 8 (2 pens), Carr 7 (2 pens), Daley 6, Kindon 5, Bell 4, Gould 3, Palmer 1.

League Cup (7): Hibbitt 3, Sunderland 2, Richards 2.

F.A. Cup (10): Richards 6, Bell, Hibbitt, Gould, Kindon.

League Cup	Second Round	Swindon T. (a)	2-2
		(h)	3-2
	Third Round	Birmingham C. (a)	2-0
	Fourth Round	Mansfield T. (a)	0-1
F.A. Cup	Third Round	Arsenal (h)	3-0
	Fourth Round	Ipswich T. (a)	0-0
		(h)	1-0
	Fifth Round	Charlton Ath. (h)	3-0
	Sixth Round	Manchester U. (a)	1-1
		(h)	2-3 (a.e.t.)

Parkes	Parkin	McNab	Bailey	Munro	McAlle	Sunderland	Carr	Richards	Kindon	Wagstaffe	Hibbitt	Farley	Taylor	Daley	Pierce	Palmer	Jefferson	Bell	Patching	Daly	Gould	Williams	O'Hara	Kelly	Match No.
1	2	3	4	5	6	7*	8	9	10	11	12														1
1	2	3	4	5	6	12	8	9	10		7*	11													2
1	2	3	4		6		8	9	10		7*	11	5	12											3
1	2	3	4	5	6	12	8	9	10		7	11*													4
		3	4	5	6	12	8	9	10*		7			11	1	2									5
	2	3	4	5	6	10	8	9			7			11	1										6
	2	3	4	5	6	10	8	9		11	7				1										7
	3*		4		6	10	8	9			7	12		11	1	2	5								8
		3	4	5	6		8		10	11	7				1	2		9							9
		3	4	5	6	12	8	9	10*		7			11	1	2									10
		3	4	5	6		8*	9	10		7			11	1	2	12								11
		3	4	5	6		8	9	10*		7			11	1	2			12						12
	3*		4	5	6	12	8	9	10		7			11	1	2									13
		3	4	5	6		8	9*	10		7	12		11	1	2									14
	2*	3	4	5	6	10	8	9			7	11		12	1										15
		3		5	6	10	8	9			7	11*		4	1	2					12				16
		3	4	5	6		12	9	10		7*	11		8	1	2									17
	3*		4	5	6		12	9	10		7	11		8	1	2									18
			4	5	6		12	9	10		7	11*		8	1	2			3						19
			4	5	6			9	12		7	11		8	1	2				3*	10				20
		3	4	5	6			9*	12		7	11		8	1	2					10				21
1		3	4	5	6	11	12	9			7			8							10*				22
1		3	4	5	6	11	10	9			7			8							10*				23
1		3	4		6	2	8		12		7	11						9		5	10*				24
1		3	4	5	6	2		9	12		7*	11		8							10				25
1		3	4	8	5	6	11		12		7					2*		9			10				26
1		3		5	6	7	8	11										9			10	2	4		27
1		3		8	5	2	6	11			4							9			10		7		28
1		3		5		6	11				4*			9		2		8	12		10		7		29
1		3		5	6	2	4	11						8				9			10		7		30
1		3		8	5	2	6	11			4							9			10		7*		31
1		3		5	6	2	8	9	12		4	11*		7							10				32
1			4	5		2	8	9	10		7				6	3								11	33
1			6	5		2	8	11	9		7				4	3								10	34
1			4	5		2	8	11	9		7				6	3								10	35
1			4	5		2	8	10	11		7*				6	3							12	9	36
1	4	5			6	2	8	9	12		7					3				11*	10				37
1		3	4*	5	6	2	8	11			7							9		12	10				38
1		3		5	6	2*	7	10			8				4			9		12				11	39
1		3		5	6	8	9				7	11*		4	2			10		12					40
		3			6*	2	7	10			8			12	1	5		9		4				11	41
	6	5				2	7	10	9		8			4	1	3					12			11*	42
23	30	13	32	30	41	24	35	38	22	3	39	13	1	27	19	26	2	11	2	3	13	1	5	9	
						+5s	+3s	+1s	+6s					+2s	+2s	+4s		+2s	+1s	+1s	+4s		+1s		

Player and position	Ht.	Wt.	Birthplace	Clubs	League Appearances	Goals
Goalkeepers						
Gary Pierce	6 2½	13 4	Bury	Huddersfield T.	23	—
				Wolverhampton W.	53	—
Phil Parkes	6 3½	13 8	W. Bromwich	Wolverhampton W.	305	—
Stuart Garnham	6 1	12 6	Selby	Wolverhampton W.	—	—
				Northampton T. (on loan)	1	—
Defenders						
Derek Parkin	5 8½	11 0	Newcastle	Huddersfield T.	60+1	1
				Wolverhampton W.	298	6
Geoff Palmer	5 10	10 5	Cannock	Wolverhampton W.	86	3
*Bob McNab (England)	5 7½	10 6	Huddersfield	Huddersfield T.	68	—
				Arsenal	277+1	4
				Wolverhampton W.	13	—
Derek Jefferson	5 11	10 2	Morpeth	Ipswich T.	163+2	1
				Wolverhampton W.	41+1	—
*Nigel Williams	5 8	9 13	Canterbury	Wolverhampton W.	11	—
*Gerald Taylor	5 10½	11 10	Hull	Wolverhampton W.	151+3	1
				Swindon T. (on loan)	19	—
John McAlle	5 11½	11 4	Liverpool	Wolverhampton W.	253+13	—
Francis Munro (Scotland)	6 0	13 1	Arbroath	Dundee U.	50	14
				Aberdeen	42+1	8
				Wolverhampton W.	257+6	13
Midfield						
Mike Bailey (England)	5 7½	11 2	Wisbech	Charlton Ath.	151	20
				Wolverhampton W.	350	19
Willie Carr (Scotland)	5 7¾	10 4	Glasgow	Coventry C.	245+5	32
				Wolverhampton W.	45+3	9
Maurice Daly	5 8	9 10	Dublin	Wolverhampton W.	3+1	—
Alan Sunderland	5 9	11 6½	Mexborough	Wolverhampton W.	85+19	12
Ken Hibbitt	5 10	11 4	Bradford	Bradford P.A.	13+3	—
				Wolverhampton W.	203+10	42
James Kelly	5 6	10 2	Aldergrove	Wolverhampton W.	10	—
				Wrexham (on loan)	4	—
Kenneth Todd	5 7	9 9	Co. Durham	Wolverhampton W.	—	—
Gerald O'Hara	5 8	10 11	Wolverhampton	Wolverhampton W.	5+1	—
Forwards						
Steve Daley	5 10½	12 0	Barnsley	Wolverhampton W.	71+20	10
*Don Gardner	5 9	10 8	Jamaica	Wolverhampton W.	1+2	—
Norman Bell	5 11	12 10	Sunderland	Wolverhampton W.	11+2	4
Sammy Wright	5 8	12 2	Belfast	Wolverhampton W.	—	—
John Richards (England)	5 9	11 1	Warrington	Wolverhampton W.	181+13	80
Steve Kindon	6 0	12 12	Warrington	Burnley	102+7	28
				Wolverhampton W.	80+23	23
John Farley	5 7	9 12	Stockton	Watford	96+8	8
				Halifax T. (on loan)	6	3
				Wolverhampton W.	31+2	—
Bobby Gould	5 10	11 5	Coventry	Coventry C.	78+3	40
				Arsenal	57+8	16
				Wolverhampton W.	39+1	18
				W.B.A.	52	18
				Bristol C.	35	15
				West Ham U.	46+5	15
				Wolverhampton W.	13+4	3
Martin Patching	5 11	11 4	Rotherham	Wolverhampton W.	2+1	—

WORKINGTON

DIV. 4

President: E. D. Smith, M.B.E., J.P.

Chairman: A. G. Perry.

Directors: D. Carruthers, D. N. Edgard, E. Firby, E. Fisher, F. L. Hill, A. J. Hughes, T. Kirkpatrick, W. Knowles, J. J. Payne, R. Tognarelli.

Manager: Alan Ashman.

Secretary: Mrs. M. Laurie.

Year Formed: 1884. Reformed 1921.

Limited Company: 1921.

Previous Ground: Lonsdale Park until 1937.

Honours: *Football League,* best season in Division 3: 5th, 1965–66. Division 4, Promoted: 1963–64 (3rd). *F.A. Cup,* best season: 4th Rd., 1934. *Football League Cup,* best season: 5th Rd., 1964, 1965.

Record Victory: 9-1 v Barrow, Football League Cup, 1st Rd., Sept. 2nd, 1964.

Record Defeat: 0-8 v Wrexham, Division 3(N), Oct. 24th, 1953.

Most League Points: 59, Division 4, 1963–64.

Most League Goals: 93, Division 3(N), 1956–57.

Highest League Scorer in Season: Jim Dailey, 26, Division 3(N), 1956–57.

Most League Goals in Total Aggregate: Jim Dailey, 84, 1953–58.

Most Capped Player: None.

Most League Appearances: Bobby Brown, 424, 1956–68.

Record Transfer Fee Received: £33,000 from Liverpool for Ian McDonald, Jan. 1974.

Record Transfer Fee Paid: £10,000 to Sunderland for Ken Chisholm and Ted Purdon together, Nov. 1956.

Managers Since the War: Bert Flatley, Ted Smith, Bill Shankly, Norman Low, Joe Harvey, Ken Furphy, Keith Burkinshaw, George Ainsley, Bill Lievers, Frank Upton, Brian Doyle, George Aitken, Colin Meldrum, John McNamee.

Address of Supporters Club: Same.

Address of Shop: Borough Park Shop, 10 The Crescent, Keswick, Cumberland.

Borough Park, Workington. Telephone Workington 2871. *Telegraphic address:* 'Borough Park, Workington'. *Ground capacity:* 21,000 (10,000 covered). *Record attendance:* 21,500 v Manchester U., F.A. Cup 3rd Rd., January 4, 1958. *Record receipts:* £2,236 v Manchester U., F.A. Cup 3rd Rd., January 4, 1958. *Pitch measurements:* 112 yds × 76 yds.

How to get there: Buses from Maryport and Carlisle to the ground. Nearest railway station, Workington.
Match tickets: Tickets can be booked in advance from the club secretary.
Car parking: Park adjacent to the ground holds 1,000 cars.
Entertainments/catering facilities: Social club under the main stand. Canteen on popular side of the ground.
Club shop: Sells all types of souvenirs.
Handbooks/programmes: Programmes not sold on subscription, but the club will supply back numbers when possible.
Extra information: Workington's best F.A. Cup run was achieved as a non-League side.

Club Colours: Red shirts, white shorts, red stockings.
Change Colour: Royal blue shirts with white collar, royal blue shorts, white stockings.
Club Captain: J. L. Ogilvie.
Coach: J. Waugh.
Club Nickname: 'The Reds'

WORKINGTON 1975–76 LEAGUE RECORD

Match No.	Date	Venue	Opponents	Result	H/T Score	League Pos'n	Goalscorers	Attendance
1	Aug 16	A	Torquay U.	L 0-1	0-0	—		2552
2	23	H	Newport Co.	L 1-2	0-1	22	Ward	1425
3	30	A	Stockport Co.	L 1-4	1-3	23	Walker	1678
4	Sept 6	H	Exeter C.	W 1-0	1-0	20	Harris	1004
5	13	A	Swansea C.	L 0-1	0-1	22		2126
6	20	H	Reading	L 0-2	0-0	24		1712
7	23	A	Northampton T.	L 1-2	0-0	—	Murray	4677
8	27	A	Barnsley	D 0-0	0-0	23		2843
9	Oct 4	H	Huddersfield T.	L 0-2	0-0	23		1158
10	11	A	Watford	L 0-2	0-0	23		3872
11	18	H	Cambridge U.	W 1-0	1-0	23	Harris	1122
12	22	H	Crewe Alex.	L 0-3	0-2	—		1333
13	24	A	Tranmere R.	L 0-6	0-4	23		4045
14	Nov 1	H	Southport	W 2-1	0-0	23	Bradley, Endean	1017
15	3	A	Brentford	L 0-4	0-2	—		5380
16	8	A	Scunthorpe U.	L 0-3	0-0	23		1506
17	15	H	Lincoln C.	L 0-3	0-2	23		1237
18	29	A	Rochdale	D 1-1	0-0	23	Ward	1361
19	Dec 6	H	AFC Bournemouth	L 1-3	0-1	23	Ellison	1219
20	20	H	Doncaster R.	W 3-1	2-0	23	Harris 2, Endean	1642
21	26	A	Darlington	L 0-1	0-1	23		2128
22	27	H	Hartlepool	L 1-2	0-1	23	Dawes	2553
23	Jan 9	H	Stockport Co.	L 1-2	1-0	23	Ellison	1917
24	14	A	Bradford C.	L 0-1	0-1	—		2567
25	17	A	Reading	L 0-1	0-1	23		7183
26	24	H	Swansea C.	D 1-1	1-0	23	Harris	1270
27	31	A	Crewe Alex.	D 0-0	0-0	23		1752
28	Feb 7	H	Brentford	D 1-1	0-1	23	Geidmintis (pen)	1231
29	14	H	Scunthorpe U.	L 2-3	2-2	23	Donaghy, Irvine (og)	1273
30	21	A	Lincoln C.	L 1-4	1-2	23	Elliss (og)	7069
31	25	H	Northampton T.	W 1-0	1-0	—	Murray	1135
32	28	H	Tranmere R.	L 0-1	0-0	23		1369
33	Mar 5	A	Southport	L 1-2	0-0	23	Murray	1226
34	9	A	Huddersfield T.	L 0-2	0-2	—		5010
35	13	H	Watford	L 1-3	0-1	23	Murray	1209
36	16	A	Cambridge U.	L 1-4	1-2	—	Murray	1415
37	20	H	Rochdale	D 0-0	0-0	24		1009
38	27	A	AFC Bournemouth	L 0-1	0-1	24		3564
39	30	A	Doncaster R.	L 0-1	0-1	—		4081
40	Apr 3	H	Torquay U.	L 1-3	0-2	24	Geidmintis	1003
41	7	H	Barnsley	L 1-7	1-4	—	Honour	1057
42	10	A	Exeter C.	L 0-1	0-0	24		2603
43	16	A	Bradford C.	L 0-3	0-0	24		1224
44	17	H	Darlington	D 0-0	0-0	24		1178
45	20	A	Hartlepool	W 2-0	1-0	—	Rylands (og), Donaghy	1731
46	24	A	Newport Co.	W 3-2	1-0	24	Murray, Donaghy, Hayes (og)	1226

Goalscorers

League (30): Murray 6, Harris 5, Donaghy 3, Ellison 2, Endean 2, Geidmintis 2 (1 a pen), Ward 2, Bradley 1, Dawes 1, Honour 1, Walker 1, own goals 4.
League Cup (1): Walker.
F.A. Cup (2): Heslop, Geidmintis.

League Cup	First Round	Oldham Ath. (a)	0-3
	Second Leg	(h)	1-3
F.A. Cup	First Round	Rochdale (h)	1-1
		(a)	1-2 (a.e.t.)

Rogan	Ellison	Ward	Geidmintis	Johnston	McNamee	Harris	Nevin	Murray	Kisby	Helliwell	Hughes	Walker	Scott	Harrison	Brown	Wood	Kavanagh	Heslop	Tyrer	Bradley	Broomfield	Jenkins	Endean	Mossop	Moore	Dawes	Donaghy	Ruggiero	Honour	Match No.
1	2	3	4	5	6	7	8	9	10	11																				1
	2	3	4			9	7	10	8	11	1	5	6*12																	2
	2			5		7*12		9	4	11	1	8			10	3	6													3
	2		5		6	7	4	9*10		11	1	8			12	3														4
	2	3*		5		12		9	8	11	1	7			6	4*10														5
	2	3*		5		12		9	8	11	1				6	4	7	10												6
1	2	3		5		11		9	8		12				6	4	7*10													7
1	2	3	5*			12		9	11		10				6	4	7	8												8
1	2	3	5			11		9	8		12				6	4*	7	10												9
1	2	8	5*			12		9	11		6				4	3	7	10												10
1	8	6		5		11		9*2			12				4	3	7	10												11
1	10	3		5		11		2							4	6	7		9	8										12
1	4			5		11		2			12				3	6	10	7	9*8											13
1				11*				2			12				5	6	4	3	7	10	8	9								14
1				11				2			12				3	5	4	6	7*10	8	9									15
1	4			11				2			12				3	6	5	7	9*	8	10								16
1	2	12		6	3*			5							4	7	10	9	8	11										17
	2	10	8*	9		7					1	5			12	4	3				11	6								18
	2	10		9		7		8*			1	5			12	4	3				11	6								19
1		8	2			9		7				6				4	5			10				3	11					20
1	11*	2				7		4			5				8	3	12				9			6	10					21
1		8*	2			9		7			6				4	5	12			10				3	11					22
1	8	11*	2			7		4	12		5				3					9				6	10					23
	8		2	9		7		4	12	1					5	11*	3							6	10					24
	8		2	9		7		4		1					5	11	3							6	10					25
1	8		2	6		7				11					4	5								3	10	9				26
1	9		4	6		7		2	11						5									3	10		8			27
1	8	12	4	6		7*		9	2						5									3	11	10				28
	8		4	6		7		9	2	1					11	5								3	10					29
	8	12	4	6		7		9	2	1					11*	5								3	10					30
	8		4	5*		7		9	2	1				12	11	3								6	10					31
	8		4*	5		7		9	2	1				12	11	3								6	10					32
	8	5	4	6		7		9	2	1					11									3	10					33
	2		8	10		7		9		1					5	4	3							6	11					34
1	2		8	6		7		9		11					5	3								3	10		4			35
1	8		4			7		9	2		5				3									6	11	10				36
1	8		4			7		9*2			5				12	3								6	11	10				37
1	8*		4			7		9	2		5				12	3								6	11	10				38
1	11	4				7		2			5				8	3								6	9	10				39
1	9	4	12			7		2			6*				11	5								3	10		8			40
1	7	4	5					9	2		8				3									6	10	11				41
1	8	4				7		9	2		5				6									3	10	11				42
1	11	4				7		9	2		5				12	3								6	10	8*				43
1	8	4				7		9	2		5	3			11									6	10					44
1	11	4				7		9	2		5				8	3								6	10					45
1	8	7	4					9	2		5				11	3								6	10					46
31	37	23	29	29	2	38	3	28	43	8	15	23	1	1	6	13	30	37	12	8	3	6	8	1	3	29	27	3	9	
			+3s	+1s		+4s	+1s				+2s		+7s	+1s	+3s		+2s	+3s		+2s										

413

Player and position	Ht.	Wt.	Birthplace	Clubs	League Appearances	Goals
Goalkeepers						
Mike Rogan	5 11	12 0	Fleetwood	Workington	350	—
Defenders						
Ray Ellison	5 7¼	11 6	Newcastle	Newcastle U.	5	—
				Sunderland	2	—
				Torquay U.	11+5	—
				Workington	37	2
John Ogilivie	6 0	12 2	Workington	Blackpool	—	—
				Workington	396+4	8
*Ronnie Walker	6 0	12 0	London	Workington	143+10	3
				Aldershot (on loan)	—	—
*Brian Helsop	5 10	11 5	Carlisle	Carlisle U.	5	—
				Sunderland	59+1	—
				Northampton	49+1	—
				Workington	139+1	5
*Tony Geidmintis	6 0	12 0	London	Workington	323+5	37
*Brian Wood	5 11	12 11	Hamworthy	W.B.A.	—	—
C. Palace 142+1(1) Orient 58(3) Colchester U. 71(1) Workington 202+2(9)						
Bobby Brown	5 10	11 6	Workington	Workington	10	—
Freddy Rose				Workington	0+2	—
*Alan Tyrer	5 5	10 3	Liverpool	Bury	2	—
				Workington	228+15	18
Malcolm Dawes	5 9	12 5	Trimdon Grange	Darlington	—	—
				Aldershot	159+4	2
				Hartlepool	192+1	12
				Workington	29	—
*David Jenkins	5 9	11 6	Bristol	Arsenal	16+1	3
Tottenham H. 11+3(2) Brentford 13+5(1) Hereford U. 18+4(3) Newport Co. (on loan) 7(1)						
Shrewsbury 2(1) Workington 6(—)						
*Peter Ward	5 9½	10 9	Rotherham	Sheffield U.	—	—
				Workington	39+4	2
Chris Kisby	5 7	10 8	Pudsey	Scunthorpe U.	30+9	2
				Workington	124+2	—
Ian Johnston	6 0	12 4	Gilcrux	Workington	29+3	—
*John McNamee	6 0	13 7	Lanark	Celtic	26	2
Hibernian 77(2) Newcastle U. 115+2(8) Blackburn R. 56(9) Hartlepool 2(—) Workington 2(—)						
Midfield						
Eamon Kavanagh	5 9	10 8	Manchester	Manchester C.	—	—
				Rochdale	2+2	—
				Workington	86+3	6
John Honour	5 7	10 7	Horden	W.B.A.	—	—
				Hartlepool	107+5	6
				Workington	9	1
Forwards						
*David Helliwell	5 8	9 12	Blackburn	Blackburn R.	15	1
				Lincoln C.	11+2	1
				Workington	183+13	20
Dave Murray	5 11	12 8	Rothbury	Workington	79+3	22
Martin Harris	5 7	10 4	Doncaster	Workington	61+6	8
*Ian Broomfield	6 0	11 1	Bristol	Bristol C.	16+3	2
				Stockport Co.	22+5	1
				Workington	3	—
Barry Donaghy	5 6	10 10	Consett	W.B.A.	4+2	1
				Workington	27	3
*David Bradley				Workington	8	1
Ridley Nevin	5 10	11 0	Liverpool	Everton	—	—
				Workington	3+1	—
*Ron Hughes	5 11	13 0	Workington	Workington	15	—
John Scott	5 9	12 1	Edinburgh	Workington	1+1	—
Ray Moore	5 10	10 7	Workington	Workington	3	—
Graham Mossop	5 9	11 2	Liverpool	Everton	—	—
				Workington	1	—
Wayne Harrison			Workington	Workington	1+3	—

WREXHAM

DIV. 3

W.F.C.

President: W. B. N. Kington, T.D.

Chairman: F. J. Tomlinson.

Directors: T. H. Dodds, H. G. Phillips, A. W. Gaade, G. Morris, R. E. A. Clark, C. E. Roberts, A. Morris.

Manager: John Neal.   *Secretary:* C. N. Wilson.

Year Formed: 1873 (oldest Club in Wales).

Turned Professional: 1912.   *Limited Company:* 1912.

Previous Ground: Acton Park.

Honours: Football League, best season in Division 3: 4th, 1973–74, 1970–71. Division 3(N), Runners-up: 1932–33. Division 4 Runners-up: 1969–70. *F.A. Cup,* best season: 5th Rd., 1973-74. *Football League Cup,* best season: 5th Rd., 1961. *Welsh Cup,* winners 20 times.

European Competition: Cup-Winners Cup: 1972–73, 1975–76 (Quarter-finals).

Record Victory: 10-1 v Hartlepools U., Division 4, Mar. 3rd, 1962.

Record Defeat: 0-9 v Brentford, Division 3, Oct. 15th, 1963.

Most League Points: 61, Division 4, 1969–70.

Most League Goals: 106, Division 3(N), 1932–33.

Highest League Scorer in Season: Tom Bamford, 44, Division 3(N), 1933–34.

Most League Goals in Total Aggregate: Tom Bamford, 175, 1928–34.

Most Capped Player: Horace Blew, 22, Wales.

Most League Appearances: Arfon Griffiths, 527, 1959-61; 1962-76.

Record Transfer Fee Received: £110,000 from Liverpool for Joey Jones, Aug. 1975.

Record Transfer Fee Paid: £15,000 to Cardiff C. for Mel Sutton, June 1972.

Managers Since the War: Tom Williams, Les McDowell, Peter Jackson, Cliff Lloyd, John Love, Bill Morris, Ken Barnes. Bill Morris, Jack Rowley, Alvan Williams.

Address of Supporters Club: Secretary, John Roberts, 10, Sandringham Rd.

Racecourse Ground, Mold Road, Wrexham. Telephone Wrexham 2414.   *Telegraphic address:* 'Football, Wrexham'.   *Ground capacity:* 30,000 (18,000 covered).   *Record attendance:* 34,445 v Manchester U., F.A. Cup 4th Rd., January 26, 1957.   *Record receipts:* £25,107 v Anderlecht, European Cup-Winners' Cup Quarter-Final, March 17 1976.   *Pitch measurements:* 117 yds × 75 yds.

How to get there: Wrexham General railway station is only 200 yards from the ground. Trains run from Chester and Shrewsbury. Bus services from outlying districts to town.

Match tickets: Stand tickets bookable in advance.

Car parking: Parking grounds at St Marks, Bodhyfryd Square, Eagles Meadows, Old Guild Hall, Hill Street, Holt Street, and Town Hill, Hill Street.

Entertainments/catering facilities: A social club and four catering kiosks at the ground.

Club shop: Situated on the Kop side of the ground; stocks all types of souvenirs.

Handbooks/programmes: No handbook at present. Programmes available on subscription.

Extra information: Season tickets available for all parts of the ground and all stands except the Crispin Lane Stand.

Club Colours: Red shirts with white facings, white shorts with red stripe.

Change Colours: Sky blue shirts, white shorts and stockings.

Club Captain: Eddie May.

Assistant Player/Manager: Arfon Griffiths.

Club Nickname: 'The Robins'.

WREXHAM 1975-76 LEAGUE RECORD

Match No.	Date	Venue	Opponents	Result	H/T Score	League Pos'n	Goalscorers	Attendance
1	Aug 16	H	Aldershot	W 3-1	1-1	—	Tinnion, Lyons, Sutton	3315
2	23	A	Millwall	L 1-2	0-1	10	Tinnion	6784
3	30	H	Chesterfield	W 1-0	0-0	5	Barlow (og)	3519
4	Sept 6	A	Sheffield W.	L 0-1	0-0	12		7585
5	13	H	Gillingham	W 2-0	0-0	8	May, Ashcroft	2654
6	20	A	Rotherham U.	L 1-2	0-1	12	Davies	3776
7	24	A	Peterborough U.	L 0-2	0-1	—		5888
8	27	H	Port Vale	W 1-0	1-0	13	Thomas	3853
9	Oct 4	A	Cardiff C.	L 0-3	0-1	17		7653
10	11	A	Hereford U.	L 0-2	0-1	21		6228
11	18	H	Swindon T.	W 2-0	0-0	17	Tinnion, Whittle	2893
12	25	A	Brighton & H. A.	L 2-3	1-1	21	Ashcroft, Sutton	12,059
13	Nov 1	H	Mansfield T.	W 1-0	0-0	19	Ashcroft	2701
14	8	A	Bury	W 1-0	0-0	16	Sutton	6063
15	11	A	Grimsby T.	L 2-3	1-1	—	Dwyer 2	4850
16	15	H	Crystal Palace	L 1-3	0-1	19	May	5878
17	29	H	Halifax T.	D 1-1	0-0	20	Lee (pen)	3063
18	Dec 6	A	Preston N. E.	W 1-0	0-0	18	Lee	7438
19	13	H	Colchester U.	D 1-1	1-0	14	Lee	2143
20	20	A	Colchester U.	W 2-0	2-0	11	Lee, Lyons	2608
21	26	H	Chester	D 1-1	1-1	11	Lyons	10,486
22	27	A	Walsall	D 2-2	1-1	12	Ashcroft, Whittle	9029
23	Jan 3	H	Millwall	D 1-1	0-1	9	Thomas	2779
24	10	A	Chesterfield	D 1-1	0-0	11	May	3732
25	17	H	Rotherham U.	W 3-0	2-0	8	Ashcroft, Whittle, Lee	2897
26	24	A	Gillingham	D 1-1	0-0	9	Whittle	5849
27	31	H	Grimsby T.	W 1-0	0-0	7	Griffiths (pen)	2808
28	Feb 6	A	Southend U.	L 1-2	0-1	8	Tinnion	4162
29	9	H	Shrewsbury T.	L 2-3	1-2	—	Lee, May	5356
30	14	H	Bury	W 2-1	1-0	8	Evans, Whittle	3109
31	21	A	Crystal Palace	D 1-1	1-1	8	Whittle	16,944
32	23	H	Peterborough U.	W 3-0	1-0	—	Ashcroft 2, Tinnion	3640
33	28	A	Brighton & H.A.	W 3-0	1-0	8	Griffiths, Ashcroft, Tinnion	4662
34	Mar 6	A	Mansfield T.	D 0-0	0-0	7		6473
35	8	H	Cardiff C.	D 1-1	0-0	—	Whittle	5674
36	13	H	Hereford U.	W 2-1	2-1	5	Sutton, Griffiths	7621
37	20	A	Halifax T.	W 1-0	0-0	6	Ashcroft	2970
38	27	H	Preston N.E.	L 1-2	1-1	8	Sutton	4906
39	Apr 3	A	Aldershot	W 3-2	1-1	7	Sutton, Tinnion, Whittle	3506
40	5	A	Port Vale	L 1-3	0-2	—	Evans	3604
41	10	H	Sheffield W.	W 3-0	0-0	7	Hull (og), Ashcroft 2	4190
42	17	A	Chester	W 3-1	1-0	6	Lee, May, Griffiths (pen)	6553
43	19	H	Walsall	L 0-3	0-1	—		5482
44	21	A	Shrewsbury T.	W 2-1	2-1	—	Ashcroft, Whittle	3097
45	27	H	Southend U.	D 2-2	1-0	—	Griffiths, Ashcroft	1965
46	29	A	Swindon T.	D 2-2	1-1	—	Ashcroft, Lee	9007

Goalscorers

League (66): Ashcroft 14, Whittle 9, Lee 8 (1 a pen), Tinnion 7, Sutton 6, May 5, Griffiths 5 (2 pens), Lyons 3, Dwyer 2, Thomas 2, Evans 2, Davies 1, Own Goals 2.
League Cup (4): Dwyer 2, Lyons, Davis.

F.A. Cup (3): Ashcroft, Dwyer, Own Goal 1.

League Cup	First Round	Chester (h)		3-0
	Second Leg	(a)		0-0
	Second Round	Mansfield T. (h)		1-2
F.A. Cup	First Round	Mansfield T. (a)		1-1
		(h)		1-1 (a.e.t.)
				1-2 (at Villa Park)

Lloyd	Davis A.	Fogg	Evans	May	Thomas	Tinnion	Sutton	Ashcroft	Lyons	Dwyer	Scott	Williams, M.	Hill	Davies	Kelly	Griffiths	Whittle	Lee	Williams, A. E.	Match No.
1	2	3	4	5	6	7	8	9	10	11										1
1	2	3	6	5	10	7	8	9*	11	4		12								2
1	2		4	5	6	7	8	9	10	3		11								3
1	2		4	5	6	7	8	9	10*	3		12	11							4
1	6	3	4	5		7	8	9	10*	11			2	12						5
1	4		6	5			8	9	12	3			2	10	7*	11				6
1	2		4	5	6		8		7	3*				9	11	10		12		7
1	4	3		5	6		8		12				2	7	10	11		9*		8
1	2		4	5	10	7	8	12	3				9*		11	6				9
1	2		4	5	6	7	8	12	3				9*		11	10				10
1	4	3		5	7	8	9						2	11	10	6				11
1	4	3		5	6	7	8	9					2	11	10					12
1	4	3		5	6	7	8	9	10				2			11				13
1	4	3		5	6	7	8	9	10				2			11				14
1	4	3		5	6	7	8	9	10				2			11				15
1	4	12	3	5	6		8	9	7	10*			2			11				16
1		3		5	6	7	8	9*	12	10	4		2			11				17
1	4	3	2	5	6	7	8		10							11	9			18
1	4	3	2	5	6	7	8	12	10*							11	9			19
1	4	3	2	5	6	7	8		10							11	9			20
1	4	3	2	5	6	10*	8	12	7							11	9			21
1	2		4	5	6	7	8	9		3						11	10			22
1	2		4	5	6		8	10	7	3						11	9			23
1	2			5	6	10	12	3	7*	4						11	8	9		24
1	4	3	2	5	6	7	10									11	8	9		25
1	4	3	2	5	6	7	8		10							11	9			26
1	4		2	5	6	7	9			3						11	8	10		27
1	4	3	2	5	6*	7	11	10	12								8	9		28
1	4	3	2	5	6	7	11	10									8	9		29
1	4	3	2	5	11	8	10	7									6	9		30
1	4	3	2	5	6	11	10	7									8	9		31
1	4	3	2	5		7	8		10							11	6	9		32
1	4	3	2	5		7	8		10	12			9*			11	6			33
1	4	3	2	5	6	12	8		10*				9			11	7			34
1	4		2	5		7	8		10	3			9			11	6			35
1	4	3	2	5	10		8	9								11	6	7		36
1	4	3	2	5		7	8		10							11	6	9		37
1	4	3	2	5		7*	8		10	12						11	6	9		38
1	4	3	2	5		7	8		10							11	6	9		39
1	4	3*	2	5		7	8	12	10							11	6	9		40
1	4		2	5		7	8		10	3						11	6	9		41
1	4		2	5		7	8	10	12	3*						11	6	9		42
1	4		2	5		7*	8	10	12	3						11	6	9		43
1	4		2	5		7	8		10	3						11	6	9		44
1	4		2	5			8	10	7	3						11	6	9		45
1	4		2	5			8	10	7	3							6	9		46
46	42	28	41	46	30	35	43	36	15	29	1	3	10	8	4	31	30	27	1	
	+1s				+1s	+1s	+6s	+4s	+3s	+2s				+1s			+1s			

417

Player and position	Ht.	Wt.	Birthplace	Clubs	League Appearances	Goals
Goalkeepers						
Brian Lloyd	6 2	12 7	Rhyl	Stockport Co.	32	—
(Wales)				Southend U.	46	—
				Wrexham	219	—
Eddie Niedzwieck	6 0	11 0	Wrexham	Wrexham	—	—
Defenders						
*David Fogg	5 9	11 4	Liverpool	Wrexham	158+2	—
Gareth Davis	5 10½	11 7	Bangor	Wrexham	282+6	6
Mickey Evans	5 9¾	11 2	Gaesws	Wrexham	303+10	18
Eddie May	6 1½	13 3½	Epping	Southend U.	107+4	3
				Wrexham	329+4	34
*Robert Scott	6 2½	13 4	Liverpool	Wrexham	14+4	—
				Reading (on loan)	5	—
Alan Hill	5 11	11 4	Chester	Wrexham	23	—
Anthony Larkin	5 11	11 12	Wrexham	Wrexham	—	—
Glyn Griffiths	5 9	11 2	Wrexham	Wrexham	—	—
Huw Williams	6 0	11 0	Wrexham	Wrexham	—	—
Midfield						
Arfon Griffiths	5 6	10 4½	Wrexham	Wrexham	42	8
(Wales)				Arsenal	15	2
				Wrexham	485	112
Graham Whittle	5 9	10 3	Liverpool	Wrexham	170+9	37
Mel Sutton	5 10	10 10	Birmingham	Cardiff C.	135+3	5
				Wrexham	159+1	15
Alan Dwyer	5 7	10 7	Liverpool	Wrexham	31+5	2
John Lyons	5 11	11 12	Buckley	Wrexham	18+5	26
Michael Williams	5 9	10 11	Wrexham	Wrexham	3	—
Michael Thomas	5 5	10 1	Colwyn Bay	Wrexham	115+11	14
Forwards						
Bill Ashcroft	6 1	12 9	Liverpool	Wrexham	153+23	50
*Geoff Davies	5 11	12 4	Ellesmere Port	Chester	18+14	5
				Wrexham	64+3	15
Brian Tinnion	5 8½	11 3	Workington	Workington	93+5	24
				Wrexham	265+14	54
				Chester (on loan)	3	—
				(Contract cancelled April 1976)		
Stuart Lee	5 7	8 11	Manchester	Bolton W.	77+8	20
				Wrexham	27	8
Everton Williams	5 10	12 0	Wrexham	Wrexham	1+1	—

YORK CITY

President: C. W. Sherrington. *Chairman:* R. B. Strachan, M.A., L.L.B., F.C.I.S.
Vice-chairman: G. S. Winters.
Directors: K. N. Lancaster, F.R.I.C.S., Dr. A. I. Macleod, M.B., Ch.B., Lt-Col. B. M. Kilner, A. G. D. Blundy, R. Myles Gibson, M.D., M.Sc., F. H. Magson.
Manager: Wilf McGuinness. *Secretary:* G. Teasdale.
Year Formed: 1922. *Turned Professional:* 1922.
Limited Company: 1922.
Previous Grounds: 1922, Fulfordgate; 1932, Bootham Crescent.
Honours: Football League: best season: 15th, div. 2, 1974–75. Division 4, Promoted 1958–59 (3rd), 1964–65 (3rd), 1970–71 (4th).
F.A. Cup, best season, semi-finalists: 1955, in Division 3.
Football League Cup, best season: 5th Rd., 1962.
Record Victory: 9-1 v Southport, Division 3(N), Feb. 2nd, 1957
Record Defeat: 0-12 v Chester, Division 3(N), Feb. 1st, 1936.
Most League Points: 62, Division 4, 1964–65.
Most League Goals: 92, Division 3(N), 1954–55.
Highest League Scorer in Season: Bill Fenton, 31, Division 3(N), 1951–52; Arthur Bottom, 31, Division 3(N), 1955–56.
Most League Goals in Total Aggregate: Norman Wilkinson, 125, 1954–66.
Most Capped Player: Peter Scott, 4, N. Ireland.
Most League Appearances: Barry Jackson, 481, 1958–70.
Record Transfer Fee Received: £30,000 from Sheffield U. for Cliff Calvert, Oct. 1975.
Record Transfer Fee Paid: £18,000 to AFC Bournemouth for Micky Cave, August 1974.
Managers Since the War: Tom Mitchell, Dick Duckworth, Charlie Spencer, Jimmy McCormack, Sam Bartram, Tom Lockie, Joe Shaw, Tom Johnston.
Address of Supporters Club: Same as Football Club.

Bootham Crescent, York. Telephone: York 24447. *Telegraphic address:* 'City Football Club, York'. *Ground capacity:* 17,000. *Record attendance:* 28,123 v Huddersfield T., F.A. Cup, 5th Rd., March 5, 1938. *Record receipts:* £9856 v Arsenal, F.A. Cup 3rd Rd. replay, January 7, 1975. *Pitch measurements:* 115 yds × 75 yds.

How to get there: Buses 2, 2a, and 8 every 10 minutes from York railway station to the ground.
Match tickets: On sale 14 days prior to match. Pre-match sales cease 48 hours before a game and unsold tickets are then sold immediately prior to game.
Car parking: Ample parking in side-streets.
Entertainments/catering facilities: Licensed Social Club open to members only. Three tea bars on the ground. Drinks available at half-time in front of the Popular Stand and in the officials' car park.
Club shop: Selling all types of souvenirs.
Handbooks/programmes: Programmes not available on subscription.
Extra information: One of only four Third Division clubs to reach the semi-finals of the F.A. Cup (in 1954–55).
Club Colours: White shirts with maroon 'Y' on front, maroon cuffs, white shorts, maroon stockings.
Change Colours: Royal blue shirts, royal blue shorts with white stripe, royal blue stockings.
Club Captain:
First Team Trainer/Coach: Clive Baker.
Club Nickname: 'Minster Men'.

YORK CITY 1975–76 LEAGUE RECORD

Match No.	Date	Venue	Opponents	Result	H/T Score	League Pos'n	Goalscorers	Attendance
1	Aug 16	H	Portsmouth	W 2-1	1-1	—	Lyons, McMordie	4602
2	23	A	Bristol R.	L 1-2	0-0	16	Downing	8142
3	30	H	Bolton W.	L 1-2	1-0	17	Jones	5640
4	Sept 6	A	W.B.A.	D 2-2	0-2	18	Seal, Jones	11,028
5	13	H	Notts Co.	L 1-2	0-1	20	McMordie	5586
6	20	A	Plymouth Arg.	D 1-1	1-0	20	Seal	12,818
7	23	A	Orient	L 0-1	0-1	—		4290
8	27	H	Oxford U.	W 2-0	0-0	15	Swallow, Wann	3190
9	Oct 4	A	Chelsea	D 0-0	0-0	16		15,323
10	11	A	Oldham Ath.	L 0-2	0-1	19		8704
11	18	H	Bristol C.	L 1-4	0-3	21	Cave	4661
12	21	A	Charlton Ath.	L 1-3	1-1	—	Jones	4345
13	25	A	Southampton	L 0-2	0-1	22		13,501
14	Nov 1	H	Sunderland	L 1-4	0-3	22	Jones	15,232
15	4	A	Luton T.	L 0-4	0-1	—		7982
16	8	A	Carlisle U.	L 0-1	0-1	22		7021
17	15	H	Fulham	W 1-0	1-0	21	Holmes (pen)	3414
18	22	A	Bristol C.	L 1-4	1-2	21	Seal	11,228
19	29	A	Nottingham F.	L 0-1	0-1	21		13,108
20	Dec 6	H	Hull C.	L 1-2	0-1	21	Seal	6657
21	13	H	Bristol R.	D 0-0	0-0	21		3112
22	20	A	Portsmouth	W 1-0	1-0	21	Hinch	7093
23	26	H	Blackburn R.	W 2-1	1-0	21	Holmes (pen), Hosker	6597
24	27	A	Blackpool	D 0-0	0-0	21		7939
25	Jan 10	A	Notts Co.	L 0-4	0-3	21		10,136
26	17	H	W.B.A.	L 0-1	0-1	21		5628
27	31	A	Charlton Ath.	L 2-3	0-1	21	Cave, Pollard	6916
28	Feb 7	H	Luton T.	L 2-3	1-2	21	Holmes (pen), Pollard	3132
29	14	H	Carlisle U.	L 1-2	0-0	22	Holmes	3850
30	21	A	Fulham	L 0-2	0-1	22		6686
31	24	H	Orient	L 0-2	0-1	—		2857
32	28	H	Southampton	W 2-1	1-1	22	Cave, Hinch	3777
33	Mar 13	A	Oldham Ath.	W 1-0	1-0	22	Cave	4132
34	20	A	Nottingham F.	W 3-2	1-0	22	Hinch, Pollard 2	5571
35	27	A	Hull C.	D 1-1	0-0	22	Cave	6306
36	30	A	Sunderland	L 0-1	0-1	—		33,462
37	Apr 3	A	Oxford U.	L 0-1	0-0	22		4926
38	10	A	Plymouth Arg.	W 3-1	1-0	21	Holmes, Pollard, Cave	3646
39	13	A	Bolton W.	W 2-1	0-0	—	Hinch, Cave	19,048
40	17	A	Blackburn R.	L 0-4	0-1	21		8952
41	19	H	Blackpool	D 1-1	0-0	—	Holmes	3800
42	24	H	Chelsea	D 2-2	1-0	21	Seal, Cave	4914

Goalscorers

League (39): Cave 8, Holmes 6 (3 pens), Pollard 5, Seal 5, Hinch 4, Jones 4, McMordie 2, Downing 1, Hosker 1, Lyons 1, Swallow 1, Wann 1.

League Cup (3): Seal 2, Jones.

F.A. Cup (2): Seal, Hosker.

League Cup	First Round	Bradford C. (a)	0-2
	Second Leg	(h)	3-0
	Second Round	Liverpool (h)	0-1
F.A. Cup	Third Round	Hereford U. (h)	2-1
	Fourth Round	Chelsea (h)	0-2

Crawford	Oliver	Downing	Holmes	Swallow	Topping	Lyons	Cave	Seal	Jones	McMordie	Woodward	Calvert	Stone	Pollard	Wann	Hinch	Hunter	Creamer	Hosker	Scott	Taylor	James	Match No.
1	2	3	4	5	6	7	8	9	10	11													1
1	2	3	4*	5	6	7	8	10	9	11	12												2
1		3	4	5	6	7	8	9	10	11		2											3
1		3		5	6	7	8	9	10	11	4	2											4
1		3	12	5	6	7	8	9	10	11	4*	2											5
1		3		5	6			9	10	7	8		2	4	11								6
1		3		5	6			9	10	11*	4		2	7	8	12							7
1		3		5	6	7		9	10	11			2	4	8								8
1		3		5	6		8	9	10	7			2	4	11								9
1		3		5	6		8	9	10*	7			2	4	11	12							10
1	2	3	4*	5	6	11	8	9		10				7		12							11
1	2	3		5		4		9	10	11	8			7		6							12
1	2	3		5			8	9	10		4			7	11	6							13
1	2	3		5			8	9	10		7			4	11	6							14
1	2	3	8	5	6		4	9	10					7	11								15
1	11	4	5	6	8			9	10*	7	3							2	12				16
1	11	4	5	6	8			9	10	7	3							2					17
1	11	4	5	6	8*			9		7	3				10			2	12				18
1	11	4	5	6	8*			9		7	3				10			2	12				19
1	11	4	5	6				9	10*	7	3				12			8	2				20
1	11*	4	5	6			12	9		7	3				10			8	2				21
1		8	5	6			11	9		4	3				10	2		7					22
1	11	8	5	6			12	9		4	3*				10	2		7					23
1	3*		5	6			8	9		7			12		10	2		4		11			24
1	11	4	5	6				9		7	3				10			8	2				25
1			6					10	12		4*	3		8		9	11	7	2	5			26
1		8*	6	11				10	9		4	3		7		12			2	5			27
1		8*	5	6				10	9	11		3	2	7				12		4			28
1		4		6			8	9	10		3			7				11	2	5			29
1		8		5	6			9	10		3			7				11	2	4			30
1		8		5	6			9	10		3			7	12			11*	2	4			31
1		3	4		6		8		10	11				7		9			2	5			32
1		3	4		6		8		11	10				7		9			2	5			33
1		3	4		6		8		10	11				7		9			2	5			34
1	2		4*		6		8		10	11	12			7		9			3	5			35
1		3	8	5				10	12	11	6			7*		9			2			4	36
1		3	4*	5			8		12	11	6			7		9			10	2			37
1		3	4*		6		8		12	11	10			7		9			2	5			38
1		3	8	5				10	4	11	6			7		9			2				39
1		3	4	5			8		10	11*	6			7		9			12	2			40
1		3	8	5				10	11		6			7		9			2			4	41
1		3	8	5				10	11		6			7		9			2			4	42
42	7	35	30	24	42	10	32	34	17	37	33	3	6	27	8	19	7	4	11	19	1	14	

+1s (Downing) +2s (Topping) +5s (Lyons) +1s (Jones) +1s (Pollard) +4s (Wann) +2s (Hinch) +5s (Creamer)

Player and position	Ht.	Wt.	Birthplace	Clubs	League Appearances	Goals
Goalkeepers						
Graeme Crawford	6 2	12 4	Falkirk	East Stirling	2	—
				Sheffield U.	2	—
				Mansfield T. (on loan)	2	—
				York C.	197	—
Stuart Walker	6 0	12 2	Leeds	York C.	—	—
Defenders						
Gordon Hunter	5 7	11 1	Lyrehan	York C.	19+2	1
*Ian Robb	6 2	12 0	Doncaster	York C.	4	—
*John Stone	6 0	12 2		Middlesbrough	2	—
				York C.	86	5
Peter Scott	5 9	11 4	Liverpool	Everton	42+2	1
(N. Ireland)				Southport (on loan)	4	—
				York C.	19	—
*Barry Swallow	6 2	12 10	Doncaster	Doncaster R.	51	10
				Crewe A.	14	—
				Barnsley	97	2
				Bradford C.	79+6	7
				York C.	269+1	21
Chris Topping	6 1	11 12	Selby	York C.	318+2	8
Derrick Downing	5 9	10 4	Frickley Colliery	Middlesbrough	171+11	39
				Orient	100+4	11
				York C.	35	1
Steve James	6 0	12 2	Coseley	Manchester U.	129	4
				York C.	14	—
Midfield						
Micky Cave	5 8	10 13	Weymouth	Torquay	106+8	17
				Plymouth Arg. (on loan)	8	4
				Bournemouth	91+8	17
				York C.	71+2	9
John Woodward	5 10	10 2	Glasgow	Arsenal	2+1	—
				York C.	128+15	6
Cliff Calvert	5 10	11 6		York C.	59+5	—
Ian Holmes	5 7	10 6	Wombwell	Sheffield U.	4+2	—
				York C.	99+5	20
Brian Pollard	5 5	9 6	York	York C.	93+9	17
Eric McMordie	5 6	9 4	Belfast	Middlesbrough	231+10	23
(N. Ireland)				Sheffield W. (on loan)	9	6
				York C.	37	2
Forwards						
Ian Butler	5 8½	11 4	Rotherham	Rotherham U.	98	28
				Hull C.	300+5	64
				York C.	43+3	2
				Barnsley (on loan)	5	—
				(contract cancelled Jan 1976)		
Jim Hinch	6 2	12 2	Sheffield	Tranmere R.	36+3	10
				Plymouth Arg.	102+5	28
				Hereford U.	22+5	7
				York C.	28+11	5
				Southport (on loan)	7	2
*Barry Lyons	5 7	10 8	Nottingham	Rotherham U.	132	24
				Nottingham F.	201+2	28
				York C.	80+5	11
*Dennis Wann	5 8	10 11	Blackpool	Blackpool	10+6	—
				York C.	65+1	7
				Southend U. (on loan)	—	—
				Chesterfield (on loan)	3	—
				Hartlepool (on loan)	2	—
Jimmy Seal	5 10	11 8	Pontefract	Wolverhampton W.	1	—
				Walsall (on loan)	40	14
				Barnsley	43	12
				York C.	147+7	42
Bobby Hosker	5 5	9 9	Cannock	Middlesbrough	—	—
				York C.	11+5	1
Chris Jones	5 10	10 12	Altrincham	Manchester C.	6+1	2
				Swindon T.	49+19	18
				Oldham Ath.	3	1
				Walsall	54+5	14
				York C.	94+1	33
Philip Taylor	5 9	10 12	Sheffield	York C.	1+1	—

FOOTBALL LEAGUE STATISTICS

FINAL FOOTBALL LEAGUE TABLES 1975-76

DIVISION 1

	P	Home					Away					Pts
		W	D	L	F	A	W	D	L	F	A	
Liverpool	42	14	5	2	41	21	9	9	3	25	10	60
Q.P.R.	42	17	4	0	42	13	7	7	7	25	20	59
Manchester U.	42	16	4	1	40	13	7	6	8	28	29	56
Derby C.	42	15	3	3	45	30	6	8	7	30	28	53
Leeds U.	42	13	3	5	37	19	8	6	7	28	27	51
Ipswich T.	42	11	6	4	36	23	5	8	8	18	25	46
Leicester C.	42	9	9	3	29	14	4	10	7	19	27	45
Manchester C.	42	14	5	2	46	18	2	6	13	18	28	43
Tottenham H.	42	6	10	5	33	32	8	5	8	30	31	43
Norwich C.	42	10	5	6	33	26	6	5	10	25	32	42
Everton	42	10	7	4	37	24	5	5	11	23	42	42
Stoke C.	42	8	5	8	25	24	7	6	8	23	26	41
Middlesbrough	42	9	7	5	23	11	6	3	12	23	34	40
Coventry C.	42	6	9	6	22	22	7	5	9	25	35	40
Newcastle U.	42	11	4	6	51	26	4	5	12	20	36	39
Aston Villa	42	11	8	2	32	17	0	9	12	19	42	39
Arsenal	42	11	4	6	33	19	2	6	13	14	34	36
West Ham U.	42	10	5	6	26	23	3	5	13	22	48	36
Birmingham C.	42	11	5	5	36	26	2	2	17	21	49	33
Wolves	42	7	6	8	27	25	3	4	14	24	43	30
Burnley	42	6	6	9	23	26	3	4	14	20	40	28
Sheffield U.	42	4	7	10	19	32	2	3	16	14	50	22

DIVISION 2

	P	Home					Away					Pts
		W	D	L	F	A	W	D	L	F	A	
Sunderland	42	19	2	0	48	10	5	6	10	19	26	56
Bristol C.	42	11	7	3	34	14	8	8	5	26	21	53
W.B.A.	42	10	9	2	29	12	10	4	7	21	21	53
Bolton W.	42	12	5	4	36	14	8	7	6	28	24	52
Notts Co.	42	11	6	4	33	13	8	5	8	27	28	49
Southampton	42	18	2	1	49	16	3	5	13	17	34	49
Luton T.	42	13	6	2	38	15	6	4	11	23	36	48
Nottingham F.	42	13	1	7	34	18	4	11	6	21	22	46
Charlton Ath.	42	11	5	5	40	34	4	7	10	21	38	42
Blackpool	42	9	9	3	26	22	5	5	11	14	27	42
Chelsea	42	7	9	5	25	20	5	7	9	28	34	40
Fulham	42	9	8	4	27	14	4	6	11	18	33	40
Orient	42	10	6	5	21	12	3	8	10	16	27	40
Hull C.	42	9	5	7	29	23	5	6	10	16	26	39
Blackburn R.	42	8	6	7	27	22	4	8	9	18	28	38
Plymouth Arg.	42	13	4	4	36	20	0	8	13	12	34	38
Oldham Ath.	42	11	8	2	37	24	2	4	15	20	44	38
Bristol R.	42	7	9	5	20	15	4	7	10	18	35	38
Carlisle U.	42	9	8	4	29	22	3	5	13	16	37	37
Oxford U.	42	7	7	7	23	25	4	4	13	16	34	33
York C.	42	8	3	10	28	34	2	5	14	11	37	28
Portsmouth	42	4	6	11	16	23	5	1	15	17	38	25

DIVISION 3

	P	W	D	L	F	A	W	D	L	F	A	Pts.
		Home					Away					
Hereford U.	46	14	6	3	45	24	12	5	6	41	31	63
Cardiff C.	46	14	7	2	38	13	8	6	9	31	35	57
Millwall	46	16	6	1	35	14	4	10	9	19	29	56
Brighton	46	18	3	2	58	15	4	6	13	20	38	53
Crystal Palace	46	7	12	4	30	20	11	5	7	31	26	53
Wrexham	46	13	6	4	38	21	7	6	10	28	34	52
Walsall	46	11	8	4	43	22	7	6	10	31	39	50
Preston N.E.	46	15	4	4	45	23	4	6	13	17	34	48
Shrewsbury T.	46	14	2	7	36	25	5	8	10	25	34	48
Peterborough U.	46	12	7	4	37	23	3	11	9	26	40	48
Mansfield T.	46	8	11	4	31	22	8	4	11	27	30	47
Port Vale	46	10	10	3	33	21	5	6	12	22	33	46
Bury	46	11	7	5	33	16	3	9	11	18	30	44
Gillingham	46	10	8	5	38	27	2	11	10	20	41	43
Chesterfield	46	11	5	7	45	30	6	4	13	24	39	43
Rotherham U.	46	11	6	6	35	22	4	6	13	19	43	42
Chester	46	13	7	3	34	19	2	5	16	9	43	42
Grimsby T.	46	13	7	3	39	21	2	3	18	23	53	40
Swindon T.	46	11	4	8	42	31	5	4	14	20	44	40
Sheffield W.	46	12	6	5	34	25	0	10	13	14	34	40
Aldershot	46	10	8	5	34	26	3	5	15	25	49	39
Colchester U.	46	9	6	8	25	27	3	8	12	16	38	38
Southend U.	46	9	7	7	40	31	6	6	14	25	44	37
Halifax T.	46	6	5	12	22	32	5	8	10	19	29	35

DIVISION 4

	P	W	D	L	F	A	W	D	L	F	A	Pts.
		Home					Away					
Lincoln C.	46	21	2	0	71	15	11	8	4	40	24	74
Northampton T.	46	18	5	0	62	20	11	5	7	25	20	68
Reading	46	19	3	1	42	9	5	9	9	28	42	60
Tranmere R.	46	18	3	2	61	16	6	7	10	28	39	58
Huddersfield T.	46	11	6	6	28	17	10	8	5	28	24	56
AFC Bournemouth	46	15	5	3	39	16	5	7	11	18	32	52
Exeter C.	46	13	7	3	37	17	5	7	11	19	30	50
Watford	46	16	4	3	38	18	6	2	15	24	44	50
Torquay U.	46	12	6	5	31	24	6	8	9	24	39	50
Doncaster R.	46	10	6	7	42	31	9	5	9	33	38	49
Swansea C.	46	14	8	1	51	21	2	7	14	15	36	47
Barnsley	46	12	8	3	34	16	2	8	13	18	32	44
Cambridge U.	46	7	10	6	36	28	7	5	11	22	34	43
Hartlepool	46	10	6	7	37	29	6	4	13	25	49	42
Rochdale	46	7	11	5	27	23	5	7	11	13	31	42
Crewe Alx.	46	10	7	6	36	21	3	8	12	22	36	41
Bradford C.	46	9	7	7	35	26	3	10	10	28	39	41
Brentford	46	12	7	4	37	18	2	6	15	19	42	41
Scunthorpe U.	46	11	3	9	31	24	3	7	13	19	35	38
Darlington	46	11	7	5	30	14	3	3	17	18	43	38
Stockport Co.	46	8	7	8	23	23	5	5	13	20	53	38
Newport Co.	46	8	8	7	35	33	5	2	16	22	57	35
Southport	46	6	6	11	27	31	2	4	17	14	46	26
Workington	46	5	4	14	19	43	2	3	18	11	44	21

LEAGUE HONOURS LIST

FOOTBALL LEAGUE

	First	Pts.	Second	Pts.	Third	Pts.
1888–89a	Preston N.E.	40	Aston Villa	29	Wolverhampton W.	28
1889–90a	Preston N.E.	33	Everton	31	Blackburn R.	28
1890–91a	Everton	29	Preston N.E.	27	Notts. Co.	26
1891–92b	Sunderland	42	Preston N.E.	37	Bolton W.	36

FIRST DIVISION

	First	Pts.	Second	Pts.	Third	Pts.
1892–93c	Sunderland	48	Preston N.E.	37	Everton	36
1893–94c	Aston Villa	44	Sunderland	38	Derby Co.	36
1894–95c	Sunderland	47	Everton	42	Aston Villa	39
1895–96c	Aston Villa	45	Derby Co.	41	Everton	39
1896–97c	Aston Villa	47	Sheffield U.	36	Derby Co.	36
1897–98c	Sheffield U.	42	Sunderland	37	Wolverhampton W.	35
1898–99d	Aston Villa	45	Liverpool	43	Burnley	39
1899–1900d	Aston Villa	50	Sheffield U.	48	Sunderland	41
1900–1d	Liverpool	45	Sunderland	43	Notts. Co.	40
1901–2d	Sunderland	44	Everton	41	Newcastle U.	37
1902–3d	The Wednesday	42	Aston Villa	41	Sunderland	41
1903–4d	The Wednesday	47	Manchester C.	44	Everton	43
1904–5d	Newcastle U.	48	Everton	47	Manchester C.	46
1905–6e	Liverpool	51	Preston N.E.	47	The Wednesday	44
1906 7e	Newcastle U.	51	Bristol C.	48	Everton	45
1907–8e	Manchester U.	52	Aston Villa	43	Manchester C.	43
1908–9e	Newcastle U.	53	Everton	46	Sunderland	44
1909–10e	Aston Villa	53	Liverpool	48	Blackburn R.	45
1910–11e	Manchester U.	52	Aston Villa	51	Sunderland	45
1911–12e	Blackburn R.	49	Everton	46	Newcastle U.	44
1912–13e	Sunderland	54	Aston Villa	50	Sheffield W.	49
1913–14e	Blackburn R.	51	Aston Villa	44	Middlesbrough	43
1914–15e	Everton	46	Oldham Ath.	45	Blackburn R.	43
1919–20f	W.B.A.	60	Burnley	51	Chelsea	49
1920–21f	Burnley	59	Manchester C.	54	Bolton W.	52
1921–22f	Liverpool	57	Tottenham H.	51	Burnley	49
1922–23f	Liverpool	60	Sunderland	54	Huddersfield	53
1923–24f	*Huddersfield	57	Cardiff C.	57	Sunderland	53
1924–25f	Huddersfield	58	W.B.A.	56	Bolton W.	55
1925–26f	Huddersfield	57	Arsenal	52	Sunderland	48
1926–27f	Newcastle U.	56	Huddersfield	51	Sunderland	49
1927–28f	Everton	53	Huddersfield	51	Leicester C.	48
1928–29f	Sheffield W.	52	Leicester C.	51	Aston Villa	50
1929–30f	Sheffield W.	60	Derby Co.	50	Manchester C.	47
1930–31f	Arsenal	66	Aston Villa	59	Sheffield W.	52
1931–32f	Everton	56	Arsenal	54	Sheffield W.	50
1932–33f	Arsenal	58	Aston Villa	54	Sheffield W.	51
1933–34f	Arsenal	59	Huddersfield	56	Tottenham H.	49
1934–35f	Arsenal	58	Sunderland	54	Sheffield W.	49
1935–36f	Sunderland	56	Derby Co.	48	Huddersfield	48
1936–37f	Manchester C.	57	Charlton Ath.	54	Arsenal	52
1937–38f	Arsenal	52	Wolverhampton W.	51	Preston N.E.	49
1938–39f	Everton	59	Wolverhampton W.	55	Charlton Ath.	50
1946–47f	Liverpool	57	Manchester U.	56	Wolverhampton W.	56
1947–48f	Arsenal	59	Manchester U.	52	Burnley	52
1948–49f	Portsmouth	58	Manchester U.	53	Derby Co.	53
1949–50f	*Portsmouth	53	Wolverhampton W.	53	Sunderland	52
1950–51f	Tottenham H.	60	Manchester U.	56	Blackpool	50
1951–52f	Manchester U.	57	Tottenham H.	53	Arsenal	53
1952–53f	*Arsenal	54	Preston N.E.	54	Wolverhampton W.	51
1953–54f	Wolverhampton W.	57	W.B.A.	53	Huddersfield	51
1954–55f	Chelsea	52	Wolverhampton W.	48	Portsmouth	48
1955–56f	Manchester U.	60	Blackpool	49	Wolverhampton W.	49
1956–57f	Manchester U.	64	Tottenham H.	56	Preston N.E.	56
1957–58f	Wolverhampton W.	64	Preston N.E.	59	Tottenham H.	51
1958–59f	Wolverhampton W.	61	Manchester U.	55	Arsenal	50
1959–60f	Burnley	55	Wolverhampton W.	54	Tottenham H.	53
1960–61f	Tottenham H.	66	Sheffield W.	58	Wolverhampton W.	57

	First	Pts.	Second	Pts.	Third	Pts.
1961–62f	Ipswich T.	56	Burnley	53	Tottenham H.	52
1962–63f	Everton	61	Tottenham H.	55	Burnley	54
1963–64f	Liverpool	57	Manchester U.	53	Everton	52
1964–65f	*Manchester U.	61	Leeds U.	61	Chelsea	56
1965–66f	Liverpool	61	Leeds U.	55	Burnley	55
1966–67f	Manchester U.	60	Nottingham F.	56	Tottenham H.	56
1967–68f	Manchester C.	58	Manchester U.	56	Liverpool	55
1968–69f	Leeds U.	67	Liverpool	61	Everton	57
1969–70f	Everton	66	Leeds U.	57	Chelsea	55
1970–71f	Arsenal	65	Leeds U.	64	Tottenham H.	52
1971–72f	Derby Co.	58	Leeds U.	57	Liverpool	57
1972–73f	Liverpool	60	Arsenal	57	Leeds U.	53
1973–74f	Leeds U.	62	Liverpool	57	Derby Co.	48
1974–75f	Derby Co.	53	Liverpool	51	Ipswich T.	51
1975–76f	Liverpool	60	Q.P.R.	59	Manchester U.	56

Maximum points: *a*, 44; *b*, 52; *c*, 60; *d*, 68; *e*, 76; *f*, 84.
No competition during 1915–19 and 1939–46.

SECOND DIVISION

	First	Pts.	Second	Pts.	Third	Pts.
1892–93a	Small Heath	36	Sheffield U.	35	Darwen	30
1893–94b	Liverpool	50	Small Heath	42	Notts. Co.	39
1894–95c	Bury	48	Notts. Co.	39	Newton Heath	38
1895–96c	*Liverpool	46	Manchester C.	46	Grimsby T.	42
1896–97c	Notts. Co.	42	Newton Heath	39	Grimsby T.	38
1897–98c	Burnley	48	Newcastle U.	45	Manchester C.	39
1898–99d	Manchester C.	52	Glossop N.E.	46	Leicester Fosse	45
1899–1900d	The Wednesday	54	Bolton W.	52	Small Heath	46
1900–1d	Grimsby T.	49	Small Heath	48	Burnley	44
1901–2d	W.B.A.	55	Middlesbrough	51	Preston N.E.	42
1902–3d	Manchester C.	54	Small Heath	51	Woolwich A.	48
1903–4d	Preston N.E.	50	Woolwich A.	49	Manchester U.	48
1904–5d	Liverpool	58	Bolton W.	56	Manchester U.	53
1905–6e	Bristol C.	66	Manchester U.	62	Chelsea	53
1906–7e	Nottingham F.	60	Chelsea	57	Leicester Fosse	48
1907–8e	Bradford C.	54	Leicester Fosse	52	Oldham Ath.	50
1908–9e	Bolton W.	52	*Tottenham H.	51	W.B.A.	51
1909–10e	Manchester C.	54	*Oldham Ath.	53	Hull C.	53
1910–11e	W.B.A.	53	Bolton W.	51	Chelsea	49
1911–12e	*Derby Co.	54	Chelsea	54	Burnley	52
1912–13e	Preston N.E.	53	Burnley	50	Birmingham C.	46
1913–14e	Notts. Co.	53	Bradford P.A.	49	Woolwich A.	49
1914–15e	Derby Co.	53	Preston N.E.	50	Barnsley	47
1919–20f	Tottenham H.	70	Huddersfield	64	Birmingham C.	56
1920–21f	*Birmingham C.	58	Cardiff C.	58	Bristol C.	51
1921–22f	Nottingham F.	56	Stoke C.	52	Barnsley	52
1922–23f	Notts. Co.	53	*West Ham U.	51	Leicester C.	51
1923–24f	Leeds U.	54	*Bury	51	Derby Co.	51
1924–25f	Leicester C.	59	Manchester U.	57	Derby Co.	55
1925–26f	Sheffield W.	60	Derby Co.	57	Chelsea	52
1926–27f	Middlesbrough	62	*Portsmouth	54	Manchester C.	54
1927–28f	Manchester C.	59	Leeds U.	57	Chelsea	54
1928–29f	Middlesbrough	55	Grimsby T.	53	Bradford	48
1929–30f	Blackpool	58	Chelsea	55	Oldham Ath.	53
1930–31f	Everton	61	W.B.A.	54	Tottenham H.	51
1931–32f	Wolverhampton W.	56	Leeds U.	54	Stoke C.	52
1932–33f	Stoke C.	56	Tottenham H.	55	Fulham	50
1933–34f	Grimsby T.	59	Preston N.E.	52	Bolton W.	51
1934–35f	Brentford	61	*Bolton W.	56	West Ham U.	56
1935–36f	Manchester U.	56	Charlton Ath.	55	Sheffield U.	52
1936–37f	Leicester C.	56	Blackpool	55	Bury	52
1937–38f	Aston Villa	57	*Manchester U.	53	Sheffield U.	53
1938–39f	Blackburn R.	55	Sheffield U.	54	Sheffield W.	53
1939–46	Competition cancelled owing to war.					
1946–47f	Manchester C.	62	Burnley	58	Birmingham C.	55
1947–48f	Birmingham C.	59	Newcastle U.	56	Southampton	52
1948–49f	Fulham	57	W.B.A.	56	Southampton	55
1949–50f	Tottenham H.	61	*Sheffield W.	52	Sheffield U.	52
1950–51f	Preston N.E.	57	Manchester C.	52	Cardiff C.	50

* Won on goal average

	First	Pts.	Second	Pts.	Third	Pts.
1951–52	Sheffield W.	53	*Cardiff C.	51	Birmingham C.	51
1952–53f	Sheffield U.	60	Huddersfield	58	Luton T.	52
1953–54f	*Leicester C.	56	Everton	56	Blackburn R.	55
1954–55f	*Birmingham C.	54	*Luton T.	54	Rotherham U.	54
1955–56f	Sheffield W.	55	Leeds U.	52	Liverpool	48
1956–57f	Leicester C.	61	Nottingham F.	54	Liverpool	53
1957–58f	West Ham U.	57	Blackburn R.	56	Charlton Ath.	55
1958–59f	Sheffield W.	62	Fulham	60	Sheffield U.	53
1959–60f	Aston Villa	59	Cardiff C.	58	Liverpool	50
1960–61f	Ipswich T.	59	Sheffield U.	58	Liverpool	52
1961–62f	Liverpool	62	Leyton O.	54	Sunderland	53
1962–63f	Stoke C.	53	*Chelsea	52	Sunderland	52
1963–64f	Leeds U.	63	Sunderland	61	Preston N.E.	56
1964–65f	Newcastle U.	57	Northampton	56	Bolton W.	50
1965–66f	Manchester C.	59	Southampton	54	Coventry C.	53
1966–67f	Coventry C.	59	Wolverhampton W.	58	Carlisle U.	52
1967–68f	Ipswich T.	59	*Q.P.R.	58	Blackpool	58
1968–69f	Derby Co.	63	C. Palace	56	Charlton Ath.	50
1969–70f	Huddersfield	60	Blackpool	53	Leicester C.	51
1970–71f	Leicester C.	59	Sheffield U.	56	Cardiff C.	53
1971–72f	Norwich C.	57	Birmingham C.	56	Millwall	55
1972–73f	Burnley	62	Q.P.R.	61	Aston Villa	50
1973–74f	Middlesbrough	65	Luton T.	50	Carlisle U.	49
1974–75f	Manchester U.	61	Aston Villa	58	Norwich C.	53
1975–76f	Sunderland	56	Bristol C.	53	W.B.A.	53

Maximum points: a, 44; b, 56; c, 60; d, 68; e, 76; f, 84.

THIRD DIVISION

	First	Pts.	Second	Pts.	Third	Pts.
1958–59	Plymouth Arg.	62	Hull C.	61	Brentford	57
1959–60	Southampton	61	Norwich C.	59	Shrewsbury T.	52
1960–61	Bury	68	Walsall	62	Q.P.R.	60
1961–62	Portsmouth	65	Grimsby T.	62	Bournemouth	59
1962–63	Northampton	62	Swindon T.	58	Port Vale	54
1963–64	*Coventry C.	60	Crystal Palace	60	Watford	58
1964–65	Carlisle U.	60	*Bristol C.	59	Mansfield T.	59
1965–66	Hull C.	69	Millwall	65	Q.P.R.	57
1966–67	Q.P.R.	67	Middlesbrough	55	Watford	54
1967–68	Oxford U.	57	Bury	56	Shrewsbury T.	55
1968–69	*Watford	64	Swindon T.	64	Luton T.	61
1969–70	Orient	62	Luton T.	60	Bristol R.	56
1970–71	Preston N.E.	61	Fulham	60	Halifax T.	56
1971–72	Aston Villa	70	Brighton	65	Bournemouth	62
1972–73	Bolton W.	61	Notts Co.	57	Blackburn R.	55
1973–74	Oldham Ath.	62	Bristol R.	61	York C.	61
1974–75	Blackburn R.	60	Plymouth Arg.	59	Charlton Ath.	55
1975–76	Hereford U.	63	Cardiff C.	57	Millwall	56

Maximum points: 92.

FOURTH DIVISION

	First	Pts.	Second	Pts.	Third	Pts.	Fourth	Pts.
1958–59	Port Vale	64	Coventry C.	60	York C.	60	Shrewsbury T.	58
1959–60	Walsall	65	Notts. Co.	60	Torquay U.	60	Watford	57
1960–61	Peterborough U.	66	C. Palace	64	Northampton	60	Bradford P.A.	60
1961–62	†Millwall	56	Colchester U.	55	Wrexham	53	Carlisle U.	52
1962–63	Brentford	62	Oldham Ath.	59	Crewe Alex.	59	Mansfield T.	57
1963–64	*Gillingham	60	Carlisle U.	60	Workington T.	59	Exeter C.	58
1964–65	Brighton	63	Millwall	62	York C.	62	Oxford U.	61
1965–66	*Doncaster R.	59	Darlington	59	Torquay U.	58	Colchester U.	56
1966–67	Stockport Co.	64	Southport	59	Barrow	59	Tranmere R.	58
1967–68	Lutor. T.	66	Barnsley	61	Hartlepools U.	60	Crewe Alex.	58
1968–69	Doncaster R.	59	Halifax T.	57	Rochdale	56	Bradford C.	56
1969–70	Chesterfield	64	Wrexham	61	Swansea C.	60	Port Vale	59
1970–71	Notts Co.	69	Bournemouth	60	Oldham Ath.	59	York C.	56
1971–72	Grimsby T.	63	Southend U.	60	Brentford	59	ScunthorpeU.	57
1972–73	Southport	62	Hereford U.	58	Cambridge U.	57	*Aldershot	56
1973–74	Peterborough U.	65	Gillingham	62	Colchester U.	60	Bury	59
1974–75	Mansfield T.	68	Shrewsbury T.	62	Rotherham U.	59	Chester	57
1975–76	Lincoln C.	74	Northampton T.	68	Reading	60	Tranmere R.	58

Maximum points: 92. †Maximum points: 88 due to Accrington Stanley's resignation.
* Won on goal average.

THIRD DIVISION—SOUTH (1921–1958)

	First	Pts.	Second	Pts.	Third	Pts.
1920–21a	C. Palace	59	Southampton	54	Q.P.R.	53
1921–22a	*Southampton	61	Plymouth Arg.	61	Portsmouth	53
1922–23a	Bristol C.	59	Plymouth Arg.	53	Swansea T.	53
1923–24a	Portsmouth	59	Plymouth Arg.	55	Millwall	54
1924–25a	Swansea T.	57	Plymouth Arg.	56	Bristol C.	53
1925–26a	Reading	57	Plymouth Arg.	56	Millwall	53
1926–27a	Bristol C.	62	Plymouth Arg.	60	Millwall	56
1927–28a	Millwall	65	Northampton	55	Plymouth Arg.	53
1928–29a	*Charlton Ath.	54	C. Palace	54	Northampton	52
1929–30a	Plymouth Arg.	68	Brentford	61	Q.P.R.	51
1930–31a	Notts. Co.	59	C. Palace	51	Brentford	50
1931–32a	Fulham	57	Reading	55	Southend U.	53
1932–33a	Brentford	62	Exeter C.	58	Norwich C.	57
1933–34a	Norwich C.	61	Coventry C.	54	Reading	54
1934–35a	Charlton Ath.	61	Reading	53	Coventry C.	51
1935–36a	Coventry C.	57	Luton T.	56	Reading	54
1936–37a	Luton T.	58	Notts. Co.	56	Brighton	53
1937–38a	Millwall	56	Bristol C.	55	Q.P.R.	53
1938–39a	Newport Co.	55	C. Palace	52	Brighton	49
1939–46	Competition cancelled owing to war.					
1946–47a	Cardiff C.	66	Q.P.R.	57	Bristol C.	51
1947–48a	Q.P.R.	61	Bournemouth	57	Walsall	51
1948–49a	Swansea T.	62	Reading	55	Bournemouth	52
1949–50a	Notts. Co.	58	Northampton	51	Southend U.	51
1950–51d	Nottingham F.	70	Norwich C.	64	Reading	57
1951–52d	Plymouth Arg.	66	Reading	61	Norwich C.	61
1952–53d	Bristol R.	64	Millwall	62	Northampton	62
1953–54d	Ipswich T.	64	Brighton	61	Bristol C.	56
1954–55d	Bristol C.	70	Leyton O.	61	Southampton	59
1955–56d	Leyton O.	66	Brighton	65	Ipswich T.	64
1956–57d	*Ipswich T.	59	Torquay U.	59	Colchester U.	58
1957–58d	Brighton	60	Brentford	58	Plymouth Arg.	58

THIRD DIVISION—NORTH (1921–1958)

	First	Pts.	Second	Pts.	Third	Pts.
1921–22b	Stockport Co.	56	Darlington	50	Grimsby T.	50
1922–23b	Nelson	51	Bradford P.A.	47	Walsall	46
1923–24a	Wolverhampton W.	63	Rochdale	62	Chesterfield	54
1924–25a	Darlington	58	Nelson	53	New Brighton	53
1925–26a	Grimsby T.	61	Bradford P.A.	60	Rochdale	59
1926–27a	Stoke C.	63	Rochdale	58	Bradford P.A.	55
1927–28a	Bradford P.A.	63	Lincoln C.	55	Stockport Co.	54
1928–29a	Bradford C.	63	Stockport Co.	62	Wrexham	52
1929–30a	Port Vale	67	Stockport Co.	63	Darlington	50
1930–31a	Chesterfield	58	Lincoln C.	57	Wrexham	54
1931–32c	*Lincoln C.	57	Gateshead	57	Chester	52
1932–33a	Hull C.	59	Wrexham	57	Stockport Co.	50
1933–34a	Barnsley	62	Chesterfield	61	Stockport Co.	54
1934–35a	Doncaster R.	57	Halifax T.	55	Chester	59
1935–36a	Chesterfield	60	Chester	55	Tranmere R.	54
1936–37a	Stockport Co.	60	Lincoln C.	57	Chester	55
1937–38a	Tranmere R.	56	Doncaster R.	54	Hull C.	53
1938–39a	Barnsley	67	Doncaster R.	56	Bradford C.	53
1939–46	Competition cancelled owing to war.					62
1946–47a	Doncaster R.	72	Rotherham U.	64	Chester	
1947–48a	Lincoln C.	60	Rotherham U.	59	Wrexham	56
1948–49a	Hull C.	65	Rotherham U.	62	Doncaster R.	50
1949–50a	Doncaster R.	55	Gateshead	53	Rochdale	50
1950–51d	Rotherham U.	71	Mansfield T.	64	Carlisle U.	51
1951–52d	Lincoln C.	69	Grimsby T.	66	Stockport Co.	55
1952–53d	Oldham Ath.	59	Port Vale	58	Wrexham	59
1953–54d	Port Vale	69	Barnsley	58	Scunthorpe U.	56
1954–55d	Barnsley	65	Accrington S.	61	Scunthorpe U.	57
1955–56d	Grimsby T.	68	Derby Co.	63	Accrington S.	58
1956–57d	Derby Co.	63	Hartlepools U.	59	Accrington S.	59
1957–58d	Scunthorpe U.	66	Accrington S.	59	Bradford C.	78

Maximum points: a, 84; b, 76; c, 80; d, 92. * Won on goal average.

LEAGUE TITLE WINS

LEAGUE DIVISION 1

Liverpool	9	Huddersfield	3	Tottenham H.	2
Arsenal	8	Wolverhampton W.	3	Leeds U.	2
Manchester U.	7	Blackburn R.	2	Derby Co.	2
Everton	7	Portsmouth	2	Chelsea	1
Aston Villa	6	Preston N.E.	2	Sheffield U.	1
Sunderland	6	Burnley	2	W.B.A.	1
Newcastle U.	4	Manchester C.	2	Ipswich T.	1
Sheffield W.	4				

LEAGUE DIVISION 2

Manchester C.	6	W.B.A.	2	Everton	1
Leicester C.	5	Aston Villa	2	Wolverhampton W.	1
Sheffield W.	5	Stoke C.	2	Fulham	1
Birmingham C. (One as		Leeds U.	2	Sheffield U.	1
Small Heath)	4	Ipswich T.	2	West Ham U.	1
Liverpool	4	Burnley	2	Newcastle U.	1
Notts. Co.	3	Manchester U.	2	Coventry C.	1
Preston N.E.	3	Huddersfield	1	Blackpool	1
Derby Co.	3	Bristol C.	1	Blackburn R.	1
Middlesbrough	3	Brentford	1	Norwich C.	1
Grimsby T.	2	Bury	1	Sunderland	1
Nottingham F.	2	Bradford C.	1		
Tottenham H.	2	Bolton W.	1		

LEAGUE DIVISION 3—Plymouth Arg., Southampton, Bury, Portsmouth, Northampton, Coventry C. Carlisle U., Hull C., Q.P.R., Oxford U., Watford, Leyton O., Preston N.E., Aston Villa, Bolton W. Oldham Ath., Blackburn R., Hereford U.

LEAGUE DIVISION 4—Doncaster R., Peterborough U. (two); Port Vale, Walsall, Millwall, Brentford, Gillingham, Brighton, Stockport Co., Luton T., Chesterfield, Notts Co., Grimsby T., Southport, Mansfield T., Lincoln C.

To 1957–58

DIVISION 3 (South): Bristol C., 3; Charlton Ath., Ipswich T., Millwall, Notts. Co., Plymouth Arg., Swansea T., 2; Brentford, Bristol R., Cardiff C., C. Palace, Coventry C., Fulham, Leyton O., Luton T., Newport Co., Nottingham F., Norwich C., Portsmouth, Q.P.R., Reading, Southampton, Brighton, 1.

DIVISION 3 (North): Barnsley, Doncaster R., Lincoln C., 3; Chesterfield, Grimsby T., Hull C., Port Vale, Stockport Co., 2; Bradford P.A., Bradford C., Darlington, Derby Co., Nelson, Oldham Ath., Rotherham U., Stoke C., Tranmere R., Wolverhampton W., Scunthorpe U., 1.

RELEGATED CLUBS

1891–92 League extended. Newton Heath, Sheffield W. and Nottingham F. admitted. *Second Division formed* including Darwen.

1892–93 In Test matches, Sheffield U. and Darwen won promotion in place of Notts. Co. and Accrington S.

1893–4 In Tests, Liverpool and Small Heath won promotion. Newton Heath and Darwen relegated.

1894–95 After Tests, Bury promoted, Liverpool relegated.

1895–96 After Tests, Liverpool promoted, Small Heath relegated.

1896–97 After Tests, Notts. Co. promoted, Burnley relegated.

1897–98 Test system abolished after success of Stoke C. and Burnley. League extended. Blackburn R. and Newcastle U. elected to First Division. *Automatic promotion and relegation introduced.*

DIVISION 1 TO DIVISION 2

1898–99 Bolton W. and Sheffield W.
1899–1900 Burnley and Glossop
1900–1 Preston N.E. and W.B.A.
1901–2 Small Heath and Manchester C.
1902–3 Grimsby T. and Bolton W.
1903–4 Liverpool and W.B.A.
1904–5 League extended. Bury and Notts. Co., two bottom clubs in First Division, re-elected.
1905–6 Nottingham F. and Wolverhampton W.
1906–7 Derby Co. and Stoke C.
1907–8 Bolton W. and Birmingham C.
1908–9 Manchester C. and Leicester Fosse

1909–10 Bolton W. and Chelsea
1910–11 Bristol C. and Nottingham F.
1911–12 Preston N.E. and Bury
1912–13 Notts. Co. and Woolwich Arsenal
1913–14 Preston N.E. and Derby Co.
1914–15 Tottenham H. and *Chelsea
1919–20 Notts. Co. and Sheffield W.
1920–21 Derby Co. and Bradford
1921–22 Bradford C. and Manchester U.

* Subsequently re-elected to Division 1 when League was extended after the War.

1922-23 Stoke C. and Oldham Ath.
1923-24 Chelsea and Middlesbrough
1924-25 Preston N.E. and Nottingham F.
1925-26 Manchester C. and Notts. Co.
1926-27 Leeds U. and W.B.A.
1927-28 Tottenham H. and Middlesbrough
1928-29 Bury and Cardiff C.
1929-30 Burnley and Everton
1930-31 Leeds U. and Manchester U.
1931-32 Grimsby T. and West Ham U.
1932-33 Bolton W. and Blackpool
1933-34 Newcastle U. and Sheffield U.
1934-35 Leicester C. and Tottenham H.
1935-36 AstonVilla and Blackburn R.
1936-37 Manchester U. and Sheffield W.
1937-38 Manchester C. and W.B.A.
1938-39 Birmingham C. and Leicester C.
1946-47 Brentford and Leeds U.
1947-48 Blackburn R. and Grimsby T.
1948-49 Preston N.E. and Sheffield U.
1949-50 Manchester C. and Birmingham C.
1950-51 Sheffield W. and Everton
1951-52 Huddersfield and Fulham
1952-53 Stoke C. and Derby Co.

1953-54 Middlesbrough and Liverpool
1954-55 Leicester C. and Sheffield W.
1955-56 Huddersfield and Sheffield U.
1956-57 Charlton Ath. and Cardiff C.
1957-58 Sheffield W. and Sunderland
1958-59 Portsmouth and Aston Villa
1959-60 Luton T. and Leeds U.
1960-61 Preston N.E. and Newcastle U.
1961-62 Chelsea and Cardiff C.
1962-63 Manchester C. and Leyton O.
1963-64 Bolton W. and Ipswich T.
1964-65 Wolverhampton W. and Birmingham C.
1965-66 Northampton T. and Blackburn R.
1966-67 Aston Villa and Blackpool
1967-68 Fulham and Sheffield U.
1968-69 Leicester C. and Q.P.R.
1969-70 Sunderland and Sheffield W.
1970-71 Burnley and Blackpool
1971-72 Huddersfield T. and Nottingham F.
1972-73 C. Palace and W.B.A.
1973-74 Southampton, Manchester U., Norwich C.
1974-75 Luton T., Chelsea, Carlisle U.
1975-76 Wolverhampton W., Burnley, Sheffield U.

DIVISION 2 TO DIVISION 3

1920-21 Stockport Co.
1921-22 Bradford and Bristol C.
1922-23 Rotherham C. and Wolverhampton W.
1923-24 Nelson and Bristol C.
1924-25 C. Palace and Coventry C.
1925-26 Stoke C. and Stockport Co.
1926-27 Darlington and Bradford C.
1927-28 Fulham and South Shields
1928-29 Port Vale and Clapton O.
1929-30 Hull C. and Notts. Co.
1930-31 Reading and Cardiff C.
1931-32 Barnsley and Bristol C.
1932-33 Chesterfield and Charlton Ath.
1933-34 Millwall and Lincoln C.
1934-35 Oldham Ath. and Notts. Co.
1935-36 Port Vale and Hull C.
1936-37 Doncaster R. and Bradford C.
1937-38 Barnsley and Stockport Co.
1938-39 Norwich C. and Tranmere R.
1946-47 Swansea T. and Newport Co.
1947-48 Doncaster R. and Millwall
1948-49 Nottingham F. and Lincoln C.
1949-50 Plymouth Arg. and Bradford
1950-51 Grimsby T. and Chesterfield
1951-52 Coventry C. and Q.P.R.

1952-53 Southampton and Barnsley
1953-54 Brentford and Oldham Ath.
1954-55 Ipswich T. and Derby Co.
1955-56 Plymouth Arg. and Hull C.
1956-57 Port Vale and Bury
1957-58 Doncaster R. and Notts. Co.
1958-59 Barnsley and Grimsby T.
1959-60 Bristol C. and Hull C.
1960-61 Lincoln C. and Portsmouth
1961-62 Brighton and Bristol R.
1962-63 Walsall and Luton T.
1963-64 Grimsby T. and Scunthorpe U.
1964-65 Swindon T. and Swansea T.
1965-66 Middlesbrough and Leyton O.
1966-67 Northampton T. and Bury
1967-68 Plymouth Arg. and Rotherham U.
1968-69 Fulham and Bury
1969-70 Preston N.E. and Aston Villa
1970-71 Blackburn R. and Bolton W.
1971-72 Charlton Ath. and Watford
1972-73 Huddersfield T. and Brighton
1973-74 C. Palace, Preston N. E., Swindon T.
1974-75 Millwall, Cardiff C., Sheffield W.
1975-76 Oxford U., York C., Portsmouth

DIVISION 3 TO DIVISION 4

1958-59 Rochdale, Notts. Co., Doncaster R. and Stockport Co.
1959-60 Accrington S., Wrexham, Mansfield T. and York C.
1960-61 Chesterfield, Colchester U., Bradford C. and Tranmere R.
1961-62 Newport Co., Brentford, Lincoln C. and Torquay U.
1962-63 Bradford, Brighton, Carlisle U. and Halifax T.
1963-64 Millwall, Crewe Alex., Wrexham and Notts. Co.
1964-65 Luton T., Port Vale, Colchester U. and Barnsley
1965-66 Southend U., Exeter C., Brentford and York C.
1966-67 Doncaster R., Workington T., Darlington and Swansea T.

1967-68 Scunthorpe U., Colchester U., Grimsby T. and Peterborough U. (demoted)
1968-69 Oldham Ath., Crewe Alex., Hartlepools U. and Northampton.
1969-70 Bournemouth, Southport, Barrow, Stockport Co.
1970-71 Reading, Bury, Doncaster R., Gillingham.
1971-72 Mansfield T., Barnsley, Torquay U., Bradford C.
1972-73 Rotherham U., Brentford, Swansea C., Scunthorpe U.
1973-74 Cambridge U., Shrewsbury T., Southport, Rochdale
1974-75 AFC Bournemouth, Tranmere R., Watford, Huddersfield T.
1975-76 Aldershot, Colchester U., Southend U., Halifax T.

APPLICATIONS FOR RE-ELECTION

FOURTH DIVISION

SEVEN: Hartlepool.
SIX: Barrow.
FIVE: Lincoln C.
FOUR: Chester, York C., Bradford P.A. (lost League place to Cambridge United 69–70), Southport, Newport Co., Stockport Co., Workington.
THREE: Crewe, Darlington
TWO: Oldham Ath., Bradford C., Rochdale, Northampton, Doncaster R.
ONE: Aldershot, Exeter C., Gateshead, Halifax T., Port Vale, Wrexham, Colchester U., Grimsby T., Swansea C., Scunthorpe U., (Gateshead were not re-elected, their place being taken by Peterborough U. Accrington S. resigned and Oxford U. were elected.) Port Vale were forced to re-apply following expulsion.

THIRD DIVISIONS NORTH & SOUTH

SEVEN: Walsall.
SIX: Exeter C., Newport Co., Halifax T.
FIVE: Accrington S., Barrow, Gillingham, New Brighton, Southport.
FOUR: Rochdale, Norwich C.
THREE: C. Palace, Crewe Alex., Darlington, Hartlepool, Merthyr T., Swindon T.
TWO: Aberdare Ath., Aldershot, Ashington, Bournemouth, Brentford, Chester, Colchester U., Millwall, Durham C., Nelson, Q.P.R., Rotherham U., Southend U., Tranmere R., Watford, Workington T.
ONE: Bradford, Bradford C., Brighton, Bristol R., Cardiff C., Carlisle U., Charlton Ath., Gateshead, Grimsby T., Mansfield T., Shrewsbury T., Torquay U., York C.

LEADING SCORERS 1975-76

(Listed in order of League goals scored)

Division 1	League	FA Cup	FL Cup	Total
MacDougall (Norwich C.)	23	2	3	28
Duncan (Tottenham H.)	20	1	4	25
Macdonald (Newcastle U.)	19	4	1	24
Richards (Wolverhampton W.)	17	6	2	25
Francis (Birmingham C.)	17	1	–	18
Gowling (Newcastle U.)	16	8	6	30
George (Derby Co.)	16	3	1	20
McKenzie (Leeds U.)	16	–	1	17
Toshack (Liverpool)	16	1	–	17
Hill (Manchester U.)	15	3	–	18
(inc. 8 League for Millwall)				
Tueart (Manchester C.)	14	2	8	24
Cross (Coventry C.)	14	1	1	16
Noble (Burnley)	13	–	4	17
Rioch (Derby Co.)	13	3	1	17
Hankin (Burnley)	13	–	1	14
Pearson (Manchester U.)	13	1	–	14
Taylor A. (West Ham U.)	13	–	1	14
Givens (Q.P.R.)	13	–	–	13
Lee (Derby Co.)	13	–	–	13
Whymark (Ipswich T.)	13	–	–	13
Royle (Manchester C.)	12	–	6	18
Graydon (Aston Villa)	12	1	–	13
Keegan (Liverpool)	12	1	–	13
Latchford (Everton)	12	–	1	13
Francis (Q.P.R.)	12	–	–	12
Macari (Manchester U.)	11	1	2	14
Clarke (Leeds U.)	11	1	1	13
Greenhoff (Stoke C.)	11	1	1	13
Lee (Leicester C.)	11	2	–	13
Boyer (Norwich C.)	11	–	–	11
Jennings (West Ham U.)	11	–	–	11
Kidd (Arsenal)	11	–	–	11
King (Everton)	11	–	–	11
(inc. 9 League for Luton T.)				
McIlroy (Manchester U.)	10	2	1	13
Peters (Norwich C.)	10	2	1	13
Pratt (Tottenham H.)	10	–	3	13
Bowles (Q.P.R.)	10	–	2	12
Gray (Aston Villa)	10	1	1	12
Mills (Middlesbrough)	10	–	2	12
Lorimer (Leeds U.)	10	–	1	11
Moores (Stoke C.)	10	1	–	11
Hamilton (Everton)	10	–	–	10
(inc. 5 League for Ipswich T.)				
Woodward (Sheffield U.)	10	–	–	10
Division 2	League	FA Cup	FL Cup	Total
Hales (Charlton Ath.)	28	–	3	31
Channon (Southampton)	19	5	–	24
Ritchie (Bristol C.)	18	–	–	18
Walsh (Blackpool)	17	–	–	17
Bradd (Notts Co.)	16	–	3	19
Cheesley (Bristol C.)	15	–	1	16
Mariner (Plymouth Arg.)	15	–	1	16
Husband (Luton T.)	14	–	–	14
Bowyer (Nottingham F.)	13	–	3	16
Robson (Sunderland)	13	2	–	15
Bannister (Bristol R.)	13	–	1	14

433

	League	FA Cup	FL Cup	Total
Shaw (Oldham Ath.)	13	–	–	13
Holden (Sunderland)	12	2	1	15
Rafferty (Plymouth Arg.)	12	1	1	14
Scanlon (Notts Co.)	12	–	2	14
Tait (Oxford U.)	12	–	–	12
Jones G. (Bolton W.)	11	2	–	13
Whatmore (Bolton W.)	11	2	–	13
Piper (Portsmouth)	11	1	–	12
Wilkins (Chelsea)	11	1	–	12
Holmes (Southampton)	11	–	–	11
Division 3	*League*	*FA Cup*	*FL Cup*	*Total*
McNeil (Hereford U.)	35	2	–	37
Buckley (Walsall)	34	–	1	35
Clarke (Mansfield T.)	24	–	3	27
Binney (Brighton & H.A.)	23	3	1	27
Evans (Cardiff C.)	21	3	–	24
Silvester (Southend U.)	19	3	1	23
Darling (Chesterfield)	18	–	1	19
Davey (Hereford U.)	18	–	–	18
Cullerton (Port Vale)	17	1	3	21
Rowland (Bury)	16	3	2	21
Swindlehurst (C. Palace)	16	2	1	19
Bruce (Preston N.E.)	16	–	–	16
(inc. 1 League for Newcastle U.)				
Alston (Cardiff C.)	15	4	–	19
(inc. 1 League for Luton T.)				
Elwiss (Preston N.E.)	15	1	–	16
Anderson (Swindon T.)	15	–	–	15
Lewis (Grimsby T.)	15	–	–	15
Shanahan (Millwall)	15	–	–	15
(inc. 15 League for Chesterfield)				
Howarth (Aldershot)	14	3	–	17
Gregory (Peterborough U.)	14	1	2	17
Syrett (Swindon T.)	14	2	–	16
Ashcroft (Wrexham)	14	1	–	15
Bell (Aldershot)	14	–	–	14
Robson (Peterborough U.)	13	–	2	15
Kearney (Shrewsbury T.)	13	1	–	14
McHale (Halifax T.)	12	4	–	16
Taylor (C. Palace)	12	4	–	16
Gough (Colchester U.)	12	–	2	14
(inc. 7 League, 1 LC for Southport)				
Wright (Walsall)	12	–	–	12
Division 4	*League*	*FA Cup*	*FL Cup*	*Total*
Moore (Tranmere R.)	34	–	3	37
Ward (Lincoln C.)	24	1	4	29
Freeman (Lincoln C.)	23	2	–	25
O'Callaghan (Doncaster R.)	22	–	6	28
Cooke (Bradford C.)	22	2	–	24
Kitchen (Doncaster R.)	22	–	2	24
Friday (Reading)	21	–	1	22
Hall (Northampton T.)	21	–	1	22
Sinclair (Darlington)	21	–	1	22
Beer (Exeter C.)	20	1	2	23
Bray (Swansea C.)	19	–	–	19
Jenkins (Watford)	19	–	–	19
James (Tranmere R.)	17	–	–	17
Stratford (Northampton T.)	16	–	–	16
Gray (Huddersfield T.)	15	2	2	19
Green (Scunthorpe U.)	15	1	–	16
Nelson (Reading)	15	–	1	16
(inc. 12 League, 1 LC for Crewe Alex.)				
Horsfall (Cambridge U.)	15	–	–	15
Murray (Reading)	15	–	–	15

CAREER RECORD OF LEAGUE GOALSCORERS

This is a list of players at present playing, who during their careers have scored 50 or more goals in Football League matches. An asterisk denotes players who retired during the past year, but whose totals have been included to provide a complete record.

270	K. Wagstaff (Hull C.)	114	R. Woodruff (Newport Co.)
253	K. Hector (Derby Co.)	113	R. Hatton (Birmingham C.)
229	F. Lee (Derby Co.)*		A. Wood (Hull C.)
215	M. Chivers (Tottenham H.)	111	J. Radford (Arsenal)
212	G. Hurst (W.B.A.)*		B. Rioch (Derby Co.)
201	A. Clarke (Leeds U.)	109	G. Ingram (Bradford C.)
199	B. Clark (Cardiff C.)	107	J. Greenhoff (Stoke C.)
198	E. MacDougall (Norwich C.)	105	D. Possee (Orient)
181	D. Rogers (Swindon T.)	104	G. Graham (Portsmouth)
180	J. Hickton (Middlesbrough)		R. Latchford (Everton)
	J. Howarth (Aldershot)	103	C. Dobson (Bristol R.)
179	T. Brown (W.B.A.)		S. Earle (Leicester C.)
178	I. Lawther (Stockport Co.)		A. Suddick (Blackpool)
170	J. Ritchie (Stoke C.)	102	P. Boyer (Norwich C.)
165	T. Paine (Hereford U.)	101	L. Bradd (Notts Co.)
164	R. Marsh (Manchester C.)		D. Shaw (Oldham Ath.)
163	R. McNeil (Hereford U.)	100	F. Casper (Burnley)
160	A. Horsfield (Watford)		E. Moss (Peterborough U.)
	B. Robson (Sunderland)	99	F. Worthington (Leicester C.)
158	J. Byrom (Bolton W.)	98	J. Giles (W.B.A.)
	A. Lochhead (Oldham Ath.)	97	J. James (Tranmere R.)
153	S. Brace (Southend U.)	96	A. Murray (Peterborough U.)
152	H. Curran (Bolton W.)		J. Tudor (Newcastle U.)
	W. Davies (Stockport Co.)	95	K. Beamish (Blackburn R.)
	J. Hall (Northampton T.)	94	R. Graydon (Aston Villa)
151	A. Ball (Arsenal)		D. Masson (Q.P.R.)
150	G. Jones (Halifax T.)		I. Butler (York C.)
149	M. Macdonald (Newcastle U.)		P. Noble (Burnley)
147	J. Galley (Hereford U.)		P. Silvester (Southend U.)
142	P. Lorimer (Leeds U.)	93	B. Owen (Carlisle U.)
141	B. Best (Northampton T.)		A. Warboys (Bristol R.)
	J. Manning (Crewe Alex.)	92	W. Bremner (Leeds U.)
140	G. Andrews (Walsall)		W. Dearden (Sheffield U.)
	C. Bell (Manchester C.)		K. Foggo (Southend U.)
138	M. Channon (Southampton)		A. Gowling (Newcastle U.)
	K. Randall (Mansfield T.)	91	C. Balderstone (Doncaster R.)
	J. Toshack (Liverpool)		J. O'Hare (Nottingham F.)
137	B. Bannister (Bristol R.)		G. Reece (Cardiff C.)
	F. Clarke (Carlisle U.)	90	D. Roberts (Scunthorpe U.)
	M. Peters (Norwich C.)	89	W. Brown (Torquay U.)
136	A. Woodward (Sheffield U.)		M. Bullock (Halifax T.)
132	F. Binney (Brighton & H.A.)	88	S. Bowles (Q.P.R.)
130	A. Durban (Shrewsbury T.)		D. Gwyther (Rotherham)
128	B. Godfrey (Newport Co.)	86	V. Halom (Sunderland)
125	L. Chappell (Doncaster R.)		R. Svarc (Blackburn R.)
	R. Gould (Wolverhampton W.)	85	M. Summerbee (Burnley)
123	P. Osgood (Southampton)	84	P. Price (Barnsley)
122	A. Griffiths (Wrexham)	83	T. Bell (Aldershot)
121	R. Hiron (Reading)		K. Weller (Leicester C.)
119	A. Field (Sheffield U.)	82	B. Kidd (Arsenal)
117	A. Provan (Torquay U.)		D. Givens (Q.P.R.)
	D. Martin (Northampton T.)		N. Piper (Portsmouth)
116	A. Hinton (Derby Co.)	81	T. Baldwin (Chelsea)
115	N. Martin (Crystal Palace)		N. Cassidy (Cambridge U.)
	T. Robson (Peterborough U.)	80	K. Peacock (Charlton Ath.)
	J. Royle (Manchester C.)		J. Richards (Wolverhampton W.)

79	P. Hubbard (Grimsby T.)	62	R. Jones (Newport Co.)
78	M. Darling (Chesterfield)		A. Mullery (Fulham)
	B. Tinnion (Wrexham)	60	M. Elwiss (Preston N.E.)
77	A. Buckley (Walsall)		N. Jennings (Exeter C.)
	C. Garwood (Colchester U.)		M. Leach (Q.P.R.)
	B. Greenhalgh (Watford)		K. McMahon (Hartlepool)
75	D. Draper (Chester)		C. Suggett (Norwich C.)
	A. Gauden (Gillingham)	59	A. Foggon (Middlesbrough)
	J. Lewis (Grimsby T.)		R. Habbin (Rotherham U.)
	D. McKenzie (Leeds U.)		D. Richardson (Gillingham)
	D. Tueart (Manchester C.)		M. Butler (Huddersfield T.)
74	A. Birchenall (Leicester C.)	58	L. Glover (Leicester C.)
	R. Cross (Brentford)		D. Hales (Charlton Ath.)
	K. Keegan (Liverpool)		M. Moore (Hartlepool)
	G. Moore (Chester)		R. Wigg (Grimsby T.)
	P. Morrissey (Aldershot)	57	W. Jennings (West Ham U.)
	S. Pearson (Manchester U.)		B. Joicey (Sheffield W.)
	A. Tarbuck (Shrewsbury T.)		C. Sinclair (Darlington)
73	E. Redrobe (Hereford U.)	56	I. Bowyer (Nottingham F.)
72	R. Treacy (Preston N.E.)		P. Fletcher (Burnley)
71	L. Barrett (Fulham)		M. Hickman (Torquay U.)
	D. Cross (Coventry C.)		G. Queen (Orient)
	W. Hughes (Sunderland)		G. Riddick (Brentford)
	J. Murray (Reading)		J. Sammels (Leicester C.)
	P. Summerill (Millwall)		S. Scullion (Watford)
	J. Ward (Lincoln C.)	55	M. Hollis (Reading)
70	L. O'Neill (Carlisle U.)		J. Robertson (Stoke C.)
69	T. Francis (Birmingham C.)	54	T. Garbett (Sheffield U.)
	P. Freeman (Lincoln C.)		R. Clarke (Mansfield T.)
	J. Husband (Luton T.)		T. Johnson (Brentford)
	J. McCalliog (Southampton)		F. McLintock (Q.P.R.)
	J. Rudge (AFC Bournemouth)		S. Melledew (Crewe Alex.)
68	P. Graham (Lincoln C.)	53	B. Butlin (Nottingham F.)
	C. Jones (York C.)		B. Endean (Hartlepool U.)
	J. Seal (York C.)		J. Sissons (Chelsea)
67	W. Garner (Chelsea)	52	T. Brooking (West Ham U.)
	W. Rudd (Bury)		M. Dobson (Everton)
66	J. Conway (Fulham)		R. Greaves (Bolton W.)
	S. Davey (Hereford U.)		I. Hamilton (Aston Villa)
	C. Garland (Leicester C.)		J. Hinch (York C.)
	M. Kitchen (Doncaster R.)		G. Hamstead (Bury)
	J. Woodward (Scunthorpe U.)		G. Thomas (Swansea C.)
64	F. Barton (Grimsby T.)	51	G. Armstrong (Arsenal)
	A. Currie (Leeds U.)		D. Downing (York C.)
	A. Harding (Lincoln C.)		R. Kerr (Sunderland)
	R. Kennedy (Liverpool)		S. Kindon (Wolverhampton W.)
	J. Laidlaw (Carlisle U.)		T. Shanahan (Millwall)
	P. Morris (Norwich C.)		G. Taylor (Blackburn R.)
	P. Thompson (Bolton W.)	50	W. Ashcroft (Wrexham)
	R. Walton (Aldershot)		A. Brown (W.B.A.)
63	M. Burns (Newcastle U.)		L. James (Derby Co.)
	G. Gilbert (Rotherham U.)		J. Martin (Southport)
	B. Lyons (York C.)		F. Saul (Millwall)
	A. Welsh (Millwall)		T. Whymark (Ipswich T.)

HAT TRICK HEROES 1975-76

Football League

August
16 David Cross 3, Coventry C. v Everton, Div. 1
23 Stan Bowles 3, Q.P.R. v Derby Co. Div. 1
    Ted MacDougall 3, Norwich C. v Aston Villa Div. 1
30 Peter Noble 3, Burnley v Middlesbrough Div. 1
    Ian Evans 3, Crystal P. v Colchester U. Div. 3

September
6   Ted MacDougall 3, Norwich C. v Everton Div. 1
    Peter Silvester 3, Southend U. v Walsall Div. 3
13 Peter Noble 4, Burnley v Norwich C. Div. 1
20 Alan Gowling 3, Newcastle U. v Wolverhampton W. Div. 1
    Micky Walsh 3, Blackpool v Southampton Div. 2
22 Jack Whitham 3, Reading v Hartlepool Div. 4
27 Mick Channon 3, Southampton v Portsmouth Div. 2
    Ray Clarke 3, Mansfield T. v Walsall Div. 3
    Mike Kitchen 3, Doncaster R. v Southport Div. 4

October
11 John Toshack 3, Liverpool v Birmingham C. Div. 1
18 Paul Cheesley 3, Bristol C. v York C. Div. 2
    Tommy Robson 3, Peterborough U. v Bury Div. 3
    Colin Sinclair 4, Darlington v Torquay U. Div. 4
21 David Shaw 3, Oldham Ath. v Southampton Div. 2
24 Steve Peplow 3, Tranmere R. v Workington Div. 4

November
1   Peter Graham 3, Lincoln C. v Crewe Alex. Div. 4
4   Dave Gregory 3, Peterborough U. v Grimsby T. Div. 3
5   Terry Shanahan 3, Chesterfield v Colchester U. Div. 3
7   Ron Moore 4, Tranmere R. v Brentford Div. 4
15 Ian Miller 3, Doncaster R. v Newport Co. Div. 4
22 Tom Ritchie 3, Bristol C. v York C. Div. 2

December
5   Peter Silvester 3, Southend U. v Grimsby T. Div. 3
6   John Murray 3, Reading v Stockport Co. Div. 4
20 Billy Jennings 3, West Ham U. v Stoke C. Div. 1
27 Ron Moore 4, Tranmere R. v Stockport Co. Div. 4

January
3   Ron Moore 4, Tranmere R. v Newport Co. Div. 4
10 Alan Gowling 3, Newcastle U. v Everton Div. 1
31 John Toshack 3, Liverpool v West Ham U. Div. 1

February
13 Alan Buckley 4, Walsall v Rotherham U. Div. 3
    John Manning 3, Crewe Alex. v Southport Div. 4
17 Derek Hales 3, Charlton Ath. v Fulham Div. 2
    Peter Silvester 4, Southend U. v Brighton & H.A. Div. 3
27 Alan Buckley 3, Walsall v Gillingham Div. 3

March
10 Dixie McNeil 4, Hereford U. v Chester Div. 3
15 Ray Clarke 3, Mansfield T. v Southend U. Div. 3
20 Brian Kidd 3, Arsenal v West Ham U. Div 1
    Alan Buckley 3, Walsall v Aldershot Div. 3
31 John Murray 3, Reading v Tranmere R. Div. 4

April
7   John Peachey 3, Barnsley v Workington Div. 4
10 John Richards 3, Wolverhampton W. v Newcastle U. Div. 1
17 Alan Green 3, Coventry C. v Wolverhampton W. Div. 1
    Tony McAndrew 3, Middlesbrough v Sheffield U. Div. 1
    Don Martin 3, Northampton T. v Hartlepool Div. 4
    Ron Moore 3, Tranmere R. v Huddersfield T. Div. 4
19 Keith Mercer 3, Watford v Exeter C. Div. 4
23 Alan Beer 3, Exeter C. v Scunthorpe U. Div. 4
    Paul Stratford 3, Northampton T. v Stockport Co. Div. 4
24 David Cross 3, Coventry C. v Burnley Div. 1
    Trevor Anderson 3, Swindon T. v Walsall Div. 3
28 Dixie McNeil 3, Hereford U. v Preston N.E. Div. 3

FA Cup

November
22 Adrian Alston 3, Cardiff C. v Exeter C. Rd. 1

December
15 Malcolm Moore 3, Hartlepool v Marine Rd. 2 re-play

January
3   Mick Lambert 3, Ipswich T. v Halifax T. Rd. 3
    Chris Garland 3, Leicester C. v Sheffield U. Rd. 3

February
14 John Richards 3, Wolverhampton W. v Charlton Ath. Rd. 5
17 Mick Channon 3, Southampton v W.B.A. Rd. 5 re-play

League Cup

August
18 Michael Cullerton 3, Port Vale v Hereford U. Rd. 1
19 George Jones 3, Oldham Ath. v Workington Rd. 1
    Bren O'Callaghan 3, Doncaster R. v Grimsby T. Rd. 1
20 John Ward 4, Lincoln C. v Chesterfield Rd. 1

September
10 Alan Gowling 4, Newcastle U. v Southport Rd. 2
    Chris Guthrie 3, Sheffield U. v Halifax T. Rd. 2
29 Dennis Tueart 3, Manchester C. v Norwich C. Rd. 2 2nd re-play

December
3   John Duncan 3, Tottenham H. v Doncaster R Rd. 5

LEADING GOALSCORERS IN EACH DIVISION OF THE FOOTBALL LEAGUE SINCE WORLD WAR II

1946-47

Division 1
D. Westcott (Wolverhampton W.)	37
D. Reid (Portsmouth)	29
F. Steele (Stoke City)	29
R. Lewis (Arsenal)	28
S. Mortensen (Blackpool)	28

Division 2
C. Wayman (Newcastle U.)	30
J. D. Walsh (W.B.A.)	28
G. Lowrie (Coventry C.)	26
G. Robledo (Barnsley)	24

Division 3 (South)
D. Clarke (Bristol C.)	36
M. G. McPhee (Reading)	31
S. Richards (Cardiff C.)	31
A. Garrett (Northampton T.)	26
J. W. Stephens (Swindon T.)	25

Division 3 (North)
C. Jordan (Doncaster R.)	41
W. Ardron (Rotherham U.)	38
R. Yates (Chester)	36
P. M. Cheetham (Lincoln C.)	28

1947-48

Division 1
R. Rooke (Arsenal)	33
M. Fenton (Middlesbrough)	28
A. Stubbins (Liverpool)	26
J. Rowley (Manchester U.)	23
S. Mortensen (Blackpool)	21

Division 2
E. Quigley (Sheffield W.)	23
A. J. Wakefield (Leeds U.)	22
D. J. Walsh (W.B.A.)	22
J. Milburn (Newcastle U.)	21
J. Downie (Bradford)	19

Division 3 (South)
L. Townsend (Bristol C.)	29
D. Milligan (Bournemouth & B.A.)	26
D. Massart (Walsall)	23
C. Hatton (Q.P.R.)	21

Division 3 (North)
J. Hutchinson (Lincoln C.)	32
W. Ardron (Rotherham U.)	27
J. Lindsay (Carlisle U.)	26
T. Wyles (Southport)	26
W. F. Tunnicliffe (Wrexham)	20

1948-49

Division 1
W. Moir (Bolton W.)	25
F. Bowyer (Stoke C.)	21
R. Bentley (Chelsea)	20
J. Rowley (Manchester U.)	20
C. Vaughan (Charlton A.)	20

Division 2
C. Wayman (Southampton)	32
T. Briggs (Grimsby T.)	26
D. Massart (Bury)	25
R. Thomas (Fulham)	23
D. J. Walsh (W.B.A.)	23

Division 3 (South)
D. McGibbon (Bournemouth & B.A.)	30
S. Richards (Swansea T.)	26
J. Sewell (Notts County)	26
P. E. Chapman (Walsall)	25
W. M. Jones (Swindon T.)	25

Division 3 (North)
W. Ardron (Rotherham U.)	29
A. Patrick (York C.)	26
A. Quinn (Darlington)	23
N. W. Moore (Hull C.)	22
E. Gemmell (Oldham A.)	19

1949-50

Division 1
D. Davis (Sunderland)	25
S. Mortensen (Blackpool)	22
J. Stamps (Derby Co.)	22
H. Goring (Arsenal)	21
J. Rowley (Manchester U.)	20

Division 2
T. Briggs (Grimsby T.)	35
C. Wayman (Southampton)	24
W. Robinson (West Ham U.)	23
J. Lee (Leicester C.)	22
L. Medley (Tottenham H.)	18

Division 3 (South)
T. Lawton (Notts Co.)	31
W. Ardron (Nottingham F.)	25
A. Wakefield (Southend U.)	23
R. Blackman (Reading)	22
J. Devlin (Walsall)	22

Division 3 (North)
P. Doherty (Doncaster R.)	26
R. Phillips (Crewe Alex.)	26
A. C. Burgess (Chester)	24
E. Dodds (Lincoln C.)	21
D. Travis (Accrington Stanley)	20

1950-51

Division 1
S. Mortensen (Blackpool)	30
J. Lee (Derby Co.)	28
N. Lofthouse (Bolton W.)	21
A. McCrae (Middlesbrough)	21
D. Reid (Portsmouth)	21

Division 2
J. McCormack (Barnsley)	33
A. Rowley (Leicester C.)	28
C. Wayman (Preston N.E.)	27
W. Robinson (West Ham U.)	26

Division 3 (South)
W. Ardron (Nottingham F.)	36
R. Blackman (Reading)	35
J. Constantine (Millwall)	27
M. Tadman (Plymouth Arg.)	23

Division 3 (North)
J. Shaw (Rotherham U.)	37
R. Crosbie (Bradford)	27
L. E. Wildon (Hartlepools U.)	26
A. Burgess (Chester)	22
J. Nuttall (Southport)	22

1951-52

Division 1
G. Robledo (Newcastle U.)	33
R. Allen (W.B.A.)	32
J. Rowley (Manchester U.)	30
J. Dixon (Aston Villa)	26
C. Wayman (Preston N.E.)	24

Division 2
D. Dooley (Sheffield W.)	46
A. Rowley (Leicester C.)	38
W. Ardron (Nottingham F.)	29
W. Grant (Cardiff C.)	26

Division 3 (South)		Division 3 (North)	
R. Blackman (Reading)	39	A. Graver (Lincoln C.)	36
V. Lambden (Bristol R.)	29	W. Cairns (Grimsby T.)	32
M. Tadman (Plymouth Arg.)	27	W. Fenton (York C.)	31
F. Ramscar (Northampton T.)	24	E. Gemmell (Oldham A.)	28
		D. Frost (Halifax T.)	24

1952-53

Division 1		Division 2	
C. Wayman (Preston N.E.)	24	A. Rowley (Leicester C.)	39
P. Harris (Portsmouth)	23	B. Jezzard (Fulham)	34
D. Lishman (Arsenal)	23	J. Glazzard (Huddersfield T.)	30
		J. Charles (Leeds United)	26
		J. Pye (Luton T.)	24

Division 3 (South)		Division 3 (North)	
G. Bradford (Bristol R.)	33	J. Whitehouse (Carlisle U.)	29
R. Collins (Torquay U.)	27	J. Connor (Stockport Co.)	26
J. English (Northampton T.)	26	W. Fenton (York C.)	24
J. Rodgers (Bristol C.)	26	E. Gemmell (Oldham A.)	24
W. O'Donnell (Northampton T.)	26	D. Travis (Chester)	24

1953-54

Division 1		Division 2	
J. Glazzard (Huddersfield T.)	29	J. Charles (Leeds U.)	42
J. Nicholls (W.B.A.)	29	B. Jezzard (Fulham)	38
R. Allen (W.B.A.)	25	T. Briggs (Blackburn R.)	32
J. Hancocks (Wolverhampton W.)	25	R. Burke (Rotherham U.)	32
D. Wilshaw (Wolverhampton W.)	25	J. W. Parker (Everton)	31

Division 3 (South)		Division 3 (North)	
J. English (Northampton T.)	28	J. Connor (Stockport Co.)	31
R. Blackman (Reading)	27	G. Ashman (Carlisle U.)	30
E. Day (Southampton)	26	C. Done (Tranmere Rovers)	25
L. Graham (Newport Co.)	24	R. Brown (Barnsley)	24
J. Atyeo (Bristol C.)	23	K. Murray (Mansfield T.)	22

1954-55

Division 1		Division 2	
R. Allen (W.B.A.)	27	T. Briggs (Blackburn R.)	33
J. Glazzard (Huddersfield T.)	26	G. Turner (Luton T.)	32
E. Firmani (Charlton A.)	25	W. Liddell (Liverpool)	30
J. Hancocks (Wolverhampton W.)	25	J. Evans (Liverpool)	29
		G. Bradford (Bristol R.)	27

Division 3 (South)		Division 3 (North)	
E. Morgan (Gillingham)	31	A. Bottom (York C.)	30
J. Atyeo (Bristol C.)	28	J. Conner (Stockport Co.)	30
E. Day (Southampton)	27	D. Travis (Oldham A.)	30
R. Hollis (Southend U.)	27	G. Stewart (Accrington S.)	28
		J. Whitehouse (Carlisle U.)	25

1955-56

Division 1		Division 2	
N. Lofthouse (Bolton W.)	33	W. Gardiner (Leicester C.)	34
C. Fleming (Sunderland)	28	R. Shiner (Sheffield W.)	33
V. Keeble (Newcastle U.)	26	T. Briggs (Blackburn R.)	31
T. Taylor (Manchester U.)	25	J. Atyeo (Bristol C.)	30
		J. Charles (Leeds U.)	30

Division 3 (South)		Division 3 (North)	
R. Collins (Torquay U.)	40	R. Crosbie (Grimsby T.)	36
R. A. R. Hunt (Norwich C.)	31	G. Stewart (Accrington Stanley)	35
T. Parker (Ipswich T.)	30	W. Sowden (Chesterfield)	32
K. McCurley (Colchester U.)	29	A. Bottom (York C.)	31
A. Mundy (Brighton & H.A.)	27	J. Connor (Stockport Co.)	30

1956-57

Division 1		Division 2	
J. Charles (Leeds U.)	38	A. Rowley (Leicester C.)	44
J. Mudie (Blackpool)	32	B. Clough (Middlesbrough)	38
G. Turner (Luton T.)	30	T. Briggs (Blackburn R.)	32
N. Lofthouse (Bolton W.)	28	J. Barrett (Nottingham F.)	27
		T. Johnston (Leyton Orient)	27

Division 3 (South)		Division 3 (North)	
E. Phillips (Ipswich T.)	42	R. Straw (Derby Co.)	37
R. Collins (Torquay U.)	30	G. Stewart (Accrington Stanley)	33
S. Newsham (Bournemouth & B.A.)	30	W. Tulip (Darlington)	32
T. Dixon (Reading)	28	R. Smith (Bradford)	28
B. Edwards (Swindon T.)	25	W. Gordon (Barrow)	27

1957-58

Division 1		Division 2	
R. Smith (Tottenham H.)	36	B. Clough (Middlesbrough)	40
T. Thompson (Preston N.E.)	34	T. Johnston (Leyton Orient)	35
G. Turner (Luton T.)	33	J. Summers (Charlton Ath.)	28
J. Murray (Wolverhampton W.)	29	R. Rafferty (Grimsby T.)	26
T. Finney (Preston N.E.)	26	J. Atyeo (Bristol C.)	23

Division 3 (South)

S. McGrory (Southend U.)	31
D. Reeves (Southampton)	31
E. Towers (Brentford)	29
W. Carter (Plymouth Arg.)	26
T. Dixon (Reading)	24

Division 3 (North)

A. Ackerman (Carlisle U.)	35
K. Williams (Tranmere R.)	28
G. Stewart (Accrington Stanley)	27
B. Jepson (Chester)	25
J. Parker (Bury)	25

1958-59

Division 1

J. Greaves (Chelsea)	33
R. Smith (Tottenham H.)	32
R. Charlton (Manchester U.)	29
N. Lofthouse (Bolton W.)	29

Division 2

B. Clough (Middlesbrough)	42
R. Shiner (Sheffield W.)	28
R. Froggatt (Sheffield W.)	26
D. Pace (Sheffield U.)	26
D. Ward (Bristol R.)	26

Division 3

E. Towers (Brentford)	32
W. Bradbury (Hull C.)	30
J. McCole (Bradford C.)	28
C. Smith (Hull C.)	26
T. Rowley (Tranmere R.)	25

Division 4

A. Rowley (Shrewsbury T.)	37
A. Woan (Northampton T.)	32
A. Richards (Walsall)	28
E. Calland (Exeter C.)	27
R. Straw (Coventry C.)	27

1959-60

Division 1

D. Viollet (Manchester U.)	32
J. Greaves (Chelsea)	29
J. Murray (Wolverhampton W.)	29
L. White (Newcastle U.)	28
D. Kevan (W.B.A.)	26

Division 2

B. Clough (Middlesbrough)	39
E. Phillips (Ipswich T.)	24
T. Johnston (Leyton Orient)	24
W. Curry (Brighton & H.A.)	23
G. Hitchens (Aston Villa)	23

Division 3

D. Reeves (Southampton)	39
R. Hunt (Grimsby T.)	33
A. Rowley (Shrewsbury T.)	32
M. King (Colchester U.)	30
D. Price (Southend U.)	28

Division 4

C. Holton (Watford)	42
E. Uphill (Watford)	30
J. Allan (Bradford)	27
H. Llewellyn (Crewe Alex.)	25

1960-61

Division 1

J. Greaves (Chelsea)	41
D. Herd (Arsenal)	29
G. Hitchens (Aston Villa)	29
J. Farmer (Wolverhampton W.)	28
R. Smith (Tottenham H.)	28

Division 2

R. Crawford (Ipswich T.)	39
B. Clough (Middlesbrough)	34
E. Phillips (Ipswich T.)	30

Division 3

A. Richards (Walsall)	36
B. Bedford (Q.P.R.)	33
C. Taylor (Walsall)	33
C. Holton (Watford)	32
J. Wheeler (Reading)	31

Division 4

T. Bly (Peterborough U.)	52
G. Hudson (Accrington Stanley)	35
P. Burridge (Millwall)	34
J. Byrne (Crystal Palace)	30
R. Summersby (Crystal Palace)	25

1961-62

Division 1

R. Crawford (Ipswich T.)	33
D. Kevan (W.B.A.)	33
R. Charnley (Blackpool)	30
E. Phillips (Ipswich T.)	28
T. R. Vernon (Everton)	28

Division 2

R. Hunt (Liverpool)	41
B. Thomas (Scunthorpe U.)	31
B. Clough (Sunderland)	29
G. O'Brien (Southampton)	28
A. Peacock (Middlesbrough)	24

Division 3

C. Holton (Northampton T. 36, plus 1 for Watford)	37
B. Bedford (Q.P.R.)	36
R. Rafferty (Grimsby T.)	34
T. Bly (Peterborough U.)	30
J. Atyeo (Bristol C.)	26

Division 4

R. R. Hunt (Colchester U.)	37
D. Layne (Bradford C.)	34
M. King (Colchester U.)	31
F. Lord (Crewe Alex.)	30
J. Weir (York C.)	28

1962-63

Division 1

J. Greaves (Tottenham Hotspur)	37
J. Baker (Arsenal)	29
D. Layne (Sheffield W.)	29
R. Crawford (Ipswich T.)	25

Division 2

R. Tambling (Chelsea)	35
A. Peacock (Middlesbrough)	31
T. Allcock (Norwich C.)	26
J. Storrie (Leeds U.)	25
B. Clough (Sunderland)	24

Division 3

G. Hudson (Coventry C.)	30
D. Ward (Watford)	29
M. King (Colchester U.)	26
A. Ashworth (Northampton T.)	25

Division 4

K. Wagstaff (Mansfield T.)	34
C. Booth (Doncaster R.)	34
R. Chapman (Mansfield T.)	31
H. Lister (Oldham Ath.)	30
F. Lord (Crewe Alex.)	30

1963-64

Division 1

J. Greaves (Tottenham H.)	35
M. McEvoy (Blackburn R.)	32
R. Hunt (Liverpool)	31
D. Law (Manchester U.)	30
R. Crawford (Wolverhampton W. 26, plus 2 for Ipswich T.)	28

Division 2

R. Saunders (Portsmouth)	33
I. Dawson (Preston N.E.)	31
D. Kevan (Manchester C.)	30
R. T. Davies (Norwich C.)	26
J. Crossan (Sunderland)	22

MEMORABLE MOMENTS 1: July 30 1966, and as Jackie Charlton sinks to his knees, Martin Peters embraces Geoff Hurst. The reason for all this emotion? England have just won the World Cup, and Peters and hat-trick hero Hurst scored the goals that sunk West Germany at Wembley.

MEMORABLE MOMENTS 2: Remember them? It's July 19 1966 at Ayresome Park, and little North Korea have just pitched the multi-million lire Italy out of the World Cup. Pak Doo Ik scored the only goal of the game – a 20-yard screamer – and the inscrutable men from the East were through to the quarter-finals.

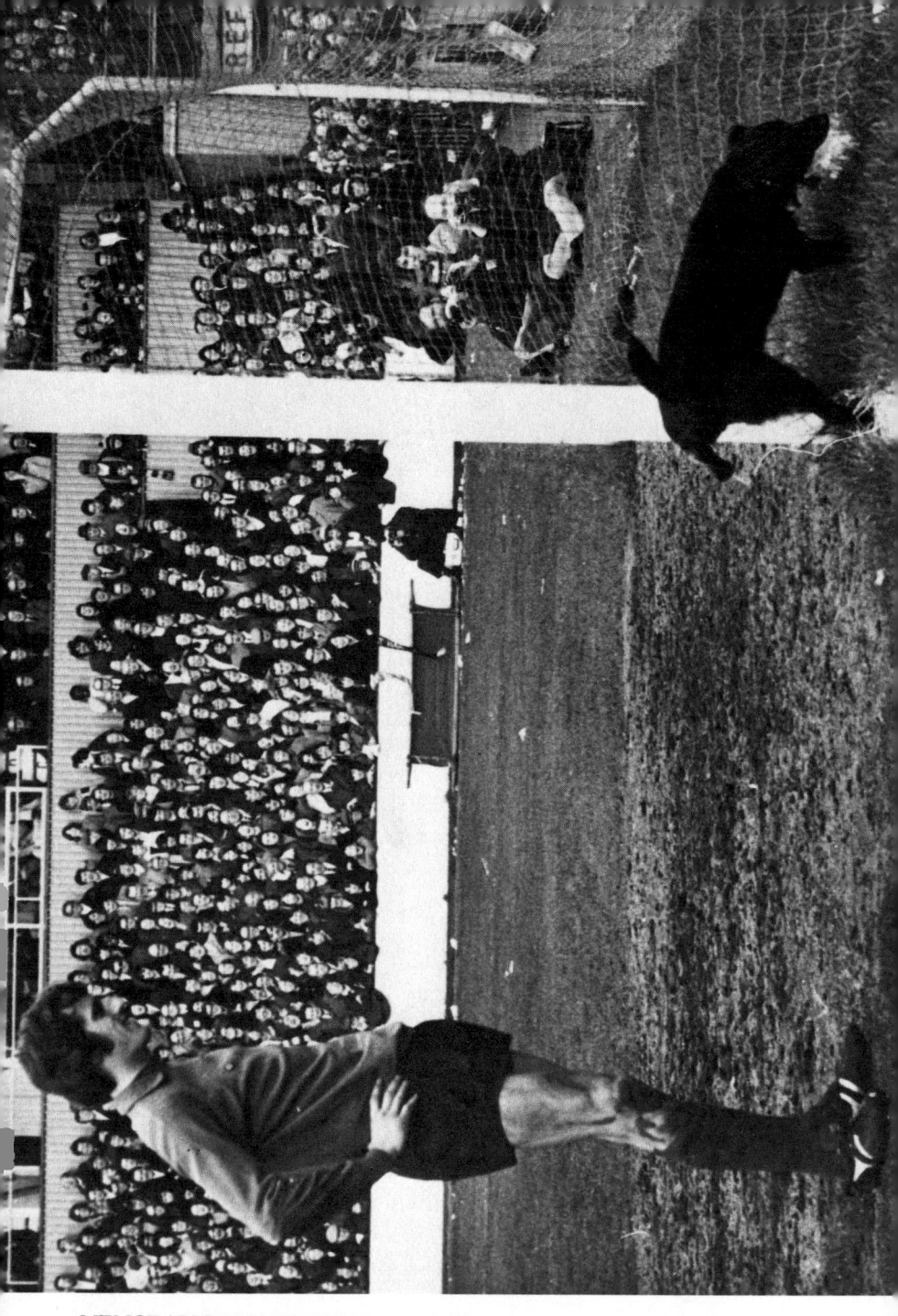

MEMORABLE MOMENTS 3: An April afternoon in 1972, and though the West Ham forwards couldn't score, Bonzo the mongrel managed to get past Ray Clemence and hit the post! The referee thought this constituted ungentlemanly conduct, and Bonzo was sent off – in the arms of a policeman.

MEMORABLE MOMENTS 4: September 1964, and a look at the sadder side of football. Dave Mackay, then with Spurs, has just broken his leg for the second time in nine months during his comeback game in the Football Combination against Shrewsbury reserves at White Hart Lane. Referee Peter Songhurst beckons for a stretcher.

MEMORABLE MOMENTS 5: The sweet smile of success from Arsenal manager Bertie Mee. Now that Bertie has retired from football, we thought the time appropriate to reprint this famous shot of the League Championship trophy and FA Cup, which Arsenal captured in 1970–71.

MEMORABLE MOMENTS 6: As England set out on another World Cup quest, we look back to their last match in a World Cup final series. They've just lost 3–2 to West Germany in the quarter-finals at Leon, Mexico, in June 1970, and England manager Alf Ramsey consoles Bobby Charlton as they leave the field.

MEMORABLE MOMENTS 7: In the 1950s, the FA Cup final always seemed to throw up a famous or controversial incident, and the Bolton v Manchester United final in 1958 was no exception. In an incident that is still being argued about nearly 20 years later, Nat Lofthouse barges United 'keeper Harry Gregg – and the ball – into the net. The goal was allowed.

MEMORABLE MOMENTS 8: Stanley Matthews looks as if he still doesn't quite believe it, but it's true. In an FA Cup final known ever since as 'Matthews' final', he at last won the winners' medal that everyone (except Bolton supporters!) thought he deserved. It was a good match to win, too, with the 4–3 scoreline reflecting one of the most exciting finals ever.

Division 3

A. Biggs (Bristol R.)	30
K. Wagstaff (Mansfield T.)	29
D. Coughlin (Bournemouth & B.A.)	28
G. Hudson (Coventry C.)	25

Division 4

H. McIlmoyle (Carlisle U.)	39
H. Green (Bradford C.)	29
A. Spence (Southport)	27
J. Dyson (Tranmere R.)	26
J. Bonson (Newport County)	25

1964-65

Division 1

J. Greaves (Tottenham H.)	29
A. McEvoy (Blackburn R.)	29
D. Law (Manchester U.)	28
F. Pickering (Everton)	27

Division 2

G. O'Brien (Southampton)	34
A. Dawson (Preston N.E.)	26
B. Godfrey (Preston N.E.)	25
A. Bennett (Rotherham U.)	24
F. Lee (Bolton W.)	23

Division 3

K. Wagstaff (Mansfield T. 8, plus 23 for Hull C.)	31
C. Chilton (Hull C.)	27
J. Atyeo (Bristol C.)	23
N. Bedford (Q.P.R.)	23
A. Clarke (Walsall)	23

Division 4

A. Jeffrey (Doncaster R.)	36
T. Harkin (Crewe Alex.)	35
R. Stubbs (Torquay U.)	31
K. Hector (Bradford)	29

1965-66

Division 1

R. Hunt (Liverpool)	30
W. Irvine (Burnley)	29
T. Hateley (Aston Villa)	27
D. Herd (Manchester U.)	24
G. Hurst (West Ham U.)	23

Division 2

M. Chivers (Southampton)	30
G. Vowden (Birmingham C.)	21
P. Knowles (Wolverhampton W.)	20
J. Atyeo (Bristol C.)	19

Division 3

L. Allen (Q.P.R.)	30
M. Tees (Grimsby T.)	28
K. Wagstaff (Hull C.)	27
B. Gibbs (Gillingham)	23

Division 4

K. Hector (Bradford)	34
J. O'Rourke (Luton T.)	32
J. Dyson (Tranmere R.)	29
L. Sheffield (Doncaster R.)	28

1966-67

Division 1

R. Davies (Southampton)	37
G. Hurst (West Ham U.)	29
A. Clarke (Fulham)	24
J. Greaves (Tottenham H.)	23
D. Law (Manchester U.)	23

Division 2

R. Gould (Coventry C.)	24
F. Lee (Bolton W.)	22
R. Crawford (Ipswich T.)	21
K. Wagstaff (Hull C.)	21
E. Hunt (Wolverhampton W.)	20

Division 3

R. Marsh (Q.P.R.)	30
J. O'Rourke (Middlesbrough)	27
I. Towers (Oldham Athletic)	27
D. Rogers (Swindon T.)	25

Division 4

E. Phythian (Hartlepools U.)	23
E. Chapman (Lincoln C.)	20
J. Mulvaney (Hartlepools U.)	19
R. Smith (Southend U.)	19

1967-68

Division 1

G. Best (Manchester U.)	28
R. Davies (Southampton)	28
J. Astle (W.B.A.)	25
R. Hunt (Liverpool)	25
J. Greaves (Tottenham H.)	23

Division 2

J. Hickton (Middlesbrough)	24
B. Bridges (Birmingham C.)	23
K. Hector (Derby Co.)	21
G. Ingram (Blackpool)	18
R. Woodruff (Crystal Palace)	18

Division 3

D. Rogers (Swindon T.)	25
R. Owen (Bury)	25
J. Fryatt (Torquay U. 2 plus 22 for Stockport County)	24
K. Napier (Brighton & H.A.)	24
G. Yardley (Tranmere R.)	23

Division 4

R. Chapman (Port Vale)	25
L. Massie (Halifax T.)	25
B. Rioch (Luton T.)	24
E. Loydon (Chester)	22
K. Randall (Chesterfield)	21

1968-69

Division 1

J. Greaves (Tottenham H.)	27
G. Hurst (West Ham U.)	25
J. Royle (Everton)	22
J. Astle (W.B.A.)	21

Division 2

J. Toshack (Cardiff C.)	22
K. Wagstaff (Hull C.)	20
J. Hickton (Middlesbrough)	18

Division 3

B. Lewis (Luton Town)	22
D. Rogers (Swindon T.)	22
G. Andrews (Southport)	19
W. Atkins (Stockport Co.)	18

Division 4

G. Talbot (Chester)	22
W. Best (Southend U.)	20
J. Howarth (Aldershot)	19
E. MacDougall (York C.)	19

1969-70

Division 1

J. Astle (W.B.A.)	25
P. Osgood (Chelsea)	23
J. Royle (Everton)	23
B. Robson (Newcastle U.)	22
H. Curran (Wolverhampton W.)	20

Division 2

J. Hickton (Middlesbrough)	24
B. Bridges (Q.P.R.)	22
J. Byrom (Bolton W.)	20

Division 3		Division 4	
G. Jones (Bury)	26	A. Kinsey (Wrexham)	27
M. MacDonald (Luton T.)	25	S. Brace (Grimsby T.)	25
L. Chappell (Reading)	24	J. Hall (Peterborough U.)	24
S. Earle (Fulham)	22		
E. MacDougall (Bournemouth & B.A.)	21		

1970-71

Division 1		Division 2	
A. Brown (W.B.A.)	28	J. Hickton (Middlesbrough)	25
M Chivers (Tottenham H.)	21	M. Macdonald (Luton T.)	24
A. Clarke (Leeds U.)	19	C. Chilton (Hull C.)	21
R. Kennedy (Arsenal)	19	R. Marsh (Q.P.R.)	21
		R. Hatton (Carlisle U.)	18

Division 3		Division 4	
G. Ingram (Preston North End)	22	E. MacDougall (Bournemouth & B.A.)	42
D. Roberts (Mansfield T.)	22	P. Aimson (York C.)	26
K. Randall (Chesterfield)	19	R. Crawford (Colchester U.)	25
		J. Fryatt (Oldham A.)	24

1971-72

Division 1		Division 2	
F. Lee (Manchester C.)	33	R. Latchford (Birmingham C.)	23
M. Chivers (Tottenham H.)	25	J. Galley (Bristol C.)	22
P. Lorimer (Leeds U.)	23	R. Hatton (Carlisle U. 7 plus 15	
M. Macdonald (Newcastle U.)	23	for Birmingham C.)	22
P. Osgood (Chelsea)	19	B. Clark (Cardiff C.)	21
		F. Casper (Burnley)	18

Division 3		Division 4	
E. MacDougall (Bournemouth & B.A	35	P. Price (Peterborough U.)	28
A. Wood (Shrewsbury T.)	35	R. McNeil (Lincoln C. 13 plus 14	
C. Gilbert (Rotherham U.)	22	for Northampton T.)	27
L. Bradd (Notts County)	21	M. Tees (Grimsby T.)	27
A. Lochhead (Aston Villa)	19	W. Garner (Southend U.)	25
		J. O'Mara (Brentford)	25

1972-73

Division 1		Division 2	
B. Robson (West Ham U.)	28	D. Givens (Q.P.R.)	23
J. Richards (Wolverhampton W.)	27	G. Bolland (Millwall)	19
W. Dearden (Sheffield U.)	20	S. Bowles (Q.P.R.)	17
R. Latchford (Birmingham C.)	19	A. Gowling (Huddersfield T.)	17
		S. Pearson (Hull C.)	11

Division 3		Division 4	
B. Bannister (Bristol R.)	25	F. Binney (Exeter C.)	28
A. Horsfield (Charlton A.)	25	J. Hall (Peterborough U.)	21
J. Byrom (Bolton W.)	20	R. McNeil (Lincoln C.)	21
E. Loyden (Tranmere R.)	19	A. Provan (Southport)	21
K. Randall (Notts County)	19	J. Fairbrother (Mansfield T.)	20

1973-74

Division 1		Division 2	
M. Channon (Southampton)	21	D. McKenzie (Nottingham F.)	26
F. Worthington (Leicester C.)	20	A. Wood (Millwall)	21
S. Bowles (Q.P.R.)	19	T. Brown (W.B.A.)	19
K. Hector (Derby Co.)	18	A. Foggon (Middlesbrough)	19

Division 3		Division 4	
W. Jennings (Watford)	26	B. Yeo (Gillingham)	31
J. Howarth (Aldershot)	25	F. Binney (Exeter C.)	25
A. Gowling (Huddersfield T.)	24	L. Chappell (Reading)	24
A. Warboys (Bristol R.)	22	R. Svarc (Colchester U.)	24
A. Buckley (Walsall)	21		

1974-75

Division 1		Division 2	
M. Macdonald (Newcastle U.)	21	A. Little (Aston Villa)	20
B. Kidd (Arsenal)	19	M. Channon (Southampton)	19
F. Worthington (Leicester C.)	18	R. Graydon (Aston Villa)	19
K. Hibbitt (Wolverhampton W.)	17	B. Robson (Sunderland)	19
R. Latchford (Everton)	17		

Division 3		Division 4	
R. McNeil (Hereford U.)	31	R. Clarke (Mansfield T.)	28
P. Eastoe (Swindon T.)	26	R. Habbin (Rotherham U. 10 plus	
R. Svarc (Colchester U.)	24	12 for Reading)	22
W. Rafferty (Plymouth Argyle)	23	R. Haywood (Shrewsbury T.)	21
		P. Kitchen (Doncaster R.)	21
		E. Woods (Newport County)	21

442

TRANSFER TRAIL 1975-76

These transfers are those which were officially registered by the Football League and the Football Association between June 1 1975 and May 30 1976.

June 1975

3	M. Burleigh	Darlington to Carlisle U.
9	N. Davids	Leeds U. to Norwich C.
11	G. Coyne	Manchester C. to Manchester U.
13	A. Evans	Blackpool to Cardiff C.
14	W. Morgan	Manchester U. to Burnley
14	N. O'Brien	Arsenal to Mansfield T.
14	R. Phillips	Bolton W. to Bury
14	M. Summerbee	Manchester C. to Burnley
16	K. Charlton	A.F.C. Bournemouth to Hereford U.
18	D. Watson	Sunderland to Manchester C.
19	J. Clarke	Manchester C. to Sunderland

July 1975

4	S. Kember	Chelsea to Leicester C.
8	C. George	Arsenal to Derby C.
8	C. Hewitt	Distillery to Middlesbrough
9	B. Daniels	Manchester C. to Chester
10	J. Hollins	Chelsea to Q.P.R.
12	J. Giles	Exeter C. to Charlton Ath.
12	W. Glazier	Coventry C. to Brentford
14	M. Horswill	Manchester C. to Plymouth Arg.
15	J. Dennehy	Nottingham F. to Walsall
15	D. Downing	Orient to York C.
15	J. Jones	Wrexham to Liverpool
15	P. Latchford	W.B.A. to Glasgow Celtic
16	D. Allder	Millwall to Orient
16	J. Giles	Leeds U. to W.B.A.
17	T. Brisley	Orient to Millwall
17	B. Fairbrother	Orient to Millwall
17	C. Wigginton	Grimsby T. to Scunthorpe U.
18	J. Hall	Peterborough U. to Northampton T.
18	G. Hope	Newcastle U. to Charlton Ath.
18	T. Lee	Tottenham H. to Torquay U.
22	B. Alderson	Coventry C. to Leicester C.
22	I. McDonald	Liverpool to Mansfield T.
29	R. Fern	Luton T. to Chesterfield

Temporary Transfers – July 1975

28	L. Bond	Bristol C. to Cardiff C.
31	D. Peacock	Nottingham F. to Doncaster R.

August 1975

6	A. Gowling	Huddersfield T. to Newcastle U.
11	S. Davey	Plymouth Arg. to Hereford U.
14	M. King	Millwall to Coventry C.
14	J. Lindsay	Colchester U. to Hereford U.
15	N. Ramsbottom	Coventry C. to Sheffield W.
18	T. Lees	Stoke C. to Port Vale
19	G. Hurst	Stoke C. to W.B.A.
22	D. Livermore	Norwich C. to Cardiff C.
22	B. Parker	Crewe Alex. to Arsenal

28	J. Bird	Preston N.E. to Newcastle U.
28	A. Bruce	Newcastle U. to Preston N.E.
28	E. Curran	Doncaster R. to Nottingham F.
28	J. Kinnear	Tottenham H. to Brighton & H.A.
28	I. Miller	Nottingham F. to Doncaster R.
28	D. Peacock	Nottingham F. to Doncaster R.
28	P. Withe	Wolverhampton W. to Birmingham C.

Temporary Transfers – August 1975

15	M. Lester	Manchester C. to Stockport Co.
15	J. O'Donnell	Cambridge U. to Colchester U.
16	J. Durrell	Bristol C. to Cardiff C.
22	K. Baker	Oxford U. to Grimsby T.
29	M. Cawston	Norwich C. to Leicester C.

September 1975

1	T. Hibbitt	Newcastle U. to Birmingham C.
3	B. Powell	Wolverhampton W. to Coventry C.
6	R. Scaife	Middlesbrough to Hartlepool
10	A. Horsfield	Charlton Ath. to Watford
11	P. Crossley	Tranmere R. to Chester
11	J. James	Chester to Tranmere R.
18	W. Young	Aberdeen to Tottenham H.
19	C. Calvert	York C. to Sheffield U.
25	J. Burridge	Blackpool to Aston Villa
25	R. Saxton	Plymouth Arg. to Exeter C.
26	D. Jones	Nottingham F. to Norwich C.

Temporary Transfers – September 1975

4	N. Davids	Norwich C. to Northampton T.
4	S. Hayes	Shrewsbury T. to Torquay U.
5	A. Merrick	W.B.A. to Peterborough U.
6	K. Griffin	Bristol C. to Cambridge U.
6	D. Irving	Everton to Sheffield U.
6	S. Litt	Luton T. to Arsenal
11	G. Hindson	Luton T. to Carlisle U.
12	J. Hemmerman	Hull C. to Scunthorpe U.
15	G. Hutt	Huddersfield T. to Blackburn R.
15	J. McIlwraith	Motherwell to Bury
16	G. Buchan	Bury to Motherwell
16	B. Butlin	Nottingham F. to Brighton & H.A.
17	J. Kelly	Wolverhampton W. to Wrexham
19	P. Hilton	Blackburn R. to Gillingham
19	B. Watling	Hartlepool to Chester
20	P. Ashworth	Blackburn R. to A.F.C. Bournemouth
20	M. Lester	Manchester C. to Stockport Co.
27	D. Syrett	Swindon T. to Wolverhampton W.

October 1975

1	A. Gray	Dundee U. to Aston Villa
3	R. Svarc	Colchester U. to Blackburn R.
17	M. Hickman	Blackburn R. to Torquay U.
23	P. Ashworth	Blackburn R. to A.F.C. Bournemouth
24	S. Baxter	Preston N.E. to Dundee U.
24	P. Hilton	Blackburn R. to Gillingham
28	J. Brown	Aston Villa to Preston N.E.
30	A. Alston	Luton T. to Cardiff C.
31	R. Delgado	Rotherham U. to Chester

Temporary Transfers – October 1975

1	I. Collard	Portsmouth to Ipswich T. (transfer back)
3	J. Hynd	Birmingham C. to Oxford U.
3	M. Martin	Manchester U. to W.B.A.
3	J. McLaughlin	Liverpool to Portsmouth
6	S. Litt	Luton T. to Arsenal
8	J. Walker	Brighton & H.A. to Peterborough U.
9	J. Brown	Aston Villa to Preston N.E.
9	G. Hindson	Carlisle U. to Luton T. (transfer back)
9	G. Hindson	Luton T. to Blackburn R.
9	D. Sunley	Sheffield W. to Nottingham F.
10	K. Ayres	C. Palace to Charlton Ath.
10	L. Bond	Bristol C. to Torquay U.
14	D. MacKinnon	Arsenal to Dundee
15	G. Shaw	W.B.A. to Oldham Ath.
17	I. Butler	York C. to Barnsley
17	S. Phillips	Birmingham C. to Northampton T.
17	T. Tynan	Liverpool to Swansea C.
21	J. McCann	Nottingham F. to Stockport Co.
23	P. Lally	Swansea C. to Aldershot
23	G. Taylor	Wolverhampton W. to Swindon T.
24	S. Deere	Hull C. to Barnsley
28	M. Smith	Middlesbrough to Bury
29	S. Taylor	Bolton W. to Port Vale
31	B. Endean	Huddersfield T. to Workington

November 1975

6	D. Simmons	Brentford to Cambridge U.
13	G. Armstrong	Bangor C. to Tottenham H.
13	G. Hill	Millwall to Manchester U.
14	K. Randall	Notts Co. to Mansfield T.
19	F. Lee	Bolton W. to Wrexham
24	D. Martin	Blackburn R. to Northampton T.
27	B. Hamilton	Ipswich T. to Everton

Temporary Transfers – November 1975

3	C. Griffiths	Manchester U. to Tranmere R.
3	I. Seddon	Chester to Stockport Co.
4	J. Hamilton	Sunderland to Plymouth Arg.
4	D. Syrett	Wolverhampton W. to Swindon T. (transfer back)
5	G. Horn	Luton T. to Brentford
6	J. Emanuel	Bristol C. to Swindon T.
7	P. Bielby	Manchester U. to Hartlepool
7	W. Coulson	Southend U. to Huddersfield T.
7	P. Creamer	Middlesbrough to York C.
7	J. Durrell	Bristol C. to Gillingham
7	J. Wann	York C. to Chesterfield
12	R. Davies	Manchester U. to Millwall
13	D. Westwood	Q.P.R. to Gillingham
14	P. Garner	Huddersfield T. to Sheffield U.
14	R. Wylde	Sheffield W. to Burnley
18	B. Watling	Hartlepool to Crewe Alex.
20	A. Macken	Derby Co. to Portsmouth
27	M. Dawes	Hartlepool to Workington
27	C. Duffey	Shrewsbury T. to Rochdale
29	K. Baker	Oxford U. to Millwall

December 1975

4	P. Boersma	Liverpool to Middlesbrough
4	R. Gould	West Ham U. to Wolverhampton W.
4	L. James	Burnley to Derby Co.

4	J. McIlwraith	Motherwell to Bury
4	G. McVitie	Oldham Ath. to Carlisle U.
4	G. Shaw	W.B.A. to Oldham Ath.
5	P. Creamer	Middlesbrough to Doncaster R.
5	B. Taylor	Middlesbrough to Doncaster R.
6	J. Hynd	Birmingham C. to Walsall
6	M. Martin	Manchester U. to W.B.A.
8	P. Scott	Everton to York C.
9	P. Bielby	Manchester U. to Hartlepool
11	P. Garner	Huddersfield T. to Sheffield U.
11	P. Marinello	Portsmouth to Motherwell
12	S. Phillips	Birmingham C. to Northampton T.
16	J. Sims	Derby Co. to Notts Co.
18	A. Evans	Aston Villa to Walsall
18	G. Lyall	Nottingham F. to Hull C.
19	M. Dawes	Hartlepool to Workington
23	S. Morgan	Aston Villa to Brighton & H.A.
24	D. Mortimer	Coventry C. to Aston Villa
30	M. Conway	Brighton & H.A. to Swansea C.

Temporary Transfers—December 1975

4	L. Bond	Bristol C. to Scunthorpe U.
4	P. Creamer	York C. to Middlesbrough (transfer back)
5	J. Peachey	Barnsley to Darlington
9	W. Woof	Middlesbrough to Brighton & H.A.
11	R. Ferguson	Sheffield W. to Scunthorpe U.
18	B. Donaghy	W.B.A. to Workington
18	J. Saunders	Huddersfield T. to Barnsley
19	S. Deere	Hull C. to Stockport Co.
19	B. Endean	Huddersfield T. to Workington
19	B. Watling	Hartlepool to Rotherham U.
20	D. McKellar	Ipswich T. to Peterborough U.
31	D. Rudge	Hereford U. to Torquay U.
31	P. Sutcliffe	Manchester U. to Stockport Co.

January 1976

8	R. Gough	Southport to Colchester U.
8	R. Walden	Aldershot to Sheffield W.
9	L. Badger	Sheffield U. to Chesterfield
9	R. Greenwood	Hull C. to Sunderland
12	J. Hamilton	Sunderland to Plymouth Arg.
14	D. Westwood	Q.P.R. to Gillingham
16	E. Moss	Chesterfield to Peterborough U.
23	S. Cammack	Sheffield U. to Chesterfield
29	M. McDonald	Stoke C. to Hibernian
30	D. Sunley	Sheffield W. to Hull C.

Temporary Transfers—January 1976

6	D. Wagstaffe	Wolverhampton W. to Blackburn R.
7	A. Mayes	Watford to Northampton T.
8	C. Griffin	Derby Co. to Shrewsbury T.
8	J. King	Derby Co. to Notts Co.
8	R. Marlowe	Brighton & H.A. to Aldershot
9	M. Cawston	Norwich C. to Newport Co.
9	H. Charlton	Middlesbrough to Hartlepool
9	I. Seddon	Chester to Chesterfield
10	W. Telford	Peterborough U. to Colchester U.
15	J. Higham	Liverpool to Southport
15	D. Johnson	Tranmere R. to Southport
15	W. Steele	Norwich C. to A.F.C. Bournemouth

16	T. McAlister	Sheffield U. to Rotherham U.
16	D. Ryan	Manchester U. to Port Vale
16	J. Wann	York C. to Hartlepool
19	L. Bond	Scunthorpe U. to Bristol C. (transfer back)
22	J. Ruggiero	Stoke C. to Workington
22	T. Sharp	Everton to Brentford
22	J. Waters	Leicester C. to Grimsby T.
23	L. Bond	Bristol C. to Colchester U.
23	W. Coulson	Southend U. to Darlington
23	J. McIntosh	Nottingham F. to Chesterfield
24	A. Glover	W.B.A. to Southend U.
28	S. Harding	Bristol C. to Southend U.
29	N. Davids	Norwich C. to Stockport Co.
29	M. Smith	Middlesbrough to Blackpool

February 1976

4	A. Morley	Preston N.E. to Burnley
6	C. Griffin	Derby Co. to Shrewsbury T.
6	V. McCarthy	Manchester U. to Waterford
9	S. Wallace	Everton to Waterford
16	P. Feely	Gillingham to Sheffield W.
17	D. Gwyther	Halifax T. to Rotherham U.
18	P. Sutcliffe	Manchester U. to Stockport Co.
19	B. Donaghy	W.B.A. to Workington
19	J. Lathan	Mansfield T. to Carlisle U.
21	M. Bullock	Orient to Halifax T.
21	J. McGill	Hull C. to Halifax T.
25	J. Higham	Liverpool to Southport
25	J. Waters	Leicester C. to Grimsby T.
26	J. Walker	Brighton & H.A. to Peterborough U.
27	G. Jones	Oldham Ath. to Halifax T.

Temporary Transfers—February 1976

5	M. Busby	Q.P.R. to Portsmouth
5	P. Spiring	Luton T. to Hereford U.
7	W. Emanuel	Bristol C. to Gillingham
9	R. Brown	Sheffield W. to Aldershot
11	D. McClatchey	Liverpool to Southport
13	G. Felton	Northampton T. to Barnsley
13	C. Garwood	Huddersfield T. to Colchester U.
13	A. Macken	Derby Co. to Portsmouth
16	I. Seddon	Chester to Cambridge U.
18	K. Blair	Halifax T. to Stockport Co.
18	R. Goldthorpe	Charlton Ath. to Aldershot
19	R. McGrath	Tottenham H. to Millwall
19	J. Seasman	Luton T. to Millwall
20	W. Dearden	Sheffield U. to Chester
20	J. Higham	Southport to Liverpool (transfer back)
20	D. Johnson	Tranmere R. to Southport
20	S. Uzelac	Doncaster R. to Mansfield T.
24	B. Bowery	Nottingham F. to Lincoln C.
24	A. Woodcock	Nottingham F. to Lincoln C.
26	R. Ferguson	Sheffield W. to Darlington
27	W. Steele	A.F.C. Bournemouth to Norwich C. (transfer back)
28	R. Dixey	Burnley to Stockport Co.

March 1976

4	A. Campbell	Birmingham C. to Cardiff C.
4	A. McCulloch	Oxford U. to Brentford
5	C. Garwood	Huddersfield T. to Colchester U.
6	T. McAlister	Sheffield U. to Rotherham U.
8	G. Oates	Blackburn R. to Newcastle U.
8	D. Rogers	Q.P.R. to Swindon T.
10	S. Aizlewood	Newport Co. to Swindon T.
10	B. Horton	Port Vale to Brighton & H.A.
10	D. Nelson	Crewe Alex. to Reading
11	P. Bonnyman	Hamilton Academicals to Carlisle U.
11	M. Butler	Barnsley to Huddersfield T.
11	P. Eastoe	Swindon T. to Q.P.R.
11	K. Hollis	Stockport Co. to Reading
11	J. Honour	Hartlepool to Workington
11	R. Jones	Blackburn R. to Newcastle U.
11	W. Morgan	Burnley to Bolton W.
11	G. O'Brien	Southampton to Swindon T.
11	J. Saunders	Huddersfield T. to Barnsley
11	G. Taylor	Birmingham C. to Blackburn R.
11	R. Train	Carlisle U. to Sunderland
11	D. Wagstaffe	Wolverhampton W. to Blackburn R.
12	F. Banks	Hull C. to Southend U.
12	G. Butler	Norwich C. to A.F.C. Bournemouth
12	R. Flavell	Burnley to Halifax T.
12	S. Goodwin	Norwich C. to Southend U.
12	J. McIntosh	Nottingham F. to Hull C.
13	B. Endean	Huddersfield T. to Hartlepool
16	T. Sharp	Everton to Brentford

Temporary Transfers—March 1976

3	D. Johnson	Southport to Tranmere R. (transfer back)
3	D. Ryan	Manchester U. to Southport
4	S. Litt	Arsenal to Luton T. (transfer back)
5	K. Hore	Plymouth Arg. to Exeter C.
9	P. Higgins	Doncaster R. to Torquay U.
10	A. Birchenall	Leicester C. to Notts Co.
10	R. Brown	Sheffield W. to Aldershot
10	P. Luckett	Halifax T. to Hartlepool
11	I. Cranstone	Tottenham H. to Charlton Ath.
11	D. Johnson	Tranmere R. to Preston N.E.
11	J. O'Keefe	Birmingham C. to Peterborough U.
11	F. Pimblett	Aston Villa to Newport Co.
12	C. Barrett	Manchester C. to Nottingham F.
12	D. Bell	Halifax T. to Sheffield W.
12	H. Charlton	Middlesbrough to Chesterfield
12	G. Cross	Leicester C. to Chesterfield
12	S. Downes	Halifax T. to Blackburn R.
12	S. Grapes	Norwich C. to A.F.C. Bournemouth
12	J. King	Derby Co. to Portsmouth
12	D. Rylands	Hereford U. to Hartlepool
13	J. Overton	Aston Villa to Halifax T.
13	T. Parkin	Ipswich T. to Grimsby T.
24	W. Telford	Peterborough U. to Crewe Alex.

April 1976

1	A. King	Luton T. to Everton
9	C. Barrett	Manchester C. to Nottingham F.

9	P. Luckett	Halifax T. to Hartlepool
14	J. Dunne	Fulham to Torquay U.
16	D. Cameron	Sheffield W. to Preston N.E.
16	J. Seasman	Luton T. to Millwall
26	P. Spiring	Luton T. to Hereford U.
28	T. Paterson	Middlesbrough to A.F.C. Bournemouth
28	H. Riley	Bury to A.F.C. Bournemouth
29	D. Richardson	Chelsea to Q.P.R.

Temporary Transfer—April 1976

| 10 | G. Felton | Barnsley to Northampton T. (transfer back) |

May 1976

3	P. Oliver	York C. to Huddersfield T.
8	M. Cawston	Norwich C. to Gillingham
17	P. Fletcher	Hull C. to Stockport Co.
25	K. Bowker	Exter C. to Cambridge U.
25	J. Collins	Burnley to Plymouth Arg.
25	K. Kennerley	Burnley to Port Vale
26	W. Rafferty	Plymouth Arg. to Carlisle U.
27	I. Macdonald	St Johnstone to Carlisle U.

FOOTBALL LEAGUE ATTENDANCES 1975-76

Division 1

	Home		Away	
	Aggregate	*Average*	*Aggregate*	*Average*
Arsenal	565,851	26,945	559,078	26,622
Aston Villa	816,355	38,874	619,106	29,481
Birmingham City	588,062	28,002	544,001	25,904
Burnley	380,514	18,119	520,902	24,804
Coventry City	406,779	19,370	531,458	25,259
Derby County	595,535	28,358	676,462	32,212
Everton	569,414	27,114	583,588	27,789
Ipswich Town	532,688	25,366	547,417	26,067
Leeds United	661,739	31,511	717,237	34,154
Leicester City	463,033	22,049	547,718	26,081
Liverpool	874,085	41,623	733,830	34,944
Manchester City	719,878	34,279	595,386	28,351
Manchester United	1,149,751	54,750	781,316	37,205
Middlesbrough	487,687	23,223	558,954	26,616
Newcastle United	694,258	33,059	588,229	28,010
Norwich City	477,952	22,759	519,093	24,718
Queen's Park Rangers	500,849	23,849	609,012	29,000
Sheffield United	494,539	23,549	517,720	24,653
Stoke City	468,595	22,314	590,133	28,101
Tottenham Hotspur	584,566	27,836	597,257	28,440
West Ham United	575,757	27,417	619,080	29,480
Wolverhampton Wanderers	481,974	22,951	532,884	25,375
Total	13,089,861		13,089,861	

Division 2

	Home		Away	
	Aggregate	*Average*	*Aggregate*	*Average*
Blackburn Rovers	220,271	10,489	249,485	11,880
Blackpool	174,451	8,307	236,155	11,245
Bolton Wanderers	407,200	19,390	325,227	15,487
Bristol City	340,281	16,203	295,234	14,058
Bristol Rovers	210,458	10,021	236,111	11,243
Carlisle United	173,859	8,279	238,636	11,363
Charlton Athletic	244,217	11,629	245,629	11,696
Chelsea	398,088	18,956	342,281	16,299
Fulham	204,556	9,740	267,843	12,754
Hull City	144,927	6,901	234,097	11,147
Luton Town	222,332	10,587	244,236	11,630
Nottingham Forest	268,908	12,805	277,241	13,201
Notts County	260,703	12,414	244,811	11,657
Oldham Athletic	219,584	10,456	229,976	10,951
Orient	134,100	6,385	220,374	10,494
Oxford United	141,464	6,736	235,187	11,199
Plymouth Argyle	310,804	14,800	241,454	11,497
Portsmouth	219,917	10,472	253,385	12,065
Southampton	370,603	17,647	300,745	14,321
Sunderland	656,257	31,250	367,443	17,497
West Bromwich Albion	361,752	17,226	286,449	13,640
York City	113,673	5,413	226,406	10,781
Total	5,798,405		5,798,405	

Division 3

	Home		Away	
	Aggregate	*Average*	*Aggregate*	*Average*
Aldershot	105,501	4,587	153,817	6,687
Brighton & Hove Albion	352,891	15,343	194,966	8,476
Bury	136,518	5,935	156,037	6,784
Cardiff City	269,146	11,702	170,225	7,401
Chester	117,360	5,102	136,643	5,941
Chesterfield	113,129	4,918	147,234	6,401
Colchester United	77,015	3,348	138,138	6,006
Crystal Palace	462,849	20,123	240,070	10,437
Gillingham	144,922	6,300	152,129	6,614
Grimsby Town	128,344	5,580	141,752	6,163
Halifax Town	57,643	2,506	151,784	6,599
Hereford United	190,280	8,273	205,111	8,917
Mansfield Town	168,921	7,344	158,191	6,877
Millwall	176,843	7,688	197,237	8,575
Peterborough United	174,951	7,606	166,113	7,222
Port Vale	95,062	4,133	154,282	6,707
Preston North End	162,596	7,069	162,012	7,044
Rotherham United	120,034	5,218	162,600	7,069
Sheffield Wednesday	258,038	11,219	186,835	8,123
Shrewsbury Town	106,989	4,651	157,882	6,864
Southend United	115,242	5,010	159,702	6,943
Swindon Town	177,417	7,713	157,053	6,828
Walsall	141,110	6,136	151,817	6,600
Wrexham	95,648	4,158	146,819	6,383
Total	3,948,449		3,948,449	

Division 4

	Home		Away	
	Aggregate	*Average*	*Aggregate*	*Average*
A.F.C. Bournemouth	102,600	4,460	77,822	3,383
Barnsley	85,280	3,707	93,037	4,045
Bradford City	67,073	2,916	79,500	3,456
Brentford	117,218	5,096	84,820	3,687
Cambridge United	59,018	2,566	75,694	3,291
Crewe Alexandra	54,601	2,373	82,538	3,588
Darlington	51,223	2,227	80,472	3,498
Doncaster Rovers	139,297	6,056	93,120	4,048
Exeter City	75,064	3,263	78,233	3,401
Hartlepool	50,194	2,182	77,643	3,375
Huddersfield Town	124,900	5,430	99,736	4,336
Lincoln City	193,230	8,401	117,518	5,109
Newport County	47,844	2,080	81,893	3,560
Northampton Town	147,560	6,415	104,249	4,532
Reading	176,936	7,692	89,361	3,885
Rochdale	36,665	1,594	74,261	3,228
Scunthorpe United	70,090	3,047	77,359	3,363
Southport	33,323	1,448	81,484	3,542
Stockport County	74,474	3,238	84,112	3,657
Swansea City	67,435	2,931	92,637	4,027
Torquay United	60,725	2,640	81,920	3,561
Tranmere Rovers	89,235	3,879	95,815	4,165
Watford	106,000	4,608	83,762	3,641
Workington	29,353	1,276	72,352	3,145
Total	2,059,338		2,059,338	

ATTENDANCES AT FOOTBALL LEAGUE MATCHES

SEASON	MATCHES	TOTAL	DIV: 1
1946/47	1848	35,604,606	15,005,316
1947/48	1848	40,259,130	16,732,341
1948/49	1848	41,271,414	17,914,667
1949/50	1848	40,517,865	17,278,625
1950/51	2028	39,584,967	16,679,454
1951/52	2028	39,015,866	16,110,322
1952/53	2028	37,149,966	16,050,278
1953/54	2028	36,174,590	16,154,915
1954/55	2028	34,133,103	15,087,221
1955/56	2028	33,150,809	14,108,961
1956/57	2028	32,744,405	13,803,037
1957/58	2028	33,562,208	14,468,652
1958/59	2028	33,610,985	14,727,691
1959/60	2028	32,538,611	14,391,227
1960/61	2028	28,619,754	12,926,948
1961/62	2015	27,979,902	12,061,194
1962/63	2028	28,885,852	12,490,239
1963/64	2028	28,535,022	12,486,626
1964/65	2028	27,641,168	12,708,752
1965/66	2028	27,206,980	12,480,644
1966/67	2028	28,902,596	14,242,957
1967/68	2028	30,107,298	15,289,410
1968/69	2028	29,382,172	14,584,851
1969/70	2028	29,600,972	14,868,754
1970/71	2028	28,194,146	13,954,337
1971/72	2028	28,700,729	14,484,603
1972/73	2028	25,448,642	13,998,154
1973/74	2027	24,982,203	13,070,991
1974/75	2028	25,577,977	12,613,178
1975/76	2028	24,896,053	13,089,861

NOTE: *From Season 1958/59 onwards for Div. 3 (S) read Div. 3 and for Div. 3 (N) read Div. 4*

ATTENDANCES AT FOOTBALL LEAGUE MATCHES

SEASON	MATCHES	DIV: 2	DIV: 3 (S)	DIV: 3 (N)
1946/47	1848	11,071,572	5,664,004	3,863,714
1947/48	1848	12,286,350	6,653,610	4,586,829
1948/49	1848	11,353,237	6,998,429	5,005,081
1949/50	1848	11,694,158	7,104,155	4,440,927
1950/51	2028	10,780,580	7,367,884	4,757,109
1951/52	2028	11,066,189	6,958,927	4,880,428
1952/53	2028	9,686,654	6,704,299	4,708,735
1953/54	2028	9,510,053	6,311,508	4,198,114
1954/55	2028	8,988,794	5,996,017	4,051,071
1955/56	2028	9,080,002	5,692,479	4,269,367
1956/57	2028	8,718,162	5,622,189	4,601,017
1957/58	2028	8,663,712	6,097,183	4,332,661
1958/59	2028	8,641,997	5,946,600	4,276,697
1959/60	2028	8,399,627	5,739,707	4,008,050
1960/61	2028	7,033,936	4,784,256	3,874,614
1961/62	2015	7,453,089	5,199,106	3,266,513
1962/63	2028	7,792,770	5,341,362	3,261,481
1963/64	2028	7,594,158	5,419,157	3,035,081
1964/65	2028	6,984,104	4,436,245	3,512,067
1965/66	2028	6,914,757	4,779,150	3,032,429
1966/67	2028	7,253,819	4,421,172	2,984,648
1967/68	2028	7,450,410	4,013,087	3,354,391
1968/69	2028	7,382,390	4,339,656	3,075,275
1969/70	2028	7,581,728	4,223,761	2,926,729
1970/71	2028	7,098,265	4,377,213	2,764,331
1971/72	2028	6,769,308	4,697,392	2,749,426
1972/73	2028	5,631,730	3,737,252	2,081,506
1973/74	2027	6,326,108	3,421,624	2,163,480
1974/75	2028	6,955,970	4,086,145	1,992,684
1975/76	2028	5,798,405	3,948,449	2,059,338

NOTE: *From Season 1958/59 onwards for Div. 3 (S) read Div. 3 and for Div. 3 (N) read Div. 4.*

English Post-War League Tables

FOOTBALL LEAGUE TABLES 1946–47

DIVISION 1

	P	W	D	L	F	A	Pts.
Liverpool	42	25	7	10	84	52	57
Manchester U.	42	22	12	8	95	54	56
Wolverhampton W.	42	25	6	11	98	56	56
Stoke C.	42	24	7	11	90	53	55
Blackpool	42	22	6	14	71	70	50
Sheffield U.	42	21	7	14	89	75	49
Preston N.E.	42	18	11	13	76	74	47
Aston Villa	42	18	9	15	67	53	45
Sunderland	42	18	8	16	65	66	44
Everton	42	17	9	16	62	67	43
Middlesbrough	42	17	8	17	73	68	42
Portsmouth	42	16	9	17	66	60	41
Arsenal	42	16	9	17	72	70	41
Derby Co.	42	18	5	19	73	79	41
Chelsea	42	16	7	19	69	84	39
Grimsby T.	42	13	12	17	61	82	38
Blackburn R.	42	14	8	20	45	53	36
Bolton W.	42	13	8	21	57	69	34
Charlton Ath.	42	11	12	19	57	71	34
Huddersfield	42	13	7	22	53	79	33
Brentford	42	9	7	26	45	88	25
Leeds U.	42	6	6	30	45	90	18

DIVISION 2

	P	W	D	L	F	A	Pts.
Manchester C.	42	26	10	6	78	35	62
Burnley	42	22	14	6	65	29	58
Birmingham C.	42	25	5	12	74	33	55
Chesterfield	42	18	14	10	58	44	50
Newcastle U.	42	19	10	13	95	62	48
Tottenham H.	42	17	14	11	65	53	48
W.B.A.	42	20	8	14	88	75	48
Coventry C.	42	16	13	13	66	59	45
Leicester C.	42	18	7	17	69	64	43
Barnsley	42	17	8	17	84	86	42
Nottingham F.	42	15	10	17	69	74	40
West Ham U.	42	16	8	18	70	76	40
Luton T.	42	16	7	19	71	73	39
Southampton	42	15	9	18	69	76	39
Fulham	42	15	9	18	63	74	39
Bradford P.A.	42	14	11	17	65	77	39
Bury	42	12	12	18	80	78	36
Millwall	42	14	8	20	56	79	36
Plymouth Arg.	42	14	5	23	79	96	33
Sheffield W.	42	12	8	22	67	88	32
Swansea T.	42	11	7	24	55	83	29
Newport Co.	42	10	3	29	61	133	23

DIVISION 3 (SOUTH)

	P	W	D	L	F	A	Pts.
Cardiff C.	42	30	6	6	93	30	66
Q.P.R.	42	23	11	8	74	40	57
Bristol C.	42	20	11	11	94	56	51
Swindon T.	42	19	11	12	84	73	49
Walsall	42	17	12	13	74	59	46
Ipswich T.	42	16	14	12	61	53	46
Bournemouth	42	18	8	16	72	54	44
Southend U.	42	17	10	15	71	60	44
Reading	42	16	11	15	83	74	43
Port Vale	42	17	9	16	68	63	43
Torquay U.	42	15	12	15	52	61	42
Notts. Co.	42	15	10	17	63	63	40
Northampton	42	15	10	17	72	75	40
Bristol R.	42	16	8	18	59	69	40
Exeter C.	42	15	9	18	60	69	39
Watford	42	17	5	20	61	76	39
Brighton	42	13	12	17	54	72	38
C. Palace	42	13	11	18	49	62	37
Leyton O.	42	12	8	22	54	75	32
Aldershot	42	10	12	20	48	78	32
Norwich C.	42	10	8	24	64	100	28
Mansfield T.	42	9	10	23	48	96	28

DIVISION 3 (NORTH)

	P	W	D	L	F	A	Pts.
Doncaster R.	42	33	6	3	123	40	72
Rotherham U.	42	29	6	7	114	53	64
Chester	42	25	6	11	95	51	56
Stockport Co.	42	24	2	16	78	53	50
Bradford C.	42	20	10	12	62	47	50
Rochdale	42	19	10	13	80	64	48
Wrexham	42	17	12	13	65	51	46
Crew Alex.	42	17	9	16	70	74	43
Barrow	42	17	7	18	54	62	41
Tranmere R.	42	17	7	18	66	77	41
Hull C.	42	16	8	18	49	53	40
Lincoln C.	42	17	5	20	86	87	39
Hortlepools U.	42	15	9	18	64	73	39
Gateshead	42	16	6	20	62	72	38
York C.	42	14	9	19	67	81	37
Carlisle U.	42	14	9	19	70	93	37
Darlington	42	15	6	21	68	80	36
New Brighton	42	14	8	20	57	77	36
Oldham Ath.	42	12	8	22	55	80	32
Accrington S.	42	14	4	24	56	92	32
Southport	42	7	11	24	53	85	25
Halifax T.	42	8	6	28	43	92	22

FOOTBALL LEAGUE TABLES 1947–48

DIVISION 1

	P	W	D	L	F	A	Pts.
Arsenal	42	23	13	6	81	32	59
Manchester U.	42	19	14	9	81	48	52
Burnley	42	20	12	10	56	43	52
Derby Co.	42	19	12	11	77	57	50
Wolverhampton W.	42	19	9	14	83	70	47
Aston Villa	42	19	9	14	65	57	47
Preston N.E.	42	20	7	15	67	68	47
Portsmouth	42	19	7	16	68	50	45
Blackpool	42	17	10	15	57	41	44
Manchester C.	42	15	12	15	52	47	42
Liverpool	42	16	10	16	65	61	42
Sheffield U.	42	16	10	16	65	70	42
Charlton Ath.	42	17	6	19	57	66	40
Everton	42	17	6	19	52	66	40
Stoke C.	42	14	10	18	41	55	38
Middlesbrough	42	14	9	19	71	73	37
Bolton W.	42	16	5	21	46	58	37
Chelsea	42	14	9	19	53	71	37
Huddersfield	42	12	12	18	51	60	36
Sunderland	42	13	10	19	56	67	36
Blackburn R.	42	11	10	21	54	72	32
Grimsby T.	42	8	6	28	45	111	22

DIVISION 2

	P	W	D	L	F	A	Pts.
Birmingham C.	42	22	15	5	55	24	59
Newcastle U.	42	24	8	10	72	41	56
Southampton	42	21	10	11	71	53	52
Sheffield W.	42	20	11	11	66	53	51
Cardiff C.	42	18	11	13	61	58	47
West Ham U.	42	16	14	12	55	53	46
W.B.A.	42	18	9	15	63	58	45
Tottenham H.	42	15	14	13	56	43	44
Leicester C.	42	16	11	15	60	57	43
Coventry C.	42	14	13	15	59	52	41
Fulham	42	15	10	17	47	46	40
Barnsley	42	15	10	17	62	64	40
Luton T.	42	14	12	16	56	59	40
Bradford P.A.	42	16	8	18	68	72	40
Brentford	42	13	14	15	44	61	40
Chesterfield	42	16	7	19	54	55	39
Plymouth Arg.	42	9	20	13	40	58	38
Leeds U.	42	14	8	20	62	72	36
Nottingham F.	42	12	11	19	54	60	35
Bury	42	9	16	17	58	68	34
Doncaster R.	42	9	11	22	40	66	29
Millwall	42	9	11	22	44	74	29

DIVISION 3 (SOUTH)

	P	W	D	L	F	A	Pts.
Q.P.R.	42	26	9	7	74	37	61
Bournemouth	42	24	9	9	76	35	57
Walsall	42	21	9	12	70	40	51
Ipswich T.	42	23	3	16	67	61	49
Swansea T.	42	18	12	12	70	52	48
Notts. Co.	42	19	8	15	68	59	46
Bristol C.	42	18	7	17	77	65	43
Port Vale	42	16	11	15	63	54	43
Southend U.	42	15	13	14	51	58	43
Reading	42	15	11	16	56	58	41
Exeter C.	42	15	11	16	55	63	41
Newport Co.	42	14	13	15	61	73	41
C. Palace	42	13	13	16	49	49	39
Northampton	42	14	11	17	58	72	39
Watford	42	14	10	18	57	79	38
Swindon T.	42	10	16	16	41	46	36
Leyton O.	42	13	10	19	51	73	36
Torquay U.	42	11	13	18	63	62	35
Aldershot	42	10	15	17	45	67	35
Bristol R.	42	13	8	21	71	75	34
Norwich C.	42	13	8	21	61	76	34
Brighton	42	11	12	19	43	73	34

DIVISION 3 (NORTH)

	P	W	D	L	F	A	Pts.
Lincoln C.	42	26	8	8	81	40	60
Rotherham U.	42	25	9	8	95	49	59
Wrexham	42	21	8	13	74	54	50
Gateshead	42	19	11	12	75	57	49
Hull C.	42	18	11	13	59	48	47
Accrington S.	42	20	6	16	62	59	46
Barrow	42	16	13	13	49	40	45
Mansfield T.	42	17	11	14	57	51	45
Carlisle U.	42	18	7	17	88	77	43
Crewe Alex.	42	18	7	17	61	63	43
Oldham Ath.	42	14	13	15	63	64	41
Rochdale	42	15	11	16	48	72	41
York C.	42	13	14	15	65	60	40
Bradford C.	42	15	10	17	65	66	40
Southport	42	14	11	17	60	63	39
Darlington	42	13	13	16	54	70	39
Stockport Co.	42	13	12	17	63	67	38
Tranmere R.	42	16	4	22	54	72	36
Hartlepools U.	42	14	8	20	51	73	36
Chester	42	13	9	20	64	67	35
Halifax T.	42	7	13	22	43	76	27
New Brighton	42	8	9	25	38	81	25

FOOTBALL LEAGUE TABLES 1948–49

DIVISION 1

	P	W	D	L	F	A	Pts.
Portsmouth	42	25	8	9	84	42	58
Manchester U.	42	21	11	10	77	44	53
Derby Co.	42	22	9	11	74	55	53
Newcastle U.	42	20	12	10	70	56	52
Arsenal	42	18	13	11	74	44	49
Wolverhampton W.	42	17	12	13	79	66	46
Manchester C.	42	15	15	12	47	51	45
Sunderland	42	13	17	12	49	58	43
Charlton Ath.	42	15	12	15	63	67	42
Aston Villa	42	16	10	16	60	76	42
Stoke C.	42	16	9	17	66	68	41
Liverpool	42	13	14	15	53	43	40
Chelsea	42	12	14	16	69	68	38
Bolton W.	42	14	10	18	59	68	38
Burnley	42	12	14	16	43	50	38
Blackpool	42	11	16	15	54	67	38
Birmingham C.	42	11	15	16	36	38	37
Everton	42	13	11	18	41	63	37
Middlesbrough	42	11	12	19	46	57	34
Huddersfield	42	12	10	20	40	69	34
Preston N.E.	42	11	11	20	62	75	33
Sheffield U.	42	11	11	20	57	78	33

DIVISION 2

	P	W	D	L	F	A	Pts.
Fulham	42	24	9	9	77	37	57
W.B.A.	42	24	8	10	69	39	56
Southampton	42	23	9	10	69	36	55
Cardiff C.	42	19	13	10	62	47	51
Tottenham H.	42	17	16	9	72	44	50
Chesterfield	42	15	17	10	51	45	47
West Ham U.	42	18	10	14	56	58	46
Sheffield W.	42	15	13	14	63	56	43
Barnsley	42	14	12	16	62	61	40
Luton T.	42	14	12	16	55	57	40
Grimsby T.	42	15	10	17	72	76	40
Bury	42	17	6	19	67	76	40
Q.P.R.	42	14	11	17	44	62	39
Blackburn R.	42	15	8	19	53	63	38
Leeds U.	42	12	13	17	55	63	37
Coventry C.	42	15	7	20	55	64	37
Bradford P.A.	42	13	11	18	65	78	37
Brentford	42	11	14	17	42	53	36
Leicester C.	42	10	16	16	62	79	36
Plymouth Arg.	42	12	12	18	49	64	36
Nottingham F.	42	14	7	21	50	54	35
Lincoln C.	42	8	12	22	53	91	28

DIVISION 3 (SOUTH)

	P	W	D	L	F	A	Pts.
Swansea T.	42	27	8	7	87	34	62
Reading	42	25	5	12	77	50	55
Bournemouth	42	22	8	12	69	48	52
Swindon T.	42	18	15	9	64	56	51
Bristol R.	42	19	10	13	61	51	48
Brighton	42	15	18	9	55	55	48
Ipswich T.	42	18	9	15	78	77	45
Millwall	42	17	11	14	63	64	45
Torquay U.	42	17	11	14	65	70	45
Norwich C.	42	16	12	14	67	49	44
Notts. Co.	42	19	5	18	102	68	43
Exeter C.	42	15	10	17	63	76	40
Port Vale	42	14	11	17	51	54	39
Walsall	42	15	8	19	56	64	38
Newport Co.	42	14	9	19	68	92	37
Bristol C.	42	11	14	17	44	62	36
Watford	42	10	15	17	41	54	35
Southend U.	42	9	16	17	41	46	34
Leyton O.	42	11	12	19	58	80	34
Northampton	42	12	9	21	51	62	33
Aldershot	42	11	11	20	48	59	33
C. Palace	42	8	11	23	38	76	27

DIVISION 3 (NORTH)

	P	W	D	L	F	A	Pts.
Hull C.	42	27	11	4	93	28	65
Rotherham U.	42	28	6	8	90	46	62
Doncaster R.	42	20	10	12	53	40	50
Darlington	42	20	6	16	83	74	46
Gateshead	42	16	13	13	69	58	45
Oldham Ath.	42	18	9	15	75	67	45
Rochdale	42	18	9	15	55	53	45
Stockport Co.	42	16	11	15	61	56	43
Wrexham	42	17	9	16	56	62	43
Mansfield T.	42	14	14	14	52	48	42
Tranmere R.	42	13	15	14	46	57	41
Crewe Alex.	42	16	9	17	52	74	41
Barrow	42	14	12	16	41	48	40
York C.	42	15	9	18	74	74	39
Carlisle U.	42	14	11	17	60	77	39
Hartlepools U.	42	14	10	18	45	58	38
New Brighton	42	14	8	20	46	58	36
Chester	42	11	13	18	57	56	35
Halifax T.	42	12	11	19	45	62	35
Accrington S.	42	12	10	20	55	64	34
Southport	42	11	9	22	45	64	31
Bradford C.	42	10	9	23	48	77	29

FOOTBALL LEAGUE TABLES 1949–50

DIVISION 1

	P	W	D	L	F	A	Pts.
Portsmouth	42	22	9	11	74	38	53
Wolverhampton W.	42	20	13	9	76	49	53
Sunderland	42	21	10	11	83	62	52
Manchester U.	42	18	14	10	69	44	50
Newcastle U.	42	19	12	11	77	55	50
Arsenal	42	19	11	12	79	55	49
Blackpool	42	17	15	10	46	35	49
Liverpool	42	17	14	11	64	54	48
Middlesbrough	42	20	7	15	59	48	47
Burnley	42	16	13	13	40	40	45
Derby Co.	42	17	10	15	69	61	44
Aston Villa	42	15	12	15	61	61	42
Chelsea	42	12	16	14	58	65	40
W.B.A.	42	14	12	16	47	53	40
Huddersfield	42	14	9	19	52	73	37
Bolton W.	42	10	14	18	45	59	34
Fulham	42	10	14	18	41	54	34
Everton	42	10	14	18	42	66	34
Stoke C.	42	11	12	19	45	75	34
Charlton Ath.	42	13	6	23	53	65	32
Manchester C.	42	8	13	21	36	68	29
Birmingham C.	42	7	14	21	31	67	28

DIVISION 2

	P	W	D	L	F	A	Pts.
Tottenham H.	42	27	7	8	81	35	61
Sheffield W.	42	18	16	8	67	48	52
Sheffield U.	42	19	14	9	68	49	52
Southampton	42	19	14	9	64	48	52
Leeds U.	42	17	13	12	54	45	47
Preston N.E.	42	18	9	15	60	49	45
Hull C.	42	17	11	14	64	72	45
Swansea T.	42	17	9	16	53	49	43
Brentford	42	15	13	14	44	49	43
Cardiff C.	42	16	10	16	41	44	42
Grimsby T.	42	16	8	18	74	73	40
Coventry C.	42	13	13	16	55	55	39
Barnsley	42	13	13	16	64	67	39
Chesterfield	42	15	9	18	43	47	39
Leicester C.	42	12	15	15	55	65	39
Blackburn R.	42	14	10	18	55	60	38
Luton T.	42	10	18	14	41	51	38
Bury	42	14	9	19	60	65	37
West Ham U.	42	12	12	18	53	61	36
Q.P.R.	42	11	12	19	40	57	34
Plymouth Arg.	42	8	16	18	44	65	32
Bradford P.A.	42	10	11	21	51	77	31

DIVISION 3 (SOUTH)

	P	W	D	L	F	A	Pts.
Notts. Co.	42	25	8	9	95	50	58
Northampton	42	20	11	11	72	50	51
Southend U.	42	19	13	10	66	48	51
Nottingham F.	42	20	9	13	67	39	49
Torquay U.	42	19	10	13	66	63	48
Watford	42	16	13	13	45	35	45
C. Palace	42	15	14	13	55	54	44
Brighton	42	16	12	14	57	69	44
Bristol R.	42	19	5	18	51	51	43
Reading	42	17	8	17	70	64	42
Norwich C.	42	16	10	16	65	63	42
Bournemouth	42	16	10	16	57	56	42
Port Vale	42	15	11	16	47	42	41
Swindon T.	42	15	11	16	59	62	41
Bristol C.	42	15	10	17	60	61	40
Exeter C.	42	14	11	17	63	75	39
Ipswich T.	42	12	11	19	57	86	35
Leyton O.	42	12	11	19	53	85	35
Walsall	42	9	16	17	61	62	34
Aldershot	42	13	8	21	48	60	34
Newport Co.	42	13	8	21	67	98	34
Millwall	42	14	4	24	55	63	32

DIVISION 3 (NORTH)

	P	W	D	L	F	A	Pts.
Doncaster R.	42	19	17	6	66	38	55
Gateshead	42	23	7	12	87	54	53
Rochdale	42	21	9	12	68	41	51
Lincoln C.	42	21	9	12	60	39	51
Tranmere R.	42	19	11	12	51	48	49
Rotherham U.	42	19	10	13	80	59	48
Crewe Alex.	42	17	14	11	68	55	48
Mansfield T.	42	18	12	12	66	54	48
Carlisle U.	42	16	15	11	68	51	47
Stockport Co.	42	19	7	16	55	52	45
Oldham Ath.	42	16	11	15	58	63	43
Chester	42	17	6	19	70	79	40
Accrington S.	42	16	7	19	57	62	39
New Brighton	42	14	10	18	45	63	38
Barrow	42	14	9	19	47	53	37
Southport	42	12	13	17	51	71	37
Darlington	42	11	13	18	56	69	35
Hartlepools U.	42	14	5	23	52	79	33
Bradford C.	42	12	8	22	61	76	32
Wrexham	42	10	12	20	39	54	32
Halifax T.	42	12	8	22	58	85	32
York C.	42	9	13	20	52	70	31

FOOTBALL LEAGUE TABLES 1950–51

DIVISION 1

	P	W	D	L	F	A	Pts.
Tottenham H.	42	25	10	7	82	44	60
Manchester U.	42	24	8	10	74	40	56
Blackpool	42	20	10	12	79	53	50
Newcastle U.	42	18	13	11	62	53	49
Arsenal	42	19	9	14	73	56	47
Middlesbrough	42	18	11	13	76	65	47
Portsmouth	42	16	15	11	71	68	47
Bolton W.	42	19	7	16	64	61	45
Liverpool	42	16	11	15	53	59	43
Burnley	42	14	14	14	48	43	42
Derby Co.	42	16	8	18	81	75	40
Sunderland	42	12	16	14	63	73	40
Stoke C.	42	13	14	15	50	59	40
Wolverhampton W.	42	15	8	19	74	61	38
Aston Villa	42	12	13	17	66	68	37
W.B.A.	42	13	11	18	53	61	37
Charlton Ath.	42	14	9	19	63	80	37
Fulham	42	13	11	18	52	68	37
Huddersfield	42	15	6	21	64	92	36
Chelsea	42	12	8	22	53	65	32
Sheffield W.	42	12	8	22	64	83	32
Everton	42	12	8	22	48	86	32

DIVISION 2

	P	W	D	L	F	A	Pts.
Preston N.E.	42	26	5	11	91	49	57
Manchester C.	42	19	14	9	89	61	52
Cardiff C.	42	17	16	9	53	45	50
Birmingham C.	42	20	9	13	64	53	49
Leeds U.	42	20	8	14	63	55	48
Blackburn R.	42	19	8	15	65	66	46
Coventry C.	42	19	7	16	75	59	45
Sheffield U.	42	16	12	14	72	62	44
Brentford	42	18	8	16	75	74	44
Hull C.	42	16	11	15	74	70	43
Doncaster R.	42	15	13	14	64	68	43
Southampton	42	15	13	14	66	73	43
West Ham U.	42	16	10	16	68	69	42
Leicester C.	42	15	11	16	68	58	41
Barnsley	42	15	10	17	74	68	50
Q.P.R.	42	15	10	17	71	82	40
Notts. Co.	42	13	13	16	61	60	39
Swansea T.	42	16	4	22	54	77	36
Luton T.	42	9	14	19	57	70	32
Bury	42	12	8	22	60	86	32
Chesterfield	42	9	12	21	44	69	30
Grimsby T.	42	8	12	22	61	95	28

DIVISION 3 (SOUTH)

	P	W	D	L	F	A	Pts.
Nottingham F.	46	30	10	6	110	40	70
Norwich C.	46	25	14	7	82	45	64
Reading	46	21	15	10	88	53	57
Plymouth Arg.	46	24	9	13	85	55	57
Millwall	46	23	10	13	80	57	56
Bristol R.	46	20	15	11	64	42	55
Southend U.	46	21	10	15	92	69	52
Ipswich T.	46	23	6	17	69	58	52
Bournemouth	46	22	7	17	65	57	51
Bristol C.	46	20	11	15	64	59	51
Newport Co.	46	19	9	18	77	70	47
Port Vale	46	16	13	17	60	65	45
Brighton	46	13	17	16	71	79	43
Exeter C.	46	18	6	22	62	85	42
Walsall	46	15	10	21	52	62	40
Colchester U.	46	14	12	20	63	76	40
Swindon T.	46	18	4	24	55	67	40
Aldershot	46	15	10	21	56	88	40
Leyton O.	46	15	8	23	53	75	38
Torquay U.	46	14	9	23	64	81	37
Northampton	46	10	16	20	55	67	36
Gillingham	46	13	9	24	69	101	35
Watford	46	9	11	26	54	88	29
C. Palace	46	8	11	27	33	84	27

DIVISION 3 (NORTH)

	P	W	D	L	F	A	Pts.
Rotherham U.	46	31	9	6	103	41	71
Mansfield T.	46	26	12	8	78	48	64
Carlisle U.	46	25	12	9	79	50	62
Tranmere R.	46	21	11	11	83	62	59
Lincoln C.	46	25	8	13	89	58	58
Bradford P.A.	46	23	8	15	90	72	54
Bradford C.	46	21	10	15	90	63	52
Gateshead	46	21	8	17	84	62	50
Crewe Alex.	46	19	10	17	61	60	48
Stockport Co.	46	20	8	18	63	63	48
Rochdale	46	17	11	18	69	62	45
Scunthorpe U.	46	13	18	15	58	57	44
Chester	46	17	9	20	62	64	43
Wrexham	46	15	12	19	55	71	42
Oldham Ath.	46	16	8	22	73	73	40
Hartlepools U.	46	16	7	23	64	66	39
York C.	46	12	15	19	66	77	39
Darlington	46	13	13	20	59	77	39
Barrow	46	16	6	24	51	76	38
Shrewsbury T.	46	15	7	24	43	74	37
Southport	46	13	10	23	56	72	36
Halifax T.	46	11	12	23	50	69	34
Accrington S.	46	11	10	25	42	101	32
New Brighton	46	11	8	27	40	90	30

FOOTBALL LEAGUE TABLES 1951–52

DIVISION 1

	P	W	D	L	F	A	Pts.
Manchester U.	42	23	11	8	95	52	57
Tottenham H.	42	22	9	11	76	51	53
Arsenal	42	21	11	10	80	61	53
Portsmouth	42	20	8	14	68	58	48
Bolton W.	42	19	10	13	65	61	48
Aston Villa	42	19	9	14	79	70	47
Preston N.E.	42	17	12	13	74	54	46
Newcastle U.	42	18	9	15	98	73	45
Blackpool	42	18	9	15	64	64	45
Charlton Ath.	42	17	10	15	68	63	44
Liverpool	42	12	19	11	57	61	43
Sunderland	42	15	12	15	70	61	42
W.B.A.	42	14	13	15	74	77	41
Burnley	42	15	10	17	56	63	40
Manchester C.	42	13	13	16	58	61	39
Wolverhampton W.	42	12	14	16	73	73	38
Derby Co.	42	15	7	20	63	80	37
Middlesbrough	42	15	6	21	64	88	36
Chelsea	42	14	8	20	52	72	36
Stoke C.	42	12	7	23	49	88	31
Huddersfield	42	10	8	24	49	82	28
Fulham	42	8	11	23	58	77	27

DIVISION 2

	P	W	D	L	F	A	Pts.
Sheffield W.	42	21	11	10	100	66	53
Cardiff C.	42	20	11	11	72	54	51
Birmingham C.	42	21	9	12	67	56	51
Nottingham F.	42	18	13	11	77	62	49
Leicester C.	42	19	9	14	78	64	47
Leeds U.	42	18	11	13	59	57	47
Everton	42	17	10	15	64	58	44
Luton T.	42	16	12	14	77	78	44
Rotherham U.	42	17	8	17	73	71	42
Brentford	42	15	12	15	54	55	42
Sheffield U.	42	18	5	19	90	76	41
West Ham U.	42	15	11	16	67	77	41
Southampton	42	15	11	16	61	73	41
Blackburn R.	42	17	6	19	54	63	40
Notts. Co.	42	16	7	19	71	68	39
Doncaster R.	42	13	12	17	55	60	38
Bury	42	15	7	20	67	69	37
Hull C.	42	13	11	18	60	70	37
Swansea T.	42	12	12	18	72	76	36
Barnsley	42	11	14	17	59	72	36
Coventry C.	42	14	6	22	59	82	34
Q.P.R.	42	11	12	19	52	81	34

DIVISION 3 (SOUTH)

	P	W	D	L	F	A	Pts.
Plymouth Arg.	46	29	8	9	107	53	66
Reading	46	29	3	14	112	60	61
Norwich C.	46	26	9	11	89	50	61
Millwall	46	23	12	11	74	53	58
Brighton	46	24	10	12	87	63	58
Newport Co.	46	21	12	13	77	76	54
Bristol R.	46	20	12	14	89	53	52
Northampton	46	22	5	19	93	74	49
Southend U.	46	19	10	17	75	66	48
Colchester U.	46	17	12	17	56	77	46
Torquay U.	46	17	10	19	86	98	44
Aldershot	46	18	8	20	78	89	44
Port Vale	46	14	15	17	50	66	43
Bournemouth	46	16	10	20	69	75	42
Bristol C.	46	15	12	19	58	69	42
Swindon T.	46	14	14	18	51	68	42
Ipswich T.	46	16	9	21	63	74	41
Leyton O.	46	16	9	21	55	68	41
C. Palace	46	15	9	22	61	80	39
Shrewsbury T.	46	13	10	23	62	86	36
Watford	46	13	10	23	57	81	36
Gillingham	46	11	13	22	71	81	35
Exeter C.	46	13	9	24	65	86	35
Walsall	46	13	5	28	55	94	31

DIVISION 3 (NORTH)

	P	W	D	L	F	A	Pts.
Lincoln C.	46	30	9	7	121	52	69
Grimsby T.	46	29	8	9	96	45	66
Stockport Co.	46	23	13	10	74	40	59
Oldham Ath.	46	24	9	13	90	61	57
Gateshead	46	21	11	14	66	49	53
Mansfield T.	46	22	8	16	73	60	52
Carslile U.	46	19	13	14	62	57	51
Bradford P.A.	46	19	12	15	74	64	50
Hartlepools U.	46	21	8	17	71	65	50
York C.	46	18	13	15	73	52	49
Tranmere R.	46	21	6	19	76	71	48
Barrow	46	17	12	17	57	61	46
Chesterfield	46	17	11	18	65	66	45
Scunthorpe U.	46	14	16	16	65	74	44
Bradford C.	46	16	10	20	61	68	42
Crewe Alex.	46	17	8	21	63	82	42
Southport	46	15	11	20	53	71	41
Wrexham	46	15	9	22	63	73	39
Chester	46	15	9	22	72	85	39
Halifax T.	46	14	7	25	61	97	35
Rochdale	46	11	13	22	47	79	35
Accrington S.	46	10	12	24	61	92	32
Darlington	46	11	9	26	64	103	31
Workington T.	46	11	7	28	50	91	29

DIVISION 1

	P	W	D	L	F	A	Pts.
Arsenal	42	21	12	9	97	64	54
Preston N.E.	42	21	12	9	85	60	54
Wolverhampton W.	42	19	13	10	86	63	51
W.B.A.	42	21	8	13	66	60	50
Charlton Ath.	42	19	11	12	77	63	49
Burnley	42	18	12	12	67	52	48
Blackpool	42	19	9	14	71	70	47
Manchester U.	42	18	10	14	69	72	46
Sunderland	42	15	13	14	68	82	43
Tottenham H.	42	15	11	16	78	69	41
Aston Villa	42	14	13	15	63	61	41
Cardiff C.	42	14	12	16	54	46	40
Middlesbrough	42	14	11	17	70	77	39
Bolton W.	42	15	9	18	61	69	39
Portsmouth	42	14	10	18	74	83	38
Newcastle U.	42	14	9	19	59	70	37
Liverpool	42	14	8	20	61	82	36
Sheffield W.	42	12	11	19	62	72	35
Chelsea	42	12	11	19	56	66	35
Manchester C.	42	14	7	21	72	87	35
Stoke C.	42	12	10	20	53	66	34
Derby Co.	42	11	10	21	59	74	32

DIVISION 2

	P	W	D	L	F	A	Pts.
Sheffield U.	42	25	10	7	97	55	60
Huddersfield	42	24	10	8	84	33	58
Luton T.	42	22	8	12	84	49	52
Plymouth Arg.	42	20	9	13	65	60	49
Leicester C.	42	18	12	12	89	74	48
Birmingham C.	42	19	10	13	71	66	48
Nottingham F.	42	18	8	16	77	67	44
Fulham	42	17	10	15	81	71	44
Blackburn R.	42	18	8	16	68	65	44
Leeds U.	42	14	15	13	71	63	43
Swansea T.	42	15	12	15	78	81	42
Rotherham U.	42	16	9	17	75	74	41
Doncaster R.	42	12	16	14	58	64	40
West Ham U.	42	13	13	16	58	60	39
Lincoln C.	42	11	17	14	64	71	39
Everton	42	12	14	16	71	75	38
Brentford	42	13	11	18	59	76	37
Hull C.	42	14	8	20	57	69	36
Notts. Co.	42	14	8	20	60	88	36
Bury	42	13	9	20	53	81	35
Southampton	42	10	13	19	68	85	33
Barnsley	42	5	8	29	47	108	18

DIVISION 3 (SOUTH)

	P	W	D	L	F	A	Pts.
Bristol R.	46	26	12	8	92	46	64
Millwall	46	24	14	8	82	44	62
Northampton	46	26	10	10	109	70	62
Norwich C.	46	25	10	11	99	55	60
Bristol C.	46	22	15	9	95	61	59
Coventry C.	46	19	12	15	77	62	50
Brighton	46	19	12	15	81	75	50
Southend U.	46	18	13	15	69	74	49
Bournemouth	46	19	9	18	74	69	47
Watford	46	15	17	14	62	63	47
Reading	46	19	8	19	69	64	46
Torquay U.	46	18	9	19	87	88	45
C. Palace	46	15	13	18	66	82	43
Leyton O.	46	16	10	20	68	73	42
Newport Co.	46	16	10	20	70	82	42
Ipswich T.	46	13	15	18	60	69	41
Exeter C.	46	13	14	19	61	71	40
Swindon T.	46	14	12	20	64	79	40
Aldershot	46	12	15	19	61	77	39
Gillingham	46	12	15	19	55	74	39
Q.P.R.	46	12	15	19	61	82	39
Colchester U.	46	12	14	20	59	76	38
Shrewsbury T.	46	12	12	22	68	91	36
Walsall	46	7	10	29	56	118	24

DIVISION 3 (NORTH)

	P	W	D	L	F	A	Pts.
Oldham Ath.	46	22	15	9	77	45	59
Port Vale	46	20	18	8	67	35	58
Wrexham	46	24	8	14	86	66	56
York C.	46	20	13	13	60	45	53
Grimsby T.	46	21	10	15	75	59	52
Southport	46	20	11	15	63	60	51
Bradford P.A.	46	19	12	15	75	61	50
Gateshead	46	17	15	14	76	60	49
Carlisle U.	46	18	13	15	82	68	49
Crewe Alex.	46	20	8	18	70	68	48
Stockport Co.	46	17	13	16	82	69	47
Chesterfield*	46	18	11	17	65	63	47
Tranmere R.*	46	21	5	20	65	63	47
Halifax T.	46	16	15	15	68	68	47
Scunthorpe U.	46	14	16	16	62	56	46
Bradford C.	46	14	18	14	75	80	46
Hartlepools U.	46	16	14	16	57	61	46
Mansfield T.	46	16	14	16	55	62	46
Barrow	46	16	12	18	66	71	44
Chester	46	11	15	20	64	85	37
Darlington	46	14	6	26	58	96	34
Rochdale	46	14	5	27	62	83	33
Workington T.	46	11	10	25	55	91	32
Accrington S.	46	8	11	27	39	89	27

* Equal.

FOOTBALL LEAGUE TABLES 1953–54

DIVISION 1

	P	W	D	L	F	A	Pts.
Wolverhampton W.	42	25	7	10	96	56	57
W.B.A.	42	22	9	11	86	63	53
Huddersfield	42	20	11	11	78	61	51
Manchester U.	42	18	12	12	73	58	48
Bolton W.	42	18	12	12	75	60	48
Blackpool	42	19	10	13	80	69	48
Burnley	42	21	4	17	78	67	46
Chelsea	42	16	12	14	74	68	44
Charlton Ath.	42	19	6	17	75	77	44
Cardiff C.	42	18	8	16	51	71	44
Preston N.E.	42	19	5	18	87	58	43
Arsenal	42	15	13	14	75	73	43
Aston Villa	42	16	9	17	70	68	41
Portsmouth	42	14	11	17	81	89	39
Newcastle U.	42	14	10	18	72	77	38
Tottenham H.	42	16	5	21	65	76	37
Manchester C.	42	14	9	19	62	77	37
Sunderland	42	14	8	20	81	89	36
Sheffield W.	42	15	6	21	70	91	36
Sheffield U.	42	11	11	20	69	90	33
Middlesbrough	42	10	10	22	60	91	30
Liverpool	42	9	10	23	68	97	28

DIVISION 2

	P	W	D	L	F	A	Pts.
Leicester C.	42	23	10	9	97	60	56
Everton	42	20	16	6	92	58	56
Blackburn R.	42	23	9	10	86	50	55
Nottingham F.	42	20	12	10	86	59	52
Rotherham U.	42	21	7	14	80	67	49
Luton T.	42	18	12	12	64	59	48
Birmingham C.	42	18	11	13	78	58	47
Fulham	42	17	10	15	98	85	44
Bristol R.	42	14	16	12	64	58	44
Leeds U.	42	15	13	14	89	81	43
Stoke C.	42	12	17	13	71	60	41
Doncaster R.	42	16	9	17	59	63	41
West Ham U.	42	15	9	18	67	69	39
Notts. Co.	42	13	13	16	54	74	39
Hull C.	42	16	6	20	64	66	38
Lincoln C.	42	14	9	19	65	83	37
Bury	42	11	14	17	54	72	36
Derby Co.	42	12	11	19	64	82	35
Plymouth Arg.	42	9	16	17	65	82	34
Swansea T.	42	13	8	21	58	82	34
Brentford	42	10	11	21	40	78	31
Oldham Ath.	42	8	9	25	40	89	25

DIVISION 3 (SOUTH)

	P	W	D	L	F	A	Pts.
Ipswich T.	46	27	10	9	82	51	64
Brighton	46	26	9	11	86	61	61
Bristol C.	46	25	6	15	88	66	56
Watford	46	21	10	15	85	69	52
Northampton	46	20	11	15	82	55	51
Southampton	46	22	7	17	76	63	51
Norwich C.	46	20	11	15	73	66	51
Reading	46	20	9	17	86	73	49
Exeter C.	46	20	8	18	68	58	48
Gillingham	46	19	10	17	61	66	48
Leyton O.	46	18	11	17	79	73	47
Millwall	46	19	9	18	74	77	47
Torquay U.	46	17	12	17	81	88	46
Coventry C.	46	18	9	19	61	56	45
Newport Co.	46	19	6	21	61	81	44
Southend U.	46	18	7	21	69	71	43
Aldershot	46	17	9	20	74	86	43
Q.P.R.	46	16	10	20	60	68	42
Bournemouth*	46	16	8	22	67	70	40
Swindon T.*	46	15	10	21	67	70	40
Shrewsbury T.	46	14	12	20	65	76	40
C. Palace	46	14	12	20	60	86	40
Colchester U.	46	10	10	26	50	78	30
Walsall	46	9	8	29	40	87	26

DIVISION 3 (NORTH)

	P	W	D	L	F	A	Pts.
Port Vale	46	26	17	3	74	21	69
Barnsley	46	24	10	12	77	57	58
Scunthorpe U.	46	21	15	10	77	56	57
Gateshead	46	21	13	12	74	55	55
Bradford C.	46	22	9	15	60	55	53
Chesterfield	46	19	14	13	76	64	52
Mansfield T.	46	20	11	15	88	67	51
Wrexham	46	21	9	16	81	68	51
Bradford P.A.	46	18	14	14	77	68	50
Stockport Co.	46	18	11	17	77	67	47
Southport	46	17	12	17	63	60	46
Barrow	46	16	12	18	72	71	44
Carlisle U.	46	14	15	17	83	71	43
Tranmere R.	46	18	7	21	59	70	43
Accrington S.	46	16	10	20	66	74	42
Crewe Alex.	46	14	13	19	49	67	41
Grimsby T.	46	16	9	21	51	77	41
Hartlepools U.	46	13	14	19	59	65	40
Rochdale	46	15	10	21	59	77	40
Workington T.	46	13	14	19	59	80	40
Darlington	46	12	14	20	50	71	38
York C.	46	12	13	21	64	86	37
Halifax T.	46	12	10	24	44	73	34
Chester	46	11	10	25	48	67	32

* Equal.

FOOTBALL LEAGUE TABLES 1954–55

DIVISION 1

	P	W	D	L	F	A	Pts.
Chelsea	42	20	12	10	81	57	52
Wolverhampton W.	42	19	10	13	89	70	48
Portsmouth	42	18	12	12	74	62	48
Sunderland	42	15	18	9	64	54	48
Manchester U.	42	20	7	15	84	74	47
Aston Villa	42	20	7	15	72	73	47
Manchester C.	42	18	10	14	76	69	56
Newcastle U.	42	17	9	16	89	77	43
Arsenal	42	17	9	16	69	63	43
Burnley	42	17	9	16	51	48	43
Everton	42	16	10	16	62	68	42
Huddersfield	42	14	13	15	63	68	14
Sheffield U.	42	17	7	18	70	86	41
Preston N.E.	42	16	8	18	83	64	40
Charlton Ath.	42	15	10	17	76	75	40
Tottenham H.	42	16	8	18	72	73	40
W.B.A.	42	16	8	18	76	96	40
Bolton W.	42	13	13	16	62	69	39
Blackpool	42	14	10	18	60	64	38
Cardiff C.	42	13	11	18	62	76	37
Leicester C.	42	12	11	19	74	86	35
Sheffield W.	42	8	10	24	63	100	26

DIVISION 2

	P	W	D	L	F	A	Pts.
Birmingham C.	42	22	10	10	92	47	54
Luton T.	42	23	8	11	88	53	54
Rotherham U.	42	25	4	13	94	64	54
Leeds U.	42	23	7	12	70	53	53
Stoke C.	42	21	10	11	69	46	52
Blackburn R.	42	22	6	14	114	79	50
Notts. Co.	42	21	6	15	74	71	48
West Ham U.	42	18	10	14	74	70	46
Bristol R.	42	19	7	16	75	70	45
Swansea T.	42	17	9	16	86	83	43
Liverpool	42	16	10	16	92	96	42
Middlesbrough	42	18	6	18	73	82	42
Bury	42	15	11	16	77	72	41
Fulham	42	14	11	17	76	79	39
Nottingham F.	42	16	7	19	58	62	39
Lincoln C.	42	13	10	19	68	79	36
Port Vale	42	12	11	19	48	71	35
Doncaster R.	42	14	7	21	58	95	35
Hull C.	42	12	10	20	44	69	34
Plymouth Arg.	42	12	7	23	57	82	31
Ipswich T.	42	11	6	25	57	92	28
Derby Co.	42	7	9	26	53	82	23

DIVISION 3 (SOUTH)

	P	W	D	L	F	A	Pts.
Bristol C.	46	30	10	6	101	47	70
Leyton O.	46	26	9	11	89	47	61
Southampton	46	24	11	11	75	51	59
Gillingham	46	20	15	11	77	66	55
Millwall	46	20	11	15	72	68	51
Brighton	46	20	10	16	76	63	50
Watford	46	18	14	14	71	62	50
Torquay U.	46	18	12	16	82	82	48
Coventry C.	46	18	11	17	67	59	47
Southend U.	46	17	12	17	83	80	46
Brentford*	46	16	14	16	82	82	46
Norwich C.*	46	18	10	18	60	60	46
Northampton	46	19	8	19	73	81	46
Aldershot	46	16	13	17	75	71	45
Q.P.R.	46	15	14	17	69	75	44
Shrewsbury T.	46	16	10	20	70	78	42
Bournemouth	46	12	18	16	57	65	42
Reading	46	13	15	18	65	73	41
Newport Co.	46	11	16	19	60	73	38
C. Palace	46	11	16	19	52	80	38
Swindon T.	46	11	15	20	46	64	37
Exeter C.	46	11	15	20	47	73	37
Walsall	46	10	14	22	75	86	34
Colchester U.	46	9	13	24	53	91	31

DIVISION 3 (NORTH)

	P	W	D	L	F	A	Pts.
Barnsley	46	30	5	11	86	46	65
Accrington S.	46	25	11	10	96	67	61
Scunthorpe U.	46	23	12	11	81	53	58
York C.	46	24	10	12	92	63	58
Hartlepools U.	46	25	5	16	64	49	55
Chesterfield	46	24	6	16	81	70	54
Gateshead	46	20	12	14	65	69	52
Workington T.	46	18	14	14	68	55	50
Stockport Co.	46	18	12	16	84	70	48
Oldham Ath.	46	19	10	17	74	68	48
Southport	46	16	16	14	47	44	48
Rochdale	46	17	14	15	69	66	48
Mansfield T.	46	18	9	19	65	71	45
Halifax T.	46	15	13	18	63	67	43
Darlington	46	14	14	18	62	73	42
Bradford P.A.	46	15	11	20	56	70	41
Barrow	46	17	6	23	70	89	40
Wrexham	46	13	12	21	65	77	38
Tranmere R.	46	13	11	22	55	70	37
Carlisle U.	46	15	6	25	78	89	36
Bradford C.	46	13	10	23	47	55	36
Crewe Alex.	46	10	14	22	68	91	34
Grimsby T.	46	13	8	25	47	78	34
Chester	46	12	9	25	44	77	33

* Equal.

DIVISION 1

	P	W	D	L	F	A	Pts.
Manchester U.	42	25	10	7	83	51	60
Blackpool	42	20	9	13	86	62	49
Wolverhampton W.	42	20	9	13	89	65	49
Manchester C.	42	18	10	14	82	69	46
Arsenal	42	18	10	14	60	61	46
Birmingham C.	42	18	9	15	75	57	45
Burnley	42	18	8	16	64	54	44
Bolton W.	42	18	7	17	71	58	43
Sunderland	42	17	9	16	80	95	43
Luton T.	42	17	8	17	66	64	42
Newcastle U.	42	17	7	18	85	70	41
Portsmouth	42	16	9	17	78	85	41
W.B.A.	42	18	5	19	58	70	41
Charlton Ath.	42	17	6	19	75	81	40
Everton	42	15	10	17	55	69	40
Chelsea	42	14	11	17	64	77	39
Cardiff C.	42	15	9	18	55	69	39
Tottenham H.	42	15	7	20	61	71	37
Preston N.E.	42	14	8	20	73	72	36
Aston Villa	42	11	13	18	52	69	35
Huddersfield	42	14	7	21	54	83	35
Sheffield U.	42	12	9	21	63	77	33

DIVISION 2

	P	W	D	L	F	A	Pts.
Sheffield W.	42	21	13	8	101	62	55
Leeds U.	42	23	6	13	80	60	52
Liverpool	42	21	6	15	85	63	48
Blackburn R.	42	21	6	15	84	65	48
Leicester C.	42	21	6	15	94	78	48
Bristol R.	42	21	6	15	84	70	48
Nottingham F.	42	19	9	14	68	63	47
Lincoln C.	42	18	10	14	79	65	46
Fulham	42	20	6	16	89	79	46
Swansea T.	42	20	6	16	83	81	46
Bristol C.	42	19	7	16	80	64	45
Port Vale	42	16	13	13	60	58	45
Stoke C.	42	20	4	18	71	62	44
Middlesbrough	42	16	8	18	76	78	40
Bury	42	16	8	18	86	90	40
West Ham U.	42	14	11	17	74	69	39
Doncaster R.	42	12	11	19	69	96	35
Barnsley	42	11	12	19	47	84	34
Rotherham U.	42	12	9	21	56	75	33
Notts. Co.	42	11	9	22	55	82	31
Plymouth Arg.	42	10	8	24	54	87	28
Hull C.	42	10	6	26	53	97	26

DIVISION 3 (SOUTH)

	P	W	D	L	F	A	Pts.
Leyton O.	46	29	8	9	106	49	66
Brighton	46	29	7	10	112	50	65
Ipswich T.	46	25	14	7	106	60	64
Southend U.	46	21	11	14	88	80	53
Torquay U.	46	20	12	14	86	63	52
Brentford	46	19	14	13	69	66	52
Norwich C.	46	19	13	14	86	82	51
Coventry C.	46	20	9	17	73	60	49
Bournemouth	46	19	10	17	63	51	48
Gillingham	46	19	10	17	69	71	48
Northampton	46	20	7	19	67	71	47
Colchester U.	46	18	11	17	76	81	47
Shrewsbury T.	46	17	12	17	69	66	46
Southampton	46	18	8	20	91	81	44
Aldershot	46	12	16	18	70	90	40
Exeter C.	46	15	10	21	58	77	40
Reading	46	15	9	22	70	79	39
Q.P.R.	46	14	11	21	64	86	39
Newport Co.	46	15	9	22	58	79	39
Walsall	46	15	8	23	68	84	38
Watford	46	13	11	22	52	85	37
Millwall	46	15	6	25	83	100	36
C. Palace	46	12	10	24	54	83	34
Swindon T.	46	8	14	24	34	78	30

DIVISION 3 (NORTH)

	P	W	D	L	F	A	Pts.
Grimsby T.	46	31	6	9	76	29	68
Derby Co.	46	28	7	11	110	55	63
Accrington S.	46	25	9	12	92	57	59
Hartlepools U.	46	26	5	15	81	60	57
Southport	46	23	11	12	66	53	57
Chesterfield	46	25	4	17	94	66	54
Stockport Co.	46	21	9	16	90	61	51
Bradford C.	46	18	13	15	78	64	49
Scunthorpe U.	46	20	8	18	75	63	48
Workington T	46	19	9	18	75	63	47
York C.	46	19	9	18	85	72	47
Rochdale	46	17	13	16	66	84	47
Gateshead	46	17	11	18	77	84	45
Wrexham	46	16	10	20	66	73	42
Darlington	46	16	9	21	60	73	41
Tranmere R.	46	16	9	21	59	84	41
Chester	46	13	14	19	52	82	40
Mansfield T.	46	14	11	21	84	81	39
Halifax T.	46	14	11	21	66	76	39
Oldham Ath.	46	10	18	18	76	86	38
Carlisle U.	46	15	8	23	71	95	38
Barrow	46	12	9	25	61	83	33
Bradford P.A.	46	13	7	26	61	122	33
Crewe Alex.	46	9	10	27	50	105	28

FOOTBALL LEAGUE TABLES 1956–57

DIVISION 1

	P	W	D	L	F	A	Pts.
Manchester U.	42	28	8	6	103	54	64
Tottenham H.	42	22	12	8	104	56	56
Preston N.E.	42	23	10	9	84	56	56
Blackpool	42	22	9	11	93	65	53
Arsenal	42	21	8	13	85	69	50
Wolverhampton W.	42	20	8	14	94	70	48
Burnley	42	18	10	14	56	50	46
Leeds U.	42	15	14	13	72	63	44
Bolton W.	42	16	12	14	65	65	44
Aston Villa	42	14	15	13	65	55	43
W.B.A.	42	14	14	14	59	61	42
Birmingham C.*	42	15	9	18	69	69	39
Chelsea*	42	13	13	16	73	73	39
Sheffield W.	42	16	6	20	82	88	38
Everton	42	14	10	18	61	79	38
Luton T.	42	14	9	19	58	76	37
Newcastle U.	42	14	8	20	67	87	36
Manchester C.	42	13	9	20	78	88	35
Portsmouth	42	10	13	19	62	92	33
Sunderland	42	12	8	22	67	88	32
Cardiff C.	42	10	9	23	53	88	29
Charlton Ath.	42	9	4	29	62	120	22

* Equal.

DIVISION 2

	P	W	D	L	F	A	Pts.
Leicester C.	42	25	11	6	109	67	61
Nottingham F.	42	22	10	10	94	55	54
Liverpool	42	21	11	10	82	54	53
Blackburn R.	42	21	10	11	83	75	52
Stoke C.	42	20	8	14	83	58	48
Middlesbrough	42	19	10	13	84	60	48
Sheffield U.	42	19	8	15	87	76	46
West Ham U.	42	19	8	15	59	63	46
Bristol R.	42	18	9	15	81	67	45
Swansea T.	42	19	7	16	90	90	45
Fulham	42	19	4	19	84	76	42
Huddersfield	42	18	6	18	68	74	42
Bristol C.	42	16	9	17	74	79	41
Doncaster R.	42	15	10	17	77	77	40
Leyton O.	42	15	10	17	66	84	40
Grimsby T.	42	17	5	20	61	62	39
Rotherham U.	42	13	11	18	74	75	37
Lincoln C.	42	14	6	22	54	80	34
Barnsley	42	12	10	20	59	89	34
Notts. Co.	42	9	12	21	58	86	30
Bury	42	8	9	25	60	96	25
Port Vale	42	8	6	28	57	101	22

DIVISION 3 (SOUTH)

	P	W	D	L	F	A	Pts.
Ipswich T.	46	25	9	12	101	54	59
Torquay U.	46	24	11	11	89	64	59
Colchester U.	46	22	14	10	84	56	58
Southampton	46	22	10	14	76	52	54
Bournemouth	46	19	14	13	88	62	52
Brighton	46	19	14	13	86	65	52
Southend U.	46	18	12	16	73	65	48
Brentford	46	16	16	14	78	76	48
Shrewsbury T.	46	15	18	13	72	79	48
Q.P.R.	46	18	11	17	61	60	47
Watford	46	18	10	18	72	75	46
Newport Co.	46	16	13	17	65	62	45
Reading	46	18	9	19	80	81	45
Northampton	46	18	9	19	66	73	45
Walsall	46	16	12	18	80	74	44
Coventry C.	46	16	12	18	74	84	44
Millwall	46	16	12	18	64	84	44
Plymouth Arg.	46	16	11	19	68	73	43
Aldershot	46	15	12	19	79	92	42
C. Palace	46	11	18	17	62	75	40
Exeter C.	46	12	13	21	61	79	37
Gillingham	46	12	13	21	54	85	37
Swindon T.	46	15	6	25	66	96	36
Norwich C.	46	8	15	23	61	94	31

DIVISION 3 (NORTH)

	P	W	D	L	F	A	Pts.
Derby Co.	46	26	11	9	111	53	63
Hartlepools U.	46	25	9	12	90	63	59
Accrington S.	46	25	8	13	95	64	58
Workington T.	46	24	10	12	93	63	58
Stockport Co.	46	23	8	15	91	75	54
Chesterfield	46	22	9	15	96	79	53
York C.	46	21	10	15	75	61	52
Hull C.	46	21	10	15	84	69	52
Bradford C.	46	22	8	16	78	68	52
Barrow	46	21	9	16	76	62	51
Halifax T.	46	21	7	18	65	70	49
Wrexham	46	19	10	17	97	74	48
Rochdale	46	18	12	16	65	65	48
Scunthorpe U.	46	15	15	16	71	69	45
Carlisle U.	46	16	13	17	76	85	45
Mansfield T.	46	17	10	19	91	90	44
Gateshead	46	17	10	19	72	90	44
Darlington	46	17	8	21	82	95	42
Oldham Ath.	46	12	15	19	66	74	39
Bradford P.A.	46	16	3	27	66	93	35
Chester	46	10	13	23	55	84	33
Southport	46	10	12	24	52	94	32
Tranmere R.	46	7	13	26	51	91	27
Crewe Alex.	46	6	9	31	43	110	21

FOOTBALL LEAGUE TABLES 1957–58

DIVISION 1

	P	W	D	L	F	A	Pts.
Wolverhampton W.	42	28	8	6	103	47	64
Preston N.E.	42	26	7	9	100	51	59
Tottenham H.	42	21	9	12	93	77	51
W.B.A.	42	18	14	10	92	70	50
Manchester C.	42	22	5	15	104	100	49
Burnley	42	21	5	16	80	74	47
Blackpool	42	19	6	17	80	67	44
Luton T.	42	19	6	17	69	63	44
Manchester U.	42	16	11	15	85	75	43
Nottingham F.	42	16	10	16	69	63	42
Chelsea	42	15	12	15	83	79	42
Arsenal	42	16	7	19	73	85	39
Birmingham C.	42	14	11	17	76	89	39
Aston Villa	42	16	7	19	73	86	39
Bolton W.	42	14	10	18	65	87	38
Everton	42	13	11	18	65	75	37
Leeds U.	42	14	9	19	51	63	37
Leicester C.	42	14	5	23	91	112	33
Newcastle U.	42	12	8	22	73	81	32
Portsmouth	42	12	8	22	73	88	32
Sunderland	42	10	12	20	54	97	32
Sheffield W.	42	12	7	23	69	92	31

DIVISION 2

	P	W	D	L	F	A	Pts.
West Hanm U.	42	23	11	8	101	54	57
Blackburn R.	42	22	12	8	93	57	56
Charlton Ath.	42	24	7	11	107	69	55
Liverpool	42	22	10	10	79	54	54
Fulham	42	20	12	10	97	59	52
Sheffield U.	42	21	10	11	75	50	52
Middlesbrough	42	19	7	16	83	74	45
Ipswich T.	42	16	12	14	68	69	44
Huddersfield	42	14	16	12	63	66	44
Bristol R.	42	17	8	17	85	80	42
Stoke C.	42	18	6	18	75	73	42
Leyton O.	42	18	5	19	77	79	41
Grimsby T.	42	17	6	19	86	83	40
Barnsley	42	14	12	16	70	74	40
Cardiff C.	42	14	9	19	63	77	37
Derby Co.	42	14	8	20	60	81	36
Bristol C.	42	13	9	20	63	88	35
Rotherham U.	42	14	5	23	65	101	33
Swansea T.	42	11	9	22	72	99	31
Lincoln C.	42	11	9	22	55	82	31
Notts. Co.	42	12	6	24	44	80	30
Doncaster R.	42	8	11	23	56	88	27

DIVISION 3 (SOUTH)

	P	W	D	L	F	A	Pts.
Brighton	46	24	12	10	88	64	60
Brentford	46	24	10	12	82	56	58
Plymouth Arg.	46	25	8	13	67	48	58
Swindon T.	46	21	15	10	79	50	57
Reading	46	21	13	12	79	51	55
Southampton	46	22	10	14	112	72	54
Southend U.	46	21	12	13	90	58	54
Norwich C.	46	19	15	12	75	70	53
Bournemouth	46	21	9	16	81	74	51
Q.P.R.	46	18	14	14	64	65	50
Newport Co.	46	17	14	15	73	67	48
Colchester U.	46	17	13	16	77	79	47
Northampton	46	19	6	21	87	79	44
C. Palace	46	15	13	18	70	72	43
Port Vale	46	16	10	20	67	58	42
Watford	46	13	16	17	59	77	42
Shrewsbury T.	46	15	10	21	49	71	40
Aldershot	46	12	16	18	59	89	40
Coventry C.	46	13	13	20	61	81	39
Walsall	46	14	9	23	61	75	37
Torquay U.	46	12	13	22	49	74	35
Gillingham	46	13	9	24	52	81	35
Millwall	46	11	9	26	63	91	31
Exeter C.	46	11	9	26	57	99	31

DIVISION 3 (NORTH)

	P	W	D	L	F	A	Pts.
Scunthorpe U.	46	29	8	9	88	50	66
Accrington S.	46	25	9	12	83	61	59
Bradford C.	46	21	15	10	73	49	57
Bury	46	23	10	13	94	62	56
Hull C.	46	19	15	12	78	67	53
Mansfield T.	46	22	8	16	100	92	52
Halifax T.	46	20	11	15	83	69	51
Chesterfield	46	18	15	13	71	69	51
Stockport Co.	46	18	11	17	74	67	47
Rochdale	46	19	8	19	79	67	46
Tranmere R.	46	18	10	18	82	76	46
Wrexham	46	17	12	17	61	63	46
York C.	46	17	12	17	68	76	46
Gateshead	46	15	15	16	68	76	45
Oldham Ath.	46	14	17	15	72	84	45
Carlisle U.	46	19	6	21	80	78	44
Hartlepools U.	46	16	12	18	73	76	44
Barrow	46	13	15	18	66	74	41
Workington T.	46	14	13	19	72	81	41
Darlington	46	17	7	22	78	89	41
Chester	46	13	13	20	73	81	39
Bradford P.A.	46	13	11	22	68	95	37
Southport	46	11	6	29	52	88	28
Crewe Alex.	46	8	7	31	47	93	23

FOOTBALL LEAGUE TABLES 1958–59

DIVISION 1

	P	W	D	L	F	A	Pts.
Wolverhampton W.	42	28	5	9	110	49	61
Manchester U.	42	24	7	11	103	66	55
Arsenal	42	21	8	13	88	68	50
Bolton W.	42	20	10	12	79	66	50
W.B.A.	42	18	13	11	88	68	49
West Ham U.	42	21	6	15	85	70	48
Burnley	42	19	10	13	81	70	48
Blackpool	42	18	11	13	66	49	47
Birmingham C.	42	20	6	16	84	68	46
Blackburn R.	42	17	10	15	76	70	44
Newcastle U.	42	17	7	18	80	80	41
Preston N.E.	42	17	7	18	70	77	41
Nottingham F.	42	17	6	19	71	74	40
Chelsea	42	18	4	20	77	98	40
Leeds U.	42	15	9	18	57	74	39
Everton	42	17	4	21	71	87	38
Luton T.	42	12	13	17	68	71	37
Tottenham H.	42	13	10	19	85	95	36
Leicester C.	42	11	10	21	67	98	32
Manchester C.	42	11	9	22	64	95	31
Aston Villa	42	11	8	23	58	87	30
Portsmouth	42	6	9	27	64	112	21

DIVISION 2

	P	W	D	L	F	A	Pts.
Sheffield W.	42	28	6	8	106	48	62
Fulham	42	27	6	9	96	61	60
Sheffield U.	42	23	7	12	82	48	53
Liverpool	42	24	5	13	87	62	53
Stoke C.	42	21	7	14	72	58	49
Bristol R.	42	18	12	12	80	64	48
Derby Co.	42	20	8	14	74	71	48
Charlton Ath.	42	18	7	17	92	90	43
Cardiff C.	42	18	7	17	65	65	43
Bristol C.	42	17	7	18	74	70	41
Swansea T.	42	16	9	17	79	81	41
Brighton	42	15	11	16	74	90	41
Middlesbrough	42	15	10	17	87	71	40
Huddersfield	42	16	8	18	62	55	40
Sunderland	42	16	8	18	64	75	40
Ipswich T.	42	17	6	19	62	77	40
Leyton O.	42	14	8	20	71	78	36
Scunthorpe U.	42	12	9	21	55	84	33
Lincoln C.	42	11	7	24	63	93	29
Rotherham U.	42	10	9	23	42	82	29
Grimsby T.	42	9	10	23	62	90	28
Barnsley	42	10	7	25	55	91	27

DIVISION 3

	P	W	D	L	F	A	Pts.
Plymouth Arg.	46	23	16	7	89	59	62
Hull C.	46	26	9	11	90	55	61
Brentford	46	21	15	10	76	49	57
Norwich C.	46	22	13	11	89	62	57
Colchester U.	46	21	10	15	71	67	52
Reading	46	21	8	17	78	63	50
Tranmere R.	46	21	8	17	82	67	50
Southend U.	46	21	8	17	85	80	50
Halifax T.	46	21	8	17	80	77	50
Bury	46	17	14	15	69	58	48
Bradford C.	46	18	11	17	84	76	47
Bournemouth	46	17	12	17	69	69	46
Q.P.R.	49	19	8	19	74	77	46
Southampton	46	17	11	18	88	80	45
Swindon T.	46	16	13	17	59	57	45
Chesterfield	46	17	10	19	67	64	44
Newport Co.	46	17	9	20	69	68	43
Wrexham	46	14	14	18	63	77	42
Accrington S.	46	15	12	19	71	87	42
Mansfield T.	46	14	13	19	73	98	41
Stockport Co.	46	13	10	23	65	78	36
Doncaster R.	46	14	5	27	50	90	33
Notts. Co.	46	8	13	25	55	96	29
Rochdale	46	8	12	26	37	79	28

DIVISION 4

	P	W	D	L	F	A	Pts.
Port Vale	46	26	12	8	110	58	64
Coventry C.	46	24	12	10	84	47	60
York C.	46	21	18	7	73	52	60
Shrewsbury T.	46	24	10	12	101	63	58
Exeter C.	46	23	11	12	87	61	57
Walsall	46	21	10	15	95	64	52
C. Palace	46	20	12	14	90	71	52
Northampton	46	21	9	16	85	78	51
Millwall	46	20	10	16	76	69	50
Carlisle U.	46	19	12	15	62	65	50
Gillingham	46	20	9	17	82	77	49
Torquay U.	46	16	12	18	78	77	44
Chester	46	16	12	18	72	84	44
Bradford C.	46	18	7	21	75	77	43
Watford	46	16	10	20	18	79	42
Darlington	46	13	16	17	66	68	42
Workington T.	46	12	17	17	63	78	41
Crewe Alex.	46	15	10	21	70	82	40
Hartlepools U.	46	15	10	21	74	88	40
Gateshead	46	16	8	22	56	85	40
Oldham Ath.	46	16	4	26	59	84	36
Aldershot	46	14	7	25	63	97	35
Barrow	46	9	10	27	51	104	28
Southport	46	7	12	27	41	86	26

FOOTBALL LEAGUE TABLES 1959–60

DIVISION 1

	P	W	D	L	F	A	Pts.
Burnley	42	24	7	11	85	61	55
Wolverhampton W.	42	24	6	12	106	67	54
Tottenham H.	42	21	11	10	86	50	53
W.B.A.	42	19	11	12	83	57	49
Sheffield W.	42	19	11	12	80	59	49
Bolton W.	42	20	8	14	59	51	48
Manchester U.	42	19	7	16	102	80	45
Newcastle U.	42	18	8	16	82	78	44
Preston N.E.	42	16	12	14	79	76	44
Fulham	42	17	10	15	73	80	44
Blackpool	42	15	10	17	59	71	40
Leicester C.	42	13	13	16	66	75	39
Arsenal	42	15	9	18	68	80	39
West Ham U.	42	16	6	20	75	91	38
Manchester C.	42	17	3	22	78	84	37
Everton	42	13	11	18	73	78	37
Blackburn R.	42	16	5	21	60	70	37
Chelsea	42	14	9	19	76	91	37
Birmingham C.	42	13	10	19	63	80	36
Nottingham F.	42	13	9	20	50	74	35
Leeds U.	42	12	10	20	65	92	34
Luton T.	42	9	12	21	50	73	30

DIVISION 2

	P	W	D	L	F	A	Pts.
Aston Villa	42	25	9	8	89	43	59
Cardiff C.	42	23	12	7	90	62	58
Liverpool	42	20	10	12	90	66	50
Sheffield U.	42	19	12	11	68	51	50
Middlesbrough	42	19	10	13	90	64	48
Huddersfield T.	42	19	9	14	73	52	47
Charlton Ath.	42	17	13	12	90	87	47
Rotherham U	42	17	13	12	61	60	47
Bristol R.	42	18	11	13	72	78	47
Leyton O.	42	15	14	13	76	61	44
Ipswich T.	42	19	6	17	78	68	44
Swansea T.	42	15	10	17	82	84	40
Lincoln C.	42	16	7	19	75	78	39
Brighton	42	13	12	17	67	76	38
Scunthorpe U.	42	13	10	19	57	71	36
Sunderland	42	12	12	18	52	65	36
Stoke C.	42	14	7	21	66	83	35
Derby Co.	42	14	7	21	61	77	35
Plymouth Arg.	42	13	9	20	61	89	35
Portsmouth	42	10	12	20	59	77	32
Hull C.	42	10	10	22	48	76	30
Bristol C.	42	11	5	26	60	97	27

DIVISION 3

	P	W	D	L	F	A	Pts.
Southampton	46	26	9	11	106	75	61
Norwich C.	46	24	11	11	82	54	59
Shrewsbury T.	46	18	16	12	97	75	52
Coventry C.	46	21	10	15	78	63	52
Grimsby T.	46	18	16	12	87	70	52
Brentford	46	21	9	16	78	61	51
Bury	46	21	9	16	64	51	51
Q.P.R.	46	18	13	15	73	54	49
Colchester U.	46	18	11	17	83	74	47
Bournemouth	46	17	13	16	72	72	47
Reading	46	18	10	18	84	77	46
Southend U.	46	19	8	19	76	74	46
Newport Co.	46	20	6	20	80	79	46
Port Vale	46	19	8	19	80	79	46
Halifax T.	46	18	10	18	70	72	46
Swindon T.	46	19	8	19	69	78	46
Barnsley	46	15	14	17	65	66	44
Chesterfield	46	18	7	21	71	84	43
Bradford C.	46	15	12	19	66	74	42
Tranmere R.	46	14	13	19	72	75	41
York C.	46	13	12	21	57	73	38
Mansfield T.	46	15	6	25	81	112	36
Wrexham	46	14	8	24	68	101	36
Accrington S.	46	11	5	30	57	123	27

DIVISION 4

	P	W	D	L	F	A	Pts.
Walsall	46	28	9	9	102	60	65
Notts. C.	46	26	8	12	107	69	60
Torquay U.	46	26	8	12	84	58	60
Watford	46	24	9	13	92	67	57
Millwall	46	18	17	11	84	61	53
Northampton T.	46	22	9	15	85	63	53
Gillingham	46	21	10	15	74	69	52
C. Palace	46	19	12	15	84	64	50
Exeter C.	46	19	11	16	80	70	49
Stockport Co.	46	19	11	16	58	54	49
Bradford	46	17	15	14	70	68	49
Rochdale	46	18	10	18	65	60	46
Aldershot	46	18	9	19	77	74	45
Crewe Alex.	46	18	9	19	79	88	45
Darlington	46	17	9	20	63	73	43
Workington T.	46	14	14	18	68	60	42
Doncaster R.	46	16	10	20	69	76	42
Barrow	46	15	11	20	77	87	41
Carlisle U.	46	15	11	20	51	66	41
Chester	46	14	12	20	59	77	40
Southport	46	10	14	22	48	92	34
Gateshead	46	12	9	25	58	86	33
Oldham Ath.	46	8	12	26	41	83	28
Hartlepools U.	46	10	7	29	59	109	27

FOOTBALL LEAGUE TABLES 1960–61

DIVISION 1

	P	W	D	L	F	A	Pts.
Tottenham H.	42	31	4	7	115	55	66
Sheffield W.	42	23	12	7	78	47	58
Wolverhampton W.	42	25	7	10	103	75	57
Burnley	42	22	7	13	102	77	51
Everton	42	22	6	14	87	69	50
Leicester C.	42	18	9	15	87	70	45
Manchester U.	42	18	9	15	88	76	45
Blackburn R.	42	15	13	14	77	76	43
Aston Villa	42	17	9	16	78	77	43
W.B.A.	42	18	5	19	67	71	41
Arsenal	42	15	11	16	77	85	41
Chelsea	42	15	7	20	98	100	37
Manchester C.	42	13	11	18	79	90	37
Nottingham F.	42	14	9	19	62	78	37
Cardiff C.	42	13	11	18	60	85	37
West Ham U.	42	13	10	19	77	88	36
Fulham	42	14	8	20	72	95	36
Bolton W.	42	12	11	19	58	73	35
Birmingham C.	42	14	6	22	62	84	34
Blackpool	42	12	9	21	68	73	33
Newcastle U.	42	11	10	21	86	109	32
Preston N.E.	42	10	10	22	43	71	30

DIVISION 2

	P	W	D	L	F	A	Pts.
Ipswich T.	42	26	7	9	100	55	59
Sheffield U.	42	26	6	10	81	51	58
Liverpool	42	21	10	11	87	58	52
Norwich C.	42	20	9	13	70	53	49
Middlesbrough	42	18	12	12	83	74	48
Sunderland	42	17	13	12	75	60	47
Swindon T.	42	18	11	13	77	73	47
Southampton	42	18	8	16	84	81	44
Scunthorpe U.	42	14	15	13	69	64	43
Charlton Ath.	42	16	11	15	97	91	43
Plymouth Arg.	42	17	8	17	81	82	42
Derby Co.	42	15	10	17	80	80	40
Luton T.	42	15	9	18	71	79	39
Leeds U.	42	14	10	18	75	83	38
Rotherham U.	42	12	13	17	65	64	37
Brighton	42	14	9	19	61	75	37
Bristol R.	42	15	7	20	73	92	37
Stoke C.	42	12	12	18	51	59	36
Leyton O.	42	14	8	20	55	78	36
Huddersfield T.	42	13	9	20	62	71	35
Portsmouth	42	11	11	20	64	91	33
Lincoln C.	42	8	8	26	48	95	24

DIVISION 3

	P	W	D	L	F	A	Pts.
Bury	46	30	8	8	108	45	68
Walsall	46	28	6	12	98	60	62
Q.P.R.	46	25	10	11	93	60	60
Watford	46	20	12	14	85	72	52
Notts. Co.	46	21	9	16	82	77	51
Grimsby T.	46	20	10	16	77	69	50
Port Vale	46	17	15	14	96	79	49
Barnsley	46	21	7	18	83	80	49
Halifax T.	46	16	17	13	71	78	49
Shrewsbury T.	46	15	16	15	83	75	46
Hull C.	46	17	12	17	73	73	46
Torquay U.	46	14	17	15	75	83	45
Newport Co.	46	17	11	18	81	90	45
Bristol C.	46	17	10	19	70	68	44
Coventry C.	46	16	12	18	80	83	44
Swindon T.	46	14	15	17	62	55	43
Brentford	46	13	17	16	56	70	43
Reading	46	14	12	20	72	83	40
Bournemouth	46	15	10	21	58	76	40
Southend U.	46	14	11	21	60	76	39
Tranmere R.	46	15	8	23	79	115	38
Bradford C.	46	11	14	21	65	87	36
Colchester U.	46	11	11	24	68	101	33
Chesterfield	46	10	12	24	67	87	32

DIVISION 4

	P	W	D	L	F	A	Pts.
Peterborough U.	46	28	10	8	134	65	66
C. Palace	46	29	6	11	110	69	64
Northampton T.	46	25	10	11	90	62	60
Bradford	46	26	8	12	84	74	60
York C.	46	21	9	16	80	60	51
Millwall	46	21	8	17	97	86	50
Darlington	46	18	13	15	78	70	49
Workington T.	46	21	7	18	74	76	49
Crewe Alex.	46	20	9	17	61	67	49
Aldershot	46	18	9	19	79	69	45
Doncaster R.	46	19	7	20	76	78	45
Oldham Ath.	46	19	7	20	79	88	45
Stockport Co.	46	18	9	19	57	66	45
Southport	46	19	6	21	69	67	44
Gillingham	46	15	13	18	64	66	43
Wrexham	46	17	8	21	62	56	42
Rochdale	46	17	8	21	60	66	42
Accrington S.	46	16	8	22	74	88	40
Carlisle U.	46	13	13	20	61	79	39
Mansfield T.	46	16	6	24	71	78	38
Exeter C.	46	14	10	22	66	94	38
Barrow	46	13	11	22	52	79	37
Hartlepools U.	46	12	8	26	71	103	32
Chester	46	11	9	26	61	104	31

FOOTBALL LEAGUE TABLES 1961–62

DIVISION 1

	P	W	D	L	F	A	Pts.
Ipswich T.	42	24	8	10	93	67	56
Burnley	42	21	11	10	101	67	53
Tottenham H.	42	21	10	11	88	69	52
Everton	42	20	11	11	88	54	51
Sheffield U.	42	19	9	14	61	69	47
Sheffield W.	42	20	6	16	72	58	46
Aston Villa	42	18	8	16	65	56	44
West Ham U.	42	17	10	15	76	82	44
W.B.A	42	15	13	14	83	67	43
Arsenal	42	16	11	15	71	72	43
Bolton W.	42	16	10	16	62	66	42
Manchester C.	42	17	7	18	78	81	41
Blackpool	42	15	11	16	70	75	41
Leicester C.	42	17	6	19	72	71	40
Manchester U.	42	15	9	18	72	75	39
Blackburn R.	42	14	11	17	50	58	39
Birmingham C.	42	14	10	18	65	81	38
Wolverhampton W.	42	13	10	19	73	86	36
Nottingham F.	42	13	10	19	63	79	36
Fulham	42	13	7	22	66	74	33
Cardiff C.	42	9	14	19	50	81	32
Chelsea	42	9	10	23	63	94	28

DIVISION 2

	P	W	D	L	F	A	Pts.
Liverpool	42	27	8	7	99	43	62
Leyton O.	42	22	10	10	69	40	54
Sunderland	42	22	9	11	85	50	53
Scunthorpe U.	42	21	7	14	86	71	49
Plymouth Arg.	42	19	8	15	75	75	46
Southampton	42	18	9	15	77	62	45
Huddersfield T.	42	16	12	14	67	59	44
Stoke C.	42	17	8	17	55	57	42
Rotherham U.	42	16	9	17	70	76	41
Preston N.E.	42	15	10	17	55	57	40
Newcastle U.	42	15	9	18	64	58	39
Middlesbrough	42	16	7	19	76	72	39
Luton T.	42	17	5	20	69	71	39
Walsall	42	14	11	17	70	75	39
Charlton Ath.	42	15	9	18	69	75	39
Derby Co.	42	14	11	17	68	75	39
Norwich C.	42	14	11	17	61	70	39
Bury	42	17	5	20	52	76	39
Leeds U.	42	12	12	18	50	61	36
Swansea T.	42	12	12	18	61	83	36
Bristol R.	42	13	7	22	53	81	33
Brighton	42	10	11	21	42	86	31

DIVISION 3

	P	W	D	L	F	A	Pts.
Portsmouth	46	27	11	8	87	47	65
Grimsby T.	46	28	6	12	80	56	62
Bournemouth	46	21	17	8	69	45	59
Q.P.R.	46	24	11	11	111	73	59
Peterborough U.	46	26	6	14	107	82	58
Bristol C.	46	23	8	15	94	72	54
Reading	46	22	9	15	77	66	53
Northampton T.	46	20	11	15	85	57	51
Swindon T.	46	17	15	14	78	71	49
Hull C.	46	20	8	18	67	54	48
Bradford	46	20	7	19	80	78	47
Port Vale	46	17	11	18	65	58	45
Notts. Co.	46	17	9	20	67	74	43
Coventry C.	46	16	11	19	64	71	43
C. Palace	46	14	14	18	83	80	42
Southend U.	46	13	16	17	57	69	42
Watford	46	14	13	19	63	74	41
Halifax T.	46	15	10	21	62	84	40
Shrewsbury T.	46	13	12	21	73	84	38
Barnsley	46	13	12	21	71	95	38
Torquay U.	46	15	6	25	76	100	36
Lincoln C.	46	9	17	20	57	87	35
Brentford	46	13	8	25	53	93	34
Newport Co.	46	7	8	31	46	102	22

DIVISION 4

	P	W	D	L	F	A	Pts.
Millwall	44	23	10	11	87	62	56
Colchester U.	44	23	9	12	104	71	55
Wrexham	44	22	9	13	96	56	53
Carlisle U.	44	22	8	14	64	63	52
Bradford C.	44	21	9	14	94	86	51
York C.	44	20	10	14	84	53	50
Aldershot	44	22	5	17	81	60	49
Workington T.	44	19	11	14	69	70	49
Barrow	44	17	14	13	74	58	48
Crewe Alex.	44	20	6	18	79	70	46
Oldham Ath.	44	17	12	15	77	70	46
Rochdale	44	19	7	18	71	71	45
Darlington	44	18	9	17	61	73	45
Mansfield T.	44	19	6	19	77	66	44
Tranmere R.	44	20	4	20	70	81	44
Stockport Co.	44	17	9	18	70	69	43
Southport	44	17	9	18	61	71	43
Exeter C.	44	13	11	20	62	77	37
Chesterfield	44	14	9	21	70	87	37
Gillingham	44	13	11	20	73	94	37
Doncaster R.	44	11	7	26	60	85	29
Hartlepools U.	44	8	11	25	52	101	27
Chester	44	7	12	25	54	96	26
Accrington S.	Resigned from League						

FOOTBALL LEAGUE TABLES 1962–63

DIVISION 1

	P	W	D	L	F	A	Pts.
Everton	42	25	11	6	84	42	61
Tottenham H.	42	23	9	10	111	62	55
Burnley	42	22	10	10	78	57	54
Leicester C.	42	20	12	10	79	53	52
Wolverhampton W.	42	20	10	12	93	65	50
Sheffield W.	42	19	10	13	77	63	48
Arsenal	42	18	10	14	86	77	46
Liverpool	42	17	10	15	71	59	44
Nottingham F.	42	17	10	15	67	69	44
Sheffield U.	42	16	12	14	58	60	44
Blackburn R.	42	15	12	15	79	71	42
West Ham U.	42	14	12	16	73	69	40
Blackpool	42	13	14	15	58	64	40
W.B.A.	42	16	7	19	71	79	39
Aston Villa	42	15	8	19	62	68	38
Fulham	42	14	10	18	50	71	38
Ipswich T.	42	12	11	19	59	78	35
Bolton W.	42	15	5	22	55	75	35
Manchester U.	42	12	10	20	67	81	34
Birmingham C.	42	10	13	19	63	90	33
Manchester C.	42	10	11	21	58	102	31
Leyton O.	42	6	9	27	37	81	21

DIVISION 2

	P	W	D	L	F	A	Pts.
Stoke C.	42	20	13	9	73	50	53
Chelsea	42	24	4	14	81	42	52
Sunderland	42	20	12	10	84	55	52
Middlesbrough	42	20	9	13	86	85	49
Leeds U.	42	19	10	13	79	53	48
Huddersfield T.	42	17	14	11	63	50	48
Newcastle U.	42	18	11	13	79	59	47
Bury	42	18	11	13	51	47	47
Scunthorpe U.	42	16	12	14	57	59	44
Cardiff C.	42	18	7	17	83	73	42
Southampton	42	17	8	17	72	67	42
Plymouth Arg.	42	15	12	15	76	73	42
Norwich C.	42	17	8	17	80	79	42
Rotherham U.	42	17	6	19	67	74	40
Swansea	42	15	9	18	51	72	39
Portsmouth	42	13	11	18	63	79	37
Preston N.E.	42	13	11	18	59	74	37
Derby Co.	42	12	12	18	61	72	36
Grimsby T.	42	11	13	18	55	66	35
Charlton Ath.	42	13	5	24	62	94	31
Walsall	42	11	9	22	53	89	31
Luton T.	42	11	7	24	61	84	29

DIVISION 3

	P	W	D	L	F	A	Pts.
Northampton T.	46	26	10	10	109	60	62
Swindon T.	46	22	14	10	87	56	58
Port Vale	46	23	8	15	72	58	54
Coventry C.	46	18	17	11	83	69	53
Bournemouth	46	18	16	12	63	46	52
Peterborough U.	46	20	11	15	93	75	51
Notts. Co.	46	19	13	14	73	74	51
Southend U.	46	19	12	15	75	77	50
Wrexham	46	20	9	17	84	83	49
Hull C.	46	19	10	17	74	69	48
C. Palace	46	17	13	16	68	58	47
Colchester U.	46	18	11	17	73	93	47
Q.P.R.	46	17	11	18	85	76	45
Brstol C.	46	16	13	17	100	92	45
Shrewsbury T.	46	16	12	18	83	81	44
Millwall	46	15	13	18	82	87	43
Watford	46	17	8	21	82	85	42
Barnsley	46	15	11	20	63	74	41
Bristol R.	46	15	11	20	70	88	41
Reading	46	16	8	22	74	78	40
Bradford	46	14	12	20	79	97	40
Brighton	46	12	12	22	58	84	36
Carlisle U.	46	13	9	24	61	89	35
Halifax T.	46	9	12	25	64	106	30

DIVISION 4

	P	W	D	L	F	A	Pts.
Brentford	46	27	8	11	98	64	62
Oldham Ath.	46	24	11	11	95	60	59
Crewe Alex.	46	24	11	11	86	58	59
Mansfield T.	46	24	9	13	108	69	57
Gillingham	46	22	13	11	71	49	57
Torquay U.	46	20	16	10	75	56	56
Rochdale	46	20	11	15	67	59	51
Tranmere R.	46	20	10	16	81	67	50
Barrow	46	19	12	15	82	80	50
Workington T.	46	17	13	16	76	68	47
Aldershot	46	15	17	14	73	69	47
Darlington	46	19	6	21	72	87	44
Southport	46	15	14	17	72	106	44
York C.	46	16	11	19	67	62	43
Chesterfield	46	13	16	17	70	64	42
Doncaster R.	46	14	14	18	64	77	42
Exeter C.	46	16	10	20	57	77	42
Oxford U.	46	13	15	18	70	71	41
Stockport Co.	46	15	11	20	56	70	41
Newport Co.	46	14	11	21	76	90	39
Chester	46	15	9	22	51	66	39
Lincoln C.	46	13	9	24	68	89	35
Bradford C.	46	11	10	25	64	93	32
Hartlepools U.	46	7	11	28	56	104	25

FOOTBALL LEAGUE TABLES 1963–64

DIVISION 1

	P	W	D	L	F	A	Pts.
Liverpool	42	26	5	11	92	45	57
Manchester U.	42	23	7	12	90	62	53
Everton	42	21	10	11	84	64	52
Tottenham H.	42	22	7	13	97	81	51
Chelsea	42	20	10	12	72	56	50
Sheffield W.	42	19	11	12	84	67	49
Blackburn R.	42	18	10	14	89	65	46
Arsenal	42	17	11	14	90	82	45
Burnley	42	17	10	15	71	64	44
W.B.A.	42	16	11	15	70	61	43
Leicester C.	42	16	11	15	61	58	43
Sheffield U.	42	16	11	15	61	64	43
Nottingham F.	42	16	9	17	64	68	41
West Ham U.	42	14	12	16	69	74	40
Fulham	42	13	13	16	58	65	39
Wolverhampton W.	42	12	15	15	70	80	39
Stoke C.	42	14	10	18	77	78	38
Blackpool	42	13	9	20	52	73	35
Aston Villa	42	11	12	19	62	71	34
Birmingham C.	42	11	7	24	54	92	29
Bolton W.	42	10	8	24	48	80	28
Ipswich T.	42	9	7	26	56	121	25

DIVISION 2

	P	W	D	L	F	A	Pts.
Leeds U.	42	24	15	3	71	34	63
Sunderland	42	25	11	6	81	37	61
Preston N.E.	42	23	10	9	79	54	56
Charlton Ath.	42	19	10	13	76	70	48
Southampton	42	19	9	14	100	73	47
Manchester C.	42	18	10	14	84	66	46
Rotherham U.	42	19	7	16	90	78	45
Newcastle U.	42	20	5	17	74	69	45
Portsmouth	42	16	11	15	79	70	43
Middlesbrough	42	15	11	16	67	52	41
Northampton T.	42	16	9	17	58	60	41
Huddersfield T.	42	15	10	17	57	64	40
Derby Co.	42	14	11	17	56	67	39
Swindon T.	42	14	10	18	57	69	38
Cardiff C.	42	14	10	18	56	81	38
Leyton O.	42	13	10	19	54	72	36
Norwich C.	4.	11	13	18	64	80	35
Bury	42	13	9	20	57	73	35
Swansea	42	12	9	21	63	74	33
Plymouth Arg.	42	8	16	18	45	67	32
Grimsby T.	42	9	14	19	47	75	32
Scunthorpe U	42	10	10	22	52	82	30

DIVISION 3

	P	W	D	L	F	A	Pts.
Coventry C.	46	22	16	8	98	61	60
C. Palace	46	23	14	9	73	51	60
Watford	46	23	12	11	79	59	58
Bournemouth	46	24	8	14	79	58	56
Bristol C.	46	20	15	11	84	64	55
Reading	46	21	10	15	79	62	52
Mansfield T.	46	20	11	15	76	62	51
Hull C.	46	16	17	13	73	68	49
Oldham Ath.	46	20	8	18	73	70	48
Peterborough U.	46	18	11	17	75	70	47
Shrewsbury T.	46	18	11	17	73	80	47
Bristol R.	46	19	8	19	91	79	46
Port Vale	46	16	14	16	53	49	46
Southend U.	46	15	15	16	77	78	45
Q.P.R.	46	18	9	19	76	78	45
Brentford	46	15	14	17	87	80	44
Colchester U.	46	12	19	15	70	68	43
Luton T.	46	16	10	20	64	80	42
Walsall	46	13	14	19	59	76	40
Barnsley	46	12	15	19	68	94	39
Millwall	46	14	10	22	53	67	38
Crewe Alex.	46	11	12	23	50	77	34
Wrexham	46	13	6	27	75	107	32
Notts. Co.	46	9	9	28	45	92	27

DIVISION 4

	P	W	D	L	F	A	Pts.
Gillingham	46	23	14	9	59	30	60
Carlisle U.	46	25	10	11	113	58	60
Workington T.	46	24	11	11	76	52	59
Exeter C.	46	20	18	8	62	37	58
Bradford C.	46	25	6	15	76	62	56
Torquay U.	46	20	11	15	80	54	51
Tranmere R.	46	20	11	15	85	73	51
Brighton	46	19	12	15	71	52	50
Aldershot	46	19	10	17	83	78	48
Halifax T.	46	17	14	15	77	77	48
Lincoln C.	46	19	9	18	67	75	47
Chester	46	19	8	19	65	60	46
Bradford	46	18	9	19	75	81	45
Doncaster R.	46	15	12	19	70	75	42
Newport Co.	46	17	8	21	64	73	42
Chesterfield	46	15	12	19	57	71	42
Stockport Co.	46	15	12	19	50	68	42
Oxford U.	46	14	13	19	59	63	41
Darlington	46	14	12	20	66	93	40
Rochdale	46	12	15	19	56	59	39
Southport	46	15	9	22	63	88	39
York C.	46	14	7	25	52	66	35
Hartlepools U.	46	12	9	25	54	93	33
Barrow	46	6	18	22	51	93	30

FOOTBALL LEAGUE TABLES 1964–65

DIVISION 1

	P	W	D	L	F	A	Pts.
Manchester U.	42	26	9	7	89	39	61
Leeds U.	42	26	9	7	83	52	61
Chelsea	42	24	8	10	89	54	56
Everton	42	17	15	10	69	60	49
Nottingham F.	42	17	13	12	71	67	47
Tottenham H.	42	19	7	16	87	71	45
Liverpool	42	17	10	15	67	73	44
Sheffield W.	42	16	11	15	57	55	43
West Ham U.	42	19	4	19	82	71	42
Blackburn R.	42	16	10	16	83	79	42
Stoke C.	42	16	10	16	67	66	42
Burnley	42	16	10	16	70	70	42
Arsenal	42	17	7	18	69	75	41
W.B.A.	42	13	13	16	70	65	39
Sunderland	42	14	9	19	64	74	37
Aston Villa	42	16	5	21	57	82	37
Blackpool	42	12	11	19	67	78	35
Leicester C.	42	11	13	18	69	85	35
Sheffield U.	42	12	11	19	50	64	35
Fulham	42	11	12	19	60	78	34
Wolverhampton W.	42	13	4	25	59	89	30
Birmingham C.	42	8	11	23	64	96	27

DIVISION 2

	P	W	D	L	F	A	Pts.
Newcastle U.	42	24	9	9	81	45	57
Northampton T.	42	20	16	6	66	50	56
Bolton W.	42	20	10	12	80	58	50
Southampton	42	17	14	11	83	63	48
Ipswich T.	42	15	17	10	74	67	47
Norwich C.	42	20	7	15	61	57	47
C. Palace	42	16	13	13	55	51	45
Huddersfield T.	42	17	10	15	53	51	44
Derby Co.	42	16	11	15	84	79	43
Coventry C.	42	17	9	16	72	70	43
Manchester C.	42	16	9	17	63	62	41
Preston N.E.	42	14	13	15	76	81	41
Cardiff C.	42	13	14	15	64	57	40
Rotherham U.	42	14	12	16	70	69	40
Plymouth Arg.	42	16	8	18	63	79	40
Bury	42	14	10	18	60	66	38
Middlesbrough	42	13	9	20	70	76	35
Charlton Ath.	42	13	9	20	64	75	35
Leyton O.	42	12	11	19	50	72	35
Portsmouth	42	12	10	20	56	77	34
Swindon T.	42	14	5	23	63	81	33
Swansea	42	11	10	21	62	84	32

DIVISION 3

	P	W	D	L	F	A	Pts.
Carlisle U.	46	25	10	11	76	53	60
Bristol C.	46	24	11	11	92	55	59
Mansfield T.	46	24	11	11	95	61	59
Hull C.	46	23	12	11	91	57	58
Brentford	46	24	9	13	83	55	57
Bristol R.	46	20	15	11	82	58	55
Gillingham	46	23	9	14	70	50	55
Peterborough U.	46	22	7	17	85	74	51
Watford	46	17	16	13	71	64	50
Grimsby T.	46	16	17	13	68	67	49
Bournemouth	46	18	11	17	72	63	47
Southend U.	46	19	8	19	78	71	46
Reading	46	16	14	16	70	70	46
Q.P.R.	46	17	12	17	72	80	46
Workington T.	46	17	12	17	58	69	46
Shrewsbury T.	46	15	12	19	76	84	42
Exeter C.	46	12	17	17	51	52	41
Scunthorpe U.	46	14	12	20	65	72	40
Walsall	46	15	7	24	55	80	37
Oldham Ath.	46	13	10	23	61	83	36
Luton T.	46	11	11	24	51	94	33
Port Vale	46	9	14	23	41	76	32
Colchester U.	46	10	10	26	50	89	30
Barnsley	46	9	11	26	54	90	29

DIVISION 4

	P	W	D	L	F	A	Pts.
Brighton	46	26	11	9	102	57	63
Millwall	46	23	16	7	78	45	62
York C.	46	28	6	12	91	56	62
Oxford U.	46	23	15	8	87	44	61
Tranmere R.	46	27	6	13	99	56	60
Rochdale	46	22	14	10	74	53	58
Bradford	46	20	17	9	86	62	57
Chester	46	25	6	15	119	81	56
Doncaster R.	46	20	11	15	84	72	51
Crewe Alex.	46	18	13	15	90	81	49
Torquay U.	46	21	7	18	70	70	49
Chesterfield	46	20	8	18	58	70	48
Notts Co.	46	15	14	17	61	73	44
Wrexham	46	17	9	20	84	92	43
Hartlepools U.	46	15	13	18	61	85	43
Newport Co.	46	17	8	21	85	81	42
Darlington	46	18	6	22	84	87	42
Aldershot	46	15	7	24	64	84	37
Bradford C.	46	12	8	26	70	88	32
Southport	46	8	16	22	58	89	32
Barrow	46	12	6	28	59	105	30
Lincoln C.	46	11	6	29	58	99	28
Halifax T.	46	11	6	29	54	103	28
Stockport Co.	46	10	7	29	44	87	27

FOOTBALL LEAGUE TABLES 1965–66

DIVISION 1

	P	W	D	L	F	A	Pts.
Liverpool	42	26	9	7	79	34	61
Leeds U.	42	23	9	10	79	38	55
Burnley	42	24	7	11	79	47	55
Manchester U.	42	18	15	9	84	59	51
Chelsea	42	22	7	13	65	53	51
W.B.A.	42	19	12	11	91	69	50
Leicester C.	42	21	7	14	80	65	49
Tottenham H.	42	16	12	14	75	66	44
Sheffield U.	42	16	11	15	56	59	43
Stoke C.	42	15	12	15	65	64	42
Everton	42	15	11	16	56	62	41
West Ham U.	42	15	9	18	70	83	39
Blackpool	42	14	9	19	55	65	37
Arsenal	42	12	13	17	62	75	37
Newcastle U.	42	14	9	19	50	63	37
Aston Villa	42	15	6	21	69	80	36
Sheffield W.	42	14	8	20	56	66	36
Nottingham F.	42	14	8	20	56	72	36
Sunderland	42	14	8	20	51	72	36
Fulham	42	14	7	21	67	85	35
Northampton T.	42	10	13	19	55	92	33
Blackburn R.	42	8	4	30	57	88	20

DIVISION 2

	P	W	D	L	F	A	Pts.
Manchester C.	42	22	15	5	76	44	59
Southampton	42	22	10	10	85	56	54
Coventry C.	42	20	13	9	73	53	53
Huddersfield T.	42	19	13	10	62	36	51
Bristol C.	42	17	17	8	63	48	51
Wolverhampton W.	42	20	10	12	87	61	50
Rotherham U.	42	16	14	12	75	74	46
Derby C.	42	16	11	15	71	68	43
Bolton W.	42	16	9	17	62	59	41
Birmingham C.	42	16	9	17	70	75	41
C. Palace	42	14	13	15	47	52	41
Portsmouth	42	16	8	18	74	78	40
Norwich C.	42	12	15	15	52	52	39
Carlisle U.	42	17	5	20	60	63	39
Ipswich T.	42	15	9	18	58	66	39
Charlton Ath.	42	12	14	16	61	70	38
Preston N.E.	42	11	15	16	62	70	37
Plymouth Arg.	42	12	13	17	54	63	37
Bury	42	14	7	21	62	76	35
Cardiff C.	42	12	10	20	71	91	34
Middlesbrough	42	10	13	19	58	86	33
Leyton O.	42	5	13	24	38	80	23

DIVISION 3

	P	W	D	L	F	A	Pts.
Hull C.	46	31	7	8	109	62	69
Millwall	46	27	11	8	76	43	65
Q.P.R.	46	24	9	13	95	65	57
Scunthorpe U.	46	21	11	14	80	67	53
Workington T.	46	19	14	13	67	57	52
Gillingham	46	22	8	16	62	54	52
Swindon T.	46	19	13	14	74	48	51
Reading	46	19	13	14	70	63	51
Walsall	46	20	10	16	77	64	50
Shrewsbury T.	46	19	11	16	73	64	49
Grimsby T.	46	17	13	16	68	62	47
Watford	46	17	13	16	55	51	47
Peterborough U.	46	17	12	17	80	66	46
Oxford U.	46	19	8	19	70	74	46
Brighton	46	16	11	19	67	65	43
Bristol R.	46	14	14	18	64	64	42
Swansea	46	15	11	20	81	96	41
Bournemouth	46	13	12	21	38	56	38
Mansfield T.	46	15	8	23	59	89	38
Oldham Ath.	46	12	13	21	55	81	37
Southend U.	46	16	4	26	54	83	36
Exeter C.	46	12	11	23	53	79	35
Brentford	46	10	12	24	48	69	32
York C.	46	9	9	28	53	106	27

DIVISION 4

	P	W	D	L	F	A	Pts.
Doncaster R.	46	24	11	11	85	54	59
Darlington	46	25	9	12	72	53	59
Torquay U.	46	24	10	12	72	49	58
Colchester U.	46	23	10	13	70	47	56
Tranmere R.	46	24	8	14	93	66	56
Luton T.	46	24	8	14	90	70	56
Chester	46	20	12	14	79	70	52
Notts Co.	46	19	12	15	61	53	50
Newport Co.	46	18	12	16	75	75	48
Southport	46	18	12	16	68	69	48
Bradford	46	21	5	20	102	92	47
Barrow	46	16	15	15	72	76	47
Stockport Co.	46	18	6	22	71	70	42
Crewe Alex.	46	16	9	21	61	63	41
Halifax T.	46	15	11	20	67	75	41
Barnsley	46	15	10	21	74	78	40
Aldershot	46	15	10	21	75	84	40
Hartlepools U.	46	16	8	22	63	75	40
Port Vale	46	15	9	22	48	59	39
Chesterfield	46	13	13	20	62	78	39
Rochdale	46	16	5	25	71	87	37
Lincoln C.	46	13	11	22	57	82	37
Bradford C.	46	12	13	21	63	94	37
Wrexham	46	13	9	24	72	104	35

DIVISION 1

	P	W	D	L	F	A	Pts.
Manchester U.	42	24	12	6	84	45	60
Nottingham F.	42	23	10	9	64	41	56
Tottenham H.	42	24	8	10	71	48	56
Leeds U.	42	22	11	9	62	42	55
Liverpool	42	19	13	10	64	47	51
Everton	42	19	10	13	65	46	48
Arsenal	42	16	14	12	58	47	46
Leicester C.	42	18	8	16	78	71	44
Chelsea	42	15	14	13	67	62	44
Sheffield U.	42	16	10	16	52	59	42
Sheffield W.	42	14	13	15	56	47	41
Stoke C.	42	17	7	18	63	58	41
W.B.A.	42	16	7	19	77	73	39
Burnley	42	15	9	18	66	76	39
Manchester C.	42	12	15	15	43	52	39
West Ham U.	42	14	8	20	80	84	36
Sunderland	42	14	8	20	58	72	36
Fulham	42	11	12	19	71	83	34
Southampton	42	14	6	22	74	92	34
Newcastle U.	42	12	9	21	39	81	33
Aston Villa	42	11	7	24	54	85	29
Blackpool	42	6	9	27	41	76	21

DIVISION 2

	P	W	D	L	F	A	Pts.
Coventry C.	42	23	13	6	74	43	59
Wolverhampton W.	42	25	8	9	88	48	58
Carlisle U.	42	23	6	13	71	54	52
Blackburn R.	42	19	13	10	56	46	51
Ipswich T.	42	17	16	9	70	54	50
Huddersfield T.	42	20	9	13	58	46	49
C. Palace	42	19	10	13	61	55	48
Millwall	42	18	9	15	49	58	45
Bolton W.	42	14	14	14	64	58	42
Birmingham C.	42	16	8	18	70	66	40
Norwich C.	42	13	14	15	49	55	40
Hull C.	42	16	7	19	77	72	39
Preston N.E.	42	16	7	19	65	67	39
Portsmouth	42	13	13	16	59	70	39
Bristol C.	42	12	14	16	56	62	38
Plymouth Arg.	42	14	9	19	59	58	37
Derby Co.	42	12	12	18	68	72	36
Rotherham U.	42	13	10	19	61	70	36
Charlton Ath.	42	13	9	20	49	53	35
Cardiff C.	42	12	9	21	61	87	33
Northampton T.	42	12	6	24	47	84	30
Bury	42	11	6	25	49	83	28

DIVISION 3

	P	W	D	L	F	A	Pts.
Q.P.R.	46	26	15	5	103	38	67
Middlesbrough	46	23	9	14	87	64	55
Watford	46	20	14	12	61	46	54
Reading	46	22	9	15	76	57	53
Bristol R.	46	20	13	13	76	67	53
Shrewsbury T.	46	20	12	14	77	62	52
Torquay U.	46	21	9	16	73	54	51
Swindon T.	46	20	10	16	81	59	50
Mansfield T.	46	20	9	17	84	79	49
Oldham Ath.	46	19	10	17	80	63	48
Gillingham	46	15	16	15	58	62	46
Walsall	46	18	10	18	65	72	46
Colchester U.	46	17	10	19	76	73	44
Leyton O.	46	13	18	15	58	68	44
Peterborough U.	46	14	15	17	66	71	43
Oxford U.	46	15	13	18	61	66	43
Grimsby T.	46	17	9	20	61	68	43
Scunthorpe U.	46	17	8	21	58	73	42
Brighton	46	13	15	18	61	71	41
Bournemouth	46	12	17	17	39	57	41
Swansea	46	12	15	19	85	89	39
Darlington	46	13	11	22	47	81	37
Doncaster R.	46	12	8	26	58	117	32
Workington T.	46	12	7	27	55	89	31

DIVISION 4

	P	W	D	L	F	A	Pts.
Stockport Co.	46	26	12	8	69	42	64
Southport	46	23	13	10	69	42	59
Barrow	46	24	11	11	76	54	59
Tranmere R.	46	22	14	10	66	43	58
Crewe Alex.	46	21	12	13	70	55	54
Southend U.	46	22	9	15	70	49	53
Wrexham	46	16	20	10	76	62	52
Hartlepools U.	46	22	7	17	66	64	51
Brentford	46	18	13	15	58	56	49
Aldershot	46	18	12	16	72	57	48
Bradford C.	46	19	10	17	74	62	48
Halifax T.	46	15	14	17	59	68	44
Port Vale	46	14	15	17	55	58	43
Exeter C.	46	14	15	17	50	60	43
Chesterfield	46	17	8	21	60	63	42
Barnsley	46	13	15	18	60	64	41
Luton T.	46	16	9	21	59	73	41
Newport Co.	46	12	16	18	56	63	40
Chester	46	15	10	21	54	78	40
Notts. Co.	46	13	11	22	53	72	37
Rochdale	46	13	11	22	53	75	37
York C.	46	12	11	23	65	79	35
Bradford	46	11	13	22	52	79	35
Lincoln C.	46	9	13	24	58	82	31

FOOTBALL LEAGUE TABLES 1967–68

DIVISION 1

	P	W	D	L	F	A	Pts.
Manchester C.	42	26	6	10	86	43	58
Manchester U.	42	24	8	10	89	55	56
Liverpool	42	22	11	9	71	40	55
Leeds U.	42	22	9	11	71	41	53
Everton	42	23	6	13	67	40	52
Chelsea	42	18	12	12	62	68	48
Tottenham H.	42	19	9	14	70	59	47
W.B.A.	42	17	12	13	75	62	46
Arsenal	42	17	10	15	60	56	44
Newcastle U.	42	13	15	14	54	67	41
Nottingham F.	42	14	11	17	52	64	39
West Ham U.	42	14	10	18	73	69	38
Leicester C.	42	13	12	17	64	69	38
Burnley	42	14	10	18	64	71	38
Sunderland	42	13	11	18	51	61	37
Southampton	42	13	11	18	66	83	37
Wolverhampton W.	42	14	8	20	66	75	36
Stoke C.	42	14	7	21	50	73	35
Sheffield W.	42	11	12	19	51	63	34
Coventry C.	42	9	15	18	51	71	33
Sheffield U.	42	11	10	21	49	70	32
Fulham	42	10	7	25	56	98	27

DIVISION 2

	P	W	D	L	F	A	Pts.
Ipswich T.	42	22	15	5	79	44	59
Q.P.R.	42	25	8	9	67	36	58
Blackpool	42	24	10	8	71	43	58
Birmingham C.	42	19	14	9	83	51	52
Portsmouth	42	18	13	11	68	55	49
Middlesbrough	42	17	12	13	60	54	46
Millwall	42	14	17	11	62	50	45
Blackburn R.	42	16	11	15	56	49	43
Norwich C.	42	16	11	15	60	65	43
Carlisle U.	42	14	13	15	58	52	41
C. Palace	42	14	11	17	56	56	39
Bolton W.	42	13	13	16	60	63	39
Cardiff C.	42	13	12	17	60	66	38
Huddersfield T.	42	13	12	17	46	61	38
Charlton Ath.	42	12	13	17	63	68	37
Aston Villa	42	15	7	20	54	64	37
Hull C.	42	12	13	17	58	73	37
Derby Co.	42	13	10	19	71	78	36
Bristol C.	42	13	10	19	48	62	36
Preston N.E.	42	12	11	19	43	65	35
Rotherham U.	42	10	11	21	42	76	31
Plymouth Arg.	42	9	9	24	38	72	27

DIVISION 3

	P	W	D	L	F	A	Pts.
Oxford U.	46	22	13	11	69	47	57
Bury	46	24	8	14	91	66	56
Shrewsbury T.	46	20	15	11	61	49	55
Torquay U.	46	21	11	14	60	56	53
Reading	46	21	9	16	70	60	51
Watford	46	21	8	17	74	50	50
Walsall	46	19	12	15	74	61	50
Barrow	46	21	8	17	65	54	50
Peterborough U.	46	20	10	16	79	67	50
Swindon T.	46	16	17	13	74	51	49
Brighton	46	16	16	14	57	55	48
Gillingham	46	18	12	16	59	63	48
Bournemouth	46	16	15	15	56	51	47
Stockport Co.	46	19	9	18	70	75	47
Southport	46	17	12	17	65	65	46
Bristol R.	46	17	9	20	72	78	43
Oldham Ath.	46	18	7	21	60	65	43
Northampton T.	46	14	13	19	58	72	41
Leyton O.	46	12	17	17	46	62	41
Tranmere R.	46	14	12	20	62	74	40
Mansfield T.	46	12	13	21	51	67	37
Grimsby T.	46	14	9	23	52	69	37
Colchester U.	46	9	15	22	50	87	33
Scunthorpe U.	46	10	12	24	56	87	32

DIVISION 4

	P	W	D	L	F	A	Pts.
Luton T.	46	27	12	7	87	44	66
Barnsley	46	24	13	9	68	46	61
Hartlepools U.	46	25	10	11	60	46	60
Crewe Alex.	46	20	18	8	74	49	58
Bradford C.	46	23	11	12	72	51	57
Southend U.	46	20	14	12	77	58	54
Chesterfield	46	21	11	14	71	50	53
Wrexham	46	20	13	13	72	53	53
Aldershot	46	18	17	11	70	55	53
Doncaster R.	46	18	15	13	66	56	51
Halifax T.	46	15	16	15	52	49	46
Newport Co.	46	16	13	17	58	63	45
Lincoln C.	46	17	9	20	71	68	43
Brentford	46	18	7	21	61	64	43
Swansea	46	16	10	20	63	77	42
Darlington	46	12	17	17	47	53	41
Notts. Co.	46	15	11	20	53	79	41
Port Vale	46	12	15	19	61	72	39
Rochdale	46	12	14	20	51	72	38
Exeter C.	46	11	16	19	45	65	38
York C.	46	11	14	21	65	68	36
Chester	46	9	14	23	57	78	32
Workington T.	46	10	11	25	54	87	31
Bradford	46	4	15	27	30	82	23

DIVISION 1

	P	W	D	L	F	A	Pts.
Leeds U.	42	27	13	2	66	26	67
Liverpool	42	25	11	6	63	24	61
Everton	42	21	15	6	77	36	57
Arsenal	42	22	12	8	56	27	56
Chelsea	42	20	10	12	73	53	50
Tottenham H.	42	14	17	11	61	51	45
Southampton	42	16	13	13	57	48	45
West Ham U.	42	13	18	11	66	50	44
Newcastle U.	42	15	14	13	61	55	44
W.B.A.	42	16	11	15	64	67	43
Manchester U.	42	15	12	15	57	53	42
Ipswich T.	42	15	11	16	59	60	41
Manchester C.	42	15	10	17	64	55	40
Burnley	42	15	9	18	55	82	39
Sheffield W.	42	10	16	16	41	54	36
Wolverhampton W.	42	10	15	17	41	58	35
Sunderland	42	11	12	19	43	67	34
Nottingham F.	42	10	13	19	45	57	33
Stoke C.	42	9	15	18	40	63	33
Coventry C.	42	10	11	21	46	64	31
Leicester C.	42	9	12	21	39	68	30
Q.P.R.	42	4	10	28	39	95	18

DIVISION 2

	P	W	D	L	F	A	Pts.
Derby Co.	42	26	11	5	65	32	63
C. Palace	42	22	12	8	70	47	56
Charlton Ath.	42	18	14	10	61	52	50
Middlesbrough	42	19	11	12	58	49	49
Cardiff C.	42	20	7	15	67	54	47
Huddersfield T.	42	17	12	13	53	46	46
Birmingham C.	42	18	8	16	73	59	44
Blackpool	42	14	15	13	51	41	43
Sheffield U.	42	16	11	15	61	50	43
Millwall	42	17	9	16	57	49	43
Hull C.	42	13	16	13	59	52	42
Carlisle U.	42	16	10	16	46	49	42
Norwich C.	42	15	10	17	53	56	40
Preston N.E.	42	12	15	15	38	44	39
Portsmouth	42	12	14	16	58	58	38
Bristol C.	42	11	16	15	46	53	38
Bolton W.	42	12	14	16	55	67	38
Aston Villa	42	12	14	16	37	48	38
Blackburn R.	42	13	11	18	52	63	37
Oxford U.	42	12	9	21	34	55	33
Bury	42	11	8	23	51	80	30
Fulham	42	7	11	24	40	81	25

DIVISION 3

	P	W	D	L	F	A	Pts.
Watford	46	27	10	9	74	34	64
Swindon T.	46	27	10	9	71	35	64
Luton T.	46	25	11	10	74	38	61
Bournemouth	46	21	9	16	60	45	51
Plymouth Arg.	46	17	15	14	53	49	49
Torquay U.	46	18	12	16	54	46	48
Tranmere R.	46	19	10	17	70	68	48
Southport	46	17	13	16	71	64	47
Stockport Co.	46	16	14	16	67	68	46
Barnsley	46	16	14	16	58	63	46
Rotherham U.	46	16	13	17	56	50	45
Brighton	46	16	13	17	72	65	45
Walsall	46	14	16	16	50	49	44
Reading	46	15	13	18	67	66	43
Mansfield T.	46	16	11	19	58	62	43
Bristol R.	46	16	11	19	63	71	43
Shrewsbury T.	46	16	11	19	51	67	43
Orient	46	14	14	18	51	58	42
Barrow	46	17	8	21	56	75	42
Gillingham	46	13	15	18	54	63	41
Northampton T.	46	14	12	20	54	61	40
Hartlepool	46	10	19	17	40	70	39
Crewe Alex.	46	13	9	24	52	76	35
Oldham Ath.	46	13	9	24	50	83	35

DIVISION 4

	P	W	D	L	F	A	Pts.
Doncaster R.	46	21	17	8	65	38	59
Halifax T.	46	20	17	9	53	37	57
Rochdale	46	18	20	8	68	35	56
Bradford C.	46	18	20	8	65	46	56
Darlington	46	17	18	11	62	45	52
Colchester U.	46	20	12	14	57	53	52
Southend U.	46	19	13	14	78	61	51
Lincoln C.	46	17	17	12	54	52	51
Wrexham	46	18	14	14	61	52	50
Swansea C.	46	19	11	16	58	54	49
Brentford	46	18	12	16	64	65	48
Workington T.	46	15	17	14	40	43	47
Port Vale	46	16	14	16	46	46	46
Chester	46	16	13	17	76	66	45
Aldershot	46	19	7	20	66	66	45
Scunthorpe U.	46	18	8	20	61	60	44
Exeter C.	46	16	11	19	66	65	43
Peterborough U.	46	13	16	17	60	57	42
Notts. Co.	46	12	18	16	48	57	42
Chesterfield	46	13	15	18	43	50	41
York C.	46	14	11	21	53	75	39
Newport Co.	46	11	14	21	49	74	36
Grimsby T.	46	9	15	22	47	69	33
Brentford	46	5	10	31	32	106	20

FOOTBALL LEAGUE TABLES 1969–70

DIVISION 1

	P	W	D	L	F	A	Pts.
Everton	42	29	8	5	72	34	66
Leeds U.	42	21	15	6	84	49	57
Chelsea	42	21	13	8	70	50	55
Derby Co.	42	22	9	11	64	37	53
Liverpool	42	20	11	11	65	42	51
Coventry	42	19	11	12	58	48	49
Newcastle U.	42	17	13	12	57	35	47
Manchester U.	42	14	17	11	66	61	45
Stoke C.	42	15	15	12	56	52	45
Manchester C.	42	16	11	15	55	48	43
Tottenham H.	42	17	9	16	54	55	43
Arsenal	42	12	18	12	51	49	42
Wolverhampton W.	42	12	16	14	55	57	40
Burnley	42	12	15	15	56	61	39
Nottingham F.	42	10	18	14	50	71	38
W.B.A.	42	14	9	19	58	66	37
West Ham U.	42	12	12	18	51	60	36
Ipswich T.	42	10	11	21	40	63	31
Southampton	42	6	17	19	46	67	29
C. Palace	42	6	15	21	34	68	27
Sunderland	42	6	14	22	30	68	26
Sheffield W.	42	8	9	25	40	71	25

DIVISION 2

	P	W	D	L	F	A	Pts.
Huddersfield T.	42	24	12	6	68	37	60
Blackpool	42	20	13	9	56	45	53
Leicester C.	42	19	13	10	64	50	51
Middlesbrough	42	20	10	12	55	45	50
Swindon T.	42	17	16	9	57	47	50
Sheffield U.	42	22	5	15	73	38	49
Cardiff C.	42	18	13	11	61	41	49
Blackburn R.	42	20	7	15	54	50	47
Q.P.R.	42	17	11	14	66	57	45
Millwall	42	15	14	13	56	56	44
Norwich C.	42	16	11	15	49	46	43
Carlisle U.	42	14	13	15	58	56	41
Hull C.	42	15	11	16	72	70	41
Bristol C.	42	13	13	16	54	50	39
Oxford U.	42	12	15	15	35	42	39
Bolton W.	42	12	12	18	54	61	36
Portsmouth	42	13	9	20	66	80	35
Birmingham C.	42	11	11	20	51	78	33
Watford	42	9	13	20	44	57	31
Charlton Ath.	42	7	17	18	35	76	31
Aston Villa	42	8	13	21	36	62	29
Preston N.E.	42	8	12	22	43	63	28

DIVISION 3

	P	W	D	L	F	A	Pts.
Orient	46	25	12	9	67	36	62
Luton T.	46	23	14	9	77	43	60
Bristol R.	46	20	16	10	80	59	56
Fulham	46	20	15	11	81	55	55
Brighton	46	23	9	14	57	43	55
Mansfield T.	46	21	11	14	70	49	53
Barnsley	46	19	15	12	68	59	53
Reading	46	21	11	14	87	77	53
Rochdale	46	18	10	18	69	60	46
Bradford C.	46	17	12	17	57	50	46
Doncaster R.	46	17	12	17	52	54	46
Walsall	46	17	12	17	54	67	46
Torquay U.	46	14	17	15	62	59	45
Rotherham U.	46	15	14	17	62	54	44
Shrewsbury T.	46	13	18	15	62	63	44
Tranmere R.	46	14	16	16	56	72	44
Plymouth Arg.	46	16	11	19	56	64	43
Halifax T.	46	14	15	17	47	63	43
Bury	46	15	11	20	75	80	41
Gillingham	46	13	13	20	52	64	39
Bournemouth	46	12	15	19	48	71	39
Southport	46	14	10	22	48	66	38
Barrow	46	8	14	24	46	81	30
Stockport Co.	46	6	11	29	27	71	23

DIVISION 4

	P	W	D	L	F	A	Pts.
Chesterfield	46	27	10	9	77	32	64
Wrexham	46	26	9	11	84	49	61
Swansea C.	46	21	18	7	66	45	60
Port Vale	46	20	19	7	61	33	59
Brentford	46	20	16	10	58	39	56
Aldershot	46	20	13	13	78	65	53
Notts. Co.	46	22	8	16	73	62	52
Lincoln C.	46	17	16	13	66	52	50
Peterborough U.	46	17	14	15	77	69	48
Colchester U.	46	17	14	15	64	63	48
Chester	46	21	6	19	58	66	48
Scunthorpe U.	46	18	10	18	67	65	46
York C.	46	16	14	16	55	62	46
Northampton T.	46	16	12	18	64	55	44
Crewe Alex.	46	16	12	18	51	51	44
Grimsby T.	46	14	15	17	54	58	43
Southend U.	46	15	10	21	59	85	40
Exeter C.	46	14	11	21	57	59	39
Oldham Ath.	46	13	13	20	60	65	39
Workington	46	12	14	20	46	64	38
Newport Co.	46	13	11	22	53	74	37
Darlington	46	13	10	23	53	73	36
Hartlepool	46	10	10	26	42	82	30
Bradford	46	6	11	29	41	96	23

FOOTBALL LEAGUE TABLES 1970–71

DIVISION 1

	P	W	D	L	F	A	Pts.
Arsenal	42	29	7	6	71	29	65
Leeds U.	42	27	10	5	72	30	64
Tottenham H.	42	19	14	9	54	33	52
Wolverhampton W.	42	22	8	12	64	54	52
Liverpool	42	17	17	8	42	24	51
Chelsea	42	18	15	9	52	42	51
Southampton	42	17	12	13	56	44	46
Manchester U.	42	16	11	15	65	66	43
Derby Co.	42	16	10	16	56	54	42
Coventry C.	42	16	10	16	37	38	42
Manchester C.	42	12	17	13	47	42	41
Newcastle U.	42	14	13	15	44	46	41
Stoke C.	42	12	13	17	44	48	37
Everton	42	12	13	17	54	60	37
Huddersfield T.	42	11	14	17	40	49	36
Nottingham F.	42	14	8	20	42	61	36
W.B.A.	42	10	15	17	58	75	35
C. Palace	42	12	11	19	39	57	35
Ipswich T.	42	12	10	20	42	48	34
West Ham U.	42	10	14	18	47	60	34
Burnley	42	7	13	22	29	63	27
Blackpool	42	4	15	23	34	66	23

DIVISION 2

	P	W	D	L	F	A	Pts.
Leicester C.	42	23	13	6	57	30	59
Sheffield U.	42	21	14	7	73	39	56
Cardiff C.	42	20	13	9	64	41	53
Carlisle U.	42	20	13	9	65	43	53
Hull C.	42	19	13	10	54	41	51
Luton T.	42	18	13	11	62	43	49
Middlesbrough	42	17	14	11	60	43	48
Millwall	42	19	9	14	59	42	47
Birmingham C.	42	17	12	13	58	48	46
Norwich C.	42	15	14	13	54	52	44
Q.P.R.	42	16	11	15	58	53	43
Swindon T.	42	15	12	15	61	51	42
Sunderland	42	15	12	15	52	54	42
Oxford U.	42	14	14	14	41	48	42
Sheffield W.	42	12	12	18	51	69	36
Portsmouth	42	10	14	18	46	61	34
Orient	42	9	16	17	29	51	34
Watford	42	10	13	19	38	60	33
Bristol C.	42	10	11	21	46	64	31
Charlton Ath.	42	8	14	20	41	65	30
Blackburn R.	42	6	15	21	37	69	27
Bolton W.	42	7	10	25	35	74	24

DIVISION 3

	P	W	D	L	F	A	Pts.
Preston N.E.	46	22	17	7	63	39	61
Fulham	46	24	12	10	68	41	60
Halifax T.	46	22	12	12	74	55	56
Aston Villa	46	19	15	12	54	46	53
Chesterfield	46	17	17	12	66	38	51
Bristol R.	46	19	13	14	69	50	51
Mansfield T.	46	18	15	13	64	62	51
Rotherham U.	46	17	16	13	64	60	50
Wrexham	46	18	13	15	72	65	49
Torquay U.	46	19	11	16	54	57	49
Swansea C.	46	15	16	15	59	56	46
Barnsley	46	17	11	18	49	52	45
Shrewsbury T.	46	16	13	17	58	62	45
Brighton	46	14	16	16	50	47	44
Plymouth Arg.	46	12	19	15	63	63	43
Rochdale	46	14	15	17	61	68	43
Port Vale	46	15	12	19	52	59	42
Tranmere R.	46	10	22	14	45	55	42
Bradford C.	46	13	14	19	49	62	40
Walsall	46	14	11	21	51	57	39
Reading	46	14	11	21	48	85	39
Bury	46	12	13	21	52	60	37
Doncaster R.	46	13	9	24	45	66	35
Gillingham	46	10	13	23	42	67	33

DIVISION 4

	P	W	D	L	F	A	Pts.
Notts. Co.	46	30	9	7	89	36	69
Bournemouth	46	24	12	10	81	46	60
Oldham Ath.	46	24	11	11	88	63	59
York C.	46	23	10	13	78	54	56
Chester	46	24	7	15	69	55	55
Colchester U.	46	21	12	13	70	54	54
Northampton T.	46	19	13	14	63	59	51
Southport	46	21	6	19	63	57	48
Exeter C.	46	17	14	15	67	68	48
Workington	46	18	12	16	48	49	48
Stockport Co.	46	16	14	16	49	65	46
Darlington	46	17	11	18	58	57	45
Aldershot	46	14	17	15	66	71	45
Brentford	46	18	8	20	66	62	44
Crewe Alex.	46	18	8	20	75	76	44
Peterborough U.	46	18	7	21	70	71	43
Scunthorpe U.	46	15	13	18	56	61	43
Southend U.	46	14	15	17	53	66	43
Grimsby T.	46	18	7	21	57	71	43
Cambridge U.	46	15	13	18	51	66	43
Lincoln C.	46	13	13	20	70	71	39
Newport Co.	46	10	8	28	55	85	28
Hartlepool	46	8	12	26	34	74	28
Barrow	46	7	8	31	51	90	22

FOOTBALL LEAGUE TABLES 1971-72

DIVISION 1

	P	W	D	L	F	A	Pts.
Derby Co.	42	24	10	8	69	33	58
Leeds U.	42	24	9	9	73	31	57
Liverpool	42	24	9	9	64	30	57
Manchester C.	42	23	11	8	77	45	57
Arsenal	42	22	8	12	58	40	52
Tottenham H.	42	19	13	10	63	42	51
Chelsea	42	18	12	12	58	49	48
Manchester U.	42	19	10	13	69	61	48
Wolverhampton W.	42	18	11	13	65	57	47
Sheffield U.	42	17	12	13	61	60	46
Newcastle U.	42	15	11	16	49	52	41
Leicester C.	42	13	13	16	41	46	39
Ipswich T.	42	11	16	15	39	53	38
West Ham U.	42	12	12	18	47	51	36
Everton	42	9	18	15	37	48	36
W.B.A.	42	12	11	19	42	54	35
Stoke C.	42	10	15	17	39	56	35
Coventry C.	42	9	15	18	44	67	33
Southampton	42	12	7	23	52	80	31
Crystal Palace	42	8	13	21	39	65	29
Nottingham F.	42	8	9	25	47	81	25
Huddersfield T.	42	6	13	23	27	59	25

DIVISION 2

	P	W	D	L	F	A	Pts.
Norwich C.	42	21	15	6	60	36	57
Birmingham C.	42	19	18	5	60	31	56
Millwall	42	19	17	6	64	46	55
Q.P.R.	42	20	14	8	57	28	54
Sunderland	42	17	16	9	67	57	50
Blackpool	42	20	7	15	70	50	47
Burnley	42	20	6	16	70	55	46
Bristol C.	42	18	10	14	61	49	46
Middlesbrough	42	19	8	15	50	48	46
Carlisle U.	42	17	9	16	61	57	43
Swindon T.	42	15	12	15	47	47	42
Hull C.	42	14	10	18	49	53	38
Luton T.	42	10	18	14	43	48	38
Sheffield W.	42	13	12	17	51	58	38
Oxford U.	42	12	14	16	43	55	38
Portsmouth	42	12	13	17	59	68	37
Orient	42	14	9	19	50	61	37
Preston N.E.	42	12	12	18	52	58	36
Cardiff C.	42	10	14	18	56	69	34
Fulham	42	12	10	20	45	68	34
Charlton Ath.	42	12	9	21	55	77	33
Watford	42	5	9	28	24	75	19

DIVISION 3

	P	W	D	L	F	A	Pts.
Aston Villa	46	32	6	8	85	32	70
Brighton & H.A.	46	27	11	8	82	47	65
Bournemouth	46	23	16	7	73	37	62
Notts Co.	46	25	12	9	74	44	62
Rotherham U.	46	20	15	11	69	52	55
Bristol R.	46	21	12	13	75	56	54
Bolton W.	46	17	16	13	51	41	50
Plymouth Arg.	46	20	10	16	74	64	50
Walsall	46	15	18	13	62	57	48
Blackburn R.	46	19	9	18	54	57	47
Oldham Ath.	46	17	11	18	59	63	45
Shrewsbury T.	46	17	10	19	73	65	44
Chesterfield	46	18	8	20	57	57	44
Swansea C.	46	17	10	19	46	59	44
Port Vale	46	13	15	18	43	59	41
Wrexham	46	16	8	22	59	63	40
Halifax T.	46	13	12	21	48	61	38
Rochdale	46	12	13	21	57	83	37
York C.	46	12	12	22	57	66	36
Tranmere R.	46	10	16	20	50	71	36
Mansfield T.	46	8	20	18	41	63	36
Barnsley	46	9	18	19	32	64	36
Torquay U.	46	10	12	24	41	69	32
Bradford C.	46	11	10	15	45	77	32

DIVISION 4

	P	W	D	L	F	A	Pts.
Grimsby	46	28	7	11	88	56	63
Southend U.	46	24	12	10	81	55	60
Brentford	46	24	11	11	76	44	59
Scunthorpe U.	46	22	13	11	56	37	57
Lincoln C.	46	21	14	11	77	59	56
Workington	46	16	19	11	50	34	51
Southport	46	18	14	14	66	46	50
Peterborough U.	46	17	16	13	82	64	50
Bury	46	19	12	15	73	59	50
Cambridge U.	46	17	14	15	62	60	48
Colchester U.	46	19	10	17	70	69	48
Doncaster R.	46	16	14	16	56	63	46
Gillingham	46	16	13	17	61	67	45
Newport Co.	46	18	8	20	60	72	44
Exeter C.	46	16	11	19	61	68	43
Reading	46	17	8	21	56	76	42
Aldershot	46	9	22	15	48	54	40
Hartlepool	46	17	6	23	58	69	40
Darlington	46	14	11	21	64	82	39
Chester	46	10	18	18	47	56	38
Northampton T.	46	12	13	21	66	79	37
Barrow	46	13	11	22	40	71	37
Stockport Co.	46	9	14	23	55	87	32
Crewe Alex.	46	10	9	27	43	69	29

FOOTBALL LEAGUE TABLES 1972-73

DIVISION 1

	P	W	D	L	F	A	Pts.
Liverpool	42	25	10	7	72	42	60
Arsenal	42	23	11	8	57	43	57
Leeds U.	42	21	11	10	71	45	53
Ipswich T.	42	17	14	11	55	45	48
Wolverhampton W.	42	18	11	13	66	54	47
West Ham U.	42	17	12	13	67	53	46
Derby Co.	42	19	8	15	56	54	46
Tottenham H.	42	16	13	13	58	48	45
Newcastle U.	42	16	13	13	60	51	45
Birmingham C.	42	15	12	15	53	54	42
Manchester C.	42	15	11	16	57	60	41
Chelsea	42	13	14	15	49	51	40
Southampton	42	11	18	13	47	52	40
Sheffield U.	42	15	10	17	51	59	40
Stoke C.	42	14	10	18	61	56	38
Leicester C.	42	10	17	15	40	46	37
Everton	42	13	11	18	41	49	37
Manchester U.	42	12	13	17	44	60	37
Coventry C.	42	13	9	20	40	55	35
Norwich C.	42	11	10	21	36	63	32
Crystal Palace	42	9	12	21	41	58	30
W.B.A.	42	9	10	23	38	62	28

DIVISION 2

	P	W	D	L	F	A	Pts.
Burnley	42	24	14	4	72	35	62
Q.P.R.	42	24	13	5	81	37	61
Aston Villa	42	18	14	10	51	47	50
Middlesbrough	42	17	13	12	46	43	47
Bristol C.	42	17	12	13	63	51	46
Sunderland	42	17	12	13	59	49	46
Blackpool	42	18	10	14	56	51	46
Oxford U.	42	19	7	16	52	43	45
Fulham	42	16	12	14	58	49	44
Sheffield W.	42	17	10	15	59	55	44
Millwall	42	16	10	16	55	47	42
Luton T.	42	15	11	16	44	53	41
Hull C.	42	14	12	16	64	59	40
Nottingham F.	42	14	12	16	47	52	40
Orient	42	12	12	18	49	53	36
Swindon T.	42	10	16	16	46	60	36
Portsmouth	42	12	11	19	42	59	35
Carlisle U.	42	11	12	19	50	52	34
Preston N.E.	42	11	12	19	37	64	34
Cardiff C.	42	11	11	20	43	58	33
Huddersfield T.	42	8	17	17	36	56	33
Brighton & H.A.	42	8	13	21	46	83	29

DIVISION 3

	P	W	D	L	F	A	Pts.
Bolton W.	46	25	11	10	73	39	61
Notts Co.	46	23	11	12	67	47	57
Blackburn R.	46	20	15	11	57	47	55
Oldham Ath.	46	19	16	11	72	54	54
Bristol R.	46	20	13	13	77	56	53
Port Vale	46	21	11	14	56	69	53
AFC Bournemouth	46	17	16	13	66	44	50
Plymouth Arg.	46	20	10	16	74	66	50
Grimsby T.	46	20	8	18	67	61	48
Tranmere R.	46	16	15	15	56	52	46
Charlton Ath.	46	17	11	18	69	67	45
Wrexham	46	14	17	15	55	54	45
Rochdale	46	14	17	15	48	54	45
Southend U.	46	17	10	19	61	54	44
Shrewsbury T.	46	15	14	17	46	54	44
Chesterfield	46	17	9	20	57	61	43
Walsall	46	18	7	21	56	66	43
York C.	46	13	15	18	42	46	41
Watford	46	12	17	17	43	48	41
Halifax T.	46	13	15	18	43	53	41
Rotherham U.	46	17	7	22	51	65	41
Brentford	46	15	7	24	51	69	37
Swansea C.	46	14	9	23	51	73	37
Scunthorpe U.	46	10	10	26	33	72	30

DIVISION 4

	P	W	D	L	F	A	Pts.
Southport	46	26	10	10	71	48	62
Hereford U.	46	23	12	11	56	38	58
Cambridge U.	46	20	17	9	67	57	57
Aldershot	46	22	12	12	60	38	56
Newport Co.	46	22	12	12	64	44	56
Mansfield T.	46	20	14	12	78	51	54
Reading	46	17	18	11	51	38	52
Exeter C.	46	18	14	14	57	51	50
Gillingham	46	19	11	16	63	58	49
Lincoln C.	46	16	16	14	64	57	48
Stockport Co.	46	18	12	16	53	53	48
Bury	46	14	18	14	58	51	46
Workington	46	17	12	17	59	61	46
Barnsley	46	14	16	16	58	60	44
Chester	46	14	15	17	61	52	43
Bradford C.	46	16	11	19	61	65	43
Doncaster R.	46	15	12	19	49	58	42
Torquay U.	46	12	17	17	44	47	41
Peterborough U.	46	14	13	19	71	76	41
Hartlepool	46	12	17	17	34	49	41
Crewe Alex.	46	9	18	19	38	61	36
Colchester U.	46	10	11	25	48	76	31
Northampton T.	46	10	11	25	40	73	31
Darlington	46	7	15	24	42	85	29

FOOTBALL LEAGUE TABLES 1973-74

DIVISION 1

	P	W	D	L	F	A	Pts.
Leeds U.	42	24	14	4	66	31	62
Liverpool	42	22	13	7	52	31	57
Derby Co.	42	17	14	11	52	42	48
Ipswich T.	42	18	11	13	67	58	47
Stoke C.	42	15	16	11	54	42	46
Burnley	42	16	14	12	56	53	46
Everton	42	16	12	14	50	48	44
Q.P.R.	42	13	17	12	56	52	43
Leicester C.	42	13	16	13	51	41	42
Arsenal	42	14	14	14	49	51	42
Tottenham H.	42	14	14	14	45	50	42
Wolverhampton W.	42	13	15	14	49	49	41
Sheffield U.	42	14	12	16	44	49	40
Manchester C.	42	14	12	16	39	46	40
Newcastle U.	42	13	12	17	49	48	38
Coventry C.	42	14	10	18	43	54	38
Chelsea	42	12	13	17	56	60	37
West Ham U.	42	11	15	16	55	60	37
Birmingham C.	42	12	13	17	52	64	37
Southampton	42	11	14	17	47	68	36
Manchester U.	42	10	12	20	38	48	32
Norwich C.	42	7	15	20	37	62	29

DIVISION 2

	P	W	D	L	F	A	Pts.
Middlesbrough	42	27	11	4	77	30	65
Luton T.	42	19	12	11	64	51	50
Carlisle U.	42	20	9	13	61	48	49
Orient	42	15	18	9	55	42	48
Blackpool	42	17	13	12	57	40	47
Sunderland	42	19	9	14	58	44	47
Nottingham F.	42	15	15	12	57	43	45
W.B.A.	42	14	16	12	48	45	44
Hull C.	42	13	17	12	46	47	43
Notts Co.	42	15	13	14	55	60	43
Bolton W.	42	15	12	15	44	40	42
Millwall	42	14	14	14	51	51	42
Fulham	42	16	10	16	39	43	42
Aston Villa	42	13	15	14	48	45	41
Portsmouth	42	14	12	16	45	62	40
Bristol C.	42	14	10	18	47	54	38
Cardiff C.	42	10	16	16	49	62	36
Oxford U.	42	10	16	16	35	46	36
Sheffield W.	42	12	11	19	51	63	35
Crystal Palace	42	11	12	19	43	56	34
Preston N.E.	42	9	14	19	40	62	31
Swindon T.	42	7	11	24	36	72	25

One point deducted from Preston N.E. for including unregistered player.

DIVISION 3

	P	W	D	L	F	A	Pts.
Oldham Ath.	46	25	12	9	83	47	62
Bristol R.	46	22	17	7	65	33	61
York C.	46	21	19	6	67	38	61
Wrexham	46	22	12	12	63	43	56
Chesterfield	46	21	14	11	55	42	56
Grimsby T.	46	18	15	13	67	50	51
Watford	46	19	12	15	64	56	50
Aldershot	46	19	11	16	65	52	49
Halifax T.	46	14	21	11	48	51	49
Huddersfield T.	46	17	13	16	56	55	47
Bournemouth	46	16	15	15	54	58	47
Southend U.	46	16	14	16	62	62	46
Blackburn R.	46	18	10	18	62	64	46
Charlton Ath.	46	19	8	19	66	73	46
Walsall	46	16	13	17	57	48	45
Tranmere R.	46	15	15	16	50	44	45
Plymouth Arg.	46	17	10	19	59	54	44
Hereford U.	46	14	15	17	53	57	43
Brighton	46	16	11	19	52	58	43
Port Vale	46	14	14	18	52	58	42
Cambridge U.	46	13	9	24	48	81	35
Shrewsbury T.	46	10	11	25	41	62	31
Southport	46	6	16	24	35	82	28
Rochdale	46	2	17	27	38	94	21

DIVISION 4

	P	W	D	L	F	A	Pts.
Peterborough	46	27	11	8	75	38	65
Gillingham	46	25	12	9	90	49	62
Colchester U.	46	24	12	10	73	36	60
Bury	46	24	11	11	81	49	59
Northampton T.	46	20	13	13	63	48	53
Reading	46	16	19	11	58	37	51
Chester	46	17	15	14	54	55	49
Bradford C.	46	17	14	15	58	52	48
Newport Co.	46	16	14	16	56	65	45
Exeter C.	45	18	8	19	58	55	44
Hartlepool	46	16	12	18	48	47	44
Lincoln C.	46	16	12	18	63	67	44
Barnsley	46	17	10	19	58	64	44
Swansea C.	46	16	11	19	45	46	43
Rotherham U.	46	15	13	18	56	58	43
Torquay U.	46	13	17	16	52	57	43
Mansfield T.	46	13	17	16	62	69	43
Scunthorpe U.	45	14	12	19	47	64	42
Brentford	46	12	16	18	48	50	40
Darlington	46	13	13	20	40	62	39
Crewe Alex.	46	14	10	22	43	71	38
Doncaster R.	46	12	11	23	47	80	35
Workington	46	11	13	22	43	74	35
Stockport Co.	46	7	20	19	44	69	34

Scunthorpe v Exeter was not played. Scunthorpe were awarded two points. One point deducted from Newport for including unregistered player.

FOOTBALL LEAGUE TABLES 1974-75

DIVISION 1

	P	W	D	L	F	A	Pts.
Derby Co.	42	21	11	10	67	49	53
Liverpool	42	20	11	11	60	39	51
Ipswich T.	42	23	5	14	66	44	51
Everton	42	16	18	8	56	42	50
Stoke C.	42	17	15	10	64	48	49
Sheffield U.	42	18	13	11	58	51	49
Middlesbrough	42	18	12	12	54	40	48
Manchester C.	42	18	10	14	54	54	46
Leeds U.	42	16	13	13	57	49	45
Burnley	42	17	11	14	68	67	45
Q.P.R.	42	16	10	16	54	54	42
Wolverhampton W.	42	14	11	17	57	54	39
West Ham U.	42	13	13	16	58	59	39
Coventry C.	42	12	15	15	51	62	39
Newcastle U.	42	15	9	18	59	72	39
Arsenal	42	13	11	18	47	49	37
Birmingham C.	42	14	9	19	53	61	37
Leicester C.	42	12	12	18	46	60	36
Tottenham H.	42	13	8	21	52	63	34
Luton T.	42	11	11	20	47	65	33
Chelsea	42	9	15	18	42	72	33
Carlisle U.	42	12	5	25	43	59	29

DIVISION 2

	P	W	D	L	F	A	Pts.
Manchester U.	42	26	9	7	66	30	61
Aston Villa	42	25	8	9	69	32	58
Norwich C.	42	20	13	9	58	37	53
Sunderland	42	19	13	10	65	35	51
Bristol C.	42	21	8	13	47	33	50
W.B.A.	42	18	9	15	54	42	45
Blackpool	42	14	17	11	38	33	45
Hull C.	42	15	14	13	40	53	44
Fulham	42	13	16	13	44	39	42
Bolton W.	42	15	12	15	45	41	42
Oxford U.	42	15	12	15	41	51	42
Orient	42	11	20	11	28	39	42
Southampton	42	15	11	16	53	54	41
Notts Co.	42	12	16	14	49	59	40
York C.	42	14	10	18	51	55	38
Nottingham F.	42	12	14	16	43	55	38
Portsmouth	42	12	13	17	44	54	37
Oldham Ath.	42	10	15	17	40	48	35
Bristol R.	42	12	11	19	42	64	35
Millwall	42	10	12	20	44	56	32
Cardiff C.	42	9	14	19	36	62	32
Sheffield W.	42	5	11	26	29	64	21

DIVISION 3

	P	W	D	L	F	A	Pts.
Blackburn R.	46	22	16	8	68	45	60
Plymouth Arg.	46	24	11	11	79	58	59
Charlton Ath.	46	22	11	13	76	61	55
Swindon T.	46	21	11	14	64	58	53
Crystal Palace	46	18	15	13	66	57	51
Port Vale	46	18	15	13	61	54	51
Peterborough U.	46	19	12	15	47	53	50
Walsall	46	18	13	15	67	52	49
Preston N.E.	46	19	11	16	63	56	49
Gillingham	46	17	14	15	65	60	48
Colchester U.	46	17	13	16	70	63	47
Hereford U.	46	16	14	16	64	66	46
Wrexham	46	15	15	16	65	55	45
Bury	46	16	12	18	53	50	44
Chesterfield	46	16	12	18	62	66	44
Grimsby T.	46	15	13	18	55	64	43
Halifax T.	46	13	17	16	49	65	43
Southend U.	46	13	16	17	46	51	42
Brighton & H.A.	46	16	10	20	56	64	42
Aldershot	46	14	11	21	53	63	38*
AFC Bournemouth	46	13	12	21	44	58	38
Tranmere R.	46	14	9	23	55	57	37
Watford	46	10	17	19	52	75	37
Huddersfield T.	46	11	10	25	47	76	32

One point deducted for playing unregistered player.

DIVISION 4

	P	W	D	L	F	A	Pts.
Mansfield T.	46	28	12	6	90	40	68
Shrewsbury T.	46	26	10	10	80	43	62
Rotherham U.	46	22	15	9	71	41	59
Chester	46	23	11	12	64	38	57
Lincoln C.	46	21	15	10	79	48	57
Cambridge U.	46	20	14	12	62	44	54
Reading	46	21	10	15	63	47	52
Brentford	46	18	13	15	53	45	49
Exeter C.	46	19	11	16	60	63	49
Bradford C.	46	17	13	16	56	51	47
Southport	46	15	17	14	56	56	47
Newport Co.	46	19	9	18	68	75	47
Hartlepool	46	16	11	19	52	62	43
Torquay U.	46	14	14	18	46	61	42
Barnsley	46	15	11	20	62	65	41
Northampton T.	46	15	11	20	67	73	41
Doncaster R.	46	14	12	20	65	79	40
Crewe Alex.	46	11	18	17	34	47	40
Rochdale	46	13	13	20	59	75	39
Stockport Co.	46	12	14	20	43	70	38
Darlington	46	13	10	23	54	67	36
Swansea C.	46	15	6	25	26	73	36
Workington	46	10	11	25	46	66	31
Scunthorpe U.	46	7	15	24	41	78	29

THE
FA CUP

Review of the FA Cup 1975-76
1975-76 results and match details
Results of every FA Cup final

THE FOOTBALL ASSOCIATION OFFICIALS

Patron: HER MAJESTY THE QUEEN

President: HRH THE DUKE OF KENT

Honorary Vice-Presidents
His Grace the Duke of Marlborough; The Rt Hon
The Earl of Derby, MC; Air Marshal Sir Ivor
Broom, KCB, CBE, DSO, DFC, AFC; General Sir
Cecil Blacker, KCB, OBE, MC; Right Hon Earl of
Harewood, LLD; Admiral Sir Edward Ashmore,
GCB, DSC, ADC; Sir Stanley Rous, CBE;
Sir Cyril Hawker; Lord Netherthorpe

Chairman of the Council
Sir Andrew Stephen

Vice-Chairman of the Council
Professor Sir Harold Thompson, CBE, MA,
DSC, FRS (Oxford University)

Life Vice-Presidents
R. H. Brough (Nottinghamshire FA);
Major J. Stewart, OBE (Public Schools);
I. Robinson (Liverpool County FA);
J. W. Bowers (Essex County FA);
G. N. Watson, JP (Nottingham Forest FC)

Vice-Presidents
Sir Andrew Stephen;
E. D. Smith, MBE, JP (Cumberland FA);
A. D. McMullen, MBE (Bedfordshire FA);
R. V. Stokes (Hampshire FA);
Professor Sir Harold Thompson, CBE, MA, DSC,
FRS (Oxford University);
F. Barrett (West Riding County FA)
Rt Hon Lord Westwood, JP, FCIS (Football
League)

Secretary
E. Croker, 16 Lancaster Gate, London W2 3LW

F.A. CUP 1975-76

The pattern of events in the 1975–76 FA Cup competition were to revive, inevitably, brisk discussion on the advisability of a ' seeded ' draw: certainly, if the pairing of clubs had been manipulated as some suggested the casualty rate among the famous would have been avoided. But then we should not have been left with a final that went so tantalisingly against all probability.

Manchester United and Southampton arrived at Wembley by vastly different routes. United, youthful, aggressive, and proponents of a new school of attack, had leapt excitingly from peak to peak, often in peril, it seemed, but sure-footed enough to maintain momentum.

They had been a goal down against Oxford in the third round, and needed two Daly penalties to pass on. Good matches with Peterborough and Leicester carried them to the sixth round, and a match with Wolves. The first clash, at Old Trafford, was drawn. In the replay Wolves fashioned two goals out of their great past – long passes to the wings, hard centres then driven home – to take what seemed a secure lead. Now United were tested to the limit, and triumphed. Pearson, Greenhoff, and McIlroy scored to reward football that was all about resilience, belief, and adventure.

United's next match, against Derby in the semi-final, was many watcher's idea of the 'real' climax of this cup. These *were* the two best sides left in, this *would* have been a magnetic match for Wembley. United, giving years away to Derby in experience, seemed least fancied, but their victory was never in doubt. Brash and aggressive, totally unflurried by the occasion, they never allowed Derby's maturity to count. Two goals by Hill saw them through.

How much less spectacular had been Southampton's route among the foothills of the competition. Their only top-class opposition came from Aston Villa in the third round. A minute of so from time, despite being at home, Southampton were a goal down. Then Fisher struck to earn them a replay, and they went on to a well-worked victory at Villa Park. Blackpool fell next – no great feat perhaps. Then West Bromwich were defeated at the second attempt, with Channon's three-goal contribution quite vital.

In the sixth round the improbable opposition of little Bradford City loomed up and was disposed of, but only by a single goal. Crystal Palace, a Third Division side whose Cup run was to cost them promotion (and, ultimately, their manager) slid through to confront them in the semi-final, and by most fans' reckoning were fancied to win. Palace, with Malcolm Allison's showmanship evident, looked to have the greater flair. Southampton, with Lawrie McMenemy maintaining the club's low profile, said little and promised nothing. But on the day their steady application did the talking for them, and Gilchrist and Peach (a penalty) took them through.

As Wembley neared, few living outside Southampton's enclave on the South Coast gave them a chance. How could you make a case for a club that had done nothing in the Cup since antiquity against the drive of United's talented youngsters, still in with a chance, remember, of a Cup and League double? The answer was that, unless you sought comfort in the knowledge of men like Rodrigues, Blyth, Steele, McCalliog and Osgood, you couldn't.

In fact, during the week of the match, most neutrals were looking back along the path of the competition, puzzled still by the absence of more suitable opponents for the overwhelming favourites, Manchester. Where had all the big clubs gone?

Their remains could be seen littering the route to Wembley from the third round on. All four London First Division clubs went out at that first hurdle, all beaten by their First Division peers. Liverpool and later Everton and Newcastle fell to Derby, Spurs and Manchester City to Stoke, Arsenal and Ipswich were gobbled by Wolves. Giant-killers, though Bradford City beat Norwich, and Palace, incredibly, beat Leeds, were hardly needed – the giants were killing themselves. At least eight non-First Division sides were suddenly, improbably, guaranteed a place in the last 16.

So that explains how Southampton got to the final, but it doesn't account for what happened then. The way most people previewed the match, Manchester United's momentum, once established, would overwhelm Southampton as it had so many teams before. Probably that was true. What Southampton achieved, in effect, was not to survive that momentum, but rather to prevent it from beginning.

Good tackling, and quietly alert concentration on cover by their defence kept United

in low gear. Southampton picked their moments to attack, then, when foiled, trotted swiftly back to regroup. Manchester's bright hope, winger Hill, disappointing on the day as to be substituted in the second half, saw little of the ball. Not because United didn't try to find him, not because his marker, Rodrigues, stamped him out, but because Southampton quietly interposed the nearest available forward between him and the pass. It was beautifully done, and such small tactical sums added up to a huge strategic advantage.

United, especially towards the end of the first half, and again deep into the second 45 minutes, shrugged free of the constraint and began to play. But all too soon McCalliog and, especially, Steele and Holmes, would bite into their rhythm, making it falter and stop.

It was never as dull as deadlock, for the quality of men like McIlroy and, persistently, Coppell, shone enough to maintain promise. It was never as sterile as stalemate, for there was an edge about Southampton's advances on the heels of Channon's running and Osgood's dribble, that kept attention alert. And seven minutes from time Bobby Stokes, among the least famous on this field, ran purposefully to McCalliog's shrewd pass and half-hit the winning goal beyond Stepney's dive. Southampton's fans boiled over, United's stood glum – but then they'd hardly been in full voice all day.

When Lawrie McMenemy recalled his words to his team: 'Never mind if the Queen *is* watching, if there's danger, belt the ball into the Tyne.' some felt he was confessing to a crime, in having reduced the final to a matter of football mathematics. That is too narrow a view: there is no obligation on any finalist team to play a match at the opposition's preferred tempo, no requirement to throw aside your own merits to provide neutrals with confirmation of their hopes. Southampton, of the Second Division, played to their limit, and prevented United from reaching theirs. The 1975–76 FA Cup honours went to an honest team, if not a great one.

Final at Wembley, May 1 1976   Southampton 1, Manchester United 0

Southampton: Turner; Rodrigues, Peach, Holmes, Blyth, Steele, Gilchrist, Channon, Osgood, McCalliog, Stokes.

Manchester United: Stepney; Forsyth, Houston, Daly, Greenhoff, Buchan, Coppell, McIlroy, Pearson, Macari, Hill (McCreery).

Scorer: Stokes.

FA CHALLENGE CUP COMPETITION 1975-76

Preliminary Round

Horden C.W. v Bridlington T.	1-1, 1-4
Evenwood T. v Bridlington T.	2-3
Crook T. v Barrow	3-0
Louth U. v Barton T.	0-0, 3-1
Mossley v Emley	2-0
Horwich RMI v Farsley Celtic	1-1, 1-1, 2-1
Gt. Harwood v Burscough	2-1
Porthmadog v Bethesda Ath.	3-2
New Brighton v Bacup Bor.	3-1
Eastwood v Buxton	2-3
Hednesford v Brereton Social	1-1, 1-1, 3-3, 2-0
Enderby T. v Atherstone T.	2-1
Hinckley Ath. v Dudley T.	0-4
Alvechurch v Evesham U.	1-1, 1-0
Llanelli v Mangotsfield U.	0-2
Coventry Sp. v Bromsgrove R.	3-0
Kidderminster H. v Bedworth U.	0-1
Milton Keynes C. v Didcot T.	3-1
Corby T. v Boston	0-0, 2-1
Kings Lynn v Gorleston	2-0
Lowestoft T. v Harwich & Parkeston	4-3
Grays Ath. v Barnet	1-2
Epsom & Ewell v Corinthian Cas.	4-2
Harrow Bor. v Barking	2-2, 0-2
Harlow T. v Clacton T.	2-3
Hertford T. v Burnham	0-2
Hatfield T. v Edmonton & Haringey	1-0
Hoddesdon T. v Dunstable T.	1-2
Gravesend & Northfleet v Chertsey T.	1-1, 2-0
Folkestone & Shepway v Canterbury C.	1-2
Maidstone U. v Eastbourne U.	5-0
Haywards Heath v Burgess Hill T.	0-4
Littlehampton T. v Chichester C.	1-1, 2-0
Guildford & Dorking U. v Arundel	7-0
Fareham T. v Bath C.	1-0
Melksham T. v Devizes T.	2-0
Penzance v Bideford	5-1

First Round Qualifying

Willington v Bridlington T.	4-2
Whitby T. v Wingate	4-0
Eppleton Colliery Wel v Ferryhill Ath.	1-0
Bishop Auckland v North Shields	0-1
Tow Law T. v Bridlington Tr.	1-0
South Bank v Weat Auckland T.	2-0
Durham C. v Easington Colliery Wel.	1-3
Billingham Synthonia v Shildon	1-1, 2-3
Spennymoor U. v Crook T.	1-1, 2-1
Penrith v Whitley Bay	1-0
Boldon Colliery Wel. v Consett	2-0
Ashington v Netherfield	0-2
Selby T. v Louth U.	1-0
Retford T. v Skegness T.	0-0, 2-0
Brigg T. v Goole T.	2-1
Ashby Inst. v Mexborough T.	0-1
Worksop T. v Mossley	1-0
Winterton R. v Yorkshire Am.	4-2
Frickley Col. v Gainsborough Tr.	3-0
Denaby U. v Stocksbridge Works Soc.	4-1
Radcliffe Bor. v Horwich R.M.I.	4-0
Leyland Motors v Rossendale U.	1-8
Fleetwood v Glossop	2-0
Clitheroe v Lancaster C.	1-2
Prestwich Heys v Gt. Harwood	0-1
Prescot T. v Stalybridge Celtic	1-1, 2-1
Darwen v Droylsden	2-3
Accrington Stanley 1968 v Hyde U.	2-3
Runcorn v Porthmadog	5-3
Rhyl v St. Helens T.	4-2
Formby v Marine	0-1
Bangor C. v Pwllheli & District	2-0
Winsford U. v New Brighton	4-1
S. Liverpool v Witton A.	0-3
Chorley v Nantwich T.	1-0
Ashton U. v Skelmersdale U.	1-2
Northwich Vic. v Buxton	2-0
New Mills v Oswestry T.	1-1, 3-5
Congleton T. v Curzon Ashton	4-3

Armitage v Leek T.	0-3
Sutton Coldfield T. v Hednesford	1-0
Macclesfield T. v Sutton T.	0-0, 4-0
Burton A. v Darlaston	1-3
Arnold v Long Eaton U.	2-1
Moor Green v Enderby T.	0-1
Heanor T. v Tividale	2-6
Bilston v Eastwood T.	3-1
Alfreton T. v Gresley R.	2-0
Stourbridge v Dudley T.	0-1
Nuneaton Bor. v Tamworth	2-1
Gornal Ath. v Highgate U.	1-0
Belper T. v Ilkeston T.	1-0
Welton R. v Alvechurch	1-3
Ton Pentre v Worcester C.	4-3
Barry T. v Everwarm	1-1, 1-0
Mangotsfield U. v Merthyr T.	0-1
Oldbury U. v Coventry Sp.	0-0, 1-3
Halesowen T. v Warley Co. Bor	2-1
Chippenham T. v Cinderford T.	2-4
Brierly Hill All. v Gloucester C.	2-1
Rothwell T. v Bedworth U.	1-0
Oxford C. v Wolverton T. & BR	2-0
Cheltenham T. v Desborough T.	1-1, 3-2
Banbury U. v Lye T.	1-0
Wellingborough T. v Milton Keynes C.	0-1
Rushden T. v Witney T.	0-3
Irthlingborough Diamonds v A.P. Leamington	1-2
Aylesbury U. v Redditch U.	2-1
Stamford v Corby T.	3-2
Parson Drove U. v Thetford T.	5-5, 0-5
Bourne T. v Chatteris T.	4-0
Bedford T. v Ely C.	2-0
Spalding U. v Kings Lynn	3-3, 1-1, 5-2
Soham T. R. v Wisbech T.	1-0
Gt. Yarmouth T. v Holbeach U.	1-0
Bury T. v St. Neots T.	1-1, 0-2
Stowmarket v Lowestoft T.	0-1
Potton U. v Sudbury T.	2-1
Hitson v Letchworth T.	0-2
Cambridge C. v March T. U.	5-1
Sutton U. v Barnet	1-1, 2-1
Staines T. v Tring T.	2-0
Chesham U. v Epping T.	3-0
Aveley v Hornchurch	1-1, 1-3
Southall & Ealing Bor. v Epsom & Ewell	1-1, 3-3, 5-1
Leyton Wingate v Tilbury	1-1, 0-11
Cray W. v Dulwich Hamlet	1-3
Bexley U. v Hillingdon Bor.	0-2
Stevenage Ath. v Barking	2-1
St. Albans C. v Tooting & Mitcham U.	3-3, 0-4
Bracknell T. v Feltham	1-1, 2-3
Ruislip Manor v Clacton T.	0-2
Romford v Ware	3-1
Clapton v Finchley	3-1
Cheshunt v Hemel Hempstead	2-2, 2-0
Windsor & Eton v Burnham	1-1, 0-1
Wealdstone v Woking	1-1, 5-3
Dagenham v Edgware	5-1
Boreham Wood v Hounslow	2-0
Tonbridge v Hatfield T.	5-0
Marlow v Wokingham T.	2-0
Egham T. v Hampton	2-0
Carshalton Ath. v Kingstonian	1-0
Vauxhall Motors v Dunstable T.	0-1
Uxbridge v Wembley	1-2
Enfield v Hayes	3-0
Biggleswade T. v Maidstone U.	0-1
Walthamstow Av. v Gravesend & Northfleet	2-1
Molesey v Willesden	4-1
Croydon v Erith & Belvedere	1-1, 3-1
Bromley v Leytonstone	3-1
Sidley U. v Canterbury C.	0-2
Sheppey U. v Whitstable T.	5-1
Deal T. v Eastbourne T.	1-1, 0-1
Bexhill T. v Margate	0-8
Ringmer v Maidstone U.	1-1, 1-3

Ramsgate v Sittingbourne 4-1
Faversham T. v Herne Bay 2-1
Dover v Peacehaven & Telscombe 4-1
Redhill v Burgess Hill T. 1-0
Medway v Tunbridge Wells 1-3
Crawley T. v Hastings U. 2-1
Ashford T. v Lewes 2-1
Waterlooville v Littlehampton T. 2-2, 3-1
Poole T. v Worthing 1-0
Cowes v Gosport Bor. 0-2
Bognor Regis T. v Newport IOW 1-3
Ryde Sports v Guildford & Dorking U. 0-4
Pagham v Southwick 1-1, 1-3
Basingstoke T. v Farnborough T. 2-1
Alton T. v Horsham 2-1
Swaythling v Fareham T. 2-0
Salisbury v Trowbridge T. 3-1
Bridport v Dorchester T. 4-3
Andover v Frome T. 1-1, 3-5
Weston-Super-Mare v Melksham T. 3-0
Stonehouse v Yeovil T. 0-6
Glastonbury v Hungerford T. 2-1
Bridgwater T. v Minehead 1-2
Tiverton T. v Penzance 1-3
Taunton T. v Wadebridge T. 2-3
Falmouth T. v Newquay 5-1
Barnstaple T. v St. Blazey 9-1

Second Round Qualifying
Willington v Whitby T. 2-0
Eppleton Colliery Wel. v North Shields 1-1, 1-0
Tow Law T. v South Bank 2-1
Easington Colliery Wel. v Shildon 1-3
Spennymoor U. v Penrith 2-0
Boldon Colliery Wel. v Netherfield 1-1, 2-3
Selby T. v Retford T. 0-2
Brigg T. v Mexborouth T. 2-3
Worksop T. v Winterton R. 4-3
Frickley Col. v Denaby U. 2-2, 2-0
Radcliffe Bor. v Rossendale U. 2-2, 1-4
Fleetwood v Lancaster C. 1-1, 1-2
Gt. Harwood v Prescot T. 5-1
Droylsden v Hyde U. 3-2
Runcorn v Rhyl 4-1
Marine v Bangor C. 1-0
Winsford U. v Witton A. 3-2
Chorley v Skelmersdale U. 3-1
Northwich Vic. v Oswestry T. 3-1
Congleton T. v Leek T. 1-3
Sutton Coldfield T. v Macclesfield T. 0-2
Darlaston v Arnold 0-1
Enderby T. v Tividale 0-1
Bilston v Alfreton T. 2-2, 1-2
Dudley T. v Nuneaton Bor. 0-1
Gornal Ath. v Belper T. 2-0
Alvechurch v Ton Pentre 1-0
Barry T. v Merthyr Tydfil 5-2
Coventry Sp. v Halesowen T. 2-0
Cinderford T. v Brielrey Hill All. 0-1
Rothwell T. v Oxford C. 0-1
Cheltenham T. v Banbury U. 2-0
Milton Keynes C. v Witney T. 2-1
AP. Leamington v Aylesbury U. 3-1
Stamford v Thetford T. 2-0
Bourne T. v Bedford T. 1-5
Spalding U. v Soham Town R. 8-2
Gt. Yarmouth T. v St. Neots T. 3-2
Lowestoft T. v Potton U. 3-3, 3-1
Letchworth T. v Cambridge C. 0-1
Sutton U. v Staines T. 5-1
Chesham U. v Hornchurch 2-0
Southall & Ealing Bor. v Tilbury 2-1
Dulwich Hamlet v Hillingdon Bor. 5-1
Stevenage Ath. v Tooting & Mitcham U. 2-2, 0-2
Feltham v Addlestone 2-6
Clacton T. v Romford 1-1, 2-3
Clapton v Cheshunt 1-2
Burnham v Wealdstone 0-2
Dagenham v Boreham Wood 4-0
Tonbridge v Marlow 2-2, 3-1
Egham T. v Kingstonian 0-2
Dunstable T. v Wembley 0-2
Enfield v Maidenhead U. 6-0

Walthamston Ave. v Molesey 1-2
Croydon v Bromley 2-1
Canterbury C. v Sheppey U. 6-2
Eastbourne T. v Margate 0-2
Maidstone U. v Ramsgate 1-2
Faversham T. v Dover 0-4
Redhill v Tunbridge Wells 4-1
Crawley T. v Ashford T. 4-1
Waterlooville v Poole T. 3-0
Gosport Bor. v Newport I.O.W. 2-2, 1-1, 2-0
Guildford & Dorking U. v Southwick 2-2, 2-3
Basingstoke T. v Alton T. 5-0
Swaythling v Salisbury 0-1
Bridgport v Frome T. 0-3
Weston-super-Mare v Yeovil T. 0-0, 0-4
Glastonbury v Minehead 0-4
Penzance v Wadebridge T. 2-1
Falmouth T. v Barnstaple T. 4-0

Third Round Qualifying
Willington v Eppleton Colliery Wel. 2-1
Tow Law T. v Shildon 4-1
Spennymoor U. v Netherfield 3-0
Retford T. v Mexborough T. 1-2
Worksop T. v Frickley Colliery 1-1, 1-1, 2-0
Rossendale U. v Lancaster C. 2-1
G. Harwood v Droylsden 1-1, 1-1, 0-1
Runcorn v Marine 0-0, 0-1
Winsford U. v Chorley 2-0
Northwich Vic. v Leek T. 1-1, 0-1
Macclesfield T. v Arnold 3-1
Tividale v Alfreton T. 0-0, 1-0
Nuneaton Bor. v Gornal Ath. 1-1, 3-0
Alvechurch v Barry T. 3-1
Coventry Sp. v Brierley Hill All. 2-1

Oxford C. v Cheltenham T. 0-0, 0-2
Milton Keynes C. v A.P. Leamington 0-1
Stamford v Bedford T. 0-2
Spalding v Great Yarmouth T. 2-0
Lowestoft T. v Cambridge C. 1-0
Sutton U. v Chesham U. 3-1
Southall & Ealing Bor. v Dulwich Hamlet 2-2, 2-1
Tooting & Mitcham U. v Addlestone 4-2
Romford v Cheshunt 1-0
Wealdstone v Dagenham 2-0
Tonbridge v Kingstonian 0-0, 1-3
Wembley v Enfield 1-0
Molesey v Croydon 0-4
Canterbury C. v Margate 0-4
Ramsgate v Dover 0-2
Redhill v Crawley T. 1-1, 0-1
Waterlooville v Gosport Bor. 4-0
Southwick v Basingstoke T. 2-1
Salisbury v Frome T. 1-0
Yeovil T. v Minehead 1-0
Penzance v Falmouth T. 0-3

Fourth Round Qualifying
Tow Law T. v Spennymoor U. 0-2
Droylsden v Gateshead U. 0-4
Blyth Spartans v Rossendale U. 0-0, 0-1
Willington v Morecambe 2-2, 1-4
Mexborough T. v Macclesfield T. 1-2
Worksop T. v Marine 0-0, 0-4
Kettering T. v Boston U. 3-4
Stafford R. v Alvechurch 1-1, 2-1
Nuneaton Bor. V Cheltenham T. 2-1
Coventry Sp. v Spalding U. 2-0
A.P. Leamington v Tividale 3-2
Telford U. v Winsford U. 1-1, 4-5
Grantham v Leek T. 4-0
Bedford T. v Lowestoft T. 6-1
Wembley v Dartford 0-1
Hitchin T. v Romford 0-1
Chelmsford C. v Bishop's Stortford 0-2
Leatherhead v Ilford 1-0
Wealdstone v Southwick 3-1
Southall & Ealing Bor. v Tooting & Mitcham U. 1-4
Slouth T. v Walton & Hersham 1-2
Wimbledon v Kingstonian 6-1
Sutton U. v Waterlooville 1-1, 3-1

Hendon v Canterbury C.   1-0
Crawley T. v Dover   0-0, 0-6
Croydon v Wycombe W.   2-2, 2-5
Falmouth T. v Yeovil T.   1-5
Salisbury v Weymouth   4-5

First Round
Aldershot v Wealdstone   4-3
A.P. Leamington v Stafford   2-3
Boston U. v Lincoln C.   0-1
Bradford C. v Chesterfield   1-0
Brentford v Northampton T.   2-0
Bury v Doncaster R.   4-2
Cardiff C. v Exeter C.   6-2
*Colchester U. v Dover   3-3, 1-4
Coventry Spts. v Tranmere R.   2-0
C. Palace v Walton   1-0
*Darlington v Chester   0-0, 0-2
Dartford v Bishops Stortford   1-4
*Grantham v Port Vale   2-2, 1-4
Grimsby T. v Gateshead   1-3
Halifax T. v Altrincham   3-1
Hartlepool v Stockport Co.   3-0
Hendon v Reading   1-0
Hereford U. v Torquay U.   2-0
Leatherhead v Cambridge U.   2-0
*Mansfield T. v Wrexham   1-1, 1-1, 2-1
Marine v Barnsley   3-1
*Newport Co. v Swindon T.   2-2, 0-3
Nuneaton v Wimbledon   0-1
Peterborough U. v. Winsford   4-1
Preston N.E. v Scunthorpe U.   2-1
Romford v Tooting & Mitcham U.   0-1
Rossendale v Shrewsbury T.   0-1
Rotherham U. v Crewe Alex.   2-1
Scarborough v Morecambe   2-0
Sheffield W. v Macclesfield   3-1
Southend U. v Swansea C.   2-0
Spennymoor v Southport   4-1
*Sutton v AFC Bournemouth   1-1, 0-1
Walsall v Huddersfield T.   0-1
Watford v Brighton & H.A.   0-3
Weymouth v Gillingham   0-2
Wigan Ath. v Matlock   4-1
*Workington v Rochdale   1-1, 1-2
Wycombe W. Bedford   0-0, 2-2, 2-1
*Yeovil v Millwall   1-1, 2-2, 0-1

Second Round
Aldershot v Bishops Stortford   2-0
*AFC Bournemouth v Hereford U.   2-2, 0-2
Bury v Spennymoor   3-0
Cardiff C. v Wycombe W.   1-0
Coventry Spts. v Peterborough U.   0-4
*Gateshead v Rochdale   1-1, 1-3
Gillingham v Brighton & H.A.   0-1
Hendon v Swindon T.   0-1
Huddersfield T. v Port Vale   2-1
*Leatherhead v Tooting & Mitcham   0-0, 1-2
Mansfield T. v Lincoln C.   1-2
*Marine v Hartlepool   1-1, 3-6
*Millwall v C. Palace   1-1, 1-2
Rotherham U. v Bradford C.   0-3
Scarborough v Preston N.E.   3-2
Sheffield W. v Wigan Ath.   2-0
Shrewsbury T. v Chester   3-1
Southend U. v Dover   4-1
Stafford v Halifax T.   1-3
Wimbledon v Brentford   0-2

Third Round
Aldershot v Lincoln C.   1-2
Blackpool v Burnley   1-0

*Brentford v Bolton W.   0-0, 0-2
Charlton Ath. v Sheffield W.   2-1
*Chelsea v Bristol R.   1-1, 1-0
Coventry C. v Bristol C.   2-1
Derby Co. v Everton   2-1
Fulham v Huddersfield T.   2-3
*Hull C. v Plymouth Arg.   1-1, 4-1
Ipswich T. v Halifax T.   3-1
Leicester C. v Sheffield U.   3-0
Luton T. v Blackburn R.   2-0
Manchester C. v Hartlepool   6-0
Manchester U. v. Oxford U.   2-1
*Middlesbrough v Bury   0-0, 2-3
*Norwich C. v Rochdale   1-1, 0-0, 2-1
Notts Co. v Leeds U.   0-1
*Nottingham F. v Peterborough U.   0-0, 0-1
Orient v Cardiff C.   0-1
*Portsmouth v Birmingham C.   1-1, 1-0
*Q.P.R. v Newcastle U.   0-0, 1-2
Scarborough v C. Palace   1-2
Shrewsbury T. v Bradford C.   1-2
*Southampton v Aston Villa   1-1, 2-1
Southend U. v Brighton & H.A.   2-1
Sunderland v Oldham Ath.   2-0
*Swindon T. v Tooting & Mitcham   2-2, 1-2
*Tottenham H. v Stoke C.   1-1, 1-2
W.B.A. v Carlisle U.   3-1
West Ham U. v Liverpool   0-2
Wolverhampton W. v Arsenal   3-0
York C. v Hereford U.   2-1

Fourth Round
Bradford C. v Tooting & Mitcham U.   3-1
*Charlton Ath. v Portsmouth   1-1, 3-0
*Coventry C. v Newcastle U.   1-1, 0-5
Derby Co. v Liverpool   1-0
Huddersfield T. v Bolton W.   0-1
*Ipswich T. v Wolverhampton W.   0-0, 0-1
Leeds U. v C. Palace   0-1
Leicester C. v Bury   1-0
Manchester U. v Peterborough U.   3-1
Norwich C. v Luton T.   2-0
Southampton v Blackpool   3-1
Southend U. v Cardiff C.   2-1
Stoke C. v Manchester C.   1-0
Sunderland v Hull C.   1-0
W.B.A. v Lincoln C.   3-2
York C. v Chelsea   0-2

Fifth Round
*Bolton W. v Newcastle U.   3-3, 0-0, 1-2
Chelsea v C. Palace   2-3
Derby Co. v Southend U.   1-0
Leicester C. v Manchester U.   1-2
Norwich C. v Bradford C.   1-2
*Stoke C. v Sunderland   0-0, 1-2
*W.B.A. v Southampton   1-1, 0-4
Wolverhampton W. v Charlton Ath.   3-0

Sixth Round
Bradford C. v Southampton   0-1
Derby Co. v Newcastle U.   4-2
*Manchester U. v Wolverhampton W.   1-1, 3-2
Sunderland v C. Palace   0-1

Semi-finals
Manchester U. v Derby Co.   2-0
Southampton v C. Palace   2-0

Final
Southampton v Manchester U.   1-0
Att. 100,000   Receipts £420,000

FA CUP DETAILS 1975-76

FIRST ROUND

NOV. 22

Aldershot (0) 4 (*Richardson, Morrissey pen., Howarth 2*)
Wealdstone (0) 3 (*Duck 2, 1 pen., Lewis*) 5225
Aldershot: Johnson; Walden, Walker, Crosby, Richardson, Jopling, Walton, Morrissey, Howarth, Bell, Warnock.
Wealdstone: Morton; Kinnear, Watson, Fairclough, McCormick, Moss, Lewis, Fulton, Byrne, Duck, Henderson.

A.P. Leamington (1) 2 (*Keeley 2*)
Stafford (1) 3 (*Jones 2, Hughes*) 3200
A.P. Leamington: Jones D.; Taylor, Kavanagh, Jones, A., Brown, Boot, Adcock, Lee, Keeley, Stewart, Talbot.
Stafford: Arnold; Ritchie, Richards, Lowe, Seddon, Morris, McLeish, Chapman, Jones, Hutchison, Hughes (Chadwick).

Boston U. (0) 0
Lincoln C. (0) 1 (*Freeman*) 6500
Boston U.: Stewart; Moyes, Taylor, Coxon, Madden, Adamson, Gallery, Symm, Reed, Kabia, Wilkinson.
Lincoln C.: Grotier; Branfoot, Leigh, Booth, Ellis, Cooper, Fleming, Freeman, Graham, Smith Harding (Ward.)

Bradford C. (0) 1 (*Hutchins*)
Chesterfield (0) 0 4352
Bradford C.: Downsborough; Podd, Cooper, Hockey, Middleton, Fretwell, McGinley, Johnson, Cooke, Ingram, Hutchins.
Chesterfield: Tingay; Welch, O'Neill, Hunter, Winstanley (McElvaney), Barlow, Moss, McEwan, Kowalski, Wann, Bentley.

Brentford (0) 2 (*Sweetzer 2*)
Northampton T. (0) 0 6640
Brentford: Priddy; Bence, Allen, French (Nelmes), Lawrence, Smith, Graham, Scales. Cross, Sweetzer, Johnson.
Northampton T.: Starling; Gregory, Tucker, Best, Robertson, Carlton, Felton, McGowan, Hall, Christie, Farrington.

Bury (2) 4 (*Riley, Hamstead, Rowland 2*)
Doncaster R. (1) 3 (*Uzelac 2*) 7094
Bury: Forrest; Hoolickin, Kennedy, Nicholson, Hulme, Bailey, Riley, Phillips, Rowland, Williams, Hamstead.
Doncaster R.: Peacock; Ternent, Robinson, Chappell, Uzelac, Brookes, Miller, Murray, O'Callaghan, Kitchen (Reed), Balderstone.

Cardiff C. (3) 6 (*Reece 2, Alston 3, Evans*)
Exeter C. (1) 2 (*Beer, Robertson*) 7532
Cardiff C.: Irwin; Dwyer, Charles, Buchanan, England, Larmour, Reece, Livermore, Alston, Evans, Anderson.
Exeter C.: Key; Rutter (Joy), Hooker, Wingate, Saxton, Hatch, Hodge, Bowker, Robertson, Beer, Moxham.

Colchester U. (2) 3 (*Leslie, Dominey, Smith*)
Dover (2) 3 (*Coupland, Waite, Rogers*) 3765
Colchester U.: Walker; Dwyer, Williams, Bunkell, Dominey, Packer, Cook, Leslie, Foley. Anderson, Smith.
Dover: Raine; Hamshire, Keeley, Reynolds, Waite, Fursdon, Coxhill, Coupland, Housdon, Light, Rogers.

Coventry Sp. (1) 2 (*Gallagher 2*)
Tranmere R. (0) 0 4565
Coventry Sp: Jeavons; Sorbie, Mundy, Dunk, Jones, Skelcey, Randle, Starkey, Gallagher, Core, Manning.
Tranmere R.: Johnson; Mathias, Griffiths, Parry, Philpotts, Young, Peplow, Mitchell (Kenny), Moore, Tynan, James.

Crystal Palace (0) 1 (*Kemp*)
Walton (0) 0 16,241
Crystal Palace: Hammond; Wall, Cannon, Holder, Jeffries, Evans, Chatterton, Johnson. Kemp, Swindlehurst, Taylor.
Walton: Bloom; Mason, Barrow, Shepherd, Hunt, Griffiths, Griffith, Burridge, Male, Horstead, Bisset (Baker).

Darlington (0) 0
Chester (0) 0 2620
Darlington: Ogley; Nattress, Lees, Craig, Noble, Cowan (Cochrane), Holbrook, Sinclair, Rowles, Lowrey, Young.
Chester: Millington; Edwards, Loska, Storton, Delgado, Pugh, Redfern, Draper, Moore, Owen, Lennard.

Dartford (0) 1 (*Reeves*)
Bishops Stortford (1) 4 (*Watson P., 3, McKenzie*) 2187
Dartford: Vasper; Payne, Mears, Gibbs, Pittaway, Sampson, Reeves, Henderson, Dudman, Mitchell, Shovelar.
Bishops Stortford: Kitson; Harris, Davis, Flack, Clark, Mulkearn, Leakey, Gaine, MacKenzie, Twigg, Watson.

Grantham (0) 2 (*Benskin, Norris*)
Port Vale (1) 2 (*Brownbill 2*) 2853
Grantham: Gardiner; Bower, Capewell G., Capewell M., Harrison, Clapham, Jackson, Nixon, Norris, Flemming, Benskin.
Port Vale: Connaughton; Tartt, Dulson (Williams), Horton, Ridley, Harris, McLaren, Lees, Cullerton, Bailey, Brownbill.

Grimsby T. (0) 1 (*Booth*)
Gateshead (2) 3 (*Common, Mutrie, Thompson*) 5120
Grimsby T.: Freeman; Marley, Booth, Barton, Jones, Gray, Hubbard, Partridge, Brown (Ford), Boylen, Lewis.
Gateshead: Nesbitt; Irwin, Guthrie, Wilson, Albeson, McLeod, Johnson, Thompson (Murray), Mutrie, Morrison, Common.

Halifax T. (2) 3 (*McHale 2, 1 pen., Rhodes*)
Altrincham (0) 1 (*Moore*) 4077
Halifax T.: Gennoe; Veitch, Collins, McHale, Rhodes, Phelan. Ford, Pugh, Bell. Gwyther, Downes.
Altrincham: Cavanagh; Allan, Brooke, Clements (Carrick), Casey, Owens, Wain, Dickinson, Moore Hughes R., Hughes J.

489

Hartlepool (1) 3 (*Smith D., McMahon, Potter*)
Stockport Co. (0) 0   3348
Hartlepool: Hope; Smith R., Goad, Potter, Rowlands, Johnson, Bielby, Smith D., Moore, McMahon, Scaife.
Stockport Co.: Hopkinson; Turner, Buckley, Bradley, Holsgrove, Fogarty, McNeill, Hollis, Massey, Lawther, Cross.

Hendon (1) 1 (*Phillips*)
Reading (0) 0   3500
Hendon: Dalrymple; Field J., Hand, Yerby, Phillips, Haider, Jeffries, Metchick, Baker, Field A., Child.
Reading: Death; Lenarduzzi, Moreline, Cumming, Barker, Youlden, Stuckey, Carnaby, Murray, Hiron, Whitham (Peters).

Hereford U. (1) 2 (*Carter, Tucker*)
Torquay U. (0) 0   6542
Hereford U.: Charlton; Emery, Ritchie, Layton, Tucker, Lindsay, Paine (Silkman), Tyler, Davey, McNeil, Carter.
Torquay U.: Lee; Lynch, Sandercock, Boulton, Kruse, Parker. Twitchin, Hickman, Lane, Kennedy, Provan (Morrall).

Leatherhead (2) 2 (*Batson o.g., Doyle*)
Cambridge U. (0) 0   2500
Leatherhead: Swannell; Sargent, Ibbitson, Woofinden, Reid, Wells, Cooper, Layers, Kelly, Smith, W., Doyle.
Cambridge U.: Smith G.; Howell, Seary, Lyon, Eades, Batson, Fallon, Spriggs, Simmons, Horsfall, Shinton.

Mansfield T. (1) 1 (*Eccles*)
Wrexham (1) 1 (*Madden o.g.*)   6279
Mansfield T.: Brown; Pate, Foster B., McDonald, Madden, Bird, Matthews (Foster C.), Eccles, Clarke, Hodgson, Mackenzie.
Wrexham: Lloyd; Hill, Evans, Davis, May, Fogg, Tinnion, Sutton, Ashcroft, Dwyer, Griffiths.

Marine (2) 3 (*Burke o.g., Glover 2*)
Barnsley (1) 1 (*Butler*)   2400
Marine: Crosbie; Pritchard, Hammill, Smith, Bennett, Edwards, Shergold, Bennie, Glover, Windsor, Morrey.
Barnsley: Springett; Yates, Chambers. Doyle, Burke, Pickering, Millar (Peachey), Price, Butler, Walker, Otulakowski.

Newport Co. (1) 2 (*Godfrey, Parsons*)
Swindon T. (0) 2 (*Moss, Syrett*)   5182
Newport Co.: Macey, Screen, Relish, Godfrey (White), Aizlewood, Hancock, Hooper, Love, Parson, Jones, Elliott.
Swindon T.: Barron; Taylor, Trollope, Emanuel, Burrows, Stroud, Moss, Dixon, Eastoe, Hubbard (Syrett), Anderson.

Nuneaton (0) 0
Wimbledon (0) 1 (*Connell*)   4425
Nuneaton: Knight; Stephens, Newton, Hankins, Bennsty, Cross, Goodwin, Sleet, Briscoe, Oakes, Matthans (Taylor).
Wimbledon: Guy; Tilley, Bryant, Donaldson, Edwards (Vansittart), Bassett, Rice, Cooke, Connell, Holmes, Mahon.

Peterborough U. (0) 4 (*Nixon, Cozens, Gregory, Turner*)
Winsford (0) 1 (*Chadwick*)   8324
Peterborough U.: Steele; Murray, Lee, Eustace, Turner, Carmichael, Nixon, Gregory, Cozens, Hughes, Robson.
Winsford: Whitlow; Harrop, Roberts, Woods, Neale, Mason, Bebbington, Chadwick, Clements, Smith, Houghton.

Preston N.E. (0) 2 (*Morley pen., Elwiss*)
Scunthorpe U. (1) 1 (*Green*)   8119
Preston N.E.: Tunks; McMahon, Williams, Brown (Smith), Sadler, Spark, Bruce, Burns, Treacy, Elwiss, Morley.
Scunthorpe U.: O'Meara; Markham, Peacock, Collier, Welbourne, Wigginton, Davidson, Money, Green, Keeley, O'Connor.

Romford (0) 0
Tooting & Mitcham U. (1) 1 (*Ives*)   2033
Romford: Lightfoot; Woodward, Tapping, Mann, Peck, Bickles, Sanders, Chandler, Lewis, Ferry, Pettit (Bishop).
Tooting & Mitcham U.: Dunn; Berrecloth, Smith, Grubb, Green, Rowan, Howell, Casey, Juneman, Glover, Ives.

Rossendale (0) 0
Shrewsbury T. (0) 1 (*Bates*)   3450
Rossendale: Foster; Hitchin, Kay, Grimshaw, Woods, Ross, Greenan, Roberts, Barker, Birtwhistle, Ryder.
Shrewsbury T.: Mulhearn; Collier, Roberts, Durban, Kearney, Turner, Irvine, O'Loughlin, Haywood, Bates, Tarbuck.

Rotherham U. (1) 2 (*Crawford, Stancliffe*)
Crewe Alex. (0) 1 (*Bevan*)   5080
Rotherham U.: McDonagh; Green, Breckin, Rhodes, Stancliffe, Spencer, Finney, Phillips, Habbin (Womble), Goodfellow, Crawford.
Crewe Alex.: Crudgington; Lowry, Kelly, Lugg, Bowles, Rimmer, Bevan, Nicholls, Humphreys, Melledew, Davies.

Scarborough (0) 2 (*Hewitt, Marshall*)
Morecambe (0) 0   2103
Scarborough: Barnard; Fountain, Barker, Dunn, H. Ayre, Dunna H. A., Jackson (Hewitt), Barmby, Woodall, Abbey, Marshall.
Morecambe: MacLachlan; Pearson, Ross, Sutton, Street, Baldwin, Done, Webber, Kershaw, Spavin, Grundy (Collingford).

Sheffield W. (1) 3 (*Proudlove, Knighton, Prendergast*)
Macclesfield (1) 1 (*Eccleshare*)   12,940
Sheffield W.: Ramsbottom; Shaw, Quinn, Thompson, Cusack, O'Donnell, Potts, Harvey, Prendergast, Proudlove, Knighton.
Macclesfield: Bailey; Eccleshare, Mobley, Collins, Fish, Lloyd, Morris, Hays, Collier, O'Connor, Coleman.

Southend U. (2) 2 (*Parker 2*)
Swansea C. (0) 0   5383
Southend U.: Webster; Worthington, Ford, Little, Townsend, Moody, Foggo, Brace, Parker, Nicholl, Silvester.
Swansea C.: Potter; Evans, Davies, Smith, Bruton, Harris, Curtis, Leitch, Bekker (Bartley), Bray, James.

Spennymoor (3) 4 (*Banks 2, Mulligan, Reilly*)
Southport (1) 1 (*O'Neil*)   1828
Spennymoor: Rowell; Simpson, Hickman, Gates, Robson, Kell, Banks, Rosethorn, Reilly, Hart, Mulligan.
Southport: Thomas; Sibbald, Snookes, Hughes, Taylor, O'Neil, Dewsnip (O'Riley), Gough, Wilson, Johnston, Martin.

Sutton (0) 1 (*Kidd*)
AFC Bournemouth (0) 1 (*Ashworth*) 2921
Sutton: Overton; Cross, Bangs, Raynes, Preston, Sorenson, Bailey, Pritchard, Kidd, Dennis, Stear.
AFC Bournemouth: Baker; Payne, Miller, Howard, Morgan, Hague, Nightingale, Reeves, Goddard, Ashworth, Buttle.

Walsall (0) 0
Huddersfield T. (1) 1 (*Belfitt*) 5506
Walsall: Kearns; Fry, Harrison, Robinson, Serella, Birch, Dennehy, Andrews, Wright, Buckley, Taylor (Saunders).
Huddersfield T.: Taylor; Sweeney, Hutt, Smith, Baines, Simpkin, Gray, O'Neil, Belfitt, Garwood, Lawson.

Watford (0) 0
Brighton & H.A. (1) 3 (*Martin, Binney 2*) 9283
Watford: Rankin; How, Akers, Joslyn, Lees, Garner, Scullion, Bond, Horsfield, Jenkins, Walsh (Greenhalgh)
Brighton & H.A.: Grummitt; Tiler, Wilson, Machin, Piper, Burnett, Fell, O'Sullivan, Binney, Martin, Mellor.

Weymouth (0) 0
Gillingham (0) 2 (*Richardson 2*) 3149
Weymouth: Fry; Lawrence, Toms, Mellor, Hobson, Bruck, Courtney, Brown, Astle, Foote (Mullins), Verity.
Gillingham: Hillyard; Davis, Ley, Wiltshire, Shipperley, Tydeman, Jacks, Knight, Richardson, Hilton, Wilks.

Wigan Ath. (1) 4 (*Rodgers 2, Wilkinson, Worswick*)
Matlock (0) 1 (*Fenoughty N.*) 4786
Wigan Ath.: Eales; Baker, Hinnegan, Gore, Molyneaux, Gillibrand, Bromley, Braithwaite, Wilkinson, Rodgers, Worswick.
Matlock: Fell (McKay); Smith, Goodwin, Fenoughty, M., Dawson, Stott, Oxley, Fenoughty, T., Fenoughty, N., Scott, Chambers.

Workington (0) 1 (*Heslop*)
Rochdale (1) 1 (*Ferguson*) 1190
Workington: Rogan; Ellison, Heslop, Kavanagh, Johnston, Walker, Tyrer, Kisby, Ward, Harris, Moore (Harrison).
Rochdale: Poole; Hallows, Lacey, Mulvaney, Summerscales, Hanvey, Ferguson, Tobin, Mountford, Cooper, Whelan.

Wycombe W. (0) 0
Bedford (0) 0 4000
Wycombe W.: Maskell; Bullock, Birsdeye, Mead, Delaney, Reardon, Anthony, Kennedy (Alexander). Evans, Holifield, Horseman.
Bedford: Peacock; Skinn, Foles, Colley, Gould, Earl, Hawkins (Burbett), Sargent, Dove, Markham Phillips.

Yeovil (1) 1 (*Brown*)
Millwall (0) 1 (*Kitchener*) 6822
Yeovil: Franklin; Thompson, Flay, Housley, Cotton, Harland, McMahon, Brown, Plumb, Adams, Clancy.
Millwall: Goddard; Evans, Donaldson, Brisley, Kitchener, Hazell, Welsh, Jones, Saul, Jones (Hart), Salvage.

FIRST ROUND REPLAYS

NOV. 24
Bedford (2) 2 (*Phillips, Folds*)
Wycombe W. (0) 2 (*Delaney, Horsman*) (*After extra time*) 4267
Bedford: Peacock; Skinn, Folds, Gould, Cooley, Earl, Hawkins, Phillips, Sargent, Markham, Burdett.
Wycombe W.: Maskell; Birdseye, Bullock, Mead, Delaney, Reardon, Anthony (Alexander), Kennedy, Evans, Holifield, Horseman.

Port Vale (1) 4 (*Cullerton, Brownbill 2, Tartt*)
Grantham (1) 1 (*Norris*) 4851
Port Vale: Connaughton; Tartt, Griffiths, Ridley, Chadwick, Horton, McLaren, Lees, Cullerton, Bailey, Brownbill.
Grantham: Gardiner; Bower, Capewell, G., Capewell, M., Shaw, Clapham, Jackson, Nixon, Norris, Flemming, Benskin.

Wrexham (0) 1 (*Ashcroft*)
Mansfield T. (1) 1 (*Eccles*) (*After extra time*) 4468
Wrexham: Lloyd; Hill, Evans (Fogg), Davis, May, Thomas, Tinnion, Sutton, Ashcroft, Dwyer, Griffiths.
Mansfield T.: Brown; Pate, Foster, B., McDonald, Madden, Bird, Matthews, Eccles, Clarke, Hodgson, Mackenzie.

NOV. 25
Millwall (2) 2 (*Salvage, Welsh*)
Yeovil (1) 2 (*Cotton, Housley*) 8285
Millwall: Goddard; Evans, Donaldson, Brisley, Kitchener, Hazell, Jones, Saul, Welsh, Dorney, Salvage.
Yeovil: Franklin; Thompson, Flay, Housley, Harland, Harrison, McMahon. Brown, Cotton, Adams, Clancy.

Rochdale (0) 2 (*Mountford, Whelan*)
Workington (1) 1 (*Geidmintis*) (*After extra time*)2354
Rochdale: Poole; Hallows, Lacey, Fielding, Mulvaney, Hanvey, Ferguson, Mountford, Cooper, Whelan, Tobin.
Workington: Hughes; Ellison, Heslop, Kavanagh, Johnston, Walker, Tyrer (Geidmintis), Kisby, Harris, Ward, Moore.

Swindon T. (0) 3 (*Syrett, Trollope, Dixon*)
Newport Co. (0) 0 7574
Swindon T.: Barron; Taylor, Trollope, Emannuel, Burrows, Stroud, Moss, Hubbard (Dixon), Eastoe, Syrett, Anderson.
Newport Co.: Macey; Screen, Relish, Godfrey, Aizlewood, Hancock, Hooper (White), Parsons, Love, Jones, Elliott.

Nov. 26
AFC Bournemouth (1) 1 (*Ashworth*)
Sutton (0) 0 4109
AFC Bournemouth: Baker; Payne, Miller, Howard, Impey, Hague, Nightingale, Reeves, Goddard, Ashworth, Buttle.
Sutton: Overton; Cross, Bangs, Rains, Preston, Sorenson, Bailey, Pritchard, Kidd, Dennis (Di Parma), Steer.

Chester (1) 2 (*Moore, Redfern*)
Darlington (0) 0 5238
Chester: Millington; Edwards, Loska, Storton, Delgado, Draper, Redfern, Pugh, Moore, Lennard, Owen.
Darlington: Ogley; Nattrass, Cochrane, Rowles, Craig, Noble, Holbrook, Sinclair, Lowrey, Lees, Young.

Dover (0) 4 (*Hamshare, Coxhill pen., Coupland 2*)
Colchester U. (0) 1 (*Packer pen.*)   3779
Dover: Raine; Reynolds, Keeley, Fursdon, Waite, Coupland, Hamshare, Coxhill, Housden, Light, Rogers.
Colchester U.: Walker; Dyer, Williams, Bunkell, Dominey, Packer, Cook, Leslie, Froggatt, Harrison (Anderson), Smith.

FIRST ROUND, SECOND REPLAYS

DEC. 1

Wycombe W. (0) 2 (*Bullock, Evans*)
Bedford (0) 1 (*Markham*)   2765
Wycombe W.: Maskell; Birdseye, Bullock. Mead, Delaney, Reardon. Anthony, Kennedy, Evans, Holifield, Horseman.
Bedford: Peacock; Skinn, Folds, Gould, Cooley, Earl, Hawkins, Campbell, Sargent, Markham, Burdett.

DEC. 3

Yeovil (0) 0
Millwall (0) 1 (*Hart*) (*at Aldershot*)   3309
Yeovil: Franklin; Thompson, Flay, Housley, Harland, Harrison, McMahon, Brown, Cotton, Adams, Clancy.
Millwall: Goddard; Evans, Hazell, Brisley, Kitchener, Dorney, Welsh, Hart, Summerill, Saul, Salvage.

DEC. 8

Mansfield T. (1) 2 (*Laverick, May o.g.*)
Wrexham (0) 1 (*Dwyer*) (*at Villa Park*)   1470
Mansfield T.: Evans; Pate, Foster B., McDonald, Mackenzie, Bird, Matthews, Laverick, Clarke, Hodgson, McCaffrey.
Wrexham: Lloyd; Evans, Fogg, Davis, May, Thomas, Tinnion, Sutton, Ashcroft, Dwyer, Griffiths.

SECOND ROUND

DEC. 13

Aldershot (0) 2 (*Warnock, Morrissey*)
Bishops Stortford (0) 0   5270
Aldershot: Johnson; Walden, Walker, Crosby, Richardson, Earls, Walton (Howitt), Morrissey, Howarth, Bell, Warnock.
Bishops Stortford: Kitson; Harris, Davis, Flack, Clarke, Mulkern, Leakey, Gaine, MacKenzie, Twigg, Watson.

AFC Bournemouth (1) 2 (*Ashworth, Goddard*)
Hereford U. (0) 2 (*McNeil, Tyler*)   6181
AFC Bournemouth: Baker; Payne, Miller, Howard, Morgan, Hague, Nightingale, Redknapp, Goddard, Ashworth, Buttle.
Hereford U. Charlton; Emery, Ritchie, Layton, Tucker, Lindsay, Paine, Tyler, Davey, McNeil, Walker.

Bury (1) 3 (*Kennedy, Buchan, Adams o.g.*)
Spennymoor (0) 0   6314
Bury: Forrest; Hoolickin, Kennedy, Nicholson, Hulme, Bailey, Buchan, Rowland, Spence, Phillips, Williams.
Spennymoor: Rowell; Simpson (Curry), Hickman, Robson, Adams, Kell, Banks, Hart, Reilly, Rosethorne, Mulligan.

Cardiff C. (1) 1 (*Evans*)
Wycombe W. (0) 0   11,607
Cardiff C.: Irwin; Dwyer, Pethard, Buchanan, England, Larmour, Reece, Livermore, Alston, Evans, Anderson.

Wycombe W.: Maskell; Birdseye, Bullock, Mead, Delaney, Reardon, Anthony, Kennedy, Evans, Holifield, Horseman (Alezander).

Coventry Sp. (0) 0
Peterborough U. (3) 4 (*Hughes, Jones M., Dones D. o.g., Nixon*)   8556
Coventry Sp: Jeavons; Mundy, Skelcey, Jones, Sorbie, Dunk, Starkey, Gore, Gallagher Muir, Brassington.
Peterborough U.: Steele; Murray, Lee, Eustace, Turner, Carmichael, Nixon, Gregory (Bradley), Jones, Hughes, Robson.

Gateshead (0) 1 (*Guthrie*)
Rochdale (1) 1 (*Albeson o.g.*)   4600
Gateshead: Clarke; Irwin, McCrudden, McLeod (Leask), Albeson, Guthrie, Johnson, Wilson, Mutrie, Morrison, Common.
Rochdale: Oliver; Hallows, Townsend, Ferguson, Summerscales, Hanvey, Sweeney, Mountford, Whelan, Cooper, Tobin.

Gillingham (0) 0
Brighton & H.A. (0) 1 (*Fell*)   10,579
Gillingham: Hillyard; Wiltshire (Gauden), Ley, Galvin, Shipperley, Fogarty, Jacks, Knight, Richardson, Weatherley, Durrell.
Brighton & H.A.: Grummitt; Tiler, Wilson, Machin, Rollings, Burnett, Fell, O'Sullivan (Kinnear), Binney, Martin, Mellor.

Hendon (0) 0
Swindon T. (0) 1 (*Moss pen.*)   3349
Hendon: Dalrymple; Field, J., Hand, Yerby, Phillips, Haider, Jeffries, Metchick. Baker, Field A. Childs.
Swindon T.: Barron; Taylor, Trollope, Emanuel, Burrows, Stroud, Moss, Dixon, Eastoe, Syrett, Anderson.

Huddersfield T. (1) 2 (*Belfitt, Baines*)
Port Vale (1) 1 (*Brownbill*)   6218
Huddersfield: Taylor; Sweeney, Hutt, Smith, Baines, Simpkin, Gray, Dolan, Belfitt, Maltland, Lawson.
Port Vale: Connaughton; Tartt, Griffiths (Williams), Ridley, Harris, Horton, McLaren, Lees, Cullerton, Bailey, Brownbill.

Leatherhead (0) 0
Tooting & Mitcham (0) 0   2500
Leatherhead: Swannell; Sargent, Ibbitson, Woffinden, Reid Wells, Cooper, Lavers Kelly, Smith, Doyle.
Tooting & Mitcham: Dunn; Berrecloth, Smith, Grubb, Green, Howell, Casey, Ford, Juneman, Glover, Ives.

Mansfield T. (1) 1 (*McDonald*)
Lincoln C. (2) 2 (*Branfoot, Freeman*)   8466
Mansfield T.: Brown; Pate, Foster B., McDonald, Mackenzie, Bird, Matthews, Randall, Clarke, Hodgson, McCaffrey.
Lincoln C.: Gordon; Branfoot, Neale, Booth, Ellis, Cooper, Fleming, Ward, Graham, Freeman, Smith.

Marine (1) 1 (*Shergold*)
Hartlepool (1) 1 (*Scaife*)   2300
Marine: Crosbie; Pritchard, Hammill, Smith, Bennett, Edwards. Shergold, Bennie, Glover, Windsor, Morrey.
Hartlepool: Hope; Smith R., Goad, Potter, Rowlands, Johnson, Spelman, Smith D., Moore, McMahon, Scaife.

Millwall (0) 1 (*Summerill*)
Crystal Palace (1) 1 (*Swindlehurst*)   14,920
Millwall: Goddard; Evans, Moore, Brisley, Kitchener, Hazell, Welsh, Hart, Summerill, Saul, Salvage.
Crystal Palace: Hammond; Wall, Cannon, Hinshelwood M., Evans, Jump, Chatterton, Johnson, Kemp, Swindlehurst, Taylor.

Rotherham U. (0) 0
Bradford C. (0) 3 (*Cooke, Ingram 2*)   7006
Rotherham U.: Haslam; Green, Breckin, Rhodes, Stancliffe, Spencer, Finney, Phillips, Habbin, Goodfellow, Crawford.
Bradford C.: Downsborough; Podd, Cooper, Johnson, Middleton, Fretwell, Hall, McGinley, Cooke, Ingram, Hutchins.

Scarborough (1) 3 (*Dunn, Woodall, Marshall*)
Preston N.E. (2) 2 (*Smith 2*)   4100
Scarborough: Barnard; Fountain, Barker, Dunn, H., Ayre, Dunn, H. A., Jackson, Barmby, Woodall, Hewitt (Abbey), Marshall.
Preston N.E.: Tunks; McMahon, Lawrenson, Williams, Sadler, Spark, Coleman, Burns, Smith, Elwiss, Morley.

Sheffield W. (0) 2 (*Sunley, Nimmo*
Wigan Ath. (0) 0   12,436
Sheffield W.: Fox; Shaw, Quinn, Thompson, Cusack, O'Donnell, Mullen, Proudlove, Prendergast (Nimmo), Sunley, Potts.
Wigan Ath.: Eales; Gore, Hinnegan, Molyneaux, Gillibrand, Garrett, Braithwaite, Wright, Wilson (Baines), Wilkinson, Rogers.

Shrewsbury T, (2) 3 (*Bates 2, Durban*)
Chester (1) 1 (*Edwards*)   6061
Shrewsbury T.: Mulhearn; King, Roberts, Durban, Kearney, Turner, Irvine, Atkins, Haywood, Bates, McGregor.
Chester: Millington; Edwards, Loska, Storton, Delgado, Mason, Pugh, Redfern (Crossley), Draper, Owen, Lennard.

Southend U. (3) 4 (*Parker, Silvester 2, Moody pen.*)
Dover (0) 1 (*Housden*)   7696
Southend U.: Webster; Worthington, Ford, Little, Townsend, Moody, Foggo, Brace, Parker, Silvester, Nicholl.
Dover: Raine; Reynolds, Keeley, Fursdon, Waite, Coupland, Wallace, Coxhill, Housden, Light, Rogers.

Stafford (0) 1 (*Sedden B.*)
Halifax T. (0) 3 (*McHale pen., Downes, Gwyther*)   4650
Stafford: Arnold; Ritchie, Richards, Seddon D. (Sargeant), Seddon B., Morris, Hutchison, Chapman, Jones, Lowe, Chadwick.
Halifax T.: Gennoe; Smith, Collins, McHale, Rhodes, Phelan, Harrold (Jones), Pugh, Bell, Gwyther, Downes.

Wimbledon (0) 0
Brentford (2) 2 (*Johnson 2, 1 pen.*)   8375
Wimbledon: Guy; Tilley, Aitken, Bryant, Donaldson, Bassett, Cooke, Holmes, Connell, Rice, Mahon.
Brentford: Priddy; Nelmes, Allen, Bence, Lawrence, Smith, Graham, Scales, Cross, Sweetzer, Johnson.

SECOND ROUND REPLAYS

DEC. 15
Hartlepool (3) 6 (*Moore 3, Johnson pen., Rowlands, Scaife*)
Marine (1) 3 (*Edwards, Smith P. pen., Shergold*) 5673
Hartlepool: Hope; Smith R., Goad, Potter, Rowlands, Johnson, Spelman, Smith D., Moore, McMahon, Scaife.
Marine: Crosbie; Pritchard, Hammill, Smith, Bennett, Edwards, Shergold, Bennie, Glover, Woosey, Morrey.

DEC. 16
Crystal Palace (2) 2 (*Kemp, Taylor pen.*)
Millwall (0) 1 (*Moore*)   18,284
Crystal Palace: Hammond; Wall, Cannon, Johnson, Jeffries, Evans, Chatterton, Hinshelwood, Kemp, Swindlehurst, Taylor.
Millwall: Goddard; Evans, Hazell, Moore, Kitchener, Brisley, Welsh (Donaldson), Hart, Summerill, Saul, Salvage.

Tooting & Mitcham (1) 1 (*Juneman pen.*)
Leatherhead (1) 1 (*Cooper*)   1500
(*match abandoned – pitch unfit, after 57 minutes*)

Rochdale (2) 3 (*Mountford, Morrison o.g., Tobin*)
Gateshead (0) 1 (*Morrison*)   2607
Rochdale: Poole; Hallows, Townsend, Lacey, Summerscales, Hanvey, Ferguson, Mountford, Cooper, Whelan, Tobin.
Gateshead: Clarke; Irwin, Brown, McCrudden, Albeson, Wilson, Leask, Morrison, Johnson, Mutrie, Common.

DEC. 17
Hereford U. (0) 2 (*Layton, McNeil*)
AFC Bournemouth (0) 0   6351
Hereford U.: Charlton; Emery, Ritchie, Layton, Tucker, Lindsay, Paine, Tyler, Davey, McNeil (Silkman), Walker.
AFC Bournemouth: Baker; Benson (Reeves), Miller, Howard, Cunningham, Impey, Nightingale, Redknapp, Goddard, Ashworth, Buttle.

DEC. 22
Tooting & Mitcham (0) 2 (*Juneman pen., Howell*)
Leatherhead (1) 1 (*Reid*) (*After extra time*)   2500
Tooting & Mitcham: Dunn; Berrecloth, Smith, Grubb, Green, Howell, Casey, Ford, Juneman, Glover, Ives.
Leatherhead: Swannell; Sargent, Ibbitson, (Page), Woffinden, Reid, Wells, Cooper, Lavers, Kelly, Smith, Doyle.

THIRD ROUND

JAN. 1
Chelsea (1) 1 (*Garner*)
Bristol R. (1) 1 (*Warboys*)   35,226
Chelsea: Bonetti; Locke, Harris, Stanley (Cooke), Droy, Wicks, Britton, Wilkins R., Maybank, Garner, Swain.
Bristol R.: Eadie; Bater, Parsons, Day, Williams, Smith (Staniforth), Stephens, Fearnley, Warboys, Bannister, Stanton.

Nottingham F. (0) 0
Peterborough U. (0) 0   31,525
Nottingham F.: Wells; O'Kane, Clark, McGovern, Chapman, Bowyer, McIntosh, Bowery, O'Hare, Butlin, Robertson.
Peterborough U.: Steele; Murray, Lee (Cozens), Eustace, Turner, Carmichael, Nixon, Gregory, Jones, Hughes, Robson.

Aldershot (0) 1 (*Howarth*)
Lincoln C. (1) 2 (*Ward, Ellis pen.*)   6825
Aldershot: Godfrey (Crosby); Walden, Walker,
Crosby (Howitt), Richardson, Jopling, Wallace R.,
Morrissey, Howarth, Bell, Brodie.
Lincoln C.: Grotier; Branfoot, Leigh, Booth, Ellis,
Cooper, Fleming, Ward, Freeman, Smith, Harding.

Blackpool (0) 1 (*Bentley*)
Burnley (0) 0   20,573
Blackpool: Wood; Hatton, Harrison, McEwan,
Suddaby, Alcock (Moore), Walsh, Weston, Hart,
Bentley, Evanson.
Burnley: Peyton; Docherty, Newton, Ingham,
Waldron, Thomson, Morgan (Loggie), Hankin,
Summerbee, Flynn, Bradshaw.

Brentford (0) 0
Bolton W. (0) 0   12,450
Brentford: Priddy; Nelmes, Allen, Bence, Lawrence,
Smith, Graham, Scales, Riddick (French), Sweet-
zer, Johnson.
Bolton W.: Siddall; Ritson, Dunne, Greaves,
Jones P., Allardyce, Byrom, Whatmore, Jones G.,
Reid, Thompson.

Charlton Ath. (1) 2 (*Peacock, Warman*)
Sheffield W. (0) 1 (*Sunley*)   12,284
Charlton Ath.: Tutt; Curtis, Warman, Bowman,
Giles, Young, Powell, Hales, Flanagan, Hunt,
Peacock.
Sheffield W.: Fox; Shaw, Quinn, Thompson,
Cusack, O'Donnell (Joicey), Potts, Henson,
Wylde, Sunley, Mullen.

Coventry C. (1) 2 (*Cross, Merrick o.g.*)
Bristol C. (0) 1 (*Brolly*)   15,653
Coventry C.: Blyth; Coop, Brogan, Craven, Dug-
dale, Holmes, Cartwright, Murphy, Cross, Green
(Oakey), Hutchison.
Bristol C.: Cashley; Sweeney, Drysdale, Gow,
Collier, Merrick, Tainton, Ritchie, Mann, Fear,
Brolly.

Derby Co. (1) 2 (*George 2*)
Everton (0) 1 (*Jones*)   31,647
Derby Co.: Boulton; Thomas, Newton, Rioch,
Daniel, Todd, Powell, Gemmill, Davies, George,
James.
Everton: Davies; Bernard, Darracott, Hurst,
Kenyon, Lyons, Hamilton, Dobson, Latchford,
Pearson (Connolly), Jones.

Fulham (1) 2 (*Conway, Busby*)
Huddersfield T. (1) 3 (*Gray 2, Lawson*) 10,299
Fulham: Mellor; Cutbush, Slough, Mullery, Lacy,
Moore, Conway, Dowie (James), Mitchell, Busby,
Barrett.
Huddersfield T.: Taylor; Sweeney, Hutt, Smith,
Baines, Simpkin, Gray, O'Neil, Belfitt, Dolan,
Lawson.

Hull C. (1) 1
Plymouth Arg. (0) 1 (*Rafferty*)   6515
Hull C.: Wealands; Banks, McGill, Galvin,
Croft, Roberts, Grimes, Lyall, Hawley, Wood,
Greenwood.
Plymouth Arg.: Aleksic; Darke, Burrows, Sutton,
Green, Delve, Randell, Johnson, Mariner, Rafferty,
McAuley.

Ipswich T. (3) 3 (*Lambert 3*)
Halifax T. (1) 1 (*McHale pen.*)   23,488
Ipswich T.: Cooper; Burley, Beattie, Talbot, Hun-
ter, Peddelty, Woods, Mills, Johnson (Austin),
Whymark, Lambert.

Halifax T.: Gennoe; Smith, Collins, McHale,
Veitch, Phelan, Jones, Pugh, Bell (Downes),
Gwyther, Blair.

Leicester C. (1) 3 (*Garland 3*)
Sheffield U. (0) 0   24,052
Leicester C.: Wallington; Whitworth, Rofe,
Kember, Blockley, Woollett, Weller, Lee, Garland,
Alderson, Worthington.
Sheffield U.: Brown; Franks, Garner, Bradford,
Colquhoun, Eddy, Johnstone, Ludlam, Edwards
(Speight), Currie, Woodward.

Luton T. (0) 2 (*Futcher R., Chambers*)
Blackburn R. (0) 0   11,195
Luton T.: Barber; John Ryan, Buckley, Chambers,
Faulkner, Futcher P., Husband, King, Futcher R.,
West, Aston.
Blackburn R.: Jones, Heaton, Wood, Metcalfe,
Waddington, Fazackerley, Hoy, Oates, Mullen,
Svarc, Parkes.

Manchester C. (3) 6 (*Oakes, Tueart 2, 1 pen., Booth 2, Hartford*)
Hartlepool (0) 0   26,863
Manchester C.: Corrigan; Clements, Donachie,
Doyle, Watson, Oakes, Power, Booth, Royle,
Hartford, Tueart.
Hartlepool: Hope; Smith R., Goad, Potter, Row-
lands, Honour, Bielby, Smith D., Moore, Mc-
Mahon, Scaife.

Manchester U. (0) 2 (*Daly 2 pens.*)
Oxford U. (1) 1 (*Clarke D.*)   41,082
Manchester U.: Stepney; Forsyth (Nicholl),
Houston, Daly, Greenhoff, Buchan, Coppell,
McIlroy, Pearson, Macari, Hill.
Oxford U.: Burton; Taylor, Shuker, Lowe, Clarke
C., Jeffrey, Houseman, Aylott, Clarke D., Mc-
Culloch, Briggs.

Middlesbrough (0) 0
Bury (0) 0   21,000
Middlesbrough: Platt; Craggs, Cooper, Boersma,
Boam, Maddren, McAndrew, Mills, Hickton
(Bailey), Foggon, Armstrong.
Bury: Forrest; Hoolickin, Kennedy, Keegan,
Hulme, Bailey, McIlwraith, Rowland, Spence
(Riley), Rudd, Williams.

Norwich C. (1) 1 (*MacDougall pen.*)
Rochdale (1) 1 (*Mullington*)   14,187
Norwich C.: Keelan; Jones, Powell, Morris, Forbes,
Stringer, Machin, MacDougall, Boyer, Suggett,
Peters.
Rochdale: Poole; Hallows, Lacey, Summerscales,
Mulvaney, Hanvey, Ferguson, Mountford, Cooper,
Whelan, Mullington.

Notts Co. (0) 0
Leeds U. (1) 1 (*Clarke*)   31,129
Notts Co.: McManus; Richards, O'Brien, Bolton
(Carter), Needham, Stubbs, Vinter, Sims, Bradd,
Mann, Scanlon.
Leeds U.: Harvey; Reaney, Gray F., Bremner,
Madeley, Hunter, Lorimer, Clarke, McKenzie,
Cherry, Yorath.

Orient (0) 0
Cardiff C. (1) 1 (*Alston*)   8031
Orient: Jackson; Fisher, Grealish, Heppolette,
Hoadley, Walley, Cunningham, Roeder, Bullock,
Allder, Queen.

Cardiff C.: Irwin; Dwyer, Charles, Reece, Morgan, Larmour, Villars, Livermore, Evans, Alston, Anderson.

Portsmouth (1) 1 (*Eames*)
Birmingham C. (1) 1 (*Francis*) 19,414
Portsmouth: Lloyd; Lawler, Mellows, Roberts, Went, Cahill, McGuinness, Piper, Graham, Reynolds, Eames.
Birmingham C.: Latchford; Osborne, Want, Kendall (Pendrey), Gallagher, Burns, Page, Francis, Withe, Hatton, Hibbitt.

Q.P.R. (0) 0
Newcastle U. (0) 0 20,102
Q.P.R.: Parkes; Clement, Gillard, Leach, McLintock, Webb, Thomas, Francis, Masson, Bowles, Givens (Hollins).
Newcastle U.: Mahoney; Nattrass, Kennedy, Nulty, Craig D. (Barrowclough), Howard, Burns, Cassidy, Macdonald, Gowling, Craig T.

Scarborough (0) 1 (*Abbey*)
Crystal Palace (1) 2 (*Taylor, Evans*) 8008
Scarborough: Barnard; Fountain, Hewitt, Dunn H., Ayre, Marshall, Jackson, Barmby (Dunn H. A.), Woodall, Abbey, Hilley.
Crystal Palace: Hammond; Wall, Cannon, Holder (Whittle), Jump, Evans, Chatterton, Hinshelwood M., Kemp, Swindlehurst, Taylor.

Shrewsbury T. (0) 1 (*Kearney*)
Bradford C. (0) 2 (*Cooke, Hutchins*) 6554
Shrewsbury T.: Mulhearn; King, Roberts, Durban, Kearney, Turner, Irvine, Atkins, Haywood, Bates, McGregor.
Bradford C.: Downsborough; Podd, Cooper, Hall, Middleton, Fretwell, McGinley (Watson), Johnson, Cooke, Ingram, Hutchins.

Southampton (0) 1 (*Fisher*)
Aston Villa (0) 1 (*Gray*) 24,138
Southampton: Turner; Rodrigues, Peach, Holmes, Blyth, Steele, Fisher, Channon, Stokes, McCalliog, Gilchrist (Earles).
Aston Villa: Burridge; Gidman, Robson, Ross, Nicholl, Phillips, Graydon, Deehan, Gray, Hamilton, Carrodus.

Southend U. (1) 2 (*Silvester, Brace*)
Brighton & H.A. (1) 1 (*Binney*) 9878
Southend U.: Rafter; Worthington, Ford, Little, Townsend, Moody, Foggo, Brace, Parker, Silvester, Nicholl.
Brighton & H.A.: Grummitt; Kinnear, Wilson, Machin, Rollings, Burnett, Fell, O'Sullivan, Binney, Martin, Mellor.

Sunderland (1) 2 (*Holden, Robson*)
Oldham Ath. (0) 0 29,226
Sunderland: Montgomery; Malone, Bolton, Towers, Clarke, Moncur, Kerr, Henderson, Holden, Robson, Finney.
Oldham Ath.: Platt; Wood, Whittle, Bell, Edwards, Hicks, Young, Blair, Shaw, Chapman, Groves (Robins).

Swindon T. (2) 2 (*Eastoe, Dixon*)
Tooting & Mitcham (0) 2 (*Glover, Casey*) 9428
Swindon T.: Barron; McLaughlin, Trollope, Stroud, Burrows, Emanuel, Moss, Dixon, Eastoe, Butler (Jenkins), Anderson.
Tooting & Mitcham: Dunn; Berrecloth, Smith, Grubb, Green, Howell, Casey, Ford, Juneman, Glover, Ives.

Tottenham H. (0) 1 (*Duncan*)
Stoke C. (1) 1 (*Mahoney*) 26,715
Tottenham H.: Jennings; Naylor, McAllister, Pratt, Young, Osgood, Coates (Jones), Perryman, Chivers, Duncan, Neighbour.

Stoke C.: Shilton; Marsh, Pejic, Mahoney, Dodd, Bloor, Robertson, Greenhoff, Moores, Hudson, Salmons.

W.B.A. (0) 3 (*Brown A., Brown T. 2, 1 pen.*)
Carlisle U. (1) 1 (*Wile o.g.*) 16,478
W.B.A.: Osborne; Mulligan, Mayo, Cantello, Wile, Robertson, Brown T., Martin, Brown A., Giles, Johnston.
Carlisle U.: Burleigh, Spearritt, Gorman, O'Neill (Owen), Carr, Parker, McVitie, Train, Clarke, Laidlaw, Martin.

West Ham U. (0) 0
Liverpool (1) 2 (*Keegan, Toshack*) 32,363
West Ham U.: Day; Coleman, Lampard, Holland, McGiven, Lock, Taylor A., Paddon, Brooking, Jennings, Curbishley.
Liverpool: Clemence; Smith, Neal, Thompson, Kennedy, Hughes, Keegan, Case, Heighway, Toshack, Callaghan.

Wolverhampton W. (2) 3 (*Bell, Richards, Hibbitt*)
Arsenal (0) 0 22,215
Wolverhampton W.: Parkes; Sunderland, Parkin, Bailey, McAlle, Carr, Hibbitt, Daley, Bell, Gould, Richards.
Arsenal: Rimmer, Rice, Nelson, Storey, O'Leary, Powling, Armstrong, Ball, Stapleton, Kidd, Brady.

York C. (2) 2 (*Seal, Hosker*)
Hereford U. (0) 1 (*Layton*) 5154
York C.: Crawford; Scott, Woodward, McMordoe, Swallow, Topping, Hosker, Holmes, Seal, Hinch, Downing.
Hereford U.: Hughes; Emery, Ritchie, Layton, Rylands, Lindsay, Paine, Tyler, Davey, McNeil, McCafferty (Carter).

THIRD ROUND REPLAYS

JAN. 3
Bristol R. (0) 0
Chelsea (0) 1 (*Swain*) 13,939
Bristol R.: Eadie; Bater, Parsons, Aitken, Day, Williams, Stephens, Fearnley, Warboys (Staniforth), Bannister, Stanton.
Chelsea: Bonetti; Locke, Harris, Stanley (Garner), Droy, Wicks, Britton, Wilkins R., Maybank, Hoy, Swain.

JAN. 6
Birmingham (0) 0
Portsmouth (1) 1 (*McGuinness*) 26,106
Birmingham C.: Latchford; Martin, Want, Pendrey, Gallagher (Calderwood), Burns, Page, Francis, Withe, Hatton, Bryant.
Portsmouth: Lloyd; Lawler, Mellows, Roberts, Went, Hand, McGuinness, Piper, Graham, Reynolds, Eames.

Bolton W. (0) 2 (*Whatmore 2*)
Brentford (0) 0 18,538
Bolton W.: Siddall; Ritson, Dunne, Greaves, Jones P., Allardyce, Byrom, Whatmore, Jones G., Reid, Thompson.
Brentford: Priddy; Nelmes, Allen, Bence, Lawrence, Smith, Graham, Scales, Cross, Sweetzer, Johnson.

Bury (1) 3 (*McIlwraith, Hulme, Rowland*)
Middlesbrough (2) 2 (*Brine, Hickton pen.*) 11,488
Bury: Forrest; Hoolickin, Kennedy, Keenan, Hulme, Bailey, McIlwraith, Rudd, Rowland, Spence, Williams.
Middlesbrough: Platt; Craggs, Bailey (Foggon), Berni, Boam, Maddren, Murdoch, Mills, Cooper, Hicktoe, Armstrong.

Plymouth Arg. (0) 1 (*Green*)
Hull C. (2) 4 (*Wood 2, Sutton o.g., Hawley*)   20,208
Plymouth Arg.: Aleksic; Darke, Burrows, Sutton, Green, Delve, Randell, Johnson, Mariner, Rafferty, McAuley.
Hull C.: Wealands; Daniel, Banks, Hawley, Croft, Roberts, Grimes, Lyall, Wood, Galvin, Greenwood.

Rochdale (0) 0
Norwich C. (0) 0 (*After extra time*)   8284
Rochdale: Poole; Hallows, Lacey, Mulvaney, Summerscales, Hanvey, Ferguson, Mountford, Whelan, Cooper (Murty) Mullington.
Norwich C.: Keelan; Powell, Sullivan, Morris, Forbes, Stringer, Machin, MacDougall, Boyer, Suggett, Peters.

Tooting & Mitcham U. (1) 2 (*Juneman, Ives*)
Swindon T. (0) 1 (*Green o.g.*)   7500
Tooting & Mitcham U.: Dunn; Berrecloth, Smith, Grubb, Green, Howell, Casey, Ford, Juneman, Glover, Ives.
Swindon T.: Barron; Taylor, Trollope, Stroud, Burrows, McLaughlin, Moss, Dixon, Eastoe, Syrett, Anderson.

JAN. 7
Aston Villa (1) 1 (*Graydon*)
Southampton (1) 2 (*McCalliog 2*) (*After extra time*)
   44,623
Aston Villa: Burridge; Gidman, Robson, Ross, Nicholl, Phillips, Graydon (Aitken), Deehan, Gray, Hamilton, Carrodus.
Southampton: Turner; Rodrigues, Peach, Holmes, Blyth, Steele, Fisher, Channon, Osgood, McCalliog, Stokes.

Newcastle U. (1) 2 (*Gowling, Craig T. pen*)
Q.P.R. (0) 1 (*Masson*)   37,225
Newcastle U.: Mahoney; Nattrass, Kennedy, Nulty, Bird, Howard, Burns, Cassidy, Macdonald, Gowling, Craig T.
Q.P.R.: Parkes, Clement, Gillard, Hollins, McLintock, Webb, Leach, Francis, Masson, Bowles (Busby), Givens.

Peterborough U. (1) 1 (*Nixon*)
Nottingham F. (0) 0   17,866
Peterborough U.: Steele; Murray, Walker, Eustace, Turner, Carmichael, Nixon, Gregory, Cozens, Hughes, Robson.
Nottingham F.: Wells; O'Kane, Clark, McGovern, Chapman, Richardson, McIntosh, Bowery, O'Hare, Butlin, Bowyer.

THIRD ROUND, SECOND REPLAY
JAN. 13
Norwich C. (1) 2 (*MacDougall pen., Suggett*)
Rochdale (0) 1 (*Mountford*)   18,868
Norwich C.: Keelan; Jones, Sullivan, McGuire, Forbes, Stringer, Machin, MacDougall, Boyer, Suggett, Peters.
Rochdale: Poole; Hallows, Lacey, Mulvaney, Summerscales, Hanvey, Ferguson, Mountford, Whelan, Fielding, Mullington.

THIRD ROUND, REPLAY
JAN. 24
Stoke C. (1) 2 (*Moores, Salmon pen.*)
Tottenham H. (1) 1 (*Perryman*)   29,538
Stoke C.: Shilton; Dodd, Bowers, Mahoney, Smith, Bloor, Robertson, Greenhoff, Moores, Hudson, Salmons.
Tottenham H.: Jennings; Naylor, McAllister, Pratt, Young, Osgood, Coates, Perryman, Duncan, Jones, Neighbour.

496

FOURTH ROUND
JAN. 24
Bradford C. (1) 3 (*Hutchins 2, Middleton*)
Tooting & Mitcham U. (0) 1 (*Juneman*)   21,152
Bradford C.: Downsborough; Podd, Cooper, Johnson, Middleton, Fretwell, McGinley, Ingram, Cooke, Hall, Hutchins.
Tooting & Mitcham U.: Dunn; Berrecloth, Smith, Grubb, Green, Casey, Howell, Ford (Dennis), Juneman, Glover, Ives.

Charlton Ath. (1) 1 (*Curtis pen.*)
Portsmouth (1) 1 (*Piper*)   26,333
Charlton Ath.: Tutt; Penfold, Warman, Hunt, Giles, Curtis, Powell, Hales, Hope, Peacock, Flanagan.
Portsmouth: Lloyd; Lawler, Mellows, Roberts, Went, Cahill, McGuinness, Piper, Graham, Reynolds, Eames.

Coventry C. (0) 1 (*Murphy*)
Newcastle U. (1) 1 (*Gowling*)   32,004
Coventry C.: King; Coop, Brogan, Craven (Powell), Dugdale, Holmes, Cartwright, Green, Cross, Murphy, Hutchison.
Newcastle U.: Mahoney; Nattrass, Kennedy, Nulty, Keeley, Howard, Burns, Cassidy, Macdonald, Gowling, Craig T.

Derby Co. (0) 1 (*Davies*)
Liverpool (0) 0   38,200
Derby Co.: Moseley; Thomas, Nish, Rioch, McFarland, Todd, Powell, Gemmill, Lee, George, James (Davies).
Liverpool: Clemence; Smith, Neal, Thompson, Kennedy, Hughes, Keegan, Case, Heighway, Toshack (Hall), Callaghan.

Huddersfield T. (0) 0
Bolton W. (0) 1 (*Reid*)   27,894
Huddersfield T.: Taylor; Sweeney, Hutt, Smith, Baines, Simpkin, Gray, O'Neil, Belfitt, Dolan, Garwood.
Bolton W.: Siddall; Ritson, Dunne, Greaves, Jones P., Allardyce, Byrom, Whatmore, Jones G., Reid, Thompson.

Ipswich T. (0) 0
Wolverhampton W. (0) 0   29,846
Ipswich T.: Cooper; Burley, Tibbott, Talbot, Hunter, Beattie, Woods, Mills, Johnson, Whymark, Lambert.
Wolverhampton W.: Parkes; Sunderland, Parkin, Bailey, McAlle, Carr, Hibbitt, Munro, Bell, Gould, Richards.

Leeds U. (0) 0
Crystal Palace (1) 1 (*Swindlehurst*)   43,116
Leeds U.: Harvey; Reaney, Gray F., Bremner (Hunter), Madeley, Cherry, Lorimer, Clarke, McKenzie, Yorath, Gray E.
Crystal Palace: Hammond; Wall, Cannon, Jeffries, Jump, Evans, Chatterton, Hinshelwood M., Whittle, Swindlehurst, Taylor.

Leicester C. (0) 1 (*Lee*)
Bury (0) 0   27,331
Leicester C.: Wallington; Whitworth, Rofe, Kember, Blockley, Woollett, Weller, Alderson, Garland, Lee, Worthington.
Bury: Forrest; Hoolickin, Kennedy, Keenan, Hulme, Bailey, McIlwraith, Rudd, Rowland, Woolfall, Phillips (Riley).

Manchester U. (2) 3 (*Forsyth, McIlroy, Hill*)
Peterborough U. (1) 1 (*Cozens*)   56,352
Manchester U.: Stepney; Forsyth, Houston, Daly, Greenhoff, Buchan, Coppell, McIlroy, Pearson, Macari, Hill.

Peterborough U.: Steele; Murray, Walker, Eustace, Turner, Carmichael, Nixon, Gregory, Cozens, Hughes, Robson (Jones).

Norwich C. (1) 2 *(Peters, Jones)*
Luton T. (0) 0   24,328
Norwich C.: Keelan; Jones, Sullivan, McGuire, Forbes, Stringer, Howell, MacDougall, Boyer, Suggett, Peters.
Luton T.: Barber; John Ryan, Buckley, Chambers, Faulkner, Futcher P., Husband, King, Futcher R., West, Aston.

Southampton (1) 3 *(Channon 2, Stokes)*
Blackpool (0) 1 *(Alcock)*   21,553
Southampton: Turner; Rodrigues, Peach, Holmes, Blyth, Steele, Fisher, Channon, Osgood, McCalliog (O'Brien), Stokes.
Blackpool: Wood; Hatton, Harrison, McEwan, Hart, Alcock, Evanson, Moore, Walsh, Bentley, Weston.

Southend U. (1) 2 *(Parker 2)*
Cardiff C. (1) 1 *(Evans)*   12,863
Southend U.: Webster; Worthington, Ford, Little, Townsend (Hadley), Moody, Foggo, Brace, Parker, Silvester, Nicholl.
Cardiff C.: Irwin; Dwyer, Charles, Reece, England, Larmour, Buchanan, Livermore, Evans, Alston, Anderson.

W.B.A. (1) 3 *(Brown T., Martin, Robson)*
Lincoln C. (2) 2 *(Ellis pen., Fleming)*   26,388
W.B.A.: Osborne; Mulligan, Mayo, Robson, Wile, Robertson, Brown T., Martin, Brown A., Giles, Johnston.
Lincoln C.: Grotier; Branfoot, Leigh, Booth, Ellis, Cooper, Fleming, Ward, Freeman, Smith (Neale), Krzywicki.

York C. (0) 0
Chelsea (1) 2 *(Garner, Hutchinson)*   9591
York C.: Crawford; Scott, Woodward, Cave, Swallow, Topping, Hosker, Hunter, Seal, Hinch, Pollard.
Chelsea: Bonetti; Locke, Harris, Cooke, Wicks, Hay, Britton, Wilkins R., Maybank, Hutchinson, Garner.

FOURTH ROUND REPLAYS
JAN. 27
Portsmouth (0) 0
Charlton Ath. (0) 3 *(Powell, Flanagan, Hope)*
                                                        31,722
Portsmouth: Lloyd; Lawler, Mellows, Roberts, Went, Cahill, McGuinness, Piper, Graham, Reynolds, Eames (Wilson).
Charlton Ath.: Tutt; Penfold, Warman, Hunt, Giles, Curtis, Powell, Hales, Hope, Peacock, Flanagan.

Wolverhampton W. (1) 1 *(Gould)*
Ipswich T. (0) 0   31,333
Wolverhampton W.: Parkes; Sunderland, Parkin, Bailey, McAlle, Carr, O'Hara, Munro, Bell, Gould (Kindon), Richards.
Ipswich T.: Cooper; Burley, Mills, Talbot, Beattie, Wark, Woods, Osborne, Johnson (Gates) Austin, Lambert.

FOURTH ROUND
JAN. 28
Stoke C. (0) 1 *(Greenhoff)*
Manchester C. (0) 0   38,072
Stoke C.: Shilton; Marsh, Pejic, Mahoney, Dodd, Bloor, Robertson, Greenhoff, Moores, Hudson, Salmons.
Manchester C.: Corrigan; Barrett, Donachie, Doyle, Booth, Oakes, Barnes (Keegan), Power, Royle, Hartford, Tueart.

FOURTH ROUND REPLAYS
Newcastle U. (2) 5 *(Burns, Gowling, Macdonald 2, Cassidy)*
Coventry C. (0) 0   43,445
Newcastle U.: Mahoney; Nattrass, Kennedy, Nulty, Keeley, Howard, Burns, Cassidy, Macdonald, Gowling, Craig T.
Coventry C.: King; Coop, Brogan, Powell, Dugdale, Holmes, Cartwright, Green, Cross, Murphy, Hutchison.

FOURTH ROUND
FEB. 2
Sunderland (1) 1 *(Finney)*
Hull C. (0) 0   32,320
Sunderland: Montgomery; Malone, Bolton, Towers, Clarke, Moncur, Kerr, Halom, Holden, Robson, Finney.
Hull C.: Wealands; Daniel, DeVries, Hawley, Croft, Roberts, Galvin, Lyall, Wood, Fletcher, Stewart (Deere).

FIFTH ROUND
FEB. 14
Bolton W. (1) 3 *(Allardyce, Jones G., Jones P.)*
Newcastle U. (2) 3 *(Macdonald 2, Gowling)* 46,584
Bolton W.: Siddall; Ritson, Dunne, Greaves, Jones P., Allardyce, Byrom, Whatmore, Jones G., Reid, Thompson.
Newcastle U.: Mahoney; Nattrass, Kennedy, Nulty (Barrowclough), Keeley, Howard, Burns, Cassidy, Macdonald, Gowling, Craig T.

Chelsea (0) 2 *(Wilkins R., Wicks)*
Crystal Palace (2) 3 *(Taylor 2, Chatterton)* 54,407
Chelsea: Bonetti; Locke, Harris, Cooke, Droy (Hay), Wicks, Britton, Wilkins R., Maybank, Swain, Garner.
Crystal Palace: Hammond; Wall, Cannon, Jeffries, Jump, Evans, Chatterton, Hinshelwood M., Whittle, Swindleshurst, Taylor.

Derby Co. (1) 1 *(Rioch)*
Southend U. (0) 0   31,918
Derby Co.: Moseley; Thomas, Nish, Rioch, McFarland, Todd, Powell, Gemmill, Davies (Lee), George, James.
Southend U.: Webster; Dyer, Ford, Little, Hadley, Moody, Foggo, Brace (Pountney), Parker, Silvester, Nicholl.

Leicester C. (0) 1 *(Lee)*
Manchester U. (2) 2 *(Macari, Daly)*   34,000
Leicester C.: Wallington; Whitworth, Rofe, Kember, Blockley, Woollett, Weller, Lee, Garland, Alderson (Sammels), Worthington.
Manchester U.: Stepney; Forsyth, Houston, Daly, Greenhoff, Buchan, Coppell, Macari, Pearson, McIlroy, Hill (McCreery).

Stoke C. (0) 0
Sunderland (0) 0   41,176
Stoke C.: Shilton; Marsh, Dodd, Mahoney, Smith, Bloor, Robertson, Greenhoff, Moores, Hudson, Salmons.
Sunderland: Montgomery; Malone, Bolton, Towers, Clarke, Moncur, Kerr, Ashurst, Holden, Robson, Finney.

W.B.A. (0) 1 *(Brown T.)*
Southampton (0) 1 *(Stokes)*   36,634
W.B.A.: Osborne; Mulligan, Mayo, Brown T., Wile, Robertson, Martin, Cantello, Brown A., Giles, Johnston.
Southampton: Turner; Rodrigues, Peach, Holmes, Blyth, Steele, Fisher, Channon, Gilchrist, McCalliog, Stokes.

Wolverhampton W. (1) 3 (*Richards 3*)
Charlton Ath. (0) 0   32,301
Wolverhampton W.: Parkes; Sunderland, Parkin,
Hibbitt, McAlle, Carr, O'Hara, Munro, Bell,
Gould, Wagstaff (Richards).
Charlton Ath.: Tutt; Penfold, Warman, Hunt,
Giles, Curtis, Powell, Hales, Hope, Peacock
(Young), Flanagan.

FIFTH ROUND REPLAYS

FEB. 17

Southampton (3) 4 (*Channon 3, 1 pen., Gilchrist*)
W.B.A. (0) 0   27,614
Southampton: Turner; Rodrigues, Peach, Holmes,
Blyth, Steele, Fisher, Channon, Gilchrist, McCal-
liog, Stokes (O'Brien).
W.B.A.: Osborne; Mulligan, Mayo, Brown T.,
Wile, Robertson, Martin, Cantello, Brown A.
(Robson), Giles, Johnston.

Sunderland (0) 2 (*Holden, Robson*)
Stoke C. (0) 1 (*Smith*)   47,583
Sunderland: Montgomery; Malone, Bolton,
Towers, Clarke, Moncur, Kerr, Ashurst, Holden,
Robson, Finney (Halom).
Stoke C.: Shilton; Marsh, Dodd, Bowers, Smith,
Bloor, Robertson, Greenhoff, Conroy, Hudson,
Salmons (Moores).

FEB. 18

Newcastle U. (0) 0
Bolton W. (0) 0 (*After extra time*)   50,381
Newcastle U.: Mahoney; Nattrass, Kennedy,
Craig D. (Barrowclough), Keeley, Howard, Burns,
Cassidy, Macdonald, Gowling, Craig T.
Bolton W.: Siddall; Ritson, Dunne, Greaves,
Jones P., Allardyce, Byrom, Whatmore, Jones G.,
Reid, Thompson.

FIFTH ROUND

FEB. 23

Norwich C. (1) 1 (*Peters*)
Bradford C. (1) 2 (*Hutchins, McGinley*)   27,047
Norwich C.: Keelan; Jones, Sullivan, McGuire,
Forbes, Stringer, Machin, MacDougall, Boyer,
Suggett, Peters.
Bradford C.: Downsborough; Podd, Cooper,
Johnson, Middleton, Fretwell, McGinley, Ingram,
Cooke, Hall, Hutchins.

FIFTH ROUND, SECOND REPLAY

FEB. 23

Bolton W. (0) 1 (*Jones G.*)
Newcastle U. (1) 2 (*Burns, Gowling*) (*at Leeds*)
                                                   42,280
Bolton W.: Siddall; Ritson (Walsh), Dunne,
Greaves, Nicholson, Allardyce, Byrom, What-
more, Jones G., Reid, Waldron.
Newcastle U.: Mahoney; Nattrass (Blackhall),
Kennedy, Barrowclough, Keeley, Howard, Burns,
Cassidy, Cannell, Gowling, Craig T.

SIXTH ROUND

MAR. 6

Bradford C. (0) 0
Southampton (1) 1 (*McCalliog*)   14,195
Bradford C.: Downsborough; Podd, Cooper,
Johnson, Middleton, Fretwell, McGinley, Ingram,
Cooke, Hall, Hutchins.
Southampton: Turner; Rodrigues, Peach, Gilchrist,
Blyth, Bennett, Fisher, Channon, Osgood,
McCalliog, Stokes.

Derby Co. (2) 4 (*Rioch 2, Newton, George*)
Newcastle U. (1) 2 (*Gowling 2*)   38,000
Derby Co.: Moseley; Thomas, Nish, Rioch,
McFarland, Todd, Newton (Davies), Gemmill,
Hector, George, James.
Newcastle U.: Edgar; Blackhall, Kennedy,
Barrowclough, Keeley, Howard, Burns, Cassidy,
Macdonald, Gowling, Hudson.

Manchester U. (0) 1 (*Daly*)
Wolverhampton W. (0) 1 (*Richards*)   59,433
Manchester U.: Stepney; Forsyth, Houston, Daly,
Greenhoff, Buchan, Coppell, McIlroy, Pearson,
Macari, Hill.
Wolverhampton W.: Parkes; Sunderland, Parkin,
Daley, Munro, McAlle, Hibbitt, Carr, Kindon,
Gould (Palmer), Richards.

Sunderland (0) 0
Crystal Palace (0) 1 (*Whittle*)   50,850
Sunderland: Montgomery; Malone, Bolton,
Towers, Clarke, Moncur, Kerr, Longhorn
(Hughes), Holden, Robson, Finney.
Crystal Palace: Hammond; Wall, Cannon,
Holder, Jeffries, Evans, Chatterton, Hinshelwood
M., Whittle, Swindlehurst, Taylor.

SIXTH ROUND REPLAY

MAR. 9

Wolverhampton W. (2) 2 (*Kindon, Richards*)
Manchester U. (1) 3 (*Pearson, Greenhoff, McIlroy*)
  (*After extra time*)   44,373
Wolverhampton W.: Parkes; Sunderland, Parkin,
Daley (Bailey), Munro, McAlle, Hibbitt, Carr,
Kindon, Gould, Richards.
Manchester U.: Stepney; Forsyth, Houston, Daly,
Greenhoff, Buchan, Coppell, McIlroy, Pearson,
Macari (Nicholl), Hill.

SEMI-FINALS

APR. 3

Manchester U. (1) 2 (*Hill 2*)
Derby Co. (0) 0 (*at Hillsborough*)   55,000
Manchester U.: Stepney; Forsyth, Houston, Daly,
Greenhoff, Buchan, Coppell, McIlroy, Pearson,
McCreery, Hill.
Derby Co.: Moseley; Thomas, Nish, Rioch,
McFarland, Todd, Powell, Gemill, Hector (Lee),
Davies, James.

Southampton (0) 2 (*Gilchrist, Peach pen.*)
Crystal Palace (0) 0 (*at Stamford Bridge*) 52,810
Southampton: Turner; Rodrigues, Peach, Holmes,
Blyth, Steele, Gilchrist, Channon, Osgood,
McCalliog, Stokes.
Crystal Palace: Hammond; Wall, Cannon, Holder,
Evans, Jeffries, Chatterton, Johnson, Whittle,
Swindlehurst, Taylor.

FINAL

MAY 1

Manchester U. (0) 0   at Wembley
Southampton (0) 1 (*Stokes*)   100,000
Manchester U.: Stepney; Forsyth, Houston, Daly,
Greenhoff, Buchan, Coppell, McIlroy, Pearson,
Macari, Hill (McCreey).
Southampton: Turner; Rodrigues, Peach, Holmes,
Blyth, Steele, Gilchrist, Channon, Osgood,
McCalliog, Stokes.

F.A. CUP FINALS 1872-1976

1872 and 1874–92	Kennington Oval	1911	Replay at Old Trafford
1873	Lillie Bridge	1912	Replay at Bramall Lane
1893	Fallowfield, Manchester	1915	Old Trafford, Manchester
1894	Everton	1920–22	Stamford Bridge
1895–1914	Crystal Palace	1923 to date	Wembley
1901	Replay at Bolton	1970	Replay at Old Trafford
1910	Replay at Everton		

Year	Winners	Runners-up	Score
1872	Wanderers	Royal Engineers	1-0
1873	Wanderers	Oxford University	2-0
1874	Oxford University	Royal Engineers	2-0
1875	Royal Engineers	Old Etonians	2-0 after 1-1 draw
1876	Wanderers	Old Etonians	3-0 after 0-0 draw
1877	Wanderers	Oxford University	2-0 after extra time
1878	*Wanderers	Royal Engineers	3-1
1879	Old Etonians	Clapham R.	1-0
1880	Clapham R.	Oxford University	1-0
1881	Old Carthusians	Old Etonians	3-0
1882	Old Etonians	Blackburn R.	1-0
1883	Blackburn Olympic	Old Etonians	2-1 after extra time
1884	Blackburn R.	Queen's Park, Glasgow	2-1
1885	Blackburn R.	Queen's Park, Glasgow	2-0
1886	†Blackburn R.	W.B.A.	2-0 after 0-0 draw
1887	Aston Villa	W.B.A.	2-0
1888	W.B.A.	Preston N E	2-1
1889	Preston N.E.	Wolverhampton W.	3-0
1890	Blackburn R.	Sheffield W.	6-1
1891	Blackburn R.	Notts. Co.	3-1
1892	W.B.A.	Aston Villa	3-0
1893	Wolverhampton W.	Everton	1-0
1894	Notts. Co.	Bolton W.	4-1
1895	Aston Villa	W.B.A.	1-0
1896	Sheffield W.	Wolverhampton W.	2-1
1897	Aston Villa	Everton	3-2
1898	Nottingham F.	Derby Co.	3-1
1899	Sheffield U.	Derby Co.	4-1
1900	Bury	Southampton	4-0
1901	Tottenham H.	Sheffield U.	3-1 after 2-2 draw
1902	Sheffield U.	Southampton	2-1 after 1-1 draw
1903	Bury	Derby Co.	6-0
1904	Manchester C.	Bolton W.	1-0
1905	Aston Villa	Newcastle U.	2-0
1906	Everton	Newcastle U.	1-0
1907	Sheffield W.	Everton	2-1
1908	Wolverhampton W.	Newcastle U.	3-1
1909	Manchester U.	Bristol C.	1-0
1910	Newcastle U.	Barnsley	2-0 after 1-1 draw
1911	Bradford C.	Newcastle U.	1-0 after 0-0 draw
1912	Barnsley	W.B.A.	1-0 after extra time
1913	Aston Villa	Sunderland	1-0
1914	Burnley	Liverpool	1-0 [after 0-0 draw]
1915	Sheffield U.	Chelsea	3-0
1920	Aston Villa	Huddersfield	1-0 after extra time
1921	Tottenham H.	Wolverhampton W.	1-0
1922	Huddersfield	Preston N.E.	1-0
1923	Bolton W.	West Ham U.	2-0
1924	Newcastle U.	Aston Villa	2-0
1925	Sheffield U.	Cardiff C.	1-0
1926	Bolton W.	Manchester C.	1-0
1927	Cardiff C.	Arsenal	1-0
1928	Blackburn R.	Huddersfield T.	3-1
1929	Bolton W.	Portsmouth	2-0
1930	Arsenal	Huddersfield	2-0
1931	W.B.A.	Birmingham C.	2-1
1932	Newcastle U.	Arsenal	2-1
1933	Everton	Manchester C.	3-0
1934	Manchester C.	Portsmouth	2-1
1935	Sheffield W.	W.B.A.	4-2
1936	Arsenal	Sheffield U.	1-0
1937	Sunderland	Preston N.E.	3-1
1938	Preston N.E.	Huddersfield	1-0 after extra time
1939	Portsmouth	Wolverhampton W.	4-1
1946	Derby Co.	Charlton Ath.	4-1 after extra time
1947	Charlton Ath.	Burnley	1-0 after extra time
1948	Manchester U.	Blackpool	4-2

Year	Winners	Runners-up	Score
1949	Wolverhampton W.	Leicester C.	3-1
1950	Arsenal	Liverpool	2-0
1951	Newcastle U.	Blackpool	2-0
1952	Newcastle U.	Arsenal	1-0
1953	Blackpool	Bolton W.	4-3
1954	W.B.A.	Preston N.E.	3-2
1955	Newcastle U.	Manchester C.	3-1
1956	Manchester C.	Birmingham C.	3-1
1957	Aston Villa	Manchester U.	2-1
1958	Bolton W.	Manchester U.	2-0
1959	Nottingham F.	Luton T.	2-1
1960	Wolverhampton W.	Blackburn R.	3-0
1961	Tottenham H.	Leicester C.	2-0
1962	Tottenham H.	Burnley	3-1
1963	Manchester U.	Leicester C.	3-1
1964	West Ham U.	Preston N.E.	3-2
1965	Liverpool	Leeds U.	2-1 after extra time
1966	Everton	Sheffield W.	3-2
1967	Tottenham H.	Chelsea	2-1
1968	W.B.A.	Everton	1-0 after extra time
1969	Manchester C.	Leicester C.	1-0
1970	Chelsea	Leeds U.	2-1 after extra time
	(after 2-2 draw, after extra time, at Wembley)		2-1 after extra time
1971	Arsenal	Liverpool	1-0
1972	Leeds U.	Arsenal	1-0
1973	Sunderland	Leeds U.	1-0
1974	Liverpool	Newcastle U.	3-0
1975	West Ham U.	Fulham	2-0
1976	Southampton	Manchester U.	1-0

*Won outright, but restored to the Association.
†A special trophy was awarded for third consecutive win.

F.A. CUP WINS

Aston Villa 7, Blackburn R. 6, Newcastle U. 6, The Wanderers 5, Tottenham H. 5, W.B.A. 5, Sheffield U. 4, Bolton W. 4, Wolverhampton W. 4, Manchester C. 4, Arsenal 4, Manchester U. 3, Sheffield W. 3, Everton 3, Bury 2, Old Etonians 2, Preston N.E. 2, Nottingham F. 2, Sunderland 2, West Ham U. 2, Liverpool 2, Barnsley 1, Blackburn Olympic 1, Blackpool 1, Bradford C. 1, Burnley 1, Cardiff C. 1, Charlton Ath. 1, Chelsea 1, Clapham R. 1, Derby Co. 1, Huddersfield T. 1, Notts Co. 1, Old Carthusians 1, Oxford University 1, Portsmouth 1, Royal Engineers 1, Leeds 1, Southampton 1.

APPEARANCES IN FINALS

Newcastle U. 11, W.B.A. 10, Aston Villa 9, Arsenal 8, Blackburn R. 8, Wolverhampton W. 8, Bolton W. 7, Preston N.E. 7, Everton 7, Manchester C. 7, Old Etonians 6, Sheffield U. 6, Manchester U. 6, Huddersfield T. 5, *The Wanderers 5, Sheffield W. 5, *Tottenham H. 5, Liverpool 5, Derby Co. 4, Oxford University 4, Royal Engineers 4, Leeds U. 4, Leicester C. 4, Blackpool 3, Burnley 3, Chelsea 3, Portsmouth 3, Sunderland 3, West Ham U. 3, Southampton 3, Barnsley 2, Birmingham C. 2, *Bury 2, Cardiff C. 2, Charlton Ath. 2, Clapham R. 2, Notts Co. 2, Queen's Park (Glas.) 2, *Nottingham F. 2, *Blackburn Olympic 1, *Bradford C. 1, Bristol C. 1, *Old Carthusians 1, Luton T. 1, Fulham 1.

*Denotes undefeated.

APPEARANCES IN SEMI-FINALS

Aston Villa 17, W.B.A. 17, Blackburn R. 16, Everton 16, Sheffield W. 13, Derby Co. 13, Manchester U. 13, Newcastle U. 13, Arsenal 12, Bolton W. 12, Wolverhampton W. 11, Sunderland 10, Preston N.E. 10, Sheffield U. 10, Chelsea 10, Liverpool 10, Nottingham F. 9, Tottenham H. 9, Manchester C. 9, Birmingham C. 9, Burnley 8, Southampton 8, Huddersfield 7, Old Etonians 6, Oxford University 6, Leeds U. 6, Leicester C. 6, The Wanderers 5, Notts. Co. 5, Fulham 5, Portsmouth 4, Queen's Park (Glasgow) 4, Royal Engineers 4, West Ham U. 4, Blackpool 3, Cardiff C. 3, Clapham R. 3, Millwall 3, Old Carthusians 3, The Swifts 3, Stoke C. 3, Barnsley 2, Blackburn Olympic 2, Bristol C. 2, Bury 2, Charlton Ath. 2, Grimsby T. 2, Swansea T. 2, Swindon T. 2, Crystal Palace 2, Bradford C. 1, Cambridge University 1, Crewe Alex. 1, Darwen 1, Derby Junction 1, Glasgow R. 1, Hull C. 1, Marlow 1, Old Harrovians 1, Oldham Ath. 1, Port Vale 1, Reading 1, Shropshire W. 1, York C. 1, Luton T. 1, Norwich C. 1, Watford 1, Ipswich T. 1.

THE FOOTBALL LEAGUE CUP

Review of the 1975-76 competition

Round-by-round match details

Team line-ups, results, and scorers of every Football League Cup final

R.F.76/77–26

THE FOOTBALL LEAGUE CUP 1975-76

Mere facts and figures can be a poor substitute for the truth. In 100 years' time, all the records will reveal of the 1976 League Cup final at Wembley was that Manchester City scored most goals and thus took the trophy and the spin-off prize of a UEFA Cup place in 1976–77. But what of the real stars of this outstandingly entertaining February afternoon – the 'black and white army' of Newcastle fans? They do not deserve to be forgotten by history.

Throughout the competition the contribution of the Geordie hordes had been significant; so marked was the effect of their unrelenting support that fewer and fewer sides began to fancy any fixture that involved a trip to St James. The Newcastle team, with the constant prowling menace of Macdonald and Gowling, was formidable, if not among the highest-ranked, but with that crowd at their backs they were to look invincible at times. As the week of the final began, with four and then six of the Newcastle team afflicted by colds and 'flu, it became obvious that Newcastle were going to need all the help they could muster if they were to withstand the assault of a better-balanced and clearly more skilled Manchester City side.

That support was instantly forthcoming. Long before the kick-off the noise of the 'black and white' brigade filled the stadium with sound and emotion. City's own 'chorus' was made to look so miserable by comparison that it was hard to believe each club had an equal ticket allocation.

Newcastle players seemed to be almost visibly thrown into the match by the volume of noise, and certainly the first quarter-hour belonged to them. Despite the presence in defence of Watson and Doyle, Oakes and Booth – tall men all – City had the most appalling problems, trying to turn away the centres with which Newcastle teased them.

Yet City scored first. Hartford's clever free kick was knocked back across goal by Doyle and young Barnes ran into score at the far post with a mid-air volley that took every ounce of his spring and agility to control. There was a pause, time perhaps to count slowly to 20, then Newcastle's bubbling mass was back in full song.

Kennedy won a good tackle on the left, thence to Craig, on to Cassidy. Macdonald took the ball driven in from the right and laid it adroitly for Gowling to equalise. Before even turning to fall upon each other, the makers and taker of this goal looked first to 'their' terraces as though to say 'thanks'. Erratic by comparison with their cool rivals, Newcastle thus came to half-time level, though Tueart, for City, and Macdonald, for Newcastle, walked to the tunnel cursing the courage of the goalkeepers who had thwarted them equally in the seconds before half time.

Tueart was not made to wait long for revenge. Seconds only after the interval he scored a goal of indelible novelty. He'd had one shot from the kick-off, and was wandering morosely along in its wake when Donachie crossed from the left. Booth headed back into the centre and Tueart – a Geordie himself – scored with a bicycle kick.

The applause for that glorious goal came dinning down from *all* parts of the ground but it was to be a long while before much else happened worth a shout. Manchester City, with Hartford taking from Watson and Doyle and feeding his wings, had control of the game; Newcastle, tiring by the minute, could neither match this command, nor overcome it. And so the game might have drifted to anti-climax . . . but for the Magpie army.

Gradually their voices swelled. Gradually the players responded. There was still no majesty in their play, but the morale was undeniable. Macdonald's cross found Burns with his back to an empty goal – a chance wasted. Macdonald's own shot had Corrigan grasping, but safe. Then Gowling, wriggling clear, spun into a shot which Corrigan turned aside. If this was vain effort, then it was, too, valiant enterprise. Merit, finally and properly, gave the Cup to City. And it was now that the Newcastle fans had their finest moment.

Unusually, Newcastle trooped up first for their medals and, with some unable to restrain tears, they did a slow lap of honour along the front of their forgiving fans. Now City's turn, and the warmth and generosity of the 'black and white army' to the side that had defeated them will long be remembered. It wasn't the mass of the Geordie crowd at Wembley that was so memorable; but their mood.

So ended a competition that, still criticised as 'upstart', had given much to many. From the first rounds to this last act, cash and glory had gone abundantly to those with the courage or resource to seek it.

From the Second Round on 'big' teams like Stoke fell to unconsidered sides like Lincoln, and football was in many senses richer for such oddities. There was a particularly steady erosion of the Second Division challenge, with Blackburn, Blackpool, Luton, and Chelsea all going down to lower-placed sides, and those who failed on the field were often compensated at the turnstile – like Charlton, who had their biggest crowd for years to see QPR overcome them.

Outstanding in the Third Round were the matches at Villa Park, where 41,000 paid to see Manchester United recover and win; at Burnley where a poor team in the League beat the fancied Liverpool, and – especially – at Mansfield, where Coventry were eliminated by a team deep in Division Three. Mansfield maintained their momentum in the Fourth round, knocking over Wolves, and so did Notts County, who had beaten Leeds at Leeds and now took on Everton and won again.

The Fifth Round saw the end of such audacious gestures. Mansfield were hit by four goals from Manchester City, who had also knocked four past Manchester United in the challenge before, and Notts County collapsed at St James through an own goal. The semi-finals will be remembered for the collapse of the steady Middlesbrough side at Maine Road – again by four goals – and the brilliant performance of Spurs' goalkeeper Jennings, who made Newcastle wait for their eventual prize of a Wembley place. Newcastle, having taken three matches to dispose of Norwich, were gaining pace, and the voice of their following was gaining power.

In the final reckoning, though, perhaps the men who had most cause to be grateful to Newcastle supporters were those who struggle to keep Southport alive. Drawn at home to Newcastle in the Second Round, Southport elected to forgo advantage to play at St James. They were smashed 6–0 for their temerity, but the gate was 23,000 – and that was almost precisely as many as the total Southport crowd for their first 18 matches in the League. From start to finish of the 1975–76 League Cup then, Newcastle supporters contributed generously – to be hideously ill-rewarded at the end.

FOOTBALL LEAGUE CUP RESULTS 1975-76

*Home team in first match

First Round

Aldershot v Portsmouth	1-1, 1-2
Bradford C. v York C.	2-0, 0-3
Brentford v Brighton & H.A.	2-1, 1-1
Bury v Rochdale	2-0, 2-0
Cambridge U. v Charlton Ath.	1-1, 0-3
Cardiff C. v Bristol R.	1-2, 1-1
Crystal Palace v Colchester U.	3-0, 1-3
Crewe Alex. v Tranmere R.	2-1, 1-2
Darlington v Sheffield W.	0-2, 2-0
Doncaster R. v Grimsby T.	3-1, 0-0
Halifax T. v Hartlepool	4-1, 1-2
Huddersfield T. v Barnsley	2-1, 1-1
Lincoln C. v Chesterfield	4-2, 2-3
Mansfield T. v Scunthorpe U.	4-0, 2-0
Newport Co. v Exeter C.	1-1, 0-2
Oldham Ath. v Workington	3-0, 3-1
Plymouth Arg. v AFC Bournemouth	2-0, 2-1
Port Vale v Hereford U.	4-2, 0-2
Preston N.E. v Blackburn R.	2-0, 0-0
Reading v Gillingham	0-1, 1-1
Rotherham U. v Nottingham F.	1-2, 1-5
Southend U. v Peterborough U.	2-0, 0-3
Southport v Stockport Co.	3-1, 2-1
Swansea C. v Torquay U.	1-2, 3-5
Swindon T. v Millwall	2-1, 1-0
Walsall v Shrewsbury T.	0-0, 1-2
Watford v Northampton T.	2-0, 1-1
Wrexham v Chester	3-0, 0-0

Second Round

Aston Villa v Oldham Ath.	2-0
Birmingham C. v Orient	4-0
Bolton W. v Coventry C.	1-3
Bury v Middlesbrough	1-2
Carlisle U. v Gillingham	2-0
*Charlton Ath. v Oxford U.	3-3, 1-1, 3-2

Crewe Alex. v Chelsea	1-0
Darlington v Luton T.	2-1
Derby Co. v Huddersfield T.	2-1
Doncaster R. v Crystal Palace	2-1
*Everton v Arsenal	2-2, 1-0
Halifax T. v Sheffield U.	2-4
Hereford U. v Burnley	1-4
Hull C. v Preston N.E.	4-2
Leeds U. v Ipswich T.	3-2
Lincoln C. v Stoke C.	2-1
Manchester U. v Brentford	2-1
*Norwich C. v Manchester C.	1-1, 2-2, 1-6
Notts Co. v Sunderland	2-1
Nottingham F. v Plymouth Arg.	1-0
Peterborough U. v Blackpool	2-0
*Portsmouth v Leicester C.	1-1, 0-1
Shrewsbury T. v Q.P.R.	1-4
Southampton v Bristol R.	0-1
Southport v Newcastle U.	0-6
*Swindon T. v Wolverhampton W.	2-2, 2-3
*Torquay U. v Exeter C.	1-1, 2-1
Watford v Tottenham H.	0-1
*W.B.A. v Fulham	1-1, 0-1
*West Ham U. v Bristol C.	0-0, 3-1
Wrexham v Mansfield T.	1-2
York C. v Liverpool	0-1

Third Round

Aston Villa v Manchester U.	1-2
Birmingham C. v Wolverhampton W.	0-2
*Bristol R. v Newcastle U.	1-1, 0-2
Crewe Alex. v Tottenham H.	0-2
Everton v Carlisle U.	2-0
Fulham v Peterborough U.	0-1
Hull C. v Sheffield U.	2-0
Leeds U. v Notts Co.	0-1
Leicester C. v Lincoln C.	2-1
*Liverpool v Burnley	1-1, 0-1

503

Manchester C. v Nottingham F.	2-1	**Fifth Round**		
Mansfield T. v Coventry C.	2-0	Burnley v Middlesbrough		0-2
Middlesborough v Derby Co.	1-0	Manchester C. v Mansfield T.		4-2
*Q.P.R. v Charlton Ath.	1-1, 3-0	Newcastle U. v Notts Co.		1-0
*Torquay U. v Doncaster R.	1-1, 0-3	Tottenham H. v Doncaster R.		7-2
West Ham U. v Darlington	3-0			

Fourth Round

Semi-Final

Burnley v Leicester Co.	2-0	Middlesbrough v Manchester C.	1-0, 0-4
Doncaster R. v Hull C.	2-1	*Manchester C. won 4-1 on aggregate.*	
*Everton v Notts Co.	2-2, 0-2	Tottenham H. v Newcastle U.	1-0, 1-3
Manchester C. v Manchester U.	4-0	*Newcastle U. won 3-2 on aggregate.*	
Mansfield T. v Wolverhampton W.	1-0		
Middlesbrough v Peterborough U.	3-0	**Final**	
Q.P.R. v Newcastle U.	1-3	Manchester C. v Newcastle U.	2-1
*Tottenham H. v West Ham U.	0-0, 2-0		

FOOTBALL LEAGUE CUP FINALS 1961-1975

Final 1960–61: Rotherham U. 2 Aston Villa 0 (First leg, Rotherham, 12,226, August 22, 1961)
Scorers: Webster, Kirkman.
Aston Villa 3 Rotherham U. 0 (after extra time) (Second leg, Villa Park, 27,000, September 5, 1961)
Scorers: O'Neill, Burrows, McParland. *Aston Villa won on aggregate 3–2.*

Final 1961–62: Rochdale 0 Norwich C. 3 (First leg, Rochdale, 11,123, April 26, 1962)
Scorers: Lythgoe 2, Punton.
Norwich C. 1 Rochdale 0 (Second leg, Norwich, 19,708, May 1, 1962)
Scorer: Hill. *Norwich C. won on aggregate 4–*

Final 1962–63: Birmingham C. 3 Aston Villa 1 (First leg, St. Andrews, 31,850, May 23, 1963)
Scorers—Birmingham C.: Leek 2, Bloomfield. Aston Villa: Thomson.
Aston Villa 0 Birmingham C. 0 (Second leg, Villa Park, 37,921, May 27, 1963)
Birmingham C. won on aggregate 3–1

Final 1963–64: Stoke C. 1 Leicester C. 1 (First leg, Stoke, 22,309, April 15, 1964)
Scorers—Stoke C.: Bebbington. Leicester C.: Gibson.
Leicester C. 3 Stoke C. 2 (Second leg, Leicester, 25,372, April 22, 1964)
Scorers—Leicester C.: Stringfellow, Gibson, Riley. Stoke C.: Viollet, Kinnell.
Leicester C. won on aggregate 4–3

Final 1964–65: Chelsea 3 Leicester C. 2 (First leg, Stamford Bridge, 20,690, March 15, 1965)
Scorers—Chelsea: Tambling, Venables (penalty), McCreadie. Leicester C.: Appleton, Goodfellow.
Leicester C. 0 Chelsea 0 (Second leg, Leicester, 26,957, April 5, 1965)
Chelsea won on aggregate 3–2

Final 1965–66: West Ham U. 2 W.B.A. 1 (First leg, Upton Park, 28,341, March 9, 1966)
Scorers—West Ham U.: Moore, Byrne. West Bromwich Albion: Astle.
W.B.A. 4 West Ham U. 1 (Second leg, W.B.A., 31,925, March 23, 1966)
Scorers—W.B.A.: Kaye, Brown, Clark, Williams. West Ham U.: Peters. *W.B.A. won on aggregate 5–3*

Final 1966–67: Q.P.R. 3 W.B.A. 2 (At Wembley, 97,952, receipts £57,000, March 4, 1967)
Scorers—Q.P.R.: Morgan (R.), Marsh, Lazarus. W.B.A.: Clark (C.) 2.

Final 1967–68: Leeds U. 1 Arsenal 0 (At Wembley, 97,887, receipts £95,000, March 2, 1968)
Scorer: Cooper.

Final 1968–69: Arsenal 1 Swindon T. 3 (At Wembley, 98,189, receipts £104,000, March 15, 1969)
Scorers—Arsenal: Gould. Swindon T.: Smart, Rogers 2.

Final 1969–70: Manchester C. 2 W.B.A. 1 (At Wembley, 97,963, receipts £123,000, March 7, 1970)
Scorers—Manchester City: Doyle, Pardoe. W.B.A.: Astle.

Final 1970–71: Aston Villa 0 Tottenham H. 2 (At Wembley, 100,000, receipts £132,000, February 27, 1971)
Scorer—Tottenham H.: Chivers 2.

Final 1971–72: Chelsea 1 Stoke City 2 (At Wembley, 100,000, receipts £132,000, March 4, 1972)
Scorers—Chelsea: Osgood. Stoke: Conroy, Eastham.

Final 1972–73: Tottenham H. 1 Norwich C. 0 (At Wembley, 100,000, receipts £132,000, March 3, 1973)
Scorer—Tottenham H.: Coates.

Final 1973–74: Wolverhampton W. 2 Manchester C. 1 (At Wembley,100,000, receipts £165,500, March 2, 1974).
Scorers—Wolverhampton W.—Hibbitt, Richards; Manchester C.—Bell.

Final 1974–75: Aston Villa 1, Norwich C. 0 (At Wembley, 100,000, receipts £196,000, March 1, 1975)
Scorer—Graydon.

FOOTBALL LEAGUE CUP DETAILS 1975-76

FIRST ROUND, FIRST LEG

AUG. 18

Port Vale (4) 4 (*Cullerton 3, 1 pen., Bailey*)
Hereford U. (0) 2 (*Lindsay*)   3787
Port Vale: Connaughton; Tartt, Dulson, Ridley, Harris, Horton, Morris (Chadwick), Lees, Cullerton, Bailey, Brownbill.
Hereford U.: Hughes; Emery, Ritchie, Tucker, Galley, Lindsay, Paine, Walker, Davey, McNeil, Layton.

AUG. 19

Brentford (0) 2 (*Johnson pen., Cross*)
Brighton & H.A. (1) 1 (*Glazier o.g.*)   5560
Brentford: Glazier; Nelmes, Allen, Bence, Lawrence, Smith, Graham, Scales, Simmons, French (Cross), Johnson.
Brighton & H.A.: Grummitt; Tiler, Wilson, Machin, Piper, Winstanley, Towner (Fell), Mellor, Binney, Martin, Walker.

Bury (2) 2 (*Nicholson 2*)
Rochdale (0) 0   4561
Bury: Forrest; Hoolickin, Kennedy, Nicholson, Hulme, Bailey, Williams, Phillips, Spence, Rowland, Hamstead.
Rochdale: Poole; Hallows, Townsend, Ferguson, Summerscales, Hanvey, Fielding, Mountford, Whelan, Lacey, Sweeney.

Cambridge U. (0) 1 (*Biley*)
Charlton Ath. (0) 1 (*Bowman*)   3328
Cambridge U.: Smith G.; Howell, Lill, Lyon, Eades, Watson, Smith P., Spriggs, Shinton, Horsfall, Biley.
Charlton Ath.: Tutt; Penfold, Warman, Bowman, Giles, Young, Powell, Flanagan, Hunt, Horsfield, Peacock.

Crystal Palace (2) 3 (*Swindlehurst, Kemp 2*)
Colchester U. (0) 0   10,006
Crystal Palace: Burns; Wall, Johnston J., Hinshelwood M., Jeffries, Evans, Hill, Chatterton, Kemp, Swindlehurst, Taylor.
Colchester U.: Walker; Thomas, Cook, Bunkell, Dominey, Packer, Roberts, Svarc, Froggatt, Dyer, Smith.

Darlington (0) 0
Sheffield W. (0) 2 (*Prendergast, Potts*)   3581
Darlington: Ogley; Nattress, Cochrane, Cattrell, Smith, Noble, Holbrook, Rowles, Webb, Crosson, Young.
Sheffield W.: Ramsbottom; Cameron, Quinn, Mullen, Dowd, McIver, Potts, Harvey, Joicey, Prendergast, Henson.

Doncaster R. (2) 3 (*O'Callaghan 3*)
Grimsby T. (1) 1 (*Wigg*)   3218
Doncaster R.: Peacock; Reed, Ternent, Chappell, Uzelac, Brookes, Curran, Alseinove (Wignall), O'Callaghan, Kitchen, Higgins.
Grimsby T.: Freeman (Hubbard); Czuczman, Booth, Gray, Young, Cumming, Hubbard (Walton), Partridge, Wigg, Boylen, Brown.

Halifax T. (3) 4 (*Phelan, Bell 2, Albeson*)
Hartlepool (0) 1 (*Johnson*)   1476
Halifax T.: Gennoe; Smith, Collins, McHale, Rhodes, Phelan, Jones, Ford, Downes, Bell (Blair), Pugh.
Hartlepool: Hope; Crowther, Smith R., Potter, Goad, Albeson, Honour (Skillen), Smith D., Moore, McMahon, Johnson.

Huddersfield T. (0) 2 (*Gray, Dolan*)
Barnsley (1) 1 (*Butler*)   4200
Huddersfield T.: Taylor; Hutt, Garner, Smith, Baines, Saunders, Gray, O'Neil, Belfitt, Campbell, Dolan.
Barnsley: Springett; Murphy, Chambers, Doyle, Burke, Pickering, Millar (Peachey), Butler, Price, Walker, Brown.

Newport Co. (1) 1 (*Love*)
Exeter C. (0) 1 (*Bowker*)   2268
Newport Co.: Macey; Screen, Bell, Love, Aizlewood, Elliott, Hooper, Jones, Woodruff, Woods, White.
Exeter C.: Wilson; Templeman, Hooker, Joy, Wingate, Hatch, Hodge, Bowker, Robertson, Beer, Jennings.

Oldham Ath. (1) 3 (*Jones 3*)
Workington (0) 0   4288
Oldham Ath.: Ogden; Wood, Whittle, Blair, Hicks, Holt, Bell, Jones, Young (Robins), Chapman, Groves.
Workington: Rogan; Ellison, Ward, Geidmintis (Nevin), Johnstone, Walker, Harris, Scott, Murray, Kisby, Helliwell.

Plymouth Arg. (1) 2 (*Rafferty, Hague o.g.*)
AFC Bournemouth (0) 0   10,849
Plymouth Arg.: Aleksic; Hore, Burrows, Randell, Green, Delve, Horswill, Foster, Pearson, Rafferty, McAuley.
AFC Bournemouth: Baker; Payne, Russo, Benson, Morgan, Hague, Nightingale, Howard, Goddard, Rickard, Cunningham.

Preston N.E. (1) 2 (*Morley, Treacy*)
Blackburn R. (0) 0   11,503
Preston N.E.: Tunks; McMahon, Williams, Baxter S., Bird, Spark, Lamb, Burns, Treacy, Elwiss, Morley.
Blackburn R.: Jones; Heaton, Burgin, Waddington, Hawkins, Fazackerley, Beamish, Bailey (Hoy), Hickman, Hird, Martin.

Rotherham U. (0) 1 (*Crawford pen.*)
Nottingham F. (2) 2 (*Chapman, McGovern*)   4912
Rotherham U.: McDonagh; Leng, Breckin, Wagstaff, Stancliffe, Spencer (Derrett), Finney, Phillips, Habbin, Goodfellow, Crawford.
Nottingham F.: Middleton; Anderson, Clark, O'Kane, Chapman, Richardson, Robertson, McGovern, O'Haire, Bowyer, Lyall.

Swansea C. (1) 1 (*Bekker*)
Torquay U. (0) 2 (*Boulton 2*)   2143
Swansea C.: Potter; Evans, Davies, Smith, Bruton, Harris, Lally, James (Leitch), Bekker, Thomas, Bartley.
Torquay U.: Lee; Parker, Sandercock, Chatterley, Kruse, Stocks, Provan, Myers, Boulton (Twitchin), Brown, Kennedy.

Swindon T. (1) 2 (*Stroud, Trollope pen.*)
Millwall (1) 1 (*Summerill*)   6164
Swindon T.: Barron; McLaughlin, Trollope, Hubbard, Burrows, Prophett, Moss, Stroud, Eastoe, Jenkins (Butler), Anderson.

Millwall: Goddard; Evans, Jones, Brisley, Kitchener, Hazell, Fairbrother, Welsh, Summerill, Saul, Salvage.

Walsall (0) 0

Shrewsbury T. (0) 0   5910

Walsall: Kearns; Fry, Harrison, Atthey, Robinson, Caswell, Dennehy, Andrews (Spinner), Wright, Buckley, Taylor.
Shrewsbury T.: Mulhearn; King, Gregory, Durban, Kearney, Turner, Irvine, O'Loughlin, Haywood, Bates, Tarbuck.

Watford (2) 2 (*Downes, Greenhalgh*)

Northampton T. (0) 0   3368

Watford: Rankin; How, Akers, Joslyn, Goodeve, Garner, Bond, Downes, Jenkins, Greenhalgh, Mayes.
Northampton T.: Parton; Tucker, Anderson, Farrington, Robertson, Gregory, Mabee, Best, Hall, Christie, Stratford.

AUG. 20

Aldershot (1) 1 (*Warnock*)

Portsmouth (1) 1 (*Graham*)   6274

Aldershot: Johnson; Walden, Wallace J., Sainty, Jopling, Walker, Walton (Bell), Morrissey, Howarth, Brodie, Warnock.
Portsmouth: Lloyd; Roberts, Ellis, Piper, Went, Hand, Marinello, Kane, Graham, McGuinness, Mellows.

Bradford C. (0) 2 (*Cooper, Johnson*)

York C. (0) 0   3190

Bradford C.: Downsborough; Podd, Cooper, Hockey, Middleton, Fretwell, McGinley, Johnson, Ingram, Hall, Hutchins.
York C.: Crawford; Oliver, Downing, Holmes, Swallow, Topping, Lyons, Cave, Seal, Jones, McMordie.

Cardiff C. (1) 1 (*Reece pen.*)

Bristol R. (1) 2 (*Warboys, Bannister*)   6688

Cardiff C.: Healey; Dwyer, Charles, Buchanan (Evans), England, Larmour, Villars, Clark, Reece, Pethard, Durrell.
Bristol R.: Eadie; Smith, Williams, Aitken, Taylor, Prince, Stephens, Stanton, Warboys, Bannister, Evans.

Crewe Alex. (1) 2 (*Nelson, Nicholls*)

Tranmere R. (0) 1 (*Moore*)   1947

Crewe Alex.: Crudgington; Lowry, Evans, Lugg, Bowles, Rimmer, Davies (Reed), Bevan, Nelson, Nicholls, Humphreys.
Tranmere R.: Johnson; Mathias, Flood, Parry, Philpotts, Palios, Peplow, Young, Moore, Tynan, Kenny.

Lincoln C. (1) 4 (*Ward 4*)

Chesterfield (1) 2 (*Cooper o.g., Darling*)   4168

Lincoln C.: Grotier; Neale, Leigh, Fleming, Branfoot, Cooper, Krzywicki, Ward, Graham, Smith, Harding.
Chesterfield: Tingay, Holmes, Burton, McEwan, Hunter, Barlow, Bellamy, Moss, Darling, Bentley, Fern.

Mansfield T. (1) 4 (*McDonald 2, Laverick, Bird*)

Scunthorpe (0) 0   4810

Mansfield T.: Arnold; Bird, Foster B., O'Brien, Mackenzie, Foster C., McCaffey (Eccles), Laverick, Clarke, McDonald, Hodgson.
Scunthorpe U.: Norris; Markham, Peacock, Money, Wigginton, Irvine, Pilling, O'Connor (Oates), Keeley, Charnley, Davidson.

Reading (0) 0

Gillingham (0) 1 (*Alleyne o.g.*)   4846

Reading: Death; Peters, Alleyne, Cumming, Hetzke, Youlden, Whitham (Murray), Hiron, Friday, Carnaby, Dunphy.
Gillingham: Hillyard; Wiltshire, Ley, Galvin, Hill, Tydeman, Gauden Jacks, Richardson, Wilks, Weatherley.

Southend U. (2) 2 (*Silvester, Little*)

Peterborough U. (0) 0   4684

Southend U.: Webster; Worthington, Moody, Dyer, Ford, Nicholl, Little, Brace, Pountney, Parker (Cunningham), Silvester.
Peterborough U.: Steele; Bradley, Oakes, Turner, Lee, Eustace, Murray, Hughes, Robson, Nixon, Gregory.

Southport (2) 3 (*Gough 2, Snookes*)

Stockport Co. (1) 1 (*Lester*)   1501

Southport: Thomas; Sibbald, Snookes, Hughes, James, O'Neil, Johnston, Gough, Wilson, O'Riley, Martin (Wain).
Stockport Co.: Brown; Smith, Cross, Lester, Holsgrove, Lawther, Price, Fogarty, Davies, Hollis Buckley.

Wrexham (1) 3 (*Dwyer 2, Lyons*)

Chester (0) 0   8267

Wrexham: Lloyd; Davis, Fogg, Evans, May, Thomas, Tinnion, Sutton, Ashcroft, Lyons, Dwyer, *Chester:* Millington; Edwards, Loska, Matthewson. Dunleavy, Seddon, Whitehead, Pugh (Daniels), Draper, James, Lennard.

FIRST ROUND, SECOND LEG

AUG. 25

Chesterfield (1) 3 (*Kowalski, Fern, Hunter*)

Lincoln C. (1) 2 (*Graham, Ellis pen*)   4500

Chesterfield: Tingay; Holmes, Burton, McEwan, Hunter, Barlow, Kowalski, Moss, Darling, Bentley, Fern.
Lincoln C.: Grotier; Neale, Leigh, Booth, Ellis, Branfoot, Fleming, Freeman, Graham, Smith, Harding.

Colchester U. (1) 3 (*Svarc 2, Smith*)

Crystal Palace (1) 1 (*Chatterton*)   3912

Colchester U.: Walker, Thomas, Williams, Bunkell, Dominey, Packer, Cook, Svarc, Froggatt, Dyer, Smith.
Crystal Palace: Burns; Wall, Johnson J., Hinshelwood M., Cannon, Evans, Hill, Chatterton (Holder), Kemp, Swindlehurst, Taylor.

Gillingham (0) 1 (*Richardson*)

Reading (0) 1 (*Friday*)   5016

Gillingham: Hillyard; Wiltshire, Ley, Galvin, Hill, O'Donnell, Jacks, Gauden, Richardson, Wilks, Weatherley.
Reading: Death; Peters, Henderson, Cumming, Hetzke, Youlden, Murray, Hiron, Friday, Moreline, Stuckey.

Grimsby T. (0) 0

Doncaster R. (0) 0   5552

Grimsby T.: Wainman; Czuczman, Booth, Gray, Young, Barton, Hubbard, Partridge, Wigg, Boylen, Lewis.
Doncaster R.: Peacock; Reed, Ternent, Chappell, Uzelac, Brookes, Curran, Alseinoye, O'Callaghan, Kitchen, Higgins.

Hartlepool (0) 2 (*McMahon, Skillen*)

Halifax T. (1) 1 (*Downes*)   1725

Hartlepool: Richardson; Smith R., Crowther, Honour, Goad, Potter, Skillen, Smith D., Moore, McMahon, Johnson.
Halifax T.: Gennoe; Smith A., Collins, McHale, Rhodes, Phelan, Jones, Ford, Downes, Gwyther, Pugh.

Millwall (0) 0

Swindon T. (0) 1 (*Moss pen.*)　　　　　　　5935

Millwall: Goddard; Evans, Jones, Brisley, Kitchener, Hazell, Hill, Welsh, Summerhill, Saul (Moore), Salvage.
Swindon T.: Barron; Dixon, Trollope, Hubbard, Stroud, Prophett, Moss, McLaughlin, Eastoe, Butler, Anderson.

Stockport Co. (1) 1 (*Massey pen.*)

Southport (1) 2 (*O'Riley, Wilson*)　　　　2484

Stockport Co.: Brown; Smith, Cross, McNeill (Hollis), Holsgrove, Lawther, Price, Massey, Davies, Fogarty, Lester.
Southport: Thomas; Sibbald, Snookes, Hughes, Jones, O'Neil, Johnston, Welbourne, Wilson, O'Riley, Wain.

AUG. 26

AFC Bournemouth (1) 1 (*Rickard*)

Plymouth Arg. (1) 2 (*Burrows, Mariner*)　　3203

AFC Bournemouth: Baker; Payne, Miller, Benson (Reeves), Morgan, Hague, Redknapp, Rickard, Goddard, Nightingale, Buttle.
Plymouth Arg.: Aleksic; Hore, Burrows, Randell, Green, Delve, Horswill (Saxton), Mariner, Pearson, Rafferty, McAuley.

Bristol R. (1) 1 (*Stephens*)

Cardiff C. (1) 1 (*Clark*)　　　　　　　　7220

Bristol R.: Eadie; Smith, Williams, Aitken, Taylor, Prince, Stephens, Stanton, Warboys, Bannister, Evans.
Cardiff C.: Healey; Attley, Charles, Dwyer, England, Larmour, Villars, Clark, Reece, Livermore, Evans.

Charlton Ath. (0) 3 (*Hope, Peacock, Giles*)

Cambridge U. (0) 0　　　　　　　　　　　6744

Charlton Ath.: Tutt; Penfold, Warman, Bowman, Giles, Young, Powell (Hope), Hunt, Hales, Flanagan, Peacock.
Cambridge U.: Smith G.; Howell, Batson, Lyon, Eades (Cassidy), Watson, Smith P., Spriggs, Shinton, Horsfall, Biley.

Exeter C. (2) 2 (*Beer, Bowker*)

Newport Co. (0) 0　　　　　　　　　　　3303

Exeter C.: Wilson; Templeman, Hooker, Joy, Wingate, Hatch, Jennings, Bowker, Robertson, Morrin, Beer.
Newport Co.: Macey; Screen, Bell, Love, Aizlewood, Elliott, Hooper, Jones, Woodruff, Woods, White.

Portsmouth (2) 2 (*Marinello, Reynolds*)

Aldershot (0) 1 (*Warnock*)　　　　　　　7409

Portsmouth: Lloyd; Reynolds, Ellis, Piper, Went, Hand, Marinello, Kane, Graham, Foster, Mellows.
Aldershot: Johnson, Walden, Wallace J., Crosby, Richardson, Jopling, Walton, Morrissey, Howarth, Bell, Warnock.

Rochdale (0) 0

Bury (0) 2 (*Rowland 2*)　　　　　　　　3725

Rochdale: Poole; Hallows, Townsend, Lacey, Summerscales, Hanvey, Ferguson, Mountford, Cooper, Whelan, Sweeney.
Bury: Forrest; Hoolockin, Kennedy, Nicholson, Hulme, Bailey, Buchan, Phillips, Spence, Rowland, Riley.

Scunthorpe U. (0) 0

Mansfield T. (0) 2 (*Lathan, Laverick*)　　1412

Scunthorpe U.: Norris; Markham, Peacock, Money, Wigginton, Oates, Collier, Pilling, Davidson, Roberts, Keeley.
Mansfield T.: Arnold; Bird, Foster B., O'Brien, Lathan, Foster C., McCaffrey (Pate), Laverick, Clarke, McDonald, Hodgson.

Shrewsbury T. (0) 2 (*Tarbuck, Duffey pen.*)

Walsall (1) 1 (*Buckley*)　　　　　　　　5933

Shrewsbury T.: Mulhearn; King, Gregory, Durban, Kearney, Turner, Irvine, McGregor (Duffey), Haywood, Bates, Tarbuck.
Walsall: Kearns; Fry, Harrison, Robinson, Saunders, Atthey, Dennehy, Andrews, Wright, Buckley, Spinner.

Tranmere R. (0) 2 (*Moore 2*)

Crewe Alex. (0) 1 (*Nicholls*)　　　　　　1856

Tranmere R.: Johnson; Mathias, Flood, Parry, Postlewhite, Palios (Crossley), Peplow, Mitchell, Moore, Tynan, Young.
Crewe Alex.: Crudgington; Lowry, Evans, Lugg, Bowles, Nicholls, Davies, Bevan, Nelson, Melldew, Humphreys.

Workington (0) 1 (*Walker*)

Oldham Ath. (1) 3 (*Robins, Groves, Holt*)　1462

Workington: Hughes; Kisby, Brown, Nevin, Johnston, Wood, Harris, Walker, Murray, Harrison, Helliwell.
Oldham Ath.: Ogden; Branagan, Whittle, Blair, Hicks, Holt, Bell (McVitie), Jones, Robins, Chapman, Groves.

York C. (1) 3 (*Seal 2, Jones*)

Bradford C. (0) 0　　　　　　　　　　　4495

York C.: Crawford, Calvert, Downing, Holmes, Swallow, Topping, Lyons, Cave, Seal, Jones, McMordie.
Bradford C.: Downsborough; Podd, Cooper, Watson, Middleton, Fretwell, Hutchins (Cooke) Johnson, Ingram, Hall, McGinley.

AUG. 27

Barnsley (0) 1 (*Price*)

Huddersfield T. (0) 1 (*Campbell*)　　　　6043

Barnsley: Springett; Murphy, Chambers, Doyle, Burke, Pickering, Millar, Butler, Price, Walker, Brown.
Huddersfield T.: Taylor; Hutt, Garner, Smith, Baines, Saunders, Gray, O'Neil, Belfitt, Campbell, Dolan.

Blackburn R. (0) 0

Preston N.E. (0) 0

Blackburn R.: Jones; Heaton, Burgin, Metcalfe, Hawkins, Fazackerley, Beamish (Hoy). Oates, Hickman, Parkes, Martin.
Preston N.E.: Tunks, McMahon, Williams, Baxter S., Bird, Spark, Lamb, Burns, Treacy, Elwiss, Morley.

Brighton & H.A. (1) 1 (*Binney pen.*)

Brentford (1) 1 (*Cross*)　　　　　　　11,000

Brighton & H.A.: Grummitt; Tiler, Wilson, Beal, Piper, Winstanley, Towner, Machin, Binney, Martin (Mellor), O'Sullivan.
Brentford: Glazier; Nelmes, Allen, Bence, Lawrence, Smith, Graham, Scales, Simmons, Cross (Riddick), Johnson.

Chester (0) 0

Wrexham (0) 0

Chester: Millington; Edwards, Mason, Storton, Dunleavy, Pugh, Redfern, Seddon, Draper, Daniels (Owen), Lennard.
Wrexham: Lloyd; Davis, Dwyer, Evans, May, Thomas, Tinnion, Sutton, Ashcroft, Lyons, Griffiths (Davies).

Hereford U. (0) 2 (*Ritchie, Carter*)

Port Vale (0) 0　　　　　　　　　　　4107

Hereford U.: Charlton; Emery, Ritchie, Layton (Paine), Tucker, Lindsay, Walker, Silkman, Davey, Redrobe, Carter.
Port Vale: Connaughton; Tartt, Dulson, Ridley, Harris, Griffiths, Morris, Lees, Cullerton, Bailey, Williams (Chadwick).

Northampton T. (1) 1 (*Hall*)
Watford (0) 1 (*Goodeve*) 4255
Northampton T.: Parton; Tucker, Anderson, Carlton, Robertson, Gregory, Farrington, Best, Hall, Christie, Stratford.
Watford: Tankin; How, Akers, Joslyn, Goodeve, Garner, Downes, Bond, Jenkins, Greenhaigh, Mayes.

Nottingham F. (2) 5 (*Lyall 2 pens, Richardson 2, Bowyer*)
Rotherham U. (0) 1 (*Goodfellow*) 7977
Nottingham F.: Middleton; Anderson, Gunn, Clark, Chapman, Richardson, Robertson. McGovern, O'Hare, Bowyer, Lyall.
Rotherham U.: Haslam; Green, Breckin, Wagstaff, Stancliffe, Derrett, Leng, Finney, Habbin, Goodfellow, Crawford.

Peterborough U. (2) 3 (*Turner, Robson, Cozens*)
Southend U. (0) 0 4828
Peterborough U.: Steele; Murray Lee, Eustace, Turner (Hodson), Carmichael, Nixon, Gregory, Cozens, Hughes, Robson.
Southend U.: Webster; Worthington, Ford, Little, Dyer. Moody, Taylor, Brace, Lamb (Cunningham), Nicholl, Silvester.

Sheffield W. (0) 0
Darlington (0) 2 (*Holbrook, Sinclair*) 7452
Sheffield W.: Ramsbottom; Cameron, Quinn (Herbert), Mullen, Dowd, McIver, Potts, Knighton, Joicey, Prendergast, Henson.
Darlington: Ogley, Nattress; Cochrane, Cattrell, Smith, Blant, Holbrook, Sinclair, Rowles, Crosson, Young.

Torquay U. (1) 5 (*Brown 2, Kennedy, Lane 2*)
Swansea C. (1) 3 (*Leitch 2, Bruton pen.*) 3197
Torquay U.: Lee; Parker, Sandercock, Chatterley (Lane), Kruse, Myers, Provan, Twitchin, Boulton, Brown, Kennedy.
Swansea C.: Potter; Evans, Davies, Smith, Bruton, Harris, Dalling, Curtis, Leitch, Bekker, Bartley.

SECOND ROUND

SEPT. 9

Birmingham C. (2) 4 (*Gallagher, Hatton, Morton, Want*)
Orient (0) 0 18,238
Bimringham C.: Latchford; Martin (Want), Pendrey, Kendall, Gallagher, Burns, Morton, Francis, Withe. Hatton, Hibbitt.
Orient: Jackson; Fisher, Roffey, Bennett, Hoadley, Walley, Cunningham (Allder), Grealish, Bullock, Roeder. Cotton.

Bury (0) 1 (*Spence*)
Middlesbrough (1) 2 (*Hickton, Mills*) 9121
Bury: Forrest; Hoolickin, Kennedy, Nicholson, Hulme (Riley), Bailey, Williams, Phillips, Spence, Rowland, Hamstead.
Middlesbrough: Platt; Craggs, Cooper, Souness, Boam, Maddren, Murdoch, Mills, Hickton, Willey (Foggon), Armstrong.

Carlisle U. (2) 2 (*Laidlaw, Knight o.g.*)
Gillingham (0) 0 5274
Carlisle U.: Burleigh; Carr, Gorman, O'Neill, Green, Parker, Martin, Barry, Clarke, Laidlaw, Prudham.
Gillingham: Hillyard; Wiltshire, Ley, Galvin, Hill, Tydeman, Jacks. Gauden, Richardson, Wilks, Fogarty.

Charlton Ath. (2) 3 (*Flanagan 2, Peacock*)
Oxford U. (2) 3 (*Foley, Aylott, Jeffrey*) 6973
Charlton Ath.: Tutt; Penfold, Warman. Bowman, Giles, Young, Peacock, Hales, Hope. Hunt, Flanagan.

Oxford U.: Milkins; Light, Shuker, Bodel, Clarke C., Jeffrey, McGrogan, Duncan, Clarke D., Foley, Aylott.

Doncaster R. (1) 2 (*O'Callaghan, Chappell*)
Crystal Palace (0) 1 (*Johnson*) 6268
Doncaster R.: Peacock; Reed, Robinson, Chappell, Uzelac. Brookes, Miller, Alseinoye, O'Callaghan, Kitchen, Balderstone.
Crystal Palace: Hammond; Wall, Cannon, Hinshelwood, Jeffries, Evans, Hill (Johnson), Holder, Kemp, Swindlehurst, Taylor.

Darlington (0) 2 (*Webb 2*)
Luton T. (1) 1 (*Futcher R.*) 6601
Darlington: Ogley; Nattress, Cochrane, Cattrell, Smith, Blant, Holbrook, Sinclair, Webb, Crosson, Young.
Luton T.: Barber; John Ryan, Buckley, Anderson, Faulkner, Futcher P., King (Jim Ryan), Spiring, Futcher R., Chambers, Aston.

Everton (1) 2 (*Smallman, Lyons*)
Arsenal (0) 2 (*Cropley, Stapleton*) 17,174
Everton: Lawson; Bernard, Clements, Pearson, Kenyon, Lyons, Buckley, Dobson, Latchford, Smallman, Jones.
Arsenal: Rimmer; Rice, Nelson, Kelly, Mancini (Stapleton), O'Leary, Ball, Cropley, Radford, Kidd, Brady.

Hull C. (2) 4 (*Lord, Greenwood 2, Wood*)
Preston N.E. (1) 2 (*Morley, Treacy*) 5095
Hull C.: Wealands; Banks, DeVries, Galvin, Croft, Roberts, Grimes, Lord, Wood, Fletcher, Greenwood.
Preston N.E.: Tunks; McMahon, Williams, Lamb, Baxter, Spark, Bruce, Burns, Treacy, Elwiss, Morley.

Leeds U. (3) 3 (*McKenzie, Lorimer, Clarke*)
Ipswich T. (1) 2 (*Johnson, Hunter*) 15,318
Leeds U.: Harvey; Cherry, Gray F., Bremner, Madeley, Hunter, Lorimer, Clarke, McKenzie, Yorath, Gray E.
Ipswich T.: Cooper; Burley, Mills, Talbot (Woods), Hunter, Beattie, Hamilton, Viljoen, Johnson, Whymark, Lambert.

Notts Co. (1) 2 (*Stubbs, Bradd*)
Sunderland (1) 1 (*Holden*) 12,500
Notts Co.: McManus; Richards, O'Brien, Bolton (Vinter), Needham, Stubbs, Carter, Probert, Bradd, McVay, Scanlon.
Sunderland: Montgomery; Ashurst, Bolton, Towers, Clarke, Moncur, Kerr, Halom, Holden (Hughes), Robson, Porterfield.

Portsmouth (0) 1 (*Eames*)
Leicester C. (0) 1 (*Garland*) 10,629
Portsmouth: Lloyd; Roberts, Ellis, Piper, Went, Hand, Marinello (Eames), Reynolds, Graham, Collard, McGuinness.
Leicester C.: Wallington; Whitworth, Rofe, Kember, Sims, Woollett, Weller, Lee, Worthington, Sammels, Garland.

Shrewsbury T. (1) 1 (*Bates*)
Q.P.R. (0) 4 (*Webb, Masson, Thomas, Leach*) 11,250
Shrewsbury T.: Mulhearn; Collier, Gregory, Durban, Kearney, Turner, Irvine (Duffey), McGregor, Haywood, Bates, Tarbuck.
Q.P.R.: Parkes; Clement, Webb, Leach, McLintock, Abbott, Thomas, Francis, Masson, Bowles, Givens.

Southampton (0) 0
Bristol R. (0) 1 (*Fearnley*) 10,257
Southampton: Middleton; Rodrigues, Steele, Holmes, Bennett, Blyth, O'Brien, Channon, Osgood, Stokes, Peach.

508

Bristol R.: Eadie; Smith, Williams, Day, Taylor, Aitken, Stephens, Prince, Warboys, Bannister, Evans (Fearnley).

Swindon T. (2) 2 (*Eastoe, Trollope*)
Wolverhampton W. (0) 2 (*Sunderland, Richards*)
                                                                12,252
Swindon T.: Barron; Dixon, Trollope, Stroud, Burrows, Prophett, Moss, McLaughlin, Eastoe, Butler, Anderson.
Wolverhampton W.: Pierce; Parkin, McNab, Bailey, Munro, McAlle, Hibbitt, Carr, Richards, Sunderland, Wagstaff.

Watford (0) 0
Tottenham H. (0) 1 (*Jones*)   14,997
Watford: Rankin; Butler (Mayes), Akers, Joslyn, Lees, Goodeve, Scullion, Bond, Jenkins, Mercer, Downes.
Tottenham H.: Daines; Pratt, Naylor, Chivers, Osgood, McAllister, Neighbour, Perryman, Duncan, Jones, McNab.

W.B.A. (1) 1 (*Johnston*)
Fulham (0) 1 (*Conway*)   10,877
W.B.A.: Osborne; Mulligan, Thompson, Cantello, Wile, Robertson, Trewick, Brown T., Hutst, Giles, Johnston.
Fulham: Mellow, Fraser, Strong, Mullery, Howe, Moore, Mitchell, Conway, Busby, Slough, Dowie.

West Ham U. (0) 0
Bristol C. (0) 0   19,837
West Ham U.: Day, McDowell, Lampard, Bonds, Taylor T., Lock, Holland (Ayris), Paddon, Jennings, Brooking, Robson.
Bristol C.: Cashley, Sweeney, Drysdale, Gow, Collier, Merrick, Tainton, Ritchie, Mann, Cheesley, Brolley (Gillies).

SEPT. 10

Aston Villa (0) 2 (*Leonard, Nicholl*)
Oldham Ath. (0) 0   23,041
Aston Villa: Cumbes, Robson, Aitken, Ross, Nichol, Phillips, Graydon, Little, Leonard, Hamilton, Carrodus.
Oldham Ath.: Ogden; Branagan, Whittle, Blair, Hicks, Holt, Bell, Jones, Wood, Chapman, Robins.

Bolton W. (1) 1 (*Bryom*)
Coventry C. (2) 3 (*Cross, Green, Ferguson*) 12,743
Bolton W.: Siddall; Ritson, Dunne, Greaves, Jones P., Allardyce, Byrom, Curran, Jones G., Reid, Thompson.
Coventry C.: King; Oakey, Brogan, Craven, Dugdale, Powell, Coop, Mortimer, Cross, Green (Ferguson), Hutchison.

Crewe Alex. (1) 1 (*Humphreys pen.*)
Chelsea (0) 0   6723
Crewe Alex.: Crudgington; Lowry, Evans, Lugg, Bowles, Nicholls, Davies, Bevan, Purdie, Nelson, Humphreys.
Chelsea: Sherwood, Harris, Sparrow, Hay, Droy, Dempsey, Britton, Wilkins R., Stanley, Swain (Bason), Garner.

Derby Co. (1) 2 (*Rioch, George*)
Huddersfield T. (1) 1 (*Gray*)   20,602
Derby Co.: Boulton; Thomas, Nish, Rioch, McFarland, Todd, Newton, Gemmill, Lee (Hinton), Hector, George.
Huddersfield T.: Taylor, Hutt, Garner, Smith, Saunders, Baines, Gray, O'Neil, Belfitt, Campbell, Dolan.

Halifax T. (1) 2 (*Rhodes, Downes*)
Sheffield U. (2) 4 (*Guthrie 3, Phelan o.g.*)   7925
Halifax T.: Gennoe; Smith (Downes), Collins, McHale, Rhodes, Phelan, Jones, Ford, Bell, Gwyther, Pugh.
Sheffield U.: Brown; Badger, Hemsley, Eddy, Colquhoun, Franks, Woodward, Garbutt, Guthrie, Currie, Speight.

Hereford U. (0) 1 (*Carter*)
Burnley (1) 4 (*Flynn 2, Noble 2*)   11,360
Hereford U.: Charlton; Emery, Ritchie, Galley, Tucker (Davey), Lindsay, Walker, Redrobe, Paine, McNeil, Carter.
Burnley: Stevenson; Newton, Brennan, Noble, Waldron, Thomson, Flynn, Hankin, Summerbee, Collins, James.

Lincoln C. (1) 2 (*Harding, Booth*)
Stoke C. (1) 1 (*Greenhoff*)   13,472
Lincoln C.: Grotier; Branfoot, Leigh, Booth, Ellis, Cooper, Fleming, Ward, Freeman, Smith, Harding.
Stoke C.: Shilton; Marsh, Pejic, Mahoney, Bloor, Dodd, Haslegrave, Greenhoff, Moorse, Hudson, Conroy.

Manchester U. (0) 2 (*Macari, McIlroy*)
Brentford (0) 1 (*Lawrence*)   25,286
Manchester U.: Stepney; Nicholl, Houston, Jackson (Grimshaw), Greenhoff, Buchan, Coppell, McIlroy, Pearson, Macari, Daly.
Brentford: Glazier; Nelmes, Allen, Bence, Lawrence, Smith, Graham, Scales, French, Cross (Simmons), Johnson.

Norwich C. (0) 1 (*MacDougall*)
Manchester C. (0) 1 (*Watson*)   18,332
Norwich C.: Keelan; Machin, Butler, Morris, Forbes, Powell, Grapes, MacDougall, Boyer, Suggett, Peters.
Manchester C.: Corrigan; Clements, Donachie, Doyle, Watson, Oakes, Hartford, Bell, Royle, Marsh, Tueart.

Nottingham F. (0) 1 (*Bowyer*)
Plymouth Arg. (0) 0   8978
Nottingham F.: Middleton; Anderson, Gunn, Clark, Chapman, Richardson, O'Neill, McGovern, O'Hare, Bowyer, Robertson.
Plymouth Arg.: Aleksic; Hore, Burrows, Horswill, Green, Delve, Randell, Johnson (Vassallo), Mariner, Rafferty, McAuley.

Peterborough U. (0) 2 (*Gregory, Robson*)
Blackpool (0) 0   6987
Peterborough U.: Steele, Murray, Lee, Eustace, Oakes, Carmichael, Nixon, Gregory, Merrick, Hughes, Robson.
Blackpool: Burridge; Curtis, Harrison (Tong), Hatton, Suddaby, Bentley, Walsh, Suddick, Dyson, Ronson, Ainscow.

Southport (0) 0
Newcastle U. (2) 6 (*Gowling 4, Cannell 2*) (*at Newcastle*)   23,352
Southport: Thomas; Sibbald, Snookes, Hughes, Jones, O'Neil, Johnston (Wain), Gough, Wilson, O'Riley, Welbourne.
Newcastle U.: Mahoney; Nattrass, Kennedy, Nulty (Barrowclough), Keeley, Howard, Cassidy, Burns, Cannell, Gowling, Craig T.

Torquay U. (1) 1 (*Provan*)
Exeter C. (0) 1 (*Hatch*)
Torquay U.: Lee; Lynch, Sandercock, Lane, Kruse, Myers, Provan, Twitchin, Boulton, Brown, Kennedy.
Exeter C.: Wilson; Templeman, Joy, Morrin, Wingate, Hatch, Hodge, Bowker, Robertson, Beer, Jennings (Moxham).

Wrexham (0) 1 (*Davis*)
Mansfield T. (1) 2 (*Clarke, Bird*)
Wrexham: Lloyd; Davis, Dwyer, Evans, May, Thomas, Lyons, Sutton, Davies, Ashcroft, Williams.
Mansfield T.: Fogg; Pate, Foster B., Bird, Mackenzie, Foster C., Lathan, O'Brien, Clarke, Hodgson, McCaffrey.

York C. (0) 0
Liverpool (0) 1 (*Lindsay*)   9421

509

York C.: Crawford; Calvert, Downing, Woodward, Swallow, Topping, Lyons, Cave, Seal, Jones, McMordie.
Liverpool: Clemence; Neal, Lindsay, Thompson, Cormack, Hughes, Keegan, McDermott, Heighway, Kennedy, Callaghan.

SECOND ROUND REPLAYS

SEPT. 16

Wolverhampton W. (0) 3 (*Sunderland, Richards, Hibbitt*)

Swindon T. (1) 2 (*Moss, Eastoe*)   14,072

Wolverhampton W.: Pierce; Parkin, McNab, Bailey, Jefferson, McAlle, Hibbitt, Carr, Richards, Sunderland. Wagstaffe.
Swindon T.: Allen; Dixon, Trollope, Stroud, Burrows, Prophett, Moss (Jenkins), McLaughlin, Eastoe, Hubbard, Anderson.

SEPT. 17

Exeter C. (0) 1 (*Beer*)

Torquay U. (1) 2 (*Twitchin, Brown*)   4707

Exeter C.: Wilson; Templeman, Joy, Morrin, Wingate, Hatch, Hodge, Bowker, Jordan, Beer, Jennings.
Torquay U.: Lee; Lynch, Sandercock, Boulton, Kruse, Myers, Provan (Morrall), Twitchin, Lane, Brown, Kennedy.

Oxford U. (0) 1 (*Heron*)

Charlton Ath. (0) 1 (*Hales*)   4761

Oxford U.: Burton; Aylott, Shuker, Lowe, Clarke C., Jeffrey, Houseman, Duncan, Clarke D., Foley, Heron.
Charlton Ath.: Tutt; Penfold, Warman, Bowman, Giles, Young, Peacock, Hales, Powell, Hunt, Flanagan.

Leicester C. (0) 1 (*Sammels*)

Portsmouth (0) 0 (*After extra time*)   11,055

Leicester C.: Wallington; Whitworth, Yates, Kember, Sims, Birchenall, Weller, Lee, Tomlin (Alderson), Sammels, Garland.
Portsmouth: Lloyd; Roberts, Cahill, Piper, Went, Hand, McGuinness (Marinello), Reynolds, Graham, Wilson, Mellows.

Manchester C. (2) 2 (*Royle, Tuart, pen.*)

Norwich C. (1) 2 (*MacDougall 2*) (*After extra time*)   29,667

Manchester C.: Corrigan; Clements, Donachie, Doyle, Watson, Oakes, Hartford, Bell, Royle (Barnes), Marsh Tueart.
Norwich C.: Keelan, Machin, Butler, Morris, Forbes, Powell, McGuire, MacDougall, Boyer, Suggett, Peters.

SEPT. 23

Arsenal (0) 0

Everton (0) 1 (*Kenyon*)   21,813

Arsenal: Rimmer; Rice, Nelson, Kelly, Mancini, O'Leary, Ball, Cropley, Stapleton, Kidd, Rostron.
Everton: Davies; Bernard, Seargeant, Pearson, Kenyon, Lyons, Buckley, Dobson, Latchford, Smallman, Jones.

SEPT. 24

Bristol C. (1) 1 (*Cheesley*)

West Ham U. (0) 3 (*Brooking, Best, Taylor A.*)   19,634

Bristol C.: Cashley, Sweeney, Drysdale, Gow, Collier, Merrick, Tainton, Ritchie, Mann, Cheesely, Brolley (Gillies).
West Ham U.: Day, McDowell, Lampard, Bonds, Taylor T., Lock, Taylor A.. Paddon, Best, Brooking, Holland.

Fulham (0) 1 (*Mullery pen.*)

W.B.A. (0) 0   10,785

Fulham: Mellor; Cutbush, Strong, Mullery, Howe, Moore, Mitchell, Conway, Busby, Slough, Lloyd.
W.B.A.: Osborne; Thompson, Wilson, Cantello, Wile, Robertson, Glover, Brown A., Hurst, Giles, Johnston.

SECOND ROUND, SECOND REPLAYS

SEPT. 29

Norwich C. (1) 1 (*Peters*)

Manchester C. (3) 6 (*Tueart 3, 2 pens. Royle, Butler o.g., Doyle*) (*At Stamford Bridge*)   6238

Norwich C.: Keelan; Machin, Butler, Morris, Forbes, Powell, Steele, MacDougall, Boyer, Suggett, Peters.
Manchester C.: Corrigan; Clements, Donachie, Doyle, Watson, Oakes, Hartford, Bell Royle, March, Tueart,

Oxford U. (1) 2 (*Lowe, Jeffrey*)

Charlton Ath. (1) 3 (*Bowman pen., Hales 2*) (*After extra time*)   3973

Oxford U.: Burton; Taylor, Shuker, Lowe, Clarke C., Jeffrey (Tait), Houseman, Aylott, Clarke D., Foley, Heron.
Charlton Ath.: Tutt; Penfold, Warman, Bowman, Giles, Young, Harrison (Berry), Hales, Flanagan, Hunt, Peacock.

THIRD ROUND

OCT. 7

Birmingham C. (0) 0

Wolverhampton W. (1) 2 (*Hibbitt 2*)   29,822

Birmingham C.: Latchford; Martin, Bryant, Kendall, Gallagher, Burns (Pendrey), Campbell, Francis, Withe, Hatton, Hibbitt.
Wolverhampton W.: Pierce; Palmer, McNab, Bailey, Munro, McAlle, Hibbitt, Carr, Richards, Kindon, Daley.

Bristol R. (1) 1 (*Staniforth*)

Newcastle U. (0) 1 (*Gowling*)   17,141

Bristol R.: Eadie; Parsons, Williams, Day, Taylor, Smith, Stephens, Prince, Staniforth, Bannister, Britten.
Newcastle U.: Mahoney; Nattrass, Kennedy, Nulty, Craig D., Howard, Burns, Barrowclough, Macdonald, Gowling, Craig T.

Hull C. (2) 2 (*Greenwood, Hawley*)

Sheffield U. (0) 0   9536

Hull C.: Wealands; Banks, DeVries, Stewart, Croft, Roberts, Hawley, McGill, Wood, Wagstaff, Greenwood.
Sheffield U.: Brown; Franks, Hemsley, Eddy, Flynn, Speight, Woodward, Cammack, Guthrie, Currie, Bradford.

Liverpool (0) 1 (*Case*)

Burnley (0) 1 (*Noble*)   24,607

Liverpool: Clemence; Neal, Lindsay, Thompson, Cormack, Hughes, Keegan, Hall, Case, Toshack, Callaghan.
Burnley: Stevenson; Docherty, Newton, Noble, Waldron, Thomson, Morgan, Hankin, Summerbee, Flynn, James.

Middlesbrough (0) 1 (*Foggon*)

Derby Co. (0) 0   25,694

Middlesbrough: Platt; Craggs, Cooper, Souness, Boam, Maddren, Murdoch, Mills, Hickton (Spraggon), Foggon, Armstrong.
Derby Co.: Boulton; Thomas, Nish, Rioch, McFarland Todd, Powell, Gemmill, Lee, Hector, George.

Q.P.R. (0) 1 (*Bowles*)

Q.P.R.: Parkes; Clement, Gillard, Leach, McLintock, Webb, Thomas, Francis, Masson, Bowles, Givens.

Charlton Ath. (1) 1 (*Powell*)   20,434

Charlton Ath.: Tutt; Penfold, Warman, Bowman, Giles, Young, Powell, Hales, Flanagan, Hunt, Peacock.

Torquay U. (1) 1 (*Lane*)

Doncaster R. (0) 1 (*Reed*)   2785

Torquay U.: Lee; Lynch, Sandercock, Chatterley, Kruse, Boulton, Provan, Kellard, Lane, Brown, Kennedy.
Doncaster R.: Peacock; Reed, Robinson, Chappell, Uzelac, Brookes, Miller, Murray, O'Callaghan, Kitchen, Balderstone.

OCT. 8

Aston Villa (0) 1 (*Gray*)

Manchester U. (0) 2 (*Macari, Coppell*)   41,447

Aston Villa: Findlay; Gidman, Aitken, Ross, Nicholl, Phillips, Graydon, Little, Gray, Hamilton, Carrodus.
Manchester U.: Stepney; Nicholl, Houston, Jackson, Greenhoff, Buchan, Coppell, McIlroy, Pearson, Macari, Daly.

Crewe Alex. (0) 0

Tottenham H. (2) 2 (*Pratt, Conn*)   10,500

Crewe Alex.: Crudgington; Lowry, Evans, Lugg, Bowles, Melledew, Reed, Bevan, Nicholls (Maguire), Nelson, Humphreys.
Tottenham H.: Jennings; Naylor, McAllister, Pratt, Young, Osgood, Duncan, Conn, Neighbour, Coates, Chivers.

Everton (1) 2 (*Latchford, Dobson*)

Carlisle U. (0) 0   20,010

Everton: Davies; Seargeant, Clements, Pearson, Kenyon, Lyons, Buckley, Dobson, Latchford, Telfer, Jones.
Carlisle U.: Burleigh; Spearritt, Gorman, Barry, Green, Carr, Martin, Owen, Laidlaw, O'Neill, McCartney.

Fulham (0) 0

Peterborough U. (0) 1 (*Gregory*)   5805

Fulham: Mellor; Cutbush, Strong, Mullery, Howe, Moore, Lloyd (Mitchell), Conway, Busby, Slough, Barrett.
Peterborough U.: Steele; Murray, Lee, Eustace, Jones, Carmichael, Nixon (Turner), Gregory, Bradley, Hughes, Robson.

Leeds U. (0) 0

Notts Co. (0) 1 (*Scanlon*)   19,122

Leeds U.: Harvey; Reaney, Cherry, Bremner, Madeley, Hunter, Lorimer, McNiven (Harris), McKenzie, Gray F., Gray E.
Notts Co.: McManus; Brindley, Richards, Bolton, Needham, Stubbs, Carter, McVay, Bradd, O'Brien, Scanlon.

Leicester C. (0) 0 (*Weller, Sammels pen.*)

Lincoln C. (1) 1 (*Smith*)   17,063

Leicester C.: Wallington; Whitworth, Rofe, Kember, Sims, Woollett, Weller, Alderson, Worthington, Sammels, Garland.
Lincoln C.: Grotier; Branfoot, Leigh, Booth, Ellis Cooper, Fleming, Ward, Freeman, Smith, Harding.

Manchester C. (1) 2 (*Royle, Bell*)

Nottingham F. (0) 1 (*Bowyer*)   26,536

Manchester C.: Corrigan; Clements, Donachie, Doyle, Watson, Oakes, Hartford, Bell, Royle, Marsh, Barnes.
Nottingham F.: Middleton; Gunn, Clark, Chapman, Cottam, Richardson, O'Neill, McGovern, O'Hare, Bowyer, Robertson.

Mansfield T. (2) 2 (*Clarke, Eccles*)

Coventry C. (0) 0   10,027

Mansfield T.: Arnold; Pate, Foster B., Laverick, Mackenzie (Foster C.), Bird, Matthews, Eccles, Clarke, Hodgson, McDonald.
Coventry C.: King; Oakey (Ferguson), Brogan, Craven, Dugdale, Holmes, Coop, Mortimer, Cross, Green, Hutchison.

West Ham U. (0) 3 (*Paddon, Bonds pen., Robson*)

Darlington (0) 0   19,844

West Ham U.: Day; McDowell, Lampard, Bonds Taylor T., Lock (Jennings), Robson, Paddon, Best, Taylor A., Holland.
Darlington: Ogley; Nattress, Cochrane, Cattrell, Noble, Blant, Holbrook (Rowles), Sinclair, Webb, Crosson, Young.

THIRD ROUND REPLAYS

OCT. 13

Doncaster R. (2) 3 (*O'Callaghan 2, Balderstone*)

Torquay U. (0) 0   9764

Doncaster R.: Peacock; Reed, Robinson, Chappell, Uzelac, Brookes, Miller, Murray, O'Callaghan, Kitchen, Balderstone.
Torquay U.: Bond; Lynch, Sandercock, Chatterley, Kruse, Boulton, Provan, Twitchin, Lane, Brown, Kennedy.

OCT. 14

Burnley (1) 1 (*Noble pen.*)

Liverpool (0) 0   19,857

Burnley: Stevenson; Docherty, Newton, Noble, Waldron, Thomson, Morgan, Hankin, Summerbee, Flynn, James.
Liverpool: Clemence; Neal, Lindsay, Thompson, Cormack, Hughes, Keegan, Hall (Boersma), Heighway, Toshack, Callaghan.

Charlton Ath. (0) 0

Q.P.R. (0) 3 (*Thomas, Masson, Bowles*)   31,583

Charlton Ath.: Tutt; Penfold, Warman, Bowman, Giles, Young, Powell, Hales, Flanagan, Hunt, Peacock.
Q.P.R.: Parkes; Clement, Gillard, Leach, McLintock (Hollins), Webb, Thomas, Francis, Masson, Bowles, Givens.

OCT. 15

Newcastle U. (0) 2 (*Craig T. pen., Nattrass*)

Bristol R. (0) 0   25,835

Newcastle U.: Mahoney; Nattrass, Kennedy, Nulty, Craig D., Howard, Burns, Barrowclough, Macdonald, Gowling, Craig T.
Bristol R.: Eadie; Williams, Parsons, Day, Taylor, Smith, Stephens (Fearnley), Prince, Warboys, Bannister, Dobson.

FOURTH ROUND

NOV. 11

Burnley (0) 2 (*Morgan pen., Hankin*)

Leicester C. (0) 0   15,113

Burnley: Stevenson; Docherty, Collins, Flynn, Waldron, Thomson, Morgan, Summerbee, Fletcher, Hankin, James.
Leicester C.: Wallington; Whitworth, Rofe (Worthington), Kember, Blockley, Woollett, Weller, Sammels, Garland, Alderson, Lee.

Doncaster R. (1) 2 (*Kitchen, Ternent*)

Hull C. (1) 1 (*Wood*)   20,476

Doncaster R.: Peacock; Reed, Robinson, Ternent, Uzelac, Brookes, Miller, Murray, O'Callaghan, Kitchen, Balderstone.
Hull C.: Wealands; Banks, DeVries, Galvin, Croft, Haigh, Grimes, Hawley, Wood, Wagstaff, Greenwood.

Everton (0) 2 (*Jones, Irving*)

Notts Co. (0) 2 (*Scanlon pen., Stubbs*)   19,169

Everton: Lawson; Darracott, Clements (Telfer), Hurst, McNaught, Lyons, Buckley, Dobson, Irving, Pearson, Jones G.
Notts Co.: McManus; Richards, O'Brien, Probert, Needham, Stubbs, Carter (Brindley), McVay, Bradd, Mann, Scanlon.

Middlesbrough (1) 3 (*Boam, Hickton pen., Armstrong*)
Peterborough U. (0) 0   17,749
Middlesbrough: Platt; Craggs, Spraggon, Souness, Boam, Maddren, Murdoch, Mills, Hickton, Cooper, Armstrong.
Peterborough U.: Steele; Murray, Bradley, Eustace, Jones, Carmichael, Nixon, Gregory, Turner (Cozens), Hughes, Robson.

Q.P.R. (1) 1 (*Leach*)
Newcastle U. (2) 3 (*Burns, Macdonald, Nulty*) 21,162
Q.P.R.: Parkes; Clement, Gillard, Leach, McLintock, Webb, Thomas, Francis, Masson, Bowles (Hollins), Givens.
Newcastle U.: Mahoney; Nattrass, Kennedy, Nulty, Craig D., Howard, Burns, Barrowclough, Macdonald, Gowling, Craig T.

NOV. 12

Manchester C. (3) 4 (*Tueart 2, Hartford, Royle*)
Manchester U. (0) 0   50,182
Manchester C.: Corrigan; Clements, Donachie, Doyle, Watson, Oakes, Barnes, Bell (Booth), Royle, Hartford, Tueart.
Manchester U.: Roche; Nicholl, Houston, Jackson (McCreery), Greenhoff, Buchan, Coppell, McIlroy, Pearson, Macari, Daly.

Mansfield T. (1) 1 (*McDonald*)
Wolverhampton W. (0) 0   12,725
Mansfield T.: Evans; Pate, Foster B., McDonald, Madden, Bird, Matthews, Eccles, Clarke, Hodgson, Mackenzie.
Wolverhampton W.: Pierce; Palmer, Parkin, Bailey, Munro, McAlle, Hibbitt, Carr (Kindon), Richards, Sunderland, Daley.

Tottenham H. (0) 0
West Ham U. (0) 0   49,125
Tottenham H.: Jennings; Naylor, McAllister, Pratt, Young, Osgood, Coates, Perryman, Duncan (Conn), Jones, Neighbour.
West Ham U.: Day; McDowell, Lock, Bonds, Taylor T., Coleman, Taylor A., Paddon, Holland, Brooking, Robson.

FOURTH ROUND REPLAYS

NOV. 24

West Ham U. (0) 0
Tottenham H. (0) 2 (*Duncan, Young*) (*After extra time*) 38,443
West Ham U.: Day; McDowell, Lampard, Bonds, Taylor T., Lock, Taylor A., Paddon, Holland, Brooking, Robson.
Tottenham H.: Jennings; Naylor, McAllister, Pratt, Young, Osgood, Coates, Perryman, Duncan, Jones, Neighbour.

NOV. 25

Notts Co. (1) 2 (*Bradd 2*)
Everton (0) 0   23,323
Notts Co.: McManus; Brindley, O'Brien, Probert, Needham, Bolton, Carter, McVay, Bradd, Mann, Scanlon.
Everton: Lawson; Sergeant, Clements, Pearson (Smallman), Kenyon, Lyons, Buckley, Dobson, Latchford, Telfer, Jones.

FIFTH ROUND

DEC. 3

Burnley (0) 0
Middlesbrough (1) 2 (*Mills, Maddren*)   15,303
Burnley: Stevenson; Docherty, Newton, Noble, Waldron, Thomson, Bradshaw, Summerbee, Hankin, Collins (Loggie), Flynn.
Middlesbrough: Platt; Craggs, Cooper, Murdoch, Boam, Maddren, Brine, Mills (McAndrew), Willey, Hickton, Armstrong.

Manchester C. (2) 4 (*Royle, Oakes, Tueart, Hartford*)
Mansfield T. (1) 2 (*Clarke, Bird*)   30,022
Manchester C.: Corrigan; Clements, Donachie, Doyle, Watson, Oakes, Barnes, Booth, Royle, Hartford, Tueart (Power).
Mansfield T.: Brown; Pate, Foster B., McDonald, Madden, Bird, Matthews, Eccles, Clarke, Hodgson, McCaffrey (Mackenzie).

Newcastle U. (1) 1 (*McManus o.g.*)
Notts Co. (0) 0   29,123
Newcastle U.: Mahoney; Nattrass, Kennedy, Nulty, Craig D., Howard, Burns, Barrowclough, Macdonald, Gowling, Craig T.
Notts Co.: McManus; Brindley, O'Brien, Probert, Needham, Stubbs, McVay, Bolton (Richards), Bradd, Mann, Scanlon.

Tottenham H. (2) 7 (*Duncan 3, Pratt, Chappell o.g., Chivers 2*)
Doncaster R. (1) 2 (*Murray, Kitchen*)   25,702
Tottenham H.: Jennings; Naylor, Knowles, Pratt, Young, Osgood, Coates, Perryman. Duncan, Chivers, Neighbour.
Doncaster R.: Peacock; Reed, Robinson, Chappell, Uzelac, Brookes, Miller, Murray, O'Callaghan, Kitchen, Balderstone.

SEMI-FINAL, FIRST LEGS

JAN. 13

Middlesbrough (0) 1 (*Hickton*)
Manchester C. (0) 0   35,000
Middlesbrough: Platt; Craggs, Bailey, Souness, Boam, Maddren, Murdoch, Mills, Hickton (Foggon), Cooper, Armstrong.
Manchester C.: Corrigan; Barrett, Donachie, Doyle, Booth, Oakes, Barnes, Power, Royle, Hartford, Tueart.

JAN. 14

Tottenham H. (1) 1 (*Pratt*
Newcastle U. (0) 0   40,215
Tottenham H.: Jennings; Naylor, McAllister, Pratt, Young, Osgood, Coates, Perryman, Chivers, Duncan, Neighbour.
Newcastle U.: Mahoney; Nattrass, Kennedy, Nulty, Keeley, Howard, Burns, Cassidy, Macdonald, Gowling, Craig T.

SEMI-FINAL, SECOND LEGS

JAN. 21

Manchester C. (2) 4 (*Keegan, Oakes, Barnes, Royle*)
Middlesbrough (0) 0   44,426
Manchester C.: Corrigan; Barrett, Donachie, Doyle, Clements, Oakes, Power. Keegan, Royle, Hartford, Barnes.
Middlesbrough: Platt; Craggs, Cooper, Souness, Boam, Maddren, Murdoch (McAndrew), Brine, Hickton, Mills, Armstrong.

Newcastle U. (1) 3 (*Gowling, Keeley, Nulty*)
Tottenham H. (0) 1 (*McAllister*)   51,000
Newcastle U.: Mahoney; Nattrass (Barrowclough) Kennedy, Nulty, Keeley, Howard, Burns, Cassidy, Macdonald, Gowling, Craig T.
Tottenham H.: Jennings; Naylor, McAllister, Pratt, Young, Osgood (Jones), Coates, Perryman, Chivers, Duncan, Neighbour.

FINAL

FEB. 28 at Wembley, receipts £299,601.16p (a record)

Manchester C. (1) 2 (*Barnes, Tueart*)
Newcastle U. (1) 1 (*Gowling*)   100,000
Manchester C.: Corrigan; Keegan, Donachie, Doyle, Watson, Oakes, Barnes, Booth, Royle, Hartford, Tueart.
Newcastle U.: Mahoney; Nattrass, Kennedy, Barrowclough, Keeley, Howard, Burns, Cassidy, Macdonald, Gowling, Craig.

SCOTTISH FOOTBALL

Review of the 1975-76 season

Full details of all Scottish League clubs, including 1975-76 records

League tables and results

Honours list from 1890-91

Scottish FA Cup full details

Scottish Football League Cup full details

Review of the Season

By Alex Cameron, of the *Daily Record*

Scottish football was given a badly needed injection of hope at international level with victories over Wales, Northern Ireland, and England in the British Championship. The title 'Champions of Britain' is not one that we wear over-modestly, particularly in the company of Englishmen! However, though Willie Ormond moves into the World Cup arena at least with hope and new skills, club football is still in a state of dilemma.

The three-division experiment of 10, 14, and 14 has been retained at least for another season, but the clubs have decided to abolish the Spring Cup, and to make up for the loss of fixtures, First and Second Division teams will play each other three times instead of twice. This presents a problem in venue-selecting for the third match, but there was no other acceptable way out.

Premier Division elitists are, in the main, content, although worry lies in the stepped-up danger of costly relegation, for in the first furious fight to stay among the top ten there were no fewer than six genuine candidates for the drop.

Competition is certainly better, but no marked overall improvement in standard was apparent. This could come when players adjust properly to the fact that clubs in the Premier Division have to meet four times. There was a fear that this would diminish crowd interest but it hasn't happened.

Rangers won handsome victories at all levels. First of all, they beat Celtic 1-0 in the League Cup Final. It was a dream way to start the more earnest business of being the first Premier League champions. This they did with 54 points from the 36 games, scoring 61 goals and conceding 25. And they rounded off the season by romping over Hearts in the Scottish Cup Final.

It was a memorable treble and established hard-talking, demanding, ex-jungle fighter Jock Wallace as Scotland's 'Manager of the Year'. The Rangers performance also helped to win for captain John Greig the honour of being the first in 10 years to be picked twice by Scotland's football writers as their 'Player of the Year'. There are no guidelines for the sports writers, but most would confirm that they chose Greig because of his ability and leadership on the field rather than as a salute to the club.

Celtic, managed by Irishman Sean Fallon in the absence of Jock Stein, who spent the season recuperating from injuries sustained in a car crash, struggled to keep pace with Rangers but fell in the critical run-in despite the individual brilliance of skipper Kenny Dalglish and full back Danny McGrain.

One thing the Premier League didn't achieve, nor will it ever, was to quell the bitter rivalry between the two big Glasgow clubs. Both of them were well ahead of Hibs and Motherwell, the only two to make a real challenge. In five meetings between Rangers and Celtic, the Ibrox club won three by a single goal and the others were drawn. Yes, it was a bad season for Parkhead supporters. Stein, however, will be back for the new season to try to guide Celtic back to glory.

The only minor concession to 'outsiders' came with Hearts reaching the Cup Final. The Edinburgh club had to struggle to get there in replays against Montrose and Dumbarton, and they went to Hampden heavily tipped to lose. They didn't let the forecasters down.

Rangers' outstanding successes were achieved in quite different style to the techniques of Celtic, who switched players about in their champion times with an eye to the opposition. Jock Wallace took the view that he wanted a settled formation and, when he found it, two of Scotland's best players – striker Derek Parlane and full back Sandy Jardine – found themselves as substitutes. On the run-in, Rangers team rarely changed and teenaged Fifer Martin Henderson could hardly credit that he was in the side and Parlane out of it.

St. Johnstone knew very early in the proceedings that they would be relegated. Manager Jackie Stewart departed the scene for the final games (later he succeeded Ian McMillan at Airdrie) and next season Saints will be run by Jim Storrie. If the blow

to Muirton Park fans was softened by expectancy, the shock of demotion rocked Dundee. It now remains to be seen if they can get back quickly. I think they will, and finance makes it essential. First Division football will cost the Dens Park club at least £100,000, for they will run with Premier Division over-heads and none of the benefits of games against Rangers and Celtic. That was why centre-half George Stewart, who handily lives in Edinburgh, was transferred to Hibs for £40,000. Manager Davie White regretted the signing as much as Eddie Turnbull at Easter Road welcomed it.

Partick Thistle and Kilmarnock are promoted to the Premier Division and it will be interesting to see how both meet the vastly stronger compeition of the top ten. Kilmarnock appear to have more problems, for they are committed to part-time football, a policy they have not the slightest intention of changing.

Interestingly, ex-Celtic men run both teams – Bertie Auld (Thistle) and Willie Fernie (Killie). They have very different approaches to the game, although they are from the same 'school', so their progress will be followed closely.

Relegation to the Second Division for Clyde and Dunfermline were hard blows. Many thought it might even finish Clyde but, happily, this is not so. The most remarkable club were Clydebank with the witty, with-it director-manager Jack Steedman at the helm. They had a full-time staff in the Second Division and were rewarded by winning the championship and, of course, promotion, along with Raith Rovers.

Ironically, possibly the most exciting game was provided by the abortive Spring Cup. Airdrie beat Clydebank in the final at Firhill by 4-2, but only after extra time. It was a thrilling night but only about 5000 fans were there so the competition was doomed.

The price of Scottish football will be increased next season by 10p for the Premier and First Divisions with 5p added for the Second. This will make no difference at the gates, for Scottish football is the cheapest in Europe, which is why gate receipts at Wembley and Hampden compare so ridiculously.

However, clubs, apart from Rangers and Celtic will have to do more to make the top ten lively and sustain the interest. Hibs and Motherwell have the greatest responsibility, although the Fir Park club are progressive and can only now improve with experience. Edinburgh, with Hearts struggling miserably, is in the doldrums, and it will be up to Hibs to do something about it. Aberdeen, now bossed by Ally MacLeod, have been active on the transfer market. They have one of the best supports, but must produce the goods – and especially in the oil-boom area. MacLeod's former club, Ayr United, continue to do well against all-comers even though all their players have other jobs.

The new league set-up now moves into a more intensive trial stage than before. The big clubs are well aware of the mechanics in voting power which they delegated to the First and Second Divisions when the leagues were re-grouped. The 28, or most of them, need only gang up and they dictate the play. Significantly, the big men behind the scenes are being rejected for high office. The best legislator, Celtic chairman Desmond White, has twice been outvoted for the SFA treasurership – although he is an accountant as well as being the most experienced club director.

At international level, Willie Ormond will try to qualify Scotland for Argentina. He has refashioned the team by making Archie Gemmill captain and calling in Don Masson, a Banchory man who is having his best footballing days with Queens Park Rangers. So long as Scots are not bewildered by super-optimism we might just make it. That 2-1 win against England is still good for a bar debate, but the memory of it is not a World Cup credential. Qualifying for the world's major football tournament, establishing the three-league set-up as a workable permanency, and reappearing as a force in Europe are the three tasks facing Scotland.

It will need skill and nerve to bring off the treble, but the chance is undoubtedly there.

ABERDEEN

Year Formed: 1903.
Ground: Pittodrie Stadium. *Size:* 110 × 71 yds. *Capacity:* 30,000 (15,000 seated).
Telephone: Aberdeen 21428, 53497.
Manager: Jimmy Bonthrone. *Coach:* George Murray.
Secretary: J. R. Rust. *Trainer:* Teddy Scott.
Club Colours: Scarlet shirts, white collars and cuffs, scarlet shorts with single white stripe, red
   stockings white tops.
Club Nickname: 'The Dons'.
Record Attendance: 45,061, v Hearts, Scottish Cup, 4th Rd., March 13th, 1954.
(Present Aberdeen F.C. have had no other home but Pittodrie.)
European Competitions Entered: Fairs Cup, 1968–69; Cup Winners Cup, 1967–68, 1970–71, UEFA Cup
   1971–72, 1972–73, 1973–74.
Record Transfer Fee Received: £180,000 from Everton for Joe Harper, December 1972.

1975–76 LEAGUE RECORD

Match No.	Date	Venue	Opponents	League Pos'n	Result	H/T Score	Goalscorers	Atten- dance
1	30	A	Dundee	—	L 2-3	2-1	Williamson, Smith	6067
2	Sep 6	H	Motherwell	9	D 2-2	2-1	Williamson, Robb	5500
3	13	H	Dundee U.	10	L 1-3	1-2	Scott	5500
4	20	A	Hearts	8	D 2-2	2-2	Williamson, Scott	9500
5	27	H	Ayr U.	7	W 3-1	1-0	Williamson, Scott 2	4500
6	Oct 4	A	Rangers	7	L 0-1	0-1		22,000
7	11	H	Celtic	9	L 1-2	0-2	Scott	18,000
8	18	H	St. Johnstone	9	W 2-0	0-0	Pirie 2	5100
9	25	A	Hibernian	9	L 1-3	0-1	Robb	11,133
10	Nov 1	H	Dundee	8	W 2-0	0-0	Williamson (pen), Scott	6312
11	8	A	Motherwell	9	L 0-3	0-2		6294
12	15	A	Dundee U.	9	W 2-1	1-0	Williamson (pen), Scott	4704
13	22	H	Hearts	8	D 0-0	0-0		11,390
14	29	A	Ayr U.	8	L 0-1	0-0		6000
15	Dec 6	H	Rangers	8	W 1-0	0-0	Jarvie	19,565
16	13	A	Celtic	7	W 2-0	2-0	Jarvie, Graham	24,000
17	20	A	St. Johnstone	7	D 1-1	0-0	Williamson	3500
18	27	H	Hibernian	6	D 2-2	1-2	Williamson, McMaster	17,630
19	Jan 1	A	Dundee	—	W 3-1	2-1	Robb, Scott, Graham	10,009
20	3	H	Motherwell	6	D 0-0	0-0		16,177
21	10	H	Dundee U.	5	W 5-3	2-0	Scott 3 (2 pens), Graham 2	9581
22	17	A	Hearts	5	D 3-3	1-1	Scott, Pirie, McMaster	10,300
23	31	H	Ayr U.	5	W 2-1	1-0	Pirie, McMaster	9920
24	Feb 7	A	Rangers	5	L 1-2	0-2	Pirie	20,000
25	21	H	Celtic	5	L 0-1	0-0		18,221
26	28	H	St. Johnstone	5	W 3-0	1-0	Scott, Pirie 2	5920
27	Mar 13	H	Dundee	5	L 0-1	0-0		6460
28	20	A	Motherwell	5	L 1-2	0-1	Fleming	5908
29	27	A	Dundee U.	5	L 0-1	0-0		4875
30	31	A	Hibernian	—	L 2-3	1-1	Scott, Fleming	7200
31	Apr 7	H	Hearts	—	L 0-3	0-2		6000
32	10	A	Ayr U.	5	D 1-1	0-0	Jarvie	5740
33	14	H	Rangers	—	D 0-0	0-0		17,968
34	17	A	Celtic	5	D 1-1	1-1	Edvaldsson (og)	29,000
35	21	A	St. Johnstone	—	L 0-2	0-1		2500
36	24	H	Hibernian	5	W 3-0	1-0	Smith, Robb, Jarvie	10,985

Final Place: 7

Goalscorers

League (49): Scott 14 (2 pens), Williamson 8 (2 pens), Pirie 7, Graham 4, Jarvie 4, Robb 4, McMaster 3,
Fleming 2, Smith 2, own goals 1.
League Cup (4): Graham 1, Hair 1, Jarvie 1, Williamson 1.
Cup (5): McMaster 1, Miller 1, Robb 1, Scott 1, Smith 1.

Honours
Scottish League: Division 1, Champions: 1954–55, Runners-up: 1910–11, 1936–37, 1955–56, 1970–71, 1971–72.
Scottish Cup: Winners: 1947, 1970, Runners-up: 1937, 1953, 1954, 1959, 1967.
Scottish League Cup: Winners: 1945–46, 1955–56. Runners-up: 1946–47. *Drybrough Cup:* Winners: 1971.

Record Victory: 13-0 v Peterhead, Feb. 9th, 1923 (Scottish Cup).
Record Defeat: 2-9 v Dundee, Apr. 17th, 1909.
Most League Points: 61, 1935–36.
Most Individual League Goals in Season: 38, Benny Yorston, Division 1, 1929–30.
Most Capped Player: Bobby Clark 17, Scotland.

Clark, R.	Geoghegan, A.	Thomson, E.	McLelland, C.	Williamson, W.	Hair, I.	Gibson, I.	Young, W.	Miller, W.	Henry, J.	Smith, J.	Robb, D.	Jarvie, A.	Scott, J.	Rougvie, D.	Street, R.	Graham, A.	Campbell, G.	Pirie, W.	McMaster, J.	Ward, N.	Hather, J.	Cooper, N.	Garner, W.	Fleming, I.	Docherty, J.	McCall, W.	Match No
1		3	10	2			5	6		7	8	12	4			11			9*								1
1	13	3	10	2*			5	6		7	8		4			11		12	9†								2
1		3	10	2			5*	6		7	8	9	4			11		12									3
1	12	3	10	2				6		7*	8	9	4			11		5									4
1		3	10	2				6		7*	8	9	4			11	5	12									5
1	7	3	10*	2				6			8	9	4			11	5	12									6
1	2	3*	12	4				6	10		8	9	7			11		5†		13							7
1	5	3		2				6		4	8	10*	7	12		11			9								8
1	5	3		2				6		4	8	10*	7			11		12	9								9
1	5	3		2				6		4	8	9	7			11		12	9*								10
1	5	3		2				6		4	8	9	7	10		11											11
1	5	3		2				6		4	8	9	7			11		12	10*								12
1	5	3		2				6		4	8*	9	7			11		12	10								13
1	5	3		2	12			6		4	8	9	7			11			10*								14
1	5	3		2				6		4	8	9	7			11			10								15
1	5	3		2	12			6		4*	8	9	7†			11			10	13							16
1	5	3		2	12			6		4	8	9	7*			11			10†	13							17
1	5	3		2				6		4	8	9	7			11			10								18
1	5	3		2				6		4	8	9	7			11			10								19
1	5	3		2	12			6		4*	8†	9	7			11			10	13							20
1	5	3		2	13			6		4*	8†	9	7			11		12	10								21
1		3		2	13			6		4	8	9*	7			11		12	10†				5				22
1	5	3		2				6		4	8	9				11		7	10								23
1	5	3		2*				6		4	8	9†	7			11		12	10	13							24
1		3	8	2				6		4	12	9*				11		7	10				5				25
1	5		8	2				6		4	12	13				11		11	9†	7*			5	10			26
1	5	3		2				6		12	8		7			11		9*				4		10			27
1	5	3	8	2	12			6		4			7			11			10*					9			28
1	5	3		2	12			6		4	8	9				11*		7						10			29
1	5	3		2	8			6		4		9	7			11								10			30
1	5	3		2	10*			6		4	12	9	7			11								8			31
1	5	3		2	8			6		4*	7	9	13			11†		12						10			32
1	4	3	8	2				6		11	7	9											5	10			33
1	4	3	8	2				6		11	7	9											5	10			34
1		3	8	2				6		11	7	9†	12					13					5	10	4*		35
1		3	8	2				6		4	7	9	12										5	10*		11	36
20	16	26	29	35	24	0	3	36	1	33	30	30	28	1	0	31	2	8	18	4	0	1	7	11	1	1	
	+2s	+1s	+1s	+5s	+2s					+2s	+2s	+4s	+1s	+1s					+10s	+3s		+1s	+1s	+1s	+1s	+1s	

AIRDRIEONIANS

Year Formed: 1878.
Ground: Broomfield Park.   *Size:* 112 × 68 yds.   *Capacity:* 26,000 (2,000 seats).
Telephone: Airdie 62067.
Manager: Jack Stewart.   *Coach:* Bobby Morrison.
Secretary: Winnie Plunkett.   *Physiotherapist:* Adam Good.
Club Colours: White shirt with red diamond, white shorts, black stockings with red and white tops.
Club Nickname: 'Diamonds' or 'Waysiders'.
Record Attendance: 24,000, v Hearts, Scottish Cup, March 8, 1952.

1975–76 LEAGUE RECORD

Match No.	Date	Venue	Opponents	League Pos'n	Result	H/T Score	Goalscorers	Attendance
1	Aug 30	A	Dunfermline Ath.	—	D 3-3	0-0	McRoberts, Wilson, Clarke	3000
2	Sep 6	H	Kilmarnock	10	L 3-4	3-2	Jonquin (pen), McRoberts, Wilson	3000
3	13	A	Queen of the S.	7	W 7-1	5-1	Jonquin (pen), Menzies, Whiteford 2, Clarke 3 (1 pen)	3000
4	20	H	Falkirk	5	W 2-0	2-0	Whiteford, Clarke	4000
5	27	A	Arbroath	6	L 0-3	0-1		1534
6	Oct 4	H	Dumbarton	3	W 3-0	2-0	Jonquin 2 (2 pens), Wilson (pen)	2500
7	11	A	Clyde	4	D 2-2	0-0	Walker, March	1500
8	18	A	Partick T.	3	W 1-0	0-0	McRoberts	6000
9	25	H	East Fife	3	W 1-0	0-0	Jonquin (pen)	3000
10	Nov 1	A	St. Mirren	3	D 2-2	1-2	McRoberts, Wilson (pen)	3600
11	8	H	Hamilton A.	3	D 2-2	0-1	Whiteford 2	4000
12	15	H	Montrose	3	D 2-2	1-1	Whiteford, McRoberts	2500
13	22	A	Morton	3	L 0-1	0-1		2000
14	29	H	Arbroath	3	D 2-2	1-1	Cowan, Reynolds	3000
15	Dec 2	A	Dumbarton	3	D 0-0	0-0		1500
16	13	H	Clyde	3	W 2-1	0-1	Jones 2	2500
17	20	H	Partick T.	3	L 2-4	1-3	Whiteford, Clarke	5000
18	27	A	East Fife	3	D 1-1	1-1	Jonquin (pen)	1770
19	Jan 1	A	Kilmarnock	—	L 1-2	1-0	Jonquin (pen)	7000
20	3	H	Queen of the S.	5	D 2-2	2-0	McCulloch, Jones	3000
21	10	A	Montrose	5	L 0-1	0-0		1200
22	17	H	Morton	4	W 2-1	0-1	McCulloch, Wilson (pen)	2000
23	31	A	Falkirk	4	D 1-1	1-1	Whiteford	3000
24	Feb 7	H	Dunfermline Ath.	4	D 1-1	0-1	Wilson (pen)	2000
25	21	H	St. Mirren	4	L 1-3	1-1	Clarke	2000
26	28	A	Hamilton A.	7	L 1-2	1-0	Lapsley	2500

Final Place: 7

Goalscorers

League (44): Whiteford 8, Clarke 7 (1 pen), Jonquin 7 (7 pens), Wilson 6 (4 pens), McRoberts 5, Jones 3, McCulloch 2, Cowan 1, Lapsley 1, March 1, Menzies 1, Reynolds 1, Walker 1.
League Cup (7): Jonquin 3 (1 pen), McCann 1, McCulloch 1, Whiteford 1, Wilson 1.
Cup (2): McRoberts 1, Whiteford 1.
Spring Cup (32): McCulloch 9, Whiteford 7, Cairney 5 (1 pen), Jonquin 2 (2 pens), McVeigh 2, Walker 2, Clarke 1, Jones 1, Wilson 1, own goals 2.

Honours

Scottish League: Division 1, Runners-up: 1922–23, 1923–24, 1924–25, 1925–26.
Division 2, Champions: 1902–03, 1954–55, 1973–74, Runners-up: 1946–47, 1949–50, 1965–66.
Scottish Cup: Winners: 1924, Runners-up 1975.
Scottish League Cup: None.
Spring Cup: Winners: 1975-76.
Record Victory: 11-1 v Falkirk, Division 1, 1950–51.
Record Defeat: 1-11 v Hibernian, Division 1, 1959–60.
Most League Points: 60, Division 2, 1973-74.
Most Individual League Goals in Season: 45, H. G. Yarnall, Division 1, 1916–17.
Most Capped Player: Jimmy Crapnell, 9, Scotland.
Highest goalscorers in British league football 1973-74 with 102 goals.

Poulton, M.	McWilliams, D.	Jonquin, P.	Lapsley, J.	Cowan, M.	Menzies, J.	Black, J.	Whiteford, D.	McRoberts, A.	Reynolds, T.	Walker, T.	McCulloch, W.	March, J. A.	Wilson, W.	Clarke, A.	Anderson, N.	Sutherland, S.	Conroy, M.	McCann, K.	Jones, J.	McVeigh, J.	Flavell, G.	Young, I.	Gallacher, S.	Match No.
	1	2	6	3	4*	5	10	13	8	11		9	12				7†							1
1	2	12	3*		5	6	7	8	11†			9	10	4				13						2
	1	2	3			8*	5	6	7	13	12	10†	11	9	4									3
	1	2	3		4	5	8†	7*	12	13	11		9	10	6									4
	1	2	3		4	6	13	7	8		11†	12	9*	10	5									5
	1	2	3		4	5	6	7			8	11	9	10										6
	1	2	3		4	5	6	7	12	8	11	13	9*	10†										7
	1	2	3		4	5	6	10	7*	8	11	12	9											8
	1	2	3		4	5	6	10	7	8	11*	12	9											9
	1	2	3	5	4	6	10	7*	8†	11	12		9					13						10
	1	2	3	8	4	5	6	7		11*	10		9				12							11
	1	2	8	3	4	5	6	7		12	10*		9				11							12
	1		3		5	8	7	10*					9	11	4			12	2	6				13
	1		3		5	8	7	11					9	10†	4		13	12	2	6*				14
	1		3		5	8	7	10					11		4		6*	9	12	2				15
	1	2	3		5	8					12	11	7*	4			6	9	10					16
	1	2	3		5	8	13				12	11	7	4*			6	9	10†					17
	1	2	11	3	4	8	7	12	13	5			9†	10			6*							18
	1	2	11*	3	4	8	7		12	5			9	10			6							19
	1	2	12	4	8	7	9*	5		10							6	11		3				20
	1	2	6	4		13	12	10	5	7	9						8	11†				3*		21
	1	2	3	4		8	7*	10	9	5	11	12					6							22
	1	2	3			5	6	7		8	9	4	11	10										23
	1	2	13	3		5	6	7*	12	8†	9	4	11	10										24
	1	2	13	3	4		7*		11	5		8†	10	9			12	6						25
	1	2	11	3	4		8	6	5	7	10							9						26
1	25	23	14	18	10	25	23	19	12	10	16	11	25	18	9	1	0	10	6	3	3	2	2	

Goal markers:
+ + / 3s 1s
+ + + + / 4s 6s 2s 3s 7s
+ / 2s
+ + + + / 1s 3s 1s 3s

ALBION ROVERS

DIV. 2

Year Formed: 1881. *Ground:* Cliftonhill Park. *Capacity:* 20,000 (580 seats) *Telephone:* Coatbridge 21865
Manager: *Secretary:* David Lyttle. *Club Colours:* Primrose shirts, white shorts, primrose stockings,
Record Attendance: 27,381 v Rangers, Scottish Cup, 2nd Rd, Feb. 8th, 1936.
Previous Grounds: Meadow Park, Whifflet, 1881–1919.
Club Nickname: "The Wee Rovers".

1975–76 LEAGUE RECORD

Match No.	Date	Venue	Opponents	League Pos'n	Result	H/T Score	Goalscorers	Atten- dance
1	Aug 30	H	Stenhousemuir	—	D 2-2	2-2	Sermanni, Paterson	800
2	Sep 6	A	Stranraer	3	W 2-1	1-0	Brogan, Dickson	1500
3	13	H	East Stirling	2	W 2-1	1-0	Shields 2	800
4	20	A	Cowdenbeath	4	L 0-3	0-2		700
5	27	H	Alloa	7	L 0-1	0-0		400
6	Oct 4	A	Berwick R.	6	W 1-0	0-0	Muldoon	350
7	11	H	Clydebank	7	L 0-4	0-1		1500
8	18	H	Stirling Albion	8	D 1-1	0-0	Brogan	500
9	25	A	Raith R.	8	D 1-1	1-1	Brogan	1782
10	Nov 1	H	Forfar Ath.	7	W 4-0	2-0	Brogan, Muldoon, Dickson 2 (1 pen)	800
11	8	A	Queen's Park	7	D 2-2	0-1	Sermanni, McGuigan	1000
12	15	A	Brechin C.	8	L 0-2	0-1		300
13	22	H	Meadowbank T.	6	W 4-0	3-0	Main, Shields, Sermanni 2	500
14	29	A	Alloa	8	L 0-2	0-1		600
15	Dec 6	H	Berwick R.	8	D 2-2	1-0	Shields, Paterson	500
16	20	A	Stirling Albion	7	D 1-1	1-0	Doherty I. (pen)	750
17	27	H	Raith R.	9	L 1-2	0-2	McGuigan	800
18	Jan 1	H	Stranraer	—	W 2-1	2-1	Brogan 2	500
19	3	A	East Stirling	7	D 0-0	0-0		500
20	17	A	Meadowbank T.	8	L 1-4	0-3	Coughlin	350
21	Feb 7	A	Stenhousemuir	9	L 2-4	2-2	McLean 2	301
22	14	A	Clydebank	8	D 2-2	1-0	Sermanni, McLean	1000
23	21	A	Forfar Ath.	9	L 0-1	0-0		250
24	25	H	Cowdenbeath	—	D 1-1	1-1	McLean	200
25	28	H	Queen's Park	9	D 0-0	0-0		400
26	Apr 26	H	Brechin C.	9	W 4-0	1-0	Doherty I., Sermanni, Brogan, McLean	350

Final Place: 9

Goalscorers

League (35): Brogan 7, Sermanni 6, McLean 5, Shields 4, Dickson P. 3 (1 pen), Doherty I. 2 (1 pen),
McGuigan 2, Muldoon 2, Paterson 2, Coughlin 1, Main 1,
League Cup: (5) Dickson P. 3 (1 pen), Coughlin 1, Muldoon 1.
Cup (6): Brogan 2, Sermanni 2 (1 pen), Franchetti 1, McLean 1.
Spring Cup (12): Doherty I. 4 (3 pens), McLean 3, Brogan 1, Main 1, Muldoon 1, Sermanni 1, Shields 1.

Honours
Scottish League: Division 2 Champions 1933–34; Runners-up: 1913–14, 1937–38, 1947–48.
Scottish Cup: Finalists 1920.

Record Victory: 10-0 v Brechin C., Division 2, 1937–38.
Record Defeat: 1-9 v Motherwell, Division 1, 1936–37.
Most League Points: 54, Division 2, 1929–30.
Most Individual League Goals in Season: Jim Renwick, 41, 1932–33.
Most Capped Player: Jock White, 1, Scotland.

Hutchison, L.	Gryzka, S.	McConville, D.	Main, D.	Shields, D.	Doherty, J.	McCue, D.	Doherty, I.	Sermanni, T.	Brogan, J.	Dickson, P.	Coughlin, J.	McGuigan, I.	Muldoon, W.	O'Connor, J.	Paterson, W.	Franchetti, R.	McLean, D.	Walker, J.	Burns, J.	Hadden, J.	
	1	13	5	2	3	6	7	11†	9		8*	4	12	10							1
	1	2	8	5	7	3	6			4	9	11		10							2
	1	2	8†	5	7*	3	6	13	4	9	11	12		10							3
	1	2	13	5	4	3	6	7	9		11†12		8	10*							4
1		11†	5	2	3	6	4	10*	7	13	8		9	12							5
	1	2	3*	5	12		6	4†	7	9	13	10	8			11					6
	1	2		5	13	3	6		4	9	11†10*	8	12		7						7
1		2	4	5	13	3	6	12	9	11*		8		10†	7						8
1		2	4	5		3	6	7*	9	8	12		10			11					9
1		2	4	5	12	3*	6		9	8	7	13	10		11†						10
1		2	4	5	13	3	6	12	9*	8	11	10†	7								11
	1		4*	5	2	3	6	8		9	10	7†11			13	12					12
	1		4	5	2	3	6	8			11		7		10	9					13
	1	13	4*	5	2	3	6	8			11		7	12	10	9†					14
	1	12	4	5	2	3	6	8				10*	7		11	9					15
	1		5	2	3	6	8	9			7	4		10	11						16
	1	2	3	5		10	6	8	9			7	4	12		11*					17
	1	12	3	5	2	10	6	8	9			7†	4*13			11					18
	1	4	3	5	2	10	6	8	9				12		11		7*				19
	1	2		5	12	3	6	8	9	11	7†		13		4*10						20
	2		5	4	3	10		9	12	11†	6*	7	13	8				1			21
	1	2	3	5	4		6	9	10		8	7			11						22
	1	2	3	5	4		6	9	10		8	7*	12	11							23
	1	2	3	5	4	13	6	7	10		12	9†		11		8*					24
	1	2	12	5	4	3	6	7	10		8*13		9	11†							25
	1	2	6	5	3		10	7	12		4†	8	13		9	11*					26
5	20	18	19	26	18	21	26	19	20	12	10	13	21	4	9	15	7	1	1	1	
		+3s	+3s		+6s	1s		+3s	1s	+4s	3s	1s	10s	1s	3s						

ALLOA

Year Formed: 1878. *Ground:* Recreation Ground. *Size:* 110×75 yds. *Capacity:* 12,000.
Telephone: Alloa 2695. *Manager:* Hugh Wilson.
Secretary: George Ormiston.
Club Colours: Gold with black trim, black shorts, gold socks with black tops.
Club Nickname: 'The Wasps'.
Record attendance: 13,000 v Dunfermline Ath., Scottish Cup 3rd Rd. replay, Feb. 26th, 1939.

1975–76 LEAGUE RECORD

Match No.	Date	Venue	Opponents	League Pos'n	Result	H/T Score	Goalscorers	Attendance
1	Aug 30	H	Meadowbank T.	—	D 1-1	1-0	Donald	359
2	Sep 6	A	Stenhousemuir	4	W 1-0	1-0	Morrison	500
3	13	H	Stranraer	4	D 3-3	2-2	Low 2, Morrison	375
4	20	A	Brechin C.	3	W 3-2	2-1	Morrison 2, Russell	350
5	27	A	Albion R.	2	W 1-0	0-0	Morrison	400
6	Oct 4	H	East Stirling	2	W 1-0	0-0	Russell	400
7	11	A	Raith R.	3	L 0-1	0-0		1756
8	18	H	Berwick R.	3	W 1-0	0-0	Russell	470
9	25	A	Stirling Albion	3	D 2-2	0-2	Campbell (pen), Wilson	1600
10	Nov 1	H	Queen's Park	3	D 3-3	0-2	Stewart, Miller, Morrison	700
11	8	A	Cowdenbeath	2	W 1-0	0-0	Low	800
12	15	H	Forfar Ath.	2	W 2-1	1-1	Thomson J. (pen), Morrison	500
13	22	A	Clydebank	3	L 1-3	0-1	Campbell (pen)	3000
14	29	H	Albion R.	2	W 2-0	1-0	Wilson, Miller	600
15	Dec 6	A	East Stirling	2	W 3-0	2-0	Morrison 3	500
16	27	H	Stirling Albion	3	L 1-2	0-0	McPhee (og)	1764
17	Jan 1	H	Stenhousemuir	—	W 4-2	3-0	Morrison 2, Thomson, Wilson	740
18	3	A	Stranraer	3	W 1-0	0-0	Low	1000
19	31	H	Brechin C.	3	D 0-0	0-0		600
20	Feb 7	A	Meadowbank T.	3	W 2-1	2-0	Morrison, Forrest	450
21	18	A	Berwick R.	—	W 3-0	1-0	Campbell 2 (2 pens), Wilson	300
22	21	A	Queen's Park	3	L 1-3	1-3	Morrison	700
23	24	A	Forfar Ath.	—	D 3-3	1-2	Wilkinson, Campbell, Wilson	350
24	28	H	Cowdenbeath	3	W 4-0	2-0	Campbell (pen), Russell, Wilson, Morrison	680
25	Mar 31	H	Raith R.	—	L 0-1	0-0		3400
26	Apr 6	H	Clydebank	3	D 0-0	0-0		1050

Final Place: 3

Goalscorers

League (44): Morrison 15, Campbell 6 (4 pens), Wilson 6, Low 4, Russell 4, Miller 2, Thomson J. 2 (1 pen), Donald 1, Forrest 1, Stewart 1, Wilkinson 1, own goal 1.
League Cup (5): Forrest 2, Campbell 1 (pen), McCann 1, Morrison 1.
Cup (7): Russell 3, Wilson 2, Low 1, Morrison 1.
Spring Cup (11): Forrest 2, Russell 2, Campbell 1 (pen), Donald 1, Low 1, Morrison 1, Thomson J. 1, Wilkinson 1, Wilson 1.

Honours

Scottish League: Division 2 Champions 1921–22; Runners up 1938–39.

Record Victory: 9-2 v Forfar, Division 2, March 18th, 1933.
Record Defeat: 0-10 v Dundee, Division 2, March 8th, 1947.
Most League Points: 60, 1921–22.
Most Individual League Goals in Season: 49, Wee Crilley, Division 2, 1921–22.
Most Capped Player: Jock Hepburn 1, Scotland.

Thomson, A.	McCann, H.	Wilkinson, W.	McGarry, B.	Stewart, E.	Watson, I.	Campbell, A.	Russell, R.	Thomson, J.	Wilson, D.	Low, K.	Miller, D.	Morrison, W.	Liddell, F.	Forrest, G.	Donald, K.	Menmuir, W.	Trail, D.	Match No.
1	2	3	4	5*12		6	11	8	7					9	10			1
1	2	3	4	5		6	9	8	7		10	11						2
1	2	3	4	5		6	9	8	7		10	11						3
1	2	3		5	4*	9	8	7†	6	11					13	12	10	4
1	2	3	4	6		10	9	8	7	5	11							5
1	2	3	4	6*		10	9	8	7†	5	11				13	12		6
1	2	3	4	12		10	9	8	7	5	6*			11				7
1	2	3	4			6	9	8	7*	5	11			10	12			8
1	2*	3	4			6		8	9	7	5	11		10	12			9
1		3	4	6	2	9	8	10	7*	5	11			12				10
1	2	3	4	5		8	7	10	9*13	6	11†			12				11
1	2*	3	4	5		12	9	8	13	7	6	11†		10				12
1	2	3	4	5		10	9	8*12	7	6	11†			13				13
1	2	3	4	5		10*	7	8	9	6	11†			12	13			14
1	2	3	4	5		10†	7	8	9	6*11				13	12			15
1	2	3	4	5		7*	8	9	12	6	10†			11	13			16
1	2†	3	4	5		10	7	8	9*12	6	11			13				17
1	2*	3	4	5		10	7	8	9	12	6	11†		13				18
1	2	3	4	5		10†11	8	9*	7	6	13			12				19
1	2	3		5		10	7*	8	9	12	4	11		6				20
1	2	3		5		10		8	9	7	4	11		6				21
1	2	3		5		10†	8	9	7*	4	11	13		6	12			22
1	2	3		5		10	7	8	9		4	11		6				23
1	2	3		5*		10	7†	8	9	13	4	11	12	6				24
1	2	3		5		10	7	8	9	12	4	11		6*				25
1	2	3		5		10	11	8	9	7	4	6						26
26	25	26	18	23	0	25	22	26	16	16	23	24	0	13	2	0	1	
			+1s	+1s	+1s				+2s	+7s			+1s	+2s	+9s	+8s	+1s	

ARBROATH   DIV. 1

Year Formed: 1878.   *Ground:* Gayfield Park.   *Capacity:* 15,000.   *Telephone:* Arbroath 2157.
Manager: Albert Henderson.
Trainer: Alan Reid.   *Club Colours:* Maroon shirts, white shorts, maroon stockings.
Club Nickname: 'Red Lichties'.
Record Attendance: 13,510 v Rangers, Scottish Cup 3rd Rd, Feb. 23rd, 1952.
Record Transfer Fee received: £35,000 from Aberdeen for W. Pirie, March 1974.

1975–76 LEAGUE RECORD

Match No.	Date	Venue	Opponents	League Pos'n	Result	H/T Score	Goalscorers	Atten-dance
1	Aug 30	A	Falkirk	—	L 0-1	0-0		2500
2	Sep 6	H	Montrose	13	L 1-2	1-0	Bone (pen)	2762
3	13	A	Morton	12	D 2-2	0-0	Bone 2	2000
4	20	H	Queen of the S.	9	W 3-2	1-2	Bone, Fletcher, Yule	1441
5	27	H	Airdrieonians	7	W 3-0	1-0	Cargill, Fletcher 2	1534
6	Oct 4	A	East Fife	8	L 1-3	0-2	Bone	1685
7	11	H	Hamilton A.	6	W 2-1	2-1	Bone, Fletcher	1550
8	18	A	Kilmarnock	8	L 1-2	0-1	Sellars	3000
9	25	H	Partick T.	8	D 0-0	0-0		2147
10	Nov 1	H	Dumbarton	12	L 1-5	0-2	McKenzie	1682
11	8	A	Clyde	13	L 2-5	1-2	Bone 2	1000
12	15	H	St. Mirren	11	W 4-1	1-0	Carson, Bone 2, Yule	1279
13	22	A	Dunfermline Ath.	8	W 1-0	0-0	Sellars	2500
14	29	A	Airdrieonians	8	D 2-2	1-1	Bone, Yule	3000
15	Dec 6	H	East Fife	6	W 3-1	2-1	Bone, Penman 2	1499
16	13	H	Hamilton A.	6	W 1-0	1-0	Mathieson	2000
17	20	H	Kilmarnock	4	W 2-0	1-0	Carson, Yule	1950
18	27	A	Partick T.	6	L 0-2	0-1		5000
19	Jan 1	A	Montrose	—	W 5-3	2-2	Mathieson 2, Sellars 2, McKenzie	3600
20	3	H	Morton	6	L 0-1	0-1		2143
21	17	H	Dunfermline Ath.	5	W 1-0	1-0	Bone	1616
22	31	A	Queen of the S.	5	L 1-2	0-0	Carson	2000
23	Feb 7	A	Falkirk	6	L 0-1	0-0		1385
24	14	A	St. Mirren	6	D 0-0	0-0		1900
25	21	A	Dumbarton	8	L 2-3	0-2	Yule, Fettes	2500
26	28	H	Clyde	5	W 3-0	1-0	Yule 2, McKenzie	1122

Final Place: 5

Goalscorers

League (41): Bone 13 (1 pen), Yule 7, Fletcher 4, Sellars 4, Carson 3, McKenzie 3, Mathieson 3, Penman 2, Cargill 1, Fettes 1.
League Cup (13): Bone 7 (4 pens), Yule 4, Rylance 1, Sellars 1,
Cup (0).
Spring Cup (9): Bone 4 (2 pens), Fletcher 1, Gavine 1, McKenzie 1, Mitchell 1, Yule 1.

Honours

Scottish League: Division 2 Runners-up 1934–35, 1958–59, 1967–68, 1971–72.

Record Victory: 36-0 v Bon Accord, Scottish Cup 1st Rd, Sep. 12th, 1885.
Record Defeat: 0-8 v Kilmarnock, Division 2, 1948–49.
Most League Points: 57, Division 2, 1966–67.
Most Individual League Goals in Season: 45, Dave Easson, Division 2, 1958–59.

Wilson, B.	Marshall, G.	Milne, J.	Mathieson, W.	Murray, C.	Wells, W.	Carson, J.	Rylance, D.	Sellars, E.	Cargill, J.	McIlravey, J.	Bone, J.	Fletcher, J.	Penman, A.	Yule, T.	Mitchell, J.	McKenzie, A.	Fettes, A.	Campbell, I.	Follon, N.	Match No.
1	2	3	4	5		6	12	8	7	9	10*		11†						13	1
1	2	3	4	5		6	13	10†	8*	9	7		11	12						2
1	2	3	12	5	10	6	13	4	8*	9	7		11†							3
1	2	3	12	5*	10	6	13	4	8†	9	7		11							4
1	2	3	4		5	6		10	8†	9	7*		11	12	13					5
1	2	3	4		5	6		8	12	9	7		10*	11						6
1	2	3	4		5	6	13	10	8*	9	7		11†		12					7
1	2	3	4		5	6	12	10	8*	9	7		11							8
1	2	3	4	5		6	7*	8	12	9	10		11†	13						9
1	2	3	4	5		6		8*		9	7	10†	13	11	12					10
	1	8	3	12		5	6	13		9	10	7			11†	4		2*		11
	1	2		6		5	3	7	4		9		8	10	11					12
	1	2	12	6		5	3	7	4		9		8	10*	11					13
	1	2*	12	6		5	3	7	4		9		8	10	11†	13				14
	1	2	12	6		5	3	7	4		9		8*	10	11					15
	1	2	8	6		5	3	7	4		9			10	11					16
	1	2	8	6		5	3	7*	4		9			11	12	10				17
	1	2	8	6		5	3	7*	4		9		10†	11	12	13				18
	1	2	8	6		5	3	7	4		9			11		10				19
	1	2	8†	6		5	3	7*	4		9		13	11	12	10				20
	1	2	8	6		5	3	7*	4		9		10†	11	12	13				21
	1	2	8	6		5	3	7*	4		9			12	11	10				22
	1	2	8	6		5	3	7*	4		9	13		12	11†	10				23
	1	2	3			5	6	7*	4		10		11	12	9	8				24
	1	2*	3	12		5	6		4		9		11†	13	7	8	10			25
	1	2*	12	6		5	3		4		9		13	11	7†	8	10			26
10	16	26	21	21	6	22	26	14	25	7	26	17	10	20	6	9	3	0	1	
	+4s	+4s					+7s		+2s		+2s	+1s	+4s	+9s	+5s		+1s			

AYR UNITED

Year Formed: 1910.
Ground: Somerset Park. *Size:* 111 × 75 yds. *Capacity:* 25,000 (1,500 seats).
Telephone: Ayr 63435.
Manager: Alex. Stuart. *Coach:* Sam McMillan.
Secretary: John Robertson.
Club Colours: White shirts with black facings, black shorts, white stockings.
Club Nickname: 'The Honest Men'.
Record Attendance: 25,225 v Rangers, Division 1, Sept 13, 1969.

1975–76 LEAGUE RECORD

Match No.	Date	Venue	Opponents	League Pos'n	Result	H/T Score	Goalscorers	Attendance
1	Aug 30	A	Motherwell	—	D 1-1	1-0	Graham (pen)	5115
2	Sep 6	H	St Johnstone	2	W 1-0	0-0	Doyle	4194
3	13	A	Hibernian	6	L 0-1	0-0		8897
4	20	H	Dundee	4	W 2-1	0-0	Graham 2 (1 pen)	4024
5	27	A	Aberdeen	6	L 1-3	0-1	Graham	4500
6	Oct 4	A	Dundee U.	6	L 2-3	0-2	Wells 2	3000
7	11	H	Rangers	4	W 3-0	2-0	Graham, Ingram, McCulloch	15,000
8	18	A	Hearts	7	L 1-2	1-0	Ingram	9000
9	Nov 1	H	Motherwell	6	W 2-0	1-0	Doyle, Phillips	6400
10	8	A	St Johnstone	5	W 1-0	1-0	Phillips	2097
11	12	H	Celtic	—	L 2-7	1-5	Doyle, Graham (pen)	15,000
12	15	H	Hibernian	6	L 1-3	1-1	Doyle	5000
13	22	A	Dundee	6	D 2-2	0-0	McDonald, Doyle	5132
14	29	H	Aberdeen	6	W 1-0	0-0	Murphy	6000
15	Dec 6	H	Dundee U.	6	D 2-2	0-2	Graham 2	4764
16	13	A	Rangers	8	L 0-3	0-0		20,000
17	20	H	Hearts	8	D 1-1	1-0	Graham (pen)	5442
18	27	A	Celtic	8	L 1-3	0-1	McCulloch	22,000
19	Jan 1	A	Motherwell	—	L 0-1	0-0		7367
20	3	H	St Johnstone	8	W 2-0	1-0	Doyle, Graham	4300
21	10	A	Hibernian	8	L 0-3	0-2		8083
22	17	H	Dundee	8	W 3-1	1-0	Graham 2, Ingram	4378
23	31	A	Aberdeen	8	L 1-2	0-1	Graham (pen)	9920
24	Feb 21	H	Rangers	8	L 0-1	0-0		15,000
25	28	A	Hearts	8	L 0-1	0-1		8000
26	Mar 3	A	Dundee U.	—	L 0-5	0-3		3300
27	20	A	St Johnstone	9	W 2-1	0-0	Robertson, 2	1500
28	27	H	Hibernian	9	W 2-0	0-0	Fleming, Robertson	4700
29	Apr 3	A	Dundee	7	W 2-1	0-0	Graham, Robertson	4149
30	10	H	Aberdeen	8	D 1-1	0-0	Graham	5740
31	14	H	Dundee U.	—	W 1-0	0-0	Ingram	5200
32	17	A	Rangers	7	L 1-2	1-1	Ingram	25,000
33	21	H	Hearts	—	L 0-1	0-0		5200
34	24	A	Celtic	7	W 2-1	0-0	Robertson 2 (1 pen)	16,000
35	May 1	H	Celtic	9	L 3-5	2-1	Graham, Phillips, McCulloch	6800
36	3	H	Motherwell	—	W 2-1	0-1	Phillips, McCulloch	6500

Final Place: 6

Goalscorers

League (46): Graham 16 (4 pens), Doyle 6, Robertson 6 (1 pen), Ingram 5, McCulloch 4, Phillips 4, Wells 2, Fleming 1, McDonald 1, Murphy 1.
League Cup (11): Graham 3 (1 pen), Fleming 2, Ingram 2, Phillips 2, Dickson 1, Doyle 1.
Cup (10): Ingram 5, Robertson 3 (1 pen), Doyle 1, McCulloch 1.

Honours

Scottish League: Division 2, Champions: 1911–12, 1912–13, 1927–28, 1936–37, 1958–59, 1965–66, Runners-up: 1910-11, 1955-56, 1968-69.
Scottish Cup: None.
Scottish League Cup: None.

Record Victory: 11-1 v Dumbarton, League Cup, Aug. 13th, 1952.
Record Defeat: 0-9 v Rangers, Division 1, Nov. 16th, 1929, and Hearts, Division 1, Feb. 28th, 1931.
Most League Points: 60, Division 2, 1958–59.
Most Individual League Goals in Season: Jim Smith 66 in 1927–28.

Sproat, H.	Wells, D.	Murphy, J.	Filippi, J.	McDonald, D.	McAnespie, A.	Fleming, R.	Paton, W.	McSherry, J.	Doyle, J.	Kelly, W.	Graham, J.	Ingram, A.	Phillips, G.	McCulloch, D.	Dickson, J.	Cameron, H.	Robertson, M.	Bell, B.	Tait, R.	Cramond, G.	Hyslop, J.	Match No.
1	2	3			4	5	6	7			8	9		10	11							1
1	2	3			4	5	6	7			8	9		10	11*12							2
1	2	3			4	5	6	7			8	9		10	11							3
1	2	3			4	5	6	7			8	9		10	11*12							4
1	2	3	12	5*	4	6	7				8	9		10	11†13							5
1	2	3	12	4	5	6*	7†				8	9		10	11	13						6
1	2	3	6	5	4			7			8	9		10	11							7
1	2	3	6		4	5		7	12		8	9		10	11*							8
1	2	3	6		4	5		7			8	9*		10		11	12					9
1		3	6	2	4	5		7			8	9		10			11					10
1		3	6*	2	4	5		7	12		8	9		10			11					11
1		3	6	2	4	5		7	12		8*	9		10			11					12
1		3	2		4	5		7	6		8	9		10			11					13
1		3	2		4	5		7	6		8	9		10*		12	11					14
1		3	6*	2	4	5		7	12		8	9	13	10			11†					15
1		3	2		4	5		7	6		8	9		10			11					16
1		3	2		4	5		7*	6		8	9		10		12	11					17
1	12	3	2		4	5		7	6		8*	9		10		13	11†					18
1		3	2		4	5		7	6		8	9*		10		12	11					19
1		3	2		4	5		7	6		8	9*		10		12	11					20
1		3	2		4	5		7	6		8	9		10			11*12					21
1	2	3	6		4	5		7	10		8	9				12	11*					22
1	2	3	6		4	5*		7	10		8	9				12	11					23
1	2	3	12	6†	4	5			10		8†	9		7		13	11					24
1	2	3	6*		4	5			10		8	9		7†13		12	11					25
1		6	2		4	5			12		3	13	9	10	8†	7*	11					26
1	2	3	6		4	5		7			8	9					11			10		27
1	2	3	6		4	5		7			8	9					11			10		28
1	2	3	6		4			7			8	9*	12				11		5	10		29
1	2	3	6		4			7			8	9*	12				11		5	10		30
1		3	6	2	4			7			8	9					11		5	10		31
1		3	6	2	4			7*			8	9	12				11		5	10		32
1		3	6	2	4	5		7			8	9					11			10		33
1		3*	2		4				6		12	8	9	10			7		5	11		34
1		3	2		4				6		8	12	9	10			7		5	11*		35
1		3	2		4						8	9	7	10					5		6	36
36	17	35	18	20	23	31	11	28	23	1	34	31	12	25	8	4	22	0	7	9	1	
+1s		+1s	+2s					+5s			+1s	+1s	+1s	+3s	+4s	+2s	+9s			+2s		

BERWICK RANGERS

DIV. 2

Year Formed: 1881. *Ground:* Sheffield Park. *Size:* 112×76 yds. *Capacity:* 16,000.
Telephone: Berwick 7424. *Manager:* Gordon Haig.
Secretary: Richard Shiel. *Assistant Secretary:* Dennis McCleary.
Club Colours: Gold with Black trimmings, black shorts, gold stockings.
Record Attendance: 13,365 v Rangers, Scottish Cup, 1st Rd, Jan. 28th, 1967.
Club Nickname: 'The Wee Rangers'.

1975–76 LEAGUE RECORD

Match No.	Date	Venue	Opponents	League Pos'n	Result	H/T Score	Goalscorers	Attendance
1	Aug 30	H	East Stirling	—	L 1-2	1-0	Georgeson	402
2	Sep 13	H	Brechin C.	7	W 2-1	0-0	Smith, Georgeson	350
3	16	A	Meadowbank T.	—	W 6-2	3-1	Jones (og), Smith 2, Welsh, Georgeson 2	500
4	20	A	Stenhousemuir	5	L 1-2	0-2	Rose (og)	301
5	27	H	Clydebank	10	L 0-4	0-1		350
6	Oct 4	H	Albion R.	11	L 0-1	0-0		350
7	11	A	Queen's Park	12	L 0-1	0-0		800
8	18	A	Alloa	13	L 0-1	0-0		470
9	25	H	Forfar Ath.	12	D 3-3	1-2	Smith, Georgeson, Tait	350
10	Nov 1	A	Cowdenbeath	12	L 2-3	0-2	Smith 2	400
11	8	H	Stranraer	13	L 1-2	0-1	Davidson	300
12	15	H	Raith R.	14	L 1-3	1-2	Georgeson	450
13	22	H	Stirling Albion	13	W 3-2	2-1	Smith, Georgeson (pen), Tait	1500
14	29	A	Clydebank	13	W 1-0	0-0	Georgeson (pen)	2000
15	Dec 6	A	Albion R.	12	D 2-2	0-1	Miller, Welsh	500
16	27	A	Forfar Ath.	10	W 3-1	2-0	Smith, Welsh, McLeod	350
'7	Jan 1	H	Meadowbank T.	—	W 1-0	0-0	Georgeson (pen)	550
8	17	A	Stirling Albion	10	L 0-2	0-1		850
19	31	H	Stenhousemuir	10	D 1-1	0-0	Laing	350
20	Feb 7	A	East Stirling	11	D 1-1	0-1	McQuade	300
21	14	H	Queen's Park	10	D 1-1	1-1	McQuade	235
22	18	H	Alloa	—	L 0-3	0-1		300
23	21	H	Cowdenbeath	11	L 0-1	0-0		220
24	28	A	Stranraer	11	W 2-1	2-1	Smith 2	850
25	Mar 17	A	Raith R.	—	L 0-3	0-2		2518
26	Apr 24	A	Brechin C.	11	L 0-1	0-1		300

Final Place: 11

Goalscorers

League (32): Smith 10, Georgeson 9 (3 pens), Welsh G. K. 3, McQuade 2, Tait 2, Davidson 1, Laing 1, McLeod 1, Miller 1, own goals 2.
League Cup (6): Georgeson 3, Laing 1, McLeod 1, Welsh G. K. 1.
Cup (4): McLeod 2, Tait 1, Welsh G. K. 1.
Spring Cup (4): McLeod 3, Welsh G. K. 1.

Honours

Record Victory: 8-1 v Forfar Athletic.
Record Defeat: 0-8 v Morton and 1-9 v Dundee United.
Most League Points: 45, Division 2, 1973-74.
Most Individual League Goals in Season: Ken Bowron, 38, Division 2, 1963-64.
Highest League Position: 6th in 1973-74 (Division 2).
Most League Goals: 83—1961-62 (Division 2).
Most League Appearances: 282 Alistair Campbell 1955-62.
Best Cup Run: 1963 League Cup Semi-Final 1-3 v Rangers (Hampden).

Lyle, J. W.	Laing, G.	McQuade, P. M.	Donaldson, P.	Davidson, T.	Cairns, R. B.	McDowell, R.	McCabe, B. J.	Tomlie, R.	Thomson, L. P.	Smith, I. R.	Miller, J. K.	Steven, T.	Welsh, G. K.	McLeod, A.	Georgeson, R.	Tait, E. J.	Donald, K.	Butler, J.	Brown, A. C.	Welsh, J. A.	Moyes, D. J.	Muir, G.	Pryde, A.	Forbes, C.	Ross, B.	Neilson, G.	Match No.
1	2	3			4	5	6*		12	7†13	8	9		10	11												1
1	2	3			4	5	6			7		8		9	10	11											2
1	2	3			4	5	6			7*12		8	11	13	9	10†											3
1	2	3			4	5	6			7	12	8	13		9	10*		11†									4
1	2	3	4			5	6			7		8	12		9	10		11*									5
1	2	3				5	4			7	10	8	11	12	9	6*											6
1	2	3				4	6			7	10	8	11		9	5											7
1	2	3	12	4		5	6			7		8	11		9*10												8
1	3		2	4		5	6			7	9	8		11	10												9
1	3		2	4		5	6			7	9	8	12	11	10*												10
1	3		2	4		5	6			7	9	8		11	10												11
1	3		2	4		5	6			7	11*		12	9	10				8								12
1	3		2			5	4			7	11†	10*13			9	6			8	12							13
1	3		2			5	4			7	10		12		9*11	6			8								14
1	3		2			5	4			7	10			11	9	6			8								15
1	3		2	4		5	6			7	10	8		11	9												16
1	3		2	4		5*	6			7†10		8			9	11	12							13			17
1	3		2			4				7	10	8		5	9	6		11									18
1	3		2			5	6			7		8	12	10	9	11*					4						19
1	3	6	2	4		5	8			7		10			9	11											20
1	3	6	2	4		5	11			7*12					9						8	10					21
1	3	6	2	4		5	12			7					9	10					8	11*					22
1	3	6	2			5				7			11	10	9						4		8				23
1	3	6	2	8		5				7	12		11		10						4				9*		24
1	3	13	2	8*	12	5	11			7					9†						4				6	10	25
12	3		2	5*				1		7		8		11	9	10					4				6		26
25	25	14	18	13	5	24	22	1	0	24	20	10	13	11	19	19	1	3	4	1	7	2	1	1	2	1	
+1s	+1s	+1s		+1s		+1s	+1s		+4s	+4s		6s				+1s					+2s						

BRECHIN CITY   DIV. 2

Year Formed: 1906.   *Ground:* Glebe Park.   *Size* 110 × 67 yds.   *Capacity:* 10,000   *Telephone:* Brechin 2856.   *Manager:* Charlie Dunn.   *Secretary:* George Johnston.   *Club Colours:* Red shirts, shorts and stockings.   *Club Nickname:* 'City'.   *Record Attendance:* 8123 v Aberdeen, Scottish Cup, 3rd round, Feb. 3rd, 1973.

1975–76 LEAGUE RECORD

Match No.	Date	Venue	Opponents	League Pos'n	Result	H/T Score	Goalscorers	Attendance
1	Aug 30	A	Clydebank	—	L 0-3	0-1		1400
2	Sep 6	H	Forfar Ath.	8	W 2-1	1-1	Weir (pen), Wilson	500
3	13	A	Berwick R.	11	L 1-2	0-0	Sime	350
4	20	H	Alloa	14	L 2-3	1-2	Weir (pen), Sutherland	350
5	27	A	East Stirling	14	L 0-1	0-0		200
6	Oct 4	H	Queen's Park	12	W 1-0	0-0	Weir	300
7	11	A	Meadowbank T.	8	W 4-0	0-0	Weir, Wilson, Robb, Rice	250
8	18	A	Stranraer	9	L 2-4	1-2	Robb, Rice	1050
9	25	H	Cowdenbeath	11	L 1-2	1-1	Rice	350
10	Nov 1	H	Stenhousemuir	11	D 1-1	0-0	Rice	300
11	8	A	Stirling Albion	11	D 1-1	0-0	Rice	1100
12	15	H	Albion R.	9	W 2-0	1-0	Wilson, Robb	300
13	22	A	Raith R.	10	D 1-1	0-0	Morton	1651
14	29	A	East Stirling	10	D 2-2	1-0	Mitchell, Rice	300
15	Dec 6	A	Queen's Park	10	L 0-1	0-0		900
16	27	A	Cowdenbeath	11	L 2-5	2-3	Reid, Morton	200
17	Jan 1	A	Forfar Ath.	—	W 1-0	1-0	Rice	800
18	17	H	Raith R.	11	L 0-4	0-2		800
19	31	A	Alloa	11	D 0-0	0-0		600
20	Feb 7	H	Clydebank	12	L 1-2	1-2	Young	400
21	14	H	Meadowbank T.	13	L 0-3	0-2		300
22	21	A	Stenhousemuir	14	L 1-4	0-2	Young	400
23	28	H	Stirling Albion	14	L 2-3	1-2	Mitchell 2 (1 pen)	300
24	Apr 17	H	Stranraer	—	L 0-4	0-3		350
25	24	H	Berwick R.	—	W 1-0	1-0	Mitchell	300
26	26	A	Albion R.	13	L 0-4	0-1		350

Final Place: 13

Goalscorers

League (28): Rice 7, Mitchell 4 (1 pen), Weir 4 (2 pens), Robb 3, Wilson 3, Morton 2, Young 2, Reid 1, Sime 1, Sutherland 1.
League Cup (7): Mitchell 3 (1 pen), Young 2, Reid 1, Weir 1.
Cup (7): Robb 4, Rice 2, Morton 1.
Spring Cup (9): Gillespie R. 2, Morton 2 (1 pen), Rice 2, Mitchell 1, Robb 1, Wilson 1.

Honours

Record Victory: 12-1 v Thornhill, Scottish Cup, 1st Rd., Jan. 28th, 1926.
Record Defeat: 1-10 v Dunfermline Ath., Division 2, 1929–30.
Most League Points: 42, Division 2, 1955–56, 1958–59.
Most Individual Goals: Davie Paris, 51 (all games), 1948–49.

Ritchie, J. B.	Beatson, J. S. M.	Brown, A.	Weir, J.	Hopcroft, R. J.	Sime, J.	Sutherland, W.	Gillespie, D.	Grier, G.	Wilson, S. R.	Souttar, J.	Mitchell, J.	Young, J.	Reid, B.	Morton, J.	Dorian, R.	Robb, R.	Rice, A.	Nicol, B.	Watt, D. C.	Gillespie, R. J.	Match No.
1	3	4	5	6*	2	8	7	12				9	11	10†	13						1
1	3	4	2	5	8	6	12	10				9*	7	11							2
1	3	4	2	5	7	6		8				9		10		11					3
1	3	4	2	5*	8	6	7	11			12	9†		10	13						4
1	3*	4	6	5	7	2		9			10†			13	11	8	12				5
1		4	5	6	7		3	9	13					10	11*	8	12†		2		6
1	3	4	5	6	7					12	8*			10		11	9		2		7
1	3	4	5	6	7					8				10		11	9		2		8
1	3	4	5	6	7					8				10		11	9		2		9
	1	3	4	5	6	12	7*	8	13					10†		11	9		2		10
1		6	4	5	3							10	8	11		7	9		2		11
	1	3	4		6			8		5	7			10		11	9		2		12
	1	6	13	3	4*	12		5	8				7	10		11†	9		2		13
1	3	4	12	6	10			13		5*	8†		7			11	9		2		14
	1	6	4	5	3			9				10	7	12		11*	8		2		15
1		6	4*	5	3	8		12	11†			13	7	10			9		2		16
	1	6		5	3	4		7	12	13		10				11†	9		2	8*	17
	1	3	4	5	6			12	7*			9		10		11†	8		2	13	18
	1	3	4	5	6							9*	7	11		12	10		2	8	19
	1	3	4	5	6							13	9†	7	10	12	11		2	8*	20
1		4	5	6	13			8		12	7*	3				11	10†		2	9	21
1	3		5	6			7					11	9	4	10				2	8	22
1	3		5	6			7					11	9	4	10*	12	8		2		23
1	3	4	5			13		12		6		7		10		11	8†		2	9*	24
1		4	5		10			8		6		11	7	3			9		2		25
1	13	4	5		10			8		6		11†	7	3			9*		2	12 6	26
16	10	22	22	23	23	15	4	7	14	7	13	9	14	23	2	16	19	0	21	6	
	+1s	+2s		+2s	+1s	+7s	+1s	+2s	+3s	+2s	+1s	+2s	+2s	+3s				+2s		+2s	

531

CELTIC

PREM. DIV.

Year Formed: 1888. *Ground:* Celtic Park. *Size:* 115×75 yds. *Capacity:* 80,000 (9,000 seats). *Telephone:* 041-554 2710. *Manager:* Jock Stein. *Coach:* Neil Mochan. *Secretary:* Desmond White C.A. *Ass. Manager:* Sean Fallon. *Club Colours:* Green and white hooped shirts, white shorts. *Club Nickname:* 'The Bhoys'. *Record Attendance:* 92,000 v Rangers, Division 1, Jan. 1st, 1938. *European Competitions Entered:* European Cup, 1966–67 (Winners); 1967–68, 1968–69, 1969–70 (Finalists), 1970–71, 1971–72, 1972–73, 1973–74, 1974–75; Cup Winners Cup, 1963–64, 1965–66; Fairs Cup, 1962–63, 1964–65. *Coronation Cup:* 1953. *Empire Exhibition Cup:* 1938.

1975–76 LEAGUE RECORD

Match No.	Date	Venue	Opponents	League Pos'n	Result	H/T Score	Goalscorers	Attendance
1	Aug 30	A	Rangers	—	L 1-2	1-0	Dalglish	69,000
2	Sept 6	H	Dundee	3	W 4-0	1-0	McNamara, Lennox 3	25,000
3	13	A	Motherwell	4	D 1-1	1-1	Dalglish	18,612
4	20	A	St. Johnstone	2	W 2-1	1-0	McCluskey 2 (2 pens)	12,000
5	27	H	Dundee U.	2	W 2-1	0-0	McDonald, Dalglish	21,000
6	Oct 4	H	Hearts	2	W 3-1	3-0	Hood, Wilson, Deans	20,000
7	11	A	Aberdeen	1	W 2-1	2-0	Dalglish, Deans	18,000
8	Nov 1	H	Rangers	1	D 1-1	0-0	Wilson	55,000
9	8	A	Dundee	3	L 0-1	0-0		16,456
10	12	A	Ayr U.	—	W 7-2	5-1	McDonald, Edvaldsson 3, Dalglish, Deans 2	15,000
11	15	H	Motherwell	3	L 0-2	0-1		33,000
12	22	H	St. Johnstone	2	W 3-2	1-2	Dalglish, Lennox 2	20,000
13	29	A	Dundee U.	1	W 3-1	1-0	Lynch, Deans, Lennox	10,000
14	Dec 6	A	Hearts	1	W 1-0	0-0	Deans	21,000
15	10	H	Hibernian	—	D 1-1	0-0	Deans	21,000
16	13	H	Aberdeen	1	L 0-2	0-2		24,000
17	20	A	Hibernian	1	W 3-1	2-1	Edvaldsson, McNamara, Deans	21,360
18	27	H	Ayr U.	1	W 3-1	1-0	Edvaldsson 2, Dalglish	22,000
19	Jan 1	A	Rangers	—	L 0-1	0-1		57,839
20	3	H	Dundee	1	D 3-3	2-1	Dalglish 2, Deans	21,000
21	10	A	Motherwell	1	W 3-1	0-0	Dalglish, Deans 2	18,092
22	17	A	St. Johnstone	2	W 4-3	2-2	McDonald, Edvaldsson, Dalglish, Deans	9915
23	31	H	Dundee U.	1	W 2-1	2-1	Dalglish, Wilson	18,000
24	Feb 7	H	Hearts	1	W 2-0	0-0	Dalglish 2	22,000
25	21	A	Aberdeen	1	W 1-0	0-0	Lennox	18,221
26	28	H	Hibernian	1	W 4-0	3-0	Dalglish, Wilson, Deans (pen), Lennox	33,000
27	Mar 20	A	Dundee	1	W 1-0	0-0	Dalglish	14,830
28	27	H	Motherwell	1	W 4-0	4-0	Dalglish 2, Deans, Lennox	29,000
29	Apr 3	H	St. Johnstone	1	W 1-0	1-0	Dalglish	16,000
30	10	A	Dundee U.	2	L 2-3	0-1	Dalglish 2	12,771
31	17	H	Aberdeen	2	D 1-1	1-1	Dalglish	29,000
32	21	A	Hibernian	—	L 0-2	0-1		17,480
33	24	H	Ayr U.	2	L 1-2	0-0	Deans (pen)	16,000
34	26	H	Rangers	—	D 0-0	0-0		51,000
35	May 1	A	Ayr U.	2	W 5-3	1-2	McCluskey (pen), Dalglish 2, Lennox, Ritchie	6800
36	3	A	Hearts	—	L 0-1	0-0		9000

Final Place: 2

Goalscorers

League (71): Dalglish 24, Deans 15 (2 pens), Lennox 10, Edvaldsson 7, Wilson 4, McCluskey P. 3 (3 pens), McDonald 3, McNamara 2, Hood 1, Lynch 1, Ritchie 1.
League Cup (21): Dalglish 4, Edvaldsson 3, Lennox 3, Wilson 3, Hood 2, Lynch 2, Callaghan 1, Glavin 1, McGrain 1, Ritchie 1.
Cup (2): Dalglish 1, Lynch 1.

Honours

Scottish League: Division 1 Champions: 1892–93, 1893–94, 1895–96, 1897–98, 1904–5, 1905–6, 1906–7, 1907–8, 1908–9, 1909–10, 1913–14, 1914–15, 1915–16, 1916–17, 1918–19, 1921–22, 1925–26, 1935–36, 1937–38, 1953–54, 1965–66, 1966–67, 1967–68, 1968–69, 1969–70, 1970–71, 1971–72, 1972–73, 1973–74. Premier Division Runners-up 1976. Runners-up: 16 times, *Scottish Cup:* Winners: 1892, 1899, 1900, 1904, 1907, 1908, 1911, 1912, 1914, 1923-1925, 1927, 1931, 1933, 1937, 1951, 1954, 1965, 1967, 1969, 1971, 1972, 1974, 1975. Runners-up: 14 times, *Scottish League Cup:* Winners: 1956-57, 1957-58, 1965-66, 1966-67, 1967-68, 1968-69, 1969-70, 1974-75. Runners-up: 5 times. *Record Victory:* 11-0 v Dundee, Division 1, Oct. 26th, 1895. *Record Defeat:* 0-8 Motherwell, Division 1, 1936-37. *Most League Points:* 67, 1915-16, 1921-22. *Most Individual League Goals in Season:* 50, James McGrory, 1935-36. *Most Goals in Total Aggregate:* 397, James McGrory, 1922-39. *Most Capped Player:* Bobby Evans, 48, Scotland.

Hunter, A.	Latchford, P.	McGrain, D.	Lynch, A.	McCluskey, P.	Murray, S.	McDonald, R.	Edvaldsson, J.	Connelly, G.	Glavin, R.	Hood, H.	McNamara, J.	Dalglish, K.	Wilson, P.	Deans, J.	Lennox, R.	Callaghan, T.	Ritchie, A.	Aitken, R.	Casey, J.	McCluskey, G.	Doyle, J.	Burns, T.	Hannah, R.	Match No.
	1	2	3	4		5	6		12	7*	9	8	11†	10			13							1
	1	2	3	4*		5	6		12	7		8	9	6	11	10								2
	1	2	3	4		5	6		12			8	7*	9	11	10								3
	1	2*	3	4		5	6		12			8	7	9	11	10								4
	1	2	3	4		5	6		12	8*			9	7	11	10								5
	1	2	3	4		5	6		12	11		8	7*	9		10								6
	1	2	3	4		5	6		12	11†		8	7	9*	10	13								7
	1	2	3	4		5	6		12			8	11	9	10				7*					8
	1	2	3	4		5	6		7*	10		8	9	11					12					9
	1	2	3	4		5	6			10		8	7	9	11									10
	1	2	3	4		5	6			10		8	7	9	11*	12								11
	1	2	3	4		5	6					8	9	11	10	7								12
	1	2	3	4		5	6					8	7	9	10									13
	1	2	3	4		5	6		7*			8	12	9	11	10								14
	1	2	3	4		5	6		7*	12		8	9	11	10									15
	1	2	3	4		5	6		12			8	7*	9	11	10								16
	1	2	3	6		5	4			7		8	9	11	10									17
	1	2	3	6		5	4			7		8	9	11	10									18
	1	2	3	6		5	4		13	7		8	12	9*	11†	10								19
	1	2	3	6	12	5*	4			7		8	11†	9	13	10								20
	1	2	6	3	8	5	4			7			10	9	11									21
	1	2	6	3	8	5	4			7			10	9	11									22
1	2	3	6			5			12	10		8	7	9	11*	4								23
	1	2	3	4		5	8			10		11	9	7	6									24
	1	2	3	4		6	10			8		11	9	12	7*	5								25
	1	2	3	4		6	10			8		7	9	11	5									26
	1	2	3	4		9	6		11	8		10	12		5				7*					27
	1	2	3	4		9*	6		8	10		12	7	11	5									28
	1	2	3	4		9*	6		8	10		12	7	11	5									29
	1	2	3	4			6	7	9*	10	12	8	11		5									30
	1	2				3	4		8	13		9	11†	6	12	5				7*	10			31
	1	2	3	4		6	8		10	7*		9	11		5					12				32
	1	2	3	4		6			8	10		9		5							7	11		33
	1	2	3	4		9	6*		12	8		11		5							7	10		34
	1	2	3	4		6			8			11	9	5							7	10*	12	35
1		2				6	10†		4	12	9*	7	3	8	5							11	13	36
1	35	35	34	34	2	27	35	1	10	7	16	35	18	29	25	22	5	12	1	2	5	5	0	
				+1s		+2s			+7s	+2s		+8s		+5s		+3s		+2s			+2s			

CLYDE

DIV. 2

Year Formed: 1878.
Ground: Shawfield Stadium, Glasgow C.5.   *Size:* 110 × 70 yds.   *Capacity:* 25,000 (2,000 seats).
Telephone: 041-647 6329.
Manager: Stan Anderson.
Secretary: John McBeth.
Coach: Jimmy Rowan.
Club Colours: White shirts with red facings, black shorts.
Club Nickname: 'The Bully Wee'.
Record Attendance: 52,000 v Rangers, Division 1, Nov. 21st, 1908.

1975–76 LEAGUE RECORD

Match No.	Date	Venue	Opponents	League Pos'n	Result	H/T Score	Goalscorers	Attendance
1	Aug 30	H	Dumbarton	—	L 1-2	1-0	Harvey	1500
2	Sept 6	A	Partick T.	14	L 0-1	0-1		5000
3	13	H	St. Mirren	9	W 3-0	2-0	Archibald 2, Boyle	1500
4	20	H	Dunfermline Ath.	12	L 0-2	0-1		800
5	27	A	Kilmarnock	13	L 0-3	0-1		3500
6	Oct 4	A	Falkirk	12	W 2-1	0-1	Boyle, Hood	1500
7	11	H	Airdrieonians	12	D 2-2	0-0	Harvey, Hood	1500
8	18	A	East Fife	13	L 3-4	1-2	John Burns, Ward, Boyle	1856
9	25	H	Montrose	11	W 3-0	2-0	Hood 3	1500
10	Nov 1	A	Hamilton A.	11	D 0-0	0-0		2500
11	8	H	Arbroath	8	W 5-2	2-1	Swan 2, Boyle, Hood 2	1000
12	15	A	Morton	7	D 1-1	0-0	Hamilton	2000
13	22	A	Queen of the S.	7	W 3-1	2-0	Ward 2, Hood	1500
14	29	H	Kilmarnock	7	L 0-2	0-1		3000
15	Dec 6	H	Falkirk	9	L 3-4	1-1	Ahern, Hood 2	1500
16	13	A	Airdrieonians	10	L 1-2	1-0	Hood	2500
17	20	H	East Fife	12	L 0-2	0-1		600
18	27	A	Montrose	13	L 3-4	1-1	Ferris, Hood 2	1400
19	Jan 1	H	Partick T.	—	L 1-2	0-1	Sullivan	3500
20	3	A	St. Mirren	14	L 0-3	0-2		4000
21	17	H	Queen of the S.	14	L 1-3	0-0	Hood	1000
22	Feb 7	A	Dumbarton	14	L 0-1	0-1		2000
23	14	H	Morton	14	L 1-2	0-1	Harvey	2300
24	18	A	Dunfermline Ath.	—	L 1-5	1-4	Boyle	3000
25	21	H	Hamilton A.	14	D 0-0	0-0		1500
26	28	A	Arbroath	14	L 0-3	0-1		1122

Final Place: 14

Goalscorers

League (34): Hood 14, Boyle 5, Harvey 3, Ward 3, Archibald 2, Swan 2, Ahern 1, John Burns 1, Ferris 1, Hamilton 1, Sullivan 1.
League Cup (4): Boyle 3, Millar 1.
Cup (2): Hood 1, Ward 1.
Spring Cup (7): Hood 3, Sullivan 2, Boyd 1, Ward 1.

Honours

Scottish League: Division 2, Champions: 1904–5, 1951–52, 1956–57, 1961–62, 1972–73. Runners-up 1903–4, 1905–6, 1925–26, 1963–64.
Scottish F.A. Cup: Winners: 1939, 1955, 1958. Runners-up: 1910, 1912, 1949.
Scottish League Cup: None.

Record Victory: 11-1 v Cowdenbeath, Division 2, Oct. 6th, 1951.
Record Defeat: 0-11 v Rangers, Scottish Cup, 4th Rd., 1880–81.
Most League Points: 64, Division 2, 1956–57.
Most Individual League Goals in Season: 32, Bill Boyd, 1932–33.

Ross, K.	Cairney, P.	Anderson, E.	Swan, A.	Boyd, J.	Burns, John	Sullivan, D.	Ahern, B.	Burns, Jim	Archibald, S.	Ward, J.	Marshall, G.	Boyle, P.	Ferris, R.	Harvey, R.	Taylor, J.	Hood, N.	Hamilton, G.	Sweeney, S.	Watchman, P.	Grant, A.	Millar, S.	Match No.
	1	2	3	5*	6	7	10	9	13			11	12		8†							1
	1	2	3	5*10	7	9	4	13	8			11	12	6†								2
	1	2	3		10	6	9	4	8	7		11*12		5								3
	1	2	3	12	10	6*	9	4	8	7	13		11†	5								4
	1	2	10	13	3	6	9	4	8*12			11†		7	5							5
	1	2	10	3*12	7	6			13			11		8†	4	9	5					6
	1	2	10*	12†	3	7	6		13			11		8	4	9	5					7
	1	2	10†	13	3	7	6		12			11		8	4	9	5*					8
	1	2	10*		3	7	6		12			11		8	4	9	5					9
	1	2	10		3	7	6		12			11		8*	4	9	5					10
	1	2	10		3	12	7*	6	13			11		8†	4	9	5					11
	1	2	10		3	7	6		8			11*	12		4	9	5					12
	1	2	10		3*12	7	6		8			11			4	9	5					13
	1	2	10		3	13	7	6	8†		12	11			4*	9	5					14
	1	2*	3		10	4	7	6	13			11		8†12		9	5					15
	1	2	3			6	7*	4	8†11	13	12				10	9	5					16
	1	2	10		3	7	6		12			11†		8	13	4*	9	5				17
	1	2	6	3	7	4	8*	10	11†13		12					9	5					18
	1	2	6	3	7	4	8	10	11							9	5					19
	1	2*	6	3	7	4	8	11	10†13		12					9	5					20
	1	2	6	3	7†	4	8	10	11	13	12					9	5*					21
	1	2	6	3		4	8	10	11†			7*12				9	5		13			22
	1	2	6	3*	7	4	8	10	11		12					9	5					23
1		2	6		7	3	4	10	13	11†						9	5		8*12			24
	1	2	6	3	10	4	8				12	11*				9	5			7		25
	1	2	6		10†	4	3	9	12	11						5	13		8*	7		26
1	25	25	16	11	18	12	25	26	14	13	4	22	1	11	16	20	21	0	2	2	1	
			+2s	+2s	+4s		+2s	+11s	+1s	+2s	+9s	+6s	+1s					+2s		+1s		

CLYDEBANK

Year Formed: 1965. *Ground:* Kilbowie Park. *Size:* 110 × 68 yds. *Capacity:* 13,500.
Telephone: 041 952 2887. *Secretary:* John S. Steedman. *Team Manager:* W. Munro.
Club Colours: Red shirts with broad white vertical stripe on front, black shorts, white stockings.
Club Nickname: The 'Bankies'.
Record Attendance: 14,900 v Hibs., Scottish Cup, 1st Rd., Feb. 10th, 1965.

1975–76 LEAGUE RECORD

Match No.	Date	Venue	Opponents	League Pos'n	Result	H/T Score	Goalscorers	Attendance
1	Aug 30	H	Brechin C.	—	W 3-0	1-0	Hall, Hay, Larnach	1400
2	Sep 6	A	Stirling Albion	1	W 1-0	1-0	McCallan	300
3	13	H	Cowdenbeath	1	W 3-0	2-0	McCallan 2, Caskie	1200
4	20	A	Stranraer	1	W 1-0	1-0	McCallan	1500
5	27	A	Berwick R.	1	W 4-0	1-0	Larnach, McCallan, Laing (og), Davidson (og)	350
6	Oct 4	H	Raith R.	1	D 1-1	0-0	Goodwin	1200
7	11	A	Albion R.	1	W 4-0	1-0	Goodwin, Cooper, Larnach 2	1500
8	18	H	Stenhousemuir	1	W 2-1	0-1	Cooper, McCallan	1500
9	25	H	Queen's Park	1	D 1-1	1-1	Cooper	1800
10	Nov 1	H	East Stirling	1	W 3-0	0-0	Hay 2, Cooper	2000
11	8	A	Forfar Ath.	1	W 2-0	1-0	Larnach, Brash (og)	490
12	15	A	Meadowbank T.	1	D 0-0	0-0		500
13	22	H	Alloa	1	W 3-1	1-0	Cooper 3 (2 pens)	3000
14	29	H	Berwick R.	1	L 0-1	0-0		2000
15	Dec 6	A	Raith R.	1	L 0-1	0-0		2526
16	13	H	Meadowbank T.	1	W 2-0	0-0	McCallan 2	1000
17	20	A	Stenhousemuir	1	L 1-2	0-2	Cooper	2500
18	27	A	Queen's Park	1	W 2-0	2-0	Cooper 2	1100
19	Jan 1	H	Stirling Albion	—	W 1-0	1-0	Cooper	1800
20	3	A	Cowdenbeath	1	D 1-1	0-1	Larnach	500
21	31	H	Stranraer	1	W 2-1	0-1	McCallan, Browning	1100
22	Feb 7	A	Brechin C.	1	W 2-1	2-1	Larnach, McCallan	400
23	14	H	Albion R.	1	D 2-2	0-1	Lumsden, Cooper	1000
24	21	A	East Stirling	1	W 1-0	1-0	McCallan	500
25	28	H	Forfar Ath.	1	W 2-0	0-0	Cooper (pen), McCallan	1100
26	Apr 6	A	Alloa	1	D 0-0	0-0		1050

Final Place: 1

Goalscorers

League (44): Cooper 13 (3 pens), McCallan 12, Larnach 7, Hay 3, Goodwin 2, Browning 1, Caskie 1, Hall 1, Lumsden 1, own goals 3.
League Cup (12): Larnach 4, McCallan 4, Cooper 2, Abel 1, own goal 1.
Cup (1): Lumsden 1.
Spring Cup (25): Cooper 7 (3 pens), McCallan 5, Hall 4, Browning 2, Larnach 2, Lumsden 2, McColl 2, Provan 1.

Scottish League: Division 2 Champions 1975-76.
Spring Cup: Runners-up 1975-76.
Record Victory: 7-1 v Hamilton, Division 2, Nov. 20th, 1971.
Record Defeat: 0-7 v Falkirk, Scottish League, Division 2, Sept. 20th, 1969
Most League Points: 44, Division 2, 1974-75.

McKenzie, R.	Hall, N.	Abel, G.	Flanning, W.	Fallon, J.	Provan, R.	Goodwin, S.	McColl, W.	Hay, D.	Lumsden, J.	Cooper, D.	Henderson, S.	Larnach, M.	McCallan, J.	Caskie, J.	Browning, I.	Match No.
1	2	3	4	5	12	6*	11	7	8	9	10					1
1	2	3	4	5		6	11	7	8	9	10					2
1	2	3		5	4	8	7	6	9	10	11					3
1	2	3	4	5		6	8	7	11	9	10					4
1	2	3	4	5		6	11	7	8	9	10					5
1	2	3	4	5		11*	6	7	8	9	10	12				6
1	2	3	4	5		6	8	7		9	10	11				7
1	2	3	4	5		6	8	7		9*	10	11	12			8
1	2	3	4	5		6	8	7		9	10	11*	12			9
1	2	3	4	5		6	11	7	8	9	10					10
1	2	3	4	12	5	6	11*	7	8	9	10					11
1	2	3	4	12	5	6	11*	7	8	9	10					12
1	2	3	4	5	12	6*	11	7	8	9	10					13
1	2	3	4	5		6	11	7	8	9	10					14
1	2	3	4	5		6	11	7	8	9	10					15
1	2		4	5	6	3		7	8	9	10	11				16
1	2		4	5	6	3	12	7	8	11*	10		9			17
1	2	3	4	5		6	11	7	8	9	10					18
1	2	3	4	5		6	11	7	8	9	10					19
1	2	3	4*12	5		6		7	8	9	10	13	11†			20
1	2	3	4	5		6	8	7		9	10	11*	12			21
1	2	3	12	4	13	5	6	8	7*		11	10†		9		22
1	2	3	4	5		6	8	11	7		9		10			23
1	2	3	4	5	12	6	11	7	8*	9	10					24
1	2	3	4	5	6	11		7	8	9	10					25
1	2	3	5	4	13	8	6	11†	7		12	10		9*		26
26	26	24	1	25	2	23	4	25	23	26	19	25	26	6	5	
			+1s		+4s	+1s	+3s	+1s				+1s		+2s	+3s	

COWDENBEATH

DIV. 2

Year Formed: 1881. *Ground:* Central Park. *Size:* 110×70 yds. *Telephone:* Cowdenbeath 511205.
Manager: Frank Conners.
Secretary: D. Fowlis. *Club Colours:* Royal blue and white vertical striped shirts, white shorts, white stockings with blue and white tops. *Club Nickname:* 'Cowden'.
Record Attendance: 25,586, v Rangers, League Cup Quarter Final, Sept. 21st, 1949.
Previous Grounds: North End Park, 1881-1917.

1975-76 LEAGUE RECORD

Match No.	Date	Venue	Opponents	League Pos'n	Result	H/T Score	Goalscorers	Atten-dance
1	Aug 30	A	Forfar Ath.	—	D 1-1	0-1	McHale	510
2	Sep 6	H	Raith R.	7	D 1-1	0-0	Murphy	1350
3	13	A	Clydebank	12	L 0-3	0-2		1200
4	20	H	Albion R.	7	W 3-0	2-0	Harrow, Murphy 2	700
5	27	A	Meadowbank T.	5	D 1-1	0-0	Harrow	300
6	Oct 4	H	Stranraer	5	W 2-1	1-1	McHale, Rae T.	250
7	11	A	Stenhousemuir	5	W 2-0	2-0	Murphy, Ross	250
8	18	H	East Stirling	5	L 0-1	0-1		400
9	25	A	Brechin C.	6	W 2-1	1-1	Reid, Harrow	350
10	Nov 1	H	Berwick R.	4	W 3-2	2-0	Laing 3 (1 pen)	400
11	8	H	Alloa	5	L 0-1	0-0		800
12	15	A	Stirling Albion	6	L 2-5	2-1	Laing (pen), Rae A.	800
13	22	A	Queen's Park	7	L 1-4	0-2	Morrison	800
14	29	H	Meadowbank T.	6	W 2-0	0-0	Murphy 2	250
15	Dec 6	A	Stranraer	4	W 4-2	1-2	Rae A., Murphy, Breen, Morrison	850
16	20	H	East Stirling	6	L 2-4	1-1	Seath, Harrow	200
17	27	H	Brechin C.	5	W 5-2	3-2	McHale 2, Harrow, Morrison 2	200
18	Jan 1	A	Raith R.	—	L 1-2	0-1	Murphy	3119
19	3	H	Clydebank	6	D 1-1	1-0	Murphy	500
20	17	H	Queen's Park	6	D 2-2	2-0	Russell, Harrow	500
21	Feb 7	H	Forfar Ath.	6	D 2-2	2-1	Hunter, Rae A.	500
22	21	A	Berwick R.	5	W 1-0	0-0	Harrow	220
23	25	A	Albion R.	—	D 1-1	1-1	Morrison	200
24	28	A	Alloa	6	L 0-4	0-2		680
25	Mar 9	H	Stenhousemuir	—	W 3-1	0-0	McHale, Hunter, Murphy	400
26	Apr 17	H	Stirling Albion	5	W 2-1	0-1	Hunter 2 (1 pen)	350

Final Place: 5

Goalscorers

League (44): Murphy 10, Harrow 7, McHale 5, Morrison 5, Hunter 4 (1 pen), Laing 4 (2 pens), Rae A. 3
Breen 1, Rae T. 1, Reid 1, Ross 1, Russell 1, Seath 1.
League Cup (15): Hunter 4 (1 pen), Harrow 3, Laing 3, Ross 3, McHale 1, Murphy 1.
Cup (5): Murphy 3, Hunter 1 (1 pen), Morrison 1.
Spring Cup (8): Harrow 3, Ross 2, Hunter 1 (1 pen), Morrison 1, Murphy 1.

Honours

Scottish League: Division 2 Champions 1913-14, 1914-15, 1938-39; Runners-up 1921-22, 1923-24, 1969-70.

Record Victory: 12-0 v St. Johnstone, Scottish Cup 1st Rd., Jan 21st., 1928.
Record Defeat: 1-11 v Clyde, Division 2, Oct. 6th, 1951.
Most League Points: 60, Division 2, 1938-39.
Most Individual League Goals in Season: Willie Devlin, 40, Division 1, 1925-26.
Most Capped Player: Alec Venters 1 (3).

Connor, F.	Wilson, W.	Callaghan, W.	Kinnell, A.	Jones, M.	Russell, R.	Seath, J.	Reid, A.	Simpson, W.	McHale, R.	Laing, W.	Hunter, G.	Harrow, A.	Murphy, J.	Ross, D.	Breen, J.	Rae, A.	Morrison, R.	Wilson, P.	Rutherford, K.	Rae, T.	Dick, G.	McPheat, W.	Match No.
1	2	3	4	5	6			7	8	9*10	11	12											1
1	2	5		4		6	7	8	11	10					3				9				2
1	2	5	8	6	4	12		11	10	7*					3				9				3
1		2	8	4	5	12	7*	6	10	11					3				9				4
1		2	8†	4	5	12	13	7*	6	10	11				3				9				5
1	2	3	5	4	6	7*12	8	11†10	13						3				9				6
1	2	13	3	5	4*	6	7†12	8		10	11								9				7
1	2	3	5	6	7	12	8*	10	11	4									9				8
1	2	3*	5	6	7†	9	8	11	10	12	13	4											9
1	2	5	4	13	6*	7	9	12	11	10†		3	8										10
1	2	5	4	6*	7	9†12	11	10	13			3	8										11
1	2	5	4	12	6*	7	9	10	11			3	8										12
1	2*	5	4	12	6	7	13	11	10	3†	8	9											13
1		5	4	8	2	7	11	9	3	6	10												14
1		5	6	4	2	7*11	10	12	3	8	9												15
1		5	6	4	2	7	11	10	3	8	9												16
1		4	5	2	8	7	10	11	3	6	9												17
1		4	5	2	8	7	11	10	3	6	9												18
1		12	4	5	2	8	7*11	10	3	6	9												19
1	2	5	6	4	7*	8	11	9	12	3	10†	13											20
1		12	5	4*	8	2	7	11	10	3	6	9											21
1*		5	4	8	2	12	7	11	10	3	6	9											22
	2	5	6	8	4		11	10	3		9	7									1		23
1*12	2	5	6	8	4		11	9	3	10	7												24
	5	6	4	2	7	12	11*10	3	8	9†13										1			25
1	2	5				7	10	11	3	6	9	4		8									26
1	23	6	4	16	18	23	19	19	13	5	18	24	24	9	21	18	13	1	1	7	1	2	
+1s		+1s	+1s	+1s		+3s	+1s	+3s	+4s	+4s				+5s	+2s				+2s				

DUMBARTON

DIV. 1

Year Formed: 1872. *Ground:* Boghead Park. *Capacity:* 18,000. *Telephone:* Dumbarton 62569.
Manager: Alex Wright.
Secretary: John Hosie.
Club Colours: White with gold horizontal band between two black bands, white shorts and stockings.
Club Nickname: 'Sons'.
Record Attendance: 18,000 v Raith Rovers, Scottish Cup 7th Rd, Mar. 2nd, 1957.
Previous Name: Dumbarton Athletic.

1975–76 LEAGUE RECORD

Match No.	Date	Venue	Opponents	League Pos'n	Result	H/T Score	Goalscorers	Atten-dance
1	Aug 30	A	Clyde	—	W 2-1	0-1	McLean 2	1500
2	Sep 6	H	Falkirk	9	L 1-4	1-3	Bourke	3000
3	13	A	Montrose	10	L 2-3	1-0	McLean 2	1100
4	20	H	Partick T.	13	L 2-3	0-2	Wallace, Bourke	4000
5	27	H	East Fife	12	D 5-5	3-3	Graham, Cook, McLean (pen), Wallace, Bourke	1500
6	Oct 4	A	Airdrieonians	13	L 0-3	0-2		2500
7	11	H	Morton	11	W 4-0	2-0	McAdam 2, Wallace, Bourke	3000
8	18	A	St Mirren	12	L 2-3	0-1	Bourke 2	3500
9	25	H	Queen of the S.	12	W 2-1	2-0	McAdam 2	1500
10	Nov 1	A	Arbroath	7	W 5-1	2-0	Cook, McLean 2, Wallace, Bourke	1682
11	8	H	Dunfermline Ath.	6	W 2-0	1-0	Wallace, Bourke	2000
12	15	H	Hamilton A.	5	W 5-1	3-1	Brown A., Muir 2, McLean, Bourke	2000
13	22	A	Kilmarnock	6	L 0-1	0-1		5000
14	29	A	East Fife	6	L 1-2	1-1	Brown A.	1493
15	Dec 6	H	Airdrieonians	7	D 0-0	0-0		1500
16	13	A	Morton	7	D 1-1	0-0	Cook	2500
17	20	H	St. Mirren	7	W 2-0	1-0	Wallace, Bourke	3000
18	27	A	Queen of the S.	7	L 2-4	2-2	McLean, Bourke	2000
19	Jan 1	A	Falkirk	—	L 2-3	2-2	Cook, Bourke	3000
20	3	H	Montrose	10	L 0-6	0-3		2000
21	17	H	Kilmarnock	9	W 3-0	1-0	Muir, Bourke 2	3500
22	31	A	Partick T.	9	D 0-0	0-0		6000
23	Feb 7	H	Clyde	7	W 1-0	1-0	Bourke	2000
24	21	H	Arbroath	6	W 3-2	2-0	Muir, McLean, Wallace	2500
25	28	A	Dunfermline Ath.	4	W 3-0	2-0	Wallace, Bourke 2	2500
26	Mar 15	A	Hamilton A.	4	W 3-2	1-1	Cook, Kane, Wallace	1500

Final Place: 4

Goalscorers

League (53): Bourke 17, McLean 10 (1 a pen), Wallace 9, Cook 5, McAdam 4, Muir 4, Brown A. 2, Graham 1, Kane 1.
League Cup (5): Bourke 1, Brown J. 1, Cook 1, McAdam 1, McLean 1.
Cup (5): Muir 2, Wallace 2, own goal 1.
Spring Cup (25): Bourke 8, Wallace 6, Brown A. 2, Graham 2, Harvey 2, Cook 1, McKinley 1, McLeod 1, Muir 1 (pen), own goal 1.

Honours

Original members of Scottish League 1890.

Scottish League: Division 1 Champions 1890–91 (shared with Rangers), 1891–92; Division 2 Champions 1910–11, 1971–72.

Scottish Cup: Winners 1883; Finalists 1881, 1882, 1887, 1891, 1897.

Record Victory: 8-0 v Cowdenbeath, Division 2, March 28th, 1964.
Record Defeat: 1-11 v Ayr United, League Cup, August 13th, 1952.
Most League Points: 52, Division 2, 1971–72.
Most Individual League Goals in Season: Kenny Wilson, 38, Division 2, 1971–72
Most Capped Player: John Lindsay, 18, Scotland; James McAulay, 18, Scotland.

Williams, L.	Brown, A.	Watt, D.	Mullen, T.	Ruddy, D.	Muir, J.	McKinley, C.	Graham, J.	Cook, J.	McLean, H.	Cushley, J.	Kane, G.	McAdam, T.	Coleman, P.	Wallace, L.	Bourke, J.	Bennett, A.	Brown, J.	McNeil, D.	Mathie, R.	Smith, W.	McLeod, M.	Brown, B.	
1	3	2		5	4	6	7	8				9		10	11								1
1	3	2*		5†	4	6	7	8				9		10	11	12	13						2
1	2	3			4†	5	6	11	10			8	13					7*	12	9			3
1		3			4	6	10	12	11			2	7	9	8*			5					4
1		3			4	6	7	8				9	2	10	11			5					5
1	3				12	13	6†	7	8	5*		9	2	10	11					4			6
1	2	3			6	7	8	9	10†				13		11			5*		4	12		7
1	2	3			5	9	7	8	4					10	11			6					8
1		3	2		5	6	7*	8				9		10	11					4	12		9
1	10	3	2		5	6	7	8						11	9					4			10
1	8	3	2		5*	6	7	11						10	9					4	12		11
1	8†	3	2		6	7*		11						10	9			5		4	12	13	12
1	8	3	2		5	6	7	11*						10	9					4	12		13
1	8	3	2		5	6		11	7					10	9					4			14
1	8	3	2		5		11*		7					10	9			6		4	12		15
1	8	3			6	5		11	7					10	9			2		4			16
1	8†	3			6	5	13	11	7*					10	9			2		4	12		17
1	8	3			6	5*	12	11	7					10	9			2		4			18
1	8	3			6*	5	12	11	7					10	9			2*		4		13	19
1	2	3	12		6		7	11						10	9			5		4	8*		20
1		3	2		6	5	11	7	8					10	9					4			21
1	8	3	2		6	5	11	7						10	9					4			22
1	8	3	2		6	5	11	7						10	9					4			23
1	3*	2			6	5	11	7	8					10	9			12		4			24
1	8	3	2		6*		11	7	13				12	10*	9			5		4			25
1	6†	3	2			5	11	7	8			12		10	9*			13		4			26
26	19	25	10	2	18	19	22	25	21	2	0	6	5	25	25	1	1	11	1	21	1	0	
	+2s	+1s	+1s	+3s	+1s	+1s		+1s						+1s	+2s	+1s	+3s			+6s	+3s		

DUNDEE

Year Formed: 1893.
Ground: Dens Park.   *Size:* 110 × 75 yds.   *Capacity:* 38,500 (4,750 seats).
Telephone: Dundee 86104.
Manager: David White.   *Coach:* Harold Davis.
Secretary: Ian Gellatly.   *Physiotherapist:* Eric Ferguson.
Club Colours: Dark blue shirts, white shorts, red stockings.
Club Nickname: 'Dark Blues' or 'The Dee'.
Record Attendance: 43,024, v Rangers, Scottish Cup, 1953.
Previous Name: East End and 'Our Boys' amalgamated to become Dundee in 1893.
Previous Ground: Caroline Park 1893–98.
European Competitions Entered: European Cup, 1962–63 (semi-final); Cup Winners Cup, 1964–65; Fairs Cup, 1967–68 (semi-final), UEFA Cup 1971–72, 1973–74, 1974–75.
Record Transfer Fee Received: £140,000 from Tottenham H. for John Duncan, Oct. 1974.

1975–76 LEAGUE RECORD

Match No.	Date	Venue	Opponents	League Pos'n	Result	H/T Score	Goalscorers	Attendance
1	Aug 30	H	Aberdeen	—	W 3-2	1-2	Gemmell (pen), Ford, Hoggan	6067
2	Sept 6	A	Celtic	8	L 0-4	0-1		25,000
3	13	H	Hearts	9	L 2-3	2-1	Johnston, Martin	6707
4	20	A	Ayr U.	10	L 1-2	0-0	Wallace	4024
5	27	H	Rangers	9	D 0-0	0-0		15,087
6	Oct 4	A	Hibernian	10	D 1-1	1-0	Wallace	8708
7	11	H	St. Johnstone	8	W 4-3	2-2	Wallace, Gordon, Hoggan 2 (2 pens)	5316
8	18	A	Dundee U.	6	W 2-1	1-1	Wallace, Hoggan (pen)	11,327
9	25	H	Motherwell	6	L 3-6	1-3	Strachan (pen), Wallace, Gordon	6853
10	Nov 1	A	Aberdeen	9	L 0-2	0-0		6312
11	8	H	Celtic	8	W 1-0	0-0	Robinson	16,456
12	15	A	Hearts	7	D 1-1	1-0	Strachan	10,000
13	22	H	Ayr U.	7	D 2-2	0-0	Strachan, Gordon	5132
14	29	A	Rangers	7	L 1-2	1-2	Wallace	15,000
15	Dec 6	H	Hibernian	7	W 2-0	0-0	Caldwell 2	7360
16	13	A	St. Johnstone	6	W 3-1	1-0	Wallace 3	3500
17	20	H	Dundee U.	6	D 0-0	0-0		9957
18	27	A	Motherwell	7	L 2-3	0-3	Laing, Wallace	7169
19	Jan 1	H	Aberdeen	—	L 1-3	1-2	Hutchinson	10,009
20	3	A	Celtic	7	D 3-3	1-2	Hoggan, McIntosh, Lynch (og)	21,000
21	10	H	Hearts	7	W 4-1	0-0	Martin, Robinson, Wallace, Hutchinson	6758
22	17	A	Ayr U.	7	L 1-3	0-1	Hutchinson	4378
23	31	H	Rangers	7	D 1-1	0-0	Johnston	14,407
24	Feb 7	A	Hibernian	7	L 0-4	0-1		9241
25	21	H	St. Johnstone	6	W 3-0	0-0	Strachan 2 (1 pen), Wallace	4114
26	28	A	Dundee U.	7	L 0-1	0-0		10,408
27	Mar 13	A	Aberdeen	6	W 1-0	0-0	Hutchinson	6460
28	20	H	Celtic	6	L 0-1	0-0		14,830
29	27	A	Hearts	7	L 0-3	0-1		8500
30	Apr 3	H	Ayr U.	9	L 1-2	0-0	Strachan (pen)	4149
31	10	A	Rangers	9	L 0-3	0-2		25,000
32	14	H	Hibernian	—	D 1-1	0-0	Ford	6054
33	17	A	St. Johnstone	9	D 1-1	0-0	Gemmell (pen)	3410
34	21	H	Dundee U.	—	W 2-1	1-0	Gemmell (pen), Sinclair	13,768
35	24	A	Motherwell	8	D 1-1	1-0	Hutchinson	4675
36	May 1	H	Motherwell	7	W 1-0	0-0	Sinclair	7661

Final Place: 9

Goalscorers
League (49): Wallace 12, Strachan 6 (3 pens), Hoggan 5 (3 pens), Hutchinson 5, Gemmell 3 (3 pens), Gordon 3, Caldwell 2, Ford 2, Johnston 2, Martin 2, Robinson 2, Sinclair 2, Laing 1, McIntosh 1, own goal 1.
League Cup (9): Gemmell 2 (1 pen), Gordon 2, Wallace 2, Caldwell 1, Hoggan 1, own goal 1.
Cup (1): Laing 1.

Honours

Scottish League: Division 1, Champions: 1961–62, Runners-up: 1902–03, 1906–07, 1908–09, 1948–49. Division 2, Champions: 1946–47.
Scottish Cup: Winners: 1910, Runners-up: 1925, 1952, 1964.
Scottish League Cup: Winners: 1951–52, 1952–53, 1973–74. Runners-up: 1967–68.

Record Victory: 10-0 v Alloa, Division 2, March 8th, 1947 and v Dunfermline, Division 2, March 22nd 1947.
Record Defeat: 0–11 v Celtic, Division 1, Oct. 26th, 1895.
Most League Points: 54, Division 1, 1961–62.
Most Individual League Goals in Season: 38, Dave Halliday, 1923–24.
Most Capped Player: Alex Hamilton, 24, Scotland.

Allan, T.	Wilson, R.	Johnston, D.	Gemmell, T.	Ford, R.	Caldwell, A.	Stewart, G.	Phillip, I.	Martin, J.	Robinson, R.	Strachan, G.	Bavidge, M.	Purdie, I.	Laing, D.	Wallace, G.	Gordon, A.	Hoggan, W.	Sinclair, E.	Anderson, I.	Hutchinson, R.	Mackie, G.	McIntosh, D.	Hendrie, T.	McPhail, J.	Match No.
1	2	3*13	4			5†	6	8				11			9	7	12	10						1
1	2	3 13	4			5	6*	8				11			9	7	12	10†						2
1		3	4 13	5	6	2		8*				11†		12	10	7	9							3
1		3	4	5	6	2		12				11		9	10	7*	8							4
1		3	4		5	2	6	12				11		9	10*	7	8							5
1	2	3	6 12	5			4					11		9	10	7	8*							6
1	2	3	6		5 12		4					11	7	9	10*	8								7
1	2	3	6		5*12		4					11	7	9	10	8								8
1	2	3	6		5 12		4*	8†				11	7	9	10				13					9
1	2	3*	6 12	5 13			4	8†				11	7	9	10									10
1		3	6	4	2	5				8	7	11		9	10									11
1		3	6	4	2	5				8	7	11		9	10									12
1		3	6	4	2*	5				8†	7	11		9	10	12			13					13
1		3	6	4	2	5					8†	11		9	10	7*			12	13				14
1		3	6	10	2	5				8		11		9		7				4				15
1		3	6	10	2	5				8		11		9		7				4				16
1		3	6	10	2	5				8†		11		9	13	7*			12	4				17
1		3*	6 12	2	5	8			13			11	9			7†			10	4				18
1			3* 4	2	5	6		12	8			7	9						11	10				19
1			8	2*	5†	6			10			7	9	13	12				11	3	4			20
1			8		5	4		2*12	10			7	9						11	3	6			21
1			8		5	4		2*13	10			7	9		12				11	3	6†			22
1		3	8	2	5	4						11	9						10	6	7			23
1		3	4		5	6	2	8	10†			12	11	9*13								7		24
1		3	4	5		6	2	8	7			11	9						10					25
1		3 5	6		4	2	8	7				12	11	9*					10					26
1	2	3	6		5		4	12				11*	9	8					10	7				27
1	2*	3 12	6		5		4					11	9	8					10	7				28
1	2	3*	6		5		4	12				11†	7	13	8				9	10				29
1	2	3	4*	5	6		8	12	13			11	9						10	7†				30
1	2	3 6	4*		5		8†	13				7	9						11	10		12		31
1	2	3 6	7		5							12	9		8				11	10*		4		32
1	2	3 6	7		5							11†13	9*	12	8				10			4		33
1	2	3 6	8		5							11			7	9			10			4		34
1	2	3 6	8		5							12 11			7*	9			10			4		35
1	2	3 6	8		5							11			7	9			10			4		36
36	17	32	16	29	18	25	23	10	17	17	0	22	18	29	17	16	9	2	18	14	4	2	5	
		+3s	+1s	+3s		+4s		+3s	+6s	+3s	+3s	+1s	+2s	+3s	+4s	+3s			+3s	+1s		+1s		

543

DUNDEE UNITED

Year Formed: 1910 as Dundee Hibernians, became Dundee U. in 1923.
Ground: Tannadice Park. *Size:* 110×74 yds. *Capacity:* 28,500 (2,500 seats).
Telephone: Dundee 86289.
Secretary: Mrs Helen Lindsay *Physiotherapist:* Andy Dickson.
Manager: Jim McLean.
Club Colours: All tangerine with black facings.
Club Nickname: 'Terrors'.
Record Attendance: 28,000, v Barcelona, Fairs Cup, 1966.
European Competitions Entered: Fairs Cup, 1966–67, 1969–70, 1970–71. European Cup Winners' Cup: 1974-75, U.E.F.A. Cup: 1975-76.
Record Transfer Fee Received: £100,000 from Aston Villa for Andy Gray.

1975–76 LEAGUE RECORD

Match No.	Date	Venue	Opponents	League Pos'n	Result	H/T Score	Goalscorers	Atten-dance
1	Aug 30	A	St. Johnstone	—	L 0-1	0-0		3300
2	Sep 6	H	Hibernian	5	W 1-0	1-0	Payne (pen)	7000
3	13	A	Aberdeen	2	W 3-1	2-1	Copland, Sturrock, Hegarty	5500
4	20	H	Motherwell	3	D 1-1	0-1	Sturrock	5600
5	27	A	Celtic	4	L 1-2	0-0	Payne (pen)	21,000
6	Oct 4	H	Ayr U.	4	W 3-2	2-0	Houston, Hall, Addison	3000
7	11	A	Hearts	5	L 0-1	0-1		9000
8	18	H	Dundee	8	L 1-2	1-1	Houston	11,327
9	Nov 1	H	St. Johnstone	7	W 3-1	1-0	Hegarty (pen), McAdam 2	4850
10	8	A	Hibernian	7	D 1-1	0-1	McAdam	10,600
11	12	A	Rangers	—	L 1-4	0-1	Sturrock	10,000
12	15	H	Aberdeen	8	L 1-2	0-1	Hegarty	4704
13	22	A	Motherwell	9	L 1-2	1-0	McAdam	6328
14	29	H	Celtic	9	L 1-3	0-1	Hegarty	10,000
15	Dec 6	A	Ayr U.	9	D 2-2	2-0	Hall, McAdam	4764
16	13	H	Hearts	9	L 0-1	0-1		4865
17	20	A	Dundee	9	D 0-0	0-0		9957
18	27	H	Rangers	9	D 0-0	0-0		11,500
19	Jan 1	A	St. Johnstone	—	D 1-1	1-0	Rolland	4825
20	10	A	Aberdeen	9	L 3-5	0-2	Hegarty, Reid 2 (1 pen)	9581
21	17	H	Motherwell	9	L 1-4	1-1	Copland	5200
22	31	A	Celtic	9	L 1-2	1-2	Hall	18,000
23	Feb 21	A	Hearts	9	W 1-0	0-0	Hall	9500
24	28	H	Dundee	9	W 1-0	0-0	McAdam	10,408
25	Mar 3	H	Ayr U.	—	W 5-0	3-0	Hegarty, McAdam 3, Reid	3300
26	20	A	Hibernian	8	W 1-0	1-0	Hall	6720
27	27	H	Aberdeen	8	W 1-0	0-0	Fleming	4875
28	31	A	St. Johnstone	—	D 1-1	0-0	Hegarty	2500
29	Apr 3	A	Motherwell	8	L 2-3	1-1	Hall, Fleming	3829
30	10	H	Celtic	7	W 3-2	1-0	Fleming, McAdam 2	12,771
31	14	A	Ayr U.	—	L 0-1	0-0		5200
32	17	H	Hearts	6	W 2-0	1-0	Hegarty, McAdam	6598
33	21	A	Dundee	—	L 1-2	0-1	Hall	13,768
34	24	H	Rangers	9	L 0-1	0-1		17,000
35	28	H	Hibernian	—	W 2-0	2-0	McAlpine (pen), Hall	6500
36	May 4	A	Rangers	—	D 0-0	0-0		40,000

Final Place: 8

Goalscorers

League (46): McAdam 12, Hall 8, Hegarty 8, Fleming 3, Reid 3 (1 pen), Sturrock 3, Copland 2, Houston 2, Payne 2 (2 pens), Addison 1, McAlpine 1 (pen), Rolland 1.
League Cup (8): Steele 3 (1 pen), Gray 2, Hall 1, Narey 1, Sturrock 1.
Cup (5): Hall 2, Hegarty 1, McAdam 1, Payne 1.

544

Honours
Scottish League: Division 2, Champions: 1924–25, 1928–29. Runners-up: 1930–31, 1959–60.
Scottish Cup: Runners-up: 1973–74.
Scottish League Cup: None.

Record Victory: 14–0 v Nithsdale Wanderers, Scottish Cup, 1st Rd. Jan. 17th, 1931.
Record Defeat: 1–12 v Motherwell, Division 2, 1953–54.
Most League Points: 51, Division 2, 1928–29.
Most Individual League Goals in Season: 41, John Coyle, Division 2, 1955–56.
Most Capped Player: Orjan Persson, 3 (11), Sweden.

McAlpine, H.	Rolland, A.	Kopel, F.	Holt, J.	Houston, D.	Smith, D.	Copland, J.	Rennie, A.	Narey, D.	Hall, H.	Smith, W.	McDonald, I.	Payne, G.	Forsyth, A.	Gray, A.	Fleming, G.	Addison, D.	Steele, W.	Sturrock, P.	Hegarty, P.	Traynor, T.	McAdam, T.	Knox, A.	Reid, A.	Match No.
1	12	2		3		4	5	6	11†						9	10	8		13	7*				1
1	2	3		10		4	7	6				5			8				9				11	2
1	2	3		10		4	7	6†				5*			8				9		11	12	13	3
1	2	3		5		4			7			10			8	6			9				11	4
1	2	3		5			7	6	10*			12			8	4			9				11	5
1	2	3		5			7	6	10						8	4			9				11	6
1	2	3		5			7	6	10*			13		12†	8	4			9				11	7
1	2	13	5				7	6					4*		8		5	12			10		11	8
1	2	13	5				4	6	7*					3	8			12	9		10†		11	9
1	2	12	7	6			5						4	3	8				9		10		11*	10
1	2	3	7	11			4	6				5*			8			12	9		10			11
1	2		7	5			4	6						3*	8	11		12	9		10			12
1	2		7	3		4	5	6				12			8		11		9		10*			13
1	2		5			4	7	6						3	8	12	11		9		10*			14
1	3	2		5		4	7	6				11			8			12	9		10*			15
1		3	12	5*		4	7	6	10			11†			8	2		13	9					16
1	2	3	7	5			4	6				11*			8			12	9		10			17
1	2	3	7	5			4	6				11*			8			12	9		10			18
1	2	3	7	5			4	6				12			8				9		10*		11	19
1	2	3	7	5			4*	6							8			12	9		10		11	20
1	2		7	3		5	4	6				12					11†	13	9		10	8*		21
1	2		8	3		5	4	6	7*			13					11†	12	9		10			22
1	2	3		5				6	7			11	4		8				9		10			23
1	2	3	11	5				6	7				4		8				9		10			24
1	2	3	13	5				6	7*				4		8			12	9		10	11†		25
1	2	3		5				6	7				4		8				9		10		11	26
1	2	3		5				6	7				4		8			12	9		10*		11	27
1	2	3		5			12	6	7			13	4*		8			10†	9				11	28
1	2	3	11	5			4	6	7			12			8				9		10*			29
1	2	3		5		11		6	7				4		8				9		10			30
1	2	3		5			11*	6	7				4		8				9		10	12		31
1	2	3		5				6	7				4		8				9		10		11	32
1	2	3		5			11*	6	7				4		8				9		10	12		33
1	2	3		5		11		6	7				4		8				9		10			34
1	2	3		5		11		6	7				4		8				9		10			35
1	2	3		5*		11	12	6	7				4		8				9		10			36
36	32	29	13	33	7	13	25	33	25	2	1	15	14	3	30	3	4	10	31	1	26	2	8	
+1s	+1s	+3s					+2s		+1s			+2s	+4s		+2s			+6s	+7s		+2s	+2s	+2s	

DUNFERMLINE ATHLETIC DIV. 2

Year Formed: 1885.
Ground: East End Park. *Size:* 112×72 yds. *Capacity:* 27,500 (3,000 seats).
Telephone: Dunfermline 24295.
Manager: Harry Melrose. *Physiotherapist* Jim Stevenson.
Secretary: Jim McConville J.P.
Club Colours: White shirts with vertical black candy stripes, black shorts.
Club Nickname: 'The Pars'.
Record Attendance: 27,816, v Celtic, Division 1, 1968.
European Competitions Entered: Cup Winners Cup, 1961–62, 1968–69; Fairs Cup, 1962–63, 1964–65, 1965–66, 1966–67, 1969–70.

1975–76 LEAGUE RECORD

Match No.	Date	Venue	Opponents	League Pos'n	Result	H/T Score	Goalscorers	Attendance
1	Aug 30	H	Airdrieonians	—	D 3-3	0-0	Markey, Mackie, Cowan (og)	3000
2	Sep 6	A	East Fife	12	L 1-5	0-2	Reid	2285
3	13	H	Hamilton A.	13	L 0-4	0-2		2500
4	20	A	Clyde	11	W 2-0	1-0	Dunn, Shaw	800
5	27	H	St. Mirren	10	D 2-2	0-2	Shaw 2	2500
6	Oct 4	A	Morton	10	D 1-1	1-0	Hunter	600
7	11	H	Queen of the S.	10	D 2-2	0-1	Adair, Hall	3000
8	18	A	Montrose	9	D 2-2	0-1	Shaw 2	1500
9	25	H	Falkirk	9	D 2-2	2-0	Scott, Hall	4000
10	Nov 1	A	Partick T.	9	D 1-1	0-1	Shaw	4000
11	8	A	Dumbarton	12	L 0-2	0-1		2000
12	15	H	Kilmarnock	10	W 1-0	0-0	Evans	3000
13	22	H	Arbroath	13	L 0-1	0-0		2500
14	29	A	St. Mirren	13	L 0-2	0-0		2500
15	Dec 6	H	Morton	12	W 1-0	0-0	Mackie	2500
16	13	A	Queen of the S.	12	L 2-5	1-1	Hall, Mackie	2000
17	20	A	Montrose	10	W 1-0	1-0	Mackie	2000
18	27	A	Falkirk	10	L 1-4	1-3	Mackie	2000
19	Jan 1	H	East Fife	—	D 1-1	1-0	Mackie (pen)	4000
20	3	A	Hamilton A.	11	D 1-1	0-0	Mackie	2000
21	10	A	Kilmarnock	11	L 0-4	0-3		4000
22	17	A	Arbroath	13	L 0-1	0-1		1616
23	Feb 7	A	Airdrieonians	13	D 1-1	1-0	Mackie	2000
24	18	H	Clyde	—	W 5-1	4-1	Mackie 2 (1 pen), Hunter, Georgeson, Taylor (og)	3000
25	21	H	Partick T.	13	L 0-3	0-2		4000
26	28	H	Dumbarton	13	L 0-3	0-2		2500

Final Place: 13

Goalscorers

League (30): Mackie 10 (2 pens), Shaw 6, Hall 3, Hunter 2, Adair 1, Dunn 1, Evans 1, Georgeson 1, Markey 1, Reid 1, Scott 1, Own Goals 2.
League Cup (4): Mackie 2, Shaw 1, Watson 1.
Cup (2): Hunter 1, Reid 1.
Spring Cup (11): Georgeson 4, Scott 2, Smith 2, Reid 1, Watson 1, Own Goal 1.

Honours

Scottish League: Division 2, Champions: 1925–26. Runners-up: 1912–13, 1933–34, 1954–55, 1957–58, 1972–73.

Scottish Cup: Winners: 1961, 1968. *Finalists:* 1965.

Scottish League Cup: Finalists: 1949–50.

Record Victory: 11-2 v Stenhousemuir, Division 2, 1930–31.

Record Defeat: 0-10 v Dundee, Division 2, March 22nd, 1947.

Most League Points: 59, Division 2, 1925–26.

Most Individual League Goals in Season: 31, Alec Ferguson, 1965–66 (Div. 1), 55, Bobby Skinner 1925–26 (Div. 2).

Most capped player: Andy Wilson, 6 (12) (Scotland); Geir Karlsen, 26 (Norway).

Barclay, G.	Scott, J.	Markey, J.	Thomson, K.	Adair, G.	Evans, A.	Kinninmonth, A.	Dunn, L.	Reid, A.	Hall, I.	Mackie, K.	Smith, D.	Shaw, G.	Cameron, R.	Watson, K.	Leishman, J.	Mercer, J.	Petrie, D.	Hunter, A.	Meakin, J.	Laing, W.	Georgeson, R.	Match No.
1	8	3	2	4	5	6	7		9		12	10			11*							1
1	8	3	2	4*	5	6	7	12	9			10		11								2
1	2	3	4	6	5	10	8		9*11					7	12							3
1	2	3	4	6	5	10	8	9				11		7								4
1	2	3	4	6	5	10	8†13	9	12			11		7*								5
1	2	3	4	6	5	10		9	7			11	12					8*				6
1	2	3	4	6	5	10*		9	12			11		7				8				7
1	2	3	4	6	5	10	7		9	8*		11	12									8
1	2	3	4	6	5	10	8		9			11		7								9
1	2	3*	4		5	10	8	12	9	13		11		7†			6					10
1	3		4	6*	5	10	8	12	9			11		7			2					11
1	2	3	4		5	10	8	6	9			11		7								12
1	2	3	4		5	10	8		9			11		7					6			13
1	2	3	4		5	10	8	12	9			11		7*					6			14
1	2	3	4	10†5		8	13		12	9*11				7					6			15
1	2	3	4		5	10	8	11	9					7					6			16
1	2	3	4		5	10	8	11	9					7					6			17
1	2	3	4	13	5*12	8		11	9					7					6†			18
1	2		4	6	5			8	9			10		7			3	12	11*			19
1	2*12		4	6	5			8†	9			10		7			3	13	11			20
1	2	12	4	6	5		8*		9					7			3	10	11			21
1	2	3	4	6	5		8		9			11		7*				10	12			22
1	2		3	6	5	8			9			11		7				4	12	10*		23
1	2		3	6*	5	8			9†			11	7	12				13	4	10		24
1	2		3	6*	5	8			9†			11	7					13	4	12	10	25
1	2		3	6	5	8	11*		9				7					12	4		10	26
26	26	18	26	19	26	16	21	3	13	18	2	18	4	24	0	0	5	3	11	3	4	
	+2s	+1s	+1s	+6s	+4s	+1s		+1s	+1s	+1s	+1s						+5s	+3s				

EAST FIFE

DIV. 1

Year Formed: 1903.
Address: Bayview Park, Methil, Fife KY8 3AG, Scotland. Capacity: 25,000.
Telephone: Leven 26323.
Manager: Frank Christie.
Secretary: Tom Clark.
Colours: Gold jerseys, black shorts, white stockings with black and gold tops.
Record Attendance: 22,515, v Raith R., Division 1, Jan. 2nd, 1950.
Club Nickname: 'The Fifers'.

1975–76 LEAGUE RECORD

Match No.	Date	Venue	Opponents	League Pos'n	Result	H/T Score	Goalscorers	Atten-dance
1	Aug 30	A	Montrose	—	L 0-3	0-2		1300
2	Sep 6	H	Dunfermline Ath.	5	W 5-1	2-0	Honeyman, O'Connor, Kinnear 3	2285
3	13	A	Falkirk	6	W 1-0	0-0	O'Connor	4000
4	20	H	Kilmarnock	7	L 2-4	2-2	McPhee, Kinnear	2344
5	27	A	Dumbarton	8	D 5-5	3-3	Miller 2, Kinnear, Hegarty 2	1500
6	Oct 4	H	Arbroath	5	W 3-1	2-0	McPhee, Miller, Hegarty	1685
7	11	A	St. Mirren	7	L 0-2	0-1		2000
8	18	H	Clyde	5	W 4-3	2-1	Rankin (pen), Rutherford, Hegarty 2	1860
9	25	A	Airdrieonians	7	L 0-1	0-0		3000
10	Nov 1	A	Queen of the S.	5	D 1-1	0-0	Gillies (pen)	2000
11	8	H	Morton	7	D 2-2	0-0	Gillies, Honeyman	1893
12	15	A	Partick T.	9	L 0-5	0-3		2500
13	22	A	Hamilton A.	12	L 2-3	2-0	Rutherford, Hegarty	1500
14	29	H	Dumbarton	9	W 2-1	1-1	Rankin (pen), Rutherford	1493
15	Dec 6	A	Arbroath	10	L 1-3	1-2	George	1499
16	13	H	St. Mirren	11	L 0-2	0-1		1548
17	20	A	Clyde	9	W 2-0	1-0	Rutherford, Hegarty	600
18	27	A	Airdrieonians	9	D 1-1	1-1	Rankin	1770
19	Jan 1	A	Dunfermline Ath.	—	D 1-1	0-1	Rutherford	4000
20	3	H	Falkirk	8	W 2-1	2-1	Rutherford, Hegarty	2177
21	10	H	Partick T.	7	D 1-1	1-0	O'Connor	2167
22	17	H	Hamilton A.	8	D 0-0	0-0		1632
23	31	A	Kilmarnock	8	L 1-2	1-1	O'Connor	4500
24	Feb 7	H	Montrose	10	L 1-7	1-4	Rutherford	1482
25	21	H	Queen of the S.	9	W 2-0	1-0	Methven, Rutherford (pen)	1462
26	28	A	Morton	12	L 0-3	0-0		2000

Final Place: 12

Goalscorers

League (39): Hegarty 8, Rutherford 8 (1 pen), Kinnear 5, O'Connor 4, Miller 3, Rankin 3 (2 pens), Gillies 2 (1 pen), Honeyman 2, McPhee 2, George 1, Methven 1.
League Cup (8): Kinnear 2, Miller 2, Gillies 1 (pen), O'Connor 1, Rankin 1, Robertson 1.
Cup (0).
Spring Cup (13): O'Connor 5, Hegarty 2, Kinnear 2, McPhee 2, Rankin 1, own goal 1.

Honours
Scottish League, Division 2, Champions: 1947–48. Runners-up: 1929–30, 1970–71.
Scottish Cup: Winners: 1938 (only Second Division winners). Runners-up: 1927, 1950.
Scottish League Cup: Winners: 1947–48 (only Second Division winners), 1949–50, 1953–54.
Record Victory: 13-2 v Edinburgh City, Division 2, Dec. 11th, 1937.
Record Defeat: 0-9 v Hearts, Division 1, Oct. 5th, 1957.
Most League Points: 57, Division 2, 1929–30.
Most Individual League Goals in a Season: Henry Morris, 41, Division 2, 1947–48.
Most Capped player: George Aitken 5 (8) Scotland.

McGarr, E.	Gillies, W.	Clarke, D.	Clougherty, M.	MacIvor, R.	Methven, C.	George, J.	Rankin, B.	McPhee, W.	Honeyman, G.	O'Connor, D.	Rutherford, A.	Robertson, J.	Miller, R.	Kinnear, H.	Hegarty, K.	Watson, J.	Love, J.	Mellon, S.	Steven, T.	Match No.
1	3	4	6	2	5			10*	8				7	9	11	12				1
1	3	4		2	5			11	8	12			7	9	10*	6				2
1	3	4		2	5			11	8	10	12		7*	9	6					3
1	3	4	13	2	5			11†	8	12	10*		7	9	6					4
1	3	4		2	5			10*	8	12			7	9	11	6				5
1	3	4	8	2	5	6		10					7	9	11					6
1	3	4	8	2	5	6*	11			12				9	7	10				7
1	3	4		2	5	12	6	10	8*					9	11	7				8
1	3	4		2	5	6	12	8	10				9*	11	7					9
1	3	4	12	2	5	6	8	9*	10					11	7					10
1	3	4	8*	2	5	6				11					7	12				11
1	3	4	13	2	5	6*	11	9	8		10				12	7†				12
1		4		2	5	3	12	10	8	9	6				11	7*				13
1		4		2	5	3	6	12	9	8	11*					7	10			14
1		4	12	2	5	3	6	13	9	8*	11†					7	10			15
1		4		2	5	3	6	12	9	8	11*					7	10			16
1		4		2	5	3	6	11*	9	8					7	12	10			17
1		4		2	5	3	6	11*	12	9	8				7		10			18
1		4		2	5	3	6	11†	9	8					7	12	13	10*		19
1	12	4		2	5	3	6	11	9	10					7	8*				20
1		4		2	5	3	6	11*	9	10					7	8	12			21
1		4			5	3	6	11†	9	10	13				7	8*	12		2	22
1		4		2	5	3	6	11†	9*	8					7	13	12	10		23
1		4	6	2	5	3				9	8				11	7*	12	10		24
1		4		2	5	3	6			9	10				11	7	8			25
1		4		2*	5	3	6	13		9	10				11	7†	8	12		26
26	12	25	6	25	26	18	14	17	9	17	19	2	6	9	24	12	7	3	9	
+1s	+4s					+3s	+1s	+4s	+1s	+2s	+3s					+2s	+4s	+4s	+2s	

EAST STIRLING

Year Formed: 1881.   *Ground:* Firs Park.   *Size:* 112×72 yds.   *Capacity:* 12,000.
Telephone: Falkirk 23583.   *Secretary:* J. C. Crawford.   *Manager:* Dan McLindon.
Club Colours: Black and white 1 inch hoops, white shorts, white stockings.   *Club Nickname:* 'The Shire'.
Record Attendance: 11,500 v Hibernian, Scottish Cup, Feb 10 1960.

1975–76 LEAGUE RECORD

Match No.	Date	Venue	Opponents	League Pos'n	Result	H/T Score	Goalscorers	Atten- dance
1	Aug 30	A	Berwick R.	—	W 2-1	0-1	Meakin, Barrowman	402
2	Sep 6	H	Queen's Park	2	W 2-1	1-0	McCulley (pen), Mullin	550
3	13	A	Albion R.	5	L 1-2	0-1	McCulley (pen)	800
4	20	A	Stirling Albion	6	L 2-3	1-0	Hart, Barrowman	930
5	27	H	Brechin C.	4	W 1-0	0-0	Mullin	200
6	Oct 4	A	Alloa	7	L 0-1	0-0		400
7	11	H	Forfar Ath.	6	D 1-1	1-1	Mullin	200
8	18	A	Cowdenbeath	6	W 1-0	1-0	Stein	400
9	25	H	Meadowbank T.	5	W 3-0	2-0	Stein, Soutar, Donnelly	250
10	Nov 1	A	Clydebank	6	L 0-3	0-0		2000
11	8	H	Raith R.	6	D 1-1	1-0	Meakin	800
12	15	A	Stranraer	7	L 1-2	1-1	Murray	1050
13	22	H	Stenhousemuir	9	L 1-3	0-2	Mullin	400
14	29	A	Brechin C.	9	D 2-2	0-1	McCulley, Mullin	300
15	Dec 6	H	Alloa	9	L 0-3	0-2		500
16	20	H	Cowdenbeath	9	W 4-2	1-1	Adams, Soutar, McCulley, Mullin	200
17	27	A	Meadowbank T.	8	W 4-0	2-0	Adams 2, McCulley, McMillan	250
18	Jan 1	A	Queen's Park	—	L 0-1	0-1		1500
19	3	H	Albion R.	8	D 0-0	0-0		500
20	17	A	Stenhousemuir	9	L 1-2	1-2	Soutar	350
21	24	H	Stranraer	7	W 3-1	1-0	Adams, Mullin 2	200
22	31	H	Stirling Albion	7	D 0-0	0-0		250
23	Feb 7	H	Berwick R.	7	D 1-1	1-0	Donnelly	300
24	14	A	Forfar Ath.	6	D 2-2	0-2	Simpson, Murray	350
25	21	H	Clydebank	7	L 0-1	0-1		500
26	28	A	Raith R.	7	D 0-0	0-0		2000

Final Place: 8

Goalscorers

League (33): Mullin 8, McCulley 5 (2 pens), Adams 4, Soutar 3, Barrowman 2, Donnelly 2, Meakin 2, Murray 2, Stein 2, Hart 1, McMillan 1, Simpson 1.
League Cup (6): Mullin 2, Stein 2, McCulley 1 (pen), Meakin 1.
Cup (0).
Spring Cup (4): Rae 3, Adams 1.

Honours
Scottish League: Division 2 Champions 1931–32; Runners-up 1962–63.
Record Victory: 8-2 v Brechin C., Division 2, March 31st, 1962.
Record Defeat: 0-10 v Dundee U., Division 2, March 25th, 1939.
Most League Points: 55, Division 2, 1931–32.
Most Individual League Goals in a Season: Malcolm Morrison, 36, Division 2, 1938–39.

Taylor, R.	Gourlay, T.	Stirling, J.	Campbell, D.	McGregor, J.	Stein, R.	Simpson, G.	Adams, G.	Dunne, P.	Soutar, G.	Hart, G.	McCulley, R.	Donnelly, T.	Meakin, J.	Mullin, J.	Barrowman, A.	Browning, L.	Murray, J.	Rae, T.	McGuiness, J.	McMillan, D.	Match No.
	1	2	12	3	5*	4				11	7	8	9	10†	13	6					1
	1	2	8	3	5					10	7	4	9	12	11*	6					2
	1	2	11	3	5*					8	7	4	9	10		6	12				3
1	2			3	5				13	8	7	4	9†	10	11	12	6*				4
1	2	13	3	12	5	4	6*				8	9	10	11	7†						5
1	2	4*	3	11	5	6	9		12		7†	8	10	13							6
	1	2	8	3	6	4	5					7	10		9	11					7
	1	2		3	6	5	4			11		7	8	9	10						8
	1	2		3	6	5	4			11		7	8	9	10						9
	1	2	13	3	6	5	4			11	8†	7*		9	10		12				10
	1	2		3	11	5	4			6		7*	8	10		9				12	11
	1	2	12	3		5	4*			6		7†	8	9	13	10				11	12
	1	2		3		5	4			6	12	7	8		9	10				11*	13
	1	8	2	3		5	9			6		7	4		10		11				14
	1	8	2	3	12	5	9			6		7	4		10		11*				15
	1	2		3	4		9	5	6	11	7	8		10							16
	1	2		3	4		9	5	6	11*	7	8		10			12				17
	1	2		3†	4	11	5	6	13	7*	8		10	12			9				18
	1	2		3	4		9	5	6	10		8	7	11							19
	1	2		3	4		9	5	6	11	7*	8		10		12					20
	1	2		3	4	8	9	5	6			7	11	10							21
	1	2		3	4		9	5	6	11	7	8		10							22
	1	2		3	4		9	5	6*11	7	8		10		12						23
	1	2		3	4		9	5	6	11*	7	8		10	12						24
	1	2		3	11	4		5	6			7	8	10		9					25
	1	2		3	8	4	10	5	6	11	7			9							26
3	23	26	6	26	17	20	20	12	20	13	23	24	11	20	8	4	6	2	1	1	
			+4s	+2s						+1s	+3s		+2s	+2s	+2s	+5s	+1s		+1s		

FALKIRK

DIV. 1

Year Formed: 1876.
Ground: Brockville Park. Size: 110 × 70 yds. Capacity: 24,000 (2,750 seats).
Telephone: Falkirk 24121.
Manager: George Miller. Physiotherapist/Trainer: Gordon Russell.
Secretary: Charles S. Taylor. P.R.O: William McFarlane.
Club Colours: white shirts, navy blue trimming, white shorts, white stockings.
Club Nickname: 'The Bairns'.
Record Attendance: 23,100, v Celtic, Scottish Cup, 3rd Rd. Feb. 21st, 1953.

1975–76 LEAGUE RECORD

Match No.	Date	Venue	Opponents	League Pos'n	Result	H/T Score	Goalscorers	Attendance
1	Aug 30	H	Arbroath	—	W 1-0	0-0	Wheatley	2500
2	Sep 6	A	Dumbarton	1	W 4-1	3-1	McCaig 2, Whiteford J., Shirra	3000
3	13	H	East Fife	4	L 0-1	0-0		4000
4	20	A	Airdrieonians	6	L 0-2	0-2		4000
5	27	A	Morton	5	W 3-2	2-2	Wheatley, Whiteford J. 2	2500
6	Oct 4	H	Clyde	7	L 1-2	1-0	Hamilton (og)	1500
7	11	A	Partick T.	9	L 2-3	0-1	McCaig, Whiteford J.	4500
8	21	H	Hamilton A.	—	W 1-0	1-0	Whiteford J.	2400
9	25	A	Dunfermline Ath.	6	D 2-2	0-2	Wilson 2	4000
10	Nov 1	H	Kilmarnock	8	L 0-1	0-0		4000
11	8	A	St. Mirren	10	L 0-1	0-0		2600
12	15	H	Queen of the S.	8	W 1-0	0-0	McCaig	2500
13	22	A	Montrose	11	L 1-2	1-0	Shirra	1450
14	29	H	Morton	11	D 3-3	1-2	Whiteford J. (pen), Shirra, Holt	1200
15	Dec 6	A	Clyde	8	W 4-3	1-1	Cameron, Whiteford J. 3 (1 pen)	1500
16	13	H	Partick T.	8	D 0-0	0-0		4000
17	20	A	Hamilton A.	8	L 0-1	0-1		1500
18	27	H	Dunfermline Ath.	8	W 4-1	3-1	Lawson, Whiteford J. 2, Shirra	2000
19	Jan 1	H	Dumbarton	—	W 3-2	2-2	Mitchell, Lawson, Whiteford J. (pen)	3000
20	3	A	East Fife	7	L 1-2	1-2	Shirra	2177
21	10	A	Queen of the S.	8	L 2-3	2-2	Whiteford J. 2 (1 pen)	2000
22	17	H	Montrose	7	W 2-0	1-0	Whiteford J., Wilson	1500
23	31	H	Airdrieonians	6	D 1-1	1-1	Whiteford J.	3000
24	Feb 7	A	Arbroath	5	W 1-0	0-0	Whiteford J.	1385
25	21	A	Kilmarnock	7	L 0-1	0-1		4000
26	28	H	St. Mirren	8	D 1-1	1-0	McLeod	2500

Final Place: 8

Goalscorers

League (38): Whiteford J. 17 (4 pens), Shirra 5, McCaig 4, Wilson 3, Lawson 2, Wheatley 2, Cameron 1, Holt 1, McLeod 1, Mitchell 1, own goal 1.
League Cup (5): Whiteford J. 3 (1 pen), Shirra 1, Wilson 1.
Cup (3): Wheatley 1, Whiteford J. 1, Wilson 1.
Spring Cup (16): Whiteford J. 5 (2 pens), Cameron 3, Fowler 2, Lawson 2, Mitchell 1, Shirra 1, Wheatley 1, own goal 1.

Honours
Scottish League: Division 1, Runners-up: 1907–08, 1909–10.
Division 2, Champions: 1935–36, 1969–70, 1974–75. Runners-up: 1904–5, 1951–52, 1960–61.
Scottish Cup: Winners: 1913, 1957. Scottish League Cup: Runners-up: 1947–48.
Record Victory: 10-0 v Breadalbane, Scottish Cup, 1st Rd. Jan. 13th, 1923 and Jan. 23rd, 1926.
Record Defeat: 1-11 v Airdrieonians, Division 1, April 28th, 1950–51.
Most League Points: 59, Division 2, 1935–36.
Most Individual League Goals in Season: 43, Evelyn Morrison, Division 1, 1928–29.
Most Capped Player: Alec Parker 14 (15), Scotland.

Watson, G.	Donaldson, A.	Kennedy, R. S.	McLeod, T.	Cameron, J.	Gibson, G.	Fowler, J.	Markie, J.	McCaig, D.	Wheatley, S.	Whiteford, D.	Mitchell, J.	Lawson, K.	Whiteford, J.	Shirra, J.	Perry, J.	Holt, A. B.	Wilson, J.	McLoughlin, J.	Match No.
1	2	3	5	9	4		6	8*			10	7	12		11				1
1	2	3	5	11	4	9†	6	8*			10	7	13	12					2
1	2	3	5	9	4	11†	6	8			10*	7	13				12		3
1	2	3	5	8	4		6	11	9		10						12	7*	4
1	2	3	5	13	4	9*	6	10†			12	8	11				7		5
1	2	10	3	5	4		9	6	7*			8	11					12	6
1	2		5	3	4		9	8			10	7	11			6			7
1	2		5	3	12	9†	6	13			10	8	11			7*	4		8
1	2		5	3		9	6				10	8	11			4	7		9
1	2		5	3*	9†	6	12	13			10	8	11			4	7		10
1	2	3	5			6			11	9	8	10				4	7		11
1	2	3	5			11	6		8	9	10					4	7		12
1	2	3	5			11	6		9	8	10					4	7		13
1	2	3	5	11		4			9	8	10					6	7		14
1	2	3	5	11		4			9	8	10					6	7		15
1	2	3	5	11	12	4			9	8*10						6	7		16
1	2	3	5	11*	12	4			9	8	10					6	7		17
1	2	3	5		4			11	10	9	8					6	7		18
1	2	3	5		4			11	9	8	10					6	7		19
1	2	3	5	9	12	4			11*10		8					6	7		20
1	2	11	3	5		4			10	9	8					6	7		21
1	2	3	5		4			11	10	9	8					6	7		22
1	2	11*	3	5		4			12	10	9	8				6	7		23
1	2	11	3	5		4		6*13	10	9	8					12	7†		24
1	2	10	3	5*13	4			11†	9	12	8					6	7		25
1	2	10*	3	5	13	4	12	11†	7	9	8					6			26
6	20	26	6	22	26	13	7	10	22	10	8	23	24	23	1	20	17	2	
			+3s	+1s	+2s	+1s	+3s	+3s	+1s	+1s	+3s					+2s	+1s	+2s	

553

FORFAR ATHLETIC

DIV. 2

Year Formed: 1884. *Ground:* Station Park. *Capacity:* 11,800 (850 seated). *Telephone:* Forfar 3576 and 2817. *Manager:* Jerry Kerr. *Secretary:* James Robertson.
Club Colours: Sky blue shirts, sky blue shorts, sky blue stockings with navy tops.
Club Nickname: 'Loons'.
Record Attendance: 10,780 v Rangers Scottish Cup 2nd Rd, Feb. 2nd, 1970.

1975–76 LEAGUE RECORD

Match No.	Date	Venue	Opponents	League Pos'n	Result	H/T Score	Goalscorers	Attendance
1	Aug 30	H	Cowdenbeath	—	D 1-1	1-0	White	510
2	Sep 6	A	Brechin C.	10	L 1-2	1-1	Hunter	500
3	13	H	Stirling Albion	10	D 0-0	0-0		460
4	20	A	Meadowbank T.	13	L 0-1	0-0		250
5	27	A	Raith R.	12	D 2-2	2-1	Bannon 2	1113
6	Oct 4	H	Stenhousemuir	8	W 3-1	1-1	Brash (pen), Kyles 2	350
7	11	A	East Stirling	10	D 1-1	1-1	Bannon	200
8	18	H	Queen's Park	7	W 4-1	3-1	Bannon, White 2, Boyle	360
9	25	A	Berwick R.	7	D 3-3	2-1	Steen, Bannon, White	350
10	Nov 1	A	Albion R.	9	L 0-4	0-2		800
11	8	H	Clydebank	10	L 0-2	0-1		490
12	15	A	Alloa	11	L 1-2	1-1	Kyles	500
13	22	H	Stranraer	11	L 0-3	0-1		360
14	29	H	Raith R.	12	D 0-0	0-0		450
15	Dec 6	A	Stenhousemuir	11	W 2-1	0-1	Brash, White	300
16	13	A	Stirling Albion	11	L 0-2	0-1		600
17	20	A	Queen's Park	12	L 0-4	0-1		800
18	27	H	Berwick R.	13	L 1-3	0-2	Bannon	350
19	Jan 1	H	Brechin C.	—	L 0-1	0-1		800
20	17	A	Stranraer	14	L 0-4	0-4		760
21	31	H	Meadowbank T.	14	D 1-1	0-0	White	175
22	Feb 7	A	Cowdenbeath	13	D 2-2	1-2	White, Brogan	500
23	14	H	East Stirling	14	D 2-2	2-0	White 2	350
24	21	H	Albion R.	12	W 1-0	0-0	White	250
25	24	H	Alloa	—	D 3-3	2-1	Bannon, Tront 2	350
26	28	A	Clydebank	12	L 0-2	0-0		1100

Final Place: 12

Goalscorers

League (28): White 10, Bannon 7, Kyles 3, Brash 2 (1 a pen), Tront 2, Boyle 1, Brogan 1, Hunter 1, Steen 1.
League Cup (9): Brogan 2, Payne 2, Bannon 1, Boyle 1, Kyles 1, Spink 1, Steen 1.
Cup (3): Brogan 1, Tront 1, White 1.
Spring Cup (5): Kyles 2, Boyle 1, Ritchie 1, Steen 1.

Record Victory: 9-1 v Stenhousemuir, Division 2, 1968–69.
Record Defeat: 2-10 v Dundee, Division 2, 1938–39.
Most League Points: 47, Division 2, 1968–69.
Most Individual League Goals in Season: Davie Kilgour, 45, Division 2, 1929–30.

Milne, J. G.	Miklinski, A.	Lowe, C.	Will, J.	Clark, D.	Ritchie, M. S.	McHugh, J.	Steen, I.	Brash, A.	Hunter, S.	Bannon, J.	Spink, J.	Kyles, J.	Payne, K. M.	White, A.	Brogan, D.	Boyle, P.	Tront, J.	Carnegie, A. S.	Dailey, D.	Match No.
1		2	3	13	4	5	6	7*	12	8†	9	10	11							1
1	13	2*	3		4	6	5	7	12	8†	9	10	11							2
1		2	3		4	5	6	9	11*	8				7		12	10			3
1		2*	3	13	4	5	6		12	8	9			7		11	10†			4
1		2			4	5	6	12	9*	3	11			7		8	10			5
1		2			4	5	6		9	3	11			7		8	10*	12		6
1		2			4	5	6	7	9	3				11		10	8			7
1		2			4	6	5	12	9*	3	11			7		8	10			8
	1	2	12		4	5	6	13	9†	3	11			7		8*	10			9
	1	2			4	5	6		9	3	11			7		8	10*	12		10
	1	2			4	6	5	12	9*	3	11			7		8	10			11
	1	2			4	5	6			3	11			7		8	10		9	12
	1	2	12	5		6		4*13		3	11			7		8	10		9†	13
	1	5	2		4		6		7	3		11				8	10		9	14
	1	5	2	3	4	11	6		9		12		7			10		8*		15
	1	5†	2	3*	4	9	6		13		11	8	7		12	10				16
1		5	2*	3	4	9	6		13		11	8†	7		12	10				17
1			2	3	4	5	6		12		9	8†11		7*10	13					18
	1	2*	3	5	4	8	6			11	12	13	9		10	7†				19
	1	2*	3	8	4	5	6		12		9	7	11		10					20
	1	2	3	4	5	6		9	12	7	10*11		8							21
1		2	3	4	5	6		8	10	11	9		7							22
1		2*	3	4	6	5		9	12	8	10	11		7						23
	1	2	3	4	5	6	9		8		11	10	7							24
	1	3		4	2	5	12		6	10	11	9*	8	7						25
	1	2	3	4	5	6		9	12		10	11	8*	7						26
12	14	7	3	26	11	26	24	26	5	14	14	21	11	25	4	14	24	1	4	
	+1s			+4s						+4s	+9s	+3s	+1s	+1s	+1s		+4s		+2s	

HAMILTON ACADEMICALS DIV. 1

Year Formed: 1875.
Ground: Douglas Park. *Size:* 110 × 72 yds. *Capacity:* 24,000 (1,600 seated).
Telephone: Hamilton 23108.
Manager: J. Eric Smith.
Secretary: Joseph Friel. *P.R.O.:* Alan Dick. *Physiotherapist:* R. Reid. *Coach:* P. Barkey.
Club Colours: Red and White striped shirts, Black shorts with Red stockings.
Club Nickname: 'The Accies'.
Record Attendance: 28,281 v Hearts, Scottish Cup, 3rd Round, Mar. 3rd, 1937.
Previous Grounds: Bent Farm, South Avenue, South Haugh.
Record Transfer Fee Received: £30,000 from Dundee United for Paul Hegarty, November, 1974.

1975–76 LEAGUE RECORD

Match No.	Date	Venue	Opponents	League Pos'n	Result	H/T Score	Goalscorers	Attendance
1	Aug 30	A	Kilmarnock	—	L 2-4	2-4	Thomas 2	4500
2	Sep 6	H	Queen of the S.	6	W 2-0	1-0	Thomas 2	2000
3	13	A	Dunfermline Ath.	3	W 4-0	2-0	Bonnyman, Thomas 2 (2 pens), Lynch	2500
4	20	H	Morton	2	W 2-0	1-0	Thomas (pen), Lynch	3000
5	27	A	Montrose	3	D 1-1	0-1	Campbell	1400
6	Oct 4	H	Partick T.	4	L 1-2	1-0	Thomas (pen)	2500
7	11	A	Arbroath	5	L 1-2	1-2	Thomas (pen)	1550
8	21	A	Falkirk	—	L 0-1	0-1		2400
9	25	H	St. Mirren	10	L 0-1	0-0		2500
10	Nov 1	H	Clyde	10	D 0-0	0-0		2500
11	8		Airdrieonians	9	D 2-2	1-0	Frew, Lynch	4000
12	15	A	Dumbarton	13	L 1-5	1-3	Taylor	2000
13	22	H	East Fife	10	W 3-2	0-2	McGrogan, Robertson, Taylor	1500
14	Dec 6	A	Partick T.	13	L 0-2	0-0		4000
15	13	H	Arbroath	13	L 0-1	0-1		2000
16	20	H	Falkirk	13	W 1-0	1-0	McNicol	1500
17	27	A	St. Mirren	11	D 2-2	1-2	McGrogan, Thomas	4000
18	Jan 1	A	Queen of the S.	—	D 2-2	2-1	McNicol 2	3000
19	3	H	Dunfermline Ath.	12	D 1-1	0-0	Lynch	2000
20	17	A	East Fife	12	D 0-0	0-0		1632
21	31	A	Morton	11	W 4-1	2-0	McGrogan, Lynch, Robertson 2	1000
22	Feb 7	H	Kilmarnock	11	D 1-1	0-0	Bonnyman	3000
23	21	A	Clyde	11	D 0-0	0-0		1500
24	23	H	Montrose	—	D 3-3	1-1	Young, Thomas, Paterson	1500
25	28	H	Airdrieonians	9	W 2-1	0-1	Thomas (pen), Paterson	2500
26	Mar 15	H	Dumbarton	9	L 2-3	1-1	Thomas 2	1500

Final Place: 9

Goalscorers

League (37): Thomas 14 (6 pens), Lynch 5, McGrogan 3, McNicol 3, Robertson 3, Bonnyman 2, Paterson 2, Taylor 2, Campbell 1, Frew 1, Young 1.
League Cup (6): Bonnyman 1 (pen), Edgar 1, Hood 1, Lannon 1, McGrogan 1, Thomas 1.
Cup (0).
Spring Cup (12): Thomas 4 (1 a pen), Hughes 3, McDougall 3, Canning 1, Lynch 1.

Honours
Scottish League: Division 2 Champions: 1903–04, Runners-up: 1952–53, 1964–65.
Scottish Cup: Runners-up; 1911, 1935.
Record Victory: 10–2 v Cowdenbeath, Division One, 1932–33.
Record Defeat: 1–11 v Hibernian, Division One, 1965–66.
Most League Points: 55, Division Two, 1973–74.
Most League Goals: 87, Division One, 1934–35.
Most Individual League Goals in a Season: 34, David Wilson, 1936–37.
Highest scorer in total aggregate: 246, David Wilson, 1928–39.
Most Capped Player: Jimmy King 2, Scotland.

Ferguson, R.	Frew, J.	McGrogan, J.	McMillan, A.	Bonnyman, P.	Lannon, B.	Young, A.	Campbell, I.	Hamilton, G.	Hughes, A.	McQuade, J.	Hood, N.	Brand, J.	Thomas, W.	Lynch, E.	Edgar, R.	Hendry, J.	McDowell, G.	Welsh, F.	McNicol, W.	Robertson, R.	Taylor, A.	Fairlie, J.	McCluskey, S.	McLean, G.	Baillie, M.	Jamieson, J.	Paterson, T.	McDougall, E.	
1	2	11†	3	5	6	13	8	4		9	12		7				10*												1
1	2	6*	3	5	10	11	8	4				13	7†	9	12														2
1	2	11	3	5	10	6	8	4					7	9															3
1	2		3	5	6	11	8	4					10*	7	9		12												4
1	2	6*	3	5	13	11	8	4				10†	12	7	9														5
1	2	3	4		5	11	6				12		10	7*	8	13	9†												6
1	2	4	3	5	12	11	8					13	7	10†	9		6*												7
1	2	8	3	4	6	11	5						10*	7†	9	13	12												8
1	2	3	5	4	10	8	6					13	12	9	11†							7*							9
1	2	6	3	4	8	11	5				12	10†	13	7	9*														10
1	2	11	3	4	8*	6	5					10†	13	9	12							7							11
1	2	11	6	4	10†	8	5					13	12	9			3					7*							12
1	2	11	3	4	5*	7	8						10	12							6	9							13
1	2	11	3*	4		7	6						10	8†			5		9	13	12								14
1	2	11†	3	5	6	7*	8						10	12			9	13			4								15
1	2	12	3	5	6		9					13							8*	11	7	10†	4						16
1	2	10	3	5	12	6	9†					13							8	11	7	4*							17
1	2	10†	3	5	4	6	9					12							8	11	7*	13							18
1	2	10	3	5	4	6	9					12							8	11	7*								19
1	2	10	3		4	6	9	5				11†							8	13	7*	12							20
1	2	10*	3	5	4	6	12	9												11	7						8		21
1	2	10	3	5	4	6	12	9				7*								11							8		22
1	2	10†	3	5	4	6	12					9								13	7*						8		23
1	2	10	3	5	4	6	13	9									11†			12	7*						8		24
1	2	10	3	5	4	6						7	9				11										8		25
1	2	6	3		4	5	13						7	9	11*	12						8†						10	26
26	26	24	26	23	12	23	26	5	0	2	1	8	13	18	3	2	6	1	5	4	8	13	1	0	2	2	5	1	

Substitute appearances: +1s, +2s +2s, +2s +3s +2s +3s +9s +2s +4s, +3s, +5s, +2s, +1s +1s +1s

HEART OF MIDLOTHIAN   PREM. DIV.

Year Formed: 1874.
Ground: Tynecastle Park.   *Size:* 110×76 yds.   *Capacity:* 49,000 (4,000 seats).
Telephone: 031-337-6132.
Manager/Coach: John Hagart.
Secretary: Janes Calder.   *Trainer:* John Cumming.   *Coach:* John Hagart.
Club Colours: Maroon shirts, white collar and cuffs, white shorts, maroon stockings with white tops.
Club Nickname: 'The Maroons'.
Record Attendance: 53,496, v Rangers, Scottish Cup, 3rd Rd. Feb. 13th, 1932.
Previous Grounds: The Meadows, 1873–78; Powderhall, 1878–81; Tynecastle 1881–86; Tynecastle Park, 1886–.
Ruropean Competitions Entered: European Cup, 1958–59, 1960–61. Fairs Cup, 1961–62, 1963–64, 1965–66.
Record Attendance: 53,496, v Rangers, Scottish Cup, 3rd Rd. Feb. 13th, 1932.
Record Transfer Fee Received: £65,000, from Manchester C. for Arthur Mann, Nov. 1968.
Record Transfer Fee Paid: £20,000, to Wolverhampton W. for George Miller, Nov. 1965.

1975–76 LEAGUE RECORD

Match No.	Date	Venue	Opponents	League Pos'n	Result	H/T Score	Goalscorers	Attendance
1	Aug 30	A	Hibernian	—	L 0-1	0-1		23,646
2	Sep 6	H	Rangers	10	L 0-2	0-2		25,000
3	13	A	Dundee	7	W 3-2	1-2	Busby, Park 2	6707
4	20	H	Aberdeen	7	D 2-2	2-2	Prentice, Gibson	9500
5	27	A	Motherwell	8	D 1-1	1-1	Busby	6073
6	Oct 4	A	Celtic	8	L 1-3	0-3	Busby	20,000
7	11	H	Dundee U.	7	W 1-0	1-0	Prentice	9000
8	18	H	Ayr U.	5	W 2-1	0-1	Brown, Busby	9000
9	25	A	St. Johnstone	5	W 1-0	0-0	Aird	4700
10	Nov 1	H	Hibernian	5	D 1-1	0-0	Callachan	25,000
11	8	A	Rangers	2	W 2-1	2-0	Gibson 2	24,000
12	15	H	Dundee	5	D 1-1	0-1	Gibson	10,000
13	22	A	Aberdeen	5	D 0-0	0-0		11,390
14	29	H	Motherwell	5	D 3-3	0-1	Brown, Aird, Busby (pen)	15,500
15	Dec 6	H	Celtic	5	L 0-1	0-0		21,000
16	13	A	Dundee U.	5	W 1-0	1-0	Callachan	4865
17	20	A	Ayr U.	5	D 1-1	0-1	Aird	5442
18	27	H	St. Johnstone	5	W 2-0	1-0	Aird, Busby (pen)	9000
19	Jan 1	A	Hibernian	—	L 0-3	0-3		32,900
20	3	H	Rangers	5	L 1-2	0-1	Forsyth (og)	23,000
21	10	A	Dundee	6	L 1-4	0-0	Shaw	6758
22	17	A	Aberdeen	6	D 3-3	1-1	Anderson, Prentice, Gibson	10,300
23	31	A	Motherwell	6	L 0-2	0-2		10,054
24	Feb 7	A	Celtic	6	L 0-2	0-0		22,000
25	21	H	Dundee U.	7	L 0-1	0-0		9500
26	28	H	Ayr U.	6	W 1-0	1-0	Gibson	8000
27	Mar 13	H	Hibernian	7	L 0-1	0-1		19,000
28	20	A	Rangers	7	L 1-3	0-1	Aird	30,000
29	27	H	Dundee	6	W 3-0	1-0	Aird, Busby (pen), Shaw	8500
30	Apr 7	A	Aberdeen	—	W 3-0	2-0	Aird, Gibson 2	6000
31	10	H	Motherwell	6	L 1-2	1-2	Busby	11,500
32	17	A	Dundee U.	8	L 0-2	0-1		6598
33	21	A	Ayr U.	—	W 1-0	0-0	Park	5200
34	24	H	St. Johnstone	6	W 1-0	1-0	Thomson (og)	8500
35	26	A	St. Johnstone	—	D 0-0	0-0		3101
36	May 3	H	Celtic	—	W 1-0	0-0	Brown	9000

Final Place: 5

Goalscorers

League (39): Busby 8 (3 pens), Gibson 8, Aird 7, Brown 3, Park 3, Prentice 3, Callachan 2, Shaw 2 Anderson 1, own goals 2.
League Cup (13): Busby 3, Hancock 3, Callachan 2, Ford 2 (1 a pen), Prentice 2, Park 1.
Cup (16): Shaw 4, Busby 3(1 a pen), Gibson 3, Callachan 2, Park 1, Prentice 1, own goals 2.

Honours

Scottish League: Division 1, Champions: 1894–95, 1896–97, 1957–58, 1959–60. Runners-up: 1893–94, 1898–99, 1903–04, 1905–06, 1914–15, 1937–38, 1953–54, 1955–56, 1956–57, 1958–59, 1964–65.
Scottish Cup: Winners 1891, 1896, 1901, 1006, 1956, Runners-up: 1903, 1907, 1968, 1976.
Scottish League Cup: Winners: 1954–55, 1958–59, 1959–60, 1962–63. Runners-up 1961–62.
Record Victory: 15–0 v King's Park, Scottish Cup, 2nd Rd. Feb. 13th, 1937.
Record Defeat: 0–7 v Hibernian, Jan. 1st, 1973, Division 1.
Most League Points: 62, Division 1, 1957–58.
Most League Goals: 132, Division 1, 1957–58. (Record for Division 1).
Most Individual League Goals in Season: 44, Barney Battles, 1930–31.
Highest Scorer in Total Aggregate: 206, Jimmy Wardhaugh, 1946–59.
Most Capped Player: Bobby Walker, 29, Scotland.

Graham, D.	Cruickshank, J.	Kay, R.	Clunie, D.	Jefferies, T.	Anderson, A.	Murray, D.	Brown, J.	Aird, K.	Busby, A.	Ford, D.	Hancock, S.	Prentice, R.	Fraser, C.	Callachan, R.	Park, D.	Gibson, W.	Burrell, A.	Gallacher, J.	Donaldson, G.	Shaw, G.	Match No.
	1	2	3	4	5	6	7	8			9	11*		10	12						1
	1	2			5	6	4	8			9*	11		12	7	10	3				2
	1	2			5	6	4	8				11		10	7	9	3				3
	1	3	2		5	6	4*	12	8			11		10	7	9					4
	1	3	2	12	5	6*	4		8			11		10	7	9					5
	1	3	2	4	5	6	8*	7	9			11†		10	12	13					6
	1	3	2*	12	5	6	4	7†	8		13	11		10		9					7
	1	3	2		5	6	4	7	8			11		10		9					8
	1	3	2		5	6	4	7	8		12	11		10		9*					9
	1	2	3		5	6	4	7	8			11		10		9					10
	1	12	2	3	5	6*	4	7	8			11		10†	13	9					11
	1	3	2	6	5		4	7	8			11		10*	12	9					12
	1	2	3		6		4		8			11*	12	10	7	9	5				13
	1	2	3		5	6	4	7	8			11		10		9					14
	1	2	3		5	6	4	7	8		12	11*		10		9					15
	1	2	3		5	6	4		8			11		10	7	9					16
	1	2	3*		5	6	4	12	8			11	9†	10	7	13					17
	1	2			5	6	3	7*	8			11	12	4	10	9					18
	1	2	12		5	6	3		8			11	7*	4	10	9					19
	1	2	3		5	6	4		8		12	11		7		9	10*				20
	1	2	3		6			7	8			11		10	5			4	9		21
1		6	2	3	5	13		7				11	12	4	8*			9	10†		22
	1	6	2	3	5		4	7	10		13	11	12			8*		9†			23
	1	2	3		6		4	7*	8			9		10	12			11	5		24
	1	6	2	3			4	7*	8			11†	13	10	12			9	5		25
	1	2	3		6		4	7	8					10	9				5		26
	1	6	2	3				7				11		10	4	8	12	9*		5	27
	1	6	2				4					11		10*	8	12	3	9		5	28
	1	6	2				4		8			11		10	3			9		5	29
	1	6*	2	3				7	8			11	12	4	10			9		5	30
	1	6	2	3				7	8			11	12	4	10*			9		5	31
	1	6	2	3			7*		8			11†	13	4	10	12		9		5	32
	1	6	2	3			7*		8			11		4	10	12		9		5	33
	1	6	2	3			7		8*			11	12	4	10	13		9†		5	34
	1	6	5		4		2	7				11	12	10	8		3	9*			35
	1	6	2	3			4	7	8			11		10				9		5	36
1	35	23	26	26	21	22	33	26	32	2	2	30	5	34	18	24	6	14	2	13	
		+1s	+3s			+1s	+2s					+2s	+3s	+10s	+1s	+9s	+4s				

HIBERNIAN

Year Formed: 1875.   *Ground:* Easter Road Park.   *Size:* 112×74yds.   *Capacity:* 50,136 (6636 seats).
Telephone: 031-661-2159.
Manager: Eddie Turnbull.   *Secretary:* C. F. Graham.   *Trainer:* Wilson Humphries.
Club Colours: Green shirts with white collars and sleeves, white shorts, green and white stockings.
Club Nickname: 'Hi-Bees'.
Record Attendance: 65,840 v Hearts, Division 1, Jan. 2nd, 1950.
Previous Names: Edinburgh Hibernians.   *Previous Ground:* Mayfield 1875-80.
European Competitions Entered: European Cup: 1955-56.   Cup Winners Cup: 1972-73.   Fairs Cup: 1960-61, 1961-62, 1962-63, 1965-66, 1967-68, 1968-69.   UEFA Cup: 1973-74.   UEFA Cup: 1974-75 and 1975-76.
Record Transfer Fee Received: £150,000 from Arsenal for Alex Cropley, Dec. 1974.
Record Transfer Fee Paid: £120,000 to Everton 1974 for Joe Harper.

1975–76 LEAGUE RECORD

Match No.	Date	Venue	Opponents	League Pos'n	Result	H/T Score	Goalscorers	Atten- dance
1	Aug 30	H	Hearts	—	W 1-0	1-0	Harper	23,646
2	Sep 6	A	Dundee U.	6	L 0-1	0-1		7000
3	13	H	Ayr. U.	3	W 1-0	0-0	Brownlie (pen)	8897
4	20	A	Rangers	5	D 1-1	0-1	Johnstone (og)	37,000
5	27	H	St. Johnstone	3	W 4-2	2-1	McLeod, Harper, Munro, Duncan	5700
6	Oct 4	H	Dundee	3	D 1-1	0-1	Edwards	8708
7	11	A	Motherwell	3	L 1-2	1-0	Harper	8207
8	25	H	Aberdeen	3	W 3-1	1-0	Jarvie (og), Bremner, Smith	11,133
9	Nov 1	A	Hearts	2	D 1-1	0-0	Stanton	25,000
10	8	H	Dundee U.	4	D 1-1	1-0	Brownlie (pen)	10,600
11	15	A	Ayr U.	4	W 3-1	1-1	McLeod, Duncan 2	5000
12	22	H	Rangers	3	W 2-1	1-0	Stanton 2	26,547
13	29	A	St. Johnstone	3	W 4-3	3-2	Brownlie (pen), Duncan 3	4484
14	Dec 6	A	Dundee	3	L 0-2	0-0		7360
15	10	A	Celtic	—	D 1-1	0-0	Schaedler	21,000
16	13	H	Motherwell	2	W 1-0	1-0	Stanton	15,991
17	20	H	Celtic	3	L 1-3	1-2	Duncan	21,360
18	27	A	Aberdeen	4	D 2-2	2-1	Bremner, Duncan	17,630
19	Jan 1	H	Hearts	—	W 3-0	3-0	Smith, Duncan 2	32,900
20	10	H	Ayr U.	3	W 3-0	2-0	Brownlie (pen), Harper 2	8083
21	17	A	Rangers	4	L 0-2	0-0		40,000
22	31	H	St. Johnstone	4	W 5-0	2-0	Brownlie, Smith, McLeod 2, Duncan	7839
23	Feb 7	H	Dundee	4	W 4-0	1-0	Stanton, Smith, McLeod, Duncan	9241
24	21	A	Motherwell	3	W 1-0	1-0	Smith	10,578
25	28	A	Celtic	3	L 0-4	0-3		33,000
26	Mar 13	A	Hearts	3	W 1-0	1-0	Duncan	19,000
27	20	H	Dundee	3	L 0-1	0-1		6720
28	27	A	Ayr U.	3	L 0-2	0-0		4700
29	31	H	Aberdeen	3	W 3-2	1-1	Blackley, Murray, Muir	7200
30	Apr 3	H	Rangers	3	L 0-3	0-1		18,820
31	10	A	St. Johnstone	3	W 2-0	2-0	Bremner, McGhee	2182
32	14	A	Dundee	—	D 1-1	0-0	McGhee	6054
33	17	H	Motherwell	3	W 2-0	1-0	McLeod, McGhee	9098
34	21	H	Celtic	—	W 2-0	1-0	Smith, McLeod (pen)	17,480
35	24	A	Aberdeen	3	L 0-3	0-1		10,985
36	28	A	Dundee U.	—	L 0-2	0-2		6500

Final Place: 3
Goalscorers

League (55): Duncan 13, McLeod 7 (1 pen), Smith 6, Brownlie 5 (4 pens), Harper 5, Stanton 5, Bremner 3, McGhee 3, Blackley 1, Edwards 1, Muir 1, Munro 1, Murray 1, Schaedler 1, own goals 2.
League Cup (16): Harper 7, Duncan 2, McLeod 2, Brownlie (1 pen), Munro 1, Smith 1, Stanton 1, own goal 1.
Cup (10): Harper 2, Spalding 2, Stanton 2, Bremner 1, Duncan 1, Edwards 1, Smith 1

Honours

Scottish League: Division 1, Champions: 1902–03, 1947–48, 1950–51, 1951–52; Runners-up: 1896–97, 1946–47, 1949–50, 1952–53, 1973–74. 1974-75 Division 2, Champions: 1893–94; 1894–95; 1932–33.
Scottish Cup: Winners: 1887, 1902; Runners-up: 1896, 1914, 1923, 1924, 1947, 1958, 1972
Scottish League Cup: Winners: 1972–73; Runners-up: 1950–51, 1968–69, 1974-75.
Drybrough Cup: Winners 1972–73, 1973–74.
Record Victory: 15–1 v Peebles Rovers, Scottish Cup, 2nd Rd. Feb. 11th, 1961.
Record Defeat: 2–9 v Morton, Division 1, 1918–19.
Most League Points: 54, Division 2, 1932–33.
Most Individual League Goals in Season: 42, Joe Baker, Division 1, 1959–60.
Most Capped Player: Lawrie Reilly, 39, Scotland.

Whyte, H.	McArthur, J.	McDonald, M.	Brownlie, J.	Schaedler, E.	Bremner, D.	Stanton, P.	Barry, R.	Blackley, J.	Edwards, A.	Smith, R.	McLeod, A.	Harper, J.	Spalding, D.	Munro, I.	Duncan, A.	Higgins, A.	Carroll, P.	Murray, W.	Wilson, M.	Muir, L.	McGhee, A.	Paterson, W.	Match No.
	1		2	3	8	4	5	6	7			9		10	11								1
	1		2	3	8	4	5	6	7			9		10	11								2
	1		2	3	8	4	5*	6	7	12		9		10	11								3
	1		2	3		4	5	6	7*	8		9		10	11	12							4
	1		2	3	4		5	6	7	8		9		10	11								5
1			2	3	4	5	6	7	8*			9		10	11	12							6
	1		2	3*	4	12	5	6	7			9		10	11	8							7
	1		2	3	8	4	5	6	12	7*		9		10	11								8
	1		2	3	8	4	5	6	7			9		10	11								9
	1		2	3	8	4	5	6				9	12	10	11			7*					10
	1		2	3	8	4	5	6	7			9		10	11								11
	1		2	3	8	4	5	6	7			9		10	11								12
	1		2	3	8	4	5	6	7			9		10	11								13
	1		2	3	8	4	5	6	7			9		10	11								14
	1		2	3	8	4	5	6	7			9		10	11								15
	1		2	3	8	4	5	6	7	9				10	11								16
	1		2	3	8	4	5	6	7	12		9		10*	11								17
	1		2	3*	8	4	5	6	7	10		9	12		11								18
	1		2		8	4	5	6	7	10		9	3		11								19
	1		2		8	4	5	6	7	10		9	3		11								20
	1		2	3	8	4	5			10	7*	9		6	11	12							21
	1		2	3	8	4*	5		7	10		9		6	11				12				22
	1		2	3	8	4	5	6	7	10		9			11								23
	1		2	3	8	4		6	7	10		9		5	11								24
	1		2	3	8	4		6	7	10		9*		5	11				12				25
	1		2		8	4	5	6		10†		9*	3		11			7	12		13		26
	1		2	3*	8	4		6	7	10		9		5	11				12				27
	1		2	3	8	4		6	7			9		5	11				10				28
	1		2	3	10	4		6	7*					5	11			8	9	12			29
	1		2	3	4	12	5*	6	7			9			11			8	10				30
	1		2	3	8	4*		6	7	10				5	11				12	9			31
	1		2	3	4*			6	7†	10		9		5	11			13	8	12			32
	1			3	4			6		10	2			5		11*		7	8	9	12		33
	1			3	4			6		10	2			5		12		7	8	9	11*		34
	1			3	4			6		10	2			5		11*		7	8	9	12		35
	1	12	2	3*	4			6		8	10			5	11			7			9		36
1	20	15	33	32	32	31	25	34	25	20	16	22	16	17	35	1	1	6	2	6	5	1	
		+1s			+2s					+3s	1s	+1s		1s		+1s	+3s		+3s	1s	+4s	1s	+2s

R.F. 7677—29 561

KILMARNOCK PREM. DIV.

Year Formed: 1869.
Ground: Rugby Park. *Size:* 115×75 yds. *Capacity:* 34,500 (4,200 seats).
Telephone: Kilmarnock 25184.
Manager: William Fernie. *Hon. Secretary:* David McCulloch.
Trainer/Physiotherapist: Hugh Allan. *Trainer:* Dave Sneddon.
Club Colours: White shirts with blue and white centre panel, white shorts, white stockings.
Club Nickname: 'the Killies'.
Record Attendance: 34,246, v Rangers, League Cup, Aug 1963.
European Competitions Entered: European Cup: 1965–66; Fairs Cup: 1964–65, 1966–67, 1969–70, 1970–71.
Record Transfer Fee Received. £75,000 from Rangers F.C. for Tommy McLean, June 1971.

1975–76 LEAGUE RECORD

Match No.	Date	Venue	Opponents	League Pos'n	Result	H/T Score	Goalscorers	Atten- dance
1	Aug 30	H	Hamilton A.	—	W 4-2	4-2	Smith (pen.), Fallis, Provan, Morrison	4500
2	Sep 6	A	Airdrieonians	3	W 4-3	2-3	Morrison 2, Fallis, Smith G.	3000
3	13	H	Partick T.	5	L 0-1	0-0		8500
4	3 20	A	East Fife	3	W 4-2	2-2	Smith 2 (1 pen), Fleming, Fallis	2344
5	27	H	Clyde	2	W 3-0	1-0	Fleming 2, Morrison	3500
6	Oct 4	H	St Mirren	2	W 3-1	3-1	McLean, Morrison 2	4000
7	11	A	Montrose	2	L 0-2	0-1		1600
8	18	H	Arbroath	2	W 2-1	1-0	Fallis, Smith	3000
9	25	A	Morton	1	W 3-1	2-1	Fleming 2, Smith	3000
10	Nov 1	A	Falkirk	1	W 1-0	0-0	Smith	4000
11	8	H	Queen of the S.	1	W 2-0	0-0	Provan, Fallis	5000
12	15	A	Dunfermline Ath.	1	L 0-1	0-0		3000
13	22	H	Dumbarton	1	W 1-0	1-0	Fallis	5000
14	29	A	Clyde	1	W 2-0	1-0	McDicken, Fallis	3000
15	Dec 6	A	St. Mirren	1	D 0-0	0-0		5800
16	13	H	Montrose	1	D 1-1	0-0	McLean	5000
17	20	A	Arbroath	2	L 0-2	0-1		1950
18	27	H	Morton	2	W 3-2	3-0	Morrison, Fallis, Smith	5000
19	Jan 1	H	Airdrieonians	—	W 2-1	0-1	Provan, Smith	7000
20	3	A	Partick T.	2	L 0-2	0-1		11,500
21	10	H	Dunfermline Ath.	2	W 4-0	3-0	Adair (og), Scott (og), Fallis, Sheed	4000
22	17	A	Dumbarton	2	L 0-3	0-1		3500
23	31	H	East Fife	2	W 2-1	1-1	Clarke, McCulloch	4500
24	Feb 7	A	Hamilton A.	2	D 1-1	0-0	Rodman	3000
25	21	H	Falkirk	2	W 1-0	1-0	Fallis	4000
26	28	A	Queen of the S.	2	L 1-2	0-2	Rodman	4500

Final Place: 2

Goalscorers

League (44): Fallis 10, Smith 9 (2 pens), Morrison E. 7, Fleming I. 5, Provan 3, McLean 2, Rodman 2
Clarke 1, McCulloch 1, McDicken 1, Sheed 1, own goals 2.
League Cup (5): Fallis 1, Fleming I. 1, McCulloch 1, Morrison E. 1, Sheed 1.
Cup (6): McDicken 2, Fallis 1, Sheed 1, Smith 1, own goal 1.
Spring Cup (5): Murdoch 2, Fleming C. 1, Maxwell 1, Smith 1.

Honour

Scottish League: Division 1, Champions: 1964-65. Runners-up: 1959-60, 1960-61, 1962-63, 1963-64, 1975-76. Division 2, Champions: 1897-98, 1898-99. Runners-up: 1953-54, 1973-74.
Scottish Cup: Winners: 1920, 1929. Runners-up: 1898, 1932, 1938, 1957, 1960.
Scottish League Cup: Runners-up: 1952–53, 1960–61, 1962–63.
Record Victory: 11–1 v Paisley Academicals, Scottish Cup, 1st Rd. Jan. 18th, 1930.
Record Defeat: 0–8 v Hibernian, Division 1, 1925–26, and v Rangers, Division 1, 1936–37.
Most League Points: 50, Division 1, 1959–60, 1960–61, 1964–65.
Most Individual League Goals in Season: 35, Peerie Cunningham, Division 1, 1927–28.
Most Capped player: Joe Nibloe 9, Scotland.

Stewart, J.	Maxwell, G.	Robertson, A.	McLean, S.	Rodman, B.	Clarke, P.	McCulloch, I.	McDicken, D.	Provan, D.	Fleming, I.	Morrison, E.	Fallis, L.	Sheed, R.	Sharp, R.	Smith, G.	Jenkins, J.	Wilson, W.	Morrison, D.	Murdoch, W.	Fleming, C.	Match No.
1	3	2	5	12	4	6*	7	9			8	10		11						1
1	3	2	5	12	4	6*	7	9†	13		8	10		11						2
1	3	2	5	6	4	13	7	12	9*		8	10†		11						3
1	6	3	2	5		4	10	7	12	9	8*			11						4
1	3	2	5		4	6	7	9			8	10		11						5
1	3	2	5		4	6	7	9			8	10		11						6
1	12	3	2	5	4	6	7*	9			8	10		11						7
1	12	3	2	5	4	6	7*	9			8	10		11						8
1	8	3	2	5	4	6*	12	9	11†	10					7	13				9
1	10	3	2	5	6	4	7*	9			8			11	12					10
1	3	2	5	6	4		7*	9			8	10		11		12				11
1	3	2	5	6	4		7	9			8	10*		11		12				12
1	12	3	2	5*	6	4	10	7	9†		8	13		11						13
1	6	3	2	5	4	9	7	12			8	10		11*						14
1	6	3	2	5	4	9	7				8	10		11						15
1	6	3	2	12	5	4	9*	7			8	10		11						16
1	6	3	2	5	4	9*	7	12			8	10		11						17
1	6	3	2	5	4	7*		9			8	10		11	12					18
1	6	3	2*	12	5	4	7	9			8	10		11						19
1	2	3	12	6*	5	4	7	9			8	10		11						20
1	2	3	12	5	6	4*	7	9			8	10		11						21
1	3	2	5	6*		4	7	9		12	8	10		11						22
1	2	3		5	6	7		9			8	10		11				4		23
1	2	3		5	6	7		9			8	10		11				4		24
1	2	3		5	6	9*	7				8	10		11			12	4		25
1	2	3		5	6	9	7				8*	10					12	4	11	26
26	15	26	20	20	18	23	16	23	9	14	26	16	4	25	0	0	0	4	1	
	+3s		+2s	+2s	+2s	+1s	+1s	+4s	+2s			+1s	+1s		+2s	+2s	+2s			

MEADOWBANK THISTLE DIV. 2

Year Formed: 1974. (Previously called Ferranti Thistle). *Ground:* Meadowbank Stadium. *Size:* 105 ×
75 yards. *Capacity* 16,000 (at present only main stand 7,500 seats is used for football). *Telephone*
(Secretary's office): 031-337 2442.
Manager: A. Ness. *Secretary:* William L. Mill.
Club Colours: Amber with black trim shirts, black shorts, amber stockings.
Record attendance: 4000 v Albion Rovers, Scottish League Cup, Aug. 9, 1974.

1975–76 LEAGUE RECORD

Match No.	Date	Venue	Opponents	League Pos'n	Result	H/T Score	Goalscorers	Attendance
1	Aug 30	A	Alloa	—	D 1-1	0-1	Fotheringham	359
2	Sep 13	A	Queen's Park	8	D 1-1	1-0	Davidson	600
3	16	H	Berwick R.	—	L 2-6	1-3	O'Rourke, Davidson	500
4	20	H	Forfar Ath.	8	W 1-0	0-0	Mackenzie	250
5	27	H	Cowdenbeath	8	D 1-1	0-0	Fotheringham	300
6	Oct 4	A	Stirling Albion	9	L 0-5	0-3		900
7	11	H	Brechin C.	11	L 0-4	0-0		250
8	18	H	Raith R.	12	L 0-1	0-1		650
9	25	A	East Stirling	13	L 0-3	0-2		250
10	Nov 1	A	Stranraer	13	L 1-5	1-1	McFarlane	900
11	8	H	Stenhousemuir	12	D 1-1	0-1	Harper	350
12	15	H	Clydebank	12	D 0-0	0-0		500
13	22	A	Albion R.	14	L 0-4	0-3		500
14	29	A	Cowdenbeath	14	L 0-2	0-0		250
15	Dec 6	H	Stirling Albion	14	W 1-0	1-0	Jones	400
16	13	A	Clydebank	14	L 0-2	0-0		1000
17	20	A	Raith R.	14	L 2-3	1-0	Fotheringham, Davidson	1578
18	27	H	East Stirling	14	L 0-4	0-2		250
19	Jan 1	A	Berwick R.	—	L 0-1	0-0		550
20	3	H	Queen's Park	14	W 1-0	0-0	Davidson	350
21	17	H	Albion R.	13	W 4-1	3-0	Mackenzie 2, O'Rourke, Davidson	350
22	31	A	Forfar Ath.	13	D 1-1	0-0	O'Rourke	175
23	Feb 7	H	Alloa	14	L 1-2	0-2	Davidson	450
24	14	A	Brechin C.	12	W 3-0	2-0	McFarlane, O'Rourke 2	300
25	21	H	Stranraer	13	L 2-3	1-2	McFarlane 2	200
26	28	A	Stenhousemuir	13	L 1-2	0-0	Davidson	309

Final Place: 14

Goalscorers

League (24): Davidson 7, O'Rourke 5, McFarlane 4, Fotheringham 3, Mackenzie 3, Harper 1, Jones 1.
League Cup (8): Davidson 2, McFarlane 2, Duthie 1, Fotheringham 1, Martin 1, O'Rourke 1.
Cup (1): Mackenzie 1.
Spring Cup (6): Davidson 3, Hancock 1, Mackenzie 1, own goal 1.

Honours

Record Victory: 3-1 v Albion Rovers, Division 2, 1974-75.
Record defeat: 0-8 v Hamilton, Division 2, 1974-75.
Most League points: 23 Division 2, 1974-75.

Honours: East of Scotland Qualifying Cup Winners 1962–63
Scottish Qualifying Cup (South) Winners 1973–74.

Gray, D.	McVay, L.	Mackenzie, D.	Printy, L	Jones, R.	Catheart, D.	Fotheringham, D.	Hogg, W.	Hancock, J.	McFarlane, J. I.	O'Rourke, T. L.	Duthie, A. G.	Davidson, K. J.	Harper, W.	Kilgour, R.	Carter, J. E.	Thomson, L.	Morgan, J.	Wight, W. D.	Williamson, A.	Martin, L	Match No.
1	2	3		4	5	6	8	9	10			11								7	1
1	2		3	4	5	6	8	9	10			11								7	2
1	2	3	13	4†	5	6	8	9	10			11	12	7*							3
1	2	3	13	4	5	6	8	9		7*		11	10†						12		4
1	2	3	4*	6	5	10	8	9	12	7		11									5
1	2*	3			5	10	4	9†	8	7		11	6	12					13		6
1	2	3	4		5	6	9	8*	7	11	10	12									7
1	2	6	4		5	8*	9	7	12	11		3	10								8
1	2	6		4	5		8	9	10			11	3	7							9
1	2	10†		4	5	6	7	9	8*	13		11	12	3							10
1	4	3	2	8*	5	9		6	10	7		11	12								11
1	4	3	2		5	9		6	8	7		11	10								12
1	4†	3*	2	12	5	9		6	8	7	13	11	10								13
1		3	2	4	5	9		6	8	7		11	10								14
1		3	2	4	5	9		6	8	7		11	10								15
1		2	4†		5	9	6	8	7*	11	10	3					13		12		16
1	7	2	4		5	9	6	8	12	11	10*	3									17
1	7†	2	4		5	9	6	8	10	12		3*					11		13		18
1	12	3	4	5	6		8	9	10	7		2					11*				19
1		3	4	6	5	8	7	9	10	11		2									20
1		3	4	8	5	9	6	10	7			2					11				21
1	7*	3	4	8	5	9	6	10	11	12		2									22
1		3	4	8	5	9	6	10	7	12		2					11*				23
1		3	4	8	5	10	9	7	11	12		2						6*			24
1		3	4		5	8	9	7	11	10		2						6			25
1	2	3	4	8		9	6	11	10			12							5	7*	26
26	17	22	18	20	23	24	8	26	18	15	6	26	11	13	1	2	4	3	1	2	
	+1s				+2s	+1s			+1s	+1s	+3s		+7s	+2s			+2s		+4s		

MONTROSE

Year Formed: 1879. *Ground:* Links Park. *Size:* 114 × 66 yards. *Capacity:* 9000. *Telephone:* Montrose 3200
Manager: Kenneth Cameron.
Secretary: William Coull.
Club Colours: Royal blue shirts, and shorts, white stockings with royal blue tops.
Club Nickname: 'Gable Endies'.
Record Attendance: 8983 v Dundee. 3rd Round Scottish Cup 17th March, 1973
Record Transfer Fee received: £20,000 for Bobby Hutchinson from Dundee, August 1974.

1975–76 LEAGUE RECORD

Match No.	Date	Venue	Opponents	League Pos'n	Result	H/T Score	Goalscorers	Atten- dance
1	Aug 30	H	East Fife	—	W 3-0	2-0	Cameron, Livingstone 2	1300
2	Sep 6	A	Arbroath	2	W 2-1	0-1	Cant, Livingstone	2762
3	13	H	Dumbarton	1	W 3-2	0-1	Barr (pen), Johnston 2	1100
4	20	A	St. Mirren	4	L 1-3	0-1	Cameron	2100
5	27	H	Hamilton A.	4	D 1-1	1-0	Cameron	1400
6	Oct 4	A	Queen of the S.	6	L 1-2	0-0	Craig	1500
7	11	H	Kilmarnock	3	W 2-0	1-0	Barr (pen), Johnston	1600
8	18	H	Dunfermline Ath.	4	D 2-2	1-0	Stewart, Cameron	1500
9	25	A	Clyde	5	L 0-3	0-2		1500
10	Nov 1	A	Morton	6	L 1-2	0-1	McNicoll	1500
11	8	H	Partick T.	5	W 2-1	1-0	Johnston, Livingstone	1750
12	15	A	Airdrieonians	6	D 2-2	1-1	Markland, Cant	2500
13	22	H	Falkirk	4	W 2-1	0-1	Barr, Livingstone	1450
14	Dec 6	A	Queen of the S.	4	W 2-1	2-0	Barr (pen), Lowe	1200
15	13	A	Kilmarnock	5	D 1-1	0-0	Livingstone	5000
16	20	A	Dunfermline Ath.	6	L 0-1	0-1		2000
17	27	H	Clyde	4	W 4-3	1-1	McNicoll, Johnston, Livingstone, Ahern (og)	1400
18	Jan 1	H	Arbroath	—	L 3-5	2-2	Lowe, Livingstone, Miller	3600
19	3	A	Dumbarton	3	W 6-0	3-0	Barr, Markland, Stewart, Miller 2, Livingstone	2000
20	10	H	Airdrieonians	3	W 1-0	0-0	Lowe	1200
21	17	A	Falkirk	3	L 0-2	0-1		1500
22	31	H	St. Mirren	3	W 2-1	1-1	Johnston, Miller	1200
23	Feb 7	A	East Fife	3	W 7-1	4-1	Livingstone 2, Miller 2, Lowe, Markland, MacIvor (og)	1482
24	21	H	Morton	3	D 1-1	0-1	Johnston	2000
25	23	A	Hamilton A.	—	D 3-3	1-1	Barr (pen), Johnston, Livingstone	1500
26	28	A	Partick T.	3	L 1-4	0-2	McNicoll	6000

Final Place: 3

Goalscorers

League (53): Livingstone 12, Johnston 8, Barr 6 (4 pens), Miller 6, Cameron 4, Lowe 4, McNicoll 3, Markland 3, Cant 2, Stewart 2, Craig 1, own goal 2.
League Cup (15): Cameron 5, Livingstone 5, Barr 4 (2 pens), Guthrie 1.
Cup (10): Cant 3, Johnston 2, Lowe 2, Barr 1 (pen), Miller 1, Stewart 1.
Spring Cup (21): Barr 5 (3 pens), Guthrie 5, Livingstone 5, Miller 2, Cant 1, Daun 1, Johnston 1, Stewart 1.

Honours

Record Victory 12-0 Vale of Leithen, 2nd Round Scot. Cup, 4th January 1975
Record Defeat: 0-13 v Aberdeen, Division C, March 17, 1951.
Most League Points: 53, Division 2, 1974-75.
Most Capped Player: A. Keillor, 2 (6) Scotland.

Gorman, D.	Barr, L.	Lowe, M.	Markland, S.	McNicholl, D.	D'Arcy, D.	Stewart, I.	Guthrie, C.	Downie, C.	Johnston, H.	Cameron, K.	Cant, J.	Livingstone, R.	Guyan, J.	Craig, G.	Miller, R.	Walker, A.	Match No.
1	2	12	3	4	5	8*	7		6	8	10	11					1
1	2		3	4	5	8	7		6	9	10	11					2
1	2	3	6	4	5	12	7		10	9	8*	11					3
1	7	2	3	4	5	12	13		6	9	8*	11	10†				4
1	2	10*	3	4	5	8	7		6	9	12	11†13					5
1	2	3	6	4	5	10	7		11	9	8*	12					6
1	2		3	4	5	8	7		6	9	12	10*			11		7
1	2		3	4	5	8	7*	12	6	9		10			11		8
1	2	3		4	5	8			6	10		11		9	7		9
1	2	3		4	5	8	12		6	10		11		9*	7		10
1	2	12	3	4	5	7*			6	10	8	9			11		11
1	2	7	3	4	5				6	10	8	9			11		12
1	2	7*	3	4	5	13	12		6	10	8†	9			11		13
1	2	7	3	4	5	12			6	10	8	9*			11		14
1	2	7	3	4	5		12		6*	10	8	9			11		15
1	2	7	3	4	5		12		6*	10	8	9			11		16
1	2	7*	3	4	5		12		6	10	8	9			11		17
1	2	7†	3	4	5	13	12		6*	10	8	9			11		18
1	2	7	3	4	5	8			10		6	9			11		19
1	2	7	3	4	5	8			10		6	9			11		20
1	2	7	3	4	5	8	12		10		6*	9			11		21
1	2	7	3	4*	5	8†13	12		10		6	9			11		22
1	2	7	3	4	5	8			10		6	9			11		23
1	2	7*	3	4	5	8†13			10		6	9			11	12	24
1	2		3	4	5	7			10		6	9			11	8	25
1	2	7	8	4	5	12	13		10		6	9			11†	3*	26
26	26	20	24	26	26	14	9	10	26	8	21	25	1	2	20	2	
		+				+	+	+			+		+	+	+		
		2s				6s	11s	2s			2s		1s	1s	1s		

Year Formed: 1874.   *Limited Company:* 1896.
Ground: Cappielow Park.   *Size:* 110×71 yds.   *Capacity:* 25,000 (2,900 seats).
Telephone: Greenock 23571.
Manager: Joe Gilroy
Secretary: Tom Robertson.
Club Colours: Blue and white vertical striped shirts, white shorts and stockings,
Club Nickname: 'Ton'.
Record Attendance: 23,500, v Celtic, Division 1, 1922.
European Competitions Entered: Fairs Cup, 1968–69.

1975–76 LEAGUE RECORD

Match No.	Date	Venue	Opponents	League Pos'n	Result	H/T Score	Goalscorers	Attendance
1	Aug 30	H	Partick T.	—	D 0-0	0-0		3000
2	Sep 6	A	St. Mirren	8	D 2-2	0-2	Irvine (pen), Sharp	3400
3	13	H	Arbroath	8	D 2-2	0-0	Reid, Brown	2000
4	20	A	Hamilton A.	10	L 0-2	0-1		3000
5	27	H	Falkirk	11	L 2-3	2-2	McIlmoyle, Sharp	2500
6	Oct 4	H	Dunfermline Ath.	11	D 1-1	0-1	Evans (og)	600
7	11	A	Dumbarton	13	L 0-4	0-2		3000
8	18	A	Queen of the S.	11	W 1-0	1-0	Sharp	1500
9	25	H	Kilmarnock	13	L 1-3	1-2	Harley	3000
10	Nov 1	H	Montrose	13	W 2-1	1-0	Reid (pen), Anderson	1500
11	8	A	East Fife	11	D 2-2	0-0	Sharp, Rae	1893
12	15	H	Clyde	12	D 1-1	0-0	Sharp	2000
13	22	H	Airdrieonians	9	W 1-0	1-0	Rankin	2000
14	29	A	Falkirk	10	D 3-3	2-1	Reid, Harley 2	1200
15	Dec 6	A	Dunfermline Ath.	11	L 0-1	0-0		2500
16	13	H	Dumbarton	9	D 1-1	0-0	Reid	2500
17	20	H	Queen of the S.	11	L 0-1	0-1		1200
18	27	A	Kilmarnock	12	L 2-3	0-3	McGhee, Harley	5000
19	Jan 1	H	St. Mirren	—	W 1-0	0-0	Goldthorp	2300
20	3	A	Arbroath	9	W 1-0	1-0	Goldthorp	2143
21	17	A	Airdrieonians	11	L 1-2	1-0	Harley	2000
22	31	H	Hamilton A.	12	L 1-4	0-2	Goldthorp	1000
23	Feb 7	A	Partick T.	12	L 0-2	0-0		5000
24	14	A	Clyde	12	W 2-1	1-0	McNeil T., Goldthorp	2300
25	21	A	Montrose	12	D 1-1	1-0	Goldthorp	2000
26	28	H	East Fife	11	W 3-0	0-0	McNeil T., Morrison 2	2000

Final Place: 11

Goalscorers

League (31): Goldthorp 5, Harley 5, Sharp 5, Reid 4 (1 pen), McNeil T. 2, Morrison 2, Anderson 1,
Brown 1, Irvine 1 (pen), McGhee 1, McIlmoyle 1, Rae 1, Rankin 1, Own Goal 1.
League Cup (11): Harley 3, Sharp 3, McNeil T. 2, Reid 2, McIlmoyle 1.
Cup (1): McGhee 1.
Spring Cup (18): Goldthorp 6, McGhee 4, McNeil T. 3 (1 pen), Brown 2 (1 pen), Harley 2, Morrison 1.

Honours

Scottish League: Division 1, Runners-up: 1916–17. Division 2, Champions: 1949–50, 1963–64, 1966–67.
  Runners-up: 1899–1900, 1928–29, 1936–37.
Scottish Cup: Winners: 1922. Runners-up: 1948.
Scottish League Cup: Runners-up: 1963–64.
Southern League Cup: Runners-up: 1941–42.
Renfrewshire Cup: 36 times winners.

Record Victory: 11-0 Carfin Shamrock, Scot. Cup 1886.
Record Defeat: 2-8 v Rangers, Division 1, Mar. 15th 1927.
Most League Points: 69, Division 2, 1966–67.
Most League Goals: 135, Division 2, 1963–64.
Most Individual League Goals in Season: 51, Allan McGraw, Division 2, 1963–64.
Most Capped Player: Jimmy Cowan, 25, Scotland.

Herriot, J.	Baines, R.	Sneddon, L.	Hayes, D.	McNeil, T.	Reid, A.	Anderson, G.	Rankin, S.	Irvine, R. G.	Brown, C.	Evans, B.	McIlmoyle, H.	Sharp, R.	Townsend, J.	McGhee, M. E.	Harley, J.	Flaherty, B.	Hepburn, M.	Taylor, R.	McNeil, J.	Nelson, J.	Rae, T.	Orr, N. I.	Goldthorp, J.	Traynor, T.	Palmer, C.	Clarke, G.	Spragia, R.	Morrison, E.	No.
	1	2	4	3	8	5	6	11			9	10			7														1
	1	2	4	3	8	5*	6†	11			9	10			7			12	13										2
	1	2	4	3	8	5	6*		13		9	10			7			12	11†										3
	1	2	5	3	8		6	4			9	10			7		11*	12											4
	1*	2	4		8	5	6	13	12		9	10*			7			3†	11										5
1		2	4	3	8	5	6	13	11†		9	10*			7			12											6
	1	2	4	3	8	5*	6	10			9	13			7			12	11†										7
	1	3	2	11	8	4	6	5			10	9			7														8
	1	2	3		5	4	11*	12		6	10	9			7			8											9
	1	2	3		8	5	4	12		6	9	10			7						11*								10
	1	2	3		8	5*	4	12		6	9	10			7						11								11
	1	2	3		8	6	4	11*		5	9				12			7			10								12
	1	2	3		8	6	4	10		5	9				12						11*	7							13
	1	2	3		8	6		10		5	9				7						11	4							14
	1	3	2	11	8	6		10		5	9				7*						12	4							15
	1	3	2	12	8	6		10		4	9				7					5	11*								16
	1	3	2	10	8	6		7		5	9				12						11	4*							17
	1	3*	2	4	8	6		10		5	9				7						11	12							18
	1	3	2	4		6	8			5	9				7*	12							10	11					19
	1	3	2	4		6	8			5	9				11								10	7					20
	1	3	2	4		6	11	8		5	9												10	7					21
	1	3	2	4*		6	8			5†	9	13											10	11	12	7			22
	1	3	2	4			11	8		5					7*	12							10				6	9	23
	1	3	2	4			11	8*		5					7	12							10				6	9	24
	1	3		4	6			8		5					7	12	11*						10				2	9	25
	1	3	2	4		6				5					7		11						10				8	9	26
1	25	20	25	24	17	9	22	11	15	21	7	19	4	2	20	0	1	6	3	1	8	4	8	4	0	1	4	4	
+1s						+2s	+4s	+1s		+1s				+3s	+5s	+1s		+2s	+2s	+1s	+2s			+1s					

MOTHERWELL

Year Formed: 1886.
Ground: Fir Park. *Size:* 110 × 72 yds. *Capacity:* 31,000 (3,300 seats).
Telephone: Motherwell 63229.
Manager: Wm. McLean
Secretary: Jack McGraw. *Trainer:* William McKenzie.
Club Colours: All amber with claret band, claret shorts and stockings.
Club Nickname: 'Well'.
Record Attendance: 35,632, v Rangers, Scottish Cup, 4th Rd. Replay, Mar. 12th, 1952.
Previous Names: Club formed following the amalgamation of Alpha and Glencairn. Known as Wee Alpha for a year before becoming Motherwell in 1886.
Previous Grounds: Roman Park, Dalziel Park.

1975–76 LEAGUE RECORD

Match No.	Date	Venue	Opponents	League Pos'n	Result	H/T Score	Goalscorers	Attendance
1	Aug 30	H	Ayr U.	—	D 1-1	0-1	Stevens	5115
2	Sept 6	A	Aberdeen	4	D 2-2	1-2	Pettigrew 2	5500
3	13	H	Celtic	5	D 1-1	1-1	Davidson	18,612
4	20	A	Dundee U.	6	D 1-1	1-0	Millar (pen)	5600
5	27	H	Hearts	5	D 1-1	1-1	Pettigrew	6073
6	Oct 4	A	St. Johnstone	5	L 1-2	0-1	Pettigrew	2600
7	11	H	Hibernian	6	W 2-1	0-1	Pettigrew, Stevens	8207
8	18	H	Rangers	3	W 2-1	0-1	Davidson, Pettigrew	18,925
9	25	A	Dundee	2	W 6-3	3-1	Pettigrew 4, Taylor 2	6853
10	Nov 1	A	Ayr U.	3	L 0-2	0-1		6400
11	8	H	Aberdeen	1	W 3-0	2-0	Millar (pen), Graham, Taylor	6294
12	15	A	Celtic	2	W 2-0	1-0	Pettigrew 2	33,000
13	22	H	Dundee U.	1	W 2-1	0-1	Davidson, McIlwraith	6328
14	29	A	Hearts	2	D 3-3	1-0	Gardner 2, Pettigrew	15,500
15	Dec 6	H	St. Johnstone	2	W 2-0	0-0	Millar (pen), Pettigrew	5632
16	13	A	Hibernian	3	L 0-1	1-0		15,991
17	20	A	Rangers	4	L 2-3	1-1	McLaren, Pettigrew	20,000
18	27	H	Dundee	3	W 3-2	3-0	Graham 2, Pettigrew	7169
19	Jan 1	H	Ayr U.	—	W 1-0	0-0	McLaren	7367
20	3	A	Aberdeen	3	D 0-0	0-0		16,177
21	10	H	Celtic	4	L 1-3	0-0	Davidson	18,092
22	17	A	Dundee U.	3	W 4-1	1-1	Watson, Graham, Pettigrew, Marinello	5200
23	31	H	Hearts	3	W 2-0	2-0	Pettigrew 2	10,054
24	Feb 7	A	St. Johnstone	3	W 3-1	2-1	Pettigrew, Taylor, Anderson (og)	3500
25	21	H	Hibernian	4	L 0-1	0-1		10,578
26	28	H	Rangers	4	L 0-1	1-0		25,241
27	Mar 20	H	Aberdeen	4	W 2-1	1-0	Davidson, Pettigrew	5908
28	27	A	Celtic	4	L 0-4	0-4		29,000
29	Apr 3	H	Dundee U.	4	W 3-2	1-1	Millar (pen), McVie, Stevens	3829
30	10	A	Hearts	4	W 2-1	2-1	Gardner, Graham	11,500
31	14	H	St. Johnstone	—	W 2-0	1-0	Pettigrew, Marinello (pen)	4334
32	17	A	Hibernian	4	L 0-2	0-1		9098
33	21	A	Rangers	—	L 1-2	0-2	Stevens	27,000
34	24	H	Dundee	4	D 1-1	0-1	Marinello	4675
35	May 1	A	Dundee	4	L 0-1	0-0		7661
36	3	A	Ayr U.	—	L 1-2	1-0	Gardner	6500

Final Place: 4

Goalscorers

League (57): Pettigrew 22, Davidson 5, Graham 5, Gardner 4, Millar 4 (4 pens), Stevens 4, Taylor 4, Marinello 3 (1 pen), McLaren 2, McIlwraith 1, McVie 1, Watson R. 1, Own Goal 1.
League Cup (10): Pettigrew 4, Davidson 1, Goldthorp 1, Millar 1 (pen), Taylor 1, Wark 1, Watson R. 1.
Cup (12): Graham 3, Marinello 3 (2 pens), Pettigrew 3, Taylor 2, McLaren 1.

Honours

Scottish League: Division 1, Champions: 1931–32. Runners-up: 1926–27, 1929–30, 1932–33, 1933–34.
Division 2 Champions: 1953–54, 1968–69.
Scottish Cup: Winners: 1952. Finalists: 1931, 1933, 1939, 1951.
Scottish League Cup: Winners: 1950–51. Finalists: 1954–55.

Record Victory: 12–1 v Dundee U., Division 2, 1953–54.
Record Defeat: 3–8 v Patrick T. Division 1, Dec 11th 1971.
Most League Points: 66, Division 1, 1931–32.
Most Individual League Goals in Season: 52, Willie McFadyen, 1931–32.
Highest Scorer in Total Aggregate: Hugh Ferguson, 283, 1916–25.
Most Capped Player: George Stevenson, 12, Scotland.

Rennie, S.	Watson, W.	Wark, J.	Millar, P.	Watson, R.	McLaren, S.	McVie, W.	Goldthorp, J.	Gardner, P.	Davidson, V.	Graham, R.	Kennedy, I.	Pettigrew, W.	Stevens, G.	McAdam, C.	Taylor, I.	McIlwraith, J.	McManus, M.	Marinello, P.		Match No.
1	2	3		4		5		7*	12	9		8	6	10	11					1
1	2	3	13	4*	12	5			10	9		8	6	7	11†					2
1	2	3	7*	4	6	5	12		10	9		8	13	11†						3
1	7	3	11†	4	2	5		12	10	9		8	6*		13					4
1	2	3	7	4		5	13		10*	9		8	6	12	11†					5
1		3	7	4*	2	5			10†	9	12	8	6	11	13					6
1		3	2	4		5	12		10	9		8	6	7	11*					7
1		3	2	4		5			10	9		8	6	7	11					8
1	13	3	2	4	6	5			10†	9		8		7*	11	12				9
1	2	3	10	4	12	5			13	9		8	6*	7†	11					10
1		3	2	4*	6	5		13		9		8		7†	11	10	12			11
1		3	2	4	10	5			12	9		8	6		11*	7				12
1		3	2	4*	10	5			12	9		8	6		11	7				13
1		3	2		4	5		7	10	9		8	6		11*	12				14
1		3	2	13	4	5*		7	10	9		8	6	12	11†					15
1		3	2	13	4	5		11†	10	9*		8	6	12				7		16
1	12	3	2*	4†	7	5			10	9		8	6	13			11			17
1	2	3			4	5		7	10*	9		8	6	12			11			18
1	2	3		12	4	5		7	10	9*		8	6				11			19
1	2	3		4	10	5			9*			8	6	7	12		11			20
1	2	3	5*	4	10				7	9		8	6	12			11			21
1	2	3	12	4*	7†	5			10	9		8	6		13		11			22
1	2	3	12		4	5			10	9		8	6		7			11*		23
1	2	3	12	4*	6	5			10	9		8		11				7		24
1	2	3		4	6				10	9		8	5	12	11*			7		25
1		3		4	6	5		7	10*	9		8	2	11	12					26
1		3	2	4		5		7*	12	9		8	6		10		11			27
1	2	3	7*	4		5			12	10	9	8	6	13			11†			28
1	2	3	7	4*	11	5			10	9		8	12	6†		13				29
1		3	2	4	6	5		7*	10	9	11†	9	12		13					30
1		3	2	4	7	5			10	9		8	6				11			31
1		3	2*	4	7	5			12	10†	9	8	6		13		11			32
1		3		4	6	5			10	12	9	8	7	2	11*					33
1		3	12	4	7	5			10	9		8	6†	2*		13	11			34
1		3	2	4	7*	5			10	9		8	6	12			11†	13		35
1	2	3		4		5			8	10	9		6	11				7		36
36	17	36	23	30	29	32	0	12	29	34	1	35	30	15	17	3	1	16		
	+		+	+	+		+	+	+			+		+	+	+	+	+	+	
	2s		5s	3s	2s		3s	4s	6s			1s		3s	9s	7s	2s	2s	2s	

571

PARTICK THISTLE   PREM. DIV.

Year Formed: 1876. *Team Manager:* Robert Auld. *Asst. Manager:* Scot Symon. *Secretary:* J. C. Monachan, C.A. *Address:* Firhill Park, Glasgow, N.W. *Size:* 110×71 yards. *Capacity:* 36,000 (3,500 seated). *Telephone:* 041-946 2673. *Previous Grounds:* Kelvingrove, 1876–81; Jordanvale Park, 1881–83; Muirpark 1883–85; Meadowside Park, 1891–1908; Firhill Park, 1909 (1908–9, Ibrox was used by Partick when they had no ground of their own, but some 'home' games still had to be played away). *Nickname:* 'The Jags'. *Colours:* Red and yellow shirts, broad vertical stripes, black shorts, red stockings with black and yellow tops.
Record Attendance: 49,838, v Rangers, Division 1, Feb. 18th, 1922.
European Competitions Entered: Fairs Cup, 1963–64; UEFA Cup, 1973–74.

1975-76 LEAGUE RECORD

Match No.	Date	Venue	Opponents	Result	Score	H/T League Pos'n	Goalscorers	Attendance
1	Aug 30	A	Morton	—	D 0-0	0-0		3000
2	Sep 6	H	Clyde	4	W 1-0	1-0	Rooney	5000
3	13	A	Kilmarnock	2	W 1-0	0-0	Somner	8500
4	20	A	Dumbarton	1	W 3-2	2-0	Joe Craig 2, Somner (pen)	4000
5	27	H	Queen of the S.	1	W 2-1	1-0	McQuade, Somner	3450
6	Oct 4	A	Hamilton A.	1	W 2-1	0-1	McQuade 2	2500
7	11	H	Falkirk	1	W 3-2	1-0	McQuade, Somner 2	4500
8	18	H	Airdrieonians	1	L 0-1	0-0		6000
9	25	A	Arbroath	2	D 0-0	0-0		2147
10	Nov 1	H	Dunfermline Ath.	2	D 1-1	1-0	John Craig	4000
11	8	A	Montrose	2	L 1-2	0-1	Hansen J.	1750
12	15	H	East Fife	2	W 5-0	3-0	Houston, Joe Craig (pen), Somner 3	2500
13	22	H	St Mirren	2	W 2-1	1-0	McQuade, Somner	4500
14	29	A	Queen of the S.	2	D 1-1	1-0	Joe Craig	1500
15	Dec 6	H	Hamilton A.	2	W 2-0	0-0	Joe Craig, Somner	4000
16	13	A	Falkirk	2	D 0-0	0-0		4000
17	20	A	Airdrieonians	1	W 4-2	3-1	Hansen A., Joe Craig 3	5000
18	27	H	Arbroath	1	W 2-0	1-0	Joe Craig, McQuade	5000
19	Jan 1	A	Clyde	—	W 2-1	1-0	Joe Craig, Somner	3500
20	3	H	Kilmarnock	1	W 2-0	1-0	Rooney, Joe Craig	11,500
21	10	A	East Fife	1	D 1-1	0-1	John Craig	2167
22	17	A	St. Mirren	1	W 3-2	2-1	Hansen A., Houston, John Craig	10,000
23	31	A	Dumbarton	1	D 0-0	0-0		6000
24	Feb 7	H	Morton	1	W 2-0	0-0	McQuade, Somner (pen)	5000
25	21	A	Dunfermline Ath.	1	W 3-0	2-0	Joe Craig 2, Somner	4000
26	28	H	Montrose	1	W 4-1	2-0	Joe Craig, Somner 3	6000

Final Place: 1

Goalscorers

League (47): Somner 16 (2 pens), Joe Craig 14 (1 pen), McQuade 7, John Craig 3, Hansen A. 2, Houston 2, Rooney 2, Hansen J. 1.
League Cup (21): Joe Craig 7, Somner 6 (1 pen), Houston 3, Hansen J. 2, Campbell 1, John Craig 1, McQuade 1.
Cup (2): Joe Craig 1, McQuade 1.
Spring Cup (15): Somner 5, McQuade 4, Melrose 2, Anderson 1, Joe Craig 1, Houston 1, Whittaker 1.

Honours

Scottish League: Division 1: Champions 1975-76, Division 2: Champions: 1896-97, 1899-1900, 1970-71. Runners-up: 1901-02. *Scottish Cup:* Winners: 1921; Runners-up: 1930. *Scottish League Cup:* Winners: 1971-72. Runners-up: 1953-54, 1956-57, 1958-59. *Most Capped player:* John McKenzie 9, Scotland. *Most League Points:* 56, Division 2, 1970-71. *Record Victory:* 16-0 v Royal Albert, Scottish Cup, 1st Rd., Jan. 17th, 1931. *Record Defeat:* 1-10 v Dunfermline Ath., Division 1, 1958-59. *Most Individual League Goals in Season:* Alec Hair, 41, Division 1, 1926-27.

Rough, A.	Hansen, J.	Kellachan, D.	Campbell, J.	Hansen, A.	Anderson, A.	Marr, J.	Houston, R.	Rooney, B.	Craig, Joe	McQuade, D.	Somner, D.	Craig, John	Lawrie, R.	Melrose, J.	Whittaker, D.	Fitzpatrick, K.	Frame, A.	Match No.
1	2*	3	4	5	6	12	7	8	9†13	10	11							1
1	2	3	4*	5	6	13	7	8†	9	12	10	11						2
1	2	3	4	5	6		7		9*	8	10	11	12					3
1	2	3	4	5	6	12	7*		9	8	10	11						4
.1	2	3	4	5	6	9†	7*			8	10	11	12	13				5
1	2	3	4	5	6	9	7			8	10	11						6
1	2	3	4		6		7	5	9	8	10	11						7
1	2		4		6		7	5*	9	8	10	11			3	12		8
1	2	3	4		6	9		5	8	7*10	11					12		9
1	2	3	4	5	6	12	7	8*	9†13	10	11							10
1	2	3	4	5	6	7	11*		8		9	10				12		11
1	2	3	4	5	13		7	8	12	11†10	6					9*		12
1	2	3	4	5	12		7	8*13	11	10	6					9†		13
1	2	3	4*	5	6	13	7		8	11†	9	10			12			14
1	2	3		5	6		7	4	9	11	8	10						15
1	2	3		5	6	9		4	8	7	10	11						16
1	2	3		5	4	7	11	8	9		10	6						17
1	2	3		5	6	7		4	8	9	10	11						18
1	2	3		5	6	7		4	8	9	10	11						19
1	2	3		5	6	9	7	4	8		10	11						20
1	2	3	5		6	9	7*	4	8	12	10	11						21
1	2	3	12	5	6	9*	7	4	8		10	11						22
1	2	3	4	5		7	6	8	9	10	11							23
1	2	3	6	5†		9	7	4*	8	12	10	11				13		24
1	2	3	4		6	7	5	10	9†	8*11	13					12		25
1	2	3	6	5		8	7†	4*10	13	9	11					12		26
26	26	25	19	21	20	14	22	20	22	16	26	26	0	0	1	0	2	
			+1s		+2s	+5s			+2s	+6s			+1s	+2s		+6s	+2s	

QUEEN OF THE SOUTH

DIV. 1

Year Formed: 1919. *Ground:* Palmerston Park. *Size:* 111×73 yds. *Capacity:* 20,000.
Telephone: Dumfries 4853.
Secretary: John Watson.
Club Colours: Royal blue shirts with white facings, white shorts, royal blue stockings with two white
hoops on top.
Club Nickname: 'Queens' or 'The Doonhamers'.
Record Attendance: 24,500 v Hearts, Scottish Cup, 3rd Rd, Feb. 23rd, 1952.

1975–76 LEAGUE RECORD

Match No.	Date	Venue	Opponents	League Pos'n	Result	H/T Score	Goalscorers	Attendance
1	Aug 30	H	St. Mirren	—	D 2-2	1-2	McLaren, Bryce	2500
2	Sep 6	A	Hamilton A.	11	L 0-2	0-1		2000
3	13	H	Airdrieonians	14	L 1-7	1-5	Reid	3000
4	20	A	Arbroath	14	L 2-3	2-1	Dempster, Bryce	1441
5	27	A	Partick T.	14	L 1-2	0-1	Donald	3450
6	Oct 4	H	Montrose	14	W 2-1	0-0	Dickson G., Reid	1500
7	11	A	Dunfermline Ath.	14	D 2-2	1-0	Reid, Bryce	3000
8	18	H	Morton	14	L 0-1	0-1		1500
9	25	A	Dumbarton	14	L 1-2	0-2	Dempster (pen)	1500
10	Nov 1	H	East Fife	14	D 1-1	0-0	Miller (pen)	2000
11	8	A	Kilmarnock	14	L 0-2	0-0		5000
12	15	A	Falkirk	14	L 0-1	0-0		2500
13	22	H	Clyde	14	L 1-3	0-2	Reid	1500
14	29	H	Partick T.	14	D 1-1	0-1	Reid	1500
15	Dec 6	A	Montrose	14	L 1-2	0-2	Clark	1200
16	13	H	Dunfermline Ath.	14	W 5-2	1-1	Reid, Bryce, Dickson P.3	2000
17	20	A	Morton	14	W 1-0	1-0	Dickson P.	1200
18	27	H	Dumbarton	14	W 4-2	2-2	Reid 2, Dickson P., Muir (og)	2000
19	Jan 1	H	Hamilton A.	—	D 2-2	1-2	Boyd, Reid	3000
20	3	A	Airdrieonians	13	D 2-2	0-2	Dempster (pen), Reid	3000
21	10	H	Falkirk	13	W 3-2	2-2	Boyd, Dempster, Dickson P.	2000
22	17	A	Clyde	10	W 3-1	0-0	Dempster (pen), Dickson P. 2	1000
23	31	H	Arbroath	10	W 2-1	0-0	McLaren, Dickson P.	2000
24	Feb 7	A	St. Mirren	9	W 2-0	1-0	Dempster, Dickson P.	3000
25	21	A	East Fife	10	L 0-2	0-1		1462
26	28	H	Kilmarnock	10	W 2-1	2-0	Reid, Dickson P.	4500

Final Place: 10

Goalscorers

League (41): Dickson P. 11, Reid 11, Dempster 6 (3 pens), Bryce 4, Boyd 2, McLaren 2, Clark 1, Dickson
G. 1, Donald 1, Miller, 1 (pen), own goal 1.
League Cup (9): Bryce 4, Reid 2, Dempster 1, Renton 1, own goal 1.
Cup (10): Dempster 3 (1 pen), Reid 3, Dickson P. 2, Clark 1, Dickson G. 1
Spring Cup (6): Bryce 3, Dempster 1 (pen), Dickson P. 1, Reid 1.

Scottish League: Division 2: Champions: 1950–51; Runners-up: 1932–33, 1961–62, 1974-75.
Record Victory: 12-1 v Whithorn, 1920.
Record Defeat: 2-10 v Dundee, Division 1, December 1, 1962.
Most League Points: 53, Division 2, 1961–62.
Most Individual League Goals in Season: Jimmy Gray, 33, Division 2, 1927–28.
Most Capped Player: Billy Houliston, 3, Scotland.

McLean, G.	Ball, A.	Miller, J.	Thorburn, R.	McChesney, I.	McLaren, W.	Clark, R.	O'Hara, T.	Boyd, C.	Dempster, J.	Donald, J.	Renton, D.	Dickson, G.	Reid, L.	Mitchell, D.	Bryce, T.	Law, A.	Lochrie, A.	Mitchell, L.	Frye, J.	Dickson, P.	Murphy, J.	Match No.
1	2	3			4	5		6	7	11	8	10		9								1
1	2*	3	12		4	5		6	7	13		10†	9		11	8						2
1	2	3	13	4		6	5	7*				10	8		11	9†12						3
1	2		3	4		6*	5	7	9			10	8		11		12					4
1	2		3	4	12	6*	5	7	9			10†	8		11		13					5
1	2		3	4	5	6		7	10			8	9		11							6
1	2		3	4	5	6		7	8			10	9		11							7
1	2	3		4		6	5*	10	7	8			9	12	11†				12			8
1	2	3		4		6	5	7*	8	13			9	10	11†				12			9
1	2		3	4		6	5		11	12	10†	9	8*					7	13			10
1	2		3	4		6*	5	8	11†12	10	9	7						13				11
1	2		3		5		6	7		10	8	9	11					4				12
1	8		3*	4		5	11		6	10	13	7†12					2		9			13
1	8	3		4	2	6	5	7		11	10							9				14
1	8*	3	12	4	2	6	5	7		11	10†		13					9				15
1	2	3		6	4	10	5	7				9	11*					8	12			16
1		3	2	6	4	10	5	7		11	9							8				17
1		3	2	6	4	10	5	7*		11	9							8	12			18
1		3	2	6	4	10	5	7*13		11†	9							8	12			19
1	12	3	2	6*	4	10	5	7	13	11†	9							8				20
1	12	3	2	6	4	10	5	7		11*	8							9				21
1		3	2	6	4	10	5	7		11	9							8				22
1	12	3	2	6	4	10	5	7		11*	9							8				23
1		3	2	6	4	10	5	7		11	9							8				24
1	4	3	2	6	5	10			7*11		9	12						8				25
1	12	3	2*	6	4	10	5	7		11	8							9				26
2	24	17	17	19	25	19	22	23	24	10	4	22	24	5	10	2	0	1	2	14	0	
			+4s		+3s		+1s			+3s	+3s		+1s	+2s	+2s		+3s	+1s	+2s		+3s	

QUEEN'S PARK　　　　　　　　　　　　DIV. 2

Year Formed: 1867.　*Ground:* Hampden Park.　*Telephone:* 041 632 1275 (ground).
Secretary: James Logan, C.A.　*Ground Secretary:* James Gillies.
Club Colours: Black and white hooped shirts, white shorts, white stockings with two black hoops on top.
Club Nickname: 'Spiders'.
　　　　　　　　　　(Only amateur club in British senior football)
Record Attendance: 97,000 v Rangers, Scottish Cup 2nd Rd, Feb. 18th, 1933.
　　　　　　　(Record for ground—149,547, Scotland v England, 1937)
Previous Grounds: Queen's Park (re-named Cathkin Park) 1868–73.

1975-76 LEAGUE RECORD

Match No.	Date	Venue	Opponents	League Pos'n	Result	H/T Score	Goalscorers	Atten-dance
1	Aug 30	H	Stirling Albion	—	W 3-1	1-0	Currie (pen), McGill 2	500
2	Sep 6	A	East Stirling	5	L 1-2	0-1	Paton	550
3	13	H	Meadowbank T.	6	D 1-1	0-1	Wilkie	600
4	20	H	Raith R.	9	L 2-3	2-2	McGill, Wilkie	600
5	27	A	Stranraer	9	D 1-1	0-0	McGill	750
6	Oct 4	A	Brechin C.	10	L 0-1	0-0		300
7	11	H	Berwick R.	9	W 1-0	0-0	Nicholson	800
8	18	A	Forfar Ath.	10	L 1-4	1-3	McGill	360
9	25	A	Clydebank	10	D 1-1	1-1	McGill	1800
10	Nov 1	A	Alloa	10	D 3-3	2-0	McKay, McNaughton, Colgan	700
11	8	H	Albion R.	9	D 2-2	1-0	Campbell (pen), McNaughton	1000
12	15	A	Stenhousemuir	10	D 2-2	2-1	Paton, Rodgers	300
13	22	H	Cowdenbeath	8	W 4-1	2-0	McGill 2, Campbell (pen) Breen (og)	800
14	29	H	Stranraer	7	W 2-0	0-0	Campbell, McNaughton	930
15	Dec 6	H	Brechin C.	5	W 1-0	0-0	McNaughton	900
16	20	H	Forfar Ath.	5	W 4-0	1-0	Campbell (pen), Paton, McNaughton, Colgan	800
17	27	H	Clydebank	6	L 0-2	0-2		1100
18	Jan 1	H	East Stirling	—	W 1-0	1-0	McKay	1500
19	3	A	Meadowbank T.	5	L 0-1	0-0		350
20	17	A	Cowdenbeath	5	D 2-2	0-2	Currie, Colgan	500
21	31	H	Raith R.	5	W 2-0	1-0	McNaughton, Colgan	2791
22	Feb 7	A	Stirling Albion	4	W 3-1	1-1	Paton, McNaughton, Dickson	850
23	14	A	Berwick R.	4	D 1-1	1-1	Rooney	235
24	21	H	Alloa	4	W 3-1	3-1	Currie, McNaughton, Wilkie	700
25	24	H	Stenhousemuir	—	L 0-3	0-2		500
26	28	A	Albion R.	4	D 0-0	0-0		400

Final Place: 4

Goalscorers

League (41): McGill 8, McNaughton 8, Campbell 4 (3 pens), Colgan 4, Paton 4, Currie 3 (1 pen), Wilkie 3, McKay 2, Dickson 1, Nicholson 1, Rodgers 1, Rooney 1, own goal 1.
League Cup (10): Rooney 3, Campbell 2 (1 pen), McWilliams 2, Currie 1, Paton 1, Wilkie 1.
Cup (0).
Spring Cup (12): Donnelly B. 3, Campbell 2 (2 pens), McNaughton 2, Rooney 2, Colgan 1, Dickson 1, Paton 1.

Honours

Scottish League: Division 2 Champions 1922–23, 1955–56.
Scottish Cup: Winners 1874, 1875, 1876, 1880, 1881, 1882, 1884, 1886, 1890, 1893; Finalists 1892, 1900.
F.A. Cup: Finalists 1884, 1885.
Record Victory: 16-0 v St. Peters, Scottish Cup, 1st Rd., 1885–86.
Record Defeat: 0-9 v Motherwell, Division 1, April 26, 1930.
Most League Points: 57, Division 2, 1922–23.
Most Individual League Goals in Season: Willie Martin, 30, Division 1, 1937–38.
Most Capped Player: Watty Arnold, 14, Scotland.

Cameron, R.	Anderson, R.	Currie, W.	Gillespie, D.	Thomson, C.	Campbell, I.	McDonald, A.	Duff, P.	Bowie, A.	Paton, J.	Rooney, J.	McKay, M.	Nicholson, J.	McNaughton, A.	McWilliams, I.	McGill, H.	Wilkie, D.	Colgan, G.	Dickson, R.	Rodgers, D.	Finnigan, J.	Kane, J.	McSkimming, R.	Donnelly, T.	Heggie, S.	Sinclair, J.	Donnelly, B.	Match No.
1	3	2						5	4	10	9				6	8	11				7						1
1	3				4			5	7	10	9				6	8		11				2					2
	3	1			4			5		10		8			6	9	7	12	11*			2					3
1	3					13		5	4	10		8	7	6†	9	11	12					2*					4
1					6			5	10		7	8			9		11			4		2	3				5
1	12				4			5	11†			9*	8	6	10	7	13					2	3				6
1	6							5	4		12			9	8	7	10	11				2*	3				7
1	6							5	4	10		9†	7	8	12	11			13			2	3*				8
1								5	4	10	8		7	6	9		11					2	3				9
1					12			5	4		8		7	6	9	11*10						2	3				10
1					10			5	4		9*		7	6	8	12	11†		13			2	3				11
1					4			5	7	10			8	6	9				11			2	3				12
1					4†			5	7	10	13		8	6	9	11	12					2	3*				13
1					4			5	7	10			8	6	9	11	3					2					14
1					4			5	7	10	12		8	6	9*11†	3		13				2					15
1	6				4			5	7	10†			8	9*	11	3					2	12	13				16
1	6				4			5†	7	10	13		8	9	11	3		12			2*						17
1	6				4			5	4	10	8			9	11	3		7			2						18
1	6				4			5	4	10	8†13	9			11	3		7*			2	12					19
1	4	6						5	11	8	9*	10				3		12			2	7					20
1	6				4			5	7	10			8			3	11				2				9		21
1	6				4			5	7	10			8			3	11				2				9		22
1	6				4			5	7	10			8		12	3	11*				2				9		23
1	6							5	4*10				8			11	3				2	7	12	9			24
1	6					13		5	4	10			8			11	3				2*	7†	12	9			25
1		6			12			5	7	10			8			3	11†		2			13	4*	9			26
25	4	13	1	1	14	1	0	26	22	24	8	5	22	15	15	15	19	7	4	1	4	21	9	3	1	6	

Substitute totals (+ ns): +1s (Anderson); +1s +1s +2s (Campbell, McDonald, Duff); +3s +2s (Nicholson, McNaughton); +3s +4s (Wilkie, Colgan); +4s +1s (Rodgers, Finnigan); +1s +3s +2s (Donnelly T., Heggie, Sinclair).

577

RAITH ROVERS

DIV. 1

Year Formed: 1893. *Ground:* Stark's Park. *Capacity:* 28,000. *Telephone:* Kirkcaldy 3514. *Manager:* R. Paton. *Club Seeretary:* Mrs. M. B. Watters. *Club Colours:* Royal blue, white. *Record Attendance:* 30,000 v Hibs, Scottish Cup 1st Rd, Jan. 26th, 1952 and v Hearts, Scottish Cup 2nd Rd, Feb. 7th, 1953. *Previous Grounds:* Robbie's Park 1883–89.

1975-76 LEAGUE RECORD

Match No.	Date	Venue	Opponents	League Pos'n	Result	H/T Score	Goalscorers	Attendance
1	Aug 30	H	Stranraer	—	D 3-3	1-2	Urquhart, Duncan, Heap (og)	1402
2	Sep 6	A	Cowdenbeath	6	D 1-1	0-0	Urquhart	1350
3	13	H	Stenhousemuir	3	W 2-0	2-0	Robertson, Duncan	1292
4	20	A	Queen's Park	2	W 3-2	2-2	Brown T., Robertson, Wallace	600
5	27	H	Forfar Ath.	3	D 2-2	1-2	Brown J., Duncan	1113
6	Oct 4	A	Clydebank	3	D 1-1	0-0	Robertson	1200
7	11	H	Alloa	2	W 1-0	0-0	Robertson (pen)	1756
8	18	A	Meadowbank T.	2	W 1-0	1-0	Cooper	650
9	25	H	Albion R.	2	D 1-1	1-1	Robertson (pen)	1782
10	Nov 1	H	Stirling Albion	2	D 2-2	1-1	Robertson 2	2145
11	8	A	East Stirling	3	D 1-1	0-1	Hislop	800
12	15	A	Berwick R.	3	W 3-1	2-1	Robertson 2 (1 pen), Hislop	450
13	22	H	Brechin C.	2	D 1-1	0-0	Duncan	1651
14	29	A	Forfar Ath.	3	D 0-0	0-0		450
15	Dec 6	H	Clydebank	3	W 1-0	0-0	Hislop	2526
16	20	H	Meadowbank T.	2	W 3-2	0-1	Brown W., Urquhart, Graham	1578
17	27	A	Albion R.	2	W 2-1	2-0	Wallace 2	800
18	Jan 1	H	Cowdenbeath	—	W 2-1	1-0	Wallace, Graham	3119
19	3	A	Stenhousemuir	2	W 3-0	2-0	Wallace 2, Hislop	1200
20	17	A	Brechin C.	1	W 4-0	2-0	Brown J., Wallace, Graham, Duncan	800
21	31	H	Queen's Park	2	L 0-2	0-1		2791
22	Feb 7	A	Stranraer	2	W 3-1	1-1	Brown J. (pen), Wallace, Hunter	1000
23	28	H	East Stirling	2	D 0-0	0-0		2000
24	Mar 6	A	Stirling Albion	—	W 1-0	1-0	Wallace	1600
25	17	H	Berwick R.	—	W 3-0	2-0	Duncan, Jobson 2	2518
26	31	A	Alloa	2	W 1-0	0-0	Hunter	3400

Final Place: 2

Goalscorers

League (45): Robertson 9 (3 pens), Wallace 9, Duncan 6, Hislop 4, Brown J. 3 (1 pen), Graham 3, Urquhart 3, Hunter 2, Jobson 2, Brown T. 1, Brown W. 1, Cooper 1, own goal 1.
League Cup (7): Robertson 5 (2 pens), Duncan 1, Hislop 1.
Cup (7): Wallace 4, Graham 2, Hunter 1.
Spring Cup (14): Wallace 5, Hislop 2 (1 pen), Urquhart 2, Brown T. 1, Duncan 1, Graham 1, Hunter 1, Jobson 1.

578

Honours:
Scottish League: Division 2 Champions 1907–08, 1909–10 (shared), 1937–38, 1948–49; Runners-up 1926-27, 1966-67, 1975-76.
Scottish Cup: Finalists 1913.
League Cup: Finalists 1948–49.
Record Victory: 10-1 v Coldstream, Scottish Cup, 2nd Rd., February 13, 1954.
Record Defeat: 2-11 v Morton, Division 2, 1935–36.
Most League Points: 59, Division 2, 1937–38.
Most Individual League Goals in Season: Norman Haywood, 39, Division 2, 1937-38.
Most Capped Player: Dave Morris, 6, Scotland.

McDermott, M.	Brown, J.	Dempster, C.	Brown, W.	Cairns, D.	Cooper, B.	Brown, T.	Taylor, J.	Urquhart, D.	Robertson, M.	Wallace, G.	Hislop, J.	Graham, R.	Duncan, R.	Hunter, D.	Jobson, J.	McFarlane, T.	Candlish, C.	Match No.
1	2		3		6	4	5	10	7	8		9	11					1
1	2		3		6	4	5	10	7	8		9	11					2
1	2		3	5	6	8	4	10	7	9			11					3
1	2		3	5	6	8†	4*10	7	9	13			11	12				4
1	2		3	5	6	8	4*10	7	9				11	12				5
1	2	3		5	6	12	4	7	8			9	11	10*				6
1	2	3		5	6	8	4	7	12			9*	11	10				7
1	2	3		5	6	8*	4	7	9	12			11	10				8
1	2		3		6	4	5	10	7	9	11		12		8*			9
1	2		3		6	8	5	4*	7	9	12		11	10				10
1	2		3		6	4	5		7	8	12	9*11	10					11
1	2		3		6	4*	5	12	7	8	9		11	10				12
1	2		3		6	4	5		7	8	9		11	10				13
1	2		3		6		5		7	8	9*		11	10	12	4		14
1	2		3		6		5	12	8	7	9	11	10*			4		15
1	2		3		6	12	5	4	8	7*	9		11	10				16
1	2		3		6	12	5*	4	8	7	9		11	10				17
1	2		3		6		5	4	8	7	9		11	10				18
1	2		3		6	12	5	4	8	7*	9†11	10	13					19
1	2		3		6	12	5	4*	8	7	9	11	10†	13				20
1	2		3		6	12	5	4	8	7*	9†11	10	13					21
1	2	3*12	6		7	5		8	13	9	11	10†	4					22
1	2	3*		6		5	7	8†13	9	11	10					4	12	23
1	2				6		5	3	8	7	9	11	10			4		24
1	2				6	13	5	3	8	7	12	11	10†	9*	4			25
1	2				6		5	3	8	7	9	11	10			4		26
26	26	3	18	8	26	13	24	19	14	25	14	16	25	20	2	7	0	
			+1s		+7s		+2s	+1s	+6s	+1s	+1s	+2s	+2s	+2s	+1s			

RANGERS

Year Formed: 1873. *Turned Professional:* 1893. *Limited Company:* 1899.
Ground: Ibrox Stadium. *Size:* 115 × 72 yds. *Capacity:* 71,000 (19,500 seated). *Telephone:* 041-427. 0159.
Manager: Jock Wallace. *Secretary:* Frank King.
Club Colours: Royal blue shirts, with white shorts. Stockings black with red tops.
Club Nicknames: 'Blues' or 'Gers'.
Record Attendance: 118,567 v Celtic, Division 1, Jan. 2nd, 1939.
Previous Grounds: Flesher's Haugh on Glasgow Green was shared with Great Eastern F.C.; Kinning Park, Burnbank; Ibrox Park since 1887.
European Competitions Entered: European Cup: 1956–57, 1957–58, 1959–60, 1961–62, 1963–64, 1964–65; European Cup Winners Cup: 1960–61 (finalists), 1962–63, 1966–67 (finalists), 1969–70, 1971–72 (winners), 1973–74; Fairs Cup: 1967–68, 1968–69.
Record Transfer Fee Received: £140,000 from Coventry C. for Colin Stein, Oct. 1972.
Record Transfer Fee Paid: £100,000 to Hibernian for Colin Stein, Oct. 1968.

1975–76 LEAGUE RECORD

Match No.	Date	Venue	Opponents	League Pos'n	Result	H/T Score	Goalscorers	Attendance
1	Aug 30	H	Celtic	—	W 2-1	0-1	Johnstone, Young	69,000
2	Sep 6	A	Hearts	1	W 2-0	2-0	Anderson (og), Murray (og)	25,000
3	13	H	St. Johnstone	1	W 2-0	0-0	Johnstone, Stein	25,000
4	20	H	Hibernian	1	D 1-1	1-0	Blackley (og)	37,000
5	27	A	Dundee	1	D 0-0	0-0		15,087
6	Oct 4	H	Aberdeen	1	W 1-0	1-0	McDougall	22,000
7	11	A	Ayr U.	2	L 0-3	0-2		15,000
8	18	A	Motherwell	2	L 1-2	1-0	Johnstone	18,925
9	Nov 1	A	Celtic	4	D 1-1	0-0	Parlane	55,000
10	8	H	Hearts	6	L 1-2	0-2	Henderson	24,000
11	12	H	Dundee U.	—	W 4-1	1-0	Jackson, MacDonald, Forsyth, Parlane	10,000
12	15	A	St. Johnstone	1	W 5-1	2-0	Jardine, McLean, Parlane, McKean, MacDonald (og)	9500
13	22	A	Hibernian	4	L 1-2	0-1	Young	26,547
14	29	H	Dundee	4	W 2-1	2-1	Henderson 2	15,000
15	Dec 6	A	Aberdeen	4	L 0-1	0-0		19,565
16	13	H	Ayr U.	4	W 3-0	0-0	Jardine (pen), McKean, Henderson	20,000
17	20	H	Motherwell	2	W 3-2	1-1	Johnstone 2, Henderson	20,000
18	27	A	Dundee U.	2	D 0-0	0-0		11,500
19	Jan 1	H	Celtic	—	W 1-0	1-0	Johnstone	57,839
20	3	A	Hearts	2	W 2-1	0-0	Henderson 2	23,000
21	10	H	St. Johnstone	2	W 4-0	1-0	Miller (pen), Johnstone, McKean, Hamilton	18,000
22	17	H	Hibernian	1	W 2-0	0-0	McLean, Parlane	40,000
23	31	A	Dundee	2	D 1-1	0-0	Johnstone	14,407
24	Feb 7	H	Aberdeen	2	W 2-1	2-0	MacDonald, Henderson	20,000
25	21	A	Ayr U.	2	W 1-0	0-0	McKean	15,000
26	28	A	Motherwell	2	W 1-0	1-0	Johnstone	25,241
27	Mar 20	H	Hearts	2	W 3-1	1-0	Jackson, Johnstone, McLean	30,000
28	27	A	St. Johnstone	2	W 3-0	1-0	Greig, Johnstone 2	9079
29	Apr 3	A	Hibernian	2	W 3-0	1-0	MacDonald, Johnstone, Henderson	18,820
30	10	H	Dundee	1	W 3-0	2-0	Greig, Johnstone, McKean	25,000
31	14	A	Aberdeen	—	D 0-0	0-0		17,968
32	17	H	Ayr U.	1	W 2-1	1-1	MacDonald, Parlane	25,000
33	21	H	Motherwell	—	W 2-1	1-0	McLean, Henderson	27,000
34	24	A	Dundee U.	1	W 1-0	1-0	Johnstone	17,000
35	26	A	Celtic	—	D 0-0	0-0		51,000
36	May 4	H	Dundee U.	—	D 0-0	0-0		40,000

Final Place: 1

Goalscorers

League (60): Johnstone 15, Henderson 10, McKean 5, Parlane 5, MacDonald 4, McLean 4, Greig 2, Jackson 2, Jardine 2 (1 a pen), Young 2, Forsyth 1, Hamilton 1, McDougall 1, Miller 1 (pen), Stein 1, own goals 4.
League Cup (27): Jardine 5 (2 pens), Johnstone 5, Miller 4 (4 pens), Parlane 4, MacDonald 3, Young 2, Greig 1, Jackson 1, Scott 1, Stein 1.
Cup (18): Johnstone 7, Henderson 3, MacDonald 3, McKean 2, Hamilton 1, Miller 1 (pen), Parlane 1.

Honours

Scottish League: Division 1, Champions: 1890–91 (shared with Dumbarton), 1898–99, 1899–1900, 1900–01, 1901–02, 1910–11, 1911–12, 1912–13, 1917–18, 1919–20, 1920–21, 1922–23, 1923–24, 1924–25, 1926–27, 1927–28, 1928–29, 1929–30, 1930–31, 1932–33, 1933–34, 1934–35, 1936–37 1938–39, 1946–47, 1948–49, 1949–50, 1952–53, 1955–56, 1956–57, 1958–59, 1960–61, 1962–63, 1963–64, 1974–75, Premier Division: 1975–76, Runners-up: 21 times.

Scottish Cup: Winners: 1894, 1897, 1898, 1903, 1928, 1930, 1932, 1934, 1935, 1936, 1948, 1949, 1950, 1953, 1960, 1962, 1963, 1964, 1966, 1973, 1976; Runners-up: 10 times.

Scottish League Cup: Winners: 1946–47, 1948–49, 1960–61, 1961–62, 1963–64, 1964–65, 1970–71, 1975–76. Runners-up: 5 times.

Record Victory: 14-2 v Blarigowrie, Scottish Cup, 1st Rd. Jan 20th, 1934. *Record Defeat:* 2-10 v Airdrie, 1886. *Most League Points:* 76, Division 1, 1920–21. *Most Individual League Goals in Season:* 44, Sam English, Division 1, 1931-32. *Highest Scorer in Total Aggregate:* Bob McPhail, 233, 1927–39. *Most Capped Player:* George Young, 53, Scotland. *Most League Appearances:* Davie Meikeljohn, 493.

McCloy, P.	Kennedy, S.	Jardine, A.	Miller, A.	Greig, J.	Jackson, C.	MacDonald, A.	Forsyth, T.	Johnstone, D.	McLean, T.	Stein, C.	Parlane, D.	McKean, R.	Denny, J.	Fyfe, G.	O'Hara, A.	Scott, A.	Young, Q.	Henderson, M.	Dawson, A.	McDougall, J.	Hamilton, J.	Boyd, G.	Match No.
1	2*		3	5	6	4	10	7	9		8					12		11					1
1		2	3	5	6	4*10	7	13	9	8†12								11					2
1		2	3	4	5	6	10		13	9†	7*12		8					11					3
1			3	4	5	6	10	7*13	9	8	2	12						11†					4
1		2	4	5	6		10	7	9									11		3	8			5
1		2	6	4	5		10	7	9									11		3	8			6
1		2	12	4	5	6	10	7	9†13			11								3	8*			7
1	2		3	5	6	4	11	7	10	9	8												8
1	2		3	5	6	4	10	7	8	9								11					9
1	2		3	5	6	4	13	12		9	8		7*					11			10†		10
1	4		3	10	5	12	6	11†	7		9	8*	2					13					11
1	4		3	5	10	6	11	7		9	8	2											12
1	4		3	5	10	6	11	7		9†	8*	2				12	13						13
1		2	3	5	6	4	11	10		7								9		8			14
1		2	3	5	6	4	11	10		7								9		8			15
1		2	3	5	6	4	11	10		7								9		8			16
1	2*12		3	5	6	4	11	10		7								9		8			17
1		2	3	5	6	4*11	10			7	12							9		8			18
1		2	3	5	6	4	11	10		7*		13	12					9		8†			19
1		2	3	5	6	4	11	10		7	12							9		8*			20
1		2	3	5	6	4	11	10		7								9		8			21
1		2	3	5	6	4		10	11	7								9		8			22
1		2	3	5	6	4	11	10	9*	7								12		8			23
1	12	2	3	5	6	4	11	10	13	7								9†		8*			24
1	12	2	3	5	6	4		10	11	7								9		8*			25
1	13	2	3	5	6	4	11	7*	12	10								9		8†			26
1		2	3	5	6	4	11	10		7								9		8			27
1	12	2	3	5	6	4	11	10	13	7*								9†		8			28
1		2	3	5	6	4	11	10	12	7								9*		8			29
1	13	2	3	5	6	4	11	10†	12	7								9		8*			30
1	13	2	3	5	6	4	11	10†	12	7*								9		8			31
1	12	2	3	5*	6	4	11	10	13	7								9†		8			32
1		4	2	3		6	5*11	10		7	12							9		8			33
1		8	3	4	5	6		11	10		7	2						9					34
1		2	3	4		6		5	10		11	7						9		8			35
1		4	2	3		6		10		11	7	5*						9		12	8		36
24	12	18	25	36	33	34	28	32	34	3	17	32	6	1	1	1	7	23	3	22		1	
	+7s	+2s		+1s		+1s	+1s	+3s	+7s	+1s	+3s	+2s	+3s	+1s	+1s	+3s			+1s				

ST. JOHNSTONE

DIV. 1

Year Formed: 1884.
Ground: Muirton Park. *Size:* 115 × 74 yds. *Capacity:* 28,000 (2,500 seats).
Telephone: Perth 26961.
Manager:
Secretary: George Bell. *Coach:* J. Lambie. *Physiotherapist:* J. Peacock.
Club Colours: Royal blue with white collar and cuffs, white shorts and white with royal blue tops stockings.
Club Nickname: 'Saints'.
Record Attendance: 29,972, v Dundee, Scottish Cup, 2nd Rd. Feb. 10th, 1952.
Previous Ground: Perth Recreation Ground.
European Competition Entered: UEFA Cup 1971–72.

1975–76 LEAGUE RECORD

Match No.	Date	Venue	Opponents	League Pos'n	Result	H/T Score	Goalscorers	Attendance
1	Aug 30	H	Dundee U.	—	W 1-0	0-0	Muir	3300
2	Sept 6	A	Ayr U.	7	L 0-1	0-0		4194
3	13	A	Rangers	8	L 0-2	0-0		25,000
4	20	H	Celtic	9	L 1-2	0-1	McCluskey (og)	12,000
5	27	A	Hibernian	10	L 2-4	1-2	O'Rourke, Lambie	5700
6	Oct 4	H	Motherwell	9	W 2-1	1-0	O'Rourke 2	2600
7	11	A	Dundee	10	L 3-4	2-2	Muir, Thomson, Cramond	5316
8	18	A	Aberdeen	10	L 0-2	0-0		5100
9	25	H	Hearts	10	L 0-1	0-0		4700
10	Nov 1	A	Dundee U.	10	L 1-3	0-1	Smith G. (pen)	4850
11	8	H	Ayr U.	10	L 0-1	0-1		2097
12	15	H	Rangers	10	L 1-5	0-2	Muir	9500
13	22	A	Celtic	10	L 2-3	2-1	O'Rourke, Smith C.	20,000
14	29	H	Hibernian	10	L 3-4	2-3	Smith G. (pen), Smith C. 2	4484
15	Dec 6	A	Motherwell	10	L 1-2	0-0	McGregor	5632
16	13	H	Dundee	10	L 1-3	0-1	O'Rourke	3500
17	20	H	Aberdeen	10	D 1-1	0-0	O'Rourke	3500
18	27	A	Hearts	10	L 0-2	0-1		9000
19	Jan 1	H	Dundee U.	—	D 1-1	0-1	O'Rourke	4825
20	3	A	Ayr U.	10	L 0-2	0-1		4300
21	10	A	Rangers	10	L 0-4	0-1		18,000
22	17	H	Celtic	10	L 3-4	2-2	Thomson, Cramond, Lambie	9915
23	31	A	Hibernian	10	L 0-5	0-2		7839
24	Feb 7	H	Motherwell	10	L 1-3	1-2	O'Rourke	500
25	21	A	Dundee	10	L 0-3	0-0		4114
26	28	A	Aberdeen	10	L 0-3	0-1		5920
27	Mar 20	H	Ayr U.	10	L 1-2	0-0	Lamie	1500
28	27	H	Rangers	10	L 0-3	0-1		9079
29	31	A	Dundee U.	—	D 1-1	0-0	McGregor	3500
30	Apr 3	A	Celtic	10	L 0-1	0-1		16,000
31	10	H	Hibernian	10	L 0-2	0-2		2182
32	14	A	Motherwell	—	L 0-2	0-1		4334
33	17	H	Dundee	10	D 1-1	0-0	Anderson	3410
34	21	H	Aberdeen	—	W 2-0	1-0	Thomson, Hotson	2500
35	24	A	Hearts	10	L 0-1	0-0		8500
36	26	H	Hearts	—	D 0-0	0-0		3101

Final Place: 10

Goalscorers

League (29): O'Rourke 8, Lambie 3, Muir 3, Smith C. 3, Thomson 3, Cramond 2, McGregor 2, Smith G. 2 (2 pens), Anderson 1, Hotson 1, own goal 1.
League Cup (6): O'Rourke 2, Thomson 2, Muir 1, Smith G. 1 (pen).
Cup (2): Anderson 1, Thomson 1.

Honours

Scottish League: Division 2, Champions: 1923–24, 1959–60, 1962–63. Runners-up: 1931–32.
Scottish League Cup: Runners-up: 1969–70.
Record Victory: 8-1 v Partick T. Scottish Cup 1969-70.
Record Defeat: 1-10 v Third Lanark, Scottish Cup 1st Round Jan. 24th, 1903.
Most League Points: 56, Division 2, 1923–24.
Most Individual League Goals in Season: Jimmy Benson 36, Dvision 2, 1931-32.
Most Capped Players: Sandy McLaren, 2, Scotland.

Nicoll, D.	Robertson, D.	Smith, G.	Smith, A.	MacLeod, D.	Ritchie, W.	Roberts, P.	Kinnell, A.	MacDonald, I.	Muir, J.	O'Rourke, J.	Thomson, R.	McGregor, G.	Cramond, G.	Lambie, D.	Smith, C.	Hamilton, L.	Hotson, J.	Henderson, A.	Stevenson, J.	Anderson, I.	McCulloch, G.	Mackay, J.	McBean, S.	Match No.
	1	2	3		4	6	5	7	8	9		10	11											1
	1	2	3	12	4	6	5	7	8	9		10*	11											2
	1	2	3		4	6	5	7	8	9						10	11							3
	1	2	3			6	5	7	8	9	12	10	11		4*									4
	1	2	3		4	6	5	7	8			10	11				9							5
	1	2	10		4	6	5	7	8	9*	12	3	11											6
1	2	10			4	6	5	7	8	9		3	11											7
	1	2	3		4*	6	5	7	8	9	11	10				12								8
	1	2			4	6	5	7	8	9		3	11			10*	12							9
	1	2	3	12	4	6	5		8†	9	13	10	11						7*					10
	1	2*	10		4	6	5	7	8	9		3	11	12										11
	1	2	10		4	6	5	7	8	9*	12	3	11											12
1	2	3			4	6*	5		8	9		10	11			7		12						13
	1	2	6		3	4*	5		8	9	12	10	11			7								14
	1	2	6		3	4	5		8	9	13	10	11†	12		7*								15
	1	2	6		3		5	7	8	9	13	10	11†		4*	12								16
	1	2	3		4		5		8	9		10	11			7		6						17
	1	2	3		4		5		8	9	12	10	11†			7*		13		6				18
	1	2	3			6	5	7	8	9		10	11							4				19
	1	2	3		4		5	7	8	9		10	11			12				6*				20
	1	2	3		4		5		8	9		10	11			7				6				21
	1	3	2*	12			5	13	8	9		10			6	11			7*	4				22
	1	3	2				5		8	9					6	11	7			4	10			23
	1	3	2				5		8	9		10	11		6		7			4				24
	1	3	2			6			8	9		10	11		5		7			4				25
	1	2	9		3	6		7	8		12	10	11*		5					4				26
	1	2	9		3	6	5		8		12	10	11*				7			4				27
	1	2	9		3*	6	5		8		13	10	11*			12	7			4				28
1	2	3				6	5		8	9		10	11				7			4				29
1	2	3				6	5		8*	9		10	11			12	7			4				30
	1	2	3*			6	5	7	8	9		10	11*			12	13			4				31
	1	2	8			6	5			9		10	11				7			4			3	32
	1	2	12			6	5*		8	9		10	11				7			4			3	33
	1	2				6	5		8	9	12	10	11				7*			4			3	34
	1	2				6	5		8	9		10	11				7*			4	12		3	35
	1	2			4	6*	5		8	9		10	11			12	7						3	36
4	32	32	23	1	21	20	25	30	24	34	23	15	25	26	8	9	13	4	1	20	1	0	5	

Goals: + 1s (Nicoll), + 1s (Robertson), + 1s (Smith, G.), + 1s (Smith, A.); + 2s (Muir); + 3s (Thomson), + 9s (McGregor); + 1s, + 1s, + 4s, + 4s, + 2s; + 1s.

ST. MIRREN DIV. 1

Year Formed: 1876. *Ground:* St. Mirren Park (Also known as Love Street). *Capacity:* 53,000.
Telephone: 041840 1337
Manager: Alex Ferguson, *Secretary:* J. Aitken. *Club Colours:* Black and white stripes, white shorts and white stockings, with two black bands. *Club Nickname:* 'The Buddies'.
Record Attendance: 47,428 v Celtic, Scottish Cup, 4th Rd, Mar. 7th, 1925.

1975-76 LEAGUE RECORD

Match No.	Date	Venue	Opponents	League Pos'n	Result	H/T Score	Goalscorers	Attendance
1	Aug 30	A	Queen of the S.	—	D 2-2	2-1	Leonard 2	2500
2	Sep 6	H	Morton	7	D 2-2	2-0	McDowell, Stark	3400
3	13	A	Clyde	11	L 0-3	0-2		1500
4	20	H	Montrose	8	W 3-1	1-0	Young, McDowell 2	2100
5	27	A	Dunfermline Ath.	9	D 2-2	2-0	McDowell 2	2500
6	Oct 4	A	Kilmarnock	9	L 1-3	1-3	Ferguson	4000
7	11	H	East Fife	8	W 2-0	1-0	McDowell, Ferguson	2000
8	18	H	Dumbarton	6	W 3-2	1-0	Reid R., McDowell, McGillivray	3500
9	25	A	Hamilton A.	4	W 1-0	0-0	McGillivray (pen)	2500
10	Nov 1	H	Airdrieonians	4	D 2-2	2-1	McDowell, McGillivray (pen)	3600
11	8	H	Falkirk	4	W 1-0	0-0	McGarvey	2600
12	15	A	Arbroath	4	L 1-4	0-1	Stark	1279
13	22	A	Partick T.	5	L 1-2	0-1	McGarvey	4500
14	29	H	Dunfermline Ath.	4	W 2-0	0-0	McGillivray, McGarvey	2500
15	Dec 6	A	Kilmarnock	5	D 0-0	0-0		5800
16	13	A	East Fife	4	W 2-0	1-0	McDowell, Stark	1548
17	20	A	Dumbarton	5	L 0-2	0-1		3000
18	27	H	Hamilton A.	5	D 2-2	2-1	Borthwick 2 (1 a pen)	4000
19	Jan 1	A	Morton	—	L 0-1	0-0		2300
20	3	H	Clyde	4	W 3-0	2-0	McDowell 2, Stark	4000
21	17	H	Partick T.	6	L 2-3	1-2	McDowell, McGarvey	10,000
22	31	A	Montrose	7	L 1-2	1-1	Borthwick (pen)	1200
23	Feb 7	H	Queen of the S.	8	L 0-2	0-1		3000
24	14	H	Arbroath	7	D 0-0	0-0		1900
25	21	A	Airdrieonians	5	W 3-1	1-1	Stark 2 (1 a pen), Mowat	2000
26	28	A	Falkirk	6	D 1-1	0-1	McGarvey	2500

Final Place: 6

Goalscorers

League (37): McDowell 12, Stark 6 (1 a pen), McGarvey 5, McGillivray 4 (2 pens), Borthwick 3 (2 pens) Ferguson 2, Leonard 2, Mowat 1, Reid R. 1, Young 1.
League Cup (5): Borthwick 2 (1 a pen), Ferguson 1, McDowell 1, McGillivray 1.
Cup (0).
Spring Cup (25): McGarvey 5, Munro 5, Stark 5, Borthwick 3 (1 a pen), McGillivray 3, Fitzpatrick 2, McDowell 1, Richardson 1.

Honours

Scottish League: Division 2 Champions 1967–68; Runners-up 1935–36.
Scottish Cup: Winners 1926, 1959; Finalists 1908, 1934, 1962.
League Cup: Finalists 1955–56.
Record Victory: 15-0 v Glasgow University, Scottish Cup 1st Rd, Jan. 30th, 1960.
Record Defeat: 2-9 v Dundee, Division 1, Feb. 29th, 1964.
Most League Points: 62, Division 2, 1967–68.
Most Individual League Goals in Season: 45 Dunky Walker, Division 1, 1921–22.
Most Capped Player: Tommy Jackson, 6, Scotland.

Morrison, A.	Hunt, J.	McConnell, D.	Reid, I.	Johnston, W.	Beckett, A.	Young, J.	Reid, R.	Fitzpatrick, R.	Borthwick, W.	Campbell, J.	Stevenson, W.	McDowell, D.	Munro, A.	McGillivray, J.	Ferguson, R.	McGarvey, F.	Leonard, P.	Stark, W.	Hyslop, D.	Kinnear, B.	Mowat, J.	Hughes, A.	Plommer, J.	Match No.
1		2	3		6	5	11	4	12			10†				7	13	9	8*					1
1		2	3*		6	5	4	11	12			10				7	13	9†	8					2
1		2*	3	12	5	4	8					10		11		7		9†	13	6				3
		1	2	3	10	5	4					8		9	11	7*	12			6				4
		1	2	3	13	5	4	8				9		10*	11†	7	12			6				5
		1	2	3	10	5	4					8		9*	11†	7	12	13		6				6
		1	2	3	10	5	4*					9		11		7	8	12		6				7
		1	2	3	10	5*	4					9	12	11		7†	8	13		6				8
		1	2	3	10	5	4					8	12	11		7*	9			6				9
		1	2	3	10	5			12			9		11		7*	8	4		6				10
		1	2*	3	10	5		13	12			9		11		7†	8	4		6				11
		1	2*	3	10	5	4	12				9		11	13	8†	7			6				12
		1	3	2	5	4*	12					9		11	7†	8		10		6		13		13
		1	3	2	5	4	12							11		8		10	9	6			7*	14
		1	3	2	5	4	10					9*		11		8		7	12	6				15
		1	3	2	5	4	10					9		11		8		7		6				16
		1	3	2	5	4	10					9		11	12	8†	7*	13		6				17
1			3	2	5	4	10					9†		11	12	8	7*	13		6				18
		1	2	3	8	5	13	4				10*		11†		7	12	9		6				19
		1	2	3*	8	5	4	12				10		13		7		11	9†	6				20
		1	2		8	5	4	13				10		12		7		11†	9*	6	3			21
		1	6	2	4		12	10†						11		7	13	9	5	3			8*	22
		1	12	2	8	5	4					10		11		7†	13	9	6*	3				23
		1	2	6	5	4		10†	9					11	13	7*	12	3		8				24
		1	2	6	5	4		7*	9	10		13				12	8	3		11†				25
		1	2	6*	5	4		7†	9	10		13				12	8	3		11				26
3	**1**	**22**	**8**	**13**	**20**	**24**	**25**	**22**	**10**	**0**	**2**	**24**	**6**	**20**	**13**	**16**	**3**	**14**	**6**	**23**	**6**	**1**	**4**	
		+1s		+2s		+2s	+7s	+3s				+2s	+2s	+3s	+9s	+1s	+7s	+3s	+1s			+1s		

585

STENHOUSEMUIR

DIV. 2

Year Formed: 1884. *Ground:* Ochilview Park. *Capacity:* 16,000 (500 seated). *Telephone:* Larbert 2299,
Team Manager: Henry Glasgow. *Secretary:* Jimmy Weir.
Club Colours: Maroon shirts with white trimmings, white shorts and stockings.
Club Nickname: 'The Warriors'.
Record Attendance: 12,500 v East Fife, Scottish Cup 4th Rd, Mar. 11th, 1950.

1975–76 LEAGUE RECORD

Match No.	Date	Venue	Opponents	League Pos'n	Result	H/T Score	Goalscorers	Atten- dance
1	Aug 30	A	Albion R.	—	D 2-2	2-2	Wight 2	800
2	Sep 6	H	Alloa	11	L 0-1	0-1		500
3	13	A	Raith R.	13	L 0-2	0-2		1292
4	20	H	Berwick R.	10	W 2-1	2-1	Wight, Steven (og)	301
5	27	H	Stirling Albion	13	L 0-1	0-1		500
6	Oct 4	A	Forfar Ath.	14	L 1-3	1-1	McLean	350
7	11	H	Cowdenbeath	14	L 0-2	0-2		250
8	18	A	Clydebank	14	L 1-2	1-0	McPaul	1500
9	25	H	Stranraer	14	L 1-2	1-1	McPaul	300
10	Nov 1	A	Brechin C.	14	D 1-1	0-0	McCullie	300
11	8	A	Meadowbank T.	14	D 1-1	1-0	Scott J.	350
12	15	H	Queen's Park	13	D 2-2	1-2	Ruddy, McCullie	300
13	22	A	East Stirling	12	W 3-1	2-0	Wight 3	400
14	29	A	Stirling Albion	11	W 2-1	1-0	McPaul 2	1000
15	Dec 6	H	Forfar Ath.	13	L 1-2	1-0	Scott J.	300
16	20	H	Clydebank	11	W 2-1	2-0	Simpson 2	2500
17	27	A	Stranraer	12	L 1-3	0-0	McPaul	900
18	Jan 1	A	Alloa	—	L 2-4	0-3	Wight 2	740
19	3	H	Raith R.	12	L 0-3	0-2		1200
20	17	H	East Stirling	12	W 2-1	2-1	Wight 2	350
21	31	A	Berwick R.	12	D 1-1	0-0	Simpson	350
22	Feb 7	H	Albion R.	10	W 4-2	2-2	Sage, Simpson, McCullie, Scott D.	301
23	21	H	Brechin C.	10	W 4-1	2-0	Rose, Halliday, Wight 2	400
24	24	A	Queen's Park	—	W 3-0	2-0	Simpson, Wight, Sinclair	500
25	28	H	Meadowbank T.	8	W 2-1	0-0	Ruddy, Wight	306
26	Mar 9	A	Cowdenbeath	—	L 1-3	0-0	Simpson	400

Final Place: 10

Goalscorers

League (39): Wight 14, Simpson 6, McPaul 5, McCullie 3, Scott J. 2, Ruddy 2, Halliday 1, McLean 1,
Rose 1, Sage 1, Scott D. 1, Sinclair 1, own goal 1.
League Cup (7): Simpson 2, Wight 2, McLean 1, Murdoch 1. Rose 1.
Cup (4): McPaul 2, Murdoch 1 (pen), Simpson 1.
Spring Cup (6): Wight 2, McPaul 1, Sage 1, Simpson 1, Sinclair 1.

Honours
Record Victory: 9-2 v Dundee U, Division 2, 1936–37.
Record Defeat: 2-11 v Dunfermline Ath. Division 2, 1930–31.
Most League Points: 50, Division 2, 1960–61.

Dunlop, R.	Fairley, H.	Rose, A.	Gordon, W.	Ruddy, D.	Murdoch, W.	Sage, J.	Simpson, A.	McLean, D.	McCullie, C.	Scott, J.	Halliday, R.	Wight, J.	Kane, A.	McPaul, J.	Sinclair, J.	Scott, D.	McAuley, J.	Bone, G.	Hill, G.	Portlovy, A.	Match No.
1		3*	5	4	6	7	2	8	13	9				12	11	10†					1
1		3	5	4	6	7*	2	8	12	9				13	11	10†					2
1	12	3	5	4*	6	11	2	8	10	9				7							3
1	8	3	5	4	6	11*	2	12	10	9				7							4
1		3	5	4	6	11	13		2	8†10	9			12	7*						5
1	12	3	5	4	6	11†	9		2	13	10			8*	7						6
1	2	3	5	4	6	11	9	13	10†		12			8*	7						7
1	2	3	8	6	4	5	13	9*				10	12	7	11†						8
1	2	3	8	5	4	6	13	9*				10	12	7	11†						9
1		4	5	6		7	8	10		9	11			3		2					10
1		4	5	12	6	7	8	10*13		9	11†			3		2					11
1	3	2	5	4	6	7	8	10	9	11											12
1		2	5	4	6	7	8	10*	9	11		12	3								13
1		2	5	4	6	7*	8	10	9	11	12		3								14
1		2	5	4	6	7	8	10	9	11			3								15
1	12	2	5		6	11	13	8	10†	9		7		3	4*						16
1	13	2	5	4	6	11	7*	8	10†	9	12			3							17
1	4	2	5	12	6	11	7†	8	10	9	13			3*							18
1	3	2	5		6	11*	12	4	10	9	8	7									19
1	2	5		12	6	11	8	10	9	4*	7		3								20
1	2	5		6	11	12	3	10	9	4	7*	8									21
1	2	5	13	6	11	7	3	10†	9	4	12	8*									22
1	2		5	6	11	12	10	9	4†	7	8	3*13									23
1	3		5	6	11	2	8	10	9	7	4										24
	3		5	6	11	2	8	10†	9	12	13	7	4*	1							25
1	3	5	12	6	11	2	8†		9	7*13	10	4									26
25	4	19	23	15	14	26	18	4	18	21	22	20	5	13	17	5	10	4	2	1	

| + | + | | + | + | | + | + | + | + | + | + | + | + | + | | + | | | | |
| 2s | 2s | | 2s | 3s | | 2s | 1s | 5s | 2s | 2s | 4s | 1s | 8s | 1s | 1s | | 1s | | | | |

STIRLING ALBION

DIV. 2

Year Formed: 1945. *Ground:* Annfield Park. *Capacity:* 25,000 (900 seated). *Telephone:* Stirling 3584.
Manager: Alex Smith. *Secretary:* Peter Gardiner. *Club Colours:* Red shirts, socks and shorts.
Record Attendance: 26,400 v Celtic, Scottish Cup 4th Rd, Mar 14th, 1959.

1975-76 LEAGUE RECORD

Match No.	Date	Venue	Opponents	League Pos'n	Result	H/T Score	Goalscorers	Attendance
1	Aug 30	A	Queen's Park	—	L 1-3	0-1	Thomson (pen)	500
2	Sep 6	H	Clydebank	14	L 0-1	0-1		300
3	13	A	Forfar Ath.	14	D 0-0	0-0		460
4	20	H	East Stirling	11	W 3-2	0-1	Nicol, Steele, Lawson	930
5	27	A	Stenhousemuir	6	W 1-0	1-0	Lawson	500
6	Oct 4	H	Meadowbank T.	4	W 5-0	3-0	Kennedy, Lawson 3, Downie	900
7	11	H	Stranraer	4	W 3-0	1-0	Thomson, Lawson 2	1100
8	18	A	Albion R.	4	D 1-1	0-0	Lawson	500
9	25	H	Alloa	4	D 2-2	2-0	Duffin, Thomson	1600
10	Nov 1	A	Raith R.	5	D 2-2	1-1	Steele, Lawson	2145
11	8	H	Brechin C.	4	D 1-1	0-0	Thomson (pen)	1100
12	15	H	Cowdenbeath	4	W 5-2	1-2	Clark 2, Thomson (pen), Lawson 2	800
13	22	A	Berwick R.	4	L 2-3	1-2	Lawson, Armstrong	1500
14	29	H	Stenhousemuir	4	L 1-2	0-1	Nicol	1000
15	Dec 6	A	Meadowbank T.	6	L 0-1	0-1		400
16	13	H	Forfar Ath.	4	W 2-0	1-0	Thomson (pen), Lawson	600
17	20	H	Albion R.	4	D 1-1	0-1	Thomson (pen)	750
18	27	A	Alloa	4	W 2-1	0-0	Lawson 2	1764
19	Jan 19	A	Clydebank	—	L 0-1	0-1		1800
20	17	H	Berwick R.	4	W 2-0	1-0	Steele, Lawson	850
21	31	A	East Stirling	4	D 0-0	0-0		250
22	Feb 7	H	Queen's Park	5	L 1-3	1-1	Gray	850
23	28	A	Brechin C.	5	W 3-2	2-1	Steele, Lawson 2	300
24	Mar 6	H	Raith R.	—	L 0-1	0-1		160
25	Apr 17	A	Cowdenbeath	—	L 1-2	1-0	McPhee	350
26	24	A	Stranraer	6	L 0-1	0-0		600

Final Place: 6

Goalscorers

League (39): Lawson 18, Thomson 7 (5 pens), Steele 4, Clark 2, Nicol 2, Armstrong 1, Downie 1, Duffin 1, Gray 1, Kennedy 1, McPhee 1.
League Cup (7): Lawson 2, McPhee 2, Clark 1, Steele 1, Thomson 1.
Cup (6): Lawson 3, Steele 2, Downie 1.
Spring Cup (6): Lawson 2, McPhee 2, Clark 1, Duffin 1.

Honours

Scottish League: Division 2 Champions 1952–53, 1957–58, 1960–61, 1964–65; Runners-up 1948–49, 1950–51.

Record Victory: 7-0 v Albion R., Division 2, 1947–48; v Montrose, Division 2, 1957–58; v St. Mirren, Division 1, 1959–60; v Arbroath, Division 2, 1960–61.

Record Defeat: 0-9 v Dundee U., Division 1, Dec. 30th, 1967.

Most League Points: 59, Division 2, 1964–65.

Most Individual League Goals in Season: Michael Lawson, 24, Division 2, 1974–75.

Howie, B.	Young, G.	Gray, R.	Nicol, G.	Dempsey, J.	Duffin, R.	Kennedy, J.	Carr, S.	Clark, J.	McPhee, M.	Steele, W.	Thomson, R.	Lawson, M.	Downie, T.	Muir, K.	Setterington, D.	Armstrong, G.	Hulston, W.	Match No.
	1	3	2	4*12	5	6	8	7†	10	11	9	13						1
	1	2	3	4 12	5	6	8	7	10	11	9*							2
	1	2	3*	4 13	5	6	8	7	9†10	11	12							3
	1		3	5 4	6	10	12	7*	9	8	2	11						4
	1	2		5 4	6	10†	7*	13	9	8	3	12	11					5
	1	2		5 4	3	6	8	7	10	11	9							6
	1		5	4 3	6	8	7*	10	11	9	2	12						7
	1		5	4 3	6	8	13	7*10	11	9†	2	12						8
	1		5	4*	6	8	7	12	10	9	2	11	3					9
	1	2	5	4	6	8	7	10	9	11	3							10
	1	2	5	4	6	8	12	7	10	9	11*	3						11
	1	2	5	4	6	8	7	10	11	9	3							12
	1		5	4	6 12	8	13	7	10†11	2*	9	3						13
	1	2	5	4	6	8	12	9	10*11	7	3							14
	1	2	5	4	6 12	10†	7*	8	13	9	11	3						15
	1	2	3	8*	5	6	4	7	9	10	11	12						16
	1	3	2	8	5	6	4	7	9	10*11	12							17
	1	3	2		5	6	4	7	9	11					8		10	18
	1	3	2	5†	6	4	7*	9	11	13					8	12	10	19
	1	3	2		5	6	4	12	8	9	7*					11	10	20
	1	3	2		5	6	4	7	8	9						11	10	21
	1	3	2	6*12	5	4	7†	8	9	13						11	10	22
	1	3			5	6	10	7	8	9	4	2				11		23
	1	3		4*	5	6	10	7	8†	9	12	2	13			11		24
1		3	2	8*	5	6	4	7	9	10†11	13				12			25
	1	2	5	4	6	8	7	9	10	11	3							26
1	25	14	20	16	17	22	19	26	18	20	16	26	9	8	3	14	12	
				+4s		+2s		+6s	+1s	+2s		+5s	+2s	+2s		+5s		

589

STRANRAER

Year Formed: 1870. *Ground:* Stair Park. *Size:* 110 × 70 yards. *Capacity:* 5,500.
Telephone: Stranraer 3271. *Manager:*   *Secretary:* James Edmunds.
Club Colours: Royal blue shirts, white shorts, blue stockings with red tops.
Record Attendance: 6,500 v Rangers, Scottish Cup 1st Rd, Jan 24th, 1948.

1975-76 LEAGUE RECORD

Match No.	Date	Venue	Opponents	League Pos'n	Result	H/T Score	Goalscorers	Attendance
1	Aug 30	A	Raith R.	—	D 3-3	2-1	Muir, McClymont 2	1402
2	Sep 6	H	Albion R.	12	L 1-2	0-1	McCabe	1500
3	13	A	Alloa	9	D 3-3	2-2	McClymont (pen), Traynor, McCabe	375
4	20	H	Clydebank	12	L 0-1	0-1		1500
5	27	H	Queen's Park	11	D 1-1	0-0	Muir	750
6	Oct 4	A	Cowdenbeath	13	L 1-2	1-1	Traynor	250
7	11	A	Stirling Albion	13	L 0-3	0-1		1100
8	18	H	Brechin C.	11	W 4-2	2-1	McClymont, Traynor 3	1050
9	25	A	Stenhousemuir	9	W 2-1	1-1	Muir, McCabe	300
10	Nov 1	H	Meadowbank T.	8	W 5-1	1-1	Hay (pen), McClymont, Coulston, Traynor 2	900
11	8	A	Berwick R.	8	W 2-1	1-0	McCabe (pen), Lawrie	300
12	15	H	East Stirling	5	W 2-1	1-1	Coulston, McCabe	1050
13	22	A	Forfar Ath.	5	W 3-0	1-0	Muir, Hay, Traynor	360
14	29	A	Queen's Park	5	L 0-2	0-0		930
15	Dec 6	H	Cowdenbeath	7	L 2-4	2-1	Traynor 2	850
16	27	H	Stenhousemuir	7	W 3-1	0-0	McClymont, Traynor, McCabe	900
17	Jan 1	A	Albion R.	—	L 1-2	1-2	McCabe	500
18	3	H	Alloa	9	L 0-1	0-0		1000
19	17	H	Forfar Ath.	7	W 4-0	4-0	McCutcheon, Traynor, McCabe, Lawrie	760
20	24	A	East Stirling	8	L 1-3	0-1	Hay (pen)	200
21	31	A	Clydebank	8	L 1-2	1-0	Goodwin (og)	1100
22	Feb 7	H	Raith R.	8	L 1-3	1-1	McCabe	1000
23	21	A	Meadowbank T.	8	W 3-2	2-1	McCutcheon 2, Lawrie	200
24	28	H	Berwick R.	10	L 1-2	1-2	Coulston	850
25	Apr 17	A	Brechin C.	—	W 4-0	3-0	Hay 3 (1 pen), McCabe	350
26	24	H	Stirling Albion	7	W 1-0	0-0	McCabe	600

Final Place: 7

Goalscorers

League (49): Traynor 12, McCabe 11 (1 pen), Hay 6 (3 pens), McClymont 6 (1 pen), Muir 4, Coulston 3, Lawrie 3, McCutcheon 3, Own Goal 1.
League Cup (13): McCabe 4, Hay 3 (1 pen), Traynor 2, Hopkins 1, McClymont 1, McCormack 1, Osborne 1.
Cup (3): McCabe 2 (1 pen), Traynor 1.
Spring Cup (7): McClymont 2, Coulston 1, Fletcher 1, McCutcheon 1, McGeehan 1, Traynor 1.

Honours
Record Victory: 7-0 v Brechin C., Division 2, 1964–65.
Record Defeat: 1-11 v Queen of the South, Scottish Cup, 1st Rd., 1931–32.
Most League Points: 44, Division 2, 1960–61, 1971–72.

Taylor, J.	Ritchie, W.	Williams, S. E.	Duffy, R.	McCormack, W.	Muir, J.	Heap, J.	Bruce, I.	Hopkins, J.	Hay, H.	McCall, R.	McCutcheon, A.	McClymont, W.	Coulston, F.	Osborne, W.	Traynor, J.	McCabe, J.	Hannah, J.	Gallacher, G.	Lawrie, R.	Fletcher, R.	Match No.
1		2	3	4*	5	10	7	6†12	13	8	11	9									1
	1		3	4	5	6	7	13		2	8	11†	9*10	12							2
	1		3*	4	5	12	2		13	7	8	11†	9	10	6						3
	1			4	5	3	2	11		7	8		9	10	6						4
		2		4	5	3	7	6			8	12	11	9*10							5
	1		2*12	4	5	3		6		13	8		11†	9	10	7					6
		1	2*	4	5	6		7	13	3	8	11	12	9†10							7
			8	2	4	5	6		7	3*10†13	12	9	11					1			8
	1		2		4	5	6		3	7		10	8	9	11						9
	1		2		4	5		3	7		6	8	9	10					11		10
	1		2		4	5		3	7		6	8	9	10					11		11
	1		2		4	5	12	3	7		6	8	9	10					11*		12
	1		2		4	5	12	3	7		6	8	9	10					11*		13
	1				4	5	2	7	3		6	8	9	10					11		14
	1		2		4	5		3	7		6	8	12	9	10*				11		15
	1		2	5	4	12	6	7*	3		11	8	9	10							16
	1		2	13	4	5	6		3		11	8*	7	9†10	12						17
	1			2	4	5	6		3	7		9	10	8					11		18
	1			2	5		3	7	6		8	9	10						11	4	19
	1			4	5	12	2*	3	11	6	8	7	9	10							20
	1		2		4	5		6	3	11	8		9	10	7						21
	1		2		4	5	12	3		6*	8	7	9	10					11		22
	1		2		4	5		3		6	8	7	9	10					11		23
	1		2		4	5		3	12	6	8	7	9	10					11*		24
	1		2			5	3	10	7*	4	6	9		12	8				11		25
	1		2			5	3	10	7	4	6	9			8				11		26
1	23	1	18	7	24	25	14	9	23	12	13	24	18	10	22	24	2	1	14	1	
			+2s			+1s	+2s	+3s	+1s	+4s	+2s			+2s	+3s	+1s	+1s		+1s		

591

SCOTTISH LEAGUE 1975-76

PREMIER DIVISION

		HOME					AWAY				
	P	W	D	L	F	A	W	D	L	F	A	Pts.
Rangers	36	15	2	1	38	12	8	6	4	21	12	54
Celtic	36	10	5	3	35	18	11	1	6	36	24	48
Hibernian	36	13	2	3	37	15	7	5	6	21	25	43
Motherwell	36	11	4	3	29	18	5	4	9	28	31	40
Hearts	36	7	5	6	23	19	6	4	8	16	25	35
Ayr U.	36	10	3	5	29	24	4	2	12	17	35	33
Aberdeen	36	8	5	5	27	19	3	5	10	22	31	32
Dundee U.	36	9	3	6	27	20	3	5	10	19	28	32
Dundee	36	8	5	5	31	26	3	5	10	18	36	32
St. Johnstone	36	3	4	11	19	34	0	1	17	10	45	11

FIRST DIVISION

		HOME					AWAY				
	P	W	D	L	F	A	W	D	L	F	A	Pts.
Partick T.	26	10	2	1	26	7	7	5	1	21	12	41
Kilmarnock	26	11	1	1	28	10	5	2	6	16	19	35
Montrose	26	9	3	1	28	18	3	3	7	25	25	30
Dumbarton	26	8	2	3	30	22	4	2	7	23	24	28
Arbroath	26	8	1	4	23	14	3	3	7	18	25	26
St. Mirren	26	6	5	2	22	14	3	3	7	15	23	26
Airdrieonians	26	5	5	3	25	22	2	6	5	19	19	25
Falkirk	26	6	4	3	18	12	4	1	8	20	23	25
Hamilton A.	26	5	4	4	18	15	2	6	5	19	22	24
Queen of the S.	26	6	4	3	26	26	3	2	8	15	21	24
Morton	26	4	5	4	16	17	3	4	6	15	23	23
East Fife	26	6	4	3	25	24	2	3	8	14	29	23
Dunfermline Ath.	26	4	5	4	18	22	1	5	7	12	29	20
Clyde	26	3	2	8	20	23	2	2	9	14	29	14

SECOND DIVISION

		HOME					AWAY				
	P	W	D	L	F	A	W	D	L	F	A	Pts.
Clydebank	26	9	3	1	25	8	8	3	2	19	5	40
Raith R.	26	6	6	1	21	14	9	4	0	24	8	40
Alloa	26	6	5	2	22	13	8	2	3	22	15	35
Queen's Park	26	8	2	3	24	14	2	7	4	17	19	29
Cowdenbeath	26	7	4	2	26	15	4	3	6	18	28	29
Stirling Albion	26	6	3	4	26	15	3	4	6	13	17	25
Stranraer	26	6	1	6	25	19	5	2	6	24	24	25
East Stirling	26	5	5	3	17	14	3	3	7	16	19	24
Albion R.	26	5	5	3	23	15	2	5	6	12	23	24
Stenhousemuir	26	6	1	6	20	20	3	4	6	19	24	23
Berwick R.	26	3	3	7	14	24	4	2	7	18	20	19
Forfar Ath.	26	3	6	4	16	18	1	4	8	12	30	18
Brechin C.	26	4	2	7	15	25	2	3	8	13	26	17
Meadowbank T.	26	4	3	6	14	23	1	3	9	10	30	16

SCOTTISH LEAGUE HONOURS LIST

PREMIER DIVISION
Maximum points 72

	First	*Pts.*	*Second*	*Pts.*	*Third*	*Pts.*
1975–76	Rangers	54	Celtic	48	Hibernian	43

FIRST DIVISION
Maximum points 52

	First	*Pts.*	*Second*	*Pts.*	*Third*	*Pts.*
1975–76	Partick T.	41	Kilmarnock	35	Montrose	30

Maximum points 52

	First	Pts.	Second	Pts.	Third	Pts.
1975–76	Clydebank	40	Raith R.	40	Alloa	35

FIRST DIVISION to 1974–75

	First	Pts.	Second	Pts.	Third	Pts.
1890–1a† †	Dumbarton	29	Rangers	29	Celtic	24
1891–2b	Dumbarton	37	Celtic	35	Hearts	30
1892–3a	Celtic	29	Rangers	28	St. Mirren	23
1893–4a	Celtic	29	Hearts	26	St. Bernards	22
1894–5a	Hearts	31	Celtic	26	Rangers	21
1895–6a	Celtic	30	Rangers	26	Hibernian	24
1896–97a	Hearts	28	Hibernian	26	Rangers	25
1897–98a	Celtic	33	Rangers	29	Hibernian	22
1898–99a	Rangers	36	Hearts	26	Celtic	24
1899–1900a	Rangers	32	Celtic	25	Hibernian	24
1900–1c	Rangers	35	Celtic	29	Hibernian	25
1901–2a	Rangers	28	Celtic	26	Hearts	22
1902–3b	Hibernian	37	Dundee	31	Rangers	29
1903–4d	Third Lanark	43	Hearts	39	*Rangers	38
1904–5d‡	Celtic	41	Rangers	41	Third Lanark	35
1905–6e	Celtic	49	Hearts	43	Airdrieonians	38
1906–7f	Celtic	55	Dundee	48	Rangers	45
1907–8f	Celtic	55	Falkirk	51	Rangers	50
1908–9f	Celtic	51	Dundee	50	Clyde	48
1909–10f	Celtic	54	Falkirk	52	Rangers	46
1910–11f	Rangers	52	Aberdeen	48	Falkirk	44
1911–12f	Rangers	51	Celtic	45	Clyde	42
1912–13f	Rangers	53	Celtic	49	*Hearts	41
1913–14g	Celtic	65	Rangers	59	*Hearts	54
1914–15g	Celtic	65	Hearts	61	Rangers	50
1915–16g	Celtic	67	Rangers	56	Morton	51
1916–17g	Celtic	64	Morton	54	Rangers	53
1917–18f	Rangers	56	Celtic	55	Kilmarnock	43
1918–19f	Celtic	58	Rangers	57	Morton	47
1919–20h	Rangers	71	Celtic	68	Motherwell	57
1920–21h	Rangers	76	Celtic	66	Hearts	56
1921–22h	Celtic	67	Rangers	66	Raith R.	56
1922–23g	Rangers	55	Airdrieonians	50	Celtic	46
1923–24g	Rangers	59	Airdrieonians	50	Celtic	41
1924–25g	Rangers	60	Airdrieonians	57	Hibernian	52
1925–26g	Celtic	58	*Airdrieonians	50	Hearts	50
1926–27g	Rangers	56	Motherwell	51	Celtic	49
1927–28g	Rangers	60	*Celtic	55	Motherwell	55
1928–29g	Rangers	67	Celtic	51	Motherwell	50
1929–30g	Rangers	60	Motherwell	55	Aberdeen	53
1930–31g	Rangers	60	Celtic	58	Motherwell	56
1931–32g	Motherwell	66	Rangers	61	Celtic	48
1932–33g	Rangers	62	Motherwell	59	Hearts	50
1933–34g	Rangers	66	Motherwell	62	Celtic	47
1934–35g	Rangers	55	Celtic	52	Hearts	50
1935–36g	Celtic	66	*Rangers	61	Aberdeen	61
1936–37g	Rangers	61	Aberdeen	54	Celtic	52
1937–38g	Celtic	61	Hearts	58	Rangers	49
1938–39g	Rangers	59	Celtic	48	Aberdeen	46
1946–47f	Rangers	46	Hibernian	44	Aberdeen	39
1947–48j	Hibernian	48	Rangers	46	Partick T.	36
1948–49j	Rangers	46	Dundee	45	Hibernian	39
1949–50j	Rangers	50	Hibernian	49	Hearts	43
1950–51j	Hibernian	48	*Rangers	38	Dundee	38
1951–52j	Hibernian	45	Rangers	41	East Fife	37
1952–53j	*Rangers	43	Hibernian	43	East Fife	39
1953–54j	Celtic	43	Hearts	38	Partick T.	35
1954–55j	Aberdeen	49	Celtic	46	Rangers	41
1955–56f	Rangers	52	Aberdeen	46	*Hearts	45
1956–57f	Rangers	55	Hearts	53	Kilmarnock	42
1957–58f	Hearts	62	Rangers	49	Celtic	46
1958–59f	Rangers	50	Hearts	48	Motherwell	44
1959–60j	Hearts	54	Kilmarnock	50	*Rangers	42
1960–61f	Rangers	51	Kilmarnock	50	Third Lanark	42

593

	First	Pts.	Second	Pts.	Third	Pts.
1961–62f	Dundee	54	Rangers	51	Celtic	46
1962–63f	Rangers	57	Kilmarnock	48	Partick T.	46
1963–64f	Rangers	55	Kilmarnock	49	*Celtic	47
1964–65f	*Kilmarnock	50	Hearts	50	Dunfermline Ath.	49
1965–66f	Celtic	57	Rangers	55	Kilmarnock	45
1966–67f	Celtic	58	Rangers	55	Clyde	46
1967–68f	Celtic	63	Rangers	61	Hibernian	45
1968–69f	Celtic	54	Rangers	49	Dunfermline Ath.	45
1969–70f	Celtic	57	Rangers	45	Hibernian	44
1970–71f	Celtic	56	Aberdeen	54	St. Johnstone	44
1971–72f	Celtic	60	Aberdeen	50	Rangers	44
1972–73f	Celtic	57	Rangers	56	Hibernian	45
1973–74f	Celtic	53	Hibernian	49	Rangers	48
1974–75f	Rangers	56	Hibernian	49	Celtic	45

Maximum points: *a*, 36; *b*, 44; *c*, 40; *d*, 52; *e*, 60; *f*, 68; *g*, 76; *h*, 84; *j*, 60.

SECOND DIVISION to 1974–75

	First	Pts.	Second	Pts.	Third	Pts.
1921–22a	†Alloa	60	Cowdenbeath	47	Armadale	48
1922–23a	Queen's Park	57	Clydebank	¶50	St. Johnstone	¶45
1923–24a	St. Johnstone	56	Cowdenbeath	55	Bathgate	44
1924–25a	Dundee U.	50	Clydebank	48	Clyde	47
1925–26a	Dunfermline Ath.	59	Clyde	53	Ayr U.	52
1926–27a	Bo'ness	56	Raith R.	49	Clydebank	45
1927–28a	Ayr U.	54	Third Lanark	45	King's Park	44
1928–29b	Dundee U.	51	Morton	50	Arbroath	47
1929–30a	*Leith Ath.	57	East Fife	57	Albion R.	54
1930–31a	Third Lanark	61	Dundee U.	50	Dunfermline Ath.	47
1931–32a	*East Stirling	55	St. Johnstone	55	*Raith Rovers	46
1932–33c	Hibernian	54	Queen of the S.	49	Dunfermline Ath.	47
1933–34c	Albion R.	45	*Dunfermline Ath.	44	Arbroath	44
1934–35c	Third Lanark	52	Arbroath	50	St. Bernard's	47
1935–36c	Falkirk	59	St. Mirren	52	Morton	48
1936–37c	Ayr U.	54	Morton	51	St. Bernard's	48
1937–38c	Raith R.	59	Albion R.	48	Airdrieonians	47
1938–39c	Cowdenbeath	60	*Alloa	48	East Fife	48
1946–47d	Dundee	45	Airdrieonians	42	East Fife	31
1947–48e	East Fife	53	Albion R.	42	Hamilton A.	40
1948–49e	*Raith R.	42	Stirling Albion	42	*Airdrieonians	41
1949–50e	Morton	47	Airdrieonians	44	*St. Johnstone	36
1950–51e	*Queen of the S.	45	Stirling Albion	45	*Ayr U.	36
1951–52e	Clyde	44	Falkirk	43	Ayr U.	39
1952–53e	Stirling Albion	44	Hamilton A.	43	Queen's Park	37
1953–54e	Motherwell	45	Kilmarnock	42	*Third Lanark	36
1954–55e	Airdrieonians	46	Dunfermline Ath.	42	Hamilton A.	39
1955–56b	Queen's Park	54	Ayr U.	51	St. Johnstone	49
1956–57b	Clyde	64	Third Lanark	51	Cowdenbeath	45
1957–58b	Stirling Albion	55	Dunfermline Ath.	53	Arbroath	47
1958–59b	Ayr U.	60	Arbroath	51	Stenhousemuir	46
1959–60b	St. Johnstone	53	Dundee U.	50	Queen of the S.	49
1960–61b	Stirling Albion	55	Falkirk	54	Stenhousemuir	50
1961–62b	Clyde	54	Queen of the S.	53	Morton	44
1962–63b	St. Johnstone	55	East Stirling	49	Morton	48
1963–64b	Morton	67	Clyde	53	Arbroath	46
1964–65b	Stirling Albion	59	Hamilton A.	50	Queen of the S.	45
1965–66b	Ayr U.	53	Airdrieonians	50	Queen of the S.	49
1966–67b	Morton	69	Raith R.	58	Arbroath	57
1967–68b	St. Mirren	62	Arbroath	53	East Fife	40
1968–69b	Motherwell	64	Ayr U.	53	*East Fife	47
1969–70b	Falkirk	56	Cowdenbeath	55	Queen of the South	58
1970–71b	Partick Thistle	56	East Fife	51	Arbroath	46
1971–72b	Dumbarton	52	Arbroath	52	Stirling Albion	50
1972–73b	Clyde	56	Dunfermline Ath.	52	*Raith R.	47
1973–74b	Airdrieonians	60	Kilmarnock	59	Hamilton A.	55
1974–75a	Falkirk	54	Queen of the S.	53	Montrose	53

Maximum points: *a*, 76; *b*, 72; *c*, 68; *d*, 52; *e*, 60.

* On goal average. † Held jointly after indecisive play-off. ‡ Won on deciding match.
†† Held jointly. ¶Two points deducted for fielding ineligible player.
Competition suspended 1940–45 during war.

594

RELEGATED FROM PREMIER DIVISION

1975–76 Dundee, St. Johnstone

RELEGATED FROM DIVISION 1

1975–76 Dumfermline Ath., Clyde

RELEGATED FROM DIVISION 1 TO 1973-74

1921–22*Queen's Park, Dumbarton, Clydebank	1951–52 Morton, Stirling Albion
1922–23 Albion R., Alloa	1952–53 Motherwell, Third Lanark
1923–24 Clyde, Clydebank	1953–54 Airdrieonians, Hamilton A.
1924–25 Third Lanark. Ayr U.	1954–55 No clubs relegated
1925–26 Raith R., Clydebank	1955–56 Stirling Albion, Clyde
1926–27 Morton, Dundee U.	1956–57 Dunfermline Ath., Ayr U.
1927–28 Dunfermline Ath., Bo'ness	1957–58 East Fife, Queen's Park
1928–29 Third Lanark, Raith R.	1958–59 Queen of the S., Falkirk
1929–30 St. Johnstone, Dundee U.	1959–60 Arbroath, Stirling Albion
1930–31 Hibernian, East Fife	1960–61 Ayr U., Clyde
1931–32 Dundee U., Leith Ath.	1961–62 St. Johnstone, Stirling Albion
1932–33 Morton, East Stirling	1962–63 Clyde, Raith R.
1933–34 Third Lanark, Cowdenbeath	1963–64 Queen of the S., East Stirling
1934–35 St. Mirren, Falkirk	1964–65 Airdrieonians, Third Lanark
1935–36 Airdrieonians, Ayr U.	1965–66 Morton, Hamilton A.
1936–37 Dunfermline Ath., Albion R.	1966–67 St. Mirren, Ayr U.
1937–38 Dundee, Morton	1967–68 Motherwell, Stirling Albion
1938–39 Queen's Park, Raith R.	1968–69 Falkirk, Arbroath
1946–47 Kilmarnock, Hamilton A.	1969–70 Raith R., Partick T.
1947–48 Airdrieonians, Queen's Park	1970–71 St. Mirren, Cowdenbeath
1948–49 Morton, Albion R.	1971–72 Clyde, Dunfermline Ath.
1949–50 Queen of the S., Stirling Albion	1972–73 Kilmarnock, Airdreonians
1950–51 Clyde, Falkirk	1973–74 East Fife, Falkirk

* Season 1921–22—only 1 club promoted, 3 clubs relegated.

The Scottish Football League was reconstructed into three divisions at the end of the 1974–75 season, so the usual relegation statistics do not apply.

SCOTTISH F.A. CUP FINALS 1874-1976

Year	Winners	Runners-up	Score
1874	Queen's Park	Clydesdale	2-0
1875	Queen's Park	Renton	3-0
1876	Queen's Park	Third Lanark	2-0 after 1-1 draw
1877	Vale of Leven	Rangers	3-2 after 0-0 and 1-1 draws
1878	Vale of Leven	Third Lanark	1-0
1879	*Vale of Leven	Rangers	
1880	Queen's Park	Thornlibank	3-0
1881	†Queen's Park	Dumbarton	3-1
1882	Queen's Park	Dumbarton	4-1 after 2-2 draw
1883	Dumbarton	Vale of Leven	2-1 after 2-2 draw
1884	‡Queen's Park	Vale of Leven	
1885	Renton	Vale of Leven	3-1 after 0-0 draw
1886	Queen's Park	Renton	3-1
1887	Hibernian	Dumbarton	2-1
1888	Renton	Cambuslang	6-1
1889	§Third Lanark	Celtic	2-1
1890	Queen's Park	Vale of Leven	2-1 after 1-1 draw
1891	Hearts	Dumbarton	1-0
1892	¶Celtic	Queen's Park	5-1
1893	Queen's Park	Celtic	2-1
1894	Rangers	Celtic	3-1
1895	St. Bernard's	Renton	2-1
1896	Hearts	Hibernian	3-1
1897	Rangers	Dumbarton	5-1
1898	Rangers	Kilmarnock	2-0
1899	Celtic	Rangers	2-0
1900	Celtic	Queen's Park	4-3
1901	Hearts	Celtic	4-3

Year	Winners	Runners-up	Score
1902	Hibernian	Celtic	1-0
1903	Rangers	Hearts	2-0 after 1-1 and 0-0 draws
1904	Celtic	Rangers	3-2
1905	Third Lanark	Rangers	3-1 after 0-0 draw
1906	Hearts	Third Lanark	1-0
1907	Celtic	Hearts	3-0
1908	Celtic	St. Mirren	5-1
1909	‖		
1910	Dundee	Clyde	2-1 after 2-2 and 0-0 draws
1911	Celtic	Hamilton A.	2-0 after 0-0 draw
1912	Celtic	Clyde	2-0
1913	Falkirk	Raith R.	2-0
1914	Celtic	Hibernian	4-1 after 0-0 draw
1920	Kilmarnock	Albion R.	3-2
1921	Partick T.	Rangers	1-0
1922	Morton	Rangers	1-0
1923	Celtic	Hibernian	1-0
1924	Airdrieonians	Hibernian	2-0
1925	Celtic	Dundee	2-1
1926	St. Mirren	Celtic	2-0
1927	Celtic	East Fife	3-1
1928	Rangers	Celtic	4-0
1929	Kilmarnock	Rangers	2-0
1930	Rangers	Partick T.	2-1 after 0-0 draw
1931	Celtic	Motherwell	4-2 after 2-2 draw
1932	Rangers	Kilmarnock	3-0 after 1-1 draw
1933	Celtic	Motherwell	1-0
1934	Rangers	St. Mirren	5-0
1935	Rangers	Hamilton A.	2-1
1936	Rangers	Third Lanark	1-0
1937	Celtic	Aberdeen	2-1
1938	East Fife	Kilmarnock	4-2 after 1-1 draw
1939	Clyde	Motherwell	4-0
1947	Aberdeen	Hibernian	2-1
1948	Rangers	Morton	1-0 after 1-1 draw
1949	Rangers	Clyde	4-1
1950	Rangers	East Fife	3-0
1951	Celtic	Motherwell	1-0
1952	Motherwell	Dundee	4-0
1953	Rangers	Aberdeen	1-0 after 1-1 draw
1954	Celtic	Aberdeen	2-1
1955	Clyde	Celtic	1-0 after 1-1 draw
1956	Hearts	Celtic	3-1
1957	Falkirk	Kilmarnock	2-1 after 1-1 draw
1958	Clyde	Hibernian	1-0
1959	St. Mirren	Aberdeen	3-1
1960	Rangers	Kilmarnock	2-0
1961	Dunfermline Ath.	Celtic	2-0 after 0-0 draw
1962	Rangers	St. Mirren	2-0
1963	Rangers	Celtic	3-0 after 1-1 draw
1964	Rangers	Dundee	3-1
1965	Celtic	Dunfermline Ath.	3-2
1966	Rangers	Celtic	1-0 after 0-0 draw
1967	Celtic	Aberdeen	2-0
1968	Dunfermline Ath.	Hearts	3-1
1969	Celtic	Rangers	4-0
1970	Aberdeen	Celtic	3-1
1971	Celtic	Rangers	2-1 after 1-1 draw
1972	Celtic	Hibernian	6-1
1973	Rangers	Celtic	3-2
1974	Celtic	Dundee U.	3-0
1975	Celtic	Airdrieonians	3-1
1976	Rangers	Hearts	3-1

* Vale of Leven awarded cup, Rangers failed to appear for replay after 1-1 draw.
† After Protest game, Queen's Park 2 Dumbarton 1.
‡ Queen's Park awarded cup, Vale of Leven failing to appear.
§ Protested replay after Third Lanark had won 3-0.
¶ After mutual protested game which Celtic won 1-0.
‖ Owing to riot, the cup was withheld after two drawn games—Celtic 2-1, Rangers 2-1.

SCOTTISH F.A. CUP 1975-76

FIRST ROUND

DEC. 13

Albion R. (0) 0
Hawick Royal Albert (0) 0   200
Albion R.: Gryzka; Doherty J., McCue, Main, Shields, Doherty I., Franchetti (McGuigan), Sermanni, O'Connor (Brogan), Paterson, Muldoon.
Hawick Royal Albert: Hunter; Oliver, Peoples, Kerr, Robertson, Darling, Brown, Smith, Blacklock, Costello, Forrest.

Brechin C. (0) 1 (*Robb*)
Berwick R. (0) 1 (*Welsh*)   421
Brechin C.: Beatson; Watt, Sime, Weir (Gillespie), Hopcroft, Brown, Reid, Mitchell (Robb), Rice, Wilson, Morton.
Berwick R.: Lyle; Donaldson, Laing, McCabe, McDowell, Tait (Davidson), Smith, Brown, Georgeson, Miller, Welsh.

East Stirling (0) 0
Alloa (2) 5 (*Russell 2, Wilson 2, Morrison*)   500
East Stirling: Gourlay; Campbell, McGregor, Donnelly, Dunne, Soutar, McCulley, Stirling, Adams, Mullin, Murray.
Alloa: Thomson A.; McCann, Wilkinson, McGarry, Stewart, Miller, Russell, Thomson J., Wilson, Campbell, Morrison.

Elgin City (0) 0
Forres Mechanics (1) 1 (*Guyan*)   2000
Elgin City: Lawtie; Richmond, McKen, Dingwell (Davidson), Douglas, Wilson, Kellas, Blacklaw, Wilkie, Bruce, Gilbert (Johnstone).
Forres Mechanics: Ross; Urquhart G., Crawford, Fraser R., McRae, Fraser D., Urquhart A., Slater, Law, Will, Guyan.

Peterhead (0) 0
Raith R. (1) 2 (*Wallace 2*)   2200
Peterhead: McHattie, Rennie, Smith (Horn), Pirie, Sievwright, Krukowski, Ross, Grant, O'Hara, Noble, Third (Esslemont).
Raith R.: McDermott; Brown J., Brown W., McFarlane (Brown T.), Taylor, Cooper, Hislop, Wallace, Graham, Hunter (Urquhart), Duncan.

Stranraer (1) 1 (*McCabe*)
Queen's Park (0) 0   1100
Stranraer: Ritchie; Duffy, Hay, Muir, McCormack, Bruce, Hopkins, Coulston, Traynor, McCabe, McClymont.
Queen's Park: Cameron; McSkimming (Finnigan), Colgan, Campbell, Bowie, McWilliams, Paton, McNaughton, McKay, Rooney, Wilkie (Currie).

FIRST ROUND REPLAYS

DEC. 18

Hawick Royal Albert (0) 0
Albion R. (1) 3 (*Brogan, Sermanni 2, I pen.*)   450
Hawick Royal Albert: Hunter; Oliver, Peoples, Kerr, Robertson, Darling, Brown, Smith, Blacklock, Costello, Forrest.
Albion R.: Gryzka; Doherty J., McCue, Main, Shields, Doherty I., Franchetti, Paterson, Sermanni, O'Connor, Brogan.

DEC. 20

Berwick R. (1) 3 (*McLeod 2, Tait*)
Brechin C. (1) 3 (*Morton, Robb 2*)   372
Berwick R.: Lyle; Donaldson, Laing, McCabe, McDowell, Tait, Smith, Brown (Davidson), Georgeson, Miller, Welsh (McLeod).
Brechin C.: Beatson; Watt, Sime, Weir, Hopcroft, Brown, Reid, Gillespie (Sutherland), Rice, Morton, Robb.

FIRST ROUND SECOND REPLAY

DEC. 22

Berwick R. (0) 0
Brechin C. (0) 1 (*Rice*)   250
Berwick R.: Lyle; Donaldson, Laing, McCabe, McDowell, Davidson, Smith, Miller, McLeod, Georgeson, Tait.
Brechin C.: Ritchie; Watt, Sime, Sutherland (Grier), Hopcroft, Brown, Reid, Gillespie, Rice, Morton, Robb.

SECOND ROUND

JAN. 10

Albion R. (1) 1 (*Brogan*)
Glasgow University (1) 1 (*Cairns*)   216
Albion R.: Gryzka; Doherty J., Main (O'Connor), McConville, Shields, Doherty I., McGuigan, Sermanni, Brogan, McCue, Franchetti (Muldoon).
Glasgow University: Caldwell; McDonald, Hannay, Watson, Fergusson, Mooney, Swan, Brannigan, Cairns, Cummings, Gemmill.

Cowdenbeath (1) 2 (*Hunter, pen., Murphy*)
Selkirk (0) 0   757
Cowdenbeath: Wilson; Simpson, Breen, Seath, Reid, Rae, Hunter, McHale, Morrison, Murphy, Harrow.
Selkirk: McMenemy; Colville, McFadyen, Whitehead, Rutherford, Fairgrieve (Brown), Watkins, Dick, McLaren, McConnell, Bell.

Forfar Ath. (0) 2 (*White, Brogan*)
Meadowbank T. (1) 1 (*McKenzie*)   301
Forfar Ath.: Miklinski; Clark, Spink, McHugh, Steen, Brash, Kyles, Ritchie, Brogan, Tront, White.
Meadowbank T.: Gray; Kilgour, McKenzie, Printy, Cathcart, Hogg, Davidson, Hancock, Fotheringham, O'Rourke, McFarlane.

Forres Mechanic (1) 1 (*Slater*)
Alloa (1) 2 (*Russell, Low*)   1600
Forres Mechanics: Ross; Urquhart G., Crawford, Fraser R., McRae, Fraser D., Slater, Urquhart A., Law, Will, Guyan.
Alloa: Thomson A.; McCann (Donald), Wilkinson, McGarry, Stewart, Miller (Low), Russell, Thomson J., Wilson, Campbell, Forrest.

Raith R. (1) 3 (*Wallace, Graham, Hunter*)
Clydebank (1) 1 (*Lumsden*)   3899
Raith R.: McDermott; Brown J., Brown W., Urquhart, Taylor, Cooper, Hislop, Wallace (McFarlane), Graham, Hunter, Duncan.
Clydebank: McKenzie; Hall, Abel, Fanning, Goodwin, Hay, Cooper, Henderson, (McColl), Larnach, McCallan, Lumsden.

Stenhousemuir (2) 2 (*Simpson, McPaul*)
Brechin C. (1) 2 (*Robb, Rice*)   409
Stenhousemuir: Dunlop; Rose, McAuley, Murdoch, Gordon, Sage, Sinclair (McCullie), McPaul, Wight, Halliday, Simpson.
Brechin C.: Beatson; Watt, Morton, Grier, Hopcroft, Sime, Reid, Mitchell, Rice, Sutherland (Weir), R bb.

Stirling Albion (1) 4 (*Lawson 2, Downie, Steele*)
Civil Service Strollers (0) 0   848
Stirling Albion: Young; Nicol, Gray, Clark, Kennedy, Carr, McPhee (Armstrong), Downie, Steele, Setterington, Lawson.
Civil Service Strollers: Arnott; Gordon, McGurk, Haggarty, Pert (Heeney), Cooper, Callaghan, Waugh, Leeles, Lamb, Gowans (McLean).

Stranraer (0) 2 (*Traynor, McCabe pen.*)
Keith (1) 3 (*Christie 2, Elvin pen.*)   1160
Stranraer: Ritchie; Bruce, Hay, Muir, Heap, McCormack (Lawrie), McCall, McClymont, Traynor, McCabe, McCutcheon (Osborne).
Keith: Gray; Martin, Maxwell, Dalgarno, Wilson, Munro, Winton, Elvin, Simmers (Curran), Duncan, Christie (Graham).

SECOND ROUND REPLAYS

JAN. 14

Brechin C. (0) 0
Stenhousemuir (0) 1 (*McPaul*)   500
Brechin C.: Beatson; Watt, Morton, Weir, Hopcroft, Sime, Reid (Gillespie), Mitchell, Rice, Sutherland (Young), Robb.
Stenhousemuir: Dunlop; Rose, McAuley, Murdock, Gordon, Sage, McPaul, Scott I., Wight, Halliday, Simpson.

Glasgow University (0) 0
Albion Rovers (0) 1 (*Franchetti*)   1300
Glasgow University: Caldwell; McDonald, Hannay (Booth), Watson, Fergusson, Mooney, Swan, Brannigan, Cairns, Cummings (Hennessy), Gemmill.
Albion R.: Gryzka; Doherty J. (McConville), McCue, Muldoon (Franchetti), Shields, Doherty I., McGuigan, Sermanni, Brogan, O'Connor, Coughlin.

THIRD ROUND

JAN. 24

Albion R. (1) 1 (*McLean*)
Partick T. (0) 2 (*Joe Craig, McQuade*)   4042
Albion R.: Gryzka; McConville, Main, Doherty J., Shields, Doherty I., McGuigan, Sermanni, Brogan, McLean (Coughlin), Muldoon (O'Connor).
Partick T.: Rough; Hansen J., Kellachan, Campbell, Hansen A., Anderson (McQuade), Houston, Joe Craig, Rooney, Somner, John Craig.

Alloa (0) 0
Aberdeen (2) 4 (*Scott, McMaster, Miller, Robb*)   6312
Alloa: Thomson A.; McCann, Wilkinson,McGarry, Stewart, Miller, Low, Thomson J., Wilson, Campbell, Russell (Morrison).
Aberdeen: Geoghegan; Williamson, McLelland, Smith, Garner, Miller, Scott, Robb, Jarvie, McMaster, Graham.

Ayr U. (2) 4 (*Ingrams 2, Doyle, Robertson*)
Airdrieonians (0) 2 (*Whiteford, McRoberts*)   6100
Ayr U.: Sproat; Wells, Murphy, McAnespie, Fleming, McDonald, Doyle, Graham, Ingram, McSherry, Robertson.
Airdrieonians: McWilliams; Jonquin, Cowan, March, Black, Whiteford, Wilson, Walker, McCulloch, Clarke, McCann (McRoberts).

598

Cowdenbeath (1) 3 (*Murphy 2, Morrison*)
St Mirren (0) 0   1242
Cowdenbeath: Wilson; Simpson, Breen, Reid, Russell, Seath, Hunter, Rae, Morrison, Murphy, Harrow.
St Mirren: McConnell; Johnston, Mowat, Fitzpatrick, Reid (Hislop), Kinnear, Borthwick, Young, McGarvey, McDowell, Stark (McGillivray).

Dumbarton (1) 2 (*Wallace, Muir*)
Keith (0) 0   2500
Dumbarton: Williams; Mullen, Watt, Smith, McKinlay, Muir, Cook, McLean, Bourke, Wallace, Graham.
Keith: Gray; Martin, Maxwell, Dalgarno, Wilson, Munro (Graham), Winton, Elvin, Simmers (Curran), Duncan, Christie.

Dundee (1) 1 (*Laing*)
Falkirk (1) 2 (*Wheatley, Wilson*)   5586
Dundee: Allan; Ford, Mackie, Robinson, Phillip, Caldwell, Hoggan (Henrie), Hutchinson, Wallace, Strachan, Laing.
Falkirk: Watson; Kennedy, Cameron, Wheatley, Gibson, Holt, Wilson, Shirra, Whiteford J., Lawson, McLeod.

Dundee U. (1) 4 (*McAdam, Hall, Payne, Hegarty*)
Hamilton A. (0) 0   3136
Dundee U.: McAlpine; Rolland, Kopel, Copland, Rennie, Houston, Hall, Payne, Hegarty, McAdam (Sturrock), Steele.
Hamilton A.: Ferguson; Frew, McMillan, Young (Lannon), Robertson, Campbell, Fairlie, Lynch, Thomas (McDowell), McGrogan, Edgar.

Hearts (2) 2 (*Gibson, Park*)
Clyde (0) 2 (*Hood, Ward*)   10,165
Hearts: Cruickshank; Clunie, Jefferies, Brown (Fraser), Anderson, Murray, Aird, Park, Gibson, Callachan, Prentice.
Clyde: Cairney; Anderson, Jim Burns, Ahern, Hamilton, Boyd, Ferris (Watchman), Archibald, Hood, Ward, Harvey (Marshall).

Hibernian (2) 3 (*Harper, Stanton, Smith*)
Dunfermline Ath. (1) 2 (*Reid, Hunter*)   10,719
Hibernian: McArthur; Brownlie, Schaedler, Stanton, Barry, Spalding, Smith, Bremner, Harper, Munro, Duncan.
Dunfermline Ath.: Barclay; Scott, Thomson, Reid, Evans, Adair, Watson, Dunn, Mackie, Meakin, Cameron (Hunter).

Motherwell (0) 3 (*Graham, Taylor, Pettigrew*)
Celtic (2) 2 (*Dalglish, Lynch*)   25,000
Motherwell: Rennie; Watson W., Wark, Watson R. (Millar), McVie, Stevens (Taylor), Marinello, Pettigrew, Graham, Davidson, McLaren.
Celtic: Latchford; McGrain, Lynch, McCluskey, McDonald, Edvaldsson, McNamara, Glavin, Deans, Dalglish, Lennox.

Morton (0) 1 (*McGhee*)
Montrose (0) 3 (*Lowe, Cant, Miller*)   1882
Morton: Baines; Hayes, Sneddon, McNeill, Evans, Rankin, Traynor (McGhee), Brown, Harley, Goldthorp, Irvine.
Montrose: Gorman; Barr, Markland, McNicoll, D'Arcy, Cant, Lowe (Guthrie), Stewart, Livingstone, Johnston, Miller.

Queen of the S. (2) 3 (*Dempster 2, Reid*)
St Johnstone (0) 2 (*Anderson, Thomson*)   3726
Queen of the S.: Ball; McChesney, Thorburn, Clark, Boyd, McLaren, Dempster, Dickson P., Reid, O'Hara, Dickson G.
St Johnstone: Robertson; Roberts, Ritchie, Anderson, MacDonald, Cramond, Hotson, O'Rourke, McGregor, Thomson, Lambie.

Raith R. (0) 1 (*Wallace*)
Arbroath (0) 0   6626
Raith R.: McDermott; Brown J., Brown W., Urquhart, Taylor, Cooper, Hislop, Wallace, Graham (McFarlane), Hunter, Duncan.
Arbroath: Marshall; Milne, Rylance, Cargill, Carson, Murray, Sellars, Mathieson, Bone, Penman (McKenzie), Yule (Mitchell).

Rangers (2) 3 (*MacDonald, Henderson, Hamilton*)
East Fife (0) 0   30,000
Rangers: McCloy; Miller, Greig, Forsyth, Jackson, MacDonald, McKean, Hamilton, Henderson, McLean, Parlane.
East Fife: McGarr; MacIvor, George, Clarke, Methven, Rankin, Hegarty, Rutherford, O'Connor (Mellon), Steven, McPhee.

Stenhousemuir (1) 1 (*Murdoch, pen.*)
Kilmarnock (1) 1 (*Sheed*)   1870
Stenhousemuir: Dunlop; Rose, McAuley, Murdoch, Gordon, Sage, McPaul (Sinclair), Scott, Wight, Halliday, Simpson.
Kilmarnock: Stewart; McLean, Robertson, McCulloch, Rodman, Maxwell, Provan, Fallis, Sharp, Sheed (Clark), Smith.

Stirling Albion (2) 2 (*Lawson, Steele*)
Forfar Ath. (0) 1 (*Tront*)   900
Stirling Albion: Young; Nicol, Gray, Clark, Kennedy, Carr, McPhee, Steele, Lawson, Hulston, Armstrong.
Forfar Ath.: Miklinski; Clark, Ritchie, McHugh, Steen (Bannon), Brash, Payne, Kyles, Brogan, Tront, White.

THIRD ROUND REPLAYS

JAN. 28

Clyde (0) 0
Hearts (0) 1 (*Gibson*)   3000
Clyde: Cairney; Anderson, Jim Burns, Ahern, Hamilton, Boyd, Ferris, Archibald, Hood, Ward, Sullivan (Marshall).
Hearts: Cruickshank; Clunie, Jefferies, Brown, Anderson, Murray, Aird, Park, Gibson, Busby, Shaw (Fraser).

Kilmarnock (0) 1 (*Smith*)
Stenhousemuir (0) 0
Kilmarnock: Stewart; Maxwell, Robertson, McCulloch, Rodman, Clark, Provan, Fallis, Sharp, Sheed, Smith.
Stenhousemuir: Dunlop; Rose, McAuley, Murdoch, Gordon, Sage, McPaul, Scott, Wight, Halliday, Simpson (McCullie).

FOURTH ROUND

Feb. 14

Ayr U. (2) 2 (*Ingram 2*)
Queen of the S. (0) 2 (*Reid, Dempster, pen.*) 8400
Ayr U.: Sproat; Wells, Murphy, McAnespie, Fleming, McDonald, Doyle, Graham, Ingram, McCulloch (McSherry), Robertson.
Queen of the S.: Ball; McChesney, Thorburn, Clark, Boyd, McLaren, Dempster, Dickson P., Reid, O'Hara, Dickson G.

Cowdenbeath (0) 0
Motherwell (1) 2 (*Graham, Marinello*)   8650
Cowdenbeath: Wilson; Simpson, Breen, Seath, Russell, Rae, Hunter, Reid, Morrison, Murphy, Harrow (McHale)
Motherwell: Rennie; Watson W., Millar (Watson R.), McLaren, McVie, Stevens, Gardner (McAdam), Pettigrew, Graham, Taylor, Marinello.

Hearts (2) 3 (*Callachan, Busby 2, 1 pen.*)
Stirling Albion (0) 0   10,396
Hearts: Cruickshank; Clunie, Jefferies, Brown, Gallacher, Murray, Aird, Busby, Ford, Callachan, Prentice.
Stirling Albion: Young; Nicol, Gray, Duffin, Kennedy, Carr, McPhee, Steele (Downie), Lawson, Clark, Armstrong.

Hibernian (0) 1 (*Bremner*)
Dundee U. (0) 1 (*Hall*)   13,682
Hibernian: McDonald; Brownlie, Schaedler, Stanton, Barry, Blackley, Edwards, Bremner, McLeod, Smith, Duncan.
Dundee U.: McAlpine; Rennie, Kopel, Copland, Houston, Narey, Hall, Fleming, Hegarty, McAdam, Reid (Rolland).

Kilmarnock (1) 3 (*McDicken 2, Holt (o.g.)*)
Falkirk (0) 1 (*Whiteford J.*)   6454
Kilmarnock: Stewart; Maxwell, Robertson, McCulloch, Rodman, Clark, Provan, Fallis, McDicken, Sheed, Smith.
Falkirk: Watson; Kennedy, Cameron, Wheatley, Gibson, Holt, Wilson, Shirra, Whiteford J., Lawson, Mitchell.

Montrose (1) 2 (*Johnston, Cant*)
Raith R. (1) 1 (*Graham*)   4170
Montrose: Gorman; Barr, Markland, McNicoll, D'Arcy, Cant, Lowe, Stewart, Livingstone, Johnston, Miller.
Raith R.: Reid; Urquhart, Cairns, McFarlane, Taylor, Cooper, Brown T. (Hislop), Wallace, Graham (Jobson), Hunter, Duncan.

Partick T. (0) 0
Dumbarton (0) 0   8300
Partick T.: Rough; Hansen J., Kellachan, Anderson (Rooney), Campbell, Marr, Houston, Joe Craig, McQuade, Somner, John Craig.
Dumbarton: McGregor; Mullen, Watt, Smith, McKinlay, Muir, Cook, Brown, Bourke, Wallace, Graham.

Rangers (1) 4 (*Johnstone, MacDonald, Henderson, Parlane*)
Aberdeen (0) 1 (*Smith*)   53,000
Rangers: McCloy; Miller, Greig, Forsyth (Parlane), Jackson, MacDonald, McKean, Hamilton (Jardine), Henderson, McLean, Johnstone.
Aberdeen: Geoghegan; Williamson, McLelland, Smith, Thomson (Hair), Miller, Scott, Robb, Jarvie, McMaster (Pirie), Graham.

FOURTH ROUND REPLAYS

Feb. 18

Queen of the S. (3) 5 (*Clark, Reid, Dickson G., Dickson P. 2*)
Ayr U. (3) 4 (*Robertson 2, 1 pen., Ingram, McCulloch*) 7000
Queen of the S.: McLean; McChesney, Miller, Clark, Boyd, McLaren, Dempster, Dickson P., Reid, Dickson G., O'Hara.
Ayr U.: Sproat; McDonald, Murphy, McAnespie, Fleming, McSherry, Doyle, Graham, Ingram, McCulloch, Robertson.

Feb. 25

Dumbarton (0) 1 (*Wallace*)
Partick T. (0) 0   8000
Dumbarton: Williams; Mullen, Watt, Smith, McKinlay, Muir, McLean, Brown, Bourke, Wallace, Graham.

Partick T.: Herriot; Hansen J., Kellachan, Campbell, Rooney, Marr, Houston, Somner, McQuade, Joe Craig, John Craig.

Dundee U. (0) 0
Hibernian (2) 2 (*Spalding, Edwards*) 13,000
Dundee U.: McAlpine; Rolland, Kopel, Forsyth (Sturrock), Houston, Narey, Hall, Fleming, Hegarty, McAdam, Reid.
Hibernian: McDonald; Brownlie, Schaedler, Stanton, Spalding, Blackley, Edwards, Bremner, McLeod, Munro (Wilson), Duncan.

FIFTH ROUND

Mar. 6

Dumbarton (0) 2 (*Clark (o.g.), Muir*)
Kilmarnock (0) 1 (*Fallis*) 7796
Dumbarton: Williams; Mullen, Watt, Smith, McKinlay, Muir, Cook, Brown A. (McLean), Bourke, Wallace, Graham.
Kilmarnock: Stewart; Maxwell, Robertson, McCulloch, Rodman, Clark, Provan, Fallis, McDicken, Sheed, Smith.

Montrose (0) 2 (*Lowe, Stewart*)
Hearts (0) 2 (*McNicoll (o.g.), Shaw*) 8200
Montrose: Gorman; Barr, Markland (Walker), McNicoll, D'Arcy, Cant, Lowe, Stewart, Livingstone, Johnstone, Miller.
Hearts: Cruickshank; Clunie, Jefferies, Brown, Gallacher, Murray, Aird, Busby, Gibson, Callachan, Shaw.

Motherwell (2) 2 (*Pettigrew, Marinello, pen.*)
Hibernian (1) 2 (*Spalding, Duncan*) 17,438
Motherwell: Rennie; Watson W., Wark, Watson R., McVie, McLaren, Gardner, Pettigrew, Graham, Davidson, Marinello.
Hibernian: McDonald; Brownlie, Schaedler, Spalding, Barry (Muir), Blackley, Smith, Bremner, McGhee, Stanton, Duncan.

Queen of the S. (0) 0
Rangers (1) 5 (*McKean 2, Johnstone 2, Henderson*) 18,700
Queen of the S.: Ball; McChesney, Thorburn, Clark, Boyd, McLaren, Dempster, Dickson P., Reid (Bryce), O'Hara, Dickson G. (Miller).
Rangers: McCloy; Miller, Greig, Forsyth, Jackson, MacDonald, McKean, Hamilton, Henderson, McLean, Johnstone.

FIFTH ROUND REPLAYS

Mar. 9

Hearts (0) 2 (*Shaw, Gibson*)
Montrose (2) 2 (*Johnstone, Barr, pen.*) (*after extra time*) 16,228
Hearts: Cruickshank; Clunie, Jefferies, Brown, Gallacher, Murray, Aird, Busby (Park), Gibson, Callachan, Shaw.
Montrose: Gorman; Barr, Walker, McNicoll, D'Arcy, Cant, Lowe, Stewart, Livingstone, Johnstone, Miller (Guthrie).

MAR. 10

Hibernian (0) 1 (*Stanton*)
Motherwell (0) 1 (*Graham*) (*after extra time*) 25,658
Hibernian: McDonald; Brownlie, Schaedler (Carroll), Muir, Spalding, Blackley, Smith, Bremner, McGhee (Murray), Stanton, Duncan.
Motherwell: Rennie; McAdam (Taylor), Wark, Watson R., McVie, Stevens, Gardner, Pettigrew, Graham, McLaren, Marinello (Davidson).

FIFTH ROUND, SECOND REPLAYS

MAR. 15

Hibernian (1) 1 (*Harper*) at Ibrox Stadium
Motherwell (0) 2 (*Marinello, pen., Taylor*) 16,000
Hibernian: McDonald; Brownlie, Schaedler, Stanton, Spalding, Blackley, Murray (Smith), Bremner, Harper, Carroll (Muir), Duncan.
Motherwell: Rennie; Dickson, Wark, Watson R. (Kennedy), McLaren, Stevens, Gardner, Pettigrew, Graham, Davidson (Marinello), Taylor.

MAR. 16

Hearts (0) 2 (*Shaw, Callachan*) at Muirton Park
Montrose (1) 1 (*Cant*) (*after extra time*) 10,047
Hearts: Cruickshank; Brown, Clunie, Callachan, Gallacher, Kay, Aird, Park, Gibson (Shaw), Fraser, Prentice.
Montrose: Gorman; Barr, Lowe, McNicoll, D'Arcy, Cant, Guthrie, Stewart (Downie), Livingstone, Johnstone, Miller.

SEMI-FINALS

At Hampden Park

MAR. 31

Motherwell (2) 2 (*McLaren, Pettigrew*)
Rangers (0) 3 (*Miller, pen., Johnstone 2*) 50,000
Motherwell: Rennie; Watson W., Wark, Watson R., McLaren, Stevens, McAdam, Pettigrew, Graham, Gardner, Marinello (Davidson).
Rangers: McCloy; Miller, Greig, Forsyth, Jackson, MacDonald, McKean (Parlane), Hamilton, Henderson (Jardine), McLean, Johnstone.

APR. 3

Dumbarton (0) 0
Harts (0) 0 16,087
Dumbarton: Williams; Brown, Watt, Smith, McKinlay, Muir, Cook, McLean, Bourke, Wallace, Graham.
Hearts: Cruickshank; Brown, Burrell, Jefferies, Gallacher, Kay, Aird, Busby, Shaw, Callachan, Prentice.

SEMI-FINAL REPLAY

APR. 14

Dumbarton (0) 0
Hearts (2) 3 (*Smith (o.g.), Prentice, Busby*) 11,273
Dumbarton: Williams; Brown, Watt (McNeill), Smith (Mullen), McKinlay, Muir, Cook, McLean, Bourke, Wallace, Graham.
Hearts: Cruickshank; Brown, Jefferies, Callachan, Gallacher, Kay, Aird, Busby, Shaw, Gibson, Prentice.

FINAL

At Hampden Park

MAY 1

Hearts (0) 1 (*Shaw*)
Rangers (2) 3 (*Johnstone 2, MacDonald*) 85,354
Hearts: Cruickshank; Brown, Burrell (Aird), Jefferies, Gallacher, Kay, Gibson (Park), Busby, Shaw, Callachan, Prentice.
Rangers: McCloy; Miller, Greig, Forsyth, Jackson, MacDonald, McKean, Hamilton (Jardine), Henderson, McLean, Johnstone.
Referee: Mr R. H. Davidson (Airdrie)

SCOTTISH LEAGUE CUP 1975-76

FIRST ROUND

AUG. 9

Albion R. (0) 0
Morton (0) 1 (*Reid*)　　　　　　　　　1000
Albion R.: Gryzka; Doherty I., Main, Paterson (O'Connor), Shields, Doherty, T., Sermanni (Coughlin), Franchetti, Dickson, McGuigan, Muldoon.
Morton: Baines; Hayes, McNeill, T., Reid, Anderson, Irvine, Brown, Evans, McIlmoyle (McGhee), Harley, Flaherty, (Taylor).

Alloa (0) 1 (*Morrison*)
Cowdenbeath (1) 3 (*Hunter, Harrow* 2)　　　495
Alloa: Thomson A.; McCann, Wilkinson, Stewart, Watson, Campbell, Russell, Thomson J., Wilson (Miller), Morrison, Forrest (Donald)
Cowdenbeath: Wilson; Callaghan, Jones, Seath, Reid, Simpson, McHale (Laing), Hunter, Harrow, Murphy (Kinnell), Ross.

Arbroath (1) 4 (*Bone* 2, *2 pens., Yule* 2)
Clydebank (0) 0　　　　　　　　　　　1817
Arbroath: Wilson; Milne, Mathieson, Murray, Wells, Rylance, Campbell (Sellars), McIlravey, Bone, Fletcher (Carson), Yule.
Clydebank: Gallacher; Hall, Abel, Fallon, Goodwin, McColl (Hay), Cooper, Henderson, Larnach (Lumsden), McCallan, Caskie.

Berwick R. (0) 1 (*Georgeson*)
East Stirling (2) 2 (*Meakin, Mullin*)　　550
Berwick R.: Lyle; Donaldson, Laing, Cairns, McCabe, Thomson, Smith, Steven, McLeod, Georgson, Welsh.
East Stirling: Gourlay; Campbell, McGregor, Simpson, Adams, Soutar, Hart, Donnelly (Stein), Meakin, Mullin, Barrowman (Murray).

Brechin C. (0) 1 (*Reid*)
Meadowbank T. (1) 1 (*Davidson*)　　　400
Brechin C.: Ritchie; Grier, Hopcroft, Weir, Souttar, Gillespie (Sutherland), Wilson, Mitchell, Young, Dorian, Reid.
Meadowbank T.: Gray; McVay, McKenzie, Jones, Cathcart, Fotheringham, Martin, Hancock, McFarlane, O'Rourke, Davidson.

Celtic (1) 1 (*Dalglish*)
Aberdeen (0) 0　　　　　　　　　　32,000
Celtic: Latchford; McGrain, Lynch, McCluskey, McDonald, Edvaldsson, Hood (McNamara), Dalglish, Wilson, Glavin, Lennox.
Aberdeen: Clark; Thomson (Williamson), McLelland, Hair, Young, Miller, Smith, Robb, Jarvie, Rougvie, Graham (Campbell).

Dumbarton (1) 2 (*McLean, Bourke*)
Hearts (1) 1 (*Callachan*)　　　　　　4000
Dumbarton: Williams; Brown A., Watt, Ruddy, Muir, Graham, Cook, McLean, McAdam (Coleman), Wallace, Bourke.
Hearts: Garland; Clunie, Jefferies, Cant, Anderson, Murray, Stevenson (Brown), Busby, Ford (Prentice), Fraser, Callachan.

Dundee U. (1) 2 (*Steele, Sturrock*)
St Johnstone (0) 1 (*Muir*)　　　　　5000
Dundee U.: McAlpine; Rolland, Holt, Houston, Smith D., Narey, Hall (McDonald), Payne, Gray, Flemming (Steele), Sturrock.
St. Johnstone: Robertson; Smith G., Smith A., MacLeod, Roberts, Kinnell, Muir, O'Rourke, Thomson, Cramond, Lambie.

Dunfermline Ath. (1) 1 (*Mackie*)
Ayr U. (0) 1 (*Fleming*)　　　　　　2000
Dunfermline Ath.: Barclay; Scott, Thomson, Adair, Evans, Kinninmonth, Dunn, Reid, Mackie (Smith), Shaw, Watson (Mercer).
Ayr U.: Sproat; Wells, Murphy (McDonald), McAnespie, Fleming, McSherry, Doyle. Graham, Ingram, Phillips (McVake), Dickson.

Falkirk (0) 0
Hamilton A. (1) 1 (*Hamilton pen.*)　　2000
Falkirk: Donaldson; Kennedy, McLeod (Cameron), Fowler, Moffat (McCaig), Wheatley, Mitchell, Markie, Lawson, Whiteford J., Wilson.
Hamilton A.: Ferguson; Frew, McGrogan, McMillan, Hamilton, Lannon, Young, Campbell, McQuade. Bonnyman (Hood), Thomas (Lynch).

Hibernian (1) 2 (*McLeod pen., Harper*)
Dundee (0) 0　　　　　　　　　　10,851
Hibernian: McArthur; Bremner, Schaedler, Stanton, Barry, Blackley, Smith, McLeod, Harper, Munro, Duncan.
Dundee: Allan; Wilson, Johnston, Ford, Caldwell, Phillip (Martin), Strachan (Bavidge), Robinson, Wallace, Gordon, Hoggan.

Kilmarnock (1) 1 (*Sheed*)
Partick T. (2) 3 (*Houston, Joe Craig* 2)　5000
Kilmarnock: Stewart; Maxwell, Robertson, McLean, Clark, McDicken (Matthews), McCulloch, Fleming, Fallis, Sheed (Ferguson), Smith.
Partick T.: Rough; Hansen J., Kellachan, Rooney (Marr), Hansen A., Campbell, McQuade, Somner, Joe Craig, John Craig, Houston (Lawrie).

Motherwell (1)2 (*Millar pen., Pettigrew*)
Clyde (0) 0　　　　　　　　　　　4256
Motherwell: Rennie; Millar, Wark, Watson R. (Kennedy), McVie, Gardner, Davidson, Pettigrew (Farrell), Stevens, Graham, Taylor.
Clyde: Cairney, Anderson, Swan, Millar, Boyd, Jim Burns, Sullivan, Archibald, Ward (Marshall), Ahern, Ferris.

Queen of the S. (1) 2 (*Bryce, Nicol (o.g.)*)
Stirling Albion (0) 0　　　　　　　2500
Queen of the S.: Ball; Miller, Thorburn, McLaren, Clark, O'Hara, Dempster, Donald (Renton), Reid (Mitchell), Boyd, Bryce.
Stirling Albion: Young; Gray, Nicol, Dempsey, Kennedy, Carr, McPhee, Clark, Steele, Thomson (Downie), Lawson.

Queen's Park (1) 5 (*Campbell* 2,1 *pen., McWilliams* 2, *Wilkie*)
Forfar Ath. (0) 0　　　　　　　　723
Queen's Park: Cameron; Currie, Anderson, Campbell, McDonald, Thomson, Paton, Rooney, Nicholson (McWilliams), McGill, Wilkie (Colgan).
Forfar Ath.: Milne; Clark (Will), Spink, McHugh, Ritchie, Steen, Hunter, Payne, Kyles, Brogan (Boyle), White.

Raith R. (1) 2 (*Robertson pen., Duncan*)
Montrose (0) 1 (*Livingstone*)　　　1613
Raith R.: McDermott; Brown J., Brown W., Brown T., Cairns, Cooper, Robertson, Wallace, Hislop, Hunter, Duncan.
Montrose: Gorman, Barr, Markland, McNicoll, D'Arcy, Watson, Guthrie, Stewart (Downie), Cameron, Cant, Livingstone.

Rangers (2) 6 (*Jardine 3, 2 pens., Miller pen., Stein, Parlane*)

Airdrieonians (1) 1 (*Jonquin pen.*   45,000

Rangers: McCloy; Jardine, Miller, Greig, Jackson, MacDonald, McLean, Stein, Parlane, Johnstone (Denny), Fyfe.
Airdrieonians: McWilliams; Jonquin, Cowan, Menzies, Black, Lapsley (McRoberts), Reynolds, Walker, McCulloch, March, Wilson (Clarke).

St Mirren (0) 2 (*Borthwick pen., McGarvey*)

East Fife (0) 1 (*Robertson*)   2200

St Mirren: McConnell; Reid I., Johnston, Fitzpatrick, Reid R., Young, Campbell (McGarvey), Borthwick, McDowell, Munro (Leonard), McGillivray.
East Fife: McGarr; MacIvor, Gillies, Clougherty, Methven, George (Frickleton), Miller, Rankin (Robertson), Kinnear, McPhee, Hegarty.

Stranraer (0) 0

Stenhousemuir (0) 0   1050

Stranraer: Taylor; Duffy, McCormack, Muir, Heap, Bruce (Hopkins), McCall (McCutcheon), McClymont, Coulston, Traynor, Hay.
Stenhousemuir: Dunlop; Gordon, Rose, Murdoch, Jamieson (McLean), Sage, McCullie, Halliday, Wight, McPaul, Sinclair.

AUG 13

Aberdeen (2) 2 (*Jarvie, Graham*)

Dumbarton (0) 0   6000

Aberdeen: Clark; Hair, McLelland, Gibson, Young, Miller, Smith, Robb, Jarvie (Williamson), Rougvie (Thomson), Graham.
Dumbarton: Williams; Brown A., Watt, Ruddy, Muir, Graham, Cook, McLean, Wallace (Coleman), McKinlay (McAdam), Bourke.

Airdrieonians (1) 2 (*McCulloch, Wilson*)

Motherwell (0) 1 (*Davidson*)   6000

Airdrieonians: McWilliams; Jonquin, Cowan, Menzies, Black, Whiteford (March), McCann, Walker, McCulloch, Reynolds, Wilson.
Motherwell: Rennie; Millar, Wark, Watson R., McVie, Stevens, Gardner, Pettigrew, Graham, Davidson, Taylor.

Ayr U. (2) 2 (*Fleming, Phillips*)

Hibernian (1) 1 (*McLeod*)   6000

Ayr U.: Sproat, Wells, Murphy, McAnespie, Fleming, McSherry, Doyle, Graham, Ingram, Phillips, Dickson.
Hibernian: McArthur; Bremner, Schaedler, Stanton, Barry, Blackley, Smith, McLeod, Harper, Munro, Duncan.

Clyde (0) 0

Rangers (0) 1 (*Johnstone*)   28,000

Clyde: Cairney; Anderson, Swan, Millar, Boyd, Jim Burns, Sullivan, Ward, Boyle, Ahern, Marshall (Archibald).
Rangers: McCloy; Jardine, Miller, Greig, Jackson, MacDonald, McLean, Stein, Parlane, Johnstone, McKean.

Clydebank (2) 3 (*Cooper, Larnach, McCallan*)

Berwick R. (0) 2 (*McLeod, Georgeson*)   800

Clydebank: Gallacher; Hall, Abel, Fallon, Goodwin, McColl, Cooper, Henderson, Larnach, McCallan, Caskie.
Berwick R.: Lyle; Donaldson, Laign, Cairns, McCabe, Thomson, Smith Steven, McLeod, Georgeson, Welsh.

Cowdenbeath (2) 5 (*Laign, Hunter 2, 1 pen., Murphy, Ross*)

Brechin C. (1) 2 (*Mitchell, Young*)   600

Cowdenbeath: Wilson; Callaghan, Jones, Seath, Reid, Simpson, McHale (Laing), Hunter, Harrow, Murphy, Ross
Brechin C.: Ritchie ; Grier, Hopcroft, Weir, Souttar, Sime, Mitchell, Sutherland, Young, Reid, Dorian.

Dundee (2) (*Gemmel 2, 1 pen., Wallace, Gordon*)

Dunfermline Ath. (0) 0   4000

Dundee: Allan; Martin, Johnston, Ford, Caldwell, Gemmell, Strachan, Robinson, Wallace, Gordon, Hoggan.
Dunfermline Ath.: Barclay; Scott, Thomson, Adair, Evans, Kinninmonth, Dunn, Reid, Mackie, Shaw, Watson.

East Fife (0) 2 (*Kinnear 2*)

Raith R. (1) 2 (*Robertson 2, 1 pen.*)   3014

East Fife: McGarr; MacIvor, Gillies, Clougherty, Methven, Rankin, Miller, Robertson (Frickleton), Kinnear, McPhee, Hegarty (George)
Raith R.: McDermott; Brown J., Brown W., Brown T., Cairns, Cooper, Robertson, Wallace, Hislop (Hunter), Graham, Duncan.

East Stirling (0) 0

Arbroath (0) 4 (*Yule, Sellars, Bone, Rylance*)   500

East Stirling: Gourlay; Campbell, McGregor, Simpson, Adams, Soutar, Hart (Stein), Donnelly (Murray), Meakin, Mullin, Barrowman.
Arbroath: Wilson; Milne, Mathieson, Murray, Wells, Rylance, Sellars (Campbell), McIlravey (Carson), Bone, Fletcher, Yule.

Forfar Ath. (1) 2 (*Payne, Brogan*)

Alloa (1) 1 (*Forrest*)   710

Forfar Ath.: Miklinski; Will, Ritchie, McHugh, Brash, Steen, Payne, Spink, Kyles, Hunter (Boyle), Brogan.
Alloa: Thomson A.; McCann, Wilkinson, Campbell, Watson, Miller, Low, Stewart, Donald, Forrest, Russell.

Hamilton A. (0) 0

Queen of the S. (0) 2 (*Reid 2*)   1600

Hamilton A.: Ferguson; Frew, McMillan, Hamilton, Bonnyman, McGrogan, Thomas, Campbell, McQuade, Lannon, Young.
Queen of the S.: Ball; Miller, Thorburn, McLaren, Clark, O'Hara, Bryce, Boyd, Reid, Mitchell, Donald.

Hearts (1) 2 (*Ford pen., Hancock*)

Celtic (0) 0   19,000

Hearts: Cruickshank; Kay, Clunie, Jefferies, Anderson, Murray, Brown, Busby, Hancock, Ford, Prentice.
Celtic: Latchford; McGrain, Lynch, McCluskey, McDonald, Edvaldsson, Hood, Glavin, Dalglish, Wilson, Lennox.

Meadowbank T. (1) 1 (*O'Rourke*)

Queen's Park (1) 2 (*Rooney, Paton*)   350

Meadowbank T.: Gray; McVay, McKenzie, Jones, Cathcart, Fotheringham, Printy, Hancock, McFarlane, O'Rourke, Davidson.
Queen's Park: Cameron; Currie, Anderson, Campbell, McDonald, Thomson, Paton, Rooney, McWilliams, McGill, Wilkie.

Montrose (1) 1 (*Guthrie*)

St. Mirren (0) 1 (*Borthwick*)   1500

Montrose: Gorman; Barr, Lowe, Markland, McNicoll, Watson, Guthrie, Stewart, Cameron, Johnston, Livingstone.
St. Mirren: McConnell; Reid I., Johnston, Fitzpatrick, Reid R., Young, Campbell, Borthwick, McDowell, Munro, McGillivray.

Morton (1) 2 (*Reid, Sharp*)
Stranraer (3) 5 (*Hay 2, 1 pen., McClymont, Traynor 2*)　　　　1000
Morton: Baines; Hayes, McNeill T., Reid, Anderson, Irvine, Brown, Sharp, McIlmoyle, Harley, McGhee.
Stranraer: Taylor; Duffy, McCormack, Muir, Heap, Hopkins, McCutcheon, McClymont, Coulston, Traynor, Hay.

Partick T. (2) 3 (*Joe Craig 2, Somner*)
Dundee U. (1) 1 (*Steele*)　　　　5500
Partick T.: Rough; Hansen J., Kellachan, Rooney, Hansen A., Campbell, Houston, Somner, Joe Craig (Marr), John Craig, McQuade.
Dundee U.: McAlpine; Rolland, Kopel, Copland, Houston, Narey, Hall (Hegarty), Payne (Steele), Gray, Fleming, Sturrock.

St Johnstone (1) 2 (*O'Rourke 2*)
Kilmarnock (1) 1 (*Fleming*)　　　　2300
St Johnstone: Robertson; Smith G., Smith A., MacLeod, Roberts Kinnell, Muir, O'Rourke, McGregor (Hotson), Smith C. (Thomson), Lambie
Kilmarnock: Stewart; McLean, Robertson, McDicken, Clark, Maxwell, McCulloch, Fleming, Fallis, Sheed, Smith

Stenhousemuir (0) 0
Albion R. (0) 0　　　　500
Stenhousemuir: Dunlop; Fairley, Rose, Murdoch, Gordon, Sage, Halliday, McLean, Wight, McPaul, Sinclair
Albion R.: Gryzka; McConville, Main, Doherty J., Shields, Doherty I., Muldoon, Brogan, Dickson, Paterson, McGuigan

Stirling Albion (0) 3 (*Clarke, McPhee, Steele*)
Falkirk (0) 0　　　　1200
Stirling Albion: Young; Gray, Nicol, Dempsey, Kennedy, Carr, McPhee, Clark, Steele, Thomson, Lawson.
Falkirk: Donaldson; Kennedy, Cameron, Fowler, Gibson, Wheatley, Whiteford D., Markie, Lawson, Whiteford J., Wilson.

AUG. 16

Aberdeen (0) 1 (*Williamson*)
Hearts (0) 2 (*Ford, Hancock*)　　　　8000
Aberdeen: Clark; Hair, McLelland, Gibson (Henry), Young, Miller, Smith, Robb, Williamson, Rougvie, Graham.
Hearts: Cruickshank; Kay (Park), Clunie, Callachan, Anderson, Murray, Brown, Busby, Hancock, Ford, Prentice.

Airdrieonians (1) 2 (*Jonquin 2*)
Clyde (0) 1 (*Boyle*)　　　　3500
Airdrieonians: McWilliams; Jonquin, Cowan, Menzies, Black, Whiteford, McCann (March), Reynolds, McCulloch, Wilson, Walker.
Clyde: Cairney; Anderson, Swan, Millar, Boyd, Jim Burns (Archibald), Sullivan, Boyle, Harvey, Ahern, Marshall (Ward).

Alloa (0) 1 (*Campbell pen.*)
Queen's Park (2) 2 (*Currie pen., Rooney*)　　　　500
Alloa: Thomson; McCann, Wilkinson, McGarry, Watson, Miller, Low, Campbell, Morrison, Russell, Forrest (Donald).
Queen's Park: Cameron; Currie, Anderson, Finnigan, McDonald, Thomson, Paton, Rooney, McWilliams (McNaughton), McGill, Wilkie (Colgan).

Ayr U. (1) 1 (*Dickson*)
Dundee (0) 1 (*Gordon*)　　　　5000
Ayr U.: Sproat; Wells, Murphy, McAnespie, Fleming, McSherry, Doyle, Graham, Ingram, Phillips, Dickson (McCulloch).
Dundee: Allan; Wilson (Purdie), Johnston, Caldwell, Stewart (Robinson), Gemmell, Strachan, Ford, Wallace, Gordon, Hoggan.

Berwick R. (0) 1 (*Georgeson*)
Arbroath (0) 0　　　　552
Berwick R.: Lyle; Donaldson, Laing, Cairns, McDowell, McCabe, Smith, Steven, McLeod, Georgeson, Welsh
Arbroath: Wilson; Milne, Mathieson, Murray, Wells, Rylance, Sellars (Campbell), McIlravey (Carson), Bone, Fletcher, Yule.

Celtic (2) 3 (*Edvaldsson, Wilson, Lennox*)
Dumbarton (0) 1 (*McAdam*)　　　　23,000
Celtic: Latchford; McGrain, Lynch, McCluskey, McDonald, Edvaldsson, McNamara (Hood), Dalglish, Wilson, Glavin, Lennox.
Dumbarton: Williams; Brown A., Watt, Cushley (Cook), Muir, Graham, Wallace, McLean, McAdam, Ruddy, Bourke.

Clydebank (0) 1 (*McCallan*)
East Stirling (0) 1 (*Stein*)　　　　900
Clydebank: McKenzie; Hall, Abel, Fallon, Goodwin, McColl, Cooper, Henderson, Larnach, McCallan, Caskie (Houston).
East Stirling: Gourlay; Campbell, McGregor, Simpson, Adams, Soutar, Hart, Donnelly, Meakin, Mullin, Barrowman (Stein).

Cowdenbeath (0) 0
Meadowbank T. (1) 2 (*McFarlane, Duthie*)　　　　600
Cowdenbeath: Wilson, Callaghan, Jones, Seath, Reid, Simpson, McHale (Laing), Hunter, Harrow, Murphy, Ross.
Meadowbank T.: Gray; McVay, McKenzie, Jones, Cathcart, Hancock, Duthie, Fotheringham, McFarlane, O'Rourke, Davidson.

Dundee U. (1) 2 (*Gray 2*)
Kilmarnock (0) 0　　　　3000
Dundee U.: McAlpine; Rolland, Kopel, Fleming, Smith D., Narey, Traynor (McDonald), Hegarty, Gray, Steele, Sturrock.
Kilmarnock: Stewart; McLean, Robertson, McDicken, Clark, Maxwell, Provan, Fleming, Smith, Sheed, McCulloch.

Falkirk (0) 0
Queen of the S. (0) 0　　　　2000
Falkirk: Donaldson; Kennedy, Cameron, Wheatley, Gibson, Whiteford D., Wilson, Fowler (Whiteford J.), McCaig, Lawson, Mitchell (Shirra).
Queen of the S.: Ball; Miller, Thorburn, McLaren, Clark, O'Hara, Bryce, Boyd, Reid, Mitchell, Donald (Dickson G.).

Forfar Ath. (2) 4 (*Bannon, Spink, Payne, Boyle*)
Brechin C. (0) 0　　　　870
Forfar Ath.: Miklinski; Will, Ritchie, McHugh, Brash, Steen, Payne, Spink, Kyles, Bannon, Boyle.
Brechin C: Ritchie; Sutherland, Brown, Weir, Sime, Gillespie, Wilson, Morton (Grier), Young, Dorian (Mitchell), Reid.

Hamilton A. (0) 0
Stirling Albion (0) 0　　　　1500
Hamilton A.: Ferguson; Frew, McMillan, Hamilton, Bonnyman, McGrogan, Thomas, Campbell, McQuade, Lannon, Young (Hood).
Stirling Albion: Young; Gray, Nicol, Dempsey, Kennedy, Carr, McPhee (Downie), Clark, Steele, Thomson, Lawson.

Hibernian (1) 3 (*Harper*, 2, *Duncan*)
Dunfermline Ath. (0) 0   9636
Hibernian: McArthur; Brownlie, Schaedler, Stanton, Barry, Blackley, Edwards, McLeod (Bremner), Harper (Smith), Munro, Duncan.
Dunfermline Ath.: Barclay; Scott, Thomson, Adair, Evans, Kinninmonth, Dunn, Reid (Smith), Mackie, Shaw, Watson.

Montrose (2) 4 (*Cameron* 2, *Livingstone* 2)
East Fife (0) 0   1100
Montrose: Gorman; Barr, Markland, McNicoll, D'Arcy, Watson, Guthrie, Cant (Stewart), Cameron (Guyan), Johnston, Livingstone.
East Fife: McGarr; MacIvor, Gillies, Clougherty, Methven. George (Frickleton), Miller, Robertson (Honeyman), Kinnear, Rankin, O'Connor.

Morton (1) 4 (*McIlmoyle, Sharp, Harley* 2)
Stenhousemuir (1) 1 (*Wight*)   800
Morton: Baines; Sneddon, Hepburn, Hayes, Irvine, Rankin, Harley, Reid, McIlmoyle, Sharp, McNeill, T.
Stenhousemuir: Dunlop; Fairley (Murdoch), Rose, Gordon, Jamieson, Sage, Sinclair, Halliday, Wight, McLean (Simpson), McPaul.

Raith R. (0) 1 (*Hislop*)
St Mirren (0) 0   2152
Raith R.: McDermott; Brown J., Brown W., Brown T., Cairns, Cooper, Robertson, Wallace (Urquhart), Hislop, Graham, Duncan.
St Mirren: Hunt; Reid I., Johnston, Fitzpatrick, Reid R., Young, McGarvey, Borthwick, McDowell (McGillivray), Munro, Campbell.

Rangers (0) 1 (*Greig*)
Motherwell (0) 1 (*Wark*)   30,000
Rangers: McCloy; Jardine, Miller, Greig, Jackson, MacDonald, McLean, Stein, Parlane, Johnstone, Young.
Motherwell: Rennie; Millar, Wark, Watson R., McVie, Stevens, Gardner (Taylor), Pettigrew, Graham, Davidson, McAdam.

St Johnstone (2) 2 (*Thomson* 2)
Partick T. (4) 4 (*Campbell, Joe Craig, Somner, John Craig*)   3000
St Johnstone: Robertson; Smith G., Smith A., Smith C. (MacLeod), Roberts, Kinnell, Muir, O'Rourke, Thomson, Cramond, Lambie.
Partick T.: Rough; Hansen J., Kellachan, Rooney, Hansen A., Campbell, Houston (Marr), Somner, Joe Craig, John Craig, McQuade (Anderson).

Stranraer (2) 3 (*McCormack, Hopkins, McCabe*)
Albion R. (0) 2 (*Dickson, Muldoon*)   1200
Stranraer: Taylor; Duffy, McCormack, Muir, Heap, Hopkins (McCabe), McCutcheon, McClymont, Coulston, Traynor, Hay.
Albion R.: Gryzka; McConville, Main, Brogan, Shields, Doherty I., McGuigan, Doherty J. (Muldoon), Dickson, Paterson, Coughlin.

AUG. 18

Meadowbank T. (0) 0
Alloa (0) 1 (*McCann*)   600
Meadowbank T.: Gray; McVay, McKenzie, Jones, Cathcart, Fotheringham Kilgour, Hancock, McFarlane, O'Rourke, Davidson.
Alloa: Thomson A.; McCann, Wilkinson, McGarry, Miller, Morrison, Low. Campbell, Donald, Forrest, Russell.

604

AUG. 20

Albion R. (0) 0
Stenhousemuir (1) 1 (*McLean*)   500
Albion R.: Gryzka; McConville, Main, Brogan, Shields, Doherty I., Sermanni, Muldoon, Dickson, McGuigan, Coughlin.
Stenhousemuir: Dunlop; McCullie, Rose, Murdoch, Gordon, Sage, Wight, Scott, McLean, McPaul, Sinclair.

Arbroath (2) 3 (*Bone* 2, 1 *pen.*, *Yule*)
East Stirling (1) 1 (*Stein*)   1614
Arbroath: Wilson; Milne, Mathieson, Murray, Wells, Rylance, Sellars, McIlravey, Bone, Fletcher (Cargill), Yule.
East Stirling: Gourlay; Stirling, McGregor, Simpson, Dunne, Soutar, Hart, Donnelly, Meakin, Mullin, Stein.

Berwick R. (0) 0
Clydebank (0) 1 (*Larnach*)   450
Berwick R.: Lyle; Donaldson, Laing, Cairns, McDowell, McCabe, Smith, Thomson, McLeod, Georgeson, Miller.
Clydebank: McKenzie; Hall, Abel, Fallon, Goodwin, McColl, Caskie, Henderson, Larnach, McCallan, Cooper.

Celtic (2) 3 (*Lynch, Edvaldsson, Glavin*)
Hearts (0) 1 (*Busby*)   28,000
Celtic: Latchford; McGrain, Lynch, McCluskey, McDonald, Edvaldsson, Glavin, Wilson, Dalglish, McNamara, Hood.
Hearts: Cruickshank; Kay, Clunie, Jefferies, Anderson, Murray, Brown, Busby, Hancock (Park), Ford, Prentice.

Dumbarton (0) 0
Aberdeen (0) 1 (*Hair*)   3000
Dumbarton: Williams; Brown A., Watt, Bennett (Ruddy), Muir, Graham, Cook, McLean, Bourke, McAdam (Coleman), Wallace.
Aberdeen: Clark; Hair, McLelland, Scott, Young, Miller, Smith, Robb, Jarvie, Williamson (Pirie), Campbell.

Dundee U. (0) 1 (*Steele pen.*)
Partick T. (1) 2 (*Joe Craig, Hansen J.*)   4500
Dundee U.: McAlpine; Rolland, Kopel, Fleming (McDonald), Smith D. (Copland), Narey, Traynor, Hegarty, Gray, Steele, Sturrock.
Partick T.: Rough; Hansen J., Kellachan, Campbell, Hansen A., Anderson, Houston, Rooney, Joe Craig, Somner, John Craig.

Dumfermline Ath. (0) 1 (*Shaw*)
Dundee (0) 1 (*Caldwell*)   3000
Dunfermline Ath.: Barclay; Scott, Thomson, Adair, Evans, Kinninmonth, Dunn, Reid, Mackie, Shaw, Watson
Dundee: Allan; Martin (Robinson), Johnston, Caldwell, Stewart, Gemmell, Hoggan, Ford, Wallace (Bavidge), Strachan, Purdie.

Falkirk (1) 2 (*Whiteford J.* 2, 1 *pen.*)
Stirling Albion (0) 1 (*Thomson*)   2200
Falkirk: Donaldson; Kennedy, Cameron, Markie, Gibson, Wheatley, Whiteford J., Whiteford D., McCaig, Lawson, Wilson.
Stirling Albion: Young, Gray, Nicol, Dempsey, Kennedy, Carr, McPhee, Clarke, Steele, Thomson, Lawson.

Hibernian (1) 2 *(Munro, Fleming (og.))*
Ayr U. (0) 1 *(Graham)* 9969
Hibernian: McArthur; Brownlie, Schaedler, Stanton, Barry, Blackley, Edwards, Bremner, Harper, Munro, Duncan.
Ayr U.: Sproat; Wells, Murphy, McAnespie, Fleming, McSherry, Doyle, Graham, Ingram, Phillips (McDonald), Dickson

Kilmarnock (0) 1 *(McCulloch)*
St Johnstone (0) 0 2000
Kilmarnock: Stewart; McLean, Robertson, McCulloch, Clark, McDicken, Provan, Fleming, Fallis, Smith (Morrison), Matthews.
St Johnstone: Robertson; Smith G., McBean, Smith C. (MacLeod), MacDonald, Roberts, Muir, O'Rourke (Hotson), Thomson, Cramond, Lambie.

Motherwell (1) 2 *(Pettigrew 2)*
Airdrieonians (0) 0 5122
Motherwell: Rennie; Watson W., Wark, Watson R., McVie, Stevens, Millar, Pettigrew, McAdam, Davidson, Taylor.
Airdrieonians: McWilliams; Jonquin, Lapsley, Menzies, Black, Whiteford, McCann, Cowan, McCulloch, Wilson, Walker.

Queen of the S. (0) 0
Hamilton A. (2) 3 *(Lannon, Thomas, Edgar)* 3000
Queen of the S.: Ball; Miller, Thorburn, McLaren, Clark, O'Hara, Bryce, Boyd, Reid, Mitchell, Donald.
Hamilton A.: Ferguson; Frew, McMillan, Hamilton, Bonnyman, McGrogan, Thomas, Campbell, McQuade, Lannon, Edgar.

Raith R. (0) 0
East Fife (1) 2 *(Rankin, Miller)*
Raith R.: McDermott; Brown J., Brown W., Brown T., Cairns, Cooper, Robertson, Wallace, Hislop, Graham, Duncan (Taylor).
East Fife: McGarr; MacIvor, Gillies, Clougherty, Methven, Rankin, Miller, Honeyman, Kinnear, McPhee, O'Connor.

Rangers (2) 6 *(Miller pen., Jackson, MacDonald, Parlane 2, Young)*
Clyde (0) 0 15,000
Rangers: McCloy; Jardine, Miller, Greig, Jackson, MacDonald, McLean, McKean, Parlane, Johnstone, Young.
Clyde: Cairney; Anderson, Swan, Millar, Boyd (Archibald), Jim Burns (Harvey), Sullivan, Ferris, Ward, Ahern, Boyle.

St Mirren (0) 1 *(McGillivray)*
Montrose (0) 2 *(Cameron, Livingstone)* 1900
St Mirren: Hunt; Beckett, Johnston, Fitzpatrick, Reid R., Young, McGarvey, Borthwick, McDowell, Munro, Campbell (McGillivray).
Montrose: Gorman; Barr, Markland, McNicoll, D'Arcy, Watson, Guthrie, Cant, Cameron, Johnston, Livingstone.

Stranraer (0) 2 *(McCabe 2)*
Morton (1) 1 *(Harvey)* 1080
Stranraer: Taylor; Duffy, McCormack, Muir, Heap, McCabe, Coulston (Hay), McClymont, Osborne, Traynor, McCutcheon (Hopkins).
Morton: Baines; Sneddon, Hepburn, Hayes, Anderson, Rankin, Harley, Reid, McIlmoyle, Sharp, McNeill T.

Albion R. (1) 2 *(Dickson 2, 1 pen.)*
Stranraer (0) 1 *(Osborne)* 400
Albion R.: Gryzka; Doherty J., McCue, Muldoon, Shields, Doherty I., Sermanni (O'Connor), McGuigan, Dickson, Brogan, Coughlin (McConville).
Stranraer: Taylor; Duffy, McCormack, Muir, Heap, McCabe (Hopkins), Coulston, McClymont, Osborne, Traynor, McCutcheon.

Arbroath (0) 2 *(Bone 2, 1 pen.)*
Berwick R. (0) 0 1833
Arbroath: Wilson; Milne, Mathieson, Murray, Wells (Carson), Rylance, Sellars, McIlravey, Bone, Cargill, Yule.
Berwick R.: Lyle; Donaldson, McQuade, Cairns, McDowell (Miller), McCabe, Welsh, Steven, McLeod, Georgeson (Thomson), Tait.

Brechin C. (0) 2 *(Mitchell 2, 1 pen.)*
Alloa (0) 1 *(Forrest)* 300
Brechin C.: Ritchie; Sutherland, Brown, Weir, Sime, Gillespie, Grier (Wilson), Mitchell, Young, Reid, Morton.
Alloa: Thomson A.; McCann, Wilkinson, McGarry, Watson, Morrison, Low, Campbell, Donald, Russell, Forrest.

Clyde (1) 2 *(Millar, Boyle)*
Airdrieonians (1) 1 *(Whiteford)* 1000
Clyde: Cairney; Anderson, Swan, Millar, Boyd, Jim Burns, Sullivan, Ferris (Archibald), Ward (Harvey), Ahern, Boyle.
Airdrieonians: McWilliams; Jonquin, Lapsley, Menzies, Black, Whiteford (Anderson), Reynolds, Cowan, Clarke, McCulloch (Walker), McCann.

Dumbarton (0) 0
Celtic (2) 8 *(McGrain, Hood 2, Wilson 2, Dalglish 2, Callaghan)* 14,000
Dumbarton: McGregor; Brown A. (Mullen), Watt, Bennett, McKinlay, Graham, Cook, McLean, McAdam, Wallace (Brown J.), Coleman.
Celtic: Latchford; McGrain, Lynch, McCluskey, McDonald, Edvaldsson, Glavin (Callaghan), Wilson, Dalglish, McNamara, Hood (Lennox).

Dundee (0) 2 *(Wallace, Hoggan)*
Ayr U. (2) 4 *(Graham 2, 1 pen., Ingram 2)* 5248
Dundee: Allan; Martin, Gemmell, Ford, Stewart, Caldwell (Wallace), Hoggan, Robinson, Gordon, Strachan, Purdie.
Ayr U.: Sproat; Wells, Murphy, McAnespie, Fleming, McSherry, Doyle, Graham, Ingram, McCulloch, Dickson.

Dunfermline Ath. (0) 0
Hibernian (1) 4 *(Stanton, Smith, Harper 2)* 8000
Dunfermline Ath.: Barclay; Scott, Thomson, Adair, Evans, Kinninmonth, Dunn, Reid, Mackie, Shaw, Watson.
Hibernian: McArthur; Brownlie, Schaedler, Stanton, Barry, Blackley, Edwards, Bremner, Harper, Munro, Smith.

East Fife (0) 1 *(O'Connor)*
Montrose (0) 1 *(Cameron)* 1844
East Fife: McGarr; MacIvor, Gillies, Clarke, Methven, Rankin, Miller, Honeyman, Kinnear (Hegarty), O'Connor, McPhee (Clougherty).
Montrose: Gorman; Barr, Markland, McNicholl, D'Arcy, Watson, Guthrie, Stewart, Cameron, Johnston, Livingstone (Cant).

605

East Stirling (0) 0
Clydebank (0) 1 (Simpson (o.g.))   600
East Stirling: Gourlay; Stirling, McGregor, Simpson, Stein, Soutar, McCulley, Donnelly, Meakin, Mullin, Browning.
Clydebank: McKenzie; Hall, Abel, Fallon, Goodwin, McColl, Caskie, Henderson, Larnach, McCallan, Cooper.

Hearts (1) 1 (Prentice)
Aberdeen (0) 0   11,000
Hearts: Cruickshank; Kay, Clunie, Jefferies, Anderson, Murray, Brown, Busby, Hancock, Ford, Prentice (Callachan),
Aberdeen: Clark; Hair, McLelland, Scott, Young, Miller, Smith, Robb, Jarvie (Rougvie) Pirie, Graham.

Kilmarnock (0) 1 (Fallis)
Dundee U. (0) 0   3500
Kilmarnock: Stewart; McLean (Ferguson), Robertson, McCulloch, Clark, McDicken, Provan, Fleming, Morrison, Smith, Fallis.
Dundee U.: McAlpine; Fleming, Kopel, Copland, Rennie, Narey, McDonald, Hegarty, Gray, Hall (Rolland), Sturrock.

Meadowbank T. (3) 4 (Fotheringham, Martin, McFarlane, Davidson)
Forfar Ath. (1) 1 (Brogan)   810
Meadowbank T.: Gray; McVay, Printy, Jones, Cathcart, Fotheringham, Martin, Hancock, McFarlane, O'Rourke, Davidson.
Forfar Ath.: Miklinski; Will (Clark), Ritchie, McHugh, Brash, Steen, Bannon, Payne (Tront), Kyles, Spink, Brogan.

Motherwell (1) 2 (Watson R., Pettigrew)
Rangers (1) 2 (Jardine, Miller pen.)   20,561
Motherwell: Rennie; Watson W., Wark, Watson R., McVie, Stevens, Millar (Davidson), Pettigrew, Graham, McAdam, Taylor.
Rangers: McCloy; Jardine, Miller, Greig, Jackson, MacDonald, McLean, McKean, Parlane, Johnstone, Young.

Partick T. (1) 3 (Hansen J., Somner 2)
St. Johnstone (0) 0   4500
Partick T.: Rough; Hansen J., Kellachan, Campbell, Hansen A., Anderson, Houston (McQuade), Rooney (Marr), Joe Craig, Somner, John Craig.
St. Johnstone: Robertson; Smith G., Smith A., Ritchie, MacDonald, Roberts, Muir, Thomson, Hotson, Cramond, Lambie.

Queen of the S. (0) 0
Falkirk (1) 1 (Whiteford J.)   2500
Queen of the S.: Ball; Miller, Thorburn, McLaren, Clark, Boyd, Donald, Dickson G., Reid, O'Hara, Bryce.
Falkirk: Donaldson; Kennedy, Cameron, Markie, Gibson, Wheatley, Whiteford J., Whiteford D., McCraig (Shirra), Lawson, Holt.

Queen's Park (0) 0
Cowdenbeath (1) 1 (McHale)   600
Queen's Park: Cameron; Currie (McNaughton), Anderson, McWilliams, McDonald, Thomson, Paton, Rooney, Finnigan, McGill, Wilkie (Dickson).
Cowdenbeath: Wilson; Callaghan. Jones, Seath, Reid, Simpson, McHale, Hunter, Harrow, Murphy, Ross (Laing).

St. Mirren (1) 1 (McDowell)
Raith R. (0) 1 (Robertson)   1700
St. Mirren: Hunt; Reid I., Johnston, Fitzpatrick, Reid R., Borthwick, McGarvey, Stark, McDowell, Campbell (Leonard), McGillivray.
Raith R.: McDermott; Brown J., Brown W. (Hislop), Taylor, Cairns, Cooper, Robertson, Brown T., Graham, Urquhart, Duncan.

Stenhousemuir (1) 2 (Rose, Simpson)
Morton (0) 1 (McNeill, T.)
Stenhousemuir: Dunlop; McCullie, Rose, Murdoch, Gordon, Sage, Wight, Scott J., McLean (Simpson), McPaul, Sinclair.
Morton: Baines; Evans (Law), McNeill T., Hayes, Anderson, Rankin, Townsend, Sharp, McIlmoyle, Harley, McNeill J.

Stirling Albion (0) 1 (Lawson)
Hamilton A. (0) 0   1200
Stirling Albion: Young; Gray, Nicol, Dempsey, Kennedy, Carr, McPhee, Clark, Steele, Thomson, Lawson.
Hamilton A.: Ferguson; Frew, McGrogan, Hamilton, Bonnyman, McMillan, Thomas, Campbell, McQuade, Lannon, Edgar (Young).

AUG. 27

Aberdeen (0) 0
Celtic (1) 2 (Lennox, Ritchie)   13,000
Aberdeen: Clark; Hair, McLelland, Scott, Young, Miller, Smith (Rougvie,) Robb, Pirie, McMaster, Graham.
Celtic: Latchford; McGrain, Lynch, McCluskey (Connelly), McDonald, Edvaldsson, Dalglish, Wilson (Ritchie), McNamara, Callaghan, Lennox.

Airdrieonians (0) 1 (McCann)
Rangers (2) 2 (Johnstone, Young)   20,000
Airdrieonians: McWilliams; Jonquin, Cowan, Menzies, Black, Lapsley, McCann, Reynolds, Wilson, Whiteford, Walker.
Rangers: McCloy; Greig, Miller, Forsyth, Jackson, MacDohald, McKean, O'Hara, Stein, Johnstone, Young.

Ayr U. (0) 2 (Doyle, Phillips)
Dunfermline Ath. (2) 2 (Watson, Mackie)   4500
Ayr U.: Sproat; Wells, Murphy, McAnespie, Fleming, McSherry, Doyle, Graham, Ingram, McCulloch, Dickson.
Dunfermline Ath.: Barclay; Thomson, Markey, Adair, Evans, Kinninmonth, Dunn, Scott, Mackie, Shaw, Watson.

Clyde (0) 1 (Boyle)
Motherwell (2) 2 (Goldthorp, Taylor)   1500
Clyde: Cairney; Anderson, Jim Burns, Ahern, Millar, Swan, Sullivan, Ferris (Harvey), Ward, Archibald, Boyle.
Motherwell: Rennie; Watson W., Wark, Gardner (Farrell), McLaren, Stevens, Millar, Pettigrew, Davidson, Goldthorp, Taylor.

Clydebank (0) 1 (Larnach)
Arbroath (0) 0   2700
Clydebank: McKenzie; Hall, Abel, Fallon, Goodwin, Hay, Cooper, Henderson, Larnach, McCallan, Lumsden.
Arbroath: Wilson; Milne, Mathieson, Murray, Wells, Rylance, Fletcher, Campbell, Bone, Cargill, Yule.

Cowdenbeath (2) 6 (*Laing, 2, Hunter, Harrow, Ross 2*)
Forfar Ath. (1) 2 (*Steen, Kyles*)   700
Cowdenbeath: Wilson; Callaghan, Jones, Seath, Reid, Simpson, Laing, Hunter, Harrow, Murphy, Ross.
Forfar Ath.: Miklinski; Will, Lowe, McHugh, Brash, Steen, Payne, Spink, Bannon, Kyles, Brogan.

Dundee (0) 1 (*Munro (o.g.*))
Hibernian (0) 2 (*Brownlie pen., Harper*)   4982
Dundee: Allan; Martin, Johnston, Robinson (Caldwell), Gemmell, Ford, Hoggan, Strachan, Bavidge (Phillip), Gordon, Purdie.
Hibernian: McArthur; Brownlie, Schaedler, Stanton, Barry, Blackley, Edwards, Bremner, Harper, Munro, Smith.

East Fife (1) 2 (*Gillies pen., Miller*)
St Mirren (0) 0   1104
East Fife: McGarr; MacIvor, Gillies, Clarke, Methven, Rankin (Watson), Miller, Honeyman, O'Connor, Rutherford (Robertson), Hegarty.
St Mirren: Hunt; Johnston, Beckett (McGarvey), Fitzpatrick, Reid R., Young, Ferguson, Stark, Leonard (Hislop), Campbell, McDowell.

East Sterling (0) 2 (*McCulley pen., Mullin*)
Berwick R. (1) 2 (*Welsh, Laing*)   500
East Sterling: Gourlay; Stirling, McGregor, Simpson, Stein, Murray, McCulley, Donnelly, Meakin, Mullin, Browning.
Berwick R.: Lyle; Laing, McQuade, Cairns, McCabe, Thomson, Miller, Steven, McLeod, Welsh, Tait.

Hamilton A. (2) 2 (*McGrogan, Hood*)
Falkirk (1) 2 (*Shirra, Wilson*)   4000
Hamilton A.: Ferguson; Frew, McMillan, Hamilton, Bonnyman, McGrogan, Thomas, Campbell, Hood, Lynch, Young.
Falkirk: Donaldson; Kennedy, Cameron, Markie, Gibson, Wheatley, Whiteford, J., Whiteford D. McCaig, Lawson, Wilson (Shirra).

Hearts (4) 6 (*Busby 2, Hancock, Prentice, Callachan, Park*)
Dumbarton (1) 2 (*Cook, Brown J.*)   6000
Hearts: Cruickshank; Kay, Clunie, Callachan, Anderson, Murray, Brown, Busby, Hancock (Gibson), Ford (Park), Prentice.
Dumbarton: McGregor; Mullen, Watt, Ruddy, McKinlay, Graham, Cook, Bennett, McAdam, McLean, Coleman (Brown J.).

Montrose (0) 2 (*Barr pen., Cameron*)
Raith R. (0) 1 (*Robertson*)   2000
Montrose: Gorman; Barr, Markland, McNicoll, D'Arcy, Johnston, Guthrie, Stewart (Lowe), Cameron, Cant, Livingstone.
Raith R.: McDermott; Brown J., Cairns, Brown T., Taylor, Cooper, Robertson, Wallace, Graham, Urquhart (Brown W.), Duncan.

Morton (1) 2 (*McNeill T., Sharp*)
Albion R. (1) 1 (*Coughlin*)   800
Morton: Baines; Hayes, McNeill T., Brown, Anderson, Rankin, Flaherty, Harley, McIlmoyle, Sharp, McNeill J.
Albion R.: Gryzka; Doherty J., McCue, Muldoon, Shields, Doherty I., Sermanni, McGuigan, Dickson, Brogan, Coughlin.

Queen's Park (0) 1 (*Rooney*)
Brechin C. (1) 2 (*Weir, Young*)   700
Queen's Park: Cameron; Currie, Colgan, Campbell, McDonald (McKay), Thomson, Paton, Rooney, McWilliams, McGill, Dickson (Wilkie).
Brechin C.: Ritchie; Sutherland, Brown, Weir, Sime, Gillespie, Grier (Hopcroft), Mitchell (Dorian), Young, Reid, Morton.

Partick T. (2) 2 (*Houston, Joe Craig*)
Kilmarnock (0) 1 (*Morrison*)   5000
Partick T.: Rough; Hansen J. (Melrose), Kellachan, Campbell, Hansen A., Houston, Lawrie (Marr), Rooney, Joe Craig, Somner, John Craig.
Kilmarnock: Stewart; Rodman, Robertson, McCulloch, Clark, McDicken, Provan, Fleming (McLean), Morrison, Smith, Fallis.

St. Johnstone (1) 1 (*Smith G. pen.*)
Dundee U. (0) 2 (*Narey, Hall*)   1800
St. Johnstone: Robertson; Smith G., Smith A., Ritchie, MacDonald, Roberts, Hotson (Muir), Henderson, Thomson, McGregor, Lambie.
Dundee U.: McAlpine; Narey, Kopel, Copland, Rennie, Houston, Traynor, Steele, Gray, Fleming, Hall.

Stenhousemuir (1) 3 (*Wight, Murdoch, Simpson*)
Stranraer (2) 2 (*Hay, McCabe*)   1000
Stenhousemuir: Dunlop; McCullie, Rose, Murdoch, Gordon, Sage, Wight, Scott J., McLean (Simpson), McPaul, Sinclair.
Stranraer: Taylor; Duffy, McCormack, Muir, Heap, Hay, Hopkins, McClymont, Osborne, McCabe, Coulston.

Stirling Albion (1) 2 (*McPhee, Lawson*)
Queen of the S. (1) 3 (*Renton, Bryce 2*)   3000
Stirling Albion: Young; Gray, Nicol, Dempsey, Kennedy, Carr, McPhee, Clark, Steele (Downie), Thomson, Lawson.
Queen of the S.: Ball; Miller, Thorburn, McLaren, Clark, O'Hara, Bryce, Boyd, Reid, Renton, Dickson G.

SUPPLEMENTARY ROUND

FIRST LEG, SEPT. 2

Cowdenbeath (0) 0
Clydebank (1) 2 (*Cooper, McCallan*)   1200
Cowdenbeath: Wilson; Callaghan, Jones, Seath, Reid, Simpson, Laing, Hunter, McHale, Murphy, Harrow.
Clydebank: McKenzie; Hall, Abel, Provan, Goodwin, Hay, Cooper, Henderson, Larnach, McCallan, Lumsden.

SECOND LEG, SEPT. 3

Clydebank (2) 2 (*Larnach, McCallan*)
Cowdenbeath (2) 0
Clydebank: McKenzie; Hall, Abel, Provan, Goodwin, Hay, Cooper, Henderson (McColl), Larnach, McCallan, Lumsden.
Cowdenbeath: Wilson; Callaghan, Jones (Breen), Seath, Reid (Ross), Simpson, Laing, Hunter, McHale, Murphy, Harrow.

	Home			Away					
	P	W	D L	W	D L		F	A	Pts

Section 1

Rangers	6	2 1 0		2 1 0			18	5	10
Motherwell	6	2 1 0		1 1 1			10	6	8
Airdrieonians	6	2 0 1		0 0 3			7	14	4
Clyde	6	1 0 2		0 0 3			4	14	2

Section 2

Hibernian	6	3 0 0		2 0 1			14	4	10
Ayr U.	6	1 2 0		1 1 1			11	9	7
Dundee	6	1 0 2		0 2 1			9	10	4
Dunfermline Ath.	6	0 2 1		0 1 2			4	15	3

Section 3

Celtic	6	3 0 0		2 0 1			17	4	10
Hearts	6	3 0/0		1 0 2			13	8	8
Aberdeen	6	1 0 2		1 0 2			4	6	4
Dumbarton	6	1 0 2		0 0 3			5	21	2

Section 4

Partick T.	6	3 0 0		3 0 0			17	6	12
Dundee U.	6	2 0 1		1 0 2			8	8	6
Kilmarnock	6	2 0 1		0 0 3			5	9	4
St Johnstone	6	1 0 2		0 0 3			6	13	2

Section 5

Queen of the S.	6	1 0 2		2 1 0			7	6	7
Hamilton A.	6	0 2 1		2 0 1			6	5	6
Falkirk	6	1 1 1		1 1 1			5	7	6
Stirling Albion	6	2 0 1		0 1 2			7	7	5

Section 6

Montrose	6	2 1 0		1 1 1			11	6	8
East Fife	6	1 2 0		1 0 2			8	9	6
Raith R.	6	2 0 1		0 2 1			7	8	6
St Mirren	6	1 1 1		0 1 2			5	8	4

Section 7

Clydebank	6	2 1 0		2 0 1			7	7	9
Arbroath	6	3 0 0		1 0 2			13	3	8
East Stirling	6	0 1 2		1 1 1			6	12	4
Berwick R.	6	1 0 2		0 1 2			6	10	3

Section 8

Stenhousemuir	6	2 1 0		1 1 1			7	7	8
Stranraer	6	2 1 0		1 0 2			13	10	7
Morton	6	2 0 1		1 0 2			11	11	6
Albion R.	6	1 0 2		0 1 2			5	8	3

Section 9

Cowdenbeath	5	2 0 1		2 0 0			15	7	8
Queen's Park	5	1 0 2		2 0 0			10	5	6
Meadowbank T.	5	1 0 2		1 1 0			8	5	5
Brechin C.	5	1 1 0		1 0 2			7	12	5
Forfar Ath.	5	2 0 0		0 0 3			9	16	4
Alloa	5	0 0 2		1 0 2			5	9	2

QUARTER-FINALS, FIRST LEG

SEPT. 10

Hibernian (0) 1 (*Harper*)

Montrose (0) 0   7650

Hibernian: McArthur; Brownlie, Schaedler (Smith),
Stanton, Barry, Blackley, Edwards, Bremner,
Harper, Munro, Duncan.
Montrose: Gorman; Barr, Lowe, McNicoll,
D'Arcy, Markland, Guthrie, Cant, Cameron,
Johnston, Livingstone.

Partick T. (3) 4 (*Houston, McQuade, Somner* 2,
1 *pen.*)

Clydebank (0) 0   4000

Partick T.: Rough; Hansen J., Kellachan, Campbell,
Hansen A., Anderson, Houston (Marr), McQuade,
Joe Craig, Somner, John Craig.
Clydebank: McKenzie; Hall, Abel, Fallon (Provan),
Goodwin, Hay (Caskie), Cooper, Henderson,
Larnach, McCallan, Lumsden.

Rangers (0) 1 (*Johnstone*)

Queen of the S. (0) 0   12,000

Rangers: McCloy; Denny, Miller, Greig. Jackson,
MacDonald, McLean (Stein), McKean (O'Hara),
Parlane, Johnstone, Young.
Queen of the S.: Ball; Miller, Thorburn, McLaren,
Boyd, O'Hara, Dempster, Law, Reid, Dickson G.,
Bryce.

Stenhousemuir (0) 0

Celtic (0) 2 (*Dalglish, Lennox*)   4701

Stenhousemuir: Dunlop; McCullie, Rose, Murdoch,
Gordon, Sage, Sinclair, Scott J. (McPaul), Wight,
Halliday, Simpson.
Celtic: Latchford; McGrain, Lynch, McNamara,
Connelly, Edvaldsson (Aitken), Glavin, Wilson,
Dalglish, Callaghan (Hood), Lennox.

QUARTER-FINALS, SECOND LEG

SEPT. 24

Celtic (0) 1 (*Lynch*)

Stenhousemuir (0) 0   6000

Celtic: Latchford; Aitken, Lynch, Edvaldsson
(Casey), McDonald, McCluskey, Dalglish, Mc-
Namara, Deans, Glavin, Lennox (Hood).
Stenhousemuir: Dunlop; McCullie, Rose, Murdoch,
Gordon, Sage, Sinclair, Scott J. (Fairley), Wight,
Halliday (Scott D.), Simpson.

Clydebank (1) 1 (*Abel*)

Partick T. (0) 0   2500

Clydebank: McKenzie; Hall, Abel, Fallon,
Goodwin, Hay (Caskie), Cooper, Henderson,
Larnach, McCallan, Lumsden.
Partick T.: Rough; Hansen J., Kellachan, Campbell,
Hansen A., Anderson, Houston, McQuade (Marr),
Joe Craig (Whittaker), Somner, John Craig.

Montrose (0) 3 (*Barr* 2, *Livingstone*)

Hibernian (1) 1 (*Duncan*) (*after extra time*)   4000

Montrose: Gorman; Barr, Lowe, McNicoll,
D'Arcy, Markland, Guthrie, Stewart (Cant),
Cameron, Johnston, Livingstone.
Hibernian: McArthur; Brownlie, Schaedler, Stan-
ton, Barry, Blackley, Edwards, Higgins (Smith),
Harper, Munro, Duncan.

Queen of the S. (1) 2 (*Dempster pen., Bryce*)

Rangers (1) 2 (*Johnstone, MacDonald*)
                                    (*after extra time*) 7500

Queen of the S.: Ball; Miller, McChesney, McLaren,
Boyd, O'Hara, Dempster, Reid, Donald (Thor-
burn), Dickson G., Bryce.
Rangers: McCloy; Miller, Dawson, Greig,
Jackson, MacDonald, McLean, McDougall,
Parlane, Johnstone, Young.

SEMI-FINALS

OCT. 6

(at Hampden Park)

Celtic (1) 1 (*Edvaldsson*)

Partick T. (0) 0   30,000

Celtic: Latchford; McGrain, Lynch, McCluskey,
McDonald, Edvaldsson, Wilson, Dalglish, Deans,
Callaghan, Hood (Lennox).
Partick T.: Rough; Hansen J., Kellachan. Camp-
bell, Hansen A. (Fitzpatrick), Anderson, Houston,
McQuade (Joe Craig), Marr, Somner, John Craig.

OCT. 8

(at Hampden Park)

Montrose (1) 1 (*Barr pen.*)

Rangers (0) 5 (*Jardine, Miller pen., Johnstone, Parlane, Scott*) 20,319
Montrose: Gorman; Barr, Lowe, McNicoll, D'Arcy, Markland, Guthrie, Stewart, Cameron, Johnston, Livingstone.
Rangers: McCloy; Jardine, Dawson, Greig, Jackson, Miller, McLean, McDougall, Parlane, Johnstone, Scott.

OCT. 25

(at Hampden Park
Celtic (0) 0
Rangers (0) 1 (*MacDonald*) 58,806
Celtic: Latchford; McGrain, Lynch, McCluskey, McDonald, Edvaldsson, Hood (McNamara), Dalglish, Wilson (Glavin), Callaghan, Lennox.
Rangers: Kennedy; Jardine, Greig, Forsyth, Jackson, MacDonald, McLean, Stein, Parlane, Johnstone, Young.
Referee: Mr W. Anderson (East Kilbride).

SCOTTISH LEAGUE CUP FINALS 1946-75

Season	Winners	Runners-up	Score
1945–46	Aberdeen	Rangers	3–2
1946–47	Rangers	Aberdeen	4–0
1947–48	East Fife	Falkirk	4–1 after 1–1 draw
1948–49	Rangers	Raith R.	2–0
1949–50	East Fife	Dunfermline Ath.	3–0
1950–51	Motherwell	Hibernian	3–0
1951–52	Dundee	Rangers	3–2
1952–53	Dundee	Kilmarnock	2–0
1953–54	East Fife	Partick T.	3–2
1954–55	Hearts	Motherwell	4–2
1955–56	Aberdeen	St. Mirren	2–1
1956–57	Celtic	Partick T.	3–0 after 0–0 draw
1957–58	Celtic	Rangers	7–1
1958–59	Hearts	Partick T.	5–1
1959–60	Hearts	Third Lanark	2–1
1960–61	Rangers	Kilmarnock	2–0
1961–62	Rangers	Hearts	3–1 after 1–1 draw
1962–63	Hearts	Kilmarnock	1–0
1963–64	Rangers	Morton	5–0
1964–65	Rangers	Celtic	2–1
1965–66	Celtic	Rangers	2–1
1966–67	Celtic	Rangers	1–0
1967–68	Celtic	Dundee	5–3
1968–69	Celtic	Hibernian	6–2
1969–70	Celtic	St. Johnstone	1–0
1970–71	Rangers	Celtic	1–0
1971–72	Partick T.	Celtic	4–1
1972–73	Hibernian	Celtic	2–1
1973–74	Dundee	Celtic	1–0
1974–75	Celtic	Hibernian	6–3
1975–76	Rangers	Celtic	1–0

SCOTTISH SPRING CUP

QUALIFYING COMPETITION

	P	W	D	L	W	D	L	F	A	Pt.
Airdrieonians	6	3	0	0	1	1	1	11	7	9
East Fife	6	3	0	0	0	1	2	10	5	7
Brechin C.	6	1	2	0	0	1	2	9	8	5
Stranraer	6	1	1	1	0	0	3	7	17	3
Falkirk	6	3	0	0	1	1	1	10	5	9
Alloa	6	2	1	0	0	2	1	10	8	7
Kilmarnock	6	1	1	1	0	2	1	5	6	5
Berwick R.	6	0	3	0	0	0	3	4	10	3
St. Mirren	6	2	0	1	3	0	0	18	3	10
Partick T.	6	2	0	1	2	0	1	14	8	8
Meadowbank T.	6	2	0	1	0	1	2	6	17	5
Forfar Ath.	6	0	1	2	0	0	3	5	15	1
Dumbarton	6	2	0	1	2	0	1	12	7	8
Arbroath	6	1	0	2	2	0	1	7	6	6
Albion R.	6	2	0	1	1	0	2	9	11	6
Stenhousemuir	6	1	0	2	1	0	2	6	10	4

	P	W	D	L	W	D	L	F	A	Pt.
Queen's Park	6	1	2	0	1	1	1	9	6	7
Dunfermline Ath.	6	2	0	1	1	1	1	7	8	7
Hamilton A.	6	1	1	1	1	1	1	5	8	6
Cowdenbeath	6	2	0	1	0	0	3	8	7	4
Raith R.	6	3	0	0	1	1	1	12	9	9
Clydebank	6	2	0	1	2	0	1	15	6	8
Clyde	6	1	1	1	0	2	1	7	11	5
Queen of the S.	6	1	0	2	0	0	3	6	14	2
Montrose	6	2	0	1	2	1	0	15	11	9
Morton	6	1	1	1	3	0	0	11	7	9
East Stirling	6	1	1	1	0	1	2	4	8	4
Stirling Albion	6	0	1	2	0	1	2	6	10	2

FIRST ROUND, FIRST LEG

APRIL 14

Arbroath (0) 2 (*Bone 2 (1 pen)*)
Falkirk (0) 1 (*Cameron*)

Clydebank (3) 4 (*McCallan, Cooper (pen), Lumsden 2*)
Albion R. (0) 1 (*Shields*)

Dunfermline Ath. (2) 4 (*Scott, Georgeson 2, Smith*)
Airdrieonians (0) 2 (*Whiteford 2*)

Montrose (1) 3 (*Bart, Guthrie, Livingstone*)
Hamilton A. (1) 1 (*Lynch*)

Morton (0) 1 (*McNeil*)
Queen's Park (0) 1 (*Colgan*)

Partick T. (1) 1 (*McQuade*)
East Fife (0) 0

St. Mirren (3) 3 (*Stark, Fitzpatrick, Richardson*)
Alloa (0) 0

APRIL 17

First Round, first leg

Raith R. (2) 2 (*Graham, Wallace*)
Dumbarton (0) 2 (*Brown, Cooper (og)*)

First Round; second leg

Airdrieonians (2) 3 (*Cairney, McCulloch, Whiteford*)
Dunfermline Ath. (0) 0

Albion R. (1) 2 (*Doherty 1, 2 (2 pens)*)
Clydebank (0) 0

Alloa (1) 1 (*Wilkinson*)
St. Mirren (1) 4 (*Munro 2, Stark, McGillivray*)

East Fife (1) 2 (*McPhee, Kinnear*)
Partick T. (0) 0

Falkirk (1) 2 (*Mitchell, Fowler*)
Arbroath (0) 0

Hamilton A. (1) 6 (*McDougall 2, Hughes 3, Thomas*)
Montrose (2) 3 (*Livingstone, Miller, Barr (pen)*)

Queen's Park (1) 2 (*Campbell 2 (2 pens)*)
Morton (2) 3 (*McGhee 2, Brown (pen)*)

APRIL 19

Dumbarton (4) 4 (*Bourke 2, Graham, Wallace*)
Raith R. (0) 0

APRIL 21

Quarter Finals; first leg

Hamilton A. (0) 0
Airdrieonians (1) 4 (*Jonquin (pen), McVeigh, McCulloch, Whiteford*)

Morton (0) 1 (*Goldthorp*)
St. Mirren (0) 0

Dumbarton (1) 4 (*Harvey 2, Graham, Bourke*)
Falkirk (0) 2 (*Whiteford J. (pen), Lawson*)

Clydebank (0) 1 (*Cooper (pen)*)
East Fife (0) 0

APRIL 24

Quarter Finals; second leg

Airdrieonians (2) 5 (*Whiteford 2, Jonquin (pen), McCulloch, Jones*)
Hamilton A. (0) 0

East Fife (1) 1 (*O'Connor*) after extra time Clydebank (0) 0   bank won 4-2 on penalties.

Falkirk (0) 1 (*Fowler*)
Dumbarton (0) 2 (*Bourke, Brown A.*)

St. Mirren (0) 0
Morton (0) 1 (*Brown C.*)

APRIL 28

Semi-finals
at Firhill Park, Glasgow

Clydebank (0) 3 (*Hall, McCallan 2*)
Dumbarton (0) 1 (*Wallace*)

at Love St., Paisley

Airdrieonians 3 (*Cairney, Hayes (og), Sneddon (og)*)
Morton 1 (*McGhee*)

MAY 3

Final: at Firhill Park, Glasgow

Airdrieonians	(0)	4	(*McCulloch 2, McVeigh, Walker*)
Clydebank	(1)	2	(*Larnach 2*) (after extra time)

Airdrieonians: Poulton; Jonquin, Lapsley, Black, March, Whiteford, Wilson, McVeigh, McCulloch, Walker, Cairney (Jones).

Clydebank, McKenzie; Hall, Abel, Fallon, Fanning, Hay (Browning) (Provan), Cooper, McColl, Larnach, McCallan, Lumsden.

Referee: Mr. W. J. Mullan (Dalkeith).

IRISH
AND WELSH
FOOTBALL

Review of the season in Northern Ireland

Honours lists and all the important statistics for Northern Ireland and Wales

Irish Football 1975-76

By Malcolm Brodie

For Northern Ireland it was a far from memorable season. Disaster struck in the British championship with defeats by Scotland, England, and Wales, and, even more depressing, not a goal was scored. And there was elimination too, from Group Three of the European championship – losing 2-1 to Sweden at Windsor Park and 1-0 against Yugoslavia at Belgrade.

After the breakthrough of the isolation barrier a year ago with the resumption of international football in Belfast, happy days appeared to lie ahead, but then came Scotland's refusal to play in Belfast on May 8 because of continuing civil unrest. So reluctantly, but fully aware of all the difficult circumstances, the Irish FA agreed to switch the venue to Hampden Park, Glasgow.

The performance of the international squad, particularly in the home series, was abysmal, with a lack of method, of planning and with many players who figure prominently throughout the season for English First Division clubs failing to make any impact. Strangely for an Irish side, there was no fight, no traditional fervour. Everything looked ponderous, predictable, lethargic.

Criticism, naturally, greeted player-manager Dave Clements who, in March, was transferred from Everton to New York Cosmos, and, although some legislators contended he could not manage the national team 3000 miles from base, the Irish FA International Committee let him continue in the job. Clements however, throughout showed a professional approach and complete dedication but unfortunately just did not get the response from the players, quite a few of whom do not measure up to this grade of football.

With his contract, on a seasonal basis, expired, a complete reappraisal of the international situation has been undertaken by the Irish FA in view of the forthcoming World Cup matches against Holland, Belgium, and Iceland.

It was a domestic season of comparative mediocrity, too. Linfield lost 10-1 on aggregate to PSV Eindhoven in the European Cup; Coleraine 11-3 to Eintracht Frankfurt in the Cup Winners Cup and Glentoran 14-1 to Ajax Amsterdam in the UEFA Cup.

Perhaps they were unfortunate to meet teams of such potency, but it pin-pointed the vast gulf between Continental football and that in the Province, a situation not helped by the persistent terrorist activities, although football has fortunately been able to avoid getting directly caught up.

Neither of Belfast's 'Big Two', Linfield and Glentoran, won a major trophy – something which has not happened for 25 years to Linfield. It was Crusaders, with a flourishing social centre from which considerable revenue is obtained, who took the Irish League title after an impressive, last-minute spurt but, unquestionably the biggest sensation of all was the Irish Cup triumph of 'B' Division Carrick Rangers, who defeated Linfield 2-1 to emulate the feat of Dundela, then an Irish Alliance side, 21 years ago.

Carrick made an unsuccessful application for admittance to the Irish League, but it would appear their chance of elevation may come in the not-too-distant future. Distillery, still searching for a ground to replace Grosvenor Park, which they were forced to evacuate four years ago at the height of the civil unrest, and Glenavon were re-elected.

Attendances at club matches have increased in provincial areas but after the euphoria of the 1974-75 season it was back to stern reality. Arduous times lie ahead. Indeed you could say it is a fight for survival.

FINAL LEAGUE TABLE 1975-76

ULSTER CUP

	P	W	D	L	F	A	Pts
Coleraine	11	8	3	0	32	5	19
Linfield	11	7	2	2	20	7	16
Glentoran	11	7	2	2	25	13	16
Portadown	11	6	1	4	22	23	13
Bangor	11	5	2	4	18	17	12
Glenavon	11	3	4	4	14	20	10
Crusaders	11	2	5	4	15	26	9
Distillery	11	2	4	5	15	24	9
Ards	11	3	3	5	15	18	8
Ballymena U.	11	3	1	7	13	18	7
Larne	11	2	3	6	24	31	7
Cliftonville	11	3	0	8	13	24	6

IRISH LEAGUE

	P	W	D	L	F	A	Pts
Crusaders	22	15	6	1	51	19	36
Glentoran	22	14	4	4	48	22	32
Coleraine	22	13	5	4	42	27	31
Linfield	22	11	5	6	43	25	27
Bangor	22	9	7	6	28	27	25
Ballymena U.	22	8	5	9	36	35	21
Ards	22	7	5	10	32	43	19
Portadown	22	7	3	12	34	39	17
Cliftonville	22	6	4	12	32	46	16
Larne	22	6	3	13	32	45	15
Glenavon	22	4	7	11	24	44	15
Distillery	22	3	4	15	24	54	10

CITY CUP SECTION A

	P	W	D	L	F	A	Pts
Bangor	5	4	1	0	12	6	9
Linfield	5	4	0	1	8	5	8
Ards	5	2	2	1	13	8	6
Portadown	5	2	0	3	12	11	4
Distillery	5	0	2	3	3	8	2
Glenavon	5	0	1	4	2	12	1

SECTION B PLAY-OFF

Play-Off

	P	W	D	L	F	A	Pts
Coleraine	5	3	2	0	16	5	8
Larne	5	2	1	2	7	13	5
Ballymena U.	5	1	3	1	7	7	5
Crusaders	5	2	0	3	7	8	4
Cliftonville	5	1	2	2	9	11	4
Glentoran	5	1	2	2	11	13	4

1974-75 PLAY-OFF
(Held over from last season)

Linfield v Glentoran　　　　　　　1-3
Windsor Park, October 15 1975
Linfield: Barclay; Fraser, McVeigh, Magee, Crozier, Porter, Nixon, Malone, M., Malone, P., Hunter, McKee.
Glentoran: McCullough; McCreery, Craig, Walsh, Robson, Dougan, Caskey, Moreland, Dickinson (Kennedy), Jamison, Feeney.
Referee: Malcolm Wright (Portadown).
Scorers: Linfield; Crozier, Glentoran: Jamison (3).

PLAY OFF

Bangor v Coleraine　　　　　　　0-0
Bangor won 3-1 on penalties at Seaview, Wednesday, December 10 1975. Receipts £475
Bangor: Addis; Feeney, Smith, McCullogh, Jeffrey, Thompson, Jamison, Whiteside, Stewart, Hume, McMullan.

Coleraine: Magee; McCurdy, McNutt, Beckett, Hutton, Murray, Tweed, Jennings, Guy, Dickson, Cochrane.
Referee: Mr. E. Smyton, Dungannon.

PREVIOUS LEAGUE CHAMPIONS

1891	Linfield	1910	Cliftonville	1933	Belfast Celtic	1959	Linfield
1892	Linfield	1911	Linfield	1934	Linfield	1960	Glenavon
1893	Linfield	1912	Glentoran	1935	Linfield	1961	Linfield
1894	Glentoran	1913	Glentoran	1936	Belfast Celtic	1962	Linfield
1895	Linfield	1914	Linfield	1937	Belfast Celtic	1963	Distillery
1896	Distillery	1915	Belfast Celtic	1938	Belfast Celtic	1964	Glentoran
1897	Glentoran	1920	Belfast Celtic	1939	Belfast Celtic	1965	Derry City
1898	Linfield	1921	Glentoran	1940	Belfast Celtic	1966	Linfield
1899	Distillery	1922	Linfield	1948	Belfast Celtic	1967	Glentoran
1900	Belfast Celtic	1923	Linfield	1949	Linfield	1968	Glentoran
1901	Distillery	1924	Queen's Island	1950	Linfield	1969	Linfield
1902	Linfield	1925	Glentoran	1951	Glentoran	1970	Glentoran
1903	Distillery	1926	Belfast Celtic	1952	Glenavon	1971	Linfield
1904	Linfield	1927	Belfast Celtic	1953	Glentoran	1972	Glentoran
1905	Glentoran	1928	Belfast Celtic	1954	Linfield	1973	Crusaders
1906	Cliftonville/Dist	1929	Belfast Celtic	1955	Linfield	1974	Coleraine
1907	Linfield	1930	Linfield	1956	Linfield	1975	Linfield
1908	Linfield	1931	Glentoran	1957	Glentoran	1976	Crusaders
1909	Linfield	1932	Linfield	1958	Ards		

IRISH CUP 1975-76

First Round, January 31
Ards v Dundela	1-0
Crusaders v Omagh T.	3-0
Distillery v Glentoran	0-2
Larne v Glenavon	2-2, 1-2
Linfield v Bangor	4-2
Limavady v Cliftonville	0-1
Portadown v Coleraine	0-0, 0-1

Second Round, February 21
Glentoran v Cliftonville	3-1
Ards v Linfield	1-1, 1-7
Coleraine v Carrick Rangers	1-1, 3-3, 2-1

Semi-Finals, March 13
Glentoran v Linfield	0-2
	(Oval)
Larne v Carrick Rangers	3-3, 2-3
	(Seaview)

FINAL, BELFAST OVAL, APRIL 10

Carrick Rangers v Lingfield　　　　2-1
Attendance 9500

Carrick Rangers: Cowan; Hamilton, Macklin, Matchett, Whiteside, Brown, Cullen, Connor, McKenzie, Prenter, Allen.

Linfield: Barclay; Fraser, McVeigh, Coyle, Rafferty, Bowyer, Nixon, Lemon (McKee), Bell, Malone, Magee.

Referee: T. Perry (Newtownabbey)

Scorers: Carrick Rangers: Prenter (25 mins, 64 mins); *Linfield:* Malone (50 seconds).

1880–81	Moyola Park 1, Cliftonville 0
1881–82	Queen's Island 2, Cliftonville 1
1882–83	Cliftonville 5, Ulster 0
1883–84	Distillery 5, Wellington Park 0
1884–85	Distillery 2, Limavady 0
1885–86	Distillery 1, Limavady 0
1886–87	Ulster 3, Cliftonville 0
1887–88	Cliftonville 2, Distillery 1
1888–89	Distillery 5, Y.M.C.A. 4
1889–90	Gordon Highlanders 3, Cliftonville 1
1890–91	Linfield 4, Ulster 2
1891–92	Linfield 7, The Black Watch 0
1892–93	Linfield 5, Cliftonville 1
1893–94	Distillery 3, Linfield 2
1894–95	Linfield 10, Bohemians 1
1895–96	Distillery 3, Glentoran 1
1896–97	Cliftonville 3, Sherwood Foresters 1
1897–98	Linfield 2, St. Columb's Hall Celtic 0
1898–99	Linfield 2, Glentoran 1
1899–1900	Cliftonville 2, Bohemians 1
1900–1	Cliftonville 1, Freebooters 0
1901–2	Linfield 5, Distillery 1
1902–3	Distillery 3, Bohemians 1
1903–4	Linfield 5, Derry Celtic 1
1904–5	Distillery 3, Shelbourne 0
1905–6	Shelbourne 2, Belfast Celtic 0
1906–7	Cliftonville 1, Shelbourne 0
1907–8	Bohemians 3, Shelbourne 1
1908–9	Cliftonville 2, Bohemians 1
1909–10	Distillery 1, Cliftonville 0
1910–11	Shelbourne 2, Bohemians 1
1911–12	Linfield were awarded Cup. Final not played.
1912–13	Linfield 2, Glentoran 0
1913–14	Glentoran 3, Linfield 1
1914–15	Linfield 1, Belfast Celtic 0
1915–16	Linfield 1, Glentoran 0
1916–17	Glentoran 2, Belfast Celtic 0
1917–18	Belfast Celtic 2, Linfield 0
1918–19	Linfield 2, Glentoran 1
1919–20	Cup awarded to Shelbourne.
1920–21	Glentoran 2, Glenavon 0
1921–22	Linfield 2, Glenavon 0
1922–23	Linfield 2, Glentoran 0
1923–24	Queen's Island 1, Willowfield 0
1924–25	Distillery 2, Glentoran 1
1925–26	Belfast Celtic 3, Linfield 2
1926–27	Ards 3, Cliftonville 2
1927–28	Willowfield 1, Larne 0
1928–29	Ballymena 2, Belfast Celtic 1
1929–30	Linfield 4, Ballymena 3
1930–31	Linfield 3, Ballymena 0
1931–32	Glentoran 2, Linfield 1
1932–33	Glentoran 3, Distillery 1
1933–34	Linfield 5, Cliftonville 0
1934–35	Glentoran 1, Larne 0
1935–36	Linfield 2, Derry City 1
1936–37	Belfast Celtic 3, Linfield 0
1937–38	Belfast Celtic 2, Bangor 0
1938–39	Linfield 2, Ballymena 0
1939–40	Ballymena 2, Glenavon 0
1940–41	Belfast Celtic 1, Linfield 0
1941–42	Linfield 3, Glentoran 1
1942–43	Belfast Celtic 1, Glentoran 0
1943–44	Belfast Celtic 2, Linfield 1
1944–45	Linfield 4, Glentoran 2
1945–46	Linfield 3, Distillery 0
1946–47	Belfast Celtic 1, Glentoran 0
1947–48	Linfield 3, Coleraine 0
1948–49	Derry City 3, Glentoran 1
1949–50	Linfield 2, Distillery 1
1950–51	Glentoran 3, Ballymena United 1
1951–52	Ards 1, Glentoran 0
1952–53	Linfield 5, Coleraine 0
1953–54	Derry City 1, Glentoran 0
1954–55	Dundela 3, Glenavon 0
1955–56	Distillery 1, Glentoran 0
1956–57	Glenavon 2, Derry City 0
1957–58	Ballymena United 2, Linfield 0
1958–59	Glenavon 2, Ballymena United 0
1959–60	Linfield 5, Ards 1
1960–61	Glenavon 5, Linfield 1
1961–62	Linfield 4, Portadown 0
1962–63	Linfield 2, Distillery 1
1963–64	Derry City 2, Glentoran 0
1964–65	Coleraine 2, Glenavon 1
1965–66	Glentoran 2, Linfield 0
1966–67	Crusaders 3, Glentoran 1
1967–68	Crusaders 2, Linfield 0
1968–69	Ards 4, Distillery 2
1969–70	Linfield 2, Ballymena United 1
1970–71	Distillery 3, Derry City 0
1971–72	Coleraine 2, Portadown 1
1972–73	Glentoran 3, Linfield 2
1973–74	Ards 2, Ballymena 1
1974–75	Coleraine 1:0:1, Linfield 1:0:0
1975–76	Carrick Rangers 2, Linfield 1

	Winners	*Runners-up*
Hennessey Gold Cup	Coleraine	Ballymena U.
Co. Antrim Shield	Ballymena U.	Distillery
Blaxnit Cup	*Not Played*	
Irish League 'B' Div	Linfield Swifts	Dungannon Swifts
George Wilson Cup	Limavady U.	Dundela
Steel Cup	Chimney Cnr.	Ballyclare C.
Intermediate Cup	Carrick R.	Dundela
IFA Junior Cup	*Withheld*	
Irish Junior Shield	44th Old Boys	Bantor Y.M.
Irish Youth Cup	Sunnyside C.	Star of the S.
Collingwood Cup (Inter Varsity Championship)	University Col. Dublin	Stranmillis
Irish Schools Cup	Glengormley	Ashfield

Ulster Footballer of the Year (promoted by Castlereagh Glentoran Supporters Club) — Warren Feeney (Glentoran)

N.I. Footballer of the Year (Football Writers Association) — Warren Feeney (Glentoran)

Young Footballer of the Year — Jim Hagan (Larne)

N.I. Professional Football Association Player of the Year — Warren Feeney (Glentoran)

Most Promising Newcome Mullan-Stewart Award for — Sam Galway (Larne)

Meritorious Service — Billy Neill (Glentoran)

CITY CUP WINNERS

Year	Winner	Year	Winner	Year	Winner	Year	Winner
1895	Linfield	1914	Glentoran	1936	Linfield	1961	Glenavon
1896	Glentoran	1915	Glentoran	1937	Derry City	1962	Linfield
1897	Glentoran	1920	Linfield	1938	Linfield	1963	Distillery
1898	Linfield	1921	Glenavon	1939	Portadown	1964	Linfield
1899	Glentoran	1922	Linfield	1940	Belfast Celtic	1965	Glentoran
1900	Linfield	1923	Queen's Island	1948	Belfast Celtic	1966	Glenavon
1901	Linfield	1924	Queen's Island	1949	Belfast Celtic	1967	Glentoran
1902	Linfield	1925	Queen's Island	1950	Linfield	1968	Linfield
1904	Linfield	1926	Belfast Celtic	1951	Glentoran	1969	Coleraine
1905	Distillery	1927	Linfield	1952	Linfield	1970	Glentoran
1906	Belfast Celtic	1928	Belfast Celtic	1953	Glentoran	1971	Bangor
1907	Belfast Celtic	1929	Linfield	1954	Coleraine	1972	Ballymena U.
1908	Linfield	1930	Belfast Celtic	1955	Glenavon	1973	Glentoran
1909	Shelbourne	1931	Belfast Celtic	1956	Glenavon	1974	Linfield
1910	Linfield	1932	Glentoran	1957	Glentoran	1975	Glentoran
1911	Glentoran	1933	Belfast Celtic	1958	Linfield	1976	Bangor
1912	Glentoran	1934	Distillery	1959	Linfield		
1913	Distillery	1935	Derry City	1960	Distillery		

WELSH CUP 1975–1976

Qualifying Round
Druids United v Hawarden	6-0
Rhosddu v Courtaulds (Greenfield)	0-1
*Machynlleth v Berriew	0-6
Montgomery T. v Guilsfield Utd.	3-2

Played on ground of second-named Club.

First Round
*Holyhead Town v Portmadog	
**Pwllheli & District v Flint Town Utd.	1-2, 2-2, 3-4
Nantlle Vale v Bethesda Athletic	1-2
Blaenau Ffestiniog v Prestatyn	1-1, 3-2
Point of Ayr v Caernarvon Town	1-1, 0-1
Colwyn Bay v Rhos United	3-1
Mold Alexandra v Chirk AAA	1-3
Welshpool v Connahs Quay Nomads	4-1
Gresford Athletic v Buckley W.	6-1
Bala Town v Ruthin	3-1
Brymbo S.W. v Courtaulds (Greenfield)	2-2, 2-3
Llay Welfare v Druids United	1-0
Berriew v Llanidloes Town	2-3
Montgomery Town v Towyn	0-2
Llandrindod Wells v Newtown	1-2
Llanfair Caereinion v Aberystwyth Town	1-1, 0-1
Talgarth v Rhayader Town	3-1
GKN Sankey v Knighton Town	0-1
Worcester City v Brierley H.A.	2-2, 3-1
Bridgnorth T. v Kidderminster H.	1-1, 2-5
Tonyrefail Welfare v Cardiff Cor.	2-3
Ebbw Vale v Caerau Athletic	2-0
Caerleon v Abermana	2-1
Spencer W. v Cardiff Coll. of Ed.	0-2
Cwymbran Town v Merthyr Tydfil	0-1
Pontardawe Athletic v Ton Pentre	1-2
Sully v Everwarm	0-0, 2-1
Ferndale Athletic v Cwmbran Celtic	3-1
Barry Town v Pontllanfraith	2-0
Llanelli v Milford United	1-0
BP Llandarcy v Ammanford Town	0-4
Pembroke Boro. v Haverfordwest C.	0-1

*Holyhead Town F.C. withdrew from the Competition
– tie awarded to Portmadog F.C.*
**1st game abandoned after 55 minutes.*

Second Round
Chirk AAA v Rhyl	2-6
Llay Welfare v Blaenau Ffestiniog	1-2
Caernarvon Town v Bala Town	1-1, 3-7
Gresford Athletic v Bethesda Ath.	1-4
Colwyn Bay v Courtaulds (Greenfield)	0-0, 2-3
Porthmadog v Flint Town United	3-1
Kidderminster H. v Newtown	1-1, 3-0
Oswestry Town v Welshpool	2-0
Knighton T. v Worcester C.	0-1
Llanidloes Town v Towyn	3-0
Stourbridge v Aberystwyth T.	5-0
Sully v Caerleon	3-0
Cardiff Cor. v Briton Ferry A.	4-2
Llanelli v Haverfordwest County	3-4

Ton Pentre v Merthyr Tydfil	4-2
Ebbw Vale v Barry Town	0-2
Cardiff Coll. of Ed. v Ammanford Town	5-1
Talgarth v Ferndale Athletic	1-2

Third Round
Llanidloes Town v Bangor City	6-1
Oswestry Town v Porthmadog	1-2
Bala Town v Courtaulds (Greenfield)	0-3
Bethesda Athletic v Rhyl	2-2, 1-5
*Blaenau Ffestiniog v Kidderminster H.	1-1, 2-2, 2-3
**Cardiff Coll. of Ed. v Worcester City	1-1, 2-4
Stourbridge v Hereford United	1-2
Cardiff Cor. v Haverfordwest Co.	4-1
Ferndale Athletic v Barry Town	1-1, 3-2
Ton Pentre v Sully	2-5

1st Match abandoned after 17 minutes.
**Both matches played at Worcester City F.C.*

Fourth Round
Chester v Kidderminster Harriers	8-1
Courtaulds Greenfield v Shrewsbury Town	0-5
Rhyl v Porthmadog	0-2
Wrexham v Llanidloes Town	8-0
Worcester City v Ferndale Ath.	4-0
Newport County v Hereford Utd.	1-2
Sully v Cardiff City	0-5
Swansea City v Cardiff Cor.	6-0

Fifth Round
Cardiff City v Swansea City	1-1, 3-0
Wrexham v Chester	0-0, 1-2
*Porthmadog v Hereford United	0-4
Worcester City v Shrewsbury T.	2-2, 0-3

Played at Hereford United F.C.

Semi-finals
Hereford United v Shrwesbury T.	1-1, 5-4
Chester v Cardiff City	0-0, 0-1

Final
First leg at Hereford, May 18 1976

Hereford U. 3
Cardiff C. 3

Hereford: Charlton, Emery, Byrne, Tucker, Galley, Lindsay, Paine, Briley, Davey, McNeil, Carter.
Cardiff: Healey, Pethard, Charles, Giles, Dwyer, Lamour, Sayer, Livermore, Evans, Showers, Clark.

Second Leg at Ninian Park, May 19 1976.

Cardiff C. 3
Hereford U. 2

Cardiff: Irwin, Pethard, Charles, Giles, Dwyer, Larmour, Sayer, Livermore, Evans, Clark, Anderson.
Hereford: Charlton, Emery, Ritchie, Tucker, Galley, Lindsay, Paine, Tyler, Davey, McNeil, Carter.

WELSH CUP FINALS 1878–1976

1877–78	Wrexham 1, Druids 0
1878–79	Newtown 1, Wrexham 0
1879–80	Druids 2, Ruthin 1
1880–81	Druids 2, Newtown White Stars 0
1881–82	Druids 2, Northwich 1
1882–83	Wrexham 1, Druids 0
1883–84	Oswestry 3, Druids 2
1884–85	Druids 2, Oswestry 0
1885–86	Druids 5, Newtown 2
1886–87	Chirk 4, Davenham 2
1887–88	Chirk 5, Newtown 0
1888–89	Bangor 2, Northwich 1
1889–90	Chirk 1, Wrexham 0
1890–91	Shrewsbury Town 5, Wrexham 1
1891–92	Chirk 2, Westminster Rovers 1
1892–93	Wrexham 2, Chirk 1
1893–94	Chirk 2, Westminster Rovers 0
1894–95	Newtown 3, Wrexham 2
1895–96	Bangor 3, Wrexham 1
1896–97	Wrexham 2, Newtown 0
1897–98	Druids 2, Wrexham 1 *(after draw 1 1)*
1898–99	Druids 1, Wrexham 0 *(after draw 2 2)*
1899–1900	Aberystwyth 3, Druids 0
1900–01	Oswestry 1, Druids 0
1901–02	Wellington 1, Wrexham 0
1902–03	Wrexham 8, Aberaman 0
1903–04	Druids 3, Aberdare 2
1904–05	Wrexham 3, Aberdare 0
1905–06	Wellington 3, Whitchurch 2
1906–07	Oswestry 2, Whitchurch 0
1907–08	Chester 3, Connah's Quay 1
1908–09	Wrexham 1, Chester 0

1909–10	Wrexham 2, Chester 1	1947–48	Lovells Ath 3, Shrewsbury T. 0
1910–11	Wrexham 6, Connah's Quay 1	1948–49	Merthyr Tydfil 2, Swansea T. 0
1911–12	Cardiff C. 3, Pontypridd 0 (*after draw* 0 0)	1949–50	Swansea T. 4, Wrexham 1
1912–13	Swansea 1, Pontypridd 0 (*after draw* 0 0)	1950–51	Merthyr Tydfil 3, Cardiff C. 2 (*after draw* 1 1)
1913–14	Wrexham 3, Llanelly 0 (*after draw* 1 1)		
1914–15	Wrexham 1, Swansea 0 (*after draw* 0 0)	1951–52	Rhyl 4, Merthyr Tydfil 3
1915–19	No competition. First World War	1952–53	Rhyl 2, Chester 1
1919–20	Cardiff C. 2, Wrexham 1	1953–54	Flint Town U. 2, Chester 0
1920–21	Wrexham 3, Pontypridd 1 (*after draw* 1 1)	1954–55	Barry T. 4, Chester 3 (*after draw* 1 1)
1921–22	Cardiff C. 2, Ton Pentre 0	1955–56	Cardiff C. 3, Swansea T. 2
1922–23	Cardiff C. 3, Aberdare 2	1956–57	Wrexham 2, Swansea T. 1
1923–24	Wrexham 1, Merthyr 0 (*after draw* 2 2)	1957–58	Wrexham 2, Chester 0 (*after draw* 1 1)
1924–25	Wrexham 3, Flint 1	1958–59	Cardiff C. 2, Lovells Athletic 0
1925–26	Ebbw Vale 3, Swansea 2	1959–60	Wrexham 1, Cardiff C. 0 (*after draw* 00)
1926–27	Cardiff C. 2, Rhyl 0	1960–61	Swansea T. 3, Bangor C. 1
1927–28	Cardiff C. 2, Bangor 0	1961–62	Bangor C. 3, Wrexham 1
1928–29	Connah's Quay 3, Cardiff C. 0	1962–63	Borough U. 2, Newport Co. 1*
1929–30	Cardiff C. 4, Rhy 2 (*after draw* 0 0)	1963–64	Cardiff C. 5, Bangor C. 3*
1930–31	Wrexham 7, Shrewsbury 0	1964–65	Cardiff C. 8, Wrexham 2*
1931–32	Swansea 2, Wrexham 0 (*after draw* 1 1)	1965–66	Swansea T. 2, Chester 1
1932–33	Chester 2, Wrexham 0	1966–67	Cardiff C. 2, Wrexham 1*
1933–34	Bristol C. 3, Tranmere R. 0 (*after draw* 1 1)	1967–68	Cardiff C. 6, Hereford U. 1*
		1968–69	Cardiff C. 5, Swansea T. 1*
1934–35	Tranmere R. 1, Chester 0	1969–70	Cardiff C. 5, Chester 0
1935–36	Crewe 2, Chester 0	1970–71	Cardiff C. 4, Wrexham 1*
1936–37	Crewe 3, Rhyl 1 (*after draw* 1 1)	1971–72	Wrexham 3, Cardiff C. 2*
1937–38	Shrewsbury 2, Swansea 1	1972–73	Cardiff C. 5, Bangor C. 1*
1938–39	South Liverpool 2, Cardiff C. 1	1973–74	Cardiff C. 2, Stourbridge 0*
1939–40	Welling Town 4, Swansea 0	1974–75	Wrexham 5, Cardiff 2*
1940–46	No competition. Second World War	1975–76	Cardiff C. 6, Hereford U. 5*
1946–47	Chester 5, Methyr Tydfil 1 (*after draw* 0 0)		* Aggregate score

THE WELSH LEAGUE FINAL TABLES 1973-74

Premier Division

	P	W	D	L	P
Swansea C.	34	22	7	5	51
Everwarm	34	20	10	4	50
Ferndale	34	17	9	8	43
Sully	34	18	7	9	43
Ammanford	34	15	12	7	42
Cardiff C.	34	15	10	9	40
Ton Pentre	34	17	4	13	38
Pontllanfraith	34	14	8	12	36
Spencer Works	34	13	9	12	35
Briton Ferry	34	14	5	15	33
Newport Co.	34	11	10	13	32
Merthyr Tydfil	34	12	7	15	31
Pembroke Boro	34	9	12	13	30
Llanelli	34	10	8	16	28
Caerleon	34	7	10	17	24
Blaenrhonnda	34	8	5	21	21
Lewistown	34	6	9	19	21
Haverfordwest	34	4	6	24	14

Division I

	P	W	D	L	P
Cardiff Coll.	34	25	4	5	54
Cwmbran	34	20	9	5	49
Afan Lido	34	19	9	6	47
Pontardawe	34	18	11	5	47
Pontlottyn	34	16	9	9	41
Blaenavon	34	15	10	9	40
Cardiff Corries	34	15	8	11	38
Caerau	34	15	8	11	38
Tonyrefail	34	12	8	14	32
Tredoman	34	11	10	13	32
Barry Town	34	11	10	13	32
Maesteg Park	34	13	5	16	31
Treharris	34	14	1	19	29
Ebbw Vale	34	11	3	20	25
Swansea Univ.	34	9	7	18	25
Carmathen	34	7	10	17	24
Tynte Rovers	34	5	6	17	16
Cardiff Univ.	34	2	8	24	12

WELSH LEAGUE (NORTH)

Division I

	P	W	D	L	P
Porthmadog	20	14	3	3	31
Nantlle Vale	20	13	4	3	30
Bethesda Ath.	20	13	4	3	30
Caernarfon Town	20	13	2	5	28
Bl. Ffestiniog	20	7	7	6	21
Wrexham	20	7	5	8	19
Pwllheli & Dst.	20	7	4	9	18
Bangor City	20	7	4	9	18
Colwyn Bay	20	4	8	8	16
Rhyl	20	3	3	14	9
Llandudno Swifts	20	0	0	10	0

WELSH INTERMEDIATE CUP 1975–1976

First Round

Courtaulds (Greenfield) v Mountain R.	2-0
Menai Bridge Tigers v Peritus	5-1
Machno Utd. v Penmaenmawr Phoenix	3-1
Caernarvon Utd. v Pilkingtons (St. Asaph)	0-5
Coedpoeth S.C. v Hawarden Rangers	4-0
Treuddyn V. v Johnstown R.G.A.	2-2, 2-1
Montgomery Town v Presteigne St.A.	3-1
Broseley Athletic v Guilsfield Utd.	4-0
Llanfair Caereinion v Snailbeach W.S.	0-0, 2-1
Bryncrug v Bont	7-1
Ffostrasol W. v New Quay & District	3-0
Newport Corinthians v Govilon	6-0
Croesyceiliog v Newport (Pill) YMCA	1-3

Second Round

Menai Bridge Tigers v Courtaulds (Greenfield)	1-2
Pilkington (St. Asaph) v Machno Utd.	4-0
Saltney Social v Rhos Aelwyd	2-1
	(after extra time)
Lex XI v Coedpoeth S.C.	1-2
New Broughton v Treuddyn Villa	2-0

Montgomery T. v Ffostrasol W.	1-3
Snailbeach White Stars v Bryncrug	5-1
Dolgellau Ath. v Broseley Ath.	1-4
Cwmbran Celtic v Rogerstone	3-6
Newport YMCA v Newport Cor.	3-3, 4-1

Third Round

Prestatyn v Rhos United	4-1
Denbigh Town v Pilkington (St. Asaph)	2-1
Nantlle Vale v Flint Town United	0-1
Holyhead Town v Llandegfan	0-4
Colwyn Bay v Llanberis Athletic	1-3
Courtaulds (Greenfield) v Point of Ayr	0-0, 2-1
Bala Town v Connah's Quay Nomads	2-1
Llay Welfare v Buckley Rovers	2-1
Druids Utd. v Buckley Wanderers	3-0
Burntwood & Drury v Hawarden (Hawarden withdrawn from Competition tie awarded to Burntwood & Drury)	
Mold Alex. v Llangollen	1-1, 2-5
Coedpoeth S.C. v New Broughton	1-0
Brymbo Steel Works v Ruthin	1-0

Gresford Ath. v Saltney Social	1-1, 1-5
Rhosddu v Chirk AAA	1-3
Shifnal T. v UCW Aberystwyth	1-1, 5-3
	(after extra time)
Caersws Amateur v Machynlleth	3-2
Wem. Town Colts v Welshpool	4-1
Belle Vue Boys v Donnington Wood	0-2
Knighton Town v Llanfyllin Town	4-0
Ffostrasol W. v Llandrindod Wells	3-2
Whitchurch Alport v Rhayader Town	5-1
GKN Sports v Towyn	2-3
Broseley Ath. v Aberysthwyth Town	2-1
Talgarth v Llanidloes Town	2-0
Harlech T. v Snailbeach W.S.	2-2, 0-4
Newtown v Berriew	3-0
Cardiff Corinthians v Ynysybwl	8-0
Rogerstone v Treharris Athletic	1-2
Aberaman v Newport YMCA	2-5
Cardiff Coll. of Ed. v Tonyrefail Welfare	0-0, 4-1
Blaenrhondda v Cwmbran Town	1-3

Fourth Round

Llandegfan v Whitchurch Alport	4-2
Llay Welfare v Bala Town	2-1
Flint Town Utd. v Coedpoeth S.C.	2-0
Llangollen v Cortaulds Greenfield	2-1
Prestatyn v Burntwood & Drury	2-1
Saltney Social v Brymbo Steel Works	1-3
Chirk AAA v Llandberis Athletic	3-1
Denbigh Town v Druids United	2-1
Cwmbran Town v Treharris Athletic	4-3
Shifnal Town v Knighton Town	1-0
Snailbeach White Stars v Towyn	2-1

Wem Town Colts v Ffostrasol Wanderers	3-0
Caersws Amateur v Cardiff Corinthinas	2-4
Cardiff Coll. of Ed. v Donnington Wood	3-1
Newport YMCA v Newtown	2-3
Broseley Athletic v Talgarth	4-2

Fifth Round

Prestatyn v Brymbo Steelworks	0-0, 2-5
	(after pen kicks)
Llay Welfare v Llangollen	1-1, 3-5
Flint Town Utd. v Llandegfan	4-2
Denbigh Town v Chirk AAA	2-1
Cardiff Coll. of Ed. v Cwmbran T.	4-0
Wem Town Colts v Newtown	2-2, 5-3
	(after pen kicks)
Cardiff Corinthians v Brosley Ath.	0-1
Shifnal Town v Snailbeach White Stars	2-0

Sixth Round

Denbigh Town v Llangollen	3-0
Wem Town Colts v Broseley Ath.	0-0, 2-1
Cardiff Coll. of Ed. v Flint Town Utd.	3-2
Shifnal Town v Brymbo Steelworks	2-0

Semi-Finals

Shifnal Town v Wem Town Colts	3-2
	(at Welshpool)
Cardiff Coll. of Ed. v Denbigh Town	1-1, 5-2
	(at Aberystwyth)

Final

| Shifnal Town v Cardiff Coll. of Ed. | 1-2 |
| | (at Knighton Town) |

WELSH AMATEUR CUP FINALS from 1902–1975

1901–02	Wrexham Victoria 1, Machynlleth 0
1902–03	Druids Res. 4, Bangor Res. 0
1903–04	Wrexham Victoria 4, Druids Res. 2
1904–05	Esclusham White Stars 4, Bangor R. 0
1905–06	Buckley Engineers 4, Portmadoc 1 (after draw 2 2)
1906–07	Buckley Engineers 4, Aberystwyth 1 (after draw 2 2)
1907–08	Esclusham White Stars 1, Brymbo 0
1908–09	Caernarvon 5, Oak Aly Rovers 1
1909–10	Johnstown Amateurs 2, Bangor 1
1910–11	Buckley 1, Aberystwyth 0
1911–12	Rhos 2, Summerhill 1 (after draw 1 1)
1912–13	Johnstown 3, Aberaman 1
1913–14	Cardiff Corinthians 1, Holywell 0
1915–19	Competition suspended through the War
1919–20	Caerau 4, Barmouth 1
1920–21	Northern Nomads 2, Cardiff Cories 0
1921–22	Llanidloes 3, Aberystwyth University 1
1922–23	Acrefair 1, Lovell's Athletic 0
1923–24	Denbigh Town 2, Lovell's Athletic 1
1924–25	Northern Nomads 5, Llanidloes 1 (after draw 1 1)
1925–26	Lovell's Athletic 2, Holywell 0
1926–27	Lovell's Athletic 2, Holywell 0
1927–28	Lovell's Athletic 1, Llanidloes 0
1928–29	Cardiff Corinthians 2, Aberystwyth 0
1929–30	Cardiff Corinthians 4, Burntwood 3
1930–31	Aberystwyth 5, Llanfairfechan 1
1931–32	Machynlleth 3, Cardiff Corinthians 0
1932–33	Aberystwyth 2, Llanidloes 1
1933–34	Cardiff Corinthians 1, Llanidloes 0
1934–35	Aberdovey 2, Flint Ath. 1
1935–36	Llay Welfare 3, Treharris 1 (after draw 1 1)
1936–37	Treharris 2, Llandudno 1
1937–38	Abercynon Athletic 2, Wem Town 1 (after draw 1 1)
1938–39	Caerau Athletic 1, Lovell's Athletic 0

1939–40	Abercynon 3, Flint Ath. 0
1940–45	No competition, Second World War
1945–46	Caerau Athletic 5, Llay United 1
1946–47	Troedyrhiw 5, Llay United 0
1947–48	Flint Town United 2, Troedyrhiw 1
1948–49	Llay United 2, Hanwood Welfare 0
1949–50	Caerau Athletic 2, Llay Welfare 0
1950–51	Treharris Athletic 3, Connah's Quay Juniors 1
1951–52	Ton Pentre 6, Chirk A.A.A. 2
1952–53	Connah's Quay Nomads 3, Caersws 2
1953–54	Lovell's Athletic 3, Overton St. Mary's 2
1954–55	Newtown 4, Chirk A.A.A. 2
1955–56	Portmadoc 5, Peritus 2
1956–57	Portmadoc 5, Druids United 2 (after draw 2 2)
1957–58	55th R.A. Tonfannau 3, Portmadoc 2
1958–59	Chirk A.A.A. 2, Whitchurch Alport 0 (after draw 2 2)
1959–60	Chirk A.A.A. 3, Caerau Ath. 2
1960–61	Caersws Am 4, Buckley W. 2
1961–62	Cardiff Corinths. 3, Holywell Town 2
1962–63	Chirk A.A.A. 2, Caersws Am. 0
1963–64	Donnington Wd. 2, Caersws Am. 1
1964–65	Llanidloes Town 3, Gwynfi Welfare 2
1965–66	Caerleon 1, Welshpool 0
1966–67	Brymbo Steel Wks. 3, Cardiff Col. of Ed. 2
1967–68	Cardiff Co., of Ed. 3, Welshpool 1
1968–69	Cardiff Col. of Ed. 2, Tonyrefail Welf. 0
1969–70	Aberystwyth T. 2, Cardiff Col. of Ed. 1
1970–71	Bridgnorth T. 2, Welshpool 1
1971–72	Welshpool 1, Aberystwyth T. 0
1972–73	Rhyl 2, G.K.N. Sankey 0
1973–74	Whitchurch Alport 2, Cardiff Col. of Ed. 0
1974–75	Donnington W. 2, Buckley W. 0

MISCELLANY

World Cup

Facts and Figures

Anglo-Scottish Cup

Charity Shield

Directory of ex-Football League clubs

Directory of Managers

THE WORLD CUP

URUGUAY 1930

POOL 1

France 4, Mexico 1
Argentina 1, France 0
Chile 3, Mexico 0
Chile 1, France 0
Argentina 6, Mexico 3
Argentina 3, Chile 1

	P	W	D	L	F	A	Pts.
Argentina	3	3	0	0	10	4	6
Chile	3	2	0	1	5	3	4
France	3	1	0	2	4	3	2
Mexico	3	0	0	3	4	13	0

POOL 2

Yugoslavia 2, Brazil 1
Yugoslavia 4, Bolivia 0
Brazil 4, Bolivia 0

	P	W	D	L	F	A	Pts.
Yugoslavia	2	2	0	0	6	1	4
Brazil	2	1	0	1	5	2	2
Bolivia	2	0	0	2	0	8	0

POOL 3

Rumania 3, Peru 1
Uruguay 1, Peru 0
Uruguay 4, Rumania 0

	P	W	D	L	F	A	Pts.
Uruguay	2	2	0	0	5	0	4
Rumania	2	1	0	1	3	5	2
Peru	2	0	0	2	1	4	0

POOL 4

United States 3, Belgium 0
United States 3, Paraguay 0
Paraguay 1, Belgium 0

	P	W	D	L	F	A	Pts.
United States	2	2	0	0	6	0	4
Paraguay	2	1	0	1	1	3	2
Belgium	2	0	0	2	0	4	0

SEMI-FINALS

Argentina 6, United States 1
Uruguay 6, Yugoslavia 1

FINAL

Uruguay 4, Argentina 2 (1-2)

Uruguay: Ballesteros; Nasazzi (capt.), Mascheroni, Andrade, Fernandez, Gestido, Dorado, Scarone, Castro, Cea, Iriarte.

Argentina: Botasso; Della Torre, Paternoster, Evaristo J., Monti, Suarez, Peucelle, Varallo, Stabile, Ferreira (capt.), Evaristo M.

Scorers: Dorado, Cea, Iriarte, Castro for Uruguay; Peucelle, Stabile for Argentina.

Leading scorer: Stabile (Argentina) 8.

ITALY 1934

FIRST ROUND

Italy 7, U.S.A. 1
Czechoslovakia 2, Rumania 1
Germany 5, Belgium 2
Austria 3, France 2
Spain 3, Brazil 1
Switzerland 3, Holland 2
Sweden 3, Argentina 2
Hungary 4, Egypt 2

SECOND ROUND

Germany 2, Sweden 1
Austria 2, Hungary 1
Italy 1, Spain 1
Italy 1, Spain 0 *replay*
Czechoslovakia 3, Switzerland 2

SEMI-FINALS

Czechoslovakia 3, Germany 1
Italy 1, Austria 0

THIRD PLACE MATCH

Germany 3, Austria 2

FINAL

Italy 2, Czechoslovakia 1 (0-0) (1-1) after extra time. *Rome.*

Italy: Combi (capt.); Monzeglio, Allemandi; Ferraris IV, Monti, Bertolini, Guaita, Meazza, Schiavio, Ferrari, Orsi.

Czechoslovakia: Planicka (capt.); Zenisek, Ctyroky, Kostalek, Cambal, Krcil; Junek, Svoboda, Sobotka, Nejedly, Puc.

Scorers: Orsi, Schiavio for Italy, Puc for Czechoslovakia.

Leading Scorers: Schiavio (Italy), Nejedly (Czechoslovakia), Conen (Germany) each 4.

FRANCE 1938

FIRST ROUND

Switzerland 1, Germany 1
Switzerland 4, Germany 2 *replay*
Cuba 3, Rumania 3
Cuba 2, Rumania 1 *replay*
Hungary 6, Dutch East Indies 0
France 3, Belgium 1
Czechoslovakia 3, Holland 0
Brazil 6, Poland 5
Italy 2, Norway 1

SECOND ROUND

Sweden 8, Cuba 0
Hungary 2, Switzerland 0
Italy 3, France 1
Brazil 1, Czechoslovakia 1
Brazil 2, Czechoslovakia 1 *replay*

SEMI-FINALS

Italy 2, Brazil 1
Hungary 5, Sweden 1

THIRD PLACE MATCH

Brazil 4, Sweden 2

FINAL

Italy 4, Hungary 2 (3-1). *Paris*

Italy: Olivieri; Foni, Rava; Serantoni, Andreolo, Locatelli; Biavati, Meazza (capt.), Piola, Ferrari. Colaussi.

Hungary: Szabo; Polgar, Biro; Szalay, Szucs, Lazar; Sas, Vincze, Sarosi (capt.), Szengeller, Titkos.

Scorers: Colaussi (2), Piola (2) for Italy, Titkos, Sarosi for Hungary.

Leadnig Scorer: Leonidas (Brazil) 8.

BRAZIL 1950

POOL 1

Brazil 4, Mexico 0
Yugoslavia 3, Switzerland 0
Yugoslavia 4, Mexico 1
Brazil 2, Switzerland 2
Brazil 2, Yugoslavia 0
Switzerland 2, Mexico 1

	P	W	D	L	F	A	Pts.
Brazil	3	2	1	0	8	2	5
Yugoslavia	3	2	0	1	7	3	4
Switzerland	3	1	1	1	4	6	3
Mexico	3	0	0	3	2	10	0

POOL 2

Spain 3, United States 1
England 2, Chile 0
United States 1, England 0
Spain 2, Chile 0
Spain 1, England 0
Chile 5, United States 2

	P	W	D	L	F	A	Pts.
Spain	3	3	0	0	6	1	6
England	3	1	0	2	2	2	2
Chile	3	1	0	2	5	6	2
United States	3	1	0	2	4	8	2

POOL 3

Sweden 3, Italy 2
Sweden 2, Paraguay 2
Italy 2, Paraguay 0

	P	W	D	L	F	A	Pts.
Sweden	2	1	1	0	5	4	3
Italy	2	1	0	1	4	3	2
Paraguay	2	0	1	1	2	4	1

POOL 4

Uruguay 8, Bolivia 0

	P	W	D	L	F	A	Pts.
Uruguay	1	1	0	0	8	0	2
Bolivia	1	0	0	1	0	8	0

Final pool replaced knock-out system.

FINAL POOL

Uruguay 2, Spain 2
Brazil 7, Sweden 1
Uruguay 3, Sweden 2
Brazil 6, Spain 1
Sweden 3, Spain 1
Uruguay 2, Brazil 1

FINAL POSITIONS

	P	W	D	L	F	A	Pts.
Uruguay	3	2	1	0	7	5	5
Brazil	3	2	0	1	14	4	4
Sweden	3	1	0	2	6	11	2
Spain	3	0	1	2	4	11	1

Leading Scorers: Ademir (Brazil) 7, Schiaffino (Uruguay), Basora (Spain) 5.

SWITZERLAND 1954

GROUP 1

Yugoslavia 1, France 0
Brazil 5, Mexico 0
France 3, Mexico 2
Brazil 1, Yugoslavia 1

	P	W	D	L	F	A	Pts.
Brazil	2	1	1	0	6	1	3
Yugoslavia	2	1	1	0	2	1	3
France	2	1	0	1	3	3	2
Mexico	2	0	0	2	2	8	0

GROUP 2

Hungary 9, Korea 0
W. Germany 4, Turkey 1
Hungary 8, W. Germany 3
Turkey 7, Korea 0

PLAY-OFF W. Germany 7, Turkey 2

	P	W	D	L	F	A	Pts.
Hungary	2	2	0	0	17	3	4
Germany	2	1	0	1	7	9	2
Turkey	2	1	0	1	8	4	2
Korea	2	0	0	2	0	16	0

GROUP 3

Austria 1, Scotland 0
Uruguay 2, Czechoslovakia 0
Austria 5, Czechoslovakia 0
Uruguay 7, Scotland 0

	P	W	D	L	F	A	Pts.
Uruguay	2	2	0	0	9	0	4
Austria	2	2	0	0	6	0	4
Czechoslovakia	2	0	0	2	0	7	0
Scotland	2	0	0	2	0	8	0

GROUP 4

England 4, Belgium 4
England 2, Switzerland 0
Switzerland 2, Italy 1
Italy 4, Belgium 1

PLAY-OFF Switzerland 4, Italy 1

	P	W	D	L	F	A	Pts.
England	2	1	1	0	6	4	3
Italy	2	1	0	1	5	3	2
Switzerland	2	1	0	1	2	3	2
Belgium	2	0	1	1	5	8	1

QUARTER-FINALS

W. Germany 2, Yugoslavia 0
Hungary 4, Brazil 2
Austria 7, Switzerland 5
Uruguay 4, England 2

SEMI-FINALS

West Germany 6, Austria 1
Hungary 4, Uruguay 2

THIRD PLACE MATCH

Austria 3, Uruguay 1

FINAL

West Germany 3, Hungary 2

West Germany: Turek; Posipal, Kohlmeyer; Eckel, Liebrich, Mai; Rahn, Morlock, Walter, O., Walter, F. (Capt.), Schaefer.

Hungary: Grosics; Buzansky, Lantos; Boszik, Lorant, Zakarias; Czibor, Kocsis, Hidegkuti, Puskas (capt.), Toth, J.

Scorers: Morlock, Rahn (2) for Germany, Puskas, Czibor for Hungary.

Leading Scorer: Kocsis (Hungary) 11.

SWEDEN 1958

GROUP 1

W. Germany 3, Argentina 1
N. Ireland 1, Czechoslovakia 0
W. Germany 2, Czechoslovakia 2
Argentina 3, N. Ireland 1
W. Germany 2, N. Ireland 2
Czechoslovakia 6, Argentina 1

	P	W	D	L	F	A	Pts.
West Germany	3	1	2	0	7	5	4
Czechoslovakia	3	1	1	1	8	4	3
Ireland	3	1	1	1	4	5	3
Argentina	3	1	0	2	5	10	2

PLAY-OFF MATCH

N. Ireland 2, Czechoslovakia 1

GROUP 2

France 7, Paraguay 3
Yugoslavia 1, Scotland 1
Yugoslavia 3, France 2
Paraguay 3, Scotland 2
France 2, Scotland 1
Yugoslavia 3, Paraguay 3

	P	W	D	L	F	A	Pts.
France	3	2	0	1	11	7	4
Yugoslavia	3	1	2	0	7	6	4
Paraguay	3	1	1	1	9	12	3
Scotland	3	0	1	2	4	6	1

GROUP 3

Sweden 3, Mexico 0
Hungary 1, Wales 1
Wales 1, Mexico 1
Sweden 2, Hungary 1
Sweden 0, Wales 0
Hungary 4, Mexico 0

	P	W	D	L	F	A	Pts.
Sweden	3	2	1	0	5	1	5
Hungary	3	1	1	1	6	3	3
Wales	3	0	3	0	2	2	3
Mexico	3	0	1	2	1	8	1

PLAY-OFF MATCH

Wales 2, Hungary 1

GROUP 4

England 2, Russia 2
Brazil 3, Austria 0
England 0, Brazil 0
Russia 2, Austria 0
Brazil 2, Russia 0
England 2, Austria 2

	P	W	D	L	F	A	Pts.
Brazil	3	2	1	0	5	0	5
England	3	0	3	0	4	4	3
Russia	3	1	1	1	2	4	3
Austria	3	0	1	2	2	7	1

PLAY-OFF MATCH

Russia 1, England 0

QUARTER-FINALS

France 4, Ireland 0
W. Germany 1, Yugoslavia 0
Sweden 2, Russia 0
Brazil 1, Wales 0

SEMI-FINALS

Brazil 5, France 2
Sweden 3, West Germany 1

THIRD PLACE MATCH

France 6, West Germany 3

FINAL

Brazil 5, Sweden 2 (2-1) *Stockholm*

Brazil: Gilmar; Santos, D., Santos, N.; Zito, Bellini, Orlando, Garrincha, Didi, Vava, Pele, Zagalo.

Sweden: Svensson; Bergmark, Axbom; Boerjesson, Gustavsson, Parling, Hamrin, Gren, Simonsson, Liedholm, Skoglund.

Scorers: Vava (2), Pele (2), Zagalo for Brazil. Liedholm, Simonsson for Sweden.

Leading Scorer: Fontaine 13 (present record total).

CHILE 1962

GROUP 1

Uruguay 2, Colombia 1
Russia 2, Yugoslavia 0
Yugoslavia 3, Uruguay 1
Russia 4, Colombia 4
Russia 2, Uruguay 1
Yugoslavia 5, Colombia 0

	P	W	D	L	F	A	Pts.
Russia	3	2	1	0	8	5	5
Yugoslavia	3	2	0	1	8	3	4
Uruguay	3	1	0	2	4	6	2
Colombia	3	0	1	2	5	11	1

GROUP 2

Chile 3, Switzerland 1
W. Germany 0, Italy 0
Chile 2, Italy 0
W. Germany 2, Switzerland 1
W. Germany 2, Chile 0
Italy 3, Switzerland 0

	P	W	D	L	F	A	Pts.
Germany	3	2	1	0	4	1	5
Chile	3	2	0	1	5	3	4
Italy	3	1	1	1	3	2	3
Switzerland	3	0	0	3	2	8	0

GROUP 3

Brazil 2, Mexico 0
Czechoslovakia 1, Spain 0
Brazil 0, Czechoslovakia 0
Spain 1, Mexico 0
Brazil 2, Spain 1
Mexico 3, Czechoslovakia 1

	P	W	D	L	F	A	Pts.
Brazil	3	2	1	0	4	1	5
Czechoslovakia	3	1	1	1	2	3	3
Mexico	3	1	0	2	3	4	2
Spain	3	1	0	2	2	3	2

GROUP 4

Argentina 1, Bulgaria 0
Hungary 2, England 1
England 3, Argentina 1
Hungary 6, Bulgaria 1
Argentina 0, Hungary 0
England 0, Bulgaria 0

	P	W	D	L	F	A	Pts.
Hungary	3	2	1	0	8	2	5
England	3	1	1	1	4	3	3
Argentina	3	1	1	1	2	3	3
Bulgaria	3	0	1	2	1	7	1

QUARTER-FINALS

Yugoslavia 1, W. Germany 0
Brazil 3, England 1
Chile 2, Russia 1
Czechoslovakia 1, Hungary 0

SEMI-FINALS

Brazil 4, Chile 2
Czechoslovakia 3, Yugoslavia 1

THIRD PLACE MATCH

Chile 1, Yugoslavia 0

FINAL

Santiago

Brazil 3, Czechoslovakia 1 (1-1)

Brazil: Gilmar; Santos, D., Mauro, Zozimo, Santos, N.; Zito, Didi; Garrincha, Vavà, Amarildo, Zagalo.

Czechoslovakia: Schroiff; Tichy, Novak; Pluskal, Popluhar, Masopust, Pospichal, Scherer, Kvasniak, Kadraba, Jelinek.

Scorers: Amarildo, Zito, Vavà for Brazil. Masopust for Czechoslovakia.

Leading Scorers: Albert (Hungary), Ivanov (Russia), Sanchez, L. (Chile), Garrincha, Vavà (Brazil), Jerkovic (Yugoslavia) each 4.

ENGLAND 1966

GROUP 1

England 0, Uruguay 0
France 1, Mexico 1
Uruguay 2, France 1
England 2, Mexico 0
Uruguay 0, Mexico 0
England 2, France 0

	P	W	D	L	F	A	Pts.
England	3	2	1	0	4	0	5
Uruguay	3	1	2	0	2	1	4
Mexico	3	0	2	1	1	3	2
France	3	0	1	2	2	5	1

GROUP 2

W. Germany 5, Switzerland 0
Argentina 2, Spain 1
Spain 2, Switzerland 1
Argentina 0, W. Germany 0
Argentina 2, Switzerland 0
W. Germany 2, Spain 1

	P	W	D	L	F	A	Pts.
West Germany	3	2	1	0	7	1	5
Argentine	3	2	1	0	4	1	5
Spain	3	1	0	2	4	5	2
Switzerland	3	0	0	3	1	9	0

GROUP 3

Brazil 2, Bulgaria 0
Portugal 3, Hungary 1
Hungary 3, Brazil 1
Portugal 3, Bulgaria 0
Portugal 3, Brazil 1
Hungary 3, Bulgaria 1

	P	W	D	L	F	A	Pts.
Portugal	3	3	0	0	9	2	6
Hungary	3	2	0	1	7	5	4
Brazil	3	1	0	2	4	6	2
Bulgaria	3	0	0	3	1	8	0

GROUP 4

Russia 3, N. Korea 0
Italy 2, Chile 0
Chile 1, N. Korea 1
Russia 1, Italy 0
N. Korea 1, Italy 0
Russia 2, Chile 1

	P	W	D	L	F	A	Pts.
Russia	3	3	0	0	6	1	6
North Korea	3	1	1	1	2	4	3
Italy	3	1	0	2	2	2	2
Chile	3	0	1	2	2	5	1

QUARTER-FINALS

England 1, Argentina 0
West Germany 4, Uruguay 0
Portugal 5, North Korea 3
Russia 2, Hungary 1

SEMI-FINALS

West Germany 2, Russia 1
England 2, Portugal 1

THIRD PLACE MATCH

Portugal 2, Russia 1

FINAL *Wembley*

England 4, West Germany 2 (1-1) (2-2) after extra time

England: Banks; Cohen, Wilson; Stiles, Charlton, J., Moore; Ball, Hurst, Hunt, Charlton, R., Peters.

West Germany: Tilkowski; Hottges, Schulz, Weber, Schnellinger; Haller, Beckenbauer; Overath, Seeler, Held, Emmerich.

Scorers: Hurst 3, Peters for England, Haller, Weber for Germany.

Leading scorer: Eusebio (Portugal) 9

MEXICO 1970

GROUP A

Mexico 0, Russia 0
Belgium 3, El Salvador 0
Russia 4, Belgium 1
Mexico 4, El Salvador 0
Russia 2, El Salvador 0
Belgium 0, Mexico 1

	P	W	D	L	F	A	Pts.
Russia	3	2	1	0	6	1	5
Mexico	3	2	1	0	5	0	5
Belgium	3	1	0	2	4	5	2
El Salvador	3	0	0	3	0	9	0

GROUP B

Uruguay 2, Israel 0
Italy 1, Sweden 0
Uruguay 0, Italy 0
Israel 1, Sweden 1
Sweden 1, Uruguay 0
Israel 0, Italy 0

	P	W	D	L	F	A	Pts.
Italy	3	1	2	0	1	0	4
Uruguay	3	1	1	1	2	1	3
Sweden	3	1	1	1	2	2	3
Israel	3	0	2	1	1	3	2

GROUP C

England 1, Rumania 0
Brazil 4, Czechoslovakia 1
Rumania 2, Czechoslovakia 1
Brazil 1, England 0
Brazil 3, Rumania 2
England 1, Czechoslovakia 0

	P	W	D	L	F	A	Pts.
Brazil	3	3	0	0	8	3	6
England	3	2	0	1	2	1	4
Rumania	3	1	0	2	4	5	2
Czechoslovakia	3	0	0	3	2	7	0

GROUP D

Peru 3, Bulgaria 2
W. Germany 2, Morocco 1
Peru 3, Morocco 0
W. Germany 5, Bulgaria 2
W. Germany 3, Peru 1
Bulgaria 1, Morocco 1

	P	W	D	L	F	A	Pts.
W. Germany	3	3	0	0	10	4	6
Peru	3	2	0	1	7	5	4
Bulgaria	3	0	1	2	5	9	1
Morocco	3	0	1	2	2	6	1

QUARTER FINALS

Uruguay 1, Russia 0
Italy 4, Mexico 1
Brazil 4, Peru 2
West Germany 3, England 2

SEMI-FINALS

Italy 4, West Germany 3
Brazil 3, Uruguay 1

THIRD PLACE MATCH

West Germany 1, Uruguay 0

FINAL *Mexico City*
Brazil 4, Italy 1.

Brazil: Felix; Carlos Alberto, Brito, Piazza, Everaldo; Gerson, Clodoaldo; Jairzinho, Pele, Tostao, Rivelino. No subs.

Italy: Albertosi; Burgnich, Cera, Rosato, Facchetti; Bertini, Riva; Domenghini, Mazzola, De Sisti, Boninsegna. Subs: Juliano for Bertini, Rivera for Boninsegna.

Scorers: Pele, Gerson, Jairzinho, Carlos Alberto for Brazil, Boninsegna for Italy.

Referee: Rudi Glockner (East Germany). Linesmen: Rudolf Scheurer (Switzerland), Angel Coerazza (Argentine).

WEST GERMANY 1974

GROUP 1

West Germany 1, Chile 0
East Germany 2, Australia 0
West Germany 3, Australia 0
East Germany 1, Chile 1
East Germany 1, West Germany 0
Chile 0, Australia 0

	P	W	D	L	F	A	Pts.
East Germany	3	2	1	0	4	1	5
West Germany	3	2	0	1	4	1	4
Chile	3	0	2	1	1	2	2
Australia	3	0	1	2	0	5	1

GROUP 2

Brazil 0, Yugoslavia 0
Scotland 2, Zaire 0
Brazil 0, Scotland 0
Yugoslavia 9, Zaire 0
Scotland 1, Yugoslavia 1
Brazil 3, Zaire 0

	P	W	D	L	F	A	Pts.
Yugoslavia	3	1	2	0	10	1	4
Brazil	3	1	2	0	3	0	4
Scotland	3	1	2	0	3	1	4
Zaire	3	0	0	3	0	14	0

GROUP 3

Holland 2, Uruguay 0
Sweden 0, Bulgaria 0
Holland 0, Sweden 0
Bulgaria 1, Uruguay 1
Holland 4, Bulgaria 1
Sweden 3, Uruguay 0

	P	W	D	L	F	A	Pts.
Holland	3	2	1	0	6	1	5
Sweden	3	1	2	0	3	0	4
Bulgaria	3	0	2	1	2	5	2
Uruguay	3	0	1	2	1	6	1

GROUP 4

Italy 3, Haiti 1
Poland 3, Argentina 2
Argentina 1, Italy 1
Poland 7, Haiti 0
Argentina 4, Haiti 1
Poland 2, Italy 1

	P	W	D	L	F	A	Pts.
Poland	3	3	0	0	12	3	6
Argentina	3	1	1	1	7	5	3
Italy	3	1	1	1	5	4	3
Haiti	3	0	0	3	2	14	0

GROUP A

Brazil 1, East Germany 0
Holland 4, Argentina 0
Holland 2, East Germany 0
Brazil 2, Argentina 1
Holland 2, Brazil 0
Argentina 1, East Germany 1

	P	W	D	L	F	A	Pts.
Holland	3	3	0	0	8	0	6
Brazil	3	2	0	1	3	3	4
East Germany	3	0	1	2	1	4	1
Argentina	3	0	1	2	2	7	1

GROUP B

Poland 1, Sweden 0
West Germany 2, Yugoslavia 0
Poland 2, Yugoslavia 1
West Germany 4, Sweden 2
Sweden 2, Yugoslavia 1
West Germany 1, Poland 0

	P	W	D	L	F	A	Pts.
West Germany	3	3	0	0	7	2	6
Poland	3	2	0	1	3	2	4
Sweden	3	1	0	2	4	6	2
Yugoslavia	3	0	0	3	2	6	0

THIRD PLACE MATCH

Poland 1, Brazil 0

FINAL

Munich, July 7, 77,833

West Germany 2, Holland 1 (2-1)

West Germany: Maier; Vogts, Schwarzenbeck, Beckenbauer, Breitner, Bonhof, Hoeness, Overath, Grabowski, Muller, Holzenbein.

Holland: Jongbloed; Suurbier, Rijsbergen (De Jong), Haan, Krol, Jansen, Van Hanegem, Neeskens, Rep, Cruyff, Rensenbrink (Van der Kerkhof R).

Scorers: Breitner (*pen*), Muller for West Germany; Neeskens (*pen*) for Holland.

Ref: J. Taylor (*England*).

FIFA WORLD CUP 1978

The following 103 National Associations have entered for the 1978 World Cup. Those marked with an asterisk did not enter for the 1974 tournament. They are grouped in confederated areas.

AFRICA (25 entries): Algeria, Cameroon, Central Africa*, AR Egypt, Ethiopia, Ghana, Guinea, Ivory Coast, Kenya, Libya*, Malawi*, Mauritania*, Morocco, Niger*, Nigeria, Senegal, Sierra Leone, Sudan, Tanzania, Togo, Tunisia, Uganda*, Upper Volta*, Zaire, Zambia.

CONCACAF (16 entries): Barbados*, Canada, Costa Rica, Cuba*, Dominican Republic*, Guatemala, Guyana*, Haiti, Jamaica, Mexico, Netherlands Antilles, Panama*, El Salvador, Surinam, Trinidad & Tobago, USA.

CONMEBOL (10 entries): Argentina, Bolivia, Brazil, Chile, Colombia, Ecuador, Paraguay, Peru, Uruguay, Venezuela.

ASIA (17 entries): Bahrain*, Hong Kong, Indonesia, Iran, Iraq, Israel, Japan, Korea DPR, Republic of Korea, Kuwait, Malaysia, Qatar*, Saudi Arabia*, Singapore*, Syria, Thailand, United Arab Emirates.

EUROPE (32 entries): Austria, Belgium, Bulgaria, Cyprus, Czechoslovakia, Denmark, England, Finland, France, East Germany, West Germany, Greece, Hungary, Iceland, Ireland (Northern), Ireland (Republic), Italy, Luxembourg, Malta, Netherlands, Norway, Poland, Portugal, Rumania, Scotland, Spain, Sweden, Switzerland, Turkey, USSR, Wales, Yugoslavia.

OCEANIA (3 entries): Australia, New Zealand, China National (Taiwan)*.

The following Associations, which had entered in 1974, are no longer on the list: *Africa:* Dahomey, Gabon, Lesotho, Madagascar, Mauritius; *Asia:* India, The Philippines, Vietnam Republic; *Concacaf:* Antigua, Puerto Rico; *Europe:* Albania.

Only South America is represented by all 10 Associations. In Europe, two are missing— Albania and Leichtenstein. In Oceania, Fiji and Papua-New Guinea are missing; in Concacaf six are missing; in Africa, 14 are missing, although South Africa and Rhodesia are both suspended, so that only 12 eligible Associations are missing. In Asia, no fewer than 17 Associations – half their FIFA membership – are missing. The holders of the World Cup, West Germany, and the host nation, Argentina, qualify automatically for the final tournament.

THE QUALIFYING TOURNAMENT

EUROPE

At least nine teams will qualify from UEFA. The holders, West Germany, qualify automatically, and there are nine qualifying groups. However, the winner of Group 9 will have to play off for a place in Argentina against the team coming third in the final South American qualifying group. The European qualifying groups and fixtures are as follows:

GROUP 1

Poland, Portugal, Denmark, Cyprus.

23.5.76	Cyprus v Denmark (*result: 1-5*)	1.5.77	Denmark v Poland
16.10.76	Portugal v Poland	15.5.77	Cyprus v Poland
27.10.76	Denmark v Cyprus	21.9.77	Poland v Denmark
31.10.76	Poland v Cyprus	9.10.77	Denmark v Portugal
17.11.76	Portugal v Denmark	29.10.77	Poland v Portugal
5.12.76	Cyprus v Portugal	16.11.77	Portugal v Cyprus

GROUP 2

Italy, England, Finland, Luxembourg.

13.6.76	Finland v England	26.5.77	Luxembourg v Finland
22.9.76	Finland v Luxembourg	8.6.77	Finland v Italy
13.10.76	England v Finland	12.10.77	Luxembourg v England
16.10.76	Luxembourg v Italy	15.10.77	Italy v Finland
17.11.76	Italy v England	16.11.77	England v Italy
30.3.77	England v Luxembourg	3.12.77	Italy v Luxembourg

GROUP 3

East Germany, Austria, Turkey, Malta.

31.10.76	Turkey v Malta	24.9.77	Austria v East Germany
17.11.76	East Germany v Turkey	12.10.77	East Germany v Austria
5.12.76	Malta v Austria	29.10.77	East Germany v Malta
2.4.77	Malta v East Germany	30.10.77	Turkey v Austria
17.4.77	Austria v Turkey	16.11.77	Turkey v East Germany
30.4.77	Austria v Malta	27.11.77	Malta v Turkey

GROUP 4

Netherlands, Belgium, Northern Ireland, Iceland.

5.9.76	Iceland v Belgium	31.8.77	Netherlands v Iceland
8.9.76	Iceland v Netherlands	4.9.77	Belgium v Iceland
13.10.76	Netherlands v Northern Ireland	21.9.77	Northern Ireland v Iceland
10.11.76	Belgium v Northern Ireland	12.10.77	Northern Ireland v Netherlands
26.3.77	Belgium v Netherlands	26.10.77	Netherlands v Belgium
11.6.77	Iceland v Northern Ireland	16.11.77	Northern Ireland v Belgium

GROUP 5

Bulgaria, France, Eire.

9.10.76	Bulgaria v France	1.6.77	Bulgaria v Eire
17.11.76	France v Eire	12.10.77	Eire v Bulgaria
30.3.77	Eire v France	16.11.77	France v Bulgaria

GROUP 6
Sweden, Switzerland, Norway.

16.6.76	Sweden v Norway	8.6.77	Sweden v Switzerland
8.9.76	Norway v Switzerland	7.9.77	Norway v Sweden
9.10.76	Switzerland v Sweden	30.10.77	Switzerland v Norway

GROUP 7
Scotland, Czechoslovakia, Wales.

13.10.76	Czechoslovakia v Scotland	21.9 77	Scotland v Czechoslovakia
17.11.76	Scotland v Wales	12.10.77	Wales v Scotland
30.3.77	Wales v Czechoslovakia	16.11.77	Czechoslovakia v Wales

GROUP 8
Yugoslavia, Spain, Rumania.

10.10.76	Spain v Yugoslavia	26.10.77	Spain v Rumania
16.4.77	Rumania v Spain	13.11.77	Rumania v Yugoslavia
8.5.77	Yugoslavia v Rumania	30.11.77	Yugoslavia v Spain

GROUP 9
USSR, Hungary, Greece.

9.10.76	Greece v Hungary	10.5.77	Greece v USSR
20.4.77	USSR v Greece	18.5.77	USSR v Hungary
30.4.77	Hungary v USSR	25.5.77	Hungary v Greece

SOUTH AMERICA

Argentina, the host nation, qualify automatically for the final tournament, and the remaining nine member nations have been divided into the following three groups. The dates of fixtures were not known at the time of going to Press.

Group 1	Group 2	Group 3
Brazil	Uruguay	Chile
Paraguay	Venezuela	Peru
Colombia	Bolivia	Ecuador

The teams in each group will play home and away games against each other, thus producing three group winners. These three winners will then play off amongst themselves in a neutral country. The first two teams in this secondary tournament will qualify for the final tournament, and the team coming third will have to play off for a place in Argentina against the winners of the European Group 9 (USSR, Hungary, Greece).

AFRICA

The first part of the qualifying system in Africa consisted of the following extra preliminary round:

7.3.76	Sierra Leone v Niger	5-1 (1-1)
21.3.76	Niger v Sierra Leone	2-1 (1-1)

Sierra Leone go through to the First Round Proper.

13.3.76	Upper Volta v Mauritania	1-1 (0-1)
28.3.76	Mauritania v Upper Volta	0-2 (0-1)

Upper Volta go through.

The African qualifying tournament now looks like this:

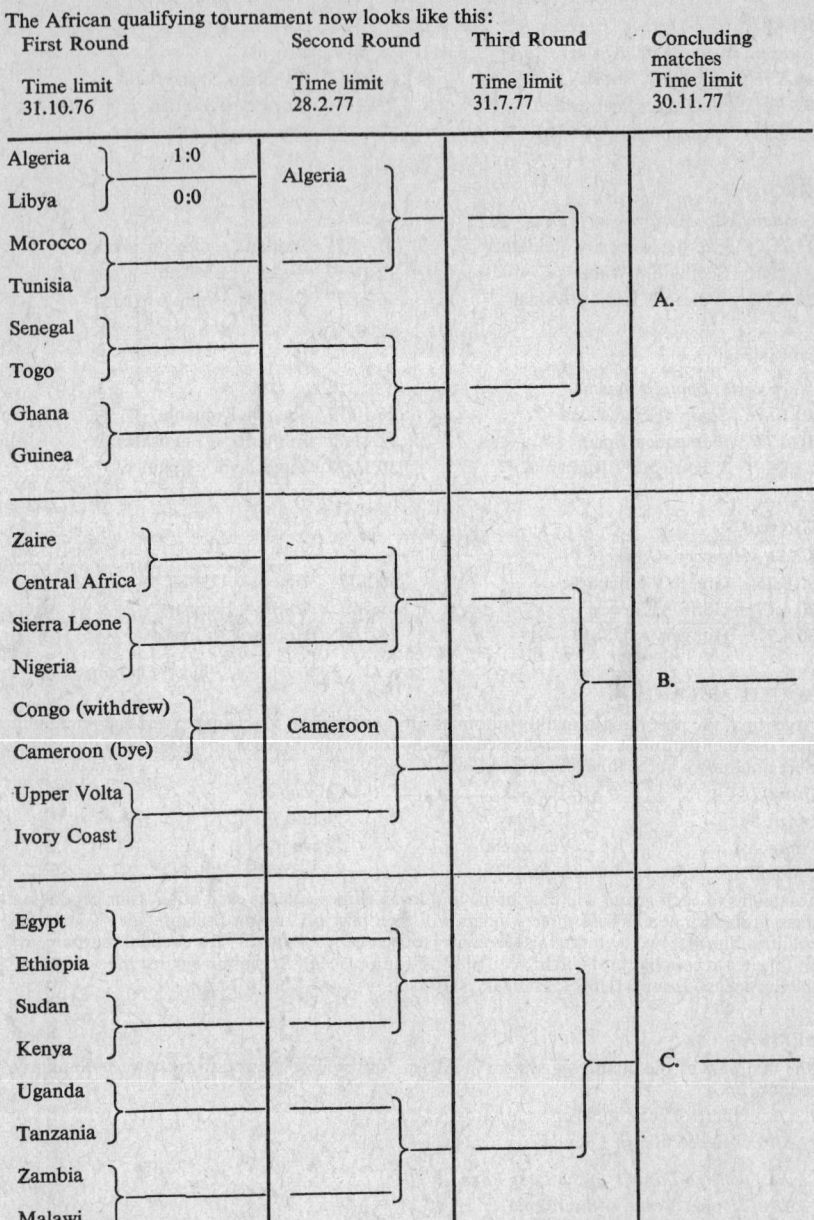

The team named first will play the first game at home. The three winning teams (A, B, C) will play off in a league, on a home and away basis, to decide the qualifier for Argentina. The time limits mentioned indicate the dates by which matches in those rounds must be completed.

ASIA/OCEANIA

The qualifier from these two areas will be decided as follows:

ASIA — Winners of Groups I to IV to be known by 31.3.77				OCEANIA — Winner to be known by 31.7.77
Group I	Group II	Group III	Group IV	
Hong Kong	Israel	Iran	Bahrain	Australia
Indonesia	Japan	Iraq	Kuwait	New Zealand
Malaysia	DPR Korea	Saudi Arabia	U.A. Emirates	Taiwan
Thailand	Rep. Korea	Syria	Qatar	
Singapore				
Winner I	Winner II	Winner III	Winner IV	Winner Oceania

Winner Asia (to be known by 31.7.77)

Qualifier for Argentina (to be known by 30.11.77)

The Group winners are to be decided on the usual home and away league basis.

CONCACAF

The Preliminary Competition will be played in three main groups as follows:

Group 1 (Northern Area): Canada
USA
Mexico

Group 2 (Central Area): Guatemala
El Salvador
Costa Rica
Panama

Group 3 (Caribbean Area): Netherlands Antilles
Barbados
Cuba
Guyana
Haiti
Jamaica
Surinam
Trinidad
Dominican Republic

There will be a preliminary round, to be completed by the end of 1976, followed by a final round, in which the two best teams from each area will play off in a tournament to be held in the northern area. The winner of this tournament will qualify for Argentina, thus making a grand total of 16 teams in the final tournament in 1978.

WORLD CUP 1930-74 FINAL SERIES

	P	W	D	L	F	A		P	W	D	L	F	A
1. Brazil	45	29	7	9	109	53	24. Wales	5	1	3	1	4	4
2. West Germany	41	27	5	9	100	63	25. Northern Ireland	5	2	1	2	6	10
3. Italy	29	16	5	8	53	34	26. Rumania	8	2	1	5	12	17
4. Uruguay	29	14	5	10	57	39	27. Scotland	8	1	3	4	7	15
5. Hungary	23	13	2	8	70	34	28. Peru	6	2	0	4	10	13
6. Sweden	25	11	5	9	47	43	29. Bulgaria	12	0	4	8	9	29
7. England	24	10	6	8	34	28	30. Cuba	3	1	1	1	5	12
8. Yugoslavia	25	11	3	11	45	34	31. North Korea	4	1	1	2	5	9
9. Russia	19	10	3	6	30	21	32. Belgium	9	1	1	7	12	25
10. Argentina	22	9	4	9	40	39	33. Turkey	3	1	0	2	10	11
11. Czechoslovakia	22	8	3	11	32	36	34. Israel	3	0	2	1	1	3
12. Chile	18	7	3	8	23	24	35. Morocco	3	0	1	2	2	6
13. France	17	7	1	9	38	33	36. Australia	3	0	1	2	0	5
14. Spain	15	6	2	7	20	23	37. Colombia	3	0	1	2	5	11
15. Austria	12	6	1	5	26	26	38. Norway	1	0	0	1	1	2
16. Poland	8	6	0	2	21	11	39. Egypt	1	0	0	1	2	4
17. Switzerland	18	5	2	11	28	44	40. Dutch East Indies	1	0	0	1	0	6
18. Holland	9	5	1	3	17	9	41. South Korea	2	0	0	2	0	16
19. Portugal	6	5	0	1	17	8	42. El Salvador	3	0	0	3	0	9
20. Mexico	21	3	4	14	19	50	43. Haiti	3	0	0	3	2	14
21. East Germany	6	2	2	2	5	5	44. Zaire	3	0	0	3	0	14
22. Paraguay	7	2	2	3	12	19	45. Bolivia	3	0	0	3	0	16
23. United States	7	3	0	4	12	21	TOTAL	540	227	86	227	948	948

Only five countries have won the World Cup: Brazil (1958, 1962 and 1970), Italy (1934 and 1938), Uruguay (1930 and 1950), West Germany (1954 and 1974) and England (1966).
948 goals have been scored in 270 matches in the 10 final tournaments for an overall average of 3.5 goals per match.

Major British Records

HIGHEST SCORES

First-Class Match		Arbroath *(Scottish Cup 1st Round)*	36	Bon Accord	0	5.9.1885
International		England	13	Ireland	0	18.2.1882
F.A. Cup Tie		Preston North End *(First Round)*	26	Hyde United	0	15.10.1887

FOOTBALL LEAGUE

Division 1	(Home)	West Bromwich Albion	12	Darwen	0	4.3.1892
		Nottingham Forest	12	Leicester Fosse	0	21.4.1909
	(Away)	Newcastle United	1	Sunderland	9	5.12.1908
		Cardiff City	1	Wolverhampton Wanderers	9	3.9.1955
Division 2	(Home)	Newcastle United	13	Newport County	0	5.10.1946
	(Away)	Burslem Port Vale	0	Sheffield United	10	10.12.1892
Division 3	(Home)	Tranmere Rovers	9	Accrington Stanley	0	18.4.1959
		Brentford	9	Wrexham	0	15.10.1963
	(Away)	Halifax Town	0	Fulham	8	16.9.1969
		Brighton	2	Bristol Rovers	8	1.12.1973
Division 3(S)	(Home)	Luton Town	12	Bristol Rovers	0	13.4.1936
	(Away)	Northampton Town	0	Walsall	8	2.2.1947
Division 3(N)	(Home)	Stockport County	13	Halifax Town	0	6.1.1934
	(Away)	Accrington Stanley	0	Barnsley	9	3.2.1934
Division 4	(Home)	Oldham Athletic	11	Southport	0	26.12.1962
	(Away)	Crewe Alexandra	1	Rotherham United	8	8.9.1973

SCOTTISH LEAGUE

Division 1	(Home)	Celtic	11	Dundee	0	26.10.1895
	(Away)	Airdrieonians	1	Hibernian	11	24.10.1959
Division 2	(Home)	East Fife	13	Edinburgh City	2	11.12.1937
	(Away)	Alloa Athletic	0	Dundee	10	8.3.1947

MOST GOALS FOR IN A SEASON

FOOTBALL LEAGUE

		Goals	Games	Season
Division 1	Aston Villa	128	42	1930–31
Division 2	Middlesbrough	122	42	1926–27
Division 3 (S)	Millwall	127	42	1927–28
Division 3 (N)	Bradford City	128	42	1928–29
Division 3	Queen's Park Rangers	111	46	1961–62
Division 4	Peterborough United	134	46	1960–61

SCOTTISH LEAGUE

Division 1	Hearts	132	34	1957–58
Division 2	Raith Rovers	142	34	1937–38

MOST GOALS AGAINST IN A SEASON

FOOTBALL LEAGUE

		Goals	Games	Season
Division 1	Blackpool	125	42	1930–31
Division 2	Darwen	141	34	1898–99
Division 3 (S)	Merthyr Town	135	42	1929–30
Division 3 (N)	Nelson	136	42	1927–28
Division 3	Accrington Stanley	123	46	1959–60
Division 4	Hartlepools United	109	46	1959–60

SCOTTISH LEAGUE

Division 1	Leith Athletic	137	38	1931–32
Division 2	Edinburgh City	146	38	1931–32

FEWEST GOALS AGAINST IN A SEASON

FOOTBALL LEAGUE (min. 42 games)		Goals	Games	Season
Division 1	Liverpool	24	42	1968–69 & 1970–71
Division 2	Manchester United	23	42	1924–25
Division 3 (S)	Southampton	21	42	1921–22
Division 3 (N)	Port Vale	21	46	1953–54
Division 3	Bristol Rovers	33	46	1973–74
Division 4	Gillingham	30	46	1963–64
SCOTTISH LEAGUE (min. 30 games)				
Division 1	Celtic	14	38	1913–14
Division 2	Morton	20	38	1966–67

MOST POINTS IN A SEASON

FOOTBALL LEAGUE		Points	Games	Season
Division 1	Leeds United	67	42	1968–69
Division 2	Tottenham Hotspur	70	42	1919–20
Division 3	Aston Villa	70	46	1971–72
Division 3 (S)	Nottingham Forest	70	46	1950–51
	Bristol City	70	46	1954–55
Division 3 (N)	Doncaster Rovers	72	42	1946–47
Division 4	Lincoln City	74	46	1975–76
SCOTTISH LEAGUE				
Division 1	Rangers	76	42	1920–21
Division 2	Morton	69	38	1966–67

FEWEST POINTS IN A SEASON

FOOTBALL LEAGUE (min. 34 games)		Points	Games	Season
Division 1	Leeds United	18	42	1946–47
	Queen's Park Rangers	18	42	1968–69
	Glossop	18	34	1899–1900
	Notts County	18	34	1904–05
	Woolwich Arsenal	18	38	1912–13
Division 2	Doncaster Rovers	8	34	1904–05
	Loughborough Town	8	34	1899–1900
Division 3	Rochdale	21	46	1973–74
Division 3 (S)	Merthyr Town	21	42	1924–25 & 1929–30
	Queen's Park Rangers	21	42	1925–26
Division 3 (N)	Rochdale	11	40	1931–32
Division 4	Bradford	20	46	1968–69
SCOTTISH LEAGUE (min. 30 games				
Division 1	Stirling Albion	6	30	1954–55

MOST WINS IN A SEASON

FOOTBALL LEAGUE		Wins	Games	Season
Division 1	Tottenham Hotspur	31	42	1960–61
Division 2	Tottenham Hotspur	32	42	1919–20
Division 3 (S)	Millwall	30	42	1927–28
	Plymouth Argyle	30	42	1929–30
	Cardiff City	30	42	1946–47
	Nottingham Forest	30	46	1950–51
	Bristol City	30	46	1954–55
Division 3 (N)	Doncaster Rovers	33	42	1946–47
Division 3	Aston Villa	32	46	1971–72
Division 4	Lincoln City	32	46	1975–76
SCOTTISH LEAGUE				
Division 1	Rangers	35	42	1920–21
Division 2	Morton	33	38	1966–67

RECORD HOME WINS IN A SEASON

Brentford won all 21 games in Division 3 (S), 1929–30

RECORD AWAY WINS IN A SEASON

Doncaster Rovers won 18 of 21 games in Division 3 (N), 1946–47

MOST DEFEATS IN A SEASON

FOOTBALL LEAGUE

		Defeats	Games	Season
Division 1	Leeds United	30	42	1946–47
	Blackburn Rovers	30	42	1965–66
Division 2	Tranmere Rovers	31	42	1938–39
Division 3	Newport County	31	46	1961–62
Division 3 (S)	Merthyr Town	29	42	1924–25
Division 3 (N)	Rochdale	33	40	1931–32
Division 4	Workington	32	46	1975–76

SCOTTISH LEAGUE

Division 1	St. Mirren	31	42	1920–21
Division 2	Lochgelly United	30	38	1923–24
	Brechin City	30	36	1962–63
	Forfar Athletic	30	38	1974–75

FEWEST DEFEATS IN A SEASON

FOOTBALL LEAGUE

		Defeats	Games	Season
Division 1	Preston North End	0	22	1888–89
	Leeds United	2	42	1968–69
Division 2	Liverpool	0	28	1893–94
	Burnley	2	30	1897–98
	Bristol City	2	38	1905–06
	Leeds United	3	42	1963–64
Division 3	Queen's Park Rangers	5	46	1966–67
Division 3 (S)	Southampton	4	42	1921–22
	Plymouth Argyle	4	42	1929–30
Division 3 (N)	Port Vale	3	46	1953–54
	Doncaster Rovers	3	42	1946–47
	Wolverhampton Wanderers	3	42	1923–24
Division 4	Lincoln City	4	46	1975–76

SCOTTISH LEAGUE

Division 1	Celtic	0	18	1897–98
	Rangers	0	18	1898–99
	Rangers	1	42	1920–21
	Hearts	1	34	1957–58
	Celtic	1	34	1967–68
	Rangers	1	34	1967–68
Division 2	Kilmarnock	0	18	1898–99
	Clyde	1	36	1956–57
	Morton	1	36	1963–64

MOST LEAGUE GOALS IN A SEASON

FOOTBALL LEAGUE

		Goals	Actual Games	Season
Division 1	Dixie Dean (Everton)	60	39	1927–28
Division 2	George Camsell (Middlesbrough)	59	37	1926–27
Division 3 (S)	Joe Payne (Luton Town)	55	39	1936–37
Division 3 (N)	Ted Harston (Mansfield Town)	55	41	1936–37
Division 3	Derek Reeves (Southampton)	39	46	1959–60
Division 4	Terry Bly (Peterborough United)	52	46	1960–61

SCOTTISH LEAGUE

Division 1	William McFadyen (Motherwell)	52	34	1931–32
Division 2	Jim Smith (Ayr United)	66	38	1927–28

FEWEST GOALS FOR IN A SEASON

FOOTBALL LEAGUE (min. 42 games)		Goals	Games	Season
Division 1	Huddersfield Town	27	42	1971–72
Division 2	Watford	24	42	1971–72
Division 3 (S)	Crystal Palace	33	42	1950–51
Division 3 (N)	Crewe Alexandra	32	42	1923–24
Division 3	Stockport County	27	46	1969–70
Division 4	Bradford	30	46	1967–68
	Workington	30	46	1975–76

SCOTTISH LEAGUE (min. 30 games)				
Division 1	Ayr United	20	34	1966–67
Division 2	Lochgelly United	20	38	1923–24

FEWEST WINS IN A SEASON

FOOTBALL LEAGUE		Wins	Games	Season
Division 1	Stoke	3	22	1899–1900
	Woolwich Arsenal	3	38	1912–13
Division 2	Loughborough Town	1	34	1899–1900
Division 3 (S)	Merthyr Town	6	42	1929–30
Division 3 (N)	Rochdale	4	40	1931–32
Division 3	Rochdale	2	46	1973–74
Division 4	Bradford	4	46	1967–68

SCOTTISH LEAGUE				
Division 1	Vale of Leven	0	22	1891–26
Division 2	East Stirlingshire	1	22	1905–90
	Forfar Athletic	1	38	1974–75

MOST DRAWN GAMES IN A SEASON

FOOTBALL LEAGUE		Draws	Games	Season
Division 3	Tranmere Rovers	22	46	1970–71

SCOTTISH LEAGUE				
Division 1	Falkirk	17	42	1921–22
Division 1	Falkirk	17	38	1922–23
Division 2	Bo'ness	17	38	1922–23

MOST GOALS IN A GAME

FOOTBALL LEAGUE

Division 1	Ted Drake (Arsenal) 7 goals v Aston Villa	14.12.1935
Division 2	Tommy Briggs (Blackburn Rovers) 7 goals v Bristol Rovers	5.2.1955
	Neville Coleman (Stoke City) 7 goals v Lincoln City	23.2.1957
Division 3 (S)	Joe Payne (Luton Town) 10 goals v Bristol Rovers	13.4.1936
Division 3 (N)	Robert Bell (Tranmere Rovers) 9 goals v Oldham Athletic	26.12.1935
Division 3	Steve Earle (Fulham) 5 goals v Halifax Town	16.9.1969
	Barrie Thomas (Scunthorpe United) 5 goals v Luton Town	24.4.1965
	Keith East (Swindon Town) 5 goals v Mansfield Town	20.11.1965
	Alf Wood (Shrewsbury Town) 5 goals v Blackburn Rovers	2.10.1971
Division 4	Herbert Lister (Oldham Athletic) 6 goals v Southport	26.12.1962

SCOTTISH LEAGUE

Division 1	Jimmy McGrory (Celtic) 8 goals v Dunfermline Athletic	14.1.1928
Division 2	Owen McNally (Arthurlie) 8 goals v Armadale	1.10.1927
	Jim Dyet (King's Park) 8 goals v Forfar Athletic	2.1.1930
	John Calder (Morton) 8 goals v Raith Rovers	18.4.1936

F.A. CUP	Ted MacDougall (Bournemouth) 9 goals v Margate	20.11.1971

SCOTTISH CUP	John Petrie (Arbroath) 13 goals v Bon Accord	5.9.1885

RECORD ATTENDANCES

Football League	83,260	Manchester United v Arsenal, Maine Road	17.1.1948
Scottish League	118,567	Rangers v Celtic, Ibrox Stadium	2.1.1939
F.A. Cup Final	126,047*	Bolton Wanderers v West Ham United, Wembley	28.4.1923
Scottish Cup Final	146,433	Celtic v Aberdeen, Hampden Park	24.4.1937
European Cup	135,826	Celtic v Leeds United, semi-final at Hampden Park	15.4.1970

* It has been estimated that as many as 70,000 more broke in without paying.

MOST CUP WINNERS' MEDALS

F.A. CUP – 5 medals each

James Forrest (Blackburn Rovers) 1884, 1885, 1886, 1890, 1891.
Hon. A. F. Kinnaird (Wanderers) 1873, 1877, 1878, (Old Etonians) 1879, 1882.
C. H. R. Wollaston (Wanderers) 1872, 1873, 1876, 1877, 1878.

SCOTTISH CUP – 7 medals each

Jimmy McMenemy (Celtic) 1904, 1907, 1908, 1911, 1912, 1914, (Partick Thistle) 1921.
Bob McPhail (Airdrieonians) 1924, (Rangers) 1928, 1930, 1932, 1934, 1935, 1936.
Billy McNeill (Celtic) 1965, 1967, 1969, 1971, 1972, 1974, 1975.

MOST LEAGUE GOALS IN A CAREER

FOOTBALL LEAGUE		Goals	Games	Season
Arthur Rowley	West Bromwich Albion	4	24	1946–48
	Fulham	27	56	1948–50
	Leicester City	251	303	1950–58
	Shrewsbury Town	152	236	1958–65
		434	619	

SCOTTISH LEAGUE				
Jimmy McGrory	Celtic	1	3	1922–23
	Clydebank	13	30	1923–24
	Celtic	396	375	1924–38
		410	408	

MOST GOALS IN AN INTERNATIONAL CAREER

		Goals	Games
England	Bobby Charlton (Manchester United)	49	106
Scotland	Denis Law (Huddersfield Town, Manchester City, Torino, Manchester United)	30	55
Ireland	Billy Gillespie (Sheffield United)	13	25
Wales	Trevor Ford (Swansea Town, Aston Villa, Sunderland, Cardiff City)	23	38

MOST GOALS IN AN INTERNATIONAL

England	Malcolm Macdonald (Newcastle United) 5 goals v Cyprus, at Wembley	16.4.1975
	Willie Hall (Tottenham Hotspur) 5 goals v Ireland, at Old Trafford	16.11.1938
	G. O. Smith (Corinthians) 5 goals v Ireland, at Sunderland	18.2.1899
	Steve Bloomer (Derby County) 5 goals* v Wales, at Cardiff	16.3.1896
Scotland	Charles Heggie (Rangers) 5 goals v Ireland, at Belfast	20.3.1886
Ireland	Joe Bambrick (Linfield) 6 goals v Wales, at Belfast	1.2.1930
Wales	James Price (Wrexham) 4 goals v Ireland, at Wrexham	25.2.1882
	Mel Charles (Cardiff City) 4 goals v Ireland, at Cardiff	11.4.1962

* There are conflicting reports which make it uncertain whether Bloomer actually scored four or five goals in this game.

Some International Records

HIGHEST SCORES

World Cup match	West Germany	12	Cyprus	0	1969
Olympic Games	Denmark	17	France	1	1908
	Germany	16	USSR	0	1912
International	Germany	13	Finland	0	1940
	Spain	13	Bulgaria	0	1933
European Cup	Feyenoord	12	Reykjavik	2	1969
Cup-Winners' Cup	Sporting Lisbon	16	Apoel Nicosia	1	1963
Fairs & UEFA Cups	1FC Cologne	13	Union		
			Luxembourg	0	1965

GOALSCORING RECORDS

World Cup Final	Geoff Hurst (England) 3 goals v West Germany	1966
World Cup Final tournament	Just Fontaine (France) 13 goals	1958
A major European cup game	Lothar Emmerich (Borussia Dortmund) v Floriana (Cup-Winners' Cup—6 goals)	1965
Career	Artur Friedenreich (Brazil) 1329 goals	1910–30
	Pele (Brazil) 1216 goals*	1956 74
	Franz 'Bimbo' Binder (Austria, Germany) 1006 goals 1930–1950	

*(Joined New York Cosmos in June 1975 after coming back from retirement)

MISCELLANEOUS

Brazil set up a record for undefeated matches in the World Cup in the 1958 and 1962 finals playing 13, winning 11, and drawing two. Their run ended when they lost 3–1 to Hungary in the 1966 World Cup.

Hungary went 13 years undefeated at home from after losing 7–2 to Sweden in 1943 until they lost 4–2 to Czechoslovakia in 1956. The Hungarians also had a run of 29 games before losing from their 5–3 defeat against Austria in May 1950 until they lost the World Cup final 3–2 to West Germany in July 1954.

Real Madrid were undefeated in League matches at home from February 1957 when they lost 3–2 to Atletico Madrid until beaten again by Atletico 1–0 in March 1965. Between these defeats they won 114 matches and drew eight.

Ferenc Deak was one of the most prolific goalscorers in League football in the years immediately after the war. In 1945–46 he scored 66 goals for Szentlorinci AC in Hungary, 48 in 1946–47, and 59 in 1948–49 when with Ferencvaros.

Players who have won international caps for three different countries are Ladislav Kubala, capped for Hungary, Czechoslovakia, and Spain in the post-war period, and Alfredo Di Stefano for Argentina, Colombia, and Spain.

The Nordahl brothers Knut, Bertil, and Gunnar won Olympic Gold medals with Sweden in 1948.

In 1955–56 Fiorentina went through 33 Italian League matches without defeat.

Thought to be the longest match on record, Santos (Brazil) and Penarol (Uruguay) played 3½ hours from August 2 to August 3 after kicking off at 9.30 a.m. The match ended 3–3 after interruptions during play, however.

The first international played in Europe other than between British teams was Austria 5 Hungary 0 on October 12 1902. The first match in South America was between Argentina and Uruguay in 1905 and drawn 1–1.

The world record transfer fee is £922,300 for Johan Cruyff from Ajax (Holland) to Barcelona (Spain) in 1973.

FIRSTS IN FOOTBALL

Football League

The first five Football League games were played on September 8 1888. Bolton Wanderers were three goals up in about six minutes against Derby County, but were eventually beaten 6-3. Cox of Aston Villa scored the first 'own goal', giving Wolverhampton Wanderers an early lead, but Villa recovered to draw 1-1.

Huddersfield Town became the first team to complete a hat-trick of League Championships — 1924-25-26.

F.A. Cup

Tottenham Hotspur was the first Southern club to win the Cup when they beat Sheffield United in 1901. Spurs were then members of the Southern League and so were the first and only non-League club to carry off the trophy.

King George V was the first reigning monarch to attend a Cup Final. He saw Burnley beat Liverpool at the Crystal Palace in 1914.

David Jack (Bolton Wanderers) scored the first goal in a Wembley Cup Final. This was in 1923 when the crowd broke in to see the Wanderers beat West Ham United 2-0.

Extra time was first played in the Cup Final in 1877. Wanderers and Oxford University were drawing 0-0 at full-time, but Wanderers scored twice in extra time.

Internationals and representative games

The first representative game was played at Battersea Park, March 31 1866, London beating Sheffield by two goals and four touch-downs to nil.

The first official England v Scotland international was played at the West of Scotland Cricket Ground, Partick, November 30 1872, and resulted in a goalless draw.

Wales played their first international in 1876, losing 4-0 to Scotland in Glasgow.

Ireland's first international was against England at Bloomfield, Belfast, in 1882 when the visitors won 13-0.

Caps were first awarded for appearances in internationals in 1886.

The Football League played their first representative game in April 1891. It was against the Football Alliance at Sheffield and resulted in a draw 1-1.

England's first defeat on foreign soil in a full international was against Spain in Madrid in 1929 when the Spaniards won 4-3.

England's first home defeat by a continental country was at Wembley in 1953 when Hungary won 6-3.

Scotland's first home defeat by a foreign team was at Hampden Park in 1950 when Austria won 1-0.

Billy Wright became the first international in Britain to gain 100 caps when he captained England against Scotland at Wembley in April 1959.

Terry Venables was the first player to win international honours for England at five levels – Schoolboy, Youth, Amateur, Under-23 and Full International. He gained his first full cap in October 1964.

Floodlit football

The first-ever game by floodlight was that between two Sheffield Association teams at Bramall Lane, October 14 1878.

The first F.A. Cup tie under floodlights was a replay between Kidderminster Harriers and Brierley Hill Alliance, September 14 1955.

Floodlights were first switched on during an international match in England in November 1955 at Wembley – England v Spain.

The first Football League game under floodlights – Portsmouth v Newcastle United, at Fratton Park, February 22 1956.

The first full international played entirely under floodlights in Britain took place at Wembley in 1963 when England beat N. Ireland 8-3.

Hat-tricks

The first hat-trick in an F.A. Cup Final was that scored by William Townley for Blackburn Rovers v Sheffield Wednesday in 1890.

Equipment, etc.

Shinguards were first introduced and registered by Sam Widdowson of Nottingham Forest in 1874. The cross-bar first replaced the tape in 1875, and the whistle was used by the referee for the first time in 1878. Goalnets were invented and patented by J. A. Brodie of Liverpool in 1890 and were first used in the F.A. Cup Final in 1892.

Substitutes

First substitute in a Football League game – Keith Peacock of Charlton Athletic, at Bolton, August 21 1965.

The first instance of a substitute in a home International Championship game was at Wrexham in 1889 when a player named Pugh of Rhostyllen, took over from the injured S. G. Gillam in the Welsh goal against Scotland.

England's first substitute in a full international was Jimmy Mullen (Wolverhampton Wanderers) who took over from the injured Jackie Milburn after 10 minutes of the game against Belgium in Brussels, May 18 1950.

The first substitute to score in a Football League game was Bobby Knox (Barrow) v Wrexham, Division 4, August 21 1965.

Transfers

The first four, five, and six-figure transfer fees between British clubs were as follows:
£1,000 – Alf Common, Sunderland to Middlesbrough, 1905.
£10,890 – David Jack, Bolton Wanderers to Arsenal, 1928.
£110,000 – Alan Ball Blackpool to Everton, 1966.

Radio and TV
The first match broadcast in England was the First Division game between Arsenal and Sheffield United at Highbury, January 22 1927.
The first Football League game to be televised was Blackpool v Bolton Wanderers, September 10 1960,
The first F.A. Cup tie to be televised – other than the Final – was Charlton Athletic v Blackburn Rovers, 5th Round, February 8 1947.

Corner-kick
Billy Smith was the first player to score direct from a corner-kick in a Football League game – Huddersfield Town v Arsenal, October 11 1924.

Limited Company
The first football club to form itself into a limited liability company was Birmingham City in 1888. At that time they were still known as Small Heath.

Penalty kick
The first player to score from a penalty kick in a Football League match was Heath of Wolverhampton Wanderers v Accrington, Division I, September 14 1891.

Professional
The identity of the first professional footballer may never be definitely established, but it was probably J.J. Lang, a Scot who joined Sheffield Wednesday in 1876 after playing for Clydesdale and Glasgow Eastern.

Tour
Oxford University were the first to send a football team on an overseas tour. This was in 1875 when they visited Germany.

Sunday Football
The first Football League game to be played on a Sunday was that between Millwall and Fulham on the morning of January 20 1974. Eleven other Football League games were played later the same day.

SOME OTHER RECORDS

The oldest player ever to appear in the Football League was Neil McBain who played in goal for New Brighton v Hartlepools United, Division 3(N), March 15 1947. He was then aged 52 years 4 months.
The oldest player ever to appear for any of the home countries in a full international was Billy Meredith. He was nearly 46 years of age when he played for Wales v England, March 15 1920.
The record for most appearances in the Football League during one season by a player over 40 years of age was created by Bob McGrory. In his last season as a player with Stoke City (1934–35) he appeared in all 42 First Division games. Bob was then 43 years of age.
The record for most consecutive appearances in the Football League was created by Harold Bell, Tranmere Rovers centre-half. Commencing with the opening game of season 1946–47 Bell did not miss a single game until August 1955 – a run of 401 consecutive Division 3(N) matches. Including F.A. Cup, Liverpool Senior Cup and Cheshire Bowl games, Bell enjoyed a run of 459 consecutive first team appearances.
Jimmy Dickinson created a club record by making 764 Football League appearances for Portsmouth between 1946 and 1965. In the Scottish League the record for most appearances for a single club was created by Bob Ferrier with a total of 626 for Motherwell between 1918 and 1937.
Billy Wright (Wolverhampton Wanderers) set up a world record by playing in 70 consecutive internationals for England, from 1951 to 1959.
Since substitutes were introduced into League football in 1965, Bristol City is the club that has played through the longest spell without calling upon one of these players – a run of 52 League games, 4 F.A. Cup, and 2 League Cup ties from February 1966 to April 1967.
The shortest player ever to appear in the Football League is outside-right Fred le May who was only 5 ft tall. He played for Thames 1930–31, Watford 1931–32, and Clapton Orient 1932–33. The tallest was Albert Iremonger, Notts County and Lincoln City goalkeeper 1904–27. He was 6 ft 5 in. tall.
The longest F.A. Cup tie was that in the 4th qualifying round between Alvechurch and Oxford City in 1971. This needed 11 hours (six games) before Oxford City won 1-0.
The longest single game on record is that between Stockport County and Doncaster Rovers, March 26 1946. In an effort to reach a decisive result this Third Division (N) cup tie continued for 205 minutes before bad light forced an abandonment.
Rochdale suffered 14 consecutive home defeats in Division 3(N) in 1931–32. This is a Football League record. After beating New Brighton 3-2 on November 7 1931, they did not get another home point until holding Barrow to a goalless draw in their second home game of season 1932–33. During that same period Rochdale suffered one run of 17 consecutive defeats (home and away) – also a Football League record.
In season 1905–06 Bristol City won 14 consecutive Division 2 games. This Football League record was equalled by Preston North End in Division 2 in 1950–51.
The Scottish League record for the longest run of consecutive victories was created by Morton in Division 2 in 1963–64 when they won 23 games in a row.
Leeds United were undefeated in a run of 34 First Division games, October 1968 to August 1969. This is a Football League record.
The longest run without defeat in a single season of Football League games is one of 30 matches by Burnley in Division 1 in 1920–21.
In the Scottish League, Celtic created a record by remaining undefeated in a run of 63 games – November 1915 to April 1917.
Blackburn Rovers hold the record for the longest run of consecutive F.A. Cup ties without defeat. From December 1883 to December 1886 they were unbeaten in 24 Cup ties and won the trophy three times during this period.
Only two players have scored two goals for each side in a Football League game. Sam Wynne did so in a Division 2 game, October 6 1923, scoring twice for Oldham Athletic as well as putting two through his own goal for Manchester United. Chris Nicholl (Aston Villa) scored all the goals in a 2-2 draw with Leicester City, Division 1, March 20 1976.

638

Arhur Chandler scored in each of 16 consecutive Football League games for Leicester City in Division 2 during season 1924–25. This is a League record.

Jimmy Cookson was the player who reached a first century of Football League goals in the shortest time. He made his debut for Chesterfield in 1925 and reached his century in December 1927 with West Bromwich Albion when figuring in his 87th Football League game.

The record number of goals scored by a player making his Football League debut is five – by George Hilsdon for Chelsea v Glossop, Division 2, September 1 1906.

The record for scoring the fastest goal in a Football League game is claimed by Jim Fryatt. According to Referee Mr. R. J. Simon this player scored for Bradford v Tranmere Rovers only four seconds after the kick-off, April 25 1964.

The fastest goals scored in the F.A. Cup Final at Wembley were obtained in the first minute. In 1928 John Roscamp put Blackburn Rovers ahead when he charged both the Huddersfield goalkeeper and the ball into the net, and in 1955 Jackie Milburn headed Newcastle United into a first-minute lead over Manchester City.

John McIntyre scored four goals in five minutes for Blackburn Rovers v Everton, Division 1, September 16 1922.

W. G. Richardson also scored four goals in five minutes for West Bromwich Albion, Division 1, November 7 1931, but this was even more remarkable because the feat was achieved in an away game – against West Ham United.

The record number of penalties missed by one side in a Football League Division 1 game is three. Manchester City (Fletcher 2 and Thornley) missed this number against Newcastle United, January 27 1912.

The most penalties scored by a player in a First Division game is three – Billy Walker for Aston Villa v Bradford City, November 12 1921; Charlie Mitten for Manchester United v Aston Villa, March 8 1950, and Ken Barnes for Manchester City v Everton, December 7 1957.

The record number of players from the same club in an England team is seven, Frank Moss, George Male, Eddie Hapgood, Wilf Copping, Raymond Bowden, Ted Drake and Clifford Bastin, all of Arsenal, played against Italy at Highbury, November 14 1934.

The England team twice included all Corinthian players in the 1890s but this cannot be considered a record because the Corinthians were a combined eleven, most of their players also appearing with other clubs.

In season 1925–26 Cardiff City created a Football League record by having as many as 17 internationals on their books. There were 9 Welsh internationals, 4 Scottish, and 4 Irish.

The England team that won the 1966 World Cup created a record for the country by remaining unchanged in six consecutive games – the quarter-final, semi-final and final of the World Cup and their next three games.

England's longest run without defeat is one of 20 games between 1889 and 1896.

The biggest championship winning margin for any division of the Football League is 15 points. Middlesbrough finished that far ahead of the runners-up in Division 2 in 1973–74.

The smallest number of players called upon by a club to complete a season of Football League games is 14 by Liverpool when winning the Championship in 1965–66. Five of their players were ever-present.

In the Scottish League, Dundee called upon only 15 players throughout season 1961–62. They also won the Championship that season and had five players ever-present.

The goalscoring record for a goalkeeper in a single season of Football League games was set up in 1923–24 by Arnold Birch of Chesterfield. In Division 3(N) games that season he scored five goals, all from penalties.

Five men have both played in and managed Football League Championship winning teams: Ted Drake, Arsenal, centre-forward, 1933–34, 1934–35, 1937–38; Chelsea, manager, 1954–55. Bill Nicholson, Tottenham Hotspur, right half-back, 1950–51, manager, 1960–61. Alf Ramsey, right-back, Tottenham Hotspur, 1950–51, Ipswich Town, manager, 1961–62. Joe Mercer, left-half, Everton 1938–39, Arsenal 1947–48, 1952–53, Manchester City, manager, 1967–68. Dave Mackay, left half, Tottenham Hotspur 1960–61, Derby County, manager, 1974–75. Bob Paisley, Liverpool left-half-back, 1946–47; manager 1975–76.

In 1973–74 Leeds United created a Football League record for the longest run without defeat from the start of a season – 29 First Division games before losing 2–3 at Stoke. It could be said that this only equalled Liverpool's run in the Second Division in 1893–94 when they were unbeaten in all 28 games. Their 29th game that season was the extra 'Test Match' to decide promotion and relegation between the First and Second Divisions.

ANGLO-SCOTTISH TOURNAMENT 1975-76

Qualifying Group final tables

Group 1	P	W	D	L	F	A	Bonus Pts.	Pts.	Total Pts.
Middlesbrough	3	2	1	0	9	5	2	5	7
Carlisle U.	3	2	0	1	4	4	0	4	4
Sunderland	3	1	0	2	4	4	0	2	2
Newcastle U.	3	0	1	2	2	6	0	1	1

Group 2	P	W	D	L	F	A	Bonus Pts.	Pts.	Total Pts.
Mansfield T.	3	2	1	0	5	2	0	5	5
W.B.A.	3	1	1	1	4	4	0	3	3
Leicester C.	3	1	1	1	3	4	0	3	3
Hull C.	3	0	1	2	3	5	0	1	1

Group 3	P	W	D	L	F	A	Bonus Pts.	Pts.	Total Pts.
Blackburn R.	3	2	0	1	5	5	1	4	5
Sheffield U.	3	1	1	1	5	5	1	3	4
Blackpool	3	1	1	1	4	4	0	3	3
Manchester C.	3	1	0	2	3	3	1	2	3

Group 4	P	W	D	L	F	A	Bonus Pts.	Pts.	Total Pts.
Fulham	3	2	1	0	5	3	0	5	5
Bristol C.	3	1	1	1	6	4	1	3	4
Chelsea	3	1	1	1	2	2	0	3	3
Norwich C.	3	0	1	2	3	7	0	1	1

A bonus point was awarded for teams scoring three or more goals in a match.
The four Scottish quarter-finalists appeared by invitation.

QUARTER-FINAL, FIRST LEG

SEPT. 15

Ayr U. (0) 0

Mansfield T. (1) 1 (*McDonald*) 3750

Ayr U.: Sproat; Wells, Murphy, Paton, McAnespie, McSherry, Doyle, Graham, Ingram, McCulloch, Phillips.
Mansfield T.: Arnold; Pate, Foster B., Lathan, Mackenzie, Foster C., O'Brien, McDonald, Eccles, Hodgson, McCaffrey (Laverick).

SEPT. 16

Fulham (3) 3 (*Mitchell 2, Busby*)

Hearts (1) 2 (*Gibson 2*) 6256

Fulham: Mellor; Cutbush, Strong, Mullery, Howe, Moore, Mitchell, Conway, Busby, Slough, Barrett.
Hearts: Cruickshank; Clunie, Burrell, Jefferies, Anderson, Murray, Park, Busby, Gibson, Brown, Callachan.

Middlesbrough (2) 2 (*Hickton pen., Mills*)

Aberdeen (0) 0 13,965

Middlesbrough: Platt; Craggs, Cooper, Souness, Boam, McAndrew, Murdoch (Charlton), Mills, Hickton, Foggon, Armstrong.
Aberdeen: Geoghegan; Hair, McLelland, Scott, Ward, Miller, Smith, Robb, Jarvie, Williamson, Graham (Pirie).

SEPT. 17

Blackburn R. (0) 0

Motherwell (0) 0 18,647

Blackburn R.: Jones; Heaton, Hutt, Hird, Hawkins, Fazackerley, Beamish, Oates, Hickman, Parkes, Hoy.
Motherwell: Rennie; McLaren, Wark, Watson B., McVie, Stevens, Watson W., Pettigrew, Graham, Davidson, Millar.

QUARTER-FINAL, SECOND LEG

SEPT. 29

Mansfield T. (2) 2 (*McDonald, Clarke*)

Ayr U. (0) 0 7149

Mansfield T.: Arnold; Pate, Foster B., Bird, Laverick, Foster C., Matthews, Eccles (McCaffrey), Clarke, Hodgson, McDonald.
Ayr U.: Sproat; Wells, Murphy, McAnespie, McDonald, McSherry, Doyle (Payton), Graham, Ingram, McCullock, Dickson.

SEPT. 30

Motherwell (1) 2 (*Davidson, Pettigrew*)

Blackburn R. (0) 1 (*Beamish*) 5962

Motherwell: Rennie; McLaren, Wark, Millar, McVie, Stevens, McAdam, Pettigrew, Graham, Davidson, Goldthorpe (Watson R.).
Blackburn R.: Jones; Wilkinson, Hutt, Metcalfe, Hawkins, Fazackerley, Kenyon, Oates, Beamish, Waddington, Parkes.

OCT. 1

Aberdeen (1) 2 (*Scott, Robb*)

Middlesbrough (2) 5 (*Mills 2, Hickton 2, Foggon*)
9000
Aberdeen: Geoghegan; Hair, McLelland, Scott, Ward, Miller, Smith, Robb, Jarvie (Henry), Williamson, Graham.
Middlesbrough: Platt (Cuff); Craggs, Cooper, Souness, Boam, Maddren, Brine, Mills, Hickton, Foggon (Murdoch), Armstrong.

Hearts (1) 2 (*Jeffries, Gibson*)

Fulham (1) 2 (*Slough, Mullery pen.*)   14,000
Hearts: Cruickshank; Clunie, Kay, Brown, Anderson, Jefferies, Aird, Busby, Gibson, Callachan, Prentice.
Fulham: Mellor; Cutbush, Strong, Mullery, Howe, Moore, Lloyd, Conway, Busby, Slough, Scrivens.

SEMI-FINAL, FIRST LEG
OCT. 21

Fulham (0) 1 (*Conway*)

Motherwell (0) 1 (*Pettigrew*)   9672
Fulham: Mellor; James, Slough, Mullery, Howe, Moore, Mitchell, Conway, Busby, Lloyd, Barrett.
Motherwell: Rennie; Watson W., Wark, Watson B., McVie, Stevens, McAdam, Pettigrew, Graham, Davidson, Millar.

Middlesbrough (0) 3 (*Armstrong 2, Hickton*)

Mansfield T. (0) 0   14,929
Middlesbrough: Platt; Craggs, Cooper, Souness, Boam, Maddren, Murdoch, Mills, Hickton, Foggon (Spraggon), Armstrong.
Mansfield T.: Arnold; Pate, Foster B., Laverick, Foster C., Bird, Matthews, Eccles (McCaffrey), Clarke, Hodgson, McDonald.

SEMI-FINAL, SECOND LEG
NOV. 3

Mansfield T. (0) 0

Middlesbrough (0) 2 (*Murdcch, Souness*)   7115
Mansfield T.: Evans; Pate, Foster B., McDonald, Madden, Bird, Matthews, Eccles (Laverick), Clarke, Hodgson, Mackenzie.
Middlesbrough: Platt; Craggs, Spraggon, Souness, Boam, Maddren, Murdoch (Brine), Mills, Hickton, Cooper, Armstrong.

NOV. 4

Motherwell (2) 2 (*Graham, Davidson*)

Fulham (2) 3 (*Watson o.g., Conway, Barrett*) 13,085
Motherwell: Rennie; Watson W., Wark, Millar, McVie, Stevens, McAdam, Pettigrew, Graham, Davidson, Taylor.
Fulham: Mellor; James, Slough, Mullery, Lacy, Moore, Dowie, Lloyd, Busby, Conway, Barrett.

FINAL, FIRST LEG
NOV. 26

Middlesbrough (0) 1 (*Armstrong*)

Fulham (0) 0   15,000
Middlesbrough: Platt; Craggs, Spraggon, Murdoch (Foggon), Boam, Maddren, Brine, Mills, Cooper, Hickton, Armstrong.
Fulham: Mellor; Fraser, Strong, Mullery, Howe, Moore, Dowie (Lloyd), Conway, Busby, Slough, Barrett.

FINAL, SECOND LEG
DEC. 9

Fulham (0) 0

Middlesbrough (0) 0   13,723
Fulham: Mellor; Howe, Strong, Mullery, Lacy, Moore, Dowie, Conway, Busby, Slough, Barrett.
Middlesbrough: Platt; Craggs, Cooper, Boersma, Boam, Maddren, Murdoch, Mills, Willey, Hickton, Armstrong.

F.A. CHARITY SHIELD WINNERS 1908-75

Year	Winners	Runners-up	Score
1908	Manchester U.	Q.P.R.	4-0 after 1-1 draw
1909	Newcastle U.	Northampton	2-0
1910	Brighton	Aston Villa	1-0
1911	Manchester U.	Swindon T.	8-4
1912	Blackburn R.	Q.P.R.	2-1
1913	Professionals	Amateurs	7-2
1919	W.B.A.	Tottenham H.	2-0
1920	Tottenham H.	Burnley	2-0
1921	Huddersfield	Liverpool	1-0
1922	No Competition		
1923	Professionals	Amateurs	2-0
1924	Professionals	Amateurs	3-1
1925	Amateurs	Professionals	6-1
1926	Amateurs	Professionals	6-3
1927	Cardiff C.	Corinthians	2-1
1928	Everton	Blackburn R.	2-1
1929	Professionals	Amateurs	3-0
1930	Arsenal	Sheffield W.	2-1
1931	Arsenal	W.B.A.	1-0
1932	Everton	Newcastle U.	5-3
1933	Arsenal	Everton	3-0
1934	Arsenal	Manchester C.	4-0
1935	Sheffield W.	Arsenal	1-0
1936	Sunderland	Arsenal	2-1
1937	Manchester C.	Sunderland	2-0
1938	Arsenal	Preston N.E.	2-1
1948	Arsenal	Manchester U.	4-3
1949	Portsmouth	Wolverhampton W.	1-1*
1950	World Cup Team	Canadian Touring Team	4-2
1951	Tottenham H.	Newcastle U.	2-1
1952	Manchester U.	Newcastle U.	4-2
1953	Arsenal	Blackpool	3-1
1954	Wolverhampton W.	W.B.A.	4-4*
1955	Chelsea	Newcastle U.	3-0
1956	Manchester U.	Manchester C.	1-0
1957	Manchester U.	Aston Villa	4-0
1958	Bolton W.	Wolverhampton W.	4-1
1959	Wolverhampton W.	Nottingham F.	3-1
1960	Burnley	Wolverhampton W.	2-2*
1961	Tottenham H.	F.A. XI	3-2
1962	Tottenham H.	Ipswich T.	5-1
1963	Everton	Manchester U.	4-0
1964	Liverpool	West Ham U.	2-2*
1965	Manchester U.	Liverpool	2-2*
1966	Liverpool	Everton	1-0
1967	Manchester U.	Tottenham H.	3-3*
1968	Manchester C.	W.B.A.	6-1
1969	Leeds U.	Manchester C.	2-1
1970	Everton	Chelsea	2-1
1971	Leicester	Liverpool	1-0
1972	Manchester C.	Aston Villa	1-0
1973	Burnley	Manchester C.	1-0
1974	Liverpool†	Leeds	1-1

* Each club retained shield for six months.   † won on penalties

F.A. Charity Shield 1975

Derby Co. (2) **2** (*Hector, McFarland*), West Ham U. (0) 0, 59,000. *Derby Co.*: Boulton; Thomas, Nish, Rioch, McFarland, Todd, Newton, Gemmill, Lee, Hector, George. *West Ham U.*: Day; McDowell, Lampard, Holland, Taylor T., Lock, Taylor A., Paddon, Jennings (Coleman), Brooking, Gould (Robson).

ENGLAND v YOUNG ENGLAND

Year	Date	Venue	England	Y.E.	Year	Date	Venue	England	Y.E.
1954	April 30	Highbury	2	1	1963	May 24	Highbury	3	2
1955	May 6	Highbury	5	0	1964	May 1	Stamford Bridge	3	0
1957	May 3	Highbury	1	2	1965	April 30	Highbury	2	2
1958	May 2	Stamford Bridge	4	1	1966	May 13	Stamford Bridge	1	1
1959	May 1	Highbury	3	3	1967	May 19	Highbury	0	5
1960	May 6	Highbury	2	1	1968	May 17	Highbury	1	4
1961	May 5	Stamford Bridge	1	1	1969	April 25	Stamford Bridge	0	0
1962	May 4	Highbury	3	2					

Directory of Ex-Football League Clubs

ABERDARE ATHLETIC
Founded: 1920. *League career:* Division 3 (S) 1921-27—not re-elected. Afterwards played in Welsh League. *Ground:* Athletic Ground, Aberdare, Glamorgan. *Colours:* Blue and gold striped shirts, white shorts.

ACCRINGTON STANLEY
Founded: 1876 as Accington. Original members of League 1888, re-formed 1919. *League career:* League 1888-92, Division 1 1892-93; resigned 1893; Division 3 (N) 1921-39, 1946-58; Division 4 1960-62—withdrew before the end of the season. Club folded up. New club Accrington Stanley (1968). Now in Lancashire Combination. *Ground:* Peel Park, Accrington, Lancs. *Colours:* Red shirts with white sleeves, white shorts.

ASHINGTON
Founded: 1888. *League career:* Division 3 (N) 1921-29 not re-elected. Later in North-Eastern League, Midland Counties League and now Rothmans Northern League. *Ground:* Portland Park, Ashington, Northumberland. *Colours:* Black and white striped shirts, blue shorts.

BARROW
Founded: 1901. *League Career:* Division 3 (N) 1921-29, 1946-58; Division 4 1958-67; Division 3 1967-70; Division 4 1970-72—not re-elected. Now in Northern Premier League. *Ground:* Holker Street, Barrow-in-Furness, Lancs. *Colours:* Blue and white striped shirts, white shorts.

BOOTLE
Founded: 1881. Original members of Division 2 1892. *League career:* Division 2 1892-93 —not re-elected. Now in Lancashire Combination. *Colours:* Blue and white shirts, blue shorts.

BRADFORD PARK AVENUE
Founded: 1907. *League career:* Division 2 1908-14; Division 1 1914-15, 1919-21; Division 2 1921-22; Division 3 (N) 1922-28; Division 2 1928-39, 1946-50; Division 3 (N) 1950-58; Division 4 1958-61; Division 3 1961-63; Division 4 1963-70—not re-elected. Afterwards played in Northern Premier League but since folded up. *Ground:* Park Avenue, Bradford, Yorks. *Colours:* White shirts, green facings, black shorts.

BURTON UNITED
Founded: 1890 as Burton Swifts. *League career:* Division 2 1892-1907—not re-elected. Later folded up. *Ground:* Peel Croft. *Colours:* Blue shirts, white shorts; then maroon and orange shirts, black shorts.

BURTON WANDERERS
Founded 1893. *League career:* Division 2 1894-97—not re-elected. Later folded up. *Ground:* Derby Turn. *Colours:* Blue and white halves.

DARWEN
Founded: 1875. *League career:* League 1891-92; Division 2 1892-93; Division 1 1893-94; Division 2 1894-99—not re-elected. *Ground:* Barley Bank. *Colours:* White shirts, navy blue shorts. Club of same name in Lancashire Combination.

GAINSBOROUGH TRINITY
Founded: 1890. *League career:* Division 2 1896-1912—not re-elected. Later in Midland League. Now Northern Premier League. *Ground:* Northolme. *Colours:* Royal blue shirts, white shorts.

GATESHEAD
Founded: 1899 as South Shields Adelaide; South Shields 1908, elected to Division 2 1919, changed name on moving to Gateshead 1930. *League career:* Division 2 1919-28; Division 3 (N) 1928-39, 1946-58; Division 4 1958-60—not re-elected. Later Northern Premier League, Midland League. Reconstructed as Gateshead United.

GLOSSOP NORTH END
Founded: 1890. *League career:* Division 2 1898-99; Division 1 1899-1900; Division 2 1900-15; resigned after World War 1. *Ground:* North Road. *Colours:* White shirts, white shorts. Club folded up.

LOUGHBOROUGH TOWN
Founded: 1890. *League career:* Division 2 1895-1900—not re-elected. *Ground:* Athletic Grounds. *Colours:* Black and white striped shirts, blue shorts. Club folded up.

MERTHYR TYDFIL (or TOWN)
Founded: 1910. *League career:* Division 3 1920-21; Division 3 (S) 1921-30—not re-elected. Now in Southern League. *Ground:* Penydarren Park, Merthyr Tydfil, Glamorgan. *Colours:* Red shirts, green collars, white shorts.

MIDDLESBOROUGH IRONOPOLIS
Founded: 1885. *League career:* Division 2 1893-94—not re-elected. Club folded up. *Colours:* Cherry and white.

NELSON
Founded: 1882. *League career:* Division 3 (N) 1921-23; Division 2 1923-24; Division 3 (N) 1924-31—not re-elected. Club of same name in Lancashire Combination. *Ground:* Park Ground, Seedhill, Nelson, Lancs. *Colours:* Royal blue shirts, white shorts.

NEW BRIGHTON
Founded: 1890. *League career:* Division 2 1898-1901—resigned; Division 3 (N) 1923-39, 1946-51—not re-elected. Later Lancashire Combination, Cheshire County League. *Ground:* Tower Ground, Wallasey, Cheshire. *Colours:* White and maroon striped shirts, white shorts.

NORTHWICH VICTORIA
Founded: 1880. *League career:* Division 2 1892-94—not re-elected. Later Cheshire County League, Northern Premier League. *Colours:* Red shirts, blue shorts.

STALYBRIDGE CELTIC
Founded: 1920. *League career:* Division 3 (N) 1921-23—resigned. Club of same name in Cheshire County League.

THAMES ASSOCIATION
Founded: 1927. *League career:* Division 3 (S) 1930-32—did not seek re-election. Club folded up. *Ground:* West Ham Stadium, Prince Regent's Lane, Custom House, London E16. *Colours:* Red and blue quarter shirts, white shorts.

WIGAN BOROUGH
Founded: 1921. League career: Division 3 (N) 1921-31—resigned. *Ground:* Springfield Park, Wigan, Lancs. *Colours:* Black and gold shirts, white shorts.

The Managers

A directory of Football League managers with biographical details.

ANDERSON, Stan. *Manager:* Middlesbrough 1966–1972; Q.P.R. (Assistant Manager) 1974; Doncaster R. 1975–. *Honours:* Division 3 runners-up 1967. *Player:* Sunderland 1951–1963; Newcastle U. 1963–1965; Middlesbrough 1965–1966. *Honours:* Four Under-23 and two full England caps; World Cup party 1962; Division 2 Champions medal 1965.

ARMFIELD, Jimmy. *Manager:* Bolton W. 1971–1974; Leeds U. 1974–. *Honours:* Division 3 Champions 1973; European Cup runners-up 1975. *Player:* Blackpool 1953–1971. *Honours:* Played in two World Cups: 1962 and 1966. Football League and Under-23 and 43 full caps for England (Captain 1962–1964).

ASHURST, Len. *Manager:* Hartlepool, Gillingham, Sheffield W. *Player:* Sunderland 1957–1971; Hartlepool 1971–1973. *Honours:* One Under-23 cap for England.

ASHMAN, Alan. *Manager:* Carlisle U. 1963–1967; W.B.A. 1967–1972; Olympiakos (Greece) 1971–1972; Carlisle U. 1972–1975; Workington 1976–. *Honours:* Carlisle U., Promotion to Division 3 1965; Division 3 Champions 1966; Promotion to Division 1 1974; W.B.A., FA Cup Winners 1968; FA Cup Semi-Finalists 1969; League Cup runners-up 1970; Olympiakos, League runners-up 1972. *Player:* Nottingham F. 1949–1951; Carlisle U. 1951–1959.

ASHMAN, Ron. *Manager:* Norwich C. 1963–1966; Scunthorpe 1967–1973; Grimsby T. 1973–1975; Scunthorpe 1976–. *Honours:* Scunthorpe, Promotion to Division 3 1973. *Player:* Norwich C. 1944–1962. *Honours:* League Cup winners medal 1962.

BALL, Alan (Snr.). *Manager:* Oswestry, Aston Utd., Nantwich, Halifax T. 1967, Preston N.E. 1971, Southport, Saab, Sirius, Uppsala (Sweden), Halifax 1976. *Honours:* Oswestry Shropshire Senior Cup, Birmingham League Championship; Halifax T. promotion to Division 3 1969; Preston N.E. Division 3 Championship 1971; Saab Swedish League runners-up; Sirius, Uppsala Third Place in League. *Player:* Southport, Birmingham C., Oldham Ath., Rochdale.

BELL, William. *Manager:* Birmingham C. 1975–. *Player:* Queen's Park 1957–1959; Leeds U. 1959–1968; Leicester C. 1968–1970; Brighton & H.A. 1970–1971. *Honours:* Amateur and two full caps for Scotland; Leeds U., FA Cup runners-up medal 1965; Fairs Cup runners-up medal 1967; Division 2 Championship medal 1964.

BENSON, John. *Manager:* A.F.C. Bournemouth 1975–. *Player:* Manchester C. 1961–1963; Torquay U. 1964–1970; A.F.C. Bournemouth 1970–1973; Norwich C. 1973–1975.

BINGHAM, Billy. *Manager:* Southport; Plymouth Arg.; Linfield; Everton 1974–; Northern Ireland; Greek National team. *Honours:* Southport, promotion to Division 3; Linfield, All Ireland Champions; Everton UEFA Cup participation 1975. *Player:* Glentoran; Sunderland 1950–1958; Luton T. 1958–1960; Everton 1960–1963; Port Vale 1963–1965. *Honours:* Everton, Division 1 Championship medal 1963; Luton T. FA Cup runners-up medal 1959.

BLOOMFIELD, Jimmy. *Manager:* Orient 1969, Leicester C. 1971. *Player:* Brentford, Arsenal, Birmingham C., West Ham U., Plymouth Arg., Orient (player-manager). *Honours:* Two Under-23 caps for England.

BOND, John. *Manager:* A.F.C. Bournemouth; Norwich C. 1974–. *Honours:* A.F.C. Bournemouth, Promotion to Division 3; Norwich C., Promotion to Division 1 1975. *Player:* West Ham U. (17 years); Torquay U. (3 years). *Honours:* West Ham U. Division 2 Championship medal 1958; FA Cup winners medal 1964; Torquay U., Promotion to Division 3 1966.

BOOK, Tony. *Manager:* Manchester C. 1975–. *Honours:* League Cup winners 1976. *Player:* Plymouth Arg. 1964–1966; Manchester C. 1967–1974. *Honours:* Manchester C., Division 1 Championship medal 1968; European Cup Winners Cup medal 1970; Football League Cup Winners medal 1970; FA Cup Winners medal 1969; 'Footballer of the Year' 1969.

BROWN, Allan. *Manager:* Luton T. 1967; Torquay U. 1969; Bury 1972; Nottingham F. 1974; Southport 1976; Blackpool. *Honours:* Luton T., Division 4 Champions 1968. *Player:* East Fife 1944–1950; Blackpool 1950–1956; Luton T. 1956–1960; Portsmouth 1960–1964. *Honours:* East Fife, League Cup Winners medal 1950; Scottish Cup runners-up medal 1950; Blackpool, Two FA Cup finals. (Injured) 1951 and 1953; Luton T., FA Cup runners-up medal 1959.

BROWN, Joe. *Manager:* Burnley 1976–. *Player:* Middlesbrough 1946–1952; Burnley 1952–1954; Bournemouth 1954–1960; Aldershot 1960–1961.

BROWN, Michael. *Manager:* Oxford U. 1975–. *Player:* Hull C. (13 years); Lincoln C. (1 year); Cambridge U. (18 months). *Honours:* Hull C., Division 3 Champions medal 1965.

CANTWELL, Noel. *Manager:* Coventry C. 1968–1972; Peterborough U. 1972–. *Honours:* Coventry C., qualifiers for Fairs Cup 1970; Peterborough U., Division 4 champions 1974. *Player:* West Ham U. 1952–1960; Manchester U. 1960–1967. *Honours:* Captain West Ham U.; Division 2 Champions 1958. Captain Manchester U.; FA Cup winners 1963; Division 1 Championship medal 1965; 32 full caps for the Republic of Ireland (Captain 20 times).

CASEY, Tom. *Manager:* Grimsby T. *Player:* Leeds U.; A.F.C. Bournemouth; Newcastle U.; Portsmouth; Bristol C. *Honours:* Newcastle U. FA Cup winners medal 1955; 14 full caps for N. Ireland. (World Cup 1958).

CATTERICK, Harry. *Player-Manager:* Crewe Alex 1951–1953. *Manager:* Rochdale 1953–1958; Sheffield W. 1958–1961; Everton 1961–1973; Preston N.E. *Honours:* Sheffield W., Division 1 runners-up 1961; Division 2 Champions 1959; Everton, Division 1 Champions 1963 and 1970; FA Cup Winners 1966, runners-up 1968. *Player:* Everton 1937-1951.

CHAPMAN, Roy. *Manager:* Lincoln C. 1965–1967; Stafford Rangers 1970–1975; Stockport Co. 1976. *Honours:* Stafford Rangers, Northern Premier League Champions 1972; Runners-up 1971; Non-League Trophy winners 1972; Staffs Senior Cup (3 times); 4th Round FA Cup 1975. *Player:* Aston Villa 1952–1957; Lincoln C. 1957–1961; Mansfield T. 1961–1965; Lincoln C. 1965–1967; Port Vale 1967–1970; Chester 1970. *Honours:* FA Eleven v. South Africa; Mansfield T., promotion to Division 3 1963.

CHARLTON, Jack O.B.E. *Manager:* Middlesbrough 1973–. *Honours:* 'Manager of the Year' 1974. *Player:* Leeds United 1952–1973. *Honours:* Division 2 Championship medal 1964; FA Cup runners-up medal 1965; World Cup winners medal 1966; Fairs Cup runners-up medal 1967; 'Footballer of the Year' 1967; League Cup winners medal 1968; Fairs Cup winners medal 1968; Division 1 championship medal 1969; FA Cup runners-up medal 1970; Fairs Cup winners medal 1971; FA Cup winners medal 1972.

DICKS, Alan. *Manager:* Bristol C. 1967–. *Honours:* Promotion to Division 1 1976. *Player:* Chelsea 1951–1958; Southend U. 1958–1962; Coventry C. 1962–1967.

DOCHERTY, John. *Manager:* Brentford. *Player:* Brentford 1959–1961; 1965–1968; 1970–1974; Sheffield U. 1961–1965; Reading 1968–1970; Q.P.R. player/coach 1974–1975.

DOCHERTY, Tommy. *Manager:* Chelsea 1962; Rotherham U. 1967; Aston Villa 1969; Porto F.C.; Scottish Team Manager; Manchester U. 1973–. *Honours:* Qualified for 1974 World Cup with Scotland; Manchester U., Division 2 Champions 1975. *Player:* Celtic 1949; Preston N.E. 1949–1958; Arsenal 1958–1962. *Honours:* Division 2 Championship medal 1951; 25 full caps for Scotland.

DODGIN, William. *Manager:* Q.P.R.; Fulham, Northampton T. *Honours:* Fulham, promotion to Division 2 1971. *Player:* Fulham 1949–1952; Arsenal 1952–1961; Fulham 1961–1965. *Honours:* One Under-23 cap for England.

DURBAN, William Alan. *Manager:* Shrewsbury T. 1973–. *Honours:* Division 4 runners-up 1975. *Player:* Cardiff C. 1959–1963; Derby Co. 1963–1973; Shrewsbury T. 1973–. *Honours:* 27 full caps for Wales; Division 2 Championship medal 1969; Division 1 Championship medal 1972; promotion to Division 3 1975.

FENTON, Ron. *Manager:* Notts Co. 1976–. *Player:* Burnley 1957–1962; W.B.A. 1962–1964; Birmingham C. 1964–1967; Brentford 1967–1969.

FRASER, Doug. *Manager:* Walsall. *Player:* Aberdeen; W.B.A.; Walsall. *Honours:* League Cup winners medal 1966; League Cup runners-up medals 1967, 1970; FA Cup winners medal 1968; 2 full caps for Scotland.

FRIZZELL, James. *Manager:* Oldham Ath. *Honours:* Winners of Ford Sporting League; Division 3 champions 1974. *Player:* Morton 1957–1960; Oldham Ath. 1960–1970. *Honours:* Promotion to Division 3 1963.

GILES, John. *Manager:* W.B.A .June 1975–. *Honours:* Promotion to Division 1 1976. *Player:* Manchester U. 1956–1963; Leeds U. 1963–1975; W.B.A. *Honours:* 44 caps for the Republic of Ireland. Manchester U. FA Cup Winners medal 1963; Leeds U. Division 1 Championship medal 1969, 1974; Fairs Cup Winners medals 1968, 1971; League Cup Winners medal 1968; FA Cup Winners medal 1972. Promotion to Division 1 1976.

GREAVES, Ian. *Manager:* Huddersfield T. 1968–1974; Bolton W. 1974–. *Honours:* Huddersfield T., Division 2 Champions 1970. *Player:* Manchester U. 1952–1960; Lincoln C. 1960–1961; Oldham Ath. 1961–1963. *Honours:* Manchester U. Division 1 Championship medal 1956, FA Cup runners-up medal 1958.

GREGG, Harry. *Manager:* Shrewsbury T., Swansea C., Crewe Alex. *Player:* Doncaster R., Manchester U., Stoke C. *Honours:* Manchester U. Division 1 Champions 1956, 1957. 24 caps for Northern Ireland.

GRIFFITHS, Harry. *Manager:* Swansea C. *Player:* Swansea C. 1945–1964; Merthyr Tydfil. *Honours:* One full cap for Wales.

HALE, Kenneth. *Manager:* Hartlepool. *Player:* Newcastle U. 1957–1963; Coventry C. 1963–1966; Oxford U. 1966–1968;Darlington 1968–1972; Halifax T. 1972–74. *Honours:* Coventry C., Division 3 Championship medal 1964; Oxford U., Division 3 Championship medal 1968.

HURLEY, Charles J. *Manager:* Reading. *Player:* Millwall 1953–1957; Sunderland 1957–1969; Bolton W. 1969–1971. *Honours:* 40 full caps for Eire.

ILEY, Jim. *Manager:* Peterborough U. 1969; Barnsley 1973–. *Honours:* Watney Cup entry 1973, 1974. *Player:* Sheffield U. 1953–1957; Tottenham H. 1958–1959; Nottingham F. 1959–1963; Newcastle U. 1963–1969; Peterborough U. 1969–1973. *Honours:* Football League XI with Sheffield U., Tottenham H. One Under-23 cap for England. FA XI.

JAGO, Gordon. *Manager:* Eastbourne U.; Q.P.R.; Millwall 1975–. *Coach/Asst. Manager:* Fulham; Baltimore Bays, (USA). *Honours:* Q.P.R., Division 2 runners-up 1973. *Player:* Charlton Ath. 1951–1962. *Honours:* 6 England Youth caps.

JOHNSTONE, Thomas D. *Manager:* Rotherham U. 1958–1962; Grimsby T. 1962–1964; Huddersfield T. 1964–1968; York C. 1968–1975; Huddersfield T. 1975–. *Honours:* Rotherham U., League Cup runners-up 1961; York C., Promotion to Division 3 1971 and to Division 2 1974. *Player:* Nottingham F. 1942–1948; Notts Co. 1948–1957. *Honours:* Scottish reserve. Notts Co. Division 3 (South) Championship medal 1950.

KEEN, Michael T. *Manager:* Watford. *Player:* Q.P.R. 1958–1969; Luton T. 1969–1972; Watford 1972–1973. *Honours:* Q.P.R., Division 3 Championship medal 1967; Division 2 runners-up medal 1968; League Cup Winners medal 1967; Luton T., Division 3 runners-up medal 1970.

KENNEDY, Robert. *Manager:* Grimsby T., Bradford C. *Player:* Kilmarnock 1956–1961; Manchester C. 1961–1969; Grimsby T. 1969–1971. *Honours:* One Under-23 cap for Scotland. Division 1 Championship medal 1968; Division 2 Championship medal 1966.

KING, John A. *Manager:* Tranmere R. *Player:* Everton; A.F.C. Bournemouth; Tranmere R.; Port Vale; Wigan Ath. *Honours:* Promoted to Captain at all clubs excluding Everton.

LEE, Gordon. *Manager:* Port Vale 1968–1973; Blackburn R. 1973–1975; Newcastle U. 1975–. *Honours:* Port Vale, promotion to Division 3 1971; Blackburn R. Division 3 Champions 1975; Newcastle U. League Cup runners-up 1976; Division 3 Manager of the Year 1975. *Player:* Aston Villa 1955–1966; Shrewsbury T. 1966–1968. *Honours:* Aston Villa, League Cup Winners medal 1961; League Cup runners-up medal 1963.

LYALL, John. *Manager:* West Ham U. 1974–. Previously Assistant Manager 1971. *Honours:* FA Cup Winners 1975. *Player:* West Ham U. 1957. *Honours:* Youth International.

MACKAY, Dave. *Manager:* Swindon T. 1971–1972; Nottingham F. 1972–1973; Derby Co. 1973–. *Honours:* Derby Co. Division 1 Champions 1975; FA Charity Shield Winners 1975. *Player:* Heart of Midlothian 1953–1959; Tottenham H. 1959–1968; Derby Co. 1968–1971. *Honours:* FA Cup Winners medal 1961, 1962, 1967; Scottish Schoolboy, Under-23 and 22 full caps; Division 2 Championship medal 1969; 'Footballer of the Year' 1969.

MADDEN, Peter. *Manager:* Darlington. *Player:* Rotherham U. 1955–1966; Bradford P.A. 1966–1967; Aldershot 1967–1968; Skegness 1968–1970. *Honours:* Rotherham U. League Cup runners-up medal 1961; 2 Lincolnshire Cup medals with Skegness.

McANEARNEY, Thomas. *Manager:* Aldershot 1966–1968; Asst. Manager Sheffield W. 1968–1970; Crewe Alex. 1970; Bury 1970–1972; Aldershot 1972–. *Honours:* Promotion to Division 3 1973. *Player:* Sheffield W. 1951–1965; Peterborough U. 1965–1966; Aldershot 1966–1968. *Honours:* Sheffield W., Division 2 Champion medals 1957 and 1959.

McCREADIE, Eddie. *Manager:* Chelsea 1975–. *Player:* East Stirling, Chelsea 1962–1975. *Honours:* 23 full caps for Scotland. FA Cup Winners medal 1970, FA Cup runners-up medal 1967.

McGARRY, William H. *Manager:* Watford; Ipswich T.; Wolverhampton W. 1968–1976. *Honours:* Ipswich T. Division 2 champions 1968; Wolverhampton W. League Cup winners 1974. *Player:* Port Vale; Huddersfield T.; A.F.C. Bournemouth. *Honours:* Four full England caps.

McGUIGAN, Jim. *Manager:* Crewe Alex. 1960; Grimsby T. 1964; Chesterfield 1967; Rotherham U. 1973. *Honours:* Crewe Alex. Promotion to Division 3 1963; Chesterfield promotion to Division 3 1970; Rotherham U. promotion to Division 3 1975. Division 4 Manager of the Year. *Player:* Hamilton Acad., Sunderland, Stockport Co., Crewe Alex., Rochdale.

McGUINESS, Wilf. *Manager:* Manchester U. 1969–1970; Aris Salonica (Greece) 1971–1973; Panachaiki Patras (Greece) 1973–1974; York C. *Player:* Manchester U. 1953–1961. *Honours:* Four Under-23 and two full England caps.

McMENEMY, Lawrie. *Manager:* Doncaster R. 1968–1971; Grimsby T. 1971–1973; Southampton 1973–. *Honours:* Doncaster R., Division 4 Championship 1969; Grimsby T., Division 4 Championship 1972, Southampton, FA Cup Winners 1976. *Player:* Newcastle U., Gateshead.

MEE, Bertie. *Manager:* Arsenal 1966–1976. *Honours:* Fairs Cup winners 1970; League Championship and FA Cup double winners 1971. *Player:* Derby Co. 1937–1939.

MEGSON, Don. *Manager:* Bristol R. *Honours:* Watney Cup winners 1972; Promotion to Division 2 1974. *Player:* Sheffield W.; Bristol R. *Honours:* Football League 1960; FA Tours 1969–1970 Far East; FA Cup runners-up medal 1966.

MILNE, Gordon. *Manager:* Coventry C. *Player:* Preston N.E. 1957; Liverpool 1960; Blackpool 1967–1970. *Honours:* 14 full caps for England; Liverpool Division 2 championship medals 1964 and 1966; FA Cup Winners medal 1965.

MUSGROVE, Malcolm. *Manager:* Torquay U. *Player:* West Ham U. 1953–1962; Orient 1962–1966. *Honours:* West Ham Division 2 championship medal 1959.

NEAL, John. *Manager:* Wrexham. *Honours:* Promotion to Division 3 1970; Welsh Cup winners 1972, 1975; Qualified for Cup Winners Cup 1973, 1976 (quarter-finalists). *Player:* Hull C. 1949–1955; Swindon T. 1956–1958; Aston Villa 1959–1963; Southend U. 1964–1967. *Honours:* Aston Villa, Division 2 championship medal 1960; League Cup winners medal 1961.

NEILL, Terry. *Manager:* Hull C.; N. Ireland; Tottenham H. 1974–. *Player:* Arsenal 1959–1970; Hull C. 1970–1974. *Honours:* Schoolboy, Youth, Under-23, 'B' and 59 full caps for Northern Ireland.

NELSON, Andrew. *Manager:* Gillingham 1971–1974; Charlton Ath. 1974–. *Honours:* Gillingham, promotion to Division 3 1974; Charlton Ath., promotion to Division 2 1975. *Player:* West Ham U. 1953–1958; Ipswich T. 1958–1963; Orient 1963–1964; Plymouth Arg. 1964–1969. *Honours:* Ipswich T., Division 2 Championship medal 1961; Division 1 Championship medal 1962.

NEWMAN, John H. G. *Manager:* Exeter C. *Player:* Birmingham C. 1951–1958; Leicester C. 1958–1960; Plymouth Arg. 1960 -1968; Exeter C. 1968–1970. *Honours:* Birmingham C., Division 2 championship medal 1955; FA runners-up 1956; Football League.

PAISLEY, Robert. *Manager:* Liverpool 1974– *Honours:* Division 1 Champions 1976; UEFA Cup winners 1976. *Player:* Bishop Auckland 1938–1939; Liverpool 1939–1954. *Honours:* Amateur Cup winners medal 1939; Division 1 Championship medal 1947.

ROBERTS, Bobby. *Manager:* Colchester U. *Player:* Motherwell; Leicester C.,; Mansfield T. *Honours:* One Under-23 cap for Scotland; Scottish League.

ROBERTS, Ken. *Manager:* Chester 1968– *Honours:* Promotion to Division 3 1975. *Player:* Wrexham 1950–1953; Aston Villa 1953–1958.

ROBSON, Bobby. *Manager:* Fulham 1968; Ipswich T. 1969– *Honours:* Ipswich T., Texaco Cup winners 1973. *Player:* Fulham 1950–1956; W.B.A. 1956–1962; Fulham 1962–1968. *Honours:* Under-23 and 20 full England caps; (World Cups 1958 and 1962); Football League.

ROWLEY, Arthur. *Manager:* Shrewsbury T. *Player/Manager* 1958–1965; *Manager* 1965–1968; Sheffield U. 1968–1969; Southend U. 1970–1976. *Honours:* Shrewsbury T., Promotion to Division 3 1959; Southend U., Promotion to Division 3 1972. *Player:* W.B.A. 1945–1948; Fulham 1948–1950; Leicester C. 1950–1958; Shrewsbury T. 1958–1965. *Honours:* Fulham, Division 2 Championship medal 1949; Leicester C., Division 2 Championship medals 1954, 1957; England "B" cap; Football League; Holder of record number of 434 goals in League football.

SAUNDERS, Ron. *Manager:* Yeovil 1967; Oxford U. 1969; Norwich C. 1969; Manchester C. 1973; Aston Villa 1974–. *Honours:* Norwich C. Champions Division 2 1972; League Cup runners-up 1973; Manchester C. League Cup runners-up 1974; Aston Villa League Cup Winners 1975; Runners-up Division 2 1975; Manager of the Year 1975.

SCOULAR, Jimmy. *Manager:* Bradford P.A. 1961–1964 (Player/Manager); Cardiff C. 1964–1973; Newport Co. *Honours:* Bradford P.A. Promotion to Division 3 1961; Cardiff C., European Cup Winners Cup Semi-Final 1968; Ten times winners Welsh cup. *Player:* Portsmouth 1944–1953; Newcastle U. 1953–1961; Bradford P.A. 1961–1964. *Honours:* Portsmouth, Division 1 Championship medals 1949 and 1950; Newcastle FA Cup winners medal 1955; 9 full caps for Scotland; One of eleven players who have played in most Division 1 Football League matches.

SEXTON, David. *Manager:* Orient 1965–1966; Chelsea 1967–1974; Q.P.R. 1974–. *Honours:* FA Cup winners 1970; European Cup Winners Cup 1971; League Cup runners-up 1972. *Player:* Chelmsford 1950–1951; Luton T. 1951–1953; West Ham U. 1953–1956; Orient 1956–1957; Brighton & H.A. 1957–1959; C. Palace 1959–1961. *Honours:* FA XI v RAF; Third Division South v Third Division North.

SHAW, Joe. *Manager:* York C. 1968–1969; Chesterfield. *Player:* Sheffield U. 1945–1966 (club record 629 appearances). *Honours:* Twice an England reserve; Football League; FA tour of Australia.

SILLETT, John C. *Manager:* Hereford U. *Honours:* Promotion to Division 2 1976. *Player:* Chelsea; Coventry C.; Plymouth Arg. *Honours:* League Championship medal with Chelsea.

SIRREL, Jimmy. *Manager:* Brentford 1965–1969; Notts Co. 1969–1975; Sheffield U. 1975– *Honours:* Notts Co., Division 4 Champions 1971; Division 3 runners-up 1973. *Player:* Glasgow Celtic 1945–1949; Bradford P.A. 1949–1951; Brighton & H. A. 1951–1954; Aldershot 1954–1955 (later trainer).

SMITH, Bobby. *Manager:* Bury. *Honours:* Promotion to Division 3 1974. *Player:* Manchester U. 1959–1964; Scunthorpe U. 1964–1966; Grimsby T. 1966–1967; Brighton & H. A. 1967–1970; Chester 1970–1971; Hartlepool 1971–1973; Bury 1973– *Honours:* England Schoolboy and Youth caps.

SMITH, Jimmy. *Manager:* Boston U. 1968–1972; Colchester U. 1972–1975; Blackburn R. 1975–. *Honours:* Boston U. Eastern Professional Floodlight Cup winners; Colchester U. Promoted from Division 4 1974. *Player:* Sheffield U. 1957–1961; Aldershot 1961–1964; Halifax T. 1964–1967; Lincoln C. 1967–1968; Boston U. 1968–1972.

SPROSON, Roy. *Manager:* Port Vale 1973–. *Player:* Port Vale 1949–1970 (Record 761 League appearances). *Honours:* FA Cup semi-finals 1954. Champions Division 3 (N) 1954. Champions Division 4 1959.

ST. JOHN, Ian. *Manager:* Motherwell 1973–1974; Portsmouth 1975–. *Player:* Motherwell, Liverpool, Coventry C., Tranmere R. *Honours:* 21 full caps for Scotland; Division 1 Championship medals 1964, 1966; Division 2 Championship medal 1962; FA Cup Winners medal 1965; Cup-Winners' Cup runners-up medal 1966.

STOCK, Alec. *Manager:* Yeovil T. 1946–1949; Leyton Orient 1949–1958; AS Roma 1958; Q.P.R. 1958–1968; Luton T. 1969–1972; Fulham 1972– *Honours:* Leyton Orient Division 3 Championship 1956; Q.P.R. Division 3 Championship 1967; League Cup winners 1967; Promotion to Division 2 1970; Fulham FA Cup runners-up 1975; *Player:* Charlton Ath. 1936–1938; Q.P.R. 1938–1946.

STOKOE, Bob. *Manager:* Charlton Ath., Rochdale, Carlisle U., Blackpool, Sunderland 1972–. *Honours:* Sunderland FA Cup Winners 1973; Division 2 champions 1976. *Player:* Newcastle U. (13 years), Bury (Player-Manager). *Honours:* FA Cup Winners medal 1955.

SUMMERS, Gerry. *Manager:* Oxford U. 1969–1975; Gillingham 1975–. *Player:* W.B.A. 1951–1957; Sheffield U. 1957–1964; Hull C. 1964–1966; Walsall 1966–1968; *Honours:* Sheffield U., promotion to Division 1 1961; FA Tour 1962, Far East and America.

TAYLOR, Graham. *Manager:* Lincoln C. *Honours:* Division 4 Championship 1976. *Player:* Grimsby T. 1962–1968; Lincoln C. 1968–1972.

WADDINGTON, Tony. *Manager:* Stoke C. 1960–. Previously Assistant Manager 1957, Coach 1952. *Honours:* Division 2 Championship 1963; League Cup Winners 1972. *Player:* Manchester United (amateur), Crewe Alex. 1946–1951.

WAITERS, Tony. *Manager:* Plymouth Arg. *Honours:* Promotion to Division 2 1975. *Player:* Blackpool 1957–1969; Burnley 1970–1972. *Honours:* Five full England caps; Football League; England Amateur Cup 1959 (Loughborough College).

WILLIAMS, Danny. *Manager:* Rotherham U. 1962–1965; Swindon T. 1965–1969; Sheffield W. 1969–1971; Mansfield T. 1971; 1974; Swindon T. 1974– *Honours:* Swindon T. Football League Cup winners 1969; promotion to Division 2 1969. *Player:* Rotherham U. 1942–1962. *Honours:* Rotherham U., promotion to Division 2 1951.

YOUNG, Dick. *Manager:* Carlisle U. *Player:* Sheffield U. 1935–1949; Lincoln C. 1949–1957. *Honours:* Sheffield U., promotion to Division 1 1939.

BRITISH INTERNATIONAL FOOTBALL

International Review of the Season

In a black year for the international hopes of Britain, only Wales lit any warming flames of success. Unlike England, Scotland, and Northern Ireland they sustained their challenge for the European Championship beyond the qualifying groups and into the quarter-finals. It was a brave tilt at such illustrious windmills and certainly the principality's finest hour since the World Cup escapades of 1958.

They began the season needing a home victory over Austria, opponents who, in the Prater Stadium, had inflicted their only defeat the previous year. But on the night Austria were no match for the passion of the Wrexham crowd, whose frenetic support eroded their confidence and willed Wales to their target. The only goal had the air of schoolboy fiction, scored yet again by the local son, Arfon Griffiths; his fourth in the competition.

In many ways it typified the strength of the squad; the abrasive Yorath, the thoughtful Mahoney, the enthusiastic Flynn, and the shrewd experience of Griffiths provided a midfield which ensured Wales more than a fair share of possession and the ability to use it. The problem lay more in installing these four in advanced positions to score when the inevitable Toshack knock-downs dropped from James' crosses.

With only a disappointing centenary match against England on a foul night to bridge the five-month gap between the Austrian success and the quarter-final first leg, Mike Smith had more time than opportunity to sharpen his resources. In the end much of the pre-match planning for the game in Yugoslavia fell to nought in the face of a goal conceded inside 45 seconds when Yorath, feeling his feet, lost them on a damp surface. Even so, without ever threatening to equalise Wales only conceded one further goal in the second-half, to Popivoda.

Recovery at Ninian Park remained a possibility. 'We have a hill to climb, but we can do it,' was Smith's battle-cry. But in a combination of lack of discipline and lack of fortune, that hill soon became an unassailable mountain. The ill-luck came when the East German referee, Rudi Glockner, allowed Yugoslavia to take a free-kick inside their own half with the ball still rolling; the speed of this illegal ploy caught the Welsh defence unprepared and Page, in attempting to put the matter to rights, collided with Popivoda inside the area. Glockner, still some distance from the incident, gave a penalty and Katalinski scored.

Wales had already shown that the passion of the occasion was ruffling any attempt to play to a pattern. Both sides flung themselves at man and ball, in that order, and even though Evans made an in-road into the deficit with their first goal of the tie, Wales lost control of the game and themselves. Toshack, quite rightly, had two goals disallowed; Flynn, who had earlier hit a post from close range, missed another opportunity; and finally Yorath fluffed the last chance of recovery when his feeble penalty was saved by Maric. Sadly, what had been a great achievement by the Welsh ended in senseless violence as spectators threw cans at players and ran onto the pitch to further blacken the name of British crowds.

England's chances of entering the quarter-final draw had evaporated in a period of defensive disaster immediately before and after half-time in their match against Czechoslovakia in Bratislava. Yet the omens had been reasonably sound. The warm-up match in Switzerland, in which Revie had attempted to fool Czech spies by issuing his players with shirts numbered at random, had been won with comparative comfort after a strong opening with goals from Channon and Keegan plus a penalty-miss from the latter, and when fog interrupted the first attempt to start the match in Bratislava, England had begun well and Macdonald's unseen scoring shot was disallowed for offside.

Moreover, when the re-run unfolded the following day Channon put England in front. But a soft header by Nehoda at the near post put a very different complexion on the game in the last minute of the first half, and before the taste of the half-time tea had dried on their lips the England defence were chasing Masny's shadow and Gallis thumped in the winner. Three weeks later, needing nothing less than a win in Portugal to retain any hope, Revie's side could only draw after a display which again called into question the international class of several of its members.

Scotland's performances on the field had virtually condemned them to a place among the also-rans when another of their self-destructive off-the-field incidents meant that they went down with ignominy. The night life of Copenhagen held too much temptation

for five of their players after the 1-0 win over Denmark. Bremner, McKluskey, Young, Harper, and Duncan were banned indefinitely by the Scottish FA, a particularly sad end to the international career of the captain, Bremner.

Though Scotland also beat Denmark at Hampden Park, a 1-1 draw with Rumania reduced them to third place in Group 4. Northern Ireland went one place better in Group 3 without seriously threatening Yugoslavia. Their season began badly with a home defeat by Sweden, and though they competently beat Norway not even the brilliance of Pat Jennings, later in the year to become the most-capped Irishman in history, could salvage anything from the visit to Belgrade.

By the time of the British International Championship, England, Scotland, and Northern Ireland had embarked on rebuilding. Facing the first World Cup qualifier in Finland in June, Revie blooded Cherry, Kennedy, Thompson, Doyle, Neal, Clement, and Taylor in the Wales Centenary game and the Manchester United pair of Pearson and Greenhoff in the opening Championship game. Willie Ormond put his faith in Rough, a new goalkeeper from Partick Thistle, Forsyth of Rangers instead of Buchan in defence and Masson, from Queens Park Rangers, in midfield.

Well served by having all their three games at Hampden, Scotland began the competition with a 3-1 win over a reserve Welsh squad, Wales being forced to play twice in 36 hours because of a fixture reorganisation necessitated by Glasgow's staging of the European Cup final. The European Championship version of Mike Smith's squad then threatened to overrun England in the first half at Ninian Park, only to fall behind to a Peter Taylor goal and never catch up. On the same day Scotland, with Masson, a late entrant at such levels, in inspirational form, annihilated Northern Ireland; player-manager Dave Clements, commuting to the job from his newly acquired New York home, referred to his side's performance as 'a shambles'.

But three days later it was little better for Ireland at Wembley, where England won at a canter; and when they lost to a James goal in Cardiff, Clements' viability as a transatlantic manager was openly questioned. With England and Scotland both on four points, the scene was set for the traditional battle of Hampden Park, though Revie had to rebuff another blow when Peter Shilton announced that he found being second-choice for his country unsatisfactory and would be leaving the squad.

The description of what followed depended on your viewpoint; for the Scots it was undoubtedly a rousing triumph; for the majority of watching Englishmen it was overwhelmingly disappointing, for Don Revie it was a praiseworthy England performance. In fact Channon put England into an eleventh minute lead after some splendidly adventurous play by the recalled, but only partially-fit, McFarland. Masson, never renowned for his aerial prowess, headed in, unmarked, a corner for the equaliser. In the second half Clemence conceded the wining goal like a parks' keeper, through his legs. But his mistake only averted the criticism from those in front of him who were more deserving of it. Though a certain amount of self-respect was re-captured on tour in America, World Cup qualification at the end of the season looked to be more a mountain than a hill.

MAY 6

Scotland (2) 3 (*Pettigrew, Rioch, Gray E.*)
Wales (0) 1 (*Griffiths pen.*) (at Hampden Park) 35,000
Scotland: Rough; McGrain, Donachie, Forsyth (T), Jackson, Rioch, Pettigrew, Masson, Jordan, Gemmill, Gray (E).
Wales: Lloyd; Jones (D), Jones (J), Roberts (D), Roberts (J), Yorath, Griffiths, Harris (Cartwright), Curtis, O'Sullivan, James.

MAY 8

Wales (0) 0
England (0) 1 (*Taylor*) (at Ninian Park, Cardiff) 24,592
Wales: Davies; Thomas (Jones, D.), Page, Mahoney, Phillips, Evans, Yorath, Flynn, Curtis (Griffiths), Toshack, James.
England: Clemence; Clement, Mills, Towers, Greenhoff, Thompson, Keegan, Francis, Pearson, Kennedy, Taylor.

Scotland (2) 3 (*Gemmill, Masson, Dalglish*)
Northern Ireland (0) 0 (*at Hampden Park*) 49,897
Scotland: Rough; McGrain, Donachie, Forsyth (T), Jackson, Rioch (Hartford), Masson, Gemmill, Pettigrew (Johnstone), Jordan, Dalglish.
Northern Ireland: Jennings; Scott, Nicholl (C), Hunter, Rice, Hamilton, Cassidy, Sharkey (McCreery), McIlroy, Morgan (Spence), Finney.

MAY 11

England (2) 4 (*Francis, Channon 2, 1 pen., Pearson*)
Northern Ireland (0) 0 (at Wembley) 50,000
England: Clemence; Todd, Mills, Thompson, Greenhoff, Kennedy, Keegan (Royle), Francis, Pearson, Channon, Taylor (Towers).
Northern Ireland: Jennings; Rice, Nelson (Scott), Clements, Hunter, Nicholl (C), Hamilton, Cassidy, McCreery, Spence, McIlroy.

MAY 14

Wales (1) 1 (*James*)
Northern Ireland (0) 0 (*at Swansea*) 10,000
Wales: Davies; Phillips, Page, Mahoney, Roberts (D), Evans, Griffiths, Flynn, Yorath, Curtis, James.
Northern Ireland: Jennings; Scott, Rice, Nicholl (C), Hunter, Clements, Hamilton, McIlroy, Spence (Morgan), Cassidy (Nicholl, J.), McCreery.

MAY 15

Scotland (1) 2 (*Masson, Dalglish*)
England (1) 1 (*Channon*) (at Hampden Park) 85,000
Scotland: Rough; McGrain, Donachie, Forsyth (T), Jackson, Rioch, Masson, Gemmill, Dalglish, Jordan, Gray (E) (Johnstone).
England: Clemence; Todd, Mills, Thompson, McFarland (Doyle), Kennedy, Keegan, Francis, Pearson (Cherry), Channon, Taylor.

FINAL TABLE

	P	W	D	L	F	A	Pts.
Scotland	3	3	0	0	8	2	6
England	3	2	0	1	6	2	4
Wales	3	1	0	2	2	4	2
Northern Ireland	3	0	0	3	0	8	0

BRITISH HOME INTERNATIONALS

INTERNATIONAL CHAMPIONSHIP WINNERS 1883-1975

Year	Champions	Pts.	Year	Champions	Pts.	Year	Champions	Pts
1883–84	Scotland	6	1912–13	England	4	1953–54	England	6
1884–85	Scotland	5	1913–14	Ireland	5	1954–55	England	6
1885–86 {	England	5	1919–20	Wales	4	1955–56 {	England	3
	Scotland	5	1920–21	Scotland	6		Scotland	3
1886–87	Scotland	6	1921–22	Scotland	4		Wales	3
1887–88	England	6	1922–23	Scotland	5		Ireland	3
1888–89	Scotland	5	1923–24	Wales	6	1956–57	England	5
1889–90 {	Scotland	5	1924–25	Scotland	6	1957–58 {	England	4
	England	5	1925–26	Scotland	6		Ireland	4
1890–91	England	6	1926–27 {	Scotland	4	1958–59 {	Ireland	4
1891–92	England	6		England	4		England	4
1892–93	England	6	1927–28	Wales	5	1959–60 {	England	4
1893–94	Scotland	5	1928–29	Scotland	6		Scotland	4
1894–95	England	5	1929–30	England	6		Wales	4
1895–96	Scotland	5	1930–31 {	Scotland	4	1960–61	England	6
1896–97	Scotland	5		England	4	1961–62	Scotland	6
1897–98	England	6	1931–32	England	6	1962–63	Scotland	6
1898–99	England	6	1932–33	Wales	5	1963–64 {	Scotland	4
1899–1900	Scotland	6	1933–34	Wales	5		England	4
1900–01	England	5	1934–35 {	England	4		Ireland	4
1901–02	Scotland	5		Scotland	4	1964–65	England	5
1902–03 {	England	4	1935–36	Scotland	4	1965–66	England	5
	Ireland	4	1936–37	Wales	6	1966–67	Scotland	5
	Scotland	4	1937–38	England	4	1967–68	England	5
1903–04	England	5	1938–39 {	England	4	1968–69	England	6
1904–05	England	5		Scotland	4	1969–70 {	England	4
1905–06 {	England	4		Wales	4		Scotland	4
	Scotland	4	1946–47	England	5		Wales	4
1906–07	Wales	5	1947–48	England	5	1970–71	England	5
1907–08 {	Scotland	5	1948–49	Scotland	6	1971–72 {	England	4
	England	5	1949–50	England	6		Scotland	4
1908–09	England	6	1950–51	Scotland	6	1972–73	England	6
1909–10	Scotland	4	1951–52 {	Wales	5	1973–74 {	England	4
1910–11	England	5		England	5		Scotland	4
1911–12 {	England	5	1952–53 {	England	4	1974–75	England	4
	Scotland	5		Scotland	4	1975–76	Scotland	6

ENGLAND v SCOTLAND

PLAYED: 94; England won 35, Scotland won 37, Drawn 22. GOALS: England 172, Scotland 161.

Year	Venue	Goals E.	S.	Year	Venue	Goals E.	S.	Year	Venue	Goals E.	S
1872	Glasgow	0	0	1896	Glasgow	1	2	1925	Glasgow	0	2
1873	Kennington Oval	4	2	1897	Crystal Palace	1	2	1926	Manchester	0	1
1874	Glasgow	1	2	1898	Glasgow	3	1	1927	Glasgow	2	1
1875	Kennington Oval	2	2	1899	Birmingham	2	1	1928	Wembley	1	5
1876	Glasgow	0	3	1900	Glasgow	1	4	1929	Glasgow	0	1
1877	Kennington Oval	1	3	1901	Crystal Palace	2	2	1930	Wembley	5	2
1878	Glasgow	2	7	1902	Birmingham	2	2	1931	Glasgow	0	2
1879	Kennington Oval	5	4	1903	Sheffield	1	2	1932	Wembley	3	0
1880	Glasgow	4	5	1904	Glasgow	1	0	1933	Glasgow	1	2
1881	Kennington Oval	1	6	1905	Crystal Palace	1	0	1934	Wembley	3	0
1882	Glasgow	1	5	1906	Glasgow	1	2	1935	Glasgow	0	2
1883	Sheffield	2	3	1907	Newcastle	1	1	1936	Wembley	1	1
1884	Glasgow	0	1	1908	Glasgow	1	1	1937	Glasgow	1	3
1885	Kennington Oval	1	1	1909	Crystal Palace	2	0	1938	Wembley	0	1
1886	Glasgow	1	1	1910	Glasgow	0	2	1939	Glasgow	2	1
1887	Blackburn	2	3	1911	Everton	1	1	1947	Wembley	1	1
1888	Glasgow	5	0	1912	Glasgow	1	1	1948	Glasgow	2	0
1889	Kennington Oval	2	3	1913	Chelsea	1	0	1949	Wembley	1	3
1890	Glasgow	1	1	1914	Glasgow	1	3	wc1950	Glasgow	1	0
1891	Blackburn	2	1	1920	Sheffield	5	4	1951	Wembley	2	3
1892	Glasgow	4	1	1921	Glasgow	0	3	1952	Glasgow	2	1
1893	Richmond	5	2	1922	Aston Villa	0	1	1953	Wembley	2	2
1894	Glasgow	2	2	1923	Glasgow	2	2	wc1954	Glasgow	4	2
1895	Everton	3	0	1924	Wembley	1	1	1955	Wembley	7	2

Year Venue	Goals E.	S.	Year Venue	Goals E.	S.	Year Venue	Goals E.	S.
1956 Glasgow	1	1	1964 Glasgow	0	1	1972 Glasgow	1	0
1957 Wembley	2	1	1965 Wembley	2	2	1973 Glasgow	5	0
1958 Glasgow	4	0	1966 Glasgow	4	3	1973 Wembley	1	0
1959 Wembley	1	0	EC1967 Wembley	2	3	1974 Glasgow	0	2
1960 Glasgow	1	1	EC1968 Glasgow	1	1	1975 Wembley	5	1
1961 Wembley	9	3	1969 Wembley	4	1	1976 Glasgow	1	2
1962 Glasgow	0	2	1970 Glasgow	0	0			
1963 Wembley	1	2	1971 Wembley	3	1			

WC = World Cup   EC = European Championship

ENGLAND v WALES

PLAYED: 89; England won 59, Wales won 11, Drawn 19. GOALS: England 232, Wales 82.

Year Venue	Goals E.	W.	Year Venue	Goals E.	W.	Year Venue	Goals E.	W.
1879 Kennington Oval	2	1	1908 Wrexham	7	1	WC1949 Cardiff	4	1
1880 Wrexham	3	2	1909 Nottingham	2	0	1950 Sunderland	4	2
1881 Blackburn	0	1	1910 Cardiff	1	0	1951 Cardiff	1	1
1882 Wrexham	3	5	1911 Millwall	3	0	1952 Wembley	5	2
1883 Kennington Oval	5	0	1912 Wrexham	2	0	WC1953 Cardiff	4	1
1884 Wrexham	4	0	1913 Bristol	4	3	1954 Wembley	3	2
1885 Blackburn	1	1	1914 Cardiff	2	0	1955 Cardiff	1	2
1886 Wrexham	3	1	1920 Highbury	1	2	1956 Wembley	3	1
1887 Kennington Oval	4	0	1921 Cardiff	0	0	1957 Cardiff	4	0
1888 Crewe	5	1	1922 Liverpool	1	0	1958 Aston Villa	2	2
1889 Stoke-on-Trent	4	1	1923 Cardiff	2	2	1959 Wembley	1	1
1890 Wrexham	3	1	1924 Blackburn	1	2	1960 Wembley	5	1
1891 Sunderland	4	1	1925 Swansea	2	1	1961 Cardiff	1	1
1892 Wrexham	2	0	1926 Crystal Palace	1	3	1962 Wembley	4	0
1893 Stoke	6	0	1927 Wrexham	3	3	1963 Cardiff	4	0
1894 Wrexham	5	1	1927 Burnley	1	2	1964 Wembley	2	1
1894 Queen's Club, Kensington	1	1	1928 Swansea	3	2	1965 Cardiff	0	0
1896 Cardiff	9	1	1929 Chelsea	6	0	EC1966 Wembley	5	1
1897 Sheffield	4	0	1930 Wrexham	4	0	EC1967 Cardiff	3	0
1898 Wrexham	3	0	1931 Liverpool	3	1	1969 Wembley	2	1
1899 Bristol	4	0	1932 Wrexham	0	0	1970 Cardiff	1	1
1900 Cardiff	1	1	1933 Newcastle	1	2	1971 Wembley	0	0
1901 Newcastle	6	0	1934 Cardiff	4	0	1972 Cardiff	3	0
1902 Wrexham	0	0	1936 Wolverhampton	1	2	WC1972 Cardiff	1	0
1903 Portsmouth	2	1	1936 Cardiff	1	2	WC1973 Wembley	1	1
1904 Wrexham	2	2	1937 Middlesbrough	2	1	1973 Wembley	3	0
1905 Liverpool	3	1	1938 Cardiff	2	4	1974 Cardiff	2	0
1906 Cardiff	1	0	1946 Manchester	3	0	1975 Wembley	2	2
1907 Fulham	1	1	1947 Cardiff	3	0	1976 Wrexham	2	1
			1948 Aston Villa	1	0	1976 Cardiff	1	0

ENGLAND v IRELAND

PLAYED: 83; England won 64, Ireland won 6, Drawn 13. GOALS: England 293, Ireland 77.

Year Venue	Goals E.	I.	Year Venue	Goals E.	I.	Year Venue	Goals E.	I.
1882 Belfast	13	0	1905 Middlesbrough	1	1	1932 Blackpool	1	0
1883 Liverpool	7	0	1906 Belfast	5	0	1933 Belfast	3	0
1884 Belfast	8	1	1907 Everton	1	0	1935 Everton	2	1
1885 Manchester	4	0	1908 Belfast	3	1	1935 Belfast	3	1
1886 Belfast	6	1	1909 Bradford	4	0	1936 Stoke	3	1
1887 Sheffield	7	0	1910 Belfast	1	1	1937 Belfast	5	1
1888 Belfast	5	1	1911 Derby	2	1	1938 Manchester	7	0
1889 Everton	6	1	1912 Dublin	6	1	1946 Belfast	7	2
1890 Belfast	9	1	1913 Belfast	1	2	1947 Everton	2	2
1891 Wolverhampton	6	1	1914 Middlesbrough	0	3	1948 Belfast	6	2
1892 Belfast	2	0	1919 Belfast	1	1	WC1949 Manchester	9	2
1893 Birmingham	6	1	1920 Sunderland	2	0	1950 Belfast	4	1
1894 Belfast	2	2	1921 Belfast	1	1	1951 Aston Villa	2	0
1895 Derby	9	0	1922 West Bromwich	2	0	1952 Belfast	2	2
1896 Belfast	2	0	1923 Belfast	1	2	WC1953 Everton	3	1
1897 Nottingham	6	0	1924 Everton	3	1	1954 Belfast	2	0
1898 Belfast	3	2	1925 Belfast	0	0	1955 Wembley	3	0
1899 Sunderland	13	2	1926 Liverpool	3	3	1956 Belfast	1	1
1900 Dublin	2	0	1927 Belfast	0	2	1957 Wembley	2	3
1901 Southampton	3	0	1928 Everton	2	1	1958 Belfast	3	3
1902 Belfast	1	0	1929 Belfast	3	0	1959 Wembley	2	1
1903 Wolverhampton	4	0	1930 Sheffield	5	1	1960 Belfast	5	2
1904 Belfast	3	1	1931 Belfast	6	2	1961 Wembley	1	1

Year	Venue	E.	I.	Year	Venue	E.	I.	Year	Venue	E.	I.
1962	Belfast	3	1	EC1967	Wembley	2	0	1973	Everton	2	1
1963	Wembley	8	3	1969	Belfas.	3	1	1974	Wembley	1	0
1964	Belfast	4	3	1970	Wembley	3	1	1975	Belfast	0	0
1965	Wembley	2	1	1971	Belfast	1	0	1976	Wembley	4	0
EC1966	Belfast	2	0	1972	Wembley	0	1				

SCOTLAND v WALES

PLAYED: 89; Scotland won 54, Wales won 15, Drawn 20. GOALS: Scotland 227, Wales 102.

Year	Venue	S.	W.	Year	Venue	S.	W.	Year	Venue	S.	W.
1876	Glasgow	4	0	1905	Wrexham	1	3	1946	Wrexham	1	3
1877	Wrexham	2	0	1906	Edinburgh	0	2	1947	Glasgow	1	2
1878	Glasgow	9	0	1907	Wrexham	0	1	1948	Cardiff	3	1
1879	Wrexham	3	0	1908	Dundee	2	1	1949	Glasgow	2	0
1880	Glasgow	5	1	1909	Wrexham	2	3	wc1950	Cardiff	3	1
1881	Wrexham	5	1	1910	Kilmarnock	1	0	1951	Glasgow	0	1
1882	Glasgow	5	0	1911	Cardiff	2	2	1952	Cardiff	2	1
1883	Wrexham	4	1	1912	Tynecastle	1	0	1953	Glasgow	3	3
1884	Glasgow	4	1	1913	Wrexham	0	0	wc1954	Cardiff	1	0
1885	Wrexham	8	1	1914	Glasgow	0	0	1955	Glasgow	2	0
1886	Glasgow	4	1	1920	Cardiff	1	1	1956	Cardiff	2	2
1887	Wrexham	2	0	1921	Aberdeen	2	1	1957	Glasgow	1	1
1888	Edinburgh	5	1	1922	Wrexham	1	2	1958	Cardiff	3	0
1889	Wrexham	0	0	1923	Paisley	2	0	1959	Glasgow	1	1
1890	Paisley	5	0	1924	Cardiff	0	2	1960	Cardiff	0	2
1891	Wrexham	4	3	1925	Tynecastle	3	1	1961	Glasgow	2	0
1892	Edinburgh	6	1	1926	Cardiff	3	0	1962	Cardiff	3	2
1893	Wrexham	8	0	1927	Glasgow	3	0	1963	Glasgow	2	1
1894	Kilmarnock	5	2	1928	Wrexham	2	2	1964	Cardiff	2	3
1895	Wrexham	2	2	1929	Glasgow	4	2	1965	Glasgow	4	1
1896	Dundee	4	0	1930	Cardiff	4	2	EC1966	Cardiff	1	1
1897	Wrexham	2	2	1931	Glasgow	1	1	EC1967	Glasgow	3	2
1898	Motherwell	5	2	1932	Wrexham	3	2	1969	Wrexham	5	3
1899	Wrexham	6	0	1933	Edinburgh	2	5	1970	Glasgow	0	0
1900	Aberdeen	5	2	1934	Cardiff	2	3	1971	Cardiff	0	0
1901	Wrexham	1	1	1935	Aberdeen	3	2	1972	Glasgow	1	0
1902	Greenock	5	1	1936	Cardiff	1	1	1973	Wrexham	2	0
1903	Cardiff	1	0	1937	Dundee	1	2	1974	Glasgow	2	0
1904	Dundee	1	1	1938	Cardiff	1	2	1975	Cardiff	2	2
				1939	Edinburgh	3	2	1976	Glasgow	3	1

SCOTLAND v IRELAND

PLAYED 81; Scotland won 57, Ireland won 13, Drawn 11. GOALS: Scotland 244, Ireland 75.

Year	Venue	S.	I.	Year	Venue	S.	I.	Year	Venue	S.	I.
1884	Belfast	5	0	1911	Glasgow	2	0	1949	Belfast	8	2
1885	Glasgow	8	2	1912	Belfast	4	1	1950	Glasgow	6	1
1886	Belfast	7	2	1913	Dublin	2	1	1951	Belfast	3	0
1887	Glasgow	4	1	1914	Belfast	1	1	1952	Glasgow	1	1
1888	Belfast	10	2	1920	Glasgow	3	0	1953	Belfast	3	1
1889	Glasgow	7	0	1921	Belfast	2	0	1954	Glasgow	2	2
1890	Belfast	4	1	1922	Glasgow	2	1	1955	Belfast	1	2
1891	Glasgow	2	1	1923	Belfast	1	0	1956	Glasgow	1	0
1892	Belfast	3	2	1924	Glasgow	2	0	1957	Belfast	1	1
1893	Glasgow	6	1	1925	Belfast	3	0	1958	Glasgow	2	2
1894	Belfast	2	1	1926	Glasgow	4	0	1959	Belfast	4	0
1895	Glasgow	3	1	1927	Belfast	2	0	1960	Glasgow	5	2
1896	Belfast	3	3	1928	Glasgow	0	1	1961	Belfast	6	1
1897	Glasgow	5	1	1929	Belfast	7	3	1962	Glasgow	5	1
1898	Belfast	3	0	1930	Glasgow	3	1	1963	Belfast	1	2
1899	Glasgow	9	1	1931	Belfast	0	0	1964	Glasgow	3	2
1900	Belfast	3	0	1932	Glasgow	3	1	1965	Belfast	2	3
1901	Glasgow	11	0	1933	Belfast	4	0	1966	Glasgow	2	1
1902	Belfast	5	1	1934	Glasgow	1	2	1967	Belfast	0	1
1903	Glasgow	0	2	1935	Belfast	1	2	1969	Glasgow	1	1
1904	Dublin	1	1	1936	Edinburgh	2	1	1970	Belfast	1	0
1905	Glasgow	4	0	1937	Belfast	3	1	1971	Glasgow	0	1
1906	Dublin	1	0	1938	Aberdeen	1	1	1972	Glasgow	2	0
1907	Glasgow	3	0	1939	Belfast	2	0	1973	Glasgow	1	2
1908	Dublin	5	0	1946	Glasgow	0	0	1974	Glasgow	0	1
1909	Glasgow	5	0	1947	Belfast	0	2	1975	Glasgow	3	0
1910	Belfast	0	1	1948	Glasgow	3	2	1976	Glasgow	3	0

WALES v IRELAND

PLAYED: 83; Wales won 39, Ireland won 26, Drawn 18. GOALS: Wales 173, Ireland 122.

Year	Venue	Goals W.	Goals L.	Year	Venue	Goals W.	Goals L.	Year	Venue	Goals W.	Goals L.
1882	Wrexham	7	1	1910	Wrexham	4	1	WC1950	Wrexham	0	0
1883	Belfast	1	1	1911	Belfast	2	1	1951	Belfast	2	1
1884	Wrexham	6	0	1912	Cardiff	2	3	1952	Swansea	3	0
1885	Belfast	8	2	1913	Belfast	1	0	1953	Belfast	3	2
1886	Wrexham	5	0	1914	Wrexham	1	2	WC1954	Wrexham	1	2
1887	Belfast	1	4	1920	Belfast	2	2	1955	Belfast	3	2
1888	Wrexham	11	0	1921	Swansea	2	1	1956	Cardiff	1	1
1889	Belfast	3	1	1922	Belfast	1	1	1957	Belfast	0	0
1890	Shrewsbury	5	2	1923	Wrexham	0	3	1958	Cardiff	1	1
1891	Belfast	2	7	1924	Belfast	1	0	1959	Belfast	1	4
1892	Bangor	1	1	1925	Wrexham	0	0	1960	Wrexham	3	2
1893	Belfast	3	4	1926	Belfast	0	3	1961	Belfast	5	1
1894	Swansea	4	1	1927	Cardiff	2	2	1962	Cardiff	4	0
1895	Belfast	2	2	1928	Belfast	2	1	1963	Belfast	4	1
1896	Wrexham	6	1	1929	Belfast	2	2	1964	Cardiff	2	3
1897	Belfast	3	4	1930	Belfast	0	7	1965	Belfast	5	0
1898	Llandudno	0	1	1931	Wrexham	3	2	1966	Cardiff	1	4
1899	Belfast	0	1	1932	Belfast	0	4	EC1967	Belfast	0	0
1900	Llandudno	2	0	1933	Wrexham	4	1	EC1968	Wrexham	2	0
1901	Belfast	1	0	1934	Belfast	1	1	1969	Belfast	0	0
1902	Cardiff	0	3	1935	Wrexham	3	1	1970	Swansea	1	0
1903	Belfast	0	2	1936	Belfast	2	3	1971	Belfast	0	1
1904	Bangor	0	1	1937	Wrexham	4	1	1972	Wrexham	0	0
1905	Belfast	2	2	1938	Belfast	0	1	1973	Everton	0	1
1906	Wrexham	4	4	1939	Wrexham	3	1	1974	Belfast	1	0
1907	Belfast	3	2	1947	Belfast	1	2	1975	Belfast	0	1
1908	Aberdare	0	1	1948	Wrexham	2	0	1976	Wrexham	1	0
1909	Belfast	3	2	1949	Belfast	2	0				

OTHER BRITISH INTERNATIONAL AND REPRESENTATIVE MATCHES 1975-76

Basle, Sept. 3 1975
Switzerland 1 (*Muller*)
England 2 (*Keegan, Channon*)   25,000
Switzerland: Burgener; Guyot, Stohler, Trinchero, Fischback, Schild, Hasler, Botterton, Pfister, Muller Jeandupeux.
England: Clemence; Whitworth, Todd, Watson, Beattie, Bell, Currie, Francis, Channon, Johnson (Macdonald), Keegan.

Tel Aviv, March 3 1976
Israel 1 (*Damti*)
N. Ireland 1 (*Lev o.g.*)   9000
Israel: Surinov; Lev, Barr, Bendor, Nimni, Schum, Oz, Schwitzer (Malmillina), Damti, Barad (Peretz), Levental.
N. Ireland: Jennings (Platt); Scott, Nicholl J., Hunter, Rice, Blair, Nelson, Hamilton, Anderson (McGrath), Spence, Feeney.

Wrexham, March 24 1976
Wales 1 (*Curtis*)
England 2 (*Kennedy, Taylor*)   20,927
Wales: Lloyd; Page, Jones, Yorath, Phillips, Evans, Harris, Flynn, Curtis, Roberts, J., Griffiths.
England: Clemence; Cherry (Clement), Mills, Neal, Thompson, Doyle, Keegan, Channon (Taylor), Boyer, Brooking, Kennedy.

Hampden Park, April 7 1976
Scotland 1 (*Pettigrew*)
Switzerland 0   10,000
Scotland: Rough; McGrain, Gray F., Forsyth, Blackley, Craig, Dalglish (Bremner D.), Pettigrew (McKean), Gray A., MacDonald, Johnstone.
Switzerland: Burgener; Stohler, Fischback, Bizzini, Guyot, Hasler (Andrey), Elsener, (Schnyder) Muller, Risi, Botteron, Jeandupeux.

Los Angeles, May 23 1976
Brazil 1 (*Roberto*)
England 0   33,000
Brazil: Leao; Orlando, Miguel, Beto, Marco Antonio (Marinho), Falcao, Rivelino, Zico, Gil, Neca (Roberto), Lula.
England: Clemence; Todd, Doyle, Thompson, Mills, Francis, Cherry, Brooking, Keegan, Pearson, Channon.

New York, May 28 1976
Italy 2 (*Graziani* 2)
England 3 (*Channon* 2, *Thompson*)   42,000
Italy: Zoff; Roggi (Maldera), Rocca, Benetti (Zaccarelli), Bellugi, Facchetti, Causio (Sala), Capello, Graziani, Antognoni, Pulici.
England: Rimmer (Corrigan); Clement, Neal (Mills), Thompson, Doyle, Towers, Wilkins, Brooking, Royle, Channon, Hill.

Philadelphia, May 31 1976
Team America 1 (*Scullion*)
England 3 (*Keegan* 2, *Francis*)   16,231
Team America: Rigby; Smith B., Jump, Eddy, England (Kowalik), Moore, Vee (Scullion), Smith T. Chinaglia, Pele, Clements (Chandler).
England: Clemence; Todd (Doyle), Mills, Thompson, Greenhoff, Cherry, Keegan (Taylor), Channon, Pearson, Brooking, Francis.

INTER-LEAGUE 1892-1976

FOOTBALL LEAGUE v SCOTTISH LEAGUE
Played 69. England won 38; Scotland 18; drawn 13

Year	Venue	Goals F.L.	S.L.	Year	Venue	Goals F.L.	S.L.	Year	Venue	Goals F.L.	SL..
1892	Bolton	2	2	1920	Glasgow	4	0	1951	Glasgow	0	1
1893	Glasgow	4	3	1921	Highbury	1	0	1952	Sheffield	2	1
1894	Liverpool	1	1	1922	Glasgow	3	0	1953	Glasgow	0	1
1895	Glasgow	4	1	1923	Newcastle	2	1	1954	Stamford Bdge	4	0
1896	Liverpool	5	1	1924	Glasgow	1	1	1955	Glasgow	2	3
1897	Glasgow	0	3	1925	Everton	4	3	1956	Sheffield	4	2
1898	Birmingham	1	2	1926	Glasgow	2	0	1957	Glasgow	2	3
1899	Glasgow	4	1	1927	Leicester	2	2	1958	Newcastle	4	1
1900	London	2	2	1928	Glasgow	6	2	1959	Glasgow	1	1
1901	Glasgow	2	6	1929	Birmingham	2	1	1960	Highbury	1	0
1902	Newcastle	6	3	1930	Glasgow	1	2	1961	Glasgow	2	3
1903	Glasgow	3	0	1931	Tottenham	7	3	1962	Birmingham	3	4
1904	Manchester	2	1	1932	Glasgow	3	4	1963	Not played		
1905	Glasgow	3	2	1933	Manchester	0	3	1964	Sunderland	2	2
1906	London	6	2	1934	Glasgow	2	2	1965	Glasgow	2	2
1907	Glasgow	0	0	1935	Stamford Bdge	2	1	1966	Newcastle	1	3
1908	Birmingham	2	0	1936	Glasgow	2	2	1967	Glasgow	3	0
1909	Glasgow	1	3	1937	Everton	2	1	1968	Middlesbrough	2	0
1910	Blackburn	2	3	1938	Glasgow	0	1	1969	Glasgow	3	1
1911	Glasgow	1	1	1939	Wolverh'ton	3	0	1970	Coventry	3	2
1912	Middlesbrough	2	0	1940–46	Not played			1971	Glasgow	1	0
1913	Glasgow	1	4	1947	Glasgow	3	1	1972	Middlesbrough	3	2
1914	Burnley	2	3	1948	Newcastle	1	1	1973	Glasgow	2	2
1915	Glasgow	4	1	1949	Glasgow	3	0	1974	Maine Road	5	0
1916–18	Not played			1950	Middlesbrough	3	1	1976	Glasgow	1	0

FOOTBALL LEAGUE v IRISH LEAGUE
Played 61. England won 54; Ireland 3; drawn 4

Year	Venue	Goals F.L.	I.L.	Year	Venue	Goals F.L.	I.L.	Year	Venue	Goals F.L.	I.L.
1894	Belfast	4	2	1916–19	Not played			1947	Everton	4	2
1895	Not played			1920	Liverpool	2	2	1948	Belfast	4	3
1896	Stoke	2	2	1921	Not played			1949	Liverpool	5	1
1897	Belfast	2	0	1922	Belfast	1	0	1950	Belfast	3	1
1898	Manchester	8	1	1923	Bolton	5	1	1951	Blackpool	6	3
1899	Belfast	5	1	1924	Belfast	9	2	1952	Belfast	9	0
1900	Bolton	3	1	1925	Belfast	5	0	1953	Wolverh'ton	7	1
1901	Belfast	4	2	1926	Liverpool	5	1	1954	Belfast	5	0
1902	Woolwich	9	0	1927	Belfast	6	1	1955	Liverpool	4	2
1903	Belfast	3	2	1928	Newcastle	9	1	1956	Belfast	2	5
1904	Bradford	2	1	1929	Belfast	5	0	1957	Newcastle	3	2
1905	Belfast	2	0	1930	Everton	5	2	1958	Belfast	4	2
1906	Manchester	4	0	1931	Belfast	2	2	1959	Liverpool	5	2
1970	Belfast	6	0	1932	Blackpool	4	0	1960	Belfast	5	0
1908	Sunderland	6	3	1933	Belfast	5	2	1961	Blackpool	5	2
1909	Belfast	5	0	1934	Preston	4	0	1962	Belfast	6	1
1910	Oldham	8	1	1935	Belfast	6	1	1963	Norwich	3	1
1911	Belfast	6	2	1936	Blackpool	1	2	1964	Belfast	4	0
1912	Liverpool	4	0	1937	Belfast	2	3	1966	Plymouth	12	0
1913	Belfast	0	0	1938	Blackpool	3	0	1968	Belfast	1	0
1914	Belfast	2	0	1939	Belfast	8	2	1970	Norwich	5	0
1915	West Bromwich	2	1	1940–46	Not played						

SCOTTISH LEAGUE v IRISH LEAGUE
Played 60. Scotland won 55, Ireland 5

Year	Venue	Goals S.L.	I.L.	Year	Venue	Goals S.L.	I.L.	Year	Venue	Goals S.L.	I.L.
1893	Belfast	2	3	1899	Belfast	1	3	1905–8	Not played		
1894	Glasgow	6	2	1900	Edinburgh	6	0	1909	Belfast	2	1
1895	Belfast	4	1	1901	Belfast	2	1	1910	Glasgow	2	0
1896	Glasgow	3	2	1902	Dundee	3	0	1911	Belfast	3	1
1897	Belfast	2	0	1903	Belfast	0	1	1912	Glasgow	3	0
1898	Dundee	5	0	1904	Paisley	3	1	1913	Belfast	3	1

Year	Venue	Goals S.L.	Goals I.L.	Year	Venue	Goals S.L.	Goals I.L.	Year	Venue	Goals S.L.	Goals I.L.
1914	Belfast	2	1	1932	Belfast	2	3	1952	Glasgow	3	0
1915	Belfast	2	1	1933	Glasgow	4	1	1953	Belfast	5	1
1916–19	Not played			1934	Belfast	0	3	1954	Glasgow	4	0
1920	Belfast	2	0	1935	Glasgow	3	2	1955	Belfast	5	1
1921	Glasgow	3	0	1936	Belfast	3	2	1956	Glasgow	3	0
1922	Glasgow	3	0	1937	Glasgow	5	2	1957	Belfast	7	1
1923	Glasgow	3	0	1938	Belfast	3	2	1958	Glasgow	7	0
1924	Belfast	1	0	1939	Glasgow	6	1	1959	Belfast	5	0
1925	Edinburgh	3	0	1939†	Belfast	3	2	1960	Glasgow	7	1
1926	Belfast	7	3	1940–46	Not played			1961	Belfast	2	1
1927	Edinburgh	5	2	1947	Belfast	7	4	1962	Glasgow	7	0
1928	Belfast	2	1	1948	Glasgow	3	0	1964	Belfast	4	1
1929	Glasgow	8	2	1949	Belfast	1	0	1966	Glasgow	6	2
1930	Belfast	4	1	1950	Glasgow	8	1	1968	Belfast	2	0
1931	Glasgow	5	0	1951	Belfast	4	0	1970	Glasgow	5	2

†Played in season 1939–40 prior to the outbreak of war.

SCOTTISH LEAGUE v LEAGUE OF IRELAND

Year	Venue	Goals S.L.	Goals L.o.I.	Year	Venue	Goals S.L.	Goals L.o.I.	Year	Venue	Goals S.L.	Goals L.o.I.
1938	Dublin	1	2	1955	Glasgow	5	0	1962	Dublin	1	1
1948	Dublin	2	0	1956	Dublin	4	2	1963	Glasgow	11	0
1949	Glasgow	5	1	1957	Glasgow	3	1	1965	Dublin	2	2
1950	Dublin	1	0	1958	Dublin	5	1	1967	Glasgow	6	0
1951	Glasgow	7	0	1959	Glasgow	1	0	1969	Dublin	0	0
1952	Dublin	2	0	1960	Dublin	4	1	1970	Glasgow	1	0
1953	Glasgow	5	1	1961	Glasgow	5	1	1971	Glasgow	1	0
1954	Dublin	3	1								

FOOTBALL LEAGUE v LEAGUE OF IRELAND

Year	Venue	Goals F.L.	Goals L.o.I.	Year	Venue	Goals F.L.	Goals L.o.I.	Year	Venue	Goals F.L.	Goals L.o.I.
1947	Dublin	3	1	1954	Manchester	9	1	1961	Dublin	4	0
1948	Preston	4	0	1955	Dublin	6	0	1962	Bristol	5	2
1949	Dublin	5	0	1956	Everton	5	1	1963	Dublin	1	2
1950	Wolverh'ton	7	0	1957	Dublin	3	3	1965	Hull	5	0
1951	Dublin	1	0	1958	Leeds	3	1	1967	Dublin	7	2
1952	Liverpool	9	1	1959	Dublin	0	0	1969	Barnsley	3	0
1953	Dublin	2	0	1960	Blackburn	2	0	1972	Dublin	2	1

THE LEAGUE v SOUTHERN LEAGUE

	T.L.	S.L.			T.L.	S.L.			T.L.	S.L.
1909–10 Chelsea	2	2	1911–12 Stoke		2	1	1913–14 Millwall		3	1
1910–11 Tottenham	2	3	1912–13 Manchester		2	1	1914–15 Highbury		2	1

FOOTBALL LEAGUE v INTERNATIONAL FOOTBALL COMBINATION OF DENMARK

	F.L.	I.F.C.
1952–53 Copenhagen	4	0

FOOTBALL LEAGUE v ITALIAN LEAGUE

Year	Venue	F.L.	I.L.	Year	Venue	F.L.	I.L.	Year	Venue	F.L.	I.L.
1961	Milan	2	4	1962	Old Trafford	0	2	1963	Highbury	3	2
								1964	Milan	0	1

FOOTBALL LEAGUE v BELGIAN LEAGUE

Year	Venue	F.L.	B.L.
1967	Brussels	2	2

OTHER BRITISH INTERNATIONAL RESULTS 1908-1976

ENGLAND

v ARGENTINA

Year	Date		Venue	Goals England	Argentina
1951	May	9	Wembley	2	1
1953	May	17	Buenos Aires	0	0
			(abandoned 21 mins)		
wc1962	June	2	Rancagua	3	1
1964	June	6	Rio de Janeiro	0	1
wc1966	July	23	Wembley	1	0
1974	May	22	Wembley	2	2

v AUSTRIA

Year	Date		Venue	Goals England	Austria
1908	June	6	Vienna	6	1
1908	June	8	Vienna	11	1
1909	June	1	Vienna	8	1
1930	May	14	Vienna	0	0
1932	Dec.	7	Chelsea	4	3
1936	May	6	Vienna	1	2
1951	Nov.	28	Wembley	2	2
1952	May	25	Vienna	3	2
wc1958	June	15	Boras	2	2
1961	May	27	Vienna	1	3
1962	April	4	Wembley	3	1
1965	Oct.	20	Wembley	2	3
1967	May	27	Vienna	1	0
1973	Sept.	26	Wembley	7	0

v BELGIUM

Year	Date		Venue	England	Belgium
1921	May	21	Brussels	2	0
1923	Mar.	19	Highbury	6	1
1923	Nov.	1	Antwerp	2	2
1924	Dec.	8	West Bromwich	4	0
1926	May	24	Antwerp	5	3
1927	May	11	Brussels	9	1
1928	May	19	Antwerp	3	1
1929	May	11	Brussels	5	1
1931	May	16	Brussels	4	1
1936	May	9	Brussels	2	3
1947	Sept.	21	Brussels	5	2
1950	May	18	Brussels	4	1
1952	Nov.	26	Wembley	5	0
wc1954	June	17	Basle	4	4*
1964	Oct.	21	Wembley	2	2
1970	Feb.	25	Brussels	3	1

v BOHEMIA

Year	Date		Venue	England	Bohemia
1908	June	13	Prague	4	0

v BRAZIL

Year	Date		Venue	England	Brazil
1956	May	9	Wembley	4	2
wc1958	June	11	Gothenburg	0	0
1959	May	13	Rio de Janeiro	0	2
wc1962	June	10	Vina del Mar	1	3
1963	May	8	Wembley	1	1
1964	May	30	Rio de Janeiro	1	5
1969	June	12	Rio de Janeiro	1	2
wc1970	June	7	Guadalajara	0	1
1976	May	23	Los Angeles	0	1

v BULGARIA

Year	Date		Venue	Goals England	Bulgaria
wc1962	June	7	Rancagua	0	0
1968	Dec.	11	Wembley	1	1
1974	June	1	Sofia	1	0

v CHILE

Year	Date		Venue	England	Chile
wc1950	June	25	Rio de Janeiro	2	0
1953	May	24	Santiago	2	1

v COLOMBIA

Year	Date		Venue	England	Colombia
1970	May	20	Bogota	4	0

v CYPRUS

Year	Date		Venue	England	Cyprus
EC1975	Apr.	16	Wembley	5	0
EC1975	May	11	Limassol	1	0

v CZECHOSLOVAKIA

Year	Date		Venue	England	Czecho-slovakia
1934	May	16	Prague	1	2
1937	Dec.	1	Tottenham	5	4
1963	May	29	Bratislava	4	2
1966	Nov.	2	Wembley	0	0
wc1970	June	11	Guadalajara	1	0
1973	May	27	Prague	1	1
EC1974	Oct.	30	Wembley	3	0
EC1975	Oct.	30	Bratislava	1	2

v DENMARK

Year	Date		Venue	England	Denmark
1948	Sept.	26	Copenhagen	0	0
1955	Oct.	2	Copenhagen	5	1
wc1956	Dec.	5	Wolverhampton	5	2
wc1957	May	15	Copenhagen	4	1
1966	July	3	Copenhagen	2	0

v ECUADOR

Year	Date		Venue	England	Ecuador
1970	May	24	Quito	2	0

v FIFA

Year	Date		Venue	England	FIFA
1938	Oct.	26	Highbury	3	0
1953	Oct.	21	Wembley	4	4
1963	Oct.	23	Wembley	2	1

v FINLAND

Year	Date		Venue	England	Finland
1937	May	20	Helsinki	8	0
195(	May	20	Helsinki	5	1
196(	June	26	Helsinki	3	0

v FRANCE

Year	Date		Venue	England	France
1923	May	10	Paris	4	1
1924	May	17	Paris	3	1
1925	May	21	Paris	3	2
1927	May	26	Paris	6	0
1928	May	17	Paris	5	1
1929	May	9	Paris	4	1
1931	May	14	Paris	2	5
1933	Dec.	6	Tottenham	4	1
1938	May	26	Paris	4	2

* After extra time.

Year	Date	Venue	Goals England	Goals France
1947	May 3	Highbury	3	0
1949	May 22	Paris	3	1
1951	Oct. 3	Highbury	2	2
1955	May 15	Paris	0	1
1957	Nov. 27	Wembley	4	0
ENC1962	Oct. 3	Sheffield	1	1
ENC1963	Feb. 27	Paris	2	5
WC1966	July 20	Wembley	2	0
1969	Mar. 12	Wembley	5	0

v EAST GERMANY

Year	Date	Venue	England	Germany
1963	June 2	Leipzig	2	1
1970	Nov. 25	Wembley	3	1
1974	May 29	Leipzig	1	1

v WEST GERMANY

Year	Date	Venue	England	Germany
1930	May 10	Berlin	3	3
1935	Dec. 4	Tottenham	3	0
1938	May 14	Berlin	6	3
1954	Dec. 1	Wembley	3	1
1956	May 26	Berlin	3	1
1965	May 12	Nuremberg	1	0
1966	Feb. 23	Wembley	1	0
WC1966	July 30	Wembley	4	2*
1968	June 1	Hanover	0	1
WC1970	June 14	Leon	2	3*
EC1972	April 29	Wembley	1	3
EC1972	May 13	Berlin	0	0
1975	Mar. 12	Wembley	2	0

v GREECE

Year	Date	Venue	England	Greece
EC1971	Apr. 21	Wembley	3	0
EC1971	Dec. 1	Athens	2	0

v HUNGARY

Year	Date	Venue	England	Hungary
1908	June 10	Budapest	7	0
1909	May 29	Budapest	4	2
1909	May 31	Budapest	8	2
1934	May 10	Budapest	1	2
1936	Dec. 2	Highbury	6	2
1953	Nov. 25	Wembley	3	6
1954	May 23	Budapest	1	7
1960	May 22	Budapest	0	2
WC1962	May 31	Rancagua	1	2
1965	May 5	Wembley	1	0

v REPUBLIC OF IRELAND

Year	Date	Venue	England	Rep. of Ireland
1946	Sept. 30	Dublin	1	0
1949	Sept. 21	Everton	0	2
WC1957	May 8	Wembley	5	1
WC1957	May 19	Dublin	1	1
1964	May 24	Dublin	3	1

v ITALY

Year	Date	Venue	England	Italy
1933	May 13	Rome	1	1
1934	Nov. 14	Highbury	3	2
1939	May 13	Milan	2	2
1948	May 16	Turin	4	0
1949	Nov. 30	Tottenham	2	0
1952	May 18	Florence	1	1
1959	May 6	Wembley	2	2
1961	May 24	Rome	3	2
1973	June 14	Turin	0	2
1973	Nov. 14	Wembley	0	1
1976	May 28	New York	3	2

v LUXEMBOURG

Year	Date	Venue	Goals England	Goals Luxembourg
1927	May 21	Luxembourg	5	2
WC1960	Oct. 19	Luxembourg	9	0
WC1961	Sept. 28	Highbury	4	1

v MALTA

Year	Date	Venue	England	Malta
EC1971	Feb. 3	Valletta	1	0
EC1971	May 12	Wembley	5	0

v MEXICO

Year	Date	Venue	England	Mexico
1959	May 24	Mexico City	1	2
1961	May 10	Wembley	8	0
WC1966	July 16	Wembley	2	0
1969	June 1	Mexico City	0	0

v NETHERLANDS

Year	Date	Venue	England	Netherlands
1935	May 18	Amsterdam	1	0
1946	Nov. 27	Huddersfield	8	2
1964	Dec. 9	Amsterdam	1	1
1969	Nov. 5	Amsterdam	1	0
1970	Jan. 14	Wembley	0	0

v NORWAY

Year	Date	Venue	England	Norway
1937	May 14	Oslo	6	0
1938	Nov. 9	Newcastle	4	0
1949	May 18	Oslo	4	1
1966	June 29	Oslo	6	1

v PERU

Year	Date	Venue	England	Peru
1959	May 17	Lima	1	4
1962	May 20	Lima	4	0

v POLAND

Year	Date	Venue	England	Poland
1966	Jan. 5	Everton	1	1
1966	July 5	Chorzow	1	0
WC1973	June 6	Chorzow	0	2
WC1973	Oct. 17	Wembley	1	1

v PORTUGAL

Year	Date	Venue	England	Portugal
1947	May 25	Lisbon	10	0
1950	May 14	Lisbon	5	3
1951	May 19	Everton	5	2
1955	May 22	Oporto	1	3
1958	May 7	Wembley	2	1
WC1961	May 21	Lisbon	1	1
WC1961	Oct. 25	Wembley	2	0
1964	May 17	Lisbon	4	3
1964	June 4	São Paulo	1	1
WC1966	July 26	Wembley	2	1
1969	Dec. 10	Wembley	1	0
1974	April 3	Lisbon	0	0
EC1974	Nov. 20	Wembley	0	0
EC1975	Nov. 19	Lisbon	1	1

v RUMANIA

Year	Date	Venue	England	Rumania
1939	May 24	Bucharest	2	0
1968	Nov. 6	Bucharest	0	0
1969	Jan. 15	Wembley	1	1
WC1970	June 2	Guadalajara	1	0

v SPAIN

Year	Date	Venue	England	Spain
1929	May 15	Madrid	3	4
1931	Dec. 9	Highbury	7	1
WC1950	July 2	Rio de Janeiro	0	1
1955	May 18	Madrid	1	1
1955	Nov. 30	Wembley	4	1

Year	Date		Venue	Goals	
1960	May	15	Madrid	0	3
1960	Oct.	26	Wembley	4	2
1965	Dec.	8	Madrid	2	0
1967	May	24	Wembley	2	0
EC1968	April	3	Wembley	1	0
EC1968	May	8	Madrid	2	1

v SWEDEN

Year	Date		Venue	England	Sweden
1923	May	21	Stockholm	4	2
1923	May	24	Stockholm	3	1
1937	May	17	Stockholm	4	0
1947	Nov.	19	Highbury	4	2
1949	May	13	Stockholm	1	3
1956	May	16	Stockholm	0	0
1959	Oct.	28	Wembley	2	3
1965	May	16	Gothenburg	2	1
1968	May	22	Wembley	3	1

v SWITZERLAND

Year	Date		Venue	England	Switz
1933	May	20	Berne	4	0
1938	May	21	Zurich	1	2
1947	May	18	Zurich	0	1
1948	Dec.	2	Highbury	6	0
1952	May	28	Zurich	3	0
wc1954	June	20	Berne	2	0
1962	May	9	Wembley	3	1
1963	June	5	Basle	8	1
EC1971	Oct.	13	Basle	3	2
EC1971	Nov.	10	Wembley	1	1
1975	Sept.	3	Basle	2	1

v USA

Year	Date		Venue	England	USA
wc1950	June	29	Belo Horizonte	0	1
1953	June	8	New York	6	3
1959	May	28	Los Angeles	8	1
1964	May	27	New York	10	0

v USSR

Year	Date		Venue	England	USSR
1958	May	18	Moscow	1	1
wc1958	June	8	Gothenburg	2	2
wc1958	June	17	Gothenburg	0	1
1958	Oct.	22	Wembley	5	0
1967	Dec.	6	Wembley	2	2
ENC1968	June	8	Rome	2	0
1973	June	10	Moscow	2	1

v URUGUAY

Year	Date		Venue	England	Uruguay
1953	May	31	Montevideo	1	2
wc1954	June	26	Basle	2	4
1964	May	6	Wembley	2	1
wc1966	July	11	Wembley	0	0
1969	June	8	Montevideo	2	1

v YUGOSLAVIA

Year	Date		Venue	England	Yugo-slavia
1939	May	18	Belgrade	1	2
1950	Nov.	22	Highbury	2	2
1954	May	16	Belgrade	0	1
1956	Nov.	28	Wembley	3	0
1958	May	11	Belgrade	0	5
1960	May	11	Wembley	3	3
1965	May	9	Belgrade	1	1
1966	May	4	Wembley	2	0
EC1968	June	5	Florence	0	1
1972	Oct.	11	Wembley	1	1
1974	June	5	Belgrade	2	2

SCOTLAND

v AUSTRIA

Year	Date		Venue	Scotland	Au
1931	May	16	Vienna	0	5
1933	Nov.	29	Glasgow	2	2
1937	May	9	Vienna	1	1
1950	Dec.	13	Glasgow	0	1
1951	May	27	Vienna	0	4
wc1954	June	16	Zurich	0	1
1955	May	19	Vienna	4	1
1956	May	2	Glasgow	1	1
1960	May	29	Vienna	1	4
1963	May	8	Glasgow	4	1
			(abandoned after 79 mins.)		
wc1968	Nov.	6	Glasgow	2	1
wc1969	Nov.	5	Vienna	0	2

v BELGIUM

Year	Date		Venue	Scotland	Belgium
1947	May	18	Brussels	1	2
1948	April	28	Glasgow	2	0
1951	May	20	Brussels	5	0
EC1971	Feb.	3	Liege	0	3
EC1971	Nov.	10	Glasgow	1	0
1974	June	2	Brussels	1	2

v BRAZIL

Year	Date		Venue	Scotland	Brazil
1966	June	25	Glasgow	1	1
1972	July	5	Rio	0	1
1973	June	30	Glasgow	0	1
wc1974	June	18	Frankfurt	0	0

v CYPRUS

Year	Date		Venue	Scotland	Cyprus
wc1968	Dec.	17	Nicosia	5	0
wc1969	May	11	Glasgow	8	0

v CZECHOSLOVAKIA

Year	Date		Venue	Scotland	Czecho-slovakia
1937	May	22	Prague	3	1
1937	Dec.	8	Glasgow	5	0
wc1961	May	14	Bratislava	0	4
wc1961	Sept.	26	Glasgow	3	2
wc1961	Nov.	29	Brussels	2	4*
1972	July	2	Porto Alegre	0	0
wc1973	Sept.	26	Glasgow	2	1
wc1973	Oct.	17	Prague	0	1

v DENMARK

Year	Date		Venue	Scotland	Denmark
1951	May	12	Glasgow	3	1
1952	May	25	Copenhagen	2	1
1968	Oct.	16	Copenhagen	1	0
EC1970	Nov.	11	Glasgow	1	0
EC1971	June	9	Copenhagen	0	1
WC1972	Oct.	18	Copenhagen	4	1
WC1972	Nov.	15	Glasgow	2	0
EC1975	Sept.	3	Copenhagen	1	0
EC1975	Oct.	29	Glasgow	3	1

v FINLAND

				Scotland	Finland
1954	May	25	Helsinki	2	1
WC1964	Oct.	21	Glasgow	3	1
WC1965	May	27	Helsinki	2	1

v FRANCE

				Scotland	France
1930	May	18	Paris	2	0
1932	May	8	Paris	3	1
1948	May	23	Paris	0	3
1949	April	27	Glasgow	2	0
1950	May	27	Paris	1	0
1951	May	16	Glasgow	1	0
WC1958	June	15	Orebro	1	2

v EAST GERMANY

				Scotland	E. Germany
1974	Oct.	30	Glasgow	3	0

v WEST GERMANY

				Scotland	West Germany
1929	June	1	Berlin	1	1
1936	Oct.	14	Glasgow	2	0
1957	May	22	Stuttgart	3	1
1959	May	6	Glasgow	3	2
1964	May	12	Hanover	2	2
WC1969	April	16	Glasgow	1	1
WC1969	Oct.	22	Hamburg	2	3
1973	Nov.	14	Glasgow	1	1
1974	Mar.	27	Frankfurt	1	2

v HUNGARY

				Scotland	Hungary
1938	Dec.	7	Glasgow	3	1
1954	Dec.	8	Glasgow	2	4
1955	May	29	Budapest	1	3
1958	May	7	Glasgow	1	1
1960	June	5	Budapest	3	3

v ITALY

				Scotland	Italy
1931	May	20	Rome	0	3
WC1965	Nov.	9	Glasgow	1	0
WC1965	Dec.	7	Naples	0	3

v LUXEMBOURG

				Scotland	Luxembourg
1947	May	24	Luxembourg	6	0

v NETHERLANDS

				Scotland	Netherlands
1929	June	4	Amsterdam	2	0
1938	May	21	Amsterdam	3	1
1959	May	27	Amsterdam	2	1
1966	May	11	Glasgow	0	3
1968	May	30	Amsterdam	0	0
1971	Dec.	1	Rotterdam	1	2

v NORWAY

Year	Date		Venue	Scotland	Norway
1929	May	28	Oslo	7	3
1954	May	5	Glasgow	1	0
1954	May	19	Oslo	1	1
1963	June	4	Bergen	3	4
1963	Nov.	7	Glasgow	6	1
1974	June	6	Oslo	2	1

v PARAGUAY

				Scotland	Paraguay
WC1958	June	11	Norrkoping	2	3

v PERU

				Scotland	Peru
1972	April	26	Glasgow	2	0

v POLAND

				Scotland	Poland
1958	June	1	Warsaw	2	1
1960	May	4	Glasgow	2	3
WC1965	May	23	Chorzow	1	1
WC1965	Oct.	13	Glasgow	1	2

v PORTUGAL

				Scotland	Portugal
1950	May	21	Lisbon	2	2
1955	May	4	Glasgow	3	0
1959	June	3	Lisbon	0	1
1966	June	18	Glasgow	0	1
EC1971	April	21	Lisbon	0	2
EC1971	Oct.	13	Glasgow	2	1
1975	May	13	Glasgow	1	0

v RUMANIA

				Scotland	Rumania
EC1975	June	1	Bucharest	1	1
EC1975	Dec.	17	Glasgow	1	1

v SPAIN

				Scotland	Spain
WC1957	May	8	Glasgow	4	2
WC1957	May	26	Madrid	1	4
1963	June	13	Madrid	6	2
1965	May	8	Glasgow	0	0
EC1974	Nov.	20	Glasgow	1	2
EC1975	Feb.	5	Valencia	1	1

v SWEDEN

				Scotland	Sweden
1952	May	30	Stockholm	1	3
1953	May	6	Glasgow	1	2
1975	April	16	Gothenburg	1	1

v SWITZERLAND

				Scotland	Switz.
1931	May	24	Geneva	3	2
1948	May	17	Berne	1	2
1950	April	26	Glasgow	3	1
WC1957	May	19	Basle	2	1
WC1957	Nov.	6	Glasgow	3	2
1973	June	22	Berne	0	1
1976	Apr.	7	Glasgow	1	0

v TURKEY

				Scotland	Turkey
1960	June	8	Ankara	2	4

v URUGUAY

Year Date	Venue	Scotland	Uruguay
wc1954 June 19	Basle	0	7
1962 May 2	Glasgow	2	3

v USA

Year Date	Venue	Scotland	USA
1952 April 30	Glasgow	6	0

v USSR

Year Date	Venue	Scotland	USSR
1967 May 10	Glasgow	0	2
1971 June 14	Moscow	0	1

v YUGOSLAVIA

Year Date	Venue	Scotland	Yugo.
1955 May 15	Belgrade	2	2
1956 Nov. 21	Glasgow	2	0
wc1958 June 8	Vasteras	1	1
1972 June 29	Belo Horizonte	2	2
wc1974 June 22	Frankfurt	1	1

v ZAIRE

Year Date	Venue	Scotland	Zaire
wc1974 June 14	Dortmund	2	0

WALES

v AUSTRIA

		Wales	Austria
1954 May 9	Vienna	0	2
1955 Nov 23	Wrexham	1	2
EC1974 Sept. 4	Vienna	1	2
EC1975 Nov. 19	Wrexham	1	0

v BELGIUM

		Wales	Belgium
1949 May 22	Liege	1	3
1949 Nov. 23	Cardiff	5	1

v BRAZIL

		Wales	Brazil
wc1958 June 19	Gothenburg	0	1
1962 May 12	Rio de Janeiro	1	3
1962 May 16	São Paulo	1	3
1966 May 14	Rio de Janeiro	1	3
1966 May 18	Belo Horizonte	0	1

v CHILE

		Wales	Chile
1966 May 22	Santiago	0	2

v CZECHOSLOVAKIA

		Wales	Czecho-slovakia
wc1957 May 1	Cardiff	1	0
wc1957 May 26	Prague	0	2
EC1971 April 21	Swansea	1	3
EC1971 Oct. 27	Prague	0	1

v DENMARK

		Wales	Denmark
wc1964 Oct. 21	Copenhagen	0	1
wc1965 Dec. 1	Wrexham	4	2

v FINLAND

		Wales	Finland
EC1971 May 26	Helsinki	1	0
EC1971 Oct. 13	Swansea	3	0

v FRANCE

		Wales	France
1933 May 25	Paris	1	1
1939 May 20	Paris	1	2
1953 May 14	Paris	1	6

v EAST GERMANY

		Wales	East Germany
wc1957 May 19	Leipzig	1	2
wc1957 Sept. 25	Cardiff	4	1
wc1969 April 16	Dresden	1	2
wc1969 Oct. 22	Cardiff	1	3

v WEST GERMANY

		Wales	West Germany
1968 May 8	Cardiff	1	1
1969 Mar. 26	Frankfurt	1	1

v GREECE

		Wales	Greece
wc1964 Dec. 9	Athens	0	2
wc1965 Mar. 17	Cardiff	4	1

v HUNGARY

		Wales	Hungary
wc1958 June 8	Sanviken	1	1
wc1958 June 17	Stockholm	2	1
1961 May 28	Budapest	2	3
ENC1962 Nov. 7	Budapest	1	3
ENC1963 Mar. 20	Cardiff	1	1
EC1974 Oct. 30	Cardiff	2	0
EC1975 Apr. 16	Budapest	2	1

v ISRAEL

		Wales	Israel
wc1958 Jan. 15	Tel Aviv	2	0
wc1958 Feb. 5	Cardiff	2	0

v ITALY

		Wales	Italy
1965 May 1	Florence	1	4
wc1968 Oct. 23	Cardiff	0	1
wc1969 Nov. 4	Rome	1	4

v LUXEMBOURG

		Wales	Luxembourg
EC1974 Nov. 20	Swansea	5	0
EC1975 May 1	Luxembourg	3	1

v MEXICO

		Wales	Mexico
wc1958 June 11	Stockholm	1	1
1962 May 22	Mexico City	1	2

v POLAND

		Wales	Poland
wc1973 Mar. 28	Cardiff	2	0
wc1973 Sept. 26	Katowice	0	3

v PORTUGAL

		Wales	Portugal
1949 May 15	Lisbon	2	3
1951 May 12	Cardiff	2	1

v REPUBLIC OF IRELAND

Year Date	Venue	Goals	
		Wales	Rep. of Ireland
1960 Sept. 28	Dublin	3	2

v RUMANIA

		Wales	Rumania
EC1970 Nov. 11	Cardiff	0	0
EC1971 Nov. 24	Bucharest	0	2

v SPAIN

		Wales	Spain
wc1961 April 19	Cardiff	1	2
wc1961 May 18	Madrid	1	1

v SWEDEN

		Wales	Sweden
wc1958 June 15	Stockholm	0	0

v SWITZERLAND

Year Date	Venue	Goals	
		Wales	Switz.
1949 May 26	Berne	0	4
1951 May 16	Wrexham	3	2

v REST OF UNITED KINGDOM

		Wales	U.K.
1951 Dec. 5	Cardiff	3	2
1969 July 28	Cardiff	0	1

v USSR

		Wales	USSR
wc1965 May 30	Moscow	1	2
wc1965 Oct. 27	Cardiff	2	1

v YUGOSLAVIA

		Wales	Yugoslavia
1953 May 21	Belgrade	2	5
1954 Nov. 22	Cardiff	1	3
EC1976 April 24	Zagreb	0	2
EC1976 May 22	Cardiff	1	1

NORTHERN IRELAND

v ALBANIA

		North. Ireland	Albania
wc1965 May 7	Belfast	4	1
wc1965 Nov. 24	Tirana	1	1

v ARGENTINA

		North. Ireland	Argentina
wc1958 June 11	Halmstad	1	3

v BULGARIA

		North. Ireland	Bulgaria
wc1972 Oct. 18	Sofia	0	3
wc1973 Sept. 26	Sheffield	0	0

v CYPRUS

		North Ireland	Cyprus
EC1971 Feb. 3	Nicosia	3	0
EC1971 April 21	Belfast	5	0
wc1973 Feb. 14	Nicosia	0	1
wc1973 May 8	London	3	0

v CZECHOSLOVAKIA

		North. Ireland	Czechoslovakia
wc1958 June 8	Halmstad	1	0
wc1958 June 17	Malmo	2	1*

v FRANCE

		North. Ireland	France
1951 May 12	Belfast	2	2
1952 Nov 11	Paris	1	3
wc1958 June 19	Norrkoping	0	4

v WEST GERMANY

		North. Ireland	West Germany
wc1958 June 15	Malmo	2	2
wc1960 Oct. 26	Belfast	3	4
wc1961 May 10	Hamburg	1	2
1966 May 7	Belfast	0	2

v GREECE

		North. Ireland	Greece
wc1961 May 3	Athens	1	2
wc1961 Oct. 17	Belfast	2	0

v ISRAEL

		North. Ireland	Israel
1968 Sept. 10	Jaffa	3	2

v ITALY

		North. Ireland	Italy
wc1957 April 25	Rome	0	1
1957 Dec. 4	Belfast	2	2
wc1958 Jan. 15	Belfast	2	1
1961 April 25	Bologna	2	3

v MEXICO

		North. Ireland	Mexico
1966 June 22	Belfast	4	1

v NETHERLANDS

		North. Ireland	Netherlands
1962 May 9	Rotterdam	0	4
wc1965 Mar. 17	Belfast	2	1
wc1965 April 7	Rotterdam	0	0

v NORWAY

		North. Ireland	Norway
EC1974 Sept. 4	Oslo	1	2
EC1975 Oct. 29	Belfast	3	0

v POLAND

		North. Ireland	Poland
ENC1962 Oct. 10	Katowice	2	0
ENC1962 Nov. 28	Belfast	2	0

v PORTUGAL

		North. Ireland	Portugal
wc1957 Jan. 16	Lisbon	1	1
wc1957 May 1	Belfast	3	0
wc1973 Mar. 28	Coventry	1	1
wc1973 Nov. 14	Lisbon	1	1

* After extra time.

v SPAIN

Year	Date		Venue	Goals North. Ireland	Spain
1958	Oct.	15	Madrid	2	6
1963	May	30	Bilbao	1	1
1963	Oct.	30	Belfast	0	1
EC1970	Nov.	11	Seville	0	3
EC1972	Feb.	16	Hull	1	1

v SWEDEN

				North. Ireland	Sweden
EC1974	Oct.	30	Solna	2	0
EC1975	Sept.	3	Belfast	1	2

v SWITZERLAND

				North. Ireland	Switzerland
wc1964	Oct.	14	Belfast	1	0
wc1964	Nov.	14	Lausanne	1	2

v TURKEY

Year	Date		Venue	Goals N. Ireland	Turkey
wc1968	Oct.	23	Belfast	4	1
wc1968	Dec.	11	Istanbul	3	0

v URUGUAY

				N. Ireland	Uruguay
1964	April	29	Belfast	3	0

v USSR

				N. Ireland	USSR
wc1969	Sept.	10	Belfast	0	0
wc1969	Oct.	22	Moscow	0	2
EC1971	Sept.	22	Moscow	0	1
EC1971	Oct.	13	Belfast	1	1

v YUGOSLAVIA

				North. Ireland	Yugoslavia
EC1975	Mar.	16	Belfast	1	0
EC1975	Nov.	19	Belgrade	0	1

REPUBLIC OF IRELAND

v ARGENTINA

				Rep. of Ireland	Argentina
1951	May	13	Dublin	0	1

v AUSTRIA

				Rep. of Ireland	Austria
1952	May	7	Vienna	0	6
1953	Mar.	25	Dublin	4	0
1958	Mar.	14	Vienna	1	3
1962	April	8	Dublin	2	3
ENC1963	Sept.	25	Vienna	0	0
ENC1963	Oct.	13	Dublin	3	2
1966	May	22	Vienna	0	1
1968	Nov.	10	Dublin	2	2
EC1971	May	30	Dublin	1	4
EC1971	Oct.	10	Linz	0	6

v BELGIUM

				Rep. of Ireland	Belgium
1928	Feb.	12	Liege	4	2
1929	April	30	Dublin	4	0
1930	May	11	Brussels	3	1
wc1934	Feb.	25	Dublin	4	4
1949	April	24	Dublin	0	2
1950	May	10	Brussels	1	5
1965	Mar.	24	Dublin	0	2
1966	May	25	Liege	3	2

v BRAZIL

				Rep. of Ireland	Brazil
1974	May	5	Rio de Janeiro	1	2

v CHILE

				Rep. of Ireland	Chile
1960	Mar.	30	Dublin	2	0
1972	Jun.	21	Recife	1	2
1974	May	12	Santiago	2	1

v CZECHOSLOVAKIA

				Rep. of Ireland	Czech.
1938	May	18	Prague	2	2
ENC1959	April	5	Dublin	2	0
ENC1959	May	10	Bratislava	0	4
wc1961	Oct.	8	Dublin	1	3
wc1961	Oct.	29	Prague	1	7
EC1967	May	21	Dublin	0	2
EC1967	Nov.	22	Prague	2	1
wc1969	May	4	Dublin	1	2
wc1969	Oct.	7	Prague	0	3

v DENMARK

				Rep. of Ireland	Denmark
wc1956	Oct.	3	Dublin	2	1
wc1957	Oct.	2	Copenhagen	2	0
wc1968	Dec.	4	Dublin	1	1

(abandoned after 51 mins.)

wc1969	May	27	Copenhagen	0	2
wc1969	Oct.	15	Dublin	1	1

v ECUADOR

				Rep. of Ireland	Ecuador
1972	June	19	Natal	3	2

v FINLAND

				Rep. of Ireland	Finland
wc1949	Sept.	8	Dublin	3	0
wc1949	Oct.	9	Helsinki	1	1

v FRANCE

				Rep. of Ireland	France
1937	May	23	Paris	2	0
1952	Nov.	16	Dublin	1	1
wc1953	Oct.	4	Dublin	3	5
wc1953	Nov.	25	Paris	0	1
wc1972	Nov.	15	Dublin	2	1
wc1973	May	19	Paris	1	1

v WEST GERMANY

				Rep. of Ireland	West Germany
1935	May	8	Dortmund	1	3
1936	May	6	Cologne	1	4
1936	Oct.	17	Dublin	5	2
1939	May	23	Bremen	1	1
1951	Oct.	17	Dublin	3	2
1952	May	4	Cologne	0	3
1955	May	28	Hamburg	1	2
1956	Nov.	25	Dublin	3	0
1960	May	11	Dusseldorf	1	0
1966	May	4	Dublin	0	4
1970	May	9	Berlin	1	2

v HUNGARY

				Rep. of Ireland	Hungary
1934	Dec.	15	Dublin	2	4
1936	May	3	Budapest	3	3
1936	Dec.	6	Dublin	2	3
1939	Mar.	19	Cork	2	2
1939	May	18	Budapest	2	2
wc1969	June	8	Dublin	1	2
wc1969	Nov.	5	Budapest	0	4

v ICELAND

				Rep. of Ireland	Iceland
ENC1962	Aug.	12	Dublin	4	2
ENC1962	Sept.	2	Reykjavik	1	1

v LUXEMBOURG

				Rep. of Ireland	Luxembourg
wc1953	Oct.	28	Dublin	4	0
wc1954	Mar.	7	Luxembourg	1	0

v IRAN

				Rep. of Ireland	Iran
1972	June	18	Recife	2	1

v ITALY

				Rep. of Ireland	Italy
1926	Mar.	21	Turin	0	3
EC1970	Dec.	8	Rome	0	3
EC1971	May	10	Dublin	1	2

v NETHERLANDS

				Rep. of Ireland	Netherlands
1932	May	8	Amsterdam	2	0
1934	April	8	Amsterdam	2	5
1935	Dec.	8	Dublin	3	5
1955	May	1	Dublin	1	0
1956	May	10	Rotterdam	4	1

v NORWAY

Year	Date		Venue	Goals Rep. of Ireland	Norway
wc1937	Oct.	10	Oslo	2	3
wc1937	Nov.	7	Dublin	3	3
1950	Nov.	26	Dublin	2	2
1951	May	30	Oslo	3	2
1954	Nov.	8	Dublin	2	1
1955	May	25	Oslo	3	1
1960	Nov.	6	Dublin	3	1
1964	May	13	Oslo	4	1
1973	June	6	Oslo	1	1

v POLAND

Year	Date		Venue	Goals Rep. of Ireland	Poland
1938	May	22	Warsaw	0	6
1938	Nov.	13	Dublin	3	2
1958	May	11	Katowice	2	2
1958	Oct.	5	Dublin	2	2
1964	May	10	Cracow	1	3
1964	Oct.	25	Dublin	3	2
1968	May	15	Dublin	2	2
1968	Oct.	30	Katowice	0	1
1970	May	6	Dublin	1	2
1970	Sept.	23	Dublin	0	2
1973	May	16	Wroclaw	0	2
1973	Oct.	21	Dublin	1	0
1976	May	26	Posnan	2	0

v PORTUGAL

				Rep. of Ireland	Portugal
1946	June	16	Lisbon	1	3
1947	May	4	Dublin	0	2
1948	May	23	Lisbon	0	2
1949	May	22	Dublin	1	0
1972	June	25	Recife	1	2

v SCOTLAND

				Rep. of Ireland	Scotland
wc1961	May	3	Glasgow	1	4
wc1961	May	7	Dublin	0	3
1963	June	9	Dublin	1	0
1969	Sept.	21	Dublin	1	1

v SPAIN

				Rep. of Ireland	Spain
1931	April	26	Barcelona	1	1
1931	Dec.	13	Dublin	0	5
1946	June	23	Madrid	1	0
1947	Mar.	2	Dublin	3	2
1948	May	30	Barcelona	1	2
1949	June	12	Dublin	1	4
1952	June	1	Madrid	0	6
1955	Nov.	27	Dublin	2	2
ENC1964	Mar.	11	Seville	1	5
ENC1964	April	8	Dublin	0	2
wc1965	May	5	Dublin	1	0
wc1965	Oct.	27	Seville	1	4
wc1965	Nov.	10	Paris	0	1
EC1966	Oct.	23	Dublin	0	0
EC1966	Dec.	7	Valencia	0	2

v SWEDEN

				Rep. of Ireland	Sweden
wc1949	June	2	Stockholm	1	3
wc1949	Nov.	13	Dublin	1	3
1959	Nov.	1	Dublin	3	2
1960	May	18	Malmo	1	4
EC1970	Oct.	14	Dublin	1	1
EC1970	Oct.	28	Malmo	0	1

v SWITZERLAND	Rep. of Ireland	Switzerland
1935 May 5 Basle	0	1
1936 Mar. 17 Dublin	1	0
1937 May 17 Berne	1	0
1938 Sept. 18 Dublin	4	0
1948 Dec. : Dublin	0	1
EC1975 May 11 Dublin	2	1
EC1975 May 21 Berne	0	1

v TURKEY	Rep. of Ireland	Turkey
EC1966 Nov. 16 Dublin	2	1
EC1967 Feb. 22 Ankara	1	2
EC1974 Nov. 20 Izmir	1	1
EC1975 Oct. 29 Dublin	4	0

v URUGUAY	Rep. of Ireland	Uruguay
1974 May 8 Montevideo	0	2

v USSR	Rep. of Ireland	USSR
WC1972 Oct. 18 Dublin	1	2
WC1973 May 13 Moscow	0	1
EC 1974 Oct. 30 Dublin	3	0
EC 1975 May 18 Kiev	1	2

v YUGOSLAVIA	Rep. of Ireland	Yugoslavia
1955 Sept. 19 Dublin	1	4

WC denotes World Cup Match.
ENC denotes European Nations Championship Match.
EC is European Championship

INTERNATIONAL SCORERS 1946-76

(Up to and including 1-6-76)
ENGLAND

49	R. Charlton		D. Kevan		A. Peacock
44	J. Greaves		Own Goals		A. Ramsey
30	T. Finney		J. Connelly		J. Sewell
	N. Lofthouse		T. Paine		W. Wright
24	G. Hurst	6	J. Charlton	3	G. Francis
23	S. Mortensen		M. Macdonald	2	R. Allen
21	M. Peters		J. Mullen		W. Bradley
18	J. Haynes		J. Rowley		P. Broadbent
	R. Hunt	5	J. Atyeo		J. Brooks
16	M. Channon		E. Baily		G. Eastham
	T. Lawton		H. Carter		J. Froggatt
	T. Taylor		D. Edwards		R. Froggatt
13	M. Chivers		G. Hitchens		J. Haines
	R. Smith		K. Keegan		J. Hancocks
11	B. Douglas		S. Pearson		N. Hunter
	W. Mannion		F. Pickering		R. Moore
10	A. Clarke	4	H. Hassall		W. Perry
	R. Flowers		D. Revie		R. Pointer
	F. Lee		R. Robson		P. Taylor
	J. Milburn		J. Baker		F. Wignall
	D. Wilshaw		W. Elliott		F. Worthington
9	C. Bell		C. Grainger	1	A. A'Court
	R. Bentley		D. Johnson		G. Astall
8	A. Ball		S. Matthews		K. Beattie
	I. Broadis		J. Morris		S. Bowles
	J. Byrne		M. O'Grady		G. Bradford

B. Bridges
R. Crawford
A. Currie
E. Hughes
A. Kay
R. Kennedy
B. Kidd
R. Langton
C. Lawler
J. Lee
R. Marsh
L. Medley
J. Melia
A. Mullery
J. Nicholls
W. Nicholson
R. Parry
S. Pearson
J. Royle
M. Summerbee
L. Shackleton
N. Stiles
R. Tambling
P. Thomson
D. Viollet
K. Weller

(Note: highest pre-war total, Steve Bloomer, 28)

N. IRELAND

10 J.Crossan	4 E. McMorran	T. Casey	R. Ferguson
J.McIlroy	B. Hamilton	T. Harkin	J. Jones
9 G. Best	W. Simpson	D.Blanchflower	S. McCrory
W. Bingham	3 M. Harvey	T. Neill	H. Barr
W. Irvine	N. Lockhart	Own Goals	W. Humphries
P. McParland	E. McMordie	1 A. Stevenson	A. Hunter
8 D. Dougan	S. Morgan	R. Brennan	E. Welsh
7 S. Wilson	M. O'Neill	K. McGarry	W. Campbell
W. Cush	T. Anderson	R. Ferris	L. O'Kane
W. McAdams	2 P. Doherty	S. D'Arcy	S. McIlroy
6 J. McLaughlin	D. Clements	R. Walker	T. Cassidy
J. Nicholson	T. Finney	J. Blanchflower	C.Nicholl
5 S. Smyth	C. Tully	A. Elder	
D. Walsh	R. Peacock	W. Johnston	

(Note: highest pre-war totals, W. Gillespie 13, J. Bambrick 11)

SCOTLAND

30 D. Law	P. Lorimer	D. Masson	T. Docherty
22 L. Reilly	J. Mason	W. Pettigrew	H. Curran
13 W. Steel	G. Hamilton	J. Harper	A. Conn
12 A. Gilzean	J. Johnstone	C. Fleming	W. Fernie
11 C. Stein	3 G. Smith	T. Ring	T. Hutchison
10 R. Collins	E. Caldow	A. Robertson	K. Burns
K. Dalglish	W. Bremner	A. Gemmill	C. Jackson
R. Johnstone	L. Macari	S. Baird	D. Parlane
9 J. Mudie	D. Mackay	J. Hewie	G. McQueen
I. St. John	D. Herd	E. Gray	P. Quinn
D. Wilson	E. MacDougall	J. Holton	A. Weir
8 R. Brand	W. McNeill	1 T. Gemmell	J. Murray
G. Leggat	H. Morris	R. Combe	G. Mulhall
7 Own Goals	J. McPhail	D. Cuncan	W. Hunter
6 A. Brown	J. Baxter	G. Herd	F. McLintock
J. Jordan	J. White	H. Howie	J. McCalliog
W. Liddell	D. Gibson	A. Linwood	R. McKinnon
W. Waddell	R. Lennox	R. Mitchell	J. Hughes
5 A. Scott	J. Greig	T. Orr	T. McLean
A. Young	S. Chalmers	W. Thornton	L. Johnstone
R. Murdoch	G. Graham	J. Henderson	R. Campbell
W. Henderson	2 W. Bauld	J. McKenzie	W. Morgan
B. Rioch	R. Flavell	W. Ormond	J. Bone
J. O'Hare	W. Houliston	J. Davidson	S. Jardine
4 A. McLaren	J. McMillan	P. Buckley	

(Note: highest pre-war total, H. Gallagher, 24)

WALES

23 T. Ford	4 D. Tapscott	G. Reece	G. Williams
22 I. Allchurch	L. James	A. Durban	T. Hockey
16 C. Jones	3 D. Palmer	1 R. Paul	D. Smallman
15 J. Charles	R. Rees	A. Powell	J. Roberts
9 J. Toshack	M. England	R. Burgess	T. Yorath
8 R. Davies	P. Woosnam	W. Foulkes	J. Mahoney
R. Vernon	2 G. Lowrie	W. Barnes	B. Flynn
6 T. Medwin	G. Edwards	D. Bowen	A. Curtis
A. Griffiths	M. Griffiths	G. Moore	I. Evans
M. Charles	B. Godfrey	R. Hewitt	
5 R. Clarke	Bryn Jones	A. Powell	
K. Leek	Barrie Jones	R. Krzywicki	

(Note: highest pre-war total, D. Astley, 12)

REPUBLIC OF IRELAND

15 D. Givens	P. Farrell	F. O'Farrell	J. Mooney
14 N. Cantwell	A. Fogarty	J. Dennehy	T. Moroney
8 D. Curtis	J. Haverty	J. Conway	P. Mulligan
A. Fitzsimons	R. Ryan	T. Eglinton	F. O'Neill
7 A. Ringstead	M. Martin	E. Hand	J. O'Reilly
6 C. Martin	R. Treacy	1 P. Ambrose	W. Sloan
A. McEvoy	2 T. Conroy	J. Carey	F. Strahan
5 G. Cummins	S. Fallon	T. Carroll	T. Mancini
F. Fagan	P. Fitzgerald	J. Dempsey	L. Brady
E. Rogers	J. Gavin	B. Duffy	J. Holmes
D. Walsh	A. Hale	J. Fitzgerald	M. Walsh
4 J. Giles	C. Hurley	J. Fullam	
L. Tuohy	M. Leech	D. Glynn	
3 P. Coad	T. O'Connor	J. McCann	

(Note: highest pre-war total, J. Dunne, 14).

International Appearances

(as at June 2 1976)

This is a list of full international appearances by Englishmen, Irishmen, Scotsmen and Welshmen in matches against the Home Countries and against Foreign Nations. It does not include matches against Commonwealth and Empire countries.

Explanatory code for matches played by all four countries: A, represents Austria; Alb, Albania; Arg, Argentine; B, Bohemia; Bel, Belgium; Br, Brazil; Bul, Bulgaria; Ch, Chile; Co, Columbia; Cy, Cyprus; Cz, Czechoslovakia; D, Denmark; Ec, Ecuador; Ei, Eire; EG, East Germany; F, France; Fi, Finland; G, Germany (pre-war); Gr, Greece; H, Hungary; Ho, Holland; I, Italy; Is, Israel; L, Luxembourg; M, Mexico; Ma, Malta; N, Norway; Ni, Northern Ireland; P, Portugal; Par, Paraguay; Pe, Peru; Pol, Poland; R, Rumania, R of E, Rest of Europe; R of W, Rest of World; S, Scotland; Se, Sweden; Sp, Spain; Sw; Switzerland; T, Turkey; U, Uruguay; UK, Rest of United Kingdom; US, United States of America; USSR, Russia; W, Wales; WG, West Germany; Y, Yugoslavia. (Note; for purposes of this code, and in order to distinguish from Eire, Northern Ireland is given throughout the series as Ni).

ENGLAND

Abbott, W. (Everton), 1902 v W (1)

A'Court, A. (Liverpool), 1958 v Ni, Br, A, USSR; 1959 v W (5)

Adcock, H. (Leicester C.), 1929 v F, Bel, Sp; 1930 v Ni, W (5)

Alcock, C. W. (Wanderers), 1875 v S (1)

Alderson, J. T. (C. Palace), 1923 v F (1)

Aldridge, A. (W.B.A.), 1888 v Ni, (with Walsall Town Swifts), 1889 v Ni (2)

Allen, A. (Stoke C.), 1960 v Se, W, Ni (3)

Allen, A. (Aston Villa), 1888 v Ni (1)

Allen, H. (Wolverhampton W.), 1888 v S, W, Ni; 1889 v S: 1890 v S (5)

Allen, J. P. (Portsmouth), 1934 v Ni, W (2)

Allen, R. (W.B.A.), 1952 v Sw; 1954 v Y, S; 1955 v WG, W (5)

Alsford, W. J. (Tottenham H.), 1935 v S (1)

Amos, A. (Old Carthusians), 1885 v S; 1886 v W (2)

Anderson, R. D. (Old Etonians), 1879 v W (1)

Anderson, S. (Sunderland), 1962 v A, S (2)

Angus, J. (Burnley), 1961 v A (1)

Armfield, J. C. (Blackpool), 1959 v Br, Pe, M, US; 1960 v Y, Sp, H, S; 1961, L, P, Sp, M, I, A, Y, W, Ni, S; 1962, A, Sw, Pe, W, Ni, S, L, P, H, Arg, Bul, Br; 1963 v F (2), Br, EG, Sw, Ni, W, S; 1964 v R of W, W, Ni, S; 1966 v Y, Fi (43)

Armitage, G. H. (Charlton Ath.), 1926 v Ni (1)

Armstrong, K. (Chelsea), 1955 v S (1)

Arnold, J. (Fulham), 1933 v S (1)

Arthur, J. W. H. (Blackburn R.), 1885 v S, W, Ni; 1886 v S, W; 1887 v W, Ni (7)

Ashcroft, J. (Woolwich Arsenal), 1906 v Ni, W, S (3)

Ashmore, G. S. (W.B.A.), 1926 v Bel (1)

Ashton, C. T. (Corinthians), 1926 v Ni (1)

Ashurst, W. (Notts. Co.), 1923 v Se (2); 1925 v S, W, Bel (5)

Astall, G. (Birmingham C.), 1956 v Fi, WG (2)

Astle, J. (W.B.A.), 1969 v W; 1970 v S, P, Br (sub), Cz (5)

Aston, J. (Manchester U.), 1949 v S, W, D, Sw, Se, N, F; 1950 v S, W, Ni, Ei, I, P, Bel, Ch. US; 1951 v Ni (17)

Athersmith, W. C. (Aston Villa), 1892 v Ni; 1897 v S, W, Ni; 1898 v S, W, Ni: 1899 v S, W, Ni; 1900 v S, W (12)

Atyeo, P. J. W. (Bristol C.), 1956 v Br, Se, Sp; 1957 v D, Ei (2) (6)

Austin, S. W. (Manchester C.), 1926 v Ni (1)

Bach, P. (Sunderland), 1899 v Ni (1)

Bache, J. W. (Aston Villa), 1903 v W; 1904 v W, Ni; 1905 v S; 1907 v Ni; 1910 v Ni; 1911 v S (7)

Baddeley, T. (Wolverhampton W.), 1903 v S, Ni; 1904 v S, W, Ni (5)

Bagshaw, J. J. (Derby Co.), 1920 v Ni (1)

Bailey, H. P. (Leicester Fosse), 1908 v W, A (2), H, B (5)

Bailey, M. A. (Charlton Ath.), 1964 v US; 1965 v W (2)

Bailey, N. C. (Clapham Rovers), 1878 v S; 1879 v S, W; 1880 v S; 1881 v S; 1882 v S, W; 1883 v S, W; 1884 v S, W, Ni; 1885 v S, W, Ni; 1886 v S, W; 1887 v S, W (19)

Baily, E. F. (Tottenham H.), 1950 v Sp; 1951 v Y, Ni, W; 1952 v A (2), Sw, W; 1953 v Ni (9)

Bain, J. (Oxford University), 1887 v S (1)

Baker, A. (Arsenal), 1928 v W (1)

Baker, B. H. (Everton), 1921 v Bel; (with Chelsea), 1926 v Ni (2)

Baker, J. H. (Hibernian), 1960 v Y, Sp, H, Ni, S; (with Arsenal) 1966 v Sp, Pol. Ni (8)

Ball, A. J. (Blackpool), 1965 v Y. WG, Se; 1966 v S, Sp, Fi, D, U, Arg, P, WG (2), Pol (2); (Everton), 1967 v W, S, Ni, A, Cz, Sp; 1968, W, S, USSR, Sp (2), Y, WG; 1969 v Ni, W, S, R (2), M, Br, U; 1970 v P, Co, Ec. R, Br, Cz (sub), WG, W, S, Bel; 1971 v Ma, EG, Gr, Ma (sub), Ni, S; 1972 v Sw, Gr; (with Arsenal) WG (2), S; 1973 v W (3), Y, S (2) Cz, Ni, Pol; 1974 v P (sub); 1975 v WG, Cy (2), Ni, W, S (72)

Ball, J. (Bury), 1928 v Ni (1)

Balmer, W. (Everton), 1905 v Ni (1)

Bamber, J. (Liverpool), 1921 v W (1)

Bambridge, A. L. (Swifts), 1881 v W; 1883 v W; 1884 v Ni (3)

Bambridge, E. C. (Swifts), 1879 v S; 1880 v S; 1881 v S; 1882 v S, W, Ni; 1883 v W; 1884 v S, W, Ni; 1885 v S, W, Ni; 1886 v S, W; 1887 v S, W, Ni (18)

Bambridge, E. H. (Swifts), 1876 v S (1)

Banks, G. (Leicester C.), 1963 v S, Br, Cz, EG; 1964 v W, Ni, S, R of W, U, P (2), US, Arg; 1965 v Ni, S, H, Y, WG, Se; 1966 v Ni, S, Sp, Pol (2), WG (2), Y, Fi, U, M, F, Arg, P; 1967 v Ni, W, S, Cz; (with Stoke C.), 1968 v W, Ni, S, USSR (2), Sp, WG, Y; 1969 v Ni, S, R (2), F, U, Br; 1970 v W, Ni, S, Ho, Bel, Co, Ec, R, Br, Cz, 1971 v Gr, Ma (2), Ni, S; 1972 v Sw, Gr, WG (2), W, S (73)

Banks, H. E. (Millwall), 1901 v Ni (1)

Banks, T. (Bolton W.), 1958 v USSR (3), Br, A; 1959 v Ni (6)

Bannister, W. (Burnley), 1901 v W; (with Bolton W.), 1902 v Ni (2)

Barclay, R. (Sheffield W.), 1932 v S; 1933 v Ni; 1936 v S (3)

671

Barkas, S. (Manchester C.), 1936 v Bel; 1937 v S; 1938 v W, Ni, Cz (5)

Barker, J. (Derby Co.), 1935 v I, Ho, S, W, Ni; 1936 v G, A, S, W, Ni; 1937 v W (11)

Barker, R. (Herts Rangers), 1872 v S (1)

Barker, R. R. (Casuals), 1895 v W (1)

Barlow, R. J. (W.B.A.), 1955 v Ni (1)

Barnet, H. H. (Royal Engineers), 1882 v Ni (1)

Barrass, M. W. (Bolton W.), 1952 v W, Ni; 1953 v S (3)

Barrett, A. F. (Fulham), 1930 v Ni (1)

Barrett, J. W. (West Ham U.), 1929 v Ni (1)

Barry, L. (Leicester C.), 1928 v F, Bel; 1929 v F, Bel, Sp (5)

Barson, F. (Aston Villa), 1920 v W (1)

Barton, J. (Blackburn R.), 1890 v Ni (1)

Barton P. H. (Birmingham), 1921 v Bel; 1922 v Ni; 1923 v F; 1924 v Bel, S, W; 1925 v Ni (7)

Bassett, W. I. (W.B.A.), 1888 v Ni; 1889 v S, W; 1890 v S; 1891 v S, Ni; 1892 v S; 1893 v S, W; 1894 v S; 1895 v S, Ni; 1896 v S, W, Ni (16)

Bastard, S. R. (Upton Park), 1880 v S (1)

Bastin, C. S. (Arsenal), 1932 v W; 1933 v I, Sw; 1934 v S, Ni, W, H, Cz; 1935 v S, Ni, I; 1936 v S, W, G, A; 1937 v W, Ni; 1938 v S, G, Sw, F (21)

Baugh, R. (Stafford Road), 1886 v Ni; (with Wolverhampton W.) 1890 v Ni (2)

Bayliss, A. E. J. M. (W.B.A.), 1891 v Ni (1)

Baynham, R. L. (Luton T.), 1956 v Ni, D, Sp (3)

Beasley, A. (Huddersfield T.), 1939 v S (1)

Beats, W. E. (Wolverhampton W.), 1901 v W; 1902 v S (2)

Beattie, T. K. (Ipswich T.), 1975 v Cy (2), S; 1976 v Sw, P (5)

Becton, F. (Preston N.E.), 1895 v Ni; (with Liverpool); 1897 v W (2)

Bedford, H. (Blackpool), 1923 v Se; 1925 v Ni (2)

Bell, C. (Manchester C.), 1968 v Se, WG; 1969 v W, Bul, F, U, Br; 1970 v Ni (sub.), Ho (2), P, Br (sub), Cz, WG (sub); 1972 v Gr, WG (2), W, Ni, S; 1973 v W (3), Y, S (2), Ni, Cz, Pol; 1974 v A, Pol, I, W, Ni, S, Arg, EG, Bul, Y; 1975 v Cz, P, WG. Cy (2), Ni, S; 1976 v Sw, C2 (48)

Bennett, W. (Sheffield U.), 1901 v S, W (2)

Benson, R. W. (Sheffield U.), 1913 v Ni (1)

Bentley, R. T. F. (Chelsea), 1949 v Se; 1950 v S, P, Bel, Ch, USA; 1953 v W, Bel; 1955 v W, WG, Sp, P (12)

Beresford, J. (Aston Villa), 1934 v Cz (1)

Berry, A. (Oxford University), 1909 v Ni (1)

Berry, J. J. (Manchester U.), 1953 v Arg, Ch, U; 1956 v Se (4)

Bestall, J. G. (Grimsby T.), 1935 v Ni (1)

Betmead, H. A. (Grimsby T.), 1937 v Fi (1)

Betts, M. P. (Old Harrovians), 1877 v S (1)

Betts, W. (Sheffield W.), 1889 v W. (1)

Beverley, J. (Blackburn R.), 1884 v S, W, Ni (3)

Birkett, R. H. (Clapham Rovers), 1879 v S (1)

Birkett R. J. E. (Middlesbrough), 1936 v Ni (1)

Birley, F. H. (Oxford University), 1874 v S; (with Wanderers), 1875 v S (2)

Bishop, S. M. (Leicester C.), 1927 v S, Bel, L, F (4)

Blackburn, F. (Blackburn R.), 1901 v S; 1902 v Ni; 1904 v S (3)

Blackburn, G. F. (Aston Villa), 1924 v F (1)

Blenkinsop, E. (Sheffield W.), 1928 v F, Bel; 1929 v S, W, Ni, F, Bel, Sp; 1930 v S, W, Ni, G, A; 1931 v S, W, Ni, F, Bel; 1932 v S, W, Ni, Sp; 1933, S W, Ni, A (26)

Bliss, H. (Tottenham H.), 1921 v S (1)

Blockley, J. P. (Arsenal), 1973 v Y (1)

Bloomer, S. (Derby Co.), 1895 v S, Ni; 1896 v W,

Ni; 1897 v S, W, Ni; 1898 v S; 1899 v S, W, Ni; 1900 v S; 1901 v S, W; 1902 v S, W, Ni; 1904 v S; 1905 v S, W, Ni; (with Middlesbrough), 1907 v S, W (23)

Blunstone, F. (Chelsea), 1955 v W, S, F, P; 1957 v Y (5)

Bond, R. (Preston N.E.), 1905 v Ni, W; 1906 v S, W, Ni; (with Bradford C.), 1910 v S, W, Ni (8)

Bonetti, P. P. (Chelsea), 1966 v D; 1967 v Sp, A; 1968 v Sp; 1970 v Ho, P, WG (7)

Bonsor, A. G. (Wanderers), 1873 v S; 1875 v S (2).

Booth, F. (Manchester C.), 1905 v Ni (1)

Booth, T. (Blackburn R.), 1898 v W; (with Everton), 1903 v S (2)

Bowden, E. R. (Arsenal), 1935 v W, I; 1936 v W, Ni, A; 1937 v H (6)

Bowser, A. G. (Corinthians), 1924 v Ni, Bel; 1925 v W, Bel; 1927 v W (5)

Bowers, J. W. (Derby Co.), 1934 v S, Ni, W (3)

Bowles, S. (Q.P.R.), 1974 v P, W, Ni (3)

Bowser, S. (W.B.A.), 1920 v Ni (1)

Boyer, P. J. (Norwich C.), 1976 v W (1)

Boyes, W. (W.B.A.), 1935 v Ho; (with Everton), 1939 v W, R of E (3)

Boyle, T. W. (Burnley), 1913 v Ni (1)

Brabrook, P. (Chelsea), 1958 v USSR; 1959 v Ni; 1960 v Sp (3)

Bradford, G. R. W. (Bristol R.), 1956 v D (1)

Bradford J. (Birmingham), 1924 v Ni; 1925 v Bel; 1928 v S; 1929 v Ni, W, F, Sp; 1930 v S, Ni, G, A, 1931 v W (12)

Bradley, W. (Manchester U.), 1959 v I, US, M (sub) (3)

Bradshaw, F. (Sheffield W.), 1908 v A (1)

Bradshaw, T. H. (Liverpool), 1897 v Ni (1)

Bradshaw, W. (Blackburn R.) ,1910 v W, Ni; 1912 v Ni; 1913 v W (4)

Brann, G. (Swifts), 1886 v S, W; 1891 v W (3)

Brawn, W. F. (Aston Villa), 1904 v W, Ni (2)

Bray, J. (Manchester C.), 1935 v W; 1936 v S, W, Ni, G; 1937 v S (6)

Brayshaw, E. (Sheffield W.), 1887 v Ni (1)

Bridges, B. J. (Chelsea), 1965 v S, H, Y; 1966 v A (4)

Bridgett, A. (Sunderland) ,1905 v S; 1908 v S, A (2), H, B; 1909 v Ni, W, H (2), A (11)

Brindle, T. (Darwen), 1880 v S, W (2)

Brittleton, J. T. (Sheffield W.), 1912 v S, W, Ni; 1913 v S; 1914 v W (5)

Britton, C. S. (Everton), 1935 v S, W, Ni, I; 1937 v S, Ni, H, N, Se (9)

Broadbent, P. F. (Wolverhampton W.) 1958 v USSR; 1959 v S, W, Ni, I, Br; 1960 v S (7)

Broadis, I. A. (Manchester C.), 1952 v S, A, I; 1953 v S, Arg, Ch, U, US; (with Newcastle U.), 1954 v S, H, Y, Bel, Sw, U (14)

Brockbank, J. (Cambridge University), 1872 v S (1)

Brodie, J. B. (Wolverhampton W.), 1889 v S, Ni; 1891 v Ni (3)

Bromilow, T. G. (Liverpool), 1921 v W; 1922 v S, W; 1923 v Bel; 1926 v Ni (5)

Bromley-Davenport, W. E. (Oxford University), 1884 v S, W (2)

Brook, E. F. (Manchester C.), 1930 v Ni; 1933 v Sw; 1934 v S, W, Ni, F, H, Cz; 1935 v S, W, Ni, I; 1936 v S, W, Ni; 1937 v H; 1938 v W, Ni (18)

Brooking, T. D. (West Ham U.), 1974 v P, Arg, EG, Bul, Y; 1975 v Cz (sub), P; 1976 v P, W, Br, I (11)

Brooks, J. (Tottenham H.), 1957 v W, Y, D (3)

Broome, F. H. (Aston Villa), 1938 v G, Sw, F; 1939 v N, I, R, Y (7)

Brown, A. (Aston Villa), 1882 v S, W, N (3)

Brown, A. S. (Sheffield U.), 1904 v W; 1906 v Ni (2)

672

Brown, A. (W.B.A.), 1971 v W (1)
Brown, G. (Huddersfield T.), 1927 v S, W, Ni, Bel, L, G; 1928 v W; 1929 v S; (with Aston Villa), 1933 v W (9)
Brown, J. (Blackburn R.), 1881 v W; 1882 v Ni; 1885 v S, W, Ni (5)
Brown, J. H. (Sheffield W.), 1927 v S, W, Bel, L F; 1930 v Ni (6)
Brown, K. (West Ham U.), 1960 v Ni (1)
Brown, W. (West Ham U.), 1924 v Bel (1)
Bruton, J. (Burnley), 1928 v F, Bel; 1929 v S (3)
Bryant, W. I. (Clapton), 1925 v F (1)
Buchan, C. M. (Sunderland), 1913 v Ni; 1920 v W; 1921 v W, Bel; 1923 v F; 1924 v S (6)
Buchanan. W. S. (Clapham R.), 1876 v S (1)
Buckley, F. C. (Derby Co.), 1914 v Ni (1)
Bullock, F.E. (Huddersfield T.), 1921 v Ni (1)
Bullock, N. (Bury), 1923 v Bel; 1926 v W; 1927 v Ni (3)
Burgess, H. (Manchester C.), 1904 v S, W, Ni; 1906 v S (4)
Burgess, H. (Sheffield W.), 1931 v S, Ni, F, Bel (4)
Burnup, C. J. (Cambridge University), 1896 v S (1)
Burrows, H. (Sheffield W.), 1934 v H, Cz; 1935 v Ho (3)
Burton, F. E. (Nottingham F.), 1889 v Ni (1)
Bury, L. (Cambridge University), 1877 v S; (with Old Etonians), 1879 v W (2)
Butler, J. D. (Arsenal), 1925 v Bel (1)
Butler, W. (Bolton W.), 1924 v S (1)
Byrne, G. (Liverpool), 1963 v S; 1966 v N (2)
Byrne, J. J. (C. Palace), 1962 v Ni; (with West Ham U.), 1963 v Sw; 1964 v S, U, P (2), Ei, Br, Arg; 1965 v W, S (11)
Byrne, R. W. (Manchester U.), 1954 v S, H, Y, Bel, Sw, U; 1955 v S, W Ni, WG, F, Sp, P; 1956 v S, W, Ni, Br, Se, Fi, WG, D, Sp; 1957 v S, W, Ni, Y D (2), Ei (2); 1958 v W, Ni, F (33)

Callaghan, I. R. (Liverpool), 1966 v Fi, F (2)
Calvey, J. (Nottingham F.), 1902 v Ni (1)
Campbell, A. F. (Blackburn R.), 1929 v W, Ni; (with Huddersfield T.), 1931 v W, S, Ni; 1932 v W, Ni, Sp (8)
Camsell, G. H. (Middlesbrough), 1929 v F, Bel; 1930 v Ni, W; 1934 v F; 1936 v S, G, A, Bel (9)
Capes, A. J. (Stoke C.), 1903 v S (1)
Carr, J. (Middlesbrough), 1920 v Ni; 1923 v W (2)
Carr, J. (Newcastle U.), 1905 v Ni; 1907 v Ni (2)
Carr, W. H. (Owlerton, Sheffield), 1875 v S (1)
Carter, H. S. (Sunderland), 1934 v S, H; 1936 v G; 1937 v S, Ni, H; (with Derby Co.), 1947 v S, W, Ni, Ei, Ho, F, Sw (13)
Carter, J. H. (W.B.A.), 1926 v Bel; 1929 v Bel, Sp (3)
Catlin, A. E. (Sheffield W.), 1937 v W, Ni, H, N, Se (5)
Chadwick, A. (Southampton), 1900 v S, W (2)
Chadwick, E. (Everton), 1891 v S, W; 1892 v S; 1893 v S; 1894 v S; 1896 v Ni; 1897 v S (7)
Chambers, H. (Liverpool), 1921 v S, W, Bel; 1923 v S, W, Ni, Bel; 1924 v Ni (8)
Channon, M. R. (Southampton), 1973 v Y, S (2), Ni, W, Cz, USSR, I; 1974 v A, Pol, I, P, W, Ni, S, Arg, EG, Bul, Y; 1975 v Cz, P, WG, Cy (2), Ni(sub), W, S; 1976 v Sw, Cz, P, W, Ni, S, Br, I (35)
Charlton, J. (Leeds U.) 1965 v S, H, Y, WG, Se; 1966 v W, Ni, S, A, Sp, Pol(2), WG (2), Y, Fi, D, U, M, F, Arg, P; 1967 v W, S, Ni, Cz; 1968 v W, Sp; 1969 v W, R, F; 1970 v Ho (2), P, Cz (35)

Charlton, R. (Manchester U.), 1958 v S, P, Y; 1959 v S, W, Ni, USSR, I, Br, Pe, M, US; 1960 v W, S, Se, Y, Sp, H; 1961 v Ni, W, S, L, P, Sp, M, I, A; 1962 v W, Ni, S, A, Sw, Pe, L, P, H, Arg, Bul, Br; 1963 v S, F, Br, Cz, EG, Sw; 1964 v S, W, Ni, R of W, U, P, Ei, Br, Arg, US (sub); 1965 v Ni, S, Ho; 1966 v W, Ni, S, A, Sp, WG (2), Y, Fi, N, Pol, U, M, F, Arg, P; 1967 v Ni, W, S, Cz; 1968 v W, Ni, S, USSR (2), Sp (2), Se, Y; 1969 v S, W, Ni, R (2), Bul, M, Br; 1970 v W, Ni, Ho (2) P, Co, Ec, Cz, R, Br, WG (106)
Charnley, R. O. (Blackpool), 1963 v F (1)
Charsley, C. C. (Small Heath), 1893 v Ni (1)
Chedgzoy, S. (Everton), 1920 v W; 1921 v W, S, Ni; 1922 v Ni; 1923 v S; 1924 v W; 1925 v Ni (8)
Chenery, C. J. (C. Palace), 1872 v S; 1873 v S; 1874 v S (3)
Cherry, T. J. (Leeds U.), 1976 v W, S (sub), Br (3)
Chilton, A. (Manchester U.), 1951 v Ni; 1952 v F (2)
Chippendale, H. (Blackburn R.), 1894 v Ni (1)
Chivers, M. (Tottenham H.), 1971 v Ma (2), Gr, Ni, S; 1972 v Sw (1+1 sub), Gr, WG (2), Ni (sub), S; 1973 v W (3), S (2), Ni, Cz, Pol, USSR, I; 1974 v A, Pol (24)
Christian, E. (Old Etonians), 1879 v S (1)
Clamp, E. (Wolverhampton W.), 1958 v USSR (2), Br, A (4)
Clapton, D. R. (Arsenal), 1959 v W (1)
Clare, T. (Stoke C.), 1889 v Ni; 1892 v Ni; 1893 v W; 1894 v S, (4)
Clarke, A. J. (Leeds U.), 1970 v Cz; 1971 v EG, Ma, Ni, W (sub). S (sub.); 1973 v S (2), W, Cz, Pol, USSR, I; 1974 v A, Pol, I; 1975 v P; 1976 v Cz, P (sub) (19)
Clarke, H. A. (Tottenham H.), 1954 v S (1)
Clay, T. (Tottenham H.), 1920 v W; 1922 v W, S, Ni (4)
Clayton, R. (Blackburn R.), 1956 v Ni, Br, Se, Fi, WG, Sp; 1957 v S, W, Ni, Y, D (2), Ei(2); 1958 v S, W, Ni, F, P, Y, USSR; 1959 v S, W, Ni, USSR, I, Br, Pe, M, US; 1960 v W, Ni, S, Se, Y (35)
Clegg, J. C. (Sheffield W.), 1872 v S (1)
Clegg, W. E. (Sheffield W.), 1873 v S; (with Sheffield Albion), 1879 v W (2)
Clemence, R. N. (Liverpool), 1973 v W (2); 1974 v EG, Bul, Y; 1975 v Cz, P, WG, Cy, Ni, W, S; 1976 v Sw, Cz, P, W (2), Ni, S, Br (20)
Clement, D. T. (Q.P.R.), 1976 v W (sub), W, I (3)
Clough, B. H. (Middlesbrough), 1960 v W, Se (2)
Coates, R. (Burnley), 1970 v Ni; 1971 v Gr (sub), (with Tottenham H.) Ma W (4)
Cobbold, W. N. (Cambridge University), 1883 v S, Ni; 1885 v S, Ni; 1886 v S, W; (with Old Carthusians, 1887 v S, W, Ni (9)
Cock, J. G. (Huddersfield T.), 1920 v Ni (with Chelsea) v S (2)
Cockburn, H. (Manchester U.), 1947 v W, Ni, Ei; 1948 v S, I; 1949 v S, Ni, D, Sw, Se; 1951 v Arg, P; 1952 v F (13)
Cohen, G. R. (Fulham), 1964 v U, P Ei, US, Br; 1965 v S, Ni, Bel, H, Ho, Y, WG, Se; 1966 v W, S, Ni, A, Sp, Pol (2), WG (2), N, D, U, M, F, Arg, P; 1967 v W, S, Ni, Cz, Sp; 1968 v W, Ni (37)
Coleclough, H. (C. Palace), 1914 v W (1)
Coleman, E. H. (Dulwich Hamlet), 1921 v W (1)
Coleman, J. (Woolwich Arsenal), 1907 v Ni (1)
Common, A. (Sheffield U.), 1904 v W, Ni; (with Middlesbrough), 1906 v W (3)
Compton, L. H. (Arsenal), 1951 v W, Y (2)
Conlin, J. (Bradford C.), 1906 v S (1)
Connelly, J. M. (Burnley), 1960 v W, N, S, Se; 1962 v W, A, Sw, P; 1963 v W, F; (with Manchester

673

U.), 1965 v H, Y, Se, 1966 v W, Ni, S, A, N, D, U (20)

Cook, T. E. R. (Brighton), 1925 v W (1)

Cooper, N. C. (Cambridge University), 1893 v Ni (1)

Cooper, T. (Derby Co.), 1928 v Ni, 1929 v W, Ni, S, F, Bel, Sp; 1931 v F; 1932 v W, Sp; 1933 v S; 1934 v S, H, Cz; 1935 v W (15)

Cooper, T. (Leeds U.), 1969 v W, S, F, M; 1970 v Ho, Bel, Co, Ec, R, Cz, Br, WG; 1971 v EG, Ma, Ni, W, S; 1972 v Sw (2); 1975 v P (20)

Copping, W. (Leeds U.), 1933 v I, Sw; 1934 v S, Ni, W, F; (with Arsenal), 1935 v Ni, I; 1936 v A, Bel; 1937 v N, Se, Fi; 1938 v S, W, Ni. Cz; 1939 v W. R of E (with Leeds U.), R (20)

Corbett, B. O. (Corinthians), 1901 v W (1)

Corbett, R. (Old Malvernians), 1903 v W (1)

Corbett, W. S. (Birmingham), 1908 v A, H, B (3)

Corrigan, J. T. (Manchester C.), 1976 v I (sub) (1)

Cotterill, G. H. (Cambridge University), 1891 v Ni; (with Old Brightonians), 1892 v W; 1893 v S, Ni (4)

Cottle, J. R. (Bristol C.), 1909 v Ni (1)

Cowan, S. (Manchester C.), 1926 v Bel; 1930 v A; 1931 v Bel (3)

Cowell, A. (Blackburn R.), 1910 v Ni (1)

Cox, J. (Liverpool), 1901 v Ni; 1902 v S; 1903 v S (3)

Cox, J. D. (Derby Co.), 1892 v Ni (1)

Crabtree, J. W. (Burnley), 1894 v Ni; 1895 v Ni, S; (with Aston Villa), 1896 v S, Ni; 1899 v S, W, Ni; 1900 v S, W, Ni; 1901 v W; 1902 v W (14)

Crawford, J. F. (Chelsea), 1931 v S (1)

Crawford, R. (Ipswich T.), 1962 v Ni, A (2)

Crawshaw, T. H. (Sheffield W.), 1895 v Ni; 1896 v S, W, Ni; 1897 v S, W, Ni; 1901 v Ni; 1904 v W, Ni (10)

Crayston, W. J. (Arsenal), 1936 v S, W, G, A, Bel; 1938, v W, Ni, Cz (8)

Creek, F. N. S. (Corinthians), 1923 v F (1)

Cresswell, W. (South Shields), 1921 v W, (with Sunderland), 1923 v F; 1924 v Bel; 1925 v Ni; 1926 v W; 1927 v Ni; (with Everton), 1930 v Ni (7)

Crompton, R. (Blackburn R.), 1902 v S, W, Ni; 1903 v S, W; 1904 v S, W, Ni; 1906 v S, W, Ni; 1907 v S, W, Ni; 1908 v S, W, Ni, A (2), H, B; 1909 v S, W, Ni, H (2), A; 1910 v S, W; 1911 v S, W, Ni; 1912 v S, W, Ni; 1913 v S, W, Ni; 1914 v S, W, Ni (41)

Crooks, S. D. (Derby Co.), 1930 v S, G, A; 1931 v S, W, Ni, F, Bel; 1932 v S, W, Ni, Sp; 1933 v Ni, W, A; 1934 v S, Ni, W, F, H, Cz; 1935 v Ni; 1936 v S, W; 1937 v W, H (26)

Crowe, C. (Wolverhampton W.), 1963 v F (1)

Cuggy, F. (Sunderland), 1913 v Ni; 1914 v Ni (2)

Cullis, S. (Wolverhampton W.), 1938 v S, W, Ni, F Cz; 1939 v S, Ni, R of E, N, I, R, Y (12)

Cunliffe, A. (Blackburn R.), 1933 v Ni, W (2)

Cunliffe, D. (Portsmouth), 1900 v Ni (1)

Cunliffe, J. N. (Everton), 1936 v Bel, (1)

Currey, E. S. (Oxford University), 1890 v S, W (2)

Currie, A. W. (Sheffield U.), 1972 v Ni; 1973 v USSR, 1; 1974 v A, Pol, I; 1976 v Sw (7)

Cursham, A. W. (Notts. Co.), 1876 v S; 1877 v S; 1878 v S; 1879 v W; 1883 v S, W (6)

Cursham, H. A. (Notts Co.), 1880 v W; 1882 v S, W, Ni; 1883 v S, W, Ni; 1884 v Ni (8)

Daft, H. B. (Notts. Co.), 1889 v Ni; 1890 v S, W; 1891 v Ni; 1892 v Ni (5)

Danks, T. (Nottingham F.), 1885 v S (1)

Davenport, J. K. (Bolton W.), 1885 v W; 1890 v Ni (2)

Davis, G. (Derby Co.), 1904 v W, Ni (2)

Davis, H. (Sheffield W.), 1903 v S, W, Ni (3)

Davison, J. E. (Sheffield W.), 1922 v W (1)

Dawson, J. (Burnley), 1922 v S, Ni (2)

Day, S. H. (Old Malvernians), 1906 v Ni, W, S (3)

Dean, W. R. (Everton), 1927 v S. W. F. Bel, L; 1928 v S, W, Ni, F, Bel; 1929 v S, W, Ni; 1931 v S; 1932 v Sp; 1933 v Ni (16)

Deeley, N. V. (Wolverhampton W.), 1959 v Br, Pe (2)

Devey, J. H. G. (Aston Villa), 1892 v Ni; 1894 v Ni (2)

Dewhurst, F. (Preston N.E.), 1886 v W, Ni; 1887 v S, W, Ni; 1888 v S, W, Ni; 1889 v W (9)

Dewhurst, G. P. (Liverpool Ramblers), 1895 v W (1)

Dickinson, J. W. (Portsmouth), 1949 v N, F; 1950 v S, W, Ei, P, Bel, Ch, US, Sp; 1951 v Ni, W, Y; 1952 v W, Ni, S, A (2), I, Sw; 1953 v W, Ni, S, Bel, Arg, Ch, U, US, 1954 v W, Ni, S, R of E, H (2), Y, Bel, Sw, U; 1955 v Sp, P; 1956 v W, Ni. S, D, Sp; 1957 v W, Y, D (48)

Dimmock, J. H. (Tottenham H.), 1921 v S; 1926 v W, Bel (3)

Ditchburn, E. G. (Tottenham H.), 1949 v Sw, Se; 1953 v US; 1957 v W, Y, D (6)

Dix, R. W. (Derby Co.), 1939 v N (1)

Dixon, J. A. (Notts. Co.), 1885 v W (1)

Dobson, A. T. C. (Notts. Co.), 1882 v Ni; 1884 v S, W, Ni (4)

Dobson, C. F. (Notts. Co.), 1886 v Ni (1)

Dobson, J. M. (Burnley), 1974 v P, EG, Bul, Y; 1975 (with Everton) v Cz (5)

Doggart, A. G. (Corinthians), 1924 v Bel (1)

Dorrell, A. R. (Aston Villa), 1925 v W, Bel, F; 1926 v Ni (4)

Douglas, B. (Blackburn R.), 1958 v S, W, Ni, F, P. Y, USSR (2), Br, A; 1959 v S, USSR; 1960 v Y, H; 1961 v Ni, W, S, L, P, Sp, M, I, A; 1962 v W, Ni, S, Pe, L, P. H, Arg, Bul, Br; 1963 v S, Br, Sw (36)

Downs, R. W. (Everton), 1921 v Ni (1)

Doyle, M. (Manchester C.), 1976 v W, S (sub), Br, I (4)

Drake, E. J. (Arsenal), 1935 v Ni, I; 1936 v W; 1937 v H; 1938 v F (5)

Ducat, A. (Woolwich Arsenal), 1910 v S, W, Ni; (with Aston Villa), 1920 v S, W; 1921 v Ni (6)

Dunn, A. T. B. (Cambridge University), 1883 v Ni; 1884 v Ni; (with Old Etonians), 1892 v S, W (4)

Earle, S. G. J. (Clapton), 1924 v F; (with West Ham U.) 1928 v Ni (2)

Eastham, G. (Arsenal), 1963 v Br, Cz, EG; 1964 v W, Ni, S, R of W, U, P, Ei, US, Br, Arg; 1965 v H, WG, Se; 1966 v Sp, Pol, D (19)

Eastham, G. R. (Bolton W.), 1935 v Ho (1)

Eckersley, W. (Blackburn R.), 1950 v Sp; 1951 v S, Y, Arg, P; 1952 v A (2), Sw; 1953 v Ni, Arg, Ch, U, US; 1954 v W, Ni, R of E, H (17)

Edwards, D. (Manchester U.), 1955 v S, F, Sp, P; 1956 v S, Br, Se, Fi, WG; 1957 v S, Ni, Ei (2), D (2); 1958 v W, Ni, F (18)

Edwards, J. H. (Shropshire Wanderers), 1874 v S (1)

Edwards, W. (Leeds U.), 1926 v S, W; 1927 v W, Ni, S, F, Bel, L; 1928 v S, F, Bel; 1929 v S, W. Ni; 1930 v W, Ni (16)

Ellerington, W. (Southampton), 1949 v N F (2)

Elliott, G. W. (Middlesbrough), 1913 v Ni; 1914 v Ni; 1920 v W(3)

674

Eliott, W. H. (Burnley), 1952 v I, A; 1953 v Ni, W, Bel (5)

Evans, R. E. (Sheffield U.), 1911 v S, W, Ni; 1912 v W (4)

Ewer, F. H. (Casuals), 1924 v F; 1925 v Bel (2)

Fairclough, P. (Old Foresters), 1878 v S (1)

Fairhurst, D. (Newcastle U.), 1934 v F (1)

Fantham, J. (Sheffield W.), 1962 v L (1)

Felton, W. (Sheffield W.) 1925 v F (1)

Fenton, M. (Middlesbrough), 1938 v S (1)

Field, E. (Clapham Rovers), 1876 v S; 1881 v S (2)

Finney, T. (Preston N.E.), 1947 v W, I, Ei, Ho, F, P; 1948 v S, W, Ni, Bel, Se, I; 1949 v S, W, Ni, Se, N, F; 1950 v S, W, Ni, Ei, I, P, Bel, Ch, US, Sp, 1951 v W, S, Arg, P, 1952 v W, Ni, S, F, I, Sw, A, 1953 v W, Ni, S, Bel, Arg, Ch, U, US; 1954 v W, S, Bel Sw, U, H, Y; 1955 v WG; 1956 v S, W, Ni; D, Sp; 1957 v S, W, Y, D (2), Ei (2); 1958 v W, S; F, P, Y, USSR (2); 1959 v Ni, USSR (76)

Fleming, H. J. (Swindon T.), 1909 v S, H (2); 1910 v W, Ni; 1911 v W, Ni; 1912 v Ni; 1913 v S, W; 1914 v S (11)

Fletcher, A. (Wolverhampton W.), 1889 v W; 1890 v W (2)

Flowers, R. (Wolverhampton W.), 1955 v F; 1959 v S, W, I, Br, Pe, US, M (sub); 1960 v W, Ni, S, Se, Y, Sp, H; 1961 v Ni, W, S, L, P, Sp, M, I, A; 1962 v W, Ni, S, A, Sw, Pe, L, P, H, Arg, Bul, Br; 1963 v Ni, W, S, F (2), Sw; 1964 v Ei, US, P; 1965 v W, Ho, WG; 1966 v N (49)

Forman, Frank (Nottingham F.), 1898 v S, Ni; 1899 v S, W, Ni; 1901 v S; 1902 v S, Ni; 1903 v W (9)

Forman, F. R. (Nottingham F.), 1899 v S, W, Ni (3)

Forrest, J. H. (Blackburn R.), 1884 v W; 1885 v S, W, Ni; 1886 v S, W; 1887 v S, W, Ni; 1889 v S; 1890 v Ni (11)

Fort, J. (Millwall), 1921 v Bel(1)

Foster, R. E. (Oxford University), 1900 v W; (with Corinthians), 1901 v W, Ni, S; 1902 v W (5)

Foulke, W. J. (Sheffield W.), 1897 v W (1)

Foulkes, W. A. (Manchester U.), 1955 v Ni (1)

Fox, F. S. (Millwall), 1925 v Se (1)

Francis, G. C. J. (Q.P.R.), 1975 v Cz, P, W, S; 1976 v Sw, Cz, P, W, Ni, S, Br (11)

Franklin, C. F. (Stoke C.), 1947 v S, W, Ni, Ei, Ho, F, Sw, P; 1948 v S, W, Ni, Bel, Se, I; 1949 v S, W, Ni, D, Sw, N, F, Se; 1950 v W, S, Ni, Ei, I (27)

Freeman, B. C. (Everton), 1909 v S, W; (with Burnley), 1912 v S, W, Ni(5)

Froggatt, J. (Portsmouth), 1950 v Ni, I; 1951 v S; 1952 v S, A (2), I, Sw; 1953 v Ni, W, S, Bel, US (13)

Froggatt, R. (Sheffield W.), 1953 v W, S, Bel, US (4)

Fry, C. B. (Corinthians), 1901 v Ni(1)

Furness, W. I. (Leeds U.), 1933 v I (1)

Galley, T. (Wolverhampton W.), 1937 v N, Se (2)

Gardner, T. (Aston Villa), 1934 v Cz; 1935 v Ho (2)

Garfield, B. (W.B.A.), 1898 v Ni(1)

Garratty, W. (Aston Villa), 1903 v W (1)

Garrett, T. (Blackpool), 1952 v S, I; 1954 v W (3)

Gay, L. H. (Cambridge University), 1893 v S; (with Old Brightonians), 1894 v S, W (3)

Geary, F. (Everton), 1890 v Ni; 1891 v S (2)

Geaves, R. L. (Clapham Rovers), 1875 v S (1)

Gee, C. W. (Everton), 1932 v W, Sp; 1937 v Ni (3)

Geldard, A. (Everton), 1933 v I, Sw; 1935 v S; 1938 v Ni(4)

George, W. (Aston Villa), 1902 v S, W, Ni (3)

Gibbins, W. V. T. (Clapton), 1924 v F; 1925 v F (2)

Gillard, I. T. (Q.P.R.), 1975 v WG, W; 1976 v Cz (3)

Gilliat, W. E. (Old Carthusians), 1893 v Ni (1)

Goodall, F. R. (Huddersfield T.), 1926 v S; 1927 v S, F, Bel, L; 1928 v S, W, F, Bel; 1930 v S, G, A; 1931 v S, W, Ni, Bel; 1932 v Ni; 1933 v W, Ni, A, I, Sw; 1934 v W, Ni, F (25)

Goodall, J. (Preston N.E.), 1888 v S, W; 1889 v S, W; (with Derby) 1891 v S, W; 1892 v S; 1893 v W; 1894 v S; 1895 v S, Ni; 1896 v S, W; 1898 v W (14)

Goodhart, H. C. (Old Etonians), 1883 v S, W, Ni(3)

Goodwyn, A. G. (Royal Engineers), 1873 v S(1)

Goodyer, A. C. (Nottingham F.), 1879 v S(1)

Gosling, R. C. (Old Etonians), 1892 v W; 1893 v S; 1894 v W; 1895 v W, S (5)

Gosnell, A. A. (Newcastle U.), 1906 v Ni (1)

Gough, H. C. (Sheffield U.), 1921 v S (1)

Goulden, L. A. (West Ham) U.), 1937 v Se, N; 1938 v W, Ni, Cz, G, Sw, F; 1939 v S, W, R of E, I, R, Y(14)

Graham, L. (Millwall), 1925 v S, W (2)

Graham, T. (Nottingham F.), 1931 v F; 1932 v Ni(2)

Grainger, C. (Sheffield U.), 1956 v Br, Se, Fi, WG; 1957 v W, Ni; (with Sunderland), 1957 v S (7)

Greaves, J. (Chelsea), 1959 v Pe, M, US; 1960 v W, Se, Y, Sp; 1961 v Ni, W, S, L, P, Sp, I, A; (with Tottenham H.), 1962 v S, Sw, Pe, H, Arg, Bul, Br; 1963 v Ni, W, S, F (2) Br, Cz, Sw; 1964 v W, Ni, R of W, P (2), Ei, Br, U, Arg; 1965 v Ni, S, Bel, Ho, H, Y; 1966 v W, A, Y, N, D, Pol, U, M, F; 1967 v S, Sp, A (57)

Green, F. T. (Wanderers), 1876 v S(1)

Green, G. H. (Sheffield U.), 1925 v F; 1926 v S, Bel, W; 1927 v W, Ni; 1928 v F, Bel(8)

Greenhalgh, E. H. (Notts.), 1872 v S; 1873 v S (2)

Greenhoff, B. (Manchester U.), 1976 v W, Ni (2)

Greenwood, D. H. (Blackburn R.), 1882 v S, Ni (2)

Grimsdell, A. (Tottenham H.), 1920 v S, W; 1921 v S, Ni; 1923 v W, Ni(6)

Grosvenor, A. T. (Birmingham), 1934 v Ni, W, F (3)

Gunn, W. (Notts. Co.), 1884 v S, W (2)

Gurney, R. (Sunderland), 1935 v S(1)

Hacking, J. (Oldham Ath.), 1929 v S, W, Ni(3)

Hadley, N. (W.B.A.), 1903 v Ni(1)

Hagan, J. (Sheffield U.), 1949 v D (1)

Haines, J. T. W. (W.B.A.), 1949 v Sw (1)

Hall, A. E. (Aston Villa), 1910 v Ni(1)

Hall, G. W. (Tottenham H.), 1934 v F; 1938 v S, W, Ni, Cz; 1939 v S, W, Ni, R of E, I, Y(11)

Hall, J.(Birmingham C.), 1956 v S, W, Ni, Br, Se, Fi, WG, D, Sp; 1957 v S, W, Ni, Y, D (2), Ei (2) (17)

Halse, H. J. (Manchester U.), 1909 v A(1)

Hammond, H. E. D. (Oxford University), 1889 v S (1)

Hampson, J.(Blackpool), 1931 v Ni, W; 1933 v A (3)

Hampton, H. (Aston Villa), 1913 v S, W; 1914 v S, W (4)

Hancocks, J. (Wolverhampton W.), 1949 v Sw; 1950 v W; 1951 v Y(3)

Hapgood, E. (Arsenal), 1933 v I, Sw; 1934 v S, Ni, W, H, Cz; 1935 v S, Ni, W, I, Ho; 1936 v S, Ni, W, G, A, Bel; 1937 v Fi; 1938 v S, G, Sw, F; 1939 v S, W, Ni, R of E, N, I, Y(30)

Hardinge, H. T. W. (Sheffield U.), 1910 v S (1)

Hardman, H. P. (Everton), 1905 v W; 1907 v S, Ni; 1908 v W (4)

Hardwick, G. F. M. (Middlesbrough), 1947 v S, W, Ni, Ei, Ho, F, Sw, P; 1948 v S, W, Ni, Bel, Se(13)

675

Hardy, H. (Stockport Co.), 1925 v Bel (1)

Hardy, S. (Liverpool), 1907 v S, W, Ni; 1908 v S; 1909 v S, W, Ni, H (2), A; 1910 v S, W, Ni; 1912 v Ni (with Aston Villa), 1913 v S; 1914 v Ni, W, S; 1920 v S, W, Ni (21)

Hargreaves, F. W. (Blackburn R.), 1880 v W; 1881 v W; 1882 v Ni (3)

Hargreaves, J. (Blackburn R.), 1881 v S, W (2)

Harper, E. C. (Blackburn R.), 1926 v S (1)

Harris, G. (Burnley), 1966 v Pol (1)

Harris, P. P. (Portsmouth), 1950 v Ei; 1954 v H (2)

Harris, S. S. (Cambridge University), 1904 v S; (with Old Westminsters) 1905 v Ni, W; 1906 v S, W, Ni (6)

Harrison, A. H. (Old Westminsters), 1893 v S, Ni(2)

Harrison, G. (Everton), 1921 v Bel; 1922 v Ni (2)

Harrow, J. H. (Chelsea), 1923 v Ni, Se (2)

Hart, E. (Leeds U.), 1929 v W; 1930 v W, Ni; 1933 v S, A; 1934 v S, H, Cz(8)

Hartley, F. (Oxford C.), 1923 v F(1)

Harvey, A. (Wednesbury Strollers), 1881 v W (1)

Harvey, J. C. (Everton), 1971 v Ma (1)

Hassall, H. W. (Huddersfield T.), 1951 v S, Arg, P; 1952 v F; (with Bolton W.), 1954 v Ni(5)

Haworth, G. (Accrington), 1887 v Ni, W, S; 1888 v S; 1890 v S (5)

Hawtrey, J. P. (Old Etonians), 1881 v S, W (2)

Hawkes, R. M. (Luton T.), 1907 v Ni; 1908 v A (2), H, B(5)

Haygarth, E. B. (Swifts), 1875 v S (1)

Haynes, J. N. (Fulham), 1955 v Ni; 1956 v S, Ni, Br, Se, Fi, WG, Sp; 1957 v W, Y, D, Ei (2); 1958 v W, Ni, S, F, P, Y, USSR (3), Br, A; 1959 v S, Ni, USSR, I, Br, Pe, M, US; 1960 v Ni, Y, Sp, H; 1961 v Ni, W, S, L, P, Sp, M, I, A; 1962 v W, Ni, S, A, Sw, Pe, P, H, Arg, Bul, Br (56)

Healless, H. (Blackburn R.), 1925 v Ni; 1928 v S (2)

Hector, K. J. (Derby Co.), 1974 v Pol (sub), I (sub, (2)

Hedley, G. A. (Sheffield U.) 1901 v Ni (1)

Hegan, K. E. (Corinthians), 1923 v Bel, F; 1924 v Ni, Bel(4)

Hellawell, M. S. (Birmingham C.), 1963 v Ni, F (2)

Henfrey, A. G. (Cambridge University), 1891 v Ni; (with Corinthians), 1892 v W; 1895 v W; 1896 v S, W (5)

Henry, R. P. (Tottenham H.), 1963 v F (1)

Heron, F. (Wanderers), 1876 v S(1)

Heron, G. H. H. (Uxbridge), 1873 v S; 1874 v S; (with Wanderers), 1875 v S; 1876 v S; 1878 v S (5)

Hibbert, W. (Bury), 1910 v S(1)

Hibbs, H. E. (Birmingham), 1930 v S, W, A, G; 1931 v S, W, Ni; 1932 v W, Ni, Sp; 1933 v S, W, Ni, A, I, Sw; 1934 v Ni, W, F; 1935 v S, W, Ni, Ho; 1936 v G, W(25)

Hill, F. (Bolton W.), 1963 v Ni, W (2)

Hill, J. H. (Burnley), 1925 v W; 1926 v S; 1927 v S, Ni, Bel, F; 1928 v Ni, W; 1929 v F, Bel, Sp (11)

Hill, G. A. (Manchester U.), 1976 v I (1)

Hill, R. H. (Millwall), 1926 v Bel (1)

Hillman, J. (Burnley), 1899 v Ni(1)

Hills, A. F. (Old Harrovians), 1879 v S (1)

Hilsdon, G. R. (Chelsea), 1907 v Ni; 1908 v S, W, Ni, A, H, B; 1909 v Ni(8)

Hine, E. W. (Leicester C.), 1929 v W, Ni; 1930 v W, Ni; 1932 v W, Ni(6)

Hinton, A. T. (Wolverhampton W.), 1963 v F; (with Nottingham F.), 1965 v W, Bel(3)

Hitchens, G. A. (Aston Villa), 1961 v M, I, A; (with Inter-Milan), 1962 v Sw, Pe, H, Br (7)

Hobbis, H. H. F. (Charlton Ath.), 1936 v A, Bel(2)

Hodgetts, D. (Aston Villa), 1888 v S, W, Ni; 1892 v S, Ni; 1894 v Ni(6)

Hodgkinson, A. (Sheffield U.), 1957 v S, Ei (2), D; 1961 v W (5)

Hodgson, G. (Liverpool), 1931 v S, Ni, W (3)

Hodkinson, J. (Blackburn R.), 1913 v W, S; 1920 v Ni(3)

Hogg, W. (Sunderland), 1902 v S, W, Ni(3)

Holdcroft, G. H. (Preston N.E.), 1937 v W, Ni (2)

Holden, A. D. (Bolton W.), 1959 v S, I, Br, Pe, M (5)

Holden, G. H. (Wednesday O.A.), 1881 v S; 1884 v S, W, Ni (4)

Holden-White, C. (Corinthians), 1888 v W, S (2)

Holford, T. (Stoke), 1903 v Ni(1)

Holley, H. (Sunderland), 1909 v S, W, H (2), A; 1910 v W; 1912 v S, W, Ni; 1913 v S (10)

Holliday, E. (Middlesbrough), 1960 v W, Ni, Se (3)

Hollins, J. W. (Chelsea), 1967 v Sp (1)

Holmes, R. (Preston N.E.), 1888 v Ni; 1891 v S; 1892 v S; 1893 v S, W; 1894 v Ni; 1895 v Ni (7)

Holt, J. (Everton), 1890 v W; 1891 v S, W; 1892 v S, Ni; 1893 v S; 1894 v S, Ni; 1895 v S; (with Reading), 1900 v Ni (10)

Hopkinson, E. (Bolton W.), 1958 v W, Ni, S, F, P, Y; 1959 v S, I, Br, Pe, M, US; 1960 v W, Se(14)

Hossack, A. H. (Corinthians), 1892 v W; 1894 v W (2)

Houghton, W. E. (Aston Villa), 1931 v Ni, W, F, Bel; 1932 v S, Ni; 1933 v A (7)

Houlker, A. E. (Blackburn R.), 1902 v S; (with Portsmouth), 1903 v S, W; (with Southampton), 1906 v W, Ni (5)

Howarth, R. H. (Preston N.E.), 1887 v Ni; 1888 v S, W; 1891 v S; (with Everton), 1894 v Ni (5)

Howe, D. (W.B.A.), 1958 v S, W, Ni, F, P, Y, USSR (3), Br, A; 1959 v S, W, Ni, USSR, I, Br, Pe, M, US; 1960 v W, Ni, Se(23)

Howe, J. R. (Derby Co.), 1948 v I; 1949 v S, Ni (3)

Howell, L. S. (Wanderers), 1873 v S(1)

Howell, R. (Sheffield U.), 1895 v Ni; (with Liverpool) 1899 v S (2)

Hudson, A. A. (Stock C.), 1975 v WG, Cy (2)

Hudson, J.(Sheffield), 1883 v Ni(1)

Hudspeth, F. C. (Newcastle U.), 1926 v Ni (1)

Hufton, A. E. (West Ham U.), 1924 v Bel; 1928 v S, Ni; 1929 v F, Bel, Sp (6)

Hughes, E. W. (Liverpool), 1970 v W, Ni, S, Ho, P, B; 1971 v EG, Ma (2), Gr, W; 1972 v Sw, Gr, WG (2), W, Ni, S; 1973 v W (3), S (2), Pol, USSR, I; 1974 v A, Pol, I, W, Ni, S, Arg, EG, Bul, Y; 1975 v Cz, P, Cy (sub), Ni(40)

Hughes, L. (Liverpool), 1950 v Ch, US, Sp (3)

Hulme, J. H. A. (Arsenal), 1927 v S, Bel, F; 1928 v S, Ni, W; 1929 v Ni, W; 1933 v S (9)

Humphreys, P. (Notts Co.), 1903 v S(1)

Hunt, G. S. (Tottenham H.), 1933 v I, Sw, S (3)

Hunt, Rev. K. R. G. (Leyton), 1911 v S, W (2)

Hunt, R. (Liverpool), 1962 v A; 1963 v EG; 1964 v S, US, P; 1965 v W; 1966 v S, Sp, Pol(2), WG (2), Fi, N, U, M, F, Arg, P; 1967 v Ni, W, Cz, Sp, A; 1968 v W, Ni, USSR (2), Sp (2), Se, Y; 1969 v R (2) (34)

Hunter, J. (Sheffield Heeley), 1878 v S; 1880 v S, W; 1881 v S, W; 1882 v S, W (7)

Hunter, N. (Leeds U.), 1966 v WG, Y, Fi, Sp (sub), 1967 v A; 1968 v Sp, Se, Y, WG, USSR; 1969 v R, W; 1970 v Ho, WG (sub); 1971 v Ma; 1972 v WG (2), W, Ni, S; 1973 v W (2), USSR (sub); 1974 v A, Pol, Ni(sub), S; 1975 v Cz(28)

Hurst, G. C. (West Ham U.), 1966 v S, WG (2), Y, Fi, D, Arg, P; 1967 v Ni, W, S, Cz, Sp, A; 1968 v

676

W, Ni, S, Se (sub), WG, USSR (2); 1969 v Ni, S, R (2), Bul, F, M, U, Br; 1970 v W, Ni, S, Ho (1 + 1 sub), Be, Co, Ec, R, Br, WG; 1971 v EG, Gr, W, S; 1972 v Sw (2), Gr, WG (49)

Iremonger, J. (Nottingham F.), 1901 v S; 1902 v Ni (2)

Jack, D. N. B. (Bolton W.), 1924 v S, W; 1928 v F, Bel; (with Arsenal), 1930 v S, G, A; 1993 v W, A (9)

Jackson, E. (Oxford University), 1891 v W (1)

Jarrett, B. G. (Cambridge University), 1876 v S; 1877 v S; 1878 v S (3)

Jefferis, F. (Everton), 1912 v S, W (2)

Jezzard, B. A. G. (Fulham), 1954 v H; 1956 v Ni (2)

Johnson, D. E. (Ipswich T.), 1975 v W, S; 1976 v Sw (3)

Johnson, E. (Saltley College), 1880 v W; (with Stoke), 1884 v Ni (2)

Johnson, J. A. (Stoke C.), 1937 v N, Se, Fi, S, Ni (5)

Johnson, T. C. F. (Manchester C.), 1926 v Bel; 1930 v W; (with Everton), 1932 v S, Sp; 1933 v Ni (5)

Johnson, W. H. (Sheffield U.), 1900 v S, W, Ni; 1903 v S, W, Ni (6)

Johnston, H. (Blackpool), 1947 v S, Ho; 1951 v S; 1953 v Arg, Ch, U, US; 1954 v W, Ni, H (10)

Jones, A. (Walsall Town Swifts), 1882 v S, W; (with Great Lever), 1883 v S (3)

Jones, H. (Blackburn R.), 1927 v S, Bel, L, F; 1928 v S, Ni, (6)

Jones, H. (Nottingham F.), 1923 v F (1)

Jones, M. D. (Sheffield U.), 1965 v WG, Se (with Leeds U.); 1970 v Ho (3)

Jones, W. (Bristol C.), 1901 v Ni (1)

Jones, W. H. (Liverpool), 1950 v P, Bel (2)

Joy, B. (Casuals), 1936 v Bel (1)

Kail, E. I. L. (Dulwich Hamlet), 1929 v F, Bel, Sp (3)

Kay, A. H. (Everton), 1963 v Sw (1)

Kean, F. W. (Sheffield W.), 1923 v S, Bel; 1924 v W; 1925 v Ni; 1926 v Ni, Bel; 1927 v L; (with Bolton W.), 1929 v F, Sp (9)

Keegan, J. K. (Liverpool), 1973 v W (2); 1974 v W, Ni, Arg, EG, Bul, Y; 1975 v Cz, WG, Cy (2), Ni, S; 1976 v Sw, Cz, P, W (2), Ni, S, Br (22)

Keen, E. R. L. (Derby Co), 1933 v A; 1937 v W, Ni, H (4)

Kelly, R. (Burnley), 1920 v S; 1921 v S, W, Ni; 1922 v S, W; 1923 v S; 1924 v Ni; 1925 v W, Ni, S; (with Sunderland), 1926 v W; (with Huddersfield T.), 1927 v L; 1928 v S (14)

Kennedy, R. (Liverpool), W (2), Ni, S (3)

Kenyon-Slaney, W. S. (Wanderers), 1873 v S (1)

Kevan, D. T. (W.B.A.), 1957 v S; 1958 v W, Ni, S, P, Y, USSR (3), Br, A; 1959 v M, US; 1961 v M (14)

Kidd, B. (Manchester U.), 1970 v Ni, Ec (sub) (2)

King, R. S. (Oxford University), 1882 v Ni (1)

Kingsford, R. K. (Wanderers), 1874 v S (1)

Kingsley, M. (Newcastle U.), 1901 v W (1)

Kinsey, G. (Wolverhampton W.), 1892 v W; 1893 v S; (with Derby Co.), 1896 v W, Ni (4)

Kirchen, A. J. (Arsenal), 1937 v N, Se, Fi (3)

Kirton, W. J. (Aston Villa), 1922 v Ni (1)

Knight, A. E. (Portsmouth), 1920 v Ni (1)

Knowles, C. (Tottenham H.), 1968 v USSR, Sp, Se, WG (4)

Labone, B. L. (Everton), 1963 v Ni, W, F; 1967 v Sp, A; 1968 v S, Sp, Se, Y, USSR, WG; 1969 v Ni,

S, R, Bul, M, U, Br; 1970 v S, W, Bel, Co, Ec, R, Br, WG (26)

Lampard, F, R, G, (West Ham U.), 1973 v Y (1)

Langley, E. J. (Fulham), 1958 v S, P, Y (3)

Langton, R. (Blackburn R.), 1947 v W, Ni, Ei, Ho, F. Sw; 1948 v Se; (with Preston N.E.) 1949 v D, Se; (with Bolton W.), 1950 v S; 1951 v Ni (11)

Latheron, E. G. (Blackburn R.), 1913 v W; 1914 v Ni (2)

Lawler, C. (Liverpool), 1971 v Ma, W, S; 1972 v Sw (4)

Lawton, T. (Everton), 1939 v S, W, Ni, R of E, N I, R, Y; (with Chelsea), 1947 v S. W, Ni, Ei, Ho, F, Sw, P; 1948 v W, Ni, Bel; (with Notts. Co.), 1948 v S, Se, I; 1949 v D (23)

Leach, T. (Sheffield W.), 1931 v W, Ni (2)

Leake, A. (Aston Villa), 1904 v S, Ni; 1905 v S, W, Ni (5)

Lee, E. A. (Southampton), 1904 v W (1)

Lee, F. H. (Manchester C.), 1969 v Ni, W, S, Bul, F, M, U; 1970 v W, Ho (2), P, Bel, Co, Ec, R, Br, WG; 1971 v EG, Gr, Ma, W, S; 1972 v Sw (2), Gr, WG (27)

Lee, J. (Derby Co.), 1951 v Ni (1)

Leighton, J. E. (Nottingham F.), 1886 v Ni (1)

Lilley, H. E. (Sheffield U.), 1892 v W (1)

Linacre, H. J. (Nottingham F.), 1905 v W, S (2)

Lindley, T. (Cambridge University), 1886 v S, W, Ni; 1887 v S, W, Ni; 1888 v S, W, Ni; (with Nottingham F.), 1889 v S; 1890 v S, W; 1891 v Ni (13)

Lindsay, A. (Liverpool) 1974 v Arg, EG, Bul, Y (4)

Lindsay, W. (Wanderers), 1873 v S (1)

Lintott, E. H. (Q.P.R.), 1908 v S, W, Ni; (with Bradford C.), 1909 v S, Ni, H (2) (7)

Lipsham, H. B. (Sheffield U.), 1902 v W (1)

Little, B. (Aston Villa), 1975 v W (sub) (1)

Lloyd, L. V. (Liverpool), 1971 v W; 1972 v Sw, Ni (3)

Lockett, A. (Stoke), 1903 v Ni (1)

Lodge, L. V. (Cambridge University), 1894 v W, 1895 v S, W; (with Corinthians), 1896 v S, Ni (5)

Lofthouse, J. M. (Blackburn R.), 1885 v S, W, Ni; 1887 v S, W; (with Accrington), 1889 v Ni; (with Blackburn R.) 1890 v Ni (7)

Lofthouse, N. (Bolton W.), 1951 v Y; 1952 v W, Ni, S, A (2), I, Sw; 1953 v W, Ni, S, Bel, Arg, Ch, U, US; 1954 v W. Ni, R of E, Bel, U; 1955 v Ni, S, F, Sp, P; 1956 v W. S, Sp, D, Fi (sub); 1959 v W, USSR (33)

Longworth, E. (Liverpool), 1920 v S; 1921 v Bel; 1923 v S, W, Bel (5)

Lowder, A. (Wolverhampton W.), 1889 v W (1)

Lowe, E. (Aston Villa), 1947 v F, Sw, P (3)

Lucas, T. (Liverpool), 1922 v Ni; 1924 v F; 1926 v Bel (3)

Luntley, E. (Nottingham F.), 1880 v S, W (2)

Lyttelton, Hon. A. (Cambridge University), 1877 v S (1)

Lyttelton, Hon. E. (Cambridge University), 1878 v S (1)

McCall, J. (Preston N.E.), 1913 v S, W; 1914 v S; 1920 v S; 1921 v Ni (5)

McDonald, C. A. (Burnley), 1958 v USSR (3), Br, A; 1959 v W, Ni, USSR (8)

McFarland, R. L. (Derby Co.), 1971 v Gr, Ma (2), Ni, S; 1972 v Sw, Gr, WG, W, S; 1973 v W (3), Ni, S, Cz, Pol, USSR, I; 1974 v A, Pol, I, W, Ni; 1976 v Cz, S (26)

McGarry, W. H. (Huddersfield T.), 1954 v Sw, U; 1956 v W, D (4)

677

McGuinness, W. (Manchester U.), 1959 v Ni, M (2)

McInroy, A. (Sunderland), 1927 v Ni (1)

McNab, R. (Arsenal), 1969 v Ni, Bul, R (1 + 1 sub) (4)

McNeal, R. (W.B.A.), 1914 v S, W (2)

McNeil, M. (Middlesbrough), 1961 v W, Ni, S, L, P, Sp, M, I; 1962 v L (9)

Macaulay, R. H. (Cambridge University), 1881 v S (1)

Macdonald, M. (Newcastle U.), 1972 v W, Ni, S (Sub); 1973 v USSR (sub); 1974 v P, S (sub), Y (sub); 1975 v WG, Cy (2), Ni; 1976 v Sw (sub), Cz, P (14)

Macrae, S. (Notts. Co.), 1883 v S. W, Ni; 1884 v S, W, Ni (6)

Maddison, F. B. (Oxford University), 1872 v S (1)

Madeley, P. E. (Leeds U.), 1971 v Ni; 1972 v Sw (2), Gr, WG (2), W, S, 1973 v S, Cz, Pol, USSR, I; 1974 v A, Pol, 1; 1975 v Cz, P, Cy; 1976 v Cz, P (21)

Magee, T. P. (W.B.A.), 1923, v W Se; 1925 v S, Bel, F (5)

Makepeace, H. (Everton), 1906 v S; 1910 v S; 1912 v S, W (4)

Male, C. G. (Arsenal), 1935 v Se, Ni, I, Ho; 1936 v S, W, Ni, G, A, Bel; 1937 v S, Ni, H, N, Se, Fi; 1939 v I, R, Y (19)

Mannion, W. J. (Middlesbrough), 1947 v S, W, Ni, Ei, Ho, F, Sw, P; 1948 v W, Ni, Bel, Se, I; 1949 v N, F; 1950 v S, Ei, P, Bel, Ch, US; 1951 v Ni, W, S, T; 1952 v F (26)

Marsden, J. T. (Darwen), 1891 v Ni (1)

Marsden, W. (Sheffield W.), 1930 v W, S, G (3)

Marsh, R. W. (Q.P.R.), 1972 v Sw (sub), (with Manchester C.) WG (sub + 1), W, Ni, S; 1973 v W (2), Y (9)

Marshall, T. (Darwen), 1880 v W; 1881 v W (2)

Martin, H. (Sunderland), 1914 v Ni (1)

Maskrey, H. M. (Derby Co.), 1908 v Ni (1)

Mason, C. (Wolverhampton W.), 1887 v Ni; 1888 v W; 1890 v Ni (3)

Matthews, R. D. (Coventry C.), 1956 v S, Br, Se, WG; 1957 v Ni (5)

Matthews, S. (Stoke C.), 1935 v W, I; 1936 v G, 1937 v S; 1938 v S, W, Cz, G, Sw, F; 1939 v S, W; Ni, R of E, N, I, Y; 1947 v S; (with Blackpool), 1947 v Sw, P; 1948 v S, W, Ni, Bel, I; 1949 v S, W, Ni, D, Sw; 1950 v Sp; 1951 v Ni, S; 1954 v Ni, R of E, H, Bel, U; 1955 v Ni, W, S, F, WG, Sp, P; 1956 v W, Br; 1957 v S, W, Ni, Y, D (2) Ei (54)

Matthews, V. (Sheffield U.), 1928 v F, Bel (2)

Maynard, W. J. (1st Surrey Rifles), 1872 v S; 1876 v S (2)

Meadows, J. (Manchester C.), 1955 v S (1)

Medley, L. D. (Tottenham H.), 1951 v Y, W; 1952 v F, A, W, Ni (6)

Meehan, T. (Chelsea), 1924 v Ni (1)

Melia, J. (Liverpool), 1963 v S, Sw (2)

Mercer, D. W. (Sheffield U.), 1923 v Ni, Bel (2)

Mercer, J. (Everton) 1939 v S, Ni, I, R, Y (5)

Merrick, G. H. (Birmingham C.), 1952 v Ni, S, A (2), I, Sw; 1953 v Ni, W, S, Bel, Arg, Ch, U; 1954 v W, Ni, S, R of E, H (2), Y, Bel, Sw, U (23)

Metcalfe V. (Huddersfield T.), 1951 v Arg. P. (2)

Mew, J. W. (Manchester U.), 1921 v Ni (1)

Middleditch, B. (Corinthians), 1897 v Ni (1)

Milburn, J. E. T. (Newcastle U.), 1949 v S, W, Ni, Sw; 1950 v W, P, Bel, Sp; 1951 v W, Arg, P; 1952 v F; 1956 v D (13)

Miller, B. G. (Burnley), 1961 v A (1)

Miller, H. S. (Charlton Ath.), 1923 v Se (1)

Mills, G. R. (Chelsea), 1938 v W, Ni, Cz (3)

Mills, M. D. (Ipswich T.), 1973 v Y; 1976 v W (2), Ni, S, Br, I (sub) (7)

Milne, G. (Liverpool), 1963 v Br, Cz, EG; 1964 v W, Ni, S, R of W, U, P, Ei, Br, Arg; 1965 v Ni, Bel (14)

Milton, C. A. (Arsenal), 1952 v A (1)

Milward, A. (Everton), 1891 v S, W; 1897 v S, W (4)

Mitchell, C. (Upton Park), 1880 v W; 1881 v S; 1883 v S, W; 1885 v W (5)

Mitchell, J. F. (Manchester C.), 1925 v Ni (1)

Moflat, H. (Oldham Ath.), 1913 v W (1)

Molyneux, G. (Southampton), 1902 v S; 1903 v S, W, Ni (4)

Moon, W. R. (Old Westminsters), 1888 v S, W; 1889 v S, W; 1890 v S, W; 1891 v S (7)

Moore, H. T. (Notts. Co.), 1883 v Ni; 1885 v W (2)

Moore, J. (Derby Co.), 1923 v Se (1)

Moore, R. F. (West Ham U.), 1962 v Pe, H, Arg, Bul, Br; 1963 v W, Ni, S, F (2), Br, Cz, EG, Sw; 1964 v W, Ni, S, R of W, U, P (2), Ei, Br, Arg; 1965 v Ni, S, Bel, H, Y, WG, Se; 1966 v W, Ni, S, A, Sp, Pol (2), WG (2), N, D, U, M, F, Arg, P; 1967 v W, Ni, S, Cz, Sp, A; 1968 v W, Ni, S, USSR (2), Sp (2), Se, Y, WG; 1969 v Ni, W, S, R, Bul, F, M, U, Br; 1970 v W, Ni, S, Ho, P, Bel, Co, Ec, R, Br, Cz, WG; 1971 v EG, Gr, Ma, Ni, S; 1972 v Sw (2), Gr, WG (2), W, S; 1973 v W (3), Y, S (2), Ni, Cz, Pol, USSR, I; 1974 v I (108)

Moore, W. G. B. (West Ham U.), 1923 v Se (1)

Mordue, J. (Sunderland), 1912 v Ni; 1913 v Ni (2)

Morice, C. J. (Barnes), 1872 v S (1)

Morley, H. (Notts. Co.), 1910 v Ni (1)

Morren, T. (Sheffield U.), 1898 v Ni (1)

Morris, F. (W.B.A.), 1920 v S; 1921 v Ni (2)

Morris, J. (Derby Co.), 1949 v N, F; 1950 v Ei (3)

Morris, W. W. (Wolverhampton W.), 1939 v S, Ni, R (3)

Morse, H. (Notts.), 1879 v S (1)

Mort, T. (Aston Villa), 1924 v W, F; 1926 v S (3)

Morten, A. (C. Palace), 1873 v S (1)

Mortensen, S. H. (Blackpool), 1947 v P; 1948 v W, S, Ni, Bel, Se, I; 1949 v S, W, Ni, Se, N; 1950 v S, W, Ni, I, P, Bel, Ch, US, Sp; 1951 v S, Arg; 1954 v R of E, H (25)

Morton, J. R. (West Ham U.), 1938 v Cz (1)

Mosforth, W. (Sheffield W.) 1877 v S; (with Sheffield Albion), 1878 v S; 1879 v S, W; 1880 v S, W; (with Sheffield W.), 1881 v W; 1882 v S, W (9)

Moss, F. (Arsenal), 1934 v S, H, Cz; 1935 v I (4)

Moss, F. (Aston Villa), 1922 v S, Ni; 1923 v Ni; 1924 v S, Bel (5)

Mosscrop, E. (Burnley), 1914 v S, W (2)

Mozley, B. (Derby Co.), 1950 v W, Ni, Ei (3)

Mullen, J. (Wolverhampton W.), 1947 v S; 1949 v N, F; 1950 v Bel (sub), Ch, US; 1954 v W, Ni, S, R of E, Y, Sw (12)

Mullery, A. P. (Tottenham H.), 1965 v Ho; 1967 v Sp, A; 1968 v W, Ni, S, USSR, Sp (2), Se Y; 1969 v Ni, S, R, Bul, F, M, U, Br; 1970 v W, Ni, S (sub), Ho (sub), Bel, P, Co, Ec, R, Cz, WG, Br; 1971 v Ma, EG, Gr; 1972 v Sw (35)

Neal, P. G. (Liverpool), 1976 v W, I (2)

Needham, E. (Sheffield U.), 1894 v S; 1895 v S; 1897 v S, W, Ni; 1898 v S, W; 1899 v S, W, Ni; 1900 v S, Ni; 1901 v S, W, Ni; 1902 v W (16)

Newton, K. R. (Blackburn R.), 1966 v S, WG; 1967 v Sp, A; 1968 v W, S, Sp, Se, Y, WG; 1969 v Ni, W, S. R, Bul, M, U, Br, F; (with Everton), 1970 v Ni, S, Ho, Co, Ec, R, Cz, WG (27)

678

Nicholls, J. (W.B.A.), 1954 v S, Y (2)
Nicholson, W. E. (Tottenham H.), 1951 v P (1)
Nish, D. J. (Derby Co.), 1973 v Ni; 1974 v P, W, Ni, S (5)
Norman, M. (Tottenham H.), 1962 v Pe, H, Arg, Bul, Br; 1963 v S, F, Br, Cz, EG; 1964 v W, Ni, S, R of W, U, P (2), US, Br, Arg; 1965 v Ni, Bel, Ho (23)
Nuttall, H. (Bolton W.), 1928 v W, Ni; 1929 v S (3)

Oakley, W. J. (Oxford University), 1895 v W; 1896 v S, W, Ni; (with Corinthians), 1897 v S, W, Ni; 1898 v S, W, Ni; 1900 v S, W, Ni; 1901 v S, W, Ni (16)
O'Dowd, J. P. (Chelsea), 1932 v S; 1933 v Ni, Sw (3)
O'Grady, M. (Huddersfield T.), 1963 v Ni; (with Leeds U.), 1969 v F (2)
Ogilvie, R. A. M. M. (Clapham R.), 1874 v S (1)
Oliver, L. F. (Fulham), 1929 v Bel (1)
Olney, B. A. (Aston Villa), 1928 v F, Bel (2)
Osborne, F. R. (Fulham), 1923 v Ni, F; (with Tottenham H.), 1925 v Bel; 1926 v Bel (4)
Osborne R. (Leicester C.), 1928 v W (1)
Osgood, P. L. (Chelsea), 1970 v Bel, R, (sub), Cz (sub), 1974 v I (4)
Ottaway, C. J. (Oxford University), 1872 v S; 1874 v S (2)
Owen, J. R. B. (Sheffield), 1874 v S (1)
Owen, S. W. (Luton T.), 1954 v H, Y, Bel (3)

Page, L. A. (Burnley), 1927 v S, W, Bel, L, F; 1928 v W, Ni (7)
Paine, T. L. (Southampton), 1963 v Cz, EG; 1964 v W, Ni, S, R of W, U, US P; 1965 v Ni, H, Y, WG, Se; 1966 v W, A, Y, N, M (19)
Pantling, H. H. (Sheffield U.), 1924 v Ni (1)
Paravacini, P. J. de (Cambridge University), 1883 v S, W, Ni (3)
Parker, T. R. (Southampton), 1925 v F (1)
Parkes, P. B. (Q.P.R.), 1974 v P (1)
Parkinson, J. (Liverpool), 1910 v S, W (2)
Parr, P. C. (Oxford University), 1882 v W (1)
Parry, E. H. (Old Carthusians), 1879 v W; 1882 v W, S (3)
Parry, R. A. (Bolton W.), 1960 v Ni, S (2)
Pawson, F. W. (Cambridge University), 1883 v Ni; (with Swifts), 1885 v Ni (2)
Payne, J. (Luton T.), 1937 v Fi (1)
Peacock, A. (Middlesbrough), 1962 v Arg, Bul; 1963 v Ni, W; (with Leeds U.), 1966 v W, Ni (6)
Peacock. J. (Middlesbrough), 1929 v F, Bel, Sp (3)
Pearson, H. F. (W.B.A.), 1932 v S (1)
Pearson, J. H. (Crewe Alex.), 1892 v Ni (1)
Pearson, J. S. (Manchester U.), 1976 v W, Ni, S, Br (4)
Pearson, S. C. (Manchester U.), 1948 v S; 1949 v S, Ni; 1950 v Ni, I, 1951 v P; 1952 v S, I (8)
Pease, W. H. (Middlesbrough), 1927 v W (1)
Pegg, D. (Manchester U.), 1957 v Ei (1)
Pejic, M. (Stoke C.), 1974 v P, W, Ni, S (4)
Pelly, F. R. (Old Foresters), 1893 v Ni; 1894 v S, W (3)
Pennington, J. (W.B.A.), 1907 v S, W; 1908 v S, W, Ni, A; 1909 v S, W, H (2), A; 1910 v S, W; 1911 v S, W, Ni; 1912 v S, W, Ni; 1913 v S, W; 1914 v S, Ni; 1920 v S, W (25)
Pentland, F. B. (Middlesbrough), 1909 v S, W, H (2) A (5)
Perry, C. (W.B.A.), 1890 v Ni; 1891 v Ni; 1893 v W (3)

Perry, T. (W.B.A.), 1898 v W (1)
Perry, W. (Blackpool), 1956 v Ni, S, Sp (3)
Peters, M. (West Ham U.), 1966 v Y, Fi, Pol, M, F, Arg, P, WG; 1967 v Ni, W, S, Cz; 1968 v W, Ni, S, USSR (2), Sp (2), Se, Y; 1969 v Ni, S, R, Bul, F, M, U, Br; 1970 v Ho (2), P (sub), Bel (with Tottenham H.), W, Ni, S, Co, Ec, R, Br, Cz, WG; 1971 v EG, Gr, Ma (2), Ni, W, S; 1972 v Sw, Gr, WG (1+1 sub.) 1973 v S (2), Ni, W, Cz, Pol, USSR, I; 1974 v A, Pol, I, P, S (67)
Phillips, L. H. (Portsmouth), 1952 v Ni 1955 v W, WG (3)
Pickering, F. (Everton), 1964 v US; 1965 v Ni, Bel (3)
Pickering, J. (Sheffield), 1933 v S (1)
Pike, T. M. (Cambridge University), 1886 v Ni (1)
Pilkington, B. (Burnley), 1955 v Ni (1)
Plant, J. (Bury), 1900 v S (1)
Plum, S. L. (Charlton Ath.), 1923 v F (1)
Pointer, R. (Burnley), 1962 v W, L. P (3)
Porteous, T. S. (Sunderland), 1891 v W (1)
Priest, A. E. (Sheffield U.), 1900 v Ni (1)
Prinsep, J. F. M. (Clapham Rovers), 1879 v S (1)
Puddefoot, S. C. (Blackburn R.), 1926 v S, Ni (2)
Pye, J. (Wolverhampton W.), 1950 v Ei (1)
Pym, R. H. (Bolton W.), 1925 v S, W. 1926 v W (3)
Quantrill, A. (Derby Co.), 1920 v S, W; 1921 v W, Ni (4)
Quixall, A. (Sheffield W.), 1954 v W, Ni, R of E; 1955 v Sp, P (sub) (5)

Radford, J. (Arsenal), 1969 v R; 1972 v Sw (sub) (2)
Raikes, G. B. (Oxford University), 1895 v W; 1896 v W, Ni, S (4)
Ramsey, A. E. (Southampton), 1949 v Sw; (with Tottenham H.), 1950 v S, I, P, Bel, Ch, US, Sp; 1951 v S, Ni, W, Y, Arg, P; 1952 v S, W, Ni, F, A (2), I, Sw; 1953 v Ni, W, S, Bel, Arg. Ch, U, US; 1954 v R of E, H (32)
Rawlings, A. (Preston N.E.), 1921 v Bel (1)
Rawlings, W. E. (Southampton), 1922 v S, W (2)
Rawlinson, J. F. P. (Cambridge University), 1882 v Ni (1)
Rawson, H. E. (Royal Engineers), 1875 v S (1)
Rawson, W. S. (Oxford University), 1875 v S; 1877 v S (2)
Read, A. (Tufnell Park), 1921 v Bel (1)
Reader, J. (W.B.A.), 1894 v Ni (1)
Reaney, P. (Leeds U.), 1969 v Bul (sub); 1970 v P; 1971 v Ma (3)
Revie, D. G. (Manchester C.), 1955 v Ni, S, F; 1956 v W, D; 1957 v Ni (6)
Reynolds, J. (W.B.A.), 1892 v S; 1893 v S, W; (with Aston Villa), 1894 v S, Ni; 1895 v S; 1897 v S, W (8)
Richards, C. H. (Nottingham F.), 1898 v Ni (1)
Richards, G. H. (Derby Co.), 1909 v A (1)
Richards, J. P. (Wolverhampton W.), 1973 v Ni (1)
Richardson, J. R. (Newcastle U.), 1933 v I, Sw (2)
Richardson, W. G. (W.B.A.), 1935 v Ho (1)
Rickaby, S. (W.B.A.), 1954 v Ni (1)
Rigby, A. (Blackburn R.), 1927 v S, Bel, L. F; 1928 v W (5)
Rimmer, E. J. (Sheffield W.), 1930 v S, G, A; 1932 v Sp (4)
Rimmer, J. J. (Arsenal), 1976 v I (1)
Robb, G. (Tottenham H.), 1954 v H (1)
Roberts, C. (Manchester U.), 1905 v Ni, W, S (3)
Roberts, F. (Manchester C.), 1925 v S, W, Bel, F (4)

Roberts, H. (Arsenal), 1931 v S (1)
Roberts, H. (Millwall), 1931 v Bel (1)
Roberts, R. (W.B.A.), 1887 v S; 1888 v Ni; 1890 v Ni (3)
Roberts, W. T. (Preston N.E.), 1924 v W, Bel (2)
Robinson, J. (Sheffield W.), 1937 v Fi; 1938 v G, Sw; 1939 v W (4)
Robinson, J. W. (Derby Co.), 1897 v S, Ni; (with New Brighton Tower), 1898 v S, W, Ni; (with Southampton), 1899 v S; 1900 v S, W, Ni; 1901 v Ni (10)
Robson, R. (W.B.A.), 1958 v F, USSR (2), Br, A; 1960 v Sp, H; 1961 v Ni, W, S, L, P, Sp, M, I; 1962 v W, Ni, Sw, L, P (20)
Rose, W. C. (Wolverhampton W.), 1884 v S, W, Ni; (with Preston N.E.) 1886 v Ni; (with Wolverhampton W.), 1891 v Ni (5)
Rostron, T. (Darwen), 1881 v S, W (2)
Rowe, A. (Tottenham H.), 1934 v F (1)
Rowley, J. F. (Manchester U.) 1949 v Sw, Se, F; 1950 v Ni, I; 1952 v S(6)
Rowley, W. (Stoke C.), 1889 v Ni; 1892 v Ni (2)
Royle, J. (Everton), 1971 v Ma; 1973 v Y; (with Manchester C.), 1976 v Ni (sub), I (4)
Ruddlesdin, H. (Sheffield W.). 1904 v W, Ni ; 1905 v S (3)
Ruffell, J. W. (West Ham U.), 1926 v S; 1927 v Ni; 1929 v S, W, Ni; 1930 v W (6)
Russell, B. B. (Royal Engineers), 1883 v W (1)
Rutherford, J. (Newcastle U.), 1904 v S; 1907 v S, Ni, W; 1908 v S, Ni, W, A (2), H, B (11)

Sadler, D. (Manchester U.), 1968 v Ni, USSR; 1970 v Ec (sub); 1971 v EG (4)
Sagar, C. (Bury), 1900 v Ni; 1902 v W (2)
Sagar, E. (Everton), 1936 v S, Ni, A, Bel (4)
Sandford, E. A. (W.B.A.), 1933 v W (1)
Sandilands, R. R. (Old Westminsters), 1892 v W; 1893 v Ni; 1894 v W; 1895 v W; 1896 v W (5)
Sands, J. (Nottingham F.), 1880 v W (1)
Saunders, F. E. (Swifts), 1888 v W (1)
Savage, A. H. (C. Palace), 1876 v S (1)
Sayer, J. (Stoke), 1887 v Ni (1)
Scattergood, E. (Derby Co.), 1913 v W (1)
Schofield, J. (Stoke), 1892 v W; 1893 v W; 1895 v Ni (3)
Scott, L. (Arsenal), 1947 v S, W, Ni, Ei, Ho, F, Sw, P; 1948 v S, W, Ni, Bel, Se, I; 1949 v W, Ni, D (17)
Scott, W. R. (Brentford), 1937 v W (1)
Seddon, J. (Bolton W.), 1923 v F, Se (2); 1924 v Bel; 1927 v W; 1929 v S (6)
Seed, J. M. (Tottenham H.), 1921 v Bel; 1923 v W, Ni, Bel; 1925 v S (5)
Settle, J. (Bury), 1899, v S, W, Ni; (with Everton), 1902 v S, Ni; 1903 v Ni (6)
Sewell, J. (Sheffield W.), 1952 v Ni, A, Sw; 1953 v Ni; 1954 v H (2) (6)
Sewell, W. R. (Blackburn R.), 1924 v W (1)
Shackleton, L. F. (Sunderland), 1949 v W, D; 1950 v W; 1955 v W, WG (5)
Sharp, J. (Everton), 1903 v Ni; 1905 v S (2)
Shaw, G. E. (W.B.A.), 1932 v S (1)
Shaw, G. L. (Sheffield U.), 1959 v S, W, USSR, I; 1963 v W (5)
Shea, D. (Blackburn R.), 1914 v W, Ni (2)
Shellito, K. J. (Chelsea), 1963 v Cz(1)
Snelton. A. (Notts. Co.), 1889 v Ni; 1890 v S, W; 1891 v S, W; 1892 v S (6)
Shelton, C. (Notts Rangers), 1888 v Ni (1)
Shepherd, A. (Bolton W.), 1906 v S; (with Newcastle U.), 1911 v Ni (2)

Shilton, P. L. (Leicester C.), 1971 v EG, W; 1972 v Sw, Ni; 1973 v Y, S (2) Ni, W, Cz, Pol, USSR, I; 1974 v A, Pol, I, W, Ni, S, Arg; (with Stoke C.) 1975 v Cy(21)
Shimwell, E. (Blackpool), 1949 v Se (1)
Shutt, G. (Stoke C.), 1886 v Ni (1)
Silcock, J. (Manchester U.), 1921 v S, W; 1923 v Se (3)
Sillett, R. P. (Chelsea), 1955 v F, Sp, P (3)
Simms, E. (Luton T.), 1922 v Ni (1)
Simpson, J. (Blackburn R.), 1911 v S, W, Ni; 1912 v S, W, Ni; 1913 v S; 1914 v W (8)
Slater, W. J. (Wolverhampton W.) ,1955 v W, WG; 1958 v S, P, Y, USSR (3), Br, A; 1959 v USSR; 1960 v S (12)
Smalley, T. (Wolverhampton W.), 1937 v W (1)
Smart, T. (Aston Villa), 1921 v S; 1924 v S, W 1926 v Ni; 1930 v W (5)
Smith, A. (Nottingham F.), 1891 v S, W; 1893 v Ni (3)
Smith, A. K. (Oxford University), 1872 v S (1)
Smith, B. (Tottenham H.), 1921 v S; 1922 v W (2)
Smith, C. E. (C. Palace), 1876 v S (1)
Smith, G. D. (Oxford University), 1893 v Ni; 1894 v W, S; 1895 v W; 1896 v Ni, W, S; (with Old Carthusians) 1897 v Ni, W, S; 1898 v Ni, W, S; (with Corinthians) 1899 v Ni, W, S; 1899 v Ni, W, S; 1901 v S (20)
Smith, H. (Reading), 1905 v W, S; 1906 v W, Ni (4)
Smith, J. (W.B.A.), 1920 v Ni; 1923 v Ni (2)
Smith, Joe (Bolton W.), 1913 v Ni; 1914 v S, W; 1920 v W, Ni (5)
Smith, J. C. R. (Millwall), 1939 v Ni, N (2)
Smith, J. W. (Portsmouth), 1932 v Ni, W, Sp (3)
Smith, Leslie (Brentford), 1939 v R (1)
Smith, Lionel (Arsenal), 1951 v W; 1952 v W, Ni; 1953 v W, S, Bel (6)
Smith, R. A. (Tottenham H.), 1961 v Ni, W, S, L, P, Sp; 1962 v S; 1963 v S, F, Br, Cz, EG; 1964 v W Ni, R of W (15)
Smith, S. (Aston Villa), 1895 v S (1)
Smith, S. C. (Leicester C.), 1936 v Ni (1)
Smith, T. (Birmingham C.), 1960 v W, Se (2)
Smith, T. (Liverpool), 1971 v W (1)
Smith, W. H. (Huddersfield T.), 1922 v W, S; 1928 v S (3)
Sorby, T. H. (Thursday Wanderers, Sheffield),1879 v W(1)
Southworth, J. (Blackburn R.), 1889 v W; 1891 v W; 1892 v S (3)
Sparks, F. J. (Herts Rangers), 1879 v S; (with Clapham Rovers) 1880 v S, W (3)
Spence, J. W. (Manchester U), 1926 v Bel; 1927 v Ni (2)
Spence, R. (Chelsea), 1936 v A, Bel (2)
Spencer, C. W. (Newcastle U.), 1924 v S; 1925 v W (2)
Spencer, H. (Aston Villa), 1897 v S, W; 1900 v W; 1903 v Ni; 1905 v W, S (6)
Spiksley, F. (Sheffield W.), 1893 v S, W; 1894 v S, Ni; 1896 v Ni; 1898 v S, W (7)
Spilsbury, B. W. (Cambridge University), 1885 v Ni; 1886 v Ni, S (3)
Spouncer, W. A. (Nottingham F.), 1900 v W (1)
Springett, R. D. G. (Sheffield W.), 1960 v Ni, S, Y, Sp, H; 1961 v Ni, S, L, P, Sp, M, I, A; 1962 v W, Ni, S, A, Sw, Pe, L, P, H, Arg, Bul, Br; 1963 v Ni, W, F (2), Sw; 1966 v W, A, N (33)
Sproston, B. (Leeds U.), 1937 v W; 1938 v S, W, Ni, Cz, G, Sw, P; (with Tottenham H.), 1939 v W, R of E; (with Manchester C.), 1939 v N (11)

Squire, R. T. (Cambridge University), 1886 v S, W, Ni (3)
Stanbrough, M. H. (Old Carthusians), 1895 v W (1)
Staniforth, R. (Huddersfield T.), 1954 v S, H, Y, Bel, Sw, U; 1955 v W, WG (8)
Starling, R. W. (Sheffield W.), 1933 v S; (with Aston Villa), 1937 v S (2)
Steele, F. C. (Stoke C.), 1937 v S, W, Ni, N, Se, Fi (6)
Stephenson, C. (Huddersfield T.), 1924 v W (1)
Stephenson, G. T. (Derby Co.), 1928 v F, Bel; (with Sheffield W.), 1931 v F (3)
Stephenson, J. E. (Leeds U.), 1938 v S; 1939 v Ni (2)
Stepney, A. C. (Manchester U.), 1968 v Se (1)
Stewart, J. (Sheffield W.), 1907 v S, W; (with Newcastle U.), 1911 v S (3)
Stiles, N. P. (Manchester U.), 1965 v S, H, Y, Se; 1966 v W, Ni, S, A, Sp, Pol (2), WG (2), N, D, U, M, F, Arg, P, 1967 v Ni, W, S, Cz; 1968 v USSR; 1969 v R; 1970 v Ni, S (28)
Stoker, J. (Birmingham), 1933 v W; 1934 v S, H (3)
Storer, H. (Derby Co.), 1924 v F; 1928 v Ni (2)
Storey P. E. (Arsenal), 1971 v Gr, Ni, S. 1972 v Sw, WG, W, Ni, S; 1973 v W (3), Y, S (2), Ni, Cz, Pol, USSR, I (19)
Storey-Moore, I. (Nottingham F.), 1970 v Ho (1)
Strange, A. H. (Sheffield W.), 1930 v S, A, G; 1931 v S, W, Ni,F, Bel; 1932 v S, W, Ni, Sp; 1933 v S, Ni, A, I, Sw; 1934 v Ni, W, F (20)
Stratford, A. H. (Wanderers), 1874 v S (1)
Streten, B. (Luton T.), 1950 v Ni (1)
Sturgess, A. (Sheffield U.), 1911 v Ni; 1914 v S (2)
Summerbee, M. G. (Manchester C.), 1968 v S, Sp, WG; 1972 v Sw, WG (sub), W, Ni; 1973 v USSR (sub) (8)
Sutcliffe, J. W. (Bolton W.), 1893 v W; 1895 v S, Ni; 1901 v S; (with Millwall), 1903 v W (5)
Swan, P. (Sheffield W.), 1960 v Y, Sp, H; 1961 v Ni, W, S, L, P, Sp, M, I, A; 1962 v W, Ni, S, A, Sw, L, P (19)
Swepstone, H. A. (Pilgrims), 1880 v S; 1882 v S, W; 1883 v S, W, Ni (6)
Swift, F. V. (Manchester C.), 1947, v S, W, Ni, Ei, Hol, F, Sw, P; 1948 v S, W, Ni, Bel, Se, I; 1949v S, W, Ni, D, N (19)

Tait, G. (Birmingham Excelsior), 1881 v W (1)
Tambling, R. V. (Chelsea), 1963 v W, F; 1966 v Y (3)
Tate, J. T. (Aston Villa), 1931 v F, Bel; 1933 v W (3)
Taylor, E. (Blackpool), 1954 v H (1)
Taylor, E. H. (Huddersfield T.), 1923 v S, W, Ni, Bel; 1924 v S, Ni, F; 1926 v S (8)
Taylor, J. G. (Fulham), 1951 v Arg, P (2)
Taylor, P. J. (C. Palace), 1976 v W (sub), W, Ni, S (4)
Taylor, P. H. (Liverpool), 1948 v W, Ni, Se (3)
Taylor, T. (Manchester U.), 1953 v Arg, Ch, U; 1954 v Bel, Sw; 1956 v S, Br, Se, Fi, WG; 1957 v Ni, Y (sub), D (2), Ei (2); 1958 v W, Ni, F (19)
Temple, D. W. (Everton), 1965 v WG (1)
Thickett, H. (Sheffield U.), 1899 v S, W (2)
Thomas, D. (Q.P.R.), 1975 v Cz (sub), P, Cy (sub + 1), W, S (sub); 1976 v Cz (sub), P (sub) (8)
Thompson, P. (Liverpool), 1964 v P (2), Ei, US, Br, Arg; 1965 v Ni, W, S, Bel, Ho; 1966 v Ni; 1968 v Ni, WG; 1970 v S, Ho (sub) (16)
Thompson, P. B. (Liverpool), 1976 v W (2), Ni, S, Br, I (6)
Thompson, T. (Aston Villa), 1952 v W; (with Preston N.E.), 1957 v S (2)

Thomson, R. A. (Wolverhampton W.), 1964 v Ni, US, P, Arg; 1965 v Bel, Ho, Ni, W (8)
Thornewell, G. (Derby Co.), 1923 v Se (2); 1924 v F; 1925 v F (4)
Thornley, I. (Manchester C.), 1907 v W (1)
Tilson, S. F. (Manchester C.), 1934 v H, Cz; 1935 v W; 1936 v Ni (4)
Titmuss, F. (Southampton), 1922 v W; 1923 v W (2)
Todd, C. (Derby Co.), 1972 v Ni; 1974 v P, W, Ni, S, Arg, EG, Bul, Y; 1975 v P (sub), WG, Cy (2), Ni, W, S; 1976 v Sw, Cz, P, Ni, S, Br (22)
Toone, G. (Notts. Co.), 1892 v S, W (2)
Topham, A. G. (Casuals), 1894 v W (1)
Topham, R. (Wolverhampton W.), 1893 v Ni; (with Casuals) 1894 v W (2)
Towers, M. A. (Sunderland), 1976 v W, Ni (sub), I (3)
Townley, W. J. (Blackburn R.), 1889 v W; 1890 v Ni (2)
Townrow, J. E. (Clapton Orient), 1925 v S; 1926 v W (2)
Tremelling, D. R. (Birmingham), 1928 v W (1)
Tresadern, J. (West Ham U.), 1923 v S, Se (2)
Tueart, D. (Manchester C.), 1975 v Cy (sub), Ni (2)
Tunstall, F. E. (Sheffield U.), 1923 v S; 1924 v S. W. Ni, F; 1925 v Ni, S (7)
Turnbull, R. J. (Bradford), 1920 v Ni (1)
Turner, A. (Southampton), 1900 v Ni; 1901 v Ni (2)
Turner, H. (Huddersfield T.), 1931 v F, Bel (2)
Turner, J. A. (Bolton W.), 1893 v W; (with Stoke) 1895 v Ni; (with Derby Co.) 1898 v Ni (3)
Tweedy, G. J. (Grimsby T.) 1937 v H (1)

Ufton, D. G. (Charlton Ath.), 1954 v R of E (1)
Underwood, A. (Stoke), 1891–2 v Ni (2)
Urwin, T. (Middlesbrough), 1923 v Se (2); (with Newcastle U.) 1924 v Bel; 1926 v W (4)
Utley, G. (Barnsley), 1913 v Ni (1)

Vaughton, O. H. (Aston Villa), 1882 v S, W, Ni; 1884 v S, W (5)
Veitch, C. C. M. (Newcastle U.), 1906 v S, W, Ni; 1907 v S, W; 1909 v W (6)
Veitch, J. G. (Old Westminsters), 1894 v W (1)
Venables, T. F. (Chelsea), 1965 v Ho, Bel (2)
Vidal, R. W. S. (Oxford University), 1873 v S (1)
Viljoen, C. (Ipswich T.), 1975 v Ni, W (2)
Viollet, D. S. (Manchester U.), 1960 v H; 1962 v L (2)
Von Donop (Royal Engineers), 1873 v S; 1875 v S (2)

Wace, H. (Wanderers), 1878 v S; 1879 v S, W (3)
Wadsworth, S. J. (Huddersfield T.), 1922 v S; 1923 v S, Bel; 1924 v S, Ni; 1925 v S, Ni; 1926 v W; 1927 v Ni (9)
Wainscoat, W. R. (Leeds U.), 1929 v S, (1)
Waiters, A. K. (Blackpool), 1964 v Ei, Br; 1965 v W, Bel, Ho (5)
Walden, F. I. (Tottenham H.), 1914 v S; 1922 v W (2)
Walker, W. H. (Aston Villa), 1921 v Ni; 1922 v Ni, W, S; 1923 v Se (2); 1924 v S; 1925 v Ni, W, S, Bel, F; 1926 v Ni, W, S; 1927 v Ni, W; 1933 v A (18)
Wall, G. (Manchester U.), 1907 v W; 1908 v Ni; 1909 v S; 1910 v W, S; 1912 v S; 1913 v Ni (7)
Wallace, C. W. (Aston Villa), 1913 v W; 1914 v Ni; 1920 v S (3)
Walters, A. M. (Cambridge University), 1885 v S, N, 1886 v S; 1887 v S, W; (Old Carthusians) 1889 v S, W; 1890 v S, W (9)

Walters, P. M. (Oxford University), 1885 v S, Ni; (Old Carthusians), 1886 v S, W, Ni; 1887 v S, W; 1888 v S, Ni; 1889 v S, W; 1890 v S, W (13)

Walton, N. (Blackburn R.), 1890 v Ni (1)

Ward, J. T. (Blackburn Olympic), 1885 v W (1)

Ward, T. V. (Derby Co.), 1948 v Bel; 1949 v W (2)

Waring, T. (Aston Villa), 1931 v F, Bel; 1932 v S, W, Ni (5)

Warner, C. (Upton Park), 1878 v S (1)

Warren, B. (Derby Co.), 1906 v S, W, Ni; 1907 v S, W, Ni; 1908 v S, W, Ni, A (2), H, B; 1909 v S, Ni, W, H (2), A; 1911 v S, Ni, W (22)

Waterfield, G. S. (Burnley), 1927 v W (1)

Watson, D. V. (Sunderland, 1974 v P, S (sub), Arg, EG, Bul, Y; 1975 v Cz, P, WG, Cy (2), Ni, W, S; 1976 v Sw, Cz (sub), P (17)

Watson, V. M. (West Ham U.), 1923 v W, S; 1930 v S, G, A (5)

Watson, W. (Burnley), 1913 v S, 1914 v Ni; 1920 v Ni (3)

Watson, W. (Sunderland). 1950 v Ni, I; 1951 v W, Y (4)

Weaver, S. (Newcastle U.), 1932 v S, 1933 v S, Ni (3)

Webb, G. W. (West Ham U.), 1911 v S, W (2)

Webster, M. (Middlesbrough), 1930 v S; A, G (3)

Wedlock, W. J. (Bristol C.), 1907 v S, Ni, W; 1908 v S, Ni, W. A (2), H, B; 1909 v S, W, Ni, H (2), A; 1910 v S, W, Ni; 1911 v S, W, Ni; 1912 v S, W Ni; 1914 v W (26)

Weir, D. (Bolton W.), 1889 v S, Ni (2)

Welch, R. de C. (Wanderers), 1872 v S; (with Harrow Chequers), 1874 v S (2)

Weller, K. (Leicester C.) 1974 v W, Ni, S, Arg (4)

Welsh, D. (Charlton Ath.), 1938 v G, Sw; 1939 v R (3)

West, G. (Everton), 1969 v W, Bul, M (3)

Westwood, R. W. (Bolton W.), 1935 v S, W, Ho; 1936 v Ni, G; 1937 v W (6)

Whatley, O. (Aston Villa), 1883 v S, Ni (2)

Wheeler, J. E. (Bolton W.), 1955 v Ni (1)

Wheldon, G. F. (Aston Villa), 1897 v Ni; 1898 v S, W, Ni (4)

White, T. A. (Everton), 1933 v Ni (1)

Whitehead, J. (Accrington), 1893 v W; (with Blackburn R.), 1894 v Ni (2)

Whitfeld, H. (Old Etonians), 1879 v W (1)

Whitham, M. (Sheffield U.), 1892 v Ni (1)

Whitworth, S. (Leicester C.), 1975 v WG, Cy, Ni, W, S; 1976 v Sw, P (7)

Widdowson, S. W. (Nottingham F.), 1880 v S (1)

Wignall, F. (Nottingham F.), 1965 v W, Ho (2)

Wilkes, A. (Aston Villa), 1901 v S, W; 1902 v S, W, Ni (5)

Wilkins, R. G. (Chelsea), 1976 v I (1)

Wilkinson, B. (Sheffield U.), 1904 v S (1)

Wilkinson, L. R. (Oxford University), 1891 c W (1)

Williams, B. F. (Wolverhampton W.), 1949 v F; 1950 v S, W, Ei, I, P, Bel, Ch, US, Sp; 1951 v Ni, W, S, Y, Arg, P; 1952 v W, F, 1955 v S, WG, F, Sp, P; 1956 v W (24)

Williams, O. (Clapton Orient), 1923 v W, Ni (2)

Williams, W. (W.B.A.), 1897 v Ni; 1898 v W, Ni, S; 1899 v W, Ni (6)

Williamson, E. C. (Arsenal), 1923 v Se (2) (2)

Williamson, R. G. (Middlesbrough), 1905 v Ni; 1911 v Ni, S, W; 1912 v S, W; 1913 v Ni (7)

Willingham, C. K. (Huddersfield T.), 1937 v Fi; 1938 v S, G, Sw, F; 1938 v S, W, Ni, R of E, N, I, Y (12)

Willis, A. (Tottenham H.), 1952 v F (1)

Wilshaw, D. J. (Wolverhampton W.), 1954 v W, Sw, U; 1955 v S, F, Sp, P; 1956 v W, Ni, Fi, WG; 1957 v Ni (12)

Wilson, C. P. (Hendon), 1884 v S, W (2)

Wilson, C. W. (Oxford University), 1879 v W; 1881 v S (2)

Wilson, G. (Sheffield W.), 1921 v S, W, Bel; 1922 v S, Ni; 1923 v S W, Ni, Bel; 1924 v W, Ni, F (12)

Wilson, G. P. (Corinthians), 1900 v S, W (2)

Wilson, R. (Huddersfield T.), 1960 v S, Y, Sp, H; 1962 v W, Ni, S, A, Sw, Pe, P, H, Arg, Bul, Br; 1963 v Ni F, Br, Cz, EG, Sw; 1964 v W, S, R of W, U, P (2), Ei, Br, Arg; (with Everton), 1965 v S, H, Y, WG, Se; 1966 v WG (sub), W, Ni, A, Sp, Pol (2), Y, Fi, D, U, M, F, Arg, P, WG; 1967 v Ni, W, S, Cz, A; 1968 v Ni, S, USSR (2), Sp (2), Y (63)

Wilson, T. (Huddersfield T.), 1928 v S (1)

Winckworth, W. N. (Old Westminsters), 1892 v W; 1893 v Ni (2)

Windridge, J. E. (Chelsea), 1908 v S, W. Ni A (2), H, B; 1909 v Ni (8)

Wingfield-Stratford, C. V. (Royal Engineers) 1877 v S (1)

Wollaston, C. H. R. (Wanderers), 1874 v S; 1875 v S; 1877 v S; 1880 v S (4)

Wolstenholme, S. (Everton), 1904 v S; (with Blackburn R.) 1905 v W, Ni (3)

Wood, H. (Wolverhampton W.), 1890 v S, W; 1896 v S (3)

Wood R. E. (Manchester U.), 1955 v Ni, W, 1956 v Fi (3)

Woodger, G. (Oldham Ath.), 1911 v Ni (1)

Woodhall, G. (W.B.A.), 1888 v S, W (2)

Woodley, V. R. (Chelsea), 1937 v S, N, Se, Fi; 1938 v S, W, Ni, Cz, G, Sw, F; 1939 v S, W, Ni, R of E, N, I, R, Y (19)

Woodward, V. J. (Tottenham H.). 1903 v S, W, Ni; 1904 v S, Ni; 1905 v S, W, Ni; 1907 v S; 1908 v S, W, Ni; 1908 v A (2), H, B; 1909 v W, Ni, H (2), A; (with Chelsea), 1910 v Ni; 1911 v W (23)

Woosnam, M. (Manchester C.), 1922 v W (1)

Worrall, F. (Portsmouth), 1935 v Ho; 1937 v Ni (2)

Worthington, F. S. (Leicester C.), 1974 v Ni (sub) S, Arg, EG, Bul, Y; 1975 v Cz, P (sub) (8)

Wreford-Brown, C. (Oxford University), 1889 v Ni; (Old Carthusians), 1894 v W; 1895 v W; 1898 v S (4)

Wright, E. G. D. (Cambridge University), 1906 v W (1)

Wright, J. D. (Newcastle U.), 1939 v N (1)

Wright, T. J. (Everton), 1968 v USSR; 1969 v R (2) M (sub), U, Br; 1970 v W, Ho, Bel, R (sub), Br (11)

Wright, W. A. (Wolverhampton W.), 1947 v S, W, Ni, Ei, Ho, F, Sw, P; 1948 v S, W, Ni, Bel, Se, I; 1949 v S, W, Ni, D, Sw, Se, N, F: 1950 v S, W, Ni, Ei, I, P, Bel, Ch, US, Sp; 1951 v Ni, S, Arg; 1952 v W, Ni, S, F, A (2), I, Sw; 1953 v Ni, W, S, Bel, Arg, Ch, U, US; 1954 v W, Ni, S, R of E, H (2), Y, Bel, Sw, U; 1955 v W, Ni, S, WG, F, Sp, P; 1956 v Ni, W, S, Br, Se, Fi, WG, D, Sp; 1957 v S, W, Ni, Y, D (2), Ei (2); 1958 v W, Ni, S, P, Y, USSR (3), Br, A, F; 1959 v W, Ni, S, USSR, I, Br, Pe, M, US (105)

Wyllie, J. G. (Wanderers), 1878 v S (1)

Yates, J. (Burnley), 1889 v Ni (1)

York, R. E. (Aston Villa), 1922 v S; 1926 v S (2)

Young, A. (Huddersfield T.), 1933 v W; 1937 v S, H, N, Se; 1938 v G, Sw, F; 1939 v W (9)

Young, G. M. (Sheffield W.), 1965 v W (1)

R. E. Evans also played for Wales against E, Ni, S; J. Reynolds also played for Ireland against E, W S.

Addis, D. J. (Cliftonville), 1922 v N (2) (2)

Aherne, T. (Belfast C.), 1947 v E; 1948 v S; 1949 v W; (with Luton T.), 1950 v W (4)

Alexander, A. (Cliftonville), 1895 v S (1)

Allen, C. A. (Cliftonville), 1936 v E (1)

Allen, J. (Limavady), 1887 v E (1)

Anderson, T. (Manchester U.) 1973 v Cy, E, S, W; 1974 v Bul, P (with Swindon T.), 1975 v S (sub); 1976 v Is (8)

Anderson, W. (Linfield), 1898 v W,E, S; 1899 v S (4)

Andrews, W. (Glentoran), 1908 v S; (with Grimsby T.), 1913 v E, S (3)

Baird, G. (Distillery), 1896 v S, E, W (3)

Baird, H. (Huddersfield T.), 1939 v E (1)

Balfe, J. (Shelbourne), 1909 v E; 1910 v W (2)

Bambrick, J. (Linfield), 1929 v W, S, E; 1930 v W, S, E; 1932 v W; (with Chelsea), 1935 v W, 1936 v E, S; 1938 v W (11)

Banks, S. J. (Cliftonville), 1937 v W (1)

Barr, H. H. (Linfield), 1962 v E; (with Coventry C.), 1963 v E, Pol (3)

Barron, H. (Cliftonville), 1894 v E, W, S; 1895 v S; 1896 v S; 1897 v E, W (7)

Barry, H. (Bohemians), 1900 v S (1)

Baxter, R. A. (Cliftonville), 1887 v S, W (2)

Bennett, L. V. (Dublin University), 1889 v W (1)

Berry, J. (Cliftonville), 1888 v S, W; 1889 v E (3)

Best, G. (Manchester U.), 1964 v W, U; 1965 v E, Ho (2), S, Sw (2), Alb; 1966 v S, E, Alb; 1967 v E; 1968 v S; 1969 v E, S, W, T; 1970 v S, E, W, USSR; 1971 v Cy (2), Sp, E, S, W; 1972 v USSR, Sp; 1973 v Bul; 1974 v P (32)

Bingham, W. L. (Sunderland), 1951 v F; 1952 v E,S, W; 1953 v E, S, F, W; 1954 v E, S, W; 1955 v E, S, W; 1956 v E, S, W; 1957 v E, S, W, P (2) I; 1958 v S, E, W, I (2), Arg, Cz (2), WG, F; (with Luton T.), 1959 v E, S, W, Sp; 1960 v S, E, W; (with Everton), 1961 v E, S, WG (2), Gr, I; 1962 v E, Gr; 1963 v E, S, Pol (2), Sp; (with Port Vale), 1964 v S, E, Sp (56)

Black, J. (Glentoran), 1901 v E (1)

Blair, H. (Portadown), 1931 v S; 1932 v S; (with Swansea) 1934 v S (3)

Blair, J. (Cliftonville), 1907 v W, E, S; 1908 v E, S (5)

Blair, R. V. (Oldham Ath.), 1975 v Se (sub), S (sub), W; 1976 v Se, Is (5)

Blanchflower, R. D. (Barnsley), 1950 v S, W; 1951 v E, S; (with Aston Villa), F; 1952 v W; 1953 v E, S, W, F; 1954 v E, S, W; (with Tottenham H.), 1955 v E, S, W; 1956 v S, W; 1957 v E, S, W, I, P (2); 1958 v E, S, W, I (2), Cz (2), Arg, F, WG; 1959 v E, S, W, Sp; 1960 v S, E, W; 1961 v E, S, W, WG (2); 1962 v E, S, W, Gr, Ho; 1963 v E, S, Pol (2) (56)

Blanchflower, J. (Manchester U.), 1954 v W; 1955 v E, S; 1956 v S, W; 1957 v S, E, P; 1958 v S, E, I (2) (12)

Bookman, L. O. (Bradford C.), 1914 v W; (with Luton T.), 1921 v S, W; 1922 v E (4)

Bothwell, A. W. (Ards), 1926 v S, E, W; 1927 v E, W (5)

Bowler, G. C. (Hull C.), 1950 v E, S, W (3)

Braithwaite, R. S. (Linfield), 1962 v W; 1963 v P, Sp; (with Middlesbrough), 1964 v W, U; 1965 v E, S, Sw (2), Ho (10)

Breen, T. (Belfast C.), 1935 v E, W; 1937 v E, S; (with Manchester U.), 1937 v W; 1938 v E, S; 1939 v W, S (9)

Brennan, B. (Bohemians), 1912 v W (1)

Brennan, R. A. (Luton T.), 1949 v v W; (with Birmingham C.), 1950 v E, S, W; (with Fulham), 1951 v E (5)

Briggs, W. R. (Manchester U.), 1962 v W; (with Swansea T.), 1965 v Ho (2)

Brisby, D. (Distillery), 1891 v S (1)

Brolly, T. (Millwall), 1937 v W; 1938 v W; 1939 v E, W (4)

Brookes, E. A. (Shelbourne), 1920 v S (1)

Brown, J, (Glenavon), 1921 v W; (Tranmere R.) 1924 v E, W (3)

Brown, J. (Wolverhampton W.), 1935 v E, W; 1936 v E; (with Coventry C.), 1937 v E. W; 1938 v S, W; (with Birmingham C.), 1939 v E, S, W (10)

Brown, W. G. (Glenavon), 1926 v W (1)

Brown, W. M. (Limavady), 1887 v E (1)

Browne, F. (Cliftonville). 1887 v E, S, W; 1888 v E, S (5)

Browne, R. J. (Leeds U.), 1936 v E, W; 1938 v E, W; 1939 v E, S (6)

Bruce, W. (Glentoran), 1961 v S, 1967 v W (2)

Buckle, H. (Cliftonville), 1882 v E (1)

Buckle, H. R. (Sunderland), 1904 v E; (with Bristol C.), 1908 v W (2)

Burnett, J. (Distillery), 1894 v E, W, S; (with Glentoran), 1895 v E, W (5)

Burnison, J. (Distillery), 1901 v E, W (2)

Burnison, S. (Distillery), 1908 v E; 1910 v E, S; with Bradford, 1911 v E, S, W; (with Distillery), 1912 v E; 1913 v W (8)

Burns, J. (Glenavon), 1923 v E (1)

Butler, M. P. (Blackpool), 1939 v W (1)

Campbell, A. C. (Crusaders), 1963 v W; 1965 v Sw (2)

Campbell, J. (Cliftonville), 1896 v W; 1897 v E, S, W; (with Distillery), 1898 v E, S, W; (with Cliftonville), 1899 v E, 1900 v E; S; 1901 v S, W; 1902 v S; 1903 v E; 1904 v S (15)

Campbell, J. P. (Fulham), 1951 v E, S (2)

Campbell, W. G. (Dundee), 1968 v S, E; 1969 v T; 1970 v S, W, USSR (6)

Carey, J. J. (Manchester U.), 1947 v E, S, W; 1948 v E; 1949 v E, S, W (7)

Carroll, E. (Glenavon), 1925 v S (1)

Casey, T. (Newcastle U.), 1955 v W; 1956 v W; 1957 v E, S, W I, P (2); 1958 v WG, F; 1959 v Sp (sub); (with Portsmouth),1959 v E (12)

Cashin, M. (Cliftonville), 1898 v S (1)

Cassidy, T. (Newcastle U.), 1971 v E (sub); 1972 v USSR (sub); 1974 v Bul (sub), S, E, W; 1975 v N; 1976 v S, E, W (10)

Chambers, J. (Distillery), 1921 v W; (with Bury) 1928 v S, W; 1929 v E, S, W; 1930 v S, W; (with Nottingham F.), 1932 v E, S, W (12)

Chatton H. A. (Partick T.), 1925 v E, S; 1926 v E (3)

Christian, J. (Linfield), 1889 v S (1)

Clarke, R. (Belfast C.), 1901 v E, S (2)

Clements, D. (Coventry C.), 1965 v W, Ho; 1966 v M; 1967 v S, W; 1968 v S, E,; 1969 v T (2), S, W; 1970 v S, E, W, USSR (2); 1971 v Sp, E, S, W, Cz; (with Sheffield W.) 1972 v USSR (2) Sp, E, S, W; 1973 v Bul, Cy (2) P, E, S, W; (with Everton) 1974 v Bul, P, S, E, W; 1975 v N, Y, E S, W; 1976 v Se, Y (with New York Cosmos), E, W (48)

Clugston, J. (Cliftonville), 1888 v W; 1889 v W, S, E; 1890 v E, S; 1891 v E, W; 1892 v E, S, W; 1893 v E, S, W (14)

Cochrane, D. (Leeds), 1939 v E, W; 1947 v E, S, W; 1949 v E, S, W; 1949 v S, W; 1950 v S, E, (12)

Cochrane, M. (Distillery), 1898 v S, W, E; 1899 v E; 1900 v E, S, W; (with Leicester Fosse), 1901 v S (8)

Cochrane, T. (Coleraine), 1976 v N (1)

Collins, F. (Glasgow C.), 1922 v S (1)

Collins, R. (Cliftonville), 1922 v N (1)

Condy, J. (Distillery), 1882 v W; 1886 v E, S (3)

Connor, J. (Glentoran), 1901 v S, E; (with Belfast C.), 1905 v E, S, W; 1907 v E, S; 1908 v E, S; 1909 v W; 1911 v S, E, W (13)

Connor, M. J. (Brentford), 1903 v S, W; (with Fulham) 1904 v E (3)

Cook, W. (Celtic), 1933 v E, W, S; (with Everton) 1935 v E; 1936 v S, W; 1937 v E, S, W; 1938 v E, S, W; 1939 v E, S, W (15)

Cooke, S. (Belfast YMCA), 1889 v E; (with Cliftonville), 1890 v E, S (3)

Coulter, J. (Belfast C.), 1934 v E, S, W; (with Everton), 1935 v E, S, W; 1937 v S, W; (with Grimsby T.), 1938 v S, W; (with Chelmsford C.), 1939 v S (11)

Cowan, J. (Newcastle U.), 1970 v E (sub)(1)

Cowan, T. S. (Queen's Island), 1925 v W (1)

Coyle, F. (Coleraine), 1956 v E, S; 1957 v P (with Nottingham F.), 1958 v Arg (4)

Coyle R. I. (Sheffield W.), 1973 v P, Cy (sub), W (sub); 1974 v Bul (sub), P (sub) (5)

Craig A. B. (Rangers), 1908 v E, S, W; 1909 v S; (with Morton), 1913 v S, W, 1914 v E, S, W (9)

Craig, D. J. (Newcastle U.), 1967 v W; 1968 v W; 1969 v T (2), E, S, W; 1970 v E, S, W, USSR; 1971 v Cy (2), S, S (sub); 1972 v USSR, S (sub); 1973 v Cy (2), E, S, W; 1974 v Bul, P; 1975 v N (25)

Crawford, S. (Distillery), 1889 v E, W; (with Cliftonville), 1891 v E, S, W; 1893 v E, W (7)

Crone, R. (Distillery), 1889 v S; 1890 v E, S, W (4)

Crone, W. (Distillery), 1882 v W; 1884 v E, S, W; 1886 v E, S, W; 1887 v E; 1888 v E, W; 1889 v S; 1890 v W (12)

Crooks, W. (Manchester U.), 1922 v W (1)

Crossan, E. (Blackburn R.), 1950 v S; 1951 v E; 1955 v W (3)

Crossan, J. A. (Sparta-Rotterdam), 1960 v E; (with Sunderland); 1963 v W, P, Sp; 1964 v E, S, W, U, Sp; 1965 v E, S, Sw (2); (with Manchester C.), v W, Ho (2), Alb; 1966 v S, E, Alb, WG; 1967 v E, S; (with Middlesbrough), 1968 v S (23)

Crothers, C. (Distillery), 1907 v W (1)

Cumming, L. (Huddersfield T.), 1929 v W, S; (with Oldham Ath.), 1930 v E (3)

Cunningham, R. (Ulster), 1892 v S, E, W; 1893 v E (4)

Cunningham, W. E. (St. Mirren), 1951 v W; 1953 v E; 1954 v S; 1955 v S; (with Leicester C.), 1956 v E, S, W; 1957 v E, S, W, I, P (2); 1958 v S, W, I, Cz (2), Arg, WG, F; 1959 v E, S, W; 1960 v E, S, W; (with Dunfermline Ath.), 1971 v W; 1962 v W, Ho (30)

Curran, S. (Belfast C.), 1926 v S, W; 1928 v S (3)

Curran, J. J. (Glenavon), 1922 v W, N (2); (with Pontypridd), 1923 v E, S; (with Glenavon), 1924 v E (6)

Cush, W. W. (Glenavon), 1951 v E, S; 1954 v S, E; 1957 v W, I, P (2); (withLeeds U.), 1958 v I (2), W, Cz (2), Arg, WG, F; 1959 v E, S, W, Sp; 1960 v E, S, W; (with Portadown), 1961 v WG, Gr; 1962 v Gr (26)

Dalrymple, J. P. (Distillery), 1922 v N (2) (2)

Dalton, W. (YMCA), 1888 v S; (with Linfield), 1890 v S, W; 1891 v S, W; 1892 v E, S,W ; 1894 v E, S, W (11)

D'Arcy, S. D. (Chelsea), 1952 v W; 1953 v E; (with Brentford), 1953 v S, W, F (5)

Darling, J. (Linfield), 1897 v E, S; 1900 v S; 1902 v E, S, W; 1903 v E, S, W; 1905 v E, S, W; 1906 v E, S, W; 1908 v W; 1909 v E; 1910 v E, S, W; 1912 v S (21)

Davey, H. H. (Reading), 1926 v E; 1927 v E, S; 1928 v E; (with Portsmouth), 1928 v W (5)

Davis, T. L. (Oldham Ath.), 1937 v E (1)

Davison, J. R. (Cliftonville), 1882 v E, W; 1883 v E, W; 1884 v E, W, S; 1885 v E (8)

Devine, W. (Limavady), 1886 v E, S; 1887 v W; 1888 v W (4)

Dickson, D. (Coleraine), 1970 v S (sub), W; 1973 v Cy, P (4)

Dickson, T. A. (Linfield), 1357 v S (1)

Dickson, W. (Chelsea), 1951 v W, F; 1952 v E, S W; 1953 v E, S, W, F; (with Arsenal); 1954 v E W; 1955 v E (12)

Diffin, W. (Belfast C.), 1931 v W (1)

Dill, A. H. (Knock and Down Ath.), 1882 v E, W; (with Cliftonville), 1883 v W; 1884 v E, S, W; 1885 v E, S, W (9)

Doherty, I. (Belfast C.), 1901 v E (1)

Doherty, J. (Cliftonville), 1933 v E, W (2)

Doherty, M. (Derry C.), 1938 v S (1)

Doherty, P. D. (Blackpool), 1935 v E, W; 1936 v E, S; (with Manchester C.), 1937 v E, W; 1938 v E, S; 1939 v E, W; (with Derby Co.), 1947 v E; (with Huddersfield T.), 1947 v W; 1948 v E, W; 1949 v S; (with Doncaster R.), 1951 v S (16)

Donnelly, L. (Distillery), 1913 v W (1)

Doran, J. F. (Brighton), 1921 v E; 1922 v E, W (3)

Dougan, A. D. (Portsmouth), 1958 v Cz; (with Blackburn R.), 1960 v S; 1961 v E, W, I, Gr; (with Aston Villa), 1963 v S, P (2); (with Leicester C.), 1966 v S, E, W, M ;Alb, WG; 1967 v E, S; (with Wolverhampton W.), 1967 v W; 1968 v S, W, Is, T (2); 1969 v E, S, W; 1970 v S, E, USSR (2); 1971 v Cy (2), Sp, E, S, W; 1972 v USSR (2), E, S, W; 1973 v Bul, Cy (43)

Douglas, J. P., (Belfast C.), 1947 v E (1)

Dowd, H. O. (Glentoran), 1974 v W; (with Glenavon), 1975 v N (sub), Se (3)

Duggan, H. A. (Leeds U.), 1930 v E; 1931 v E, W; 1933 v E; 1934 v E; 1935 v S, W; 1936 v S (8)

Dunne, J. (Sheffield U.), 1928 v W; 1931 v W, E; 1932 v E, S; 1933 v E, W (7)

Eames, W. L. E. (Dublin U.), 1885 v E, S, W (3)

Eglington, T. J. (Everton), 1947 v S, W; 1948 v E, S, W; 1949 v E (6)

Elder, A. R. (Burnley), 1960 v W; 1961 v S, E, W, WG (2), Gr; 1962 v E, S, Gr; 1963 v E, S, W, P (2), Sp; 1964 v W, U; 1965 v E, S, W, Sw (2), Ho (2), Alb; 1966 v E, S, W, M, Alb; 1967 v E, S, W (with Stoke C.), 1968 v E, W; 1969 v E (sub), S, W; 1970 v USSR (40)

Elleman, A. R. (Cliftonville), 1889 v W; 1890 v E (2)

Elwood, J. H. (Bradford), 1929 v W; 1930 v E (2)

Emerson, W. (Glentoran), 1920 v E, S, W; 1921 v E; 1922 v E, S; (with Burnley), 1922 v W; 1923 v E, S, W; 1924 v E (11)

English, S. (Glasgow R.), 1933 v W, S (2)

Enright, J. (Leeds C.), 1912 v S (1)

Fallon, E. (Aberdeen), 1931 v S; 1933 v S (2)

Farquharson, T. G. (Cardiff C.), 1923 v S, W; 1924 v E, S, W; 1925 v E, S (7)

Farrell, P. (Distillery), 1901 v S, W (2)
Farrell, P. (Hibernian), 1938 v W (1)
Farrell, P. D. (Everton), 1947 v S, W; 1948 v E, S, W; 1949 v E, W (7)
Feeney, J. M. (Linsfield), 1947 v S; (with Swansea T.), 1950 v E (2)
Feeney, W. (Glentoran), 1976 v Is (1)
Ferguson, W. (Linfield), 1966 v M; 1967 v E (2)
Ferris, J. (Belfast Celtic), 1920 v E, W; (with Chelsea), 1921 v S, E, (with Belfast C.), 1928 v S (5)
Ferris, R. O. (Birmingham), 1950 v S; 1951 v F; 1952 v S (3)
Finney, T. (Sunderland), 1975 v N, E (sub), S, W; 1976 v N, Y, S (7)
Fitzpatrick, J. C. (Bohemians), 1896 v E, S (2)
Flack, H. (Burnley), 1929 v S (1)
Forbes, G. (Limavady), 1888 v W; (with Distillery), 1891 v E, S (3)
Forde, J. T. (Ards), 1959 v Sp; 1961 v E, S, WG (4)
Foreman, T. A. (Cliftonville), 1899 v S (1)
Forsyth, J. (YMCA), 1888 v E, S (2)
Fox, W. (Ulster), 1887 v E, S (2)
Fulton, R, P. (Belfast C.), 1930 v W; 1931 v E, S, W; 1932 v W, E; 1933 v E, S; 1934 v E, W, S; 1935 v E, W, S; 1936 v S, W; 1937 v E, S, W; 1938 v W (20)

Gaffikin, J. (Linfield Ath.), 1890 v S, W; 1891 v S, W; 1892 v E, S, W; 1893 v E, S, W; 1894 v E, S, W; 1895 v E, W (15)
Galbraith, W. (Distillery), 1890 v W (1)
Gallagher, P. (Celtic), 1920 v E, S; 1922 v S; 1923 v S, W; 1924 v S, W; 1925 v S, W, E; (with Falkirk), 1927 v S (11)
Gallogly, C. (Huddersfield T.), 1951 v E, S (2)
Gara, A. (Preston N.E.), 1902 v E, S, W (3)
Gardiner, A. (Cliftonville), 1930 v S, W; 1931 v S; 1932 v E, S (5)
Garrett, J. (Distillery), 1925 v W (1)
Gaston, R. (Oxford U.), 1969 v Is (sub) (1)
Gaukrodger, G. (Linfield), 1895 v W (1)
Gaussen, A. W. (Moyola Park), 1884 v E, S; 1888 v E, W; 1889 v E, W (6)
Geary, J. (Glentoran), 1931 v S; 1932 v S (2)
Gibb, J. T. (Wellington Park), 1884 v S, W; 1885 v S, E, W; 1886 v S; 1887 v S, E, W; 1889 v S (10)
Gibb, T. J. (Cliftonville), 1936 v W (1)
Gibson, W. K. (Cliftonville), 1894 v S, W, E; 1895 v S; 1897 v W; 1898 v S, W, E; 1901 v S, W, E; 1902 v S, W (13)
Gillespie, R. (Hertford), 1886 v E, S, W; 1887 v E, S, W (6)
Gillespie, W. (Sheffield U.), 1913 v E, S; 1914 v E, W; 1920 v S, W; 1921 v E; 1922 v E, S, W; 1923 v E, S, W; 1924 v E, S, W; 1925 v E, S; 1926 v S, W; 1927 v E, W; 1928 v E; 1929 v E; 1931 v E (25)
Gillespie, W. (West Down), 1889 v W (1)
Goodall, A. L. (Derby Co.), 1899 v S, W; 1900 v E, W; 1901 v E; 1902 v S; 1903 v E, W; (with Glossop), 1904 v E, W (10)
Goodbody, M. F. (Dublin University), 1889 v E; 1891 v W (2)
Gordon, H. (Linfield), 1891 v S; 1892 v E, S, W 1893 v E, S, W; 1895 v E, W; 1896 v E, S (11)
Gordon, T. (Linfield), 1894 v W; 1895 v E (2)
Gorman, W. C. (Brentford), 1947 v E, S, W; 1948 v W (4)
Gowdy, J. (Glentoran), 1920 v E; (with Queen's Island), 1924 v W; (with Falkirk), 1926 v E, S; 1927 v E, S (6)
Gowdy, W. A. (Hull C.), 1932 v S; (with Sheffield

W.), 1933 v S; (with Linfield), 1935 v E, S, W; (with Hibernian), 1936 v W (6)
Graham, W. G. L. (Doncaster R.), 1951 v W, F; 1952 v E, S, W; 1953, v S, F; 1954 v E, W; 1955 v S, W; 1956 v E, E, S; 1959 v E (14)
Greer, W. (Q.P.R.), 1909 v E, S, W (3)
Gregg, H. (Doncaster R.), 1954 v W; 1957 v E, S, W, I, P; 1958 v E, I; (with Manchester U.), 1958 v Cz, Arg, WG, F, W; 1959 v E, W; 1960 v S, E, W; 1961 v E, S; 1962 v S, Gr; 1964 v S, E (24)
Hall, G. (Distillery), 1897 v E (1)
Halligan, W. (Derby Co.), 1911 v W; (with Wolverhampton W.), 1912 v E (2)
Hamil, M. (Manchester U.), 1912 v E; 1914 v E, S; (with Belfast C.), 1920 v E, S, W; (with Manchester C.), 1921 v S (7)
Hamilton, B. (Linfield), 1969 v T; 1971 Cy (2) E, S, W; (with Ipswich T.), 1972 v USv1 (1+1 sub), Sp; 1973 v Bul, Cy (2), P, E, S, WS974 v Bul, S, E, W; 1975 v N, Se, Y, E; 1976 v Se, N, Y (with Everton), Is, S, E, W (31)
Hamilton, J. (Knock), 1882 v E, W (2)
Hamilton, R. (Distillery), 1908 v W (1)
Hamilton, R. (Glasgow R.), 1928 v S; 1929 v E; 1930 v S, E; 1932 v S (5)
Hamilton, W. D. (Dublin Association), 1885 v W (1)
Hamilton, W. J. (Dublin Association), 1885 v W (1)
Hampton, H. (Bradford C.), 1911 v E, S, W; 1912 v E, W; 1913 v E, S; W; 1914 v E (9)
Hanna, D. R. A. (Porstmouth), 1899 v W (1)
Hanna, J. (Nottingham), 1912 v S, W (2)
Hannon, D. J. (Bohemian), 1908 v E, S; 1911 v E, S; 1912 v W; 1913 v E (6)
Harkin, J. T. (Southport), 1968 v W; (with Shrewsbury), 1969 v T, W (sub); 1970 v USSR; 1971 v Sp (5)
Harland, A. I. (Linfield), 1922 v N (2), 1923 v E (3)
Harris, J. (Cliftonville), 1921 v W (1)
Harris, V. (Shelbourne), 1906 v E; 1907 v E, W; 1908 v E, W, S; (with Everton); 1909 v E, W, S; 1910 v E, S, W; 1911 v E, S, W; 1912 v E; 1913 v E, S; 1914 v S, W (20)
Harvey, M. (Sunderland), 1961 v I; 1962 v Ho; 1963 v W Sp; 1964 v S, E, W, U, Sp; 1965 v E, S, W, Sw (2), Ho (2), Alb; 1966 v S, E, W, M; Alb, WG; 1967 v E, S; 1968 v E, W,; 1969, Is, T (2) v E; 1970 v USSR; 1971 v Cy, W (sub) (33)
Hastings, J. (Knock), 1882 v E, W; (with Ulster), 1883 v W; 1884 v E, S; 1886 v E, S (7)
Hatton, S. (Linfield), 1963 v S, Pol (2)
Hayes, W. E. (Huddersfield T.), 1938 v E, S,; 1939 v E, S (4)
Hegan, D. (W.B.A.), 1970 v USSR (with Wolverhampton W.); 1972 v USSR, E, S, W; 1973 v Bul, Cy (7)
Henderson, A. W. (Ulster), 1885 v E, S, W (3)
Hewison, G. (Moyola Park), 1885 v E, S (2)
Hill, M. J. (Norwich C.), 1959 v W; 1960 v W; 1961 v WG; 1962 v S (with Everton), 1964 v S, E, Sp (7)
Hinton, E. (Fulham), 1947 v S, W; 1948 v S, E, W; (Millwall), 1951 v W, F (7)
Hopkins, J. (Brighton), 1926 v E (1)
Houston, J. (Linfield), 1912 v S, W; 1913 v W, (with Everton), 1913 v E, S; 1914 v S (6)
Houston, W. (Linfield), 1933 v W (1)
Houston, W. G. (Moyola Park), 1885 v E, S (2)
Hughes, W. (Bolton W.), 1951 v W (1)
Humphries, W. (Ards), 1962 v W; (with Coventry C.), 1962 v Ho; 1963 v E, S, W, Pol, Sp; 1964 v S, E, Sp; 1965 v S; (with Swansea T.), 1965 v W, Ho, Alb (14)

Hunter, A. (Blackburn R.), 1970 v USSR, 1971 v
Cy (2), E, S, W; (with Ipswich T.), 1972 v USSR
(2), Sp, E, S, W; 1973 v Bul, Cy. (2), P, E, S,
W; 1974 v Bul, S, E, W; 1975 v N, Se, Y, E, S, W
1976 v Se, N, Y, Is, S, E, W (36)
Hunter, A. (Distillery), 1905 v W; 1906 v W, E, S;
(with Belfast C.), 1908 v W: 1909 v W, E, S (8)
Hunter, R. J. (Cliftonville), 1884 v E, S, W (3)
Hunter, V. (Coleraine), 1962 v E; 1964 v Sp (2)

Irvine, R. W. (Everton), 1922 v S; 1923 v E, W; 1924
v E, S; 1925 v E; 1926 v E; 1927 v E, W; 1928 v
E, S; (with Portsmouth), 1929 v E; 1930 v S;
(with Connah's Quay), 1931 v E; (with Derry
C.), 1932 v W (15)
Irvine, R. J. (Linfield), 1962 v Ho; 1963 v E, S, W,
Pol (2), Sp; (with Stoke C.), 1965 v W (8)
Irvine, W. J. (Burnley), 1963 v W, Sp; 1965 v S, W,
Sw, Ho (2), Alb; 1966 v S, E, W, M, Alb; 1967 v
E, S, 1968 v E, W; (with Preston N.E.), 1969 v
Is, T, E; (with Brighton), 1927 v E, S, W (23)
Irving, S. J. (Dundee), 1923 v S, W; 1924 v S, E,
W; 1925 v S, E, W; 1926 v S, W; (with Cardiff
C.), 1927 v S, E, W; 1928 v S, E, W; (with
Chelsea), 1929 v E; 1931 v W (18)

Jackson, T. (Everton), 1969 v Is, E, S, W; 1970 v
USSR (1+1 sub); (with Nottingham F.), 1971
v Sp; 1972 v E, S, W; 1973 v Cy, E, S, W;
1974 v Bul, P, S (sub), E (sub), W (sub); 1975 v
N (sub), Se, Y, E, S, W; (with Manchester U.);
1976 v Se, N, Y (28)
Jamison, J. (Glentoran), 1976 v N (1)
Jennings, P. A. (Watford), 1964 v W, U; (with
Tottenham H.), 1965 v E, S, Sw (2), Ho, Alb;
1966 v S, E, W, Alb, WG; 1967 v E, S; 1968 v S,
E, W; 1969 v Is, T (2), E, S, W; 1970 v S, E,
USSR (2); 1971 v Cy (2), E, S, W; 1972 v USSR,
Sp, S, E, W; 1973 v Bul, Cy, P, E, S, W; 1974 v
P, S, E, W; 1975 v N, Se, Y, E, S, W; 1976 v Se,
N, Y, Is, S, E, W (61)
Johnston, H. (Portadown), 1927 v W (1)
Johnston, R. (Old Park), 1885 v S, W (2)
Johnston, S. (Distillery), 1882 v W; 1884 v E;
1886 v E, S (4)
Johnston, S. (Linfield), 1890 v W; 1893 v S, W;
1894 v E (4)
Johnston, S. (Distillery), 1905 v W (1)
Johnston, W. C. (Glenavon), 1962 v W; (with
Oldham), 1966 v M (sub) (2)
Jones, J. (Linfield), 1930 v S, W; 1931 v S, W, E;
1932 v S, E; 1933 v S, E, W; 1934 v S, E, W;
1935 v S, E, W; 1936 v E, S; (with Hibernian),
1936 v W; 1937 v E, W, S; (with Glenavon),
1938 v E (23)
Jones, J. (Glenavon), 1956 v W; 1957 v E, W (3)
Jones, S. (Distillery), 1934 v E; (with Blackpool),
1934 v W (2)
Jordan, T. (Linfield), 1895 v E, W (2)

Kavanagh, P. J. (Glasgow C.), 1930 v E (1)
Keane, T. R. (Swansea T.), 1949 v S (1)
Kearns, A. (Distillery), 1900 v E, S, W; 1902 v
E, S, W (6)
Keith, R. M. (Newcastle U.), 1958 v E, W, Cz (2),
Arg, I, WG, F; 1959 v E, S, W, Sp; 1960 v S, E;
1961 v S, E, W, I, WG (2), Gr; 1962 v W, Ho (23)
Kelly, H. R. (Fulham), 1950 v E, W; (with
Southampton), 1951 v E, S (4)
Kelly, J. (Glentoran), 1896 v E (1)
Kelly, J. (Derry C.), 1932 v E, W; 1933 v E, W, S;
1934 v W; 1936 v E, S, W; 1937 v S, E (11)

Kelly, P. (Manchester C.), 1921 v E (1)
Kelly, P. M. (Barnsley), 1950 v S (1)
Kennedy, A. L. (Arsenal), 1923 v W; 1925 v E (2)
Kernaghan, N. (Belfast C.), 1936 v W; 1937 v S;
1938 v E (3)
Kirkwood, H. (Cliftonville), 1904 v W (1)
Kirwan, J. (Tottenham H.), 1900 v W; 1902 v E,
W; 1903 v E, S, W; 1904 v E, S, W; 1905 v
E, S, W; (with Chelsea), 1906 v E, S, W; 1907 v
W; (with Clyde), 1909 v S (17)

Lacey, W. (Everton), 1909 v E, S, W; 1910 v E, S,
W; 1911 v E, S, W; 1912 v E; (with Liverpool),
1913 v W; 1914 v E, S, W; 1920 v E, S, W;
1921 v E, S, W; 1922 v E, S; (with New Brighton),
1925 v E (3)
Lawther, W. I. (Sunderland), 1960 v W; 1961 v I;
(with Blackburn R.) 1962 v S, Ho (4)
Leatham, J. (Belfast C.), 1939 v W (1)
Ledwidge, J. J. (Shelbourne), 1906 v S, W (2)
Lemon, J. (Glentoran), 1886 v W; 1888 v S; (with
Belfast YMCA), 1889 v W (3)
Leslie, W. (YMCA), 1887 v E (1)
Lewis, J. (Glentoran), 1889 v S, E, W; (with
Distillery), 1900 v S (4)
Little, J. (Glentoran), 1898 v W (1)
Lockhart, H. (Rossall School), 1884 v W (1)
Lockhart, N. (Linfield), 1947 v E; (with Coventry
C.), 1950 v W; 1951 v W; 1952 v W; (with Aston
Villa), 1954 v S, E; 1955 v W; 1956 v W (8)
Lowther, R. (Glentoran), 1888 v E, S (2)
Loyal, J. (Clarence), 1891 v S (1)
Lutton, R. J. (Wolverhampton W.), 1970 v S, E
1973 (with West Ham U.), Cy (sub), S (sub), W
(sub); 1974 v P (6)
Lyner, D. (Glentoran), 1920 v E, W; 1922 v S, W;
(with Manchester U.), 1923 v E; (with Kilmar-
nock), 1923 v W (6)

McAdams, W. J. (Manchester C.), 1954 v W; 1955 v
S; 1957 v E; 1958 v S, I; (with Bolton W.), 1961 v
E, S, W, I, WG (2), Gr; 1962 v E, Gr, (with
Leeds U.), Ho (15)
M'Alery, J. M. (Cliftonville), 1882 v E, W (2)
M'Alinden, J. (Belfast C.), 1938 v S; 1939 v S;
(with Portsmouth), 1947 v E; (with Southend
U.), 1949 v E (4)
M'Allen, J. (Linfield), 1898 v E; 1899 v E, S, W;
1900 v E, S, W; 1901 v W; 1902 v S (9)
M'Alpine, W. J. (Cliftonville), 1901 v S (1)
M'Arthur, A. (Distillery), 1886 v W (1)
McAuley, P. (Belfast C.), 1900 v S (1)
M'Cabe, J. J. (Leeds U.), 1949 v S; 1950 v E;
1951 v W; 1953 v W; 1954 v S (6)
M'Cabe, W. (Ulster), 1891 v E (1)
M'Cambridge, J. (Ballymena), 1930 v S, W; (with
Cardiff C.), 1931 v W; 1932 v E (4)
M'Candless, J. (Bradford), 1912 v W; 1913 v W;
1920 v W, S; 1921 v E (5)
McCandless, W. (Linfield), 1920 v E, W; 1921 v E;
(with Rangers), 1921 v W; 1922 v S; 1924 v W,
S; 1925 v S; 1929 v W (9)
M'Cann, P. (Belfast C.), 1910 v E, S, W; 1911 v E,
(with Glentoran), 1911 v S; 1912 v E; 1913 v W
(7)
M'Cashin, J. (Cliftonville), 1896 v W; 1898 v S, W;
1899 v S (4)
M'Cavana, W. T. (Coleraine), 1955 v S; 1956 v E,
S (3)
M'Caw, D. (Distillery), 1882 v E (1)
M'Caw, J. H. (Linfield), 1927 v W; 1930 v S; 1931 v
E, S, W (5)

686

M'Clatchey, J. (Distillery), 1886 v E, S, W (3)
M'Clatchey, R. (Distillery), 1895 v S (1)
M'Cleary, J. W. (Cliftonville), 1955 v W (1)
M'Cleery, W. (Cliftonville), 1922 v N; 1930 v E, W; 1931 v E, S, W; 1932 v S, W; 1938 v E, W (10)
McClelland, J. (Arsenal), 1961 v W, I, WG (2), Gr; (with Fulham), 1967 v M (6)
M'Cluggage, A. (Cliftonville), 1922 v N (2) (with Bradford), 1924 v E; (with Burnley), 1927 v S, W; 1928 v S, E, W; 1929 v S, E, W; 1930 v W; 1931 v E, W (14)
M'Clure, G. (Cliftonville), 1907 v S, W; 1908 v E; (with Distillery), 1909 v E (4)
M'Connell, E. (Cliftonville), 1904 v S, W; (with Glentoran), 1905 v S; (with Sunderland), 1906 v E; 1907 v E; 1908 v S, W; (with Sheffield W.), 1909 v S, W; 1910 v S, W, E (12)
M'Connell, W. G. (Bohemians), 1912 v W; 1913 v E, S; 1914 v E, S, W (6)
M'Connell, W. H. (Reading), 1925 v W; 1926 v E, W; 1927 v E, S, W; 1928 v E, W (8)
M'Court, F. J. (Manchester C.), 1952 v E, W; 1953 v E, S, W, F (6)
M'Coy, J. (Distillery), 1896 v W (1)
McCracken, R. (Linfield) 1922 v N (2)
M'Cracken, R. (C. Palace), 1921 v E; 1922 v E, S, W (4)
M'Cracken, W. (Distillery), 1902 v E, W; 1903 v E; 1904 v E, S, W; (with Newcastle U.), 1905 v E, S, W; 1907 v E; 1920 v E; 1922 v E, S, W; (with Hull C.), 1923 v S (15)
McCreery, D. (Manchester U.), 1976 v S (sub), E, W (3)
McCrory, S. (Southend U.), 1958 v E (1)
M'Cullough, K. (Belfast C.), 1935 v W; 1936 v E; (with Manchester C.), 1936 v S; 1937 v E, S (5)
McCullough, W. J. (Arsenal), 1961 v I; 1963 v Sp; 1964 v E, W, U, Sp; 1965 v E, Sw; (with Millwall), 1967 v E (10)
M'Donald, R. (Glasgow R.), 1930 v S; 1932 v E (2)
M'Donnell, J. (Bohemians), 1911 v E, S; 1912 v W; 1913 v W (4)
M'Faul, W. S. (Linfield), 1967 v E (sub); (with Newcastle U.) 1970 v W; 1971 v Sp; 1972 v USSR; 1973 v Cy; 1974 v Bul (6)
M'Garry, J. K. (Cliftonville), 1951 v W, F, S (3)
M'Gee, G. (Willington Park), 1885 v E, S, W (3)
M'Grath, R. C. (Tottenham H.), 1974 v S, E, W; 1975 v N; 1976 v Is (sub), (5)
M'Gregor, S. (Glentoran), 1921 v S (1)
M'Grillen, J. (Clyde), 1924 v S; (with Belfast C.) 1927 v S (2)
M'Ilroy, H. (Cliftonville), 1906 v E (1)
McIlroy, J. (Burnley), 1952 v E, S, W; 1953 v E, S, W; 1954 v E, S, W; 1955 v E, S, W; 1956 v E, S, W; 1957 v E, S, W, I, P (2); 1958 v E, S, W, I (2), Cz (2), Arg, WG, F; 1959 v E, S, W, Sp; 1960 v E, S, W; 1961 v E, W, WG (2) Gr; 1962 v E, S, Gr, Ho; 1963 v E, S, Pol (2); (with Stoke C.), 1963 v W; 1966 v S, E, A, (55)
McIlroy, S. B. (Manchester U.), 1972 v Sp, S (sub); 1974 v S, E, W; 1975 v N, Se, Y, E, S, W; 1976 v Se, N, Y, S, E, W (17)
M'Ilvenny, J. (Distillery). 1890 v E; 1891 v E (2)
M'Ilvenny, P. (Distillery), 1924 v W (1)
McKeag, W. (Glentoran), 1968 v S, W (2)
M'Kee, F. W. (Cliftonville). 1906 v S, W; (with Belfast C.), 1914 v E, S, W (5)
M'Kelvie, H. (Glentoran), 1901 v W (1)
McKenna, J. (Huddersfield), 1950 v E, S, W; 1951 v E, S, F; 1952 v E (7)

M'Kenzie, H. (Distillery), 1922 v N (2); 1923 v S (3)
McKenzie, R. (Airdrie), 1967 v W (1)
M'Keown, H. (Linfield), 1892 v E, S, W; 1893 v S, W; 1894 v S, W (7)
M'Kie, H. (Cliftonville), 1895 v E, S, W (3)
M'Kinney, D. (Hull C.), 1921 v S; (with Bradford C.), 1924 v S (2).
McKinney, V. J. (Falkirk), 1966 v WG (1)
M'Knight, J. (Preston N.E.), 1912 v S; (with Glentoran), 1913 v S (2)
McLaughlin, J. C. (Shrewsbury T.), 1962 v E, S, W, Gr; 1963 v W; (with Swansea T.), 1964 v W, U; 1965 v E, W, Sw (2); 1966 v W (12)
M'Lean. T. (Limavady), 1885 v S (1)
M'Mahon, J. (Bohemians), 1934 v S (1)
M'Master, G. (Glentoran), 1897 v E, S, W (3)
McMichael, A. (Newcastle U.), 1950 v E, S; 1951 v E, S, F; 1952 v E, S, W; 1953 v E, S, W, F; 1954 v E, S, W; 1955 v E, W; 1956 v W; 1957 v E, S, W, I, P (2); 1958 v E, S, W, I (2), Cz (2), Arg, WG, F; 1959 v S, W, Sp; 1960 v E, S, W (40)
M'Millan, G. (Distillery), 1903 v E; 1905 v W (2)
McMillan, S. (Manchester U), 1963 v E, S (2)
M'Millen, W. S. (Manchester U.), 1934 v E; 1935 v S; 1937 v S; (with Chesterfield), 1938 v S, W; 1939 v E, S (7)
McMordie, A. S. (Middlesbrough), 1969 v Is, T (2), E, S, W; 1970 v E, S, W, USSR; 1971 v Cy (2) E, S, W; 1972 v USSR, Sp, E, S, W; 1973; v Bul (21)
McMorran, E. J. (Belfast C.), 1947 v E; (with Barnsley), 1951 v E, S, W; 1952 v E, S, W; 1953 v E, S, F; (with Doncaster R.), 1953 v W; 1954 v E; 1956 v W; 1957 v I, P (15)
M'Mullan, D. (Liverpool), 1926 v E, W; 1927 v S (3)
M'Ninch, J. (Ballymena), 1931 v S; 1932 v S, W (3)
McParland, P. J. (Aston Villa), 1954 v W; 1955 v E, S; 1956 v E, S; 1957 v E, S, W, P; 1958 v E, S, W, I (2), Cz (2), Arg, WG, F; 1959 v E, S, W, Sp; 1960 v E, S, W; 1961 v E, S, W, I, WG (2), Gr; (with Wolverhampton W.); 1962 v Ho (34)
M'Shane, J. (Cliftonville), 1899 v S; 1900 v E, S, W (4)
M'Vickers, J. (Glentoran), 1888 v E; 1889 v S (2)
M'Wha, W. B. R. (Knock), 1882 v E, W; (with Cliftonville) 1883 v E, W; 1884 v E; 1885 v E, W (7)
Macartney, A. (Ulster), 1903 v S, W; (with Linfield) 1904 v S, W; (with Everton) 1905 v E, S; (with Belfast C.), 1907 v E, S, W; 1908 v E, S, W; (with Glentoran) 1909 v E, S, W (15)
Macauley, J. L. (Huddersfield T.) 1911 v E, W; 1912 v E, S; 1913 v E, S(6)
Mackie, J. (Arsenal), 1923 v W; (with Portsmouth), 1935 v S, W (3)
Madden, O. (Norwich C.), 1938 v E (1)
Magill, E. J. (Arsenal), 1962 v E, S, Gr; 1963 v E, S, W, Pol (2), Sp; 1964 v E, S, W, U, Sp; 1965 v E, S, Sw (2), Ho, Alb; 1966 v S, Alb; (with Brighton), 1966 v E, W, WG, M (26)
Maginnis, H. (Linfield), 1900 v E, S, W; 1903 v S, W; 1904 v E, S, W (8)
Maguire, E. (Distillery) 1907 v S (1)
Mahood, J. (Belfast C.), 1926 v S; 1928 v E, S. W; 1929 v E, S, W; 1930 v W; (with Ballymena), 1934 v S (9)
Manderson, R. (Glasgow R.), 1920 v W, S; 1925 v S, E; 1926 v S (5)
Mansfield, J. (Dublin Freebooters), 1901 v E (1)
Martin, C. (Bo'ness), 1925 v S (1)

687

Martin, C. J. (Glentoran), 1947 v S; (with Leeds U), 1948 v E, S, W; (with Aston Villa), 1949 v E; 1950 v W (6)

Martin, D. (Bo'ness), 1925 v S (1)

Martin, D. C. (Cliftonville), 1882 v E, W; 1883 v E (3)

Martin, D. K. (Belfast C.), 1934 v E, S, W; 1935 v S; (with Wolverhampton W.), 1935 v E; 1936 v W; (with Nottingham F.), 1937 v S; 1938 v E, S; 1939 v S (10)

Mathieson, A. (Luton T.), 1921 v W; 1922 v E (2)

Maxwell, J. (Linfield), 1902 v W; 1903 v W, E; (with Glentoran), 1905 v W, S; (with Belfast C.), 1906 v W; 1907 v S (7)

Meek, H. L. (Glentoran), 1922 v N (2); 1925 v W (3)

Mehaffy, J. A. C. (Queen's Island), 1922 v W (1)

Meldon, J. (Dublin Freebooters), 1899 v S, W (2)

Mercer, H. V. A. (Linfield), 1908 v E (1)

Mercer, J. T. (Distillery), 1898 v E, S, W; 1899 v E; (with Linfield), 1902 v E, W; (with Distillery), 1903 v S, W; (with Derby Co.), 1904 v E, W; 1905 v S (11)

Millar, W. (Barrow), 1932 v W; 1933 v S (2)

Miller, J. (Middlesbrough), 1929 v W, S; 1930 v E (3)

Milligan, D. (Chesterfield), 1939 v W (1)

Milne, R. G. (Linfield), 1894 v E, S, W; 1895 v E, W; 1896 v E, S, W; 1897 v E, S; 1898 v E, S, W; 1899 v E, W; 1901 v W; 1902 v E, S, W; 1903 v E, S; 1904 v E, S, W; 1906 v E, S, W (27)

Mitchell, C. (Glentoran), 1934 v W (1)

Mitchell, E. J. (Cliftonville), 1933 v S (1)

Mitchell, W. (Distillery), 1932 v E, W; 1933 v E, W; (with Chelsea), 1934 v W, S; 1935 v S, E; 1936 v S, E; 1937 v E, S, W; 1938 v E, S (15)

Molyneux, T. B. (Ligoniel), 1883 v E, W; (with Cliftonville) 1884 v E, W, S; 1885 v E, W; 1886 v E, W, S; 1888 v S (11)

Montgomery, F. J. (Coleraine), 1955 v E (1)

Moore, C. (Glentoran), 1949 v W (1)

Moore, J. (Linfield Ath.), 1891 v E, S, W (3)

Moore, P. (Aberdeen), 1933 v E (1)

Moore, T. (Ulster), 1887 v S, W (2)

Moorhead, F. W. (Dublin University), 1885 v E (1)

Moorhead, G. (Linfield); 1923 v S; 1928 v S; 1929 v S (3)

Moran, J. (Leeds C.), 1912 v S (1)

Morgan, F. G. (Linfield), 1922 v N (2); 1923 v E; (with Nottingham F.), 1924 v S; 1927 v E; 1928 v E, S, W; 1929 v E (9)

Morgan, S. (Port Vale), 1972 v Sp; 1973 v Bul (sub) P, Cy, E, S, W; (with Aston Villa) 1974 v Bul, P, S, E; 1975 v Se; 1976 v Se, N, Y (with Brighton & H.A.), S, W (sub) (17)

Morrison, J. (Linfield Ath.), 1891 v E, W (2)

Morrison, T. (Glentoran), 1895 v E, S, W; (with Burnley); 1899 v W; 1900 v W; 1902 v E, S (7)

Morrogh, E. (Bohemians), 1896 v S (1)

Morrow, W. J. (Moyola Park), 1883 v E, W; 1884 v S (3)

Muir, R. (Old Park), 1885 v S, W (2)

Mulholland, S. (Celtic), 1906 v S, E (2)

Mulligan, J. (Manchester C.), 1921 v S (1)

Murphy, J. (Bradford C.), 1910 v E, S, W (3)

Murphy, N. (Q.P.R.), 1905 v E, S, W (3)

Murray, J. M. (Motherwell), 1910 v E, S; (with Sheffield W.), 1910 v W (3)

Napier, R. J. (Bolton W.), 1966 v WG (1)

Neill, W. J. T. (Arsenal), 1961 v I, Gr, WG; 1962 v E, S, W, Gr; 1963 v E, W, Pol, Sp; 1964 v S, E, W, U, Sp; 1965 v E, S, W, Sw, Ho (2), Alb; 1966 v S,

E, W, Alb, WGM; 1967 v S, W; 1968 v S, E) 1969 v E, S, W, Is, T (2); 1970 v S, E, W, USSR (2); (with Hull C.), 1971 v Cy, Sp; 1972 v USSR (2), Sp, S, E, W; 1973 v Bul, Cy, (2), P, E, S, W (59)

Nelis, P. (Nottingham F.), 1923 v E (1)

Nelson, S. (Arsenal), 1970 v W, E (sub); 1971 v Cy, Sp, E, S, W; 1972 v USSR (2), Sp, E, S, W; 1973 v Bul, Cy, P; 1974 v S, E; 1975 v Se, Y; 1976 v Se, N, Is, E (24)

Nicholl, C. J. (Aston Villa), 1975 v Se, Y, E, S, W; 1976 v Se, N, Y, S, E, W (11)

Nicholl, J. M. (Manchester U.), 1976 v Is, W (sub) (2)

Nicholl, H. (Belfast C.), 1902 v E, W; 1905 v E (3),

Nicholson, J. J. (Manchester U.), 1961 v S, W; 1962 v E, W, Gr, Ho; 1963 v E, S, Pol (2); (with Huddersfield T.), 1965 v W, Ho (2); Alb; 1966 v S, E, W, Alb, M; 1967 v S, W; 1968 v S, E, W; 1969 v S, E, W, T (2); 1970 v S, E, W, USSR (2); 1971 v Cy (2), E, S, W; 1972 v USSR (2) (41)

Nixon, R. (Linfield), 1914 v S (1)

Nolan-Whelan, J. V. (Dublin Freebooters), 1901 v E, W; 1902 v S, W (4)

O'Brien, M. T. (Q.P.R.), 1921 v S; (with Leicester C.), 1922 v S, W; 1924 v S, W; (with Hull C.), 1925 v S, E, W; 1926 v W; (with Derby Co.), 1927 v W (10)

O'Connell, P. (Sheffield W.), 1912 v E, S; (with Hull C.), 1914 v E, S, W (5)

O'Doherty, A. (Coleraine), 1970 v E, A, W (sub) (2)

O'Driscoll, J. F. (Swansea T.), 1949 v E, S, W (3)

O'Hagan, C. (Tottenham H.), 1905 v S, W; 1906 v S, W, E; (with Aberdeen), 1907 v E, S, W; 1908 v S, W; 1909 v E (11)

O'Hagan, W. (St. Mirren), 1920 v E, W (2)

O'Hehir, J. C. (Bohemians), 1910 v W (1)

O'Kane, W. J. (Nottingham F.), 1970 v E, W, S (sub); 1971 v Sp, E, S, W; 1972 v USSR (2), 1973 v P, Cy; 1974 v Bul, P, S, E, W; 1975 v N; Se, E, S (20)

O'Mahoney, M. T. (Bristol R.), 1939 v S (1)

O'Neill, J. (Sunderland), 1962 v W (1)

O'Neill, M. H. (Distillery), 1972 v USSR (sub); (with Nottingham F.) Sp (sub), W (sub); 1973 v P, Cy, E, S, W; 1974 v Bul, P, E (sub), W; 1975 v Se, Y, E, S; 1976 v Y (17)

O'Reilly, H. (Dublin Freebooters), 1901 v S, W; 1904 v S (3)

Parke, J. (Linfield), 1964 v S; (with Hibernian), 1964 v E, Sp; (with Sunderland), 1965 v Sw; 1965 v S, W, Ho (2), Alb; 1966 v WG; 1967 v E, S; 1968 v S, E (14)

Peacock, R. (Celtic), 1952 v S; 1953 v F; 1954 v W; 1955 v E, S; 1956 v E, S; 1957 v W, I, P; 1958 v S, E, W, I (2), Arg, Cz (2) WG; 1959 v E, S, W, Sp; 1960 v S, E; 1961 v E, S, I, WG (2), Gr; (with Coleraine, 1962 v S (32)

Peden, J. (Linfield), 1887 v S, W; 1888 v W, E; 1889 v S, E; 1890 v W, S; 1891 v W, E; 1892 v W, E; 1893 v E, S, W; (with Distillery), 1896 v W, E, S; 1897 v W, S; 1898 v W, E, S; (with Linfield), 1899 v W (24)

Percy, J. C. (Belfast YMCA), 1889 v W (1)

Platt, J. A. (Middlesbrough), 1976 v Is (sub) (1)

Posonby, J. (Distillery), 1895 v S; 1896 v E, S, W; 1897 v E, S, W; 1899 v E (8)

Potts, R. M. C. (Cliftonville), 1833 v E, W (2)

Priestley, T. J. (Coleraine), 1933 v S; (with Chelsea), 1934 v E (2)

Pyper, Jas. (Cliftonville), 1897 v S, W; 1898 v E, S, W; 1899 v S; 1900 v E (7)
Pyper, John (Cliftonville), 1897 v E, S, W; 1899 v E, W; 1900 v E, W, S; 1902 v S (9)
Pyper, M. (Linfield), 1931 v W (1)

Rankine, J. (Alexander), 1883 v E, W (2)
Raper, E. O. (Dublin University), 1886 v W (1)
Rattray, D. (Avoniel), 1882 v E; 1883 v E, W (3)
Rea, B. (Glentoran), 1901 v E (1)
Redmond, J. (Cliftonville), 1884 v W (1)
Reid, G. H. (Cardiff C.), 1923 v S (1)
Reid, J. (Ulster), 1883 v E; 1884 v W; 1887 v S; 1889 v W; 1890 v S, W (6)
Reid, S. E. (Derby Co.), 1934 v E, W; 1936 v E (3)
Reid, W. (Hearts), 1931 v E (1)
Reilly, J. (Portsmouth), 1900 v E; 1902 v E (2)
Renneville, W. T. (Leyton), 1910 v S, E, W; (with Aston Villa), 1911 v W (4)
Reynolds, J. (Distillery), 1890 v E, W; (with Ulster), 1891 v ES, W (5)
Reynolds, R. (Bohemians), 1905 v W (1)
Rice, P. J. (Arsenal), 1969 v Is; 1970 v USSR; 1971 v E, S, W; 1972 v USSR, Sp, E, S, W; 1973 v Bul, Cy, E, S, W; 1974 v Bul, P, S, E, W; 1975 v N, Y, E, S, W; 1976 v Se, N, Y, Is, S, E, W (32)
Roberts, F. C. (Glentoran), 1931 v S (1)
Robinson, P. (Distillery), 1920 v S; (with Blackburn R.), 1921 v W (2)
Rollo, D. (Linfield), 1912 v W; 1913 v W; 1914 v W, E; (with Blackburn R.), 1920 v S, W; 1921 v E, S, W; 1922 v E; 1923 v E; 1924 v S, W; 1925 v W; 1926 v E; 1927 v E (16)
Rosbotham, A. (Cliftonville), 1887 v E, S, W; 1888 v E, S, W; 1889 v E (7)
Ross, W. E. (Newcastle U.), 1969 v Is (1)
Rowley, R. W. M. (Southampton), 1929 v S, W; 1930 v W, E; (with Tottenham H.), 1931 v W; 1932 v S (6)
Russell, A. (Linfield), 1947 v E (1)
Russell, S. R. (Bradford C.), 1930 v E, S; (with Derry C.), 1932 v E (3)
Ryan, R. A. (W.B.A.), 1950 v W (1)

Scott, E. (Liverpool), 1920 v S; 1921 v E, S, W; 1922 v E; 1925 v W; 1926 v E, S, W; 1927 v E, S, W; 1928 v E, S, W; 1929 v E, S, W; 1930 v E; 1931 v E; 1932 v S; 1933 v E, S, W; 1934 v E, S, W; (with Belfast C.), 1935 v S; 1936 v E, S, W (30)
Scott, J. (Grimsby), 1958 v Cz, F (2)
Scott, J. E. (Cliftonville), 1901 v S (1)
Scott, L. J. (Dublin University), 1895 v S, W (2)
Scott, P. W. (Everton), 1975 v W; 1976 v Y (with York C.), Is, S, E (sub), W (6)
Scott, T. (Cliftonville), 1894 v E, S; 1895 v S, W; 1896 v S, E, W; 1897 v E, W; 1988 v E, S, W; 1900 v W (13)
Scott, W. (Linfield), 1903 v E, S, W; 1904 v E, S, W; (with Everton) 1905 v E, S; 1907 v E, S; 1908 v E, S, W; 1909 v E, S, W; 1910 v E, S; 1911 v E, S, W; 1912 v E; (with Leeds City) 1913 v E, S, W (25)
Scraggs, M. J. (Glentoran), 1921 v W; 1922 v E (2)
Seymour, H. C. (Bohemians), 1914 v W (1)
Seymour, J. (Cliftonville), 1907-9 v W (2)
Shanks, T. (Woolwich Arsenal), 1903 v S; 1904 v W; (with Brentford), 1905 v E (3)
Sharkey, P. (Ipswich T.), 1976 v S (1)
Sheehan, Dr. G. (Bohemians), 1899 v S; 1900 v E, W (3)
Sheridan, J. (Everton), 1903 v W, E, S; 1904 v E, S;

(with Stoke C.), 1905 v E (6)
Sherrard, J. (Limavady), 1885 v S; 1887 v W 1888; v W (3)
Sherrard, W. (Cliftonville), 1895 v E, W, S (3)
Sherry, J. J. (Bohemians), 1906 v E; 1907 v W (2)
Shields, J. (Southampton), 1957 v S (1)
Silo, M. (Belfast YMCA), 1888 v E (1)
Simpson, W. J. (Glasgow R.), 1951 v W, F; 1954 v E, S; 1955 v E; 1957 v I, P; 1958 v S, E, W, I; 1959 v S (12)
Sinclair, J. (Knock), 1882 v E, W (2)
Slemin, J. C. (Bohemians), 1909 v W (1)
Sloan, A. S. (London Caledonians), 1925 v W (1)
Sloan, D. (Oxford U.), 1969 v Is; 1971 v Sp (2)
Sloan, H. A. de B. (Bohemians), 1903 v E; 1904 v S; 1905 v E; 1906 v W; 1907 v E, W; 1908 v W; 1909 v S (8)
Sloan, J. W. (Arsenal), 1947 v W (1)
Sloan, T. (Cardiff C.), 1926 v S, W. E; 1927 v W, S; 1928 v E, W; 1929 v E; (with Linfield), 1930 v W, S; 1931 v S (11)
Small, J. (Clarence), 1887 v E (1)
Small, J. M. (Cliftonville) 1893 v E, S, W (3)
Smith, E. E. (Cardiff C.), 1921 v S; 1923 v W, E; 1924 v E (4)
Smith, J. (Distillery), 1901 v S, W (2)
Smyth, R. H. (Dublin University), 1886 v W (1)
Smyth, S. (Wolverhampton W.), 1948 v E, S, W; 1949 v W; 1950 v E, S, W; (with Stoke C.), 1952 v E (9)
Smyth, W. (Distillery), 1949 v E, S; 1954 v S, E (4)
Snape, A. (Airdrie), 1920 v E (1)
Spence, D. W. (Bury), 1975 v Y, E, S, W; 1976 v Se, Is, E, W, S (sub) (9)
Spencer, S. (Distillery), 1890 v E, S; 1892 v E, S, W; 1893 v E (6)
Spiller, E. A. (Cliftonville), 1883 v E, W; 1884 v E, W, S (5)
Stanfield, O. M. (Distillery), 1887 v E, S, W; 1888 v E, S, W; 1889 v E, S, W; 1890 v E, S; 1891 v E, S, W; 1892 v E, S, W, 1893 v E, W; 1894 v E, S, W; 1895 v E, S; 1896 v E, S, W; 1897 v E, S, W (30)
Steele, A. (Charlton Ath.), 1926 v W, S; (with Fulham), 1929 v W, S (4)
Stevenson, A. E. (Rangers), 1934 v E, S, W; (with Everton), 1935 v E, S; 1936 v S, W; 1937 v E, W; 1938 v E, W; 1939 v E, S, W; 1947 v S, W; 1948 v S (17)
Stewart, A. (Glentoran), 1967 v W; 1968 v S, E; (with Derby Co.), 1968 v W; 1969 v Is, T (1 + 1 sub) (7)
Stewart, R. H. (St. Columbia Court), 1890 v E, S, W; (with Cliftonville), 1892 v E, S, W; 1893 v E, W; 1894 v E, S, W (11)
Stewart, T, C, (Linfield), 1961 v W (1)
Swan, S. (Linfield), 1899 v S (1)

Taggart, J. (Walsall), 1899 v W (1)
Thompson, F. W. (Cliftonville), 1910 v E, S, W; (with Bradford C.), 1911 v E, (with Linfield), v W; 1912 v E, W; 1913 v E, S, W; (with Clyde), 1914 v v E, S (12)
Thompson, J. (Distillery), 1897 v S (1)
Thompson, J. (Belfast Ath.), 1889 v S (1)
Thunder, P. J. (Bohemians), 1911 v W (1)
Todd, S. J. (Burnley), 1966 v M (sub); 1967 v E; 1968 v W; 1969 v E, S, W; 1970 v S, USSR (Sheffield W.), 1971 v Cy (2) Sp (sub) (11)
Toner, J. (Arsenal), 1922 v W; 1923 v W; 1924 v W, E; 1925 v E, S; (with St. Johnstone), 1927 v E, S (8)

Torrans, R. (Linfield), 1893 v S (1)
Torrans, S. (Linfield), 1889 v S; 1890 v S, W; 1891 v S, W; 1892 v E, S, W; 1893 v E, S; 1894 v E, S, W; 1895 v E; 1896 v E, S, W; 1897 v E, S, W; 1898 v E, S, W; 1899 v E; 1901 v S, W (26)
Trainor, D. (Crusaders), 1967 v W (1)
Tully, C. P. (Glasgow C.), 1949 v E; 1950 v E; 1952 v S; 1953 v E, S, W, F; 1954 v S; 1956 v E; 1959 v Sp (10)
Turner, E. (Cliftonville), 1896 v E, W (2)
Turner, W. (Cliftonville), 1886 v E; 1886 v S; 1888 v S (3)
Twoomey, J. F. (Leeds U.), 1938 v W; 1939 v E (2)

Uprichard, W. N. M. C. (Swindon T.), 1952, v E, S, W; 1953 v E, S; (with Portsmouth), 1963 v W, F; 1955–6 v E, S, W; 1956 v E, S, W; 1958 v S, I, Cz; 1959 v S, Sp (18)

Vernon, J. (Belfast C.), 1947 v E, S; (with W.B.A.), 1947 v W; 1948 v E, S, W; 1949 v E, S, W; 1950 v E, S; 1951 v E, S, W, F; 1952 v S, E (17)

Waddell, T. M. R. (Cliftonville), 1906 v S (1)
Walker, J. (Doncaster R.), 1955 v W (1)
Walker, T. (Bury), 1911 v S (1)
Walsh, D. J. (W.B.A.), 1947 v S, W; 1948 v E, S, W; 1949 v E, S, W; 1950 v W (9)
Walsh, W. (Manchester C.), 1948 v E, S, W; 1949 v E, S (5)
Waring, R. (Distillery), 1899 v E (1)
Warren, P. (Shelbourne), 1913 v E, S (2)
Watson, J. (Ulster), 1883 v E, W; 1886 v E, S, W; 1887 v S, W; 1889 v E, W (9)
Watson, P. (Distillery) v Cy (sub), (1)
Watson, T. (Cardiff C.), 1926 v S (1)
Wattle, J. (Distillery), 1899 v E (1)
Webb, C. G. (Brighton), 1909 v S, W; 1911 v S (3)
Weir, E. (Clyde), 1939 v W (1)
Welsh, E. (Carlisle U.), 1966 v W, WG, M; 1967 v W (4)
Whiteside, T. (Distillery), 1891 v E (1)
Whitfield, E. R. (Dublin University), 1886 v W (1)
Williams, J. R. (Ulster), 1886 v E, W (2)
Williamson, J. (Cliftonville), 1890 v E; 1892 v S, 1893 v S (3)
Willigham, T. (Burnley), 1933 v W; 1934 v S (2)
Willis, G. (Linfield), 1906 v S, W; 1907 v S; 1912 v S (4)
Wilson, H. (Linfield), 1925 v W (1)
Wilson, M. (Distillery), 1884 v E, S, W (3)
Wilson, R. (Cliftonville), 1888 v S (1)
Wilson, S. J. (Glenavon), 1962 v S; 1964 v S; (with Falkirk), 1964 v E, W, U, Sp; 1965 v E, Sw; (with Dundee), 1966 v W, WG; 1967 v S; 1968 v E (12)
Wilton, J. M. (St. Columbia Court), 1888 v E, W; 1889 v S, E; (with Cliftonville), 1890 v E; (with St. Columbia Court), 1892 v W; 1893 v S (7)
Wright, J. (Cliftonville), 1906 v E, S, W; 1907 v E, S, W (6)
Young, S. (Linfield), 1907 v E, S; 1908 v E, S; (with Airdrie), 1909 v E; 1912 v S; (with Linfield), 1914 v E, S, W (9)

SCOTLAND

Adams, J. (Hearts), 1889 v Ni; 1892 v W; 1893 v Ni (3)

690

Agnew, W. B. (Kilmarnock), 1907 v Ni; 1908 v W Ni (3)
Aird, J. (Burnley), 1954 v N (2), A, U (4)
Aitken, A. (Newcastle U.), 1901 v E; 1902 v E; 1903 v E, W; 1904 v E; 1905 v E, W; 1906 v E; (with Middlesbrough), 1907 v E, W; 1908 v E; (with Leicester Fosse), 1910 v E; 1911 v E, Ni(14)
Aitken, G. G. (East Fife), 1949 v E, F; 1950 v W, Ni, Sw; (with Sunderland), 1953 v W, Ni; 1954 v E (8)
Aitken, R. (Dumbarton), 1886 v E; 1888 v Ni (2)
Aitkenhead, W. A. C. (Blackburn R.), 1912 v Ni (1)
Alexander, D. (East Stirlingshire), 1894 v W, Ni (2)
Allan, D. S. (Queen's Park), 1885 v E, W; 1886 v W (3)
Allan, G. (Liverpool), 1897 v E (1)
Allan, H. (Hearts), 1902 v W (1)
Allan, J. (Queen's Park), 1887 v E, W (2)
Allan, T. (Dundee) 1974 v WG, N (2)
Ancell, R. F. D. (Newcastle U.), 1937 v W, Ni (2)
Anderson, A. (Hearts), 1933 v E; 1934 v A, E, W, Ni; 1935 v E, W, Ni; 1936 v E, W, Ni, 1937 v G, E, W, Ni, A; 1938 v E, W, Ni, Cz, Ho; 1939 v W, H (23)
Anderson, F. (Clydesdale), 1874 v E (1)
Anderson G. (Kilmarnock), 1901 v Ni (1)
Anderson, H. A. (Raith R.), 1914 v W (1)
Anderson, J. (Leicester C.), 1954 v Fi (1)
Anderson, K. (Queen's Park), 1896 v Ni; 1898 v E Ni (3)
Anderson, W. (Queen's Park), 1882 v E; 1883 v E, W; 1884 v E; 1885 v E, W (6)
Andrews, P. (Eastern), 1875 v E (1)
Archibald, A. (Rangers), 1921 v W; 1922 v W, E; 1923 v Ni; 1924 v E, W; 1931 v E; 1932 v E (8)
Armstrong, M. W. (Aberdeen), 1936 v W, Ni; 1937 v G (3)
Arnott, W. (Queen's Park), 1883 v W; 1884 v E, Ni; 1885 v E, W; 1886 v E; 1887 v E, W; 1888 v E; 1889 v E; 1890 v E; 1891 v E; 1892 v E; 1893 v E (14)
Auld, J. R. (Third Lanark), 1887 v E, W; 1889 v W (3)
Auld, R. (Celtic), 1959 v H, P; 1960 v W (3)

Baird, A. (Queen's Park), 1892 v Ni; 1894 v W (2)
Baird, D. (Hearts), 1890 v Ni; 1891 v E; 1892 v W (3)
Baird, H. (Airdrie), 1956 v A (1)
Baird, J. C. (Vale of Leven), 1876 v E; 1878 v W; 1880 v E (3)
Baird, S. (Rangers), 1957 v Y, Sp (2), Sw, WG; 1958 v F, Ni (7)
Baird, W. U. (St. Bernard), 1897 v Ni (1)
Barbour, A. (Renton), 1885 v Ni (1)
Barker, J. B. (Rangers), 1893 v W; 1894; v W (2)
Barrett, F. (Dundee), 1894 v Ni; 1895 v W (2)
Battles, B. (Celtic), 1901 v E, W, Ni (3)
Battles, B. jun. (Hearts), 1931 v W (1)
Bauld, W. (Hearts), 1950 v E, Sw, P (3)
Baxter, J. C. (Rangers), 1961 v Ni, Ei (2), Cz; 1962 v Ni, W, E, Cz (2), U; 1963 v W, Ni, E, A, N, Ei, Sp; 1964 v W, E, N, WG; 1965 v W, Ni, Fi; (with Sunderland), 1966 v P, Br, Ni, W, E, I; 1967 v W, E, USSR; 1968 v W (34)
Baxter, R. D. (Middlesbrough), 1939 v E, W, H (3)
Beattie, A. (Preston N.E.), 1937 v E, A, Cz; 1938 v E; 1939 v W, Ni, H (7)
Beattie, R. (Preston N.E.), 1939 v W (1)
Begbie, I. (Hearts), 1890 v Ni; 1891 v E; 1982 v W; 1894 v E (4)

Bell, A. (Manchester U.), 1912 v Ni (1)
Bell, J. (Dumbarton), 1890 v Ni; 1892 v E; (with Everton), 1896 v E; 1897 v E; 1898 v E; (with Celtic), 1899 v E, W, Ni; 1900 v E, W (10)
Bell, M. (Hearts), 1901 v W (1)
Bell, W. J. (Leeds U.), 1966 v P, Br (2)
Bennett, A. (Celtic), 1904 v W; 1907 v Ni; 1908 v W; (with Rangers), 1909 v W, Ni, E; (1910 v E, W; 1911 v E, W; 1913 v Ni (11)
Bennie, R. (Airdrieonians), 1925 v W, Ni; 1926 v Ni (3)
Berry, D. (Queen's Park), 1894 v W; 1899 v W, Ni (3)
Berry, W. H. (Queen's Park), 1888 v E; 1889 v E; 1890 v E; 1891 v E (4)
Beveridge, W. W. (Glasgow University), 1879 v E, W; 1880 v W (3)
Black, A. (Hearts), 1938 v Cz, Ho; 1939 v H (3)
Black, D. (Hurlford), 1889 v Ni (1)
Black, I. H. (Southampton), 1948 v E (1)
Blackburn, J. E. (Royal Engineers), 1873 v E (1)
Blacklaw, A. S. (Burnley), 1963 v N, Sp; 1966 v I (3)
Blackley, J. (Hibernian), 1974 v Cz, E, Bel, Z; 1976 v Sw (5)
Blair, D. (Clyde), 1929 v W, Ni; 1931 v E, A, I; 1932 v W, Ni; (with Aston Villa), 1933 v W (8)
Blair, J. (Sheffield W.), 1920 v E, Ni; (with Cardiff C.), 1921 v E; 1922 v E; 1923 v E, W, Ni; 1924 v W (8)
Blair, J. (Motherwell), 1934 v W (1)
Blair, J. A. (Blackpool), 1947 v W (1)
Blair, W. (Third Lanark), 1896 v W (1)
Blessington J. (Celtic), 1894 v E, Ni; 1896 v E, Ni (4)
Bone, J. (Norwich C.), 1972 v Y (sub); 1973 v D (2)
Bowie, J. (Rangers), 1920 v E, Ni (2)
Bowie, W. (Linthouse), 1891 v Ni (1)
Bowman, G. A. (Montrose), 1892 v Ni (1)
Boyd, J. M. (Newcastle U.), 1934 v Ni (1)
Boyd, R. (Mossend Swifts), 1889 v Ni; 1891 v W (2)
Boyd, W. G. (Clyde), 1931 v I, Sw (2)
Brackenbridge, T. (Hearts), 1888 v Ni (1)
Bradshaw, T. (Bury), 1928 v E (1)
Brand, R. (Rangers), 1961 v Ni, Ei (2); 1962 v Ni, W, Cz, U (8)
Branden, T. (Blackburn R.), 1896 v E (1)
Bremner, D. (Hibernian), 1976 v Sw (1)
Bremner, W. J. (Leeds U.), 1965 v Sp; 1966 v E, Pol, P, Br, I (2); 1967 v W, Ni, E; 1968 v W, E; 1969 v W, E, Ni, D, A, WG, Cy (2); 1970 v Ei, WG, A; 1971 v W, E; 1972 v P, Bel, Ho, Ni, W, E, Y, Cz, Br; 1973 v D (2), E (2), Ni (sub), Sw, Br; 1974 v Cz, WG, Ni, W, E, Bel, N, Z, Br, Y; 1975 v Sp (2); 1976 v D (54)
Brennan, F. (Newcastle U.), 1947 v W, Ni; 1953 v W, Ni, E; 1954 v Ni, E (7)
Breslin, B. (Hibernian), 1897 v W (1)
Brewster, G. (Everton), 1921 v E (1)
Brogan, J. (Celtic), 1971 v W, Ni, P, E (4)
Brown, A. (Middlesbrough), 1904 v E (1)
Brown, A. (St. Mirren), 1890 v W; 1891 v W (2)
Brown, A. D. (East Fife), 1950 v Sw, P, F; (with Blackpool), 1952 v U.S.A., D. Se; 1953 v W; 1954 v W, E, N (2), Fi, A, U (14)
Brown, G. C. P. (Rangers), 1931 v W; 1932 v E, W, Ni; 1933 v E; 1935 v A; E, W; 1936 v E, W; 1937 v G, E, W, Ni, Cz; 1938 v E, W, Cz, Ho (19)
Brown, H. (Partick T.), 1947 v W, Bel, L (3)
Brown, J. (Cambuslang), 1890 v W (1)
Brown, J. B. (Clyde), 1939 v W (1)
Brown, J. G. (Sheffield U.), 1975 v R (1)

Brown, R. (Dumbarton), 1884 v W, Ni (2)
Brown, R. (Rangers), 1947 v Ni; 1949 v Ni; 1952 v E (3)
Brown, R. jun. (Dumbarton), 1885 v W (1)
Brown, W. D. F. (Dundee), 1958 v F; 1959 v E, W, Ni; (with Tottenham H.), 1960 v W, Ni, Pol, A, H, T; 1962 v Ni, W, E, Cz; 1963 v W, Ni, E, A; 1964 v Ni, W, N; 1965 v E, Fi, Pol, Sp; 1966 v Ni, Pol, I (28)
Browning, J. (Celtic), 1914 v W (1)
Brownlie, J. (Hibernian), 1971 v Rus; 1972 v Pe, Ni, E; 1973 v D (2); 1976 v R (7)
Brownlie, J. (Third Lanark), 1909 v E, Ni; 1910 v E, W, Ni; 1911 v W, Ni; 1912 v W, Ni, E; 1913 v W, Ni, E; 1914 v W, Ni, E (16)
Bruce, D. (Vale of Leven), 1890 v W (1)
Bruce, R. F. (Middlesbrough), 1934 v A (1)
Buchan, M. M. (Aberdeen), 1972 v P (sub), Bel; (with Manchester U.), W, Y, Cz, Br; 1973 v D (2), E; 1974 v WG, Ni, W, N, Br, Y; 1975 v EG, Sp, P; 1976 v D, R (20)
Buchanan, J. (Cambuslang), 1889 v Ni (1)
Buchanan, J. (Rangers), 1929 v E; 1930 v E (2)
Buchanan, P. S. (Chelsea), 1938 v Cz (1)
Buchanan, R. (Abercorn), 1891 v W (1)
Buckley, P. (Aberdeen), 1954 v N; 1955 v W, Ni (3)
Buick, A. (Hearts), 1902 v W, Ni (2)
Burns, F. (Manchester U.), 1970 v A (1)
Burns, K. (Birmingham C.), 1974 v WG; 1975 v EG (sub), Sp (2)/(4)
Busby, M. W. (Manchester C.), 1934 v W (1)

Cairns, T. (Rangers), 1920 v W; 1922 v E; 1923 v E, W; 1924 v Ni; 1925 v W, E, Ni (8)
Calderhead, D. (Queen of the South W.), 1889 v Ni (1)
Caldow, E. (Rangers), 1957 v Sp (2), Sw, WG; v E, 1958 v Ni, W, Sw, Par, H, Pol, Y, F; 1959 v E, W, Ni, WG, Ho, P; 1960 v E, W, Ni, A, H, T; 1961 v E, W, Ni, Ei (2), Cz; 1962 v Ni, W, E, Cz (2), U; 1963 v W, Ni, E (40)
Callaghan, P. (Hibernian), 1900 v Ni (1)
Callaghan, W. (Dunfermline), 1970 v Ei (sub), W (2)
Cameron, J. (St. Mirren), 1904 v Ni; (with Chelsea), 1909 v E (2)
Cameron, J. (Queen's Park), 1896 v Ni (1)
Cameron, J. (Rangers), 1886 v Ni (1)
Campbell, C. (Queen's Park), 1874 v E; 1877 v E, W; 1878 v E, W; 1879 v E,; 1880 v E; 1881 v E; 1882 v E, W; 1884 v E; 1885 v E; 1886 v E (13)
Campbell, H. (Renton), 1889 v W (1)
Campbell, Jas. (Sheffield W.), 1913 v W (1)
Campbell, J. (South Western), 1880 v W (1)
Campbell, J. (Kilmarnock), 1891 v Ni; 1892 v W (2)
Campbell, John (Celtic), 1893 v E, Ni; 1898 v E, Ni; 1900 v E, Ni; 1901 v E, W, Ni; 1902 v W, Ni; 1903 v W (12)
Campbell, John (Rangers), 1899 v E, W, Ni; 1901 v Ni (4)
Campbell, K. (Liverpool), 1920 v E, W, Ni; (with Partick T.), 1921 v W, Ni; 1922 v W, Ni, E (8)
Campbell, P. (Rangers), 1878 v W; 1879 v W (2)
Campbell, P. (Morton), 1898 v W (1)
Campbell, R. (Chelsea), 1947 v Bel, L; 1950 v Sw, P, F (5)
Campbell, W. (Morton), 1947 v Ni; 1948 v E, Bel, Sw, F (5)
Carabine, J. (Third Lanark), 1938 v Ho; 1939 v E, Ni (3)

Carr, W. M. (Coventry C.), 1970 v Ni, W, E; 1971 v D; 1972 v Pe; 1973 v D (sub) (6)

Cassidy, J. (Celtic), 1921 v W, Ni; 1923 v Ni; 1924 v W (4)

Chalmers, S. (Celtic), 1965 v W, Fi; 1966 v P (sub), Br; 1967 v Ni (5)

Chalmers, W. (Rangers), 1885 v Ni (1)

Chalmers, W. S. (Queen's Park), 1929 v Ni (1)

Chambers, T. (Hearts), 1894 v W (1)

Chaplin, G. D. (Dundee), 1908 v W (1)

Cheyne, A. G. (Aberdeen), 1929 v E, N, G, Ho; 1930 v F (5)

Christie, A. J. (Queen's Park) 1898 v W; 1899 v E, Ni (3)

Christie, R. M. (Queen's Park), 1884 v E (1)

Clark, J. (Celtic), 1966 v Br.; 1967 v W, Ni, USSR (4)

Clark, R. B. (Aberdeen), 1968 v W, Ho; 1970 v Ni; 1971 v W, Ni, E, D, P, USSR; 1972 v Bel, Ni, W, E, Cz, Br; 1973 v D, E (17)

Cleland, J. (Royal Albert), 1891 v Ni (1)

Clements, R. (Leith Ath.), 1891 v Ni (1)

Clunas, W. L. (Sunderland), 1924 v E; 1926 v W (2)

Collier, W. (Raith R.), 1922 v W (1)

Collins, R. Y. (Celtic), 1951 v W, Ni, A; 1955 v Y, A, H; 1956 v Ni, W; 1957 v E, W, Sp (2), Sw, WG; 1958 v Ni, W, Sw, H, Pol, Y, F, Par; (with Everton), 1959, v E, W, Ni, WG, Ho, P; (with Leeds U.); 1965 v E, Pol, Sp (31)

Collins, T. (Hearts), 1909 v W (1)

Colman, D. (Aberdeen), 1911, v E, W, Ni; 1913 v Ni (4)

Colquhoun, E. P. (Sheffield U.), 1972 v P, Ho, Pe, Y, Cz, Br; 1973 v D (2), E (9)

Combe, J. R. (Hibernian), 1948 v E, Bel, Sw (3)

Conn, A. (Hearts), 1956 v A (1)

Conn, A. (Tottenham H.), 1975 v Ni (sub), E (2)

Connachan, E. D. (Dunfermline A.), 1962 v Cz, U (2)

Connelly, G. (Celtic), 1974 v Cz, WG (2)

Connolly, J. (Everton), 1973 v Sw (1)

Connor, J. (Airdrieonians), 1886 v Ni (1)

Connor, J. (Sunderland), 1930 v F; 1932 v Ni; 1934 v E; 1935 v Ni (4)

Cook, W. L. (Bolton W.), 1934 v E; 1935 v W, Ni (3)

Cooke, C. (Dundee), 1966 v W, I; (with Chelsea), P, Br; 1968 v E, Ho; 1969 v W, Ni, A, WG (sub), Cy (2); 1970 v A; 1971 v Bel; 1975 v Sp, P (16)

Cormack, P. B. (Hibernian), 1966 v Br; 1969 v D (sub); 1970 v Ei, WG; (with Nottingham F.), 1971 v D (sub), W, P, E; 1972 v Ho (sub 9)

Cowan, J. (Aston Villa), 1896 v E; 1897 v E; 1898 v E (3)

Cowan, J. (Morton), 1948 v Bel, Sw, F; 1949 v E, W, F; 1950 v E, W, Ni, Sw, P, F; 1951 v E, W, Ni, A (2), D, F, Bel; 1952 v Ni, W, USA, D, Se (25)

Cowan, W. D. (Newcastle U.), 1924 v E (1)

Cowie, D. (Dundee), 1953 v E, Se; 1954 v Ni, W, Fi, N, A, U; 1955 v W, Ni, A, H; 1956 v W, A; 1957 v Ni, W; 1958 v H, Pol, Y, Par (20)

Cox, C. J. (Hearts), 1948 v F (1)

Cox, S. (Rangers), 1949 v E, F; 1950 v E, F, W, Ni, Sw, P; 1951 v E, D, F, Bel, A; 1952 v Ni, W, USA, D, Se; 1953 v W, Ni, E; 1954 v W, Ni, E (24)

Craig, A. (Motherwell), 1929 v N, Ho; 1932 v E (3)

Craig, J. P. (Celtic), 1968 v W (1)

Craig, T. (Rangers), 1927 v Ni; 1928 v Ni; 1929 v N, G; 1930 v Ni, E, W (7)

Craig, T. B. (Newcastle U.), 1976 v Sw (1)

Crapnell, J. (Airdrieonians), 1929 v E, N, G; 1930 v F; 1931 v Ni, Sw; 1932 v E, F; 1933 v Ni (9)

Crawford, D. (St. Mirren), 1894, v W, Ni; 1900 v W (3)

Crawford, J. (Queen's Park), 1932 v F, Ni; 1933 v E, W, Ni (5)

Crerand, P. T. (Celtic), 1961 v Ei (2), Cz; 1962 v Ni, W, E, Cz (2), U; 1963 v W, Ni; (with Manchester U.), 1964 v Ni; 1965 v E, Pol, Fi; 1966 v Pol (16)

Cringan, W. (Celtic), 1920 v W; 1922 v E, Ni; 1923 v W, E (5)

Crosbie, J. A. (Ayr U.), 1920 v W; (with Birmingham); 1922 v E (2)

Croal, J. A. (Falkirk), 1913 v Ni; 1914 v E, W (3)

Cropley, A. J. (Hibernian), 1972 v P, Bel (2)

Cross, J. H. (Third Lanark), 1903 v Ni (1)

Cruickshank, J. (Hearts), 1964 v WG; 1970 v W, E; 1971 v D, Bel; 1976 v R (6)

Crum, J. (Celtic), 1936 v E; 1939 v Ni (2)

Cullen, M. J. (Luton T.), 1956 v A (1)

Cumming, D. S. (Middlesbrough), 1938 v E (1)

Cumming, J. (Hearts), 1955 v E, H, P, Y; 1960 v E, Pol, A, H, T (9)

Cummings, G. (Partick T.), 1935 v E; 1936 v W, Ni, (with Aston Villa), G, E; 1938 v W, Ni, Cz; 1939 v E (9)

Cunningham, A. N. (Rangers), 1920 v Ni; 1921 v W, E; 1922 v Ni; 1923 v E, W; 1924 v E, Ni; 1926 v E, Ni; 1927 v E, W (12)

Cunningham, W. C. (Preston N.E.), 1954 v N (2), U, Fi, A; 1955 v W, E, H (8)

Curran, H. P. (Wolverhampton W.), 1970 v A; 1971 v Ni, E, D, USSR (sub) (5)

Dalglish, K. (Celtic), 1972 v Bel (sub), Ho; 1973 v D (1 + 1 sub), E (2), W, Ni, Sw, Br; 1974 v Cz (2), WG (2), Ni, W, E, Bel, N (sub), Z, Br, Y; 1975 v EG, Sp (sub + 1), Se, P, W, Ni, E, R; 1976 v D (2), R, Sw, Ni, E (37)

Davidson, D. (Queen's Park), 1878 v W; 1879 v W; 1880 v W; 1881 v E, W (5)

Davidson, J. A. (Partick T.), 1954 v N (2), A, U; 1955 v W, Ni, E, H (8)

Davidson, S. (Middlesbrough), 1921 v E (1)

Dawson, J. (Rangers), 1935 v Ni; 1936 v E; 1937 v G, E, W, Ni, A, Cz; 1938 v W, Ho, Ni; 1939 v E, Ni, H (14)

Deans, J. (Celtic), 1975 v EG, Sp (2)

Delaney, J. (Celtic), 1936 v W, Ni; 1937 v G, E, A, Cz; 1938 v Ni; 1939 v W, Ni; (with Manchester U.), 1947 v E; 1948 v E, W, Ni (13)

Devine, A. (Falkirk), 1910 v W (1)

Dewar, G. (Dumbarton), 1888 v Ni; 1889 v E (2)

Dewar, N. (Third Lanark), 1932 v E, F; 1933 v W (3)

Dick, J. (West Ham U.), 1959 v E (1)

Dickie, M. (Rangers), 1897 v Ni; 1899 v Ni; 1900 v W (3)

Dickson, W. (Kilmarnock), 1970 v Ni, W, E; 1971 v D, USSR (5)

Dickson, W. (Dumbarton), 1888 v Ni (1)

Divers, J. (Celtic), 1895 v W (1)

Divers, J. (Celtic), 1939 v Ni (1)

Docherty, T. H. (Preston N.E.), 1952 v W; 1953 v E, Se; 1954 v N (2), A, U; 1955 v W, E, H (2), A; 1957 v E, Y, Sp (2), Sw, WG; 1958 v Ni, W, E, Sw; (with Arsenal), 1959 v W, E, Ni (25)

Dodds, J. (Celtic), 1914 v E, W, Ni (3)

Doig, J. E. (Arbroath), 1887 v Ni; 1889 v Ni;

(with Sunderland), 1896 v E; 1899 v E; 1902 v E; 1903 v E (6)

Donachie, W. (Manchester C.), 1972 v Pe, Ni, E, Y, Cz, Br; 1973 v D, E, W, Ni; 1974 v Ni; 1976 v R, Ni, W, E (15)

Donaldson, A. (Bolton W.), 1914 v E, Ni, W; 1920 v E, Ni; 1922 v Ni (6)

Donnachie, J. (Oldham Ath.), 1913 v E; 1914 v E, Ni (3)

Dougall, C. (Birmingham C.), 1947 v W (1)

Dougall, J. (Preston N.E.), 1939 v E (1)

Dougan, R. (Hearts), 1950 v Sw (1)

Douglas, A. (Chelsea), 1911 v Ni (1)

Douglas, J. (Renfrew), 1880 v W (1)

Dowds, P. (Celtic), 1892 v Ni (1)

Downie, R. (Third Lanark), 1892 v W (1)

Doyle, D. (Celtic), 1892 v E; 1893 v W; 1894 v E; 1895 v E, Ni; 1897 v E; 1898 v E, Ni (8)

Doyle, J. (Ayr U.), 1976 v R (1)

Drummond, J. (Falkirk), 1892 v Ni; (with Rangers), 1894 v Ni; 1895 v Ni, E; 1896 v E, Ni; 1897 v Ni; 1898 v E; 1900 v E; 1901 v E; 1920 v E, W, Ni; 1903 v Ni (14)

Dunbar, M. (Cartvale), 1886 v Ni (1)

Duncan, A. (Hibernian), 1975 v P (sub), W, Ni, E, R; 1976 v D (6)

Duncan, D. (Derby Co.), 1933 v E, W; 1934 v A, W; 1935 v E, W; 1936 v E, W, Ni; 1937 v G, E, W, Ni; 1938 v W (14)

Duncan, D. M. (East Fife), 1948 v Bel, Sw, F (3)

Duncan, J. (Alexandra Ath.), 1878 v W; 1882 v W (2)

Duncan, J. (Leicester C.), 1926 v W (1)

Duncanson, J. (Rangers), 1947 v Ni (1)

Dunlop, J. (St. Mirren), 1890 v W (1)

Dunlop, W. (Liverpool), 1906 v E (1)

Dunn, J. (Hibernian), 1925 v W, Ni; 1927 v Ni; 1928 v Ni, E; (with Everton), 1929 v W (6)

Dykes, J. (Hearts), 1938 v Ho; 1939 v Ni (2)

Easson, J. F. (Portsmouth), 1931 v A, Sw; 1934 v W

Ellis, J. (Mossend Swifts), 1892 v Ni (1)

Evans, R. (Celtic), 1949 v E, W, Ni, F; 1950 v W, Ni, Sw, P; 1951 v E, A; 1952 v Ni; 1953 v Se; 1954 v Ni, W, E, N, Fi; 1955 v Ni, P, Y, A, H; 1956 v E, Ni, W, A; 1957 v WG, Sp; 1958 v Ni, W, E, Sw, H, Pol, Y, Par, F; 1959 v E, WG, Ho, P; 1960 v E, Ni, W, Pol; (with Chelsea), 1960 v A, H, T (48)

Ewart, J. (Bradford C.), 1921 v E (1)

Ewing, T. (Partick T.), 1958 v W, E (2)

Farm, G. N. (Blackpool), 1953 v W, Ni, E, Se; 1954 v Ni, W, E; 1959 v WG, Ho, P (10)

Ferguson, J. (Vale of Leven), 1874 v E; 1876 v E, W; 1877 v W; 1878 v W (6)

Ferguson, R. (Kilmarnock), 1966 v W, E, Ho, P, Br; 1967 v W, Ni (7)

Fernie, W. (Celtic), 1954 v Fi, A, U; 1955 v W, Ni; 1957 v E, Ni, W, Y; 1958 v W, Sw, Par (12)

Findlay, R. (Kilmarnock), 1898 v W (1)

Fitchie, T. T. (Woolwich Arsenal), 1905 v W; 1906 v W, Ni; (with Queen's Park), 1907 v W (4)

Flavell, R. (Airdrieonians), 1947 v Bel, L (2)

Fleming, C. (East Fife), 1954 v Ni (1)

Fleming, J. W. (Rangers), 1929 v G, Ho; 1930 v E (3)

Fleming, R. (Morton), 1886 v Ni (1)

Forbes, A. R. (Sheffield U.), 1947 v Bel, L, E; 1948 v W, Ni; (with Arsenal), 1950 v E, P, F; 1951 v W, Ni, A; 1952 v W, D, Se (14)

Forbes, J. (Vale of Leven), 1884 v E, W, Ni; 1887 W, E (5)

Ford, D. (Hearts), 1974 v Cz (sub), WG (sub), W (3)

Forrest, J. (Rangers), 1966 v W, I; (with Aberdeen), 1971 v Bel (sub), D, Rus (5)

Forrest, J. (Motherwell), 1958 v E (1)

Forsyth, A. (Partick T.), 1972 v Y, Cz Br; 1973 v D; (with Manchester U.), E; 1975 v Sp, Ni (sub), R, EG; 1976 v D (10)

Forsyth, C. (Kilmarnock), 1964 v E; 1965 v W Ni, Fi (4)

Forsyth, T. (Motherwell), 1971 v D; (with Rangers) 1974 v Cz; 1976 v Sw, Ni, W, E (6)

Foyers, R. (St. Bernards), 1893 v W; 1894 v W (2)

Fraser, D. M. (W.B.A.), 1968 v Ho; 1969 v Cy (2)

Fraser, J. (Moffat), 1891 v Ni (1)

Fraser, M. J. E. (Queen's Park), 1880 v W; 1882 v W, E; 1883 v W, E (5)

Fraser, J. (Dundee), 1907 v Ni (1)

Fraser, W. (Sunderland), 1955 v W, Ni (2)

Fulton, W. (Abercorn), 1884 v Ni (1)

Fyle, J. H. (Third Lanark), 1895 v W (1)

Gabriel, J. (Everton), 1961 v W; 1964 v N (sub) (2)

Gallacher, H. K. (Airdrieonians), 1924 v Ni; 1925 v E, W, Ni; 1926 v W; (with Newcastle U.), 1926 v E, Ni; 1927 v E, W, Ni; 1928 v E, W; 1929 v E, W, Ni: 1930 v W, Ni, F; (with Chelsea), 1934 v E; (with Derby Co.), 1935 v E (20)

Gallacher, P. (Sunderland), 1935 v Ni (1)

Galt, J. H. (Rangers), 1908 v W, Ni (2)

Gardiner, I. (Motherwell), 1958 v W (1)

Gardner, D, R. (Third Lanark), 1897 v W (1)

Gardner, R. (Queen's Park), 1872 v E; 1873 v E; (with Clydesdale), 1874 v E; 1875 v E; 1878 v E (5)

Gemmell, T. (St. Mirren), 1955 v P, Y (2)

Gemmell, T. (Celtic), 1966 v E; 1967 v W, Ni, E, USSR; 1968 v Ni, E; 1969 v W, Ni, E, D, A, WG, Cy; 1970 v E, Ei, WG; 1971 v Bel (18)

Gemmill, A. (Derby Co.), 1971 v Bel; 1972 v P, Ho, Pe, Ni, W, E; 1976 v D, R, Ni, W, E (12)

Gibb, W. (Clydesdale), 1873 v E (1)

Gibson, D. W. (Leicester C.), 1963 v A, N, Ei, Sp; 1964 v Ni; 1965 v W, Fi (7)

Gibson, J. D. (Partick T.), 1926 v E; 1927 v E, W, Ni; (with Aston Villa), 1928 v E, W; 1930 v W, Ni (8)

Gibson, N. (Rangers), 1895 v E, Ni; 1896 v E, Ni; 1897 v E, Ni; 1898 v E; 1899 v E, W, Ni; 1900 v E, Ni; 1901 v W; (with Partick T.), 1905 v Ni (14)

Gilchrist, J. E. (Celtic), 1922 v E (1)

Gilhooley, M. (Hull C.), 1922 v W (1)

Gillespie, G. (Rangers), 1880 v W; 1881 v E, W; 1882 v E; (with Queen's Park), 1886 v W; 1890 v W; 1891 v Ni (7)

Gillespie, Jas. (Third Lanark), 1898 v W (1)

Gillespie, Jno. (Queen's Park), 1896 v W (1)

Gillespie, R. (Queen's Park), 1927 v W; 1931 v W; 1932 v F; 1933 v E (4)

Gillick, T. (Everton), 1937 v A, Cz; 1939 v W, Ni, H (5)

Gilmour, J. (Dundee), 1931 v W (1)

Gilzean, A. J. (Dundee), 1964 v W, E, N, WG; 1965 v Ni; (with Tottenham H.), Sp; 1966 v Ni, W, Pol, I; 1968 v W; 1969 v W, E, WG, Cy (2), A (sub); 1970 v Ni, E (sub) WG, A; 1971 v P (22)

Glen, A. (Aberdeen), 1956 v E, Ni (2)

Glen, R. (Renton), 1895 v W; 1896 v W; (with Hibernian), 1900 v Ni (3)

Gordon, J. E. (Rangers), 1912 v E, Ni; 1913 v E, Ni, W; 1914 v E, Ni; 1920 v W, E, Ni (10)

Gossland, J. (Rangers), 1884 v Ni (1)
Goudle, J. (Abercorn), 1884 v Ni (1)
Gourlay, J. (Cambuslang), 1886 v Ni (1)
Govan, J. (Hibernian), 1948 v E, W, Bel, Sw, F; 1949 v Ni (6)
Gow, D. R. (Rangers), 1888 v E (1)
Gow, J. J. (Queen's Park), 1885 v E (1)
Gow, J. R. (Rangers), 1888 v Ni (1)
Graham, J. A. (Arsenal), 1921 v Ni (1)
Graham, G. (Arsenal), 1972 v P, Ho, Ni, Y, Cz, Br; 1973 v D (2); (with Manchester U.), E, W, Ni, Br (sub) (12)
Graham, J. (Annbank), 1884 v Ni (1)
Grant, J. (Hibernian), 1959 v W, Ni (2)
Gray, A. (Hibernian), 1903 v Ni (1)
Gray, A. M. (Aston Villa), 1976 v R, Sw (2)
Gray, D. (Rangers), 1929 v W, Ni, G, Ho; 1930 v W, Ei, Ni; 1931 v W; 1933 v W, Ni (10)
Gray, E. (Leeds U.), 1969 v E, Cy; 1970 v WG, A; 1971 v W, Ni; 1972 v Bel, Ho; 1976 v W, E (10)
Gray, F. T. (Leeds U.), 1976 v Sw (1)
Gray, W. (Pollokshields Ath.), 1886 v E (1)
Green, A. (Blackpool), 1971 v Bel (sub), P (sub), Ni, E; 1972 v W, E, (sub) (6)
Greig, J. (Rangers), 1964 v E, WG; 1965 v W, Ni, E, Fi (2), Sp, Pol; 1966 v Ni, W, E, Pol, I (2), P, Ho, Br; 1967 v W, Ni, E; 1968 v Ni, W, E, Ho; 1969 v W, Ni, E, D, A, WG, Cy (2), 1970 v W, E, Ei, WG, A; 1971 v D, Bel, W (sub), Ni, E; 1976 v D (44)
Groves, W. (Hibernian), 1888 v W; (with Celtic), 1889 v Ni; 1890 v E (3)
Guilliland, W. (Queen's Park), 1891 v W; 1892 v Ni; 1894 v E; 1895 v E (4)

Haddock, H. (Clyde), 1955 v E, H (2), P, Y; 1958 v E (6)
Haddow, D. (Rangers), 1894 v E (1)
Haffey, F. (Celtic), 1960 v E; 1961 v E (2)
Hamilton, A. (Queen's Park), 1885 v E, W; 1886 v E; 1888 v E (4)
Hamilton, A. W. (Dundee), 1962 v Cz, U, W, E; 1963 v W, Ni, E, A, N, Ei; 1964 v Ni, W, E, N, WG; 1965 v Ni, W, E, Fi (2), Pol, Sp; 1966 v Pol, Ni (24)
Hamilton, G. (Aberdeen), 1947 v Ni; 1951 v Bel, A; 1954 v N (2) (5)
Hamilton, G. (Port Glasgow Ath.), 1906 v Ni (1)
Hamilton, J. (Queen's Park), 1892 v W; 1893 v E, Ni (3)
Hamilton, J. (St. Mirren), 1924 v Ni (1)
Hamilton, R. C. (Rangers), 1899 v E, W, Ni; 1900 v W; 1901 v E, Ni; 1902 v W, Ni; 1903 v E; 1904 v Ni; (with Dundee), 1911 v W (11)
Hamilton, T. (Hurlford), 1891 v Ni (1)
Hamilton, T. (Rangers), 1932 v E (1)
Hamilton, W. M. (Hibernian), 1965 v Fi (1)
Hannah, A. B. (Renton), 1888 v W (1)
Hannah, J. (Third Lanark), 1889 v W (1)
Hansen, J. (Partick T.), 1972 v Bel (sub), Y (sub) (2)
Harkness, J. D. (Queen's Park), 1927 v E, Ni; 1928 v E; (with Hearts), 1929 v W, E, Ni; 1930 v E, W; 1932 v W, F; 1934 v Ni (11)
Harper, J. M. (Aberdeen), 1973 v D (1+1 sub) (with Hibernian); 1976 v D (3)
Harper, W. (Hibernian), 1923 v E, Ni, W; 1924 v E, Ni, W; 1925 v E, Ni, W; (with Arsenal), 1926 v E, Ni (11)
Harris, J. (Partick T.), 1921 v W, Ni (2)
Harris, N. (Newcastle U.), 1924 v E (1)

Harrower, W. (Queen's Park), 1882 v E; 1884 v Ni; 1886 v W (3)
Hartford, R. A. (W.B.A.), 1972 v Pe, W (sub), E, Y, Cz, Br; 1976 v D, R, Ni (sub) (9)
Harvey, D. (Leeds U.), 1973 v D; 1974 v Cz, WG, Ni, W, E, Bel, Z, Br, Y; 1975 v EG, Sp (2); 1976 v D (2) (15)
Hastings, A. C. (Sunderland), 1936 v Ni; 1938 v Ni (2)
Haughney, M. (Celtic), 1954 v E (1)
Hay, D. (Celtic), 1970 v Ni, W, E; 1971 v D, Bel, W, P, Ni; 1972 v P, Bel, Ho; 1973 v W, Ni, E, Sw, Br; 1974 v Cz (2), WG, Ni, W, E, Bel, N, Z, Br, Y (27)
Hay, J. (Celtic), 1905 v Ni; 1909 v Ni; 1910 v W, Ni, E; 1911 v Ni, E; (with Newcastle U.), 1912 v E, W; 1914 v E, Ni (11)
Heggie, C. (Rangers) 1886 v Ni (1)
Henderson, G. H. (Rangers), 1904 v Ni (1)
Henderson, J. G. (Portsmouth), 1953 v Se; 1954 v Ni, E, N; 1956 v W; (with Arsenal), 1959 v W, Ni (7)
Henderson, W. (Rangers), 1963 v W, Ni, E, A, N, Ei, Sp; 1964 v W, Ni, E, N, WG; 1965 v Fi, Pol, E, Sp; 1966 v Ni, W, Pol, I, Ho; 1967 v W, Ni; 1968 v Ho; 1969 v Ni, E, Cy; 1970 v Ei; 1971 v P (29)
Hepburn, J. (Alloa Ath.), 1891 v W (1)
Hepburn, R. (Ayr U.), 1932 v Ni (1)
Herd, A. C. (Hearts), 1915 v Ni (1)
Herd, D. G. (Arsenal), 1959 v E, W, Ni; 1961 v Ei, Cz (5)
Herd, G. (Clyde), 1958 v E; 1960 v H, T; 1961 v W, N (5)
Herriot, J. (Birmingham C.), 1969 v Ni, E, D, Cy (2), W (sub); 1970 v Ei (sub), WG (8)
Hewie, J. D. (Charlton Ath.), 1956 v E, A; 1957 v E, Ni, W, Y, Sp (2), Sw, WG; 1958 v Pol, W, Y, F; 1959 v Ho, P; 1960 v Ni, W, Pol (19)
Higgins, A. (Kilmarnock), 1885 v Ni (1)
Higgins, A. (Newcastle U.), 1910 v E, Ni; 1911 v E, Ni (4)
Highet, T. C. (Queen's Park), 1875 v E; 1876 v E, W; 1878 v E (4)
Hill, D. (Rangers), 1881 v E, W; 1882 v W (3)
Hill, D. A. (Third Lanark), 1906 v Ni (1)
Hill, F. R. (Aberdeen), 1930 v F; 1931 v W, Ni (3)
Hill, J. (Hearts), 1891 v E, 1892 v W (2)
Hogg, G. (Hearts), 1896 v E, Ni (2)
Hogg, J. (Ayr U.), 1922 v Ni (1)
Hogg, R. M. (Celtic), 1937 v Cz (1)
Holm, A. H. (Queen's Park), 1882 v W; 1883 v E, W (3)
Holt, D. D. (Hearts), 1963 v A, N, Ei, Sp; 1964 v WG, (sub) (5)
Holton, J. A. (Manchester U.), 1973 v W, Ni, E, Sw, Br; 1974 v Cz, WG, Ni, W, E, N, Z, Br, Y; 1975 v EG (15)
Hope, R. (W.B.A.), 1968 v Ho; 1969 v D (2)
Houliston, W. (Queen of the South), 1949 v E, Ni, F (3)
Houston, S. M. (Manchester U.), 1976 v D (1)
Howden, W. (Partick T.), 1905 v Ni (1)
Howe, R. (Hamilton A.), 1929 v N, Ho (2)
Howie, J. (Newcastle U.), 1905 v E; 1906 v E; 1908 v E (3)
Howie, H. (Hibernian), 1949 v W (1)
Howieson, J. (St. Mirren), 1927 v Ni (1)
Hughes, J. (Celtic), 1965 v Pol, Sp; 1966 v Ni, I (2), 1968 v E; 1969 v A; 1970 v Ei (8)
Hughes, W. (Sunderland), 1975 v Se (sub) (1)
Humphries, W. (Motherwell), 1952 v Se (1)

Hunter, A. (Kilmarnock), 1972 v Pe, Y; (with Celtic), 1973 v E; 1974 v Cz (4)

Hunter, J. (Dundee), 1909 v W (1)

Hunter, J. (Third Lanark), 1874 v E; (with Eastern), 1875 v E; (with Third Lanark), 1876 v E; 1877 v W (4)

Hunter, R. (St. Mirren), 1890 v Ni (1)

Hunter, W. (Motherwell), 1960 v H, T; 1961 v W (3)

Husband, J. (Partick T.), 1947 v W (1)

Hutchison. T, (Coventry C.), 1974 v Cz (2), WG (2), Ni, W, Bel (sub), N, Z (sub), Y (sub) 1975 v; EG, Sp (2), P, E (sub), R (sub); 1976 v D (17)

Hutton, J. (Aberdeen), 1923 v E, W, Ni, 1924 v Ni; 1926 v W, E, Ni; (with Blackburn R.), 1927 v Ni; 1928 v W, Ni (10)

Hutton, J. (St. Bernards), 1887 v Ni (1)

Hyslop, T. (Stoke C.), 1896 v E; (with Rangers), 1897 v E (2)

Imlach, J. J. S. (Nottingham F.), 1958 v H, Pol, Y, F (4)

Imrie, W. N. (St. Johnstone), 1929 v N, G, (2)

Inglis, J. (Kilmarnock Ath.), 1884 v Ni (1)

Inglis, J. (Rangers), 1883 v E, W (2)

Irons, J. H. (Queen's Park), 1900 v W (1)

Jackson, A. (Cambuslang), 1886 v W; 1888 v Ni (2)

Jackson, A. (Aberdeen), 1925 v E, W, Ni; (with Huddersfield T.), 1926 v E, W, Ni; 1927 v W, Ni; 1928 v E W; 1929 v E, W, Ni; 1930 v E, W, Ni, F (17)

Jackson, C. (Rangers), 1975 v Se, P (sub), W; 1976 v D, R, Ni, W, E (8)

Jackson, J. (Partick T.), 1931 v A, I, Sw; 1933 v E; (with Chelsea), 1934 v E; 1935 v E; 1936 v W, Ni(8)

Jackson, T. A. (St. Mirren), 1904 v W, E, Ni; 1905 v W; 1907 v W, Ni (6)

James, A. W. (Preston N.E.), 1926 v W; 1928 v E; 1929 v E, Ni; (with Arsenal), 1930 v E, W, Ni; 1933 v W (8)

Jardine, A. (Rangers), 1971 v D (sub); 1972 v P, Bel, Ho; 1973 v E, Sw, Br; 1974 v Cz (2), WG (2), Ni, W, E, Bel, N, Z, Br, Y; 1975 v EG, Sp (2), Se, P, W, Ni, E (27)

Jarvie, A. (Airdrieonians), 1971 v P (sub), Ni (sub), E (sub) (3)

Jenkinson, T. (Hearts), 1887 v Ni (1)

Johnston, L. H. (Clyde), 1948 v Bel, Sw (2)

Johnston, R. (Sunderland), 1938 v Cz (1)

Johnston, W. (Rangers), 1966 v W, E, Pol, Ho; 1968 v W, E; 1969 v Ni (sub); 1970 v Ni; 1971 v D (9)

Johnston, D. (Rangers), 1973 v W, Ni, E, Sw, Br; 1975 v EG (sub), Se (sub); 1976 v Sw, Ni (sub), E (sub) (10)

Johnstone, J. (Abercorn), 1888 v W (1)

Johnstone, J. (Celtic), 1965 v W, Fi; 1966 v E; 1967 v W, USSR; 1968 v W; 1969 v A, WG; 1970 v E, WG; 1971 v D, E; 1972 v P, Bel, Ho, Ni, E (sub); 1974 v W, E, Bel, N; 1975 v EG, Sp (23)

Johnstone, Jas (Kilmarnock), 1894 v W (1)

Johnstone, J. A. (Hearts), 1930 v W; 1933 v W, Ni (3)

Johnstone, R. (Hibernian), 1951 v E, D, F; 1952 v Ni, E; 1953 v E, Se; 1954 v W, E, N, Fi; 1955 v Ni, H; (with Manchester C.) 1955 v E; 1956 v E, Ni, W (17)

Johnstone, W. (Third Lanark), 1887 v Ni; 1889 v W; 1890 v E (3)

Jordan, J. (Leeds U.), 1973 v E (sub), Sw (sub), Br; 1974 v Cz (sub + 1), WG (sub), Ni (sub),

W, E, Bel, N, Z, Br, Y; 1975 v EG, Sp (2); 1976 v Ni, W, E (20)

Kay, J. L. (Queen's Park), 1880 v E; 1882 v E, W; 1883 v E, W; 1884 v W (6)

Keillor, A. (Montrose), 1891 v W; 1892 v Ni; (with Dundee), 1894 v Ni; 1895 v W; 1896 v W; 1897 v W (6)

Keir, L. (Dumbarton), 1885 v W; 1886 v Ni; 1887 v E, W; 1888 v E (5)

Kelly, H. T. (Blackpool), 1952 v USA (1)

Kelly, J. (Renton), 1888 v E; (with Celtic), 1889 v E; 1890 v E; 1892 v E; 1893 v E, Ni; 1894 v W; 1896 v Ni (8)

Kelly, J. C. (Barnsley), 1949 v W, Ni (2)

Kelso, R. (Renton), 1885 v W, Ni; 1886 v W; 1887 v E, W; 1888 v E; (with Dundee), 1898 v Ni (7)

Kelso, T. (Dundee), 1914 v W (1)

Kennaway, J. (Celtic), 1934 v A, W (2)

Kennedy, A. (Eastern), 1875 v E; 1876 v E, W; (with Third Lanark), 1878 v E; 1882 v W; 1884 v W (6)

Kennedy, J. (Celtic), 1964 v W, E, WG; 1965 v W, Ni, Fi (6)

Kennedy, J. (Hibernian), 1897 v W (1)

Kennedy, S. (Partick T.), 1905 v W (1)

Kennedy, S. (Rangers), 1975 v Se, P, W, Ni, E (5)

Ker, G. (Queen's Park), 1880 v W; 1881 v E, W; 1882 v W, E (5)

Ker, W. (Granville), 1872 v E; (with Queen's Park), 1873 v E (2)

Kerr, A. (Partick T.), 1955 v A, H (2)

Kerr, P. (Hibernian), 1924 v Ni (1)

Key, G. (Hearts), 1902 v Ni (1)

Key, W. (Queen's Park), 1907 v Ni (1)

King, A. (Hearts), 1896 v E, W; (with Celtic), 1897 v Ni; 1898 v Ni; 1899 v Ni, W (6)

King, J. (Hamilton A.), 1933 v Ni; 1934 v Ni (2)

King, W. S. (Queen's Park), 1929 v W (1)

Kinloch, J. D. (Partick T.), 1922 v Ni (1)

Kinnaird, A. F. (Wanderers), 1873 v E (1)

Kinnear, D. (Rangers), 1938 v Cz (1)

Lambie, J. A. (Queen's Park), 1886 v Ni; 1887 v Ni; 1888 v E (3)

Lambie, W. A. (Queen's Park), 1892 v Ni; 1893 v W; 1894 v E; 1895 v E, Ni; 1896 v E, Ni; 1897 v E, Ni (9)

Lamont, D. (Pilgrims), 1885 v Ni (1)

Lang, A. (Dumbarton), 1880 v W (1)

Lang, J. J. (Clydesdale), 1876 v W; (with Third Lanark), 1878 v W (2)

Latta, A. (Dumbarton), 1888 v W; 1889 v E (2)

Law, D. (Huddersfield T.), 1959 v W, Ni, Ho, P; 1960 v Ni, W; (with Manchester C.), 1960 v E, Pol, A; 1961 v E, Ni; (with Torino), 1961 v Cz (2); 1962 v E; (with Manchester U.), 1963 v W, Ni, E, A, N, Ei, Sp; 1964 v W, E, N, WG; 1965 v W, Ni, E, Fi (2), Pol, Sp; 1966 v Ni, E, Pol; 1967 v W, E, USSR; 1968 v Ni; 1969 v Ni, A, WG; 1972 v Pe, Ni, W, E, Y, Cz, Br; (with Manchester C.) 1974 v Cz (2), WG (2), Ni, Z (55)

Law, G. (Rangers), 1910 v E, Ni, W (3)

Law, T. (Chelsea), 1928 v E; 1930 v E (2)

Lawrence, J. (Newcastle U.), 1911 v E (1)

Lawrence, T. (Liverpool), 1963 v Ei; 1969 v W, WG (3)

Lawson, D. (St. Mirren), 1923 v E (1)

Leckie, R. (Queen's Park), 1872 v E (1)

Leggat, G. (Aberdeen), 1956 v E; 1957 v W; 1958 v Ni, H, Pol, Y, Par; (with Fulham), 1959 v E, W,

Ni, WG, Ho; 1960 v E, Ni, W, Pol, A, H (18)
Lennie, W. (Aberdeen), 1908 v W, Ni (2)
Lennox, R. (Celtic), 1967 v Ni, E, USSR; 1968 v W, E; 1969 v D, A, W G, Cy(sub); 1970 v W(sub)(10)
Leslie, L. G. (Airdrieonians), 1961 v W, Ni, Ei (2), Cz(5)
Liddell, W, (Liverpool), 1947 v W, Ni; 1948 v E, W, Ni; 1950 v E, W, P, F; 1951 v W, Ni, E, A; 1952 v W, Ni, E, USA, D, Se; 1953 v W, Ni, E; 1954 v W; 1955 v P, Y, A, H; 1956 v Ni (28)
Liddle, D. (East Fife),)1931 v A, I, Sw (3)
Lindsay, D. (St. Mirren), 1903 v Ni (1)
Lindsay, J. (Dumbarton), 1880 v W; 1881 v W, E; 1884 v W, E; 1885 v W, E; 1886 v E (8)
Lindsay, J. (Renton), 1888 v E; 1893 v E, Ni (3)
Linwood, A. B. (Clyde), 1950 v W (1)
Little, R. J. (Rangers), 1953 v Se (1)
Livingstone, G. T. (Manchester C.), 1906 v E; (with Rangers), 1907 v W (2)
Lochhead, A. (Third Lanark), 1889 v W (1)
Logan, J. (Ayr U.), 1891 v W (1)
Logan, T. (Falkirk), 1913 v Ni (1)
Logie, J. T. (Arsenal), 1953 v Ni (1)
Loney, W. (Celtic), 1910 v W, Ni (2)
Long, H. (Clyde), 1947 v Ni (1)
Longair, W. (Dundee), 1894 v Ni (1)
Lorimer, P. (Leeds U.), 1970 v A (sub); 1971 v W, Ni, 1972 v Ni (sub), W, E; 1973 v D (2), E (2); 1974 v WG (sub), E, Bel, N, Z, Br, Y; 1975 v Sp (sub); 1976 v D (2), R (21)
Love, A. (Aberdeen), 1931 v A, I, Sw (3)
Low, A. (Falkirk), 1934 v Ni (1)
Low, T. P. (Rangers), 1897 v Ni (1)
Low, W, L. (Newcastle U.), 1911 v E. W; 1912 v Ni; 1920 v E, Ni (5)
Lowe, J. (Cambuslang), 1891 v Ni (1)
Lowe, J. (St. Bernards), 1887 v Ni (1)
Lundle, J. (Hibernian), 1886 v W (1)
Lyall, J. (Sheffield W.), 1905 v E (1)

M'Adam, J. (Third Lanark), 1880 v W (1)
M'Arthur, D. (Celtic), 1895 v E, Ni; 1899 v W (3)
M'Atee, A. (Celtic), 1913 v W (1)
Macari, L. (Celtic), 1972 v W (sub), E, Y, Cz, Br; 1973 v D; (with Manchester U.) E (2), W (sub), Ni (sub); 1975 v Se, P (sub), W, E (sub), R (15)
Macauley, A. R. (Brentford), 1947 v E; (with Arsenal), 1948 v E, W, Ni, Bel, Sw, F (7)
M'Aulay, J. (Dumbarton), 1882 v W; (with Arthurlie), 1884 v Ni (2)
M'Aulay, J. (Dumbarton), 1883 v E, W; 1884 v E; 1885 v E, W; 1886 v E; 1887 v E, W (8)
M'Auley, R. (Rangers), 1932 v Ni, W (2)
M'Bain, E. (St. Mirren), 1894 v W (1)
M'Bain, N. (Manchester U.), 1922 v E; (with Everton), 1923 v Ni; 1924 v W (3)
McBride, J. (Celtic), 1967 v W Ni (2)
M'Bride, P. (Preston N.E.), 1904 v E; 06 v 19E; 1907 v E, W; 1908 v E; 1909 v W (6)
M'Call, J. (Renton), 1886 v W; 1887 v E, W; 1888 v E; 1890 v E (5)
McCalliog, J. (Sheffield W.), 1967 v E, USSR; 1968 v Ni; 1969 v D; (with Wolverhampton W.), 1971 v P (5)
McCallum, N. (Renton), 1888 v Ni (1)
McCann, R. J. (Motherwell), 1959 v WG; 1960 v E, Ni, W; 1961 v E (5)
McCartney, W. (Hibernian), 1902 v Ni (1)
McClory, A. (Motherwell), 1927 v W; 1928 v Ni; 1935 v W (3)
McCloy, P. (Ayr U.), 1924 v E; 1925 v E (2)

McCloy, P. (Rangers), 1973 v W, Ni, Sw, Br (4)
McColl, A. (Renton), 1888 v Ni (1)
McColl, I. M. (Rangers), 1950 v E, F; 1951 v W, Ni, Bel; 1957 v E, Ni, W, Y, Sp, Sw, WG; 1958 v Ni, E (14)
McColl, R. S. (Queen's Park), 1896 v W, Ni; 1897 v Ni, 1898 v Ni; 1899 v Ni, E, W; 1900 v E; W; 1901 v E, Ni; (with Newcastle U.), 1902 v E; (with Queen's Park), 1908 v Ni (13)
M'Coll, W. (Renton), 1895 v W (1)
M'Combie, A. (Sunderland), 1903 v E, W; (with Newcastle U.), 1905 v E, W (4)
M'Corkindale, J. (Partick T.), 1891 v W (1)
M'Cormick, R. (Abercorn), 1886 v W (1)
McCrae, D. (St. Mirren), 1929 v N, G (2)
M'Creadie, A. (Rangers), 1893 v W; 1894 v E (2)
McCreadie, E. G. (Chelsea), 1965 v E, Sp, Fi, Pol; 1966 v P, Ni, W, Pol, I; 1967 v E, USSR; 1968 v Ni, W, E, Ho; 1969 v W, Ni, E, D, A, WG, Cy (2) (23)
McCulloch, D. (Hearts), 1935 v W; (with Brentford), 1936 v E; 1937 v W, Ni; 938 v Cz;1 (with Derby Co.), 1939 v H, W (7)
MacDonald, A. (Rangers), 1976 v Sw (1)
M'Donald, J. (Edinburgh University), 1886 v E (1)
M'Donald, J. (Sunderland), 1956 v W, Ni (2)
MacDougall, E. J. (Norwich C.), 1975 v Se, P, W Ni, E; 1976 v D, R (7)
McDougall, J. (Liverpool), 1931 v I (2)
McDougall J. (Airdrieonians), 1926 v Ni (1)
M'Dougall, J. (Vale of Leven), 1877 v E, W; 1878 v E; 1879 v E, W (5)
McFayden, W. (Motherwell), 1934 v A, W (2)
Macfarlane, A. (Dundee), 1904 v W; 1906 v W; 1908 v W; 1909 v Ni; 1911 v W (5)
M'Farlane, R. (Greenock Morton), 1896 v W (1)
Macfarlane, M. (Hearts), 1947 v L (1)
McGarr, E. (Aberdeen), 1970 v Ei, A (2)
M'Geoch, A. (Dumbreck), 1876 v E, W; 1877 v E, W (4)
McGhee, J. (Hibernian), 1886 v W (1)
McGonagle, W. (Celtic), 1933 v E; 1934 v A, E, Ni; 1935 v Ni, W (6)
McGrain, D. (Celtic), 1973 v W, Ni, E, Sw, Br; 1974 v Cz (2), WG, W (sub), E, Bel, N, Z, Br, Y; 1975 v Sp, Se, P, W, Ni, E, R; 1976 v D (2), Sw, Ni, W, E (28)
M'Gregor, J. C. (Vale of Leven), 1877 v E, W; 1878 v E; 1880 v E (4)
McGrory, J. E. (Kilmarnock), 1965 v Ni, Fi; 1966 v P (3)
M'Grory, J. (Celtic), 1928 v Ni; 1931 v E; 1932 v Ni, W; 1933 v E, Ni; 1934 v Ni (7)
M'Guire, W. (Beith), 1881 v E, W (2)
M'Gurk, F. (Birmingham), 1934 v W (1)
M'Hardy, H. (Rangers), 1885 v Ni (1)
M'Inally, T. B. (Celtic), 1926 v Ni; 1927 v W (2)
M'Innes, T. (Cowlairs), 1889 v Ni (1)
M'Intosh, W. (Third Lanark), 1905 v Ni (1)
M'Intyre, A. (Vale of Leven), 1878 v E; 1882 v E (2)
M'Intyre, H. (Rangers), 1880 v W (1)
M'Intyre, J. (Rangers), 1884 v W (1)
McKay, D. (Celtic), 1959 v E, WG, Ho, P; 1960 v E, Pol, A, H, T; 1961 v W, Ni; 1962 v Ni, Cz, U (sub) (4)
Mackay, D. C. (Hearts), 1957 v Sp; 1958 v F; 1959 v. W, Ni; (with Tottenham H.), 1959 v WG, E; 1960 v W, Ni, A, Pol, H, T; 1961 v W, Ni, E; 1963 v E, A, N; 1964 v Ni, W, N; 1966 v Ni (22)
M'Kay, J. (Blackburn R.), 1924 v W (1)
M'Kay, R. (Newcastle), 1928 v W (1)

McKean, R. (Rangers), 1976 v Sw (1)
M'Kenzie, D. (Brentford), 1938 v Ni (1)
Mackenzie, J. A. (Partick T.), 1954 v W, E, N, Fi, A, U; 1955 v E, H; 1956 v A (9)
M'Keown, M. (Celtic), 1889 v Ni ;1890 v E (2)
M'Kie, J. (East Stirling), 1898 v W (1)
McKillop, T. R. (Rangers), 1938 v Ho (1)
M'Kinlay, D. (Liverpool), 1922 v W, Ni (2)
McKinnon, A. (Queen's Park), 1874 v E (1)
McKinnon, R. (Rangers), 1966 v W, E, I (2), Ho, Br; 1967 v W, Ni, E; 1968 v Ni, W, E, Ho; 1969 v D, A, WG, Cy; 1970 v Ni, W, E, Ei, WG, A; 1971 v D, Bel, P, Rus, D (28)
M'Kinnon, W. (Dumbarton), 1883 v E, W; 1884 v E, W (4)
M'Kinnon, W. W. (Queen's Park), 1872 v E; 1873 v E; 1874 v E; 1875 v E; 1876 v E, W; 1877 v E; 1878 v E; 1879 v E (9)
McLaren, A. (St. Johnstone), 1929 v N, G, Ho; 1933 v W, Ni (5)
McLaren, A. (Preston N.E.), 1947 v E, Bel, L; 1948 v W (4)
M'Laren, J. (Hibernian), 1888 v W; (with Celtic), 1889 v E; 1890 v E (3)
M'Lean, A. (Celtic), 1926 v W, Ni; 1927 v W, E (4)
M'Lean, D. (St. Bernard,s) 1896 v W; 1897 v Ni (2)
M'Lean, D. (Sheffield W.), 1912 v E (1)
McLean, G. (Dundee) 1968 v Ho (1)
M'Lean, T. (Kilmarnock), 1969 v D, Cy, W; 1970 v Ni, W; 1971 v D (6)
M'Leod, D. (Celtic), 1905 v Ni; 1906 v E, W, Ni (4)
M'Leod, J. (Dumbarton), 1888 v Ni; 1889 v W; 1890 v Ni; 1892 v E; 1893 v W (5)
MacLeod, J. M. (Hibernian), 1961 v E, Ei (2), Cz; 4
M'Leod, W. (Cowlairs), 1886 v Ni (1)
McLintock, A. (Vale of Leven), 1875 v E; 1876 v E; 1880 v E (3)
McLintock, F. (Leicester C.). 1963 v N (sub) Ei, Sp; (with Arsenal), 1965 v Ni; 1967 v USSR; 1970 v Ni; 1971 v W, Ni, E (9)
McLuckie, J. S. (Manchester C.), 1934 v W (1)
M'Mahon, A. (Celtic), 1892 v E; 1893 v E, Ni; 1894 v E; 1901 v Ni; 1902 v W (6)
M'Menemy, J. (Celtic), 1905 v Ni; 1909 v Ni; 1910 v E, W; 1911 v Ni, W, E; 1912 v W; 1914 v W, Ni, E; 1920 v Ni (12)
M'Menemy, J. (Motherwell), 1934 v W (1)
McMillan, J. (St. Bernards), 1897 v W (1)
McMillan, J. L. (Airerieonians), 1952 v E, USA, D; 1955 v E; 1956 v E; (with Rangers), 1961 v Cz (6)
McMillan, T. (Dumbarton), 1897 v Ni (1)
McMullan, J. (Partick T.), 1920 v W; 1921 v W, Ni, E; 1924 v E Ni; 1925 v E; 1926 v W; (with Manchester C.), 1926 v E; 1927 v E, W; 1928 v E, W; 1929 v W, E, Ni (16)
McNab, A. (Morton), 1921 v E, Ni (2)
McNab, A. (Sunderland), 1937 v A; (with W.B.A.), 1939 v E (2)
McNab, C. D. (Dundee), 1931 v E, W, A, I, Sw; 1932 v E (6)
McNab, J. S. (Liverpool), 1923 v W (1)
M'Nair, A. (Celtic), 1906 v W; 1907 v Ni; 1908 v E, W; 1909 v E; 1910 v W; 1912 v E, W, Ni; 1913 v E; 1914 v E, Ni; 1920 v E, W Ni (15)
McNaught, W. (Raith R.), 1951 v A, W, Ni; 1952 v E; 1955 v Ni (5)
McNeil, H. (Queen's Park), 1874 v E; 1875 v E; 1876 v E, W; 1877 v W; 1878 v E; 1879 v E, W; 1881 v E, W (10)
M'Neil, M. (Rangers), 1876 v W; 1880 v E (2)
McNeill, W. (Celtic), 1961 v E, Ei (2), Cz; 1962 v

Ni, E, Cz, U; 1963 v Ei, Sp; 1964 v W, E, WG; 1965 v E, Fi, Pol. Sp; 1966 v Ni, Pol; 1967 v USSR; 1968 v E; 1969 v Cy, W, E, Cy (sub); 1970 v WG; 1972 v Ni, W, E (29)
McPhail, J. (Celtic), 1950 v W; 1951 v W, Ni, A; 1954 v Ni (5)
McPhail, R. (Airdrieonians), 1927 v E; (with Rangers), 1929 v W; 1931 v E, Ni; 1932 v W, Ni, F; 1933 v E, Ni; 1934 v A, Ni; 1935 v E; 1937 v G, E, Cz; 1938 v W, Ni (17)
McPherson, D. (Kilmarnock), 1892 v Ni (1)
McPherson, J. (Kilmarnock), 1888 v W; (with Cowlairs), 1889 v E; 1890 v Ni, E; (with Rangers), 1892 v W; 1894 v E; 1895 v E, Ni; 1897 v Ni (9)
McPherson, J. (Clydesdale), 1875 v E (1)
McPherson, J. (Vale of Leven), 1879 v E, W; 1880 v E; 1881 v W; 1883 v E, W; 1884 v E; 1885 v Ni (8)
McPherson, J. (Hearts), 1891 v E (1)
McPherson, R. (Arthurlie), 1882 v E (1)
McQueen, G. (Leeds U.), 1974 v Bel; 1975 v Sp (2), P, W, Ni, E, R; 1976 v D (9)
M'Queen, M. (Leith Ath.), 1890 v W; 1891 v W (2)
M'Rorie, D. M. (Morton), 1931 v W (1)
McSpadyen, A. (Partick T.), 1939 v E, H (2)
M'Stay. W. (Celtic), 1921 v W, Ni; 1925 v E, Ni, W; 1926 v E, Ni ,W; 1927 v E, Ni, W; 1928 v W, Ni (13)
M'Tavish, J. (Falkirk), 1910 v Ni (1)
M'Wattie, G. C. (Queen's Park), 1901 v W, Ni (2)
M'William P. (Newcastle U.), 1905 v E; 1906 v E; 1907 v E, W; 1909 v E, W; 1910 v E; 1911 v W (8)
Madden, J. (Celtic), 1893 v W; 1895 v W (2)
Main, F. R. (Rangers), 1938 v W (1)
Main, J. (Hibernian), 1909 v Ni (1)
Maley, W. (Celtic), 1893 v E, Ni (2)
Marshall, H. (Celtic). 1899 v W; 1900 v Ni (2)
Marshall, J. (Rangers), 1932 v E; 1933 v E; 1934 v E (3)
Marshall, J. (Middlesbrough), 1921 v E, W, Ni; 1922 v E, W, Ni; (with Llanelly), 1924 v W (7)
Marshall, J. (Third Lanark), 1885 v Ni; 1886 v W; 1887 v E, W (4)
Marshall, R. W. (Rangers), 1892 v Ni; 1894 v Ni (2)
Martin, F. (Aberdeen), 1954 v N (2), A, U; 1955 v E, H (6)
Martin, N. (Hibernian), 1965 v Fi, Pol; (with Sunderland), 1966 v I (3)
Martis, J. (Motherwell), 1961 v W (1)
Mason, J. (Third Lanark), 1949 v E, W, Ni; 1950 v Ni; 1951 v Ni, Bel, A (7)
Massie, A. (Hearts), 1932 v Ni, W, F; 1933 v Ni; 1934 v E, Ni; 1935 v E, Ni, W; 1936 v W, Ni; (with Aston Villa), 1936 v E; 1937 v G, E, W, Ni, A; 1938 v W (18)
Masson, D. S. (Q.P.R.), 1976 v Ni, W, E (3)
Mathers, D. (Partick T.), 1954 v Fi (1)
Maxwell, W. S. (Stoke C.), 1898 v E (1)
May, J. (Rangers), 1906 v W, Ni; 1908 v E, Ni; 1909 v W (5)
Meechan, P. (Celtic), 1896 v Ni (1)
Meiklejohn, D. D. (Rangers), 1922 v W; 1924 v W; 1925 v W, Ni, E; 1928 v W, Ni; 1929 v E, Ni; 1930 v E, Ni; 1931 v E; 1932 v W, Ni; 1934 v A (5)
Menzies, A. (Hearts), 1906 v E (1)
Mercer, R. (Hearts), 1912 v W; 1913 v Ni (2)
Middleton, R. (Cowdenbeath), 1930 v Ni (1)
Millar, J. (Rangers), 1897 v E; 1898 v E, W (3)
Millar. J. (Rangers), 1963 v A, Ei (2)
Miller, A. (Hearts), 1939 v W (1)

Miller, J. (St. Mirren), 1931 v E, I Sw; 1932 v F; 1934 v E (5)

Miller, P. (Dumbarton), 1882 v E; 1883 v E, W (3)

Miller, T. (Liverpool), 1920 v E; (with Manchester U.), 1921 v E, Ni (3)

Miller, W. (Third Lanark), 1876 v E (1)

Miller, W. (Celtic), 1947 v E, W, Bel, L; 1948 v W, Ni (6)

Miller, W. (Aberdeen), 1975 v R (1)

Mills, W. (Aberdeen), 1936 v W, Ni; 1937 v W (3)

Milne, J. V. (Middlesbrough), 1938 v E; 1939 v E (2)

Mitchell, D. (Rangers), 1890 v Ni; 1892 v E; 1893 v E, Ni; 1894 v E (5)

Mitchell, J. (Kilmarnock), 1908 v Ni; 1910 v Ni, (3)

Mitchell, R. C. (Newcastle U.), 1951 v D, F (2)

Mochan, N. (Celtic), 1954 v N, A, U (3)

Moir, W. (Bolton W.), 1950 v E (1)

Moncur, R. (Newcastle U.), 1968 v Ho; 1970 v Ni, W, E, Ei; 1971 v D, Bel, W, P, Ni, E, D; 1972 v Pe, Ni, W, E (16)

Morgan, H. (St. Mirren), 1898 v W; (with Liverpool), 1899 v E (2)

Morgan, W. (Burnley), 1968 v Ni; (with Manchester U.) 1972, v Pe, Y, Cz, Br; 1973 v D (2), E (2), W, Ni, Sw, Br; 1974 v Cz (2), WG (2), Ni, Bel (sub), Br, Y (21)

Morris, D. (Raith R.), 1923 v Ni; 1924 v E, Ni; 1925 v E, W, Ni (6)

Morris, H. (East Fife), 1950 v Ni (1)

Morrison, T. (St. Mirren), 1927 v E (1)

Morton, A. L. (Queen's Park), 1920 v W, Ni; (with Rangers), 1921 v E; 1922 v E, W; 1923 v E, W, Ni; 1924 v E, W, Ni; 1925 v E, W, Ni; 1927 v E, Ni; 1928 v E, W, Ni; 1929 v E, W, Ni; 1930 v E, W, Ni; 1931 v E, W, Ni; 1932 v E, W, F (3l)

Morton, H. A. (Kilmarnock), 1929 v G, Ho (2)

Mudie, J. K. (Blackpool), 1957 v W, Ni, E, Y, Sw, Sp, (2) WG; 1958 v N, E, W, Sw, H, Pol, Y, Par, F (17)

Muir, W. (Dundee), 1907 v Ni (1)

Muirhead, T. A. (Rangers), 1922 v Ni; 1923 v E; 1924 v W; 1927 v Ni; 1928 v Ni; 1929 v W, Ni; 1930 v W (8)

Mulhall, G. (Aberdeen). 1960 v Ni; (with Sunderland), 1963 v Ni; 1964 v Ni (3)

Munro, A. D. (Hearts), 1937 v W, Ni; (with Blackpool), 1938 v Ho (3)

Munro, F. M. (Wolverhampton W.), 1971 v Ni (sub), E (sub), D, USSR; 1975 v Se, W (sub), Ni, E, R (9)

Munro, N. (Abercorn), 1888 v W; 1889 v E (2)

Murdoch, J. (Motherwell), 1931 v Ni (1)

Murdoch, R. (Celtic), 1966 v W, E, I (2); 1967 v Ni; 1968 v Ni; 1969 v W, Ni, E, WG, Cy; 1970 v A (12)

Murphy, F. (Celtic), 1938 v Ho (1)

Murray, J. (Renton), 1895 v W (1)

Murray, J. (Hearts), 1958 v E, H, Pol, Y, F (5)

Murray, J. W. (Vale of Leven), 1890 v W (1)

Murray, P. (Hibernian), 1896 v Ni; 1897 v W (2)

Murray, S. (Aberdeen), 1972 v Bel(1)

Mutch, G. (Preston N.E.) 1938 v E (1)

Napier, C. E. (Celtic), 1932 v E; 1935 v E, W; (with Derby Co.), 1937 v Ni, A (5)

Neil, R. G. (Hibernian), 1896 v W; (with Rangers), 1900 v W (2)

Neill, R. W. (Queen's Park), 1876 v W; 1877 v E, W; 1878 v W; 1880 v E (5)

Neilles, P. (Hearts), 1914 v W, Ni (2)

Nelson, J. (Cardiff C.), 1922 v W, Ni; 1928 v E;

1930 v F (4)

Niblo, T. D. (Aston Villa), 1904 v E (1)

Nibloe, J. (Kilmarnock), 1929 v E, N, Ho; 1930 v W; 1931 v E, Ni, A, I, Sw; 1932 v E, F (11)

Nisbert, J. (Ayr U.), 1929 v N, G, Ho (3)

Niven, J. B. (Moffatt), 1885 v Ni (1)

O'Donnell, F. (Preston N.E.), 1937 v E, A, Cz; 1938 v E, W (with Blackpool), Ho (6)

Ogilvie, D. H. (Motherwell), 1934 v A (1)

O'Hare, J. (Derby Co.), 1970 v W, Ni, E; 1971 v D, Bel, W, Ni; 1972 v P, Bel, Ho (sub), Pe, Ni, W (13)

Ormond, W. E. (Hibernian), 1954 v E, N, Fi, A, U; 1959 v E (6)

O'Rourke, F. (Airdrieonians), 1907 v Ni (1)

Orr, J. (Kilmarnock), 1892 v W (1)

Orr, R. (Newcastle U.), 1902 v E; 1904 v E (2)

Orr, T. (Morton), 1952 v Ni, W (2)

Orr, W. (Celtic), 1900 v Ni; 1903 v Ni; 1904 v W; (3)

Orrock, R. (Falkirk), 1913 v W (1)

Oswald, J. (Third Lanark), 1889 v E; (with St. Bernards), 1895 v E; (with Rangers); 1897 v W (3)

Parker, A. H. (Falkirk), 1955 v P, Y, A; 1956 v E, Ni, W, A; 1957 v Ni, W, Y; 1958 v Ni, W, E, Sw, (with Everton) Par (15)

Parlane, D. (Rangers), 1973 v W, Sw, Br; 1975 v Sp (sub), Sc, P, W, Ni, E, R; 1976 v D (11)

Parlane, R. (Vale of Leven), 1878 v W; 1879 v E, W (3)

Paterson, G. D. (Celtic), 1939 v Ni (1)

Paterson, J. (Leicester C.), 1920 v E (1)

Paterson, J. (Cowdenbeath), 1931 v A, I, Sw (3)

Paton, A. (Motherwell), 1952 v D, Se (2)

Paton, D. (St. Bernards), 1896 v W (1)

Paton, M. (Dumbarton), 1883 v E; 1884 v W; 1885 v W, E; 1886 v E (5)

Paton, R. (Vale of Leven), 1879 v E, W (2)

Patrick, J. (St. Mirren), 1897 v E, W (2)

Paul, H. McD. (Queen's Park), 1909 v E, W, Ni (3)

Paul, W. (Partick T.), 1888 v W; 1889 v W; 1890 v W (3)

Paul, W. (Dykebar), 1891 v Ni (1)

Pearson, T. (Newcastle U.), 1947 v E, Bel (2)

Penman, A. (Dundee), 1966 v Ho (1)

Pettigrew, W. (Motherwell), 1976 v Sw, Ni, W (3)

Phillips, J. (Queen's Park), 1877 v E, W; 1878 v W (3)

Plenderleith, J. B. (Manchester C.), 1961 v Ni (I)

Porteous, W. (Hearts), 1903 v Ni (1)

Pringle, C. (St. Mirren), 1921 v W (1)

Provan, D. (Rangers), 1964 v Ni, N; 1966 v I (2), Ho (5)

Pryce, J. (Hibernians), 1897 v W (1)

Pursell, P. (Queen's Park), 1914 v W (1)

Quinn, J. (Celtic), 1905 v Ni; 1906 v Ni, W; 1908 v Ni, E; 1909 v E, 1910 v E, Ni, W; 1912 v E, W(11)

Quinn, P. (Motherwell), 1961 v E, Ei (2); 1962 v U (4)

Rae, J. (Third Lanark), 1889 v W; 1890 v Ni (2)

Raeside, J. S. (Third Lanark), 1906 v W (1)

Raisbeck, A. G. (Liverpool), 1900 v E; 1901 v E; 1902 v E; 1903 v E, W; 1904 v E; 1906 v E; 1907 v E (8)

Rankin, G. (Vale of Leven), 1890 v Ni; 1891 v E (2);

Rankin, R. (St. Mirren), 1929 v N, G, Ho (3)

Redpath, W. (Motherwell), 1949 v W, Ni; 1951 v E, D, F, Bel, A; 1952 v Ni, E (9)

Reid, J. G. (Airdrieonians), 1914 v W; 1920 v W; 1924 v Ni (3)
Reid, R. (Brentford), 1938 v E, Ni (2)
Reid, W. (Rangers), 1911 v E, W, Ni; 1912 v Ni; 1913 v E, W, Ni; 1914 v E, Ni (9)
Reilly, L. (Hibernian), 1949 v E, W, F; 1950 v W, Ni, Sw, F; 1951 v W, E, D, F, Bel. A; 1952 v Ni, W, E, USA, D, Se; 1953 v Ni, W, E, Se; 1954 v W; 1955 v H (2), P, Y, A, E; 1956 v E, W, Ni, A; 1957 v E, Ni, W, Y (38)
Rennie, H. G. (Hearts), 1900 v E, Ni; (with Hibernian), 1901 v E; 1902 v E, Ni, W; 1903 v Ni, W; 1904 v Ni; 1905 v W; 1906 v Ni; 1908 v Ni, W (13)
Renny-Tailyour, H. W. (Royal Engineers), 1873 v E (1)
Rhind, A. (Queen's Park), 1872 v E (1)
Richmond, A. (Queen's Park), 1906 v W (1)
Richmond, J. T. (Clydesdale), 1877 v E; (with Queen's Park), 1878 v E; 1882 v W (3)
Ring, T. (Clyde), 1953 v Se; 1955 v W, Ni, E, H; 1957 v E, Sp (2), Sw, WG; 1958 v Ni, Sw (12)
Rioch, B. D. (Derby Co.), 1975 v P, W, Ni, E, R; 1976 v D (2), R, Ni, W, E (11)
Ritchie, A. (East Stirlingshire), 1891 v W (1)
Ritchie, H. (Hibernian), 1923 v W; 1928 v Ni (2)
Ritchie, J. (Queen's Park), 1897 v W (1)
Ritchie, W. (Rangers) 1962 v U (sub) (1)
Robb, D. T. (Aberdeen), 1971 v W, E, P, D (sub), USSR (5)
Robb, W. (Rangers), 1926 v W; (with Hibernian), 1928 v W (2)
Robertson, A. (Clyde), 1955 v P. A. H; 1958 v Sw, Par (5)
Robertson, G. (Motherwell), 1910 v W; (with Sheffield W.), 1912 v W; 1913 v E, Ni (4)
Robertson, G. (Kilmarnock), 1938 v Cz (1)
Robertson, H. (Dundee), 1962 v Cz (1)
Robertson, J. (Dundee), 1931 v A, I (2)
Robertson, J. G. (Tottenham H.), 1965 v W (1)
Robertson, J. T. (Everton), 1898 v E; (with Southampton), 1899 v E; (with Rangers); 1900 v E, W; 1901 v W, Ni, E; 1902 v W, Ni, E; 1903 v E, W; 1904 v E, W, Ni; 1905 v W (16)
Robertson P. (Dundee), 1903 v Ni (1)
Robertson, T. (Queen's Park), 1889 v Ni; 1890 v E; 1891 v W; 1892 v Ni (4)
Robertson, T. (Hearts), 1898 v Ni (1)
Robertson, W. (Dumbarton), 1887 v E, W (2)
Robinson, R. (Dundee); 1974 v WG (sub); 1975 v Se, Ni, R (sub) (4)
Rough, A. (Partick T.), 1976 v Sw, Ni, W, E (4)
Rowan, A. (Caledonian), 1880 v E; (with Queen's Park), 1882 v W (2)
Russell, D. (Hearts), 1895 v E, Ni; (with Celtic), 1897 v W; 1898 v Ni: 1901 v W, Ni (6)
Russell, J. (Cambuslang), 1890 v Ni (1)
Russell, W. F. (Airdrieonians), 1924 v W; 1925 v E (2)
Rutherford, E. (Rangers), 1948 v F (1)

St. John, I. (Motherwell), 1959 v WG; 1960 v E, Ni W, Pol, A; 1961 v E; (with Liverpool), 1962, v Ni, W, E, Cz (2), U; 1963 v W, Ni, E, N, Ei (sub) Sp; 1964 v I; 1965 v E (21)
Sawers, W. (Dundee), 1895 v W (1)
Scarff, P. (Celtic), 1931 v Ni (I)
Schaedler, E. (Hibernian), 1974 v WG (1)
Scott, A. S. (Rangers), 1957 v Ni, Y, WG; 1958 v W, Sw; 1959 v P; 1962 v Ni, W, E, Cz, U; (with Everton), 1964 v W, N; 1965 Fi; 1966 v P, Br (16)
Scott, J. (Hibernian), 1964 v Ho (1)

Scott, J. (Dundee), 1971 v D (sub), USSR (2)
Scott, M. (Airdrieonians), 1898 v W (1)
Scott, R. (Airdrieonians), 1894 v Ni (1)
Scoular, J. (Portsmouth), 1951 v D, F, A; 1952 v E, USA, D, Se; 1953 v W, Ni (9)
Sellar, W. (Battlefield), 1885 v E; 1886 v E; 1887 v E, W; 1888 v E (with Queen's Park), 1891 v E; 1892 v E; 1893 v E, Ni (9)
Semple, W. (Cambuslang), 1886 v W (1)
Shankly, W. (Preston N.E.), 1938 v E; 1939 v E, W, Ni H (5)
Sharp, J. (Dundee), 1904 v W; (with Woolwich Arsenal), 1907 v W, E; 1908 v E; (with Fulham), 1909 v W (5)
Shaw, D. (Hibernian), 1947 v W, Ni; 1948 v E, Bel, Sw, F; 1949 v W, Ni (8)
Shaw, F. W. (Pollockshields Ath.), 1884 v E, W (2)
Shaw, J. (Rangers), 1947 v E, Bel, Lux; 1948 v Ni (4)
Shearer, R. (Rangers), 1961 v E, Ei (2), Cz (4)
Sillars, D. C. (Queen's Park), 1891 v Ni; 1892 v E; 1893 v W; 1894 v E; 1895 v W (5)
Simpson, J. (Third Lanark), 1895 v E, W, Ni (3)
Simpson, J. (Rangers), 1935 v E, W, Ni; 1936 v E, W, Ni; 1937 v G, E, W, Ni; A, Cz; 1938 v W, Ni, (14)
Simpson, R. C. (Celtic), 1967 v E, USSR; 1968 v Ni, E; 1969 v A (5)
Sinclair, G. L. (Hearts), 1910 v Ni; 1912 v W, Ni (3)
Sinclair, J. W. E. (Leicester C.), 1966 v P (1)
Skene, L. H. (Queen's Park), 1904 v W (1)
Sloan, T. (Third Lanark), 1904 v W (1)
Smellie, R. (Queen's Park), 1887 v Ni; 1888 v W; 1889 v E; 1891 v E; 1893 v E, Ni (6)
Smith, A. (Rangers), 1898 v E; 1900 v E, Ni, W; 1901 v E, Ni, W; 1902 v E, Ni, W; 1903 v E, Ni, W; 1904 v Ni; 1905 v W; 1906 v E, Ni; 1907 v W; 1911 v E, Ni (20)
Smith, D. (Aberdeen), 1966 v Ho; (with Rangers), 1968 v Ho (2)
Smith, G. (Hibernian), 1947 v E, Ni; 1948 v W, Bel, Sw, F; 1952 v E, USA; 1955 v P, Y, A, H; 1956 v E, Ni, W; 1957 v Sp (2), Sw (18)
Smith, J. (Rangers), 1935 v Ni; 1938 v Ni (2)
Smith, J. (Ayr U.), 1924 v E (1)
Smith, J. (Aberdeen), 1968 v Ho (sub); (with Newcastle U.), 1974 v WG, Ni (sub), W (sub) (4)
Smith, J. E. (Celtic) 1959 v H, P (2)
Smith, Jas. (Queen's Park), 1872 v E; 1873 v E, (2)
Smith, Jno. (Mauchline), 1877 v E, W; 1879 v E, W; (with Edinburgh University), 1880 v E; (with Queen's Park), 1881 v W, E; 1883 v E, W; 1884 v E (10)
Smith, N. (Rangers), 1897 v E; 1898 v W; 1899 v E, W, Ni; 1900 v E, W, Ni; 1901 v Ni, W; 1902 v E, Ni (12)
Smith, R. (Queen's Park), 1872 v E (1)
Smith, T. M. (Kilmarnock), 1934 v E; (with Preston N.E.), 1938 v E (2)
Somers, P. (Celtic), 1905 v E, Ni; 1907 v Ni; 1909 v W (4)
Somers, W. S. (Third Lanark), 1879 v E, W; (with Queen's Park), 1880 v W (3)
Somerville, G. (Queen's Park), 1886 v E (1)
Souness, G. J. (Middlesbrough), 1975 v EG, Sp, Se (3)
Speedle, F. (Rangers), 1903 v E, W, Ni (3)
Speirs, J. H. (Rangers), 1908 v W (1)
Stanton, P. (Hibernian), 1966 v Ho; 1969 v Ni; 1970 v Ei, A; 1971 v D, Bel, P, USSR, D; 1972 v P, Bel, Ho, W; 1973 v W, Ni; 1974 v WG (16)
Stark, J. (Rangers), 1909 v E, Ni (2)
Steel, W. (Morton), 1947 v E, Bel, L; (with Derby

Co.), 1948 v F, E, W, Ni; 1949 v E, W, Ni, F; 1950 v E, W, Ni, Sw, P, F; (with Dundee), 1951 v W, Ni, E, A (2), D, F, Bel; 1952 v W; 1953 v W, E, Ni Se (30)

Steele, D. M. (Huddersfield), 1923 v E, W, Ni (3)

Stein, C. (Rangers), 1969 v W, Ni, D, E, Cy (2); 1970 v A (sub), Ni (sub), W, E, Ei, WG; 1971 v D, USSR, Bel, D; 1972 v Cz (sub); (with Coventry C) 1973 v E (2 subs), W (sub) Ni (21)

Stephen, J. F. (Bradford), 1947 v W; 1948 v W (2)

Stevenson, G. (Motherwell), 1928 v W, Ni; 1930 v Ni, E, F; 1931 v E, W; 1932 v W, Ni; 1933 v Ni; 1934 v E; 1935 v Ni (12)

Stewart, A. (Queen's Park), 1888 v Ni; 1889 v W (2)

Stewart, A. (Third Lanark), 1894 v W (1)

Stewart, D. (Dumbarton), 1888 v Ni (1)

Stewart, D. (Queen's Park), 1893 v W; 1894 v Ni; 1897 v Ni (3)

Stewart, G. (Hibernian), 1906 v W, E; (with Manchester C.), 1907 v E, W (4)

Stewart, W. E. (Queen's Park), 1898 v Ni; 1900 v Ni (2)

Storrier, D. (Celtic), 1899 v E, W, Ni (3)

Summers, W. (St. Mirren), 1926 v E (1)

Symon, J. S. (Rangers), 1939 v H (1)

Tait, T. S. (Sunderland), 1911 v W (1)

Taylor, J. (Queen's Park), 1872 v E; 1873 v E; 1874 v E; 1875 v E; 1876 v E, W (6)

Taylor, J. D. (Dumbarton), 1892 v W; 1893 v W; 1894 v Ni; (with St. Mirren), 1895 v Ni (4)

Taylor, W. (Hearts), 1892 v E (1)

Telfer, W. (Motherwell), 1933 v Ni; 1934 v Ni(2)

Telfer, W. D. (St. Mirren), 1954 v W (1)

Templeton, R. (Aston Villa), 1902 v E; (with Newcastle U.), 1903 v E, W; 1904 v E; (with Woolwich Arsenal), 1905 v W; (with Kilmarnock), 1908 v Ni; 1910 v E, Ni; 1912 v E, Ni; 1913 v W (11)

Thomson, A. (Arthurlie), 1886 v Ni (1)

Thomson, A. (Airdrieonians), 1909 v Ni (1)

Thomson, A. (Celtic), 1926 v E; 1932 v F; 1933 v W (3)

Thomson, A. (Third Lanark), 1889 v W (1)

Thomson, C. (Hearts), 1904 v Ni; 1905 v E, Ni, W; 1906 v W, Ni; 1907 v E, W, Ni; 1908 v E, W, Ni; (with Sunderland), 1909 v W; 1910 v E; 1911 v Ni; 1912 v E, W; 1913 v E, W; 1914 v E, Ni(21)

Thomson, C. (Sunderland), 1937 v Cz (1)

Thomson, D. (Dundee), 1920 v W (1)

Thomson, J. (Celtic), 1930 v F; 1931 v E, W, Ni (4)

Thomson, J. J. (Queen's Park), 1872 v E; 1873 v E; 1874 v E (3)

Thomson, J. R. (Everton), 1933 v W (1)

Thomson, R. (Celtic), 1932 v W (1)

Thomson, R. W. (Falkirk), 1927 v E (1)

Thomson, S. (Rangers), 1884 v W, Ni (2)

Thomson, W. (Dumbarton), 1892 v W; 1893 v W; 1898 v Ni, W (4)

Thomson, W. (Dundee), 1896 v W (1)

Thornton, W. (Rangers), 1947 v W, Ni; 1948 v E, Ni; 1949 v F; 1952 v D, Se (7)

Toner, W. (Kilmarnock), 1959 v W, Ni (2)

Townsley, T. (Falkirk), 1926 v W (1)

Troup, A. (Dundee), 1920 v E; 1921 v W, Ni; 1922 v Ni; (with Everton), 1926 v E (5)

Turnbull, E. (Hibernian), 1948 v Bel, Sw; 1951 v A; 1958 v H, P, Y, Par, F (8)

Turner, T. (Arthurlie), 1884 v W (1)

Turner, W. (Pollockshields), 1885 v Ni; 1886 v Ni(2)

Ure, J. F. (Dundee), 1962 v W, Cz; 1963 v W, Ni ,E, A, N, Sp; (with Arsenal), 1964 v Ni, N; 1968 v Ni (11)

Urquhart, D. (Hibernian), 1934 v W (1)

Vallance, T. (Rangers), 1877 v E, W; 1878 v E 1879 v E, W; 1881 v E, W (7)

Venters, A. (Cowdenbeath). 1934 v Ni; (with Rangers), 1936 v E; 1939 v E (3)

Waddell, T. S. (Queen's Park), 1891 v Ni; 1892 v E; 1893 v E, Ni; 1895 v E, Ni (6)

Waddell, W. (Rangers), 1947 v W; 1949 v E, W, Ni, F; 1950 v E, Ni; 1951 v E, D, F, Bel, A; 1952 v Ni, W; 1954 v Ni; 1955 v W, Ni (17)

Wales, H. M. (Motherwell), 1933 v W (1)

Walker, F. (Third Lanark), 1922 v W (1)

Walker, G. (St. Mirren), 1930 v F; 1931 v Ni, A, Sw (4)

Walker, J. (Hearts), 1895 v Ni; 1897 v W; 1898 v Ni; (with Rangers), 1904 v W, Ni (5)

Walker, J. (Swindon T.), 1911, E, W, Ni; 1912 v E, W, Ni; 1913 v E, W, Ni(9)

Walker, R. (Hearts), 1900 v E, Ni; 1901 v E, W; 1902 v E, W, Ni; 1903 v E, W, Ni; 1904 v E, W, Ni; 1905 v E, W, Ni; 1906 v Ni; 1907 v E, Ni; 1908 v E, W, Ni; 1909 v E, W; 1912 v E, W, Ni; 1913 v E, W (29)

Walker, T. (Hearts), 1935 v E, W; 1936 v E, W, Ni; 1937 v G, E, W, Ni, A, Cz; 1938 v E, W, Ni Cz, H; 1939 v E, W, Ni, H (20)

Walker, W. (Clyde), 1909 v Ni; 1910 v Ni(2)

Wallace, W. S. B. (Hearts), 1965 v Ni; 1966 v E, Ho; (with Celtic), 1967 v E, USSR (sub); 1968 v Ni; 1969 v E (sub) (7)

Wardhaugh, J. (Hearts), 1955 v H; 1957 v Ni(2)

Watson, A. (Queen's Park), 1881 v E, W; 1882 v B (3)

Watson, J. (Sunderland), 1903 v E, W; 1904 v E; 1905 v E; (with Middlesbrough), 1909 v E, Ni(5)

Watson, J. (Motherwell), 1948 v Ni; (with Huddersfield T.), 1954 v Ni (2)

Watson, J. A. K. (Rangers), 1878 v W (1)

Watson, P. R. (Blackpool), 1934 v A (1)

Watson, R. (Motherwell), 1971 v USSR (1)

Watson, W. (Falkirk), 1898 v W (1)

Watt, F. (Kilbirnie), 1889 v W, Ni; 1890 v W; 1891 v E (4)

Watt, W. W. (Queen's Park), 1887 v Ni (1)

Waugh, W. (Hearts), 1938 v Cz (1)

Weir, A. (Motherwell), 1959 v WG; 1960 v E, P, A. H, T (6)

Weir, J. (Third Lanark), 1887 v Ni (1)

Weir, J. B. (Queen's Park), 1872 v E; 1874 v E; 1875 v E; 1878 v W (4)

White, John (Albion R.). 1922 v W; (with Hearts), 1923 v Ni (2)

White, J. A. (Falkirk), 1959 v WG, Ho, P; 1960 v Ni; (with Tottenham H.), 1960 v W, Pol, A, T; 1961 v W; 1962 v Ni, W, E, Cz(2); 1963 v W, Ni, E; 1964 v Ni, W, E, N, WG (22)

White, W. (Bolton W.), 1907 v E; 1908 v E (2)

Whitelaw, A. (Vale of Leven), 1887 v Ni; 1890 v W (2)

Wilson, A. (Sheffield W.), 1907 v E; 1908 v E; 1912 v E; 1913 v E, W; 1914 v Ni(6)

Wilson, A. (Portsmouth), 1954 v Fi (1)

Wilson, A. N. (Dunfermline), 1920 v E, W, Ni; 1921 v E, W, Ni; (with Middlesbrough), 1922 v E, W, Ni; 1925 v E, W, Ni (12)

Wilson, D. (Queen's Park), 1900 v W (1)

Wilson ,D. (Oldham Ath.), 1913 v E (1)

700

Wilson, D. (Rangers), 1961 v E, W, Ni, Ei (2), Cz; 1962 v Ni, W, E, Cz, U; 1963 v W, E, A, N, Ei, Sp; 1964 v E, WG; 1965 v Ni, E, Fi (22)

Wilson, G. W. (Hearts), 1904 v W; 1905 v E. Ni; 1906 v W; (with Everton), 1907 v E; (with Newcastle U.) 1909 v E (6)

Wilson, Hugh, (Newmilns), 1890 v W; (with Sunderland), 1897 v E; (with Third Lanark), 1902 v W; 1904 v Ni (4)

Wilson, J. (Vale of Leven), 1888 v W; 1889 v Ni; 1890 v Ni; 1891 v Ni (4)

Wilson, P. (Celtic), 1926 v Ni; 1930 v F; 1931 v Ni; 1933 v E (4)

Wilson, P. (Celtic), 1975 v Sp (sub) (1)

Wilson, R. P. (Arsenal), 1972 v P. Ho (2)

Wiseman, W. (Queen's Park), 1927 v W; 1930 v Ni (2)

Woodburn, W. A. (Rangers), 1947 v E, Bel, L; 1948 v W, Ni; 1949 v E, F; 1950 v E, W, Ni, P, F; 1951 v E, W, Ni, A (2), D, F, Bel; 1952 v E, W, Ni. USA (24)

Wotherspoon, D. N. (Queen's Park), 1872 v E; 1873 v E (2)

Wright, T. (Sunderland), 1953 v W, Ni, E (3)

Wylie, T. G. (Rangers), 1890 v Ni (1)

Yeats, R. (Liverpool), 1965 v W; 1966 v I (2)

Yorston, B. C. (Aberdeen), 1931 v NI (1)

Yorston, H. (Aberdeen), 1955 v W (1)

Young, A. (Hearts), 1960 v E, A (sub), H, T; 1961 v W, Ni; (with Everton), Ei; 1966 v P (8)

Young, A. (Everton), 1905 v E; 1907 v W (2)

Young, G. L. (Rangers), 1947 v E, Ni, Bel, L; 1948 v E, Ni, Bel, Sw, F; 1949 v E, W, Ni, F; 1950 v E, W, Ni, Sw, P, F, 1951 v E, W, Ni, A (2), D, F, Bel; 1952 v E, W, Ni, USA, D, Se; 1953 v W, E, Ni, Se; 1954 v Ni, W; 1955 v W, Ni, P, Y; 1956 v Ni, W, E, A; 1957 v E, Ni, W, Y, Sp, Sw (53)

Young, J. (Celtic), 1906 v Ni (1)

Younger, T. (Hibernian), 1955 v P, Y, A, H; 1956, v E, Ni, W, A; (with Liverpool), 1957 v E, Ni, W, Y, Sp (2), Sw, WG; 1958 v Ni, W, E, Sw, H, Pol, Y, Par (24)

WALES

Adams, H. (Berwyn Rangers), 1882 v Ni, E; (with Druids) 1883 v Ni, E (4)

Allchurch, I. J. (Swansea T.), 1951 v E, Ni, P, Sw; 1952 v E, S, Ni, R of UK; 1953 v S, E, Ni, F, Y; 1954 v S, E, Ni, A; 1955 v S, E, Ni, Y; 1956 v E, S, Ni, A; 1957 v E, S; 1958 v Ni, Is (2), H (2), M, Sw, Br; (with Newcastle U.), 1959 v E, S, Ni; 1960 v E, S; 1961 v Ni, H, Sp (2); 1962 v E, S, Br (2), M; (with Cardiff C.), 1963 v S, E, Ni, H (2); 1964 v E; 1965 v S, E, Ni, Gr, I, Ru; 1966 (with Swansea T.), v USSR, E, S, D, Br (2), Ch (68)

Allchurch, L. (Swansea T.), 1955 v Ni; 1956 v A; 1958 v S, Ni, EG, Is; 1959 v S; (with Sheffield U.), 1962 v S, Ni, Br; 1964 v E (11)

Allen, B. W. (Coventry C.), 1951 v S, E (2)

Arridge, S. (Bootle), 1892 v S, Ni; (with Everton), 1894 v Ni; 1895 v Ni; 1896 v E; (with New Brighton Tower), 1898 v E, Ni; 1899 v E (8)

Astley, D. J. (Charlton Ath.), 1931 v Ni; (with Aston Villa), 1932 v E; 1933 v E, S, Ni; 1934 v E, S; 1935 v S; 1936 v E, Ni; (with Derby Co.), 1939 v E, S; (with Blackpool), F, (13)

Atherton, R. W. (Hibernian), 1899 v E, Ni; 1903 v E, S, Ni; (with Middlesbrough), 1904 v E, S, Ni; 1905 v Ni (9)

Bailiff, W. E. (Llanelly), 1913 v E, S, Ni; 1920 v Ni (4)

Baker, C. W. (Cardiff C.), 1958 v M; 1960 v S, Ni 1961 v S, E, Ei; 1962 v S (7)

Baker, W. G. (Cardiff C.), 1948 v Ni (1)

Bamford, T. (Wrexham), 1931 v E, S, Ni; 1932 v Ni; 1933 v F (5)

Barnes, W. (Arsenal), 1948 v E, S, Ni; 1949 v E, S, Ni ; 1950 v E, S, Ni, Bel; 1951 v E .S, Ni, P; 1952 v E, S. Ni, R of UK; 1954 v E, S; 1955 v S, Y (22)

Bartley, T. (Glossop N.E.), 1898 v E (1)

Beadles, G. H. (Cardiff C.), 1925 v E, S (2)

Bell, W. S. (Shrewsbury Engineers), 1881 v E, S; (with Crewe Alex.), 1886 v E, S, Ni (5)

Bennion, S. R. (Manchester U.), 1926 v S; 1927 v S; 1928 v S, E, Ni; 1929 v S, E, Ni; 1930 v S; 1932 v Ni (10)

Blew, H. (Wrexham), 1899 v S, Ni; 1902 v S, Ni; 1903 v E, S; 1904 v E, S, Ni; 1905 v S, Ni; 1906 v E, S, Ni; 1907 v S; 1908 v E, S, Ni; 1909 v E, S; 1910 v E (22)

Boden, T. (Wrexham), 1880 v E (1)

Bostock, A. M. (Shrewsbury), 1892 v Ni (1)

Boulter, L. M. (Brentford), 1939 v Ni (1)

Bowdler, H. E. (Shrewsbury), 1893 v S (1)

Bowdler, J. C. H. (Shrewsbury), 1890 v Ni; (with Wolverhampton W.), 1891 v S; 1892 v Ni; (with Shrewsbury), 1894 v E (4)

Bowen, D. L. (Arsenal), 1955 v S, Y; 1957 v Ni, Cz, EG; 1958 v E, S, Ni. EG. Is (2), H (2), M, Se, Br; 1959 v E, S, Ni (19)

Bowen, E. (Druids), 1880 v S; 1883 v S, (2)

Bowsher, S. J. (Burnley), 1929 v Ni (1)

Britten, T. J. (Parkgrove), 1878 v S; (with Presteigne), 1880 v S (2)

Brookes, S. J. (Llandudno), 1900 v E, Ni (2)

Brown, A. I. (Aberdare Ath.), 1926 v Ni (1)

Bryan, T. (Oswestry), 1886 v E, Ni (2)

Buckland, T. (Bangor), 1899 v E (1)

Burgess, W. A. R. (Tottenham H.), 1947 v E, S, Ni; 1948 v E, S; 1949 v E, S, Ni, P, Bel, Sw; 1950 v E, S, Ni, Bel; 1951 v S, Ni, P, Sw; 1952 v E, S, Ni, R of UK; 1953 v S, E, Ni, F, Y; 1954 v S, E, Ni A (32)

Burke, T. (Wrexham), 1883 v E; 1884 v S; 1885 v E, S, Ni; (with Newton Heath), 1887 v E, S; 1888 v S (8)

Burnett, T. B. (Ruabon), 1877 v S (1)

Burton, A. D. (Norwich C.), 1963 v Ni, H; (with Newcastle U.), 1964 v E; 1969 v S, E, Ni, I, EG; 1972 v Cz (9)

Butler, A. (Druids), 1900 v S, Ni (2)

Butler, J. (Chirk), 1893 v E, S, Ni (3)

Cartwright, L. (Coventry C.), 1974 v E (sub), S, Ni; 1976 v S (sub) (4)

Carty, T. (Wrexham), 1889 v Ni (1)

Challen, J. B. (with Corinthians), 1887 v E, S; 1888 v E; (Wellingborough G. S.), 1890 v E (4)

Chapman, T. (Newtown), 1894 v E, S, Ni; 1895 v S, Ni; (with Manchester C.), 1896 v E; 1897 v E (7)

Charles, M. (Swansea T.), 1955 v Ni; 1956 v E, S, A; 1957 v E, Ni, Cz (2), EG; 1958 v E, S, EG, Is (2). H (2), M, Se. Br; 1959 v E, S; (with Arsenal), 1961 v Ni. H, Sp (2); 1962 v E, S, (with Cardiff C.), 1962 v Br, Ni; 1963 v S, H (31)

Charles, W. J. (Leeds U.), 1950 v Ni; 1951 v Sw; 1953 v Ni, F, Y; 1954 v E, S, Ni, A; 1955 v S, E, Ni, Y; 1956 v E, S, A, Ni; 1957 v E, S, Ni; 1957 v Cz (2), EG; (with Juventus), 1958 v Is (2), H (2), M, Se; 1960 v S; 1962 v E, Br (2), M; (with

Leeds U.), 1963 v S; (with Cardiff C.), 1964 v S; 1965 v S. USSR (38)

Clarke, R. J. (Manchester C.), 1949 v E; 1950 v S, Ni, Bel; 1951 v E, S, Ni, P, Sw; 1952 v S, E, Ni, R of UK; 1953 v S, E; 1954 v E, S, Ni; 1955 v Y, S E; 1956 v Ni (22)

Collier, D. J. (Grimsby T.), 1921 v S (1)

Collins, W. S. (Llanelly), 1931 v S (1)

Conde, C. (Chirk), 1884 v E, S, Ni (3)

Cook, F. C. (Newport Co)., 1925 v E, S; (with Portsmouth), 1928 v E, S; 1930 v E, S, Ni; 1932 v E, (8)

Crompton, W. (Wrexham), 1931 v E, S, Ni (3)

Cross, E. A. (Wrexham), 1876 v S; 1877 v S (2)

Cross, K. (Druids), 1879 v E, S (3)

Crowe, V. H. (Aston Villa), 1959 v E, Ni; 1960 v E, Ni; 1961 v S, E, Ni, Ei, H, Sp (2); 1962 v E, S, Br, M; 1963 v H (16)

Cumner, R. H. (Arsenal), 1939 v E, S, Ni (3)

Curtis, A. (Swansea C.), 1976 v E, Y, S, Ni, Y (sub), E (6)

Curtis, E. R. (Cardiff C.), 1928 v S; (with Birmingham), 1932 v S; 1934 v Ni (3)

Daniel, R. W. (Arsenal), 1951 v E, Ni, P; 1952 v E, S, Ni, R of UK; 1953 v S, E, Ni, F, Y; (with Sunderland), 1954 v E, S, Ni; 1955 v E, Ni; 1957 v S, E, Ni, Cz (21)

Darvell, S. (Oxford University), 1897 v S, Ni (2)

Davies, A. (Wrexham), 1876 v S; 1877 v S (2)

Davies, A. (Shrewsbury), 1891 v Ni (1)

Davies, A. (Druids), 1904 v S; (with Middlesbrough), 1905 v S (2)

Davies, A. O. (Barmouth), 1885 v Ni; 1886 v E, S; (with Swifts), 1887 v E, S; 1888 v E, Ni; (with Wrexham), 1889 v S; (with Crewe Alex.,) 1890 v E (9)

Davies, C. (Brecon), 1899 v Ni; (with Hereford), 1900 v Ni (2)

Davies, C. (Charlton Ath.), 1972 v R (sub) (1)

Davies, D. (Bolton W.), 1904 v S, Ni; 1908 v E (sub) (3)

Davies, D. W. (Treharris), 1912 v Ni; (with Oldham Ath.), 1913 v Ni (2)

Davies, E. Lloyd (Stoke C.), 1904 v E; 1907 v E, S, Ni; (with Northampton), 1908 v S; 1909 v Ni; 1910 v Ni; 1911 v E, S; 1912 v E, S; 1913 v E, S; 1914 v Ni, E, S (16)

Davies, E. R. (Newcastle U.), 1953 v S, E; 1954 v E, S; 1958 v E, EG (6)

Davies, Rev. H. (Wrexham), 1928 v Ni (1)

Davies, Idwal (Liverpool Marine), 1923 v S (1)

Davies, J. E. (Oswestry), 1885 v E (1)

Davies, Jas. (Wrexham), 1878 v S (1)

Davies, Jno. (Wrexham), 1879 v S (1)

Davies, Jos. (Everton), 1889 v S, Ni; (with Chirk), 1891 v Ni, (with Ardwick), v E, S; (with Sheffield U.), 1895 v E, S, Ni; (with Manchester C.), 1896 v E; (with Millwall). 1897 v E; (with Reading), 1900 v E (11)

Davies, Jos. (Newton Heath), 1888 v E, S, Ni; 1889 v S; 1890 v E; (with Wolverhampton W.), 1892 v E; 1893 v E (7)

Davies, J. P. (Druids), 1883 v E, Ni (2)

Davies, Ll. (Wrexham), 1907 v Ni; 1910 v Ni, S, B; (with Everton), 1911 v S, Ni; 1912 v Ni, S, E; 1913 v Ni, S, E; 1914 v Ni (13)

Davies, L. S. (Cardiff C.), 1922 v E. S, Ni; 1923 v E, S, Ni; 1924 v E, S, Ni; 1925 v S, Ni; 1926 v E, Ni; 1927 v E, Ni; 1928 v S, Ni, E; 1929 v S, Ni, E; 1930 v E, S (23)

Davies, O. (Wrexham), 1890 v S (1)

Davies, R. (Wrexham), 1883 v Ni; 1884 v Ni; 1885 v Ni (3)

Davies, R. (Druids), 1885 v E (1)

Davies, R. L. (Wrexham), 1892 v Ni (1)

Davies, R. O. (Wrexham), 1892 v Ni, E (2)

Davies, R. T. (Norwich C.), 1964 v Ni; 1965 v E; 1966 v Br (2), Ch; (with Southampton), 1967 v S, E, Ni; 1968 v S, Ni, WG; 1969 v S, E, Ni, I, WG, R of UK; 1970 v E, S, Ni; 1971 v Cz, S, E, Ni; 1972 v R, E, S, N; (with Portsmouth) 1974 v E (29)

Davies, R. W. (Bolton W.), 1964 v E; 1965 v E, S, Ni, D, Gr, USSR; 1966 v E, S, Ni, USSR, D, Br (2), Ch (sub); 1967 v S (with Newcastle U.), E; 1968 v S, Ni, WG; 1969 v S, E, Ni, I; 1970 v EG; 1971 v R, Cz; (with Manchester C.) 1972 v E, S, N; (with Manchester U.) 1973 v E, S (sub), Ni; (with Blackpool), 1974 v Pol (34)

Davies, Stanley (Preston N.E.), 1920 v E, S, Ni; (with Everton), 1921 v E, S, Ni; (with W.B.A.), 1922 v E, S, Ni; 1923 v S; 1925 v S, Ni; 1926 v S, E, Ni; 1927 v S; 1928 v S; (with Rotherham U.), 1930 v Ni (18)

Davies, T. (Oswestry), 1886 v E (1)

Davies, T. (Druids), 1903 v E, Ni, S; 1904 v S (4)

Davies, W. (Swansea T.), 1924 v E, S, Ni; (with Cardiff C.), 1925 v E, S, Ni; 1926 v E, S, Ni; 1927 v S; 1928 v Ni; (with Notts. Co.), 1929 v E. S. Ni; 1930 v E. S. Ni (17)

Davies, W. (Wrexham), 1884 v Ni (1)

Davies, William (Wrexham), 1903 v Ni; 1905 v Ni; (with Blackburn R.), 1908 v E, S; 1909 v E, S, Ni; 1911 v E, S, Ni; 1912 v Ni (11)

Davies, W. C. (C. Palace), 1908 v S; (with W.B.A.), 1909 v E; 1910 v S; (with C. Palace), 1914 v E (4)

Davies, W. D. (Everton), 1975 v H, L, S, E, Ni; 1976 v Y (2), E, Ni (9)

Davies, W. H. (Oswestry), 1876 v S; 1877 v S; 1879 v E; 1880 v E (4)

Davies, W. O. (Millwall Ath.), 1913 v E, S, Ni; 1914, v S, Ni (5)

Day, A. (Tottenham H.). 1934 v Ni (1)

Dearson, D. J. (Birmingham), 1939 v S Ni, F (3)

Derrett, S. C. (Cardiff C.), 1969 v S, WG; 1970 v I; 1971 v Fi (4)

Dewey, F. T. (Cardiff Corinthians), 1931 v E, S (20)

Doughty, J. (Druids), 1886 v S; (with Newton Heath), 1887 v S, Ni; 1888 v E, S, Ni; 1889 v S, 1890 v E (8)

Doughty, R. (Newton Heath and Druids), 1888 vS Ni; (2)

Durban, A. (Derby Co.), 1966 v Br (sub); 1967 v Ni; 1968 v E, S, Ni, WG; 1969 v EG, S, E, Ni, WG; 1970 v E, S, Ni, EG, I; 1971 v R, S, E, Ni, Cz, Fi; 1972 v Fi, Cz, E, S, Ni (27)

Edwards, C. (Wrexham), 1878 v S (1)

Edwards, G. (Birmingham), 1947 v E, S, Ni; 1948 v E, S, Ni; (with Cardiff C.), 1949 v Ni, P, Bel, Sw; 1950 v E, S (12)

Edwards, H. (Wrexham Civil Service), 1878 v S; 1880 v E; 1882 v E, S; 1883 v S; 1884 v Ni; 1887 v Ni (7)

Edwards, J. H. (Owestry), 1895 v Ni; 1897 v E, Ni; (with Aberystwyth), 1898 v Ni (4)

Edwards, J. H. (Wanderers), 1876 v S (1)

Edwards, L. T. (Charlton Ath.), 1957 v Ni, EG (2)

Edwards, T. (Linfield), 1932 v S (1)

Egan, W. (Chirk), 1892 v S (1)

Ellis, B. (Motherwell), 1932 v E; 1933 v E, S; 1934 v S; 1936 v E; 1937 v S (6)

Ellis, E. (Nunhead), 1931 v E (with Oswestry), S; 1932 v Ni (3)
Emanuel, W. J. (Bristol C.), 1973 v E (sub), Ni (sub) (2)
England, H. M. (Blackburn R.), 1962 v Ni, Br, M; 1963 v Ni, H; 1964 v E, S, Ni; 1965 v E, S, D, Gr (2), USSR, I; 1966 v E, S, Ni, USSR, D; (with Tottenham H.), 1967 v S, E; 1968 v E, Ni, WG; 1969 v Ei; 1970 v R of UK, EG E, S, Ni, I; 1971 v R; 1972 v Fi, E, S, Ni; 1973 v E (3), S; 1974 v Pol; 1975 v H, L (44)
Evans, B. C. (Swansea C.), 1972 v Fi, Cz; 1973 v E (2), Pol, S; (with Hereford U.), 1974 v Pol (7)
Evans, D. G. (Reading), 1926 v Ni; 1927 v Ni, E; (with Huddersfield T.), 1929 v S (4)
Evans, H. P. (Cardiff C.), 1922 v E, S, Ni; 1924 v E, S, Ni (6)
Evans, I. (C. Palace), 1976 v A, E, Y (2), E, Ni (6)
Evans, J. (Cardiff C.), 1912 v Ni; 1913 v Ni; 1914 v S; 1920 v S, Ni; 1922 v Ni; 1923 v E, Ni (8)
Evans, J. (Oswestry), 1893 v Ni; 1894 v E, Ni (3)
Evans, J. H. (Southend U.). 1922 v E, S, Ni; 1923 v S (4)
Evans, Len (Cardiff C.), 1931 v E, S; (with Birmingham), 1934 v Ni (3)
Evans, L. H. (Aberdare Ath.), 1927 v Ni (1)
Evans, M. (Oswestry), 1884 v E (1)
Evans, R. (Clapton), 1902 v Ni (1)
Evans, R. E. (Wrexham), 1906 v E, S; (with Aston Villa), Ni; 1907 v E; 1908 v E, S; (with Sheffield U.), 1909 v S; 1910 v E, S, Ni (10)
Evans, R. O. (Wrexham), 1902 v Ni; 1903 v E,S, Ni; (with Blackburn R.), 1908 v Ni; (with Coventry C.), 1911 v E, Ni; 1912 v E, S, Ni (10)
Evans, R. S. (Swansea T.), 1964 v Ni (1)
Evans, T. J. (Clapton Orient), 1927 v S; 1928 v E, S; (with Newcastle U.), 1928 v Ni (4)
Evans, W. (Tottenham H.), 1933 v Ni; 1934 v E, S; 1935 v E; 1936 v E, Ni (6)
Evans, W. A. W. (Oxford University), 1876 v S; 1877 v S (2)
Evans, W. G. (Bootle), 1890 v E; 1891 v E; (with Aston Villa), 1892 v E (3)
Evelyn, E. C. (Crusaders), 1887 v E (1)
Eyton-Jones, J. A. (Wrexham), 1883 v Ni; 1884 v Ni, E, S (4)

Farmer, G. (Oswestry), 1885 v E, S (2)
Finnigan, R. J. (Wrexham), 1930 v Ni (1)
Flynn, B. (Burnley), 1975 v L (2 subs), H (sub), S, E, Ni; 1976 v A, E, Y (2), E, Ni (12)
Ford, T. (Swansea T.), 1947 v S; (with Aston Villa), 1947 v Ni; 1948 v S, Ni; 1949 v E, S, Ni P, Bel, Sw; 1950 v E, S, Ni, Bel; 1951 v S; (with Sunderland), 1951 v E, Ni, P, Sw; 1952 v E, S, Ni, R of UK; 1953 v S, E, Ni, F, Y; (with Cardiff C.), 1954 v A; 1955 v S, E, Ni, Y; 1956 v S, Ni, E, A; 1957 v S (38)
Foulkes, H. E. (W.B.A.), 1932 v Ni (1)
Foulkes, W. I. (Newcastle), 1952 v E, S, Ni, R of UK; 1953 v E, S, F, Y; 1954 v E, S, Ni (11)
Foulkes, W. T. (Oswestry), 1884 v Ni; 1885 v S (2)
Fowler, J. (Swansea T.), 1925 v E; 1926 v E, Ni; 1927 v S; 1928 v S; 1929 v E (6)

Garner, J. (Aberystwyth), 1896 v S (1)
Gillam, S. G. (Wrexham), 1889 v S, Ni; (with Shrewsbury), 1890 v E, Ni; (with Clapton), 1894 v S (5)
Glascodine, G. (Wrexham), 1879 v E (1)
Glover, E. M. (Grimsby T.), 1932 v S; 1934 v Ni;

1936 v S; 193 7 v E, S, Ni; 1939 v Ni (7)
Godding, G. (Wrexham), 1923 v S, Ni (2)
Godfrey, B. C. (Preston N.E.), 1964 v Ni; 1965 v D, I (3)
Goodwin, U. (Ruthin), 1881 v E (1)
Gough, R. T. (Oswestry White Star), 1883 v S, (1)
Gray, A. (Oldham Ath.), 1924 v E, S, Ni; 1925 v E, S, Ni; 1926 v E, S; 1927 v S; (with Manchester C.), 1928 v E, S; 1929 v E, S, Ni; (with Manchester Central), 1930 v S; (with Tranmere R.), 1932 v E, S, Ni; (with Chester), 1937 v E, S, Ni; 1938 v E, S, Ni (24)
Green, A. W. (Aston Villa), 1901 v Ni, (with Notts. Co.), 1903 v E; (with Notts. Co.), 1904 v S, Ni; 1906 v Ni, E, (with Nottingham F.), 1907 v E; 1908 v S (8)
Green C. R. (Birmingham C.), 1965 v USSR, I; 1966 v E, S, USSR, Br (2); 1967 v E; 1968 v E, S, Ni, WG; 1969 v S, I, Ni (sub) (15)
Green, G. H. (Charlton Ath.), 1938 v Ni; 1939 v E, Ni, F (4)
Grey, Dr. W. (Druids), 1876 v S; 1878 v S (2)
Griffiths, A. T. (Wrexham) 1971 v Cz (sub); 1975 v A, H (2), L (2), E, Ni; 1976 v A, E, S, E (sub), Ni, Y (2) (15)
Griffiths, F. J. (Blackpool), 1900 v E, S (2)
Griffiths, G. (Chirk), 1887 v Ni (1)
Griffiths, J. H. (Swansea T.), 1953 v Ni (1)
Griffiths, M. W. (Leicester C.), 1947 v Ni; 1949 v P, Bel; 1950 v E, S, Bel; 1951 v E, Ni, P, Sw; 1954 v A (11)
Griffiths, P. (Chirk), 1884 v E, Ni; 1888 v E; 1890 v S, Ni; 1891 v Ni (6)
Griffiths, S. (Wrexham), 1902 v S (1)
Griffiths, T. P. (Everton), 1927 v E, Ni; 1929 v E; 1930 v E; 1931 v Ni; 1932 v Ni, S, E; (with Bolton W.), 1933 v F, E, S, Ni; (with Middlesbrough), 1934 v E, S; 1935 v E, Ni; 1936 v S, (with Aston Villa), Ni; 1937 v E, S, Ni (21)

Hallam, J. (Oswestry), 1889 v E (1)
Hanford, H. (Swansea T.), 1934 v Ni; 1935 v S; 1936 v E; (with Sheffield W.), 1936 v Ni; 1938 v E, S; 1939 v F (7)
Harrington, A. C. (Cardiff C.), 1956, v Ni; 1957 v E, S; 1958, v S, Ni, Is (2); 1961 v S, E; 1962 v E, S (11)
Harris, C. S. (Leeds U.), 1976 v E, S (2)
Harris, W. C. (Middlesbrough), 1954 v A; 1957 v EG, Cz; 1958 v E, S, EG (6)
Harrison, W. C. (Wrexham), 1899 v E; 1900 v E, S, Ni; 1901 v Ni (5)
Hayes, A. (Wrexham), 1890 v Ni; 1894 v Ni (2)
Hennessey, W. T. (Birmingham), 1962 v Ni Br (2) 1963 v S, E, H (2); 1964 v E, S; 1965 v S, E, D, Gr, R; 1966 v E, USSR; (with Nottingham F.), 1966 v S, Ni, D, Br (2), Ch; 1967 v S, E; 1968 v E, S, Ni; 1969 v WG, EG, R of UK, EG; (with Derby Co.), 1970 v E, S, Ni; 1972 v Fi, Cz, E, S; 1973 v E (39)
Hersee, A. M. (Bangor), 1886 v S, Ni (2)
Hersee, R. (Llandudno), 1886 v Ni (1)
Hewitt, R. (Cardiff C.), 1958 v Ni, Is, Sc. H, Br (5)
Hewitt, T. J. (Wrexham), 1911 v E, S, Ni; (with Chelsea), 1913 v E, S, Ni; (with South Liverpool), 1914 v E, S (8)
Heywood, D. (Druids), 1879 v E (1)
Hibbott, H. (Newtown Excelsior), 1880 v E, S (2)
Hibbott, R. (Newtown), 1885 v S (1)
Higham, G. G. (Oswestry), 1878 v S; 1879 v E (2)
Hill, M. R. (Ipswich T.), 1972 v Cz, R (2)

703

Hockey, T. (Sheffield U.), 1972, Fi, R; 1973 v E (2); (with Norwich C.) Pol, S, E, Ni; (with Aston Villa), 1974 v Pol (9)

Hoddinott, T. F. (Watford), 1921 v E, S (2)

Hodgkinson, A. V. (Southampton), 1908 v Ni (1)

Hole, B. G. (Cardiff C.), 1963 v Ni: 1964 v Ni; 1964 v S, E, Ni, D, Gr (2), R, I; 1966 v E, S, Ni, R, D, Br (2), Ch; (with Blackburn R.), 1967 v S, E, Ni; 1968 v E, S, Ni, WG; (with Aston Villa), 1969 v I, WG, EG; 1970 v I; (with Swasnea C.), 1971 v R (30)

Hole, W. J. (Swansea T.), 1921 v Ni; 1922 v E; 1923 v E, Ni; 1928 v E, S, Ni; 1929 v E, S (9)

Hollins, D. M. (Newcastle U.), 1962 v Br (sub), M; 1963 v Ni, H; 1964 v E; 1965 v Ni, Gr, I; 1966 v S, D. Br (11)

Hopkins, I. J. (Brentford), 1935 v S, Ni; 1936 v E, Ni; 1937 v E, S, Ni; 1938 v E, Ni; 1939 v E, S, Ni (12)

Hopkins, M. (Tottenham H.), 1956 v Ni; 1957 v Ni, S, E, Cz (2), EG; 1958 v E, S, Ni, EG, Is (2), H(2), M, Se, Br; 1959 v E, S, Ni; 1960 v E, S; 1961 v Ni, H, Sp (2); 1962 v Ni, Br (2), M; 1963 v S, Ni, H (34)

Howell, E. G. (Builth), 1888 v Ni; 1890 v E; 1891 v E (3)

Howells, R. G. (Cardiff C.), 1954 v E, S (2)

Hugh, A. R. (Newport Co.), 1930 v Ni (1)

Hughes, A. (Rhos), 1894 v E, S (2)

Hughes, A. (Chirk), 1907 v Ni (1)

Hughes, A. J. (Aberystwyth), 1879 v S (1)

Hughes, E. (Everton), 1899 v S, Ni; (with Tottenham H.), 1901 v E, S; 1902 v Ni; 1904 v E, Ni, S; 1905 v E, Ni, S; 1906 v E, Ni; 1907 v E (14)

Hughes, B. (Wrexham), 1906 v S; (with Nottingham F.), 1906 v Ni; 1908 v S, E; 1910 v Ni, E, S; 1911 v Ni, E, S; (with Wrexham), 1912 v Ni, E, S; (with Manchester C.), 1913 v E, S; 1914 v Ni (16)

Hughes, F. W. (Northwich Victoria), 1882 v E, Ni; 1883 v E, Ni, S; 1884 v S (6)

Hughes, I, (Luton T.), 1951 v E, Ni, P, Sw (4)

Hughes, J. (Cambridge University), 1877 v S (1)

Hughes, J. (Liverpool), 1905 v E, S, Ni (3)

Hughes, J. I. (Blackburn R.), 1935 v Ni (1)

Hughes, P. W. (Bangor), 1887 v Ni; 1889 v Ni, E(3)

Hughes, W. (Bootle), 1891 v E; 1892 v S, Ni (3)

Hughes, W. A. (Blackburn R.), 1949 v E. Ni, P, Bel, Sw (5)

Hughes, W. M. (Birmingham), 1938 v E, Ni, S, 1939 v E, Ni, S, F; 1947 v E, S, Ni (10)

Humphreys, J. V. (Everton), 1947 v Ni (1)

Humphreys, R. (Druids), 1888 v Ni (1)

Hunter, W. H. (North End, Belfast), 1887 v Ni (1)

Jackson, W. (St. Helens Rec.), 1899 v Ni (1)

James, E. (Chirk), 1893 v E, Ni; 1894 v E, S, Ni; 1898 v E; 1899 v Ni (7)

James, E. G. (Blackpool), 1966 v Br (2), Ch; 1967 v Ni; 1968 v S; 1971 v Cz, S, E, Ni (9)

James, L. (Burnley), 1972 v Cz, R, S (sub); 1973 v E (3), Pol, S, Ni; 1974 v Pol, E, S, Ni; 1975 v A, H (2), L (2), S, E, Ni; 1976 v A, S, E, Y (2), Ni (27)

James, W. (West Ham U.), 1931 v Ni; 1932 v Ni(2)

Jarrett, R. H. (Ruthin), 1889 v Ni; 1890 v S (2)

Jarvis, A. L. (Hull C.), 1967 v S, E, Ni (3)

Jenkins, R. W. (Rhyl), 1902 v Ni (1)

Jenkins, J. (Brighton), 1924 v Ni, E, S; 1925 v S, Ni; 1926 v E, S; 1927 v S (8)

Jenkins, R. W. (Rhyl), 1902 v Ni (1)

Jenkyns, C. A. L. (Small Heath), 1892 v E, S, Ni; 1895 v E; (with Woolwich Arsenal), 1896 v S; (with Newton Heath), 1897 v Ni; (with Walsall), 1898 v S, E (8)

Jennings, W. (Bolton W.), 1914 v E, S; 1920 v S; 1923 v Ni, E; 1924 v E, S, Ni; 1927 v S, Ni; 1929 v S (11)

John, R. F. (Arsenal), 1923 v S, Ni; 1925 v Ni; 1926 v E; 1927 v E; 1928 v E, Ni; 1930 v E, S; 1932 v E; 1933 v F, Ni; 1935 v Ni; 1936 v S; 1937 v E (15)

John, W. R. (Walsall), 1931 v Ni; (with Stoke C.) 1932 v E, S, Ni; 1933 v F; 1934 v E, S; (with Preston N.E.), 1935 v E, S; (with Sheffield U.), 1936 v E, S, Ni; (with Swansea T.), 1939 v E, S (14)

Johnson, M. G. (Swansea T.), 1964 v Ni (1)

Jones, A. F. (Oxford University), 1877 v S (1)

Jones, A. T. (Nottingham F.), 1905 v E; (with Notts Co.), 1906 v E (2)

Jones, Bryn (Wolverhampton W.), 1935 v Ni; 1936 v E, S, Ni; 1937 v E, S, Ni; 1938 v E, S, Ni; (with Arsenal), 1939 v E, S, Ni; 1947 v S, Ni; 1948 v E 1949 v S (17)

Jones, B. S. (Swansea T.), 1963 v S, E, Ni, H (2); 1964 v S, Ni; (with Plymouth Arg.), 1965 v D; (with Cardiff C.), 1969 v S, E, Ni, I (sub), WG, EG, R of UK (15).

Jones, Charlie (Nottingham F.), 1926 v E; 1927 v S, Ni; 1928 v E; (with Arsenal), 1930 v E, S; 1932 v E; 1933 v F (7)

Jones, Cliff (Swansea T.), 1954 v A; 1956 v E, Ni, S, A; 1957 v E, S, Ni, Cz (2), EG; 1958 v EG, E, S, Is (2); (with Tottenham H.), 1958 v Ni, H (2), M, Se, Br; 1959 v Ni; 1960 v E, S, Ni; 1961 v S, E, Ni, Sp, H, Ei; 1962 v E, Ni, S, Br (2), M; 1963 v S, Ni, H; 1964 v E, S, Ni; 1965 v S, Ni, D, Gr (2), USSR, I; 1967 v S, E; 1968 v E, S, WG; (with Fulham), 1969 v I, R of UK (59)

Jones, C. W. (Birmingham), 1935 v Ni; 1939 v F (2)

Jones, D. (Chirk), 1888 v S, Ni; (with Bolton W), 1889 v E, S, Ni; 1890 v E, Ni; 1891 v S; 1892 v Ni; 1893 v E; 1894 v E; 1895 v E; 1898 v S; (with Manchester C.), 1900 v E, Ni (15)

Jones, D. E. (Nrwich C.), 1976 v S, E (sub) (2)

Jones, D. O. (Leicester C.), 1934 v E, Ni; 1935 v E, S; 1936 v E, Ni; 1937 v Ni (7)

Jones, Evan (Chelsea), 1910 v S, Ni; (with Oldham Ath.), 1911 v E, S; 1912 v E, S; (with Bolton W.), 1914 v Ni (7)

Jones, F. R. (Bangor), 1885 v E, Ni; 1886 v S (3)

Jones, F. W. (Small Heath), 1893 v S (1)

Jones, G. P. (Wrexham), 1907 v S, Ni (2)

Jones, H. (Aberaman), 1902 v Ni (1)

Jones, Humphrey (Bangor), 1885 v E, Ni, S; 1886 v E, Ni, S; (with Queen's Park), 1887 v E; (with East Stirlingshire), 1889 v E, Ni; 1890 v E, S, Ni; (with Queen's Park), 1891 v E, S (14)

Jones, Ivor (Swansea T.), 1920 v S, Ni; 1921 v Ni, E; 1922 v S, Ni, (with W.B.A.), 1923 v E, Ni; 1924 v S; 1926 v Ni (10)

Jones, J. (Druids), 1876 v S (1)

Jones, J. (Berwyn Rangers), 1883 v S, Ni; 1884 v S (3)

Jones, J. (Wrexham), 1925 v Ni (1)

Jones, Jeffrey (Llandrindod Wells), 1908 v Ni; 1909 v Ni; 1910 v S (3)

Jones, J. L. (Sheffield U.), 1895 v E, S, Ni; 1896 v Ni, S, E; 1897 v Ni, S, E; (with Tottenham H.), 1898 v Ni, E, S; 1899 v S, Ni; 1900 v S; 1902 v E, S, Ni; 1904 v E, S, Ni (21)

Jones, J. Love (Stoke C.), 1906 v S; (with Middlesbrough), 1910 v Ni (2)

Jones, J. O. (Bangor), 1901 v S, Ni (2)

Jones, J. P. (Liverpool), 1976 v A, E, S (3)

Jones, J. T. (Stoke C.), 1912 v E, S, Ni; 1913 v E, Ni; 1914 v S, Ni; 1920 v E, S, Ni; (with C. Palace), 1921 v E, S; 1922 v E, S, Ni (15)

Jones, K. (Aston Villa), 1950 v S (1)

Jones, Leslie J. (Cardiff C.), 1933 v F; (with Coventry C.), 1935 v Ni; 1936 v S; 1937 v E, S, Ni; (with Arsenal), 1938 v E, S, Ni; 1939 v E, S (11)

Jones, P. W. (Bristol R.), 1971 v Fi (1)

Jones, R. (Bangor), 1887 v S; 1889 v E; (with Crewe Alex.), 1890 v E (3)

Jones, R. (Bangor), 1900 v S, Ni (2)

Jones, R. (Druids), 1899 v S; (with Millwall), 1906 v S, Ni (3)

Jones, R. A. (Druids), 1884 v E, Ni, S; 1885 v S (4)

Jones, R. S. (Everton), 1894 v Ni; (with Leicester Fosse), 1898 v S (2)

Jones, S. (Wrexham), 1887 v Ni; (with Chester), 1890 v S (2)

Jones, S. (Wrexham), 1893 v S, Ni; (with Burton Swifts), 1895 v S; 1896 v E, Ni (5)

Jones, T. (Manchester U.), 1926 v Ni; 1927 v E, Ni; 1930 v Ni (4)

Jones, T. D. (Aberdare), 1908 v Ni (1)

Jones, T. G. (Everton), 1938 v Ni; 1939 v E, S, Ni; 1947 v E, S; 1948 v E, S, Ni; 1949 v E, Ni, P, Bel, Sw; 1950 v E, S, Bel (17)

Jones, T. J. (Sheffield W.), 1932 v Ni; 1933 v F (2)

Jones, W. (Druids), 1899 v E (1)

Jones, W. E. A. (Swansea T.), 1947 v E, S; (with Tottenham H.), 1949 v E, S (4)

Jones, W. J. (Aberdare), 1901 v E, S; (with West Ham U.), 1902 v E, S (4)

Jones. W. Lot (Manchester C.), 1905 v E, Ni; 1906 v E, S, Ni; 1907 v E, S, Ni; 1908 v S; 1909 v E, S, Ni; 1910 v E; 1911 v E; 1913 v E, S; 1914 v S, Ni; (with Southend U.), 1920 v E, Ni (20)

Jones, W. P. (Druids), 1889 v E, Ni; (with Wynstay), 1890 v S, Ni (4)

Jones, W. R. (Aberystwyth), 1897 v S (1)

Keenor, F. C. (Cardiff C.), 1920 v E, Ni; 1921 v E, Ni, S; 1922 v Ni; 1923 v E, Ni, S; 1924 v E, Ni, S; 1925 v E, Ni, S; 1926 v S; 1927 v E, Ni, S; 1928 v E, Ni, S; 1929 v E, Ni, S; 1930 v E, Ni, S; 1931 v E, Ni, S; (with Crewe Alex.), 1933 v S (32)

Kelly, F. C. (Wrexham), 1899 v S, Ni; (with Druids), 1902 v Ni (3)

Kelsey, A. J. (Arsenal), 1954 v E, A; 1955 v S, Ni, Y; 1956 v E, Ni, S, A; 1957 v E, Ni, S, Cz (2), EG; 1958 v E, S, Ni, Is (2), H (2), M, Se, Br; 1959 v E, S; 1960 v E, Ni, S; 1961 v E, Ni, S, H, Sp (2); 1962 v E, S, Ni Br (2) (41)

Kenrick, S. L. (Druids), 1876 v S; 1877 v S; (with Oswestry), 1879 v E, S; (with Shropshire Wanderers), 1881 v E (5)

Ketley, C. F. (Druids), 1882 v Ni (1)

King, J. (Swansea T.), 1955 v E (1)

Kinsey, N. (Norwich C.), 1951 v Ni, P, Sw; 1952 v E; (with Birmingham), 1954 v Ni; 1956 v E, S (7)

Krzywicki, R. L. (Huddersfield T.), 1970 v E, S, (with W.B.A.), Ni, EG, I; 1971 v R, Fi; 1972 v Cz (sub) (8)

Lambert, R. (Liverpool), 1947 v S; 1948 v E; 1949 v P, Bel, Sw (5)

Lathom, G. (Liverpool), 1905 v E, S; 1906 v S; 1907 v E, S, Ni; 1908 v E; 1909 v Ni; (with

Southport Central), 1910 v E; (with Cardiff C.), 1913 v Ni (10)

Lawrence, E. (Clapton Orient), 1930 v Ni; (with Notts. Co.), 1932 v S (2)

Lawrence, S. (Swansea T.), 1932 v Ni; 1933 v F; 1934 v S, E, Ni; 1935 v E, S; 1936 v S (8)

Lea, A. (Wrexham), 1889 v E; 1891 v S, Ni; 1893 v Ni (4)

Lea, C. (Ipswich T.), 1965 v Ni, I (2)

Leary, P. (Bangor), 1889 v Ni (1)

Leek, K. (Leicester C.), 1961 v S, E, Ni, H, Sp (2); (with Newcastle U.), 1962 v S; (with Birmingham C.), v Br (sub), M; 1963 v E; 1965 v S, Gr; (with Northampton T.), 1965 v Gr (13)

Lever, A. R. (Leicester C.), 1953 v S (1)

Lewis, B. (Wrexham), 1891 v Ni; 1892 v S, E, Ni; (with Middlesbrough), 1893 v S, E; (with Wrexham), 1894 v S, E, Ni; 1895 v S (10)

Lewis, D. (Arsenal), 1927 v E; 1928 v Ni; 1930 v E (3)

Lewis, D. (Bangor), 1890 v Ni (1)

Lewis, D. J. (Swansea T.), 1933 v E, S (2)

Lewis, J. (Bristol R.), 1906 v E (1)

Lewis, J. (Cardiff C.), 1926 v S (1)

Lewis, T. (Wrexham), 1881 v E, S (2)

Lewis, W. L. (Swansea T.), 1927 v E, Ni; 1929 v S; (with Huddersfield T.), 1930 v E (4)

Lewis, W. (Bangor), 1885 v E; 1886 v E, S; 1887 v E, S; 1888 v E; 1889 v E, Ni, S; (with Crewe Alex.), 1890 v E, S; 1891 v E, S; 1892 v E, S, Ni; (with Chester), 1894 v E, S, Ni; (with Chester), 1895 v S, Ni, E; 1896 v E, S, Ni; (with Manchester C.), 1897 v E, S; (with Chester), 1898 v N, (30)

Lloyd, B. W. (Wrexham), 1976 v A, E, S (3)

Lloyd, J. W. (Wrexham). 1879 v S; (with Newtown), 1885 v S (2)

Lloyd, R. A. (Ruthin), 1891 v Ni; 1895 v S (2)

Lockley, A. (Chirk), 1898 v Ni (1)

Lowrie, G. (Coventry C.), 1948 v E, S, Ni; (with (Newcastle U.), 1949 v P (4)

Lucas, P. M. (Leyton Orient), 1962 v Ni, M; 1963 v S, E (4)

Lucas, W. H. (Swansea T.), 1949 v S, Ni, P, Bel, Sw; 1950 v E; 1951 v E (7)

Lumberg, A. (Wrexham), 1929 v Ni; 1930 v E, S; (with Wolverhampton W.), 1932 v S (4)

McMillan, R. (Shrewsbury Engineers), 1881 v E, S (2)

Mahoney, J. F. (Stoke C.), 1968 v E; 1969 v EG; 1971 v Cz; 1973 v E (3), Pol, S, Ni; 1974 v Pol, E, S, Ni; 1975 v A, H (2), L (2), S, E, Ni; 1976 v A, Y (2), E, Ni (26)

Martin, T. J. (Newport Co.), 1930 v Ni (1)

Mates, J. (Chirk), 1891 v Ni; 1897 v E, S (3)

Mathews, R. W. (Liverpool), 1921 v Ni; (with Bristol C), 1923 v E; (with Bradford), 1926 v Ni(3)

Matthews. W. (Chester), 1905 v Ni; 1908 v E (2)

Matthias, J. S. (Brymbo), 1896 v S, Ni; (with Shrewsbury), 1897 v E, S; (with Wolverhampton W.), 1899 v S (5)

Matthias, T. J. (Wrexham), 1914 v S, E; 1920 v Ni, S, E; 1921 v S, E, Ni; 1922 v S, E, Ni; 1923 v S, (12)

Mays, A. W. (Wrexham), 1929 v Ni (1)

Medwin, T. C. (Swansea T.), 1953 v Ni, F, Y; (with Tottenham H.), 1957 v E, S, Ni, Cz (2), EG; 1958 v E, S, Ni, Is (2), H (2), M, Br; 1959 v E, S, Ni; 1960 v E, S, Ni; 1961 v S, E, Ei, Sp; 1963 v E, H (30)

Meredith, S. (Chirk), 1900 v S; 1901 v S, E, Ni;

(with Stoke C.), 1902 v E; 1903 v Ni; 1904 v E; (with Leyton), 1907 v E (8)

Meredith, W. H. (Manchester C.), 1895 v E, Ni; 1896 v E, Ni; 1897 v E, Ni, S; 1898 v E, Ni; 1899 v E; 1900 v E, Ni; 1901 v E, Ni; 1902 v E, S; 1903 v E, S, Ni; 1904 v E; 1905 v E, S; (with Manchester U.), 1907 v E, S, Ni; 1908 v E, Ni; 1909 v E, S, Ni; 1910 v E, S, Ni; 1911 v E, S, Ni; 1912 v E, S, Ni; 1913 v E, S, Ni; 1914 v E, S, Ni; 1920 v E, S, Ni (48)

Mielczarek, R. (Rotherham), 1971 v Fi (1)

Millership, H. (Rotherham Co.), 1920 v E, S, Ni; 1921 v E, S, Ni (6)

Millington, A. H. (W.B.A.), 1963 v S, E, H; (with C. Palace), 1965 v E, USSR; (with Peterborough U.), 1966 v Ch, Br; 1967 v E, Ni; 1968 v Ni, WG; 1969 v I, EG (with Swansea); 1970 v E, S, Ni; 1971 v Cz, Fi; 1972 v Fi (sub), Cz, R (21)

Mills, T. J. (Clapton Orient), 1934 v E, Ni; (with Leicester C.), 1935 v E, S (4)

Mills-Roberts, R. H. (St. Thomas' Hospital), 1885 v E, S, Ni; 1886 v E; 1887 v E; (with Preston N.E.), 1888 v E, Ni; (with Llanberis), 1892 v E (8)

Moore, G. (Cardiff C.), 1960 v E, S, Ni; 1961 v Ei, Sp; (with Chelsea), 1962 v Br; 1963 v Ni, H; (with Manchester U.), 1964 v S, Ni; (with Northampton T.), 1966 v Ni, Ch; (with Charlton Ath.), 1969 v S, E, Ni, R of UK; 1970 v E, S, Ni, I; 1971 v R (21)

Morgan, J. R. (Cambridge U.), 1877 v S; (with Swansea), 1879 v S; (with Derby School Staff); 1880 v E, S; 1881 v E, S; 1882 v E, S, Ni; (with Swansea), 1883 v E (10)

Morgan, J. T. (Wrexham), 1905 v Ni (1)

Morgan-Owen, H. (Oxford University), 1901 v E, S; 1902 v S; 1906 v E, Ni; (with Welshpool), 1907 v S (6)

Morgan-Owen, M. M. (Oxford University), 1897 v S, Ni; 1898 v E, S; 1899 v S; 1900 v E; (with Corinthians), 1903 v S; 1906 v S, E, Ni; 1907 v E (11)

Morley, E. J. (Swansea T.), 1925 v E; (with Clapton Orient), 1929 v E, S, Ni (4)

Morris, A. G. (Aberystwyth), 1896 v E, Ni, S; (with Swindon T.), 1897 v E; 1898 v S; (with Nottingham F.), 1899 v E, S; 1903 v S; 1905 v E, S; 1907 v E, S; 1908 v E; 1910 v E, S, Ni; 1911 v E, S, Ni; 1912 v E (21)

Morris, C. (Chirk), 1900 v E, S, Ni; (with Derby Co.), 1901 v E, S, Ni; 1902 v E; 1903 v E, S, Ni; 1904 v Ni; 1905 v E, S, Ni; 1906 v S; 1907 v S; 1908 v E, S; 1909 v E, S, Ni; 1910 v E, S, Ni; (with Huddersfield T.), 1911 v E, S, Ni (27)

Morris, E. (Chirk), 1893 v E, S, Ni (3)

Morris H. (Sheffield U.), 1894 v S; (with Manchester C.), 1896 v E; (with Grimsby T.), 1897 v E (3)

Morris, J. (Oswestry), 1887 v S (1)

Morris, J. (Chirk), 1898 v Ni (1)

Morris, R. (Chirk), 1900 v E, Ni; 1901 v Ni; 1902 v S; (with Shrewsbury T.), 1903 v, E, Ni (6)

Morris, R. (Druids), 1902 v E, S; (with Newtown), 1902 v Ni; (with Liverpool), 1903 v S, Ni; 1904 v E, S, Ni; (with Leeds C.), 1906 v S; (with Grimsby T.), 1907 v Ni; (with Plymouth Arg.), 1908 v Ni (11)

Morris, S. (Birmingham), 1937 v E, S; 1938 v E, S; 1939 v F (5)

Morris, W. (Burnley), 1947 v Ni; 1949 v E; 1952 v S, Ni, R of UK (5)

Moulsdale, J. R. B. (Corinthians), 1925 v Ni (1)

Murphy, J. P. (W.B.A.), 1933 v F, E, Ni; 1934 v E, S; 1935 v E, S, Ni; 1936 v E, S, Ni; 1937 v S, Ni; 1938 v E, S, (15)

Neal, J. E., (Colwyn Bay), 1931 v E, S (2)

Newnes, J. (Nelson), 1926 v Ni (1)

Newton, L. F. (Cardiff Corinthians), 1912 v Ni (1)

Nicholas, D. S. (Stoke C.), 1923 v S; (with Swansea T.), 1927 v E, Ni (3)

Nicholls, J. (Newport Co.), 1924 v E, Ni; (with Cardiff C.), 1925 v E, S (4)

Nock, W. (Newtown), 1897 v Ni (1)

Nurse, M. T. G. (Swansea T.), 1960 v E, Ni; 1961 v S, E, H, Ni, Ei, Sp (2); (with Middlesbrough), 1963 v E, H; 1964 v S (12)

O'Callaghan, E. (Tottenham H.), 1929 v Ni; 1930 v S; 1932 v S, E; 1933 v Ni, S, E; 1934 v Ni, S, E; 1935 v E (11)

Oliver, A. (Blackburn R.), 1905 v E (with Bangor), S (2)

O'Sullivan, P. A. (Brighton), 1973 v S (sub); 1976 v S (2)

Owen, D. (Oswestry), 1879 v E (1)

Owen, E. (Ruthin Grammar School), 1884 v E, Ni, S (3)

Owen, G. (Chirk), 1888 v S; (with Newton Heath), 1889 v S, Ni; 1892 v E; 1893 v Ni (5)

Owen, T. (Oswestry), 1879 v E (1)

Owen, Trevor (Crewe Alex.), 1899 v E, S (2)

Owen, W. (Chirk), 1884 v E; 1885 v Ni; 1887 v E; 1888 v E; 1889 v E, Ni, S; 1890 v S, Ni; 1891 v E, S, Ni; 1892 v E, S; 1893 v S, Ni (16)

Owen, W. P. (Ruthin), 1880 v E, S; 1881 v E, S; 1882 v E, S, Ni; 1883 v E, S; 1884 v E, S, Ni (12)

Owens, J. (Wrexham), 1902 v S (1)

Page, M. E. (Birmingham C.), 1971 v Fi; 1972 v S Ni; 1973 v E (1 + 1 sub), Ni; 1974 v S, Ni; 1975 v H, L, S, E, Ni; 1976 v E, Y (2), E, Ni (18)

Palmer, D. (Swansea T.), 1957 v Cz; 1958 v E, EG (3)

Parris, J. E. (Bradford), 1932 v Ni (1)

Parry, B. J. (Swansea T.), 1951 v S (1)

Parry, C. (Everton), 1891 v E, S; 1893 v E; 1894 v E; 1895 v E, S; (with Newtown), 1896 v E, S, Ni; 1897 v Ni; 1898 v E, S, Ni (13)

Parry, E. (Liverpool), 1922 v S; 1923 v E, Ni; 1925 v Ni; 1926 v Ni (5)

Parry, H. (Newtown), 1895 v Ni (1)

Parry, M. (Liverpool), 1901 v E, S, Ni; 1902 v E, S, Ni; 1903 v E, S; 1904 v E, Ni; 1906 v E; 1908 v E, S, Ni; 1909 v E, S (16)

Parry, T. D. (Oswestry), 1900 v E, S, Ni; 1901 v E, S, Ni; 1902 v E (7)

Paul, R. (Swansea T.), 1949 v E, S, Ni, P, Sw; 1950 v E, S, Ni, Bel; (with Manchester C.), 1951 v S, E, Ni, P, Sw; 1952 v E, S, Ni, R of UK; 1953 v S, E, Ni, F, Y; 1954 v E, S, Ni; 1955 v S, E, Y; 1956 v E, Ni, S, A (33)

Peake, E. (Aberystwyth), 1908 v Ni; (with Liverpool), 1909 v Ni, S, E; 1910 v S, Ni; 1911 v Ni; 1912 v E; 1913 v E, Ni; 1914 v Ni (11)

Peers, E. J. (Wolverhampton W.), 1914 v Ni, S, E; 1920 v E, S; 1921 v S, Ni, E; (with Port Vale), 1922 v E, S, Ni; 1923 v E (12)

Perry, E. (Doncaster R.), 1938 v E, S, Ni (3)

Phennah, E. (Civil Service), 1878 v S (1)

Phillips, C. (Wolverhampton W.), 1931 v Ni; 1932 v E; 1933 v S; 1934 v E, Ni; 1935 v E, S, Ni; 1936 v S; (with Aston Villa), 1936 v E, Ni; 1938 v S (13)

Phillips, L. (Cardiff C.), 1971 v Cz, S, E, Ni; 1972 v Cz, R, S, Ni; 1973 v E; 1974 v Pol (sub), Ni; 1975 v A (with Aston Villa), H (2), L (2), S, E, Ni; 1976 v A, E, Y (2), E, Ni (25)

Phillips, T. J. S. (Chelsea), 1973 v E; 1974 v E; 1975 v H (sub) (3)

Phoenix, H. (Wrexham), 1882 v S (1)

Poland, G. (Wrexham), 1939 v Ni, F (2)

Powell, A. (Leeds U.), 1947 v E, S; 1948 v E, S, Ni; (with Everton), 1949 v E; 1950 v Bel; (with Birmingham), 1951 v S (8)

Powell, D. (Wrexham), 1968 v WG; (with Sheffield U.), 1969 v S, E, Ni, I, WG; 1970 v E, S, Ni, EG; 1971 v R (11)

Powell, I. V. (Q.P.R.), 1947 v E; 1948 v E, S, Ni; (with Aston Villa), 1949 v Bel; 1950 v S, Bel; 1951 v S (8)

Powell, J. (Druids), 1878 v S; 1880 v E, S; 1882 v E, S, Ni; 1883 v E, S, Ni; (with Bolton W.), 1884 v E; (with Newton Heath), 1887 v E, S; 1888 v E, S, Ni (15)

Powell, Seth (W.B.A.), 1885 v S; 1886 v E, Ni; 1891 v E, S; 1982 v E, S (7)

Price, H. (Aston Villa), 1907 v S; (with Burton U.), 1908 v Ni; (with Wrexham), 1909 v S, E, Ni (5)

Price, J. (Wrexham), 1877 v S; 1878 v S; 1879 v E; 1880 v E, S; 1881 v E, S; (with Druids), 1882 v S, E, Ni; 1883 v S, Ni (12)

Pring, K. D. (Rotherham), 1966 v Ch, D; 1967 v Ni (3)

Pryce-Jones, A. W. (Newtown), 1895 v E (1)

Pryce-Jones, W. E. (Cambridge University), 1887 v S; 1888 v S, E, Ni; 1890 v Ni (5)

Pugh, A. (Rhostyllen), 1889 v S (sub) (1)

Pugh, D. H. (Wrexham), 1896 v S, Ni; 1897 v S, Ni; (with Lincoln C.), 1900 v S; 1901 v S, E (7)

Pugsley, J. (Charlton Ath.), 1930 v Ni (1)

Pullen, W. J. (Plymouth Arg.), 1926 v E (1)

Rankmore, F. E. J. (Peterborough), 1966 v Ch (sub) (1)

Rea, J. C. (Aberystwyth), 1894 v Ni, S, E; 1895 v S; 1896 v S, Ni; 1897 v S, Ni; 1898 v Ni (9)

Reece, G. I. (Sheffield U.), 1966 v E, S, Ni, USSR; 1967 v S; 1969 v R of UK (sub); 1970 v I (sub); 1971 v S, E, Ni, Fi; 1972 v Fi, R, E (sub), S, Ni; (with Cardiff C.), 1973 v E (sub), Ni; 1974 v Pol (sub), E, S, Ni; 1975 v A, H (2), L (2), S, Ni (29)

Reed, W. G. (Ipswich T.), 1955 v S, Y (2)

Rees, R. R. (Coventry C.) 1965 v S, E, Ni, D, Gr (2), I, R; 1966 v E, S, Ni, R, D, Br (2), Ch; 1967 v E, Ni; 1968 v E, S, Ni (with W.B.A.), WG; 1969 v I; (with Nottingham F.), 1969 v WG, EG, S (sub), R of UK; 1970 v E, S, Ni, EG, I; 1971 v Cz, R, E (sub), Ni (sub), Fi; 1972 v Cz (sub), R (39)

Rees, W. (Cardiff C.), 1949 v Ni, Bel, Sw; (with Tottenham H.), 1950 v Ni (4)

Richards, A. (Barnsley), 1932 v S (1)

Richards, D. (Wolverhampton W.), 1931 v Ni; 1933 v E, S, Ni; 1934 v. E, S, Ni; 1935 v E, S, Ni; 1936 v S; (with Brentford), 1936 v E, Ni; 1937 v S, E; (with Birmingham), 1937 v Ni; 1938 v E, S, Ni; 1939 v E, S (21)

Richards, G. (Druids), 1899 v E, S, Ni; (with (Oswestry), 1903 v Ni; (with Shrewsbury), 1904 v S; 1905 v Ni (6)

Richards, R. W. (Wolverhampton W.), 1920 v E, S; 1921 v Ni; 1922 v E, S; (with West Ham U.), 1924 v E, S, Ni; (with Mold), 1926 v S (9)

Richards, S. V. (Cardiff C.), 1947 v E (1)

Richards, W. E. (Fulham), 1933 v Ni (1)

Roach, J. (Oswestry), 1885 v Ni (1)

Robbins, W. W. (Cardiff C.), 1931 v E, S; 1932 v Ni, E, S; (with W.B.A.), 1933 v F, E, S, Ni; 1934 v S; 1936 v S (11)

Roberts, D. F. (Oxford U.), 1973 v Pol, E (sub), Ni; 1974 v E, S; 1975 v A; (with Hull C.), L, Ni; 1976 v S, Ni, Y (11)

Roberts, J. G. (Arsenal), 1971 v S, E, Ni, Fi; 1972 v Fi, E, Ni; (with Birmingham C.), 1973 v E (2), Pol, S, Ni; 1974 v Pol, E S, Ni; 1975 v A, H, S, F; 1976 v E, S (22)

Roberts, J. H. (Bolton), 1949 v Bel (1)

Roberts, J. (Corwen), 1879 v S; 1880 v E, S; 1882 v E, S, Ni; (with Berwyn R.), 1883 v E (7)

Roberts, J. (Ruthin), 1881 v S; 1882 v S (2)

Roberts, J. (Bradford C.), 1906 v Ni; 1907 v Ni (2)

Roberts, Jas. (Chirk), 1898 v S (1)

Roberts, Jas. (Wrexham), 1913 v S, Ni (2)

Roberts, P. S. (Portsmouth), 1974 v E; 1975 v A, H, L (4)

Roberts, R. (Rhos), 1891 v Ni; (with Crewe Alex.) 1893 v E (2).

Roberts, R. (Druids), 1884 v S; (with Bolton W.); 1887 v S; 1888 v S, E; 1889 v S, E; 1890 v S; 1892 v Ni; (with P.N.E.) v S (9)

Roberts, R. (Wrexham), 1886 v Ni; 1887 v Ni; 1891 v Ni (3)

Roberts, W. (Llangollen), 1879 v E, S; 1880 v E, S; (with Berwyn R.), 1881 v S; 1883 v E, S (7)

Roberts, W. (Wrexham), 1886 v E, S, Ni; 1887 v Ni (4)

Roberts, N. H. (Ruthin), 1882 v E, S; 1883 v E, S, N; (with Rhyl), 1884 v S (6)

Rodrigues, P. J. (Cardiff C.), 1965 v Ni, Gr (2), 1966 v R, E, S, D; (with Leicester C.), v Ni, Br (2), Ch; 1967 v S; 1968 v E, S, Ni; 1969 v E, Ni, EG, R of UK; 1970 v E, S, Ni, EG; (with Sheffield W.) 1971 v R, E, S, Cz, Ni; 1972 v Fi, Cz, R, E, Ni (sub); 1973 v E (3), Pol, S, Ni; 1974 v Pol (40)

Rogers, J. P. (Wrexham), 1896 v E, S, Ni (3)

Rogers, W. (Wrexham), 1931 v E, S (2)

Roose, L. R. (Aberystwyth), 1900 v Ni; (with London Welsh), 1901 v E, S, Ni; (with Stoke C.), 1902 v E, S; 1904 v E; (with Everton), 1905 v S, E; (with Stoke C.), 1906 v E, S, Ni; 1907 v E, S, Ni; (with Sunderland), 1908 v E, S; 1909 v E, S, Ni; 1910 v E, S, Ni; 1911 v S (24)

Rouse, R. V. (C. Palace), 1959 v Ni (1)

Rowlands, A. C. (Tranmere R.), 1914 v E (1)

Rowley, T. (Tranmere R.), 1959 v Ni (1)

Russell, M. R. (Merthyr T.), 1912 v S, Ni; 1914 v E; (with Plymouth Arg.), 1920 v E, S, Ni; 1921 v E, S, Ni; 1922 v E, Ni; 1923 v E, S, Ni; 1924 v E, S, Ni; 1925 v E, S; 1926 v E, S; 1928 v S; 1929 v E (23)

Sabine, H. W. (Oswestry), 1887 v Ni (1)

Savin, G. (Oswestry), 1878 v S (1)

Scrine, F. H. (Swansea T.), 1950 v E, Ni (2)

Sear, C. R. (Manchester C.), 1963 v E (1)

Shaw, E. G. (Oswestry), 1882 v Ni; 1884 v S, Ni (3)

Sherwood, A. T. (Cardiff C.), 1947 v E, Ni; 1948 v S, Ni; 1949 v E, S, Ni, P, Sw; 1950 v E, S, Ni, Bel; 1951 v E, S, Ni, P. Sw; 1952 v E, S, Ni, R of UK; 1953 v S, E, Ni, F, Y; 1954 v E, S, Ni, A; 1955 S, E, Y, Ni; 1956 v E, S, Ni, A; (with Newport Co.), 1957 v E, S (41)

Shone, W. W. (Oswestry), 1879 v E (1)

Shortt, W. W. (Plymouth Arg.), 1947 v Ni; 1950 v

Ni, Bel; 1952 v E, S, Ni, R of UK; 1953 v S, E, Ni, F. Y (12)

Showers, D. (Cardiff C.), 1975 v E (sub), Ni (2)

Sidlow, C. (Liverpool), 1947 v E, S; 1948 v E. S, Ni; 1949 v S, 1950 v E (7)

Sisson, H. (Wrexham Olympic), 1885 v Ni; 1886 v S, Ni (3)

Smallman, D. P. (Wrexham), 1974 v E (sub), S (sub), Ni; (with Everton) 1975 v H (sub), E, Ni (sub); 1976 v A (7)

Sprake, G. (Leeds U.), 1964 v S, Ni; 1965 v S, D, Gr; 1966 v E, Ni, USSR; 1967 v S; 1968 v E, S; 1969 v S, E, Ni, WG, R of UK; 1970 v EG, I; 1971 v R, S, E, Ni; 1972 v Fi, E, S, Ni; 1973 v E (2), Pol, S, Ni; 1974 v Pol (with Birmingham C.) S. Ni; 1975 v A, H, L (37)

Stanfield, F. (Cardiff C.), 1949 v S (1)

Stitfall, R. F. (Cardiff C.), 1953 v E; 1957 v Cz (2)

Sullivan, D. (Cardiff C.), 1953 v Ni, F, Y; 1954 v Ni; 1955 v E, Ni; 1957 v E, S; 1958 v Ni, H (2), Se, Br; 1959 v S, Ni; 1960 v E, S (17)

Tapscott, D. R. (Arsenal), 1954 v A; 1955 v S, E, Ni, Y; 1956 v E, Ni, S. A; 1957 v Ni, Cz, EG; (with Cardiff C.), 1959 v E, Ni (14)

Taylor, J. (Wrexham), 1898 v E (1)

Taylor, O. D. S. (Newtown), 1893 v S, Ni; 1894 v S, Ni (4)

Thomas, C. (Druids) 1899 v Ni; 1900 v S (2)

Thomas, D.A. (Swansea T.), 1957 v Cz; 1958 v EG (2).

Thomas, D. S. (Fulham), 1948 v E, S, Ni; 1949 v S (4)

Thomas, E. (Cardiff Corinthians), 1925 v E (1)

Thomas, G. (Wrexham), 1885 v E, S (2)

Thomas, H. (Manchester U.), 1927 v E (1)

Thomas, R. J. (Swindon T.), 1967 v Ni; 1968 v WG; 1969 v E, Ni, I, WG, R of UK; 1970 v E, S, Ni, EG, I; 1971 v S, E, Ni, R, Cz; 1972 v Fi, Cz, E, S, Ni; 1973 v E (3), Pol, S, Ni; 1974 v Pol; (with Derby Co.), E, S Ni; 1975 v H (2), L (2), S, E, Ni; 1976 v A, Y, E (43)

Thomas, T. (Bangor), 1898 v S, Ni (2)

Thomas, W. R. (Newport Co.), 1931 v E, S (2)

Thomson, D. (Druids), 1876 v S (1)

Thomson, G. F. (Druids), 1876 v S; 1877 v S (2)

Toshack, J. B. (Cardiff C.), 1969 v S, E, Ni, WG, EG, R of UK; 1970 v EG, I; (with Liverpool), 1971 v S, E, Ni, Fi; 1972 v Fi, E; 1973 v E (3). Pol, S; 1975 v A, H (2), L (2), S, E; 1976 v Y (2), E (29)

Townsend, W. (Newtown), 1887 v Ni; 1893 v Ni (2)

Trainer, H. (Wrexham), 1895 v E, S, Ni (3)

Trainer, J. (Bolton W.), 1887 v S; (with Preston N.E.), 1888 v S; 1889 v E; 1890 v S; 1891 v S; 1892 v Ni, S; 1893 v E; 1894 v Ni, E; 1895 v Ni, E; 1896 v S; 1897 v Ni, S, E; 1898 v S, E; 1899 v Ni, S (20)

Turner, H. G. (Charlton Ath.), 1937 v E, S, Ni; 1938 v E, S, Ni; 1939 v Ni, F (8)

Turner, J. (Wrexham), 1892 v E (1)

Turner, R. E. (Wrexham), 1891 v E, Ni (2)

Turner, W. H. (Wrexham) 1887 v E, Ni; 1890 v S; 1891 v E, S (5)

Vaughan, Jas. (Druids), 1893 v E, S, Ni; 1899 v E (4)

Vaughan, John (Oswestry), 1879 v S; 1880 v S; 1881 v E, S; 1882 v E, S, Ni; 1883 v E, S, Ni; (with Bolton W.), 1884 v E (11)

Vaughan, J. O. (Rhyl), 1885 v Ni; 1886 v Ni, E, S (4)

Vaughan, T. (Rhyl), 1885 v E (1)

Vearncombe, G. (Cardiff C.), 1958 v EG; 1961 v Ei (2)

Vernon, T. R. (Blackburn R.), 1957 v Ni, Cz (2), EG; 1958 v E, S, EG, Se; 1959 v S; (with Everton) 1960 v Ni; 1961 v S, E, Ei; 1962 v Ni, Br (2), M; 1963 v S, E, H; 1964 v E, S; (with Stoke C.) 1965 v Ni, Gr, I; 1966 v E, S, Ni, USSR, D; 1967 v Ni; 1968 v E (32)

Villars, A. K. (Cardiff C.), 1974 v E, S, Ni (sub) (3)

Vizard, E, T. (Bolton W.), 1911 v E, S, Ni; 1912 v E, S; 1913 v S; 1914 v E, Ni; 1920 v E; 1921 v E, S, Ni; 1922 v E, S; 1923 v E, Ni; 1924 v E, S, Ni; 1926 v E, S; 1927 v S (22)

Walley, J. T. (Watford), 1971 v Cz (1)

Ward, D. (Bristol R.), 1959 v E; (with Cardiff C.), 1962 v E (2)

Warner, J. (Swansea T.), 1937 v E; (with Manchester U.), 1939 v F (2)

Warren, F. W. (Cardiff C.), 1929 v Ni; (with Middlesbrough), 1931 v Ni; 1933 v F, E; (with Hearts), 1937 v Ni; 1938 v Ni (6)

Watkins, A. E. (Leicester Fosse), 1898 v E, S; (with Aston Villa) 1900 v E, S; (with Millwall), 1904 v Ni (5)

Watkins, W. M. (Stoke), 1902 v E; 1903 v E, S; (with Aston Villa); 1904 v E, S, Ni; (with Sunderland), 1905 v E, S, Ni (with Stoke C.) 1908 v Ni (10)

Webster, C. (Manchester U.), 1957 v Cz; 1958 v H, M, Br (4)

Whatley, W. J. (Tottenham H.), 1939 v E, S (2)

White, P. F. (London Welsh), 1896 v Ni (1)

Wilcocks, A. R. (Oswestry), 1890 v Ni (1)

Wilding, J. (Wrexham O.), 1885 v E, S, Ni; 1886 v E, Ni; (with Bootle), 1887 v E; 1888 v S, Ni; (with Wrexham) 1892 v S (9)

Williams, A. L. (Wrexham) 1931 v E (1)

Williams, B. D. (Swansea T.), 1928 v Ni, E; 1930 v E, S; (with Everton), 1931 v Ni; 1932 v E; 1933 v E, S, Ni; 1935 v Ni (10)

Williams, B. (Bristol C.), 1930 v Ni (1)

Williams, D. R. (Merthyr T.), 1921 v E, S; (with Sheffield W.), 1923 v S; 2926 v S; 1927 v E, Ni; (with Manchester U.), 1929 v E, S (8)

Williams, E. (Crewe Alex.), 1893 v E, S (2)

Williams, E. (Druids) 1901 v E, Ni, S; 1902 v E, Ni (5)

Williams, G. (Chirk), 1893 v S; 1894 v S; 1895 v E, S, Ni; 1898 v Ni (6)

Williams, G. E. (W.B.A.), 1960 v Ni; 1961 v S, E, Ei; 1963 v Ni, H; 1964 v E, S, Ni; 1965 v S, E, Ni, D, Gr (2), R. I. 1966 v Ni, Br (2), Ch; 1967 v S, E, Ni; 1968 v Ni; 1969 v I (26)

Williams, G. G. (Swansea T.), 1961 v Ni, H, Sp (2); 1962 v E (5)

Williams, G. J. J. (Cardiff C.), 1951 v Sw (1)

Williams, G. O. (Wrexham), 1907 v Ni (1)

Williams, H. J. (Swansea), 1965 v Gr (2); 1972 v R (3)

Williams, H. T. (Newport Co), 1949 v Ni, Sw; (with Leeds U.), 1950 v Ni; 1951 v S (4)

Williams, J. T. (Wrexham), 1939 v F (1)

Williams, J. H. (Oswestry), 1884 v E (1)

Williams, J. T. (Middlesbrough), 1925 v Ni (1)

Williams, J. W. (C. Palace), 1912 v S, Ni (2)

Williams, R. (Newcastle U.), 1935 v S, E (2)

Williams, R. P. (Caernarvon), 1886 v S (1)

Williams, S. G. (W.B.A.), 1954 v A; 1955 v E, Ni 1956 v E, S, A; 1958 v E, S, Ni, Is (2), H (2), M, Se, Br; 1959 v E, S, Ni; 1960 v E, S, Ni; 1961 v Ni, Ei, H, Sp (2); 1962 v E, S, Ni, Br (2), M; (with Southampton), 1963 v S, E, H (2); 1964 v E, S; 1965 v S, E, D; 1966 v D (43)

Williams, W. (Druids), 1876 v S; 1878 v S; (with Oswestry), 1879 v E, S; (with Druids), 1880 v E, S; 1881 v E, S; 1882 v E, S, Ni; 1883 v Ni (12)
Williams, W. (Northampton), 1925 v S (1)
Witcomb, D. F. (W.B.A.), 1947 v E, S; (with Sheffield W.), 1947 v Ni (3)
Woosnam, A. P. (Leyton Orient), 1959 v S; (with West Ham U.) v E; 1960 v E, S, Ni; 1961 v S, E, Ni, Ei, Sp, H; 1962 v E, S, Ni, Br; (with Aston Villa), 1963 v Ni H (17)

Woosnam, G. (Newton White Star), 1879 v S (1)
Worthington, T. (Newtown), 1894 v S (1)
Wynn, G. A. (Chirk), 1903 v Ni; (with Wrexham) 1909 v E, S, Ni; (with Manchester C.), 1910 v E; 1911 v Ni; 1912 v E, S; 1913 v E, S; 1914 v E, S 12)
Yorath, T. C. (Leeds U.), 1970 v I; 1971 v S, E, Ni; 1972 v Cz, E, S, Ni; 1973 v E, Pol, S; 1974 v Pol, E, S, Ni; 1975 v A, H (2), L (2), S; 1976 v A, E, S, Y (2), E, Ni (28)

REPUBLIC OF IRELAND

Aherne, T. (Belfast Celtic), 1946 v P, Sp; (Luton T) 1950 v Fi, E, Fi, Se, Bel; 1951 v N, Arg, N; 1952 v WG (2), A, Sp; 1953 v F; 1954 v F (16)
Ambrose, P. (Shamrock R.), 1955 v N, Ho; 1964 v Pol, N, E (5)
Andrews, P. (Bohemians) 1936 v Ho (1)
Arrigan, T. (Waterford), 1938 v N (1)

Bailham, E. (Shamrock R), 1964 v E (1)
Barber, E. (Shelbourne), 1966 v Sp; (Birmingham City) 1966 v Bel (2)
Barry, P. (Fordsons), 1928 v Bel; 1929 v Bel (2)
Bermingham, J. (Bohemians), 1929 v Bel (1)
Bermingham, P. (St James' Gate), 1935 v H (1)
Bradshaw, P. (St James' Gate), 1939 v Sw, Pol, H (2) G (5)
Brady, F. (Fordsons), 1926 v I; 1927 v I (2)
Brady, T. R. (Q.P.R.), 1964 v A (2), Sp (2), Pol, N (6)
Brady, W. L. (Arsenal), 1975 v USSR, T, Sw, USSR, Sw; 1976 v T, N, Pol (8)
Breen, T. (Manchester U.), 1937 v Sw, F; (Shamrock R.), 1947 v E, Sp, P (5)
Brennan, F. (Drumcondra), 1965 v Bel (1)
Brennan, S. A. (Manchester U.), 1965 v Sp; 1966 v Sp, A, Bel; 1967 v Sp, T, Sp; 1969 v Cz, D, H; 1970 v S, Cz, D, H, Pol (sub), WG; (Waterford), 1971 v Pol, Se, I, (19)
Brown, J. (Coventry C.) 1937 v Sw, F (2)
Browne, W. (Bohemians), 1964 v A, Sp, E (3)
Burke, F. (Cork), 1934 v Bel (1)
Burke, F. (Cork Ath.), 1952 v WG (1)
Burke, J. (Shamrock R.), 1929 v Bel (1)
Byrne, A. B. (Southampton), 1970 v D, Pol, WG, 1971 v Pol, Se (2), 1 (2), A; 1973 v F, USSR (sub), F, N; 1974 v Pol (14)
Byrne, D. (Shelbourne), 1929 v Bel; (Shamrock R.), 1932 v Sp; (Coleraine), 1934 v Bel (3)
Byrne, J. (Bray Unknowns), 1928 v Bel (1)
Byrne, P. (Shelbourne), 1931 v Sp; 1932 v Ho; (Drumcondra), 1934 v Ho (3)
Byrne, S. (Bohemians), 1931 v Sp (1)

Campbell, N. (St Patrick's Ath.), 1971 v A (sub); (Fortuna, Cologne), 1972 v Iran, Ec, Ch, P; 1973 v USSR, F (sub); 1976 v N (8)
Cannon, H. (Bohemians), 1926 v I; 1928 v Bel (2)
Cantwell, N. (West Ham U.), 1954 v L; 1956 v Sp, Ho; 1957 v D, WG, E (2), 1958 v D, Pol, A; 1959 v Pol, Cz (2); 1960 v Se, Ch, Se; 1961 v N; (Manchester United), 1961 v S (2); 1962 v Cz (2), A; 1963 v Ic (2), S; 1964 v A, Sp, E; 1965 v Pol, Sp, 1966 v Sp (2); A, Bel; 1967 v Sp, T (36)
Carey, J. J. (Manchester U.) 1938 v N, Cz, Pol; 1939 v Sw, Pol, H (2), G; 1946 v P, Sp; 1947 v E, Sp P; 1948 v P, Sp; 1949 v Sw, Bel, P, Se, Sp; 1950 v Fi, E, Fi, Se; 1951 v N, Arg, N; 1953 v F, A (29)

Carolan, J. (Manchester U.), 1960 v Se, Ch (2)
Carroll, B. (Shelbourne), 1949 v Bel; 1950 v Fi (2)
Carroll, T. R. (Ipswich T.), 1968 v Pol; 1969 v Pol, A, D; 1970 v Cz, Pol, WG; 1971 v Se; (Birmingham C.), 1972 v Iran, Ec, Ch, P; 1973 v USSR (2), Pol, F, N (17)
Chatton, H. A. (Shelbourne), 1931 v Sp; Dumbarton), 1932 v Sp; (Cork), 1934 v Ho (3)
Clarke, K. (Drumcondra), 1948 v P, Sp (2)
Clarke, M. (Shamrock R.), 1950 v Bel (1)
Clinton, T. J. (Everton), 1951 v N; 1954 v F, L (3)
Coad, P. (Shamrock R), 1947 v E, Sp, P; 1948 v P, Sp; 1949 v Sw, Bel, P, Se, 1951 v N (sub); 1952 v Sp (11)
Coffey, T. (Drumcondra), 1950 v Fi (1)
Colfer, M. D. (Shelbourne), 1950 v Bel; 1951 v N (2)
Collins, F. (Jacobs), 1927 v I (1)
Conmy, O. M. (Peterborough U.), 1965 v Bel; 1967 v Cz; 1968 v Cz, Pol; 1970 v Cz (5)
Connolly, J. (Fordsons), 1926 v I (1)
Connolly, N. (Cork), 1937 v G (1)
Conroy, G. A. (Stoke C.), 1970 v Cz, D, H, Pol, WG; 1971 v Pol, Se (2), I; 1973 v USSR, F, USSR, N; 1974 v Pol, Br, U, Ch; 1975 v T, Sw, USSR, Sw; 1976 v T (sub), Pol (23)
Conway, J. P. (Fulham), 1967 v Sp, T, Sp, 1968 v Cz; 1969 v A (sub), H; 1970 v S, Cz, D, H, Pol, WG; 1971 v I, A; 1974 v U, Ch; 1976 v N, Pol (18)
Corr, P. J. (Everton), 1949 v P, Sp; 1950 v E, Se (4)
Courtney, E. (Cork U.), 1946 v P (1)
Cummins, G. P. (Luton T.), 1954 v L (2); 1955 v N (2), WG; 1956 v Y, Sp; 1958 v D, Pol, A; 1959 v Pol, Cz (2); 1960 v Se, Ch, WG, Se; 1961 v S (2) (19)
Cuneen, T. (Limerick), 1951 v N (1)
Curtis, D. P. (Shelbourne) 1957 v D, WG; (Bristol C.), 1957 v E (2); 1958 v D, Pol, A; (Ipswich T.), 1959 v Pol; 1960 v Se, Ch, WG, Se; 1961 v N, S; 1962 v A; 1963 v Ic (Exeter C.), 1964 v A (17)
Cusack, S. (Limerick), 1953 v F (1)

Daly, G. A. (Manchester U.), 1973 v Pol (sub), N; 1974 v Br (sub), U (sub); 1975 v Sw (sub) (5)
Daly, J. (Shamrock R.), 1932 v Ho; 1935 v Sw (2)
Daly, P. (Shamrock R.), 1950 v Fi (sub) (1)
Davis, T. L. (Oldham Ath.), 1937 v G, H, (Tranmere R.), 1938 v Cz, Pol (4)
Dempsey, J. T. (Fulham), 1967 v Sp, Cz; 1968 v Cz, Pol; 1969 v Pol, A, D; (Chelsea), 1969 v Cz, D; 1970 v H, WG; 1971 v Pol, Se (2), I; 1972 v Iran, Ec, Ch, P (19)
Dennehy, J. (Cork Hibernians), 1972 v Ec (sub), Ch; (Nottingham F.), 1973 v USSR (sub), Pol, F, N; 1974 v Pol (sub); 1975 v T (sub); (with Walsall) 1976 v Pol (sub) (9)
Desmond, P. (Middlesbrough), 1950 v Fi, E, Fi, Se (4)
Donnelly, J. (Dundalk), 1935 v H, Sw, G; 1936 v Ho, Sw, H, L; 1937 v G, H, 1938 v N (10)

Donnelly, T. (Drumcondra) 1938 v N; (Shamrock R), 1939 v Sw (2)

Donovan, D. C. (Everton), 1955 v N, Ho, N, WG; 1957 v E (5)

Dowdall, C. (Fordsons), 1928 v Bel; (Barnsley), 1929 v Bel; (Cork) 1931 v Sp (3)

Doyle, C. (Shelbourne), 1959 v Cz (1)

Doyle, D. (Shamrock R.), 1926 v I (1)

Doyle, L. (Dolphin), 1932 v Sp (1)

Duffy, B. (Shamrock R.), 1950 v Bel (1)

Duggan, H. A. (Leeds U.), 1927 v I; 1930 v Bel; 1936 v H, L, (Newport Co.), 1938 v N (5)

Dunne, A. P. (Manchester U.), 1962 v A; 1963 v Ic, S; 1964 v A, Sp, Pol, N, E; 1965 v Pol, Sp; 1966 v Sp (2), A, Bel; 1967 v Sp, T, Sp; 1969 v Pol, D, H; 1970 v H; 1971 v Se, I, A; (Bolton W),1974 v Br (sub), U, Ch; 1975 v T, Sw, USSR, Sw; 1976 v T (32)

Dunne, J. (Sheffield U.), 1930 v Bel; (Arsenal), 1936 v Sw, H, L; (Southampton), 1937 v Sw, F; (Shamrock R.),1938 v N (2), Cz, Pol; 1939 v Sw, Pol, H (2), G (15)

Dunne, J. C. (Fulham), 1971 v A (1)

Dunne, L. (Manchester C.), 1935 v Sw, G (2)

Dunne, P. A. J. (Manchester U.), 1965 v Sp; 1966 v Sp (2), WG; 1967 v T (5)

Dunne, S. (Luton T.), 1953 v F, A; 1954 v F, L; 1956 v Sp, Ho; 1957 v D, WG, E; 1958 v D, Pol, A; 1959 v Pol; 1960 v WG, Se (15)

Dunne, T. (St Patrick's Ath.), 1956 v Ho; 1957 v D, WG (3)

Dunning, P. (Shelbourne), 1971 v Se, I (2)

Dunphy, E. M. (York C.), 1966 v Sp; (Millwall), 1966 v WG; 1967 v T, Sp, T, Cz; 1968 v Cz, Pol; 1969 v Pol, A, D (2), H; 1970 v D, H, Pol, WG (sub); 1971 v Pol; Se, (2), I (2), A (23)

Dwyer, N. M. (West Ham U.), 1960 v Se, Ch, WG, Se; (Swansea T.), 1961 v W, N, S (2); 1962 v Cz (2); 1964 v Pol (sub), N, E; 1965 v Pol (14)

Egan, R. (Dundalk), 1929 v Bel (1)

Eglington, T. J. (Shamrock R.), 1946 v P, Sp; Everton), 1947 v E, Sp, P; 1948 v P, 1949 v Sw, P, Se; 1951 v N, Arg; 1952 v WG (2), A, Sp; 1953 v F, A; 1954 v F, L, F; 1955 v N, Ho, WG; 1956 v Sp (24)

Ellis, P. (Bohemians), 1935 v Sw, G; 1936 v Ho, Sw, L; 1937 v G, H (7)

Fagan, E. (Shamrock R.), 1973 v N (sub) (1)

Fagan, F. (Manchester C.), 1955 v N; 1960 v Se; (Derby Co.), 1960 v Ch, WG, Se; 1961 v W, N, S (8)

Fagan, K. (Shamrock R.), 1926 v I (1)

Fallon, S. (Celtic), 1951 v N; 1952 v WG (2), A, Sp; 1953 v F; 1955 v N, WG (8)

Fallon, W. J. (Notts Co.), 1935 v H; 1936 v H; 1937 v H, Sw, F; 1939 v Sw, Pol; (Sheffield W.), 1939 v H, G (9)

Farquharson, T. G. (Cardiff C.), 1929 v Bel; 1930 v Bel; 1931 v Sp; 1932 v Sp (4)

Farrell, P. (Hibernian), 1937 v Sw, F (2)

Farrell, P. D. (Shamrock R.), 1946 v P, Sp; (Everton), 1947 v Sp, P; 1948 v P, Sp; 1949 v Sw, P (sub), Sp; 1950 v E, Fi, Se; 1951 v Arg, N; 1952 v WG (2), A, Sp; 1953 v F, A; 1954 v F (2); 1955 v N, Ho, WG; 1956 v Y, Sp; 1957 v E (28)

Feenan, J. J. (Sunderland), 1937 v Sw, F (2)

Finucane, A. (Limerick), 1967 v T, Cz; 1969 v Cz, D, H; 1970 v S, Cz; 1971 v Se, I, I (sub); 1972 v A (11)

Fitzgerald, F. J. (Waterford), 1955 v Ho; 1956 v Ho (2)

Fitzgerald, P. J. (Leeds U.), 1961 v W, N, S; 1962 v Cz (2) (5)

Fitzpatrick, K. (Limerick), 1970 v Cz (1)

Fitzsimons, A. G. (Middlesbrough), 1950 v Fi, Bel; 1952 v WG (2), A, Sp; 1953 v F, A; 1954 v F, L, F; 1955 v Ho, N, WG; 1956 v Y, Sp, Ho, 1957 v D, WG, E (2); 1958 v D, Pol, A; 1959 v Pol; (Lincoln C.), 1959 v Cz (26)

Flood, J. J. (Shamrock R.), 1926 v I; 1929 v Bel; 1930 v Bel; 1931 v Sp; 1932 v Sp (5)

Fogarty, A. (Sunderland), 1960 v WG, Se; 1961 v S; 1962 v Cz (2); 1963 v Ic (2), S (sub); 1964 v A (2), Sp (11)

Foley, J. (Cork), 1934 v Bel, Ho; (Celtic), 1935 v H, Sw, G; 1937 v G, H (7)

Foley, M. (Shelbourne), 1926 v I (1)

Foley, T. C. (Northampton T.), 1964 v Sp, Pol, N; 1965 v Pol, Bel; 1966 v Sp (2), WG; 1967 v Cz (9)

Foy, T. (Shamrock R.), 1938 v N; 1939 v H (2)

Fullam, J. (Preston N.E.), 1961 v N; (Shamrock R.), 1964 v Sp, Pol, N; 1966 v A, Bel; 1968 v Pol; 1969 v Pol, A, D; 1970 v Cz (sub) (11)

Fullam, R. (Shamrock R.), 1926 v I; 1927 v I (2)

Gallagher, C. (Celtic), 1967 v T, Cz (2)

Gallagher, M. (Hibernian), 1954 v L (1)

Gallagher, P. (Falkirk), 1932 v Sp (1)

Gannon, E. (Notts Co.) 1949 v Sw; (Sheffield W.), 1949 v Bel, P, Se, Sp; 1950 v Fi; 1951 v N; 1952 v G, A; 1954 v L, F; 1955 v N; (Shelbourne), 1955 v N, WG (14)

Gannon, M. (Shelbourne) 1972 v A (1)

Gaskins, P. (Shamrock R.), 1934 v Bel, Ho; 1935 v H, Sw, G; (St James' Gate), 1938 v Cz, Pol (7)

Gavin, J. T. (Norwich C.), 1950 v Fi (2); 1953 v F; 1954 v L; (Tottenham H.), 1955 v Ho, WG; (Norwich C.), 1957 v D (7)

Geoghegan, M. (St James' Gate), 1937 v G; 1938 v N (2)

Gibbons, A. (St Patrick's Ath.), 1952 v WG; 1954 v L; 1956 v Y, Sp (4)

Gilbert, R. (Shamrock R.), 1966 v WG (1)

Giles, C. (Doncaster R.), 1951 v N (1)

Giles, M. J. (Manchester U.), 1960 v Se, Ch; 1961 v W, N, S (2); 1962 v Cz (2), A; 1963 v Ic, S; (Leeds U.), 1964 v A (2), Sp (2), Pol, N, E; 1965 v Sp; 1966 v Sp (2), A, Bel; 1967 v Sp, T (2); 1969 v A, D, Cz; 1970 v S, Pol, WG; 1971 v I; 1973 v F USSR; 1974 v Br, U, Ch; 1975 v USSR, T, Sw, USSR, Sw; (with W.B.A.) 1976 v T (44)

Givens, D. J. (Manchester U.), 1969 v D, H; 1970 v S, Cz, D, H; (Luton T.), 1970 v Pol, WG; 1971 v Se, I (2), A; 1972 v Iran, Ec, P; 1973 v F, USSR, Pol, F, N; (QPR), 1974 v Pol, Br, U, Ch; 1975 v USSR, T, Sw, USSR, Sw; 1976 v T, N, Pol (32)

Glen, W. (Shamrock R.), 1927 v I; 1929 v Bel; 1930 v Bel; 1932 v Sp; 1936 v Ho, Sw, H, L (8)

Glynn, D. (Drumcondra), 1952 v WG; 1955 v N (2)

Godwin, T. F. (Shamrock R.), 1949 v P, Se, Sp; 1950 v Fi, E; (Leicester C.), 1950 v Fi, Se, Bel; (Bournemouth & Boscombe Ath.), 1951 v N; 1956 v Ho; 1957 v E; 1958 v D, Pol (13)

Golding, L. (Shamrock R.), 1928 v Bel; 1930 v Bel (2)

Gorman, W. C. (Bury), 1936 v Sw, H, L; 1937 v G, H; 1938 v N, Cz, Pol; 1939 v Sw, Pol, H; (Brentford), 1947 v E, P (13)

Grace, J. (Drumcondra), 1926 v I (1)
Grealish, A. (Orient), 1976 v N, Pol (2)
Griffith, R. (Walsall), 1935 v H (1)

Hale, A. (Aston Villa), 1962 v A; (Doncaster R.) 1963 v Ic; 1964 v Sp (2); (Waterford), 1967 v Sp; 1968 v Pol (sub); 1969 v Pol, A, D; 1970 v S, Cz; 1971 v Pol (sub); 1972 v A (sub (13)
Hamilton, T. (Shamrock R.), 1959 v Cz (2) (2)
Hand, E. K. (Portsmouth), 1969 v Cz (sub); 1970 v Pol, WG; 1971 v Pol, A; 1973 v USSR, F, USSR, Pol, F; 1974 v Pol, Br, U, Ch; 1975 v T, Sw, USSR, Sw; 1976 v T (19)
Harrington, W. (Cork), 1936 v Ho, Sw, H, L (4)
Hartnett, J. B. (Middlesbrough), 1949 v Sp; 1954 v L (2)
Haverty, J. (Arsenal), 1956 v Ho, 1957 v D, WG, E (2); 1958 v D, Pol, A; 1959 v Pol; 1960 v Se, Ch; 1961 v W, N, S (2); (Blackburn R.), 1962 v Cz (2); (Millwall), 1963 v S; 1964 v A, Sp, Pol, N, E; (Celtic), 1965 v Pol; (Bristol R.), 1965 v Sp; (Shelbourne), 1966 v Sp (2), WG, A, Bel; 1967 v T, Sp (32)
Hayes, W. E. (Huddersfield T.), 1947 v E, P (2)
Hayes, W. J. (Limerick), 1949 v Bel (1)
Heighway, S. D. (Liverpool), 1971 v Pol, Se (2), I, A; 1973 v USSR; 1975 v USSR, T, USSR; 1976 v T, N (11)
Henderson, B. (Drumcondra), 1948 v P, Sp (2)
Hennessy, J. (Shelbourne), 1956 v Pol, B, Sp; 1966 v WG; (St Patrick's Ath.), 1969 v A (5)
Herrick, J. (Cork Hibernians), 1972 v A, Ch (sub); Shamrock R.), 1973 v F (sub) (3)
Higgins, J. (Birmingham C.), 1951 v Arg (1)
Holmes, J. (Coventry C.), 1971 v A (sub); 1973 v F, USSR, Pol, F, N; 1974 v Pol, Br; 1975 v USSR, Sw; 1976 v T, N, Pol (13)
Horlecher, A. F. (Bohemians), 1930 v Bel; 1932 v Sp, Ho; 1935 v H; 1936 v Ho, Sw (6)
Hoy, M. (Dundalk), 1938 v N; 1939 v Sw, Pol, H (2), G (6)
Hurley, C. J. (Millwall), 1957 v E; 1958 v D, Pol, A; (Sunderland), 1959 v Cz (2); 1960 v Se, Ch, WG, Se; 1961 v W, N, S (2); 1962 v Cz (2), A; 1963 v Ic (2), S; 1964 v A (2), Sp (2), Pol, N; 1965 v Sp; 1966 v WG, A, Bel; 1967 v T, Sp, T, Cz; 1968 v Cz, Pol (2); (Bolton W.), 1969 v D, Cz, H (40)
Hutchinson, F. (Drumcondra), 1935 v Sw, G (2)

Jordan, D. (Wolverhampton W.), 1937 v Sw, F (2)
Jordan, W. (Bohemians), 1934 v Ho; 1938 v N (2)

Kavanagh, P. J. (Celtic), 1931 v Sp; 1932 v Sp (2)
Keane, T. R. (Swansea T.), 1949 v Sw, P, Se, Sp (4)
Kearin, M. (Shamrock R.), 1972 v A (1)
Kearns, F. T. (West Ham U.), 1954 v L (1)
Kearns, M. (Oxford U.), 1970 v Pol (sub), (Walsall), 1974 v Pol (sub), U, Ch; 1976 v N, Pol (6)
Kelly, J. (Derry C.), 1932 v Ho; 1934 v Bel; 1936 v Sw, L (4)
Kelly, J. A. (Drumcondra), 1957 v WG, E; (Preston N. E.), 1962 v A; 1963 v Ic (2), S; 1964 v A (2), Sp (2), Pol; 1965 v Bel; 1966 v A, Bel; 1967 v Sp (2), T, Cz (2), Pol; 1968 v Pol, A, D, Cz, D, H; 1970 v S, D, H, Pol, WG; 1971 v Pol, Se (2), I (2), A; 1972 v Iran, Ec, Ch, P; 1973 v USSR, F, USSR, Pol, F, N, (47)
Kelly, J. P. V. (Wolverhampton W.), 1961 v W, N, S; 1962 v Cz (2) (5)
Kelly, N. (Nottingham F.), 1954 v L (1)

Kendrick, J. (Everton), 1927 v I; 1934 v Bel, Ho; 1936 v Ho (4)
Kennedy, W. (St. James' Gate), 1932 v Ho; 1934 v Bel, Ho (3)
Keogh, J. (Shamrock R.), 1966 v WG (sub) (1)
Keogh, S. (Shamrock R.), 1959 v Pol (1)
Kiernan, F. W. (Shamrock R.), 1951 v Arg, N; (Southampton), 1952 v WG (2), A (5)
Kinnear, J. P. (Tottenham H.), 1967 v T; 1968 v Cz; Pol; 1969 v A; 1970 v Cz, D, H, Pol; 1971 v Se (sub), I; 1972 v Iran, Ec, Ch, P; 1973 v USSR, F; 1974 v Pol, Br, U, Ch; 1975 v USSR, T, Sw, USSR; (with Brighton) 1976 v T (sub) (25)
Kinsella, J. (Shelbourne), 1928 v Bel (1)
Kinsella, P. (Shamrock R.), 1932 v Ho; 1938 v N (2)
Kirkland, A. (Shamrock R.), 1927 v I (1)

Lacey, W. (Shelbourne), 1927 v I; 1928 v Bel; 1930 v Bel (3)
Lawler, J. F. (Fulham), 1953 v A; 1954 v L, F; 1955 v N, H, N, WG; 1956 v Y (8)
Lawlor, J. C. (Drumcondra), 1949 v Bel; (Doncaster R.), 1951 v N, Arg (3)
Lawlor, M. (Shamrock R.), 1971 v Pol; Se (2), I (sub); 1973 v Pol (5)
Leech, M. (Shamrock R.), 1969 v Cz, D, H; 1972 v A, Iran, Ec, P; 1973 v USSR (sub) (8)
Lennon, C. (St. James' Gate), 1935 v H, Sw, G (3)
Lennox, G. (Dolphin), 1931 v Sp; 1932 v Sp (2)
Lowry, D. (St. Patrick's Ath.), 1962 v A (sub) (1)
Lunn, R. (Dundalk), 1939 v Sw, Pol (2)
Lynch, J. (Cork Bohemians), 1934 v Bel (1)

McAlinden, J. (Portsmouth), 1946 v P, Sp (2)
McCann, J. (Shamrock R.), 1957 v WG (1)
McCarthy, J. (Bohemians), 1926 v I; 1928 v Bel; 1930 v Bel (3)
McCarthy, M. (Shamrock R.), 1932 v Ho (1)
McConville, T. (Dundalk), 1972 v A; (Waterford), 1973 v USSR, F, USSR, Pol, F (6)
McEvoy, M. A. (Blackburn R.), 1961 v S (2); 1963 v S; 1964 v A, Sp (2), Pol, N, E; 1965 v Pol, Bel, Sp; 1966 v Sp (2); 1967 v Sp, T, Cz (17)
McGowan, D. (West Ham U.), 1949 v P, Se, Sp (3)
McGowan, J. (Cork U.), 1947 v Sp (1)
McGrath, M. (Blackburn R.), 1958 v A; 1959 v Pol, Cz (2); 1960 v Se, WG, Se; 1961 v W; 1962 v Cz (2); 1963 v S; 1964 v A (2), E; 1965 v Pol, Bel, Sp; 1966 v Sp; (Bradford), 1966 v WG, A, Bel; 1967 v T (22)
McGuire, W. (Bohemians) 1936 v Ho (1)
McKenzie, G. (Southend U.), 1938 v N (2), Cz, Pol; 1939 v Sw, Pol, H, (2), G (9)
Mackey, G. (Shamrock R.), 1957 v D, WG, E (3)
McLoughlin, F. (Fordsons), 1930 v Bel; (Cork), 1932 v Sp (2)
McMillan, W. (Belfast Celtic), 1946 v P, Sp (2)
McNally, J. B. (Luton T.), 1959 v Cz; 1961 v Sp; 1963 v Ic (3)
Madden, O. (Cork), 1936 v H (1)
Maguire, J. (Shamrock R.), 1929 v Bel (1)
Malone, G. (Shelbourne), 1949 v Bel (1)
Mancini, T. J. (QPR), 1974 v Pol, Br, U, Ch; (Arsenal), 1975 v USSR (5)
Martin, C. (Bo'ness), 1927 v I (1)
Martin, C. J. (Glentoran), 1946 v P (sub), Sp; 1947 v E; (Leeds U.), 1947 v Sp; 1948 v P, Sp; (Aston Villa), 1949 v Sw, Bel, P, Se, Sp; 1950 v Fi, E, Fi, Se, Bel; 1951 v Arg; 1952 v WG, A, Sp; 1954 v F (2), L; 1955 v N, Ho, N, WG; 1956 v Y, Sp, Ho (30)

Martin, M. P. (Bohemians), 1972 v A, Iran, Ec, Ch, P; 1973 v USSR; (Manchester U.), 1973 v USSR, Pol, F, N; 1974 v Pol, Br, U, Ch; 1975 v USSR, T, Sw, USSR, Sw; (with W.B.A.) 1976 v T, N, Pol (22)

Meagan, M. K. (Everton), 1961 v S; 1962 v A; 1963 v Ic; 1964 v Sp; (Huddersfield T.), 1965 v Bel; 1966 v Sp (2), A, Bel, 1967 v Sp, T, Sp, T, Cz; 1968 v Cz, Pol; (Drogheda), 1970 v S (17)

Meehan, P. (Drumcondra), 1934 v Ho (1)

Monahan, P. (Sligo R.), 1935 v Sw, G (2)

Mooney, J. (Shamrock R.), 1965 v Pol, Bel (2)

Moore, P. (Shamrock R.), 1931 v Sp; 1932 v Ho; (Aberdeen), 1934 v Bel; Ho; 1935 v H, G, (Shamrock R.), 1936 v Ho; 1937 v G, H (9)

Moroney, T. (West Ham U,), 1948 v Sp; 1949 v P, Se, Sp; 1950 v Fi, E, Fi, Bel; 1951 v N (2); 1952 v WG; 1954 v F (12)

Moulson, C. (Lincoln C.), 1936 v H. L; (Notts Co.), 1937 v H, Sw, F (5)

Moulson, G. B. (Lincoln C.), 1948 v P, Sp; 1949 v Sw (3)

Muldoon, T. (Aston Villa), 1927 v I (1)

Mulligan, P. M. (Shamrock R.), 1969 v Cz, D, H; 1970 v S, Cz, D; (Chelsea) 1970 v H, Pol, WG; 1971 v Pol, Se, I; 1972 v A, Iran, Ec, Ch, P; 1973 v F, USSR, Pol, F, N; 1974 v Pol, Br, U, Ch; 1975 v USSR, T, Sw, USSR, Sw; (with W.B.A.) 1976 v T, N, Pol (34)

Munroe, L. (Shamrock R.), 1954 v L (1)

Murphy, A. (Clyde), 1956 v Y (1)

Murray, T. (Dundalk), 1950 v Bel (1)

Newman, W. (Shelbourne), 1969 v D (1)

Nolan, R. (Shamrock R.), 1957 v D, WG, E; 1958 v Pol; 1960 v Ch, WG, Se; 1962 v Cz (2); 1963 v Ic (10)

O'Brien, M. T. (Derby Co.), 1927 v I; (Walsall), 1929 v Bel; (Norwick C.), 1930 v Bel; (Watford), 1932 v Ho (4)

O'Brien, R. (Notts Co.), 1976 v N, Pol (2)

O'Byrne, L. B. (Shamrock R.), 1949 v Bel (1)

O'Connell, A. (Dundalk), 1967 v Sp; (Bohemians), 1971 v Pol (sub) (2)

O'Connor, T. (Shamrock R.), 1950 v Fi, E, Fi, Se (4)

O'Connor, T. (Fulham), 1968 v Cz; (Dundalk), 1972 v A, Iran (sub), Ec (sub), Ch; (Bohemians), 1973 v F (sub), Pol (sub) (7)

O'Driscoll, J. F. (Swansea T.), 1949 v Sw, Bel, Se (3)

O'Farrell, F. (West Ham U.), 1952 v A; 1953 v A; 1954 v F; 1955 v Ho, N; 1956 v Y, Ho; (Preston N.E.), 1958 v D; 1959 v Cz (9)

O'Flanagan, K. P. (Bohemians), 1938 v N, Cz, Pol; H (2), G; (Arsenal), 1947 v E, Sp, P (10)

O'Flanagan, M. (Bohemians), 1947 v E (1)

O'Kane, P. (Bohemians), 1935 v H, Sw, G (3)

O'Keefe, T. (Cork), 1934 v Bel; (Waterford), 1938 v Cz, Pol (3)

O'Mahoney, M. T. (Bristol R.), 1938 v Cz, Pol; 1939 v Sw, Pol, H, G (6)

O'Neill, F. S. (Shamrock R.), 1962 v Cz (2); 1965 v Pol, Bel, Sp; 1966 v Sp (2), WG, A; 1967 v Sp, T, Sp, T; 1969 v Pol, A, D, Cz, D (sub), H (sub); 1972 v A (20)

O'Neill, J. (Everton), 1952 v Sp; 1953 v F, A; 1954 v F, L, F; 1955 v N, Ho, N, WG; 1956 v Y, Sp; 1957 v D; 1958 v M; 1959 v Pol, Cz (2) (17)

O'Neill, J. (Preston N.E.), 1961 v W (1)

O'Neill, W. (Dundalk), 1936 v Ho, Sw, H, L; 1937 v G, H, Sw, F; 1938 v N; 1939 v H, G (11)

O'Reilly, J. (Brideville), 1932 v Ho; (Aberdeen), 1934 v Bel, Ho; (Brideville), 1936 v Ho; Sw, H, L, (St. James' Gate), 1937 v G, H, Sw, F; 1938 v N (2), Cz, Pol; 1939 v Sw, Pol, H (2), G (20)

O'Reilly, J. (Cork U.), 1946 v P, Sp (2)

Peyton, N. (Shamrock R.), 1957 v WG; (Leeds U.), 1960 v WG, Se (sub); 1961 v W; 1963 v Ic, S (6)

Reid, C. (Brideville)k, 1931 v Sp (1)

Richardson, D. J. (Shamrock R.), 1972 v A (sub); (Gillingham), 1973 v N (sub) (2)

Rigby, A. (St. James' Gate), 1935 v H, Sw, G (3)

Ringstead, A. (Sheffield U.), 1951 v Arg, N; 1952 v WG (2), A, Sp; 1953 v A; 1954 v F; 1955 v N; 1956 v Y, Sp, Ho; 1957 v E (2)0; 1958 v D, Pol, A;1 959 v Pol, Cz (2) (20)

Robinson, J. (Bohemians), 1928 v Bel; (Dolphin), 1931 v Sp (2)

Roche, P. J. (Shelbourne), 1972 v A; (Manchester U.), 1975 v USSR, T, Sw, USSR, Sw; 1976 v T (7)

Rogers, E. (Blackburn R.), 1968 v Cz, Pol; 1969 v Pol, A, D, Cz, D, H; 1970 v S, D, H; 1971 v I (2), A; (Charlton Ath.), 1972 v Iran, Ec, Ch, P; 1973 v USSR (19)

Ryan, R. A. (W.B.A.), 1950 v Se, Bel; 1951 v N, Arg N; 1952 v WG (2), A, Sp; 1953 v F, A; 1954 v F, L, F; 1955 v N; (Derby Co.), 1956 v Sp (16)

Saward, P. (Millwall), 1954 v L; (Aston Villa), 1957 v E (2); 1958 v D, Pol, A; 1959 v Pol, Cz; 1960 v Se, Ch, WG, Se; 1961 v W, N; (Huddersfield T.), 1961 v S; 1962 v A; 1963 v Ic (2) (18)

Scannell, T. (Southend U.), 1954 v L (1)

Sloan, J. W. (Arsenal), 1946 v P, Sp (2)

Smyth, M. (Shamrock R.), 1969 v Pol (sub) (1)

Squires, J. (Shelbourne), 1934 v Ho (1)

Stevenson, A. E. (Dolphin), 1932 v Ho; (Everton), 1947 v E, Sp, P; 1948 v P, Sp; 1949 v Sw (7)

Strahan, F. (Shelbourne), 1964 v Pol, N, E; 1965 v Pol; 1966 v WG (5)

Sullivan, J. (Fordsons), 1928 v Bel (1)

Swan, M. M. G. (Drumcondra), 1960 v Se (sub) (1)

Thomas, P. (Waterford), 1974 v Pol, Br (2)

Traynor, T. J. (Southampton), 1954 v L; 1962 v A; 1963 v Ic (2), S; 1964 v A (2), Sp (8)

Treacy, R. C. P. (W.B.A.), 1966 v WG; 1967 v Sp, Cz; 1968 v Cz; (Chartlon Ath.), 1968 v Pol; 1969 v Pol, Cz, D; 1970 v S, D, H (sub), Pol (sub), WG (sub); 1971 v Pol, Se (sub), Se, I, A; (Swindon T.), 1972 v Iran, Ec, Ch, P; 1973 v USSR, F, USSR, Pol, F, N; 1974 v Pol; (Preston N.E.), 1974 v Br; 1975 v USSR, Sw (2); 1976 v T, N (sub), Pol (sub) (36)

Tuohy, L. (Shamrock R.), 1956 v Y; 1959 v Cz (2); (Newcastle U.), 1962 v A; 1963 v Ic (2); (Shamrock R.), 1964 v A; 1965 v Bel (8)

Turner, A. (Celtic), 1963 v S; 1964 v Sp (2)

Turner, C. J. (Southend U.), 1936 v Sw; 1937 v G, H, Sw, F; (West Ham U.), 1938 v N (2), Cz, Pol; 1939 v H (10)

Vernon, J. (Belfast Celtic), 1946 v P, Sp (2)

Walsh, D. J. (W.B.A.), 1946 v P, Sp; 1947 v Sp, P; 1948 v P, Sp; 1949 v Sw, P, Se, Sp; 1950 v E, Fi,

Se; 1951 v N; (Aston Villa), v Arg, N; 1952
  v Sp; 1953 v A; 1954 v F (2) (20)
Walsh, M. (Blackpool), 1976 v N, Pol (2)
Walsh, W. (Manchester C.), 1947 v E, Sp, P; 1948 v
  P, Sp; 1949 v Bel, 1950 v E; Se, Bel (9)
Watters, F. (Shelbourne), 1926 v I (1)
Weir, E. (Clyde), 1939 v H (2), G (2)

Whelan, R. (St. Patrick's Ath.), 1964 v A, E (sub)
  (2)
Whelan, W. (Manchester U.), 1956 v Ho; 1957 v
  D, E (2) (4)
White, J. J. (Bohemians), 1928 v Bel (1)
Whittaker, R. (Chelsea), 1959 v Cz (1)
Williams, J. (Shamrock R.), 1938 v N (1)

British International Teams since 1970

ENGLAND

1970 Netherlands	1970 Belgium	1970 Wales	1970 N. Ireland	1970 Scotland
1 Banks, G.	1 Banks, G.	1 Banks, G.	1 Banks, G.	1 Banks, G.
2 Newton, K.	2 Wright, T.	2 Wright, T.	2 Newton, K. (Bell)	2 Newton, K.
3 Cooper	3 Cooper	3 Hughes, E.	3 Hughes, E.	3 Hughes, E.
4 Peters	4 Moore	4 Mullery	4 Mullery	4 Stiles
5 Charlton, J.	5 Labone	5 Labone	5 Moore	5 Labone
6 Hunter	6 Hughes, E.	6 Moore	6 Stiles	6 Moore
7 Lee, F. (Mullery)	7 Lee, F.	7 Lee, F.	7 Coates	7 Thompson, P. (Mullery)
8 Bell	8 Ball	8 Ball	8 Kidd	8 Ball
9 Jones, M. (Hurst, G.)	9 Osgood	9 Charlton, R.	9 Charlton, R.	9 Astle
10 Charlton, R.	10 Hurst, G.	10 Hurst, G.	10 Hurst, G.	10 Hurst, G.
11 Moore, I.	11 Peters	11 Peters	11 Peters	11 Peters
Wembley Jan 14: 0-0	Brussels Feb 25: 3-1 *Ball 2, Hurst, G.*	Cardiff Spril 18: 1-1 *Lee, F.*	Wembley April 21: 3-1 *Peters, Hurst, G. Charlton, R.*	Glasgow April 25: 0-0

1970 Colombia	1970 Ecuador	1970 Rumania†	1970 Brazil†	1970 Czechoslovakia†
1 Banks, G.	1 Banks, G.	1 Banks, G.	1 Banks, G.	1 Banks, G.
2 Newton, K.	2 Newton, K.	2 Newton, K. (Wright, T.)	2 Wright, T.	2 Newton, K.
3 Cooper	3 Cooper	3 Cooper	3 Cooper	3 Cooper
4 Mullery	4 Mullery	4 Mullery	4 Mullery	4 Mullery
5 Labone	5 Labone	5 Labone	5 Labone	5 Charlton, J.
6 Moore	6 Moore	6 Moore	6 Moore	6 Moore
7 Lee, F.	7 Lee, F. (Kidd)	7 Lee, F. (Osgood)	7 Lee, F. (Astle)	7 Bell
8 Ball	8 Ball	8 Ball	8 Ball	8 Charlton, R. (Ball)
9 Charlton, R.	9 Charlton, R.	9 Charlton, R.	9 Charlton, R. (Bell)	9 Astle (Osgood)
10 Hurst, G.	10 Hurst, G.	10 Hurst, G.	10 Hurst, G.	10 Clarke, A.
11 Peters	11 Peters	11 Peters	11 Peters	11 Peters
Bogota May 20: 4-0 *Peters 2 Charlton, R., Ball*	Quito May 24: 2-0 *Lee, F., Kidd*	Guadalajara June 2: 1-0 *Hurst, G.*	Guadalajara June 7: 0-1	Guadalajara June 11: 1-0 *Clarke (pen.)*

1970 W. Germany†	1970 E. Germany	1971 Malta	1971 Greece	1971 Malta
1 Bonetti	1 Shilton	1 Banks, G.	1 Banks, G.	1 Banks, G.
2 Newton, K.	2 Hughes	2 Reaney	2 Storey	2 Lawler
3 Cooper	3 Cooper	3 Cooper	3 Hughes	3 Cooper
4 Mullery	4 Mullery	4 Mullery	4 Mullery	4 Moore
5 Labone	5 Sadler	5 McFarland	5 McFarland	5 McFarland
6 Moore	6 Moore	6 Hunter	6 Moore	6 Hughes
7 Lee, F.	7 Lee, F.	7 Ball	7 Lee, F.	7 Lee, F.
8 Ball	8 Ball	8 Chivers	8 Ball (Coates)	8 Coates
9 Charlton, R. (Bell)	9 Hurst, G.	9 Royle	9 Chivers	9 Chivers
10 Hurst, G.	10 Clarke, A.	10 Harvey	10 Hurst, G.	10 Clarke
11 Peters (Hunter)	11 Peters	11 Peters	11 Peters	11 Peters (Ball)
Leon June 14: 2-3 (after extra time) *Mullery, Peters*	Wembley Nov 25: 3-1 *Lee, F. Peters, Clarke*	Valletta Feb 3: 1-0 *Peters*	Wembley April 21: 3-0 *Chivers, Hurst, G. Lee, F.*	Wembley May 12: 5-0 *Chivers 2, Lee Clarke (pen.) Lawler*

1971 N. Ireland	1971 Wales	1971 Scotland	1971 Switzerland	1971 Switzerland
1 Banks, G.	1 Shilton	1 Banks, G.	1 Banks, G.	1 Shilton
2 Madeley	2 Lawler	2 Lawler	2 Lawler	2 Madeley
3 Cooper	3 Cooper	3 Cooper	3 Cooper	3 Cooper
4 Storey	4 Smith	4 Storey	4 Mullery	4 Storey
5 McFarland	5 Lloyd	5 McFarland	5 McFarland	5 Lloyd
6 Moore	6 Hughes	6 Moore	6 Moore	6 Moore
7 Lee, F.	7 Lee, F.	7 Lee, F. (Clarke)	7 Lee, F.	7 Summerbee (Chivers)
8 Ball	8 Coates	8 Ball	8 Madeley	8 Ball
9 Chivers	9 Hurst, G.	9 Chivers	9 Chivers	9 Hurst, G.
10 Clarke	10 Brown, A.	10 Hurst, G.	10 Hurst, G. (Radford)	10 Lee, F. (Marsh)
11 Peters	11 Peters	11 Peters	11 Peters	11 Hughes
Belfast May 15: 1-0 Clarke	Wembley May 19: 0-0	Wembley May 22: 3-1 Peters Chivers 2	Basle Oct 13: 3-2 Hurst, Chivers Weibel (o.g.)	Wembley Nov 10: 1-1 Summerbee

1971 Greece	1972 W. Germany	1972 W. Germany	1972 Wales	1972 N. Ireland
1 Banks, G.	1 Banks, G.	1 Banks, G.	1 Banks, G.	1 Shilton
2 Madeley	2 Madeley	2 Madeley	2 Madeley	2 Todd
3 Hughes	3 Hughes	3 Hughes	3 Hughes	3 Hughes
4 Bell	4 Bell	4 Storey	4 Storey	4 Storey
5 McFarland	5 Moore	5 McFarland	5 McFarland	5 Lloyd
6 Moore	6 Hunter	6 Moore	6 Moore	6 Hunter
7 Lee, F.	7 Lee, F.	7 Ball	7 Summerbee	7 Summerbee
8 Ball	8 Ball	8 Bell	8 Bell	8 Bell
9 Chivers	9 Chivers	9 Chivers	9 Macdonald	9 Macdonald (Chivers)
10 Hurst, G.	10 Hurst, G. (Marsh)	10 Marsh (Summerbee)	10 Marsh	10 Marsh
11 Peters	11 Peters	11 Hunter (Peters)	11 Hunter	11 Currie (Peters)
Athens Dec 1: 2-0 Hurst, Chivers	Wembley April 29: 1-3 Lee, F.	Berlin May 13: 0-0	Cardiff May 20: 3-0 Hughes, Bell, Marsh	Wembley May 23: 0-1

1972 Scotland	1972 Yugoslavia	1972 Wales	1973 Wales	1973 Scotland
1 Banks, G.	1 Shilton	1 Clemence	1 Clemence	1 Shilton
2 Madeley	2 Mills	2 Storey	2 Storey	2 Storey
3 Hughes	3 Lampard	3 Hughes	3 Hughes	3 Hughes
4 Storey	4 Storey	4 Hunter	4 Hunter	4 Bell
5 McFarland	5 Blockley	5 McFarland	5 McFarland	5 Madeley
6 Moore	6 Moore	6 Moore	6 Moore	6 Moore
7 Ball	7 Ball	7 Keegan	7 Keegan	7 Ball
8 Bell	8 Channon	8 Chivers	8 Bell	8 Channon
9 Chivers	9 Royle	9 Marsh	9 Chivers	9 Chivers
10 Marsh (Macdonald)	10 Bell	10 Bell	10 Marsh	10 Clarke
11 Hunter	11 Marsh	11 Ball	11 Ball	11 Peters
Hampden May 27: 1-0 Ball	Wembley Oct 11: 1-1 Royle	Cardiff Nov 15: 1-0 Bell	Wembley Jan. 24: 1-1 Hunter	Glasgow Feb 14: 5-0 Lorimer (o.g.) Clarke 2 Channon, Chivers

1973 N. Ireland	1973 Wales	1973 Scotland	1973 Czechoslovakia	1973 Poland
1 Shilton	1 Shilton	1 Shilton	1 Shilton	1 Shilton
2 Storey	2 Storey	2 Storey	2 Madeley	2 Madeley
3 Nish	3 Hughes	3 Hughes	3 Storey	3 Hughes
4 Bell	4 Bell	4 Bell	4 Bell	4 Storey
5 McFarland	5 McFarland	5 McFarland	5 McFarland	5 McFarland
6 Moore	6 Moore	6 Moore	6 Moore	6 Moore
7 Ball	7 Ball	7 Ball	7 Ball	7 Ball
8 Channon	8 Channon	8 Channon	8 Channon	8 Bell
9 Chivers	9 Chivers	9 Chivers	9 Chivers	9 Chivers
10 Richards	10 Clarke	10 Clarke, A.	10 Clarke, A.	10 Clarke, A.
11 Peters	11 Peters	11 Peters	11 Peters	11 Peters
Liverpool May 12: 2-1 *Chivers 2*	Wembley May 15: 3-0 *Chivers, Channon Peters*	Wembley May 19: 1-0 *Peters*	Prague May 27: 1-1 *Clarke*	Chorzow June 6: 0-2

1973 USSR	1973 Italy	1973 Austria	1973 Poland	1973 Italy
1 Shilton	1 Shilton	1 Shilton	1 Shilton	1 Shilton
2 Madeley	2 Madeley	2 Madeley	2 Madeley	2 Madeley
3 Hughes	3 Hughes	3 Hughes	3 Hughes	3 Hughes
4 Storey	4 Storey	4 Bell	4 Bell	4 Bell
5 McFarland	5 McFarland	5 McFarland	5 McFarland	5 McFarland
6 Moore	6 Moore	6 Hunter	6 Hunter	6 Moore
7 Currie	7 Currie	7 Currie	7 Currie	7 Currie
8 Channon (Summerbee)	8 Channon	8 Channon	8 Channon	8 Channon
9 Chivers	9 Chivers	9 Chivers	9 Chivers (Hector)	9 Osgood
10 Clarke, A. (Macdonald)	10 Clarke, A.	10 Clarke	10 Clarke	10 Clarke (Hector)
11 Peters (Hunter)	11 Peters	11 Peters	11 Peters	11 Peters
Moscow June 10: 2-1 *Chivers, Khurtislava (o.g.)*	Turin June 14: 0-2	Wembley Sept 26: 7-0 *Channon 2, Clark 2, Chivers, Currie, Bell*	Wembley Oct 17: 1-1 *Clarke, pen*	Wembley Nov 14: 0-1

1974 Portugal	1974 Wales	1974 N. Ireland	1974 Scotland	1974 Argentina
1 Parkes	1 Shilton	1 Shilton	1 Shilton	1 Shilton
2 Nish	2 Nish	2 Nish	2 Nish	2 Hughes
3 Pejic	3 Pejic	3 Pejic	3 Pejic	3 Lindsay
4 Dobson	4 Hughes	4 Hughes	4 Hughes	4 Todd
5 Watson	5 McFarland	5 McFarland (Hunter)	5 Hunter (Watson)	5 Watson
6 Todd	6 Todd	6 Todd	6 Todd	6 Bell
7 Bowles	7 Keegan	7 Keegan	7 Channon	7 Keegan
8 Channon	8 Bell	8 Weller	8 Bell	8 Channon
9 Macdonald (Ball)	9 Channon	9 Channon	9 Worthington (Macdonald)	9 Worthington
10 Brooking	10 Weller	10 Bell	10 Weller	10 Weller
11 Peters	11 Bowles	11 Bowles (Worthington)	11 Peters	11 Brooking
Lisbon April 3: 0-0	Cardiff May 11: 2-0 *Bowles, Keegan*	Wembley May 15: 1-0 *Weller*	Hampden Park May 18: 0-2	Wembley May 22: 2-2 *Channon, Worthington*

716

1974 East Germany	1974 Bulgaria	1974 Yugoslavia	1974 Czechoslovakia	1974 Portugal
1 Clemence	1 Clemence	1 Clemence	1 Clemence	1 Clemence
2 Hughes	2 Hughes	2 Hughes	2 Madeley	2 Madeley
3 Lindsay	3 Todd	3 Lindsay	3 Hughes	3 Watson
4 Todd	4 Watson	4 Todd	4 Dobson (Brooking)	4 Hughes
5 Watson	5 Lindsay	5 Watson	5 Watson	5 Cooper (Todd)
6 Dobson	6 Dobson	6 Dobson	6 Hunter	6 Brooking
7 Keegan	7 Brooking	7 Keegan	7 Bell	7 Francis
8 Channon	8 Bell	8 Channon	8 Francis	8 Bell
9 Worthington	9 Keegan	9 Worthington (Macdonald)	9 Worthington (Thomas)	9 Thomas
10 Bell	10 Channon	10 Bell	10 Channon	10 Channon
11 Brooking	11 Worthington	11 Brooking	11 Keegan	11 Clarke (Worthington)
Leipzig May 29: 1-1 *Channon*	Sofia June 1: 1-0 *Worthington*	Belgrade June 5: 2-2 *Channon, Keegan*	Wembley Oct. 30: 3-0 *Channon, Bell 2.*	Wembley Nov. 20: 0-0

1975 West Germany	1975 Cyprus	1975 Cyprus	1975 N. Ireland	1975 Wales
1 Clemence	1 Shilton	1 Clemence	1 Clemence	1 Clemence
2 Whitworth	2 Madeley	2 Whitworth	2 Whitworth	2 Whitworth
3 Gillard	3 Watson	3 Beattie (Hughes)	3 Hughes	3 Gillard
4 Bell	4 Todd	4 Hudson	4 Bell	4 Francis
5 Watson	5 Beattie	5 Todd	5 Watson	5 Watson
6 Todd	6 Bell	6 Bell	6 Todd	6 Todd
7 Ball	7 Ball	7 Thomas	7 Ball	7 Ball
8 Macdonald	8 Hudson	8 Ball	8 Viljoen	8 Channon (Little)
9 Channon	9 Channon (Thomas)	9 Channon	9 Macdonald (Channon)	9 Johnson
10 Hudson	10 Macdonald	10 Macdonald	10 Keegan	10 Viljoen
11 Keegan	11 Keegan	11 Keegan (Tueart)	11 Tueart	11 Thomas
Wembley March 12: 2-0 *Bell, Macdonald*	Wembley April 16: 5-0 *Macdonald 5*	Limassol May 11: 1-0 *Keegan*	Belfast May 17: 0-0	Wembley May 21: 2-2 *Johnson 2*

1975 Scotland
1 Clemence
2 Whitworth
3 Beattie
4 Bell
5 Watson
6 Todd
7 Ball
8 Channon
9 Johnson
10 Francis
11 Keegan (Thomas)
Wembley May 24: 5-1 *Francis 2, Beattie, Bell, Johnson*

NORTHERN IRELAND

1970 Scotland	1970 England	1970 Wales	1970 Spain	1971 Cyprus
1 Jennings	1 Jennings	1 McFaul	1 McFaul	1 Jennings
2 Craig	2 Craig	2 Craig	2 Craig	2 Craig
3 Clements	3 Clements	3 Nelson	3 Nelson	3 Nelson
4 Todd (O'Kane)	4 O'Kane	4 O'Kane	4 Jackson	4 Hunter
5 Neill	5 Neill	5 Neill	5 Neill	5 Neill
6 Nicholson	6 Nicholson	6 Nicholson	6 O'Kane	6 Todd
7 Campbell (Dickson)	7 McMordie	7 Campbell (O'Doherty)	7 Sloan	7 Hamilton
8 Lutton	8 Best	8 Best	8 Best	8 McMordie
9 Dougan	9 Dougan	9 Dickson	9 Dougan (Todd)	9 Dougan
10 McMordie	10 O'Doherty (Nelson)	10 McMordie	10 Harkin	10 Nicholson
11 Best	11 Lutton (Cowan)	11 Clements	11 Clements	11 Best
Belfast April 18: 0-1	Wembley April 21: 1-3 *Best*	Swansea April 25: 0-1	Seville Nov 11: 0-3	Nicosia Feb 3: 3-0 *Nicholson, Dougan Best*

1971 Cyprus	1971 England	1971 Scotland	1971 Wales	1971 USSR
1 Jennings	1 Jennings	1 Jennings	1 Jennings	1 McFaul
2 Craig	2 Rice	2 Rice	2 Rice	2 Craig (Hamilton)
3 Clements	3 Nelson	3 Nelson	3 Nelson	3 Neill
4 Harvey	4 O'Kane	4 O'Kane	4 O'Kane	4 Hunter
5 Hunter	5 Hunter	5 Hunter	5 Hunter	5 Nelson
6 Todd (Watson)	6 Nicholson	6 Nicholson	6 Nicholson (Harvey)	6 Hegan
7 Hamilton	7 Hamilton	7 Hamilton	7 Hamilton	7 Clements
8 McMordie	8 McMordie (Cassidy)	8 McMordie (Craig)	^ McMordie	8 Nicholson
9 Dougan	9 Dougan	9 Dougan	9 Dougan	9 O'Kane
10 Nicholson	10 Clements	10 Clements	10 Clements	10 Dougan
11 Best	11 Best	11 Best	11 Best	11 Best
Belfast April 21: 5-0 *Dougan, Best* 3 *Nicholson*	Belfast May 15: 0-1	Hampden May 18: 1-0 *opponent o.g.*	Belfast May 22: 1-0 *Hamilton*	Moscow Sept 22: 0-1

1971 USSR	1972 Spain	1972 Scotland	1972 England	1972 Wales
1 Jennings	1 Jennings	1 Jennings	1 Jennings	1 Jennings
2 Rice	2 Rice	2 Rice	2 Rice	2 Rice
3 Nelson	3 Nelson	3 Nelson	3 Nelson	3 Nelson
4 Nicholson	4 Neill	4 Neill	4 Neill	4 Neill
5 Hunter	5 Hunter	5 Hunter	5 Hunter	5 Hunter
6 O'Kane	6 Clements	6 Clements (Craig)	6 Clements	6 Clements
7 McMordie	7 Hamilton (O'Neill)	7 Hegan	7 Hegan	7 Hegan
8 Hamilton (O'Neill)	8 McMordie	8 McMordie (McIlroy)	8 McMordie	8 McMordie
9 Neill	9 Morgan	9 Dougan	9 Dougan	9 Dougan (O'Neill)
10 Dougan (Cassidy)	10 McIlroy	10 Irvine	10 Irvine	10 Irvine
11 Clements	11 Best	11 Jackson	11 Jackson	11 Jackson
Belfast Oct 13: 1-1 *Nicholson*	Hull Feb 16: 1-1 *Morgan*	Hampden May 20: 0-2	Wembley May 23: 1-0 *Neill*	Wrexham May 27: 0-0

1972 Bulgaria	1973 Cyprus	1973 Portugal	1973 Cyprus	1973 England
1 Jennings	1 Jennings	1 Jennings	1 McFaul	1 Jennings
2 Rice	2 Rice	2 O'Kane	2 O'Kane	2 Rice
3 Nelson	3 Neill	3 Nelson	3 Hunter (Coyle)	3 Craig
4 Hunter	4 Hunter	4 Neill	4 Neill	4 Neill
5 Neill	5 Graig	5 Hunter	5 Craig	5 Hunter
6 Clements	6 Hegan	6 Clements	6 Hamilton (Lutton)	6 Clements
7 Hamilton (Morgan)	7 Clements	7 Hamilton	7 Jackson	7 Hamilton
8 Hegan	8 Hamilton	8 Coyle	8 Clements	8 Jackson
9 McMordie	9 Dickson	9 Morgan	9 Morgan	9 Morgan
10 Dougan	10 Dougan	10 Dickson	10 O'Neill	10 O'Neill
11 Best	11 Nelson	11 O'Neill	11 Anderson	11 Anderson
Sofia Oct 18: 0-3	Nicosia Feb 14: 0-1	Coventry Mar 28: 1-1 O'Neill	London May 8: 3-0 Morgan, Anderson 2	Liverpool May 12: 1-2 Clements, pen

1973 Scotland	1973 Wales	1973 Bulgaria	1973 Portugal	1974 Scotland
1 Jennings	1 Jennings	1 McFaul	1 Jennings	1 Jennings
2 Rice	2 Rice	2 Rice	2 Rice	2 Rice
3 Craig	3 Craig	3 Craig	3 Craig	3 Nelson
4 Neill	4 Neill	4 O'Kane	4 Lutton	4 O'Kane
5 Hunter	5 Hunter	5 Hunter	5 O'Kane	5 Hunter
6 Clements	6 Clements	6 Clements	6 Clements	6 Clements
7 Hamilton	7 Hamilton (Lutton)	7 Hamilton	7 Jackson	7 Hamilton (Jackson)
8 Jackson	8 Jackson	8 Jackson (Coyle)	8 O'Neill	8 Cassidy
9 Morgan	9 Morgan	9 Morgan	9 Morgan	9 Morgan
10 O'Neill	10 O'Neill	10 Anderson	10 Anderson	10 McIlroy
11 Anderson (Lutton)	11 Anderson (Coyle)	11 O'Neill (Cassidy)	11 Best	11 McGrath
Glasgow May 16: 2-1 O'Neill, Anderson	Liverpool May 19: 1-0 Hamilton	Hillsborough Sept 26: 0-0	Lisbon Nov 14: 1-1 O'Kane	Hampden May 11: 1-0 Cassidy

1974 England	1974 Wales	1974 Norway	1974 Sweden	1975 Yugoslavia
1 Jennings	1 Jennings	1 Jennings	1 Jennings	1 Jennings
2 Rice	2 Rice	2 Rice	2 O'Kane	2 Rice
3 Nelson (Jackson)	3 Dowd	3 Craig (Dowd)	3 Nelson (Blair)	3 Nelson
4 O'Kane	4 O'Kane	4 O'Kane	4 Dowd	4 Nicholl
5 Hunter	5 Hunter	5 Hunter	5 Hunter	5 Hunter
6 Clements	6 Clements	6 Clements	6 Nicholl	6 Clements
7 Hamilton (O'Neill)	7 Hamilton (Jackson)	7 Hamilton	7 Jackson	7 Hamilton
8 Cassidy	8 Cassidy	8 Cassidy	8 O'Neill	8 O'Neill
9 Morgan	9 McIlroy	9 Finney	9 Morgan	9 Spence
10 McIlroy	10 McGrath	10 McIlroy	10 McIlroy	10 McIlroy
11 McGrath	11 O'Neill	11 McGrath (Jackson)	11 Hamilton	11 Jackson
Wembley May 15: 0-1	Wrexham May 18: 0-1	Oslo Sept 4: 1-2 Finney	Solna Oct 30: 2-0 O'Neill, Nicholl	Belfast March 16: 1-0 Hamilton

1975 England	1975 Scotland	1975 Wales
1 Jennings	1 Jennings	1 Jennings
2 Rice	2 Rice	2 Scott
3 O'Kane	3 O'Kane	3 Rice
4 Nicholl	4 Nicholl	4 Nicholl
5 Hunter	5 Hunter	5 Hunter
	(Blair)	
6 Clements	6 Clements	6 Clements
7 Hamilton	7 Finney	7 Blair
(Finney)		
8 O'Neill	8 O'Neill	8 Jackson
	(Anderson)	
9 Spence	9 Spence	9 Spence
10 McIlroy	10 McIlroy	10 McIlroy
11 Jackson	11 Jackson	11 Finney
Belfast	Hampden	Belfast
May 17: 0-0	May 20: 0-3	May 23: 1-0
		Finney

SCOTLAND

1970 N. Ireland	1970 Wales	1970 England	1970 Denmark	1971 Belgium
1 Clark	1 Cruickshank	1 Cruickshank	1 Cruickshank	1 Cruickshank
2 Hay	2 Callaghan	2 Gemmell	2 Hay (Jardine)	2 Hay
3 Dickson	3 Dickson	3 Dickson	3 Greig	3 Gemmell
4 McLintock	4 Greig	4 Greig	4 Stanton	4 Stanton (Green)
5 McKinnon	5 McKinnon	5 McKinnon	5 McKinnon	5 McKinnon
6 Moncur	6 Moncur	6 Moncur (Gilzean)	6 Moncur	6 Moncur
7 McLean	7 McLean (Lennox)	7 Johnstone	7 Johnstone	7 Gemmill
8 Carr	8 Hay	8 Hay	8 Carr	8 Greig
9 O'Hare	9 O'Hare	9 Stein	9 Stein	9 Stein (Forrest)
10 Gilzean (Stein)	10 Stein	10 O'Hare	10 O'Hare (Cormack)	10 O'Hare
11 Johnston	11 Carr	11 Carr	11 Johnston	11 Cooke
Belfast	Hampden	Hampden	Hampden	Liege
April 18: 1-0	April 22: 0-0	April 25: 0-0	Nov 11: 1-0	Feb 3: 0-3
O'Hare			*O'Hare*	

1971 Portugal	1971 Wales	1971 N. Ireland	1971 England	1971 Denmark
1 Clark	1 Clark	1 Clark	1 Clark	1 Clark
2 Hay	2 Hay	2 Hay	2 Greig	2 Munro
3 Brogan	3 Brogan	3 Brogan	3 Brogan	3 Dickson
4 Stanton (Green)	4 Bremner (Grieg)	4 Greig	4 Bremner	4 Stanton
5 McKinnon	5 McLintock	5 McLintock (Munro)	5 McLintock	5 McKinnon
6 Moncur	6 Moncur	6 Moncur	6 Moncur	6 Moncur
7 Henderson	7 Lorimer	7 Lorimer	7 Johnstone	7 McLean
8 McCalliog (Jarvie)	8 Robb	8 Green	8 Robb	8 Forsyth (Robb)
9 Robb	9 O'Hare	9 O'Hare (Jarvie)	9 Curran (Munro)	9 Stein
10 Cormack	10 Cormack	10 Curran	10 Green (Jarvie)	10 Curran
11 Gilzean	11 Gray	11 Gray	11 Cormack	11 Forrest (Scott)
Lisbon	Cardiff	Hampden	Wembley	Copenhagen
April 21: 0-2	May 15: 0-0	May 18: 0-1	May 22: 1-3	June 9: 0-1
			Curran	

1971 USSR	1971 Portugal	1971 Belgium	1971 Netherlands	1972 Peru
1 Clark	1 Wilson	1 Clark	1 Wilson	1 Hunter
2 Brownlie	2 Jardine	2 Jardine	2 Jardine	2 Brownlie
3 Dickson	3 Colquhoun (Buchan)	3 Hay	3 Hay	3 Donachie
4 Munroe	4 Stanton	4 Bremner	4 Bremner	4 Carr
5 McKinnon	5 Hay	5 Buchan	5 Colquhoun	5 Colquhoun
6 Stanton	6 Bremner	6 Stanton	6 Stanton	6 Moncur
7 Forrest	7 Cropley	7 Johnstone (Hansen)	7 Johnstone (O'Hare)	7 Morgan
8 Watson	8 Graham	8 Murray	8 Gemmill	8 Hartford
9 Stein (Curran)	9 Johnstone	9 O'Hare	9 Dalglish	9 O'Hare
10 Robb	10 O'Hare	10 Gray	10 Graham	10 Law
11 Scott	11 Gemmill	11 Cropley (Dalglish)	11 Gray (Cormack)	11 Gemmill
Moscow June 14: 0-1	Hampden Oct 13: 2-1 *O'Hare, Gemmill*	Aberdeen Nov 10: 1-0 *O'Hare*	Amsterdam Dec 1: 1-2 *Graham*	Hampden April 26: 2-0 *O'Hare, Law*

1972 N. Ireland	1972 Wales	1972 England	1972 Yugoslavia	1972 Czechoslovakia
1 Clark	1 Clark	1 Clark	1 Hunter	1 Clark
2 Brownlie	2 Stanton	2 Brownlie	2 Forsyth	2 Forsyth
3 Donachie	3 Buchan	3 Donachie (Green)	3 Buchan	3 Colquhoun
4 Bremner	4 Bremner	4 Bremner	4 Hansen	4 Buchan
5 McNeill	5 McNeill	5 McNeill	5 Donachie	5 Donachie
6 Moncur	6 Moncur	6 Moncur	6 Bremner	6 Bremner
7 Johnstone (Lorimer)	7 Lorimer	7 Gemmill (Johnstone)	7 Hartford	7 Graham
8 Gemmill	8 Green	8 Hartford	8 Graham	8 Law
9 O'Hare	9 O'Hare (Macari)	9 Lorimer	9 Morgan	9 Hartford
10 Law	10 Law	10 Macari	10 Law (Bone)	10 Morgan
11 Graham	11 Gemmill (Hartford)	11 Law	11 Macari	11 Macari
Hampden May 20: 2-0 *Law, Lorimer*	Hampden May 24: 1-0 *Lorimer*	Hampden May 27: 0-1	Belo Horizonte June 29: 2-2 *Macari 2*	Porto Alegre July 2: 0-0

1972 Brazil	1972 Denmark	1972 Denmark	1973 England	1973 Wales
1 Clark	1 Clark	1 Harvey	1 Clark	1 McCloy
2 Forsyth	2 Brownlie	2 Brownlie	2 Forsyth	2 McGrain
3 Colquhoun	3 Forsyth	3 Donachie	3 Donachie	3 Donachie
4 Buchan	4 Bremner	4 Bremner	4 Bremner	4 Graham
5 Donachie	5 Colquhoun	5 Colquhoun	5 Colquhoun	5 Holton
6 Bremner	6 Buchan	6 Buchan	6 Buchan	6 Johnstone
7 Graham	7 Lorimer	7 Lorimer	7 Lorimer	7 Dalglish (Macari)
8 Hartford	8 Macari (Dalglish)	8 Dalglish (Carr)	8 Dalglish	8 Stanton
9 Morgan	9 Bone	9 Harper	9 Macari	9 Parlane (Stein)
10 Law	10 Graham	10 Graham	10 Graham	10 Hay
11 Macari	11 Morgan	11 Morgan	11 Morgan (Stein)	11 Morgan
Rio July 5: 0-1	Copenhagen Oct 18: 4-1 *Macari, Bone, Harper, Morgan*	Glasgow Nov 15: 2-0 *Dalglish, Lorimer*	Glasgow Feb 14: 0-5	Wrexham May 12: 2-0 *Graham 2*

1973 N. Ireland	1973 England	1973 Switzerland	1973 Brazil	1973 Czechoslovakia
1 McCloy	1 Hunter	1 McCloy	1 McCloy	1 Hunter
2 McGrain	2 Jardine	2 Jardine	2 Jardine	2 Jardine
3 Donachie	3 McGrain	3 McGrain	3 McGrain	3 McGrain
4 Graham (Macari)	4 Bremner	4 Bremner	4 Bremner	4 Bremner
5 Holton	5 Holton	5 Holton	5 Holton	5 Holton
6 Johnstone	6 Johnstone	6 Johnstone	6 Johnstone	6 Connelly
7 Dalglish	7 Morgan	7 Dalglish	7 Morgan	7 Hay
8 Stanton (Bremner)	8 Macari (Jordan)	8 Hay	8 Hay	8 Law
9 Stein	9 Dalglish	9 Parlane	9 Parlane	9 Morgan
10 Hay	10 Hay	10 Connolly	10 Jordan	10 Dalglish (Jordan)
11 Morgan	11 Lorimer (Stein)	11 Morgan	11 Dalglish (Graham)	11 Hutchison
Glasgow May 16: 1-2 *Dalglish*	Wembley May 19: 0-1	Berne June 22: 0-1	Glasgow June 30: 0-1	Hampden Park Sept. 26: 2-1 *Holton, Jordan*

1973 Czechoslovakia	1973 West Germany	1974 West Germany	1974 N. Ireland	1974 Wales
1 Harvey	1 Harvey	1 Allan	1 Harvey	1 Harvey
2 Jardine	2 Jardine	2 Jardine	2 Jardine	2 Jardine
3 McGrain	3 McGrain	3 Schaedler	3 Donachie (Smith)	3 Hay
4 Forsyth	4 Bremner	4 Hay	4 Bremner	4 Bremner
5 Blackley	5 Holton	5 Buchan	5 Holton	5 Holton
6 Hay	6 Connelly	6 Stanton	6 Buchan	6 Buchan (McGrain)
7 Morgan	7 Morgan	7 Morgan	7 Morgan	7 Johnstone
8 Jordan	8 Smith (Lorimer)	8 Dalglish	8 Hay	8 Dalglish
9 Law (Ford)	9 Law (Jordan)	9 Law (Ford)	9 Law (Jordan)	9 Ford
10 Dalglish	10 Dalglish	10 Hutchinson	10 Dalglish	10 Jordan
11 Hutchison	11 Hutchison	11 Burns (Robinson)	11 Hutchison	11 Hutchison (Smith)
Bratislava Oct 17: 0-1	Hampden Nov 14: 1-1 *Holton*	Frankfurt March 27: 1-2 *Dalglish*	Hampden May 11: 0-1	Hampden May 14: 2-0 *Dalglish, Jardine*

1974 England	1974 Belgium	1974 Norway	1974* Zaire	1974* Brazil
1 Harvey	1 Harvey	1 Allan	1 Harvey	1 Harvey
2 Jardine	2 Jardine	2 Jardine	2 Jardine	2 Jardine
3 McGrain	3 McGrain	3 McGrain	3 McGrain	3 McGrain
4 Bremner	4 Bremner	4 Bremner	4 Bremner	4 Holton
5 Holton	5 McQueen	5 Holton	5 Holton	5 Buchan
6 Blackley	6 Blackley	6 Buchan	6 Blackley	6 Bremner
7 Lorimer	7 Johnstone (Morgan)	7 Johnstone (Dalglish)	7 Dalglish (Hutchison)	7 Hay
8 Johnstone	8 Dalglish (Hutchison)	8 Lorimer	8 Hay	8 Dalglish
9 Jordan	9 Jordan	9 Jordan	9 Lorimer	9 Morgan
10 Dalglish	10 Hay	10 Hay	10 Jordan	10 Jordan
11 Hay	11 Lorimer	11 Hutchison	11 Law	11 Lorimer
Hampden May 18: 2-0 *Jordan, Todd og*	Bruges June 1: 1-2 *Johnstone*	Oslo June 6: 2-1 *Jordan, Dalglish*	Dortmund June 14: 2-0 *Lorimer, Jordan*	Frankfurt June 18: 0-0

1974* Yugoslavia	1974 East Germany	1974 Spain	1975 Spain	1975 Sweden
1 Harvey	1 Harvey	1 Harvey	1 Harvey	1 Kennedy
2 Jardine	2 Jardine	2 Jardine	2 Jardine	2 Jardine
3 McGrain	3 Forsyth A.	3 Forsyth	3 McQueen	3 McGrain
4 Holton	4 Souness	4 McQueen	4 Buchan	4 Munro
5 Buchan	5 Holton (Burns)	5 Burns	5 McGrain	5 Jackson
6 Bremner	6 Buchan	6 Bremner	6 Bremner	6 Robinson
7 Dalglish (Hutchison)	7 Johnstone J.	7 Souness	7 Cooke	7 Dalglish
8 Hay	8 Dalglish (Johnstone D.)	8 Hutchison (Dalglish)	8 Hutchison	8 Souness (Johnstone D.)
9 Morgan	9 Deans	9 Johnstone	9 Dalglish	9 Parlane
10 Jordan	10 Jordan	10 Deans (Lorimer)	10 Jordan (Parlane)	10 MacDougall
11 Lorimer	11 Hutchison	11 Jordan	11 Burns (Wilson)	11 Macari (Hughes)
Frankfurt June 22: 1-1 *Jordan*	Hampden Park Oct 30: 3-0 *Hutchison (pen), Burns, Dalglish*	Hampden Nov 20: 1-2 *Bremner*	Valencia Feb 5: 1-1 *Jordan*	Gothenburg April 16: 1-1 *MacDougall*

1975 Portugal	1975 Wales	1975 N. Ireland	1975 England	1975 Rumania
1 Kennedy	1 Kennedy	1 Kennedy	1 Kennedy	1 Brown
2 Jardine	2 Jardine	2 Jardine (Forsyth)	2 Jardine	2 McGrain
3 McGrain	3 McGrain	3 McGrain	3 McGrain	3 Forsyth
4 Buchan (Jackson)	4 Jackson (Munro)	4 Munro	4 Munro	4 Munro
5 McQueen	5 McQueen	5 McQueen	5 McQueen	5 McQueen
6 Rioch	6 Rioch	6 Rioch	6 Rioch	6 Rioch (Hutchison)
7 Cooke (Macari)	7 Macari	7 Dalglish	7 Dalglish	7 Dalglish
8 Dalglish	8 Dalglish	8 Robinson (Conn)	8 Conn	8 Miller
9 Parlane	9 Parlane	9 Parlane	9 Parlane	9 Parlane
10 MacDougall	10 MacDougall	10 MacDougall	10 MacDougall (Macari)	10 Macari (Robinson)
11 Hutchison (Duncan)	11 Duncan	11 Duncan	11 Duncan (Hutchison)	11 Duncan
Hampden Park May 13: 1-0 *Artur o.g.*	Cardiff May 17: 2-2 *Jackson, Rioch*	Hampden May 20: 3-0 *MacDougall, Dalglish, Parlane*	Wembley May 24: 1-5 *Rioch, pen*	Bucharest June 1: 1-1 *McQueen*

WALES

1970 England	1970 Scotland	1970 N. Ireland	1970 Rumania	1971 Czechoslovakia
1 Millington	1 Millington	1 Millington	1 Sprake	1 Millington
2 Rodrigues	2 Rodrigues	2 Rodrigues	2 Rodrigues	2 Rodrigues
3 Thomas	3 Thomas	3 Thomas	3 Thomas	3 Thomas
4 Hennessey	4 Hennessey	4 Hennessey	4 Powell	4 Phillips
5 England	5 England	5 England	5 England	5 James
6 Powell	6 Powell	6 Powell	6 Hole	6 Walley
7 Kryzwicki	7 Krzywicki	7 Krzywicki	7 Krzywicki	7 Rees
8 Durban	8 Durban	8 Durban	8 Durban	8 Durban
9 Davies, R.	9 Davies, R.	9 Davies, R.	9 Davies, W.	9 Davies, R.
10 Moore	10 Moore	10 Moore	10 Moore	10 Davies, W.
11 Rees	11 Rees	11 Rees	11 Rees	11 Mahoney
Cardiff April 18: 1-1 *Krzywicki*	Hampden April 22: 0-0	Swansea April 25: 1-0 *Rees*	Cardiff Nov 11: 0-0	Swansea April 21: 1-3 *Davies, R.*

1971 Scotland	1971 England	1971 N. Ireland	1971 Finland	1971 Finland
1 Sprake	1 Sprake	1 Sprake	1 Millington	1 Sprake (Millington)
2 Rodrigues	2 Rodrigues	2 Rodrigues	2 Page	2 Rodrigues
3 Thomas	3 Thomas	3 Thomas	3 Derrett	3 Thomas
4 James	4 James	4 James	4 Durban	4 Roberts
5 Roberts	5 Roberts	5 Roberts	5 Roberts	5 England
6 Yorath	6 Yorath	6 Yorath	6 Mielczarek	6 Hennessey
7 Phillips	7 Phillips	7 Phillips (Rees)	7 Krzywicki	7 Evans
8 Durban	8 Durban	8 Durban	8 Jones, W.	8 Reece
9 Davies, R.	9 Davies, R.	9 Davies, R.	9 Rees	9 Toshack
10 Toshack	10 Toshack	10 Toshack	10 Toshack	10 Durban
11 Reece	11 Reece (Rees)	11 Reece	11 Reece	11 Hockey
Cardiff May 15: 0-0	Wembley May 18: 0-0	Belfast May 22: 0-1	Helsinki May 26: 1-0 Toshack	Swansea Oct 13: 3-0 Durban, Toshack, Reece

1971 Czechoslovakia	1971 Rumania	1972 England	1972 Scotland	1972 N. Ireland
1 Millington	1 Millington	1 Sprake	1 Sprake	1 Sprake
2 Rodrigues	2 Rodrigues	2 Rodrigues	2 Page	2 Page
3 Phillips	3 Thomas	3 Thomas	3 Thomas	3 Thomas
4 Burton	4 Phillips	4 Hennessey	4 Hennessey (James)	4 Yorath (Rodrigues)
5 Thomas	5 Williams	5 England	5 England	5 England
6 Yorath	6 Hockey	6 Roberts (Reece)	6 Yorath	6 Roberts
7 Hennessey (Rees)	7 James	7 Yorath	7 Durban	7 Durban
8 Durban	8 Hill (Davies, C.)	8 Davies, R.	8 Davies, W.	8 Davies, W.
9 Evans (Krzywicki)	9 Davies, R.	9 Davies, W.	9 Reece	9 Reece
10 Hill	10 Reece	10 Toshack	10 Davies, R.	10 Davies, R.
11 James	11 Rees	11 Durban	11 Phillips	11 Phillips
Prague Oct 27: 0-1	Bucharest Nov 24: 0-2	Cardiff May 20: 0-3	Hampden May 24: 0-1	Wrexham May 27: 0-0

1972 England	1973 England	1973 Poland	1973 Scotland	1973 England
1 Sprake	1 Sprake	1 Sprake	1 Sprake	1 Phillips
2 Rodrigues (Reece)	2 Rodrigues (Page)	2 Rodrigues	2 Rodrigues	2 Rodrigues
3 Thomas	3 Thomas	3 Thomas	3 Thomas	3 Thomas
4 Hennessey	4 Hockey	4 Roberts, D.	4 Hockey	4 Hockey
5 England	5 England	5 Roberts, J.	5 England	5 England (Roberts, D.)
6 Hockey	6 Roberts, J.	6 Hockey	6 Roberts, J.	6 Roberts, J.
7 Phillips	7 Evans	7 James	7 James	7 James
8 Mahoney	8 Mahoney	8 Yorath	8 Mahoney	8 Mahoney
9 Davies	9 Toshack	9 Toshack	9 Toshack	9 Toshack
10 Toshack	10 Yorath	10 Mahoney	10 Yorath (Davies, W.)	10 Page (Emanuel)
11 James	11 James	11 Evans	11 Evans (O'Sullivan)	11 Evans
Cardiff Nov 15: 0-1	Wembley Jan 24: 1-1 Toshack	Cardiff Mar 28: 2-0 James, Hockey	Wrexham May 12: 0-2	Wembley May 15: 0-3

1973 N. Ireland	1973 Poland	1974 England	1974 Scotland	1974 N. Ireland
1 Sprake	1 Sprake	1 Phillips	1 Sprake	1 Sprake
2 Rodrigues	2 Rodrigues	2 Roberts P. (Cartwright)	2 Thomas	2 Page
3 Thomas	3 Thomas	3 Thomas	3 Page	3 Thomas
4 Hockey (Emanuel)	4 Mahoney (Phillips)	4 Mahoney	4 Mahoney	4 Mahoney
5 Roberts, D.	5 England	5 Roberts, J.	5 Roberts, J.	5 Roberts J.
6 Roberts, J.	6 Roberts, J.	6 Roberts, D.	6 Roberts, D.	6 Reece
7 James	7 Evans (Reece)	7 Reece	7 Reece (Smallman)	7 Yorath
8 Mahoney	8 Yorath	8 Villars	8 Villars	8 James
9 Reece	9 Davies, W.	9 Davies, R. (Smallman)	9 Yorath	9 Smallman (Villars)
10 Page	10 Hockey	10 Yorath	10 Cartwright	10 Phillips
11 Davies, W.	11 James	11 James	11 James	11 Cartwright
Liverpool May 19: 0-1	Chorzow Sept. 26: 0-3	Cardiff May 11: 0-2	Hampden Park May 14: 0-2	Wrexham May 18: 1-0 *Smallman*

1974 Austria	1974 Hungary	1974 Luxembourg	1975 Hungary	1975 Luxembourg
1 Sprake	1 Sprake (Phillips, J.)	1 Sprake	1 Davies	1 Davies
2 Roberts, P.	2 Thomas	2 Thomas	2 Thomas	2 Page
3 Phillips	3 Roberts, P.	3 England	3 Page	3 Yorath
4 Roberts, D.	4 Mahoney	4 Roberts, P.	4 Phillips, L.	4 Thomas
5 Roberts, J.	5 England	5 Phillips, L.	5 Roberts, J.	5 Roberts, D.
6 Yorath	6 Phillips, L.	6 Mahoney (Flynn)	6 Yorath	6 Mahoney
7 Mahoney	7 Griffiths	7 Yorath	7 Mahoney	7 Phillips
8 Griffiths	8 Yorath	8 Griffiths	8 Griffiths	8 Griffiths (Flynn)
9 Reece	9 Reece	9 James	9 Reece (Smallman)	9 Reece
10 Toshack	10 Toshack	10 Reece	10 Toshack	10 Toshack
11 James	11 James	11 Toshack	11 James (Flynn)	11 James
Vienna Sept. 4: 1-2 *Griffiths*	Cardiff Oct. 30: 2-0 *Griffiths, Toshack*	Swansea Nov. 20: 5-0 *Toshack, England, Roberts, P., Griffiths, Yorath*	Budapest April 16: 2-1 *Toshack, Mahoney*	Luxembourg May 1: 3-1 *Reece, James 2 1 pen)*

1975 Scotland	1975 England	1975 N. Ireland
1 Davies	1 Davies	1 Davies
2 Thomas	2 Thomas	2 Thomas
3 Page	3 Page	3 Page
4 Yorath	4 Mahoney	4 Mahoney
5 Roberts, J.	5 Roberts, J.	5 Roberts, D.
6 Phillips	6 Phillips	6 Phillips
7 Mahoney	7 Griffiths	7 Griffiths
8 Flynn	8 Flynn	8 Flynn
9 Reece	9 Smallman (Showers)	9 Reece (Smallman)
10 Toshack	10 Toshack	10 Showers
11 James	11 James	11 James
Cardiff May 17: 2-2 *Toshack, Flynn*	Wembley May 21: 2-2 *Toshack, Griffiths*	Belfast May 23: 0-1

DENMARK 0, SCOTLAND 1 (in Fredrikshavn, September 2 1975, 5000)
Denmark: Kjaer; Hoejaard, Hansen Sorensen, Andersen, Lorentzen, Rasmussen, Christensen, Bastrup, Petersen, Skov.
Scotland: Rough; Smith, Gray (F), Narey, Young, McCluskey, Pearson, Bremner, Pettigrew, Craig (Joe), Craig (T).
Scorer: Scotland: Bremner

CZECHOSLOVAKIA 1, ENGLAND 1 (at Trnava, October 28 1975, 4000)
Czechoslovakia: Michalik; Lipnicky, Barmos, Sajenek, Hamrik, Stany, Herda, Kozak, Kroupa, Stambacher, Hajsky
England: Parkes; Gidman, Kennedy, Dodd, Lyons, Towers, Buckley, Mills, Boyer, Moores (Taylor), Armstrong.
Scorers: Czechoslovakia: Kroupa, England: Taylor.

SCOTLAND 4, DENMARK 1 (at Edinburgh, October 28 1975, 16,500)
Scotland: Rough; Smith, Gray F., Narey (Prentice), McDonald, Miller, Conn, Bremner, Pettigrew, Gray A., Craig T.
Denmark: Poulsen; Hoigaard, Hansen A., Sorensen, Steffensen, Lorentzen, Bertelsen, Nielsen, Hansen J., Arnesen, Skov.
Scorers: Scotland: Gray A. 3, Prentice. Denmark: Hansen.

ENGLAND 2, PORTUGAL 0 (at Selhurst Park, November 18 1975, 19,472)
England: Day; Gidman, Kennedy, Towers, Taylor T., Dodd, Wilkins, Francis (Mills), Johnson, Taylor P., Armstrong.
Portugal: Meireles; Ramalho, Francisco (Pereira), Mendes, Cardoso, Teixeira, Viera, Vital, Gomes, Abrev, Han.
Scorers: England: Taylor P., Mills.

SCOTLAND 4, RUMANIA 0 (at Falkirk, December 16 1975, 7000)
Scotland: Rough; Smith, Gray F., Bremner, Hansen, Miller, Conn, Pettigrew, Joe Craig, Craig T., Prentice.
Rumania: Morau (Stefan); Poratchi, Clocan, Bobrau, Purima, Maizer, Gligore, Muresan, Troi, Raducanu, Vrinceanu.
Scorers: Scotland: Pettigrew 2, Craig T. pen., Bremner.

WALES 2, SCOTLAND 3 (at Wrexham, February 4 1976, 2222)
Wales: Letheran; Dwyer, Jones, Johnson, Aizlewood, Williams (Aitken), Cartwright (Thomas), Lewis (Curtis), Deacy, O'Sullivan, Harris.
Scotland: Rough (Stewart); Brownlie, McLelland, Miller, McVie (Hansen A.), Craig T., Johnstone, Bremner, Pettigrew, Craig J., Prentice (Smith G.).
Scorers: Wales: Thomas, Deacy pen. Scotland: Craig T. Pettigrew 2.

HOLLAND 2, SCOTLAND 0 (at Breda, February 18 1976, 14,000)
Holland: Ruiter; Meutstege, Van Kraay, Rijsbergen, Everse, Willy van der Kerkhof, Peters, Arntz, Kist, Rene van der Kerkhof, Jansen (van Densen).
Scotland: Rough; Brownlie, McLelland, Miller, McVie, Souness, Burns, Bremner, Joe Craig, Dalglish, Johnstone.
Scorers: Holland: Van Deinsen, Kist.

HUNGARY 3, ENGLAND 0 (at Budapest, March 10 1976, 22,000)
Hungary: Gujdar; Paroczai, Balint, Rab, Lukacs, Nyilasi, Ebedli, Zombori (Csapo), Pusztai, Varadi (Fekete), Szabo.
England: Wallington; Gidman, Thompson, Dodd, Kennedy, Hudson, Towers, Francis G., Francis T. (Mills), Greenhoff, Johnson.
Scorers: Hungary: Nyilasi 2, Szabo.

ENGLAND 3, HUNGARY 1 (at Old Trafford, March 23 1976, 33,410)
England: Wallington; Nattrass, Kennedy, Greenhoff, Lock, Wilkins, R. Coppell, Case, Pearson, Paddon, Hill.
Hungary: Gujdar; Paroczai, Balint, Lukacs, Ebedli, Rab, Fekete (Kereki), Weimper, Kovacs (Zombori) Magyar, Pinter.
Scorers: England: Case, Hill, Paddon, Hungary: Fekete.

SCOTLAND 2, HOLLAND 0 (at Easter Road, March 24 1976, 32,593)
(After extra time)
Scotland: Rough; Brownlie, Gray F., Jackson, Miller, Craig, Bremner, Pettigrew, Jordan, Smith (Dickson), Johnstone.
Holland: Schellekens; Meustege, Lacroix (Van Rijnsoever), Balkenstein, Everse, Kila, Lubse, Hovenkamp (Van Marwijk), Kist, Nanninga, Van Deinsen.
Scorers: Scotland: Johnstone, Jackson.
(Holland won this European Championship tie on penalties.)

UNDER-23 INTERNATIONAL MATCHES 1954-76

ENGLAND v AUSTRIA

			England	Austria
1965	June	2	Vienna	0	0
1967	May	10	Hull	3	0

ENGLAND v BELGIUM

				England	Belgium
1962	Nov.	7	Plymouth	6	1
1969	May	25	Ostend	1	0

ENGLAND v BULGARIA

				England	Bulgaria
1957	May	19	Sofia	1	2
1957	Sept.	25	Chelsea	6	2
1967	June	3	Sofia	1	1
1970	Apr.	8	Plymouth	4	1

ENGLAND v CZECHOSLOVAKIA

				England	Czecho.
1957	May	30	Bratislava	2	0
1958	Oct.	15	Norwich	3	0
1965	April	7	Leeds	0	0
1965	May	29	Liberec	0	0
1973	Mar.	7	Villa Park	1	0
1973	June	1	Bratislava	0	3
1974	Oct.	29	Selhurst Park	3	1
1975	Oct.	28	Trnava	1	1

ENGLAND v DENMARK

				England	Denmark
1955	Sept.	28	Portsmouth	5	1
1956	Sept.	26	Copenhagen	3	0
1973	May	24	Naestved	1	1
1973	Nov.	13	Portsmouth	1	1

ENGLAND v FRANCE

				England	France
1956	Oct.	17	Bristol	0	0
1959	Mar.	18	Lyons	1	1
1959	Nov.	11	Sunderland	2	0
1964	April	8	Rouen	2	2
1965	Nov.	3	Norwich	3	0
1974	May	19	Valence	2	2

ENGLAND v EAST GERMANY

				England	East Germany
1960	May	15	Berlin	4	1
1972	Mar.	22	Bristol	0	1
1972	June	1	Leipzig	2	2

ENGLAND v WEST GERMANY

				England	West Germany
1959	May	10	Bochum	2	2
1961	Mar.	15	Tottenham	4	1
1963	Nov.	27	Liverpool	4	1
1965	May	25	Frieberg	0	1
1968	June	3	Kassel	1	0
1970	Oct.	14	Leicester	3	1

ENGLAND v GREECE

				England	Greece
1962	Nov.	28	Birmingham	5	0
1967	May	31	Athens	0	0

ENGLAND v HUNGARY

				England	Hungary
1959	Sept.	23	Liverpool	0	1
1964	May	13	Budapest	1	2
1968	May	1	Everton	4	0
1968	May	30	Budapest	0	1
1976	Mar.	10	Budapest	0	3
1976	Mar	23	Old Trafford	3	1

ENGLAND v ISRAEL

				England	Israel
1960	May	22	Tel Aviv	0	4
1961	Nov.	9	Leeds	7	1
1964	May	17	Tel Aviv	4	0

ENGLAND v ITALY

				England	Italy
1954	Jan.	20	Bologna	0	3
1955	Jan.	19	Chelsea	5	1
1959	May	7	Milan	3	0
1960	Nov.	2	Newcastle	1	1
1967	Dec.	20	Nottingham	1	0
1968	May	25	Trieste	1	1

ENGLAND v NETHERLANDS

				England	Netherlands
1960	Mar.	16	Sheffield	5	2
1961	Nov.	29	Rotterdam	5	2
1968	Nov.	13	Birmingham	2	2
1969	May	22	Deventer	1	2
1973	Jan.	2	Highbury	3	1
1973	May	29	Maastricht	0	1

ENGLAND v POLAND

				England	Poland
1958	Sept.	24	Sheffield	4	1
1960	May	18	Warsaw	3	2
1972	June	4	Warsaw	3	0

ENGLAND v PORTUGAL

				England	Portugal
1969	April	16	Coventry	4	0
1969	May	28	Funchal	1	1
1973	Oct.	16	Plymouth	0	0
1974	Nov.	19	Lisbon	3	2
1975	Nov.	18	Selhurst Park	2	0

ENGLAND v RUMANIA

				England	Rumania
1957	May	26	Bucharest	1	0
1957	Oct.	16	Wembley	3	2
1963	June	2	Bucharest	0	1
1964	Nov.	25	Coventry	5	0

ENGLAND v SCOTLAND

				England	Scotland
1955	Feb.	8	Glasgow	6	0
1956	Feb.	8	Sheffield	3	1
1957	Feb.	26	Glasgow	1	1
1958	Jan.	15	Everton	3	1
1960	Mar.	2	Glasgow	4	4
1961	Mar.	1	Middlesbrough	0	1
1962	Feb.	28	Aberdeen	4	2
1964	Feb.	5	Newcastle	3	2
1965	Feb.	24	Aberdeen	0	0
1967	Mar.	1	Newcastle	1	3
1968	Feb.	7	Glasgow	2	1
*1970	Mar.	4	Sunderland	3	1
1971	Feb.	24	Glasgow	2	3
1972	Feb.	16	Derby	2	2
1973	Feb.	13	Kilmarnock	2	1
1974	Mar.	13	Newcastle	2	0
1974	Dec.	18	Aberdeen	3	0

Abandoned, snow, after 62 minutes.

ENGLAND v SWEDEN

	England	Sweden
1970 Nov. 11 Hull	2	0

ENGLAND v SWITZERLAND

	England	Switzer-land
97 1 Nov. 24 Ipswich	1	1

ENGLAND v TURKEY

	England	Turkey
1962 Mar. 22 Southampton	4	1
1964 May 20 Istanbul	0	3
1966 April 20 Blackburn	2	0
1967 June 7 Ankara	3	0
†1974 May 11 Ankara	0	0

ENGLAND v USSR

	England	USSR
1969 Oct. 22 Manchester	2	0
1972 June 7 Kiev	0	0

ENGLAND v WALES

	England	Wales
1958 April 23 Wrexham	1	2
1961 Feb. 8 Everton	2	0
1963 Nov. 13 Bristol	1	1
1964 Nov. 4 Wrexham	3	2
1966 Oct. 12 Wolverhampton	8	0
1967 Nov. 1 Swansea	2	1
1968 Oct. 2 Wrexham	3	1
1969 Oct. 1 Bristol	2	0
1970 Dec. 2 Wrexham	0	0
1972 Jan. 5 Swindon	2	0
1972 Nov. 29 Wrexham	3	0
1974 Jan. 16 Bristol	0	0
1975 Jan. 21 Wrexham	2	0

ENGLAND v YUGOSLAVIA

	England	Yugo-slavia
1963 Mar. 21 Manchester	0	0
1963 May 29 Belgrade	4	2
1965 Nov. 24 Southampton	2	1
1974 May 15 Zrenjanin	0	1

SCOTLAND v WALES

	Scotland	Wales
1959 Nov. 25 Wrexham	1	1
1962 Dec. 5 Aberdeen	2	0
1966 Nov. 30 Wrexham	6	0
1968 Dec. 10 Edinburgh	0	1
1970 Jan. 14 Aberdeen	1	1
1971 Jan. 13 Swansea	0	1
1972 Jan. 26 Aberdeen	2	0
1973 Mar. 14 Swansea	2	1
1974 Feb. 27 Aberdeen	3	0
1975 Feb. 25 Swansea	0	2
1976 Feb. 4 Wrexham	3	2

SCOTLAND v BRITISH ARMY

	Scotland	Army
1961 Feb. 13 Motherwell	3	2

SCOTLAND v BELGIUM

	Scotland	Belgium
1960 April 20 Ghent	1	1

SCOTLAND DENMARK

	Scotland	Denmark
1975 Oct. 28 Edinburgh	4	1

SCOTLAND v FRANCE

	Scotland	France
1964 May 24 Nantes	0	0
1969 Dec. 3 Glasgow	4	0

SCOTLAND v HOLLAND

	Scotland	Holland
1957 Oct. 24 Edinburgh	4	1
1958 Oct. 30 Amsterdam	2	1
1976 Feb. 18 Breda	0	2
1976 Mar. 24 Easter Road	2	0

SCOTLAND v SWEDEN

	Scotland	Sweden
1975 Apr. 16 Gothenburg	2	1

SCOTLAND v RUMANIA

	Scotland	Ru-mania
1975 May 31 Bucharest	2	1
1975 Dec. 16 Falkirk	4	0

WALES v NORTHERN IRELAND

	Wales	N. Ireland
1962 Feb. 7 Belfast	0	0
1963 Feb. 27 Swansea	5	1
1964 Feb. 5 Belfast	3	3
1965 Feb. 10 Cardiff	2	2
*1967 Feb. 22 Belfast	1	2
1968 Mar. 20 Cardiff	0	1
1969 Mar. 3 Wrexham	—	—
(post. through snow)		

* Abandoned 73 minutes, waterlogged.
† Abandoned half-time, rain.

ENGLISH UNDER-23 GOALSCORERS

---

13 Greaves; 11 Tambling; 8 Haynes; 7 Chivers, Clarke; 6 Byrne (J.), Hill (F.), Hinton (A.); 5 Charlton, Edwards (D.), Kidd; 4 Baker, Currie, Farmer, Jones (M.), Macdonald, Osgood, Pickering, Royle; 3 Blunstone, Channon, Eastham, Hollins, Johnson, Mills (D.), Paine, Pointer, Taylor; 2 Armstrong, Atyeo, Ball, Chisnall, Coates, Clough, Crowe, Greenhoff, Harrison, Holliday, Hooper, Latchford (R.), Marsh, Morgan, Mortimer, Murray (J.), Peters, Radford, Smith (T.), Stokes (A.), Stokes (D.), Tueart, Whymark; 1 A'Court, Ayre, Barrowclough, Beattie, Bell, Birchenall, Blockley, Bloomfield, Brabrook, Brooking, Case, Cross, Curry, Dobing, Dyson, Fletcher, George, Gillard, Harris (G.), Harris (J.), Hayes, Hill (G.), Hill (S.), Hitchens, Hurst (G.), Hurst (J.), Husband, Kay, Keegan, Kendall, Knowles (C.), Knowles (P.), Lloyd, Mannion, Moore, Murray (A.), Newton (H.), Nish, O'Grady, O'Rourke, Opponents, Paddon, Parry, Richards, Robson (B.), Robson (J.) (Burnley), Robson (J.) (Derby Co.), Robson (R.), Rodgers, Sammels, Setters, Shawcross, Sissons, Suddick, Whitworth, Worthington.

ENGLAND

A'Court, A. (Liverpool): 1957 v F, Bul, Cz; 1958 v Bul, R, S, W. (7)

Allen, A. (Stoke C.): 1959, v P, Cz, F, It, WG; 1960 v Hun, S. (7)

Allen, L. (Tottenham H.): 1961 v W. (1)

Anderson, S. (Sunderland): 1955 v S (sub); 1956 v D; 1957 v F, Bul. (4)

Angus, J. (Burnley): 1959 v WG; 1960 v EG, P, Is; 1961 v It, W; 1962 v S. (7)

Armfield, J. (Blackpool): 1957 v D, Bul, R, Cz; 1958 v R; 1959 v P, Cz, F, It. (9)

Armstrong, D. (Middlesbrough): 1975 v P, W; 1976 v Cz, P (4)

Armstrong, G. (Arsenal): 1965 v Cz, WG, A; 1966 v Y, T. (5)

Ashurst, L. (Sunderland): 1961 v WG (1)

Aston J. (Manchester U.) 1970 v W. (1)

Atyeo, J. (Bristol C.): 1955 v It, S. (2)

Ayre, R. (Charlton Ath.): 1955 v It, S. (2)

Badger, L. (Sheffield U.): 1964 v S, Hun, Is, T; 1965 v W, R, S, Cz, A; 1966 v T; 1968 v W, Hun (sub), WG. (13)

Bailey, M. (Charlton Ath.): 1964 v S, F, Hun, Is, T. (5)

Baker, J. (Hibernian): 1959 v P Cz; 1960 v F, Ho; 1961 v It; (Arsenal) 1963 v Y. (6)

Baldwin, T. (Chelsea): 1968 v It, WG. (2)

Ball, A. (Blackpool): 1965 v W, R, S, Cz, WG, Cz, A; 1966 v F. (8)

Banks, G. (Leicester C.): 1961 v W, S. (2)

Barnwell, J. (Arsenal): 1961 v WG. (1)

Barrett, L. (Fulham): 1967 v G. (1)

Barrowclough, S. (Newcastle U.): 1973 v W, S, Cz, D, Ho. (5).

Beattie, K. (Ipswich T.): 1973 v W, Ho, S; 1974 v Pol, W, T, Y, F; 1975 v W (9)

Bell, C. (Manchester C.): 1968 v S, Hun. (2)

Bennett, A. (Rotherham): 1965 v W. (1)

Bernard, M. (Stoke C.): 1971 v WG (sub), Se (sub), W. (3)

Birchenall, A. (Sheffield U.): 1966 v T; 1968 v W, (Chelsea) It, WG. (4)

Blockley, J. (Coventry C.): 1972 v Sw, W, S, EG, Pol; (Arsenal 1973 v S, D, Ho, Cz. (10)

Bloomfield, J. (Arsenal): 1957 v D, Bul. (2)

Blunstone, F. (Chelsea): 1954 v It; 1955 v It, S; 1956 v D; 1957 v D. (5)

Bonds, W. (West Ham U.): 1969 v W, Ho. (2)

Bonetti, P. (Chelsea): 1962 v S, T; 1963 v Bel, G, Y, Y, R; 1964 v F, Hun, Is, T; 1965 v A. (12)

Booth, C. (Wolverhampton W.): 1957 v F. (sub) (1)

Booth, T. (Manchester C.): 1969 v Pt; 1972 v Sw, W, S. (4)

Boyer, P. (Norwich C.): 1975 v S; 1976 v Cz (2)

Brabrook, P. (Chelsea): 1958 v Bul, R, S; 1959 v P, Cz, It, WG; 1960 v Hun; 1961 v S. (9)

Broadbent, P. (Wolverhampton W.): 1954 v It. (1)

Brooking, T. (West Ham U.): 1972 v Sw. (1)

Buckley, M. (Everton); 1975 v P; 1976 v Cz (2)

Burnside, D. (W.B.A.): 1962 v T. (1)

Burrows, H. (Aston Villa): 1963 v G. (1)

Byrne, G. (Liverpool): 1961 v W. (1)

Byrne, J. (C. Palace): 1961 v W, S, WG; 1962 v Is, Ho, S; (West Ham U.) T. (7)

Callaghan, I. (Liverpool): 1963 v G, Y, Y, R. (4)

Cantello, L. (W.B.A.): 1972 v EG; 1973 v W, Ho (2), D, Cz; 1974 v Pol, D. (8)

Case, J. (Liverpool): 1976 v H (1)

Cattlin, C. (Coventry C.): 1969 v W, Ho. (2)

Channon, M. (Southampton: 1971 v Se, W, S; 1972 v Sw, W, S, EG (2) USSR (sub) (9)

Charlton, R. (Manchester U.): 1959 v P, Cz, F; 1960 v Hun, S; 1961 v It. (6)

Cheesebrough, A. (Burnley): 1957 v F. (1)

Chisnall, P. (Manchester U.): 1964 v W, WG, S, F. (4)

Chivers, M. (Southampton): 1964 v F (sub), Hun; 1965 v W, R (sub), S, Cz, WG, Cz, A (sub); 1966 v F, Y; 1968 v It, (Tottenham H.) S, Hun, It, Hun, WG. (17)

Clark, C. (W.B.A.): 1961 v W. (1)

Clarke, A. (Fulham): 1967 v W, A, G, Bul, T; (Leicester) 1969 v Pt. (6)

Clayton, R. (Blackburn R.): 1956 v D, S; 1957 v D, S, R, Cz. (6)

Clemence, R. (Liverpool): 1968 v W; 1971 v Se, W. S. (4)

Clough, B. (Middlesbrough): 1957 v S, Bul; 1958 v W. (3)

Coates, R. (Burnley): 1967 v W, G, Bul, T; 1969 v Ho, Pt, N, Bel. (8)

Cohen, G. (Fulham): 1960 v Hun, F, S, Ho; 1961 v S, WG; 1963 v Y, R. (8)

Connelly, J. (Burnley): 1961 v It. (1)

Coppell, S. (Manchester U.): 1976 v H (1)

Corrigan, J. (Manchester C.): 1970 v USSR (1)

Crawford, B. (Blackpool): 1962 v S. (1)

Cross, G. (Leicester C.): 1963 v Y, Y, R; 1964 v W, WG, S, F, Hun, Is, T; 1966 v T. (11)

Crowe, C. (Leeds U.): 1960 v F, S; (Blackburn) 1961 v W, S. (4)

Crowther, S. (Aston Villa): 1958 v Bul, R, S. (3)

Currie, A. (Sheffield U.): 1970 v W, Bul; 1971 v WG, S; 1972 v W, S, EG, Pol, USSR; 1973 v W, Ho, S, Cz (13)

Curry, W. (Newcastle): 1958 v R. (1)

Davies, R. (Derby Co.): 1974 v S. (sub) (1)

Day, M. (West Ham U.): 1974 v Y, F (sub): 1975 v S, W; 1976 v P (5)

Deakin, A. (Aston Villa): 1962 v Is, T; 1963 v Y (2), R; 1964 v T (sub) (6)

Dobing, P. (Blackburn): 1959 v WG; 1960 v F, EG, P, Is; 1961 v It, S. (7)

Dobson, C. (Sheffield W.): 1963 v Y (sub), R. (2)

Dobson, M. (Burnley): 1970 v Bul. (1)

Dodd, A. (Stoke C.): 1975 v Cz, P, S; 1976 v Cz, P, H (6)

Dodgin, W. (Arsenal): 1954 v It. (1)

Douglas, B. (Blackburn): 1957 v D, F, Bul, R, Cz (5)

Doyle, M. (Manchester C.): 1968 v Hun, It, Hun, WG; 1969 v Pt, Ho, Bel, Pt. (8)

Dyson, J. (Manchester C.): 1957 v S. (1)

Dyson, K. (Newcastle U.): 1970 v Bul. (1)

Eastham, G. (Newcastle U.): 1960 v F, S, Ho, EG, P, Is. (6)

Edwards, D. (Manchester U.): 1954 v It; 1955 v It, S; 1956 v S; 1957 v R, Cz. (6)

Edwards, P. (Manchester U.): 1970 v Bul (sub); 1971 v WG, Se. (3)

Ellis, S. (Sheffield W.): 1969 v W; 1970 v W, USSR (3)

Ellis, S. (Charlton Ath.): 1954 v It. (1)

Evans, A. (Liverpool): 1969 v Ho, Pt, Bel, Pt. (4)

Fantham, J. (Sheffield W.): 1961 v It. (1)

Farmer, E. (Wolverhampton W.): 1962 v Is, Ho. (2).

Farmer, J. (Stoke C.): 1967 v W. (1)

Finney, A. (Sheffield W.): 1954 v It; 1956 v S; 1957 v S. (3)

Fletcher, P. (Burnley): 1974 v D (sub),W,Y,F(sub)(4)

Flowers, R. (Wolverhampton W.): 1955 v It, S. (2)

Ford, D. (Sheffield W.): 1967 v W, S. (2)

Foulkes, W. (Manchester U.): 1955 v It, S. (2)

Francis, G. (Q.P.R.): 1974 v D, S, T, Y, (sub), F; 1976 v H (6)

Francis, T. (Birmingham C.): 1974 v Pol, D, W; 1976 v P, H (5)

Garland, C. (Bristol C.): 1970 v Bul (sub). (1)

George, C. (Arsenal): 1973 v W, Ho, Cz; 1974 v Pol, D. (5)

Gidman, J. (Aston Villa): 1975 v Cz; 1976 v Cz, P, H (4)
Gillard, I. (Q.P.R.): 1974 v S, T, Y, F: 1975 c S (5)
Glazier, W. (Coventry C.): 1965 v R, S, Cz. (3)
Gowling, A. (Manchester U.): 1972 v Sw. (1)
Greaves, J. (Chelsea): 1958 v Bul, R, S, W; 1959 v P, Cz, F, It; 1960 v Hun, S, Ho; (Tottenham H.) 1962 v S. (12)
Greenhoff, B. (Manchester U.): 1974 v Y, F (sub); 1975 v Cz; 1976 v H (4)
Greenhoff, J. (Birmingham C.): 1969 v W, Ho, Ho (sub), Bel; 1976 v H (5)
Groves, V. (Arsenal): 1957 v F. (1)
Grummitt, P. (Nottingham F.): 1962 v Ho; 1964 v W, WG. (3)
Gunter, P. (Portsmouth): 1954 v It. (1)

Hankin, R. (Burnley): 1975 v Cz (sub), S, W (3)
Harris, Gordon (Burnley): 1962 v Is; 1963 v Y. (2)
Harris, Gerry (Wolverhampton W.): 1958 v Bul, R, S. W. (4)
Harris, J. (Everton): 1956 v S. (1)
Harris, R. (Chelsea): 1967 v W.; 1968 v It, Hun, WG. (4)
Harrison, M. (Chelsea): 1961 v WG; 1962 v S, T. (3)
Harvey, J. (Everton): 1967 v S, A, G, Bul, T. (5)
Hayes, J. (Manchester C.): 1958 v S, W. (2)
Haynes, J. (Fulham): 1955 v It, S; 1956 v D, S; 1957 v S, R, Cz; 1958 v Bul. (8)
Hibbitt, K. (Wolverhampton W.): 1971 v W (sub) (1)
Hill, F. (Bolton W.): 1961 v WG; 1962 v Is, Ho, S, T; 1963 v Bel, G, Y, Y, R. (10)
Hill, G. (Manchester U.): 1976 v H (1)
Hill, S. (Blackpool): 1962 v Is, Bel, S, T. (4)
Hindley, P. (Nottingham F.): 1967 v G. (1)
Hinton, A. (Wolverhampton W.): 1963 v Y, R; 1964 v W, (Nottingham F.) Hun, Is, T; 1965 v R. (7)
Hinton, M. (Charlton Ath.): 1962 v S, T; 1963 v Bel (3)
Hitchens, G. (Cardiff C.): 1957 v D.(1)
Hodgkinson, A. (Sheffield U.): 1957 v D, F, S; 1958 v R, W; 1959 v P, Cz. (7)
Holiday, E. (Middlesbrough): 1960 v Hun, Ho, EG, P, Is. (5)
Hollins, J. (Chelsea): 1965 v W, Cz, A; 1966 v F, Y; 1967 v W, S, A; 1968 v W, It, S, Hun. (12)
Hooper, H. (West Ham U.): 1955 v It, S. (2)
Hopkinson, E. (Bolton W.): 1957 v Bul, R, Cz; 1958 v Bul, S; 1959 v F. (6)
Howe, D. (W.B.A.): 1956 v S; 1957 v F, S; 1958 v Bul, S, W. (6)
Hudson, A. (Chelsea): 1970 v S; 1971 v W, S; 1972 v S, EG; (with Stoke C.), 1974 v S, T, Y, F; 1976 v H (10)
Hughes, E. (Liverpool): 1968 v W, It, S; 1969 v Ho, Bel, Pt (sub); 1970 v R, Bul. (8)
Hunt, R. P. (Swindon T.): 1963 v R ;(Wolverhampton W.) 1966 v Y, T. (3)
Hunter, N. (Leeds U.): 1965 v W R, S. (3)
Hurst, G. (West Ham U.): 1964 v W, F, Is, T. (4)
Hurst, J. (Everton): 1967 v G, Bul, T; 1969 v W, Ho, Ho, Bel, Pt; 1970 v USSR (9)
Husband, J. (Everton): 1967 v A (sub), G, Bul.; 1970 v USSR, S. (5)
Hutchinson, I. (Chelsea): 1971 v W, S. (2)

Iley, J. (Tottenham H.): 1958 v W. (1)

Jeffrey, A. (Doncaster R.): 1957 v D, F. (2)
Jeffries, D. (Manchester C.): 1972 v EG. (1)
Johnson, D. (Ipswich T.): 1973 v Cz (2), Ho; 1974 v Pol; 1975 v Cz, P, W; 1976 v P, H (9)
Jones, G. (Middlesbrough): 1962 v Is, Ho, S, T; 1963 v Bel, G, Y: 1974 v W, WG. (9)
Jones, M. (Sheffield U.): 1965 v R, S, Cz, WG, A; 1966 v F, Y, T; 1967 v A. (9)
Jones, R. (Bournemouth): 1968 v Hun. (1)

Kay, A. (Sheffield W.): 1959 v It, WG; 1960 v S, Ho, EG, P, Is. (7)
Kaye, A. (Barnsley: 1956 v D. (1)

Keegan, K. (Liverpool): 1972 v S, EG (2), Pol, USSR. (5)
Kember, S. (C. Palace): 1971 v WG; (Chelsea) 1972 v Sw, EG. (3)
Kendall, H. (Everton): 1968 v W, It, It, Hun; 1969 v W, Ho. (6)
Kennedy, A. (Newcastle U.): 1975 v Cz, P; 1976 v Cz, P, H (2) (6)
Kennedy, R. (Arsenal): 1972 v W; 1973 v Ho, (1 +1 sub), D, Cz (sub); 1974 v Pol (6)
Kevan, D. (W.B.A.): 1957 v Bul, R, Cz; 1958 v Bul. (4)
Kidd, B. (Manchester U.): 1968 v W, It, S; 1969 v Ho, Bel (sub); 1970 v W, USSR, S; 1971 v WG, Se (10)
Kirkham, J. (Wolverhampton W.): 1961 v W, S. (2)
Kirkup, J. (West Ham U.): 1962 v Is, Ho, T. (3)
Knowles, C. (Tottenham H.): 1965 v W; 1967 v W, S, G, Bul, T. (6)
Knowles, P. (Wolverhampton W.): 1968 v W, It; 1969 v W, Ho. (4)

Labone, B. (Everton): 1961 v It, W, S; 1962 v Is, Ho; 1963 v Y. R. (7)
Lampard, F. (West Ham U.): 1972 v Sw EG, Pol, USSR. (4)
Latchford, P. (W.B.A.): 1974 v Pol, W (2)
Latchford, R. (Birmingham C.): 1974 v D, W (Everton), S, T, Y, F (6)
Lawler, C. (Liverpool): 1966 v F, Y; 1967 v S, A. (4)
Leary, S. (Charlton Ath.): 1954 v It. (1)
Le Flem, R. (Nottingham F.): 1962 v Ho. (1)
Lloyd, L. (Liverpool): 1971 v WG, Se, W, S; 1972 v EG (2), Pol, USSR. (8)
Lock, K. (West Ham U.): 1973 v D, Ho, Cz; 1976 v H (4)
Lyons, M. (Everton): 1975 v Cz, P, S, W (sub); 1976 v Cz (5)

Maddren, W. (Middlesbrough): 1973 v Cz; 1974 v D, S, Y (sub), F (5)
Macedo, E. (Fulham): 1959 v It, WG; 1960 v Hun, F, Ho, EG, P, Is; 1961 v It, WG. (10)
Mannion, G. (Wolverhampton W.): 1960 v P, Is. (2)
Marsh, R. (Q.P.R.): 1968 v S, Hun. (2)
Marshall, G. (Hearts): 1960 v S. (1)
Matthews, R. (Coventry C.): 1955 v It, S; 1965 v D, S. (4)
McDermott, T. (Newcastle U.): 1974 v W (1)
Macdonald, M. (Newcastle U.): 1972 v W, S, EG; 1973 v W (4)
McDowell, J. (West Ham U.): 1973 v W, Ho (2), S, Cz (2), D; 1974 v Pol, D, S, T, Y (sub), F (13)
McFarland, R. (Derby Co.): 1969 v Ho (2), Bel, Pt; 1970 v S. (5)
McGrath, J. (Newcastle U.): 1961 v WG. (1)
McGuinness, W. (Manchester U.): 1959 v P, Cz, F; 1960 v Hun. (4)
McNeil, M. (Middlesbrough): 1960 v F, Ho, EG, P, Is; 1961 v It, S; 1963 v Bel, G. (9)
Miller, B. (Burnley): 1960 v EG, P, Is. (3)
Mills, D. (Middlesbrough): 1974 v S, T, Y, F; 1975 v Cz; 1976 v Cz, P (sub), H (sub) (8)
Mills, M. (Ipswich T.): 1971 v W; 1972 v S, EG Pol, USSR. (5)
Mills, S. J. (Southampton), 1974 v W (1)
Mobley, V. (Sheffield W.): 1965 v W, R, S, Cz, WG, Cz, A; 1966 v F, Y; 1967 v A, G, Bul, T. (13)
Montgomery, J. (Sunderland): 1964 v S; 1967 v S, A, G, Bul, T. (6)
Moore, I. (Nottingham F.): 1967 v S, A. (2)
Moore, R. (West Ham U.): 1961 v It, W, S, WG, 1962 v Is, Ho, S, T. (8)
Moores, I. (Stoke C.): 1975 v W; 1976 v Cz (2)
Morgan, R. (Tottenham R.): 1970 v Bul. (1)
Morley, M. (Preston N.E.): 1975 v W (sub) (1)
Mortimer, D. (Coventry C.): 1973 v W, Ho (2), S, Cz (2) (6)
Mullery, A. (Fulham): 1961 v It; 1962 v Ho; 1963 v Bel (3)
Murray, A. (Chelsea): 1965 v R, S, Cz, WG, Cz, A. (6)

730

Murray, J. (Wolverhampton W.): 1958, v S; 1959 v F. (2)

Nattrass, I. (Newcastle U.): 1976 v H (1)
Neal, R. (Lincoln): 1957 v D. F, S, (Birmingham C.) Bul. (4)
Newton, H. (Nottingham F.): 1965 v R, Cz; 1967 v Bul, T. (4)
Newton, K. (Blackburn R.): 1964 v S, Hun, Is, T. (4)
Nicholls, J. (W.B.A.): 1954 v It. (1)
Nisbet, G. (W.B.A.): 1972 v EG. (1)
Nish, D. (Leicester C.): 1969 v Pt (sub), Bel, Pt; 1970 v W, USSR, S, Bul; 1971 v Se, W, S. (10)
Norman, M. (Tottenham H.): 1956 v S; 1957 v R, Cz. (3)

O'Grady, M. (Huddersfield): 1961 v S; 1963 v Bel; (Leeds) 1966 v F. (3)
O'Neil, B. (Burnley): 1966 v T. (1)
O'Rourke, J. (Middlesbrough): 1967 v T. (1)
Osgood, P. (Chelsea): 1968 v W, S, Hun; 1970 v W, USSR, S. (6)

Pacey, D. (Luton T.): 1959 v WG. (1)
Paine, T. (Southampton): 1960 v Ho, EG; 1961 v WG; 1962 v T (sub). (4)
Paddon, G. (West Ham U.): 1976 v H (1)
Palmer, G. (Wolverhampton W.): 1974 v W; 1975 v P (2)
Pardoe, G. (Manchester C.): 1968 v Hun; 1969 Pt, Bel, Pt. (4)
Parkes, P. (Q.P.R.): 1972 v W, S, EG; 1973 v D, Cz; 1976 v Cz (6)
Parkin, D. (Wolverhampton W.): 1970 v W, USSR, Bul, S; 1971 v S. (5)
Parry, R. (Bolton): 1958 v R; 1959 v F, It, WG. (4)
Payne, D. (C. Palace): 1968 v W (sub). (1)
Pearson, S. (Manchester U.): 1976 v H (1)
Pegg, D. (Manchester U.): 1956 v S; 1957 v S, R. (3)
Pejic, M. (Stoke C.): 1972 v Pol, USSR; 1973 v W, Ho (2), S, D, Cz (8)
Perryman, S. (Tottenham H.): 1972 v EG, Pol, USSR; 1973 v S, D, Ho, Cz; 1974 v Pol, D, W, S, T, Y; 1975 v Cz, P, S, W (17)
Peters, M. (West Ham U.): 1963 v Bel, G; 1964 v W, WG; 1966 v T. (5)
Pickering, F. (Blackburn R.): 1964 v W; WG, S. (3)
Piper, N. (Plymouth Arg.): 1970 v Bul; (Portsmouth) 1971 v WG, Se, S. (4)
Pointer, R. (Burnley): 1959 v It; 1960 v Hun, EG, P, Is. (5)
Powell, B. (Wolverhampton W.): 1974 v S; 1975 v Cz, P (sub), S (4)
Powell, S. (Derby Co.): 1975 v S (1)
Pugh, J. (Sheffield W.): 1970 v W. (1)

Quixall, A. (Sheffield W.): 1956 v S. (1)

Radford, J. (Arsenal): 1969 v W, Ho (2), Pt. (4)
Rankin, A. (Everton): 1965 v W. (1)
Reaney, P. (Leeds U.): 1964 v F; 1965 v S, WG, Cz; 1967 v S. (5)
Richards, J. (Wolverhampton W.): 1972 v EG, Pol, USSR; 1973 v S; 1974 v Pol (sub), W (6)
Riley, H. (Leicester C.): 1958 v W; 1961 v W. (2)
Robson, B. (Newcastle U.): 1967 v S; 1969 v Pt. (2)
Robson, Jimmy (Burnley): 1959 v WG. (1)
Robson, John (Derby): 1971 v WG, Se, S; 1972 v W, S, EG; (Aston Villa) 1973 v Cz(7)
Robson, R. (Fulham): 1956 v D. (1)
Rofe, D. (Leicester C.): 1973 v Cz (sub) (1)
Rogers, D. (Swindon T.): 1966 v Y; 1968 v W. (2)
Royle, J. (Everton): 1968 v Hun (sub), Hun; 1969 Ho, Bel (sub), Pt; 1970 v USSR, S (sub); 1971 v WG, Se; 1972 v Sw. (10)

Sadler, D. (Manchester U.): 1967 v S; 1968 v W; 1969 v Pt. (3)
Sammels, J. (Arsenal): 1967 v W, A, G, Bul, T; 1968 v It, It, Hun, WG. (9)
Scanlon, A. (Manchester U.): 1959 v P. Cz. F, It, WG. (5)
Scott, M. (Chelsea): 1959 v P, Cz, F; 1960 v Hun. (4)

Setters, M. (W.B.A.): 1958 v Bul, R, S, W; 1959 v P, Cz, F, It, WG; 1960 v Hun. F, (with Manchester U.) S, Ho, EG, P, Is. (16)
Shaw, B. (Sheffield U.): 1968 v It, Hun. (2)
Shaw, G. (Sheffield U.): 1956 v D; 1957 v D, F, S, Bul. (5)
Shawcross, D. (Manchester C.): 1961 v WG. (1)
Shellito, K. (Chelsea): 1963 v Y. (1)
Shilton, P. (Leicester C.): 1969 v W, Ho, Pt, Ho, Pt; 1970 v W, Bul, S; 1971 v WG; 1972 v Sw, EG, Pol. USSR. (13)
Sillett, P. (Chelsea): 1955 v It, S; 1956 v D. (3)
Sissons, J. (West Ham U.): 1965 v W, S; 1967 v W; 1968 v Hun, WG; 1969 v W, Pt, Ho, Bel, Pt. (10)
Sleeuwenhoek, J. (Aston Villa): 1963 v G, Y. (2)
Smith, J. (West Ham U.): 1960 v F. (1)
Smith, Tommy (Liverpool): 1965 v Cz, WG, Cz, A; 1966 v F, Y; 1967 v S, A; 1968 v It, S. (10)
Smith, Trevor (Birmingham C.): 1955 v It, S; 1956 v D, S; 1957 v D, F, S, Bul, R, Cz; 1958, v Bul, R, S, W; 1959 v It. (15)
Smith, W. (Sheffield W.): 1969 v Pt, Ho, Pt; 1970 v W, Bul, S. (6)
Springett, P .(Sheffield W.): 1968 v It, S, Hun, It, WG; 1969 v Bel. (6)
Stephenson, A. (C. Palace): 1967 v W; 1968 v It, S, (West Ham U.) Hun, It, Hun, WG. (7)
Stepney, A. (Millwall): 1966 v F, Y, T. (3)
Stevens, D. (Bolton W.): 1957 v R, Cz. (2)
Stevenson, A. (Burnley): 1973 v W, Ho (2), S, Cz; 1974 v D, S, T, F; 1975 v Cz, P (11)
Stiles, N. (Manchester U.): 1965 v S, WG, Cz. (3)
Stokes, A. (Tottenham): 1956 v D. (1)
Stokes, D. (Huddersfield): 1963 v Bel, G, Y, R (sub), (4)
Suddick, A. (Newcastle U.): 1963 v Bel, Y, (2)
Suddick, A. (Newcastle U.): 1963 v B, Y, (2)
Sullivan, C. (Plymouth A.): 1974 v Pol, D (2)
Summerbee, M. (Manchester C.): 1966 v T. (1)
Sunderland, A. (Wolverhampton W.): 1974 v S, (sub) (1)
Swan, P. (Sheffield W.): 1960 v F, S, Ho. (3)
Sydenham, J. (Southampton): 1960 v F, S. (2)

Talbut, J. (Burnley): 1964 v W, WG, S, F, Hun, Is, T. (7)
Tambling, R. (Chelsea): 1963 v Bel, G, Y; 1964 v WG, S, F, Hun, Is, T; 1965 v W (sub), R, Cz, A. (13)
Taylor, P. (C. Palace): 1975 v Cz, P; 1976 v Cz (sub), P (4)
Taylor, T. (West Ham U.): 1972 v EG (sub); 1973 v W, Ho, Cz; 1974 v Pol, D, W, S, T, Y; 1976 v P(11)
Thomas, D. (Burnley): 1970 v Bul, S; 1971 v WG, Se, W; 1972 v Sw, S, EG; (with Q.P.R.) 1974 v D(sub), T, F.(11)
Thompson, P. (Liverpool): 1964 v WG, S, F; 1966 v F. (4)
Thompson, P. B. (Liverpool): 1975 v W; 1976 v H.(2)
Thomson, R. (Wolverhampton W.): 1963 v Y, R; 1964 v W, WG, F; 1965 v R, Cz, WG, Cz, A: 1966 v F, Y, T; 1967 v W. A. (15)
Todd, C. (Sunderland): 1968 v Hun, Hun (sub), WG; 1969 v W, Ho (sub); 1970 v W, USSR, S; 1971 v WG, Se, W (Derby) S; 1972 v W; 1975 v W. (14)
Towers, A. (Manchester C.): 1972 v USSR, R (sub); 1973 v D, Cz (with Sunderland); 1975 v W; 1976 v Cz, P, H (8)
Tueart, D. (Manchester C.): 1975 v S (1)

Usher, B. (Sunderland): 1964 v F. (1)

Venables, T. (Chelsea): 1963 v G; 1964 v Hun, Is, T. (4)

Wallington, M. (Leicester C.): 1976 v H (2) (2)
West, A. (Burnley): 1972 v W. (1)
West, D. (Blackpool): 1962 v Is; (Everton) 1965 v WG, Cz. (3)
Whitefoot, G. (Manchester U.): 1954 v It. (1)

Whitham, J. (Sheffield W.): 1969 v W (sub). (1)
Whittle, A. (Everton): 1971 v W, (1)
Whitworth, S. (Leicester C.): 1972 v Sw; W; 1974 v Y, F; 1975 v S, S, W (6)
Whymark, T. (Ipswich T.): 1973 v Ho (2), S, Cz, (2), D; 1975 v P (7)
Wilkins, R. (Chelsea): v P, H (2)

Wilson, D. (Preston N.E.): 1964 v W, WG, S.Hun, Is, T; 1965 v W. (7)
Wood, R. (Manchester U.): 1954 v It. (1)
Worthington, F. (Huddersfield T.): 1972 v Pol, USSR. (2)
Wright, T. (Everton): 1967 v Bul T; 1968 v It S, Hun, It, Hun. (7)

NORTHERN IRELAND
(all matches against Wales)

Briggs, R. (Manchester United): 1962; (with Swansea T.), 1965. (2)
Burke, (Portadown): 1963. (1)

Campbell, W. (Distillery): 1964; (with Sunderland) 1965 (with Dundee): 1967. (3)
Clarke, F. (Arsenal): 1962, 1963, 1964, 1965. (4)
Clarke, N. (Ballymena): 1962; (with Sunderland) 1963. (2)
Clements, D. (Coventry C.): 1965, 1967, 1968. (3)
Craig, D. (Newcastle U.): 1965, 1967. (1)
Craig, W. (Linfield): 1965. (1)

Dunlop, J. (Coleraine): 1965, 1968. (2)

Elder, A. (Burnley): 1964. (1)
Elwood, J. (L. Orient): 1962. (1)

Hamilton B. (Linfield): 1968. (1)
Harkin, T. (Port Vale): 1963. (1)
Harvey, M. (Sunderland): 1962, 1963, 1964. (3)

Irvine, R. (Linfield): 1963. (1)
Irvine, W. (Burnley): 1963, 1964, 1965. (3)

Jackson, T. (Everton): 1968. (1)
Jennings, P. (Watford): 1964. (1)
Johnston, W. (Glenavon): 1962. (1)

Magill, J. (Arsenal): 1962. (1)
McAvoy, W. (Ards.): 1968 (1)
McCaffrey W. (Leicester C.): 1963. (1)
McIlroy (Burnley): 1968. (1)
McKeag, W. (Glentoran): 1967, 1968. (2)
McKenzie, R. (Airdrieonians): 1967, 1968. (2)
McKinney (Falkirk): 1967. (1)
McLaughlin, J. (Shrewsbury T.): 1963 (with Swansea T.), 1964. (2)
McMillan, S. (Wrexham): 1964. (1)

McMordie, E. (Middlesbrough): 1967. (1)
McNeill, M. (Middlesbrough): 1968. (1)
Morrow (Glentoran): 1968. (1)

Napier, J. (Bolton W.): 1967; (with Brighton) 1968. (2)
Neill, T. (Arsenal): 1962, 1963, 1964, 1965. (4)
Nicholson, J. (Manchester U.): 1962, 1963, 1964, (with Huddersfield T.), 1965. (4)

O'Neill, J. Sunderland): 1962. (1)

Rice, P. (Arsenal): 1968. (1)
Ross E. (Glentoran): 1967. (1)

Sloan, D. (Scunthorpe U.): 1964. (1)

Todd, S. (Burnley): 1965, 1967, 1968. (3)
Trainor, D. (Crisaders): 1967. (1)

Welsh, E. (Distillery): 1962. (1)

Ireland also played an under 23 international v Italy on 26 March, 1969 at Brescia losing 1-2.

Team:—
Gaston, R. (Oxford United)
Hamilton, B. (Linfield)
Hunter, A. (Oldham Athletic)
Johnston, J. (Blackpool)
McKenzie, R. (Airdrieonians)
Morrow, T. (Glentoran)
Mullan B. (Fulham)
Nelson, S. (Arsenal)
O'Doherty, A. (Coleraine)
Rice, P. (Arsenal)
Todd, S. (Burnley)

SCOTLAND

Aitken, C. (Aston Villa): 1962 v E, W; 1963 v W. (3)
Alderson, B. (Coventry C.): 1973 v E (1)
Allan, W. (Aberdeen): 1963 v W. (1)
Anderson, G. (Morton): 1973 v W (1)

Baillie, D. (Airdreionians): 1955 v E; 1959 v W. (2)
Baird, D. (Partick T.): 1959 v W. (1)
Baxter, James (Raith R.): 1959 v W. (1)
Baxter, John (Hibernian): 1959 v W. (1)
Baxter, T. (Queen of the South): 1956 v E. (1)
Beattie, R. (Celtic): 1958 v Ho (2), E. (3)
Blacklaw, A. (Burnley): 1960 v E, W. (2)
Blackley, J. (Hibernian): 1970 v F, E, W; 1971 v E. (4)
Bone, J. (Norwich C.): 1972 v E, W; 1973 v E (3)
Brand, W. (Rangers): 1958 v E. (1)
Bremner, D. (Hibernian): 1975 v E, W, Se; 1976 v D (2), R, W, Ho (2) (9)
Bremner, W. (Leeds U.): 1964 v E, F; 1965 v W, E. (4)
Brown, H. (Kilmarnock): 1963 v W. (1)
Brown, J. (Chesterfield): 1974 v W (sub), E (sub) (with Sheffield U.); 1975 v E (sub), Se (sub) (4)
Brownlie, J. (Hibernian): 1972 v E, W; 1976 v W, Ho (2) (5)
Bruce, A. (Newcastle U.): 1974 v E (1)
Buchan, M. (Aberdeen): 1971 v W; 1972 v W, E. (3)
Burley, G. (Ipswich T.): 1975 v E, Se (2)
Burns, F. (Manchester U.): 1968 v E. (1)

Burns, K. (Birmingham C.): 1974 v W; 1976 v Ho (2)

Calderwood, R . (Birmingham C.): 1974 v E (1)
Caldow, E. (Rangers): 1955 v E; 1957 v E. (2)
Campbell, A. (Charlton): 1970 v W. (1)
Carr, W. (Coventry C.): 1970 v F, W; 1971 v W; 1972 v E. (4)
Clark, R. (Aberdeen): 1967 v W, E. (2)
Clunie (Hearts): 1970 v E, W. (2)
Colquhoun (W.B.A.): 1968 v E. (1)
Colrain (Celtic): 1958 v Ho. (1)
Conn, A. (Tottenham H.): 1975 v R; 1976 v D, R (3)
Connelly, G. (Celtic): 1970 v E; 1971 v E; 1972 v E (3)
Connolly, J. (Everton): 1971 v W; 1973 v W (2)
Cooke, A. (Aberdeen): 1963 v W; 1964 v W; 1965 v W; (with Dundee) 1965 v E. (4)
Cormack, P. (Hibernian): 1965 v W, E; 1967 v W, E; 1968; v E (5)
Cousin, A. (Dundee): 1958 v Ho; 1960 v E, Bel. (3)
Craig, J. (Partick T.): 1976 v D, R, W, Ho. (4)
Craig, T. (Sheffield W.): 1974 v E (with Newcastle U): 1975 v W, Se, R; 1976 v D (2), R. W, Ho (9).
Crawford, I. (Hearts): 1957 v E. (1)
Crerand, P. (Celtic): 1961 v E. (1)
Cropley, A. (Hibernian): 1972 v W; 1973 v E; 1974 v W (3)
Cruickshank, J. (Quee'n's Park): 1960 v Bel; (with Hearts): 1964 v W. E. (3)
Currie, D. (Clyde): 1958 v Ho (2), E. 1959 v W. (47

732

Dalglish, K. (Celtic): 1972 v W, E; 1973 v W; 1976 v H. (4)
Davie, A. (Dundee U.): 1964 v F. (1)
Dickson, P. (Q.o.S.): 1976 v H. (sub) (1)
Dickson, W. (Kilmarnock): 1970 v E. (1)
Donachie, W. (Manchester C.): 1972 v W, E (2)
Donaldson, A. (Dundee): 1965 v W E,. (2)
Doyle, J. (Ayr U.): 1973 v E, W; 1974 v W (sub) (3)
Duff, W. (Hearts): 1955 v E. (1)
Duncan, A. (Hibernian): 1971 v E. (1)

Eston, J. (Hibernian): 1964 v W. (1)
Edwards, A. (Dunfermline Ath.): 1976 v W. (1)
Ewen, R. (Aberdeen): 1959 v W. (1)

Ferguson, R. (West Ham U.): 1968 v E. (1)
Forrest, J. (Rangers): 1964 v W; 1965 v E. (2)
Forsyth, A. (Manchester U.): 1974 v W (1)
Forsyth, C. (St. Mirren): 1957 v E. (1)
Forsyth, T. (Motherwell): 1971 v E. (1)
Fraser, C. (Dunfermline Ath.): 1962 v W; (with Aston Villa) 1963 v W. (2)

Gabriel, J. (Dundee): 1960 v W (with Everton), E, Bel; 1962 v W; 1963 v W, E. (6)
Gemmill, A. (Preston N.E.): 1970 v E. (1)
Gibb, T. (Partick T.): 1968 v E (sub) (1)
Gibson, I. (Middlesbrough): 1964 v W, F. (2)
Gillies, D. (Bristol C.): 1974 v E (1)
Gilzean, A. (Dundee): 1961 v E; 1962 v W, E. (3)
Glen, A. (Queen's Park): 1957 v E. (1)
Gow, G. (Bristol C.): 1974 v E (sub) (1)
Graham, A. (Aberdeen): 1975 v E, Se, R (sub) (3)
Graham, G. (Chelsea): 1965 v W, E. (2)
Gray, A. (Dundee U.): 1975 v E, W, R; (with Aston Villa), 1976 v D. (4)
Gray, E. (Leeds U.): 1967 v W, E. (2)
Gray, F. (Leeds U.): 1974 v E; 1976 v D (2), R, Ho. (5)
Greig, J. (Rangers): 1964 v W, E.(2)

Hamilton, J. (Hearts): 1956 v E; 1957 v E. (2)
Hamilton, R. (Kilmarnock): 1965 v W. (1)
Hansen, A. (Partick T.): 1975 v Se; 1976 v R, W. (sub) (3)
Harper, J. (Aberdeen): 1970 v W (sub); 1971 v W. (2)
Harrower, J. (Hibernian): 1958 v Ho. (1)
Hartford, A. (W.B.A.): 1970 v W; 1971 v W; 1972 v E; 1973 v E, W. (5)
Hay, D. (Celtic): 1970 v F; 1971 v E. W, (3)
Henderson, W. (Rangers): 1962 v W, E. (2)
Herd, G. (Clyde): 1958 v Ho. (2)
Hermiston, J. (Aberdeen): 1971 v W. (1)
Hewie, J. (Charlton Ath.): 1957 vE. (1)
Higgins, W. (Hearts): 1960 v E, W, Bel; 1962 v E. (4)
Hill, A. (Clyde): 1955 v E. (1)
Hilley, D. (Third Lanark): 1961 v E. (1)
Hogan, J. (Partick T.): 1961 v E. (1)
Hollywood, D. (Southampton): 1965 v E. (1)
Holmes, R. (St. Mirren): 1955 v E. (1)
Holt, D. (Queen's Park): 1958 v Ho; (with Hearts) (1)
Holton, J. (Manchester U.): 1973 v W (1)
Hood, H. (Clyde): 1968 v E. (1)
Hope, R. (W.B.A.): 1967 v W. (1)
Houston, S. (Manchester U.): 1975 v Se, R (2)
Hughes, J. (Celtic): 1961 v E; 1962 v W, E; 1964 v E. (4)
Hughes, T. (Chelsea): 1970 v F, E. (2)
Hunter, A. (Kilmarnock): 1971 v E (sub); 1972 v W, E. (3)
Hunter, W. (Motherwell): 1960 v W, E, Bel; 1962 v E. (4)
Hutchison, T. (Blackpool): 1971 v W. (1)

Jackson, C. (Rangers): 1976 v Ho. (1)
Jardine, S. (Rangers): 1971 v E, W (sub); 1972 v W, E. (4)
Jarvie, A. (Airdreionians): 1971 v E. (1)
Jeffrey, R. (Celtic): 1963 v W. (1)
Jordan, J. (Leeds U.): 1976 v Ho (1)
Johnston, W. (Rangers): 1970 v F, E. (2)
Johnstone, D. (Rangers): 1974 v W. E; 1975 v E; 1976 v W, Ho (2) (6).

Johnstone, J. (Celtic): 1964 v F, E. (2)

Kelly, E. (Arsenal): 1971 v E, W; 1974 v W (3)
Kennedy, J. (Kilmarnock): 1958 v N. (1)
Kennedy, S. (Falkirk): 1973 v E, W; 1975 v W (3)
Kennedy, S. (Rangers): 1975 v W (1)
King, A. (Kilmarnock): 1964 v W, F; 1965 v W. (3)

Lamb, A. (P.N.E.): 1974 v E (sub) (1)
Law D. (Huddersfield T.): 1960 v W, E; 1961 v E, (3)
Lawrence, T. (Liverpool): 1963 v W. (1)
Leggat, G. (Aberdeen): 1955 v E. (1)
Lochhead, A. (Burnley): 1963 v W. (1)
Lorimer, P. (Leeds U.): 1970 v W, F. (2)

Macari, L. (Celtic): 1972 v W, E. (2)
Mackay, D. (Hearts): 1955 v E; 1957 v E; 1958 v Ho, E. (4)
Mackay, D. (Celtic): 1959 v W; 1960 v E, W, Bel. (4)
Malone, D. (Ayr U.): 1970 v F. (1)
Martin, N. (Hibernian): 1964 v F. (1)
Martis, J. (Motherwell): 1960 v E. (1)
Marinello, P. (Hibernian): 1970 v F (sub), (with Arsenal) v E (sub), (2)
McCalliog, J. (Sheffield W.): 1967 v W, E. (2)
McCluskey, P. (Celtic): 1973 v E, W (sub); 1975 v E, W, R; 1976 v D. (6)
McCulloch, W. (Cardiff C.): 1973 v W (sub) (1)
McDonald, I. (St. Johnstone): 1974 v E (1)
McDonald, R. (Celtic)
MacDonald, A. (Rangers): 1975 v E
McDougall, I. (Rangers): 1975 v W (1)
McGillivray, A. (Third Lanark): 1962 v E (1)
McGovern (Derby Co.): 1972 v W; 1973 v W. (2)
McGrain, D. (Celtic): 1973 v W, E (2)
McGrory, J. (Kilmarnock): 1964 v F. E; 1965 v W. (3)
McIntosh, J. (Falkirk): 1956 v E; 1958 v E, Ho. (3)
McLelland, C. (Aberdeen): 1976 v W, Ho. (2)
McLeod, J. M. (Hibernian): 1961 v E. (1)
McLintock, F. (Leicester C.): 1962 v E. (1)
McMillan, T. (Aberdeen): 1967 v W, E. (2)
NcNeill, W. (Celtic): 1960 v Bel; 1961 v E; 1962 v W. E; 1963 v W. (5)
McParland, D. (Partick T.): 1955 v E. (1)
McQuade, D. (Partick T.): 1972 v W (sub). (1)
MacRae, K. (Motherwell): 1971 v E, W. (2)
McVie, W. (Motherwell): 1976 v W, Ho. (2)
Milne, A. (Cardiff C.): 1960 v W. (1)
Mitchell, I. (Dundee U.): 1967 v W, E. (2)
Morgan, W. (Burnley): 1968 v E. (1)
Miller, W. (Aberdeen): .1974 v E; 1975 v E, W, Se; 1976 v D, R, W, Ho. (2) (9)
Morrison, R. (Aberdeen): 1956 v E. (1)
Moncur, R. (Newcastle U.): 1968 v E, (1)
Munro, F. (Wolverhampton W.): 1970 v F, E, W (sub). 1971 v W. (4)
Murdoch, R. (Celtic): 1964 v E. (1)
Murray, D. (Cardiff C.): 1965v E. (1)
Murray, G. (Motherwell): 1964 v F; 1965 v W. E. (3)
Murray, M. (Rangers): 1956 v E; 1957 v E. (2)
Murray, S. (Dundee): 1968 v E. (1)

Narey, D. (Dundee U.): 1975 v R; 1976 v D. (2) (3)
Nicol, R. (Hibernian): 1956 v E, 1958 v Ho. (2)

Ogston, J. (Aberdeen): 1961 v E; 1962 v W, E. (3)
O'Hara, E. (Falkirk): 1958 v Ho (2), E. (3)
O'Hare, J. (Derby Co.): 1970 v F, E, W. (3)
Oliver, J. (Hearts): 1971 v W (sub). (1)

Parker, A. (Falkirk): 1955 v E; 1956 v E; 1957 v E; 1958 v Ho (2). E. (6)
Parlane, D. (Rangers): 1973 v E (sub), W; 1974 v W; 1975 v E, W. (5)
Pearson, J. (St. Johnstone): 1974 v W, E; 1975 (with Everton) v W (sub), Se, R; 1976 v D. (6)
Penman, A. (Dundee): 1960 v Bel; 1962 W; 1964 v v W; 1965 v E. (4)
Pettigrew, W. (Aberdeen): 1975 v Se, R; 1976 v D (2), R, W, Ho. (7)
Phillip, I. (Crystal P.): 1973 v E (1)

Plenderleith, J. (Hibernian): 1957 v E; 1958 v Ho (2), E; 1960 v W. (5)
Prentice, R. (Hearts): 1974 v W; 1976 v D (sub), R. (3)
Price, W. (Airdrieonians): 1956 v E; 1958 v Ho. (2)
Provan, D. (Rangers): 1964 v E. (1)
Purdie, I. (Aberdeen): 1975 v E (sub)

Rae, I. (Falkirk): 1956 v E. (1)
Reilly, F. (Dunfermline Ath.): 1957 v E. (1)
Riddell, I. (St. Mirren): 1960 v E; 1961 v E. (2)
Robb, D. (Aberdeen): 1970 v F, W; 1971 v E. (3)
Roberts, R. (Motherwell): 1962 v W. (1)
Robertson, H. (Dundee): 1962 v W. (1)
Robertson, J. (St. Mirren): 1964 v W; (with Tottenham H.) 1964 v F; 1965 v W; 1968 v E. (4)
Robinson, R. (Dundee): 1974 v W. (1)
Rough, A. (Partick T.): 1973 v E; 1975 v Se, R; 1976 v D (2), R, W, Ho (2), (9)

St. John, i. (Motherwell): 1960 v E, Bel. (2)
Scott, A. (Rangers): 1958 v E. (1)
Sharkey, D. (Sunderland): 1964 v F, E (2)
Shevlane, C. (Hearts): 1964 v W, F, E; 1965 v W. (4)
Slater R. (Falkirk): 1959 v W. (1)
Smith, D. (Aberdeen): 1963 v W; 1964 v W. (2)
Smith, G. (Kilmarnock): 1975 v W, Se, R (sub); 1976 v W (sub) (4)
Smith, G. (St. Johnstone): 1975 v R; 1976 v D (2), R (4)

Smith, J. (Aberdeen): 1967 v E. (1)
Smith, J. (Aberdeen): 1976 v Ho (1)
Sneddon, D. (Dundee): 1959 v W. (1)
Souness, G. (Middlesbrough): 1974 v E.; 1976 v Ho. (2)
Stanton, P. (Hibernian): 1967 v W, E; 1968 v E. (3)
Stein, C. (Hibernian): 1968 v E. (1)
Stewart, D. (Ayr U.): 1970 v W (1).
Stewart, J. (Kilmarnock): 1973 v W; 1974 v W, E; 1975 v E; 1976 v W (sub). (5)
Sullivan, D. (Clyde): 1975 v E, W (sub) (2)

Thomson, A. (Hearts): 1970 v F, E, W. (3)
Thomson, J. (Hearts): 1958 v E; 1960 v Bel. (2)
Tinney, H. (Partick T.): 1967 v W, E. (2)

Ure, I. (Dundee): 1961 v E. (1)

Wallace, J. (Dunfermline Ath.): 1974 v W. (1)
Walsh, J. (Celtic): 1955 v E. (1)
Weir, A. (Motherwell): 1960 v E, Bel, W. (3)
White, J. (Tottenham H.): 1960 v W. (1)
Whyte, J. (Aberdeen): 1967 v W, E. (2)
Wilson, R. (W.B.A.): 1970 v W. (1)
Wilson, D. (Rangers): 1959 v W. (1)
Wishart, R. (Aberdeen): 1955 v E; 1956 v E. (2)

Young, A. (Hearts): 1956 v E; 1957 v E; 1958 v E, Ho; 1959 v W; 1960 v W. (6)
Young, I. (Celtic): 1965 v E. (1)
Young Q, (Ayr U.): 1971 v E. (1)
Young, W. (Aberdeen): 1972 v W; 1973 v E; 1975 v W. R; 1976 v D

WALES

Aitken, P. (Bristol R.): 1975 v E, S; 1976 v S (sub), (3)
Aizlewood, S. (Newport Co.): 1972 v E, S; 1973 v S; 1974 v E; 1976 v S. (5)

Baker, C. (Cardiff C.): 1958. (1)
Baker, T. (Plymouth Arg.): 1958 v E; 1959 v S. (2)
Barry, M. (Carlisle U.): 1975 v E (sub) (1)
Blore, R. (Southport): 1962 v S; (with Blackburn R.) 1965 v E, S, Ni. (4)
Burton, O. (Newport Co.): 1961 v E; (with Norwich C.), 1963 v S, Ni; (with Newcastle U.) 1965 v E, S. (5)
Cartwright, L. (Coventry C.): 1974 v S; 1975 v E, S; 1976 v S (4)
Charles, M. (Swansea T.): 1958 v E. (1)
Coldrick, G. (Cardiff C.): 1967 v S; 1968 v E. (2)
Collins, J. (Portsmouth): 1967 v E, Ni; (with Tottenham) 1968 v E, Ni; 1969 v E; (with Portsmouth) 1972 v E, S. (7)
Curtis, A. (Swansea C.): 1976 v S (sub) (1)

Davies, C. (Charlton Ath.): 1971 v E, S; 1972: v E, S (sub). (4)
Davies, D. (Swansea C.): 1971 v E, (with Everton) S; 1975 v E. (3)
Davies, D. L. (Cardiff C.): 1967 v E. (1)
Davies, R. (Norwich C.): 1964 v S, Ni; 1965 v S, Ni. (4)
Davies, W. (Bolton W.): 1963 v S; 1964 v E; 1965 v S, Ni. (4)
Davis, G. (Wrexham): 1970 v E, S; 1971 v E, S. (4)
Deacy, N. (P.S.V. Eindhoven): 1976 v S. (1)
Derrett, S. (Cardiff C.): 1970 v E; 1971 v E, S. (3)
Draper, D. (Swansea T.): 1965 v E. (1)
Durban, A. (Cardiff C.): 1963 v Ni; (with Derby Co.) 1964 v E, S, Ni. (4)
Dwyer, P. (Cardiff C.): 1974 v E, S; 1975 v E, S; 1976 v S (5)

Edwards, M. (Bolton W.): 1958 v E; 1959 v S. (2)
Edwards, N. (Chester): 1973 v E. S; 1974 v E. (3)
Edwards, T. (Charlton Ath.): 1958 v E; 1959 v S. Ni. (2)
Emmanuel, G. (Birmingham C.): 1975 v S (1)
England, M. (Blackburn R.): 1960 v S; 1961 v E; 1962 v S, Ni; 1963 v Ni; 1964 v E, S, Ni; 1965 v E, S, Ni. (11)

Evans, B. C. (Swansea T.): 1965 v E, S. (2)
Evans, I. (Q.P.R.): 1973 v E; 1974 v S. (2)
Evans, M. (Wrexham): 1967 v Ni; 1970 v E. (2)
Evans, R. (Swansea T.): 1963 v Ni; 1964 v E, Ni. (3)

Flynn, B. (Burnley): 1975 v E, S (2)
Fox, A. (Wrexham): 1959 v S. (1)

Gammon, S. (Cardiff C.): 1960 v S; 1962 v Ni. (2)
Green, C. (Everton): 1962 v S. Ni; 1963 v S (with Birmingham C.) Ni; 1964 v E, S; 1965 v Ni. (7)
Griffiths, A. (Arsenal): 1961 v E (sub) 1962 v Ni; 1963 v S; (with Wrexham) 1964
Griffiths, C. (Manchester U.): 1974 v E, S. (2)
Godfrey, B. (Scunthorpe U.): 1962 v Ni. (1)
Gwyther, D. (Swansea C.): 1972 v E, S. (2)

Harris, C. (Leeds U.): 1976 v S. (1)
Hawkins, D. (Leeds U.): 1967 v S, Ni; 1968 v E, Ni; 1969 v E; (with Shrewsbury T.) 1970 v S. (6)
Hennessey, T. (Birmingham C.): 1962 v Ni; 1963 v Ni; 1964 v S, Ni; 1965 v E, S. (6)
Hole, B. (Cardiff C.): 1961 v S; 1962 v S; 1963 v S; 1965 v S, Ni. (5)
Hollins, D. (Brighton): 1960 v S; 1961 v E. (2)
Hopkins, M. (Tottenham H.): 1958 v E. (1)
Hubbard, T. (Swindon T.): 1973 v S. (sub); 1974 v E. (2)
Hughes, B. (Swansea T.): 1960 v S; 1961 v E. (2)
Hughes, J. (Blackpool): 1971 v E (sub) S. (2)
Humphreys, G. (Everton): 1965 v Ni; 1967 v E, S, Ni; 1969 v E. (5)

James, G. (Blackpool): 1965 v E, Ni. (2)
James, L. (Burnley): 1972 v E, S; 1973 v E, S; 1974 v E; 1975 v E, S (7)
John, D. (Cardiff C.): 1965 v S. (1)
Johnson, J. (C. Palace): 1974 v S; 1976 v S. (2)
Johnson, M. (Swansea T.): 1963 v S; 1964 v E. (2)
Jones, A. (Swansea T.): 1967 v E. (1)
Jones, B. (Bristol R.): 1971 v E. (1)
Jones, B. (Swansea T.): 1961 v E; 1962 v S, Ni; 1963 v S, Ni; 1964 v E, Ni; (with Plymouth Arg.) 1965 v S. (8)
Jones, C. (Tottenham H.): 1958 v E. (1)
Jones, D. (Bournemouth): 1973 v S; 1974 v E. S. (4)

Jones, F. (Brighton): 1959 v S; (with Swindon) 1961 v E. (2)
Jones, J. (Wrexham): 1974 v S; 1975 v E , S (with Liverpool); 1976 v S (4)
Jones, K. (Cardiff C.): 1958 v E. (1)
Jones, W. (Bristol R.): 1968 v E, Ni; 1969 v E; 1970 v S; 1971 v E, S. (6)
Jones, T. L. (Wrexham), 1963 v S. (1)

Krzywicki, R. (W.B.A.): 1967 v E, S; 1970 v S. (3)

Leek, K. (Northampton T.): 1958 v E. (1)
Letheran, G. (Leeds U.): 1976 v S. (1)
Lewis, B. (Cardiff C.): 1965 v Ni; 1967 v E, S; 1968 v E; (with Watford) 1968 v Ni. (5)
Lewis, J. (Grimsby T.): 1976 v . (1)
Llewellyn, D. (West Ham U.): 1972 v S. (1)
Lloyd, B. (Southend U.): 1970 v E, S. (2)
Lucas, A. (Wrexham): 1967 v S. (1)
Lucas M. (Leyton O.): 1962 v S.

Mahoney, J. (Crewe Alex.): 1967 v Ni; (with Stoke C.) 1969 v E; 1970 v E. (3)
Mielczarek, R. (Huddersfield T.): 1968 v E, Ni. (2)
Millington T. (W.B.A.): 1962 v S, Ni; 1963 v S, Ni. (4)
Moore, G. (Cardiff C.): 1960 v S; 1961 v E; 1962 v S; (with Chelsea) 1962 v Ni; 1963 v S, Ni; (with Manchester U.) 1964 v E, S, Ni. (9)
Morgan, R. (Cardiff): 1970 v S. (1)
Morgans, K. (Manchester U.): 1959 v S; 1960 v S. (2)

Nurse, M. (Swansea T.): 1960 v S; 1961 v E. (2)

Orritt, B. (Birmingham C.): 1958 v E; 1959 v S; 1960 v S. (3)
O'Sullivan, P. (Brighton): 1971 v S (sub), 1972 v E, S; 1973 v E, S; 1976 v S. (6)

Page, M. (Birmingham C.): 1967 v E, S; 1968 v Ni; 1969 v E; 1970 v E, S. (6)
Parton, J. (Burnley): 1972 v E, S; 1974 v E. (3)
Pearson, D.; 1970 v S. (1)
Phillips, J. (Chelsea): 1973 v E. S; 1974 v S; 1975 v S. (4)
Phillips, L. (Cardiff C.): 1971 v S; 1972 v S; 1973 v E, S (with Aston Villa). (4)
Powell, D. (Wrexham): 1967 v E, Ni; 1968 v E, Ni. (4)
Price, P. (Peterborough U.): 1970 v E, S; 1971 v E, S. (4)
Prince, F. (Bristol Rovers): 1971 v S; 1972 v E, S; 1973 v E. (4)
Pugh, D. (Newport Co.): 1967 v E, S. (2)

Randell, C. (Plymouth Arg.): 1975 v E (1)

Rankmore, F. (Cardiff C.): 1962 v S, Ni. (2)
Rees, R. (Coventry C.): 1963 v S, Ni; 1964 v E, S, Ni; 1965 v E, Ni. (7)
Rodrigues, P. (Cardiff C.): 1964 v S, Ni; 1965, v E, S, Ni. (5)
Roberts, D. (Oxford U.): 1973 v E, S; 1975 v E, (with Hull C.) S. (4)
Roberts, J. (Swansea T.): 1967 v Ni; 1968 v E; (with Northampton T.) 1968 v Ni (sub); 1969 v E; 1970 v E. (5)
Roberts, P. (Bristol R.): 1971 v E, S; 1972 v E, S.; 1973 v E, S. (6)
Roberts, R. (Wrexham): 1962 v S, Ni. (2)
Rouse, V. (C. Palace): 1959 v S. (1)
Rowland, J. (Newport Co.): 1959 v S. (1)
Ryan, J. (Charlton Ath.): 1965 v E. (1)

Screen, A. L. (Swansea C.); 1971 v S (sub). (1)
Screen, W. (Swansea T.): 1968 v Ni; 1969 v E. (2)
Sear, C. (Manchester C.): 1959 v S; 1960 v S. (2)
Showers, J. (Cardiff C.): 1973 v E, S; 1974 v E, S; 1975 v E, S (6)
Simpkins, K. (Hartlepools U.): 1967 v S. (1)
Smallman, D. (Wrexham): 1973 v S; 1974 v E, S, 1975 v E, (with Everton) S (5)
Sprake, G. (Leeds U.): 1964 v E, S, Ni; 1965 v E, Ni. (5)
Stephens, J. (Hull C.): 1958 v E. (1)
Summerhayes, D. (Cardiff C.): 1967 v S. (1)

Thomas, G. (Swansea T.): 1968 v E; 1971 v E, S. (3)
Thomas, M. (Wrexham): 1976 v S (sub). (1)
Thomas, J. (Newport Co.): 1967 v Ni. (1)
Thomas, J. (Swindon T.): 1967 v S, Ni; 1968 v Ni; 1969 v E; 1970 v E, S. (6)
Todd, K. H. (Swansea T.): 1963 v Ni (1)
Toshack, J. (Cardiff C.): 1967 v E. (with Liverpool) 1971 v E; 1972 v E. (3)

Vernon, R. (Blackburn R.): 1959 v S. (2)
Villars, A. (Cardiff C.): 1974 v E, S. (2)

Walker, M. (York C.): 1967 v Ni; 1968 v E, Ni. (3) (Watford) 1969 v E. (4)
Walley, T. (Arsenal): 1967 v E; Ni; (with Watford) 1968 v E, Ni. (4)
Williams, D. (Bristol R.): 1976 v S. (1)
Williams, G. (Swansea T.): 1960 v S. (1)
Williams, G. E. (W.B.A.): 1960 v S; 1961 v E. (2)
Williams, H. (Swansea T.): 1961 v E; 1962 v S; 1964 v S, E, Ni. (5)

Yorath, T. (Leeds U.): 1969 v E; 1970 v E, S; 1971 v E; 1972 v E, S; 1973 v E. (7)
Young, G. (Newport Co.): 1970 v E. (1)

'B' INTERNATIONAL MATCHES

ENGLAND v FINLAND

	England	Finland
1949 May 15 Helsinki	4	0

ENGLAND v FRANCE

	England	France
1952 May 22 Le Havre	1	7

ENGLAND v WEST GERMANY

	England	West Germany
1954 Mar. 24 Gelsenkirchen	4	0
1955 Mar. 23 Sheffield	1	1

ENGLAND v ITALY

	England	Italy
1950 May 11 Milan	0	5

ENGLAND v LUXEMBOURG

	England	Luxembourg
1950 May 21 Luxembourg	2	1

ENGLAND v NETHERLANDS

	England	Netherlands
1949 May 18 Amsterdam	4	0
1950 Feb. 22 Newcastle	1	0
1950 Mar. 17 Amsterdam	0	3
1952 Mar. 26 Amsterdam	1	0

ENGLAND v SCOTLAND

	England	Scotland
1953 Mar. 11 Edinburgh	2	2
1954 Mar. 3 Sunderland	1	1
1956 Feb. 29 Dundee	2	2
1957 Feb. 6 Birmingham	4	1

ENGLAND v SWITZERLAND

	England	Switzerland
1950 Jan. 18 Sheffield	5	0
1954 May 22 Basle	0	2
1956 Mar. 21 Southampton	4	1

ENGLAND v YUGOSLAVIA

	England	Yugoslavia
1954 May 16 Lubljana	1	2
1955 Oct. 19 Manchester	5	1

UNOFFICIAL INTERNATIONAL MATCHES

ENGLAND v SCOTLAND

Year	Date	Venue	England	Scotland
D1902	April 5	Glasgow	1	1
†1919	April 26	Everton	2	2
†1919	May 3	Glasgow	4	3
J1935	Aug. 21	Glasgow	2	4
*1939	Dec. 2	Newcastle	2	1
*1940	May 11	Glasgow	1	1
*1941	Feb. 8	Newcastle	2	3
*1941	May 3	Glasgow	3	1
*1941	Oct. 4	Wembley	2	0
*1942	Jan. 17	Wembley	3	0
*1942	April 18	Glasgow	4	5
*1942	Oct. 10	Wembley	0	0
*1943	April 17	Glasgow	4	0
*1943	Oct. 16	Manchester	8	0
*1944	Feb. 19	Wembley	6	2
*1944	April 22	Glasgow	3	2
*1944	Oct. 14	Wembley	6	2
*1945	Feb. 3	Aston Villa	3	2
*1945	April 14	Glasgow	6	1
†1946	April 13	Glasgow	0	1

ENGLAND v SWITZERLAND

	England	Switzerland
†1946 May 11 Chelsea	4	1

ENGLAND v FRANCE

	England	France
*1945 May 26 Wembley	2	2

ENGLAND v WALES

Year	Date	Venue	England	Wales
†1919	Oct. 11	Cardiff	1	2
†1919	Oct. 18	Stoke	2	0
*1939	Nov. 11	Cardiff	1	1
*1939	Nov. 18	Wrexham	3	2
*1940	April 13	Wembley	0	1
*1941	April 26	Nottingham	4	1
*1941	June 7	Cardiff	3	2
*1941	Oct. 25	Birmingham	2	1
*1942	May 9	Cardiff	0	1
*1942	Oct. 24	Wolverhampton	1	2
*1943	Feb. 27	Wembley	5	3
*1943	May 8	Cardiff	1	1
*1943	Sept. 25	Wembley	8	3
*1944	May 6	Cardiff	2	0
*1944	Sept. 16	Liverpool	2	2
*1945	May 5	Cardiff	3	2
†1945	Oct. 20	West Bromwich	0	1

ENGLAND v IRELAND

	England	Ireland
†1945 Sept. 15 Belfast	1	0

ENGLAND v BELGIUM

	England	Belgium
†1946 Jan. 19 Wembley	2	0

ENGLAND v TEAM AMERICA

	England	Team America
B1976 May 30 Philadelphia	3	1

D Declared unofficial owing to disaster at ground.
   † Victory.   J Jubilee.   * War-time.
B American Bicentennial Tournament

736

EUROPEAN FOOTBALL

EUROPEAN REVIEW

by Leslie Vernon

Tactical planning has become the key to success in international club football. Leading managers travel to watch the opposition not just once as they used to in order to give token notice of their respect and interest, but practically every week between the draw and the actual matches. Before each West Ham game, a member of the Greenwood-Lyall-Nicholson trio spied on their foes. Dettmar Cramer has been a regular visitor almost everywhere, and Miljan Miljanic must be the best customer the international airlines ever had. In itself, this search for information could be charitably described as 'thorough preparation', but for me it represents a regrettably negative philosophy. Managers, consciously or not, have decided that football is nothing but an animated chess-game, and if the pawns, masquerading as players, are pushed the right way on the board, the result ought to be favourable.

Such a clinical, scientific approach robs the game of its irresistible appeal. Football, at its best, is an incomparable drama, unscripted, spontaneous, full of invention, individuality, and surprise. Over-planning cannot ruin it entirely (nothing can!), but by legislating for all possibilities, it attempts to make the predictable inevitable! Tommy Docherty, who of course wasn't involved in European football this season, refuses to be drawn into this web of conformist conspiracy. He never looks at the opposition, hardly talks to his players about them, and allows free reign to off-the-cuff football. But the tactically 'more mature' Southampton took advantage of this idealistic attitude, and outmanoeuvred Manchester United in the Cup Final.

So, who was right? That is the dilemma facing the camp of 'progressive thinkers' who are eager to put 'entertainment' back into soccer. Patience was another hackneyed virtue which became eminently respectable during the season. Patience with a bunch of players who performed like cart-horses, patience in the build-up of attacks, patience to hold the ball until a telling pass was 'on'. In several games I have seen, the crowd needed the patience of Job to endure all the rubbish disguised as 'patience' which was served up to them.

The showgame of the year, the European Cup Final, was the most lurid example of the unholy matrimony between tactical overplanning and 'patience'. Bayern Munich took the enormous risk of not risking anything. Against the exuberant St. Etienne, they played with such cautious circumspection that no pass was ever longer than 10 yards, Beckenbauer ventured over the halfway line only twice, and the entire display lacked passion. One felt instinctively sorry for the green-shirted, small-town French team, as they hurled themselves towards the goal occupied by the implacable Maier. And if Sarramagna's finishing would have matched his speed and inventiveness, if Patrick Revelli's heading would have been more accurate, and if Rocheteau would have been introduced earlier, then perhaps . . . After all, the Bayern full-backs looked slow and ponderous, and especially in the first half, Larque was the best midfielder on the Hampden pitch. But Janvion did foul Muller, and from the resulting free-kick a Beckenbauer touch-on to Roth was fatal, when he hammered the ball past the gallant Curkovic.

Notwithstanding Bayern's technical excellence, I was disappointed with the European Cup treble winners. Indeed, of all their finals, only the second match against Atletico Madrid measured up to their lofty position as reigning monarchs of our continent. In the interview room after the Final, Dettmar Cramer – morose as ever – defended his team's strategy with this significant statement: 'Cups are there to be won. Our job was to hold on to this one, no other consideration entered into my calculations.'

In fact, Robert Herbin, the St Etienne boss, seemed the happier of the two because his boys at least tried to inject the game with some commendable adventure. Despite a 'cool Press', the experts were highly delighted with the match. It is true that compared with the hurly-burly of the Scotland v England game which was played at the same venue three days later, it was a monument to artistry and skill, but compared with the Real v Eintracht crescendo at Glasgow 16 years earlier, it was a testimony of the deterioration of football as a spectator sport.

Bill Shankly said: 'This was great football! The Continentals play fast, we are in a hurry!' I rest my case and confess that the earlier rounds of the tournament produced some remarkable encounters. Derby were perhaps fortunate to gain a three-goal advantage over Real Madrid at home, but the Spaniards were equally blessed with a co-operative referee in the second match. However, Santillana's extra-time goal deserved to win any game. Real's tie against Moenchengladbach brought the darker side of the coin into focus. With the overall score delicately poised at 3-3, the Germans had two 'goals' disallowed by the Dutch ref., Van Der Kroft. The second of these certainly looked perfectly legitimate, and one had the impression that no matter what 'Gladbach did, they wouldn't be permitted to KO the hosts. This is a sad indictment on the standard of refereeing, and indeed, in all three competitions one came across the same frustrating phenomenon time and again.

Glockner's senseless handling of the Den Haag v West Ham game, a doubtful penalty given to Liverpool by Biwersi against Bruges, Bayern's assisted passage into the next round against Malmoe, were the other depressing examples. Rangers were deservedly beaten by St. Etienne, in a year when the Scottish clubs failed to make any impression in Europe.

The Cup-Winners' Cup was crowned by a glorious final in Brussels. West Ham, always positive, always sportsmanlike, allowed Anderlecht to parade all their skills in this thrilling finale. The old adage that bad defences provide good football matches worked once again as the scoreline fluctuated. The Londoners dominated the first half partly because the limping Coeck was kept on the field by the Belgians' manager, Hans Croon. 1-1 at half-time with the injured Lampard off, and the West Ham defence even more disorganised than usual. Led by the mercurial (I cannot find a more original adjective) Rensenbrink, Anderlecht took the Hammers apart in the second half, and the finishing of Francois Van Der Elst brought back the blessed memory of an Irish pixie called George Best. West Ham earlier beat Eintracht Frankfurt and Ararat amongst others, while the Belgians were given an easy passage into the final. Perhaps the blind-folded virgin who pulls the numbers out of an opera hat in these UEFA draws knew that the final was scheduled for Brussels, and a large crowd would be financially desirable!

Wrexham deserve a mention for the efforts in this competition, but Celtic couldn't get past the East Germans, Sachsenring Zwickau – later beaten by Anderlecht 5-0! I have already mentioned Liverpool's luck when Steve Highway was grounded at Anfield a yard outside the box, and Keegan scored from the resulting penalty. But what a game, what a final! Bruges played magnificently for 30 minutes, scoring twice, and then in the second half, got run over by the irresistible Red steamroller. The return game was a less romantic affair, with the home team netting from the obligatory penalty, and Keegan equalizing after Herr Glockner gave a free-kick for dangerous play. (He is very keen on that. Just ask John Mahoney!)

However, Liverpool fully deserved their UEFA-Cup triumph. To remain unbeaten in Dresden, Barcelona, and Bruges is no small achievement. Aston Villa, below par, went out against Antwerp, Everton had no answers to Milan's man-to-man marking, and Ipswich were annihilated at Bruges 4-0 after beating the same team 3-0 at home. So, Bayern are once again on the zenith of the European plateau, Anderlecht have become the first Belgian club to win a major international tournament, and Liverpool have brought home the UEFA Cup after a three years' absence – the seventh win for England, if we count, as we should, the Fairs Cup as well.

I talked about tactics earlier in this review. Let's pose these questions. What would have happened in Glasgow if the half-fit Rocheteau would have been selected to play for St Etienne? What would have happened in Brussells if Coeck had gone off immediately after he was injured? What would have happened at Anfield, if at half-time, Bruges brought on an extra defender, and tried to sit on their lead? We shall never know, and that is what makes football such a glorious game!

EUROPEAN FOOTBALL CHAMPIONSHIP
(formerly EUROPEAN NATIONS' CUP)

Year	Winners		Runners-up		Venue
1960	USSR	2	Yugoslavia	1	Paris
1964	Spain	2	USSR	1	Madrid
1968	Italy	2	Yugoslavia	0	Rome
			After 1-1 draw		
1972	West Germany	3	USSR	0	Brussels

EUROPEAN NATIONS CUP 1958–60

PRELIMINARY ROUND
Eire 2, Czechoslovakia 0
Czechoslovakia 4, Eire 0

FIRST ROUND
France 7, Greece 1
Greece 1, France 1
USSR 3, Hungary 1
Hungary 0, USSR 1
Rumania 3, Turkey 0
Turkey 2, Rumania 0
Norway 0, Austria 1
Austria 5, Norway 2
Yugoslavia 2, Bulgaria 0
Bulgaria 1, Yugoslavia 1
Portugal 3, East Germany 2
East Germany 0, Portugal 2
Denmark 2, Czechoslovakia 2
Czechoslovakia 5, Denmark 1
Poland 2, Spain 4
Spain 3, Poland 0

QUARTER-FINALS
Portugal 2, Yugoslavia 1
Yugoslavia 5, Portugal 1
France 5, Austria 2
Austria 2, France 4
Rumania 0, Czechoslovakia 2
Czechoslovakia 3, Rumania 0
Russia w.o. Spain withdrew

SEMI-FINALS
Yugoslavia 5, France 4 (in Paris)
USSR 3, Czechoslovakia 0 (in Marseilles)

THIRD PLACE MATCH
Czechoslovakia 2, France 0

FINAL
(Paris, July 10, 1960)
USSR 2, Yugoslavia 1 after extra time
USSR: Yachin; Tchekeli, Kroutikov; Voinov, Maslenkin, Netto; Metreveli, Ivanov, Ponedelnik, Bubukin, Meshki.
Yugoslavia: Vidinic; Durkovic, Jusufi; Zanetic, Miladinovic, Perusic; Sekularac, Jerkovic, Galic, Matus, Kostic.
Scorers: Metreveli, Ponedelnik for USSR, Netto (own goal) for Yugoslavia.

EUROPEAN NATIONS CUP 1962–64

FIRST ROUND
Spain 6, Rumania 0
Rumania 3, Spain 1
Poland 0, Northern Ireland 2
Northern Ireland 2, Poland 0
Denmark 6, Malta 1
Malta 1, Denmark 3

Eire 4, Iceland 2
Iceland 1, Eire 1
Greece withdrew against Albania
East Germany 2, Czechoslovakia 1
Czechoslovakia 1, East Germany 1
Hungary 3, Wales 1
Wales 1, Hungary 1
Italy 6, Turkey 0
Turkey 0, Italy 1
Holland 3, Switzerland 1
Switzerland 1, Holland 1
Norway 0, Sweden 2
Sweden 1, Norway 1
Yugoslavia 3, Belgium 2
Belgium 0, Yugoslavia 1
Bulgaria 3, Portugal 1
Portugal 3, Bulgaria 1
Bulgaria 1, Portugal 0
England 1, France 1
France 5, England 2

SECOND ROUND
Spain 1, Northern Ireland 1
Northern Ireland 0, Spain 1
Denmark 4, Albania 0
Albania 1, Denmark 0
Austria 0, Eire 0
Eire 3, Austria 2
East Germany 1, Hungary 2
Hungary 3, East Germany 3
USSR 2, Italy 0
Italy 1, USSR 1
Holland 1, Luxembourg 1
Luxembourg 2, Holland 1
Yugoslavia 0, Sweden 0
Sweden 3, Yugoslavia 2
Bulgaria 1, France 0
France 3, Bulgaria 1

QUARTER-FINALS
Luxembourg 2, Denmark 2
Denmark 3, Luxembourg 3
Denmark 1, Luxembourg 0
Spain 5, Eire 1
Eire 0, Spain 2
France 1, Hungary 3
Hungary 2, France 1
Sweden 1, USSR 1
USSR 3, Sweden 1

SEMI-FINALS
USSR 3, Denmark 0 (in Barcelona)
Spain 2, Hungary 1 (in Madrid)

THIRD PLACE MATCH
Hungary 3, Denmark 1 after extra time

FINAL
(Madrid, June 21, 1964)
Spain (1) 2, USSR (1) 1
Spain: Iribar; Rivilla, Calleja; Fuste, Olivella, Zoco; Amancio, Pereda, Marcellino, Suarez, Lapetra.
USSR: Yachin; Chustikov, Mudrik; Voronin, Shesternjev, Anitchkin; Chislenko, Ivanov, Ponedelnik, Kornaev, Khusainov.
Scorers: Pereda, Marcellino for Spain, Khusainov for USSR.

GROUP 1

Eire 0, Spain 0
Eire 2, Turkey 1
Spain 2, Eire 0
Turkey 0, Spain 0
Turkey 2, Eire 1
Eire 0, Czechoslovakia 2
Spain 2, Turkey 0
Czechoslovakia 1, Spain 0
Spain 2, Czechoslovakia 1
Czechoslovakia 3, Turkey 0
Turkey 0, Czechoslovakia 0
Czechoslovakia 1, Eire 2

GROUP 2

Norway 0, Bulgaria 0
Portugal 1, Sweden 2
Bulgaria 4, Norway 2
Sweden 1, Portugal 1
Norway 1, Portugal 2
Sweden 0, Bulgaria 2
Norway 3, Sweden 1
Sweden 5, Norway 2
Bulgaria 3, Sweden 0
Portugal 2, Norway 1
Bulgaria 1, Portugal 0
Portugal 0, Bulgaria 0

GROUP 3

Finland 0, Austria 0	Austria 2, Finland 1
Greece 2, Finland 1	Greece 4, Austria 1
Finland 1, Greece 1	Austria 1, USSR 0
USSR 4, Austria 3	Greece 0, USSR 1
USSR 2, Finland 0	Austria 1, Greece 1
Finland 2, USSR 5	USSR 4, Greece 0

GROUP 4

Albania 0, Yugoslavia 2
West Germany 6, Albania 0
Yugoslavia 1, West Germany 0
West Germany 3, Yugoslavia 1
Yugoslavia 4, Albania 0
Albania 0, West Germany 0

GROUP 5

Holland 2, Hungary 2
Hungary 6, Denmark 0
Holland 2, Denmark 0
East Germany 4, Holland 3
Hungary 2, Holland 1
Denmark 0, Hungary 2
Denmark 1, East Germany 1
Holland 1, East Germany 0
Hungary 3, East Germany 1
Denmark 3, Holland 2
East Germany 3, Denmark 2
East Germany 1, Hungary 0

GROUP 6

Cyprus 1, Rumania 5
Rumania 4, Switzerland 2
Italy 3, Rumania 1
Cyprus 0, Italy 2
Rumania 7, Cyprus 0
Switzerland 7, Rumania 1
Italy 5, Cyprus 0
Switzerland 5, Cyprus 0
Switzerland 2, Italy 2

Italy 4, Switzerland 0
Cyprus 2, Switzerland 1
Rumania 0, Italy 1

GROUP 7

Poland 4, Luxembourg 0
France 2, Poland 1
Luxembourg 0, France 3
Luxembourg 0, Belgium 5
Luxembourg 0, Poland 0
Poland 3, Belgium 1
Belgium 2, France 1
Poland 1, France 4
Belgium 2, Poland 4
France 1, Belgium 1
Belgium 3, Luxembourg 0
France 3, Luxembourg 1

GROUP 8

Ireland 0, England 2
Wales 1, Scotland 1
England 5, Wales 1
Scotland 2, Ireland 1
Ireland 0, Wales 0
England 2, Scotland 3
Wales 0, England 3
Ireland 1, Scotland 0
England 2, Ireland 0
Scotland 3, Wales 2
Scotland 1, England 1
Wales 2, Ireland 0

QUARTER-FINALS

England 1, Spain 0
Spain 1, England 2
Bulgaria 3, Italy 2
Italy 2, Bulgaria 0
France 1, Yugoslavia 1
Yugoslavia 5, France 1
Hungary 2, USSR 0
USSR 3, Hungary 0

SEMI-FINALS

Yugoslavia 1, England 0 (in Florence)
Italy 0, USSR 0 (Italy won toss) (in Naples)

THIRD-PLACE MATCH (Rome)

England 2, USSR 0

FINAL (Rome, June 8, 1968)

Italy (0) 1 Yugoslavia (1) 1

Italy: Zoff; Burgnich, Facchetti; Ferrini, Guarneri, Castano; Domenghini, Juliano, Anastasi, Lodetti, Prati.

Yugoslavia: Pantelic; Fazlagic, Damjanovic; Pavlovic, Paunovic, Holcer; Petkovic, Acimovic, Musemic, Trivic, Dzajic.

Scorers: Italy, Domenghini. Yugoslavia, Dzajic.

REPLAYED FINAL (Rome, June 10, 1968)

Italy (2) 2, Yugoslavia (0) 0

Italy: Zoff; Burgnich, Facchetti; Rosato, Guarneri, Salvadore; Domenghini, Mazzola, Anastasi, De Sisti, Riva.

Yugoslavia: Pantelic; Fazlagic, Damjanovic; Pavlovic, Paunovic, Holcer; Hosic, Acimovic, Musemic, Trivic, Dzajic.

Scorers: Riva, Anastasi for Italy.

EUROPEAN CHAMPIONSHIP 1970–72

GROUP 1

Czechoslovakia 1, Finland 1
Rumania 3, Finland 0
Wales 0, Rumania 0
Wales 1, Czechoslovakia 3
Finland 0, Wales 1
Czechoslovakia 1, Rumania 0
Finland 0, Czechoslovakia 4
Finland 0, Rumania 4
Wales 3, Finland 0
Czechoslovakia 1, Wales 0
Rumania 2, Czechoslovakia 1
Rumania 2, Wales 0

GROUP 2

Norway 1, Hungary 3
France 3, Norway 1
Bulgaria 1, Norway 1
Hungary 1, France 1
Bulgaria 3, Hungary 0
Norway 1, Bulgaria 4
Norway 1, France 3
Hungary 2, Bulgaria 0
France 0, Hungary 2
Hungary 4, Norway 0
France 2, Bulgaria 1
Bulgaria 2, France 1

GROUP 3

Greece 0, Switzerland 1
Malta 1, Switzerland 2
Malta 0, England 1
England 3, Greece 0
Switzerland 5, Malta 0
England 5, Malta 0
Malta 1, Greece 1
Switzerland 1, Greece 0
Greece 2, Malta 0
Switzerland 2, England 3
England 1, Switzerland 1
Greece 0, England 2

GROUP 4

Spain 3, Northern Ireland 0
Cyprus 0, Northern Ireland 3
Northern Ireland 5, Cyprus 0
Cyprus 1, USSR 3
Cyprus 0, Spain 2
USSR 2, Spain 1
USSR 6, Cyprus 1
USSR 1, Northern Ireland 0
Northern Ireland 1, USSR 1
Spain 0, USSR 0
Spain 7, Cyprus 0
Northern Ireland 1, Spain 1

GROUP 5

Denmark 0, Portugal 1
Scotland 1, Denmark 0
Belgium 2, Denmark 0
Belgium 3, Scotland 0
Belgium 3, Portugal 0
Portugal 2, Scotland 0
Denmark 1, Scotland 0
Portugal 5, Denmark 0
Denmark 1, Belgium 2
Scotland 2 Portugal 1
Scotland 1, Belgium 0
Portugal 1, Belgium 1

GROUP 6

Eire 1, Sweden 1
Sweden 1, Eire 0
Austria 1, Italy 2
Italy 3, Eire 0
Eire 1, Italy 2
Eire 1, Austria 4
Sweden 1, Austria 0
Sweden 0, Italy 0
Austria 1, Sweden 0
Italy 3, Sweden 0
Austria 6, Eire 0
Italy 2, Austria 2

GROUP 7

Holland 1, Yugoslavia 1
East Germany 1, Holland 0
Luxembourg 0, East Germany 5
Yugoslavia 2, Holland 0
East Germany 2, Luxembourg 1
Luxembourg 0, Yugoslavia 2
Holland 6, Luxembourg 0
East Germany 1, Yugoslavia 2
Holland 3, East Germany 2
Yugoslavia 0, East Germany 0
Yugoslavia 0, Luxembourg 0
Luxembourg 0, Holland 8

GROUP 8

Poland 3, Albania 0
West Germany 1, Turkey 1
Turkey 2, Albania 1
Albania 0, West Germany 1
Turkey 0, West Germany 3
Albania 1, Poland 1
West Germany 2, Albania 0
Poland 5, Turkey 1
Poland 1, West Germany 3
Albania 3, Turkey 0
West Germany 0, Poland 0
Turkey 1, Poland 0

QUARTER-FINALS

England 1, West Germany 3
Italy 0, Belgium 0
Hungary 1, Rumania 1
Yugoslavia 0, USSR 0
West Germany 0, England 0
Belgium 2, Italy 1
USSR 3, Yugoslavia 0
Rumania 2, Hungary 2
Play-off: Hungary 2, Rumania 1

SEMI-FINALS

USSR 1, Hungary 0 (in Brussels)
West Germany 2, Belgium 1 (in Antwerp)

THIRD-PLACE MATCH (Liege)

Belgium 2, Hungary 1

FINAL (Brussels, June 18, 1972)

West Germany (1) 3 (*Muller* 2, *Wimmer*)

USSR (0) 0

West Germany: Maier, Hottges, Schwarzenbeck, Beckenbauer, Breitner, Hoeness, Wimmer, Netzer, Heynkes, Muller, Kremers.

USSR: Rudakov; Dzodzuashvili, Khurtsilava, Kaplichny, Istomin, Troshkin, Kolotov, Baidachni, Konkov (Dolmatov), Banishevski (Kozinkievits), Onishenko.

EUROPEAN CHAMPIONSHIP 1974-76

(Henri Delaunay Cup)

Qualifying Competition

GROUP 1

October 30 1974, Wembley
England (0) 3 (*Channon, Bell* 2)
Czechoslovakia (0) 0   86;000
England: Clemence; Madeley, Hughes, Dobson (Brooking), Watson, Hunter, Bell, Francis, Worthington (Thomas), Channon, Keegan.
Czechoslovakia: Viktor; Pivarnik, Varadin, Bicovsky (Kuna), Capkovic (Vojacek), Ondrus, Masny, Pekarik, Svehlik, Gajdusek, Stratil.

November 20 1974, Wembley
England (0) 0
Portugal (0) 0   85,700
England: Clemence; Madeley, Watson, Cooper (Todd), Brooking, Francis, Bell, Thomas, Channon, Clarke (Worthington).
Portugal: Damas; Artur, Humberto, Alhinho, Osvaldinho, Teixeira, Alves, Octavio, Martins, Nene (Romeu), Chico (Oliveira).

April 16 1975, Wembley
England (2) 5 (*Macdonald* 5)
Cyprus (0) 0   68,000
England: Shilton; Madeley, Watson, Todd, Beattie, Bell, Ball, Hudson, Channon (Thomas), Macdonald, Keegan.
Cyprus: Alkiviades (Constantinou I); Kovis, Zyzas, Koureas, Pantzarau, Michael, Savva, Theodorou, Stylianou, Charalambous (Constantinou II), Marcou.

April 20 1975, Prague
Czechoslovakia (2) 4 (*Panenka* 3, *Masny*)
Cyprus (0) 0   5000
Czechoslovakia: Viktor; Ondrus, Pivarnik, Capkovic (Petras), Koubek, Panenka, Bicovsky, Gajdusek, Masny, Svehlik, Nehoda.
Cyprus: Panos; Kovis, Zyzas, Stavros, Pantzarau, Gregory, Melis (Pnikos), Stefanis (Yolidis), Markos, Charalambous, Stylianou.

April 30 1975, Prague
Czechoslovakia (3) 5 (*Bicovsky* 2, *Nehoda* 2, *Petras*)
Portugal (0) 0   25,000
Czechoslovakia: Viktor; Ondrus, Pivarnik, Capkovic, Koubek (Svoboda), Bicovsky, Knapp (Medvid), Gajdusek, Masny, Petras. Nehoda.
Portugal: Damas; Rebelo, Humberto, Alhinho, Barros, Toni (Pietra), Fragito, Octavio, Alves, Marinho, Nene (Gomes).

May 11 1975, Limassol
Cyprus (0) 0
England (0) 1 (*Keegan*)   20,000
Cyprus: Constantinou; Kovis, Kyzas, Stylianou, Pantziaras, Michaél, Constantinou T., Miamilliotis, Savva, Charalambous, Panayotou.
England: Clemence; Whitworth, Beattie (Hughes), Hudson, Todd, Bell, Thomas, Ball, Channon, Macdonald, Keegan (Tueart).

June 8 1975, Limassol
Cyprus (0) 0
Portugal (1) 2 (*Nene, Moinhos*)   11,000

Cyprus: Stylianou F.; Nicolaou, Pantzaras, Stylianou S., Kyzas, Savva A., Michael, Charalambous (Economou), Marcou, Savva G., Papezzas (Kanaris).
Portugal: Damas; Artur, Humberto, Freitas, Barros, Toni, Octavio, Alves, Godinho, Nene (Moinhos), Marinho (Francisco Mario).

October 30 1975, Bratislava
Czechoslovakia (1) 2 (*Nehoda, Gallis*)
England (1) 1 (*Channon*)   45,000
Czechoslovakia: Viktor; Gogh (Dobias), Jurkemik, Ondrus, Pivarnik, Knapp, Bivocsky, Gallis, Pollak, Masny, Nehoda.
England: Clemence; Madeley, Gillard, Francis, McFarland (Watson,) Todd, Keegan, Channon (Thomas), Macdonald, Clarke, Bell.

November 12 1975, Porto
Portugal (1) 1 (*Nene*)
Czechoslovakia (1) 1 (*Ondrus*)   45,000
Portugal: Damas; Rebelo, Humberto, Freitas, Artur, Octavio, Alves, Toni, Moinhos, Vitor Baptista, Nene (Oliveira) (Marinho).
Czechoslovakia: Viktor; Pivarnik, Jurkemik, Ondrus, Gogh, Bicovsky, Pollak, Moder, Masny (Dobias), Gallis (Vesely), Nehoda.

November 19 1975, Lisbon
Portugal (1) 1 (*Rodrigues*)
England (1) 1 (*Channon*)   40,000
Portugal: Damas; Rebelo (Tai), Rodrigues (Carolina), Freitas, Artur, Toni, Alves, Octavio, Nene, Vitor Baptista, Moinhos.
England: Clemence; Whitworth, Beattie, Francis, Watson, Todd, Keegan, Channon, Macdonald (Thomas), Brooking, Madeley (Clarke).

November 23 1975, Limaso
Cyprus (0) 0   15,000
Czechoslovakia (3) 3 (*Nehoda, Bicovsky, Masny*)
Cyprus: Alkiviades; Fokkis (Kovis), Stylianou, Pantzares, Mertakkas, Michael, Savva, Marcou, Kaiafas (Miamiliotis), Papettas, Kanaris.
Czechoslovakia: Viktor; Pivarnik, Jurkemik, Ondrus, Gogh, Moder, Bicovsky, Pollak (Medvid), Masny, Svehlik (Vesely), Nehoda.

December 3 1975, Setubal
Portugal (1) 1 (*Alves*)
Cyprus (0) 0   4000
Portugal: Botelho; Artur, Mendes, Freitas, Lima, Toni, Octavio, Alves, Oliveira, Vitor Baptista Moinhos (Fernandes).
Cyprus: Stylianou F.; Stylianou S., Constantinou K., Pantzaras, Mertakkas, Christou, Michael, Kanaris (Panayiotou), Papezzas (Efthymiades), Savva G., Marcou.

	P	W	D	L	F	A	Pts.
Czechoslovakia	6	4	1	1	15	5	9
England	6	3	2	1	11	3	8
Portugal	6	2	3	1	5	7	7
Cyprus	6	0	0	6	0	16	0

GROUP 2

September 4 1974, Vienna
Austria (0) 2 (*Kreuz, Krankl*)
Wales (1) 1 (*Griffiths*)   34,000
Austria: Rettensteiner; Eigenstiller, Winkelbauer, Krieger, Kriess, Walzer, Stering, Kreuz, Krankl, Starek, Schlagbauer (Koglberger).
Wales: Sprake; Roberts P., Phillips, Roberts D., Roberts J., Yorath, Mahoney, Griffiths, Reece, Toshack, James.

October 13 1974, Luxembourg
Luxembourg (2) 2 (*Dussier* 2, 1 *pen.*)
Hungary (2) 4 (*Horvath, Nagy* 2, *Balint*)   3000
Luxembourg: Moes; Fandel, Flenghi, Hansen, De Grava, Philipp, Zwang, Trierweiler, Dussier, Braun, Langers.
Hungary: Meszaros; Torok, Harsanyi, Kantor, Balint, Horvath, Penzes, A. Toth, Kiss, Fazekas, L. Nagy.

October 30 1974, Cardiff
Wales (0) 2 (*Griffiths, Toshack*)
Hungary (0) 0   8445
Wales: Sprake (Phillips J.); Thomas, Roberts P., Mahoney, England, Phillips L., Griffiths, Yorath, Reece, Toshack, James.
Hungary: Meszaros; Torok, Balint, Kantor, Halmosi, Mucha, Fekete, A. Toth (Poczik), Fazekas, Kiss, L. Nagy.

November 20 1974, Swansea
Wales (1) 5 (*Toshack, England, Roberts P., Griffiths, Yorath*)
Luxembourg (0) 0   10,530
Wales: Sprake; Thomas, England, Roberts, P. Phillips, L., Mahoney (Flynn), Yorath, Griffiths, James, Reece, Toshack.
Luxembourg: Thill; Fandel, Flenghi, Hansen, Da Grava (Roemer), Trierweiler, Pilot, Zuang, Langers (Martin), Dussier, Phillip.

March 16 1975, Luxembourg
Luxembourg (1) 1 (*Braun*)
Austria (0) 2 (*Koglberger, Krankl*)   6000
Luxembourg: Moes; Fandel, Pilot, Hansen, Marque, Trierweiler, Philipp, Zuang, Zender (Gorres), Dussier, Braun.
Austria: Koncilla; Eigenstiller, Pajenk, Hof, Prohaska, Hickersberger, Hattenberger (Koglberger), Gombasch, Stering, Welzl, Krankl.

April 2 1975, Vienna
Austria (0) 0
Hungary (0) 0   70,000
Austria: Koncilla; Eigenstiller, Winkelbauer, Obermayer, Strasser, Hattenberger, Kreuz, Prohaska, Koglberger (Pirkner), Krankl, Jara.
Hungary: Meszaros; J. Toth, Balint, Horvath, Torok, A. Toth (Pinter), J. Nagy, Kocsis, Csapo, Branikovits (Fekete), Bene.

April 16 1975, Budapest
Hungary (0) 1 (*Branikovits*)
Wales (1) 2 (*Toshack, Mahoney*)   30,000
Hungary: Meszaros; Torok, J. Nagy, Balint, J. Toth, Csapo (Bene), Kocsis, Horvath (Horvath), Kozma, Branikovits, Mate.
Wales: Davies; Thomas, Page, Phillips L., Roberts J., Yorath, Mahoney, Griffiths, Reece (Smallman), Toshack, James (Flynn).

744

May 1 1975, Luxembourg
Luxembourg (1) 1 (*Philipp pen*)
Wales (2) 3 (*Reece, James* 2, 1 *pen*)   5000
Luxembourg: Moes; Pilot, Fandel, Hansen, Margue, Trierweiler, Zwang, Philipp, Martin (Krecke) (Roemer), Zender, Braun.
Wales: Davies; Page, Yorath, Thomas, Roberts D., Mahoney, Phillips, Griffiths (Flynn), Reece, Toshack, James.

September 24 1975, Budapest
Hungary (2) 2 (*Nyilasi, Pusztai*)
Austria (1) 1 (*Krankl pen.*)   30,000
Hungary: Kovacs; Nagy J., Balint, Rab (Varadi), Lukacs, Nyilasi, Kocsis, Toth A. (Pinter), Pusztai, Fazekas, Nagy L.
Austria: Koncilia F.; Obermayer (Winkelbauer), Sara, Pezzey, Kriess, Koncilia P. Prohaska (Steiner), Jara, Rinker, Welzl, Krankl.

October 15 1975, Vienna
Austria (3) 6 (*Welzl* 2, *Krankl* 2, 1 *pen., Jara, Prohaska*)
Luxembourg (2) 2 (*Braun, Phillip*)
Austria: Koncilia F.; Kriess, Winkelbauer, Pezzey, Strasser, Prohaska, Koncilia P., Ettmayer, Welzl, Krankl, Jara.
Luxembourg: Hoffmann; La Hure, Pilot, Hansen, Margue, Trierweiler, Zuang, Philipp, Langers (Krecke) Dussier (Hauer), Braun.

October 19 1975, Szombathely
Hungary (4) 8 (*Pinter, Nyilasi* 5, *Wollek, Varadi*)
Luxembourg (0) 1 (*Dussier*)   15,000
Hungary: Rothermel; Nagy J., Balint, Rab, Lukacs, Nyilasi, Kovacs J., Pinter, Fazekas, Varadi, Nagy L. (Wollek).
Luxembourg: Zender; Schmit, Pilot, Hansen, La Hure, Trierweiler (Flenghi), Zuang, Philipp, Langers (Krecke), Dussier, Braun.

November 19 1975, Wrexham
Wales (0) 1 (*Griffiths*)
Austria (0) 0   30,000
Wales: Lloyd; Thomas, Jones, Mahoney, Evans, Phillips, Griffiths, Flynn, Yorath, Smallman, James.
Austria: Koncilia F.; Sara, Winkelbauer, Pezzey, Kriess (Strasser), Prohaska, Steiner, Ettmayer, Welzl (Stering), Krankl, Jara.

	P	W	D	L	F	A	Pts.
WALES	6	5	0	1	14	4	10
Hungary	6	3	1	2	15	8	7
Austria	6	3	1	2	11	7	7
Luxembourg	6	0	0	6	7	28	0

GROUP 3

September 4 1974, Oslo
Norway (0) 2 (*Lund* 2)
Northern Ireland (1) 1 (*Finney*)   6585
Norway: Karlsen; Goa, Brakstad, Birkelund, Grondalen, Austboe, Johansen, Kvia, Fuglset, Lund, Hestad.
Northern Ireland: Jennings; Rice, Craig (Dowd), O'Kane, Hunter, Clements, Hamilton, Cassidy, Finney, McIlroy, McGrath (Jackson).

October 30 1974, Belgrade
Yugoslavia (1) 3 (*Vukotic, Katalinski* 2)
Norway (1) 1 (*Lund*)   9100
Yugoslavia: O. Petrovic; Dzoni, Buljan, Katalinski, Hadziabdic, Jerkovic, Zungul, Vukotic, Surjak, Vladic (Rajkovic), Dzajic.

Norway: Karlsen; Wormdal, Birkelund, Brakstad, Grondalen, Austboe, Kvia (Fuglset), Johansen, Olsen, Lund, Hestad.

October 30 1974, Solna
Sweden (0) 0
Northern Ireland (0) 2 (*O'Neill, Nicholl*)   16,657
Sweden: Hellstrom; Andersson B., Karlsson, Nordqvist, Andersson R., Tapper, Bo Larsson, Torstensson (Mattsson), Kindvall (Nordahl), Edstrom, Sandberg.
Northern Ireland: Jennings; O'Kane, Nelson (Blair), Dowd, Hunter, Nicholl, Jackson, O'Neill, Morgan, McIlroy, Hamilton.

March 16 1975, Belfast
Northern Ireland (1) 1 (*Hamilton*)
Yugoslavia (0) 0   30,000
Northern Ireland: Jennings; Rice, Nelson, Nicholl, Hunter, Clements, Hamilton, O'Neill, Spence, McIlroy, Jackson.
Yugoslavia: O. Petrovic; Muzinic, Katalinski, Peruzovic, Hadziabdic, Buljan, Oblak, Jerkovic (Milkovio), Danovic, Vukotic (Vladic), Surjak.

June 4 1975, Solna
Sweden (1) 1 (*Edstrom*)
Yugoslavia (1) 2 (*Katalinksi, Ivezic*)   27,250
Sweden: Hellstrom (Hagberg); Roland Andersson, Karlsson, Nordqvist, Augustsson, Frederiksson, Grahn, Edstrom, Sandberg, Sjoberg (Nordahl), Wendt.
Yugoslavia: Petrovic; Buljan, Muzinic, Katalinski, Hadziabdic, Oblak, Bogicevic, Vladic, Popivoda, Savic (Ivezic), Surjak.

June 9 1975, Oslo
Norway (0) 1 (*Thunberg*)
Yugoslavia (3) 3 (*Buljan, Bogicevic, Surjak*) 21,700
Norway: Johannessen; Meirik, Goa (Pedersen), Birkelund, Grondalen, Hested, Johanessen, Kvia, Thunberg, Lund, Hoyland.
Yugoslavia: Petrovic O.; Katalinski, Buljan, Muzinic, Hadziabdic, Bogicevic, Oblak, Vladic (Petrovic V.), Popivoda, Savic, Surjak.

June 30 1975, Solna
Sweden (1) 3 (*Nordahl 2, Grahn pen.*)   9580
Norway (0) 1 (*Olsen*)
Sweden: Hellstrom; Roland Andersson, Karlsson, Roy Andersson, Augustsson, Linderoth, Grahn, Fredriksson (Olsberg) Sandberg, Nordahl, Wendt (Mattsson).
Norway: Johannesen (Antonsen); Meirik, Karlsen, Grondalen, Pedersen, Johansen, Kvia, Olsen, Larsen (Thunberg) Skuseth, Hoyland.

August 13 1975, Oslo
Norway (0) 0
Sweden (1) 2 (*Sandberg, Sjoberg*)   18,011
Norway: Antonsen; Pedersen, Karlsen, Grondalen, Slinning, Hansen, Kvia, Thunberg (T. E. Johansen), Larsen, Skuseth, Hoyland (Mathisen).
Sweden: Hellstrom; Roland Andersson, Karlsson, Nordqvist, Augustsson Grahn, Linderoth, Edstrom, Sandberg, Sjoberg, Wendt (Mattsson).

September 3 1975, Belfast
Northern Ireland (1) 1 (*Hunter*)
Sweden (1) 2 (*Sjoberg, Torstensson*)   12,000
Northern Ireland: Jennings; Rice, Nelson, Clements, Hunter, Nicholl, Blair, Hamilton (Morgan), Spence, McIlroy, Jackson.

Sweden: Hellstrom; Andersson, Karlsson, Nordqvist, Augustsson, Fredriksson, Torstensson, Linderoth, Sjoberg, Mattson, Olsberg (Tapper).

October 15 1975, Zagreb
Yugoslavia (1) 3 (*Oblak, Vladic, Vabec*)
Sweden (0) 0   45,000
Yugoslavia: Petrovic; Buljan, Katalanski, Vabec, Hadziabdic, Muzinic, Oblak, Vladic, Surjak, Jerkovic, Dzajic.
Sweden: Hellstrom, Roland Andersson, Nordqvist, Karlsson, Augustsson, Tapper, Torstensson, Lineroth, Sjoberg (Matsson), Edstrom, Sandberg.

October 29 1975, Belfast
Northern Ireland (2) 3 (*Morgan, McIlroy, Hamilton*)
Norway (0) 0   8000
Northern Ireland: Jennings; Rice, Nelson, Nicholl, Hunter, Jackson, Hamilton, McIlroy, Morgan (Cochrane), Jamison, Finney.
Norway: Karlsen G. (Jacobsen T.); Petersen, Grondalen (Josefsen), Karlsen H., Slinning, Hansen, Kvia, Skuseth, Hoyland, Jacobsen P., Hestad.

November 19 1975, Belgrade
Yugoslavia (1) 1 (*Oblak*)
Northern Ireland (0) 0   30,000
Yugoslavia: Petrovic; Buljan, Hadziabdic, Oblak, Katalinski, Muzinic, Jerkovic, Vukotic, Surjak, Vladic, Dzajic.
Northern Ireland: Jennings; Rice, Scott, Nicholl, Hunter, Clements, Hamilton, McIlroy, Morgan, Jackson (O'Neill), Finney.

	P	W	D	L	F	A	Pts.
YUGOSLAVIA	6	5	0	1	11	4	10
Northern Ireland	6	3	0	3	8	4	6
Sweden	6	3	0	3	8	9	6
Norway	6	1	0	5	5	15	2

GROUP 4
September 25 1974, Copenhagen
Denmark (0) 1 (*Nygaard pen*)
Spain (2) 2 (*Claramunt pen, Roberto Martinez*) 27,300
Denmark: Larsen, Mortensen, Munk Jensen, Seneca, Rasmussen, Sorensen, (Jorgensen) John Olsen, Nygaard, Simonsen, Henning Jensen, Holmstrom (Flindtbjerg).
Spain: Iribar; Sol, Benito, Capon, Jesus Martinez, Castellanos, Roberto Martinez (Garcia Soriano) Claramunt, Asensi, Marcial, Quini.

October 13 1974, Copenhagen
Denmark (0) 0
Rumania (0) 0   15,700
Denmark: Larsen; Mortensen, Munk Jensen, Danielsen, Rasmussen, John Olsen, Le Fevre, Jorgensen, Nielsen, Lund, Holmstrom.
Rumania: Raducanu; Cheran, Antonescu, Satmareanu, Anghelini, Dinu, Nunweiler, Kun, Jordanescu, Dumitru, Lucescu (Troi).

November 20 1974, Glasgow
Scotland (1) 1 (*Bremner*)
Spain (1) 2 (*Quini 2*)   92,000
Scotland: Harvey; Jardine, Forsyth, McQueen, Burns, Bremner, Souness, Hutchison (Dalglish), Johnstone, Deans (Lorimer), Jordan.
Spain: Iribar; Castellanos, Benito, Costas, Capon, Migueli (Sol), Villar, Planas, Roberto Martinez, Quini, Rexach.

February 5, 1975, Valencia

Spain (0) 1 (*Megido*) 60,000

Scotland (1) 1 (*Jordan*)

Spain: Iribar; Sol, Benito, Costas, (Migueli) Camacho, Claramunt, Villar, Asensi, Rexach, Garate (Megido), Quini.

Scotland: Harvey; Jardine, McQueen, Buchan, McGrain, Bremner, Cooke, Hutchison, Dalglish, Jordan (Parlane), Burns (Wilson).

April 17 1975, Madrid

Spain (1) 1 (*Velasquez*)

Rumania (0) 1 (*Crisan*) 100,000

Spain: Iribar; Camacho, Capon, Benito, De Bosque, Pirri, Velazquez (Irureta), Santillana Rexach, Rojo, Garate.

Rumania: Raducanu; Cheran, Sandu, Satmareanu, Anghelini, Balaci, Georgescu, Dumitru, Nunweiler (Crisan), Kun (Jordanescu), Lucescu.

May 11 1975, Bucharest

Rumania (2) 6 (*Georgescu* 2, *Crisan* 2, *Lucescu*, *Dinu*)

Denmark (0) 1 (*Dahl*) 60,000

Rumania: Raducanu; Cheran, Sandu, Satmareanu, Anghelini, Dumitru (Balaci), Dinu, Georgescu, Crisan, Dobrin (Kun), Lucescu.

Denmark: Bent Larsen (Poulsen); Mortensen, Jensen, Lars Larsen, Rasmussen, Sorensen (F. Nielsen), Olsen, Jorgensen, Mauritzen, Dahl, E. Nielsen.

June 1 1975, Bucharest

Rumania (1) 1 (*Georgescu*)

Scotland (0) 1 (*McQueen*) 80,000

Rumania: Raducanu; Cheran, Sandu, Anghelini (Kun), Satmareanu, Dinu, Crisan, Georgescu (Balaci), Dobrin, Dumitru, Lucescu.

Scotland: Brown; McGrain, Forsyth, Munro, McQueen, Rioch (Hutchison), Dalglish, Miller, Parlane, Macari (Robinson), Duncan.

September 3 1975, Copenhagen

Denmark (0) 0

Scotland (0) 1 (*Harper*) 40,300

Denmark: Jensen B.; Mortensen, Jensen M., Larsen, Thune, Flindtberg, Simonsen, Neilsen B., Bjornmose, Jensen H., Le Fevre.

Scotland: Harvey; McGrain, Forsyth, Bremner, McQueen, Buchan, Lorimer, Dalglish, Harper, Rioch, Hutchison (Duncan).

October 12 1975, Barcelona

Spain (1) 2 (*Pirri, Capon*)

Denmark (0) 0 20,000

Spain: Miguel Angel; Ramos, Benito, Marcial, Capon, Migueli, Solsona, Pirri, Santillana, Del Bosque (Asensi), Rexach (Churruca).

Denmark: Bo Larsen; Johnny Hansen, Andersen, Munk Jensen, Lars Larsen, Flindt, Hansen H., Sorensen (Nielsen C.), Rasmussen, Bastrup, Dahl.

October 29 1975, Glasgow

Scotland (0) 3 (*Dalglish, Rioch, MacDougall*)

Denmark (1) 1 (*Bastrup*) 48,021

Scotland: Harvey; McGrain, Houston, Greig, Jackson, Rioch, Lorimer, Dalglish, MacDougall (Parlane), Hartford, Gemmill.

Denmark: Ben Larsen; Andersen, Jensen, Lars Larsen, Hansen J., Sorensen, Hansen H., Thune (Nielsen F.), Nygaard, Bastrup, Kolding.

November 16 1975, Bucharest

Rumania (0) 2 (*Georgescu pen., Jordanescu*)

Spain (1) 2 (*Villar, Santillana*) 50,000

Rumania: Raducanu; Angelini, Sandu G., Satmareanu, Lucuta, Georgescu, Dobrin, Dinu, Sandu M. (Jordanescu), Zamfir (Crisan), Lucescu.

Spain: Miguel Angel; Sol, Benito, Pirri, Camacho, Migueli, Del Bosque, Villar, Quini (Satrustegui), Santillana, Rojo (Fortes).

December 17 1975, Glasgow

Scotland (1) 1 (*Rioch*)

Rumania (0) 1 (*Hainal*) 11,375

Scotland: Cruickshank; Brownlie, Donachie, Buchan, Jackson, Rioch, Doyle (Lorimer), Hartford, Gray, Dalglish (MacDougall), Gemmill.

Rumania: Raducanu; Cheran, Sandu, Anghelini, Satmareaunu, Dinu, Lucescu (Hainal), Romila, Georgescu, Boloni, Jordanescu.

	P	W	D	L	F	A	Pts.
SPAIN	6	3	3	0	10	6	9
Rumania	6	1	5	0	11	6	7
Scotland	6	2	3	1	8	6	7
Denmark	6	0	1	5	3	14	1

GROUP 5

September 1 1974, Helsinki

Finland (1) 1 (*Rahja*)

Poland (1) 2 (*Szarmach, Lato*) 19,000

Finland: Alaja; Forsell, Tolsa, Vihtila, Ranta, Soumalainen, (Nikkanen) Rahja, Heiskanen, Tiovola, Paatelainen, (Manninen) Laine.

Poland: Tomaszewski; Symanowski, Gorgon, Musial, Bulzacki, Maszczyk, Kasperczak (Kusto) Cmikievicz, Lato, Szarmach, Gadocha.

September 25 1974, Helsinki

Finland (1) 1 (*Rahja*)

Holland (2) 3 (*Cruyff* 2, *Neeskens*) 20,449

Finland: Holli; Saari, Tolsa, Vihtila, Ranta, Suomalainen, Heiskanen (Rissanen), Hukka (Toivola), Rahja, Petterson, Laine.

Holland: Jongbloed; Van Ierssel, De Jong, Haan, Krol, Jansen, Neeskens, Van Hanegem, (Notten) (Geels) Rep, Cruyff, Ressel.

October 9 1974, Poznan

Poland (2) 3 (*Kasperczak, Gadocha, Lato*)

Finland (0) 0 40,000

Poland: Tomaszewski; Szymanowski, Ostafinski, Wybrobek, Drzewiecki, Kasperczak, (Jakobczak), Deyna, Bula, Lato, Szarmach (Marx), Gadocha.

Finland: Holli, Saari, Tolsa, Vihtila, Ranta, Suomalainen, Heiskanen, (Laine) Rakja, Rissanen, (Pettersson) Toivola, Paatelainen.

November 20 1974, Rotterdam

Holland (1) 3 (*Resenbrink, Cruyff* 2)

Italy (1) 1 (*Boninsegna*) 60,000

Holland: Jongbloed; Suurbier, Haan, Rijsbergen, Krol, Van der Kuylen, Neeskens, Van Hanegem, Rep (Willy van Der Kerkhof), Cruyff, Resenbrink.

Italy: Zoff; Rocca, Zecchini, Orlandini, Roggi-Juliano, Morini, Antognoni, Causio, Boninsegna, Anastasi.

April 19 1975, Rome

Italy (0) 0

Poland (0) 0 90,000

Italy: Zoff; Facchetti, Gentile, Bellugi, Rocca, Cordova, Antognoni, G. Morini, Graziani, Chinaglia, Pulici.

Poland: Tomaszewski; Gorgon, Szymanovski, Zmuda, Wawrowski, Kasperczak (Cmikiewicz) Deyna, Maszczyk, Lato, Szarmach, Gadocha,

June 5 1975, Helsinki
Finland (0) 0
Italy (1) 1 (*Chinaglia*)   17,700
Finland: Enckelman; Vihtila, Tolsa, Paatelainen, Ranta, Suomalainen, Kymalainen (Rissanen), Heiskanen, Manninen, Laine (Nieminen), Toivola.
Italy: Zoff; Gentile, Bellugi, Facchetti, Rocca, Cordova (Orlandini), Antognoni, Capello, Graziani, Chinaglia, Bettega.

September 3 1975, Nijmegen
Holland (2) 4 (*Van der Kuylen* 3, *Lubse*)
Finland (1) 1 (*Paatelainen*)   28,000
Holland: Van Beveren; Van Kraay, Suurbier, Overweg, Krol, Peters, Jansen, Van Hanegem, Rene van der Kerkhof, Lubse, Van der Kuylen.
Finland: Enckelmann; Vihtila, Makinen, Forssel, Eskoranta, Rissanen E., Hamalainen, Suomalainen (Laine), Heiskanen (Suhonen), Rissanen O., Paatelainen.

September 10 1975, Chorzow
Poland (2) 4 (*Lato, Gadocha* 2, *Szarmach*)
Holland (0) 1 (*Van de Kerkhof*)   100,000
Poland: Tomaszewski; Zmuda, Szymanowski, Bulzacki, Wawrowski, Kasperczak, Deyna, Maszczyk, Lato, Szarmach, Gadocha.
Holland: Van Beveren; Van Kraay, Suurbier, Overweg, Krol, Jansen, Neeskens, Van Hanegem (Geels), Rene van der Kerkhof, Cruyff, Van der Kuylen.

September 27 1975, Rome
Italy (0) 0
Finland (0) 0   29,000
Italy: Zoff; Rocca, Roggi, Benetti, Bellugi, Facchetti, Graziani, Pecci, Savoldi, Antognoni, Morini G.
Finland: Enckelman; Vihtala, Paatelainen, Tolsa, Ranta, Suomalainen, Jantunen, Heiskanen, Rissanen (Hamalainen), Makynen (Kantonen), Toivola

October 15 1975, Amsterdam
Holland (1) 3 (*Neeskens, Geels, Thijssen*)
Poland (0) 0   60,000
Holland: Schrijvers; Suurbier, Krijgh, Van Kraay, Krol, Neeskens, Jansen, Thijssen, Geels, Cruyff, Rene van der Kerkhof.
Poland: Tomaszewski; Szymanowski, Bulzacki, Zmuda, Wawrowski, Maszczyk, Deyna (Bula), Kasperczak, Lato, Szarmach, Gadocha.

October 26 1975, Warsaw
Poland (0) 0
Italy (0) 0   70,000
Poland: Tomaszewski; Szymanowski, Ostafinski, Zmuda, Wawrowski, Kasperczak, Bula (Marx), Deyna, Lato, Szarmach, Gadocha (Kmiecik).
Italy: Zoff; Gentile, Bellugi, Facchetti, Rocca, Benetti, Causio, Cuccureddu, Antognoni (Zaccarelli), Anastasi (Bettega), Pulici.

November 22 1975, Rome
Italy (1) 1 (*Capello*)
Holland (0) 0   80,000
Italy: Zoff; Gentile, Bellugi, Facchetti, Rocca, Benetti, Capello, Antognoni, Causio, Savoldi, Pulici.
Holland: Schrijvers; Suurbier, Krijgh, Van Kraay, Krol, Peters, Jansen, Thijssen, Rene van der Kerkhof, Geels, Willy van der Kerkhof (Notten).

	P	W	D	L	F	A	Pts.
HOLLAND	6	4	0	2	14	8	8
Poland	6	3	2	1	9	5	8
Italy	6	2	3	1	3	3	7
Finland	6	0	1	5	3	13	1

GROUP 6

October 30 1974, Dublin
Eire (2) 3 (*Givens* 3)
Russia (0) 0   32,000
Eire: Roche; Kinnear, Mulligan, Mancini, Holmes, Martin, Giles, Brady, Heighway, Givens, Treacy.
Russia: Pilgui; Nikolini, Olshansky, Matvienko, Kaplichny, Lovchev, Veremeyev, Onischenko, Kolotov Fedotov (Feodorov). Blokhin.

November 20 1974, Izmir
Turkey (0) 1 (*Conroy og*)
Eire (0) 1 (*Givens*)   67,000
Turkey: Yasin; Alpasian, Ziya, Ismail, Zekeriya, Engin, Selcuk, Fuji Mehmet (Osman), Buyuk Mehmet, Cemil, Metin.
Eire: Roche; Kinnear, Mulligan, Hand, Dunne, Brady, Martin, Giles, Heighway, Conroy (Dennehy), Givens.

December 1 1974, Izmir
Turkey (1) 2 (*Ismail, Buyuk Mehmet*)
Switzerland (1) 1 (*Schild*)   51,410
Turkey: Yasin; Alpasian, Ismail, Ziya, Zekediya, Kucuk Mehmet, Selcuk (Rasit), Engin, Osman (Buyuk Mehmet), Cemil, Metin.
Switzerland: Burgener; Hasler, Guyot, Bizzini, Botteron, Schild, Kuhn, Schneeberger, Pfister (Rutschmann), Jeandupeux, Muller.

April 2 1975, Kiev
Russia (1) 3 (*Kolotov* 2, *Blokhin*)
Turkey (0) 0   100,000
Russia: Rudakov; Troschkin, Fomenko, Reshko, Matvienko, Konkov (Burjak), Muntian, Veremeyev, Kolotov. Onishenko (Feodorov), Blokhin.
Turkey: Sabri; Alpaslan, Zafer, Ismail, Kemal, Siya, Rashit, Metin (Turgay), Engin, Ali-Kemal, Cemil.

April 30 1975, Zurich
Switzerland (1) 1 (*Muller*)
Turkey (0) 1 (*Alpasian*)   23,000
Switzerland: Kunz; Guyot, Heer, Bizzini, Fischbach, Hasler (Schild), Botteron, Rutschmann (Pfister), Muller, Jeandupeux, Elsener.
Turkey: Yasin; Ziya, Alpasian, Ismail, Fatih, Zekeriya, Engin, Nikola, Ali-Kemal (Aydin), Gokmen, Cemil.

May 11 1975, Dublin
Eire (2) 2 (*Martin, Treacy*)
Switzerland (0) 1 (*Muller*)   50,000
Eire: Roche; Kinnear, Mulligan, Hand, Dunne, Martin, Giles, Brady, Conroy, Treacy, Givens.
Switzerland: Burgener; Guyot, Bizzini, Heer, Hasler, Schild, Kuhn, Botteron, Rutschmann, Muller, Jeandupeux.

May 18 1975, Kiev
Russia (2) 2 (*Blokhin, Kolotov*)
Eire (0) 1 (*Hand*)   100,000
Russia: Rudakov; Fomenko, Troschkin, Konkov, Matvienko, Burjak, Muntian (Reshko), Kolotov, Onishenko, Veremeyev (Feodorov), Blokhin.
Eire: Roche; Kinnear, Mulligan, Hand, Dunne, Martin, Giles, Brady, Conroy, Givens, Heighway.

May 21 1975, Berne
Switzerland (0) 1 (*Elsener*)
Eire (0) 0   15,000
Switzerland: Burgener, Guyot, Bizzini, Trinchero, Fischbach, Kuhn, Hasler, Botteron, Rutschmann (Pfister), Muller (Elsener), Jeandupeux.
Eire: Roche; Dunne, Mulligan, Hand, Holmes, Martin, Giles (Daly), Brady, Conroy, Treacy, Givens.

October 12 1975, Zurich
Switzerland (0) 0
Russia (0) 1 (*Muntjan*)   18,000
Switzerland: Burgener; Bizzini, Guyot, Trinchero (Schneeberger), Fischbach, Muller, Kuhn, Botteron (Schwiwiler), Pfister, Risi, Jeandupeux.
Russia: Rudakov; Fomenko, Troschkin (Reschko), Zwianguentsev, Lovchev, Konkov, Muntian, Burjak (Sacharov), Onischenko, Veremejev, Blokhin.

October 29 1975, Dublin
Eire (3) 4 (*Givens* 4)
Turkey (0) 0   25,000
Eire: Roche, Dunne (Kinnear); Holmes, Mulligan, Hand, Martin, Brady, Giles, Treacy, Givens, Heighway (Conroy).
Turkey: Yasin (Rasin); Sabhattin, Ismail (Zafer), Alpasian, Fatih, Kadir, Engin, Nocati, Gokmen, Kemal, Cemil.

November 12 1975, Kiev
Russia (2) 4 (*Konkov, Onischenko* 2, *Veremejev*)
Switzerland (1) 1 (*Risi*)   40,000
Russia: Rudakov; Fomenko, Troschkin, Zwianguentsev, Lovchev, Konkov (Sacharov), Burjak, Muntian (Kolotov), Onischenko, Veremejev, Blokhin.
Switzerland: Burgener; Trinchero, Bizzini, Guyot, Fischbach, Botteron, Kuhn, Schneeberger, Muller, Risi, Jeandupeux.

November 23 1975, Ankara
Turkey (1) 1 (*Cemil*)
Russia (0) 0   80,000
Turkey: Rasim; Turgay, Fatih, Ismail, Sabahattin F., Mehmet (Eser), Ali, Kadir A., Kemal, Gokmen (Borhan), Cemil.
Russia: Rudakov; Konkov, Fomenko, Reschko, Sujev, Muntian (Burjak), Zwianguentsev, Veremejev, Onischenko, Kolotov, Blokhin.

	P	W	D	L	F	A	Pts.
RUSSIA	6	4	0	2	10	6	8
Eire	6	3	1	2	11	5	7
Turkey	6	2	2	2	5	10	6
Switzerland	6	1	1	4	5	10	3

GROUP 7
September 8 1974, Reykjavik
Iceland (0) 0
Belgium (1) 2 (*Van Moer* 2, 1 *pen*)   7,600
Iceland: Olaffsson; Torfasson, Petursson, Sigurvinsson, Geirsson, Elvadsson, Leifsson, Magnusson, Thoradsson (Hallgrimsson), Eliassonn, Hermasson.
Belgium: Piot; Van Binst, Broos, Van Den Daele, Coeck (Cools), Van Himst, Verheyen, Van Moer, Van Der Elst, Janssens (Teugels), Henrotay.

October 12 1974, Magdeburg
East Germany (1) 1 (*Hoffmann*)
Iceland (1) 1 (*Hallgrimsson*)   16,000
East Germany: Schulze; Weise, Zapt, Bransch, Watzlich (Dorner), Kubjuweit, Decker, Pommerenke (Vogel), Ducke, Streich, Hoffmann.
Iceland: Olaffsson; Torasson (Thorsteinsson), Petursson, Sigurvinsson, Geirsson, Evaldsson, Leifsson, Magnusson, Thoradsson (Hedinsson), Hallgrimsson, Eliasson.

October 12 1974, Brussels
Belgium (1) 2 (*Martens, Van der Elst*)
France (1) 1 (*Coste*)   50,000
Belgium: Piot; Van Binst, Broos, Van Den Daele, Martens, Van Moer, Verheyen, Van Himst (Dockx), Van der Elst, Lambert, Teugels.
France: Bartelli; Jodar, Adams, Tresor, Bracci, Huck, Michel, Guillou, Coste, Lacombe (Gallice), Bereta.

November 16 1974, Paris
France (0) 2 (*Guillou, Gallice*)
East Germany (1) 2 (*Sparwasser, Kreische*)   50,000
France: Bertrand; Demanes, Jodar, Tresor, Adams, Bracci, Michel (Synaeghel), Huck, Guillou, Soler, Coste (Gallice), Bereta.
East Germany: Croy; Kische, Dorner, Weise, Watzlich, Kurbjuweit, Lauck, Hafner, Kreische (Seguin), Sparwasser, Hoffmann.

December 7 1974, Leipzig
East Germany (0) 0
Belgium (0) 0   50,000
East Germany: Croy; Dorner, Kische, Weise, Watzlich (Kreische), Hafner, Lauck, Kurbjuweit, Hoffmann, Streich, Vogel.
Belgium: Piot; Broos, Van Binst, Van Den Daele, Martens, Verheyen, Dewalque, Van Himst (Van der Elst), Cools, Lambert, Teugels.

May 25 1975, Reykjavik
Iceland (0) 0
France (0) 0   11,000
Iceland: Dagsson; Torfasson, M. Geirsson, Edwaldsson, Petursson, Hermansson (Magnusson), Sigurvinsson, Juliusson, Leifsson, Hallgrimsson (E. Geirsson), Thordesson.
France: Baratelli; Lopez, Adams, Tresor, Bracci, Michel, Larque, Guillou, Gallice (Parizon), Berdoll, Bereta.

June 5 1975, Reykjavik
Iceland (2) 2 (*Edvaldsson, Sigurvinsson*)
East Germany (0) 1 (*Pommerenke*)   11,500
Iceland: Dagsson; Edvaldsson, Geirsson M., Torfasson, Petursson, Sigurvinsson, Hilmarsson (Hermannsson), Leifsson, Thordarsson, Geirsson E. (Hallgrimsson), Juliusson.
East Germany: Croy; Zapf (Riediger), Kische, Weise, Watzlich, Pommerenke, Schnuphase (Dorner), Kurbjuweit, Hoffman, Streich, Vogel.

September 3 1975, Nantes
France (1) 3 (*Guillou* 2, *Berdoll*)
Iceland (0) 0   20,000
France: Baratelli; Domenech, Adams, Tresor, Bracci, Michel, Huck, Guillou, Rocheteau, Molitor (Berdoll), Emon.
Iceland: Stefansson; Sigurvinsson O., Torfasson, Geirsson, Petursson, Hilmarsson (Thordarsson K.), Leifsson, Sigurvinsson A., Edvaldsson, Thordarsson T., Halgrimsson (Geirsson M.).

September 6 1975, Liege
Belgium (1) 1 (*Lambert*)
Iceland (0) 0   9000
Belgium: Piot; Van Binst, Broos, Dewalque, Martens, Cools, Verheyen (Coeck), Polleunis, Lambert, Devrindt, Teugels.
Iceland: Stafansson; Sigurvinsson O., Petursson, Geirsson M., Larusson, Torfasson, Leifsson, Hallgrimsson, Thordarsson T. (Sveinsson), Sigurvinsson A., Geirsson E.

September 27 1975, Anderlecht
Belgium (0) 1 (*Puis*)
East Germany (0) 2 (*Ducke, Hafner*)   26,000
Belgium: Piot; Gerets Dewalque, Van den Daele, Martens, Polleunis (Janssens), Cools, Coeck, Teugels, Devrindt, Puis.
East Germany: Croy (Grapenthin); Fritsche, Weise, Dorner, Kurbjuweit, Lauck, Weber, Hafner, Ducke, Riediger, Hoffmann.

October 12 1975, Leipzig
East Germany (0) 2 (*Streich, Vogel*)
France (0) 1 (*Batheney*)   30,000

748

East Germany: Croy; Fritsch, Weise, Dorner, Weber, Lauck, Schade, Hafner, Streich (Hoffmann), Ducke, Vogel.
France: Baratelli; Janvion, Bracci, Adams, Tresor, Batheney, Rocheteau, Michel, Gallice, Guillou, Emon.

November 15 1975, Paris
France (0) 0
Belgium (0) 0   47,500
France: Baratelli; Domenech, Tresor, Orlanducci, Bracci, Huck (Larque), Michel, Guillou, Rocheteau, Coste (Gallice), Emon.
Belgium: Piot; Van Binst, Vandendaale, Dockx, Leekens, Cools, Verheyen, Coeck, Van der Eycken. Van Gool, Lambert (Teugels).

	P	W	D	L	F	A	Pts.
BELGIUM	6	3	2	1	6	3	8
East Germany	6	2	3	1	8	7	7
France	6	1	3	2	7	6	5
Iceland	6	1	2	3	3	8	4

GROUP 8
October 13 1974, Sofia
Bulgaria (3) 3 (*Bonev, Denev* 2)
Greece (1) 3 (*Antoniadis, Papaionnou, Glezos*)
                                                35,000
Bulgaria: Jordanov; Zafirov, Penev, Dimitrov, Kolev, Borisov, Voinov, Bonev, Sokolov (Panov), Denev, Tzvetkov (Barsov).
Greece: Ikonomopoulos; Palas, Iosifidis, Firos, Glezos, Tersanidis, Eleftherakis, Sarafis (Dimitriou), Antonidis, Delikaris, Papaioannou.

November 24 1974, Piraeus
Greece (1) 2 (*Delikaris, Eleftherakis*)
West Germany (0) 2 (*Cullmann, Wimmer*)   11,000
Greece: Ikonomopoulos; Kyrastas, Siokos, Glezos (Fyros), Iossifidis, Tersanidis, Domazos, Eleftherakis, Sarafis, Delikaris, Papaioannou (Aslanidis).
West Germany: Maier; Vogts, Beckenbauer, Schwarzenbeck, Helmut Kremers, Wimmer, Hoeness, Cullmann (Kapellmann), Geye, Holzenbein, Heynckes (Pirrung).

December 18 1974, Piraeus
Greece (2) 2 (*Sarafis, Antoniadis*)
Bulgaria (0) 1 (*Kolev*)   22,300
Greece: Konstantinou; Elefteriadis, Siokos, Glezos, Pallas, Tersanidis, Eleftherakis, Sarafis, Aslanidis, Antoniadis, Papaioannou (Kyrastas).
Bulgaria: Filipov; Vassilov, Aladjov, Kolev, Ivkov, Flanke, Christov (Svedkov), Bonev, Volnov (Anghelov), Denev, Kourbanov.

December 29 1974, Gzira
Malta (0) 0
West Germany (1) 1 (*Cullmann*)   12,535
Malta: Debono; Borg, Holland, Darmanin, Vella, R. Zuereb, Vassallo, E. Aquilina (R. Aquilina), Margo, Camilleri, Seychell.
West Germany: Nigbur; Vogts, Beckenbauer, Korbel, Dietz, Bonhof, Flohe, Cullmann (Seliger), Pirrung (Nickel), Kostedde, Holzenbein.

February 23 1975, Valetta
Malta (1) 2 (*Aquilina, Magro*)
Greece (0) 0   20,000
Malta: Gatt; Ciantar, Vella, Darmanin, Holland, Vassallo, Azzopardi (Seychell), Camilleri, Magro, Xuereb, Aquilina.
Greece: Konstantinou; Pallas, Iossifidis, Siokos, Firos, Dimitriou (Paridis), (Nikolaiou), Papaioannou, Domazos, Sarafis, Antoniadis, Kritikopoulos.

April 27 1975, Sofia
Bulgaria (0) 1 (*Kolev, pen*)
W. Germany (0) 1 (*Ritschel, pen*)   50,000

Bulgaria: Filipov; Zafirov, Rangelov, Marev, Eftimov, Kolev, Dimitrov, Panov, Alexandrov (Zdravkov), Jeliaskov, Denev.
W. Germany: Maier; Beckenbauer, Vogts, Schwarzenbeck, Breitner, Bonhof, Hoeness (Korbel), Netzer, Ritschel, Seel, Heynckes (Holzenbein).

June 4 1975, Salonika
Greece (2) 4 (*Mavros, Antoniadis pen., Iosifidis, Papaoiannou*)
Malta (0) 0   15,000
Greece: Papstratos; Pallas, Pellias (Nikalaou), Foiros, Iosifidis, Apostalides, Papaioannou, Mavros, Anastasiadis, Antoniadis (Kalambakas), Aslanidis.
Malta: Gatt (Debono); Borg, Varrugia, Vassalo, Parmanin, Holland, Magrou, Asoparelli, Aguillina E., Seychell (Camilieri), Huerid.

June 11 1975, Sofia
Bulgaria (3) 5 (*Dimitrov, Denev, Panov, Bonev, Milanov*)
Malta (0) 0   35,000
Bulgaria: Filipov; Zafirov, Marev, Evtimov, Dimitrov, Issakidis (Milanov), Kurbanov (Alexandrov), Bonev, Jeliaskov, Panov, Denev.
Malta: Debono; Ciantar, Farrugia, Vella E., Holland, Darmanin, Magro, Borg, Aquilina E., Vasallo, Aquiliana R.

October 11 1975, Dusseldorf
West Germany (0) 1 (*Heynckes*)
Greece (0) 1 (*Delikaris*)   65,000
West Germany: Maier; Korbel, Kaltz, Beckenbauer, Vogts, Beer, Netzer, Breitner, Holzenbein, Kostedde, Heynckes.
Greece: Kelesidis; Kyrastas, Synetopoulos (Apostolidis), Forios, Pallas, Tersanidis, Sarafis, Koudas (Aslanidis), Papaioannu, Kritikopoulos, Delikaris.

November 19 1975, Stuttgart
West Germany (0) 1 (*Heynckes*)
Bulgaria (0) 0   73,000
West Germany: Maier; Vogts, Beckenbauer, Dietz, Wimmer, Danner, Stielike, Holzenbein, Beer, Heynckes, Schwarzenbeck.
Bulgaria: Filipov; Zafirov, Ivkov, Angelov, Vassilov, Kolev (Panov), Bonev, Rangelov, Alexandrov (Voinov), Zvetkov, Milanov.

December 21 1975, Gzira
Malta (0) 0
Bulgaria (0) 2 (*Panov, Jordanov*)   7000
Malta: Debono; Farrugai, Gouder (Vella E.), Azzorpardi, Holland, Darmanin, Magro (Vella C.), Vassallo, Vellar, Aquilina, Seychell.
Bulgaria: Tichonov; Zafirov (Joronov), Ivkov, Vassilev, Angelov, Rangelov, Alexandrov, Bonev, Milanov, Panov, Tsvetkov (Alexandrov).

February 28 1976, Dortmund
West Germany (4) 8 (*Worm 2, Heynckes 2, Beer 2, 1 pen., Vogts, Holzenbein*)
Malta (0) 0   54,000
West Germany: Maier; Vogts, Schwarzenbeck, Beckenbauer, Dietz, Stielike (Cullmann), Wimmer (Bongartz), Beer, Holzenbein, Worm, Heynckes.
Malta: Scibberas; Losko, Holland, Gouder, Garrugia, Vassalo, Feneck, Aquilina R., Magro (Seychell), Xuereb, Loporto (Aquilina S.).

	P	W	D	L	F	A	Pts.
WEST GERMANY	6	3	3	0	14	4	9
Greece	6	2	3	1	12	9	7
Bulgaria	6	2	2	2	12	7	6
Malta	6	1	0	5	2	20	2

QUARTER-FINALS FIRST LEG
April 24 1976, Madrid
Spain (1) 1 (*Santillana*)
West Germany (0) 1 (*Beer*)   63,000
Spain: Iribar; Sol, Benito, Migueli (Alabanda),
Capon, Camacho, Villar, Del Bosque, Churruca,
Santillana, Quini (Satrustegui).
West Germany: Maier; Beckenbauer, Vogts,
Schwarzenbeck (Cullmann), Dietz (Reichel),
Wimmer, Danner, Beer, Bonhof, Holzenbein,
Worm.

April 24 1976, Zagreb
Yugoslavia (1) 2 (*Vukotic, Popivoda*)
Wales (0) 0   55,000
Yugoslavia: Petrovic O.; Buljan, Hadziabdic,
Katalinski, Muzinic, Oblak, Acimovic, Vukotic
(Jerkovic), Popivoda, Surjak, Vabec.
Wales: Davies; Thomas, Page, Mahoney, Phillips,
Evans, James (Curtis), Flynn, Yorath, Toshack,
Griffiths.

April 24 1976, Bratislava
Czechoslovakia (1) 2 (*Moder, Panenka*)
USSR (0) 0   52,000
Czechoslovakia: Viktor; Dobias, Capkovic, Ondrus,
Gogh, Pollak, Moder (Knapp), Panenka, Masny,
Nehoda, Petras (Kroupa).
USSR: Prochorov; Reschko, Zwianguentsev,
Fomenko, Lovchev (Veremejev), Konkov, Trosh-
kin, Kolotov, Matvienko, Onishenko (Nasarenko),
Blokhin.

April 25 1976, Rotterdam
Holland (2) 5 (*Rensenbrink* 3, *Rijsbergen, Neeskens
pen.*)
Belgium (0) 0   58,000
Holland: Schrijvers; Suurbier, Van Kraay, Rijs-
bergen, Krol, Neeskens (Peters), Jansen, W. Van
der Kerkhof, Rep, Cruyff, Rensenbrink.
Belgium: Piot; Van Binst, Martens, Leekens,
Gerets, Cools (Van der Elst), Coeck, Verheyen,
Van der Eyken, Van Gool, Lambert (Teugels).

QUARTER-FINALS SECOND LEG
May 22 1976, Munich
West Germany (2) 2 (*Hoeness, Toppmoller*)
Spain (0) 0   77,600
West Germany: Maier; Beckenbauer, Vogts,
Schwarzenbeck, Dietz, Wimmer, Bonhof, Beer,
Hoeness, Toppmoller, Holzenbein.
Spain: Miguel Angel; Pirri, Capon, Sol (Porta-
berria), Camacho, Villar (Remos), Asensi, Del
Bosque, Churruca, Santillana, Quini.

May 22 1976, Kiev
USSR (0) 2 (*Burjak, Blokhin*)
Yugoslavia (1) 2 (*Moder* 2)   100,000
USSR: Rudakov; Fomenko, Konkov (Minejev),
Zwianguentsev, Lovchev, Troshkin, Muntian,
Veremejev, Onishenko, Burjak, Blokhin.
Czechoslovakia: Viktor; Ondrus, Pivarnik, Cap-
kovic (Jurkemik), Gogh, Dobias, Pollak, Moder,
Masny, Gallis (Svehlik), Nehoda.

May 22 1976, Cardiff
Wales (1) 1 (*Evans*)
Yugoslavia (1) 1 (*Katalinski pen.*)   30,000
Wales: Davies; Phillips, Roberts D., Evans, Page,
Griffiths (Curtis), Yorath, Mahoney, Flynn,
Toshack, James.
Yugoslavia: Maric; Buljan, Muzinic, Katalinski,
Hadziabdic, Zungul (Vladic), Jerkovic, Oblak,
Surjak, Djordjevic, Popivoda.

May 22 1976, Brussels
Belgium (1) 1 (*Van Gool*)
Holland (0) 2 (*Rep, Cruyff*)   45,000
Belgium: Pfaff; Van Binst, Renquin, Dalving,
Martens, Van der Elst, Cools, Verheyen, Van der
Eycken, Van Gool (Delesie), Wellens.
Holland: Schrijvers; Van Kraay, Suurbier, Rijs-
bergen, Krol, W. Van der Kerkhof, Neeskens, Van
Hanegem (Peters), Rep, Cruyff, Rensenbrink.

SEMI-FINALS
June 16 1976, Zagreb
Czechoslovakia (1) 3 (*Ondrus, Nehoda, Vesely F.*)
Holland (0) 1 (*Ondrus og*) (*after extra time, 90
minutes:* 1-1)   40,000
Czechoslovakia: Viktor; Dobias, Pivarnik, Ondrus,
Capkovic (Jurkemik), Pollak, Gogh, Moder
(Vesely F.), Panenka, Masny, Nehoda.
Holland: Schrijvers; Suurbier, Rijsbergen (Van
Hanegem), Van Kraay, Krol, Jansen, W. van der
Kerkhof, Neeskens, Rep (Geels), Cruyff, Rensen-
brink.

June 17 1976, Belgrade
West Germany (0) 4 (*Flohe, Muller* 3)   75,000
Yugoslavia (2) 2 (*Popivoda, Dzajic*) (*after extra
time,* 90 *minutes:* 2-2)
West Germany: Maier; Vogts, Beckenbauer,
Schwarzenbeck, Dietz, Bonhof, Wimmer (Muller
D.), Danner (Flohe), Beer, Hoeness, Holzenbein.
Yugoslavia: Petrovic O.; Buljan, Katalinski,
Muzinic, Oblak (Vladic), Zungul, Jerkovic, Surjak,
Acimovic (Peruzovic), Popivoda, Dzajic.

THIRD PLACE PLAY-OFF
June 19 1976, Zagreb
Holland (2) 3 (*Geels* 2, *W. Van der Kerkhof*)
Yugoslavia (1) 2 (*Katalinski, Dzajic*) (*after extra
time,* 90 *minutes:* 2-2)   18,000
Holland: Schrijvers; Suurbier, Jansen (Meutstege),
Van Kraay, Krol, Arntz (Kist), W. Van der
Kerkhof, R. Van der Kerkhof, Geels, Peters,
Rensenbrink.
Yugoslavia: Petrovic O.; Buljan, Katalinski,
Muzinic, Oblak, Zungul (Vladic), Jerkovic, Surjak,
Acimovic (Halilhodzic), Popivoda, Dzajic.

FINAL
June 20 1976, Belgrade
Czechoslovakia (2) 2 (*Svehlik, Dobias*)
West Germany (1) 2 (*Muller, Holzenbein*) (*after
extra time,* 90 *minutes:* 2-2. *Czechoslovakia won
5-3 on penalties*)   45,000
Czechoslovakia: Viktor; Dobias (Vesely F.), Pivarnik,
Ondrus, Capkovic, Gogh, Moder, Panenka,
Svehlik (Jurkemik), Masny, Nehoda.
West Germany: Maier; Vogts, Beckenbauer,
Schwarzenbeck, Dietz, Bonhof, Wimmer (Flohe),
Muller D., Beer (Bongartz), Hoeness, Holzenbein.

EUROPEAN CHAMPIONSHIP FOR UNDER-23 TEAMS 1974-76

GROUP 1

England	3	Czechoslovakia	1
Portugal	2	England	3
Portugal	2	Czechoslovakia	0
Czechoslovakia	1	England	1
Czechoslovakia	1	Portugal	1
England	2	Portugal	0

	P	W	D	L	F	A	Pts.
England	4	3	1	0	9	4	7
Portugal	4	1	1	2	5	6	3
Czechoslovakia	4	0	2	2	3	7	2

GROUP 2

Luxembourg	0	Hungary	3
Luxembourg	1	Austria	3
Austria	2	Hungary	2
Hungary	2	Austria	0
Austria	1	Luxembourg	1
Hungary	4	Luxembourg	0

	P	W	D	L	F	A	Pts.
Hungary	4	3	1	0	11	2	7
Austria	4	1	2	1	6	6	4
Luxembourg	4	0	1	3	2	11	1

GROUP 3

Yugoslavia	2	Norway	0
Sweden	1	Yugoslavia	1
Norway	0	Yugoslavia	0
Norway	0	Sweden	2
Sweden	2	Norway	1
Yugoslavia	4	Sweden	1

	P	W	D	L	F	A	Pts.
Yugoslavia	4	2	2	0	7	2	6
Sweden	4	2	1	1	6	6	5
Norway	4	0	1	3	1	6	1

GROUP 4

Rumania	6	Denmark	2
Denmark	1	Rumania	1
Rumania	1	Scotland	2
Denmark	0	Scotland	1
Scotland	4	Denmark	1
Scotland	4	Rumania	0

	P	W	D	L	F	A	Pts.
Scotland	4	4	0	0	11	2	8
Rumania	4	1	1	2	8	9	3
Denmark	4	0	1	3	4	12	1

GROUP 5

Holland	3	Finland	0
Holland	3	Italy	2
Italy	3	Finland	0
Finland	0	Holland	3
Finland	2	Italy	3
Italy	1	Holland	1

	P	W	D	L	F	A	Pts.
Holland	4	3	1	0	10	3	7
Italy	4	2	1	1	9	6	5
Finland	4	0	0	4	2	12	0

GROUP 6

Turkey	2	Russia	1
Russia	3	Turkey	0

GROUP 7

France	1	Belgium	0
East Germany	1	France	1
Belgium	0	East Germany	0
East Germany	1	Belgium	2
France	1	East Germany	2
Belgium	2	France	3

	P	W	D	L	F	A	Pts.
France	4	2	1	1	6	5	5
East Germany	4	1	2	1	4	4	4
Belgium	4	1	1	2	4	5	3

GROUP 8

Greece	0	Bulgaria	2
Bulgaria	2	Greece	1
Poland	2	Bulgaria	1
Poland	4	Greece	1
Greece	2	Poland	1
Bulgaria	1	Poland	0

	P	W	D	L	F	A	Pts.
Bulgaria	4	3	0	1	6	3	6
Poland	4	2	0	2	7	5	4
Greece	4	1	0	3	4	9	2

Quarter-finals

Holland v Scotland   2-0,   0-2
(*Holland won on penalties*)

Hungary v England   3-0,   1-3

France v Russia   2-1,   1-2
(*Russia won on penalties*)

Bulgaria v Yugoslavia   2-3,   1-2

Semi-finals

Hungary v Yugoslavia   3-2,   1-1

Russia v Holland   3-0,   0-1

Final

European Club Tournaments 1975-76

EUROPEAN CUP

First Round, First Leg

Benfica 7 (*Sheu, Nene 3, Jordao 3*)
Fenerbahce 0
Borussia Moenchengladbach 1 (*Simonsen pen.*)
Swarowski Innsbruck 0 (*Welzl*)
KB Copenhagen 0
St. Etienne 2 (*P. Revelli, Larque*)
CSKA Sofia 2 (*Denev, Marashliev*)
Juventus 1 (*Anastasi*)
Floriana 0
Hajduk Split 5 (*Zungul 3, Buljan, Surjak*)
Jeunesse D'Esch 0
Bayern Munich 5 (*Wunder, Schuster 2, Rummenigge 2*)
Linfield 1 (*P. Malone*)
PSV Eindhoven 2 (*Rene Van der Kerkhof, Edstrom*)
Malmo 2 (*Cervin, Bo Larsson*)
Magdeburg 1 (*Hoffmann*)
Olympiakos 2 (*Kritikopoulos, Aidiniou*)
Dynamo Kiev 2 (*Kolotov, Burjak*)
Rangers 4 (*Fyfe, Burge o.g,, O'Hara, Johnstone*)
Bohemians 1 (*Flanagan*)
Real Madrid 4 (*Santillana 2, Roberto Martinez, Netzer*)
Dinamo Bucharest 1 (*Lucescu*)
Ruch Chorzow 5 (*Marx 2, Bula, Beniger, Kopicera*)
Kuopion Palloseura 0
Slovan Bratislava 1 (*Masny*)
Derby County 0
Ujpest Dozsa 4 (*Fazekas, Dunai, Toth, pen., Keleman*)
Zurich 0
RWD Molenbeek 3 (*Boskamp, Teugals, Wellens*)
Viking Stavanger 2 (*Johansson, Kvia*)
Omonia Nicosia 2 (*Philippou 2*)
Akranes 1 (*Alfredsson*)

First Round, Second Leg

Akranes 4 (*M. Hallgrimsson 2, T. Thordarson, K. Thordarson*)
Omonia Nicosia 0
Viking Stavanger 0
RWD Molenbeek 1 (*Neilsen*)
Bayern Munich 3 (*Schuster 3*)
Jeunesse D'Esch 1 (*Zwally*)
Bohemians 1 (*T. O'Connor*)
Rangers 1 (*Johnstone*)
Derby County 3 (*Bourne, Lee 2*)
Slovan Bratislava 0
Dinamo Bucharest 1 (*Satmareanu*)
Real Madrid 0
Dynamo Kiev 1 (*Onishenko*)
Olympiakos 0
Fenerbahce 1 (*Engin*)
Benfica 0
Hajduk Split 3 (*Buljan, Djordjevic, Salvov*)
Floriana 0
Juventus 2 (*Furino, Anastasi*)
CSKA Sofia 0
Kuopion Palloseura 2 (*Toernroos, Heiskanen*)
Ruch Chorzow 2 (*Chojnacki, Faber*)
Magdeburg 2 (*Hoffmann, Streich*)
Malmo 1 (*Andersson*)
PSV Eindhoven 8 (*Lubse 2, Dahlqvist, Willy Van der Kerkhof, Van der Kuylen, Edstrom, Deacy 2*)
Linfield 0
St. Etienne 3 (*Rocheteau, Patrick Revelli, Larque*)
KB Copenhagen 1 (*Petersen*)

Swarowski Innsbruck 1 (*Flindt*)
Borussia Moenchengladbach 6 (*Stielike, Simonsen, Heynckes 4*)
Zurich 5 (*Katic, Risi 3, Kuhn*)
Ujpest Dozsa 1 (*Nagy*)

Second Round, Second Leg

Benfica 5 (*Moinhos, Sheu, Vitor Baptista 2, Toni*)
Ujpest Dozsa 2 (*Dunai A., Fazekas*)
Borussia Moenchengladbach 2 (*Heynckes, Simonsen*)
Juventus 0
Derby County 4 (*George 3, 2 pens., MNish*)
Real Madrid 1 (*Pirri*)
Dynamo Kiev 3 (*Burjak 2, Blokhin*)
Akranes 0
Hajduk Split 4 (*Zungul, Rozic, Surjak, Mijak*)
RWD Molenbeek 0
Malmo 1 (*Andersson T.*)
Bayern Munich 0
Ruch Chorzow 1 (*Bula*)
PSV Eindhoven 3 (*Lubse, Edstrom, Rene Van der Kerkhof*)
St. Etienne 2 (*Patrick Revelli, Bathenay*)
Rangers 0

Second Round, Second Leg

Akranes 0
Dynamo Kiev 2 (*Onischenko, Gunnlaugsson o.g.*)
Bayern Munich 2 (*Durnberger pen, Torstensson*)
Malmo 0
Juventus 2 (*Gori, Bettega*)
Borussia Moenchengladbach 2 (*Danner, Simonsen*)
PSV Eindhoven 4 (*Rene Van der Kerkhof, Van der Kuylen 2, Lubse*)
Ruch Chorzow 0
Rangers 1 (*MacDonald*)
St. Etienne 2 (*Rocheteau, Herve Revelli*)
Real Madrid 5 (*Roberto Martinez 2, Santillana 2, Pirri pen.*)
Derby County 1 (*George*)
RWD Molenbeek 2 (*Teugels, Nielsen pen.*)
Hajduk Split 3 (*Surjak, Zungul, Jovanic*)
Ujpest Dozsa 3 (*Bene 2, Nagy L.*)
Benfica 1 (*Nene*)

Quarter-finals, First Leg

Benfica 0
Bayern Munich 0
Borussia Moenchengladbach 2 (*Jensen, Wittkamp*)
Real Madrid 2 (*Roberto Martinez, Pirri*)
Dynamo Kiev 2 (*Konkov, Blokhin*)
St. Etienne 0
Hajduk Split 2 (*Mijac, Surjak*)
PSV Eindhoven 0

Quarter-finals, Second Leg

Bayern Munich 5 (*Durnberger 2, Rummenigge, Muller 2*)
Benfica 1 (*Barros*)
PSV Eindhoven 3 (*Dahlqvist, Lubse, Van der Kuylen*)
Hajduk Split 0
Real Madrid 1 (*Santillana*)
Borussia Moenchengladbach 1 (*Heynckes*)
St. Etienne 3 (*Herve Revelli, Larque, Rocheteau*)
Dynamo Kiev 0 (*after extra time*)

753

Semi-finals, First Leg

Real Madrid 1 (*Roberto Martinez*)
Bayern Muni ι 1 (*Muller*)
St. Etienne 1 (*Larque*)
PSV Eindhoven 0

Semi-finals, Second Leg

Bayern Munich 2 (*Muller* 2)
Real Madrid 0
PSV Eindhoven 0
St. Etienne 0

Final 1975–76: Bayern Munich 1 St. Etienne 0
(at Hampden Park, May 12 1976, 54,864)

Bayern: Maier; Hansen, Schwarzenbeck, Becken-
bauer, Horsmann, Roth, Durnberger, Kapellmann,
Rummenigge, Muller, Hoeness.
St. Etienne: Curkovιc; Repellini, Piazza, Lopez
Janvioh, Bathenay, Santini, Larque, Patrick
Revelli, Herve Revelli, Sarramagna (Rocheteau).
Scorer: Bayern: Roth

EUROPEAN CUP WINNERS' CUP

First Round, First Leg

Ararat Erevan 9 (*Markarov 5, 1 pen, Oganiesian 2,
Petrosian S., Bondarenko*)
Anorthosis 0
Basel 1 (*Schoenberger*)
Atletico Madrid 2 (*Garate, Ayala*)
Besiktas 0
Fiorentina 3 (*Caso 2, Casarsa*)
Borac Banja Luka 9 (*Cetina 3, Ibrahimbegovic 5
Jurkovic*)
US Rumelange 0
Eintracht Frankfurt 5 (*Korbel, Beverungen
Holzenbein, Nickel 2*)
Coleraine 1 (*Cochrane*)
Haladas Szombathely 7 (*Fedor 2, Horath 2, Frakas,
Halmosi*)
Valetta 0
Home Farm 1 (*Brophy*)
Lens 1 (*Hopquin*)
Lahden Reipas 2 (*Lindholm, Tupasela*)
West Ham 2 (*Brooking, Bonds*)
Panathinaikos 0
Sachsenring Zwicau 0
Rapid Bucharest 1 (*Thissen o.g.*)
Anderlecht 0
Spartak Trnava 0
Boavista 0
Skeid Oslo 1 (*B. Skjoensberg*)
Stal Rzeszow 4 (*Kozierski 2, Curylo, Krawczyk*)
Sturm Graz 3 (*Stendal 2 pens, Kulmer*)
Slavia Sofia 1 (*Kostov*)
Valur Reykjavik 0
Celtic 2 (*Dalglish, McDonald*)
Vejle 0
Den Haag 2 (*Jol, Van Leeuwen*)
Wrexham 2 (*Griffiths, Davis*)
Djurgaardens 1 (*Krantz*)

First Round, Second Leg

Anderlecht 2 (*Van Binst, Rensenbrink*)
Rapid Bucharest 0
Anorthosis 1 (*Fivos pen*)
Ararat Erevan 1 (*Bondarenko*)
Atletico Madrid 1 (*Becerra*)
Basel 1 (*Demarmels*)
Boavista 3 (*Mane, Celse, Salvador*)
Spartak Trnava 0
Celtic 7 (*Edvaldsson, Dalglish, McCluskey pen.,
Hood 2, Deans, Callaghan*)
Valur 0
Den Haag 2 (*Perazic, Mansveld*)
Vejle 0
Djurgaarden 1 (*Lovfors*)
Wrexham 1 (*Whittle*)
Lens 6 (*Northeaux, Mujica pen., Kaiser 3, Llorens*)
Home Farm 0
Sachsenring Zwickau 2 (*Schykowski, Dietzsch pen.*)
Panathininaikos 0
Slavia Sofia 1 (*Kostov*)
Sturm Graz 0
West Ham 3 (*Robson 2, Jennings*)
Reipas Lahden 0
US Rumelange 1 (*Rohmann*)
Borac Banja Luka 5 (*Smilevski, Reso, Kovahevic,
Vidacek, Marjonaovic*)

Coleraine 2 (*McCurdy, Cochrane*)
Eintracht Frankfurt 6 (*Grabowski 3, Nickel,
Lorenz, Holzenbein*)
Valetta 1 (*Giglio*)
Haladas Szombathely 1 (*Karaci*)
Fiorentina 3 (*Caso 2, Casarsa*)
Besiktas 0
Stal Rzeszow 4 (*Kozierski, Miler, Krawczyk,
Napieracz*)
Skeid Oslo 0

Second Round, First Leg

Anderlecht 3 (*Rensenbrink 2, Coeck*)
Borac Banja Luka 0
Ararat Erevan 1 (*Petrosian S.*)
West Ham 1 (*Taylor, A.*)
Atletico Madrid 1 (*Bacerra*)
Eintracht Frankfurt 2 (*Holzenbein 2*)
Boavista 0
Celtic 0
Den Haag 3 (*Schoenmaker, Van Vliet, Van Leeawen*)
Lens 2 (*Zuraszek, Janovic*)
Fiorentina 1 (*Speggiorin*)
Sachsenring Zwickau 0
Sturm Graz 2 (*Stendal, Steiner pen.*)
Haladas Szombathely 0
Wrexham 2 (*Ashcroft 2*)
Stal Rzeszow 0

Second Round, Second Leg

Borac Banja Luka 1 (*Ibrahimbegovic*)
Anderlecht 0
Celtic 3 (*Dalglish, Edvaldsson, Deans*)
Boavista 1 (*Mane*)
Eintracht Frankfurt 1 (*Reichel*)
Atletico Madrid 0
Haladas Szombathely 1 (*Horvath*)
Sturm Graz 1 (*Jurtin*)
Lens 1 (*Mujica pen.*)
Den Haag 3 (*Schoenmaker 2, Van Leeuwen*)
Sachsenring Zwickau 1 (*Schykowski, J.*)
Fiorentina 0
Stal Rzeszow 2 (*Kozierski*)
Wrexham 1 (*Sutton*)
West Ham 3 (*Paddon, Robson, Taylor A.*)
Ararat Erevan 1 (*Petrosian, N.*)

Quarter-finals, First Leg

Anderlecht 1 (*Van Binst*)
Wrexham 0
Celtic 1 (*Dalglish*)
Sachsenring Zwickau 1 (*Blank*)
Den Haag 4 (*Mansveld 3, 2 pens., Schoenmaker*)
West Ham 2 (*Jennings 2*)
Sturm Graz 0
Eintracht Frankfurt 2 (*Holzenbein, Wenzel*)

Quarter-finals, Second Leg

Eintracht Frankfurt 1 (*Holzenbein*)
Sturm Graz 0
Sachsenring Zwickau 1 (*Blank*)
Celtic 0
West Ham 3 (*Taylor A., Lampard, Bonds pen.*)
Den Haag 1 (*Schoenmaker*)
Wrexham 1 (*Lee*)
Anderlecht 1 (*Rensenbrink*)

Semi-finals, First Leg

Eintracht Frankfurt 2 (*Neuberger, Kraus*)
West Ham 1 (*Paddon*)
Sachsenring Zwickau 0
Anderlecht 3 (*Van der Elst* 2, *Rensenbrink*)

Semi-finals, Second Leg

Anderlecht 2 (*Rensenbrink, Van der Elst*)
Sachsenring Zwickau 0
West Ham 3 (*Brooking* 2, *Robson*)
Eicntraht Frankfurt 1 (*Beverungen*)

Final 1975-76: Anderlecht 4 West Ham United 2

(at Heysel Stadium, Brussels, 5 May 1976, 58,000)
Anderlecht: Ruiter; Lomme, Broos, Van Binst, Thissen, Dockx, Coeck (Vercauteren), Van der Elst, Ressel, Haan, Rensenbrink
West Ham: Day; Coleman, Bonds, Taylor (T), Lampard (Taylor A.), McDowell, Brooking, Paddon, Holland, Jennings, Robson
Scorers: Anderlecht: Rensenbrink 2, 1 pen, Van der Elst 2). West Ham: Holland, Robson.

UEFA CUP

First Round, First Leg

Duisberg 7 (*Mertakas o.g., Lehmann* 3, *Worm* 2, *Thies*)
Paralimni 1 (*Chatzyannis*)

Glentoran 1 (*Jamieson*)
Ajax 6 (*Geels,* 4 *Meyer, Notten*)

Grasshoppers 3 (*Elsener, Santrac, Bosco*)
Real Sociedad 3 (*Satrustegui* 2, *Murillo*)

PAOK Salonika 1 (*Koudas*)
Barcelona 0

AIK Stockholm 1 (*Leback pen.*)
Spartak Moscow 1 (*Lovchev*)

Antwerp 4 (*Heylingen, Kodat* 3)
Aston Villa 1 (*Graydon*)

Bohemians Prague 1 (*Masnik*)
Honved 2 (*Pinter, Toth*)

Carl Zeiss Jena 3 (*Sengewald* 2, *Kurbjuweit*)
Marseille 0

Uni Craiova 1 (*Oblemenco*)
Red Star Belgrade 3 (*Filipovic* 2, *Savic*)

Everton 0
AC Milan 0

Feyenoord 1 (*De Jong*)
Ipswich 2 (Whymark, Johnson)

GAIS Gothenburg 2 (*Palsson* 2, 1 *pen.*)
Slask Wroclaw 1 (*Kwaitkowski*)

Hertha Berlin 4 (*Kostedde* 2, *Hoor* 2)
HJK Helsinki 1 (*Kangaslorpi*)

Hibernian 1 (*Harper*)
Liverpool 0

Holbaek 0
Stal Mielec 1 (*Domarski*)

Cologne 2 (*Glowacz, Lohr*)
B1903 Copenhagen 0

Lyon 4 (*Jodar, Millard* 2, *Mihajlovic*)
Bruges 3 (*Van der Eycken,* 3, 1 *pen.*)

Molde 1 (*Wetterdahl*)
Oesters Vaxjo 0

Tirgu Mures 2 (*Muresan, Faxekas*)
Dynamo Dresden 2 (*Schade, Heidler*)

Chernomonretz Odessa 1 (*Doroschenko*)
Lazio 0

Porto 7 (*Julio, Cubillas* 3, 1 *pen., Oliveira, Octavio, Gomes*)
Avenir Beggen 0

Rapid Vienna 1 (Widmann)
Galatasaray 0

Roma 2 (*Pellegrini, Petrini*)
Dounav Russe 0

Moscow Torpedo 4 (*Grishken* 2, *Sakharov pen., Belenkov*)
Napoli 1 (*Savoldi*)

VOEST Linz 2 (*Scharmann, Stering*)
Vasas Budapest 0

Vojvodina 0
AEK Athens 0

Young Boys 0
Hamburg 0

Athlone Town 3 (*Martin, Davis* 2)
Valerengen 1 (Olsen)

Inter Bratislava 5 (*Levicky, Luprich, Petras, Jurkemik, Sajanek*)
Zaragoza 0

Keflavik 0
Dundee Utd. 2 (*Narey* 2)

Levski Spartak 3 (*Spassov* 2, *Panov*)
Eskisehirspor 0

Sliema Wanderers 1 (*Azzopardi*)
Sporting Lisbon 2 (*Marinho, Fernandez*)

First Round, Second Leg

Paralimni 2 (*Konstantinou A., Mertakas*)
Duisburg 3 (*Dietz, Krause, Seliger*)

Dundee Utd 4 (*Hall,* 2 *Hegarty pen., Sturrock*)
Keflavik 0

Liverpool 3 (*Toshack* 3)
Hibernian 1 (*Edwards*)

AEK Athens 3 (*Papaioannou, Papadopoulos, Wagner*)
Vojvodina 1 (*Buikov*)

Ajax 8 (*Notten, Van Dord, Geels* 3, *G. Muhren, Brokamp* 2)
Glentoran 1

Aston Villa 0
Antwerp 1 (*Kodat*)

Barcelona 6 (*Neeskens* 2 *pens., Rexach* 3, *Cruyff*)
PAOK Salonika 1 (*Anastasiadis*)

Bruges 3 (*Van der Eycken, Valette o.g., Chnier, o.g.*)
Lyon 0

Avenir Beggen 0
Porto 3 (*Julio, Grilli o.g., Seninho*)

Marseille 0
Carl Zeiss Jena 1 (*Irmscher*)

B1903 Copenhagen 2 (*Christiansen* 2)
Cologne 3 (*Brucken* 3)

Dounav Russe 1 (Ivanov)
Roma 0

Dynamo Dresden 4 (*Heidler,* 3, *Kreische*)
Tirgu Mures 1 (*Muresan*)

Eskisehirspor 1 (*Mehmet*)
Levski Spartak 4 (*Spassov* 2, *Panov, Milanov*)

Galatasaray 3 (*Sevkı, Gokmen* 2)
Rapid Vienna 1 (*Krankl*)

Hamburg 4 (*Reimann, Bertl* 2, *Bjornmose*)
Young Boys 2 (*Siegenthaler* 2)

HJK Helsinki 1 (*Salo*)
Hertha Berlin 2 (*Sidka, Grau*)

Honved 1 (*Kocsis pen.*)
Bohemians Prague 1 (*Panenka*)

Ipswich 2 (*Woods, Whymark*)
Feyenoord 0

Lazio 3 (*Chinaglia* 3, 1 *pen.*)
Chernomoretz Odessa 0

AC Milan 1 (*Calloni pen.*)
Everton 0

Napoli 1 (*Braglia*)
Moscow Torpedo 1 (*Filatov*)

Oesters Vaxjo 6 (*Svensson, Matsson*, 2 *Evesson, Ejderstedt, Isaxsson*)
Molde 0

Red Star Belgrade 1 (*Filipovic pen.*)
Uni. Craiova 1 (*Krizan*)

Real Sociedad 1 (*Urreisti*)
Grasshoppers 1 (Santrac)

Slask Wroclaw 4 (*Sybis* 3, *Pawlowski*)
GAIS Gothenburg 2 (*Hans Johanson* 2)

Moscow Spartak 1 (*Andreyev*)
AIK Stockholm 0

Sporting Lisbon 3 (*Baltazar, Da Costa, Manuel Fernandez pen.*)
Sliema Wanderers 1 (*Loporto*)

Stal Mielec 2 (*Karas, Krawczyk*)
Holbaek 1 (*Torben Hansen*)

Valerengen 1 (*Dag Olvavason*)
Athlone Town 1 (*Martin*)

Vasas Budapest 4 (*Varadi* 2, *Kovacs, Izso*)
VOEST Linz 0

Zaragoza 2 (*Pepe Gonzalez pen, Arrua*)
Inter Bratislava 3 (*Jurkemik, Petras, Mraz*)

Second Round, First Leg

Duisburg 3 (*Schneider W., Worm, Krause*)
Levski Spartak 2 (*Panov* 2)

Athlone Town 0
AC Milan 0

Carl Zeiss Jena (*Kurbjuweit*)
Stal Mielec 0

Dundee Utd 1 (*Rennie*)
Porto 2 (*Oliveira, Seninho*)

Galatasaray 2 (*Sevki, Gokmen*)
Moscow Torpedo 4 (*Enver o.g., Hrobroskin, Sakharov pen., Maksimenkov*)

Hertha Berlin 1 (*Kostedde*)
Ajax 0

Honved 2 (*Weimper* 2)
Dynamo Dresden 2 (*Heidler* 2)

Inter Bratislava 2 (*Luprich pen., Mraz*)
AEK Athens 0

Ipswich 3 (*Gates, Peddelty, Austin*)
Bruges 0

Spartak Moscow 2 (*Lovchev* 2)
Cologne 0

Oesters Vaxjo 1 (*Evansson*)
Roma 0

Real Sociedad 1 (*Amas*)
Liverpool 3 (*Heighway, Callaghan, Thompson*)

Red Star Belgrade 1 (*Susic*)
Hamburg 1 (*Bjornmose*)

Slask Wroclaw 1 (*Pawlowski*)
Antwerp 1 (*Houwaart*)

Vasas Budapest 3 (*Kovacs* 2, *Varadi pen.*)
Sporting Lisbon 1 (*Chico*)

Lazio 0
Barcelona 3 (*Lazio refused to play because of possible political demonstrations against the Spaniards. FIFA thus awarded the game to Barcelona 3–0*).

Second Round, Second Leg

Levski Spartak 2 (*Ivkov, Panov pen.*)
Duisburg 1 (*Worm*)

Liverpool 6 (*Toshack, Kennedy* 2, *Fairclough, Heighway, Neal*)
Real Sociedad 0

Ajax 4 (*Brokamp, Geels* 2, 1 *pen., Meyer*)
Hertha Berlin 1 (*Kostedde*)

Antwerp 1 (*De Schrijver*)
Slask Wroclaw 2 (*Sybis, Pawlowski*)

AEK Athens 3 (*Tassos* 2, 1 *pen., Wagner*)
Inter Bratislava 1 (*Novotny*)

Barcelona 4 (*Sotil, Cruyff, Neeskens, Fortes*)
Lazio 0

Bruges 4 (*Lambert* 1 *pen., De Cubber, Le Fevre, Van der Eycken*)
Ipswich 0

Dynamo Dresden 1 (*Dorner pen.*)
Honved 0

Hamburg 4 (*Reimann* 2, *Ettmayer, Memering*)
Red Star Belgrade 0

Cologne 1
Moscow Spartak 1 (*Andreyev*)

AC Milan 3 (*Vincenzi, Benetti* 2, 1 *pen.*)
Athlone Town 0

Moscow Torpedo 3 (*Degtyarev, Sahkarov pen., Budulakin*)
Galatasaray 0

Porto 1 (*Seninho*)
Dundee Utd 1 (*Hegarty*)

Roma 2 (*Pellegrini, Boni*)
Oesters Vaxjo 0

Sporting Lisbon 2 (*Manuel Fernandez* 2)
Vasas Budapest 1 (*Gass*)

Stal Mielec 1 (*Karas*)
Carl Zeiss Jena 0

Third Round, First Leg

Ajax 2 (*Geels, Steffenhagen*)
Levski Spartak 1 (*Voinov*)

Barcelona 3 (*Migueli, Rexach, Neeskens*)
Vasas Budapest 1 (*Muller*)

Bruges 1 (*Cools*)
Roma 0

Dynamo Dresden 3 (*Riedel* 2, *Kreische*)
Moscow Torpedo 0

Hamburg 2 (*Zaczyk, Volkert pen.*)
Porto 0

Inter Bratislava 1 (*Saljanek*)
Stal Mielec 0

Slask Wroclaw 1 (*Pawlowski*)
Liverpool 2 (*Faber o.g., Toshack*)

AC Milan 4 (*Calloni* 2, *Bigon, Maldera*)
Moscow Spartak 0

Third Round, Second Leg

Levski Spartak 2 (*Panov* 2)
Ajax 1 (*Geels*)

Liverpool 3 (*Case* 3)
Slask Wroclaw 0

Moscow Spartak 2 (*Papayev, Ovchev*)
AC Milan 0

Moscow Torpedo 3 (*Dedtyaryov* 2, *Petrenko*
Dynamo Dresden 1 (*Heidler*)

Porto 2 (*Julio, Cubillas*)
Hamburg 1 (*Reimann*)

Roma 0
Bruges 1 (*Lambert*)

Stal Mielec 2 (*Sekulski, Karas*)
Inter Bratislava 0

Vesas Budapest 0
Barcelona 1 (*Fortes*)

Quarter-finals, First Leg

Barcelona 4 (*Neeskens pen., Marcial, Asensi, Heredia*)
Levski Spartak 0

Bruges 2 (*Le Fevre, Krieger*)
AC Milan 0

Dynamo Dresden 0
Liverpool 0

Hamburg 1 (*Bertl*)
Stal Mielec 1 (*Oratowski*)

Quarter-finals, Second Leg

Levski Spartak 5 (*Panov* 2, 1 *pen., Yordanov* 2, *Spassov*)
Barcelona 4 (*Marcial, Asensi, Heredia, Neeskens pen.*)

Liverpool 2 (*Case, Keegan*)
Dynamo Dresden 1 (*Heidler*

AC Milan 2 (*Chiarugi* 2)
Bruges 1 (*Sanders*)

Stal Mielec 0
Hamburg 1 (*Nogly*

Semi-finals, First Leg

Barcelona 0
Liverpool 1 (*Toshack*)

Hamburg 1 (*Reimann*)
Bruges 1 (*Lambert*)

Semi-finals, Second Leg

Bruges 1 (*Kaltz o.g.*)
Hamburg 0

Liverpool 1 (*Thompson*)
Barcelona 1 (*Rexach*)

Final 1975-76: Liverpool 3, Bruges 2
(First leg at Anfield, April 28 1976, 56,000

Liverpool: Clemence; Smith, Neal, Thompson, Kennedy, Hughes, Keegan, Fairclough, Heighway, Toshack (Case), Callaghan).

Bruges: Jensen; Bastyns, Krieger, Leekens, Volders, Cools, Van der Eycken, De Cubber, Van Gool, Lambert, Le Fevre.

Scoreres: Liverpool: Kennedy, Case, Keegan pen. Bruges: Lambert, Cools.

Bruges 1, Liverpool 1
(Second leg at Olympia Stadium, Bruges, May 19 1976, 32,000)

Bruges: Jensen; Bastyns, Krieger, Leekens, Volders, Cools, Van der Eycken, Van Gool, Lambert (Sanders), De Cubber (Hinderyckx), Le Fevre.

Liverpool: Clemence; Smith, Neal, Thompson, Kennedy, Hughes, Keegan, Case, Heighway, Toshack (Fairclough), Callaghan.

Scorers: Bruges: Lambert, pen. Liverpool: Keegan,

EUROPEAN CUP 1975-76
BRITISH CLUBS FULL RECORD

FIRST ROUND, FIRST LEG

Linfield (1) 1 (*Malone, P.*)
PSV Eindhoven (2) 2 (*R. Vander Kerkhof,
Edstrom*)   8000
Linfield: Barclay; McVeigh, Porter, Fraser,
Bowyer, Bell (Paterson), Malone, M., Magee,
Campbell, Malone P., Rafferty.
PSV Eindhoven: Van Beveren; Deykers, Portvliet,
Edstrom, Strik, Lubse, Rene Van der Kerkhof
(Francois), Willy Van der Kerkhof, Van Kraay,
Krijgh, Van der Kuylen (Quaars).

Slovan Bratislava (0) 1 (*Masny*)
Derby Co. (0) 0   45,000
Slovan Bratislava: Vencel; Pivarnik, Ondrus, Jozef
Capkovic, Gogh, Medvid, Pekarik (Haraslin),
Novotny, Masny, Svehlik, Jan Capkovik.
Derby Co.: Boulton; Thomas, Todd, McFarland,
Nish, Powell, Newton, Gemmill, Rioch, Lee
(Bourne), George.

Rangers (2) 4 (*Fyfe* 2, *Burke o.g., Johnstone*)
Bohemians (1) 1 (*Flanagan*)   20,000
Rangers: McCloy; Denny, Miller, Greig, Jackson,
Johnstone, Fyfe, O'Hara, Parlane, Stein, Young.
Bohemians: Smyth; Doran, O'Brien, Kelly, Burke,
Fullam, Byrne, O'Connor P., O'Connor T.,
Flanagan, Mitten.

FIRST ROUND, SECOND LEG

Derby Co. (1) 3 (*Bourne, Lee* 2)
Slovan Bratislava (0) 0   30,888
Derby Co.: Boulton; Thomas, Nish, Rioch,
McFarland, Todd, Newton, Gemmill, Lee, Hector,
George.
Slovan Bratislava: Vencel; Elefant, Jozef Capkovic,
Ondrus, Gogh, Medvid (Haraslin), Masny,
Svehlik, Pekarik, Novotny, Jan Capkovic.

Bohemians (0) 1 (*O'Connor T.*)
Rangers (1) 1 (*Johnstone*)   8000
Bohemians: Smith; Gregg, O'Brien, Kelly, Burke,
Fullam, Byrne, O'Connor P., O'Connor T., Martin,
Mitten.
Rangers: McCloy; Miller, Dawson, Greig, Jackson,
Young, McLean, McDonald, Parlane, Johnstone,
Fyfe.

PSV Eindhoven (5) 8 (*Edstrom, Deacy* 2, *Lubse* 2,
Dahlqvist, Van der Kuylen, Willy Van der Kerkhof)
Linfield (0) 0   15,000
PSV Eindhoven: Van Beveren; Krijgh, Portvliet,
Van Kraay, Deykers, Willy Van der Kerkhof, Van
der Kuylen, Lubse, Rene Van der Kerkhof,
Edstrom, Dahlqvist (Deacy).
Linfield: Barclay; Fraser, McVeigh, Campbell,
Crozier, Bowyer, Bell, Porter, Malone M., Magee,
McKee.

SECOND ROUND, FIRST LEG

Derby Co. (3) 4 (*George* 3. 2 *pens., Nish*)
Real Madrid (1) 1 (*Pirri*)   34,839
Derby Co.: Boulton; Thomas, Nish, Rioch,
McFarland, Todd, Newton, Gemmill, Lee, Hector,
(Bourne), George (Davies).
Real Madrid: Miguel Angel; Sol, Rubinan, Pirri,
Camacho, Velazquez, Amancio, Breitner, Del
Bosque, Netzer, Roberto Martinez.

St. Etienne (1) 2 (*Patrick Revelli, Bathenay*)
Rangers (0) 0
St. Etienne: Curkovic; Janvion, Piazza, Lopez,
Farison, Larque, Bathenay, Synaeghel, Rochteau,
Herve Revelli, Patrick Revelli.
Rangers: Kennedy; Jardine, Miller, Greig, Jackson,
Forsyth, McLean, Stein, Parlane, MacDonald,
Johnstone.

SECOND ROUND, SECOND LEG

Rangers (0) 1 (*MacDonald*)
St. Etienne (0) 2 (*Rocheteau, Herve Revelli*) 45,000
Rangers: Kennedy; Jardine, Greig, Forsyth,
Jackson, MacDonald, McLean, Stein, Parlane,
Johnstone, Young.
St. Etienne: Curkovic; Janvion, Farison (Repellini),
Piazza, Lopez, Bathenay, Rocheteau, Larque
Herve Revelli, Synaeghel, Schaer (Santini).

Real Madrid (1) 5 (*Martinez* 2, *Santillana* 2, *Pirri
pen.*)
Derby Co. (0) 1 (*George*) (*after extra time*) 120,000
Real Madrid: Miguel Angel; Sol, Camacho, Pirri,
Benito, Del Bosque, Amancio (Rubinan), Breitner,
Santillana, Netzer, Roberto Martinez.
Derby Co.: Boulton; Thomas, Nish, Powell,
McFarland, Todd, Newton, Gemmill, Davies,
Hector (Bourne) (Hinton), George.

EUROPEAN CUP-WINNERS' CUP 1975-76
BRITISH CLUBS FULL RECORD

FIRST ROUND, FIRST LEG

Valur Reykjavik (0) 0
Celtic (1) 2 (*Wilson, McDonald*)   9000
Valur: Dagsson; Alfonsson, Samundsen, Kjartans-
son, Gudmundsson, Bergs, Porbjonsson, Hilmars-
son, Gunnarsson, Albertsson, Edvaldsson.
Celtic: Latchford; McGrain, Lynch, McCluskey,
McDonald, Edvaldsson, Hood (Glavin),
McNamara, Dalglish, Callaghan, Wilson.

Eintracht Frankfurt (5) 5 (*Korbel, Beverungen,
Holzenbein, Nickel* 2)
Coleraine (0) 1 (*Cochrane*)   11,000
Eintracht: Wienhold; Reichel, Neuberger, Krob-
bach, Muller, Korbel, Beverungen, Nickel,
Holzenbein (Wenzell), Grabowski (Stradt), Lorenz.
Coleraine: Magee; Gordon (McIntyre), McNutt,
Beckett, Jackson, Murray, Cochrane, Jennings,
Guy (Moffatt), Dickson, Simpson.

Home Farm (1) 1 (*Brophy*)
Lens (1) 1 (*Hopquin*)
Home Farm: Grace; Daly, Cregan, Kelly, Brophy,
O'Dea, Hughes, King, Higgins, Devlin, Murray.
Lens: Lannot; Hopquin, Winkler, Cieselski,
Mujica, Northeaux, Leclerq, Jankovic, Elie,
Bousidra, Kaiser.

Reipas Lahti (1) 2 (*Lindholm, Tupasela*)
West Ham U. (1) 2 (*Brooking, Bonds*)   4587
Reipas Lahti: Holli; Kosonen, Kautonen M.,
Riutto, Repo, Toivanen, Kautonen T., Tupasela,
Jantunen, Hamalainen, Lindholm.
West Ham U.: Day; McDowell, Lampard, Bonds,
Taylor T., Lock, Holland, Paddon, Taylor A.,
Brooking, Robson (Jennings).

Wrexham (1) 2 (*Griffiths, Davis*)
Djurgaarden (0) 1 (*Krantz*)   9002

Wrexham: Lloyd; Hill, Fogg (Lyons), Evans, May, Davis, Tinnion, Sutton, Ashcroft, Dwyer, Griffiths.
Djurgaarden: Alkeby; Andersson, Davidsson, Jakobsson, Berggren, Lindman, Samuelsson, Svensson, Stenback, Karlsson, Krantz.

FIRST ROUND, SECOND LEG

Coleraine (1) 2 (*McCurdy, Cochrane*)
Eintracht Frankfurt (3) 6 (*Grabowski 3, Nickel, Lorenz, Holzenbein*)   4000
Coleraine: Magee; McCurdy, McNutt, Beckett, Jackson, Simpson (Gordon), Cochrane, Jennings, Guy, Dickson, Moffatt (Tweed).
Eintracht: Kunter; Muller, Korbel, Beverungen, Neuberger, Weidle, Grabowski, Wenzel (Stradt), Holzenbein, Nickel, Lorenz.

Celtic (5) 7 (*Edvaldsson, Dalglish,McCluskey P.pen. Hood 2, Deans, Callaghan*)
Valur Reykjavik (0) 0   16,000
Celtic: Latchford; McGrain, Lynch, Edvaldsson, McDonald, McCluskey P., Wilson (McCluskey G.), Dalglish, Deans, Callaghan (Casey), Hood.
Valur: Dagsson; Alfonsson, Samundsen, Kjartansson, Gudmundsson, D., Bergs, Porbjonsson, Hilmarsson, Gunnarsson, Albertsson, Edvaldsson.

Djurgaarden (0) 1 (*Lovfors*)
Wrexham (1) 1 (*Whittle*)   1769
Djurgaarden: Alkeby; Ericsson, Berggren, Davidsson, Jakobsson, Lovfors, Lindman, Samuelsson, Karlsson (Olsberg), Svensson, Krantz (Stenback).
Wrexham: Lloyd; Hill, Evans, Davis, May, Thomas, Tinnion, Sutton, Davies, Whittle, Griffiths.

Lens (3) 6 (*Northeaux, Mujica pen., Kaiser 3, Llorens*)
Home Farm (0) 0   25,000
Lens: Lannoy; Hopquin, Winkler, Stassiewicz (Cieselski), Mujica, Elie, Bousdira, Leclerq, Jankovic, Notheaux (Llorens), Kaiser.
Home Farm: Grace; Daly, Cregan, Devlin, Brophy, O'Dea, Hughes, King, Higgins, Breslin, Murray.

West Ham U. (0) 3 (*Robson, Holland, Jennings*)
Reipas Lahti (0) 0   24,131
West Ham U.: Day; McDowell, Lampard, Bonds, Taylor T., Lock, Taylor A. (Jennings), Paddon, Robson, Brooking, Holland.
Reipas Lahti: Holli; Kosonen, Kautonen M., Riutto, Repo, Toivanen (Nordman), Kautonen T., Tupasela, Jantunen, Hamalainen, Lindholm.

SECOND ROUND, FIRST LEG

Ararat Erevan (0) 1 (*Petrosian S.*)
West Ham U. (0) 1 (*Taylor A.*)   70,000
West Ham U.: Day; McDowell, Lampard, Bonds, Taylor T., Coleman, Taylor A., Paddon, Gould, Holland, Robson.
Ararat Erevan: Abramian; Gevorkian, Sarkissian, Martirosian, Mesropian, Andreassian, Azarian (Bondarenko), Oganesian, Markarov, Petrosian S., Petrosian N. (Pogosian) S.)

Boavista (0) 0
Celtic (0) 0   25,000
Boavista: Botelho; Trindade, Mario Joao, Carolino, Tai, Celso, Alves, Acacio (Rufino), Mario, Mane, Salvador.
Celtic: Latchford; McGrain, Lynch, McCluskey G., McDonald, Edvaldsson, Hood, McNamara, Wilson, Callaghan, Lennox.

Wrexham (2) 2 (*Ashcroft 2*)
Stal Rzeszow (0) 0   9598
Wrexham: Lloyd; Hill, Evans, Davis, May,Thomas (Dwyer), Tinnion, Sutton, Ashcroft, Whittle, Griffiths.
Stal Rzeszow: Jalocha; Steniawski, Kawalec, Biel, Gawlik, Michaliszyn, Kozerski, Curvlo, Krawczyk, Napieracz (Jamiszewski), Miler.

SECOND ROUND, SECOND LEG

Celtic (2) 3 (*Dalglish, Edvaldsson, Deans*)
Boavista (1) 1 (*Mane*)   37,000
Celtic: Latchford; McGrain, Lynch, McCluskey P., McDonald, Edvaldsson, McCluskey G., Dalglish, Deans, McNamara, Callaghan (Lennox)
Boavista: Botelho; Trindade, Mario Joao, Carolino, Tai, Barbosa (Rufino), Alves, Mario, Salvador, Acacio (Zezinho), Mane.

Stal Rzeszow (0) 1 (*Kozerski*)
Wrexham (0) 1 (*Sutton*)   20,000
Stal Rzeszow: Jalocha; Blaga, Rosot, Biel, Gawlik (Janiszewski), Dziama, Kozerski, Curylo, Krawczyk, Napieracz, Krysinski.
*Wrexham:*Lloyd; Hill, Dwyer, Davis, May, Evans, Tinnion, Sutton, Ashcroft, Thomas, Griffiths.

West Ham U. (2) 3 (*Paddon, Robson, Taylor A.*)
Ararat Erevan (0) 1 (*Petrosian N.*)   30,399
West Ham U.: Day; McDowell, Lampard, Bonds, Taylor T., Coleman, Taylor A., Paddon, Holland, Brooking, Robson.
Ararat Erevan: Abramian; Martirosian, Sarkissian, Gevorkian, Mesropian, Andreassian, Azarian, Oganesian, Markarov (Ishtoyan), Petrosian S., Petrosian N. (Bondarenko).

QUARTER FINALS, FIRST LEG

Anderlecht (1) 1 (*Van Binst*)
Wrexham (0) 0   30,000
Anderlecht: Ruiter; Van der Elst, Broos, Vandendaele (Andersen), Dockx, Haan, Lomme, Ressel, Van Binst, Coeck (De Groome,) Rensenbrink.
Wrexham: Lloyd; Evans, Fogg, Davis, May, Thomas, Whittle, Sutton, Lee, Ashcroft, Griffiths.

Celtic (1) 1 (*Dalglish*)
Sachsenring Zwickau (0) 1 (*Blank*)   46,000
Celtic: Latchford; McGrain, Lynch, McCluskey, Aitken, Edvaldsson, Wilson, Dalglish, Deans, Hood, Lennox.
Sachsenring Zwickau: Croy: Lippman, Schykowski H., Stemmler, Reicheit, Leuschner, Schwemmer, Blank, Schykowski J., Dietzsch, Braun.

Den Haag (4) 4 (*Mansveld 3, 2 pens., Schoenmaker*)
West Ham U. (0) 2 (*Jennings 2*)   26,000
Den Haag: Thie; Mansveld, De Caluwe, Van Vliet, Korevaar, Kila, Perazic, Schoenmaker, Ouwenhand, Van Leeuwen, Swanenburg.
West Ham U.: Day; McGiven (Coleman), Lampard, Bonds, Taylor T., Lock, Taylor A., Paddon, Jennings, Curbishley, Robson.

QUARTER FINALS, SECOND LEG

Wrexham (0) 1 (*Lee*)
Anderlecht (0) 1 (*Rensenbrink*)   19,668
Wrexham: Lloyd; Evans, Fogg, Davis, May, Whittle, Tinnion, Sutton, Lee, Ashcroft, Griffiths.
Anderlecht: Ruiter; Van der Elst, Broos, Vandendaele, Dockx, Haan, Lomme, Ressel, Van Binst, Coeck, Rensenbrink.

West Ham U. (3) 3 (*Taylor A., Lampard, Bonds pen.*)
Den Haag (0) 1 (*Schoenmaker*)   29,829
West Ham U.: Day; Coleman, Lampard, Bonds, Taylor T., (McGiven), Lock, Taylor A., Paddon (Curbishley), Jennings, Brooking, Robson.
Den Haag: Thie; Mansveld, Ouwehand, Van Vliet, Korevaar, Kila (Jol), Perazic, Schoenmaker, Bres, Van Leeuwen, Albertsen (Swanenburg).

Sachsenring Zwickau (1) 1 (*Blank*)
Celtic (0) 0   40,000
Sachsenring Zwickau: Croy; Lippman, Schykowski H., Stemmler, Schykowski J., Schwemmer, Leuschner, Blank, Brautigam (Eichelt,) Dietzsch, Braun.
Celtic: Latchford; McGrain, Callaghan, McDonald, Aitken, McCluskey, Wilson (Casey), Glavin, (McNamara), Evaldsson, Dalglish, Hood.

SEMI FINAL, FIRST LEG

Eintracht Frankfurt (1) 2 (*Neuberger, Kraus*)
West Ham U. (1) 1 (*Paddon*)   60,000
Eintracht: Kunter; Reichel, Neuberger, Simons,
Beverungen, Kraus (Weidle), Korbel, Holzenbein,
Wenzel, Grabowski, Nickel.
West Ham U.: Day; Coleman, Lampard, Bonds,
Taylor T., McDowell, Holland, Paddon, Jennings,
Brooking, Robson.

SEMI FINAL, SECOND LEG

West Ham U. (0) 3 (*Brooking* 2, *Robson*)
Eintracht Frankfurt (0) 1 (*Beverungen*)   39,202
West Ham U.: Day; Coleman, Lampard, Bonds,
Taylor T., McDowell, Holland, Paddon, Jennings,
Brooking, Robson.

Eintracht: Kunter; Reichel, Neuberger, Lorenz,
Beverungen, Weidle, Korbel, Holzenbein, Wenzel,
Grabowski, Nickel.

FINAL

Anderlecht (1) 4 (*Rensenbrink* 2, 1 *pen., Van der
Elst* 2)
West Ham U. (1) 2 (*Holland, Robson*) at Heysel
Stadium, Brussels   58,000
Anderlecht: Ruiter; Lomme, Broos, Van Binst,
Thissen, Dockx, Coeck (Vercauteren), Van der Elst,
Ressel, Haan, Rensenbrink
West Ham U.: Day; Coleman, Bonds, Taylor (T),
Lampard (Taylor A.), McDowell, Brooking,
Paddon, Holland, Jennings, Robson.

UEFA CUP 1975-76
BRITISH CLUBS FULL RECORD

FIRST ROUND, FIRST LEG

Glentoran (0) 1 (*Jamison*)
Ajax (3) 6 (*Geels* 4, *Meyer, Notten*)   8000
Glentoran: McCullough; McCreery, Craig, Walsh,
Stewart, Jamison, Caskey, Moreland, Robson
(Dougan), Kennedy (Dickinson), Feeney.
Ajax: Schrijvers; Suurbier, Hulshoff, Dusbaba,
Krol, Notten (Helling), Muhren, Van Dord, Geels,
Meyer, Steffenhagen.

Antwerp (4) 4 (*Kodat* 3, *Heyligen*)
Aston Villa (0) 1 (*Graydon*)
Antwerp: Trappeniers; Lieben, Velser, Geens,
Caers, De Schrijver, Van Gaal, Heyligen, Lund,
Kodat (Wilmsen), Deraeve.
Aston Villa: Cumbes; Gidman, Aitken, Ross,
Nicholl, Phillips, Graydon, McDonald (Robson),
Morgan, Hamilton (Hunt), Carrodus.

Everton (0) 0
A.C. Milan (0) 0   31,917
Everton: Lawson; Bernard, Seargeant, Pearson,
Kenyon, Lyons, Buckley (Clements), Dobson,
Latchford, Smallman (Hurst), Jones.
A.C. Milan: Albertosi; Anquilletti, Zecchini,
Turone, Bet, Maldera, Gorin, Bennetti, Bigon,
Scala, Chiarugi.

Hibernian (1) 1 (*Harper*)
Liverpool (0) 0   12,219
Hibernian: McArthur; Brownlie, Schaedler,
Stanton, Barry, Blackley, Edwards, Smith, Harper,
Munro, Duncan.
Liverpool: Clemence; Neal, Jones, Lawler, Cor-
mack, Hughes, Keegan, Hall, Heighway (Boersma),
Kennedy (Toshack), Callaghan.

Feyenoord (0) 1 (*De Jong*)
Ipswich T. (1) 2 (*Whymark, Johnson*)   17,000
Feyenoord: Treytel; Schneider, Ramljak, Van
Daele, Everse, De Jong (Wegerie S.), Rijsbergen
(Olsen), Jansen, Vreysen, Kreuz, Kristensen.
Ipswich T.: Cooper; Burley, Mills, Osborne,
Hunter, Beattie, Hamilton, Viljoen, Johnson
(Lambert), Whymark (Austin), Woods.

Athlone (1) 3 (*Martin. Davis* 2)
Valerengen (0) 0   4,000
Athlone: E'Brien; Duffy, Smith, Wood, Stephen-
son, Larkin, Minnock, Humphries. Martin (Healy),
Davis, Daly.
Valerengen: Blomfeldt; Hansen (Skojli), Brekke,
Haslie, Jorgensen, Edner, Eriksen, Hoetfedr,
Olavson (Foss), Karlsen, Olsen.

Keflavik (0) 0
Dundee U. (2) 2 (*Narey* 2)
Keflavik: Olafsson; Jonsson G., Zakariasson,
Torfasson, Gunnarsson A., Gunnarsson E.,
Jonsson O., Magnusson, Johannesson, Hjalmars-
son, Juliusson.

Dundee U.: McAlpine; Rolland, Kopel, Copland,
Houston, Fleming, Rennie, Payne, Hegarty, Narey,
Gray.

FIRST ROUND, SECOND LEG

Dundee U. (1) 4 (*Hall* 2, *Hegarty pen., Sturrock*)
Keflavik (0) 0   4,500
Dundee U.: McAlpine; Rolland, Kopel, Addison,
Houston (Knox), Narey, Rennie, Payne, Hegarty,
Hall, Sturrock (McDonald).
Keflavik: Olafsson; Jonsson G., Zakariasson,
Gunnarsson E., Torfasson, Gunnarsson A.,
Hjalmarsson, Magnusson, Ragnarsson A.,
Juliusson, Jonsson J.

Liverpool (1) 3 (*Toshack* 3)
Hibernian (1) 1 (*Edwards*)   29,963
Liverpool: Clemence; Neal, Lindsay, Thompson,
Cormack, Hughes, Keegan, Hall, Heighway
(Case), Toshack, Callaghan.
Hibernian: McArthur; Brownlie, Schaedler,
Bremner, Barry, Blackley, Edwards, McLeod,
Harper, Munro, Duncan.

Aston Villa (0) 0
Antwerp (1) 1 (*Kodat*)   31,513
Aston Villa: Findlay; Gidman, Aitken, Ross,
Nicholl, Phillips, Graydon, Little, Robson (Mor-
gan), Hamilton, Carrodus.
Antwerp: Trappeniers; Lieben Velser, Geens,
Caers, De Schrijver, Van Gaal, Heyligen, Lund,
Kodat (Wilmsen), Deraeve.

A.C. Milan (0) 1 (*Calloni pen.*)
Everton (0) 0   60,000
A.C. Milan: Albertosi; Anquilletti, Sabadini,
Turone, Bet, Maldera, Gorin, Benetti, Calloni,
Bigon, Chiarugi.
Everton: Davies; Seargeant, Clements, Pearson,
Kenyon, Lyons, Buckley (Darracott), Dobson,
Latchford, Telfer, Jones.

Ajax (2) 8 (*Notten, Van Dord, Geels* 3, *Muhren,
Brokamp* 2)
Glentoran (0) 0   15,000
Ajax: Schrijvers; Suurbier, Dusbaba, Krol. Van
Dord, Notten, Hulshoff, Muhren, Brockamp,
Geels, Meyer.
Glentoran: McCullough; McCreery, Craig, Walsh,
Robson, Dougan, Caskie, Moreland, Dickinson,
Jamison. Feeney.

Ipswich T. (2) 2 (*Woods, Whymark*)
Feyenoord (0) 0
Ipswich T.: Cooper; Burley, Mills, Osborne (Gates),
Hunter, Beattie, Hamilton, Viljoen, Johnson
(Lambert), Whymark, Woods.
Feyenoord: Treytel; Schneider, Van Daele, Raml-
jak, Everse (Vos), Kreuz, Jansen, Wegerie S.,
Vreysen, Van Hanegem, Kristensen.

Valerengen (0) 1 (*Eriksen*)
Athlone (1) 1 (*Martin*)   747
Valerengen: Blomfeldt; Hansen, Brekke, Haslie, Jorgensen, Edner, Eriksen, Foss, Olavson (Hyving), Karlsen, Olsen.
Athlone: O'Brien; Duffy, Smith, Healy, Stephenson, Larkin, Minnock, Humphries, Martin (Wood), Davis, Daly.

SECOND ROUND, FIRST LEG
Athlone (0) 0
A.C. Milan (0) 0   12,000
Athlone: O'Brien; Duffy, Smith, Wood, Stephenson, Larkin (Barnicle), Minnock, Humphries, Martin (Healy), Davis, Daly.
A.C. Milan: Albertosi; Anquilletti, Maldera, Bet, Turone, Scala, Gorin, Benetti, Calloni (Sabadini), Bigon, Vincenzi.

Dundee U. (0) 1 (*Rennie*)
Porto (1) 2 (*Oliveira, Seninho*)   6500
Dundee U.: McAlpine; Rolland, Kopel, Houston, Forsyth, Narey, Rennie, Payne, Hall, Fleming, Sturrock.
Porto: Tibi; Murca, Ronaldo, Simoes, Gabriel Oliveira, Cubillas, Octavio, Seninho, Rodolfo, Dinis.

Ipswich T. (1) 3 (*Gates, Peddelty, Austin*)
Bruges (0) 0   28,617
Ipswich T.: Cooper; Mills, Beattie, Osborne, Hunter, Peddelty, Hamilton, Gates (Lambert), Johnson (Austin), Whymark, Woods.
Bruges: Jensen; Bastyns, Krieger, Leekens, Volders, Van der Eycken, Cools, Van Gool, Lambert (Sanders), De Cubber, Le Fevre.

Real Sociedad (0) 1 (*Amas*)
Liverpool (1) 3 (*Heighway, Callaghan, Thompson*)
                                           30,000
Liverpool: Clemence; Neal, Thompson, Hughes, Lindsay, Cormack, Hall, Callaghan, Keegan, Toshack, Heighway.
Real Sociedad: Arconada; Cortabarria, Uranga, Amas, Urreisti, Boronat, Murillo (Araquistain), Satrustegui, Idigoras (Martinez); Gaztelu, Zamora,

SECOND ROUND, SECOND LEG
Liverpool (2) 6 (*Toshack, Kennedy 2, Fairclough, Heighway, Neal*)
Real Sociedad (0) 0   23,796
Liverpool: Clemence; Neal, Kettle (Thompson M.), Thompson P., Smith, Callaghan (Fairclough), Keegan, Hall, Heighway, Toshack, Kennedy.
Real Sociedad: Vruti; Cochea, Gaztelu (Esnaola), Uranga, Urreisti, Martinez, Elcoro, Amas Murillo, Satrustegui, Zamora, Idigoras (Araquistain).

A.C. Milan (0) 3 (*Vincenzi, Benetti 2*)
Athlone (0) 0   80,000
A.C. Milan: Albertosi; Sabatini, Maldera, Turone, Bet, Scala, Gorin, Benetti, Bigon, Rivera, Vincenzi.
Athlone: O'Brien; Duffy, Smith, Wood, Stevenson, Larkin, Minnock, Humphries, Martin, Davis, Daly.

Bruges (3) 4 (*Lambert, De Cubber, Le Fevre, Van der Eycken*)
Ipswich T. (0) 0   30,000
Bruges: Jensen; Bastyns, Krieger, Leekens, Volders, Cools, Van der Eycken, Van Gool, Lambert, De Cubber, Le Fevre.
Ipswich T.: Cooper; Burley, Mills, Osborne, Hunter, Peddelty, Hamilton, Viljoen (Gates), Johnson, Whymark, Woods.

Porto (0) 1 (*Seninho*)
Dundee U. (0) 1 (*Hegarty*)   35,000
Porto: Tibi; Murca, Ronaldo, Simoes, Gabriel, Octavio, Teixeria (Rodolfo), Cubillas, Oliveira, Deninho, Dinis.
Dundee U.: McAlpine; Rolland, Fleming, Rennie, Smith D., Houston, Holt, Payne, Hegarty, Knox (Traynor), Sturrock.

THIRD ROUND, FIRST LEG
Slask Wroclaw (0) 1 (*Pawlowski*)
Liverpool (0) 2 (*Kennedy, Toshack*)   40,000
Slask Wroclaw: Kalinowski; Balcerzak, Kowalcyzk, Karpinski, Erlich, Kopycki, Pawlowski, Faber, Garlowski, Kwiatkowski (Olesiak), Sybis.
Liverpool: Clemence; Smith, Neal, Thompson, Kennedy, Hughes, Case, Hall, Heighway, Toshack, Callaghan.

THIRD ROUND, SECOND LEG
Liverpool (2) 3 (*Case 3*)
Slask Wroclaw (0) 0   17,886
Liverpool: Clemence; Smith, Neal, Thompson, Kennedy (Cormack), Hughes, Keegan, Hall, Case, Toshack, Callaghan.
Slask Wroclaw: Kalinowski; Balcerzak, Kowlcyzk, Karpinski, Erlich, Kopycki, Pawlowski, Faber, Garlowski, Olesiak, Sybis.

QUARTER FINALS, FIRST LEG
Dynamo Dresden (0) 0
Liverpool (0) 0   33,000
Dynamo Dresden: Boden; Muller M., Ganzera, Schmuck, Muller K., Hafner, Schade, Riedel, Sachse (Richter), Kotte, Heidler.
Liverpool: Clemence; Smith, Neal, Thompson, Kennedy, Hughes, Keegan, Case, Heighway, Fairclough (Hall), Callaghan.

QUARTER FINALS, SECOND LEG
Liverpool (1) 2 (*Case, Keegan*)
Dynamo Dresden (0) 1 (*Heidler*)   39,300
Liverpool: Clemence; Smith, Neal, Thompson, Kennedy, Hughes, Keegan, Case, Heighway (Fairclough), Toshack, Callaghan.
Dynamo Dresden: Boden; Muller M., Ganzera, Schmuck, Muller K., Hafner, Weber, Kreische, Riedel, Kotte, Heidler.

SEMI FINAL, FIRST LEG
Barcelona (0) 0
Liverpool (1) 1 (*Toshack*)   80,000
Barcelona: Mora; Tome, Migueli, Marcial, Corominas, Neeskens, Rexach, Cruyff, Mir (Clares), Asensi, Fortes.
Liverpool: Clemence; Smith, Neal, Thompson, Kennedy, Hughes, Keegan, Case (Hall), Heighway, Toshack, Callaghan.

SEMI FINAL, SECOND LEG.
Liverpool (0) 1 (*Thompson*)
Barcelona (0) 1 (*Rexach*)   55,104
Liverpool: Clemence; Smith, Neal, Thompson, Kennedy, Hughes, Keegan, Case (Hall), Heighway, Toshack, Callaghan.
Barcelona: Mora; Costas, Migueli, Rife, Albaladejo (Tome), Corominas (De la Cruz), Rexach, Neeskens, Cruyff, Marcial, Heredia.

FINAL, FIRST LEG
Liverpool (0) 3 (*Kennedy, Case, Keegan pen.*)
Bruges (2) 2 (*Lambert, Cools*)   56,000
Liverpool: Clemence; Smith, Thompson, Hughes, Neal, Callaghan, Kennedy, Fairclough, Keegan, Toshack (Case), Heighway
Bruges: Jensen; Bastyns, Krieger, Leekens, Volders, Cools, Vander Eycken, De Cubber, Van Gool, Lambert, Le Fevre.

FINAL, SECOND LEG
Bruges (1) 1 (*Lambert pen.*)
Liverpool (1) 1 (*Keegan*)   32,000
Bruges: Jensen; Bastyns, Krieger, Leekens, Volders Cools, Vander Eycken, Van Gool, Lambert (Sanders); De Cubber (Hinderyckx), Le Fevre.
Liverpool: Clemence; Smith, Neal, Thompson, Kennedy, Hughes, Keegan, Case, Heighway, Toshack (Fairclough), Callaghan.

PROGRESS OF BRITISH AND
IRISH CLUBS IN EUROPE

1955–56
EUROPEAN CUP   Hibernian (Semi-Final)

1955–58
EUROPEAN
INTER-CITIES   London beat Basle, Frankfurt and Lausanne before losing to Barcelona 2-2, 2-6
in the Final.
FAIRS CUP   Birmingham C. knocked out Inter and Zagreb before losing to Barcelona 4-3, 0-1
and 1-2 at Basle.

1956–57

EUROPEAN CUP	Manchester U. (Semi-Final)	Rangers (First Round Proper)

1957–58

EUROPEAN CUP	Manchester U. (Semi-Final)	Glenavon (Preliminary Round)
	Rangers (First Round Proper)	Shamrock R. (Preliminary Round)

1958–60

FAIRS CUP	Birmingham C. (Runners-Up)	Chelsea (Second Round)

1958–59

EUROPEAN CUP	Wolverhampton W. (First Round)	Drumcondra (Preliminary Round)
	Ards (Preliminary Round)	Hearts (Preliminary Round)
	Manchester U. were invited to compete, but were withdrawn by the Football League.	

1959–60

EUROPEAN CUP	Rangers (Semi-Final)	Linfield (Preliminary Round)
	Wolverhampton W. (Quarter-Final)	Shamrock R. (Preliminary Round)

1960–61

EUROPEAN CUP	Burnley (Quarter-Final)	Limerick (Preliminary Round)
	Hearts (Preliminary Round)	Glenavon—Withdrew
EUROPEAN CUP-WINNERS' CUP	Rangers (Runners-Up)	Wolverhampton W. (Semi-Final)
FAIRS CUP	Birmingham C. (Runners-Up)	Hibernian (Semi-Final)

1961–62

EUROPEAN CUP	Tottenham H. (Semi-Final)	Drumcondra (Preliminary Round)
	Rangers (Quarter-Final)	Linfield (Preliminary Round)
EUROPEAN CUP-WINNERS' CUP	Dunfermline Ath. (Quarter-Final)	Swansea T. (First Round)
	Leicester C. (Second Round)	Glenavon (First Round)
		St Patrick's Ath. (Preliminary Round)
FAIRS CUP	Sheffield W. (Quarter-Final)	Nottingham F. (First Round)
	Hearts (Second Round)	Birmingham C. (Second Round)
		Hibernian (Second Round)

1962–63

EUROPEAN CUP	Dundee (Semi-Final)	Shelbourne (Preliminary Round)
	Ipswich T. (First Round)	Linfield (Preliminary Round)
EUROPEAN CUP-WINNERS' CUP	Tottenham H. (Winners)	Shamrock R. (Second Round)
	Rangers (Second Round)	Bangor C. (First Round)
		Portadown (First Round)
FAIRS CUP	Hibernian (Quarter-Final)	Everton (First Round)
	Dumfermline Ath. (Second Round)	Celtic (First Round)
	Glentoran (First Round)	Drumcondra (Second Round)

1963–64

EUROPEAN CUP	Rangers (Preliminary Round)	Dundalk (Preliminary Round)
	Everton (Preliminary Round)	Distillery (Preliminary Round)
EUROPEAN CUP-WINNERS' CUP	Celtic (Semi-Final)	Borough U. (Second Round)
	Manchester U. (Quarter-Final)	Tottenham H. (Second Round)
	Linfield (Second Round)	Shelbourne (First Round)
FAIRS CUP	Partick T. (Second Round)	Hearts (First Round)
	Arsenal (Second Round)	Glentoran (First Round)
	Sheffield W. (Second Round)	Shamrock R. (First Round)

1964–65

EUROPEAN CUP	Liverpool (Semi-Final) Rangers (Quarter-Final)	Shamrock R. (Preliminary Round) Glentoran (Preliminary Round)
EUROPEAN CUP-WINNERS' CUP	West Ham U. (Winners) Cardiff C. (Quarter-Final) Dundee (Second Round)	Cork Celtic (First Round) Derry C. (First Round)
FAIRS CUP	Manchester U. (Semi-Final) Dunfermline Ath. (Third Round) Everton (Third Round)	Celtic (Second Round) Shelbourne (Second Round) Kilmarnock (Second Round)

1965–66

EUROPEAN CUP	Manchester U. (Semi-Final) Derry C. (First Round)	Kilmarnock (First Round) Drumcondra (Preliminary Round)
EUROPEAN CUP-WINNERS' CUP	Liverpool (Runners-Up) Celtic (Semi-Final) West Ham U. (Semi-Final)	Limerick (First Round) Cardiff C. (First Round) Coleraine (First Round)
FAIRS CUP	Leeds U. (Semi-Final) Chelsea (Semi-Final) Dunfermline Ath. (Quarter-Final) Hearts (Third Round)	Everton (Second Round) Glentoran (First Round) Hibernian (First Round) Shamrock R. (Second Round)

1966–67

EUROPEAN CUP	Celtic (Winners) Linfield (Quarter-Final)	Liverpool (First Round) Waterford (Preliminary Round)
EUROPEAN CUP-WINNERS' CUP	Rangers (Runners-Up) Everton (Second Round) Shamrock R. (Second Round)	Glentoran (First Round) Swansea T. (First Round)
FAIRS CUP	Leeds U. (Runners-Up) Kilmarnock (Semi-Final) Burnley (Quarter-Final) Dundee U. (Third Round)	W.B.A. (Third Round) Dunfermline Ath. (Second Round) Drumcondra (First Round)

1967–68

EUROPEAN CUP	Manchester U. (Winners) Dundalk (First Round)	Celtic (First Round) Glentoran (First Round)
EUROPEAN CUP-WINNERS' CUP	Cardiff C. (Semi-Final) Aberdeen (Second Round) Tottenham H. (Second Round)	Crusaders (First Round) Shamrock R. (First Round)
FAIRS CUP	Leeds U. (Winners) Dundee (Semi-Final) Hibernian (Third Round) Liverpool (Third Round)	Rangers (Quarter-Final) Nottingham F. (Second Round) Linfield (First Round) St. Patricks (First Round)

1968–69

EUROPEAN CUP	Manchester U. (Semi-Final) Celtic (Quarter-Final) Manchester C. (First Round)	Glentoran (First Round) Waterford (First Round)
EUROPEAN CUP-WINNERS' CUP	Dunfermline Ath. (Semi-Final) W.B.A. (Quarter-Final) Crusaders (First Round)	Cardiff C. (First Round) Shamrock R. (First Round)
FAIRS CUP	Newcastle U. (Winners) Rangers (Semi-Final) Leeds U. (Quarter-Final) Hibernian (Third Round) Aberdeen (Second Round)	Chelsea (Second Round) Dundalk (Second Round) Liverpool (First Round) Linfield (First Round) Morton (First Round)

1969–70

EUROPEAN CUP	Celtic (Runners-Up) Leeds U. (Semi-Final)	Waterford (First Round) Linfield (First Round)
EUROPEAN CUP-WINNERS' CUP	Manchester C. (Winners) Rangers (Second Round) Cardiff C. (Second Round)	Ards (First Round) Shamrock R. (First Round)
EUROPEAN FAIRS CUP	Arsenal (Winners) Newcastle U. (Quarter-Finals) Dunfermline Ath. (Third Round) Southampton (Third Round) Liverpool (Second Round)	Kilmarnock (Third Round) Dundee U. (First Round) Coleraine (Second Round) Dundalk (First Round) Glentoran (First Round)

763

1970–71

| EUROPEAN CUP | Celtic (Quarter Final)
Everton (Quarter Final) | Waterford (Second Round)
Glentoran (First Round) |

EUROPEAN CUP — Celtic (Quarter Final), Everton (Quarter Final) — Waterford (Second Round), Glentoran (First Round)

EUROPEAN CUP-WINNERS' CUP — Manchester C. (Semi-Final), Chelsea (Winners), Cardiff C. (Quarter Final) — Linfield (First Round), Aberdeen (First Round), Bohemians (Preliminary Round)

EUROPEAN FAIRS CUP — Leeds U. (Winners), Arsenal (Quarter Final), Liverpool (Semi-Final), Newcastle U. (Second Round), Coleraine (Second Round) — Dundee U. (Second Round), Coventry C. (Second Round), Cork Hibernians (First Round), Rangers (First Round), Kilmarnock (First Round), Hibernian (Third Round)

1971–72

EUROPEAN CUP — Arsenal (Quarter-Final), Celtic (Semi-Final) — Linfield (First Round), Cork Hibs. (First Round)

EUROPEAN CUP-WINNERS' CUP — Liverpool (Second Round), Chelsea (Second Round), Cardiff C. (First Round) — Rangers (Winners), Distillery (First Round), Limerick (First Round)

UEFA CUP — Tottenham H. (Winners), Wolverhampton W. (Runners-up), Leeds (First Round), Southampton (First Round), Shelbourne (First Round), Glentoran (First Round) — Dundee (Third Round), Aberdeen (Second Round), St. Johnstone (Third Round)

1972–73

EUROPEAN CUP — Derby Co. (Semi-Final), Celtic (Second Round) — Waterford (First Round)

EUROPEAN CUP-WINNERS' CUP — Leeds U. (Runners-up), Hibernian (Quarter-Final) — Wrexham (Second Round), Cork Hibs. (Second Round)

UEFA CUP — Liverpool (Winners), Tottenham H. (Semi-Final), Stoke C. (First Round), Manchester C. (First Round) — Aberdeen (First Round), Partick T. (First Round), Bohemians (First Round)

1973-74

EUROPEAN CUP — Liverpool (Second Round), Celtic (Semi-Final) — Waterford (First Round), Crusaders (First Round)

EUROPEAN CUP-WINNERS' CUP — Sunderland (Second Round), Rangers (Second Round), Cardiff C. (First Round) — Glentoran (Quarter-Finals), Cork Hibs. (First Round)

UEFA CUP — Tottenham H. (Runners-up), Ipswich T. (Quarter-Finals), Leeds U. (Third Round), Wolverhampton W. (Second Round) — Aberdeen (Second Round), Hibernian (Second Round), Finn Harps (First Round), Ards (First Round)

1974–75

EUROPEAN CUP — Leeds U. (Runners-up), Celtic (First Round) — Coleraine (First Round), Cork Celtic (Second Round)

EUROPEAN CUP-WINNERS' CUP — Liverpool (Second Round), Ards (First Round), Cardiff (First Round) — Finn Harps (First Round), Dundee U. (Second Round)

UEFA CUP — Derby Co. (Third Round), Ipswich T. (First Round), Stoke C. (First Round), Wolverhampton W. (First Round) — Bohemians (First Round), Dundee (First Round), Portadown (Second Round), Hibernian (Second Round)

1975-76

EUROPEAN CUP — Derby Co. (Second Round), Linfield (First Round) — Rangers (Second Round), Bohemians (First Round)

EUROPEAN CUP-WINNERS' CUP — West Ham U. (Runners-up), Celtic (Quarter-Final), Home Farm (First Round) — Wrexham (Quarter-Final), Coleraine (First Round)

UEFA CUP — Liverpool (Winners), Aston Villa (First Round), Glentoran (First Round), Athlone T. (Second Round) — Ipswich T. (Second Round), Everton (First Round), Hibernian (First Round), Dundee U. (Second Round)

764

SUMMARY OF APPEARANCES BY BRITISH AND IRISH CLUBS IN EUROPE

THE EUROPEAN CUP (1955–76)

English clubs	Appearances	Clubs from Northern Ireland	Appearances
Manchester U.	5	Linfield	7
Liverpool	3	Glentoran	4
Derby Co.	2	Glenavon	1
Wolverhampton W.	2	Ards	1
Everton	2	Distillery	1
Leeds U.	2	Derry C.	1
Burnley	1	Crusaders	1
Tottenham H.	1	Coleraine	1
Ipswich T.	1		
Manchester C.	1	**Clubs from Eire**	
Arsenal	1	Waterford	6
		Drumcondra	3
		Shamrock R.	3
		Dundalk	2
Scottish clubs		Limerick	1
Celtic	9	Shelbourne	1
Rangers	7	Cork Hibs.	1
Hearts	2	Cork Celtic	1
Dundee	1	Bohemians	1
Kilmarnock	1	Winners: Celtic 1966–67; Manchester U. 1967–68	
Hibernian	1	Finalists: Celtic 1969–70; Leeds U. 1974–75	

THE EUROPEAN CUP-WINNERS' CUP (1960–76)

English clubs	Appearances	Clubs from Northern Ireland	Appearances
Tottenham H.	3	Crusaders	2
Liverpool	3	Glentoran	2
West Ham U.	3	Ards	2
Chelsea	2	Linfield	2
Manchester C.	2	Coleraine	2
Wolverhampton W	1	Glenavon	1
Leicester C.	1	Derry C.	1
Manchester U.	1	Distillery	1
Everton	1	Portadown	1
W.B.A.	1		
Leeds U.	1		
Sunderland	1	**Clubs from Eire**	
		Shamrock R.	5
Scottish clubs		Limerick	2
Rangers	6	Cork Hibs.	2
Celtic	3	Shelbourne	1
Dunfermline Ath.	2	Cork Celtic	1
Aberdeen	2	St. Patrick's Ath.	1
Dundee	1	Bohemians	1
Dundee U.	1	Finn Harps	1
Hibernian	1	Home Farm	1
		Winners: Tottenham H. 1962–63; West Ham U.	
Welsh clubs		1964–65; Manchester C. 1969–70; Chelsea 1970–71;	
Cardiff C.	9	Rangers 1971–72	
Swansea City (then Town)	2		
Wrexham	2	Finalists: Liverpool 1965–66; Rangers 1960–61;	
Bangor C.	1	1966–67; Leeds U. 1972–73; West Ham U. 1975–76	

THE EUROPEAN FAIRS CUP & UEFA CUP (1955–76)

English clubs
7 Leeds U.
6 Liverpool
4 Birmingham C., Everton
3 Chelsea, Arsenal, Newcastle U., Tottenham H., Wolverhampton W., Ipswich
2 Sheffield W., Nottingham F., Southampton, Stoke C.
1 Manchester U., Burnley, W.B.A., Coventry C., London Rep. XI, Manchester C., Derby Co., Aston V.

Scottish clubs
10 Hibernian
5 Dunfermline Ath.
4 Kilmarnock, Aberdeen, Dundee U.
3 Hearts, Rangers, Dundee
2 Partick T., Celtic
1 Morton, St. Johnstone

Clubs from Northern Ireland
6 Glentoran
2 Linfield, Coleraine
1 Ards, Portadown

Clubs from Eire
2 Dundalk, Shelbourne, Shamrock R., Drumcondra, Bohemians
1 St. Patrick's Ath., Cork Hibs, Finn Harps, Athlone T.

Winners: Leeds U. 1967–68, 1970–71; Newcastle U. 1968–69; Arsenal 1969–70; Tottenham H. 1971–72; Liverpool 1972–73, 1975–76

Finalists: Leeds U. 1966–67; Birmingham C. 1958–60, 1960–61; Wolverhampton W. 1971–72; Tottenham H. 1973–74

EUROPEAN CHAMPIONS CUP FINALS 1956–76

Year	Winners		Runners-up		Venue
1956	Real Madrid	4	Stade de Rheims	3	Paris
1957	Real Madrid	2	AC Fiorentina	0	Madrid
1958	Real Madrid	3	AC Milan	2	Brussels
1959	Real Madrid	2	Stade de Rheims	0	Stuttgart
1960	Real Madrid	7	Eintracht Frankfurt	3	Glasgow
1961	Benfica	3	Barcelona	2	Berne
1962	Benfica	5	Real Madrid	3	Amsterdam
1963	AC Milan	2	Benfica	1	London
1964	Inter-Milan	3	Real Madrid	1	Vienna
1965	Inter-Milan	1	Benfica	0	Milan
1966	Real Madrid	2	Partizan Belgrade	1	Brussels
1967	Celtic	2	Inter-Milan	1	Lisbon
1968	Manchester U.	4	Benfica	1	London
1969	AC Milan	4	Ajax Amsterdam	1	Madrid
1970	Feyenoord	2	Celtic	1	Milan
1971	Ajax Amsterdam	2	Panathinaikos	0	London
1972	Ajax Amsterdam	2	Inter-Milan	0	Rotterdam
1973	Ajax Amsterdam	1	Juventus	0	Belgrade
1974	Bayern Munich	4	Atletico Madrid	0	Brussels
	(after 1-1 draw in Brussels)				
1975	Bayern Munich	2	Leeds U.	0	Paris
1976	Bayern Munich	1	St. Etienne	0	Glasgow

EUROPEAN CUP-WINNERS' CUP FINALS 1961–76

Year	Winners		Runners-up		Venue
1961	AC Fiorentina	4	Rangers	1	on aggregate
1962	Atletico Madrid	3	AC Fiorentina	0	Stuttgart
	(after 1-1 draw in Glasgow)				
1963	Tottenham H.	5	Atletico Madrid	1	Rotterdam
1964	Sporting Club Lisbon	1	MTK Budapest	0	Antwerp
	(after 3-3 draw in Brussels)				
1965	West Ham U.	2	TSV Munich 1860	0	London
1966	Borussia Dortmund	2	Liverpool	1	Glasgow
1967	Bayern Munich	1	Rangers	0	Nuremberg
1968	AC Milan	2	SV Hamburg	0	Rotterdam
1969	Slovan Bratislava	3	Barcelona	2	Basel
1970	Manchester C.	2	Gornik Zabrze	1	Vienna
1971	Chelsea	2	Real Madrid	1	Athens
	(after 1-1 draw in Athens)				
1972	Rangers	3	Dynamo Moscow	2	Barcelona
1973	AC Milan	1	Leeds U.	0	Salonika
1974	FC Magdeburg	2	AC Milan	0	Rotterdam
1975	Dynamo Kiev	3	Ferencvaros	0	Basel
1976	Anderlecht	4	West Ham U.	2	Brussels

EUROPEAN FAIRS CUP FINALS 1958–71

1958 Barcelona 8, London 2*	1966 Barcelona 4, Real Zaragoza 3*
1960 Barcelona 4, Birmingham C. 1*	1967 Dynamo Zagreb 2, Leeds U. 0*
1961 A. S. Roma 4, Birmingham C. 2*	1968 Leeds U. 1, Ferencvaros 0*
1962 Valencia 7, Barcelona 3*	1969 Newcastle U. 6, Ujpest Dozsa 2*
1963 Valencia 4, Dynamo Zagreb 1*	1970 Arsenal 4, Anderlecht 3*
1964 Real Zaragoza 2, Valencia 1	1971 Leeds U. 3, Juventus 3*
1965 Ferencvaros 1, Juventus 0	(Leeds won on away goals)

UEFA CUP 1972–76

1972 Tottenham H. 3, Wolverhampton W. 2*
1973 Liverpool 3, Bor. Moenchengladbach 2*
1974 Feyenoord 4, Tottenham H. 2*
1975 Bor. Moenchengladbach 5, Twente Enschede 1*
1976 Liverpool 4, FC Bruges 3*
*aggregate scores

EUROPEAN NATIONS SECTION

Details have been listed for all European footballing nations, but unfortunately due to other countries seasons finishing at different times from our own, some league champions and cup winners are unknown for the current season. Total number of championship and cup wins is given with winners' present names, with previous names in brackets. In the tables of league champions and cup winners, contemporary names are used.

ALBANIA

President: Besim Fagu
Secretary: Ilia Shuke.
Address of Association: Federation Albanaise de Football, Rruga, Kongresi I Permetit, 41 Tirana.
Telephone: 41–70, 24–26, 28–55, 34–89.
Cable: Albsport Tirana.
Area: 11,100 square miles.
Population: 1,872,000. *Number of Clubs:* 33.
Teams: 130
Number of Players: 4,070.
Year of Formation: 1932.
National Colours: Red shirts, black shorts, black stockings with red stripe.
Second Choice of Colours: White shirts, white shorts, white stockings.
Name, Address and Capacity of National Stadium: Qemal Stafa, Tirana, 24,000.
Names and Capacity of Other Principal Football Grounds: Dinamo, 15,000; Shkodra, 13,000; Durresi, 15,000; Korca, 13,000; Fier, 10,000; Vlora, 13,000.

International matches 1975
Jan. 2, Algiers: v Algeria (a) lost 2-4

League Championship wins (1945–75)
Dinamo Tirana 11; Partizan Tirana 10; 17 Nendori 5; Vlaznia 4.
Cup wins (1948–74)
Dinamo Tirana 11; Partizan Tirana 8; 17 Nendori 2; Besa 1; Vlaznia 1.

	League Champions	Cup Winners
1945	Vlaznia	
1946	Vlaznia	
1947	Partizan Tirana	
1948	Partizan Tirana	Partizan Tirana
1949	Partizan Tirana	Partizan Tirana
1950	Dinamo Tirana	Dinamo Tirana
1951	Dinamo Tirana	Dinamo Tirana
1952	Dinamo Tirana	Dinamo Tirana
1953	Dinamo Tirana	Dinamo Tirana
1954	Partizan Tirana	Dinamo Tirana
1955	Dinamo Tirana	No competition
1956	Dinamo Tirana	No competition
1957	Partizan Tirana	Partizan Tirana
1958	Partizan Tirana	Partizan Tirana
1959	Partizan Tirana	No competition
1960	Dinamo Tirana	Dinamo Tirana
1961	Partizan Tirana	Partizan Tirana
1963*	Dinamo Tirana	17 Nendori
1964	Partizan Tirana	Partizan Tirana
1965	17 Nendori	Dinamo Tirana
1966	17 Nendori	Dinamo Tirana
1967	Dinamo Tirana	Vlaznia
1968	17 Nendori	Dinamo Tirana
1969	17 Nendori	17 Nendori
1970	17 Nendori	Partizan Tirana
1971	Partizan Tirana	Dinamo Tirana
1972	Vlaznia	Besa
1973	Dinamo Tirana	Partizan Tirana
1974	Vlaznia	Dinamo Tirana
1975	Dinamo Tirana	

* Changed from calendar season to overlapping season from autumn to spring.

AUSTRIA

President: Karl Sekanina.
Secretary: Otto Demuth.
Address of Association: Oesterreichischer Fussball-Bund, Mariahilferstrasse Postfach 161, Wien 56.
Telephone: 57–15–36.
Cable: Football Wien.
Telex: 01 3232-h Sport.
Area: 32,374 square miles.
Population: 7,000,000.
Number of Clubs: 1,918. *Teams:* 6,380.
Number of Players: 267,000.
Year of Formation: 1904.
National Colours: White shirts, black shorts, black stockings.
Second Choice of Colours: Red shirts, white shorts, red stockings.
Name, Address and Capacity of National Stadium: Wiener Stadion, Prater, Vienna, 72,500.
Names, Addresses and Capacities of Other Principal Football Grounds: Linzer Stadion, Linz, 22,100; Stadion Liebenau, Graz, 19,000; Tivoli Stadion, Innsbruck, 14,000; Stadion, Wiener Neustadt, 12,600; Bodenseestadion, Bregenz, 12,000; Stadion Klagenfurt, Klagenfurt, 11,000; Hohe Warte, Wien, 32,000.

Principal Honours
Olympic Games: runners-up 1936

International matches 1975

March 16, Luxembourg: v Luxembourg (a) won 2-1 (EC) (*Koglberger, Krankl*)

April 2, Vienna: v Hungary (h) drew 0-0 (EC).

June 7, Vienna: v Czechoslovakia (h) drew 0-0.

Sept. 3, Vienna: v West Germany (h) lost 0-2.

Sept. 24, Budapest: v Hungary (a) lost 1-2 (EC) (*Krankl pen.*).

Oct 15, Vienna: v Luxembourg (h) won 6-2 (EC) (*Welzl 2, Krankl 2, 1 pen, Jara, Prohaska*).

Nov. 19, Wrexham: v Wales (a) lost 0-1 (EC).

League Championship wins (1912–76)

Rapid Vienna 25; Austria/WAC (previously FK Austria) 12; Admira-Energie-Wacker (prev. Sportklub Admira & Admira-Energie) 8; First Vienna 5; Wiener Sportklub 3; Tirol-Svarowski-Innsbruck (prev. Wacker Innsbruck) 4; FAC 1; Hakoah 1; Linz ASK 1; Wacker Vienna 1; WAF 1; Wiener AC 1; Voest Linz 1.

Cup wins (1919–76)

FK Austria 14; Rapid Vienna 9; Admira-Energie-Wacker (prev. Sportklub Admira & Admira-Energie) 5; First Vienna 3; Wiener AC 3; Tirol-Svarowski-Innsbruck (prev. Wacker Innsbruck) 3; Linz ASK 1; Wacker Vienna 1; WAF 1; Wiener Sportklub 1; Austria WAC 1.

League Champions	Cup Winners
1946 Rapid Vienna	Rapid Vienna
1947 Wacker Vienna	Wacker Vienna
1948 Rapid Vienna	FK Austria
1949 FK Austria	FK Austria
1950 FK Austria	No competition
1951 Rapid Vienna	No competition
1952 Rapid Vienna	No competition
1953 FK Austria	No competition
1954 Rapid Vienna	No competition
1955 First Vienna	No competition
1956 Rapid Vienna	No competition
1957 Rapid Vienna	No competition
1958 Wiener Sportklub	No competition
1959 Wiener Sportklub	Wiener AC
1960 Rapid Vienna	FK Austria
1961 FK Austria	Rapid Vienna
1962 FK Austria	FK Austria
1963 FK Austria	FK Austria
1964 Rapid Vienna	Admira-Energie
1965 Linz ASK	Linz ASK
1966 Admira-Energie	Admira-Energie
1967 Rapid Vienna	FK Austria
1968 Rapid Vienna	Rapid Vienna
1969 FK Austria	Rapid Vienna
1970 FK Austria	Wacker Innsbruck
1971 Wacker Innsbruck	FK Austria
1972 T.-S. Innsbruck	Rapid Vienna
1973 T.-S. Innsbruck	T.-S. Innsbruck
1974 Voest Linz	Austria WAC
1975 T.-S. Innsbruck	T.-S. Innsbruck
1976 Austria/WAC	Rapid Vienna

League Table 1975–76
(up to and including June 13, 1976)

	P	W	D	L	F	A	Pts.
Austria/WAC	34	20	10	4	73	25	50
SW Innsbruck	34	17	9	8	66	36	43
Rapid Vienna	34	17	6	11	55	44	40
Admira/Wacker	34	13	10	11	51	50	36
Austria Salzburg	34	12	11	11	44	47	35
Voest Linz	34	11	9	14	39	44	31
Sturm Graz	34	11	8	15	36	46	30
Linz ASK	34	8	11	15	38	51	27
Graz AK	34	7	11	16	32	60	25
Austria Klagenfurt	34	6	11	17	30	61	23

BELGIUM

President: M. Louis Wouters.
Secretary: Albert Roosens.
Address of Association: Union Royale Belge des Sociétés de Football Association, 14 Rue Guimard, Bruxelles 4.
Telephone: 02/12.98.50.
Cable: UBSFA Bruxelles.
Area: 11,779 square miles.
Population: 9,250,000.
Number of Clubs: 3,071. *Teams:* 8,694.
Number of Players: 197,065.
Year of Formation: 1895.
National Colours: White shirts with tricoloured (black-yellow-red) collar and cuffs, white shorts, white stockings with tricoloured (black-yellow-red) tops.
Second Choice of Colours: White shirts with tricoloured (black-yellow-red) collar and cuffs, black shorts, white stockings with tricoloured (black-yellow-red) tops.

Name, Address and Capacity of National Stadium: Centenary Stadium, Marathon Avenue, Brussels (Heysel), 70,000.
Names, Addresses and Capacities of Other Principal Football Grounds: R. Antwerp F.C.-Bosuilbaan, at Deurne (Antwerp), 62,000; R.F.C. Liégeois-Chaussée de Tongres, at Rocourt (Liège), 43,000; R. Standard C. Liégeois-2 rue de la Centrale at Sclessin (Liège), 35,000; R.S.C. Anderlechtois-2, avenue Théo Verbeeck, Anderlecht (Brussels), 38,000.
Season: September–May.

Principal Honours

Olympic Games: winners 1920
Fairs Cup: runners-up Anderlecht 1970
European Cup Winners Cup: winners Anderlecht 1976
UEFA Cup: runners-up F.C. Bruges 1976

International matches 1975
April 30, Antwerp: v Netherlands (h) won 1-0 (*Lambert*).
Sept. 6, Liege: v Iceland (h) won 1-0 (EC) (*Lambert*).
Sept. 27, Brussels: v East Germany (h) lost 1-2 (*Puis*).
Nov. 15, Paris: v France (a) drew 0-0 (EC).

League Championship wins (1896–1976)
Anderlecht 16; Union St. Gilloise 11; Beerschot 7; Standard Liege 6; RC Brussels 6; FC Liege 5; Daring Brussels 5; Antwerp 4; Lierse SK 3; Malines 3; CS Bruges 3; FC Bruges 3; R.W.D. Molenbeek 1.

Cup wins (1954–76)
Anderlecht 5; Standard Liege 3; FC Bruges 2; Antwerp 1; Beerschot 1; La Gantoise 1; Lierse SK 1; Tournai 1; Waregem 1.

League Champions	Cup Winners
1946 Malines	
1947 Anderlecht	
1948 Malines	
1949 Anderlecht	
1950 Anderlecht	
1951 Anderlecht	
1952 FC Liege	
1953 FC Liege	
1954 Anderlecht	Standard Liege
1955 Anderlecht	Antwerp
1956 Anderlecht	Tournai
1957 Antwerp	No competition
1958 Standard Liege	No competition
1959 Anderlecht	No competition
1960 Lierse S.K.	No competition
1961 Standard Liege	No competition
1962 Anderlecht	No competition
1963 Standard Liege	No competition
1964 Anderlecht	La Gantoise
1965 Anderlecht	Anderlecht
1966 Anderlecht	Standard Liege
1967 Anderlecht	Standard Liege
1968 Anderlecht	FC Bruges
1969 Standard Liege	Lierse SK
1970 Standard Liege	FC Bruges
1971 Standard Liege	Beerschot
1972 Anderlecht	Anderlecht
1973 FC Bruges	Anderlecht
1974 Anderlecht	Waregem
1975 R.W.D. Molenbeek	Anderlecht
1976 FC Bruges	Anderlecht

Final League Table 1975–76

	P	W	D	L	F	A	Pts.
FC Bruges	36	22	8	6	81	38	52
Anderlecht	36	19	10	7	65	36	48
RWD Molenbeek	36	18	11	7	60	30	47
Lokeren	36	19	7	10	58	33	45
SV Waregem	36	16	12	8	61	39	44
Beveren-Waas	36	15	14	7	41	24	44
Beerschot Antwerp	36	17	9	11	59	54	41
Standard Liege	36	15	9	12	53	46	39
Lierse SK	36	14	11	11	59	44	39
Liege	36	12	11	13	59	62	35
Antwerp	36	10	14	12	40	55	34
AS Ostend	36	10	11	15	42	61	31
CS Bruges	36	8	13	14	41	52	31
La Louviere	36	7	16	13	42	59	30
FC Malines	36	9	11	16	45	62	29
SC Charleroi	36	9	9	18	47	62	27
Beringen	36	7	13	16	27	50	27
Berchem Sport	36	5	11	20	22	57	21
Racing Malines	36	6	8	22	27	65	20

BULGARIA

President: Danayl Nikolov.
Secretary: Nikola Mollov.
Address of Association: Federation Bulgare de Football, Stade-v-Levsky, Sofia.
Telephone: 87 53 91–4. *Cable:* Besefese Sofia.
Area: 42,830 square miles.
Population: 8,500,000.
Number of Clubs: 2,307. *Teams:* 5,312.
Number of Players: 109,722.
Year of Formation: 1923.
National Colours: White shirts, green shorts, red stockings.
Second Choice of Colours: Red shirts, white shorts, white stockings.
Name, Address and Capacity of National Stadium: "Vassil Levski", Sofia, 60,000.
Names, Addresses and Capacities of Other Principal Football Grounds: Stade Narodna Armia, Parc de la Liberté, Sofia, 30,000; Stade Slavia, Ovtcha Koupel, Sofia, 30,000; Stade Rakovski, quartier Ivan Vasoc, Sofia, 29,000; Stade Guerena, quartier Podouene, Sofia, 33,000; Stade 9 Septembre, Plovdiv, 25,000; Stade Christo Botev, Plovdiv, 30,000; Stade Yuri Gagarine, Varna, 40 000;

Stade de la ville de Rousse, 20,000; Stade 9 Septembre, Bourgass, 15,000.

Principal Honours
Olympic Games: runners-up 1968

International matches 1975
March 26, East Berlin: v East Germany (a) drew 0-0.
April 27, Sofia: v West Germany (h) drew 1-1 (EC) (*Kolev pen*).
June 11, Sofia: v Malta (h) won 5-0 (EC) (*Dimitrov, Denev, Panov, Bonev, Milanov*).
Nov. 19, Stuttgart: v West Germany (a) lost 0-1 (EC).
Dec. 21, Valetta: v Malta (a) won 2-0 (EC) (*Panov, Jordanov*).

League Championship wins (1925–76)
CSKA Sofia (prev. CDNA) 19; Levski Spartak (prev. Levski Sofia) 11, Slavia Sofia 6; Vladislav Varna 3; Lokomotiv Sofia 2; AS 23 Sofia 1; Botev Plovdiv 1; SC Sofia 1; Sokol Varna 1; Spartak Plovdiv 1; Tichka Varna 1; Trakia Plovdiv 1; ZSK Sofia 1.

Cup wins (1946–76)
Levski Spartak (prev. Levski Sofia) 11;
CSKA Sofia (prev. CDNA) 10; Slavia Sofia
5; Lokomotiv Sofia 2; Botev Plovdiv 1;
Spartak Plovdiv 1; Spartak Sofia 1.

League Champions	Cup Winners
1946 Levski Sofia	Levski Sofia
1947 Levski Sofia	Levski Sofia
1948 CDNA Sofia	Lokomotiv Sofia
1949 Levski Sofia	Levski Sofia
1950 Levski Sofia	Levski Sofia
1951 CDNA Sofia	CDNA Sofia
1952 CDNA Sofia	Slavia Sofia
1953 Levski Sofia	Lokomotiv Sofia
1954 CDNA Sofia	CDNA Sofia
1955 CDNA Sofia	CDNA Sofia
1956 CDNA Sofia	Levski Sofia
1957 CDNA Sofia	Levski Sofia
1958 CDNA Sofia	Spartak Plovdiv
1959 CDNA Sofia	Levski Sofia
1960 CDNA Sofia	CDNA Sofia
1961 CDNA Sofia	CDNA Sofia
1962 CDNA Sofia	Botev Plovdiv
1963 Spartak Plovdiv	Slavia Sofia
1964 Lokomotiv Sofia	Slavia Sofia
1965 Levski Sofia	CSKA Sofia
1966 CSKA Sofia	Slavia Sofia
1967 Trakia Plovdiv	Levski Sofia
1968 Levski Sofia	Spartak Sofia
1969 CSKA Sofia	CSKA Sofia
1970 Levski Spartak	Levski Spartak
1971 CSKA Sofia	Levski Spartak
1972 CSKA Sofia	CSKA Sofia
1973 CSKA Sofia	CSKA Sofia
1974 Levski Spartak	CSKA Sofia
1975 CSKA Sofia	Slavia Sofia
1976 CSKA Sofia	Levski Spartak

Final League Table 1975–76

	P	W	D	L	F	A	Pts.
CSKA Sofia	30	17	9	4	61	30	43
Levski Spartak	30	16	9	5	58	33	41
Akademik Sofia	30	14	9	7	35	25	37
Lokomotiv Plovdiv	30	12	9	9	43	33	33
Slavia Sofia	30	11	10	9	43	41	32
Trakia Plovdiv	30	10	12	8	24	26	32
Sliven	30	13	5	12	29	30	31
Lokomotiv Sofia	30	9	11	10	35	33	29
Dunav Russe	30	11	7	12	32	38	29
Beroe Stara Zagora	30	8	12	10	35	39	28
Spartak Varna	30	10	7	13	32	33	27
Pirin Blagoevgrad	30	7	13	10	24	28	27
Botev Vratza	30	11	5	14	30	36	27
Mineur Pernik	30	8	10	12	30	46	26
Tchernomore Varna	30	7	10	13	35	44	24
Spartak Pleven	30	4	6	20	32	63	14

CYPRUS

President:
Secretary: Demetrakis Stephanides.
Address of Association: Cyprus Football
Association, Stasinos Street I, Engomi 114,
P.O. Box 1471, Nicosia.
Telephone: 65341, 72136.
Cable: Kop Nicosia.
Area: 3,572 square miles.
Population: 600,000.
Number of Clubs: 41.   *Teams:* 40.
Number of Players: 11,850.
Year of Formation: 1934.
National Colours: Blue shirts, white shorts,
blue and white stockings.
Second Choice of Colours: White shirts, blue
shorts, white stockings.
*Name, Address and Capacity of National
Stadium:* G.S.P., Nicosia, 20,000.
*Names, Addresses and Capacities of Other
Principal Football Grounds:* G.S.E., Fama-
gusta, 10,000; G.S.O., Limassol, 10,000;
G.S.Z., Larnaca, 18,000.
Season: October–June.
All Players are Amateurs.

International matches 1975

April 1, Nicosia: v Greece (h) lost 1-2.
April 16, Wembley: v England (a) lost 0-5
(EC).
April 20, Prague: v Czechoslovakia (a)
lost 0-4 (EC).
May 11, Limassol: v England (h) lost 0-1
(EC).
June 8, Limassol: v Portugal (h) lost 0-2
(EC).
Nov 5, Limassol: v Greece (Amat.) (h) won
1-0.
Nov 23, Limassol: v Czechoslovakia (h)
lost 0-3 (EC).
Dec. 3, Setubal: v Portugal (a) lost 0-1.

League Championship wins (1935–75)
Apoel 11; Anorthosis 6; Omonia 5; AEL 5;
EPA 3; Olympiakos 3; Chetin Kaya 1;
Pezoporikos 1; Trast 1

Cup wins (1935–75)
Apoel 7; EPA 5; AEL 3; Trast 3; Chetin
Kaya 2; Omonia 2; Apollon 2; Pezoporikos
2; Anorthosis 2; Paralimni 1.

League Champions	Cup Winners
1946 EPA	EPA
1947 Apoel	Apoel
1948 Apoel	AEL
1949 Apoel	Anorthosis
1950 Anorthosis	EPA
1951 Chetin Kaya	Apoel
1952 Apoel	Chetin Kaya
1953 AEL	EPA
1954 Pezoporikos	Chetin Kaya
1955 AEL	EPA
1956 AEL	No competition
1957 Anorthosis	No competition
1958 Anorthosis	No competition
1959 No competition	No competition

1960 Anorthosis	No competition	1968 AEL	Apoel
1961 Omonia	No competition	1969 Olympiakos	Apoel
1962 Anorthosis	Anorthosis	1970 EPA	Pezoporikos
1963 Anorthosis	Apoel	1971 Olympiakos	Anorthosis
1964 No competition	No competition	1972 Omonia	Omonia
1965 Apoel	Omonia	1973 Apoel	Pezoporikos
1966 Omonia	Apollon	1974 Omonia	Paralimni
1967 Olympiakos	Apollon	1975 Omonia	Anorthosis

CZECHOSLOVAKIA

President: Ing-Ladislav Sarosi.
Secretary: Jan Fabera.
Address of Association: Czechoslovak Football, 12, Na Porící, Prague, 1.
Telephone: 249–841.
Cable: Sportsvaz.
Area: 49,370 square miles.
Population: 14,000,000.
Number of Clubs: 6,776. *Teams:* 26,847.
Number of Players: 348,000.
Year of Formation: 1906.
National Colours: Red shirts, white shorts, blue stockings.
Second Choice of Colours: White shirts, white shorts, red stockings.
Name, Address and Capacity of National Stadium: Stadion ceskoslovenské armády, Praha-Strahov, 60,000.
Names, Addresses and Capacities of Other Principal Football Grounds: Slovan Bratislava, Bratislava-Tehelné pole, 63,000; Spartak Brno, Brno, 70,000; Slavia Prague, Prague, 43,000; Sparta Praha, Prague, 38,000.

Principal Honours
World Cup: runners-up 1934, 1962
Olympic Games: runners-up 1964
Cup-Winners Cup: winners Slovan Bratislava (1969)

International matches 1975
March 31, Prague: v Rumania (h) drew 1-1 (*Nehoda*).
April 20, Prague: v Cyprus (h) won 4-0 (EC) (*Panenka 3, Masny*).
April 30, Prague: v Portugal (h) won 5-0 (EC) (*Bicovsky 2, Nehoda 2, Petras*).
June 7, Vienna: v Austria (a) drew 0-0.
Sept 24, Brno: v Switzerland (h) drew 1-1 (*Masny*).
Oct. 15, Prague: v Hungary (h) drew 1-1 (*Nehoda*).
Oct. 30, Bratislava: v England (h) won 2-1 (EC) (*Nehoda, Gallis*).
Nov. 12, Oporto: v Portugal (a) drew 1-1 (EC) (*Ondrus*).
Nov. 23, Limassol: v Cyprus (a) won 3-0 (EC) (*Nehoda, Bicovsky, Masny*).

League Championship wins (1926–76)
Sparta Prague 13; Slavia Prague 12; Dukla Prague (prev. UDA) 8; Slovan Bratislava 6; Spartak Trnava 5; Inter-Bratislava 1; Spartak Hradec Kralove 1; Viktoria Zizkov 1; Banik Ostrava 1.

Cup wins (1961–75)
Dukla Prague 4; Slovan Bratislava 4; Sparta Trnava 3; Sparta Prague 2; TJ Gottwaldov 1; Banik Ostrava 1.

League Champions	Cup Winners
1946 Sparta Prague	
1947 Slavia Prague	
1948 Sparta Prague	
1949 Slovan Bratislava	
1950 Slovan Bratislava	
1951 Slovan Bratislava	
1952 Sparta Prague	
1953 Dukla Prague	
1954 Sparta Prague	
1955 Slovan Bratislava	
1956 Dukla Prague	
1957 No competition	
1958 Dukla Prague	
1959 Inter-Bratislava	
1960 Hradec Kralove	
1961 Dukla Prague	Dukla Prague
1962 Dukla Prague	Slovan Bratislava
1963 Dukla Prague	Slovan Bratislava
1964 Dukla Prague	Sparta Prague
1965 Sparta Prague	Dukla Prague
1966 Dukla Prague	Dukla Prague
1967 Sparta Prague	Spartak Trnava
1968 Spartak Trnava	Slovan Bratislava
1969 Spartak Trnava	Dukla Prague
1970 Slovan Bratislava	TJ Gottwaldov
1971 Spartak Trnava	Spartak Trnava
1972 Spartak Trnava	Sparta Prague
1973 Spartak Trnava	Banik Ostrava
1974 Slovan Bratislava	Slovan Bratislava
1975 Slovan Bratislava	Spartak Trnava
1976 Banik Ostrava	

Final League Table 1975–76

	P	W	D	L	F	A	Pts.
Banik Ostrava	30	14	9	7	37	29	37
Slovan Bratislava	30	15	6	9	49	25	36
Slavia Prague	30	16	4	10	50	33	36
Dukla Prague	30	15	5	10	52	36	35
Union Teplice	30	12	8	10	36	44	32
Inter Bratislava	30	12	7	11	34	27	31
Zbrojovka Brno	30	11	9	10	35	28	31
Lokomotiv Kosice	30	12	6	12	55	50	30
Bohemians Prague	30	10	10	10	35	31	30
Spartak Trnava	30	12	5	13	35	32	29
VSS Kosice	30	11	6	13	45	42	28
ZVL Zilina	30	12	4	14	38	42	28
Skoda Plzen	30	10	7	13	34	48	27
Jednota Trencin	30	9	8	13	23	53	26
LIAZ Jablonec	30	7	10	13	28	51	24
TZ Trinec	30	8	4	18	22	37	20

DENMARK

President: Vilhelm Skousen.
Secretary: Erik Hyldstorp.
Address of Association: Danish Football Association, P.H.-Lings-Allé 4, Copenhagen, 2100.
Telephone: Tria 4540.
Cable: Danksboldspil.
Area: 17,159 square miles.
Population: 5,000,000.
Number of Clubs: 1,390. *Teams:* 7,400.
Number of Players: 208,000.
Year of Formation: 1889.
National Colours: Red shirts, white shorts, red/white stockings.
Second Choice of Colours: Blue shirts, white shorts, blue/white stockings.
Name, Address and Capacity of National Stadium: Kobenhavns Idraetspark, P.H.-Lings-Alle 2, 50,000.
Names, Addresses and Capacities of Other Principal Football Grounds: Odense stadium, Odense, 20,000; Aarhus stadium, Aarhus, 24,000; Aalborg stadium, Aalborg, 22,000; Esbjerg stadium, Esbjerg, 18,000; Vejle stadium, Vejle, 18,000.
Season: April–November. Break: December to March.

Principal Honours
Olympic Games: runners-up 1908, 1912, 1960

International matches 1975
May 10, Bucharest: v Rumania (a) lost 1-6 (EC) (*Dahl*)
June 25, Copenhagen: v Finland (h) won 2-0 (*Bjornmose, Mehtinen o.g.*).
Sept. 3, Copenhagen: v Scotland (h) lost 0-1 (EC).
Sept. 25, Malmo: v Sweden (a) drew 0-0,
Oct 12, Barcelona: v Spain (a) lost 0-2 (EC).
Oct. 29, Glasgow: v Scotland (a) lost 1-3 (EC) (*Bastrup*).

League Championship wins (1913–75)
KB Copenhagen 15; B 93 Copenhagen 9; AB (Akademisk) 9; Frem 6; B 1903 Copenhagen 6; AGF Aarhus 4; Esbjergs FK 4; Vejle BK 3; B 1909 Odense 2; Hvidovre 2; Koge BK 2.

Cup wins (1955–76)
Aarhus GF 5; Vejle 4; BK 09 Odense 3; Randers Freja 3; Aalborg BK 2; Esbjerg BK 2; Frem 1; KB Copenhagen 1; Vanlose 1.

League Champions	Cup Winners
1946 BK 93	
1947 Akademisk	
1948 KB Copenhagen	
1949 KB Copenhagen	
1950 KB Copenhagen	
1951 Akademisk	
1952 Akademisk	
1953 KB Copenhagen	
1954 Koge BK	
1955 Aarhus GF	Aarhus GF
1956 Aarhus GF	Frem
1957 Aarhus GF	Aarhus GF
1958 Vejle	Vejle
1959 BK 09 Odense	Vejle
1960 Aarhus GF	Aarhus GF
1961 Esbjerg BK	Aarhus GF
1962 Esbjerg BK	BK Odense 09
1963 Esbjerg BK	BK Odense 09
1964 BK 09 Odense	Esbjerg
1965 Esbjerg BK	Aarhus GF
1966 Hvidovre	Aalborg BK
1967 Akademisk	Randers Freja
1968 KB Copenhagen	Randers Freja
1969 BK 03 Copenhagen	KB Copenhagen
1970 BK 03 Copenhagen	Aalborg BK
1971 Vejle	BK 09 Odense
1972 Vejle	Vejle
1973 Hvidovre	Randers Freja
1974 KB Copenhagen	Vanlose
1975 Koge BK	Vejle
1976	Esbjerg

Final League Table 1975

	P	W	D	L	F	A	Pts.
Koge	30	17	7	6	61	31	41
Holbaek	30	18	5	7	59	37	41
Naestved	30	15	8	7	56	42	38
KB Copenhagen	30	17	3	10	67	42	37
Esbjerg	30	10	14	6	38	34	34
B 1903 Copenhagen	30	13	7	10	52	36	33
Aalborg	30	14	5	11	63	49	33
Vanlose	30	13	7	10	49	54	33
B 1901 Nykobing	30	12	6	12	43	55	30
Vejle	30	9	8	13	46	53	26
Frem Copenhagen	30	10	6	14	43	52	26
Randers Freja	30	8	9	13	46	53	24
Fremad Amager	30	10	4	16	45	54	24
B 93 Copenhagen	30	6	10	14	33	47	22
Slagelse	30	8	4	18	35	58	20
B 1909 Odense	30	8	1	21	47	78	17

FINLAND

President: Ove H. Rehn.
Secretary: Erkki Poroila.
Address of Association: Suomen Palloliitto—Finlands Bollförbund, Bulevardi 28, Helsinki.
Telephone: 634932, 669025.
Cable: Suomi Fotboll.
Area: 130,119 square miles.
Population: 6,000,000.
Number of Clubs: 750. *Teams:* 1,828.
Number of Players: 35,500.
Year of Formation: 1908.
National Colours: White shirts, blue shorts, white stockings.
Second Choice of Colours: Blue shirts, white shorts, blue stockings.
Name, Address and Capacity of National

Stadium: Olympiastadion, Helsinki, 48,000.
Names, Addresses and Capacities of Other Principal Football Grounds: the most important football grounds are in the cities mentioned below, their capacity being about 10,000–20,000 spectators.

Kotka, Urheilukeskus, Kuopio, Väinölänniemen kenttä, Lahti, Kisapuisto, Lappeenranta, Kimpisen kenttä, Mikkeli, Urheilupuisto, Oulu, Raatin kenttä, Pori, Herralahden kenttä, Tampere, Ratinan kenttä, Turku, Kupittaan kenttä, Vaasa, Hietalahden kenttä, Valkeakoski, Tehtaan kenttä.

All Amateur Players.

International matches 1975
June 5, Helsinki: v Italy (h) lost 0-1 (EC).
June 25, Copenhagen: v Denmark (a) lost 0-2.
Sept. 3, Nijmegen: v Netherlands (a) lost 1-4 (EC) (Paatelainen).
Sept. 29, Rome: v Italy (a) drew 0-0 (EC).

Championship wins (1949–75)
Turun Palloseura 5; Kupion Palloseura 4; Valkeakosken Haka 3; Lahden Reipas 3; IF Kamraterna 2; Kotkan TP 2; Helsinki JK 2; Turun Pyrkivä 1; IF Kronohagens 1; Helsinki PS 1; Ilves-Kissat 1; Kokkolan PV 1; IF Kamraterna I Vasa 1.

Cup wins (1955–75)
Valkeakosken Haka 5; Lahden Reipas 5; Kotkan TP 3; Mikkelin 2; IFK Abo 1; Drott 1; Helsinki JK 1; Helsinki PS 1; Kuopion Palloseura 1; Pallo-Peikot 1.

League Champions	Cup Winners
1949 Turun Palloseura	
1950 Ilves-Kissat	
1951 Kotkan TP	
1952 Kotkan TP	
1953 IF Kamraterna I Vasa	
1954 Turun Pyrkivä	
1955 IF Kronohagens	Valkeakosken Haka
1956 Kuopion Palloseura	Pallo-Peikot
1957 Helsinki PS	Drott
1958 Kuopion Palloseura	Kotkan TP
1959 IF Kamraterna	Valkeakosken Haka
1960 Valkeakosken Haka	Valkeakosken Haka
1961 IF Kamraterna	Kotkan TP
1962 Valkeakosken Haka	Helsinki PS
1963 Lahden Reipas	Valkeakosken Haka
1964 Helsinki JK	Lahden Reipas
1965 Valkeakosken Haka	IFK Abo
1966 Kuopion Palloseura	Helsinki JK
1967 Lahden Reipas	Kotkan TP
1968 Turun Palloseura	Kuopion Palloseura
1969 Kokkolan PV	Valkeakosken Haka
1970 Lahden Reipas	Mikkelin
1971 Turun Palloseura	Mikkelin
1972 Turun Palloseura	Lahden Reipas
1973 Helsinki JK	Lahden Reipas
1974 Kuopion Palloseura	Lahden Reipas
1975 Turun Palloseura	Lahden Reipas

Final League Table 1975

	P	W	D	L	F	A	Pts.
Turun Palloseura	22	13	6	3	34	18	32
Kuopion Palloseura	22	12	6	4	40	24	30
Kokkolan Palloveikot	22	11	5	6	31	21	27
Mikkelin Pallokissat	22	10	6	6	40	27	26
Kuopion Pallotoverit	22	10	6	6	32	22	26
Lahden Reipas	22	10	3	9	47	35	23
Vaasan Palloseura	22	8	6	8	29	28	22
Helsingin	22	8	2	12	29	37	18
Mikkelin Palloilijat	22	6	6	10	23	36	18
Valkeakosken Haka	22	6	3	13	21	36	15
Oulun	22	5	5	12	19	38	15
Myllykosken Pallo	22	4	4	14	22	45	12

FRANCE

President: Fernand Sastre.
Secretary: Michel Cagnion (Dir. Gen.)
Address of Association: Federation Francaise de Football, 60 bis, Avenue d'Iena, Paris 16e.
Telephone: 720 65–40.
Cable: CEFI Paris 034.
Telex: 62–837 Football Paris.
Area: 209,454 square miles.
Population: 46,700,000.
Number of Clubs: 16,242. Teams: 62,000.
Number of Players: 1,007,422.
Year of Formation: 1919.
National Colours: Blue shirts, white shorts, red stockings.
Second Choice of Colours: Red shirts, white shorts, blue stockings.
Name, Address and Capacity of National Stadium: Stade du Parc de Princes, 24 rue du Commandant Guilbaud, 75, Paris, 16ème, 50,000.

Names, Addresses and Capacities of Other Principal Football Grounds: Stade Vélodrome Municipal de Marseille, Boulevard Michelet, 13, Marseille, 45,000; Stade Municipal de Bordeaux, Avenue de la Côte d'Argent, 33, Bordeaux, 33,000; Stade Municipal de Gerland, Lyon, 30,000; Stadium Municipal de Toulouse, Parc des Sports, 31 Toulouse, 30,000; Parc de Princes, Paris, 50,000.
Season: September to June.

Principal Honours
European Champions Cup: runners-up Stade de Reims (1956, 1959), St. Etienne (1976)

International matches 1975

March 26, Paris: v Hungary (h) won 2-0 (*Michel, Parizon*).
April 26, Paris: v Portugal (h) lost 0-2.
May 25, Reykjavik: v Iceland (a) drew 0-0 (EC).
Sept. 3, Nantes: v Iceland (h) won 3-0 (EC) (*Guillou 2, Berdoll*).
Oct. 12, Leipzig: v East Germany (a) lost 1-2 (EC) (*Bathenay*).
Nov. 15, Paris: v Belgium (h) drew 0-0 (EC).

League Championship wins (1933-75)

Saint Etienne 8; Stade de Reims 6; OGC Nice 4; Lille OSC 2; Olympique Marseilles 4; Nantes 3; FC Sete 2; Sochaux 2; AS Monaco 2; Racing Club Paris 1; Roubaix-Tourcoing 1; Girondins Bordeaux 1; Olympique Lillois 1.

Cup wins (1918-76)

Olympique Marseilles 9; Lille OSC 5; Racing Club Paris 5; Red Star 5; Saint Etienne 5; Olympique Lyon 3; CAS Genereaux 2; AS Monaco 2; OGC Nice 2; Racing Club Strasbourg 2; Sedan 2; FC Sete 2; Stade de Reims 2; Stade Rennes 2; AS Cannes 1; Club Francais 1; Excelsior Roubaix 1; Girondins Bordeaux 1; Le Havre 1; SO Montpelier 1; Nancy-Lorraine 1; Olympique de Pantin 1; CA Paris 1; Sochaux 1; Toulouse 1.

League Champions	Cup Winners
1946 Lille OSC	Lille OSC
1947 Roubaix-Tourcoing	Lille OSC
1948 Ol. Marseilles	Lille OSC
1949 Stade de Reims	Racing Paris
1950 Girondins Bordeaux	Stade de Reims
1951 OGC Nice	Racing Strasbourg
1952 OGC Nice	OGC Nice
1953 Stade de Reims	Lille OSC
1954 Lille OSC	OGC Nice
1955 Stade de Reims	Lille OSC
1956 OGC Nice	Sedan
1957 Saint Etienne	Toulouse
1958 Stade de Reims	Stade de Reims
1959 OGC Nice	Le Havre
1960 Stade de Reims	AS Monaco
1961 AS Monaco	Sedan
1962 Stade de Reims	Saint Etienne
1963 AS Monaco	AS Monaco
1964 Saint Etienne	Ol. Lyon
1965 Nantes	Stade Rennes
1966 Nantes	Racing Strasbourg
1967 Saint Etienne	Ol. Lyon
1968 Saint Etienne	Saint Etienne
1969 Saint Etienne	Ol. Marseilles
1970 Saint Etienne	Saint Etienne
1971 Ol. Marseilles	Stade Rennes
1972 Ol. Marseilles	Ol. Marseilles
1973 Nantes	Ol. Lyon
1974 Saint Etienne	Saint Etienne
1975 Saint Etienne	Saint Etienne
1976	Ol. Marseilles

League Table 1975-76
(up to and including June 13 1976)

	P	W	D	L	F	A	Bonus Pts.	Pts
St. Etienne	36	17	15	4	62	36	5	54
Nice	36	16	12	8	58	49	6	51
Sochaux	36	16	12	8	58	49	6	50
Nantes	36	14	14	8	65	42	6	48
Reims	36	16	8	12	65	46	5	45
Nancy	36	14	9	13	65	55	7	44
Bastia	36	14	12	10	55	48	4	44
Metz	36	16	4	16	67	60	7	43
Marseilles	36	19	1	16	55	55	1	40
Nimes	36	14	8	14	48	50	3	39
Paris St. Germain	36	13	10	13	61	57	2	38
Valenciennes	36	12	10	14	42	50	4	38
Lille	36	13	7	16	54	69	4	37
Bordeaux	36	13	9	14	55	58	1	36
Lens	36	9	16	11	56	64	2	36
Lyon	36	12	7	17	52	58	4	35
Troyes	36	8	16	12	44	52	2	34
Monaco	36	11	9	16	48	68	2	33
Strasbourg	36	9	11	16	39	53	3	32
Avignon	36	6	6	24	28	75	0	18

EAST GERMANY

President: Helmut Riedel.
Secretary: Gunter Schneider.
Address of Association: Deutscher Fussball-Verband, Storkower Strasse 118, Berlin No. 18. *Telephone:* 53 07 11/App 388.
Cable: Fussball Verband Berlin.
Telex: 0112119. *Area:* 41,802 square miles.
Population: 20,000,000.
Number of Clubs: 4,880. *Teams:* 26,022.
Number of Players: 487,570.
Year of Formation: 1952.
National Colours: White shirts, blue shorts, white stockings.
Name, Address and Capacity of National Stadium: Sportforum-Leipzig, 100,000.
Names, Addresses and Capacities of Other Principal Football Grounds: Walter-Ulbricht-Stadion, Berlin, 65,000; Heinz-Steyer-Stadion, Dresden, 55,000; Ernst-Thälmann-Stadion, 55,000; Karl-Marx-Stadt, 55,000; Georg-Dimitroff-Stadion, Erfurt, 50,000; Kurt-Wabbel-Stadion, Halle, 50,000; Ernest-Abbe-Stadion, Jena, 30,000; Ostsee-Stadion, Rostock, 30,000; Friedrich-Ludwig-Jahn-Sportpark, Berlin, 25,000; Ernest-Grube-Stadion, Magdeburg, 45,000.

Principal Honours:

Cup-Winners' Cup
Winners: FC Magdeburg 1974.

International matches 1975

March 26, East Berlin: v Bulgaria (h) drew 0-0.

May 28, Halle: v Poland (h) lost 1-2 (*Vogel*).
June 5, Reykjavik: v Iceland (a) lost 1-2 (EC) (*Pommerenke*).
July 29, Toronto: v Canada (a) won 3-0 (*Vogel o.g., Bransch*).
July 31, Ottawa: v Canada (a) won 7-1 (*Vogel 3, Streich 2, Riediger, Pommerenke*).
Sept. 3, Moscow: USSR (a) drew 0-0.
Sept. 27, Brussels: v Belgium (a) won 2-1 (EC) (*Ducke, Hafner*).
Oct. 12, Leipzig: v France (h) won 2-1 (EC) (*Streich, Vogel pen.*).

League Championship wins (1950–76)

ASK Vorwaerts 6; Wismut Karl-Marx-Stadt 4; Dynamo Dresden 4; Carl Zeiss Jena (prev. Motor Jena) 3; FC Magdeburg 3; Chemie Leipzig 2; Turbine Erfurt 2; Turbine Halle 1; Zwickau Horch 1; Empor Rostock 1.

Cup wins (1949–76)

Carl Zeiss Jena (prev. Motor Jena) 4; Chemie Leipzig 2; FC Magdeburg 2; Magdeburg Aufbau 2; Motor Zwickau 2; ASK Vorwaerts 2; Lokomotiv Leipzig 2; Dynamo Dresden 1; Dresden Einheit SC 1; Dresden VP 1; Dynamo Berlin 1; Halle Chemie SC 1; North Dessau Waggonworks 1; Thale EHW 1; Union East Berlin 1; Wismut Karl-Marx-Stadt 1; Sachsenring Zwickau 1.

League Champions	Cup Winners
1949	North Dessau Waggonworks
1950 Zwickau Horch	Thale EHW
1951 Chemie Leipzig	No competition
1952 Halle Turbine	Dresden VP
1953 Dynamo Dresden	No competition

	League Champions	Cup Winners
1954	Turbine Erfurt	ASK Vorwaerts
1955	Turbine Erfurt	Wismut Karl-Marx-Stadt
1956	Wismut Karl-Marx-Stadt	Chemie Leipzig
1957	Wismut Karl-Marx-Stadt	Lokomotiv Leipzig
1958	ASK Vorwaerts	Dresden Einheit SC
1959	Wismut Karl-Marx-Stadt	Dynamo Berlin
1960	ASK Vorwaerts	Motor Jena
1961	Empor Rostock	Motor Jena
1962	ASK Vorwaerts	Halle Chemie SC
1963	Motor Jena	Motor Zwickau
1964	Leipzig Chemie	Magdeburg Aufbau
1965	ASK Vorwaerts	Magdeburg Aufbau
1966	ASK Vorwaerts	Chemie Leipzig
1967	Wismut Karl-Marx-Stadt	Motor Zwickau
1968	Carl Zeiss Jena	Union East Berlin
1969	ASK Vorwaerts	FC Magdeburg
1970	Carl Zeiss Jena	ASK Vorwaerts
1971	Dynamo Dresden	Dynamo Dresden
1972	FC Magdeburg	Carl Zeiss Jena
1973	Dynamo Dresden	FC Magdeburg
1974	FC Magdeburg	Carl Zeiss Jena
1975	FC Magdeburg	Sachsenring Zwickau
1976	Dynamo Dresden	Lokomotiv Leipzig

Final League Table 1975–76

	P	W	D	L	F	A	Pts.
Dynamo Dresden	26	19	5	2	70	23	43
Dynamo Berlin	26	17	3	6	67	34	37
Magdeburg	26	15	6	5	59	33	36
Lokomotiv Leipzig	26	13	5	8	40	34	31
Carl Zeiss Jena	26	11	7	8	50	43	29
Wismut Aue	26	9	9	8	30	35	27
Rot-Weiss Erfurt	26	8	10	8	44	36	26
Chemie Halle	26	9	7	10	37	35	25
Sachsenring Zwickau	26	7	8	11	29	43	22
Stahl Riesa	26	7	7	12	35	46	21
Karl-Marx-Stadt	26	7	7	12	25	41	21
Vorwaerts Frankfurt	26	8	4	14	41	57	20
Chemie Leipzig	26	4	6	16	25	62	14
Energie Cottbus	26	3	6	17	23	63	12

WEST GERMANY

President: Dr. Hermann Gossmann.
Secretary: Hans Passlak.
Address of Association: Deutscher Fussball-Bund, Zeppelinallee 77, 6, Frankfurt/Main, 90.
Telephone: (0611) 770568.
Cable: Fussball, Frankfurt.
Telex: 041 2500 dfbd.
Area: 95,097 square miles.
Population: 55,000,000.
Number of Clubs: 16,890. *Teams:* 98,911.
Number of Players: 3,199,569
Year of Formation: 1904–45; 1950.
National Colours: White shirts, black shorts, black stockings with white tops.
Second Choice of Colours: Green shirts, white shorts, white stockings.
Name, Address and Capacity of National Stadium: There is no stadium which could be considered as the National Stadium.
Names, Addresses and Capacities of Principal Football Grounds: Olympiastadion Berlin, 85,000 (61,800 seats); Olympiastadion München, 74,500 (44,200 seats); Neckarstadion Stuttgart, 72,200 (34,400 seats); Parkstadion Gelsenkirchen, 70,000 (36,000 seats); Rheinstadion Düsseldorf, 69,600 (31,800 seats); Waldstadion Frankfurt 62,200 (29,900 seats); Volksparkstadion Hamburg, 60,600 (27,800 seats); Niedersachsenstadion Hannover 58,700 (39,000 seats); Westfalen stadion Dortmund 53,600 (16,600 seats). Müngersdorfer Stadion, Cologne 60,000 (28,000 *seats*).

Season: August to June.

775

Principal Honours

World Cup: winners 1954, 1974; runners-up 1966
European Championship: winners 1972
European Champions Cup: winners, Bayern Munich 1974, 1975, 1976, runners-up Eintracht Frankfurt (1960)
Cup-Winners' Cup: winners Borussia Dortmund (1966), Bayern Munich (1967); runners-up Munich 1860 (1965), SV Hamburg (1968)
UEFA Cup:
Borussia Moenchengladbach winners (1975) runners-up (1973)

International matches 1975

March 12, Wembley: v England (a) lost 0-2
April 27, Sofia: v Bulgaria (a) drew 1-1 (EC) (*Ritschel pen.*)
May 18, Frankfurt: v Netherlands (h) drew 1-1 (*Wimmer*)
Sept. 3, Vienna: v Austria (a) won 2-0 (*Beer 2*)
Oct. 11, Dusseldorf: v Greece (h) drew 1-1 (EC) (*Heynckes*)
Nov. 19, Stuttgart: v Bulgaria (h) won 1-0 (EC) (*Heynckes*)
Dec. 21, Istanbul: v Turkey (a) won 5-0 (*Worm 2, Heynckes 2, Beer*)

League Championship wins (1903–76)

1FC Nuremberg 9; Schalke 7; Bayern Munich 5; Borussia Moenchengladbach 4; VfB Leipzig 3; SpV Früth 3; SV Hamburg 3; Borussia Dortmund 3; Viktoria Berlin 2; Hertha Berlin 2; Hanover 96 2; Dresden SC 2; VfB Stuttgart 2; 1FC Kaiserslautern 2; 1FC Cologne 2; Munich 1860 1; SV Werder Bremen 1; Union Berlin 1; FC Freibourg 1; Phoenix Karlsruhe 1; Karlsruher FV 1; Holstein Kiel 1; Fortuna Düsseldorf 1; Rapid Vienna 1; VfR Mannheim 1; Rot-Weiss Essen 1; Eintracht Frankfurt 1; Eintracht Brunswick 1.

Cup wins (1935–75)

Bayern Munich 5; 1FC Nuremberg 3; Dresden SC 2; Karlsruher SC 2; Munich 1860 2; Schalke 04 2; VfB Stuttgart 2; Borussia Moenchengladbach 2; Eintracht Frankfurt 2; Borussia Dortmund 1; IFC Cologne 1; First Vienna 1; SV Hamburg 1; VfB Leipzig 1; Offenbach Kickers 1; Rapid Vienna 1; Rot-Weiss Essen 1; Schweiss Essen 1; Werder Bremen 1.

776

	League Champions	Cup Winners
1948	1FC Nuremberg	No competition
1949	VfR Mannheim	No competition
1950	VfB Stuttgart	No competition
1951	1FC Kaiserslautern	No competition
1952	VfB Stuttgart	No competition
1953	1FC Kaiserslautern	Rot-Weiss Essen
1954	Hanover 96	VfB Stuttgart
1955	Rot-Weiss Essen	Karlsruhe SC
1956	Borussia Dortmund	Karlsruhe SC
1957	Borussia Dortmund	Bayern Munich
1958	Schalke 04	VfB Stuttgart
1959	Eintracht Frankfurt	Schweiss Essen
1960	SV Hamburg	Borussia Moenchengladbach
1961	1FC Nuremberg	Werder Bremen
1962	1FC Cologne	IFC Nuremberg
1963	Borussia Dortmund	SV Hamburg
1964	1FC Cologne	Munich 1860
1965	Werder Bremen	Borussia Dortmund
1966	Munich 1860	Bayern Munich
1967	Eintracht Brunswick	Bayern Munich
1968	1FC Nuremberg	IFC Cologne
1969	Bayern Munich	Bayern Munich
1970	Borussia Moenchengladbach	Offenbach Kickers
1971	Borussia Moenchengladbach	Bayern Munich
1972	Bayern Munich	Schalke 04
1973	Bayern Munich	Borussia Moenchengladbach
1974	Bayern Munich	Eintracht Frankfurt
1975	Borussia Moenchengladbach	Eintracht Frankfurt
1976	Borussia Moenchengladbach	

Final League Table 1975–76

	P	W	D	L	F	A	Pts.
Borussia Moenchengladbach	34	16	13	5	66	37	45
Hamburg	34	17	7	10	59	32	41
Bayern Munich	34	15	10	9	72	50	40
Cologne	34	14	11	9	62	45	39
Eintracht Brunswick	34	14	11	9	52	48	39
Schalke 04	34	13	11	10	76	55	37
Kaiserslautern	34	15	7	12	66	60	37
Rot-Weiss Essen	34	13	11	10	61	67	37
Eintracht Frankfurt	34	13	10	11	79	58	36
Duisburg	34	13	7	14	55	62	33
Hertha Berlin	34	11	10	13	59	61	32
Fortuna Dusseldorf	34	10	10	14	47	57	30
Werder Bremen	34	11	8	15	44	55	30
VfL Bochum	34	12	6	16	49	62	30
Karlsruhe	34	12	6	16	46	59	30
Hannover 96	34	9	9	16	48	60	27
Kickers Offenbach	34	9	9	16	40	72	27
Bayer Uerdingen	34	6	10	18	28	69	22

GREECE

President: Lucas Panourgias.
Secretary: Basile Andrianopoulos.
Address of Association: Federation Hellenique de Football Association, 93 Rue de L'Académie, Athénes.
Telephone: 622 202/203. *Cable:* Football Athenes. *Telex:* 5328. *Area:* 50,547 square miles. *Population:* 9,000,000. *Number of Clubs:* 1,758. *Teams:* 1,638. *Number of Players:* 87,050. *Year of Formation:* 1926.
National Colours: White shirts, blue shorts, white stockings.
Second Choice of Colours: Blue shirts, white shorts.
Name, Address and Capacity of National Stadium: Karaïskaki, Neon Faliron, 42,000.
Names, Addresses and Capacities of Other Principal Football Grounds: Kaftatzoglion, Salonique, 45,000; A.E.K., Athens, 35,000; Panathinaïkos, Athénes, 25,000; PAOK, Salonique, 35,000.

Principal Honours

European Champions Cup: runners-up Panathinaikos (1971)

International matches 1975

Feb. 23, Valetta: v Malta (a) lost 0-2 (EC).
April 1, Nicosia: v Cyprus (a) won 2-1.
June 4, Salonika: v Malta (h) won 4-0 (EC) (*Mavros, Antoniadis pen., Iosifides, Papaioannou*).
Sept. 24, Salonika : v Rumania (h) drew 1-1 (*Sarafis*).
Oct. 11, Dusseldorf: v West Germany (a) drew 1-1 (EC) (*Delikaris*).
Nov. 5, Limassol: (Amat.) v Cyprus (a) lost 0-1.
Dec. 30, Florence: v Italy (a) lost 2-3 (*Kritikopoulos, Sarafis*).

League Championship wins (1928-76)

Olympiakos 20; Panathinaikos 11; AEK Athens 5; Aris Salonika 3; PAOK Salonika 1.

Cup wins (1932-75)

Olympiakos 17; AEK Athens 7; Panathinaikos 5, PAOK Salonika 2; Aris Salonika 1; Ethnikos 1; Iraklis 1.

	League Champions	Cup Winners
1946	Aris Salonika	No competition
1947	Olympiakos	Olympiakos
1948	Olympiakos	Panathinaikos
1949	Panathinaikos	AEK Athens
1950	No competition	AEK Athens
1951	Olympiakos	Olympiakos
1952	No competition	Olympiakos
1953	Panathinaikos	Olympiakos
1954	Olympiakos	Olympiakos
1955	Olympiakos	Panathinaikos
1956	Olympiakos	AEK Athens
1957	Olympiakos	Olympiakos
1958	Olympiakos	Olympiakos
1959	Olympiakos	Olympiakos
1960	Panathinaikos	Olympiakos
1961	Panathinaikos	Olympiakos
1962	Panathinaikos	Olympiakos
1963	AEK Athens	Olympiakos
1964	Panathinaikos	AEK Athens
1965	Panathinaikos	Olympiakos
1966	Olympiakos	AEK Athens
1967	Olympiakos	Panathinaikos
1968	AEK Athens	Olympiakos
1969	Panathinaikos	Panathinaikos
1970	Panathinaikos	Aris Salonika
1971	AEK Athens	Olympiakos
1972	Panathinaikos	PAOK Salonika
1973	Olympiakos	Olympiakos
1974	Olympiakos	PAOK Salonika
1975	Olympiakos	Olympiakos
1976	PPAOK Salonika	Iraklis

Football League Table 1975-76

	P	W	D	L	F	A	Pts.
PAOK Salonika	30	21	7	2	60	17	49
AEK Athens	30	18	8	4	57	18	44
Olympiakos	30	16	9	5	48	28	41
Panathinaikos	30	14	10	6	47	28	38
Iannina	30	15	6	9	40	33	36
Aris Salonika	30	13	9	8	50	27	35
Ethnikos *	30	12	8	10	43	39	29
Iraklis	30	9	9	12	33	39	27
Atromitos *	30	9	11	10	27	33	26
Panachaiki	30	7	11	12	22	35	25
Pierikos	30	5	13	12	26	38	23
Panionios	30	5	12	13	15	36	22
Kastoria	30	4	14	12	21	45	22
Apollon	30	6	9	15	26	49	21
Panaitolikos	30	3	13	14	17	41	19
Panseraikos	30	5	7	18	21	47	17

*Three points deducted.

HUNGARY

President: Istvan Kutas.
Secretary: Jozsef Krizsan.
Address of Association: Fédération Hongroise de Football, Népköztársaság utja 47, Budapest VI.
Telephone: 225-817 421-316.
Cable: MLSZ-Budapest.
Area: 35,919 square miles.

Population: 10,000,000.
Year of Formation: 1901
Number of Clubs: 2,915. *Teams:* 5,087
Number of Players: 157,102.
National Colours: Red shirts, white shorts, green stockings.
Name, Address and Capacity of National Stadium: Népstadion Budapest XIV, István

Mezei ut 3/5, 80,000.

Names, Addresses and Capacities of Other Principal Football Grounds: Ferencvaros, Budapest IX Ullgi-ut, 30,000; BP. Vasas SC. Budapest XIII. Fay-u. 58, 30,000; Ujpesti Dozsa SE. Budapest IV. Mergyeri ut 13, 40,000; MTK-VM Budapest VIII. Hungaria krt. 6, 37,000; Csepel SE. Budapest XXI. Béke tér, 22,000; Györi Vasas ETO Györ, 20,000; Pécs MSC. Pécs, 25,000; Szegedi Egyetemi OL. Szeged, 25,000; Djösgyöri VTK Diösgyör, 25,000.

Season: August–June. Break between December–February.

Principal Honours

World Cup: runners-up 1938, 1954

Olympic Games: winners 1952, 1964, 1968; runners-up 1972

Cup-Winners' Cup: runners-up MTK Budapest (1964); Ferencvaros (1975)

Fairs Cup: winners Ferencvaros (1965); runners-up Ferencvaros (1968), Ujpest Dozsa (1969)

International matches 1975

March 26, Paris: v France (a) lost 0-2

April 2, Vienna: v Austria (a) drew 0-0 (EC)

April 16, Budapest: v Wales (h) lost 1-2 (EC) (*Branikovits*)

Aug. 10, Teheran: v Iran (a) won 2-1

Sept. 24, Budapest: v Austria (h) won 2-1 (EC) (*Nyilasi, Pusztai*)

Oct 8, Lodz: v Poland (a) lost 2-4 (*Nagy, Pusztai*)

Oct. 15, Prague: v Czechoslovakia (a) drew 1-1 (*Varadi*)

Oct. 19, Szombathely: v Luxembourg (h) won 8-1 (EC) (*Pinter, Nyilasi 5, Wollek, Varadi*)

League Championship wins (1901–76)

Ferencvaros (prev FTC.) 23; MTK-VM Budapest (prev. Hungaria, Bastay, & Vörös Lobogo) 18; Ujpest Dozsa 16; Vasas Budapest 5; Honved 5; Csepel 4; BTC 2; Nagyvarad 1; Vasas Györ 1.

Cup wins (1910–76)*

Ferencvaros (prev. FTC) 13; MTK-VM Budapest (prev. Hungaria, Bastya, & Vörös Lobogo) 9; Ujpest Dozsa 4; Vasas Györ 3; Vasas Budapest 1; Bocskai 1; Honved 1; III Ker 1; Kispesti AC 1; Soroksar 1; Szolnoki MAV 1.

*Cup not held regularly until 1964

League Champions	Cup Winners
1946 Ujpest Dozsa	No competition
1947 Ujpest Dozsa	No competition
1948 Vasas Csepel	No competition
1949 Ferencvaros	No competition
1950 Honved	No competition
1950*Honved	No competition
1951 Bastya	No competition
1952 Honved	Bastya
1953 Vörös Lobogo	No competition
1954 Honved	No competition
1955 Honved	Vasas Budapest
1956 Champ. abandoned	No competition
1957 Vasas Budapest	No competition
1958 MTK Budapest	Ferencvaros
1959 Vasas Csepel	No competition
1960 Ujpest Dozsa	No competition
1961 Vasas Budapest	No competition
1962 Vasas Budapest	No competition
1963 Ferencvaros	No competition
1963*Vasas Györ	
1964 Ferencvaros	Honved
1965 Vasas Budapest	Vasas Györ
1966 Vasas Budapest	Vasas Györ
1967 Ferencvaros	Vasas Györ
1968 Ferencvaros	MTK Budapest
1969 Ujpest Dozsa	Ujpest Dozsa
1970 Ujpest Dozsa	Ujpest Dozsa
1971 Ujpest Dozsa	Ujpest Dozsa
1972 Ujpest Dozsa	Ferencvaros
1973 Ujpest Dozsa	Vasas Budapest
1974 Ujpest Dozsa	Ferencvaros
1975 Ujpest Dozsa	Ujpest Dozsa
1976 Ferencvaros	Ferencvaros

*(short season)

League Table 1975-76
(up to and including June, 13, 1976)

	P	W	D	L	F	A	Pts.
Ferencvaros	29	19	6	4	62	37	44
Videoton	29	17	8	4	57	24	42
Ujpest Dozsa	29	17	6	6	74	47	40
Honved	29	14	8	7	47	31	36
Vasas Budapest	29	15	4	10	64	39	34
MTK/VM	29	13	3	13	49	36	29
Haladas	29	11	7	11	36	40	29
Zalaegerszeg	29	9	9	11	46	46	27
Salgotarjan	29	7	12	10	37	45	26
Tatabanya	29	10	6	13	40	50	26
Raba ETO Gyor	29	7	11	11	36	44	25
Diosgyor	29	6	12	11	25	42	24
Csepel	29	7	9	13	33	47	23
Kaposvar	29	5	12	12	36	52	22
Bekescsaba	29	7	8	14	23	44	22
Szeged	29	5	5	19	25	66	15

ICELAND

President: Ellert B. Schram.
Secretary: Bjarni Felixson.
Address of Association: Football Association of Iceland, P.O. Box 1011, Reykjavik.
Telephone: 8–4444. *Cable:* KSI Reykjavik.
Area: 39,768 square miles.
Population: 300,000. *Number of Clubs:* 65.

Teams: 396. *Number of Players:* 11,456
Year of Formation: 1929.
National Colours: Red shirts, white shorts and blue stockings. *Second Choice of Colours:* A variation of the above colours.
Name, Address and Capacity of National Stadium: Laugardalsvöllur, Reykjavik, 15,000.

*Names and Addresses of Other Principal
Football Grounds:* Melavöllur, Reykjavik.
Ibrottavöllurinn, Akureyri. Ibróttavöllurinn,
Akranesi. Ibrottavollurinn, Keflavik 10,000.
Season: April–September.

International matches 1975

May 25, Reykjavik: v France (h) drew 0-0
(EC)
June 5, Reykjavik: v East Germany (h) won
2-1 (EC) (*Edvaldsson, Sigurvinsson*)
Sept. 3, Nantes: v France (a) lost 0-3 (EC)
Sept. 6, Liege: v Belgium (a) lost 0-1 (EC)

League Championship wins (1912–75)

KR 20; Fram 15; Valur 14; IA Akranes 9;
IBK Keflavik 3; Vikingur 2; IBV Vestmann 1

Cup wins (1960–75)

KR 7; IBV Vestmann 2; Fram 2; Valur 2;
IBA Akureyri 1; Vikingur; IBK Keflavik 1.

League Champions	Cup Winners
1946 Fram	
1947 Fram	
1948 KR	
1949 KR	
1950 KR	
1951 IA Akranes	
1952 KR	
1953 IA Akranes	
1954 IA Akranes	
1955 KR	
1956 Valur	
1957 IA Akranes	
1958 IA Akranes	
1959 KR	
1960 IA Akranes	KR
1961 KR	KR
1962 Fram	KR
1963 KR	KR
1964 IBK Keflavik	KR
1965 KR	Valur
1966 Valur	KR
1967 Valur	KR
1968 KR	IBV Vestmann
1969 IBK Keflavik	IBV Akureyri
1970 IA Akranes	Fram
1971 IBV Vestmann	Vikingur
1972 Fram	IBV Vestmann
1973 IBK Keflavik	Fram
1974 IA Akranes	Valur
1975 IA Akranes	IBK Keflavik

Final League Table 1975

	P	W	D	L	F	A	Pts.
IA Akranes	14	8	3	3	28	13	19
IA Fram	14	8	1	5	19	17	17
Valur	14	7	2	5	20	16	16
Vikingur	14	6	3	5	17	10	15
IB Keflavik	14	4	5	5	13	12	13
Hafnarfjordur	14	4	5	5	9	20	13
KR Reykjavik	14	3	4	7	11	16	10
IB Vestmannaeyjar	14	2	5	7	13	21	9

REPUBLIC OF IRELAND

President: C. H. Walsh.
Secretary: P. J. O'Driscoll P.C.
Address of Association: The Football
Association of Ireland, 80 Merrion Square,
Dublin 2
Telephone: 6 68 64
Cable: Soccer Dublin
Population: 2,855,500
Year of formation: 1921
Number of Clubs: 2,716. *Teams:* 3,180.
Number of Players: 50,328.
National colours: Green and white
Second Choice of Colours: White
*Name, Address and Capacity of National
Stadium:* Dalymount Park, Dublin, 50,000
*Names, Addresses and Capacities of Other
Principal Football Grounds:* Glenmalure
Park, Milltown, Dublin, 25,000; Flower
Lodge, Cork, 25,000; Lourde Stadium,
Drogheda, 25,000; Tolka Park, Dublin,
20,000; Oriel Park, Dundalk, 15,000;
Richmond Park, Dublin, 10,000; Markeis
Field, Limerick, 10,000; Kilcohan Park,
Waterford, 15,000.

International matches 1976

May 11, Dublin: v Switzerland (h) won 2-1
(EC) (*Martin, Treacy*)
May 18, Kiev: v USSR (a) lost 1-2 (EC)
(*Hand*)
May 21, Berne: v Switzerland (a) lost 0-1
(EC)
Oct. 29, Dublin: v Turkey (h) won 4-0 (EC)
(*Givens 4*)

League Championship wins (1922-76)

Shamrock Rovers 10; Shelbourne 7; Waterford
6; Bohemians 6; Cork United 5; Drumcondra
5; Dundalk 4; St. Patrick's Athletic 3; St.
James's Gate 2; Cork Athletic 2; Dolphin 1;
Sligo Rovers 1; Limerick 1; Cork Hibernians 1; Cork Celtic 1.

Cup wins (1922-76)

Shamrock Rovers 20; Drumcondra 5;
Dundalk 4; Bohemians 4; Shelbourne 3;
Cork Athletic 2; Cork United 2; St. James's
Gate 2; St. Patrick's Athletic 2; Cork
Hibernians 2; Alton United 1; Athlone
Town 1; Cork 1; Fordsons 1; Limerick 1;
Transport 1; Waterford 1; Finn Harps 1;
Home Farm 1.

League Champions	Cup Winners
1946 Cork United	Drumcondra
1947 Shelbourne	Cork United
1948 Drumcondra	Shamrock Rovers
1948 Drumcondra	Shamrock Rovers
1949 Drumcondra	Dundalk
1950 Cork Athletic	Transport
1951 Cork Athletic	Cork Athletic
1952 St. Patrick's Ath.	Dundalk
1953 Shelbourne	Cork Athletic
1954 Shamrock Rovers	Drumcondra
1955 St. Patrick's Ath.	Shamrock Rovers
1956 St. Patrick's Ath.	Shamrock Rovers
1957 Shamrock Rovers	Drumcondra
1958 Drumcondra	Dundalk
1959 Shamrock Rovers	St. Patrick's Ath.
1960 Limerick	Shelbourne
1961 Drumcondra	St. Patrick's Ath.
1962 Shelbourne	Shamrock Rovers
1963 Dundalk	Shelbourne
1964 Shamrock Rovers	Shamrock Rovers
1965 Drumcondra	Shamrock Rovers
1966 Waterford	Shamrock Rovers
1967 Dundalk	Shamrock Rovers
1968 Waterford	Shamrock Rovers
1969 Waterford	Shamrock Rovers
1970 Waterford	Bohemians
1971 Cork Hibernians	Limerick
1972 Waterford	Cork Hibernians
1973 Waterford	Cork Hibernians
1974 Cork Celtic	Finn Harps
1975 Bohemians	Home Farm
1976 Dundalk	Bohemians

Final League Table 1975-76

	P	W	D	L	F	A	Pts.
Dundalk	26	15	10	1	54	26	40
Finn Harps	26	15	6	5	57	35	36
Waterford	26	13	8	5	54	37	34
Bohemians	26	10	12	4	44	25	32
Cork Hibs	26	11	9	6	37	24	31
Drogheda United	26	11	6	9	42	45	28
Athlone Town	26	12	4	10	40	49	28
Cork Celtic	26	11	5	10	41	34	27
Shelbourne	26	7	7	12	42	44	21
Sligo Rovers	26	6	8	12	32	49	20
St. Patrick's Ath.	26	7	5	14	31	53	19
Home Farm	26	4	9	13	35	54	17
Limerick	26	6	4	16	37	49	16
Shamrock Rovers	26	4	7	15	27	49	15

ITALY

President: Dr. Artemio Franchi.
Secretary: Dr. Dario Borgogno.
Address of Association: Federazione Italiana Giuoco Calcio, via Gregorio Allegri, 14, Rome.
Telephone: 8449841, 853541.
Cable: Federcalcio Roma
Area: 97,068 square miles.
Population: 50,000,000.
Number of Clubs: 16,307. *Teams:* 17,210.
Number of Players: 710,040.
Year of Formation: 1905.
National Colours: Blue shirts, white shorts, blue stockings with white tops.
Second Choice of Colours: White with light blue stripe.
Name, Address and Capacity of National Stadium: Stadio Olimpico, Roma, 90,000.
Names, Addresses and Capacities of Other Principal Football Grounds: Bologna, Stadio Comunale, Via A. Costa 176, 50,000; Firenze, Stadio Comunale, Viale M. Fanti 4/6, 52,000; Milano, Stadio Comunale San Siro, Via Fetonte, 79,000; Torino, Stadio Comunale, Corso Sebatopoli 123, 71,000; Napoli, Stadio S. Paolo, Fuorigrotta, 82,000; Genova, Stadio Luigi, Ferraris, Via del Piano, 64,000.

Principal Honours

World Cup: winners 1934, 1938; runners-up 1970
European Championship: winners 1968
Olympic Games: winners 1936
World club champions: Inter-Milan (1964, 1965), AC Milan (1969)

European Champions Cup: winners AC Milan (1963, 1969), Inter-Milan (1964, 1965); runners-up Fiorentina (1957), AC Milan (1958), Inter-Milan (1967, 1972), Juventus (1973)
Cup-Winners' Cup: winners Fiorentina (1961), AC Milan (1968, 1973); runners-up Fiorentina (1962), A. C. Milan (1974)
Fairs Cup: winners AS Roma (1961); runners-up Juventus (1965, 1971)

International matches 1975

Feb. 19, Florence: v Norway (h) won 4-1 (*Graziani, Chinaglia, Savoldi, Cordova*)
April 2, Rome: v USA (h) won 10-0 (*Graziani 3, Rocca 2, Cordova, Chinaglia 2, Savoldi 2*)
April 19, Rome: v Poland (h) drew 0-0 (EC)
June 5, Helsinki: v Finland (a) won 1-0 (EC) (*Chinaglia pen.*)
June 8, Moscow: v USSR (a) lost 0-1
Sept. 27, Rome: v Finland (h) drew 0-0 (EC)
Oct. 26, Warsaw: v Poland (a) drew 0-0 (EC)
Nov. 22, Rome: v Netherlands (h) won 1-0 (EC) (*Capello*)
Dec. 30, Florence: v Greece (h) won 3-2 (*Pulici 2, Savoldi pen.*)

League Championship wins (1898-1976)

Juventus 16; Inter-Milan 11; Genoa 9; AC Milan 9; Torino 8; Pro Vercelli 7; Bologna 7; Fiorentina 2; Casale 1; Novese 1; AS Roma 1; Cagliari 1; Lazio 1.

Cup wins (1922–75)

Juventus 5; Torino 4; Fiorentina 4; AC Milan 3; AS Roma 2; Bologna 2; Atalanta 1; Genoa 1; Inter-Milan 1; Lazio 1; Napoli 1; Vado 1; Venezia 1.

League Champions	Cup Winners
1946 Torino	No competition
1947 Torino	No competition
1948 Torino	No competition
1949 Torino	No competition
1950 Juventus	No competition
1951 AC Milan	No competition
1952 Juventus	No competition
1953 Inter-Milan	No competition
1954 Inter-Milan	No competition
1955 AC Milan	No competition
1956 Fiorentina	No competition
1957 AC Milan	No competition
1958 Juventus	Lazio
1959 AC Milan	Juventus
1960 Juventus	Juventus
1961 Juventus	Fiorentina
1962 AC Milan	Napoli
1963 Inter-Milan	Atalanta
1964 Bologna	AS Roma
1965 Inter-Milan	Juventus
1966 Inter-Milan	Fiorentina
1967 Juventus	AC Milan
1968 AC Milan	Torino
1969 Fiorentina	AS Roma
1970 Cagliari	Bologna
1971 Inter-Milan	Torino
1972 Juventus	AC Milan
1973 Juventus	AC Milan
1974 Lazio	Bologna
1975 Juventus	Fiorentina
1976 Torino	

Final League Table 1975-76

	P	W	D	L	F	A	Pts.
Torino	30	18	9	3	49	22	45
Juventus	30	18	7	5	46	26	43
AC Milan	30	15	8	7	42	28	38
Inter-Milan	30	14	9	7	36	28	37
Napoli	30	13	10	7	40	27	36
Cesna	30	9	14	7	39	35	32
Bologna	30	9	14	7	32	32	32
Perugia	30	10	11	9	31	34	31
Fiorentina	30	9	9	12	39	39	27
Roma	30	6	13	11	25	31	25
Verona	30	8	8	14	35	46	24
Sampdoria	30	8	8	14	21	32	24
Lazio	30	6	11	13	35	40	23
Ascoli	30	4	15	11	19	34	23
Como	30	5	11	14	28	36	21
Cagliari	30	5	9	16	25	52	19

LIECHTENSTEIN

President: Herbert Moser.
Secretary: Werner Ospelt.
Address of Association: Liechtensteiner, Fussball-Verband, 9490 Vaduz.

Number of Clubs: 7. *Teams:* 59.
Number of Players: 1,103.

LUXEMBOURG

President: M. Rene van den Bulcke.
Secretary: Mlle Eliane Cremona.
Address of Association: Fédération Luxembourgeoise de Football, 50 Rue de Strasbourg, Luxembourg.
Telephone: 48–86–61.
Area: 999 square miles.
Population: 330,000.
Number of Clubs: 203. *Teams:* 484.
Number of Players: 12,047.
Year of Formation: 1908.
National Colours: Red shirts, white shorts, blue stockings.
Second Choice of Colours: White shirts, white shorts, blue stockings.
Name, Address and Capacity of National Stadium: City Stadium Luxembourg, 18,000.
Names, Addresses and Capacities of Other Principal Football Grounds: Stade E. Mayrisch, Esch-sur-Alzette, 11,000; Stade Municipal, Differdange, 10,000.
Season: August – June.

International matches 1975
March 16, Luxembourg: v Austria (h) lost 1-2 (EC) (*Braun*)
May 1, Luxembourg: v Wales (h) lost 1-3 (EC) (*Philipp pen.*)
Oct. 15, Vienna: v Austria (a) lost 2-6 (EC) (*Braun, Philipp*)
Oct. 19, Szombathely: v Hungary (a) lost 1-8 (EC) (*Dussier*)

League Championship wins (1910–76)
Jeunesse Esch 15; Spora Luxembourg 10; Stade Dudelange 10; US Hollerich-Bonnevoie 5; Fola Esch 5; Red Boys Differdange 5; US Luxembourg 3; Sporting Luxembourg 2; Aris Bonnevoie 3; Racing Luxembourg 1; National Schifflge 1; Progres Niedercorn 1; Avenir Beggen 1.

Cup wins (1922–76)
Red Boys Differdange 13; Spora Luxembourg 7; Jeunesse Esch 7; US Luxembourg 6; Stade Dudelange 4; Fola Esch 3; Alliance Dudelange 2; Progres Niedercorn 2; US Rumelange 2; Aris Bonnevoie 1; US Dudelange 1; Jeunesse Hautcharage 1; National Schifflge 1; Racing Luxembourg 1; SC Tetange 1.

League Champions	Cup Winners
1946 Stade Dudelange	Jeunesse Esch
1947 Stade Dudelange	US Luxembourg
1948 Stade Dudelange	Stade Dudelange
1949 Spora Luxembourg	Stade Dudelange
1950 Stade Dudelange	Spora Luxembourg
1951 Jeunesse Esch	SC Tetange
1952 National Schifflge	Red Boys Differdange
1953 Progres Niedercorn	Red Boys Differdange
1954 Jeunesse Esch	Jeunesse Esch
1955 Stade Dudelange	Fola Esch
1956 Spora Luxembourg	Stade Dudelange
1957 Stade Dudelange	Spora Luxembourg
1958 Jeunesse Esch	Red Boys Differdange
1959 Jeunesse Esch	US Luxembourg
1960 Jeunesse Esch	National Schifflge
1961 Spora Luxembourg	Alliance Dudelange
1962 US Luxembourg	Alliance Dudelange
1963 Jeunesse Esch	US Luxembourg
1964 Aris Bonnevoie	US Luxembourg
1965 Stade Dudelange	Spora Luxembourg
1966 Aris Bonnevoie	Spora Luxembourg
1967 Jeunesse Esch	Aris Bonnevoie
1968 Jeunesse Esch	US Rumelange
1969 Avenir Beggen	US Luxembourg
1970 Jeunesse Esch	US Luxembourg
1971 US Luxembourg	Jeunesse Hautcharage
1972 Aris Bonnevoie	Red Boys Differdange
1973 Jeunesse Esch	Jeunesse Esch
1974 Jeunesse Esch	Jeunesse Esch
1975 Jeunesse Esch	US Rumelange
1976 Jeunesse Esch	Jeunesse Esch

Final League Table 1975-76

	P	W	D	L	F	A	Pts.
Jeunesse Esch	22	14	6	2	50	24	34
Differdingen	22	12	6	4	46	24	30
Rumelingen	22	9	7	6	32	21	25
Etzella Ettelbruck	22	10	5	7	39	29	25
Aris Bonneweg	22	10	4	8	31	23	24
Progres Niedercorn	22	9	4	9	30	37	22
Chiers Rodange	22	9	3	10	36	39	21
Avenir Beggen	22	6	8	8	28	29	20
Alliance Dudelingen	22	7	6	9	36	39	20
Stade Dudelingen	22	5	8	9	27	31	18
Union Luxembourg	22	5	7	10	20	35	17
Fola Esch	22	2	4	16	14	58	8

MALTA

President: Dr. Gius Mifsud Bonnici H.D.
Secretary: Frank Attard.
Address of Association: Malta Football Association, 84 Old Mint Street, Valetta, Malta.
Telephone: 22697, 74372.
Cable: Football Malta 1960.
Area: 122 square miles.
Population: 335,000.
Number of Clubs: 238.
Number of Players: 8,164.   *Teams:* 362.
Year of Formation: 1900.
National Colours: Red.
Second Choice of Colours: White.
Name, Address and Capacity of National Stadium: Malta F.A. Ground, Gzira, 15,000.
Name, Address and Capacity of Other Principal Football Ground: Schreiber Sports Ground, Paola, 8,000.

International matches 1975
Feb. 23, Valetta: v Greece (h) won 2-0 (EC)
   (*Aquilina, R., Magro*)
June 4, Salonika: v Greece (a) lost 0-4 (EC)
Aug. 11, Sofia: v Bulgaria (a) (EC) lost 0-5
Dec. 21, Valetta: v Bulgaria (h) lost 0-2 (EC)

League Championship wins
Floriana 23; Sliema Wanderers 21; Valletta 9; Hamrun Spartans 3; Hibernians 3; St. George's 1; K.O.M.R. 1.

Cup wins
Sliema Wanderers 15; Floriana 14; Hibernians 3; Valletta 3; Gzira United 1; Melita 1.

League Champions	Cup Winners
1946 Valletta	Sliema Wanderers
1947 Hamrun Spart.	Floriana
1948 Valletta	Sliema Wanderers
1949 Sliema Wand.	Floriana
1950 Floriana	Floriana
1951 Floriana	Sliema Wanderers
1952 Floriana	Sliema Wanderers
1953 Floriana	Floriana
1954 Sliema Wand.	Floriana
1955 Floriana	Floriana
1956 Slieme Wand.	Sliema Wanderers
1957 Sliema Wand.	Floriana
1958 Floriana	Floriana
1959 Valletta	Sliema Wanderers
1960 Valletta	Valletta
1961 Hibernians	Floriana
1962 Floriana	Hibernians
1963 Valletta	Sliema Wanderers
1964 Sliema Wand.	Valletta
1965 Sliema Wand.	Sliema Wanderers
1966 Sliema Wand.	Floriana
1967 Hibernians	Floriana
1968 Floriana	Sliema Wanderers
1969 Hibernians	Sliema Wanderers
1970 Floriana	Hibernians
1971 Sliema Wand.	Hibernians
1972 Sliema Wand.	Floriana
1973 Floriana	Gzira
1974 Valletta	Sliema Wanderers
1975 Floriana	Valletta
1976 Sliema Wand.	

NETHERLANDS

President: W. A. G. M. Menleman.
Secretary: H. A. Brugwal.
Address of Association: Koninklijke Nederlandsche Voetbalbond, (KNVB) Woudenbergseweg 56-58, Zeist Netherlands.
Telephone: 03439 922
Area: 12,616 square miles.
Population: 12,000,000.
Number of Clubs: 6,665. *Teams:* 38,843.
Number of Players: 882,835.
Year of Formation: 1904.
National Colours: Orange shirts, white shorts, blue stockings.
Name, Address and Capacity of National Stadium: "Olympisch Stadion", Stadionplein, 20, Amsterdam, 67,000
Names, Addresses and Capacities of Other Principal Football Grounds: Stadion Feijenoord, Olympiaweg 50, Rotterdam, 63,923; Stadion De Vliert (F.C. Den Bosch) Graafseweg, 's-Hertogenbosch, 35,000; Ground of F.C. Tubantia, Krabbenbosweg 227, Hengelo, 34,750; Ground of Sparta, Spartastraat 5, Rotterdam, 30,000; Stadium De Goffert, Nijmegen, 30,000; Sportpark Diekman, J. J. van Deinselaan 30, Enschede, 27,564.
Season: August–June.

Principal Honours

World Cup: Runners-up 1974.
World club champions: Feyenoord (1970), Ajax Amsterdam (1972).
European Champions Cup: winners Feyenoord (1970), Ajax Amsterdam (1971, 1972, 1973); runners-up Ajax (1969).
UEFA-Cup winners Feyenoord (1974). runners-up Twente Enschede (1975).

International matches 1975

April 30, Antwerp: v Belgium (a) lost 0-1
May 18, Frankfurt: v West Germany (a) drew 1-1 *(Van Hanegem)*
May 31, Belgrade: v Yugoslavia (a) lost 0-3
Sept. 3, Nijmegen: v Finland (h) won 4-1 (EC) *(Van der Kuylen 3, Lubse)*
Sept. 10, Chorzow: v Poland (a) lost 1-4 (EC) *(Rene Van der Kerkhof)*
Oct. 15, Amsterdam: v Poland (h) won 3-0 (EC) *(Neeskens, Geels, Thijssen)*
Nov. 22, Rome: v Italy (a) lost 0-1 (EC)

League Championship wins (1898-1976)

Ajax Amsterdam 16; Feyenoord 12; HVV The Hague 8; Sparta Rotterdam 6; PSV Eindhoven 6; Go Ahead Deventer 4; HBS The Hague 3; Willem II Tilburg 3; RCH Haarlem 2; RAP 2; Heracles 2; ADO The Hague 2; Quick The Hague 1; BVV Scheidam 1; NAC Breda 1; Eindhoven 1; Enschede 1; Volewijckers Amsterdam 1; Limburgia 1; Rapid JC Haarlem 1; DOS Utrecht 1; DWS Amsterdam 1; Haarlem 1; Be Quick Groningen 1; SVV Scheidam 1.

Cup wins (1899-1976)

Ajax Amsterdam 7; Feyenoord 4; Quick The Hague 4; PSV Eindhoven 4; HEC 3; Sparta Rotterdam 3; DFC 2; Fortuna Geleen 2; Haarlem 2; HBS The Hague 2; RCH 2; VOC 2; Wageningen 2; Willem II Tilburg 2; F.C. Den Haag 2; Concordia Rotterdam 1; CVV 1; Eindhoven 1; HVV The Hague 1; Longa 1; Quick Njimegen 1; RAP 1; Roermond 1; Schoten 1; Velocitas Breda 1; Velocitas Groningen 1; VSV 1; VUC 1; VVV 1; ZFC 1; N.A.C. Breda 1.

	League Champions	Cup Winners
1946	Haarlem	No competition
1947	Ajax Amsterdam	No competition
1948	BVV Scheidam	Wageningen
1949	SVV Scheidam	Quick Njimegen
1950	Limburgia	PSV Eindhoven
1951	PSV Eindhoven	No competition
1952	Willem II Tilburg	No competition
1953	RCH Haarlem	No competition
1954	Eindhoven	No competition
1955	Willem II Tilburg	No competition
1956	Rapid JC Haarlem	No competition
1957	Ajax Amsterdam	Fortuna Geleen
1958	DOS Utrecht	Sparta Rotterdam
1959	Sparta Rotterdam	VVV Groningen
1960	Ajax Amsterdam	No competition
1961	Feyenoord	Ajax Amsterdam
1962	Feyenoord	Sparta Rotterdam
1963	PSV Eindhoven	Willem II Tilburg
1964	DWS Amsterdam	Fortuna Geleen
1965	Feyenoord	Feyenoord
1966	Ajax Amsterdam	Sparta Rotterdam
1967	Ajax Amsterdam	Ajax Amsterdam
1968	Ajax Amsterdam	ADO The Hague
1969	Feyenoord	Feyenoord
1970	Ajax Amsterdam	Ajax Amsterdam
1971	Feyenoord	Ajax Amsterdam
1972	Ajax Amsterdam	Ajax Amsterdam
1973	Ajax Amsterdam	N.A.C. Breda
1974	Feyenoord	P.S.V. Eindhoven
1975	P.S.V. Eindhoven	F.C. Den Haag.
1976	P.S.V. Eindhoven	P.S.V. Eindhoven

	P	W	D	L	F	A	Pts.
PSV Eindhoven	34	24	5	5	89	27	53
Feyenoord	34	23	6	5	88	40	52
Ajax Amsterdam	34	21	8	5	74	38	50
Twente Enschede	34	19	8	7	64	32	46
AZ 67 Alkmaar	34	15	9	10	46	39	39
Den Haag	34	15	7	12	65	51	37
NEC Nijmegen	34	11	15	8	43	38	37
Roda JC Kerkrade	34	13	11	10	40	36	37
Telstar Velsen	34	7	15	12	42	48	29
Sparta Rotterdam	34	7	15	12	32	42	29
NAC Breda	34	9	10	15	26	53	28
DE Graafschap	34	7	14	13	41	69	28
Go Ahead Deventer	34	6	15	13	43	58	27
Utrecht	34	9	9	16	36	57	27
EEV Eindhoven	34	9	9	16	40	63	27
Amsterdam	34	7	10	17	39	52	24
MVV Maastricht	34	8	7	19	34	64	23
Excelsior Rotterdam	34	7	5	22	24	59	19

NORWAY

President: Einar Jorum.
Secretary: Nicolaij Johansen.
Address of Association: Norges Fotball-forbund, Ulleval Stadion, Sognsun 75, Post Boks 603, Tasen, Oslo 8.
Telephone: 46.98.30.
Cable: Fotballforbund Oslo.
Area: 125,064 square miles.
Population: 3,700,000.
Number of Clubs: 2,850. *Teams:* 5,100.
Number of Players: 84,000.
Year of Formation: 1908.
National Colours: Red shirts, white shorts, blue and white stockings.
Second Choice of Colours: Blue shirts, white shorts.
Name, Address and Capacity of National Stadium: Ulleval Stadium, Sognsveien 75, Oslo, 24,500
Names, Addresses and Capacities of Other Principal Football Grounds: Bislett Stadium, Oslo, 24,000; Brann Stadium, Bergen, 26,000; Lerkendal Stadium, Trondheim, 30,000; Stavanger Stadium, Stavanger, 19,800
Season: April-October.

International matches 1975

Feb. 19, Florence: v Italy (a) lost 1-4 (*Fuglset pen.*)
June 9, Oslo: v Yugoslavia (h) lost 1-3 (EC) (*Thunberg*)
June 30, Solna: v Sweden (a) lost 1-3 (EC) (*Erik Just Olsen*)
Aug. 13, Oslo: v Sweden (h) lost 0-2 (EC)
Oct. 29, Belfast: v Northern Ireland (a) lost 0-3 (EC)

League Championship wins (1938-75)

Fredrikstad 9; Viking Stavanger 5; Rosenborg Trondheim 3; Larvik Turn 3; Brann Bergen 2; Lyn Oslo 2; Valerengen 1; Friedig 1; Fram 1; Lillestroem 1; Skeid Oslo 1; Stromgodset Drammen 1.

Cup wins (1902-75)

Odds Bk, Skien 11; Fredrikstads Fk 9; Lyn Oslo 8; Skeid Oslo 8; Sarpsborgs Fk 6; Ørn Fk Horten 4; Brann Bergen 3; Mion-dalens IF 3; Rosenborgs BK Trondheim 3; Strömgodset IF Drammen 3; Mercantile 2; Viking Stavanger 2; Grane Nordstrand 1; Kvik Halden 1; Sparta 1; Gjovik 1; Bodo-Glimt 1. (*Until* 1937 *the cup-winners were regarded as champions.*)

	League Champions	Cup Winners
1946	No competition	Lyn Oslo
1947	No competition	Skeid Oslo
1948	Freidig	Sarpsborg FK
1949	Fredrikstad	Sarpsborg FK
1950	Fram	Fredrikstad
1951	Fredrikstad	Sarpsborg FK
1952	Fredrikstad	Sparta Sarpsborg
1953	Larvik Turn	Viking Stavanger
1954	Fredrikstad	Skeid Oslo
1955	Larvik Turn	Skeid Oslo
1956	Larvik Turn	Skeid Oslo
1957	Fredrikstad	Fredrikstad
1958	Viking Stav.	Skeid Oslo
1959	Lillestroem	Viking Stav.
1960	Fredrikstad	Rosenborg Tr.
1961	Fredrikstad	Fredrikstad
1962	Brann Bergen	Gjovik Lyn
1963	Brann Bergen	Skeid Oslo
1964	Lyn Oslo	Rosenborg Tr.
1965	Valerengen	Skeid Oslo
1966	Skeid Oslo	Fredrikstad
1967	Rosenborg Tr.	Lyn Oslo
1968	Lyn Oslo	Lyn Oslo
1969	Rosenborg Tr.	Strömgodset Dr.
1970	Strömgodset Dr.	Strömgodset Dr.
1971	Rosenborg Tr.	Rosenborg Tr.
1972	Viking Stav.	Brann Bergen
1973	Viking Stav.	Strömgodset Dr.
1974	Viking Stav.	Skeid Oslo
1975	Viking Stav.	Bodo-Glimt

Final League Table 1975

	P	W	D	L	F	A	Pts.
Viking Stavangar	22	12	6	4	38	20	30
SK Brann	22	10	7	5	36	27	27
IK Start	22	11	5	6	29	20	27
Rosenborg	22	11	5	6	36	28	27
Stromgodset	22	10	4	8	39	27	24
Mjondalen	22	9	6	7	21	21	24
Lillestrom	22	10	3	9	27	20	23
Molde	22	7	8	7	27	29	22
Fredrikstadt	22	8	6	8	21	25	22
Skeid	22	5	7	10	18	23	17
Valerengens	22	3	10	9	19	36	16
Os	22	0	5	17	15	50	5

POLAND

President: Jan Maj.
Secretary: Piotr Sniadowski.
Address of Association: Polish Football Association, Al. Ujazdowskie 22, Warszawa.
Telephone: 28–93–44: 28–58–21: 29–24–89.
Area: 120,359 square miles.
Population: 31,500,000.
Number of Clubs: 4,702. *Teams:* 11,223.
Number of Players: 188,585.
Year of Formation: 1923.
National Colours: White shirts, red shorts, white and red stockings.
Second Choice of Colours: Red shirts, white shorts, red stockings.
Name, Address and Capacity of National Stadium: Stadium of the "X Anniversary" Warszawa, 100,000.
Names, Addresses and Capacities of Other Principal Football Grounds: Stadium Slaski, Chorzów, 100,000; Stadium "Warta", Poznan, 45,000; Stadium "Olimpijski", Wroclaw, 72,000; Stadium "Wisla" Kraków 40,000; Stadium "Ruch", Chorzów, 40,000; Stadium "Legia", Warszawa, 35,000; Stadium "Piast", Gliwice, 55,000; Stadium "Pogon", Szczecin, 36,000; Stadium "Polonia", Bytom, 35,000.
Season: March–November.

Principal Honours
Olympic Games: winners 1972
Cup-Winners' Cup: runners-up Gornik Zabrze (1970)

International matches 1975
March 26, Posnen: v USA (h) won 7-0 (*Deyna 3, Szarmach 2, Lato 2*)
April 19, Rome: v Italy (a) drew 0-0 (EC)
May 28, Halle: v East Germany (a) won 2-1 (*Lato, Marx*)
June 24, Seattle: v USA (a) won 4-0 (*Bula, Lato, Szarmach, Wyrobek*)
July 6, Montreal: v Canada (a) won 8-1 (*Marx, Lato 3, Deyna 2, Bula, Szarmach*)
July 9, Toronto: v Canada (a) won 4-1 (*Kwiatkowski, Szarmach 2, Deyna*)
Sept. 10, Chorzow: v Netherlands (h) won 4-1 (EC) (*Szarmach 2, Lato, Gadocha*)
Oct. 8, Lodz: v Hungary (h) won 4-2 (*Kasperczak, Kmiecik, Marx 2*)
Oct. 15, Amsterdam: v Netherlands (a) lost 0-3 (EC)
Oct. 26, Warsaw: v Italy (h) drew 0-0 (EC)

League Championship wins (1921–76)
Ruch Chorzow 11; Gornik Zabrze 10; Cracovia 5; Pogon Lwow 4; Wisla Krakow 5; Legia Warsaw 4; Warta Poznan 2; Polonia Bytom 2; Stal Mielec 2; Garbarnia Krakow 1; Polonia Warsaw 1; LKS Lodz 1.

Cup wins (1951–75)
Gornik Zabrze 6; Legia Warsaw 4; Zaglebie Sosnowiec 2; Ruch Chorzow 2; Gwardia Warsaw 1; LKS Lodz 1; Polonia Warsaw 1; Wisla Krakow 1; Stal Rzeszow 1.

	League Champions	Cup Winners
1946	Polonia Warsaw	
1947	Warta Poznan	
1948	Cracovia	
1949	Wisla Krakow	
1950	Wisla Krakow	
1951	Wisla Krakow	Ruch Chorzow
1952	Ruch Chorzow	Polonia Warsaw
1953	Ruch Chorzow	No competition
1954	Polonia Bytom	Gwardia Warsaw
1955	Legia Warsaw	Legia Warsaw
1956	Legia Warsaw	Legia Warsaw
1957	Gornik Zabrze	LKS Lodz
1958	LKS Lodz	No competition
1959	Gornik Zabrze	No competition
1960	Ruch Chorzow	No competition
1961	Gornik Zabrze	No competition
1962	Polonia Bytom	Zaglebie Sosnowiec
1963	Gornik Zabrze	Zaglebie Sosnowiec
1964	Gornik Zabrze	Legia Warsaw
1965	Gornik Zabrze	Gornik Zabrze
1966	Gornik Zabrze	Legia Warsaw
1967	Gornik Zabrze	Wisla Krakow
1968	Ruch Chorzow	Gornik Zabrze
1969	Legia Warsaw	Gornik Zabrze
1970	Legia Warsaw	Gornik Zabrze
1971	Gornik Zabrze	Gornik Zabrze
1972	Gornik Zabrze	Gornik Zabrze
1973	Stal Mielec	Legia Warsaw
1974	Ruch Chorzow	Ruch Chorzow
1975	Ruch Chorzow	Stal Rzeszow
1976	Stal Mielec	

Final League Table 1975-76

	P	W	D	L	F	A	Pts.
Stal Mielec	30	13	12	5	45	23	38
GKS Tychy	30	15	8	7	38	34	38
Wisla Krakow	30	15	7	8	39	19	37
Ruch Chorzow	30	12	13	5	34	24	37
Widzew Lodz	30	10	12	8	33	33	32
Pogon Szczecin	30	13	5	12	46	41	31
Slask Wroclaw	30	11	9	10	36	33	31
Legia Warsaw	30	12	5	13	44	46	29
Gornik Zabrze	30	10	8	12	38	39	28
Zaglebie Sosnowiec	30	12	4	14	37	38	28
ROW Rybnik	30	11	6	13	30	40	28
Lech Poznan	30	9	9	12	33	46	27
LKS Lodz	30	8	10	12	27	33	26
Szombierki Bytom	30	10	5	15	37	42	25
Stal Rzeszow	30	8	8	14	23	35	24
Polonia Bytom	30	6	9	15	19	33	21

President: Dr. Jorge H. Fagundes.
Secretary: Manuel Correia Arrabaca.
Address of Association: Federação Portuguesa de Futebol, Praça de Alegria, 25, Lisboa.
Telephone: 328207—8–9.
Cable: Futebol Lisboa.
Area: 34,139 square miles.
Population: 10,000,000.
Number of Clubs: 880. *Teams:* 248.
Number of Players: 45,947.
Year of Formation: 1914.
National Colours: Red shirts, white shorts, green stockings.
Second Choice of Colours: White shirts, blue shorts, blue stockings.
Name, Address and Capacity of National Stadium: National Stadium, Lisboa, 54,000.
Names, Addresses and Capacities of Other Principal Football Grounds: Estadio de Luz, Lisboa, 69,000; Estadio José Alvalade, Lisboa, 47,000; Estadio do Restelo, Lisboa, 35,000; Estadio das Antas, Porto, 40,000; Estadio 28 de Maio, Braga, 30,000; Estadio Bonfim, Setubal, 20,000; Estadio Alfredo da Silva, 23,000; Estadio Municipal, Coimbra, 25,000; Estadio Municipal, Guimaraes, 25,000.

Season: September–May.

Principal Honours

European Champions Cup: winners Benfica (1961, 1962); runners-up Benfica (1963, 1965, 1968)
Cup-Winners' Cup: winners Sporting Lisbon (1964)

International matches 1975

April 26, Paris: v France (a) won 2-0 (*Nene, Marinho*).
April 30, Prague: v Czechoslovakia (a) lost 0-5 (EC).
May 13, Glasgow: v Scotland (a) lost 0-1.
June 8, Limassol: v Cyprus (a) won 2-0 (EC) (*Nene, Moinhos*).
Nov. 12, Oporto: v Czechoslovakia (h) drew 1-1 (EC) (*Nene*).
Nov. 19, Lisbon: v England (h) drew 1-1 (EC) (*Rui Rodrigues*).
Dec. 3, Setubal: v Cyprus (h) won 1-0 (EC) (*Alves*)

League Championship wins (1935–76)

Benfica 22; Sporting Lisbon 14; FC Porto 5; Belenenses 1.

Cup wins (1939–76)

Benfica 15; Sporting Lisbon 8; FC Porto 3; Belenenses 2; Boavista 2; Vitoria Setubal 2; Academica Coimbra 1; Leixoes Porto 1; Sporting Braga 1.

League Champions	Cup Winners
1946 Belenenses	Sporting Lisbon
1947 Sporting Lisbon	No competition
1948 Sporting Lisbon	Sporting Lisbon
1949 Sporting Lisbon	Benfica
1950 Benfica	No competition
1951 Sporting Lisbon	Benfica
1952 Sporting Lisbon	Benfica
1953 Sporting Lisbon	Benfica
1954 Sporting Lisbon	Sporting Lisbon
1955 Benfica	Benfica
1956 FC Porto	FC Porto
1957 Benfica	Benfica
1958 Sporting Lisbon	FC Porto
1959 FC Porto	Benfica
1960 Benfica	Belenenses
1961 Benfica	Leixoes
1962 Sporting Lisbon	Benfica
1963 Benfica	Sporting Lisbon
1964 Benfica	Benfica
1965 Benfica	Vitoria Setubal
1966 Sporting Lisbon	Sporting Braga
1967 Benfica	Vitoria Setubal
1968 Benfica	FC Porto
1969 Benfica	Benfica
1970 Sporting Lisbon	Benfica
1971 Benfica	Sporting Lisbon
1972 Benfica	Benfica
1973 Benfica	Sporting Lisbon
1974 Sporting Lisbon	Sporting Lisbon
1975 Benfica	Boavista
1976 Benfica	Boavista

Final League Table 1975-76

	P	W	D	L	F	A	Pts.
Benfica	30	23	4	3	94	20	50
Boavista Porto	30	21	6	3	65	23	48
Belenenses	30	16	8	6	45	28	40
Porto	30	16	7	7	73	33	39
Sporting Lisbon	30	16	6	8	54	28	38
Vitoria Guimaraes	30	13	10	7	49	32	36
Braga	30	9	10	11	35	43	28
Estoril Praia	30	10	8	12	31	45	28
Vitoria Setubal	30	8	10	12	39	42	26
Academico	30	7	9	14	32	47	23
Atletico	30	9	5	16	23	49	23
Leixoes Porto	30	8	6	16	30	65	22
Beira-Mar	30	6	9	15	28	47	21
Tomar	30	7	7	16	32	61	21
Farense	30	8	3	19	33	65	19
CUF Barreiro	30	4	10	16	15	50	18

RUMANIA

President: Mircea Angelescu.
Secretary: Florea Tanasescu.
Address of Association: Federatia Romana de Fotbal, 16 Rue Vasile Conta, Bucaresti.
Telephone: 12–13–31. Cable: Sportrom Bucaresti. Telex: 180 Bucaresti. Area: 91,699 square miles. Population: 19,000,000. Number of Clubs: 5,214. Teams: 5,343. Number of Players: 102,727.
Year of Formation: 1908.
National Colours: Yellow shirts, blue shorts, red stockings.
Second Choice of Colours: Blue shirts, red shorts, yellow stockings.
Name, Address and Capacity of National Stadium: 23 August, Bucuresti, 95,000.
Names, Addresses and Capacities of Other Principal Football Grounds: Republicii, Bucuresti, 37,000; Giulesti, Bucuresti, 20,000; Municipal, Cluj, 25,000; 1 Mai, Timisoara, 30,000; 23 August, Iasi, 20,000; 1 Mai, Constanta, 20,000; Petrolul, Ploiesti, 20,000; 1 Mai, Pitesti, 20,000.
Season: March–July; September–December.

International matches 1975
March 19, Istanbul: v Turkey (a) drew 1-1 (Lucescu).
March 31, Prague: v Czechoslovakia (a) drew 1-1 (Kun).
April 17, Madrid: v Spain (a) drew 1-1 (EC) (Crisan).
May 10, Bucharest: v Denmark (h) won 6-1 (EC) (Georgescu 2, Crisan 2, Lucescu, Dinu).
June 1, Bucharest: v Scotland (h) drew 1-1 (EC) (Georgescu).
Sept. 24, Salonika: v Greece (a) drew 1-1 (Dimitru).
Oct 12, Bucharest: v Turkey (h) drew 2-2 (Jordanescu, Dinu).
Nov. 16, Bucharest: v Spain (h) drew 2-2 (EC) (Georgescu pen., Jordanescu).
Nov. 30, Bucharest: v USSR (h) drew 2-2.
Dec. 17, Glasgow: v Scotland (a) drew 1-1 (EC) (Hainal).

League Championship wins (1910–76)
Dynamo Bucharest 8; Steaua Bucharest (prev. CCA) 8; Venus Bucharest 7; CSC Temesvar 6; UT Arad 6; Rapid Bucharest Ripensia Temesvar 3; Petrolul Ploesti 3; Olimpia Bucharest 2; CAC Bucharest 2; Soc. RA Bucharest 1; Prahova Ploesti 1; CSC Brasov 1; Juventius Bucharest 1; SSUD Reita 1; Craiova Bucharest 1; Progresul 1; Arges 1; Ploesti United 1; Uni. Craiova 1.

Cup wins (1934–75)
Steaua Bucharest (prev. CCA) 11; Rapid Bucharest 7; Dynamo Bucharest 3; UT Arad 2; CFR Bucharest 2; Progresul 2; RIP Timisoara 2; ICO Oradeo 1; Metal Ochimia Resita 1; Petrolul Ploesti 1; Stinta Cluj 1; Stinta Timisoara 1; Turnu Severin 1; Chimia Ramnicu 1; Jiul Petroseni 1.

	League Champions	Cup Winners
1947	UT Arad	No competition
1948	UT Arad	UT Arad
1949	Progresul	CCA Bucharest
1950	UT Arad	CCA Bucharest
1951	CCA Bucharest	CCA Bucharest
1952	CCA Bucharest	CCA Bucharest
1953	CCA Bucharest	UT Arad
1954	UT Arad	Metal Och. Resitta
1955	Dynamo Bucharest	CCA Bucharest
1956	CCA Bucharest	ICO Oradea
1957	No competition	No competition
1958	Petrolul Ploesti	Stinta Timisoara
1959	Petrolul Ploesti	Dynamo Buchares
1960	CCA Bucharest	Progresul
1961	CCA Bucharest	Progresul
1962	Dynamo Bucharest	Steaua Bucharest
1963	Dynamo Bucharest	Petrolul Ploesti
1964	Dynamo Bucharest	Dynamo Bucharest
1965	Dynamo Bucharest	Stinta Cluj
1966	Petrolul Ploesti	Steaua Bucharest
1967	Rapid Bucharest	Steaua Bucharest
1968	Steaua Bucharest	Dynamo Bucharest
1969	UT Arad	Steaua Bucharest
1970	UT Arad	Steaua Bucharest
1971	Dynamo Bucharest	Steaua Bucharest
1972	Arges Pitesti	Rapid Bucharest
1973	Dynamo Bucharest	Chimia Ramnicu
1974	Uni Craiova	Jiul Petroseni
1975	Dynamo Bucharest	Rapid Bucharest
1976	Steaua Bucharest	

League Table 1975-76

	P	W	D	L	F	A	Pts.
Steaua Bucharest	31	19	9	3	75	31	47
Dynamo Bucharest	31	16	7	8	59	33	39
AS Armata	31	16	4	11	44	35	36
Poli. Timisoara	31	13	9	9	49	44	35
Sportul Stud.	31	12	9	10	44	40	33
SC Bacau	31	14	5	12	36	33	33
Uni. Craiova	31	11	9	11	36	32	31
Resita	31	13	5	13	36	51	31
Constanta	31	12	6	13	33	33	30
Bihor	31	13	4	14	39	43	30
Jiul	31	11	8	12	32	45	29
Rapid Bucharest	31	12	5	14	39	45	29
Arges	31	10	8	13	27	38	28
Olimpija	31	11	6	14	33	53	28
Poli. Iassi	31	11	5	15	42	46	27
CFR Cluj	31	9	9	13	29	36	27
UT Arad	31	11	5	15	40	52	27
Uni. Cluj	31	7	3	21	29	41	17

President: Jose Luis Perez-Paya.
Secretary: Andres Ramirez Pardinas.
Address of Association: Real Federación Española de Futbol, Calle Alberto Bosch 13, Apartado 347, Madrid 14.
Telephone: 2391000, 2391008, 2391009.
Cable: Futbol.
Area: 190,115 square miles.
Population: 34,000,000.
Number of Clubs: 5,344.   *Teams:* 5,344.
Number of Players: 164,588.
Year of Formation: 1913.
National Colours: Red shirts, dark blue shorts, black with yellow border stockings.
Second Choice of Colours: Blue shirts, dark blue shorts.
No National Stadium.
Names, Addresses and Capacities of Principal Football Grounds: Santiago Bernabeu, Madrid, 125,000; Campo nuevo, Barcelona, 100,000; Manzanares, Madrid, 70,000; Mestalla, Valencia, 53,100; Sánchez Pizjuan, Sevilla, 46,000; San Mamés, Bilbao, 45,000; Sarriá, Barcelona, 38,295; Riazor, La Coruña, 35,860; La Romareda, Zaragoza, 32,416.
Season: September–June.

Principal Honours
European Nations Cup: winners 1964
Olympic Games: runners-up 1920
European Champions Cup: winners Real Madrid (1956, 1957, 1958, 1959, 1960, 1966); runners-up Real Madrid (1962, 1964), Barcelona (1961), Atletico Madrid (1974)
World club champions: Real Madrid (1960), Atletico Madrid (1975).
Cup-Winners Cup: winners Atletico Madrid (1962); runners-up Atletico Madrid (1963), Barcelona (1969), Real Madrid (1971)
Fairs Cup: winners Barcelona (1958, 1960, 1966), Valencia (1962, 1963), Zaragoza (1964); runners-up Barcelona (1962), Valencia (1964), Zaragoza (1966)

International matches 1975
Feb. 5, Valencia: v Scotland (h) drew 1–1 (EC) (*Megido*).
April 17, Madrid: v Rumania (h) drew 1–1 (EC) (*Velazquez*).
Oct. 12, Barcelona: v Denmark (h) won 2–0 (EC) (*Pirri, Capon*).
Nov. 16, Bucharest: v Rumania (a) drew 2–2 (EC) (*Villar, Santillana*).

League Championship wins (1929–76)
Real Madrid 17; Barcelona 9; Atletico Madrid 7; Atletico Bilbao 6; Valencia 4; Betis 1; Seville 1.

Cup wins (1902–75)
Atletico Bilbao 22; Barcelona 17; Real Madrid 13; Atletico Madrid 4; Valencia 4; Real Union de Irun 3; Seville 3; Espanol 2; Real Zaragoza 2; Arenas 1; Ciclista Sebastian 1; Racing de Irun 1; Vizcaya Bilbao 1.

League Champions		Cup Winners
1946	Seville	Real Madrid
1947	Valencia	Real Madrid
1948	Barcelona	Seville
1949	Barcelona	Valencia
1950	Atletico Madrid	Atletico Bilbao
1951	Atletico Madrid	Barcelona
1952	Barcelona	Barcelona
1953	Barcelona	Barcelona
1954	Real Madrid	Valencia
1955	Real Madrid	Atletico Bilbao
1956	Atletico Bilbao	Atletico Bilbao
1957	Real Madrid	Barcelona
1958	Real Madrid	Atletico Bilbao
1959	Barcelona	Barcelona
1960	Barcelona	Atletico Madrid
1961	Real Madrid	Atletico Madrid
1962	Real Madrid	Real Madrid
1963	Real Madrid	Barcelona
1964	Real Madrid	Real Zaragoza
1965	Real Madrid	Atletico Madrid
1966	Atletico Madrid	Real Zaragoza
1967	Real Madrid	Valencia
1968	Real Madrid	Barcelona
1969	Real Madrid	Atletico Bilbao
1970	Atletico Madrid	Real Madrid
1971	Valencia	Barcelona
1972	Real Madrid	Atletico Madrid
1973	Atletico Madrid	Atletico Bilbao
1974	Barcelona	Real Madrid
1975	Real Madrid	Real Madrid
1976	Real Madrid	

Final League Table 1975–76

	P	W	D	L	F	A	Pts.
Real Madrid	34	20	8	6	54	26	48
Barcelona	34	18	7	9	61	41	43
Atletico Madrid	34	18	6	10	60	38	42
Espanol	34	18	4	12	48	45	40
Atletico Bilbao	34	14	11	9	43	38	39
Hercules	34	12	12	10	33	37	36
Real Betis	34	15	5	14	34	49	35
Real Sociedad	34	12	10	12	45	45	34
Salamanca	34	12	10	12	31	33	34
Valencia	34	12	8	14	43	41	32
Seville	34	13	6	15	35	39	32
Racing Santander	34	14	4	16	45	56	32
Real Zaragoza	34	11	8	15	45	43	30
Las Palmas	34	12	6	16	38	43	30
Elche	34	8	12	14	38	49	28
Oviedo	34	11	5	18	41	45	27
Granada	34	8	10	16	29	50	26
Sporting Gijon	34	9	6	19	41	46	24

President: Gunnar Ericsson.
Secretary: Tore Brod.
Address of Association: Svenska Fotboll-förbundet, Box 1216, S-171 23, Solna.
Telephone: 08/27 25 00.
Cable: Fotball. *Telex:* 17711 Fotball S.
Area: 173,665 square miles.
Population: 8,200,000.
Number of Clubs: 3,016. *Teams:* 6,011.
Number of Players: 127,655.
Year of Formation: 1904.
National Colours: Yellow shirts, blue shorts, yellow and blue stockings.
Second Choice of Colours: Blue shirts, white shorts, white stockings.
Name, Address and Capacity of National Stadium: Fotbollstadion, Solna, 52,000.
Names, Addresses and Capacities of Other Principal Football Grounds: Nya Ullevi, Göteborg, 52,000; Malmö stadion, Malmö, 35,000; Idrottsparken, Norrköping, 35,000; Olympia, Helsingborg, 25,000.
Season: April–October.

Principal Honours

Olympic Games: winners 1948
World Cup: runners-up 1958

International matches 1975

April 16, Gothenburg: v Scotland (h) drew 1-1 (*Sjoberg*).
May 19, Halmstadt: v Algeria (h) won 4-0 (*Sandberg, Edstrom, Grahn, Sjoberg*).
June 4, Solna: v Yugoslavia (h) lost 1-2 (EC) (*Edstrom*).
June 30, Solna: v Norway (h) won 3-1 (EC) (*Nordahl 2, Grahn*).
Aug. 13, Oslo: v Norway (a) won 2-0 (EC) (*Sandberg, Andersson*).
Sept. 3, Belfast: v Northern Ireland (a) won 2-1 (EC) (*Sjoberg, Torstensson*).
Sept. 25, Malmo: v Denmark (h) drew 0-0.
Oct. 15, Zagreb: v Yugoslavia (a) lost 0-3 (EC)

League Championship wins (1896–1975)

Oergryte IS Gothenburg 11; IFK Norrköping 11; Malmö FF 10; Djurgaarden 8; IFK Gothenburg 8; AIK Stockholm 8; GAIS Gothenburg 4; Boras IF Elfsborg 4; IF Halsingborg 3; Atvidaberg 2; IFK Ekilstune 1; IF Gavle Brynas 1; IF Gothenburg Fassbergs 1; Norrköping IK Sleipner 1; Oester Vaexjoe 1.

Cup wins (1941–76)

Malmö FF 9; IFK Norrköping 3; AIK Stockholm 3; Atvidaberg 2; GAIS Gothenburg 1; IFK Halsingborg 1; Raa 1; Landskrona 1.

Year	League Champions	Cup Winners
1946	IFK Norrköping	Malmö FF
1947	IFK Norrköping	Malmö FF
1948	IFK Norrköping	Raa
1949	Malmö FF	AIK Stockholm
1950	Malmö FF	AIK Stockholm
1951	Malmö FF	Malmö FF
1952	IFK Norrköping	No competition
1953	Malmö FF	Malmö FF
1954	GAIS Gothenburg	No competition
1955	Djurgaarden	No competition
1956	IFK Norrköping	No competition
1957	IFK Norrköping	No competition
1958	IFK Gothenburg	No competition
1959	Djurgaarden	No competition
1960	IFK Norrköping	No competition
1961	Boras Elfsborg	No competition
1962	IFK Norrköping	No competition
1963	IFK Norrköping	No competition
1964	Djurgaarden	No competition
1965	Malmö FF	No competition
1966	Djurgaarden	No competition
1967	Malmö FF	Malmö FF
1968	Oester Vaexjoe	No competition
1969	IFK Gothenburg	IFK Norrköping
1970	Malmö FF	Atvidaberg
1971	Malmö FF	Atvidaberg
1972	Atvidaberg	Landskrona
1973	Atvidaberg	Malmö FF
1974	Malmö FF	Malmö FF
1975	Malmö FF	Malmö FF
1976		AIK Stockholm

Final League Table 1975

	P	W	D	L	F	A	Pts.
Malmö FF	26	18	6	2	53	17	42
Osters Vaxjo	26	16	5	5	66	26	37
Djurgaarden	26	13	8	5	36	25	34
Landskrona	26	9	12	5	32	32	30
AIK	26	12	5	9	43	30	29
Atvidaberg	26	10	6	10	31	39	26
Orebro	26	8	9	9	34	35	25
IFK Norrkoping	26	8	7	11	44	49	23
Elfsborg Boras	26	8	7	11	35	45	23
Hammarby	26	8	6	12	39	44	22
Orgryte	26	7	7	12	31	42	21
Halmstad	26	5	9	12	28	36	19
GAIS	26	6	7	13	24	41	19
Sundsvall	26	4	6	16	21	56	14

President: Victor de Werra.
Secretary: Edgar Obertufer.
Address of Association: Schweizerischer Fussballverband, Laubeggstrasse 70 B.P. 24, 3000 Berne 32.
Telephone: (031) 44–62–23.
Cable: Fussballverband Berne.
Area: 15,941 square miles.
Population: 5,500,000.
Number of Clubs: 1,313. *Teams:* 5,754.
Number of Players: 131,500.
Year of Formation: 1895.
National Colours: Red jerseys, white shorts, white stockings.
Second Choice of Colours: White jersey, white shorts, red stockings.
Name, Address and Capacity of National Stadium: Wankdorf Stadium, Berne, 60,000 (the biggest stadium)
Names, Addresses and Capacities of Other Principal Football Grounds: St. Jakob Stadium, Basel, 48,600; Stade Olympique, Lausanne, 41,600; Parc des Sports des Charmilles, Genève, 38,800; Sportplatz Hardturm, Zurich, 37,200.
Season: September–May.

Principal Honours

Olympic Games: runners-up 1924

International matches 1975

April 30, Zurich: v Turkey (h) drew 1-1 (EC) (*Muller*).
May 11, Dublin: v Eire (a) lost 1-2 (EC) (*Muller*).
May 21, Berne: v Eire (h) won 1-0 (EC) (*Elsener*).
Sept. 3, Basle: v England (h) lost 1-2 (*Muller*)
Sept. 24, Brno: v Czechoslovakia (a) drew 1-1 (*Risi pen.*).
Oct 12, Zurich: v USSR (h) lost 0-1 (EC).
Nov 12, Kiev: v USSR (a) lost 1-4 (EC) (*Risi*).

League Championship wins (1898–1976)

Grasshoppers 16; Servette 13; Young Boys Berne 10; FC Zurich 8; Lausanne 7; FC Basle 6 ; La Chaux-de-Fonds 3; FC Lugano 3; Winterthur 3; FC Aarau 2; FC Anglo-Americans 1; St. Gallen 1; FC Brühl 1; Cantonal-Neuchatel 1; Biel 1; Bellinzona 1; FC Etoile la Chaux de Fonds 1.

Cup wins (1926–76)

Grasshoppers 13; La Chaux-de-Fonds 6; Lausanne 6; FC Basle 5; FC Zurich 5; Young Boys Berne 4; Servette 3; FC Lugano 2; FC Sion 2; FC Granges 1; Lucerne 1; St. Gallen 1; Urania Geneva 1; Young Fellows Zurich 1.

League Champions	Cup Winners
1946 Servette	Grasshoppers
1947 Biel	FC Basle
1948 Bellinzona	La Chaux-de-Fonds
1949 FC Lugano	Servette
1950 Servette	Lausanne
1951 Lausanne	La Chaux-de-Fonds
1952 Grasshoppers	Grasshoppers
1953 FC Basle	Young Boys Berne
1954 La Chaux-de-Fonds	La Chaux-de-Fonds
1955 La Chaux-de-Fonds	La Chaux-de-Fonds
1956 Grasshoppers	Grasshoppers
1957 Young Boys, Berne	La Chaux-de-Fonds
1958 Young Boys, Berne	Young Boys, Berne
1959 Young Boys, Berne	FC Granges
1960 Young Boys, Berne	Lucerne
1961 Servette	La Chaux-de-Fonds
1962 Servette	Lausanne
1963 FC Zurich	FC Basle
1964 La Chaux-de-Fonds	Lausanne
1965 Lausanne	FC Sion
1966 FC Zurich	FC Zurich
1967 FC Basle	FC Basle
1968 FC Zurich	FC Lugano
1969 FC Basle	St. Gallen
1970 FC Basle	FC Zurich
1971 Grasshoppers	Servette
1972 FC Basle	FC Zurich
1973 FC Basle	FC Zurich
1974 FC Zurich	FC Sion
1975 FC Zurich	FC Basle
1976 FC Zurich	FC Zurich

Final League Table 1975–76

	P	W	D	L	F	A	Pts.
Zurich	26	19	6	1	69	26	44
Servette	26	16	7	3	50	14	39
Basle	26	13	8	5	59	38	34
Grasshoppers	26	14	4	8	54	37	32
Young Boys	26	11	9	6	41	27	31
Neuchatel Xamax	26	11	8	7	37	25	30
St. Gallen	26	8	11	7	41	39	27
Lausanne	26	10	6	10	35	39	26
Sion	26	6	9	11	40	54	21
Chenois	26	5	9	12	30	42	19
Winterthur	26	8	2	16	34	65	18
Lugano	26	5	6	15	19	37	16
La Chaux-de-Fonds	26	5	4	17	27	61	14
Biel	26	5	3	18	26	58	13

TURKEY

President: Hasan Polat.
Secretary: Ibrahim Onuk.
Address of Association: Fédération Turque de Football, Fevzi Cakmak Sokak 35, Yenisehir, Ankara.
Telephone: 123240, 129623, 178818.
Cable: Futbolsport.
Area: 296,185 square miles.
Population: 32,000,000.
Number of Clubs: 1,432.   *Teams:* 1,540.
Number of Players: 43,229.
Year of Formation: 1923.
National Colours: White shirts with white crescent and star on red hoop, white shorts, red and white stockings.
Name, Address and Capacity of National Stadium: Stade 19, Mayis, Ankara, 35,000.
Names, Addresses and Capacities of Other Principal Football Grounds: Stade Ali Sam, Yen Istanbul, 40,000; Stade Mithatpasat Istanbul, 50,000; Stade Alsancak, Izmiri 30,000; Stade d'Ataturk, Eskisehir, 35,000; Stade d'Ataturk, Adana, 30,000; Stade de Ville, Kayseri, 25,000; Stade d'Ataturk Bursa, 25,000.

International matches 1975

March 19, Istanbul: v Rumania (h) drew 1-1 (*Cemil*).
April 2, Kiev: v USSR (a) lost 0-3 (EC).
April 30, Zurich: v Switzerland (a) drew 1-1 (EC) (*Alpaslan*).
Oct. 12, Bucharest: v Rumania (a) drew 2-2 (*Cemil 2*).
Oct. 29, Dublin: v Eire (a) lost 0-4 (EC).
Nov. 23, Ankara: v USSR (h) won 1-0 (EC) (*Cemil*).
Dec. 21, Istanbul: v West Germany (h) lost 0-5.

League Championship wins (1960–1976)

Fenerbahce 7; Gatatasaray 5; Besiktas 3; Trabzonspor 1.

Cup wins (1963–1976)

Galatasaray 6; Goztepe Izmir 2; Fenerbahce 2; Altay Izmir 1; Ankaragücü 1; Eskisehirspor 1; Besiktas 1.

	League Champions	Cup Winners
1960	Besiktas	
1961		
1962	Fenerbahce	
1963	Galatasaray	Galatasaray
1964	Fenerbahce	Galatasaray
1965	Fenerbahce	Galatasaray
1966	Besiktas	Galatasaray
1967	Besiktas	Altay Izmir
1968	Fenerbahce	Fenerbahce
1969	Galatasaray	Goztepe Izmir
1970	Fenerbahce	Goztepe Izmir
1971	Galatasaray	Eskisehirspor
1972	Galatasaray	Ankaragücü
1973	Galatasaray	Galatasaray
1974	Fenerbahce	Fenerbahce
1975	Fenerbahce	Besiktas
1976	Trabzonspor	Galatasaray

Final League Table 1975-76

	P	W	D	L	F	A	Pts.
Trabzonspor	30	17	9	4	36	14	43
Fenerbahce	30	14	12	4	40	18	40
Galatasaray	30	12	13	5	36	23	37
Adanaspor	30	13	10	7	36	27	36
Altay Izmir	30	9	12	9	31	32	30
Giresunspor	30	8	12	10	27	27	28
Boluspor	30	9	10	11	34	38	28
Adanademirspor	30	10	8	12	32	36	28
Eskisehirspor	30	8	11	11	29	29	27
Bursaspor	30	9	9	12	30	33	27
Besiktas	30	5	17	8	25	32	27
Orduspor	30	7	13	10	20	27	27
Zonguldakspor	30	7	12	11	25	25	26
Goztepe Izmir	30	7	12	11	31	32	26
Ankaragucu	30	8	9	13	33	48	25
Balikesir	30	9	7	14	18	39	25

USSR

President: Boris Fedosov.
Secretary: Anatoly Chetirko.
Address of Association: Federation De Football De L'URSS, Skatertnyi, Pereulok 4, Moscow, 69.
Telephone: 290–24–90. *Cable:* Sportkomitet USSR. *Area:* 8,598,678 square miles. *Population:* 210,000,000. *Number of Clubs:* 180. *Teams:* 50,163. *Number of Players:* 4,300,000. *Year of Formation:* 1934.
National Colours: Red shirts, white shorts, red stockings.
Second Choice of Colours: White.
Name, Address and Capacity of National

Stadium: Lenin Stadium, Moscow, 102,000.
Names, Addresses and Capacities of Other Principal Football Grounds: Kirov Stadium, Victory Park, Leningrad, 84,000; "Pakhtakov" Central Stadium, Tashkent, Socialism Street 23, 60,000; Ukraine Republic Stadium, Kiev, Krasnoarmeiskaya Street 51, 90,000; Dynamo Stadium, Moscow, Leningrad Prospect 36, 54,000; Dynamo Stadium, Tbilisi, Tseretely Street 2, 60,000.

Season: South: March–December.
Central: April–October.
North: May–September.

Principal Honours

Olympic Games: winners 1956
European Nations Cup: winners 1960; runners-up 1964
European Championship: runners-up 1972
Cup-Winners' Cup: winners Dynamo Kiev (1975); runners-up Dynamo Moscow (1972)
Super Cup: Dynamo Kiev (1975)

International matches 1975

April 2, Moscow: v Turkey (h) won 3-0 (EC) (*Kolotov 2 pens, Blokhin*).
May 18, Kiev: v Eire (h) won 2-1 (EC) (*Blokhin, Kolotov*).
June 8, Moscow: v Italy (h) won 1-0 (*Konkov*)
Sept. 3, Moscow: v East Germany (h) drew 0-0.
Oct. 12, Zurich: v Switzerland (a) won 1-0 (EC) (*Muntian*).
Nov. 12, Kiev: v Switzerland (h) won 4-1 (EC) (*Konkov, Onischenko 2, Veremejev*).
Nov. 23, Ankara: v Turkey (a) lost 0-1 (EC).
Nov. 30, Bucharest: v Rumania (a) drew 2-2

League Championship wins (1936-75)

Dynamo Moscow 10; Spartak Moscow 9; Dynamo Kiev 7; CSKA Moscow 6; Torpedo Moscow 2; Dynamo Tbilisi 1; Saria Voroshilovgrad 1; Ararat Erevan 1.

Cup wins (1936-75)

Spartak Moscow 9; Torpedo Moscow 5; CSKA Moscow 4; Dynamo Moscow 4; Dynamo Kiev 4; Donets Shaktyor 2; Lokomotiv Moscow 2; Ararat Erevan 2; Karpaty Lvov 1; Zenit Leningrad 1.

League Champions	Cup Winners
1946 CSKA Moscow	Spartak Moscow
1947 CSKA Moscow	Spartak Moscow
1948 CSKA Moscow	CSKA Moscow
1949 Dynamo Moscow	Torpedo Moscow
1950 Dynamo Moscow	Spartak Moscow
1951 CSKA Moscow	CSKA Moscow
1952*Spartak Moscow	Torpedo Moscow
1953 Spartak Moscow	Dynamo Moscow
1954 Dynamo Moscow	Dynamo Kiev
1955 Dynamo Moscow	CSKA Moscow
1956 Spartak Moscow	No competition
1957 Dynamo Moscow	Lokomotiv Moscow
1958 Spartak Moscow	Spartak Moscow
1959 Dynamo Moscow	No competition
1960 Torpedo Moscow	Torpedo Moscow
1961 Dynamo Kiev	Donets Shaktyor
1962 Spartak Moscow	Donets Shaktyor
1963 Dynamo Moscow	Spartak Moscow
1964 Dynamo Tbilisi	Dynamo Kiev
1965 Torpedo Moscow	Spartak Moscow
1966 Dynamo Kiev	Dynamo Kiev
1967 Dynamo Kiev	Dynamo Moscow
1968 Dynamo Kiev	Torpedo Moscow
1969 Spartak Moscow	Karpaty Lvov
1970 CSKA Moscow	Dynamo Moscow
1971 Dynamo Kiev	Spartak Moscow
1972 Saria Voroshilov-grad	Torpedo Moscow
1973 Ararat Erevan	Ararat Erevan
1974 Dynamo Kiev	Dynamo Kiev
1975 Dynamo Kiev	Ararat Erevan

* Short league season

Final League Table 1975

	P	W	D	L	F	A	Pts.
Dynamo Kiev	30	17	9	4	53	30	43
Schachtjor Donezk	30	15	8	7	45	23	38
Dynamo Moscow	30	13	12	5	39	23	38
Torpedo Moscow	30	13	8	9	42	33	34
Ararat Erevan	30	15	4	11	40	38	34
Karpaty Lvov	30	11	10	9	36	28	32
Dnjepropetrovsk	30	10	11	9	33	30	31
Dynamo Tbilisi	30	11	9	10	32	32	31
Saria Voroschilovgrad	30	10	11	9	32	37	31
Spartak Moscow	30	9	10	11	27	30	28
Lokomotiv Moscow	30	7	12	11	28	33	26
Tchernomorets Odessa	30	8	10	12	27	35	26
CSKA Moscow	30	6	13	11	29	36	25
Zenit Leningrad	30	7	10	13	27	42	24
Pachtakor Taschkent	30	8	7	15	31	44	23
SKA Rostov	30	4	8	18	23	50	16

YUGOSLAVIA

President: Pero Korobar.
Secretary: Vasilije Stojkovic.
Address of Association: Yugoslav Football Association, Terazije No. 35, BP 263, Belgrade.
Telephone: 333343, 333447.
Cable: Jugofutbal.
Area: 98,766 square miles.
Population: 19,000,000.
Number of Clubs: 7,455. *Teams:* 4,029.
Number of Players: 122,372.
Year of Formation: 1919.
National Colours: Blue shirts, white shorts, red stockings.

Second Choice of Colours: White shirts, white shorts, white stockings.
No National Stadium.
Names, Addresses and Capacities of Principal Football Grounds: Crvena Zvezda Stadium, Beograd, 95,000; Yugoslav National Army, Beograd, 55,000; Yuth Stadium, Beograd, 25,000; Dinamo, Zagreb, 55,000; Kosevo, Sarajevo, 40,000.

Principal Honours

Olympic Games: winners 1960; runners-up 1948, 1952, 1956
European Nations Cup: runners-up 1960

European Championship: runners-up 1968
European Champions Cup: runners-up
Partizan Belgrade (1966)
Fairs Cup: winners Dynamo Zagreb (1967);
runners-up Dynamo Zagreb (1966)

International matches 1975

April 16, Belfast: v Northern Ireland (a)
lost 0-1 (EC).
May 31, Belgrade: v Netherlands (h) won 3-0
(*Savic, Popivoda, Ivejic*).
June 4, Solna: v Sweden (a) won 2-1 (EC)
(*Katalinski, Ivejic*)
June 9, Oslo: v Norway (a) won 3-1 (EC)
(*Buljan, Bogicevic, Surjak*).
Oct. 15, Zagreb: v Sweden (h) 3-0 (EC)
(*Vabec, Oblak, Vladic*).
Nov. 19, Belgrade: v Northern Ireland (h)
won 1-0 (EC) (*Oblak*).

League Championship wins (1923–75)

Red Star Belgrade 11; Hajduk Split 8;
Partizan Belgrade 6; Gradjanski Zagreb 5;
BSK Belgrade 5; Dynamo Zagreb 3;
Jugoslovija Belgrade 2; Concordia Zagreb 2;
HASK Zagreb 1; Vojvodina Novi Sad 1;
F.C. Sarajevo 1, Zeljeznicar 1.

Cup wins (1947–76)

Red Star Belgrade 9; Partizan Belgrade 4;
Dynamo Zagreb 6; Hajduk Split 5;
BSK Belgrade 2; FK Belgrade 2; Vardar
Skoplje 1.

League Champions	Cup Winners
1947 Partizan Belgrade	Partizan Belgrade
1948 Dynamo Zagreb	Red Star Belgrade
1949 Partizan Belgrade	Red Star Belgrade
1950 Hajduk Split	Red Star Belgrade
1951 Red Star Belgrade	Dynamo Zagreb
1952 Hajduk Split	Partizan Belgrade
1953 Red Star Belgrade	BSK Belgrade
1954 Dynamo Zagreb	Partizan Belgrade
1955 Hajduk Split	BSK Belgrade
1956 Red Star Belgrade	No competition
1957 Red Star Belgrade	Partizan Belgrade
1958 Dynamo Zagreb	Red Star Belgrade
1959 Red Star Belgrade	Red Star Belgrade
1960 Red Star Belgrade	Dynamo Zagreb
1961 Partizan Belgrade	Vardar Skoplje
1962 Partizan Belgrade	OFK Belgrade
1963 Partizan Belgrade	Dynamo Zagreb
1964 Red Star Belgrade	Red Star Belgrade
1965 Partizan Belgrade	Dynamo Zagreb
1966 Vojvodina Novi Sad	OFK Belgrade
1967 FC Sarajevo	Hajduk Split
1968 Red Star Belgrade	Red Star Belgrade
1969 Red Star Belgrade	Dynamo Zagreb
1970 Red Star Belgrade	Red Star Belgrade
1971 Hajduk Split	Red Star Belgrade
1972 Zeljeznicar	Hajduk Split
1973 Red Star Belgrade	Dynamo Zagreb
1974 Hajduk Split	Hajduk Split
1975 Hajduk Split	Hajduk Split
1976	Hajduk Split

League Table 1975-76
(up to and including June 13, 1976)

	P	W	D	L	F	A	Pts.
Hajduk Split	30	17	9	4	49	20	43
Partizan Belgrade	30	18	6	6	49	28	42
Dinamo Zagreb	30	15	9	6	33	20	39
Red Star Belgrade	30	15	7	8	52	27	37
Vojvodina Novi Sad	30	9	12	9	35	34	30
Celik Zenica	30	10	10	10	24	26	30
Velez Mostar	30	9	11	10	35	32	29
Borac Banja Luka	30	9	11	10	32	35	29
Sloboda Tuzla	30	10	8	12	38	35	28
Rijeka	30	9	10	11	30	31	28
Sarajevo	30	10	8	12	39	43	28
Olimpija Ljubljana	30	10	8	12	36	40	28
OFK Belgrade	30	11	5	14	31	44	27
Buducnost Titograd	30	10	7	13	24	37	27
Vardar Skoplje	30	8	9	13	26	33	25
Radnicki Nis	30	6	13	11	25	37	25
Zeljeznicar Sarajevo	30	8	8	14	32	44	24
Radnicki Kragujevac	30	7	7	16	24	48	21

WORLD CLUB CHAMPIONSHIP

Played annually up to 1974 between the winners of the European Cup and the winners of the South American Champions Cup—known as the Copa Libertadores de America.

1960   Real Madrid beat Penarol 0-0, 5-1
1961   Penarol beat Benfica 0-1, 5-0, 2-1
1962   Santos beat Benfica 3-2, 5-2
1963   Santos beat AC Milan 2-4, 4-2, 1-0
1964   Inter-Milan beat Independiente 0-1, 2-0, 1-0
1965   Inter-Milan beat Independiente 3-0, 0-0
1966   Penarol beat Real Madrid 2-0, 2-0
1967   Racing Club beat Celtic 0-1, 2-1, 1-0
1968   Estudiantes beat Manchester United 1-0, 1-1
1969   AC Milan beat Estudiantes 3-0,1-2
1970   Feyenoord beat Estudiantes 2-2, 1-0
1971   Nacianal beat Panathinaikos 1-1, 2-1
1972   Ajax beat Independiente 1-1, 3-0
1973   Independiente beat Juventus 1-0
1974   Atlético Madrid beat Independiente 0-1, 2-0

SUPER CUP and ANGLO-ITALIAN CUP

1975   Super Cup: Dynamo Kiev beat Bayern Munich 1-0, 2-0
1975   Anglo-Italian: Fiorentina beat West Ham United 1-0, 1-0

SOUTH AMERICAN FOOTBALL

Ten countries are affiliated to the South American Football Confederation (CONME-BOL): Argentina, Bolivia, Brazil, Chile, Colombia, Ecuador, Peru, Paraguay, Uruguay and Venezuela. The principal competition for national teams is the South American Championship, which has been played infrequently in recent years but was revived in 1975 with Peru as the winners.

Unfortunately, Brazil, with the best record in the World Cup, have not always either competed or sent her strongest team. In 1975 for instance, they were represented by the Minas Gerais state selection. Some of the lesser countries have not always been able to afford to compete.

Between the start of the tournament and 1920 only Argentina, Brazil, Chile, and Uruguay entered. In 1921 Paraguay was added and by 1967 only Venezuela had not previously competed. Argentina and Uruguay have dominated the competition throughout its history.

There are many other competitions between the various South American countries. In 1976 the Atlantic Cup was revived between Argentina, Brazil, Paraguay, and Uruguay with the Brazilians emerging as the undefeated winners. This same competition was also used to decide the Rio Branco Cup between Brazil and Uruguay; the Colonel Bogado Cup between Argentina and Paraguay; the Roca Cup between Argentina and Brazil and the General Artigas Cup between Paraguay and Uruguay.

Others have included the Carlos Dittborn Cup (Argentina and Chile); Lipton Cup (Argentina and Uruguay); Newton Cup (Argentina and Uruguay), O'Higgins Cup (Brazil and Chile) and Oswaldo Cruz Cup (Brazil and Paraguay).

Organised on similar lines to the European Champions Cup, the Copa Liberatadores caters for international competition at club level. But the qualifying rounds are played off in groups, not on a knock-out basis.

Again Brazilian clubs have not been as interested as the teams of Argentina and Uruguay. The distances involved in travelling, and the unlikelihood of large attendances in the smaller centres have often deterred them. But Uruguay in particular have taken more interest in this than even their own domestic competition, which is invariably contested between their two leading clubs, Penarol and Nacional.

SOUTH AMERICAN CHAMPIONSHIPS

1916	Uruguay	1941	Argentina
1917	Uruguay	1942	Uruguay
1919	Brazil	1945	Argentina
1920	Uruguay	1946	Argentina
1921	Argentina	1947	Argentina
1922	Brazil	1949	Brazil
1923	Uruguay	1953	Paraguay
1924	Uruguay	1955	Argentina
1925	Argentina	1956	Uruguay
1926	Uruguay	1957	Argentina
1927	Argentina	1959	Argentina
1929	Argentina	1959	Uruguay
1935	Uruguay	1963	Bolivia
1937	Argentina	1967	Uruguay
1939	Peru	1975	Peru

N.B. Regional League titles for Brazilian clubs only given up to start of National Championship in 1971.

ATLETICO MINEIRO (Brazil)

Founded: 1908. *Ground:* Mineirao Stadium.
Colours: Black and white striped shirts, black shorts.
Honours: Brazilian Championship 1971. Minas Gerais League: 1915, 1926, 1927, 1931, 1932, 1936, 1938, 1939, 1941, 1942, 1946, 1947, 1949, 1950, 1952, 1953, 1954, 1955, 1956, 1958, 1962, 1963, 1970.

BOCA JUNIORS (Argentina)

Founded: 1905. *Ground:* Estadio Bonbonera.
Colours: Dark blue shirts with broad yellow hoop, dark blue shorts.
Honours: Argentine League: 1919, 1920, 1923, 1924, 1926, 1930, 1931, 1934, 1935, 1940, 1943, 1944, 1954, 1962, 1964, 1965. National Championship: 1969, 1970.

BOTAFOGO (Brazil)

Founded: 1904. *Ground:* General Severiano.
Colours: Black and white striped shirts, black shorts.
Honours: Rio League: 1907 (joint), 1910, 1930, 1932, 1933, 1935, 1948, 1957, 1961, 1962, 1967, 1968.

CRUZEIRO (Brazil)

Founded: 1921. *Ground:* Mineirao Stadium.
Colours: Blue shirts, white shorts.
Honours: Minas Gerais League: 1928, 1929, 1930, 1940, 1943, 1944, 1945, 1959, 1960, 1961, 1965, 1966, 1967, 1968, 1969.

ESTUDIANTES DE LA PLATA (Argentina)

Founded: 1905. *Ground:* Paseo del Bosque.
Colours: Red and white striped shirts, black shorts.
Honours: World Club Championship 1968. South American Cup: 1968, 1969, 1970. Argentine League: 1931, 1967.

FLAMENGO (Brazil)

Founded: 1895. *Ground:* Estadio da Gavea.
Colours: Red and black hooped shirts, white shorts.
Honours: Rio League: 1914, 1915, 1920, 1921, 1925, 1927, 1939, 1942, 1943, 1944, 1953, 1954, 1955, 1963, 1965.

FLUMINENSE (Brazil)

Founded: 1902. *Ground:* Alvaro Chaves.
Colours: Red, white and green striped shirts, white shorts.
Honours: Rio League: 1906, 1907 (joint), 1908, 1909, 1911, 1917, 1918, 1919, 1924, 1936, 1937, 1938, 1940, 1941, 1946, 1951, 1959, 1964, 1969.

INDEPENDIENTE (Argentina)

Founded: 1905. *Ground:* Avellaneda.
Colours: Red shirts and shorts.
Honours: South American Cup: 1964, 1965, 1972. Argentine League: 1922, 1926, 1938, 1939, 1948, 1960, 1963, 1970, 1971. National Championship: 1967.

NACIONAL (Uruguay)

Founded: 1899. *Ground:* Estadio Centenario.
Colours: White shirts with red and blue striped collar and sleeves, blue shorts.
Honours: World Club Championship 1971. South American Cup 1971 Uruguayan League: 1902, 1903, 1912, 1915, 1916, 1917, 1919, 1920, 1922, 1923, 1924, 1933, 1934, 1939, 1940, 1941, 1942, 1943, 1946, 1947, 1950, 1952, 1955, 1956, 1957, 1963, 1966, 1969, 1970, 1971, 1972.

PALMEIRAS (Brazil)

Founded: 1914. *Ground:* Parque Antartica.
Colours: Green shirts, white shorts.
Honours: Sao Paulo League: 1920, 1926, 1927, 1932, 1933, 1934, 1936, 1940, 1942, 1944, 1947, 1950, 1959, 1963, 1966. Brazilian Championship: 1972, 1973.

PENAROL (Uruguay)

Founded: 1891. *Ground:* Estadio Centenario.
Colours: Black and yellow striped shirts, black shorts.
Honours: World Club Championship: 1961, 1966. South American Cup: 1960, 1961, 1966. Uruguayan League: 1900, 1901, 1905, 1907, 1911, 1918, 1921, 1926, 1928, 1929, 1932, 1935, 1936, 1937, 1938, 1944, 1945, 1949, 1951, 1953, 1954, 1958, 1959, 1960, 1961, 1962, 1964, 1965, 1967, 1968, 1973, 1974, 1975.

RIVER PLATE (Argentina)

Founded: 1901. *Ground:* Estadio Monumental.
Colours: White shirts with red diagonal stripes, black shorts.
Honours: Argentine League: 1920, 1932, 1936, 1937, 1941, 1942, 1945, 1947, 1952, 1953, 1955, 1956, 1957, 1975. National Championship: 1975. Uruguayan League: 1908, 1910, 1913, 1914.

SANTOS (Brazil)

Founded: 1912. *Ground:* Estadio Urbano Caldeira, Vila Belmiro.
Colours: White shirts and shorts.
Honours: World Club Championships: 1962, 1963. South American Cup: 1962, 1963. Sao Paulo League: 1935, 1955, 1956, 1958, 1960, 1961, 1962, 1964, 1965, 1967, 1968, 1969.

SAO PAULO (Brazil)

Founded: 1930. *Ground:* Morumbi (Estadio Cicero Pompeu de Toledo).
Colours: White shirts with one red and black band separated by white, white shorts.
Honours: Sao Paulo League: 1931, 1943, 1945, 1946, 1948, 1949, 1953, 1957, 1970.

VASCO DA GAMA (Brazil)

Founded: 1898. *Ground:* Estadio de Sao Januario.
Colours: Black shirts with white diagonal band, white shorts.
Honours: Rio League: 1923, 1929, 1934, 1936, 1945, 1947, 1949, 1950, 1952, 1956, 1958, 1970. Brazilian Championship: 1974.

SOUTH AMERICAN CHAMPIONSHIP RECORD 1917-1975

	P	W	D	L	F	A
Argentina	87	61	11	15	243	84
Uruguay	92	56	7	29	230	122
Brazil	76	43	9	24	207	106
Paraguay	88	42	9	37	164	175
Peru	73	31	13	29	123	125
Chile	81	23	15	43	129	180
Bolivia	48	11	6	31	56	157
Colombia	35	8	5	22	37	91
Ecuador	51	2	9	40	48	163
Venezuela	9	1	0	8	8	42

Table includes only 23 championships considered as 'official' tournaments

COPA LIBERTADORES RECORD 1960-1975

	P	W	D	L	F	A
Penarol (U)	130	66	30	34	228	135
Nacional (U)	107	54	27	26	189	103
Universitario (Pe)	91	35	24	32	123	119
Independiente (A)	67	35	15	17	102	62
River Plate (A)	54	27	12	15	113	67
Olimpia (Pa)	64	24	18	22	90	82
Boca Juniors (A)	47	27	8	12	76	41
Cerro Portena (Pa)	64	22	18	24	93	97
Palmeiras (Br)	44	28	4	12	73	43
Guarani (Pa)	59	21	17	21	78	74
Universidad Catolica (Ch)	52	23	10	19	91	79
Estudiantes (A)	31	22	3	6	44	20
Colo Colo (Ch)	51	19	9	23	87	95
Emelec (E)	51	17	10	24	62	81
Deportivo Cali (Co)	41	16	9	16	62	66
Barcelona (E)	45	15	11	19	53	60
Rosario Central (A)	30	16	7	7	44	29
Sporting Cristal (Pe)	42	12	15	15	49	60
Racing Club (A)	27	16	6	5	54	26
Universidad de Chile (Ch)	44	15	8	21	64	70
Deportivo Italia (V)	44	14	9	21	44	81
Millonarios (Co)	38	13	8	17	46	50
Union Espanola (Ch)	35	12	9	14	46	51
Santos (Br)	22	14	3	5	60	32
Sao Paulo (Br)	23	12	7	4	39	18
Jorge Wilsterman (Bo)	38	11	9	18	39	70
Cruzeiro (Br)	22	14	2	6	42	27
Botafogo (Br)	17	10	3	4	30	23
Liga Deportiva U. (E)	20	8	6	6	31	25
Nacional (E)	24	8	6	10	27	30
Bolivar (Bo)	23	5	9	9	25	40
San Lorenzo (A)	15	7	4	4	26	10
Alianza (Pe)	24	6	5	13	24	37
Indep. Santa Fe (Co)	22	5	6	11	30	44
Nacional Medellin (Co)	18	5	5	8	18	24
Dep. Municipal (Bo)	20	6	3	11	39	49
Galicia (V)	36	5	5	26	30	64
Huracan (A)	11	6	2	3	19	12
Portuguesa (V)	12	3	6	3	9	13
The Strongest (Bo)	16	4	4	8	18	39
Wanderers (Ch)	12	4	3	5	20	22
America (E)	12	4	2	6	13	22
Defensor Lima (Pe)	10	4	1	5	8	12
Dep. Ind. Medellin (Co)	10	4	1	5	15	21
Fluminense (Br)	6	4	0	2	16	6
Newell's Old Boys (A)	7	3	2	2	9	9
Oriente Petroleo (Bo)	12	3	2	7	15	26
Deportivo Por. (V)	12	3	2	7	8	23
Valencia (V)	16	2	4	10	16	35
Huachipato (Ch)	6	2	2	2	10	10
Juan Aurich (Pe)	8	2	2	4	14	20
Deportivo Quito (E)	10	1	4	5	7	19
Vasco da Gama (Br)	6	1	3	2	7	7
Union Magdalena (Co)	6	2	1	3	7	8
Defensor Arica (Pe)	6	1	3	2	5	6
Sport Boys (Pe)	8	2	1	5	10	11
America (Co)	10	1	3	6	12	22
31st October (Bo)	10	2	1	7	11	28
Chaca Petroleo (Bo)	12	2	1	9	8	22
Nautico (Br)	6	1	2	3	7	8
Atletico Mineiro (Br)	6	0	4	2	5	6
Union San Felipe (Ch)	6	1	2	3	5	8
Univer. Catolica (E)	6	1	2	3	2	5

	P	W	D	L	F	A
Atletico Junior (Co)	6	1	2	3	5	9
U.D. Canarias (V)	6	1	2	3	3	7
Deportivo Lara (V)	10	1	2	7	5	16
Bahia (Br)	4	1	1	2	4	7
Wanderers (U)	6	1	1	4	8	10
Union Huaral (Pe)	6	0	3	3	8	17
Libertad (Pa)	6	1	1	4	2	13
Ninth October (E)	10	1	1	8	14	28
Rangers (Ch)	10	1	1	8	11	26
Club Always Ready (Bo)	6	0	2	4	2	17
Universitario (Bo)	6	0	2	4	2	19
Aurora (Bo)	4	0	1	3	2	14
Litoral (Bo)	6	0	1	5	1	14
Everest (E)	2	0	0	2	1	14

(Penarol (Uruguay) have competed in the highest number of competitions – 15; Nacional (Uruguay) and Universitario (Peru) in 11 each; Olimpia (Paraguay) in 10.)

RECORD OF SOUTH AMERICAN COUNTRIES 1975

	P	W	D	L	F	A
Brazil	6	5	0	1	16	4
Argentina	8	5	1	2	29	7
Colombia	9	6	0	3	11	5
Peru	11	6	1	4	14	14
Uruguay	7	4	0	3	8	8
Ecuador	6	2	1	3	11	10
Paraguay	7	2	1	4	6	8
Chile	6	1	1	4	8	10
Bolivia	4	1	0	3	3	9
Venezuela	4	0	0	4	1	26

COPA LIBERTADORES (South American Cup)

Year	Winners	Runners-up	Year	Winners	Runners-up
1960	Penarol (Uruguay)	Olimpia (Paraguay)	1968	Estudiantes	Palmeiras
1961	Penarol	Palmeiras (Brazil)		(Argentina)	
1962	Santos (Brazil)	Penarol	1969	Estudiantes	Nacional
1963	Santos	Boca Juniors	1970	Estudiantes	Penarol
		(Argentina)	1971	Nacional	Estudiantes
1964	Independiente	Nacional (Uruguay)	1972	Independiente	Universitario (Peru)
	(Argentina)		1973	Independiente	Colo Colo (Chile)
1965	Independiente	Penarol	1974	Independiente	Sao Paulo (Brazil)
1966	Penarol	River Plate	1975	Independiente	Union Espanola
		(Argentina)			(Chile)
1967	Racing (Argentina)	Nacional			

OTHER LEAGUE, YOUTH, AND SCHOOLS FOOTBALL

Rothmans Sponsored Football 1975-76

Two champions (Blyth Spartans and Falmouth Town) retained their titles in the Northern League and Western League respectively, but whereas Blyth edged ahead of Spennymoor United and Willington on the last day of the season, Falmouth cruised through the season with comparative ease.

Enfield, beaten by Wycombe Wanderers on goal average for the Isthmian Championship last season, reversed the position in fine style by winning their title by five points. The North London Club had an eventful season in the Cups as well, winning the London Senior Cup and finishing as runners-up in the Middlesex Senior Cup while also reaching the semi-finals of the FA Trophy. Burnham enjoyed a great season in the Hellenic League, where they emulated Thatcham's performance the previous season in winning the cup and league 'double'.

All four leagues produced a high percentage of county cup finalists and once again league goals were in abundance, especially in the Western League, while discipline was seen at its best in the North. The Jersey Football Combination and the Guernsey Priaulx League joined 'The Family' last season and both upheld the aims and principles of sporting positive football in the best possible way.

Final league tables for the sponsored leagues can be found between pages 823 and 827.

Rothmans Isthmian League Prize Money 1975-76

	Champions	*2nd*	*3rd*
Division 1	£1,000 (Forfeited by Enfield)	£500 (Wycombe Wanderers)	£300 (Dagenham)
Division 2	£500 (Tilbury)	£250 (Croydon)	£150 (Carshalton Athletic)
	Highest Goalscorers	*2nd Highest*	*3rd Highest*
Division 1	£300 (Forfeited by Tooting & Mitcham)	£200 (Sutton United)	£100 (Forfeited by Dulwich Hamlet)
Division 2	£150 (Forfeited by Chesham United)	£100 (Forfeited by Harwich & Parkeston)	£50 (Forfeited by Hampton)

Rothmans Isthmian Football League Total Sponsorship 1975-76

DIVISION ONE

League Position		League awards £	Goal-scoring awards £	Sportsman-ship awards £	Three goal awards £	TOTAL £
3	Dagenham	300.00	—	465.72	400.00	1,165.72
2	Wycombe Wanderers	500.00	—	465.72	200.00	1,165.72
11	Sutton United	—	200.00	388.10	240.00	828.10
16	Hitchin Town	—	—	543.34	80.00	623.34
12	Bishop's Stortford	—	—	465.72	80.00	545.72
9	Staines Town	—	—	232.86	200.00	432.86
19	Southall & Ealing Boro.	—	—	232.86	160.00	392.86
1	Enfield	—	—	—	320.00	320.00
20	Leytonstone	—	—	155.24	120.00	275.24
18	Kingstonian	—	—	232.86	40.00	272.86
5	Dulwich Hamlet	—	—	—	240.00	240.00
7	Tooting & Mitcham United	—	—	—	240.00	240.00
10	Slough Town	—	—	—	200.00	200.00
6	Hendon	—	—	77.62	80.00	157.62
15	Barking	—	—	—	120.00	120.00
4	Ilford	—	—	—	120.00	120.00
14	Woking	—	—	—	120.00	120.00
17	Hayes	—	—	—	80.00	80.00
8	Leatherhead	—	—	—	80.00	80.00
13	Walthamstow Avenue	—	—	—	80.00	80.00
22	Clapton	—	—	—	—	—
21	Oxford City	—	—	—	—	—

£40 bonuses (Div. 1) and £25 (Div. 2) were awarded to clubs each time they recorded a league victory by three or more goals. 42 shares of the Division One Sportsmanship Pool (£2000) remained intact at the end of the season and the pool was supplemented by the prize money forfeited by Enfield, Tooting & Mitcham and Dulwich Hamlet so each share was worth £77.62. In Division Two, 26 shares remained and the pool (£1000) was supplemented by the prize money forfeited by Chesham United, Harwich & Parkeston and Hampton, so each share was worth £48.85. Each club started the season with eight sportsmanship points, and lost one for each caution and four for each dismissal. Clubs who lost all eight points forfeited the right to claim league position and goalscoring awards.

DIVISION TWO

League Position		League awards £	Goal-scoring awards £	Sportsman-ship awards £	Three goal awards £	TOTAL £
1	Tilbury	500.00	—	195.40	225.00	920.40
2	Croydon	250.00	—	341.95	125.00	716.95
3	Carshalton Athletic	150.00	—	293.10	175.00	618.10
7	St. Albans City	—	—	146.55	100.00	246.55
4	Clapham United	—	—	—	200.00	200.00
9	Harrow Borough	—	—	97.70	100.00	197.70
11	Horsham	—	—	97.70	100.00	197.70
10	Hornchurch	—	—	97.70	75.00	172.70
8	Boreham Wood	—	—	—	100.00	100.00
6	Hampton	—	—	—	75.00	75.00
5	Harwich & Parkeston	—	—	—	75.00	75.00
14	Walton & Hersham	—	—	—	75.00	75.00
13	Wokingham Town	—	—	—	75.00	75.00
16	Bromley	—	—	—	50.00	50.00
14	Finchley	—	—	—	50.00	50.00
18	Harlow Town	—	—	—	50.00	50.00
17	Aveley	—	—	—	25.00	25.00
20	Ware	—	—	—	25.00	25.00
12	Wembley	—	—	—	25.00	25.00
22	Corinthian-Casuals	—	—	—	—	—
21	Hertford Town	—	—	—	—	—
19	Maidenhead Utd.	—	—	—	—	—

Rothmans Isthmian League Leading Goalscorers 1975-76

DIVISION ONE
A. Morton (*Woking*) 25, R. C. Kidd (*Sutton United*) 24, N. Glover (*Tooting & Mitcham*) 22, M. Harkins (*Dagenham*) 20, K. Searle (*Enfield*) 19. C. Proctor (*Kingstonian*) 19, D. Evans (*Wycombe Wanderers*) 18, A. Jackson (*Dulwich Hamlet*) 17, D. Baker (*Enfield*) 15, J. Baker (*Hendon*) 15, T. Brown (*Slough Town*) 15, J. Ritchie (*Staines Town*) 15, A. Hunter (*Walthamstow Avenue*) 15, S. Cosham (*Woking*) 15, A. Horseman (*Wycombe Wanderers*) 15, G. Dennis (*Sutton United*) 14.

DIVISION TWO
S. Atkins (*Chesham United*) 32, E. Whittington (*Horsham*) 25, A. Walker (*Carshalton Athletic*) 21, G. Gilbert (*Harrow Borough*) 20, G. Tibbals (*Ware*) 20, G. Allen (*Carshalton Athletic*) 18, A. Coppin (*Hampton*) 18, J. Griffith (*Walton & Hersham*) 18, D. Hutchins (*Hampton*) 17, A. Noonan (*Hornchurch*) 17, B. Merron (*Croydon*) 16, B. Walder (*Tilbury*) 16, M. O'Donoghue (*St. Albans City*) 15, V. Cotter (*Tilbury*) 15, C. Duggan (*Boreham Wood*) 14, R. Robinson (*Harwich & Parkeston*) 14.

Rothmans Northern League 1975-76 Total Sponsorship Awards

League Position		League awards £	Goal-scoring awards £	Sportsman-ship awards £	Three goal awards £	TOTAL £
1	Blyth	1000	—	211.95	400	1611.95
2	Willington	500	—	181.66	320	1001.66
3	Spennymoor	300	—	211.95	280	791.95
5	Tow Law	—	300	242.23	240	782.23
4	Bishop Auckland	—	100	90.83	240	430.83
9	Consett	—	—	242.23	120	362.23
8	North Shields	—	—	121.11	240	361.11
6	Whitby	—	—	—	320	320.00
14	Billingham	—	—	211.95	80	291.95
7	Ashington	—	—	90.83	200	290.83
19	South Bank	—	—	211.95	40	251.95
16	Shildon	—	—	121.11	80	201.11
17	Whitley Bay	—	—	90.83	80	170.83
15	Crook	—	—	—	160	160.00
10	Evenwood	—	—	30.29	120	150.29
13	Durham	—	—	90.83	40	130.83
12	Penrith	—	—	—	120	120.00
18	Ferryhill	—	—	—	40	40.00
11	Horden	—	—	30.27	—	30.27
20	West Auckland	—	—	—	—	—

Poskett (*Whitby Town*) 33, Ogden (*Willington*) 24, Slane (*Blyth Spartans*) 23, Banks (*Spennymoor*) 22, Shoulder (*Bishop Auckland*) 21, Hart (*Spennymoor*) 21, Mills (*West Auckland*) 19, Holden (*Willington*) 18, Parkinson (*Consett*) 17, Jones (*Tow Law*) 17, Cochrane (*Willington*) 16, Dixon (*Ashington*) 15.

Rothmans Western League 1975-76 Total Sponsorship Awards

League Position		League awards £	Goal-scoring awards £	Sportsman-ship awards £	Three goal awards £	TOTAL £
1	Falmouth Town	1000	—	201.81	640	1,841.81
2	Taunton Town	500	—	115.32	480	1,095.32
6	Barnstaple Toen	—	300	144.15	360	804.15
19	Devizes Town	—	—	230.64	160	390.64
12	Exeter City	—	—	144.15	240	384.15
4	Bridgwater Town	—	100	28.83	240	368.83
15	Westland Yeovil	—	—	201.81	160	361.81
11	Frome Town	—	—	172.98	160	332.98
9	Mangotsfield United	—	—	201.81	120	321.81
20	Chippenham Town	—	—	115.32	200	315.32
14	Weston-Super-Mare	—	—	115,32	200	315.32
17	Bridport	—	—	172.98	120	292.98
5	Glastonbury	—	—	—	280	280.00
21	Melksham Town	—	—	172.98	40	212.98
13	St. Lukes College	—	—	86.49	120	206.49
18	Dawlish	—	—	115.32	80	195.32
7	Tiverton Town	—	—	28.83	160	188.83
23	Exmouth Town	—	—	144.15	40	184.15
8	Paulton Rovers	—	—	57.66	120	177.66
10	Bideford	—	—	—	160	160.00
3	Clevedon	—	—	—	160	160.00
22	Keynsham Town	—	—	—	160	160.00
16	Welton Rovers	—	—	—	160	160.00

Rothmans Hellenic League Premier Division

PREMIER DIV.SiON

League Position		League awards £	Goal-scoring awards £	Sportsman-ship awards £	Three goal awards £	TOTAL £
1	Burnham	500.00	—	173,28	220.00	893.28
4	Forest Green	—	150,00	202.16	140.00	492.16
13	Pinehurst	—	—	231.04	60.00	291.04
3	Clanfield	—	—	144.40	80.00	224.40
7	Hungerford Town	—	—	144.40	80.00	224.40
12	Cirencester	—	—	144.40	20.00	164.40
14	Didcot Town	—	—	144.40	20.00	164.40
8	Thame Utd.	—	—	86.64	40.00	126.64
9	Thatcham Town	—	—	28.88	20.00	48.88
2	Moreton Town	—	—	—	80.00	80.00
5	Newbury Town	—	—	—	60.00	60.00
6	Chipping Norton	—	—	—	40.00	40.00
10	Stratford Town	—	—	—	40.00	40.00
16	Bicester Town	—	—	—	20.00	20.00
11	Wallingford Town	—	—	—	20.00	20.00
15	Wantage Town	—	—	—	—	—

Rothmans Hellenic Premier Division Leading Goalscorers (*League games only*)

J. Evans (*Forest Green*) 24, K. Prue (*Forest Green*) 18, J. Harris (*Burnham*) 14, M. Palmer (*Hungerford T.*) 14, J. Rose (*Ch. Norton T.*) 14, L. Wenban (*Cirencester T.*) 14, N. Hiscock (*Pinehurst*) 13, C. Josey (*Thatcham T.*) 13, G. Medcroft (*Forest Green*) 11, E. Nicklin (*Moreton T.*) 11, M. Green (*Moreton T.*) 10, D. Ingram (*Newbury T.*) 10, F. Hughes (*Burnham*) 10.

Rothmans Guernsey Priaulx League

	P	W	D	L	F	A	Pts.	C	D
Vale Rec.	21	19	2	0	91	21	59	5	0
St. Martin's	21	16	2	3	69	17	50	7	0
Belgraves	21	11	2	8	54	39	35	3	4
Northerners	21	10	4	7	45	42	34	2	4
Rangers	21	6	5	10	36	46	23	0	0
Sylvans	21	5	6	10	39	63	21	3	0
Centrals	21	2	3	16	22	82	9	4	4
Rovers	21	2	2	17	21	67	8	4	0

Leading goalscorers:
Nigel Le Page (*Vale Rec.*) 25; Brian Robson (*St. Martin's*) 18; Alan Bougourd (*Vale Rec.*) 15; Ray Blondel (*Vale Rec.*) 14; Rodney Webb (*North*) 14; Peter Allen (*Belgraves*) 13; Phil Brehaut (*Rangers*) 13; Colin Fallaize (*North*) 12; Colin Reeve (*Belgraves*) 11; Alan Le Moury (*Sylvans*) 11; Andy McMillan (*Belgraves*) 10.

Rothmans Jersey Football Combination

DIVISION ONE

	P	W	D	L	F	A	Pts.	C	D
First Tower United	18	15	2	1	44	11	47	2	4
St. Ouens F.C.	18	10	3	5	35	23	33	1	0
St. Paul's F.C.	18	9	3	6	35	29	30	0	4
Georgetown S.C.	18	9	1	8	39	29	28	0	0
St. Peter F.C.	18	7	7	4	27	25	28	0	0
Oaklands F.C.	18	6	6	6	33	34	24	1	4
Trinity F.C.	18	5	5	8	24	29	20	1	4
Beeches O.B.	18	6	2	10	25	29	20	0	4
Old Victorians	18	5	0	13	20	46	15	0	0
Grouville F.C.	18	2	3	13	25	52	9	0	0

Leading goalscorers:
A. Baillie (*St. Ouens F.C.*) 14, P. Dunford (*Georgetown S.C.*) 11, R. Crick (*First Tower*) 10, B. Pitman (*First Tower*) 10, J. McKenna (*St. Paul's*) 10, R. Pollock (*Oaklands*) 10.

Rothmans Inter-League Representative Tournament

Hellenic League	3	Western League	0
Northern League	2	Western League	1
Northern League	2	Hellenic League	0

	P	W	D	L	F	A	Pts.
Northern League	2	2	0	0	4	1	4
Hellenic League	2	1	0	1	3	2	2
Western League	2	0	0	2	1	5	0

Channel Islands touring party selected from the above leagues: Mr. A. Harrison (RNL), Mr. S. Bradley (RNL), Mr. L. Phillips (RWL), Mr. N. Matthews (RHL), A. Hickman (*Spennymoor U*) captain, C. Palmer (*Hungerford T*), I. Harrison (*Blyth Spartans*), B. Perrett (*Glastonbury*), S. Foster (*Hungerford T*), C. Hallimond (*Evenwood T*), A. Hurford (*Bridgwater T*), Ray Shinners (*St. Lukes College*), Gavin Brown (*Hungerford T*), K. Houghton (*North Shields*), John Meggett (*Frome T*), J. Kelman (*Newbury T*), C. Shepherd (*Moreton T*), T. Holden (*Willington*), Mike Jordan (*Exeter C*), K. Reilly (*Spennymoor U*).

Rothmans National XI 3   Rothmans Jersey Football Combination 1

Rothmans JFC: Matthews (D), Blampied (J), A'Court, Cooper (M), Corfield, Gasston (W), Le Cornu, Guegan, Addison, Watson, Pitman (B).
Subs: O'Boyle and Appleton.

Scorer: Addison

Rothmans National XI: Palmer, Foster, Perrett, Hallimond, Hickman, Meggett, Shepherd, Houghton, Reilly, Jordan, Holden.
Subs: Kelman, Shinners.

Scorers: Holden, Shepherd, Hallimond.

Rothmans National XI 3   Rothmans Priaulx League 1

Rothmans Priaulx League: Hamon, Reid, P. Blondel, Rowe, Pollock, R. Brehaut (C. Le Page), Thoume, Graham, Fallaize, Webb (Queripel), Bougourd.

Scorer: Bougourd.

Rothmans National XI: Palmer (*Hungerford*), Harrison (*Blyth Spartans*), Hurford (*Bridgwater*), Shinners (*St. Lukes College*), Hickman (*Spennymoor*), Houghton (*North Shields*), Kelman (*Newbury*), Brown (*Hungerford*), Holden (*Willington*), Jordan (*Exeter*), Reilly (*Spennymoor*),
Subs: Foster (*Hungerford*), Hallimond (*Evenwood*).

Scorers: Holden 2, Hallimond.

Basic Sponsorship Awards for Rothmans Football League Season 1976-77

Prize Money

	Champions	Second	Third
Division 1 RIL, North & West (Premier Division)	£1000	£500	£300
Division 2 RIL	£500	£250	£150
Rothmans Hellenic League	£500	£200	
Rothmans Western League (Division One)	£400	£150	
Rothmans Jersey Football Combination	£300		
Rothmans Priaulx League (Guernsey)	£200	£100	

Clubs with most goals in a season who had not won league prize money

	Highest Scorers	Second Highest	Third Highest
Division 1 RIL, North & West (Premier Division)	£300	£200	£100
Division 2 RIL	£150	£100	£50
Rothmans Hellenic League	£150	£100	
Rothmans Western League (Division One)	£125	£75	
Rothmans Jersey Football Combination	£100		
Rothmans Guernsey Priaulx	£100		

Sportsmanship Pool

Division 1 RIL, Northern & Western (Premier Division)	£2000
Division 2 RIL	£1000
Rothmans Hellenic League	£1000
Rothmans Western League (Division One)	£750
Rothmans Jersey Combination	£500
Rothmans Guernsey Priaulx League	£500

Teams will lose four points if a player is sent off, and one point if a player is cautioned. If a team loses eight points or more in the course of a season it will not qualify for a share of the Sportsmanship Pool or prize money as shown above.

Match by Match Incentives—Victories by Three Clear Goals

Division 1 RIL, Northern & Western (Premier Division)	£40
Division 2 RIL	£25
Rothmans Western League (Division One)	£17·50
Rothmans Hellenic League	£20
Rothmans Jersey Football Combination and Rothmans Guernsey Praiulx League	£10

Three points are awarded for a win, and one for a draw in all sponsored Leagues.

UEFA YOUTH TOURNAMENT 1975-76

GROUP A

			Final Table						
Wales	v Yugoslavia	2-1		P	W	D	L	F	A	Pts
Hungary	v Italy	2-1	Hungary	3	2	—	1	6	5	4
Italy	v Yugoslavia	2-1	Wales	3	2	—	1	3	2	4
Hungary	v Wales	1-0	Yugoslavia	3	1	—	2	6	7	2
Yugoslavia	v Hungary	4-3	Italy	3	1	—	2	3	4	2
Wales	v Italy	1-0								

GROUP B

			Final Table						
Spain	v Turkey	2-0		P	W	D	L	F	A	Pts
Switzerland	v Iceland	0-0	Spain	3	2	1	—	5	0	5
Turkey	v Iceland	0-0	Switzerland	3	1	2	—	1	0	4
Spain	v Switzerland	0-0	Iceland	3	—	2	1	0	3	2
Spain	v Iceland	3-0	Turkey	3	—	1	2	0	3	1
Switzerland	v Turkey	1-0								

GROUP C

			Final Table						
W. Germany	v Finland	2-1		P	W	D	L	F	A	Pts
France	v Czechoslovakia	2-1	France	3	2	1	—	5	1	5
France	v W. Germany	3-0	W. Germany	3	2	—	1	5	6	4
Czechoslovakia	v Finland	1-0	Czechoslovakia	3	1	—	2	4	5	2
W. Germany	v Czechoslovakia	3-2	Finland	3	—	1	2	1	3	1
France	v Finland	0-0								

GROUP D

			Final Table						
USSR	v Holland	3-0		P	W	D	L	F	A	Pts
Denmark	v N. Ireland	5-3	USSR	3	3	—	—	8	0	6
Holland	v N. Ireland	3-0	Denmark	3	2	—	1	8	7	4
USSR	v Denmark	3-0	Holland	3	1	—	2	4	6	2
Denmark	v Holland	3-1	N. Ireland	3	—	—	3	3	10	—
USSR	v N. Ireland	2-0								

SEMI-FINALS

Hungary	v France	1-1

(Hungary win on penalties)

USSR	v Spain	3-0

THIRD PLACE PLAY-OFF

Spain	v France	3-0

FINAL

USSR	v Hungary	1-0

UEFA YOUTH TOURNAMENT FINALS 1948-76

Year	Winners		Runners-up		Venue
1948	England	3	Netherlands	2	London
1949	France	4	Netherlands	1	Rotterdam
1950	Austria	3	France	2	Vienna
1951	Yugoslavia	3	Austria	2	Cannes
1952	*Spain	0	Belgium	0	Barcelona
1953	Hungary	2	Yugoslavia	0	Brussels
1954	*Spain	2	West Germany	2	Cologne
1955-56	Played in groups only				
1957	Austria	3	Spain	2	Madrid
1958	Italy	1	England	0	Luxembourg
1959	Bulgaria	1	Italy	0	Sofia
1960	Hungary	2	Rumania	1	Vienna
1961	Portugal	4	Poland	0	Lisbon
1962	Rumania	4	Yugoslavia	1	Bucharest
1963	England	4	Northern Ireland	0	London
1964	England	4	Spain	0	Amsterdam
1965	East Germany	3	England	2	Essen
1966	†Italy	0	USSR	0	Belgrade
1967	U.S.S.R.	1	England	0	Istanbul
1968	Czechoslovakia	2	France	1	Cannes
1969	*Bulgaria	1	East Germany	1	Leipzig
1970	*East Germany	1	Holland	1	Glasgow
1971	England	3	Portugal	0	Prague
1972	England	2	West Germany	0	Barcelona
1973	England	3	East Germany	2	Florence
1974	Bulgaria	1	Yugoslavia	0	Malmoe
1975	England	1	Finland	0	Berne
1976	U.S.S.R.	1	Hungary	0	Budapest

* Won on toss of a coin   † Joint holders.

ENGLISH YOUTH INTERNATIONAL MATCHES 1975-76

February 11 1976

Wales 0

England 1 (*Langley*)   860

England: Richardson; Kerslake, Owens, Curbishley, McCaffery, Walford, Hoddle, Deehan, Patching, Langley, Owen.

March 3 1976

England 2 (*Deehan, Langley*)

Wales 3   1168

England: Richardson; Kerslake, Owens, Reeves, McCaffery, Martin, Hoddle, Deehan, Patching, Langley (Geddis), Owen.

YOUTH INTERNATIONAL MATCHES 1947-76

ENGLAND v SCOTLAND	Eng-land	Scot-land
1947 Oct. 25 Doncaster	4	2
1948 Oct. 30 Aberdeen	1	3
UYT1949 April 21 Utrecht	0	1
1950 Feb. 4 Carlisle	7	1
1951 Feb. 3 Kilmarnock	6	1
1952 Mar. 15 Sunderland	3	1
1953 Feb. 7 Glasgow	4	3
1954 Feb. 6 Middlesbrough	2	1
1955 Mar. 5 Kilmarnock	3	4
1956 Mar. 3 Preston	2	2
1957 Mar. 9 Aberdeen	3	1
1958 Mar. 1 Hull	2	0
1959 Feb. 28 Aberdeen	1	1
1960 Feb. 27 Newcastle	1	1
1961 Feb. 25 Elgin	3	2
1962 Feb. 24 Peterborough	4	2
*UYT1963 April 19 White City	1	0
1963 May 18 Dumfries	3	1
1964 Feb. 22 Middlesbrough	1	1
1965 Feb. 27 Inverness	1	2
1966 Feb. 5 Hereford	5	3
1967 Feb. 4 Aberdeen	0	1
*UYT1967 Mar. 1 Southampton	1	0
*UYT1967 Mar. 15 Dundee	0	0
1968 Feb. 3 Walsall	0	5
1969 Feb. 1 Stranraer	1	1
1970 Jan. 31 Derby	1	2
1971 Jan. 30 Greenock	1	2
1972 Jan. 30 Bournemouth	2	0
1973 Jan. 20 Kilmarnock	3	2
1974 Jan. 26 Brighton	2	2

ENGLAND v WALES	Eng-land	Wales
1948 Feb. 28 High Wycombe	4	2
UYT1948 April 15 Shepherds Bush	4	0
1949 Feb. 26 Swansea	0	0
1950 Feb. 25 Worcester	1	0
1951 Feb. 17 Wrexham	1	1
1952 Feb. 23 Plymouth	6	0
1953 Feb. 21 Swansea	4	2
1954 Feb. 20 Derby	2	1
1955 Feb. 19 Milford Haven	7	2

	Eng-land	Scot-land
1956 Feb. 18 Shrewsbury	5	1
1957 Feb. 9 Cardiff	7	1
1958 Feb. 15 Reading	8	2
1959 Feb. 14 Portmadoc	3	0
1960 Mar. 19 Canterbury	1	1
1961 Mar. 18 Newtown	4	0
1962 Mar. 17 Swindon	4	0
1963 Mar. 16 Haverfordwest	1	0
1964 Mar. 15 Leeds	2	1
1965 Mar. 20 Newport	2	2
1966 Mar. 19 Northampton	4	1
1967 Mar. 18 Cwmbran	3	3
1968 Mar. 16 Watford	2	3
1969 Mar. 15 Haverfordwest	3	1
*UYT1970 Feb. 25 Newport	0	0
*UYT1970 Mar. 18 Leyton	1	2
1970 April 20 Reading	0	0
1971 Feb. 20 Aberystwyth	1	2
1972 Feb. 19 Swindon	4	0
1973 Feb. 24 Portmadoc	4	1
*UYT1974 Jan. 9 West Bromwich	1	0
1974 Mar. 2 Shrewsbury	2	1
*UYT1974 Mar. 13 Cardiff	0	1
UYT1976 Feb. 11 Cardiff	1	0
UYT1976 Mar. 3 Maine Rd.	2	3

ENGLAND v IRELAND	Eng-land	Ire-land
1948 May 15 Belfast	2	2
UYT 1949 April 18 Haarlem	3	3
1949 May 14 Hull	4	2
1950 May 6 Belfast	0	1
1951 May 5 Liverpool	5	2
1952 April 19 Belfast	0	2
1953 April 11 Wolverhampton	0	0
UYT1954 April 10 Bruehl	5	0
1954 May 8 Newtownards	2	2
1955 May 14 Watford	3	0
1956 May 12 Belfast	0	1
1957 May 1 Leyton	6	2
1958 May 10 Bangor	2	4
1959 May 9 Liverpool	5	0

UYT UEFA Youth Tournament.   † Abandoned.   * Professionals.

Year	Date	Venue	Goals	
1960	May 14	Portadown	5	2
1961	May 13	Manchester	2	0
1962	May 12	Londonderry	1	2
*UYT1963	April 23	Wembley	4	0
1963	May 11	Oldham	1	1
1964	Jan. 25	Belfast	3	1
1965	Jan. 22	Birkenhead	2	3
1966	Feb. 26	Belfast	4	0
1967	Feb. 25	Stockport	3	0
1968	Feb. 23	Belfast	0	2
1969	Feb. 28	Birkenhead	0	2
1970	Feb. 28	Lurgan	1	3
1971	Mar. 6	Blackpool	1	1
1972	Mar. 11	Chester	1	1
UYT1972	May 17	Sabadell	4	0
1973	Mar. 24	Telford	3	0
1974	April 19	Birkenhead	1	2
*UYT1975	May 13	Kriens	3	0

ENGLAND v AUSTRIA

			England	Austria
UYT1949	April 19	Zeist	4	2
UYT1952	April 17	Barcelona	5	5
UYT1957	April 16	Barcelona	0	3
1958	Mar. 4	Highbury	3	2
1958	June 1	Graz	4	3
UYT1960	April 20	Vienna	0	1
*UYT1964	April 1	Rotterdam	2	1

ENGLAND v BELGIUM

			England	Belgium
UYT1948	April 16	West Ham	3	1
UYT1951	Mar. 22	Cannes	1	1
UYT1953	Mar. 31	Brussels	2	0
†1956	Nov. 7	Brussels	3	2
1957	Nov. 13	Sheffield	2	0
*UYT1965	April 15	Ludwigshafen	3	0
*UYT1969	Mar. 11	West Ham	1	0
*·UYT1969	Mar. 26	Waregem	2	0
UYT1972	May 13	Palma	0	0
*UYT1973	June 4	Viareggio	0	0

ENGLAND v BULGARIA

			England	Bulgaria
UYT1956	Mar. 28	Salgotarjan	1	2
UYT1960	April 16	Graz	0	1
UYT1962	April 24	Ploesti	0	0
*UYT1968	April 7	Nimes	0	0

ENGLAND v CZECHOSLOVAKIA

			England	Czechoslovakia
UYT1955	April 7	Lucca	0	1
*UYT1966	May 21	Rijeka	2	3
*UYT1969	May 20	Leipzig	3	1

ENGLAND v DENMARK

			England	Denmark
*1955	Oct. 1	Plymouth	9	2
1956	May 20	Esbjerg	2	1

ENGLAND v FINLAND

			England	Finland
*UYT1975	May 19	Berne	1	0

ENGLAND v FRANCE

Year	Date	Venue	Goals	
			England	France
1957	Mar. 24	Fontainebleau	1	0
1958	Mar. 22	Eastbourne	0	1
*UYT1966	May 23	Rijeka	1	2
*UYT1967	May 11	Istanbul	2	0
*1968	Jan. 25	Paris	0	1

ENGLAND v EAST GERMANY

			England	East Germany
UYT1958	April 7	Neunkirchen	1	0
1959	Mar. 8	Zwickau	3	4
1960	April 2	Portsmouth	1	1
*UYT1965	April 25	Essen	2	3
*UYT1969	May 22	Magdeburg	0	4
*UYT1973	June 10	Florence	3	2

ENGLAND v WEST GERMANY

			England	West Germany
UYT1953	April 4	Boom	3	1
UYT1954	April 15	Gelsenkirchen	2	2
UYT1956	April 1	Sztalinvaros	2	1
1957	Mar. 31	Oberhausen	4	1
1958	Mar. 12	Bolton	1	2
1961	Mar. 12	Flensberg	0	2
*1962	Mar. 31	Northampton	1	0
*1967	Feb. 14	Moenchengladbach	1	0
UYT1972	May 22	Barcelona	2	0
1975	Jan. 25	Las Palmas	4	2

ENGLAND v GREECE

			England	Greece
UYT1957	April 18	Barcelona	2	3
UYT1959	April 2	Dimitrovo	4	0

ENGLAND v HUNGARY

			England	Hungary
UYT1954	April 11	Dusseldorf	1	3
UYT1956	Mar. 31	Tatabanya	2	4
*1956	Oct. 23	Tottenham	2	1
*1956	Oct. 25	Sunderland	2	1
*UYT1965	April 21	Wuppertal	5	0
*UYT1975	May 16	Olten	3	1

ENGLAND v ICELAND

			England	Iceland
*UYT1973	May 31	Viareggio	2	0

ENGLAND v REPUBLIC OF IRELAND

			England	Rep. of Ireland
UYT1953	April 5	Leuven	2	0
*UYT1964	Mar. 30	Middelburg	6	0
*UYT1968	Feb. 7	Dublin	0	0
*UYT1968	Feb. 28	Portsmouth	4	1
*UYT1970	Jan. 14	Dublin	4	1
*UYT1970	Feb. 4	Luton	10	0
*UYT1975	May 9	Brunnen	1	0

ENGLAND v ISRAEL

			England	Israel
*1962	May 20	Tel Aviv	3	1
*1962	May 22	Haifa	1	2

ENGLAND v ITALY

Year	Date	Venue	England	Italy
UYT1958	April 13	Luxembourg	0	1
UYT1959	Mar. 25	Sofia	0	3
UYT1961	April 4	Braga	2	3
*UYT1965	April 23	Marl-Huels	3	1
*UYT1966	May 25	Rijeka	1	1
*UYT1967	May 5	Izmir	1	0
1973	Feb. 14	Cava dei Tirreni	0	1
1973	Mar. 14	Highbury	1	0
*UYT1973	June 6	Viareggio	1	0

ENGLAND v LUXEMBOURG

Year	Date	Venue	England	Luxembourg
UYT1950	May 25	Vienna	1	2
UYT1954	April 17	Bad Neuenahr	0	2
1957	Feb. 2	West Ham	7	1
1957	Nov. 17	Luxembourg	3	0
UYT1958	April 9	Eschsalzette	5	0

ENGLAND v MALTA

Year	Date	Venue	England	Malta
*UYT1969	May 18	Wolfen	6	0

ENGLAND v NETHERLANDS

Year	Date	Venue	England	Netherlands
UYT1948	April 17	Tottenham	3	2
UYT1951	Mar. 26	Cannes	2	1
*1954	Nov. 21	Arnhem	2	3
*1955	Nov. 5	Norwich	3	1
1957	Mar. 2	Brentford	5	5
UYT1957	April 14	Barcelona	1	2
1957	Oct. 2	Amsterdam	3	2
1961	Mar. 9	Utrecht	0	1
*1962	Jan. 31	Brighton	4	3
UYT1962	April 22	Ploesti	0	3
*UYT1963	April 13	Wimbledon	5	0
*UYT1968	April 9	Nimes	1	0
*UYT1974	Feb. 13	West Bromwich	1	1
*UYT1974	Feb. 27	The Hague	1	0

ENGLAND v POLAND

Year	Date	Venue	England	Poland
UYT1960	April 18	Graz	4	2
*UYT1964	Mar. 26	Breda	1	1
*UYT1971	May 26	Presov	0	0
UYT1972	May 20	Valencia	1	0
1975	Jan. 21	Las Palmas	1	1

ENGLAND v PORTUGAL

Year	Date	Venue	England	Portugal
UYT1954	April 18	Bonn	0	2
UYT1961	April 2	Lisbon	0	4
*UYT1964	April 3	The Hague	4	0
*UYT1971	May 30	Prague	3	0

ENGLAND v RUMANIA

Year	Date	Venue	England	Rumania
1957	Oct. 15	Tottenham	4	2
UYT1958	April 11	Luxembourg	1	0
UYT1959	Mar. 31	Pazardjic	1	2
*UYT1963	April 15	Highbury	3	0

ENGLAND v SAAR

Year	Date	Venue	England	Saar
UYT1954	April 13	Dortmund	1	1
UYT1955	April 9	Prato	3	1

ENGLAND v SPAIN

Year	Date	Venue	England	Spain
UYT1952	April 15	Barcelona	1	4
1957	Sept. 26	Birmingham	4	4
UYT1958	April 5	Saarbrucken	2	2
*1958	Oct. 8	Madrid	4	2
UYT1961	Mar. 30	Lisbon	0	0
*1964	Feb. 27	Murcia	2	1
*UYT1964	April 5	Amsterdam	4	0
*UYT1965	April 17	Heilbronn	0	0
*1966	Mar. 30	Swindon	3	0
*UYT1967	May 7	Manisa	2	1
*1971	Mar. 31	Pamplona	2	3
*1971	April 20	Luton	1	1
1972	Feb. 9	Alicante	0	0
1972	Mar. 15	Sheffield	4	1
*UYT1975	Feb. 25	Bristol	1	1
*UYT1975	Mar. 18	Madrid	1	0

ENGLAND v SWEDEN

Year	Date	Venue	England	Sweden
*UYT1971	May 24	Poprad	1	0

ENGLAND v SWITZERLAND

Year	Date	Venue	England	Switzerland
UYT1950	May 26	Stockerau	2	1
UYT1951	Mar. 27	Nice	3	1
UYT1952	April 13	Barcelona	4	0
UYT1955	April 11	Florence	0	0
1956	Mar. 11	Schaffhausen	2	0
1956	Oct. 13	Brighton	2	2
1958	May 26	Zurich	3	0
*1960	Oct. 8	Leyton	4	3
*†1962	Nov. 22	Coventry	1	0
*1963	Mar. 21	Bienne	7	1
*UYT1973	June 2	Forte dei Marim	2	0
*UYT1975	May 11	Buochs	4	0

ENGLAND v TURKEY

Year	Date	Venue	England	Turkey
UYT1959	Mar. 29	Dimitrovo	1	1

ENGLAND v USSR

Year	Date	Venue	England	USSR
*UYT1963	April 17	Tottenham	2	0
*UYT1967	May 13	Istanbul	0	1
*UYT1968	April 11	Nimes	1	1
*UYT1971	May 28	Prague	1	1

ENGLAND v YUGOSLAVIA

Year	Date	Venue	England	Yugoslavia
UYT1953	April 2	Liege	1	1
1958	Feb. 4	Chelsea	2	2
UYT1962	April 20	Ploesti	0	5
*UYT1967	May 9	Izmir	1	1
*UYT1971	May 22	Bardejor	1	0
UYT1972	May 18	Barcelona	1	0

FA YOUTH CHALLENGE CUP 1975-76

First Round Qualifying

New Hartley Jun. v Annfield Plain	3-0
North Shields v Whitley Bay	1-3
Gateshead U. v Farsley Celtic	3-1
Nunthorpe Ath. v Yorkshire Am.	2-0
Leeds Ashley R. v G. Harwood	3-1
Rochdale v Skelmersdale U.	16-1
Kirkby T. v Chester	2-1
Macclesfield T. v S. Liverpool	2-3
Lincoln U. v Lincoln C.	0-3
Louth U. v Spalding	10-1
Gorleston v Ely Crusaders	2-3
Parson Drove U. v Wisbech T.	0-5
Cambridge U. v Cambridge C.	2-6
Letchworth T. v March T. U.	2-1
Chingford v Chelmsford C.	4-3
Colchester U. v Edmonton & Haringey	8-0
Carlton v Bedmond	3-2
North Greenford U. v Barnet	2-0
The '61' v Wealdstone	4-0
Fareham T. v Camberley T.	3-4
Maidenhead U. v Staines T.	3-2
Hampton v Croydon	2-2, 0-5
Kingstonian v Welling U.	2-0
Horsham v Eastbourne T.	0-2
Ringmer v Tonbridge	
Tonbridge withdrawn, w.o. for Ringmer	
Folkestone & Shepway v Dover	0-3
Maidstone U. v Penhill Standard	0-0, 4-0
Exeter C. v Bath C.	2-4
Mangotsfield U. v Torquay U.	7-5
Gloucester C. v Cheltenham T.	1-4
AP Leamington v Worcester C.	
w.o. for Worcester City	
Coventry Sp. v Coalville T.	3-1
Valley Sports Rugby v Wigston Fields	2-5
Long Eaton U. v Aylestone Park Youth	2-4
Nuneaton Bor. v Sutton Coldfield T.	0-0, 0-1
Kidderminster H. v Hednesford	2-0
Oldswinford v West Bromwich YMCA	2-4

Second Round Qualifying

Whitley Bay v New Hartley Jun.	0-0, 1-2
Nunthorpe Ath. v Gateshead U.	2-1
Rochdale v Leeds Ashley R.	3-0
S. Liverpool v Kirkby T.	2-0
Louth U. v Lincoln C.	2-2, 3-1
Wisbech T. v Ely Crusaders	1-1, 3-5
Letchworth T. v Cambridge C.	3-3, 0-3
Colchester U. v Chingford	3-1
Icknield v Carlton	2-1
The '61' v North Greenford U.	2-4
Maidenhead U. v Camberley T.	0-6
Kingstonian v Croydon	1-6
Ringmer v Eastbourne T.	2-3
Maidstone U. v Dover	1-1, 0-1
Mangotsfield U. v Bath C.	4-6
Worcester C. v Cheltenham T.	1-2
Wigston Fields v Coventry Sp.	3-2
Sutton Coldfield T. v Aylestone Park Youth	1-2
West Bromwich YMCA v Kidderminster H.	2-1

First Round Proper

Consett v Nunthorpe Ath.	0-3
Hartlepool v New Hartley Jun.	1-3
Grimsby T. v Louth U.	5-1
York C. v Scunthorpe U.	2-0
Barnsley v Doncaster R.	3-0
Oldham Ath. v Bradford C.	1-0
Rochdale v Blackburn R.	0-1
Blackpool v Altrincham	3-0
Tranmere R. v Bolton W.	0-1
S. Liverpool v Wrexham	2-3
Manchester C. v Shrewsbury T.	3-0
Port Vale v Rotherham U.	0-1
Clifton v Mansfield T.	0-2
Leicester C. v Chesterfield	1-1, 1-2
West Bromwich YMCA v Wigston Fields	0-6
Aylestone Park Youth v Northfield Jun.	0-2

Hereford U. v Kettering T.	3-2
Cambridge C. v Peterborough U.	3-3, 1-3
Ely Crusaders v Norwich C.	0-0, 0-6
Q.P.R. v Watford	1-0
Southend U. v Colchester U.	1-0
Northampton T. v North Greenford U.	2-0
Oxford C. v Luton T.	1-3
Orient v Viking Sports	3-2
Eastbourne T. v Dover	0-0, 1-3
Fulham v Gillingham	6-3
Croydon v Portsmouth	2-0
Millwall v Brighton & H. A.	3-1
A.F.C. Bournemouth v Southampton	2-1
Camberley T. v Bognor Regis T.	3-0
Cardiff C. v Swindon T.	2-2, 3-4
Oxford U. v Bath C.	1-1, 1-5
Cheltenham T. v Swansea C.	3-1
Newport Co. v Bristol R.	2-1

Second Round

Middlesbrough v Nunthorpe Ath.	2-1
New Hartley Jun. v Sunderland	1-4
Newcastle U. v Barnsley	4-1
Hull C. v Leeds U.	0-1
York C. v Grimsby T.	0-3
Preston N. E. v Liverpool	1-2
Everton v Blackpool	2-1
Blackburn R. v Burnley	0-0, 2-1
Bolton W. v Wrexham	2-0
Manchester C. v Oldham Ath.	1-2
Sheffield W. v Nottingham F.	1-1, 0-1
Manchester U. v Derby Co.	4-0
Mansfield T. v Chesterfield	5-1
Huddersfield T. v Stoke C.	2-0
Rotherham U. v Sheffield U.	3-1
Hereford U. v Swindon T.	2-4
Northampton T. v Wigston Fields	1-2
Cheltenham T. v Northfield Jun.	1-0
Birmingham C. v Wolverhampton W.	1-1, 1-2
Oxford U. v Aston Villa	0-1
W.B.A. v Coventry C.	3-0
Tottenham H. v Peterborough U.	6-0
Orient v Norwich C.	0-3
Arsenal v Luton T.	7-0
Ipswich T. v West Ham U.	1-0
Q.P.R. v Southend U.	1-1, 2-1
Millwall v Camberley T.	2-0
Fulham v Dover	5-1
Crystal Palace v Croydon	6-1
Charlton Ath. v Chelsea	2-1
A.F.C. Bournemouth v Newport Co.	1-1, 1-2
Bristol C. v Plymouth Arg.	2-0

Third Round

Huddersfield T. v Mansfield T.	1-0
Everton v Oldham Ath.	1-2
Rotherham U. v Bolton W.	1-0
Manchester U. v Grimsby T.	8-0
Blackburn R. v Liverpool	0-0, 2-2, 0-3
Leeds U. v Sunderland	1-1, 0-1
Middlesbrough v Newcastle U.	2-3
Q.P.R. v Nottingham F.	2-0
Fulham v Wolverhampton W.	1-1, 2-3
Norwich C. v Tottenham H.	3-3, 0-2
W.B.A. v Charlton Ath.	3-1
Ipswich T. v Millwall	4-0
Crystal Palace v Aston Villa	1-0
Bristol C. v Swindon T.	4-2
Cheltenham T. v Newport Co.	1-3
Arsenal v Wigston Fields	4-1

Fourth Round

Manchester U. v Rotherham U.	5-0
Sunderland v Bristol C.	2-2, 2-6
W.B.A. v Ipswich T.	1-1, 2-1
Newport Co. v Newcastle U.	1-2
Tottenham H. v Wolverhampton W.	2-2, 0-4
Oldham Ath. v Liverpool	3-0
Huddersfield T. v Q.P.R.	1-2
Arsenal v Crystal Palace	0-2

FA YOUTH CHALLENGE CUP 1975-76—*continued*

Fifth Round

W.B.A. v Manchester U.	2-2, 4-1
Q.P.R. v Wolverhampton W.	0-1
Crystal Palace v Oldham Ath.	2-1
Bristol C. v Newcastle U.	1-1, 1-6

Semi-finals (2 legs)

W.B.A. v Crystal Palace	3-2, 2-0
Newcastle U. v Wolverhampton W.	1-2, 1-2

Final (2 legs)

W.B.A. v Wolverhampton W.	2-0, 3-0

F.A. YOUTH CHALLENGE CUP 1953-76

Year	Winners	Runners-up	Score
1953	Manchester United	Wolverhampton Wanderers	7-2, 2-2
1954	Manchester United	Wolverhampton Wanderers	4-4, 1-0
1955	Manchester United	West Bromwich Albion	4-1, 3-0
1956	Manchester United	Chesterfield	3-2, 1-1
1957	Manchester United	West Ham United	3-2, 4-0
1958	Wolverhampton Wanderers	Chelsea	1-5, 6-1
1959	Blackburn Rovers	West Ham United	1-1, 1-0
1960	Chelsea	Preston North End	1-1, 4-1
1961	Chelsea	Everton	4-1, 1-2
1962	Newcastle United	Wolverhampton Wanderers	1-1, 1-0
1963	West Ham United	Liverpool	1-3, 5-2
1964	Manchester United	Swindon Town	1-1, 4-1
1965	Everton	Arsenal	0-1, 3-1
1966	Arsenal	Sunderland	1-2, 4-1
1967	Sunderland	Birmingham City	1-0, 1-0
1968	Burnley	Coventry City	1-2, 2-0
1969	Sunderland	West Bromwich Albion	0-3, 6-0
1970	Tottenham Hotspur	Coventry City	1-0, 0-1, 2-2, 1-0
1971	Arsenal	Cardiff City	0-0, 2-0
1972	Aston Villa	Liverpool	0-3, 4-2
1973	Ipswich Town	Bristol City	3-0, 1-1
1974	Tottenham Hotspur	Huddersfield Town	1-1, 1-0
1975	Ipswich Town	West Ham United	3-1, 2-0
1976	W.B.A.	Wolverhampton Wanderers	2-0, 3-0

F.A. COUNTY YOUTH CHALLENGE CUP 1975-76

First Round

Cumberland v Westmorland	3-3
Westmorland v Cumberland	2-1
North Riding v West Riding	0-1
Liverpool v Sheffield & Hallamshire	1-2
Lincolnshire v Nottinghamshire	5-0
Cheshire v Shropshire	2-0
Staffordshire v Birmingham	2-3
Suffolk v Huntingdonshire	0-1
Cambridgeshire v Hertfordshire	2-0
Kent v Surrey	2-4
Sussex v Royal Navy	3-1
Northamptonshire v Oxfordshire	2-0
Gloucestershire v Somerset	2-5
Herefordshire v Wiltshire	1-6
Devon v Cornwall	4-2

Second Round

Northumberland v Durham	3-1
Westmorland v Lancashire	2-4
Manchester v Cheshire	2-1
West Riding v Sheffield & Hallamshire	0-8
East Riding v Lincolnshire	0-1
Derbyshire v Birmingham	1-2
Leicestershire v Worcestershire	3-1
Northamptonshire v Bedfordshire	2-0
Huntingdonshire v Berk & Bucks	2-1
Norfolk v Cambridgeshire	1-2
Essex v London	1-0

Middlesex v Army	1-2
Surrey v Sussex	5-1
Wiltshire v R.A.F.	3-1
Hampshire v Dorset	2-0
Somerset v Devon	2-1

Third Round

Lancashire v Northumberland	4-5
Manchester v Sheffield	0-1
Leicestershire v Lincolnshire	1-2
Birmingham v Northamptonshire	0-3
Huntingdonshire v Cambridgeshire	1-3
Essex v Surrey	0-5
Hampshire v Army	1-2
Somerset v Wiltshire	1-3

Fourth Round

Sheffield & Hallamshire v Northumberland	2-0
Lincolnshire v Northamptonshire	0-2
Surrey v Cambridgeshire	2-0
Army v Wiltshire	3-4

Semi-finals

Northamptonshire v Sheffield & Hallamshire	4-3
Wiltshire v Surrey	1-4

Final

Surrey v Northamptonshire	1-7

813

THE SOUTHERN FOOTBALL LEAGUE 1975-76

PREMIER DIVISION

	P	W	D	L	F	A	Pts.
Wimbledon	42	26	10	6	74	29	62
Yeovil T.	42	21	12	9	68	35	54
Atherstone T.	42	18	15	9	56	55	51
Maidstone U.	42	17	16	9	52	39	50
Nuneaton Bor.	42	16	18	8	41	33	50
Gravesend & Northfleet	42	16	18	8	49	47	50
Grantham	42	15	14	13	56	47	44
Dunstable	42	17	9	16	52	43	43
Bedford T.	42	13	17	12	55	51	43
Burton Albion	42	17	9	16	52	53	43
Margate	42	15	12	15	62	60	42
Hillingdon Bor.	42	13	14	15	61	54	40
Telford U.	42	14	12	16	54	51	40
Chelmsford C.	42	13	14	15	52	57	40
Kettering T.	42	11	17	14	48	52	39
Bath C.	42	11	16	15	62	57	38
Weymouth	42	13	9	20	51	67	35
Dover	42	8	18	16	51	60	34
Wealdstone	42	12	9	21	61	82	33
Tonbridge A.F.C.	42	11	11	20	45	70	33
Cambridge C.	42	8	15	19	41	67	31
Stourbridge	42	10	9	23	38	72	29

FIRST DIVISION NORTH

	P	W	D	L	F	A	Pts.
Redditch U.	42	29	11	2	101	39	69
A.P. Leamington	42	27	10	5	85	31	64
Witney T.	42	24	9	9	66	40	57
Worcester C.	42	24	8	10	90	49	56
Cheltenham T.	42	20	10	12	87	55	50
Barry T.	42	19	10	13	52	47	48
King's Lynn	42	17	14	11	52	48	48
Tamworth	42	18	11	13	65	43	47
Barnet	42	15	12	15	56	56	42
Oswestry T.	42	16	8	18	63	71	40
Enderby T.	42	16	6	20	48	51	38
Banbury U.	42	15	8	19	58	67	38
Merthyr Tydfil	42	11	15	16	59	67	37
Bromsgrove R.	42	13	11	18	49	65	37
Milton Keynes C.	42	15	6	21	51	63	36
Bury T.	42	12	11	19	52	72	35
Gloucester C.	42	13	9	20	49	78	35
Kidderminster H.	42	13	8	21	54	70	34
Bedworth U.	42	8	18	16	41	66	34
Corby T.	42	11	10	21	50	65	32
Wellingborough T.	42	9	11	22	42	68	29
Stevenage Ath.	42	6	6	30	46	105	18

FIRST DIVISION SOUTH

	P	W	D	L	F	A	Pts.
Minehead	38	27	8	3	102	35	62
Dartford	38	26	4	8	84	46	56
Romford	38	21	9	8	66	37	51
Salisbury	38	17	11	10	73	53	45
Hastings U.	38	15	15	8	67	51	45
Poole T.	38	20	2	16	57	57	42
Bexley U.	38	14	13	11	62	53	41
Waterlooville	38	13	13	12	62	54	39
Basingstoke T.	38	13	12	13	69	71	38
Ashford T.	38	14	8	16	67	73	36
Canterbury C.	38	11	13	14	53	60	35
Folkestone & Shepway	38	10	14	14	36	51	34
Metropolitan Police	38	9	14	15	46	58	32
Trowbridge T.	38	11	10	17	48	75	32
Guildford & Dorking U.	38	9	13	16	43	50	31
Bognor Regis T.	38	6	17	15	44	72	29
Ramsgate	38	9	10	19	57	76	28
Crawley T.	38	9	10	19	46	66	28
Andover	38	9	10	19	42	62	28
Dorchester T.	38	11	6	21	45	69	28

Leading Goalscorers (League and League Cup)

PREMIER DIVISION
28 Gregory (Margate)
25 Stonebridge (Tonbridge A.F.C.)
24 Adams (Dunstable)
24 Astle (Weymouth)
21 Clayton (Kettering T.)
20 Plumb (Yeovil T.)
20 Sargent (Bedford T.)
19 Duck (Wealdstone)

FIRST DIVISION NORTH
39 Shaw (Redditch U.)
39 Stewart (A.P. Leamington)
30 Inglis (Worcester C.)
27 Lenihan (Merthyr Tydfil)
24 Jones (Oswestry T.)
24 Williams (Worcester C.)
22 Lewis (Cheltenham T.)
21 Griffiths (Kidderminster Harriers)

FIRST DIVISION SOUTH
31 Henderson (Dartford)
22 Green (Salisbury)
20 Bryant (Minehead)
20 Guy (Salisbury)
19 Jenkins (Minehead)

THE NORTHERN PREMIER FOOTBALL LEAGUE 1975-76

	P	W	D	L	F	A	Pts.
Runcorn	46	29	10	7	95	42	68
Stafford Rangers	46	26	15	5	81	41	67
Scarborough	46	26	10	10	84	43	62
Matlock T.	46	26	9	11	96	63	61
Boston U.	46	27	6	13	95	58	60
Wigan Ath.	46	21	15	10	81	42	57
Altrincham	46	20	14	12	77	57	54
Bangor C.	46	21	12	13	80	70	54
Mossley	46	21	11	14	70	58	53
Goole T.	46	20	13	13	58	49	53
Northwich Vic.	46	17	17	12	79	59	51
Lancaster C.	46	18	9	19	61	70	45
Worksop T.	46	17	10	19	63	56	44
Gainsborough Tr.	46	13	17	16	58	69	43
Macclesfield T.	46	15	12	19	50	64	42
Gateshead U.	46	17	7	22	64	63	41
Buxton	46	11	13	22	37	62	35
Skelmersdale U.	46	12	10	24	45	74	34
Netherfield	46	11	11	24	55	76	33
Morecambe	46	11	11	24	47	67	33
Great Harwood	46	13	7	26	58	86	33
South Liverpool	46	12	9	25	45	78	33
Barrow	46	12	9	25	47	84	33
Fleetwood	46	3	9	34	36	131	15

Leading Goalscorers (League and League Cup)
35, Rolland (Northwich Victoria); 34, Finnigan (Runcorn); 32, Kabia (Boston U.); 26, Rogers (Wigan Ath.); 25, Scott (Matlock T.); 24 Moore (Mossley); 22, Thompson (Goole T.); 22, Woodall (Scarborough); 21, Whitbread (Runcorn); 20, Thomas (Lancaster C.); 19, Grogan (Great Harwood); 18, Broadhead (Bangor C.); 18 Hutchison (Stafford Rangers); 18, Moore (Altrincham).

SOUTHERN LEAGUE – PREMIER DIVISION – 1975-76

Home \ Away	Atherstone T.	Bath C.	Bedford T.	Burton A.	Cambridge C.	Chelmsford C.	Dover	Dunstable T.	Grantham	Gravesend & Northfleet	Hillingdon Bor.	Kettering T.	Maidstone U.	Margate	Nuneaton Bor.	Stourbridge	Telford U.	Tonbridge	Wealdstone	Weymouth	Wimbledon	Yeovil T.
Atherstone T.	—	3-2	2-0	0-1	2-1	3-1	1-0	1-0	0-3	1-1	0-0	1-1	1-0	1-1	0-0	3-1	1-1	2-2	3-1	1-1	2-1	4-3
Bath C.	1-1	—	1-0	2-1	3-1	1-1	1-2	3-3	0-1	1-1	1-1	4-0	0-0	3-0	1-1	5-1	2-1	6-1	2-2	3-0	0-1	1-2
Bedford T.	1-1	0-0	—	0-0	0-0	1-0	3-1	3-1	2-0	3-0	4-1	1-0	0-1	2-2	4-0	1-2	1-1	2-2	2-1	2-0	0-1	3-2
Burton A.	3-1	1-0	1-2	—	3-0	1-1	2-2	1-0	1-0	1-1	3-1	4-1	2-1	0-1	1-1	2-0	1-0	0-0	2-1	1-1	1-2	3-1
Cambridge C.	1-1	4-3	1-1	2-1	—	1-1	2-1	0-4	1-1	0-0	0-1	1-1	1-2	1-1	1-1	2-3	2-0	1-2	4-1	1-3	1-1	1-1
Chelmsford C.	2-1	1-1	3-1	3-1	1-0	—	2-2	0-2	2-3	1-2	2-2	1-1	0-2	0-1	1-1	0-0	2-1	2-0	4-0	3-1	3-0	1-1
Dover	1-2	2-2	1-2	2-2	1-0	2-2	—	1-0	1-1	1-1	0-0	0-0	0-0	3-0	0-1	3-0	3-3	0-2	4-1	3-1	1-2	1-1
Dunstable T.	0-1	0-0	5-1	3-1	3-0	3-2	1-0	—	2-2	1-1	1-0	3-1	0-0	3-0	0-1	3-0	0-1	2-0	2-0	2-1	1-0	1-2
Grantham	4-0	2-1	2-2	0-0	1-1	0-2	1-0	0-1	—	2-2	1-0	1-1	1-0	3-3	2-0	1-2	1-0	2-3	3-0	1-3	0-1	1-0
Gravesend & Northfleet (formerly Yiewsley)	3-3	2-0	1-0	2-1	2-1	2-2	1-0	2-0	0-0	—	2-0	3-1	1-0	3-3	0-0	1-1	0-0	1-1	2-0	2-0	0-0	0-0
Hillingdon Bor.	6-1	1-1	1-1	3-1	4-1	1-2	3-3	0-0	2-2	0-0	—	5-4	0-1	1-0	2-0	1-0	1-1	3-1	4-1	2-3	0-1	0-0
Kettering T.	0-1	2-2	0-0	0-1	1-1	4-2	1-1	1-0	1-0	1-1	1-0	—	0-0	2-2	1-0	2-0	1-2	4-0	2-0	1-0	3-3	0-0
Maidstone U.	1-1	3-1	2-0	1-0	6-2	0-0	2-2	1-5	1-3	1-0	3-1	2-1	—	0-2	0-0	1-1	1-0	2-1	1-1	3-2	2-4	2-1
Margate	0-1	4-1	0-0	0-1	0-2	2-0	1-1	2-1	1-2	3-1	3-1	0-1	2-2	—	0-1	1-0	1-2	1-1	0-0	3-1	2-0	1-1
Nuneaton Bor.	1-1	0-1	1-1	1-1	1-1	2-0	3-3	0-2	0-0	1-0	1-0	2-0	0-0	1-2	—	2-1	1-1	1-1	2-1	1-1	1-0	0-2
Stourbridge	3-0	1-1	2-6	2-0	0-0	0-0	3-0	0-2	1-4	1-3	0-1	0-0	1-1	1-0	0-1	—	1-1	3-0	4-0	2-1	0-6	0-0
Telford U. (formerly Wellington T.)	0-2	4-1	4-1	1-1	2-0	2-0	0-0	1-0	2-2	6-2	1-0	1-4	3-3	3-1	0-1	0-1	—	0-0	2-1	2-4	0-0	0-1
Tonbridge	3-1	1-0	1-3	3-1	0-1	1-2	0-0	1-1	2-0	1-1	1-3	2-1	1-1	1-1	0-2	2-1	1-0	—	3-3	1-0	1-2	1-2
Wealdstone	1-2	3-1	1-1	1-1	0-1	4-0	3-4	3-0	2-2	3-1	2-1	1-0	2-1	1-4	1-4	4-0	3-2	2-1	—	3-1	1-2	0-2
Weymouth	0-2	0-0	2-2	3-1	4-0	1-1	1-0	0-0	1-0	2-1	0-4	1-1	1-1	2-0	1-4	2-1	0-1	5-2	0-2	—	0-2	0-1
Wimbledon	1-1	0-2	0-0	4-0	0-0	2-0	3-0	3-0	2-0	2-1	2-2	2-0	1-0	2-1	1-0	4-0	3-0	3-0	4-1	4-0	—	1-2
Yeovil T.	2-0	2-1	3-0	4-0	2-0	3-0	5-1	0-1	2-0	3-1	1-1	1-1	2-1	3-1	0-1	4-0	2-0	1-0	1-1	3-1	1-2	—

815

SOUTHERN LEAGUE – FIRST DIVISION (NORTH) – 1975-76

	Automotive Products Leamington	Banbury U.	Barnet	Barry T.	Bedworth U.	Bromsgrove R.	Bury T.	Cheltenham T.	Corby T.	Enderby T.	Gloucester C.	Kidderminster Harriers	King's Lynn	Merthyr Tydfil	Milton Keynes C.	Oswestry T.	Redditch U.	Stevenage Ath.	Tamworth	Wellingborough T.	Witney T.	Worcester C.
Automotive Products Leamington (formerly Lockheed Leamington)	—	5-0	1-0	1-1	3-0	4-0	3-1	1-1	4-0	3-1	2-1	0-0	1-1	2-2	3-2	2-0	2-3	3-1	3-2	3-0	1-1	4-0
Banbury U.	0-2	—	1-1	0-3	2-2	2-2	4-1	3-3	0-0	0-1	3-0	0-2	1-2	1-1	2-0	1-0	2-2	3-0	1-0	4-2	0-1	2-0
Barnet	0-0	4-1	—	1-1	4-1	1-2	1-1	2-1	1-0	3-1	1-2	3-1	2-0	1-2	1-1	2-0	0-1	2-1	2-1	0-1	0-1	2-2
Barry T.	0-1	1-0	3-1	—	1-1	1-0	0-1	1-1	3-0	1-0	0-2	2-0	4-1	0-2	1-2	1-1	2-3	2-1	0-0	2-1	0-1	1-0
Bedworth U.	1-2	1-1	2-0	1-0	—	0-1	1-1	1-2	1-4	0-0	2-0	2-2	0-0	3-1	1-0	0-3	5-0	1-0	0-1	1-3	0-1	0-0
Bromsgrove R.	3-2	1-0	3-1	5-1	1-1	—	2-2	2-3	1-4	1-1	2-0	2-2	0-0	0-0	1-0	2-0	0-2	2-0	0-1	2-1	1-2	0-3
Bury T.	0-1	0-1	1-1	0-1	4-2	0-2	—	3-2	3-2	1-2	3-0	2-1	1-1	2-1	1-2	4-0	0-3	5-2	1-1	0-0	0-3	0-0
Cheltenham	2-2	2-4	5-2	2-3	2-0	2-0	3-1	—	5-1	2-0	5-0	3-0	3-2	2-1	4-1	3-3	3-1	6-0	1-1	2-0	1-1	1-2
Corby T.	0-1	2-3	2-1	3-3	1-2	1-1	3-1	0-1	—	2-0	5-0	1-2	2-0	0-0	1-0	1-0	1-3	1-2	3-0	2-1	1-1	1-2
Enderby T.	0-1	0-2	0-2	1-1	0-0	1-1	2-1	0-3	0-1	—	1-2	3-0	1-1	1-0	3-1	2-0	1-3	3-1	1-0	1-0	0-1	2-3
Gloucester C.	0-3	1-0	2-2	1-0	1-3	2-0	3-1	3-2	2-2	2-1	—	4-3	2-1	1-0	0-1	0-0	0-4	1-1	0-4	3-1	1-2	4-2
Kidderminster H.	1-3	0-2	3-1	2-2	4-2	1-3	2-0	3-0	2-1	4-3	4-1	—	1-0	1-1	5-0	2-0	0-4	1-0	2-1	0-0	1-2	1-0
King's Lynn	1-0	1-3	2-0	4-1	0-0	0-0	1-1	3-2	1-1	3-0	1-0	3-3	—	1-1	5-0	0-1	0-1	3-1	2-1	4-1	1-1	0-1
Merthyr Tydfil	1-4	2-0	1-1	3-1	2-1	0-0	2-1	2-1	0-0	1-0	1-0	3-3	5-1	—	5-1	0-1	1-1	0-0	4-0	1-0	3-1	4-3
Milton Keynes C. (formerly Bletchley T.)	0-2	1-1	1-1	1-2	1-0	1-0	1-2	4-1	1-0	3-1	0-1	5-0	5-1	5-1	—	3-0	3-2	4-1	0-0	2-1	3-1	2-1
Oswestry T.	3-2	3-2	1-1	1-1	2-3	3-4	7-1	1-0	1-0	1-3	0-0	2-0	0-1	3-1	3-0	—	3-1	3-4	0-1	3-1	3-1	1-0
Redditch U.	1-1	4-2	2-2	2-2	5-1	3-2	4-0	1-0	3-1	4-2	2-0	1-2	0-0	5-1	3-2	3-1	—	2-4	1-1	3-0	1-0	1-1
Stevenage Ath.	1-0	2-3	2-1	2-1	2-2	4-1	0-2	2-3	1-2	1-4	2-2	1-0	3-4	1-4	1-1	3-4	2-4	—	2-2	4-0	0-4	1-3
Tamworth	0-2	0-1	3-4	3-0	2-0	2-0	1-2	1-1	3-0	1-0	3-0	2-1	2-1	4-0	3-1	0-1	1-1	2-2	—	0-0	0-4	0-0
Wellingborough T.	0-1	1-0	0-1	1-1	1-1	0-1	2-2	2-0	3-1	1-3	2-3	0-0	4-1	1-0	3-1	3-1	3-0	4-0	1-3	—	1-1	1-2
Witney T.	0-0	5-2	1-0	2-0	2-0	1-1	0-2	0-3	4-0	3-1	3-0	1-2	1-1	3-1	1-1	3-1	1-0	0-4	0-4	1-1	—	3-1
Worcester C.	0-4	1-0	5-1	2-1	5-1	4-1	6-1	2-1	4-0	0-2	3-0	1-0	0-1	4-3	2-1	1-0	1-1	1-3	0-0	1-2	3-1	—

SOUTHERN LEAGUE – FIRST DIVISION (SOUTH) – 1975-6

	Andover	Ashford T.	Basingstoke T.	Bexley U.	Bognor Regis T.	Canterbury C.	Crawley T.	Dartford	Dorchester T.	Folkestone and Shepway (formerly Folkestone)	Guildford and Dorking U. (formerly Guildford C.)	Hastings U.	Metropolitan Police	Minehead	Poole T.	Ramsgate	Romford	Salisbury	Trowbridge	Waterlooville
Andover	—	2-3	2-0	0-2	2-2	1-0	2-2	0-1	0-4	0-0	1-2	1-1	0-0	4-0	0-2	2-0	1-3	0-2	0-3	2-0
Ashford T.	2-4	—	0-2	6-1	5-1	4-3	0-0	3-5	2-0	4-1	1-1	4-0	1-1	1-1	3-0	2-2	1-2	3-1	5-0	2-1
Basingstoke T.	2-0	0-1	—	2-1	3-0	7-2	5-0	2-0	5-3	2-3	2-2	1-1	3-3	0-3	2-1	2-2	0-3	4-3	1-1	3-2
Bexley U.	1-1	2-1	1-1	—	1-2	2-2	3-0	4-0	1-0	0-0	2-2	2-2	2-2	0-4	4-1	2-3	1-1	0-2	3-0	0-0
Bognor Regis T.	0-4	0-0	1-1	2-0	—	0-0	1-0	4-0	1-0	1-1	1-3	0-0	0-3	3-4	1-5	2-2	1-1	0-2	1-1	1-0
Canterbury C.	4-1	0-0	3-1	2-0	5-2	—	0-1	0-1	3-0	2-2	2-0	0-2	3-0	1-1	4-1	0-1	0-0	1-5	1-1	0-0
Crawley T.	3-0	3-1	3-3	2-1	1-1	2-5	—	1-3	1-1	5-1	2-0	1-4	3-0	1-1	3-1	3-1	2-1	1-1	0-0	0-0
Dartford	1-0	4-1	4-1	2-1	3-1	4-0	2-1	—	4-1	5-1	2-0	1-4	0-2	1-4	3-1	2-2	2-1	1-1	4-5	0-0
Dorchester T.	1-4	2-1	1-1	1-1	2-0	4-0	2-1	0-2	—	2-1	2-0	3-3	6-2	0-2	1-2	2-2	1-0	0-1	3-0	5-1
Folkestone and Shepway (formerly Folkestone)	0-0	1-0	0-2	0-0	1-1	0-1	3-0	1-2	0-2	—	1-0	1-1	1-3	0-2	1-0	2-1	2-1	0-3	0-0	0-3
Guildford and Dorking U. (formerly Guildford C.)	3-1	1-2	2-0	0-1	1-1	4-1	0-0	0-2	0-1	1-1	—	0-2	4-1	1-1	4-1	2-4	1-1	1-2	2-2	3-3
Hastings U.	0-0	3-1	3-3	2-2	2-2	1-2	2-1	3-1	1-0	3-0	1-0	—	0-0	3-2	2-0	4-5	1-1	2-1	0-1	1-0
Metropolitan Police	2-2	2-2	1-0	0-2	1-1	3-0	1-0	0-2	2-0	0-1	1-1	1-4	—	1-1	2-4	2-1	0-1	2-2	0-0	2-2
Minehead	3-0	5-0	7-2	1-0	2-1	3-0	1-0	2-0	5-1	4-0	1-0	2-2	2-1	—	1-0	4-2	4-1	2-2	3-1	1-1
Poole T.	4-0	3-1	2-1	0-4	4-3	1-0	0-0	2-1	2-0	0-2	3-0	2-1	2-0	0-1	—	3-1	2-4	2-1	1-0	5-1
Ramsgate (formerly Ramsgate Ath.)	1-1	1-2	1-1	3-5	0-0	1-2	0-0	1-1	2-0	2-1	2-4	4-5	2-1	0-1	4-2	—	1-0	1-3	5-1	2-2
Romford	1-0	4-0	1-0	1-3	2-1	1-1	2-0	2-3	2-1	0-0	2-0	1-0	2-0	1-1	2-1	5-3	—	2-1	5-0	1-3
Salisbury	2-0	6-1	3-3	0-1	3-3	3-1	1-0	1-3	3-2	2-1	0-0	3-3	0-0	1-5	0-1	3-1	1-1	—	4-2	1-1
Trowbridge	2-4	3-0	0-1	1-2	1-2	2-1	2-1	1-3	1-0	2-0	1-1	1-0	0-2	0-7	4-0	2-0	1-3	1-1	—	4-4
Waterlooville	3-0	5-1	5-0	2-2	0-1	1-1	4-2	1-2	2-1	1-1	1-1	1-0	0-2	2-1	0-1	3-1	1-0	2-1	4-0	—

NORTHERN PREMIER LEAGUE – 1975-76

	Altrincham	Bangor C.	Barrow	Boston U.	Buxton	Fleetwood	Gainsborough Tr.	Gateshead U.	Goole T.	Great Harwood	Lancaster C.	Macclesfield T.	Matlock T.	Morecambe	Mossley	Netherfield	Northwich Vic.	Runcorn	Scarborough	Skelmersdale U.	S. Liverpool	Stafford R.	Wigan Ath.	Worksop T.
Altrincham	—	1-0	4-0	1-0	4-0	2-1	3-0	3-0	1-1	3-2	2-2	3-2	1-2	4-1	0-0	2-2	1-1	3-1	0-1	3-1	1-1	5-2	1-0	0-1
Bangor C.	0-3	—	3-1	2-2	4-1	0-1	4-2	4-0	2-1	2-3	2-1	0-1	5-1	1-1	3-3	1-0	1-1	0-3	4-1	4-0	5-1	1-0	2-2	3-2
Barrow	1-1	1-2	—	2-3	1-0	4-0	1-1	1-0	1-2	0-2	1-0	2-0	3-1	1-0	2-0	3-1	1-6	0-2	2-1	0-2	0-1	0-0	0-4	1-1
Boston U.	4-1	4-1	8-0	—	3-1	2-1	1-2	1-0	1-0	4-0	4-2	6-0	2-1	4-1	0-1	3-1	4-1	0-1	2-0	3-0	3-0	2-2	2-1	3-1
Buxton	1-1	0-1	0-0	0-1	—	1-1	2-2	1-0	3-4	4-1	1-4	1-1	0-1	0-1	0-1	0-4	0-6	2-2	0-2	3-0	2-1	1-0	2-0	0-0
Fleetwood	0-1	1-1	0-0	0-1	0-0	—	0-2	1-0	1-1	2-2	1-3	1-2	1-2	1-0	0-3	0-4	0-6	0-2	0-2	1-4	3-1	0-2	0-4	1-7
Gainsborough Tr.	5-0	2-1	4-2	1-2	0-0	5-1	—	3-3	0-1	0-2	0-0	0-2	1-0	2-1	1-3	3-1	2-2	0-2	1-1	2-1	3-0	1-1	0-0	1-1
Gateshead U. (formerly South Shields)	0-2	4-2	1-0	1-0	0-1	8-1	0-0	—	0-0	1-0	2-1	0-2	5-1	2-0	2-2	1-0	0-1	2-3	2-0	2-2	2-0	0-2	1-2	3-0
Goole T.	0-3	1-2	1-0	0-0	3-1	5-0	1-0	3-0	—	1-0	1-1	2-1	1-1	1-1	2-1	2-0	0-3	0-2	2-1	1-0	1-2	1-0	0-0	2-1
Great Harwood	0-3	2-4	3-2	0-1	0-1	2-2	2-0	1-3	—	—	2-3	2-1	0-1	0-1	2-2	2-4	0-4	0-3	1-2	1-0	2-1	0-1	3-7	1-0
Lancaster C.	2-1	0-2	1-0	2-3	0-0	7-1	1-5	0-1	1-2	1-5	—	0-1	4-2	3-2	2-0	3-2	0-0	0-4	2-2	1-0	1-0	0-2	0-0	1-0
Macclesfield T.	2-1	3-1	1-1	1-0	2-1	0-0	2-0	3-0	4-3	3-0	0-1	—	1-1	0-1	1-1	2-1	1-1	1-2	1-1	0-1	2-0	1-1	1-1	0-0
Matlock T.	4-3	1-1	2-0	4-1	3-1	4-2	5-0	2-1	3-1	3-1	2-0	1-0	—	4-1	3-0	2-0	2-1	1-0	1-2	2-1	2-2	3-2	2-2	1-0
Morecambe	0-0	3-1	1-2	1-2	1-0	0-0	5-0	2-1	0-1	3-1	1-0	2-0	0-1	—	0-2	2-1	1-0	1-0	2-3	0-0	2-0	3-3	3-0	6-2
Mossley	0-1	3-1	1-1	1-0	3-0	3-2	0-1	2-1	0-1	4-1	1-0	4-0	0-4	2-2	—	2-1	1-0	1-0	2-3	0-0	6-0	3-3	1-1	1-3
Netherfield	1-1	0-1	1-1	1-4	0-0	2-1	2-2	1-6	0-2	0-0	0-0	1-1	1-3	2-0	2-0	—	0-0	0-1	1-1	2-0	6-0	0-1	0-2	1-3
Northwich Vic	0-0	1-2	1-3	1-3	3-0	4-0	2-1	1-1	0-2	0-0	2-1	4-0	5-3	2-0	5-3	1-2	—	0-2	1-1	1-1	0-0	3-3	1-3	1-3
Runcorn	6-2	4-1	3-1	1-3	3-0	2-1	1-0	1-1	2-0	2-1	4-0	3-1	1-1	1-1	1-0	4-4	0-1	—	1-1	6-0	4-2	2-2	2-0	1-2
Scarborough	1-0	4-1	5-0	4-1	1-0	6-1	3-0	2-0	1-0	1-0	3-0	5-2	4-2	1-1	0-0	2-1	1-2	2-0	—	2-0	4-3	0-1	0-0	3-0
Skelmersdale	2-2	3-1	2-1	3-1	1-2	1-0	2-1	3-0	1-1	2-1	0-1	2-0	1-6	0-0	0-1	0-2	2-0	1-0	0-1	—	0-0	0-1	1-2	0-3
S. Liverpool	1-1	1-1	2-0	2-0	1-2	1-0	3-0	2-1	2-1	3-0	2-1	1-2	0-3	2-1	1-0	4-1	1-1	2-1	0-2	3-2	—	3-0	2-2	1-0
Stafford R.	2-1	3-2	1-0	2-0	1-0	4-0	1-1	4-0	1-3	1-1	4-0	0-1	1-0	0-0	2-3	5-2	1-2	2-1	1-0	4-1	3-0	—	2-2	1-2
Wigan Ath.	4-1	2-0	1-0	6-0	6-0	3-0	0-0	1-0	1-3	0-0	1-1	2-0	1-0	0-0	2-3	1-1	1-1	2-0	0-0	4-1	3-0	1-2	—	2-1
Worksop T.	0-0	1-1	3-1	1-1	0-0	5-0	1-3	3-0	0-0	1-3	1-2	3-1	0-2	3-0	1-2	1-0	3-1	3-0	0-1	2-0	2-0	0-2	0-1	—

SOUTHERN LEAGUE CUP 1975-76

First Round

Ashford T. v Ramsgate	3-1, 0-1
A.P. Leamington v Atherstone T.	2-4, 4-3
Barry T. v Cheltenham T.	0-2, 3-2
Basingstoke T. v Romford	2-2, 1-1
Bedford T. v Chelmsford C.	0-2, 0-0
Bedworth U. v Tamworth	2-1, 0-0
Bexley U. v Maidstone U.	0-1, 3-1
Burton A. v Nuneaton Bor.	2-0, 2-4
Bury T. v Banbury U.	0-2, 1-2
Canterbury C. v Folkestone & Shepway	2-0, 0-1
Crawley T. v Hastings U.	1-1, 0-4
Dartford v Guildford & Dorking U.	3-1, 4-2
Dover v Margate	2-0, 2-1
Dunstable T. v Barnet	2-0, 2-1
Enderby T. v Kettering T.	1-2, 0-3
Gloucester C. v Dorchester T.	0-2, 1-2
Gravesend & Northfleet v Bognor Regis	8-2, 1-3
Kidderminster H. v Oswestry T.	2-1, 0-4
King's Lynn v Corby T.	2-0, 2-1
Merthyr Tydfil v Waterlooville	1-2, 5-1
Metropolitan Police v Tonbridge	0-5, 0-2
Milton Keynes C. v Grantham	2-1, 0-1
Minehead v Weymouth	1-1, 0-2
Poole T. v Salisbury	1-1, 0-1
Redditch U. v Bromsgrove R.	2-1, 2-1
Stevenage Ath. v Wealdstone	1-3, 1-4
Trowbridge T. v Andover	0-3, 2-3
Wellingborough T. v Cambridge C.	1-2, 0-2
Wimbledon v Hillingdon Bor.	3-0, 2-0
Witney T. v Stourbridge	1-1, 1-2
Worcester C. v Telford U.	4-0, 1-1
Yeovil T. v Bath C.	4-0, 1-2

First Round Replays

Basingstoke T. v Romford	0-2
*Milton Keynes C. v Grantham	0-0
Nuneaton Bor. v Burton A.	1-2

First Round Second Replay

Grantham v Milton Keynes C.	0-1

Second Round

Ashford T. v Tonbridge	1-1
Bedworth U. v Burton A.	0-2
Canterbury C. v Bexley U.	1-2
Chelmsford C. v Banbury U.	6-1
Cheltenham T. v Stourbridge	1-3
Gravesend & Northfleet v Dartford	2-1
Hastings U. v Dover	1-1
Kettering T. v King's Lynn	3-0

Milton Keynes C. v Cambridge C.	0-2
Oswestry T. v Atherstone T.	3-1
Redditch U. v Worcester C.	1-1
Salisbury v Dorchester T.	1-3
Wealdstone v Dunstable T.	3-1
Weymouth v Andover	5-0
Wimbledon v Romford	4-1
Yeovil T. v Merthyr Tydfil	3-0

Second Round Replays

Dover v Hastings U.	2-0
*Tonbridge v Ashford T.	3-2
*Worcester C. v Redditch U.	1-1

After extra time

Second Round Second Replay

Redditch U. v Worcester C.	3-1

Third Round

Bexley U. v Gravesend & Northfleet	0-0
Burton A. v Oswestry T.	1-0
Cambridge C. v Wealdstone	0-0
*Dorchester T. v Yeovil T.	1-1
Kettering T. v Redditch U.	5-2
Stourbridge v Weymouth	1-1
Tonbridge v Dover	0-3
Wimbledon v Chelmsford C.	1-1

Played at Yeovil, as Dorchester Town have no lights.

Third Round Replays

*Chelmsford C. v Wimbledon	2-2
*Gravesend & Northfleet v Bexley U.	1-0
Wealdstone v Cambridge C.	2-0
Weymouth v Stourbridge	2-1
Yeovil Town v Dorchester T.	3-1

After extra time

Third Round Second Replay

Chelmsford C. v Wimbledon	1-2

Fourth Round

Dover v Wealdstone	2-1
Weymouth v Kettering	1-5
Wimbledon v Burton A.	2-0
Yeovil T. v Gravesend & Northfleet	1-0

Semi-finals (2 legs)

Wimbledon v Dover	3-0
†Dover v Wimbledon	1-1
Yeovil T. v Kettering T.	3-0
Kettering T. v Yeovil T.	0-0

†*Played at Wimbledon in order to obtain a larger gate.*

Final 1975-76

First-Leg: Yeovil T. 1 Wimbledon 1
(April 3 1976, Att. 2441)

Yeovil T.: Franklin; Thompson B, Cottle, McMahon, Harland, Harrison, Adams, Brown, Cotton, Thompson K, Clancy (Plumb).
Scorer: Cotton.

Wimbledon: Guy; Tilley, Bryant, Donaldson, Edwards, Bassett, Rice, Cooke, Connell, Holmes, Leslie.
Scorer: Holmes (pen).

Second Leg: Wimbledon 2 Yeovil T. 1
(April 10 1976, Att. 3350)

Wimbledon: Guy; Tilley, Bryant, Donaldson, Edwards, Bassett, Rice, Cooke, Connell, Leslie, Holmes.
Scorers: McMahon (o.g.), Cooke.

Yeovil: Franklin; Thompson B, Cottle, McMahon, Cotton, Harrison, Harland, Brown, Plumb, Thompson K, Clancy (Adams).
Scorer: Edwards (o.g.).

CHAMPIONSHIP MATCH

Wimbledon 1 Kettering T. 0 (a.e.t.)
(Played at Wimbledon on 19 August 1975, Attendance 1739)
This is a match played between the League winners (Wimbledon) and the Cup winners (Kettering Town).

GREENALL'S NORTHERN PREMIER LEAGUE CHALLENGE CUP
1975-76

Firs Round

The following clubs received byes into the Second Round: Fleetwood, Gateshead U., Mossley, Netherfield, Runcorn, Scarborough, S. Liverpool, and Worksop T.

Boston U. v Gainsborough Tr.	1-1
Goole T. v Matlock T.	4-2
Great Harwood v Northwich Vic.	2-1
Macclesfield T. v Bangor C.	2-2
Morecambe v Barrow	0-1
Skelmersdale U. v Altrincham	0-2
Stafford R. v Buxton	2-2
Wigan Ath. v Lancaster C.	3-2

First Round Replays

*Bangor C. v Macclesfield T.	1-1
*Buxton v Stafford Rangers	0-0
Gainsborough Trinity v Boston U.	2-3

After extra time

First Round Second Replays

Macclesfield T. v Bangor C.	2-1
Stafford Rangers v Buxton	1-0

Second Round

Barrow v Fleetwood	4-1
Gateshead U. v Boston U.	1-2

Goole T. v Altrincham	0-3
Great Harwood v Netherfield	5-2
Macclesfield T. v Worksop T.	1-2
Scarborough v Wigan Ath.	1-0
South Liverpool v Runcorn	4-3
Stafford Rangers v Mossley	1-1

Second Round Replay

*Mossley v Stafford Rangers	2-1

After extra time

Third Round

Altrincham v Great Harwood	5-1
Barrow v Boston U.	0-0
South Liverpool v Mossley	1-3
Worksop T. v Scarborough	2-1

Third Round Replay

Boston U. v Barrow	1-0

Semi-finals

Altrincham v Boston U.	3-4
Worksop T. v Mossley	1-2

Final 1975-76

First Leg: Boston U. 4 Mossley 0

(April 22 1976, Att. 1820)

Boston U.: Stewart; Moyes, Taylor, Coxon, Madden, Adamson. Callery, Symm, Reid, Kabia, Wilkinson.
Scorers: Callery, Kabia 2, Reid.

Mossley: Fitton; Brown, Sleight, Fletcher, Boslem, Pollitt, Ash, Moore, Williams, Bell, Brodie.

Second Leg: Mossley 2 Boston U. 1

(April 28 1976, Att. 821)

Mossley: Fitton; Brown, Sleight, Fletcher, Boslem, Pollitt, Brodie, Moore, Skeete, Williams, Bell (Cook).
Scorers: Fletcher, Moore.

Boston U.: Stewart; Moyes, Taylor, Bolland, Madden, Adamson, Callery, Symm, Reid, Kabia, Wilkinson.
Scorer: Kabia.

NORTHERN PREMIER CHALLENGE SHIELD 1975

Wigan Ath. 3 Runcorn 1

(Played at Wigan on 18 August Att. 1289)

This is a match between the League Champions, Wigan Ath. and the Cup winners, Runcorn for the previous season.

NORTHERN PREMIER LEAGUE CHAMPIONS v SOUTHERN FOOTBALL LEAGUE CHAMPIONS

Wigan Ath. v Wimbledon 1–0 on 24 September 1975

Wimbledon v Wigan Ath. 2–0 on 11 November 1975 (a.e.t.)

FA CHALLENGE TROPHY COMPETITION 1975-76

Preliminary Round

Clitheroe v Nelson	0-1
Crook T. v Ferryhill Ath.	1-0
Bridlington Tr. v Accrington Stanley 1968	2-0
Evenwood T. v Billingham Synth.	3-1
Tow Law T. v Boldon Colliery Wel.	3-2
Annfield Plain v West Auckland T.	2-2, 0-4
Horden Colliery Wel. v Thackley	2-2, 0-0, 1-0
Emley v Shildon	4-2
Bacup Bor. v Consett	0-2
Penrith v City of Leeds & Carnegie Coll.	2-0
Ossett A. v Whitley Bay	1-2
Frickley Coll. v Hatfield Main	2-4
Willington v Rossendale U.	7-3
Eastwood T. v Congleton T.	3-1
Leek T. v Prestwich Heys	0-0, 2-0
Denaby U. v Ashton U.	1-2
Kimberley T. v Heanor T.	1-0
Droylsden v Retford T.	0-2
Radcliffe Bor. v New Mills	1-1, 2-2, 5-2
Blackpool Mech. v Eastwood (Hanley)	4-0
Alfreton T. v Darwen	2-2, 3-3, 1-0
Rhyl v Blaenau Ffestiniog	2-1
St. Helens T. v Kirkby T.	1-2
Witton A. v Marine	2-3
New Brighton v Stalybridge Celtic	0-0, 0-4
Horwich R.M.I. v Middlewich Ath.	2-1
Hyde U. v Bethesda Ath.	1-1, 0-0, 3-0
Formby v Nantwich T.	0-1
Oswestry T. v Caernarvon T.	0-1
Skegness T. v Arnold	1-0
Spalding U. v Hednesford	1-2
Wellingborough T. v Irthlingborough Diamonds	0-2
Louth U. v Sutton Coldfield T.	1-1, 0-1
Corby T. v Long Eaton U.	1-0
Enderby T. v Armitage	2-0
Boston v A.P. Leamington	1-2
Moor Green v Bedworth U.	0-1
St. Neots T. v Gt. Yarmouth T.	0-2
Histon v Lowestoft T.	0-3
Wisbech T. v Gorleston	4-1
Stowmarket v Harwich & Parkeston	0-4
Ely C. v Bury T.	2-0
Harlow T. v Letchworth T.	0-5
Barking v Milton Keynes C.	0-0, 3-0
Uxbridge v Cheshunt	0-0, 0-3
Biggleswade T. v Tilbury	0-10
Grays Ath. v Ware	2-1
Walthamstow Av. v Hornchurch	3-2
Hertford T. v Ruislip Manor	1-0
Boreham Wood v Clapton	0-0, 1-0
Wembley v Stevenage Ath.	1-2
Harrow Bor. v Hayes	1-3
Bromley v Guildford & Dorking U.	1-2
Ramsgate v Medway	4-2
Lewes v Redhill	0-0, 2-0
Corinthian Cas. v Crawley T.	1-1, 0-2
Carshalton Ath. v Sittingbourne	1-1, 2-1
Sheppey U. v Folkestone & Shepway	0-1
Croydon v Erith & Belvedere	2-0
Metropolitan Police v Waterlooville	2-0
Hounslow v Chesham U.	0-0, 0-2
Hampton v Frome T.	0-1
Maidenhead U. v Fareham T.	0-2
Staines T. v Andover	3-0
Wokingham T. v Salisbury	0-2
Basingstoke T. v Kingstonian	5-5, 5-1
Devizes T. v Southall	1-1, 0-1
Bognor Regis T. v Horsham	0-3
Mangotsfield U. v Welton R.	0-1
Alvechurch v Paulton R.	0-1
Lye T. v Weston-Super-Mare	1-0
Trowbridge T. v Cinderford T.	1-0
Barry T. v Llanelli	5-1
Dudley T. v Redditch U.	1-1, 0-1
Chippenham T. v Darlaston	2-5
Gloucester C. v Everwarm	1-1, 4-2
Oldbury U. v Brierley Hill All.	2-0
Taunton T. v Dawlish	2-1
Falmouth T. v Glastonbury T.	4-0
Westland-Yeovil v Bridgwater T.	5-2
Bideford v Barnstaple T.	0-2

First Round Qualifying

Horden C. W. v Fleetwood	0-0, 1-1, 1-2
Bishop Auckland v South Bank	4-0
Hatfield Main v Blackpool Mech.	1-1, 1-0
Goole T. v Tow Law T.	1-0
Evenwood T. v Penrith	1-1, 0-2
Bridlington Tr. v West Auckland T.	6-0
Whitley Bay v Crook T.	0-0, 0-1
Durham C. v Willington	0-2
Great Harwood v Consett	1-0
Ashby Inst. v Emley	1-2
Nelson v Winterton R.	5-1
Netherfield v Whitby T.	5-4
Alfreton T. v Belper T.	2-0
Retford T. v Sutton T.	3-2
Ilkeston T. v Kimberley T.	1-1, 2-3
Leek T. v Ashton U.	2-1
Worksop T. v Ratcliffe Bor.	6-1
Leyland Motors v Eastwood T.	1-2
Brereton Social v Caernarvon T.	4-0
Rhyl v Skelmersdale U.	2-0
Kirkby T. v Marine	0-1
Nantwich T. v Horwich RMI	1-1, 3-0
Winsford U. v Pwllheli & District	2-0
Stalybridge Celtic v Hyde U.	2-2, 1-2
Louth U. v Rushden T.	2-1
Atherstone T. v Hednesford	3-1
Oldbury U. v Bedworth U.	1-1, 2-0
Enderby T. v A.P. Leamington	2-1
Skegness T. v Corby T.	1-1, 0-2
Darlaston v Lye T.	0-1
Warley Co. Bor. v Tamworth	0-3
Irthlingborough Diamonds v Bilston	3-1
Stevenage Ath. v Letchworth T.	1-1, 0-2
Dunstable T. v Hertford T.	1-0
Wisbech T. v Ely C.	3-0
Walthamstow Av. v Grays Ath.	2-2, 2-0
Aveley v Leytonstone	0-0, 2-1
Boreham Wood v Finchley	0-0, 2-2, 0-1
Hitchin T. v St. Albans C.	1-1, 0-1
Lowestoft T. v Cambridge C.	0-2
Tilbury v Barking	0-0, 2-3
Gt. Yarmouth T. v Harwich & Parkeston	0-0, 0-4
Lewes v Ramsgate	0-1
Canterbury C. v Guildford & Dorking U.	0-1
Metropolitan Police v Carshalton Ath.	0-2
Gravesend & Northfleet v Horsham	3-1
Tonbridge v Croydon	5-1
Folkestone & Shepway v Maidstone U.	0-1
Walton & Hersham v Tooting & Mitcham U.	0-5
Hayes v Crawley T.	3-0
Alton T. v Basingstoke T.	1-6
Cheshunt v Wealdstone	1-2
Chesham U. v Oxford C.	0-1
Poole T. v Southall & Ealing Bor.	0-2
Witney v Staines T.	0-2
Salisbury v Fareham T.	1-1, 0-1
Paulton R. v Redditch U.	0-3
Cheltenham T. v Barry T.	3-2
Ton Pentre v Gloucester C.	2-0
Ferndale Ath. v Frome T.	2-0
Welton R. v Dorchester T.	1-2
Barnstaple T. v Bath C.	3-1
Westland-Yeovil v Taunton T.	3-1
Falmouth T. v Trowbridge T.	7-1

Second Qualifying Round

Crook T. v Penrith	1-1, 2-0
Hatfield Mann v Bishop Auckland	0-1
Emley v Nelson	2-1
Goole T. v Gt. Harwood	4-0
Willington v Fleetwood	3-1
Bridlington Tr. v Netherfield	2-1
Worksop T. v Kimberley T.	3-1

Alfreton T. v Retford T.	0-0, 0-2
Corby T. v Louth U.	4-0
Winsford U. v Marine	1-1, 1-2
Brereton Social v Rhyl	0-0, 0-2
Hyde U. v Nantwich T.	5-2
Enderby T. v Irthlingborough Diamonds	1-0
Eastwood T. v Atherstone T.	0-1
Tamworth v Leek T.	1-4
Lye T. v Oldbury U.	2-1
Harwich & Parkeston v Aveley	3-3, 2-1
St. Albans C. v Cambridge C.	1-1 ,3-1
Dunstable T. v Letchworth T.	3-0
Finchley v Walthamstow Av.	2-2, 0-2
Barking v Wisbech T.	4-2
Guildford & Dorking U. v Ramsgate	0-1
Gravesend & Northfleet v Carshalton Ath.	1-0
Tooting & Mitcham U. v Hayes	2-0
Maidstone U. v Tonbridge	2-1
Wealdstone v Oxford C.	4-0
Basingstoke T. v Southall & Ealing Bor.	2-1
Staines T. v Fareham T.	0-0, 2-0
Redditch U. v Cheltenham T.	5-0
Ferndale Ath. v Ton Pentre	2-1
Falmouth T. v Barnstaple T.	6-2
Dorchester T. v Westland-Yeovil	1-0

Third Round Qualifying

Ashington v North Shields	3-2
Willington v Blyth Spartans	3-2
Crook T. v Spennymoor U.	2-1
Bishop Auckland v Emley	3-2
Goole T. v Bridlington Tr.	3-0
Chorley v Lancaster C.	2-2, 0-4
Rhyl v Northwich Vic.	1-1, 1-2
Mossley v Runcorn	2-2, 1-2
Hyde U. v Marine	2-0
Altrincham v Gainsborough Tr	2-2, 1-4
Retford T. v Worksop T.	2-4
Mexborough T. v Leek T.	3-1
Lye T. v Enderby T.	2-2, 1-2
Redditch U. v Kidderminster H.	1-2
Corby T. v Nuneaton Bor.	1-1, 1-1, 3-0
Highgate U. v Atherstone	1-2
Kings Lynn v Dunstable T.	3-0
Chelmsford C. v St. Albans C.	1-0
Barnet v Harwich & Parkeston	2-2, 0-5
Bishops Stortford v Ilford	1-1, 1-1, 3-1
Barking v Dagenham	1-1, 0-5
Walthamstow Av. v Enfield	1-1, 0-4
Hendon v Basingstoke T.	6-1
Maidstone U. v Tooting & Mitcham U.	0-2
Dorchester T. v Dulwich Hamlet	3-4
Gravesend & Northfleet v Staines T.	0-0, 1-4
Slough T. v Wycombe W.	1-0
Ramsgate v Bexley U.	3-0*, 1-1, 1-3
Wealdstone v Leatherhead	2-2, 0-1
Woking v Sutton U.	2-4
Ferndale Ath. v Yeovil T.	1-3
Minehead v Falmouth T.	0-0, 0-0, 1-2

Abandoned after 70 minutes.

First Round Proper

Morecambe v Crook T.	5-2
Gateshead U. v Bishop Auckland	0-1
Lancaster C. v Barrow	4-0
Scarborough v Willington	3-2
Ashington v Goole T.	2-2, 1-3
Hyde U. v S. Liverpool	3-3, 2-0
Northwich Vic. v Wigan Ath.	0-2
Macclesfield v Runcorn	1-3
Stafford R. v Burscough	4-0
Bangor C. v Telford U.	1-2
Worksop T. v Matlock T.	3-5
Buxton v Atherstone T.	0-0, 0-3
Mexborough T. v Grantham	0-0, 1-2
Kings Lynn v Burton A.	0-5
Gainsborough Tr. v Boston U.	0-0, 4-2
Chelmsford C. v Bedford T.	0-1
Bromsgrove R. v Worcester C.	2-0
Harwich & Parkeston v Stourbridge	3-0
Enfield v Banbury U.	3-0
Corby T. v Kidderminster H.	2-0
Bishops Stortford v Enderby T.	1-1, 1-1, 1-0
Hendon v Kettering T.	1-0

Slough T. v Dover	2-1
Margate v Dulwich Hamlet	2-0
Hastings U. v Bexley U.	4-0
Hillingdon Bor. v Ashford T.	4-0
Leatherhead v Staines T.	2-2, 1-1, 1-0
Romford v Tooting & Mitcham U.	1-1, 1-4
Dartford v Dagenham	1-3
Sutton U. v Wimbledon	0-0, 1-3
Merthyr Tydfil v Yeovil T.	1-0
Falmouth T. v Weymouth	2-3

Second Round

Hyde U. v Morecambe	2-2, 2-3
Lancaster C. v Corby T.	3-3, 1-0
Goole T. v Scarborough	1-1, 1-3
Runcorn v Gainsborough Tr.	1-1, 1-0
Matlock T. v Bishop Auckland	1-0
Wigan Ath. v Grantham	1-1, 2-1
Atherstone T. v Telford U.	1-1, 2-1
Burton Albion v Stafford R.	0-1
Bedford T. v Hastings U.	2-0
Enfield v Bishops Stortford	2-1
Merthyr Tydfil v Tooting & Mitcham U.	1-3
Margate v Hillingdon Bor.	1-2
Harwich & Parkeston v Weymouth	4-1
Hendon v Slough T.	2-2, 0-0, 0-1
Wimbledon v Dagenham	0-0, 0-2
Bromsgrove R. v Leatherhead	1-0

Third Round

Scarborough v Dagenham	3-0
Runcorn v Slough T.	2-0
Wigan Ath. v Hillingdon Bor.	1-3
Stafford R. v Matlock T.	2-1
Harwich & Parkeston v Bedford T.	1-2
Lancaster C. v Enfield	0-1
Atherstone T. v Bromsgrove R.	1-1, 0-1
Tooting & Mitcham U. v Morecambe	2-0

Fourth Round

Stafford R. v Hillingdon Bor.	2-0
Bromsgrove R. v Enfield	0-0, 1-2
Scarborough v Tooting & Mitcham U.	1-0
Bedford T. v Runcorn	1-2

Semi-finals (2 legs)

| Scarborough v Enfield | 1-0, 0-0 |
| Stafford R. v Runcorn | 1-0, 0-0 |

Final at Wembley

Scarborough 3 (*Woodall, Abbey, Marshal pen.*)
Stafford R. 2 (*Jones 2*)   21,000
Scarborough: Barnard; Jackson, Marshall, H. Dunn, Ayre, H. A. Dunn, Dale, Barnaby, Woodall, Abbey, Hilley. *Sub:* Donoughie.
Stafford R.: Arnold; R. Ritchie, Richards, Sargeant, Seddon, Morris, Chapman, Lowe, Jones, Hutchison, Chadwick. *Sub:* J. Ritchie.
After extra time.

Previous Finals

1970	Macclesfield Town 2; Telford United 0; (28,000)
1971	Telford United 3; Hillingdon 2; (29,500)
1972	Stafford Rangers 3; Barnet 0; (24,000)
1973	Scarborough 2; Wigan Athletic 1; (23,000)
1974	Morecambe 2; Dartford 1; (19,000)
1975	Matlock T 4; Scarborough 0; (21,000)

822

OTHER LEAGUE TABLES 1975-76

Rothmans Isthmian League

Division 1	P	W	D	L	F	A	Pts	Sportsmanship Points lost	
								C	D
Enfield	42	26	9	7	83	38	87	5	8
Wycombe W.	42	24	10	8	71	41	82	2	0
Dagenham	42	25	6	11	89	55	81	2	0
Ilford	42	22	10	10	58	39	76	11	4
Dulwich Hamlet	42	22	5	15	67	41	71	8	8
Hendon	42	20	11	11	60	41	71	3	4
Tooting & Mitcham U.	42	19	11	12	73	49	68	14	0
Leatherhead	42	19	10	13	63	53	67	8	0
Staines T.	42	19	9	14	46	37	66	5	0
Slough T.	42	17	12	13	58	45	63	5	4
Sutton U.	42	17	11	14	71	60	62	3	0
Bishop's Stortford	42	15	12	15	51	47	57	2	0
Walthamstow Av.	42	14	11	17	47	60	53	11	0
Woking	42	14	9	19	58	62	51	8	4
Barking	42	15	6	21	57	70	51	7	8
Hitchin T.	42	13	11	18	45	57	50	1	0
Hayes	42	10	19	13	44	48	49	9	8
Kingstonian	42	13	8	21	53	87	47	5	0
Southall & Ealing Bor.	42	11	9	22	56	69	42	5	0
Leytonstone	42	10	10	22	41	63	40	6	0
Oxford C.	42	9	8	25	29	65	35	5	4
Clapton	42	3	3	36	19	112	12	10	0

Division II	P	W	D	L	F	A	Pts	C	D
Tilbury	42	32	6	4	97	30	102	4	0
Croydon	42	28	14	0	81	27	98	1	0
Carshalton Ath.	42	28	6	8	75	37	90	2	0
Chesham U.	42	21	12	9	91	51	75	9	0
Harwich & Parkeston	42	21	11	10	78	56	74	8	8
Hampton	42	21	9	12	72	52	72	14	0
St. Albans C.	42	18	12	12	59	48	66	5	0
Boreham Wood	42	17	12	13	68	50	63	19	4
Harrow Bor.	42	15	12	15	71	74	57	6	0
Hornchurch	42	15	11	16	61	61	56	6	0
Horsham	42	14	13	15	60	55	55	6	0
Wembley	42	14	13	15	51	54	55	7	1
Wokingham T.	42	13	16	13	45	52	55	6	4
Walton & Hersham	42	14	12	16	61	56	54	11	0
Finchley	42	14	11	17	52	53	53	11	8
Bromley	42	11	11	20	64	86	44	33	0
Aveley	42	11	9	22	34	51	42	11	4
Harlow T.	42	11	9	22	50	73	42	10	4
Maidenhead U.	42	6	17	19	32	65	35	9	4
Ware	42	7	12	23	50	95	33	9	0
Hertford T.	42	5	9	28	32	87	24	5	4
Corinthian-Casuals	42	4	7	31	42	113	19	5	4

C = Caution (one sportsmanship point deducted)
D = Dismissal (four sportsmanship points deducted)
Three points are awarded for a win and one for a draw in all sponsored leagues.

Rothmans Western League

	P	W	D	L	F	A	Pts
Falmouth T.	44	35	5	4	134	43	110
Taunton T.	44	27	8	9	86	43	89
Clevedon	44	27	6	11	77	51	87
Bridgwater T.	44	25	10	9	81	44	85
Glastonbury	44	23	10	11	84	49	79
Barnstaple T.	44	21	9	14	95	66	72
Tiverton T.	44	20	12	12	73	70	72
Paulton R.	44	19	12	13	60	58	69
Mangotsfield U.	44	18	10	16	63	63	64
Bideford	44	17	12	15	60	56	63
Frome T.	44	17	10	17	76	61	61
Exeter C.	44	16	10	18	64	69	57*
St. Luke's Coll.	44	16	7	21	60	70	55
Weston-super-Mare	44	13	15	16	52	57	54
Westland Yeovil	44	14	11	19	66	82	53
Welton R.	44	14	9	21	57	71	51
Bridport	44	13	11	20	49	72	50
Dawlish	44	13	10	21	51	69	49
Devizes T.	44	10	15	19	45	59	45
Chippenham T.	44	12	7	25	66	94	43
Melksham T.	44	12	7	25	66	106	43
Keynsham T.	44	8	6	30	50	86	30
Exmouth T.	44	5	10	29	38	114	25

*One Point deducted for playing an ineligible Player.

Rothmans Hellenic League

Premier Division	P	W	D	L	F	A	Pts.	C	D
Burnham	30	19	8	3	62	20	65	2	—
Moreton T.	30	15	9	6	52	34	54	5	2
Clanfield	30	14	10	6	47	29	52	3	—
Forest Green Rvs.	30	14	10	6	82	53	52	1	—
Newbury T.	30	14	9	7	54	37	51	12	1
Ch. Norton T.	30	14	8	8	46	37	50	7	1
Hungerford T.	30	11	12	7	40	31	45	3	—
Thame Utd.	30	11	10	9	43	44	43	5	—
Thatcham T.	30	12	7	11	36	45	43	7	—
Stratford T.	30	9	11	10	49	44	38	5	2
Wallingford T.	30	9	9	12	33	44	36	5	2
Cirencester T.	30	9	6	15	41	59	33	3	—
Pinehurst	30	8	7	15	43	50	31	—	—
Didcot T.	30	6	8	16	27	39	26	3	—
Wantage U.	30	3	11	16	29	62	20	—	2
Bicester T.	30	2	5	23	29	85	11	4	1

Sportsmanship Points Lost

Divison 1	P	W	D	L	F	A	Pts.	C	D
Abingdon T.	26	22	3	1	53	12	69	1	0
Fairford T.	26	19	4	3	52	12	61	2	0
Hazells	26	15	5	6	53	23	50	2	4
Rivets Spts.	26	14	7	5	40	31	49	2	4
Abingdon Utd.	26	11	3	12	46	45	36	3	8
Pressed Steel	26	11	3	12	41	56	36	4	0
Maidenhead T.	26	9	5	12	37	49	33	3	0
Morris Motors	26	7	9	10	33	32	30	0	4
Watlington T.	26	9	3	14	50	57	30	3	0
Easington	26	8	5	13	43	52	29	3	0
Kidlington	26	8	4	14	37	50	28	1	0
M.C. Ath.	26	6	7	13	24	34	25	15	0
Aston Clinton	26	6	6	14	37	53	24	3	4
Buckingham Ath.	26	4	2	20	26	66	14	0	4

Sportsmanship Points Lost

Rothmans Northern League

	P	W	D	L	F	A	Pts.	C	D
Blyth Spartans	38	28	4	5	88	36	88	1	0
Willington	38	27	6	5	102	43	87	2	0
Spennymoor U.	38	27	6	5	90	43	87	1	0
Bishop Auckland	38	25	8	5	75	32	83	5	0
Tow Law T.	38	22	8	8	102	60	74	0	0
Whitby T.	38	21	11	6	76	36	72*	4	4
Ashington	38	18	4	16	60	52	58	1	4
North Shields	38	15	7	16	57	49	52	4	0
Consett	38	15	6	17	53	56	51	0	0
Evanwood T.	38	11	11	16	50	58	44	3	4
Horden Colliery Welfare	38	11	10	17	42	62	43	7	0
Penrith	38	11	10	17	49	89	43	8	0
Durham C.	38	10	10	18	36	57	40	1	4
Billingham Synthonia	38	10	8	20	39	67	38	1	0
Crook T.	38	9	10	19	55	68	37	5	4
Shildon	38	9	10	19	43	61	37	4	0
Whitley Bay	38	8	11	19	41	74	35	5	0
Ferryhill Ath.	38	8	9	21	51	73	33	4	8
South Bank	38	7	8	23	41	80	29	1	0
West Auckland T.	38	7	5	26	44	98	26	6	4

Sportsmanship Points Lost

*2 points deducted for playing an ineligible player.

Spartan League

SENIOR SECTION, DIV. 1

	P	W	D	L	F	A	Pts
Farnborough T.	30	22	5	3	85	23	49
Bracknell T.	30	21	7	2	73	39	49
Alma Swanley	30	19	8	3	75	38	46
Swanley T.	30	16	8	6	62	44	40
East Ham U.	30	13	7	10	43	36	33
Cray W.	30	11	9	10	55	54	31
Kingsbury T.	30	11	7	12	44	43	29
Hoddesdon T.	30	9	8	13	31	33	26
Farnham T.	30	10	6	14	47	61	26
Heathside Sports	30	9	8	13	26	35	26
Chingford	30	9	7	14	34	47	25
Penhill Standard	30	10	4	16	41	53	24
Hatfield T.	30	8	8	14	49	69	24
Banstead Ath.	30	6	7	17	39	64	19
Berkhamstead T.	30	5	8	17	28	59	18
Chertsey T.	30	6	3	21	32	65	15

Cheshire County League

	P	W	D	L	F	A	Pts
Marine	42	28	8	6	94	34	64
Chorley	42	29	5	8	88	33	63
Leek Town	42	27	7	8	74	33	61
Winsford United	42	24	10	8	83	44	58
Witton Albion	42	20	14	8	71	37	54
Nantwich Town	42	23	8	11	88	54	54
Middlewich Ath.	42	20	8	14	61	51	48
Stalybridge Celtic	42	20	6	16	67	47	46
Droylsden	42	17	11	14	66	55	45
New Brighton	42	19	7	16	59	57	45
Rossendale Utd.	42	17	9	16	69	62	43
Burscough	42	16	10	16	68	73	42
Hyde United	42	15	11	16	73	75	41
St. Helens Town	42	14	11	17	54	57	39
Formby	42	10	15	17	44	59	35
Ashton United	42	13	8	21	50	63	34
Radcliffe Borough	42	13	5	24	56	94	31
Horwich R.M.I.	42	8	13	21	42	90	29
Rhyl	42	8	10	24	46	83	26
Darwen	42	9	7	26	49	89	25
New Mills	42	8	6	28	47	95	22
Prestwich Heys	42	6	7	29	39	103	19

Athenian League

DIVISION ONE

	P	W	D	L	F	A	Pts
Cheshunt	30	18	5	7	66	31	41
Egham	30	17	7	7	46	28	39
Addlestone	30	15	7	8	40	30	37
Grays Ath.	30	15	6	9	39	29	36
Rainham	30	15	3	12	52	37	33
Erith & Belvedere	30	11	10	9	29	28	32
Alton T.	30	14	4	12	37	42	32
Worthing	30	12	7	11	42	35	31
Hounslow	30	11	7	12	50	43	29
Lewes	30	9	11	10	45	45	29
Letchworth	30	10	9	11	31	38	29
Redhill	30	10	7	13	31	34	27
Ruislip Manor	30	9	8	13	39	41	26
Leyton-Wingate	30	8	8	14	37	41	24
Marlow	30	6	6	18	27	61	18
Edmonton	30	5	7	18	31	79	17

Highland League

	P	W	D	L	F	A	Pts
Nairn Co.	30	19	6	5	75	35	44
Fraserburgh	30	20	4	6	66	35	44
Peterhead	30	19	5	6	85	42	43
Keith	30	19	5	6	65	30	43
Inverness Th.	30	15	7	8	69	41	37
Inverness Cal.	30	15	7	8	52	49	37
Elgin C.	30	11	11	8	57	48	33
Ross Co.	30	12	9	9	64	62	33
Rothes	30	13	3	14	57	57	29
Inverness Clach.	30	8	10	12	38	43	26
Buckie Th.	30	9	6	15	31	48	24
Huntly	30	8	7	15	31	46	23
Brora R.	30	9	5	16	39	57	23
Lossiemouth	30	4	8	18	34	73	16
Forres Mechs.	30	4	7	19	53	74	15
Deveronvale	30	3	4	23	29	105	10

Challenge Match for the championship: Nairn County 2; Fraserburgh 1 (after extra time).

United Counties League

PREMIER DIVISION

	P	W	D	L	F	A	Pts
Stamford A.F.C.	38	27	7	5	106	33	61
Spalding U.	38	21	11	6	65	38	53
Kempston R.	38	17	12	9	54	40	46
Potton U.	38	20	5	13	58	39	45
Irthlingborough Diamonds	38	18	9	11	65	46	45
Wolverton T.	38	16	12	10	58	43	44
Long Buckby A.F.C.	38	19	5	14	75	48	43
Ampthill T.	38	15	12	11	64	60	42
Desborough T.	38	14	13	11	49	43	41
Vauxhall Motors	38	15	10	13	61	55	40
Bourne T.	38	15	9	14	62	50	39
Stewart & Lloyds	38	15	9	14	60	56	39
Rothwell T.	38	10	17	11	42	54	37
Rushden T.	38	14	9	15	70	46	35
Holbeach U.	38	12	10	16	57	79	34
Wootton Blue Cross	38	12	9	17	43	56	33
St. Neots T.	38	12	7	19	41	57	31
Northampton Spencer O.B.	38	7	11	20	36	65	25
Olney T.	38	7	7	24	38	80	21
Biggleswade T.	38	1	2	34	22	13	34

Midland Counties League

PREMIER DIVISION

	P	W	D	L	F	A	Pts
Eastwood T.	34	23	6	5	70	36	52
Arnold	34	20	9	5	74	44	49
Long Eaton U.	34	17	12	5	47	31	46
Alfreton T.	34	19	6	9	76	41	44
Bridlington Tr.	34	18	6	10	56	36	40
Mexborough T.	34	15	10	9	71	45	40
Boston F.C.	34	14	8	12	54	47	36
Frickley Ath.	34	10	16	8	50	45	36
Belper T.	34	14	8	12	36	32	36
Kimberley T.	34	14	6	14	47	56	34
Ilkeston T.	34	12	8	14	52	61	32
Skegness T.	34	11	9	14	41	40	31
Louth U.	34	10	10	14	57	60	30
Sutton T.	34	9	12	13	39	46	30
Clifton F.C.	34	5	12	17	37	63	22
Retford T.	34	6	7	21	37	79	19
Heanor T.	34	4	9	21	33	69	17
Ashby F.C.	34	4	8	22	28	74	16

Football Combination

	P	W	D	L	F	A	Pts
Ipswich T.	42	25	10	7	91	46	60
Birmingham C.	42	24	11	7	53	23	59
Southampton	42	22	11	9	76	44	55
West Ham U.	42	24	4	14	89	51	52
Bristol C.	42	20	11	11	74	44	51
Chelsea	42	20	10	12	81	51	50
Luton T.	42	19	8	15	75	60	46
Arsenal	42	16	14	12	54	42	46
Plymouth Arg.	42	17	12	13	51	51	46
Cardiff C.	42	17	8	17	54	62	42
Tottenham H.	42	14	13	15	69	62	41
Q.P.R.	42	15	11	16	60	62	41
Oxford U.	42	15	9	18	42	62	39
Fulham	42	10	18	14	47	55	38
Norwich C.	42	14	9	19	46	58	37
Leicester C.	42	13	10	19	56	55	36
Orient	42	10	16	16	50	63	36
Crystal Palace	42	12	12	18	49	64	36
Reading	42	13	9	20	50	78	35
Swindon T.	42	11	9	22	40	77	31
AFC Bournemouth	42	6	14	22	40	67	26
Bristol Rovers	42	8	5	29	46	116	21

The Central League

	P	W	D	L	F	A	Pts
Liverpool	42	31	5	6	94	32	67
W.B.A.	42	25	13	4	83	35	63
Derby Co.	42	21	13	8	81	40	55
Wolverhampton W.	42	21	11	10	82	54	53
Leeds U.	42	21	9	12	76	52	51
Aston Villa	42	17	13	12	57	51	47
Coventry C.	42	16	13	13	54	46	45
Everton	42	18	8	16	70	57	44
Bury	42	14	16	12	64	66	44
Manchester U.	42	18	7	17	65	55	43
Stoke C.	42	16	10	16	60	55	42
Sheffield U.	42	15	11	16	54	56	41
Burnley	42	15	10	17	64	71	40
Newcastle U.	42	14	11	17	53	58	39
Nottingham F.	42	14	11	17	51	64	39
Manchester C.	42	11	16	15	47	54	38
Sheffield W.	42	9	15	18	42	60	33
Blackburn R.	42	12	8	22	58	85	32
Bolton W.	42	10	9	23	40	72	29
Huddersfield T.	42	8	13	21	41	75	29
Preston N.E.	42	10	8	24	36	88	28
Blackpool	42	5	12	25	37	83	22

The Leicestershire Senior League

DIVISION ONE

	P	W	D	L	F	A	Pts
Friar Lane O.B.	30	18	8	4	65	25	44
Jones & Shipman	30	18	6	6	71	34	42
Thringstone M.W.	30	18	5	7	53	29	41
Oadby Town	30	16	6	8	61	29	38
Newf'dpool W.M.C.	30	17	3	10	58	35	37
Anstey Nomads	30	16	4	10	51	30	36
Enderby Town	30	14	7	9	53	39	35
Wigston Fields	30	11	9	10	34	37	31
Harborough Town	30	10	6	14	39	57	26
Stapenhill	30	9	6	15	31	49	24
Earl Shilton Albion	30	9	6	15	35	62	24
Hinckley Town	30	8	6	16	34	52	22
Leicester Y.M.C.A.	30	8	6	16	31	52	22
Ibstock Pen. Rovers	30	7	8	15	29	52	22
Whetstone Athletic	30	8	5	17	34	58	21
Midland Athletic	30	4	7	19	23	62	15

Lancashire Combination

	P	W	D	L	F	A	Pts
Bootle	34	28	3	3	82	29	59
Acc. Stanley (1968)	34	25	5	4	104	36	55
Kirkby Town	34	18	9	7	69	38	45
Blackpool Mechs.	34	18	9	7	48	32	45
Nelson	34	18	5	11	59	35	41
Colne Dynamos	34	13	10	11	59	55	36
Maghull	34	14	6	14	54	62	34
Lytham	34	11	9	14	53	54	31
Clitheroe	34	11	9	14	51	54	31
Bacup Borough	34	9	12	13	44	59	30
Ford Motors	34	10	10	14	37	50	30
Wren Rovers	34	10	10	14	37	51	30
Skelmersdale United	34	11	8	15	35	56	30
Morecambe	34	12	3	19	50	57	27
Leyland Motors	34	9	9	16	46	54	27
Wigan Athletic	34	11	3	20	37	57	25
Atherton Collieries	34	6	8	20	48	72	20
Ashton Town	34	6	4	24	33	95	16

West Midlands Regional League

PREMIER DIVISION

	P	W	D	L	F	A	Pts
Alvechurch	36	29	3	4	74	20	61
Bilston	36	24	6	6	74	25	54
Dudley T.	36	19	11	6	61	34	49
Tividale	36	21	7	8	75	46	49
Lye T.	36	16	13	7	60	36	45
Darlaston	36	18	9	9	59	42	45
Bereton Social	36	16	7	13	42	33	39
Armitage	36	15	9	12	64	52	39
Hednesford T.	36	12	13	11	61	52	37
Coventry Sporting	36	13	9	14	41	42	35
Eastwood (Hanley)	36	12	10	14	46	45	34
Brierley Hill All.	36	14	6	16	53	63	34
Halesowen T.	36	10	9	17	46	59	29
Gresley R.	36	8	11	17	51	65	27
V.S. Rugby	36	9	7	20	26	57	25
Gornal Ath.	36	10	5	21	32	71	25
Hinckley Ath.	36	6	9	21	21	69	21
Staffs Police	36	7	5	24	38	74	19
Warley County Bor.	36	5	7	24	30	64	17

The South Midlands League

PREMIER DIVISION

	P	W	D	L	F	A	Pts
Barton R.	30	22	7	1	72	22	51
Winslow U.	30	17	7	6	57	28	41
Electrolux	30	12	11	7	45	28	35
Pirton	30	11	12	7	53	38	34
Stotfold	30	13	8	9	33	37	34
Sandy Alb.	30	12	8	10	55	43	32
Welwyn Garden	30	12	7	11	42	32	31
Arlesey T.	30	11	9	10	36	34	31
Selby	30	8	11	11	41	53	27
Towcester T.	30	9	8	13	38	40	26
Langford	30	8	10	12	40	43	26
Eaton Bray U.	30	10	4	14	33	44	26
Baldock T.	30	11	4	15	35	53	26
Harpenden T.	30	8	9	13	41	42	25
Shefford T.	30	8	8	14	39	52	24
Lucas Sports	30	2	7	21	25	96	11

Yorkshire League
DIVISION ONE

	P	W	D	L	F	A	Pts
Emley	30	21	7	2	68	25	49
North Ferriby U.	30	21	4	5	70	25	46
Hallam	30	15	4	11	58	44	34
Bridlington T.	30	14	6	10	41	38	34
Leeds Carnegie Col.	30	14	5	11	52	40	33
Thackley	30	10	13	7	28	26	33
Hatfield Main	30	11	10	9	48	45	32
Redfearn N.G.	30	11	10	9	45	47	32
Ossett Albion	30	12	6	12	46	43	30
Winterton R.	30	10	8	12	44	44	28
Lincoln U.	30	10	7	13	41	50	27
Pickering T.	30	9	8	13	36	49	26
Farsley Celtic	30	7	9	14	28	46	23
Maltby M.W.	30	9	3	18	45	70	21
Worsbrough Bridge M.W.	30	8	1	21	41	60	17
Frecheville C.A.	30	6	3	21	44	83	15

South East Counties League
DIVISION ONE

	P	W	D	L	F	A	Pts
Ipswich T.	30	23	4	3	83	31	50
Southend U.	30	21	4	5	65	27	46
Chelsea	30	19	3	8	63	26	41
Fulham	30	16	6	8	51	36	38
Portsmouth	30	15	2	13	52	46	32
Gillingham	30	12	7	11	46	50	31
Arsenal	30	12	7	11	44	56	31
West Ham U.	30	11	7	12	42	36	29
Q.P.R.	30	11	7	12	52	50	29
Tottenham H.	30	11	4	15	51	44	26
Norwich C.	30	10	5	15	29	57	25
Crystal P.	30	9	4	17	46	57	22
Charlton A.	30	7	5	18	50	68	19
Millwall	30	5	9	16	25	55	19
Watford	30	9	6	15	47	61	18*
Orient	30	6	6	18	32	69	18

*Points deducted

Lancashire League
DIVISION ONE

	P	W	D	L	F	A	Pts
Oldham Athletic	30	23	2	5	101	32	48
Liverpool	30	21	3	6	86	40	45
Everton	30	18	5	7	62	37	41
Manchester U.	30	15	6	9	82	48	36
Bradford C.	30	14	7	9	51	44	35
Tranmere R.	30	12	8	10	55	46	32
Manchester C.	30	12	8	10	43	40	32
Stockport Co.	30	12	7	11	49	36	31
Macclesfield T.	30	13	5	12	48	61	31
Rochdale	30	12	5	13	53	53	29
Altrincham	30	10	8	12	56	63	28
Crewe Alexandra	30	12	3	15	58	73	27
Chester	30	9	7	14	39	55	25
Blackpool	30	4	7	19	21	78	15
South Liverpool	30	4	5	21	29	73	13
Southport	30	4	4	22	35	89	12

Midland Football Combination
DIVISION ONE

	P	W	D	L	F	A	Pts
Northfield T.	34	23	5	6	63	30	51
Moor Green	34	20	10	4	72	39	50
Malvern T.	34	20	9	5	66	30	49
Paget R.	34	19	7	8	50	39	45
Racing Warwick	34	17	8	9	42	29	42
Sutton Coldfield T.	34	16	9	9	57	33	41
West Midlands Police	34	14	10	10	46	40	38
Blakenall	34	12	13	9	54	33	37
Bridgnorth T.	34	9	18	7	48	45	36
Evesham U.	34	12	11	11	51	40	35
Solihull Bo.	34	9	15	10	41	43	33
Cadbury Heath	34	11	8	15	47	47	30
Highgate U.	34	11	8	15	46	53	30
Cinderford T.	34	8	8	18	40	60	24
Oldbury U.	34	6	10	18	35	57	22
Boldmere St. Michaels	34	5	12	17	23	49	22
Coleshill T.	34	2	11	21	26	72	15
Knowle	34	2	8	24	21	89	12

The Mid-Week Football League

	P	W	D	L	F	A	Pts
Watford	26	16	5	5	55	29	37
Cambridge U.	26	13	8	5	42	32	34
Peterborough U.	26	14	5	7	59	34	33
Charlton Ath.	26	15	3	8	65	42	33
Southend U.	26	13	4	9	37	28	30
Gillingham	26	11	7	8	52	33	29
Brighton & H.A.	26	10	7	9	48	44	27
Luton T.	26	9	8	9	35	39	26
Orient	26	10	4	12	36	37	24
Portsmouth	26	9	4	13	33	45	22
Millwall	26	7	5	14	43	59	19
Brentford	26	6	7	13	36	54	19
Colchester U.	26	7	4	15	34	63	18
Northampton T.	26	6	1	19	39	75	13

Manchester League

	P	W	D	L	F	A	Pts
Salford Amateurs	34	23	8	3	70	23	54
Curzon Ashton	34	22	9	3	84	38	53
O. Altrinchamians	34	21	9	4	83	47	51
Irlam T.	34	19	9	6	63	32	47
Glossop	34	18	5	11	53	41	41
Wythenshaw Am.	34	16	8	10	65	43	40
Little Lever	34	15	10	9	56	43	40
Abbey Hey	34	14	6	14	62	62	34
Anson Villa	34	12	8	14	64	67	32
Chadderton	34	13	6	15	54	57	32
Chloride Recs	34	12	5	17	55	61	29
North Withington	34	11	7	16	46	54	29
Sale	34	9	7	18	55	78	25
Milton	34	9	7	18	45	68	25
Maine Road	34	9	6	19	44	64	24
Northern Nomads	34	9	6	19	48	76	24
Hollang U.	34	5	6	23	37	79	16
Man. University	34	5	6	23	47	98	16

OLYMPIC FOOTBALL 1908-1972

LONDON 1908

Semi-Finals
Gt. Britain v Holland	4-0
Denmark v France 'A'	17-1

Third Place Final
Holland v Sweden*	2-1

Final
Gt. Britain v Denmark	2-0

Sweden were nominated for the third-place final in preference to France 'A', who had been awarded a bye into the semis.

STOCKHOLM 1912

Semi-Finals
Gt. Britain v Finland	4-0
Denmark v Holland	4-1

Third Place Final
Holland v Finland	9-0

Final
Gt. Britain v Denmark	4-2

ANTWERP 1920

Semi-Finals
Belgium v Holland	3-0
Czechoslovakia v France	4-1

Play-off for Second and Third Places
Spain v Holland	3-1

Final
Belgium v Czechoslovakia	2-0

(Czechoslovakia were disqualified for walking off during the Final. Placings Belgium – Olympic Champions, Spain – Second, Holland – Third, France – Fourth.)

PARIS 1924

Semi-Finals
Uruguay v Holland	2-1
Switzerland v Sweden	2-1

Third Place Final
Sweden v Holland	1-1, 3-1

Final
Uruguay v Switzerland	3-0

AMSTERDAM 1928

Semi-Finals
Uruguay v Italy	3-2
Argentina v Egypt	6-0

Third Place Final
Italy v Egypt	11-3

Final
Uruguay v Argentina	1-1, 2-1

BERLIN 1936

Semi-Finals
Italy v Norway (after extra time)	2-1
Austria v Poland	3-1

Third Place Final
Norway v Poland	3-2

Final
Italy v Austria (after extra time)	2-1

LONDON 1948

Semi-Finals
Sweden v Denmark	4-2
Yugoslavia v Gt. Britain	3-1

Third Place Final
Denmark v Gt. Britain	5-3

Final
Sweden v Yugoslavia	3-1

HELSINKI 1952

Semi-Finals
Hungary v Sweden	6-0
Yugoslavia v West Germany	3-1

Third Place Final
Sweden v West Germany	2-0

Final
Hungary v Yugoslavia	2-0

MELBOURNE 1956

Semi-Finals
USSR v Bulgaria (after extra time)	2-1
Yugoslavia v India	4-1

Third Place Final
Bulgaria v India	3-0

Final
USSR v Yugoslavia	1-0

ROME 1960

Semi-Finals
Yugoslavia v Italy	1-1

(Yugoslavia won on toss-up)
Denmark v Hungary	2-0

Third Place Final
Italy v Hungary	2-1

Final
Yugoslavia v Denmark	3-1

TOKYO 1964

Semi-Finals
Czechoslovakia v East Germany	2-1
Hungary v United Arab Republic	6-0

Third Place Final
East Germany v U.A.R.	3-1

Final
Hungary v Czechoslovakia	2-1

MEXICO CITY 1968

Semi-Finals
Hungary v Japan	5-0
Bulgaria v Mexico	3-2

Third Place Final
Japan v Mexico	2-0

Final
Hungary v Bulgaria	4-1

MUNICH 1972

Second round qualifiers
Hungary, East Germany, Poland, USSR

Third Place Final
USSR v East Germany	2-2

Final
Poland v Hungary	2-1

F.A. REPRESENTATIVE MATCHES 1934-76

F.A. XI v ROYAL NAVY

Year	Date	Venue	F.A.	R.N.
1934	Dec.	Portsmouth	0	0
1935	Dec.	Plymouth	3	4
1936	Dec.	Chatham	7	0
1937	Dec.	Devonport	5	0
1938	Dec.	Portsmouth	6	2
1947	Feb.	Portsmouth	3	0
1947	Dec.	Portsmouth	4	0
1948	Dec.	Plymouth	1	1
1949	Dec.	Plymouth	4	1
1950	Dec.	Portsmouth	1	2
1951	Dec.	Portsmouth	4	1
1952	Dec.	Plymouth	4	0
1953	Dec.	Portsmouth	1	0
1954	Dec.	Portsmouth	2	1
1955	Dec.	Portsmouth	5	5
1957	Jan.	Portsmouth	5	1
1957	Dec.	Portsmouth	5	2
1958	Dec.	Portsmouth	4	1
1959	Dec.	Portsmouth	5	3
1960	Dec.	Portsmouth	6	2
1961	Dec.	Portsmouth	7	3
1962	Dec.	Portsmouth	4	0
1963	Dec.	Portsmouth	2	0
1964	Dec.	Portsmouth	4	1
1965	Dec.	Portsmouth	9	1
1966	Nov.	Portsmouth	1	0
1967	Nov.	Portsmouth	3	0
1968	Nov.	Portsmouth	2	0
1969	Nov.	Portsmouth	1	0
1970	Dec.	Portsmouth	2	2
1971	Dec.	Portsmouth	3	2
1972	Nov.	Portsmouth	2	1
1973	Nov.	Portsmouth	2	0
1969	Oct.	Aldershot	3	0
1970	Oct.	Aldershot	2	0
1972	Oct.	Aldershot	3	2
1973	Oct.	Bordon	0	4

F.A. XI v OXFORD UNIVERSITY

Year	Date	Venue	F.A.	O.U.
1934	Nov.	Oxford	6	1
1935	Nov.	Oxford	3	2
1936	Nov.	Oxford	5	1
1937	Nov.	Oxford	6	2
1938	Nov.	Oxford	2	0
1945	Nov.	Oxford	7	0
1946	Nov.	Oxford	4	3
1947	Nov.	Oxford	2	0
1948	Nov.	Oxford	1	1
1949	Nov.	Oxford	2	1
1950	Nov.	Oxford	3	3
1951	Nov.	Oxford	2	1
1952	Nov.	Oxford	4	2
1953	Nov.	Oxford	4	2
1954	Nov.	Oxford	5	0
1955	Nov.	Oxford	2	1
1956	Nov.	Oxford	3	0
1957	Nov.	Oxford	1	1
1958	Nov.	Oxford	5	0
1959	Nov.	Malvern	4	1
1960	Nov.	Eastbourne	3	1
1961	Nov.	Oxford	6	0
1962	Nov.	Eastbourne	3	3
1963	Nov.	Oxford	4	0
1964	Oct.	Eastbourne	4	1
1965	Nov.	Oxford	6	0
1966	Nov.	Eastbourne	3	0
1967	Nov.	Oxford	6	0
1968	Nov.	Eastbourne	5	0
1969	Nov.	Oxford	0	1
1970	Nov.	Eastbourne	1	0
1971	Nov.	Oxford	1	0
1972	Nov.	Eastbourne	5	0
1973	Nov.	Oxford	5	0

F.A. XI v THE ARMY

Year	Date	Venue	F.A.	Army
1934	Nov.	Tidworth	1	1
1935	Nov.	Colchester	4	4
1936	Nov.	Aldershot	6	3
1937	Nov.	Aldershot	4	2
1938	Nov.	Colchester	1	1
1946	Nov.	Stoke	3	8
1947	Nov.	Brighton	4	0
1948	Nov.	Ipswich	0	2
1949	Nov.	Charlton	4	1
1950	Nov.	Highbury	3	2
1951	Nov.	Highbury	4	2
1952	Nov.	Leeds	4	1
1953	Nov.	Newcastle	3	1
1954	Nov.	Sheffield	1	1
1955	Nov.	Newcastle	2	2
1956	Nov.	Manchester	7	3
1957	Oct.	Manchester	6	3
1958	Oct.	Newcastle	4	1
1959	Oct.	Newcastle	3	1
1960	Oct.	Sheffield	2	1
1961	Oct.	Sunderland	1	2
1962	Oct.	Aldershot	6	2
1963	Oct.	Aldershot	4	2
1964	Feb.	Catterick	2	2
1964	Oct.	Aldershot	1	4
1965	Feb.	Catterick	1	2
1965	Oct.	Aldershot	1	1
1966	Oct.	Aldershot	1	1
1967	Oct.	Aldershot	3	1
1968	Oct.	Aldershot	1	1

F.A. XI v UNIVERSITIES ATHLETIC UNION

Year	Date	Venue	F.A.	U.A.U.
1934	Feb.	Newcastle	5	2
1935	Feb.	Manchester	0	5
1936	Feb.	Manchester	2	2
1937	Feb.	Exeter	1	4
1938	Feb.	Leeds	4	1
1939	Feb.	Southampton	0	2
1946	Feb.	Darlington	10	1
1947	Feb.	Southampton	4	1
1948	Feb.	Bristol	2	1
1949	Feb.	Sheffield	2	0
1950	Feb.	Exeter	4	0
1951	Feb.	Hull	2	1
1952	Mar.	Doncaster	1	4
1953	Feb.	Nottingham	4	1
1954	Feb.	Bristol	3	1
1955	Feb.	Sheffield	5	0
1956	Feb.	Reading	0	3
1957	Mar.	Stoke	4	1
1958	Mar.	Leicester	1	1
1959	Mar.	Peterborough	1	2
1960	Mar.	Norwich	3	0
1961	Feb.	Reading	1	2
1963	Apr.	Sheffield	3	0

Year	Date	Venue		
1964	Feb.	Birmingham	8	0
1965	Mar.	Coventry	1	3
1966	Mar.	Rugby	5	0
1967	Mar.	Sheffield	2	1
1968	Feb.	Nottingham	1	1
1969	Apr.	Sheffield	6	0
1970	Feb.	Morecambe	3	1
1971	Apr.	Durham	1	1
1971	Oct.	Aldershot	0	2
1973	Feb.	Newcastle	2	3
1974	Feb.	Nuneaton	2	2
1976	Feb.	York	2	2

F.A. XI v ROYAL AIR FORCE

			F.A.	R.A.F
1934	Jan.	Cranwell	2	0
1935	Jan.	Watford	4	0
1936	Jan.	Uxbridge	3	3
1937	Jan.	Uxbridge	9	1
1937	Nov.	Uxbridge	4	4
1938	Dec.	Cranwell	3	2
1946	Oct.	Reading	4	1
1947	Oct.	Highbury	3	0
1948	Oct.	Highbury	9	2
1949	Oct.	Fulham	2	1
1950	Oct.	Fulham	6	1
1951	Oct.	Stamford Bridge	4	0
1952	Oct.	Stamford Bridge	8	1
1953	Oct.	Tottenham	4	0
1954	Oct.	Highbury	3	1
1955	Oct.	Bristol	9	0
1956	Oct.	Sheffield	2	1
1957	Oct.	Nottingham	5	2
1958	Oct.	Bristol	1	4
1959	Oct.	Norwich	9	2
1960	Oct.	Manchester	2	2
1961	Oct.	Peterborough	13	0
1962	Oct.	Uxbridge	4	2
1963	Oct.	Uxbridge	4	2
1964	Sept.	Uxbridge	5	1
1969	Oct.	Halton	2	2
1970	Oct.	Halton	5	0
1971	Oct.	Halton	1	0
1972	Oct.	Uxbridge	2	1
1973	Oct.	Uxbridge	4	0
1976	Jan.	Wealdstone	2	1

F.A. XI v CAMBRIDGE UNIVERSITY

			F.A.	C.U.
1934	Nov.	Cambridge	5	0
1935	Nov.	Cambridge	6	1
1936	Nov.	Cambridge	5	0
1937	Nov.	Cambridge	3	1
1938	Nov.	Cambridge	6	2
1946	Feb.	Cambridge	5	1
1946	Nov.	Cambridge	3	2
1947	Nov.	Cambridge	6	1
1948	Nov.	Cambridge	7	1
1949	Nov.	Cambridge	3	1
1950	Nov.	Cambridge	4	2
1951	Nov.	Cambridge	4	1
1952	Nov.	Cambridge	8	0
1953	Nov.	Cambridge	2	3
1954	Nov.	Cambridge	4	2
1955	Nov.	Cambridge	5	1
1956	Nov.	Cambridge	6	1

Year	Date	Venue		
1957	Nov.	Cambridge	5	0
1958	Nov.	Cambridge	1	1
1959	Nov.	Eastbourne	1	2
1960	Nov.	Cambridge	3	4
1961	Nov.	Eastbourne	3	2
1962	Nov.	Cambridge	abandoned	
1963	Oct.	Eastbourne	2	0
1964	Nov.	Cambridge	3	1
1965	Nov.	Eastbourne	4	0
1966	Nov.	Cambridge	5	1
1967	Nov.	Eastbourne	1	1
1968	Nov.	Cambridge	2	1
1969	Nov.	Eastbourne	3	0
1970	Nov.	Cambridge	7	0
1971	Nov.	Eastbourne	4	0
1972	Nov.	Cambridge	1	0
1973	Nov.	Eastbourne	3	0

F.A. XI v LONDON UNIVERSITY

			F.A.	L.U.
1958	Mar.	Motspur Park	7	1
1959	Mar.	Motspur Park	0	1
1960	Mar.	Motspur Park	5	1
1961	Mar.	Kingston	2	2
1962	Mar.	Motspur Park	7	0
1964	Mar.	Kingston	5	1
1965	Mar.	Motspur Park	6	2
1966	Mar.	Motspur Park	2	1
1967	Mar.	Hayes	3	1
1968	Mar.	Motspur Park	3	0
1969	Mar.	Motspur Park	3	0
1970	Mar.	Woking	9	0
1971	Mar.	Motspur Park	4	0
1973	Mar.	Motspur Park	4	1
1974	Mar.	Motspur Park	8	1
1976	Mar.	Kingston	4	1

F.A. XI v AMATEUR FOOTBALL ALLIANCE

			F.A.	A.F.A.
1958	Jan.	Maidstone	4	2
1959	Jan.	Barking	3	1
1960	Feb.	Maidstone	5	0
1961	Feb.	Bromley	2	2
1962	Feb.	Wimbledon	3	1
1963	Feb.	Kingston	7	1
1964	Feb.	Tooting	3	0
1965	Feb.	Wealdstone	2	2
1966	Feb.	Kingston	3	0
1967	Feb.	Bromley	1	2
1968	Feb.	Enfield	1	0
1969	Feb.	Dulwich	Ground unfit	
1970	Feb.	Clapton	2	2
1971	Feb.	Tooting	4	0
1973	Feb.	B. Stortford	3	1
1974	Feb.	Leytonstone	2	1
1976	Apr.	Dulwich	4	0

F.A. XI v BRITISH COLLEGES SPORTS ASSOCIATION

			F.A.	B.C.
1972	Dec.	Chorley	2	1
1973	Dec.	Spennymoor	0	1
1976	Mar.	Cheltenham	0	1

F.A. XI v SUNDERLAND

			F.A.	Sund.
1973	Dec.	Sunderland	0	4

F.A. CHALLENGE VASE COMPETITION

Preliminary Round

Wallsend T. v Annan Ath.	4-0
Whitkirk W. v Hall Road R.	2-0
Whalley Range Am. v Milton U.	0-3
Worsborough Bridge MW v Chloride Rec.	1-3
Sheffield v Glossop	3-0
Swallownest MW v Barton T.	0-2
Players Ath. v Clay Cross Works	1-1, 1-6
Sohan Town R. v City of Norwich School OBU	0-5
Tividale v Blakenall	1-2
Thringstone v Gresley R.	3-2
Walsall Wood v Astwood Bank R.	2-0
Lutterworth T. v Buckingham T.	0-2
Wolverton T. & BR v Long Buckby	3-2
Welwyn Garden v Clacton T.	2-3
Knebworth v Basildon U.	0-1
Shefford T. v Aylesbury U.	1-3
Thame U. v Didcot T.	2-1
Wantage T. v Burnham	0-2
Willesden v Cobham	4-0
Chingford v Kingsbury T.	0-1
Royal Arsenal Sports v Old Salesians	0-1
Egham T. v Malden T.	3-2
Three Bridges v Eastbourne U.	1-3
Seaford T. v Cowes	2-4
Ringmer v Burgess Hill T.	2-1
Wigmore Ath. v Camberley T.	0-2
Stratford v Chipping Norton T.	4-2
Thatcham T. v Bemerton Ath.	3-1
Stonehouse v Bromham	6-1

First Round

Wallsend T. v Eppleton C.W.	2-1
Wingate v South Shields Mariners	1-1, 2-3
Gretna Ath. v Alnwick T.	1-3
Heaton Stannington v Blue Star	2-2, 1-3
Whitkirk W. v Leeds Ashley R.	0-1
Yorkshire Am. v Pickering T.	1-2
North Ferriby U. v Guiseley	1-2
Norton Cricket Club v Harrogate T.	1-2
Anson Villa v Chadderton	1-2
Old Blackburnians v Liversedge	0-3
Corinthians (Milnthorpe) v Birkenshaw R.	3-1
Little-Lever v Brook Sports	2-1
Milton U. v Old Altrinchamians	0-3
Wigan R. v Warrington T.	1-0
Prescot T. v Hoylake Ath.	6-0
Stork v North Withington	1-2
Chloride Rec. v Frecheville Community	3-2
Wythenshawe Am. v Sheffield Univ.	2-1
Hallam v BSC Parkgate	1-0
Maltby M.W. v Curzon Ashton	0-1
Sheffield v Manchester YMCA	6-1
Woolley M.W. v Rawmarsh Wel.	3-1
Northern Nomads v East Chorlton Am.	2-3
Norton Woodseats v Irlam Town Am.	1-0
Barton T. v Brigg T.	0-2
Wombwell & District v Redfearn National Glass	2-1
Immingham T. v Barton R.	0-1
Kiveton Park v Bentley Vic.	3-1
Claycross Works v Clipstone Wel.	2-2, 0-3
Stamford v Oakham U.	4-0
Lincoln T. v Bourne T.	2-0
Loughborough Coll. v Clifton All Whites	1-2
City of Norwich School O.B.U. v Holt U.	4-2
Warboys T. v Peterborough R.	0-3
March T. U. v Bungay T.	5-2
Parson Drove U. v Holbeach U.	0-3
Blakenall v Chelmsley T.	4-0
West Midlands Police v Mile Oak R. & Youth	2-1
Coleshill T. v Bermuda WMC	0-1
Halesowen T. v Bridgnorth T.	0-2
Thringstone v Knowle	1-0
Whitmore O.B. v Paget R.	1-2
Newfoundpool WMC v Gornal Ath.	4-2
Northfield T. v Hinckley Ath.	2-2, 3-3, 4-1

Walsall Wood v Hinckley T.	3-1
Wickman v Solihull Bor.	2-3
Oadby T. v Anstey Nomads	0-3
Pershore U. v Friar Lane O.B.	0-2
Buckingham T. v Coventry Sp.	2-3
Rothwell T. v Kempston R.	2-1
Desborough T. v Bicester T.	5-1
Jones-Shipman v Burton Park W.	3-0
Wolverton T. v Potton U.	2-1
Wootton Blue Cross v Stotfold	0-1
Raunds T. v Hazells	1-0
Royston v Northampton Spencer	1-1, 0-3
Clacton T. v Hoddesdon T.	1-0
Witham T. v Stansted	3-0
Maldon T. v Brightlingsea U.	4-1
Saffron Walden T. v Epping T.	1-2
Basildon U. v Braintree & Crittall Ath.	1-0
Tiptree U. v Heybridge Sw.	1-2
Coggeshall T. v Arlesey T.	0-2
Hatfield T. v Billericay T.	1-1, 0-2
Aylesbury U. v Harpenden T.	3-1
Tring T. v Rolls Royce Engines	2-1
Hemel Hempstead v Ampthill	7-2
Leighton T. v Baldock T.	0-1
Thame U. v Maidenhead T.	2-0
Vauxhall Motors v Shillington	w.o. for Vauxhall
Marlow v Berkhamsted T.	2-0
Selby v Leggatts O.B.	0-2
Burnham v Chobham	5-1
Windsor & Eton v Newbury T.	2-0
Farnborough T. v Amersham T.	3-2
Fleet T. v Chalfont St. Peter	1-2
Addlestone v Banstead Ath.	3-1
Old Salesians v Feltham	1-3
Civil Service v Crown & Motor	1-2
Swanley T. v Cray W.	2-1
Eton Manor v Willesden	2-1
Ulysses v Virginia Water	2-3
Edmonton & Haringey v Borough R. Coll.	w.o. for Edmonton
Egham T. v Whyteleafe	2-0
Harefield U. v East Barnet O.G.	4-1
B.A.C. (Weybridge) v Westfield	1-2
Kingsbury T. v Crockenhill	0-1
Thames Polytechnic v Rainham T.	0-4
Bexley v Leyton-Wingate	1-2
Rayners Lane v Molesey	0-1
Lion Sports v Ford U.	0-3
Chessington U. v Epsom & Ewell	2-2, 2-3
Bexhill T. v Faversham T.	2-3
Whitstable T. v Slade Green Ath.	2-0
Herne Bay v Deal T.	3-2
Merstham v East Grinstead	2-1
Eastbourne U. v Horley T.	0-2
Tunbridge Wells v Sidley U.	3-2
Horsham YMCA v Dartford Am.	2-2, 0-2
Reigate Priory v Heathside Sp.	0-1
Cowes v Farnham T.	0-1
Shoreham v Pagham	3-3, 2-0
Gosport Bor. v Arundel	5-1
Lancing v Eastbourne T.	1-4
Ringmer v East Cowes Victoria Ath.	2-3
Swaythling v Portfield	4-0
Frimley Green v Brockenhurst	1-3
Havant & Leigh Park v Chichester C.	1-1, 2-3
Camberley T. v Moneyfield Sp.	0-1
Worthing v Whitehawk	2-1
Portsmouth R.N. v Bracknell T.	2-3
Selsey v Chertsey T.	3-1
Stratford T. v Longlevens Star	5-0
Valley Sports v Pegasus Jun.	2-0
Malvern T. v Alcester T.	3-1
Moreton T. v Evesham U.	0-2
Thatcham T. v Cirencester T.	1-2
Wallingford T. v Melksham T.	2-0
Clanfield v Abingdon T.	1-3
Hungerford T. v Calne T.	1-0
Stonehouse v Forest Green R.	2-1
Yate T. v Radstock T.	0-2
Hanham Ath. v Avon	2-1

Malmesbury Vic. v Cadbury Heath	0-1
Bridport v Glenside Hospital	1-0
Westbury U. v Tiverton T.	3-1
Ottery St. Mary v Bristol St. George	1-2
Shepton Mallet T. v Exmouth T.	3-1

Second Round

Wallsend T. v Blue Star	3-1
Alnwick T. v South Shields Mariners	1-2
Pickering T. v Liversedge	2-3
Guiseley v Leeds Ashley Rd.	2-3
Harroga.e T. v Woolley Miners Wel.	2-1
Wythenshawe Am. v Chloride Rec.	5-1
Little Lever v East Chorlton Am.	5-3
Prescot T. v Wigan R.	3-2
Chadderton v N. Withington	2-1
Old Altrinchamians v Corinthians (Milnthorpe)	1-0
Maltby M.W. v Hallam	1-4
Wombwell & District v Brigg T.	0-1
Norton Woodseats v Lincoln U.	2-2, 1-3
Kiveton Park v Sheffield	1-1, 0-1
Newfoundpool W.M.C. v Clifton	2-3
Friar Lane O.B. v Clipstone Wel.	5-0
Anstey Nomads v Thringstone	1-3
March T. U. v Holbeach U.	2-0
City of Norwich School O.B.U. v Peterborough R.	6-0
Raunds T. v Coventry Sp.	0-3
Valley Sports (Rugby) v Bermuda W.M.C.	0-3
Rothwell T. v Jones-Shipman	1-2
Desborough T. v Stamford	0-2
West Midlands Police v Bridgnorth T.	1-4
Northfield T. v Malvern T.	0-3
Stratford T. v Walsall Wood	1-0
Blakenell v Paget R.	1-2
Solihull Bor. v Evesham U.	1-2
Northampton Spencer v Aylesbury U.	1-2
Wolverton T. & BR v Arlesey T.	2-2, 2-0
Stotfold v Barton R.	1-2
Baldock T. v Vauxhall Motors	1-2
Maldon T. v Epping T.	0-1
Heybridge Sw. v Clacton T.	1-4
Basildon U. v Witham T.	1-1, 2-1
Tring T. v Marlow	2-0
Thame U. v Hemel Hempstead	1-2
Abingdon T. v Wallingford T.	2-0
Tunbridge Wells v Herne Bay	2-0
Dartford Am. v Faversham T.	2-1
Eastbourne T. v Whitstable T.	2-0
Swaythling v Selsey	0-1
Brockenhurst v Worthing	1-0
Chichester C. v Moneyfield Sp.	4-2
Gosport Bor. v East Cowes Vic. Ath.	6-1
Farnham T. v Shoreham	2-3
Leggatts O.B. v Addlestone	0-2
Windsor & Eton v Virginia Water	4-0
Rainham T. v Farnborough T.	0-3
Crown & Manor v Billericay T.	0-2
Bracknell T. v Swanley T.	2-1
Horley T. v Chalfont St. Peter	0-1
Heathside Sp. v Edmonton & Haringey	4-3
Feltham v Westfield	3-0
Egham T. v Leyton-Wingate	4-0
Epsom & Ewell v Merstham	4-5
Crockenhill v Ford U.	1-0
Burnham v Harefield U.	2-0
Eton Manor v Molesey	0-1
Hungerford T. v Hanham Ath.	1-0
Cirencester T. v Stonehouse	6-1
Shepton Mallet T. v Cadbury Heath	1-2
Radstock T. v Bristol St. George	2-3
Bridport v Westbury U.	5-2

Third Round

Wallsend T. v South Shields Mariners	1-3
Brigg T. v Sheffield	7-1
Leeds Ashley Rd. v Chadderton	2-0
Harrogate T. v Lincoln U.	0-1
Hallam v Liversedge	2-1
Little-Lever v Wythenshawe Amateurs	0-2
Prescot T. v Old Altrinchamians	3-3, 1-2
Clifton v Stamford	1-2
Jones-Shipman v Friar Lane OB	1-1, 0-3
Bermuda W.M.C. v Thringstone	4-2
Paget R. v Stratford T.	2-3
Bridgnorth T. v Coventry Sp.	1-0
Malvern T. v Evesham U.	3-3, 1-3
March T. U. v City of Norwich School OBU	1-4
Billericay T. v Epping T.	1-0
Basildon U. v Clacton T.	1-0
Tring T. v Hemel Hempstead	3-1
Barton R. v Chalfont St. Peter	4-0
Wolverton T. & BR v Aylesbury U.	2-3
Abingdon T. v Vauxhall Motors	2-1
Farnborough T. v Merstham	2-0
Egham T. v Molesey	1-2
Addlestone v Dartford Am.	2-1
Feltham v Heathside Sp.	2-3
Burnham v Crockenhill	2-0
Bracknell T. v Windsor & Eton	3-2
Eastbourne T. v Selsey	5-1
Shoreham v Tunbridge Wells	1-4
Gosport Bor. v Bridport	2-0
Brockenhurst v Chichester C.	2-0
Cirencester T. v Cadbury Heath	2-2, 1-5
Bristol St. George v Hungerford T.	3-4

Fourth Round

Prescot T. v Hallam	1-0
Leeds Ashley Rd. v Wythenshawe Am.	1-1, 2-1
South Shields Mariners v Brigg T.	3-1
Stamford v Bermuda WMC	5-0
Friar Lane OB v Lincoln U.	2-1
Stratford T. v Cadbury Heath	0-1
Evesham U. v Bridgnorth T.	0-2
Barton R. v Basildon U.	3-2
Billericay T. v City of Norwich School OBU	2-1
Tunbridge Wells v Addlestone	0-3
Eastbourne T. v Heathside Sp.	1-0
Abingdon T. v Tring T.	1-0
Bracknell T. v Aylesbury U.	2-0
Molesey v Burnham	1-0
Hungerford T. v Brockenhurst	2-1
Gosport Bor. v Farnborough T.	1-4

Fifth Round

Leeds Ashley Rd. v Friar Lane OB	1-2
Stamford v Prescot T.	3-1
Bridgnorth T. v South Shields	0-2
Billericay T. v Hungerford T.	2-0
Cadbury Heath v Molesey	2-0
Barton R. v Eastbourne T.	1-0
Addlestone v Abingdon T.	5-2
Farnborough T. v Bracknell T.	3-0

Sixth Round

Friar Lane OB v South Shields	2-0
Stamford v Addlestone	3-0
Farnborough T. v Barton R.	2-0
Cadbury Heath v Billericay T.	0-3

Semi-Finals (2 legs)

Billericay T. v Farnborough T.	2-1, 0-0
Friar Lane OB v Stamford	1-2, 1-3

Final at Wembley

Billericay T. 1, Stamford 0 (*after extra time*) 12,000

Billericay T.: Griffiths; Foreman, Bone, Payne, Pullin, Coughlin, Geddes, Aslett, Claydon, Scott, Smith.
Stamford: Johnson; Kwiatkowski, Marchant, Crawford, Downs, Hird, Barnes, Walpole, Smith, Russell, Broadhurst.

F.A. AMATEUR CUP WINNERS 1894-1974

Year	Venue	Winners	Runners-up	Score	
1894	Richmond	Old Carthusians	Casuals	2-1	
1895	Leeds	Middlesbrough	Old Carthusians	2-1	
1896	Leicester	Bishop Auckland	R.A. (Portsmouth)	1-0	
1897	Darlington	Old Carthusians	Stockton	4-1	after 1-1 draw at Tufnell Park
1898	Crystal Palace	Middlesbrough	Uxbridge	2-1	
1899	Middlesbrough	Stockton	Harwich & Parkeston	1-0	
1900	Leicester	Bishop Auckland	Lowestoft T.	5-1	
1901	Ipswich	Crook T.	King's Lynn	3-0	after 1-1 draw at Harwich
1902	Leeds	Old Malvernians	Bishop Auckland	5-1	
1903	Darlington	Stockton	Oxford C.	1-0	after 0-0 draw at Reading
1904	Bradford	Sheffield	Ealing	3-1	
1905	Shepherds Bush	West Hartlepool	Clapton	3-2	
1906	Stockton	Oxford C.	Bishop Auckland	3-0	
1907	Chelsea	Clapton	Stockton	2-1	
1908	Bishop Auckland	Depot Bn. R.E.	Stockton	2-1	
1909	Ilford	Clapton	Eston U.	6-0	
1910	Bishop Auckland	R.M.L.I. (Gosport)	South Bank	2-1	
1911	Herne Hill	Bromley	Bishop Auckland	1-0	
1912	Middlesbrough	Stockton	Eston U.	1-0	after 0-0 draw at Middlesbrough
1913	Bishop Auckland	South Bank	Oxford C.	1-0	after 1-1 draw at Reading
1914	Leeds	Bishop Auckland	Northern Nomads	1-0	
1915	Millwall	Clapton	Bishop Auckland	1-0	
1920	Millwall	Dulwich Hamlet	Tufnell Park	1-0	after extra time
1921	Middlesbrough	Bishop Auckland	Swindon Victoria	4-2	
1922	Middlesbrough	Bishop Auckland	South Bank	5-2	after extra time
1923	Crystal Palace	London Caledonians	Evesham T.	2-1	after extra time
1924	Millwall	Clapton	Erith & Belvedere	3-0	
1925	Millwall	Clapton	Southall	2-1	
1926	Sunderland	Northern Nomads	Stockton	7-1	
1927	Millwall	Leyton	Barking T.	3-1	
1928	Middlesbrough	Leyton	Cockfield	3-2	
1929	Arsenal	Ilford	Leyton	3-1	
1930	West Ham	Ilford	B'mouth Gasw'ks Ath.	5-1	
1931	Arsenal	Wycombe W.	Hayes	1-0	
1932	West Ham	Dulwich Hamlet	Marine (Liverpool)	7-1	
1933	Darlington	Kingstonian	Stockton	4-1	1-1 at Dulwich
1934	West Ham	Dulwich Hamlet	Leyton	2-1	
1935	Chelsea	Bishop Auckland	Wimbledon	2-1	after 0-0 draw at Middlesbrough
1936	West Ham	Casuals	Ilford	2-0	after 1-1 draw at Selhurst Park
1937	West Ham	Dulwich Hamlet	Leyton	2-0	
1938	Milfwall	Bromley	Erith & Belvedere	1-0	
1939	Sunderland	Bishop Auckland	Willington	3-0	after extra time
1946	Chelsea	Barnet	Bishop Auckland	3-2	
1947	Arsenal	Leytonstone	Wimbledon	2-1	
1948	Chelsea	Leytonstone	Barnet	1-0	
1949	Wembley	Bromley	Romford	1-0	
1950	Wembley	Willington	Bishop Auckland	4-0	
1951	Wembley	Pegasus	Bishop Auckland	2-1	
1952	Wembley	Walthamstow Av.	Leyton	2-1	after extra time
1953	Wembley	Pegasus	Harwich & Parkeston	6-0	
1954	Middlesbrough	Crook T.	Bishop Auckland	1-0	after two draws: at Wembley (2-2) Newcastle (2-2)
1955	Wembley	Bishop Auckland	Hendon	2-0	
1956	Middlesbrough	Bishop Auckland	Corinthian-Casuals	4-1	1-1 at Wembley
1957	Wembley	Bishop Auckland	Wycombe W.	3-1	
1958	Wembley	Woking	Ilford	3-0	
1959	Wembley	Crook T.	Barnet	3-2	
1960	Wembley	Hendon	Kingstonian	2-1	
1961	Wembley	Walthamstow Av.	W. Auckland T.	2-1	
1962	Middlesbrough	Crook T.	Hounslow T.	4-0	1-1 at Wembley
1963	Wembley	Wimbledon	Sutton U.	4-2	
1964	Wembley	Crook T.	Enfield	2-1	
1965	Wembley	Hendon	Whitby T.	3-1	
1966	Wembley	Wealdstone	Hendon	3-1	
1967	Manchester	Enfield	Skelmersdale U.	3-0	0-0 at Wembley
1968	Wembley	Leytonstone	Chesham U.	1-0	
1969	Wembley	North Shields	Sutton U.	2-1	
1970	Wembley	Enfield	Dagenham	5-1	
1971	Wembley	Skelmersdale U.	Dagenham	4-1	
1972	Wembley	Hendon	Enfield	2-0	
1973	Wembley	Walton & Hersham	Slough Town	1-0	
1974	Wembley	Bishop's Stortford	Ilford	4-1	

FA SUNDAY CUP WINNERS 1965-76

Year	Winners		Runners-up		Venue
1965	*London	6	Staffordshire	2	—
1966	Ubique United	1	Aldridge Fabrications	0	Dudley
1967	Carlton United	2	Stoke Works	0	Hendon
1968	Drovers	2	Brook United	0	Cambridge
1969	Leigh Park	3	Loke United	1	Romford
1970	Vention United	1	Ubique United	0	Corby
1971	Becontree Rovers	2	Saltley United	0	Leamington
1972	Newton U.	4	Springfield Colts	0	Dudley
1973	Carlton United	2	Wear Valley	1	Spennymoor
1974	Newtown Unity	3	Brentford East	0	Moor Green
1975	Fareham T. Centipedes	1	Players Athletic Engineers	0	—
1976	Brandon U.	2	Evergreen	1	—

*Aggregate score.

FA SUNDAY CUP 1975-76

First Round
Middlestone Moor v Brandon U.	2-4
Wheatley Hill WMC v Pioneer	5-2
Hull Fruit Trades v Black Bull Taverners	0-3
Rochdale Nomads v Magnet Joinery	0-8
Railway Ath. v Lobster	2-2, 1-4
Rylands v Raysel	1-2
John Player v Adelaide Park	1-0
Taverners v Sutton Sports	2-1
Kingstanding Ex-Service v Cotgrave Wel.	1-5
Poplar Ath. v Old Horns	2-2, 3-5
Kingswinford Ath. v Arley Rectory	2-5
Olympic Star v Lodge Cottrell	1-3
Halesowen H. v Byron Ath.	3-1
Sandwell v Newtown Unity	1-2
Westfields v Lion R.	2-1
Springfield Social v Club Lafayette	0-1
Rydell Mount v Pinvin U.	0-2
Stewartby v Bedford Midlanders	3-1
Thameside Wandsworthians v Billericay T.	1-2
Crossness Sports v Basildon U.	1-2
Roman U. v Croxley Cas.	0-2
Woodford T. v Bankside	4-0
Oxford Rd. v Carlton U.	1-2
Southern Arg. v St. James	4-0
Minley U. v Durrington Youth	2-0
Test Valley Select v North Stoneham	2-0
Tally Ho v Embassy 2	1-5

Second Round
Wheatley Hill WMC v Carlisle United Supporters	2-1
Brandon U. v Willington Market Blue Star	4-3
Magnet Joinery v Hull Fish Trades	1-0
Black Bull Taverners v Swanfield	1-2
Raysel v Music Hall	3-0
Lobster v Standish	4-1
Taverners v Athletico Imperials	5-1
John Player v Woodhouse R.	4-2
Old Horns v Enderby R.	0-2
Cotgrave Wel. v Selston Co-op	2-3
Lodge Cottrell v Counts XI	0-2
Arley Rectory v Three Tuns	2-1
Newtown Unity v Dulwich	4-0
Halesowen H. v Wombourne WMC	5-0
Club Lafayette v Jumbos XI	4-2
Westfields v Pinvin U.	0-1
Queens Arms v Girton Eagles	5-6
Stewartby v Loke U.	1-2
Sawbridgeworth v Evergreen	2-3
Arras v Queensmen	3-2
Sun v Buxton Ath.	0-2
Billericay T. v Rainham WMC	2-1

Third Round — Croxley Cas. etc.
Croxley Cas. v Clifda	0-2
Basildon U. v Two Seven-Nine	1-2
Ship & Anchor v Brentford E.	3-1
Woodford T. v Pools U.	4-2
Southern Arg. v Newick R.	4-3
Carlton U. v Theale	1-2
Test Valley Select v Fareham T. Centipedes	0-3
Minley U. v Wildern	1-2
Sawyers v Prince Albert	0-1
Embassy 2 v Robin Hoods Retreat	0-4

Third Round
Wheatley Hill E.M.C. v Swanfield	2-5
Magnet Joinery v Brandon U.	0-1
Lobster v Raysel	2-3
Newtown Unity v Halesowen H.	2-0
Club Lafayette v Pinvin U.	1-0
Counts XI v Arley Rectory	1-5
John Player v Taverners	0-3
Selston Co-op v Enderby R.	2-1
Clifda v Loke U.	1-1, 1-2
Girton Eagles v Billericay T.	0-2
Two-Seven-Nine v Southern Arg.	1-0
Woodford T. v Arras	3-3, 5-4
Ship & Anchor v Theale	2-0
Buxton Ath. v Evergreen	0-4
Wildern v Robin Hoods Retreat	0-3
Prince Albert v Fareham T. Centipedes	0-2

Fourth Round
Brandon U. v Raysel	5-0
Selston Co-op v Swanfield	2-1
Newtown Unity v Taverners	2-0
Club Lafayette v Arley Rectory	3-0
Loke U. v Two-Seven-Nine	1-2
Ship and Anchor v Billericay T.	4-0
Woodford T. v Robin Hoods Retreat	1-2
Fareham T. Centipedes v Evergreen	0-2

Fifth Round
Newtown Unity v Brandon U.	0-0, 1-5
Club Lafayette v Selston Co-op	1-0
Two-Seven-Nine v Robin Hoods Retreat	1-0
Ship & Anchor v Evergreen	1-2

Semi-finals
Club Lafayette v Brandon U. (at Dudley Town FC)	1-3
Two-Seven-Nine v Evergreen (at Dulwich Hamlet FC)	1-2

Final
Brandon U. v Evergreen (at Spennymoor)	2-1

A.F.A. FOOTBALL 1975-76

AMATEUR FOOTBALL ALLIANCE SENIOR CUP FINAL 1975-76

Old Aloysians 2 West Wickham 1
(at Witan FC Sports Ground, Sutton, Surrey)

Old Aloysians: Osman; Macauley, Murty, Doherty, Fleming, Morrissey, Allpress, Reed (capt.), Brooks, Quaid, Glover.
West Wickham: Open; Reeves, Miller, Lawson (capt.), Ross, Pearce, Childs, Osborne, Harding, Dash, Fudge.

OTHER COMPETITION WINNERS 1975-76

A.F.A. Middlesex Senior Cup: East Barnet Old Grammarians (*beat Old Actonians 1-0*)

A.F.A. Surrey Senior Cup: Carhsalton (*beat Old Westminster Citizens 2-1*)

A.F.A. Essex Senior Cup: Old Fairlopians (*beat Old Parmiterians 2-0*)

Arthur Dunn Cup: Old Malverians (*beat Old Brentwoods 5-3*)

Southern Amateur League: Midland Bank

Southern Olympian League: Old Fairlopians

Arthurian League: Old Brentwoods

Nemean League: Old Actonians

Old Boys League: East Barnet Old Grammarians

THE OLD BOYS LEAGUE

Premier Division

	P	W	D	L	F	A	Pts.
East Barnet O.G.	20	12	4	4	35	19	28
Old Suttonians	20	10	4	6	44	23	24
Old Salesians	20	9	5	6	29	24	23
Old Manorians	20	8	7	5	27	25	23
Old Aloysians	20	7	7	6	25	21	21
Old Sinjuns	20	8	3	9	30	29	19
Old Fincunians	20	7	5	8	33	35	19
Old Strandians	20	7	4	9	37	42	18
Old Uffingtonians	20	6	5	9	19	33	17
Enfield O.G.	20	5	5	10	35	42	15
Old Tenisonians	20	4	5	11	21	42	13

Senior Division One

	P	W	D	L	F	A	Pts.
Old Minchendenians	20	11	7	2	41	19	29
Old Ignatians	20	11	6	3	38	20	28
Old Edmontonians	20	9	5	6	40	34	23
Old Addeyans	20	8	4	8	30	31	20
Old Westhamians	20	8	3	9	45	40	19
Glyn Old Boys	20	6	6	8	33	32	18
Old Uxonians	20	6	6	8	31	38	18
Shene O.G.	20	5	8	7	25	45	18
Old Wokingians	20	7	3	10	25	32	17
Old Paludians	20	5	6	9	23	33	16
East Barnet O.G. Res.	20	5	4	11	34	41	14

UNIVERSITY FOOTBALL 1975-76

UNIVERSITY MATCH

Oxford (1) 2 (*Smith, Thomas*)

Cambridge (0) 0   at Wembley   8000

Oxford: M. Wickham; D. Kay, I. Barr, B. Thomas, M. Morowiec, P. Kent (capt), J. Herlihy, J. Lever, M. Feely, D. Smith, S. Ryan. Sub: P. White.

Cambridge: B. Jones; E. Jackson, C. Walters, E. Evans, I. Poslethwaite, G. Allcott (capt), J. Little, S. Smith, P. Roberts, A. Fitchie, J.Wilks. Sub: I. Swalwell.

BRITISH UNIVERSITIES GROUP TOURNAMENT 1975/6

(at Edinburgh University))

March 29, 1976					March 31, 1976			
Scotland II	5	Oxford	0		London	4	Scotland I	3
N. Ireland	1	London	0		N. Ireland	3	Cambridge	2
U.A.U.	1	Wales	0		Wales	4	Oxford	1
Scotland I	2	Cambridge	1		U.A.U.	1	Scotland II	0

March 30, 1976					PLACE	April 1, 1976			
N. Ireland	0	Scotland I	0		Final	U.A.U.	4	N. Ireland	3
Cambridge	3	London	1		3rd and 4th	Scotland I	5	Scotland II	1
Oxford	1	U.A.U.	1		5th and 6th	Wales	4	Cambridge	2
Wales	1	Scotland II	1		7th and 8th	London	2	Oxford	1

UNIVERSITIES, POLYTECHNICS AND COLLEGES TRIANGULAR TOURNAMENT 1975-76

(MADELEY COLLEGE)

British Universities	2	British Polytechnics	3
British Universities	2	British Colleges	1
British Polytechnics	0	British Colleges	1

Universities won on number of goals scored, teams finished with same points and goal difference.

UNIVERSITIES ATHLETIC UNION TOURNAMENT

Quarter Final					Semi-Final			
U.W.I.S.T.*	1	Durham	1		Aston	2	The City	0
The City	1	Bradford	1*		Durham	3	Leicester	2
Bristol	1	Leicester	2					
Aston	2	Swansea	2					

*eliminated on penalties.

Final (at Coventry City F.C.)
Aston 2 v Durham 0

Representative Fixtures

U.A.U.	2	British Colleges	3
U.A.U.	3	British Polytechnics	3
U.A.U.	2	F.A. XI	2

SCHOOLS' INTER-ASSOCIATION TROPHY 1975-76

Fifth Round

Oxford v Hereford	3-2
Barking v North Herts	3-1
Blackpool v Liverpool	2-2, 0-1
Leicester v Walsall	3-0
Reading v Merton	1-1, 2-4
Cambridge v Swindon	1-0
Rotherham v Birkenhead	2-1
Chesterfield v Grimsby & Cleethorpes	1-1, 0-1
Slough v Waltham Forest	4-1
Bristol v Plymouth	1-0
South Suffolk v Hillingdon	1-0
Havering v Hackney	0-1
Manchester v Nuneaton	6-1
Middlesbrough South v Northumberland	4-0
Sheffield v Stockport	1-0
Warley v Leeds	1-0

Sixth Round

Oxford v Barking	0-2
Liverpool v Leicester	3-0

Merton v Cambridge	0-1
Rotherham v Grimsby & Cleethorpes	2-0
Slough v Bristol	4-1
South Suffolk v Hackney	0-2
Manchester v Middlesbrough	4-2
Sheffield v Warley	2-1

Seventh Round

Barking v Liverpool	1-2
Cambridge v Rotherham	0-0, 1-2
Slough v Hackney	4-1
Manchester v Sheffield	1-1, 2-2, 2-1

Semi-finals

Liverpool v Rotherham	0-0, 3-0
Slough v Manchester	2-0

Final

Liverpool v Slough	4-2, 0-1

ENGLISH SCHOOLS' TROPHY WINNERS 1975-76

	Winners	Runners up		Winners	Runners up
1905	London	Sheffield	1940	Abandoned	
1906	Sheffield	Manchester	1941-5	No Competition	
1907	West Ham	Sunderland	1946	Leicester	Stockton-on-Tees
1908	Derby	Oxford	1947	Salford	Leicester
1909	Sheffield	Birmingham N.	1948	*Stockport	*Liverpool
1910	Sunderland	Walsall	1949	Barnsley	Derby County
1911	Chester-le-S.	Tottenham	1950	Swansea	Manchester
1912	West Ham	Birkenhead	1951	Liverpool	Brierley Hill &
1913	Watford	Sunderland			Sedgeley
1914	Sheffield	West Ham	1952	Ilford	Swansea
1915	Cardiff	Manchester	1953	Swansea	Chesterfield
1916	Bradford	West Ham	1954	Liverpool	Southampton
1917	West Ham	Grimsby	1955	Swansea	Manchester
1918	Liverpool	West Ham	1956	Liverpool	Brighton
1919	Grimsby	Sunderland	1957	*Southampton	*Barnsley
1920	Reading	Grimsby	1958	Bristol	Swansea
1921	Liverpool	West Ham	1959	*Brierley Hill, Sedgeley	
1922	S. London	Grimsby		& Tipton	*Doncaster
1923	Sheffield	Birmingham	1960	Manchester	East London
1924	N. Staffs.	Reading	1961	Barnsley	Liverpool
1925	Sheffield	Brighton	1962	Stoke	Liverpool
1926	Grimsby	Liverpool	1963	Stoke	Bristol
1927	E. Northumberland	Rotherham	1964	Erdington and Saltley	Chester-le-St.
1928	N. Staffordshire	Brighton	1965	*Swansea	*Leicester
1929	S. Northumberland	Southampton	1966	East London	Oxford
1930	Newcastle	Chesterfield	1967	Liverpool	East London
1931	Islington	Wolverhampton	1968	*Manchester	*Waltham Forest
1932	*Manchester	*Southampton	1969	Liverpool	Swindon
1933	Sunderland	Edmonton	1970	Liverpool	East London
1934	Manchester	Swansea	1971	Huyton	Stoke
1935	Manchester	Swansea	1972	Chelmsford	Oxford
1936	*Preston	*West Ham	1973	Liverpool	Chelmsford
1937	Liverpool	Blyth (N'th'bld)	1974	Manchester	Oxford
1938	Manchester	Bootle	1975	Barking	Havering
1939	Swansea	Chesterfield	1976	Liverpool	Slough

*Joint Winners

INDIVIDUAL SCHOOLS CHAMPIONSHIP 1975-76

Preliminary Round

Durham v Cumbria	1-0
Cleveland v Yorkshire	1-1, 1-1, 2-3
Greater Manchester v Merseyside	2-5
Clwyd v Shropshire	2-3
Lincolnshire v Humberside	0-1
Leicestershire v Staffordshire	3-1
West Midlands Met v Warwickshire	1-1, 0-0, 1-2
Buckinghamshire v Bedfordshire	3-3, 0-5
Avon v Gloucestershire	1-3
West Glamorgan v South Glamorgan	7-0
Cambridgeshire v Norfolk	2-5
Hertfordshire v Middlesex	1-3
Surrey v Sussex	3-1
Oxfordshire v Inner London	1-1, 1-5
Cornwall v Devon	1-0
Hampshire v Dorset	3-2

First Round

Yorkshire v South Yorkshire	2-3
Durham v Northumberland	0-1
Merseyside v Lancashire	9-3
Shropshire v Cheshire	2-0
Warwickshire v Hereford & Worcs.	3-1
Northants v Bedfordshire	1-1, 0-3
Nottinghamshire v Humberside	4-0
Derbyshire v Leicestershire	0-0, 3-1
Wiltshire v Hampshire	4-0
Somerset v Cornwall	0-1
West Glamorgan v Mid Glamorgan	5-1
Gwent v Gloucestershire	4-4, 1-2
Surrey v Kent	2-0

Inner London v Berkshire	1-0
Suffolk v Norfolk	0-1
Middlesex v Essex	1-1, 2-0

Second Round

South Yorkshire v Northumberland	2-2, 1-2
Merseyside v Shropshire	4-2
Warwickshire v Bedfordshire	0-3
Nottinghamshire v Derbyshire	2-2, 1-4
Wiltshire v Cornwall	5-3
West Glamorgan v Gloucestershire	5-2
Surrey v Inner London	4-0
Norfolk v Middlesex	1-0

Third Round

Northumberland v Merseyside	1-0
Bedfordshire v Derbyshire	6-1
Wiltshire v West Glamorgan	0-2
Surrey v Norfolk	3-3, 3-1

Semi-finals

Northumberland v Bedfordshire	5-1
West Glamorgan v Surrey	3-2

Final

Northumberland v West Glamorgan	1-0

VICTORY SHIELD AND FRIENDLY INTERNATIONALS

Victory Shield (U15)

Wales v Scotland	2-2
England v N. Ireland	5-0
England v Wales	1-1
Wales v N. Ireland	2-0
Scotland v N. Ireland	4-1
Scotland v England	1-3

	P	W	D	L	F	A	Pts.
England	3	2	1	0	9	2	5
Wales	3	1	2	0	5	3	4
Scotland	3	1	1	1	7	6	3
N. Ireland	3	0	0	3	1	11	0

Other Under-15 International matches

England v Wales	4-1
Netherlands v England	0-4
West Germany v England	3-1
West Germany v England	3-3
England v France	6-1

Centenary Shield (U18)

Scotland v Wales	3-0
Wales v England	0-4
England v Scotland	2-2

	P	W	D	L	F	A	Pts.
England	2	1	1	0	6	2	3
Scotland	2	1	1	0	5	2	3
Wales	2	0	0	2	0	7	0

Trophy Shared

INFORMATION

LAWS OF THE GAME

The Laws of the Game and Decisions of the International Board that follow are reproduced with the special permission of FIFA, and the text is the official text as published by FIFA.

LAW 1
THE FIELD OF PLAY

The Field of Play and appurtenances shall be as shown in the following plan:

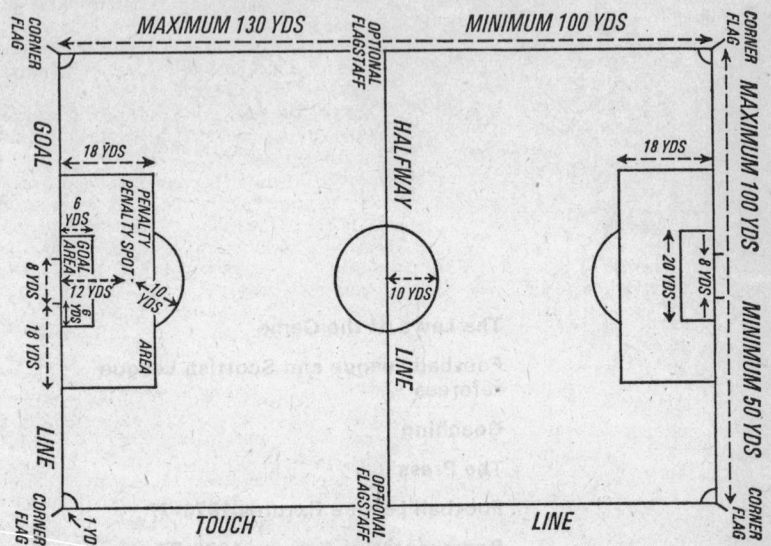

(1) **Dimensions.** The field of play shall be rectangular, its length being not more than 130 yards nor less than 100 yards and its breadth not more than 100 yards nor less than 50 yards. (In International Matches the length shall be not more than 120 yards nor less than 110 yards and the breadth not more than 80 yards nor less than 70 yards.) The length shall in all cases exceed the breadth.

(2) **Marking.** The field of play shall be marked with distinctive lines, not more than 5 inches in width, not by a V-shaped rut, in accordance with the plan, the longer boundary lines being called the touch-lines and the shorter the goal-lines. A flag on a post not less than 5 ft. high and having a non-pointed top, shall be placed at each corner; a similar flag-post may be placed opposite the halfway line on each side of the field of play, not less than 1 yard outside the touch-line. A halfway-line shall be marked out across the field of play. The centre of the field of play shall be indicated by a suitable mark and a circle with a 10 yards radius shall be marked round it.

(3) **The Goal-Area.** At each end of the field of play two lines shall be drawn at right-angles to the goal-line, 6 yards from each goal-post. These shall extend into the field of play for a distance of 6 yards and shall be joined by a line drawn parallel with the goal-line. Each of the spaces enclosed by these goal lines and the goal-line shall be called a goal-area.

(4) **The Penalty-Area.** At each end of the field of play two lines shall be drawn at right-angles to the goal-line, 18 yards from each goal-post. These shall extend into the field of play for a distance of 18 yards and shall be joined by a line drawn parallel with the goal-line. Each of the spaces enclosed by these lines and the goal-line shall be called a penalty-area. A suitable mark shall be made within each penalty-area, 12 yards from the mid-point of the goal-line, measured along an undrawn line at right-angles thereto. These shall be the penalty-kick marks. From each penalty-kick mark an arc of a circle, having a radius of 10 yards, shall be drawn outside the penalty-area.

(5) **The Corner-Area.** From each corner-

flag post a quarter circle, having a radius of 1 yard, shall be drawn inside the field of play.

(6) **The Goals.** The goals shall be placed on the centre of each goal-line and shall consist of two upright posts, equidistant from the corner-flags and 8 yards apart (inside measurement), joined by a horizontal cross-bar the lower edge of which shall be 8 ft from the ground. The width and depth of the goal-posts and the width and depth of the cross-bars shall not exceed 5 inches (12 cm). The goal-posts and the cross-bars shall have the same width.

Nets may be attached to the posts, cross-bars and ground behind the goals. They should be appropriately supported and be so placed as to allow the goal-keeper ample room.

Footnote

Goal nets. The use of nets made of hemp, jute or nylon is permitted. The nylon strings may, however, not be thinner than those made of hemp or jute.

Decisions of the International Board

(1) In International matches the dimensions of the field of play shall be: maximum 110 x 75 metres; minimum 100 x 64 metres.

(2) National Associations must adhere strictly to these dimensions. Each National Association organising an International Match must advise the visiting Association, before the match, of the place and the dimensions of the field of play.

(3) The Board has approved this table of measurements for the Laws of the Game:

130 yards	120 Metres
120 yards	110
110 yards	100
100 yards	90
80 yards	75
70 yards	64
50 yards	45
18 yards	16.50
12 yards	11
10 yards	9.15
8 yards	7.32
6 yards	5.50
1 yard	1
8 feet	2.44
5 feet	1.50
28 inches	0.71
27 inches	0.68
9 inches	0.22
5 inches	0.12
3/4 inch	0.019
1/2 inch	0.0127
3/8 inch	0.010

14 ounces	396 grams
16 ounces	453 grams
15 lb./sq.in.	1 kg/cm^2

(4) The goal-line shall be marked the same width as the depth of the goal-posts and the cross-bar, so that the goal-line and goal-post will conform to the same interior and exterior edges.

(5) The 6 yards (for the outline of the goal-area) and the 18 yards (for the outline of the penalty-area) which have to be measured along the goal-line, must start from the inner sides of the goal-posts.

(6) The space within the inside areas of the field of play includes the width of the lines marking these areas.

(7) All Associations shall provide standard equipment, particularly in International Matches, when the Laws of the Game must be complied with in every respect and especially with regard to the size of the ball and other equipment which must conform to the regulations. All cases of failure to provide standard equipment must be reported to FIFA.

(8) In a match played under the Rules of a Competition if the cross-bar becomes displaced or broken play shall be stopped and the match abandoned unless the cross-bar has been repaired and replaced in position or a new one provided without such being a danger to the players. A rope is not considered to be a satisfactory substitute for a cross-bar.

In a Friendly Match, by mutual consent, play may be resumed without the cross-bar provided it has been removed and no longer constitutes a danger to the players. In these circumstances, a rope may be used as a substitute for a cross-bar. If a rope is not used and the ball crosses the goal-line at a point which in the opinion of the Referee is below where the cross-bar should have been he shall award a goal.

The game shall be restarted by the Referee dropping the ball at the place where it was when play was stopped.

(9) National Associations may specify such maximum and minimum dimensions for the cross-bars and goal-posts, within the limits laid down in Law I, as they consider appropriate.

(10) Goal-posts and cross-bars must be made of wood, metal or other approved material as decided from time to time by the International F.A. Board. They may be square, rectangular, round, half-round or elliptical in shape. Goal-posts and cross-bars made of other materials and in other shapes are not permitted.

(11) 'Curtain-raisers' to International

matches should only be played following agreement on the day of the match, and taking into account the condition of the field of play, between representatives of the two Associations and the Referee (of the International Match).

(12) National Associations, particularly in International Matches, should
— restrict the number of photographers around the field of play,
— have a line ("photographers' line") marked behind the goal-lines at least two metres from the corner flag going through a point situated at least 3.5 metres behind the intersection of the goal-line with the line marking the goal area to a point situated at least six metres behind the goal-posts,
— prohibit photographers from passing over these lines,
— forbid the use of artificial lighting in the form of "flashlights".

LAW II.—THE BALL

The ball shall be spherical; the outer casing shall be of leather or other approved materials. No material shall be used in its construction which might prove dangerous to the players.

The circumference of the ball shall not be more than 28 in and not less than 27 in. The weight of the ball at the start of the game shall not be more than 16 oz nor less than 14 oz. The pressure shall be equal to 0.6-0.7 atmosphere, which equals 9.0-10.5 lb/sq in (= 600-700 gr/cm^2) at sea level. The ball shall not be changed during the game unless authorised by the Referee.

Decisions of the International Board

(1) The ball used in any match shall be considered the property of the Association or Club on whose ground the match is played, and at the close of play it must be returned to the Referee.

(2) The International Board, from time to time, shall decide what constitutes approved materials. Any approved material shall be certified as such by the International Board.

(3) The Board has approved these equivalents of the weights specified in the Law: 14 to 16 ounces = 396 to 453 grammes.

(4) If the ball bursts or becomes deflated during the course of a match, the game shall be stopped and restarted by dropping the new ball at the place where the first ball became defective.

(5) If this happens during a stoppage of the game (place-kick, goal-kick, corner-kick, free-kick, penalty-kick or throw-in) the game shall be restarted accordingly.

LAW III.—NUMBER OF PLAYERS

(1) A match shall be played by two teams, each consisting of not more than eleven players, one of whom shall be the goalkeeper.

(2) Substitutes may be used in any match played under the rules of a competition, subject to the following conditions:
(a) that the authority of the international association(s) or national association(s) concerned, has been obtained,
(b) that, subject to the restriction contained in the following paragraph (c) the rules of a competition shall state how many, if any, substitutes may be used, and
(c) that a team shall not be permitted to use more that two substitutes in any match.

(3) Substitutes may be used in any other match, provided that the two teams concerned reach agreement on a maximum number, not exceeding five, and that the terms of such agreement are intimated to the Referee, before the match. If the Referee is not informed, or if the teams fail to reach agreement, no more than two substitutes shall be permitted.

(4) Any of the other players may change places with the goalkeeper, provided that the Referee is informed before the change is made, and provided also, that the change is made during a stoppage in the game.

(5) When a goalkeeper or any other player is to be replaced by a substitute, the following conditions shall be observed:
(a) the Referee shall be informed of the proposed substitution, before it is made,
(b) the substitute shall not enter the field of play until the player he is replacing has left, and then only after having received a signal from the Referee,
(c) he shall enter the field during a stoppage in the game, and at the half-way line.
Punishment:
(a) Play shall not be stopped for an infringement of paragraph 4. The players concerned shall be cautioned immediately the ball goes out of play.
(b) For any other infringement of this law, the player concerned shall be cautioned, and if the game is stopped by the Referee, to administer the caution, it shall be re-started by an indirect free-kick, to be taken by a player of the opposing team, from the place where the ball was, when play was stopped.

Decisions of the International Board

(1) The minimum number of players in a team is left to the discretion of National Associations.

(2) The Board is of the opinion that a match should not be considered valid if there are fewer than seven players in either of the teams.

(3) A competition may require that the referee shall be informed, before the start of the match, of the names of not more than five players, from whom the substitutes (if any) must be chosen.

(4) A player who has been ordered off before play begins may only be replaced by one of the named substitutes. The kick-off must not be delayed to allow the substitute to join his team.

A player who has been ordered off after play has started may not be replaced.

A named substitute who has been ordered off, either before or after play has started, may not be replaced (this decision only relates to players who are ordered off under Law XII. It does not apply to players who have infringed Law IV.)

(5) A player who has been replaced shall not take any further part in the game.

(6) A substitute shall be deemed to be a player and shall be subject to the authority and jurisdiction of the Referee whether called upon to play or not. For any offence committed on the field of play a substitute shall be subject to the same punishment as any other player whether called upon or not.

LAW IV.—PLAYERS' EQUIPMENT

(1) A player shall not wear anything which is dangerous to another player.

(2) Footwear (boots or shoes) must conform to the following standard:

(a) Bars shall be made of leather or rubber and shall be transverse and flat, not less than half an inch in width and shall extend the total width of the sole and be rounded at the corners.

(b) Studs which are independently mounted on the sole and are replaceable shall be made of leather, rubber, aluminium, plastic or similar material and shall be solid. With the exception of that part of the stud forming the base, which shall not protrude from the sole more than one quarter of an inch, studs shall be round in plan and not less than half an inch in diameter. Where studs are tapered, the minimum diameter of any section of the stud must not be less than half an inch. Where metal seating for the screw type is used, this seating must be embedded in the sole of the footwear and any attachment screw shall be part of the stud. Other than the metal seating for the screw type of stud, no metal plates even though covered with leather or rubber shall be worn, neither studs which are threaded to allow them to be screwed on to a base screw that is fixed by nails or otherwise to the soles of footwear, nor studs which, apart from the base, have any form of protruding edge rim or relief marking or ornament should be allowed.

(c) Studs which are moulded as an integral part of the sole and are not replaceable shall be made of rubber, plastic, polyurethane or similar soft materials. Provided that there are no fewer than ten studs on the sole, they shall have a minimum diameter of three eighths of an inch (10 mm). Additional supporting material to stabilise studs of soft materials, and ridges which shall not protrude more than 5 mm from the sole and moulded to strengthen it, shall be permitted provided that they are in no way dangerous to other players. In all other respects they shall conform to the general requirements of this Law.

(d) Combined bars and studs may be worn, provided the whole conforms to the general requirements of this Law. Neither bars nor studs on the soles shall project more than three-quarters of an inch. If nails are used they shall be driven in flush with the surface.

(3) The goalkeeper shall wear colours which distinguish him from the other players and from the referee.

Punishment: For any infringement of this Law, the player at fault shall be sent off the field of play to adjust his equipment and he shall not return without first reporting to the Referee, who shall satisfy himself that the player's equipment is in order; the player shall only re-enter the game at a moment when the ball has ceased to be in play.

Decisions of the International Board

---

(1) The usual equipment of a player is a jersey or shirt, shorts, stockings and footwear. In a match played under the rules of a competition, players need not wear boots or shoes, but shall wear jersey or shirt, shorts, or track suit or similar trousers, and stockings.

(2) The Law does not insist that boots or shoes must be worn. However, in competition matches Referees should not allow one or a few players to play without footwear when all the other players are so equipped.

(3) In International Matches, International Competitions, International Club Competitions and friendly matches between clubs of different National Associations, the Referee, prior to the start of the game, shall inspect the players' footwear, and prevent any player whose footwear does not conform to the requirements of this Law from playing until such time as it does comply,

The rules of any competition may include a similar provision.

(4) If the Referee finds that a player is wearing articles not permitted by the Laws and which may constitute a danger to other players, he shall order him to take them off. If he fails to carry out the Referee's instruction, the player shall not take part in the

match.

(5) A player who has been prevented from taking part in the game or a player who has been sent off the field for infringing Law IV must report to the Referee during a stoppage of the game and may not enter or re-enter the field of play unless and until the Referee has satisfied himself that the player is no longer infringing Law IV.

(6) A player who has been prevented from taking part in a game or who has been sent off because of an infringement of Law IV, and who enters or re-enters the field of play to join or re-join his team, in breach of the conditions of Law XII, shall be cautioned. If the Referee stops the game to administer the caution, the game shall be restarted by an indirect free-kick, taken by a player of the opposing side, from the place where the offending player was when the Referee stopped the game.

LAW V.—REFEREES

A Referee shall be appointed to officiate in each game. His authority and the exercise of the powers granted to him by the Laws of the Game commence as soon as he enters the field of play.

His power of penalising shall extend to offences committed when play has been temporarily suspended, or when the ball is out of play. His decision on points of fact connected with the play shall be final, so far as the result of the game is concerned. He shall:

(a) Enforce the Laws.

(b) Refrain from penalising in cases where he is satisfied that, by doing so, he would be giving an advantage to the offending team.

(c) Keep a record of the game, act as timekeeper and allow the full or agreed time, adding thereto all time lost through accident or other cause.

(d) Have discretionary power to stop the game for any infringement of the Laws and to suspend or terminate the game whenever, by reason of the elements, interference by spectators, or other cause, he deems such stoppage necessary. In such a case he shall submit a detailed report to the competent authority, within the stipulated time, and in accordance with the provisions set up by the National Association under whose jurisdiction the match was played. Reports will be deemed to be made when received in the ordinary course of post.

(e) From the time he enters the field of play, caution any player guilty of misconduct or ungentlemanly behaviour and, if he persists, suspend him from further participation in the game. In such cases the Referee shall send the name of the offender to the competent authority, within the stipulated time, and in accordance with the provisions set up by the National Association under whose jurisdiction the match was played. Reports will be deemed to be made when received in the ordinary course of post.

(f) Allow no person other than the players and linesmen to enter the field of play without his permission.

(g) Stop the game if, in his opinion, a player has been seriously injured; have the player removed as soon as possible from the field of play, and immediately resume the game. If a player is slightly injured, the game shall not be stopped until the ball has ceased to be in play. A player who is able to go to the touch or goal-line for attention of any kind, shall not be treated on the field of play.

(h) Send off the field of play, any player who, in his opinion, is guilty of violent conduct, serious foul play, or the use of foul or abusive language.

(i) Signal for recommencement of the game after all stoppages.

(j) Decide that the ball provided for a match meets with the requirements of Law II.

Decisions of the International Board

(1) Referees in International Matches shall wear a blazer or blouse the colour of which is distinct from the colours worn by the contesting teams.

(2) Referees for International Matches will be selected from a neutral country unless the countries concerned agree to appoint their own officials.

(3) The Referee must be chosen from the official list of International Referees. This need not apply to Amateur and Youth International Matches.

(4) The Referee shall report to the appropriate authority misconduct or any misdemeanour on the part of spectators, officials, players, named substitutes or other persons which take place either on the field of play or in its vicinity at any time prior to, during, or after the match in question so that appropriate action can be taken by the Authority concerned.

(5) Linesmen are assistants of the Referee. In no case shall the Referee consider the intervention of a Linesman if he himself has seen the incident and from his position on the field, is better able to judge. With this reserve, and the Linesman neutral, the Referee can consider the intervention and if the information of the Linesman applies to that phase of the game immediately before the scoring of a goal, the Referee may act thereon and cancel the goal.

(6) The Referee, however, can only reverse his first decision so long as the game has not been restarted.

(7) If the Referee has decided to apply the advantage clause and to let the game proceed, he cannot revoke his decision if the presumed advantage has not been realised, even though he has not, by any gesture, indicated his decision. This does not exempt the offending player from being dealt with by the Referee.

(8) The Laws of the Game are intended to provide that games should be played with as little interference as possible, and in this view it is the duty of Referees to penalise only deliberate breaches of the Law. Constant whistling for trifling and doubtful breaches produces bad feeling and loss of temper on the part of the players and spoils the pleasure of spectators.

(9) By para. (d) of Law V the Referee is empowered to terminate a match in the event of grave disorder, but he has no power or right to decide, in such event, that either team is disqualified and thereby the loser of the match. He must send a detailed report to the proper authority who alone has power to deal further with this matter.

(10) If a player commits two infringements of a different nature at the same time, the Referee shall punish the more serious offence.

(11) It is the duty of the Referee to act upon the information of neutral Linesmen with regard to incidents that do not come under the personal notice of the Referee.

(12) The Referee shall not allow any person to enter the field until play has stopped, and only then, if he has given him a signal to do so, nor shall he allow coaching from the boundary lines.

LAW VI.—LINESMEN

Two Linesmen shall be appointed, whose duty (subject to the decision of the Referee) shall be to indicate when the ball is out of play and which side is entitled to the corner-kick, goal-kick or throw-in. They shall also assist the Referee to control the game in accordance with the Laws. In the event of undue interference or improper conduct by a Linesman, the Referee shall dispense with his services and arrange for a substitute to be appointed. (The matter shall be reported by the Referee to the competent authority.) The Linesmen should be equipped with flags by the Club on whose ground the match is played.

Decisions of the International Board

(1) Linesmen, where neutral, shall draw the Referee's attention to any breach of the Laws of the Game of which they become aware if they consider that the Referee may not have seen it, but the Referee shall always be the judge of the decision to be taken.

(2) National Associations are advised to appoint official Referees of neutral nationality to act as Linesmen in International Matches.

(3) In International Matches Linesmen's flag shall be of a vivid colour, bright reds and yellows. Such flags are recommended for use in all other matches.

(4) A Linesman may be subject to disciplinary action only upon a report of the Referee for unjustified interference or insufficient assistance.

LAW VII.—DURATION OF THE GAME

The duration of the game shall be two equal periods of 45 minutes, unless otherwise mutually agreed upon, subject to the following: (a) Allowance shall be made in either period for all time lost through accident or other cause, the amount of which shall be a matter for the discretion of the Referee; (b) Time shall be extended to permit a penalty-kick being taken at or after the expiration of the normal period in either half.

At half-time the interval shall not exceed five minutes except by consent of the Referee.

Decisions of the International Board

(1) If a match has been stopped by the Referee, before the completion of the time specified in the rules, for any reason stated in Law V it must be replayed in full unless the rules of the competition concerned provide for the result of the match at the time of such stoppage to stand.

(2) Players have a right to an interval at half-time.

LAW VIII.—THE START OF PLAY

(a) At the beginning of the game, choice of ends and the kick-off shall be decided by the toss of a coin. The team winning the toss shall have the option of choice of ends or the kick-off. The Referee having given a signal, the game shall be started by a player taking a place-kick (i.e., a kick at the ball while it is stationary on the ground in the centre of the field of play) into his opponents' half of the field of play. Every player shall be in his own half of the field and every player of the team opposing that of the kicker shall remain not less than 10 yards from the ball until it is kicked-off; it shall not be deemed in play until it has travelled the distance of its own

circumference. The kicker shall not play the ball a second time until it has been touched or played by another player.

(b) **After a goal is scored,** the game shall be restarted in like manner by a player of the team losing the goal.

(c) **After half-time:** when restarting after half-time, ends shall be changed and the kick-off shall be taken by a player of the opposite team to that of the player who started the game.

Punishment. For any infringement of this Law, the kick-off shall be retaken, except in the case of the kicker playing the ball again before it has been touched or played by another player; for this offence, an indirect free-kick shall be taken by a player of the opposing team from the place where the infringement occurred. A goal shall not be scored direct from a kick-off.

(d) **After any other temporary suspension:** when restarting the game after a temporary suspension of play from any cause not mentioned elsewhere in these Laws, provided that immediately prior to the suspension the ball has not passed over the touch or goal-lines, the Referee shall drop the ball at the place where it was when play was suspended and it shall be deemed in play when it has touched the ground; if, however, it goes over the touch or goal-lines after it has been dropped by the Referee, but before it is touched by a player, the Referee shall again drop it. A player shall not play the ball until it has touched the ground. If this section of the Law is not complied with the Referee shall again drop the ball.

Decisions of the International Board

(1) If, when the Referee drops the ball, a player infringes any of the Laws before the ball has touched the ground, the player concerned shall be cautioned or sent off the field according to the seriousness of the offence, but a free-kick cannot be awarded to the opposing team because the ball was not in play at the time of the offence. The ball shall therefore be again dropped by the Referee.

(2) Kicking-off by persons other than the players competing in a match is prohibited.

LAW IX.—BALL IN AND OUT OF PLAY

The ball is out of play:

(a) When it has wholly crossed the goal-line or touch-line, whether on the ground or in the air.

(b) When the game has been stopped by the Referee.

The ball is in play at all other times from the start of the match to the finish including:

(a) If it rebounds from a goal-post, cross-bar or corner-flag post into the field of play.

(b) If it rebounds off either the Referee or Linesmen when they are in the field of play.

(c) In the event of a supposed infringement of the Laws, until a decision is given.

Decisions of the International Board

(1) The lines belong to the areas of which they are the boundaries. In consequence, the touch-lines and the goal-lines belong to the field of play.

LAW X.—METHOD OF SCORING

Except as otherwise provided by these Laws, a goal is scored when the whole of the ball has passed over the goal-line, between the goal-posts and under the cross-bar, provided it has not been thrown, carried or intentionally propelled by hand or arm, by a player of the attacking side, except in the case of a goalkeeper, who is within his own penalty-area.

The team scoring the greater number of goals during a game shall be the winner; if no goals, or an equal number of goals are scored, the game shall be termed a "draw".

Decisions of the International Board

(1) Law X defines the only method according to which a match is won or drawn; no variation whatsoever can be authorised.

(2) A goal cannot in any case be allowed if the ball has been prevented by some outside agent from passing over the goal-line. If this happens in the normal course of play, other than at the taking of a penalty-kick: the game must be stopped and restarted by the Referee dropping the ball at the place where the ball came into contact with the interference.

(3) If, when the ball is going into goal, a spectator enters the field before it passes wholly over the goal-line, and tries to prevent a score, a goal shall be allowed if the ball goes into goal unless the spectator has made contact with the ball or has interfered with play, in which case the Referee shall stop the game and restart it by dropping the ball at the place where the contact or interference occurred.

LAW XI.—OFF-SIDE

A player is off-side if he is nearer his opponents' goal-line than the ball **at the moment the ball is played** unless:

(a) He is in his own half of the field of play.

(b) There are two of his opponents nearer to their own goal-line than he is.

(c) The ball last touched an opponent or

846

was last played by him.

(d) He receives the ball direct from a goal-kick, a corner-kick, a throw-in, or when it was dropped by the Referee.

Punishment. For an infringement of this Law, an indirect free-kick shall be taken by a player of the opposing team from the place where the infringement occurred.

A player in an off-side position shall not be penalised unless, in the opinion of the Referee, he is interfering with the play or with an opponent, or is seeking to gain an advantage by being in an offside position.

Decisions of the International Board

(1) Off-side shall not be judged at the moment the player in question receives the ball, but at the moment when the ball is passed to him by one of his own side. A player who is not in an off-side position when one of his colleagues passes the ball to him or takes a free-kick, does not therefore become off-side if he goes forward during the flight of the ball.

LAW XII.—FOULS AND MISCONDUCT

A player who intentionally commits any of the following nine offences:

(a) Kicks or attempts to kick an opponent;

(b) Trips an opponent, i.e., throwing or attempting to throw him by the use of the legs or by stooping in front of or behind him;

(c) Jumps at an opponent;

(d) Charges an opponent in a violent or dangerous manner;

(e) Charges an opponent from behind unless the latter be obstructing;

(f) Strikes or attempts to strike an opponent;

(g) Holds an opponent;

(h) Pushes an opponent;

(i) Handles the ball, i.e., carries, strikes or propels the ball with his hand or arm. (This does not apply to the goalkeeper within his own penalty-area)

shall be penalised by the award of a direct free-kick to be taken by the opposing side from the place where the offence occurred.

Should a player of the defending side intentionally commit one of the above nine offences within the penalty-area he shall be penalised by a **penalty-kick**.

A penalty-kick can be awarded irrespective of the position of the ball, if in play, at the time an offence within the penalty-area is committed.

A player committing any of the five following offences:

(1) Playing in a manner considered by the Referee to be dangerous, e.g., attempting to kick the ball while held by the goalkeeper;

(2) Charging fairly, i.e., with the shoulder, when the ball is not within playing distance of the players concerned and they are definitely not trying to play it;

(3) When not playing the ball, intentionally obstructing an opponent, i.e., running between the opponent and the ball, or interposing the body so as to form an obstacle to an opponent;

(4) Charging the goalkeeper except when he

(a) is holding the ball;

(b) is obstructing an opponent;

(c) has passed outside his goal-area;

(5) When playing as goalkeeper,

(a) takes more than 4 steps whilst holding, bouncing or throwing the ball in the air and catching it again without releasing it so that it is played by another player, or

(b) indulges in tactics which, in the opinion of the Referee, are designed merely to hold up the game and thus waste time and so give an unfair advantage to his own team—

shall be penalised by the award of an **indirect free-kick** to be taken by the opposing side from the place where the infringement occurred.

A player shall be **cautioned** if:

(j) he enters or re-enters the field of play to join or rejoin his team after the game has commenced, or leaves the field of play during the progress of the game (except through accident) without, in either case, first having received a signal from the Referee showing him that he may do so. If the Referee stops the game to administer the caution the game shall be restarted by an indirect free-kick taken by a player of the opposing team from the place where the ball was when the Referee stopped the game. If, however, the offending player has committed a more serious offence he shall be penalised according to that section of the law he infringed;

(k) he persistently infringes the Laws of the Game;

(l) he shows by word or action, dissent from any decision given by the Referee;

(m) he is guilty of ungentlemanly conduct.

For any of these last three offences, in addition to the caution, an **indirect free-kick** shall also be awarded to the opposing side from the place where the offence occurred unless a more serious infringement of the Laws of the Game was committed.

A player shall be **sent off** the field of play, if:

(n) in the opinion of the Referee he is guilty of violent conduct or serious foul play;

(o) he uses foul or abusive language;

(p) he persists in misconduct after having received a caution.

If play be stopped by reason of a player being ordered from the field for an offence

without a separate breach of the Law having been committed, the game shall be resumed by an **indirect free-kick** awarded to the opposing side from the place where the infringement occurred.

Decisions of the International Board

(1) If the goalkeeper either intentionally strikes an opponent by throwing the ball vigorously at him or pushes him with the ball while holding it, the Referee shall award a penalty-kick, if the offence took place within the penalty-area.

(2) If a player deliberately turns his back to an opponent when he is about to be tackled, he may be charged but not in a dangerous manner.

(3) In case of body-contact in the goal-area between an attacking player and the opposing goalkeeper not in possession of the ball, the Referee, as sole judge of intention, shall stop the game if, in his opinion, the action of the attacking player was intentional, and award an indirect free-kick.

(4) If a player leans on the shoulders of another player of his own team in order to head the ball, the Referee shall stop the game, caution the player for ungentlemanly conduct and award an indirect free-kick to the opposing side.

(5) A player's obligation when joining or rejoining his team after the start of the match to 'report to the Referee' must be interpreted as meaning 'to draw the attention of the Referee from the touch-line'. The signal from the Referee shall be made by a definite gesture which makes the player understand that he may come into the field of play; it is not necessary for the Referee to wait until the game is stopped (this does not apply in respect of an infringement of Law IV), but the Referee is the sole judge of the moment in which he gives his signal of acknowledgement.

(6) The letter and spirit of Law XII do not oblige the Referee to stop a game to administer a caution. He may, if he chooses, apply the advantage. If he does apply the advantage, he shall caution the player when play stops.

(7) If a player covers up the ball without touching it in an endeavour not to have it played by an opponent, he obstructs but does not infringe Law X11 para. 3 because he is already in possession of the ball and covers it for tactical reasons whilst the ball remains within playing distance. In fact, he is actually playing the ball and does not commit an infringement; in this case, the player may be charged because he is in fact playing the ball.

(8) If a player intentionally stretches his arms to obstruct an opponent and steps from one side to the other, moving his arms up and down to delay his opponent, forcing him to change course, but does not make "bodily contact" the Referee shall caution the player for ungentlemanly conduct and award an indirect free-kick.

(9) If a player intentionally obstructs the opposing goalkeeper, in an attempt to prevent him from putting the ball into play in accordance with Law XII, 5(a), the Referee shall award an indirect free-kick

(10) If after a Referee has awarded a free-kick a player protests violently by using abusive or foul language and is sent off the field, the free-kick should not be taken until the player has left the field.

(11) Any player, whether he is within or outside the field of play, whose conduct is ungentlemanly or violent, whether or not it is directed towards an opponent, a colleague, the Referee, a linesman or other person, or who uses foul or abusive language, is guilty of an offence, and shall be dealt with according to the nature of the offence committed.

(12) If, in the opinion of the Referee a goalkeeper intentionally lies on the ball longer than is necessary, he shall be penalised for ungentlemanly conduct and

(a) be cautioned and an indirect free-kick awarded to the opposing team;

(b) in case of repetition of the offence, be sent off the field.

(13) The offence of spitting at opponents, officials or other persons, or similar unseemly behaviour shall be considered as violent conduct within the meaning of section (n) of Law XII.

(14) If, when a Referee is about to caution a player, and before he has done so, the player commits another offence which merits a caution, the player shall be sent off the field of play.

LAW XIII. – FREE-KICK

Free-kicks shall be classified under two headings: "Direct" (from which a goal can be scored direct against the offending side), and "Indirect" (from which a goal cannot be scored unless the ball has been played or touched by a player other than the kicker before passing through the goal).

When a player is taking a direct or an indirect free-kick inside his own penalty-area, all of the opposing players shall remain outside the area, and shall be at least ten yards from the ball whilst the kick is being taken. The ball shall be in play immediately it has travelled the distance of its own circumference and is beyond the penalty-area. The goalkeeper shall not receive the ball into his hands, in order that he may there-

after kick it into play. If the ball is not kicked direct into play, beyond the penalty-area, the kick shall be retaken.

When a player is taking a direct or an indirect free-kick outside his own penalty-area, all of the opposing players shall be at least ten yards from the ball, until it is in play, unless they are standing on their own goal-line, between the goal-posts. The ball shall be in play when it has travelled the distance of its own circumference.

If a player of the opposing side encroaches into the penalty-area, or within ten yards of the ball, as the case may be, before a free-kick is taken, the Referee shall delay the taking of the kick, until the Law is complied with.

The ball must be stationary when a free-kick is taken, and the kicker shall not play the ball a second time, until it has been touched or played by another player.

Punishment. If the kicker, after taking the free-kick, plays the ball a second time before it has been touched or played by another player an indirect free-kick shall be taken by a player of the opposing team from the spot where the infringement occurred.

Decisions of the International Board
---

(1) In order to distinguish between a direct and an indirect free-kick, the Referee, when he awards an indirect free-kick, shall indicate accordingly by raising an arm above his head. He shall keep his arm in that position until the kick has been taken.

(2) Players who do not retire to the proper distance when a free-kick is taken must be cautioned and on any repetition be ordered off. It is particularly requested of Referees that attempts to delay the taking of a free-kick by encroaching should be treated as serious misconduct.

(3) If, when a free-kick is being taken, any of the players dance about or gesticulate in a way calculated to distract their opponents, it shall be deemed ungentlemanly conduct for which the offender(s) shall be cautioned.

LAW XIV – PENALTY-KICK

A penalty-kick shall be taken from the penalty-mark and, when it is being taken, all players with the exception of the player taking the kick, and the opposing goalkeeper, shall be within the field of play but outside the penalty-area, and at least 10 yards from the penalty-mark. The opposing goalkeeper must stand (without moving his feet) on his own goal-line, between the goal-posts, until the ball is kicked. The player

taking the kick must kick the ball forward; he shall not play the ball a second time until it has been touched or played by another player. The ball shall be deemed in play directly it is kicked, i.e., when it has travelled the distance of its circumference, and a goal may be scored direct from such a penalty-kick. If the ball touches the goalkeeper before passing between the posts, when a penalty-kick is being taken at or after the expiration of half-time or full-time, it does not nullify a goal. If necessary, time of play shall be extended at half-time or full-time to allow a penalty-kick to be taken.

Punishment

For any infringement of this Law:

(a) by the defending team, the kick shall be retaken if a goal has not resulted.

(b) by the attacking team other than by the player taking the kick, if a goal is scored it shall be disallowed and the kick retaken.

(c) by the player taking the penalty-kick, committed after the ball is in play, a player of the opposing team shall take an indirect free-kick from the spot where the infringement occurred.

Decisions of the International Board
---

(1) When the Referee has awarded a penalty-kick, he shall not signal for it to be taken, until the players have taken up position in accordance with the Law.

(2) (a) If, after the kick has been taken, the ball is stopped in its course towards goal, by an outside agent, the kick shall be retaken.

(b) If, after the kick has been taken, the ball rebounds into play, from the goalkeeper, the cross-bar or a goal-post, and is then stopped in its course by an outside agent, the Referee shall stop play and restart it by dropping the ball at the place where it came into contact with the outside agent.

(3) (a) If, after having given the signal for a penalty-kick to be taken, the Referee sees that the goalkeeper is not in his right place on the goal-line, he shall, nevertheless, allow the kick to proceed. It shall be retaken, if a goal is not scored.

(b) If, after the Referee has given the signal for a penalty-kick to be taken, and before the ball has been kicked, the goalkeeper moves his feet, the Referee shall, nevertheless, allow the kick to proceed. It shall be retaken, if a goal is not scored.

(c) If, after the Referee has given the signal for a penalty-kick to be taken, and before the ball is in play, a player of the defending team encroaches into the penalty-area, or within ten yards of the penalty-mark, the Referee shall, nevertheless, allow

the kick to proceed. It shall be retaken, if a goal is not scored.

The player concerned shall be cautioned.

(4) (a) If, when a penalty-kick is being taken, the player taking the kick is guilty of ungentlemanly conduct, the kick, if already taken, shall be retaken, if a goal is scored.

The player concerned shall be cautioned.

(b) If, after the Referee has given the signal for a penalty-kick to be taken, and before the ball is in play, a colleague of the player taking the kick encroaches into the penalty-area or within ten yards of the penalty-mark, the Referee shall, nevertheless, allow the kick to proceed. If a goal is scored, it shall be disallowed, and the kick retaken.

The player concerned shall be cautioned.

(c) If, in the circumstances described in the foregoing paragraph, the ball rebounds into play from the goalkeeper, the crossbar or a goal-post, the Referee shall stop the game, caution the player and award an indirect free-kick to the opposing team from the place where the infringement occurred.

(5) (a) If, after the referee has given the signal for a penalty-kick to be taken, and before the ball is in play, the goalkeeper moves from his position on the goal-line, or moves his feet, and a colleague of the kicker encroaches into the penalty-area or within 10 yards of the penalty-mark, the kick, if taken, shall be retaken.

The colleague of the kicker shall be cautioned.

(b) If, after the Referee has given the signal for a penalty-kick to be taken, and before the ball is in play, a player of each team encroaches into the penalty-area, or within 10 yards of the penalty-mark, the kick, if taken, shall be retaken.

The players concerned shall be cautioned.

(6) When a match is extended, at half-time or full-time, to allow a penalty-kick to be taken or retaken, the extension shall last until the moment that the penalty-kick has been completed, i.e. until the Referee has decided whether or not a goal is scored.

A goal is scored when the ball passes wholly over the goal-line.

(a) direct from the penalty-kick,

(b) having rebounded from either goal-post or the cross-bar, or

(c) having touched or been played by the goalkeeper.

The game shall terminate immediately the Referee has made his decision.

(7) When a penalty-kick is being taken in extended time:

(a) the provisions of all of the foregoing paragraphs, except paragraphs (2) (b) and (4) (c) shall apply in the usual way, and

(b) in the circumstances described in paragraphs (2) (b) and (4) (c) the game shall terminate immediately the ball rebounds from the goalkeeper, the cross-bar or the goalpost.

LAW XV – THROW-IN

When the whole of the ball passes over a touch-line, either on the ground or in the air, it shall be thrown in from the point where it crossed the line, in any direction, by a player of the team opposite to that of the player who last touched it. The thrower at the moment of delivering the ball must face the field of play and part of each foot shall be either on the touch-line or on the ground outside the touch-line. The thrower shall use both hands and shall deliver the ball from behind and over his head. The ball shall be in play immediately it enters the field of play, but the thrower shall not again play the ball until it has been touched or played by another player. A goal shall not be scored direct from a throw-in.

Punishment:

(a) If the ball is improperly thrown in the throw-in shall be taken by a player of the opposing team.

(b) If the thrower plays the ball a second time before it has been touched or played by another player, an indirect free-kick shall be taken by a player of the opposing team from the place where the infringement occurred.

Decisions of the International Board

---

(1) If a player taking a throw-in, plays the ball a second time by handling it within the field of play before it has been touched or played by another player, the Referee shall award a direct free-kick.

(2) A player taking a throw-in must face the field of play with some part of his body.

(3) If, when a throw-in is being taken, any of the opposing players dance about or gesticulate in a way calculated to distract or impede the thrower, it shall be deemed ungentlemanly conduct, for which the offender(s) shall be cautioned.

LAW XVI – GOAL-KICK

When the whole of the ball passes over the goal-line excluding that portion between the goal-posts, either in the air or on the ground, having last been played by one of the attacking team, it shall be kicked direct into play beyond the penalty-area from a point within that half of the goal-area nearest to where it crossed the line, by a player of the defending team. A goalkeeper shall not receive the ball into his hands from a goal-kick in order that he may thereafter kick it into play. If the ball is not kicked

beyond the penalty-area, i.e., direct into play, the kick shall be retaken. The kicker shall not play the ball a second time until it has touched – or been played by – another player. A goal shall not be scored direct from such a kick. Players of the team opposing that of the player taking the goal-kick shall remain outside the penalty-area whilst the kick is being taken.

Punishment:

If a player taking a goal-kick plays the ball a second time after it has passed beyond the penalty-area, but before it has touched or been played by another player, an indirect free-kick shall be awarded to the opposing team, to be taken from the place where the infringement occurred.

Decisions of the International Board

(1) When a goal-kick has been taken and the player who has kicked the ball touches it again before it has left the penalty-area, the kick has not been taken in accordance with the Law and must be retaken.

LAW XVII – CORNER-KICK

When the whole of the ball passes over the goal-line, excluding that portion between the goal-posts, either in the air or on the ground, having last been played by one of the defending team, a member of the attacking team shall take a corner-kick, i.e., the whole of the ball shall be placed within the quarter circle at the nearest corner-flag-post, which must not be moved, and it shall be kicked from that position. A goal may be scored direct from such a kick. Players of the team opposing that of the player taking the corner-kick shall not approach within 10 yards of the ball until it is in play, i.e., it has travelled the distance of its own circumference, nor shall the kicker play the ball a second time until it has been touched or played by another player.

Punishment:

(a) If the player who takes the kick plays the ball a second time before it has been touched or played by another player, the Referee shall award an indirect free-kick to the opposing team, to be taken from the place where the infringement occurred.

(b) For any other infringement the kick shall be retaken.

FOOTBALL LEAGUE REFEREES 1976-77

Ashley, N. J. (Nantwich)
Baker, K. W. (Rugby)
Baker, M. R. (Wolverhampton)
Bent, J. E. (Hemel Hempstead)
Biddle, D. J. (Bristol)
Bosi, T. P. (Codsall)
Bune, T. G. (Billingshurst)
Burden, L. F. (Broadstone, Dorset)
Burns, K. H. (Stourbridge)
Butcher, J. K. (Kendal)
Capey, R. (Madeley Heath, Nr. Crewe)
Chadwick, R. (Darwen)
Challis, R. C. (Tonbridge, Kent)
Civil, D. W. (Birmingham)
Courtney, G. (Spennymoor)
Crabb, R. C. (Exeter)
Daniels, B. H. (Brentwood)
Farley, T. (Newton Aycliffe)
Flint, G. E. (Kirkby-in-Ashfield)
Garner, E. R. (Maghull)
Glasson, A. R. (Salisbury)
Gow, W. J. (Swansea)
Grey, A. W. (Great Yarmouth)
Hackett, K. S. (Sheffield)
Hackney, H. P. (Barnsley)
Hamil, A. J. (Wolverhampton)
Hayes, L. (Doncaster)
Homewood, B. J. (Sunbury-on-Thames)
Hough, J. D. (Macclesfield)
Hughes, A. (West Kirby)
Hughes, E. O. (Weston-Super-Mare)
Hunting, J. (Leicester)
James, B. M. L. (South Croydon)
Johnson, W. B. (Kendal)
Jones, A. W. S. (Orsmkirk)
Kew, G. C. (Amersham)
Kirkpatrick, R. B. (Leicester)
Lees, A. R. (Bridgwater)
Lewis, R. S. (Great Bookham, Surrey)
Lloyd, D. W. (Fernhill Heath)
Lowe, M. (Sheffield)
McNally, K. (Hooton, Cheshire)
Martin, B. (Keyworth, Notts.)
Maskell, C. A. (Cambridge)

Matthewson, R. (Bolton)
Mills, T. (Barnsley)
Morris, T. L. (Leeds)
Morrissey, A. E. (Bramhall)
Newsome, C. L. (Broseley, Salop)
Nippard, D. R. G. (Christchurch, Dorset)
Nolan, G. (Hazel Grove)
Partridge, P. (Cockfield, Co. Durham)
Perkin, R. N. (Stafford)
Porter, A. (Bolton)
Read, E. A. (Bristol)
Reeves, D. V. (Uxbridge, Middlesex)
Reeves, P. G. (Leicester)
Reynolds, T. H. C. (Swansea)
Rice, J. (Leyland)
Richardson, D. (Great Harwood)
Richardson, D. T. (Lincoln)
Richardson, P. J. (Lincoln)
Ridden, K. W. (Shrewsbury)
Robinson, A. (Waterlooville)
Robinson, H. R. (Norwich)
Salmon, K. G. (Barnet)
Seel, C. N. (Carlisle)
Sewell, J. (Birstall, Leicester)
Shapter, L. C. (Paignton)
Shaw, D. (Sandbach)
Sinclair, M. V. (Guildford)
Smith, D. (Hornchurch)
Spencer, T. D. (Wootton Bassett)
Stevens, B. T. (Stonehouse, Glos.)
Styles, K. (Barnsley)
Taylor, J. K. (Wolverhampton)
Taylor, M. J. (Deal)
Thomas, C. (Treorchy)
Toseland, R. W. (Kettering)
Turner, D. (Cannock)
Turvey, A. C. F. (Basingstoke)
Walmsley, K. (Blackpool)
White, C. B. (Harrow)
Willis, P. N. (Meadowfield)
Worrall, J. B. (Warrington)
Wrennall, J. (Eccleston)
Yates, J. H. (Redditch)

SUPPLEMENTARY REFEREES

Bates, S. G. (Bristol)
Bevan, M. K. D. (Melksham)
Challinor, A. (Rotherham)
Davies, J. G. P. (Swansea)
Downey, C. (Isleworth, Middlesex)
Gardner, C. W. J. (Gloucester)
Glover, N. H. (Chorley)
Gunn, A. (Southwick, Sussex)
Harvey, W. C. (Redditch)
Horner, R. J. (Halifax)
Jackson, D. T. (Water Orton, W. Mid.)

Jenkins, A. F. (Scunthorpe)
McDonald, A. (Birmingham)
Midgley, N. (Salford)
Owen, G. P. (Pentraeth, Anglesey)
Peck, M. G. (Lancaster)
Roost, J. (Bath)
Saunders, A. (Newcastle-upon-Tyne)
Seville, A. (Birmingham)
Suter, P. (Liverpool)
Totney, P. (Wombourne, W. Mid.)

SCOTTISH LEAGUE REFEREES 1976-77

H. Alexander (Kilmarnock)
W. Anderson (East Kilbride)
R. H. Davidson (Airdrie)
D. S. Downie (Edinburgh)
A. Ferguson (Giffnock)
I. M. D. Foote (Glasgow)
J. R. P. Gordon (Newport-on-Tay)
K. J. Hope (Clarkston)
R. M. Hopkins (Markinch)
C. H. Hutton (Dunfermline)
R. D. Keggie (Edinburgh)
T. Kellock (East Kilbride)
T. R. Kyle (Glasgow)
B. R. McGinlay (Glasgow)

A. McGunnigle (Glasgow)
A. McKenzie (Larbert)
R. Marshall (Clydebank)
T. Muirhead (Stenhousemuir)
W. J. Mullan (Dalkeith)
A. Paterson (East Kilbride)
J. W. Paterson (Bothwell)
E. H. Pringle (Edinburgh)
D. Ramsay (Edinburgh)
W. D. Reid (Aberdeen)
G. B. Smith (Edinburgh)
D. F. T. Syme (Rutherglen)
E. Thomson (Edinburgh)
R. B. Valentine (Dundee)

Coaching and Coaches

In recent years it has become fashionable to blame coaches for all the ills that befall football. Negative tactics which some clubs employ, which ensnare others, are always laid directly at the door of their coaches. In the majority of cases nothing could be further from the truth. The job of the coach is to organize, put right faults, teach skills and techniques, and basically to transform kick and rush into push and run.

Coaches, of course, come in all varieties and types but invariably they all want to win by playing open attacking football and the Football Association through its top National Coaches are intent on advocating these principles.

The Football Association are in fact the governing body for coaching in this country with the Director of Coaching, Mr. Allen Wade, carrying overall responsibility for the implementation of the various coaching schemes and policies. He is supported by the Assistant Director of Coaching, Mr. Charles Hughes, both of whom can be located at the Football Association headquarters at 16 Lancaster Gate London, W.2.

There are four regional coaches who are responsible for their particular areas and look after the needs and problems which attach to coaching and coaches in those areas. The four regional coaches are:—

(1) *The North Region*—Mr. Keith Wright, 22 High Street, Sheffield, S1 2JE, Telephone No. Sheffield 874108.

(2) *The North West Region*—Mr Terry Casey, 31a Wellington Street, St Johns, Blackburn, BB18 8AU, Telephone No. Blackburn 51642.

(3) *The Midland Region*—Mr Kevin Verity, 25 Gresham Chambers, 14 Lichfield Street, Wolverhampton, WV1 1DG, Telephone No. Wolverhampton 27407.

(4) *London and South East Region*—Mr Colin Murphy, 16 Lancaster Gate, London, W.2.

Each County has its own County Association which has a coaching committee to help oil the wheels and provide much needed revenue and support; while coaching associations which are situated up and down the country collect together coaches who have passed the appropriate examinations and others interested in coaching in order to promote refresher courses, demonstrations of coaching and training ideas, and put on lectures by those involved in teaching the game.

In addition to the above, there are the FA Staff coaches appointed by the FA for their dedication to and work for the coaching scheme and the ability that they have shown in being involved in it.

At the moment one qualifies as a coach by passing the FA preliminary certificate and thereafter the qualifying certificate. It is understood there will be sweeping changes in the coaching scheme over the next few years but details are not as yet available. There is however a course for teachers which although called a teachers award provides only a certificate after satisfactory attendance on a recognised course but there is no examination.

FIFA runs its own courses in various countries and the qualification for a FIFA Certificate are attendance on a preliminary course followed by an intermediate course followed by a final course having in each case passed the appropriate tests.

There are two coaching magazines available for purchase as follows:—

(1) *Football Insight* published by the Football Association. Editor, Keith Wright. Available four times per year obtainable from the North Regional Coaching Office at 22 High Street, Sheffield, S1 2GE, subscription £1·50 pa and;

(2) *Soccer Coach*, produced by the London Football Coaches Association, editor Kenneth Goldman. Available three times per year, price 20 pence per copy plus 10 pence p&p available from Mr. J. Keen, 21 Haynes Park Court, Slewins Close, Hornchurch, Essex.

The present list of FA Staff Coaches consists of:—

J. W. ADAMS	Sports Executive and Radio
J. ADAMSON	Manager
G. E. AINSLEY	On Staff of Crystal Palace NRC

J. ARMFIELD	Manager, Leeds United
E. W. BEAGLEHOLE	School Headmaster
E. B. BLENKINSOP	University Lecturer
K. R. W. BLUNT	Coach, Plymouth Argyle
C. E. BOND	College of Education Lecturer
A. BROWN	University Lecturer
A. W. BROWN	Manager, Blackpool F.C.
K. BURTON	Business Executive
J. S. CALVERT	University Lecturer
S. T. CANN	Car Firm Executive
T. CASEY	FA North West Regional Coach
J. CHARLTON	Manager, Middlesbrough FC
T. CHURCHILL	Organizer of PE, Wolverhampton
G. CURTIS	National Coach, Norway
F. FORD	Club Official
K. FURPHY	Coach, New York Cosmos
J. W. GOODWIN	Vice Chairman, London Football Coaches Association
J. GORDON	Club Coach
D. GRADI	Coach, Chelsea FC
R. GREENWOOD	General Manager, West Ham United
J. R. E. HARDISTY	College Head of PE Dept., County Durham
H. W. HASSALL	College of Education Lecturer
J. R. HENDERSON	Housemaster, School in Newcastle
J. W. T. HILL	Sports Agency and Television
D. HOWE	Club Coach, Leeds United
C. F. C. HUGHES	Assistant Director of Coaching, the FA
G. JAGO	Manager, Millwall FC
J. JARMAN	Director of Coaching, FA of Ireland
C. JONES	University Lecturer
M. KELLY	Player, Birmingham City
T. E. LAWRENCE	Travel Executive
B. R. LEE	Director, Bisham Abbey NSC
R. LEWIN	Football Club Coach
J. McANEARNEY	Club Coach
J. MANSELL	Football Club Manager, Greece
D. H. MEGSON	Manager, Bristol Rovers
J. MERCER	Director, Coventry FC
R. MINSHULL	Coach, Everton FC
W. E. NICHOLSON	Assistant to West Ham United FC
E. W. POWELL	Manager, Wycombe Wanderers
R. W. ROBSON	Manager, Ipswich Town
T. W. SAUNDERS	Coach, Liverpool FC
C. SAYER	Co-ordinator, Sports Council
D. J. SEXTON	Manager, Q.P.R.
L. SHANNON	Club Manager in Greece
J. SIRREL	Manager, Sheffield United
W. J. SLATER	Director, Department of PE, Birmingham University
G. C. SMITH	Ex-manager
M. J. SMITH	Director of Coaching and Team Manager of Wales
G. SUMMERS	Manager, Gillingham
G. TAYLOR	Club Manager, Lincoln City
T. TRANTOR	Lecturer, Borough Road College, London
J. B. TRUMAN	National Coach of New Zealand
A. WADE	Director of Coaching, the FA
A. K. WAITERS	Manager, Plymouth Argyle
G. WARDLE	Head of PE, Durham College
P. WELTON	Coach, Tottenham Hotspur
S. T. WIGMORE	Senior Lecturer in PE, Loughborough College
H. WILKINSON	Club Coach
B. WILLIAMS	Lecturer, Barking, Essex
P. WOOSNAM	Commissioner, North American Soccer League
E. WORTHINGTON	National Coach, Australia
W. A. WRIGHT	Head of Sport, ATV Network

I.P.C. National Press Awards

SPORTS WRITER CATEGORY

David Gray, former tennis correspondent of *The Guardian*, was chosen as Sports Writer of the Year, 1975. This is one of the awards originally instituted in memory of the brilliant journalist, Hannen Swaffer.

From August 1976, Gray takes over from Basil Reay as secretary of the International Lawn Tennis Federation, a difficult job which he looks forward to with relish. Unless the Federation finds new strength, there is a danger that the United States will monopolise the world's best players, and this problem is probably the biggest challenge that Gray will have to face.

Born a few minutes before midnight on New Year's Eve 1928, Gray went on to graduate with an English degree from Birmingham University in 1951, and then went to work as a journalist. He worked first on the *Evening Telegraph* in Blackburn, then the *News Chronicle* in Manchester, and finally on *The Guardian*. He has been reporting tennis since 1956, and has said that there is only one job he would prefer – editor of the Good Food Guide!

Politics – both of tennis and governments – has always fascinated him, and he has been known to take time off from the professional circuit to report on the American Primaries, but it is in the field of tennis that he has made his name as one of the most respected sports writers in Fleet Street, and when he announced his three-year contract with the ILTF, he said: 'I feel like a drama critic who has been called on the stage to play Hamlet!'

The President of the ILTF – farmer Derek Hardwick – is another Briton, and it will now be the responsibility of these two men to take the ever more popular game of tennis into the 80s. Good luck to them both.

Previous winners of the award:
1963: J. L. Manning; 1964: George Whiting; 1965: Peter Wilson; 1966: Hugh McIlvanney; 1967: Sam Leitch; 1968: Chris Brasher; 1969: Hugh McIlvanney; 1970: Frank Butler; 1971: Ian Wooldridge; 1972: John Morgan; 1973: Peter Batt; 1974: Ian Wooldridge.

FOOTBALL PUBLICATIONS

Monthlies (Address, size, Editor, Year first published)

Football News, 53, Hampstead High Street, London N.W.3. (8¼" by 11"), 48 pages, 25p, Don Aldridge, 1974.

World Soccer, 79, Temple Chambers, London E.C.4. (8¼" by 11¾"), 52 pages, 40p, Philip Rising, 1959.

Football, 79, Baker Street, London W.1 (8⅜" by 11¼"), 48 pages, 20p, Phil Osborn, 1974.

The A.F.A. Record, Room 724, Cecil Chambers, 86, The Strand, London W.C.2. (7" by 9½"), 40 pages, 20p, Jack Perry, 1963.

Sports Review, P.O. Box 4EA, London W1A 4EA. (8¼" by 11¾"), 52 pages, 30p, Peter West, 1976. (All sports magazine.)

Weeklies

Shoot/Goal, Fleetway House, Farringdon Street, London E.C.4. (9" by 11½"), 40 pages, 12p, David Gregory 1969.

THE NATIONAL PRESS

These are the names of the men who spend most of their working lives in the newspaper, TV, and Radio world reporting football matches and generally covering the game:

Daily Express
David Miller
Jim Lawson
Alan Thompson
Alan Williams
Steve Curry
Malcolm Folley

Daily Mail
Brian James
Jeff Powell
Ronald Crowther
Brian Scovell
Bill Mallinson
Ian Wooldridge

Daily Mirror
Frank McGhee
Harry Miller
Derek Wallis
Kevin Moseley
Frank Taylor
Nigel Clarke

Daily Telegraph
Donald Saunders
Bob Oxby
Denis Lowe
Roger Malone

The Times
Norman Fox
Tom Freeman

The Guardian
David Lacey
John Arlott
Eric Todd
Paul Wilcox

Sporting Life
Derrick Shaw

Financial Times
Trevor Bailey

Belfast Telegraph
Malcolm Brodie
Bill Ireland

Radio
Bryon Butler
John Camkin
Peter Jones
Alan Parry
Norman De Mesquito

Manchester Evening News
David Meek
Peter Gardner

The Sun
Frank Clough
Bob Driscoll
Mike Ellis
Alex Montgomery
Brian Woolnough
Alasdair Ross
Roy Bentley

Sunday Mirror
Ken Jones
Ken Montgomery
Vince Wilson
Rodger Baillie

Sunday Express
Alan Hoby
Danny Blanchflower
James Connolly
James Mossop
Ray Bradley

Sunday Telegraph
Colin Malam
John Moynihan
Alun Rees
Jack Rollin

The Observer
Hugh McIlvanney
Julie Welch
Peter Corrigan
Tony Pawson

News of the World
Frank Butler
Reg Drury
Patrick Collins
Terry McNeill
Don Evans
Martin Frizell

The Sunday People
Mike Langley
Brian Madley
Sam Bartram

The Sunday Times
Brian Glanville
James Wilson
Rob Hughes
Jason Tomas

BBC TV
David Coleman
Jimmy Hill
Barry Davies
John Motson
Bob Wilson
Frank Bough

Radio Times
Brian Gearing

Evening News
Victor Railton
Peter Batt
John Oakley
Steve Stammers

Evening Standard
Bernard Joy
Peter Blackman
Michael Hart

Exchange Telegraph Co. Ltd.
Ken Mays
John Bowles

Reuters Limited
John F. Davis
Morley Myers
John Freeman

Press Association
Michael Gee
Tony Smith
Barry Pedley

Reg Hayter Ltd., Sports Services
Albert Sewell
Tony Roche

Associated Press
Geoff Miller
Colin Frost

Thomson Regional Newspapers, London
Basil Easterbrook
Bob Harris

D. C. Thomson
Charles Holloway
Bob Hammond

ITV
Brian Moore
Hugh Johns
Gerry Harrison
Keith Macklin
Gerald Sinstadt
Paul Doherty
Martin Tyler
Kenneth Wolstenholme
Dickie Davies

Visnews
Neil Mallard

Freelance
Eric Batty
Eric Nicholls
Pat Collins
Lionel Francis
Dennis Signy
Norman Giller
Tony Pullein
Steve Richards
Arthur Rotmil
Leslie Vernon
Leslie Yates
Max Marquis
Harold Mayes

FOOTBALL LEAGUE FIXTURES 1976-77

Saturday, August 21 1976
DIVISION ONE
Arsenal v Bristol C.
Aston Villa v West Ham U.
Ipswich T. v Tottenham H.
Leeds U. v W.B.A.
Leicester C. v Manchester C.
Liverpool v Norwich C.
Manchester U. v Birmingham C.
Middlesbrough v Coventry C.
Newcastle U. v Derby Co.
Q.P.R. v Everton
Stoke C. v Sunderland

DIVISION TWO
Blackburn R. v Bolton W.
Bristol R. v Blackpool
Charlton Ath. v Cardiff C.
Fulham v Nottingham F.
Hereford U. v Hull C.
Luton T. v Sheffield U.
Notts Co. v Millwall
Oldham Ath. v Plymouth Arg.
Orient v Chelsea
Southampton v Carlisle U.
Wolverhampton W. v Burnley

DIVISION THREE
Brighton & H.A. v Oxford U.
Bury v Grimsby T.
Chesterfield v Northampton T.
Crystal Palace v York C.
Gillingham v Reading
Lincoln C. v Shrewsbury T.
Mansfield T. v Preston N.E.
Peterborough U. v Rotherham U.
Sheffield W. v Walsall
Swindon T. v Port Vale
Tranmere R. v Chester
Wrexham v Portsmouth

DIVISION FOUR
Aldershot v Bradford C.
Brentford v Barnsley
Cambridge U. v Colchester U.
Halifax T. v AFC Bournemouth
Hartlepool v Exeter
Newport Co. v Stockport Co.
Scunthorpe U. v Rochdale
Southend U. v Watford
Southport v Doncaster R.
Swansea C. v Darlington
Torquay U. v Huddersfield T.
Workington v Crewe Alex.

Monday, August 23 1976
DIVISION ONE
W.B.A. v Liverpool
West Ham U. v Q.P.R.

DIVISION THREE
Portsmouth v Chesterfield

DIVISION FOUR
Darlington v Newport Co.
Rochdale v Cambridge U.
Stockport Co. v Brentford

Tuesday, August 24 1976
DIVISION ONE
Birmingham C. v Leeds U.
Bristol C. v Stoke C.
Coventry C. v Manchester U.

Everton v Ipswich T.
Sunderland v Leicester C.

DIVISION TWO
Blackpool v Oldham Ath.
Bolton W. v Orient
Burnley v Fulham
Carlisle U. v Hereford U.
Hull C. v Luton T.
Plymouth Arg. v Blackburn R.
Sheffield U. v Wolverhampton W.

DIVISION THREE
Chester v Brighton & H.A.
Grimsby T. v Crystal Palace
Northampton T. v Sheffield W.
Oxford U. v Mansfield T.
Portsmouth v Swindon T.
Preston N.E. v Peterborough U.
Rotherham U. v Bury
Shrewsbury T. v Gillingham
Walsall v Lincoln C.
York C. v Tranmere

DIVISION FOUR
Barnsley v Torquay U.
Colchester U. v Halifax T.
Doncaster R. v Aldershot
Huddersfield T. v Southport
Watford v Hartlepool

Wednesday, August 25 1976
DIVISION ONE
Derby Co. v Middlesbrough
Manchester C. v Aston Villa
Norwich C. v Arsenal
Tottenham H. v Newcastle U.

DIVISION TWO
Cardiff C. v Bristol R.
Chelsea v Notts Co.
Millwall v Southampton
Nottingham F. v Charlton Ath.

DIVISION THREE
Reading v Wrexham

DIVISION FOUR
A.F.C. Bournemouth v Workington
Bradford C. v Swansea C.
Crewe Alex. v Southend U.
Exeter C. v Scunthorpe U.

Saturday, August 28 1976
DIVISION ONE
Birmingham C. v Liverpool
Coventry C. v Leeds U.
Derby Co. v Manchester U.
Everton v Aston Villa
Ipswich T. v Q.P.R.
Manchester C. v Stoke C.
Newcastle U. v Bristol C.
Sunderland v Arsenal
Tottenham H. v Middlesbrough
W.B.A. v Norwich C.
West Ham U. v Leicester C.

DIVISION TWO
Blackpool v Orient
Bolton W. v Millwall
Bristol R. v Oldham Ath.
Burnley v Luton T.
Cardiff C. v Blackburn R.
Charlton Ath. v Fulham

Chelsea v Carlisle U.
Hull C. v Southampton
Nottingham F. v Wolverhampton W.
Plymouth Arg. v Notts Co.
Sheffield U. v Hereford U.

DIVISION THREE
Chester v Oxford U.
Grimsby T. v Peterborough U.
Northampton T. v Lincoln C.
Portsmouth v Chesterfield
Port Vale v Sheffield W.
Preston N.E. v Brighton & H.A.
Rotherham U. v Mansfield T.
Shrewsbury T. v Reading
Swindon T. v Wrexham
Tranmere R. v Crystal Palace
Walsall v Gillingham
York C. v Bury

DIVISION FOUR
Aldershot v Southport
Barnsley v Newport Co.
AFC Bournemouth v Southend U.
Bradford C. v Darlington
Crewe Alex. v Hartlepool
Doncaster R. v Torquay U.
Exeter C. v Cambridge U.
Huddersfield T. v Brentford
Rochdale v Colchester U.
Stockport Co. v Swansea C.
Watford v Scunthorpe U.
Workington v Halifax T.

Friday, September 3 1976
DIVISION FOUR
Darlington v Stockport Co.
Newport Co. v Huddersfield
Southport v Bradford C.

Saturday, September 4 1976
DIVISION ONE
Arsenal v Manchester C.
Aston Villa v Ipswich T.
Bristol C. v Sunderland
Leeds U. v Derby Co.
Leicester C. v Everton
Liverpool v Coventry C.
Manchester U. v Tottenham H.
Middlesbrough v Newcastle U.
Norwich C. v Birmingham C.
Q.P.R. v W.B.A.
Stoke C. v West Ham U.

DIVISION TWO
Blackburn R. v Blackpool
Carlisle U. v Hull C.
Fulham v Bristol R.
Hereford U. v Burnley
Luton T. v Nottingham F.
Millwall v Chelsea
Notts Co. v Bolton W.
Oldham Ath. v Cardiff C.
Orient v Plymouth Arg.
Southampton v Sheffield U.
Wolverhampton W. v Charlton Ath.

DIVISION THREE
Brighton & H.A. v Rotherham U.
Bury v Tranmere R.
Chesterfield v Swindon T.
Crystal Palace v Chester
Gillingham v Northampton T.
Lincoln C. v Port Vale
Mansfield T. v Grimsby T.
Oxford U. v Preston N.E.
Peterborough U. v York C.
Reading v Walsall
Sheffield W. v Portsmouth
Wrexham v Shrewsbury T.

DIVISION FOUR
Brentford v Doncaster R.
Cambridge U. v Watford

Colchester U. v Exeter C.
Halifax T. v Rochdale
Hartlepool v AFC Bournemouth
Scunthorpe U. v Crewe Alex.
Southend U. v Workington
Swansea C. v Barnsley
Torquay U. v Aldershot

Friday, September 10 1976
DIVISION TWO
Charlton Ath. v Luton T.
Oldham Ath. v Blackburn R.

DIVISION FOUR
Aldershot v Brentford
Southend U. v Halifax T.

Saturday, September 11 1976
DIVISION ONE
Birmingham C. v W.B.A.
Coventry C. v Norwich C.
Derby Co. v Liverpool
Everton v Stoke C.
Ipswich T. v Leicester C.
Manchester C. v Bristol C.
Middlesbrough v Sunderland
Newcastle U. v Manchester U.
Q.P.R. v Aston Villa
Tottenham H. v Leeds U.
West Ham U. v Arsenal

DIVISION TWO
Blackpool v Millwall
Bolton W. v Hull C.
Bristol R. v Orient
Burnley v Southampton
Cardiff C. v Notts. Co.
Fulham v Wolverhampton W.
Nottingham F. v Hereford U.
Plymouth Arg. v Chelsea
Sheffield U. v Carlisle U.

DIVISION THREE
Chester v Preston N.E.
Chesterfield v Wrexham
Crystal Palace v Bury
Grimsby T. v Brighton & H.A.
Northampton T. v Reading
Portsmouth v Lincoln C.
Port Vale v Gillingham
Rotherham U. v Oxford U.
Swindon T. v Sheffield W.
Tranmere R. v Peterborough U.
Walsall v Shrewsbury T.
York C. v Mansfield T.

DIVISION FOUR
Barnsley v Darlington
AFC Bournemouth v Scunthorpe U.
Bradford C. v Stockport Co.
Crewe Alex. v Cambridge U.
Doncaster R. v Newport Co.
Halifax T. v Rochdale
Hartlepool v A.F.C. Bournemouth
Southport v Torquay U.
Watford v Colchester U.
Workington v Hartlepool

Friday, September 17 1976
DIVISION ONE
W.B.A. v Coventry C.

DIVISION TWO
Hull C. v Sheffield U.

DIVISION FOUR
Newport Co. v Aldershot
Stockport Co. v Barnsley

Saturday, September 18 1976
DIVISION ONE
Arsenal v Everton
Aston Villa v Birmingham C.
Bristol C. v West Ham U.
Leeds U. v Newcastle U

Leicester C. v Q.P.R.
Liverpool v Tottenham H.
Manchester U. v Middlesbrough
Norwich C. v Derby Co.
Stoke C. v Ipswich T.
Sunderland v Manchester C.

DIVISION TWO
Blackburn R. v Bristol R.
Carlisle U. v Burnley
Chelsea v Bolton W.
Hereford U. v Charlton Ath.
Luton T. v Fulham
Millwall v Plymouth Arg.
Notts Co. v Blackpool
Orient v Cardiff C.
Southampton v Nottingham F.
Wolverhampton W. v Oldham Ath.

DIVISION THREE
Brighton & H.A. v York C.
Bury v Chester
Gillingham v Portsmouth
Lincoln C. v Swindon T.
Mansfield v Tranmere R.
Oxford U. v Grimsby T.
Peterborough U. v Crystal Palace
Preston N.E. v Rotherham U.
Reading v Port Vale
Sheffield W. v Chesterfield
Shrewsbury T. v Northampton T.
Wrexham v Walsall

DIVISION FOUR
Brentford v Southport
Cambridge U. v AFC Bournemouth
Colchester U. v Crewe Alex.
Darlington v Huddersfield T.
Halifax T. v Exeter C.
Hartlepool v Southend U.
Rochdale v Watford
Scunthorpe U. v Workington
Swansea C. v Doncaster R.
Torquay U. v Bradford C.

Friday, September 24 1976
DIVISION TWO
Cardiff C. v Millwall
Charlton Ath. v Southampton

DIVISION FOUR
Halifax T. v Hartlepool
Southend U. v Scunthorpe U.

Saturday, September 25 1976
DIVISION ONE
Aston Villa v Leicester C.
Coventry C. v Birmingham C.
Derby Co. v W.B.A.
Everton v Bristol C.
Ipswich T. v Arsenal
Manchester C. v Manchester U.
Middlesbrough v Leeds U.
Newcastle U. v Liverpool
Q.P.R. v Stoke C.
Tottenham H. v Norwich C.
West Ham U. v Sunderland

DIVISION TWO
Blackpool v Chelsea
Bristol R. v Notts Co.
Burnley v Hull C.
Fulham v Hereford U.
Nottingham F. v Carlisle U.
Oldham Ath. v Orient
Plymouth Arg. v Bolton W.
Sheffield U. v Blackburn R.
Wolverhampton W. v Luton T.

DIVISION THREE
Bury v Peterborough U.
Chesterfield v Lincoln C.
Crystal Palace v Mansfield T.

Grimsby T. v Preston N.E.
Northampton T. v Walsall
Portsmouth v Reading
Port Vale v Shrewsbury T.
Rotherham U. v Chesster
Swindon T. v Gillingham
Tranmere R. v Brighton & H.A.
Wrexham v Sheffield W.
York C. v Oxford U.

DIVISION FOUR
Aldershot v Swansea C.
Barnsley v Bradford C.
AFC Bournemouth v Colchester U.
Crewe Alex. v Rochdale
Doncaster R. v Darlington
Huddersfield T. v Stockport Co.
Southport v Newport Co.
Torquay U. v Brentford
Watford v Exeter C.
Workington v Cambridge U.

Friday, October 1 1976
DIVISION THREE
Oxford U. v Tranmere R.

DIVISION FOUR
Bradford C. v Brentford
Newport Co. v Torquay U.

Saturday, October 2 1976
DIVISION ONE
Arsenal v Q.P.R.
Birmingham C. v Derby Co.
Bristol C. v Ipswich T.
Coventry C. v Leicester C.
Leeds U. v Manchester U.
Liverpool v Middlesbrough
Manchester C. v West Ham U.
Norwich C. v Newcastle U.
Q.P.R. v Aston Villa
Sunderland v Everton
W.B.A. v Tottenham H.

DIVISION TWO
Bolton W. v Blackpool
Carlisle U. v Charlton Ath.
Chelsea v Cardiff C.
Hereford U. v Wolverhampton W.
Hull C. v Nottingham F.
Millwall v Bristol R.
Notts Co. v Oldham Ath.
Orient v Blackburn R.
Plymouth Arg. v Luton T.
Sheffield U. v Burnley
Southampton v Fulham

DIVISION THREE
Brighton & H.A. v Crystal Palace
Chester v Peterborough U.
Gillingham v Chesterfield
Lincoln C. v Sheffield W.
Mansfield T. v Bury
Northampton T. v Wrexham
Preston N.E. v York C.
Reading v Swindon T.
Rotherham U. v Grimsby T.
Shrewsbury T. v Portsmouth
Walsall v Port Vale

DIVISION FOUR
Barnsley v Huddersfield T.
Cambridge U. v Southend U.
Colchester U. v Workington
Darlington v Aldershot
Exeter C. v Crewe Alex.
Rochdale v AFC Bournemouth
Scunthorpe U. v Hartlepool
Stockport Co. v Doncaster
Swansea C. v Southport
Watford v Halifax

Friday, October 8 1976
DIVISION FOUR
Southend U. v Colchester U.

Saturday, October 9 1976
DIVISION ONE
Aston Villa v Arsenal
Derby Co. v Coventry C.
Everton v Manchester C.
Ipswich T. v Sunderland
Leicester C. v Stoke C.
Manchester U. v Liverpool
Middlesbrough v Norwich C.
Newcastle U. v W.B.A.
Q.P.R. v Bristol C.
Tottenham H. v Birmingham C.
West Ham U. v Leeds U.

DIVISION TWO
Blackburn R. v Notts Co.
Blackpool v Plymouth Arg.
Bristol R. v Chelsea
Burnley v Orient
Cardiff C. v Bolton W.
Charlton Ath. v Hull C.
Fulham v Carlisle U.
Luton T. v Hereford U.
Nottingham F. v Sheffield U.
Oldham Ath. v Millwall
Wolverhampton W. v Southampton

DIVISION THREE
Bury v Brighton & H.A.
Chesterfield v Reading
Crystal Palace v Oxford U.
Grimsby T. v Chester
Peterborough U. v Mansfield T.
Portsmouth v Walsall
Port Vale v Northampton T.
Sheffield W. v Gillingham
Swindon T. v Shrewsbury T.
Tranmere R. v Preston N.E.
Wrexham v Lincoln C.
York C. v Rotherham U.

DIVISION FOUR
Aldershot v Stockport Co.
AFC Bournemouth v Exeter C.
Brentford v Newport Co.
Crewe Alex. v Watford
Doncaster R. v Barnsley
Halifax T. v Scunthorpe
Hartlepool v Cambridge U.
Huddersfield T. v Bradford C.
Southport v Darlington
Torquay U. v Swansea C.
Workington v Rochdale

Saturday, October 16 1976
DIVISION ONE
Arsenal v Stoke C.
Birmingham C. v Middlesbrough
Bristol C. v Leicester C.
Coventry C. v Newcastle U.
Derby Co. v Tottenham H.
Liverpool v Everton
Manchester C. v Q.P.R.
Norwich C. v Leeds U.
Sunderland v Aston Villa
W.B.A. v Manchester U.
West Ham U. v Ipswich T.

DIVISION TWO
Blackpool v Nottingham F.
Bolton W. v Birstol R.
Burnley v Charlton Ath.
Carlisle U. v Luton T.
Chelsea v Oldham Ath.
Hull C. v Wolverhampton W.
Millwall v Blackburn R.
Notts. Co. v Orient
Plymouth Arg. v Cardiff C.
Sheffield U. v Fulham
Southampton v Hereford U.

DIVISION THREE
Brighton & H.A. v Peterborough U.

Chester v Mansfield T.
Gillingham v Lincoln C.
Grimsby T. v York C.
Northampton T. v Portsmouth
Oxford U. v Bury
Port Vale v Wrexham
Preston N.E. v Crystal Palace
Reading v Sheffield W.
Rotherham U. v Tranmere R.
Shrewsbury T. v Chesterfield
Walsall v Swindon T.

DIVISION FOUR
Barnsley v Aldershot
Bradford C. v Newport Co.
Cambridge U. v Scunthorpe U.
Colchester U. v Hartlepool
Crewe Alex. v Halifax T.
Darlington v Torquay U.
Exeter C. v Workington
Huddersfield T. v Doncaster R.
Rochdale v Southend U.
Stockport Co. v Southport
Swansea C. v Brentford
Watford v AFC Bournemouth

Friday, October 22 1976
DIVISION TWO
Orient v Millwall

DIVISION FOUR
Doncaster R. v Bradford C.
Newport Co. v Swansea C.

Saturday, October 23 1976
DIVISION ONE
Aston Villa v Bristol C.
Everton v West Ham U.
Ipswich T. v Manchester C.
Leeds U. v Liverpool
Leicester C. v Arsenal
Manchester U. v Norwich C.
Middles_rough v W.B.A.
Newcastle U. v Birmingham C.
Q.P.R. v Sunderland
Stoke C. v Derby Co.
Tottenham H. v Coventry C.

DIVISION TWO
Blackburn R. v Chelsea
Bristol R. v Plymouth Arg.
Cardiff C. v Blackpool
Charlton Ath. v Sheffield U.
Fulham v Hull C.
Hereford U. v Notts. Co.
Luton T. v Southampton
Nottingham F. v Burnley
Oldham Ath. v Bolton W.
Wolverhampton W. v Carlisle U.

DIVISION THREE
Bury v Preston N.E.
Chesterfield v Walsall
Crystal Palace v Rotherham U.
Lincoln C. v Reading
Mansfield T. v Brighton & H.A.
Peterborough U. v Oxford U.
Portsmouth v Port Vale
Sheffield W. v Shrewsbury T.
Swindon T. v Northampton T.
Tranmere R. v Grimsby T.
Wrexham v Gillingham
York C. v Chester

DIVISION FOUR
Aldershot v Huddersfield T.
AFC Bournemouth v Crewe Alex.
Brentford v Darlington
Halifax T. v Cambridge U.
Hartlepool v Rochdale
Scunthorpe U. v Colchester U.
Southend U. v Exeter C.
Southport v Barnsley
Torquay U. v Stockport Co.
Workington v Watford

Monday, October 25 1976
DIVISION THREE
Mansfield T. v Reading
Tranmere R. v Port Vale

DIVISION FOUR
Brentford v Workington
Darlington v AFC Bournemouth
Stockport Co. v Exeter

Tuesday, October 26 1976
DIVISION THREE
Brighton & H.A. v Walsall
Bury v Swindon T.
Chester v Gillingham
Crystal Palace v Shrewsbury T.
Grimsby T. v Wrexham
Oxford U. v Lincoln C.
Preston N.E. v Sheffield W.
Rotherham U. v Portsmouth
York C. v Northampton T.

DIVISION FOUR
Barnsley v Southend U.
Doncaster R. v Colchester U.
Huddersfield T. v Watford
Newport Co. v Hartlepool
Southport v Cambridge U.
Swansea C. v Scunthorpe U.

Wednesday, October 27 1976
DIVISION THREE
Peterborough U. v Chesterfield

DIVISION FOUR
Aldershot v Rochdale
Bradford C. v Halifax
Torquay U. v Crewe Alex.

Friday, October 29 1976
DIVISION TWO
Orient v Hull C.

Saturday, October 30 1976
DIVISION ONE
Birmingham C. v Q.P.R.
Coventry C. v Sunderland
Derby Co. v Bristol C.
Leeds U. v Arsenal
Liverpool v Aston Villa
Manchester U. v Ipswich T.
Middlesbrough v Leicester C.
Newcastle U. v Stoke C.
Norwich C. v Manchester C.
Tottenham H. v Everton
W.B.A. v West Ham U.

DIVISION TWO
Blackburn R. v Luton T.
Blackpool v Wolverhampton W.
Bolton W. v Fulham
Bristol R. v Charlton Ath.
Cardiff C. v Sheffield U.
Chelsea v Southampton
Millwall v Hereford
Notts Co. v Carlisle U.
Oldham Ath. v Nottingham F.
Plymouth Arg. v Burnley

DIVISION THREE
Chesterfield v York C.
Gillingham v Preston N.E.
Lincoln C. v Rotherham U.
Northampton T. v Brighton & H.A.
Portsmouth v Peterborough U.
Port Vale v Grimsby T.
Reading v Chester
Sheffield W. v Mansfield T.
Shrewsbury T. v Oxford U.
Swindon T. v Tranmere R.
Walsall v Crystal Palace
Wrexham v Bury

DIVISION FOUR
AFC Bournemouth v Aldershot
Cambridge U. v Torquay U.
Colchester U. v Brentford
Crewe Alex. v Swansea C.
Exeter C. v Southport
Halifax T. v Stockport Co.
Hartlepool v Huddersfield T.
Rochdale v Doncaster R.
Scunthorpe U. v Darlington
Southend U. v Newport Co.
Watford v Barnsley
Workington v Bradford C.

Monday, November 1 1976
DIVISION THREE
Port Vale v Preston N.E.
Wrexham v York C.

DIVISION FOUR
Hartlepool v Stockport Co.
Rochdale v Darlington

Tuesday, November 2 1976
DIVISION THREE
Gillingham v Grimsby T.
Northampton T. v Peterborough U.
Portsmouth v Chester
Sheffield W. v Rotherham U.
Shrewsbury T. v Mansfield T.
Swindon T. v Crystal Palace
Walsall v Oxford U.

DIVISION FOUR
Cambridge U. v Huddersfield T.
Colchester U. v Torquay U.
Halifax T. v Doncaster R.
Scunthorpe U. v Southport
Southend U. v Swansea
Watford v Aldershot

Wednesday, November 3 1976
DIVISION THREE
Chesterfield v Tranmere R.
Lincoln C. v Bury
Reading v Brighton & H.A.

DIVISION FOUR
AFC Bournemouth v Newport Co.
Crewe Alex. v Bradford C.
Exeter C. v Brentford
Workington v Barnsley

Friday, November 5 1976
DIVISION TWO
Charlton Ath. v Plymouth Arg.

DIVISION FOUR
Aldershot v Southend U.
Newport Co. v Colchester U.

Saturday, November 6 1976
DIVISION ONE
Arsenal v Birmingham C.
Aston Villa v Manchester U.
Coventry C. v Sunderland
Derby Co. v Bristol C.
Ipswich T. v W.B.A.
Leicester C. v Norwich C.
Manchester C. v Newcastle U.
Q.P.R. v Derby Co.
Stoke C. v Middlesbrough
Sunderland v Liverpool
West Ham U. v Tottenham H.

DIVISION TWO
Burnley v Oldham Ath.
Carlisle U. v Bolton W.
Fulham v Cardiff C.
Hereford U. v Chelsea
Hull C. v Blackpool
Luton T. v Bristol R.
Nottingham F. v Blackburn R.

Sheffield U. v Notts Co.
Southampton v Orient
Wolverhampton W. v Millwall

DIVISION THREE
Brighton & H.A. v Swindon T.
Bury v Sheffield W.
Chester v Walsall
Crystal Palace v Reading
Grimsby T. v Chesterfield
Mansfield T. v Lincoln C.
Oxford U. v Portsmouth
Peterborough U. v Gillingham
Preston N.E. v Northampton T.
Rotherham U. v Shrewsbury T.
Tranmere R. v Wrexham
York C. v Port Vale

DIVISION FOUR
Barnsley v Scunthorpe U.
AFC Bournemouth v Cambridge U.
Bradford C. v AFC Bournemouth
Darlington v Halifax T.
Doncaster R. v Hartlepool
Huddersfield T. v Workington
Southport v Rochdale
Stockport Co. v Crewe Alex.
Swansea C. v Exeter C.
Torquay U. v Watford

Friday, November 12 1976
DIVISION TWO
Orient v Nottingham F.

Saturday, November 13 1976
DIVISION ONE
Birmingham C. v Ipswich T.
Coventry C. v Q.P.R.
Derby Co. v Arsenal
Leeds U. v Stoke C.
Liverpool v Leicester C.
Manchester U. v Sunderland
Middlesbrough v Manchester C.
Newcastle U. v Everton
Norwich C. v West Ham U.
Tottenham H. v Bristol C.
W.B.A. v Aston Villa

DIVISION TWO
Blackburn R. v Hull C.
Blackpool v Sheffield U.
Bolton W. v Burnley
Bristol R. v Hereford U.
Cardiff C. v Southampton
Chelsea v Charlton Ath.
Millwall v Luton T.
Notts Co. v Wolverhampton W.
Oldham Ath. v Carlisle U.
Plymouth Arg. v Fulham

DIVISION THREE
Chesterfield v Chester
Gillingham v Mansfield T.
Lincoln C. v Tranmere R.
Northampton T. v Oxford U.
Portsmouth v Bury
Port Vale v Brighton & H.A.
Reading v Preston N.E.
Sheffield W. v Crystal Palace
Shrewsbury T. v Grimsby T.
Swindon T. v Rotherham U.
Walsall v York C.
Wrexham v Peterborough U.

DIVISION FOUR
AFC Bournemouth v Southport
Cambridge U. v Barnsley
Colchester U. v Stockport Co.
Crewe Alex. v Darlington
Exeter C. v Huddersfield T.
Halifax T. v Swansea C.
Hartlepool v Brentford
Rochdale v Newport Co.
Scunthorpe U. v Aldershot

Southend U. v Bradford C.
Watford v Doncaster
Workington v Torquay U.

Saturday, November 20 1976
DIVISION ONE
Arsenal v Liverpool
Aston Villa v Coventry C.
Bristol C. v Norwich C.
Everton v Derby Co.
Ipswich T. v Leeds U.
Leicester C. v Manchester U.
Manchester C. v W.B.A.
Q.P.R. v Middlesbrough
Stoke C. v Birmingham C.
Sunderland v Tottenham H.
West Ham U. v Newcastle U.

DIVISION TWO
Burnley v Bristol R.
Carlisle U. v Millwall
Charlton Ath. v Blackpool
Fulham v Notts Co.
Hereford U. v Oldham Ath.
Hull C. v Plymouth Arg.
Luton T. v Cardiff C.
Nottingham F. v Chelsea
Sheffield U. v Orient
Southampton v Bolton W.
Wolverhampton W. v Blackburn R.

DIVISION TWO
Friday, November 26 1976
Orient v Wolverhampton W.

DIVISION THREE
Bury v Gillingham
Tranmere R. v Reading

DIVISION FOUR
Huddersfield T. v Rochdale

Saturday, November 27 1976
DIVISION ONE
Birmingham C. v Manchester C.
Coventry C. v Arsenal
Derby Co. v Sunderland
Leeds U. v Leicester C.
Liverpool v Bristol C.
Manchester U. v West Ham U.
Middlesbrough v Ipswich T.
Newcastle U. v Q.P.R.
Norwich C. v Aston Villa
Tottenham H. v Stoke C.
W.B.A. v Everton

DIVISION TWO
Blackburn R. v Hereford U.
Blackpool v Fulham
Bolton W. v Charlton Ath.
Bristol R. v Hull C.
Cardiff C v Nottingham F.
Chelsea v Burnley
Millwall v Sheffield U.
Notts Co. v Luton T.
Oldham Ath. v Southampton
Plymouth Arg. v Carlisle U.

DIVISION THREE
Brighton & H.A. v Wrexham
Chester v Northampton T.
Crystal Palace v Chesterfield
Grimsby T. v Portsmouth
Mansfield T. v Swindon T.
Oxford U. v Port Vale
Peterborough U. v Sheffield W.
Preston N.E. v Lincoln C.
Rotherham U. v Walsall
York C. v Shrewsbury T.

DIVISION FOUR
Aldershot v Hartlepool
Barnsley v Colchester U.
AFC Bournemouth v Watford

Bradford C. v Cambridge U.
Darlington v Exeter C.
Doncaster R. v Crewe Alex
Newport Co. v Halifax T.
Southport v Southend U.
Stockport Co. v AFC Bournemouth
Swansea C. v Workington
Torquay U. v Scunthorpe

Friday, December 3 1976
DIVISION TWO
Sheffield U. v Chelsea

DIVISION THREE
Port Vale v Chester
Swindon T. v Grimsby T.
Walsall v Peterborough U.

Saturday, December 4 1976
DIVISION ONE
Arsenal v Newcastle U.
Aston Villa v Tottenham H.
Bristol C. v Leeds U.
Everton v Norwich C.
Ipswich T. v Liverpool
Leicester C. v Birmingham C.
Manchester C. v Derby Co.
Q.P.R. v Manchester U.
Stoke C. v Coventry C.
Sunderland v W.B.A.
West Ham U. v Middlesbrough

DIVISION TWO
Burnley v Cardiff C.
Carlisle U. v Orient
Charlton Ath. v Blackburn R.
Fulham v Oldham Ath.
Hereford U. v Bolton W.
Hull C. v Millwall
Luton T. v Blackpool
Nottingham F. v Bristol R.
Southampton v Notts Co.
Wolverhampton W. v Plymouth Arg.

DIVISION THREE
Chesterfield v Bury
Gillingham v Rotherham U.
Lincoln C. v Crystal Palace
Northampton T. v Mansfield T.
Portsmouth v Preston N.E.
Reading v York C.
Sheffield W. v Tranmere R.
Shrewsbury T. v Brighton & H.A.
Wrexham v Oxford U.

DIVISION FOUR
AFC Bournemouth v Bradford C.
Cambridge U. v Stockport Co.
Colchester U. v Darlington
Crewe Alex. v Newport Co.
Exeter C. v Doncaster R.
Halifax T. v Torquay
Hartlepool v Southport
Rochdale v Barnsley
Scunthorpe U. v Brentford
Southend U. v Huddersfield T.
Watford v Swansea C.
Workington v Aldershot

Saturday, December 11 1976
DIVISION ONE
Birmingham C. v Sunderland
Coventry C. v Everton
Derby Co. v West Ham U.
Leeds U. v Aston Villa
Liverpool v Q.P.R.
Manchester U. v Bristol C.
Middlesbrough v Arsenal
Newcastle U. v Ipswich T.
Norwich C. v Stoke C.
Tottenham H. v Manchester C.
W.B.A. v Leicester C.

DIVISION TWO
Blackburn R. v Southampton

Blackpool v Hereford U.
Bolton W. v Luton T.
Bristol R. v Carlisle U.
Cardiff C. v Hull C.
Chelsea v Wolverhampton W.
Millwall v Nottingham F.
Notts Co. v Burnley
Oldham Ath. v Charlton Ath.
Orient v Fulham
Plymouth Arg. v Sheffield U.

Saturday, December 18 1976
DIVISION ONE
Arsenal v Manchester U.
Aston Villa v Newcastle U.
Bristol C. v Middlesbrough
Everton v Birmingham C.
Ipswich T. v Derby Co.
Leicester C. v Tottenham H.
Manchester C. v Coventry C.
Q.P.R. v Leeds U.
Stoke C. v W.B.A.
Sunderland v Norwich C.
West Ham U. v Liverpool

DIVISION TWO
Burnley v Millwall
Carlisle U. v Cardiff C.
Charlton Ath. v Notts Co.
Fulham v Blackburn R.
Hereford U. v Orient
Hull C. v Chelsea
Luton T. v Oldham Ath.
Nottingham F. v Plymouth Arg.
Sheffield U. v Bristol R.
Southampton v Blackpool
Wolverhampton W. v Bolton W.

DIVISION THREE
Brighton & H.A. v Chesterfield
Bury v Walsall
Chester v Swindon T.
Crystal Palace v Northampton T.
Grimsby T. v Reading
Mansfield T. v Wrexham
Oxford U. v Sheffield W.
Peterborough U. v Lincoln C.
Preston N.E. v Shrewsbury T.
Rotherham U. v Port Vale
Tranmere R. v Gillingham
York C. v Portsmouth

DIVISION FOUR
Aldershot v Exeter C.
Barnsley v Hartlepool
Bradford C. v Colchester U.
Brentford v Rochdale
Darlington v Watford
Doncaster R. v AFC Bournemouth
Huddersfield T. v Crewe Alex.
Newport Co. v Workington
Southport v Halifax T.
Stockport Co. v Scunthorpe U.
Swansea C. v Cambridge U.
Torquay U. v Southend U.

Monday, December 27 1976
DIVISION ONE
Birmingham C. v West Ham U.
Coventry C. v Ipswich T.
Derby Co. v Leicester C.
Leeds U. v Manchester C.
Liverpool v Stoke C.
Manchester U. v Everton
Middlesbrough v Aston Villa
Newcastle U. v Sunderland
Norwich C. v Q.P.R.
Tottenham H. v Arsenal
W.B.A. v Bristol C.

DIVISION TWO
Blackburn R. v Burnley
Blackpool v Carlisle U.
Bolton W. v Nottingham F.

863

Bristol R. v Wolverhampton W.
Cardiff C. v Hereford U.
Chelsea v Fulham
Millwall v Charlton Ath.
Notts Co. v Hull C.
Oldham Ath. v Sheffield U.
Orient v Luton T.
Plymouth Arg. v Southampton

DIVISION THREE
Chesterfield v Mansfield T.
Gillingham v Crystal Palace
Lincoln C. v Grimsby T.
Northampton T. v Rotherham U.
Portsmouth v Brighton & H.A.
Port Vale v Bury
Reading v Peterborough U.
Sheffield W. v York C.
Shrewsbury T. v Tranmere R.
Swindon T. v Oxford U.
Walsall v Preston N.E.
Wrexham v Chester

DIVISION FOUR
AFC Bournemouth v Swansea
Cambridge U. v Newport Co.
Colchester U. v Aldershot
Crewe Alex. v Barnsley
Exeter C. v Torquay U.
Halifax T. v Huddersfield
Hartlepool v Darlington
Rochdale v Bradford C.
Scunthorpe U. v Doncaster R.
Southend U. v Brentford
Watford v Stockport Co.
Workington v Southport

Tuesday, December 28 1976
DIVISION ONE
West Ham U. v Coventry C.

DIVISION TWO
Burnley v Blackpool
Fulham v Millwall
Hull C. v Oldham Ath.
Sheffield U. v Bolton W.

DIVISION THREE
Bury v Northampton T.
Chester v Shrewsbury T.
Grimsby T. v Sheffield W.
Mansfield T. v Port Vale
Rotherham U. v Chesterfield
Tranmere R. v Walsall

DIVISION FOUR
Darlington v Workington
Doncaster R. v Southend U.
Huddersfield T. v Scunthorpe U.

Wednesday, December 29 1976
DIVISION ONE
Arsenal v W.B.A.
Aston Villa v Derby Co.
Bristol C. v Birmingham C.
Everton v Middlesbrough
Ipswich T. v Norwich C.
Leicester C. v Newcastle U.
Manchester C. v Liverpool
Q.P.R. v Tottenham H.
Stoke C. v Manchester U.
Sunderland v Leeds U.

DIVISION TWO
Carlisle U. v Blackburn R.
Charlton Ath. v Orient
Hereford U. v Plymouth Arg.
Luton T. v Chelsea
Nottingham F. v Notts Co.
Southampton v Bristol R.
Wolverhampton W. v Cardiff C.

DIVISION THREE
Brighton & H.A. v Gillingham

Crystal Palace v Portsmouth
Oxford U. v Reading
Peterborough U. v Swindon T.
Preston N.E. v Wrexham
York C. v Lincoln C.

DIVISION FOUR
Aldershot v Cambridge U.
Barnsley v Halifax T.
Bradford C. v Hartlepool
Brentford v Watford
Newport Co. v Exeter C.
Southport v Crewe Alex.
Stockport Co. v Rochdale
Swansea C. v Colchester U.
Torquay U. v AFC Bournemouth

Saturday, January 1 1977
DIVISION ONE
Birmingham C. v Arsenal
Coventry C. v Bristol C.
Derby Co. v Q.P.R.
Leeds U. v Everton
Liverpool v Sunderland
Manchester U. v Aston Villa
Middlesbrough v Stoke C.
Newcastle U. v Manchester C.
Norwich C. v Leicester C.
Tottenham H. v West Ham U.
W.B.A. v Ipswich T.

DIVISION TWO
Blackburn R. v Nottingham F.
Blackpool v Hull C.
Bolton W. v Carlisle U.
Bristol R. v Luton T.
Cardiff C. v Fulham
Chelsea v Hereford U.
Millwall v Wolverhampton W.
Notts Co. v Sheffield U.
Oldham Ath. v Burnley
Orient v Southampton
Plymouth Arg. v Charlton Ath.

DIVISION THREE
Chesterfield v Grimsby T.
Gillingham v Peterborough U.
Lincoln C. v Mansfield T.
Northampton T. v Preston N.E.
Portsmouth v Oxford U.
Port Vale v York C.
Reading v Crystal Palace
Sheffield W. v Bury
Shrewsbury T. v Rotherham U.
Swindon T. v Brighton & H.A.
Walsall v Chester
Wrexham v Tranmere R.

DIVISION FOUR
AFC Bournemouth v Brentford
Cambridge U. v Bradford C.
Colchester U. v Newport
Crewe Alex. v Stockport Co.
Exeter C. v Swansea C.
Halifax T. v Darlington
Hartlepool v Doncaster R.
Rochdale v Southport
Scunthorpe U. v Barnsley
Southend U. v Aldershot
Watford v Torquay
Workington v Huddersfield T.

Monday, January 3 1977
DIVISION ONE
Arsenal v Leeds U.
Aston Villa v Liverpool
Bristol C. v Derby Co.
Everton v Tottenham H.
Ipswich T. v Manchester U.
Leicester C. v Middlesbrough
Manchester C. v Norwich C.
Q.P.R. v Birmingham C.
Stoke C. v Newcastle U.
Sunderland v Coventry C.
West Ham U. v W.B.A.

DIVISION TWO
Burnley v Plymouth Arg.
Carlisle U. v Notts. Co.
Charlton Ath. v Bristol R.
Fulham v Bolton W.
Hereford U. v Millwall
Hull C. v Orient
Luton T. v Blackburn R.
Nottingham F. v Oldham Ath.
Sheffield U. v Cardiff C.
Southampton v Chelsea
Wolverhampton W. v Blackpool

DIVISION THREE
Brighton & H.A. v Northampton T.
Bury v Wrexham
Chester v Reading
Crystal Palace v Walsall
Grimsby T. v Port Vale
Mansfield T. v Sheffield W.
Oxford U. v Shrewsbury T.
Peterborough U. v Portsmouth
Preston N.E. v Gillingham
Rotherham U. v Lincoln C.
Tranmere R. v Swindon T.
York C. v Chesterfield

DIVISION FOUR
Aldershot v AFC Bournemouth
Barnsley v Watford
Bradford C. v Workington
Brentford v Colchester U.
Darlington v Scunthorpe U.
Doncaster R. v Rochdale
Huddersfield T. v Hartlepool
Newport Co. v Southend U.
Southport v Exeter C.
Stockport Co. v Halifax T.
Swansea C. v Crewe Alex.
Torquay U. v Cambridge U.

Saturday, January 8 1977
DIVISION THREE
Lincoln C. v Chester
Northampton T. v Tranmere R.
Oxford U. v Chesterfield
Portsmouth v Mansfield T.
Port Vale v Peterborough U.
Preston N.E. v Swindon T.
Reading v Rotherham U.
Sheffield W. v Brighton & H.A.
Shrewsbury T. v Bury
Walsall v Grimsby T.
Wrexham v Crystal Palace
York C. v Gillingham

DIVISION FOUR
AFC Bournemouth v Huddersfield T.
Colchester U. v Southport
Crewe Alex. v Brentford
Darlington v Southend
Doncaster R. v Cambridge U.
Exeter C. v Barnsley
Halifax T. v Aldershot
Hartlepool v Torquay U.
Rochdale v Swansea C.
Scunthorpe U. v Bradford C.
Stockport Co. v Workington
Watford v Newport Co.

Friday, January 14 1977
DIVISION TWO
Charlton Ath. v Nottingham F.

DIVISION THREE
Tranmere R. v York C.

DIVISION FOUR
Newport Co. v Darlington
Southport v Huddersfield

Saturday, January 15 1977
DIVISION ONE
Arsenal v Norwich C.

Aston Villa v Manchester C.
Ipswich T. v Everton
Leeds U. v Birmingham C.
Leicester C. v Sunderland
Liverpool v W.B.A.
Manchester U. v Coventry C.
Middlesbrough v Derby Co.
Newcastle U. v Tottenham H.
Q.P.R. v West Ham U.
Stoke C. v Bristol C.

DIVISION TWO
Blackburn R. v Plymouth Arg.
Bristol R. v Cardiff C.
Fulham v Burnley
Hereford U. v Carlisle U.
Luton T. v Hull C.
Notts Co. v Chelsea
Oldham Ath. v Blackpool
Orient v Bolton W.
Southampton v Millwall
Wolverhampton W. v Sheffield U.

DIVISION THREE
Brighton & H.A. v Chester
Bury v Rotherham U.
Chesterfield v Port Vale
Crystal Palace v Grimsby T.
Gillingham v Shrewsbury T.
Lincoln C. v Walsall
Mansfield T. v Oxford U.
Peterborough U. v Preston N.E.
Sheffield W. v Northampton T.
Swindon T. v Portsmouth
Wrexham v Reading

DIVISION FOUR
Aldershot v Doncaster R.
Brentford v Stockport Co.
Cambridge U. v Rochdale
Halifax T. v Colchester U.
Hartlepool v Watford
Scunthorpe U. v Exeter C.
Southend U. v Crewe Alex.
Swansea C. v Bradford C.
Torquay U. v Barnsley
Workington v AFC Bournemouth

Saturday, January 22 1977
DIVISION ONE
Birmingham C. v Manchester U.
Bristol C. v Arsenal
Coventry C. v Middlesbrough
Derby Co. v Newcastle U.
Everton v Q.P.R.
Manchester C. v Leicester C.
Norwich C. v Liverpool
Sunderland v Stoke C.
Tottenham H. v Ipswich T.
W.B.A. v Leeds U.
West Ham U. v Aston Villa

DIVISION TWO
Blackpool v Bristol R.
Bolton W. v Blackburn R.
Burnley v Wolverhampton W.
Cardiff C. v Charlton Ath.
Carlisle U v Southampton
Chelsea v Orient
Hull C. v Hereford U.
Millwall v Notts Co.
Nottingham F. v Fulham
Plymouth Arg. v Oldham Ath.
Sheffield U. v Luton T.

DIVISION THREE
Chester v Tranmere R.
Grimsby T. v Bury
Northampton T. v Chesterfield
Oxford U. v Brighton & H.A.
Portsmouth v Wrexham
Port Vale v Swindon T.
Preston N.E. v Mansfield T.

Reading v Gillingham
Rotherham H.A. v Peterborough U.
Shrewsbury T. v Lincoln C.
Walsall v Sheffield W.
York C. v Crystal Palace

DIVISION FOUR
Barnsley v Brentford
AFC Bournemouth v Halifax T.
Bradford C. v Aldershot
Colchester U. v Cambridge U.
Crewe Alex. v Workington
Darlington v Swansea C.
Doncaster R. v Southport
Exeter C. v Hartlepool
Huddersfield T. v Torquay U.
Rochdale v Scunthorpe U.
Stockport Co. v Newport Co.
Watford v Southend U.

Saturday, January 29 1977
DIVISION THREE
Brighton & H.A. v Lincoln C.
Bury v Reading
Chester v Sheffield W.
Chesterfield v Preston N.E.
Crystal Palace v Port Vale
Gillingham v Oxford U.
Grimsby T. v Northampton T.
Mansfield T. v Walsall
Peterborough U. v Shrewsbury T.
Rotherham U. v Wrexham
Swindon T. v York C.
Tranmere R. v Portsmouth

DIVISION FOUR
Aldershot v Crewe Alex.
Barnsley v AFC Bournemouth
Bradford C. v Exeter C.
Brentford v Halifax T.
Cambridge U. v Darlington
Huddersfield T. v Colchester U.
Newport Co. v Scunthorpe U.
Southend U. v Stockport Co.
Southport v Watford
Swansea C. v Hartlepool
Torquay U. v Rochdale
Workington v Doncaster R.

Friday, February 4 1977
DIVISION TWO
Fulham v Charlton Ath.

DIVISION FOUR
Darlington v Bradford C.
Newport Co. v Barnsley
Southport v Aldershot

Saturday, February 5 1977
DIVISION ONE
Arsenal v Sunderland
Aston Villa v Everton
Bristol C. v Newcastle U.
Leeds U. v Coventry C.
Leicester C. v West Ham U.
Liverpool v Birmingham C.
Manchester U. v Derby Co.
Middlesbrough v Tottenham H.
Norwich C. v W.B.A.
Q.P.R. v Ipswich T.
Stoke C. v Manchester C.

DIVISION TWO
Blackburn R. v Cardiff C.
Carlisle U. v Chelsea
Hereford U. v Sheffield U.
Luton T. v Burnley
Millwall v Bolton W.
Notts Co. v Plymouth Arg.
Oldham Ath. v Bristol R.
Orient v Blackpool
Southampton v Hull C.
Wolverhampton W. v Nottingham F.

DIVISION THREE
Brighton & H.A. v Preston N.E.
Bury v York C.
Chesterfield v Portsmouth
Crystal Palace v Tranmere R.
Gillingham v Walsall
Lincoln C. v Northampton T.
Mansfield T. v Rotherham U.
Oxford U. v Chester
Peterborough U. v Grimsby T.
Reading v Shrewsbury T.
Sheffield W. v Port Vale
Wrexham v Swindon T.

DIVISION FOUR
Brentford v Huddersfield
Cambridge U. v Exeter C.
Colchester U. v Rochdale
Halifax T. v Workington
Hartlepool v Crewe Alex.
Scunthorpe U. v Watford
Southend U. v AFC Bournemouth
Swansea C. v Stockport Co.
Torquay U. v Doncaster R.

Friday, February 11 1977
DIVISION ONE
Sunderland v Bristol C.

Saturday, February 12 1977
DIVISION ONE
Birmingham C. v Norwich C.
Coventry C. v Liverpool
Derby Co. v Leeds U.
Everton v Leicester C.
Ipswich T. v Aston Villa
Manchester C. v Arsenal
Newcastle U. v Middlesbrough
Tottenham H. v Manchester U.
W.B.A. v Q.P.R.
West Ham U. v Stoke C.

DIVISION TWO
Blackpool v Blackburn R.
Bolton W. v Notts Co.
Bristol R. v Fulham
Burnley v Hereford U.
Cardiff C. v Oldham Ath.
Charlton Ath. v Wolverhampton W.
Chelsea v Millwall
Hull C. v Carlisle U.
Nottingham F. v Luton T.
Plymouth Arg. v Orient
Sheffield U. v. Southampton

DIVISION THREE
Chester v Crystal Palace
Grimsby T. v Mansfield T.
Northampton T. v Gillingham
Portsmouth v Sheffield W.
Port Vale v Lincoln C.
Preston N.E. v Oxford U.
Rotherham U. v Brighton & H.A.
Shrewsbury T. v Wrexham
Swindon T. v Chesterfield
Tranmere R. v Bury
Walsall v Reading
York C. v Peterborough U.

DIVISION FOUR
Aldershot v Torquay U.
Barnsley v Swansea C.
AFC Bournemouth v Hartlepool
Bradford C. v Southport
Crewe Alex. v Scunthorpe U.
Doncaster R. v Brentford
Exeter C. v Colchester U.
Huddersfield T. v Newport Co.
Rochdale v Halifax T.
Stockport Co. v Darlington
Watford v Cambridge U.
Workington v Southend U.

Friday, February 18 1977
DIVISION ONE
W.B.A. v Birmingam C.

DIVISION THREE
Shrewsbury T. v Walsall

DIVISION FOUR
Newport Co. v Doncaster R.
Stockport Co. v Bradford C.

Saturday, February 19 1977
DIVISION ONE
Arsenal v West Ham U.
Aston Villa v Q.P.R.
Bristol C. v Manchester C.
Leeds U. v Tottenham H.
Leicester C. v Ipswich T.
Liverpool v Derby Co.
Manchester U. v Newcastle U.
Norwich C. v Coventry C.
Stoke C. v Everton
Sunderland v Middlesbrough

DIVISION TWO
Blackburn R. v Oldham Ath.
Carlisle U. v Sheffield U.
Chelsea v Plymouth Arg.
Hereford U. v Nottingham F.
Hull C. v Bolton W.
Luton T. v Charlton Ath.
Millwall v Blackpool
Notts Co. v Cardiff C.
Orient v Bristol R.
Southampton v Burnley
Wolverhampton W. v Fulham

DIVISION THREE
Brighton & H.A. v Grimsby T.
Bury v Crystal Palace
Gillingham v Port Vale
Lincoln C. v Portsmouth
Mansfield T. v York C.
Oxford U. v Rotherham U.
Peterborough U. v Transmere R.
Preston N.E. v Chester
Reading v Northampton T.
Sheffield W. v Swindon T.
Wrexham v Chesterfield

DIVISION FOUR
Brentford v Aldershot
Cambridge U. v Crewe Alex.
Colchester U. v Watford
Darlington v Barnsley
Halifax T. v Southend U.
Hartlepool v Workington
Rochdale v Exeter C.
Scunthorpe U. v AFC Bournemouth
Swansea C. v Huddersfield T.
Torquay U. v Southport

Friday, February 25 1977
DIVISION TWO
Charlton Ath. v Hereford U.
Fulham v Luton T.

Saturday, February 26 1977
DIVISION ONE
Birmingham C. v Aston Villa
Coventry C. v W.B.A.
Derby Co. v Norwich C.
Everton v Arsenal
Ipswich T. v Stoke C.
Manchester C. v Sunderland
Middlesbrough v Manchester U.
Newcastle U. v Leeds U.
Q.P.R. v Leicester C.
Tottenham H. v Liverpool
West Ham U. v Bristol C.

DIVISION TWO
Blackpool v Notts. Co.
Bolton W. v Chelsea

Bristol R. v Blackburn R.
Burnley v Carlisle U.
Cardiff v Orient
Nottingham F. v Southampton
Oldham Ath. v Wolverhampton W.
Plymouth Arg. v Millwall
Sheffield U. v. Hull C.

DIVISION THREE
Chester v Bury
Chesterfield v Sheffield W.
Crystal Palace v Peterborough U.
Grimsby T. v Oxford U.
Northampton T. v Shrewsbury T.
Portsmouth v Gillingham
Port Vale v Reading
Rotherham U. v Preston N.E.
Swindon T. v Lincoln C.
Tranmere R. v Mansfield T.
Walsall v Wrexham
York C. v Brighton & H.A.

DIVISION FOUR
Aldershot v Newport Co.
Barnsley v Stockport Co.
AFC Bournemouth v Cambridge U.
Bradford C. v Torquay U.
Crewe Alex. v Colchester U.
Doncaster R. v Swansea C.
Exeter C. v Halifax T.
Huddersfield T. v Darlington
Southend U. v Hartlepool
Southport v Brentford
Watford v Rochdale
Workington v Scunthorpe U.

Friday, March 4 1977
DIVISION THREE
Preston N.E. v Grimsby T.

DIVISION FOUR
Hartlepool v Halifax T.
Newport Co. v Southport
Stockport Co. v Huddersfield T.

Saturday, March 5 1977
DIVISION ONE
Arsenal v Ipswich T.
Birmingham C. v Coventry C.
Bristol C. Everton
Leeds U. v Middlesbrough
Leicester C. v Aston Villa
Liverpool v Newcastle U.
Manchester U. v Manchester C.
Norwich C. v Tottenham H.
Stock C. v Q.P.R.
Sunderland v West Ham U.
W.B.A. v Derby Co.

DIVISION TWO
Blackburn R. v Sheffield U.
Bolton W. v Plymouth Arg.
Carlisle U. v Nottingham F.
Chelsea v Blackpool
Hereford U. v Fulham
Hull C. v Burnley
Luton T. v Wolverhampton W.
Millwall v Cardiff C.
Notts Co. v Bristol R.
Orient v Oldham Ath.
Southampton v Charlton Ath.

DIVISION THREE
Brighton & H.A. v Tranmere R.
Chester v Rotherham U.
Gillingham v Swindon T.
Lincoln C. v Chesterfield
Mansfield T. v Crystal Palace
Oxford U. v York C.
Peterborough U. v Bury
Reading v Portsmouth
Sheffield W. v Wrexham
Shrewsbury T. v Port Vale
Walsall v Northampton T.

DIVISION FOUR
Bradford C. v Barnsley
Brentford v Torquay U.
Cambridge U. v Workington
Colchester U. v AFC Bournemouth
Darlington v Doncaster R.
Exeter C. v Watford
Rochdale v Crewe Alex.
Scunthorpe U. v Southend U.
Swansea C. v Aldershot

Saturday, March 12 1977
DIVISION ONE
Aston Villa v Stoke C.
Derby Co. v Birmingham C.
Everton v Sunderland
Ipswich T. v Bristol C.
Leicester C. v Coventry C.
Manchester U. v Leeds U.
Middlesbrough v Liverpool
Newcastle U. v Norwich C.
Q.P.R. v Arsenal
Tottenham H. v W.B.A.
West Ham U. v Manchester C.

DIVISION TWO
Blackburn R. v Orient
Blackpool v Bolton W.
Bristol R. v Millwall
Burnley v Sheffield U.
Cardiff C. v Chelsea
Charlton Ath. v Carlisle U.
Fulham v Southampton
Luton T. v Plymouth Arg.
Nottingham F. v Hull C.
Oldham Ath. v Notts. Co.
Wolverhampton W. v Hereford U.

DIVISION THREE
Bury v Mansfield T.
Chesterfield v Gillingham
Crystal Palace v Brighton & H.A.
Grimsby T. v Rotherham U.
Peterborough U. v Chester
Portsmouth v Shrewsbury
Port Vale v Walsall
Sheffield W. v Lincoln C.
Swindon T. v Reading
Tranmere R. v Oxford U.
Wrexham v Northampton T.
York C. v Preston N.E.

DIVISION FOUR
Aldershot v Darlington
AFC Bournemouth v Rochdale
Brentford v Bradford C.
Crewe Alex. v Exeter C.
Doncaster R. v Stockport Co.
Halifax T. v Watford
Hartlepool v Scunthorpe U.
Huddersfield T. v Barnsley
Southend U. v Cambridge U.
Southport v Swansea C.
Torquay U. v Newport Co.
Workington v Colchester U.

Friday, March 18 1977
DIVISION FOUR
Bradford C. v Huddersfield T.
Newport Co. v Brentford

Saturday, March 19 1977
DIVISION ONE
Arsenal v Aston Villa
Birmingham C. v Tottenham H.
Bristol C. v Q.P.R.
Coventry C. v Derby Co.
Leeds U. v West Ham U.
Liverpool v Manchester U.
Manchester C. v Everton
Norwich C. v Middlesbrough
Stoke C. v Leicester C.
Sunderland v Ipswich T.
W.B.A. v Newcastle U.

DIVISION TWO
Bolton W. v Cardiff C.
Carlisle U. v Fulham
Chelsea v Bristol R.
Hereford U. v Luton T.
Hull C. v Charlton Ath.
Millwall v Oldham Ath.
Notts. Co. v Blackburn R.
Orient v Burnley
Plymouth Arg. v Blackpool
Sheffield U. v Nottingham F.
Southampton v Wolverhampton W.

DIVISION THREE
Brighton & H.A. v Bury
Chester v Grimsby T.
Gillingham v Sheffield W.
Lincoln C. v Wrexham
Mansfield T. v Peterborough U.
Northampton T. v Port Vale
Oxford U. v Crystal Palace
Preston N.E. v Tranmere R.
Reading v Chesterfield
Rotherham U. v York C.
Shrewsbury T. v Swindon T.
Walsall v Portsmouth

DIVISION FOUR ·
Barnsley v Doncaster R.
Cambridge U. v Hartlepool
Colchester U. v Southend U.
Darlington v Southport
Exeter C. v AFC Bournemouth
Rochdale v Workington
Scunthorpe U. v Halifax T.
Stockport Co. v Aldershot
Torquay U. v Swansea C.
Watford v Crewe Alex.

Friday, March 25 1977
DIVISION TWO
Charlton Ath. v Burnley
Orient v Notts Co.

DIVISION FOUR
Doncaster R. v Huddersfield T.
Newport Co. v Bradford C.

Saturday, March 26 1977
DIVISION ONE
Aston Villa v Sunderland
Everton v Liverpool
Ipswich T v West Ham U.
Leeds U. v Norwich C.
Leicester C. v Bristol C.
Manchester U. v W.B.A.
Middlesbrough v Birmingham C.
Newcastle U. v Coventry C.
Q.P.R. v Manchester C.
Stoke C. v Arsenal
Tottenham H. v Derby Co.

DIVISION TWO
Blackburn R. v Millwall
Bristol R. v Bolton W.
Cardiff C. v Plymouth Arg.
Fulham v Sheffield U.
Hereford U. v Southampton
Luton T. v Carlisle U.
Nottingham F. v Blackpool
Oldham Ath. v Chelsea
Wolverhampton W. v Hull C.

DIVISION THREE
Bury v Oxford U.
Chesterfield v Shrewsbury T.
Crystal Palace v Preston N.E.
Lincoln C. v Gillingham
Mansfield T. v Chester
Peterborough U. v Brighton & H.A.
Portsmouth v Northampton T.
Sheffield W. v Reading
Swindon T. v Walsall
Tranmere R. v Rotherham U.

Wrexham v Port Vale
York C. v Grimsby T.

DIVISION FOUR
Aldershot v Barnsley
AFC Bournemouth v Watford
Brentford v Swansea C.
Halifax T. v Crewe Alex.
Hartlepool v Colchester U.
Scunthorpe U. v Cambridge U.
Southend U. v Rochdale
Southport v Stockport Co.
Torquay U. v Darlington
Workington v Exeter

Saturday, April 2 1977
DIVISION ONE
Arsenal v Leicester C.
Birmingham C. v Newcastle U.
Bristol C. v Aston Villa
Coventry C. v Tottenham H.
Derby Co. v Stoke C.
Liverpool v Leeds U.
Manchester C. v Ipswich T.
Norwich C. v Manchester U.
Sunderland v Q.P.R.
W.B.A. v Middlesbrough
West Ham U. v Everton

DIVISION TWO
Blackpool v Cardiff C.
Bolton W. v Oldham Ath.
Burnley v Nottingham F.
Carlisle U. v Wolverhampton W.
Chelsea v Blackburn R.
Hull C. v Fulham
Millwall v Orient
Notts Co. v Hereford U.
Plymouth Arg. v Bristol R.
Sheffield U. v Charlton Ath.
Southampton v Luton T.

DIVISION THREE
Brighton & H.A. v Mansfield T.
Chester v York C.
Gillingham v Wrexham
Grimsby T. v Tranmere R.
Northampton T. v Swindon T.
Oxford U. v Peterborough U.
Port Vale v Portsmouth
Preston N.E. v Bury
Reading v Lincoln C.
Rotherham U. v Crystal Palace
Shrewsbury T. v Sheffield W.
Walsall v Chesterfield

DIVISION FOUR
Barnsley v Southport
Bradford C. v Doncaster R.
Cambridge U. v Halifax T.
Colchester U. v Scunthorpe U.
Crewe Alex. v AFC Bournemouth
Darlington v Brentford
Exeter C. v Southend U.
Huddersfield T. v Aldershot
Rochdale v Hartlepool
Stockport Co. v Torquay U.
Swansea C. v Newport Co.
Watford v Workington

Friday, April 8 1977
DIVISION ONE
Sunderland v Newcastle U.
West Ham U. v Birmingham C.

DIVISION TWO
Charlton Ath. v Millwall
Fulham v Chelsea
Hereford U. v Cardiff C.
Hull C. v Notts Co.
Nottingham F. v Bolton W.
Southampton v Plymouth Arg.

DIVISION FOUR
Aldershot v Colchester U.
Bradford C. v Rochdale
Brentford v Southend U.
Darlington v Hartlepool
Newport Co. v Cambridge U.
Southport v Workington
Torquay U. v Exeter C.

Saturday, April 9 1977
DIVISION ONE
Birmingham C. v Bristol C.
Coventry C. v West Ham U.
Derby Co. v Aston Villa
Leeds U. v Sunderland
Liverpool v Manchester C.
Manchester U. v Stoke C.
Middlesbrough v Everton
Newcastle U. v Leicester C.
Norwich C. v Ipswich T.
Tottenham H. v Q.P.R.
W.B.A. v Arsenal

DIVISION TWO
Blackburn R. v Carlisle U.
Blackpool v Burnley
Bolton W. v Sheffield U.
Bristol R. v Southampton
Cardiff C. v Wolverhampton W.
Chelsea v Luton T.
Millwall v Fulham
Notts Co. v Nottingham F.
Oldham Ath. v Hull C.
Orient v Charlton Ath.
Plymouth Arg. v Hereford U.

DIVISION THREE
Chesterfield v Rotherham
Gillingham v Brighton & H.A.
Lincoln C. v York C.
Northampton T. v Bury
Portsmouth v Crystal Palace
Port Vale v Mansfield T.
Reading v Oxford U.
Sheffield W. v Grimsby T.
Shrewsbury T. v Chester
Swindon T. v Peterborough U.
Walsall v Tranmere R.
Wrexham v Preston N.E.

DIVISION FOUR
AFC Bournemouth v Torquay U.
Cambridge U. v Aldershot
Colchester U. v Swansea C.
Crewe Alex. v Southport
Exeter C. v Newport Co.
Halifax T. v Barnsley
Hartlepool v Bradford C.
Rochdale v Stockport Co.
Scunthorpe U. v Huddersfield
Southend U. v Doncaster
Watford v Brentford
Workington v Darlington

Friday, April 8 1977
DIVISION THREE
Brighton & H.A. v Portsmouth
Bury v Port Vale
Chester v Wrexham
Crystal Palace v Gillingham
Grimsby T. v Lincoln C.
Oxford U. v Swindon T.
Peterborough U. v Reading
Tranmere R. v Shrewsbury T.

Monday, April 11 1977
DIVISION ONE
Arsenal v Tottenham H.
Aston Villa v W.B.A.
Everton v Newcastle U.
Ipswich T. v Birmingham C.
Leicester C. v Derby Co.
Manchester C. v Middlesbrough
Q.P.R. v Coventry C.

Stoke C. v Liverpool
Sunderland v Manchester U.
West Ham U. v Norwich C.

DIVISION TWO
Burnley v Blackburn R.
Carlisle U. v Blackpool
Charlton Ath. v Chelsea
Fulham v Plymouth Arg.
Hereford U. v Bristol R.
Luton T. v Orient
Sheffield U. v Oldham Ath.
Southampton v Cardiff C.
Wolverhampton W. v Notts Co.

DIVISION THREE
Bury v Lincoln C.
Chester v Portsmouth
Grimsby T. v Gillingham
Mansfield T. v Chesterfield
Preston N.E. v Walsall
Rotherham U. v Northampton T.
York C. v Sheffield W.

DIVISION FOUR
Barnsley v Workington
Bradford C. v Crewe Alex.
Doncaster R. v Scunthorpe U.
Huddersfield T. v Halifax T.
Stockport Co. v Watford
Swansea C. v AFC Bournemouth
Torquay v Colchester U.

Tuesday, April 12 1977
DIVISION ONE
Arsenal v Derby Co.
Aston Villa v Middlesbrough
Bristol C. v Tottenham H.
Ipswich T. v Coventry C.
Leicester C. v Liverpool
Q P.R. v Norwich C.
Stoke C. v Leeds U.

DIVISION TWO
Burnley v Bolton W.
Carlisle U. v Oldham Ath.
Hull C. v Blackburn R.
Luton T. v Millwall
Nottingham F. v Orient
Sheffield U. v Blackpool
Wolverhampton W. v Bristol R.

DIVISION THREE
Brighton & H.A. v Reading
Crystal Palace v Swindon T.
Mansfield T. v Shrewsbury T.
Oxford U. v Walsall
Peterborough U. v Northampton T.
Preston N.E. v Port Vale
Rotherham U. v Sheffield W.
Tranmere R. v Chesterfield
York C. v Wrexham

DIVISION FOUR
Aldershot v Watford
Barnsley v Crewe Alex.
Brentford v Exeter C.
Darlington v Rochdale
Doncaster R. v Halifax T.
Huddersfield T. v Cambridge U.
Newport Co. v AFC Bournemouth
Southport v Scunthorpe U.
Stockport Co. v Hartlepool
Swansea C. v Southend

Saturday, April 16 1977
DIVISION ONE
Birmingham C. v Stoke C.
Coventry C. v Aston Villa
Derby Co. v Everton
Leeds U. v Ipswich T.
Liverpool v Arsenal
Manchester U. v Leicester C.
Middlesbrough v Q.P.R.

Newcastle U. v West Ham U.
Norwich C. v Bristol C.
Tottenham H. v Sunderland
W.B.A. v Manchester C.

DIVISION TWO
Blackburn R. v Wolverhampton W.
Blackpool v Charlton Ath.
Bolton W. v Southampton
Bristol R. v Burnley
Cardiff C. v Luton T.
Chelsea v Nottingham F.
Millwall v Carlisle U.
Notts Co. v Fulham
Oldham Ath. v Hereford U.
Orient v Sheffield U.
Plymouth Arg. v Hull C.

DIVISION THREE
Chesterfield v Peterborough U.
Gillingham v Chester
Lincoln C. v Oxford U.
Northampton T. v York C.
Portsmouth v Rotherham U.
Port Vale v Tranmere R.
Reading v Mansfield T.
Sheffield W. v Preston N.E.
Shrewsbury T. v Crystal Palace
Swindon T. v Bury
Walsall v Brighton & H.A.
Wrexham v Grimsby T.

DIVISION FOUR
AFC Bournemouth v Darlington
Cambridge U. v Southport
Colchester U. v Doncaster R.
Crewe Alex. v Torquay U.
Exeter C. v Stockport Co.
Halifax T. v Bradford C.
Hartlepool v Newport Co.
Rochdale v Aldershot
Scunthorpe U. v Swansea C.
Southend U. v Barnsley
Watford v Huddersfield T.
Workington v Brentford

Monday, April 18 1977
DIVISION THREE
Port Vale v Crystal Palace
Wrexham v Rotherham U.

DIVISION FOUR
Darlington v Cambridge U.
Hartlepool v Swansea C.
Rochdale v Torquay U.
Southport v Southend U.

Tuesday, April 19 1977
DIVISION THREE
Northampton T. v Grimsby T.
Oxford U. v Gillingham
Portsmouth v Tranmere R.
Preston N.E v Chesterfield
Sheffield W. v Chester
Shrewsbury T. v Peterborough U.
Walsall v Mansfield T.
York C. v Swindon T.

DIVISION FOUR
Colchester U. v Huddersfield T.
Doncaster R. v Workington
Halifax T. v Brentford
Scunthorpe U. v Newport Co.
Watford v Southport

Wednesday, April 20 1977
DIVISION THREE
Lincoln C. v Brighton & H.A.
Reading v Bury

DIVISION FOUR
AFC Bournemouth v Barnsley
Crewe Alex. v Aldershot
Exeter C. v Bradford C.

Friday, April 22 1977
DIVISION TWO
Charlton Ath. v Bolton W.

DIVISION FOUR
Newport Co. v Rochdale

Saturday, April 23 1977
DIVISION ONE
Arsenal v Coventry C.
Aston Villa v Norwich C.
Bristol C. v Liverpool
Everton v W.B.A.
Ipswich T. v Middlesbrough
Leicester C. v Leeds U.
Manchester C. v Birmingham C.
Q.P.R. v Newcastle U.
Stoke C. v Tottenham H.
Sunderland v Derby Co.
West Ham U. v Manchester U.

DIVISION TWO
Burnley v Chelsea
Carlisle U. v Plymouth Arg.
Fulham v Blackpool
Hereford U. v Blackburn R.
Hull C. v Bristol R.
Luton T. v Notts. Co.
Nottingham F. v Cardiff C.
Sheffield U. v Millwall
Southampton v Oldham Ath.
Wolverhampton W. v Orient

DIVISION THREE
Brighton & H.A. v Port Vale
Bury v Portsmouth
Chester v Chesterfield
Crystal Palace v Sheffield W.
Grimsby T. v Shrewsbury T.
Mansfield T. v Gillingham
Oxford U. v Northampton T.
Peterborough U. v Wrexham
Preston N.E. v Reading
Rotherham U. v Swindon T.
Tranmere R. v Lincoln C.
York C. v Walsall

DIVISION FOUR
Aldershot v Scunthorpe U.
Barnsley v Cambridge U.
Bradford C. v Southend U.
Brentford v Hartlepool
Darlington v Crewe Alex.
Doncaster R. v Watford
Huddersfield T. v Exeter C.
Southport v AFC Bournemouth
Stockport Co. v Colchester U.
Swansea C. v Halifax T.
Torquay U. v Workington

Saturday, April 30 1977
DIVISION ONE
Birmingham C. v Leicester C.
Coventry C. v Stoke C.
Derby Co. v Manchester C.
Leeds U. v Bristol C.
Liverpool v Ipswich T.
Manchester U. v Q.P.R.
Middlesbrough v West Ham U.
Newcastle U. v Arsenal
Norwich C. v Everton
Tottenham H. v Aston Villa
W.B.A. v Sunderland

DIVISION TWO
Blackburn R. v Charlton Ath.
Blackpool v Luton T.
Bolton W. v Hereford U.
Bristol R. v Nottingham F.
Burnley v Cardiff C.
Chelsea v Sheffield U.
Millwall v Hull C.
Notts. Co. v Southampton
Oldham Ath. v Fulham

Orient v Carlisle
Plymouth Arg. v Wolverhampton W.

DIVISION THREE
Chesterfield v Crystal Palace
Gillingham v Bury
Lincoln C. v Preston N.E.
Northampton T. v Chester
Portsmouth v Grimsby T.
Port Vale v Oxford U.
Reading v Tranmere R.
Sheffield W. v Peterborough U.
Shrewsbury T. v York C.
Swindon T. v Mansfield T.
Walsall v Rotherham U.
Wrexham v Brighton & H.A.

DIVISION FOUR
AFC Bournemouth v Stockport Co.
Cambridge U. v Brentford
Colchester U. v Barnsley
Crewe Alex. v Doncaster R.
Exeter C. v Darlington
Halifax T. v Newport Co.
Hartlepool v Aldershot
Rochdale v Huddersfield
Scunthorpe U. v Torquay U.
Southend U. v Southport
Watford v Bradford
Workington v Swansea C.

Monday, May 2 1977
DIVISION THREE
Mansfield T. v Portsmouth
Tranmere R. v Northampton T.

DIVISION FOUR
Brentford v Crewe Alex.

Tuesday, May 3 1977
DIVISION THREE
Brighton & H.A. v Sheffield W.
Bury v Shrewsbury T.
Chester v Lincoln C.
Crystal Palace v Wrexham
Gillingham v York C.
Grimsby T. v Walsall
Rotherham U. v Reading
Swindon T. v Preston N.E.

DIVISION FOUR
Barnsley v Exeter C.
Cambridge U. v Doncaster R.
Huddersfield T. v AFC Bournemouth
Newport Co. v Watford
Southend U. v Darlington
Southport v Colchester U.
Swansea C. v Rochdale

Wednesday, May 4 1977
DIVISION THREE
Chesterfield v Oxford U.
Peterborough U. v Port Vale

DIVISION FOUR
Aldershot v Halifax T.
Bradford C. v Scunthorpe U.
Torquay U. v Hartlepool
Workington v Stockport Co.

Saturday, May 7 1977
DIVISION ONE
Arsenal v Middlesbrough
Aston Villa v Leeds U.
Bristol C. v Manchester U.
Everton v Coventry C.
Ipswich T. v Newcastle U.
Leicester C. v W.B.A.
Manchester C. v Tottenham H.
Q.P.R. v Liverpool
Stoke C. v Norwich C.
Sunderland v Birmingham C.
West Ham U. v Derby Co.

DIVISION TWO
Burnley v Notts Co.
Carlisle U. v Bristol R.
Charlton Ath. v Oldham Ath.
Fulham v Orient
Hereford U. v Blackpool
Hull C. v Cardiff C.
Luton T. v Bolton W.
Nottingham F. v Millwall
Sheffield U. v Plymouth Arg.
Southampton v Blackburn R.
Wolverhampton W. v Chelsea

DIVISION THREE
Brighton & H.A. v Shrewsbury T.
Bury v Chesterfield
Chester v Port Vale
Crystal Palace v Lincoln C.
Grimsby T. v Swindon T.
Mansfield T. v Northampton T.
Oxford U. v Wrexham
Peterborough U. v Walsall
Preston N.E. v Portsmouth
Rotherham U. v Gillingham
Tranmere R. v Sheffield W.
York C. v Reading

DIVISION FOUR
Aldershot v Workington
Barnsley v Rochdale
Bradford C. v AFC Bournemouth
Brentford v Scunthorpe U.
Darlington v Colchester U.
Doncaster R. v Exeter C.
Huddersfield T. v Southend U.
Newport Co. v Crewe Alex.
Southport v Hartlepool
Stockport Co. v Cambridge U.
Swansea C. v Watford
Torquay U. v Halifax T.

Saturday, May 14 1977
DIVISION ONE
Birmingham C. v Everton
Coventry C. v Manchester C.
Derby Co. v Ipswich T.
Leeds U. v Q.P.R.
Liverpool v West Ham U.

Manchester U. v Arsenal
Middlesbrough v Bristol C.
Newcastle U. v Aston Villa
Norwich C. v Sunderland
Tottenham H. v Leicester C.
W.B.A. v Stoke C.

DIVISION TWO
Blackburn R. v Fulham
Blackpool v Southampton
Bolton W. v Wolverhampton W.
Bristol R. v Sheffield U.
Cardiff C. v Carlisle U.
Chelsea v Hull C.
Millwall v Burnley
Notts Co. v Charlton Ath.
Oldham Ath. v Luton T.
Orient v Hereford U.
Plymouth Arg. v Nottingham F.

DIVISION THREE
Chesterfield v Brighton & H.A.
Gillingham v Tranmere R.
Lincoln C. v Peterborough U.
Northampton T. v Crystal Palace
Portsmouth v York C.
Port Vale v Rotherham U.
Reading v Grimsby T.
Sheffield W. v Oxford U.
Shrewsbury T. v Preston N.E.
Swindon T. v Chester
Walsall v Bury
Wrexham v Mansfield T.

DIVISION FOUR
AFC Bournemouth v Doncaster R.
Cambridge U. v Swansea C.
Colchester U. v Bradford C.
Crewe Alex. v Huddersfield T.
Exeter C. v Aldershot
Halifax T. v Southport
Hartlepool v Barnsley
Rochdale v Brentford
Scunthorpe U. v Stockport Co.
Southend U. v Torquay U.
Watford v Darlington
Workington v Newport Co.

August 1976
14 Charity Shield, Liverpool v Southampton
    League Cup 1st Round (1st leg)
18 League Cup 1st Round (2nd leg)

September 1976
1 League Cup 2nd Round
4 FA Cup Preliminary Round
8 England v Eire (friendly)
11 FA Challenge Vase Preliminary Round
15 European Club tournaments Preliminary
    Rounds (1st leg)
18 FA Cup 1st Round Qualifying
22 League Cup 3rd Round
25 FA Challenge Trophy Preliminary Round
29 European Club tournaments Preliminary
    Rounds (2nd leg)

October 1976
2 FA Challenge Vase 1st Round
9 FA Cup 2nd Round Qualifying
10 FA Sunday Cup 1st Round
20 European Cup, European Cup-Winners' Cup
    eighth-final ties (1st leg)
    UEFA Cup sixteenth-final ties (1st leg)
23 FA Cup 3rd Round Qualifying
27 League Cup 4th Round
30 FA Challenge Trophy 1st Round Qualifying

November 1976
3 European Cup, European Cup-Winners' Cup
    eighth-final ties (2nd leg)
    UEFA Cup sixteenth-final ties (2nd leg)
6 FA Cup 4th Round Qualifying
7 FA Sunday Cup 2nd Round
20 FA Cup 1st Round proper
    FA Challenge Vase 2nd Round
24 UEFA Cup eighth-final (1st leg)
    FA Challenge Trophy 2nd Round Qualifying

December 1976
1 League Cup 5th Round
5 FA Sunday Cup 3rd Round
8 UEFA Cup eighth-final (2nd leg)
11 FA Cup 2nd Round
13 FA Challenge Trophy 3rd Round Qualifying

January 1977
3 FA Cup 3rd Round
15 FA Challenge Trophy 1st Round proper
16 FA Sunday Cup 4th Round
19 League Cup Semi-finals (1st leg)
29 FA Cup 4th Round
    FA Challenge Vase 4th Round

February 1977
9 England v Netherlands (friendly)
13 FA Sunday Cup 5th Round
16 League Cup Semi-finals (2nd leg)
19 FA Challenge Vase 5th Round
26 FA Cup 5th Round
    FA Challenge Trophy 3rd Round

March 1977
2 European Club tournaments Quarter-finals
    (1st leg)
12 League Cup Final
    FA Challenge Vase 6th Round
13 FA Sunday Cup Semi-finals
16 European Club tournaments Quarter-finals
    (2nd leg)
19 FA Cup 6th Round
    FA Challenge Trophy 4th Round

April 1977
2 FA Challenge Vase Semi-finals (1st leg)
6 European Club Tournaments Semi-finals
    (1st leg)
9 FA Challenge Trophy Semi-finals (1st leg)
    FA Challenge Vase Semi-finals (2nd leg)
16 FA Challenge Trophy Semi-finals (2nd leg)
20 European Club tournaments Semi-finals (2nd
    leg)
23 FA Cup Semi-finals
    FA Challenge Vase Final

May 1977
4 UEFA Cup Final (1st leg)
8 FA Sunday Cup Final
11 European Cup-Winners' Cup Final
14 FA Challenge Trophy Final
18 UEFA Cup Final (2nd leg)
21 FA Cup Final
25 European Cup Final

BRITISH CHAMPIONSHIP 1977

May 28: Northern Ireland v England, Wales v
    Scotland
May 31: Scotland v Northern Ireland
June 1: England v Wales
June 4: England v Scotland, Northern Ireland v
    Wales.

STOP PRESS

World Cup Qualifying match June 13 Helsinki 25,000

FINLAND 1 ENGLAND 4

Finland; Enckelman; Vihtila, Tolsa, Makynen, Ranta, Jantunen, Suomalainen, (Pyykka), Esa Heiskanen, Rissanen, Aki Heiskanen, Paatelainen

England: Clemence; Todd, Mills, Thompson, Madeley, Cherry, Keegan, Channon, Pearson, Brooking, Francis

IMPORTANT FOOTBALL ADDRESSES

The Football Association: 16, Lancaster Gate, London, W2 3LW

Scotland—W. P. Allan, C.B.E., J.P., 6, Park Gardens, Glasgow G3 7YE

Northern Ireland (Irish FA)—W. J. Drennan, J.P., 20 Windsor Avenue, Belfast BT9 6EG

Wales—Trevor Morris, O.B.E., 3, Fairy Road, Wrexham LL13 7PS

Republic of Ireland (FA of Ireland)—P. J. O'Driscoll, 80, Merrion Square, Dublin, 2

International Federation (FIFA)—Dr. H. Käser, FIFA House, Hitzigweg 11, 8032 Zurich, Switzerland

Union of European Football Associations—Mr. H. Bangerter, PO Box 16, CH-3000 Berne 15, Switzerland

THE LEAGUES

The Football League—A. Hardaker, O.B.E., The Football League, Lytham St Annes, Lancs. FY8 1JG. *St Annes 22161/4. Telex 67675*

The Scottish League—T. Maule, 188, West Regent Street, Glasgow G2 4RY. *041-248 3844/5*

The Irish League—J. H. Long, 16 Donegall Square South, Belfast.

Athenian League—G. G. Dell, 'Ardranech', Monument Lane, Chalfont St Peter, Bucks. *Chalfont St Giles 3819*

Central League—D. J. Grimshaw, 118, St Stephens Road, Deepdale, Preston, Lancs., PR1 6TD. *Preston 55898*

Cheshire County League—R. C. Bayley, 228, Grove Lane, Hale, Altrincham, Cheshire. *061-980 7007*

Eastern Counties League and East Anglian Cup— A. W. G. Rudd, 'Heathercliff', Gunton Cliff, Lowestoft. *Lowestoft 5996*

Football Combination—T. P. R. Kirkup, 95, Barking Road, London, E16. *01-476 1151*

Rothmans Hellenic League—N. A. S. Matthews, Cedar Court, Steeple Aston, Oxford. *Steeple Aston 347*

Lancashire Amateur League—H. Heap, 'Maraldo', Carlton Road, Hale, Altrincham, Cheshire, WA15 8RH. *061-980 2344*

Lancashire Combination—K. H. Dean, 61, Queens Road, Blackburn, Lancs. BB1 1QF

Lancashire Football League—H. E. Lambert, 3, Cravans Avenue, Ewood, Blackburn BB2 4LB. *Blackburn 58561*

Leicestershire Senior League—P. Henwood, 63, Carisbrooke Rd., Leicester LE2 3PF. *Leicester 705475*

Manchester League—T. W. Gilgryst, 7, Bowlee Close, Unsworth, Bury, Lancs. *061-766 3082*

Metropolitan London Football League—H. S. Bearman, 142, St Alban's Rd., Seven Kings, Ilford, Essex 1G3 8NP. *01-590 5506*

Midland Counties League—R. Russell-Louden, 44, Exeter Road, Scunthorpe, Lincs. DN15 6PN. *Scunthorpe 4685*

Midland Intermediate—J. B. Holmes, 492, Melton Rd., Leicester, LE4 7SP. *Leicester 63968*

Midweek Football League—F. P. White, 19, Harrow Drive, Edmonton, London N9 9EQ, *01-807 5771*

Nemean Amateur League—W. Chivers, 58 Laurel Avenue, Potters Bar, Herts. EN6 2AB. *Potters Bar 54969*

Northern Intermediate League—F. R. Vicary, 12, Holmefield Avenue, Thornes, Wakefield, Yorks WF2 7AF. *Wakefield 75013*

Rothmans Northern League—G. Nicholson, 99, Watling Road, Bishop Auckland, Co. Durham. *Bishop Auckland 2167*

Northern Premier League—G. B. Graham, 36, Foregate, Highgate Park, Fullwood, Preston PR2 4LA.

North Midlands League—T. Garnett, 14, Brierley Road, Bessacarr, Doncaster DN4 7EE. *Doncaster 56002*

Old Boys' Football League—D. C. Northwood, 94, Ripon Way, Boreham Wood, Herts. *01-953 4597*

Peterborough and District League—A. V. Brown, 27, Gloucester Road, Old Fletton, Peterborough

Plymouth Combination League—J. Holywell, 110, Browning Road, Mile House, Plymouth, Devon PL2 3AR. *Plymouth 52408*

Plymouth and District League—R. J. Smith, 29, Jephson Road, Mount Gold, Plymouth. *Plymouth 61734*

Premier Midweek Floodlight League—N. Hornby, 45, Bishops Avenue, Bromley, Kent BR1 3ET.

Rothmans Isthmian League—M. I. Whittingham, 18, Tudor Close, Hampstead, London NW3 4AB. *01-794 5850 (home) 01-735 3001 (Bus.)*

Southern Amateur League—F. J. Banner, 307D, Crofton Road, Locks Bottom, Orpington, Kent BR6 8EZ. *01-365 8720*

South-East Counties League—R. A. Bailey, 10, Highlands Road, New Barnet, Herts. EN5 5AB. *01-449 5131*

Southern League—W. E. Dellow, FCCS, 1, Cartmel Close, Great Tylers, Wray Common, Reigate, Surrey RH2 0LS. *Redhill 62585*

South Midlands League—C. Moyse, 33, Markham Crescent, Dunstable, Beds. LU5 4SS. *Dunstable 64682*

South-Western League—A. Jewells, 9, Sunway Close, Tavistock, Devon PL19 8LU. *Tavistock 3004*

South Yorkshire Amateur League—A. Bottom, 2, Melbourne Avenue, Aston, Sheffield S31 0BW. *Sheffield 872426*

Spartan League—J. H. Wills, 64, Bellclose Road West Drayton, Middx. *West Drayton 3972*

United Counties League—E. W. Evans, 97, Littlewood Street, Rothwell, Kettering, Northants. *Kettering 710108*

Rothmans Western League—J. Veale, 5, Everest Road, Bristol BS16 2BX. *0272-652699*

The Welsh League—J. T. Burrows, 16, Meyer Street, Thomastown, Tonyrefail, Glam.

West Midland League—C. Gordon Davis, "Roselawns", 42, Ridgewood Avenue, Wollaston, Stourbridge, West Midlands DY8 4QH. *Stourbridge 73241*

West Yorkshire League—W. Keyworth, 2, Hill Court Grove, Branley, Yorks. L13 2AP. *Pudsey 74465*

Yorkshire League—B. Wood, 5, Restmore Avenue, Guiseley, Nr. Leeds, LS20 9DG. *Guiseley 4558 (home); Bradford 29595 (9 a.m. to 5 p.m.)*

Bedfordshire—P. Burns, 13, Wendover Way, Luton, Beds. LU2 7LS

Berks and Bucks—C. J. Twelftree, 42, Bourton-ville, Buckingham, Bucks. *Buckingham 2137*

Birmingham County—W. F. Pennick, County F.A. Offices, Rayhall Lane, Great Barr, Birmingham B43 6JE

Cambridgeshire—R. E. Rogers, 20, Aingers Road, Histon, Cambridge

Cheshire—F. Foden, 549, Crewe Road, Wistaston, Crewe, CW2 6PU

Cornwall—W. Parnell, 12, Higher Tremena, St Austell PL25 5QQ

Cumberland—E. D. Smith, MBE, 4, High Rigg, Brigham, Cickermouth, Cumberland CA13 0TA

Derbyshire—H. L. P. Holmes, 82, Friar Gate, Derby

Devon County—C. H. Norsworthy, 8, Belair Road, Peverell, Plymouth PL2 3QH. *Plymouth 73550*

Dorset County—G. Mitchell, 4, Beaufoys Close, Ferndown, Dorset

Durham—R. D. Lyons, 'Codeslaw', Ferens Park, Durham DH1 1JZ

East Riding County—C. Branton, 83, Belvedere Road, Hessle, Hull HU13 9JH

Essex County—R. G. Melton, 55, Swallowdale, Clacton-on-Sea, Essex CO15 4HG. *Clacton 24116*

Gloucestershire—E. J. Marsh, 12, Down View, Ashley Down Road, Bristol BS7 9BP

Guernsey—L. A. De La Mare, Rosemount Private Hotel, Ruette Des Emrais, Castel, Guernsey, C.I.

Hampshire—R. G. Barnes, 367, Winchester Road, Southampton

Herefordshire—E. G. Powell, 7, Greyfriars Road, Hereford HR4 0BE. *Hereford 2572*

Hertfordshire—F. Holloway, 115, Tile Kiln Lane, Leverstock Green, Hemel Hempstead HP3 8NX

Hunts County—K. T. Masters, 142, Miller Way, Brampton, Hunts. PE18 8UA

Isle of Man—R. Raley, 120, Bucks Road, Douglas, I.O.M.

Jersey—W. A. Nicole, 1, Les Chalets, Queen's Road, St Helier, Jersey, C.I.

Kent County—R. H. Speake, 69, Maidstone Road, Chatham, Kent ME4 6DT. *Medway 43824*

Lancashire—J. Kenyon, 31A, Wellington St., St John's, Blackburn, Lancs. BB1 8AU

Leicestershire and Rutland—J. B. Holmes, 492, Melton Road, Leicester LE4 7SP. *Leicester 63968*

Lincolnshire—B. Webster, 31, Chantry Lane, Grimsby, DN31 2LP

Liverpool County—S. A. Rudd, Barclays Bank Building, 99, Bold Street, Liverpool L1 4HN

London—A. F. Monger, Association House, 88, Lewisham High Street, London SE13 5LL. *01-852 4777*

Manchester County—W. Jackson, 92, Appleby Lodge, Wilmslow Road, Rusholme, Manchester 14

Middlesex County—A. L. Smith, 68, Squires Lane, London N3 2AP

Norfolk County—B. G. Smith, 64, Gunton Lane, Costessey, Norwich, NOR 32K

Northamptonshire—N. W. Hillier, 36, Watkin Terrace, Northampton NN1 3ER. *Northampton 37071*

North Riding County—T. H. Harper, 125, Westbury Street, Thornaby-on-Tees, Cleveland TS17 6NF

Northumberland—J. Laidler, 80, Riding Dene, Mickley, Stocksfield-on-Tyne, Northumberland. *Stocksfield 2360*

Nottinghamshire—W. T. Annable, 34, Castle Gate, Nottingham NG1 7AU. *Nottingham 53753*

Oxfordshire—S. W. Jacobs, 9, Burrows Close, Headington, Oxford. *Oxford 61187*

Sheffield and Hallamshire—E. Kangley, 40, Wain-gate, Sheffield S3 8LB. *Sheffield 27817*

Shropshire—W. B. Jones, 146, Whitchurch Road, Shrewsbury SY1 4EJ

Somerset County—L. G. Webb, 32, North Road, Midsomer Norton, Bath BA3 2QQ. *Midsomer Norton 3176*

Staffordshire—H. Goodall, Winton House, Stoke Road, Hanley, Stoke-on-Trent ST4 2RW

Suffolk County—E. A. Brown, 'Shobdon', 68, Fairfield Road, Saxmundham IP17 1BB

Surrey County—L. F. J. Smith, 2, Fairfield Avenue, Horley, Surrey RH6 7PD

Sussex County—R. F. Reeve, 56, Hawkins Crescent, Shoreham-by-Sea, Sussex BN4 6TP. *Southwick 3444*

Westmorland—J. R. Plumbe, 24, Crescent Green, Kendal LA9 6DR

West Riding County—R. M. Robin, 47, Park Square, Leeds LS1 2NJ. *Leeds 22444*

Wiltshire—F. J. Peart, 161, Grange Drive, Stratton St Margaret, Swindon. *Stratton St Margaret 2239*

Worcestershire—P. Rushton, 84, Windermere Drive, Warndon, Worcester WR4 9JB

OTHER USEFUL ADDRESSES

Amateur Football Alliance—A. J. Hutchinson, Room 724, 7th Floor, Cecil Chambers, 86, The Strand, London W.C.2. *01-240 3837/8*

English Schools FA—G. Evans, 4A, Eastgate Street, Stafford ST16 2NN

Oxford University—P. J. Harding, Hertford College, Oxford

Cambridge University—S. J. Smith, St. Catherine's College, Cambridge

Army—Major A. Dobson, M.B.E., Ministry of Defence (A.S.C.B.), Clayton Barracks, Aldershot, Hants.

Royal Air Force—S/Ldr. D. R. Stewart, R.A.F., PG4A (RAF), Ministry of Defence, Adastral House, Theobalds Road, London WC1X 8RU

Royal Navy—Lt.-Cdr. H. A. Sheppard, R.N. Sports Office, H.M.S. Nelson, Portsmouth, Hants. PO1 3HH

Universities Athletic Union—B. Byrne, U.A.U., 28 Woburn Square, London W.C.1. *01-580 7870*

Central Council of Physical Recreation—General Secretary, 70, Brompton Road, London, SW3 1HE. *01-584 6651*

British Olympic Association—K. S. Duncan, MBE, 12, Buckingham Street, London W.C.2

National Federation of Football Supporters' Clubs—The Secretary, 44, Buxton Road, Luton, Beds.

National Playing Fields Association—Captain Roy Harry, CBE, RN, 578, Catherine Place, London, S.W.1

Professional Footballers' Association—C. Lloyd, 124, Corn Exchange Buildings, Hanging Ditch, Manchester M4 3BN. *061-834 7554*

Referees' Association—R. G. Warnke, 7 Ferndale Road, Binley Woods, Nr. Coventry, CV3 2BG

The Association of Football League Referees and Linesmen—R. Hall, Secretary, 59, Woodcock Hill, Kenton, Harrow, Middlesex HA3 0JH

Football League Managers and Secretaries Association—K. Friar, c/o Arsenal FC, Highbury, London, N5.

Women's Football Association—Miss P. Gregory, 7, Mayfield Road, London, N.8

FINNEGAN

self-portrait of a fighting man

Dateline: October 26 1968. The Mexico Olympics have meant two weeks of all-night television for sports fans throughout Europe, and tonight a little-known boxer named Chris Finnegan is representing Great Britain in the middleweight final. No-one in the world of boxing has given him much chance, for this is a man who only just made the Olympic team and allegedly puts booze before boxing. Born into a London-Irish family with five brothers, who all liked a fight, and two sisters, Finnegan, at 24, has already done his share of blood-letting both in and out of the ring, and as he faces up to the Russian Alexei Kiselyev in the early hours of this October morning he is a penniless building labourer with a wife, daughter, and debts back in England. Eleven minutes later he is a star.

This is Chris Finnegan's own story—the story of a resilient, happy-go-lucky fighter who gained a permanent place in our affections on that October night in Mexico and went on fighting until an eye injury ended his career as the British professional light-heavyweight champion almost eight years later. He didn't win all the time —there was a classic battle with Bob Foster for the world title—but he never admitted defeat, and his story will be enjoyed by sports fans and others everywhere.

Published in September   **£3·95**

Available from bookshops everywhere or from QAP Direct Sales, 9 Partridge Drive, Orpington, Kent BR6 8PE.

PREVIOUS EDITIONS OF ROTHMANS FOOTBALL YEARBOOK

This is the seventh edition of Rothmans Football Yearbook. Because of the limitation on space and the need to revise and broaden the scope of the work, some items that appeared in previous years have been omitted. In previous years we have invited readers to apply direct to the publisher for back issues of the yearbook, and the response has been so great that we are now able only to offer the fifth and sixth editions in this way. You can obtain copies of the editions mentioned below by writing to:

Department QAP, 9 Partridge Drive, Orpington, Kent

enclosing a cheque or PO together with your name and address.

ROTHMANS FOOTBALL YEARBOOK 1974-75

Amongst items included, which are not in the 1976-77 edition are:
Full details of the 1974 World Cup qualifying competition and final tournament; an appreciation of Dennis Follows; pen pictures of 100 international stars of the past; a complete list of British international team line-ups from 1872 to 1973 — never before published in one book.

Standard Edition £1.50 + 40p p&p

ROTHMANS FOOTBALL YEARBOOK 1975-76

Amongst items included, which are not in the 1976-77 edition are:
A tribute to Pele; a tribute to Sir Stanley Rous; all the FA Cup final team line-ups from 1872; Scottish stars of the past; the All-Time Football League tables; a full statistical history of European club football; a European club directory.

Standard Edition £2.25 + 40p p&p